Handbook of Public Administration

Third Edition

PUBLIC ADMINISTRATION AND PUBLIC POLICY

A Comprehensive Publication Program

Executive Editor

JACK RABIN
Professor of Public Administration and Public Policy
School of Public Affairs
The Capital College
The Pennsylvania State University—Harrisburg
Middletown, Pennsylvania

Assistant to the Executive Editor
T. Aaron Wachhaus, Jr.

Available Electronically

Principles and Practices of Public Administration, edited by
Jack Rabin, Robert F. Munzenrider, and Sherrie M. Bartell

PublicADMINISTRATION*netBASE*

Handbook of Public Administration

Third Edition

edited by

Jack Rabin
Pennsylvania State University
Harrisburg, Pennsylvania, U.S.A.

W. Bartley Hildreth
Wichita State University
Wichita, Kansas, U.S.A.

Gerald J. Miller
Rutgers University
Newark, New Jersey, U.S.A.

Taylor & Francis
Taylor & Francis Group
Boca Raton   London   New York

CRC is an imprint of the Taylor & Francis Group,
an informa business

Published in 2007 by
CRC Press
Taylor & Francis Group
6000 Broken Sound Parkway NW, Suite 300
Boca Raton, FL 33487-2742

International Standard Book Number-10: 1-57444-560-X (Hardcover)
International Standard Book Number-13: 978-1-57444-560-2 (Hardcover)
Library of Congress Card Number 2006008566

Library of Congress Cataloging-in-Publication Data

Handbook of public administration / editors, Jack Rabin, W. Bartley Hildreth, and Gerald Miller. -- 3rd ed.
    p. cm. -- (Public administration and public policy ; 124)
  ISBN-13: 978-0-57444-560-2 (alk. paper)
  ISBN-10: 1-57444-560-X (alk. paper)
  1. Public administration--Handbooks, manuals, etc. I. Rabin, Jack, 1945- II. Hildreth, W. Bartley, 1949- III. Miller, Gerald. IV. Series.

JF1351.H275 2006
351--dc22
                                                  2006008566

informa
Taylor & Francis Group
is the Academic Division of Informa plc.

Visit the Taylor & Francis Web site at
http://www.taylorandfrancis.com

and the CRC Press Web site at
http://www.crcpress.com

Dedication

This book is dedicated to:
Dr. Joseph T. Acri
Rhonda N. Hildreth
Reba and Cecil Miller

Preface

What better way could there be to commemorate the three-decade collaboration of our editorial team than to bring forth this third edition?

We have been faithful to the original model of presenting a review of the literature by major subfields of public administration. For each subfield, there are two bibliographic treatises written by subject matter experts from one of these different perspectives:

- Starting in 1880, the development of the field's literature, decade by decade
- Author opinion and analysis of the five great theories, concepts, or ideas that describe the field's literature

In addition to updated chapters, we have added two new units, one on information technology and the other on conduct of inquiry.

We editors are grateful to each chapter author, not only for their willingness to share their intellectual contributions, but also for their diligent labors. We hope that this book will be as well received by the profession as were the previous two—in sum, the industry standard as is befitting the first attempt to develop a comprehensive volume dealing with the vast field of public administration.

We all welcome your comments and suggestions.

Jack Rabin
W. Bartley Hildreth
Gerald J. Miller

Editors

Jack Rabin is a professor of public administration and public policy at The Pennsylvania State University—Harrisburg, Middletown, Pennsylvania. Previously, he was an associate professor and chair in the graduate program in human services administration at Rider College in Lawrenceville, New Jersey. He serves as editor/coeditor of seven journals: the *International Journal of Organization Theory and Behavior* and the *International Journal of Public Administration* (both journals, Marcel Dekker, Inc.), *Public Administration Quarterly*, the *Journal of Health and Human Services Administration*, the *Journal of Public Budgeting Accounting, and Financial Management*, the *Journal of Management History*, and *Public Administration and Management: An Interactive Journal*. Dr. Rabin is author, editor, or coeditor of 25 books, including the *Handbook of Public Budgeting*, the *Handbook of Public Personnel Administration*, the *Handbook of Public Sector Labor Relations*, *Politics and Administration*, *Managing Administration*, *State and Local Government Administration*, the *Handbook of Information Resource Management*, the *Handbook on Human Services Administration*, the *Handbook of Strategic Management*, and *Public Budgeting and Finance* (all book titles, Marcel Dekker, Inc.). Dr. Rabin, moreover, was a consultant in budgeting and strategic planning in the executive office of the President of the United States. He also serves as executive editor of the Public Administration and Public Policy Series (Marcel Dekker, Inc.). Dr. Rabin received a Ph.D. (1972) in political science from the University of Georgia, Athens.

W. Bartley Hildreth is regents distinguished professor of public finance at the Hugo Wall School of Urban and Public Affairs and the W. Frank Barton School of Business, and director of the Kansas Public Finance Center, Wichita State University, Kansas. Dr. Hildreth has served as director of finance for the city of Akron, Ohio; associate professor of finance and public administration in the graduate school of management at Kent State University, Ohio; professor of public administration in the College of Business Administration at Louisiana State University, Baton Rouge; and former chair of the Association for Budgeting and Financial Management, a section of the American Society for Public Administration. Currently, he serves as editor-in-chief of the *Municipal Finance Journal*, book review editor of the *International Journal of Public Administration* (Marcel Dekker, Inc.), member of the National Advisory Council on State and Local Budgeting as well as the Council on Certification for the Certified Public Finance Officer program of the Government Finance Officers' Association, and board member of PFP Publishers. His work has been published in numerous journals, such as the *Public Administration Review*, the *American Review of Public Administration*, the *Public Administration Quarterly*, *Public Budgeting & Finance*, *Public Budgeting and Financial Management*, the *Journal of Applied Behavioral Science*, the *Review of Public Personnel Administration*, *Public Personnel Management*, and *Public Productivity Review*. His publications also include *State and Local Government Debt Issuance and Management Service*. In addition, he is the coauthor of the *State and Local Government Budgeting Practices Handbook* and *Public Budgeting Laboratory, Second Edition* as well as coeditor of the *Handbook of Public Personnel Administration*, the *Handbook of Public Sector Labor Relations*, the *Handbook of Strategic Management* (edited titles, Marcel Dekker, Inc.), *Case Studies in Public Budgeting and Financial Management*, and *Budgeting: Formulation and Execution*. In 1995, Dr. Hildreth received the Donato J. Pugliese Award from the Southeastern Conference for Public Administration for his contributions to public service and administration. A former member of the Governor's Tax Equity Task Force and director of research for the 1995 Kansas tax reform study,

Dr. Hildreth received a B.A. (1971) in political science from the University of Alabama, an M.P.A. (1974) from Auburn University at Montgomery, Alabama, and a D.P.A. (1979) from the University of Georgia, Athens.

Gerald J. Miller is a professor of public administration, Rutgers, the State University of New Jersey in Newark. The author of over fifty research articles, his work has been published in numerous journals in the United States and abroad, including *Public Administration Review*, *Policy Studies Journal*, *Public Budgeting & Finance*, *Journal of Public Budgeting, Accounting & Financial Management*, *Public Productivity and Management Review*, *International Journal of Public Administration*, *Public Integrity*, and *Public Administration Quarterly*. Having published over twenty books, he is the author of *Government Financial Management Theory* and coauthor of the *Public Budgeting Laboratory*. He is the editor of the *Handbook of Debt Management* and coeditor of the *Handbook of Public Policy Analysis* (with Frank Fischer and Mara Sidney), *Handbook of Research Methods in Public Administration* (2d ed. forthcoming with Kaifeng Yang), *Handbook of Strategic Management* (with Jack Rabin and W. Bartley Hildreth), the *Handbook of Public Personnel Administration and Labor Relations*, and the *Handbook of Public Sector Labor Relations* (both with Jack Rabin, Thomas Vocino and W. Bartley Hildreth). In addition, he has published *Managerial Behavior and Organization Demands* (edited with Robert T. Golembiewski and Frank K. Gibson), *Budget Management*, and *Budgeting: Formulation and Execution* (both edited with Jack Rabin and W. Bartley Hildreth). He is an editorial board member of the *International Journal of Public Administration*, *Journal of Accounting, Public Budgeting & Financial Management*, *Municipal Finance Journal*, *Public Productivity and Management Review*, *Journal of Public Management*, and *Journal of Health and Human Resources Administration*. He serves as a book review editor for the *Public Administration Quarterly*. As a former investment banker with the firm of Rauscher, Pierce, Refsnes, Inc. in Phoenix, Arizona, Dr. Miller continues an active consulting practice in the United States, Canada and Western Europe with clients including national, state, and local government organizations in legislative, executive and judicial branches of government, as well as private businesses and business and public sector associations such as the Chartered Institute of Public Finance and Accountancy (England and Wales), the Government Finance Officers Association of the U.S. and Canada, the World Bank, and the International City and County Management Association. His research centers on resource allocation in nonmarket organizations; his work has received continuous and substantial support from government and private donors in the United States, Canada, England and Wales, and the European Union. Dr. Miller received a B.S. in economics and an M.P.A. from Auburn University. He received a Ph.D. in political science from the University of Georgia.

Contributors

Matthew R. Auer
Indiana University
Bloomington, Indiana

David L. Baker
Arizona State University
Tempe, Arizona

Julia Beckett
University of Akron
Akron, Ohio

Luther F. Carter
Francis Marion University
Florence, South Carolina

N. Joseph Cayer
Arizona State University
Tempe, Arizona

David Coursey
Florida State University
Tallahassee, Florida

Peter deLeon
University of Colorado
Denver, Colorado

Robert B. Denhardt
Arizona State University
Tempe, Arizona

James W. Douglas
University of South Carolina
Columbia, South Carolina

David John Farmer
Virginia Commonwealth University
Richmond, Virginia

Howard A. Frank
Florida International University
Miami, Florida

Vache Gabrielyan
American University of Armenia &
    Central Bank of Armenia
Yerevan, Armenia

John J. Gargan
Kent State University
Kent, Ohio

G. David Garson
North Carolina State University
Raleigh, North Carolina

James A. Gazell
San Diego State University
San Diego, California

Robert T. Golembiewski
University of Georgia
Athens, Georgia

George M. Guess
Open Society Institute
Local Government and
    Public Service Initiative
Budapest, Hungary

Steven W. Hays
University of South Carolina
Columbia, South Carolina

Ferrel Heady
University of New Mexico
Albuquerque, New Mexico

Marc Holzer
Rutgers University
Newark, New Jersey

Jonathan B. Justice
University of Delaware
Newark, Delaware

Lawrence F. Keller
Cleveland State University
Cleveland, Ohio

Kenneth D. Kitts
Francis Marion University
Florence, South Carolina

Dale Krane
University of Nebraska at Omaha
Omaha, Nebraska

Eleanor V. Laudicina
Kean University
Union, New Jersey

Richard H. Leach
Duke University
Durham, North Carolina

Carol W. Lewis
University of Connecticut
Storrs, Connecticut

Robert P. McGowan
University of Denver
Denver, Colorado

James Melitski
Marist College
Poughkeepsie, New York

Gerald J. Miller
Rutgers University
Newark, New Jersey

Vincent Ostrom
Indiana University
Bloomington, Indiana

Alexei Pavlichev
North Carolina State University
Raleigh, North Carolina

Bruce Perlman
University of New Mexico
Albuquerque, New Mexico

Norma M. Riccucci
Rutgers University
Newark, New Jersey

Mario Rivera
University of New Mexico
Albuquerque, New Mexico

David H. Rosenbloom
American University
Washington, District of Columbia

Carl W. Stenberg
University of North Carolina
Chapel Hill, North Carolina

Fred Thompson
Willamette University
Salem, Oregon

Danielle M. Vogenbeck
University of Colorado
Denver, Colorado

Robert K. Whelan
University of New Orleans
New Orleans, Louisiana

Dennis P. Wittmer
University of Denver
Denver, Colorado

Deil S. Wright
University of North Carolina
Chapel Hill, North Carolina

Kaifeng Yang
Florida State University
Tallahassee, Florida

Samuel J. Yeager
Wichita State University
Wichita, Kansas

Table of Contents

Unit 1

Public Administration History

1 Public Administration and the American Republic: The Continuing Saga of Management and Administration in Politics

Lawrence F. Keller

CONTENTS

I. INTRODUCTION

In light of the numerous significant political and economic issues, one would expect public administration also to experience a variety of issues. It is, after all, in if not of politics. The study and practice of public administration are indeed under scrutiny. Concerns range from the nature of its managerial premises to its ability to carry out the affairs of state for which it was created. A continuing populism (Rosenbloom 1993a) fed by Americans' distrust of government as well as advances in information technology provide for instant popular opinion and government by initiative. The Internet along with cable television provides a venue for all types of groups to advocate for their own interests and ideologies. Starting with the presidency of Richard Nixon, political executives see less and less value in a high level civil service. Consequently, the recently created Department of Homeland Security does not provide civil service to its employees. National level politics continue to become increasingly partisan, sometimes exacerbated by adherence to strongly expressed, if not strident, ideologies. At the municipal level, elected officials increasingly question the executive authority of city managers, apparently elevating election as empowerment rather than a method of selecting an officeholder. These developments question the degree to which independent and professionally trained administrators can provide responsive and responsible government. They also raise important questions about some fundamental premises upon which the study and evolution of public administration has been based. Within the field, many scholars, following in the footsteps of Dwight Waldo (1948), continue to question the foundations of both the study and the practice, critically examining its so-called scientific roots and an often implicit political philosophy (Farmer 1998; Fox and Miller 1995; Spicer 1995).

This chapter is organized, as were previous editions of the chapter, to review, decade by decade, the history and organization of the study and practice of public administration. This history illustrates the peculiar mix of events and people that influenced the direction of a practice, if not a profession, and a field of study.* Major highlights are preserved, although some illustrative materials have been deleted and others arranged differently. Events and people in public administration are linked to contemporary events and trends. Thus, the chapter starts with major political issues, as the field and profession are part of the larger society. All is organized by ascertaining the influence of three models of governance on the field. These are explicated in the following section.

The importance of public administration derives from its crucial role in the governing of a society (Rohr 1986). Governance is best illuminated by examining politico-administrative systems. Accordingly, viable images or models are important tools to guide research and reflect practice (Boulding 1956; Kass and Catron 1990; Morgan 1986). For example, Bailey (1968) and Henry (1975) suggest that the scope of public administration concerns normative questions about the "oughts" of administration, an openness to technology and management, and regard for the impacts of individuals and organizations on public sector policy and management. In addition, the "refounding" movement has refocused attention to the role of public administration in governance. Others call attention to the role of Law and the Constitution in the practice (Cook 1996; Cooper 1992; Rohr 1986; Rosenbloom, Carroll and Carroll 2000; Wamsley and Wolf 1996). In international affairs, a scholar has pungently questioned how global economic development has been pursued. He argues forcefully that many lessons of Public Administration have been ignored (Fukuyama 2004). Emphatically, he noted that current efforts in global economic development were based on a "black hole of public administration." These ignored seventy years of literature in Public Administration.

Historically, as politico-administrative systems, three rather distinct American models can be identified, with each having widely different roles for public administration. Each connects with the normative sides of different disciplines. Thus, to understand the history requires a brief examination of the rise and content of the three models.

---

*Michael Foucault, in another context, described the utility of such an approach in the following way: [T]o follow the complex course of descent is to maintain passing events in their proper dispersion; it is to identify the accidents, the minute deviations—or conversely, the complete reversals—the errors, the false appraisals, and the faulty calculations that gave birth to those things that continue to exist and have value for us; it is to discover that truth or being do not lie at the root of what we know and what we are but the exteriority of accidents (Foucault 1976, 146).

II. ADMINISTRATION, POLITICS, AND HISTORY: THREE LEGACIES OF REPUBLICAN GOVERNANCE

Three models of politico-administrative systems have driven the evolution of public administration.[*] Philosophically, the models can be traced to the founding of the republic, greatly modified over time. These models illustrate variations in how governments control conflicting interests and govern a society. They include both descriptive analyses and normative assessments. The scope and nature of public administration is defined in light of the assumptions behind these models.

Many of the founding fathers perceived people as inherently corruptible, analogous to what Christian theology denotes as being in a state of original sin. This assumption is significant because for the founding fathers it suggested that public power must be allocated in ways that avoid tempting people with opportunities for personal corruption. From this perspective, the founding fathers' concern with checks and balances is understandable; it is a structural hedge against the foibles of innately fallible humankind.

A second assumption dealt with the control of official authority in a republic. The purpose was to create a limited government, with no official able to exercise public authority without approval from representatives of the people and/or the specification of the authority in a constitutional provision. Government consisted of a variety of public offices sharing public authority. The offices were filled by very different methods. By dispersing authority through a fragmented governmental structure (checks and balances as well as federalism), the design limited opportunities for tyranny. Tyranny, as James Madison's research prior to the Constitutional Convention noted, was often an outcome of badly designed offices, particularly the office of the main executive.

A third assumption anticipated the participation and conflict of individuals and groups around public bodies. Madison's *Federalist* No. 10 reflected a belief in the inevitable evil of factions and the need to control them. Madison assumed that factions seek favorable governmental action with control best achieved by balancing the factions against each other. Although some faction might pursue a more elitist and general public interest (Redford 1969), this would not rectify the tendency of the rest to follow their special interests. Thus our first model, the *conflict of factions* (COF) model, assumes that a jostling of interests would be an enduring, yet deplorable, characteristic of a polity. In the Constitutional Convention, public offices were designed to respond to and dominate differing mixes of interests, thus assuring that no one interest or related interests alone could determine policy.

On the other hand, Hamilton, among others (Caldwell 1944, 1987), urged that some public offices be rooted in the Constitution and empower the incumbent to exercise considerable discretion. These offices could provide energy and direction that might counter current desires of even those interests that had been instrumental in their selection. Other founding fathers coupled this capability to an ethical demand, calling for holders of public office to seek fame; that is, to act in a way that would be judged by future generations as working for a better society generally (Hart 1984). Fame-seeking individuals would moderate conflicts among factions and promote a disinterested sharing of authority. Nevertheless, most of the founders, and with exceptions such as many of the reformers who founded modern public administration, succeeding generations preferred separation of powers so as to dilute the effects of factions and thus protect the system.

---

[*] Several others have commented on three models or variables. The model in this chapter differs by looking at broad political patterns over all of American history. In essence, the models are three distinct philosophies on governance with direct implications for public administration. In contrast, Stillman (1982) examined the conceptions of three of the founding fathers and ascertained three different models of government. In his classic piece, Kaufman (1956) identified three core values around which the field of public administration has oscillated.

Soon afterward, elements for a second model, the *rule of factions* (ROF) model began to draw attention. Within this model public authority and legitimacy were grounded on direct election. Parties, which arose relatively rapidly but which did not become important until decades later, emphasized the representative function and made the "fame-worthiness" call more difficult to implement (Hofstadter 1969). Using its integrative tendencies, the political party became a vehicle for governance by uniting various factions. Party and policy loyalty among officeholders became critical. Offices were often allocated to secure votes or other resources for elected officials. However, the basic political structures created under the COF model were not dramatically changed. Particularly at the municipal level, the outcome seemed to personify Aristotle's classification of a democracy as the degenerative form of a republic. This same perspective compelled many founding fathers to condemn Andrew Jackson, including Thomas Jefferson whose name later often became coupled with Jackson's (Wills 2003).

The ROF model focused on election as the foundation of public authority. The electorate and the number of elected offices were expanded. Governmental behavior was to reflect electoral results. Normatively, with a successful election went the right, if not the responsibility to implement a proposed program, platform, or mandate. Officeholders were selected according to either their agreement to the policy preferences of elected officials, or the utility of their appointment in securing votes or other political resources necessary to implement a program. In reality, such dynamics frequently enriched individuals or supported parties with little regard for the impact of public programs. Ironically, as Crenson (1975) noted, the need to supervise these political appointees, who had little, if any, specialized knowledge or commitment to any notion of a public interest, created the impetus toward an expanded government bureaucracy.

Late in the nineteenth century, contending with a rapidly urbanizing and industrializing country energized by an accelerating technological revolution, a movement of reformers called for basic changes in American government. Although reformers battled over specific elements (Holli 1969), most shared basic assumptions and their beliefs directly influenced the development of American public administration (Crunden 1984; Haber 1964; Keller 1989).

In the third model, the *public interest* (PI) model, the efficacy of science formed the cornerstone of governance. The application of science, the reformers believed, would solve current public problems and inculcate morality.[*] The need was to create governmental structures that empower experts: people who possessed relevant scientific knowledge. Educational credentials indicated expertise. In many ways, this began the American concern, if not obsession, with academic degrees.

The reformers conceptualized science as a cumulative and growing body of knowledge. This concept of science that many Americans still possess is more correctly termed technology (Merton 1970). Many reformers expressed faith in the acquisition of total knowledge through the careful and consistent application of the scientific method. They perceived few limits to the efficacy of science and its ability to solve all current problems by the application of unbiased general laws.[†] Philosophically, this belief derived from the Enlightenment movement. Scientific

---

[*] The spoils system had some ironic outcomes. Surprisingly the use of unfit and unmotivated people for public service required considerable supervision. This extensive supervision helped to bureaucratize public service (Crenson 1975). As a result, a citizen may have difficulty distinguishing a complex public agency created to implement expertise from one that is staffed by patronage. Both seem baffling, emphasizing procedures and certainly not appearing transparent to citizens. All too often desired action only occurs after the discovery of the right person. Interestingly, the belief in a science-based management has waned but such a belief drives much of the public policy perspective. In fact, candidates for public office seek out policy works to forge a platform based on effective policies.

[†] The novel *Philip Dru, Administrator*, published in 1912, captures this belief and its expression in administration. Philip Dru is the appointed Administrator of the United States in the wake of the Second Civil War. He solves all problems, even seemingly intractable social problems. He sails for the Soviet Union to become their administrator, bringing universal science to solve public problems regardless of political or cultural context. The book was published anonymously, but was later attributed to Colonel House, chief advisor to Woodrow Wilson (Haber 1964).

rationality was seen as not only desirable but also feasible in an era of urban-centered technology. A crucial element of the new politico-administrative system was management because science enables administrators to be rational. Appropriately trained experts, administrators, empowered by appointment to public office by representatives of the people, would exercise all administrative authority and be answerable only to the appointing body that would follow their expert advice. These revisions, among others, found a home in the council-manager form of government, the only significant new structure in the American politico-administrative system since the writing of the Constitution. At the national level, the reformers such as Brownlow advocated placing the experts in the executive branch, where they would report to the president (President's Committee on Administrative Management 1937).

By separating politics from administration, reformers believed that scientific rationality would eliminate political conflict. Any conflict over issues that could be resolved by research obviously would be dysfunctional, or as some of the reformers stated, inefficient. The nonpolitical application of knowledge would gain public interest, a state of affairs in which all would be better (Brownell and Stickle 1973; Haber 1964; Hofstadter 1955; see Spicer 1995, for an insightful comparison of the founders and reformers beliefs). Interestingly, this distinction between politics and governing is similar to how a recent biography on Napoleon summarized his views on politics. According to Englund (2004), Napoleon hated politics—particularly, as a review put it, "the freewheeling clash of interests found in America and Britain"—but loved the political, the governing of the state and community. Napoleon also reflected rational systems, implementing a code of law and the metric system.

This PI model assumed perfectibility of people through knowledge.[*] Rationality not only increases the ability to shape reality, but perfects individuals morally. To increase rationality the reformers were willing to grant extensive public authority to experts. Formal education was broadly mandated at least through high school. Education not only sharpened cognitive skills, but it infused a scientifically based morality. In retrospect, this approach to education sadly overlooked Horace Mann's (Antioch College 1937) concern for training citizens for a democratic republic.

The ROF and PI models came to the fore after the Civil War. The ROF model was to serve as the pattern for presidential reform, while the PI model initially influenced civil service reform and local government. Placing civil servants under the president at the national level can be seen as a compromise between the two. Although no one model was able to assert sole influence, at different times one would be more significant than the other. The PI model has guided public management for most of the twentieth century. Social and political events during the 1980s and 1990s, however, suggest a resurgence in the support for the ROF model, with considerable skepticism regarding the future of the PI model for providing for the public's needs without significant attention to demands for change.

---

[*] Plato was one of the first to express a relationship between knowledge and virtue. The concept of philosopher kings certainly reflects a belief in this relationship. During the American reform era, the moral nature of the politico-administrative system, and life in general, was inculcated in the capstone courses of colleges. In his study of the Mugwumps, James McLachlan found that they were predominantly college educated. The capstone course at the time was moral philosophy, taught by the university president who typically connected the moral imperatives of philosophy to the problems of the time. In contrast, the industrial elite and New York City officials, the groups to which he compared the Mugwumps, typically had no college education (McLachlan 1974). Karl Marx's methodology and his utopian beliefs are also reflective of the moral nature of knowledge. Thus, after the inevitable revolution, he predicted the withering away of the state as conflict would disappear (Feuer 1969). A similar outlook fueled Thomas Jefferson's concern over public education. For him, education of independent yeoman minimized the need for government as well as called into question the necessity of the state. The yeoman would be both informed and moral, thanks to education. The view ironically compelled Jefferson, particularly when holding an executive office, often to act differently from his stated philosophy. The original administrative structure for the University of Virginia is a clear example of what Jefferson expected education to achieve morally and politically. The University had no president until the early years of the twentieth century (Ellis 1996).

III. THE 1880s: INTIMATIONS AND FOUNDATIONS

During the 1880s, the United States became an urban industrial society with laborers replacing farmers as the modal occupational category by 1900 (Naisbitt 1982; Toffler 1980). Unfortunately the political system was not ready to handle the increased demand for the necessary traditional public works, much less the social needs of an urban nation. Many cities became domains of political machines, where partisanship and corruption controlled most aspects of public policy (Bridges 1984). A concern for a public interest was scarcely evident in those locales of the ROF model. However, it should be noted that public had a much narrower definition at that time, with most of what is now identified as public services provided by private, for-profit firms (Callow 1976; Riordon 1948; in contrast, see Dewey 1927).

The 1880s were the seedtime of contemporary public administration (Peterson 1961; White 1957). City growth and governance was the focus of political action (Howe 1925). The decade was marked by an explosion of immigration from overseas and from the rural countryside to the cities. Large industrial firms and their international markets played a catalytic role (Chandler 1984; Degler 1959; Hofstadter 1963), often in combination with corrupt political machines. The often naked use of political power by private interests helped spawn reform efforts, one branch of which created the field of public administration (Croly 1909).

The first theoretical piece on public administration is attributed to Woodrow Wilson, written while he was a young and reform-minded professor (Stillman 1973; Wilson 1887; for a dissenting but discerning view, see Hoffman 1998, 2002). Though Wilson's essay is traditionally cited as the intellectual cornerstone of public administration, it later influenced theory rather than contemporary practice. As Van Riper (1984) observed, citing Waldo, the earliest contribution to public administration as a "scientific practice" may be the work of Dorman Eaton, a New York lawyer who produced a civil service study for President Hayes. Eaton later became a major figure in the municipal reform movement (Van Riper 1983). In this decade, Johns Hopkins, one of the first modern research universities, established a program in what would later be called public administration. Interestingly, its curriculum was a broad social approach that was lost to a later, narrower management focus (Hoffman 2002).

Wilson (1984) did, however, identify how assumptions and substantive concerns drive the practice of administration. He visualized a government independent of the culture and time. He called for a businesslike approach to government with an administrative technology that could overcome the partisan nature of American politics.[*] The modern civil service, created in 1883 (prior to Wilson's published essay), was an early reform illustrative of the PI model. Though it initially applied to only 12% of the federal workforce, the reformers were sufficiently shrewd enough to provide for its expansion by permitting presidents to protect their appointees by converting the positions to civil service. By 1900, over 100,000 federal employees were covered (Hoogenboom 1961; Van Riper 1958).

The development of government regulatory agencies, such as the Interstate Commerce Commission (ICC) in 1887, exemplified the reformers' belief in the efficacy of the specially educated to lead an industrial democracy. Though initially given limited power, and for a long time hindered by an unsympathetic Supreme Court, the ICC eventually became the prototype for other government regulatory initiatives. For those who saw separation of powers and factionalized politics as a handicap in dealing with the social and economic problems of a complex society, regulatory agencies manned by experts and divorced from the traditional political bodies were the answer (Landis 1938; Rosenbloom 1983). These agencies deliberately violated separation of powers and mobilized the expertise necessary to end corruption, implement policies in the public interest, and monitor the results to ensure proper outcomes. The reassertion of interest

---

[*] This was originally published in 1912 in the *Woman's Home Companion*, indicating the persistence and diffusion of reform efforts. See Bok (1920) for the story of the leading women's publications during the reform era.

group politics during the 1980s and 1990s would question many of these assumptions and lead to major efforts to reduce the regulatory roles of the national government.

The reform effort was active on a broad front starting from this period. Social organizations had long been a facet of American life, as observers from as early as DeTocqueville had noted. The groups that emerged after the Civil War, however, often pursued policies that went beyond the needs of their own members. The American Economic Association, for example, created in 1885, espoused the goal of positive aid from the state to help meet broader societal needs. Among its founding members were Andrew Carnegie, Woodrow Wilson, and Henry Adams, who shared an interest in expanding public responsibility (Commager 1950). At the local level, social movements such as settlement houses were fertile grounds for what was later considered local public administration. As Cam Stivers pointedly noted, these tended to be lost in official histories that emphasized management rather than social policies (Stivers 2000). Thus, municipal bureaus of research were perceived as the legitimate ancestors of modern managers. These typified the PI model with its emphasis on science and downplayed several community-oriented philosophies that were significant seedbeds for public administration[*] (Hoffman 1998; Stivers 2000).

IV. THE 1890s: PRELUDE CONTINUED

Although fewer innovations in public administration occurred in the 1890s, this decade was critical to the general development of American thought and culture. The role of Congress in urging administrative reform grew and the contest between the ROF model and the emerging PI model continued. The 1890 Sherman Anti-Trust Act and earlier interstate commerce legislation emphasized reform policies; nonetheless, these actions were often frustrated by the rulings of a conservative Supreme Court.

During this period there was a slow but steady evolution of the administrative apparatus, often designed to cope with immediate political issues. Reformers were strategic in attaching administrative reforms to as many issues as they could. For example, because of scandals over the quality of pork shipped to Europe and the 50% decline of domestic sales, the inspection of pork by the national government started in 1890. The industry clamored for government inspection as a way to rebuild consumer confidence (Schlesinger 1983). The period also saw major improvements in urban governance. Reform management practices were applied to problem areas such as public health, housing, and water and sewage treatment systems (Bettmans 1974). Frank Goodnow's *Comparative Administrative Law* (1893), the first American treatise on public administration, was written during this decade. It was a forerunner for those noting the growing significance of administration to modern government and society (Haines and Dimock 1935 cited in Van Riper 1984).

In the mid-1890s, the country entered a major depression. With few exceptions, the public sector was not mobilized to combat the economic downturn as in the later depression of the 1930s. In fact, governments at both the state and national levels were more often used to quell labor disputes than to meet social needs. These failures spurred efforts aimed at reform and professional development. By 1894, more than 80 citizens' associations and groups in various cities were attacking abuses. The American Society for Municipal Development was established. The first national conference for good city government was also held, a forerunner to the National Municipal League (NML) (Stewart 1950; Stone and Stone 1975). The thrust toward municipal reform was spearheaded by urban business interests who desired a more businesslike and politically restrained approach to governance (Hays 1964; Weinstein 1962). However, the movement, and the NML, also included reformers such as Frederick Law Olmsted and Theodore Roosevelt (Morris 1979;

---

[*] Stivers critiques the rise and emphasis on management as part of consciously diminishing women if not writing them out of history and disciplines. She insightfully delineates the masculine metaphors that permeate political philosophy and which cast public administration as a male domain. This distorts the history of the field and thus unfortunately reinforces its overly rational, nearly anti-political perspective (Stivers 2000).

Stevenson 1977). In some cities, such as those in the South-west, the council-manager plan was adopted as a strategy for capital investment (Bridges 1992, 1997) These initiatives were indicative of later efforts to operationalize a functional separation between governmental management and the political process (Svara 1990).

V. THE 1900s: TRANSFORMATIONS IN PRACTICE

In 1900, a hurricane struck the city of Galveston, Texas, claiming 6000 lives. Reconstruction was facilitated by a new form of city government called the commission form. Reflecting a more practical focus for public management, policy matters were decided by a seven-member commission initially appointed by the state. Each commissioner was also the director of an executive department or departments. A later form of the commission plan that provided for elected commissioners spread rapidly and within a decade hundreds of cities had adopted some version of it (Rice 1977; Schiesl 1977).

Soon afterward, Richard Child's commission-manager form of government was developed (Stillman 1974). This significant amendment of the commission form retained a small legislative body armed with all of the policy-making powers of government. The separation of powers was effectively eliminated at the local level and a politics–administration dichotomy was implemented by vesting a city manager appointed by the commission with all of the administrative power.* The only nonelected chief executive in American political history (the president is indirectly elected via the electoral college) was to be filled on the basis of demonstrated competence that would increase the scope of administration and dramatically reduce that of politics (Childs 1952; East 1965) all in the name of community-wide interest. The form became operational in 1908, although the first city to actually utilize the form is disputed (one claims priority by evolution of the office of city engineer and the other by establishing the system; Stone et al. 1940).

The early city managers were almost solely engineers by profession, in large part a response to the extensive public works needs of expanding cities. The city manager system also implemented other components of the PI model, such as the efficacy of science and the supplanting of partisan politics with at-large and nonpartisan elections. Combined with the public planning profession, the vision was of cities expertly run, morally uplifting to the citizens, and more responsive to the needs of the community (Boyer 1983; Crunden 1982; White 1927; White 1937). In fact, some new cities were designed to be symbols of progress and centers of morality (Buder 1967; Mumford 1961; Scott 1971). These practical concerns of the municipal reformers were perhaps more instrumental in the call for a politics–administration dichotomy than was Wilson's essay (Van Riper 1984).

Later, critics would suggest that professional government was a variant on the machine model, citing the granting of contracts on a sole source basis to "friends" (see Lowi's introduction in Gosnell 1968). For these critics, the values derived from business interests reflected an emerging factional interest, in spite of the beliefs and rhetoric of the reformers suggesting a community interest. Arthur Bentley's focus on interest groups expressed a somewhat different interpretation. In what would later be identified as pluralism, Bentley (1908) captured the dynamics of group participation in public affairs that was to continue and even accelerate in an increasingly organizationally based polity. It was not until David Truman's (1951) classic, *The Governmental Process*, however, that this version of the COF model became a normative base for government studies in American political science. To be sure, Truman took a much more positive view of the results of competing factions than did Madison, who viewed it as an evil influence to be minimized.

---

* Richard Childs with his typical bluntness characterized separation of powers and checks and balances as "ancient superstitions" (East 1965). He also opposed less than pure forms of the city management system and even debated managers on this point. Banfield, in *Urban Government* (1969), cites additional arguments articulated by reformers against separation of powers.

By 1903, the steady growth of interest in governmental studies that began with the founding of the initial chair in political economy at the University of North Carolina, Chapel Hill, in the decade of the Civil War resulted in the organization of the American Political Science Association (APSA). With the exception of individuals such as Wilson and Willoughby, however, most of the developing discipline focused on abstract issues of political theory and philosophy rather than practical applications (Stone and Stone 1975).

This decade saw bureaus of governmental research become centers of applied research, dedicated to science as a tool in political reform at the local level. The bureaus were important training grounds for many of the reformers, such as Robert Moses (Caro 1974; Upson 1947). For example, the tracking of local finances not only aided in identifying miscreants and peculators, but also created the basis for budgetary and accounting reforms. Moreover, the training and educational programs found in the bureaus later developed into programs of graduate study in public administration, one example being the transfer of some of the training and educational programs of the New York Bureau to Syracuse University. Within a few months a similar program was initiated at the University of Southern California (Goodsell 1986).

VI. THE 1910s: REFORM CONTINUED AND INTENSIFIED

The pace of political and administrative reform began to quicken during the next decade. In 1913, the city managers formed their own professional association, the International City Managers Association. At its annual meetings, managers not only shared mundane experiences, but debated their roles in urban governance.* City planners formed the American Institute of Planners in 1917 (Scott 1971), while at the state level, leagues of municipalities grew in number and eventually organized the National League of Cities (Stone and Stone 1975).

Frederick Taylor's (1923) authoritative writings on scientific management published in 1911 and originally aimed at the private sector gave rise to a technology-based management in the public sector. Scientific management formed the basis of the recommendations of the President's Commission on Economy and Efficiency (1912), better known as the Taft Commission. Both were full of normative fervor and generalizations and illustrated the hopes of the reformers to implement scientific management in a public setting (Caiden 1969).

The same impetus led to the creation, in 1911, of the *Municipal Research Journal* by the New York Bureau's Training School. The concern for research was matched by a concern for training and education for public service. Shortly thereafter the APSA established a Committee on Practical Training for Public Service, leading in 1914 to their issuance of an all but forgotten report calling for separate schools in public administration within universities (Caldwell 1965). The most consistent speaker for specialized professional education in separate university units was Charles A. Beard. He urged professional education much along the lines of many contemporary MPA programs (Caldwell 1965). The curriculum he initiated while director at the Training School was remarkably similar to those endorsed by later National Association of Schools of Public Affairs and Administration (NASPAA) standards (Goodsell 1986).

By 1917, the NML, largely comprised of municipal administrators, published a model city charter to guide the legal reform of city government. The commission-manager form of government was advocated with a unification of powers within the commission and with no provision for an office of mayor. (However, many cities allowed for the position, often conferred on the member of the council with the highest number of votes in the last election.) To ensure adequate representation of varying interests in the community and justify the commission's broad powers, it recommended proportional representation, a method for election of commission members based on only a specific

---

*Transcripts of the early meetings were printed for many years in the yearbooks published by ICMA. These are interesting glimpses into the experiences and thinking of appointed chief executives on their roles and responsibilities.

number (proportion) of votes.* This recommendation, however, was short lived as it detracted from the community-wide preferences of the business groups supporting reform (Hays 1964).

Reform efforts at the national level were exemplified by the passage of the Federal-Aid Highway Act of 1916. Demanding fiscal responsibility and compliance with scientifically established standards, this categorical grant program carved out an active administrative role for the national government based on the PI model (Uveges 1963). In addition, the Federal Highway Research Board was created and was an early example of the national government's interest in supporting research and its practical application to public problems.

These basic innovations in government, especially at the local level, catalyzed academic degree and public service-type programs in the next decade. The many studies completed and implemented during this period demonstrated the value of professional training and informed analysis to the amelioration of public problems. The resulting administrative needs of expanding government required executive leadership and specialized training, thereby creating a fertile field for the reform and growth in university-based programs.

VII. THE 1920s: MATURATION OF THE PUBLIC INTEREST MODEL

The rapid and geographically dispersed adoption of these administrative innovations justified belief in the public interest model. The early textbooks captured this spirit, as did the first academic portrait of the city manager (White 1927; Willoughby 1927; Storing 1965). Though not as narrowly conceived or as dogmatic as later scholars often stated, they continued to develop and support the public interest model. Reformers encouraged the development of university programs to educate public administration professionals. The University of Michigan started its program in 1914. Later the University of California at Berkeley, Stanford, Syracuse, Cincinnati, Southern California, and the University of Chicago also initiated relevant programs. Local members of the Women's Civic Action League were instrumental in the creation of an Institute of Government at the University of Southern California in 1926. Eventually, in 1929, the university's School of Public Administration was an outgrowth of the reformer's activities.

Though of good intent, many of the developing university programs were comprised largely of a few training courses added to liberal arts curricula. While keeping the reform motif alive, they contributed little to the practical education of managers (Stone and Stone 1975). The failure to establish more focused programs and a research community around public administration may account for the inability to incorporate the findings of research into basic management practices. For example, Mary Parker Follet (1918) created useful management technologies in this regard by the mid-1920s, but they were not a valued component in public management education until many years later (Fox 1968; Metcalf and Urwick 1940).

Some universities also established what would later be called public service units. Efforts such as those by the University of Chicago's "1313" Public Administration Center (Brownlow 1958; Stone and Stone 1975) often reflected the dedication of specific scholars such as Charles Merriam. Unfortunately, the university connection often failed to survive the key actors in academe. Nevertheless, the grouping of such organizations had a high payoff for creating and maintaining networks within the profession. The locus of such activities would eventually move to Washington, DC by the 1960s, thus reflecting the rise of federal programs in all levels of government and the concomitant need for networking in Washington.

At the national level, two staff reforms were initiated that had long-term impacts. The Budgeting and Accounting Act of 1921 implemented many of the reforms called for by the Taft Commission.

---

* The city of Cincinnati continued to elect their councils at large by a complicated version of proportional representation until the late 1950s. It was only stopped with the election of a black vice-mayor in 1957, an innovation not desired in a city that had recently caused its baseball team to change its moniker from Reds to Redlegs to avoid the taint of Communism. See Miller (1980) and Straetz (1958) for interesting details of this period.

The Bureau of the Budget and the General Accounting Office were both created, though the former was a part of the Department of the Treasury until the creation of the Executive Office of the President in 1939. These two organizations personified the PI model with its emphasis on scientific management through staff units manned by experts. The Bureau of the Budget, later the Office of Management and Budget, was an early example of the administrative infrastructure that would later support what some termed the "imperial presidency" (Reedy 1970; Schlesinger 1973).

If the 1920s was the zenith of both the practice and theory based on the PI model, then the 1930s provided a severe test of these theories and practices. The national government expanded both the variety and level of services offered. The application of scientific management to large-scale government organizations with broad social mandates quickly illuminated theoretical and practical shortcomings. One apparent shortcoming was an inability to handle the political context of public management. Another weakness was the lack of sensitivity to research findings from human relations research. Incorporation would await further experience with and discussion about management of the modem state. Even then, the models of politico-administrative systems did not easily facilitate the melding of politics, administration, and management.

VIII. THE 1930s: THE RISE OF THE ADMINISTRATIVE STATE

By the 1930s, the identification of public administration in terms of scientific management principles was well established. The work of the Social Science Research Council, the Public Administration Clearing House, and the Advisory Committee on Public Administration formed the core of public administration. With funding support from several Rockefeller philanthropies, who insisted their support be seen as nonpolitical, this core group of administrators blended governmental research and scientific management with a distinctly technical and local governmental orientation. This, according to Roberts (1994), provided great reinforcement for the politics–administration dichotomy during the rise of academic public administration programs.

Although identified by pragmatic governmental concerns, the advocates for training for public service were mostly academics. They were committed to the progressive vision of an administrative government capable of resolving societal problems (Mosher 1937). As the depression deepened, people like Luther Gulick, Frederick Cleaveland, William Mosher, and William Willoughby readjusted their focus from the municipal to the national level, applying scientific management principles to the growing public role undertaken by the Roosevelt administration. Leonard D. White had earlier called for a unity for public administration, based on scientific management, and aimed at coping with social change through administrative processes (Merriam 1937; White 1926). Moreover, these academics were not naive about practicing the political arts and often helped transform the practice by "besting" politicos (Gaus 1931, 1947).

An example of these principles in practice was the Tennessee Valley Authority (TVA). Created in 1933, it utilized professional management and appointed administrators to attempt the social and economic transformation of a region (Clapp 1955; Lilienthal 1944; Schlesinger 1958). Ironically the TVA was later depicted as preeminently political in one of the first studies of public organizations (Selznick 1949). Looking back, most see the TVA as a step forward in professional public management but seem to ignore its commitment to developing a more inclusive community.

Governmental management from this perspective sought to limit, if not preclude, political influences in solving public problems. The writings of John Pfiffner (1935) Fritz Morstein-Marx (1940), and Harvey Walker (1937) exemplified this anti-political philosophy centered on solving political problems with administrative techniques. Gulick and Urwick's *Papers on the Science of Administration* and The President's Commission on Administrative Management, the Brownlow Commission Report, both published in 1937, became the high points of the public interest orthodoxy in public administration theory (Gulick and Urwick 1937; Sayre 1958). Later critics claimed this weakened individual choice and democratic responsibility as people could neither register preferences nor meaningfully participate (Denhardt 1981; Schick 1975; Stivers 1990).

Although several early university programs, such as the ones at the University of Cincinnati and the University of Michigan, ceased to exist, the decade of the 1930s saw a continuation of the study of public administration within university-based programs. Soon after its creation in 1926, the Public Administration Clearing House (PACH) became a most effective research center for collecting and sharing public sector research and expertise on a nationwide basis (Stillman 1982). Political scientists, however, found it increasingly difficult to accept a separate training role for public administration. They were establishing an academic discipline. At a conference sponsored by the PACH in 1935 at Princeton, public administration was perceived as needing a university-wide approach. Students could then gain "an appreciation of the responsibilities of public officers, their environment, relationships among agencies, and the political, financial, and legal foundations of public offices" (Caldwell 1965, 57). In contrast to Beard's earlier call for practical training for public service, political science now altered its normative focus. Beginning in the late 1930s, it took an increasingly pluralistic approach to governmental studies (Gaus et al. 1936; Herring 1936). Building on the ROF model of governance, though often unconcerned with governance per se, political scientists began to question the role of a "professionalized" public administration.

Ironically, however, the national government's social and economic responsibilities accelerated the demand for a more professionalized public service. The demand for a proactive public service required human relations and broad administrative and managerial skills (Egger 1975). In 1934, the US Civil Service Commission scheduled examinations for "professional positions" that provided career opportunities for college graduates in administration (Van Riper 1958). A series of treatises published in 1937 by the American Academy of Political and Social Sciences on "Improved Personnel in Government Service" underscored the need for a professional identity for public personnel and management (Dimock 1937; Gulick 1933, 1935).

By late in the decade, the unplanned explosion of the executive branch resulted in an institutional and managerial crisis (Egger 1975). Some called for legal and judicial controls on the expanding administrative process, ultimately leading to the passing of an Administrative Procedures Act in the following decade. Others focused on the managerial role of the president. The President's Committee on Administrative Management (Brownlow Commission) extensively analyzed it. Their conclusions in 1937 emphasized the critical role of scientific study for governmental administration. The Commission recommended replacing uninformed judgment and political expediency in the planning and managing of public agencies in the new era (President's Commission on Administrative Management 1937). They called for executive empowerment, suggesting a leadership style aware of, yet independent from, overt, pluralistic pressures (Karl 1963; Polenberg 1966). This reform recalled the ROF model by expressing a concern for the role of experts, but only as staff to an elected executive.

At the same time, Chester Barnard's seminal work on executive roles provided a bridge between public administration and a more generic approach to management (Barnard 1938). It was the first conceptual piece to note the importance of the social side of management and to integrate it into the fabric of organizational administration. Management processes and activities, such as leadership and decision making, were seen as functional linkages between traditional scientific and more recent behavioral approaches. The organizational setting of modern management was perceived as both task and social system (Golembiewski 1977; Selznick 1949).

By 1939, seeing that academic trends in political science would not provide a suitable foundation for the growth and development of public administration, leaders of academic programs, training institutes, and professional associations met to establish national organization for improving the relationships between the academic and practitioner segments of the field. The resultant American Society for Public Administration (ASPA) sought not only to address the lack of identity for public administration, academically and professionally, but also to develop a body of knowledge for the analysis, evaluation, and improvement of public sector management. Embracing both practitioners and academics, the ASPA provided for more effective applied research and increased communication about public administration issues.[*] Its publication, the *Public Administration Review*, provided a national forum for the exchange of ideas and research findings and an academically and professionally recognized voice to support and promote its goals and objectives (Martin 1952; Mosher 1975; Stone 1975). An organization separate from political science, yet inclusive of political scientists, ASPA provided a supportive environment for political scientists, other academics, and field professionals interested in the academic development and training of public managers.

IX. THE 1940s: REFLECTION ON THE ADMINISTRATIVE STATE

The decade of the 1940s saw public administration groping for an identity and significance apart from both the orthodoxy of the principles school and the increasingly pluralistic emphasis of political science. Early in the decade the application of scientific management principles, specifically, and the PI model, generally, to the public sector fell under increased questioning (Stene 1940). Many called for more information and data on the state of public administration education and its ability to address the needs of public sector management. Active collaboration between academics and public officials were advocated through innovative educational and training programs (Graham 1941). There was an explicit recognition of the role of democratic values in public management as well as an interest in how public management practices might be reconciled with those values (Appleby 1945; Beard 1941; Gaus 1955; Levitan 1943; Wengert 1942).

World War II accelerated several trends begun during the depression. One trend was the broad laboratory exposure of a large number of academics to actual government work in public agencies. This introduction to the realities of line management rather than staff responsibilities led to significant changes in the perception of public administration. Greater involvement with the natural science community was evident, starting with the Manhattan Project and its success in building nuclear weapons; the national government utilized natural scientists in university laboratories, especially in the area of national defense. These continued to grow in an era of cold war, as did the governmental use of the products of science (Price 1965). The expansion of government investment in social science research and its application during the 1960s and beyond would find a somewhat different reception given the emerging debate over the efficacy of science for dealing with social issues and the perceived different cultures of science and government (Snow 1959, 1961).

By the late 1940s, several shifts occurred in the basic orientation of the field. These emphasized (1) a shift from administrative specialties to line operations aimed at achieving public purposes; (2) a shift from the chief executive and auxiliary and control agencies to activities at the departmental or bureau level; (3) a shift from general, abstract principles to the varying contexts of individual departments and programs; and (4) a lessening of concern for efficiency and economy and more concern about the links between democratic values and administrative processes (Fesler 1975). Appleby (1945) formulated a new approach to leadership, building upon the traditional management norms, but recognizing their roles and limitations in the politico-administrative system. These reformulations reflected greater participation in an enlarged, intellectually driven national government.

An acceptance, albeit implicit, of the inevitability of big government prevailed. Not all, however, were pleased with this trend. Perhaps anticipating later difficulties, some questioned the excesses of governmental authority that they believed threatened democratic and individualistic

---

[*] Note the preposition is "for" not "of." Its use indicates an intention to emphasize the relations of the study to the practice as well as a more avocational stance toward the promotion of professional goals.

values. Their concern centered on the consequences of social and economic control in the hands of technically trained professionals (Hayek 1944; Von Mises 1944).

Such a view did not predominate, however. University research centers were again becoming active and their scientific and technological findings found application in the public sector. Stillman (1982) suggests that the arrival of the "professional state" (Mosher 1968) heralded a shift in thinking in public administration from a concern about the practical problems of government to a more detached, analytical, and process-oriented approach. Public and business management were seen as distinct concerns involving varying expectations about public agency ends and, therefore, not amenable to the same administrative practices or evaluations (Appleby 1945, 1949; Dimock 1945). The old politics–administration dichotomy was now inappropriate; public administration was increasingly viewed as a combination of individual and group behavior based on the interaction of social, economic, and political influences on policy and management decisions (Schick 1975). Case studies were gaining favor as an approach for analyzing administrative behavior within this new awareness (Stein 1952).

During the 1940s, serious discussion arose over the applicability of a science of administration. The critique was exemplified by Robert Dahl's suggestion that a science of administration was questionable, especially if based on a mechanistic assumption about behavior. According to Dahl (1947), universal laws of a science of administration existed primarily in textbooks of public administration.

Herbert Simon argued further that the so-called principles of administration were nothing more than proverbs and, as such, provided little scientific basis for public administration. A logical positivist, Simon suggested an intensified effort to identify empirically based principles. The determination of such principles required a separation of fact and values (Simon 1946, 1947), a logical separation that produced echoes similar to those regarding the politics–administration dichotomy.

Dwight Waldo (1948) took a somewhat different approach. He reviewed the roots and developments of public administration within the framework of western and democratic values. In *The Administrative State*, Waldo demonstrated that there were fundamental flaws in the classical orthodoxy of public administration and suggested that significant problems arose from the application of those "principles" to public sector situations. He argued that there was little basis for a primacy of administration over the political process and urged a recognition of public administration within the context of a democratic governmental process.

With the demise of the classical orthodoxy in the 1940s came an increased awareness of the broader perspectives of the field. Interdisciplinary approaches gained importance. For example, the influence of sociological and psychological research on public administration was strengthened by the translation of the works of Max Weber (Gerth and Mills 1946). The relationships among organizational structure, authority, and individual behavior in large-scale, complex governmental organizations became evident. Unfortunately, Weber was read prescriptively, not descriptively. His research design and intent were lost in his conclusions about the efficacy of bureaucracy. These developments reinforced prescriptions for formal, inflexible governmental structures at the same time that the new field of organization theory was first applied to public administration (Blau 1956; Merton 1957; Selznick 1949, 1957). Later, organizational theorists would question the notion of a universal formal model and concentrate on specific contingencies (Koontz 1980; Scott 1961; Thompson 1967).

This decade saw the end of a tumultuous debate about regulation of the administrative process that had begun in the flurry of administrative action in the Roosevelt New Deal. The debate included a presidential veto of the first proposed Administrative Procedures Act in 1938 and ended, in essence, with a codification of the minority dissent to the recommendations of the Attorney General's Committee on Administrative Procedure (1941). Later, in 1946, Congress passed the Administrative Procedures Act by an overwhelming margin, thereby clarifying congressional–executive relationships and suggesting that the administrative process reflected an intermingling of political and administrative processes (Rosenbloom 1993a).

Federal and state judicial interpretations of the acts, however, often dulled some of their cutting edges. Amendments on items such as public access to official documents illustrated the inherent limitations of judicial control over the practicalities of administration (Schwartz and Wade 1972; Shapiro 1968; Warren 1982). A greater partnership between the courts and agencies (Cooper 1985; Melnick 1985), if not a "juridical" polity (Lowi 1979), was hoped for as the courts began to exert influence on many policy areas.

At the end of the decade, in 1949, the first Hoover Commission filed its final report. Officially called The Commission on the Organization of the Executive Branch, its ostensible purpose was to reduce the number of agencies. In the end, however, the report called for increased professional management and greater executive control over administration. Many of its recommendations were eventually adopted (Arnold 1976).

Many of the developments in this decade raised questions about the central unifying theme of public administration—the PI model—that had endured for nearly 40 years. No satisfactory replacement was offered, however, especially not one that could incorporate empirical analyses with the realities of administrative practice. More significantly, the demise of the old orthodoxy left the field without a normative base just as it encountered the first determined opposition to the enlarged functions of the administrative state.

X. THE 1950s: THE BEGINNINGS OF SELF-AWARENESS

The discrediting of the principles approach during the 1940s created a vacuum. Major effects to reshape the field arose during the 1950s. A central theme for these efforts was the recognition of the interdependence between political values and the administrative process (Caro 1974; Martin 1952; Sayre 1958; Waldo 1952; Waldo 1955; Waldo 1956; Willbern 1957). Some attempted to return to the earlier models of COF and ROF. The scope of public administration was enlarged, but little coherence for consolidating the study or the practice of public administration emerged (Landau 1962; Mosher 1956).

University research in public administration and policy increased as the academic community became more active in shaping and defining the field. The intellectual grounds existed for a rapprochement between political science and public administration, especially because the impact of political values and special interests (factions) on governmental administration was now widely acknowledged. Such did not occur. As public administration moved toward a more interdisciplinary and open-ended identity, political science became enamored of pluralism and behavioralism. Neither of these themes provided a suitable base for the nurturing of public administration with its institutional and professional concerns. Political science completed the normative shift begun in the 1930s; public administration lost its image as a "lusty young giant" (Landau 1962) and seemed awash in the non-training, pluralistic mode now dominating political science.

Pluralism, for example, left no normative role to public administration. It was only one of many governmental processes subject to the influence of political factions (Dahl and Lindblom 1953; Truman 1951). Like the legislative and executive processes, the administrative process was simply another pressure point for political influences seeking to serve their own particular interests. In essence, public management in the administrative state was added to the rule of interests *dramatae personis*. A public administration concerned about the ways in which policy was implemented or how public policy might reflect a public interest that went beyond the rule of factions seemed out of place (Fesler 1975).

Behavioralism further isolated public administration from the mainstream of political science. Building, in part, upon Simon's call for increased efforts to use scientific inquiry based on a particular philosophy of science, the behavioralists severely circumscribed roles for political science. They focused their research on inputs, aggregates, voting behavior, and other quantifiable facts rather than on the somewhat less empirically ascertainable behavior of individuals and institutions responsible for public policy. Behavioralism became the new orthodoxy for political science. Public administration, with its nonscientific concern with institutional dynamics and management training, was not political science.

Public administration, without its former principles, seemed increasingly unable or unwilling to construct a viable alternative to the behavioralists. It lacked both a sense of self-awareness and an intellectual substance (Martin 1952; Siffin 1956). A science of public administration became an endangered species in a discipline that would, later in the 1960s, virtually deny its existence (Landau 1962; Waldo 1968).

Nevertheless because most public administration programs were located within political science departments, the development of a self-aware, interdisciplinary public administration sensitive to political and societal values depended on frameworks developed within political science. Textbooks written during this period, principally by political scientists, began to include materials reflecting pluralistic and behavioral influences (Pfiffner and Presthus 1953; Simon et al. 1950). Early roots of a public policy focus were developed as attention was directed toward the politics of the policy-making process and the implementation of specific public programs. The mechanistic for was de-emphasized and the impact of values on public administration was highlighted (Golembiewski 1977). The increased use of the case study approach typified efforts to identify and explore specific administrative activities. The work of Lasswell suggested an interdisciplinary policy science focused on the concept of a policy system transcending both political science and public administration and thereby illustrated the emphasis on the policy process (Dror 1967, 1971; Lerner and Lasswell 1951).

The absence of a central dominant theme enabled public administration during the 1950s to absorb ideas and influences from a variety of sources. Modern public administration became concerned with any and all fields of knowledge appropriate to the functioning of individuals and organizations vested with a public purpose (Dimock 1958; Stover 1958). The more broadly written and methodologically sound research of sociologists like Merton (1957) and Selznick (1957) provided insights into large formal organizations characteristic of the administrative state. Moreover, the socio-psychological approach to face-to-face relationships and an appreciation of the informal organization increased the relevance of the human dimension in the study of public organizations. For the moment, at least, this dampened concerns about converting business and industrial models into public sector applications and permitted acceptance of much of the proliferating research pertinent to the study of contemporary organizations (Argyris 1957; Golembiewski 1962; Katz and Khan 1966; Likert 1961; March and Simon 1958; McGregor 1960).

When Herbert Simon (1946, 1947) identified the "decision" as the central event in administration, an interdisciplinary and generic focus for explaining organizational behavior was suggested. The location of some public administration programs in generic schools of management may reflect the impact of this approach (Caldwell 1965; Schick 1975). Although Dahl's criticism of Simon's "decisionmaking schema" questioned its suitability to public organizations and their decision-making processes, it still became a major consideration for the field (Dahl 1947).

A contrasting, though certainly compatible, rationale for public sector decision making was presented by Lindblom (1959). He identified the public decision maker as one who made decisions conditioned by a practical and "achieveable" rationality (Lindblom 1959). In their own ways, both Simon and Lindblom depicted a process with a multiplicity of decision points, high degrees of fragmentation, and bounded rationality (Caiden 1991). In essence, administrative decision-makers sought to reconcile values of social harmony, stability, and unity within a fluid, unstable environment of competing political interests (Stillman 1982); in Lindblom's famous phrase, they "muddled through."

By the end of the 1950s public administration remained troubled by its lack of identity and focus, yet poised to clarify and renew its self-awareness. Pluralism and behavioralism created both opportunities and problems. Demands for systematic, empirical analyses of organizational behavior within highly pluralistic settings energized an active research agenda. The findings emphasized variability and adaptability in public organizations. But when questions about actual administrative problems arose, the temptation to fall back on simpler prescriptive remedies remained strong (Divine 1955).

As the number of governmental functions expanded, demands for cooperation and integration grew. The need for competent professional public managers spurred an increase in the number of courses and programs offered in public administration (Somit 1956). Those providing academic and professional training became more self-conscious about the field. There was a greater sharing of information between university-based programs and public sector practitioners (Mosher 1956).

Yet concerns about the size and scope of government remained. The second Hoover Commission, created in 1953, called for the elimination of many government services, especially those it saw competing with the private sector (Mansfield 1969). In contrast to the experience of the first Hoover Commission, few of the recommendations of the second were ever accepted.

With the publication of the *Administrative Science Quarterly* in 1955, research on organizations and their behaviors became readily available. The research emphasized the interactions of organizations and their environments. Public administration seemed ready to end its culture-bound perspective. The interdependencies and linkages between economic development and comparative politico-administrative systems were gaining recognition (Etzioni 1961; Lawson 1959; Riggs 1956; Siffin 1957).

XI. THE 1960s: BEYOND POLITICAL SCIENCE

Entering the 1960s, many thought that policy analysis could guide selection among program alternatives. Others believed that a maturing scientific and technological base opened the door for a public administration that could be both rational and pluralistic (Campbell 1972). Similarly the application of operations research and systems analysis to public problems (Quade 1975) opened new managerial insights and applications.

Unfortunately these hopes were limited by the realities of the political process (Lindblom 1965; Schattschneider 1960; Schlesinger 1967; Waldo 1961). The largely incremental legislative decision-making processes, for example, limited the use of planning–programming–budgeting (PPBS) at the national level (Botner 1970; Schick 1966, 1973) as it did later efforts to apply rational financial decision making through zero-base budgeting in the 1970s. Nonetheless, benefits for administration came through the greater participation of program managers in a more decentralized process (Moore 1980; Draper and Pitsvada 1981).

President John F. Kennedy's pledge that the United States would go to the moon in the 1960s was fulfilled by the National Aeronautics and Space Administration (NASA). When fulfilled, this boost to the national psyche did more than catch up with the Soviets. NASA's focus on project management, the organization of the task system around jobs rather than a hierarchy, moved public management toward increased flexibility (Cleland 1983; Martin 1976). Theoretically, organizing around projects mixed people based on skills and remixed them upon completion of the project. Most fully conceptualized as matrix management or matrix organization (Davis and Lawrence 1977), the lessons from NASA have seldom been applied generally to the movement for public–private partnership, even though NASA and private contractors were intertwined in its project matrix. Conceptually, project management was an updating of organizational principles based on the premises of the PI model.

The increased acceptance of science and technology fostered a relationship between public administration and the use of that technology to assist in cross-national development. The comparative and development administration movements of the late 1950s grew out of the effort to provide technical assistance to developing nations. Young behavioralists in political science, under the direction of change-oriented academics, formed the Comparative Administration Group (CAG) as part of ASPA in 1970 (Jones 1976; Savage 1976). CAG spearheaded the publication of the

Journal of Comparative Administration and promoted a cross-disciplinary approach to the analysis of govern mental bureaucracies (Riggs 1964; Heady 1996).

Largely theoretical in its emphasis, the CAG faltered in the aftermath of the doubt and pessimism that arose later in the decade and existed throughout most of the 1970s (Heady 1979; Waldo 1976). Vietnam, increasing uncertainty about the environment, perceived failures in the Great Society programs, Watergate, and a general antipathy about the efficacy of science and technology, as well as the government's ability to apply it effectively, removed much of the basis for its promise (Waldo 1971; Waldo 1984). Although comparative administration remained on the agenda of public administration into the 1970s, the focus became more middle range and institutional (Jreisat 1975). The change in the name of the *Journal of Comparative Administration* to *Administration and Society* in 1972 was indicative of the declining interest in the area. The general turmoil of the decade, from civil rights demonstrations to anti-war activities, affected general Public Administration as well. The responses to these events upfolded in the 1970s and later as a new generation entered the academy and the practice. The era was indeed a discontinuity from the past (Drucker 1969).

Others based in political science built upon a policy process approach to public administration and sought to bring about a merging of the systems approach (Churchman 1968; Kast and Rosenzweig 1970; Schoderbek 1971) with science and technology (Denny 1967). The application of operations research and the desire to quantify research on administrative behavior are specific examples (Campbell 1972). Some, like Dror (1967, 1968), took exception to the domination of policy analysis by economic decision theory and behavioralism. He suggested that the use of such techniques be tempered by the inclusion of qualitative factors and their impacts on public policy processes. At the same time, Downs' application of economic principles to bureaucratic structures and behaviors suggested a relationship between economic norms and individual value choices (Downs 1957). He later illustrated the relation of bureaucratic policies and practices to individual norms and attitudes (Downs 1967). Building on the view that public administration was part of a generic approach to organization and management, others noted that individual values and roles were significant factor in determining organizational behavior (Bennis 1966; Likert 1961; Prethus 1965).

Although the number of schools and colleges of administration peaked in the 1960s (Caldwell 1965; Schick 1975), efforts to clarify the identity of public administration led a new generation of academicians to articulate an approach reflecting previous developments, while seeking independence from both political science and the administrative management school (Frederickson 1976). Like their counterparts in the CAG (Najjar 1974), they were frustrated with the apparent intellectual estrangement of public administration within political science and the lack of attention to values in the administrative management approach (Marini 1971). At a conference called by Dwight Waldo at Minnowbrook, they argued for a separate identity for public administration based on relevance, participation, change, values, and social equity. Their new public administration (NPA) was policy centered, projecting a normative, proactive role for public managers (Barton 1980; Ramos 1972; Richter 1970). Drastic changes in the established procedures and outcomes of public policy were advocated (Frederickson 1974; Schick 1975). The NPA challenged public administration's commitment to professionalism, credentialing, hierarchy, and value neutral management. Their normative commitment to democratic values promoted client control, decentralization, and value consensus (Bennis 1965, 1969; Campbell 1972). The prescriptive thrust of Minnowbrook expressed some of the themes that later reemerged in the electoral trends of the mid-1990s and subsequent efforts to redirect the focus of public administration (cf., Drucker 1954, 1959).

Indicative of a reawakening of public administration to a rapidly changing and politically volatile society, the values promoted by the NPA were difficult to translate into the practice of public administration. However, increasing numbers began to voice concern about the relevancy of professional education and training to the needs and aspirations of organizational members, clients, and even society. Later generations would raise similar concerns and issue a call for reinventing government.

As early as 1959, public administration education leaders demonstrated their concern for the nature and quality of professional public service education by organizing the Council on Graduate Education for Public Administration (CGEPA). The CGEPA authorized an omnibus report on the status of education for public service. Completed in 1967, the Honey Report documented the inadequacy of public service education, especially in a time of increased opportunities and demands for public service professionals (Honey 1967). The report offered numerous suggestions and identified a need for remedying many problems. It also emphasized developing a coherence and identity for public administration, both as a discipline and as a focus for professional development. Honey reiterated and expanded the call for change in public service education along the lines suggested earlier by Dwight Waldo (1965).

The debate and dialogue over educational programs for public service rekindled interest in the development of an identity for public administration (Miles 1967). The hope was for a broad reconciliation among the many interests of the field. Academic program content, the creation of a disciplinary focus, and effective career development were prioritized. Forums for the discussion of the "scope, objectives, and methods" of public administration were held (Charlesworth 1968). Political science came under increasing attack as an unsuitable "homebase" for public administration (Hinderaker 1963; Charlesworth 1966, 1968). Waldo, among others, made the point clearly by suggesting that public administration needed to identify its central core and to recognize that its future lay in the development of a "professional" stance, broad and flexible enough to encompass the diversity of interests found in public administration, yet firm and understandable enough to provide unity and a sense of purpose and direction (Waldo 1968).

At this early juncture, however, efforts to clarify public administration's identity were limited. Most public administration programs were still located in political science departments. Many lacked the needed enthusiasm for supporting visible, high-quality professional programs. Also, the traditional political science base for public administration was eroding under the expanded roles played by other academic disciplines within public administration (Waldo 1975). The results left an increasingly eclectic public administration in search of new footings. Waldo's call for public administration to "act like it was a profession" even though it might not really be one was insufficient in this regard. Critics underscored the lack of the trappings of a profession, such as codes of conduct, the ability to control membership entry, and the absence of a recognized body of research and writing specifically related to professional concerns (Schick 1975; Schott 1976). Later studies attacked what they termed "sociological" definitions of profession. Using a more traditional notion of profession, they urged public administration to become truly professional (Green et al. 1993).

By the end of the decade, however, there were several unmistakable trends. The need for and interest in providing an identity for public administration and understanding better its roles and substance was generally accepted. The neutral competent, value-free emphasis of public administration as conceptualized in the PI model was functionally reinterpreted. The debate over values in public administration was now focused on their nature and direction rather than on whether or not values properly had a place in the field (Gawthrop 1970; Hart and Scott 1971; Redford 1969). Some perceived the development of public administration as a craft more so than either an art or a science (Campbell 1972; Berkeley 1975). Lastly, questions of identity were not answered solely on the basis of particular disciplinary characteristics, but also on the basis of program content and professional responsibilities.

XII. THE 1970s: IDENTITY REVISITED, NEW CURRENTS AND CURRICULUM

Society and government during the 1970s reflected ambivalence about the future. Differences over civil rights, Vietnam, Watergate, and the energy crisis questioned previously held assumptions about the relationship between individuals and governments, intergovernmental responsibilities, and international relations. Public administration would bear the blame for many perceived governmental weaknesses, while being expected to herald positive changes in administrative patterns (Waldo 1972).

Both academics and practitioners felt increased stress and pressure. The need for a merging of the scientific and the political became more explicit. For the practitioner, critical issues included public productivity during a time of decreasing resource availability, the need for reorganizing administrative structures and delivery systems, greater attention to the needs and interests of clients, and the relevance of policy outputs to societal needs (Campbell 1972; Etzioni 1967). Pressures grew for diversity in the practice of public administration as well as for the development of a more visible and consensual academic view of the field.

Suggestions for change ranged from those proposing new central theories to replace the old "orthodoxy" (Landau 1972; Ostrom 1974) to those urging a multi-disciplinary, pluralistic focus (Waldo 1975; Frederickson 1976). Others called for a concern with social equity and justice, often based on Rawls' (1971) work. Contradictory views were common (O'Toole 1977). Those supporting the interests of the NPA movement proposed to discredit the value-free rational bureaucratic approach and urged the opening of the study and practice of public administration to humanistic and democratic influences (Crozier 1964; LaPorte 1971; Levine et al. 1975; Price 1975; Savage 1976; Wilson 1975). Others resisted such efforts, claiming that the rule of law should not be replaced by a system of administration based on the rule of men (Thompson 1975). Bureaucracy's death was forecast by some (Denhardt 1981), while others predicted it a more positive outcome (Miewald 1970). Professional managers and other leaders in public affairs indicated some acceptance of the NPA agenda as they saw a need to shift priorities. They recognized the worth of the individual, the need for public service to become more sympathetic and responsive to heterogeneous political and social desires (Berkeley 1971), and the need for increased attention to professional career development programs to handle technological change and innovation (Chapman and Cleaveland 1973). A major career development program was the Federal Executive Institute (FEI) and its sister agencies, the East and West Management Development Centers (Buchanan 1973). FEI helped to spawn similar efforts in many states.

Out of the civil rights movement of the 1960s came new criticisms of the PI model and its merit system. Equal employment opportunity and affirmative action initiatives sought to eliminate discriminatory practices and enhance opportunities for the disadvantaged by opening up the recruitment and advancement processes to more minorities and women (Nigro 1974). Although the initiatives were based more on legal mandates than on calls for popular sovereignty or individual values, supporters of the PI model questioned the long-term consequences of such changes. Others, in contrast, stressed the compatibility of a merit system and equal employment opportunity (Kranz 1974; Reeves 1970).

In the early 1970s, Vincent Ostrom called for a shift in focus from bureaucracy and the Wilsonian model (that he argued was biased in favor of a strong, centralized executive system) to a decentralized, dispersed service delivery system somewhat akin to the COF or ROF models (Ostrom 1974). He envisioned public administration as a responsive service delivery system, a multiplicity of democratic decision points as well as a dispersed system of administrative authority with overlapping jurisdictions and fragmented organizational patterns. By including the work of political economists in explaining public administrative behavior, Ostrom believed decisions about administrative policies should include concern about competition and alternative delivery systems (Ostrom and Ostrom 1971).

Along related lines, another effort to develop a central theory was concerned with agency outputs and the trade-offs between public and private goods. Questions about the boundaries between public and private were partially delineated through the use of economic concepts (Wamsley and Zald 1973a, 1973b; Caiden 1991). A variety of paradigms for the field appeared as the search for central theories continued (Ostrom 1974; Henry 1975; Golembiewski 1977). Though these seldom reached scientific maturity, they invigorated the search for an academically acceptable identity. One paradigm calling for a merger of pluralism and political economy was timely, though its feasibility was subject to question. Critics of Ostrom's thesis pointed out its apparent inability to explore and explain the complexities of the field (Ostrom 1977; Stillman 1976). Furthermore, its methodological approach was deemed simplistic and somewhat unrealistic in its assumptions about the outcomes of democratic administration (Golembiewski 1977). Moreover, what some termed "policy subsystems," a relatively small group of administrators, legislators, and lobbyists who controlled basic public policies (Freeman 1952; Kingdon 1984; Seidman 1970; Walker 1974) seemed to be legitimated by Ostrom. Some researchers examined public administration in terms of networks of organizations. This perspective focused on how organizations of all types were connected to policy making and implementation (Keller 1984; Milward and Wamsley 1985).

During the 1970s, efforts increased to incorporate more systematic and applied research methods to solve governmental problems (Eddy and Saunders 1972). Knowledge management was promoted as a tool for providing a more responsive and responsible public management (Bowman 1978; Henry 1974). Public productivity (Balk 1978) and the development of theoretical and practical approaches for dealing with a public sector facing declining resources and stable, if not increasing, service demands became agenda items (Levine 1978). Policy analysis was touted as a way to sort out priorities, avoiding the "muddling through" that Lindblom trumpeted (Beckman 1977). Once again private sector management techniques were deemed desirable and applicable for public sector use. To improve the quality of work-life while also increasing employee and agency productivity, organization development was identified and promoted (Golembisewki 1978, 1980; Golembiewski and Eddy 1978; McGill 1974).

The federal government expanded its role in shaping state and local policies during this decade. Many federal grant programs required the use of a merit system. Also, the federal government called for coordination of grants and policies at the regional level. They required a regional body, a Council of Governments, to review grants in many areas. In some cases, these bodies assumed considerable authority over time, such as the Greater Minneapolis COG. Most became heavily involved with transportation and environmental policies, helping to prioritize projects among local governments.

As pressures mounted for a more representative public service, so did calls for a review and reform of the leadership and accountability aspects of the merit system. Presidential frustrations with a career service seemingly immune to executive leadership, an enlarged manpower pool, and the need to enhance the image and responsibilities of the professional career service prompted President Carter's initiatives for merit system reform. On the advice of leaders in public service education and practice, President Carter applied contemporary management techniques to federal management. The roles of executive leadership and responsibility were strengthened (Beam 1978; Campbell 1978). At the onset of the reforms, few perceived conflicts between expanded executive control of the public service and continued professionalization at the highest levels.

By virtue of the Civil Service Reform Act of 1978, public service professionals were less constrained by a process-oriented personnel system. Merit-based pay provisions and a Senior Executive Service emphasizing productivity and flexibility were mandated. The hope was to reverse the "triumph of technique over purpose" lamented by Sayre (1948) in his examination of personnel administration. Following the 1980 election, the Reagan administration, sensing a mandate for less government, used the provisions of the reform mandate for the selection of political appointees who pushed for limited, if not scaled down, government programs and a diminished influence of professional managers in policy making (Carroll et al. 1985). Once again, the ROF model seemed to gain new life.

The efforts by the Reagan administration provided a fertile environment for those public administrationists and public interest adherents who questioned the reforms. Their fears that political values might again become the criteria for decisions in public personnel management (Thayer 1978) seemed to be supported. Even those in the public service were somewhat reserved in their support of the reforms. Not surprisingly, public support for reform seemed to be greater than that found among professional public employees (Lynn and Vaden 1979).

While the applied side of public administration struggled with changes in expectations during the 1970s, efforts to move forward with an agenda for public service education flowered. The NASPAA succeeded CGEPA in 1970. Working with the insights of the Honey Report and considering other studies identifying the future needs for public service (Chapman and Cleaveland 1973), NASPAA set about to create an educational and professional base for the development of public sector managers. NASPAA focused on building an identity based on a consensus regarding educational curricula and programmatic characteristics. The consensus would provide coherence in the field and empower organizational authority for a professional approach to public administration education and training (Uveges 1987). NASPAA's development and support of curriculum components representative of the cross-disciplinary character of the field was generally welcomed by those providing professional education for public service. NASPAA's "Guidelines and Standards for Master's Degree Programs" were broad and flexible, providing identity as well as responsibility to public administration programs. They included major academic and professional features found in most programs (NASPAA 1974, 1976). The university's role in clarifying the nature of the field was strengthened, as was the special relationship between the Master of Public Administration (MPA) degree and professional career development for public service (Grode and Holzer 1975; for an earlier analysis, see Walker 1945).

Field identity and coherence were substantially reinforced during the 1970s by the introduction of new scholarly journals. Regional journals such as the *Midwest Review of Public Administration* and the *Southern Review of Public Administration* began. By the early 1980s, however, interest in public administration research had grown to the extent that these journals adopted new names more indicative of a larger audience: the *American Review of Public Administration* and the *Public Administration Quarterly*, respectively.

Amid the support for NASPAA's efforts, questions still remained. To bring conformity among MPA programs, NASPAA approved a process of voluntary peer review. Some concern was evidenced about the link between the peer review process and some possible future effort to enter into a formal accreditation process (Engelbert 1977; Thayer 1976). Additional cautionary issues included how the standards and NASPAA's role would impact the relationship between NASPAA and ASPA (Thayer 1976); whether or not the standards focused attention too heavily on techniques and pedagogy, foreclosing diversity and innovation (Howard 1975); and the issue of professionalism and its relationship to public administration curriculum (Schott 1976). On the whole, however, considerable support was generated for NASPAA's initiative and for realistic efforts to ascertain the parameters of the field. The need to measure quality profession-oriented education for the public service was increasingly acknowledged.

XIII. THE 1980s: CROSSCURRENTS AND A RETURN TO BASICS

Professionalism in governmental administration came under increased scrutiny during the 1980s. Although the initial skepticism was most evident at the national level, even state and local governments faced increasing pressure to make administrative policies more responsive and reflective of societal and political trends.

Early on, the Reagan administration initiated controls on the size and scope of the national government. The Grace Commission called for a distinctly businesslike approach to governmental management and a limitation on the degree to which professional public managers, as opposed to political executives, were exposed to direct political pressures (Goodsell 1984). Some saw this as requiring a more active and interchangeable role for the private sector in meeting public sector needs (Savas 1982). Boulding (1981) inferred that the future shape of both government and non-government could dramatically change through short-term incremental shifts that would evolve into new "niches." The outcome would create multiple opportunities for administrative diversity and provide a basis for the private sector to offer public services (Behn 1980; Ingraham and Barrilleuax 1983; Lewis and Logalbo 1980; Schacter 1983).

The effort to offer public services through nonpublic privatization gained the most momentum at the local level, especially in metropolitan areas. Central cities found it an attractive alternative in light of increasingly tight budgets and prospects of less federal aid. Their efforts often met with opposition from well-organized unionized employees often represented by very strong traditional groups such as the Fraternal Order of Police. Where such employee organizations were more limited, such as in suburban cities, privatization gained greater momentum. However, in most cases, the gains from privatization were minimal: in some cases, the public employees organized and made lower bids than private firms. Nevertheless, as a result of the bidding process, governments did realize some savings, as in Cleveland where public employees won a bid against outsiders, lowering the cost by $2 million (Janik 1995). In the 1990s the call for privatization directly fed a growing movement to reinvent government.

In the 1980s, state and local governments were called on to bear increased responsibility for their administrative policies. Bureaucracy was no longer, if it ever was, primarily a national phenomenon. Between 1950 and 1980, state and local bureaucracies went from 4 million to more than 13 million employees (Van Riper 1983). Much of this growth was financed by the national government. Now state and local governments were asked to assume greater responsibility for policies and financial support for public programs.

In addition, the continued growth of the national debt and demands for less national bureaucracy seriously curtailed national efforts to assist state and local efforts. To adjust for these changes, in 1989, Mississippi's governor, William F. Winter, was authorized to chair the National Commission on the State and Local Public Service (Winter Commission), aimed at recommending reforms in state and local administrative practices (see Winter 1993).

At a time when the need for increased formal training for managers was mandated (Newland 1979) and when decentralization and productivity were trumpeted as effective ways to resolve the problems of the 1980s (Gulick 1983), public administration faced new challenges. These challenges helped feed a growing interest in strategic planning for governmental administration. Originally conceived as establishing direction for a corporation, the planning perspective was vitally important for public administration.[*] This perspective helped sort out alternative policy directions and was applied in tandem with organizational development (Eadie and Steinbacher 1985; Olsen and Eadie 1982). Even states noted for the partisan nature of their politics, such as Ohio, implemented strategic planning on a broad scale. At the local level, it tended to be used selectively, aimed at priority items such as police services (Levine 1985). Strategic planning was often combined with innovative procedures, such as negotiation techniques, to ensure that those responsible for implementation buy into the process (Fisher and Ury 1981; Gargan and Moore 1984) with issues analysis (House of Representatives 1983).

The 1980s also reflected efforts to resolve problems of low esteem and professional identity for career public servants (Riggs 1983). Productivity and accountability measures were developed in ways to increase flexibility and effectiveness (Pfiffner 1983). Professionalism and ethics took on added importance (Bowman 1982; Frederickson 1993; Golembiewski 1983; Rabin 1981, 1985). Increased professionalism and ethics were seen as the key to a more knowledgeable and responsible career executive at the state level (Daley 1983; Mertins and

---

[*] Jim Paisley, who worked with the strategic Management Group at Deloitte, Haskins and Sells, used the phrase "direction establishment" to capture the purpose of strategic planning for the private sector. Given the fact that for public agencies the legislature and other external bodies often establish much of the direction for a public agency, it has been difficult to transfer the technology of strategic planning from the private to the public sector. However, the strategic perspective is useful to public administration, although it would seem to unnecessarily limit its potential by combining it with the budgetary process (Olsen and Eadie 1982).

Hennigan 1982). In 1984, ASPA approved a code of ethics that further narrowed the gap between the practice of public administration and its status as a profession. By 1985, public administration was seen to possess many of the trappings of a profession (Daniels and Johansen 1985). Later, a reconceptualization of professionalism would be formulated, one that better comports with the original meaning of profession and to a public sector profession of governance (Green et al. 1993).

Field identity and recognition continued high on the agenda of public administration academics. The availability of resource materials and literature in public administration was at an all-time high (Rouse 1982). NASPAA's peer review process gained general acceptance. By 1985, 81 master's degree programs had achieved roster status, with the impact of the process most important in curriculum content and program jurisdiction issues (Uveges 1987). NASPAA was recognized by the Council on Professional Accreditation in 1986 as the accreditation unit for master's degree programs in public administration.

Interestingly, just at the time when it seemed likely that the issues of field identity and professional responsibilities were on the way toward resolution, efforts by the Reagan administration to reshape the administrative state appear to have reignited an age-old controversy within the field: the politics–administration dichotomy. His vision of the American politico-administrative system did not have Bill Bureaucrat as an active policy player (see Appleby 1945). President Reagan saw the relationship between politics and administration (though as much rhetoric as program statement) as being based on the individual independence that Jefferson saw in "yeoman" and a private sector along the lines that the liberals in Europe supported (see Stillman 1982, in Uveges 1982).

While emphasizing the rights of individuals, the Reagan administration paradoxically pursued economic policies that threatened a classical, free enterprise system. The implicit vision was of a government that would serve only as the infrastructure for independent and sturdy Americans and their international corporations. There was little recognition that independent individuals and international economic organizations may have inherent conflicts. In essence, a limited role for the national government in social and economic affairs was the aim.

Professional (career) administrators' discretionary powers were more limited. Operationally, both Presidents Carter and Reagan attempted to reduce the presence of civil service appointees in policy making. They increased the number of appointments based on political (value consistent) rather than career (merit) bases. The movement was back toward a separation of political and administrative roles, with the policy questions answered by politically appointed officials. Carroll et al. (1985) called these new types of managers supply-side managers, and noted "[s]upply-side theorists in administration will almost certainly be disappointed, however, by their efforts to revive the politics-administration dichotomy." Others called for the revitalization of public service (National Commission on the Public Service 1989).

In like manner, Burke (1983) suggested that the realities of the politico-administrative system may not limit professional influences on public sector policy and management. However, a clarification of their roles and expectations within the politico-administrative system was required. Svara (1985) sees such clarification as better recognizing contemporary trends in the more sensitized political and professional roles of governmental managers.

The reemergence of the politics–administration dichotomy may have deeper roots. Though practitioners and theorists in the field recognized a need for change, calls for less activism on the part of public administrators and other experts may represent a basic shift away from the PI model. The Reagan–Bush administrations reflected a greater openness to the ROF model, although modified for the realities of the professionalization of American life. The demand for less expert-objective-dominated administration seemed to be a reaction to the degree to which professionalism increased organizational performance, while generating a psychological longing for more socially intimate contacts (Broder 1980; Naisbitt 1982; see Green et al. 1993). The demand for more "human centered" workplaces and more responsiveness to shifts in political values asserted the "values" of a democratically oriented public service (Frederickson and Hart 1985) where "benevolence" was related to "patriotism" as an appropriate method for serving a political community.

It is sobering to note that some research has found an irony in democratic administration by suggesting that the satisfaction of the workforce may be inversely related to the satisfaction of the clients (Katz 1975). More interesting, however, may be to note that as early as 1902, Jane Addams foresaw much of the behavioral and political consequences of a professionalized public administration as defined by the public interest model.

> ...The well-to-do men of the community think of politics as something off by itself; they may conscientiously recognize political duty as part of good citizenship, but political effort is not the expression of their moral or social life. As a result of this detachment, "reform movements", started by business men and the better element, are almost wholly occupied in the correction of political machinery and with a concern for the better method of administration, rather than with the ultimate purpose of securing the welfare of the people. They fix their attention so exclusively on methods that they fail to consider the final aims of ... government. This accounts for the growing tendency to put more and more responsibility upon executive officers and appointed commissions at the expense of curtailing the power of the direct representatives of the voters ... [T]hey speak and write of the purification of politics as of a thing set apart from daily life.
> On the other hand, the real leaders of the people are part of the entire life of the community they control, and so far as they are representative at all, are giving a social expression to democracy. They are often politically corrupt, but in spite of this they are proceeding upon a sounder theory [than the reformers]. [...] living near to the masses of voters, and knowing them intimately, [they] recognize this and act upon it; they minister directly to life and to social needs. They realize that the people as a whole are clamoring for social results, and they hold their power because they respond to that demand. They are corrupt and often do their work badly; but they at least avoid the mistake of a certain type of business men who are frightened by democracy, and have lost faith in the people. (Addams 1902:223-225)

The feelings of exclusion and lack of control by clients and citizens evidenced as the 1990s began could also account for the renewed legislative interest to review and change structures that under the PI model were considered the essence of administration (Yates 1982).

Some public administrationists perceived the problem and sought explanations and resolutions (Stever 1988). For example, the Public Administration Network was started toward the end of the decade as a counterrevolution to the dominance of behavioral methods in research. Some believed the detachment of public administration resulted in great part from how science was defined under behavioralism. They called for a redefinition of science and knowledge that could tie public administration to the community. This perspective echoed the concerns of the earlier Minnowbrook conferences that had criticized public administrators for refraining from correcting social problems (Bailey and Mayer 1992; Frederickson 1980; Marini 1971). The reaction to behavioralism was also based in part on the inability of research from that perspective to handle issues such as professionalism and the role of public administrators in the governance process (Adams and White 1994; for an early reaction to behavioralism in politics, see Dahl 1961).

Concerned with a dearth of normative theory in the discourse about governance, the network facilitated a 1987 conference at Lewis and Clark College, from which a set of papers was published looking at how to conceptualize public administrators (Kass and Catron 1990). The volume borrowed its methodology from Gareth Morgan (1986), who advocated a new methodology called *imaginization*. This methodology analyzed organizations in terms of the images created by different theories. For those writing papers for the conference, the roles and even the nature of public administration were developed in a series of images, such as the administrator as tortured soul (Harmon 1995). The conference demonstrated the utility of nonbehavioral methodology and the necessity of examining the origins and contexts of views of public administrators (Waugh 1992).

XIV. PUBLIC ADMINISTRATION IN THE 1990s: RESHAPING MANAGEMENT, SEARCHING FOR MACRO LEGITIMACY

The 1990s followed a decade of major transitions, especially in how the field was viewed by the public and many elected officials at all levels of government. Elected officials increasingly questioned the utility of dealing with professional administrators. This skepticism was especially new at the national level. Previously, presidents had often found utility in having the bureaucracy staffed by professionals, perhaps to avoid the adverse consequences of patronage best expressed by Lincoln. Lincoln sarcastically noted that patronage tended to produce one ingrate and ten enemies. In spite of the difficulty of filling high-level appointments, and of keeping incumbents for any period of time in such positions, presidents in the 1980s and 1990s resorted more and more to policy, if not patronage, appointments. (Of course, some agencies had earlier experienced such political utility, especially the General Services Administration and the Post Office. These agencies have offices in most congressional districts and are therefore most amenable to patronage opportunities.)

At the state and local levels, the animosity to professional public administrators was less new. In many cases professional appointments had never occurred or were relegated to clerical and other positions that had limited utility for patronage purposes. Sadly many in the public did not distinguish professional from nonprofessional administrators and had an all too ready propensity to lump all those who worked in government into the hated category of bureaucrat.

In light of these difficulties, the search for more secure foundations took several different forms. Some criticized the attitude of elected officials and the public, while others advocated changes in public administration based on the criticisms voiced by some elected officials, the media, and the public. As with most controversies in a modern extended republic, knowing who the public was and what their concerns were was difficult to discern. Further complicating these issues was the manner in which contemporary media reflected and influenced the agendas identified as being relevant for discussion. Nevertheless, the opposition to government was palpable and growing, with few in the media and the public apparently distinguishing professional from nonprofessional administration. Some opposed taxes per se, disregarding the purposes for which the taxes were raised and the economic and social policies a tax may involve (Steuerle 1992).

Two camps emerged in the reaction to the discipline and the profession. One concentrated on the governance roles of public administration, recalling older arguments and recasting new approaches to the administrative state. Rosenbloom argued that Congress and the Judiciary were helping to "retrofit" the administrative state to the Constitution (Rosenbloom 2000a, 2000b). Some critiques followed in the footsteps of Waldo, examining how managerialism promoted a perverse political philosophy. Stivers and King (1998), for example, opined about the stifling effects of professionalism qua expertise on an active citizenship. Such perspectives, however, were seldom informed by political history (Morgan 1988). Others warned about generally treating citizens as customers (Frederickson and Chandler 1984; Perlmutter and Cnaan 1995). Some of the critiques appeared to deviate from Waldo's general support of an active field, if not a governing profession (Adams and Balfour 1998, 2004; Farmer 1998).

The second camp followed in the footsteps of Herbert Simon. They called for a new public management, one that eschewed the exposed homilies of the traditional public management and implemented a science driven service delivery that was effective and efficient (Brudney et al. 2000; Dilulio et al. 1993) for a range of views, some of considerable vintage, on management and administration, but emphasizing the latter, see Stivers 2001). In the same general vein, many championed e-government, the offering of services over the Internet. Many in this camp prophesized that the harnessing of technology would achieve both robust management and convenient democracy (Garson 1999; Accenture 2001). For example, the 2004 website of a major consulting organization for e-government, Accenture, formerly the consulting partners of Arthur Andersen, touted:

From the United Kingdom to the United States, Belgium to Brazil and Malaysia to Mexico, governments are talking about the significant benefits that can be realized by migrating traditionally paper-based and face-to-face services to the Internet. Governments also understand these services must be customer focused, cost effective, easy to use and value-added for citizens, businesses and the governments themselves.

Those concerned with the administrative state and the governing function of public administration addressed several issues. For example, the politics–administration dichotomy that had reappeared in a new garb was reexamined critically. In his intriguing piece, Roberts (1994) traced the rise and persistence of the dichotomy to a strategy of the Rockefeller Foundation for funding government research. Fearing the backlash that would likely happen if the Rockefeller money was perceived as spent in a political fashion, the Foundation could support public administration if it were divorced from politics and empowered to deal with a broad range of public policy. The Foundation was highly supportive of people, such as Brownlow, who advocated the desirable dichotomy by empowering administrators in the making of policy.

For some, the doctrine was not a romantic relic of a distant past, but a highly useful guide to administrators in dealing with current issues and problems. Montjoy and Watson (1995) honed the concept by noting it had both policy and institutional implications. They found the doctrine useful in dealing with "particularisms," such as patronage, in local politics. Their reconceptionalization reinforced Svara's (1985) revision of the dichotomy, where he pointed out that the dichotomy was part of a larger division of functions. Svara perceived four functions (mission, policy, administration, and management) that were performed in an effective governmental system. He criticized how existing notions ignored the mission duties of government and the roles of public administrators in defining mission. The traditional myopic view of the dichotomy reduced the capacity of government to plan strategically and create policies reflecting visions of desirable futures. It also prompted elected officials to spend inappropriate time on management. Svara concluded that the four functions were shared in council-manager systems, contrary to the neat separation envisioned by the dichotomy. Thus, one reaction to the increasingly anti-professional politics was to interpret the past more carefully and create powerful, normative guides for professional administrators as well as clarify the historical record.

More fundamentally, the refounding movement that surfaced in the mid-1980s when a group of faculty at Virginia Tech issued their Blacksburg Manifesto took on additional importance (Wamsley 1985). The manifesto aggressively defended a policy role for public administrators. The book, *Refounding Public Administration*, when published early in the 1990s, built on earlier efforts such as John Rohr's award winning volume, *To Run a Constitution*. Rohr (1986) argued for constitutionally based policy roles for administrators by tracing the foundations for these roles to both the Federalist and anti-Federalist perspectives at the time of the founding of the republic (See also Cook 1992, a more realist view is Riggs 1994). Others saw peril in such roots because they were packaged with slavery and other undesirable values (Spicer and Terry 1993).

Refounding for these intrepid academics was a process, or dialogue, aimed at critically evaluating foundations and past practices. The focus was more on current norms and ethics than accurate portraits of past systems or a concern for improving managerial techniques. The politics–administration dichotomy was of minor interest and was perceived as having, at best, some utility for administrators if their policy roles were questioned. Gary Wamsley (1990), for example, argued for an agency perspective. For him, administrators were agents for a variety of principals. The tension produced by multiple principals both enlarged and confined the domain of administration. Since recent history indicates a primacy for presidential administrative dominance, a more effective administration would allow administrators to avoid control by only one principal. A more constitutionally based system, according to Wamsley, would remove administrators from domination by the presidency; however, it also exposes them to the problem of multiple principals, a not insignificant concern when the branches are controlled by different parties, and more importantly, different ideologies (Public Administration and the Constitution 1993). It also raises critical issues of ethics to which the field responded (Bowman 1991; Cooper 1994; Rohr 1976,1989).

Another contribution to the refounding literature was Terry's (1995) argument for redefining leadership. Terry uses Selnick's notion of institution as an organization endowed with values of the community, and his argument that leadership in administration should focus on turning organizations—instrumental entities—into institutions, or value-laden enterprises. He further asserts that a public leader should "conserve" those values central to his/her agency. Such a leadership concern does not rule out change; however, change is supported according to whether core values are furthered.

Furthermore, Goodsell's resounding defense of bureaucracy notes its functional aspects. Further building on his popular book, *The Case for Bureaucracy* (1994), he sees the bureaucracy as a desirable necessity insofar as it provides accountability for the actions of public servants. Bringing credibility back to government is seen more as a process of rediscovery than one of reinvention (Goodsell 1993; Moe 1994).

The citizen's place in defining public administration is identified when Cam Stivers (1996) incisively questions how citizens are viewed by our political and administrative theories. As she insightfully observes, most theories presume a quiescent citizen, contented to be led by those who hold key positions in government and left with no functions to perform other than the selection of some leaders who will be humbly served once they are installed. Similarly, she suggests, the field is burdened by underlying and only haltingly recognized problems with race and gender, particularly the latter (Gallas 1976; Guy 1993; Meyer-Emerick 2001; Naff 1994; Stivers 1993). Interestingly, affirmative action has seemed to create a more diversified federal service (Keller et al. 1994).

All in all, the refounding movement attempts to protect, if not enhance, the policy roles of public administration in the administrative state by more carefully conceptualizing these and creating appropriate norms based on the Constitution. In the process, key components of public administration have been reinterpreted (Terry 1995) and/or called into question (Lane and Wolf 1990; Luton 1994; Stivers 1994). In addition, some, in particular David Rosenbloom, recalled the importance of law to public administration (Cooper 1988). Rosenbloom interpreted the Administrative Procedures Act (APA), adopted overwhelmingly by Congress in 1946, as part of creating a "legislatively centered Public Administration" (Rosenbloom 2000b). This approach complemented calls for a more broadly rooted public administration, going beyond traditional administration centered on the chief executive. Interestingly, Rosenbloom (2000a) noted that the empowerment of the Office of President by public administrationists such as Brownlow was the result of erroneously perceiving public administration as universally applicable in any system and thus the president, charged with the executive function, should oversee administration at the national level. In essence, the perception of public administration as outside of politics mooted the issue of its constitutional position within the American system. Wamsley and Schoeder (1996) analyzed the "quagmire" of emergency policies and pointedly noted how modern media can further enhance the Presidency at the expense of constitutional and institutional design. In contrast to Behn's (1995) list of the three big questions of public management, John Kirlin (1996) emphasized the seven big questions of public administration in a democracy and Neumann (1996) emphasized more enduring quetions of the practice. Terry (1998) cautioned that the assumptions of the new public management could promote managerial behavior that conflicts with constitutional and democratic values. Both the calls for law and the design of governing systems emphasized the importance of structure to politics and administration (Elkin and Soltan 1996).

Unfortunately, the focus of much of the refounding effort has been almost entirely on the national level and does not note the very different conditions of state and local government (Winter 1969). In contrast to the highly philosophical and theoretical questioning of basic values and institutions of the refounding movement, the focus at the local level has proceeded mainly from a managerial perspective, the Simonian legacy, concentrating on improving service delivery and measuring if the improvements did in fact occur. Almost two years after the publication of the refounding volume, a former city manager and a consultant argued that public administration needed to be reinvented (Gaebler and Osborne 1992). They found administrative stagnation, along with a largely ineffective and inefficient delivery of public services. This unfortunate state of affairs, they suggested, derives from a refusal to reconsider the tenets of the field and to update these by liberating managers from the heavy hand of unexamined tradition. Unless we liberate, the authors argued, public services shall lag far behind what they could be and continue to foster negative feelings among citizens. The solution is to rethink how government is structured and empower the service provider, perhaps by having nongovernmental organizations offer the service or services (Bellone and Goerl 1992; Nathan 1995; Perlmutter and Cnaan 1995; Terry 1993). Others noted the need for, and improvements in, measuring the effects and assessing the success of local policies (Ammons 1995; Behn 1995; Poister and Streib 1995; for an overview of public management at this time, see Bozeman, 1993).

More ominously for the governance functions of public administration, the role of the city manager continued to be a major concern. ICMA itself became split on the issue of whether the office of city manager as traditionally developed could, or should, be sustained. Some argued for transforming the office into more of an executive partnership, involving the office of mayor in a serious manner (Frederickson 1995; Frederickson and Nalbandian 2002; Svara 1994). Cincinnati, long one of the most traditional council-manager cities, amended its charter to enlarge the role of the mayor in the selection process of the city manager and, more generally, in the political process. Though ICMA did not oppose the change in the Cincinnati charter, the Ohio City Management Association publicly opposed it. In addition, some managers called for the creation of a Staunton Society, dedicated to supporting a more traditional model of the city manager. The issue, though centered on the council-manager form of government, is similar to those involving high-level public servants in all levels of American government.

The Clinton administration joined the effort to transform the national bureaucracy. Vice President Al Gore, a person long interested in the application of technology to improving government, was placed in charge of the reinvention effort. He approached the task as a true believer, aiming at permanent changes in how services are offered (Executive Office of the President 1993, 1995). Access to the process was broadly expanded through the use of modern telecommunication facilities such as the Internet. In fact, by the mid-1990s, many aspects of the national government, and a growing number of state and local governments, were on the Net, complete with home pages that permitted those who surfed the Net to peruse many documents and use e-mail to interact with those engaged in the effort to change government. Such access promised to make government more available to citizens, though some questioned who the users were and how representative they were of citizens in general.

The diversity of issues and approaches appear, on the surface, to lack unity in either scope or method. Those refounding the field question the desirability of reinventing government (see Goodsell 1993), but seldom engage in meaningful dialogue. Those intent on reinventing appear uninterested in the larger philosophical issues around the public sector and its reform. However, progress in both cases may require conceptually relating these and other movements, such as the extent to which public administration has an adequate conception of the state (Stillman 1991) or adequate conceptions of professionalism (Gazell and Pugh 1993; Green et al. 1993). In addition, it may require a more unified conception of the environment (Etzioni and Lawerence 1991). Yet, NASPAA continued to review and accredit programs at the graduate level in public administration (Williams 1994). In a most unexpected manner, the debate was pre-empted in early 2001 with a direct and devastating attack on American soil. Ironically, the reactions to that attack may require public administration to turn serious attention to governance on the basis of political philosophy as well as efficient management. To this event and its aftermath we now turn.

XV. CONCLUSION: PUBLIC ADMINISTRATION AND THE SEARCH FOR GOVERNANCE IN A GLOBAL SECURITY STATE

September 11, 2001, threatened to change the face of American government. President Bush announced we were in a state of war and requested the creation of a Department of Homeland Security.* American troops were quickly dispatched to Afghanistan and toppled the Taliban regime. The resulting reorganization of the national government was the most extensive in our history. Public administrationists quickly theorized about its implications, for a variety of issues from management to civil liberties (see the Special Issue of the *Public Administration Review* 2001). Spicer and Gould worried about the implications for civil liberties and even the basic nature of our government. Frederickson and LaPorte questioned the capability of a rationally driven traditional management to accomplish security while Wise and Nader as well as Kincaid and Cole explored the effects on federalism. O'Toole and Hanf provided the broadest perspective, analyzing the effects of international governance on the American system. The range of concerns about the effects of what came to be called 9/11 indicates the scope of change the event wrought, and may yet wrought, on the American republic.

Whether the changes will continue for the long term is an open issue. However, as the theory on complex systems notes, changes are irreversible. Systems cannot "go home again"—that is, return to their original states (Holland 1995; Prigogine and Stengers 1997). However, the eventual outcome is seldom predictable as a range of outcomes is possible. This theoretical approach will be returned to later as it promises to help public administration avoid the determinism of some scientific paradigms while applying a robust theoretical framework. The stakes are indeed perilously high for where the American system may go under pressure of a global concern with terrorism. Much may depend upon the extent to which public administration can articulate and implement a public management attuned to core political and constitutional values in the context of a community as well as organizational efficiency (Newland 1984).

In essence, the discipline and profession of public administration will have to make stronger connections between the Waldo and Simon legacies (Kaufman 1996). This will be a difficult task. However, some public administrationists are responding to the task, analyzing management in the political context of constitutional government. Bertelli and Lynn (2003) phrased the issue pointedly:

> ... a central theoretical (but also quite practical) problem of Public Administration: deriving   from our historical experience a role for administrative officers as practitioners of statecraft..., rather than politicians, clerks or anything else of lesser constitutional significance.

However, to achieve this noble and what many would agree is a necessary goal requires a clear understanding of the shortcomings of many aspects of current public administration. More importantly, the field must communicate those shortcomings to the public, eschewing what seems to be an American penchant for believing in technical silver bullets. Too often, Americans expect science to deliver a solution that requires no trade-offs and blessedly bypasses the messy politics that seem unnecessary in an age of sophisticated technology and wide-spread, if costly, higher education. Public administration must assume its constitutional role in systemic politics without losing its expertise in management or supplanting other constitutional actors.

---

*The irony of calling a federal agency Homeland Security in a nation built on immigration and replacement of those inhabiting the land at the time of immigration seemed to escape notice. Moreover, the name has a chilling resemblance to European ministries, such as the infamous Ministry of Interior, which often became the point of attack for those wanting to take over a state. In any event, it is an unfortunate name for a federal agency. Some of the content recalls the ill-fated Alien and Sedition Acts that helped to undo the administration of John Adams and the Federalists generally.

Similarly, many have hopes that the technical efficiency can be tamed by placing it under the discipline of the market and the logic of economics generally. This logic of economics, particularly in terms of comparing costs with benefits of public policy, has assumed a large role in many forms of policy analysis (McKean 1958). At the national level, it was first mandated in the case of water resource projects. By the 1980s, some advocated the privatization of public services (Savas 1982). Politically, the market was promoted in developed and developing countries, apparently fulfilling both the yearning for material well-being and the hope for democratic politics. In essence, public administration was to be a player in the service market, competing with not-for-profit and for-profit firms. The result was to be both efficiency at the organizational level and democracy at the systemic level (Donahue and Nye 2002). Similar hopes exist for utilizing technology in public management and service delivery (West 2004). However, even the World Bank has cautioned about ignoring the governance capacity when implementing market and other reforms (Kaufman 2005).

Surprisingly, Jefferson's hopes for small-scale democracy, one that he perceived as threatened by urban and other forms of complex development, is now visualized by some as the outcome of technology and management in a complex society. It is not that these efforts have no merit; the concern is a tendency to promote them as panaceas, total solutions to what is often perceived as a malfunctional system. They ignore, as Goodsell (2004) continues to point out, that the system is healthier than many understand and that any thrust painted as a systemic solution ignores the inevitable trade-offs of any vision or the dark-side of the "iron cage" of organizational efficiency, if it is elevated above other political values and designed beyond constitutional restraints (Bendix 1960).

As emphasized in the second edition, difficult questions may be posed for public administration as the republic enters its second century. It was noted that the foundations—the PI model—must be tempered by connecting professional concerns with social needs, while avoiding the corruption and petty partisanship that Addams (1902) noted around the turn of the century. It was stressed that this requires an emphasis on governance by placing administration in our politics. Such a focus facilitates the incorporation of many lessons from other fields into public administration for example, quoting from that edition,

> Michael Saranson (1972) expanded the prescriptions from organizational development into more general ones on the nature of societies and their futures. Similarly, Cobb and Elder (1972) emphasized the importance of agenda building, an activity obviously important for public administration, but one that has eluded conceptual inclusion (Allison 1971; Cobb and Rochefort 1994; Kingdon 1984). Most importantly, a focus on governance can provide a constitutional foundation to an active public administration. As Lowi (1995) notes, we have in many ways failed to conceptualize adequately the constitutional context of our politics. Without more robust conceptualizations, we will fail to ground public administration constitutionally and deny it a meaningful role in governance (Freedman 1977).

Not surprisingly, the current field, reflecting social and unconventional political struggles across the globe, resists classification in a classically rational manner. Intellectual synthesis is unlikely to succeed if it is conceptualized as creating a dominant and all-explaining theory.* As

---

* A pertinent parallel may be the inability of Albert Einstein to create a unified field theory for physics. In fact, he opposed the approach of Niels Bohr who explained micro level events from a statistical perspective. For Einstein, this nullified the potential of a robust science and in a quaint metaphor, Einstein opined that "God does not play dice." For all his contributions and even charisma, Einstein lost the argument over the nature of science within physics. Ilya Prigogine (1997) sees the integrated notions of a science from a traditional rational perspective as erroneous. Prigogine notes that the Newtonian explanations may be appropriate for a subset of systems but not for the general ones. Thus, complex systems of any type may preclude easy generation of universal laws and thwart attempts to comprehend complex systems with traditional logic, or even non-traditional logic (Holland 1995). Several approaches from this perspective, such as Holland's, have much promise for a more robust empirical picture of public administration and better capture the nuances of the normative side. ASPA recently created a section on complex systems and named it in honor of Sam Overman. This illustrates that many see the utility of the perspective for understanding American public administration.

Burrell and Morgan (1979) note, one's journey has a start that in many ways determines routing and destinations. Paradigmatic assumptions vary according to the assumptions researchers make and create a diversity of scientific methodologies. Particularly important in terms of intellectual starts is how one sees human nature and the resulting social system. If one starts with assumption of innately good people, one will propound a very different public administration than if one starts with a notion of people as equally likely to do evil as good. For a most interesting study of dramatically different outcomes based on how administrators are perceived, see Anechiarico and Jacob's examination of anti-corruption strategies and their influence on public administration (Anechiarico and Jacob, 1994). These incompatible paradigmatic assumptions, and similar ones about basic notions of linear cause and effect, are likely to continue in public administration. In fact, they may be necessary to understand the state in a complex global system with a technological base that can threaten the system itself. (See Jun 2002 for readings on these topics; Sorensen 2004).

A revealing episode is the clash around administrative responsibility triggered by reviews of Michael Harmon's (1995) book. *Responsibility as Paradox: A Critique of Rational Discourse on Government*. In a spirited dialogue on the book, Terry Cooper and Harmon in particular engage is a ringing debate over the issue (1996). The dispute is not just over reaching different conclusions; it also involved quite different paradigmatic assumptions. The inability to reach an accommodation in that dialogue reflects that fundamental assumptions lead to incompatible outcomes, even in traditional areas of public administration.

Ironically, the resulting messy intellectual landscape may prove most useful to governing a diverse and ever-changing global society. The utility requires creation of, and incorporation into, academic degree programs, of the products of science defined as a process of inquiry rather than any particular paradigm (Mesaros and Balfour 1993). In essence, students must be paradigmatically aware and able to gather lessons from a variety of perspectives without oversimplification or a belief in the dominance for all public administration of one particular approach. In addition, students must have a fuller understanding of our actual history and the resulting lessons for the systemic importance of administration (Hoffman 1998, 2002; Lynn 2001; Riccucci 2001; Rutgers 2003). These lessons must be integrated at the organizational level with public management theory and at the systemic level with political philosophy. Similarly, informed comparative studies from a more philosophical perspective may prove very useful (Rohr 2002).

Theoretically, approaches such as complex adaptive systems may be quite useful. Emanating from places of intellectual investigation such as the Santa Fe Institute, researchers perceived similarities among systems, whether natural or social, if they were complex. Such systems behaved quite differently than simpler systems and demanded newer methodologies reflecting more complex behaviors. John Holland (1995), for example, argued that urban history could be usefully understood from this perspective. He regretted that most of our mathematics were based on linear assumptions and thus of limited utility for investigating the behavior of complex systems. Political systems certainly qualify as complex and the application of CAS may help to delineate the roles of public administration in such complex systems. Most usefully, the theory relegates the often deterministic nature of many social science epistemologies to simple systems. Complex systems may have a limited domain but the outcomes and evolution are not easily predictable and result from the action of numerous agents who are significant information centers of the system. The perspective is obviously relevant to the systems in which public administration is often embedded and notes the importance of how administrators act, even on what may seem minor issues.

Without such conceptual integration, public administration will be unable to perform its indispensable role of facilitating the governing of the state in a democratic constitutional manner (Newland 2000). Anything less would be to leave the administrative state in peril, as the rule of faction, thanks to the rise of a fearfully effective organization of political campaigns, may well create a coalition of factions that endangers democratic politics itself. Only a more robust public administration, incorporating the norms of its actual public interest heritage, can help to maintain, and ideally enhance, the constitutional foundations of the administrative state.

XVI. DEDICATION

I dedicate this history to those who toiled in the field, often with little acknowledgment but with a burning commitment to robust research, empowered teaching, and public service to American communities. Dr Joseph Uveges, who co-authored this chapter for the first two editions and who enlisted my services, is an exemplar of those who created and moved our field. I dedicate this version to him and them with thanks and gratitude.

REFERENCES

Accenture, *eGovernment Leadership: Rhetoric vs Reality—Closing the Gap*, Accenture, New York, 2001.

Adams, G. and Balfour, D., *Unmasking Administrative Evil*, M.E. Sharpe, Armonk, NY, 1998, 2004.

Adams, G. B. and White, J. D., *Research in Public Administration: Reflections on Theory and Practice*, Sage Publications, Thousand Oaks, CA, 1994.

Addams, J., *Democracy and Social Ethics*, Macmillan, New York, 1902.

Allison, G., *The Essence of Decision: Explaining the Cuban Missile Crisis*, Little, Brown, Boston, MA, 1971.

Ammons, D., Overcoming the inadequacies of performance measurement in local government: the case of libraries and leisure services, *Public Admin. Rev.*, 37–47, January/February, 1995.

Anechiarico, F. and Jacob, J. B., Visions of corruption, control and the evolution of american public administration, *Public Admin. Rev.*, 465–474, September/October, 1994.

Antioch College, *Educating for Democracy: A Symposium*, Antioch College, Antioch, OH, 1937.

Appleby, P. H., *Big Democracy*, Knopf, New York, 1945.

Appleby, P. H., *Policy and Administration*, University of Alabama Press, Tuscaloosa, AL, 1957.

Argyris, C., *Personality and Organization*, Harper & Row, New York, 1957.

Arnold, P. E., The first hoover commission and the managerial presidency, *J. Politics*, 38, 46–70, 1976.

Attorney General's Committee on Administrative Procedure, *Final Report*, US Government Printing Office, Washington, DC, 1941.

Bailey, M. T. and Mayer, R. T., *Public Management in an Interconnected World: Essays in the Minnowbrook Perspective*, Greenwood Press, New York, 1992.

Bailey, S. K., Objectives of the theory of public administration, In *Theory and Practice of Public Administration: Scope, Objectives, Methods*, Charlesworth, J. C., Ed., American Academy of Political and Social Sciences, Philadelphia, PA, pp. 128–139, 1968.

Balk, W. A., A symposium: productivity in government, *Public Admin. Rev.*, 1–51, January/February, 1978.

Banfield, E. C., *Urban Government: A Reader in Administration and Politics*, 2nd ed., Free Press, New York, 1969.

Barnard, C. I., *Functions of the Executive*, Harvard University Press, Cambridge, MA, 1938.

Barton, R., Roles advocated for administrators by the new public administration, *South. Rev. Public Admin.*, 3, 463–486, 1980.

Beam, D. R., Public administration is alive and well—and living in the White House, *Public Admin. Rev*, 72–77, January/February, 1978.

Beard, C. A., *Public Policy and General Welfare*, Holt, Rinehart, and Winston, New York, 1941.

Beckman, N. Ed., A symposium: policy analysis in government: alternatives to "muddling through," *Public Admin. Rev.*, 221–263, May/June, 1977.

Behn, R. D., The big questions of public management, *Public Admin. Rev*, 313–324, July/August, 1955.

Behn, R.D, Ed., A symposium: leadership in an era of retrenchment. *Public Admin. Rev.*, 603–626, November/December, 1980.

Bellone, C. J. and Goerl, G. F., Reconciling public entrepreneurship and democracy, *Public Admin. Rev*, 130–134, March/April, 1992.

Bendix, Reinhard, *Max Weber: An Intellectual Portrait*, Doubleday, Garden City, New York, 1960.

Bennis, W., Beyond bureaucracy, *Transaction*, 44–51, 1965.

Bennis, W., *Changing Organizations*, McGraw-Hill, New York, 1966.

Bennis, W., *Organizational Development: Its Nature, Origins, and Prospects*, Addison-Wesley, Reading, MA, 1969.

Bentley, A. F., *Process of Government: A Study of Social Pressures*, University of Chicago Press, Chicago, IL, 1908.

Berkeley, G., *The Administrative Revolution: Notes on the Passing of Administrative Man*, Prentice Hall, Englewood Cliffs, NJ, 1971.

Berkeley, G., *The Craft of Public Administration*, Allyn and Bacon, Boston, MA, 1975.

Bertelli, A. M. and Lynn, L. E., Managerial responsibility, *Public Admin. Rev.*, 259–268, May/June, 2003.

Bettmans, O. L., *The Good Old Days—They Were Terrible*, Random House, New York, 1974.

Blau, P., *The Dynamics of Bureaucracy*, University of Chicago Press, Chicago, IL, 1956.

Bok, W., *The Americanization of Edward Bok: The Autobiography of a Dutch Boy Fifty Years After*, C. Scribner's Sons, New York, 1920.

Botner, S. B., Four years of ppbs: an appraisal, *Public Admin. Rev.*, 423–431, July/August, 1970.

Boulding, K. E., *The Image: Knowledge and Life in Society*, University of Michigan Press, Ann Arbor, MI, 1956.

Boulding, K. E., *Ecodynamics: A New Theory of Societal Evolution*, Russell Sage, Beverly Hills, CA, 1981.

Bowman, J. S., Managerial theory and practice: the transfer of knowledge in public administration, *Public Admin. Rev.*, 563–570, November/December, 1978.

Bowman, J. S., A professional perspective for public administration, *Bureaucrat*, 49–52, November, 1982.

Bowman, J. S., *Ethical Frontiers in Public Management*, Jossey-Bass, San Francisco, CA, 1991.

Boyer, M. C., *Dreaming the Rational City: The Myth of American City Planning*, MIT Press, Cambridge, MA, 1983.

Bozeman, B., *Public Management: The State of the Art*, Jossey-Bass, San Francisco, CA, 1993.

Bridges, A., *A City in the Republic: Antebellum New York and the Origins of Machine Politics*, Cambridge University Press, New York, 1984.

Bridges, A., Winning the west to reform, *Urban Affairs Quarterly*, 494–518, 1992.

Bridges, A., *Morning Glories: Municipal Reform in the Southwest*, Princeton University Press, Princeton, NJ, 1997.

Broder, D. S., *Changing of the Guard: Power and Leadership in America*, Simon and Schuster, New York, 1980.

Brownell, B. A. and Stickle, W., *Bosses and Reformers: Urban Politics in America, 1880–1920*, Houghton-Mifflin, Boston, MA, 1973.

Brownlow, L., *A Passion for Anonymity: The Autobiography of Louis Brownlow, Second Half*, University of Chicago Press, Chicago, IL, 1958.

Brudney, J. L., O'Toole, L. J., and Rainey, H., *Advancing Public Management: New Developments in Theory, Practice and Methods*, Georgetown University Press, Washington, DC, 2000.

Buchanan, P., Ed., *An Approach to Executive Development in Government*, National Academy of Public Administration, Washington, DC, 1973.

Buder, S., *Pullman: An Experiment in Industrial Order and Community Planning, 1880–1930*, Oxford University Press, New York, 1967.

Burke, C.G., *Stratified Systems Theory: Politics and Administration Revisited*, Unpublished paper presented at the annual meeting, American Society for Public Administration, Chicago, IL, 1983.

Burrell, G. and Morgan, G., *Sociological Paradigms and Organisational Analysis: Elements of the Sociology of Corporate Life*, Heinemann, London, 1979.

Caiden, G., Ed., *Administrative Reform*, Aldine, Chicago, IL, 1969.

Caiden, G., Ed., *Administrative Reform Comes of Age*, W. de Gruyter, New York, 1991.

Caldwell, L. K., *The Administrative Theories of Hamilton and Jefferson: Their Contribution to Thought on Public Administration*, University of Chicago Press, Chicago, IL, 1944.

Caldwell, L. K., March Public administration and the universities: a half century of development, *Public Administration Review*, 52–60, March, 1965.

Caldwell, L. K., *The Administrative Theories of Hamilton and Jefferson: Their Contribution to Thought on Public Administration*, 2nd ed., Holmes and Meier, New York, 1987.

Callow, A. B., Ed., *The City Bosses in America: An Interpretative Reader*, Oxford University Press, New York, 1976.

Campbell, A. K., Old and new public administration in the 1970's, *Public Admin. Rev.*, 343–347, July/August, 1972.

Campbell, A. K., Civil service reform: a new commitment, *Public Admin. Rev.*, 99–103, March/April, 1978.

Caro, R. A., *The Power Broker: Robert Moses and the Fall of New York*, Knopf, New York, 1974.

Carroll, J. D., Fritscher, A. L., and Smith, B. L. R., Supply-side management in the Reagan administration, *Public Admin. Rev.,* 805–814, November/December, 1985.

Chandler, A. D., Jr., *The Visible Hand: The Managerial Revolution in American Business*, Harvard University Press, Cambridge, MA, 1984.

Chapman, R. L. and Cleaveland, F. N., The changing character of the public service and the administrator of the 1980's, *Public Admin. Rev.,* 358–366, July/August, 1973.

Charlesworth, J. C., Ed., *A Design for Political Science: Scope, Objectives, Methods*, American Academy of Political and Social Sciences, Philadelphia, PA, p. 1, 1966.

Charlesworth, J. C., Ed., *Theory and Practice of Public Administration: Scope, Objectives, Methods*, American Academy of Political and Social Sciences, Philadelphia, PA, 1968.

Childs, R. S., *Civil Victories: The Story of an Unfinished Revolution*, Harper, New York, 1952.

Churchman, C. W., *The Systems Approach*, Delacorte, New York, 1968.

Clapp, G., *TVA and its Critics*, University of Chicago Press, Chicago, IL, 1955.

Cleland, D. I., *Systems Analysis and Project Management*, 3rd ed., McGraw-Hill, New York, 1983.

Cobb, R. and Elder, C., *Participation in American Politics: The Dynamics of Agenda Building*, Allyn and Bacon, Boston, MA, 1972.

Cobb, R. and Rochefort, D., *The Politics of Problem Definition: Shaping the Policy Agenda*, University of Kansas Press, Lawrence, KS, 1994.

Commager, H. S., *The American Mind: An Interpretation of American Thought and Character Since the 1880's*, Yale University Press, New Haven, CT, 1950.

Cook, B. J., Subordination or independence for administrators: the decision of 1789 reexamined, *Public Admin. Rev,* 497–503, September/October, 1992.

Cook, B. J., *Bureaucracy and Self-Government: Reconsidering the Role of Public Administration in American Politics*, Johns Hopkins Press, Baltimore, MD, 1996.

Cooper, P. J., Conflict or constructive tension: the changing relationship of judges and administrators, *Public Admin. Rev.,* 643–652, 1985.

Cooper, P. J., *Hard Judicial Choices: Federal District Court Judges and State and Local Officials*, Oxford University Press, New York, 1988.

Cooper, T. L. and Wright, N. D., Eds., *Exemplary Public Administrators: Character and Leadership in Government*, Jossey-Bass, San Francisco, CA, 1992.

Cooper, T. L., Ed., *Handbook of Administrative Ethics*, Marcel Dekker, New York, 1994.

Crenson, M. A., *The Federal Machine: Beginnings of Bureaucracy in Jacksonian America*, John Hopkins University Press, Baltimore, MD, 1975.

Croly, H. D., *The Promise of American Life*, Macmillan, New York, 1909.

Crozier, M., *The Bureaucratic Phenomenon*, University of Chicago Press, Chicago, IL, 1964.

Crunden, R. M., *Ministers of Reform: The Progressives' Achievement in American Civilization, 1889–1920*, Basic Books, New York, 1982.

Crunden, R. M., *Ministers of Reform: The Progressives' Achievement in American Civilization, 1889–1920*, University of Illinois Press, Urbana, IL, 1984.

Dahl, R. A., The science of public administration: three problems, *Public Admin. Rev.,* 1–11, January/February, 1947.

Dahl, R. A., The behavioral approach in political science: epitaph for a monument to a successful protest, *Am. Politi. Sci. Rev.*, 55, 763–772, 1961.

Dahl, R. A. and Lindblom, C. E., *Politics, Economics and Welfare: Planning and Politico-Economic Systems Resolved into Basic Social Processes*, Harper, New York, 1953.

Daley, D., Support for professionalism in the states: an examination of administrative, executive and legislative attitudes, *Am. Rev. Public Admin.*, 17, 102–114, 1983.

Daniels, M. R. and Johansen, E., Role of accreditation in the development of public administration: a theoretical and empirical assessment, *Public Admin. Q*, 8, 419–441, 1985.

Davis, S. M. and Lawrence, P. R., *Matrix*, Addison-Wesley, Reading, MA, 1977.

Degler, C. N., *Out of Our Past: The Forces that Shaped Modern America*, Harper, New York, 1959.

Denhardt, R. B., *In the Shadow of Organization*, University Press of Kansas, Lawrence, KS, 1981.

Denhardt, R.B., *Theories of Public Organization*, 4th ed., Thomson/Wadsworth, Belmont, CA.

Denny, B. C., Science and public policy: a symposium, *Public Admin. Rev.,* 95–161, June, 1967.

Dewey, J., *The Public and its Problems*, H. Holt, New York, 1927.

Dilulio, J., Garvey, G., and Kettl, D., *Improving Government Performance*, Brookings Institution, Washington, DC, 1993.

Dimock, M. E., The study of administration, *Am. Politic. Sci. Rev.*, 31, 28–40, 1937.

Dimock, M. E., *Administrative efficiency within a democratic polity New Horizons in Public Administration: A Symposium*, University of Alabama Press, Tuscaloosa, AL, 1945.

Dimock, M. E., *A Philosophy of Administration*, Harper, New York, 1958.

Divine, W. R., The second Hoover commission report: an analysis, *Public Admin. Rev.*, 263–270, Autumn, 1955.

Donahue, J. D. and Nye, J. S., Jr., *Market Based Governance: Supply Side, Demand Side, Upside and Downside*, Brookings Institution, Washington, DC, 2002.

Downs, A., *An Economic Theory of Democracy*, Harper & Row, New York, 1957.

Downs, A., *Inside Bureaucracy*, Little, Brown, Boston, MA, 1967.

Draper, F. O. and Pitsvada, B. T., ZBB—looking back after ten years, *Public Admin. Rev.*, 41, 76–83, 1981.

Dror, Y., Policy analysts: a new professional role in government service, *Public Admin. Rev.*, 197–203, September, 1967.

Dror, Y., *Public Policy-Making Reexamined*, Chandler, San Francisco, CA, 1968.

Dror, Y., *Ventures in Policy Sciences: Concepts and Applications*, Elsevier American, New York, 1971.

Drucker, P., *The Practice of Management*, Harper, New York, 1954.

Drucker, P., *Landmarks of Tomorrow*, Harper, New York, 1959.

Drucker, P., *The Age of Discontinuity*, Harper, New York, 1969.

Eadie, D. C. and Steinbacher, R., Strategic agenda management: a marriage of organizational development and strategic planning, *Public Admin. Rev.*, 424–430, May/June, 1985.

East, J. P., *Council-Manager Government: The Political Thought of Its Founder, Richard S. Childs*, University of North Carolina Press, Chapel Hill, NC, 1965.

Eddy, W. B. and Saunders, R. J., Applied behavioral sciences in urban administrative/political systems, *Public Admin. Rev.*, 1–11, January/February, 1972.

Egger, R., The period of crisis: 1933–1945, In *American Public Administration: Past, Present, and Future*, Mosher, F. C., Ed., University of Alabama Press, Tuscaloosa, AL, 1975.

Elkin, S. L. and Soltan, K. E., Eds., *The Constitution of Good Societies*, Penn State Press, University Park, PA, 1996.

Ellis, J. H., *The American Sphinx: The Character of Thomas Jefferson*, Knopf, New York, 1996.

Engelbert, E. A., The findings and implications of a survey of standards and accreditation for education programs in public administration, *Public Admin. Rev.*, 520–527, September/October, 1977.

Englund, S., *Napoleon: A Political Life*, Scribner, New York, 2004.

Etzioni, A., *A Comparative Analysis of Complex Organizations*, Free Press, New York, 1961.

Etzioni, A., Mixed scanning: a third approach to decision-making, *Public Admin. Rev.*, 385–392, December, 1967.

Etzioni, A. and Lawrence, P., *Socio-Economics: Toward a New Synthesis*, M.E. Sharpe, Armonk, NY, 1991.

Executive Office of the President, *From Red Tape to Results: Creating a Government that Works Better and Costs Less*, U.S. Government Printing Office, Washington, DC, 1993.

Executive Office of the President, *Common Sense Government, Works Better and Costs Less*, US Government Printing Office, Washington, DC, 1995.

Farmer, J. D., Ed., *Papers on the Art of Anti-Administration*, Chatelaine Press, Burke, VA, 1998.

Fesler, J. W., Public administration and the social sciences: 1946–1960, In *American Public Administration: Past, Present, and Future*, Mosher, F. C., Ed., University of Alabama Press, Tuscaloosa, AL, 1975.

Feuer, L. S., *Marx and the Intellectuals: A Set of Post-Ideological Essays*, Doubleday, New York, 1969.

Fisher, R. and Ury, W., *Getting to Yes: Negotiating Agreement Without Giving in*, Houghton-Mifflin, Boston, MA, 1981.

Follet, M. P., *The New State*, Longmans, Green, New York, 1918.

Foucault, M., *The Archaeology of Knowledge, Trans. A.M.S. Smith*, Harper & Row, Ithaca, NY, 1976.

Fox, E. M., Mary parker Follet: the enduring contribution, *Public Admin. Rev.*, 520–529, November/December, 1968.

Fox, C. and Miller, H. T., *Postmodern Public Administration: Towards Discourse*, Sage Publications, Thousand Oaks, CA, 1995.

Frederickson, H. G., Social equity and public administration: a symposium, *Public Admin. Rev.,* 1–51, January/February, 1974.

Frederickson, H. G., The lineage of new public administration, *Admin. Soc.,* 8, 149–174, 1976.

Frederickson, H. G., *New Public Administration,* University of Alabama Press, University, AL, 1980.

Frederickson, H. G., Ed., *Ethics and Public Administration,* M.E. Sharpe, Armonk, NY, 1993.

Frederickson, H. G., *Ideal and Practice in Council-Management Government,* 2nd ed., ICMA, Washington, DC, 1995.

Frederickson, H. G. and Chandler, R., *Citizenship and Public Administration: Proceedings of the National Conference on Citizenship and Public Service,* American Society for Public Administration, Washington, DC, 1984.

Frederickson, H. G. and Hart, D. K., The public service and the patriotism of benevolence, *Public Admin. Rev.,* 547–553, September/October, 1985.

Frederickson, H. G. and Nalbandian, J., *The Future of Local Government Administration: The Hansell Symposium,* ICMA, Washington, DC, 2002.

Freedman, J. O., *Crisis and Legitimacy: The Administrative Process and American Government,* Cambridge University Press, New York, 1977.

Freeman, A. L., *The Political Process: Executive Bureau–Legislative Committee Relationships,* Random House, New York, 1952.

Fukuyama, F., *State-Building: Governance and World Order in the 21st Century,* Cornell University Press, New York, 2004.

Gaebler, T. and Osborne, D., *Reinventing Government: How the Entrepreneurial Spirit is Transforming the Public Sector,* Addison-Wesley, Reading, MA, 1992.

Gallas, N., Ed. Women in public administration: a symposium, *Public Admin. Rev.,* 347–389, July/August, 1976.

Gargan, J. J. and Moore, C. M., Enhancing local government capacity in budget decision making: the use of group process techniques, *Public Admin. Rev.,* 504–511, November/December, 1984.

Garson, G. D., Ed., *Information Technology and Computer Applications in Public Administration: Issues and Trends,* Idea Group, Hershey, PA, 1999.

Gaus, J. M., The present status of the study of public administration, *Am. Politic. Sci. Rev.,* 25, 120–134, 1931.

Gaus, J. M., *Reflections on Public Administration,* University of Alabama Press, University, AL, 1947.

Gaus, J. M., Public participation in federal programs, In *Democracy in Federal Administration,* US Department of Agriculture, Washington, DC, 1955.

Gaus, J. M., White, L. D., and Dimock, M. E., *The Frontiers of Public Administration,* University of Chicago Press, Chicago, IL, 1936.

Gawthrop, L., *The Administrative Process and Democratic Theory,* Houghton-Mifflin, Boston, MA, 1970.

Gazell, J. A. and Pugh, D. L., The future of professionalization and professionalism in public administration: advancements, barriers, and prospects, *Int. J. Public Admin.,* 16, 1933–1965, 1993.

Gerth, H. H. and Mills, C. W., *From Max Webber: Essays in Sociology,* Oxford University Press, New York, 1946.

Golembiewski, R. T., *The Small Group,* University of Chicago Press, Chicago, 1962.

Golembiewski, R. T., *Public Administration as a Developing Discipline,* Marcel Dekker, New York, 1977.

Golembisewki, R. T., Perspectives on public sector OD: a symposium, *South Rev. Public Admin.,* 1, 406–502, 1978.

Golembisewki, R. T., Perspectives on public sector OD: II, *South Rev. Public Admin.,* 4, 136–252, 1980.

Golembiewski, R. T., Toward professional certification, *Bureaucrat,* 12, 50–55, 1983.

Golembiewski, R. T. and Eddy, W. B., *Organization Development and Public Administration,* Marcel Dekker, New York, 1978.

Goodnow, F. J., *Comparative Administration Law,* Putman's Sons, New York, 1893.

Goodnow, F. J., *Policy and Administration,* Macmillan, New York, 1900.

Goodsell, C. T., The grace commission: seeking efficiency for the whole people, *Public Admin. Rev.,* 196–204, May/June, 1984.

Goodsell, C. T., Re-invent government or re-discover it?, *Public Admin. Rev.,* 85–87, January/February, 1993.

Goodsell, C. T., *The Case for Bureaucracy: A Public Administration Polemic,* 3rd ed., Chatham House, Chatham, NJ, 1994, 2004.

Goodsell, C. T. and Charles, A., Beard, prophet for public administration, *Public Admin. Rev.,* 105–106, March/April, 1986.

Gosnell, H. F., *Machine Politics: Chicago Model*, University of Chicago Press, Chicago, IL, 1937. 1968

Graham, G., *Education for Public Administration*, Public Administration Service, Chicago, IL, 1941.

Green, B. and Feerick, J. D., *Government Ethics Reform for the 1990's: The Collected Reports of the New York State Commission on Government Integrity*, Fordham University Press, New York, 1991.

Green, R. T., Keller, L. F., and Wamsley, G. L., Reconstituting a profession for American public administration, *Public Admin. Rev.,* 516–524, November/December, 1993.

Grode, G. and Holzer, M., The perceived utility of MPA degrees, *Public Admin. Rev.,* 403–412, July/August, 1975.

Gulick, L. H., Politics, administration and the new deal, *Ann. Am. Acad. Politic. Soc. Sci.*, 169, 55–66, 1933.

Gulick, L. H., *Better Government Personnel: Report of the Commission of Inquiry on Public Service Personnel*, McGraw-Hill, New York, 1935.

Gulick, L. H., The dynamics of public administration today as guidelines for the future, *Public Admin. Rev,* 193–198., May/June, 1983.

Gulick, L. H. and Urwick, L., Eds., *Papers on the Science of Administration*, Institute of Public Administration, New York, 1937.

Guy, M. E., Three steps forward, two steps backward: the status of women's integration into public management, *Public Admin. Rev.,* 285–291, July/August, 1993.

Haber, S., *Efficiency and Uplift: Scientific Management in the Progressive Era, 1890–1920*, University of Chicago Press, Chicago, IL, 1964.

Haines, C. G. and Dimock, M. E., *Essays on the Law and Practice of Governmental Administration*, Johns Hopkins University Press, Baltimore, MD, 1935.

Harmon, M. M., *Responsibility as Paradox: A Critique of Rational Discourse on Government*, Sage Publications, Thousand Oaks, CA, 1995.

Hart, D. K., The virtuous citizen, the honorable bureaucrat, and "public" administration, *Public Admin. Rev.*, Special Issue 111–120, 1984.

Hart, D. K. and Scott, W. G., The moral nature of man in organization: a comparative analysis, *Acad. Manage. J.*, 14, 241–255, 1971.

Hayek, F. A., *The Road to Serfdom*, University of Chicago Press, Chicago, IL, 1944.

Hays, S. P., The politics of reform in municipal government in the progressive era, *Pacific Northwest Q.*, 55, 157–166, 1964.

Heady, F., *Public Administration: A Comparative Perspective*, 2nd ed., Marcel Dekker, New York, 1966, 1979.

Henry, N. L., Knowledge management: a new concern for public administration, *Public Admin. Rev.,* 189–196, May/June, 1974.

Henry, N. L., Paradigms of public administration, *Public Admin. Rev.*, 35, 378–386, 1975.

Herring, E. P., *Public Administration and the Public Interest*, McGraw-Hill, New York, 1936.

Hinderaker, I., The study of administration: interdisciplinary dimensions, *West Politic. Q.*, 16, 5–12, 1963.

Hoffman, M.C., City republic, civil religion, and the single tax: the progressive-era founding of public administration in cleveland, 1901–1915, Ph.D. diss., Cleveland State University, Cleveland, OH, 1998.

Hoffman, M. C., Paradigm lost: Public administration at Johns Hopkins University, *1884–1996, Public Admin. Rev.,* 12–23, January/February, 2002.

Hofstadter, R., *The Age of Reform: From Bryant to F.D.R*, Knopf, New York, 1955.

Hofstadter, R., *The Progressive Movement, 1900–1915*, Prentice Hall, Englewood Cliffs, NJ, 1963.

Hofstadter, R., *The Idea of a Party System: The Rise of Legitimate Opposition in the United States, 1780–1840*, University of California Press, Berkeley, CA, 1969.

Holland, J. H., *Hidden Order: How Adaptation Builds Complexity*, Addison-Wesley, Reading, MA, 1995.

Holli, M. G., *Reform in Detroit: Hazen S. Pingree and Urban Politics*, Oxford University Press, New York, 1969.

Honey, J. C., A report: higher education for the public service, *Public Admin. Rev.,* Special Issue, 294–321, November, 1967.

Hoogenboom, A., *Outlawing the Spoils: A History of the Civil Service Reform Movement*, University of Illinois Press, Urbana, IL, 1961.

Howard, L. C., Education for the public interest: a critique and a projection of the NAPA view of meeting the needs of tomorrow's public service, *Public Admin. Rev.,* 173–180, March/April, 1975.

Howe, F. C., *Confessions of a Reformer*, Scribner's Sons, New York, 1925.

Ingraham, P. W. and Barrilleaux, C., Motivating government managers for retrenchment: some possible lessons from the senior executive service, *Public Admin. Rev.*, 393–402, September/October, 1983.

Janik, D., $2 million blown, $2 million saved, *Cleveland Plain Dealer*, 11B, October 11, 1995.

Jones, G. N., Frontiersman in search for the 'lost horizon': the state of development administration in the 1960's, *Public Admin. Rev.*, 99–110, January/February, 1976.

Jreisat, J. E., Synthesis and relevance in comparative public administration, *Public Admin. Rev.*, 663–671, November/December, 1975.

Jun, J. S., In *Rethinking Administrative Theory: The Challenge of a New Century*, Jun, J. S., Ed., Praeger, Westport, CT, 2002.

Karl, B. D., *Executive Reorganization and Reform in the New Deal*, Harvard University Press, Cambridge, MA, 1963.

Kass, H. D. and Catron, B., Eds., *Images and Identities in Public Administration*, Sage Publications, Newbury Park, CA, 1990.

Kast, E. E. and Rosenzweig, J. E., *Organization and Management: A Systems Approach*, McGraw-Hill, New York, 1970.

Katz, D., *Bureaucratic Encounters: A Pilot Study in the Evaluation of Government Services*, Institute for Social Research, Ann Arbor, MI, 1975.

Katz, D. and Kahn, R., *The Social Psychology of Organizations*, Wiley, New York, 1966.

Kaufman, H. A., Emerging conflicts in the doctrine of public administration, *Am. Politic. Sci. Rev.*, 50, 1057–1073, 1956.

Kaufman, H. A., The paradox of excellence: remarks on receiving the Dwight Waldo Award of ASPA 30 June 1996, ii, November/December, 1996.

Keller, L. F., The political economy of public management: an interorganizational network perspective, *Admin. Society*, 15, 455–474, 1984.

Keller, L. F., Public administration, city management, and the American enlightenment, *Int. J. Public Admin.*, 20, 213–249, 1989.

Keller, L. F., Murray, S., Terry, L., and Washington, C., The role demands and dilemmas of minority public administrators: The Herbert thesis revisited, *Public Admin. Rev*, 409–417, September/October, 1994.

King, C. S. and Stivers, C., Eds., *Government is us: Public Administration in an Anti-Government Era*, Sage, Thousand Oaks, CA, 1998.

Kingdon, J. W., *Agendas, Alternatives and Public Policies*, Little, Brown, Boston, MA, 1984.

Kirlin, J. J., The big questions of public administration in a democracy, *Public Admin. Rev.*, 416–423, September/October, 1996.

Koontz, H., The management theory jungle revisited, *Acad. Manage. Rev.*, 5, 175–187, 1980.

Kranz, H., Are merit and equity compatible?, *Public Admin. Rev.*, 434–440, September/October, 1974.

Landau, M., Political science and public administration: 'Field' and the concept of decisionmaking, In *Concepts and Issues in Administrative Behavior*, Mailick, S. and Van, E. H., Eds., Prentice-Hall, Englewood Cliffs, NJ, 1962.

Landau, M., *Political Theory and Political Science: Studies in the Methodology of Political Inquiry*, Macmillan, New York, 1972.

Landis, J. M., *The Administrative Process*, Yale University Press, New Haven, CT, 1938.

Lane, L. M. and Wolf, J. E., *The Human Resource Crisis in the Public Sector: Rebuilding the Capacity to Govern*, Quorum Books, New York, 1990.

LaPorte, T., The recovery of relevance in the study of public organization, In *Toward a New Public Administration: The Minnowbrook Perspective*, Marini, F., Ed., Chandler, Scranton, PA, 1971.

Lawson, G. W., Technical cooperation for administrative improvement, *Ann. Am. Acad. Politic. Social Sci.*, 323, 111–119, 1959.

Lerner, D. and Lasswell, H., Eds., *The Policy Sciences*, Stanford University Press, Stanford, CA, 1951.

Levitan, D. M., Political ends and administrative means, *Public Admin. Rev.*, 353–359, Autumn, 1943.

Levine, C. H., A symposium: organizational decline and cutback management, *Public Admin. Rev.*, 315–357, July/August, 1978.

Levine, C. H., Police management in the 1980's: from decrementalism to strategic thinking, *Public Admin. Rev.*, 45, 691–700, 1985.

Levine, C. H., Backoff, R. W., Cahoon, A. R., and Siffin, W. J., Organizational design: a post-Minnowbrook perspective for the 'new' public administration, *Public Admin. Rev.*, 425–435, July/August, 1975.

Lewis, C. W. and Logalbo, A. T., Cutback principles and practices: a checklist for managers, *Public Admin. Rev.*, 184–188, March/April, 1980.

Likert, R., *The Human Organization: Its Management and Ealue*, McGraw-Hill, New York, 1961.

Lilienthal, D., *TVA—Democracy on the March*, Harper & Row, New York, 1944.

Lindblom, C. E., The science of 'muddling through,' *Public Admin. Rev.*, 79–88, Spring, 1959.

Lindblom, C. E., *The Intelligence of Democracy: Decision Making Through Mutual Adjustment*, Free Press, New York, 1965.

Lowi, T. J., *The End of Liberalism: The Second Republic of the U.S.*, 2nd ed., W.W. Norton, New York, 1979.

Lowi, T. J., *The End of the Republican Era*, University of Oklahoma Press, Norman, OK, 1995.

Luton, L. S., To run this democracy: reflections on American public administration and the constitution, *Admin. Theory Praxis*, 16, 31–43, 1994.

Lynn, N. and Vaden, R., Bureaucratic responses to civil service reform, *Public Admin. Rev.*, 333–343, July/August, 1979.

Lynn, L. E., The myth of the bureaucratic paradigm: what traditional public administration really stood for, *Public Admin. Rev.*, 144–160, March/April, 2001.

Mansfield, H. C., *Federal Executive Reorganization: Thirty Years of Experience*, Brookings Institution, Washington, DC, 1969.

March, J. G. and Simon, H. A., *Organizations*, Wiley, New York, 1958.

Marini, F., Ed., *Toward a New Public Administration: The Minnowbrook Perspective*, Chandler, Scranton, PA, 1971

Martin, C. C., *Project Management: How to Make it Work*, AMACON, New York, 1976.

Martin, R. C., Political science and public administration—a note on the state of the union, *Am. Politic. Sci. Rev.*, 46, 660–676, 1952.

McGill, M. E., *Training for Action Research*, National Training and Development Service, Washington, DC, 1974.

McGregor, D., *The Human Side of Enterprise*, McGraw-Hill, New York, 1960.

McKean, R. N., *Efficiency in Government Through Systems Analysis*, Wiley, New York, 1958.

McLachlan, J., American colleges and the transmission of culture: the case of the mugwumps, In *The Hofstadter Aegis: A Memorial*, Elkins, S. and McKitrick, E., Eds., Knopf, New York, 1974.

Melnick, R. S., The politics of partnership, *Public Admin. Rev.*, 45, 653–660, 1985.

Merriam, L., The trend toward professionalization, *Ann. Am. Acad. Politic. Social Sci.*, 189, 71–77, 1937.

Mertins, H. and Hennigan, P. J., *Applying Professional Standards and Ethics in the '80s*, American Society for Public Administration, Washington, DC, 1982.

Merton, R. K., *Social Theory and Social Structure*, Rev. ed., Free Press, Glencoe, IL, 1957.

Merton, R. K., *Science, Technology and Society in Seventeenth Century England*, H. Fertig, New York, 1970. Reprinted from vol. IV, p. II, Osiris: Studies on the history and philosophy of science and on the history of learning and culture, 1938.

Mesaros, W. and Balfour, D. L., Hermeneutics, scientific realism, and social research: toward a unifying paradigm for public administration, *Admin. Theory Praxis*, 15, 25–36, 1993.

Metcalf, H. C. and Urwick, L., Eds., *Dynamic Administration: The Collected Papers of Mary Parker Follet*, Harper & Brothers, New York, 1940.

Meyer-Emerick, N., *The Violence Against Women Act of 1994: An Analysis of Intent and Perception*, Praeger, Westport, CT, 2001.

Miewald, R., The greatly exaggerated death of bureaucracy, *Calif. Manage. Rev.*, 65–69, 1970.

Miles, R., The search for identity of graduate schools of public affairs, *Public Admin. Rev.*, Special Issue, November 343–356, 1967.

Miller, H. T., *Postmodern Public Policy*, State University of New York Press, Albany, NY, 2002.

Miller, Z. L., *Boss Cox's Cincinnati: Urban Politics in the Progressive Era*, University of Chicago Press, Chicago, IL, 1968.

Milward, H. B. and Wamsley, G. L., Policy Subsystems, Networks and the Tools of Public Management, In *Policy Systems in Federal and Unitary Systems*, Hankf, K and Toonen, T. A. J., Eds., Martinus Nijhoff, Dordrecht, Netherlands, 1985.

Moe, R. C., The re-inventing government exercise: misinterpreting the problem, misjudging the consequences, *Public Admin. Rev.,* 111–122, March/April, 1994.

Montjoy, R. S. and Watson, D. J., A case for a reinterpreted dichotomy of politics and administration as a professional standard in council-manager government, *Public Admin. Rev.,* 231–239, May/June, 1995.

Moore, P., Zero base budgeting in American cities, *Public Admin. Rev.,* 253–258, May/June, 1980.

Morgan, E. S., *Inventing the People: The Rise of Popular Sovereignty in England and America*, Norton, New York, 1988.

Morgan, G., *Images of Organization*, 2nd ed., Sage Publications, Beverly Hills, CA, 1986.

Morris, E., *The Rise of Theodore Roosevelt*, Coward, McCann & Geoghegan, New York, 1979.

Morstein-Marx, F, Ed., *Public Management in the New Democracy*, Harper & Brothers, New York, 1940.

Morstein-Marx, F., Ed., *Elements of Public Administration*, Prentice Hall, Englewood Cliffs, NJ, 1946.

Mosher, F. C., Research in public administration: some notes and suggestions, *Public Admin. Rev.*, 169–179, 1956.

Mosher, F. C., Ed., *Democracy and the Public Service*, Oxford University Press, New York, 1968.

Mosher, F. C., Ed., *American Public Administration: Past, Present, and Future*, University of Alabama Press, Tuscaloosa, AL, 1975.

Mosher, F. C., Ed., *Basic Documents of American Public Administration: 1776–1950*, Holmes and Meier, New York, 1976.

Mosher, W. E., Government without patronage, *Ann. Am. Acad. Politic. Social Sci.*, 189, 35–41, 1937.

Mumford, L., *The City in History: Its origins, Its Transformations, and Its Prospects*, Harcourt Brace Javanovich, New York, 1961.

Naff, K. C., Through the glass ceiling, prospects for the advancement for women in the federal civil service, *Public Admin. Rev.,* 505–517, November/December, 1994.

Naisbitt, J., *Megatrends*, Warner Books, New York, 1982.

Najjar, G. K., Development administration and the 'new' public administration: a convergence of perspectives, *Public Admin. Rev.,* 584–587, November/December, 1974.

NASPAA, *Guidelines and Standards for Professional Masters Degree Programs in Public Affairs/Administration*, National Association of Schools of Public Affairs and Administration, Washington, DC, 1974.

NASPAA, *Guidelines and Standards for Baccalaureate Degree Programs in Public Affairs–Public Administration*, National Association of Schools Public Affairs and Administration, Washington, D.C., 1976.

NASPAA, *1994 Directory of Programs*, National Association of Schools of Public Affairs and Administration, Washington, DC, 1994.

Nathan, R. P., Re-inventing government: what does it mean?, *Public Admin. Rev.,* 213–215, March/April, 1995.

National Commission on the Public Service, *Leadership for America: Rebuilding the Public Service*, National Commission on the Public Service, Washington, DC, 1989.

Neumann, F. X., What makes public administration a science? Or is its "big questions" really big?, *Public Admin. Rev.,* 409–415, September/October, 1996.

Newland, C. A., Ed., Public sector training: diversity, dispersion, discipline: a symposium, *South. Rev. Public Admin.*, 2, 402–510, 1979.

Newland, C. A., Ed., *Public Administration and Community: Realism in the Practice of Ideals*, Public Administration Service, MacLean, VA, 1984.

Newland, C. A., Ed., The public administration review and ongoing struggles for connectedness, *Public Admin. Rev.*, 20–38, January/February, 2000.

Nigro, L. C., Ed., Affirmative action in public employment: a mini-symposium, *Public Admin. Rev.*, 234–246, May/June, 1974.

Olsen, J. B. and Eadie, D. C., *The Game Plan: Governance with Foresight*, Council of State Planning Agencies, Washington, DC, 1982.

Osborne, D. and Gaebler, T., *Re-inventing Government: How The Enterpreneurial Spirit Is Transforming the Public Sector*, Addison-Wesley, Reading, MA, 1992.

Ostrom, V., *The Intellectual Crisis in American Public Administration*, Rev. ed., University of Alabama Press, Tuscaloosa, AL, 1974.

Ostrom, V., The undisciplinary discipline of public administration: a response to Stillman's critique, *Midwest Rev. Public Admin.*, 11, 304–308, 1977.

Ostrom, V. and Ostrom, E., Public choice: a different approach to the study of public administration, *Public Admin. Rev.*, 203–216, March/April, 1971.

O'Toole, L., Lineage, continuity, Federickson, and the new public administration, *Admin. Society*, 9, 223–253, 1977.

Perlmutter, F. D. and Cnaan, R. A., Entrepreneurship in the public sector: the horns of a dilemma, *Public Admin. Rev.*, 29–36, January/February, 1995.

Peterson, L., *The Day of the Mugwump*, Random House, New York, 1961.

Pfiffner, J. P., *Public Administration*, Macmillan, New York, 1935.

Pfiffner, J. P., The challenge of federal management in the 1980's, *Public Admin. Q.*, 7, 162–182, 1983.

Pfiffner, J. P. and Presthus, R., *Public administration*, 3rd ed., Ronald Press, New York, 1953.

Polenberg, R., *Reorganizing Roosevelt's Government*, Harvard University Press, Cambridge, MA, 1966.

Poister, T. H. and Streib, G., MBO in municipal government: variations on a traditional management tool, *Public Admin. Rev.*, 48–56, January/February, 1995.

President's Commission on Administrative Management, *Report of the Commission*, US Government Printing, Washington, DC, 1937.

President's Commission on Economy and Efficiency, *Report of the Commission*, US Government Printing Office, Washington, DC, 1912.

Prethus, R., *The Organizational Society*, Random House, New York, 1965.

Price, D. K., *The Scientific Estate*, Harvard University Press, Cambridge, MA, 1965.

Price, D. K., 1984 and beyond: social engineering or political values, In *American Public Administration: Past, Present, and Future*, Mosher, F. C., Ed., University of Alabama Press, Tuscaloosa, AL, 1984.

Prigogine, I. and Stengers, I., *The End of Certainty: Time, Chaos and the New Laws of Nature*, Free Press, New York, 1997.

Public Administration Review, Public administration and the constitution: a forum, *Public Admin. Rev.*, 237–267, May/June, 1993.

Quade, E. S., *Analysis for Public Decisions*, American Elsevier, New York, 1975.

Rabin, J., Ed., Public administration as a profession: a symposium, *South. Rev. Public Admin.*, 5, 237–391, 1981.

Rabin, J., Ed., Public administration professionalism: has it a future?. A symposium, part one, *Public Admin. Q.*, 8, 398–508, 1985.

Ramos, A. G., Models of man and administrative theory, *Public Admin. Rev.*, 241–246, May/June, 1972.

Rawls, J., *A Theory of Justice*, Harvard University Press, Cambridge, MA, 1971.

Redford, E., *Democracy in the Administrative State*, Oxford University Press, Cambridge, MA, 1969.

Reedy, G. E., *The Twilight of the Presidency*, World Publishing, New York, 1970.

Reeves, E. J., Making equality of employment opportunity a reality in the federal service, *Public Admin. Rev.*, 43–49, January/February, 1970.

Riccucci, N. M., The old public management versus the new public management: where does public administration fit in?, *Public Admin. Rev.*, 172–175, March/April, 2001.

Rice, B. R., *Progressive Cities: The Commission Government Movement in America, 1901–1920*, University of Texas Press, Austin, TX, 1977.

Richter, A., The existentialist executive, *Public Admin. Rev.*, 415–422, July/August, 1970.

Riggs, F. W., Public administration: a neglected factor in economic development, *Ann. Am. Acad. Politic. Social Sci.*, 305, 70–80, 1956.

Riggs, F. W., *Administration in Developing Countries*, Houghton Mifflin, Boston, MA, 1964.

Riggs, F. W., Bureaucracy and the constitution, *Public Admin. Rev.*, 65–72, January/February, 1994.

Riggs, R. R., PA's public image, *Bureaucrat*, 12, 38–40, 1983.

Riordon, W. L., *Plunkitt of Tammany Hall: A Series of Very Plain Talks on Very Practical Politics, Delivered by Ex-Senator George Washington Plunkitt, the Tammany Philosopher, from His Rostrum, the New York County Court-House Bootblack Stand*, Knopf, New York, 1948.

Roberts, A., Demonstrating neutrality: the Rockefeller philanthropies and the evolution of public administration, 1927–1936, *Public Admin. Rev.*, 54, 221–228, 1994.

Rohr, J. A., The study of ethics in public administration curriculum, *Public Admin. Rev.*, 398–406, July/August, 1976.

Rohr, J. A., *To Run a Constitution: The Legitimacy of the Administrative State*, University Press of Kansas, Lawrence, KS, 1986.

Rohr, J. A., *Ethics for Bureaucrats: An Essay on Law and Values*, 2nd ed., Marcel Dekker, New York, 1989.

Rohr, J. A., *Civil Servants and Their Constitutions*, University Press of Kansas, Lawrence, KS, 2002.

Rosenbloom, D. H., Public administrative theory and the separation of powers, *Public Admin. Rev.*, 219–227, May/June, 1983.

Rosenbloom, D. H., Have an administrative Rx: don't forget the politics, *Public Admin. Rev.*, 53, 503–507, 1993a.

Rosenbloom, D. H., Prescriptive public administration theory as a product of political dominance, *Admin. Theory Praxis*, 15, 1–10, 1993b.

Rosenbloom, D. H., Retrofitting the administrative state to the constitution: congress and the judiciary's twentieth century progress, *Public Admin. Rev.*, 39–46, January/February, 2000a.

Rosenbloom, D. H., *Building a Legislatively-Centered Public Administration: Congress and the Administrative state 1946–1999*, University of Alabama Press, Tuscaloosa, AL, 2000b.

Rouse, J. E., Jr., Boundaries of an emerging superdiscipline: a review of recent and selected older bibliographic material in public administration, *Public Admin. Rev.*, 390–398, July/August, 1982.

Rutgers, M., Ed., *Retracing Public Administration*, Elsevier, Boston, 2003.

Saranson, M., *The Creation of Settings and the Future Societies*, Jossey-Bass, San Francisco, CA, 1972.

Savage, P., Optimism and pessimism in comparative administration, *Public Admin. Rev.*, 415–423, July/August, 1976.

Savas, E. S., *Privatizing the Public Sector*, Chatham House, Chatham, NJ, 1982.

Sayre, W. S., The triumph of techniques over purpose, *Public Admin. Rev.*, 134–137, Spring, 1948.

Sayre, W. S., Premises of public administration: past and emerging, *Public Admin. Rev.*, 102–105, Spring, 1958.

Schacter, H. L., Retroactive seniority and agency retrenchment, *Public Admin. Rev.*, 77–81, January/February, 1983.

Schattschneider, E. E., *The Semi-Sovereign People: A Realist's View of Democracy in America.*, Rinehart and Winston, New York, 1960.

Schick, A., The road to PPB: the stages of budget reform, *Public Admin. Rev.*, 243–258, December, 1966.

Schick, A., A death in the bureaucracy: the demise of federal PPB, *Public Admin. Rev.*, 145–156, March/April, 1973.

Schick, A., The trauma of politics, In *American Public Administration: Past, Present, and Future*, Mosher, F. C., Ed., University of Alabama Press, Tuscaloosa, AL, 1975.

Schiesl, M. J., *The Politics of Efficiency: Municipal Administration and Reform in America: 1880–1920*, University of California Press, Berkeley, CA, 1977.

Schlesinger, A. M., *The Age of Roosevelt: The Coming of the New Deal*, Houghton Mifflin, Boston, MA, 1958.

Schlesinger, A. M., *The Imperial Presidency*, Houghton Mifflin, Boston, MA, 1973.

Schlesinger, A. M., Ed., *The Almanac of American History*, Putnam, New York, 1983.

Schlesinger, A. M., *The Disuniting of America: Reflections on a Multicultural Society*, Whittle Direct Books, Knoxville, TN, 1991.

Schlesinger, J. R., *Systems Analysis and the Political Process Rand Paper P-3464*, Rand Corporation, Santa Monica, CA, 1967.

Schoderbek, P. P., *Management Systems*, 2nd ed., Wiley, New York, 1971.

Schott, R., Public administration as a profession: problems and prospects, *Public Admin. Rev.*, 253–259, May/June, 1976.

Schwartz, B. and Wade, H. W. R., *Legal Control of Government: Administrative Law in Britain and the United States*, Oxford University Press, New York, 1972.

Scott, M., *American City Planning*, American Planning Association, Washington, DC, 1971.

Scott, W. G., Organization theory: an overview and an appraisal, *Acad. Manage. J.*, 4, 7–26, 1961.

Seidman, H., *Politics, Position and Power: The Dynamics of Federal Organization*, Oxford University Press, New York, 1970.

Selznick, P. A., *TVA and the Grass Roots*, Harper & Row, New York, 1949.

Selznick, P. A., *Leadership and Administration*, Row Peterson, Evanston, IL, 1957.

Shapiro, M. M., *The Supreme Court and Administrative Agencies*, Free Press, New York, 1968.

Siffin, W. J., The new public administration: its study in the U.S., *Public Admin*, 34, 365–376, 1956.

Siffin, W. J., *Toward the Comparative Study of Public Administration*, Department of Government, Indiana University, Bloomington, IN, 1957.

Simon, H. A., The proverbs of administration, *Public Admin. Rev.*, 53–67, Winter, 1946.

Simon, H. A., *Administrative Behavior*, Macmillan, New York, 1947.

Simon, H. A., Smithburg, D. W., and Thompson, V. A., *Public Administration*, Knopf, New York, 1950.

Snow, C. P., *The Two Cultures and the Scientific Revolution*, Cambridge University Press, New York, 1959.

Snow, C. P., *Science and Government*, Oxford University Press, New York, 1961.

Somit, A., Bureaucratic real politic and the teaching of administration, *Public Admin. Rev.*, 292–296, Autumn, 1956.

Sorensen, Georg, *The Transformation of the State: Beyond the Myth of Retreat*, Plagrave McMillan, New York, 2004.

Spicer, M. W., *The Founders, the Constitution, and Public Administration: A Conflict in World Views*, Georgetown University Press, Washington, DC, 1995.

Spicer, M. W. and Terry, L. D., Legitimacy, history and logic: public administration and the constitution, *Public Admin. Rev.*, 239–246, May/June, 1993.

Spirited dialogue: michael harmon's responsibility as paradox, *Public Admin. Rev.*, 593–610, November/December, 1996.

Stein, H., *Public Administration and Policy Development*, Harcourt Brace, New York, 1952.

Stene, E. O., An approach to a science of administration, *Am. Politic. Sci. Rev.*, 34, 1124–1137, 1940.

Stewart, F. M., *A Half Century of Municipal Reform: The History of the National Municipal League*, University of California Press, Berkeley, CA, 1950.

Steuerle, C. E., *The Tax Decade: How Taxes Came to Dominate the Public Agenda*, Urban Institute Press, Washington, DC, 1992.

Stever, J., *The End of Public Administration: Problems of the Profession in the Post-Progressive Era*, Transnational Publishers, Dobbs Ferry, NY, 1988.

Stillman, R. J., Woodrow Wilson and the study of administration: a new look at an old essay, *Am. Politic. Sci. Rev.*, 67, 582–588, 1973.

Stillman, R. J., *The Rise of the City Manager*, University of New Mexico Press, Albuquerque, NM, 1974.

Stillman, R. J., Ostrom's new paradigm for American public administration—adequate or antique?, *Midwest Rev. Public Admin.*, 10, 179–192, 1976.

Stillman, R. J., The changing patterns of public administration theory in America, In *Public Administration: History and Theory in Contemporary Perspective*, Uveges, J. A., Ed., Marcel Dekker, New York, 1982.

Stillman, R. J., *Preface to Public Administration*, St. Martins Press, New York, 1991.

Stivers, C., Active Citizenship and Public Administration, In *Refounding Public Administration*, Wamsley, G., et al., Ed., Sage Publications, Newbury Park, CA, 1990.

Stivers, C., *Gender Images in Public Administration: Legitimacy and the Administrative Atate*, Sage Publications, Newbury Park, CA, 1993.

Stivers, C., The listening bureaucrat: responsiveness in public administration, *Public Admin. Rev.*, 364–369, July/August 1994.

Stivers, C., Refusing to get it right: citizenship, difference and the refounding project, In *Refounding Democratic Public Administration: Modern Paradoxes, Postmodern Challenges*, Wamsley, G., Ed., Sage Publications, Thousand Oaks, CA, 1996.

Stivers, C., *Bureau Men, Settlement Women: Constructing Public Administration in the Progressive Era*, University Press of Kansas, Lawrence, KS, 2000.

Stivers, C., Ed., *Democracy, Bureaucracy and the Study of Administration*, Westview Press, Boulder, CO, 2001.

Stevenson, E., *Park Maker: A Life of Frederick Law Olmsted*, Transaction Publishers, Brunswick, NJ, 2000 (first printed in 1977).

Stone, A. B. and Stone, D. C., Early development of education in public administration, In *American Public Administration: Past, Present, and Future*, Mosher, F. C., Ed., University of Alabama Press, Tuscaloosa, AL, 1975.

Stone, D. C., Birth of ASPA—a collective effort in institution building, *Public Admin. Rev.*, 83–93, January/February, 1975.

Stone, H. A., Price, D. K., and Stone, K. H., *City Manager Government in Nine Cities*, Public Administration Service, Chicago, IL, 1940.

Storing, H. J. and Leonard, D., White and the study of public administration, *Public Admin. Rev.*, 25, 38–51, March, 1965.

Stover, C. F., Changing patterns in the philosophy of management, *Public Admin. Rev.*, 21–27, Winter, 1958.

Straetz, R. A., *PR Politics in Cincinnati: Thirty-Two Years of City Government Through Proportional Representation*, New York University Press, New York, 1958.

Sundquist, J. L., The concept of governmental management: or what's missing in the Gore report, *Public Admin. Rev.*, 398–399, July/August, 1995.

Svara, J. H., Dichotomy and duality: reconceptualizing the relationship between policy and administration in council-manager cities, *Public Admin. Rev.*, 221–232, January/February, 1985.

Svara, J. H., *Official Leadership in the City: Patterns of Conflict and Cooperation*, Oxford University Press, New York, 1990.

Svara, J. H., *Facilitative Leadership in Local Government: Lessons from Successful Mayors and Chair-Persons*, Jossey-Bass, San Francisco, CA, 1994.

Taylor, F. W., *Scientific Management*, Harper & Row, New York, 1923.

Terry, L. D., Why we should abandon the misconceived quest to reconcile public entrepreneurship with democracy, *Public Admin. Rev.*, 393–395, July/August, 1993.

Terry, L. D., *Leadership of Public Bureaucracies: The Administrator as Conservator*, Sage Publications, Thousand Oaks, CA, 1995.

Terry, L. D., Ed., Spirited dialogue: theodore lowi's the end of the republican era, *Public Admin. Rev.*, 475–494, September/October, 1995.

Terry, L. D., Administrative leadership, neo-managerialism and the public management movement, *Public Admin. Rev.*, 194–200, May/June, 1998.

Thayer, F., The NASPAA threat, *Public Admin. Rev.*, 85–90, January/February, 1976.

Thayer, F., The president's management reforms: theory x triumphant, *Public Admin. Rev.*, 309–314, July/August, 1978.

Thompson, J., *Organizations in Action: The Social Science Basis of Administrative Theory*, McGraw-Hill, New York, 1967.

Thompson, V., *Without Sympathy or Enthusiasm: The Problem of Administrative Compassion*, University of Alabama Press, Tuscaloosa, AL, 1975.

Toffler, A., *The Third Wave*, William Morrow, New York, 1980.

Truman, D. B., *The Governmental Process*, Knopf, New York, 1951.

U.S. House of Representatives, Committee on Energy and Commerce, *Foresight in the Private Sector: How Can Government Use it?*, U.S. Government Printing Office, Washington, DC, 1983.

Upson, L. D., *Letters on Public Administration, From a Dean to His Graduates*, Detroit Citizens Research Council of Michigan, Detroit, MI, 1947.

Uveges, J. A. Jr., *Federal–State Relationships in Interstate Highway Administration: A Case Study of Florida*, Public Administration Clearing Service, Gainesville, FL, 1963.

Uveges, J. A., Ed, *Public Administration: History and Theory in Contemporary Perspective*, Marcel Dekker, New York, 1982.

Uveges, J. A., Identifying the impacts of NASPAA's MPA standards and peer review process on education for the public service: 1975–1985, *Int. J. Public Admin.*, 9, 193–227, 1987.

Van Riper, P. P., *History of the United States Civil Service*, Row, Peterson, Evanston, IL, 1958.

Van Riper, P. P., The American administrative state: Wilson and the founders—an unorthodox view, *Public Admin. Rev.*, 477–490, November/December, 1983.

Van Riper, P. P., The politics-administration dichotomy: concept for reality?, In *Politics and Administration: Woodrow Wilson and American Public Administration*, Rabin, J. and Bowman, J. S., Eds., Marcel Dekker, New York, 1984.

Von Mises, L., *Bureaucracy*, Yale University Press, New Haven, CT, 1944.

Waldo, D., *The Administrative State*, Ronald Press, New York, 1948.

Waldo, D., Development of theory of democratic administration, *Am. Politic. Sci. Rev.*, 46, 81–103, 1952.

Waldo, D., *The Study of Public Administration*, Doubleday, New York, 1955.

Waldo, D., *Perspectives on Administration*, University of Alabama Press, Tuscaloosa, AL, 1956.

Waldo, D., Organization Theory: An Elephantine Problem, *Public Admin. Rev.*, 210–225, Autumn, 1961.

Waldo, D., The administrative state revisited, *Public Admin. Rev.*, 5–30, March, 1965.

Waldo, D., Scope of the theory of public administration, In *Theory and Practice of Public Administration: Scope, Objectives, Methods*, Charlesworth, J. C., Ed., American Academy of Political and Social Sciences, Philadelphia, PA, 1968.

Waldo, D., Ed., *Public Administration in a Time of Turbulence*, Chandler, San Francisco, CA, 1971.

Waldo, D., Developments in public administration, *Ann. Am. Acad. Politic. Social Sci.*, 404, 217–245, 1972.

Waldo, D., Education for public administration in the seventies, In *American Public Administration: Past, Present, and Future*, Mosher, F. C., Ed., University of Alabama Press, Tuscaloosa, AL, 1975.

Waldo, D., Symposium on comparative and development administration: retrospect and prospect, *Public Admin. Rev.*, 36, 615–654, 1976.

Waldo, D., *The Administrative State*, 2nd ed., Homes and Meier, New York, 1984.

Walker, H., *Public Administration in the U.S.*, Farrar and Rinehart, New York, 1937.

Walker, J. L., Performance gaps, policy research, and political entrepreneurs, *Policy Stud. J.*, 3, 112–116, 1974.

Walker, R. A., Public administration: the universities and the public service, *Am. Politic. Sci. Rev.*, 39, 926–933, 1945.

Wamsley, G. L. *et al.*, *The Blacksburg manifesto*, Center for Public Administration and Policy, Virginia Polytechnic Institute and State University, Blacksburg, VA, 1985.

Wamsley, G. L. *et al.*, *Refounding Public Administration*, Sage Publications, Newbury Park, CA, 1990.

Wamsley, G. L. and Wolf, J. F., *Refounding Democratic Public Administration: Modern Paradoxes, Modern Challenges*, Sage Publications, Newbury Park, CA, 1996.

Wamsley, G. L. and Schoeder, A. D., Escalating in a quagmire: the changing dynamics of the emergency management policy subsystem, *Public Admin. Rev.*, 56, 235–244, 1996.

Wamsley, G. and Zald, M., *The Political Economy of Public Organizations*, D.C. Heath, Lexington, MA, 1973.

Wamsley, G. and Zald, M., The political economy of public organizations, *Public Admin. Rev.*, 62–73, January/February, 1973.

Warren, K. F., *Administrative Law in the American Political System*, West Publishing, St. Paul, MN, 1982.

Waugh, P., Ed., *Postmodernism: A Reader*, E. Arnold, New York, 1992.

Weinstein, J., Organized business and the city commission and manager movements, *J. South. Hist.*, 28, 166–182, 1962.

Wengert, E., The study of public administration, *Am. Politic. Sci. Rev.*, 36, 313–322, 1942.

West, D. M., E-Government and the transformation of service delivery and citizen attitudes, *Public Admin. Rev.*, 15–27, 2004.

White, L. D., *Introduction to the Study of Public Administration*, Macmillan, New York, 1926.

White, L. D., *The City Manager*, University of Chicago Press, Chicago, IL, 1927.

White, L. D., Administration as a profession, *Ann. Am. Acad. Politic. Social Sci.*, 189, 90–94, 1937.

White, M. G., *Social thought in America*, Beacon Press, Boston, MA, 1957.

Willbern, Y., The broadening concerns of administration, *Public Admin. Rev.*, ii–iii, Autumn, 1957.

Williams, D. G., *Applying Public Management Concepts to Ourselves: Accreditation Under the New Master Degree Minimum Standards*, National Association of Schools of Public Affairs and Administration, Washington, DC, 1994.

Willoughby, W. F., *Principles of Public Administration*, Johns Hopkins Press, Baltimore, MD, 1927.

Wilson, J. Q., The rise of the bureaucratic state, *Public Interest*, 41, 77–103, 1975.

Wilson, W., The study of administration, *Politic. Sci. Q.*, 2, 197–222, 1887.

Wilson, W., The new meaning of government, *Public Admin. Rev.*, 44, 193–195, 1984.

Winter, W. O., *The Urban Polity*, Dodd, Mead and Co, New York, 1969.

Winter, W. F., *Hard Truths/Tough Choices: An Agenda for State and Local Reform*, National Commission on the State and Local Public Service, Washington, DC, 1993.

Wills, Garry, *Negro President: Jefferson and the Slave Power*, Houghton Mifflin, Boston, MA, 2003.

Yates, D., *Bureaucratic Democracy: The Search for Democracy and Efficiency in American Government*, Harvard University Press, Cambridge, MA, 1982.

2 Five Great Ideas in American Public Administration

Marc Holzer, Vache Gabrielyan, and Kaifeng Yang

CONTENTS

I. INTRODUCTION

Public administration is a subject of human inquiry with ancient roots. Contrary to present practice, the ancients were preoccupied with governance of the public as affairs, not business. As found in Greece, they disdained commerce and management of business enterprise. Ancient empires created elaborate state structures and effectively operated an apparatus overseeing huge territories.

49

China gave the world the first civil service system some two thousand years ago, and the Roman Empire set the structures of governance (e.g., the organization of the executive branch into five main agencies) that many modern European states borrowed in their development (see e.g., Heady 1996; Wren 1994).

The study and systematic development of public administration in America, however, is scarcely more than a century-old phenomenon. It is a field of study that continuously adapts, both in practice and theory, to the government's and the society's changing nature. Often, public administration is characterized as an application of social and other sciences to public problems, which allows it to bridge disciplines (Frederickson 1976, 152). Constantly trying to define itself, public administration draws from multiple sources with an effort to reconcile often contradicting views.

Coping with the field's perpetual "identity crisis" (as coined by Dwight Waldo in the 1960s) and in search of answers that are in step with the times, academics and practitioners of public administration consistently reflect on several key issues: Where does politics stop and adminis-tration begin? How can employees be led, motivated, and protected from political excesses? How different is public management from private management? What is the necessary scope of govern-ment's services? What, and how much, should be centralized or decentralized? How can the public sector achieve efficiency and effectiveness while balancing those concerns with equity in service delivery? Who should govern, and what is the role of experts and expertise in the process of governance? What is the nature of public interest if there is one? Some questions pertain to the realm of political theory that underlies the field, and others refer to more pragmatic concerns of public administration's applied practice.

During the evolution of American public administration, these questions were often framed through public discourse in a much simpler, sharper, and sometimes conflicting pattern. The discourses often rejected established mentalities and are cast it in dichotomous terms (i.e., admini-stration is *different* from politics, public management is *different* from private management). They were often used as powerful rhetoric to advance the development of the field (Roberts 1994).

In some form, during the century-long development of American public administration theory, key issues were articulated by scholars of administration from different perspectives. Several ideas caught the spirit of the times, although they never received simple or final answers in adminis-trative studies. Catalyzed by events and problems that caught the public's attention, such ideas were able to command significant amounts of scientific effort and advocacy. Each marked an era in the evolution of the field. For example, Frederick Taylor's system of industrial shop management was viewed by Progressives such as Louis Brandeis (who coined the term "scientific manage-ment") as a means to improve railroads' productivity, helping prevent fare increases. Following Congressional hearings on Taylor's methods that resulted in their banishment from the federal government, Taylor and others continued to publicize the concepts of scientific management. The concepts were widely embraced by many in the private sector (Wren 1994). Similarly, Whiting Williams' pioneering work in developing the human relations model (i.e., industrial sociology) in the 1920s did not take hold until the social sciences were an established, significant field of study in the 1930s. At this point, the academic credentials of researchers at Harvard and M.I.T. made the case for that model through the Hawthorne studies (Wren 1994). It is useful to study the evolution of thought about public administration through the prism of the issues and concerns that shape the field.

As a relatively new and applied field, management and public administration are always adapting to changing socio-political and economic conditions. As a result, they are difficult to classify. The most popular and fruitful approach to teaching public administration theory is to trace its evolution through time and by putting different theories in their historical context. As Gulick comments, "the global content of the field of public administration is set by the environment, not by logic; if government does it, it is 'public administration'" (1990, 602). The pursuit of effective public sector administration may be explained as a series of ideas, each representing a step or increment toward a complete theory of public administration. None is comprehensive or complete. Taken as a whole, they do not preempt possible future insights. With each successive limited emphasis, public administration is a closer approximation to desirable administration. Taken separately, each emphasis may be considered more as a complement to, rather than a substitution for, others. Viewed over time, they helped build a substantial reservoir of knowledge. Although the history of insights into public administration is neatly divided into discrete periods, that neatness can be unnecessarily arbitrary, seeming to confine any one idea or perspective to certain years. For example, the following approaches are often confined to certain dates (e.g., McCurdy 1972; Nigro and Nigro 1973):

- Administrative Reform Movement: 1870–1926
- Orthodox Period: Administrative Science Movement: 1906–1952
- Politics Period: 1936–1967
- Human Relations and Behavioral Science: 1933–present
- Program Effectiveness 1964–present

Hard and fast divisions are also misleading if students then presume that each successive school displaced its predecessor based on the correct core idea of an emerging new school. Public administration might be more clearly described as a series of continuing and overlapping insights with none that have been supplanted. From the rise of the administrative state to date, society's governance has become more and more complex with old problems unresolved and new issues emerging. New insights or new theories of public administration are constructed to reflect new aspects of changing administrative practice. Working together, they demonstrate a whole and real public administration.

Since the 1960s, rigorous theoretical attempts have developed taxonomies of management theories according to their approaches and emphases on different aspects of management (both public and private). Perhaps the most basic division of management theories, one that in some form is acknowledged by every student of organizational theory, is to emphasize either general, scientific principles of management (basically structure and process) or to emphasize human behavior in organizations. Koontz (1961) was credited with the concept of the "management theory jungle," wherein he identified six schools: (1) the *management process* school, (2) the *empirical* school, (3) the *human behavior* school, (4) the *social system* school, (5) the *decision theory* school, and (6) the *mathematical* school. Although clear, this taxonomy of approaches to management was neither systematic nor based upon consistent criteria. For example, an empirical (research methodology) study can be mathematical (tools) and focus on human behavior (content). A 1962 symposium at UCLA addressing Koontz's article questioned the universality of management theory (including public and private spheres). It concluded that there were language differences in different schools that drew from different sources (Wren 1994, 355–357).

In pursuit of a more rigorous taxonomy of the field, organizational science drew from the work of Burrell and Morgan in *Sociological Paradigms in Organizational Analysis* (1979). They classified all theories of organization (Figure 2.1) according to their approach to science (along the continuum subjective–objective) and approach to society (along the continuum of radical change–regulation). Burrell and Morgan (1979, 3) define a subjective viewpoint as focusing on "an understanding of the way in which the individual creates, modifies, and interprets the world in which he or she finds himself," and an objective viewpoint as looking for "universal laws which explain and govern the reality which is being observed." The other dimension stems from what Burrel and Morgan call "order–conflict" debate in sociology. This refers to whether the theory tries to explain the order of cohesive human systems or it tries to account for radical change. Later, Morgan (1997) identifies eight theoretical frameworks as eight metaphors in organizational theory: organization as machines, brains, cultures, political systems, psychic prisons, flux and transformation, and instruments of domination.

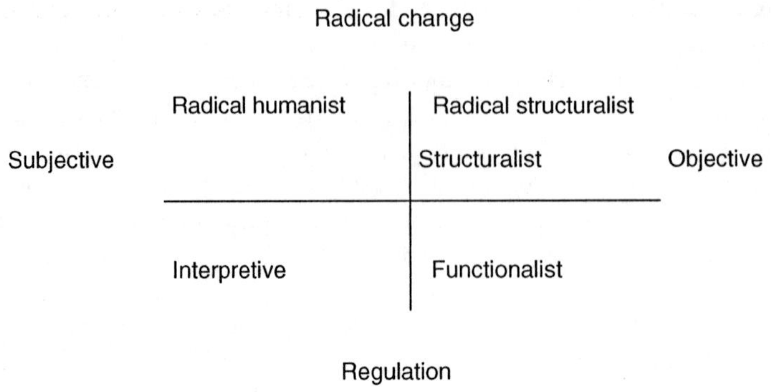

Radical change

Radical humanist	Radical structuralist	
Subjective	Structuralist	Objective
Interpretive	Functionalist	

Regulation

FIGURE 2.1 Burrel and Morgan's classification of organization theories. (From Burrell, G, and G. Morgan, *Sociological Paradigms in Organizational Analysis*, Heinemann, London, 1979. With permission.)

In the 1980s, Quinn (1988) developed a competing values framework (Figure 2.2) classifying management theories according to their approaches toward control or decentralization (along the axis control–flexibility) and their focus on the organization's internal or external endeavors (along the axis internal–external). Quinn's holistic approach to the competing theories asserts that successful organizations and managers should balance capacities that reinforce each model rather than excel at one of them; otherwise, narrowness will leave them vulnerable to competing claims that organizations typically encounter. Since the 1970s, such calls for a holistic approach have been a part of mainstream organizational thought. Here, the public productivity movement was launched to synthesize different schools of management in the context of enhanced organizational practice.

One problem with Quinn's methodology is that Taylor's and other studies in the category of the rational goal model are not exclusively externally oriented. Additionally, all classifications have characterized Taylor's model and the internal process model as being essentially the same—the classic bureaucratic or closed model. Perhaps, instead of the control–flexibility differentiation, rewording of that dimension to certain–uncertain (simple–complex; structured–loosely coupled) will better explain the stress of Taylor's scientific management on getting the most out of a

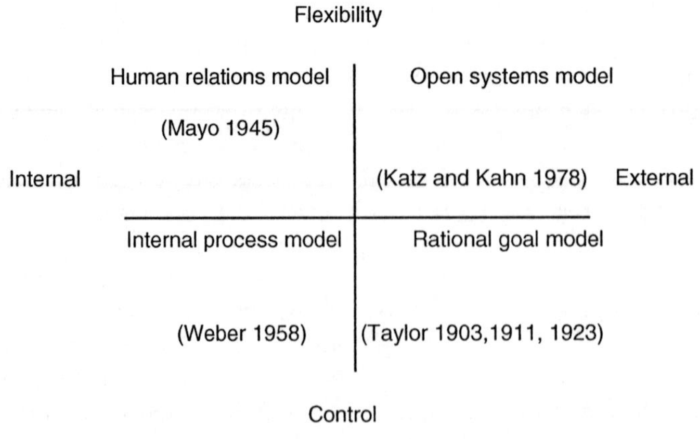

Flexibility

Human relations model	Open systems model	
(Mayo 1945)		
Internal	(Katz and Kahn 1978)	External
Internal process model	Rational goal model	
(Weber 1958)	(Taylor 1903,1911, 1923)	

Control

FIGURE 2.2 Quinn's classification of organization theories. (From Quinn, R.E., *Beyond Rational Management*, Jossey-Bass, San Francisco, 1988. With permission.)

given stable set of conditions as well as Weber's emphasis on coordination in large and complex organizations.

More theoretical attempts at multi-paradigm or meta-paradigm theory-building exist (e.g., Gioia and Pitre 1990). Although the problem of theoretical reconciliation of conflicting paradigms is not an easy one, it is a problem with a solution. Each of the paradigms addresses a separate field of activities or the same activity in different situations; therefore, different approaches are complementary or can coexist. Each theory or paradigm draws from a set of core beliefs or a certain ideology. Without discussing these ideologies, conflicting beliefs can peacefully coexist (albeit with tension). In Mary Douglas' group-grid typology of culture, four basic and exclusive cultural assumptions about society—hierarchy, egalitarianism, fatalism, and individualism—can be held by the same person or organization (e.g., as a parent, one may be a hierarchist; as a citizen, an individualist; as a religious person, a fatalist; as a professional, a egalitarianist) because they are context-specific (Thompson et al. 1990).

Within public administration literature, there are classification attempts as well. Because of its multi-disciplinary nature, public administration resists classification. Along with a multiplicity of perspectives from general organization studies, it also has legal and political frameworks of reference. Because of diverse and often conflicting perspectives, Waldo (1961) calls organization theory in the context of public administration an "elephantine problem." Notwithstanding the variety of approaches to the field, theories of public administration can be broadly classified as coming from two directions—administration or politics—or as having micro and macro concerns: management of public organizations and the role of bureaucracy in the framework of constitutional democracy.

In the first direction, management of public organizations, two basic models can be recognized: the classic administrative model (from Taylor, Wilson, and Weber to Simon and March) and the human relations model (from Mayo and Follett to Golembiewski and Argyris).

The second direction, bureaucracy in the framework of constitutional democracy, is more diverse because of its close bonds to the fields of political science, economics, and sociology as well as its larger scope (society at large). For instance, Hill (1991) classifies theories of bureaucracy according to the end result—the impact they prescribe to bureaucracy in governance. This classification has three main categories or theories: (1) bureaucracies are (or should be) weak and instrumental; (2) they are significant actors in political process; and (3) they dominate the policy process. Each of these perspectives has its variations from pure pluralism to interest-group liberalism to Marxism and elitism. Cook (1992) classifies theories of bureaucracy's role along institutionalist (hierarchist) and functionalist lines. Wood and Waterman (1994) distinguish between normative and empirical research. Despite the diversity of approaches, only a few resulted in a shaping influence on the field. One influential stream of thought in this direction is the public choice school (Niskanen 1971; Ostrom 1977; 1989b; Ostrom and Ostrom 1971; Williamson 1975) with its application of economic logic to political and social life. To this line of argument, there has also been the constant reminder that a theory of public administration is a theory of politics and society (Waldo 1990).

Most attempts to classify public administration theory have been positivistic. Frederickson (1976, 153), for example, argues for a more critical "new public administration," yet he still recognizes five models of public administration based on a definition of theory as "positive or empirically based knowledge." The models he identifies are classic bureaucratic (Gulick and Urwick 1937), neo-bureaucratic (Simon 1947), institutional (Lindblom 1959), human relations (McGregor 1960), and public choice (Ostrom 1989b) as well as the new public administration with more humanistic, equitable, and democratic values as opposed to the previous ones that focused primarily on efficiency and effectiveness. Rosenbloom (1983) distinguishes the three historical approaches to the theory of public administration as *managerial*, *political*, and *legal*. Based on stratified systems theory, Burke (1989) suggests the following essential themes for the development of the field: the relationship between theory and administration; employment; bureaucracy; public interest; and a definition of public administration. Stillman (1995) identifies six schools of the "refounding public administration" movement developed since the 1970s: (1) the "reinventors" who use an eclectic approach catalyzed by Osborne and Gaebler (1992); (2) "the communitarians" who emphasize citizenship, family values, and civic participation; (3) the Blacksburg Manifesto (Wamsley 1990) "refounders" who try to extend the meaning of public administration from mere management of public organizations to a larger and more legitimate understanding of it as a part of governance; (4) the interpretive theorists and post-modernists who emphasize the human condition in a society dominated by organizations; (5) the "tools approach"—with a leading theme that today, with a burgeoning of the not-for-profit sector in delivery of public services, there is no one best way of approaching the administration of services, even at the federal level; and (6) the new bureaucratic perspective whose main emphasis is on bureaucratic accountability in a constitutional democracy.

Along with these divergent approaches, there is also a sub-surface stream of comparative public administration (e.g., Heady 1996; Riggs 1994a; 1994b; Willoughby 1919). Although the American public administration community has been distinctly myopic and self-centered, the comparative public administrationists persevere in demonstrating the utility of cross-cultural studies.

Since the 1970s, scholars acknowledge that the field of public administration is very complex and must satisfy multiple, often competing, values. Frederickson (1976), for example, notes that models of public administration have tried to maximize some values at the expense of the others, while other values were also legitimate. In the tradition of Waldo, Stillman (1976, 1991, 1995) argues for multiple perspectives in the field. Since the 1970s, there has also been the growth of postmodern, interpretive, and critical analysis of public administration (Denhardt 1981; Farmer 1995a; Fox and Miller 1995; Harmon 1981; Hummel 1994; Jun 1986; Kass and Catron 1990) with a focus on human experience in organizations and bureaucracy. Fox and Miller (1995) discussing public administration in the postmodern tradition, distinguish three discourses that shaped public administration: orthodox, constitutional, and communitarian.

Some fundamental ideas or values have been identified as major forces shaping the field. Gulick (1990) contends that American public administration is fundamentally tied to four, sometimes inconsistent, principles of social organization: democracy, individualism, specialization, and the market. Kettl (2000) emphasizes an understanding of how political traditions shape administrative theory and how administrative theory brings political traditions to life. Kettl identifies the Hamiltonian, Jeffersonian, Wilsonian, and Madisonian traditions as major bedrocks of American public administration (Figure 2.3). As Kettl argues, most administrative approaches flow out of these traditions one way or another.

	Wilsonian Hierarchical	Madisonian Balance of Power
Hamiltonian	Strong executive	Non-bureaucratic institutions
Strong executive/Top–down	Top–down accountability	Focus on political power
	Hierarchical authority	Top–down accountability
Jeffersonian	Weak executive	Non–bureaucratic institution
Weak executive/Bottom–up	Bottom–up accountability	Focus on local control
	Responsiveness to citizens	Bottom–up responsiveness

FIGURE 2.3 Administrative ideas in the American political tradition. (From Kettl, D.F., *J. Public Admin. Research Theory*, 10(1):7–34, 2000. With permission.)

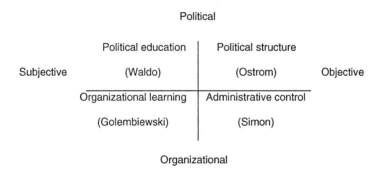

FIGURE 2.4 Denhardt's classification of public administration theories. (From Denhardt, R.B., *Theories of Public Organization*, 2nd ed., Wadsworth, Belmont, CA, 1993. With permission.)

Denhardt (1990, 1993) provides the most sophisticated analytical typology of public administration theories. Drawing from Burrell and Morgan (1979) typology for organization theories, Denhardt develops a typology for public administration. Denhardt's classification (Figure 2.4) abandons the radical change–regulation (or normalization) dimension, and instead introduces the more relevant politics–administration dimension. This classification significantly improves Burrel and Morgan's classification in terms of its applicability to public administration. This substitution of dimension can be justified on different grounds. For example, some theorists argue that public administration theory is geared to the production (or efficiency) ethic, and it is aimed at normalization of the society and the bureaucracy. However, it fails to discuss alternative liberation ethics (Farmer 1995b). Public administration theories in the United States, though always concerned with a good life and more democratic administration, were based on the premise of a democratic political system (the US ideal-type model) and never espoused an ideology of radical change based on Marxist or other understandings of politics. Instead, the politics–administration dimension highlights the unique character of public administration (the difference from generic management) and the central dilemma of its identity. One problem with Denhardt's classification is that, as opposed to Burrell and Morgan's typology, the criteria involved are heterogeneous, for subjectivity or objectivity (as well as change or adaptation) is a matter of general methodology while organizations or politics are more objects of study than mode of analysis.

Denhardt's model also resembles Quinn's (1988) competing values model with the possibility that one can be translated into another. Assuming that (1) public agencies are political in their nature in that they carry out a political function in their external activities with regard to other agencies, legislatures, people (clients), and organizations, and (2) knowledge of objective reality (certainty) enables us to plan and control while subjective understanding supposes multiple and competing interpretations of reality (uncertainty) and calls for a more flexible approach. These two typologies can be juxtaposed. Of course, these assumptions are good for drawing parallels only; the criteria do not translate into each other directly and should not be treated literally.

The resulting double classification (Figure 2.5) provides a rich analysis of public administration theories. First, it indicates the link between public administration to management and organization studies. Second, it helps to underscore the difference between public and private management, and it hints to where they may be more alike. Third, it helps to explore, compare, and contrast epistemological underpinnings of theory (subjective–objective) with its more pragmatic concerns (control–flexibility) as well as to look behind what seem to be instrumental categories (e.g., what type of rationality is implied in the rational goal model). Fourth, one aspect of the criteria employed (political–organizational and control–flexibility) is more homogeneous, and they both relate to the

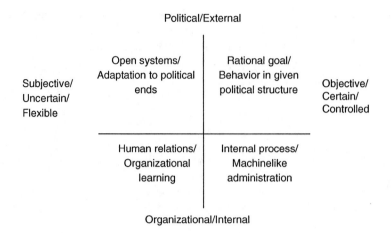

FIGURE 2.5 Dual classification of public administration theories.

object of study. It once again shows that different approaches to administrative theory can and should be reconciled on a practical level, encompassing elements from each quadrant of the diagram. Productive public agencies should carry out the political function they are created for and behave politically (e.g., clientele building for political support); rationally and honestly deal within an established political, social, and economic structure (e.g., accountability to Congress, the President, and the public through different mechanisms); constantly improve the internal organization and technologies (e.g., measurement techniques); and develop human resources and maintain a creative social atmosphere in the workplace.

This double structure highlights the themes the public choice school shares with the intellectual tradition of Finer (1941) who, reflecting on Wilson (1887) and perceiving the political system as a certain and fixed set of principles (assumptions it shares with public choice theory), argued in the famous debate with Friedrich (1940) that "the servants of the public are not to decide their own course; they are to be responsible to the elected representatives of the public, and these are to determine the course of action of the public servants to the most minute degree that is technically feasible" (Finer 1941, 335). In the same manner, Waldo's study of intellectual currents that shaped the field of public administration has common characteristics with studies that examine the impact of social and political forces on the structure of different agencies (e.g., DiTomaso 1994).

Of course, any single framework can hardly capture the complexity and diversity of public administration. First, human cognitive capacity is limited when describing and analyzing a field that is actively evolving. Second, many terms that are routinely used in administrative theories have multiple, context-specific meanings. For example, Dunsire (1973) identifies 15 meanings for the word *administration*. Third, there are other dimensions of scientific inquiry that are closely related, but not identical to, the above-mentioned dimensions (e.g., normative versus empirical research, qualitative versus quantitative research, comparative/international versus US-specific research). And finally, each dichotomous classification (e.g., politics–administration) is a crude approximation of a much subtler continuum ranging from one ideal (e.g., politics) to another ideal (e.g., administration) with real-world phenomena always containing elements of both.

For a better understanding of the different theories of public administration and the reasons why they were able to command so much attention, it is important to situate the theories in their historical context. Very often, looking beyond the immediate features of the theories allows a look into what events shaped them. For example, despite an always existing legalistic stream of thought in the Unites States, public administration in this country never acquired a legalistic bent (as in France) for several reasons: (1) the absence of a tradition of state in the United States

(Stillman 1991); (2) the American inclination towards universalism (Hampden-Turner and Trompenaars 1993), which in this particular situation resulted in treating public administration as generic management; (3) a limited and decentralized government. Administrative law in the United States began to emerge as a full-fledged discipline only in the twentieth century as a result of tensions between a modern administrative state and a constitutional democracy (Rosenbloom 1989). Whatever the reasons for this development, the argument is that although some of them can be analyzed through a proposed framework by distinguishing differences in theory (e.g., limited and decentralized government as a form of political structure), phenomena like the absence of a tradition of state (in the European sense) can be assessed only through historical analysis.

Therefore, it is important to discuss theories and ideas (i.e., tenets) of public administration not only from the viewpoint of their theoretical distinctiveness and rigor, but also from the viewpoint of their impact on the development of the field, the rhetoric that justified their embrace by the public, and the factors that shaped them. For this reason we find it useful to present five great ideas that shaped the field in the following framework, combining their historical importance and theoretical distinctiveness. Several ideas will be emphasized, while others will be barely mentioned. For example, subjective treatments of organizational issues (e.g., phenomenological, critical studies), although theoretically rigorous and distinctive as well as growing rapidly since the 1970s, still do not have the same impact on the field of public administration as do the schools of scientific management and human relations. Of course, overlaps are possible, but this framework is believed to be very useful in presenting ideas that have had a lasting impact upon the field.

Five great ideas (or sets of ideas) of American public administration based on epistemological and content-based criteria identified in our dual classification scheme are distinguished below. Based on the suggested link between epistemology and content, it is possible to show that theoretical concerns cast in more pragmatic terms (e.g. control vs. flexibility) were able to capture not only the attention of scholars of public administration but also the imagination of the public as well. Becoming part of public rhetoric at certain periods of history, the five great ideas shaped the field.

First, there is the idea of honest and businesslike government. It is assumed that the rules of the game and the goals of the actors are certain and stable—everyone knows what people, public officials, and politicians should strive for in this political environment. Then there is the idea of efficient administration of an organization. The tasks and roles are clear and certain again, and the system is closed—interaction with the outside world is often out of the focus. The third approach holds that political structure and goals change, and much like politicians, public agencies have to respond and adapt to change. The fourth approach is concerned with human interaction within organizations—how people reconcile multiple perspectives and interests in pursuit of organizational ends. Finally, the last idea is concerned with overall program effectiveness, recognizing limitations of the previous approaches and integrating all of the perspectives. The assumption here is that reality has multiple tenets, and each should be approached with a different focus in mind and employ various analytical tools; however, this should not be at the expense of the others. To be successful, public organizations should excel in all directions: execute functions within accepted structures and rules; adapt to emergent political structures and interests; motivate and lead employees; and strive for the most efficient use of internal resources. The five ideas that comprise this framework and that continue to serve as a foundation block for modern public administration are

1. *Honest, Non-partisan and Businesslike Government*: The idea of honest, efficient, partisan-free government administration is the single most important concept in the establishment of the field of American public administration. This stream of thought is based on two basic assumptions—that there are clear-cut, "divine laws of social order and well-being" (G. L. Prentiss 1877, as quoted in Waldo 1984, 28), and there are primarily two ultimate functions of government—"expression of will and execution of

that will" (Goodnow 1900, 22). In other words, there is an established and stable political framework that public administration should be assigned within its proper, unambiguous place. The Progressive Movement not only separated administration from politics, but by attaching the label of notoriety to virtually everything political, it also started the relentless drive of looking to the private sector for best practices. It ignored legalistic management as too bookish, and public administration did not develop within a legal framework. One reason for this ignorance was angst against bookishness, and another reason was case law that differs from continental European (France's) codes of law. As today's calls for privatization and more market structure in the provision of public services show, this drive to borrow from the private sector is not limited to internal organizational processes, but it relates to political and economic structures as well. Interestingly enough, analysis of public administration theories from this perspective (based on objectivity and external focus) brings Wilson's theory of public administration and public choice theory under the same conceptual umbrella, however strange it may seem.

2. *Classic Management Models*: After administration was legitimately accepted as separate from politics and functionally identical to business, the dominant ideal became machinelike efficiency in getting the job done with a minimum of wasted energy. The focus shifted from the political question of the place of public administration in society to a more micro-concern—effective management of an organization premised upon the idea of clearly recognizable, scientific laws describing reality. This direction drew heavily from the scientific management school and reached a peak in the more sophisticated analyses of administrative decision-making. Studies of the business organization gave rise to a number of supposedly universal laws or principles of administration and to a procedure, scientific management, by which optimum efficiency could be achieved. It was no more than logical to borrow these discoveries for application to the management of public sector organizations; as such, management was defined within the closed model.

3. *Politics and Policy Making*: After the field of public administration was already established and the emergent welfare state began its extensive programs, it became evident that the dichotomy between politics and administration was no longer realistic. As government intervention became common and as interest-group liberalism took hold, it became obvious that public agencies were reaching to different constituencies, influencing them, and adapting to their needs. This meant change in one of the assumptions upon which the field had been founded—clear, fixed laws of democratic structure where every institution is assigned its specific and exclusive role. It was recognized that there is no set role for public administration in a democratic political system; rather, public administration reflects changes in the society and simultaneously shapes them. Thus, a major trend in public administration has been the movement away from the idea of neutrality and toward the idea of politics. Although early advocates of administrative neutrality argued that administrators merely implement public policies, that assumption now was seen as naive. It was recognized that values intrude on administration from many external sources and are also present in even supposedly objective internal decisions as to policy implementation. Also recognized was the idea that bureaucrats are necessarily policymakers as much as any other participants in the process.

4. *Human Behavior*: The classical school of management had its roots in Taylor's scientific management school and an engineering conception of efficiency: getting the job done with a minimum of wasted energy. Although management theories primarily derived from the private sector did provide an understanding of the organizational skeleton, they proved to be inadequate for explaining behavior in public or private

organizations. In particular, they failed to account for the complexity of human nature or for the impact of an uncertain and changing environment. Following the much publicized Hawthorne (i.e., Western Electric) experiments in the late 1920s and 1930s as well as introduction of a sociological approach to organizations (organizations as social systems), a new school of management thought was formed. The behavioral model emphasizes the importance of human relations and personal goals. If the closed model concentrates primarily on a technical system of organization—a system that produces products or services or that maintains operations—then the behavioral model recognizes the equal importance of the social system that is comprised of uninstitutionalized, multidimensional, and nebulous networks of relationships between individuals or groups within an organization. While preserving the focus on intraorganizational management, this school focused on multiple meanings and uncertainties that people have in coping with any human organization.

5. *Program Effectiveness*: As a result of government programs' growth with new missions, combined with the rapid technological and demographic changes experienced since the turn of the twentieth century, and the shrinking of public resources (in constant dollars), the effectiveness or productivity of public organizations has become a primary concern of the American public. Notions of the one best way of administration have been criticized, and more inclusive approaches to administration have been advocated. This is true not only of practical tools and techniques, but also of a theoretical understanding of the field. By and large, public administration began to view itself as a synthetic field that has to balance competing, and often contradicting, values and that is open to continuous adaptation and improvement in pursuit of productive performance.

II. IDEA ONE: HONEST, NEUTRAL, BUSINESSLIKE GOVERNMENT

One of the continuing tug-of-wars in American public administration has been credentials (which imply competence) versus representativeness (which implies responsiveness). Even in the relatively small bureaucracies presided over by presidents from George Washington to John Quincy Adams, qualifications were highly valued. Although there certainly existed political patronage, such patronage was not elevated to the level of political philosophy. George Washington claimed that government jobs should be given to "those who seem to have the greatest fitness for public office" (Tolchin and Tolchin 1971, 323). But in 1828, the influx of previously disenfranchised, propertyless masses into politics through the elevation of Andrew Jackson to the Presidency initiated a new administrative philosophy—spoils. As opposed to government by the elite, that system emphasized rotation in office as a means to achieving politically responsive administration. Almost any citizen was considered fit to carry out the simple duties of public management, which were, after all, just a matter of common sense. In his first annual message to Congress in 1829, Jackson declared, "The duties of all public offices are ... so plain and simple that men of intelligence may readily qualify themselves for their performance; and I cannot but believe that more is lost by the long continuance of men in office than is generally to be gained by their experience. They are apt to acquire a habit of looking with indifference upon the public interest" (Hofstadter 1954, 51).

Unfortunately, the price of responsiveness was high. Although the offering of gifts as corrupting bribes is a practice that dates back to the establishment of the first ancient public organizations, it was particularly rampant under Jackson's spoils system. During much of the nineteenth century, at all levels of government, graft was widespread; scandals were frequent. It was not unusual for a public official to receive very large sums for reasons of influence, not friendship. Such behavior is still not unusual in many developing societies. But corruption had high indirect costs. Inefficiency became endemic; graft widespread; scandals frequent—not only at the federal level but also at the state and municipal levels where the spoils system prevailed. A large, increasingly industrialized and more complex nation could not tolerate such poor public service administration just as government was taking on new responsibilities. Municipalities had to deliver water, assure public safety, maintain smooth streets, fight fires, and, by the end of the century, provide public education and regulate private utilities or mass transit systems.

Waste and dishonesty had to be curbed if government and a growing society were to function efficiently. In the post–Civil War period, reform movements appealed directly to the public for efficiency and honesty in both politics and administration. A common theme of reform emerged in the 1870s and dominated politics for half a century. Known as the Progressive Era, reforms would bring about significant changes in the administrative functions of government. Between 1875 and 1920, economic progress and turbulence changed the context of politics, stirring citizens to replace the corrupt machines and install administrators who would improve the cities' atmosphere for commerce and the quality of life. Old machine politics and the spoils system were blamed for every ill in society—inefficiency, injustice, corruption, and prostitution (Kaufman 1965, 129). Attacking the spoils system, reformers did succeed in defining *conflict of interest* as an immoral situation. It is now common to find such constraints on officials since the prohibition against having a financial interest in any company that their agency regulates or has commercial dealings with. Similar situations that are considered ethical within the letter of the law are increasingly coming into question on moral grounds.

The reaction—the first great theoretical foundation stone of American public administration—was a reform movement that appealed for efficiency and honesty in government. The Pendleton Civil Service Act of 1883 created a neutral, bipartisan Civil Service Commission—the beginning of the system that now covers more than 90% of public employees. The establishment of a civil service system amid a prevailing atmosphere of reform provided both the means and the impetus for getting the job done with a minimum of wasted effort.

As a function of the reform movement, jurisdictions within the United States began to establish codes of ethics, which were written into law; today, those laws typically require that public services should be provided honestly, openly, fairly, and without discrimination. In short, citizens expect bureaucrats to act within the law, not as a law unto themselves. Although compliance with the law is often cumbersome, members of a society are willing to accept some inefficiency as the price of freedom. They recognize that one of the basic strengths of democracy is concern with the means as much as with the ends of government. To the public and the press, however, the rules and regulations that result from the necessity to administer laws equitably are merely manifested as the frustrating red tape they so often deride.

The clear separation between politics and administration was demanded by reformers such as Woodrow Wilson (1887) (in his role as professor), who suggested a dichotomy between (1) policy determination via politics and (2) policy implementation via nonpolitical administration.[*] Implementation of public policy in government would, according to Wilson, follow principles of more businesslike management. To do so, those managing governments needed to devote greater attention to the science of administering government (i.e., administrative principles and sound management). According to Wilson, "Organization and methods of government should determine first, what government can properly and successfully do, and secondly, how it can do these things with the utmost efficiency... America needs to develop an administrative organization and skills for proper administration" (Wilson 1887). Only through competent, uncorrupted administration would government carry out the people's wishes and those of their representatives. Public servants would be perceived as professionals, administration as efficient, and government as trustworthy. This reflected a second distinctive feature of the movement—belief in a science of administration

---

[*] For Wilson's role in formation of public administration in the United States, see Cook (1995), Stillman (1973), and Van Riper (1984).

(or the one best way of doing things), in addition to a belief in expertise, which nonpolitical public servants were to represent.

Later Frank Goodnow (1900, 22) reinforced Wilson's points, interpreting the Constitution as a statement of "two distinct functions of government." Policy was centered in the legislative and judicial branches, and it was to be administered only by the executive. Policy was an expression of state will, depoliticized administration the execution of that will. The thrust of the turn-of-the-century reform movement was captured in the saying: There is neither a Democratic nor a Republican way to build a road, just the right way. Thus the Reform Movement was evolving in two main directions: (1) neutrality of personnel and (2) improvement of efficiency, mostly on a local level.

In 1894, the First Annual Conference for Good City Government organized the National Municipal League as a forum and coordinating body with the objective of formulating a plan that could be supported nationally (Shafritz and Hyde 1991). Two hundred affiliated societies developed a theory of good government that rested on four fundamental elements and associated reforms that held:

- The efficient delivery of public services is central to the public interest.
- Administration of public services must be separated from politics and would operate through independently elected boards and commissions.
- Experts with specialized training, appointed under a civil service merit system, would comprise a permanent civil service and could implement scientific methods.
- Government would be operated as a business by applying principles of scientific management, including proper budgeting and accounting procedures and competitive bidding.

By the turn of the century, the Reform Movement had achieved significant changes in the practice of public administration, particularly in the areas of fiscal and personnel management. Galveston, Texas, for example, become the first city to be run on the business model, and this model was subsequently adopted by more than 450 municipalities prior to World War I (ICMA 1994). The city manager model was implemented in the first decade of the century in several municipalities. With the advance of reforms, the rhetoric of reform also began to change. If personnel reform was seen by many in the 1880s as a high moral endeavor, by the beginning of the century, it was mostly seen as a more pragmatic "matter of improving the quality of administration" (Waldo 1984, 29).

In the century intervening since Wilson's call for more businesslike public administration, the public sector has certainly adopted many private sector techniques. Nevertheless, such improvements in public administration have had one ultimate objective—improved productivity. However, public service has lost much of the public's confidence. Despite a century of systematic efforts to improve the delivery of government services and despite great progress, the public is frustrated and angry, and it continues to demand that government personnel be smarter and work harder. The lack of confidence evident in the latter third of the nineteenth century has not dissipated. In 1926, Leonard D, White (1979), a noted analyst of American government, observed that

> Two ideas are widely held by the American taxpayer. He believes that there is an extraordinary number of useless or overpaid public officials and he is convinced that most government employees are lazy and incompetent.... The city, state, or federal employee... thinks of the years of faithful service which he has performed, well hidden from the windows where "the public" peers in... and is not unlikely to shrug his shoulders, thinking, "What's the use."

And almost six decades later, Kaufman (1981) concluded that public administration had not made any headway with the populace.

Over the course of more than a century, the idea of honest, neutral, businesslike government did not die in public administration studies or in popular rhetoric. Although many concepts preoccupied generations of scholars, such as the more responsive and just, value-driven perspective of the New Public Administration in the 1970s (Frederickson 1971; Marini 1971), the idea of situating public administration within an objective, clear notion of governance did not vanish. A major intellectual development in the field of public administration in the early 1970s was the emergence of the public choice School of thought. The methodological emphasis of public choice theory is on more or less objective and stable knowledge from which to draw and a preoccupation as to the place of public administration in constitutional government. Drawing from the public choice school in economics, Ostrom (1989b, 16) argues for a new concept in American public administration that is based on the theory of public goods rather than the theory of bureaucracy with which, he suggested, American public administration was preoccupied. The public choice school can be best characterized by its proposed foci of study (Ostrom 1989a, 876): "multiple levels, facets, and foci of analysis that relate to: (1) human valuation, (2) production possibilities, (3) arrays of goods and services, (4) rule-oriented relationships, and (5) shared levels of common understanding that enable people to communicate, and act meaningfully, to one another." As Vincent Ostrom (1977, 1510) explains, "the subject matter of political inquiry is the allocation, exercise and control of decision-making capabilities among people in human societies. Decisions are ordered by reference to rules." This attention to rules squarely stands in the tradition of public choice. After Arrow (1951) demonstrated that in a rational-voting collective system it is possible not to achieve a collective choice that is consistent with diverse preferences of the individuals comprising the collective, the process of inquiry focused on making the process fair. Buchanan and Tullock (1962) shifted the analysis to the rules of the game instead of the outcome because some inevitably would win and others would lose, as Arrow demonstrated. This type of analysis has paid attention to the rules of aggregation of preferences in the society. Elinor Ostrom (1991) took the analysis of this mode farther, drawing on game-theoretical traditions, and identified a minimal set of rules that are important to governance of democratic societies, which includes information rules, boundary rules, scope rules, authority rules, and aggregation rules. As for every major intellectual achievement, it is difficult to put the work of Vincent and Elinor Ostrom and other representatives of the public choice school into procrustean cells of classification schemes. Based on tenets of public choice theory such as multiple arrangements of service provision, the importance of voting for service delivery and flexibility in its approach, many may see the public choice school as closer to the political adaptation category. This may have been the approach if the classification followed the flexibility–control nexus instead of the subjectivity–objectivity nexus. But, as mentioned above, these classifications do not translate into each other directly. In this case, the classification on the objective nature of knowledge is based in public choice theory. The importance of the public choice school also rests on the fact that, on a theoretical level, it reintroduced and facilitated the idea of multiple arrangements for provision of public goods, including, among others, privatization. These ideas have become so strong a political theme that the field of public administration has been forced to accede to an almost irrational rush to privatization. The enduring nature of the privatization movement remains in question, however, to the extent that the unanticipated, and often negative, consequences of so fundamental a shift in service provision become evident.

The ideas of neutrality, competence, and businesslike behavior have their manifestations and critics in contemporary terms. The citizens' distrust toward government, lamented by White (1979) and Kaufman (1981), has not been alleviated. Instead, it has worsened. Since the 1950s, there has been an increase in distrust of the government (Kass and Newton 1995; Nye et al. 1997) and a decline in voter turnout because of an increasing sense of alienation by the people. The increase in distrust has been used by many politicians to promote an anti-government or a smaller government agenda. Whatever the reasons for the distrust, government faces more and more pressure in terms of its performance and accountability. As Gulick (1990, 602) assesses: "the turn of the century to the twenty-first century needs much of the same reforming energy that the turn of the century to the twentieth generated."

Businesslike government is prescribed in the reform programs guided by the New Public Management philosophy. One aspect of the idea, borrowing management practices from the private sector, has been evident for the past two decades. For example, strategic planning, especially the Harvard Business School model, has been widely adopted in public agencies. Performance measurement techniques have been implemented widely too. Of particular interest now is the balanced-scorecard model made popular in the private sector. The general idea of re-inventing government originated in the business process re-engineering model that become popular in the late 1980s. The new fanfare of e-commerce has spilled into government operations, which IT managers are called upon to develop e-government.

The privatization and out-sourcing practice and theory can be related to this idea of businesslike government from a seemingly shared assumption: business organizations are better managed with higher level of efficiency, economy, and effectiveness. The difference with government is that privatization advocates go much farther than the Progressive reformers: because business organizations presumably generate greater efficiency, let them do the job and shrink the government. The idea of businesslike government remains active; however, coupled with the current political environment and ideologies, its practical meaning has changed from reforming government to make it work to shrink government. Progressive reformers at the beginning of the twentieth century valued efficiency, but they placed efficiency under a democratic framework supporting active citizenship. As Sayre (1958, 103) explains, "The responsibility of administrative agencies to popular control was a value taken-for-granted." White (1926, 419) acknowledges that means must be found to "ensure that the acts of administrative officers shall be consistent not only with the law but equally with the purposes and temper of the mass of citizens." It is clear for Willoughby that "efficient bureaucracy was a solution to the manifold problems of democratic governance" (Lynn 2001, 149). The contemporary re-inventors, however, tend to achieve efficiency at the price of democratic accountability and governance.

The endurance of the old idea and the change of its practical meaning also apply to other aspects of businesslike neutral government: expertise and competence. These aspects may be more important than being businesslike because, as Gulick (1990, 600) says, "the drive for specialization and professionalization of management came first from the municipal research and reform forces, well before schools of management were initiated for private business." The call for more professional expertise has never been abated in the United States, but the dominance of expertise has also been increasingly criticized for ignoring citizens and their local knowledge. On the one hand, Dewey's observation in the 1920s that the public's problem is the dilemma between the increasing complexity of the society and the limitation of human beings is still sound today. The government needs more qualified professionals to solve complex changing problems. On the other hand, since the 1920s, government policies have increasingly been formulated by a network of policy elites, researchers, and administrators with the advent of a technocracy dominated by a world view in favor of positivistic, objective knowledge over local, subjective understanding (Fischer 1995). The unexpected consequence is that average citizens are left out in the administrative decision process because of a lack of professional knowledge (Hummel and Stivers 1998; Zanetti 1998).

Another major tenet associated with this first idea, the politics–administrative dichotomy, is also still alive. Although vehemently attacked by the advocates of a political theory of public administration as illustrated later in the third idea, it has been reinterpreted as a professional standard (Rosenbloom 1993), an institutional ban on particularism (Montjoy and Watson 1995), an ideological doctrine (Lee 1995), a structural tension (Skok 1995), a complementarity (Svara 2001), and an ideal type (Rutgers 2001). In practice, politics and administration are still considered as separate ways of thinking and decision-making (Klingner et al. 2002), which differentiates non-career and career executives (Dolan 2000). In management capacity studies, Ingraham and Donahue (2000, 294) differentiate administrative functions and policy implementation, a move appearing to revive the politics–administration dichotomy. Although they argue that their intention is not to revive the dichotomy, their statement testifies to the dichotomy's analytical relevance: "the staff functions and program-policy functions also have independent effects on government performance, and thus should be distinguished to develop a richer understanding of government management."

More efforts have been made to probe early writers such as Wilson and Goodnow's meaning of the dichotomy with the assumption that they have been misinterpreted or distorted by their followers and critics. Lynn (2001) makes a significant contribution in arguing that traditional thought shows great respect for law, politics, citizens, and values. For example, Goodnow is often considered as a proponent of a stark dichotomy of politics and administration, but, as interpreted by Merriam (1926, 142), Goodnow "drew a line between political officials, who are properly elective and the administrative officials, who are properly appointive. 'Politics' should supervise and control 'administration,' but should not extend this control farther than is necessary for the main purpose." This idea is summarized by Van Riper (1983): "As we all know by now, politics and administration are inextricably intermixed. Both are central to effective action. One problem is to bring them together in a symbiotic association yet keep each in its proper place. The other is to understand that the 'proper place' of each will vary through time. There is no permanent solution, no fixed paradigm, to this or any other ends–means continuum."

To many contemporary writers, the rereading of this first idea and its historical context is of great relevance. For example, the New York Bureau of Municipal Research was traditionally viewed as a major implementer of scientific management principles in government. A re-examination shows that what the center stands for is professionalization and informed citizenship (Schachter 1997; Stivers 2000). A study traces to the center the use of performance measurement techniques to improve government responsiveness and democratic governance (Williams 2003). These studies do not nullify the importance of the first great idea; on the contrary, they make it currently more useful by demonstrating its context and by balancing efficiency and neutrality with democratic values such as accountability and citizenship.

III. IDEA TWO: CLASSIC MANAGEMENT MODELS

The establishment of a civil service system amid a prevailing atmosphere of reform provided both the means and the impetus for more businesslike government. Following Wilson and other reformers who suggested that the running of government needed to be made more businesslike, the dominant ideal became machinelike efficiency in getting the job done with a minimum of wasted energy. Although the business sector was often pointed to by government's critics as a model of efficiency, neither businesslike management nor common sense was an adequate guide in these complex matters. The business model (whether applied by public or private organizations) still came up short; the right way to run an organization was simply neither self-evident nor intuitive. Honest common sense proved inadequate as an efficient, productive guide to managing complicated systems in complex organizations. Paradigms were needed.

Studies of the business organization had given rise to a number of universal laws or principles of administration and to a procedure—scientific management—by which optimum efficiency could be achieved. It was only logical to borrow these discoveries for application to the management of public sector organizations, and such management was defined within the closed model. Or, as Willoughby (1927) writes, "…in administration, there are certain fundamental principles of general application analogous to those characterizing any science which must be observed if the end of administration, efficiency in operation, is to be secured." Urwick (1937, 49) concurs:

There are principles which can be arrived at inductively from the study of human experience of organization, which should govern arrangements for human association of any kind. These principles can be studied as a technical question, irrespective of the purpose of it, or any constitutional, political or social theory underlying its creation.

Generic principles or organization were considered applicable to the management of public sector organizations within the closed model (administrative, bureaucratic, mechanistic) that describes organizations where organizational interests dominate the individual's interests. These organizations' interests are concentrated on efficiency and effectiveness as well as specialization and obedience to authority. The closed model of organizations is described by such terms as bureaucracy, hierarchy, pyramid, or vertical, formal, rational, and mechanistic.

Under the scientific management rubric, the works of Taylor (1903, 1911, 1923) and his followers demonstrated the efficiencies of having management study, identify, and teach workers the one best way to perform each task. However, these management theories proved to be inadequate for explaining organizations. They failed to account for the complexity of human nature or for the impact of an uncertain and changing environment. But if they omitted the muscle and the flesh, they did provide an understanding of the skeleton: organizations are made up of certain parts and processes that have to be managed. Taylor assumed that a manager's job is a result of the division of labor, and it is a separate full-time job to manage. Thus, Taylor's theoretical framework included the notion that management has: (1) the responsibilities for discovering the best ways to plan and perform all aspects of operations and (2) is charged with selecting, training, developing, and monitoring each individual in the establishment [organization] to enable that worker to do the highest class of work to the limit of his natural abilities.

Although his principles were resisted by organized labor within government, Taylor's work helped to set a model for government by defining the formal model of organization as a rational, legitimate, institutionalized relationship of people formally managed or coordinated from one center to accomplish certain common predetermined goals, objectives, or purposes.

According to Fayol (1949) and others, working in an industrial context, basic elements of formal or administrative organization are specialization, authority, hierarchy, division of labor, communication, standard procedures of operations, and management. The combination of these elements, and the relationships between them, defines the organizational structure.

Within the public sector, the types of organizations that Taylor and Fayol helped to define, in industrial terms, fit within the bureaucratic model defined by German sociologist and political scientist Max Weber. The basic prototype of such a model was described by Weber as an "ideal-type" bureaucracy (1958). Weber's ideal type, or model of bureaucracy, describes an arrangement of positions that he considered to be the "most rational known means" of accomplishing objectives. According to Weber, the bureaucratic form routinizes the process of administration exactly as the machine routinizes production. Efficiency is achieved through the creation of a fixed division of tasks, a well-defined hierarchy of authority, impersonality, and detailed rules and regulations. Weber viewed bureaucracy as based on a more progressive type of authority than did previous historical formations. As opposed to kings who held traditional power and extraordinary leaders who wielded charismatic power, bureaucracy was based on legal-rational authority. This approach made it both more vital and more efficient although the popular understanding of *bureaucracy* is associated with no response, red tape, and inefficiency.

The chief characteristics of the Weber model include universal rules impersonally carried out, use of written records, division of duties into spheres of competence, training for each position, selection on the basis of competence, hierarchical arrangement of offices, salary based on position, and tenure of office. These characteristics make for an enduring, predictable, efficient, organized machine. In a well-run bureaucracy, of which the best military divisions and agencies are the most appropriate examples, operations are managed in a way that the best compliment is like clockwork. It is often the most efficient model in terms of logic, cost, speed, control, and operational stability. Basic features of this model include politically predetermined and clearly stated goals, centralized authority, a strict chain of command, and a prescribed set of impersonal and interconnected regulations for all aspects of the organization's activities (management's and employees' rights and duties, punishments and benefits, operating and managerial procedures, etc.). The core element of the structure of every public bureaucracy is strict hierarchy with a single chief executive on the top. Each position is under the direct administrative control of the supervisor one level above. Functions, rights, and duties are assigned to the positions, not to persons. Each member of the organization has limited and clearly defined rights, duties, powers, and expertise fixed in written instructions. Vacancies are filled and promotions are accomplished because of formal technical qualifications (certificates, degrees), seniority, or achievement.

Whereas Taylor (an American) emphasized more of an engineering understanding of efficiency—performing a particular job in one best, scientific way as to produce maximum output from each worker—Fayol (a Frenchman) and Weber (a German) placed more emphasis on coordination and control as to produce maximum output from an organization. It is often argued that this difference was a result of different American and European experiences (Hofstede 1993).

Building on the type of work and principles that Taylor, Fayol, and others developed in the industrial context, Gulick and Urwick (1937) identified a set of processes that take place in every organization. They used the acronym POSDCORB (Planning, Organizing, Staffing, Directing, Controlling, Reporting, and Budgeting). Each of these processes was linked to rules for their healthy conduct. For example, Gulick and Urwick identified and advanced the concept of specialization so to better utilize the varying skills and aptitudes of different workers. With the advance of specialization, they also recognized a heightened need for coordination of work. Coordination was to be achieved by (1) a structure of hierarchical authority and (2) the development of a singleness of purpose in the minds and wills of those who are working together. Organizations should always adhere to the (scalar) principle of a chain of command with unity of command. Urwick's (1952) Ten Principles describe guidelines for organizational design that should be used in building up any formal organization:

1. *Principle of the Objective*: Every organization and every part of every organization must be an expression of the purpose of the undertaking concerned, or it is meaningless and redundant. Organization cannot be found in a vacuum; it must be for something.
2. *Principle of Specialization*: The activities of every member of any organized group should be confined, as far as possible, to the performance of a single function.
3. *Principle of Coordination*: The purpose of organizing, as distinguished from the purpose of the undertaking, is to facilitate coordination or unity of effort.
4. *Principle of Authority*: In every organized group, the supreme authority must rest somewhere. There should be a clear line of authority from supreme authority to every individual in the group.
5. *Principle of Responsibility*: The responsibility of the superior for the acts of his subordinate is absolute.
6. *Principle of Definition*: The function of each position, the duties involved, the authority and the responsibility contemplated, and the relationships with other positions should be clearly defined in writing and published to all that are concerned.
7. *Principle of Correspondence*: In every position, the responsibility and the authority should correspond.
8. *The Span of Control*: No person should supervise more than six direct subordinates whose work interlocks.
9. *Principle of Balance*: It is essential that the various units of an organization should be kept in balance.
10. *Principle of Continuity*: Reorganization is a continuous process; in every undertaking, specific provision should be made for it.

In 1937, President Roosevelt charged the Brownlow Committee with seeing that American democracy can efficiently do the job required of it. The Brownlow Report (Brownlow Committee 1937), under Gulick's direction, represents the high point of an impetus for scientific management in government. As opposed to the *Papers on the Science of Administration* (1937) that did not elaborate on political assumptions and the implications of generic administrative science (Golembiewski 1989), the Brownlow Report was more forthcoming on this issue. According to Rohr (1986) it "attempts to ground scientific management in constitutional theory and fundamental principles of American government."

To the field's credit, principles of management were not naively accepted as universal absolutes. Simon (1946) challenged the concept of principles in administration, likening them to proverbs. He identified contradictions, and he suggested that these so-called principles should be treated as possible prescriptions, depending on a situation. In his landmark study, Simon (1997 [1947]) reoriented inquiry in the field of public administration, and organizational science in general, to decision-making. Drawing from the philosophy of logical positivism, Simon distinguished between values and facts, and he identified a value–fact chain as a knowledge basis for different levels of the organization where the means for a higher level could be interpreted as ends for the lower levels. This leads to rational decision-making based on limited, but more or less unambiguous, knowledge. Rationality is not comprehensive, but bounded—by both human cognitive abilities and costs related to acquiring that knowledge. Analyzing the decision-making process, Simon showed that human decisions are not based on the principle of maximizing results; it would be too ambitious and costly a task. Rather, people "satisfice" (a term coined by Simon from *satisfy* and *suffice*). Simon's and his colleagues' work (e.g., March and Simon 1958; Simon et al. 1950) is considered to be the peak of the classic school, or as it is often branded, constitutes the neoclassical school in management.

Classic management models set the basis for many modern management techniques such as management by objectives (MBO), and planning, programming, budgeting systems (PPBS). But they have also been criticized for underplaying the human aspects and the uncertain environments of an organization, for resulting in mindless bureaucracy and dehumanizing human beings, and for endorsing monopoly over knowledge to control execution. A contingency view considers, at best, that the models work well only in situations with a stable environment, easy tasks, standard production, and where precision and efficiency are at a premium.

To some extent, the limitations of the classic models are the limitations of modernity and rationality. The mechanization of life and bureaucratization of organization was, and still is, a broad social trend or underlying social force. Modernity and rationality cannot be escaped for the time being, and the classic models cannot be thrown away. One simple fact is the terminologies used in the models are still the basis for communication on managing and organizing. Some researchers have attempted to recover a certain ethical dignity for bureaucracies, countering romantic critiques from radical humanists and the ahistorical allegations from new manageralists (e.g., Du Gay 2000). In organizational research, Scott (1996) shows that Weber's legacy and mandate is still being honored in the field. Sharp and Housel (2004) validate Fayol and Gulick's approach with a case study on the Oklahoma Health Department. Taylor, for example, has been depicted as authoritarian and reductionistic, equating employees with economic man and motivation with pay incentives. But his theory is still relevant, far beyond the football field, gymnasium, and McDonald's (e.g., Morgan 1997). Taylor had many supporters in the early twentieth century and has many modern defenders (Drucker 1976; Fry 1976; Hodgetts and Greenwood 1995; Martin 1995). Drucker (1976) welcomes a rediscovery of scientific management, arguing that Taylor's motivational strategies provided the worker with an opportunity for full personality development. Hodgetts and Greenwood (1995) find that Taylor's principles of scientific management are alive, well, and ready for the twenty-first century, and organizations adopting total quality management (TQM) practices are employing concepts espoused by Taylor. Their latter point is also confirmed by Martin (1995) who sees much continuity between scientific management and modern TQM in terms of fundamental issues (meeting the needs of external and internal customers) and methods of decision-making (group research and continuous improvement) and implementation.

In public administration, Schachter (1989) shows that the loss of autonomy in a working place, a common critique on Taylorism, occurred before Taylor was born; Taylor was not oblivious to social relations, but he had an innate concern with improving worker participation. Schachter identifies a prewar appreciation of Taylor in local reformers assuming that "adapting his methodologies to city bureaucracies can increase their responsiveness and accountability" (111). The denigration of Taylor is partly caused by misinterpretation that "focuses on a narrow range of quotations or confuses his own ideas with their purported application by people he specifically repudiated" (Schachter 1989, 1). This misinterpretation manifests the field's weakness of theorizing, writing, and teaching.

Another powerful defense of scientific management comes from a publication by Van Riper (1995) who presents Gulick's only known speech (in 1931) on the place of scientific management in public administration. In this speech, Gulick admits that it is more difficult to apply scientific management in government than it is in industry because of politics' presence, the democracy controlled by the many, the complex environment, the home rule in local affairs, and the teleological enigma of government. But Gulick goes on to defend scientific management: "It is because of all these difficulties that scientific management in public affairs is of supreme necessity. The very fact that government enterprises are larger in manpower and more complex in function than private industries makes scientific management the more essential" (in Van Riper 1995, 7). In a similar vein, Weber's conception of administrators as neutral servants to political masters is reviewed to examine its relevance for American public administration (Fry and Nigro 1996).

IV. IDEA THREE: POLITICS AND POLICY MAKING

Idea One underscored competence emphasized competence that was premised on neutrality, and Idea Two that was on efficiency. Inflexible adherence to assumptions of neutrality, businesslike management, and the one best way, however, leaves little room for compromise between the competing values that characterize the environment public agencies work in. Contemporary public administration must stress the interaction of political values and administration: the exercise of administrative discretion in interpreting policy directives, the need to decide between countervailing values and interests, and the relation between external and administrative advocates of policies. Idea Three critiques each aspect of the policy process: the need to decide, the need for information and the role of the expert, and the rational and incremental decision styles.

As opposed to the relatively naive assumptions of nineteenth century reformers, twentieth century analysts accept the reality that major appointed administrative officials often take the lead in making policy, and officials at lower levels must be involved in interpreting policies. Policies in the nineteenth century were predominantly distributive—in the framework of limited government—and did not require as much interpretation as regulatory and redistributive policies that became prevalent with the welfare state.[*] With the advent of Depression-era big government, with the blossoming of New Deal programs, public administration has recognized that the assumed dichotomy between politics and administration is not realistic. A major trend has been the movement away from the preoccupation with neutrality and toward realization of the politics aspect of administration. Although early advocates of administrative neutrality argued that administrators merely implement public policies, that assumption now seems naive. The idea that values intrude on administration from many external sources and are also present in supposedly objective internal

---

*For typology of public policies, see Lowi and Ginsberg (1992).

decisions as to policy implementation is now recognized. Bureaucrats are policymakers as much as other participants in the process. A more realistic concept is public administration equals politics plus management.

Although there were always voices against the naiveté of viewing public administrators as neutral, the frontal assault on the subject began in earnest in the 1940s, gathering momentum by the end of World War II. Appleby (1949, 43) argued that "arguments about the application of policy are essentially arguments about policy." Waldo (1984) found studies of public administration to be grounded in political theory. Long (1949) argued that "the lifeblood of administration is power," and called everyone's attention to such aspects of administrative agencies as political survival and cultivating of clientele. Selznick (1949) showed how the Tennessee Valley Authority (TVA), an independent public agency, was able to survive and achieve its mission by adapting to local interests. Simon (1997) showed that every decision is based not only on facts derived from administrative realities, but also on values. Elaborating on this later, Simon (1967) declared Wilson's postulate "the field of administration is field of business. It is removed from the hurry and strife of politics" simply wrong not only in the present, but also in the past. Simon insisted that Wilson's postulate is rather normative than descriptive, and it should be understood as "the field of administration *ought to be* a field of business." Simon proposed to discuss the issues of power of a bureaucratic office not in terms of neutrality, but in terms of autonomy, predictability, and reliability. Simon proposed that when neutrality is discussed, the predictability of the values that will be achieved by impartial actions of the bureaucracy must be taken into account. As long as values are not questioned, neutrality can be insisted. But when values change, it cannot be ensured that the neutral routine of the bureaucracy is taking society to predictable, reliable, and societal values it endorses.

In 1957, Glendon Schubert (1957), butchered the idea of public interest, showing that each approach to public interest that ought to guide neutral public servants in their activities had underlying political philosophy (implications).

There are many theories prescribing different roles to administrators (bureaucrats) in a system of governance (Hill 1991). Some argue that bureaucracy is an instrument (e.g., a tool of economic elites in Marxist interpretation), some argue that it is a major player in a policy process (e.g., in Dahl's and Lindblom's (1953) "polyarchy"), and some see it as a predominant actor (e.g., the bureaucratic politics model of Allison (1971)). Particularly popular is the literature on policy subsystems.

The most common image of the subsystem is that of an iron (or cozy) triangle where the interest groups, congressional committees, or subcommittees and the executive branch agencies decide policies in a closed consensual manner. But this is only one conceptualization—the simplest form of policy subsystems. Such subsystems range from (1) closed entities that are termed iron triangles* to (2) the still structured, but more open and knowledge-based, advocacy coalition framework of Sabatier (1988) to (3) the even looser structured policy issue networks of Heclo (1978) "where it is almost impossible to say where a network leaves off and its environment begins," to (4) the garbage can model of Kingdon (1984) where public policy agendas are formed by random coupling of solutions, problems, and participants (with their resources) in a period when choice opportunities occur. The portrayal of loose structures of policy processes, such as Kingdon's model, are often criticized on the basis that they disregard the institutional basis of politics because "institutions are more than simple mirrors of social forces" and that "political institutions define the framework within which politics takes place" (March and Olsen 1989, 18). The argument is often made that policy subsystems differ across policy types (Ripley and Franklin 1991). An important aspect of policy subsystems models more complete than the iron triangle is their closer attention to

---

*The term has been used since 1964 by Douglas Cater (1964), but it gained prominence in the 1970s by Gordon Adams' (1982) study of defense contractors.

knowledge and argumentation, and they are based on more sophisticated models of decision-making than rationalistic and incrementalist approaches.

For considerations of space and simplicity of the argument, focus will be on a more balanced view of the politics school, arguing that in a political system where many groups have a voice (pluralism), bureaucrats with substantial expertise play key roles. Indeed, legislation is written as often by bureaucrats as by legislators. The bureaucracy is as capable as any other participant in the political process of mobilizing support for its interests, and it is as likely as any to become part of a policy-making coalition. Laws are administratively interpreted in their execution. Written in only a few pages, they must be interpreted in many, often unanticipated, specific situations. Therefore, as the final step in the policy-making process, administration is the last chance to influence policy, which is the ultimate focal point of the process. Administrative discretion, then, is a fact necessitated, rather than precluded, by the law.

It follows that administrative agencies are the objects of outside pressures, often by interest groups and legislators, because administrative initiative in drafting policy and administrative discretion in interpreting policy inherently include value preferences, and even so-called technical decisions are actually value laden.

After a policy is formulated, its implementation is far from assured. Interest pressure fields are also to be found inside public organizations. Rourke (1984) argues that administrators should play active roles in policy development and implementation; because of their powers of discretion—creating favorable attitudes among the public, organizing clientele, and cultivating goodwill with legislatures—agencies become the objects of policy preferences from external sources—interest groups, legislators, the media, individuals. Within an agency, officials become advocates for the external pressures that the organization is subjected to—arguing for or against certain positions and interpretations, for or against strict standards, advocating or disparaging the necessity for tighter controls. Having won policy victories in the legislatures and the courts, representatives of those groups have shifted their efforts and tactics to the less glamorous bureaucracy to achieve effective policy implementation. External groups are increasingly sophisticated enough to appreciate the need for political support—the need to mobilize external forces for supposed internal decisions. Of course, some groups may work to weaken implementation; after an initial decision to tighten standards, an industry may place direct pressure on the bureaucracy to reverse or weaken the decision. And, within the bureaucracy, top-level officials may reflect those arguments.

The budget is a particularly important policy arena. It is one where the roles and skills of administrators are critically important. Every government, city, county, state, and national, operates under an authorized spending plan—a budget. Because budget documents are massive tomes filled with figures, they are commonly thought to be dry, dull, and unexciting. But nothing could be farther from the truth. Money is the lifeblood of an agency or a program; its budget will determine how many people will work and what facilities will be available to them. The struggle for such allocations is a life-and-death struggle and a struggle over values. Should the available dollars go for police patrol or for ambulance drivers or for a remedial reading program? As Key (1940) argued, the answer is not a matter of logic, but of preferences and priorities. Key (1940) posed the question of normative budgetary theory: "on what basis shall it be decided to allocate X dollars to activity A instead of activity B?" His answer was that in public budgeting it will be hard to find such criteria, because it becomes "a matter of value preferences between ends lacking a common denominator. As such, the question is a problem in political philosophy." Later, elaborating on this question, Wildavsky (1961, 184) concluded that "a normative theory of budgeting, therefore, is utopian in the fullest sense of the word; its accomplishment and acceptance would mean the end of conflict over the government's role in society."

Any seasoned bureaucrat will readily admit that bureaucratic decisions—budgetary or otherwise—are often political decisions. Employees are hired to appease one or another influential individual; contracts are awarded to relatives of high officials; ex-officials become consultants at lucrative salaries. Complicity in such actions is not for personal gain but for the sake of keeping peace. One of the first laws of bureaucracy is to not make enemies. Sometimes bureaucrats avoid making enemies by avoiding hard decisions, although a decision not to decide is still a decision, albeit a non-decision. Sometimes their interests are so threatened, as at the height of financial crises when they have been hard put to stave off severe budget cuts, that they become overtly political. To demonstrate their program's importance and to demonstrate the political costs of slashing their funds, they enlist their natural allies—worker organizations such as a fireman's union, client groups such as commuters, or a neighborhood such as that around a hospital. The representatives of special interest groups lobby vigorously, and often with the active cooperation of the bureaucracy involved, to restore budget cuts that a chief executive or legislative committee has proposed. The resulting budget document reflects the relative successes and failures of the various contenders. The same dynamics are at work on the federal, state, and local levels.

Bureaucratic discretion is often condemned as permitting uncontrolled actions by the bureaucracy, actions that may be considered unintended by policy makers or illegal by the courts. Should bureaucrats be able to make decisions with potentially important political consequences? The political power of the bureaucracy has not only been acknowledged as real, but, in the tradition of Finer (1941), was criticized on the grounds that too broad an assumption of power to administrative agencies is unconstitutional. An important critic of too broad administrative discretion is Theodore Lowi (1979). Since his *The End of Liberalism* first appeared in the late 1960s, Lowi has repeated that until the rise of the administrative state, the United States was a republic dominated by the legislature. This statement is true to the letter and ideology of the Constitution, claiming that all the power should reside in Congress (Article I). Because new interventionist programs of the government gave discretionary powers to bureaucracy and were tailored to specific groups, they soon became captive to these interest groups. This new phenomenon is called *interest-group liberalism*, and it is based on its optimism, faith in government, fragmentation, and proliferation of interest groups. Such government is not very effective, and ideology is only important to the extent that it shows which politician is related to what group. This "delegation of broad and undefined discretionary power from the legislature to the executive branch" leads to "legiscide" (Lowi 1991) and ultimately deranges virtually all constitutional relationships and prevents attainment of the constitutional goal of balanced power, substantive calculability, and procedural calculability (Lowi 1993, 151). Lowi (1991) also criticized the open-ended entitlement legislation on epistemological grounds, arguing that instead of holistic, comprehensive solutions to problems that always snowball to more legislation with even wider discretionary power, a pragmatic piecemeal approach to every problem should be applied.

In response to criticism by Lowi and others, there have also been arguments for discretionary powers of public agencies, for delegating authority to experienced bureaucrats, for implementing and interpreting legislation under principles of administrative law. For example, taking a step beyond the thesis of Long (1952) that bureaucracy is the most representative American governmental institution, John Rohr justifies public administration on the grounds of truly microcosmic representation of the American public (because there are no elections, public administration can be rational and implement policies like affirmative action) (Rohr 1990, 72). Warren (1993) does not see a point in debating the legitimacy of public administration—it is more than legitimate. Warren sees the administrative state as legitimate for two reasons: it is a response to people's non-decreasing demand for services; its legitimacy of the administrative state was upheld by the courts. A defense of administrative discretion based on empirical evidence is offered by Brower and Abolafia (1996) who consider procedural entrepreneurship as resisting established routines and enacting alternative channels to accomplish an organization's work. They see procedural entrepreneurship as more than necessary to cope with the tension between the normative pressures for administrative neutrality and the pressure to innovate to accommodate changing demands.

One way to make this policy-making process more objective is to make it more logical. Furthermore, perspectives on how decisions are made are often the framework for fuller models of policy-making. The rational-comprehensive school, for instance, argues that the best decisions are made logically. Advocates of rational-comprehensive decision-making hold that all consequences of a decision should be accounted for and that making policy in bits and pieces may blind policymakers to the overall consequences of their decisions. However, even the advocates of this school do not speak about absolute, all-encompassing rationality; rather, they discuss the concept of "bounded rationality" (Simon 1997). They hold that although rational-comprehensive decision-making is impossible, one should approach it as closely as possible.

Alternatively, incrementalists defend the muddling through process as more realistic, as being able to respond to the interests of many groups without freezing out any, as being able to respond to crisis pressures and deadlines, and as not requiring the massive investments of time and effort that logical decisions necessitate (Lindblom 1959). Decisions to implement policy are usually made in small steps, incrementally, rather than through an all-encompassing, rational plan. Incrementalists argue that crisis pressures and deadlines limit the amount of time that can be devoted to analysis. The incremental approach constitutes muddling through, selecting alternatives that are simply satisfactory and sufficient.

Incrementalism is criticized from many angles. It is often attacked on the grounds that it justifies the status quo and ignores the possibility of fundamental change (Dror 1964). Critics of incremental decision-making also question the consequences of such a mode of action. They ask: Do programs that develop incrementally tend to persist and grow over the years without any real scrutiny? Does incremental policy-making obscure the overall perspective? One response to incrementalism has been sunset laws that mandate periodic evaluation and weeding out of programs. In the 1970s, Colorado pioneered in passing a sunset law at the urging of the citizens' organization, Common Cause. Under sunset legislation, an agency or program automatically goes out of business at the end of a given period unless the legislature acts specifically to renew or modify it.

Another perspective on the decision-making process has been Amitai Etzioni's "mixed scanning" approach, which tried to "explicitly combine (a) high-order, fundamental policy-making processes which set basic directions and (b) incremental ones which prepare for fundamental decisions and work them out after they have been reached" (Etzioni 1967, 385).

Decision-making is far less rationalistic in the garbage-can model of decision-making where problems, solutions, decision makers, and choice opportunities are independent, exogenous streams flowing through a system that couple randomly (Cohen et al. 1972). As previously argued, these models of decision-making often serve as a framework for explaining the political role of bureaucracy in the process of governance. For example, both Kingdon's (1984) study of agenda setting and March and Olsen's (1989) neo-institutionalist model of politics are based on the garbage-can model of decision-making (though different readings of it); likewise, the iron triangle model is based on Lindblom's incrementalism.

Theorizing public administration more consciously in a political democratic framework is the main thrust of Idea Three, which has been gaining more and more attention in the field. The big questions identified by Kirlin (1996, 2001) fall within this line of literature that is in contrast to the big questions identified by Behn (1995) from a more public management perspective (micromanagement, motivation, and measurement). Kirlin (1996) proposes seven big concepts for the field: (1) tools of collective action supporting a democratic polity; (2) appropriate roles of nongovernmental collective action; (3) tradeoffs between designs based on function versus geography; (4) national versus local political arenas; (5) decisions isolated from politics; (6) balance among neutral competence, representativeness, and leadership; and (7) societal learning. Cook (1998) argues, from the belief that public administration is a political institution, that the conception of public management should be grounded in regime politics and the education and leadership of public administrators should consider this political standard. The "bring politics back" voice has never disappeared (e.g., Mayer and Khademian 1996).

⌇ V. IDEA FOUR: HUMAN BEHAVIOR

Turn-of-the-century reformers were concerned with the means to efficiency: getting the job done with a minimum of wasted energy. Although management theories primarily derived from the private sector did provide an understanding of the organizational skeleton, they proved to be inadequate for satisfactorily explaining behavior in organizations, public or private. In particular, they failed to account for the complexity of human nature or for the impact of an uncertain and changing environment.

An important tenet of the management model was the assumption that in exchange for a fair day's pay, someone competent could always be found to fill any vacant slot in the organization or to complete any task. Classical administrative theory assumed that the only factor that motivated people to work was money. Money would be a sufficient motivator, whereas personality, individuality, and social interests were irrelevant to job performance. That theory is still held by many managers today.

Human behavior theorists maintain that in their actions people are encouraged and discouraged by many other incentives and stimuli in this action; they have needs other than remuneration. For example, in the most popular theory of motivation, Maslow (1943) identified five levels of needs: (1) physiological needs, such as food and shelter; (2) safety needs; (3) belongingness or a desire to be part of an informal social group; (4) esteem and status needs; and finally, beyond these needs, the most powerful motivator may be (5) a need or desire to self-actualize—to do work that is personally meaningful or fulfilling. Of these needs, the lowest dissatisfied need was suggested to be the strongest motivation of a human being. Of course, Maslow's as well as others' theories of motivation (e.g., Herzberg et al. 1959; McClelland 1961; Vroom 1964) did not deny that money motivates. Rather, they underscored the complexity of human nature, and they pointed out many other mechanisms of motivation.

The behavioral model stresses the importance of human relations and personal goals. If the closed model concentrates primarily on a technical system of organization—a system that produces products or services or maintains operations—the behavioral model recognizes the equal importance of the social system—a system composed of the employees who operate the technical system. This model is a modification of the closed model that brings to management's attention the social and psychological sides of organization. The focus of the model is still internally directed as in the classical model insofar as it is mostly concerned with internal management of an organization. But it recognizes that people in organizations often interpret things differently and have different concerns and worries. So, in essence, this approach is more flexible and accommodating.

The majority of organizations in modern society follow this model. Most managers understand that, first of all, they deal with people; therefore, they are concerned with the employees' emotional and psychological well being. Any technical system can fail, and often does, when the social and psychological needs of the people operating the system are neglected. There is a need to look behind the formal structural charts of an organization to the informal organization to grasp the complexity of cooperative human endeavor. This perspective has gained hold in organizational science in the United States since the 1940s, especially when the Hawthorne Studies became widely publicized prior to World War II.[*] This was partially due to social science's establishing itself as a legitimate field of study, which facilitated a more human perspective on such concerns as organizational effectiveness.

The term *informal organization* was introduced to the management literature by Barnard (1938) who defines formal organizations as cooperative systems and appreciates the importance of common purpose, cooperation, communication, informal organization, and dynamic equilibrium. The first documented study of the phenomenon by management specialists was known

---

[*] Hawthorne studies were not embraced by all. Organized labor long disregarded or opposed to it, and many studies questioned its basic assumptions. See Wren (1994) for details.

as the Hawthorne Studies. In their experiments in the late 1920s and 1930s, in Western Electric's Hawthorne, Illinois plant, Mayo (1945) and Roethlisberger (1941) revealed that the primary working group (or the arrangement of everyday, routine working relations in the group) was as important for productivity as physical facilities and monetary remuneration. As the Hawthorne Studies indicated, a group has its norms as to appropriate attitudes and behavior on the part of its members. These norms are enforced through sanctions in the form of social and other informal pressures on deviant members. In general, groups serve the organization by providing social satisfactions and control. But it can also happen that the selfish goals of a group displace the goals of the overall organization. As critics of the Weber model have pointed out, the actual functioning of a real-life bureaucracy leads to situations of goal displacement where members treat the rules as if they were major ends in themselves; sometimes, they take goal displacement to the point of suboptimization, regarding their departmental interests as more important than broader organizational goals.

Barnard (1938) argued that the informal organization was fulfilling necessary functions for the organization (which, in Barnard's definition, is a cooperative endeavor), namely, communicating, maintaining cohesiveness in a formal organization, and supporting the employees' feelings of self-respect and integrity. Barnard also argued that as formal organizations create informal ones, informal organizations give rise to some form of formal organization that makes explicit relationships and attitudes that have developed informally.

An informal organization system is considered to fulfill the following functions: (1) augment, interpret, speed up, or alter the formal communication system (or lack of it); (2) regulate the flow, extent, manner, and enforcement of formal authority; (3) humanize the formal organization by helping to maintain a feeling of individuality of the members while providing some security, unity, and integrity at the same time; and (4) meet related psychological and social needs to such an extent as to give the impression of being the organization (Banki 1981).

Informal organizations can soothe frictions that arise in formal organizations. Although, as a function of inertia, they may resist change, informal organizations are agents of change. As such, the informal organization may be considered as a modified and advanced form of task force and team-building activities. It deals with those urgent problems or opportunities that affect the organization as a whole and which involve more than one unit of organization. Usually, these are problems focused on the future; they are new to an organization and extremely complex. In informal organization, hierarchy-based relationships and attitudes are set aside to facilitate creative problem solving (although unintended outcomes may be dysfunctional). In such an interpretation, the informal organization uses task-oriented, team-building activities that involve a change agent, data gathering, feedback, and process consultation. Informal organizations can identify and solve systemic problems which have not been solved by the formal organization, therefore creatively complementing it. Both organizations contain the same people. The output of the informal organization represents an input to the formal one. The success of the former is linked to that of the latter (Huczynski 1987; Zaud 1981).

The behavioral model also stresses the responsiveness of organization to internal conditions and to the external environment. It underscores the need for more decentralization and less hierarchy, weaker chain of command, and more freedom for lower-level managers in the decision-making process. Not only managers but also other employees are expected to be part of decision-making. They are encouraged to work in problem-solving teams led by people who do not occupy high positions in the hierarchy but who are recognized (because of their personal accomplishments and ability) as able to build successful relationships. Constant training and learning of both employees and administrators is supposed to be one of the major concerns of management. The idea that use of informal structures can lead to better performance is not new. In 1951, researchers at the Tavistock Institute in England studied the adjustment problems of informal work organizations when the ownership and technology of the coal mines changed (Trist 1963).

This five-year study illustrated that sizable informal work groups in several mines, when allowed to be self-regulating, were more capable of adapting to changes in the technology of work.

The behavioral model is a transition from a closed to open model. The open model (organic, systemic) is a concept describing organizations where authority and expertise are shared, hierarchy is less important, horizontal lines of communications dominate, and immediate response to environmental change is one of the basic managerial strategies. Essentially, organization is viewed as a social system of human interaction rather than group of humans attached to a certain technology. Though some routinization and standardization are essential components of effectiveness in any formal organization, the open model gives priority to creativity and innovativeness.

In the open model, an organization's decision-making process is totally decentralized and is by consensus rather than by individual judgment of the formal (or even informal) leader; formal rules and instructions are almost eliminated; broad cross-disciplinary skills are of great importance; and the number of managerial levels is held down to the minimum.

Studies of behavior within organizations have consistently found that the most productive employees do not function optimally under a-man-as-machine model that presumes laziness and irresponsibility and is prevalent in many areas of the world. Wages and fear are obvious motivators and widely utilized. But they are productive only at relatively low limits. Research and experience found that even organizations with well-paid employees could not expect high productivity unless they took higher order psychological needs into account. Simple, fear-based assumptions were not valid; people remain individuals, even in the workplace, and are affected and moved by many forces. Money is only one. As individuals, they can be turned on or turned off by their organizational roles, depending on what the situation offers them psychologically, and whether the organization treats them as mature, vibrant adults or as lazy, dependent drones. Management theorists have come to realize that people tend to join social groups on the job, and these groups develop production-oriented norms of their own to which the individual is expected to adhere. In particular, public servants may have more intrinsic motivations than their extrinsically motivated private sector counterparts. Human behavior, therefore, reflects not only organizational but also personal and group pressures.

Douglas McGregor, Rensis Likert, and Chris Argyris contributed to defining the theory of *Organizational Humanism*. Differing from the simpler perspectives of scientific management and the human relations school, they held that work could serve as a source of motivation and satisfaction to the worker. Building on Maslow's theory of human needs, McGregor (1960) classified managerial assumptions about human nature into Theory X and Theory Y—the hierarchical and the interpersonal. Theory X assumes that people do not like work, shun responsibility, and prefer to be led. Motivation is in response to threat or punishment. Theory Y holds that people are intrinsically motivated, have the potential for self-development, and a capacity to assume responsibility. They prefer, and can provide, self-control in achieving organizational goals. According to McGregor, management practices are largely shaped by these diametrically different views. Depending on the circumstances, success can be reached through either approach. As organizations become more complex, however, managing becomes more complicated. Theory X assumptions are less helpful; Theory Y styles of management recognize that delegation of authority, job enlargement, and participation must get more recognition.

The model of effective organizational structure, developed by Likert (1961), consists of participative work groups as an important source of individuals' need satisfaction. By creating supportive relationships, managers can facilitate the productivity of such groups. Likert also constructed a typology of organizational leadership. He distinguished four types of leadership style: (1) exploitative authoritative, (2) benevolent authoritative, (3) participative consultative, and (4) participative management systems. Research found systems 3 and 4 to be more productive (Hollway 1991). On the other hand, critics of this theory argue that whereas managers' preferences are invariably with system 4 (democratic participative management), in reality, most organizations practice the benevolent authoritarianism of system 2 with success (Perrow 1987).

Argyris (1957) also emphasizes the human condition's importance where the individual and the formal organization as two elements are often in conflict, seeking separate goals. Argyris (1957) contends that "the formal organization creates in a healthy individual feelings of failure and frustration, short time perspective and conflict." The management model's chain of command, unity of direction, span of control, and task specialization are repressive and restrictive devices that are dysfunctional insofar as they deprive individuals of their potential for growth and self-actualization. Argyris suggests that individuals' participation in decisions affecting their work will give them greater job satisfaction and generate higher productivity.

From a systemic perspective, however, individual motivational factors are necessary, but insufficient. Recognizing that insufficiency, the Organization Development school has as its goal the integration of individual and organizational objectives in "a long-range effort to improve an organization's problem-solving and renewal processes, particularly through a more effective and collaborative management of organization culture." It takes the "ongoing work team, including supervisor and subordinates" as its foundation and "puts a primary emphasis on human and social relationships" (French and Bell 1973, 15–20).

As a function of Idea Three, these theories of individual and group behavior are widely taught in public administration programs and are adopted within many government agencies. Psychological motivators are particularly important in an arena where pay lags behind the private sector. For many people, government is where the meaningful action is, not necessarily where the pay is. Civil servants often feel they are a part—however, small—of something worthwhile (Rainey 1997).

But government has also begun to recognize that an unanticipated consequence of the bureaucracies established to serve the public is their disservice to their own employees. In place of incentives to produce, there are often pressures to be mediocre. Somehow a new, bright, eager public servant quickly receives messages not to work too hard, not to outperform his or her superiors, and not to rock the boat. He or she becomes an individual who has bartered conscience for security, a survivor, a faceless product of the necessity to go along to get along. In short, they are successful bureaucrats who maximize their individual benefits while giving minimal attention to client responsibilities. A lackadaisical attitude is often reinforced by the knowledge that nonperformers are seldom fired.

Following this line of reasoning, Merton (1940) discusses the impact of bureaucratic structure on personality and points out some bureaucratic dysfunctions: trained incapacity, goal displacement, overconformity, and impersonality. Hummel (1994) outlines several effects of bureaucratic organization on people:

- The top-down structuring of work creates the kind of passivity where employees wait for the hierarchy to tell them what to do.
- The self-concept of the functionary in bureaucracy develops in terms of organizational identity, integration and similarity in relation to the rest of organization. In this way, bureaucracy creates dependency of the individual self on structures of the organization.
- People are viewed as interchangeable, functional elements of a system and qualitative differences between them do not make a functional difference. Quantitative measurement is a standard for what is real.
- By instilling the practice of analogous thinking, bureaucrats are trained to act only when they recognize aspects of reality matching predefined models for action.

Several other theorists have analyzed human experience in organizations from subjective interpretative perspectives. Denhardt (1981) applied a critical perspective for analyzing human existence in the shadow of organization, referring to unrecognized or unwanted drives and desires as the other side of the conscious ego. The phenomenological approach has been applied to studying political aspects of bureaucratic life (Harmon 1981; Jun 1986) and internal workings of bureaucracy. It often uncovers the patterns of organizational control that trap people in unsatisfactory modes of existence. Focusing on cognitive processes that are related to death, family, sexuality, anxiety, greed, fear, hate, and libidinal drives, this line of research illustrates that rationality is disguised irrationality and human beings are often trapped in a world of their own creation, as labeled by Morgan (1997) with a "psychic prison" metaphor.

Theorists of organizational learning and learning organization have constructed a contemporary behavioral model of human performance. According to Chawla and Renesch (1995, 243): "An organization's ability to survive and prosper in our turbulent age requires new ways of thinking and organizing... It demands the confluence of two streams of thought...continuous improvement (Kaizen) and continuous learning." The concept of learning was made popular by Argyris and Schön (1974) and Argyris and Schön (1978). They differentiate single-loop learning, referring to detecting and correcting error within a given set of operating norms, from double-loop learning, referring to questioning the relevance of the operating norms. Their work shows that bureaucratic organizations, because of the fragmentation and bureaucratic accountability systems, tend to create defensive routines that obstruct the learning process. Senge (1990) popularizes the concept of "learning organizations" from a nonlinear perspective of system dynamics and complexity theory. He urges people to renew their vision and commitment, reexamine their relationship with the environment, and develop an ability of questioning, challenging, and changing operating norms and assumptions. These concepts have been adopted in public administration research (Brown and Brudney 2003; Leeuw et al. 1994; Little and Cayer 1996).

Efforts have been made to demonstrate the difference in organizational behaviors between public and private organizations. In general, many studies find a lower valuation of monetary incentives and a higher level of public service motivation in public employees. Many studies also find that public employees have lower levels of job satisfaction and organizational commitment than their private counterparts (Rainey 1997). However, studies about publicness of this sort usually have mixed results because of issues related to sampling and measurement. One significant theory is about public service motivation proposed by Perry and Wise (1990) who argue that people with high public service motivation are more likely to choose government jobs, to perform better on the job, and to respond more to nonutilitarian incentives. Although Alonso and Lewis (2001) find mixed results in terms of Perry and Wise's theory, Brewer et al. (2000) identify four distinct conceptions of public service motivation in practice: samaritans, communitarians, patriots, and humanitarians. Whether the concept of public service motivation is valid seems to be a debatable question, but it holds true that the distinctive mission, value orientation, and democratic control of public organizations influence the emotions, cognitions, attitudes, and behaviors of public employees. Such a behavioral perspective can provide valuable insights for public administration researchers and practitioners (Denhardt et al. 2002).

VI. IDEA FIVE: PROGRAM EFFECTIVENESS

In the era of Weber and Taylor, the environment that an organization functioned in was relatively steady, and the government's tasks were limited and simpler than today. The years since have seen rapid change, and the demands upon government have become multidimensional. Although not always very timely and state of the art, the response of public administration has been more than adequate; through building and reinforcing multiple capacities, it has managed the American welfare state successfully. World War II gave rise to operations research, a science of maximizing allocation of limited resources for attaining maximum benefit that emerged as a policy tool useful in coordinating large-scale logistic efforts of the armed forces. Since the 1950s, the systems approach has become a framework for analyzing public programs. Versions of this approach include cost-benefit analysis, institutionalized use of which, in the United States, is often traced back to the Flood Control Act of 1936 (Hatry 1982, 167). By the 1950s, it had become an established feature of water-resources policy. Cost-effectiveness analysis gained momentum in the Department of Defense at the beginning of the 1960s when the Secretary of Defense Robert McNamara initiated the Planning Programming Budgeting System (PPBS)—a programmatic approach of systematic comparison of different programs in terms of their unit costs or effectiveness per dollar spent. To put the massive governmental effort of the War on Poverty on scientific rails and to answer questions about the effectiveness and efficiency of Great Society programs, President Johnson ordered the use of PPBS for all executive agencies in 1965 (it was officially terminated in 1971). An entire cottage industry of policy analysis and program evaluation emerged.

A variety of approaches have been proposed for program evaluation (e.g., Chelimsky 1989). Although these studies have been largely cast in terms of economic efficiency and effectiveness, they also incorporated some perspectives from organizational sociology and other related disciplines. An influential study of public policy implementation in Oakland, California, by Pressman and Wildavsky (1984) gave rise to yet another stream in this direction for public administration: how programs are implemented and these processes' obstacles. In their analysis, Pressman and Wildavsky (1984) not only paid attention to the program's economic benefits, but they also underscored the importance of the complexity of joint action. Implementation studies have since proliferated, and many frameworks have been proposed (e.g., Alexander 1985; McLaughlin 1976; Sabatier and Mazmanian 1979).

Post-World War II expansion of government services and a growth of knowledge in public administration and in the field of social science in general were proceeding against the background of rapid change in society—technological, social, and legal. Such rapid change means less predictability in the life of governmental agencies. Worker skills and expectations have changed; technology has changed; neighborhoods and cities have changed; and clients' needs are constantly changing. The policies, programs, or procedures that were appropriate even five years ago may no longer suit an agency's clientele today. Currently, it is not possible to develop slowly the one best way and then continue to use that way without question. Instead, activities must be constantly monitored and questioned in terms of their effectiveness.

In response to this change and armed with a wide range of existing theories of public administration (which, as argued above, usually concentrated on limited aspects of concerns), public administrators have tried to develop more holistic approaches that would address public problems in their complexity and in a systemic manner since the late 1960s and early 1970s. The idea of Program Effectiveness was built not only on the productivity movement, but also on other integrative approaches. In particular, the notion of effectiveness has expanded to include such concerns as unintended consequences, misuse and abuse of power, and ethical stops ranging from the inner check to whistle blowing. One such attempt at having a more holistic and ethical science of administration was the New Public Administration (NPA), which was born at the Minnowbrook I Conference held by Syracuse University in 1968 (and reevaluated twenty years later at Minnowbrook II), and other symposia that helped develop a concept of effectiveness linked to ethics and responsiveness.

Responding to social unrest and political change during the 1960s, NPA emphasized participation, decentralization, and representative bureaucracy. The NPA, as defined by young public administration scholars, was rooted in the experience of the 1960s, and in particular, a belief that public administrators could solve the country's technological and social problems (LaPorte 1971; Marini 1971). It was argued that public administrators should and could act as agents of change (Crenson 1971). As conceptualized, the "New Public Administration seeks not only to carry out legislative mandates as efficiently and economically as possible, but also to both influence and execute policies which more generally improve the quality of life for all" (Paynter 1971). Frederickson (1971, 1976) argued that, "It's abundantly clear that administrators are not neutral. They should be committed to both good management and social equity as values, things to be achieved."

The NPA held that (Marini 1971):

- Ethics, honesty, and responsibility in government had returned to the forefront of public administration. Career service bureaucrats were no longer considered to be merely implementors, but to hold a public trust to provide the best possible public service.
- Social equity was increasingly complementing efficiency and economy as the rationale or justification for policy positions.
- Questions of public policy were becoming as significant as those of public management.
- The rational model and the usefulness of the strict concept of hierarchy were severely challenged.
- Government should be responsive to the needs of the public. Unneeded and ineffective organizations or programs should be discontinued.
- Effective public administration had to be defined in the context of an active and participative citizenry.

Participation was supported both as a political process and as an organizational process. Political participation was viewed as a mechanism for dispersing power and increasing citizen involvement in government (Waldo 1984). Organizational participation was to be a means for procuring change and dispersing power within the organization. Representative bureaucracy was meant to produce client-centered administration and representation of clientele interests by administrators.

The movement to revitalize government and to reverse pressures toward centralization of power, passivity, and mediocrity developed within the federal government. A decade after Minnowbrook I, President Carter initiated major reforms to the federal civil service system in 1978, including provisions for individual incentives and greater accountability. Similar programs are instituted at the state and local levels. Commissions on public service have continued the impetus to revitalize it. The National Commission on the State and Local Public Service, chaired by former Governor William Winter, following the lead of the Volcker Commission (1989) delivered *Hard Truths/Tough Choices: An Agenda for State and Local Reform* (Winter 1993). The Volcker and Winter Commission reports define an ambitious agenda—dozens of basic changes for improving federal, state, and local government.

The recommendations of the Winter Commission present a fundamental agenda for changing the way state and local governments relate to, as well as deliver services to, their citizens. According to Chairman Winter:

> Making democracy work is what state and local public service must be about. It is here that the actual delivery of the most basic and essential services take place.... An obvious part of the process of addressing the problems that face us as a society is examining the structure of government and determining how it can be better organized to do its job more efficiently. This must be a continuous activity, and one sufficiently dynamic and broadly based to resist those defenders of political turf who would argue for maintaining the status quo. But there is another measure of governmental performance that is even more important: the human dimensions of public service (Winter 1993, vii).

Richard Nathan's[*] commenting on the report argues that there are five central values that should be pursued by governmental reinventors in the 1990s: (1) advancing political accountability and responsiveness to citizens; (2) strengthening the capability of government to make and

---

[*] Richard Nathan's comments were made during the National Center for Public Productivity Annual Conference in Scottsdale, Arizona 1993.

implement tough choices; (3) providing fresh talent to government; (4) reducing the unhealthy power of special interest groups; and (5) bringing about a more honest dialogue between citizens and their governments.

Symposia and reports, however, created insufficient momentum to maintain support for government at the level of the New Deal and Great Society programs. From the perspective of citizens, at the bottom of the political structure, the public sector had to deliver as promised. Concurrent with the development of theories of responsiveness and implementation of civil service reforms, the productivity movement developed as a means of integrating and implementing all ideas (i.e., Ideas 1–4) initiated in the development of public administration to date. Its goal was to achieve tangible improvements in service delivery, especially in outcomes as opposed to an emphasis on outputs.

The improvement of public sector productivity, so that public organizations might more readily achieve their goals, became an interdisciplinary concern. The necessity for productivity improvement is a recurring theme in economic, technological, and social arguments, as they are emphasized by chief executives (elected and appointed), media, corporations, economists, public administrators, and public citizens. Improved standards of living and sociopolitical stability are closely linked to improved productivity.

In this context, *productivity improvement* is taken to mean capacity building (i.e., infrastructure and knowledge which are the prerequisites for expected performance) and actual performance improvement. Productivity improvement is a complex undertaking. Productive management, public and private, has evolved from simple common sense in the late nineteenth century to complex systems in the late twentieth century. To produce public services, the best public organizations have developed multiple, reinforcing capacities, integrating advanced management techniques, applying quality management principles, using measurement as a decision-making tool, working hard to motivate employees, adapting new technologies, and developing public–private partnerships.

In Figure 2.6, a systematic scheme for diagnosing productive improvement is proposed. It is a comprehensive framework where identifying critical problems and opportunities may begin. The four major elements of the framework are informational, social, technological, and managerial. Political (in terms of Idea 3), although not one of these four elements, should not be dismissed as a

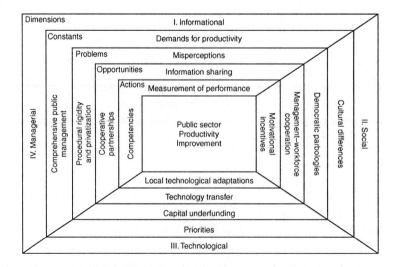

FIGURE 2.6 Public sector productivity improvement.

pertinent concern. Rather, it is a permanent environmental condition that pervades, or surrounds, the other four.

Across each of the four elements, four categorical bands emerge from the literature:

1. Constants or factors that are not amenable to change in the short run (one to three years). These include: demands for productivity; cultural differences; state priorities; and public management's scope.
2. Problems or obstacles to capacity building that must be addressed in a comprehensive productivity program. These include: misperceptions of productivity; bureaucratic pathologies; capital management; and large organizations' stereotypical rigidity.
3. Opportunities or positive approaches to capacity building. These include: information sharing; management–workforce cooperation; technology transfer; and organizational structures, systems, or controls.
4. Actions or specific programs. These include: measurements of quantity and quality; motivational incentives; local technological adaptations; and management–workforce training.

A. INFORMATIONAL FACTORS

1. Constants: Demands for Productivity Improvement

Government's customers are increasingly questioning the efficiency and effectiveness of public services. Terms such as *productivity*, *productive*, and *produce* are achieving greater prominence as progress is demanded by impatient constituencies: citizens seeking higher standards of living, corporations seeking investment opportunities, financial institutions seeking to safeguard their investments and loans, news media seeking to ferret out problems, and politicians or policy-makers seeking national self-reliance. Despite their diversity of interests, all such constituencies seem to agree that governments, public enterprises, and non-profit organizations should produce the same services or goods with fewer resources or higher levels of output with the same resources. They are asking for better information to judge progress against.

2. Problems: Misperceptions

Regardless of the functional bounds of the public sector, the concept of productivity suffers from misperceptions, fears, and myths: outputs and outcomes cannot be measured; workers will not cooperate with labor-saving technologies; productivity improvement will automatically mean a loss of jobs; managerial risks will outweigh rewards. Because the term and its derivatives almost automatically meet with such objections, productivity programs must operate under other titles: efficiency, management, performance, capacity building, capital investment, quality control, etc. (Holzer and Halachmi 1988). Through whatever means, programs to improve public sector efficiency and effectiveness by increasing worker motivation and skills, by strengthening management and measurement, by reorganizing jobs and work processes, by technological and operational innovation, or by any array of approaches, they are, indeed, productivity programs.

Despite government's considerable accomplishments, popular images reinforce the misperception of bureaucratic incompetence. Press reports are almost uniformly negative, shaping a bias against public bureaucrats that is reinforced daily by the image merchants. Public servants are stereotyped as bumbling bureaucrats. They are perceived as underworked and overpaid for jobs that anyone can do. They are unbusinesslike, and they lack ambition and common sense.

The public sector does improve its performance. In the United States, thousands of entrepreneurial, award-winning programs are successes in stretching resources, in building problem-solving capacities, and in helping solve some of society's most difficult problems (EXSL 1989–1995). They are not unusual. Government quietly harbors thousands of innovative projects, and it has accomplished much over decades. Pressured public administration is continuing to improve in pragmatic, productive terms. There is an increasingly sizable and sophisticated body of knowledge about effective productivity improvement programs, a body that is cumulative and that dates back several decades (Holzer and Halachmi 1988).

3. Opportunities: Information Sharing

A prerequisite to improved productivity, therefore, is improved information. It is freely shared and transferred on a mutually advantageous basis between sectors, organizational decision makers, and the workforce. Such interconnections between knowledge and productivity are perhaps clearest in the agricultural sector: America's best-educated farmers are the world's most productive.

Society expects professionals to be current. Yet, where there is a great deal of innovation in government, there is also a great deal of ignorance of innovation. Some cases are reported widely, but too few of the many successful projects have been widely replicated despite the appropriate adage that plagiarism is a virtue. In part, the fault lies with myopic professionals who do not search beyond the borders of their own disciplines, or who are lethargic or smug about the knowledge base they might tap to improve their performance. In large part the fault is also with a budget process that is political and shortsighted with regard to intangible investments. Frills such as conferences, journals, and professional memberships are viewed as irrelevant or as having indefinite payoffs; they do not tend to survive the budgeting process, losing out to the more immediate needs of crumbling public works or weak crime control. At best, professional knowledge is usually treated as a discretionary expenditure rather than viewed as a necessary investment. Without access to the relevant analyses and case studies, public administrators keep making the same mistakes, reinventing the same wheels, and missing the same possibilities. For example, most public managers are unaware of models that have been painstakingly developed in other jurisdictions or research centers, models which can be adapted for comprehensive productivity improvement in an environment of increasing demands and reduced resources. One example is the Ten Step Model (Holzer 1994) that was synthesized from examinations of scores of cases:

1. Clarifying goals with, and obtaining support from, top management and elected officials.
2. Locating models as successful blueprints to modify and as warnings of potential mistakes.
3. Identifying promising areas, such as those functions faced with large backlogs, slipping deadlines, high turnover, or many complaints.
4. Building a team through which all interested parties—particularly management, labor, and clients as well as possible partners in provision of the service—can identify obstacles and suggest improvements.
5. Planning the project, including objectives, tasks, responsibilities, and time frames.
6. Collecting program data and measuring progress against financial and service data.
7. Modifying project plans based upon periodic and continuing discussion of problems, opportunities, and priorities.
8. Expecting and addressing potential and actual problems such as misunderstandings, misconceptions, resistance, and slippage.
9. Implementing improvement actions on a routine basis, without fanfare and unnecessarily raising expectations.
10. Evaluating and publicizing results, building political and professional support that will justify the program and its expansion to meet increased demand of services.

As with any other generic recipe, this type of model should be modified and adapted to a specific organizational context. Real cases will always be slightly different than the model; in some cases, one or two steps would be missing because of the organizational and cultural assumptions of the situation. In other cases, several steps can be combined in one. Because the steps of the model are analytically distinguishable, the model is useful for analyzing real organizations and programs as a means of highlighting the strengths and illuminating the weaknesses of cases under discussion.

Government needs to be aware of, and then apply, its own successes, models, and conceptual roadmaps. Strategies for public performance improvement are being reported analytically and clearly in hundreds of publications and conferences (Cherry and Holzer 1991). Public organizations need to mine the mountain of knowledge—join computerized networks, share successful and unsuccessful experiences, attend conferences, and treat their managers as professionals by making it easier to do so.

4. Actions: Measurements of Performance

In an environment of tax revolts and fiscal crises, questions of measurement are implicit in citizen complaints: "The neighborhood is more dangerous." "The streets are dirtier." "The schools are worse." They often answer their own questions with dramatic stories, rumors, and personal experiences. Public executives should be able to answer those charges with data. But answers are only a black-and-white snapshot of a problem-solving attempt; more data can help diagnose a problem–response pattern.

It is often argued that measurement is a requisite tool—or pressure—for accountability and improvement, including improvement in shared access to information between units of government (as suggested above) and between decision makers and stakeholders (Fountain 1992). The goal of service delivery would be well served if debates about service allocation and resource utilization were guided by objective criteria. Perhaps the most valuable and specific forms of information are contained in measures of service or product quantity and quality. Productivity's state-of-the-art measurement is such that policy-making and policy-implementing officials no longer need bow to casual assumptions that government's productivity cannot be measured or evaluated. Quantitative approaches to the objective evaluation of government programs are especially evidenced by work throughout the United States. Taken as a whole, the literature defines a compendium of sophisticated measures for public sector outputs *and* outcomes.

Productivity measures help answer such questions as: Is an organization doing its job? Is it creating unintended side effects or producing unanticipated impacts? Is it responsive to the public? Is it fair to all, or does it inadvertently or deliberately favor certain groups? Does it keep within its proper bounds of authorized activity? Is it productive?

Management often has the hard data to construct those objective measures. If it does not, it can develop the information. As award-winning cases suggest, measurement of public services is conceptually sound and feasible: outputs and outcomes are measurable, data are readily available, and the results are not too complicated to use (EXSL 1989–1995). A measurement program offers an opportunity to develop and present feedback in place of generalized perceptions. According to a study by the US Government Accountability Office:

> Managers can use the data that performance measures provide to help them manage in three basic ways: to account for past activities, to manage current operations, or to assess progress toward planned objectives. When used to look at past activities, performance measures can show the accountability of processes and procedures used to complete a task, as well as program results. When used to manage current operations, performance measures can show how efficiently resources, such as dollars and staff, are being used. Finally, when tied to planned objectives, performance measures can be used to assess how effectively an agency is achieving the goals stated in its long-range strategic plan. Having well-designed measures that are timely, relevant, and accurate is important, but it is also important that the measures be used by decision makers (GAO 1992).

While productivity measurement is useful to the entire range of organizational actors, it is especially useful in staff analysts' and auditors' hands. Measures can be useful not just to internal decision makers, (i.e., managers and policy-level appointees). Mesaures can also help external groups, and even the press, improve their analyses by clarifying real, as opposed to suspected, problems.

That the momentum for measurement has advanced significantly is evidenced by a critical mass of research (e.g., Epstein 1988; Holzer 1992; Washnis 1980). Perhaps the most important and sustained effort has been by Harry Hatry and his colleagues at the Urban Institute (Hatry 1974, 1977, 1979; Urban Institute 1980). Here, the nuts and bolts of measurement are readily available.

The dialogue on public sector productivity measurement has continued quarterly since 1975 through the *Public Productivity and Management Review* (*PPMR*), formerly *Public Productivity Review*, which emphasizes implementation of organizational goals and objectives; measurement of efficiency and effectiveness levels; cooperation between management, labor, and clients; and recognition of the fiscal, legal, political, and technological constraints to productivity enhancement. For example, the *PPMR* published measurement-related research on "governmental efficiency" (Rabin 1990), where Miller argues that "efficiency, equity and parsimony dictate government financial innovations, [and] that efficiency is (a) basic beliefs underlying public financial management" (Miller 1990, 333).

Productivity measurement is an important drive for quality initiatives such as TQM (Milakovich 1992). The Government Accounting Standards Board (GASB) has made major progress toward the development of objective measures. In 1987, the GASB adopted Concepts Statement No. 1 which addressed the need for financial reporting to assist in fulfilling government's duty to be publicly accountable (GASB 1987). The impetus for this research, carried out by GASB, was widespread concern that the financial reports of governmental entities do not go far enough in providing "complete information to management, elected officials and the public about the 'results of the operations' of the entity or its programs" (Fountain 1992). Public organizations routinely use measurement as a decision-making tool although application of these measures is uneven (GAO 1992; GASB 1990). Responding to the pressures of citizens, elected officials, and professional associations, governments have begun to develop programmatic measures of efficiency, effectiveness, quality, and outcomes (ASPA 1992, 1996; Bowsher 1992; Christopher 1986; GAO 1992).

B. SOCIAL FACTORS

1. Constants: Cultural Differences

Classical productivity models patterned on traditional private sector models, such as scientific management, view workers as inherently economic beings behaving productively because they are motivated primarily by a desire for wages. Adherents of traditional management principles presume that individuals want to retain their positions, are fearful of being fired, and will willingly follow the dictates of centralized authority, top-down communications, and other scientific management paradigms. But views of workers as economic animals do not always coincide with the reality that forces not evident on organizational charts do indeed control employees' actions. The complexities of motivation have been discussed in detail in such work as the Hawthorne Experiments, Theory Y, TQM, and the learning organization. Such forces may, for example, include religion (holidays and prayer periods), custom (working hours and breaks which differ from the 8-to-4 or 9-to-5 day), or reference group (family, friends, village).

2. Problems: Bureaucratic Pathologies

Although public bureaucracies are under increasing pressures to be productive, several tensions tend to subvert productivity improvement efforts. One such tension is bureaucracy's unanticipated pathological consequences. Large private and public organizations share an underlying ill—bureaucratic stagnation—that current, technologically oriented policy and research virtually ignore. Although bureaucracy is an efficient tool for both public and private organizations, it is apparent that unintended consequences of the bureaucratic structure have a very limiting effect on productivity. Too often bureaucracy is epitomized by the sufficiency of mediocrity, the "Don't rock the boat" adage, a stifling loss of independence, a misdirection of energies to solving personal problems of promotion, playing office politics, and abusing or discrediting fellow employees. Bureaucracies have degenerated into machines that may be too impersonal and too insensitive for effective, productive responses to public demands. Fueled by fears, such machines produce at very low levels and with many errors.

Messages that bureaucracy stifles productivity cannot be dismissed as simplistic, for many social science theories are grounded in the same assumptions. Osborne and Gaebler (1992) argued that the old bureaucratic model must give way to an entrepreneurial approach to public administration. The same tensions—bureaucratic control versus individual initiative—have been resurfacing for decades. They have staying power because the problems of bureaucracy are still unsolved, because the organizational sciences have not been able to change most organizations, and because bureaucracy is still perceived as violating the public trust.

Bureaucracies can be run by fear, but they run at a very low level of productivity. In the long run, if control versus dishonesty is the dominant mode, organizations fail—in a crisis, a crunch, or a competition.

3. Opportunities: Management–Workforce Cooperation

One means of overcoming such pathologies is joint management–workforce cooperation. Pressured public organizations are now recognizing that a prerequisite to productivity improvement and a counterforce to negative and misleading assumptions is cooperation between the organization's decision-makers and the workforce (defined as labor and middle management). It is by no means the traditional suggestion box. Under various rubrics the premises are that productive ideas are equally distributed within organizations, the top-down characteristics of bureaucracy must be replaced by an equal relationship that draws as much of its creative energy from the bottom as from the top, innovation and risk taking are made possible, all members of the organization are rewarded, and labor and middle management are given a major psychological stake in organizational improvement (Grace and Holzer 1992).

The cooperation of middle management is minimized if internal management consulting resources are overlooked. Hoover (1992) argues that change agents can perform a number of roles within the organization as a cost-efficient alternative to the use of external consultants for improvement projects. His premises are that the internal consultant is an important resource for improving organizational performance, there should be more internal consultants within governmental organizations, and they should be put to better use. According to Hoover:

> Using existing staff to fill internal consulting positions has been quite successful when those staff are properly prepared for the task. Existing employees bring their experience and knowledge of the organizations and the operating procedures. They may be known by others within the organization, and particularly by those with whom they will have to work to perform successfully their assigned tasks. They will not be seen as outsiders by existing managers and employees (Hoover 1992).

But management does not have a monopoly on imagination or innovation. Productive ideas are distributed throughout the hierarchy. All organizations (in this case, public organizations), need to recognize that a requisite element of productivity improvement is cooperation between the organization's leaders and its workforce (defined as labor and middle management). As TQM and other earlier strategies suggest, the top-down characteristics of bureaucracy can be replaced by an equal relationship that draws as much of its creative energy from the bottom and middle as from the top, makes innovation and risk-taking possible, and gives labor and middle management a major psychological stake in organizational improvement.

Bowman (1992) recommends one particular form of labor–management cooperation—quality circles that came into vogue during the 1980s and have been in the vanguard of the employee involvement movement.

To the extent that labor and middle management are treated as an agency's internal consultants, they are buying into the process of change. Although the costs are minimal, the potential payoffs are substantial: improved performance and cost savings; a workforce–management dialogue built on a continuing stream of reasonable ideas, without the expense of external consultants or interveners; positive feelings about being treated as problem-solving adults; and an enhanced sense of professional commitment at all levels.

4. Actions: Motivational Incentives

It is widely recognized that productivity is achieved only by tapping an organization's human potential. Guy (1992), for example, points out that many interdependent factors contribute to creating a productive work environment: organizational culture, team building that maximizes the employees' strengths while compensating for their weaknesses, open communication channels, flexibility in the midst of predictability, and balancing the needs of the organization with the needs of employees. Nonmonetary incentives that can reinforce a worker's natural desire (i.e., eagerness) to contribute to the solution of productivity problems are widely available: job rotation, enlargement, and enrichment; quality circles and joint labor–management committees; career ladders; awards and other forms of recognition; flexible working hours and job sharing; and improved working conditions among dozens of others.

Government's most extensive and expensive investment is people—most public organizations devote from 50 to 85% of their budgets to employee salaries and benefits. Because those human resources have complicated needs, the most progressive public organizations have adopted enlightened human resource practices, rejecting an authoritarian, bureaucratic style. Typically, they:

- Recognize that motivation requires management of many interrelated elements. Ban et al. (1992) hold that to achieve their goals, public organizations need to take an integrated approach to personnel management, linking workforce planning, recruitment, hiring, training, and other personnel policies. Building and maintaining a productive work force includes: (1) developing a formal work force plan; (2) actively recruiting job applicants; (3) redesigning tests or developing creative alternatives to written tests; (4) linking training and development activities to organizational mission; and (5) revising personnel policies to meet the needs of employees.
- Understand that money can be an important motivator, but it is not the only motivational option. A sense of being able to make a difference in the organization is more important to the job satisfaction of public sector managers than to that of private managers (Balfour and Wechsler 1991).
- Carefully apply performance appraisal systems. Daly (1992) points out that productivity is a function of motivation, and motivation—extrinsic or intrinsic—is itself a function of the recognition of an individual's work effort. Such recognition can come from a well-conceived and well-managed system of performance appraisal.

C. Technological Factors

1. Constants: Priorities

A third productivity building block rests on technology. A prerequisite for the peaceful, productive use of technology is a clear definition of priorities. Scarce capital is often spent to improve security in the form of police and prisons. But in a more productive environment, it is more likely to be directed to reinvestment for educational, scientific, and technical purposes.

2. Problems: Capital Underfunding

It is difficult to secure financing for public sector investments as elected officials are more concerned with minimizing short-term budgets than maximizing long-term productivity pay backs. Financing is an especially difficult constraint when public policies employ as many workers as possible (including seasonal use of the unemployed) and stress the use of human capital while mitigating against capital expenditures for new machinery, facilities, or equipment. Furthermore, investments are unavailable under the pressures of agreements to tighten belts, to cutback, to economize; it then becomes difficult to acquire resources for productive opportunities.

One problem is that public organizations are tremendously under capitalized. They lack the capacity to invest in such productive technologies as computers, telecommunications, vehicles, maintenance facilities, energy-saving devices, and energy-efficient buildings. In the long run, they may also lack the capacity to make investments in the workforce (i.e., in human capital) related to such internal capacities as training, education, and medical support services. In the long run they may also lack the capacity to invest in information-sharing mechanisms such as databases, clearing-houses, publications, research, and case lessons.

3. Opportunities: Technology Transfer

Productivity improvement is a matter of organizational technology as much as industrial technology. Such organizational machinery includes simple records of finances, time, and materials; organizational charts; job descriptions; written instructions; etc. Those suffice for productivity at an acceptably low level. But higher aspirations also require more sophisticated systems: computerized records, tracking systems, matrix organizations, Internet-based communications, etc. The extent an organization can move from the simple to the sophisticated, yet still provide fast, responsive action, is the extent it can be a productive model.

A predisposition toward labor-intensive organizations and cutback management should not be allowed to preclude appropriate technology (hardware and software) as a vehicle for productivity improvement. Complex technologies such as computers, telecommunications, remote sensing devices, and systems based on Intranet and the Internet as well as simpler devices such as hand tools, trucks, and telephones, may have appropriate and specific applications. The appreciation of such opportunities is, however, contingent upon diffusion of innovations.

In the United States, some government programs are effective vehicles for the diffusion of technology transfer (there are technology transfer programs within the Commerce and Defense Departments). A not-for-profit organization, Public Technology, Inc., is devoted to the development and diffusion of productive technologies for the public sector. Private sector vendors are another avenue of diffusion. Despite those efforts, even in the US, technological and other innovations may take decades before they are widely known or before adoption is relatively pervasive.

4. Actions: Technological Adaptations

Technology is only productive if viewed as part of an organizational system and installed in synch with appropriate changes in, or accommodations for, that system's workforce, environment, tasks, and information. For example, in implementing e-government transformation, Fountain (2001) concludes that organizations have a tendency to "implement new IT in ways that reproduce, indeed strengthen, institutionalized sociostructural mechanisms even when such enactments do not use technology rationally or optimally" (90).

Advanced technologies are as important to the public as to the private sectors, and the public sector pioneers new systems. In the United States, government employees have invented (or contributed to the invention of) lasers, solid-state technology, the basic design of most commercial and military aircraft, instrument landing systems, the first modern computer, titanium (and other stronger and lighter materials), the Cat scan, plastic corneas, advanced fishing nets, nuclear power, Teflon, wash-and-wear fabric, resuscitation devices, and plastic wrap (Public Employees Round-table 1990). NASA, for example, has a continuing program to help the private sector exploit innovations resulting from the space program.

Technology is not limited to computer applications. In an area as mundane as refuse collection, for example, departments of sanitation in New York City, Scottsdale, Arizona, and Phoenix Arizona, have developed and applied numerous technological changes (Holzer and Callahan 1993). As these examples indicate, the improvement of government performance may be contingent on the identification and adaptation of mundane technologies.

D. MANAGERIAL FACTORS

1. Constants: Comprehensive Public Management

A fourth requisite for improved productivity is competent public management of the infrastructure that makes productive work possible in the public and private sectors: schools, financial institutions, health care, telephones and telecommunications, airports, railroads, ports, roads, postal services, etc. An educated middle class is a prerequisite for training new first-line supervisors. Efficient postal services and communications networks are prerequisites for timely decision making. Reliable financial institutions are prerequisites for capital formation and investments in plants and equipment.

Although TQM and similar efforts are popularly associated with the private sector (Crosby 1979; Imai 1986; Juran 1988), elected and appointed officials have come to recognize that traditional, comprehensive, management-oriented productivity efforts alone may not lead to sufficient improvements in service quality as perceived by the public. According to Milakovich (1992), decades of improvements in public management have been insufficient, "despite the best intentions, the application of these [traditional] methods has not eliminated complaints of inefficient or ineffective services, wasted resources, or lack of responsiveness by public employees." TQM, directed at public or private sector productivity improvement, is one of the reformulations of management theory (Hyde 1992). It is a theory-based improvement strategy that allows public managers to increase the capacity for agency-wide cooperation, responsiveness to customer needs, and process improvement. TQM is not, however, a new invention for the public sector. Rather, it is an innovative repackaging of several decades of public sector productivity improvement (see e.g., Holzer 1992; Hunt 1993; Washnis 1980). Although neither TQM nor quality improvement were terms generally found in the public sector literature as late as 1988, the 1990s witnessed an accelerated improvement and publication movement under this terminology (e.g., Boyne and Walker 2002; Connor 1997; Poister and Harris 1997). In many cases, what had been formerly productivity projects were redescribed as quality efforts.

There are many definitions of TQM. Cohen and Brand (1993: xi–xii) define TQM as follows:

- *Total* implies applying the search for quality to every aspect of work from identifying customer needs to aggressively evaluating whether the customer is satisfied.
- *Quality* means meeting and exceeding customer expectations.
- *Management* means developing and maintaining the organizational capacity to constantly improve quality.

Cohen and Brand argue that "the same principles of total quality management used in private industry are creating a quiet revolution in the public sector…. To improve quality of service, increase productivity, and reduce waste, more and more government managers—from Little Rock to Washington—are turning to TQM." In fact, quality improvement has become a central goal for public services across the world (Pollitt and Bouckaert 2000). In the United States, TQM is used in many public organizations as one of many improvement strategies (Berman and West 1995; Chackerian and Mavima 2001). Although a meta-analysis finds that current evidences do not provide comprehensive support for the argument that TQM leads to organizational success (Boyne and Walker 2002), many researchers have documented the positive impact of TQM on organizational culture and service delivery (e.g., Poister and Harris 1997).

2. Problems: Procedural Rigidity and Privatization

Despite productivity and quality efforts such as TQM, laws and regulations that reduce management's discretion and flexibility are, unfortunately, pervasive. An overemphasis on top-down oversight—for example, the laborious approval process for contracts or for hiring new staff—delays improvements and discourages capable vendors or job seekers from competing for public contracts or positions. Similarly, nationally funneled, locally administered programs require multiple sets of overseers to have their say. At each level, watchdogs win points for raising questions and obstacles in the public interest. Yet the sum of those hurdles is a failure to improve productivity. Unfortunately, the ethic for which they are rewarded may often be one of minimizing expenditures (no matter the loss of necessary services caused by unnecessary delays) rather than investing in or facilitating productive actions. It is also important to recognize the use-it-or-lose-it syndrome built into most public budgeting and financial management systems that discourages managers from saving resources through innovation or any other means.

A structural alternative to government—privatization—has gained momentum since the late 1980s. Privatization is a contemporary reincarnation of businesslike management. The term *privatization*, as it is commonly used, is actually a bifurcated concept (Donahue 1989; Rainey 1997; Wamsley and Zald 1973). One meaning of the term is the shift of government services to the private sector, establishing a direct relationship between the private provider and the private consumer. That shift may include the divestment or sale of government enterprises and assets; load shedding; and demonopolization of government services to allow private alternatives to emerge (Savas 1992). In these public-to-private shifts, privatization signifies moving services from government provision to a direct relationship between the service provider (a firm) and the consumer or client; the financial relationship is between the two as private parties, without a payment through government. No contract with the government entity is involved, although government may have a regulatory, policing, or indirect financing role.

In its alternative usage, privatization is contracting out or moving services from direct supply by government to an indirect relationship between the service provider (a firm acting on behalf of government as a formal contractor) and the consumer/client. The financial relationship is then between three parties: government as the conduit and monitor; the firm as the service provider; and the customer/client as the service recipient. The premise is that contractors are more innovative and frugal than government; they have greater incentives and fewer obstacles to delivering services.

Touted regularly by politicians and emphasized by the media, it may now be the most popular argument for public sector productivity improvement. Their logic is that contracting out or turning over services to the private sector produces large savings with virtually no loss of quality or reduction in service levels (Savas 1992). Advocates hold that privatization can deliver a much greater portion of services that are now public. But skeptics hold that many services are necessarily government's responsibility, and a public-to-private shift will not automatically enhance productivity in a jurisdiction or department (Barnekov and Raffel 1992). A recurring theme in the privatization literature is that what makes a difference is competition, not the fact of privatization by itself, and that private monopolies are no better than the public ones (e.g., Donahue 1989). Therefore, privatization is productive as long as it assumes competition.

3. Opportunities: Cooperative Partnerships

While the competition on which privatization is based is certainly an important opportunity for improvement, cooperation is also an essential productivity enhancement strategy that is overlooked. Cooperative arrangements of service provision today may be a more accurate characterization of emerging day-to-day relationships. Joint public–private initiatives are options that innovative public officials often turn to. Rather than privatizing, raising taxes, or soliciting donations for visible projects (i.e., tax supplements), these new relationships are joint problem-solving efforts that may be initiated by either side. Cooperation between labor and management, different public agencies, neighboring local governments, government and voluntary organizations, executive and legislative branches, or governmental entities of different levels have proven to be effective arrangements aimed at improving government service and cutting costs. The ability to think and act outside the rigid but familiar bureaucratic box can be essential for pooling resources and improving productivity in an increasingly resource-scarce atmosphere. There are many successful cases of partnerships—public and private—between labor and management, between different public organizations, etc. (Holzer and Gabrielian 1996).

According to Fosler and Berger (1982), "local initiative supported by a strong civic foundation can give a community the ability to mobilize its public and private resources to improve community conditions." Typically, joint public–private ventures strengthen government's capacity to deliver services by

- Providing personnel or equipment donations
- Supplementing services such as schools, parks, and libraries
- Jointly developing strategies to ameliorate emerging problems such as homelessness or crime
- Stimulating economic development

Private partners will generally expect their investment to provide some indirect return such as a better-educated labor force or a safer neighborhood to do business in. But the private partner may also begin to act as a public-serving institution, directly investing for the general public good rather than for any specific, short-term, bottom-line gain.

4. Actions: Competency

Competition and cooperation may be productive concepts, but only to the extent that the public sector workforce is competently trained. In many governments, on-the-job training is still considered sufficient preparation for public sector responsibilities. Governments suffer from the assumption that the duties of public office are so simple that anyone can perform them. If public management responsibilities were once that simple, they are no longer. In an industrial and now post-industrial society, on-the-job training is insufficient preparation for increasingly complex public (and private) sector responsibilities. Yet the management of many public organizations is entrusted to amateurs with virtually no professional management training other than on the job. These situations create managerially illiterate politicians and political appointees as well as professionals with technical, not management, expertise. Too many people who manage public agencies have inadequate management skills, especially at the higher policy levels. Elected executives may be sensitive to the political dimension of public management, but they may not have an appreciation for management methods or personnel and budget systems. A political connection may mean that the appointee is devoid of any training other than experienced political sensitivity.

Political appointees may supervise professionals, but they may have far fewer or no professional credentials.

In terms of program effectiveness, a similar model would be Syracuse's model of government management capacity that is viewed as the black box linking inputs and outputs or outcomes. Ingraham and Donahue (2000) outline a framework: the inputs include policy design, political commitment, and resources; the outputs and outcomes include government performance and policy outcomes; they are linked by management capacity and implementation technology; all are affected by environmental contingencies. They call for the use of managing for results to integrate financial management, human resource management, capital management, and information technology management that is influenced by exercise of leadership, use of information, and allocation of resources.

In the literature and in the classroom, old, casual assumptions to the validity of on-the-job training are superseded by an appreciation for the complexity of managerial skills, the trained competence necessary to the management of public services, and the managerial differences in initiating, maintaining, and controlling systems. In search of more productive approaches, both sectors have complemented good intentions with good insights: technical approaches used by other organizations; enlightened leadership grounded in the social and psychological realities of groups and individuals; and comprehensive management systems drawn from other public and private sector organizations.

As a profession, public administration/management has a well-defined body of knowledge to draw upon. At least four dozen comprehensive handbooks on public administration provide guidance on such topics as improving accountability, reforming bureaucracies, managing information, enhancing communications, implementing strategic management, managing financial and human resources, improving labor relations, and increasing productivity. Just one series of bibliographies annotates over five thousand publications which are pertinent to the delivery of public services (Bowman 1980–1995), highlighting such problems as: equal employment opportunity, ethics, professional dissent, civil service reform, political corruption, the media and public opinion, public policy analysis, pay inequity, and the turbulence of gubernatorial and Presidential transitions. The unique problems of managing the public sector are critiqued in hundreds of periodicals.

VII. CONCLUSION

The five ideas outlined in this chapter are valuable theoretical lenses through which the dynamics of public administration can be observed. Public administration students use them continuously in theorizing and reflection, either consciously or unconsciously. This chapter concludes by illustrating how the popular reinvention literature can be analyzed with the five ideas, considering that the re-inventing government (Osborne and Gaebler 1992) and the National Performance Review (NPR), as well as the more general terms such as the New Public Management and New Managerialism, have gained much currency in public administration.

The reinventing government paradigm provides an eclectic synthesis of different approaches. Its ten tenets state that government should be: steering rather than rowing; community owned; competitive; mission driven; result oriented; customer driven; enterprising; anticipatory; decentralized; and market oriented. These tenets are in line with the New Public Management that promotes downsizing, reengineering, continuous improvement, privatization, contracting out, decentralization, deregulation, empowerment, marketization, and entrepreneurship. These elements are not new to the field of public administration; therefore, some commentators have argued that the NPM and reinventing government are old wine in new bottles. It is far from a new invention.

The NPM and NPR share a businesslike orientation with Idea One. The NPR clearly resuscitated the politics administration as its basis: "this performance review is not about politics.... We want to make improving the way government does business a permanent part of how government works, regardless of which party is in power" (NPR 1993, iv). Their rationale is borrowed from public choice theories and neoinstitutional economics. Based on Savas (1987), distinction between types of goods (private, toll, common, and collective) and types of service arrangements (government service, government vending, intergovernmental agreement, contracts, franchises, grants, vouchers, market systems, voluntary service, and self-service), and his criteria for choosing best mode of service arrangement, Osborne and Gaebler (1992) propose a framework for tasks that are best suited for different sectors. They argue that the tasks best suited for the public sector are policy management, regulation, enforcement of equity, prevention of discrimination, prevention for exploitation, and promotion of social cohesion. The tasks best suited for the private sector include economic and investment tasks, profit generation, and promotion of self-sufficiency. The tasks more appropriate for the third sector are social tasks: tasks requiring volunteer labor, generating little profit, promoting individual responsibility, promoting community, and promoting commitment to the welfare of others. This typology is abstract and vague, because almost every endeavor the government pursues has multiple goals, and terms such as *economic tasks* are too broad. Unlike the Progressive reformers who were pro-government, most of the NPM and NPR advocates hold a government-bashing ideology (Carroll and Lynn 1996; Frederickson 1996). Progressives intend to borrow business practices to strengthen government, yet NPM and NPR advocates aim to expand markets and shrink government.

Some elements of the NPM and NPR can be found in Ideas Two, Four, and Five. They share a focus on efficiency, economy, and effectiveness with Idea Two. The idea of re-engineering, although touted as a revolution against Taylorism, has much continuity with scientific management: both study and reform organizational processes in a scientific way to achieve the greatest efficiency and cooperation. But they have different democratic meanings. The classic management models treat bureaucracies as closed systems in the sense that bureaucracies and bureaucrats cannot formulate their own goals because they should be controlled by political leaders. Therefore, hierarchical control is the major accountability assurance. In contrast, the NPM and NPR consider bureaucracies as open systems that should be more autonomous and independent from Congressional control. Outcome accountability is offered as a replacement to a traditional procedural accountability system, but its effectiveness is highly questionable, especially in contracting-out situations. Rosenbloom (2001) concludes that the reinvention movement "is older than it knows" (163), sharing many common elements with Wilson and Brownlow. The terminological similarities between the NPR (NPM) and Ideas Four and Five are also evident. For example, continuous improvement, one of the major proposals of the NPR, could be viewed as an incarnation of the human relations school (Theories Y and Z) and TQM. The NPR discussed participative management, intrinsic motivation, employee empowerment, bottom-up reform, and communitarian values, which are related to Ideas Four and Five. However, these elements should not be understood as substantive reforms; rather, they constitute a postmodern type of symbolic politics (Fox 1996): a metaphorical category is introduced (rowing and steering), good managerial terms are assembled rhetorically, and anecdotal evidence and examples are gathered as support.

The major critique of the NPR comes from scholars who hold Idea Three's view in one form or another. Wilson (1994) contends that the most striking feature of the NPR is the absence of reference to democratic accountability. Moe (1994) criticizes the NPR on the institutionalist grounds that it disregards the public law foundation of public administration and endangers the accountability process in government. Rosenbloom views the key reinvention literature as "deeply flawed" and advances "no connection between their prescriptions and more effective representative democracy" (Rosenbloom 2001, 164). With an anti-bureaucratic ideological connotation (Frederickson 1996), the NPR was less responsive to democratic values than the traditional ideas (Riccucci 2001). The political objective of the NPR was to change the balance of power, control, and authority over the federal government with the constitutional doctrine of separation of powers giving way to absolute executive power over Congress (Carroll 1995). Carroll (1995) concludes, "In treating government as a Wal-Mart, the NPR ignored the fact that many operational assumptions based on customer service had implications for broader systems of values such as the rule of law, representative government, separated and shared powers, and individual liberty" (310). As advocates of Idea Three criticize Ideas One and Two, Rosenbloom (1993) notes that the problem of the NPR is it ignored the old lesson "if we want better government, we better talk politics" (506). Government and administrative agencies cannot be reformed alone as entrepreneurial organizations, given legislative self-interest.

In reviewing the reinvention literature, society must look back to prevent those vague, anti-, or pseudo-democratic ideas from gaining currency in public administration (Lynn 2001; Rosenbloom 2001). Public administration is an actively evolving field that tries to adapt to and reflect upon a constantly changing, complex web of relationships of interactions between government and society. Theoretical frameworks, such as the NPR (NPM), no matter how comprehensive and insightful they may appear, are always incomplete. First, in a democratic society, the role of government will always be a matter of heated public debate. Second, there will always be new developments in the society that the discipline of public administration will try to respond and incorporate. With increasing international cooperation and a trend toward globalization of world governance, international and comparative administration may experience a revival. The welfare state may narrow the scope of services or ration them more carefully by outsourcing and privatizing them. With awareness of new hazards from some type of industries, the regulatory activities of the state may increase. With adoption of term limits, iron triangles will definitely be altered (perhaps still as triangles, but not of iron; perhaps still of iron, but more than triangles). With critical approaches gaining more momentum in mainstream social thought, public administrators may lean toward more participatory approaches in addressing public issues. All of these, as well as a variety of others, sometimes totally surprising, developments may occur. To predict the future is an ungrateful task, but at least one thing can be predicted with confidence—changes in general will definitely happen. Public administration has always proved to be flexible and vital so as to incorporate diverse streams of social thought into its realm, and it will do so in the future. Public sector administrators will continue to grapple with issues of citizen participation, professional responsibility, and efficient service delivery. And public administration will face the same old administrative questions that it faced yesterday and is facing today: Where does politics stop and administration begin? How can employees be led, motivated, and protected (from political excesses)? How different is public management from private management? What is the necessary scope of government's services? What, and how much, should be centralized or decentralized? How can the public sector achieve efficiency and effectiveness while balancing those concerns with equity in service delivery? Who should govern, and what is the role of experts and expertise in the process of governance? What is the nature of public interest, if there is one?

REFERENCES

Adams, G., *The Politics of Defense Contracting: The Iron Triangle*, Transaction Press, New Brunswick, NJ, 1982.

Alexander, E. R., From idea to action: notes for a contingency theory of the public implementation process, *Administration & Society*, 16(4), 481–504, 1985.

Allison, G., *Essence of Decision: Explaining the Cuban Missile Crisis*, Little, Brown, Boston, MA, 1971.

Alonso, P. and Lewis, G. B., Public service motivation and job performance: evidence from the federal sector, *American Review of Public Administration*, 31(4), 363–380, 2001.

Appleby, P., *Policy and Administration*, University of Alabama Press, Tuscaloosa, AL, 1949.

Argyris, C., *Personality and Organization*, Harper, New York, 1957.

Argyris, C. and Schön, D. A., *Theory in Practice: Increasing Professional Effectiveness*, Jossey-Bass, San Francisco, CA, 1974.

Argyris, C. and Schön, D. A., *Organizational Learning*, Addison-Wesley Pub., Reading, MA, 1978.

Arrow, K., *Social Choice and Individual Values*, Wiley, New York, 1951.

ASPA (American Society for Public Administration), Guidelines for developing government performance measurement and reporting programs: resolution encouraging the use of performance measurement and reporting by government organizations, American Society for Public Administration, Washington, DC, Resolution adopted April 14, 1992.

ASPA (American Society for Public Administration), Performance measurement training, Government Accomplishment and Accountability Task Force of the American Society for Public Administration, Washington, DC, 1996.

Balfour, D. L. and Wechsler, B., Commitment, performance, and productivity in public organizations, *Public Product Manage. Rev.*, 15(1), 355–368, 1991.

Ban, C., Faerman, S. R., and Riccucci, N. M., Productivity and the personnel process, In *Public Productivity Handbook*, Holzer, M., Ed., Marcel Dekker, New York, pp. 401–423, 1992.

Banki, I. S., *Dictionary of Administration and Management*, Systems Research Institute, Los Angeles, CA, 1981.

Barnard, C. I., *Functions of the Executive*, Harvard University Press, Cambridge, MA, 1938.

Barnekov, T. K. and Raffel, J. A., Public management of privatization, In *Public Productivity Handbook*, Holzer, M., Ed., Marcel Dekker, New York, pp. 99–115, 1992.

Behn, R. D., The big question of public management, *Public Admin. Rev.*, 55(4), 313–324, 1995.

Berman, E. M. and West, J. P., Municipal commitment to total quality management: a survey of recent progress, *Public Admin. Rev.*, 55(1), 57–66, 1995.

Bowman, J. S., Ed., *The Public Affairs and Administration Series*, Garland Press, New York, 1980.

Bowman, J. S., Quality circles for the 1990s, In *Public Productivity Handbook*, Holzer, M., Ed., Marcel Dekker, New York, pp. 499–517, 1992.

Bowsher, C.A., Performance measurement: an important tool in managing for results. Testimony before the Committee on Governmental Affairs, United States Senate, May 5, GAO/T-GGD-92-35, 1992.

Boyne, G. A. and Walker, R. M., Total quality management and performance: an evaluation of the evidence and lessons from research on public organizations, *Public Performance & Management Review*, 26(2), 111–131, 2002.

Brewer, G. A., Selden, S. C., and Facer, R. L., Individual conceptions of public service motivation, *Public Admin. Rev.*, 60(3), 254–264, 2000.

Brower, R. S. and Abolafia, M. Y., Procedural entrepreneurship: enacting alternative channels to administrative effectiveness, *American Review of Public Administration*, 26(3), 287–308, 1996.

Brown, M. M. and Brudney, J. L., Learning organizations in the public sector?, *Public Admin. Rev.*, 63(1), 30–43, 2003.

Buchanan, J. and Tullock, G. A., *The Calculus of Consent: Logical Foundations of Constitutional Democracy*, University of Michigan Press, Ann Arbor, MI, 1962.

Burke, C. G., Themes from the history of American public administration: rethinking our past, In *Handbook of Public Administration*, Rabin, J., Hildreth, W. B., and Miller, G. J., Eds., Marcel Dekker, New York, pp. 43–104, 1989.

Burrell, G. and Morgan, G., *Sociological Paradigms in Organizational Analysis*, Heinemann, London, 1979.

Carroll, J. D., The rhetoric of reform and political reality in the national performance review, *Public Admin. Rev.*, 55(3), 302–312, 1995.

Carroll, J. D. and Lynn, D. B., The future of federal reinvention: congressional perspectives, *Public Admin. Rev.*, 56(3), 213–215, 1996.

Cater, D., *Power in Washington*, Random House, New York, 1964.

Chackerian, R. and Mavima, P., Comprehensive administrative reform implementation: moving beyond single issue implementation research, *J Public Admin Res & Theory*, 11(3), 379–402, 2001.

Chawla, S. and Renesch, J. Eds., *Learning Organizations: Developing Cultures for Tomorrow's Workplace*, Productivity Press, Portland, OR, 1995.

Chelimsky, E., Ed., *Program Evaluation: Patterns and Directions* 2nd ed., American Society for Public Administration, Washington, DC, 1989.

Cherry, V. R. and Holzer, M., *Research Guide to Public Administration*, Garland Press, New York, 1991.

Christopher, W. F., *Productivity Measurement Handbook*, 2nd ed., Productivity Press, Cambridge, MA, 1986.

Cohen, M. D., March, J. D., and Olsen, J. P., A garbage-can model of organizational choice, *Admin. Sci. Q*, 17, 1–25, 1972.

Cohen, S. and Brand, R., *Total Quality Management in Government: A Practical Guide for the Real World*, Jossey-Bass, San Francisco, CA, 1993.

Connor, P. E., Total quality management: a selective commentary on its human dimensions, *Public Admin. Rev.*, 57(6), 501–509, 1997.

Cook, B. J., The representative function of bureaucracy: public administration in constitutive perspective, *Administration & Society*, 23(4), 403–429, 1992.

Cook, B. J., At the crossroads of real and ideal: Woodrow Wilson's theory of administration, *Admin. Theory and Praxis*, 17(2), 15–29, 1995.

Cook, B. J., Politics, political leadership, and public management, *Public Admin. Rev.*, 58(3), 225–230, 1998.

Crenson, M. A., Comment: Contract, law & character building, In *Toward a New Public Administration: The Minnowbrook Perspective*, Marini, F., Ed., Chandler Publishing, Scranton, PA, pp. 83–89, 1971.

Crosby, P. B., *Quality is Free: The Art of Making Quality Certain*, McGraw-Hill, New York, 1979.

Dahl, R. A. and Lindblom, C., *Politics, Economics and Welfare*, Harper and Brothers, New York, 1953.

Daly, D. M., Pay for performance, performance appraisal and total quality management, *Public Product. Management Review*, 16(2), 39–52, 1992.

Denhardt, R. B., *In the Shadow of Organization*, University of Kansas Press, Lawrence, KS, 1981.

Denhardt, R. B., Public administration theory: the state of the discipline, In *Public Administration: The State of the Discipline*, Lynn, N. and Wildavsky, A., Eds., Chatham House, Chatham, NJ, pp. 32–72, 1990.

Denhardt, R. B., *Theories of Public Organization*, 2nd ed., Wadsworth, Belmont, CA, 1993.

Denhardt, R. B., Denhardt, J. V., and Aristigueta, M. P., *Managing Human Behavior in Public & Nonprofit Organizations*, Sage, Thousand Oaks, CA, 2002.

DiTomaso, N., Class and politics in the organization of public administration: the US department of labor, In *Critical Studies in Organization and Bureaucracy*, Fischer, F. and Sirianni, C., Eds., Temple University Press, Philadelphia, PA, 1994.

Dolan, J., Influencing policy at the top of the federal bureaucracy: a comparison of career and political senior executives, *Public Admin. Rev.*, 60(6), 573–581, 2000.

Donahue, J. D., *The Privatization Decision: Public Ends, Private Means*, Basic Books, New York, 1989.

Dror, Y., Muddling through—"science" or inertia?, *Public Admin. Rev.*, 24, 153–157, 1964.

Drucker, P., The coming rediscovery of scientific management, *Conference Board Record*, June, 25–37, 1976.

Du Gay, P., *In Praise of Bureaucracy*, Sage, Thousand Oaks, CA, 2000.

Dunsire, A., *Administration: The Word and Science*, Wiley, New York, 1973.

Epstein, P. D., *Using Performance Measurement in Local Government: A Guide to Improving Decisions, Performance, and Accountability*, National Civic League Press, New York, 1988.

Etzioni, A., Mixed scanning: a "third" approach to decision-making, *Public Admin. Rev.*, 27, 385–392, 1967.

EXSL (Exemplary State and Local Awards Program), *National Center for Public Productivity*, Rutgers University, Newark, NJ, 1989–1995.

Farmer, D. J., Kill the king: foucault and public administration theory, *Admin. Theory Praxis*, 17(2), 78–83, 1995.

Farmer, D. J., *The Language of Public Administration: Bureaucracy, Modernity and Postmodernity*, University of Alabama Press, Tuscaloosa, AL, 1995b.

Fayol, H., *General and Industrial Management*, Pitman Publishing, London, 1949.

Fischer, F., *Evaluating Public Policy*, Nelson-Hall, Chicago, IL, 1995.

Finer, H., Administrative responsibility in democratic government, *Public Admin. Rev.*, 1, 335–350, 1941.

Fosler, R. S. and Berger, R. A., *Public-Private Partnerships in American Cities: Seven Case Studies*, D.C. Heath, Lexington, MA, 1982.

Fountain, J., Ed., *Service Effort and Accomplishment Project*, Government Accounting Standards Board, Norwalk, CT, 1992.

Fountain, J., *Building the Virtual State*, Brookings Institution Press, Washington, DC, 2001.

Fox, C. J. and Miller, H. T., *Postmodern Public Administration*, Sage, Thousand Oaks, CA, 1995.

Fox, C. J. and Miller, H. T., Reinventing government as postmodern symbolic politics, *Public Admin. Rev.*, 56(3), 256–262, 1996.

Frederickson, H. G., Toward a new public administration, In *Toward a New Public Administration: The Minnowbrook Perspective*, Marini, F., Ed., Chandler Publishing, Scranton, PA, 1971.

Frederickson, H. G., The lineage of new public administration, *Administration & Society*, 8, 144–174, 1976.

Frederickson, H. G., Comparing the reinventing government movement with the new public administration, *Public Admin. Rev.*, 56(3), 263–270, 1996.

French, W. O. and Bell, C. H., *Organization Development: Behavioral Science Intervention for Organization Improvement*, Prentice Hall, Englewood Cliffs, NJ, 1973.

Friedrich, C. J., Public policy and the nature of administrative responsibility, *Public Policy*, 1, 3–24, 1940.

Fry, B. R. and Nigro, L. G., Max Weber and US public administration: the administrator as neutral servant, *J. Manage. History*, 2(1), 37–46, 1996.

Fry, L., The maligned F.W. Taylor: a reply to his many critics, *Acad. Manage. Rev.*, 1, 124–129, 1976.

GAO (Government Accountability Office), Program performance measures: federal agency collection and use of performance data, *Report to the Chairman and Ranking Minority Member*, Committee on Government Affairs, U.S. Senate, U.S. Government Accountability Office, Washington, DC, 1992.

GASB (Government Accounting Standards Board), *An Overview: Service Efforts and Accomplishments Reportings: Its Time has Come*, U.S. Government Accounting Standards Board, Norwalk, CT, 1990.

GASB (Government Accounting Standards Board), *Concepts Statement No. 1, Objectives of Financial Reporting*, U.S. Government Accounting Standards Board, Norwalk, CT, 1987.

Gioia, D. and Pitre, E., Multi-paradigm perspectives in theory building, *Acad. Manage. J.*, 15(4), 584–602, 1990.

Golembiewski, R. T., The papers and productivity: posterity's guidance for today's challenges, *Public Product Rev*, 13(3), 283–301, 1989.

Goodnow, F. J., *Politics and Administration*, Macmillan, New York, 1900.

Grace, S. L. and Holzer, M., Labor-management cooperation: an opportunity for change, In *Public Productivity Handbook*, Holzer, M., Ed., Marcel Dekker, New York, pp. 487–498, 1992.

Gulick, L. H., Reflections on public administration, past and present, *Public Admin. Rev.*, 50(6), 599–604, 1990.

Gulick, L. H. and Urwick, L., Papers on the science of administration, See especially: "Notes on the Theory of Organization," Institute for Public Administration, New York, 1937, 1–46.

Guy, M. E., Productive work environment, In *Public Productivity Handbook*, Holzer, M., Ed., Marcel Dekker, New York, pp. 321–335, 1992.

Hampden-Turner, C. and Trompenaars, A., *The Seven Cultures of Capitalism*, Currency Doubleday, New York, 1993.

Harmon, M. M., *Action Theory for Public Administration*, Longman, New York, 1981.

Hatry, H. P., Cost-benefit and cost-effectiveness analysis, In *The Encyclopedia of Management*, Heyel, C., Ed., 3rd ed., Van Nostrand Reinhold, New York, pp. 167–171, 1982.

Hatry, H. P., *Measuring the Effectiveness of Basic Municipal Services*, The Urban Institute, Washington, DC, 1974.

Hatry, H. P., *How Effective are your Community Services?*, The Urban Institute, Washington, DC, 1977.

Hatry, H. P., *Efficiency Measurement for Local Government Services*, The Urban Institute, Washington, DC, 1979.

Heady, F., *Public Administration: A Comparative Perspective*, 5th ed., Marcel Dekker, New York, 1996.

Heclo, H., Issue networks and the executive establishment, In *The New American Political System*, King, A., Ed., American Enterprise Institute, Washington, DC, pp. 307–328, 1978.

Herzberg, F., Mausner, B., and Snyderman, B., *The Motivation to Work*, Wiley, New York, 1959.

Hill, L. B., Who governs the American administrative state?, *J. Public Admin. Res. Theory*, 1(3), 261–294, 1991.

Hodgetts, R.M. and Greenwood, R., *Frederick Taylor: Alive and Well and Ready for the 21st century. Academy Management J.*, Best Paper Proceedings, 1995.

Hofstadter, R., *The American Political Tradition*, Vintage Books, New York, 1954.

Hofstede, G., Cultural constraints in management theories, *Academy of Management Executive*, 7(1), 81–94, 1993.

Hollway, W., *Work Psychology and Organizational Behavior*, Sage Publications, Newbury Park, CA, 1991.

Holzer, M., Ed., *Public Productivity Handbook*, Marcel Dekker, New York, 1992.

Holzer, M., Building capacity for productivity improvement, In *Competent Government: Theory and Practice*, Halachmi, A. and Holzer, M., Eds., Chatelaine Press, Burke, VA, pp. 457–467, 1994.

Holzer, M. and Callahan, K., Fiscal pressures and productive solutions, *Public Product Manage. Rev.*, 16(4), 331–348, 1993.

Holzer, M. and Gabrielian, V., Eds., *Cases in Productive Public Management*, Chatelaine Press, Burke, VA, 1996.

Holzer, M. and Halachmi, A., *Public Sector Productivity*, Garland Press, New York, 1988.

Hoover, D.F., Internal consulting, In *Productivity Handbook*, Marc, H., Ed., Marcel Dekker, New York, pp. 565–576, 1992.

Huczynski, A., *Encyclopedia of Organizational Change Methods*, Gower Publishing Company, Brookfield, VT, 1987.

Hummel, R. P., *The Bureaucratic Experience*, 4th ed., St. Martin's Press, New York, 1994.

Hummel, R. P. and Stivers, C., Government isn't us: the possibility of democratic knowledge in representative government, In *Government is us*, King, C. S. and Stivers, C., Eds., Sage, Thousand Oaks, CA, 1998.

Hunt, V. D., *Quality Management for Government: A Guide to Federal, State and Local Implementation*, ASQC Quality Press, Milwaukee, WI, 1993.

Hyde, A. C., The proverbs of total quality management, *Public Product Manage. Rev.*, 16(1), 25–38, 1992.

ICMA (International City Managers Association), Issue Brief #93–18973, International City Managers Association, Washington, DC, 1994.

Imai, M., *Kaizen: The Key to Japan's Competitive Success*, Random House, New York, 1986.

Ingraham, P. and Donahue, A. K., Dissecting the black box revisited, In *Governance and Performance*, Heinrich, C. J. and Lynn, L. E., Eds., Georgetown University Press, Washington, DC, pp. 235–252, 2000.

Jun, J., *Public Administration: Design and Problem Solving*, Macmillan, New York, 1986.

Juran, J. M., *Juran on Planning for Quality*, Free Press, New York, 1988.

Kass, H. D. and Catron, B. L., Eds., *Images and Identities in Public Administration*, Sage, Newbury Park, CA, 1990.

Kass, M. and Newton, K., *Beliefs in Government*, Vol. 5, Oxford University Press, New York, 1995.

Katz, D. and Kahn, R. L., *The Social Psychology of Organizations*, 2nd ed., Wiley, New York, 1978.

Kaufman, H., The growth of federal personnel system, In *Bureaucratic Power in National Politics*, Rourke, F. E., Ed., Little, Brown, Boston, MA, pp. 129–140, 1965.

Kaufman, H., Fear of bureaucracy: a raging pandemic, *Public Admin. Rev.*, 41(1), 1–9, 1981.

Kettl, D. F., Public administration at the millennium: the state of the field, *J. Public Admin. Res. Theory*, 10(1), 7–34, 2000.

Key, V. O., Jr., The lack of budgetary theory, *Am. Politic. Sci. Rev.*, 34, 1137–1144, 1940.

Kingdon, J. W., *Agendas, Alternatives and Public Solicies*, Harper Collins, New York, 1984.

Kirlin, J. J., The big questions of public administration in a democracy, *Public Admin. Rev.*, 56(5), 416–423, 1996.

Kirlin, J. J., Big questions for a significant public administration, *Public Admin. Rev.*, 61(2), 140–143, 2001.

Klingner, D. E., Nalbandian, J., and Romzek, B. S., Politics, administration, and markets, *Am Rev Public Admin*, 32(2), 117–144, 2002.

Koontz, H., The management theory jungle, *J. Acad. Manage.*, 4(3), 175–187, 1961.

LaPorte, T., The recovery of relevance in the study of public organization, In *Toward a New Public Administration: The Minnowbrook Perspective*, Marini, F., Ed., Chandler Publishing, San Francisco, CA, 1971.

Lee, E. W., Political science, public administration, and the rise of the American administrative state, *Public Admin. Rev.*, 55(6), 538–546, 1995.

Leeuw, F. L., Rist, R. C., and Sonninchsen, R. C., *Can Governments Learn?*, Transaction Publishers, New Brunswick, NJ, 1994.

Likert, R., *New Patterns of Management*, McGraw-Hill, New York, 1961.

Lindblom, C. E., The science of muddling through, *Public Admin. Rev.*, 19, 79–88, 1959.

Little, J. C., Jr. and Cayer, N. J., Experiences of a learning organization in the public sector, *Inter. J. Public Admin.*, 19(5), 711–730, 1996.

Long, N. E., Power and administration, *Public Admin. Rev.*, 9, 257–264, 1949.

Long, N. E., Bureaucracy and constitutionalism, *Am. Politic. Sci. Rev.*, 46, 808–818, 1952.

Lowi, T. J., *The End of Liberalism: The Second Republic of United States*, 2nd ed., Norton, New York, 1979.

Lowi, T. J., Toward a legislature of the first kind, In *Knowledge, Power, and the Congress*, Robinson, W. H. and Wellborn, C. H., Eds., *Congressional Quarterly* pp. 9-37, 1991.

Lowi, T. J., Two roads to serfdom: liberalism, conservatism and administrative power, In *A New Constitutionalism: Designing Political Institutions for a Good Society*, Elkin, S. L. and Soltan, K. E., Eds., University of Chicago Press, Chicago, IL, pp. 149–174, 1993.

Lowi, T. J. and Ginsberg, B., *American Government: Freedom and Power*, 2nd ed., Norton, New York, 1992.

Lynn, L. E., The myth of the bureaucratic paradigm: what traditional public administration really stood for, *Public Admin. Rev.*, 61(2), 144–160, 2001.

March, J. G. and Olsen, J. P., *Rediscovering Institutions: The Organizational Basis of Politics*, Free Press, New York, 1989.

March, J. G. and Simon, H. A., *Organizations*, Wiley, New York, 1958.

Marini, F., Ed., *Toward a New Public Administration: The Minnowbrook Perspective*, Chandler Publishing, Scranton, PA, 1971.

Martin, D., From mechanical engineering to re-engineering: would Taylor be pleased with modern management, *J. Manage. History*, 1(2), 38–51, 1995.

Maslow, A. H., A theory of human motivation, *Psychol. Rev.*, 50, 370–396, 1943.

Mayer, K. R. and Khademian, A. M., Bringing politics back in: defense policy and the theoretical study of institutions and processes, *Public Admin. Rev.*, 56(2), 180–190, 1996.

Mayo, E., *The Social Problems of Industrial Civilization*, Harvard University Press, Cambridge, MA, 1945.

Merriam, C. E., *American Political Ideas: Studies in the Development of American Political Thought 1865–1917*, Macmillan, New York, 1926.

Merton, R. K., Bureaucratic structure and personality, *Social Forces*, 18(4), 560–568, 1940.

McClelland, D., *The Achieving Society*, D. Van Nostrand, Princeton, NJ, 1961.

McCurdy, H. E., *Public Administration: A Bibliography*, American University, School of Government and Public Administration, Washington, DC, 1972.

McGregor, D., *The Human Side of Enterprise*, McGraw-Hill, New York, 1960.

McLaughlin, M., Implementation as mutual adaptation, In *Social Program Implementation*, Williams, W. and Ellmore, R., Eds., Academic Press, New York, pp. 167–180, 1976.

Milakovich, M.E., Total quality management for public service productivity improvement, In *Public Productivity Handbook*, Holzer, M., Ed., New York: Marcel Dekker, 1992.

Miller, G. J., Efficiency as a competing principle in public financial management, *Public Product Management Review*, XIII(4), 331–351, 1990.

Moe, R. C., The "reinventing government" exercise: misinterpreting the problems, misjudging the consequences, *Public Admin. Rev.*, 54(2), 111–123, 1994.

Montjoy, R. S. and Watson, D. J., A case for reinterpreted dichotomy of politics and administration as a professional standard in council-manager government, *Public Admin. Rev.*, 55(3), 231–239, 1995.

Morgan, G., *Images of Organization*, 2nd ed., Sage, Thousand Oaks, CA, 1997.

NPR (National Performance Review), *Creating a Government That Works Better and Costs Less*, U.S. Government Printing Office, Washington, DC, 1993.

Nigro, F. A. and Nigro, L. G., *Modern Public Administration*, Harper & Row, New York, 1973.

Niskanen, W. A., *Bureaucracy and Representative Government*, Aldine Altherton, Chicago, IL, 1971.

Nye, J. S., Zelikow, P. D., and King, D. C., *Why People Don't Trust Government*, Harvard University Press, Cambridge, MA, 1997.

Osborne, D. and Gaebler, T., *Reinventing Government: How the Entrepreneurial Spirit is Transforming the Public Sector*, Addison-Wesley, Reading, MA, 1992.

Ostrom, V., Some problems in doing political theory: a response to Golembiewski's "critique," *Am Politic Sci Rev*, 71, 1508–1525, 1977.

Ostrom, V., Some developments in the study of market choice, public choice and institutional choice, In *Handbook of Public Administration*, Rabin, J., Hildreth, W. B., and Miller, G. J., Eds., Marcel Dekker, New York, pp. 861–883, 1989a.

Ostrom, V., *Intellectual Crisis in American Public Administration*, University of Alabama Press, Tuscaloosa, AL, 1989b.

Ostrom, E., A method of institutional analysis and an application to multiorganizational arrangements, In *The Public Sector: Challenge for Coordination and Learning*, Kaufman, F., Ed., Walter de Gruyter, Berlin, pp. 501–525, 1991.

Ostrom, E. and Ostrom, V., Public choice: a different approach to the study of public administration, *Public Admin. Rev.*, 31, 203–216, 1971.

Paynter, J., Comment: on a redefinition of administration responsibility, In *Toward A New Public Administration: The Minnowbrook Perspective*, Marini, F., Ed., Chandler Publishing, Scranton, PA, pp. 185–189, 1971.

Perrow, C., *Complex Organizations*, Random House, New York, 1987.

Perry, J. L. and Wise, L. R., The motivational bases of public service, *Public Admin. Rev.*, 50(3), 367–373, 1990.

Poister, T. H. and Harris, R. H., The impact of TQM on highway maintenance: benefit/cost implications, *Public Admin. Rev.*, 57(4), 294–302, 1997.

Pollitt, C. and Bouckaert, G., *Public Management Reform: A Comparative Analysis*, Open University Press, Oxford, UK, 2000.

President's Committee on Administrative Management (Brownlow Committee), *Report with Special Studies*, U.S. Government Printing Office, Washington, DC, 1937.

Pressman, J. L. and Wildavsky, A., *Implementation*, 3d ed., University of California Press, Berkeley, CA, 1984.

Public Employees Roundtable, *Unsung Heroes (Newsletter)*, Public Employees Roundtable, Washington, DC, 1987–1990.

Quinn, R. E., *Beyond Rational Management*, Jossey-Bass, San Francisco, CA, 1988.

Rabin, J., Ed., *Governmental Efficiency Symposium in Public Product Management Review*, XIII(4), 331–396, 1990.

Rainey, H. G., *Understanding and Managing Public Organizations*, 2nd ed., Jossey-Bass, San Francisco, CA, 1997.

Riccucci, N. M., The "old" public management versus the "new" public management: where does public management administration fit in?, *Public Admin. Rev.*, 61(2), 172–175, 2001.

Riggs, F. W., *Prismatic Society Revisited*, General Learning Press, Morristown, NJ, 1994.

Riggs, F. W., Bureaucracy and the constitution, *Public Admin. Rev.*, 54(1), 65–72, 1994.

Ripley, R. and Franklin, G., *Congress, the Bureaucracy and Public Policy*, Brooks/Cole, Publishing, Pacific Grove, CA, 1991.

Roberts, A., Demonstrating neutrality: the Rockfeller philanthropies and the evolution of public administration, *Public Admin. Rev.*, 54(3), 221–228, 1994.

Roethlisberger, F. J., *Management and Morale*, Harvard University Press, Cambridge, MA, 1941.

Rohr, J. A., *To Run a Constitution: The Legitimacy of the Administrative State*, University Press of Kansas, Lawrence, KS, 1986.

Rohr, J. A., The constitutional case for public administration, In *Refounding Public Administration*, Wamsley, G., Ed., Sage Publications, Newbury Park, CA, pp. 52–96, 1990.

Rosenbloom, D. H., Public administration theory and the separation of powers, *Public Admin. Rev.*, 43(3), 219–226, 1983.

Rosenbloom, D. H., Public law and regulation, In *Handbook of Public Administration*, Rabin, J., Hildreth, W. B., and Miller, G. J., Eds., Marcel Dekker, New York, pp. 523–577, 1989.

Rosenbloom, D. H., Editorial: Have an administrative Rx? Don't forget the pol, *Public Admin. Rev.*, 53(6), 503–507, 1993.

Rosenbloom, D. H., History lessons for reinventors, *Public Admin. Rev.*, 61(2), 161–1651, 2001.

Rourke, F. E., *Bureaucracy, Politics and Public Policy*, Little, Brown, Boston, MA, 1984.

Rutgers, M. R., Splitting the universe: on the relevance of dichotomies for the study of public administration, *Admin. Society*, 33(1), 3–20, 2001.

Sabatier, P., An advocacy coalition framework of policy change and the role of policy oriented learning therein, *Policy Sci.*, 21, 129–168, 1988.

Sabatier, P. and Mazmanian, D., The conditions of effective implementation: a guide to accomplishing policy objectives, *Policy Analysis*, 5(4), 481–504, 1979.

Savas, E. S., *Privatization: The Key to Better Government*, Chatham House, Chatham, NJ, 1987.

Savas, E. S., Privatization and productivity, In *Public Productivity Handbook*, Holzer, M., Ed., Marcel Dekker, New York, pp. 79–98, 1992.

Sayre, W. S., Premises of public administration: past and emerging, *Public Admin. Rev.*, 18(2), 102–105, 1958.

Schachter, H. L., *Frederick Taylor and the Public Administration Community*, State University Press, Albany, NY, 1989.

Schachter, H. L., *Reinventing Government or Reinventing Ourselves: The Role of Citizen Owners in Making a Better Government*, State University of New York Press, Albany, NY, 1997.

Schubert, G. A., Jr., The public interest in administrative decision-making: theorem, theosophy, or theory, *Am. Politic. Sci. Rev*, 51, 346–348, 1957.

Scott, W. R., The mandate is still being honored: in defense of Weber's disciples, *Admin. Sci. Q.*, 41(1), 163–171, 1996.

Selznick, P. A., *TVA and the Grass Roots*, Harper and Row, New York, 1949.

Senge, P. M., *The Fifth Discipline*, Doubleday/Currency, New York, 1990.

Shafritz, J. M. and Hyde, A. C., *Classics of Public Administration*, 3rd ed., Wadsworth Publishing, Belmont, CA, 1991.

Sharp, B. S. and Housel, S. W., Ghosts in the bureaucratic machine, *Am. Rev. Public. Admin.*, 34(1), 20–35, 2004.

Simon, H. A., The proverbs of administration, *Public Admin. Rev.*, 6, 53–67, 1946.

Simon, H. A., The changing theory and changing practice of public administration, In *Contemporary Political Science: Towards Empirical Theory*, de Sola, P., Ed., McGraw-Hill, New York, 1967.

Simon, H. A., *Administrative Behavior: A Study of Decision-Making Process in Administrative organizations*, 4th ed., Free Press, New York, 1947.

Simon, H. A., Smithburg, D. W., and Thompson, V. A., *Public Administration*, Alfred A. Knopf, New York, 1950.

Skok, J. E., Policy issue networks and the public policy cycle: a structural-functional framework for public administration, *Public Admin. Rev.*, 55(4), 325–332, 1995.

Stillman, R. J., Woodrow Wilson and the study of administration: a new look at an old essay, *Am Politic Sci Rev*, 67, 582–588, 1973.

Stillman, R. J., Professor Ostrom's new paradigm for American public administration—adequate or antique?, *Midwest Rev Public Admin*, 10, 179–182, 1976.

Stillman, R. J., *Preface to Public Administration Theory: A Search for Themes and Directions*, St. Martin's Press, New York, 1991.

Stillman, R. J., The refounding movement in American public administration, *Admin Theory Praxis*, 17(1), 29–45, 1995.

Stivers, C., *Bureau Men, Settlement Women: Constructing Public Administration in the Progressive Era*, University Press of Kansas, Lawrence, KA, 2000.

Svara, J. H., The myth of the dichotomy: complementarity of politics and administration in the past and future of public administration, *Public Admin. Rev.*, 61(2), 176–183, 2001.

Taylor, F., *Shop Management*, Harper & Row, New York, 1903.

Taylor, F., *The Principles of Scientific Management*, Norton, New York, 1911.

Taylor, F., *Scientific Management*, Harper & Row, New York, 1923.

Thompson, M., Ellis, R., and Wildavsky, A., *Cultural Theory*, Westview, Boulder, CO, 1990.

Tolchin, M. and Tolchin, S., *To the Victor*, Random House, 1971.

Trist, E. L., Higgin, G., Murray, H., and Pollock, A., *Organizational Choice*, Tavistock Publications, London, 1963.

Urban Institute, *Performance Measurement: A Guide for Local Elected Officials*, Urban Institute, Washington, DC, 1980.

Urwick, L. F., *Notes on the Theory of Organization*, American Management Association, New York, 1952.

Urwick, L. F., Organization as a technical matter, In *Papers on the Science of Administration*, Gullick, L. and Urwick, L., Eds., Augustus M. Kelley, New York, pp. 47–88, 1937.

Van Riper, P. P., The American administrative state: Wilson and the founders—an unorthodox view, *Public Admin. Rev.*, 43, 477–490, 1983.

Van Riper, P. P., The politics-administration dichotomy: concept or reality?, In *Politics and Administration: Woodrow Wilson and American Public Administration*, Rabin, J. and Bowman, J., Eds., Marcel Dekker, New York, pp. 203–218, 1984.

Van Riper, P. P., Luther Gulick on Frederick Taylor and scientific management, *J Manage History*, 1(2), 6–7, 1995.

Volcker Commission, *Report of the National Commission on the Public Service*, Volcker Commission, Washington, DC, 1989.

Vroom, V. H., *Work and Motivation*, Wiley, New York, 1964.

Waldo, D., Organization theory: an elephantine problem, *Public Administration Review*, 21(4), 210–225, 1961.

Waldo, D., *The Administrative State*, 2nd ed., Holmes and Meier, New York, 1984 [1948].

Waldo, D., A theory of public administration means in our time a theory of politics also, In *Public Administration: The State of the Discipline*, Lynn, N. and Wildavsky, A., Eds., Chatham House, Chatham, NJ, pp. 73–84, 1990.

Wamsley, G., Goodsell, C., Rohr, J., Stivers, C., White, O., and Wolf, J., Public administration and the governance process: shifting the political dialogue (the Blacksburg Manifesto), In *Refounding Public Administration*, Wamsley, G. et al., Eds., Sage Publications, Newbury Park, CA, pp. 31–52, 1990.

Wamsley, G. and Zald, M. N., *The Political Economy of Public Organizations*, D.C. Heath, Lexington, MA, 1973.

Warren, K., We have debated ad nauseam the legitimacy of the administrative state—but why?, *Public Admin. Rev.*, 53(3), 249–253, 1993.

Washnis, G. J., Ed., *Productivity Improvement Handbook for State and Local Government*, Wiley, New York, 1980.

Weber, M., Bureaucracy, In *From Max Weber: Essays in Sociology*, Gerth, H. H. and Mills, C. W., Eds., Oxford University Press, New York, pp. 196–244, 1958.

White, L. D., *Introduction to the Study of Public Administration*, Macmillan, New York, 1926.

White, L. D., The personnel problem, In *Classics of Public Personnel Policy*, Thompson, F. J., Ed., Moore Publishing, Oak Park, IL, 1979.

Wildavsky, A., Political implications of budget reform, *Public Admin. Rev.*, 21, 183–190, 1961.

Williams, D. W., Measuring government in the early twentieth century, *Public Admin. Rev.*, 63(6), 643–659, 2003.

Williamson, O. E., *Markets and Hierarchies*, Free Press, New York, 1975.

Willoughby, W. F., *The Government of Modern States*, D. Appleton–Century, New York, 1919.

Willoughby, W. F., *Principles of Public Administration*, Johns Hopkins Press, Baltimore, MD, 1927.

Wilson, J. Q., Reinventing public administration, *PS: Politic Sci Politic*, 22, 667–673, 1994.

Wilson, W., The study of administration, *Politic Sci Q*, 2, 197–222, 1887.

Winter, W. F., The first report of the National Commission on the State and Local Public Service. *Hard Truths/Tough Choices: An Agenda for State and Local Reform*, Nelson A. Rockefeller Institute of Government, The State University of New York at Albany, New York, 1993.

Wood, B. D. and Waterman, R. W., *Bureaucratic Dynamics: The Role of Bureaucracy in Democracy*, Westview Press, Boulder, CO, 1994.

Wren, D. A., *The Evolution of Management Thought*, 4th ed., Wiley, New York, 1994.

Zanetti, L. A., At the nexus of state and civil society: the transformative practice of public administration, In *Government Is Us*, King, C. S. and Stivers, C., Eds., Sage, Thousand Oaks, CA, pp. 102–121, 1998.

Zaud, D. E., *Information, Organization and Power*, McGraw-Hill, New York, 1981.

Unit 2

Organization Theory

3 Further Trends toward the Development of the Organizational Sciences

Robert T. Golembiewski

CONTENTS

This chapter builds around a metaphor, and adds to the substance of a contribution to an earlier edition of this work (Rabin et al. 1998, 103–115). The title here thus emphasizes this extension in the term "further toward" the organization sciences, which essentially appears in the last section of this essay.

The metaphorical story regarding rules of thumb about getting things done in public administration may be apocryphal, but perhaps not. The task there involved estimating the new year's crop of Chinese ring neck pheasants on the midwestern plains, and a convenient approach proved serviceable. Enumeration followed a trigger event: when the corn crop in selected fields grew to about a foot in height, and when pheasants went about their new happy hunting ground harvesting insects drawn to the growing corn. Economical and reasonably accurate assessments of the new population of growing birds were possible, given a certain timeline and some ingenuity. The critical period did not last long. The rising corn plants would soon hide all easily observable traces of the pheasants.

True or not, this metaphor—of the pheasant heads highlighted against a green background during the brief interval of moving from sprouts to corn-bearing stalks—focuses this essay, which highlights several trends in the development of the organizational sciences. In addition, here note only that organizational sciences (OS) is a label convenient for present purposes, and roughly relates to the analytical arena encompassed by three conventional labels: organization behavior, organization theory, and organization development.

I. SIX TRENDS AND TOPICS

To begin highlighting the key metaphor, six trends/topics in the development of the OS encompass any analysis, and this sextet may be considered as an analogue of the heads in the underlying metaphors, birds moving against the background of the growing cornfield that represents OS. More specificity may be in order.

Since World War II, especially, the simple and sovereign structure (SSS) has been specific (e.g. Simon 1946), and despite that worldview losing significant ground, it nonetheless often still remains in place, if uneasily. For example, my best estimate was that OS was stuck (e.g. Golembiewski 1986), while other voices despaired that OS was rather more a tangled jungle (e.g. Koontz 1961) than farmland ready to burst forth with fruit. Both views come to the same bottom line.

Whether one inclines toward stuckness or jungle, however, choices have to be made. What is to be nurtured, and what is to be weeded out lest it merely crowd out the more fruitful?

Now, then, seems like a good time to have a look at OS to check for heads above the conceptual crowd. A sense of that will be useful, and perhaps never more than today.

Which OS approaches have special promise in loosening the stuckness or taming the jungle? Let me emphasize six trends, even as I acknowledge several caveats; the formidable challenges implied two limits—the appreciable tentativeness appropriate to the future detailed development of these promising candidates, and the highly arbitrary focus on six candidates. Here, your commentator cannot even take refuge in the dodge illustrated by an Audi automobile commercial attempting to explain why the then-new model had five cylinders. "Six was too many," a precise Teutonic engineer soothed the viewer, "and four cylinders were too few."

Such concerns deter but they do not force a detour. In sum, six reasonable candidates for enhancing OS's cost/benefit ratio include:

- Simple and sovereign structure (SSS)
- Environmental and technological contingencies that moderate SSS applications
- Strategy = structural contingencies, divisional model
- Horizontal approaches to structuring organizations
- Organization development and change
- A primer on methodology

II. SIMPLE AND SOVEREIGN STRUCTURE

To begin, real progress will depend on taking a giant step backward. As with real cornfields, what one sees depends on when one looks. Going back in time less than a quarter century or so, the OS often were seen as an analogue of the well-tended lawn: uniform, and governed by quite direct

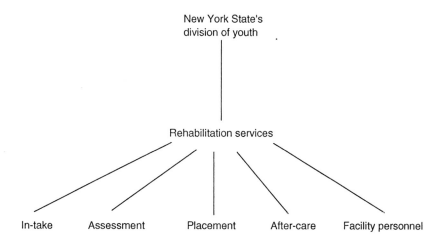

FIGURE 3.1 A skeletal bureaucratic structure in government.

principles which might not yet be fully known, but were nonetheless knowable, and in any case were universally applicable. Thus, Fayol in 1916 wrote of "acknowledged truths" that are "flexible and capable of adaptation to every need," and his orientation stuck in people's minds, more rather than less. The key to application was in the confidence of the applier, rather than in the sensitivity of the purported truths to changing environments. As Fayol notes: "It is a matter of knowing how to make use of [these acknowledged truths], which is a difficult art requiring intelligence, experience, decisions and proportion" (quoted in Shafritz and Ott 1992, 56).

The basic product of this worldview might well be called SSS, and it appears in starkest form in the bureaucratic model. Bureaucracies look like the structure in Figure 3.1 (Carew et al. 1977), to simplify a bit by not differentiating line and staff (Golembiewski 1967). Put into words, such traditional structures emphasize:

- Departmentalization around the parts of work—typically called functions at top levels.
- The aggregation of like activities into departments or work units.
- Vertical relationships of authority and responsibility to induce the required integration between units.
- Narrow control and, if necessary, coercion in authority/responsibility linkages.
- Narrow spans of control (i.e., few individuals report to a single authority figure) and hence such organizations get tall as they grow in size, and quickly.
- Close replicas of SSS spread almost everywhere, and in a brief period of time (Jacoby 1973).

III. ENVIRONMENTAL AND TECHNOLOGICAL CONTINGENCIES

At least three clusters of observers cast doubt on the SSS by emphasizing differences in environments and technologies, with a clear general point in mind. If environments and technologies do differ, in brief overview, then different structures seem more appropriate than a single structure. That is, multiple structures increase the possibility of a good fit, or even a better fit with changing contexts.

The focus here will be direct, and even elemental. The three exemplars below could be fitted within the confines of the organization ecology approach to OS, and with plenty of room left to spare (e.g., Cameron et al. 1988). Organization ecology covers a vast range—from simple notions that organizations go through elemental birth–death stages of development (e.g., Bernstein 1955) to subtle theoretical and even metaphysical treatments (e.g., Kaufman 1985, 1991). That range would overwhelm this essay, and constitutes a place where readers motivated by this essay might go next for greater attention to environmental and technological contingencies.

Simplicity, however, remains paramount in the current discussion.

A. Environmental Turbulence Versus Placidity

One direct but useful way to conceive of good fit possibilities focuses on the causal texture: stripped to essentials, environments clearly can differ in what might be called their "velocity of change" (Emery and Trist 1965). If so, mechanistic structures like the bureaucratic model seem more appropriate for low velocities, while organic structures have a greater affinity for high velocities of change facing an organization. In academic lingo, high-velocity environments usually are labeled turbulent.

The underlying rationale for relating structures to the environments surrounding them is quite straightforward. Think of a broken clock, which is clearly out of close synchronization with its environment. That clock nonetheless will provide the exact time twice during each day, as well as close approximations of the correct time at several positions clustered around those two points. But that constitutes a poor fit, as well as a bad bet, except for very limited purposes.

B. Generic Technologies

Technologies clearly differ, and this fact also challenges the sense of a SSS.

To elaborate a bit on the present point, consider the two dimensions in Figure 3.2: the variability of problems encountered in organizations, and the character of the search procedures associated with each of them. They generate four basic kinds of organizational missions to which different structures would seek good fits. For example, bureaucratic structures seem to fit best with Mission III.

Similarly, Woodward (1958) distinguishes three other kinds of technologies: crafts, large batches of identical end-items, and continuous processes. She also provides empirical data about associated differences in structural and managerial features. For example, bureaucratic structures would be less well adapted—if for different reasons—to crafts and to continuous processes than to large batch technologies. Why? Simply, reliance on crafts implies self-discipline by the

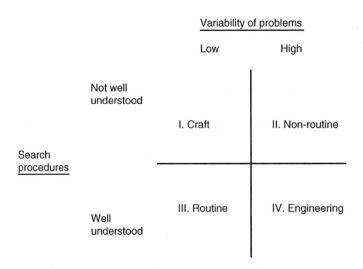

FIGURE 3.2 Four classes of organizational missions.

craftspersons and decreases the need for tall bureaucratic hierarchies. For continuous processes, the bureaucratic model also provides a poor fit because that model focuses on the components of work, when a holistic emphasis is far more appropriate for continuous processes like oil refining. The latter falls in cell IV of Figure 3.2, to be specific.

C.　Environments and Technologies

Other students (e.g., Lawrence and Lorsch 1967; Lawrence and Dyer 1983) have proposed good-fit models that relate to both environmental and technological features. Broadly, they propose that all organizations have to balance two basic tendencies:

1. Toward *differentiation*, which refers to the differences between an organization's functional departments—differences relating to both cognitive and emotional orientations.
2. Toward *integration*, which refers to the unity of effort required, between as well as within departments, by the demands of the environments within which their organization operates. Environments encompass differences in markets, product lines, technologies, and so on.

In short, bureaucratic structures are based on the differentiation of separate functions, which facilitates narrow control and specialization but also exacerbates cognitive and emotional differences between specialists and the separate units into which they are departmentalized, from the very top to the bottom. This is tolerable—perhaps even necessary—in environments such as the cardboard carton industry characterized by well-known technologies, low rates of innovation, simple product lines, and long reaction times. Moreover, operations will tend to have shorter times of development. More or less, such differences can be accommodated by various simple integrative mechanisms, in a basic bureaucratic model, given stable technology and a simple product line.

On the other hand, bureaucratic structures constitute a poor fit with other environments and technologies, and sooner or later, the costs of SSS begin to outweigh the benefits. For example, the plastics industry requires a high degree of integration of complex chains of functions based on advanced and changing technologies. Here, the heightening of differentiation by the bureaucratic model wrong-headedly impedes the higher degree of required integration.

IV.　STRATEGY = STRUCTURE CONTINGENCIES

A.　Divisional Model

It soon became commonly clear that absent change of bureaucratic structures in advanced technologies matters would trend from bad to worse, and fast. In the early 1900s in a few businesses, and perhaps a half-century later in the federal government, environmental and technological demands evolved to the point that a new organizing strategy became widely perceived as appropriate.

There are many ways to illustrate this new strategy, and Table 3.1 depicts a convenient one. Broadly, organizations could adopt one of several strategies for growth, more or less in the order given. The most direct strategy, expanding volume at a central site, permits some organizations to grow to very substantial sizes with minimal organizational complications, but only as long as technological change is slow paced and product lines limited. This situation is reflected in the inherent wisdom of Henry Ford's dictum: "You can have any kind of a Ford that you like, as long as it's a black Model T." The bureaucratic model dominated, and with reasonable fit, when the first strategy for growth dominated.

TABLE 3.1
Strategies for Growth

Expand volume at a central site
Add field units
Add functions and activities
Diversity products and product lines

Source: Based on from Chandler, *Strategy and Structure*, MIT Press,
Cambridge, MA, 1962. With permission.

Complications set in with more advanced strategies for growth, however, and especially so for diversification. And then the wisdom of Ford's insight became his downfall. He could still make Model T's cheaply and expeditiously, but he simply could not sell enough of them. In a few words, the automobile market reflected consumer demands for sophisticated wants and needs. Hence, for Ford as well as for a large number of organizations, the choice became clear: structurally adapt, or wither and die.

The detailed story has been told well, especially by Chandler (1962), so we can be satisfied with a bare sketch of the basic structural adaptation—commonly called the divisional model at high levels of organization. Analogs also apply at medium and low levels (Golembiewski 1994).

Generally, business adaptations came earlier and far outnumbered those in government. We can illustrate the genre with the late 1970s post-bureaucratic version of the New York State organization whose earlier bureaucratic structure fits Figure 3.1. Figure 3.3 depicts the basic structural change, conveniently omitting details that would burden this narrative more than enlighten it.

Rationales for the structural change from Figure 3.1 to Figure 3.3 vary in many details, but they share some dominant features. To illustrate briefly, the focus in Figure 3.3 shifts from the parts of the task to the whole—from the several activities to the holistic care of specific clients; hence the basic structuring around teams in Figure 3.3, as contrasted with separate functions in Figure 3.1. In effect, each Youth Service Team (YST) there now encompasses enough of the activities to be held

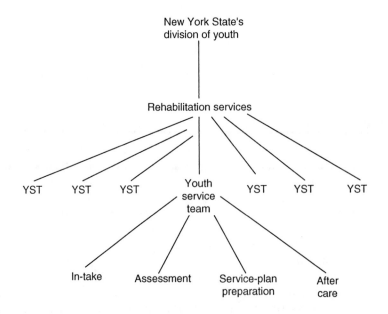

FIGURE 3.3 A divisional structure in government.

responsible for a specific cohort of clients. Some Figure 3.1 activities are reserved for assignment to overhead supervision, in part to facilitate oversight but also because of convenience.

Even these few structural details suggest some central tendencies in opposition. In Figure 3.1, if something goes wrong for a particular client, finger-pointing by the several activities is common, is moreover often necessary to maintain political leverage, and perhaps is even appropriate. "What we did was right," the associated defensiveness would go, "but *they* messed up the client." More broadly, in Figure 3.3, various opportunities to compare the several YSTs become available—for example, recidivism rates of the several cohorts of clients. This structural feature helps target responsibility and also encourages resolution of any conflicts within each YST, as contrasted with tension between units with specialized functions. This difference in tendency often can induce a significant difference in kind. It constitutes the difference between dealing with a "dead cat"—that is, any problem—in one's own yard, as contrasted with the temptation to toss that problem into the backyard of other functional specialists, as the bureaucratic model often tempts one to do.

Space does not permit detailing the whole story, of course, nor is the divisional experience all of a piece. Details are available elsewhere (e.g., Golembiewski 1995a, chaps. 7–9), both about the advantages of the divisional model, as well as about some surprises that have characterized experience with the innovation, especially in business.

Here, let us take the easy way out. Five features of the divisional model contrast both subtly and sharply with the words attached to Figure 3.1. In sum, the structures in Figure 3.3 emphasize:

- Departmentalizing around the whole, around the needs of clients.
- The aggregation of related activities, that is, those required for some complete flow of work.
- Integration via the horizontal relationships of those contributing to a common flow of work, with vertical relationships still being maintained.
- Self-control and self-discipline of members of each basic unit—that is, every YST in Figure 3.3.
- A possibly very wide span of control, due to ease in assessing performance; such organizations can be flat, even if very large. Usefully, circumstances there also can encourage a narrow span of control, as start-up or when inexperience prevails.

V. STRUCTURAL CONTINGENCIES: ALTERNATIVE MODELS

Alternative models for organizing that extend far beyond the bureaucratic and divisional structures also hold major promise for moving OS in public administration beyond the present stuckness. For example, only confusion can be expected in panels of studies that do not differentiate kinds of organizations. Absent a great deal of good fortune, undifferentiated studies are likely to generate conflicting results; relationships that exist in bureaucratic structures, for example, probably will not exist in divisional models. And there may well be several varieties of each of the two basic models.

Nevertheless, the OS literature typically does not differentiate types of organizations, and consequently, research findings often are unfocused, if not outright muddled. Typically, in effect, the OS literature risks comparing proverbial apples with oranges or even watermelons. Hence the probability of stuckness is high because the units in research can differ in many relevant particulars.

Essentially, only a substantially complete taxonomy or typology of organizations will get us out of this self-imposed analytic hole (e.g., Golembiewski 1987). This taxonomic progress is not only Hydra-headed, but also exists in diverse stages of in-process development (e.g., Selznick 1957; Worthy 1958). Four varieties of this work on structural contingencies are briefly reviewed below, with each being labeled a treatment.

A. ANALYTIC OR SYNTHETIC TREATMENTS

The longest-lived approach to structural contingencies seeks to extract alternative structural models from the rich but amorphous descriptive literature, as well as from more rigorous but narrowly focused empirical studies, both in the field and in laboratories. Basically, such analytic or synthetic efforts seek to highlight alternative structural forms and to emphasize their strengths and weaknesses. Therefore, it is difficult to say much of substance about the literature on organization types without detailed qualifications, but perhaps an attempt is nonetheless warranted.

Basically, such efforts point out the inadequacy of any simple and sovereign approach to organization design. Organization worlds are complex and turbulent, and organization structures could hardly be monolithic.

However, no agreement has been reached about a necessary and sufficient list of the basic alternative structures, or about the variables in terms of which organizations should be differentiated. Thus, the National Organizations Study (Spaeth and O'Rourke 1994) of US "work establishments" isolated five configurations, two being variations on "simple structure" and three being varieties of bureaucracy (Marsden et al., 1994). Relatedly, Golembiewski (1987) distinguishes three basic structural models as well as several subtypes, and tends to focus on contrasts/comparisons between two of them. In contrast, Mintzberg (1989) focuses on a growing family of models. In a recent form, his list included:

- The entrepreneurial structure, which resolves around a charismatic central person who directly supervises an organization with little middle management or staff services.
- The machine bureaucracy, much like Figure 3.1 but tailored to industrial or thing making contexts, with large staff services, and many hierarchical levels.
- Professional bureaucracy, much like Figure 3.1 but with the addition of complex staff and professional services.
- The diversified or divisional form on the order of Figure 3.3.
- The professional organization, in which professionals work with substantial vigor and degrees of autonomy, ideally with standards for guiding behavior.
- The innovative organization or "ad hocracy", which means what it says: structures are often temporary, sparse, as well as spontaneous, and evolve for very specific purposes.

B. STATISTICAL TREATMENTS

Powerful statistical treatments permit judgments about the number of types of organizations necessary to account for the differences and similarities within any populations of establishments. For example, the National Organizations Study (Spaeth and O'Rourke 1994) of U.S. work organizations isolated five statistically isolated configurations in their preliminary taxonomy, with two being variations on SSS and three being variants of somewhat differentiated bureaucracies (Marsden et al., 1994). Other students using similar methods isolated much larger typologies (Miller and Friessen 1984).

This integrative approach is most highly developed for differentiating individuals. That is, detailed analysis of biographical differences and similarities between people implies that more than twenty subgroups are statistically required to provide a serviceable taxonomy of people (e.g., Stokes et al., 1994). Early rounds of analysis focus on the stability of such subgroups for different populations as well as for different kinds of biographical information. Subsequent rounds of analysis can determine how such subgroups relate to numerous variables of interest: performance in schools or at work (e.g., Golembiewski 1977), or numerous behavioral and attitudinal measures. In the long run, analytic energy and intelligence may succeed in characterizing subgroups in terms of variegated clusters of marker variables. Later, such research may develop labels that identify content-filled units of a more than statistical typology.

Organizational science researchers have suggestively but infrequently explored the promise of such statistical approaches, as in the useful with organizational archetypes (e.g., Miller and Friessen 1984). This original work focuses on business firms, but the general principles apply broadly. Powerful statistical analysis of thirty-one variables concerning eighty-one organizations suggests that at least ten archetypes are necessary to encompass the full panel of differences or similarities measured. To illustrate, the archetypes describing a firm's condition include the impulsive firm, the stagnant bureaucracy, as well as the adaptive firm in a very challenging environment. In sum, archetypes seek holistic distinctions within a batch of organizations, as contrasted with focusing on covariation with one or more variables. The trap to be avoided is obvious, although the goal is far from an easy piece. Focusing on a few differences or similarities typically leaves many features free to vary in unknown ways, and this makes interpretations of findings dependent on the unlikely condition that all other things are more or less equal.

Clearly, generalizations about one organizational archetype would apply poorly, or not at all, to some or all of the others. Miller and Friessen highlight this central point by isolating nine different transitions that various archetypal firms might go through in moving beyond some original archetypal position.

The recent National Organizations Study at once builds upon and beyond the initial work with archetypes (e.g., Marsden et al., 1994). The study also relies on statistical analysis of eight variables—formalization, decentralization, vertical levels, and so on—to generate five structural configurations. These five basic types are then utilized in two basic ways: to test such proposed theoretical networks as that between size and measures of structure (e.g., Blau and Schoenherr 1971), and to test for differences among for-profit, public sector, and nonprofit organizations. Generally, large and small organizations differed on measures of structure, and contextual differences were associated with appreciable structural differences, even after controlling for differences in size and complexity between organizations (Marsden et al., 1994, 924–927).

C. Clinical Treatments

A third approach to structural contingencies sees organizations as reflecting the characteristics of their elites or even more specifically, of their founder(s). The breadth of relevant literature is vast and grows steadily. Analytic targets often have been political figures—for example, how Hitler's powers and sexual perversions influenced the development of National Socialist cadres in World War II Germany (Waite 1977, 286–294), or how the personalities of public figures like Edgar Hoover (Powers 1987) profoundly impacted the character of the agencies that developed under their influences. Targets also have been businesspersons like Sam Walton, with observers relating his indefatigable ebullience to the commercial Wal-Mart empire, which he not only built but seems to be sustaining even from beyond the grave (e.g., Huey 1991).

These may be called clinical treatments, and are usefully illustrated by one exemplar that also combines some elements of a typology. Thus, Kets de Vries and Miller and Friessen (1984) propose that organizations tend to reflect the dominant emotionalities, or even pathologies of their founder(s) or dominant members. To illustrate, five basic kinds of neurotic organizations have received attention: the dynamic, the paranoid, the schizoid, the compulsive, and the depressive.

In effect, each type is singular: each has different advantages, and each type gets out of control in its own ways. In the case of the schizoid organization, trends in opposed directions can appear at the same time. This much seems reasonable enough; few generalizations will apply more or less equally to organizations of different neurotic types.

In summary, despite its numerous attractions in theory, the development of organization taxonomy remains rare. Most observers have been content to begin their analysis from the other end, as it were. That is, the all-but-universal practice takes this procedure: an analyst selects one or more variables, and (at best) tests for a few hypotheses in a convenient sample of organizations whose individual properties are neither specified nor known. In such an approach, absent great fortune, no one can reasonably interpret results, given that no one really expects that generalization will occur across panels whose component organizations probably differ in many significant particulars, as this and the previous section suggests. Fortunately, a few exceptions indicate that greater explicit empirical attention to organizational taxonomies may well be in the future (e.g., Facer 2000).

VI. HORIZONTAL APPROACHES TO STRUCTURING ORGANIZATIONS

Another useful OS approach for special emphasis essentially replaces the vertical preoccupation of the bureaucratic model with a horizontal orientation to structuring work. For example, the divisional model retains vertical features such as up-and-down reporting relationships, but seeks to augment them with horizontal features in basic units for departmentalization. A comparison of Figure 3.1 and Figure 3.3 supports this point. The horizontal forces in Figure 3.3 include shared loyalties to, and responsibility for, the activities related to a total flow of work (e.g., each YST in Figure 3.3). The basic departments in a bureaucratic model, oppositely, tend to fragment such loyalties and responsibilities.

The horizontal orientation to structuring organizations has taken many forms, at both low levels as well as high, as Table 3.2 shows. Conveniently, the table adopts a here → there format to indicate the direction of vertical → horizontal shifts or changes. Here → there movements typically are ones of degree rather than all or none, but their combined effects can produce organizations starkly different from the bureaucratic model (e.g., Golembiewski and Kiepper 1988; Perkins et al. 1983).

TABLE 3.2
Some Developmental Tendencies in the Horizontal Structuring of Work

Features of Structures and Roles	Appropriate Behaviors and Attitudes
From particularistic activities or functions to holistic bundles of activities or functions required	From protection of narrowly specialized self-interests to enhanced performance on total flows of work, which requires appropriate cultures and values
From tall structures to flat structures with fewer levels	From focus on activities/functions to focus on customers or clients, whether internal to organization or external
From numerous narrowly specialized jobs to a much smaller number of integrative jobs (job enrichment)	From workers implementing detailed directions to a broad range of participation in making decisions within a broad context of missions/roles
From checks and controls by external units to growing reliance on internal checks and controls	From one size fits all to multiple ways of development for same/similar units in response to specific histories, mixes of personnel, etc.
From a bureaucratic monopoly to flow of work structures that can encompass numerous structural forms, including bureaucratic ones	From up-over-and-down communication, often languid, between narrowly specialized units in tall organizations to intense, flash communication within an integrative unit in flat structures
Roles transition from the controlled to the empowered, from those who control to those who empower	From competition to gain greater shares of resources to competition to reduce costs and raise quality, as facilitated by direct comparisons of several integrative units
Management orientations shift from the transactional (like scorekeeping structures in a bureaucracy) to the transformational, which involves appropriate cultural and normative changes in turbulent environments	From complicated and often political reconciliations of conflict between narrowly specialized units to straight forward reconciliations within integrative units

---

Table 3.2 seeks to illustrate a basic approach rather than to exhaust its details. Table 3.2 is largely self-explanatory, but remains incomplete in two major senses. Thus, the exemplars of vertical→horizontal shifts can be multiplied, and easily. In addition, a fuller development of the basic point would emphasize infrastructure involving politics, practices, and procedures, as well as structural patterns (e.g., Perkins et al., 1983).

A. Organization Development and Change

Finally, if only for the present short list of approaches prominent in OS, what is here labeled organization development and change (ODC) has demonstrated substantial performance and also holds great promise. ODC has two basic forms, organization development (OD) and quality of working life (QWL). See work at the state level of government (e.g., Barzelay 1991), which complements nicely the synthesis of observers like Carnavale (2003). Other sources provide generic perspective (e.g., Golembiewski, 2003). Both forms have received fulsome attention in many places (e.g., Golembiewski 1995b), but here space permits descriptions of only three features.

B. ODC Values

Both OD and QWL rest on related sets of values whose shared thrust is toward greater need satisfaction in work that is intended to encourage greater commitment and higher performance at work. Organization development tends to emphasize the character and quality of the patterns of interaction at the worksite, although QWL tends to emphasize procedural and structural issues. Both approaches share basic values (e.g., Skelley 1989), which contrast sharply with those underlying bureaucratic forms. These differences include the high degrees of participation and involvement that QWL and especially OD seek.

C. ODC's Reach

ODC applies to the full range of organization levels and activities. Thus, OD has more of an executive focus, in general, and QWL tends to emphasize operation levels; however, overlap does occur, and numerous prominent practitioners and theorists work both sides of the ODC street, as it were. In approximate order of their complexity and subtlety, ODC applications can be assigned to the following categories (Golembiewski 1990, 19–21):

- Process analysis, which involves the application of behavioral science theories and perspectives to diagnose complex and dynamic situations—interpersonal, in groups, and in systems of groups
- Skill-building consistent with ODC values, as in giving and receiving feedback, or in conflict resolution
- Diagnosis, which usually involves process analysis but can also rely on various other data-gathering and interpretive approaches, as via survey/feedback, sensing groups, or interviews
- Coaching or counseling, as in third-party conflict resolution
- Team building or development, which focuses on the efficiency and effectiveness of small task groups
- Inter-team building or development, which focuses on the relationships between two or more units in a broader system—for example, departments, projects, or task groups.
- Technostructural activities that seek to build need-satisfying roles, jobs, policies/ procedures, and structures
- System renewal or system building, which has comprehensive goals in large systems relating to culture, values, and structures

Two or more of the categories may be employed in any single ODC application. Indeed, system renewal or system building typically includes complex combinations of all seven categories of activities in building toward ODC values. Relatedly, the last ODC category may have an operating time frame of 2 to 5 years, although applications of other categories can take only days or even hours.

D. ODC's Grasp

How successful were attempts to act on these levels? Substantial confidence is possible in estimating this grasp. In sum, success rates in both OD as well as QWL are substantial in both highly developed economies as well as in third-world settings (e.g., Golembiewski 1990, 11–43).

Evaluative studies support high success rates in aggregates of studies of several thousand cases (e.g., Golembiewski 2003). Generally, but not exclusively, the cases deal with applications in English-language studies of applications in approximately 65 countries.

The cautious observer will not assume that this newly available literature says it all, of course. Rather, the available evaluations of planned change applications differ in many particulars: the number of cases dealt with, measures of success, concern for methodological rigor, and so on. As a ballpark figure, estimates of success rates seldom fall below 50%, and usually cluster in the 70%-plus range. Success rates in third-world settings are a bit lower in all available cases (e.g., Golembiewski and Luo 1994), but even there the rates are attractive.

Without a doubt, much remains to be learned about ODC success rates, but evidence suggests that no big critical surprises are likely. For example, the basic criticism of ODC applications emphasizes that they usually rely on self-report measures, which some observers see as unreliable or as mere opinions. However, ODC also has high success rates when its effects are estimated in terms of objective reports or hard data—cost of production and waste, absenteeism, and so on (e.g., Nicholas 1982). Indeed, in one large batch of QWL studies (Golembiewski and Sun 1990), success rates were greater for hard data rather than for self-report data.

VII. GUIDES FOR EMPIRICAL ANALYSIS

The trends above cannot be allowed to find their own ways—as unguided missiles, as it were; hence the crucial relevance of a great and growing respect for adherence to guidelines for empirical analysis as they underlay useful theoretical progress. This theme reaches far beyond the present confines, of course, because some useful (even if limited) things can be said here. Two foci suffice to illustrate present purposes. First, OS will experience enhanced empirical development to the extent that it follows quite specific guidelines. Second, several varieties of this development will be signaled by reliance on distinct but related types of theoretical development.

A. Criteria for Empirical Development

Progress in the development of OS as science will be no slam-dunk, to be sure, but practice from many arenas of inquiry provides some useful guidance. Table 3.3 provides a summary of these guides, with details being available elsewhere (Bozeman 1999, 221–235).

B. Types of Theoretical Development

Along with the guides in Table 3.3, and reasonable products of them, the successful development of OS in public administration will be sensitive to several kinds of theories, and not just because of fussiness. Directly, the failure to recognize and respect differences between types of theories often has proved troublesome in all areas of OS.

TABLE 3.3
Summary of Guides for Scientific Development in Public Administration

Development will be aided by ideational bases that:

- Relate directly to prevailing practical challenges facing public agencies, as sharply opposed in significant particulars to its developments as a satellite in (let us say) political science in the context of the basic politics vs. administrative distinction
- Avoid resolutions-by-definition
- Support the development of a field linking analysis and application
- Respect both task and maintenance aspects of a field, with the former relating to analytic issues and the latter relating to related-but-distinct issues such as loyalty to colleagues and respect of their approaches, however limiting
- Are tied to values external to public agencies, at constitutional, cultural, and organizational levels
- Frame useful attention to multiple organizational and analytical levels (individuals, interpersonal relationships, small groups, and large organizations)
- Take advantage of law of tactical convenience in prescribing reasonable next steps for both application and analysis
- Require and permit testing of empirical covariants, as well as the empirical consequences of value aspects, which open-system perspectives imply a self-correcting potential

Source: Adapted from Golembiewski, R. T., in *Public Management*, Bozeman, B., Ed., Gossey-Bass, San Francisco pp. 91–105, 1999. With permission.

Three types of theory get attention here, although their characters can only be illustrated, and even so, they constitute only a sampler. In outline form, these types include:

1. *Empirical theory*: This details that (for example) A is directly related to B and C under conditions x, y, and z. Great care must be given to conceptual and operational definition of all components, with the latter detailing valid and reliable ways of measuring proposed features of reality. Critically, as Table 3.3 proposes, empirical testing of hypothetical relationships is central to the development of theoretical fragments, and especially to their continuous extension to encompass broadening patches of the empirical world. Failure at such broadening implies inadequate foundations for inquiry—perhaps in conceptual definition, operational definition, or both. OS variants often neglected this central requirement, and assumptions were allowed to suffice as long as observers did not look too long or too hard.

   Despite the obvious complexity of satisfying what amounts to tridimensional chess, one central point is crystal clear. Ultimately, there can be only one empirical theory relevant to organizations, but typically, there will be several fragments of empirical theory. These fragments are not only incomplete, but they may in practice be variously at odds with one another, and even contrary.

   Awkwardly, OS variants typically propose that they are an empirical theory, as in Organization Theory. This was not only presumptuous, but also led to much wasted effort both in trying to uphold that assertion as well as deny it. Neither effort was determinative in empirical inquiry, but the former had more practical value than the latter.

2. *Goal-based, empirical theories*: In prototypic form, this type of theory proposes to develop propositions such as this one: if you want some specific desired or desirable conditions, you should induce conditions such as high A and low B. The section above on OD, ODC, and QWL illustrates examples of the reliance on goal-based, empirical theories. Thus, specific values are targeted, and ways to approach these normative states are detailed, hopefully with growing precision over time.

   Obviously, there can be many goal-based, empirical theories, one theoretical variant for each set of goals. OS research caused much mischief by neglecting this crucial point.

   Again, OS often neglects the testing of such sets of goals-and-approaches, with few exceptions, such as those sketched in the sections above on OD.

3. *Action theories*: This discussion may read so far as if those in OS encouraged us to sit around and wait for the grand breakthrough, which was at best unlikely. Not so. An important class of theoretical development involves action theories, which relate to systems of generalizations about how to attain specific values at specific locations, as is the case with such interventions as flexible workhours programs. These programs were initially applied to ease traffic congestion, and provided that employees begin and end work within some extended period, varying at their initiative on a daily basis—employees could either work the normal 8:00–5:00 h, or they could daily start and stop within limits at both ends of the total workday. These limited effects did tend to occur, but so did many others, e.g., heightened employee satisfaction, improved family relationships, and often even improved productivity (e.g., Golembiewski 2003, chap. 7). Theoretical knowledge of specifically when, where, and how flexible workhours will work is hardly complete, but it tends to work in almost every application and hence has spread broadly in both business and public settings.

Practically, good things happen with sufficient frequency to encourage reliance on the intervention, if with care to anticipate employee malingering which could terminate any program. At the same time, students see, to add to the list of factors positively affected by flexible workhour programs as well as to behavioral conditions and consequences.

Significantly, action theories can also have broadening uses. Specifically, detailed research on flexible work hours has isolated some fragments of goal-based, empirical theories, such as those related to participation, involvement, and empowerment. All of these have normative implications, of course.

Furthermore, consistent results with applications of action theories might also suggest the development of empirical theory fragments, or the linking of existing patches of theory, both of which in turn might also lead to useful developments. Thus, such developments might enhance novel goal-based, empirical theories. Moreover, even small fragments of empirical theory might be tested, if cautiously, by interventions at the level of action research.

VIII. IN-PROCESS CONCLUSION

This essay can be summarized in terms of two generalizations. To recall the early metaphor of pheasants in the cornfield, some attractive heads seem to be working their way through OS acres. Six exemplars get attention here, but more could qualify. Second, real progress in the development of PA is shown to depend upon certain guidelines which emphasize distinctions between kinds of theory development.

This essay will have achieved its highest purpose if readers gain a sense of the ways in which the first generalization applies, and also if they are motivated to employ the details of the second generalization via further reading and additional reflection of experience. Further additions to the second point are possible, but they remain objectives for a later time.

REFERENCES

Barzelay, M., *Breaking through Bureaucracy*, University of California Press, Berkeley, CA, 1991.

Bernstein, M. H., *Regulating Business by Independent Commission*, Princeton University Press, Princeton, NJ, 1955.

Blau, P. M. and Schoenherr, R. A., *The Structure of Organizations*, Basic Books, New York, 1971.

Bozeman, B., *Public Management: The State of the Art*, Jossey-Bass, San Francisco, CA, 1999.

Cameron, K. S., Sutton, R. I., and Whetten, D. A., Eds., *Readings in Organizational Decline*, Ballinger, Cambridge, MA, 1988.

Carew, D. K., Carter, S. I., Gamache, J. M., Hardiman, R., Jackson III, B., and Parisi, E. M., New York State division of youth, *J. Appl. Behav. Sci.*, 13, 327–339, 1977.

Carnavale, D. G., *Organization Development in the Public Sector*, Westview Press, Boulder, CO, 2003.

Chandler, A. D., Jr., *Strategy and Structure,* MIT Press, Cambridge, MA, 1962.

Chandler, R. C. Ed., *A Centennial History of the American Administrative State*, Free Press, New York, 1987.

Emery, F. and Trist, E. L., The causal texture of organizational environments, *Hum. Relat.*, 18, 21–31, 1965.

Facer, R., *The National Organization Study: A Review and an Extension*, Ph.D. Diss., University of Georgia, Athens, 2000.

Fayol, H. *General Administration*, Trans. C. Storrs, Pittman and Sons, London, 1954.

Golembiewski, R. T., *Men, Management, and Morality*, Transaction Publishers, New Brunswick, NJ, 1965/1989.

Golembiewski, R. T., *Organizing Men and Power*, Rand McNally, Chicago, IL, 1967.

Golembiewski, R. T., *Public Administration as a Developing Discipline*, Vols. 1 and 2, Marcel Dekker, New York, 1977.

Golembiewski, R. T., *Humanizing Public Organizations*, Lomond Publications, Mt. Airy, MD, 1985.

Golembiewski, R. T., Organization analysis and praxis: prominences of progress and stuckness, In *Review of Industrial and Organizational Psychology*, Cooper C. L. and Robertson I., Eds., John Wiley & Sons, London, pp. 279–304, 1986.

Golembiewski, R. T., Public-sector organization: Why theory and practice should emphasize purpose, and how to do so, In *A Centennial History of the American Administrative State*, Chandler R. C., Ed., Free Press, New York, pp. 433–474, 1987.

Golembiewski, R. T., *Managing Diversity in Organizations*. University of Alabama Press, University, AL, 1995a.

Golembiewski, R. T., *Practical Public Management*. Marcel Dekker, New York, 1995b.

Golembiewski, R. T., A critical appraisal of refounding public administration, In *Public Management*, Bozeman, B., Ed., Gossey-Bass, San Francisco, pp. 91–105, 1999.

Golembiewski, R. T., *Ironies in Organization Development*, Marcel Dekker, New York, 2003.

Golembiewski, R. T. and Kiepper A., *High Performance and Human Costs*, Praeger, New York, 1988.

Golembiewski, R. T. and Luo H., OD applications in developmental settings, *J.Org. An.*, 2, 295-308, 1994.

Golembiewski, R. T. and Sun B. C., Positive bias in QWL studies, *J Mgt.*, 9, 665-674, 1990.

Huey, J., America's most successful merchant, 27, September 1973, 23:46-37, 1991.

Jacoby, H., *The Bureaucratization of the World*, University of California Press, Berkeley and Los Angeles, CA, 1973.

Kaufman, H., *Time, Chance, and Organizations*, Chatham House, Chatham, NJ, 1985, 1991.

Koontz, H., The management theory jingle, *J. Acad. Mgt.*, 4, 174-189, 1961.

Lawrence, P. R. and Dyer, D., *Renewing American Industry*, Free Press, New York, 1983.

Lawrence, P. F. and Lorsch, J. W., *Organization and Environment*, Irwin, Homewood, IL, 1967.

Marsden, P. V., Kalleberg A. I., and Knoke, D., Surveying organization structures and human resource practices, In *Handbook of Organizational Behavior*, Golembiewski, R.T. Ed., Marcel Dekker, New York, 1994.

Miller, D. and Friessen, *Organizations: A Quantum View*, Prentice Hall, Englewood Cliffs, NJ, 1984.

Mintzberg, H., The design school, *Strat. Mgt.*, 11, 171-195, 1989.

Nicholas, J. M., The comparative impact of organization development interventions, *Acad. Mgt Rev.*, 7:531-542, 1982.

Perkins, D. N. T., Nieva, V. F., and Lawler, E. E., III, *Managing Creation*, Wiley–Interscience, New York, 1985.

Powers, R. G., *Secrecy and Power*, Free Press, New York, 1987.

Rabin, J., Hildreth, B., and Miller, G., Eds., *Handbook of Public Administration*. Marcel Dekker, New York, 1998.

Selznick, P., *Leadership in Administration*, Row Peterson, Evanston, IL, 1957.

Shafritz, J. M. and Ott, J. S., Eds., *Classics in Organization Theory*, Moore, Oak Park, IL, 1992.

Simon, H. A., The proverbs of public administration, *Pub. Adm. R.*, 4, 33–57, 1946.

Spaeth, J. L. and O'Rourke, D. P., Designing and implementing National Organization Study, *Am. J. Soc.*, 99, 944-971, 1994

Skelley, R. D., Workplace democracy, *Pub. Adm. Q.*, 13, 176-195.

Stokes, G. S., Mumford, M. D., and Owens, W. A., *Biodata Handbook*, Consulting Psychologists Press, Palo Alto, CA, 1994.

Waite, R. G., *The Psychopathic God*, Mentor Book, New York, 1977.

Woodward, J., The effect of technological innovation on management administration, *Intern. Conf. Econ. Soc. Aspects Automat.*, Namur, Belgium, 1958.

Worthy, J. C., *Big Business and Free Men*, Harper & Row, New York, 1958.

4 Five Great Issues in Organization Theory

Robert B. Denhardt and David L. Baker

CONTENTS

Public administration theorists have included scholars and practitioners with many different viewpoints and objectives. Most have drawn important material from the more general field of organization theory, though political theory has made important contributions as well. Indeed, as will be demonstrated near the end of this chapter, the question of whether or not a theory of public organization (bringing together organizational and political perspectives) is even possible must occupy some attention.

The first concern here, however, is to examine those developments in the field of organization theory that have been most relevant to the study of public administration. The approach here is to identify issues largely drawn from organization theory that have proven to be of interest to a wide variety of theorists and practitioners in public administration, issues that have been sources of continued controversy within the field of public administration, and issues that remain largely unresolved even today. The five great issues discussed in this chapter, each of which meets the three criteria just mentioned, are

    I. Politics and administration
    II. Bureaucracy and democracy
    III. Organization and management
    IV. Theory and practice
    V. Theories of public organization

I. POLITICS AND ADMINISTRATION

Though the dichotomy between politics and administration is unquestionably one of the oldest issues in the field of public administration, the relationship between politics and administration remains one of the most contemporary. Woodrow Wilson's (1887) essay is taken by most commentators as the first major work in public administration. In that essay, Wilson laid the groundwork for the self-conscious study of public administration by pointing out the increasing difficulties faced by public agencies, saying, "It is getting harder to run a constitution than to frame one" (Wilson 1887, 200).

His solution was to operate the agencies of government on a businesslike basis, following accepted principles of management in the private sector and seeking the utmost in efficiency. But in Wilson's view, this could never be accomplished as long as public agencies were subject to the corrupting influence of politics. For this reason, Wilson made a distinction between politics and administration: in the political realm, issues of public policy were to be formulated; in the administrative realm, they were to be implemented. Wilson's dictum was clear: "Administration lies outside the proper sphere of politics. Administrative questions are not political questions. Although politics sets the tasks for administration, it should not be suffered to manipulate its offices" (Wilson 1887, 210).

Two important concerns are raised by Wilson's argument: one, the empirical question of whether politics and administration are (or can be) separated; the other the normative question of how to maintain the accountability of administrative agencies. The first of these questions was addressed at the turn of the century by Goodnow (1900), whose book, *Policy and Administration*, was (and is) taken by many to be a defense of the Wilsonian distinction between politics and administration. In fact, Goodnow's book argues that the formalistic separation of legislative and executive functions is often violated in practice. Though Goodnow holds that it is analytically possible to distinguish between the "expression" and the "execution" of the will of the state, he argues that these two functions cannot be clearly assigned to one branch of government or another.

Similar arguments were developed by other writers, including Appleby (1949), Gulick (1933), White (1936), and Willoughby (1936). All acknowledge the difficulty of separating politics (or policy) and administration, with both Gulick and White providing specific illustrations of the role of civil servants in developing policy, either through their exercise of discretion in carrying out policy or through their advice to policy makers. For example, Gulick (1933, 561) describes the work of the public employee as involving "a seamless web of discretion and action." Similarly, White (1936) notes the increasing "executive initiative in public policy," even arguing at one point that those who staff the bureaucracy may be in the best position to make recommendations free of political influence. In these ways, the dichotomy of politics and administration, if it ever existed in either theory or practice, was quickly eroded. Indeed, by the time of Appleby's writing, it had apparently disappeared. He said simply, "public administration is policy-making" (Appleby 1949, 170). More recently, Svara suggests that the politics–administration dichotomy "should be viewed as an aberration that departed from the ideas that preceded and followed it rather than defended and reinterpreted to make it relevant to current practice" (1998, 51). The more historically accurate recognition of the interdependent relationship between elected officials and administrators "leads to a model of complementarity rather than a dichotomy" (51).

One reason scholars began to assert more straightforwardly the involvement of bureaucrats in policy making was that bureaucrats were becoming involved in more policy making (Dunn 1994; Peters 1989; Ripley and Franklin 1986; Seidman and Gilmour 1986; Wildavsky 1987). Certainly, Wilson's work itself was encouraged by the fact that those staffing public agencies were no longer merely clerks, but were increasingly technicians and professionals from a variety of substantive backgrounds. That trend has continued as government in this country has grown and has become more and more complex. Those in public agencies are a source of expertise with respect to public policy matters and consequently are called on to present their ideas. Moreover, the scope and complexity of government today make it more difficult for the legislative branch to specify every detail of newly enacted policies. Consequently, there is increasing dependence on administrators throughout public agencies to exercise their discretion and to shape public policies as they see fit (Gilmour and Halley 1994; Stillman 1991, 1996). Indeed, Maass and Radway found "public policy is being formed as it is being executed, and it is being executed as it is being formed" (2001, 165).

The increasing role of the bureaucracy in public policy, however, does not make the question of politics and administration less difficult. If the bureaucracy is in policy making to stay, how can the public make sure that the policies arrived at are responsive to the public interest? How can the public ensure democratic accountability? Wilson's answer, and the answer of most early theorists in the emerging field of public administration, was that managers in public agencies should ultimately be accountable to the legislature, which is in turn accountable to the people, thus satisfying the requirement of democracy. In this hierarchical view of accountability, the separation of politics and administration is essential—the political neutrality of appointed officials must be preserved.

Many recent studies have indicated the difficulties with such a position (see Thompson 1983, 245). Bureaucrats not only exercise discretion and provide advice: they shape public opinion through the information they provide, mobilize support for their issues (and their agencies), and bargain with numerous groups both within and outside government to achieve their objectives. Under such circumstances, it is obviously difficult to speak of an adequate measure of accountability lying solely within the hierarchical relationship between the agency and the legislature (Lynn 1981; Thompson 1980, 1985).

For this reason, more contemporary discussions of responsiveness have cast the relationship between politics and administration in a new light: by what measures might society supplement hierarchical accountability so as to ensure a "correspondence between the decision of bureaucrats and the preferences of the community" (Rourke 1984, 4)? In general, the answers have taken two forms: the first seeking to instill a sense of subjective responsibility in those who staff public agencies, and the second seeking formal or objective mechanisms to ensure responsibility (Rosen 1998).

Hoping to develop a strong sense of responsibility on the part of civil servants, especially administrators, numerous writers through the decades have commented on those qualities they found desirable. Dimock (1936, 132) hoped for "loyalty, as well as honesty, enthusiasm, humility, and all the other attributes of character and conduct which contribute to effectual and satisfying service." Appleby (1945, 4) spoke of "a special attitude of public responsibility." Bailey (1966, 24) sought moral qualities of "(1) optimism, (2) courage, (3) fairness tempered by charity."

Harmon's *Action Theory for Public Administration* (1981) uses an "active-social paradigm" to argue that public administration theory must address the relationship between substance and process and between individual and collective values. This leads to tension between hierarchical accountability and discretion. Harmon concludes in a later book, *Responsibility as Paradox* (1995), that responsibility is paradoxical. It involves the opposing ideas of moral agency, the individual's own sense of responsibility, and the accountability of institutional authority.

More recently, Dobel (1999, 21) builds a theoretical argument leading to the following commitments for public administrators:

- Be truthfully accountable to relevant authorities and publics
- Address the public values of the political regimes
- Build institutions and procedures to achieve goals
- Ensure fair and adequate participation of the relevant stakeholders
- Demand competent performance effectiveness in the execution of policy
- Work for efficiency in the operation of government
- Connect policy and program with self-interest of the public and stakeholders in such as way that the purposes are not subverted

Several efforts have been made to bring these rather abstract qualities into existence. One stream of thought, associated primarily with Friedrich (1972) and Mosher (1982), argues that the emergence of professionalism within the bureaucracy should aid in the establishment of a proper set of values among bureaucrats. Friedrich felt that professionals, whatever their technical area, were likely to be more attuned to questions of administrative responsibility. Mosher focused more on those preparing specifically for administrative careers in government. As a part of their professional training, he argued, future administrators should be imbued with a sense of democratic responsibility. In Mosher's words, "the universities offer the best hope of making the professions safe for democracy" (Mosher 1982, 219).

Another stream of thought focuses on the kinds of commitments or oaths that are required of public servants. Many professional associations, including the American Society for Public Administration, have developed codes of ethics to which their members subscribe. Some, like the International City Management Association, have developed mechanisms for punishing violators of the code. Indeed, as Rohr (1989) points out, public employees take an oath to uphold the Constitution and, in his view, are therefore bound to support "regime values." These values can be determined best through a careful review of the interpretations given the Constitution by the Supreme Court (see also Rohr 1986). This position is elaborated upon in Rohr's more recent book, *Public Service, Ethics, and Constitutional Practice* (1998).

Other studies in public administration ethics have followed other paths. Cooper views "the citizenship role as an appropriate normative foundation for the public administration role" (1991, x) with both rights and obligations. The virtuous administrator forgoes self-interest for the common good. Later, Cooper (1998) describes the responsible administrator as "a juggler managing a multitude of competing obligations and values" (Cooper 1998, 244). Cooper discusses four levels of reflection and deliberation on ethical issues: the expressive level (the emotions), the level of moral rules (of the organization or policy), the level of ethical analysis, and the postethical level (addressing basic assumptions about human nature). Cutting across these are issues of responsible conduct and individual autonomy, all of which must be balanced or combined successfully in administrative action.

From a different perspective, Burke (1986) argues that bureaucrats must be made accountable to the society they serve, but that this can occur in several ways. Formal legal definitions of responsibility are desirable, but perhaps too tinged with obedience to hierarchy and the strict rule of law. Such definitions must be balanced with attention to the individual's sense of personal responsibility as that is developed through participation in a democratic society.

Finally, Denhardt (1988) seeks to balance a philosophical and practical approach to the ethics of public service. She defines administrative ethics as "a process of independently critiquing decision standards, based on core social values that can be discovered, within reasonable organizational boundaries that can be defined, subject to personal and professional accountability" (Denhardt 1988, 26). Her approach is one that emphasizes reflection and dialogue in making ethical decisions. In a later work (Denhardt 1994) she extends this idea to support the importance of character ethics in molding the administrator's role.

Others have found dependence on the ethical commitment on the individual administrator insufficient as a device to ensure responsiveness. Among these, Finer (1972) and Lowi (1979) have both argued for greater legislative detail and increased supervision of administrative activities as means of limiting the choices bureaucrats might make. Finer (1972, 238) stated his position in this way: "Are the servants of the public to decide their own course, or is their course of action to be decided by a body outside themselves?" Feeling that bureaucrats holding a minority opinion might force their view on an unsuspecting public, Finer argued for the latter; specifically that the legislature should engage in detailed consideration of its intent in formulating public policy and that it should exercise detailed supervision of the agencies of government.

Lowi (1979) argued from a quite different perspective, but came to a similar conclusion. His concern was the fact that certain agencies of government seemed to develop a special relationship with certain private interests, often the very interests they were designed to regulate. In such cases, the bureaucracy may exercise discretion to favor certain private interests to the neglect of the larger public interest. Lowi's solution, "juridical democracy," envisions more detailed legislative action combined with more complete administrative rule making, both designed to eliminate discretion through the codification of as many relationships between agencies and their constituents as possible.

In addition to more specific legislation and greater legislative review of administrative actions, other suggestions designed to increase responsiveness have been proposed. Cooper (1998), for example, discussed the numerous roles, obligations, and objective responsibilities that provide boundaries for administrative action; Gawthrop (1984) explores the use of systems theory as a basis for redesigning organizational structures so as to fully incorporate ethical concerns. More recently, Gawthrop argues that administrators should focus "on the ethical-moral values and virtues that pervade the spirit of democracy and constitute the pathways of the common good" (1998, xii). These function as guideposts to public service.

Others have described various structural mechanisms that might be employed to ensure responsiveness on the part of administrators. Among these are devices such as sunshine and sunset laws, surveys of citizen opinion, administrative hearings, and ombudsman programs. However, the two proposals most widely discussed are representative bureaucracy and public participation in administrative decision-making. Proponents of representative bureaucracy argue that bureaucratic decisions are more likely to represent the general will of the people if government agencies are staffed in such a way as to reflect significant characteristics of the population. In its earliest applications, the notions of representative bureaucracy meant representation of various geographical constituencies (primarily the states) or, in its English version, the representation of social classes (Kingsley 1944). In more contemporary times, representative bureaucracy is more likely to refer to representation based on race or sex (Krislov 1974). Unfortunately, studies have shown mixed results in terms of responsiveness (Meier 1993).

Public participation, employed as a device to ensure correspondence between the actions of civil servants and the wishes of the people, has an equally long, if not longer, history; however, it was given special emphasis in the 1960s and 1970s. Especially in what was called the "New Public Administration" (Bellone 1980; Frederickson 1971, 1980; Marini 1971; Waldo 1971), the notion of public involvement was heralded. Through the creation of forums for citizen input ranging from open hearings to advisory boards to elected or appointed commissions, more information was sought from those likely to be affected by the decisions of the agency (see also King et al. 1998; King and Stivers 1998; Nalbandian 1999; Skocpol and Fiorina 1999).

Box (1998) outlined a model of "citizen governance" that moves citizens into the roles of creating and implementing policy. Bryson and Crosby (1992) developed a methodology for bringing together diverse groups willing to share power in the pursuit of common goals. In addition there have been a wide variety of experiences with participation and civic involvement, some initiated by government, others based in neighborhood citizen action (Barber 1992; Lappe and Du Bois 1994; Mathews 1994). In many cases, however, what appeared to be participation was better described as co-optation—"the process of absorbing new elements into the leadership or policy-determining structure or existence" (Selznick 1949, 13)—and many government agencies remain quite insulated from the public. The issue of public participation will be later addressed in the discussion of the "New Public Service."

The questions of politics and administration clearly connect with concerns about the legitimacy of public administration, an idea pursued by a group of scholars from Virginia Tech in what was first termed "The Blacksburg Manifesto" and later published in book form (Wamsley et al. 1990). The Blacksburg viewpoint suggests that the legitimacy of public administration is in question, and only through a refounding of the field can its legitimacy be restored. Such a task requires attention to such wide-ranging issues as governance and citizenship, but centers on establishing what the authors call "an agency perspective." While it remains unclear how this agency perspective is to restore legitimacy to the field, it is apparent that the authors wish to see the public bureaucracy move to a far more central role in the democratic system than is currently the case. Obviously, in such an effort, serious questions concerning politics and administration must be addressed.

Along similar lines, Stever (1988) has also called for increasing legitimacy for public organizations. In his view, "Public administration must appear to both elected officials and the public as a crucial function to the maintenance of society. Furthermore, the civil servant must achieve a certain mystique in the performance of these crucial functions" (Stever 1988, 175). While few would disagree that establishing such confidence in the public bureaucracy would help its legitimacy, how public administrators are to do that remains no clearer than before.

Why has the issue of politics versus administration continued to play a prominent role in discussions of public administration even today? At least three reasons come to mind. First, although the early writers on public administration did not argue for as strict a dichotomy of politics and administration as many people think, they did soon come to define their own subject matter in terms that seemed to imply such a distinction. By defining public administration as the work of government agencies (Willoughby 1927), these writers quickly abandoned the notion of public administration as a function occurring throughout government and pursued instead an institutional view of public administration occurring within a certain setting, the agency. The implication, of course, was that such a study could be developed independent of studies of legislative processes and that a distinction could be made between legislation and implementation, between politics and administration.

Second, the urging of Wilson and others for government agencies to pursue the kind of efficiency modeled in private industry required some distinction between politics and administration. In order for agencies to be efficient, they could not be contaminated by either the corruption or dishonesty that often crept into the political process or the concern for responsiveness that, it was felt, was the prerogative of the legislature. Moreover, the early writers, just as many today, wanted to operate government more like a business—although no one has ever been perfectly clear about what that means. The slogan, however, required then and requires today a separation.

Finally, questions about the proper relationship (not dichotomy) between politics and administration have continued simply because defining that relationship goes to the heart of what public administration is all about. If the governance and management of public organizations differ from others in society, that difference must lie in the proper role of such organizations in defining and responding to the public interest. As will be seen later, it is indeed the resulting tension, perhaps the inevitable tension between efficiency and responsiveness, that best characterizes work in public organizations.

II. BUREAUCRACY AND DEMOCRACY

As has been discussed, the question of how to reconcile a concern for efficiency with a concern for responsiveness was treated by many early writers simply in terms of legislative control. The logic seemed to be that once the responsiveness of the agency to legislative mandate was assured, the agency should concentrate on operating in the most efficient manner possible. It was natural, therefore, that the scholars and practitioners would be drawn to the best contemporary model for achieving organizational efficiency—the industrial or bureaucratic model. Therefore, despite the fact that this model had certain autocratic features considerably at odds with democratic theory, it became the standard for administrative management in the public sector.

This position, however, skirted the question of whether an administrative body organized on nondemocratic lines is consistent with the notion of a democratic society. Certainly there were many who felt there was little problem here. For example, Cleveland (1920, 15) wrote that "the difference between an autocracy and a democracy lies not in the administrative organization but in the absence or presence of a controlling electorate or representative body outside of the administration with power to determine the will of the membership and to enforce its will on the administration." On the other hand, there were many who argued, "a democratic state must be not only based on democratic principles but also democratically administered, the democratic philosophy permeating its administrative machinery" (Levitan 1943, 359). These opposing arguments typify continuing discussions about the relationship between bureaucracy and democracy.

Just as discussion of politics and administration inevitably begins with the work of Woodrow Wilson, analysis of the concept of bureaucracy inevitably begins with the German sociologist Max Weber. In his classic examination of the concept of authority, he noted the importance of bureaucratic administration in supporting legal authority (as opposed to traditional or charismatic). The concept of bureaucracy, which is applied as easily to industrial and religious organizations as to those in governments, contains several elements, among them the following: "(1) [Officials] are personally free and are subject to authority only with respect to their impersonal official obligations, (2) they are reorganized in a clearly defined hierarchy of offices, (3) each office has a clearly defined sphere of competence..., (4) officials work entirely separated from ownership of the means of administration..., (5) they are subject to strict and systematic discipline and control in the conduct of the office" (Weber 1947, 328). In slightly more modern language, bureaucracy is characterized by hierarchical patterns of authority, a division of labor and specialization of tasks, and an impersonal arrangement of offices.

To Weber, and to many later writers, bureaucracy permits the greatest degree of efficiency in the conduct of human affairs and is therefore the most "rational" mode of social organization. Again Weber writes, "Experience tends universally to show that the purely bureaucratic type of administration... is, from a purely technical point of view, capable of attaining the highest degree of efficiency and is in this sense formally the most rational known means of carrying out imperative control over human beings" (Weber 1947, 333–334). In another passage, he writes, "Bureaucratic administration is, other things being equal, always, from a formal technical point of view, the most rational type" (Weber 1947, 337).

For those early students of public administration seeking the greatest possible efficiency in government agencies, the bureaucratic model, already becoming entrenched in industry, proved an attractive model. Fayol's (1949) scalar principle, for example, depicted the levels of authority in an organization as links forming a pattern of communication. (Note, however, that Fayol did not argue for rigid adherence to hierarchical communications.)

Similarly, Willoughby (1927, 37) sought to make the executive branch into a "single, integrated piece of administrative machinery," while Gulick (1937, 44) praised the principles of hierarchical organization as the "bootstraps by which mankind lifts itself in the process of civilization." However, it was in the work of Herbert Simon that rationality in the field of administration received its most extensive treatment.

Simon began his analysis by noting the limits of human rationality, that human beings make decisions not on the basis of pure reason, as the classic model of economic man posits, but with the constraints of "bounded rationality." Indeed, it is because human beings are limited in their capacities that they join together in complex organizations. "The rational individual," according to Simon, "is, and must be, an organized and institutionalized individual" (Simon 1957, 102). It is through joining together in organizations that people can attain the kind of rationality (read "efficiency") that escapes them elsewhere.

As members of complex organizations, however, individuals tend to behave in response to their own needs and interests. For example, Simon's discussion of why people respond to organizational authority is based on an "inducement–contributions" formula—a calculus in which certain inducements are offered to individuals so that they contribute the desired actions. In making such decisions to contribute, individuals may not fully "maximize" their interests, but rather they "satisfice"; they select what they consider to be a satisfactory alternative (Simon 1957, xxvi). While "administrative man" is not fully rational, he does the best he can.

In contrast to the position that bureaucratic organization is the most rational form of social organization, others have argued that equating rationality and efficiency is not only theoretically incorrect, but it also leads to structures and behaviors antithetical to important norms of a democratic society (Fischer and Sirianni 1994; Hummel 1994). More than a few critiques of bureaucratic life have appeared over the years (Scott and Hart 1979; Thayer 1973; Whyte 1956; but see also Goodsell 1994). Several books written by theorists in the field of public administration pointed out the major difficulties that seem to accompany bureaucratic organization.

In *The New Science of Organizations* (1981), Ramos argued that a market-centered society, based on the idea of instrumental rationality, the coordination of means to given ends, has come to dominate the way people think about organizing to the exclusion of other possibilities. In contrast, Ramos argues for a new science of organizations that would enable one to envision alternative organizational designs, leading in turn to a "multicentric" or "reticular" society in which differing forms of organization would be applied to different purposes. The dehumanizing aspect of modern bureaucratic thought was further examined in Denhardt's *In the Shadow of Organization* (1981). Denhardt suggests a radical reordering of priorities so as to give primacy to the growth of the individual rather than to the efficiency of the productive process, something that would require an alternative, personalist approach to life in an organizational society. Harmon's *Action Theory for Public Administration* (1981), while equally critical of the influence of instrumental rationality in structuring our understanding of organizational life, focuses more on ways of achieving responsible human action in organizational settings. Harmon sees the individual as an intentional being, acting so as to bestow meaning on human action.

More recently, McSwite's *Invitation to Public Administration* (2002) calls for the avoidance of the "anti-human culture" of technical rationality that downplays values. Technical efficiency, as a basis for social decisions and action, clouds other civil and social relationships. A society must "continue to express and engage each other through our differences" (112). This means that a society must consider values and be responsive to issues. To do this, public administrators must provide a forum to sort differences about how people live together, rather than simply viewing themselves as public services managers. Peter deLeon (1997) contributes to this thinking by suggesting that policy sciences have strayed from their original intent of supporting democratic processes. He suggests "participatory policy analysis" to engage analysts and citizens in a mutual quest for solutions to public problems.

These general critiques apply with even greater force when one considers the value context of public administration. Whereas Gulick (1937), White (1936), and Willoughby (1927) held efficiency to be the primary objective of the study of public administration, Dimock challenged the mechanical application of the criterion of efficiency in public organizations, holding that efficiency alone is "coldly calculating and inhuman," whereas "successful administration is warm and vibrant. It is human" (Dimock 1936, 120).

Others pointed out that efficiency was only one of many criteria by which the work of public organizations might be evaluated, especially in a democratic society. For example, Dahl (1947), in an important debate with Simon, suggested that public administration in a democratic society is almost by definition committed to values such as responsiveness, compassion, and concern. Efficiency may indeed be important, but it is often less important than the concerns of democracy. How would one evaluate the German prison camps of World War II, organizations that were marked by their efficiency?

A similar theme was developed by Redford (1969) in his book *Democracy in the Administrative State*. Redford (1969, 8) suggests that democracy rests on the concepts of individuality, equality, and participation, the latter including "(1) access to information, (2) access, direct or indirect, to forums of decision, (3) ability to open any issue to public discussion, (4) ability to assert one's claim without fear of coercive retaliation, and (5) consideration of all claims asserted." However, when one examines the way in which government agencies operate, one finds a far different set of assumptions in operation. The goals of the individual are subordinate to those of the organization, authority is distributed in a vastly uneven fashion, and there is relatively little opportunity for the participation of either those lower in the organization or clients of the organization in its decision processes. Redford concludes that attainment of the democratic ideal in the field of administration depends on the representation of many and diverse interests among decision makers.

The classic treatment of these issues, however, remains Waldo's (1948) book, *The Administrative State*. In this work and in other materials, Waldo (1952, 1980) pursues the notion that, without conscious intent, those who developed various approaches to organizational design and conduct were engaging in the creation of political theory. That is, the materials they developed for use in organization circles had direct implications for the political values of the society. Specifically, Waldo argued that the selection of efficiency as the primary value of public administration led to the development of bureaucratic structures and practices, inconsistent with the normal standards of democracy. Indeed, it appeared that the earlier writers were arguing "'Autocracy' at work is the unavoidable price for 'Democracy' after hours" (Waldo 1948, 75).

The message of Waldo's work seemed clear: that an uncritical acceptance of the bureaucratic outlook constitutes a rejection of democratic theory. In contrast, Waldo called for a more democratic mode of organization, one consistent with the ideals of a democratic society. Such an alternative, he suggested, would necessarily involve a "substantial abandonment of the authority–submission, superordinate–subordinate thought patterns which tend to dominate our administrative theory" (Waldo 1952, 103). The mode of organization consistent with principles of democracy would necessarily be "postbureaucratic."

One final variant of the bureaucracy–democracy question asks whether democratic principles should be extended through many organizations in our society, not merely those in government. Certainly major aspects of public policy are being decided today by organizations that have traditionally been privately run. Moreover, there is no question that such organizations have a tremendous impact on the lives of individuals throughout the society, a point that has been made by various "communitarian" scholars (Bellah 1985; Etzioni 1993; Selznick 1992). Under such conditions, one might well ask whether all organizations, not just those in the public sector, should be evaluated by the degree of their publicness, the degree to which they are responsive to the needs and interests of an informed citizenry (Bozeman 1987). "Such a viewpoint directly suggests what public administration theorists in the past have often resisted: that public organizations should be required by definition to act in accord with democratic procedures and to seek democratic outcomes" (Denhardt 2004, 192–193).

III. ORGANIZATION AND MANAGEMENT

Our discussion of both politics and administration and bureaucracy versus democracy has emphasized the moral and political basis of work in public organizations. But what of the way in which public administration theorists have approached questions of organization and management? Have those theories and approaches that have been most influential in the field of public administration been distinctive in any way? Specifically, have they emphasized the values and concerns one would associate with democratic morality?

For the most part, the answer to these questions has been no. Theorists and practitioners in public administration have largely depended on the same approaches to organization and management as those in the private sector (see Vasu et al. 1998). However, there is some support for the view that those in public administration have been more interested in humanizing relationships, both internal and external, and have historically been far more responsive to client needs and interests than their counterparts in business. Interestingly enough, these are just the features that are being heralded in modern studies of business practice (see, for example, Block 1993; Milakovich 1995).

Certainly, as has been discussed, the early writers in the field of public administration were encouraged to follow the industrial or bureaucratic model of organization. Indeed, what came to be called the administrative management movement in public administration followed quite closely the recommendations of those in business that managers give priority in thought and action to structural concerns such as hierarchical authority, unity of command, span of control, line–staff relations, and the division of labor. Gulick's (1937) well-known essay "Notes on the Theory of Organization" exemplified the administrative management orientation. Gulick described the problems of management as those of creating an appropriate division of labor, then imposing on that division of labor mechanisms for coordination and control. He suggested four steps: (1) to define the job to be carried out, (2) to select a director, (3) to determine the nature and number of units required, and (4) to establish a structure of authority through which coordination and control can be achieved (Gulick 1937, 7).

An even more direct merging of public and private management occurred with the development of a generic orientation toward the study of management and organization. One major figure in this development was the public administrationist Herbert A. Simon, who joined others in pursuing a scientific study of administrative behavior. In pursuing regularities in human behavior in complex organization, these generic theorists came to argue that such regularities were largely independent of their context, that, for example, the exercise of power and the capacity to motivate or delegate are much the same whether one is describing a family, an industrial organization, or a government agency. From this viewpoint, there emerged a new social science, organizational analysis, drawing on work in business and public administration as well as sociology, psychology, and other disciplines.

This approach is well illustrated in Simon's own analysis of decision-making processes. As a generic phenomenon, Simon contends, decision-making consists of intelligence (finding opportunities for decision-making), design (developing alternatives), and choice (choosing from among these). Again, consistent with Simon's interpretation of human rationality, the decision maker hopes to maximize outcomes but is typically found to suffice.

Despite the appeal of the generic approach and its apparently closed system of decision-making, public administration theorists were quick to point out certain limitations. For example, Lindblom (1959) suggested that in actual practice Simon's model of decision-making was rarely used. Instead, administrators typically chose an incremental approach, setting limiting objectives and making limited comparisons based on experience and personal values. Similarly, Allison and Zelikow (1999) argued that major policy decisions, such as those involved in the Cuban missile crisis of the Kennedy administration, do not follow either the classical rational actor model or that contained in theories of organization. Rather, he argued, decisions result from a political process of bargaining and negotiation played out in a rapidly changing environment.

Other scholars pursued the idea of environmental uncertainty, noting that open systems of organization cannot be guided by strict notions of efficiency in pursuit of their objectives, simply because environmental shifts mean things are always changing. Selznick's (1949) study of the TVA examined the policy of decentralization and involvement of local groups that was employed by that agency in its early days. He pointed out that the key criterion for evaluating organizations in fluctuating environments is not necessarily their efficiency but their adaptability and their capacity to remain stable in the face of environmental changes. Similarly, Kaufman (1967) examined the environmental influences on rangers in the U.S. Forest Service, highlighting the efforts designed to maintain the loyalty and consistency of forest rangers in spite of the various environmental pressures placed on them at the local level.

Some time ago, Rainey and Milward (1983) discussed policy networks that cut across various specific organizations in the delivery of public programs. This work suggests that programs cut across agencies based on the kinds of organized interests that are involved. "Since programs are usually the focus for networks, program networks are the most important type of network for policy making. These are networks that form among groups, individuals and organizations on the basis of their interest in a particular program" (Rainey and Milward 1983, 143). More recently, Nelissen (2002) notes that new types of governance have emerged to tackle specific problems.

In this network perspective, there is an evolving dispersion of power. This recognizes the interconnectedness of the policy process with others—business, associations, nonprofit organizations, and citizens at large. Consequently, it makes more sense to talk not just about government, but also about governance. Governance can be defined as the traditions, institutions, and processes having to do with the exercise of power in society (Peters 2001). The governance process has to do with the way decisions are made in a society and how citizens and groups interact in the formulation of public purposes and the implementation of public policy. Today this process involves many different groups and organizations.

A concern for the influence of environmental factors on agency performance has also marked the work of those interested in implementation issues. Pressman and Wildavsky examined the failure of a particular economic development project, concluding that "what had looked like a relatively simple, urgent, and direct program—involving one federal agency, one city, and a substantial and immediate funding commitment—eventually involved numerous diverse participants and a much longer series of decisions than was planned" (1979, 113). In part, their recommendation was for legislative bodies to pay greater attention to creating organizational mechanisms for effective implementations as a part of policy formation; in part, it was a recommendation to scholars to consider more carefully the way in which implementation efforts affect or even determine policy outcomes (see also Bardach 1977; Wholey et al. 1986; Wildavsky, 1979).

An interesting and related interpretation of the work of public agencies was contained in Wamsley and Zald's (1973) *The Political Economy of Public Organizations*. Wamsley and Zald propose a framework for analyzing administrative bodies by focusing on the juxtaposition of political factors and economic factors, in each case both those internal to the organization and those external to the group. Political factors are those involving power and interests, and economic factors are those affecting the market and its exchange of goods and services. It is the interaction of these various factors that establishes the capacity of the organization, including its organizational power structure (Downs 1967).

Wamsley and Zald's emphasis on exchange mechanisms seems clearly related to Vincent Ostrom's important work on public choice. Ostrom's work is based on the assumption that rational individuals exercise their rationality with respect to public goods as well as private goods and that an analysis of public choices from this perspective will lead to important lessons for the design of public organizations. In this view, "Public agencies are not viewed simply as bureaucratic units which perform those services which someone at the top instructs them to perform. Rather, public agencies are viewed as means for allocating decision-making capabilities in order to provide public goods and services responsive to the preferences of individuals in different social contexts" (Ostrom and Ostrom 1971, 207). Ostrom pursues the logic of public choice to the point of identifying cases in which public enterprises can be operated within specific domains, thus opening the possibility for greater decentralization of power and authority. Ultimately his proposal is for a form of democratic administration based on multiorganizational relationships and intentional fragmentation, something the logic of public choice would see not only as more responsive, but also as more efficient (Ostrom 1973). (We should note that Ostrom's work was criticized by Golembiewski (1977), who indicated that individuals may seek to maximize values that do not necessarily enhance a democratic society and may even corrupt it. See also Ostrom's (1977) response.)

Unlike other writers with a primary interest in policy development (Edwards 1980; Kingdon 1984; Nagel 1980), Ostrom puts policy analysis to work in the critique rather than the justification of bureaucratic structures, thus connecting him to an otherwise quite distinct group of theorists interested in organizational humanism. The work of this group is usually traced back to the well-known Hawthorne experiments of the 1920s and 1930s. These experiments, basically begun as efforts to examine how favorable working conditions might influence worker productivity, resulted in documentation of the importance of social and psychological factors in the productivity of American workers. Specifically the research team found that in addition to creating goods or services, organizations also serve the purpose of "creating and distributing satisfactions among the individual members of the organization" (Roethlisberger and Dickson 1940, 562).

The Hawthorne conclusions were reaffirmed in the work of Chester Barnard, who, based on his career of executive service, wrote eloquently of the informal or social aspect of organizational work. To achieve cooperation, Barnard wrote, one must take into account the many and often contradictory forces operating on the individual organizational member. "Cooperation and organization as they are observed and experienced are concrete syntheses of opposed facts and of opposed thoughts and emotions of human beings. It is precisely the function of the executive to facilitate the synthesis in concrete action of contradictory forces, to reconcile conflicting forces, instincts, interests, conditions, positions, and ideals" (Barnard 1938, 21).

Similarly, theorists such as Blake and Mouton (1981) and McGregor (1960) argued for a more humanistic approach to management, the former writing that a combination of high concern for productivity combined with a high concern for people is "positively associated with success, productivity, and profitability in comparison with any other theory" (Blake and Mouton 1981, 128). Most noteworthy, however, was the work of Chris Argyris, whose *Personality and Organization* (1957) was highly influential. Argyris noted that contemporary management practices, which tended to emphasize highly directive, control-oriented behavior on the part of managers, was actually counterproductive, for it was at odds with the basic striving of the adult personality. Argyris emphasized instead a style of management that stressed the manager's understanding and facilitating of human development within the organization and eventually led to a strong concern for combining personal learning and organization development.

Among students of public administration, these various themes have been advanced most ably by Golembiewski (1972, 1985, 1995a, 1995b, 2001). Golembiewski's work is most important for its infusion of moral considerations into discussions of organizational development and change. Golembiewski's early work makes an important connection between humanistic approaches to management and questions of morality, holding that moral sensitivity can be associated with satisfactory output and employee satisfaction (1967, 53). His later efforts explored organization development as an approach to understanding and improving the work of complex organizations. Yet, even here, his concern for morality was evident. For example, he describes five "metavalues" that guide the laboratory approach to organizational change and development: (1) mutual accessibility and open communications, (2) willingness to experiment with new behaviors, (3) a collaborative concept of authority, (4) establishing mutual helping relationships, and (5) developing authenticity in interpersonal relationships (Golembiewski 1972, 60–66).

The humanistic tendencies of modern students of public administration were emphasized in the "New Public Administration," a series of papers brought together at a conference at Syracuse University (Marini 1971). These papers, although hardly uniform in content or perspective, did tend to emphasize a more active role for public administrators in the development of public policy and a more equitable and participative approach to the management of public organizations. Perhaps most notable in the latter area were the articles of Kirkhart (1971) and White (1971), both of whom emphasized open communications, greater equality of power, and the importance of consensus building in organizations.

Public administration theorists in a variety of different works pursued these same themes through the 1980s and early 1990s. As noted earlier, Harmon (1981) examined the concept of the "proactive" administrator and has been joined by Hart (1974) in applying the philosophical approach of Rawls (1999) to public administration; Lipsky (1980) and Vinzant and Crothers (1998) emphasized street-level action; Baum (1983, 1987) employed psychoanalytic insight in attempting to understand the actions of public managers; though none so completely as Diamond (1993) in *The Unconscious Life of Organizations*. In this work, Diamond explores the unconscious dimensions of both hierarchic and other relationships in complex organizations, suggesting that these hold a key to understanding organizational culture and identity. Finally, Denhardt (1993) and Forester (1983) have reviewed earlier work exploring the implications of critical social theory for educative approaches to management.

In parallel to these themes, a feminist critique of bureaucracy emerged. Denhardt and Perkins (1976) foreshadowed the "coming death of administrative man" by observing "some feminist theorists are developing alternative models of organization" (379). Ferguson's (1984) book, *The Feminist Case against Bureaucracy*, discussed bureaucracy as gendered, manifesting masculine approaches to power and authority. Stivers (2002) refers to the "masculinization of thought" that drives public administration theory to conceive of control in administrative development in a distinctly masculine way. Some studies analyze differences in leadership styles of men and women (Bartunek et al. 2000). Other studies suggest greater attention to gendered perspectives offers the opportunity to rethink organizational structures (Buzzanell 2001).

Meanwhile, organization theorists only marginally connected to the field of public administration have set a high standard for public administration students interested in management concerns. The related concepts of culture and learning have perhaps been most noteworthy in their recent applications. Perhaps the best introduction to the notion of organization culture is provided by Schein (1997) (see also Deal and Kennedy 1982; Kilman et al. 1985; Ott 1989; Ritti 1998; Smircich 1983; Trice and Beyer 1993). Schein notes that the term culture can have a number of different meanings, including the dominant values espoused by an organization, the philosophy that guides an organization's policy toward its employees and its customers, the feeling or climate that is conveyed in an organization, the rules of the game for getting along, the norms within working groups, and the behavioral regularities that are observed when people interact. None of these, however, captures the fullness of Schein's description of culture as "the deeper level of basic assumptions and beliefs that are shared by members of the organization, that operate unconsciously, and that define... an organization's view of itself and its environment" (12).

More recently, Khademian's (2002) book, *Working with Culture*, raises the issue of public sector managers using organizational culture to transform an organization's results. She argues that "tending to culture is an essential responsibility of top managers" (x) since it represents "the less tangible and less formal dimension of an organization that can support or sabotage change" (7). Using the idea of organizational culture, one can presumably understand more clearly the interactions among individuals who share a culture or participate either in subcultures or opposition cultures.

The recent emphasis on organizational learning directly follows earlier work by Argyris and Schon (1978) that suggests learning is the key to organizational change. Argyris and Schon argue that individuals hold espoused theories (those theories of action people profess to follow in their behaviors) and "theories-in-use" (those people actually follow). The typical discrepancy between the two is obviously destructive to the learning process and must be overcome for the most effective learning to occur. Such learning may be directed toward removing problems that limited a group's theories-in-use, which is called "single-loop learning," or it may be directed toward shifting the basic norms and values of a group, which is called "double-loop learning." Beyond that, individuals and groups can also engage in "deutero learning," that is, learning about learning.

The work of Argyris and Schon has been extended in numerous ways. However, some of the most interesting recent applications have been those of Peter Senge and his associates at MIT. Senge (1990) suggests that many organizations today suffer from learning disabilities that prevent them from being able to identify opportunities as well as the factors potentially threatening to them (see also Dibella and Nevis 1998; Garvin 2000; Oshry 1995; Schein 1999). In order to transform an organization into a "learning organization," one that prevents learning disabilities from occurring, Senge suggests that five disciplines be used.

The first discipline, personal mastery, is described as an essential cornerstone to the learning organization. It is the discipline of constantly clarifying and deepening one's personal vision, focusing energies, developing patience, and seeing reality objectively. A second discipline is involved in analyzing one's own mental models, deeply ingrained assumptions, generalizations, or images that influence how one understands the world and how one takes action. Once the mental models have been unveiled, they ought to be scrutinized so that alternative ways of thinking about the world can be considered.

The third discipline espoused by Senge concerns the idea of building a shared vision. Organizations need to bring people together around a common identity and a common sense of destiny: "When there is a genuine vision, people excel and learn, not because they are told to, but because they want to" (Senge 1990, 9).

The fourth discipline, team learning, stresses the importance of dialogue and the capacity of members to genuinely think together.

The fifth discipline, systems thinking, integrates all of the other disciplines together into a coherent body of theory and practice. According to Senge, learning disabilities related to any of the other disciplines stem from the inability to think systematically. Organizations need to think about and understand the forces and interrelationships that shape the behavior of systems. Change within organizations will come about more effectively if individuals understand and act more in tune with the larger processes around them.

Among public administration theorists dealing with management change, Denhardt's (1993) *The Pursuit of Significance* closely parallels private sector works examining the best practices among the top managers. Based on interviews with highly progressive public managers, Denhardt identifies five strategies or approaches that seem to underlie the success of these managers. Denhardt proposes that public organizations should be driven by a commitment to a common purpose, by a concern for serving the public promptly and well, by empowerment and shared leadership, by pragmatic incrementalism, and by a dedication to public service. Utilizing these approaches, managers can make dramatic improvements to the quality and productivity of their organizations.

From this brief summary, it is clear that those in public administration have relied heavily on private sector work in their approach to organization and management. But one also gets a sense that among writers in public rather than business administration, humanistic considerations are not simply "useful," but in fact are morally correct. It should not be surprising that such a feeling would prevail in public administration, marked as it is by concern for the public service. Interestingly, as noted above, while several recent books about management for the private sector have espoused a service orientation and a participative approach to shared power in organizations, exactly such tendencies have marked public administration theory for the past several decades. While often seen as copying the best practices of private sector managers, those in the public sector may, in the long run, provide some important lessons for those in business.

IV. THEORY AND PRACTICE

Whatever values and approaches researchers have endorsed, the communication of their findings has led to difficulties. The relationship between theory and practice, between knowledge and action, has been especially troublesome to those in the field of public administration for the last several decades. Practitioners have questioned the relevance of obscure research findings to the "real world" of public administration; they have objected to the elaborate and unnecessary jargon of academic research; and they have noted the apparent penchant of researchers for excessively detailed data analysis. Academics, on the other hand, have complained that practitioners are sometimes too shortsighted and too quick to dismiss findings that may be of value, and that they fail to see the long-term implications of research for practice. In either case, the result is an apparent gap between theory and practice.

In part, the theory–practice issue is a practical one—how can research findings be made available in an appropriate form to those in the field of practice? But the issue is also a theoretical one—in what way does the structure of knowledge acquisition affect the congruence of theory and practice? It is this latter question that remains an issue in the development of public administration theory.

It is interesting to note that the theory–practice issue was not a special concern for the early writers in the field of public administration. Many of these individuals moved back and forth between administrative posts at the federal, state, and local level and research positions in the universities. A great deal of the public administration research that occurred during this period was generated within the newly formed institutes of government, university-based programs with a highly practical orientation toward administrative issues. When differences between theory and practice appeared, they were likely to center around normative issues rather than around questions of relevance.

It was only with the development of a "scientific" approach to public administration that questions about the relationship between theory and practice arose. Notable in this respect was the scientific management school associated with Frederick W. Taylor (1923). Even within the field of public administration there were efforts to establish scientific respectability. Both Willoughby (1927) and White (1936) argued for the possibility of an administrative science that would provide guides to action and in turn increase the efficiency of public organizations. Similarly, Stene (1940) argued that such an approach could be built by identifying propositions that could be tested scientifically.

As noted, the most significant move in the direction of developing a science of public administration occurred in the work of Herbert Simon in the late 1940s. Simon (1957) rejected the earlier principles or proverbs of public administration as being both naive and contradictory. To replace these principles, Simon sought to lay the groundwork for a truly scientific study of administrative behavior. His interpretation of science was that of logical positivism, a movement gaining prominence in the social sciences during this period. The key to this approach was the argument that facts and values could be separated, and that science is concerned with facts, not values. The advantage of studying facts, Simon said, was that propositions based on facts can be "tested to determine whether they are true or false—whether what they say about the world actually occurs or whether it does not" (Simon 1957, 45–46). In this view, scientific theories are general frameworks built on the objective observation of manifest behavior.

Simon's view was clearly consistent with the emerging orthodoxy of the social sciences generally and soon became the mainstream orientation of research in public administration. However, such a development did not occur without criticism. Several scholars in the field of public administration joined Dahl (1947) in pointing out the important role of values in public administration and arguing that a pure science of administration was therefore inappropriate for the field. Again, the question of efficiency was raised. Simon, while maintaining the objectivity of his approach, continued to espouse the value of efficiency, writing that "the theory of administration is concerned with how an organization should be constructed and operated in order to accomplish its work efficiently" (Simon 1957, 38).

In his critique of this view, Waldo warned of the messianic tendencies of empirical social science, tendencies that led away from moral concerns. In his words, "So far did [political scientists writing on public administration] advance from the old belief that the problem of good government is the problem of moral men that they arrived at the opposite position: that morality is irrelevant..." (Waldo 1948, 23). To Waldo, the separation of fact and value would eventually lead to a disregard for questions of value.

More generally, critics of positivism raised several specific concerns about both the validity and the impact of the new approach (Fischer 1980). First, the separation of facts and values was attacked as unrealistic, perhaps even dangerous. Facts and values, it was held, are so intertwined that their separation for scientific purposes is artificial at best. Moreover, even the scientist, in choosing a topic to study, employs values, thus undercutting the claim to a "value-free" social science. Even more important, some argued that eliminating the study of values from public administration would lead to the objectification of organizational members and reinforce the image of a rigid and impersonal bureaucracy.

Second, many questioned the deterministic tendencies of positivist science. The new science of administration implied that human behavior followed certain predetermined laws that, once discovered, would enable the explanation, prediction, and control of human behavior. Such a perspective, however, did not seem to allow for the variability of human behavior, that human beings can and do change their patterns of behavior through learning and adaptation. Indeed, it was pointed out that the simple transmission of research results to those in the field of practice might lead them to new patterns of behavior.

Most important for our present purposes, the positivist orientation toward social science research created a distance between the researcher and the practitioner. This occurred in several different ways. First, the focus of mainstream social science on the observation of behavior from the outside, was at odds with the administrator's view of organizational life from the inside. Specifically the administrator views the world subjectively as a combination of facts and values, neither in isolation from the other. Consequently human beings do not react to one another as billiard balls on a table, but through exchanges of meanings and values. Research results that attempted to isolate the objective core of human interaction simply seemed out of touch. Second, the positivist interpretation of the scientist's role as simply that of theory builder left all the details of application to the practitioner. This placed an extraordinary burden on the practitioner, but it also allowed the scientist to avoid any sense of responsibility for the use of research results. Obviously such a situation seemed most unfair to nonscientists.

Over the past several decades, public administration theorists have joined other social scientists in examining alternative epistemological positions that would correct some of the deficiencies of positivism, especially its separation of theory from practice (Burrell and Morgan 1979). Among these alternatives, phenomenology (or interpretive theory) and critical theory have drawn the greatest attention from scholars in the field, though several other approaches have been explored (Harmon and Mayer 1986; Morgan 1983). Each of these approaches will be examined and the ways in which they help resolve the theory–practice dilemma will be noted.

Interpretive social theory—or action theory as some scholars in public administration have come to call it—has its toots in phenomenological studies early in this century. The phenomenological approach seeks to strip away the presuppositions that might bias the observation of behavior from the outside and instead focuses on the world as it is experienced from the inside. Subjective experience is seen to depend on human beings endowing their world with meaning; it is through people's actions and our intentions that they give shape to the world (Schultz 1967). In contrast to the positivist model, the interpretivist recognizes the inherent subjectivity of all human interactions, that all human beings as they live and work together are constantly constructing and reconstructing social reality (Berger and Luckman 1966).

As applied to organization studies, the phenomenological approach emphasizes "the typical actions of different actors and the meaning which they attach to their action" (Silverman 1971, 154). Specifically in the field of public administration, Kirkhart (1971) set the stage for interpretivist work with his proposal for a consociated model of organization. Kirkhart's model is based on the mutual disclosure and mutual recognition that underlie every reciprocal interaction, what phenomenologists call the "we" relationship. The result is a model of organization stressing adaptability, mutual disclosure, and noncompetitive trusting relationships.

Similar efforts have been made by Harmon (1981), Hummel (1984), and Jun (1986). Each of their works rests on a distinction between behavior (that observable to the outside world) and action (that intended from the inside). The development of action theories of public administration then builds on the meanings that are established by administrative actors. Interestingly, in such a study, the role of the theorist is to assist in clarifying the meanings and intentions of various actors, presumably resulting in consensual decision-making (Harmon 1981).

Such an interpretive perspective on organizational life is well characterized in a more recent collection of essays by Kass and Catron (1990). In this work, a variety of scholars explore the difficulties of establishing legitimacy in the field of public administration under circumstances in which the basic images of the field may be flawed. In more practical terms, these suggestions might lead to an examination of those conditions of domination and dependency that often make public organizations unresponsive both to their members and to their clients. A representative work here is Camilla Stivers's (2002) book, *Gender Images in Public Administration*, in which Stivers argues that the prevailing images that underlie the defense of administrative power can be found in a masculine understanding of power and achievement. Only as the field is able to release itself from these gender-bound images will it he able to achieve substantial legitimacy. Finally, Ingersoll and Adams (1992) explore dimensions of myth and mythmaking in their study of *The Tacit Organization*.

A second alternative to positivist thought is critical social theory. Critical theory traces its roots back to Hegel's view of history as the unfolding of reason, something accomplished through the critique and elimination of those forces that limit the development of reason and freedom in society. As developed by the Frankfurt school of social thought, critical theory has pointed out the narrowing of the concept of reason in modern society from an earlier interpretation of reason as offering guiding principles in the process of enlightenment to a narrow contemporary version of rationality concerned only with the proper means toward given ends. This latter preoccupation with efficiency, critical theorists argue, not only restricts the possibility for individuals to act creatively and developmentally, but also reduces the kind of dialogue about values that is an essential component of a free society. The alternative sought by critical theory is one emphasizing "public, unrestricted discussion, free from domination, of the suitability and desirability of action-oriented principles and norms" (Habermas 1979, 118–119).

In applications to public organizations, Denhardt (1981, 1993, 2004), Dunn and Fozouni (1976), Forester (1983, 1993), and Hummel (1994) have argued for an approach that would establish a value-critical basis for the study of the formulation and implementation of public policy. Surely one aspect of such a study would be an examination of communications patterns within the public bureaucracy (Garnett 1992). Obviously, hierarchical patterns of communications restrict the possibility for undistorted communications among organizational members, in turn limiting the creativity and adaptability of organizations; creating greater opportunities for undistorted communications would be an essential corrective.

More recently, postmodernism critiques provide a new approach to analyzing the "real." Generally, postmodernists view knowledge, being based on language, as bounded by historical circumstances and an environmental context (see Spicer 2000). Postmodernists "deconstruct" the flaws underlying social, cultural, or political tendencies. Because of the limitations of language, reality is fluid, all interpretations are of equal validity. "Modernity... reflect[s] a complete faith in the capacity of reasoned language to capture the world. It... reflect[s] optimism, claiming the potential for complete understanding. Postmodernists would renounce this faith, this optimism, and this claim to power" (Farmer 1995, 47; see also Fox and Miller 1995; Miller 2002; Miller and Fox 1997; White and Adams 1995). Postmodernists reject what they see as the false hope of modern rational understanding (Denhardt, 2004).

In applying the postmodern perspective to public administration theory, Fox and Miller (1995) observe "that American representative democracy today is neither representative nor democratic" (Denhardt 2004, 168). Policy discourse is inherently political and dominated by symbols and socially created hierarchical bureaucracy. To redirect public policy considerations toward "authentic discourse," public administration must facilitate citizen discourse.

In a different approach, Farmer's (1995) book, *The Language of Public Administration*, argues the limitations of traditional public administration theory. Traditional public administration theory emphasizes instrumental rationality and hierarchical authority. To enhance public service, Farmer suggests a "reflexive" approach to revitalizing public administration theory.

The postmodernist approach to public administration is also present in McSwite's (1997) *Legitimacy in Public Administration*. McSwite concludes that public administration in America is unlikely to change until people learn (1) how it is possible to act without relying on reason, and

(2) how to come to terms with the idea of "otherness" (Denhardt 2004). In McSwite's view, progress begins with opening ourselves to engagement with one another.

Common themes emanating from the postmodernist literature are skepticism of rationality, the need for authentic discourse in governance, and enhanced public dialogue. All three themes are required to reinvigorate public bureaucracy and reconstruct public administration's legitimacy (Denhardt 2004).

As will be seen later, these perspectives have implications for the way public administrators approach the task of management itself. One alternative form of management, suggested by Denhardt (1994), would be "educative" in perspective, assisting organizational members and clients in identifying their true needs and in eliminating social conditions that prevent fulfillment of those needs. Such an effort, which would necessarily be accompanied by a greater democratization of organizational structures throughout society, should enhance democratic discourse. "Under such conditions, the public bureaucracy might even become a primary vehicle for societal self-reflection and critique" (Denhardt 2004, 165).

The more practical aspect of the issue still needs attention, both in an institutional sense (how can research findings be transmitted?) and in a more personal sense (how can receptivity to theory be increased?). With respect to the latter, two comments may be made. First, practitioners must recognize that whether they consciously construct theories of public organization or not, such theories at least implicitly guide their every action. Obviously, to the extent that such theories can be articulated, discussed, and clarified, they will provide a sounder basis for effective and responsible human action. In this sense, theory and practice are tied together through a process of learning. Second, both interpretive and critical theory suggest both the responsibility of the practitioner for thought as well as action and the responsibility of the theorist for action as well as thought. Whatever ways are found to employ the insights of the various approaches to knowledge acquisition reviewed here, the question of responsibility cannot be avoided.

Before leaving the issue of theory and practice, it is important to note a recent turn toward much more practical works in public administration, works lacking the strong theoretical basis of earlier work but having substantial impact on the field. Clearly most notable in this regard is the Osborne and Gaebler (1992) volume, *Reinventing Government*, a book that guided a great deal of thinking about management in the public sector including President Clinton's National Performance Review (NPR) (see also Kaboolian 1998; Osborne and Plastrik 1997).

Osborne and Gaebler propose to reorganize government by creating entrepreneurial incentives for the purpose of giving priority to the consumer, reducing bureaucracy, and empowering employees. By doing this the authors hope to create a "governmental market" that will (1) save the government money and significantly decrease wasteful spending or bad investment choices, (2) increase the efficiency of governmental employees and the entire system of government, and (3) reduce the amount of red tape within the system. In theory these proposed changes will result in a consumer-empowered, competitive, and market-oriented government that will reduce regulations, create revenue through fees and charges, and concentrate on the decentralization of authority, the privatization of management, and quality improvement in public agencies (see also Lynn 1996; Pollitt 1990).

Although *Reinventing Government* was used as a model by Vice President Al Gore and the NPR, there are a host of critiques to this proposed way of reorganizing government. For instance, Frederickson (1992) states that the major problem areas of the book are the idea that the government is a "market" and the citizens are the "customers," that downsizing will decrease the size and cost of government without diminishing its effective level of functioning, and the assumption that the employees of government are the primary problem. Moe (1994) states that Osborne and Gaebler emphasize economically based issues over legally based values, use unsubstantiated and irrelevant statistics to support major changes in laws and government, and misunderstand the role of law within administration of the executive branch. These critiques suggest that government could possibly become more complicated, less effective and authoritative, and ultimately weaker and unsuccessful in serving its citizens.

In an even more practical description, Linda Kaboolian notes that the new public management advocates administrative technologies such as customer service, performance-based contracting, competition, market incentives, and deregulation. "Market-like arrangements such as competition within units of government and across government boundaries to the non-profit and for-profit sectors, performance bonuses, and penalties loosen the inefficient monopoly franchise of public agencies and public employees" (Kaboolian 1998, 190; see also Barzelay 2000; DiIulio 1994; Kearns 1996; Kettl 2000; Kettl and Milward 1996; Light 1997; Peters 2001; Pollitt and Bouckert 2000). Correspondingly, the new public management emphasizes approaches such as privatization, performance measurement, strategic planning, and other managerialist approaches. Obviously, there are implications of this move for governmental efficiency, but there are also implications for issues of responsiveness as well. Christopher Hood writes that the new public management moves away from traditional modes of legitimizing the public bureaucracy, such as procedural safeguards on administrative discretion, in favor of "trust in the market and private business methods... The ideas... [are] couched in the language of economic rationalism" (Hood 1995, 94). Similarly, Kettl writes, "Painted with the broadest brush, these reforms sought to replace the traditional rule-based, authority driven processes with market-base, competition-drive tactics" (Kettl 2000, 3).

In contrast to the New Public Management, the recent book by Denhardt and Denhardt (2003), *The New Public Service: Serving, Not Steering*, stands on a much stronger theoretical footing. Denhardt and Denhardt "reject the notion... [of] the reinvented, market-oriented New Public Management" (24). Instead, they offer an alternative set of unifying themes and principles about the role of public administration in governance. This organizing framework features public service, democratic governance, and civic engagement aimed at advancing the dignity and the values of citizenship and the public interest. The distinguishing characteristics of this emerging perspective are summarized as follows (Denhardt and Denhardt 2003, 42–43):

1. *Serve Citizens, Not Customers.* The public interest is the result of a dialogue about shared values rather than the aggregation of individual self-interests. Therefore, public servants do not merely respond to the demands of customers, but rather focus on building relationships of trust and collaboration with and among citizens.
2. *Seek the Public Interest.* Public administrators must contribute to building a collective, shared notion of the public interest. The goal is not to find quick solutions driven by individual choices. Rather, it is the creation of shared interests and shared responsibility.
3. *Value Citizenship over Entrepreneurship.* The public interest is better advanced by public servants and citizens committed to making meaningful contributions to society than by entrepreneurial managers acting as if public money were their own.
4. *Think Strategically, Act Democratically.* Policies and programs meeting public needs can be most effectively and responsibly achieved through collective efforts and collaborative processes.
5. *Recognize That Accountability Is Not Simple.* Public servants should be attentive to more than the market: they should also attend to statutory and constitutional law, community values, political norms, professional standards, and citizen interests.
6. *Serve Rather than Steer.* It is increasingly important for public servants to use shared, value-based leadership in helping citizens articulate and meet their shared interests rather than attempting to control or steer society in new directions.
7. *Value People, Not Just Productivity.* Public organizations and the networks in which they participate are more likely to be successful in the long run if they are operated through processes of collaboration and shared leadership based on respect for all people.

V. THEORIES OF PUBLIC ORGANIZATION

While a number of important theoretical issues have faced the field of public administration over its relatively short history, the question of whether there is such a thing as public administration theory has proven one of the most difficult. Certainly those attempting to answer theoretical questions related to the conduct of public organizations have drawn material from political theory, organizational theory, social theory, economic theory, ethical theory, and more. They have come to this study from a variety of perspectives—as practitioners interested in finding answers to specific problems, as empirical social scientists seeking to contribute results that would build a body of theory, and as self-conscious theorists hoping to construct a broad framework for understanding life in public organizations. Given the diversity of backgrounds and interests represented in the development of public administration theory, it is not surprising that there is little agreement in the field, even about what constitutes good theory.

The question of whether a theory of public administration is possible is closely related to the question of whether a separate and identifiable discipline of public administration is possible, since presumably one mark of the disciplinary status is the development of a coherent and integrated theoretical viewpoint. A brief historical review will clarify the issues here. Obviously the early development of the study of public administration occurred within the discipline of political science, and indeed there are many today who argue that public administration is merely one subfield of political science. From this perspective public agencies play an important role in the governance process, in what Easton (1965, 50) called the "authoritative allocation of values." Such agencies are seen to affect the decisions of government in many ways, ranging from their influencing the formulation of public policy to their exercising discretion in the implementation of policy. If this is the case, it is argued, public administration is a part of political science and the theory appropriate to its study and practice is political theory. In this view, theoretical dialogue in the field of public administration should focus on issues such as freedom, justice, and equality.

Exactly such focus was found in early studies of public administration, but more recently a different perspective has emerged. As previously discussed, others have argued that public organizations are first and foremost organizations and therefore are confronted with questions having to do with their managerial efficiency. Issues surrounding the exercise of delegation, for example, are much the same whether one is a manager in a private corporation or in a federal government agency. If this is the case, it is argued, public administration is a part of management and the theory appropriate to its study and practice is generic management theory. In this view, theoretical dialogue in the field of public administration should focus on such issues as communications, motivation, and group dynamics.

Somewhere between these two views is the view expressed most prominently by Dwight Waldo that public administration is a profession, drawing from many different disciplines and many different theoretical perspectives. This view is probably the prevailing view in the field today. However, it presents several difficulties. On the one hand, there is the practical problem of employing theories oriented to other fields as guides to practice. From the viewpoint of the administrative practitioner, neither political theory nor organization theory directly matches the concerns of the real world; they simply are not directed to the specific questions administrators face. They leave out essential components. This leads to a second question, the theoretical problem of reconciling theories generated out of widely varying disciplinary perspectives. For example, how is it possible to bring together the interests of political theory in equality and freedom and the interest of organization theory in hierarchy and control?

If one takes the position that political science fails to comprehend the full range of concerns of those in public organizations by failing to give full consideration to organizational and managerial concerns; if one takes the position that organizational analysis is also limited through its failure to adequately comprehend the moral and political context of work in public organizations; and if one takes the position that a view of public administration as a professional field of study fails in that it must always borrow from other disciplines and never address the concern of public administration directly—is there any hope of developing a coherent theory of public organizations and consequently a discipline suited to the interests of those in such organizations?

Denhardt (2004) argues that a redefinition of the field might enable such a development. Specifically, in his view, such a revised definition should focus on public organizations generally rather than on the administration of governmental agencies and should see public administration as a process rather than as an activity occurring within a particular type of institution (e.g., a bureaucratic agency). The definition chosen should bring together the concerns of political theory for justice, equality, and responsiveness with the concerns of organization theory for effective change processes. As a tentative definition, Denhardt suggests that public administration is concerned with "managing change processes in pursuit of publicly defined societal values" (Denhardt, 2004, 16).

This view of the public manager suggests an individual sensitive to the impact of interpersonal and structural relationships on the development of stable or changing patterns of organizations, some one able to recognize and respond to the subtleties of organizational change processes. It also acknowledges that the public manager stands in a special relationship to the design and implementation of societal values, a relationship that provides an ethical basis for public management. "The [public] manager lives in the nexus of a political and administrative world and therefore is neither an independent actor nor solely an instrument of the political system. In this singular position, the manager accepts, interprets, and influences the values which guide the application of skills and knowledge" (Denhardt and Nalbandian 1980).

This new definition brings together the insights of political science and organizational analysis (while allowing for the contribution of other disciplines as well). In this way, it becomes possible to develop theories of public organization rather than merely theories related to public administration. Moreover, the new definition suggests the important role of those in public organizations in influencing public life and their responsibility to manage their activities in a way consistent with the standards of democracy. In this way, the various issues that have been discussed previously take on different dimensions about the role of public administration in governance. This opens the way for unifying themes and principles, like the New Public Service, focused on a reinvigorated public service, democracy, and civic engagement.

For example, the new definition suggests a resolution of the politics–administration dichotomy by acknowledging that the public manager is in a position not only to respond to legislative mandates but also to articulate, in a more direct fashion, the needs and interests of individuals in the society in a more direct fashion. Such a position suggests an active role for the administrator, but at the same time underscores both the moral and political basis of work in public organizations. This new approach to the field acknowledges that since the public manager is to be actively involved in the public expression of societal values, an active and continuing concern for democracy must be given priority over the values of bureaucracy, and even efficiency.

Similarly, the way in which people understand the relationship between questions of organization and management may be affected. By focusing on processes rather than structures, this approach suggests the necessity of understanding the role of the individual in effecting organizational and social changes. Such an approach, one might note, is consistent with the demands of a rapidly changing society requiring organizations to be especially adaptive, something that can only occur under conditions that encourage and indeed enable individuals to exercise both creativity and responsibility.

Finally, by emphasizing once again the moral and political basis of work in public organizations, this approach suggests a joining of knowledge and action, of learning and change. In turn, it suggests a new role for those in public administration theory, a role that recognizes that public administration theorists share a moral obligation with those who practice. The responsibility of the theorists has in the past been minimal, the escape to the ivory tower all too easy. Recognizing, in fact emphasizing, the moral and political nature of the public service makes that escape more difficult, but it also makes the enterprise of developing theories of public organization one of great significance.

REFERENCES

Allison, G. T. and Zelikow, P., *Essence of Decision: Explaining the Cuban Missile Crisis*, 2nd ed., Addison Wesley Longman, New York, 1999.

Appleby, P., *Big Democracy*, Alfred A. Knopf, New York, 1945.

Appleby, P., *Policy and Administration*, University of Alabama Press, Tuscaloosa, AL, 1949.

Argyris, C., *Personality and Organization*, Harper & Row, New York, 1957.

Argyris, C. and Schon, D., *Organizational Learning*, Addison-Wesley, Reading, MA, 1978.

Bailey, S., Ethics and the public service, In *Public Administration: Readings in Institutions, Processes, Behavior*, Golembiewski, R. T., Gibson, F., and Cornog, G. Y., Eds., Rand McNally, Chicago, IL, pp. 22–31, 1966.

Barber, B., *An Aristocracy of Everyone: The Politics of Education and the Future of America*, Ballantine Books, New York, 1992.

Bardach, E., *The Implementation Game*, MIT Press, Cambridge, MA, 1977.

Barnard, C., *The Functions of the Executive*, Harvard University Press, Cambridge, MA, 1938.

Bartunek, J. M., Walsh, K., and Lacey, C. A., Dynamics and dilemma of women leading women, *Organizational Science*, 11(6), 589–610, 2000.

Barzelay, M., *The New Public Management*, University of California Press, Berkeley, CA, 2000.

Baum, H. S., *Planners and Public Expectations*, Schenkman, Cambridge, MA, 1983.

Baum, H. S., *The Invisible Bureaucracy: Problem Solving in Bureaucratic Organizations*, Oxford University Press, New York, 1987.

Bellah, R. N., *Habits of the Heart: Individualism and Commitment in American Life*, University of California Press, Berkeley, CA, 1985.

Bellone, C., Ed., *Organization Theory and the New Public Administration*, Allyn and Bacon, Boston, MA, 1980.

Berger, P. L. and Luckman, T., *The Social Construction of Reality*, Doubleday, New York, 1966.

Blake, R. and Mouton, J., *The Academic Administrator Grid*, Jossey-Bass, San Francisco, CA, 1981.

Block, P., *Stewardship: Choosing Service over Self Interest*, Berrett-Koehier, San Francisco, CA, 1993.

Box, R. C., *Citizen Governance: Leading American Communities into the 21st Century*, Sage Publications, Thousand Oaks, CA, 1998.

Bozeman, B., *All Organizations are Public: Bridging Public and Private Organizational Themes*, Jossey-Bass, San Francisco, CA, 1987.

Bryson, J. M. and Crosby, B. C., *Leadership for the Common Good: Tackling Public Problems in a Shared-Power World*, Jossey-Bass, San Francisco, CA, 1992.

Burke, J., *Bureaucratic Responsibility*, John Hopkins University Press, Baltimore, MD, 1986.

Burrell, G. and Morgan, G., *Sociological Paradigms and Organizational Analysis*, Heinemann, London, 1979.

Buzzanell, P., Gendered practices in the workplace, *Management Communication Quarterly*, 14(3), 517–537, 2001.

Cleveland, F. A., *The Budget and Responsible Government*, Macmillan, New York, 1920.

Cooper, T. L., *An Ethic of Citizenship for Public Administration*, Prentice Hall, Englewood, NJ, 1991.

Cooper, T. L., *The Responsible Administrator: An Approach to Ethics for the Administrative Role*, 4th ed., Jossey-Bass, San Francisco, CA, 1998.

Dahl, R. A., The science of public administration, *Public Administration Review*, 7, 1–11, 1947.

Deal, T. E. and Kennedy, A. A., *Corporate Culture*, Addison-Wesley, Reading, MA, 1982.

deLeon, P., *Democracy and the Policy Sciences*, State University of New York Press, Albany, NY, 1997.

Denhardt, J. V. and Denhardt, R. B., *The New Public Service: Serving, Not Steering*, M.E. Sharpe, Armonk, NY, 2003.

Denhardt, K. G., *The Ethics of Public Service*, Greenwood Press, New York, 1988.

Denhardt, K. G., Character ethics and the transformation of governance, *International Journal of Public Administration*, 17(12), 2165–2193, 1994.

Denhardt, R. B., *In the Shadow of Organization*, Regents Press, Lawrence, KS, 1981.

Denhardt, R. B., *The Pursuit of Significance: Strategies for Managerial Success in Public Organizations*, Wadsworth, Belmont, CA, 1993.

Denhardt, R. B., *Theories of Public Organization*, 4th ed., Wadsworth Group, Belmont, CA, 2004.

Denhardt, R. B., and Nalbandian, J., Teaching public administration as a vocation, Paper presented at the annual meeting of the American Society for Public Administration, 1980.

Denhardt, R. B. and Perkins, J., The coming death of administrative man, *Public Administration Review*, 36, 379–384, 1976.

Diamond, M. A., *The Unconscious Life of Organizations*, Quorum Books, Westport, CT, 1993.

Dibella, A. J. and Nevis, E. C., *How Organizations Learn: An Integrated Strategy for Building Learning Capability*, Jossey-Bass, San Francisco, CA, 1998.

DiIulio, J. J., Ed., *Deregulating the Public Service*, Brookings Institution, Washington, DC, 1994.

Dimock, M. E., Criteria and objectives of public administration, In *The Frontiers of Public Administration*, Gaus, J. M., White, L. D., and Dimock, M. E., Eds., University of Chicago Press, Chicago, IL, pp. 116–132, 1936.

Dobel, J. P., *Public Integrity*, John Hopkins University Press, Baltimore, MD, 1999.

Downs, A., *Inside Bureaucracy*, Little, Brown, Boston, 1967.

Dunn, W. N., *Public Policy Analysis*, 2nd ed., Prentice-Hall, Englewood Cliffs, NJ, 1994.

Dunn, W. N. and Fozouni, B., *Toward a Critical Administrative Theory*, Sage Publications, Beverly Hills, CA, 1976.

Easton, D., *A Framework for Political Analysis*, Prentice-Hall, Englewood Cliffs, NJ, 1965.

Edwards, G. C., *Implementing Public Policy*, Congressional Quarterly Press, Washington, DC, 1980.

Etzioni, A., *The Spirit of Community*, Crown Books, New York, 1993.

Fayol, H., *General and Industrial Management,* Storrs C, Trans, Pittman, London, 1949.

Farmer, J. D., *The Language of Public Administration*, University of Alabama Press, Tuscaloosa, AL, 1995.

Ferguson, K. E., *The Feminist Case Against Bureaucracy*, Temple University Press, Philadelphia, PA, 1984.

Finer, H., Administrative responsibility in democratic government, In *Bureaucratic Power in National Politics*, Rourke, F., Ed., Little, Brown, Boston, MA, pp. 326–337, 1972.

Fischer, F., *Politics, Values, and Public Policy: The Problem of Methodology*, Westview Press, Boulder, CO, 1980.

Fischer, F. and Sirianni, C., Ed.s., *Critical Studies in Organizational bureaucracy*, Temple University Press, Philadelphia, PA, 1994.

Forester, J., Critical theory and organizational analysis, In *Beyond Method*, Morgan, G., Ed., Sage Publications, Beverly Hills, CA, pp. 234–246, 1983.

Forester, J., *Critical Theory, Public Policy and Planning Practice*, State University of New York Press, Albany, NY, 1993.

Fox, C. J. and Miller, H. T., *Postmodern Public Administration*, Sage Publications, Thousand Oaks, CA, 1995.

Frederickson, H. G., Toward a new public administration, In *Toward a New Public Administration*, Marini, F., Ed., Chandler, San Francisco, CA, pp. 309–331, 1971.

Frederickson, H. G., *New Public Administration*, University of Alabama Press, Tuscaloosa, AL, 1980.

Frederickson, H. G., Painting bull's-eyes around bullet holes, *Governing*, 13, October, 1992.

Friedrich, C. J., Public policy and the nature of administrative responsibility, In *Bureaucratic Power in National Politics*, Rourke, F., Ed., Little, Brown, Boston, MA, pp. 165–175, 1972.

Garnett, J. L., *Communicating for Results in Government: A Strategic Approach for Public Managers*, Jossey-Bass, San Francisco, CA, 1992.

Garvin, D. A., *Learning in Action: A Guide to Putting the Learning Organization to Work*, Harvard Business School Press, Boston, MA, 2000.

Gawthrop, L. C., *Public Sector Management Systems and Ethics*, Indiana University Press, Bloomington, IN, 1984.

Gawthrop, L. C., *Public Service and Democracy: Ethical Imperatives for the 21st Century*, Chatham House Publishers, New York, 1998.

Gilmour, R. S. and Halley, A. A., Ed.s., *Who Makes Public Policy?*, Chatham House, Chatham, NJ, 1994.

Golembiewski, R. T., *Men, Management, and Morality*, McGraw-Hill, New York, 1967.

Golembiewski, R. T., *Renewing Organizations*, Peacock, Ithaca, IL, 1972

Golembiewski, R. T., A critique of "Democratic Administration" and its supporting ideation, *American Political Science Review*, 71, 1488–1507, 1977.

Golembiewski, R. T., *Humanizing Public Organizations*, McGraw Hill, New York, 1985.

Golembiewski, R. T., *Managing Diversity in Organizational Development*, Transaction, New Brunswick, NJ, 1995a.

Golembiewski, R. T., *Practical Public Management*, Marcel Dekker, New York, 1995b.

Golembiewski, R. T., *Handbook of Organizational Behavior*, Marcel Dekker, New York, 2001.

Goodnow, F., *Policy and Administration*, Macmillan, New York, 1900.

Goodsell, C. T., *The Case for Bureaucracy: A Public Administration Polemic*, 3rd ed., Chatham House, Chatham, NJ, 1994.

Gulick, L., Politics, administration, and the new deal, *Annals of the American Academy of Political and Social Science*, 169, 545–566, 1933.

Gulick, L., Notes on the theory of organization, In *Papers on the Science of Administration*, Gulick, L. and Urwick, L., Eds., Institute of Public Administration, New York, pp. 1–46, 1937.

Habermas, J., *Communication and the Evolution of Society Trans.* McCarthy T.J., Beacon, Boston, MA, 1979.

Harmon, M. M., *Action Theory for Public Administration*, Longman, New York, 1981.

Harmon, M. M., *Responsibility as Paradox: A Critique of Rational Discourse on Government*, Sage Publications, Thousand Oaks, CA, 1995.

Harmon, M. M. and Mayer, R. T., *Organization Theory for Public Administration*, Little, Brown, Boston, MA, 1986.

Hart, D. K., Social equity, justice, and the equitable administrator, *Public Administration Review*, 34, 3–10, 1974.

Hood, C., The 'new public management' in the 1980s, *Accounting Organization and Society*, 20(2–3), 93–100, 1995.

Hummel, R., *The Bureaucratic Experience*, 4th ed., St Martin's Press, New York, 1994.

Ingersoll, V. H. and Adams, G. B., *The Tacit Organization*, JAI Press, Greenwich, CT, 1992.

Jun, J. S., *Public Administration: Design and Problem Solving*, MacMillan, New York, 1986.

Kaboolian, L., The new public management, *Public Administration Review*, 53(3), 189–193, 1998.

Kaufman, H., *The Forest Ranger: A Study in Administrative Behavior*, Johns Hopkins University Press, Baltimore, MD, 1967.

Kass, H. D. and Catron, B. L., *Images and Edentities in Public Administration*, Sage Publications, Newbury Park, CA, 1990.

Kearns, K., *Managing for Accountability*, Jossey-Bass, San Francisco, CA, 1996.

Kettl, D. F., *The Global Public Management Revolution*, Brookings Institution, Washington, DC, 2000.

Kettl, D. and Milward, H. B., Ed.s., *The State of Public Management*, Johns Hopkins University Press, Baltimore, MD, 1996.

Khademian, A. M., *Working with Culture: The Way the Job Gets done in Public Programs*, CQ Press, Washington, DC, 2002.

Kilman, R. H., Saxon, M. J., and Serpa, R., *Gaining Control of the Corporate Culture*, Jossey-Bass, San Francisco, CA, 1985.

King, C. S., Feltey, K. M., and O'Neill, B., The question of participation: toward authentic public participation in public administration, *Public Administration Review*, 58(4), 317–326, 1998.

King, C. S. and Stivers, C., *Government is US: Public Administration in an Anti-Government Era*, Sage Publications, Thousand Oaks, CA, 1998.

Kingdon, J. W., *Agendas, Alternatives, and Public Policies*, Little, Brown, Boston, MA, 1984.

Kingsley, D., *Representative Democracy: An Interpretation of the British Civil Service*, Antioch University Press, Yellow Springs, OH, 1944.

Kirkhart, L., Toward a theory of public administration, In *Toward a New Public Administration*, Marini, F., Ed., Chandler, San Francisco, CA, pp. 127–164, 1971.

Krislov, S., *Representative Bureaucracy*, Prentice Hall, Englewood Cliffs, NJ, 1974.

Lappe, F. M. and Du Bois, P. M., *The Quickening of America*, Jossey-Bass, San Francisco, CA, 1994.

Levitan, D. M., Politics ends and administration means, *Public Administration Review*, 3, 353–359, 1943.

Light, P., *The Tides of Reform*, Yale University Press, New Haven, CT, 1997.

Lipsky, M., *Street-Level Bureaucracy*, Russell Sage, New York, 1980.

Lindblom, C. E., The science of muddling through, *Public Administration Review*, 19, 79–88, 1959.

Lowi, T., *The End of Liberalism*, 2nd ed., W.W. Norton, New York, 1979.

Lynn, L. E., Jr., *Managing the Public's Business*, Basic Books, New York, 1981.

Lynn, L. E., Jr., *Public Management as Art, Science, and Profession*, Chatham House, Chatham, NJ, 1996.

Marini, F., Ed., *Toward a New Public Administration: The Minnowbrook Perspective*, Chandler, San Francisco, CA, 1971.

Maass, A. A. and Radway, L. I., Gauging administrative responsibility, In *Democracy, Bureaucracy, and the Study of Administration*, Stivers, C., Ed., Westview Press, Boulder, CO, pp. 163–181, 2001.

Mathews, F. D., *Politics for People: Finding a Responsible Public Voice*, University of Illinois Press, Urbana, IL, 1994.

McGregor, D., *The Human Side of Enterprise*, McGraw-Hill, New York, 1960.

McSwite, O. C., *Legitimacy in Public Administration: A Discourse Analysis*, Sage Publications, Thousand Oaks, CA, 1997.

McSwite, O. C., *Invitation to Public Administration*, Sharpe, Armonk, NY, 2002.

Meier, K. J., *Politics and the Bureaucracy: Policymaking in the Fourth Branch of Government*, 3rd ed., Wadsworth, Belmont, CA, 1993.

Milakovich, M. E., *Improving Service Quality*, St. Lucie Press, Delray Beach, FL, 1995.

Miller, H. T., *Postmodern Public Policy*, State University of New York, New York, 2002.

Miller, H. T. and Fox, C. J., Ed.s., *Postmodernism, "Reality", and Public Administration: A Discourse*, Chatelaine Press, Burke, VA, 1997.

Moe, R. C., The reinventing government exercise: misinterpreting the problems, misjudging the consequences, *Public Administration Review*, 54(2), 111–122, 1994.

Morgan, G., *Beyond Method*, Sage Publications, Beverly Hills, CA, 1983.

Mosher, F., *Democracy and the Public Service*, 2nd ed., Oxford University Press, New York, 1982.

Nagel, S. and Neef, M., What's New about Policy Analysis Research?, In *Improving Policy Analysis*, Nagel, S., Ed., Sage Publications, Beverly Hills, CA, 1980.

Nalbandian, J., Facilitating community, enabling democracy: new roles for local government managers, *Public Administration Review*, 59(3), 187–197, 1999.

Nelissen, N., The administrative capacity of new types of governance, *Public Organization Review*, 2(1), 5–22, 2002.

Osborne, D. E. and Gaebler, T., *Reinventing Government*, Addison-Wesley Publishing Co., Reading, MA, 1992.

Osborne, D. and Plastrik, P., *Banishing Bureaucracy*, Addison-Wesley, Reading, MA, 1997.

Oshry, B., *Unlocking the Mysteries of Organizational Life*, Berrett-Koehler, San Francisco, CA, 1995.

Ostrom, V., *The Intellectual Crisis in American Public Administration*, University of Alabama Press, Tuscaloosa, AL, 1973.

Ostrom, V., Some problems in doing political theory, *American Political Science Review*, 71, 1508–1525, 1973.

Ostrom, V. and Ostrom, E., Public choice: a different approach to the study of public administration, *Public Administration Review*, 31, 203–216, 1971.

Ott, J. S., *The Organizational Culture Perspective*, Brooks-Cole, Pacific Grove, CA, 1989.

Peters, B. G., *The Politics of Bureaucracy*, 3rd ed., Longman, New York, 1989.

Peters, B. G., *The Future of Governing*, 2nd ed., University Press of Kansas, Lawrence, KS, 2001.

Pollitt, C., *Managerialism and the Public Service*, Basil-Blackwell, Cambridge, UK, 1990.

Pollitt, C. and Bouckert, G., *Public Management Reform*, Oxford University Press, Oxford, UK, 2000.

Pressman, J. and Wildavsky, A., *Implementation: How Great Expectations in Washington are Dashed in Oakland: Or, Why it's Amazing that Federal Programs Work at all*, University of California Press, Berkeley, CA, 1979.

Rainey, H. G. and Milward, H. B., Public organizations: policy networks and environments, In *Organizational Theory and Public Policy*, Hall, R. H. and Quinn, R. E., Eds., Sage Publications, Beverly Hills, CA, pp. 133–146, 1983.

Ramos, A. G., *The New Science of Organizations*, University of Toronto Press, Toronto, Canada, 1981.

Rawls, J., *A Theory of Justice*, Rev. ed., Belnap Press of Harvard University, Cambridge, MA, 1999

Redford, E. S., *Democracy in the Administrative State*, Oxford University Press, New York, 1969.

Ripley, R. B. and Franklin, G. A., *Bureaucracy and Policy Implementation*, 2nd ed., Dorsey Press, Homewood, IL, 1986.

Ritti, R. R., *The Ropes to Skip and the Ropes to Know*, 5th ed., Wiley, New York, 1998.

Roethlisberger, F. and Dickson, W., *Management and the Worker*, Harvard University Press, Cambridge, MA, 1940.

Rohr, J. A., *To Run a Constitution*, University Press of Kansas, Lawrence, KS, 1986.

Rohr, J. A., *Ethics for Bureaucrats,* 2nd ed., Marcel Dekker, New York, 1989.

Rohr, J. A., *Public Service, Ethics, and Constitutional Practice*, University Press of Kansas, Lawrence, KS, 1998.

Rosen, B., *Holding Government Bureaucracies Accountable*, 3rd ed., Praeger, Westport, CN, 1998.

Rourke, F. E., *Bureaucracy, Politics, and Public Policy*, 3rd ed., Little, Brown, Boston, MA, 1984.

Schein, E. H., Empowerment, coercive persuasion and organizational learning: do they connect?, *The Learning Organization*, 6(4), 163–172, 1999.

Schein, E. H., *Organizational Culture and Leadership*, 2nd ed., Jossey-Bass, San Francisco, CA, 1997.

Schultz, A., *The Phenomenology of the Social World*, Translated by Walsh, G. and Lehnert, F., Eds., Northwestern University Press, Evanston, IL, 1967.

Scott, W. G. and Hart, D. K., *Organizational America*, Houghton Mifflin, Boston, MA, 1979.

Seidman, H. and Gilmour, R., Eds., *Politics, Position, and Power: From the Positive to the Regulatory State*, 4th ed., Oxford University Press, New York, 1986.

Selznick, P., *TVA and the Grass Roots*, Harper & Row, New York, 1949.

Selznick, P., *The Moral Commonwealth*, University of California Press, Berkeley, CA, 1992.

Senge, P. M., *The Fifth Discipline*, Double Day, New York, 1990.

Silverman, D., *The Theory of Organizations*, Basic Books, New York, 1971.

Simon, H. A., *Administrative Behavior: A Study of Decision-Making Processes in Administrative Organization*, 2nd ed., Free Press, New York, 1957.

Skocpol, T. and Fiorina, M. P., *Civic Engagement in American Democracy*, Brookings Institution Press, Washington, DC, 1999.

Smircich, L., Concepts of culture and organizational analysis, *Administrative Science Quarterly*, 28, 339–358, 1983.

Spicer, M., *Public Administration and the State*, University of Alabama Press, Tuscaloosa, AL, 2000.

Stene, E. O., An approach to a science of administration, *American Political Science Review*, 34, 1124–1126, 1940.

Stever, J. A., *The End of Public Administration*, Transnational, Dobbs Ferry, NY, 1988.

Stillman, R. J., III, *A Preface to Public Administration*, St Martin's Press, New York, 1991.

Stillman, R. J., III, *The American Bureaucracy: The Core of Modern Government*, 2nd ed., Nelson-Hall Publishers, Chicago, IL, 1996.

Stivers, C., *Gender Images in Public Administration: Legitimacy and the Administrative State*, 2nd ed., Sage Publications, Thousand Oaks, CA, 2002.

Svara, J. H., Politics-administration dichotomy model as aberration, *Public Administration Review*, 58(1), 51–58, 1998.

Taylor, F., *Scientific Management*, Harper & Row, New York, 1923.

Thayer, F., *An End to Hierarchy! An End to Competition!* New Viewpoints, New York, 1973.

Thompson, D. F., Moral responsibility of public officials: the problem of many hands, *American Political Science Review*, 74, 905–916, 1980.

Thompson, D. F., Bureaucracy and democracy, In *Democractic Theory and Practice*, Duncan, G., Ed., Cambridge University Press, Cambridge, MA, 1983.

Thompson, D. F., The possibility of administrative ethics, *Public Administration Review*, 45, 555–562, 1985.

Trice, N. M. and Beyer, J. M., *The Culture of the Work Organization*, Prentice Hall, Englewood Cliffs, NJ, 1993.

Vasu, M. L., Stewart, D. W., and Garson, G. D., *Organizational Behavior and Public Management*, 3rd ed., Marcel Dekker, New York, 1998.

Vinzant, J. and Crothers, L., *Street-Level Leadership: Discretion and Legitimacy in Front-Line Public Service*, Georgetown University Press, Washington, DC, 1998.

Waldo, D., *The Administrative State*, Ronald Press, New York, 1948.

Waldo, D., The development of a theory of public administration, *American Political Science Review*, 46, 81–103, 1952.

Waldo, D., *Public Administration in a Time of Turbulence*, Chandler, San Francisco, CA, 1971.

Waldo, D., *The Enterprise of Public Administration*, Chandler & Sharp, Novato, CA, 1980.

Wamsley, G. and Zald, M., *The Political Economy of Public Organization*, Oxford University Press, New York, 1973.

Wamsley, O., Bacher, R. N., Goodsell, C. T., Kronenburg, P. S., Rohr, J. A., Stivers, C. M., White, O. F., and Wolf, J. F., *Refounding Public Administration*, Sage Publications, Newbury Park, CA, 1990.

Weber, M., *The Theory of Social and Economic Organization*, Oxford University Press, New York, 1947.

White, J. D. and Adams, G., *Reason and Postmodernity: Administrative Theory and Praxis*, 17(1), 1–18, 1995.

White, L.D., The meaning of principles in public administration. In *The Frontiers of Public Administration*, Gaus, J. M., White, L. D., and Dimock, M. E., Eds., Univeristy of Chicago Press, Chicago, pp.13–25.

White, O. F. Jr., Administrative adaptation in a changing society, In *Toward a New Public Administration: The Minnowbrook Perspective*, Marini, F, Ed., Chandler, San Francisco, CA, pp. 59–62, 1971.

Wholey, J. S., Abramson, M. A., and Bellavita, C., *Performance and Credibility: Developing Excellence in Public and Nonprofit Organizations*, Heath, D.C., Lexington, MA, 1986.

Whyte, W. H., Jr., *The Organization Man*, Simon and Schuster, New York, 1956.

Wildavsky, A., *Speaking Truth to Ower: The Art and Craft of Policy Analysis*, Transaction Books, New Brunswick, Canada, 1987.

Willoughby, W. F., *Principles of Public Administration*, Johns Hopkins University Press, Baltimore, MD, 1927.

Willoughby, W. F., *The Government of Modern States*, Appleton-Century-Crofts, New York, 1936.

Wilson, W., The study of administration, *Political Science Quarterly*, 2, 197–232, 1887.

Unit 3

Public Budgeting and Financial Management

5 The Field of Public Budgeting and Financial Management, 1789–2004

Carol W. Lewis

CONTENTS

I. INTRODUCTION

A. PURPOSE

1. Chronological Approach

This historical and bibliographic essay presents chronologically the major documents, publications, and theoretical and empirical developments most enduring in the literature and most influential in the profession of American public budgeting and financial management.* The diversity of sources reflects the fact that the field itself has emerged and evolved from the concerns and contributions of both practitioners and academics, as well as from the interplay among theoretical and applied research and analyses (Rubin 1990). Enduring commitments to limited government and to flexible federalism have also been critical, as they nurture the adaptive transfer of ideas, experiences, and innovations among national, state, and local governmental units and between governmental and nongovernmental institutions.

History is not the only legitimate point of reference, but it is the conventional one (McCaffery 1987; Webber and Wildavsky 1986). It is the overall organizing element for this chapter. Because the effects of some ideas or developments may be intermittent, recursive, continuous, delayed, or of such magnitude that they defy a simple timeline, periodization by calendar years and decades imposes an artificial coherence on a complex story. Moreover, a historical analysis requires that attention be paid to both historical continuity and disjuncture. Recurring themes such as federalism, separation of powers, and administrative capacity underscore the former, but only the latter appears in a chronology (see Table 5.1).

2. Federal Emphasis

The historical emphasis here is on the federal government because it currently dominates the system financially, economically, and intellectually. It offers the only nationally applicable model we have. Furthermore, federal practices and processes are relatively sophisticated and are therefore interesting to scholars and practitioners. Considering the variety and number of experiences and experiments associated with state and local governments, a federal focus allows some analytical order to be imposed on what could easily become a complicated, even chaotic story. For the most part, the contemporary literature reflects this same analytical choice. From a systemic perspective, a chronology of pivotal developments primarily at the federal level is best linked to significant state and local trends and the literature.

3. Bibliographic Criteria

The bibliographic component is a composite of official and unofficial publications, practitioner and academic writings, and major events and trends at various levels of government (most of the numerous court decisions impinging on practice in the field are excluded for reasons of space and clarity). A diverse, mushrooming literature—the size, variety, and technical language of which probably threaten as much as entice the uninitiated—compels compassionate and responsible selectivity. It is useful to repeat an observation by Frederick A. Cleveland, then director of New York City's influential Bureau of Municipal Research: "Difficulty in tracing the evolution of the 'budget idea' in the United States lies not so much in the historical material to be mastered as in decision as to what 'idea' is to be discussed" (Cleveland 1915, 15). For our purposes, choices are drawn from four standard categories, including statutes and other sources of the major legal

---

* The author extends her appreciation to the University of Connecticut's Political Science Department for its ongoing research support and to Zsolt Nyiri and Jason hiulietti for their research assistance.

TABLE 5.1
Chronology of Federal Budgeting, 1789–1995

From the Constitution through World War II

1789	U.S. Constitution, Art. 1, Sec. 7, revenue bills originate in House (and appropriations, by custom); Art. 1, Sec. 9, appropriation needed for expenditure and public receipts and expenditures
1789	An Act to Establish the Treasury Department (I Stat. 12). Established elements underlying federal financial system including disbursements, accounting, and reporting and offices of Secretary of the Treasury, Comptroller, and Auditor
1791	First internal tax—on distilled spirits—passed by Congress
1802	Ways and Means Committee established as standing committee
1816	Senate Committee on Finance established
1819	In *McCulloch v. Maryland*, the U.S. Supreme Court established federal government's immunity from state taxation
1837	House Rule XXI. Unauthorized appropriations and appropriations in legislation barred
1850	Senate Rule XV. Unauthorized appropriations barred
1865	House Appropriations Committee established
1867	House Appropriations Committee created
1871	First Civil Service Commission (1872–1873) created through rider to appropriations bill
1894	Dockery Act. Established fiscal accounting practices
1906	Antideficiency Act (31 U.S.C. 1511 et seq.). Initiated apportionment of funds (amended in 1950 to allow budgetary reserves and in 1974 to restrict budgetary reserves).
1906	Government Finance Officers Association (GFOA) established as professional association of state/provincial and local finance officers in U.S. and Canada
1912	Report of the (Taft) Commission on Economy and Efficiency. Expressed need for national budget and executive budget
1913	US Constitution, Amendment Act. XVI. Congress fully empowered to tax income
1913	Federal Reserve Act. Established institutions and system for national monetary policy; for first time Congress delegated considerable power over the federal budget and national economy
1917	Liberty Bond Acts. Authorized Treasury to pay debts and borrow on US credit to specified amount ("debt ceiling")
1921	Budget and Accounting Act (31 U.S.C. 1101 et seq.). Established executive budget system, Bureau of the Budget, and Government Accountability Office (GAO, now Government Accountability Office)
1933	Congress created independent public corporation, Tennessee Valley Authority (TVA)
1935	Social Security program established
1937	Report of the President's Committee on Administrative Management (Brownlow Committee). Expressed President's managerial role in executive branch and need for powers and staff.
1937	Tax Foundation founded as an organization which, though research and analysis, would inform and education Americans using objective, reliable data on government sources
1939	Reorganization Plan No. 1 (Executive Order 8284). Transferred Bureau of the Budget with expanded role to new Executive Office of the President
The postwar period 1945–1949	
1945	Government Corporation Control Act. First attempt to regularize and control government corporations' financial activities
1946	Employment Act of 1946. Established Council of Economic Advisors and Economic Report of the President
1946	Administrative Procedure Act. Standardized administrative practices among agencies
1946	Legislative Reorganization Act. Established legislative budget (discarded in 1949)
1949	Concluding Report of the Commissions on Organization of the Executive branch of the Government (first Hoover Commission). Emphasized presidential role in executive management and "management movement" made recommendations for reorganization of the executive branch, and called for performance budgeting
The 1950s	
1950	Budget and Accounting Procedures Act. Aimed at control and accountability in executive agencies' funds, established requirements for budgeting, accounting, financial reporting, and auditing, and mandated performance budgeting
1950	Omnibus Appropriations Act. All regular spending in a single appropriation bill for first time (but return to separate bills in 1951)
1953–1955	Second Hoover Commission. Recommended limiting government activities that compete with private sector and other recommendations on budgetary and financial practices

(Continued)

TABLE 5.1 *(Continued)*

From the Constitution through World War II

The 1960s

1961	Planning–programming–budgeting system (PPBS) adopted in Department of Defense
1962	Executive Order 10988. Unionization of federal employees encouraged
1965	Bureau of the Budget's bulletin no. 66-3. Provided for PPBS in executive departments and agencies (until abandoned in 1971)
1965	Amendment to Social Security Act created Medicare
1966	BOB circular A-76. Implemented government policy to use private suppliers that are competitive on a cost comparison basis; expanded in 1979
1967	President's Commission on Budget Concepts. Unified budget adopted

The 1970s

1970	Legislative Reorganization Act. Expanded role of Government Accountability Office (program evaluation) and provided for five-year budget projections
1970	Reorganization Plan No. 2. Reconstituted Bureau of the Budget as Office of Management and Budget (OMB) and reemphasized management role
1971	Requirements for PPBS formally voided
1972	Nixon administration made use of unprecedented, massive rescissions and impoundments in domestic programs
1972	State and Local Fiscal Assistance Act (P. L. 92-512). Established general revenue sharing and inaugurated "new federalism." Terminated in 1986
1972	Government Accountability Office issued comprehensive statement of standards for governmental audits
1972	Joint Study Committee on Budget Control established. With significant modifications, 1973 report to emerge as 1974 budget act
1973	Comprehensive Employment and Training Act (CETA). Created financial assistance to state and local governments for training and employment
1974	Congressional Budget and Impoundment Control Act. (P. L. 93-344). Established congressional budget process and timetable. House and Senate Budget Committees, Congressional Budget Office, and procedures for reviewing recisions and deferrals
1974	Automatic cost-of-living adjustments (COLA) added by amendment to Social Security Act
1977	Office of Management and Budget's bulletin no. 77-9. Zero-base budgeting introduced into executive departments and agencies (and officially terminated in 1981)
1978	Full Employment and Balanced Growth Act (Humphrey-Hawkins Act). Congress authorized president to propose and initiate action with respect to production, prices, and employment
1978	Inspector General Act. Created independent units in major domestic agencies to conduct audits and investigations to reduce fraud, waste, and abuse

The 1980s

1980	Reconciliation process. First use as part of first budget resolution after change allowing use at beginning of congressional budget process
1981	Reagan administration abandoned zero-base budgeting through OMB circular A-11
1981	Omnibus Reconciliation Act. Use of reconciliation in first resolution
1981	Economic Recovery Tax Act. ERTA introduced major tax cuts, including reducing highest individual tax bracket
1981	Executive Order 12291 required new, major regulations with annual economic impact of $100 million or more be subjected to cost-benefit analysis
1981	In November, when President Reagan vetoed a continuing resolution, 400,000 federal employees told not to come back when they went for lunch; a few hours later, President Reagan signed a new version of the continuing resolution and the workers were back the next morning
1982	Balanced budget amendment approved in Senate but not in House
1982	In *Immigration and Naturalization Service v. Chadha*, U.S. Supreme Court undermined legislative veto
1982	Federal Managers' Financial Integrity Act (31 U.S.C. 3512). Intended to reduce fraud, waste, and abuse in agency operations by requiring assessment and reporting annually on internal controls and accounting systems
1982	Tax Equity and Fiscal Responsibility Act (TEFRA). TEFRA instituted significant changes in medical and casualty deductions and pensions and retirement plans
1982	OMB stipulated guidelines for evaluating internal controls in accordance with OMB circular A-123
1983	Comptroller General issued standards for internal controls in federal agencies
1984	Report of the President's Private Sector Survey on Cost Control (Grace Commission). Emphasizing efficiency and savings, issued 47 reports including almost 2500 recommendations and concluded that federal reporting and accounting systems are inadequate

(Continued)

TABLE 5.1 *(Continued)*

From the Constitution through World War II

1984	Single Audit Act. Streamlined intergovernmental financial system by establishing uniform requirements for comprehensive, single audit of federal grant recipients
1984	Federal Capital Investment Program Act. As of 1985, the president's annual budget submission is required to highlight capital investment expenditures within the unified budget
1984	The Governmental Accounting Standards Board (GASB) organized to establish standards of financial accounting and reporting for state and local government entities
1984	Fiscal year starts without a budget and, in October, 500,000 federal workers are sent home; an emergency spending bill has them all back at work the next day
1985	Balanced Budget and Emergency Deficit Control Act (GRH, P.L. 99-177, the Gramm-Rudman-Hollings Act). Provided for annual reductions in the budget deficit from fiscal 1986 to zero in fiscal 1991 (balanced budget) through mandatory sequestration (canceled budget resources) if projected deficit exceeded target; legislative vehicle was debt limit extension
1985	Executive Order 12498 established OMB's clearance of regulations, including agencies' regulatory policy and proposals
1985	General revenue sharing for local governments not reauthorized in reconciliation bill for fiscal 1986
1986	In *Bowsher v. Synar* (106 S.Ct. 3181), Supreme Court invalidated *GRH's* automatic trigger mechanism for sequestration as violation of separation of powers
1986	Tax Reform Act (P.L. 99-514). Introduced the Internal Revenue Code of 1986 with major overhaul of tax system including reduced individual tax rates and number of brackets, elimination of many tax deductions and preferences, and reinstatement of standard deduction (1944–1977)
1986	Amendment to Defense Authorization Act for fiscal 1987 (P.L. 99-145, Sec. 1405). Congress mandated that president submit first biennial defense budget for fiscal 1988 and 1989
1986	Balanced budget amendment fails by one vote in Senate
1986	500,000 workers are out for a half day in October; President Reagan signs final appropriations bill and the workers are ordered back for the next shift
1987	Following stock market's plunge in October, successful executive–legislative negotiations led to two-year budget agreement
1987	Balanced Budget and Emergency Deficit Control Reaffirmation Act (P.L. 100-119). Amended 1985 GRH to reset deficit reduction targets and postpone balanced budget to 1993; automatic sequestration trigger restored and responsibility assigned to OMB; legislative vehicle was debt limit extension
1988	Accepting Republican nomination, George Bush promised no tax increases in his "read my lips" pledge
1988	*South Carolina v. Baker.* Upholding sec. 310(b)(I) of 1982 TEFRA, Supreme Court found that there is no constitutional entitlement not to pay taxes on income earned from state and local bonds
1988	Passage of Indian Gaming Regulatory Act permits casino gambling on reservations
1989	In effort to reduce pork-barrel politics, independent commission was established by law to recommend closing or downsizing obsolete military bases
1989–1990	Deficit exceeded GRH deficit targets each fiscal year
The 1990s	
1990	President Bush's submitted budget included proposal for constitutional amendment on balanced budget, item veto authority, biennial budgeting, and more
1990	For second time in history, House considered a balanced budget amendment to the Constitution and it fell seven votes short of requisite two-thirds majority; Senate Judiciary Committee reported balanced budget amendment
1990	Federal employees temporarily furloughed during budget impasse
1990	Federal Credit Reform Act changed budgetary treatment of loans and loan guarantees through government-owned and government-sponsored corporations to subsidize cost of loans for which funds must be budgeted and appropriated
1990	Chief Financial Officers (CFO) Act assigned responsibility for federal financial management to OMB's deputy director for management and the Office of Federal Financial Management; provided for appointing CFOs in 23 major departments and CFO council; effort to establish integrated financial management systems linking budgeting and accounting and monitoring budgetary execution; requires agencies prepare auditable financial statements
1990	OMB, Treasury, and GAO establish Federal Accounting Standards Advisory Board (FASAB) to develop uniform accounting standards
1990	Omnibus Budgeting Reconciliation Act (P.L. 101-508) for fiscal 1991 raised income tax rates for high-income earners, incorporated five-year spending reduction aimed at saving approximately $500 billion, and effectively repealed GRH; subsequent appropriations passed, many without final legislative text in hand

(Continued)

TABLE 5.1   *(Continued)*

From the Constitution through World War II

1990	Budget Enforcement Act of 1990 (BEA; Title XIII of 1990 OBRA) made major changes in GRH and 1974 Congressional Budget Act; shifted focus from fixed deficit limits to spending control; created new deficit controls based on variable deficit targets extended through fiscal 1995; established caps on discretionary spending and the "pay-as-you-go" rule (deficit neutral) for revenues and direct spending; and revised sequestration procedures (mini-sequesters)
1992	Multiple versions of balanced budget amendments proposed but fail to pass Congress
1993	President Clinton's deficit reduction package increased the marginal tax rate for high-income earners
1993	OMB revised its 1984 circular A-127, "Financial Management Systems," and required that each agency create a single, integrated system of financial management
1993	National Performance Review (NPR) included budgetary and financial management recommendations, including increased managerial discretion (e.g., lapses, staffing ceilings, restrictive itemization) and biennial budget cycle
1993	Executive Order 12839 instructed agencies to cut employment by 5% or about 100,000 employees from 1993 to 1995
1993	Government Performance and Results Act of 1993 (GPRA; P.L. 103-62). On an eight-year implementation schedule, required federal agencies to set annual performance targets; OMB to submit government-wide performance plan budget beginning for fiscal 1999
1993–1994	President Clinton adjusted maximum deficit amount under BEA when budget submitted
1994	In his budget message for fiscal 1995, President Clinton claimed cuts in approximately 340 discretionary programs in 1994 and proposed cuts in approximately 300 nondefense programs, including termination of more than 100 programs
1994	Federal Acquisition Streamlining Act updated and simplified procurement procedures
1994	*Contract with America* signed by 376 Republican candidates, including many congressional candidates; with accent on accountability and reduced governmental role, proposals encompassed independent, comprehensive audit of Congress; supermajority for passing tax increases; zero-baseline budgeting; balanced budget and tax limit amendment; line-item veto; regulatory reform including use of risk assessment and cost-benefit analysis; and unfunded mandate reform
1994	OMB's circular A-34, "Instructions on Budget Execution," revised to account for changes in laws and practices since last major revision in 1985
1994	OMB's circular A-ll, "Preparation and Submission of Budget Estimates," revised to account for Government Performance and Results Act of 1993
1995	Line-item veto and balanced budget amendment again defeated
1995	Unfunded Mandates Reform Act (P.L. 104-4). With emphasis on disclosure and accountability, required that CBO provide cost estimates to authorizing committee for government mandates over $50 million threshold ($100 million for private sector mandates), excluding categories such as constitutionally guaranteed civil rights; created point of order against considering a bill without CBO's cost estimate and against unfunded mandate with aggregate cost in excess of threshold; in effect, Congress must go on record as endorsing the mandate
1995	Under federal legislation, a financial oversight entity (control board) is established for Washington, DC
1995	OMB issued final revisions to circular A-87, "Cost Principles for States, Local and Tribal Governments," thereby setting costing standards for grants, reimbursements, and contracts
1995	Bills introduced to require use of risk assessment and cost-benefit analysis in federal agencies enlivened but left unsettled methodological issues in budgeting and policy making
1995	Moratorium on regulatory rule making passed House and Senate
1995	Congress moved to terminate as entitlements and devolve program responsibility to states Aid to Families with Dependent Children, food stamps, and Medicaid by approving dollar caps on block grants to states
1995	Debt ceiling held hostage (at $4.9 trillion) in budget standoff between president and Congress; federal agencies closed and 800,000 "nonessential" employees temporarily furloughed in November
1995	More than one-half of states' budgets use effectiveness and/or productivity measures
1996	On July 18, House of Representatives passes (by vote of 256 to 170) its budget reconciliation package, H.R. 3734, containing a modified version of the Personal Responsibility and Work Opportunity Act of 1996, H.R. 3507. The Personal Responsibility and Work Opportunity Reconciliation Act of 1996 (PRWORA) (Pub. L. 104-193), as amended, is the welfare reform law that established the Temporary Assistance for Needy Families (TANF) program. TANF is a block grant program designed to make dramatic reforms to the welfare system by moving recipients into work and turning welfare into a program of temporary assistance. TANF replaced the national welfare program known as Aid to Families with Dependent Children (AFDC) and the related programs known as the Job Opportunities and Basic Skills Training (JOBS) program and the Emergency Assistance (EA) program

(Continued)

TABLE 5.1   *(Continued)*

From the Constitution through World War II

1996	Line Item Veto Act of 1996 (P.L. 104-130) authorized the president to cancel discretionary budget authority, new entitlements, and limited tax benefits
1997	The Budget Enforcement Act of 1997 (BEA of 1997) required OMB to issue an end-of-session report after Congress adjourns *sine die* to determine whether or not a sequester is required
1997	Government Performance and Results Act requires federal agencies to prepare strategic plans starting with fiscal year 1997
1998	In *Clinton v. City of New York*, 524 U.S. 417 (1998), the US Supreme Court declared the Line Item Veto Act of 1996 in violation of Article I, Section 7, Clause 2 of the Constitution
1998	The first surplus since 1969 is reported for federal budget reported under Franklin D. Raines, OMB Director under President Clinton
1999	Government Performance and Results Act requires federal agencies to prepare annual performance plans starting with fiscal year 1999
The Twenty-First Century	
2000	Government Performance and Results Act requires federal agencies to submit to the President and Congress an annual program performance report comparing actual performance with their plans beginning in fiscal year 2000
2001	Economy entered official recession in March
2001	On September 11, four hijacked airplanes are used in an attack of international terrorism at World Trade Center, the Pentagon and Shankesville, Pennsalvania; immediate budgetary ramifications include federal aid to New York City, rebuilding the Pentagon, $40 billion aid to airlines and insurance bailouts, and economic loss to New York City and the travel, tourist and other industries
2001	Three days after the attack, Congress, at request of President Bush, votes $40 billion in emergency funds
2001	Tax cuts enacted in 2001 reduced individual income taxes as a share of GDP from an all-time high
2001	When Enron collapsed and is declared bankrupt in December, it had about $5 billion in outstanding "prepays" that were virtually unknown to the company's creditors, investors and business associates; report of Senate Governmental Affairs Committee's Permanent Subcommittee on Investigations found that the board had failed in its fiduciary duty to protect Enron shareholders and that it shares responsibility for Enron's deceptions and its bankruptcy
2002	Texas jury finds the audit firm of Arthur Andersen guilty of obstruction of justice for destroying documents during Security and Exchange Commission's investigation of Enron
2002	Sarbanes-Oxley Act is signed into law in July in response to numerous accounting scandals that led to bankruptcy filings of Enron, WorldCom and Global Crossing; corporate responsibility legislation provides tougher penalties for fraud and holds executives personally responsible for their corporate financial statements
2002	Overall discretionary spending caps expired on September 30 and the pay-as-you-go (PAYGO) requirement expired at year's end
2002	A majority of the states face budget shortfalls
2002	In March, the White House promoted proposed pension changes and partial privatization of Social Security as part of an overhaul of retirement financing
2002	On November 25, President Bush signed the "Homeland Security Act of 2002" that restructures the executive branch to meet the threat posed by terrorism by creating the cabinet-level Department of Homeland Security
2002	Budget Enforcement Act (BEA) expired on September 30 and the pay-as-you-go (PAYGO) requirement expired at the end of the year
2002	The budget deficit in FY 2002 is the first since 1998
2004	In a 7-2 decision in *Tennessee Student Assistance Corp. v. Hood*, the Supreme Court affirmed the decision of the US Court of Appeals for the Sixth Circuit and held that an adversary proceeding filed against a state entity was not barred by the doctrine of sovereign immunity
2004	OMB revised Circular A-11
2004	The GAO Human Capital Reform Act of 2004, Pub. L. 108-271, 118 Stat. 811 (2004), changed the GAO's legal name to the Government Accountability Office, decoupled GAO employees from the federal employee pay system and established a performance-based compensation system

parameters that practically and significantly affect the field; those publications that epitomize orthodox doctrine and traditional practices, including model legislation and authoritative statements defining professional standards; publications representing innovations in thought or practice that have been particularly influential intellectually or historically; and frequency of reference—the "classics."* These criteria of selection allow that a particular choice of inclusion or omission be mistaken, but not capricious or arbitrary.

B. CONTEXT

1. Public Administration

American budgeting and financial management have developed in tandem with the broader field of public administration. The context of the American administrative system is the combined legacy of Western political thought and a historically dynamic but stable system, the contours of which we bend to fit the times. We have adopted, adapted, rejected, and revised our interpretation of our history and experiences as we respond and adjust to change and integrate it into our polity and thinking. War, macroeconomic changes such as depression and global interdependencies, ideas such as scientific management and professional ideals, demographic change generating political and administrative demands, and technological advances from the telephone to computers—reflected in heightened administrative and analytical capacity (and speed!)—have spurred modifications in the system and in budget theory and practice.

2. Dynamism and Stability

Despite the importance—and drama—of change, an accurate portrayal also stresses those threads of continuity that tie the system and the field together over time and across the continent. Control is a significant concern that warrants separate treatment in some detail; so too is our developing understanding of the way in which decisions are made and a changing administrative and technological capacity. Yet another theme and, in this author's view, the core of the American budgetary system, is continued reliance on a governmental structure built on democratic principles, a federal republic, checks and balances, and separation of powers. Consequently and notwithstanding the fact that it predates the emergence of the modern administrative era emphasized in this chapter, we turn initially to the US Constitution. As the central thematic, historical, and legal document of the system, it is a logical beginning to the history that appropriately serves as the backdrop to our current and still evolving system.

II. HISTORICAL ANTECEDENTS

A. U.S. CONSTITUTION

1. Hamiltonian Perspective

The US Constitution is an experiment that emerged from the inadequacies of the Articles of Confederation. Arguing on behalf of ratification by states in 1789, Alexander Hamilton explained his view of the budget issue and the Confederation's lack of centralized resources and powers in *The Federalist Papers*. This source is a series of essays crucial to an understanding of the intent behind the Constitution and the political system based on it (Mosher 1976, 10; Rossiter 1961). Hamilton phrased the issue elegantly:

> Money is, with propriety, considered as the vital principle of the body politic; as that which sustains its life and motion and enables it to perform its most essential functions. A complete power, therefore, to procure a regular and adequate supply of revenue, as far as the resources of the community will permit, may be regarded as an indispensable ingredient in every constitution. From a deficiency in this particular, one of two evils must ensue; either the people must be

---

* Several collections of the literature of public administration in general and public budgeting in particular are available, including Hyde and Shafritz (1978), Hyde (1992), Mosher (1976), Sharfritz and Hyde (1978, 1987), and Schick (1987).

subjected to continual plunder, as a substitute for a more eligible mode of supplying the public wants, or the government must sink into a fatal atrophy, and, in a short course of time, perish (*Federalist* No. 30).

Hamilton, later to become the first Secretary of the Treasury, further contributed the cogent observation that "in political arithmetic, two and two do not always make four" (*Federalist* No. 21).[*]

The American version of the colonial legacy, with conflict between the Crown and Parliament dating at least to the Magna Carta, developed in terms of the institutions and processes represented by and created through the Constitution. The machinery of government is built on checks and balances and separation of powers, and it is within the context of jealously guarded constitutional powers that executive–legislative prerogatives are played out. This theme endures and dominates: "The fundamental struggle over the budget is thus between the president and the Congress. The politics of the budget are dominated by the saga of that struggle" (Shuman 1984, 16).[†]

2.   Article I and Amendments

Initially, budget and governmental economic powers rested wholly with Congress, which still retains the constitutional power to authorize spending through appropriations. Budgetary powers are enumerated in the Constitution as follows:

- Article I, Sec. 7:

  All Bills for raising Revenue shall originate in the House of Representatives; but the Senate may propose or concur with Amendments as in other Bills...

- Article I, Sec. 8:

  The Congress shall have the Power to lay and collect Taxes, Duties, Imports and Excise, to pay the Debts and provide for the common Defense and general Welfare of the United States; but all Duties, Imports and Excises shall be uniform throughout the United States;
  To borrow Money on the credit of the United States;

  To regulate Commerce with foreign Nations, and among the several States, and with the Indian Tribes;

  To establish an uniform Rule of Naturalization, and uniform Laws on the subject of Bankruptcies throughout the United States;

  To coin Money, regulate the Value thereof, and of foreign Coin, and fix the Standard of Weights and Measures;...

  To raise and support Armies, but no Appropriation of Money to that Use shall be for a longer Term than two Years;....

  To make all Laws which shall be necessary and proper for carrying into Execution the foregoing Powers, and all other Powers vested by this Constitution in the Government of the United States, or in any Department or Officer thereof.

---

[*] Before ascribing excessive authority to authoritative pronouncements, it may be worthwhile to note Hamilton's preference for indirect taxation, especially duties, excises, and taxes on consumption, expressed in *Federalist* No. 12, and his prediction in No. 21 that indirect taxes "must always constitute the chief part of the revenue in this country."

[†] Major budget reforms of 1921, 1974, 1985, and 1990, discussed in detail in this chapter, illustrate the continuing importance of executive–legislative relations and constitutional authority in the development of American budgeting and financial management.

- Article I, Sec. 9:

  … No Capitation, or other direct, Tax shall be laid, unless in Proportion to the Census or Enumeration herein before directed to be taken. [See Sixteenth Amendment.]
  No Tax or Duty shall be laid on Articles exported from any State….

  No Money shall be drawn from the Treasury, but in Consequence of Appropriations made by Law; and a regular Statement and Account of the Receipts and Expenditures of all public Money shall be published from time to time….

- Amendment XIV, Sec. 4:

  The validity of the public debt of the United States, authorized by law, including debts incurred for payment of pensions and bounties for services in suppressing insurrection or rebellion, shall not be questioned…[1868]

- Amendment XVI:

  The Congress shall have power to lay and collect taxes on incomes, from whatever source derived, without apportionment among the several States, and without regard to any census or enumeration. [1913]

3. Treasury Department

One of the first steps under the new governmental arrangements was An Act to Establish the Treasury Department (1 Stat. 12 [1789]).[*] This created the rudimentary model or "basic elements of the federal financial system" (Mosher 1976, 8). The act also clearly articulated that system's emphasis on control by establishing mechanisms that are, in principle, still relied on today, including the specific and detailed division of responsibilities among the Secretary of the Treasury, Comptroller, Auditor, Treasurer, Register, and Assistant to the Secretary; countersigning by the Comptroller of warrants drawn by the Secretary; a requirement that the Treasurer report to every session of Congress "a true and perfect account of the state of the Treasury"; and a prohibition of "conflict of interest" in Sec. 8, which states that "no person appointed to any office instituted by this act shall directly or indirectly be concerned or interested in carrying on the business of trade or commerce." It was through his office as Secretary of the Treasury that Hamilton devised the strategy to manage the federal debt, which the Revolutionary War had pushed to over $70 million by 1790 (Swan, in Rabin and Lynch 1983, 12); current observers can empathize with the problem, if not with the dollar figure.

By the end of the eighteenth century, therefore, some of the institutions and concerns that continue to play a vital role in the contemporary era were already in place. Congress temporarily established a Ways and Means Committee in 1796; it was to become permanent in 1802 (Smithies 1955, 51). The new Treasury Department was destined to become, over one and one-third centuries later, the first home of the new Bureau of the Budget. Annual appropriation acts under Secretary Hamilton amounted to a few lump-sum appropriations, with one appropriation covering Treasury warrants, another the civil list, a third the Department of War, and a fourth other expenditures in 1791–1794 (Smithies 1955, 50). But from 1795 on, the new machinery turned as it would during the next century; in another important respect, Congress exercised its constitutional powers and guarded against executive excess by voting detailed and usually nontransferable appropriations.

B. Legislative Budgeting of the Nineteenth Century

1. Imposition of Subnational Debt Limits

For some, a historical perspective may serve to blend and smooth events into of little more than an even flow time disturbed only by great events such as civil war. Nonetheless, the nineteenth century

---

[*] Basic documents in public budgeting are available in several collections, including Mosher (1976) and Stillman (1982).

was an era of change and turmoil, of the frontier, urban growth and squalor, labor unrest, and partisan excess, corruption, and bossism. It was punctuated by significant developments in public financial arrangements (see Table 5.1), such as the state financing of major public works that ultimately led to debt limits.

> In the 1820s, a great drive was undertaken to provide internal improvements for the expansion of the economic infrastructure of the states by providing financial institution and transportation links.... States actively borrowed to finance canals, banks, railroads, roads, and other ventures.... Debts began to grow very rapidly.... In theory, the borrowings were to be repaid from income derived on the investments rather than from tax levies. The building boom, however, led to gross overinvestment in projects, and outright fraud was common.... The borrowing bubble burst in the panic of 1837.... To avoid future excesses, soothe taxpayer frustrations, and restore investor confidence in their bonds, constitutional limits on debt were imposed at the state level.... Such impediments to borrowing still exist (Bennett and DiLorenzo 1983, 13–15).

The pattern was repeated during the post-Civil War era by local governments, for which indebtedness climbed from $151 million in 1860 to $900 million by 1890 (Friedman 1985, 528). The result was that states then moved to clamp restrictions on local borrowing (Moak and Hillhouse 1975, 262). These developments affecting state and local finances were all the more important because of these governments' role in the system; measured by both number of employees and percentage of government spending, they dominated the US system during this period.

2. Congressional Domination of Federal Budgeting

At the federal level, "during the nineteenth century, except for short period of war, Congress dominated the American government and its budget and budget procedures" (Shuman 1984, 17–18). That domination was exercised throughout the nineteenth century by the use of detailed appropriations, largely nontransferable among accounts. Furthermore, until after World War I, all of this operated against the background of a system in which agencies prepared their estimates and transmitted them through the Treasury Department to Congress; with the president bypassed, there was no overall governmental plan. In the words of one authority on the subject, "It is important to note that from 1789 to 1884 the Congress in legislation was primarily concerned with the legality of expenditures rather than with an understandable record of what was bought with the money spent" (Smithies 1955, 63). Thus it developed that "when the Congress wishes to assert its authority over the Executive, it returns to restrictions on the use of appropriations with unvarying monotony" (Smithies 1955, 49).

3. Appropriations Process

While legislative–executive tensions, moves, and countermoves tell some of the story, much was going on within Congress, the dominant branch, that spoke of continuing adjustments in budgetary procedures and powers. The two-step, authorization–appropriation process began in the House of Representatives in 1837, and in 1850 in the Senate (Shuman 1984, 57); separate appropriations committees were established, first in the House in 1865 and in the Senate two years later (although authority over important appropriations would go to substantive committees 20 years later). Jurisdiction over credit issues shifted from the Ways and Means Committee to the Banking and Currency Committee in 1865. This period is marked, too, by some of the notorious budgetary practices that are familiar to contemporary observers of the Potomac scene, such as the handling of substantive matters in financial bills. For example, in response to the abuses associated with the Grant administration, Congress established the first Civil Service Commission as a rider to an appropriations bill in 1871.

For a synoptic description of the nineteenth-century appropriations process that proceeded without an overall plan or executive orchestration, we turn to the 1912 Report of the

Taft Commission, according to which:

> in the United States the Book of Estimates, our nearest approach to a budget, is rather a more or less well-digested mass of information submitted by agents of the Legislature to the Legislature for the consideration of legislative committees to enable the Legislature both to originate and to determine the policy which is to be carried out by the Executive during the budgetary period.

These, then, are the terms on which we meet the modern era of budgeting and financial management.

III. THE EMERGENCE OF THE MODERN ERA

A. CONTINUITY AND DISJUNCTURE

1. Changing Role of Government

The modern era in American budgeting and financial management is characterized by several significant changes which reflect developments in the larger polity. Perhaps foremost among these is the changing role of government itself. In the twentieth century, the public sector has been subjected to systemic pressures, such as the severe economic dislocation and political threat of the Great Depression, global wars, and civil unrest in an interdependent urban society. The response, broadly defined, has been a shift from a relatively minor, sometimes even residual forum to an integral part of the socioeconomic system. The patterns of growth and change can be succinctly summarized by the fact that, whereas total government expenditures accounted for one-tenth of the nation's gross national product in 1929, that percentage has increased to the point at which, over one-half century later, total government spending amounts to approximately one-third of the country's economic activity.[*]

The broad pattern of growth masks or ignores other significant trends, not least of which is the turnabout in the relative weights of the various governmental levels that constitute the federal system. The national level came to dominate the system in terms of spending. Whereas employment has been relatively stable in percentage terms, with local governments accounting for approximately three-fifths of civilian government employees over the last half century, local governments fell from first to last among the three predominant governmental levels in terms of own-source expenditures. The financial dependency implied by this change is underscored by the importance of intergovernmental transfers and aid programs. One study pinpoints intergovernmental constraints and "fiscal atrophy" as among the dominant features of municipal budgeting (Friedman 1980); similarly, but in different language, another source identifies poverty and certainty as the two features of municipal budgeting (Wildavsky 1975, 114–135). Speaking directly to the continued salience of these same trends, attention shifted from an emphasis on retrenchment in the early years of the 1980s (Burchell and Listokin 1981; Carr 1984; Clark and Ferguson 1983; Levine 1980; Levine et al. 1981; Rubin 1979) to studies of the impact of changes in federal policies and funding (Nathan 1983; Palmer and Sawhill 1982).[†] More conflict, new rules, and probably different winners were forecast (Caiden 1981) and subsequent developments bore out these predictions (Gold 1995b;

---

[*] The patterns of growth and change are summarized in the statistics available in indispensable periodical statistical sources such as the compendia of federal, state, and local financial data from the Bureau of the Census of the US Department of Commerce.

[†] Demographic change (Peterson 1976), tax policy (Samuelson 1969; Tiebout 1956), and variations in expenditures related to political culture (Morris 1980; Wilson and Banfield 1958) or government structure (Lineberry and Fowler, 1967), as well as routine political and administrative decision making (Crecine 1969; Levy et al. 1974; Lineberry 1977; Meltsner 1971; and, with respect to the states, Bingham et al. 1978, 193–211; Sharkansky 1970, 13) are also among the independent variables associated with changes in subnational and especially municipal finance. For studies of the impact of intergovernmental transfers and policies (e.g., state constraints), see reference citations including Aronson and Hilley (1986); Bahl (1981); Bingham et al. (1978, 55–70); CBO (1983), Friedman (1980); Gold (1995b); Sbragia (1983), and Walker (1995).

Walker 1995). Practitioner and scholarly studies of state and local budgeting encompass procedural variations, federal aid, political and socioeconomic variables, state policies, mandates and other legal constraints, fiscal stress, the effects of recession, and more.[*]

2. Shifts in Federal Budgeting

As the federal level of government has come to dominate governmental budgeting (measured in standard terms as percentage of total government spending), the executive has come to dominate the federal process. In point of fact, the move to executive budgeting characterizes budgeting at all levels of government in the modem era; for example, Ohio adopted executive budgeting a decade before Washington. Illustrating the importance of a systemic perspective, the impetus behind executive budgeting can frequently be traced to the municipal reform agenda of the Progressive Era, as well as to the developing sophistication of public administration and administrative capacity. Nonetheless, the shift at the federal level is vitally important to an understanding of the literature and history of the field.

The modern era in public administration was ushered in, according to academic consensus, by the publication in 1887 of Woodrow Wilson's article "The Study of Administration" (Wilson 1887). While it is important to note that the budget function was not specifically discussed, Wilson's remarks on public opinion and his conclusions that "principles on which to base a science of administration for America must be principles which have democratic policy very much at heart," and that "our duty is to supply the best possible life to a *federal* organization, to systems within systems," underscore the continuities (such as constitutionalism, federalism, accountability and control) that connect the modern administrative era with its predecessor. (It is ironic that later, as president, Woodrow Wilson would veto an early version of what can be described without hyperbole as one of the major reforms and documents in US history, the Budget and Accounting Act of 1921.)

B. To Executive Budgeting in Slow Motion

1. Municipal Sources of Executive Budgeting

Public budgeting and financial management in the twentieth century is largely a story of executive–legislative relations, efforts to control government spending and curb corruption and abuse, intergovernmental relations, and changing ideas and technology in administration. These all came together in the early years of the century in the move toward executive budgeting and other governmental reforms. One important source of reform, the National Municipal League, a nongovernmental organization with the explicit purpose of governmental reform, was organized in the decade that saw publication of Wilson's article. The league's second Model City Charter of 1916 called for strict separation between policy (council) and administration (city manager) and an executive budget, to wit, from Section 36 of the Annual Budget:

> The city manager shall prepare and submit to the council the annual budget after receiving estimates made by the directors of the departments [Sec. 37 creates six administrative departments, one of which is finance; Sec. 51 calls for uniform classification] (Mosher 1976, 82–89).

---

[*] Among the innumerable sources on state practices and problems are the publications listed in Table 5.2; the US Advisory Commission on Intergovernmental Relations (defunct for about a decade); National Association of State Budget Officers; National Conference of State Legislatures; Cranford 1992; Eckl et al. 1993; GAO 1992b, 1993a, 1993b; Gold 1995a, 1995b; Gold and McCormick 1994; Lee 1991; Mackey 1993; Public Budgeting and Financial Management 1993; Snell 1993; Thompson 1993; and Walker 1995. In a highly selective listing of the extensive literature on municipal budgeting, see publications of the Government Finance Officers Association, International City/County Association; specialized journals such as *Urban Affairs Quarterly* and *Municipal Finance*; Bland and Nunn 1992; Botner 1989; Cope 1992; Dearborn et al. 1992; Forrester and Mullins 1992; Glick 1986; Gold and Ritchie 1994; Kantor and David 1992; Lewis 1994; MacManus et al. 1989; O'Toole and Marshall 1987; Rubin 1993; and Strachota 1994.

New York City's Bureau of Municipal Research, probably the best known of its type, was originally founded in 1906 under articles of incorporation that explicitly defined its values as efficient and economic government; these values, along with standardization and "professionaliza-tion," like the reforms that were to ensure their vitality, came to dominate the ensuing period in public administration. Perhaps the new catechism was most evident in the push toward reform in public budgeting and financial management, in the research, training, and practice of which the bureau had a determining influence (Dahlberg 1966).[*]

2. Taft Commission

While the idea of a single, comprehensive budget plan routinely and uniformly formulated by the executive and submitted for legislative review and appropriation emerged primarily from the urban arena—this was the muckracker's era of scandal, corruption, excesses, and abuses—the idea readily took root at the other government levels. President Taft established the Commission on Economy and Efficiency in 1910, and the 1912 report of the Taft Commission broke with the precedent of four congressional committees examining administrative issues between the Civil War and the turn of the century. It "endorsed the concept of Presidential responsibility for administration" (Mosher 1976, 49), a budget bureau reporting to the president along with staff and an executive budget, and uniform, object classification in all federal departments.[†] The 1912 report of the Taft Commission redefined the budget and its purpose in these words:

> As used in this report the budget is considered as a proposal to be prepared by the administration and submitted to the legislature. The use of a budget would require that there be a complete reversal of procedure by the Government—that the executive branch submit a statement to the Legislature which would be its account of stewardship as well as its proposals for the future. A national budget thus prepared and presented would serve the purposes of a prospectus. Its aim would be to present in summary form the facts necessary to shape the policy of the Government as well as to provide financial support.

Despite the congressional failure to immediately embrace the commission's recommendations, President Taft attempted to act on the new ideas. In 1911, he distributed centralized forms to department heads for reclassifying the data in estimate preparation. He even went so far as to submit an executive-type budget to Congress, which responded by referring it to the Appropriations Committee, "and there it lay without consideration, action, or report" (Cleveland 1915, 28).

3. Apportionment

The Taft Commission's report was not issued in isolation, but in a context supported by several other significant events of the period. The Antideficiency Act of 1906 (34 Stat. L. 40) pointed to the continuing interest in and recognized need for planning and control in budgeting and financial management. In a major departure from past practice, it provided for apportionment to combat the

---

[*] An early and influential text—cited in V. O. Key, Jr.'s 1940 article, for example—on public budgeting was written by a bureau staff member, A. E. Buck (1929).

[†] The members of the first comprehensive commission on national budgeting in the United States are a list of luminaries in the field and include Frederick A. Cleveland, commission chairman and director of the Bureau of Municipal Research; Frank J. Goodnow, a professor of administrative law at Columbia University who went on to the presidency of Johns Hopkins University; William F. Willoughby, whose varied career in government service ultimately saw him as consti-tutional advisor to the ill-fated Chinese Republic; Walter W. Warwick; and Merritt O. Chance. In light of the administration-versus-politics debate that was to mark the developmental phase of public administration as a field of inquiry, it is worthwhile noting that Woodrow Wilson, Frank Goodnow, W. F. Willoughby, Charles Merriam, Charles Beard, and Luther Gulick contributed to the practice and literature of public budgeting and became presidents of the American Political Science Association as well.

use of deficiency appropriations. According to the Act, appropriations "shall... be so apportioned by monthly or other allotments as to prevent expenditures in one portion of the year which may necessitate deficiency or additional appropriations ..." (in Smithies 1955, 56–57).[*]

4. Initial Steps toward Delegating Authority

The first congressional delegation of considerable power over the federal budget and national economy occurred in 1913, when Congress passed the Federal Reserve Act. Congress delegated power not to the president but to a regulatory agency and thereby established a "quasiprivate, quasipublic institution which the Federal Reserve Act made independent of the president but an agent of Congress" (Shuman 1984, 18). Yet another example is the passage of the two Liberty Bond Acts (1917), which gave the Treasury Department authority to pay debts and borrow money on the credit of the United States to a specified amount or "debt ceiling"; amendments to the second Liberty Bond Act of 1917 are still used to increase the debt limit. These congressional acts began the overall pattern that is to be identified as a hallmark of modern budgeting, that is

> In the twentieth century there has been a steady delegation by Congress of its power over the budget to the president. This has ordinarily not been the result of conspiracy or usurpation but of deliberate delegation, atrophy, or shunning of power by Congress (Shuman 1984, 17–18).

What, then, are the reasons? In the words of one answer, "Each act and each, transfer of power was preceded by economic problems, panics, wars, depression, or constitutional crisis" (Shuman 1984, 20). In sum, external or environmental factors press in on the system and force adaptive responses.

5. Influence of Public Administration

The development and refinement of innovative ideas were—and are—an important part of that environment. Frederick W. Taylor gave testimony on "scientific management" before the US House of Representatives on January 25, 1912. A few years later, in 1915, the American Academy of Political and Social Science published a landmark volume entitled *Public Budgets*. It contributed a coherent statement by leading academics and practitioners in support of an analytical, systematic, executive approach to budgeting; its scope is national (California, Massachusetts, New York, Illinois, Cleveland, New York City, Chicago) and comparative (Germany, France, England), and its list of authors and represented organizations reads like a 'who's who' in the new field of public administration; it includes Frederick A. Cleveland, chairman of the 1912 Taft Commission and director of the Bureau of Municipal Research, Charles A. Beard, the Columbia University professor, and the renowned University of Chicago professor and member of Chicago's city council, Charles E. Merriam.

In "Evolution of the Budget Idea in the United States," one of the foremost classics in the field, Cleveland discusses the Taft Commission, his ideas on administration, and the executive budget. In words with a contemporary ring, he describes a budget as "a plan for financing an enterprise or government during a definite period, which is prepared and submitted by a responsible executive to a representative body (or other duly constituted agent) whose approval and authorization are necessary before the plan may be executed" (Cleveland 1915, 15). He further clarifies what he means by a budget as a "plan of financing": Every year in every jurisdiction we have had "estimates" of both revenues and expenditures. But estimates in themselves do not constitute a budget.

---

[*] Apportionment, a recognized, standard building block of preaudit financial controls, became the responsibility of the Bureau of the Budget in 1933. On apportionment, see Fisher (1975, 38–40) and GAO's glossary (1981, 34).

They only serve the purpose of laying the foundation for work plans and financial plans (Cleveland 1915, 16).

Another contribution in that same volume is Rider's partially annotated, selective bibliography, which combines "the most important material" from academic and practitioner sources (Rider 1915, 277–287). Its references describe a field already taking shape, and include the *American Political Science Review*, which would remain a preeminent journal in the field (as would the *Journal of Accountancy*, responsible for many citations in Rider's bibliography); and contributions by members of the Taft Commission. Over the ensuing years, the leading circle of thinkers, writers, and doers would broaden, additional works would be added to the list of acknowledged classics in the literature, and the pace of publication would pick up, but these were to remain names recognized and admired by students, practitioners, and scholars for three-quarters of a century and still counting.

And the pace of publication did pick up. A straight count of published articles is surely a gross, oversimplified, and fully non-qualitative tool, but it does provide a sense of the quantity and timing of publications. One index of journal articles published from 1886 to 1974 shows only a little more than one-fifth of all the articles concerning budgeting[*] cited as published in the first five decades (1886–1935) and almost four-fifths as published in the next 38 years (1936–1974). Moreover, over two-thirds of the citations are dated in the postwar period, 1946 to 1974. A total of 218 sources are noted for 1886 to 1974 (Wile 1978). Another index (and because of different coverage and citation methods that general different results on counts, not comparable with the first) shows a total of 476 articles published from 1975 to 1985, meaning that this decade alone witnessed a minimum annual average of forty-three journal additions to the literature and the field (see Table 5.2.)

C. THE 1921 REFORM

The report of the Taft Commission and several other important events and publications of this period built to a crescendo within a few years. What resulted is second only to the US Constitution in importance to contemporary public budgeting at the federal level (even considering subsequent acts and modifications), and is usually awarded a singular place in US administrative history. After Woodrow Wilson's earlier veto on constitutional grounds,[†] Congress passed and President Harding signed the Budget and Accounting Act of 1921 (42 Stat. 18). Authoritative documents emanating from the institutions founded by the act stress its importance.

The budget system of the Federal Government rests on the Budget and Accounting Act, approved June 10, 1921. This act is a milestone on the road to effective public management in the United States. As the foundation of budgetary planning and control, the act not only fostered responsible determination of the Government's financial needs, but also committed the executive branch to a higher standard of administration in all its activities.

"For the accomplishment of both ends, full responsibility was vested in the President. What is more, he was also equipped to discharge this responsibility" (OMB/BOB 1958, 1). "The basic purposes of this act were to provide for an independent review of executive expenditures and to fill the need for a national budget system" (General Accounting Office (GAO, now Government Accountability Office) 1965, 1-1).

---

[*] Citations are limited to those in categories budget, budgetary, budgeting, budgets, and bureau of budgets to minimize double counting of entries under multiple categories.

[†] Wilson's objection about the power to remove the comptroller general would arise again 65 years later in litigation over the constitutionality of provisions of the Balanced Budget and Emergency Deficit Control Act of 1985, popularly referred to under the name of its sponsors, Gramm-Rudman-Hollings.

TABLE 5.2
Selected Contemporary Periodicals

American Political Science Review
The Public Manager
Congressional Quarterly
Governmental Finance Review
Journal of Public Budgeting, Accounting and Financial Management
Municipal Finance Journal
National Journal
National Tax Journal
Public Administration Quarterly
Public Administration Review
Public Budgeting & Finance

1. New Institutions

The Act established the Bureau of the Budget (BOB), a new staff office in the Treasury Department, which would develop into one of the true centers of power in the government in Washington.[*] The staff and informational base of the budget function was extended dramatically (see Figure 5.1). The act required that a budget officer be appointed in each department; that BOB have access to departmental information, records, and books; and that BOB be obligated to respond to requests for information from congressional revenue and appropriations committees. According to Sec. 207,

> The Bureau, under such rules and regulations as the President may prescribe, shall prepare for him the Budget, the alternative Budget, and any supplemental or deficiency estimates, and to this end shall have authority to assemble, correlate, revise, reduce, or increase the estimates of the several departments or establishments.

Counterbalancing the newly authorized staff capacity for the executive branch, the same act created a new congressional office that was "independent of the executive departments" (Sec. 301) and responsible for oversight (audit) functions. Title III established the Government Accountability Office (GAO), headed by the comptroller general, who was appointed by the president with Congress's advice and consent for a single, fixed term of 15 years and subject to removal only by joint resolution of Congress. (The comptroller was thereby removed from Treasury, where it had been since 1789.) The GAO was to perform basic audit functions (e.g., certify balances), and the comptroller general, in the language of Sec. 309, was to "prescribe forms, systems, and procedures for administrative appropriation and fund accounting in the several departments and establishments, and for the administrative examination of fiscal officers' account and claims against the United States." According to the GAO,

> The authority and responsibility of the General Accounting Office for making audits and investigations of Government agencies are stated in a number of laws. The Budget and Accounting Act, 1921, which created the General Accounting Office, vested in it all the powers and duties of the six auditors and the

---

[*] The BOB was transferred to the Executive Office of the President in 1939 and renamed the Office of Management and Budget in 1970. For a history of this agency, see Berman (1979), Congressional Research Service (CRS, 1986), LeLoup (1986, 95–119); Mosher (1984), and BOB's 1958 staff orientation manual (now OMB). For one person's view of the agency and its director's contemporary impact, see Stockman (1986); another personal history is told in McOmber (1981, 78–84); and for a collection of perspectives from numerous sources, see Schick (1980, 134–192).

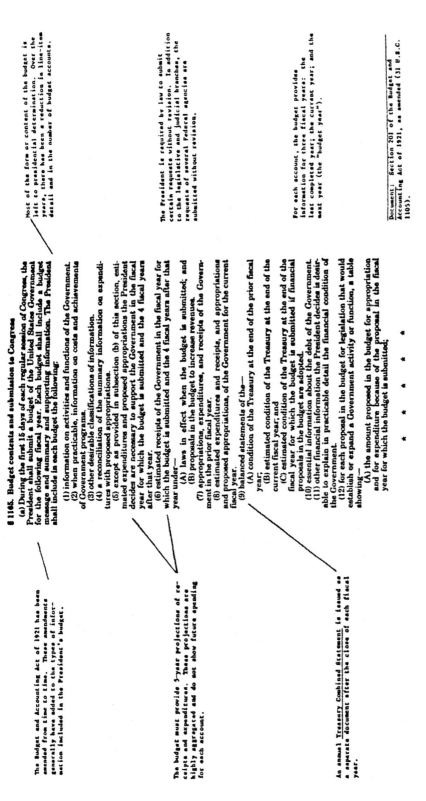

FIGURE 5.1 The Budget and Accounting Act of 1921. (From Schick, A. and Keith R., *Manual on the Federal Budget Process*, Congressional Research Service, Library of Congress, Washington, DC, 23, 1982.)

Comptroller of the Treasury as stated in the Dockery Act of July 31, 1894, and other statutes extending back to the original Treasury Act of September 2, 1789, as well as new duties. Since the passage of the organic act creating the General Accounting Office under the control and direction of the Comptroller General of the United States, the scope of its activities has been widened through subsequent legislation (including the Budget and Auditing Act of 1950, clarifying existing audit authority in Sec. 117[a]) (General Accounting Office 1965 revised, 1-1).

2. Institutional Issues

These arrangements for enhanced, executive staff capacity and congressional oversight made eminently good sense in light of the increasing scope and complexity of the government and the increasing budget numbers reflecting that development. Executive budgeting, with its centralized procedures, technical analyses, coordinated timetables, and consolidated figures, depends on central staff, just as the growth in staff awaited executive decision making in a complex environment. The two go hand in hand. Development of administrative capacity is so influential that it is identified as one of the basic elements useful for delineating budget systems or patterns (Caiden 1978).

The creation of the BOB and GAO also institutionalized one of the important sources of continuing tension between professionalism and expertise on the one hand and political accountability and responsiveness on the other, a tension that is probably inherent in the modern system and that speaks to the intimate connection between the budget function and public administration more generally. As expressed by a senior budget official, "It is the president's budget.... To have been steeped in this philosophy from the beginning of our institutional lives—to always be conscious of that 'office across the street'—is the paramount factor of our working lives" (McOmber 1981, 79). The excerpt from Office of Management and Budget 1994, illustrates that the tension generates important 'rules of the game' in contemporary budgeting (see Figure 5.2).

3. Executive Budgeting—Title II

The BOB and GAO were the institutional components of a historical turnaround in the federal budget process—from legislative budgeting to authorization of an executive budget under the aegis of the president, as enacted in Title II—The Budget:

- Section 201:

  The President shall transmit to Congress on the first day of each regular session, the Budget, which shall set forth in summary and in detail:
  (a) Estimates of the expenditures and appropriations necessary in his judgment for the support of the Government for the ensuing fiscal year...;
  (b) His estimates of the receipts of the Government...;
  (c) The amount of annual, permanent, or other appropriations...;
  (d) Balanced statements...;
  (e) All essential facts regarding the bonded and other indebtedness of the government; and
  (f) Such other financial statements and data as in his opinion are necessary or desirable to make known in all practicable detail the financial conditions of the Government.[*]

---

[*] For "Evolution of Budget Concepts in the President's Message: 1923–1968," see R. W. Johnson in President's Commission on Budget Concepts (1967, 93–103).

12.9. Responsibilities for disclosure with respect to the budget.

(a) Agency testimony before and communications with Congress on budgetary matters.-- The nature and amounts of the President's decisions are confidential and will not be released until the budget is transmitted formally to Congress. The executive branch communications that have led to the budget will not be disclosed either by the agencies or by those who have prepared the budget. . . .

Following formal transmittal of the budget, an amendment, or a supplemental appropriation request, agency representatives will be guided by the following policies pertaining to budgetary matters when testifying before any congressional committee or communicating with Members of Congress:

　　(1) Witnesses will give frank and complete answers to all questions.

　　(2) Witnesses will avoid volunteering personal opinions that reflect positions inconsistent with the program or appropriations request the President has transmitted to Congress.

　　(3) If statutory provisions exist for the direct submission of agency budget estimates to Congress, OMB may provide agencies with additional materials supporting the President's budget request to be forwarded by the agency to Congress with agency testimony., Witnesses for such agencies will be prepared to explain the agency submission, the request in the President's budget, and any justification material.

　　(4) In responding to specific questions on program and appropriations requests, witnesses will refrain from providing the agency request to OMB as well as plans for the use of appropriations that exceed the President's request. Witnesses typically bear responsibility for the conduct of one or a few programs, whereas the President must weigh carefully all of the needs of the Federal Government, and compare them against each other and against the revenues available to meet such needs. Where appropriate witnesses should call attention to this difference in scope of responsibility in explaining why it is not proper to them to support efforts to raise appropriations above the amounts requested by the President. . . .

(b) Clearance of budget-related materials for Congress and the media.--Policy consistency is essential among the various sections of the President's budget , and the budget-related materials prepared by the agencies for Congress and the media. Agencies are responsible for ensuring that these budget-related materials are consistent with the President's budget and are submitted for clearance to OMB, unless a specific exemption from clearance is approved by OMB.

Agencies will submit all proposed budget justification materials to OMB for clearance prior to transmittal to congressional committees or individual Members of Congress or their staff. Agencies also will submit to OMB for clearance budget-related oversight materials. . . .

FIGURE 5.2 Rules of the Game (Exert from OMB circular A-11, Preparation, Submission, and Execution of the Budget, rev. July 2004 (http://www.whitehouse.gov/omb/circulars/a11/04toc.html).

- Section 202 (a):

  … The President in the Budget shall make recommendations to Congress for new taxes, loans, or other appropriate action to meet the estimated deficiency.

- Section 206:

  No estimate or request for an appropriation and no request for an increase in an item of any such estimate or request, and no recommendation as to how the revenue needs of the Government should be met, shall be submitted to Congress or any committee thereof by any officer or employee of any department or establishment, unless at the request of either House of Congress.

4. Meaning of Budget Reform

New institutions, new information, and a different process for formulation made significant changes in the system. Had they not, there would have been no point in effecting the change. As Aaron Wildavsky explains in an influential examination of budget reform forty years later, "A large part of the literature on budgeting in the United States is concerned with reform… any effective change in budgetary relationships must necessarily alter the outcomes of the budgetary process. Otherwise why bother?" He goes on to point out that "no significant change can be made in the budgetary process without affecting the political process" (Wildavsky 1961, 183–190).

5. Continuities

Some fundamental features of the budget process were not wiped away by this or later changes. Domination of the budget process continues to translate into an important source of power. Constitutionally authorized appropriations still characterize the process (see Figure 5.3 and Figure 5.4.). In sum, the 1921 act

> created the major statutory basis for executive domination of the federal budgetary process. By authorizing the president and his budget director to compile a budget for all federal agencies except Congress and the Supreme Court, the act ensured that a president bent on domination had an important basis of power. Congress assumed that because it retained full authority to increase or decrease estimates, this did not constitute a surrender of power.... That assumption was proven erroneous in the following decades (Duncombe and Heffron, in Rabin and Lynch 1983, 419).

D. THE INFORMATION INDUSTRY

1. OMB and GAO Data and Documents

For students of federal budgeting as well as participants, the 1921 act's creation of two agencies devoted at least in part to nonpartisan analysis and research produced a steady stream of documents and publications that have been widely used and are considered highly reliable. Perhaps foremost among the Office of Management and Budget's (OMB, previously BOB) contributions is the president's budget request itself.* *The Budget in Brief* and its more detailed companion, *Special Analyses, Budget of the United States* (OMB, annual), are annual publications used in the legislature, media, and classroom (see Table 5.3.). To this abbreviated list should be added OMB's circulars detailing regulations and procedures (for example, Office of Management and Budget 1986a, b, 1994a, b, 2004), data collections, and individual studies and reports. The OMB generates the sophisticated graphics that frequently appear in presidential speeches and media reports. The task of coordinating federal statistical and fact-collecting services was assigned the director by virtue of the Federal Reports Act of 1942.

The GAO is also a prodigious source of data and documents. In keeping with its role as the federal audit agency, the GAO monitors and reports on regulatory and statutory compliance of other agencies and submits its own statutorily required reports. Covering management studies, cost analyses, budget studies, and more, the GAO's reports range from budget and management concerns, such as training, inventory, assets, and pension administration, to substantive issues, such as environmental protection, foreign aid, and national security.† There are publications of more general interest, including the useful and much-quoted *Glossary of Terms Used in the Federal Budget Process*. This source defines many potentially confusing aspects of the federal process. For example, "budget authority" is defined as

> [authority] provided by law to enter into obligations that will result in immediate or future outlays involving Federal Government funds, except that budget authority does not include authority to insure

---

* For an introduction to the mystifying documents known as the US budget, see especially Collender (1984–1998, 2000, and 2003).
† With respect to budgeting and financial management, GAO also produces many case studies, other sources of which include Harvard's Case Clearinghouse, Lewis and Walker (1984), and the Office of Personnel Management's training materials (1986).

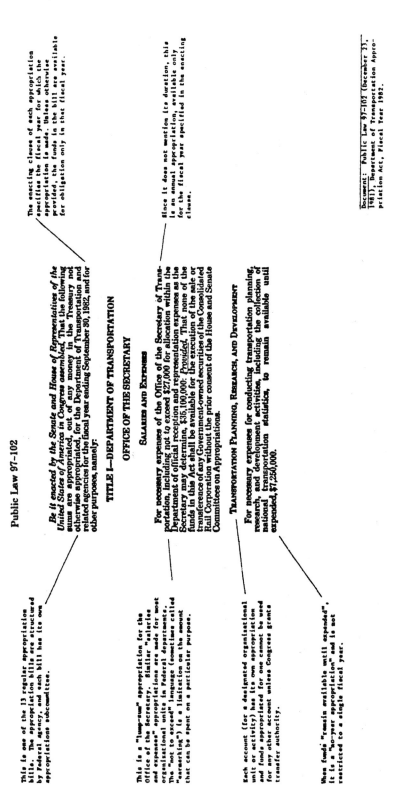

FIGURE 5.3 Regular appropriation bills. (From Schick, A. and Keith R., *Manual on the Federal Budget Process*, Congressional Research Service, Library of Congress, Washington, DC, 1982, 50–51.)

PUBLIC LAW 97-102.

URBAN MASS TRANSPORTATION ADMINISTRATION

For necessary expenses for research and training, as authorized by the Urban Mass Transportation Act of 1964, as amended (49 U.S.C. 1601 et seq.), to remain available until expended, $61,600,000: Provided, That $58,600,000 shall be available for research, development, and demonstrations, $2,000,000 shall be available for university research and training and not to exceed $1,000,000 shall be available for managerial training as authorized under the authority of said Act.

*   *   *   *

For necessary expenses for urban discretionary grants (including section 21) as authorized by the Urban Mass Transportation Act of 1964, as amended (49 U.S.C. 1601 et seq.), to remain available until September 30, 1985, $1,479,000,000, together with $11,000,000 to be derived from the appropriation "Rail service operating payments":

*   *   *   *

For payment to the urban mass transportation fund, for liquidation of contractual obligations incurred under authority of the Urban Mass Transportation Act of 1964, as amended (49 U.S.C. 1601 et seq.), and 23 U.S.C. 142(c) and of obligations incurred for projects substituted for Interstate System segments withdrawn prior to enactment of the Federal-Aid Highway Act of 1976, $1,200,000,000, to remain available until expended:

*   *   *   *

For payment to the Corporation for Public Broadcasting, as authorized by the Communications Act of 1934 as amended, an amount which shall be available within limitations specified by said Act, for the fiscal year 1984, $110,000,000:

Annual Appropriation

This appropriation allocates the total amount for three purposes. The earmarked amounts are the amounts available for each of the designated purposes. But the "not to exceed" appropriation of $1 million for managerial training means that a portion of this amount can be used for the two other purposes.

Advance Appropriation

An advance appropriation is different from "forward funding." The latter is an appropriation whose funds are available before the start of the fiscal year for which the appropriation is made.

An advance appropriation is made for one or more years beyond the current or next fiscal year. In this illustration, an appropriation bill for the 1982 fiscal year contained an appropriation to the Corporation for Public Broadcasting for the 1984 fiscal year.

Transfer

Transfers are funds shifted from one appropriation account to another. In this case, the transfer is specified in the appropriation act, but sometimes authority is given to executive officials to transfer a portion of an appropriation.

Liquidating Appropriation

When an appropriation is to pay an existing contract or obligation, it is termed a "liquidating appropriation," and is not computed as budget authority. The budget authority was provided when Congress authorized the obligation.

Documents: Public Law 97-102 (December 21, 1981), Department of Transportation Appropriation Act, Fiscal Year 1982; and H.R. 4360 (97th Cong.), Labor-Health-Education Appropriation Act, Fiscal Year 1982.

FIGURE 5.3   (Continued)

This exhibit provides an illustration of the final reports of budget execution for an annual appropriation of $200,000,000. The appropriation expires on September 30, 1994 and is canceled on September 30, 1999. Each column represents a report for a succeeding fiscal year. Appropriate S.F. 133 line numbers are denoted in parentheses ( ).

Column 1. Final end-of-year S.F. 133 that is submitted to OMB for the period ending September 30, 1994. In FY 1994, actual disbursements of $199,760,000 were made (outlays, line 14). $110,000 in unobligated balances (line 9.A) and $130,000 in obligated balances (line 13.C) remained when the appropriation expired. Unobligated balances are listed on line 9.A in the year an appropriation expires to show that balances are available for obligation before the account expired.

Column 2. Final end-of-year S.F. 133 that is submitted to OMB for the period ending September 30, 1995. In FY 1995, $110,000 in expired unobligated balances (line 2.A) were carried forward from FY 1994 (column 1, line 9.A). During FY 1995, the year-end unobligated balance increased from $110,000 to $140,000 (line 10.E). The $30,000 increase resulted from the collection of $18,000 in refunds (line 3.A) and a $12,000 recovery of a prior year obligation from the downward adjustment of a contract (line 4.A), which was obligated for $80,000, but only cost $68,000. The initial obligated balance of $130,000 (line 13.A) decreased by $68,000 for the payment of the contract obligation and $12,000 for the downward adjustment that was reclassified as an unobligated balance.

The year-end obligated balance was $50,000. Total disbursements were $68,000, but net outlays were $50,000 (line 14), since the $18,000 refund offset the same amount of outlays.

Column 3. Shows the final end-of-year S.F. 133 that is submitted to OMB for the period ending September 30, 1996. In FY 1996, $140,000 in expired unobligated balances (line 2.A) were carried forward from FY 1995 (column 2, line 10.E). During FY 1996, it was discovered that no obligations were recorded for a grant of $65,000, which was made on April 15, 1994. The unrecorded obligation is treated as an upward adjustment. It is counted as an incurred obligation (line 8, 12) and subtracted from the initial unobligated balance (line 2.A) to get the year-end unobligated balance (line 10.E).

The unobligated balance fell $65,000 (line 8) from $140,000 (line 2.A) to $75,000 (line 10.E). The initial obligated balance of $50,000 (line 13.A) decreased to $40,000 (line 13.C), since $10,000 of existing obligations were paid. Net outlays were $75,000 (line 14), which represents $65,000 for the unrecorded grant and $10,000 for existing obligations.

Column 4. Final end-of-year S.F. 133, submitted to OMB for the period ending September 30, 1997. In FY 1997, $75,000 in expired unobligated balances (line 2.A) were carried forward from FY 1996 (column 3, line 10.E). During FY 1997, the bill for a cost-plus-fixed-fee contract originally obligated at $15,000 was actually $60,000. The $45,000 upward adjustment is added as an incurred obligation (lines 8, 12) and subtracted from the

initial unobligated balance (line 2.A) to get the year-end unobligated balance (line 10.E). The unobligated balance decreased $45,000 from $75,000 (line 2.A) to $30,000 (line 10.E).

The initial obligated balance of $40,000 (line 13.A) decreased $15,000 for payment of the contract obligation and $5,000 for payment of other existing obligations. The final obligated balance was $20,000 (line 13.C). Net outlays were $65,000 (line 14), which represents $15,000 for the contract obligation, $5,000 for other obligations, and $45,000 for the upward adjustment of the contract obligation.

Column 5. Final end-of-year S.F. 133, submitted to OMB for the period ending September 30, 1998. In FY 1998, $30,000 in expired unobligated balances (line 2.A) are carried forward from FY 1997 (column 4, line 10.E). During FY 1998, actual bills received totaled $27,000 more than the previously reported obligations. The $27,000 upward adjustment is added as an incurred obligation (lines 8, 12) and subtracted from the initial unobligated balance (line 2.A) to get the year-end unobligated balance (line 10.E). The unobligated balance fell $27,000 (line 8) from $30,000 (line 2.A) to $3,000 (line 10.E). Only $3,000 is now available for further upward adjustments.

The initial obligated balance of $20,000 (line 13.A) decreased to $15,000 (line 13.C) from the payment of $5,000 in existing obligations. Net outlays were $32,000 (line 14), which represents a $27,000 upward adjustment and $5,000 in existing obligations.

Column 6. Final end-of-year S.F. 133, submitted to OMB for the period ending September 30, 1999. In FY 1999, $3,000 in expired unobligated balances (line 2.A) are carried forward from FY 1998 (column 4, line 10.E). During FY 1999, actual bills received totalled $2,000 more than the previously reported obligations. The $2,000 upward adjustment is added as an obligation incurred (lines 8, 12) and subtracted from the initial unobligated balance (line 2.A) to get to the year end unobligated balance of $1,000 before the amount was cancelled. Net outlays were $16,900 (line 14), which is comprised of $2,000 for the upward adjustment and $14,900 for existing obligations, which left $100 in obligated balances before the amount was cancelled.

To cancel the balances at the end of the fiscal year, the unobligated balances of $1,000 is cancelled, as a negative, on line 6 and a zero is recorded on line 10.E. The obligated balance of $100 for which no disbursements were made is cancelled also. First, a positive amount is recorded on line 4.A, recovery of prior year obligations. This amount is cancelled, as a negative, on line 6. The $100 in obligated balances is subtracted from the $2,000 upward adjustment, and the net amount of $1,900 is included on line 12. The total unexpended balances cancelled is shown as −$1,100, on line 6.

The account is now closed.

FIGURE 5.4 Life cycle of appropriation. (From OMB Circular A-34, *Instructions on Budget Execution*, OMB, Washington, DC, 1994, Exhibit 111.)

Illustration of a 1994 Annual Appropriation During the Unexpired Year and Each Expired Year

REPORT ON BUDGET EXECUTION

AGENCY: Department of Government
BUREAU: Office of the Secretary

DESCRIPTION	SF 133 dated 9/30/94 1994 Unexpired	SF 133 dated 9/30/95 1994 Expired	SF 133 dated 9/30/96 1994 Expired	SF 133 dated 9/30/97 1994 Expired	SF 133 dated 9/30/98 1994 Expired	SF 133 dated 9/30/99 1994 Cancelled
BUDGETARY RESOURCES						
1. Budget authority:						
A. Appropriations realized	200,000,000					
B. Appropriations anticipated (indefinite)						
C. Other new authority						
D. Net transfers						
2. Unobligated balances:						
A. Brought forward October 1	0	110,000	140,000	75,000	30,000	3,000
B. Net transfers						
3. Reimbursements and other income:						
A. Earned ($)		18,000				
B. Change in unfilled customers' orders (+ or −)						
C. Anticipated for rest of year						
4. Recoveries of prior year obligations:						
A. Actual	0	12,000				100
B. Anticipated for the rest of the year						
5. Portion not available pursuant to P.L. (−)						
6. Restorations (+) and writeoffs (−)						−1,100
7. TOTAL BUDGETARY RESOURCES	200,000,000	140,000	140,000	75,000	30,000	2,000
STATUS OF BUDGETARY RESOURCES						
8. Obligations incurred	199,890,000	0	65,000	45,000	27,000	2,000
9. Unobligated balances available:						
A. Apportioned, Category A	110,000					
B. Apportioned, Category B						
C. Other balances available						
10. Unobligated balances not available:						
A. Apportioned for subsequent periods *						
B. Withheld pending rescission *						
C. Deferred *						
D. Unapportioned balance of revolving fund *						
E. Other balances not available		140,000	75,000	30,000	3,000	0
11. TOTAL BUDGETARY RESOURCES	200,000,000	140,000	140,000	75,000	30,000	2,000
RELATION OF OBLIGATIONS TO OUTLAYS AND ACCRUED EXPENDITURES						
12. Obligations incurred, net (8−3A−3B−4A)	199,890,000	−30,000	65,000	45,000	27,000	−1,900
13. Net unpaid obligations:						
A. Obligated balance, as of October 1	0	130,000	50,000	40,000	20,000	15,000
B. Obligated balance transferred, net (+ or −)	0	0	0	0	0	0
C. Obligated balance, end of year	130,000	80,000	40,000	20,000	15,000	0
14. Outlays (12+13A−13B−13C)	199,760,000	50,000	75,000	65,000	32,000	16,900
15. Change in accounts payable, net:						
A. Accounts payable, net, as of October 1						
B. Accounts payable, transferred, net						
C. Accounts payable, net, end of period						
16. Accrued expenditures (14−15A 15B+15C)						
17. Other						
18. Other						
19. Other						
20. Other						

Lines 15 and 16 are optional.

* From the SF 132.

Shaded data should be included in the actual year column of the FY 1996 Budget.	Shaded data should be included in the actual year column of the FY 1997 Budget.	Shaded data should be included in the actual year column of the FY 1998 Budget.	Shaded data should be included in the actual year column of the FY 1999 Budget.	Shaded data should be included in the actual year column of the FY 2000 Budget.	Shaded data should be included in the actual year column of the FY 2001 Budget.

Note: This exhibit represents a series of SF 133s for the same account from 1994–1999.

FIGURE 5.4   *(Continued)*

TABLE 5.3
Standard Federal Budget Documents Available from the US Government Printing Office

Budget of the US government, fiscal year
- Contains the budget message of the president
- Presents the president's budget proposals

Analytical perspectives, budget of the US government, fiscal year
- Highlights selected program areas
- Shows other significant analyses, including economic and accounting, spending, revenues, borrowing, current service estimates, and more

Historical tables, budget of the US government, fiscal year

Budget of the US government, fiscal year—appendix
- Shows most detailed information on appropriations and funds
- Includes proposed appropriation language, legislative proposals, and certain off-budget activities
- Electronic sources of budget information are available via Internet (OMB, GPO)

---

or guarantee the repayment of indebtedness incurred by another person or government. The basic forms of budget authority are appropriations, authority to borrow, and contract authority. Budget authority may be classified by the period of availability (1-year, multiple-year, no-year), by the timing of congressional action (current or permanent), or by the manner of determining the amount available (definite or indefinite) (General Accounting Office 1981, 41).

2. Other Federal Sources

These and other federal sources of nonpartisan information and data—the Treasury Department, especially for revenue statistics; the Congressional Research Service of the Library of Congress; the Bureau of the Census of the Department of Commerce; the Council of Economic Advisors with its annual report; the Congressional Budget Office (pursuant to the 1974 act, discussed below); and other federal agencies such as Labor and Housing and Urban Development—have contributed mightily to the status and workload of the Government Printing Office. So too had Washington's nonpartisan Advisory Commission on Intergovernmental Relations (ACIR), founded in 1959 and publisher of many studies and series including over two decades of the data series *Significant Features of Fiscal Federalism* and, initiated in 1975, the journal *Intergovernmental Perspective*. Since 1972, annual surveys of public attitudes had been conducted for the Commission, first by Opinion Research Corporation and then by the Gallup Organization, and published in *Changing Public Attitudes on Governments and Taxes*. The ACIR had analyzed a large body of information pertaining to federal, state, and local fiscal relations.

Slating ACIR for termination in spring 1996, the 104th Congress began a reversal of the trend toward more information, analysis, and staff support. It took steps to abolish the congressional Office of Technology Assessment and deeply cut the Congressional Budget Office (CBO), Congressional Research Service (CRS), and GAO. Although cuts in congressional offices amount to relatively few dollars—Congress accounts for less than one-tenth of 1% of federal spending— some observers note a potential weakening of Congress and its ability to make informed budgetary decisions (Carney 1995, 2354–2355). For example, because CBO's expanded analytic role under the 1996 Unfunded Mandates Reform Act is funded at only a fraction of the original estimate, the CBO was especially hard pressed just when congressional leaders were relying on its numbers on deficit reduction, health care, and other budgetary and policy debates. Budget cutters also targeted some executive statistical agencies, including Commerce's Census Bureau and Labor's Bureau of Labor Statistics (Stanfield 1995, 2408). Among the many agencies whose mission is gathering demographic, economic, business, and other data important to budgeting are OMB (http://www.whitehouse.gov/omb),Treasury (http://www.ustreas.gov), GAO (http://www.gao.gov), CBO (http://www.cbo.gov), and the Bureaus of Labor Statistics (http://www.bls.gov) and Census (http://www.census.gov).

3. New Kinds of Information

Technical analysis and information have become a major industry throughout the nation, and it is unlikely that efforts to reverse the trend will succeed. Even so, it is ironic that the threat to data availability and integrity runs counter to contemporary management approaches' emphases on hard data in decision making and the use of quantified, analytic tools in budgeting. The moves toward performance and outcome measures and cost-benefit analysis are cases in point that purportedly address governmental accountability and disclosure (or transparency).

The same purposes drove the Governmental Accounting Standards Board's (GASB) efforts to introduce Service Efforts and Accomplishments Reporting (SEA) at the subnational level. According to GASB's concept statement (1992, iii), "The measurement of a governmental entity's performance requires information not only on the acquisition and use of resources but also on the outputs and outcomes of the services provided and the relationship between the use of resources and outputs and outcomes." The GASB (1992, 111) notes that "The objective of SEA reporting is to provide more complete information about a governmental entity's performance than can be provided by the operating statement, balance sheet, and budgetary comparison statements and schedules."

In GAO's 1992 survey of the use of performance data, 102 federal agencies reported using performance measures. Even with overstated frequencies due to the research methodology (General Accounting Office 1993a, 30), only about 50% indicated that the measures are used to gauge progress in achieving strategic goals; 70% of responding managers reported that performance measures aid budgetary decision making, program management, and more. To more accurately assess practices, Congressional Budget Office (1993b) conducted detailed case studies of six agencies and confirmed "the importance of having a clearly defined mission, the difficulty of developing outcome measures for many government functions, and the often tenuous ties between budgeting and measures of performance.... Basic aspects of agencies' budgets are not determined by the relationship between inputs and outputs" (Congressional Budget Office 1993b, 35–36).

The 1993 Government Performance and Results Act (GPRA, P.L. 103-62) requires agencies to develop strategic plans prior to FY 1998, prepare annual plans setting performance goals beginning in FY 1999, and, starting in March 2000, report annually on actual performance compared with these goals. Using an eight-year implementation schedule, the GPRA requires federal agencies to set annual performance targets and OMB to submit a government-wide performance plan budget beginning for FY 1999 (see Table 5.1). Emphasizing GPRA's implementation, Office of Management and Budget (1994, 24) contains the definitions of key terms such as outcome and output measures and performance goal and indicator. The A-ll summary (1994) states that "The 1996 budget process will take an important step in the direction of presenting more program performance measures—outputs and outcomes—in the budget and of linking goals to the resources required to produce them. This year's revision of circular no. A-11 reflects this new direction."

Cost-benefit analysis has been uses for many decades by the US Army Corps of Engineers, but its role beyond capital projects dates to the Reagan administration. Issued in 1981, Executive Order 12291 required that new, major regulations with annual economic impact of $100 million or more be subjected to cost-benefit analysis. It appears that its role will expand still further. Proposals for regulatory reform in *Contract with America* (Gillespie and Schellhas 1994) include the use of risk assessment and cost-benefit analysis. Methodological issues in budgeting and policy making were enlivened but left unsettled by 1995 bills that would require use of risk assessment and cost-benefit analysis in federal agencies.

4. State Information Producers

State counterparts of federal information producers generate studies and publications, as do privately sponsored and university-associated bureaus of government research in many states, including but not limited to Idaho, California, New York, New Jersey, Georgia, and Connecticut. These organizations constitute an excellent source of readily available, timely, frequently state-specific data and analyses. Other producers include central staff offices such as budget and personnel, audit offices, labor and health departments, and even state-level analogs of ACIR.

5. Nongovernmental Information Producers

a. Public Interest Organizations

An impressive array of nongovernmental organizations generate publications that are frequently cited in government documents as well as academic works (see references). These organizations fall primarily into four categories: public interest organizations, research organizations, professional associations and organizations, and the purely or mainly academic organizations and publications. The first category includes the National Municipal League, the National League of Cities, the League of Women Voters, and a variety of others, some of which focus on state and local concerns. The Tax Foundation started publishing its monthly newsletter, *Tax Features*, in 1957, twenty years after its founding as a nonprofit organization, and its biennial volume, *Facts and Figures on Government Finance*, is a useful data collection (Sagoo, 2005). Among state-oriented organizations in this same category are the Council of State Governments (CSG, annual; Howard 1973) and the National Conference of State Legislatures, which publishes studies and surveys relating to budgeting and financial matters (Mackey 1993; NSCL 1981, 1983, 1986, 1994, 2006) and State Legislatures Magazine available online (1999-current).

b. Research Organizations

Several research organizations or think tanks are known for their highly reputed analyses and studies, many of which are funded as contract research under grants. The Brookings Institution was organized in its present form in 1927 as, by its own description, "an independent organization devoted to nonpartisan research, education, and publication in economics, government, foreign policy, and the social sciences generally." The American Enterprise Institute, the Cato Institute, the Heritage Foundation, the Institute of Public Administration (responsible for publishing Gulick and Urwick 1937), the Rand Corporation, and the Urban Institute also fall in the category of research organizations, and are represented by citations in the references.

c. Professional Associations and Organizations

The number of professional associations, the third category of nongovernmental members of the information industry, necessitates an abbreviated introduction here. The Government Finance Officers Association, (GFOA, http://www.gfoa.org), founded in 1903 as the Municipal Finance Officers Association, started publishing its *Journal of Municipal Finance* in the 1920s; today it publishes the *Government Finance Review*. As its many widely used sources illustrate (GFOA 1994; Glick 1986; MFOA 1979; Miller 1984; Moak and Hillhouse 1975; Moak and Killian 1963; Strachota 1994), the GFOA's publications program is geared toward practitioners. Similarly, the National Association of State Budget Officers (NASBO, http://www.nasbo.org) has published the State Expenditure Report annually since 1987 and, with the National Governors Association (NGA), publishes The Fiscal Survey of States twice annually since 1979, along with other resources. The American Society for Public Administration (http://www.aspnanet.org), the national organization for both practitioners and academics in public administration, first published the journal *Public Administration Review* in 1940; its role is apparent from the number of citations (Goodsell 1984; Gore 1994; Lewis 1994; Lindblom 1959, 1979; Mani 1995; Pyhrr 1977; Rubin 1990; Schick 1966, 1973; Wildavsky 1961), and it led to editions of "PAR Classics" on budgeting in 1980 and 1987 (Schick 1987). The Association for Budgeting and Financial Management of the American Society for Public Administration publishes *Public Budgeting & Finance* (e.g., Bland and Nunn 1992; Botner 1989), which first appeared in 1981. The International City/and most recently County Management Association (ICMA), whose focus is expressed in its title, is responsible for numerous publications, including the *Municipal Year Book* (annual) the periodical *Public Management*, and other resources (http://www.icma.org).

d. Academic Organizations and Publications

The scope and number of academic publications are simply too great to conform to the format of an introductory overview; the reference list is a better guide to this category (along with indexes to journals). Other bibliographies, some general and others tailored to specific aspects of the field of budgeting and financial management, are available in many other sources (e.g., Aronson and Schwartz (1987); Rabin and Lynch (1983)). The American Political Science Association's journal, *American Political Science Review*, has been central to the develop ment of the field, and a bibliography on budgeting dating to 1915 cites an early contribution (Rider 1915).[*]

The historical reach of other journals also amounts to an impressive testimony on behalf of continuity; for example, the *National Tax Journal* can be traced to 1907 as the *National Tax Association Bulletin*. Other journals speak to the continued vibrancy of the field. Examples include *The Public Manager* (formerly, *The Bureaucrat*), which has an orientation toward the concerns of federal practitioners, and *Public Budgeting & Finance*, which is directed towards academic and practitioner interests. (This essay includes a list of selected contemporary journals that are or have been especially influential in the field of American public budgeting and financial management. See Table 5.2.)

6. Growth Industry

The ensuing years saw the addition of information reflecting new responsibilities, concerns, and demands made on budget processes and budget documents. Performance and program measures, the packages for zero-base budgeting, forecasting models, and multiyear costing are but a few examples. Their avowed, pragmatic purpose is to provide better, more useful information for decision making and for scholarly and applied analyses. It is for history to judge whether this purpose has been served, but it can be said with confidence that information is still a growth industry and that budget documents themselves get longer and more complex.

---

[*] The American Political Science Association is the professional association for political scientists, and both practitioners and academics may and do join. Yet because the journal is geared to theoretical concerns and research rather than to the applied aspects of political science, the academic category seems most appropriate.

IV. PERFECTING THE PROTOTYPE

A. Pursuing the Classical and Radical

1. Time Horizon

One of the advantages of participating in so-called modern times is that tinkering and adjustments can be called modernization and reform. An obvious disadvantage is that the short time horizon inevitably distorts evaluation. It appears that the more recent the event, the more important it is judged as a matter of course rather than as a matter of judicious assessment. Moreover, individual and institutional memories are fresh enough to recall each effort, each error, and each minor swerve on a road that appears straightforward only from the secure distance of history. Nonetheless, it is already conventional to affirm that the prolonged, deep depression and the governmental responses that preceded World War II sufficiently altered the budgetary landscape we are viewing to evoke the cliché the Second American Revolution.

2. Second American Revolution

Governmental roles and responsibilities were redefined in terms of new demands and new theory:

> Backed by the dire economic experiences of the Great Depression, John Maynard Keynes challenged the classical economists' position with *The General Theory of Employment, Interest and Money (1936)*. The challenge was successful and the resulting Keynesian theory dramatically altered legislators' behavior toward budgeting and economic policy. Under the influence of Keynesian theory, fiscal policy has come to mean deliberate government utilization of public spending and financing in the development and stabilization of the economy.

A massive, unprecedented, domestic spending program took place at the federal level. With respect to the budgetary details of that spending program, it is useful to note that appropriations for some New Deal programs occurred outside the regular budget process. State and local governments became more dependent on Washington while simultaneously enlarging their responsibilities in a pattern that would be repeated in its broad outlines in the late 1960s and 1970s.

3. Accounting and Audit Standards

Financial crises, defaults, and concerns over financial management led to the imposition of limitations on taxes, expenditures, and indebtedness in many states and localities, a that would movement also be repeated at the end of the 1970s (ACIR 1977; Peterson et al. 1977). Furthermore, professional accounting and auditing standards began to develop rapidly and be applied to governmental operations. Starting in 1934, the National Council on Governmental Accounting (1968, 1980) saw many of its works published under the auspices of the Municipal Finance Officers Association (later the Government Finance Officers Association). Similarly, rapid development occurred in the 1970s subsequent to the publication of authoritative standards, coupled with financial difficulties in New York City and elsewhere. While periodization may vary according to emphasis and author, according to one source:

> The first historically significant movement to reform municipal accounting began in the 1890s and came to an end with the founding of the first national municipal accounting board in 1934. The initial push for reform was provided by the National Municipal League and its backers in business, academia and government.... In January 1934, a National Committee on Municipal Accounting was formed and in 1935 the Committee approved accounting principles.... The stimulus for the two waves of reform [1890s– 1934, 1977 current] came from similar economic and political trends.... Both came after a crisis of confidence in the municipal bond market (Rousmaniere and Guild 1981, 66–67).

4.   Brownlow Committee

In 1936, at the same time that Keynes was revolutionizing classical economics, President Roosevelt appointed a three-member committee to comprehensively examine the president's management functions. What emerged the next year from the Brownlow Committee was the "Report of the President's Committee on Administrative Management." It was built on the premise that the "efficiency of government rests upon two factors: the consent of the governed and good management" (Mosher 1976, 113). The latter required that the president be given the staff necessary for the managerial task, along with the power to reorganize the executive branch of government. In 1939, a modified version of the Brownlow Committee's recommendations was enacted in the Reorganization Act, authorizing the president to reorganize on a temporary basis, subject to legislative veto. With respect to fiscal management, the report recommended that the BOB be used as central staff and an informational center of the executive branch. The BOB was transferred from the Treasury to the Executive Office of the President, created under the 1939 Reorganization Plan (53 Stat. Reorganization Plan No. 1) and fine-tuned under Executive Order 8248 that same year.

The Brownlow Committee's recommendations suggest the extent to which seemingly innovative concepts and extraordinary events may coexist with or even be grounded in accepted wisdom and orthodox thinking. One outstanding and often-cited example of that orthodoxy, perhaps even its epitome, was published in 1937 under the title *Papers on the Science of Administration* (Gulick and Urwick 1937). Suffice it to note that budgeting figures was among the seven activities of a chief executive that were formulated into POSDCORB.[*] According to Gulick, "Efficiency is... axiom number one in the value scale of administration" (Gulick, in Gulick and Urwick 1937). This era of supposedly radical change is marked, then, by an underlying, prevailing faith: the belief that much can be accomplished through correct structure and correct principles, both of which can be identified and implemented, and both of which are justified on the grounds of a predominant value, efficiency.

5.   The "Key" Question

The apparent conceptual and normative consensus obscured a matter that emerged only a year after the Reorganization Act in an article by the eminent political scientist V. O. Key, Jr. (Key 1940). If one were asked to select the single most important journal article published in budgeting and financial management, one would be well advised to avoid the task-perhaps at any cost! The choice, any choice, would simply generate protestations, raise forefingers in warning, and set heads to shaking in reproof by proponents devoted to another selection and for reasons as compelling as one's own. However, Key's "Lack of a Budgetary Theory" no doubt would make a short list, were one devised (Mosher 1976, 190–195; Shafritz and Hyde 1978; Shafritz and Hyde 1987). By eloquently and pointedly bemoaning a tendency in the literature to evade questions of allocations, he set the terms for discussion for decades to come:

> On the most significant aspect of public budgeting, *i.e.*, the allocation of expenditures among different purposes so as to achieve the greatest return, American budgetary literature is singularly arid. Toilers in the budgetary field have busied themselves primarily with the organization and procedure for budget preparation, the forms for the submission of requests for funds, the form of the budget document itself, and like questions [here he cites Buck 1929, among others]... the absorption of energies in the establishment of the mechanical foundations for budgeting has diverted attention from the basic budgeting problem (on the expenditure side), namely: On what basis shall it be decided to allocate X dollars to activity A instead of activity B?

---

[*]The seven "principles" of POSDCORB include planning, organizing, staffing, directing, coordinating, reporting, and budgeting (Gulick and Urwick 1937).

The most advantageous utilization of public funds resolves itself into a matter of value preferences between ends lacking a common denominator. As such, the question is a problem in political philosophy.... In detail, what forces go into the making of state budgets? What factors govern decisions of budgetary officials? Precisely what is the role of the legislature?.... For the working budget official, the implications of the discussion rest primarily in a point of view in the consideration of estimates in terms of alternatives-decisions which are always made, but not always consciously.... The thousands of little decisions made in budgetary agencies grow by accretion into formidable budgetary documents which from their sheer mass are apt often to overwhelm those with the power of final decision (Key 1940, 1137–1144).

Replies to Key's question encompass a variety of factors, including economic principles, taxes, and politics. Verne Lewis termed Key's question the "$64 question on the expenditure side of public budgeting" (and that is in current dollars!), and responded to it in terms of relative value, marginal utility, and relative effectiveness (Lewis 1952, 42–54). In his study of the history of federal budgeting, which emphasized the nineteenth century's reliance on the customs tariff as the major revenue source, Arthur Smithies, chairman of the Economics Department at Harvard University some forty years ago, wrote as if in response to V. O. Key, Jr., "And the ultimate criterion for the worthiness of expenditures is whether they warrant the taxes the Government must levy or the debt it must incur to finance them (Smithies 1955, xiii–xiv).[*] Key's article was quoted over two decades after its publication in another likely candidate for that same short list, Wildavsky's discussion of budget reform:

In 1940, in what is still the best discussion of the subject, V. O. Key lamented "The Lack of a Budgetary Theory." He called for a theory which would help answer the basic question of budgeting on the expenditure side.... A theory which contains criteria for determining what ought to be in the budget is nothing less than a theory stating what government ought to do... a normative theory of budgeting would be a comprehensive and specific political theory... utopian in the fullest sense of that word; its accomplishment and acceptance would mean the end of conflict over the government's role in society. Perhaps the 'study of budgeting' is just another expression for the 'study of politics'... (Wildavsky 1961, 183–190).

6. Immediate Postwar Years

a. Fiscal Policy

The impact of the depression, the war, and conceptual developments is evident in the Employment Act of 1946 (60 Stat. 33 [1946]), in which federal responsibility for economic and social goals was recognized and the Council of Economic Advisors created.[†] Comprising three members appointed by the president with the Senate's advice and consent, the council was to submit an economic report to each regular session of Congress. The purpose was "to develop and recommend to the President

---

[*] There are many studies of decision making about taxes, tax administration, and tax policy. They are not marked by consensus. One author concludes that public opinion is irrelevant to decisions about taxing and that these are not associated with spending decisions (Hansen 1983). According to a contrary thesis, "Expenditures are increased only to the point where the vote gained by the additional dollar spent is more than cancelled out by the vote lost by the additional dollar taxed. The budget is established where the tradeoff between spending money and raising revenues is equal" (Friedman 1980, 169). It has been suggested that environmental, legal, revenue-raising, and other factors affect tax decisions (Bingham et al. 1978, 193–211).

[†] Other legislation affecting the budget function and/or agencies include the Federal Reports Act of 1942, which gave the BOB statistical and data-collecting responsibilities; the Government Corporation Control Act of 1945, which extended the BOB's budget authority to wholly owned government corporations; the Classification Act of 1949, charging the BOB's director with regulatory duties; and the General Appropriation Act of 1950, which restated statutory authority for the apportionment procedure.

national economic policies to foster and promote free competitive enterprise, to avoid economic fluctuations or to diminish the effects thereof, and to maintain employment, production, and purchasing power..." (Mosher 1976, 180). Congress also established the Joint Economic Committee (Joint Committee on the Economic Report), and fiscal policy formally came into its own.[*]

b. First Hoover Commission

With the "Report of the Commission on Organization of the Executive Branch of the Government" in 1949, the decade drew to a close with a relapse to orthodoxy in high places. The report of the first Hoover Commission (so called after the chairman, ex-President Herbert Hoover) has been described as an expression of "the hard core of fundamentalist dogma" (Seidman and Gilmour 1986, 4).

Akin to the Brownlow Report in management philosophy and in making recommendations that would be repeated for decades, the report called for performance budgeting as preferable to the customary line-item format. Adamant on the subject at hand—the "budget and appropriation process is the heart of the management and control of the executive branch"—it announced that the "all-important thing in budgeting is the work or the service to be accomplished, and what that work or service will cost." The report recommended

> that the whole budgetary concept of the Federal Government should be refashioned by the adoption of a budget based upon functions, activities, and projects; this we designate as a "performance budget."... Such an approach would focus attention upon the general character and relative importance of the work to be done, or upon the service to be rendered, rather than upon the things to be acquired, such as personal service, supplies, equipment, and so on.... Under performance budgeting, attention is centered on the function or activity—on the accomplishment of the purpose....

Some of the first Hoover Commission's recommendations were enacted in the Budget and Accounting Procedures Act of 1950 (Stillman 1982, 180–183). According to a 1958 BOB manual,

> this act explicitly recognized the President's authority to determine the content, order, and arrangement of the proposed appropriations and statements of expenditures in the budget; pointed the presentation of financial needs in the budget toward the activities to be performed;... lent special support to the improvement of governmental accounting and auditing procedures;... and strengthened the Budget Bureau's work in the field of administrative analysis and integration of Federal statistical plans and operations. This law as well as the Budget and Accounting Act [1921] were amended in 1956 to improve further governmental budgeting and accounting methods and procedures (OMB BOB 1958, 22).

B. INCREMENTALISTS AND RATIONALISTS

1. Incrementalism

Charles Lindblom published his profoundly influential "The Science of 'Muddling Through'" in a 1959 issue of *Public Administration Review*, and much of the literature in public administration for the next two decades was devoted to an examination of decision making by "successive, limited comparison" (Lindblom 1959, 1979), critiques and rebuttals, empirical research, and explorations of alternative models. "Taken together, Lindblom's criticism of the wave of rationalism that swept

---

[*] Pointing to the passage of the Humphrey–Hawkins Act in 1978 and to the debate and legislation on deficits and taxes in the 1980s, some observers argued that fiscal policy crowds out other concerns. This concern intensified during the next two decades.

across government in the 1960s and 1970s help us to understand not simply the limitations of our budgetary practice, but the assumptions and implications that undergird them" (Plant 1986, 76).

Ideas about limits on cognitive capacity and decision-making strategies emanated from calculations of organizational and political feasibility and competitive advantage. Politics emerged as the dominant explanatory factor, rather than ideal and perhaps idealized versions of management principles and prescriptions. These ideas were injected into the way budgeting was thought about under the rubric of incrementalism. The path-breaking work of Aaron Wildavsky in the 1960s is most closely associated with this description of budgetary decision making (Davis et al. 1966; Wildavsky 1964, 1968). His *The Politics of the Budgetary Process* has gone through many editions since 1964 to become one of the most widely read books in the field, and was subsequently recast to account for changes in federal budgeting (Wildavsky 1992). In it, Wildavsky describes numerous strategies and counterstrategies that go into formulating budget requests and congressional appropriations. Succintly defined, "incrementalism" is

> a theory of the budgetary process proposing that policy makers give only limited consideration to small parts of the budget and arrive at decisions by making marginal adjustments in last year's budget... participants [in different roles] make decisions through a process of bargaining and negotiation.... The budget as a whole is not considered.... Instead, participants make marginal changes on an already existing base (LeLoup 1988, 13).

Incremental budgeting "focuses upon the current year budget request with emphasis on increases from the current year" (Lynch 1979, 316).

Another way of stating the thrust of incrementalism is through the idea that the single best predictor of an agency's budget request is history, in the form of last year's appropriation or current services. (Historical comparison is built right into many budget justifications and requests by virtue of the forms themselves, the columns of which array prior years' appropriations and actuals against this year's request and appropriation.) From this vantage point, budgets are built out of many interactive, recursive judgments, sequential decisions, and past political accommodations. The three central aspects on which to focus are the base (last year's appropriation), an expectation of fair share (maintaining budget share), and increment (a small, marginal change). Ordinarily, sweeping alterations in the percentage of the total budget going to any particular agency (budget share) are not to be expected, but the iterative nature of the process does allow for substantial change over several budget rounds. Thus, change in the short term is routinely expected to occur at the margins, affecting a relatively small proportion of the total budget in any given fiscal year.

2. Debate over Theories

The debate raged, with allegations of inherent conservatism, normative bias, limited applicability (only part of federal spending goes through the appropriations process and a large proportion of spending—for example, entitlements and other uncontrollables—is dedicated by previous decisions and laws), and budget data so highly aggregated so as to obscure important changes at the subagency and program levels. The issue of explanatory validity versus descriptive potency was raised as well (Gist 1977; LeLoup 1975, 1978; Moreland 1975; Natchez and Bupp 1973; Shull 1979; Wanat 1974, 1978). Criticism notwithstanding, Wildavsky's work defined the research task in much the same way that Key's earlier article framed the research question.

3. Rationalist Reforms

At the same time, efforts to improve the goal-setting and managerial functions of budgeting in Washington and in states and localities around the country continued, and found their way into the history via acronyms: PPBS, MBO, ZBB. It appears that even if routine decision making is incremental, reform efforts will seek to expand the potential for the rational-comprehensive approach to decision making (Lindblom 1959; LeLoup 1986, 16; Wildavsky and Hammond 1965). Closely related to the economist's concept of rationality, this decision-making model led to budget procedures supposing a step-by-step elaboration of explicit (program) goals, consideration of the universe of alternatives, selection based on feasibility, costs, and benefits, planned implementation, and systematic evaluation. "These theories or conceptual models are important because many people take them seriously and try to reform public budgeting using one of the theories as their guide" (Lynch 1979, 22). If participants in budgeting tend to behave as they believe they ought and others do, then the theory to which the individual and the general literature subscribe plays an important role in the interaction of belief and behavior, termed self-fulfilling prophecy.

a. Johnson Administration and PPBS

President Lyndon B. Johnson's administration introduced the planning–programming–budgeting system (PPBS) into federal budgeting, first in the Defense Department and then more broadly throughout federal departments and agencies.[*] Attempting to integrate planning and budgeting functions through modern systems analysis and cost-benefit analysis, PPBS is a comprehensive and systematic approach to the analysis of alternatives, costs, and consequences. It is marked by a voluminous and important literature that provides more or less stringent definitions, including BOB's bulletin no. 66-3 of October 1965.[†]

The grandiose, perhaps unattainable goals, included precisely identifying national goals, choosing among them, selecting the most effective and efficient means, and measuring performance.

To these specifications, he added something with which few would quarrel, that "It is important to remember one thing: no system, no matter how refined, can make decisions for you. But our judgment is not better than our information" (in Subcommittee on National Security 1967, 1–2).

b. Nixon Administration, GRS, and MBO

In 1970, President Nixon reorganized the Executive Office and created a Domestic Council that was expected to absorb the goal-oriented, planning function integrated by PPBS with the budget process in the renamed Office of Management and Budget (OMB). The next year, an OMB memorandum relieved federal agencies of the task of preparing program-related submissions and memoranda, and Allen Schick shortly recorded "A Death in the Bureaucracy" (Schick 1973). It bears noting that program budgeting enjoyed widespread adoption among state and local governments. A majority of states used a program format for appropriations to agencies (NASBO 1981, 14).

President Nixon also began the shift from the short-lived Great Society of his predecessor and centralization of the New Deal by inaugurating the new federalism in intergovernmental relations. This represents a reorientation of roles and responsibilities, coupled with a comprehensive reform of the confusing, often overlapping, numerous, and increasingly costly grant-in-aid programs. In a televised presidential speech in August 1969, the president enunciated his purpose and intent by proposing revenue sharing:

---

[*] The references include a few of the more frequently cited studies of PPBS (Hinrich and Taylor 1969; Lyden and Miller 1972; Merewitz and Sosnick 1971; Mosher 1969; Schick 1966, 1973; Rabin, in Golembiewski and Rabin 1975, 427–446); these and other sources (such as Grafton and Permaloff, in Rabin and Lynch 1983, 118–124) provide extensive bibliographies on this subject specifically.

[†] This administration was also responsible for introducing the "unified" federal budget and retaining the "cash" budget, based on the recommendations of the President's Commission on Budget Concepts (1967). The "unified budget" refers to the "present form of the budget of the Federal Government adopted beginning with the 1969 budget, in which receipts and outlays from Federal funds and trust funds are consolidated.... By law, budget authority and outlays of off-budget entities are excluded from the unified budget, but data relating to off-budget entities are displayed in the budget documents" (Committee on the Budget 1981, 133). See treatment of Social Security under GRH and BEA (herein) as examples.

We come now to a proposal which I consider profoundly important to the future of our Federal system of shared responsibilities....

For a third of a century, power and responsibility have flowed toward Washington, and Washington has taken for its own the best sources of revenue.... We intend to reverse this tide, and to turn back to the States a greater measure of responsibility—not as a way of avoiding problems, but as a better way of solving problems.

The entitlement program, general revenue sharing (GRS), was enacted in October 1972 by passage of Public Law 92-512, the State and Local Fiscal Assistance Act (Caputo and Cole 1976). The audit requirement in the 1976 reauthorization would introduce a new element of financial control and responsibility in many localities. Moreover (and unabashedly drawing on hindsight), the effort to shift the arena from Washington and to use more permissive financial arrangements (e.g., block grants) hinted at what was to come a decade later. General revenue sharing was completely terminated by fiscal year 1986.

The Nixon administration passed through a stage of management by objectives (MBO), attributed to Drucker's (1954) *The Practice of Management*. According to one assessment,

The purpose behind the federal MBO program was to develop consensus around presidential policy goals and then measure the degree of progress toward those goals.... The focus is on government actions and their consequences, not their costs.... When a new president came to office in 1977, MBO faded from view (Grafton and Permaloff, in Rabin and Lynch 1983, 101–102).

c. Carter Administration and ZBB

By virtue of bulletin no. 77-9, zero-base budgeting (ZBB) became the Carter administration's contribution to the rationalist reform litany repeated on the executive side for over a decade (Carter, 1977). The approach is credited to Pyhrr (1977), with whom Carter implemented ZBB while he was governor of Georgia (Lauth 1978; Pyhrr 1977).[*] Carter announced his own comprehensive goals in a press release on February 14, 1977. Working from a hypothetical zero base, analysts were, among other things, supposed to devise options for alternative funding levels for "decision units," package and rank them, and reconcile these with the operating budgets to be appropriated (Office of Management and Budget 1977). This reform fared little better, and was officially laid to rest in Washington with OMB's circular A-11 in 1981. Even so, it made a significant contribution to the literature and understanding of contemporary budgeting (Grafton and Permaloff, in Rabin and Lynch 1983, 118–124; Hyde and Shafritz 1978, 252–323; Positer and McGowan 1984).

d. Reform Assessed

The "judgment of history" may very well conclude that fifteen years of unsuccessful spurts of reform, aimed at clarifying systematic and comprehensive choice, left an indelible mark on the myth rather than on the practice of budgeting. Unrealistic expectations, burdensome paperwork, increased potential for conflict, bureaucratic resistance and entrenched routines, faltering executive interest, and a variety of environmental factors are among the many reasons cited for failure. Given that the most likely potential outcome is shortfall if not outright failure, why do moves toward rationally oriented reform at the federal, state, and local levels of public budgeting recur continuously, if not always zealously or sustained? Perhaps part of the answer lies in the continuing

[*] One source traces ZBB in the literature to 1924 and to the Department of Defense in the early 1960s (Merewitz and Sosnick 1971, 62). See also Wildavsky and Hammond (1965).

commitment of the budgeters' profession to rationalism and improvement. But the federal experience just recounted suggests that part of that answer lies also with a new executive's interest in announcing that the new boss has arrived in town—there may be no more efficient way of commanding the bureaucracy's immediate attention than by changing budget forms.

C. CONTROL!—ACCOUNTABILITY AND ECONOMY

1. Historical Perspective

American budgeters have been fascinated by control since Isabella and Ferdinand dispatched "the royal controller of accounts, sent along to keep tabs on Columbus's swindle sheet when he started to figure the cost of the gold and the spices he would accumulate" (Cooke 1973, 33). In that tradition, according to the Commonwealth of Massachusetts' archives, the routines and procedures that constituted controls even in colonial times were not even waived for revolutionary exigency. Paul Revere's bill for "riding for the Committee of Safety" and printing "soldier notes" was duly submitted; the House of Representatives approved payment in August 1775—"in full discharge of the written account"—for seven shillings less than the sum of the illustrious patriot's expense account (see Figure 5.5 and Figure 5.6).

Reasonable assurance that public monies are being spent as intended is by no means a concern unique to the United States or to the modern era. The insistence on evidential verification and separation of duties, both standard techniques in contemporary control systems, has been traced back five and one-half millennia to Mesopotamian records showing various marks alongside financial records. "One scribe prepared summaries of transactions; another verified them. It was probably here that the control systems of verification and division of duties originated" (Sawyer 1981, 3). The word *audit* is derived from the Latin *auditus*, referring to the oral verification of one official's accounts by another (Sawyer 1981, 4).

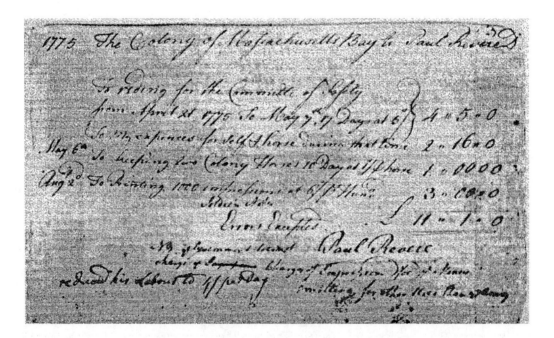

FIGURE 5.5 Paul Revere's expense account.

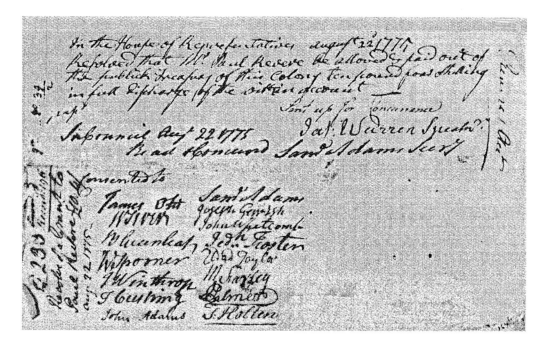

FIGURE 5.6 1775 Resolution of the Massachusetts House of Representatives.

2. Control-cum-Accountability

a. Procedures

In its accountability connotation, control conjures up all the safeguards protecting the fiduciary (or "prudent steward") aspect of handling public money. In practice, it means procedures and records routinely required on financial transactions. Controls are categorized by the source of oversight authority (internal and external controls), and whether they occur before or after the financial transaction (preaudit and postaudit controls). A number of safeguards integrated into a systematic approach are designed to reduce the risk of fraud, waste, abuse, loss, and inefficiency. The detailed, line-item appropriation is the most important preaudit control exercised by the legislature, and as such has remained a characteristic feature of US public budgeting for two centuries. Apportionment, a twentieth-century development (see above), is the preeminent external, preaudit control emanating from the executive. Its counterpart after the transaction has taken place is the postaudit, representing either a legislative or an executive function or both; the postaudit is an independent verification of the financial condition and operating results according to professional standards. Other control devices include procurement invoices and vouchers, appropriations accounts, encumbrances, personnel schedules, and the like. Taken as an aggregate, these procedures, papers, rules, and records are time-consuming, expensive, and cumbersome. Individually, some are trivial, others inexplicable without reference to historical legacy; many are annoying to those compelled to abide by them. Sometimes the efforts made to circumvent them are of heroic caliber, but nevertheless illegal; other times, these efforts are simply pursued for fraudulent purposes or personal gain.

b. And Politics

Control is not a small matter on the periphery of budgeting and thus suitably left to subordinates or financial managers. It is rather a mainstay of the budget process and a guardian of the political relationships and goals embedded in that process.[*] For example, the continuing saga of legislative–executive conflict has been played out in terms of mundane details such as appropriations accounts. This point is emphasized in A. E. Buck's discussion of control-cum-accountability in the special studies accompanying the Brownlow Report submitted to President Roosevelt in 1937.[†] According to Buck, "The itemization of appropriations has gone so far that it often enables Congress to brush aside the Executive and to control the administration directly through detailed specifications in the granting of money" (President's Committee on Administrative Management 1937, 144). Buck goes on to quote from Cleveland's paper on "Detailed Versus Lump-Fund Appropriations" delivered to the 1913 meeting of the Association of Public Accounting Officers, in which Cleveland argues that "legislative control over the administration through detailed appropriations is a device adopted for use of a political institution...." Buck's introductory statement, still relevant more than one-half century after it was written, sums up the issue nicely: "The working basis of the national fiscal system is found in certain political and administrative controls that emanate from the Congress and from the President."

Mary Parker Follett focuses directly on the control issue in her 1932 lecture, published in the famous collection edited by Gulick and Urwick, Papers on the Science of Administration (1937, 161–169). In "The Process of Control," she asks, "... what can we say are the principles of control? This is the same as asking what are the principles of organization. For the object of organization is control, or we might say that organization is control" (Follett, in Gulick and Urwick 1937, 161). In her usage, control is defined broadly as a process of coordination.

c. As Budget Function

Almost one-half century later, in an especially influential examination of the budgetary functions, Allen Schick argued that different emphases or "orientations" and their related concerns and processes vie with each other for predominance in different periods (Schick 1966). Accordingly, budget systems contain three contending functions—planning, management, and control—and are distinguished by the tilt in overall direction. Strongly supporting contemporary rationalist reforms (PPBS), the author concludes, "All the differences may be summed up in the statement that the ethos of budgeting will shift from justification to analysis." According to Schick,

> Control refers to the process of binding operating officials to the policies and plans set by their superiors... predominant during the execution and audit stages, although the form of budget estimates and appropriations often is determined by control considerations. The assorted controls and reporting procedures that are associated with budget execution... have the purpose of securing compliance with policies made by central authorities.
>
> A control orientation deals with a relatively narrow range of concerns: How can agencies be held to the expenditure ceilings established by the legislature and chief executive? What reporting procedures...: What limits... on agency spending personnel and equipment? (Schick 1966, 244–245)

Because each orientation builds on the other in successive stages of reform (and of information, analysis, and decision-making requirements and capacity), one may infer from Schick's analysis that the control orientation is a necessary part of all subsequent systems and a permanent fixture in budgeting. It is on this foundation that later additions rest. Thus it is readily understandable that

---

[*] Control is a topic that has occupied great minds or at least much time, as suggested in the exhibit from the Massachusetts House of Representatives, wherein consenting participants included James Otis, John Winthrop, Sam Adams, and others.

[†] Written by A. E. Buck, the study is entitled "Financial Control and Accountability" and is part of the report of the President's Committee on Administrative Management (1937, 137–168). Committee members included Louis Brownlow, Charles E. Merriam, and Luther Gulick.

fiduciary responsibility, the accountability aspect of control, has been and continues to be a dominant theme in the history of US budgeting and financial management.

d. Professional Standards

Perhaps no one would agree more than the players: the professional accountants, auditors, and budgeters who have developed professional standards over the last half century. One source of these standards is the GAO, which issued statements of principles and concepts of internal auditing for federal agencies in 1957 and 1968, and published a comprehensive statement of standards for governmental audits in 1972 in Standards for Audit of Governmental Organizations, Programs, Activities, and Functions, called "the yellow book." In 1974, the American Institute of Certified Public Accountants (AICPA) issued its industry audit guide, Audits of State and Local Government Units. Despite serious ongoing professional efforts to establish and abide by accepted procedures, it appears that practice has not yet been perfected. A GAO review of audits performed on recipients of federal assistance found that CPAs did not satisfactorily meet generally accepted government auditing standards in 34% of the governmental audits (GAO 1986c). As summarized by the GAO, generally accepted audit standards (GAAS) require professional proficiency, independence of attitude and appearance, due professional care, and removal or reporting of limitations on the scope or comprehensiveness of the audit (GAO 1986c, appendix 1).

Generally accepted accounting practices (GAAP) were developed under the auspices of the National Council on Government Accounting (NCGA), and published by the Government Finance Officers Association (GFOA, formerly MFOA). The NCGA's thirteen basic principles were published in 1968 in Governmental Accounting, Auditing, and Financial Reporting, the "blue book," or GAAFR. (According to the foreword of the 1980 edition, more than 40,000 copies of the 1968 edition were distributed!) It achieved authoritative status when the 1974 AICPA Audit Guide acknowledged GAAFR as the GAAP for state and local governments. The 1980 edition of GAAFR included the NCGA's 1979 "Statement I," the very foundation of contemporary standards for accounting and financial reporting, and details about its application. Statement I was recognized as GAAP by AICPA in 1980. Thus GAAP and authoritative standards emanated from NCGA and were subsequently confirmed by virtue of AICPA's acceptance. In 1984, NCGA was supplanted by the Governmental Accounting Standards Board, which continues to propose statements and interpretations that are incorporated into professional accounting standards. The most recent GAAFR (GFOA 1994) includes the twenty-four GASB pronouncements issued as of June 1994.

It is useful to make note of the fact that GAAFR's perspective on electoral politics and politicians smacks of the old dichotomy between administration and politics. It is especially important because it is impossible to overstate the impact of politics and politicians—as well as the accounting profession—on budgeting and financial management.

The governmental atmosphere is greatly influenced by the political process. Elected officials selected on the basis of popularity or political ties may not possess the management skills necessary for their positions. Elected government officials are generally interested in being elected. Unfortunately, the financial management activities most likely to enhance their re-election chances may not be optimally consistent with the efficient attainment of governmental social service organizational objectives.

> … Both the formal and informal political structures of governments affect their accounting and financial reporting activities and needs. (MFOA 1980, 2)

e. Fiscal Crisis

Perhaps the single strongest impetus behind the renewed attention directed toward accountability elements has been the New York City fiscal crisis of the 1970s. When the financial markets closed on the city in 1975, the lesson for the budgeting and financial management community was more than the "streets were [no longer] paved with gold" (Auletta 1980); alarm over financial management, accounting and auditing practices, financial reporting, and public disclosure, especially with respect to bond offerings, spilled beyond the city boundaries. New York City's experience (and, subsequently, that of other jurisdictions including Yonkers and Cleveland) affected reporting and accounting nationwide.* While New York City was restructuring its debt under the auspices of the state-established Municipal Assistance Corporation and revamping its financial and budgetary practices, other changes were visible on a national scale: the reauthorization of general revenue sharing instituted audit requirements, bond prospectuses grew in length and detail, and newspapers and periodicals including the New York Times, the Wall Street Journal, Intergovernmental Perspective, and even the Congressional Record reported the unease and demand for more and better management, accounting, and disclosure procedures. If an incentive was needed to back up conformance, then New York City provided it. After being somewhat ignored, perhaps as a realistic response to the grants game, control issues and concerns were revived in state and local budgeting and in intergovernmental finance (Dirsmith and Simon 1983; NCGA 1980).

Concern over financial practices resurfaced in December 1994, when California's wealthy (in terms of residents' income) Orange County became the largest municipal bankruptcy in history. Responsible for an investment pool worth $7.5 billion for 187 government participants, including 34 cities and 38 school districts, the county's treasurer used reverse repurchase arrangements for leveraging and derivatives in a high-risk investment strategy. Upon incurring a $1.7 billion loss, the county petitioned for bankruptcy relief. In June 1995, voters among the 2.6 million residents rejected the tax increase in a referendum held in compliance with the 1978 tax and expenditure limitation (TEL), proposition 13.

f. Recent Federal Moves

The US Congress enacted the Federal Managers' Financial Integrity Act (31 U.S.C. 3512[b] and [c]) in 1982. Aimed at reinforcing accounting and internal control requirements dating from the 1950s, the act underscores the continuing concern with accountability for all funds. The act requires each agency to establish and maintain its internal controls in accordance with the Comptroller General's standards, issued in June 1983 in Standards for Internal Controls in the Federal Government. The OMB issued guidelines for evaluating controls in executive departments and agencies in December 1982, building on the prescriptions and standards in OMB circular A-123, Internal Control Systems. These developments turned attention to annually assessing and reporting on the adequacy of internal controls and accounting systems.

Accurate disclosure of financial data is critical to performance assessment, and sound financial management systems are central to that performance. In response to grave inadequacies in both areas, serious efforts have been undertaken to improve and modernize financial reporting and management. Highlights include the Chief Financial Officers Act of 1990, which clarified responsibility for financial management, aimed at integrated financial systems, and created a coordinating council, and the establishment of the Federal Accounting Standards Advisory Board in 1990 to develop uniform accounting principles and standards. In 1991, the US Treasury's Financial Management Service published its prototype Consolidated Financial Statements of the United States Government. In 1993 the OMB revised its 1984 circular A-127, Financial Management Systems, and required that each agency create a single, integrated system of financial management. According to GAO's Joint Financial Management Improvement Program, the Chief Financial Officers Council adopted a vision statement in 1994 that avowed, "Enabling government to work better and cost less requires program and financial managers, working in partnership using modern

---

* In 1983, the Washington Public Power Supply System, derisively referred to as "Whoops," defaulted on $2.2 billion in revenue bonds.

management techniques and integrated financial management systems, to ensure the integrity of information, make decisions, and measure performance to achieve desirable outcomes and real cost effectiveness" (GAO 1995b, 1–2).

3. Control-cum-Economy

Prudence has another meaning, related to some sense of the appropriate amount or level of spending. This aspect of control, related to economy, is also important to an understanding of developments in US budgeting. Even before the acceptance of executive budgeting in Washington, Frederick A. Cleveland observed, "But it was the uncontrolled and uncontrollable increase in the cost of government that had finally jostled the public into an attitude of hostility to a system which was so fondly called the 'American system'" (Cleveland 1915, 22). Ceilings, caps, and freezes have been familiar tools in budget shops, whether in Washington, state offices, or town halls (Ceilings 1975; Lewis and Logalbo 1980).

a. Spending Patterns

During the postwar period, the state and local public sector was a high-growth industry, with spending increasing at rates several times that of the economy. Then in the 1970s, a reversal began. In 1974 local spending in real terms began to decline; in 1976 state spending exhibited the same pattern. This "rediscovery of the revenue constraint" (Peterson, in Gorham arid Glazer 1976, 35–118) is explained by a confluence of factors, including recession, double-digit inflation, managerial and political action and inaction, public opinion (especially about taxes), structural adjustments in the economy, and a turnabout in federal funds (reinforced by changes in federal policy and funding). It was soon learned that New York City was not an isolated case but the epicenter of shockwaves that rippled across the country. The outcomes included a slowdown in the growth of real spending at the state and local levels, improved financial management practices (or at least standards), more numerous restrictions on local budgets (see below), some hard choices, and the demise of some political careers.

b. Retrenchment

These experiences also generated a literature on retrenchment, or cutback management, represented by the influential article, "Organizational Decline and Cutback Management" (Levine 1978). If one accepts Levine's conclusion that the "world of the future is uncertain, but scarcity and tradeoffs seem inevitable," then the analytical contributions emerging from this period will continue to be practically important and analytically relevant. As Levine warns,

> Government organizations are neither immortal nor unshrinkable. Like growth, organizational decline and death, by erosion or plan, is a form of organizational change; but all the problems of managing organizational change are compounded by a scarcity of slack resources. This feature of declining organizations—the diminution of the cushion of sparse resources necessary for coping with uncertainty, risking innovation, and rewarding loyalty and cooperation—presents for government a problem that simultaneously challenges the underlying premises and feasibility of both contemporary management systems and the institutions of pluralist liberal democracy (Levine 1978, 316, citations omitted).

More recent studies of fiscal stress are cited in the references.

c. Proposition 13 and TELs

Contemporary insistence on economy as a decisive value in public budgeting at the state and local levels is best illustrated by Proposition 13, an initiative amendment to the California constitution passed by referendum in June 1978 (see Figure 5.7). Its provisions called for limiting taxes on property to no more than 1% of its estimated 1975–1976 market value, and for capping each annual increase in assessment at 2% (unless sold, whereupon market value applies). Moreover, the Jarvis–Gann amendment, so called after its sponsors, subjected the imposition of local tax increases and new taxes to stringent electoral approval (two-thirds of qualified voters) and required the approval of two-thirds of both houses of the state legislature for additional state taxes.

The popular, professional, and academic presses announced that the tax revolt was on.* Conferences, press releases, and entire journal issues (e.g., Intergovernmental Perspective 1978) were devoted to the hotly debated issue. For purposes of historical accuracy, however, one should note that tax and expenditure limitations (TELs) hardly constituted a new phenomenon or a new response to perceived profligacy or abuse (Bennett and DiLorenzo 1983). Limitations on operating budgets date to the 1930s and on capital budgets to a century before that. The Advisory Commission on Intergovernmental Relations found that fourteen states and Washington, DC, enacted some new control on local powers to spend and tax during the years 1970 to 1977, prior to the passage of Proposition 13. Tax and/or expenditure constraints of various types currently operate in most states. Relating TELs to state-imposed spending mandates, ACIR attributed this "recent upsurge" to several factors, including "public demand for property tax relief" (Shannon and Gabler 1997).

Several statistics are relevant to an understanding of the current role of property taxes in budgeting and in politics more broadly. Reliance on property taxes hit a "historic low" in 1981, falling to less than 31% of state and local tax revenues, and forty-six states have provided some sort of property tax relief (e.g., "circuit breaker") since the late 1960s (Walker 1986, 74). However, the property tax is still a vital component of the state and local tax structure and a volatile issue in local politics.† It is also necessary to consider public attitudes towards property taxes, especially in relation to other taxes. According to ACIR's "Changing Public Attitudes," the local property tax only lost its preeminent position as "the worst tax—that is, the least fair" in 1979, when the federal income tax won this dubious distinction, which it retained through 1985 (ACIR 1985, 1). In 1994, the local property tax and federal income tax tied as the worst tax (ACIR 1994).

d. Grace Commission

Federal offices have not been immune to the paroxysm of control-cum-economy. The President's Private Sector Survey on Cost Control (PPSS) was initiated by Executive Order 12369 in 1982 to "identify and suggest remedies for waste and abuse." The Grace Commission, named after the chairman, J. Peter Grace, reported its survey results on ways to cut costs and enhance revenues in January 1984, with almost 2500 recommendations purported to amount to $424 billion in savings in three years… or $1.9 trillion annually by the end of the century! According to the transmittal letter of January 12, 1984, recommendations with respect to system failures and personnel mismanagement account for almost three-fifths of the potential savings, a finding that elicits the conclusion that "they are at the foundation of inefficiencies in the Federal Government" (Grace Commission 1984, 6). Making a point also emphasized in the popularized version of the report (Fitzgerald and Lipson 1984), the letter dismisses traditional political considerations as legitimate criteria for decision making about public spending. It states,

> We found Congressional interference to be a major problem. For example, because Congress obstructs the closing of bases that the military wants to close, the three-year waste is $367 million. In total, PPSS

---

* In another well-publicized manifestation, the tax revolt struck Massachusetts in the form of Proposition 2, which limited property tax and property tax increases.
† The Tax Foundation's *Tax Features* is an influential source of current data and opinion on taxes.

The initiative proposes adding Article XIII A to the Constitution to read:

Section 1.
(a) The maximum amount of any ad valorem tax on real property shall not exceed one percent (1%) of the full cash value of such property. The one percent (1%) tax to be collected by the counties and apportioned according to law to the districts within the counties.

(b) The limitation provided for in subdivision (a) shall not apply to ad valorem taxes or special assessments to pay the interest and redemption charges on any indebtedness approved by the voters prior to the time this section becomes effective.

Section 2.
(a) The full cash value means the County Assessors valuation of real property as shown on the 1975-76 tax bill under "full cash value", or thereafter, the appraised value of real property when purchased, newly constructed, or a change in ownership has occurred after the 1975 assessment. All real property not already assessed up to the 1975-76 tax levels may be reassessed to reflect that valuation.

(b) The fair market value base may reflect from year to year the inflationary rate not to exceed two percent (2%) for any given year or reduction as shown in the consumer price index or comparable data for the area under taxing jurisdiction.

Section 3.
From and after the effective date of this article, any changes in State taxes enacted for the purpose of increasing revenues collected pursuant thereto whether by increased rates or changes in methods of computation must be imposed by an Act passed by not less than two-thirds of all members elected to each of the two houses of the Legislature, except that no new ad valorem taxes on real property, or sales or transaction taxes on the sales of real property may be imposed.

Section 4.
Cities, Counties and special districts, by a two-thirds vote of the qualified electors of such district, may impose special taxes on such district, except ad valorem taxes on real property or a transaction tax or sales tax on the sale of real property within such City, County or special district.

Section 5.
This article shall take effect for the tax year beginning on July 1 following the passage of this Amendment, except Section 3, which shall become effective upon the passage of this article.

Section 6.
If any section, part, clause, or phrase hereof is for any reason held to be invalid or unconstitutional, the remaining sections shall not be affected but will remain in full force and effect.

FIGURE 5.7 Proposition 13: property tax limitation.

recommends three-year savings of $3.1 billion by closing excess military bases, equivalent to the three-year income taxes of 466,000 median income families (Grace Commission 1984, 5).

The rhetoric and the recommendations elicited commentary and criticisms. The CBO and GAO, admittedly targets of some of the proposals, reviewed nearly 400 recommendations, accounting for almost 90% of the potential savings over the three-year period. This review "found that the potential deficit reductions that might result for 1985 to 1987 from implementing most of these recommendations would be much smaller than… projected" (CBO–GAO 1984, 1). Perhaps even more serious is the following observation:

> Although the majority of the Grace Commission recommendations can be characterized as management proposals to achieve greater efficiencies or to operate on a more business-like basis, the bulk of the cost savings estimated by the PPSSCC are associated with proposals to change policies or to restructure programs. All of these proposals would require Congressional action (CBO–GAO 1984, 2).

Nonetheless, about two-thirds of the revised recommendations were found to have some merit, according to GAO, which had made "similar or related recommendations" in well over one-half the cases. Another analysis broadly concurs and concludes,

> In two major respects the Grace Commission misrepresented what it did and what it accomplished. First, the savings it claims would be achieved by adoption of its recommendations are grossly exaggerated. Second, its mandate and posture of improving efficiency and not proposing new policy were widely ignored (Goodsell 1984, 199).

Reminiscent of earlier presidential commissions, this more recent one also emphasized efficient management. In what may evolve into its most significant legacy, the commission recommended a more centralized approach toward an acknowledged role for management concerns. Specifically, it suggested that an Office of Federal Management be created in the Executive Office of the President to encompass OMB, GSA, and OPM to oversee management systems throughout the government.

Efficiency, a business posture, cost cutting, and outright economy represent enduring values in US public budgeting and financial management. While one may not wish to fault this commission any more than its predecessors for pursuing these or other selected values, neither custom nor consensus alters their ideological origin. The value-laden, interpretive approach to budgeting reflects what is probably inherent in the general field of public administration:

> A final business-oriented bias of the Grace Commission is the insistence on an integrated, centralized, tightly controlled approach to public administration. The government is viewed not as a series of many organizations but as a single organization…. One must generally conclude that while the PPSSCC worked hard and produced a number of good ideas, its blizzard of paper, uneven quality of analysis, dubious savings estimates, business bias, centralization mania, anti-public service posture, and penchant for stealth make the liabilities of such an operation far outweigh its worth (Goodsell 1984, 201, 203).

e. National Performance Review

The concepts and practices associated with total quality management (TQM) formally began their penetration into federal agencies when the Internal Revenue Service embraced TQM in 1986 (Mani 1995). Adapting TQM principles to government and coupling them with state and local governments' experiences with innovative techniques and processes, Osborne and Gaebler took center stage with the publication of their *Reinventing Government* in 1992. Defining "the problem" as neither too much nor too little government but rather "the wrong kind of government" (Osborne and Gaebler 1992, 23, italics omitted), the authors argue on behalf of decentralized, innovative, adaptive, competitive, effective, creative, market-oriented, and customer-focused public institutions. Among the specific techniques advocated are quantifiable data such as performance measures and budgeting with an eye on the mission and a focus on outcomes.

With President Clinton's administration committed to reinventing principles, the vice president undertook leadership of the National Performance Review (NPR), a government-wide examination of operations with the aim of developing recommendations to, for example, cut "unnecessary" spending and implement outcome budgeting (Gore 1993, xl–xli). The first step: "streamlining the budget process" (Gore 1993, 7). Describing a process lacking strategic thinking, critical debate, and useful information, Vice President Al Gore's NPR report (1993) recommended an executive budget resolution to set broad policy and allocate funds by function, biennial budgeting and appropriations, expedited rescission, increased managerial discretion and reduced restrictions in matters such as apportionments, allotments, personnel ceilings, line items, and year-end lapses. In a statement targeted to federal managers, he stressed accountability (Gore 1994, 318): "It is now possible for a president... to decentralize, yet at the same time keep field operations fully informed and accountable for results. It is this concept—accountability—that links the federal manager of the Clinton era to the role of federal managers in earlier eras." Elaborating the concept in a way with obvious implications for budgeting, he writes,

> In the old way, federal executives were expected to use hierarchical arrangements, with checks and controls over every input, elaborate reporting mechanisms, and extensive use of rules and regulations.... In the new way, federal executives will be expected to concentrate on performance and carefully measure results—outcomes and outputs, not just inputs (Gore 1994, 320, note omitted).

Parallel recommendations from the National Commission on the State and Local Public Service called for accelerating procurement, eliminating lapses ("spend-it-or-lose-it" budget systems), and making the budgeting process more flexible (Thompson 1993).

Some observers warned that the NPR proposals would "fundamentally shift the relations between Congress and the executive branch" (Fisher and Kliman 1994, 19). While that has not yet occurred, "reinventing" and the NPR received enough attention to warrant, for example, numerous articles in the *Public Administration Review* (Gore 1994), *PA Times*, and an issue of *The Public Manager* (Fisher and Kliman 1994). One achievement is the Federal Acquisition Streamlining Act of 1994, designed to simplify and update notoriously cumbersome and expensive procedures.

In both corporate and governmental settings, TQM and reinvention/reengineering are so closely associated with downsizing that skeptics abound. Indeed, in February 1993, President Clinton issued Executive Order 12839, thereby instructing agencies to cut employment by 5% or approximately 100,000 positions from 1993 to 1995, and saving an estimated $16 billion through 1998; the NPR translated its recommendations into an additional reduction of 150,000 employees from 1996 to 1999 (CBO 1993a, 2). Note that the NPR is not the only instance of staff cuts; more than 71,000 full-time positions were eliminated and the equivalent of 11,600 full-time workers laid off from 1981 to 1983 (CBO 1993a, 18). With options including attrition, furlough, and reductions in force or RIFs, reducing the civilian workforce is a difficult, complex undertaking that ripples throughout the federal bureaucracy through bumping and other procedures. The NPR's 1995 status report claimed 160,000 federal jobs eliminated, $58 billion in cost savings, $70 billion in newly recommended cost savings, and the elimination of numerous federal regulations (Brace 1995, 1).

D. THE 1974 CONGRESSIONAL BUDGET ACT

1. Sources of Reform

The signing of P.L. 93-344, the Congressional Budget and Impoundment Control Act (31 U.S.C. 1331), in July 1974 introduced substantial change in the congressional budget process. New procedures and institutions were established and new information made available. Most importantly, from a historical perspective, the budget act reiterated two preoccupations of US budgeting: efforts at budgetary control and contention between the executive and legislative branches over budgetary dominance. The events presaging its passage can be compared with the events leading to the 1921 act, from which executive budgeting dates; however,

> in two major respects conditions and goals were very different in 1974 as compared to 1921. First, the 1974 act was not only the product of a budget crisis but a constitutional crisis. Involved were the secret and unauthorized use of funds to bomb and invade Cambodia. In addition, money appropriated by Congress for farm and city programs was impounded by President Nixon on a grandiose and unprecedented scale.
>
> Second, in 1974 Congress sought to retrieve power and authority it had delegated to the president (Shuman 1984, 183).

The issue of power and the institutional prerogatives through which power is exercised are preeminent in other analyses of the 1974 act as well (Pfiffner 1979). One observer writes, "The Constitution notwithstanding, Congress had yielded its power over the purse to the president" (Havemann 1978, 4). Phrasing the issue in terms of impoundments,[*] Schick (1980, 45) explains that, "More than any of the other budget disputes that racked Congress between 1967 and 1973, the impoundment controversy incited Congress to devise its own budget process."

The Committee on the Budget of the US House of Representatives concurs. "Despite the constitutional restriction that 'No money shall be drawn from the Treasury but in consequence of appropriations made by law,' the Congress had, in the eyes of many, lost the power of the purse to the Executive Branch" (Committee on the Budget 1981, 3). Reviewing the genesis of this act, the Committee's *General Explanation* argues[†] that

> The causes were deep and long standing, mirroring in many ways the growth and complexity of American society itself.
>
> *First*, the size of the Federal budget and its impact on the Nation's economy [emphasis added]. In little more than half a century, the budget had grown from $3 billion to over $400 billion; and since the turn of the century, the national debt had risen from $1 billion to more than $700 billion....
>
> *Second*, past budget reform efforts which enhanced and centralized budget authority in the executive branch while permitting increased fragmentation of spending authority within Congress.... [emphasis added]

---

[*] "Impoundment" is any "action or inaction by an officer or employee of the US Government that precludes the obligation or expenditure of budget authority approved by Congress" (Committee on the Budget 1981, 119). If unrestricted, its potential effect on policy and programs is comparable to the line-item veto. Schick explains that Nixon's 1972–1973 impoundments "were designed to rewrite national policy at the expense of congressional power and intent" (1980, 46). In contrast to an "impoundment," "rescission" is the "consequence of enacted legislation that cancels budget authority previously provided by Congress before the time when the authority would otherwise lapse (i.e., cease to be available for obligation)" (Committee on the Budget 1981, 128).

[†] "Controllability" refers to the "ability of Congress and the President to increase and decrease budget outlays or budget authority in the year in question.... Relatively uncontrollable refers to spending that the Federal Government cannot increase or decrease without changing existing substantive law. For example, outlays in any one year are considered to be relatively uncontrollable when the program level is determined by existing statute or by contract or other obligation." Other examples include permanent budget authority; interest on the public debt ("for which budget authority is automatically provided under a permanent appropriation enacted in 1847"); and open-ended entitlement programs mandated by law (Committee on the Budget 1981, 110). Controllable versus relatively uncontrollable spending remained an important issue in the 1970s (Ogilvie, in Penner, 1981, 101–134), and emerged as an important distinction in the sequestration process associated with the 1985 Gramm-Rudman-Hollings Act.

Third, the nature and timing of congressional budget actions [emphasis added]. About 75 percent of the budget was regarded as "relatively uncontrollable" under existing law, and uncontrollables had become the fastest rising part of the total budget. Backdoor spending—that is, spending outside the regular appropriation process—represented more than half of all spending. [emphasis added]

Appropriation bills were seldom completed by the beginning of the fiscal year for which funds were to be provided, causing many Federal agencies to operate on continuing resolutions for part, and in some cases, all of the year.

And Fourth, the increasing use of impoundments by the Executive, which directly challenged Congress' constitutional power to establish spending priorities [emphasis added] (Committee on the Budget 1981, 3–4).

Placing "the chaos that was congressional budget-making" among "the roots of budget reform," Joel Havemann quotes Senator Sam J. Ervin, Jr.:

Congress never decides how much total expenditures should be, nor does it go on record as to whether the budget should have a surplus or a deficit. The total seems to just happen, without anyone being responsible for it, or knowing with much confidence what it will be (Havemann 1978, 4).

The 1974 legislation attempted to supplant a fragmented, dispersed, decision-making process with a systematic, coordinated, legislative budget process.

This was not the first attempt to move in this direction. The Legislative Reorganization Act of 1946 called for the adoption of a legislative budget as recommended by a joint committee, but in 1949, after two unsuccessful rounds, the legislative budget was abandoned. The Omnibus Appropriations Bill of 1950 sought to integrate all regular appropriation bills, but the attempt did not survive a second budget year. A Joint Study Committee on Budget Control was established in 1972 as part of legislation on the debt limit, and its 1973 report emerged with significant modifications as the 1974 act.

2. Congressional Budget Process and Procedures

The 1974 act did not provide for a congressional budget per se but for a congressional budget process—a systematic, routine, comprehensive procedure of initial targets, then binding targets, and subsequent reconciliation (see below), all scheduled against the deadline of the rapidly approaching fiscal year. As illustrated by the 1975 concurrent resolution, the budget resolutions were designed principally to elicit agreement on five figures, including total outlays, new budget authority, the deficit, total revenues, and public debt (see Figure 5.8). Together they add up to important, new information in the decision-making process. These numbers mean that the act "required Congress twice each year to do what it had never done before—to decide the totals of the federal budget" (Havemann 1978, 4).

Considering that congressional experience with temporary or partial appropriations dates to at least 1798 (GAO 1986a, 14), the probability was high that the procedural requirements of budget resolutions and timetables would slip into temporary funding measures and piecemeal budgeting. Bipartisan commitment among leaders in both houses held Congress to the procedures for a few years. Factors contributing to the eventual reversion to old habits included the retention of the committee structure (separating appropriations and substantive committees) and the thirteen appropriations bills that needed to be passed, coupled with the diminished authority of the House Ways and Means Committee. GAO's 1986 study of continuing resolutions states that "Increased reliance on continuing resolutions and the incidence of funding gaps caused by late enactment of appropriations are serious problems associated with decision-making in the federal

Calendar No. 71

94TH CONGRESS
1ST SESSION

S. CON. RES. 32

[Report No. 94-77]

IN THE SENATE OF THE UNITED STATES

APRIL 15, 1975

Mr. MUSKIE, from the Committee on the Budget, reported the following concurrent resolution; which was ordered to be placed on the calendar

---

CONCURRENT RESOLUTION

Relating to a determination of the Congressional Budget for the United States Government for the fiscal year beginning July 1, 1975.

1   *Resolved by the Senate (the House of Representatives*

2   *concurring)*, That the Congress hereby determines, pursuant

3   to section 301 (a) of the Congressional Budget Act of 1974,

4   that for the fiscal year beginning on July 1, 1975—

5   (1) the appropriate level of total budget outlays is

6   $365,000,000,000;

7   (2) the appropriate level of total new budget au-

8   thority is $388,600,000,000;

9   (3) the amount of deficit in the budget which is

10   appropriate in the light of economic conditions and all

    V

FIGURE 5.8   1975 Concurrent resolution.

2

1   other relevant factors is $67,200,000,000 under existing

2   law, and $69,600,000,000 if the revenue measures re-

3   ferred to in paragraph (4) are extended and enacted;

4   (4) the recommended level of Federal revenues

5   under existing law is $297,800,000,000 and, if certain

6   provisions of the Federal Tax Reduction Act of 1975

7   are extended to 1976 and additional taxes on energy are

8   enacted, the level of Federal revenues will be $295,-

9   400,000,000; and

10   (5) the appropriate level of the public debt is

11     $617,600,000,000 under existing law and $620,000,-

12   000,000 if the revenue measures referred to in para-

13   graph (4) are extended and enacted.

14   Sec. 2. The Congress, in setting forth the amounts con-

15   tained in the first section of this resolution, estimates that

16   Federal receipts from the leasing of the Outer Continental

17   Shelf for oil exploration purposes will be $4,000,000,000,

18   rather than the $8,000,000,000 estimated in the budget sub-

19   mitted by the President. If the $8,000,000,000 estimated is

20   realized, the deficit set forth in paragraph (3) of the first

21   section is $63,200,000,000 under existing law and $65,-

22   600,000,000 if the revenue measures referred to in para-

23   graph (4) of such section are extended and enacted.

FIGURE 5.8   (*Continued*)

budget process" (GAO 1986a, 10).[*] The study found that the "resolutions have been used in place of regular appropriations bills and are so broad in scope as to resemble omnibus appropriations bills" (GAO 1986a, 14). With a certain delicacy, the study observed, "The underlying causes for these changes are certain inherent problems in the political decision-making process which affect budget choices" (GAO 1986a, 14).

New institutions were added to supplement the venerable ones already on guard against jurisdictional incursions and responsible in no small measure for the fragmented decision-making characteristic of Congress. The act established committees on the budget in the House and Senate, each with a staff, and a nonpartisan CBO to provide information and analyses on a par with OMB's (Titles I–II). The CBO not only joined the information industry (see above), but the availability of alternative numbers—predictions, projections, estimates, and "technical adjustments" in the mid-1980s when attention focused on deficit projections—altered the terms and participants of the traditional annual debate (Blustein and Shribman 1986). One of the consequences of the increased administrative capacity and information is that the technical aspects of the discussion put it even further beyond the reach of many, even well-informed, laymen.

The 1974 act laid out a timetable and set procedures for the congressional budget process (Titles III–IV). The Budget and Accounting Act of 1921 and the Legislative Reorganization Act of 1946 and 1970 were amended by the 1974 act, thereby creating a new fiscal year adjusted to begin on October 1, changes in budget terminology, and changes in the information provided in presidential submissions (Titles V–IX). The president was required to submit a "current services" budget as well as a presidential budget.[†] In effect, a new baseline was provided against which to measure spending needs and proposals. The new procedures called for recursive crosswalks between broad functional categories and appropriations committees, in no small measure designed to prevent the usurpation of existing committees' powers by the budget committees.[‡]

By the terms of the act, prospective new budget authority is reported and the first concurrent resolution or target is completed in mid-May; Congress completes action on new spending and new budget authority in early September; this is followed by the second concurrent resolution (binding target or ceiling) in mid-September (eliminated by the Balanced Budget and Emergency Deficit Control Act of 1985); by the end of the month, prior to the beginning of the new fiscal year, a reconciliation bill or resolution (or both) implements the second concurrent resolution. The resolutions are not laws, do not take presidential signature, and "only" affect Congress internally. According to one assessment,

> The congressional budget resolution does not actually create programs or appropriate funds. It is, however, the single most important budget decision Congress makes each year and the foremost expression of congressional spending priorities (Collender 1986, 31).

---

[*] "Continuing resolution" refers to legislation providing budget authority for ongoing activities when the regular appropriations are not enacted by the beginning of the new fiscal year. It usually states a maximum rate at which an agency may incur obligations. Although Congress enacts continuing resolutions as joint resolutions, they must be passed by both houses and approved by the president. Procedurally the House's restrictions on general appropriations do not apply; the Senate considers them to be the same, and standard procedures apply (GAO 1986a, 10–11).

[†] "Current services estimates" refer to estimated "budget authority and outlays for the ensuing fiscal year based on continuation of existing levels of service… ignoring all new initiatives, presidential or congressional that are not yet law. These estimates of budget authority and outlays, accompanied by the underlying economic and programmatic assumptions upon which they are based (such as the rate of inflation, the rate of real economic growth, the unemployment rate, program caseload, and pay increases) are required to be transmitted by the President to the Congress with the President's budget" (Committee on the Budget 1981, 111).

[‡] "Crosswalk" is any "procedure for expressing the relationship between budgetary data from one set of classifications to another, such as between appropriation accounts and authorizing legislation or between the budget functional structure and the congressional committee spending jurisdictions" (Committee on the Budget 1981, 111).

The 1974 act also spelled out procedures for congressional review of presidential impoundments (Title X), which had been the source of sufficient contention to lead to court action; this conflict peaked during the Nixon Administration in 1972. The impoundment procedures established by the act are comprised of four elements: an executive report to Congress of the budget authority permanently or temporarily withheld from obligation or expenditure; the release of proposed rescissions if Congress fails to approve within 45 days, meaning that no action is necessary to uphold existing statutory budget authority; the progression of deferrals if Congress fails to override, though either house may release funds by passing a resolution; and the empowerment of the comptroller general to seek court enforcement. According to one assessment, "The system has worked reasonably well until relatively recently" (GAO 1986d, 2). In 1983, as a result of the Supreme Court's decision in *Immigration and Naturalization Service v. Chadha*, the one-house veto provision lost reliability. Consequently, deferrals were disapproved by legislative enactment and impoundments continued to be a source of congressional frustration and executive-legislative friction.

3. Reconciliation

Ironically, while the 1974 budget act did indeed realign the balance of budgetary power between the branches and initiate an era of legislative budgeting, it also set in place the reconciliation procedure used by President Reagan and OMB Director David Stockman to capture the 1981 budget round by converting a congressional procedure into a presidential tool. Reconciliation initially provided for the House and Senate Budget Committees to instruct their appropriations committees to come up with cuts or revenues to meet the second concurrent resolution's binding targets. Reconciliation was changed in 1980 so that it could be brought into play as a part of the first budget resolution, at the beginning of the process. This is precisely what occurred in the Omnibus Reconciliation Act of 1981 (Collender 1986, 39–42; CRS 1981; Shuman 1984, 246–274; Stockman 1986). (By virtue of the 1985 act, reconciliation instructions are mandatory in the budget resolution (Collender 1986, 40).)

The only balance that was addressed was that between the branches (although statutory requirements for a balanced budget had previously been passed (Ceilings 1975; Stine 1985, 2038).[*] The act also set the stage for the next change in federal budgeting, the passage of the Balanced Budget and Emergency Deficit Control Act in 1985, by not attending to the economic aspect of control, by not providing for a mechanism to deal with deficits or debt, and by not introducing mechanisms or incentives for prudence if not balanced budgets (Wildavsky, in Penner 1981, 87–100).

E. THE GRAMM-RUDMAN-HOLLINGS ACT OF 1985

1. Sources of Reform

On December 12, 1985, the president signed P.L. 99–177, the Balanced Budget and Emergency Deficit Control Act, commonly referred to as the Gramm-Rudman-Hollings Act (GRH). This was the response of the 99th Congress to the increasing imbalance between federal revenues and expenditures and the pressure to do something about deficits. What Congress did was to amend the Congressional Budget and Impoundment Control Act of 1974 via an amendment to legislation on the debt ceiling. The structural and political circumstances behind passage have been called "America's great consumption binge" (Courant and Gramlich 1986), and can be traced to any or all of the following: tax cuts and indexing that reduced revenues; increased spending on defense and

---

[*] Because the 1985 act had no automatic revenue consequences, the deficit ceiling, in effect, became a spending ceiling. Tracing earlier efforts at controlling spending from fiscal 1968 through 1976, one assessment concluded that "spending ceilings have a record of consistent failure as a means of controlling the growth of federal spending" (Ceilings 1975, 1624).

interest combined with inadequate cuts in other areas; economic conditions that failed to support the demands made on the federal treasury in response to demographic and other changes; and a lack of political will. If the issue can be reduced to one number, it is an impressive one; the statutory limit on the public debt was raised to over $2 trillion in the fall of 1985. The purpose of the 1985 act was to reduce the federal deficit by interim targets to zero by fiscal year 1991. If the issue is one of perception, then the sense of pressure is communicated by Senator Domenici's statement in the *Congressional Record* of December 11, 1985. He remarked,

> I think the American people sense that something evil is occurring right now, if we cannot get the deficit down. That is why they support this legislation.... It [GRH] is not the greatest way to manage a magnificent country. But we have political gridlock at this point, and the existing processes of our Government, executive and legislative, invite the continuation of the gridlock (S 17386).

2. Deficit Ceiling and Sequestration

The major provisions raised the debt limit, established deficit ceilings (in presidential submission as well), revised the budget process and accelerated the timetable, and required budget cuts to achieve the set deficit limits. In the words of the act, "The term 'deficit' means, with respect to any fiscal year, the amount by which total budget outlays for such fiscal year exceed total revenues for such fiscal year." The act required the president to submit a budget with a deficit in line with the maximum specified for that fiscal year, and required Congress to proceed similarly on its budget resolution, which was to include reconciliation instructions.

The deficit reduction procedure was to be triggered by deficit estimates, an automatic feature that was designed to substitute for political will and deliberation. (With Social Security removed from the budget for all purposes except calculating the deficit and all other off-budget entities now on the budget, the reach of the "unified" budget was altered (Schick 1986, 21) If the deficit was projected to exceed the target established for each of the five years until reaching zero in FY 1991, then automatic, across-the-board reductions (substituting for program-by-program decisions) would occur unless other selected cuts were made. One-half of the cuts were to occur in defense and one-half in domestic programs, although the interest on the national debt, Social Security, Medicaid, Aid to Families with Dependent Children Food Stamps, veterans' pensions, Supplemental Security Income, and other programs were completely exempted or protected by limited percentage cuts (Schick 1986).

The automatic deficit reduction mechanism was "sequestration," meaning permanent cancellation of budget authority and budgetary resources. Some saw it as possibly "the most innovative, far-reaching, and controversial change in the congressional budget process" (Collender 1986, 49). It was mandatory, nondiscretionary, and followed upon the issue of a sequester order by the president (see Figure 5.9).

Sequestration was triggered five times from 1986 to 1993, "once each for fiscal years 1986, 1988, 1990, and twice for fiscal 1991. The sequestration reductions made for fiscal year 1986 were voided by court action and later reaffirmed, the reductions for fiscal year 1988 were later rescinded, the reductions for fiscal year 1990 were modified substantially, and the reductions for fiscal year 1991 were applied in one instance to domestic discretionary programs and in another to international discretionary programs (the latter reductions were later rescinded)" (Committee on Ways and Means 1993, 84).

3. Constitutional Issues

Serious constitutional questions were raised about the provisions of the 1985 act and the procedures under which it was adopted (CRS 1985; Hoadley 1986). The constitutional insistence on separation of powers exerted its force on the federal budget process again when in 1986, in *Bowsher v. Synar*

SECTION 10—OVERVIEW OF THE BUDGET PROCESS

MAJOR STEPS IN THE FORMULATION PHASE

What happens?	When?
OMB issues Spring planning guidance to Executive Branch agencies for the upcoming budget. The OMB Director issues a letter to the head of each agency providing policy guidance for the agency's budget request. Absent more specific guidance, the outyear estimates included in the previous budget serve as a starting point for the next budget. This begins the process of formulating the budget the President will submit the following February.	Spring
OMB and the Executive Branch agencies discuss budget issues and options. OMB works with the agencies to: Identify major issues for the upcoming budget; Develop and analyze options for the upcoming Fall review; and Plan for the analysis of issues that will need decisions in the future.	Spring and Summer
OMB issues Circular No. A–11 to all Federal agencies. This Circular provides detailed instructions for submitting budget data and materials.	July
Executive Branch agencies (except those not subject to Executive Branch review) make budget submissions. See section 25.	Fall*
Fiscal year begins. The just completed budget cycle focused on this fiscal year. It was the "budget year" in that cycle and is the "current year" in this cycle.	October 1
OMB conducts its Fall review. OMB staff analyze agency budget proposals in light of presidential priorities, program performance, and budget constraints. They raise issues and present options to the Director and other OMB policy officials for their decisions.	October–November
OMB briefs the President and senior advisors on proposed budget policies. The OMB Director recommends a complete set of budget proposals to the President after OMB has reviewed all agency requests and considered overall budget policies.	Late November
Passback. OMB usually informs all Executive Branch agencies at the same time about the decisions on their budget requests.	Late November
All agencies, including Legislative and Judicial Branch agencies, enter MAX computer data and submit print materials and additional data. This process begins immediately after passback and continues until OMB must "lock" agencies out of the database in order to meet the printing deadline.	Late November to early January *
Executive Branch agencies may appeal to OMB and the President. An agency head may ask OMB to reverse or modify certain decisions. In most cases, OMB and the agency head resolve such issues and, if not, work together to present them to the President for a decision.	December *
Agencies prepare and OMB reviews congressional budget justification materials. Agencies prepare the budget justification materials they need to explain their budget requests to the responsible congressional subcommittees.	January
President transmits the budget to the Congress.	First Monday in February

*OMB provides specific deadlines for this activity.

FIGURE 5.9 Federal Budget Process, 2004. (From OMB, Revisions to OMB Circular No. A-11, July 2004, http://www.whitehouse.gov/omb/circulars/a11/04toc.html.)

MAJOR STEPS IN THE CONGRESSIONAL PHASE

What happens?	When?
Congressional Budget Office (CBO) reports to Budget Committees on the economic and budget outlook.	January
CBO reestimates the President's Budget based on their economic and technical assumptions.	February
Other committees submit "views and estimates" to House and Senate Budget Committees. Committees indicate their preferences regarding budgetary matters for which they are responsible.	Within 6 weeks of budget transmittal
The Congress completes action on the concurrent resolution on the budget. The Congress commits itself to broad spending and revenue levels by passing a budget resolution.	April 15
The Congress needs to complete action on appropriations bill for the upcoming fiscal year. The Congress completes action on regular appropriations bills or provides a "continuing resolution" (a stop-gap appropriation law).	September 30

MAJOR STEPS IN THE EXECUTION PHASE

What happens?	When?
Fiscal year begins.	October 1
OMB apportions funds made available in the budget process and other available funds. Agencies submit apportionment requests to OMB for each budget account by *August 21* or within *10 calendar days* after the approval of the appropriation, whichever is later. OMB approves or modifies the apportionment specifying the amount of funds agencies may use by time period, program, project, or activity.	September 10 (or within 30 days after approval of a spending bill)
Agencies incur obligations and make outlays to carry out the funded programs, projects, and activities. Agencies hire people, enter into contracts, enter into grant agreements, etc., in order to carry out their programs, projects, and activities.	Throughout the fiscal year
Agencies record obligations and outlays pursuant to administrative control of funds procedures (see Appendix H), report to Treasury (see the Treasury Fiscal Requirements Manual and section 130), and prepare financial statements.	
Fiscal year ends.	September 30
Expired phase (no-year funds do not have an expired phase). Agencies disburse against obligated balances and adjust obligated balances to reflect actual obligations during the period of availability.	Until September 30, fifth year after funds expire.
Agencies continue to record obligations and outlays pursuant to administrative control of funds procedures, report to Treasury, and prepare financial statements.	

FIGURE 5.9 *(Continued)*

(106 S. Ct. 3181), the Supreme Court invalidated the automatic trigger mechanism for sequestration as violating the separation of powers. The effect of the court invalidation was contained because the act included a severability clause and provided for legislative enactment as an alternative route.

4. GRH II and III

The Balanced Budget and Emergency Deficit Control Reaffirmation Act (P.L. 100-119), passed in 1987 with the debt limit extension as the legislative vehicle, amended the 1985 GRH to reset deficit reduction targets. Budgetary balance was postponed to 1993. The automatic sequestration trigger was restored, this time with responsibility assigned to OMB. Following the stock market's plunge in October 1987, successful executive–legislative negotiations led to a two-year budget agreement.

GRH was yet again revised in 1990 (GRH III). The president and the Congress agreed to abandon the GRH II targets. Although the new system of deficit reduction was built on a more solid foundation and was more realistic, it was still labeled as "extremely complicated" by Donald F. Kettl and contained more realistic targets, including (Kettl 2003, 113–116):

1. Separate spending ceilings were established for the three major discretionary programs such as defense, international programs including foreign aid, and domestic programs.
2. The financing of the social security programs were separated from other parts of the budget through a so-called "firewall."
3. The overall deficit targets of the previous GRHs were reduced to $82 billion for FY1985.
4. Federal direct loan and loan guarantee credit programs, previously rarely included fully on the budget, were now required to be fully recorded on the budget and were part of the ceilings.
5. Congress was forbidden to make program changes that exceeded the ceilings within program categories.
6. The Office of Management and Budget became the scorekeeper for determining whether spending was kept within the ceiling or not.

F. THE BUDGET ENFORCEMENT ACTS OF 1990 AND 1997

Passed in 1990, the Budget Enforcement Act (BEA; Title XIII of the 1990 Omnibus Budget Reconciliation Act) made major changes in the 1974 and 1985–1987 budget reforms (see Table 5.1). The Congressional Research Service's summary (Davis 1991, 1) states:

> The major purpose of the Budget Enforcement Act is to establish temporary procedures to enforce the deficit reductions made by the 1990 Reconciliation Act and other laws, but the Act makes other permanent changes in budget procedures as well. The Budget Enforcement Act establishes discretionary spending limits for FY 1991–1995 and requires direct spending and revenue legislation to be deficit neutral (under a process referred to as "pay-as-you-go") throughout the same period. In general, if discretionary spending exceeds any of the established limits for a fiscal year, or direct spending (mainly entitlement) or revenue legislation increases the deficit, so-called "mini-sequesters" will be triggered at the end of the congressional session to reduce spending across-the-board within the affected categories. The Act also revises and extends the Gramm-Rudman-Hollings deficit targets through FY 1995, and removes Social Security from the sequestration deficit calculations.

The BEA shifted gears from fixed deficit limits to spending control. It created new deficit controls based on variable deficit targets, and caps on discretionary spending (subject to annual appropriations, including defense) enforced through revised sequestration procedures (mini-sequesters). Revenues and direct or backdoor spending (meaning spending outside appropriation committees' jurisdiction and determined by substantive legislation) were subject to the pay-as-you-go rule to ensure deficit neutrality.

Exemplifying the possibilities and complexities associated with off-budget financing, Social Security trust funds, off-budget since 1985, were counted in sequestration deficit estimates under BEA, while benefits were exempted from sequestration reduction (Davis 1991, 7). In other words, the BEA reaffirmed Social Security's off-budget status and removed the trust funds from deficit estimates in the sequestration process (see Collender (1992 and later), and Schick (1995) for detailed descriptions of the BEA and its application). The debate over BEA was revived later when the problem of budget deficit was so central that President Clinton signed The Balanced Budget Act (BBA 1997) to balance the federal budget by FY2002. The two most important aspects of BEA 1990—discretionary spending limit caps and pay-as-you-go (PAYGO) requirement—are also at the center for BBA 1997. The latter permitted more discretionary spending under the limits such as defense and non-defense for FY1998 and FY1999; violent crime reduction for FY1998–FY2000; and discretionary (a single category) for FY2000–FY2002.

The major points of BEA 1997 are summarized as follows (H.R. 898—Balanced Budget Enforcement Act of 1997):

1. The bill sets deficit reduction targets in addition to the amounts required by then-current law to reach balance in 2002.
2. The bill sets the institutional framework for sound economic estimates by establishing the Board of Estimates, consisting of the Chairman of the Federal Reserve and four private citizens nominated by House and Senate party leaders. The board must choose either the CBO's or the OMB's estimates of how much deficit reduction is needed in that legislative session. The Board's choice would be binding on the president and Congress, so that the deficit reduction requirement for each would be identical. Finally, the Board would meet again after adjournment to pick either CBO's or OMB's estimates of how much deficit reduction was actually accomplished by Congress during the Session.
3. The bill requires the president to submit a balanced budget and propose a budget that would reach balance by 2002.
4. Finally, the bill requires budget committees to report balanced budget and the congressional budget resolution must lay out a plan to reach balance by 2002. Under the bill, budget resolutions must use the estimating assumptions chosen by the Board of Estimates, meet all discretionary caps and entitlement and/or revenue deficit reduction targets, and achieve balance by 2002 and each year thereafter (http://www.house.gov/viscloscky/hr898.htm).

Although there was substantial support for a balanced budget in theory, there are negatives to consider as well:

A balanced budget rule could make it even harder to conduct discussions of policies on their own merits, and could lead to distortions of policies simply to meet budget goals.... [In addition,] burdens might be shifted to state and local governments (through unfunded mandates) or to the private sector (through regulation or trade policy) even when the public good would be enhanced by keeping the programs at the federal level. And spending cuts that would result in immediate savings most likely would be made first, without much consideration of the long-run merits of the programs. Major deficit reduction surely entails spending cuts, but the reductions should be based on the long-run effectiveness of the benefits provided, not on meeting a rigid annual dollar target (Reischauer 1992).

Several seasoned participants in the budget process have noted the major reasons why, although a balanced budget commonly is thought of as a good idea, a constitutional amendment requiring balanced budget may not be (Greenspan 1997). Robert Greenstein, founder and executive director of the Center on Budget and Policy Priorities, underscore the political and financial role of budget deficits. A balanced budget amendment would: heighten the risk of recession by disallowing deficits to stimulate the economy for purposes of fiscal policy; increase the risk of default on US debt; enable congressional minorities to hold the Congress hostage if the amendment requires a supermajority (e.g., three-fifths) to approve a deficit; contradict intergenerational equity by shifting the Medicare and Medicaid burdens onto future taxpayers; make it harder to raise revenues and close tax loopholes that cut programs and thereby shift the tax burden to the middle class and the poor and away from the wealthy; and represent a risk to the banking system if the Federal Deposit Insurance Program could not make insurance payments in a banking crisis (Greenstein 1997).

According to Collender's view, the BBA was not a radical departure from BEA by any means. The BBA became anachronistic and inappropriate in his view when the budget deficit turned into surplus during fiscal year 1998 (Collender 1999, 24).

G. The Elusive Balanced Budget

1. Resistance to Budget Reform

The reforms of the Reagan and Bush administrations did not succeed in achieving the fundamental goals of deficit reduction and budgetary balance. The deficit exceeded GRH targets for each fiscal year from 1985 to 1990. With a zero deficit easier to achieve in the future because current political agreement could be purchased with postponed political costs and programmatic cuts, budgetary balance became a moving target. In the 1985 GRH, the target date was 1990; the 1987 revised target pushed the deadline to 1993. The BEA again revised deficit targets for fiscal 1991–1995 and did not specify a target date for achieving a zero deficit (and the changed treatment of Social Security trust funds in effect enlarged the targets). When submitting his budget proposals in 1993 and 1994, President Clinton took the opportunity provided by the BEA rules to adjust the maximum deficit amount in accord with economic and technical assumptions. Moreover, during the 1995 budget stalemate, advocates pushed for their preferred target dates for a balanced budget—2002 or 2005— and budgetary balance was again a fundamental goal to be deferred.

2. Political Significance

Accumulated deficits translate into national debt, which historically has played an important role in US politics. In fact, the debt as a contentious issue dates back to the republic's founding and the Assumption Plan. The United States completely paid off the national debt only once, in the second term of President Andrew Jackson (Watson 1990, 162). For state and local governments, budgetary balance is viewed as the chief disciplinarian, "the most important constraint on budgeting" (Rubin 1993, 164).[*]

Public opinion polls trace public support for balanced federal budgets for over half a century. When in 1936 the Gallup Poll posed the question, "Do you think it necessary at this time to balance the budget and start reducing the national debt?" 70% of respondents answered affirmatively. The preferred tactic to accomplish this was governmental economies, favored by 80% of poll respondents (Gallup Poll 1972, 12, survey 16). In 1953, a majority of respondents favored balancing the federal budget, even in preference to tax reductions (Gallup Poll 1972, survey 510-K). In 1976, 78% of respondents indicated that they favored a constitutional amendment to balance the federal budget (Gallup Poll 1978, 679, survey 947-K). Similar questions on balancing the federal budget were posed in 1980, when 67% favored the amendment (Gallup Poll 1981, survey 150-G), and again in 1985, when support fell to 49% of respondents (Gallup Poll, 1986, special telephone survey). Respondents were asked in March 1995 whether they "favor or oppose a balanced budget amendment to the U.S. Constitution," and 71% responded in favor (Public Opinion Online, question 026). But consider that when, in January 2002, Gallup asked, "Which of the following comes closer to

---

[*] On budgetary balance at the subnational level, see especially Cranford 1992; GAO 1993a; Lewis 1994; National Association of State Budget Officers 1992; Rubin 1993, 164–206; and Snell 1993

your view of the budget deficit—the government should run a deficit if necessary when the country is in a recession and is at war, or the government should balance the budget even when the country is in a recession and is at war?," 51% of respondents opted for a necessary deficit, compared to 46% preferring a balanced budget (and 3% indicating no opinion).

What is noteworthy about federal budgetary imbalance in contemporary politics is its repetition each year for over a generation and the size and attributed impact of the accumulated national debt. Also, net interest payments accounted for approximately 14% of federal outlays by the mid-1990s. As annual deficits soared and the national debt accumulated over the past decade, raising the debt limit and reducing the deficit increasingly dominated the budget debate. The legislative vehicle for both 1985 and 1987 GRH versions was an extension of the debt limit (initiated when Congress delegated authority to borrow under the Liberty Bonds Act of World War I). "[T]he politics of budget making was the central preoccupation of the Reagan presidency," and "the budget policies of the Reagan years are directly responsible for the deficit-driven agenda.... of George Bush's presidency.... [B]udget problems remain in the center—and at the bottom—of most Washington debates in the 1990s" (Fenno 1991, ix–x). Balancing the budget and/or limiting its growth also dominated the Clinton administration's budgets and domestic policy (see Figure 5.9).[*] Driven by a downturn in income tax receipts, the 2001 tax cuts, and the cost of war, the deficit scenario was repeated at the beginning of the twenty-first century. The turnabout was from a surplus of 1.1% of GDP in 2000 to a deficit of −2.8% of GDP in 2003 and CBO's projections (http://www.cbo.gov/showdoc.cfm?index = 1944&sequence = 0#table1) show an accumulated deficit in 2004–2009 topping $1.5 trillion. According to OMB, the 40-year historical average for the deficit is 2.2% of the GDP (see Figure 5.10). The concern over the federal deficit continues to sound at a roar in the popular press, including major daily newspapers, and Washington sources such as the Congressional Quarterly (http://www.cq.com/corp/login.do?jumpto=http%3A//www.cq.com/home.do) and National Journal (www.nationaljournal.com).

3. Constitutional Amendments

Among the several tools of budgetary balance are deficit reduction through specified, scheduled targets (described above), spending cuts and spending caps, the line-item veto, and proposals to amend the Constitution to require a balanced budget (see Table 5.1). An amendment calling for a balanced budget was approved in the Senate in 1982, but not in the House. In 1990, President Bush's budget proposal included a constitutional amendment for a balanced budget. That same year, and for the second time in its history, the US House of Representatives considered a balanced budget amendment to the Constitution, but the joint resolution failed to muster the requisite two-thirds majority. Also in 1990, the Senate Judiciary Committee reported out a balanced budget amendment, and the BEA redirected efforts from deficit reduction to spending control. Multiple versions of balanced budget amendments were proposed in 1992, but failed to pass Congress (A Balanced Budget Amendment 1992). In 1994, 376 Republican candidates, including many congressional candidates, signed on to support the *Contract with America* (Gillespie and Schellhas 1994), which included a commitment to a constitutional amendment requiring a balanced budget, but the amendment failed to pass in 1995. The debt ceiling again occupied center stage in 1995, and this time was hostage to a budget standoff marked by executive–legislative conflict, partisan

---

[*] On the Reagan and Bush administrations, see especially Collender 1983–1992; Fenno, 1991; Franklin, 1993; Schick 1995; Shuman 1992; White 1988; and Wildavsky 1992. On the Clinton administration, see Collender 1993–1998, 2000; Kettl 1995, 2003; Kettl and Dilulio 1995; and Schick 1995. On the George W. Bush administration, his Stanley Collender's column, Budget Battles, in the National Journal (http://nationaljournal.com). See also annual articles on the president's budget in *Public Budgeting & Finance* and the many resources available through the Brookings Institution (http://www.brookings.edu), Tax Foundation (http://www.taxfoundation.org), Washington Post (http://www.washingtonpost.com), among others.

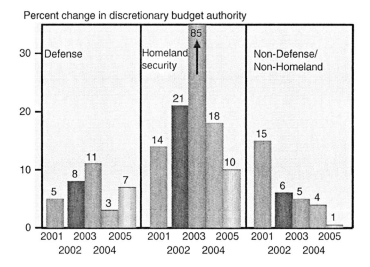

FIGURE 5.10.   Changing federal budget priorities. Growth rates exclude supplemental appropriations. Supplementals increase defense and homeland security growth rates dramatically (these categories received 90% of supplemental funding). (From OMB, Overview of the President's 2005 Budget, Dec. 1, 2004 http:// www.whitehouse.gov/omb/budget/fy2005/overview.html.)

contention, and notably different domestic political agendas. After his electoral victory in 2004, President George W. Bush and the Republican majority in Congress raised the debt limit in anticipation of higher deficits.

4. Line-Item Veto

Many presidents, including Reagan, Bush, and Clinton, have advocated giving the chief executive the authority to veto portions of appropriations bills as another tool to reduce pork-barrel spending and therefore, under current conditions, the deficit. The *Contract with America* (Gillespie and Schellhas 1994) included the line-item veto power among its objectives. Varying in specifics, this executive power is held by numerous governors and subnational chief executives.

Evidence of public support for giving the president the line-item veto dates at least to 1945, when 57% of respondents answered affirmatively to the Gallup Poll's survey question (Gallup Poll 1972, survey 356-K). In January 1995, the Gallup Poll asked, "Do you favor or oppose giving the President a line-item veto, which would allow him to reject individual parts of a spending bill, rather than having to accept or reject the entire bill as current law requires?" Fully 73% responded in favor, 20% opposed (and 7% don't know) (Public Opinion Online, question 005).

Congress has guarded its appropriating prerogatives against presidential rescissions and impoundments, effectively another vehicle to the same end. Presidential refusal to spend monies appropriated was a major factor in the adoption of the 1974 budget reform. After a serious debate over constitutional and other issues, the line-item veto was defeated in Congress in 1995, then subsequently enacted.

The use of line-item veto as a tool in reducing deficit is quite controversial. Governors in forty-three states have been using line-item veto but there is no clear evidence that it cut spending in an efficient way (Calmes and Barrett 1996). Moreover, pork-barrel spending itself, against which line-item veto is geared toward, plays an important role in budgetary politics. Donald F. Kettl notes,

Often such projects are the glue that holds together congressional compromises and the deals that presidents strike with members of the Congress.... If the president were to promise all such projects, the loss of this glue of compromise would make it far harder to produce key legislative packages (Kettl 2003, 188).

The symbolic meaning and the prospective political ramifications of the Line Item Veto Act of 1996 (P.L. 104-130) was much more important than its actual potential to reduce the deficit.

It authorized the president to cancel discretionary budget authority, new entitlements, limited tax benefits, and raised constitutional and statutory questions.

The life of the presidential line-item veto was short and US District Court Judge Thomas Hogan declared it unconstitutional on February 12, 1998. The case, *Clinton v. City of New York*, 524 US 417 (1998), argued that the presidential power to unilaterally amend or repeal parts of statutes that had already been accepted violated the Presentment Clause of the Constitution that prescribes a specific process for enacting a statute. Decisions over spending priorities have thus been placed back into the hands of Congress.

5. The Death of Sacred Cows

The paradox of efforts aimed at budgetary balance and deficit reduction is that they reveal both the power and impotence of the contemporary budget process. Allen Schick has described it as a more powerful, more encompassing budgetary process, but one constrained by "zero-sum competition for scarce federal dollars," in which historical priorities preempt current choices (Association for Budgeting & Financial Management 1994, 2). The title of GAO's *Budget Policy: Prompt Action Necessary to Avert Long-Term Damage to the Economy* (1992a) testified to an emerging and alarmed preoccupation with a problem that was increasingly framing public policy debates.

The consensus broadened and deepened around the proposition that almost three decades of annual budgetary imbalance and the resulting aggregate public debt were unsustainable and undesirable. In his budget message for fiscal 1994, President Clinton noted, "To ensure that our children's generation is not the first generation of Americans to do worse in life than their parents, we must restore the American dream." Tightening budget constraints pushed the expansion of politically admissible remedies, and policy options, and programs once deemed untouchable— the so-called sacred cows—came under scrutiny.

The GRH and BEA protected entitlement programs by according them special status under budgetary procedures such as sequestration. Their political status was undoubtedly related in part to electoral arithmetic. According to Census data, in 1980 almost 47 million people or 20.5% of the US population received Social Security or Aid to Families with Dependent Children (AFDC) benefits. By 1992 the 55.5 million beneficiaries of these two programs represented almost 22% of the population. This means that more than one in every five residents was a direct recipient of one of these two entitlements.

The CBO's report to the Senate House Committees on the Budget, *Reducing the Deficit: Spending and Revenue Options*, is published annually. A comparison of the 1989, 1993, and 1995 reports suggests some significant shifts in the budgetary agenda. In 1989, the relatively few options laid out for consideration focused primarily on program reductions; outlay options included decreasing public consumption, devolution of programs to states and localities, and progressive redistribution; revenue options included broadening the income tax base, increasing its rate, and increasing the use of consumption taxes and user fees. By 1993, the CBO presented a far larger array and the focus had expanded to add termination options (which would recur in 1995). Attention in the 1993 report turned to discretionary spending, the item veto, spending caps, and cuts in formula-driven programs. Along with terminations and reductions, the 1995 report also examined the enforcement of BEA's existing limits on discretionary spending, the possibility of increasing efficiency through restructuring, and a balanced budget plan to reduce the deficit to zero by 2002. The number of options for terminating entitlements was five in 1989, 13 in 1993, and 13 in 1995; there were eight reduction options for entitlements 1989, 21 in 1993, and 19 in 1995.

The CBO options illustrate how once-protected programs surfaced as analytical, if not political, options by the early 1990s. The entitlements' emergence as potential targets was pushed by budgetary arithmetic: direct payments to individuals were projected to reach almost one-half of all federal outlays by mid-decade. The budget process was captured by budget cutters, and the advocacy role was left by and large to nonauthoritative players, such as public interest organizations and lobbyists. In his budget message for fiscal year 1995, President Clinton claimed cuts in approximately 340 discretionary programs in 1994 and proposed cuts in approximately 300 nondefense programs, including termination of more than 100 programs. Describing this "spending restraint" in his budget message of February 2, 2004, President George W. Bush said,

> We must continue to evaluate each Federal program, to make sure that it meets its goals, and produces the desired results. I propose to hold discretionary spending growth below four percent, less than the average rate of growth of American family incomes. And spending unrelated to defense and homeland security will be held below one percent growth—less than the rate of inflation—while continuing to meet education, health care, and other priorities of this Nation.

6. Spending Cuts through Devolution: Block Grants

Replacing existing federal programs or grants, block grants represent a compromise between a wholly federal response to a national problem and federal withdrawal from a policy arena. Block grants were pivotal to congressional efforts to reduce the federal government's role in domestic policy in 1995, when three major entitlements (Medicaid, food stamps, and AFDC) were revamped into proposed block grants by the Republican Congress. Although the first block grant was enacted under President Johnson, most are associated with Republicans. President Nixon succeeded in establishing two block grants as part of his new federalism. In 1981 President Reagan led the effort to consolidate more than 50 categorical grants into nine block grants. Spending increased in real terms for only two of the nine from 1983 to 1993. Although block grants account for only $32 billion of the $206 billion and 15 of the 593 federal aid programs to the states by 1993, they are likely to play a larger role in federal aid to the states (Gold 1995a; see also GAO 1995a).

H.   Budget Surplus and Its Disappearance

1.   The Federal Budget Surplus of 1999–2001

The late 1990s brought something much unexpected to the history of the US federal budget: FY1998 saw a budget surplus for the first time in 29 years. The Congressional Budget Office reported around $70 billion surplus instead of the projected $5 billion deficit in 1998. Surpluses resulted in the next three fiscal years, through FY2001. The surpluses cannot be attributed to the success of any specific budgetary concept. Instead, it is largely derived from the economic boom of the late 1990s. Nevertheless, the end of the Cold War, tax changes, and caps on discretionary spending set forth in the 1997 Balanced Budget Act had contributed to the surpluses to some extent. There was an important change in the regular workings of the federal budget for these years: revenues grew beyond predictions and outlays decreased.

With regard to the 1999 budget surplus, Wildavsky and Caiden (2004, 207) mention that the growth of entitlement spending slowed down more than expected as early as 1996. While Medicaid, for example, was exploding at 20–30% per year in 1990–1992, by 1996 the growth slowed considerably to 3%. Discretionary spending also slowed down during these years.

The budget surplus was greeted with great fanfare, but most observers recognized that it was unlikely to last long, especially given the looming retirement of the baby-boomer generation. According to one prediction by the CBO (2000, 2–3), the cumulative on-budget surplus could total nearly $2 trillion in the next ten years. In the spirit of the predicted bright future, Congress started to spend more. The year 2001 was marked by pork-barrel projects at a record high of approximately $24 billion.

Robert D. Reischauer, President of the Urban Institute and the Director of the Congressional Budget Office in 1989–1995, warned lawmakers relatively early of the dangers of losing the surplus if it was accompanied by a splurge in spending. In a *New York Times* article entitled "The Phantom Surplus," Reischauer noted that the "surplus will materialize only if Congress adheres to the spending caps enacted in 1997 or freezes discretionary spending for 10 years" (Reischauer 2000, A27).

After four years with surpluses, the undisciplined spending spree and an economic downturn ended the budget surplus. Tax cuts compounded the problem. Taking office in 2001, President George W. Bush proposed a significant tax cut for FY2002. It was not surprising that a president would propose a $1.6 trillion dollar 10-year tax cut when experts predicted a multi-trillion dollar surplus. Some analysts argue that the 2001 tax cut proved unwise in the long run (Wildavsky and Caiden 2004, 213). The idea to cut taxes and preserve the surplus at the same time was a low-risk choice, given that increased revenues were the main reason for the surplus. Moreover, George W. Bush promised not to touch the off-budget Social Security part of the surplus. In addition to the tax cut and the slowing down of the economy, the terrorist acts of September 11, 2001 triggered a new emergency spending bill of $40 billion to defend the country and fight terrorists abroad. Quickly, the budget surplus of 1998–2001 was history.

2. What Happened to the Surplus? The Reemergence of Federal Budget Deficit

Wildavsky and Caiden (2004, 215) point out that, with his budget for fiscal year 2003, President Bush returned to deliberate deficit spending without even trying to balance the budget to increase defense, bolster homeland security, and stimulate the economy. However, Bush's earlier tax cut was untouched. Although the economy improved during 2004, according to the congressional testimony of Alan Greenspan, Chairman of the Federal Reserve Board, early in 2004, a better economic outlook will not be likely to translate to a smaller deficit in the near future:

> This favorable short-term outlook for the U.S. economy, however, is playing out against a backdrop of growing concern about the prospects for the federal budget. As you are well aware, after having run surpluses for a brief period around the turn of the decade, the federal budget has reverted to deficit. The unified deficit swelled to $375 billion in fiscal 2003 and continued to widen in the next several fiscal years. According to the projections from the Administration and the Congressional Budget Office (CB), if current policies remain in place, the budget will stay in deficit for some time (Greenspan 2004).

The fact that baby boomers will reach retirement age starting in 2008 and become eligible for Medicare and Medicaid remains the major reason for anticipating increasing budgetary pressure. Although in 2004, federal outlays under Social Security and Medicare amounted to less than 7% of GDP, the CBO projected that these outlays will increase to 12% of GDO by 2030 under then-current law. The future will require serious rethinking of the role of the federal government in providing medical services and how those are paid for. Greenspan's testimony on future budget deficits and how to handle them point out a very important aspect of the politics of the federal budget:

> The one certainty is that the resolution of this situation will require difficult choices and that the future performance of the economy will depend on those choices. No changes will be easy, as they all will involve lowering claims on resources or raising financial obligations. It falls on the eCongress to determine how best to address the competing claims. In doing so, you will need to consider not only

the distribution effects of policy change but also the broader economic effects on labor supply, retirement behavior, and private saving (Greenspan 2004).

3. The Federal Budget and Homeland Security

The terrorist attacks of September 11, 2001 fundamentally changed many federal budget priorities (see Figure 5.11). The fear that such events can happen again triggered a multifaceted government response often referred to as homeland security. The CBO defines homeland security as "a concerted national effort to prevent terrorist attacks within the United States, reduce America's vulnerability to terrorism, and minimize the damage and recover from attacks that do occur" (Office of Homeland Security 2002, 2). However, the funding of Homeland Security reveals a very complex web of activities split among 200 different appropriation accounts. For FY2004, the Congressional Budget Office estimated that $41 billion dollars were dedicated to these activities (see Figure 5.9).

I. OVERVIEW

Prevailing federal budget dynamics reflect a cumbersome process built up layer by layer, institution by institution, and procedure by procedure over two centuries. Each step represents a deliberate response to governmental challenges. The process is structured and constrained by arcane rules that have become increasingly complex, especially during the last two decades. Fenno (1991, 135) suggests that the process may be thought of as a set of variable "governing rules," under which substantial variations in procedures and sequencing are possible. McCaffery (1987, 373) depicts the process as "a resilient and flexible procedure able to accommodate changing conditions." Describing the many developments in federal budgeting, including new budgetary procedures,

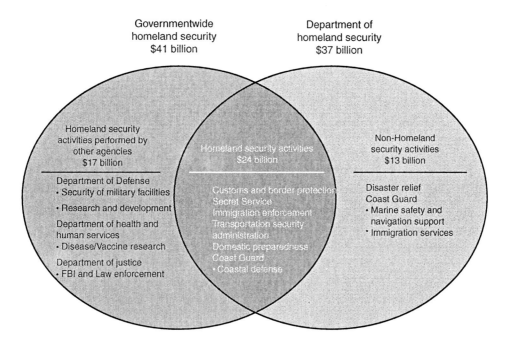

FIGURE 5.11 Funding Homeland Security, 2004. (From CBO, Federal Funding for Homeland Security, Economic and Budget Issue Brief, April 30, 2004. (http://www.cbo.gov/showdoc.cfm?index= 5414&sequence=0.)

Schick (1995, 48) comments, "[T]he cumulative effect is to overload the process with more than it can handle in the time that is available." OMB circular A-11 (1994) gives an overview of the current, formal process (see Figure 5.9).

Surely many concur with McCaffery (1987, 373), who points out that "history teaches us that techniques of budgeting are not as important as the purpose for which the money is spent." White (1998, 165) argues that "[t]he budget process collapsed in the 1980s ..." and concludes that "pressures on budgeting will approach bursting, if the stakes of partisan battle are high enough" (White 1988, 194). That is what happened in 1990, when the government closed temporarily and the process again "reformed." Several years later, in his budget message for fiscal 1995, President Clinton said, "We have ended drift and broken the gridlock of the past. A Congress and President are finally working together to confront our country's problems." Events again moved quickly, in a contrary direction. Discord and discontent over purposes and government's proper role, coupled with institutional and partisan friction over policy and prerogatives, again led to a budget impasse in 1995 and the temporary shutdown of the US government.

The purpose of the federal budget process, laboring under paradoxical public attitude where by the public advocates specific programs but rejects the aggregate cost, evidently came to this: to oblige a feeding frenzy of pluralism, unfettered by the concept of public interest. Today, the process is both captive and creator of zero-sum realities and diminished play, and also victim of deliberate institutional fragmentation. It has been observed that "the federal budget is ... a sort of skeletal structure of our political system and public philosophy" (Franklin 1993, 9). In sum, a system designed for failure is succeeding.

J. CONCLUDING COMMENTS

Public opinion has judged government spending as wasteful and inefficient since 19768 (Ladd and Bowman 1998, 102–104 and National Election Studies, 2000, http://www.umich.edu/~nes/nesguide/toptable/tab5a_3.htm). The Pew Research Center (1998) reports that a majority of respondents agreed that "government is inefficient and wasteful": 1990, 67%; 1992, 70%; 1994, 69%; and 1997, 64%. Testifying before a House subcommittee in 1996, US Comptroller General Charles Bowsher (1996, 2) said,

> Today there is widespread frustration with the budget process. It is attacked as confusing, time-consuming, burdensome, and repetitive. In addition, the results are often disappointing to both participants and observers. Although frustration is nearly universal, there is less agreement on what specific changes would be appropriate. This is not surprising. It is in the budget debate that the government determines in which areas it will be involved and how it will exercise that involvement. Disagreement about the best process to reach such important decisions and how to allocate previous resources is to be expected.

Neither increasingly stringent professional standards nor advances in technology and technique appear to have altered public perceptions. Neither have they fundamentally addressed the underlying challenge of systemic change at increased transparency, comprehensibility, and responsiveness.

> Public budgeting is adaptive, responding to social, economic, political, intellectual, and technological influences. It tends to adapt in small steps, apparently in slow motion, and generally by piling new rules, statutes, and institutions on top of the old.... The picture drawn is of a federal budgeting system that, to the uninitiated, is complex, cumbersome, convoluted, and perhaps even mysterious. Budget systems in many other large, complex jurisdictions also fit this description. Incomprehensibility and obscurity in this core decision-making process promote neither accountability nor trust in governmental institutions.

Trust and effectiveness speak directly to the role and function of budgeting ina democratic polity. Survey data show that trust in government is low compared to several decades ago; the average score on the National Election Studies' Trust in Government Index peaked at 61 in 1966, declined to 26 in 1994, rebounded somewhat to 32 in 1996, and reached 43 in 2002 (NES, http://www.umich.edyu/~nes/nesguide/toptable/tab5a_5.htm). A broad gauge of the public's assessment of responsiveness, the National Election Studies' Government Responsiveness Index showed an average score of 57 in 2000, down from its high of 78 in 1966, but well above the 1982 low of 34 (NES, http://www.umich.edu/~nes/nesguide/toptable/tab5c_3.htm).

Public budgeting most likely will continue developing its multiple aspects, and in many directions. Perhaps its future will develop in tandem with other facets of public sector management; perhaps not. Surely theory will continue to draw attention from many in the discipline and professional practitioners will continue their refining best practices and techniques. What is unlikely to change is the heart and purpose of the matter: the allocation of scarce resources through democratic political processes. It is also unlikely that the future of public budgeting will be without new priorities to address and new challenges to confront.

REFERENCES

Advisory Commission on Intergovernmental Relations, *State Limitations on Local Taxes and Expenditures*, ACIR, Washington, DC, A-64, 1977.

Advisory Commission on Intergovernmental Relations, *Changing Public Attitudes on Governments and Taxes, S Series*, ACIR, Washington, DC, 1985–1994.

Aronson, J. R. and Schwartz, E., *Management Politics in Local Government Finance*, Municipal Management Series, 3rd ed., International City Management Association, Washington, DC, 1987.

Auletta, K., *The Streets Were Paved with Gold*, Random House, New York, 1980.

Bahl, R. M., Ed., Urban government finance, emerging trends, *Urban Affairs Annual Review*, Vol. 20, Sage, Beverly Hills, CA, 1981.

Bennett, J. T. and DiLorenzo, T. J., *Underground Government: The Off-Budget Public Sector*, Cato Institute, Washington, DC, 1983.

Berrman, L., *The Office of Management and Budget and the Presidency, 1921–1979*, Princeton University Press, Princeton, NJ, 1979.

Bingham, R. D., Hawkins, B. W., and Hebert, F. T., *The Politics of Raising State and Local Revenue*, Praeger, New York, 1978.

Bland, R. B. and Nunn, S., Municipal operating budgets, *Public Budgeting and Finance*, 12(2), 32–45, 1992.

Blustein, P. and Shribman, D., Lawmakers say two rosier forecasts on deficit don't ease need for hard decisions on budget, *Wall Street Journal*, 50, February 24, 1986.

Botner, S. B., Trends and developments in budgeting and financial management in large cities of the United States, *Public Budget Finance*, 9(3), 37–42, 1989.

Brace, P., NPR saves $58 billion, outlines more plans, *PA Times*, 18(10), 1–20, 1995.

Buck, A. E., *Public Budgeting*, Harper & Row, New York, 1929.

Burchell, R. W. and Listokin, D., Eds., *Cities Under Stress*, Center for Urban Policy Research, New Brunswick, NJ, 1981.

Caiden, N., Patterns of budgeting, *Public Administration Review*, 38, 539–544, 1978.

Caiden, N., Public budgeting amidst uncertainty and instability, *Public Budget Finance*, 1, 6–19, 1981.

Caputo, D. A. and Cole, R. L., *Revenue Sharing*, D.C. Heath, Lexington, MA, 1976.

Carney, E. N., Losing support, *National Journal*, 27(38), 2353–2357, 1995.

Carr, J. H., Ed., *Crisis and Constraint in Municipal Finance*, Center for Urban Policy Research, New Brunswick NJ, 1984.

Carter, J., Jimmy Carter tells why he will use zero-base budgeting, *National Business*, 65, 24–26, 1977.

Ceilings are made to be broken, *National Journal*, 7, 1624–1625, 1975.

Congressional Budget Office (CBO), *Federal Funding for Homeland Security, Economic and Budget Issue Brief*, April 30, 2004, http://www.cbo.gov/showdoc.cfm?index=5414&sequence=0

Congressional Budget Office, *The Federal Government in a Federal System: Current Intergovernmental Programs and Options for Change*, US Government Printing Office, Washington, DC, 1983.

Congressional Budget Office, *The Economic and Budget Outlook: Fiscal Years 1986–1990, A Report to the Senate and House Committees on the Budget, Part I, as Required by P.L. 93-344*, Congressional Budget Office, Washington, DC, 1985.

Congressional Budget Office, *Reducing the Size of the Federal Civilian Work Force*, US Government Printing Office, Washington, DC, 1993.

Congressional Budget Office, *Using Performance Measures in the Federal Budget Process*, Congressional Budget Office, Washington, DC, 1993.

Congressional Budget Office, Annual. *Reducing the Deficit: Spending and Revenue Options, A Report to the Senate and House Committees on the Budget*, Government Printing Office, Washington, DC.

Congressional Budget Office, Annual. *The Economic and Budget Outlook*, Government Printing Office, Washington, DC.

CBO and GAO, *Analysis of the Grace Commission's Major Proposals for Cost Control*, CBO/GAO, Washington, DC, 1984.

Clark, T. N. and Ferguson, L. C., *City Money, Political Processes, Fiscal Strain, and Retrenchment*, Columbia University Press, New York, 1983.

Cleveland, F. A., Evolution of the budget idea in the United States, *The Annals*, 62, 15–35, 1915.

Collender, S. E., Ed., *The Guide to the Federal Budget, Fiscal 1984–2001*, Urban Institute Press, Washington, DC, 1983–1998, 2000.

Committee on the Budget, U.S. House of Representatives, *The Congressional Budget Process: A General Explanation*, Government Printing Office, Washington, DC, 1981.

Cooke, A., *Alistair Cooke's America*, Knopf, New York, 1973.

Cope, G. H., Walking the fiscal tightrope: local budgeting and fiscal stress, *International Journal of Public Administration*, 5, 1097–1120, 1992.

Council of State Governments, Annual. *Book of the States*, CSG, Lexington, KY.

Courant, P. N. and Gramlich, E. M., *Federal Budget Deficits*, Prentice Hall, Englewood Cliffs, NJ, 1986.

Cranford, J. R., State budgets: deceptive models, *Congressional Quarterly*, 50(24), 1686, 1992.

Crecine, J. P., *Governmental Problem Solving: A Computer Simulation of Municipal Budgeting*, Rand McNally, Chicago, IL, 1969.

Congressional Research Service, Library of Congress, for Committee on Governmental Affairs of U.S. Senate, *Guide to the Conference Report on H.R. 3982, The Omnibus Budget Reconciliation Act of 1981 (P.L. 97-35)*. By Robert A. Keith, CRS, Washington, DC, 1981.

Congressional Research Service, Library of Congress, for Committee on Governmental Affairs of U.S. Senate, *The Federal Budget Process: Selected References*. By Kurt E. Beske, CRS, Washington, DC, 1984.

Congressional Research Service, Library of Congress, for Committee on Governmental Affairs of U.S. Senate, *Selected Constitutional Questions Raised by Gramm–Rudman Deficit Reduction Proposal*. By Richard Ehlke, CRS, Washington, DC, 1985.

Congressional Research Service, Library of Congress, for Committee on Governmental Affairs of U.S. Senate, *Office of Management and Budget: Evolving Roles and Future Issues*, Government Printing Office, Washington, DC, 1986.

Dahlberg, J., *The New York Bureau of Municipal Research*, New York University Press, New York, 1966.

Davis, E., *Congressional Budget Process Reform: 101st Congress*, Congressional Research Service, Library of Congress, Washington, DC.

Davis, O. A., Dempster, M. A. H., and Wildavsky, A., A theory of the budgetary process, *American Political Science Review*, 60, 529–547, 1966.

Dearborn, P. M., Peterson, G. E., and Kirk, R. H., *City Finances in the 1990s*, Urban Institute, Washington, DC, 1992 (draft).

Dirsmith, M. W. and Simon, A. J., *Local Government Internal Controls, A Guide for Public Officials*, Council on Municipal Performance, New York, 1983.

Drucker, P., *The Practice of Management*, Harper & Row, New York, 1954.

Economic Report of the President, US Government Printing Office, Washington, DC, http://www.gpoaccess.gov/cop/index.html

Eckl, C. L., Hayes, K. C., and Perez, A., *State Budget Actions 1993*, National Conference of State Legislatures, Denver, CO, 1993.

Fenno, R. F. Jr., *The Emergence of a Senate Leader: Pete Domenici and the Reagan Budget*, Congressional Quarterly, Washington, DC, 1991.

Fisher, L., *Presidential Spending Power*, Princeton University Press, Princeton, NJ, 1975.

Fisher, L. and Kliman, A. J., The Gore report on budgeting, *Public Manager*, 22(4), 19–22, 1994.

Fitzgerald, R. and Lipson, G., *Pork Barrel, The Unexpurgated Grace Commission Story of Congressional Profligacy*, Cato Institute, Washington, DC, 1984.

Forrester, J.P. and Mulins, D.R., *Rebudgeting in Larger U.S. Municipalities*, International City/County Management Association, Washington, DC, 1992.

Franklin, D. P., Making ends meet: congressional budgeting in the age of deficits, *Congressional Quarterly*, 1, Washington, DC, 1993.

Friedman, L., City budgets, In *Managing State and Local Government: Cases and Readings*, Lane, F. S., Ed., St. Martin's Press, New York, pp. 167–213, 1980.

Friedman, L. M., *A History of American Law*, 2nd ed, Simon & Schuster, New York, 1985.

General Accounting Office (Now Government Accountability Office), *Comprehensive Audit Manual*, GAO, Washington, DC, 1965. 1965 revision and subsequent update transmittals of 1960 manual, first issued 1952.

General Accounting Office, *Standards for Audit of Governmental Organizations, Programs, Activities, and Functions*, GAO, Washington, DC, 1972.

General Accounting Office, *Internal Auditing in Federal Agencies*, US Government Printing Office, Washington, DC, 1974.

General Accounting Office, *Streamlining Zero-Base Budgeting will Benefit Decisionmaking*, GAO, Washington, DC, 1979.

General Accounting Office, *A Glossary of Terms Used in the Federal Budget Process, and Related Accounting, Economics, and Tax Terms*, 3rd ed., GAO, Washington, DC, 1981.

General Accounting Office, *HUD's First-Year Implementation of the Federal Managers'*, GAO, Washington, DC, 1984.

General Accounting Office, *Appropriations, Continuing Resolutions and an Assessment of Automatic Funding Approaches*, GAO, Washington, DC, 1986a.

General Accounting Office, *Compliance Report for FY 1986, Balanced Budget and Emergency Deficit Control Act of 1985*, GAO, Washington, DC, 1986b.

General Accounting Office, *CPA Audit Quality, Many Governmental Audits Do Not Comply with Professional Standards*, GAO, Washington, DC, 1986c.

General Accounting Office, *Testimony of Milton J. Socolar, Special Assistant to the Comptroller General before the House Committee on Government Operations, on the Impoundment Control Process*, Government Printing Office, Washington, DC, 1986d.

General Accounting Office, *Budget Policy, Prompt Action Necessary to Avert Long-Term Damage to the Economy, GAO/OCG-92-2*, GAO, Washington, DC, 1992b.

General Accounting Office, *Intergovernmental Relations, Changing Patterns in State–Local Finances*, GAO/HRD-92–87FS, GAO, Washington, DC, 1992a.

General Accounting Office, *Program Performance Measures: Federal Agency Collection and Use of Performance Data*, GAO/GGD-92-65, GAO, Washington, DC, 1992c.

General Accounting Office, *Balanced Budget Requirements, State Experiences and Implications for the Federal Government*, GAO/AFMD-93–58BR, GAO, Washington, DC, 1993a.

General Accounting Office, *State and Local Finances, Some Jurisdictions Confronted by Short- and Long-Term Problems*, GAO/HRD094–1, GAO, Washington, DC, 1993b.

General Accounting Office, *Block Grants: Characteristics, Experience and Lessons Learned*, GAO, Washington, DC, 1995a.

General Accounting Office, *GAO's Joint Financial Management Improvement Program. Core Financial System Requirements*, FFMSR-1, GAO, Washington, DC, 1995b.

Gallup Poll, *Public Opinion 1935–1971*, Vol. 1–2, Random House, New York, 1972.

Gallup Poll, *Public Opinion 1972–1977*, Wilmington, DE, Scholarly Resources, 1978.

Gallup Poll, Annual. *Public Opinion 1980–1985*, Scholarly Resources, Wilmington, DE, 1985.

Gallup Poll, *Special telephone survey, January 1995, March 1995, and January 2002*. Data provided courtesy of the Roper Center, University of Connecticut, 1986.

Gillespie, E. and Schellhas, B., Eds., *Contract with America, The Bold Plan by Representative Newt Gingrich, Representative Dick Armey and the House Republicans to Change the Nation*, Random House, New York, 1994.

Governmental Accounting Standards Board, Financial Accounting Foundation, Periodic, *Governmental Accounting Standards Series pronouncements and Exposure Drafts*, GASB, Stamford, CT, http://72.3.167.244.

Governmental Accounting Standards Board, Financial Accounting Foundation, *Statement No. I: Authoritative Status of NCGA Pronouncements and AICPA Audit Guide*, GASB, Stamford, CT, 1984.

Governmental Accounting Standards Board, Financial Accounting Foundation, *Service Efforts and Accomplishments Reporting, No. 093-A (Preliminary Views)*, Financial Accounting Foundation, Norwalk, CT, 1992.

Government Finance Officers Association, *Governmental Accounting, Auditing and Financial Reporting*, GFOA, Chicago, IL, 1994.

Gist, J., Increment and base in the Congressional appropriations process, *American Journal of Political Science*, 21, 341–352, 1977.

Glick, P. E., *How to Understand Local Government Financial Statements: A User's Guide*, Government Finance Officers Association, Chicago, IL, 1986.

Gold, S., *The ABCs of Block Grants. Vol. 28 of State Fiscal Briefs*, Center for the Study of the States, Nelson A. Rockefeller Institute of Government, State University of New York, Albany, NY, 1995a.

Gold, S., Ed, *The Fiscal Crisis of the Sates*, Georgetown University Press, Washington, DC, 1995b.

Gold, S. and McCormick, J., *State Tax Reform in the Early 1990s*, Center for the Study of the States, Nelson A. Rockefeller Institute of Government, State University of New York, Albany, NY, 1994.

Gold, S. and Ritchie, S., *State Actions Affecting Cities and Counties, 1990–1993: De facto Federalism*, Center for the Study of the States, Nelson A. Rockefeller Institute of Government, State University of New York, Albany, NY, 1994.

Golembiewski, R. T. and Rabin, J., Eds., *Public Budgeting and Finance*, 2nd ed., Peacock, Itasca, IL, 1975.

Goodsell, C. T., The Grace commission: seeking efficiency for the whole people?, *Public Administration Review*, 44, 196–204, 1984.

Gore, A., *Creating a Government that Works Better and Costs Less, the Report of the National Performance Review*, Penguin, New York, 1993.

Gore, A., The new job of the federal executive, *Public Administration Review*, 54(5), 317–321, 1994.

Grace Commission, *President's Private Sector Survey on Cost Control. A Report to the President, as Submitted to the Executive Committee for Consideration at its Meeting on January 15*, U.S. Government Printing Office, Washington, DC, 1984.

Greenspan, A., Testimony of Chairman Alan Greenspan, *Economic Outlook and Current Fiscal Issues*, before the Committee on the Budget, U.S. House of Representatives February 25, 2004

Greenstein, R., *If Everyone Agrees We Should Balance the Budget by 2002, What's the Problem with a Constitutional Amendment?*, Center on Budget and Policy Priorities, January 28, 1997.

Greenstein, R., The Balanced Budget Constitutional Amendment: An Overview, 1997, http://www.cbpp.org/Bbaovrvw.htm

Gulick, L. and Urwick, L., Eds., *Papers on the Science of Administration*, Institute of Public Administration, New York, 1937.

Hansen, S. B., *The Politics of Taxation: Revenue without Representation*, Praeger, New York, 1983.

Havemann, J., *Congress and the Budget*, Indiana University Press, Bloomington, IN, 1978.

Hinrich, H. H. and Taylor, G. M., Eds., *Program Budgeting and Benefit–Cost Analysis*, Goodyear, Santa Monica, CA, 1969.

Hoadley, J. F., Easy riders: Gramm–Rudman–Hollings and the legislative fast track, *Political Science and Politics*, 19(1986), 30–36, 1986.

Howard, S. K., *Changing State Budgeting*, Council of State Governments, Lexington, KY, 1973.

Hyde, A. C., Ed., *Government Budgeting: Theory, Process, Politics*, 2nd ed., Brooks/Cole, Pacific Grove, 1992.

Hyde, A. C. and Shafritz, J. M., Eds., *Government Budgeting: Theory, Process, Politics*, Moore, Oak Park, IL, 1978.

International City/County Management Association (ICMA), *The Municipal Year Book, ICMA*, Washington, DC, annual, http://www.icma.org/main/sc.asp

Kantor, P. and David, S., The political economy of change in urban budgetary politics: a framework for analysis and a case study, In *Enduring Tensions in Urban Politics*, Judd, D. and Kantor, P., Eds., Macmillan, New York, pp. 564–583, 1992. Originally published in *British Journal of Political Science*, 13, 254–274, 1983.

Kettl, D. F., *Fine Print, the Contract with America, Devolution, and the Administrative Realities of American Federalism*, Brookings Institution, Washington, DC, 1995.

Kettl, D. F., *Deficit Politics: The Search for Balance in American Politics*, 2nd ed., Longman Classics of Pearson Education, Upper Saddle River, NJ, 2003

Kettl, D. F. and Dilulio, J.J. Jr., Eds., *Cutting Government*, Brookings Institution, Washington, DC, 1995.

Key, V.O. Jr., The lack of a budgetary theory, *American Political Science Review*, 34, 1137–1144, 1940.

Keynes, J. M., *The General Theory of Employment, Interest and Money*, Harcourt, Brace & World, New York, 1936, 1965.

Ladd E. C. and Bowman, K. H., *What's Wrong, A Survey of American Satisfaction and Complaint*, AEI Press, Washington, DC, 1998.

Lauth, T. P., Zero-base budgeting in Georgia state government: myth and reality, *Public Administration Review*, 38, 420–430, 1978.

Lee, R. D., Developments in state budgeting: trends of two decades, *Public Administration Review*, 51(3), 254–262, 1991.

LeLoup, L. T., Agency policy actions: determinants of nonincremental change, In *Policy-Making in the Federal Executive Branch*, Ripley, R. B. and Franklin, G. A., Eds., Free Press, New York, pp. 65–90, 1975.

LeLoup, L. T., The myth of incrementalism. Analytic choices in budgetary theory, *Polity*, 10, 488–509, 1978.

LeLoup, L. T., *Budgetary Politics*, 4th ed., King's Court Communications, Brunswick, OH, 1986, 1988.

Levine, C. H., Organizational decline and cutback management, *Public Administration Review*, 4, 316–325, 1978.

Levine, C.H., Ed., Managing fiscal stress. *The Crisis in the Public Sector*, Chatham House, Chatham, NJ, 1980.

Levine, C. H., Rubin, I. W., and Wolohojian, G. G., *The Politics of Retrenchment*, Sage, Beverly Hills, CA, 1981.

Levy, F., Meltsner, A. J., and Wildavsky, A., *Urban Outcomes, Schools, Streets, and Libraries*, University of California Press, Berkeley, CA, 1974.

Lewis, C., Budgetary balance: the norm, concept, and practice in large U.S. cities, *Public Administration Review*, 54(6), 515–542, 1994.

Lewis, C. W. and Logalbo, A., Cutback principles and practices, a checklist for managers, *Public Administration Review*, 40, 184–188, 1980.

Lewis, C. W. and Walker III, A. G., Eds., *Casebook in Public Budgeting and Financial Management*, Prentice Hall, Englewood Cliffs, NJ, 1984.

Lewis, V. B., Toward a theory of budgeting, *Public Administration Review*, 12, 42–54, 1952.

Lindblom, C. E., The science of "muddling through," *Public Administration Review*, 19, 79–88, 1959.

Lindblom, C. E., Still muddling, not yet through, *Public Administration Review*, 39, 517–526, 1979.

Lineberry, R. L., *Equality and Urban Policy*, Sage, Beverly Hills, CA, 1977.

Lineberry, R. L. and Fowler, E., Reformism and public policies in American cities, *American Political Science Review*, 61, 701–716, 1967.

Lutz, M. A., *Taxpayer's Guide to Federal Spending, Fiscal 2004*, Tax Foundation, Washington, DC, 2003.

Lyden, G. J. and Miller, E. G., Eds., *Planning Programming Budgeting: A Systems Approach to Management* 2nd ed., Markham, Chicago, IL, 1972.

Lynch, T. D., *Public Budgeting in America*, Prentice Hall, Englewood Cliffs, NJ, 1979.

Mackey, S. R., *State Programs to Assist Distressed Local Governments*, National Conference of State Legislatures, Denver, CO, 1993.

McCaffery, J. L., The development of public budgeting in the United States, In *A Centennial History of the American Administrative State*, Chandler, R. C., Ed., Macmillan, New York, pp. 345–373, 1987.

Mani, B. G., Old wine in new bottles tastes better: a case study of TQM implementation in the IRS, *Public Administration Review*, 5(2), 147–158, 1995.

McOmber, D., An OMB retrospective, *Public Budget Finance*, 1, 78–84, 1981.

Meltsner, A.J., *The Politics of City Revenue*, University of California Press, Berkeley, CA, 1971.

Merewitz, L. and Sosnick, S. H., *The Budget's New Clothes*, Markham, Chicago, IL, 1971.

Municipal Finance Officers Association, *Disclosure Guidelines for State and Local Governments*, MFOA [now Government Finance Officers Association], Chicago, IL, 1979.

Municipal Finance Officers Association, *Government Accounting Auditing and Financial Reporting*, 2nd ed., MFOA [now Governmental Finance Officers Association], Chicago, IL, 1980.

Miller, G., *Capital Budgeting: Blueprints for Change*, GFOA, Washington, DC, 1984.

Moak, L. L. and Hillhouse, A. M., *Concepts and Practices in Local Government Finance*, Municipal Finance Officers Association [now Government Finance Officers Association], Chicago, IL, 1975.

Moak, L. L. and Killian, K. W., *Operating Budget Manual, A Manual of Techniques for the Preparation, Consideration, Adoption, and Administration of Operating Budgets*, Municipal Finance Officers Association [now Government Finance Officers Association], Chicago, IL, 1963.

Moreland, W. B., A nonincremental perspective on budgetary policy actions, Ripley, R. B. and Frank, G. A. Eds., *Policy-Making in the Federal Executive Branch*, Free Press New York, pp. 45–64, 1975.

Morris, C. R., *The Cost of Good Intentions*, W.W. Norton, New York, 45–64, 1980.

Mosher, F. C., Limitations and problems of PPBS in the states, *Public Administration Review*, 29, 160–167, 1969.

Mosher, F. C., Ed., *Basic Documents of American Public Administration, 1776–1950*, Homes & Meier, New York, 1976.

Mosher, F. C., *A Tale of Two Agencies: A Comparative Analysis of the General Accounting Office and the Office of Management and Budget*, Louisiana State University Press, Baton Rouge, LA, 1984.

Natchez, P. B. and Bupp, I. C., Policy and priority in the budgetary process, *American Political Science Review*, 67, 951–963, 1973.

National Association of State Budget Officers (NASBO), *State Expenditure Report*, annual 1987–2006.

National Association of State Budget Officers (NASBO) and the National Governors Association (NGA), *The Fiscal Survey of States*, biannual, 1979–2006.

National Council on Governmental Accounting, *Governmental Accounting, Auditing, and Financial Reporting (GAAFR)*, Municipal Finance Officers Association, Chicago, IL, 1968, 1980

National Conference of State Legislatures (NCSL), *Budget Procedures*, NCSL, Denver, CO, 2006, http://www.ncsl.org/programs/fiscal/budproced.htm

National Conference of State Legislatures, *Fiscal Survey of the States*, NCSL, Denver, CO, 1986.

National Conference of State Legislatures, *Budget Practices*, NCSL, Denver, CO, 1981.

National Conference of State Legislatures, *Legislative Budget Procedures in the 50 States, Legislative Finance Papers No. 21*, NCSL, Denver, CO, 1983.

National Conference of State Legislatures, *State Budget Update: March 1994 Legislative Finance Papers No. 93*, NCSL, Denver, CO, 1994.

Office of Management and Budget, *Budget in Brief and Special Analyses, Budget of the United States Government*, U.S. Government Printing Office, Washington, DC, annual.

Office of Management and Budget, *Budget of the United States, Analytical Perspectives*, U.S. Government Printing Office, Washington, DC, annual.

Office of Management and Budget, *Staff Orientation Manual*, Executive Office of the President, BOB, Washington, DC, 1958.

Office of Management and Budget, Bulletin 77-9, *Zero Base Budgeting*, OMB, Washington, DC, 1977.

Office of Management and Budget, Circular A-123, *Internal Control Systems. Requirements for Agency Implementation of Federal Manager's Financial Integrity Act*, OMB, Washington, DC, 1982.

Office of Management and Budget, Bulletin 86-6, *Incorporating the Effects of Sequestration into the Current Services Baseline*, OMB, Washington, DC, 1986a.

Office of Management and Budget, Bulletin 86-7, *Implementing the President's Order under the Balanced Budget and Emergency Deficit Control Act and Supplement No. 1 of Jan. 30, 1986*, OMB, Washington, DC, 1986b.

Office of Management and Budget, Circular A-11, *Preparation and Submission of Budget Estimates*, OMB, Washington, DC, 1994a.

Office of Management and Budget, Circular A-34, *Instructions on Budget Execution*, OMB, Washington, D.C, 1994b.

Office of Management and Budget OMB Circular A-11, *Preparation, Submission, and Execution of the Budget*, rev. July 2004, http://www.whitehouse.gov/omb/circulars/all/04toc.html.

Office of Management and Budget (OMB), *Overview of the President's 2005 Budget*, Dec. 1, 2004, http://www.whitehouse.gov/omb/budget/fy2005/overview.html

Office of Personnel Management, Office of Training and Development, *Financial Management Courses, FY 1986 and FY 1987*, OPM, Washington, DC, 1986.

Osborne, D. and Gaebler, T., *Reinventing Government, How the Entrepreneurial Spirit is Transforming the Public Sector*, Addison-Wesley, Reading, MA, 1992.

O'Toole, D. E. and Marshall, J., Budgeting practices in local government: the state of the art, *Government Finance Review*, 3(1), 11–16, 1987.

Ott, D. J. and Ott, A. F., *Federal Budget Policy*, 3rd ed., Brookings Institution, Washington, DC, 1977.

Palmer, J. L. and Sawhill, I. V., Eds., *The Reagan Experiment,* Changing Domestic Priorities Series, Urban Institute Press2, Washington, DC, 1982.

Penner, R. G., Ed., *The Congressional Budget Process after Five Years*, American Enterprise Institute, Washington, DC, 1981.

Peterson, G., Finance, In *The Urban Predicament*, Gorham, W. and Glazer, N., Eds., Urban Institute, Washington, DC, pp. 35–118, 1976.

Peterson, J. D., Cole, L. A., and Petrillo, M. L., *Watching and Counting: A Survey of State Assistance to and Supervision of Local Debt and Financial Administration*, NCSL MFOA, 1977.

Pfiffner, J. P., *The President, the Budget, and Congress: Impoundment and the 1974 Budget Act*, Westview Press, Boulder, CO, 1979.

Plant, J.F., Ed. Charles E. Lindblom's "decision-making" in taxation and expenditures, *Public Budget Finance*, 6, 76–86, 1986.

Poister, T. H. and McGowan, R. P., The use of management tools in municipal government: a national survey, *Public Administration Review*, 44, 215–223, 1984.

President's Commission on Budget Concepts, *Staff Papers and Other Materials Reviewed by the President's Commission*, U.S. Government Printing Office, Washington, DC, 1967.

President's Committee on Administrative Management, *Report with Special Studies (Brownlow Committee)*, U.S. Government Printing Office, Washington, DC, 1937.

Public Budgeting and Financial Management, Special issue on theory, research, and practice in state budgeting, *Public Budgeting and Financial Management*, 5(1), 1993.

Pyhrr, P. A., The zero-base approach to governmental budgeting, *Public Administration Review*, 37, 1–8, 1977.

Rabin, J. and Lynch, T. D., Eds., *Handbook on Public Budgeting and Financial Management*, Marcel Dekker, New York, 1983.

Rider, H. A., Select list of references on national state, county and municipal budgets in the United States, *The Annals*, 62, 277–287, 1915.

Rossiter, C., Ed., *The Federalist Papers*, New American Library, New York, 1961.

Rousmaniere, P. F. and Guild, N. B., The second wave of municipal accounting reform, *Public Budget Finance*, 1, 66–77, 1981.

Rubin, I., *Running in the Red*, State University of New York Press, Albany, NY, 1979.

Rubin, I., Budget theory and budget practice: how good the fit?, *Public Administration Review*, 50(2), 179–189, 1990.

Rubin, I., *The Politics of Public Budgeting*, 2nd ed., Chatham House, Chatham, NJ, 1993.

Sagoo, S., *Facts & Figures on Government Finance*, 38th ed., Tax Foundation, Washington, DC, 2005.

Samuelson, P., Pure theory of public expenditure and taxation, In *Public Economics*, Margolis, J. and Guitton, H., Eds., St. Martin's Press, New York, pp. 98–123, 1969.

Sawyer, L. B., *The Practice of Modern Internal Auditing*, Institute of Internal Auditors, Altamonte Springs, FL, 1981.

Sbragia, A. M., Ed., *The Municipal Money Chase: The Politics of Local Government Finance*, Westview Press, Boulder, CO, 1983.

Schick, A., The role to PPB: the stages of budget R, *Public Administration Review*, 26, 243–258, 1966.

Schick, A., A death in the bureaucracy: the demise of federal PPB, *Public Administration Review*, 3, 146–156, 1973.

Schick, A., *Congress and Money, Budgeting, Spending and Taxing,* Urban Institute, Washington, DC, 1980.

Schick, A., *Explanation of the Balanced Budget and Emergency Deficit Control Act of 1985—Public Law 99–177 (The Gramm–Rudman–Hollings Act)*, Congressional Research Service, Library of Congress, Washington, DC, 1986.

Schick, A., Ed., *Perspectives on Budgeting,* 2nd ed., PAR Classics Series, American Society for Public Administration, Washington, DC, 1987.

Schick, A., *The Federal Budget, Politics, Policy, Process,* Brookings Institution, Washington, DC, 1995.

Schick, A. and Keith, R., *Manual on the Federal Budget Process,* Congressional Research Service, Library of Congress, Washington, DC, 1982.

Seidman, H. and Gilmour, R., *Politics, Position, and Power, from the Positive to the Regulatory State,* 4th ed., Oxford University Press, New York, 1986.

Shafritz, J. M. and Hyde, A. C., Eds., *Classics of Public Administration,* Dorsey Press, Chicago, IL, 1978, 1987

Shannon, J. and Gabler, L. R., Tax lids and expenditure mandates: the case for fiscal fair play, *Intergovernmental Perspective,* 3, 7–13, 1997.

Sharkansky, I., *Spending in the American States,* Rand McNally, Chicago, IL, 1970.

Shull, S. A., Budgetary policy making: congress and the president compared, *Presidential Studies Quarterly,* 9, 180–191, 1979.

Shuman, H. E., *Politics and the Budget: The Struggle between the President and the Congress,* Prentice Hall, Englewood Cliffs, NJ, 1984.

Shuman, H. E., *Politics and the Budget: The Struggle between the President and the Congress,* Prentice Hall, Englewood Cliffs, NJ, 1992.

Smithies, A., *The Budgetary Process in the United States,* McGraw-Hill, New York, 1955.

Snell, R., *Do State Balanced Budgets Really Happen?,* National Conference of State Legislatures, Denver, CO, 1993.

Stanfield, R. L., Losing numbers, *National Journal,* 27(39), 2408–2411, 1995.

Stillman, R. J., Ed., *Basic Documents of American Public Administration Since 1950,* Holmes & Meier, New York, 1982.

Stine, S. F., Controlling the budgeting: an old idea, *Congressional Quarterly,* 2038, October 12, 1985.

Stockman, D. A., *The Triumph of Politics: Why the Reagan Revolution Failed,* Harper & Row, New York, 1986.

Strachota, D., *The Best of Governmental Budgeting, A Guide to Preparing Budget Documents,* GFOA, Chicago, IL, 1994.

Subcommittee on National Security and International Operations, Committee on Government Operations, US Senate, 1967, *Planning–Programming–Budgeting,* Committee Print, US Government Printing Office, Washington, DC, 1967.

Taylor, F. W., Scientific Management. Testimony before the U.S. House of Representatives, January 25, 1912, In *Classics of Public Administration,* Shafritz, J. M. and Hyde, A. C., Eds., Moore Publishing, Oak Park, IL, 1978.

Thompson, F. J., Ed., *Revitalizing State and Local Public Service, Strengthening Performance, Accountability, and Citizen Confidence,* Jossey-Bass, San Francisco, CA, 1993.

Tiebout, C. M., A pure theory of local expenditures, *Journal of Political Economy,* 64, 416–424, 1956.

U.S. Census Bureau, *Statistical Abstract of the United States,* 2000, http://www.census.gov/compendia/statab

US Treasury, Department of Financial Management Service, *Consolidated Financial Statements of the United States Government, Prototype 1991,* Government Printing Office, Washington, DC, 1991.

Walker, D. B., Intergovernmental relations and the well-governed city: cooperation, confrontation, clarification, *National Civic Review,* 75, 65–87, 1986.

Walker, D. B., *The Rebirth of Federalism, Slouching Toward Washington,* Chatham House, Chatham, NJ, 1995.

Wanat, J., The bases of budgetary incrementalism, *American Political Science Review,* 68, 1221–1228, 1974.

Wanat, J., *Introduction to Budgeting,* Duxburya, North Scituate, MA, 1978.

Webber, C. and Wildavsky, A., *A History of Taxation and Expenditure in the Western World,* Simon & Schuster, New York, 1986.

White, J., What budgeting cannot do: lessons of Reagan's and other years, In *New Directions in Budget Theory,* Rubin, I., Ed., State University of New York, Albany, NY, pp. 165–202, 1988.

Wildavsky, A., Political implications of budgetary reform, *Public Administration Review,* 21, 183–190, 1961.

Wildavsky, A., *The Politics of the Budgetary Process,* 1st ed., Little, Brown, Boston, MA, 1964, 1968.

Wildavsky, A., *Budgeting, a Comparative Theory of Budgetary Processes,* Little, Brown, Boston, MA, 1975.

Wildavsky, A., *The New Politics of the Budgetary Process,* 2nd ed., HarperCollins, New York, 1992.

Wildavsky, A. and Caiden, N., *The New Politics of the Budgetary Process,* 5th ed., Longman of Pearson Education, Upper Saddle River, NJ, 2004.

Wildavsky, Á. and Hammond, A., Comprehensive versus incremental budgeting in the Department of Agriculture, *Administrative Science Quarterly*, 10, 321–346, 1965.

Wile, A. N., Ed., *The Combined Retrospective Index Set to Journals in Political Science, 1886–1974*, Carollton Press, Washington, DC, 1978.

Willoughby, W. F., *The Movement for Budgetary Reform in the Sates*, D. Appleton, New York, 1918.

Wilson, J. Q. and Banfield, E. C., Public regardingness as a value premise in voting behavior, *American Political Science Review*, 4, 876–887, 1958.

Wilson, W. W., The study of administration, *Political Science Quarterly*, 2, 197–222, 1887.

6 Budget Theory: New Perspectives for a New Millennium

Howard A. Frank

CONTENTS

I. INTRODUCTION

The discussion of broad-gauged budget theories that seek to describe the annual budget in public entities has been ongoing for nearly a century. These theories have met with mixed acceptance from both academics and practitioners. Scholars from a number of disciplines (public administration, political science, and economics among others) have sought to explain the enormously complex budgetary process via a relatively small number of propositions—some testable, some not—that provide budgetary actors and scholars with an analytic framework for their actions. The question of whether or not these theories have value to practitioners or whether they serve as "tenure producing capital" (Neuby 1997, 139) for academics lies in the background in the study of budget theory. Budgeting may be too complex for any one set of theoretical propositions to explain. But an era of cutback management and enhanced interest in government performance suggest that as a new millennium begins, the search for tools that enhance the rationality of government expenditures—or justification for reducing government—will keep the search for a budget theory alive and well. A cautionary note is offered at the onset. Budget theory at the start of the new century is considerably different from that espoused during much of the last half of the previous century. Grand schemes of budgetary optimization put forward by economists and a wide range of budgetary formats such as zero-based budgeting, planning programming, and budgeting have gone by the wayside. In their place is a broadly defined theory in performance management and measurement that is intended to foster greater effectiveness in program delivery. Old budget theory might have suggested to a city manager that there was an optimal level of recreation services, road repair, and policing in a particular jurisdiction. The new budget theory would focus on whether the current levels of recreation, road repair, and policing in the city are consistent with mission, customer (i.e., citizen) expectations, and cost and quality in peer jurisdictions. Equally important, city managers (and the elected representatives under whom they serve) might ask if such services should be delivered by the public sector or by some alternative providers. In essence, the new theories of budgeting at the onset of the new millennium have a different fit and feel from their predecessors, and as will be seen below, have not yet been systematically articulated. And if there is a message from both academic and practitioner ranks, budget theory in our epoch is the theory of agency performance—how it is measured and enhanced over time. The first part of this chapter reviews what might be termed the classic or traditional budgetary theories that dominated discussion in this realm from the immediate post-World War II era to the 1990s. In part two, the various strains of thought associated with what might be termed the Performance Measurement Revolution and related topics such as benchmarking and re-engineering are explored. These approaches are contrasted and compared to see how and in what ways they overlap or differ from their predecessors. Perhaps more importantly, questions are raised regarding the study of performance measurement and its relation to methodological shortcomings inherent in public administration as a discipline. Lastly, some alternative approaches to the study of public budgeting are explored that might prove valuable to both practitioners and academics.

II. CLASSIC BUDGETING THEORIES

A. INCREMENTALISM

Incrementalism might be considered the grandparent of budget theory. As has been noted elsewhere (Frank 1998), many public administration students and scholars can peg their matriculation in public affairs programs to the *Politics of the Budgeting Process* (Wildavsky 1964) or one of its succeeding editions, a work thought to be the exemplar of incrementalist thinking. Indeed, for many, budget theory, incrementalism, and Aaron Wildavsky are nearly synonymous.

What are incrementalism's major tenets? Taking a cue from the work of Lindblom (1980), Wildavsky and his colleagues (Davis, Dempster and Wildavsky 1971) contended the following:

1. Time and cognitive constraints preclude a rational assessment of the benefits and costs of all but a handful of budgetary and policy alternatives; decision makers are forced to utilize a handful of simple budgetary rules to address the political and technical complexity of the budgetary process.

2. With point one in mind, decision makers are likely to anoint a budgetary base or locus of programs that remain essentially untouched in the annual budget process; changes to this base are likely to be small or incremental in size.

3. During hard financial times, rules of fairness will dictate across-the-board budget cuts rather than careful prioritization; these budget cuts might lead to wholesale elimination of some programs as a means of preserving or enhancing others.

4. Line-item budgeting will be a preferred format. Rational budget types such as program budgeting, zero-based budgeting, or management by objectives, introduce too much political conflict by clearly specifying intended program outcomes. Equally important, the bureaucracy is generally ill-equipped to implement these intelligent forms of budgets, which elected officials fail to understand in the first place (Pilegge 1989).

The inescapable conclusion of incremental thought is that budgeting is essentially a sub-optimization effort in which the typical agency accepts a small increment (perhaps as little as 3%) in any given budget year. This increment is more likely than not the outcome of a gaming process in which the agency requests an amount in excess of what is expected with the knowledge that the amounted requested will be reduced by the budget office or by some other actors. But this cooling out process will result in a budget that remains more or less static over time. The incremental mindset connotes a downplaying, if not derision, of rational analytic techniques such as benefit-cost analysis or program evaluation. From the incrementalist perspective, many view these as pseudo-scientific accoutrements of think-tankers rather than as the essential tools of budgetary trench warfare in which program reputation and lobbying strength are primary determinants of budgetary outcomes.

In retrospect, it is easy to understand the reasons how and why incrementalism was a victim of the zeitgeist from which it was born. Davis, Dempster, and Wildavsky (1971) operationalized and empirically tested their incremental model with data drawn from the middle and late 1950s through the early 1960s. This was an American era of good feeling (Halberstam 1994), when Americans' real wages were increasing and social issues such as race and crime were relatively moot. Against this backdrop, a theory of budgeting based on essentially inviolate budget bases and limited political conflict made eminent sense.

This era of social tranquility and economic growth coupled with low inflation came to a painful end in the 1970s when America was confronted with a previously unheard of combination of economic stagnation and high inflation known as stagflation (Eisner 1995; Thurow 1980). As Americans' real earnings shrank, their anti-tax sentiments grew (Kirlin 1982). The incrementalist mindset of a stable budgetary base came to an abrupt end in an era typified by increased political conflict and decreased financial resources: budget cuts as well as specific legislation, such as California's Proposition 13 which was passed in 1978, limited government's ability to raise revenue or increase expenditures even in the best of economic circumstances.

It was at this time that a number of scholars (Gist 1977; LeLoup 1988; Rubin 1990) began to question the value of incremental thinking. One aspect of the critique was normative. Is incrementalism prescriptive or descriptive? Another was technical. Empirical investigation of budgets at the department or divisional level may appear stable; however, closer examination at the departmental or program level might reveal a far greater level of instability and change. Still another technical question concerned the role of inflation: a small budgetary cut or increment may be augmented or eliminated when inflation is factored into the model. Consecutive cuts or increments in the context of price instability may add to significant cuts or may create a virtual standstill in real dollars, a fact that was neglected in much of the empirical work undertaken in support of the theory.

The advent of the Reagan era, with its widespread dismantling of domestic social programs (Stockman 1987), laid to rest the widespread belief in an incremental world whose foundation was a permanent budget base. At the local level, near-bankruptcies and wholesale reengineering efforts that resulted in significant reductions in force engendered a mindset that could not be typified as decrementalism. Instead, it was an era in which governments at all levels had to do more with less or had to make intelligent decisions about what functions to eliminate (Caroley 1982; Ukeles 1982). In *The New Politics of the Budgetary Cut*, Wildavsky and Caiden (1997) acknowledge that the incremental world of the early 1960s with stable budgets and ideological consensus was replaced with a much more fluid budgetary environment where the annual budget process was a principal ideological battleground.

Despite the change in environment, incrementalist budget theory cannot be dismissed altogether. First, a closer examination of Davis, Dempster, and Wildavsky's (1971) work indicates that while year-to-year changes of budgets were very highly correlated, those comparisons showed considerable variation two or more years out. In essence, the budgetary base may have never been as inviolate as some of incrementalism's critics assert. Second, legal obligations, union contracts, program commitments, and politics suggest that a budget process for year X cannot ignore year $X-1$. Year-to-year uncontrollability is an ever-present reality; the past simply cannot be denied. And lastly, the incrementalist skepticism regarding rational analytic tools—including the current emphasis on performance budgeting—has a rightful place in the intellectual quiver used to understand budget process and outcome.

B. ECONOMIC-BASED MODELS

As noted at the outset, economics has been the keystone in budgeting theory. This is to be expected given that budgeting ultimately deals with the allocation of scarce resources, and the *raison d'etre* of economics is how to answer the questions concerning resource allocation. The economic approaches that have dominated budgetary thinking are embedded in diametrically opposite views of government's potential as a service provider. Notwithstanding this difference, economic thinking lies at the core of classic and contemporary budget theory.

1. Models of Optimization: Budgeting at the Pigovian Margins

Assume for a moment that you are a city commissioner or city manager deliberating on the coming fiscal year's budget. Should you, for example, put incremental dollars into police or recreation? If you say the former, should the money be spent on enhanced street patrols or new data-sharing computers? If the latter, should it be for more midget league football or more day care? Presumably, these choices are not all-or-nothing in nature: street patrols would not be eliminated to enhance computing; midget league football would not be eliminated altogether to enhance day care; nor would the opposite be the case. The question would be decided at the margin with economic tools related to estimation of benefits and costs making the allocation simpler. The end result is an optimal allocation in which the marginal benefits and costs of a number of programs would be maximized at levels which maximize social welfare. This optimization is normally associated with welfare economics and the work of Musgrave (1980) and Pigou (1947).

This mindset may seem strange, indeed almost religious, to readers who have come of age in an era of governmental restraint and frequent doubt about government's ability to deliver what it promises. But as Howard McCurdy (1986) notes, the early 1960s marked a heyday for governmental intervention in the economy, and the applied microeconomic theories (as well as macroeconomic theories of full employment) were driven by optimization of government output based on marginal analysis.

The Pigovian perspective laid the groundwork for two major theories in budgeting: planning, programming, and budgeting systems (PPBS) and zero-based budgeting (ZBB). PPBS was an outgrowth of Rand Corporation thinktanking, an outgrowth that was applied to the allocation of resources for the American armed forces during World War II. Its introduction into the federal budget in the Defense Department in the 1960s was spearheaded by Robert McNamara and other whiz kids (1990) who were responsible for Cold War defense policies—most notably for the creation of credible nuclear deterrents and at the same time for the maintenance of non-nuclear capabilities in potential theatres of operation around the world. While not as deeply rooted in applied microeconomics as PPBS and undertaken from a bottoms up perspective, ZBB is also rooted in the assumption that rational analysis at the margin can deliver answers to V.O. Key's "$64.00 question on the expenditure side of public budgeting.... On what basis shall it be decided to allocate X dollars to Activity A instead allocating them to Activity B, or instead of allowing the taxpayer to use the money for his individual purposes?" (1148). In PPBS, this question is answered in the language of benefit-cost analysis and program evaluation; in ZBB, decision packages sent through the bureaucratic channels lead to senior executives and elective officials divining appropriate mixes and levels of public good and service delivery (Lewis 1952, 43). The success of PPBS and ZBB was short-lived in the hands of the federal government, and their imitators at the state level did not fare much better (Lynch 1995). Nonetheless, as ideal types in a Weberian sense, these budget formats represent the belief that rationality rather than politics can triumph in governmental resource allocation. As naive as this may appear, it is a powerful vision that has survived in a number of forms: program evaluation, performance measurement, and results-oriented governance. For better or worse, budgeting is political as well as technical. But if technocracy, though presaged by Pigovian thinking, was not altogether successful, elements of it remain in contemporary practice.

2. Public Choice

The rationality that informs the welfare economics and general equilibrium-driven models such as PPBS and ZBB also breathes life into another economic approach to budgeting. In this case, however, it takes up a political perspective at the opposite end of the spectrum from the 1960s-style optimization. Public choice adherents hold rationality of behavior and constrained choice in the same high esteem as their more politically liberal colleagues, but there the similarity ends. Adherents of the New Political Economy see government as a poor service provider at best, a threat to individual freedom at worst, and a meddler in a market system that needs little public intervention (Buchanan and Musgrave 1999) to function appropriately.

At the core of the public choice belief system is a fundamental mistrust of bureaucracy and its connection with elected officials. It can be sketched in the following interrelated propositions (Buchanan and Tullock 1962; Niskanen 1971; Ostrom 1989; Wagner 1983):

- The bureaucrat has critical knowledge of governmental operations that a cadre of predominantly part-time elected officials lack; this information asymmetry allows government agencies to overproduce public goods at wasteful prices.
- Elected officials' incentive structures make re-election paramount; this is the impetus for bureaucratic overcharging and oversupply through a bias towards increased size of the public sector.
- Operating out of self-interest, bureaucrats are predominantly members of the liberal parties of major democracies; hence political influence, particularly at the local level, can add to the oversupply of government with strong government unionization enhancing this accretion.
- Representative democracy is a messy means of translating collective desires into optimal levels of government service provision; the absence of referenda and direct forms of balloting for specific goods and services leads to an oversupply of government.
- Fiscal illusion allows current voters to consume in the present via the issuance of debt which will be paid for by future voter-consumers; these consumers will be represented by an ostensibly different generation of elected officials. This seemingly painless consumption in the present leads to over-expansion of the public service.

- Decentralized governance structures and multiple, competing jurisdictions allow voter-consumers to choose between jurisdictions that provide them with the best mix of goods and services for a given tax price; inefficient or oversupply jurisdictions will lose residents or businesses. Voting with their feet (the so-called Tiebout hypothesis) places a check on bureaucratic growth and oversupply of government services.
- A necessary check on the growth of government and the bureaucratic-elected official nexus is discernible in the constitutional limitation on revenue and expenditure. These tax and expenditure limitations (Advisory Commission on Intergovernmental Relations 1995) are, from the public choice perspective, the most effective means of thwarting the growth of government.

One could argue that public choice is not so much a budget theory as it is a theory of the bureaucracy or a theory of government in general. This line of reasoning is valid but nonetheless misses the point. The fact of the matter is that the public choice perspective of government and bureaucracy is probably the dominant mindset of governance over the past quarter century. As Rosenbaum and Gajdosova (2003) note, the growth of government and its capacity to effectively deliver public goods and services are front-burner issues in both the developed and less-developed nations. Recent efforts by the bureaucracy to shed its image as an inept oversupplier of public goods, efforts echoed in the many attempts to rebrand it re-engineering, comparative performance measurement, and customer-oriented governance, must be seen as direct reactions to the challenges that public choice has made to mainstream public administration and the Weberian bureaucratic model upon which it rests.

It matters little that many of public choice's tenets fail to hold up under careful empirical scrutiny. Service delivery in smaller, competing jurisdictions is not always perceived to be better than in larger, consolidated ones (Lyons and Lowery 1989). Movement of people and businesses between communities is not as frictionless as public choice adherents suggest (Raimondo 1992), and high tax jurisdictions that offer commensurately high quality of life may attract people and businesses (Bartik 1991; Savigeau 2000). Unfortunately, stagnation of real earnings since the oil shocks of the seventies has placed government at a relative disadvantage—people are unwilling to contribute to collective consumption when keeping roofs over their own heads becomes more difficult (Peterson 1994). This stagnation, coupled with what Aaron Wildavsky (1988, 753) terms the "ubiquitous anomie" of the American bureaucracy (i.e., the fundamental mistrust that Americans feel about government), suggests that from an operational perspective, government will be under constant pressure to deliver more with less and to prove that its services meet the needs of its customer taxpayers. This has created a double-barreled impetus to provision by private or non-profit providers (Osborne and Plastrik 2000). Within this context, public choice must be seen as a driving, if not dominant, budget theory as the new millennium is entered.

Incrementalism and both the liberal and conservative branches of economics applied to budgeting represent intellectual bookends along a continuum of thinking that can be seen in practice. Lynch (1995) correctly asserts that those who create and utilize budget theories must adopt a catholic view of major budgetary schemes if they are to be effective practitioners. History cannot be ignored; hence incrementalism will always have at least some validity in explaining budget behavior. Contrariwise, the fact that many federal, state, and local agencies have research, planning, and development division, suggests that the notion of getting the biggest bang for your buck with its associated benefit-cost mindset carries on even if PPBS is essentially dead. A strong reaction to the public choice critique of mainstream public administration is the driving force for much of the contemporary reengineering movement. The upshot is that incrementalist and economic approaches to budgeting provide much of the intellectual underpinning for the study of public budgeting despite the controversies surrounding their explanatory power and normative assumptions.

C. The Performance Measurement and Budgeting Paradigm: Budgeting Theory and Intelligent Suboptimization of Public Budgeting in the New Millenium

The sheer volume of writing in the performance measurement arena (Frank and D'Souza 2004) suggests that a new era in the arena of public budgeting has arrived. Lawrence Martin (2002) contends that the heightened emphasis on performance and outcome-related budgeting and management represents a break with the past in the study of budget theory. The intellectual warfare between incrementalists and non-incrementalists has been supplanted with the following question: Can governments begin to assess their provision of goods and services in a manner analogous to that of private entities (Kelly 2002)? The publication of *Service Efforts and Accomplishments Reporting: Its Time Has Come* (Hatry et al. 1990) by the Governmental Accounting Standards Board of the Financial Accounting Foundation will probably be remembered as a seminal event in budget theory history. This work established the need for state and local governments to systematically report on the quantity and effectiveness of their service delivery. Its publication was roughly contemporaneous with similar efforts made by the Government Performance and Results Act at the federal level as well as those by other organizations (e.g., the University of North Carolina-Chapel Hill, the International City and County Managers Association) devoted to systematic interjurisdictional comparison of performance. Osborne and Gaebler's *Reinventing Government: How the Entrepreneurial Spirit Is Transforming the Public Sector* (1993) and, more broadly, the movement towards more responsive, customer-oriented public service delivery are also a product of the early 1990s. Service effort and accomplishment reporting are an integral part of the reengineering model. In sum, Hatry et al.'s (1990) opus represents an exemplar (Ritzer 1975) in an emerging public productivity paradigm; as such it may very well dominate the study of contemporary budgeting.

Much of the public performance movement focuses on whether organizations are doing the thing right. Such an approach is in opposition to the aforementioned economic approaches to budgeting that were focused on answering whether or not governments were doing the right thing. This is unsurprising. In McLean's (1987) view, most public organizations are confronted with questions that deal with x efficiency related to execution of policies rather than y efficiency related to macro policy choices. Twenty-five years of cutback management and reengineering efforts have led to a public sector with wage gains and salary fringes on par with private sector standards. Since 1993, public sector job growth outside of education and criminal justice has been around 8%. By contrast, the private sector has seen a 19% gain (Mandel 2003, 16). On the other hand, to the extent that they can be measured, productivity gains in the public sector lag behind those of the private sector. This suggests that while the public sector does not suffer from the bloat imputed to it by public choice economists, its underlying processes and organizational design are problematic (National Commission on the Public Service 2002).

Public management scholars have long maintained the need for performance measurement and accountability in the administration of public programs (Murphy and Carnevale 2001, 2002). The last twenty years of research and implementation in the performance measurement (PM) arena is pregnant with the promise of improved practice. Reflecting a private sector mindset (Kelly 2002), PM implementation has brought systematic assessment of cost, quality, and citizen satisfaction to a number of venues in the United States at all levels of government as well as throughout government in Canada, Australia, New Zealand, and Western Europe (Dluhy et al. 2000).

The diffusion of PM utilization has many roots (Halachmi 2002) from economics and the public sphere to government, telecommunications, and beyond. The need to do more with less has spurred interest in ascertaining the value of taxpayer return on investment. A better educated public demands more information on how its money is spent. The legislative branch wants to enhance its relevance and credibility while in office, both of which are made more difficult with the increasing prevalence of term limits. The increased use of advanced telecommunications and information technology has put the once novel processes of benchmarking and cross-jurisdictional comparisons within the grasp of many practitioners. Training in PM and budgeting is becoming a staple of Master of Public Administration (MPA) curriculums (Frank 2002; Rivenbark 2001). Survey results suggest that in many jurisdictions, PM plays an important role in identifying funding alternatives and establishing service funding levels (Gianakis and Wang 1999).

Simply put, the tenets of Hatry et al. (1990) and those of Osborne and Gaebler (1993) appear to be flourishing throughout the public sector, here and abroad. The provision of systematic performance measurement—an integral part of the Reinventing Government movement that focuses on results-oriented public management—is here to stay. The movement and its tenets have been institutionalized in the federal government via the Government Performance and Results Act (GPRA) of 1993, which has been emulated by other governments (Ogata and Goodkey 2002) and sponsored by respected professional associations like the American Society for Public Administration, the Government Finance Officers Association, and Governmental Accounting Standards Board (Dluhy et al. 2000).

On the face of things, the utilization of PM has deep roots and strong support. But upon closer examination of its implementation, a picture emerges that many describe as bimodal in a number of ways. At the municipal level, half the nation's jurisdictions still deploy the line-item budget (Gianakis and Wang 1999; O'Toole and Stipak 2002). Local governments that have deployed PM have tended to focus on widget counting and workload measures with little done to measure efficiency and effectiveness. Virtually identical findings have been noted at the county level (Berman and Wang 2000). At the state level, Melkers and Willoughby (1998) note that 47 of the 50 states surveyed employed what they termed performance-based budgeting. But none had clear penalties or rewards for substandard or above-standard performance and, in a topic that will be returned to shortly, allocation decisions and linkages with larger strategic issues appeared tenuous. Grizzle's (1999) findings reinforce those of Melkers and Willoughby. She found that after nearly a decade of program budgeting in Florida, there was a substantial difference between agencies and their respective legislative oversight committees in terms of implementation: most remained wedded to traditional line-items and budgetary control, and a small handful utilized performance data for tie-in with agency-wide budget allocation and individual performance appraisal. Nearly a decade after the GPRA (Hatry 2002), this bifurcated pattern has finally been noted in many federal agencies.

The possibility that the rhetoric of PM has outstripped the reality of implementation (O'Toole and Stipak 2002) is not surprising to at least some observers. The line-item budget is a very hardy perennial (Pilegge 1989) that is simply produced and easily understood. Furthermore, it readily facilitates the most elementary of budget functions control. Ammons (1999, 2002) and Behn (2002) note that many jurisdictions do not have an organizational culture that fosters critical assessment of service cost and quality. The widespread perception in the public sector is that good performance goes unheralded, while substandard effort, to speak in mafia jargon, gets whacked. The authors' experience in applied work and technical assistance in two large urban counties in Florida suggests that public managers may support PM as a generic concept but remain highly skeptical about implementation in their respective communities. While a sense of professional best practice leads them to embrace PM, managers' past experience with prior budget reforms and management tools (e.g., ZBB, quality circles, MBO) fosters a sense of déjà vu. In short, a strong veneer of support for PM implementation masks deep misgivings about its staying power and ultimate value to practice.

This dual mindset may be a function of unsubstantiated claims made by PM adherents. No doubt research of PM has been unsystematic. Practitioners have been surprisingly lax in evaluating PM implementation (Andrews 2002), generally failing to specify clear-cut goals, outcomes, and expectations of the institution of formal PM. Academics have aided and abetted this by failing to address critical normative issues regarding PM implementation. Even worse, academic treatment has been methodologically inappropriate. A plethora of survey-based work provides the backbone of public administration's PM knowledge base. It is unlikely that these surveys will provide satisfactory answers to implementation issues in PM. Valid social science research, be it qualitative or quantitative, should align research purpose with the appropriate method (Ritzer 1975). To my mind, PM implementation and its research coverage have been poorly matched. The study of PM, as is the case any subject, should address fundamental, intertwined questions within the context of appropriate methods. In the social and managerial sciences, research substance, method, and paradigm are inextricably interconnected (Burrell and Morgan 1979; Ritzer 1975). PM in the public sector is currently pre-paradigmatic (which is to say, ill-defined in terms of means, ends, and analytic framework) and the predominance of one-shot case studies and surveys pertaining to this subject matter are both cause and effect of the pre-paradigmatic status.

As Andrews (2002) notes, academics strongly support program evaluation. Yet most PM implementation fails to specify organizational expectations regarding its roll-out. There appears to be a groundswell of support for PM, but its would-be implementers have only a vague idea of what they expect from it. From a workaday vantage point, a basic tenet of operations management is that the benefits of obtaining information should at least equal the costs of obtaining it (McKenna 1980). As will be shown below, there appears to be very little hard evidence that the expensive and time-consuming process of developing and utilizing PM really pays off in tangible or intangible benefits to public organizations and the citizens they serve. A likely prerequisite of achieving paradigmatic status in PM research will be the focus on a handful of big questions regarding, among other things, intended audience and the standards for good measures. For example, do they need an external referent such as professional standards or benchmarks with peer organizations (Frank 2002; Harris 1995)? Without widespread agreement on the critical means and ends of PM, implementation research may be circular at best, misleading and contradictory at worst. Indeed, failing to address PM implementation in a systematic manner without a minimal benefit-cost analysis of both pecuniary and non-pecuniary aspects could be construed as a moral breach in the study of public budgeting (Lewis 1992). Why is that the case? Failing to provide a preliminary benefit-cost assessment of PM implementation would only reinforce a belief held by many practitioners that PM is a feel-good exercise done to assuage an angry public's anti-government sentiment (Glaser and Denhardt 2000; Shelton and Albee 2000), rather than a *modus operandi* designed to address the strengths and weaknesses of public management. Seen in this light, honest efforts at assessing the benefits and costs of PM square with a basic tenet of organizational design and intervention called for by Swanson (1994), who notes that significant organization investment (e.g., new computers, enhanced training, expanded facilities) require careful analysis of costs and consequences.

One could argue that defining best or even effective practice in the PM arena may be premature. The Governmental Accounting Standards Board (GASB) published *Service Efforts and Accomplishments Reporting* in 1990. Perhaps more time is needed before researchers and practitioners alike adhere to an agreed upon set of expectations for PM implementation. Moreover, some might dismiss a benefit-cost framework out of hand as being too cumbersome to implement, particularly in light of the fact that very few governments have the capacity to apply activity-based costing to their activities. Nonetheless, as Robert Behn (2002) notes, it is important to begin separating the hype from the reality in the PM realm. At present, PM is portrayed as a worthwhile endeavor, but there is increasing evidence that the reality of implementation is nowhere near what many expect of how it will perform in practice. Many public organizations are simply not ready to undertake serious PM (Ammons 1999, 2002; Berman and Wang 2000) in terms of organizational climate, personnel, or information technology infrastructure. If research in the PM realm is intended to inform practice, it needs to account for these shortcomings and to help organizations develop their PM capacity.

Improving organizational capacity to implement PM is likely to require two things. First, it suggests that researchers in the PM realm need to answer some fundamental normative questions about good PM practice. Second, it requires a wholesale change in what constitutes admissible evidence in PM research. Granted, achieving these ends will not be easy. As noted earlier, research in PM has not focused on a set of big questions which might allow for accumulation of knowledge. More importantly, multi-jurisdictional, longitudinal research has been the exception rather than the norm in public administration (Forrester 1997). Without such research, it may be difficult to answer some of the more critical issues facing PM implementation. These limitations nothwithstanding, it may be appropriate to examine some potential big questions and methodological expectations that might contribute to the making of a PM implementation paradigm.

1. Do Real Performance Measures Require an External Referent or Standard to Be Valid?

Assume for a moment that a fire battalion chief informs her superiors that over the past two years, average response time at her station for the most critical calls has trended down from nine minutes to seven. *Prima facie*, a 22.2% reduction in response time might sound impressive. But what if other stations in the same city averaged five and one-half minutes? And what if national standards suggested that when life is at stake, emergency response should be under five minutes? In light of these comparisons, does the 22.2% reduction sound all that impressive?

Elaine Morley, Scott Bryant, and Harry Hatry (2001) follow this line of reasoning. It is evident in their assertion that legitimate performance measures must be developed with comparisons to professional standards, peer organizations, other communities, or sister organizations occupying different geographical or organizational space (e.g., different schools in the same district, different regions of a state department of transportation). Simply put, without an external referent, public agencies will develop self-justifying, easily attained standards that may mask objectively subpar performance.

The logic behind their assertion is difficult to refute. Theoretically, private entities are obligated to compete; hence, their PM is automatically driven by market forces. Public entities may implicitly compete with neighboring jurisdictions (Raimondo 1992), but such competition takes place in the context of a bundle of public goods and services sold at a tax price. It is not likely, however, to impact public production costs as directly or immediately as a market model. Further, it is widely believed that if left to their repose, most public managers will set easily achieved benchmarks for success. The belief that performance standards will be used asymmetrically (i.e., as a means of punishment rather than a mechanism for reward; Ammons 1999; Osborne and Plastrik 2000) appears to be particularly true in the context of external benchmarks. This anxiety over the need for an external standard is frequently dismissed by those who assert that every jurisdiction is unique and therefore unripe for what Morley, Bryant, and Hatry (2001) term "comparative performance measurement." With this fear handily repressed, it is unsurprising that very few public entities engage in cross-jurisdictional comparison (Berman and Wang 2000) or belong to PM consortiums such as those sponsored by the University of North Carolina or International City/County Management Association (Coe 1999).

In reply, one might argue that for many communities it would be a sea change to move beyond an item-of-expenditure budget. Many in the public service are still unsure about the difference between inputs, outputs, and outcomes; this is particularly the case with the latter (Frank 2002). Thus, the development of in-house measures without external referent may be a bridge to more advanced measures that would account for outside benchmarks (Ammons 1999). Unfortunately, our lack of longitudinal research in the PM realm makes it impossible to specu- late if the crawl before you can walk progression to PM implementation ever takes place. Regardless, what Morley and colleagues have suggested amounts to a more scientific approach to PM development. Their model effectively requires PM designers to research and import extant measures in particular service delivery areas. It also lends itself to systematic comparison with peer organizations.

Morley, Bryant, and Hatry (2001) have thrown down an important intellectual gauntlet that effectively tiers PM implementation. In-house PM measures are lower tier; benchmarked measures are higher. Morley and Hatry are long-time researchers in the PM arena—arguably two of its earliest and strongest promoters. Their call for externally referenced performance measures cannot be easily dismissed. This is because Morley, Bryant, and Hatry call into question much of what many practitioners would deem performance measures.

2. Is It Realistic to Expect PM Systems to Be Integrated with Strategic Planning Efforts, Individual Performance Appraisals, and Budgetary Resource Allocation?

In the best of all possible worlds, PM utilization should be connected to strategic planning, individual performance appraisal, and budgetary resource allocation (Bowsher 1985; Osborne and Plastrik 2000). Performance measures at the operational level would be aligned with broader strategic aims. These, in turn, would be linked to inducements and rewards at the individual level. In theory, superior organizational (and individual) performance should be rewarded with enhanced budgetary resources; less than satisfactory performance would be punished. This alignment of broad social aims, organizational goals, and individual-level performance appraisals is consistent with a reinventing government model in which the legislative branch focuses on policy outcomes as opposed to organizational inputs (Osborne and Gaebler 1992; Osborne and Plastrik 2000)

Evidence suggests that the marriage of PM, strategic planning, individual performance appraisal, and resource allocation is seldom consummated (Behn 2002; de Julnes and Holzer 2001). Some observers (Grizzle 1999; Melkers and Willoughby 1998) have noted this absence and the serious questions it raises regarding the true intent of PM utilization. If PM is not a linchpin for these critical functions, what then is it good for? This line of questioning is bolstered by the fact that most PM are output- as opposed to outcome-oriented (Gianakis and Wang 1999; Mikesell 1999) and offer limited information regarding program cost-effectiveness. The absence of alignment coupled with PM's limited use as an allocation tool suggests to at least some observers that PM is at best a tool for justifying the budgetary status quo and at worst a set of numbers published by governments to placate an angry, tax-averse public (Shelton and Albee 2000). Under this scenario, implementing PM can be delegitimated as oversold and, worse still, as that which increases the very public cynicism that it is ostensibly intended to reduce.

That PM has again and again been found to be linked to what might be termed higher level organizational functions raises the real possibility that PM study and implementation may be negatively impacted by a number of longstanding dysfunctions in public management. For example, are public personnel systems so slow in hiring and disciplinary actions (Lewis and Frank 2002; Ukeles 1982) that linkages to PM may be entirely unrealistic? And do limitations to strategic planning in the public sector (e.g., frequent turnover of senior managers, limited legal or administrative ability to lock-in strategic changes) crimp potential links with PM? Simply defining good performance might be a huge step in many public organizations. Linking this operationalization to other facets of the organization and ultimately tying PM to resource allocation may be beyond the capacity of many public organizations. Is the normative assumption that PM should be aligned with strategic aims and individual performance appraisals realistic? Is the linkage needed to improve service quality or reduce cost? Evidence from the performance consortium at the University of North Carolina's Institute of Government suggests that such linkages are the second or even the third things on the minds of many participants: obtaining useful information on service delivery expectations and unit costs is primary (W. Rivenbark, personal communications, 2000). Linking PM to broader strategic aims and individual appraisal may not be as necessary as some PM researchers seem to believe.

3. Who Is the Principal Beneficiary of PM Development—The Public, the Bureaucracy, or Elected Officials?

The easy and perhaps overly simplistic answer would be to reply: "all of the above." In terms of ultimate beneficiaries, this is probably the case. But in terms of PM implementation, delineating a primary beneficiary may be a significant step forward.

The presence of a "troublesome cleft" (Whicker, Strickland, and Olfshski 1993, 531) between political science and public administration is clearly evident in our unwillingness or inability to satisfactorily address this question. Research since the seminal *The American Voter* (Campbell et al. 1980) has led to the development of a critical analytic framework; this research suggests that few Americans would have the time, inclination, or cognitive capacity to understand a PM system with detailed inputs, outputs, and outcomes. It may be one thing to tell parents that their children's elementary school rates a B on a statewide, standardized test. It is still another to engage them with detailed cost and performance data on local garbage collection or waste water treatment. Indeed, as Coplin, Merget, and Bourdeaux (2002) make clear with respect to the Community Benchmark Program at Syracuse University, "In our experience, we have found the term 'benchmarking' is mentioned in discussions by citizens and government officials. In contrast, we have yet to find an editorial or public statement by a government official that uses the phrase 'government-performance' measure" (708). As these authors note, the public and elected officials find it difficult to deal with what might be termed the minutiae of performance time series or cross-sectional comparisons. In light of our knowledge regarding the American public and its relatively limited cognition of the political scene, this finding is anything but surprising.

This line of reasoning has two important corollaries. First, it speaks to the oft-noted frustration among elected and senior administrative staff regarding the public's disinterest in PM development and reporting (Gianakis and Wang 1999). However, rather than being frustrated, perhaps would-be PM implementers should adopt the stance of North Carolina–Chapel Hill Institute of Government staff (W. Rivenbark, personal communication, 2000) who assert that a PM system which obviates tax or fee increases, reduces citizen complaints, or maintains superior bond ratings is effective; these actions speak louder than any detailed public reporting. Second, a private-sector analog to government performance reporting that includes detailed quarterly or annual reports may constitute an unnecessary administrative and cost burden. An annual performance report on a handful of key aggregate measures (e.g., bond rating, tax burden, service quality assessment) is probably more than sufficient; under these measures, the citizenry would be adequately informed about government performance. Even though Internet posting or dissemination of such information may lower distribution costs, neither can change the fact that a detailed breakdown of service effort by function, with interjurisdictional comparisons, may be too much for the average citizen to comprehend. In a word, it may be time to acknowledge that developing and reporting of PM may be the province of the technocracy; citizens and their elected officials may benefit from spillovers emanating from a relatively cloistered existence. Determining the appropriate primary audience for PM goes hand-in-hand with the concern about cost-effectiveness noted above. As Rivenbark and Kelly (2000) note, PM development and reporting are an expensive undertaking. Well-intended efforts that waste time, money, and effort on measures that are too complex for cognitively challenged recipients will do little to increase the public's faith in government. Indeed, circulating overly complex PM material to the public could simply incur anger because it may appear exceptionally wasteful or unnecessarily obfuscating.

In the final analysis, PM may assist communities with strategic goal setting or citizen outreach, but it cannot be a substitute for sound planning or effective communications to citizens. Effective PM may or may not contribute to best practice in human resource management. But it is unlikely to make the public sector more attractive to potential applicants (arguably the central issue in public human resources management) or make it easier to discipline or remove unsatisfactory employees. This is particularly true if managers are unwilling to undertake the arduous path needed for such action. In short, without some intellectual boundaries, PM potential may be oversold with unrealistic expectations. Hence, addressing fundamental normative questions such as those raised here has real world implications for PM implementation.

III. BUILDING A PM PARADIGM: MATCHING APPROPRIATE METHODOLOGY TO PM IMPLEMENTATION DESIGN QUESTIONS

Developing a paradigm within the social sciences generally implies linking an agreed upon base of knowledge with research methods necessary for building upon that base (Ritzer 1975). In economics and anthropology, for example, there is general agreement about both the knowledge base and the tools used for its expansion. Yet in political science or sociology, there tends to be a rift between disciplinary scope and research methods. As noted earlier, the "performance measurement revolution" only began a few years ago. Hence, it may be too soon to expect a clear preference of method and substance for research in the PM realm. As a result, it may be appropriate to typify PM development as pre- or multi-paradigmatic (Frank 2002).

Notwithstanding the relative newness of PM implementation research, competent practice in social science dictates that researchers match appropriate methodology to the question at hand (Judd, Smith, and Kidder 1991). Unfortunately, as Robert Stallings (1986) observed in his critique of PhD programs in public administration, research in the discipline often suffers from a serious method–substance mismatch. In addition, Thompson et al. (1998) asserted that the discipline's absence of extramural funding led to serious methodological and substantive shortcomings. Public administration's chronic research shortcomings are clearly evident in the PM realm, limiting our ability to answer implementation research questions.

Generally, there have been only two types of research in PM: one-jurisdiction case studies or fixed-response mail surveys. The deployment of one-jurisdiction case studies is typical of the discipline (Forrester 1997) and reflects a research ethos and lack of extramural funding that fail to sustain multi-site, longitudinal findings. The ubiquitous surveys are more surprising and even more disappointing. As Wang (1997) has noted, a comparison of mail surveys, content analysis, and face-to-face interviews in the same community shows that survey results grossly overstate PM utilization. Despite this, researchers—and the journal editors who publish their results—continue to produce findings that may be quite misleading for pedagogy and practice (Gianakis and Frank 1998). Because validity is one of the foremost criteria for evaluating the value of a performance measure (Grizzle 1985), the ongoing utilization of fixed-response mail surveys to build the PM knowledge base becomes all the more disturbing.

What methodology would foster a more valid knowledge base that begins to make possible a PM research paradigm which would produce usable knowledge and reality-based pedagogy? Those who were first privy to this problem (Hatry et al. 1990) advocated adoption of service efforts and accomplishment reporting: "Governmental entities should undertake experimentation to develop and test indicators that relate cost (dollars and/or employee-hours) to measures of service results, especially indicators that consider the quality and outcomes of the service" (36–37). Clearly, the beta testing of PM in vitro would provide the best answers to the normative questions posed earlier. Such testing would also facilitate a more generic benefit-cost assessment of PM utilization. As Behn (2002) notes, the glaring lack of carefully enumerated benefits (tangible or intangible) remains a stumbling block to more widespread utilization. Beta testing various reporting models could provide such insights on the benefits of PM implementation. Winston-Salem's $400,000 annual savings which came as a result of participation in the North Carolina IOG consortium is illustrative of how this approach can be implemented (Jones 1997).

In the absence of real world experimentation, it appears that PM researchers should rely more on open-ended questionnaires, personal interviews, or historiography than on fixed-response surveys.[*] Contextually rich, longitudinal studies will foster a deeper understanding of successful and unsuccessful PM implementation than simplistic (and frequently one-shot) fixed-choice surveys which tell us little more than that "X percent of respondents feel performance information helps them manage better" or that "Y percent feel PM cannot work in their jurisdiction." These responses will not provide scholars the knowledge base necessary to advance practice or teaching and indeed may simply do more harm than good by providing a distorted picture of real-world behavior.

PM research which is driven by normative questions and which utilizes an evaluative framework is far more likely to advance practice than the simple reporting of survey results. Those engaged in PM research should take great pains to address the shortcomings of the current research and endeavor to partner with practitioners and their colleagues in other institutions to build a better-grounded knowledge base, one that has a much better chance of advancing practice.

IV. BUDGET THEORY: NEW DIRECTIONS AND REORIENTATION

As long as there are public budgets, there will be academicians who wish to develop theoretical frameworks that describe budget development and execution. With billions of dollars allocated and spent annually, there will almost certainly be successive generations of Antons, Lauths, and Wildavskys seeking to reduce the complexities of the budget process to a set of propositions or axioms. But as mentioned at the onset, a nagging question remains: Is the pursuit of budget theory an exercise designed to inform practitioners and practice, or is it merely something that goes into a good academic curriculum vitae? This question is not meant to trivialize the study of budgetary theory. Moreover, it is not simply a matter of deciding whether budget theory is prescriptive or descriptive. This question alludes in part to a normative problem concerning whether social science is primarily intended to produce usable knowledge for those in the endeavor being studied or whether it is an exercise intended to illuminate behavior that actors may not see without academic intervention (Ritzer 1975). This, in turn, begs another question: how and in what ways can budget theory foster the economic wellbeing and fiscal survival of the institutions and managers who deploy it (Gianakis and McCue 1999, 2002)?

Gianakis and McCue's normative assumption is that budget theory should indeed help practitioners operate in a more efficient and effective manner and thus should enhance their respective organizations' chance for survival and long-term growth and stability. Accepting the Gianakis–McCue proposition requires embracing a pragmatic view of the future of budget theory. In addition, one must subscribe to the normative assumption that budget theory's propositions should assist those in practice with their operations, providing them with usable knowledge. Of course, doing so means opposing a view of theory development that may seem utterly divorced from the reality it ostensibly describes or explains.

In what follows, I propose some potential avenues of budget theory research that would be beneficial to academicians and practitioners alike—of intellectual interest for the former, of practical service for the latter. No doubt these options are far from exhaustive. But they represent intellectual pathways that could move the theoretical discussion into new directions beyond the dead ends of budget theory research (Rubin 1990).

A. BUDGETING AS A CULTURAL EXPRESSION

In 1975, the City of New York was nearly bankrupt, with over \$13 billion of outstanding debt coming due. Many observers felt that without state or federal takeover, the city would effectively collapse. Within two years, the city's finances were righted (albeit with federal loan guarantees),

---

[*] On assessing the progress of performance budgeting in Florida, see, e.g., Grizzle (1999).

and municipal services were more effective than prior to the near-bankruptcy, despite a nearly 75,000 reduction in employee headcount. New York went on to become the first large city to adopt GAAP accounting, and its performance measurement system became a national model (Caroley 1982; Ukeles 1982). Fast forward to 1994, and consider a very different case. Orange County, California, declared bankruptcy largely as a result of imprudent cash management policies that went awry when rising interest rates proved ineffectual Treasurer Robert Citron's strategy of gambling on future interest rates (Baldassare 1998; Jorion 1995). Within two years of bankruptcy, the County effected a workout plan with nearly 200 creditors and reestablished AAA bond ratings for its debt. Almost two years to the day after Orange County declared bankruptcy, the City of Miami, with a $68 million deficit, rampant mismanagement, and deep-seated corruption in its senior management and elected officials, found itself on the verge of insolvency (Dluhy and Frank 2002). Even though its problems, though severe, were not on par with the cataclysms of New York City or Orange County, Miami went through five years, six city managers, two mayoral elections (one ordered by judicial fiat as a result of voting fraud), and extensive administrative turnover to overcome its administrative and fiscal woes.

Why did Miami take half a decade to straighten out its fiscal and administrative mess, while New York City and Orange County took less than half as long? The answer is simple: culture matters. After the shock of their respective fiscal meltdowns, leadership in New York and Orange came to painful realizations regarding maintaining a balanced budget and mustered the political, administrative, and technocratic resources needed to implement sound fiscal and administrative practice. An educated upper-middle class, coupled with an alert business elite, contributed human resources and political capital needed to spearhead profound administrative change—a "Crisis Regime" (Bailey 1985). In Miami, no such regime existed. Indeed, as Dluhy and Frank (2002) have noted, many of the city's business leaders were so disaffected with Miami's leadership that they wanted nothing to do with its administration. Meanwhile, an extremely poor electorate, whose primary focus is Latin and Cuban politics, continued to see the city's administration as a conduit for spoils rather than as a mechanism for efficient and effective service delivery. It was only when the state threatened takeover of the city in 2000 that a maverick, reform-minded mayor could begin to make the necessary changes in city administration.

Certainly, discussing culture—defined here in a traditional sociological sense as opposed to a narrower, organizational one—is often difficult. According to Harrison (1992), the concept of culture is viewed with trepidation in certain academic and practitioner circles. Proffering culture as a determinant of policy outcomes inevitably raises questions about which cultural norms are preferable; such a discourse in which these questions are raised makes some queasy. Discomfort notwithstanding, it would be impossible to understand Miami's fiscal crisis without interpreting it through the prism of a predominantly poor, Hispanic population, over 60% of whom were born outside of the United States. (Miami is the second poorest big city in the US; nearly a third of its residents live below the poverty line.) The onset of Miami's crisis—despite long-standing indicators of its financial deterioration coupled with its relatively long climb back to stability was a direct result of its demographics. Unlike New York or Orange County, Miami had no viable middle or upper-middle class that could hold its leadership accountable for honest, competent government (Frank and Dluhy 2003). Add to that traditional Hispanic antipathy towards civic, reformed political culture (Harrison 1992; Huntington and Harrison 2000), and Miami soon came to look like a perfect candidate for anti-best practice in public management.

There is a tradition in budget theory, albeit a relatively new one, which links culture to administrative and fiscal matters. Steven Koven (1999), for one, has deployed the notion of culture in his discussion of tax, economic development, and administrative reforms in local and state governments. Koven draws from Daniel Elazar's (1966) moralistic/individualistic and traditionalistic typology as a basis for his work. In essence, states or cities with immigration paths from Northern European or Anglo-Saxon countries would more likely than not adopt moralistic/individualistic norms, which support reformed government funded via income taxes that are more progressive than their property or sales-tax alternatives. Contrariwise, states or cities with immigration patterns from Southern Europe or Africa would show more traditionalistic norms—higher levels of corruption, less governmental reform, and greater dependence on regressive forms of taxation. While Koven's empirical studies show mixed results for his hypothesized behaviors and outcomes, the work is a milestone for taking culture out of the closet and integrating it into the study of public budgeting.

Culture at the level of the organization may also play a significant role in whether a state or community adopts and utilizes performance measurement (Ammons 1999, 2000; Grizzle 1999; deLancer Julnes, and Holzer 2001; Behn 2002). It seems clear that without sufficient political and technical support, PM will be difficult to implement. Moreover, organizational readiness for change is itself a primary determinant of success in this arena. Stated differently, many public organizations may be poor candidates for PM implementation. Research that provided successful benchmarks or indicators of organizational readiness could be a boon for potential implementers. Understanding successful organizational determinants of PM appears to be an intriguing and useful matter in the budget theory realm.

B. Budget Format and Allocations as Independent Variables

Research in the budget theory realm has often focused on the budget format as a target or dependent variable that reflects the politics and operating culture of the polity or organization. But what if the tables were turned: Can budget format be seen as an independent or causal variable? Do cities, states, or other organizations that adopt performance-oriented budgets achieve better fiscal performance (e.g., larger than peer fund balances, higher bond ratings) over time? Do the entities that adopt high-end use of PM (i.e., linkages with strategic plans, budget allocations, and personnel appraisals) obtain better bond ratings and higher citizen satisfaction with services? These questions require careful consideration.

Klay (1987) asserts that agencies which take the risk of articulating clear program theories and outcomes should be rewarded for these actions with enhanced appropriations. These agencies should also be allowed to retain all or part of their unexpended balances and offer bonuses to employees as they see fit. By way of example, recent experience in Coral Springs, Florida, suggests that adoption of a performance-based budget and management system has paved the way for change in the municipal organization and its politics. Elected officials adopted a less parochial perspective on allocations, coming to understand that good performance was good politics. At the same time, employee performance and enthusiasm took a significant upswing. And the results were significant: Coral Springs became the first public entity in Florida to win the Sterling Award, Florida's equivalent of the federal Baldridge Award. What was once a city with marginal reserves and non-rated debt had now achieved AAA ratings from Standard & Poor's (M. Levinson, personal communications, 2002; City of Coral Springs).

Thus the question: can performance-oriented budgets be a catalyst for organizational development? As demonstrated earlier, the costs and benefits of PM remain largely unsubstantiated. Even so, this line of questioning might provide practitioners with the right outlook for investing the time and effort needed to adopt performance-based budgeting and management in their communities.

Timothy Bartik (1991) and Rauch (1995) have illuminated another aspect of the budget as independent variable—the long-term economic impact of expenditure configurations. Specifically, they have asked: do certain budgetary allocations, particularly in the realm of physical and human capital (i.e., in the realm of education), lead to improved economic development outcome variables such as lowered unemployment and higher growth in real personal income? Their work suggests that investment does matter and that state and local governments which consistently spend more money relative to how much their peers spend in these areas reap significant rewards in the aforementioned economic outcomes. When one considers that shrinking real income is often thought to be the catalyst for the public's antipathy towards government and tax rebellion attitudes of the last quarter century (Kirlin 1982), one should welcome Bartik and Rauch's findings which are of great importance to public administrators. Unfortunately, academic public administration has paid limited attention to the connections between macroeconomic conditions and the administrative state (Carroll 1992; Frank 1992; Klay 1981). Whether this blindness is the result of ideological biases in the discipline against wealth generation of market forces or whether it is the result of impermeable disciplinary boundaries remains an open question. If Kirlin's (1982) assertion is correct and real wages are a prime determinant of the public attitudes toward government, then neglecting longitudinal studies of the linkages between expenditure patterns and economic outcomes would amount to a lost opportunity for a more relevant, practitioner-oriented study of budget theory.

This argument is in line with Gianakis and McCue's proposition (1998, 2002) that the budget process is perhaps the ultimate driver of organizational stability and growth. What this suggests is that linking budget allocations to economic development outcomes could confirm the suspicions of those who assert that government investment in people and places plays a critical role in economic competitiveness (Carroll 1992; Thurow 1980). Such studies could, in turn, provide at least some countervailing intellectual rationale for government intervention at a time when government is viewed as the enemy in a number of circles. This would be a positive spillover for budget theory development.

V. CONCLUSION

However it morphs in coming years, inquiry in public budgeting theory is likely to be right in the middle of two intellectual tugs-of-war: the first, political rationality versus analytic prowess; the second, socioeconomic stasis versus historical dynamics. The budget process reflects a synthesis of economics, ideology, history, and technocracy. None in public budgeting can afford to neglect these determinants of the budget process; nor can they afford to neglect its outcomes.

The widespread use of microcomputers in government and at home is likely to improve the quality of analysis deployed in the budgetary process. Virtually every major trade and professional association has a website that provides surfers with information on best practice. Elected officials, citizens, and civil servants alike have access to a wealth of knowledge unfathomable to prior generations. Asking the question—how and in what ways the Internet changes discourse in the budget process and how it changes the expectations of its many actors—is likely to be bear fruit for those who study the development and execution of budgets.

Computerization aside, it is noteworthy that a conservative, Republican-controlled Congress and President saw fit to extend the Government Results and Performance Act (The Mercatus Center 2006), first passed under President Clinton in 1993. While GPRA has been inconsistently implemented by federal agencies, its continuation symbolizes that enhanced accountability is increasingly embedded in the body politic. The era of fiscal constraint that commenced with Proposition 13 in 1978 has not ended. Those who see the current broad-based interest in PM as a fad should think again. There is no doubt that PM as an ideal type supersedes current facts on the ground. Nonetheless, the groundswell of support for PM at all levels of government suggests that a bottom line orientation is slowly but surely coming to the fore in the public sector worldview. In theory as well as in practice, PM is likely to play a dominant role in government operations in the coming years. Those engaged in the study of public budget theory will feel obligated to study its implementation in a structured, theory-driven manner (Martin 2002).

Regardless of substantive direction, researchers in the budget theory realm should heed the advice of Forrester (1997) and Yeager (1992) and recognize that much of the research in public administration shows little accumulation and often fails to gel with practitioners. This shortcoming may not be easy to resolve given the discipline's chronic lack of external funding and our predilection for survey-driven, one-shot case studies. But if we fail to diversify our methodological portfolio, there is a real possibility that scholars in the budget theory realm will fail to correctly represent the reality they are studying. In a professional discipline, this failure is doubly important as it heightens the risk of steering pedagogy and practice in the wrong direction. With this cautionary note, we conclude by asserting that the study of budget theory presents both a challenge and an opportunity to scholars and the discipline.

REFERENCES

Ammons, D. N., A proper mentality for benchmarking, *Public Administration Review*, 59, 105–109, 1999.

Ammons, D. N., Performance measurement and managerial thinking, *Public Performance and Management Review*, 25, 344–347, 2002.

Andrews, Matthew, A theory-based approach to evaluating budget reforms, *International Public Management Journal*, 5, 135–154, 2002.

Armstrong, J. S., *Long-Range Forecasting from Crystal Ball to Computer*, Wiley, New York, 1985.

Averch, H. A., *Private Markets and Public Intervention*, University of Pittsburgh, Pittsburgh, PA, 1990.

Bailey, R., *The Crisis Regime: The MAC, the EFCB, and the Political Impact of the New York City Financial Crisis*, State University of New York Press, Albany, NY, 1985.

Baldassare, M., *When Governments Fail: The Orange County Bankruptcy*, University of California, Berkeley, CA, 1998.

Behn, R. D., Barriers to performance management, *Public Performance and Management Review*, 26, 5–25, 2002.

Berman, E. M. and Wang, X., Performance measurement in U.S. Counties: capacity for reform, *Public Administration Review*, 60(5), 409–420, 2000.

Bowsher, C. A., Governmental financial management at the crossroads, *Public Budgeting and Finance*, 5, 9–22, 1985.

Buchanan, J. M. and Musgrave, R. A., *Public Finance and Public Choice: Two Contrasting Visions of the State*, MIT Press, Cambridge, MA, 1999.

Buchanan, J. M. and Tullock, G., *The Calculus of Consent: Logical Foundations of Constitutional Democracy*, University of Michigan, Ann Arbor, MI, 1962.

Burrell, G. and Morgan, G., *Sociological Paradigms and Organizational Analysis: Elements of the Sociology of Corporate Life*, Heinemann, London, 1979.

Caroley, D., *Doing More with Less: Cutback Management in New York City*, Columbia University Press, New York, 1982.

Carroll, J. D., The public administration of investment: grappling with the blind men and the elephant, *Public Administration Review*, 52, 223–239, 1992.

Campbell, A. et al., *The American Voter: Unabridged Version*, University of Chicago, Chicago, IL, 1980.

City of Coral Springs http://www.ci.coral-springs.fl.us/businessplan

Coe, C. K., Local government benchmarking: lessons from two major multigovernmental efforts, *Public Administration Review*, 59, 110–123, 1999.

Coplin, W. D. et al., The professional researcher as change agent in the government-performance movement, *Public Administration Review*, 62, 699–711, 2002.

Davis, O. H. et al., A theory of the budget process, *American Political Science Review*, 60, 529–547, 1966.

Davis, O. A., Dempster, M. A. H., and Wildavsky, A. B., On the process of budgeting II: an empirical study of congressional appropriations, In *Studies in Budgeting*, Byrne, R. F., Charnes, A., Cooper, W. W., Davis, A. A., and Dorothy Gifford, Eds., North Holland, Amsterdam, 1971.

De Lancer Julnes, P. and Holzer, M., Promoting the utilization of performance measures in public organizations: an empirical study of factors affecting adoption and implementation, *Public Administration Review*, 61(6), 693–708, 2001.

Dluhy, M. J. and Frank, H. A., *The Miami Fiscal Crisis: Can a Poor City Regain Prosperity?*, Praeger, Westport, CT, 2002.

Dluhy, M. J., Frank, H. A., Guerra, C., Newell, A. L., and Topinka, J. P., *Handbook on Performance Measurement for Cities in Florida: Indicators of Best Practice and Successful Implementation*, Florida Institute of Government at Florida International University, Miami, FL, 2000.

Eisner, M. A., *The State in the American Political Economy*, Prentice Hall, Englewood Cliffs, NJ, 1995.

Elazar, D., *American Federalism*, Crowel, New York, 1966.

Forrester, J. P., The rich diversity of public administration journals: departments and institutional settings— part 2, *Public Administration Quarterly*, 21, 209–226, 1997.

Frank, H. A., Book review: public financial management by Reed, B. J. and Swain, J. W., Who bears the lifetime tax burden by Don Fullerton and Diane Lim Rogers; The new politics of the budgetary process by Aaron Wildavsky and Naomi Caiden; and The federal budget: politics, policy, and process by Allen Schick, *The American Review of Public Administration*, 28, 213–220, 1998.

Frank, H. A., Public financial management in the 1990s: new directions for research and pedagogy, *The American Review of Public Administration*, 22, 190–205, 1992.

Frank, H. A., Refocusing local productivity efforts: four points of departure, *Journal of Management Science and Policy Analysis*, 6, 73–81, 1989.

Frank, H. A., Teaching performance measurement in a core MPA budgeting class, *Journal of Public Affairs Education*, 8, 141–150, 2002.

Frank, H. A. and Dluhy, M. J., Miami's fiscal crisis (1996–2001): lessons for practice in American cities, *Municipal Finance Journal*, 23, 17–44, 2003.

Frank, H. A. and D'Souza, J., Twelve years into the performance measurement revolution: where do we need to be in implementation research? *International Journal of Public Administration*, 27(8/9), 701–718, 2004.

Gianakis, G. A. and Frank, H. A., Assessing public administration practice: the case of revenue forecasting, In *Research in Public Administration*, White, J. D., Ed., Vol. 4, JAI Press, Stamford, CT, pp. 51–64, 1998.

Gianakis, G. A. and McCue, C. P., Budget theory for public administration ... and public administrators, In *Budget Theory in the Public Sector*, Khan, A. and Hidreth, W. B., Eds., Quorum, Westport, CT, pp. 158–171, 2002.

Gianakis, G. A. and McCue, C. P., *Local Government Budgeting: A Managerial Approach*, Praeger, Westport, CT, 1999.

Gianakis, G. A. and Wang, X., Public officials' attitudes toward subjective performance measures, *Public Productivity and Management Review*, 22, 537–553, 1999.

Gist, J. R., "Increment" and "base" in the Congressional appropriations process, *American Journal of Political Science*, 21, 341–352, 1977.

Glaser, M. A. and Denhardt, R. B., Local government performance through the eyes of citizens, *Journal of Public Budgeting, Accounting and Financial Management*, 12, 49–73, 2000.

Grizzle, G. A., Performance measures for budget justifications: developing a selection strategy, *Public Productivity Review*, 9, 328–341, 1985.

Grizzle, G. A., Implementing Florida's government performance and accountability act: introduction and overview, *Journal of Public Budgeting, Accounting and Financial Management*, 11, 554–558, 1999.

Halachmi, A., Performance measurement, accountability and improved performance, *Public Performance and Management Review*, 25, 370–374, 2002.

Halberstam, D., *The Fifties*, Fawcett, New York, 1994.

Harris, J., Services efforts and accomplishments reporting: fundamental questions of an emerging concept, *Public Budgeting and Finance*, 15, 18–37, 1995.

Harrison, L. E., *Who Prospers? How Cultural Values Shape Economic and Political Success*, Basic Books, New York, 1992.

Harrison, L. E. and Huntington, S. P., Eds., *Culture Matters: How Values Shape Human Progress*, Basic Books, New York, 2000.

Hatry, H. P., Performance measurement: fashion and fallacies, *Public Performance and Management Review*, 25, 352–358, 2002.

Hatry, H. P., Sullivan, J. M., Fountain, J. R., and Kremer, L., Eds., *Service Efforts and Accomplishments Reporting: Its Time has Come*, Governmental Accounting Standards Board, Norwalk, CT, 1990.

Jones, A., Winston-Salem's participation in the North Carolina performance measurement project, *Government Finance Review*, 13, 35–42, 1997.

Jorion, P., *Big Bets Gone Bad: Derivatives and Bankruptcy in Orange County*, Academic Press, New York, 1995.

Judd, C. M., Smith, E. R., and Kidder, L. H., *Research Methods in Social Relations*, 6th ed., Holt, Rinehart, and Winston, Fort Worth, TX, 1991.

Kelly, J. A., Why we should take performance measurement on faith (facts being hard to come by and not terribly important), *Public Performance and Management Review*, 25, 375–380, 2002.

Kirlin, J. E., *The Political Economy of Fiscal Limits*, Lexington Books, Lexington, MA, 1982.

Klay, W. E., Combating inflation through wage negotiations: a strategy for public administration, *Public Administration Review*, 41, 520–525, 1981.

Klay, W. E., Management through budgetary incentives, *Public Productivity Review*, 41, 59–71, 1987.

Koven, S. G., *Public Budgeting in the United States: The Cultural and Ideological Setting*, Georgetown University Press, Washington, DC, 1999.

LeLoup, L., From micro-budgeting to macro-budgeting evolution in theory and practice, In *New Directions in Budgeting Theory*, Rubin, I. S., Ed., State University of New York Press, Albany, NY, pp. 15–44, 1988.

Lewis, C. W., Public budgeting: unethical in purpose, product, and promise, *Public Budgeting and Financial Management*, 4, 667–680, 1992.

Lewis, G. B. and Frank, S. A., Who wants to work for government?, *Public Administration Review*, 62, 395–404, 2002.

Lewis, V. B., Toward a theory of budgeting, *Public Administration Review*, 12(1), 43–54.

Lindblom, C. E., *The Policy Making Process*, 2nd ed., Prentice Hall, Englewood Cliffs, NJ, 1980.

Lynch, T. D., *Public Budgeting in America*, 4th ed., Prentice Hall, Englewood Cliffs, NJ, 1995.

Lyons, W. E. and Lowery, D., Governmental fragmentation versus consolidation: five public-choice myths about how to create informed, involved, and happy citizens, *Public Administration Review*, 49, 533–543, 1989.

McKenna, C. K., *Quantitative Methods for Public Decision Making*, McGraw Hill, New York, 1980.

Mandel, M. J., Spending isn't the problem: state and local governments need productivity gains, *Business Week*, June 16, 72–73, 2003.

Martin, L. L., Budgeting for outcomes, In *Budget Theory in the Public Sector*, Khan, A. and Hildreth, W. B., Eds., Quorum, Westport, CT, pp. 246–260, 2002.

McCurdy, H. E., *Public Administration: A Bibliographic Guide to the Literature*, Marcel Dekker, New York, 1986.

McLean, I., *Public Choice: An Introduction*, Basil Blackwell, New York, 1987.

Melkers, J. E. and Willoughby, K. G., The state of the states: performance-based budgeting requirements in 47 out of 50, *Public Administration Review*, 58, 66–73, 1998.

Mikesell, J. L., *Fiscal Administration: Analysis and Applications for the Public Sector*, 5th ed., Harcourt Brace, Ft. Worth, TX, 1999.

Morley, E., Bryant, S. P., and Harty, H. P., *Comparative Performance Measurement*, The Urban Institute, Washington, DC, 2001.

Murphy, P. and Carnevale, J., *The Challenge of Developing Cross-Agency Measures: a Case Study of the Office of National Drug Control Policy Managing for Results*, Rowman and Littlefield, Oxford, 2002.

Musgrave, R. A., *Public Finance in Theory and Practice,* 3rd ed., McGraw Hill, New York, 1980.

National Commission on the Public Service, *Urgent Business for America*, Brookings Institution, Washington, DC, 2002.

Neuby, B. L., On the lack of a budget theory, *Public Administration Quarterly*, 21, 131–142, 1997.

Niskanen, W. J., *Bureaucracy and Representative Government*, Aldine, Chicago, IL, 1971.

Ogata, K. and Goodkey, R., *Redefining Government Performance, Business Performance Measurement*, Cambridge University Press, Cambridge, 2002.

Osborne, D. E. and Gaebler, T., *Reinventing Government: How the Entrepreneurial Spirit is Transforming the Public Sector*, Penguin, New York, 1993.

Osborne, D. and Plastrik, P., *The Reinventor's Fieldbook: Tools for Transforming your Government*, Josey Bass, San Francisco, CA, 2000.

Ostrom, V., *The Intellectual Crisis in American Public Administration*, 2nd ed., University of Alabama Press, Tuscaloosa, AL, 1989.

O'Toole, D. E. and Stipak, B., Productivity trends in local government budgeting, *Public Performance and Management Review*, 26, 190–203, 2002.

Peterson, W. C., *Silent Depression: Twenty-Five Years of Wage Squeeze and Middle-Class Decline*, W.W. Norton, New York, 1994.

Pigou, A. C., *A Study of Public Finance*, Macmillan, London, 1947.

Pilegge, J. C., From accounting to ZBB: trends in budgetary research, *Public Budgeting and Financial Management*, 1, 239–246, 1989.

Rauch, J. E., Bureaucracy, infrastructure, and economic growth: evidence from U.S. cities during the progressive era, *American Economic Review*, 85, 968–979, 1995.

Raimondo, H. J., *Economics of State and Local Government*, Praeger, New York, 1992.

Ritzer, G. A., *Sociology: A Multiple Paradigm Science*, Allyn and Bacon, Boston, MA, 1975.

Rivenbark, W. C., Teaching performance management in public affairs education, *Journal of Public Affairs Education*, 7, 261–266, 2001.

Rivenbark, W. C. and Kelly, J. M., Performance measurement: a local government response, *Journal of Public Budgeting, Accounting, and Financial Management*, 12, 74–86, 2000.

Rosenbaum, A. and Gajdosova, L., State modernization and the new public administrator, In *State Modernization and Decentralization—Implications for Education and Training in Public Administration*, Rosenbaum, A. and Gajdosova, L., Eds., United Nations, New York, pp. 3–11, 2003.

Rubin, I. S., Budget theory and practice: how good the fit, *Public Administration Review*, 50, 179–189, 1990.

Rutman, L., *Planning Useful Evaluations: Evaluability Assessment*, Sage, Beverly Hills, CA, 1980.

Savageau, D., *Places Rated Almanac*, IDG Books, Foster City, CA, 2000.

Shelton, M. W. and Albee, T., Financial performance monitoring and customer-oriented government: a case study, *Journal of Public Budgeting, Accounting & Financial Management*, 12, 87–105, 2000.

Stallings, R. A., Doctoral programs in public administration: an outsider's perspective, *Public Administration Review*, 46, 235–240, 1986.

Stockman, D. A., *The Triumph of Politics: why the Reagan Revolution Failed*, Avon, New York, 1987.

Swanson, R. A., *Analysis for Improving Performance: Tools for Diagnosing Organizations and Documenting Workplace Expertise*, Berrett Koehler, San Francisco, CA, 1994.

The Mercatus Center, Governmental Accountability, http://www.mercatus.org/governmentaccountability, Last accessed 6/18/06.

Thompson, F. J., Brintnall, M., Durant, R. F., Kettl, D. F., Radin, B. A., and Wise, L. R., *Report of the ASPA–NASPAA Committee on the Advancement of Public Administration*, American Political Science Association Conference, September 3–6, Boston, MA, 1998.

Thurow, L. C., *The Zero-Sum Society: Distribution and the Possibilities for Economic Change*, Basic Books, New York, 1980.

Ukeles, J., *Doing More with Less: Turning Public Management Around*, ANACOM, New York, 1982.

Wagner, R. E., *Public Finance: Revenues and Expenditures in Democratic Society*, Little, Brown, Boston, MA, 1983.

Wang, X., *Local Officials' Preferences of Performance Measurements: A Study of Local Police Services*, Doctoral Dissertation, Florida International University, Miami, FL, 1997.

Wildavsky, A. B., *The Politics of the Budgetary Process*, Brown, Little, Boston, MA, 1964.

Wildavsky, A. B., Ubiquitous anomie: public service in an era of ideological dissensus, *Public Administration Review*, 48(4), 753–755, 1988.

Wildavsky, A. B. and Caiden, N., *The New Politics of The Budgetary Process*, 3rd ed., Longman, New York, 1997.

Yeager, S. J., Introduction, *Public Administration Quarterly*, 16, 3–5, 1992.

Unit 4

Decision Making

7 Decision Making, Institutions, Elite Control, and Responsiveness in Public Administration History

Jonathan B. Justice and Gerald J. Miller

CONTENTS

I. INTRODUCTION

Without constraints on length and time, a chapter on the history of decision making might well encompass thousands of years of human history and a dizzying array of approaches to the challenges of uncertainty and ambiguity. If the scope of goals and tasks for practice and research in public administration decision making proves vast, individual and collective decision making is important enough that the realization of those goals and tasks has value.

Recognizing such limits, a more parochial approach is adopted in this chapter, restricting our discussion to post-colonial public administration decision making in the United States. Even within this constraint, this chapter offers an overview of portions of a vast body of practice and scholarship. Moreover, this section serves as a starting point for further investigation.

Our presentation follows a broad chronology. Our selection of particular developments reflects a concern with the nexus of individual and collective decisions. The discussion has concerns for rationality in public and administrative decision making and the balance among elites and publics as the legitimate force behind binding, collective decisions. This introductory section offers a rationale for our focus and selection; a framework for organizing the analysis of decision making problems, practice, and research; and an outline of the specific topics to be covered.

Our concern with the interrelationship of individual and collective decision making has roots in the nature of public administration research and practice. Public administration has developed to become an endeavor to find and achieve rational ways to maximize collective welfare. While it is surely true that: "Administration is ordinarily discussed as the art of 'getting things done'" (Simon 1997, 1), it is accepted that public administration is policy making (Appleby 1949, 169). Public administration inescapably centers on collective efforts to sort ends and means at a variety of social and organizational scales of common interest. Research in public administration also analyzes individual administrators' decisions that ultimately determine what collective decisions are made and how effectively and efficiently they are carried out. These questions of *for whom* and *by whom* decisions are and should be made are central to two of the long-running concerns of American public administration: centralization versus decentralization and the effort to reconcile democracy and efficiency. Relevant theories and practices of decision making, therefore, cover the formation and aggregation of individual decisions. Theories and practices also concentrate on steering individual decisions toward the faithful execution of the common interest. Developments are emphasized that enhance our understanding of the interdependencies of individual and collective decision. Particular attention is paid to the question of how society has allocated legitimacy and actual decision making authority among elites and masses as American Public Administration scholarship and practice have portrayed them. Within those boundaries, this presentation emphasizes three major analytic themes. First, it adopts the distinction between the judgment and choice aspects of decisions as articulated by Goldstein and Hogarth (1997) and uses it as a way to understand the concept of decisions. Second, it adopts James March's (1994) formulation of ambiguity and uncertainty as two pervasive and fundamentally different ways in which limited knowledge creates challenges for decision makers. Our third, and in some ways most fundamental concern, is the ways in which institutions structure both individual and collective decisions. Each of these themes will be briefly discussed below.

Our first theme looks at the decomposition of decisions into judgments and choices, or conversely with the composition of decisions out of judgments and choices. The body of psychological research on decision making can be divided according to whether it focuses more on judgment or choice (Goldstein and Hogarth 1997), and this analytic distinction can readily be extended to apply to decision making research and practice more generally. Judgment involves arriving at some understanding of situations, probabilities, causes, and consequences—the psychological appraisal of information—and implicates problems of knowledge, learning, and the discrepancies between the objective environment and human perceptions of those objective conditions (Simon 1997). Preferential choice involves the selection of courses of action, whether to achieve some expected utility or consequences in accordance with given preferences and an instrumentally rational "logic of consequences," or else the selection of a course suggested by a less instrumental "logic of appropriateness" that emphasizes the inherent rightness of choice over calculations of consequences (March 1978, 1994). Goldstein and Hogarth trace contemporary research into intended rational-instrumental choice to the specification of utility by von Neumann and Morgenstern in the 1947 second edition of their seminal *Theory of Games and Economic Behavior, 1972*.

We define a decision to be a complex of some combination of one or more judgments and one or more choices. The combination of judgments has both positive, or descriptive, and normative, or evaluative, facets. Our sense of decision making lies in its being an inherently normative procedure overall with deliberate aims. Decision making can intend to achieve a better state of the world or to preserve an existing, desirable state of the world. Decision making can entail pursuing an appropriate course of action, rejecting available choices that lead to undesirable states, or simply failing to choose or act. The making of decisions, whether by individuals or collective parties, is significantly complicated by the twin challenges of uncertainty about the probabilities of events and consequences and ambiguity concerning causes, effects, and preferences. Uncertainty and ambiguity challenge the decision maker in both judgment and choice. Uncertainty proves the more tractable of the two, because it can be reduced or at least partially accommodated through the judgment-enhancing systematic collection of information about reality and about the probabilities of events and effects. Developments from the early formulations of probability theory in the 16th century, to the post-WWII boom in applications of operations research and formal analysis, to recent developments in computer-assisted data mining and decision-support systems, have sought to enhance rationality in the face of uncertainty by providing more and better information and analysis. At the same time, uncertainty or vagueness about the precise nature or likely consequences of certain policy decisions or states of the world may facilitate agreement among decision makers. Ambiguity resists systematic solutions. Ambiguous circumstances do require orderly discernment, despite a lack of clarity or consistency about reality and preferences (March 1994). Together with the usual multiplicity and incommensurability of goals and preferences associated with collective decision making, ambiguity poses challenges for both judgment and choice that are not readily addressed by additional ex-ante factual information or analysis. Rational models of decision making, for example, presume stable and relatively well-behaved utility functions that can serve as the basis for preferential choice, and additionally presume that actors possess adequate judgment about at least their own wants. Ambiguity, rooted in the boundedness of human rationality as well as in the tendency for human knowledge of reality, identity, and preferences to be constructed at least in part through social processes, undermines the foundations of rational judgment and choice and points to the employment of practical reasoning and logics of appropriateness (Berger and Luckman 1967; March 1978; Scott 1995). In plain language, the problem of ambiguity in decision making is that even as individuals, we cannot always know exactly what we prefer, or that we will always want what we want now. For some understandings, such as conventional policy analysis, this is troublesome, while for others, such as the zone of acceptance central to Simon's (1997) conception of decisions in and by organizations, it is part of what makes cooperation possible. By decomposing decision making into the two sub-activities of judgment and choice, and by recognizing that decisions are made under conditions of both uncertainty and ambiguity, the technical problem of decision can be represented as comprising four basic elements, as depicted in Table 7.1. Judgments involve both positive and normative assessments of actual and possible states of the world. Tasks of positive judgment include determining what the actual state of the world is, at least in relevant part, and what causal relationships pertain to transform states of the world. Normative judgments are required to establish whether, for instance, current states are desirable and whether alternative states can be imagined that might be more or less desirable. Similarly, choices can be calculative, based on instrumental logics, or practical, based on logics of appropriateness. Uncertainty complicates positive judgment and the calculations of causality that undergird calculative choice. Ambiguity undermines our certainty about normative judgments and conceivably also our determinations concerning the inherent appropriateness of a particular choice. Administrative and policy decisions by their nature involve all four elements, because they involve evaluations of the desirability of actual and imagined states of the world as well as assessments of the actual characteristics of the world and the causes of alternative states, and choices grounded in logics of appropriateness as well as in logics of consequences. Thus, administrative and policy decisions are also subject to both uncertainty and ambiguity.

Finally, our concern with the interdependence of individual and collective decision making necessarily involves some degree of attention to social institutions—the shared systems of rules by which action is structured and order made possible (DiMaggio and Powell 1991)—because it is institutions that link the two, whether by design, accident, or both. Scott (1995) describes three broad ways in which institutions are understood to mediate the relationship between individual and collective decisions. First, institutions may operate in *regulative* fashion, employing coercion to make rationally self-interested individuals behave in accordance with rules meant to advance collective rationality *in spite of* individual rationalities seeking to advance exogenously formed individual preferences. Alternatively, institutions can operate through *normative* or *cognitive* mechanisms. These understandings place institutions as the antecedents of individual preferences

---

TABLE 7.1
Generic Problems, Elements, and Sub-Elements of Decision Making

	Judgment	Choice
Uncertainty	Positive judgments about the probabilities of current or future existence of particular states of the world; judgments as to the causes and effects of particular events and choices	Choices of means and ends based on instrumental logics of consequences: seeking to select the (best) means most likely to result in the most desired (best) ends
Ambiguity	Normative judgments about the desirability of particular states of the world; judgments about the appropriateness or inherent desirability of specific means to those ends	Choices of means and ends based on practical logics of appropriateness: seeking to select the means and ends that are the right ones, often as determined by institutions

Source: From Goldstein, W. M. and Hogarth, R. M., Eds., *Research on Judgment and Decision Making: Currents, Connections, and Controversies*, Cambridge University Press, Cambridge, 1997; March, J. G., *Bell Journal of Economics*, 9(2), 587–608, 1978; March, J. G., *A Primer on Decision Making*, Free Press, New York, 1994.

and judgments: institutions influence not just individual behavior, but the beliefs individuals hold about what is true and what is desirable. In this social-constructionist perspective, institutions are held to shape not just decisions but more fundamental decision premises as well. That is, they operate to influence the underlying logics of appropriateness that govern many aspects of judgment and choice, including choices about appropriate methods of, and participation in, decision making.

Additionally, the rules that constitute institutions operate in three interdependent "worlds" or levels of institutional rules: the "world of action," or operational level, in which action is pursued and strategies about future choices and actions adopted; the "world of collective choice," in which binding collective decisions are made about policies and operational arrangements; and the "world of constitutional choice," in which rules are formulated to govern the process of arriving at collective decisions—"decisions about decision rules" (Kiser and Ostrom 1982). The design of constitutions, public policies, and administrative procedures can be understood as collective decisions. Collective decisions on these designs are premised, alone or as a group, on the ways in which individuals form judgments and make choices. The judgments and choices are bound by particular human institutions useful in compressing, extrapolating, or projecting individuals' interpretation of particular states of the world.

The problems of decision making for public administration, then, implicate questions about the desirability of both the ends and means of making decisions, both states of the world and the ways in which our judgments and choices are developed. Thus, the problems of decisions for public administration entail matters of allocative as well as productive efficiency in the achievement of governance and policy outcomes. They also involve the effort to provide efficient processes for arriving at collective decisions and reconciling them with individual ones. Indeed much of the scholarly normative concern with decision making in public administration since the emergence of public administration as a self-conscious field of study has had to do with problems of efficiency in decision processes and outcomes, and of reconciling efficiency with popular democracy. For present purposes, the task in this essay is bounded by focusing on the question of balancing elite and mass roles in decision making. The question focuses on how prevailing institutional arrangements have balanced influence among elites and among publics in efforts to respond to the public interest by achieving desirable outcomes and processes of decision making. Elites include those whom any observer could identify as empowered by heredity and birthright, wealth and economic position, political power or electoral success, or professional training, markers that set them apart from the mass of humanity in terms of their ability or fitness to decide public questions. These elites may serve in administrative positions to decide matters in their own or the public interest. This essay will attend to the history of United States administrative decision making. In doing so, how the relationship among various elites and publics was created, defined, and institutionalized within the separation of powers, how those elites have responded to collective needs and priorities, and how they have made decisions to promote good governance, are described. It is argued here that—at least up until the end of the twentieth century—a progression can be traced both in the actual influence of various elites and in the degree of legitimacy accorded to the dominance of public decision making by them. The first part of our history traces the expanding power of the presidency from the Washington administration to the beginning of the reform era after the Civil War. The second section covers the period from the start of the reform era to the end of World War II. The third section depicts events from the end of World War II to the present. Each part narrates the primary events and the climactic trend, and each scrutinizes the role of administrative decision makers and what was expected of them. In particular, the definition of elites and their relationship to governance is examined and elite definitions of responsiveness and public interest are discussed. For example, the first section covering roughly the period 1787–1883 asks whether the rise of mass politics led to the overthrow of one elite—drawn from those who deserved to rule because they were born with the right or came to it through social position or wealth—only to replace it with another, one based on political success. In the second section on the reform era to the end of World War II, evidence is sought of institution building to bound political decision making and free administrators to become a technocratic elite entitled to decide policy alongside political elites. In the final section, the period after World War II, the managerial approach to decision making is examined. This approach may not answer fully the responsiveness question—who should respond to whom in governance—but it does try to perfect decision making as a technique and as a science.

II. FEDERALISM AND SEPARATED POWERS

The separation of powers formed the basic decision making institutions in the US Constitution. The separation of powers operates through the checks and balances provided in duties and opportunities given to leaders in the three major branches of government: legislative, executive, and judicial. Separation of powers operates at two sovereign levels in a federal structure. The branch and level structure of separation predicts the existence of randomness and conflict. The structure has constants nevertheless. The most important constant is the one-office limit in which the Constitution and later statutes forbade a person holding more than one office at once in the three branches of national government and the two levels of national and state government. Unless elected, that person assumed office through the actions of at least two of the three national branches.

Reflecting the liberal democratic theory argument that separation of power permits representation of values in society (Hill 2004), the decision makers in government also stand for institutional values. Kaufman (1956) outlined three elements of the doctrine of public administration that can also serve as institutional values. Representativeness refers to a legislative body, politically neutral competence to administrative agencies or bodies expected to have specialized expertise, and strong central leadership to the executive—president or governor. As for representativeness, the people through their elected representatives know best. The State or nation can have no kings or tyrannical executives; no taxation without representation; and "no money … drawn from the Treasury, but in Consequence of Appropriations made by law." This tendency toward representativeness is also a tendency to have elections. Everybody who holds office should stand before the people election, reelection or recall, it was thought. As for politically neutral competence or expertise, those reformers who argued in favor of taking the spoils system, the corruption, the politics out of administrative management professed belief in neutral competence or the value of expertise in decision making. Let honest experts find the best way to executive the laws or implement the programs the legislative body created, they said. The core value lay in letting the work of government be done expertly—experts chosen on the basis of merit—and do it according to explicit, objective standards rather than personal or party or other obligations and loyalties. As for executive leadership, fragmentation of interests and government structures demands efficiency and effectiveness. Only strong leadership—the idea of unity of command—can effectively deal with large problems like natural disaster, war, or economic depression.

The limits on power to act, to risk stalemate, balanced with responsiveness, have led to a good governance emphasis on decision making by neutral competent authorities. Growing from efforts to balance the risk of stalemate with the growth of power, and also with a will to be responsive and accountable to both the public interest and the people, bureaucracy has become, many find, the center of power. There one can see combined managerial, political, and legal forms of decision making once thought to risk tyranny when not separated, checked, and balanced (Rosenbloom 1983). In any case, the separation of powers offers an institutional way of explaining decision making. Separation of powers offers researchers a basis for a claim of legitimacy in its elaboration of formal powers, a necessary element of traditional institutionalism (Wilson 1885). Separation of powers may or may not exist for either functional or legitimacy reasons. Observers contest the function the separation of powers serves. Consider Vile (1967) whose emphasis on values to embody in procedure-governed administrative agency governance has much to offer a study of the history of decision making in the United States. He argues that ideas about equilibrium and balance dominated thought about government power during the time leaders debated the provisions of a Constitution. Moreover, Vile believes the eighteenth century emergence of concepts like division of labor and specialization gave debates about balancing power some depth. Both balance and specialization led to the ideas in the nineteenth and twentieth centuries of a frame of reference institution brought to decision making (Schön and Rein 1994). Vile (1967, 15) defines the frame of reference idea as "the demand for different sets of values to be embodied in the procedures of the different agencies." Thus, "the diffusion of authority among different centers of decision making is the antithesis of totalitarianism or absolutism," (15) Vile could argue, and the separation of powers functions to control power.

Freedom is a second function of the separation of powers. Hill (2004) argues that the separation of powers facilitates pluralism of interests and helps guarantee the checking and balancing of any one by the others. The pluralism idea Hill has in mind is one of different groups of people voting and controlling by balancing or even exploiting the clash of interests represented by different aspects of society. He elaborates on the liberal idea that a balanced diversity of interests serves to preserve liberty. The idea, he says, "underlies both the horizontal division of powers between the three branches of government, and the vertical distribution of power between the federal government and the states" (582–583). Freedom and liberty, Federalist No. 51 argued (Hamilton et al. 1961; Kurland and Lerner 1987), developed from the policy of supplying, by opposite and rival interests, the defect of better motives, and the division of power between the national government and the states provides double security... [so that] the different governments will control each other, at the same time that each will be controlled by itself. Therefore, Hill argues: "Counterbalanced interests throughout society serve as a corrective to democracy by controlling the majoritarian tyranny that can endanger it" (2004, 583).

Beyond the control of government, separation of powers also brings about the control of the governed, Hill says, especially in the strength of the factionalizing tendency among people in the United States but also in making a majority on more than a limited number of issues less likely.

Hill further argues that the checks and balances, separation of powers idea exerts an extended influence over other areas of society. Mimicry or simply the same tendency toward factional interests pervades sectarian and other social relationships. Hill points out that tyranny becomes less likely as other representative institutions compete, creating religious freedom and valued diversity, a wider distribution of property, freedom of speech and of the press, as well as trial by jury.

Hill raises interesting questions about the downside of diversity and the acceptable limits of association. He asks whether a sense of community develops as a way "to give the individual a meaningful sense of participation, thereby fostering the virtues of positive freedom, and as a buffer against expansion of the political sphere ..." (Goodhart 2004, 585). Or does the sheer diversity and intensity of individual interests dampen a will to participate communally, to give up to the community a good part of one's authenticity as an individual?, Hill asks. If control of power and liberty do qualify as functional arguments for the decision making underlying the separation of powers and federalism, what about efficiency? The efficiency idea has haunted discussion of basic institutional structure at least since Woodrow Wilson (1887), if not directly in *The Federalist Papers* written by Alexander Hamilton. Gwyn (1965) sees a basis for efficiency in arguments about the separation of powers. In history:

> The answer of Charles I to the Nineteen Propositions, without actually mentioning the term executive power, was very similar ... [to the idea] that those activities called legislative can best be performed by one kind of institution while those called executive can best be performed by another... (32).

Should the legislative body serve with no executive, naturally, a smaller committee of the legislature would take executive powers. Gwyn argued that legislative organization evolved because expeditious pursuit of legislative and executive duties required it. The view of separation of powers Gwyn relates has only an incidental concern with maintaining liberty. Rather, efficiency in the making of decisions underlay Charles I's advocacy of an independent executive.

The version retold by Gwyn implies a reactive role for a legislature and even a judiciary rather than one balanced with the role of the executive. Such a natural role may exist in the United Kingdom, from which vantage point Gwyn writes, but history does not clearly side with that natural role in the United States (Wilson 1885).

Efficiency has often become an irrelevant consideration in judging the institutional decision making derived from separation of powers and federalism. Popular credit goes to President Harry Truman for the comment that whenever one finds an efficient government, one finds a dictatorship.

Lewis (2004) gives further support by recalling Supreme Court Justice Louis D. Brandeis' views. Brandeis made the argument that the separation of powers, including the creation of an executive "with great powers of initiative" was meant "not to promote efficiency but to preclude the exercise of arbitrary power" in his dissenting opinion in *Myers v. United States* (272 US 52, 293, 1926). The relegation of efficiency to some lower status may have posed a problem and explains why concern arose as executive power and administrative agent discretion grew (Peabody and Nugent 2003).

A. THE FEDERALISTS AND THE GOVERNING CLASS

The well-known debate between Alexander Hamilton and Thomas Jefferson about the powers of executives and the national government consequently has masked the real achievements of the Federalists, the original ruling group in the United States. White (1978) contrasted the Confederation with the constitutional government that existed at the beginning of Washington's second and last term as president. White said that when Washington took office as chief executive, practically nothing existed as a government. When Washington's two terms ended, he left a vigorous government. White noted: "The departments of [the national government] had been established and each was making its contribution to national unity ..., revenue ... [was] flowing into the coffers ..., the credit of the country had been restored ..., a diplomatic and consular service was stationed abroad ..., the Post Office was steadily extending its routes ..., [and] laws and revenue collections were being enforced in federal courts" (2–3). What institutions and decisions, what process of decision making, had led from almost nothing across tall, strong barriers to this happier state?

The question "What decision making?" has less to do with specific battles won than with the victory of a ruling class. White (1951, vii) gives the credit to fundamental agreement won about Federalist ideals and practice. The first ruling group, composed of Jefferson, Hamilton, and supporters of both their points of view, differed internally on political differences but decided with more ease "the manner and spirit of conducting the public business," so much so that Jefferson inherited "a going concern" from Adams and Washington. Did executive and national decision making power win over legislative and local power? Clear-thinking historians agree that the initiative in the executive branch, perhaps aided by a strong Hamilton treasury, and the strong national responsibility Jefferson as president accepted and advanced, won and, Jefferson found, made sense.

The more important lesson for decision making may lie in the covariates or even the seeds out of which the Federalist decisions grew. Consider White's (1978, 6–8) view of the first administrations as growing out of ideas about human beings' indefinite perfectibility and their control of their fate through institutions.

In control of one's own fate, energetic, perfectible—all seemed to describe an individualistic political culture. The culture rewarded individual merit and effort (Webber and Wildavsky 1986). However, groups at the turn of the eighteenth century contested the process of reaching perfection. Federalists, history tells, regarded an elite as rightful process designer and leader—defending a hierarchical culture. The Federalist elite approached governance with energy, decisive action, creativity, willingness to experiment, and pragmatism. The Federalist approach may help explain the wellsprings of success in the first Federalist administrations. Most of these qualities correspond commonly to executive action, not legislative consensus building or reactive judicial scrutiny or rumination. These qualities correspond to a top-down, national government-dominated society, not a bottom-up federalist one. White (1978) always associates Hamilton with energy and decisive action, quoting him to the effect that: "Whenever the government appears in arms [and probably in every other role], it ought to appear like a Hercules, and inspire respect by the display of strength. The consideration of expense is of no moment compared with the advantages of energy" (511). Some hierarchy emerges from almost all analyses of the Federalist party's administrations under Washington and Adams.

Bailyn (2003) connects the founders with provincialism as well as elitism. This provincialism is an extremely creative sort. The founders, he says, are like provincial artists who use their "simplicity and common sense ... [who are] concrete in their visualization, committed to the ordinary facts of life as they knew them ... have fresh energies [and lack] affectation and cynicism" (6–8). The founders, and especially the Federalists, Bailyn believes, felt they could question old-world assumptions and unless shown proof otherwise, try what no cultivated European thought possible. For example, Montesquieu and his admiration of the English constitution led him to admire also a separation of crown, nobility, and commons (Bailyn 2003; Montesquieu 1748). The provincial founders would experiment with the separation of powers in government itself.

Experimental the Federalists may have been, but they were not naive. A government could grow corrupt unless led by those superior in education, in economic standing, and in native ability (White 1978). Energy, decisiveness, creativity, readiness to experiment, and pragmatism were the required characteristics for the governing elite.

Only the able might bound the energy of the masses within a set of rules that ensured decisive action. The idea of merit had a specific meaning for the Federalists. Nevertheless, the distrust of the masses led the Federalists to the Sedition Act and the destruction of their political party. The distrust of the masses came from the feeling that the masses easily become "the dupe and tool" of a domineering faction (Washington 1939–1940 (1793)). The domineering purposes to the Federalists were the goals of groups who aimed to subvert the government and Constitution, hence "sedition" (Prince 1970; Smelser 1954, 1958; Smith 1966).

1. Jefferson

Jefferson commanded an era that projected Federalist ideals and practice, White argues. Jefferson himself calls his approach logical (Lipscomb and Bergh 1905):

> Difficulties indeed sometimes arise; but common sense and honest intentions will generally steer through them, and, where they cannot be surmounted, I have ever seen the well-intentioned part of our fellow citizens sufficiently disposed not to look for impossibilities (112).

White, using this wisdom as a contrast, observes that Jefferson was skillful in using his decision making power for "far-reaching political ends" (White 1951, 4) and found himself forced to exercise [power] ruthlessly (White 1951). Jefferson, and the Democrat-Republicans who followed, Madison, Monroe, and Adams, became strong executive-centered presidents. Jefferson's view of national power may lie in both opposition to the Sedition Act and pursuit of the Louisiana Purchase, Madison's in the war of 1812 and realization of nationhood, Monroe's and Adams's in defense of national power even with a share given to Congress, especially in all cases in knitting together geographic sections of the country with canals, roads, and other internal improvements financed by the national government (Forsythe 1977; Larson 2001; White 1951). White argues that Congress became more assertive and the Jeffersonians more solicitous of state agreement in national measures. However, war as well as geographic and economic growth forced the hand of government so that the Jeffersonians ... carried the Federalist [institutional] machine forward without substantial alternation in form of in spirit for nearly three decades (White 1951).

Along with assertiveness by Congress and the President, the judiciary became powerful through Chief Justice John Marshall. His work in *Marbury v. Madison* (1 Cr. 137, 1803) created what

Corwin (1973, 173) called "that highly distinctive feature of American Government, Judicial Review." The distinction lies in the power of the US Supreme Court to review state laws and acts of Congress on a case-by-case basis. Chief Justice Marshall seems to have ruled in a manner similar to Hamilton's arguments in *Federalist* No. 78:

> The interpretation of the laws is the proper and peculiar province of the courts. A constitution is, in fact, and must be regarded by the judges as a fundamental law. It therefore belongs to them to ascertain its meaning as well as the meaning of any particular act proceeding from the legislative body. If there should happen to be any irreconcilable variance between the two, that which has the superior obligation and validity ought to be the course preferred; or in other words, the constitution ought to be preferred to the statute, the intention of the people to the intention of their agents.

In the separation of powers sense, Marshall claimed a position for the courts as equal to the other branches, establishing a check over the acts of Congress. By implication, the decision established a check for the courts on the implementation of them by the President. Future decisions starting with *The Genessee Chief* (12 How. 443, 1851) gave the doctrine of stare decisis some flexibility by establishing for the Court the right to review and overturn previous Court decisions. The chief justice also claimed a position of strength for the national government relative to the states. *Marbury v. Madison* established the US Supreme Court's dominance over state courts, especially when the Supremacy Clause of the Constitution (Article VI, Section 2) supplements the precedent set by the case.

III. THE MID-EIGHTEENTH CENTURY

Andrew Jackson came to the presidency as a war leader, a strong executive. Yet, more aptly he rode the swell of rapid change. Jackson gained the presidency as a result of a popular vote for electors in all states but Delaware and South Carolina, having done so due to widespread abolition of property and tax-paying requirements for voter participation.

The industrial expansion of the country had begun as well. As White describes the scene in 1829 when Jackson became President, steam railroad construction began an industrial revolution. The revolution propelled the growth of the United States through a rise in manufacturing, cities, and corporations.

Economic and social development had effects in political life as well. The right to vote spread rapidly, according to White (1954, vii), as wide enfranchisement of adult white male citizens and their taste for electing most, if not all, officials "rapidly became the rule ... [and] democratic dogmas overwhelmed Federalist and Jeffersonian ideas of a governing elite, and the mass political party replaced the congressional caucus as the means of selecting candidates for the White House."

The impact of representativeness on public administration was a step in another direction from a ruling elite. If everyone need be elected, almost everyone had a right to vote, and everyone not elected had a right to a government job. White calls the practice of filling the bureaucracy with political supporters "the rule of rotation." The practice clearly gained acceptance, as rotation took place not only when one political party succeeded another but when one faction within a party defeated another. White (1954, vii) recalls substantial "constitutional debate, party conflict, and sectional strife, comprising an era of tension that overshadowed the steady normal operations of government" during the Jacksonian era. The period also had "a remarkable stability in the structure of government and at the same time a profound change in its quality and its standards."

Where did remarkable stability and profound change in government quality and standards come from? White (1954, 3) argued that Jackson inherited and accepted Jefferson's political views: "The views led Jackson to a strict construction of federal powers, to reliance on the states, and to a guarded use of authority found in the Constitution ... that matters went well when the government left people alone ... [and] frugality and economy in governmental operations, ... as well as the final discharge of the public debt."

Despite his war experience and comfort with command, Jackson was not the civil administrator that his successor James Knox Polk became. According to White (1954, 69), Polk "devoted himself to detail not only by preference, but on grounds of principle, and great was his satisfaction when he could record at the end of an evening's labor that he had cleared his table... ." "I prefer to supervise the whole operations of the Government myself rather than entrust the public business to subordinates, and this makes my duties very great," Polk once wrote (Quaife 1910, 130–131).

Along with dutiful and duty-oriented presidents and stable government, the Jacksonian period saw the birth and development of a national political party system. White (1954) remembers Tocqueville's opinion (1899, I, 254) that adults who were not slaves took pleasure in politics and debated issues at length in every hamlet. With the end of the Congressional party caucus in 1824, White argues, the political party system that began at the state level informally and then formally began to serve as the national nominating device for the presidency. Certainly a centralizing force, the party system overcame or counterbalanced some of the restraints imposed by separation of powers and the strong separation of national and state governments.

The biggest issue of all was rotation. White justifies it as the biggest issue (1954) because rotation contrasted so clearly with the Federalist-Jeffersonian practice that "no man was subject to discharge for difference in political opinion or for a free expression of his political views." The view lasted through Jefferson's replacement of Federalists with Republicans. In fact, White (301) recalls Jefferson's warning "about the 'rottenness' that begins in a man's conduct when he casts a longing eye on office." White concludes, "[The] expectation of federal office was held down by the scarcity of vacancies in a stable service, by choice from among those holding a 'respectable' station in social life, [and] by presidential success in holding off congressional interference... ." The times changed and, White (1954, 301) says, "in the turmoil of ... politics a strident, pushing, and insistent type of office seeker took the place of the respectable sons of Federalist or Republican families." The rotation led to changes among administrator jobs as one party succeeded the other but also from succession of one faction by another within parties. One observer noted that the desire for office had led patronage to threaten the popularity of any president despite his talent or accomplishments. Rather, office seekers as a group held the balance of power between the two political parties (White 1954).

Rotation grew with the length of the ballot, and one tendency reinforced the other. Democratic sentiment led voters to demand the election rather than the appointment of more leaders. Kaufman (1956) observes the rather uncritical faith in the electoral principle. Belief in elections took the form of universal adult male suffrage and an increase in the number of offices filled by competitive elections. Hundreds of names on the ballot meant that change in parties led to an almost complete turnover of the administrator corps. Each leader also commanded a certain amount of patronage, and leader succession helped rotation grow.

"Efficient?" we ask today. Probably not, White relates. Political parties, the long ballot, and rotation increased decentralization by investing power locally rather than nationally. More decisions, White says, were made by officeholders based on the advantage provided in controlling office and power than on the analysis and debate about policy. Political obligation became the basis for most decisions in the legislative and executive branch and at both national and state levels.

Consider rotation in terms of Rourke's ideas about responsiveness before ceding rotation away as inefficient and thus useless or wasteful (1992). Jacksonian democracy has often paralleled thinking about the Reagan era (1980–1988) of the presidency and beyond that to the early part of the twenty-first century. Some have called the Reagan era and beyond neo-Jacksonian democracy (Kelly 2005). The argument is one of blunting distrust of government by placing in office individuals with whom citizens, voters, and taxpayers identify personally. The average, or the median voter or householder or consumer is the best to serve as a public administrator. If the median voter is in office, the thinking goes, discretion is used as the voter intends or would use it if he or she were in office. The median voter in office as public administrator also speaks to Rourke's ideas of responsiveness. If responsiveness, the argument holds, may be defined as the change from the status quo in policy development and if the median voter is largely indifferent to change, the nation needs no independent public administrator to apply expertise with partisan neutrality. Rather, change comes from the political entrepreneur to whom the public administrator owes deference, because the political entrepreneur is a partisan, achieving office through election. A modern representation of political responsiveness in allegiance to a politically elected leader, allegiance felt by both the indifferent-to-change median voter and the deferential public administrator who resembles the median voter in thought and deed is found in the argument. In other words, in neo-Jacksonian democracy, a reprise of the politics–administration dichotomy is found. The political draws deference from the administrative activities in government based not so much on bureaucratic specialization as belief in the moral superiority of politics.

The Jacksonian period could be called a populist one, given the controversies over the Bank of the United States and the theory of nullification. In the bank case, economic power came from the bank's ability to issue promissory notes that some thought of as soft money. Hard money believers opposed the banks, whether the bank was a national one or was one of many state banks because they created inflation, sooner or later economic contractions, financial servitude, and disruption. During the early 1800s, people in the Western states felt that interests in the Eastern states benefited from banks at their expense. State rights advocates believed in state banks but not the national bank. Jackson's war against the national bank, one he eventually won, may have strengthened the states rights advocates. In the nullification controversy, Jackson opposed Calhoun's states rights doctrine, based as it was on the argument that states could nullify a federal law because the origin of the Constitution lay in the will of the states, rather than the people, in ratifying the Constitution. Issuing his Nullification Proclamation in 1832 (Wilentz 2005), he argued that the origin of the Constitution lay in the will of the people; that the nation existed before the states ratified the Constitution.

With both controversies, the national bank and the theory of nullification, one might understand that Jackson argued populism at the expense of major, powerful institutions, the national government and the national bank. Yet, following Riker (1982), one might see Jackson as opposed to any elite, whether state-related or merely institutionalized, but supporting the Constitution. One might see Jackson as supporting the will of the people to have the right to elect whom they please and replace them at the next election. Riker defines the populist view to follow the rule: "the opinions of the majority must be right and must be respected because the will of the people is the liberty of the people" (14). Voting is not simply another institution, Riker's populists would say; it is the judgment of right and wrong.

In this sense of populism held by Riker, rotation in office, in the context of the bank and nullification controversies, suggests the populist theory of administration. In staffing the administrative agencies, Jackson's populism, Karl (1976) observes, follows the idea that administration is a public service and politically appointed administrators are a more accurate reflection of the public, its needs as well as its desires, than any administrative professional would be likely to be. The Jacksonian theory of administration complements a bigger theory of strong national government in neutralizing the rule of an elite, whether that elite was Eastern business interests or the interests allied against the tariff and favoring state nullification of laws creating the tariff.

IV. THE CIVIL WAR AND RECONSTRUCTION

Between Jacksonian democracy and the reform era lies an era of institutional development ignored by public administration. Leonard D. White provides no guide, and the literature of public administration history has no major champion of the period other than Karl (1976), yet Alexander (1981) calls the era pivotal in the history of institutions. He argues for a reassessment of the role of the Civil War in any analysis of "the efficacy, even viability, of our political institutions" because the

Civil War "is not some monstrous [bloodletting or] extreme value that has to be excluded to make possible a sane weighing of the pros and cons of institutional performance, [rather] it was a fulfillment of our political institutions."

What political institutions and how fulfilled, anyone can ask; Karl (1976) provides an answer. He describes the Civil War as a period of growth of presidential power as well as astute use of spoils as Cayer does (this volume). Karl emphasizes both the admirable and irredeemable in the era overlooked or neglected by a serious analysis of administration. Karl (500) argues, "No presidency since Lincoln's has managed to reach such levels of unconstitutionality." Karl mentions Lincoln's call for troops to go to war without Congress' initial consent, spending money from the Treasury without appropriation, the suspension of habeas corpus, "and Lincoln's use of military force to assure his re-election in 1864." Karl judges Lincoln's use of power one that makes the "hanky-panky" of modern-day scandals involving presidential power look amateurish and "even more childish."

Justification for executive power is not hard to find. Karl says that both Lincoln and Roosevelt get admiration for refusing to let legal principles stand in the way of compassionate or emergency use of their offices.

Bensel (1991) places Karl's view in the perspective of preceding events. He describes the earlier time as one in which the Federalists such as Hamilton had attempted to establish a strong executive, but the national government was one dominated by the states with only a relatively weak presidency and Congress, one favoring Southern interests in free trade and low protectionist barriers relying on tariffs and "… a mere shell by 1860—a government with only a token administrative presence in most of the nation and whose sovereignty was interpreted by the central administration as contingent on the consent of the individual states." That situation quickly changed and then unraveled with the Civil War and Reconstruction.

From the Civil War until the end of Reconstruction, DiLorenzo (2002) points out that Republican party and state were the same. Monopoly in the form of the Republican party expanded the power of the state and Northern industrial and financial interests. In turn, these interests provided the money for the party's activities.

Policy followed the outlines of mercantilism and protectionism, dictatorship, and total war. Tariff rates increased. A federal income tax bureaucracy came into being. Federal government leaders levied excise taxes and repealed few after the Civil War. They also established a national bank system and, with taxes on state bank notes, tried to drive state banks into bankruptcy. Congress financed even more internal improvements and financially aided the new corporations and railroads. Agriculture aid and military pensions, DiLorenzo says, created strong interest groups in addition to corporations lobbying for favor in Congress. On the economic side, Republican party Congressional power forced policy toward intense economic development through necessity.

To some, including DiLorenzo (1998), President Lincoln imposed dictatorship and total war. As DiLorenzo observes, Lincoln initiated and conducted a war by decree for months without the consent or advice of Congress. As well, DiLorenzo relates other of Lincoln's dictatorial acts: "declaring martial law; confiscating private property; suspending habeas corpus, conscripting the railroads and censoring telegraph lines; imprisoning as many as 30,000 Northern citizens without trial; … and shutting down … Northern newspapers" (DiLorenzo 1998, 263, citing Randall 1951). DiLorenzo accuses the Republican party of creating "three new states—Kansas, West Virginia, and Nevada—[to help] them rig the 1864 elections" (DiLorenzo 1998, 263, citing Donald 1956, 79). Lincoln's presidency marked the intense development of the institution's powers.

Reconstruction and the near-conviction of President Andrew Johnson after impeachment left Congress with substantial power. The freedom experiment or an experiment without race as the basis for liberty unfolded. Emancipated slaves gained freedom, some small amount of economic independence, and Congress and the states added the Constitution's 13th, 14th, and 15th amendments. Yet, the experiment provoked "a ferocious reaction," and in "the face of fraud and terror, the freedmen's white allies, north and south, abandoned them" (Goodman 2006, 23;

Foner 1988, 2005). Government corruption increased and the Crédit Mobilier scandal came to represent the impact of Congressional supremacy. Bensel (1991) suggests that financiers stopped a prolonged reconstruction that would have confiscated and redistributed land to build a stronger Republican party in the South. Bensel contends that financiers opted instead for financial and social stability, further investment in the West, and less state direction of the economy anywhere.

Understanding the influence of business interests, was the United States a corporate state? The period between the Civil War and World War I represented the rise and interconnection of business taxation, activist government, and corporate capitalism. As Higgens-Evenson (2003) interpreted the period, some states and the federal government followed the vision of Alexander Hamilton, while other states followed a path advocated by Thomas Jefferson with the Hamilton group undertaking many large, ambitious tasks and the Jefferson group offering limited public services. As a way of understanding the origin and development of the relationship between government and business, Higgens-Evenson suggests the fundamental differences in the approaches the states took.

The development of transcontinental railroads stimulated the transformation. Again, Higgens-Evenson (2003) observes how many other industries developed and began to depend on nationwide markets and, therefore, railroad transportation. The telegraph system relied upon railroad lines for lines and further consolidated national markets through the communications system.

The internal improvements placed governments in the role of stimulus for economic development. Governments had played that role in the Jacksonian era, only to run up debt and often default during the 1837 economic depression. The stimulus effort began as the Civil War's need for railroads prompted further investment, growing still further with the investment in the race between the Union Pacific and the Central Pacific to join in Utah.

The railroads influenced much more than government investment. Most important, says Higgens-Evenson (2003), were the techniques that helped railroad administrators manage their vast enterprises including everything from capital equipment to timetables.

These techniques along with financial ones bred mimicry and a definite following among other industries and eventually government. Higgens-Evenson also points to the size and scope they permitted, especially the introduction of mass production and a survival of the fittest mentality in business. Higgens-Evenson points out that "firms ... integrated vertically, by buying up their suppliers and distributors, as well as horizontally, by buying up their competitors [and economic contractions or] depressions in 1873, 1893, and 1907 [allowed] well-positioned firms to buy out their weaker competitors and increase market share" (3). Bigger and bigger, corporations grew.

Hamilton-inspired business aggrandizement prompted Jeffersonian suspicion among farmers, laborers, and small business people. The suspicion grew to the point that government regulation became a reality. The first regulation of railroad rates and business practices grew into its institutionalization through the creation of the Interstate Commerce Commission in 1886. The Commission became a regulator to the Jeffersonians and, to the others, a national method of regularizing the varied paths the states took in dealing with railroad impacts and the unpredictability state efforts created for business expansion. Such national regulation would further competition with the institutionalization of antitrust efforts in the Sherman Act of 1890, some argued. Regulation crested in Wilson's presidency with the 1914 Federal Trade Commission Act and the Clayton Act.

Shortly after the regulatory crest, business got bigger and government financing needs for World War I prompted a major compromise between business and government. Henry Ford's success in mechanizing assembly line auto manufacture created mass production for mass consumption, and ideas spread across firms, leading to an ever-higher rate of growth among businesses. World War I created a worldwide demand for US products. The war also led to windfall business profits. Business efforts to gain a financial stake in the war prompted further government regulation of railroads, a takeover, and heavy taxation of business windfall profits.

Revolutionary change occurred in government as well. Women gained the vote. Open primaries, initiative, and referendum affected political parties, helping prompt the growth of interest groups and the dwindling interest in voting. Interest group representation of business and government regulation grew to an accommodation in what became the American corporate state. Such a state represented the responsiveness of government to influence by labor and the Progressives as well as the willingness of governments at all levels to tax business firms. The state also represented the smart decision by business leaders to cooperate with institution of corporate taxes and in so doing, become the major interest group in favor of tax reform and granting government a stake in business profits. Higher taxes led to pressure by business people to persuade government regulators to grant higher rate charges and to outlaw their competitors on the grounds that such competition would diminish their profits and hence the state's revenues (Higgins-Evenson 2003).

Progressivism led to growing government activity—positive government—institutionalizing public infrastructure construction, public education, and public welfare. Each level of government retained the power to borrow and the power to tax. Business leaders, probably gladly, agreed to concede responsibility for local infrastructure, schools, and income relief for their employees and families in return for paying taxes, chief among them the national personal income tax created through the ratification of the 16th Amendment to the Constitution.

What can anyone say about the American corporate state? Higgens-Evenson (2003) does not hesitate to recall the legacies of Hamilton and Jefferson. He points out that the rise of the corporate state fundamentally altered the relationship between government and business. For example, he argues that government administration drew much of its efficiency logic from business practices. Government also gained expertise (9) as "Business officials had gone from bribing and black-mailing state legislators to helping them run government on a paying basis." Government deferred to business as "state officials … abandoned their biennial attempts to soak the corporations and instead asked them to set their own tax rates" (9). The states also pursued business in characteristically Federalist or Republican ways as the state's political culture dictated, starkly differing but with some declaring, as Higgens-Evenson recalls, that that the new methods of government were using "Hamiltonian means" to accomplish "Jeffersonian ends."

The most important insight gained from the era relates to institutionalism. National government regulation and taxation institutionalized the vision of interstate commerce prompted by the Constitution. Yet, states created institutions as well, from regulation and taxation to those giving them the lead in providing roads and canals, and the primary role in establishing public education and public welfare systems. Business firms depended on governments to regulate business competition and promote economic development. Governments depended on business firms for cooperation in a policy making process centered on an institutionalized, symbiotic relationship between business and government (Lindblom 1977).

V. THE ERA OF ADMINISTRATIVE REFORM

The period of administrative reform followed the resurgence of Congress. History marks this period as reactionary, with action countering the rise of political parties. The response to political parties' subversion of the electoral process lay in creating and building civil service and budget institutions to prevent political party entrenchment in office and corruption of elections (Frant 1993, 994; Milward 1978, 393). Kaufman (1956, 1059) argues that the long ballot and the rotation system led to confusion among voters. He observes that confusion "opened the way to power to political bosses who, while providing a measure of integration in the bewildering pullulation of government, often [advanced] their personal interests and the interests of the [political] organizations they headed [heedlessly]" (1059–1060). Disillusionment resulted, Kaufman relates, and the disillusioned called for reform.

The history of decision making to this time can suggest three ways in which anyone might understand administrative reform. First, the establishment of national power over the states, in the Civil War and Reconstruction through the principle that the union of states had a greater legitimacy than any state or group of states, through the evident superior force that might be brought to bear on major issues of state versus union, but also through the larger resources that lay at the national government's disposal. The power of the national government also had become evident as a force to balance national elites, especially a business elite. Second, events through history established a strong, unitary executive branch with the president as chief user of national power, checked by Congressional appropriation power and the right of litigants to contest the president's use of power in the courts. Third, the establishment of rotation in office, the spoils system, as a means of selection of the "good administrative decision maker" became a time bomb to go off after the Civil War.

The upshot of the three forces was the focus on the deliberate use of national power, rational, considered, and thoughtful. The unitary nature of the executive branch made administrative institutions inevitable. The spoils system became the focal reason for disillusionment.

Consider also a few lessons from the previous century. The administrative apparatus was small through the first century, and more, the government was small at all levels. The primary job was protecting the growth of the US economy through tariffs. Government leaders also allocated the revenue from tariffs and taxes as well as borrowed money to be able to make internal improvements. Improvements aimed to grow the economy further, to expand the country to provide still further growth. Leaders had the responsibility to protect the country from threats external and internal—and keep the country united.

In the previous century, the greatest struggle was the need for protective tariffs against the need for external markets, forcing a struggle to keep the country united even as the states contested the federalist structure and tried pull the country apart. Skowronek (1982, 29) called the early US history a period of "statelessness." He said that the national government left governing and any substantive task to the states.

Government size was the most important feature during the period before administrative reform took place. According to Wilson (1975):

1. At first, the federal government grew slowly with the State Department having ten employees, the Attorney General, close to the same number, War, 80, and only a few thousand soldiers, and Treasury several hundred employees.
2. Only the post office grew, accounting for 86% of the growth in federal employment to 36,672 by 1861.

Wilson (1975) explains that until the Civil War, the number of federal government administrative employees grew because public demand for government services increased, not because government assumed new tasks or administrative imperialism reigned. Rather, the increased demand existed for what were "bureaus of personnel performing essentially routine, repetitive tasks for which the public demand was great and unavoidable ... [responding only as] as population and commerce expanded" (81). The national government had little administrative capacity, and even more important, had few functions, Wilson observes. Small government persisted for almost a century after ratification of the Constitution. Stillman (1987) reported that federal government employment exceeded 50,000 in 1871.

The question then becomes: what decision making might be studied, institution or no institution binding it, when there is almost no one to decide or at least very little discretion? Certainly, dual federalism, the compact, or states rights meant something before the Civil War.

What these terms may have meant was distrust for any elite and opposition to government power. Skowronek (1982) argues that Jacksonian democracy led to the breakdown of the professional class, the burgeoning aristocracy of merit on which the Federalists might have built a state and local government administrator class. He noted that the Jacksonian era's reaction to elites

> rekindled America's anti-institutionalism and ... anti-intellectualism. The result was a ... nightmare come true. State legislatures swept aside the protective bulwark of the early bar by establishing general criteria for recruitment into the professions. Barriers on entry to legal practice were relaxed, local controls wee nullified, and recruitment into the professions was opened wide. By 1850 formal professional associations had virtually disappeared from the American scene (33–34).

With a decline in professions, little apparent need for government administration, and a clear preference for infrequent government intervention in social and economic affairs, one might ask what happened.

Bustle and a survival of the fittest attitude among the movers and shakers is one way to describe the time. Consider the evidence:

1. The internal improvements encouraged by state governments, as well as the bonded debt for transportation and banking (English 1996)
2. Pet banks that developed as a result of President Jackson's removal of federal deposits from the national bank (Scheiber 1963)
3. The development of the railroad corporation through state debt
4. The development of both massive wealth among corporation leaders and stockholders and calls for control of the economic chaos resulting from railroad competition

The latter competition led to "dangerous chaos" with aggressive pricing and efforts at "ruining a business rival, forcing a merger, building up or tearing down a city, or punishing a state that threatened to impose restrictions on the managers of railroad corporations" (Larson 2001). The bustle led to calls for change.

The president and governors were relatively strong in exploiting situations within their control, the Louisiana Purchase, the national bank, and the military and diplomatic efforts in the Civil War. They were relatively weak given the nature of governmental decision making, that is, creating and enforcing the protection for the internal economy, making internal improvements, and pursuing Reconstruction, all of which were matters for Congress or state legislatures. Only in times of war, defensive wars and then expansive wars, did the president have control of an administration.

What changed everything? First, the rise of the presidency to activism with few limits to its power to decide matters related to his role as chief diplomat (Jefferson and the Louisiana Purchase), chief executive (Jackson, the spoils system, and the national bank), and commander in chief (Lincoln) mattered. The activist presidency implied the administrative capacity to fulfill those roles with administrators chosen on the basis the president required. Second, the rise of the market system as a result of almost continuous investment in improvements in the nation required an infrastructure of laws and regulations to enforce property rights and the right to contract as well as prevent collusion and to encourage, sooner or later, free trade. Finally, the administrative state developed on the basis of good administrators as experts and specialists responsive to the institutional imperatives designed by the president, Congress, and the courts after experiment and rejection of both an aristocratic elite and rotation in office.

Therefore, one of the reforms dealt with the definition of a good administrative decision maker. The content of the definition amounted to the substitution of merit as the basis of appointment to subordinate offices, at best an avenue for expert judgment rather than political loyalty. At worst, the definition heralded a return to the Federalist idea of a ruling class, the sanctification of business expertise, or a substitution of ideological loyalty for political party membership (Villanueva 1993; Waldo 1948).

A. NEUTRAL COMPETENCE OF EXPERTISE

The desire for competence and expertise created the need for a non-partisan source. Kaufman (1956) defined the need as "the ability to do the work of government expertly... according to explicit, objective standards rather than to personal or [political] party... ." At the same time, the fundamental institution to which neutral competence and expertise should answer as the rules of game did not change. Kaufman (1060) says that the promise of institutionalized expertise would not "demean representative institutions [but would] strengthen those institutions by rationalizing governmental operations and improving their quality to such an extent that elected officers would be in a position to exert greater control over policy than they ever could hope to do in the prevailing political jungle." Competent administrators could help fulfill the promise and purpose of representative institutions.

The case for expertise held that individual representatives through their consensus building decision making regimes set the goal of government work, and neutral competent administrators did the work of government. Yet, the case had its disdainful side as Kaufman points out. Some argued that the aristocracy of talent was a necessary reform, because rule by the masses had failed. The patricians issuing from generations before joined the urban mercantile and professional groups to support civil service reform. Hamilton and the Federalists reemerged in spirit.

B. A RULING CLASS

Waldo (1948) discussed the idea that public administrators should have "a place in and claim upon the exercise of modern governmental functions... ." Why? He reiterates this ruling class argument as a high-stakes one (93):

> In general the claim is that the conditions of the modern world require a large and skilful body of bureaucrats, administrators, or experts; that the scientific method and the vast changes which it has brought about in the externals of life, the existence of the nation-state (or hope of a world-state) system, and the demand by all classes of society that government be used as an instrument for achieving the Good Life—that these stupendous factors compel us to recognize the necessity for a "governing class."

Waldo reflects the idea that the scientific method, or positivism, will open vistas for change more probably than political consensus building or political competition. Frames, reformers might argue, have very little to do with scientific investigation; only attention to method assures "the Good Life" through either "a Philosopher-King or a Communist or Fascist Party charged with a greater responsibility than preserving civilization" (91).

C. BUSINESS EXPERTISE

Strangely or not so strangely, expertise took on the modifier "business" to suggest the self-explanatory source. Waldo (1948, 91) senses this unmistakable, unarguable source in the early writings of the reformers as "a strong presumption that the businessman is the "expert" who is entitled to rule. The businessman has built this civilization; so he is morally entitled and mentally equipped to run it." Waldo recognizes dissents from the "business is sole source for administrative expertise" view, including Wilson (1887) when closely read. Rather than a business manager, public administration required a non-partisan administrator, one whose primary loyalty was not to a political party, and a person not elected to office, one steeped in the value of efficiency "whose responsibility can be unmistakably fixed" (1887, 213). With the twin emphases on efficiency and responsibility, Wilson continued (1887, 213):

> If administrative study can discover the best principles upon which to base [a distribution of authority in government], it will have done ... an invaluable service. Montesquieu did not, I am convinced, say the

last word.... All sovereigns are suspicious of their servants, and the sovereign people are no exception to the rule; but how is this suspicion to be allayed by knowledge? If that suspicion could be clarified into wise vigilance, it would be altogether salutary; if that vigilance could be aided by the unmistakable placing of responsibility, it would be altogether beneficent. Suspicion in itself is never healthful either in the private or the public mind. Trust is strength in all relations of life; and, as it is the office of the ... reformer to create conditions of trustfulness, so it is the office of the administrative organizer to fit administration with conditions of clear cut responsibility which shall insure trustworthiness.

Wilson builds a theory of public administration on efficiency, expertise, and clear-cut authority aimed toward the ultimate object of trust by the sovereign people. However efficiency, expertise and clear-cut authority may be defined, the trust of the sovereign in the administrator is Wilson's ultimate objective. In this way, Holzer et al. (in press) have noted the strange complement public choice theory provides to Wilson's theory, that efficiency as an independent variable makes more sense than as a dependent variable, that trust in public administrators makes far more sense and difference. Wilson's (1887) metaphorical explanation has a large participatory element, and he explains:

The ideal for us is a civil service cultured and self-sufficient enough to act with sense and vigor, and yet so intimately connected with the popular thought, by means of elections and constant public counsel, as to find arbitrariness or class spirit quite out of the question (217).

The Wilsonian ideal administrator takes the best from the Federalists and adds the essence of someone aware and responsive, one-person political leaders and citizens can trust. Our interest in Wilson's view relates to how much more closely his comment implies a Jacksonian model, rather than the model of expertise and specialization described by others such as Heclo (2002). Wilson's comment does reveal the quintessential expression of an irresolvable tension between democracy and expertise.

The trust lies in the administrator and not the efficiency with which an administrator does the job and, most of all, not in elected officials. Frant (1993, 994) argues just this point when he says. "Statements of the late nineteenth-century civil service reformers do not reveal great concern about the difficulty of measuring output in the public sector, nor do they generally evince great disdain for the public sector as such. They do show a strong distrust of elected officials, but this distrust was far from irrational. It was based on an established fact of life: that elected chief executives could use their control of the political process to entrench themselves (or their party) in office, thereby subverting the electoral process." The distrust of elected officials hit a high mark in the civil service reforms. Milward (1978, 393), reflecting the feeling of the period in accounting for the reform causes and consequences, says, "... it was necessary to take politics out of the civil service and vice versa [and only] through depoliticization would it be possible to deny the spoilsmen patronage, their chief political resource, and thereby relegate the bosses to a minor role in the political system." Getting rid of corruption, rather than achieving efficient administration, dominated concern during the reform era. Rosenbloom and Obuchowski's (1977, 9) review of thinking in the era led them to argue that the civil service reform movement was only a part of an entire political system that reformers wanted to change. Efficiency became an intermediate goal, subordinate to the replacement of an entire class of politicians exploiting the masses.

Loyalty might be an underlying force, however, behind civil service reform. Patronage may have survived as a value in public administration. Villanueva (1993, 276–277) points out that, in hindsight, civil service reform has become an entry point for a "new patronage system." Recruitment may take place among those "who were ideologically compatible with policy objectives [of the president] ... whose views were compatible with his ideas on how foreign [or domestic, fiscal, monetary, or executive branch management] affairs should be managed." Early, reform era administrators may have supported reforms, and later the public policy aims of strong government presidents (Rourke 1992, 541–542). Patronage changed to loyalty in political ideology from loyalty in political party membership.

D. BUDGET REFORM

The executive budget reform movement resolved the conceptual conflict between a ruling class of neutral, competent, business-oriented experts and the ideologically loyal presidential followers in public administration. In this movement, different groups vied for the normative high ground. The competition took place with different metaphors of governance, as well as distinctive ways to build a budget institution, and alternative explanations for the institutional constraints on individual decisions. Reformers also created the local and national budget systems as now known.

The budgeting literature, from its early reform period to the present, has elaborated a normative model of what should take place among government agencies and between branches of government as well as within government agencies. In this section, this model is reviewed in the forms it took in the municipal reform movement, the state reorganization movement, and the national government's executive budget movement.

1. The Municipal Reform Movement

The traditional history of the reform period, from 1890 to 1920, draws a picture of reaction. Reformers reacted to a situation in which immigrants voted on long ballots for bundled groups of machine candidates who assumed office in a fragmented structure and then went about processing voter demands and lining their own and their cronies' pockets, driving up taxes and expenditures to the detriment of the middle and old-moneyed, patrician classes (e.g., Adrian 1987; Hofstader 1955; Schiesl 1977).

Reformers reacted with a call for representativeness in political structures of a different sort. A genuine political community, not merely coalitions on both sides of a partisan struggle, would be achieved (MacDonald 1988). Specifically, according to Lineberry and Sharkansky (1971) the reformers had:

1. An aversion to "politics" as a means of arriving at public-policy decisions and specifically to political parties and organized interest groups
2. An holistic conception of the community, a belief that there is a single interest of the "community as a whole" to which "special interests" should be clearly subordinated
3. A strong preference for professional management of community affairs, implying preference for public policy-making by technical experts like the city manager
4. A strong faith in the efficacy of structural reform

At the root of the problem of partisanship was the ward election system in city governments of the time. Through divisions of the area, machine candidates could directly cultivate and exploit the new immigrant blocks, usually in homogeneous blocks of people who arrived from the same country. The machine politicians could then bundle their own ward candidates and run them without fear of their being able to be contested as a slate (Adrian 1987). The reformers tackled the problem head-on. They proposed at-large political offices that would be filled through non-partisan elections. The reform produced the desired results, a dramatic fall-off in participation (Lineberry and Fowler 1967).

The reformers also proposed a centralization of power in the form of strong mayors with executive powers. These powers included the ability to appoint, through a combination of political appointments and a merit system, the most qualified experts and specialists to run city departments. This departmentalization of expertise would be coordinated through principles of orthodox management, narrow spans of control, and a chain of command. The work of the city government would be financed by a budget in which the various needs of departments as determined by experts would be presented and deliberated over by the mayor and a council of at-large elected council members. The responsible administration that was created as a result would be held accountable on the basis of economy and efficiency by the electorate (Adrian 1987; Schiesl 1977). In summary, the municipal reform model is the clearest normative model of budgeting today. The model views a genuine political community as operating with leaders elected at-large to represent the community's interest as a whole, an administration staffed by experts headed by a strong mayor with executive powers, including a budget through which process the work of the city could be financed economically and efficiently.

2. The State Reorganization Movement

The reforms at the state level generally reacted to legislative supremacy and its problems. As White (1933, 207–208) has pointed out before reform, "the typical state agency or institution prepared its own estimates, submitted them directly to the appropriations committee, ultimately received an independent appropriation, and spent its funds without supervision other than that provided by the auditor." Such a system had led to an increase in total expenditure of the states by almost 650% over two decades, muckraking that revealed public ineptitude and corruption, and a growing following for "the new gospel" being spread by scientific management proponents (Cleveland 1915; Schick 1971):

> The new gospel's provisions included an executive budget that resembled that developed in the munici-
> pal reform movement and included three perspectives. The first or planning perspective enabled the
> governor to use the status of sole representative of all the people to produce an authoritative statement of
> policies and programs (15).

From the second or management perspective, partisans argued that the governor be chief coordinator. The executive would "standardize and consolidate agency estimates and... ensure that the budget facilitated the efficient conduct of the public business" (Schick 1971, 16). The management perspective linked the budget with the reorganization movement itself, the chief goal of which was to functionally consolidate fragmented agencies and strengthen the executive's appointive and removal powers.

The third or control perspective would deter waste and fraud. The governor would become the state's chief controller, installing centralized purchasing, accounting, personnel, and internal audit controls to protect against corrupt or inept officials.

The tradition that developed as executive budgets were installed, however, limited executives' roles in the process. The legislative bodies guarded their constitutional duty and prerogative to appropriate by trading some of their former financial powers for control over expenditures. Schick observes (1971, 18):

> De facto, the governor became the control agent of the legislature; his job was to present the budget
> accounts in a way that facilitated detailed legislative scrutiny of agency requests and enabled the
> legislature to intervene when it wanted to. The conception of the governor as active policymaker fell
> by the wayside, although his potential for this role remained.

In fact, Schick argues, prior unfettered agency initiative in the preparation of estimates did not change; rather, it provoked the creation of a centralized control role for the executive in checking unconstrained spending requests. Unchanged agency initiative and the new centralized check over it also displaced a policy and planning role.

3. The National Executive Budget Movement

The federal executive budget followed lines similar to that in the municipal reform and state reorganization movements. The movement at the national level emerged from the confluence of seven factors. First, Progressives wanted to head off the agrarian radicals and their proposals for greater levels of government spending (Savage 1988). Second, Republicans wanted but did not have enough support to pass the Payne-Aldrich Tariff. Third, Progressives wanted but did not have enough support to pass the income tax. Fourth, Republicans blamed the panic of 1907 on spending and on the deficits of 1908, 1909, and 1910. Fifth, agrarian populism led to a widespread demand for schools, roads, and other government services. Sixth, the idea of centralized administration as essential to promote efficiency and accountability caught on as a result of the efforts of members of the Bureau movement (Waldo 1948). Finally, alarms were raised over World War I spending.

In reaction, over a period from 1907 to 1921, four major financial management events cascaded. First, centralization developed in the Treasury and in the Congressional appropriations process in the collection, reporting, and consideration of expenditure and revenue measures. Second, Congress passed parts of the Payne-Aldrich tariff that placed a 1% tax on corporate incomes above $5000. Third, Congress passed the individual income tax. Finally, Congress passed the Budget and Accounting Act of 1921.

For budgeting, the 1921 Act brought centralized management into being, and it created a balance between the legislative and executive branches in pursuit of financial management as a whole. Mosher (1984, 33), following Stourm (1917), divides the ideal budget process into four steps and assigns responsibility in this system to a branch. These steps appear in Table 7.2 as a picture of the ideal budget system.

The ideal system balanced the branches and provided checks of one over the other. The creation of the income tax, despite its later dilution and laggardly implementation (Savage 1988), complemented the budget act and led to the maintenance of balanced budget symbols. The ideal budget system created an answer to the economic question in providing that the chief executive steer the economy. The ideal also answered the accountability question in providing responsible, hierarchically oriented management. Finally, the rational decision making approach offered a technically elegant way of joining steering to responsibility.

If neutral competence and expertise guided recruitment and retention of government administrators, that expertise became the hammer to the nail of fiscal problems. Through reform, the idea took seed that (Kahn 1997, 1) "A program may be good or it may be bad, but if it does not pass budgetary muster, it is dead." The budget criterion served legislators who found the fiscal impact of a program easier to evaluate than policy or simply merit. The downside for decision making became clear. Information about a program's advantages would come from a reading of the values and needs of constituents, but a program's fiscal impact could come only from the analyses done by experts. These experts were steeped in an ethos of fiscal control—accounting detail and government revenue limits. More important, Kahn's budget experts personified basic Progressive era

TABLE 7.2
The Ideal Budget System

Step	Branch	1921 Act
Preparation	Executive	Bureau of the Budget (BoB)
Appropriation	Legislative	Congress through appropriations committees
Execution and control	Executive and legislative	Agencies, BoB, General Accounting Office (GAO)
Post audits	Legislative	GAO

Source: Adapted from Mosher, F. C., *A Tale of Two Agencies: A Comparative Analysis of the General Accounting Office and the Office of Management and Budget*, Louisiana State University Press, Baton Rouge, LA. With permission.

values—"efficiency, responsibility, accountability, politically neutral professionalism, management skill, fiscal integrity, parsimony" (Kahn 1997, 2).

Before reform, many observed an agglomeration of administrative fiefdoms serving members of Congress and their committees or local political machines with limited constituencies. The agglomeration of particularistic interests took public money and used it for the gain of each member of the committee or the political machine (Fisher 1975, 21–27). The national government collected revenue from a tariff and followed a policy of protectionism in trade internationally. Smithies (1955, 59–60) explained that:

> a government that could rely on customs revenues enjoyed special privileges. The political pressures were in the direction of higher taxes rather than lower.... Revenues flooded the Treasury.... [Fears] that embarrassingly large surpluses should be used as arguments for lower protective tariffs ... [outweighed concern] about high expenditures [and extravagance].... There was no process whereby the benefit of expenditures was weighed against costs in terms of taxation.... It is straining human nature too far to expect economy in the face of a budget surplus.

The revenue flood continued through the 1800s, except for a brief Civil War interruption. Congressional fragmentation, post-Civil War corruption (Dunning 1907, 229–293), and the appearance of deficits in 1903—due to pension bills, rivers and harbors projects, the Spanish-American War costs, and the cost of constructing the Panama Canal—brought Congressional inquiries, recognition of municipal reforms, and a realization that the president was the "protector of the purse" (Fisher 1975, 25–35). After reform, Kahn says that budgets became institutions. Budget institutions, he says (119), came to demarcate the public sphere of government action and thereby became indispensable referents for public discussion ["should this go into the budget?"] ... a coherent, interrelated, and unitary state ... [;] "imagining" the state, political actors were able to proceed to conceiving of more activist possibilities for the development and application of its power.

After the early twentieth century, Kahn notes (1997, 119), as budget reform extended to all governments in the US, the budget became "the ultimate means both to identify social problems—[if it gets into the budget, it's a significant social problem]—and to represent what government could and should do." Budget reform institutionalized action for the common good, and it identified the budget expert as the key decision maker in connecting public problems with government-administered solutions.

Reform, Kahn says, created a new theory of executive power, one in which accountability played the largest part. Kahn depicts a complex, growing federal government and a Congress without the institutional ability to take the leadership role. Realizing that the president had a far better institutional capacity for management and even leadership, members of Congress delegated. The thinking in Congress, Kahn said, amounted to the sense that only a hierarchy, a unitary government with "a single chief executive sitting atop a pyramid of bureaucratic authority" could produce a responsible and efficient government. If the practices of budget reform hold true to their promises, the Congress would become the principal and the president Congress' agent. The delegation of authority from Congress to the president would work if members of Congress could define the task clearly and determine whether the task was completed successfully.

Kahn recognizes the logic in Congressional delegation of power leading to a gain in Congressional control. Congressional oversight, and accountability, lay in clear, certain delegations of authority. The system would create efficiency and responsibility in a strong executive who must account for his actions to Congress. The logic and the executive budget system could institutionalize Congressional or representative government's control over a potential tyrant, and the logic and system could transform an elite corps of bureaucratic experts into a set of agents working in the interest of executives as leaders and ultimately of the people through Congress.

E. The Rise of the Budget Idea

Four different models vied for hegemony among reformers; we have begun to understand. One model is democracy. The model develops from the New England town meeting dealing with the tragedy of the commons (Hardin 1968). The model provides for wide participation among those with a stake in the outcome of decision making. All who participate have sufficient knowledge, and all, more or less, see the world in the same way, else they would not have a reason to participate. All have equal rights to participate, although some of the more able and respected take leadership roles. The purpose of the budget lies in proper use of the commons, the economic and social use of common resources. Finally, the purpose of the institution, all agree, is to represent "mutual coercion mutually agreed upon" (Hardin 1968, 1247–1248).

A second pro-business or corporate model exists. In this model, only taxpayers and bondholders vote. Organization managers maximize the use of taxpayers' and bondholders' resources, again pursuing economic development as a goal. Managers account for the returns from development to taxpayers and bondholders. Therefore, taxpayers and bondholders are consumers of private and public goods provided by government and must receive value for money.

A third progressive, positive government model competes (Dahlberg 1966; Kahn 1997; Schiesl 1977). Decision making may or may not include anyone other than managers and analysts. These legitimate decision makers take goals as given, represented in what taxpayers presently finance and for what purpose. The decision makers determine how well the costs and benefits of the work are distributed in terms of a decision rule such as: from each according to his or her wealth, to each according to need. Decision makers measure how well the government work is done—how well the work done in one program compares with the work done in others, the marginal rate of return. Decision makers believe in the fundamental proposition that government institutions are instruments for doing good, the common good, for solving social problems that developed as a result of industrialization and urbanization. Decision makers believe in the need for publicity of what the experts find important. Strong executives must order the work to make it efficient, thus they dominate government institutions. Decision makers, finally, believe that what government institutions do, when publicized, shows what the public responsibility is—what the responsibility for and to the commons is and that all with a stake in the commons delegate to government responsibility for efficient action.

The fourth model is a settlement house government model. Following (Addams 1902, 1905; Stivers 2000) and borrowing some from the Progressive Positive government group—government is an instrument for doing good, the common good, for solving social problems that developed as a result of industrialization, urbanization, and immigration. Social analysts conduct scientific surveys of social conditions. The surveys help determine the breadth and depth of social problems by talking with the poor and having the poor shape the interpretation and convey the significance of the social problems. Another survey or investigation helps the capacity of government departments to deal with the social problems. The capacity is found by talking with public managers, but the analyst interprets the information and conveys its significance. Analysts make the case for the budget to build capacity and direct that capacity to solve social problems based on data from the surveys. The analyst also reminds public managers and leaders of the citizen's right to information and keeps efforts at oversight and surveillance going with strong citizen participation.

The models represent elements of need, merit, and mutuality. The models represent different ways to define the idea serving the common good. The actors represent the models as well.

Kahn (1997) describes the primary actors—the ABCs—and two other influential ones in budget reform and the evolution of government institutions and individual decision making during this intense reform period. First, William Allen was (1997, 47) "the publicist, focused on using budgets to create an educated citizenry capable of exercising intelligent control over their elected officials." Allen was also "… an advocate, exhorting the general public to educate itself to full citizenship… ." He urged and motivated members of the public to transform themselves into a kind of mass elite.

Second, Frederick Cleveland (47) was "the technical expert, [an accounting and finance professor at New York University who] concentrated more on educating public officials and devoted his time to the mechanics of administrative reform (47)". Cleveland was " … a dispassionate investigator, addressing fellow experts and bringing the tools of scientific reasoning to bear on discrete problems of administration" (47).

Third, Henry Bruere was "the administrator, sought to maintain a balance between the two tendencies (and the two men)" (47). Bruere " … succeeded at building bridges between the bureau and government officials."

Two others amplified the themes of the ABCs. John D. Rockefeller, Kahn argues (1997), wanted no work done by the Bureau of Municipal Research with his money outside New York State and no dabbling in issues that other experts might deal with better. Rockefeller, according to Kahn, wanted the Bureau to be a useful, local, fiscal, and technical advisory institution. At a financially sensitive time, Rockefeller offered $10,000 for five years and help in raising another $100,000. The sensitivity arose from the expiration of several substantial five-year grants the Bureau depended upon would expire and, when the principals at the Bureau accepted Rockefeller's offer, effectively curbed Allen's efforts to identify social problems and utilize budgets as solutions.

William F. Willoughby was an academic public administration figure, a Princeton University political scientist, skilled in practical public administration as a Department of Labor statistician, with experience on the governing board of Puerto Rico, in the US Bureau of Census, and as legal advisor to the Chinese government. Willoughby, according to Kahn, believed that government should run efficiently. He distrusted popular democracy and thought publicity like Allen's of small importance, too technical. A more effective and realistic reform strategy, he believed, lay in concentrating on informing Congress as the people's representative, than to address the people themselves.

The Bureau men had seen improved administration as a means to restore some measure of popular control over government and to address the dangers of a disaffected citizenry. Willoughby saw the public simply as a mass whose opinion might on occasion be aroused to support the institute's independent goal of improving government administration. In Willoughby's hands, the people became instruments of expert reform rather than its intended beneficiaries, Kahn argues.

F. THE 1921 ACT

The Budget and Accounting Act of 1921 (P. L. 67-13, 42 Stat. 20–27) created an executive budget process, the Bureau of the Budget, and the General Accounting Office. The budget became a set of "[e]stimates of the expenditures and appropriations necessary in his judgment for the support of the government for the ensuing fiscal year" (42 Stat., 20) transmitted to Congress on the first day of each regular session. The estimates included those on receipts for the ensuing fiscal year under current law and under the revenue proposals the president made. Also, the president included the "expenditures and receipts of the Government during the last completed fiscal year" as well as those estimated "during the fiscal year in progress" (42 Stat., 20). The president would also report to Congress on deficiencies in financing spending due to inadequate revenues or due to laws enacted after the transmission of the budget, including recommendations to Congress for new taxes, loans, or "other appropriate action to meet the estimated deficiency" (42 Stat., 21). The budget curtailed direct requests by agencies to members of Congress:

> No estimate or request for an appropriation and no request for an increase in an item of any such estimate or request and no recommendation as to how the revenue needs of the government should be met, shall be submitted to Congress or any committee thereof by any officer or employee of any department or establishment, unless at the request of either House of Congress (42 Stat., 21–22).

The Act gave clear guidance on the nature of executive budgeting. The Bureau of the Budget in the Treasury Department (in the Reorganization Act of 1939, 1423 in the Executive Office of the President, renamed Office of Management and Budget in July 1970 Executive Order 11541), had clear authority as well. The top managers of the Bureau gained appointment by the president. Under rules the president prescribed, the Bureau staff "shall prepare for him the budget ... and any supplemental or deficiency estimates, and to this end shall have authority to assemble, correlate, revise, reduce, or increase the estimates of the several departments or establishments" (Budget and Accounting Act of 1921, 22). The Bureau had a constituency of one, the president. The Bureau gave the president the means to centralize budget control as well as to direct and manage agencies insofar as the budget could work instrumentally to gain management control.

Finally, the Act created the General Accounting Office (GAO, which in 2004 was renamed the Government Accountability Office). The Act made the office "independent of the executive departments and under the control and direction of the Comptroller General of the United States" (23). The Act located the office in the Treasury Department. However, the Act also moved the settlement of accounts, accounting and auditing to the Comptroller General from the Secretary of the Treasury and while giving the appointment of the Comptroller General to the President, provided for confirmation by the Senate and removal only by a joint resolution of Congress. Smithies (1955, 76) observes that Congress has regarded the General Accounting Office "as its own agency.... [and] has viewed its creation with jealous pride."

Few if any have viewed with satisfaction the organizational arrangement given GAO. The 'too much power, too little power' problem lay in failing to distinguish between accounting and auditing as well as the proper functions of the president and Congress. Smithies explained:

> The settlement of accounts can be regarded as exclusively an Executive function.... On the other hand, the Congress has a responsibility to review Executive performance and to do so it needs to prescribe the form [nature, and subject of the review. In giving the president the executive budget, the GAO section of the Act also] hampers Executive performance, reduces Executive responsibility, and gives the Congress more power than it requires to discharge its proper functions (1955, 76).

The two problems, who should account and who should audit, came out of Gladstone's prime ministry in the "charter of the English financial system" (Wilmerding 1943, 252, footnote 9) and the Exchequer and Audit Departments Act of 1866. Wilmerding (1943, 252–253) noted that by 1921 the members of Congress had agreed with the reasons the English had long abandoned "complicated checks imposed before expenditure takes place." The principle held that a "system of retrospective control" in the form of an audit, done independently of the president subject instead to Congress' control, created a greater power over the purse and one that complemented the power of appropriation. Such a system had important support in the private sector, among advocates of the 1921 Act as well as among members of the president's cabinet at the time (Wilmerding 1943).

The control emphasis in the 1921 Act did not give support to reform as much as a planning emphasis. Cleveland (1915) justified the budget idea as a plan, the lack of which had led to invisible, irresponsible government. Before, he said, estimates served the purpose of laying the foundation for work plans and financial plans that did not exist. Plans and thought about the responsibility for them marked the undeveloped idea of modern government. Centralized effort, he further argued, must bring together expenditure, revenue, and economic activity estimates so that someone can think in terms of the institution as a whole and the common good rather than the good of particularistic interests. The executive, the one actually implementing a plan, could be the only person held responsible for the success or failure of the plan. Therefore, the executive must exert leadership, Cleveland argued. Kaufman's (1956) thinking suggests that besides strong executive leadership, the 1921 Act gave support to strengthened administrative expertise and political neutrality, and the Act weakened the idea of Congress' representativeness relative to that of the president.

G. THE REFORM MOVEMENT AS INSTITUTIONALIZED VALUES

The reform movement represented many specialized movements, and the conflict among these movements and their constituencies resonates through subsequent events to reveal how institutions affect individual decisions. The movement created the institution of citizenship, and the movement changed the terms of debate about the appropriate size of the national and state governments in the federalist system as well as the hierarchy of status and representativeness among the three branches of national government.

Consider the Waldo (1948) study of the reform movement. The Progressive movement produced, through the National Municipal League and the New York Bureau of Municipal Research, the idea of a budget and a principle by which to unify all aspects of financial management. According to Waldo (1948, 32–33) the product was "efficient citizenship":

1. Progressives grew sensitive to the appeals and promises of science, and put a simple trust in discovery of facts as the way of science and as a sufficient mode for solution of human problems.
2. Progressives accepted and even urged a new positive conception of government that resembled the idea of a planned and managed society.
3. The progressive reformers found in business organization and procedures an acceptable way to conduct the business of government, becoming evangelists for efficient administration of government.
4. They sensed that civic awareness and militancy, efficiency, and useful education would work to create an Efficient Citizenship movement.

Involved in this movement were three basic groups: positive government proponents usually called *progressives*, governmental research bureau professionals or the *analysts*, and *business interests* to which openness provided a way to check large increases in tax bills. The movement produced the principle that a well-informed citizenry, provided information through easily understood financial management procedures—line-itemized budgets, competitively bid purchases, and audited financial statements—could check the moves of detested politicians. Openness of government yielded a rudimentary medium through which action might follow. Efficiency stood as a scientific check on processes used in government, by providing a performance standard.

Openness became the great unifying principle that drew support and led to the coalition of interests supporting reform. The coalition that produced the reforms implementing efficient citizenship combined business interests, research movement principals, and positive government proponents. All of the goals were complementary only when the open government issue provided context. At other times, business favored restrained taxation. The researchers promoted the secular notion that "proper institutions and expert personnel" could create "good" government (Waldo 1948, 23). The positive government proponents sought to use government authority to provide services needed as a result of the demand for more roads and schools.

With restrained taxation, responsible procedures, and government leadership in economic and social development as fundamental positions of members of the original coalition, changes in the size of government could continually pull the coalition apart. In fact, the later developments integrating financial management derive from variations of these three goals: parsimony, efficiency, and equity.

The upshot of the Efficient Government movement efforts to add procedure to government administration for accountability sake led to the widespread institution of organizations for the purpose. The insistence on openness gave the institutionalizing movement momentum. The Budget and Accounting Act of 1921 became the major achievement. The Act created a budget office and an auditing agency, both of which would open government to scrutiny through publication of a unified budget. Unification and openness put the spotlight on the executive; all could follow the decisions being made because they all took place in public view. Moreover, the other half of the Act's purview could check the implementation of these decisions: the expenditure audit.

The other members of the original coalition came off somewhat less well, even poorly. Researchers could look to the budget bureau and the accounting office as places where analysis might take hold. Greater faith in government decisions might come out of greater openness and might also lead to equity in vigorous government, a position of positive government proponents. Oddly enough, business interests, and parsimony, lost the biggest fight, that over the income tax when it was established just before the 1921 Act, and their share of the outcomes of the Efficient Citizenship movement was earned from the movement's acceptance of business operations as the standard to be observed.

H. Coalition Convergence and Divergence

The leaders of the successive movements that have swayed thinking in public financial management shared one important belief—that openness in government's financial dealings served their own interests, whether they were efficiency, equity, or parsimony. Those interests might be very different—progressives wanted positive government, business interests low taxes, research bureaus analysis, and muckrakers punishment for thieves. However, the coalition built to pursue openness believed the basic currency of financial management to be procedures and routines that were able to be both observed and evaluated. Observable and able to be evaluated *for what* remained to be seen.

Openness was the currency among the members of the reform coalition. It united them all in opposition to what were referred to as political forces widely known as the political clubs that controlled local and often state government and which were themselves controlled by a political boss.

Openness was also the plateau to be reached before any of the beliefs of any of the reform coalition members could be realized. Positive government types had to have some measure of goodness and the data besides to determine equity, and to counter the effects of discrimination and less-than-ideal levels of political participation. Only openness could provide this measure and the necessary data. Analysts had to have openness to determine efficiency. Business interests had to have openness to pinpoint the threats to parsimony and the sources of inequity in their taxes. Muckrakers, finally, had to have openness to root out thievery.

Openness itself was not accountability. It was the necessary basis on which to build accountable systems of work. Accountability was the belief, the vision to be fulfilled, while openness was a way of employing technology and management to achieve the vision.

I. Systems of Accountability as Sources of Divergence

Reform coalition members held different beliefs, advocated different management systems, and advanced the use of different technologies, all of which implied different systems of accountability. If one considers muckraking as essentially the primary position of all members of the coalition, three major, sometimes overlapping, groups and systems of accountability are left: positive government types—more government as service needs expanded; analytical and research types—efficient government first and foremost; and pro-business types—low taxes for greater returns on investment in private enterprise. Consider Table 7.3 below and its portrayal of these systems.

Among the members of the group, differences existed over the *accountability premise*. Positive government advocates and pro-business interests tended to see needs outside the organization as having primary control over what the organization did; they saw responsibility in equity. This responsiveness to clients or taxpayers tended to outweigh the need for responsibility, especially that premised on the efficiency calculations esteemed by analyticals, and that premised on the parsimony arguments advanced by business interests.

TABLE 7.3
Comparison of Accountability Systems Implied by Reform Coalition Members in Government Financial Management

Group	Analyticals	Positive Government Believers[a]	Pro-Business
Accountability Premise	Efficiency	Equity	Parsimony
Technology	Productivity	Marginality	Monetized utility
Organization Theory	Hierarchical	Negotiated	Privatization
Belief System	Government as fixed sphere, neither expanding nor contracting necessarily	Government as expanding sphere	Government as contracting sphere

[a] Waldo defines their views: "They accepted—they urged—the new positive conception of government, and verged upon the idea of a planned and managed society" (1948, 32); "they look favorably upon government, regard it as a desirable instrument for the accomplishment of individual and community purposes, profess indifference or express favor at proposal to extend the range of its operation or control" (1948, 68). Waldo subsequently cites Henry Bruere's *New City Government* (1913) and Frederick A. Cleveland's *Organized Democracy* (1913).

Source: From Waldo, D., *The Administrative State*, Ronald Press, New York, 1948; Schiesl, M. J., *The Politics of Efficiency: Municipal Administration and Reform in America, 1800–1920*, University of California Press, Berkeley, CA, 1977. With permission.

Technologies of analysis and decision making differed as well. Positives tended to compare programs with other programs, defining the best programs as those whose rates of return at the margin outweighed others. Efficiency as technology demanded a calculation of material inputs and outputs with effort taken to assure minimum loss in between. Typically, pro-business interests determined the worthiness of effort based on its perceived utility expressed in money terms and discounted for loss of value over time; the value of the preferred effort exceeded that of alternative ones.

Members of the coalition differed in their approach to the problems of management, in their *organization theories*. Positive government types wanted the goals and methods of organizations to be matters of cooperation reached through negotiation (Golembiewski 1977). Analyticals, from the Brownlow Committee on, tended towards hierarchy (Gulick and Urwick 1937). The pro-business interests favored private sector provision of most services that had before been produced by government (Wolf 1988).

Finally, the *belief systems* of the three elements of the reform coalition differed. Positive government types, by definition, believed in government as an expanding sphere of influence in direct proportion to the demand for public services. In contrast, pro-business interests lay in shrinking government's sphere for the sake of both increasing business opportunity and decreasing taxes. Analyticals, however, tended to waffle on the size of government issue, emphasizing the efficiency issue whatever the sphere of government.

J. CONVERGENCE ON INSTITUTIONS THROUGH REORGANIZATION

The high point in reform took place after the 1921 Act in the first Hoover Commission. Gist (1998, 267) argues that after the 1921 Act, among reformers stress lay "almost exclusively [on] the themes of efficiency, centralization of administrative power, expertise, and the professionalization of administrators." Expertise could check the power of politicians and gain the public interest (Keller, this volume).

The need for expertise rather than politics became evident as the US and then the world economy contracted during the period from 1929 to 1933. With efforts through government programs to deal with the consequences of the Great Depression, especially in the steady increase in government agencies, and president-centered reorganization and management study commissions that began in the 1930s, a consensus on institutions emerged. That consensus reasoned toward reforms to control the institutions that, in turn, control and apply technology, expertise, and knowledge.

Engineering institutions became a major effort. The first of these engineering efforts came with the work of John Maynard Keynes. In *The General Theory*, Keynes (1936, 378) reasoned "The State will have to exercise a guiding influence on the propensity to consume partly through its scheme of taxation, partly by fixing the rate of interest, and partly, perhaps, in other ways.... If the State is able to determine the aggregate amount of resources devoted to augmenting the instruments [of production] and the basic rate of reward to those who own them, [the State] will have accomplished all that is necessary" to achieve an optimum rate of investment, economic output, and full employment.

The second engineering effort came through the President's Committee on Administrative Management or the Brownlow Committee. The reorganization efforts required study and a staff. The Committee staff did study and published the papers that became the essence of an engineering theory of institutions.

The *Papers on the Science of Administration* that emerged from the Brownlow Committee also continued in another form separation of administration and politics. Instruction comes in the last chapter (Gulick and Urwick 1937, 191–195):

> Administration has to do with getting things done; with the accomplishment of defined objectives. The science of administration is thus the system of knowledge whereby men may understand relationships, predict results, and influence outcomes in any situation where men are organized at work together for a common purpose" (191).

> It thus behooves the student of administration ... to acquire the habit of separating (a) relationships and (b) value judgments as far as is possible in his work.... [The student of administration] should endeavor to say, 'Under conditions x, y, and z conduct A will produce B; and conduct A′ will produce C.' He may have discovered this because he feels that B is desirable and C is undesirable, but if another student, or a statesman, confronts the same problem he may none the less be able to build upon and make use of the scientific work of the first student even though he has a reversed scale of values. Whenever a student of government says: 'The mayor should now do A,' this is to be interpreted:

> 1. Present conditions are xyz
> 2. Under conditions xyz, A gives B
> 3. B is good, therefore
> 4. Do A

> [If in the science of administration] the basic good is "efficiency" ... we are in the end compelled to mitigate the pure concept of efficiency in the light of the value scale of politics and the social order (192–193).

The Papers immediately became a source for orthodox decision making (Miller 1991, 33–50). At about the same time, a more organic, textural explanation for administrative decision making emerged in the work by Chester Barnard.

1.   Chester Barnard

Chester Barnard's *Functions of the Executive* (1938) was significant as a bridge between the scientific management (Taylor 1911, 1947) and principles approaches and the groundbreaking work of Herbert Simon (1947); in fact, Simon acknowledged his debt to Barnard in *Administrative Behavior*). Barnard's work has some of the strengths and weaknesses one might expect, taking into account that it is the work of a reflective practitioner attempting to explicate systematically his experiential knowledge and to integrate that experience with his informal studies in the social sciences. Barnard's writing is difficult; he never really delivers on his promise to describe in detail the actual functions of the executive, and he is occasionally inconsistent (e.g., his conflicting definitions of efficiency—first defined as being an absence of unanticipated outcomes from an activity, and only later defined as representing the equilibrium required for organizational mainten-ance). One might also take exception to his arguments in favor of informal executive organizations whose membership is based on uniformity of race, gender and religion: deliberately exclusionary elites. That said, one must be grateful for the fruit of Barnard's many years of keen observation of individuals and groups in actual organizations, his plainly deep and careful thought about those observations, and his humanizing ideal of executive leadership, particularly his emphasis on leader-ship by moral example.

One could speculate that Barnard did not seek to demolish scientific management, but only to put it in its place by articulating a range of criteria for deciding among means and ends beyond that of pure efficiency. His conception of organizational efficiency as an inducement/contribution equi-librium, after all, implicitly incorporates both the productive efficiency that was everything for Taylor and the allocative efficiency concept articulated in economic theory by Vilfredo Pareto. Rational productive efficiency is useful in helping to maximize the generation of surplus value, but cannot be an exclusive purpose in a complex organization based on systems of human cooperation. Perhaps most significantly, by introducing the allocative concepts of Pareto and other then-contem-porary economists, Barnard thus offered a precedent for the application of microeconomic theory to the analysis of individual choices (that through aggregation form collective decisions and behaviors) in organizations. The literature on the economics of organization blossomed decades later, as discussed by Moe (1984), and continues to thrive. Barnard also adapted the then-recent development of indifference curve analysis to the internal economy of organizations as systems of cooperation. His concept of the "zone of indifference" (1968, 167) within which members of an organization are most easily influenced, because they are equally ready to accept any of the alternatives within the bounded set, formed the basis for Simon's (1947) later articulation of the "zone of acceptance," similarly grounded in a framework of viewing administrative organization as equilibrating the individual desires and contributions of its members.

K. MARY PARKER FOLLETT

Barnard's formulation of the economics of organization, with its reliance on a balance of induce-ments, shares with later rational choice-based models a presumption of relatively fixed rationality on the part of individual decisions makers. At about the same time budget and administrative reformers were remaking the federal government, however, Mary Parker Follett proposed an approach to organizations that was grounded in altering rather than accommodating individual judgments.

Widely cited in recent years as an underappreciated political and administrative thinker of the early twentieth century, Mary Parker Follett identified herself as a proponent of scientific manage-ment, but articulated a conception of the interaction of managerial with rank-and-file decisions that was considerably more nuanced than, and in some cases provided directly contrary solutions to, Frederick Taylor's attempts to prevent "soldiering" and other forms of inefficient behavior by subordinates. Her work illustrates a concern with making best use of the ways in which organizations' stakeholders form judgments about the world and about their own interests, and contrasts sharply in several ways with Taylor's ideal of supplanting the unscientific judgments and choices of non-managerial members. She went further, too, in anticipating stakeholder constructs of organization, by identifying consumers and other ostensibly external parties as concerned with the results of organizational decision making. The core of her theory of human relations in administration can be found in four papers on "The Psychological Foundations of Business Administration," presented in January 1925 under the auspices of the Bureau of Personnel Administration (Follett 1940). Some of the ideas in these papers were articulated in earlier works, however, including the book *Creative Experience* (Follett 1924).

In "Constructive Conflict," Follett argued that because conflict or difference is inevitable in any organization, it ought to be put to advantageous use as much as possible. This could be accomplished, by seeking an "integration" of conflicting interests rather than simple domination or compromise, so that the conflict is exploited as a stimulus to the devising of new solutions rather than as a hindrance to resolution. Follett's integration would resolve conflict by devising solutions that respond to all parties' real interests. This requires bringing the differences causing a conflict into the open, focusing on the most significant rather than the most dramatic features of those differences to facilitate useful analysis of the problem at hand, and—by understanding the "circular" nature of human interactions—anticipating the responses of other parties and how those responses will in turn affect subsequent responses through the process of interpersonal "interpenetration." This approach to reconciling interests finds a more recent expression in the Harvard model of interest-based negotiation (Fisher and Ury 1983). In terms of our present analytic framework, it could be seen either as a way of incorporating multiple stakeholders' judgments and preferences into the premises each employs for preferential choice, or as a way of exploiting ambiguity by steering individuals' preferences in such a way as to yield compatible choices. In "The Giving of Orders," Follett asserted," … orders will not take the place of training," and proposed that the most effective employees would be those who were induced to "work with" rather than "work under" organizational management, because this allows management and workers to reconcile the receipt of orders with the taking of responsibility and the ingrained "habit-patterns" and beliefs of the workers. This was to be accomplished by focusing on the requirements of the whole of a given situation to "depersonalize" the orders given, so that they clearly reflected the "law of the situation" rather than seeming to reflect only the arbitrary requirements of a supervisor. In this way, the organization could more readily secure what 50 years later would be termed "consummate" as opposed to "perfunctory" cooperation (Williamson 1975). Follett herself acknowledged that this required a faith in the possibility that calm, rational consideration would reveal common interests that might well be regarded as utopian. Again Follett emphasized the importance of understanding "circular behavior": the way in which the effect of the changing situation on the actors changes that situation and so on.

Responding to the increasing technical complexity and size of contemporary organizations, Follett (1940) emphasized the need to make all of the parts of an enterprise work together as a "functional whole," or "integrative unity." She asserted in "Business as an Integrative Unity" that the central responsibility of business administration was to integrate the interests of the range of its stakeholders, including owners, managers, workers, and customers. Making stakeholders see the ways in which all their interests can be simultaneously satisfied could allow the organization most effectively to make use of the abilities and knowledge of all its members. She noted too that in contemporary organizations the increased role of specialization and technical expertise had rendered the distinction between managers and the managed contingent at times unclear. In contrast with Taylor, then, Follett here suggested that managerial elites themselves could or should find themselves relying on the judgments of people with a more hands-on form of knowledge. This too may have been somewhat utopian, judging by some recent evidence about the use of production workers' knowledge (Schmidt 1993). In "Power," Follett advocated seeking a co-active "power-with" rather than a coercive "power-over" within an organization or society. She argued here in favor of the careful and thoughtful integration of multiple viewpoints through circular behavior and the interpenetration of ideas, together with submission to the law of the situation and the creation of the desired "functional unity" within an organization. The use of indisputable facts ascertained through scientific methods of inquiry can build up power-with and so reduce the scope for adversarial bargaining and power-over. This is meant to create an environment in which all members of the organization gain power together, through active cooperation and participation rather than mere consent or acquiescence. Here are echoes of scientific management's search for the one best way, but Follett proposes to rely on a variety of stakeholders' judgments to identify the one best choice for any situation. Again, there is also a possibility that this exploits ambiguity by providing opportunities for actors to understand their own preferences in more compatible ways.

Taken as a whole, Follett's work in administration and her earlier work in political theory (Follett 1918) revealed a combination of normative commitment to popular self-government and confidence in the possibility for science to find win–win solutions to conflicts that in some ways anticipated the development of the policy sciences several decades later. Allowing for the open discussion of interests among the full range of those holding stakes in the outcomes of decisions (although she does not employ the term stakeholder) and the application of scientific models of problem solving might identify ways in which mutually advantageous decisions could be achieved without coercion—although not without conflict. The potential in her proposals for taking advantage of ambiguity to reconfigure individuals' judgments and choices prefigures in some ways McGregor's Theory Y (1960).

VI. WORLD WAR II TO THE END OF THE TWENTIETH CENTURY

Over the first half of the twentieth century, the development of systematic, executive-centered budgeting; the New Deal and its dramatic expansion of positive, activist government; and the growth of technical approaches to organizational management and decision making transformed the landscape of public policy and public administration. By the 1940s, it had become clear that as a result of these parallel trends, "Public administration is policy-making" (Appleby 1949, 169). Bureaucrats and technical experts had come to be a new elite, making policy from within the executive branch as well as implementing it. Paul Appleby argued that it is not possible to separate policy from administration, and that the separation of powers itself is not impermeable. Administrators make rules for the future, thus performing a legislative function, and interpret rules in the present, thus performing a judicial function. They also shape policy by making specific recommendations for legislation. At the same time, Congress intervenes in administration in a number of ways. While there is a continuum from policy to administration, the questions of "what to do" and "how to do it" are at all times intertwined, according to Appleby, and it is also possible for large policy changes to occur administratively. The politics–administration dichotomy, with its reservation of collective choice- and constitutional-level decision making for citizens and their elected representatives, is descriptively inadequate in the era of big, activist governments, whatever one may think of it as an inspirational ideal or as a formerly accurate description of limited government. The role of technical elites can no longer be confined to purely operational decisions.

A. The Dichotomy Updated: The Friedrich–Finer Debate

The famous Friedrich–Finer debate framed the implications of this emerging expert, administrative elite in terms of the problem of administrative discretion and its implications for institutional arrangements. Friedrich (1940) argued in favor of expanded discretion for executive-branch bureaucrats, asserting that the increasing scope and complexity of modern government together with legislative delegation militated in favor of increasing reliance on expertise and professional norms. This, according to Friedrich, would achieve greater responsiveness of government to the actual needs of the public. Finer (1941) objected, arguing that traditional legal, political, and hierarchical standards, with their established mechanisms for sanctions, still needed to be pre-eminent. Administrators are rightly the agents of the citizenry and their elected representatives. As such, it is their responsibility to carry out the expressed wishes of those principals, not to decide on their own what is best for the public. The legislative delegation that can occur in the face of technical complexity or irreconcilable political conflict, he argued, could and should be remedied by greater specificity. The judgments and preferred choices of experts must be subordinated to the wants—as distinguished from the needs identified by experts—of the people. The solution is not for the principals' roles of citizens and legislators to be usurped by administrators' specialized expertise, but rather to provide technical support that will enable non-specialists to evaluate the claims of technical elites.

The question of how much and what kind of discretion to grant administrators over decisions at all three levels remains an unresolved one, and an often unacknowledged problem in the schemes of reformers. For instance, Theodore Lowi argued that members of the Public Choice school, although normatively committed to limited government and the consumer sovereignty of the citizen, also favored technical expertise over representative democracy in the formulation of collective choices, abhorring as they did the "irrational inefficiency of politics" as a way to make decisions (Lowi and Simon 1992). The New Public Administration and the more recent reinventing government and New Public Management models of reform similarly have espoused in varying ways active roles for administrators in making discretionary decisions based on their own judgment and expertise at the same time as they avowed a commitment to serving the public—whether as citizens or customers— better.

B. Efforts to Enhance Rationality

The Friedrich–Finer debate and its continuations concern the appropriate locus of discretionary authority and the allocation by institutional arrangements of the authority to propose normative judgments and adopt preferential choices. The 1940s also saw the publication by Herbert Simon of a self-consciously revolutionary approach to understanding the interaction of individual and administrative rationality, Management Science, and the early stirrings of an attempt to eliminate the need for normative conflict in policy rationality, the Policy Sciences or Policy Analysis. Each approach held out hope for making its side of the politics–administration division more scientific and so more efficient, by replacing imprecise logics of appropriateness, such as that represented by the "principles of administration" Simon (1947, 1997) demolished in his second chapter, with more calculative logics grounded in the specification of ends and the discernment of the best means to those ends.

1. The Roots of Management Science: *Administrative Behavior*

Herbert Simon, for his part, proclaimed that decision was at the heart of administration and suggested that the politics–administration dichotomy be reconceived, but without abandoning the notion that the legitimate provinces of administrative and political decision could be distinguished. Instead of an abrupt dichotomy, a continuum extending from the purely factual to the purely ethical can be seen as a basis for sorting the experts' and popular representatives' realms of decision. The role of administrators is to arrange to realize the values selected in political institutions and to provide legislators with the information on which political judgments and choices can be based, and the role of administrative institutions in turn is to guide the choices of individual administrators and to perfect their judgments to facilitate both the implementing and informing functions of administration. Although his full explication of the problem of bounded rationality and the satisficing model of decision—limited search for alternatives and the adoption of a simple level of aspiration as a target rather than optimality or maximization—was still in the future, by the time of his doctoral dissertation, published as *Administrative Behavior* (1947, 1997), the outlines were visible. Organizations, Simon suggested, serve to steer the choices of rank-and-file organizational members toward the most appropriate of the possibilities within the "zones of acceptance" constituted by their inherent knowledge, skills, abilities, and predilections. That is, they simplify decision making for individuals by reducing the number of alternative judgments and choices organizational members must evaluate to do their work. Administrative organizations also serve to enhance the rationality of strategic and tactical decisions made by individuals on behalf of the public by providing systematic supports to extend individual, bounded rationality so that it might more closely approximate synoptic or complete rationality aimed at optimal choices. The human mind and attention are among the scarcest of all resources (Simon 1978), so that even considering uncertainty alone as a challenge to decision (the reliance on extra-administrative political value judgments as the sole source of policy direction served here to simplify problems of administrative decision by essentially leaving major sources of ambiguity outside the model), fully rational decisions by unaided individuals are improbable at best. Even operational decisions tend to be so complex that organizational supports for rationality are required if one hopes to approximate complete rationality.

This reliance on organizational or managerial direction of individual workers' behavioral choices and on technical expertise and administrative organization to structure the managers' judgments and choices threatened to bump up against the challenge that "The central problem of democratic administrative theory ... is how to reconcile the desire for democracy ... with the demands of authority" (Waldo 1952, 102). Indeed, according to Waldo, self-conscious public administration shared a core set of values with private, business administration, and "the theory and practice of private administration were shaped in a context that was in very important respects undemocratic" (83).

To reduce the difficulty involved in reconciling democracy and administrative hierarchy, Simon strategically simplified the second-order analytic tasks entailed in making administrative decisions and improving the processes by which those decisions are made. He carefully bounded the scope of administrative decision treated by his work to exclude the policy, ideological, and partisan political decisions for which democracy—rather than analysis by or obedience to technical and administrative elites—was the normatively desired mode of decision making. Managerial elites could govern operational decision making, but would reserve to the citizenry as much as possible decisions at the collective-choice level—the selection of the political values in the service of which administrators would seek the instrumental value of efficiency. This would be accomplished partly as a result of institutional divisions between the realms of policy and administration and partly through their own efforts not to overstep the bounds of an intention to maintain an approximation of dichotomy. If it is true that administrative decisions bear consequences for policy, it is also true that scrupulous administrators can attempt to uphold rather than undermine policy decisions to the extent those decisions are relatively certain and unambiguous. Even so, Simon acknowledged, "In practice, the separation between the ethical [deeming states of the world "good" or not] and factual ["true" or "false"] elements in judgment can usually be carried only a short distance" (61).

Simon would continue to pursue a better understanding of actual human instrumental rationality and the ways in which it could be enhanced by and within administrative organization, including exploration of decision-support techniques, expert systems, and other aids to judgment and choice. Still, his focus on administrative choice in the context of an aspiration to maintain some form of distinction between the acts of selecting authoritative values and of getting things done implied an acceptance of partisan politics and other messy and likely inefficient means of generating public decisions at the constitutional and collective-choice levels. Decades later, Simon claimed the mantle of the Framers for his own insights, remarking that his works "proclaim a very limited form of human rationality ... that acknowledges the whole person: values, emotions, stupidities, ignorance, and all. Madison, Hamilton, and Jay would have had no difficulty seeing in the administrator of *Administrative Behavior* the same *homo politicus* that they described in the pages of *The Federalist* (Lowi and Simon 1992, 111).

2. Policy Analysis and Its Discontents

The same post-World War Two period, however, also saw the emergence of a technocratic approach that, with the best of intentions, hoped to render inefficient and contestable political means of policy decision obsolete by substituting scrupulous techniques of scientific policy analysis that could help legislative and executive decision makers select objectively correct policies. The policy sciences were to be objective but also unabashedly normative, placing technical specialists from a range of disciplines in the role of intermediaries to democratic policy decisions, with the responsibility of "locating data and providing interpretations that are relevant to the policy problems of a given period" (Lasswell 1951). In the context of the continuing expansion in the size and scope of the federal government occasioned by the war, a problem-solving model placed government at the center of collective life, with a responsibility to identify and solve collective problems, with few limits other than those imposed by fiscal constraints. By systematizing value-based judgments and choices according to a rigorous logic of social efficiency, policy analysis appeared to some advocates to be a way to render politics and ideology less important than technical analysis in identifying and solving those policy problems and to overcome the limitations of individual and political rationality through science. Many of the analytic techniques of policy analysis had their origins in the decision sciences developed during the war, particularly operations research, adapting to matters of selecting public ends and the means thereto the problem-solving orientation used to support military logistics (DeLeon 1988). Economic theories and techniques of analysis formed another core set of procedures for conventional policy-analytic procedures of judgment and choice, amounting to what Lowi would later describe as "the new language of the state" (Lowi and Simon 1992). Lowi's critique suggested that rather than serving as public-empowering intermediaries, policy analysts had instead become a technical elite whose judgments and recommended choices dominated even those of the political elite comprising the public's elected representatives:

> When the key elements of a policy problem have been defined tightly in economic terms, and when the proposal comes supported with elaborate methodology, such as cost/benefit analysis, legislators find themselves voting Yes or No on whether the costs outweigh the benefits [rather than setting the terms of the policy debate themselves] (108).

Heclo's (1978) naming and analysis of the "issue networks" that by the late 1970s had come to share policy space with and even in some areas supplant the older "iron triangles" consisting of bureaucrats, congressional committees, and special-interest representatives, revealed another aspect of the inadvertently elitist implications of specialized policy analysis. Heclo argued further from the example of the Carter administration that issue-network membership rather than traditional political and ideological affiliations had come to be the requisites for appointment to key federal political-administration positions. For Heclo, the very real benefits of this arrangement—it mirrored the general public's decreasing alignment with political parties, linked Congress and the executive in new and useful ways through shared understandings and vocabularies, and allowed for greater maneuverability by public managers—were not quite sufficient to dismiss the disadvantages. Those disadvantages included the loss of democratic legitimacy through too much complexity, too little consensus, too little evident self-confidence in prescriptions, and no closure to policy problems (in large part consequences of the academic orientation of the networks and their members who now fill the appointive posts); the diminution of the president's political leadership, and potentially severe problems of "the accountability of a political technocracy" (122). Heclo's issue networks are in fact a form of institution, helping their members know what is important and true, and defining their interests in specific ways (Scott 1994, 1995). "Network members reinforce each other's sense of issues as their interests, rather than (as standard political or economic models would have it) interests defining positions on issues" (Heclo 1978, 102). "Sharing policy knowledge, the networks provide a minimum common framework for political debate and decision in the two branches.... Like experienced party politicians of earlier times, policy politicians in the knowledge networks may not agree; but they understand each other's way of looking at the world and arguing about policy choices" (117). While the parallel is not exact, to some extent this echoes the concern expressed by Waldo (1984) that administrators in a large and activist public sector tend by default to construct a particular political philosophy grounded in precepts of efficiency, possibly at the expense of other societal values and goals that might otherwise be identified and pursued in a democracy. The 1980s, however, saw an appreciable increase in the degree of partisanship of expert analysis applied to policy problems, so that some degree of ideological competition of ideas began to occur in and around policy networks, moving the system at least to some degree from elite consensus toward a real competition of ideas (Fischer 1993).

C. THE GREAT INCREMENTALISM DEBATE

Another critique of the policy analytic model, or at least of a straw-man version of the policy sciences, was presented by Charles Lindblom in the form of a defense of the more traditional "muddling through" model of administrative decision making (Lindblom 1959). In the traditions of both Plato's *Republic* and neoclassical economics, Lindblom generalized from a descriptive portrayal of the decision making procedures employed by individual public administrators, first to a similarly patterned depiction of collective decision practices and then to a claim that "incrementalism" was both accurate description and reasonable prescription for collective decisions, employing marginal reasoning, and continuous incremental adjustments of policy based on learning from previous adjustments. Rather than attempt, and fail, to identify global values, corresponding policy ends, and optimal means thereto—a model of what would later be termed synoptic rationality—actual political and administrative decision makers tended to mix ends and means, limit the scope of values and alternatives included in the analysis, and conduct policy as a series of small and easily amplified or corrected experiments. This was not only how it was, but also as it should be, given the practical limitations on individual and collective analytic capabilities and the incommensurability of many social values. In the face of what might be termed uncertainty and ambiguity, incremental analysis and change, and the "mutual adjustment" of competing interests and ideas, made it possible for actors to reach agreement and to continue pursuing policies with favorable results while changing course before undesirable results accumulated to an unacceptable degree if policy changes proved to have undesired results.

Weighing in several years later on what had by then become a voluminous and contentious literature debating the descriptive and prescriptive validity of incremental versus synoptic rationality, at both the individual and collective levels of analysis, Amitai Etzioni (1967) proposed to resolve the debate by suggesting in effect, "all of the above," with his "mixed-scanning" model of collective decision. "Mixed-scanning provides both a realistic description of the strategy used by actors in a large variety of fields and the strategy for effective actors to follow" (388–389). Etzioni argued that actual individual approaches to decision do, and processes of collective decision making ought to, combine relatively comprehensive but not highly detailed "scanning" of a broad range of values, means, and ends to "set basic directions" with "incremental processes which prepare for fundamental decisions and work them out after they have been reached" (388). Further, Etzioni claimed, "Incrementalism was shown to overlook opportunities for significant innovations" (1986, 8). This effectively presumed the desirability of a "more active approach" to the selections of values and policies and the possibility that such a more active approach could improve on incremental models by establishing a larger perspective and encouraging decision makers consciously and strategically to allocate attention and analytic resources between comprehensive and incremental analyses. Implicitly echoing Keynes's interventionist dictum that "in the long run (over which incremental adjustments through market mechanisms achieve optimal results), we're all dead," Etzioni further suggested that a mixed approach could reach preferred states more efficiently than purely incremental models, in part by working to specify actively desired states rather than just reacting to problems. "Often what from an incremental viewpoint is a step away from the goal ('worsening') may from a broader perspective be a step in the right direction" (1967, 389).

Two decades after his initial exposition, Lindblom (1979) clarified and elaborated upon his notion of incrementalism, identifying four related aspects of incrementalism and articulating its relationship with pluralist models of political decision. Political incrementalism—"political change in small steps," not to be confused with pluralism and its reliance on partisan mutual adjustment for the reconciliation of conflicts of ideology and interests—is distinct from incrementalism as an approach to policy analysis. As an analytic approach, incrementalism encompasses "simple incremental analysis," which considers as alternatives only incremental changes from current conditions, "disjointed incrementalism," which employs "a mutually supporting set of simplifying and focusing stratagems" including the "fragmentation of analytical work to many (partisan) participants," and "strategic analysis" (517–518). Analytic incrementalism and pluralism are not ideal procedures for collective decision, Lindblom argued, but they are better than the realistically available alternatives such as totalitarian centralized decision and/or inevitably failed attempts at comprehensive scientific rationality. Further, they could be improved through the application of "strategic analysis," the systematic and conscious simplification of problems in order to achieve a collective version of individuals' bounded rationality through "skillful incompleteness" (524). Lindblom concluded this article by promising to develop further inquiry into the use of knowledge and analysis in social problem solving, beginning with *Usable Knowledge* (Lindblom and Cohen, 1979).

Lindblom and Cohen's book was prompted by their "dissatisfaction with social science and social research as instruments of social problem solving." Where Heclo (1978) expressed concern about the loss of democratic legitimacy associated with an essentially academic approach to solving policy problems, Lindblom and Cohen pointed out that there were fundamental problems of usefulness as well. Professional social inquiry (PSI), they argued, was useful only insofar as it was integrated into a larger process that also included ordinary knowledge, social learning, and interactive problem solving of which political bargaining is one variety. Such an approach would accept PSI as an increment of knowledge but not one that is distinctively authoritative, and would not necessarily privilege understanding above simply arriving at agreed and agreeable solutions to problems: "agreement is the test of 'best' policy" (Lindblom 1959, 84).

By 1990, however, Lindblom's continuing investigations appeared to have rendered him somewhat more pessimistic about the use of scientific techniques to guide collective policy decisions. In effect, he argued in *Inquiry and Change* (1990) that society has serious problems of impairment in its collective ability to learn that cannot be solved merely through improvements in professional scientific inquiry. Elite models of decision making were no less subject to inconclusiveness of judgment than lay probing by non-specialists and in fact were likely to contribute to greater "impairment" of social problem-solving abilities.

These critiques of synoptic rationality as realistically descriptive of individual decision making (Simon 1959, 1997) or usefully prescriptive for collective decision making (Lindblom 1959, 1979; Lindblom and Cohen 1979) suggested that sequential and bounded models of rationality were more realistic both as description and prescription. Limited search and satisficing, and incremental choices allowing for redirection without excessive disruption, can be seen as responding to the ambiguity associated with the endogenous and emergent qualities of individual and collective preferences as well as to the uncertainty associated with the constrained rationality of both scientific and ordinary knowledge.

Processes of interaction and mutual adjustment facilitate the discovery of values and of what one might call social zones of acceptance as an alternative to the central specification, or worse, the taking for granted, of values, ends, and means thereto in an effort to seek rationality in spite of politics (Waldo 1984). But this in turn requires significant improvements in the capacities of both practitioners of PSI and ordinary citizens, involving significant changes in power relations as well as expertise and factual knowledge (Lindblom 1990). By 1990 in fact, Lindblom was fairly explicitly advocating some approximation of radically egalitarian direct democracy, of better informed lay citizens, as a means to reducing the present impairment of social decision making by establishing a genuine competition of ideas. In light of the chicken-and-egg problem of "mutual interaction between improvements in inquiry and improvements in social structure" (287), this would require addressing problems of inequality and propaganda as well as the centralizing tendencies of the policy sciences and the Progressive-era legacy in public administration (also see Schneider and Ingram 1997). Interestingly, Lindblom's (1990) work offered a program for social learning and problem-solving with marked similarities to Fay's (1976) call for a critical social science, albeit without the explicit focus on bettering the circumstances of traditionally repressed groups in particular.

D. FORMS OF INDIVIDUAL AND COLLECTIVE IRRATIONALITY

The period from the 1960s to date has seen a wide range of work produced exploring individual and collective rationality, or irrationality, in decision making. Scholars of organizations attended to some of the ways in which actual organizations failed to produce collective decisions that improved on individual bounded rationality in the way that Herbert Simon's work suggested would be desirable. Actual collective decision making, in organizations and in polities, it seemed, diverged from the idealized rational model of problem identification and goal setting, comprehensive identification and analysis of alternatives, and optimal choice, at least as much as Simon's bound-edly rational individuals—or even more so, to the extent that collectives may fail even to satisfice by working toward an initially stipulated objective or objectives. Public-choice economists and political scientists identified a number of theoretical grounds for predicting that representative democracies might readily transform individual rationality into irrational and inefficient collective decisions. As if that were not bad enough, psychologists identified a number of ways in which individual judgments tend to be biased, or simply incorrect, to an extent that results in distinctly irrational choices at the individual level as well.

1. Organizational Decision Making

In the fourth century BC, Plato famously presented the psychological makeup of individuals as a suitable analogy for the ideal structure of political collectives (Plato 1979). The three competing parts of an individual mind—appetite, reason, and passion—were paralleled by three proposed classes to discharge the basic social functions of production, reasoning and governing, and imple-menting governance—craftsmen, rulers, and auxiliaries in Cornford's translation. In both the individual and the *polis*, Socrates and his interlocutors agreed, it was best for reason to rule, so that a well-governed person or state could expected to behave rationally rather than responding merely to appetites and passions.

Two millennia later, Allison (1971) pointed out that—unlike Plato, who offered his unified, rational-state conception as an ideal at odds with the actual Athens of his day—observers of organizations fell into a trap of mistakenly assuming that organizations would inevitably act rationally and with unity of direction. Allison concluded from his examination of the Cuban missile crisis that the assumption by foreign-policy officials and analysts that governments could be understood to decide to behave as monolithic, self-interestedly rational actors led them to misinterpret actions and so misunderstand situations and their risks. "The 'maker' of government policy is not one calculating decision maker but is rather a conglomerate of large organizations and political actors" (3). Allison proposed two alternative ways of understanding how organizational decisions were made, each of which, he argued, could better account for actual responses and decisions than the black-box rational-actor presumption.

Essence of Decision (Allison 1971; and see subsequent commentary and updates by Allyn et al. 1989) examined the mechanisms of political-administrative formulation of government policy and responses to events, through an examination of the Cuban Missile Crisis of October 1962. Allison contrasted three alternative models of organizational decision making. Model I, the classical rational-actor model, presumes that governments' and agencies' decisions can be understood as responding rationally to circumstances to maximize some value or set of objectives, just as *homo economicus* is presumed to decide and act. This model takes into account uncertainty as a problem at the organizational level, but not ambiguity, and logics of consequences are presumed to dominate. Model II, the organizational-process model, depicts organizational decision as governed largely by routines and standard operating procedures of the component units that make up a government best depicted as a "conglomerate of semi-feudal loosely allied organizations" (67), such as the Navy, the State Department, and various sub-units within them. Model II is grounded extensively in the work of Chester Barnard (1938) and the Management Science researchers of the so-called Carnegie School (Cyert and March 1963; March and Simon 1958; Simon 1997) and depicts organizational behavior as composed in significant part of the sum of numerous, loosely coordinated incremental decisions by sub-organizations. Here, logics of appropriateness are important determinants of choice, and organizational judgments are subject to considerable ambiguity. Allison's Model III, the governmental politics model, focused on bargaining and power within governments among elected officials, appointees, and administrators, and borrowed some of Lindblom's (1959) argument that agreement on a course of action is a central criterion for assessing the merits of a policy. Model III also relies on Neustadt's (1960) examination of federal executive authority, and Almond's (1950) application of political pluralist analysis to foreign policy with its attention to the interactions and competition among general and attentive publics, policy and opinion elites, and official policy leadership. Here, even if individual members of the organization are invariant in their normative judgments and preferences, ambiguity exists at the organizational level.

Models II and III helped to explain the behavior of both the US and Soviet governments during the crisis in ways that Model I could not. On the other hand, they also required much more information to be collected and analyzed: at the time he wrote his book, Allison was unable to collect enough information about the Soviets to perform an effective analysis of their behavior using Model III. Understanding the practical implications of constrained organizational rationality to predict behavior in actual policy settings ironically requires more extensive rationality and analytic capacity than simply treating organizations as if they were monolithically, strategically rational. Organizational inertia, challenges of communication, parochial interests within organizations, and the use of informal channels and forums for decision making all undermine the rationality of governments as decision making entities. Allison concluded by calling for greater attention in policy analysis to implementation, bureaucratic politics, and administrative feasibility.

Also emphasizing the complexity and non-linearity of decision making processes was the garbage-can model of decision and the theories of agenda-setting and policy formation that descended from it. In its initial formulation, this model took the example of decision processes in universities, an example of *organized anarchies*, "organizations characterized by problematic preferences, unclear technology, and fluid participation," to "suggest that such organizations can be viewed for some purposes as collections of choices looking for problems, issues and feelings looking for decision situations in which they might be aired, solutions looking for issues to which they might be an answer, and decision makers looking for work" (Cohen et al. 1972, 1). As Cohen, March, and Olsen noted, the three properties that characterize organized anarchies are common in public as well as educational organizations. They suggested that in such organizations, traditional theories of management control and coordination were less useful, because they typically assumed firmer knowledge of goals and technologies, and more dependable engagement of organizational members, than exist in organized anarchies. Choice opportunities, the recurrent "occasions when the organization is expected to produce behavior that can be called a decision" (3), can be viewed as garbage cans into which people toss problems and solutions as they arise. Thus the flow volume and timing of the streams of attentive people, problems, and solutions, and the access of particular solutions and problems to choice opportunities, can be expected to influence decisions. Garbage cans are not necessarily a consistently effective means for solving particularly identified problems in a structured, instrumental fashion—in fact they often result in a choice being made before a problem has reached the choice opportunity (by oversight) or after it has left it (by flight)—but they do allow decisions to be made and problems dealt with even when the organization is plagued with goal ambiguity and conflict, with poorly understood problems that wander in and out of the system, with a variable environment, and with decisions makers who may have other things on their minds (16). In short, although Cohen, March, and Olsen did not press normative claims for the superiority of the form of decision making they described and modeled in this work, the garbage can does allow for decisions to be made and problems to be dispensed with in complex environments characterized by pervasive ambiguity and uncertainty that may stymie more structured and strategic models of problem solving and analysis.

2. Multiple Streams in Policy Making

Whereas the initial formulation of the garbage-can model generated a computer model and a series of hypotheses, Kingdon (1984) applied the model to a conceptually elegant and empirically rich descriptive/explanatory analysis of the selection and matching of policy problems and solutions in the US federal government. Kingdon modeled the policy process as broadly divisible into agenda-setting, alternative-specification, policy-choice, and implementation components. His focus was on how the attention of decision makers came to be focused on particular issues, and how issues and solutions did, or did not, move from the "specialized" agendas of particular issue networks and interests, to the "governmental" agendas of recognized public concerns, and finally to the "decision" agendas from which particular policies are adopted, or aborted, by mating issues, solutions, and politics. Kingdon framed his question as "How does an idea's time come?" Incremental models, he argued, were more accurate as descriptions of the federal policy process than models presuming comprehensive rationality and systematic, top-down analysis. Ideas for policies, he observed, can come from a variety of sources, such as interest groups, the media, elected officials, bureaucrats, academics and other professional researchers, and generalized public opinion, with no particular set of participants consistently leading with their ideas. In fact, he argued, the garbage-can model was more apt descriptively for characterizing the diverse origins and development of policies in a fragmented government with its diffuse and complex flows of information.

Kingdon operationalized the issues–solutions–people–garbage cans model by specifying three distinct and partially independent processes, the fortuitous combinations of which into "policy windows" he hypothesized to yield policy change or action: problem recognition, policy formulation, and electoral politics. Problems are constructed by normatively redefining observed conditions, so that a given condition may be viewed as any number of problems or as completely unproblematic for different observers and at different times. Crises and disasters help to focus attention, and the ability to quantify or explicitly model a problem can be a significant factor. In keeping with the original formulation of the garbage-can model, problems can go away even if they are not solved, including through inattention or calculated neglect (if, for instance, the expected costs of solving a defined problem seem unacceptable). Policies emerge from the "primeval soup" of ideas floating around in policy communities of content-area specialists. Among the participants in policy communities are policy entrepreneurs who assume the role of advocates for particular policy solutions and actively seek problems to which those solutions may be attached. Policies are more likely to emerge from the soup and rise to the public decision agenda if they are matched with problems and so "ready to go," and value acceptability within the policy community is among the other criteria for survival. The political stream involves electoral and legislative politics, with competition among jurisdictions and among branches of government, bargaining and logrolling, and the play of perceived public moods and organized lobbying all influencing the setting of the agenda for policy adoption.

Kingdon cited an informant's analogy of surfers gathered waiting for a big wave to ride in describing the policy windows that briefly present policy entrepreneurs and other attentive partici-pants with opportunities to join the three streams to move bundles of problems and solutions onto the decision agenda. Windows are amenable to being opened up when changes occur in the political stream, such as perceptions of urgency or the turnover of political actors, and can occur fortuitously, such as in response to a natural disaster, or predictably as a result of elections or the routine budget cycle. They close when participants feel they have resolved a problem, or that they cannot get action on a policy, or when events or personnel change again before action is taken. Limits of time and of individual and systemic attention are important and not always predictable factors in the outcome of a window's opening. One of the ways in which action can fail to be achieved during a window's opening is if too many solutions get stuffed into the same window, and the "entire complex of issues falls of its own weight" before issues and solutions can be joined together (185).

Returning to his larger model of the overall policy process, Kingdon concluded that the agenda-setting sub-process is driven primarily by (a) the emergence of problems, (b) the course of politics, and (c) the activities of the process's visible participants—elected officials and their key appointees, the media, and the political parties. Alternative specification is more the work of the hidden participants—policy communities of issue-area specialists, such as bureaucrats, analysts, Congres-sional staffers, consultants, and professional researchers—who generate and evaluate the solutions in the evolving primeval soup of the policy stream. Once a window opens, it becomes possible for policy entrepreneurs to promote the joining of problems and politics from the governmental agenda with policies, to move a bundle composed from all three streams onto the decision agenda for action, or rejection. Throughout the process, Kingdon is clear, alternatives precede agendas: the normative model of strategic problem selection and solution is not adhered to in practice. On balance, Kingdon's research indicated that the central active participants in the policy process are members of a variety of elites, political, professional, and to some extent economic. The general public plays a role primarily insofar as elected officials and others are alert to shifts in the public mood or attention, so that matter of deciding what public problems are to be solved and by what means is one that involves only indirect involvement by non-specialists and depends in large measure upon the solutions advanced by specialists. Kingdon's multiple-streams model of agenda setting has been examined and formalized by Zahariadis (1999), who concluded that "ambiguity is a fact of policy making" (89) that presents both costs and benefits for policy design/choice. Ambiguity (Zahariadis cites March 1978) renders the importance, meaning, and value of solutions and problems difficult to ascertain precisely and invariantly. Thus, "Choice becomes less an exercise in solving problems and more an attempt to make sense of a partially comprehensible world" (Weick 1979, 175) (75). Further, Zahariadis suggested, there are very real advantages to policy makers of selecting solutions first, rather than attempting to solve problems directly (83). Zahariadis also provided in this chapter an extensive review of policy literature grounded in Kingdon's model, and proposed a policy-research agenda centered on three questions: (1) how is the attention of policymakers rationed; (2) how are issues framed; and (3) how and where is the search for solutions and problems conducted?

3. Framing

Questions about the dominance of either institutions or individuals in decision making can consider the power of either to limit the other, the impact separation of powers and federalism have on the balance between the two, and the implicit view of each of the other. First, institutions emerge as a result of the careful cultivation of a frame of reference toward society (Schön and Rein 1994). For example, Schön and Rein (1994, 129–161) discuss the problem of homelessness in Massachusetts in the 1980s and contrast the frames brought to the problem—market, social welfare, and social control by different staff members from state departments asked by the governor to pool expertise and help solve the problem. An institution's frame of reference deliberately excludes many other frames, asserting primacy for a frame that accords with the institution's history, member training and socialization, and the expectations of society (White 1951, 1954, 1958, 1978; Krasner 1988; March and Olsen 1984; Kaufman 1969; Scott 2001, 58–61). The frame of reference may have developed as individuals shaped institutions with policy choices, but the continuing influence of those first choices have a large, perhaps decisive impact on future choices (Skocpol 1992; King 1995; Krasner 1988). Future choices include the alternatives considered by individuals. Schattschneider (1960, 66, 102) understood that a person, party, or institution that dominates choice alternatives dominates the entire decision making process. Institutions, it is argued, dominate individual decisions.

4. Public Choice Theory and the Irrationality of Politics

One institution that dominates individual decisions is the requirement of some degree of consensus for collective choice (Miller and Robbins 2004). The degree of consensus and process for obtaining it characterize fundamental rules of US governance and decision making. Consider the theory. Voting analysis demands that individuals' preferences toward a project be known. Obviously, 100% voting participation resulting in a consensus decision on a matter would guide decision makers or provide evidence of a valid decision. The first variable in voting analysis, therefore, is the probability of violating validity as the vote allowed for decisions departs from unanimity. Such a problem occurs in sampling as well as in choosing majority rule over consensus.

Gaining unanimity has drawbacks, not the least of which is the cost entailed in cajoling participation and informing voting. The counterbalance to total participation and consensus is the cost that both would entail. The closer to total participation and consensus in voting, the higher the cost of the voting process. The lower the cost of the voting process, the less likely decision making has any validity. That is, the majority of votes of the number of voters may not be valid expressions of the preferences of the total population even though such an election may cost less than any methods that could be used to secure unanimity.

The appropriate system of voting involves trading off the cost of exclusion against the cost of the election, a calculation easier than it looks. No issues exist in which an individual has choices and perfect information about them all. Rather, a continuous stream of issues appears, and individuals have varying levels of intensity of preferences.

The intensity of preferences among voters tends to form a regular pattern. Very few voters feel intensely either way about an issue. The vast majority, the middle, have no feeling at all about an issue and probably do not find the issue itself salient.

Arrays of preferences yield themselves to vote trading—logrolling—as well as coalition building. In cases of public provision of goods, conditions for bargaining emerge: costly participation, isolated issue salience, and unclear estimates of who benefits or pays for policies and by how much. These conditions can create inefficient government action or waste and overspending (Buchanan and Tullock 1962) or just as much inefficiency in solving public problems and achieving the common good through underspending (Downs 1960).

Consider an example Buchanan and Tullock (1962) offer as support for the idea that logrolling tends to create more expenditure than would ordinarily be the case if economic efficiency controlled. Consider the case of 100 farmers in a locality, each of whom is served by a separate access road requiring maintenance. Maintenance of a specific road must have the consent of a majority of voters and, if so, is financed out of general tax revenues levied on all 100 farmers equally. If each road's maintenance is voted on separately and no logrolling takes place, no road improvements would pass under general tax financing. Each road improvement benefits only one person but the cost is borne by several.

Suppose vote-trading agreements can take place. To have his or her road repaired, each farmer must agree to support the road repairs of fifty other farmers to get the fifty-one votes required for his/her own road repairs. The benefit to one farmer is having his own road repaired. The cost to the farmer willing to trade votes is his/her share of the repairs to be done on the other fifty roads he/she agrees to support. In the general case, each of the farmers will attempt to secure an agreement with fifty other farmers and the agreements will probably be overlapping, because all 100 farmers want to get their own roads repaired. In the end each farmer will have secured agreement to have his/her road repaired. In determining the level of road repairs on each road, the benefit to the farmer whose road is being repaired is weighted against the costs of fifty farmers of repairing it. The costs incurred by the other forty-nine farmers not included in that particular agreement are neglected. Overall, the cost to all farmers will exceed the benefits from the chosen level of repairs in each road. The logrolling process results in over-expenditure.

Anthony Downs (1960) demonstrates the opposite case, the case for spending less than would be necessary. Considering the same example above but substitute higher education for road repair, it might be found that the calculation of benefits each farmer made would result in undervaluing the public expenditure. Arguments, except for the agricultural experiment station, the cooperative extension service, and the college of agriculture at the state land grant university, would probably tend toward belittling most benefits and stressing higher education's costs because the farmers believe the funding should support farming activities. In the end, higher education might be under-funded, given some notion of adequate or efficient funding, and the entire government budget made smaller than economic efficiency might otherwise dictate.

Decision making may be approached through legislative-style logrolling or through executive-centered, means-ends analysis. Logrolling—using the political process to allocate—examines a project in the context of all projects on the agenda for study at one time. The supporters of a project ultimately get their way only because they trade favors with supporters of other projects. The result is a sharing of benefits, costs, knowledge and preference for technique, and collaboration or compromise on goals so that all sets of supporters, as a whole, are better off. Analysis is that allocation principle in which decision makers select a program or project when the benefits and costs are weighted and the result makes society better off. Analysis may take the form of cost-effective-ness analysis or risk-benefit analysis. Cost-effectiveness analysis collects and arranges data to facilitate a comparison of the costs of achieving a desired public program objective required by various alternative treatments, interventions, programs, or policy designs. The criterion for judging the best alternative is either least cost for a given level of effectiveness or greatest effectiveness for a given level of spending. In risk analysis or risk-benefit analysis, risk—the probability of an event multiplied by the event's severity—takes the place cost holds in other forms of analysis. The benefit calculation rests on an estimate of society's willingness to pay to reduce a risk or to forego a benefit.

The problems with logrolling tend to be those related to overspending, a condition supporters of logrolling think is a function of viewing of the needs of the individual as greater than the needs of society. That is, those who favor analysis, and who believe logrolling results in overspending, tend to be those who favor the right of individuals to reach their goals in competition with others without help from government. Those who favor logrolling rather than benefit-cost analysis see the needs of society as paramount, at least those needs that, in the end, are believed to make social benefits greater than the costs to society. The problem with analysis lies in implementing shared benefits in such a way that those who bear most of the costs get enough of the benefits to offset their losses.

5. Individual Irrationality

Public choice theories, like economics-based approaches to policy analysis, depend in both their positive analyses and normative prescriptions on a presumption that individuals behave in largely rational, *homo-economicus*, fashion, at least on average: narrowly self-interested and instrumen-tally employing logics of consequences in making choices, with the ability to form good factual judgments including accurate estimates of probabilities, and possessed of stable preferences not overly burdened by ambiguity. Even conceptions of bounded rationality, although implicitly allowing for some ambiguity in the form of Simon's (1947, 1997) zone of acceptance, take limits on attentiveness and ability to calculate, rather than instability or ignorance of preferences and self-interest, to be the fundamental weakness of individual decision rationality. These assumptions, while leading ineluctably to the conclusion that individual rationality tends to produce collective irrationality if left unchecked by coercive institutions (Elster 1989) as well as to the public choice theorists' pessimism about democracy, does at least provide a stable base for analyzing decision problems and prescribing more efficient models of collective decision. Researchers examining individual judgment and choice, however, have identified a number of ways in which the mutability of preferences and tendencies toward biased or otherwise erroneous judgments create significant challenges of ambiguity and uncertainty for individual decisions. Perhaps most widely cited is the work done during the 1970s and early 1980s by Daniel Kahneman and Amos Tversky, for which Kahneman won a Nobel Prize in 2002 (Tversky died in 1996, and Nobels are awarded only to living recipients). In a series of empirical studies and literature reviews, Tversky and Kahneman demonstrated that very small risks are given disproportionate weight, that prospective losses and gains are not treated symmetrically, that the presence or absence of non-selected alternatives can reverse preference orderings, and that the manner in which options are semantically or mathematically framed can exert undue influence on decision makers. These violations of normative standards, in turn, are apt to distort private decisions and public policy alike (Arrow et al. 1998).

An early collaborative article by Kahneman and Tversky reviewing their own and others' empirical work (Tversky and Kahneman 1974) identified three common heuristics that facilitate decision by conserving individuals' attention, but also act as sources of systematically erroneous biased judgments in the face of uncertainty. Many of the observations in this article turn on the reality that probability theory and its implications for statistical analysis are not highly intuitive, but some also identify pervasive challenges to the assumptions that underlie both descriptive and normative theories based on rational-actor models. *Representativeness* heuristics lead decision makers to focus on the degree to which one thing resembles another, and in so doing to neglect more useful information about actual probabilities of occurrence. Thus, in an example offered elsewhere, intuitive thinking leads people to presume that Linda, an intelligent woman concerned with issues of social justice, is more likely to be a bank teller and active feminist than simply to be a bank teller. *Availability* heuristics lead to biases favoring reliance on more readily recalled or located information or more readily imagined possible states of the of the world, or illusory correlations, rather than correct probabilities. *Anchoring* and *adjustment* produce bias when subjective assessments of probability distributions or of the likelihood of sequential events are based on adjustments to an initial point estimate or other starting point. Although Tversky and Kahneman do not say so in so many words, their findings here are consistent with bounded rationality and the conservation of attention: intuitive heuristics "are highly economical and usually effective" (1974, 1131) but they produce errors in individual judgments that in turn threaten the usefulness of analytic models that presume unbiased rationality of individual judgments in calculating the likelihood or usefulness of particular collective decisions or institutional arrangements. To the extent such biases are in fact systematic rather than random errors and so can be estimated and factored into calculations, of course, it may be possible to account for them in modeling (or manipulating) collective behaviors. In subsequent collaborations, Kahneman and Tversky identified further biases in individual judgment as well as—somewhat more problematically for modeling—ways in which not only positive judgments about objective states of the world but individuals' normative judgments about their own preferences, and hence their choices, could vary according to context.

Still in the category of systematic bias, or at least of errors that are relatively predictable and therefore could potentially be accounted for in economics-based policy analysis or other efforts to structure collective decisions by employing instrumental logics, were the formulations of *prospect theory* (Kahneman and Tversky 1979) and *loss aversion* (Tversky and Kahneman 1991). The 1979 article extended and refined the formulations from the authors' 1974 work, identifying ways in which individuals' choices between alternatives tended to violate the model of decision implied by expected utility theory. First, they found that evaluative judgments of alternative financial gambles tend systematically to underweight outcomes that have probabilities of less than 1 compared to events believed to be certain. This *certainty effect*, together with a *reflection effect*, causes individuals to tend to be risk-averse facing gains—settling for a smaller but perfectly certain gain over a risky gain with a higher expected value—but risk-preferring when facing losses—choosing a probabilistic outcome with a greater loss over a smaller but certain loss. The *isolation effect* describes the way judgments of value tend to use a simplifying strategy of eliminating from consideration the common features of alternatives to concentrate on the differences. This can result in different choices between alternatives, depending on how they are decomposed into common and different elements. This treatment was extended by their analysis of loss aversion (Tversky and Kahneman 1991) that describes the phenomenon that individuals tend consistently to weight losses more heavily than equal-sized gains. This helps to explain other researchers' findings that individuals often are willing to pay less for a good than they would be willing to accept to surrender it. For an application of prospect theory to the analysis of voting, see Quattrone and Tversky (1988). Somewhat more troublesome for the normative decision theory supporting conventional economic policy and organizational analyses are some of the implications of the ambiguity associated with framing effects (Tversky and Kahneman 1981, 1986) related to heuristic decision processes that rely on the simplifying editing and decision-weighting intuitions identified in prospect theory, and the potential for preference reversal or other effects of context on individual preferences (Tversky and Simonson 1993; Tversky et al. 1990). Different descriptions of decision problems, the use of different procedures for making decisions, and different orders of presentation of alternatives all can alter the choices made independently of the values of the options from which the choice is made. This presents complications for efforts to perform value-neutral policy analysis and even for efforts to direct individual decisions toward organizational purposes. At least as troublesome are the implications that both predictable decision biases and the susceptibility of preferential choices to manipulation by framing. For example, if the public choice theorists' presumptions about the motivations of bureaucrats are correct, this susceptibility of decision to manipulation by framing presents abundant opportunity for manipulations by self-interested administrators. On the other hand, consciousness of the central role of framing effects in the construction of individual and collective judgments can also be seen as offering a way to begin resolving differences toward the adoption of more satisfying collective decisions (Schön and Rein 1994). Additionally, there is at least some evidence that public administrators are on average more motivated to service than exploitation of the public (Heclo 2002). Responding in part to the findings of cognitive psychologists as well as to Simon's insights about the boundedness of irrationality, contemporary work in the field of behavioral economics has begun extending formal neoclassical models for economic analysis by explicitly incorporating various forms of individual irrationality and biases in judgment. Prominent scholars in this area include Thaler (1991) and Matthew Rabin (see Camerer et al. 2004, as well as his prolific output of working papers and journal articles) among others. Colin Camerer (1999) offers a convenient article review of the nascent sub-discipline, and recent articles by Kahneman (2003a, 2003b) explicitly draw together his work with Tversky and other descriptive analyses of decision making psychology, behavioral economics, and bounded rationality. Empirical work by Elinor Ostrom and others has demonstrated, too, that appropriate institutional designs can structure individual judgments and choices, or at least the premises underlying them, in such a way as to suggest that the constructability and manageability of preferences (Slovic 1995) may in fact provide opportunities to enhance collective rationality rather than necessarily diminishing it (Justice 2003).

E. THE NEW INSTITUTIONALISMS

The 1970s also brought renewed interest in the explicit examination of the implications of social institutions for individual judgment and choice and for the aggregation and interaction of individual decisions into collective action and outcomes. Following Scott (1995) these new-institutionalist frameworks may be grouped broadly into those that emphasize the importance of social institutions as constraints on the decisions and actions of rationally self-interested individuals (the social-realist approach), and those that emphasize the role of institutions in shaping the knowledge, values, and interests—and so the decisions and actions—of individuals and groups (the social-constructionist approach). While the wellsprings of the various new-institutionalist approaches are numerous, the analyses of the Public Choice theorists, agency theory, Mancur Olson's *Logic of Collective Action* (1971), the cognitive revolution in psychology, and the attention of Berger and Luckman (1967) to the social construction and institutionalization of knowledge may be seen as antecedents.

1. Institutional Rational-Choice Frameworks

Rational-actor frameworks build on economic models of human motivation and methodological individualism to analyze descriptively the structures of choice-directing incentives and constraints embodied in particular institutional design features. This analysis in turn leads to prescriptions for the design of institutions meant to improve the likelihood of efficiently and reliably achieving collective rationality in spite of individual rationality. Transaction-costs analysis and agency theory direct the analyst's attention to the roles of costly information and bounded rationality in structuring judgment. The meta-theoretical institutional analysis and development framework (IADF) extends those insights and attempts to identify a comprehensive set of institutional design characteristics and extra-institutional variables that structure individuals' judgments and decision rules in collective action settings. The IADF is grounded in part in a critique of the tendency of some rational-choice frameworks to emphasize hierarchy as the primary means to collective rationality (see, for example, Ostrom 1990).

a. Transaction Costs and Agency Theory

Moe (1984) recognized the emergence over the 1970s of a "new economics of organization." He suggested the "new" would be the primary alternative to "the behavioral tradition," that tradition he associated with Simon (1997), March and Simon (1958), Cyert and March (1963), and Cohen, March, and Olsen (1972) for the examination of organizational decisions and behavior relevant to the formation and operation of public bureaucracies (1984, 740; 1995). Moe noted that the development in the 1970s and 1980s of transaction-costs and principal-agent theory approaches to understanding organizational formation and decision could be traced to Coase (1937) but were rooted more immediately in the work of Alchian and Demsetz (1972). Both approaches apply fundamentally neoclassical assumptions about individual self-interest-maximizing motivations and the centrality of incentives to direct individual choice in ways that promote optimal collective efficiency, or inefficiency, but with somewhat more realistic assumptions about information availability, human rationality, and judgment, and the complexity of social interactions. Each has generated an abundant literature of prescription and description, with an emphasis on the analysis and design of organizational incentive structures meant to solve problems of cooperation and hierarchical control.

Like Olson's (1971) analysis, the seminal formulations of transaction-costs approaches emphasized the need for centralized, hierarchical solutions to the coordination of cooperation in the face of presumed tendencies to shirk. Because individual contributions to joint production can be difficult and costly to assess, information and monitoring deficiencies are likely to facilitate shirking, as members of a collective realize that their individual shares of collective surplus may not be closely correlated with their individual contributions. The problem is compounded by the fact that the monitoring of contributions is effectively a collective good, costly to produce but with diffuse and non-appropriable benefits in a hypothetical state of nature, so that there is little incentive for individuals to perform it. Alchian and Demsetz (1972) developed an argument that business firms arise to facilitate the efficient elicitation of individual contributions towards "team" production. By mutual consent or contract, cooperators select an entrepreneur to specialize in monitoring individual contributions and distributing rewards accordingly, thus maintaining a balance of contributions from, and inducements to, contingently attached cooperators reminiscent of Barnard's (1968) formulation. Being granted a transferable property right in the net earnings of collective output (the residual) motivate the entrepreneur. This effectively internalizes the externality associated with costly performance monitoring. Williamson's (1975, 1981) formulations of the transaction costs approach developed more extensively the implications of bounded rationality, environmental complexity, and the costliness of information for buyers' (we might say principals') judgments and of human opportunism ("self-interest with guile"), repeated tasks' "information impactedness," and small-numbers bargaining for sellers' (or agents') choices within transactional relations. Williamson argued that hierarchies are often a more efficient solution than markets in cases of information-related market failures, or "organizational failures." Bounded rationality and environmental complexity and uncertainty render the formulation and enforcement of "complete" contracts stipulating responses to every conceivable contingency very costly, if not impossible. Opportunistic agents can further take advantage of the "information impactedness" created when repeated contracting for a specialized service enables them to gain unique knowledge of the tasks involved. This reduces the number of competitors at the same time as it makes possible the concealment of true costs and contingencies from buyers, thus facilitating shirking and "perfunctory" rather than "consummate" cooperation by sellers. At the same time, however, the specific expertise acquired in repeat performance of similar transactions, like site- and physical capital-related forms of asset specificity, can create reciprocal dependencies or long-term bilateral relations between buyers and seller (Williamson 1981). An extensive and growing literature in public administration examines the implications of the transactional dimensions of information asymmetry, uncertainty, frequency, and asset specificity, together with the human characteristics of bounded rationality and opportunism for judgments and choices by political principals and agents about operational rules, collective choices, and constitutional arrangements in such areas as legislature–bureau relations (Horn 1995), budgeting (Bartle and Jun 2001; Patashnik 1996), local economic development (Clarke 1998; Feiock 2002), policy implementation (Calista 1994), and the analysis of policy and administrative networks and partnerships (Hindmoor 1998; Jessop 1998; Milward and Provan 1998).

Principal–agent frameworks, or agency theory, also emerged during the 1970s, and have served as vehicles for examining conflict-of-interest-generated problems in aligning the choices of principals (buyers of services) and agents (sellers of services) in the face of information asymmetries that tend to impair principals' abilities to form accurate judgments about the knowledge, motivations, traits, and performance of agents. These information problems give agents whose interests conflict with those of their principals incentives to shirk (moral hazard), and may even lead to the selection of precisely those agents least suited to a principal's needs (adverse selection). Halachmi (2003) offers a good summary of the content of agency theory, some issues in the application of agency-theoretic frameworks, and a useful list of references for further reading.

As Moe (1984) noted, there are significant difficulties in translating economic approaches to organizational analysis to the distinctive operating and task environment of the public sector, however. What Moe describes as a central strength of economic approaches—their use of the optimizing logic and many of the parsimony-promoting assumptions of neoclassical economics—can also be seen as making them less realistic descriptively and so somewhat less useful prescriptively in a world of multiple principals, ambiguous goals, and labile preferences. Although attentive to nuances in questions of incentive- and constraint-responsive choice on the part of agents and factor owners seeking to advance their own interests in maximizing personal utility, these frameworks treat principals' or employers' choices of goals largely as unitary and unproblematic. They do, however, offer a powerful complement to the behavioral approach for those seeking to understand how the interaction of organizational designs and task structures can influence individual decisions, and how those individual decisions in turn influence organization-level processes and outcomes.

b. The Institutional Analysis and Design Framework

The IADF (Kiser and Ostrom 1982; Ostrom 1986, 1990, 1999b; Ostrom and Walker 1997) retains the core premises of methodological individualism and rational choice in understanding people's responses to collective action dilemmas while expanding the scope of analysis to understand better how the interactions of multiple rules and multiple levels of rules work in specific social and physical contexts to shape individual judgment and choice and thereby influence collective decisions and outcomes. The IADF also differs from other rational-choice frameworks in avoiding the implicit or explicit presumption that hierarchy is necessarily the most efficient design for reducing uncertainty, opportunism, and the resulting collective irrationality in the face of joint production or consumption. Among the innovations of the IADF is its explicit attention to the interdependence, or configurational nature, of rules governing decisions and actions. Like those considered above, this framework attends closely to the effects of operational rules governing monitoring and enforcement, but it also takes account of the ways in which their effects are mediated by the nature of rules governing policy making and management in a variety of formal (such as courts and legislatures) and informal (such as teams and committees) arenas at the collective choice level of analysis, and by the rules determining how collective choices will be made at the constitutional level of analysis. The configuration of rules at all three levels is understood to structure the decision situation faced by an individual and thereby to influence his/her judgment about the consequences of alternative choices, and thereby his/her choices among alternative courses of action.

Empirical applications of the IADF have led to a number of insights into the contextual factors that increase the likelihood of successful self-governance and self-organization, and to a range of institutional-design prescriptions for effective and sustainable collective action. Paralleling some of the extensions of transaction-costs analysis that suggest hierarchies need not be the most effective devices of social coordination (Calista 1994; Frances et al. 1991; Hindmoor 1998), research using the IADF to analyze common resource-management regimes has demonstrated that in fact self-governance is often more effective than hierarchical control for securing collective action and collective rationality (Ostrom 1990; Ostrom and Walker 1997; Tang 1992). These findings prove challenging to reconcile with traditional rational-choice assumptions about self-interested preferential choice, however. Potential explanatory mechanisms, such as social capital (Ostrom 1995), the centrality of trust and reciprocity as well as mutual expectations (Ostrom 1998), the evolution and individual adoption of norms and beliefs (Ostrom 2000), and the possibility that self-governing institutions function as complex adaptive systems (Ostrom 1999a), suggest even to committed rational-choice scholars the need for "second-generation models of empirically grounded, boundedly rational, and moral decision making" (Ostrom 1998, 15).

2. Social-Constructionist Approaches to Institutional Analysis

An alternative group of institutional analysts focus more on the cognitive and normative consequences of institutions than on their rational-individual-constraining designs and incentive structures. "Social constructionists embrace the most far-reaching and all-encompassing version of institutions: institutions are seen as constituting the rules, defining the players, and framing the situations. The interests and identities of the principal actors are socially defined and expected to vary across place and time" (Scott 1995, 137). Preferences and meanings, rather than being stable and exogenous are in fact institutionally contingent and endogenous (March and Olsen 1984, 1989), decisions and policies can aim at symbolic as well as instrumental ends (Yanow 2000), choices can reflect practical logics of appropriateness as well as instrumental logics of consequences, and "decision structures themselves create the premises of decision" (March 1994). From this perspective, the task of institutional analysis is to understand how social institutions constitute individual and collective rationality, judgment, and choice. Although there are examples of constructionist analyses of instrumentally constructed institutions (DiMaggio 1991; Galaskiewicz 1991), the constructionist perspective has not to date generated as large a body of prescriptively oriented institutional-design studies as has the realist perspective.

An example of a mixed realist–constructionist descriptive analysis is Searing's (1991) examination of the decisions and behavior of British members of Parliament (MPs) extended a rational-actor framework that assumed self-interested individuals pursued instrumental maximizing strategies by also taking into account the mediating effects of coercive institutional-role-specific rules and sanctions (such as those governing ministerial assignments) as well as "informal" institutional rules that established norms of appropriateness for MPs who accepted roles such as "constituency member" or ministerial aspirant." In another example, Miller found that the judgments informing capital financing decisions by public financial managers were structured by their ongoing relationships within debt management networks (Miller 1993).

Recent work by Klijn (2001) also indicates some of the potential for synthesizing social-realist and social-constructionist approaches to understanding the implications of institutional characteristics for decisions and formulating second-generation models of decision making. Klijn's research examined both the behavior-regulating rules (governing such actions as policy setting entry/exit, positions, interactions, distribution of rewards, and so forth) and the reality-constituting rules (such as actor identities and professional standards) at work within a policy network. Although this research was not prescriptively design-oriented, it demonstrated the configurational effects of rules governing cognitive and normative premises as well as those regulating behavior. Cognitive, normative, and regulative rules proved interdependent and to some degree mutually constitutive, and differences in the configurations of rules accounted for differences in the decision processes and outcomes associated with different policy networks. Another synthesis of realist and constructionist perspectives, in an institutional analysis of business improvement district governing bodies, found that greater levels of cooperation resulted from the cognitive and normative effects of behavioral constraints stipulating both compulsory finance and self-governance (Justice 2003). At the same time, the design of the behaviorally coercive elements of institutional rule configurations reflected normative and cognitive bases for judgment and choice as well as rational calculations of efficacy. Individual judgments and choices at the operational and collective choice levels were observed to mix rational and practical bases inseparably.

3. Summary

A number of frameworks for institutional analysis have been developed, elaborated, and tested from the 1970s to the present. The rational-choice frameworks complement the insights of the behavioral and psychological understandings of judgment and choice by offering a guide to the analysis and design of structures to constrain the choices of self-interestedly rational individuals and thereby to simplify judgment by reducing uncertainty. The social constructionist perspective helps to elucidate the ways in which institutional structures shape the cognitive and normative premises of decisions.

Synthesis of the two thus holds the potential to facilitate the effective integration of insights into individual decision and choice derived from psychological decision research as well as insights into the collective consequences of individual decisions drawn from the behavioral approach and economic analyses of collective action problems. Systematic attention to the decisional contexts created by configurations of cognitive, normative, and regulative institutional rules can elucidate their implications for individual decision premises and choices as well as for the ways in which deliberation and other forms of collective choice interaction alter individual and collective decision premises and preferences.

Institutional arrangements are important determinants of the bases for individual judgment and choice and can increase or decrease uncertainty and ambiguity as well as conflicts of interest, with consequences for collective decisions. Intended rationality in decision employs preferential and judgmental elements that are in significant part institutionally created, and practical logics can supplement or supplant intended rationality as the basis of choice. Systematic analysis of institutional design properties and their effects thus can advance the larger project of using social structures to enhance collective rationality in decision making by both constraining and constituting individual rationality.

VII. CONTEMPORARY DEVELOPMENTS AND TRENDS OF THE EARLY TWENTY-FIRST CENTURY

Over the past two decades or so, decision makers and decision researchers have integrated previous experience with, and study of, decision making in a variety of ways. A number of techniques have been developed that integrate normative and intuitive judgments with more systematic and technical approaches to rational decision making. At the same time, dramatic developments in digital computer and telecommunications technology have facilitated the storage, transmission, and use of vast quantities of data and transactional records for inductive analysis to support decisions and enhance their rationality. Contemporary instruments have also made possible the study of human physiological processes of decision making in a variety of laboratory settings. The resulting explosion of new techniques for making and understanding decisions is too vast to be addressed comprehensively here, but the following section attempts to identify very briefly some recent developments of interest for public administration and sources for further reading.

A. INTEGRATIVE MODELS OF DECISION

A number of recent developments involve proposals or practical attempts to transform the making of policy-related decisions by better or more explicitly integrating aspects of public policy and administrative decision, as advocated 80 years ago by Mary Parker Follett (1924, 1940). Some efforts to promote the integration of practical knowledge within organizations, negotiation and conflict resolution, the integration of normative and instrumentally rational logics of policy analysis, and the integration of expert and lay preferences and knowledge through models of collective decision making that employ technology to mitigate traditional obstacles to direct participatory democracy are noted here. Within organizations, efforts to enhance decisions over the past half-century or so have included attempts to integrate the knowledge of multiple members of organizational elites, such as the Delphi techniques, and efforts to bring the knowledge of rank-and-file members of organizations to bear in the analysis and improvement of production processes, such as Edward Deming's total quality management (TQM; White and Wolf 1995a, 1995b). As with management by objectives (MBO; Drucker 1976)—an approach to eliciting organizational members' knowledge of both production processes and their own capabilities—TQM was understood and implemented in a vast range of ways over the second half of the twentieth century, including many that proved to work in ways that countered their inventor's intentions to foster relatively more egalitarian and empowering modes of decision, and often with results considerably different from expectations. More recently, researchers and practitioners have been explicitly attentive to the problem of knowledge management, often advocating the nurturing of communities of practice as ways to ensure that individuals' knowledge of organizational processes and environments is systematically available to other members whose judgments and choices can thereby be enhanced (Newcombe 2002; Wenger et al. 2002).

The last quarter of the twentieth century also saw the burgeoning of a literature concerned with integrative approaches to resolving disputes; reaching mutually agreeable negotiated choices, and collaborative decision making. Like McGregor's Theory Y, the method of integrative, interested-based, "principled" negotiation articulated by Fisher and Ury (1983) is nearly ubiquitous by now as an espoused norm, although perhaps less frequently observed in practice. In a related vein, a substantial literature has developed that offers favorable assessments of the value of, and suggestions for, the implementation of collaborative forms of decision making.

Collaborative models seek to promote multi-party models of integration and interest-based efforts to identify and realize common goals among multiple sectors, organizations, and individuals (Chrislip and Larson 1994; Gray 1989, 1996; Gregory et al. 2001; Huxham 1996). Chrislip and Larson in particular set out to answer the question, "Can civic community be created?" beginning with the premise that "if you bring together the appropriate people in constructive ways with good information, they will create authentic visions and strategies for addressing the shared concerns of the organization or community." Stakeholder participation of the type advocated by Chrislip and Larson has been found empirically to foster better quality decisions in the area of environmental policy by at least one researcher (Beierle 2002).

In the realm of policy analysis, integrative models seek, if not necessarily to transcend, at least to take explicitly into account the critiques of purposely value-neutral and self-consciously scientific policy analysis by allowing for the consideration of biases introduced by economic techniques of analysis (Tribe 1972) or other forms of institutionalized knowledge that structure judgment and choice by narrowing the range of perspectives and evidence employed by analysts and other decision makers (Forester 1999; Schön and Rein 1994). One elaborately worked out framework for policy decisions is Fischer's (1995) model for explicitly integrating "politics and science," or values and facts, across multiple levels of technical analysis and normative judgment and choice. Fischer identifies four discourses within two levels of social decision making. At the more specific level, a normative discourse concerns the desirability and relevance to particular problems of the programmatic outcomes identified through "technical-analytic" methods such as evaluation research and cost-benefit analysis. At the level of social choice, a "systems discourse" involves empirical consideration of the broad societal consequences of policies, while an "ideological" discourse concerns the appropriateness of the broad social values embodied in the social outcomes. Bogason's (2000) institutional model of "collective public action" seeks to reconcile post-modern fragmentation with the need for cooperation. To make sense of the complex, "post-modern" mix of interacting public and private decisions in local governance, Bogason urges analysts to use both top-down and bottom-up understandings of how individuals use "public means to pursue their own course of action" (173). Interpretive models of analysis are needed for this because policy actors make instrumentally rational decisions, but also tend to reformulate their goals and preferences in response to their judgments of what is attainable (175). A complementary argument, from an avowedly rational-choice perspective is offered by Elinor Ostrom (1999), who echoes Lindblom's incrementalist claims in arguing that the three core assumptions of conventional policy analysis—short-term economic rationality, susceptibility of systems to comprehensive analysis, and equation of organization with central direction—are empirically unsupported. Instead, policy should be understood as an experiment, and the broadly polycentric complex-adaptive-systems concept should be considered a desirable approach to the organization of decision making for responding to policy problems and conceivably achieving "better than rational" decisions.

B. Technology-Facilitated Decision Making

It is easy for those born in the last quarter-century to take for granted the extent to which contemporary computer and telecommunications technology facilitates the management, exchange, and utilization of information in many forms. While digital computers have been available since the 1940s and electronic communications media since the nineteenth century (if one includes basic telegraph and telephone service), in the last part of the twentieth century the development of powerful desktop computers and the Internet transformed the technology of computing and communications yet again.

In the early years of the twenty-first century, e-government—the use of computing and tele-communications technology to transform the relationship between government administrators and citizens—has been the topic of considerable attention by academics (e.g., Justice et al. forthcoming; Melitski et al. 2005; West 2004). While e-government appears in its successful implementations to have made information more readily available to citizens and specialist decision makers and to have made many routine transactions vastly more convenient by making it possible, for instance, to purchase a dog license at 3 a.m. without leaving your apartment, there is little evidence as yet that the more dramatic claims about e-government's potential qualitatively to transform the citizen–government relationship have been borne out. Within administrative organizations, contemporary computing, and communications technology unquestionably increases the speed and quantity of communication and data gathering, although those gains may be balanced by reductions in quality and by strains on the allocation of human attention, the scarcest of all resources (Simon 1978). Even before the ubiquity of personal computers and their interconnection through the World Wide Web, however, researchers in public administration and other fields concerned with decision worked to exploit the potential of digital computing within administrative organizations. Computers have been routinely used by public and private organizations alike for several decades now to process basic transactions, to maintain records of those transactions and the entities involved in those transactions, and to analyze and reduce the resulting vast collections of data by means of management information systems (MIS) and decision support systems (DSS) that seek to digest large quantities of data into concise, structured, decision-relevant information for use by organizational decision makers. Recent developments in this area include the development of software and techniques to facilitate data mining, the identification of relevant patterns or exceptions among large quantities of data.

Other uses of computers seek to transform the study of decisions and intelligence and the making of decisions in and by organizations altogether. In keeping with his concern for systematically working to expand the boundaries of individual rationality, Herbert Simon was among the pioneers in researching the application of computing technology to expert systems and other forms of artificial intelligence (AI), that involve "the phenomena that appear when computers perform tasks that, if performed by people, would be regarded as requiring intelligence—thinking" (Simon 1995, 95).

Finally, the emergence of efforts to use information technology to realize new forms of participatory democracy are noted. At the turn of the century, a number of attempts have been undertaken to integrate directly the judgments of multiple lay and specialist actors by using contemporary information technology to overcome the scale-based obstacles to mass participation that have traditionally made republican or elite-governed forms of collective decision seem necessary (see Madison, *Federalist* No. 10) or inevitable (Nie et al. 1996; Michels [1911] 1999) in collectivities of more than minimal size, even when democratic norms are espoused. The use of large numbers of trained facilitators and computer technology has been employed to structure a form of mass deliberation. An early demonstration of the technique by one firm, AmericaSpeaks, took place in 2002, when several thousand people in New York City participated in discussions about how to redevelop the site of the destroyed World Trade Center (Harmon 2002; Lowe 2004). The format involved 4000 citizens grouped around hundreds of round tables in the Javits Convention Center, with technology used to facilitate brainstorming and display participants' responses to several proposed development plans on screens visible to all participants. Several hundred others participated online. Although the arrangements for collecting and filtering individual tables' ideas before displaying them for general consideration mediated the directness of the mass discourse (see Civic Alliance to Rebuild Downtown New York 2002), and the role of the participants was advisory and based on proposals already formulated, the method still provided what one participant described as a rude awakening for the public officials who had overseen the development of the plans proposed up to that time. By the end of the long day, there were signs that the 'decision makers,' as the men in charge of rebuilding were called, realized that the original program needed some reassessment (Szenazy 2002, A19). Other projects seeking to take advantage of contemporary information technology in promoting various forms of deliberation and collaborative decision making include the Deliberative Democracy Consortium (Lukensmeyer 2006) and the Institute for Contemporary Agoras (Christakis 2006).

VIII. CONCLUSION

We now return to the original questions about elites and their responsiveness to the public interest through governance institutions. What is known about decision making when framed through the question: who should respond to whom? Our three sections deliver some answers. From the Federalist Party domination of government to the Lincoln administration, few can doubt the three trends—expanding presidential power, a growing system of spoils in determining who might be a good administrative decision maker, and an increasing need for administrative capacity in national, state, and local governments. The trends in this initial period led to the dominance of administrative reform in the second era. Administrative institutions—a civil service system and an executive budget system—heralded the beginning of the administrative state. The second period matured with a strong sense of need for government institutions to manage while many who belonged to elites that conformed to religions based on efficiency, progressive government, or market primacy coalesced to engineer the institutions of government to produce good administrative decisions. The third period after World War II has a strong scent of managerialism. Decision making gained a primary role in what became management, a social science with the emphasis on science. To many, the victory of technique over purpose enslaved both the administrative decision maker and the citizen, taxpayer, and client to administrative institutions and their logic of appropriateness, if not the logic of consequence. At the end, it is still asked: who should respond to whom? What does the future hold? And who—which elite or subgroup of citizens—rules? As for what the future holds, we see better description of the decision making process surely, enhanced decision support systems for uncontested decisions probably, but easier or more efficient ways to accomplish contested collective decisions maybe or maybe not. Researchers have not thoroughly evaluated facilitated group decision making, experimentally or otherwise, and fundamental problems of incommensurability of competing values and pervasiveness of ambiguity will always remain.

As for who decides, both Kaufman (1969) and Rourke (1992) argue there is a succession of values that provide a reason to wrest power to decide from one decision making institution and give that power to another. They document periods in US history when events and dominant, popular views of how government should perform have led the people to place one of the three values ahead of the others: representativeness, strong executive leadership, or neutral, competent, expertise. Rourke (1992) points to a recent trend toward executive leadership and away from neutral competence, especially in the new importance of political responsiveness and the availability of expertise outside the public service. He asks (539–546) whether a neutrally competent bureaucracy has lost its relevance and provides the answer: "In ... American politics, bureaucrats are ... suspected of being biased rather than neutral in their policy perspectives or even of trying to sabotage policy proposals that political leaders want to put into effect." Rourke sees bias as a poison that "threatens to undermine the legitimacy of bureaucratic participation in national policy making [especially as] courts have always regarded the professional expertise of bureaucrats as the chief justification ... in a democracy for allowing... unelected officials to ... [help shape] the country's policy decisions." The bias may lie in parochial views, ideology, professionalism or, most importantly, institutional values. Bias is no more or less than an instance where institutions constrain individual views, decisions, and actions.

To bias, Rourke adds dispensability instead of indispensability and ordinariness instead of uniqueness. Rourke (540) argues that policy makers turn more and more frequently to private organizations for help in designing organizations and policies. These leaders have privatized bureaucratic expertise by using "former government officials [and those] working in universities, think tanks, or private consulting firms" as well as better equipped and staffed in-house expertise.

This wariness or irrelevance of neutral competents and their expertise in administrative agencies may be good and bad for decision making. Rourke remembers the legitimacy issue in arguing (540) that administrators in government never had any constitutional role. Administrators relied on the willingness of leaders to consult them. Yet, leader willingness comes with a price in political responsiveness, Rourke points out.

What has decision making in institutions lost? Rourke notes (545) that neutral and expert public administration has become a form of professionalism, especially in giving first loyalty to one's knowledge base and code of proper practice. The professional administrator practiced the belief that analysis could not be shaped by political pressure. Rourke illustrates (545) the professional–political tension as "an endemic problem for scientists working for the federal government, but it is a difficulty that [lawyers] in the Justice Department, for example, have sometimes had to [face in choosing] between their responsibility to serve the president and their professional obligation to abide by the laws they have sworn to uphold, not least of all the Constitution of the United States."

Professionalism, neutrality, and expertise compete with political responsiveness, nevertheless. From Rourke's stand point, the competition puts the non-partisan professional at risk. The American public wants expertise held responsible by political controllers that voters can reward and punish. He also believes we will continue to value responsiveness and professionalism, if sometimes favoring one, sometimes the other. Neutral competence, Rourke says, has proved valuable enough to continue revering whether dominated by political controllers or professions at any particular time. Good governance could not be so without the non-partisan sources of knowledge and savvy about the social and technological worlds.

Political responsiveness, whether to Congress, which votes program authority and appropriations, or the president, who directs analysis for formulation and implementation, will energize cross pressures for neutral competence, Rourke says. Kaufman agrees that as one value dominates, the other two form a set of contending, competing alternatives to its dominance.

Within the succession of values lies the answer to the "Who rules?" question and the method by which decision making may be understood in an historic context. Each of the values Kaufman and Rourke have observed—representativeness, strong executive leadership, and non-partisan expertise competently applied—has for a time been the espoused ideal for administrative decision making, whether because of its presumed efficiency in keeping with a constitutional-level logic of consequence or because of their presumed closeness to the inherent ideals of democracy, a logic of appropriateness. At the same time, each has always been present to some degree in American governing institutions, and often in the makeup of individual administrative decision makers. The dynamics of value succession provide researchers a value path to understand institutions and decision making at both the individual and aggregate levels. Democratic administration may be understood as an elusive ideal or even as a contradiction in terms, but it remains central to the expressed values of American public administration.

REFERENCES

Addams, J., *Democracy and Social Ethics*, Belknap, Cambridge, MA, 1902.

Addams, J., Problems of municipal administration, *American Journal of Sociology*, 10(4), 425–444, 1905.

Adrian, C. R., *A History of American City Government: The Emergence of the Metropolis, 1920–1945*, Lanham, New York, 1987.

Alchian, A. A. and Demsetz, H., Production, information costs, and economic organization, *American Economic Review*, 62(5), 777–795, 1972.

Alexander, T. B., The civil war as institutional fulfillment, *Journal of Southern History*, 47(1), 3–32, 1981.

Allison, G. T., *Essence of Decision: Explaining the Cuban Missile Crisis*, Little, Brown, Boston, MA, 1971.

Allyn, B. J., Blight, J. G., and Welch, D. A., Essence of revision: Moscow, Havana, and the Cuban missile crisis, *International Security*, 14(3), 136–172, 1989.

Almond, G. A., *The American People and Foreign Policy*, Harcourt, New York, 1950.

Appleby, P. H., *Policy and Administration*, University of Alabama Press, Tuscaloosa, AL, 1949.

Arrow, K., Bower, G., Efron, B., Maccoby, E., and Ross, L., Memorial resolution for Amos Tversky, http://www.stanford.edu/dept/facultysenate/archive/1997_1998/reports/105949/106013.html (accessed Febuary 7, 2006), 1998.

Bailyn, B., *To begin the World Anew: The Genius and Ambiguities of the American Founders*, Knopf, New York, 2003.

Barnard, C., *The Functions of the Executive*, Harvard University Press, Cambridge, MA, 1938.

Bartle, J. R. and Jun, M., *Applying Transaction Cost Theory to Public Budgeting and Finance Evolving Theories of Public Budgeting*, JAI Press, New York, 2001.

Beierle, T. C., The quality of stakeholder-based decisions, *Risk Analysis*, 22(4), 739–749, 2002.

Bensel, R. F., *Yankee Leviathan*, Cambridge University Press, New York, 1991.

Berger, P. L. and Luckman, T., *The Social Construction of Reality: A Treatise in the Sociology of Knowledge*, Anchor Books, Garden City, NY, 1967.

Bogason, P., *Public Policy and Local Governance: Institutions in Postmodern Society*, Edward Elgar, Northampton, MA, 2000.

Bruere, H. J., *New City Government*, Apple, New York, 1913.

Buchanan, J. M. and Tullock, G., *The Calculus of Consent*, University of Michigan Press, Ann Arbor, MI, 1962.

Budgeting and Accounting Act of 1921, PL 67-13, 42 Stat. 20–27.

Calista, D. J., Policy implementation, In *Encyclopedia of Policy Studies*, Nagel, S., Ed., 2nd ed., Marcel Dekker, New York, 1994.

Camerer, C., Behavioral economics: reunifying psychology and economics, *Proceedings of the National Academy of Science*, 96, 10575–10577, 1999.

Camerer, C., Loewenstein, G., and Rabin, M., *Advances in Behavioral Economics*, Russell Sage Foundation, Princeton University Press, New York, 2004.

Cayer, N. J., Public Personal and Labor Relations, this volume.

Chrislip, D. D. and Larson, C. E., *Collaborative Leadership: How Citizens and Civic Leaders Can Make a Difference*, Jossey-Bass Publishers, San Francisco, CA, 1994.

Christakis, A. N., Institute for 21st century agoras: what does agoras mean? (http://www.globalagoras.org/about_us.html, accessed February 12, 2006), 2006.

Civic Alliance to Rebuild Downtown New York, Listening to the city: report of proceedings. http://www.listeningtothecity.org/background/final_report_9_20.pdf (accessed February 1, 2006), 2002.

Clark, T. N. and Ferguson, L. C., *City Money*, Columbia University Press, New York, 1983.

Clarke, S. E., Economic development roles in American cities: a contextual analysis of shifting partnership arrangements, In *Public–Private Partnerships for Local Economic Development*, Walzer, N. and Jacobs, B. D., Eds., Praeger, Westport, CT, pp. 19–45, 1998.

Cleveland, F. A., *Organized Democracy*, Longman, Green, New York, 1913.

Cleveland, F. A., Evolution of the budget idea in the United States, *Annals of the American Academy of Political and Social Science*, 62, 1–23, 1915.

Coase, R., The nature of the firm, *Economica*, 4, 386–405, 1937.

Cohen, M. D., March, J. G., and Olsen, J. P., A garbage can model of organizational choice, *Administrative Science Quarterly*, 17(1), 1–25, 1972.

Corwin, E. S., In *The Constitution and What It Means Today*, Chase, H. W. and Ducat, C. R., Eds., 13th ed., Princeton University Press, Princeton, NJ, 1973.

Cyert, R. M. and March, J. G., *A Behavioral Theory of the Firm*, Prentice Hall, Englewood Cliffs, NJ, 1963.

Dahlberg, J. S., *The New York Bureau of Municipal Research*, New York University Press, New York, 1966.

DeLeon, P., *Advice and Consent: The Development of the Policy Sciences*, Russell Sage Foundation, New York, 1988.

DiLorenzo, T. J., The great centralizer: Abraham Lincoln and the war between the states, *Independent Review*, 3(2), 243–271, 1998.

DiLorenzo, T. J., The consolidation of state power via reconstruction, 1865–1890, *Journal of Libertarian Studies*, 16(2), 139–161, 2002.

DiMaggio, P. J., Constructing an organizational field as a professional project, In *The New Institutionalism in Organizational Analysis*, Powell, W. W. and DiMaggio, P. J., Eds., University of Chicago Press, Chicago, IL, pp. 267–292, 1991.

DiMaggio, P. J. and Powell, W. W., Introduction, In *The New Institutionalism in Organizational Analysis*, Powell, W. W. and DiMaggio, P. J., Eds., University of Chicago Press, Chicago, IL, pp. 1–38, 1991.

Donald, D., *Lincoln Reconsidered*, Vintage, New York, 1956.

Downs, A., Why the government budget is too small in a democracy, *World Politics*, 12, 541–563, 1960.

Drucker, P. F., What results should you expect? A users' guide to MBO, *Public Administration Review*, 36(1), 12–19, 1976.

Dunning, W. A., *Reconstruction Political and Economic 1865–1877*, Harper & Brothers, New York, 1907.

Elster, J., *Nuts and Bolts for the Social Sciences*, Cambridge University Press, New York, 1989.

English, W. B., Understanding the costs of sovereign default: American state debts in the 1840s, *American Economic Review*, 86(1), 259–275, 1996.

Etzioni, A., Mixed-scanning: a 3rd approach to decision-making, *Public Administration Review*, 27(5), 385–392, 1967.

Etzioni, A., Mixed scanning revisited, *Public Administration Review*, 46(1), 8–14, 1986.

Fay, B., *Social Theory and Political Practice*, Holmes & Meier, New York, 1976.

Feiock, R. C., A quasi-market framework for development competition, *Journal of Urban Affairs*, 24(2), 123–142, 2002.

Finer, H., Administrative responsibility in democratic government, *Public Administration Review*, 1(4), 335–350, 1941.

Fischer, F., Policy discourse and the politics of Washington think tanks, In *The Argumentative Turn in Policy Analysis and Planning*, Fischer, F. and Forester, J., Eds., Duke University Press, Durham, NC, pp. 21–42, 1993.

Fischer, F., *Evaluating Public Policy*, Nelson-Hall Publishers, Chicago, IL, 1995.

Fisher, L., *Presidential Spending Power*, Princeton University Press, Princeton, NJ, 1975.

Fisher, R. and Ury, W., *Getting to Yes: Negotiating Agreement Without Giving in*, Penguin Books, New York, 1983.

Follett, M. P., *The New State: Group Organization the Solution of Popular Government*, Longmans, Green and Co., New York, 1918.

Follett, M. P., *Creative Experience*, Longmans, Green and Co., New York, 1924.

Follett, M. P., *Dynamic Administration: The Collected Papers of Mary Parker Follett*, Harper, New York, 1940.

Foner, Eric, *Reconstruction*, Harper & Row, New York, 1988.

Foner, Eric, *Forever Free*, Knopf, New York, 2005.

Forester, J., *The Deliberative Practitioner: Encouraging Participatory Planning Processes*, MIT Press, Cambridge, MA, 1999.

Forsythe, D. W., *Taxation and Political Change in the Young Nation 1781–1833*, Columbia University Press, New York, 1977.

Frances, J., Levacic, R., Mitchell, J., and Thompson, G., Introduction, In *Markets, Hierarchies and Networks: The Coordination of Social Life*, Thompson, G., Frances, J., Levacic, R., and Mitchell, J., Eds., Sage Publications, London, pp. 1–19, 1991.

Frant, H., Rules and governance in the public sector: the case of the civil service, *American Journal of Political Science*, 37(4), 990–1007, 1993.

Friedrich, C. J., Public policy and the nature of administrative responsibility, *Public Policy*, 1, 3–24, 1940.

Galaskiewicz, J., Making corporate actors accountable: institution-building in Minneapolis-St. Paul, In *The New Institutionalism in Organizational Analysis*, Powell, W. W. and DiMaggio, P. J., Eds., University of Chicago Press, Chicago, IL, pp. 293–310, 1991.

Gist, J. R., Decision making in public administration, In *Handbook of Public Administration*, Rabin, J., Hildreth, W. B., and Miller, G. J., Eds., 2nd ed., Dekker, New York, pp. 265–291, 1998.

Goldstein, W. M. and Hogarth, R. M., Judgment and decision research: some historical context, In *Research on Judgment and Decision Making: Currents, Connections, and Controversies*, Goldstein, W. M. and Hogarth, R. M., Eds., Cambridge University Press, Cambridge, 1997.

Golembiewski, R. T., *Public Administration as a Developing Discipline, Part 1: Perspectives on Past and Present*, Dekker, New York, 1977.

Goodhart, D., Is Britain becoming too diverse to sustain the mutual obligations behind a good society and the welfare state? Prospect 95, http://www.prospectmagazine.co.uk/article_details.php?id = 5835 (accessed February 4, 2005), 2004.

Goodman, J., Reconstruction revisited, *New York Times Book Review*, 29, 23, January, 2006.

Gould, J. D., Hypothetical history, *Economic History Review*, 22(2), 195–207, 1969.

Gray, B., *Collaborating: Finding Common Ground for Multiparty Problems*, Jossey-Bass, San Francisco, CA, 1989.

Gray, B., Cross-sectoral partners: collaborative alliances among businesses, government and communities, In *Creating Collaborative Advantage*, Huxham, C., Ed., Sage Publications, London, pp. 57–79, 1996.

Gregory, R., McDaniels, T., and Fields, D., Decision aiding, not dispute resolution: creating insights through structured environmental decisions, *Journal of Policy Analysis and Management*, 20(3), 415–432, 2001.

Gulick, L. and Urwick, L., *Papers on the Science of Administration*, Institute of Public Administration, New York, 1937.

Gwyn, W. B., *The Meaning of the Separation of Powers: An Analysis of the Doctrine from Its Origin to the Adoption of the United States Constitution*, Martinus Nijhoff, The Hague, Netherlands, 1965.

Halachmi, A., In *Principal-agent Perspective*, Rabin, J., Ed., Online ed., *Encyclopedia of Public Administration and Public Policy*, Vol. 2, Marcel Dekker, New York, pp. 956–958, 2003.

Hamilton, A., Madison, J., and Jay, J., In *The Federalist*, Cooke, J. E., Ed., Wesleyan University Press, Middletown, CT, 1961.

Hardin, G., The tragedy of the commons, *Science*, 162, 1243–1248, 1968.

Harmon, A., Vox populi, online, *New York Times*, 26, G1, September, 2002.

Harriman, L. and Straussman, J. D., Do judges determine budget decisions? Federal court decisions in prison reform and state spending for corrections, *Public Administration Review*, 43, 343–351, 1983.

Harrison, J. R. and March, J. G., Decision making and postdecision surprises, *Administrative Science Quarterly*, 29(1), 26–42, 1984.

Hayek, F., *The Road to Serfdom*, University of Chicago Press, Chicago, IL, 1944.

Heclo, H., Issue networks and the executive establishment, In *The New American Political System*, King, A., Ed., American Enterprise Institute, Washington, DC, pp. 87–124, 1978.

Heclo, H., John Gaus lecture: the spirit of public administration, *PS: Political Science and Politics*, 35(4), 689–694, 2002.

Higgens-Evenson, R. R., *The Price of Progress*, Johns Hopkins University Press, Baltimore, MD, 2003.

Hill, J. L., The five faces of freedom in American political and constitutional thought, *Boston College Law Review*, 45, 499–594, 2004.

Hindmoor, A., The importance of being trusted: transaction costs and policy network theory, *Public Administration*, 76(1), 25–43, 1998.

Hofstadter, R., *The Age of Reform*, Vintage Books, New York, 1955.

Holzer, M., Gabrielian V., and Yang K., Five great ideas in American public administration. In *Handbook of Public Administration*, Rabin, J., Hildreth, W. B., Miller. G. J., Eds., Taylor & Francis, New York, in press.

Horn, M. J., *The political Economy of Public Administration*, Cambridge University Press, New York, 1995.

Huxham, C., Ed., *Creating Collaborative Advantage*, Sage Publications, London, 1996.

Jessop, B., The rise of governance and the risks of failure: the case of economic development, *International Social Science Journal*, 50(155), 29–45, 1998.

Justice, J. B., Business improvement districts, reasoning, and results: collective action and downtown revitalization, *Dissertation Abstracts International*, 64(08), 3064, 2003.

Justice, J. B., Melitski, J., and Smith, D.L., Forthcoming, e-government as an instrument of fiscal accountability and responsiveness: do the best practitioners employ the best practices? *American Review of Public Administration*.

Kahn, J., *Budgeting Democracy*, Cornell University Press, Ithaca, NY, 1997.

Kahneman, D., Maps of bounded rationality: psychology for behavioral economics, *American Economic Review*, 93(5), 1449–1475, 2003a.

Kahneman, D., A psychological perspective on economics, *American Economic Review*, 93(2), 162–168, 2003b. (Papers and Proceedings of the One Hundred Fifteenth Annual Meeting of the American Economic Association, Washington, DC, January 3–5, 2003)

Kahneman, D. and Tversky, A., Prospect theory: an analysis of decision under risk, *Econometrica*, 47(2), 263–292, 1979.

Karl, B. D., Public administration and American history: a century of professionalism, *Public Administration Review*, 36, 489–503, 1976 (5, Special Bicentennial Issue)

Kaufman, H., Emerging conflicts in the doctrine of public administration, *American Political Science Review*, 50(4), 1057–1073, 1956.

Kaufman, H., Administrative decentralization and political power, *Public Administration Review*, 29(1), 3–15, 1969.

Kelly, J. M., A century of public budgeting reform: the "key" question, *Administration and Society*, 37(1), 89–109, 2005.

Keynes, J. M., *The General Theory of Employment, Interest, and Money*, Harcourt Brace Jovanovich, New York, 1936, 1964.

King, D. S., *Actively Seeking Work?*, University of Chicago Press, Chicago, IL, 1995.

Kingdon, J. W., *Agendas, Alternatives, and Public Policies*, Harper Collins, New York, 1984.

Kiser, L. L. and Ostrom, E., The three worlds of action: a meta-theoretical synthesis of institutional approaches, In *Strategies of Political Inquiry*, Ostram, E., Ed., Sage Publications, Beverly Hills, CA, pp. 179–222, 1982.

Klijn, E.-H., Rules as institutional context for decision making networks: the approach to postwar housing districts in two cities, *Administration and Society*, 33(2), 133–164, 2001.

Krasner, S., Sovereignty: an institutional perspective, *Comparative Political Studies*, 21, 66–94, 1988.

Kurland, P.B. and Lerner R., The founder's Constitution, University of Chicago Press, Chicago, http://press-pubs.uchicago.edu/founders, 1987.

Larson, J. L., *Internal Improvement*, University of North Carolina Press, Chapel Hill, 2001.

Lasswell, H. D., The policy orientation, In *The Policy Sciences: Recent Developments in Scope and Methods*, Lerner, D. and Lasswell, H., Eds., Stanford University Press, Stanford, CA, pp. 3–15, 1951.

Lewis, A., Bush and the lesser evil [Review of two books by Michael Ignatieff, The lesser evil: Political ethics in an age of terror and the year of living dangerously: a liberal supporter of the war looks back]. The New York Review of Books 51(9), http://www.nybooks.com/articles/17111 (accessed August 7, 2004), 2004.

Lindblom, C. E., The science of 'muddling through', *Public Administration Review*, 19(2), 79–88, 1959.

Lindblom, C., *Politics and Markets*, Basic Books, New York, 1977.

Lindblom, C. E., Still muddling, not yet through, *Public Administration Review*, 39(6), 517–526, 1979.

Lindblom, C. E., *Inquiry and Change: The Troubled Attempt to Understand and Shape Society*, Yale University Press, New Haven, CT, 1990.

Lindblom, C. E. and Cohen, K. D., *Usable Knowledge: Social Science and Social Problem Solving*, Yale University Press, New Haven, 1979.

Lineberry, R. L. and Fowler, E. P., Reformism and public policies in American cities, *American Political Science Review*, 61, 701–716, 1967.

Lineberry, R. L. and Sharkansky, I., *Urban Politics and Public Policy*, Harper and Row, New York, 1971.

Lipscomb, A. A. and Bergh, A. E., *The Writings of Thomas Jefferson*, Vol. 15, Thomas Jefferson Memorial Association, Washington, DC, 1905.

Lowe, W., Helping the masses find their way, *Group Facilitation*, 6, 37, 2004.

Lowi, T. J. and Simon, H. A., Lowi and Simon on political science, public administration, rationality and public choice, *Journal of Public Administration Research and Theory: J-PART*, 2(2), 105–112, 1992.

Lukensmeyer, C., About the consortium, http://www.deliberative-democracy.net/about/ (accessed February 12, 2006), 2006.

MacDonald, T. J., A history of urban fiscal politics in America, 1830–1930: what was supposed to be versus what was and the difference it makes, In *Review of Public Budgeting and Financial Management*, Rabin, J., Hildreth, W. B., and Miller, G. J., Eds., *International Journal of Public Administration* 11, pp. 679–712, 1988.

March, J. G., Bounded rationality, ambiguity, and the engineering of choice, *Bell Journal of Economics*, 9(2), 587–608, 1978.

March, J. G., *A Primer on Decision Making*, Free Press, New York, 1994.

March, J. G. and Olsen, J. P., The new institutionalism: organizational factors in political life, *American Political Science Review*, 78, 734–749, 1984.

March, J. G. and Olsen, J. P., *Rediscovering Institutions: The Organizational Basis of Politics*, Free Press, New York, 1989.

March, J. G. and Simon, H. A., *Organizations*, with the collaboration of Harold Guetzkow Wiley, New York, 1958.

McGregor, D., *The Human Side of Enterprise*, McGraw-Hill, New York, 1960.

Meier, K., Political economy and cost-benefit analysis: problems of bias, In *Political Economy of Public Policy*, Stone, A. and Harpham, E. J., Eds., Sage Publications, Beverly Hills, CA, 1986.

Melitski, J., Holzer, M., Kim., S. T., Kim., C. G., and Rho, S. Y., Digital government worldwide: an e-government assessment of municipal web sites throughout the world, *International Journal of E-Government Research*, 1(1), pp. 1–19, 2005.

Michels, R., *Political Parties*, Transaction, New Brunswick, NJ, 1999 [1911].

Miller, G. J. and Robbins, D. J., Benefit cost analysis, In *Public Productivity Handbook*, Holzer, M. and Lee, S., Eds., Dekker, New York, pp. 405–430, 2004.

Miller, G. J., *Government Financial Management Theory*, Dekker, New York, 1991.

Miller, G. J., Dept management networks, *Public Administration Review*, 53(1), 50–58, 1993.

Milward, H. B., Politics, personnel and public policy, *Public Administration Review*, 38(4), 391–396, 1978.

Milward, H. B. and Provan, K. G., Principles for controlling agents: the political economy of network structure, *Journal of Public Administration Research and Theory*, 8(2), 203–221, 1998.

Moe, T. M., The new economics of organization, *American Journal of Political Science*, 78, 739–777, 1984.

Moe, T. M., Toward a theory of public bureaucracy, In *Organization Theory*, Williamson, O. E., Ed., Oxford University Press, New York, pp. 116–153, 1995.

Montesquieu, C. de S., Baron de la Brède et de, *The Spirit of the Laws*, Trans. Thomas Nugent (1750), The Founders Constitution, Kurland, P. B., and Lerner, R., Eds., Vol. 1, chapter 10, document 5. The University of Chicago Press, Chicago, http://press-pubs.uchicago.edu/founders/documents/v1ch10s5.html (accessed September 9, 2005), 1748.

Mosher, F. C., *A Tale of Two Agencies: A Comparative Analysis of the General Accounting Office and the Office of Management and Budget*, Louisiana State University Press, Baton Rouge, LA, 1984.

Myers, v. United States, 272 US 52, 1926.

Neustadt, R. E., *Presidential Power, the Politics of Leadership*, Wiley, New York, 1960.

Newcombe, T., The art of knowledge sharing, *Government Technology*, 19–20, 49, 2002.

Nie, N. H., Junn, J., and Stehlik-Barry, K., *Education and Democratic Citizenship in America*, University of Chicago Press, Chicago, IL, 1996.

Olson, M., *The Logic of Collective Action: Public Goods and the Theory of Groups*, Harvard University Press, Cambridge, MA, 1971.

Ostrom, E., An agenda for the study of institutions, *Public Choice*, 48, 3–25, 1986.

Ostrom, E., *Governing the Commons: The Evolution of Institutions for Collective Action*, Cambridge University Press, Cambridge, 1990.

Ostrom, E., Self-organization and social capital, *Industrial and Corporate Change*, 4(1), 131–159, 1995.

Ostrom, E., A behavioral approach to the rational choice theory of collective action, *American Political Science Review*, 92(1), 1–22, 1998.

Ostrom, E., Coping with tragedies of the commons, *Annual Review of Political Science*, 2, 493–535, 1999a.

Ostrom, E., Institutional rational choice: an assessment of the institutional analysis and development framework, In *Theories of the Policy Process*, Sabatier, P. A., Ed., Westview, Boulder, CO, pp. 35–71, 1999b.

Ostrom, E., Collective action and the evolution of social norms, *Journal of Economic Perspectives*, 14(3), 137–158, 2000.

Ostrom, E. and Walker, J., Neither markets nor hierarchies: linking transformation processes in collective action arenas, In *Perspectives on Public Choice: A Handbook*, Mueller, D. C., Ed., Cambridge University Press, Cambridge, pp. 35–72, 1997.

Patashnik, E. M., The contractual nature of budgeting: a transaction cost perspective on the design of budgeting institutions, *Policy Sciences*, 29, 189–212, 1996.

Peabody, B. G. and Nugent, J. D., Toward a unifying theory of the separation of powers, *American University Law Review*, 52, 1–64, 2003.

Pfiffner, J., *Public Administration*, Ronald Press, New York, 1935.

Plato, *The Republic of Plato*, Trans Cornford, F. M., Oxford University Press, New York, 1979.

Prince, C. E., The passing of the aristocracy: Jefferson's removal of the Federalists, 1801–1805, *Journal of American History*, 57(3), 563–575, 1970.

Quaife, M. M., *The Diary of James K. Polk During His Presidency, 1845–1849*, Vol. 4, A.C. McClurg, Chicago, IL, 1910.

Quattrone, G. A. and Tversky, A., Contrasting rational and psychological analyses of political choice, *The American Political Science Review*, 82(3), 719–736, 1988.

Randall, J. G., *Constitutional Problems Under Lincoln*, University of Illinois Press, Urbana, IL, 1951.

Reorganization Act of 1939, 53 Stat. 813, (Reorganization Plan No. 1 of 1939, 53 Stat. 1423).

Riker, W., *Liberalism Against Populism*, W.H. Freeman, San Francisco, CA, 1982.

Rosenbloom, D. H. and Obuchowski, C. C., Public personnel examinations and the constitution: emergent trends, *Public Administration Review*, 37(1), 9–18, 1977.

Rosenbloom, D. H., Public administration theory and the separation of powers, *Public Administration Review*, 43(3), 219–227, 1983.

Rourke, F. E., Responsiveness and neutral competence in American bureaucracy, *Public Administration Review*, 52(6), 539–546, 1992.

Savage, J. D., *Balanced Budgets and American Politics*, Cornell University Press, Ithaca, NY, 1988.

Schattschneider, E. E., *The Semi-Sovereign People*, Dryden Press, New York, 1960.

Scheiber, Harry N., The pet banks in Jacksonian politics and finance, 1833–1841, *Journal of Economic History*, 23(2), 196–214, 1963.

Schick, A., *Budget Innovation in the States*, Brookings Institution, Washington, DC, 1971.

Schiesl, M. J., *The Politics of Efficiency: Municipal Administration and Reform in America, 1800–1920*, University of California Press, Berkeley, CA, 1977.

Schmidt, M. R., Grout: alternative kinds of knowledge and why they are ignored, *Public Administration Review*, 53(6), 525–530, 1993.

Schneider, A. L., and Ingram, H. M., *Policy Design for Democracy*, University Press of Kansas , Lawrence, 1997.

Schön, D. A. and Rein, M., *Frame Reflection: Toward the Resolution of Intractable Policy Controversies*, Basic Books, New York, 1994.

Scott, W. R., Institutions and organizations: toward a theoretical synthesis, In *Institutional Environments and Organizations: Structural Complexity and Individualism*, Scott, W. R. and Meyer, J. W., Eds., Sage, Thousand Oaks, CA, pp. 55–80, 1994.

Scott, W. R., *Institutions and Organizations*, Sage, Thousand Oaks, CA, 1995.

Scott, W. R., *Institutions and Organizations*, 2nd ed., Sage, Thousand Oaks, CA, 2001.

Searing, D. D., Roles, rules, and rationality in the new institutionalism, *American Political Science Review*, 85(4), 1239–1260, 1991.

Simon, H., *Administrative Behavior*, Macmillan, New York, 1947.

Simon, H. A., Theories of decision-making in economics and behavioral science, *American Economic Review*, 49(3), 253–283, 1959.

Simon, H. A., Rationality as process and product of thought, *American Economic Review*, 68(2), 1–16, 1978.

Simon, H. A., Artificial intelligence: an empirical science, *Artificial Intelligence*, 77, 95–127, 1995.

Simon, H. A., *Administrative Behavior: A Study of Decision-Making Processes in Administrative Organizations*, 4th ed., Free Press, New York, 1997.

Skocpol, T., *Protecting Soldiers and Mothers*, Belknap Press of Harvard University Press, Cambridge, MA, 1992.

Skowronek, Stephen, *Building a New American State*, Cambridge University Press, Cambridge, UK, 1982.

Slovic, P., The construction of preference, *American Psychologist*, 50(5), 364–371, 1995.

Smelser, Marshall, George Washington and the Alien and Sedition acts, *American Historical Review*, 59(2), 322–334, 1954.

Smelser, Marshall, The Federalist period as an age of passion, *American Quarterly*, 10(4), 391–419, 1958.

Smith, James Morton, *Freedom's Fetters: The Alien and Sedition Laws and American Civil Liberties*, Cornell University Press, Ithaca, NY, 1966.

Smithies, Arthur, *The Budgetary Process in the United States Committee for Economic Development*, McGraw-Hill, New York, 1955.

Stillman, Richard J., *American Bureaucracy*, Nelson-Hall, Chicago, IL, 1987.

Stivers, C., *Bureau Men and Settlement Women*, University of Kansas Press, Lawrence, KS, 2000.

Stourm, R., *The Budget,* Trans. T. Plazinski, Appleton, New York, 1917.

Szenazy, S. S., Back to the drawing board, *New York Times*, 23, A19, July, 2002.

Tang, S. Y., *Institutions and Collective Action: Self-Governance in Irrigation*, ICS Press, San Francisco, CA, 1992.

Taylor, F. W., *Scientific Management, Comprising Shop Management, The Principles of Scientific Management [and] Testimony Before the Special House Committee*, Harper, New York, 1911.

Thaler, R. W., *Quasi Rational Economics*, Russell Sage Foundation, New York, 1991.

Tocqueville, Alexis de, In *Democracy in America*, Trans. Henry Reeve, Vol. 2, Colonial Press, New York, 1899.

Tribe, L. H., Policy science: analysis or ideology?, *Philosophy and Public Affairs*, 2(1), 66–110, 1972.

Tversky, A. and Kahneman, D., Judgment under uncertainty: heuristics and biases, *Science*, 185, 1124–1131, 1974.

Tversky, A. and Kahneman, D., The framing of decisions and the psychology of choice, *Science*, 211, 453–458, 1981.

Tversky, A. and Kahneman, D., Rational choice and the framing of decisions, *Journal of Business*, 59(4), Part 2, S251–S278, 1986.

Tversky, A. and Kahneman, D., Loss aversion in riskless choice: a reference-dependent model, *Quarterly Journal of Economics*, 106(4), 1039–1061, 1991.

Tversky, A. and Simonson., I., Context-dependent preferences, *Management Science*, 39(10), 1179–1189, 1993.

Tversky, A., Slovic, P., and Kahneman, D., The causes of preference reversa, *American Economic Review*, 80(1), 204–217, 1990.

Vile, M. J. C., *Constitutionalism and the Separation of Powers*, Clarendon, Oxford, UK, 1967.

Villanueva, A. B., American civil service reform in historical perspective, *Public Administration Review*, 53(3), 276–277, 1993.

Von Neumann, J. J. and Morgenstern, O., *Theory of Games and Economic Behavior*, 3rd ed., Princeton University Press, Princeton, NJ, 1972.

Waldo, D., *The Administrative State*, Ronald Press, New York, 1948.

Waldo, D., Development of theory of democratic administration, *American Political Science Review*, 46(4), 81–103, 1952.

Waldo, D., *The Administrative State: A Study of the Political Theory of American Public Administration*, 2nd ed., Holmes & Meier, New York, 1984.

Washington, George, Letter to Richard Henry Lee, October 24, In *The Writings of George Washington, No. 33 of Numbers 30–37, 138*, Fitzpatrick, John C., Ed., US Government Printing Office, Washington, DC, pp. 1939–1940, 1793.

Webber, Carolyn and Wildavsky, Aaron, *A History of Taxation and Expenditure in the Western World*, Simon and Schuster, New York, 1986.

Weick, K. E., Cognitive processes in organizations, In *Research in Organizational Behavior*, Staw, B. M., Ed., Vol. 1, JAI Press, Greenwich, CT, pp. 41–74, 1979.

Weick, K. E., *The Social Psychology of Organizing*, 2nd ed., Random House, New York, 1979.

Wenger, E., McDermott, R., and Snyder, W., *Cultivating Communities of Practice*, Harvard Business School Press, Cambridge, MA, 2002.

West, D., E-government and the transformation of service delivery and citizen attitudes, *Public Administration Review*, 64(1), 15–27, 2004.

White, L. D., *Trends in Public Administration*, McGraw-Hill, New York, 1933.

White, L. D., *The Jeffersonians*, Macmillan, New York, 1951.

White, L. D., *The Jacksonians*, Macmillan, New York, 1954.

White, L. D., *The Republicans*, Macmillan, New York, 1958.

White, L. D., *The Federalists*, Greenwood, Westport, CT, 1978 [1948].

White, O. and Wolf, J., Deming's total quality management and the Baskin Robbins problem, part 1: is it time to go back to vanilla?, *Administration and Society*, 27, 203–225, 1995a.

White, O. and Wolf, J., Deming's total quality management and the Baskin Robbins problem, part 2: is this ice cream American?, *Administration and Society*, 27, 307–321, 1995b.

Wilentz, Sean, *The Rise of American Democracy*, W.W. Norton, New York, 2005.

Williamson, O. E., *Markets and Hierarchies: Analysis and Antitrust Implications*, Free Press, New York, 1975.

Williamson, O. E., The economics of organization: the transaction cost approach, *American Journal of Sociology*, 87(3), 548–577, 1981.

Wilmerding, L., *The Spending Power*, Yale University Press, New Haven, CT, 1943.

Wilson, James Q., The risk of the bureaucratic state, *Public Interest*, 41(Fall), 77–103, 1975.

Wilson, W., *Congressional Government*, Houghton Mifflin, Boston, MA, 1885.

Wilson, W., The study of administration, *Political Science Quarterly*, 2(2), 197–222, 1887.

Wolf, Charles Jr., *Markets or Governments: Choosing Between Imperfect Alternatives*, MIT Press, Cambridge, MA, 1988.

Yanow, D., *Conducting Interpretive Policy Analysis*, Sage, Thousand Oaks, CA, 2000.

Zahariadis, N., Ambiguity, time, and multiple streams, In *Theories of the Policy Process*, Sabatier, P. A., Ed., Westview, Boulder, CO, pp. 73–93, 1999.

8 Five Conceptual Tools for Decision-Making

Dennis P. Wittmer and Robert P. McGowan

CONTENTS

I. INTRODUCTION

The field of decision-making in public administration and public affairs frequently defies clear-cut definition and categorization, yet it has particular bearing for public administrators today and in the future. In the complex field of program and service delivery, managers are often put in the position of having to make a variety of decisions—ranging from routine, structured situations, such as the processing of payroll, to highly unstructured, nonroutine situations, such as making trade-off decisions among a variety of programs (Simon 1973). The purpose of this chapter is to examine five tools, concepts, or strategies that can be useful to managers in terms of effective decision-making.

II. DECISION TYPES

Distinct from the concept of policy, which is generally defined as a principle or rule, is a decision, which can be defined as the exercise of judgment in any particular situation. A useful distinction can be drawn between routine and nonroutine decision types. Herbert Simon, who defines the two types as "programmed" and "ill-structured," views routine decisions as those that can be made in a prescribed manner (Simon 1973, 1980). Often of an administrative or procedural nature, these decisions are governed by the traditional mores of the organization: the public agency has histori-cally operated in a particular manner, the clients or constituent groups have grown to expect a fixed pattern of behavior, or the agency is governed by established rules and legislative mandates that circumscribe its activities.

Conversely, nonroutine or ill-structured decision types involve complex problems and issues for which no precedent or pattern exists. Kenneth J. Radford describes some of their primary characteristics:

- Only limited information is available with regard to the problem.
- The individual facing the problem may have more than one objective—some of which may be in conflict.
- More than one participant in the decision process may have the power to influence the choice among alternatives.
- Disagreement may exist over the priority to be assigned to various objectives as well as over methods of evaluating progress.
- The particular problem being discussed may be linked to other problem situations. (Radford 1977)

As Radford points out, one of the distinctions between programmed and nonprogrammed decisions is the amount of information that is available to assist the decision maker. For routine administrative decisions, information is processed to the extent that it matches the required input format. In a social service agency, for example, the caseworker frequently enters the relevant information about a client on forms which, in turn, are entered into a reporting system. Based on this data, levels of eligibility and availability of service are determined. Information that does not fall within the present reporting categories is not used. Benefits of a system of this kind are: decision criteria are unambiguous and applied to cases by class of problem, an increased number of clients are serviced, and caseworkers do not reach decisions on a case-by-case or idiosyncratic bias. There are limitations as well to such systems. There is little or no room left for including additional information that the client feels is important to his or her case. The caseworker often becomes frustrated by the process—performing a processing role as opposed to a professional service activity.

At the opposite extreme, individuals in a public agency may be required to make decisions based on limited information. Returning to our social service agency, we see problems that arise for which no procedures or documentation exist. A program to establish counseling for unwed mothers is one example of this decision situation. Although the funding for the program comes from the federal level, state and local social service agencies must often operate on limited or nonexistent information in establishing standards and monitoring progress. Should the program be relatively passive in nature (i.e., providing service to those individuals who contact the agency)? Or should an active search program be enacted by contacting recipients through school districts and community groups? What, in fact, is the estimated number of individuals who would participate, and over what period of time? These questions illustrate the nature of a nonprogrammed or ill-structured decision situation.

III. DECISION-MAKING STYLES AND PROCESSES

In addition to different decision types—structured versus unstructured—the context of decision-making in public organizations also involves alternative decision styles as well as approaches. These must be carefully weighed when considering which tool or technique should be utilized.

Briefly, decision styles can be classified in three ways: autocratic, democratic, or laissez-faire. An *autocratic* decision style would be one in which the individual makes the decision with little or no consultation from others. Naturally, this approach makes implementation more difficult because those charged with implementation must be convinced of the relative worth of the decision itself. In certain circumstances, this form of approach is necessary; military exercises or crisis situations necessitate this form as time becomes a critical factor. Other situations may arise in which the individual making the decision may have greater insight or access to crucial information that must be factored into the decision itself. Finally, there are instances in which legal or statutory constraints must be considered. Problems arise in using the autocratic approach when managers have not been adept at communicating the broader context of the situation. Others tend to view such an approach as either heavy-handed or capricious.

Different from the previous approach, the *democratic* style emphasizes decision-making in which all parties to the situation seek to come up with a mutually agreed-upon outcome. The benefits of such an approach are several. Implementation becomes easier because all concerned parties have provided some degree of input—in a sense they have bought into the decision itself. Other benefits include the incorporation of multiple points of view and the integration of several sources of information. Finally, communication is greatly facilitated in this approach. One word of caution is in order. The democratic approach may not be suitable in certain situations, particularly those in which time efficiency is critical.

The final decision style, *laissez-faire*, is an approach in which final decision outcomes emerge with little or no direction from those in leadership positions. Examples of the laissez-faire approach are often found in matters that may be politically sensitive—the public desires action but to act may be damaging, either to the individual or to the organization overall. One way of addressing the issue is to postpone direct action—arguing instead for further analysis, public testimony, or some independent committee action. The use of this particular decision style is not strongly advocated because it tends to be highly risky and there is no sound method for gauging anticipated reactions from postponing action.

In sum, the use of any of three decision styles is contingent on a number of factors: (1) the extent to which legal, statutory, or programmatic constraints preclude making any additional adjustments, (2) the available time in which the decision must be made and implemented, and (3) the balance between the quality of the decision and acceptance by others, and finally, the expectations of those involved (Fiedler 1967).

The decision process is concerned with various steps that are involved in progressing from the issue or problem to final implementation (Dunn 1981; Kingdon 1984). One of the distinguishing features of this approach is the emphasis on the *process* of decision-making, whereas others often focus on the institutional or behavioral elements involved in reaching decisions (Cohen and March 1986; Selznick 1957). Figure 8.1 provides a rough schematic of this process.

The first stage of the process, *problem or issue identification*, involves several elements. Of primary concern is the necessity of differentiating symptoms from causes. An example of this would be a marked increase in incidences of alcohol and drug abuse for a particular region. There may be several causes for this marked increase—ranging from the fact that more individuals may have been identified to a sharp increase in the unemployment rate in the area. It is therefore

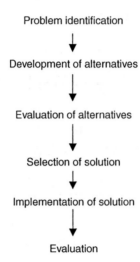

Problem identification

Development of alternatives

Evaluation of alternatives

Selection of solution

Implementation of solution

Evaluation

FIGURE 8.1 The decision process.

critical that managers take into consideration patterns of cause and effect; to overlook this distinction may mean inefficient use of agency resources and energies.

Another factor to consider in the area of problem identification is reliance on historical data. Those involved in efforts to resolve the particular problem or issue must be sensitive to the fact that historical data may be limited in scope; certain problems or issues are often unique or may occur infrequently. Other methods of correcting for this include the use of brainstorming techniques or Delphi (Worsham 1980). A brainstorming tool is the use of Paramind Brainstorming Software, created to gather every useful idea possible by the "exhaustion of the interaction of words" (ParaMind Brainstorming 2005).

The use of brainstorming is particularly effective when defining the nature of the problem or issue. The brainstorming technique requires participants to list their ideas in a free-form manner as quickly as possible. This avoids any attempt to bias the particular listing or preclude any suggestion—no matter how seemingly radical. This listing is subsequently analyzed, and through an iterative process, a key set of issues or problem areas is derived.

The Delphi method involves a different approach. Rather than have free-flowing input by all, a core group of experts on a particular set of issues is identified. This panel of experts then provides input (independently) as to the probability of certain events taking place, the nature of issues that will be unfolding, solutions to the problem posed, and the like. The results are then collected, tabulated in some form, and then transmitted back to the experts for further clarification or reduction to a manageable number. The critical variables in this process are the selection of the panel of experts and the rationale used to reduce/consolidate the results. But used correctly, the Delphi method is an effective tool for forecasting those problems or issues for which little historical data exist.

The second stage in the decision process involves the *development of alternatives*. This is closely linked with the prior stage of problem or issue identification, as the manner in which the problem or issue is defined will influence how alternatives are generated. For example, the development of a major metropolitan airport is an issue that many jurisdictions now face. Defining this issue as one involving strictly transportation policy would limit further analysis to various tradeoff analyses of one mode of transportation versus another. Broadly defining the airport development as encompassing economic development brings demographic, social, and technological factors into the process.

In addition to the issue of scope, the development of alternatives in the public sector surfaces the debate as to rationalism versus incrementalism (Wildavsky 1964). The rationalist argument states that all alternatives are considered. No alternatives are dismissed, and it is the subsequent analysis which will determine the optimal approach. Conversely, the incremental approach holds that, particularly in the public sector where many interests are involved, it is extremely inefficient to both generate a list of alternatives and achieve consensus on them.

Whether the rationalist or incremental approach is utilized depends on several factors, not the least of which is the amount of time and resources available as well as the complexity of the particular issue. Suffice it to say, the rationalist approach is perhaps better suited to more compartmentalized units or divisions in which managers have some degree of discretionary authority and control. As problems or issues unfold at the interagency or interdepartmental levels, the ability of managers to develop a degree of consensus on the range of alternatives to be considered is limited at best.

However, there are ways to merge aspects of both rationalism and incrementalism. James Brian Quinn (1980) refers to this approach as "logical incrementalism". One way of defining this approach is to consider the manner in which most of us make decisions. Rather than concentrate on a few select alternatives, we tend to focus on a range—excluding, for the most part, the extremes. We avoid the expenditure of time in analyzing all of the possibilities, but, at the same time, we have some degree of choice or options. The third stage of the decision approach, the *evaluation of alternatives*, is the area in which a great deal of the balance of this chapter will focus, for it is at this stage that we often associate the use of analytical tools and techniques for making decisions. Yet it is also important that we consider the broader context which precedes and follows this particular stage. Analytical tools and techniques should not be viewed as a replacement for managers; rather, they are supportive methods for allowing managers to make better decisions—the end result being increased productivity (qualitatively and quantitatively).

The evaluation of alternatives involves two additional concerns. First, evaluation should consider a mix of both the qualitative and quantitative aspects of program or service delivery. Susan and Martin Tolchin, in *Dismantling America: The Rush to De-Regulate,* bring this point out vividly when they examine controversies over the use of cost-benefit analysis in implementing regulation (Tolchin and Tolchin 1983). Their argument is that because agency regulators face difficult tasks in substantively articulating the qualitative aspects of a particular program or service, the courts have increasingly excluded its use in analysis, in a sense leading to least-cost analysis. Naturally, this puts a greater burden on the public manager to further develop and refine qualitative measures (Haberman 1978).

A second concern on the evaluation of alternatives involves the use of standards or criteria. Frequently, alternatives are evaluated with little or no attention devoted to standards for judging performance or adherence to the overall goal. One means of remedying this situation is the development of specific and verifiable standards. These may range from such rudimentary standards as citizen satisfaction (however defined) to program cost maintenance or recovery. In addition, such standards should be viewed as dynamic in nature, because as external events or donations change, so too should standards (Simon 1978).

The fourth stage of the process, the *selection of solution*, is largely dependent on the method of evaluation that has been utilized in the prior stage. For example, the nature of the critical path method (CPM) is to select the optimal path (or approach) based on the allocation of resources as well as time. Cost-benefit analysis should similarly select the program or service option that yields the greatest net benefit to net cost. The increasing introduction of computer-based models into the office and work setting has also greatly contributed to selection of solutions, due principally to their ability to process a great deal of information in a rapid fashion (Kraemer and King 1977). Perhaps one aside here is that administrators, those in upper levels of management, have a tendency to also rely on their own intuition and experience in selecting and backing a particular solution (McGowan and Loveless 1982). It would be interesting to note how many would alter their choice when faced with a solution that is contrary to their intuitive sense or experience. Finally, selection of the solution, particularly in the public sector, involves the necessity for a tradeoff between efficiency and equity.

The fifth and sixth stages of the decision approach primarily involve the *implementation process and follow-up* (Mazmanian and Sabatier 1981; Williams et al. 1982). As previously noted in the discussion of decision styles, a manager who adopts either an autocratic or democratic style may be faced with a different set of issues in implementation. If his or her priority is the relative quality of the decision as opposed to its likelihood of acceptance, then an autocratic approach is called for. This would entail an additional expenditure of time in the implementation phase by having to convince others that the decision is necessary and should be followed. On the other hand, if the priority is acceptance of the decision as opposed to its quality, then a democratic approach is appropriate. In this case, implementation is significantly eased as others are brought into the decision process. In both cases, the individual may be trading off time at certain phases of the process.

The final stage of the process, *evaluation and feedback*, is perhaps the weakest phase of the entire process. In the public sector, this is particularly critical as tools of formal program and service evaluation still tend to be rudimentary and under the control of such groups as the Office of Management and Budget, the United States General Accountability Office, and the Congressional Budget Office. Certain states and localities also have companion organizations (e.g., legislative post-audit organizations), but in general, formal feedback and evaluative mechanisms for most public managers are not widely in place, giving way in most instances to such evaluative means as legislative oversight, hearings, and the like. To improve this last phase, effort is needed to tie such evaluation to the previously articulated standards as well as the initial problem or issue.

Understanding differences in decision-making styles may be enlightening, and having a rational framework to guide the decision-making process may provide useful structure for resolving and solving problems. However, most complex decisions are messy and require real trade-offs. One method has been suggested for simplifying the complexity of decisions (Hammond, Keeney, and Raiffa 1998).

IV. FIVE MAJOR CONTRIBUTIONS TO DECISION-MAKING

Attempting to select five tools, concepts, or frameworks that are current and useful for decision-making in public administration is difficult at best. Others might select a different set of tools. We have selected three recent and emerging tools for management, which include value chain analysis, knowledge management, and e-government. In addition, we have included two older tools that have important staying power for managers: benefit-cost analysis, and strategic planning and management. The tools will be discussed in this order. Our intent is to provide a brief overview, including some references and Web links that will be useful to readers so they might conduct their own more in-depth searches.

A. SUPPLY CHAIN MANAGEMENT

The field of supply chain management has contributed a great deal to the field of public sector decision-making. Yet, prior to looking to its various applications, it must be clearly defined. Actually, the concept and roots of its origin are embedded in systems logic and theory (Simon 1973, 1980). This would entail such notions as: holism, synergy, feedback, and negative entropy. Of particular note is the fact that subsequent decision-making tools, such as total quality management, management by objectives, and even re-engineering, utilize similar systems logic concepts.

The concept of *holism* implies that one examine the entire enterprise and not simply a singular aspect. As an example, for a transit authority in a municipality to assess the effectiveness of its bus system without looking at the trade-offs in highways, subways, light-rail etc., means that the analysis would be inherently flawed. Indeed, most jurisdictions today adopt a multimodal approach—particularly given the costs associated with upgrading the overall transportation infrastructure. To put it in more basic terms, one wants to look at the forest as opposed to the trees. Supply chain management emphasizes a similar point.

Synergy is another concept that is basic to supply chain management as well as the other techniques that were previously listed. To paraphrase the infamous $1 + 1 = 3$, synergy addresses the issue of how one leverages resources in the most cost-effective manner. Given the pressure on the public sector to do more with less, this becomes more acute. For example, a number of jurisdictions have changed their voting systems. Rather than go to a designated polling precinct that needs to be staffed and operated under established dates and times, one can vote by mail or at their neighborhood grocery store. Indeed, voting by the Internet is not too far from becoming a common reality. The direct relevance to supply chain management is the fact that managers are learning to transfer best practices from one area to another. The key will be to develop the best mechanisms for doing so—ranging from formal suggestion systems to informal word-of-mouth or anecdotal evidence.

Feedback systems provide another vital component from systems logic and theory. As such, the notion is that any effective system—whether a municipality, federal agency, or state entity—receives information from its constituency and responds accordingly. For governmental organizations, feedback has tended to be reactive in nature. Constituents vote in someone else or decide to litigate. But governmental bodies, in some cases as a result of this passive approach, have made significant strides to be proactive. The Internal Revenue Service, for a long time the target of politicians' as well as taxpayers' wrath, has made a concerted effort to strengthen its image by utilizing focus groups, soliciting feedback, and providing taxpayers with the name and identification of its personnel. Building code inspectors in several municipalities now provide cards to their clients for a contact point if any difficulties are encountered.

The final systems concept is *negative entropy*. What this refers to is the fact that entropic organizations exhaust all of their resources and eventually cease to exist. Negative entropy, obviously, is the reverse. This means that organizations will do whatever it takes to survive and, hopefully, grow. This can be done through a variety of means—engaging in strategic alliances, finding a partner, merging resources with another enterprise, and the like. Indeed, the classic example is the March of Dimes. It was originally established in the 1950s to cure polio, which, at the time, was a serious illness affecting the population. A cure (i.e., vaccine) for polio was developed and the disease was eradicated. The March of Dimes, based on its mission, should have ceased to exist. Rather than terminating the organization, those in the lead chose to broaden its mission to work toward the eradication of birth defects. In other words, it engaged in a form of goal displacement—broadening its mission and goal to capture new opportunities, funding sources, and additional constituents. In terms of governmental organizations, Henry Kaufman (1968) observed the same phenomenon. Kaufman examined several agencies over a period of decades and administrations. He found that, on balance, very few federal agencies were terminated. Rather, they were subsumed by other branches and divisions or changed their goal or mission (i.e., goal displacement) as a survival mechanism.

To summarize then, the concept of supply chain management is not something that is relatively new. While the specific name may be unique, its roots are embedded in a number of long-held concepts.

1. Origins of Supply Chain Management

The exact origins and roots of the concept of supply chain management are somewhat murky. Some professionals and academics trace its roots to the Malcolm Baldrige Award in which organizations developed several metrics related to total quality management and competed for national and international recognition. Others claim that national competitiveness was a driving factor—as the emphasis for public productivity became the touchstone of federal, state, and local governments. Still others feel that the concept was a fundamental strategic issue—one that could be applied to any organization, public or private. Indeed, this last observation probably has the most merit and is based on the works of Michael Porter (1983, 1985).

One of the issues that Porter raises is that the concept of supply chain management is misleading and implies that the focus of the organization should be on suppliers and vendors. Porter expands this notion to a concentration on *value systems*. As such, the organization looks at the broader concept of how to achieve value—upstream, internally, and downstream—consistent with the systems logic emphasis on holism and synergy. Value can also be viewed in broader terms. Indeed, Porter states that every facet of the organization should be providing value; if it isn't, it should be changed or eliminated. In considering any governmental organization, value could be several things: having skilled personnel, delivering a service in a timely or cost-effective manner, reducing waste or duplication, budgetary savings, and the like.

A value system can also be fairly simple or complex, depending on the organization. For example, if it is the Division of Parks and Recreation, the suppliers and vendors may be those that provide recreation equipment, nursery stock, etc. The Division then provides a variety of programs and services to multiple constituents, such as private individuals, school districts, or clubs. The value system becomes fairly straightforward and routine. Conversely, the Department of Health and Human Services would have multiple suppliers and vendors as well as a more complex set of constituents, such as individuals, Health Maintenance Organizations, nursing establishments, or businesses.

Embedded in value systems are *value chains*. The value chain consists of three primary areas: primary activities, support activities, and margin. The sector of *margin* is really the residual of both the support and primary activities. Simply stated, margin refers to the fact that whatever savings in efficiencies occur in either primary or secondary sectors, the savings go straight to the bottom line. In other words, it reduces your cost of operations—the lower the cost of operation, the greater the difference. For private sector organizations, this translates to margins which can either be passed along to the customer, reinvested in the enterprise, or paid as dividends to investors. For public organizations, the gain in margin presents a different scenario. This could mean that they will need to ask for fewer resources in the future, or the gains would revert back to the general revenue. Several years ago, the Public Works Department for the City of Detroit actually adopted the intriguing concept of *productivity bargaining*. Productivity bargaining, which was actually included in the collective bargaining agreement, referred to the fact that portions of whatever savings that were incurred as a result of productivity suggestions would be allocated both to the workers in pay increases and to the department. Two departments, solid waste disposal and snow removal, were cited as examples of this initiative. This concept also has roots in the notion of *gainsharing*, a concept popularized in the United States in the 1930s with the Scanlon Plan. Gainsharing received attention with the popularity of Japanese management techniques. Briefly stated, productivity improvement suggestions and gains are distributed both to the team that originated and implemented the suggestions as well as to the organization itself. This makes it an obvious win–win situation. In sum, then, margins are a result of adding value to the organization.

The other key sector in value chain management is *primary activity*. Primary activity refers to the core organizational activity. In the Department of Motor Vehicles, the primary activity is issuing licenses and titles. In the Internal Revenue Service, the primary activity is collecting taxes from individuals and corporations. Primary activities include: inbound logistics, operations, outbound logistics, marketing and sales, and service.

Inbound logistics refers to those value activities associated with getting and receiving raw goods and supplies. Drawing heavily from the concept of supply chain, a number of organizations have achieved significant efficiencies in this area:

> The commercial airline industry, including certain manufacturers, suppliers, and airlines, are using leading-edge practices to improve logistics operations and reduce costs. Some manufacturers are providing aircraft parts to their customers on a just-in-time basis, and suppliers are assuming inventory management responsibilities for airlines and manufacturers ... In recognition of increasing budgetary pressures, the changing global threat, and the need for radical improvements in its logistics system, the Air Force has begun a reengineering program aimed at redesigning its logistics operations (US General Accounting Office 1996).

Recalling the earlier discussion on value systems, organizations are seeking to develop a strong relationship with their suppliers and vendors. This is in stark contrast to previous practices in which agencies put items out for bid. While often achieving low prices, quality was often sacrificed; and, ironically, more costs were incurred to correct the deficiencies in quality. Several value activities are possible in inbound logistics—ranging from certification of suppliers for Six Sigma, negotiating volume discounts, training suppliers, or having suppliers visit the organization. A few organizations, such as National Cash Register (NCR), have taken this one step further. Several years ago, NCR introduced the practice of *stakeholder alliances.* They would invite their key suppliers to the business and share their strategy for the future. This practice not only enabled them to forge a closer relationship, but it forced their suppliers to think of where they were going. If they wanted to do future business, they had to become a value-added partner and share ideas and suggestions for mutual benefit. There is nothing to prohibit this from taking place in the public sector. For several years, public entities had to place their supply and vendor needs out for competitive bidding. Many agencies have now changed this practice, and they now can engage in a no-bid contract as long as there is a demonstrated need for doing so.

Operations, the second activity in the primary sector, is what Porter refers to as the transformation phase. In this area, raw goods are transformed into a product and service. For most service organizations, e.g., public works, this is one of the more critical areas. In terms of specific value activities, it can involve several actions. Automating a process that was previously done manually is a classic transformation activity. Indeed, technology can also be leveraged here—witness the use of the Internet to do a variety of activities. Renewing driver licenses through the Web has allowed many jurisdictions to save dollars in staffing several offices. At the same time, individuals do not have to take time off or re-arrange schedules. The State of Colorado enhanced their air emissions program by providing drive-through portable monitoring stations, often located near a major highway intersection, for those renewing auto emissions tests. Rather than drive to one of a number of emission station locations, drivers can perform their emissions test on the way to work. Operations also involve a number of *quality assurance* and *quality control* activities. Indeed, many organizations have now shifted the focus from quality control procedures, whose emphasis was on monitoring and corrective action, to quality assurance. Quality assurance is more of an educational process in which employees are trained on the importance of doing it right the first time. It also seeks to empower employees to take corrective action on the spot and to be proactive.

Outbound logistics, the third sector in primary activities, involves the mechanics of delivering the product. For service organizations, this will usually entail payment for services already delivered in the operations stage. For others, this entails achieving efficiencies in packaging, tracking, and timely delivery. For private sector organizations, close ties with their distribution channels can give them a competitive advantage—witness the use of UPS and FedEx by many businesses to ensure on-time shipping and delivery. For the public sector, the United States Postal Service best emulates this—with different forms of express delivery, depending on the needs of the client. Again, organizations need to clearly articulate their needs in the value delivery system.

Marketing and sales, the fourth sector in primary activities, is particularly unique in the public sector. Many critics feel that the public sector does not need to market itself—given the fact that it is a monopoly and has a captive constituency. In today's environment of restricted resources and, in many cases, voter referendums and ballot initiatives, the need to be proactive in image management is a necessity. Value activities here may entail several actions. For example, a local Parks and Recreation Department may publicize the activities they provide for after-school hours and weekend events. In several states, a portion of revenue from lotteries is allocated to a number of public organizations. Therefore, states will actively market their respective lotteries. This can raise state governments to a different level of activity as they engage in active economic development activities—trying to attract various businesses. Or consider the various tourism ads that states are running to promote recreation and tourism in their locality.

Service, the final sector, should be expanded to include service and support. What this means is that once a service is provided, the organization's involvement is not finished; it may still provide follow-up, complaint resolution, or further support. Many public sector organizations are beginning to realize that the support from their constituents can give them a competitive advantage in securing support as well as justifying future expenditures. One recommendation here is that there should be more proactive measures in this value activity. Rather than assume that the service is necessary, public entities should solicit formal feedback that can further assist service delivery.

The final sector of the value chain, *support activities*, typically is referred to as overhead. While many view this area as an added cost of doing business, a number of organizations have achieved value in this area as well. First of all, this area has a number of activities that are critical—human resources management, finance, accounting, procurement, research and development, and the like. The organization needs to determine how they can give greater value to their primary activities. In addition, several agencies have decided to outsource a few of their support functions—finding a partner who can provide the support service more efficiently:

> Between now and 2007, the federal government will spend $56 billion on outsourcing its information technology services. During this period, IT outsourcing is expected to grow 18% annually, from $8 billion in fiscal 2002 to $14.8 billion in 2007.... This involves a commitment from the program offices to performance-based contracting (Washington Technology 2003).

2. Practices and Applications

There is a robust and growing community of practices regarding supply chain management. Professional groups include the Supply Chain Council and the Institute for Supply Chain Management. Professional journals include the *Journal of Supply Chain Management*, the *Supply Chain Management Review*, *Supply Chain Management: An International Journal*, *Supply Chain Forum: An International Journal*, and *Supply Chain Systems Magazine*. Besides degree programs with specializations in supply chain management, there are centers and research groups focusing on supply chain management. For example, the Center for Public Policy and Private Enterprise at the University of Maryland includes as one of its program areas the modernization of government supply chain management. Another such center is the Supply Chain Management Research Center, which includes a number of topic areas related to supply chain management.

Adoption by government units has been more problematic. The shift to information-based supply chain systems in the public sector has met with more resistance and has moved far more slowly than in the private sector. *Transforming Government Supply Chain Management* (Gesler and Luby 2003) is an example of research directed to promote and enhance the adoption of supply chain systems in government. Korosec (2003) provides guidance in terms of identifying the components of supply chain management and suggests how it may be used to enhance productivity in public procurement. Other countries are also making efforts to adopt supply chain management systems. For example, Parker (2005) assesses the acceptance of e-procurement in the public sector in Great Britain, while Stringer (2004) examines the challenges faced by the National Health Service in Great Britain.

3. Future Trends and Implications

Clearly, supply chain management is not a fad that will quickly disappear. As previously mentioned, it is imbedded in a number of critical activities and processes. Public sector managers need to make a concerted effort to do the following:

Educate employees and stakeholders. One of the cardinal principles of any quality improvement effort is that people need to understand what quality and value look like. Most people tend to view it either in terms of financial returns or cost savings. It is much broader than this. It can include quality in our operating systems, the people that are hired, skills training and development, the manner in which we are structured, and similar efforts.

Closely examine the current processes and systems. Too often, we assume that the current delivery system is the only way or manner in which the process can be done. Many organizations and agencies are re-examining this and are seeking to explore new delivery systems—witness the use today of the Internet to replace the method of many transactions. This is not to imply that this should replace human interaction. Yet, it can be utilized to enhance many functions and activities.

Institute changes quickly and openly communicate. Whether it is re-engineering, total quality management, or supply chain management, most professionals advocate that radical changes should be made quickly, rather than drawn out over a protracted period of time. This accomplishes several objectives. First, employees realize that management is indeed serious about making significant changes to current organizational processes and systems. Second, if the change is made quickly, employees will not be able to resist such change or wait it out. Finally, open communication about the broader context that requires the change will allow employees to understand the motivating factors. Absent this communication, there is a tendency to develop wild fantasies and motives—based on false information.

Continually assess and evaluate activities. Finally, any manager must view supply chain management as a continuous process—in which activities are examined constantly for further improvement. Many managers make the mistake of seeing this as a one-time effort that the organization engages in. Rather, employees must always look for further ways in which activities can be improved and ways to add (rather than subtract) value. The organization must also be willing to experiment with change and innovate. If it works fine the first time, that is great. If not, one should evaluate what didn't work and learn from it.

B. KNOWLEDGE MANAGEMENT

Knowledge management (KM) is not a single algorithm or a simple linear process for making decisions, but it is a concept or tool that is becoming increasingly recognized as valuable and useful for organizations. KM might be thought of generally as an array of strategies or tools to capture, protect, and expand what is being recognized as the most valuable asset of organizations, the intellectual capital or knowledge in the organization. The techniques in use are often associated with e-government and new digital technologies. The core idea, like many other decision-making tools, however, is not entirely new. Any good organization has always recognized the importance and value of preserving and expanding the know-how of those in the organization. But knowledge was typically not treated as a fundamental asset like capital and labor. Today, however, there is growing awareness that the funded experience and knowledge of those in the organization is perhaps the most important asset, and that systematic efforts should be taken to protect and enhance this knowledge asset.

1. Definitions and Elements

As far back as 1975, the *Public Administration Review* published a symposium on KM, in which the authors stated, "The authors share a conviction that man's ability to manage knowledge is of central importance in contemporary public administration" (Carroll and Henry, 567). Many have provided various definitions and statements to capture the basic idea in either business or government contexts.

The editors of *Knowledge Praxis* state:

> At *Knowledge Praxis*, we define knowledge management as a business activity with two primary aspects:
>
> - Treating the knowledge component of business activities as an explicit concern of business reflected in strategy, policy, and practice at all levels of the organization.
> - Making a direct connection between an organization's intellectual assets—both explicit [recorded] and tacit [personal know-how]—and positive business results (Barclay and Murray 2006).

In practice, knowledge management often encompasses identifying and mapping intellectual assets within the organization, generating new knowledge for competitive advantage within the organization, making vast amounts of corporate information accessible, sharing of best practices, and technology that enables all of the above—including groupware and intranets.

Several concepts or elements are useful and important for understanding knowledge management. The concepts are discussed in various contexts, but the following are drawn largely from Grover and Davenport (2001) and Zack (1999a, b).

Knowledge. Philosophers have engaged in debates and analyses as far back as Plato and Aristotle in terms of understanding knowledge, whether it is possible to achieve knowledge, different types of knowledge, and the process by which humans may achieve or approximate knowledge (central questions of epistemology). Sidestepping those debates, in the context of KM, knowledge can generally be understood at the end of a continuum that begins with data, moves to information, and then to knowledge as the highest and most complex terminus of the continuum. Data might be all the transactions, including date and time, for all payments of tax bills. Information can be thought of as the aggregation of the data in terms of general payment patterns of the public in terms of predicting revenue streams. Knowledge might be a broad understanding of the likely reasons for these payment patterns and the implications for cash flow in the organization.

Explicit and tacit knowledge. This distinction has its origins with the philosopher Michael Polyanyi (1962), but it has been notably applied to business by Nonaka and Takeuchi, among others (Nonaka 1991, 1994; Nonaka and Takeuchi 1995). *Explicit knowledge* is characterized by being able to be codified, documented, transferred, and shared. Examples of explicit knowledge include business plans, patents, customer lists, procedure manuals for employees, or product manuals for customers. *Tacit knowledge*, on the other hand, is more subjectively and subconsciously understood and applied. It is more difficult to articulate, formalize, and codify. It is developed more from direct and interactive experience and shared more from interactive conversation. An example might be how to effectively navigate a desired change in the organization, knowing all the subtleties and key players in the organization. KM tries to leverage both explicit and tacit knowledge in organizations.

Knowledge processes. Included here would be *knowledge generation*, or processes by which knowledge is created and acquired in the organization. *Knowledge codification* "involves the conversion of knowledge into accessible and applicable formats" (Grover and Davenport 2001, 7–8). *Knowledge transfer* can be considered the process by which knowledge is shifted from one group to another or from generation to application or codification.

Communities of practice. The idea here is that knowledge is generated by individuals who form communities with shared interests. Organizations are advanced by fostering such *communities of practice*, either formally or simply by creating environments where such creation and sharing can occur.

Knowledge markets. This concept simply recognizes that knowledge is an asset or a good that is valued, may be protected by its possessors in organization, and may be exchanged for other goods such as money, position, or even other knowledge in a barter-like arrangement.

2. Practices and Applications

KM is typically associated with information technology tools that increase collaboration and information sharing in organizations, but KM should perhaps be thought of as a business practice concept rather than a technology-based concept (Santosus and Surmac 2004). Moreover, because "... all new knowledge stems from people" (Grover and Davenport 2001), it can be argued that KM must fundamentally be about managing people rather than technology tools.

KM practices have focused on developing and using information technologies that relate to acquiring, categorizing, storing, and distributing knowledge in organizations. These KM tools might include collaborative tools for identifying and sharing knowledge in organizations. Categories of such KM tools include: "knowledge repositories, expertise access tools, e-learning applications, discussion and chat technologies, synchronous interaction tools, and search and data mining tools" (Santosus and Surmacz 2004). But to reiterate, all the practices are directed toward identifying, codifying, sharing, and utilizing knowledge in organizations.

One can categorize different organizational approaches to KM (Rubenstein-Montano et al. 2001). One approach is to distinguish between codification and personalization (Hansen et al. 1999). *Codification* involves those strategies to capture knowledge of those who possess it and formally codify the knowledge for others to use in the organization. *Personalization* strategies, on the other hand, involve leaving knowledge with those who possess it but creating systems, networks, or interactions that will provide for that knowledge to be transferred or exchanged when it is needed in the organization. Organizations may propose to adopt some combination of these approaches, as suggested for federal government agencies (Buchwalter 2000). Another way to think about KM approaches is to distinguish technology-based, culture-based, or information-based strategies (Alavi and Leidner 1999). The fundamental idea here is the relative emphasis that organizations adopt in managing knowledge, i.e., technology infrastructure, the culture and interactions of individuals, or the actual information or knowledge in the system.

It is estimated that the US government will increase spending at a compound growth rate of 9% on knowledge management products, growing from $820 million in Fiscal Year (FY) 2003 to $1.3 billion in FY 2008. The growth will occur to a great degree in the Department of Homeland Security, but the Department of State and the Department of Justice also plan heavy investments in KM (D'Alessandro 2003). The Department of Homeland Security is a natural fit for adopting KM strategies. Tools to share information and knowledge quickly become critical when responding quickly to terrorist threats. Other agencies face different kinds of reasons for adopting KM strategies. For example, there is an intellectual capital crisis in the federal government due to retirements, early retirements, unfilled vacancies, and hiring freezes (Barr 2000). Hence, KM becomes an important tool for stemming the flow of valuable knowledge from organizations, and by implication, from the public communities that depend on those government agencies. Various examples of KM strategies can be seen in government.

The US Navy created Navy Knowledge Online (NKO), which is an enterprise KM and learning portal that serves as a vehicle for sailors to find the information and knowledge they need to further their careers. The Social Security Administration conducted a survey of KM awareness as well as an audit that included a set of recommendations for improving KM in the organization

(Rubenstein-Montano et al. 2001). Not surprisingly, the recommendations incorporated technology-based, culture-based, and information-based strategies. The recommendations included: the possible establishment of a Knowledge Transfer Department, the creation of yellow pages of individuals with expertise in the organization, the formation of knowledge repositories of best and worst practices in the organization, and the establishment of a Knowledge Exchange as a way of creating communities of practice within the organization. Other efforts focus on establishing a formal position to champion KM.

One of the increasingly common organizational approaches is to create Chief Knowledge Officers (CKO) to oversee KM efforts in organizations. The first US government official to be given such a title was Dr. Shereen Remez, Chief Knowledge Officer of the General Services Administration (Yu and Hartman 2000). Such CKOs can be found at the US Coast Guard, Veteran Affairs, the General Services Administration, the military services, and some smaller agencies. Distinct from Chief Information Officers (CIOs), CKOs focus on leveraging the tacit and explicit knowledge in organizations, rather than record keeping and keeping hardware and software systems secure and up to date. Other examples of success for KM can be seen in government in the US and elsewhere around the world.

The Federal Highway Administration created a community of practice around the issue of rumble strips, the bumps on the sides of highways designed to reduce off-road crashes. At a cost of $75,000 the FHA estimates that 50 crashes were prevented at a cost savings to society of $2.6 million. The United Kingdom (UK) has developed a Knowledge-Enhanced Government strategy that involves the UK Knowledge Network. One use of the network has been the Networked Learning Communities, created by the UK National College for School Leadership. The purpose is to share learning, experiences, and knowledge among 600 schools in the UK (Neilson and McCrea 2002). The National Informatics Center in India is involved in steering information in over 500 districts. An Intranet portal (Offerings) was created to facilitate a knowledge sharing culture. The portal includes a search engine, a document-sharing feature, mailing lists, yellow pages that identify personnel with expertise, online chats, and other functions. Offerings is accessed by more than 3000 employees from over 600 locations (Misra et al. 2003). In Canada the Treasury Board Secretariat has created a position of executive director of Corporate Renewal and Knowledge Management. Among the activities is a notable meta-knowledge-like application. The organization consults with other knowledge officers around the world in terms of best practices and strategies for knowledge sharing and creation. One of their initiatives is the creation of a best kept secrets site (Nicholson-O'Brien 2000). Yet other applications have been to police practices in Singapore (Luen and Al-Hawamdeh 2001), as well as urban poverty (Hjorth 2003).

3. Benefits, Challenges, Keys to Success, and Further Sources

The benefits of successful KM can be many and varied. Benefits can include the following: fostering innovation through the free flow of ideas, improving customer service, enhancing employee retention, and streamlining operations and reducing the associated costs (Santosus and Surmacz 2004).

In terms of factors that are important for the success of KM, Han (2001) identifies effective leadership, the commitment of resources, alignment of KM with the organizational strategy, and a focus on people rather than technology as those that are most important.

Some challenges of implementing KM have been suggested by Santosus and Surmacz (2004). One challenge is getting employees on board. Asking employees to surrender their tacit knowledge can be a significant challenge, because it is this very knowledge that may make these individuals valuable in the organization. Another challenge involves allowing technology to determine or drive KM. As has been stated above, KM should be driven by the people and strategy of the organization. Yet there is a great temptation to simply implement a set of new technologies that may or may not be appropriate in creating an effective KM system. Another challenge is to keep KM evolving and fluid. Knowledge is constantly changing in relation to the organization, and so there needs to be an attitude and system that embraces change and new knowledge, including systems to facilitate and capture knowledge.

Web searches will yield a considerable body of sites and sources. A resource recommended as the best resource site by *KM World* is WWW Virtual Library on Knowledge Management. Periodicals include *KM World, Knowledge Management Magazine, KM Review, the Journal of Knowledge Management,* and *Knowledge Praxis.* There is a growing wealth of information available related to this concept and approach that managers may find useful.*

C. e-GOVERNMENT

Since the mid-1990s, governments have been executing major initiatives in order to tap the vast potential of the Internet for the distinct purpose of improving and perfecting the governing process. Like the personal computer, the Internet has become an indispensable tool in the day-to-day administration of government.

Both government and industry today are waging a fierce inner battle to provide efficient and cost-effective services, solutions, and products to their respective customers (Association for Federal Information Resources Management 2001). To do otherwise in this cost-conscious era would be viewed by some as tantamount to failure—at a minimum it would certainly be subject to review.

Broadly defined, e-government can include virtually all information and communication technology platforms and applications in use by the public sector. For the purpose of this chapter, e-government is defined as: "utilizing the internet and the world-wide-web for delivering government information and services to citizens" (United Nations Division for Public Economics and Public Administration and American Society for Public Administration 2002).

1. Existing Environment

E-government is not about technology or hosting thousands of Web sites with millions of pages. It is about providing services and products to citizens when and where they want them. It is about creating greater efficiencies across government and about citizen access and government accountability.

Yet, e-government is replete with obstacles. First and foremost, funding is an issue— particularly when additional funds are being used to solve similar problems repetitively. Second, industry is offering expensive e-government solutions; given the constraint on most budgets today, finding discretionary funds becomes a Herculean task. Third, top management leadership has not done an effective job of articulating its vision as well as a clear set of priorities. The federal government has several e-government success stories, but unfortunately, they are relatively limited to accessing and sharing information. What are really needed are success stories where agencies are making the transformation to realize the potential of e-government.

The greatest return on e-government is realized when similar functions in an organization are combined and put online. Employees, customers, and business partners have easy access to the same information and systems are not duplicated for each division, bureau, or office. However, the primary obstacle to implementing agency-wide and government-wide electronic services and practices is the stove-piped organization of agencies. In addition, the business processes that agencies have created match those stovepipes (Association for Federal Information Resources Management 2002).

---

*Other Web sites include www.brint.com and www.kmresource.com (locating the Knowledge Management Resource Center), and www.km.gov, which is the official KM site of the US government, supported by the Federal CIO Council. For case studies and examples one might visit www.kmresource.com/exp_cases.htm that includes cases on the Tennessee Valley Authority the US Department of Defense.

The stovepipes are promoted through the congressional agency funding process, which only fund individual programs. This process does not promote cross-agency programs, which are typically the e-government services and practices. In addition, incentives—such as financial rewards or performance measures—for government employees to reach across stovepipes to work with colleagues on e-government services do not exist.

In five years, agencies will be less bound by stovepipes and better able to work more easily with colleagues to develop and deploy electronic services and applications. This collaboration will be facilitated by a capital funding process that allows cross-agency, cross-government e-government functions to be created and funded.

To transform the organizational structure so that e-government implementation is more successful, the Federal government must institute a combination of employee and managerial rewards for those who encourage out-of-the-stovepipe e-government application development. New organizations that permit cross-agency funding for e-government solutions should be created. Stovepipes are institutionalized, and only with strong incentives and recognition will the obstacles be removed.

One suggestion is to create a clearinghouse for e-government projects. These projects would be thoroughly analyzed and funded. This clearinghouse would help determine which projects would warrant funding, based on performance measures and capital planning mechanisms. Congress would have a corresponding group to discuss and analyze the proposals.

In general, there appears to be an insufficient number of qualified personnel at both the technical and management levels to accelerate the transition to e-government. This can be attributed to natural market forces; that is, such skilled personnel can receive higher compensation and benefits in the private sector. Further, most managers in the public sector (as well as the private sector) have not been able to keep pace with the rapid pace of technology. This is not an indictment of the system. Rather, most managers are dealing with the vagaries of organizational policies and procedures. Finally, the entire annual budget process and lack of local agency control also hinders transformation.

2. Practices and Applications

In spite of the various obstacles to the promise of e-government, the UN Global E-Government Readiness Report of 2004 ranks the United States at the top their list, based on the state of e-government readiness and the extent of e-government participation (Swartz 2005). Of the 191 member states assessed, Denmark and Great Britain followed the US, and generally the report concluded that governments worldwide had made rapid progress in terms of embracing e-government technologies. A case study in the UK details the process of constructing an e-government organization and the attendant issues related to constructing an e-government identity (Beynon-Davis 2005). Asian countries are moving forward with e-government initiatives. South Korea, for example, has begun an e-government for foreigners, available to both businesses and individuals by 2007 (Swartz 2005).

In terms of e-government initiatives in the US, it is estimated that $4 billion was spent on e-government solutions in 2004 (Aitoro 2005). And that amount is expected to skyrocket, one estimate putting the increase at 38% by 2009 (Public Administration Times 2005). Yet, in spite of such spending, a study by Brown University found that issues of broken links and accessibility were all too common (Aitoro 2005). At the local level there are initiatives to make digital cities. An interview with the chief financial officer of Virginia City Beach, Virginia, revealed various initiatives both to cut costs and improve government efficiencies. However, once moving in the e-government direction, one of the liabilities is that expectations increase and demand for IT is outstripping their ability to deliver. Virginia Beach alone is operating some 4000 computers and 250 software packages (McEachern 2005). Other studies examine issues such as the usability and accessibility of e-government to different populations. For example, one project looked at web pages for 50 state and 50 federal agencies, in terms of potential barriers for older adults (Communications of the ACH 2005).

Interest in e-government has spawned a series of articles on E-Government II in the *Bulletin of the American Society for Information Science and Technology*, including topics regarding best practices for digital government (Brueckner 2005), best practices in Michigan local government (Hammerman 2005), user-centered design for e-government software (Boersma 2005), and impact on openness, transparency, and interactivity (Porte 2005). The impact of e-government on citizen trust and democratic institutions is a crucial issue for the design and implementation of e-government strategies (Carter and Belanger 2005; West 2004). And the International City Managers Association (ICMA, 2005) has conducted a survey of cities and counties on their e-government initiatives. Because of the disparate initiatives and lack of structure, some have argued for and offered a framework for assessing, categorizing, and comparing e-government initiatives (Grant and Chau 2004). Others have begun to examine the general benefits and advantages of e-government (Foley 2005) and the effect on democracy or the movement toward e-democracy (Maher and Krimmer 2005).

There are numerous government and private organizations emerging to deal with issues related to e-government. The Center for Digital Government, for example, is a national research and advisory institute focused on information technology policies and best practices in state and local government. The University of Southern California has a Center for E-Government that publishes the *Journal of E-Government*. There is a President's Management Council Subcommittee on E-Government. The Cyberspace Policy Research Group (CyPRG), at the University of Arizona, Tucson and George Mason University, "studies diffusion and use of World Wide Web in governments worldwide, particularly in terms of organizational openness and internal effectiveness" (Cyberspace Policy Research Group 2005). Other relevant publications include *Electronic Journal of E-Government*, *Government Computer News,* and *Government Technology Magazine.* The number of organizations and professional publications seems to be growing as fast as e-government itself.

3. Going Forward

A new wave of people with e-government experience will enter the public service. By 2007, the budget process will be modified at the federal level to provide multi-year funding for e-government initiatives, both internal to an agency and cross-agency. In addition, funding for e-government must become a priority. Once funded, and to prove that the money was well spent, matrices must be in place against which gathered data and results can be measured.

Up to this point, legislative actions such as the Government Performance and Results Act and the Government Paperwork Elimination Act have not had a significant impact on successful e-government implementations. What is needed is concerted leadership. The technology is available; enabling of the technology is critical. Congress is still unsure of agency capabilities to properly execute an e-government vision. Agencies will have to develop and present a solid business case to aggressively pursue true transformational initiatives.

Immediate initiatives that should be implemented to resolve resource issues include hiring new managers who have a broad range of IT and organizational skills; increasing job exchange programs with industry; creating a mechanism to fund government/industry R&D e-business collaboration; and creating an Office of Management and Budget (OMB) centered working group comprised of agency change e-government agents.

D. Cost-Benefit Analysis

Benefit-cost analysis or cost-benefit analysis (the terms are frequently interchanged) is an analytical technique that has had a significant impact on decision-making in the public sector. One primary reason for this is that cost-benefit analysis forces managers to articulate the quantitative as well as qualitative aspects of a program or service. Naturally, this process has its limitations and these will be further addressed.

1. Origins

The exact origin of the use of cost-benefit analysis is generally considered to lie within the Army Corps of Engineers in which, according to the Rivers and Harbors Act of 1902, the cost of projects had to be less than the benefits (Meier 1984). The application of this technique to dam and reclamation projects tended to be reasonably straightforward with a clear articulation of the costs associated with actual construction and maintenance. These were subsequently balanced with current and future benefits, usually discounted back to present value. As to the effectiveness of this specific method, little evidence remains today.

Cost-benefit analysis remained fairly dormant until the post-World War II emergence of operations research and management science. It was at this stage that quantitative methods and techniques began to take hold and were applied to a variety of events and situations, ranging from scheduling issues to large-scale project and program planning. As Kenneth Meier notes, the second threshold event for the use of cost-benefit analysis was the formal introduction of program planning and budgeting systems (PPBS) in the federal government—beginning initially within the Defense Department and expanding, by executive order, to other federal agencies. Cost-benefit analysis was frequently used to either justify the expansion/continuation of *specific* programs or make trade-off decisions.

With the phasing out of PPBS after the Johnson administration, the use of cost-benefit analysis became largely dormant until the Carter and Reagan administrations. Two critical events signaled its return. The first was the Federal Paperwork Control Act of 1980:

> The Paperwork Control Act was intended to correct a number of deficiencies in information *manage-ment*. Specifically, it attempted to reduce the burden of information processing on the public and private industry by implementing standards for collecting information (for example, prior approval by the Office of Management and Budget of agency forms). In addition, it established an Office of Federal Information Policy in the OMB to monitor and direct, if necessary, information practices by government agencies (Stevens and McGowan 1985).

With the passage of this legislation, agencies had to carefully assess and justify the paperwork cost of compliance associated with their program or service delivery function.

The second event during this time was the establishment of the Regulatory Analysis Review Group (RARG), which was intended to examine the effects of federal regulation, particularly as it affected smaller businesses. Formed in 1978, RARG represented a concerted effort on the part of the executive branch to exercise control over agency regulatory activities by requiring agencies to formally document and justify new regulations *prior to implementation*. Yet it was not without detractors:

> For their part, critics [of RARG] feared the effects of the new supremacy of economists who, they felt, were bound by their discipline into a new rigidity in which "sound analysis" was equated solely with economic analysis. Capitulating to the RARG standards of balancing costs against benefits meant viewing regulatory policy strictly through the context of White House economists, and in that frame-work, they predicted, cost factors would invariably take precedence over social concerns (Tolchin and Tolchin 1983, 49–50).

As Tolchin and Tolchin go on to explain, the position taken by most critics was that the use of cost-benefit analysis could be supported in selective areas where benefits are difficult to articulate. Under this approach, benefits that cannot be quantified, and subsequently justified, are eliminated from the analysis, resulting in least-cost analysis. Tolchin and Tolchin (1983) cite such extreme examples as attempting to assess the value of the view of the Grand Canyon. Regulatory agencies are now placed in the defensive position of attempting to quantify program areas or elements that involve a high degree of subjective judgment.

Following this effort to use cost-benefit analysis in the regulatory arena are two additional key pieces of legislation: Public Law 96-354, "The Analysis of Regulatory Functions," and Executive Order 12291 (1981). Public Law 96-354 was passed in 1980 and represented an effort by the Carter administration to provide regulatory relief to small entities (i.e., small business). It is significant to the extent to which the OMB is granted direct oversight control of agency regulatory functions and is further charged with ensuring the application of cost-benefit analysis.

Crucial portions of this law include the requirement that agencies must publish a regulatory flexibility agenda in the *Federal Register* twice a year. The purpose of this agenda is for the agency to announce forthcoming rules that are "likely to have a *significant economic impact* on small entities." In addition, regulatory agencies are required to conduct a "regulatory flexibility analysis," which includes: (1) a statement of the need for the rule, (2) a summary of the issues related by public comments, and (3) a description of significant alternatives to the rule that are designed to *minimize* any significant economic impact. Finally, in preparing the flexibility analysis, the agency must provide either a "quantifiable or numerical description of the effects of a proposed rule...or more general descriptive statements if quantification is not practicable or reliable" (Public Law 96-354 1980). The latter descriptive statements have been strongly contested in agency hearings and court proceedings.

Executive Order 12291, which was signed by Ronald Reagan on February 17, 1981, closely followed Public Law 96-354. Also intended as a device to reign in regulatory agency activities, it clearly signaled to executives the approach that was to be adopted. The critical section (Section Two) requires agencies to consider the following when issuing new regulations:

1. Decisions shall be based on adequate information concerning the need for and consequences of proposed government action.
2. Regulatory action shall not be undertaken unless the potential benefits to society from the regulation outweigh the potential costs to society.
3. Regulatory objectives shall be chosen to maximize the net benefits to society.
4. Among the alternative approaches to any given regulatory objective, the alternative involving the least net costs to society shall be chosen.
5. Agencies shall set priorities with the aim of maximizing the aggregate net benefits to society, taking into account the condition of the particular industries affected by regulations, the condition of the national economy, and other regulatory actions contemplated for the future.

Parts three and four above are the critical areas. The executive order not only required agencies to seek to maximize benefits, but they must take into consideration least net costs *at the same time*. The implications of this are clear; a cost-benefit ratio of 1:2 must take precedence over a 2:6 ratio even though the yield of the latter is on the order of threefold as opposed to twofold. In this case, cost considerations are paramount.

2. Applications

The process of applying cost-benefit analysis tends to be fairly straightforward. As Meier (1984) notes, this involves approximately three steps. First, the impacts (direct or indirect) of a program or service are determined. These are generally classified along the lines of either benefits or costs and are subsequently defined as direct (first-order) or indirect (second-order). Let us take, for example, the reduction of air pollution in a metropolitan region. Without listing all possible benefits and costs, a number of principal ones come to mind. The reduction in the number of lung-related incidents could be classified as a direct benefit. The improved health, as a result of the reduction in air pollution, would also translate to such second-order impacts as lower absenteeism and higher productivity.

On the costs side, the immediate costs of compliance (e.g., installation of emission control equipment, oversight, and enforcement) are usually considered first-order costs. Second-order costs may include lost companies or employment opportunities as businesses are either forced to close, move out of the region, or fail to locate in the area as a result of the enforcement program.

Second, a dollar estimate of each benefit and each cost is made. For most costs and benefits, a market price is assigned; those that will occur in the future are subsequently discounted using present-value techniques. The purpose of this technique is to determine what today's dollar investment will yield in the future. In addition, the opportunity costs of investing in the particular program or service should be reflected. This generally refers to the *other* opportunities for the use of those funds which would be foregone as a result. For example, the opportunity costs of the expenditure of $250 million for a dam project would perhaps include $50 million for expanding the power generation capabilities of another existing site.

Perhaps one of the most controversial aspects involved in the assignment of dollars to cost-benefit analysis revolves around the benefits for which there is no clear market value. Here, Meier (1984) suggests several remedies. First, so-called shadow prices can be assigned. Such prices are used when a competitive market does not exist, and the prices are generally higher when the market is subsidized, lower when the market is oligopolistic. So a dollar value is assigned that is either slightly higher or lower than in a competitive market—thereby shadowing the competitive market condition. Another technique is the assignment of value based on a public good. The public good associated with the building of an outer-loop interstate system may be less central-city congestion and, as a consequence, lower rates of automobile accidents.

Finally, certain benefits defy such efforts to be quantified yet are an integral part of the analysis. In our earlier example of the reduction of air pollution in a metropolitan region, a major benefit is improvement of the overall quality of life. Although this concept has as many definitions as people who are asked, it is a factor that must be considered. There are a number of unobtrusive ways of measuring this—ranging from selected neighborhood surveys to determining willingness to pay on the part of the citizenry (Hatry et al. 1973; Webb and Hatry 1973). Unfortunately, this last element has been the most controversial, as previously discussed.

An example of employing cost-benefit analysis is whether to raise federal excise taxes on alcoholic beverages. Adverse effects of alcohol consumption could be improved by raising taxes (cost). Higher taxes should decrease consumption, which will lead to fewer highway fatalities, nonfatal injures, and reductions in health and productivity losses (benefits). This analysis can be found in "An Illustration: Taxing Alcohol to Save Lives" (Weiner and Vining 1989).

3. The Future of Cost-Benefit Analysis

It is difficult to fully address the subtleties of a technique such as cost-benefit analysis. As with any technique or tool, its usefulness comes from the extent to which it is commonly accepted and used. Cost-benefit analysis is not without its critics, and there are those who see its use as one of attempting to limit agency power. Regardless of one's position, there is little doubt that the contribution of cost-benefit has been dramatic (Tolchin and Tolchin 1983). It has challenged public administrators to examine both sides of a program or service, to look at the long-term effects, and finally, to articulate its impact in quantitative as well as qualitative terms.

E.   Strategic Planning and Management

Strategic planning has been considered one of the hot innovations in public and nonprofit management (Berry and Wechsler 1995). While strategic planning and strategic management may be used interchangeably, one can distinguish strategic management as the implementation of strategic plans or the outcomes of strategic planning. Whether planning or implementing, a strategic approach will take a systems perspective by examining essential functions and goals, by analyzing the internal and external conditions and forces on an organization, and by assuming a decision-making framework that uses a time horizon of 1–5 years.

The term strategy has ancient Greek origins having to do with leading an army. What is conveyed by the term is the "idea of critical goals achieved under battle conditions" (Anderson 1994, 339). Business and government managers face some similar issues. They both function in increasingly turbulent environments, both have to manage external and internal conditions, both must design systems and determine directions to achieve goals and objectives. Yet, there are important differences. For business managers the battlefield can be thought of as the marketplace of competition for customers, while government managers compete for a limited pool of public funds. If government agencies follow a competitive business approach, it can lead to "inefficient turf-protecting behavior rather than to better, more cost-effective services" (Anderson 1994, 340). This fundamental difference can have significant impacts on the appropriate model and approach to strategic planning.

1. Definition and Essential Elements

Various definitions have been offered from a variety of sources, including:

> Strategic planning is defined as a systematic process for managing the organization and its future direction in relation to its environment and the demands of external stakeholders, including strategy formulation, analysis of agency strengths and weaknesses, identification of agency stakeholders, implementation of strategic actions, and issue management (Berry and Wechsler 1995).

> Strategic management is … the process for implementing a strategic plan which integrates the organization's goals, policies, and action sequences into a cohesive whole (Halachmi 1992).

> … we define strategic management as a disciplined effort to produce fundamental decisions and actions that shape and guide what an organization (or other entity) is, what it does, and why it does it (Bryson 1989).

Regardless of the specific definition one finds most appealing, there are several elements that any strategic planning approach will contain. We have chosen to focus on three of them.

Assessment of the external environment. Strategic planning will involve an environmental scan that examines the opportunities and threats to the basic mission and goals of the organization (Eadie 1983; Halachmi 1992). Given the turbulent conditions of most organizational environments, the strategic approach will systematically assess the conditions that provide new opportunities or pose new threats to the accomplishment of fundamental goals, if not basic survival, of the organization. This often involves examining the broad economic, political, social, and technological trends influencing developments in today's environment. For example, a university will monitor demographic trends, changing job profiles, and new entrants or competitors in the market.

Assessment of the internal environment. Strategic planning will also involve an assessment of the organization in terms of its strengths and weaknesses. This can be thought of as a resource audit that analyzes the particular assets and liabilities of the organization as they relate to the strategic choices and actions contemplated (Eadie 1983). Such information becomes essential if the choices and implementation of future directions are to be successful. For example, a decision by a university to develop a new degree program without adequate faculty expertise or the resources to acquire expertise in the needed areas is destined to failure. Strategic planning should identify such needs before making such program changes.

Selection of strategic objectives using a systems perspective. Given an awareness of the environments of the organization and a sense of the basic function or purpose of the organization, choices about specific courses of action can be made so that there is a better fit between the organization and the environmental realities. For example, regarding the situation mentioned above, rather that decide to expand degree offerings, a university may redesign the curriculum of an existing program in order to respond to the need for change while drawing upon particular assets of its faculty.

Though we have mentioned only three essential elements, there are other elements of strategic planning and management. For example, another element of strategic planning might be the identification of fundamental goals or a reassessment of the basic mission of the organization. Some argue for goal definition as part of the strategic planning process (e.g., Steiner 1979), while others argue that goal selection and strategy formulation should be separated. Differences between government and business must be considered, however. The ability to change mission in the public sector is more problematic in the public sector because managers are not in a position to make changes in fundamental goals (Stevens and McGowan 1983).

Another analysis (Anderson 1994) identifies five features of a strategic orientation, suggesting that the government or business organization would be: (1) concerned with mission-critical activities, (2) long range in time orientation, (3) looking outward from the organizational boundaries to stakeholders or customers, (4) seeking maximum return on investment rather than minimum economic cost, and (5) placing a high value on technological, human, and information resources.

Strategic planning has emerged as a widely used management tool, with increasing numbers of government agencies adopting some form of strategic planning. Strategic planning is being used at all levels of government. Independent surveys of both municipal managers and state agency managers reported very similar rates of use. Approximately 60% of managers at both state and municipal levels of government reported using some form of strategic planning (Berry and Wechsler 1995). Strategic planning and management has also been aligned with the role of government managers as leaders (Moore 1995).

Citing but a few examples of applications in the public and nonprofit sectors of strategic planning, we include: local economic development (Liou 2000); the development of information technologies in the public sector (Andersen 1994); strategic management at EEOC (Kemp, Funk, and Eadie 1993); city and county planning (Sorkin, Ferris, and Hudak 1984; Thomas, Means, and Grieve 1988; Wheeland 1993); performance measurement and human resource management (Kerr 1994); and applications to nonprofit or third sector organizations (Nutt and Backoff 1992).

2. Approaches to Strategic Planning

While there are common elements of strategic planning, a variety of approaches have been developed. Bryson (1989) has summarized the major private sector approaches to strategic planning. He divides these approaches into process and content. Content approaches include:

1. *Portfolio methods.* Various business of the company is assessed in terms of strategies in relation to each business or part of the portfolio (e.g., MacMillan 1983).
2. *Competitive analysis.* Key forces that shape the business are assessed in terms of developing strategic options (e.g., Porter 1985).
3. *Strategic issues management.* The focus here is on identifying issues that can have a major influence on the business. Strategy development becomes selecting effective ways of managing those issues (e.g., King 1982).

Process approaches, on the other hand, include:

1. *Harvard policy model.* This approach uses strengths, weaknesses, opportunities, and threats (SWOT) analysis, identifying the strengths and weaknesses of the internal elements of the organization, while examining the external environment for opportunities and threats to achieving organizational goals (e.g., Andrews 1980).
2. *Strategic planning systems.* Here managers generally make important decisions across functions and level of the organization. The focus is thought to be on mission, strategies, budgets, and control (e.g., Lorange and Vancil 1976).
3. *Stakeholder management.* This approach identifies critical stakeholders (internal and external) and formulates strategies to deal with each stakeholder group (e.g., Freeman 1984).
4. *Strategic negotiations.* Bargaining and negotiating are used as a process among players for identifying and resolving strategic issues for the organization (e.g., Pettigrew 1977).
5. *Logical incrementalism.* This approach focuses on the importance of small changes in developing and implementing strategies for the organization (e.g., Quinn 1980).
6. *Frameworks for innovation.* The emphasis here is on innovation as a strategy (e.g., Taylor 1984).

As discussed by Galloway (1990) the analysis of the current situation is critical in beginning a meaningful strategic plan. Galloway cites Floyd and Palmer (1985), who argue that a strategic plan should begin with a descriptive account of the mission, objectives, and strategies that characterize the organization. This approach insures that planners begin with how the organization is actually operating, rather than considering what the organization should be without a context. Moreover, they argue for involvement of staff in the early stages of developing a strategic plan. Such an approach emphasizes the importance of maintaining a reality check on what actually characterizes the organization and the importance of involvement and buy-in from employees and staff.

Based on his review of private sector approaches to strategic planning, Bryson draws several conclusions concerning strategic planning in the public and nonprofit sectors. First, strategic planning is not a single concept, procedure, or tool. Second, public sector strategic planning will have to allow for a wide range of planning activities. Third, strategic planning should be tailored to the situation, usually creating a hybrid of other approaches. Fourth, all public and nonprofit planners should possess an awareness and knowledge of strategic planning tools and approaches. Fifth, planners should encompass both the technical and political sides of issues. Sixth, research is needed to increase knowledge of strategic planning in the public and nonprofit sectors.

Bryson (1989) does present a general approach that combines aspects of the private sector approaches discussed above. He presents an approach that he believes is appropriate for public and nonprofit organizations. This approach includes the following eight steps: (1) initiating and agreeing on a strategic planning process, (2) identifying organizational mandates, (3) clarifying organizational mission and values, (4) assessing the external environment: opportunities and threats, (5) assessing the internal environment: strengths and weaknesses, (6) identifying the strategic issues facing an organization, (7) formulating strategies to manage the issues, and (8) establishing an effective organizational vision for the future.

In one other approach, Halachmi (1992) identifies seven steps in a simple model of strategic planning: (1) developing the plan, (2) taking stock, (3) strategic analysis, (4) alternative generation, (5) strategic choices, (6) organization leadership and support, and (7) review and evaluation. Public sector organizations may have to tailor-fit their particular approach to strategic planning and management, especially because many of the strategic approaches were developed for business applications. For example, Andersen (1994) modifies Porter's competitive strategic analysis by developing a collaborative model of analysis that includes providers, clients, entrants, and substitutions in the service environment. Andersen then combines this collaborative analysis with another business approach, the strategic options generator (Wiseman 1985), in creating a strategic approach suitable for public information management applications to public organizations. Hendrick (2003) provides an account of implementing strategic planning at the city level in Milwaukee. Llewellyn and Tappin (2003) explore the growth of strategic planning in the national parks. Irwin (2002) explores the use of strategy mapping and Balanced Scorecard in a public agency. And Kloot and Martin (2000) relate strategic plans and performance measures.

The important point here is that there are a variety of approaches to strategic planning and management, and creative modifications may be necessary for applications to public organizations, depending on the level of government, the kind of service provided, and other relevant factors. Poister and Streib (2005) studied the use of strategic planning in municipal governments of over 25,000 in population. While they did not find a significant increase in the use of strategic management, there was some evidence of a growing sophistication with regard to using strategic planning. Moreover, many European states are now using strategic planning among local governments in their efforts to coordinate and democratize local government (Abram and Cowell 2004). Yet Stewart (2004) argues the strategic management remains under-theorized in the public sector because the issues raised relate to different fields of analysis, namely the political, the policy-related, and the managerial.

V. CONCLUSION

Attempting to identify and summarize five tools in decision-making is a challenging but interesting task. Others would, no doubt, have a different list of decision-making tools and frameworks. Perhaps the key underlying feature of these tools is that they are all created to assist the decision making process to arrive at sound, rational decisions for the organization and its stakeholders. In an environment of constant change and challenge, no single aid for decision-making will be adequate. Managers will need to assess the strengths of various approaches and be prepared to custom design their own particular models and approaches for organizational success (Johnston 1995).

REFERENCES

Abram, S. and Cowell, R., Learning policy—The contextual curtain and conceptual barriers, *European Planning Studies*, 12(2), 209–229, 2004.
Aitoro, J., Redux gov, *VAR Business*, 21, 18–21, 2005.
Alavi, M. and Leidner, D. E., Knowledge management systems: issues, challenges, and benefits, *Communications of the Association for Information Systems*, 1(7), 2–41, 1999.
Andersen, D. F., Strategic information management: conceptual frameworks for the public sector, *Public Productivity and Management Review*, XVII(4), 335–353, 1994.
Andrews, K., *The Concept of Corporate Strategy*, Irwin, Homewood, IL, 1980.
Association for Federal Information Resources Management, *A Blueprint for Successful E-Government Implementation: Steps to Accelerate Cultural Change and Overcome Stakeholder Resistance*, Washington, DC, 2002.
Association for Federal Information Resources Management, *Transformation to an Electronic Environment: The Promise and the Challenge, A Resource Paper*, Washington, DC, 2001.
Barclay, R. and Murray, P., What is Knowledge Management?, http://www.mediaaccess.com/whatis.html (accessed June 22, 2006).
Barr, S., Retirement wave creates vacuum, *The Washington Post*, May 7, 2000.
Beynon-Davies, P., Constructing electronic government: the case of the UK inland revenue, *International Journal of Information Management*, 25(1), 3–21, 2005.
Berry, F. S. and Wechsler, B., State agencies' experience with strategic planning: findings from a national survey, *Public Administration Review*, 55(2), 159–168, 1995.

Boersma, P., E-government II: introducing user-centered design to an e-government software development company, *Bulletin of the American Society for Information Science and Technology*, 31(3), 20–23, 2005.

Brueckner, A., E-government II best practices for digital government, *Bulletin of the American Society for Information Science and Technology*, 31(3), 16–17, 2005.

Bryson, J. M., *Strategic Planning for Public and Nonprofit Organizations*, Jossey-Bass, San Francisco, 1989.

Buchwalter, J., Knowledge management in US federal government agencies: can it work?, In *Proceedings of Information Resources Management Association*, Khosrowpour, M., Ed., Idea Group, Hershey, PA, pp. 465–467, 2000.

Carter, L. and Belanger, F., The utilization of e-government services: citizen trust, innovation, and acceptance factors, *Information Systems Journal*, 15(1), 5–26, 2005.

Cohen, M. and March, J., *Leadership and Ambiguity: The American College President*, Harvard Business School Press, Boston, MA, 1986.

Cyberspace Policy Research Group, http://www.cyprg.arizona.edu/ (accessed March 30, 2005).

Dale, A., Letters from the corporian war zone, *Journal of Information Science*, 27(5), 351–355, 2001.

D'Alessandro, J., Gearing Up to remain on guard, *VAR Business*, 19 (suppl.), 3, 2003.

Dannenbring, D. and Starr, M., *Management Science: An Introduction*, McGraw-Hill, New York, 1981.

Dunn, W., *Public Policy Analysis*, Prentice Hall, Englewood Cliffs, NJ, 1981.

Eadie, D. C., Putting a powerful tool to practical use: the application of strategic planning in the public sector, *Public Administration Review*, 43, 447–452, 1983.

E-Government usability for older adults, *Communications of the ACM*, 48(2), 102–105, 2005.

Federal e-gov spending to increase by 38% over next five years, *PA Times*, 28(2), 1–3, 2005.

Fiedler, F. A., *Theory of Leadership Effectiveness*, McGraw-Hill, New York, 1967.

Floyd, J. and Palmer, D., *Corporate Management in Local Government*, Hargreen Publishing, North Melbourne, Australia, 1985.

Foley, P., The real benefits, beneficiaries, and value of e-government, *Public Money and Management*, 25(1), 4–7, 2005.

Freeman, R. E., *Strategic Management: A Stakeholder Approach*, Pitman, Boston, MA, 1984.

Galloway, I., Strategic management in public sector research organizations: a critical review, *International Journal of Public Sector Management*, 3(1), 5–24, 1990.

Gansler, J. and Luby, R., *Transforming Government Supply Chain Management*, Rowman and Littlefield, Eds., Lanham, MD, 2003.

Gilbert, G. R., Quality improvement in a federal defense department, *Public Productivity and Management Review*, XVI(1), 65–75, 1992.

Grant, G. and Chau, D., Developing a generic framework for e-government, *Journal of Global Information Management*, 13(1), 1–31, 2004.

Grover, V. and Davenport, T.H., Special issue: knowledge management, *Journal of Management Information Systems*, 18(1), 5–21, 2001.

Haberman, S. J., *Analysis of Qualitative Data*, Academic Press, New York, 1978.

Halachmi, A., Strategic management and productivity, In *Public Productivity Handbook*, Holzer, M., Ed., Marcel Dekker, New York, 1992.

Halachmi, A., Strategic planning and management? Not necessarily, *Public Productivity Review*, 20, 35–50, 1986.

Hammerman, C., E-government II: lessons learned in Michigan: best practices for local government, *Bulletin of the American Society for Information Science and Technology*, 31(3), 17–20, 2005.

Hammond, J. S., Keeney, R., and Raiffa, H., Even swaps: a rational method for making trade-offs, *Harvard Business Review*, 137–149, Mar./Apr. 1998.

Han, F., Understanding knowledge management, *Public Manager*, 30(2), 34–36, 2001.

Hansen, M. T., Nohria, H., and Tierney, T., What's your strategy for managing knowledge?, *Harvard Business Review*, 77(2), 106–118, 1999.

Hatry, H., Winnie, R., and Fisk, D., *Practical Program Evaluation for State and Local Government Officials*, The Urban Institute, Washington, DC, 1973.

Hendrick, R., Strategic planning environment, process, and performance in public agencies: a comparative study of departments in Milwaukee, *Journal of Public Administration Research and Theory*, 13(4), 491–520, 2003.

Hjorth, P., Knowledge development and management for urban poverty alleviation, *Habitat International*, 27(3), 381–393, 2003.

ICMA: E-government improves communication and customer service, *Government Finance Review*, 21(1), 5–7, 2005.

Irwin, D., Strategy mapping in the public sector, *Long Range Planning*, 35(6), 637–648, 2002.

Johnston, V. R., Increasing quality and productivity: strategic planning, TQM, and beyond, In *Public Productivity through Quality and Strategic Management*, Halachmi, A. and Bouchaert, G., Eds., IOS Press Amsterdam, 1995.

Kaufman, Henry, *Are Government Organizations Immortal?*, Brookings Institution, Washington, DC, 1968.

Kemp, E. J., Funk, R. J., and Eadie, D. C., Change in chewable bites: applying strategic management at EEOC, *Public Administration Review*, 53(2), 129–134, 1993.

Kerr, D. L., Managing Rosie the Riveter: the work between strategic planning and performance measurement, *Public Productivity and Management Review*, XVII(3), 215–221, 1994.

King, W. R., Using strategic issue analysis, *Long Range Planning*, 15(4), 45–49, 1982.

Kingdon, J., *Agendas, Alternatives, and Public Policies*, Little, Brown, Boston, MA, 1984.

Kloot, L. and Martin, J., Strategic performance management: a balanced approach to performance management issues in local government, *Management Accounting Research*, 11(2), 231–252, 2000.

Korosec, R., Assessing the feasibility of supply chain management within purchasing and procurement, *Public Performance and Management Review*, 27(2), 92–110, 2003.

Kraemer, K. and King, J. L., *Computers and Local Government: A Manager's Guide*, Vol. 2, Praeger, New York, 1977.

Lorange, P. and Vancil, R. F., How to design a strategic planning system, *Harvard Business Review*, 54(5) 75–82, 1976.

Llewellyn, S. and Tappin, E., Strategy in the public sector: management in the wilderness, *Journal of Management Studies*, 40(4), 955–983, 2003.

Liou, K. T., Applying strategic management to economic development: benefits and challenges, *International Journal of Public Administration*, 23(9), 1621–1679, 2000.

Luen, T. W. and Al-Hawamdeh, S., Knowledge management in the public sector: principles and practices in police work, *Journal of Information Science*, 27(5), 311–318, 2001.

Mani, B. G., Old wine in new bottles tastes better: a case study of TQM implementation in the IRS, *Public Administration Review*, 55(2), 147–158, 1995.

McGowan, R. P. and Loveless, S., Strategies for information: the administrator's perspective, *Public Administration Review*, 41, 331–339, 1982.

MacMillan, I., Competitive strategies for not-for-profit agencies, *Advances in Strategic Management*, 1, 61–82, 1983.

Mahrer, H. and Krimer, R., Towards the enhancement of e-democracy: identifying the notion of the middleman paradox, *Information Systems Journal*, 15(1), 27–43, 2005.

Mazmanian, D. and Sabatier, P., *Effective Policy Implementation*, Eds., Lexington Books, Lexington, MA, 1981.

McEachern, C., Beyond web services, *VAR Business*, 21, 12–14, 2005.

Meier, K., The limits of cost–benefit analysis, In *Decision-Making in the Public Sector*, Nigro, L., Ed., Marcel Dekker, New York, pp. 43–63, 1984.

Misra, D. C., Hariharan, R., and Khaneja, M., E-Knowledge management framework for government organizations, *Information Systems Management*, 20(2), 38, 2003.

Moore, M. H., *Creating Public Value: Strategic Management in Government*, Harvard University Press, Cambridge, MA, 1995.

Morrisey, G., *Management by Objectives and Results*, Addison-Wesley, Reading, MA, 1970.

Neilson, R. E. and McCrea, J., US and UK governments size up their KM efforts, *KM Review*, 5(5), 4, 2002.

Nicholson-O'Brien, D., Government in the knowledge age, *Knowledge Management Review*, 3(1), 30, 2000.

Nonaka, I., The knowledge creating company, *Harvard Business Review*, 69, 96–104, 1991.

Nonaka, I., A dynamic theory of organizational knowledge creation, *Organization Science*, 5, 14–37, 1994.

Nonaka, I. and Takeuchi, H., *Knowledge-Creating Company: How Japanese Companies Create the Dynamics of Innovation*, Oxford University Press, New York, 1995.

Nutt, P. C. and Backoff, R. W., *Strategic Management of Public and Third Sector Organizations: A Handbook for Leaders*, Jossey-Bass, San Francisco, CA, 1992.

As outsourcing grows, administration pushes performance-based contracting to ensure quality, *Washington Technology*, 18(2), 3–5, 2003.

ParaMind Brainstorming Software (n.d.), http://www.paramind.net (accessed March 27, 2005).

Parker, G., A purchase in government, *Supply Management*, 10(4), 17–20, 2005.

Pettigrew, A. M., Strategy formulation as a political process, *International Studies in Management and Organization*, 7(2), 78–87, 1977.

Poister, T. H. and Streib, G., Elements of strategic planning and management in municipal government: status after two decades, *Public Administration Review*, 65(1), 45–57, 2005.

Polyani, M., *Personal Knowledge*, University of Chicago Press, Chicago, IL, 1962.

Porte, T., E-government II: being good and doing well: organizational openness and government effectiveness on the world wide web, *Bulletin of the American Society for Information Science and Technology*, 31(3), 23–28, 2005.

Porter, Michael, *Competitive Strategy: Techniques for Analyzing Industries and Competitors*, Lexington Books, Lexington, MA, 1983.

Porter, M., *Competitive Advantage: Creating and Sustaining Superior Performance*, Free Press, New York, 1985.

Porter, M., *Competition in Global Industries*, 1085, Harvard Graduate School of Business Administration, Cambridge, MA, 1985.

Public Law, *USC 604*, 5, 96–354, September 19, 1980.

Quinn, J. B., *Strategies for Change: Logical Incrementalism*, Irwin, Homewood, IL, 1980.

Radford, K., *Complex Decision Problems: An Integrated Strategy for Resolution*, Reston Publishing, Reston, VA, 1977.

Rubenstein-Montano, B., Buchwalter, J., and Liebowitz, J., Knowledge management: a US social security administration case study, *Government Information Quarterly*, 18(3), 223–254, 2001.

Santosus, M. and Surmacz, J., The ABCs of knowledge management, Knowledge Management Research Center, http://www.cio.com/research/knowledge/edit/kmabcs.html (accessed January 26, 2004).

Selznick, P., *Leadership in Administration: A Sociological Interpretation*, Row, Peterson, Evanston, IL, 1957.

Simon, H., The new science of management decision, In *Management Decision-Making*, Cyert, R. and Welsch, L., Eds., Penguin Books, New York, pp. 13–16, 1980.

Simon, H., *Centralization vs. Decentralization in Organizing the Controller's Department: A Research Study and Report Prepared for Controllership Foundation*, Scholarly Books, Houston, TX, 1978.

Simon, H., The structure of ill-structured decision processes, *Artificial Intelligence*, 4, 181–201, 1973.

Sorkin, D. L., Ferris, N. B., and Hudak, J., *Strategies for Cities and Counties: A Strategic Planning Guide*, Public Technology, Washington, DC, 1984.

Steiner, G. A., *Strategic Planning: What Every Manager Must Know*, Free Press, New York, 1979.

Stevens, J. M. and McGowan, R. P., *Information Systems and Public Management*, Praeger, New York, 1985.

Stevens, J. M. and McGowan, R. P., Managerial strategies in municipal government organizations, *Academy of Management Journal*, 26(3), 527–534, 1983.

Stewart, J., The meaning of strategy in the public sector, *Australian Journal of Public Administration*, 63(4), 16–22, 2004.

Swartz, N., UN report ranks e-gov readiness, *Information Management Journal*, 39(2), 6–11, 2005.

Swartz, N., Vietnam launches e-gov initiatives, *Information Management Journal*, 39(2), 8–13, 2005.

Stringer, J., Confusing diagnoses, *Supply Management*, 9(23), 19–23, 2004.

Taylor, B., Strategic planning—which style do you need?, *Long Rang Planning*, 17(3), 51–62, 1984.

Thomas, R. L., Means, M. C., and Grieve, M., *Taking Charge: How Communities are Planning their Futures*, International City Management Association, Washington, DC, 1988.

Tolchin, S. and Tolchin, M., *Dismantling America: The Rush to Deregulate*, Houghton-Mifflin, Boston, MA, 1983.

United Nations—Division for Public Economics and Public Administration and American Society for Public Administration, *Benchmarking E-Government: A Global Perspective*, United Nations, New York, 2002.

US General Accounting Office, *Best Management Practices: Reengineering the air Force's Logistics systems can yield substantial savings*, GAO/NSIAD-96-5, US General Accounting Office, Washington, DC, 1996.

Webb, K. and Hatry, H., *Obtaining Citizen Feedback: The Application of Citizen Surveys to Local Governments*, The Urban Institute, Washington, DC, 1973.

Weiner, D. L. and Vining, A. R., *Policy Analysis: Concepts and Practices*, Prentice Hall, Englewood Cliffs, NJ, 1989.

West, D., E-government and the transformation of service delivery and citizen attitudes, *Public Administration Review*, 64(1), 15–27, 2004.

West, J. P., Berman, E. M., and Milakovich, M. E., Implementing TQM in local government: the leadership challenge, *Public Productivity and Management Review*, XVII(2), 175–189, 1993.

Wheeland, C. M., Citywide strategic planning: an evaluation of Rock Hill's empowering the vision, *Public Administration Review*, 53(1), 65–72, 1993.

Wildavsky, A., *The Politics of the Budgetary Process*, Little, Brown, Boston, 1964.

Williams, W. et al., *Studying implementation: Methodological and Administrative Issues*, Chatham House, Chatham, NJ, 1982.

Wiseman, C., *Computers and Strategy: Information Systems as Competitive Weapons*, Dow Jones-Irwin, Homewood, IL, 1985.

Worsham, J. P., *Application of the Delphi Method: A Selected Bibliography*, Vance Bibliographies, Monticello, IL, 1980.

Yu, D. and Hartman, C., Washington's knowledge management pioneer, *Knowledge Management Review*, 3(1), 14, 2000.

Zack, M. H., Managing codified knowledge, *Sloan Management Review*, 40(4), 45–58, 1999a.

Zack, M. H., Developing a knowledge strategy, *California Management Review*, 41(3), 125–145, 1999b.

Unit 5

Public Personnel Management

9 Public Personnel and Labor Relations

N. Joseph Cayer

CONTENTS

I. INTRODUCTION: DEVELOPMENT OF THE PUBLIC SERVICE

The United States public service reflects changing values and concerns of the society as a whole. Shifts in social, economic, and political values influence the issues addressed in the personnel system. To understand the dynamics of public personnel management, it is necessary to understand the basic ideals that underpin public personnel policy making. Therefore, the public service as it evolved from the beginnings of our federal system of government will be examined.

A.   1789–1800: THE FEDERALIST PERIOD

In establishing his administration, President George Washington had the opportunity to create a new public service. While precedents from the Articles of Confederation experience certainly played some role, the new administration actually had little to guide it. The pressures of pulling together a new nation and getting the government off to a strong start dictated some of the decisions that had to be made. Thus, the first administration made efforts to include those who were politically important and accommodated interests of the Congress, Revolutionary War veterans, and others who had a stake in the workings of the new government (Ingraham 1995; Kaufman 1965; Mosher 1982; Van Riper 1958).

One of the most elementary credentials for serving in the public service was support for the new political system. Thus, Washington appointed fellow Federalists to the public service. While there was no strict test of political views, the administration obviously needed to assure that its employees would not be working to undermine the new system. During the administration of John Adams, partisan politics became more important. Because of some conflicts within Federalist ranks and with the differences developing between the Federalists and the Jeffersonians, President Adams experienced pressure to consider partisan politics when appointing or replacing public officers (White 1948). Still, during the first twelve years of the new nation, partisanship played a minor role in public service staffing decisions (Kaplan 1940).

More important than partisan politics was social status. The Federalist public service clearly represented the aristocracy. As Leonard White (1948) notes, Washington had a very high standard of fitness for his appointees. However, fitness did not relate entirely to the ability to do the work. Instead, fitness also included such things as standing in the community as evidenced by having held other offices in the person's community. Place of residence also mattered, as did service in the Revolutionary War.

All of these considerations were calculated to bolster public support for the new government. Because the aristocracy held political power, appointing members of the aristocracy to government service was an effective way of gaining their support. Similarly, appointing people from all regions of the country facilitated attempts to assure the allegiance of disparate parts of the new nation. These very pragmatic considerations of President Washington are enduring elements of the personnel system (Van Riper 1958). Many of these considerations were formalized in law or civil service policy later.

Because the Republican Party competed strongly in the 1796 elections, President John Adams faced more purely partisan concerns than Washington ever did. Consequently, Adams looked more closely at political party affiliation as a criterion for appointment to office. While Washington was sensitive to the issue primarily at the highest levels, Adams carried the concern to lower levels of the public service. Attention to partisanship in selection became so intense that the Republicans began to protest what they considered discrimination against them (White 1948).

The Federalists and Republicans also clashed on the level of pay for public servants. While the Federalists favored paying public officials a salary, which would take into consideration the need for leaving property and income behind and establishing residence in the capital, the Republicans supported a more parsimonious approach. Neither side won clear-cut victories in the dispute, and commentaries of the time indicated that public servants felt underpaid.

B.   THE JEFFERSONIANS: 1801–1829

The election of Thomas Jefferson in 1800 represented the first succession of power from one political party to another in United States history. Not surprisingly, some partisan issues surfaced in staffing the public service. Thomas Jefferson inherited a public service filled with Federalists whom his party had just defeated in the election. Members of his own party wanted opportunity to serve (White 1951). As a result, Jefferson had to find some way to staff the government with employees more sensitive to his political concerns. At the same time, he did not seem interested in a complete overhaul of the public service.

To deal with the dilemma of making government more responsive to his party while maintaining some stability, Jefferson developed the doctrine that there should be a balance between the political parties in offices held (Van Riper 1958). Of course, he wished to be able to appoint members of his own political party to office and did so in a modest fashion. He began by removing high-level officials and replacing them with Republicans. The removals and replacements continued until 1803, when he achieved a balance to suit his views.

Aside from the partisanship issue, Jefferson used standards similar to the Federalists. People appointed to public office still reflected the aristocracy and powerful elements of society. During Jefferson's administration, agricultural interests seemed to fare better in representation. Otherwise, his appointments were strikingly similar to the Federalists in coming from the gentleman class. Most appointees just happened also to be Republicans.

Jefferson also introduced the first cutback management in personnel (Van Riper 1958). The Republicans distrusted big government and attempted to reduce the size of government by not filling positions and by consolidating others. While their efforts were not entirely successful, they established a precedent followed by many administrations since. The growing nation and expanding government activity made their efforts short-lived.

Madison and Monroe followed the Jeffersonian tradition of appointing people from the upper classes and generally favored Republicans. However, because partisan activity was declining during this period, there was less of a sense of urgency to partisan representation. Prior to the Madison and Monroe administrations, Jefferson had balanced the public service in favor of Republicans. One significant development during this period was the passage of the Four Years Law of 1820 (also referred to as the Tenure of Office Act of 1820), which limited the terms of public officials to four years. The effect was to open the doors to new appointments for each president. Both Madison and Monroe tended to reappoint incumbents as their terms expired.

John Quincy Adams came to office with a very divided electorate and electoral college. As a result, he was under great pressure to satisfy varying political factions. He was insistent on maintaining the same principles that had guided Washington and Jefferson in appointing people to office. Thus, he insisted on fitness for office and continued to choose from the upper socioeconomic groups when appointing public servants. His resistance to political pressures did not broaden his political support, and the stage was set for the election of Andrew Jackson and a major change in the public service.

During the Jeffersonian period, predecessors of the union movement in the public sector also emerged. Surgeons and assistant surgeons in the United States Navy became so disenchanted with their pay and working conditions that some of them got together and sent a petition to Congress for relief in 1828 (White 1951). Similarly, Army captains sought higher pay in 1826 with a petition to Congress. In 1918, Congress created the Provident Association of Clerks to provide for families of deceased members of the organization. As a benefit association, it performed many of the functions unions would later perform. As White (1951) indicates, these organizations had economic interests and represented attempts to secure their interests in a fashion similar to those of unions of the present day.

Pay remained relatively low during the Jeffersonian era, especially because the Federalist party dwindled away and there was little formal opposition to Republican policies. Despite low pay, the public service seems to have been remarkably free of corruption and collusion during this and the Federalist eras. The focus on fitness for office as defined by the early presidents appears to have been effective in assuring that public servants were of high integrity. Government service was truly a respected calling during our early history (Goodsell 2003; Newland 1984b).

State and local governments went through many of the same experiences as the national government. In some instances, the state and local governments led the way. Such is apparently the case regarding the more partisan considerations used in the appointive process. While most of the states used the model of staffing the public service with the aristocracy, some of them were much more specifically partisan in their approach (Fish 1905). New York and Pennsylvania, in particular, started using the spoils system during the first decade of the nineteenth century. Although they used Jefferson's justification for balancing the service, they demonstrated none of the restraint implicit in his approach. New York and Pennsylvania were models of what the national level was to experience in the middle of the century.

Along with the patronage issues, the Congress and president competed for control over the public service during the 1820s. Senator Thomas H. Benton (US Senate, 1826) set the tone for the conflict with his recommendations for curtailing executive control over appointments and removals. Specifically, he recommended that the president be required to justify the removal of officials, Senate confirmation of postmasters, and apportioning appointment of cadets and midshipmen by Congressional district and state.

C. THE ERA OF SPOILS: 1829–1865

The aforementioned development of spoils in state and local government during the early part of the nineteenth century enveloped the national government after the election of 1829. President Andrew Jackson came to office with the support of a much more varied electorate than any of his predecessors. Because the nation had by now grown to 24 states and was spreading westward, the nature of the electorate changed. Suffrage was extended to non-landholding men; thus, the upper economic class was not the only group voting. The rise of the Democratic party, based on the belief that the common man should be able to participate in government, provided the base of support for Jackson's administration.

Coming to office, Jackson found the system in which only the elite had access to public office offensive to democratic (and Democratic) ideals. Therefore, he favored making public service available to everyone, but especially to the common man. The result was a very strong justification for replacing office holders with partisan supporters. Jackson believed that his loyal supporters deserved the opportunity to serve in appointive positions. He also believed that public officers lost touch with their fellow citizens by being in their positions for too long (Ingraham 1995). Most importantly, he believed that the aristocracy had no right to a monopoly on government jobs (White 1954).

To remedy the situation he inherited, he proposed rotation in office, intending to implement the Tenure of Office Act of 1820 that his predecessors had not faithfully executed. He also appointed common people to government positions. While President Jackson is identified with rotation in office, the fact of the matter is that he did not remove a lot of incumbents. The evidence suggests that he removed perhaps 20%, but more likely no more than 10%, of all public servants during his administration (Crenson 1975; Eriksson 1927).

Even though the image of spoils in the Jackson administration exaggerates reality, his approach had very significant effects (Kaplan 1940; Mosher 1982). For the first time, the public service was democratized and reflected the interests and status of a large spectrum of American society (Aronson 1964). Because it was still only males who had the vote, women were not included among those who received public appointments to any significant degree.

While Jackson was restrained in his use of spoils, the fact that he used it so openly led to a great deal of criticism of his administration (Fish 1905). The nation was yet to see the worst of it. The election of 1840, in which Benjamin Harrison was elected president, only to die after one month in office, demonstrated that the Democrats were not the only ones with an interest in patronage. Hordes of office-seekers descended on Washington, establishing a trend that survived until the 1883 reform. Although Tyler, Harrison's successor, attempted to resist pressures for spoils appointments, he was unsuccessful, as electoral supporters of successful candidates considered public appointments a benefit due them for their support. Because of political instability and the rotation of the Presidency between the Democrats and Whigs until the 1860s, rotation in office was standard procedure. Even the election of a president of the same party as his predecessor did not protect public servants from removal and replacement.

The experience at the state and local levels was similar to that at the national level. As noted above, many states preceded the national government in the establishment of patronage. A notable exception to the use of patronage at the state level was in the South (Fish 1905). The landed aristocracy never lost its hold on politics in the South before the Civil War and thus was able to forestall the march of spoils. It is ironic that the South later became a stronghold of patronage in the wake of twentieth century reform efforts.

The spoils system came under severe criticism, even during the time when it was at its zenith. Spoils were dysfunctional to the public service over the long term. While the early use of spoils democratized the public service and gave the common people access to government jobs and decision making, later experiences were not so beneficial. The constant rotation of people in office led to inefficiency in operation. The scandals associated with spoils also damaged the good image the public service had during the first forty years of our nation's history. Of course, the excesses of post-Civil War days also led to corruption and coercion of employees. At the same time, patronage is considered an important element in the success of the Union in the Civil War (Van Riper 1958; White 1958).

Despite the wide use of spoils during the Jacksonian era, some developments actually helped establish the base upon which our modern personnel system was built. The Jacksonians extended the use of examinations that began with the Jeffersonians (White 1954). By 1853, all Washington departmental offices used examinations for clerk positions. Earlier, specialized exams had been developed for military medical personnel. While the use of exams was not extensive, it did provide experience that would be valuable later in the reform effort. These early features of a personnel system served as precedent for later decisions.

D. The Road to Reform: 1865–1883

The Civil War demonstrated the effectiveness of spoils for a president with a divided country. Lincoln astutely used patronage to assure loyalty to the Union. Without spoils, it is not certain that the United States would have been kept together. In his effort to consolidate the support of the Republican party, Lincoln swept people from office in unprecedented numbers (Fish 1905). The party, in disarray, was only one of his concerns. He also had to find a way of holding the nation together. As a result, office holders from the South were purged and loyalists to the Union cause replaced them (Van Riper 1958; White 1958).

Lincoln's supporters expected him to again sweep people from office when he was reelected. He resisted the pressure and set a precedent that would be used by successors. His immediate successor, Andrew Johnson, faced severe political problems and was unable to withstand the same pressures, but Lincoln's steadfastness gave hope to reformers, who were beginning to be heard. Spoils had become marked for change and slow but steady progress was made in reform from 1865 to 1883.

Lincoln's administration consolidated a lot of power in the executive branch at the expense of Congress. When Andrew Johnson succeeded him in office, Congress saw the opportunity for reclaiming some of that power. Control over the personnel system became a major test of that attempt. Johnson was faced with opposition from within his own party and used his powers to remove many of those not loyal to him. Predictably, he angered many Republicans and lost much of his own party support.

To gain control over patronage, Congress passed the Tenure of Office Act of 1867, limiting presidential removal power. Johnson defied the act and Congress retaliated by impeaching him. By one vote, he avoided conviction and removal from office. The stage had been set for Congress to attempt to exercise its power, and for the next couple decades, Congress succeeded. Johnson and two weak successors, Grant and Hayes, could do little to stem the tide.

The Grant administration was tainted with serious corruption and scandal among many of its members. A similar situation also existed in most state and local governments. The result was a public image of government as hopelessly corrupt. The prestige of the public service was severely strained. To the surprise of many, President Grant actually supported personnel reform. Congress passed the Civil Service Reform Act of 1871 as a rider to an appropriation bill. Grant attempted to establish a merit system pursuant to the act and was successful for a couple years.

However, the scandals of his administration and political infighting led him to abandon the effort. Nonetheless, the Grant administration did provide a civil service experiment that actually laid out the basic principles on which much of the 1883 reform was built (Murphy 1942).

Part of the reason for Grant's abandonment of the reform effort was that it rekindled the conflict between Congress and the president over personnel. The 1871 act provided the president with authority over the public service that Congress was unwilling to accept. Thus, Grant's effort had to be abandoned in order for his administration to accomplish other objectives. The experiment did encourage reformers and their supporters to press their cause. Grant's successor, Rutherford B. Hayes, was unable to accomplish much, although he supported reform.

Public support for change contributed to the success of reformers (Hoogenboom 1964). Civic leaders and prominent politicians began efforts to bring about change. The New York Civil Service Reform Association (established in 1877) and the National Civil Service Reform League (established in 1881) were two of many organizations formed to rally public support for reform. The news media picked up on the concerns of the reformers and highlighted the abuses of the spoils system (Hoogenboom 1961, 1964; Nelson 1973). Garfield's assassination gave the press a dramatic event on which to base a lot of its call for reform, especially because his assassin was a disgruntled unsuccessful seeker of government appointment.

An 1876 Congressional act prohibiting assessment of government workers also fueled reform support. Assessments were contributions, or kickbacks employees were expected to make to their benefactors for getting a government job. Often, it took the form of a percentage of the employee's salary and may have been turned over to the political party. Under the patronage system, if employees refused to pay the assessment, they could be removed. Newton Curtis, an employee of the Treasury Department and Treasurer of the New York Republican party, was convicted of violation of the law. The United States Supreme Court decision upholding his conviction in *Ex parte Curtis* (1882) gave support to the reform movement.

As the Republicans saw their chances of retaining the White House in 1884 slipping, they considered methods of preventing the Democrats from making a clean sweep of government employees. Support of reform in the public service was viewed as the most viable approach, and the Pendleton Civil Service Act of 1883 was passed. The hopes of those who wanted to rescue the public service from the evils of spoils rested upon the implementation of the new law.

II. THE CIVIL SERVICE SYSTEM

Even with their victory in Congress, proponents of reform still had a lot of work to do. The Civil Service Act covered only a small part of the public service; approximately 90% remained subject to patronage (Hoogenboom 1958–1959, 1961). The act represented a partial victory by Congress in its struggle for control over the public service. While providing guidelines for the president, the act had to be worded very carefully so as to make sure that it did not violate the separation of powers provisions of the Constitution. To accommodate that issue, Congress authorized the president to establish a civil service commission to develop rules and regulations for personnel management and to implement those rules and regulations. The act avoided directing the president to do so (Ingraham 1995; Siciliano no date).

The act covered a variety of issues, including use of competitive exams, apportioning positions around the country, an open entry system, and presidential extension of coverage through blanketing-in of positions. There were also provisions to protect the political neutrality of the service, prohibition of assessments, and penalties for violating rules. The newly established Civil Service Commission moved slowly in establishing its authority and scope. Recognizing political reality, it did what it could to avoid major controversy in its early existence. As a result, it gradually acquired prestige and influence, so that it became the major actor in public personnel management in the United States for ninety-five years before it was dissolved and other organizations were created in its place in the 1978 reforms (Rosenbloom 1982; US Civil Service Commission 1974, 1978; US Office of Personnel Management 2002).

A. IMPLEMENTING REFORM

The early years of the civil service system were difficult because opponents continued to attempt to weaken or destroy it. Leonard White (1958) reports that efforts to undermine the civil service included evasion of rules by public officials, giving it limited resources, reducing its powers, and renewing proposals for a four-year term for all public servants. Many members of Congress introduced bills to repeal the Pendleton Act during the first decade and a half of its existence.

Despite the conflicts it had to endure, the civil service system gained status gradually and by the turn of the century was well established. Each president encouraged the supporters of the system through extension of coverage to larger numbers of employees. President Cleveland went furthest, as he issued executive orders at the end of each of his terms that brought large numbers of employees under the jurisdiction of the Civil Service Commission.

His inclusion of 30,000 positions under civil service in the last year of his administration resulted in many complaints from the incoming Republicans. This episode actually brought to the forefront a discussion about the relationship of the political and career public service. Debate centered on the distinction between the two. Woodrow Wilson (1885), soon to become a major figure in that intellectual stream of thought, wrote about the difficulties in distinguishing between the political and nonpolitical in government service. Of course, later, Wilson (1887) was to make a strong defense for the separation of the two. The Civil Service Commission took the position that the vast majority of positions in the public service were nonpolitical, and that view has been reflected in most of the history of the civil service.

The appointment of Theodore Roosevelt as a member of the Civil Service Commission in 1889 was probably one of the most important factors in the Commission's early ability to withstand the pressures surrounding it (White 2003). Roosevelt became a very outspoken and articulate spokesperson for the civil service and broadened its popular appeal. When Roosevelt assumed office as President in 1901, the debate over whether the civil service would continue to exist ended.

At the same time the Commission was struggling for its survival, it also developed a basic set of guidelines separating politics and administration. The Commission drew up rules and guidelines for public servants that generally prohibited partisan political participation by government employees. These guidelines eventually became the rules that govern employees today. The policy included prohibition of assessment of public employees.

Examinations constituted a large part of the work of the Civil Service Commission in its early days, but it made progress in other areas, as well. The Commission took steps made in setting up a classification and pay system for many national government employees. Basically, the Commission assumed the role of ensuring implementation of the Pendleton Act of 1883. In assuming that role, it established the policing or monitoring function of personnel agencies that has been the subject of much disagreement over the years (Sayre 1948). Operating departments often resent the role, while employees and unions often view that role as one that protects their interests. Policy makers also like to see the personnel agency enforcing the policies they develop.

At the same time the civil service system was becoming institutionalized, there were many changes in society that presaged future developments. Among the most important for public personnel management was the development of unions among public employees (Brooks 1971; Coleman 1990; Kearney 2001; Moskow et al. 1970; Rabin et al. 1994; Stieber 1973). While reference to public employees meeting and pressing their grievances has already been made, the organization of unions involved a more important symbol of public employee concerns. The National Association of Letter Carriers was organized in 1889, and others followed. These developments led to pressure on the political system to consider the needs of employees. Subsequently, benefits packages and other perquisites for employees became part of the public personnel system.

While these developments were taking place in the national civil service system, state and local governments experienced pressures for the same types of changes (Aronson 1974; Dilts et al. 1992; Pynes and Lafferty 1993; Rabin et al. 1994). As noted above, some civic groups and leaders emerged at the local level, and they resulted in the national model being adopted for state and local governments as well, although reform came very slowly.

B. CONSOLIDATION OF REFORM PRINCIPLES

During the first four decades of the twentieth century, the civil service system successfully institutionalized a politically neutral public service (US Civil Service Commission, 1974; Van Riper, 1958). The succession of Theodore Roosevelt to the presidency after McKinley's assassination provided a much-needed stimulus to the efforts. McKinley had acceded to political party pressure and utilized much patronage in his personnel decisions. Much to the dismay of civil service partisans, he removed approximately 6000 positions from the coverage of the merit system. His action was in response to Cleveland's blanketing-in of nearly 30,000 positions. Nonetheless, it troubled those who had worked to develop a nonspoils approach to staffing the public service.

President Roosevelt was a friend of the civil service. Having been a very active Civil Service Commissioner, Roosevelt was outspoken in his efforts to put the public service on a sound merit basis (Kaufman 1965; White 2003). Roosevelt also reflected the moralistic fervor of the nineteenth century reformers in believing that the public service should be based on honor and integrity. Making it politically neutral was an important part of giving it a positive and moral image (Van Riper 1958; White 2003). His sincere effort to rid the government of corruption is reflected in his administration's investigation of scandals in various parts of the civil service.

In addition to his commitment to the ideals of the civil service, Roosevelt's close working relationship with the Civil Service Commission helped institutionalize the system. Because of his previous membership on the Commission and interest in its work, he was very knowledgeable about the civil service. Additionally, he appointed close friends to the Commission and developed a very close working relationship between the system and the rest of his administration.

Roosevelt was uncompromising in his dealings with opponents, and that approach led to conflicts with members within his own party as well as with Congress. For example, Roosevelt forbad federal employees from communicating directly with Congress regarding working conditions and pay. While he was successful in prohibiting such direct contact, it also inspired Congress to react. During Taft's administration, Congress passed the Lloyd–LaFollette Act of 1912, which guaranteed the right of federal employees to petition Congress and also guaranteed them the right to organize. This was the first statutory recognition of the right to organize, and was important in the development of public sector unions. Congress did impose a condition: that the union and employees could not advocate the use of strikes.

Roosevelt also was instrumental in establishing the open shop as a part of public employment. In a case involving reinstatement of an individual who had been fired because he was expelled from a union of which he had been a member, Roosevelt stated that the rules of a union could not supersede the law of the nation (US Civil Service Commission 1903). While the person could be a member of the union, the union could not require membership as a condition for employment. That doctrine has persisted in public employment through right-to-work laws.

During Roosevelt's administration, departments and agencies constantly violated the rules prohibiting political participation by public employees. Because of the difficulty in enforcing those rules, Roosevelt issued orders that separated parts of the service for that purpose. He distinguished between the classified and nonclassified service, and thus the distinction between political and career servants emerged. Again, the innovation resulted from the president's commitment to a neutral service and recognition of practical limitations. He insisted upon enforcement of the partisan political participation ban on classified servants but recognized the need for some freedom in appointing loyal supporters in policy positions.

As the twentieth century began, journalists exposed corruption in American institutions, both public and private. Roosevelt termed these journalistic advocates of reform "Muckrakers" (Weinberg and Weinberg 2001). The Muckrakers put state and local government, in particular, under the spotlight. Led by Lincoln Steffens (1904), these proponents of reform exposed corruption and spoils in major cities and in state government. The results of their publicity and reform efforts were policies adopted at the state and municipal levels to place personnel management on a more nonpartisan, merit basis (Aronson 1974). Civil service systems were adopted in states such as Wisconsin and Illinois in 1905, as well as Colorado (1907) and New Jersey (1908). In the next decade, several more states followed suit.

Between 1900 and 1910, cities such as San Francisco, Los Angeles, Philadelphia, Tacoma, Des Moines, Cleveland, and Newark also adopted civil service systems. Some cities developed civil service systems only for their police and fire departments, and vestiges of that approach still exist in many places, as police and fire departments are treated separately from the rest of the personnel system. Most cities in Texas, for example, have separate personnel systems for public safety services. While state and local governments had led the way in development of spoils, they experimented with civil service after the national civil service system was relatively well developed.

From 1910 to 1920, there were not many major changes from the pattern established by the Roosevelt administration at the national level. At the state and local levels, the number of jurisdictions adopting some form of civil service gradually increased. While there were not a lot of major developments, there were some very significant ones that would have an impact on public personnel management for a long time to come.

Wages and salary were always issues of concern to public policy makers. The civil service system attempted to provide some rational basis for establishing pay. In the national government, distinctions between levels of clerks, for example, were used for differentiating pay. As public employment became more and more professional, it became necessary to develop a formal system for distinguishing jobs. Chicago created the classification system in 1912, leading the way in formal job analysis and classification (Civil Service Assembly 1941). It was not until eleven years later that the national government adopted such a system, but state and local governments experimented with it during the intervening years. Position classification became a major tool in the institutionalization of a formal management system in personnel and is one of the most persevering elements of the early civil service system.

The veterans' preference system is another legacy of this period that has proved extremely durable. The Veterans' Preference Act of 1919 provided preference to all honorably discharged veterans in the federal classified service. While the public service had few veterans prior to the adoption of this act, their number increased to 13.6% in 1920–1921 and to 28.9% the following year. It peaked once, at 34.1% in 1922–1923, and again after World War II, when it reached 50%, a level that was maintained until the 1980s (Emmert and Gregory 1982). In 2005, the percentage of veterans in federal employment was 25%, approximately where it has been since the early 1990s (US Office of Personnel Management 2005). The important legacy for public personnel management was that this policy has persisted with very few modifications (Davis 1982). In 1923, President Harding made one major modification by establishing the five- and ten-point preference system to distinguish between disabled and nondisabled veterans, respectively. That distinction remains today, and actually was strengthened in the 1978 Civil Service Reform Act, which allowed appointment of disabled veterans without competitive exams and gave them retention rights in reductions-in-force.

Collective bargaining also has important roots during this period (Dickerson and Cayer 1994; Kearney 2001; Nesbitt 1976; Spero 1927; Stieber 1973). At the national level, the Federal Employees Union was organized in 1916 among clerks in the War Department. In 1917, the American Federation of Labor (AFL) granted various local organizations a charter as the National Federation of Federal Employees, which still exists. Finally, events in 1918 and, especially, 1919 set precedents for public sector collective bargaining—or labor–management relations, as many public officials prefer to call it (Ziskind 1971). Police strikes occurred in cities such as Cincinnati (1918) and Boston (1919). The Boston strike was especially bitter, and the Governor of Massachusetts, Calvin Coolidge, took command of the situation by dismissing all the striking officers. He asserted that no one had the right to strike against the public safety and became a hero and Republican candidate for president. The next year, Congress passed legislation prohibiting the Washington, DC police and fire officers from striking. The doctrine that public employees have no right to strike emerged from the actions in these two instances. The tarnished image of public employees and unions that accompanied the situations created a resistance to public employee collective bargaining that held until the 1960s.

President Taft appointed the Commission on Economy and Efficiency in 1910 to analyze the public service and make recommendations for its improvement. This Commission reflected a business approach to management and attempted to evaluate all aspects of the civil service for purposes of determining the most effective way of conducting its work. The Commission's recommendations were consistent with the scientific management approach that was beginning to influence public personnel management. Many of the recommendations were adopted in later decades, but the Commission's recommendations had very little immediate impact. It did establish an agenda that has been important for much of the twentieth century, though. That agenda includes centralizing the personnel function and making it a tool of the chief executive. The analysis of pay rates and other problems in working conditions focused attention on those issues in a systematic manner and eventually contributed to efforts to make the system more rational, consistent, and equitable.

The second decade of the twentieth century came to an end with Woodrow Wilson as president. His views on politics and administration were well known from his nineteenth century writings. He had been active in the National Civil Service Reform League and supported merit during his tenure as New Jersey's governor. However, he faced strong pressure from his political party because it had been out of power for a long time and wanted the spoils that went with its victory. Wilson attempted to resist the demands of his party, but he was not very successful. Nonetheless, he maintained his strong support of the merit system and mitigated the worst effects of patronage through his strong-willed support of his ideals. Out of necessity, he had to make accommodations to partisan politics.

The United States' entry into World War I in 1917 had a profound effect on the public service. The need for employees expanded quickly and the Civil Service Commission found it necessary to recruit outside the merit system. Many exceptions to merit procedures were made to staff new and growing agencies. While many merit proponents were critical of these changes, they did not have much of an impact, as the attention of the nation was focused on the war effort. In a particularly important action during the war, Wilson issued an executive order providing for the removal of federal government employees who were considered disloyal to the nation. While the executive order did not have much immediate effect, it became an important precedent for the post-World War II era.

The 1920s witnessed continual but gradual entrenchment of the civil service system. The Harding administration, known not for its strong efforts in personnel management, but rather for being scandal-ridden, got Congress to pass the Budget and Accounting Act of 1921, which affected personnel significantly. Creation of the Bureau of the Budget and other features of the act placed a focus on improving management coordination of government activities. A major element of that management was personnel, and the effect was to centralize the personnel function more. The Budget and Accounting Act of 1921 is the major achievement of the Harding administration.

In 1920, the Retirement Act was passed, establishing a precedent for public employee retirement pensions. Congress passed the law but provided no public funding for it. Rather, employee contributions funded the system.

When Calvin Coolidge succeeded Harding, he inherited the breaking scandals. He toned down the patronage process to a great extent, but did use it effectively in consolidating his own control over the party. Committed to the merit system, Coolidge sought to bring business practices and perspectives to the public service. During his administration, the Classification Act of 1923 was passed, establishing the concept of classification in the federal service. It had limited impact in that it was restricted to public servants in the Washington, DC area, but it did set salary ranges and made provisions for determining raises for employees. Like many other actions during the early twentieth century, this act was probably more important in the long run than at the time it was passed. It provided the model for future expansion of the classification system that would become a critical element of traditional civil service systems.

Overall, the 1920s were good years for the civil service system. While there were not many dramatic developments, neither were there major setbacks. The Civil Service Commission received increasingly more support over the decade and continued to establish itself as a leading management organization in the federal government. It worked with departments to develop more management-oriented approaches. Some departments, such as Agriculture, began to develop their own personnel offices for day-to-day personnel functions. The Commission continued to focus on examinations as a major activity and worked on improvements in exam procedures.

As Newland (1976) suggests, the bureaucratic model of personnel was complete in the federal service by the 1930s. In fact, during the 1930s, many of the more bureaucratic elements of the personnel system were targets of criticism. Some changes resulted from those criticisms, but it was not until the 1970s that many of the major recommendations of critics were taken to heart (Morse 1976; Rosenbloom 1982). The bureaucratic elements were advocated as a way of separating politics and administration (Barnard 1968; Goodnow 1900; White 1926). To the extent that personnel during this period focused on management, it emphasized techniques and finding the best way of doing things as outlined by the Scientific Management School. During the late 1930s, the concept of management was to undergo a change as applied to the public service.

C. THE 1930S: THE RISE OF ADMINISTRATORS

The 1930s represent two very different traditions in public personnel management, yet the two traditions also worked together. Mosher (1982) refers to the years before 1937 as part of the era of government by the efficient and the post-1937 years as government by administrators. The beginning of the 1930s, with Hoover as president, continued the pattern of the Coolidge years, when business efficiency was of paramount importance to the administration. The depression, of course, added some new concerns, but had little effect on personnel practices as such. The election of President Franklin Roosevelt, however, was to have major implications.

Roosevelt's first term was discouraging to the proponents of merit systems (Harvey 1970; Kaufman 1965). The administration elevated the use of patronage to a new high. After decades of Republican government, the new Democratic president felt that his hands were tied in reorienting government to new values. The fact that a major emergency existed in the form of the Depression made it possible for Roosevelt to get his way. One of the most effective ways of reintroducing patronage was to get Congress to create new agencies outside the protected service. The so-called alphabet agencies of the Roosevelt administration were created in just this way. By 1934, some sixty agencies had been created outside the coverage of the civil service, while only five were placed under jurisdiction of the Civil Service Commission (Van Riper 1958). Congress willingly went along because it was now controlled by Democrats, who were hungry for spoils. The president espoused the principles of merit during this time but acted to gain control over programs and agencies.

One new departure during this time was the creation of the Tennessee Valley Authority (TVA) with a personnel system of its own (Selznick 1949). Its system was based on merit. A few other agencies eventually developed along the same line.

While patronage was ascendant, the Civil Service Commission was losing support. Its budget had been cut during the Depression and it had little power to stem the tide of the new administration's efforts. It contented itself with refining the examination function for those agencies under its jurisdiction.

Roosevelt's second term represented a major shift in the outlook on the public service (Harvey 1970). By then the patronage system had accomplished its purpose and public sentiment began to reflect some of the concerns of critics of the administration's use of patronage. Roosevelt was now able to act on the ideals he espoused concerning merit. He appointed the President's Committee on Administrative Management in 1937, popularly known as the Brownlow Committee. The committee was charged with examining government with an eye to reorganization and improved management. The Brownlow Committee made many recommendations that related directly to the public service (President's Committee on Administrative Management 1937). The report had the effect of elevating personnel management to a high level of consideration in the administration and in Congress, although immediate action on recommendations was not forthcoming. The Committee recommended that the Civil Service Commission be reorganized so that there be a single personnel director whose operations would be closely integrated with the rest of the administration. Furthermore, it was critical of the centralization of many personnel activities by the civil service, and the president directed departments to develop personnel units to handle day-to-day responsibilities.

Many of the other recommendations found their way into specific legislation. The Ramspeck-O'Mahoney Postmaster Act (1938), for example, went a long way toward bringing merit to postal appointments. The postal service had been the epitome of spoils. The Hatch Acts of 1939 and 1940 also incorporated some of the Committee's recommendations into statute (Kaplan 1940; Kirchheimer 1941). The 1939 act codified prohibited political activities for federal employees, while the 1940 act extended the prohibitions to state and local government employees working in programs funded by federal monies. The 1940 act also forbad employment of individuals advocating overthrow of the government through violent means. Members of Congress became suspicious of the president's intentions in the upcoming elections. Fearing that Roosevelt would have a vast army of partisan public employees to use in the reelection effort in 1940, the Congress found good reason to institutionalize partisan political participation prohibitions (Nelson 1958; Rose 1962).

In 1938, Roosevelt blanketed-in many employees in the alphabet agencies, partly in response to the Brownlow Committee suggestions. Congress passed the Ramspeck Act of 1940 to control blanketing-in. While the act actually encouraged blanketing-in of employees, it required noncompetitive examinations for those being blanketed in, thus reinforcing the concept of merit or competence as necessary for public employment (Harvey 1970). Additionally, the Ramspeck Act of 1940 encouraged the Civil Service Commission to analyze the civil service through pay and classification studies. It also prohibited discrimination in employment on the basis of race, religion, or color.

The Social Security Act of 1939 also directly affected public personnel management by establishing standards for state and local government merit systems (Aronson 1940). These standards applied to agencies and programs funded by federal government monies. Employees in those programs covered had to be governed by a merit system, and these standards established minimum requirements for such systems.

Congress passed many significant labor laws during the 1930s and 1940s, as well (Brooks 1971; Cayer 2003; Dickerson and Cayer 1994; Kearney 2001). Establishing a trend that survived until the 1960s, the National Labor Relations Act of 1935 specifically excluded most public employees from its coverage. Thus, while the rights of private sector employees were protected, public employees were not accorded the same type of coverage. Nonetheless, other developments did work to the benefit of public employees. The American Federation of State, County, and Municipal Employees (AFSCME) was founded in 1935 and had a major impact on state and local governments (Kramer 1962). It was an outspoken supporter of the merit system in state and local governments, believing that it protected employees from the ravages of spoils manipulation. Beginning in 1939, the City of Philadelphia negotiated agreements with its employees.

Thus, while national legislation was not supportive of public employee collective bargaining, unions were making their marks elsewhere.

III. BIG GOVERNMENT

With the programs of the 1930s to deal with the depression and social problems, the nation moved from a limited government perspective to one in which government was viewed as having responsibility for solving a wide range of social and economic problems. The passage of the Social Security Act amendments of 1939 was especially symbolic because it became the foundation of much social legislation for the next thirty years.

A. MEETING WARTIME AND PEACETIME PERSONNEL NEEDS: THE 1940s

The first half of the 1940s continued the policies of President Roosevelt, although there were some specific new developments. In essence, the idea of personnel management being a positive management force and providing assistance to operating departments rather than only negative policing forces took hold. Characterizing the development of much of personnel up to this time, Sayre (1948) referred to it as a triumph of technique over purpose. Rules and procedures were streamlined during this period and greater flexibility in recruitment developed. In particular, a junior management exam was created to recruit college-educated generalists into the public service.

Between 1939 and 1941, recruitment skyrocketed. The workforce doubled from approximately 900,000 to 1.8 million employees. This massive recruitment led to greater flexibility in the process and much decentralization of responsibility to operating departments. The Civil Service Commission acted increasingly as a coordinator of activities and this activity enhanced its status and authority. To avoid some of the problems faced after the Civil War and First World War, these recruitments were considered temporary, to last during the war and for six months afterwards. The jobs of those who went to war were protected by this provision. The Veterans' Preference Act of 1944 provided more protection by putting into statute many of the practices that had been stimulated by the 1919 Veterans' Preference Act. State and local governments followed suit.

Not surprisingly, loyalty and security became issues during the war as well, although the post-World War II era brought much greater attention to those issues (Bar of the City of New York, 1956; Latham 1966; Morganthau 1955). The House Un-American Activities Committee (HUAC) created in 1939, conducted some investigations during the early 1940s. The administration also paid attention to the issue in the form of executive orders and directives.

When Harry Truman assumed the presidency, there were many conflicts to be addressed. Of course, the difficulties of demobilization and dealing with the post-World War II balance of power occupied much of his time. These concerns affected his ability to attend to domestic affairs. The death of Roosevelt also left a void in political leadership that Truman had to try to fill. The public and Congress were not eager to make his job easy. While Truman was a strong supporter of the merit system, he also had to deal with internal political conflicts in the Democratic party; pressures for patronage were strong. Nonetheless, on that score, the Truman administration did not significantly change the Roosevelt policies. The administration was fraught with minor scandals that fueled the fires of Congressional wrangling with the president. The public service was often the scapegoat for much of the conflict.

The new administration faced the immediate challenge of absorbing the military personnel into the domestic work force. To do that, and to reinstate those whose jobs had been protected as they went to war, required development of rules and regulations. Reduction-in-force policies were developed to separate those employed on a temporary basis from the service. Processing the paperwork to reemploy those whose jobs had been protected was a massive endeavor, but because of careful planning by the administration and the Civil Service Commission, the effort went smoothly. A major feature of its postwar effort involved reinstitution of competitive recruitment and selection procedures to replace the more flexible policies that were used during the war build-up.

While providing for the adjustment to peacetime, the Civil Service Commission benefited from good appointments by both Roosevelt and Truman. Taking their responsibilities seriously, the commissioners developed a blueprint for managing the public service in peacetime. Their plans emphasized the expansion of the merit concept and improved techniques throughout the organization of the public service (Harvey 1970). The Commission also worked toward cooperation with operating agencies, with the Commission having responsibilities for setting standards and the operating departments assuming responsibility for implementing the standards (McDiarmid 1946). The Civil Service Commission also assumed monitoring responsibilities to insure proper implementation of its guidelines. Thus, the work of the Commission became more service-oriented than action-oriented as it related to specific departmental personnel.

Truman directed the Civil Service Commission to extend its classification policies to the entire civil service in 1945. The Commission dealt with a great deal of conflict in attempting to get field offices around the country to comply with the system. The Classification Act of 1949 resulted in part from that conflict. The act consolidated the Commission's authority and strengthened its role, especially in terms of auditing classifications.

Partially in response to the conflicts between the executive and congressional branches over control of the government and its employees, Congress created the First Hoover Commission in 1947. The recommendations of this Commission reflected many of the same concerns as those of the Brownlow Committee of 1937. In particular, the Commission strongly recommended greater decentralization of personnel functions and called for reorganization of pay and classification policies (Hoover Commission 1949). The Commission's report, like reports of such bodies before, helped set the agenda for public personnel policy decisions for a long time in the future. The immediate impact, however, was piecemeal and limited. It did stimulate a great deal of discussion of the role of personnel management in the federal government, thereby focusing attention on the service.

The Truman administration also took tentative steps toward development of employee relations programs. Many agencies addressed the health and welfare of employees. The Commission evaluated national government contributions to retirement systems and recommended changes, although it was not until later that much would be accomplished in this regard. Powers and functions of the Board of Appeals and Review of the Civil Service expanded in an effort to protect employee rights. The board had been created in 1930 but had very limited authority.

Among the more controversial elements of the immediate postwar personnel issues were loyalty and security. Because both the executive branch and Congress dabbled in loyalty and security issues, they became political hot potatoes (Latham 1966). The Truman administration was able to contain the issue for the most part, but in the 1950s, politics took over and the system ran amok. Truman created a loyalty program by executive order in 1947. The order gave the Civil Service Commission responsibility for the program. Loyalty investigations were developed and loyalty boards created to review cases. Generally, these programs cooled down the atmosphere, but Congress stirred things up occasionally (Bar of the City of New York, 1956). The Senate Investigation Subcommittee began investigations after 1948, and by 1954 was making vitriolic attacks on the public service.

President Truman's actions regarding equality of treatment and opportunity in the federal service represent some of his most significant and controversial contributions to public personnel management (Axelrod 2004; Gardner 2003). In 1946, he created the President's Committee on Civil Rights to study and make recommendations to him regarding racial discrimination in federal employment. Based on the Committee's recommendations, he sent a message to Congress in February 1948, requesting it to adopt legislation to end all racial discrimination, including discrimination in employment. Predictably, Congress did not act on his request, and he issued Executive Order 9980 on July 26, 1948, requiring each cabinet officer to integrate his/her workforce.

The order also detailed an implementation process and created the Fair Employment Board within the Civil Service Commission to review employment discrimination. It permitted employees or applicants to appeal decisions by employment officers directly to cabinet officials. On the same day, Truman issued Executive Order 9981, which required the military to provide equal treatment and opportunity to all personnel, thus integrating the Armed Forces. These actions by President Truman were not popular with Congress, military officers, or much of the electorate. Nonetheless, his policies prevailed and began the slow process of desegregation and anti-discrimination efforts in the federal and military services. These actions also started the push for broader social justice that took hold in the 1960s.

The United States' entry into the Korean War stimulated another buildup in the public service. The World War II experience served the nation well, and the buildup went relatively smoothly. The controversy over participation in the Korean War, however, had effects for all of the administration's domestic affairs. The public service tended to lose stature and got caught in the middle of the political conflicts. There were few specific personnel actions or policies that emerged from the conflict, but the Civil Service Commission once again had to use its expertise in recruiting large numbers of personnel. The flexibility developed during World War II returned to the recruitment and selection processes, as appointments once again were made temporary for the duration of the emergency.

B. Slowing Government Growth: The 1950s

The Eisenhower administration brought a business orientation back to government and the public service. It also represented the Republicans' opportunity to recapture some patronage after twenty years out of office. The administration was committed to economy and efficiency in government, and that translated into pressure on the public service. While Eisenhower was not particularly strongly patronage-oriented, he did experience pressures to reward the party, and in higher-level positions, patronage was evident. Otherwise, though, he was committed to the merit system. The biggest problem faced by the administration was that in bringing many people from the business world into public service, there was often insensitivity to expectations concerning public officials' conduct. Practices common in business were often frowned upon in the public service. As a result, the administration was plagued by conflicts of interest and other minor scandals that affected the public image of government in general. The civil service suffered in status and the morale of the public service was low (Kilpatrick et al. 1964).

The relationship of the Civil Service Commission to the administration changed during the Eisenhower administration (Harvey, 1970). The president made the chair of the Commission his assistant for personnel administration, thus giving the appearance that the Commission was more involved in political patronage issues as well as civil service concerns. That relationship further clouded the image of the public service.

The president also proposed the development of Schedule C to provide opportunities for utilizing high-level officials in a variety of positions. They would serve at the pleasure of the administration and would not have civil service protection. Schedule C was the predecessor to the Senior Executive Service, established at the end of the 1970s. While the administration experimented with the concept, it never was actually implemented.

The loyalty and security issues erupted into a major conflict during the Eisenhower years. An executive order in 1953 allowed departments to administer loyalty and security programs. The order also included a more vague standard for loyalty and security. Departments could separate employees for inconsistency with national security interests. That criterion was subject to much discretion and abuse (Rosenbloom 1971). At the same time, Senator Joseph McCarthy of Wisconsin began targeting individuals in department agencies, especially the State Department, for attack (Morganthau 1955). As Chair of the Senate Committee on Government Operations and its Permanent Subcommittee on Investigations, McCarthy launched vitriolic attacks on the public service, using anti-Communism as his justification. Many people had their careers ruined because the Senator accused them of having Communist sympathies. The administration did little to defend public servants. Predictably, morale sank to new lows. In 1954, the celebrated Army hearings during the summer were conducted in a circus atmosphere and McCarthy finally went too far for his Senate colleagues, who voted to censure him in December. Things calmed down somewhat, but the HUAC continued investigations into the 1960s. The vitriol of these activities did nothing to improve the status of the public service.

In 1955, the second Hoover Commission published its recommendations after examining the organization of the executive branch. Once again, its recommendations paralleled those of earlier committees and commissions. The distinguishing features of its recommendations were a call for more distinction between policy and administration as far as personnel was concerned and the call for creation of a Senior Civil Service along the lines of Eisenhower's Schedule C. The Commission also criticized the red tape in the personnel process and called for more flexibility and accountability (Commission on the Organization of the Executive Branch of Government 1955). Eisenhower proposed the creation of a Career Executive Program in 1957 and actually went so far as to create it by executive order, but political opposition in Congress ultimately thwarted the effort.

Collective bargaining continued to spread during the 1950s, especially at the state and local levels (Brooks 1971; Coleman 1990; Dickerson and Cayer 1994; Dilts et al. 1992; Kearney 2001; Stieber 1973; Wellington and Winter 1971). The Eisenhower administration was unsympathetic to collective bargaining; therefore, there were few developments at the national level. New York City began bargaining with its employees pursuant to an executive order issued by Mayor Robert Wagner in 1958. Wisconsin became the first state to provide for collective bargaining for public employees with the passage of legislation in 1959. These developments set the stage for a surge in such activity in the 1960s (Grodin and Wollett 1974; Hanslowe 1967; Moskow et al. 1970).

Concerns with employee welfare were not high on the agenda during the 1950s, but the government began to develop policies to better utilize human resources. The Government Employees Training Act of 1958 signaled recognition that it was necessary to deal with employee development. While the act focused on specific skills training, it represented an important step in working with employees. Many state and local governments followed suit.

C. Accountability, Equity and Justice: The 1960s

The early 1960s represented a period of idealism, epitomized by the Kennedy administration's mystique. A new image of the public service as being able to do anything it set its mind to encouraged many young people to pursue public service careers. Recruitment on college campuses was stepped up and the Peace Corps brought many people into that special segment of the public service.

The idealism of the 1960s was infused with a sense of social justice and fairness. The civil rights issue began to develop as a national agenda in the early 1960s and by the middle of the decade had become the major item on the agenda (Dye 1971; Galbraith 1973; Gardner 1961). Similarly, the plight of the poor and downtrodden received a great deal of attention. The Kennedy administration provided the philosophical thrust to these issues, along with many groups in the society. It was not until after John F. Kennedy's assassination, though, that many programs to address these issues were actually implemented.

With attention turning to social justice, the hold loyalty and security issues upon the national attention weakened. As a result, the public service was less a target of Congressional investigation. The role of the Civil Service Commission changed somewhat during the Kennedy years, as well (Harvey 1970). The chair of the Commission was actually made manager of the work of the Civil Service Commission. The Commission as a whole became the policy makers. The thrust was to make the Commission more cognizant of the integration of its policy with management, and the chair became more powerful than in earlier administrations.

Probably the biggest legacy of the Kennedy administration was in collective bargaining. Executive Order 10988 (1962) recognized, for the first time, the right of federal government employees to engage in negotiations with their employers. Agencies were directed to develop procedures for bargaining. This executive order set the tone for much of the country. As has been noted earlier, some state and local governments had already developed similar policies, but after 1962, the collective bargaining movement gained legitimacy and momentum. During the rest of the 1960s and into the 1970s, public sector collective bargaining grew phenomenally (Kearney 2001; Warner 1963; Wellington and Winter 1971). The Kennedy order was revised by later orders and finally by the Civil Service Reform Act of 1978, but its basic assumptions continue to serve as the foundation for federal service and much of state and local labor management relations (Horton 1973; Piskulich 1992; Sulzner 1982).

The Federal Salary Reform Act of 1962 and the Equal Pay Act of 1963 reflect the interest in equity and justice that affected the personnel system. The 1962 act made comparability with the private sector a feature of the compensation system, and the equal pay legislation required equal pay for equal work, thus focusing on internal equity. The Pay Comparability Act of 1970 refined the comparability issue and actually specified a process for determining comparability. This process was refined further by the Federal Employees Pay Comparability Act of 1990. The Bureau of Labor Statistics now conducts a national survey of professional, technical, and clerical pay for purposes of comparing national compensation with the private sector. This annual review is used to determine federal service pay levels.

The assassination of President Kennedy and succession of President Johnson presaged a period of intense conflict. The new president utilized his legislative skills to get Congress to pass a lot of social legislation. Among the most significant was the Civil Rights Act of 1964 (Gutman 2000). Although the employment part of the act applied only to the private sector, it set a tone for employment practices generally (Dye 1971). Governments at all levels were under pressure to conduct personnel processes in a nondiscriminatory manner. The act eventually was extended to the public service by the Equal Employment Opportunity Act of 1972 (actually an amendment to the 1964 act). Equal employment opportunity and affirmative action were to dominate the 1970s agendas and had their impetus in the 1960s (Glazer 1975; Gutman 2000; Hudson and Broadnax 1982; Kranz 1976; Krislov and Rosenbloom 1984; Rosenbloom 1977). Arising from similar values, the Age Discrimination in Employment Act of 1967 set limits on age discrimination.

The legislation and other policies focusing on equity issues stimulated a great deal of litigation during the late 1960s. The tendency to litigate issues continues to this day. Plaintiffs litigated not only issues of equal opportunity, but all types of employee rights issues (Baird et al. 1995; Jaegal and Cayer 1991; O'Neill 1993; Roberts 1985; Rosenbloom 1970, 1971, 1981; Rosenbloom and Caroll 1995). Litigation concerning the Hatch Act and its state counterparts was also frequent during this time (Martin 1973). Similarly, there were many challenges (generally unsuccessful) to veterans' preference policies at the national and state levels.

The dynamism and idealism of the 1960s had conflicting impacts on the public service. The early years of the Kennedy administration had an aura of optimism about them that gave the public service a good image, especially among young people. The morale problems of the public service during the 1950s faded. With the social upheaval of the middle of the decade, there were many conflicts with established values that strained the public service. Many critics of the conservatism of bureaucracy aimed their attacks at the public service. At the same time, there was a sense that government could accomplish anything it set out to do. The results were reflected in a developing distrust of the establishment (including the public bureaucracy) and a yearning for change.

The New Public Administration was born in the 1960s and found expression in the Minnow-brook conference in 1970 (Marini 1971). The New Public Administration focused on the need for public administrators to be change agents and was infused with a great deal of idealism about the mission and integrity of the public service (Bellone 1980; Frederickson 1980; Waldo 1971). Advocates of the New Public Administration suspected the existing bureaucracy of serving the interests of the economically and politically powerful. Some students of bureaucracy also characterized the system as a new machine politics, serving the interests of the professional bureaucrat rather than the citizen (Lowi 1967). Consistent with emphases on social justice and equity, the New Public Administrationists were supposed to become the advocates for the clientele of agencies and programs and particularly for the powerless and downtrodden. While it is not surprising that public bureaucracy did not openly embrace the New Public Administration perspective, it is also clear that the movement has sensitized the bureaucracy, policy makers, and the general public to the issues it raised.

IV. RETRENCHMENT AND REFORM

Since 1970, political values have moved away from the idea that government intervention is the answer to all societal problems and toward a calculated evaluation of what government should be doing. The result has been a focus on economizing in government and in reducing its size (Levine 1978, 1979; Nathan et al. 1983; Rubin 1985). Evaluation of programs and activities is also a major objective in much of government policy since the early 1970s.

A. SETTING THE STAGE FOR REFORM: THE 1970S

The early 1970s were troubled times for the nation as a whole and the public service in particular. With the election of President Richard Nixon in 1968, political party control of the presidency once again changed hands. Unfortunately for the Nixon administration, control of the Congress did not change. Thus, a struggle was inevitable, especially because there was also much personal distrust and animosity between the leadership of the administration and leaders in Congress.

The Nixon administration clearly wanted to cut back on government activity and deemphasize social issues, but these objectives were virtually impossible to accomplish, given Congressional opposition. Consequently, many of the social equity issues of the 1960s carried over and were reflected in such acts as the Equal Employment Opportunity Act of 1972, the Comprehensive Employment Training Act of 1973, and the Rehabilitation Act of 1973. These laws promoted employment opportunity for groups that had earlier been the target of discriminatory practices. For the most part, the administration did not actively support these programs.

Social equity issues continued to be addressed in the courts and by the Equal Employment Opportunity Commission, among other agencies. Actually, many conflicts developed. Much of the litigation centered around examination issues, although court action also addressed pay issues (Kearney and Hays, 1985). Reflecting concerns with equity, the Equal Employment Opportunity Commission (EEOC) published guidelines for state and local governments and contractors to use in selecting employees in 1970. The Departments of Justice and Labor and the Civil Service Commission promulgated separate guidelines in 1976. After much confusion about the two sets of guidelines, the two were compromised and a single set was developed in 1978. These guidelines had a great impact on state and local governments. Many grants were awarded on the condition that the grantee have an affirmative action plan. Similarly, individuals who felt they had been discriminated against were able to bring charges against employers to contract compliance offices or the EEOC. Employers found to be discriminatory could be subject to a variety of remedies, including back pay and employment of the individual discriminated against. Usually, the guilty party would also be required to develop and implement an affirmative action plan.

Examinations came under a great deal of scrutiny in this period as well. The Federal Service Entrance Examination (FSEE) was criticized for not being job-specific enough, and thus subject to equal employment suspicion. The Professional and Administrative Careers Exam (PACE) was developed in 1974 to replace FSEE. PACE was criticized on the same grounds and was discontinued in 1984. Each department is now responsible for developing its own exams relevant to the jobs for which it is recruiting. Assessment centers for the selection of employees or for promotion became popular during the 1970s (Ross 1979; Sackett 1982). They replaced traditional exams in many decisions.

Nixon advocated general revenue sharing as a way of loosening the federal government's control over activities at the state and local levels. The Revenue Sharing Act of 1972 distributed money to state and local governments with few strings attached, although a significant personnel issue was addressed by the prohibition of discrimination in jurisdictions using the revenue-sharing funds. The attempt to weaken the federal government's influence over other units of government set the stage for further developments in that direction during the 1980s.

The administration also ordered absolute veterans' preference for Vietnam veterans in grades 1 through 5 of the federal service. The Vietnam Veterans Readjustment Act (1974) required government contractors to give special consideration to those veterans.

The Nixon administration is probably best remembered in personnel management for direct challenges to the merit system. Frustrated by a bureaucracy the administration perceived as unsympathetic to its values, the administration developed an elaborate system for selecting people who were more politically supportive. A document known as the Malek Manual (Federal Political Personnel Manual 1976) was used by political operatives in the administration. Its use, along with the Watergate scandal of 1974, undermined the integrity of the public service and the public image of it again sank (Panetta and Gall 1971; Weisband and Franck 1975). As a result of these problems, ethics in the public service received a high level of attention (Bowman 1977; Stewart 1984).

Reflecting growing concerns with training and development, the Intergovernmental Personnel Act of 1970 provided money to state and local governments for training purposes. At the same time, organizational humanists were influential in training circles (Argyris 1973a, 1973b, 1983; Bennis 1973; Berkley 1971; Golembiewski and Eddy 1978; Golembiewski et al. 1981; Harmon 1981; Kaplan and Tausky 1977; Presthus 1978; Simmons 1981). The money funded many behaviorally oriented training programs at all levels of government. While specific skill training was done in some programs, the emphasis was clearly on more behavioral considerations. Motivation and productivity were central themes, along with organizational development (Newland 1972).

The capstone to the 1970s was the Civil Service Reform Act (CSRA) of 1978, the only major reform in ninety-five years (Ingraham and Ban 1984). The Carter administration was not like the Democratic administrations of the 1960s, or even those of the 1930s and 1940s, in its approach to government responsibilities. Like the Republican Nixon administration preceding it, the Carter administration wanted a reduction in the size of government. Carter came to the presidency viewed as an outsider by Washingtonians. He did little to ingratiate himself to those who wielded power and influence. As a result, his relationship with the civil service was not a very good one. Despite strong dissent from some (Rosen 1978, 1983), many in the public service supported his efforts for reform. A major cornerstone of his effort to make government more efficient and responsive was the Civil Service Reform Act, which he convinced Congress to pass.

The president set up a task force to conduct a thorough examination of all aspects of federal government personnel. The task force made its recommendations in 1977 and Congress passed many of them into law in the 1978 act (Ingraham and Rosenbloom 1992; President's Reorganization Project 1977). CSRA strengthened personnel management and integrated it more closely with the rest of the executive branch. Personnel was once again viewed as part of management.

At the same time, the act reorganized the personnel function by eliminating the Civil Service Commission and replacing it with several agencies. Three major agencies emerged in the reorganization. The Office of Personnel Management (OPM) became the major policy making arm of personnel and was directly responsible to the president. The Federal Labor Relations Authority (FLRA) was made a separate agency with responsibility for administration of the federal service's labor management relations program. The Merit Systems Protection Board (MSPB) was created to protect employees from prohibited personnel practices. It served as an appeals board for employees but also monitored the overall implementation of personnel policies. It was charged with making annual reports on problems in the system.

The 1978 act also established the Senior Executive Service (SES). A concept going back at least as far as the Brownlow Committee, the SES allowed for flexibility in assignment of high-level employees. They could be assigned to take advantage of their special expertise wherever it was needed. The idea behind the system was to more effectively use the talent available and to avoid some of the red tape associated with the civil service system (Buchanan 1981; Colby and Ingraham 1982; Huddleston 1992; Long 1981; Pagano 1984; Rosen 1981; Waldby and Hartsfield 1984).

At the same time the CSRA was being passed, President Carter proposed stronger rules on conflicts of interest and other behavior of public employees. The Ethics in Government Act was passed in 1978, placing restrictions on post-government employment and requiring many public employees to divest themselves of investments, make public their financial statements, and refrain from participation in decisions in which a conflict of interest might appear (Walter 1981). The act was stimulated in part by the fallout from the Watergate scandal (Bowman 1977; Plant and Gortner 1981).

The reforms in civil service and the concern with ethics stimulated many state and local governments to action (Plant and Gortner 1981). While some predated the federal service in reorganization, most undertook studies of their systems after the 1978 act, and many made changes modeled on the new federal system (Dressang 1982). Many also adopted more stringent ethics laws (Hays and Gleissner 1981; Maletz and Herbel 2000). Open meeting laws and freedom of information or open access legislation were also part of the sunshine legislation movement to make government more accountable (Feinberg 1997).

The state and local levels were the leaders in another area of activity with important public service implications. Proposition 13, passed by California voters in 1978, stimulated the era of cutback management that is felt to this day. Taxpayer revolts spread across the country and governments suddenly found themselves under pressure to cut back expenditures. Because personnel costs represented the largest expenditure item for most governments, cutback meant reductions in personnel. Reductions-in-force, layoffs, and other forms of cuts forced a new examination of public services and the bases on which they operated (Koteen 1997; Lewis et al. 1983; Rubin 1985). Productivity improvement gained increasing attention as one means of coping with reductions.

B. More Retrenchment: The 1980s

The plight of the public service took a turn for the worse in the 1980s. The Reagan administration came to office partly on the basis of an attack on the public service. The attack was part of a larger broadside against big government (Levine 1986). Not surprisingly, the morale of the public service plummeted. In addition to portraying the civil service as a main culprit in what the administration considered to be wasteful government activity, the administration attempted to make the public service over in an ideological sense (Newland 1983). Congress and the courts became the sources of support for public employees.

The 1981 PATCO strike and the administration's handling of it symbolized the Reagan administration's approach. Although the Professional Air Traffic Controllers had endorsed Reagan in his bid for the presidency, it bore the brunt of the new values. Upon going on strike, the union was informed that employees would be fired if they did not return to work. That is just what happened after the administration succeeded in making the union appear unreasonable because of its pay demands. The union never could capture the attention of the public with what it considered to be its more important issues. With public opinion securely on his side, Reagan used PATCO as an example of how his administration would play hardball with public employees. Of course, because the strike was illegal, the union had no solid ground to stand on, despite the fact that strikes throughout the public sector had been handled differently in the past, with employees being welcomed back after a settlement of the issues. The Reagan administration stood firm and PATCO was decertified. The message to public employee unions was clear, and they have not been very effective in pressing their demands at any level of government since. The phenomenal growth of public employee unions and collective bargaining was brought to an abrupt halt.

The insensitivity of many of Reagan's appointments to conflicts of interest further disheartened the public service (Newland 1983, 1987; Pfiffner 1987; Rosen 1983). Like Eisenhower in the 1950s, Reagan seemed to have a penchant for appointing people whose backgrounds had not been carefully checked or who behaved in office as if the department or agency with which they were associated was their own private domain. Once again, practices acceptable in private business proved to be unacceptable in the public service. Many of the appointees seemed not to be able to understand this, resulting in embarrassing episodes for the administration. The image of unethical behavior rubbed off on the public service as a whole. In 1989, the Ethics Reform Act was passed, strengthening some of the rules governing employee behavior.

The administration also made a major issue of deemphasizing equal employment opportunity and affirmative action (Krislov and Rosenbloom 1984; Thompson 1984). It entered court cases in support of overturning such efforts, thereby alienating many state and local governments that earlier had established equal employment opportunity and affirmative action programs at the demand of the federal government. Many also felt that such efforts were right, given concerns with equity and justice and recognition of demographic changes. They resented having to now defend against efforts by the administration and others to dismantle the programs they had been pressured to develop in the first place. Employee organizations and unions began to embrace affirmation action and equal employment opportunity.

Comparable worth has been described as the issue of the 1980s and was an extension of the equal employment opportunity commitments of three decades earlier (Doherty and Harriman 1981; Johanson 1984a, 1984b; Moore and Abraham 1994; Neuse 1982; Remick 1981; Steel and Lovrich 1987; Tompkins 1987). Among the leading proponents of comparable worth are employee unions, especially the American Federation of State, County, and Municipal Employees.

The Reagan administration also was a strong advocate of government cutback (Levine 1986; Rubin 1985). Along with that went personnel cuts. While the national government was able to cut back on many programs, and particularly the funding of social programs, state and local governments were forced to take up the slack (Ciglar 1994; Conlan 1998; Hulten and Sawhill 1984; Nathan et al. 1983; Palmer and Sawhill 1984; Rivlin 1992; Wallin 1998). Many state and local government officials supported the idea of cuts, but the fact is that public agencies at those levels had to deal with increased demands for services while having fewer resources with which to deliver them. They faced issues concerning their capacity to perform the functions devolved to them. Capacity remains an issue for state and local governments.

Sexual harassment is another concern that received increasing attention as a result of changes in the workforce (Dressang and Stuiber 1991; MacKinnon 1979; Neugarten and Shafritz 1981; Ross and England 1987). In 1986, the US Supreme Court explicitly accepted *quid pro quo* and *hostile environment* harassment as illegal (*Meritor Savings Bank v. Vinson*1986). *Quid pro quo* harassment refers to situations in which employment decisions are dependent upon sexual favors, and *hostile environment* harassment refers to a work environment in which such things as suggestive comments, touching, leering, and offensive materials make individuals uncomfortable or create feelings of intimidation (MacKinnon 1979).

Rights issues are always important concerns with public employees because of the need of public agencies for public support. In the 1980s, drug use among public employees led to suggestions for testing all public employees or for random testing. Similarly, polygraph tests were suggested as screening devices for potential employees. Of course, employees and their unions usually were hesitant to accept such proposals. Civil liberties questions concerning such programs received a great deal of attention (Elliott 1989; O'Neill 1993; Thompson et al. 1991). Public and private employers also created employee assistance programs, in part to address problems identified by substance abuse tests (Johnson 1986; Kemp 1985). These programs dealt with problems employees had that might affect their abilities to be productive.

The Civil Service Reform Act of 1978 laid the groundwork for innovation and experimentation in public personnel management during the 1980s. For example, some federal agencies and many state and local governments experimented with merit pay or pay-for-performance systems. Pay-for-performance appealed to many public officials. It was difficult to imagine anyone not wanting to reward performance. However, implementation was another story. Lack of agreement on what constituted meritorious performance and reluctance of political decision makers to dedicate the kinds of funds to make merit pay significant led to lack of success of most pay-for-performance systems. The promise of such systems was much greater than the reality of their implementation (Bernadin et al. 1998; Ingraham 1993; Kellough 2002; Kellough and Lu 1993; National Research Council 1991; Perry 2003).

Experiments in classification reform and pay banding also emerged during the 1980s. In several federal installations, efforts were made to find ways of making classification and compensation systems more flexible. While the experiments led to some successes, efforts to broaden their use have not been readily accepted (Ban, 1991; Beecher, 2003; National Academy of Public Administration 1983, 1991, 1995; Risher and Schay 1994).

As the 1980s ended, George H. W. Bush was president and generally followed the approaches developed by the Reagan administration. However, the rhetoric bashing of the public service was noticeably lacking in his administration. While the conservative wing of his political party pressured him to maintain many of the policies of his predecessor, the tone of his administration was much less harsh.

V. THE 1990s AND BEYOND: REINVENTION, REENGINEERING, AND DOWNSIZING

The 1990s began with a continuation of the retrenchment and cutback focus of the 1980s. As the decade progressed, the attacks on government escalated and the political environment also generated reactions to many programs fostering social equity. While Bill Clinton retook the presidency for the Democrats running for office on a platform that included reaching out to all segments of society, he quickly encountered resistance. The midterm elections of 1994 resulted in a Republican majority in Congress controlled by the conservative wing of the party. Anti-government rhetoric dominated the political agenda, and the president began wavering in his support of moderate and liberal policies. For public personnel management, the implications were and are many. While the major focus was on cutting back the scope and size of government, many activities have been aimed at improving government performance and achieving savings through such efforts. Thus, reinvention and reengineering became the fads of the 1990s, using Total Quality Management and variations of it as the tool for accomplishing the objectives.

In 1989, the National Commission on the Public Service (Volcker Commission) issued a report entitled *Leadership for the Public Service* that stimulated much analysis of personnel systems, especially at the national level. It was followed by the National Commission on the State and Local Public Service, which published a report in 1993 paralleling the Volcker Commission's recommendations. President Clinton appointed Vice President Al Gore to head the National Performance Review, which issued reports in 1993 and 1994 focusing on approaches to reinventing and reengineering government agencies and programs. All of these reports incorporated elements of quality management approaches. Streamlining and cutting back were results of the efforts, but the primary focus was on improving performance of agencies and personnel

(Ingraham et al. 1994). Studies of and recommendations for improving all aspects of personnel administration continue (Light 1999; National Academy of Public Administration 2004).

Changing demographics put new pressures on personnel systems to accommodate a workforce that was increasingly older, better educated, more diverse, and more white collar (Dolan 2004; Dolan and Rosenbloom 2003; Hudson Institute 1988; Light 1999; Pomerleau 1994; US Office of Personnel Management 1993). The changing nature of the workforce challenged public personnel management in many ways. Organizations found that they had to sensitize managers and employees to the diverse workforce and ensure that the work environment was comfortable for all. The contemporary workforce had very different expectations of the employer organization. They expected more opportunity for participation in decisions affecting them. They also expected to change jobs/careers several times in their lives. These expectations created major challenges for employers (Light 1999).

Equal employment opportunity and affirmative action programs were major elements of public personnel systems by the early 1990s. The Civil Rights Act of 1991 strengthened enforcement of anti-discrimination policies and permitted collection of compensatory and punitive damages for discrimination. It also called for establishment of a Glass Ceiling Commission to deal with lack of advancement opportunities of women and minorities above certain levels in management (Guy 1993).

Starting in the mid-1990s, opponents of affirmative action programs launched an all-out assault. As the political system approached the 1996 presidential elections, candidates staked out their positions in response to the conservative swing apparent in the 1994 midterm elections. Republican candidates attacked affirmative action programs, with Governor Pete Wilson of California leading the way. He convinced the University of California Board of Regents to abandon affirmative action programs for their campuses. President Clinton, mindful of the saliency of the issue, ordered a review of affirmative action programs in the federal government and eventually went on record in strong support of improving but not abandoning affirmative action. The courts became more open to challenges to such programs as well.

George W. Bush became president after the 2000 election. Clearly, he did not support affirmative action and worked to undermine its use. Some states, such as California and Washington, adopted policies prohibiting use of affirmative action, and court decisions generally applied a very strict scrutiny standard. However, the US Supreme Court did approve of affirmative action in law school admissions at the University of Michigan (*Grutter v. Bollinger* 2003). Scholars debate the applicability of the decision to personnel matters, but clearly, the Court has indicated that some forms of affirmative action are acceptable (Sisneros 2004).

As part of the equal opportunity debate, people with disabilities have pressed for their rights. The Americans with Disabilities Act of 1990 was passed and has had immense implications for public personnel (Cozzetto 1994; Crampton and Hodge 2003; Kellough 2000; Mani 2003). All aspects of personnel systems are subject to analysis to ensure that they are not discriminatory against those with disabilities.

Gays and lesbians also began asserting their rights as American citizens. They were encouraged by candidate Clinton, who promised to support their interests and to lift the ban on gays and lesbians in the military. President Clinton, however, backed down from his position in the face of major political opposition, including opposition in his own party in Congress. A compromise allowed gays and lesbians to serve in the military as long as they did not publicly discuss the fact that they were gay or lesbian. Their superiors were not supposed to ask about sexual orientation either. Many state and local governments are now the arenas for policy on the issue. Many jurisdictions have passed laws or ordinances protecting gays and lesbians against discrimination, but some have generated citizen initiatives that rescind such policies or prohibit establishment of them. In 2004, gay marriage arose as a hot-button issue in the election campaigns and is having implications for personnel policies, especially regarding benefits. Litigation over the policies is prevalent; thus, there is as yet no definitive approach to dealing with the rights of gays and lesbians in public employment (Lee and Greenlaw 1995; McNaught 1993; Simon and Daly 1992). Domestic partnership policies extending to domestic partners the same benefits provided to spouses often are debated with major gay and lesbian undertones, although the policies often extend to heterosexual relationships as well (Gossett 1994; IPMA HR Center 1996).

Harassment is another equity issue that has been highly visible. Harassment is "repeated and persistent attempts to torment, wear down, frustrate, or get a reaction from another. It is treatment that persistently provokes, pressures, frightens, intimidates, or otherwise discomforts another person" (Brodsky 1976). Employees may experience harassment because of their race, ethnicity, religion, gender, or sexual orientation. Women have been subjected to harassment since they became part of work forces (Newman et al. 2003). The Civil Rights Act of 1964 and the Equal Employment Opportunity Act of 1972 dealt with broad aspects of harassment in the workplace, but it took much effort on the part of organizations such as the National Organization for Women to draw attention to the sexual exploitation of women in the workplace. Eventually, the Equal Employment Opportunity Commission defined sexual harassment as a violation of federal law and published guidelines defining sexual harassment as "unwelcome advances, requests for sexual favors, and other verbal or physical conduct of a sexual nature…when submission to or rejection of this conduct explicitly or implicitly affects an individual's employment, unreasonably interferes with an individual's work performance or creates an intimidating, hostile or offensive work environment" (US Equal Opportunity Commission, 1980).

The extent of sexual harassment is difficult to measure, but various surveys and studies indicate that it is a serious problem in employment, with as many as 50% of women and 40% of men reporting having been the victim of sexual harassment (Gutek 1985; Hoyman 1998; Reese and Lindenberg 1997; Selden 2003; US General Accounting Office 1995; US Merit Systems Protection Board 1995). Employers have a responsibility to develop a policy on sexual harassment and to communicate it clearly to everyone in the organization. The courts often hold employers liable for damages if they do not make good faith efforts to prevent sexual harassment and/or to correct it if it has occurred (*Harris v. Forklift Systems* 1993; *Meritor Savings Bank v. Vinson* 1986; *Ellison v. Brady* 1991). The Civil Rights Act of 1991 allows harassed employees to sue for as much as $300,000 in punitive damages in addition to any back pay and attorney's fees. In 1998, the Supreme Court ruled that same-sex harassment also is covered under the Civil Rights Act (*Oncale v. Sundowner Offshore Services, Inc.*, 1998).

Employee benefits emerged as a major personnel issue in the 1990s (Cayer 2003). The costs of health care benefits increased dramatically during the 1990s and continue unabated. Employers responded by redesigning health care benefits. Health Maintenance Organizations (HMO) and Preferred Provider Organizations (PPO) became the dominant health care plans, displacing the traditional indemnity insurance plans. Employers also now increasingly require employees to share in the cost of premiums and include fees (copays) for services as a way of reducing costs. Flexible plans also have become staples, as employees can choose only the benefits of most value to them.

Employers now offer many benefits as family-friendly benefits packages (Cayer 2003). The Family and Medical Leave Act of 1993 requires all employers of at least 50 people to allow up to twelve weeks of unpaid family and medical leave in any twelve-month period. In 2002, California adopted the first paid family leave policy, providing employees 55% of their pay for up to six weeks.

Violence in the workplace now costs employers more than $40 billion annually, with more than two million victims (Injury Prevention Research Center, 2001; *IPMA News*, 1999). Employees and employers experience attacks from stressed colleagues, family members, and clients (Elliot and Jarrett 1994; Johnson and Indvik 1994). Employers find it necessary to implement programs to help avoid the violence and to deal with the aftermath of incidents of violence (Bowman and Zigmond 1997; Chernier 1998). The issue has spawned efforts to assess the potential for violence and what steps might be taken to prevent it. Training programs help supervisors and employees to recognize the signs of stress and behavior that can lead to violence. Employers also now have to provide security and support for employees who work with victims of such violence.

The challenges for personnel management in the contemporary workplace are many. The political and demographic shifts keep public personnel a dynamic field. The image of the public service continues to suffer, especially because presidential administrations seem to have a penchant for getting mired in controversies over the actions of many of their appointees and nominees. In the George W. Bush administration, investigations concerning influence by special interests in energy and environmental policy have tainted the public service. The scandals involving abuse of prisoners in Iraq and contracts for rebuilding and other activities in Iraq have further demeaned the public service as questions arise as to who approved such actions. While the focus is on elected and politically appointed officials, the general public rarely makes a distinction between them and the public service overall. The result is a lessening of confidence in the public service, making it more difficult for it to fulfill its role.

The Bush administration developed "Strategic Management of Human Capital" as the theme for its approach to public personnel management (Abramson 200217; US General Accounting Office 2002). The approach focuses on recruiting high-quality employees and creating strategies for motivation and performance. Part of the strategy is to reduce the rules protecting public employees, including collective bargaining rights, and make them more responsive to elected officials, as was done with the creation of the Department of Homeland Security.

The Bush administration has also promoted privatization, promising to privatize as much as 50% of public employment. Many state and local governments also engage in contracting or privatization of public services, often because they anticipate savings on personnel costs (Brown and Potoski 2003; Chi et al. 2004). Privatization presents many challenges, as employers need new sets of tools to develop requests for proposals, evaluate bids, and negotiate and monitor contracts (Cooper 2003; Kettl 1993; Van Slyke 2003). Unions also generally oppose privatization; thus, employers have labor relations issues to address as well.

Reform is a constant for personnel systems. Some contemporary reforms have replaced civil service systems with performance-based approaches (Chi 2004; Scott 2004). The idea is to reduce the protections to public employees and focus on performance outcomes. Thus, Georgia and Florida have eliminated their civil service systems, and other states, such as Texas, have made major changes to their systems. The reforms reignite the debate about the proper balance between a neutral service and political partisanship because of the potential for political abuse (Condrey and Maranto 2001; Kellough and Selden 2003).

VI. SUMMARY

Public personnel management in the United States has undergone continual change (Ingraham et al. 1994; Lane and Wolf 1990; Light 1999; McEnery and Lifter 1987; Rothwell et al. 2000; Wooldridge and Wester 1991). The change is usually in response to changing political values. The political values of the very first administrations involved gaining support for the new system, and every administration since has had some concern with getting public employees to buy into its value system. Otherwise, it is very difficult to have a responsive public service. The extent to which the public service should be responsive to the administration has been continually debated. The nation has swung from extremes of responsiveness (unmitigated spoils) to extreme neutrality (the early twentieth century). Each time, there is a reaction that swings the pendulum back to some extent.

The early literature of public personnel management focused on descriptions and analyses of specific personnel systems or problems. Thus, the civil service system might have been examined or spoils might have been profiled. However, there was very little in the way of formal consideration of the role of personnel in overall management. Woodrow Wilson (1885) provided an intellectual justification for the reform movement of four years earlier and has been used as a major centerpiece of the civil service system. The literature of the early nineteenth century built upon that approach, along with the scientific management principles of management approach. Until the 1960s, separation of politics and administration was accepted as a given in public personnel management (Rosenbloom 1982).

The literature of the 1960s began to question the separation of politics and administration or policy and administration. With that change came recognition of the fact that public personnel management was shaped by political values. Mosher (1968) led the way, and Thompson's (1975) classic *Personnel Policy in the City* made one of the most articulate cases for the premise. Criticism of the field as being devoid of theory and dull and plodding, among other things, was a challenge to public personnel management as well (Klingler and Nalbandian 1978; Milward 1978; Rosenbloom 1973; Shafritz 1975). The literature of the 1970s and 1980s represents a much more research-oriented approach and is based on placing public personnel management into the context of the politics and public policy in which it operates (Cayer 2003; Elliot 1985; Klingner 1981; Mainzer 1973; Nalbandian and Klingner 1982; Rich 1982; Rosenbloom 1973; 1982; Stein 1987; Thompson 1975, 1991, 1995).

In modern-day recognition of the centrality of politics in the personnel process, we have come full circle from the beginning days of the nation. Public personnel management is both politics and administration, with the balance between the two being one of the central questions for scholars and personnel managers (Ingraham and Kettl 1992; Ingraham et al. 1994; Klay 1983; Macy et al. 1983; Newland 1984a; O'Toole 1987; Thompson 1995). Building an effective organization requires both internal and external political skills (Carnevale 1995). Contemporary challenges arise from the changing values of the population served by and making up the public service (Light 1999). Public personnel management must accommodate high expectations for performance with changing employee expectations about their participation in decision-making and recognition of their needs as well. Governments at all levels continually reform their systems to accommodate changing values and political forces (Beecher 2003; Butcher and Massey 2003; Condrey and Maranto 2001).

REFERENCES

Argyris, C., Some limits of rational man organizational theory, *Public Administration Review*, 33, 253–267, 1973a.

Argyris, C., Organization man: rational and self-actualizing, *Public Administration Review*, 33, 354–357, 1973b.

Argyris, C., *Reasoning, Learning, and Action: Individual and Organizational*, Jossey-Bass, San Francisco, CA, 1983.

Aronson, A. H., Merit systems under the social security act, *Public Personnel Review*, 1, 20–24, 1940.

Aronson, A. H., *States and Kinship in the Higher Civil Service*, Harvard University Press, Cambridge, MA, 1964.

Aronson, A. H., State and local personnel administration, In *Biography of an Ideal, by the United States Civil Service Commission*, US Government Printing Office, Washington, DC, 1974.

Axelrod, A., *When the Buck Stops with You*, Portfolio/Penguin, New York, 2004.

Baird, J., Kadue, D. D., and Sulzer, K. D., *Public Employee Privacy: A Legal and Practical Guide to Issues Affecting the Workplace*, The American Bar Association, Chicago, IL, 1995.

Ban, C., The Navy demonstration project: an experiment in experimentation, In *Public Personnel Management: Current Concerns, Future Challenges*, Ban, C. and Riccucci, N., Eds., Longman, New York, pp. 31–41, 1991.

Bar of the City of New York, *Report of the Special Committee on the Federal Loyalty Security Program*, Dodd Mead, New York, 1956.

Barnard, C. I., *The Functions of the Executive*, Harvard University Press, Cambridge, MA, 1968.

Beecher, D. B., The next wave of civil service reform, *Public Personnel Management*, 32, 457–474, 2003.

Bellone, C., Ed., *Organization Theory and the New Public Administration*, Allyn and Bacon, Boston, MA, 1980.

Bennis, W., *Beyond Bureaucracy*, McGraw-Hill, New York, 1973.

Berkley, G. R., *The Administrative Revolution*, Prentice Hall, Englewood Cliffs, NJ, 1971.

Bernadin, H. J., Hagan, C. M., Kane, J. S., and Villanova, P., Effective performance management: a focus on precision, customers, and constraints, In *Performance Appraisal*, Smither, J. W., Ed., Jossey-Bass, San Francisco, CA, pp. 3–48, 1998.

Bowman, J. S., Ethics in the federal service: a post-watergate view, *Midwest Review of Public Administration*, 11, 3–20, 1977.

Bowman, J. S. and Zigmond, C. J., State government responses to violence, *Public Personnel Management*, 29, 289–300, 1997.

Brodsky, C. M., *The Harassed Worker*, Lexington Books, Lexington, MA, 1976.

Brooks, T. R., *Toil and Trouble*, 2nd ed., Dell, New York, 1971.

Brown, T. L. and Potoski, M., Contract management capacity in municipal and county governments, *Public Administration Review*, 63, 153–163, 2003.

Buchanan, B., The senior executive service: how we can tell if it works, *Public Administration Review*, 41, 349–358, 1981.

Butcher, T. and Massey, A., *Modernizing Civil Service*, Edward Elgar, Northampton, MA, 2003.

Carnevale, D. G., *Trustworthy Government: Leadership and Management Strategies for Building Trust and High Performance*, Jossey-Bass, San Francisco, CA, 1995.

Cayer, N. J., *Public Personnel Administration in the United States*, 4th ed., Wadsworth/Thomson, Belmont, CA, 2003.

Chernier, E., The workplace: a battleground for violence, *Public Personnel Management*, 27, 557–568, 1998.

Chi, K. S., Trends in state civil service systems: personnel agencies, reform efforts, classification and workforce planning, In *The Book of the States*, Vol. 36, The Council of State Governments, Lexington, KY, pp. 405–432, 2004.

Chi, K. S., Arnold, K. A., and Perkins, H. M., Privatization in state government: trends and issues, In *The Book of the States*, Vol. 36, The Council of State Governments, Lexington, KY, pp. 465–482, 2004.

Ciglar, B. A., State–local relations: a need for reinvention?, *Intergovernmental Perspective*, 20, 20–23, 1994.

Civil Service Assembly, *Position Classification in the Public Service*, Civil Service Assembly, Chicago, IL, 1941.

Colby, P. W. and Ingraham, P. W., Individual motivation and institutional changes under the senior executive service, *Review of Public Personnel Administration*, 2, 101–118, 1982.

Coleman, C. J., *Managing Labor Relations in the Public Sector*, Jossey-Bass, San Francisco, CA, 1990.

Commission on the Organization of the Executive Branch of Government, *Personnel and Civil Service: A Report to Congress*, U.S. Government Printing Office, Washington, DC, 1955.

Conlan, T., *From New Federalism to Devolution—Twenty-Five Years of Intergovernmental Reform*, Brookings, Washington, DC, 1998.

Condrey, S. E. and Maranto, R., Eds., *Radical Reform of Civil Service*, Lexington Books, New York, 2001.

Cooper, P. J., *Governing by Contract: Challenges and Opportunities for Public Managers*, CQ Press, Washington, DC, 2003.

Cozzeto, D. A., Implications of ADA for state and local government: judicial activism reincarnated, *Public Personnel Management*, 23, 105–116, 1994.

Crampton, S. M. and Hodge, J. W., The ADA and disability accommodations, *Public Personnel Management*, 32, 143–154, 2003.

Crenson, M. A., *The Federal Machine: Beginning of a Bureaucracy in Jacksonian America*, Johns Hopkins University Press, Baltimore, MD, 1975.

Davis, C. E., Veterans' preference and civil service employment: issues and policy implications, *Review of Public Personnel Administration*, 2, 57–65, 1982.

Dickerson, S. D. and Cayer, N. J., The environmental context of public labor relations, In *Handbook of Public Sector Labor Relations*, Rabin, J., Vocino, T., Hildreth, W. B., and Miller, G. J., Eds., Marcel Dekker, New York, 1994.

Dilts, D., Deitsch, C., and Rassuli, A., *Labor Relations Law in State and Local Government*, Quorum Books, Westport, CT, 1992.

Doherty, M. H. and Harriman, A., Comparable worth: the equal employment issue of the 1980s, *Review of Public Personnel Administration*, 1, 11–31, 1981.

Dolan, J., Gender equity: illusion or reality for women in the federal executive service?, *Public Administration Review*, 64, 299–306, 2004.

Dolan, J. and Rosenbloom, D. H., Eds., *Representative Bureaucracy: Classic Readings and Continuing Controversies*, M.E. Sharpe, Armonk, NY, 2003.

Dressang, D. L., Diffusion of civil service reform: the federal and state governments, *Review of Public Personnel Administration*, 2, 35–47, 1982.

Dressang, D. L. and Stuiber, P. J., Sexual harassment: challenges for the future, In *Public Personnel Management: Current Concerns, Future Challenges*, Ban, C. and Riccucci, N., Eds., Longman, New York, pp. 114–125, 1991.

Dye, T. R., *The Politics of Equality*, Bobbs-Merrill, Indianapolis, IN, 1971.

Elliot, R. H., *Public Personnel Administration: A Values Perspective*, Reston, VA, 1985.

Elliot, R. H., Drug testing and public personnel administration, *Review of Public Personnel Administration*, 9, 15–31, 1989.

Elliot, R. H. and Jarrett, D. T., Violence in the workplace: the role of human resource management, *Public Personnel Management*, 23, 287–289, 1994.

Emmert, M. A. and Gregory, B. L., Veterans' preference and the merit system, In *Centenary Issues of the Pendleton Act of 1883*, Rosenbloom, D. H., Ed., Marcel Dekker, New York, pp. 45–61, 1982.

Eriksson, E. M., The federal civil service under President Jackson, *Mississippi Valley Historical Review*, 13, 527–528, 1927.

Federal personnel manual: the Malek manual, *The Bureaucrat*, 4, 429–508, 1976.

Feinberg, L., Open government and freedom of information: fishbowl accountability?, In *Handbook of Public Law and Administration*, Cooper, P. J. and Newland, C. A., Eds., Jossey-Bass, San Francisco, CA, pp. 376–399, 1997.

Fish, C. R., *The Civil Service and the Patronage*, Longmans, Green, New York, 1905.

Frederickson, H. G., *New Public Administration*, University of Alabama Press, Tuscaloosa, AL, 1980.

Galbraith, J. K., *Economics and the Public Purpose*, Houghton Mifflin, Boston, MA, 1973.

Gardner, J., *Excellence: Can We Be Equal and Excellent Too?*, Harper & Row, New York, 1961.

Gardner, M. R., *Harry Truman and Civil Rights: Moral Courage and Political Risk*, Southern Illinois University Press, Carbondale, IL, 2003.

Glazer and Nathan, *Affirmative Discrimination: Ethnic Inequality and Public Policy*, Basic Books, New York, 1975.

Golembiewski, R. T. and Eddy, W., Eds., *Organization Development in Public Administration, Part I*, Marcel Dekker, New York, 1978.

Golembiewski, R. T., Proehl, C. W., and Sink, D., Success of OD applications in the public sector: toting up the score for a decade, more of less, *Public Administration Review*, 41, 679–682, 1981.

Goodnow, F. J., *Politics and Administration: A Study in Government*, Macmillan, New York, 1900.

Goodsell, C. T., *The Case for Bureaucracy*, 4th ed., CQ Press, Washington, DC, 2003.

Gossett, C. W., Domestic partnership benefits: patterns in the public sector, *Review of Public Personnel Administration*, 14, 64–84, 1994.

Grodin, J. R. and Wollett, D. H., *Collective Bargaining in Public Employment*, 2nd ed., Bureau of National Affairs, Washington, DC, 1974.

Grutter v. Bollinger, 123 U.S. 2325, 2003.

Gutek, B. A., *Sex and the Workplace*, Jossey-Bass, San Francisco, CA, 1985.

Gutman, A., *EEO Law and Personnel Practices*, 2nd ed., Sage, Thousand Oaks, CA, 2000.

Guy, M. E., Three steps forward, two steps backward: the status of women's integration into public management, *Public Administration Review*, 53, 285–292, 1993.

Hanslowe, K. L., *The Emerging Law of Labor Relations in Public Employment*, New York State School of Industrial and Labor Relations, Cornell University, Ithaca, NY, 1967.

Harmon, M. M., *Action Theory for Public Administration*, Longman, New York, 1981.

Harris v. Forklift Systems, 114 S. Ct. 367, 1993.

Harvey, D. R., *The Civil Service Commission*, Praeger, New York, 1970.

Hays, S. and Gleissner, R., Codes of ethics in state government: a nationwide survey, *Public Personnel Management*, 10, 48–68, 1981.

Hoogenboom, A., The Pendleton Act and the civil service, *American Historical Review*, 64, 301–318, 1958–1959.

Hoogenboom, A., *Outlawing the Spoils: A History of the Civil Service Reform Movement*, 1865–1883, University of Illinois Press, Urbana, IL, 1961.

Hoogenboom, A., Ed., *Spoilsmen and Reformers*, Rand McNally, Chicago, IL, 1964.

Hoover Commission, *The Hoover Commission Report*, McGraw-Hill, New York, 1949.

Horton, R. D., *Municipal Labor Relations in New York City*, Praeger, New York, 1973.

Hoyman, M. M., Sexual harassment in the workplace, In *Handbook of Human Resource Management in Government*, Condrey, S. E., Ed., Jossey-Bass, San Francisco, CA, pp. 183–198, 1998.

Huddleston, M., To the threshold of reform: the senior executive service, In *The Promise and Paradox of Civil Service Reform*, Ingraham, P. W. and Rosenbloom, D. H., Eds., University of Pittsburgh Press, Pittsburgh, PA, pp. 165–197, 1992.

Hudson Institute, *Civil Service 2000*, U.S. Office of Personnel Management, Washington, DC, 1988.

Hudson, W. T. and Broadnax, W. D., Equal opportunity as public policy, *Public Personnel Management*, 11, 268–276, 1982.

Hulten, C. R. and Sawhill, I., Ed., *The Legacy of Reaganomics*, Urban Institute Press, Washington, DC, 1984.

Ingraham, P. W., Of pigs in pokes and policy diffusion: another look at pay-for-performance, *Public Administration Review*, 53, 348–356, 1993.

Ingraham, P. W., *The Foundation of Merit: Public Service in American Democracy*, Johns Hopkins University Press, Baltimore, MD, 1995.

Ingraham, P. W. and Ban, C., Ed., *Legislating Bureaucratic Change: The Civil Service Reform Act of 1978*, State University of New York Press, Albany, NY, 1984.

Ingraham, P. W. and Kettl, D. F., *Agenda for Excellence: Public Service in America*, Chatham House, Chatham, NJ, 1992.

Ingraham, P. W. and Rosenbloom, D. H., Ed., *The Promise and Paradox of Civil Service Reform*, University of Pittsburgh Press, Pittsburgh, PA, 1992.

Ingraham, P. W., Romzek, B. S. *et al.*, *New Paradigms for Government: Issues for the Changing Public Service*, Jossey-Bass, San Francisco, CA, 1994.

Injury Prevention Research Center, *Workplace Violence: A Report to the Nation*, University of Iowa, Iowa City, IA, 2001.

IPMA HR Center, *Personnel Practices: Domestic Partners*, International Personnel Management Association, Washington, DC, 1996.

IPMA News, Workplace violence costs U.S. employers nearly $40 billion annually, *IPMA News*, November 25, p. 6, 1999.

Jaegal, D. and Cayer, N. J., Public personnel administration by lawsuit, *Public Administration Review*, 51, 211–221, 1991.

Johanson, E., *Comparable Worth: The Myth and the Movement*, Westview, Boulder, CO, 1984a.

Johanson, E., Managing the revolution: the case of comparable worth, *Review of Public Personnel Administration*, 4, 14–27, 1984b.

Johnson, A. T., A comparison of employee assistance programs in corporate and government organization contexts, *Review of Public Personnel Administration*, 6, 28–42, 1986.

Johnson, P. R. and Indvik, J., Workplace violence: an issue of the nineties, *Public Personnel Management*, 23, 515–523, 1994.

Kaplan, H. E., Political neutrality of the public service, *Public Personnel Review*, 1, 10–23, 1940.

Kaplan, H. R. and Tausky, C., Humanism in organizations: a critical appraisal, *Public Administration Review*, 37, 171–180, 1977.

Kaufman, H., The growth of the federal government service, In *The Federal Government Service: Its Character, Prestige, and Problems*, 2nd ed., Sayre, W., Ed., Prentice Hall, Englewood Cliffs, NJ, pp. 7–69, 1965.

Kearney, R. C., *Labor Relations in the Public Sector*, 3rd ed., Marcel Dekker, New York, 2001.

Kearney, R. C. and Hays, S. W., The politics of selection: spoils, merit, and representative bureaucracy, In *Public Personnel Policy: The Politics of Civil Service*, Rosenbloom, D. H., Ed., Associated Faculty Press, Port Washington, NY, pp. 89–104, 1985.

Kellough, J. E., The Americans with Disabilities Act—a note on personnel policy, *Public Personnel Management*, 29, 211–224, 2000.

Kellough, J. E., Employee performance appraisal and pay-for-performance in the public sector, In *Public Personnel Management: Current Concerns, Future Challenges*, 3rd ed., Longman, New York, 2002.

Kellough, J. E. and Lu, H., The paradox of merit pay in the public sector: persistence of a problematic procedure, *Review of Public Personnel Administration*, 13, 45–64, 1993.

Kellough, J. E. and Selden, S. J., The reinvention of public personnel administration: an analysis of personnel reform in the states, *Public Administration Review*, 63, 165–176, 2003.

Kemp, D., Employee assistance programs: organization and services, *Public Administration Review*, 45, 378–382, 1985.

Kettl, D. F., *Sharing Power: Public Governance and Private Markets*, Brookings Institution, Washington, DC, 1993.

Kilpatrick, F. P., Cummings, M. C., and Jennings, M. K., *The Image of the Federal Service*, Brookings Institution, Washington, DC, 1964.

Kirchheimer, O., The historical and comparative background of the Hatch Act, *Public Policy*, 2, 341–373, 1941.

Klay, W. E., Fiscal constraints, trust and the need for a new politics/administration dichotomy, *Review of Public Personnel Administration*, 4, 44–54, 1983.

Klingler, D. E., Political influences on the design of state and local personnel systems, *Review of Public Personnel Administration*, 3, 1–10, 1981.

Klingler, D. E. and Nalbandian, J., Personnel management by whose objectives, *Public Administration Review*, 38, 366–372, 1978.

Koteen, J., *Strategic Management in Public and Nonprofit Organizations, Managing Public Concerns in an Era of Limits*, 2nd ed., Praeger, Westport, CT, 1997.

Kramer, L., *Labor's Paradox: The American Federation of State, County, and Municipal Employees, AFL–CIO*, Wiley, New York, 1962.

Kranz, H., *The Participatory Bureaucracy: Women and Minorities in a More Representative Public Service*, Lexington Books, Lexington, MA, 1976.

Krislov, S. and Rosembloom, D. H., *Representative Bureaucracy and the American Political System*, 2nd ed., Praeger, New York, 1984.

Lane, L. M. and Wolf, J. E., *The Human Resource Crisis in the Public Sector: Rebuilding the Capacity to Govern*, Quorum Books, Westport, CT, 1990.

Latham, E., *The Communist Controversy in Washington: From the New Deal to McCarthy*, Harvard University Press, Cambridge, MA, 1966.

Lee, R. D. and Greenlaw, P. S., The legal evolution of sexual harassment, *Public Administration Review*, 55, 357–364, 1995.

Levine, C. H., Organizational decline and cutback management, *Public Administration Review*, 38, 316–325, 1978.

Levine, C. H., More on cutback management: hard questions for hard times, *Public Administration Review*, 39, 179–189, 1979.

Levine, C. H., The federal government in the year 2000: administrative legacies of the Reagan years, *Public Administration Review*, 46, 195–205, 1986.

Lewis, C. W., Shannon, W. W., and Ferree, G. D. Jr., The cutback issue: administrators' perceptions, citizen attitudes, and administrative behavior, *Review of Public Personnel Administration*, 4, 12–27, 1983.

Light, P., *The New Public Service*, Brookings, Washington, DC, 1999.

Long, N. E., The S.E.S. and the public interest, *Public Administration Review*, 41, 305–312, 1981.

Lowi, T. J., Machine politics—old and new, *The Public Interest*, 9, 83–92, 1967.

McDiarmid, J., The changing role of the U.S. Civil Service Commission, *American Political Science Review*, 40, 1067–1096, 1946.

McEnery, J. M. and Lifter, M. L., Demands for change: interfacing environmental pressures and the personnel process, *Public Personnel Management*, 16, 61–87, 1987.

MacKinnon, C. A., *Sexual Harassment of Working Women: A Case of Sex Discrimination*, Yale University Press, New Haven, CT, 1979.

McNaught, B., *Gay Issues in the Workplace*, St. Martin's, New York, 1993.

Macy, J. W., Adams, B., and Walter, J. J., *America's Unelected Government: Appointing the President's Team*, Ballinger, Cambridge, MA, 1983.

Mainzer, L. C., *Political Bureaucracy*, Scott, Foresman, Glencoe, IL, 1973.

Maletz, D. J. and Herbel, J., Beyond idealism: democracy and ethics reform, *The American Review of Public Administration*, 30, 19–45, 2000.

Mani, G. M., Disabled or not disabled: how does the Americans with Disabilities Act affect employment policies?, In *Public Personnel Administration: Problems and Prospects*, 4th ed., Hays, S. W. and Kearney, R. C., Eds., Prentice Hall, Upper Saddle River, NJ, 2003.

Marini, F., Ed., *Toward a New Public Administration*, Chandler, San Francisco, CA, 1971.

Martin, P. L., The Hatch Act in court: some recent developments, *Public Administration Review*, 33, 443–447, 1973.

Meritor Savings Bank v. Vinson, 106 S.Ct. 2399, 1986.

Milward, H. B., Politics, personnel and public policy, *Public Administration Review*, 38, 391–396, 1978.

Moore, M. V. and Abraham, Y. T., Comparable worth: is it a moot issue? Part II: the legal and judicial posture, *Public Personnel Management*, 23, 263–286, 1994.

Morganthau, H. J., The impact of the loyalty and security measures on the State Department, *Bulletin of the Atomic Scientists*, 11, 134–140, 1955.

Morse, M. M., We've come a long way, *Public Personnel Management*, 5, 218–224, 1976.

Mosher, F. C., *Democracy and the Public Service,* 2nd ed., Oxford University Press, New York, 1982.

Moskow, M. H., Loewenberg, J. J., and Koziara, E. C., *Collective Bargaining in Public Employment*, Random House, New York, 1970.

Murphy, L. V., The first civil service commission: 1871–1875, *Public Personnel Review*, 3, 29–39, 218–231, and 299–323, 1942.

Nalbandian, J. and Klingner, D., The politics of public personnel administration: towards theoretical understanding, *Public Administration Review*, 41, 541–549, 1982.

Nathan, R. P., Doolittle, F. C., and Associates, *The Consequences of Cuts: The Effects of the Reagan Domestic Program on State and Local Governments*, Princeton University Urban and Regional Research Center, Princeton, NJ, 1983.

National Academy of Public Administration, *Revitalizing Federal Management: Managers and Their Overburdened Systems*, National Academy of Public Administration, Washington, DC, 1983.

National Commission on the Public Service, *Leadership for the Public Service*, National Commission on the Public Service, Washington, DC, 1989.

National Academy of Public Administration, *Modernizing Federal Classification: An Opportunity for Excellence*, National Academy of Public Administration, Washington, DC, 1991.

National Academy of Public Administration, *Modernizing Federal Classification: Operational Broadbanding Systems Alternatives*, National Academy of Public Administration, Washington, DC, 1995.

National Academy of Public Administration, *Recommending Performance-Based Federal Pay*, National Academy of Public Administration, Washington, DC, 2004.

National Commission on the State and Local Public Service, *Hard Truths/Tough Choices: An Agenda for State and Local Reform*, Rockefeller Institute of Government, Albany, NY, 1993.

National Performance Review, *From Red Tape to Results: Creating a Government that Works Better and Costs Less*, U.S. Government Printing Office, Washington, DC, 1993.

National Performance Review, *Creating a Government that Works Better and Costs Less: Status Report*, U.S. Government Printing Office, Washington, DC, 1994.

National Research Council, *Pay for Performance: Evaluating Performance Appraisal and Merit Pay*, National Academy Press, Washington, DC, 1991.

Nelson, C. J., The press & civil service reform, *Civil Service Journal*, 13, 1–3, 1973.

Nelson, D. C., Political expression under the Hatch Act and the problem of statutory ambiguity, *Midwest Journal of Political Science*, 2, 82–85, 1958.

Nesbitt, M. M., *Labor Relations in the Federal Government Service*, Bureau of National Affairs, Washington, DC, 1976.

Neugarten, D. A. and Shafritz, J. M., Eds., *Sexuality in Organizations: Romantic and Coercive Behaviors at Work*, Moore, Oak Park, IL, 1981.

Neuse, S., A critical perspective on the comparable worth debate, *Review of Public Personnel Administration*, 3, 1–20, 1982.

Newland, C. A., Symposium on productivity in government, *Public Administration Review*, 32, 739–850, 1972.

Newland, C. A., Public personnel administration: legalistic reforms vs. effectiveness, efficiency, and economy, *Public Administration Review*, 36, 529–537, 1976.

Newland, C. A., A midterm appraisal—the Reagan presidency: limited government and political administration, *Public Administration Review*, 43, 1–21, 1983.

Newland, C. A., Crucial issues for public personnel professionals, *Public Personnel Management*, 13, 15–46, 1984a.

Newland, C. A., *Public Administration and Community: Realism in the Practice of Ideals*, Public Administration Service, McClean, VA, 1984b.

Newland, C. A., Public executives: imperium, sacerdotium, collegium? Bicentennial leadership challenges, *Public Administration Review*, 47, 45–56, 1987.

Newman, M. A., Jackson, R. A., and Baker, D. D., Sexual harassment in the federal workforce, *Public Administration Review*, 63, 472–483, 2003.

Oncale v. Sundowner Offshore Services, Inc., 523 U.S. 75, 1998.

O'Neill, R. M., *The Rights of Employees*, 2nd ed., Southern Illinois University Press, Carbondale, IL, 1993.

OPM Director Makes Special Veterans Hiring DVD Available to Chief Human Capital Officers, US Office of Personnel Management, Washington, DC, http://www.opm.gov/viewDocument.aspx?q = 778 (accessed March 2, 2005), 2005.

O'Toole, L. J., Doctrines and developments: separation of powers, the politics-administration dichotomy, and the rise of the administrative state, *Public Administration Review*, 47, 17–25, 1987.

Pagano, M. A., The SES performance management system and bonus awards, *Review of Public Personnel Administration*, 4, 40–56, 1984.

Palmer, J. L. and Sawhill, I., *The Reagan Record*, Ballinger, New York, 1984.

Panetta, L. E. and Gall, P., *Bring us Together*, Lippincott, Philadelphia, PA, 1971.

Perry, J. L., Compensation, merit pay, and motivation, In *Public Personnel Administration: Problems and Prospects*, 4th ed., Hays, S. W. and Kearney, R. C., Eds., Prentice Hall, Upper Saddle River, NJ, pp. 143–153, 2003.

Pfiffner, J. D., Political appointees and career executives: the democracy-bureaucracy nexus in the third century, *Public Administration Review*, 47, 57–65, 1987.

Piskulich, J. P., *Collective Bargaining in State and Local Government*, Praeger, New York, 1992.

Plant, J. and Gortner, H. F., Ethics, personnel management, and civil service reform, *Public Personnel Management*, 10, 3–10, 1981.

Pomerleau, R., A desideratum for managing the diverse workplace, *Review of Public Personnel Administration*, 14, 85–100, 1994.

President's Committee on Administrative Management, *Report with Special Studies*, US Government Printing Office, Washington, DC, 1937.

President's Reorganization Project, *Personnel Management Project, Volume I, Final Staff Report*, Government Printing Office, Washington, DC, 1977.

Presthus, R., *The Organizational Society*, Rev. ed., St. Martin's Press, New York, 1978.

Pynes, J. E. and Lafferty, J. M., *Local Government Labor Relations: A Guide for Public Administrators*, Quorum, Westport, CT, 1993.

Rabin, J., Vocino, T., Hildreth, W. B., and Miller, G. J., *Handbook of Public Sector Labor Relations*, Marcel Dekker, New York, 1994.

Reese, L. A. and Lindenberg, K. E., Victimhood and the implementation of sexual harassment policy, *Review of Public Personnel Administration*, 17, 37–57, 1997.

Remick, H., The comparable worth controversy, *Public Personnel Management*, 10, 371–383, 1981.

Rich, W. C., *The Politics of Urban Personnel Policy: Reformers, Politicians and Bureaucrats*, Kennikat, Port Washington, NY, 1982.

Risher, H. H. and Schay, B. W., Grade banding: the model for future salary programs?, *Public Personnel Management*, 23, 187–199, 1994.

Rivlin, A. M., *Reviving the American Dream: The Economy, the States and the Federal Government*, Brookings Institution, Washington, DC, 1992.

Roberts, R. N., The public law litigation model and *Memphis v Stotts*, *Public Administration Review*, 45, 527–532, 1985.

Rose, H., A critical look at the Hatch Act, *Harvard Law Review*, 75, 510–526, 1962.

Rosen, B., Merit and the president's plan for changing the civil service system, *Public Administration Review*, 38, 301–304, 1978.

Rosen, B., Uncertainty in the senior executive service, *Public Administration Review*, 41, 203–207, 1981.

Rosen, B., Effective continuity of U.S. government operations in jeopardy, *Public Administration Review*, 43, 383–392, 1983.

Rosenbloom, D. H., The Constitution and the civil service: some recent developments: judicial and political, *Kansas Law Review*, 18, 839–869, 1970.

Rosenbloom, D. H., *Federal Service and the Constitution*, Cornell University Press, Ithaca, NY, 1971.

Rosenbloom, D. H., Public personnel administration and politics: toward a new public personnel administration, *Midwest Review of Public Administration*, 7, 98–110, 1973.

Rosenbloom, D. H., *Federal Equal Employment Opportunity in Politics and Public Personnel Administration*, Praeger, New York, 1977.

Rosenbloom, D. H., The sources of continuing conflict between the constitution and public personnel management, *Review of Public Personnel Administration*, 2, 3–18, 1981.

Rosenbloom, D. H.,Ed., *Centenary Issues of the Pendleton Act of 1883: The Problematic Legacy of Civil Service Reform*, Marcel Dekker, New York, 1882.

Rosenbloom, D. H. and Carroll, J. D., Public personnel administration and the law, In *Handbook of Public Personnel Administration*, Rabin, J., Vocino, T., Hildreth, W. B., and Miller, G. J., Eds., Marcel Dekker, New York, pp. 71–113, 1995.

Ross, C. S. and England, R. B., State government's sexual harassment policy initiatives, *Public Administration Review*, 47, 259–262, 1987.

Ross, J. D., A current review of public-sector assessment centers: cause for concern, *Public Personnel Management*, 8, 41–46, 1979.

Rothwell, W. J., Prescott, B. K., and Taylor, M. W., *Strategic Human Resource Management: How to Prepare Your Organization for The Six Key Trends Shaping The Future*, Davies-Black, Palo Alto, CA, 2000.

Rubin, I., *Shrinking the Federal Government*, Longman, New York, 1985.

Sackett, P. R., A critical look at some common beliefs about assessment centers, *Public Personnel Management*, 11, 140–147, 1982.

Sayre, W., The triumph of technique over purpose, *Public Administration Review*, 8, 134–137, 1948.

Scott, L., Trends in state personnel administration, In *The Book of the States*, Vol. 36, The Council of State Governments, Lexington, KY, 2004.

Selden, S. C., Sexual harassment in the workplace, In *Public Personnel Administration: Problems and Prospects*, 4th ed., Hays, S. W. and Kearney, R. C., Eds., Prentice Hall, Upper Saddle River, NJ, 2003.

Selznick, P., *TVA and the Grass Roots*, University of California Press, Berkeley, CA, 1949.

Shafritz, J. M., *Public Personnel Management: The Heritage of Civil Service Reform*, Praeger, New York, 1975.

Siciliano, R. C. no date, The federal personnel system under scrutiny, In *The Personnel Agency and the Chief Executive*, T. Page, Ed., Public Personnel Association, Chicago, IL, pp.12–18.

Simmons, R. H., *Achieving Humane Organizations*, Daniel Spencer Publications, Malibu, CA, 1981.

Simon, H. A. and Daly, E., Sexual orientation and workplace rights: a political land mine for employers?, *Employee Relations Law Journal*, 18, 29–60, 1992.

Sisneros, A., Marching in the procession of precaution: a rebuttal to Martin D. Carcieri's the affirmative action cases and public personnel decisions, *Review of Public Personnel Administration*, 24, 175–182, 2004.

Spero, S. D., *The Labor Movement in Government Industry: A Study of Employee Organization in the Postal Service*, Macmillan, New York, 1927.

Steel, B. S. and Lovrich, N. P., Comparable worth: the problematic politicization of a public personnel issue, *Public Personnel Management*, 16, 23–36, 1987.

Steffens, J. L., *The Shame of the Cities*, McClure, Phillips, New York, 1904.

Stein, L., Merit systems and political influence: the case of local government, *Public Administration Review*, 47, 262–271, 1987.

Stewart, D. W., Managing competing claims: an ethical framework for human resource decision making, *Public Administration Review*, 44, 14–22, 1984.

Stieber, J., *Public Employee Unionism: Structure, Growth and Policy*, Brookings, Washington, DC, 1973.

Sulzner, G. T., Politics, labor relations and public personnel management: retrospect and prospect, *Policy Studies Journal*, 11, 279–289, 1982.

Thompson, F. J., *Personnel Policy in the City*, University of California Press, Berkeley, CA, 1975.

Thopmson, F. J., Deregulation at the EEOC: prospects and implications, *Review of Public Personnel Administration*, 4, 41–56, 1984.

Thompson, F. J., Ed., *Classics of Public Personnel Policy*, 2nd ed., Brooks/Cole, Belmont, CA, 1991.

Thompson, F. J., The politics of public personnel administration, In *Public Personnel Administration: Problems and Prospects*, 3rd ed., Hays, S. W. and Kearney, R. C., Eds., Prentice Hall, Englewood Cliffs, NJ, 1995.

Thompson, F. J., Riccucci, N., and Ban, C., Biological testing and personnel policy: drugs and the federal workplace, In *Public Personnel Management: Current Concerns, Future Challenges*, Ban, C. and Riccucci, N. M., Eds., Longman, New York, pp. 156–171, 1991.

Tompkins, J., Comparable worth and job evaluation validity, *Public Administration Review*, 47, 254–258, 1987.

US Civil Service Commission, *Twentieth Report*, US Government Printing Office, Washington, DC, 1903.

US Civil Service Commission, *Biography of an Ideal*, 2nd ed., US Government Printing Office, Washington, DC, 1974.

US Civil Service Commission, *Introducing the Civil Service Reform Act*, US Government Printing Office, Washington, DC, 1978.

US Equal Employment Opportunity Commission, *Final Guidelines on Sexual Harassment in the Workplace*, US Government Printing Office, Washington, DC, 1980.

US General Accounting Office, *NIH's Handling of Alleged Sexual Harassment and Sex Discrimination Matters*, US Government Printing Office, Washington, DC, 1995.

US General Accounting Office, *Human Capital: Effective Use of Flexibilities can Assist Agencies in Managing Their Workforces*, US General Accounting Office, Washington, DC, 2002.

US Merit Systems Protection Board, *Sexual Harassment in the Federal Workplace*, Government Printing Office, Washington, DC, 1995.

US Office of Personnel Management, *Revisiting Civil Service 2000: New Policy Direction Needed*, US Office of Personnel Management, Washington, DC, 1993.

US Office of Personnel Management, *Biography of an Ideal: A History of the Federal Civil Service*, US Government Printing Office, Washington, DC, 2002.

US Senate, *Report on the Reduction of Executive Patronage*, 19th Congress, 1st sess., 1826. Senate Doc. 88.

Van Riper, P. P., *History of the United States Civil Service*, Row, Peterson, Evanston, IL, 1958.

Van Slyke, D. M., The mythology of privatization in contracting for social services, *Public Administration Review*, 63, 296–315, 2003.

Waldby, H. O. and Hartsfield, A. M., The senior management service in the United States, *Review of Public Personnel Administration*, 4, 28–39, 1984.

Waldo, D., *Public Administration in a Time of Turbulence*, Chandler, Scranton, PA, 1971.

Wallin, B. A., *From Revenue Sharing to Deficit Sharing: General Revenue Sharing and Cities*, Brookings, Washington, DC, 1998.

Walter, J. J., The Ethics in Government Act, conflict of interest laws and presidential recruiting, *Public Administration Review*, 41, 659–666, 1981.

Warner, K. O., Ed., *Management Relations with Organized Public Employees: Theory, Policies, Programs*, Public Personnel Association, Chicago, IL, 1963.

Weinberg, A. and Weinberg, L. S., Eds., *The Muckrakers*, University of Illinois Press, Urbana, IL, 2001.

Weisband, E. and Franck, T. M., *Resignation in Protest*, Penguin, New York, 1975.

Wellington, H. H. and Winter, R. K., *The Unions and the Cities*, Brookings Institution, Washington, DC, 1971.

White, L. D., *Public Administration*, Macmillan, New York, 1926.

White, L. D., *The Federalists: A Study in Administrative History*, Macmillan, New York, 1948.

White, L. D., *The Jeffersonians: A Study in Administrative History, 1801–1829*, Macmillan, New York, 1951.

White, L. D., *The Jacksonians: A Study in Administrative History, 1829–1861*, Macmillan, New York, 1954.

White, L. D., *The Republican Era: 1869–1901: A Study in Administrative History*, Macmillan, New York, 1958.

White, R. D. Jr., *Roosevelt the Reformer: Theodore Roosevelt as Civil Service Commissioner*, University of Alabama Press, Tuscaloosa, AL, 2003.

Wilson, W., *Congressional Government: A Study in American Politics*, Houghton Mifflin, Boston, 1885.

Wilson, W., The study of administration, *Political Science Quarterly*, 2, 197–220, 1887.

Wooldridge, B. and Wester, J, The turbulent environment of public personnel administration: responding to the challenge of the changing workplace of the twenty-first century, *Public Personnel Management*, 20, 207–224, 1991.

Ziskind, D., *One Thousand Strikes of Government Employees*, Arno and the New York Times, New York, 1971.

10 Managing Public Personnel: A Turn-of-the-Century Perspective

Luther F. Carter and Kenneth D. Kitts

CONTENTS

I. INTRODUCTION

Two ideas are widely held by the American taxpayer. He believes there is an extraordinary number of useless or overpaid public officials, and he is convinced that most government employees are lazy or incompetent, and secured their positions only by 'pull.' Two ideas are likewise held by civil servants. They assert that they are underpaid, and they believe that the value of their work is neither understood nor appreciated by the public (White 1926).

Leonard White's description of the divisiveness in opinion over public employment during the first quarter of the twentieth century is timeless: the public's lament over the bureaucracy versus the administrator's anguish over the thankless nature of the job. Yet over the course of the last one hundred years, few professions have undergone such substantial change, definition, and redefinition. At the beginning of the twentieth century, the understanding of structure, process, and behavior in complex organizations was rudimentary and intuitive. Yet with each successive decade, the criticality of managing such organizations and their personnel has become increasingly manifest. This quest has spawned numerous theories, concepts, and controversies, many of which have been seminal in their impact. This chapter will undertake to identify those major concepts that have most profoundly affected the scope and substance of the public personnel function.

As is usual with such a venture, all academic caveats regarding objectivity apply. Identifying the major concepts or themes as the most illustrious achievement managerially is an exercise fraught with bias and speculation. Each generation of scholars and practitioners has championed their own thematic agenda, with only a few ideas receiving enduring attention. Still, across the years, certain core tenets have survived intergenerational scrutiny and served to shape the study and practice of public personnel.

First, a word of explanation should be offered regarding the criteria used to select these themes or issues. As with previous versions of this chapter, each issue presented is assessed on the basis of its ability to satisfy four requisites: permanent impact, application to the practitioner as well as the academic community, a predominantly public sector focus, and a lasting contribution in furthering personnel thought and practice.

Since the beginning of the previous century, five visible themes in public personnel administration have met these criteria. Chronologically, these are (1) the establishment and refinement of the civil service and merit concepts, (2) the development of the human relations and workplace quality movements, (3) the emergence of public bilateralism, (4) the quest for representativeness, and (5) the recognition of the professional public administrator.

The five issues collectively define the essence of contemporary public personnel administration. Individually, however, each issue represents a curious view of the frequently incongruous values and principles reflected in the development of this country's public employee systems.

II. THE ESTABLISHMENT AND REFINEMENT OF THE CIVIL SERVICE AND MERIT CONCEPTS

The theme of civil service development and reform defines the very essence of the modern public personnel system, with the merit principle serving as its core component. While there are many historical antecedents for such reform, the wellspring legislation in the American experience was the Pendleton Civil Service Act of 1883. In addition to recognizing merit as the compelling criterion for personnel decisions, the act initiated the advent of the bipartisan personnel commission, a concept designed to moderate the influence of overt patronage pressures. The commission bestowed a modicum of impartiality, or at the very least balanced partiality, on the governance of the civil service system (Van Riper 1958).

Mosher (1968, 65–66), contends that there were three basic themes comprising the campaign that led to the adoption of the Pendleton Act. These themes explain the genesis of civil service, as well as governmental, reform. First, he argues that personnel administration, or what passed for it at the time, was associated with the concept of morality. Second, and a distant second according to Mosher, its adoption was influenced by a concern for more efficiency. Finally, the movement for civil service reform was an effort "to eradicate evil." The first and third themes illustrated the tendency to elevate public personnel to a higher plane by legislating away corrupt influences. The second theme, arguably the least visible of the three, represented an attempt to select more capable personnel for government employment.

While these two intentions were certainly not antithetical, each accentuated a distinctly separate pattern characteristic of subsequent reform efforts. In the case of the purification orientation, emphasis was placed on controlling the personnel system in order to eliminate such negative forces as corruption, as well as the destabilizing influence of political pressure. The second orientation focused more deliberately on improving the personnel system through developmental change. In the years following, efforts were undertaken to arrive at a workable concept of merit and to apply this concept to selection and promotion decisions. On the whole, the successes related to both pursuits have been both systematic and sustained, although not without an occasional setback.

Wilson's (1887) classic essay, "The Study of Administration," published in the wake of the Pendleton Act, perpetuated the purification theme by drawing a conceptual distinction between the avocation of politics and the profession of administration. Of the latter, Wilson wrote:

> The field of administration is a field of business. It is removed from the hurry and strife of politics; it at most points stands apart even from the debatable ground of constitutional study. It is a part of political life only as the methods of the counting-house are a part of the life of society; only as machinery is a part of the manufactured product. But it is, at the same time, raised very far above the dull level of mere technical detail by the fact that through its greater principles it is directly connected with the lasting maxims of political wisdom, the permanent truths of political progress (Wilson 1887).

As to the difficulty and value of administrative as compared to political labors, Wilson advised that:

> This is the reason why administrative tasks have nowadays to be so studiously and systematically adjusted to carefully tested standards of policy, the reason why we are having now what we never had before, a science of administration. The weightier debates of constitutional principle are even yet by no means concluded; but they are no longer of more immediate practical moment than questions of administration. It is getting to be harder to run a constitution than to frame one (Wilson 1887).

Within two decades, Frank Goodnow had joined this argument by calling for the removal of politics from administration in his aptly-titled book, *Politics and Administration*. Goodnow viewed the functional distinction between the two as an extension of the structural division between the legislative and the executive branches. Thus politics involved "policies or expressions of the state will," while administration involved the "execution of these policies" (Goodnow 1900, 10–11).

Both of these viewpoints conveyed an explicit assumption regarding public personnel and the civil service system. Such a system, in order to be effective, must enjoy considerable autonomy from political decision-making. Wilson summed it up adequately in his remarks on civil service reform:

> Most important to be observed is the truth already so much and so fortunately insisted upon by our civil-service reformers; namely, that administration lies outside the sphere of politics. Administrative questions are not political questions. Although politics sets the tasks for administration, it should not be suffered to manipulate its offices (Wilson 1887).

The purification theme dominated throughout the latter part of the 19th century, and became one of the more visible issues advocated by municipal reform proponents. Martin Schiesl's history of the municipal reform movement, *The Politics of Efficiency*, discusses in detail the emphasis placed on the development of nonpartisan employee systems during this era. However, Schiesl is careful to point out that political reformers were hesitant to extend the argument for nonpartisanship beyond appointive positions to include elected officials. Wary of the constraints imposed by nonpartisan restrictions, "reformers chose to be the sponsors of the new system rather than the tools of it" (Schiesl 1977, 34–36). Presumably, there was a juncture at which politics and administration merged; perhaps in the appointment of public employees, perhaps in their removal. Any effective civil service system must, on the one hand, shield appointed employees from obtrusive political pressure and yet, on the other hand, ensure that elected officials possess sufficient authority to direct these employees.

The topic of political control became the subject of intense debates within the National Municipal League and other regional reformist organizations such as the Massachusetts Reform Club, New York's Constitution Club, and the Chicago Civil Service Reform League (Schiesl 1977, 25–45). The various organizations uniformly agreed that efficiency and responsiveness were the virtues to be acquired; the dilemma was how to obtain both while eliminating the spoils system. Gradually, but perceptibly, the concept of merit became recognized as an instrument for depoliticizing public personnel systems. Although subsequent efforts at modeling the theoretical underpinnings of merit have identified certain tenuous, yet inextricable, linkages between political pressure and merit adaptability (Nalbandian and Klingner 1981), reformists at the time argued vehemently for merit-based rules, regulations, and procedures.

The concept of merit in personnel administration has been poorly defined and largely misunderstood. At various times the term has been used interchangeably with terms such as qualification, ability, and competition. O. Glenn Stahl, in his classic text on personnel administration, defines the merit system as "a personnel system in which comparative merit or achievement governs each individual's selection or progress in the service and in which the conditions and rewards of performance contribute to the competency and continuity of the service" (Stahl 1976). From the passage of the Pendleton Act, the presence of merit in a personnel system has been traditionally confirmed through a reliance on open and formal examinations. The implication was apparent: whatever merit encompassed and however it worked, the concept could be realized best through the imposition of objective measures. In view of the highly subjective hiring and promotion decisions made in spoils administrations, it is not surprising that the examination would be viewed as a panacea for eliminating patronage and favoritism.

Although the use of examinations to hire civil servants was distinctly British in origin, the examinations required by the Pendleton Act were to be "practical in character," thus providing a uniquely American perspective to this concept (Henry 1986). The practical examination was certainly intended to make selection decisions on the basis of some type of work-related knowledge or skills, however ill-defined. Unfortunately, the early tests were so primitive that they fell considerably short of fulfilling most merit-based expectations. They simply served to affirm the contention of the reformers that "chance selection is better than patronage selection" (Wentworth 1968).

In time, the administrative benefits of examinations were more fully realized, as personnel specialists better understood the concepts of test validity and reliability. The creation of the Federal Service Entrance Examination in 1955 and its successor, the Professional Career Administration Examination in 1974, typified the attempt to develop more sophisticated and accurate test instruments. Despite the trend in the past few years to move away from the written examination because of methodological concerns and accusations of racial bias (Rosenbloom and Obuchowski, 1977), tests played a key role in the early development of the merit principle.

In a similar vein, standardized classification and compensation systems lent substance to the merit idea by creating uniformity in titles, position responsibilities, and pay. The Classification Act of 1923 was responsible for incorporating this essential component into the federal civil service system, while the Social Security Act, as amended in 1939, led to the creation of a number of state merit systems. Subsequent legislation, such as the Fair Labor Standards Act of 1938 with its various amendments, attempted to establish an equitable basis for remuneration. While this act, in particular, has pursued a circuitous route in addressing this issue, both in the Congress and in the courts, (Davis and Murphy 1985; Elder and Miller 1979), it signifies an effort at compensatory reform nonetheless.

The evolution of the personnel department itself should not be overlooked as a critical element in the maturation of the civil service system. Despite the fact that Congress in 1937 rejected the Brownlow Committee's recommendation for a single, appointed civil service administrator (President's Committee on Administrative Management 1937), Roosevelt did create personnel departments in the major federal agencies the following year. In the post-World War II years, these departments were delegated increased authority, and finally, the Classification Act of 1949 ceded them the responsibility for allocating individual positions within the standards set by the Civil Service Commission (Siegel and Myrtle 1985).

Of course, no discussion of civil service reform initiatives would be complete without a consideration of one of the more controversial reforms of the twentieth century, the Civil Service Reform Act of 1978. According to Alan Campbell, then-chairman of the Civil Service Commission and subsequently director of the Office of Personnel Management, the act was designed in such a manner as "to improve management, stimulate performance and efficiency, provide needed protections for employees, and help achieve the equal employment expectations to which the federal service is committed and the public is entitled" (Campbell 1978).

In essence, the act effectively restructured the federal personnel system by eliminating the archaic Civil Service Commission and splitting its functions between two new agencies: the Office of Personnel Management (OPM), the administrative element, and the Merit Systems Protection Board (SPB), the body for hearing and resolving personnel grievances. Also included was the provision for a special counsel who would serve a five-year fixed term. The special counsel would investigate federal agencies who allegedly engaged in prohibited personnel practices. In addition, the act established a new personnel system for senior policy-making administrators, the Senior Executive Service (SES). New performance standards and evaluative processes were created for these executives, and merit-pay incentives were developed for them, as well as for senior-level managers in levels GS 13–15.

Almost immediately, a number of criticisms arose over various aspects of the act. Among the criticisms were the contentions that the valuation system provided political appointees too much power over career executives (Rosen 1978), that the act did not enumerate priority concerns for minorities and women (Howard 1978), and that it placed a "narrowly-based emphasis upon efficiency" (Thayer 1978).

The criticisms of legal, political science, and public administration researchers have become even more intense with the passage of time. Pearce and Perry (1983) concluded, as a result of longitudinal analyses, that the merit pay concept "at grades 13–15 has not been sufficiently successful to proceed with plans to include employees in grades 1–12." In a survey of SES executives in the period immediately after the act's passage, Lynn and Vaden (1979) found that a substantial percentage of the career bureaucrats were uncertain about job security, thus producing a potentially demoralizing situation. Others, including Huddleston (1982), have continued to question the power of political appointees over career administrators. Huddleston, in fact, characterized the OPM as a "partisan political organization that has a partisan political function." Charles Levine has also deplored the "increased 'politicization' of the higher civil service and the more extensive use of central controls by OMB to shape the policy agendas of departments and agencies" (Levine, 1986, 201).

Defenders of the Civil Service Reform Act have become increasingly vocal in responding to these charges. Dwight Ink, a Carter administration official with key responsibility for the legislation, points out that the reform measures were developed through an open, deliberative process that focused on the ills of the existing personnel system. He blames many of the problems associated with the act on "poor agency management and weak leadership," rather than on the legislation itself (Ink 2000, 55). Ink argues that evaluation of the CSRA should be based on facts, not assumptions, and that critics should focus less heavily on specific passages and more on the overarching objectives of the Act's creators.

A recent Princeton survey of federal employees found that concerns regarding the civil service are not limited to academicians. Paul Light (2001) has used the survey data to chronicle the growing gap in job satisfaction between the public and private sectors. He attributes much of the organizational ennui to a "personnel system last overhauled in 1978 based on ideas from the 1950s that were built on research conducted in the 1930s, using data collected in the 1920s by scholars trained in the 1910s."

In light of these concerns, civil service reform has emerged as a major issue at the state and local government level since the passage of the Civil Service Reform Act. In the past few years the reform of archaic and obsolete state and municipal personnel systems has been of particular interest to a growing number of elected officials (Nigro and Nigro 1981). A number of such jurisdictions have completed, or are presently in the process of completing, reform initiatives, such as the repeal of nepotism laws and the adoption of merit-based compensatory and evaluative processes. These initiatives have, in turn, generated scholarly efforts to rank the states based on innovation in public personnel administration (Kellough and Selden 2003). Such rankings are watched with great interest by the state practitioners.

Of continuing concern, however, is the politicization reflected in the substantial number of elected executive officials at the state and local levels. The long ballot concept has continued to impede systemic reform of the truncated and fragmented personnel fiefdoms that such officials direct. Even in those instances in which employees are ostensibly afforded merit protection, electoral cycles introduce unique stresses in which the distinction between political loyalty and managerial accountability is blurred.

While research, such as that conducted by Conant (1988), affirms the success in achieving executive branch reorganization at the state level, questions remain as to the degree of administrative efficiency and effectiveness achieved in these efforts. Yet, as Conant points out, in the absence of "a definitive answer to the perplexing question about the bottom-line results of comprehensive reorganization... no compelling reason exists for reformers to abandon the pursuit of a modernized, streamlined, executive branch or strong executive leadership." Indeed, the lessons of the past clearly illustrate the necessity for executive centralization and leadership as a prerequisite for meaningful civil service reform.

During the waning decades of the late twentieth century, two presidential study initiatives raised the specter of federal government reform in differing, although compatible contexts. Additionally, both examined the public personnel function and its relationship to governmental reform sui generis. The first of these, Ronald Reagan's Private Sector Survey on Cost Control, was chaired by business executive J. Peter Grace. This initiative, conducted from 1982 to 1984, produced over 47 reports and was an unabashed critique of governmental process and function. The final Grace Commission report stated that as much as 21.4% in projected savings could be derived by correcting personnel mismanagement problems (Goodsell 1984). However, by the late 1980s, few of the Grace Commission recommendations had been implemented. Perhaps, as Arnold (1995) subsequently observed, "because they were really intended to castigate government and not change it."

A markedly different tack was attempted with Bill Clinton's National Performance Review in 1993. Chaired by Al Gore, this panel embarked on a reform planning effort intended to examine both the ends and means of government. The tone of the panel was less caustic than that of the Grace Commission, but its final messages and symbolism were no less pejorative:

> *From Red Tape to Results* was issued on September 7, 1993. The semiotics of its public presentation offers a glimpse into the implicit political goals of the National Performance Review. With officials and press present on the White House lawn, President Clinton and Vice President Gore stood against a backdrop of forklift trucks loaded with volumes of federal budget rules, procurement rules and personnel rules (Arnold 1995).

The ensuing reform effort was not well received by those on the federal payroll. Fully half of all general schedule employees reported that the Clinton-era initiative made their jobs *more* difficult. As Light (2001) notes, "[S]o much for reinvention's promise of empowerment and efficiency on the front lines of government."

The move to streamline government and to downsize public payrolls, although checked somewhat by expansion of the national security agencies in the wake of the terrorist attacks of September 11, 2001, continued under the administration of George W. Bush. *The President's Management Agenda*, released in 2002, repeated the well-worn call to reduce middle-management positions in government and to accelerate the trend toward outsourcing federal functions. These recommendations were hardly surprising, given the prevailing political climate and Bush's status as America's first MBA president.

Whatever the value of these initiatives, it is clear that they are not without consequence for the public employee striving for merit excellence. Arnold (1995) warned that "the contemporary use of reorganization to displace political disquiet about big government only serves to undermine the legitimacy of public administration." At the very least, such efforts appear only too willing to sacrifice merit-based systems on the altar of political expediency. On the related issue of down-sizing the public sector workforce, Kettl et al. (1996) suggest that "tallying the body counts" has become a political end in itself. Consequently, there is little discussion about the deeper problems that inhibit the ability of public sector organizations to function effectively.

As an enduring issue, civil service/merit/personnel reform has resulted in consistent and systematic change in the perception of the public servant. Over the past century, the selection and promotion criteria for public employment have tightened, and the demands placed on the public employee have intensified. It is nevertheless disconcerting to note that the three persistent challenges remain: the need to control political influence, the question for a better realization of the elusive notion of merit, and a more refined appreciation for the use of reform as a viable change strategy.

III. THE DEVELOPMENT OF THE HUMAN RELATIONS AND WORKPLACE QUALITY MOVEMENTS

The second notable issue involves the collection of theories and concepts which the social sciences have generally referred to as the human relations movement. While the effects of civil service reform were realized primarily as a result of legislative action, the human relations movement has evolved as a progression of scholarly ideas and opinions. As a consequence, the impact of human relations is better understood as a process of challenge and counterchallenge to orthodox thought rather than as a process of orderly and systematic change.

Of no less importance over the past decade has been the advent of the quality movement in American public administration. Distinctly humanistic in its orientation toward both subordinate employees and clientele (customers), the movement has attempted to undertake a no less ambitious task than the "reinvention" of government itself to produce more anticipatory and more entrepreneurial processes (Osborne and Gaebler 1992).

The departure point for the human relations perspective and much of the change that it produced was the Western Electric experiments, conducted at the Hawthorne Works in Cicero, Illinois, from 1929 to 1932. In the course of these experiments, Elton Mayo and a team of researchers from the Harvard Business School redefined the basic assumptions pertaining to worker productivity in complex organizations. In the process, they enhanced our understanding of the informal group and taught the importance of unobtrusive employee reward structures (Roethlisberger, 1941; Roethlisberger and Dickson 1939). Fortunately for successive generations of academic consultants, their efforts also served to affirm the value of the university as a center for applied behavioral research.

In many ways, the Western Electric studies substantiated the earlier contentions of scholars such as Mary Parker Follet and Henri DeMan. In arguing against the mechanistic-oriented "scientific management" approach prescribed by Taylor (1911), Follett urged that "one person should not give orders to another person, but both should agree to take their orders from the situation" (Follett 1926). Follett clearly viewed individual workers as being participants in determining their own work environment and, ultimately, their organizational destiny. Just as importantly, Follett viewed the needs of the organization and the needs of the individual as being compatible. Consequently, the wills evident at each of the two levels, individual and organization, had to be integrated in a manner that would allow both to be addressed through routine work processes. This task of integration was the responsibility of leadership, and according to Follett, a successful leader "knows how to relate these wills so that they will have a driving force" (Follett 1940).

Henri DeMan's work was focused more specifically on analyzing the attitudes of German workers toward their daily labor. Relying heavily on the interview technique, DeMan concluded that the attempt to find "joy in work" was a natural instinct, influenced by both positive and negative factors in the workplace (DeMan 1929). DeMan's findings have been favorably compared with the "hygiene-motivation" theory espoused by Frederick Herzberg three decades later (Wren 1972).

The issue of compatibility, primarily compatibility between organizational and individual needs, wants, and goals, has been an essential facet of the human relations approach. From the perspective of personnel administration and labor relations, such compatibility serves as a constant reminder that the organization need not be antithetical to the natural human experience; instead, it should be a meaningful part of that experience. The Western Electric researchers foresaw a new era of "collaborative" relationships between employees and organizations. However, as Roethlisberger cautioned, this was a form of collaboration quite different from that to which management had become accustomed:

> Too often we think of collaboration as something which can be logically or legally contrived. The Western Electric studies indicate that it is far more a matter of sentiment than a matter of logic. Workers are not isolated, unrelated individuals; they are social animals and should be treated as such.
>
> This statement—the worker is a social animal and should be treated as such—is simple, but the systematic and consistent practice of this point of view is not. If it were systematically practiced, it would revolutionize present-day personnel work (Roethlisberger, 1941).

As a result of the controversial nature of the research, the Western Electric studies produced a fair number of critics, both in the immediate aftermath and in the years following. At various times, Robert S. Lynd, Reinhard Bendix, Herbert Blumer, Clark Kerr, C. Wright Mills, Wilbert E. Moore, Harold Wilensky, and Daniel Bell have joined the debate questioning the design of the research or the interpretation of the findings.[*] Most of the major criticisms have centered around the pejorative connotation assigned to organizational conflict by the researchers and the disruption attributed to social groups within the Hawthorn plant. No allowance was made, contended the critics, for the dissension and inherent conflict that is naturally a part of the management–labor relationship. The goals and processes of "management [were] seen as rational while the worker [was] seen as nonrational" (Perrow, 1986, 83).

The human relations movement hardly revolutionized personnel work. It has, however, raised questions about orthodox management approaches and offered fresh ideas regarding new approaches. The movement has been less successful in offering empirical support for its basic contention, namely, that there is a direct relationship between social factors and productivity. Perrow contends that this may be due to an inherent shortcoming of social science methodology as applied to complex organizations:

> The social sciences, at least in the area of complex organizations, have been desperate for ideas, not data. The practitioners seize upon concepts that will make sense of the world; if the concepts make sense, the social sciences do not inquire too carefully into the empirical support for these ideas or concepts. For those who find the idea as repugnant, the most pressing thing is to respond on ideological grounds; only later do some have the "luxury" of patiently reexamining the empirical documentation of the new idea (Perrow, 1986).

Despite this criticism, the human relations movement has contributed substantially to the knowledge and practice within the field of personnel administration. The research undertaken by the generations of psychologists, sociologists, and political scientists associated with the movement can be categorized into the areas discussed in the following two sections.

A. LEADERSHIP, MOTIVATION, AND PRODUCTIVITY

The relationship between leadership, motivation, and performance in work organizations has been the single largest research focus to emerge from the Western Electric studies. The presumption has

---

[*] For a comprehensive discussion of the criticisms of the Western Electric research, see Perrow (1979, 82–84).

generally been that "good" leadership will lead to greater motivation which will subsequently result in greater productivity (Perrow 1979). Despite uncertainty over the direction and strength of the linkage, a great deal of research has focused on this relationship during the past 60 years. Stogdill's (1974) *Handbook of Leadership: A Survey of Theory and Research* provides the most exhaustive one-volume treatment of this research written to date.

In a survey essay reviewing leadership studies undertaken over this 60-year period, Schriesheim et al. (1978) categorized the leadership research into three phases: the trait phase (up to the late 1940s), the behavioral phase (late 1940s to early 1960s), and the situational phase (early 1960s to present). Regardless of the phase, they concluded that leadership could never be properly understood when studied apart from broader, more environmentally induced concerns.

Other studies, examining more directly the relationship between employee attitudes and performance, have examined a range of issues without producing remarkable conclusions. Brayfield and Crockett (1955) reviewed the results of approximately 50 such studies and found little evidence of this presumed relationship. In subsequent years, a number of the premiere names in organization theory and behavior, including Vroom (1964) and Lawler and Porter (1967), completed similar studies with only moderately conclusive results.[*] In the 1980s, Cavanagh (1984), Cummings (1984), and Milbourn (1980) examined the effect of compensation on worker motivation and performance. As a collection, this research has produced findings of limited applicability to organizations or management, although the phenomenon continues to be of interest to a few social scientists.

B. GROUPS, GROUP PROCESSES, AND ORGANIZATIONAL ENVIRONMENTS

This aspect of the human relations movement also focused on performance and productivity, but with more concern for the influences of groups, both formal and informal, and organizational environments than for the attitudes and approaches of individual leaders. Although the research in this area has been less prolific than research on leadership and productivity, it has on the whole produced more tangible benefits.

As with the leadership–motivation–productivity research, a number of luminaries in the behavioral sciences have contributed to an understanding of the issues surrounding group and climatic influences. Barnard (1938) pioneered the study of the informal group in his seminal book, *The Functions of the Executive*. Most importantly, Barnard identified its major effects as establishing "attitudes, understanding, customs, habits, (and) institutions" and creating "the conditions under which formal organizations may arise."

Maslow (1943) examined various factors shaping human needs in an effort to rank those needs in order of relative importance. McGregor (1960) explored managerial attitudes in relationship to employee typologies and produced the contrasting concepts of "Theory X" and "Theory Y" management. Likert (1961, 1967) structured four types of organizational "systems" and posited the "values" that each would produce with regard to various aspects of the organizational environment. Emery and Trist (1965) also dealt with organizational environments in order to identify the varying types of "causal textures."

The group and environmental research led to a much broader appreciation of the complexities of life with organizations. Moreover, it has called to question many of the simplistic assumptions underlying both the scientific management approach and the leadership–motivation–productivity work. Finally, and perhaps most importantly, the research has served to legitimize the use of empirical studies, with an array of methodological approaches, in studying administrative and organizational phenomena.

Beyond the two areas addressed above, the work of human relations theorists has focused on numerous other themes, such as organizational and individual conflict (Argyris 1957, 1964, 1970), the development of democratic bureaucracies (Bennis 1966; Waldo 1952, 1980), and the pursuit of

---

* See Perrow (1979, chap. 3, 98–112).

social equity through administration (Frederickson 1971, 1980), to name but a few. Harmon and Mayer (1986, 197–239) provide a comprehensive review and critique of the work of the later human relations theorists.

Over the decades, the human relations movement has produced a vocal collection of opponents and proponents alike. Human relations opponents have criticized its inconclusive and often contradictory research findings, the absence of an integrated body of theory, and the tendency of its disciples to accept too much on the basis of ideological belief. Perrow (1979, 137), in particular, has criticized the movement's tendency to counter "the extreme rationality of scientific management with a romantic rationality sometimes grounded in Freudian psychology."

The majority of scholars, however, are more likely to agree with the assessment of Hannon and Mayer (1986, 239) that while later human relations theorists "have raised far more questions than they have answered," the "theory of public organization has been greatly enriched as a result." Their efforts have certainly enhanced our understanding of work situations in complex organizations and inexorably altered many managerial philosophies. Just as importantly, the human relations movement has taught organizations to reject any and all truisms regarding human behavior.

C. THE QUALITY WORKPLACE MOVEMENT

Gradually, although consistently since 1985, total quality management (TQM) proponents have worked to challenge the administrative orthodoxy of government at all levels. It would be erroneous to characterize the quality movement as a logical extension of the human relations movement. Yet both movements are heavily value laden with a strong emphasis on goal-directed rather than process-directed behavior. Indeed, they advocate many of the same institutional values: participatory processes, decentralized decision-making, and flattened organizational structures (Osborne and Gaebler 1992).

In the rich and varied array of ideas progressing from Deming's work in post-World War II Japan to Brian Joiner's (1994) *Fourth Generation Management*, the quality movement has raised serious questions about the efficiency and effectiveness of the contemporary complex organization. Given that admonitions are delivered equally to the public and private sector and that a common model is advocated, the movement has great appeal for students of the generic organization.

Skepticism exists among those scholars and practitioners who regard government as serving a different, arguably higher end. Fundamental differences between entrepreneurial autonomy versus democratic accountability (Bellone and Goerl 1992) and service to the customer versus service to the broader public (Boyne et al. 1999; Swiss 1992) have been offered as basic incompatibilities. Indeed, the existence of a "public service ethos" (Pratchett and Wingfield 1996) might go far in explaining why predictions of a homogenized private–public personnel function have yet to materialize.

The private sector bias in the literature on administrative and managerial techniques has led some observers to wonder about the attendant neglect of public sector success stories. Ingraham speculates that cases of superlative work by government agencies often go unrecognized or unreported:

> There are lessons to be learned from private-sector techniques and experience. There are also, however, lessons to be learned from excellent *public* organizations, and those lessons have been far more rare in the reform tradition. Organizations such as the Internal Revenue Service, many agencies in the Department of Defense, and the Forest Service have a long tradition of creative and farsighted management. Their experience with change and with the translation of other models of change to a public context can provide guidelines for other public organizations. ... How they did it and what they learned should be a part of the public-reform tradition (Ingraham 1995, 141).

Whatever the resolution, this debate promotes introspection and serious discourse on the nature and essence of public service. The quality movement should be credited in no small part for re-engendering such a debate at a time when public administration at all levels seeks to revalidate its societal worth.

IV. THE QUEST FOR REPRESENTATIVENESS

Few issues in public personnel during the past century have been as vehemently argued as the necessity for achieving a representative bureaucracy. Even the definition of what constitutes representativeness in public organizations has been open to debate. One of its earliest advocates, J. Donald Kingsley (1944), viewed the concept as a class issue, particularly within the context of the British Civil Service, the principal focus of his thesis. Kingsley generally contended that members of underrepresented groups should be vertically promoted to an elite status. Other scholars have argued stringently that the concept requires bureaucratic participation in direct proportion to the group's size in society (Kranz 1976). Still others have argued more moderately for simple equality of opportunity in entry and promotion. Krislov and Rosenbloom (1981) have advanced an even broader view of the representative bureaucracy that includes representation by personnel, representation by administration organization, and representation through citizen participation.

As a personnel issue, representativeness has been a vitally important, yet exceptionally sensitive, concern since the early 1940s. Of critical importance has been the necessity for preserving the merit idea while at the same time advocating preferential hiring. From a legal perspective, the role of public personnel administration in pursuing such representativeness has been problematic. Until 1972, the federal personnel system produced little beyond a series of well-intentioned, but largely symbolic, executive orders.

In 1972, the passages of the Equal Employment Opportunity Act (EEOA) reflected a determined, but tempered commitment to achieving broader representation in the public workforce. During this same period, the judiciary was active in championing the means, if not always the ends, of affirmative action. The decisions in court cases such as *Griggs vs. Duke Power Company*,[*] *Carter vs. Gallagher*,[†] and *LeFleur vs. Cleveland Board of Education*[‡] served to restrict the use of discriminatory practices or processes, although frequently in the most circuitous manner.

How should scholars assess the effects of such change? Despite nearly unanimous appreciation for the approach taken by the EEOA and the courts, research on its effects has produced limited findings. Rose and Chia (1978), in examining black employment in the federal service during the period 1969–1974, concluded that "slow but steady progress" was being made, but they found the change occurring primarily at the bottom of the federal schedules. The problem continues in the 21st century. In 2003, an OPM official appeared before a congressional committee to warn of the difficulty in diversifying the SES due to the dearth of minorities in the GS 14 and 15 classifications which have traditionally served as the "feeder pools" for senior positions (U.S. House, Committee on Government Reform 2003).

Rogers (1984) has contended that the federal government did not realize more progress before 1978[¶] largely as a result of the Office of Personnel Management's (OPM's) resistance to affirmative action. He reasoned that such resistance stemmed from a commitment to strict merit hiring and an

---

*US 861, 27 L. Ed. 2d 101, 91 5.Ct. 98 (1971).

†L. Ed. 2d 338, 92 S. Ct. 2045 (1971).

‡US 632 (1974).

¶The federal reorganization plan of 1978 transferred OPM's responsibility for affirmative action oversight to the Equal Employment Opportunity Commission (EEOC).

aversion to "special training programs" and "qualification exceptions for women and minorities" (Rogers 1984, 100). Beyond OPM's resistance, Rogers (1984, 114–115) identified seven problems contributing to the obstruction of progress:

1. An ill-defined policy goal and no quantitative standard by which to measure progress
2. Passive monitoring and enforcement of nondiscrimination efforts
3. Varying commitments from federal agencies for the concept
4. Reluctant support from Presidents Nixon, Ford, and Reagan
5. Little coordination among the enforcement agencies
6. Wavering pressure from minorities to force compliance
7. A cost-benefit implementation ratio that favors noncompliance

In analyzing the percentages of black males and females employed in the total workforce between 1958 and 1977, Rodgers did find evidence of employment gains. Similarly, Rodgers' analysis of the federal workforce during this same period revealed moderate gains in black employment. Unfortunately, the gains were so minimal and so compressed at the lower end of the schedules that, in Rodgers' (1984, 103) view, it would "take decades for blacks to obtain parity in the top positions within the federal government." Stewart's (1976) analysis of women in top federal jobs reflected a similar trend.

In an interesting development, however, the move to downsize government agencies in the 1990s gave a substantial boost to the percentage of women and minorities in the federal work force. Lane et al. (2003) attribute the increase to "a concerted effort... to retain minorities and women through the use of buyouts and early retirements in lieu of reductions-in-force." By the close of the twentieth century, white males accounted for a shrinking portion of government jobs. Most observers expect the trend toward diversification to continue well into the new century (Lewis and Frank 2002). But in a survey of public personnel administrators and academicians, Hays and Kearney (2001) discovered that the latter were less optimistic that the quest for representativeness would continue to enjoy broad political support.

At the state and local government level, researchers found that these governments were generally doing a good job at increasing the number of blacks in their workforces (Dometrius and Sigelman 1984; Elling 1983). Moreover, blacks at these governmental levels were receiving salaries more comparable to those of white males (Dometrius and Sigelman 1984).

The struggle between merit and affirmative action principles has been the subject of extensive discussion. Livingston (1979) argues that the concept of meritocracy is deceptively racist, for both ideological and social reasons:

> This capacity for self-deception increases as a society moves closer to the requirements of meritocracy. As legally sanctioned inequalities of opportunity to demonstrate merit are eliminated, and as effort and luck play a diminished role in determining life chances, it becomes easier to image that privately enforced group justice is inconsequential. This group disadvantage rooted in racism can be made to appear as individual moral failure (Livingston 1979, 154).

A more pragmatic critique of merit is offered by Krislov and Rosenbloom (1981, 52–57). In considering a number of factors influencing merit hiring, including education, they caution that "in simple, real world situations, an open meritocratic system is not pure." Frequently, merit systems reflect biases on the basis of other than ability:

> Information available to high status persons on opportunities and how to use them, informal access to gatekeepers or persons who can influence gatekeepers, and the fiscal opportunities to take advantage of education opportunities are usually classbound factors (Krislov and Rosenbloom 1981, 55).

Certain scholars, however, have maintained a wariness toward affirmative action, at least as it applies to preferential hiring. O. Glenn Stahl, in equating such hiring to "quotaism," has condemned its potential effect on public personnel systems:

> The danger is not merely the direct damage to the quality of administrative performance; the danger is equally the bad image of the public service created—one that public jobs are by nature rewards, or worse still, welfare dispensations created for the purposes of providing incomes to the needy or the deserving. The moral fabric of the society is surely in less danger by resort to the 'negative income tax,' a guaranteed income tax, or any other such device than it is by a corrosion in the public mind of the prestige of government employment (Stahl 1976, 24–25).

Zashin (1981, 380) agreed that affirmative action brought about "important deviations from ostensibly meritocratic standards in the public service," but he also contended that no one had demonstrated that its success came "at the cost of deteriorating the quality of federal personnel."

Glazer (1977), in his polemic against affirmative action entitled *Affirmative Discrimination*, expressed similar reservations:

> To say that no policies have worked would be a simple error; everything, or almost everything, 'works' to some extent or another. But we have been crushingly disappointed by all our policies.

> Have goals and quotas helped? Perhaps. It was my argument in this book that they help those who do not need help and hardly reach those who do. I am not sure I am right. Complex econometric analyses come out with different stories. If we take as a measure the condition of the black lower class, certainly goals and quotas have been no marked success (Glazer 1978, xii–xiii).

Partisan clashes over affirmative action in recent decades have ensured that representativeness remains a prominent topic of scholarly concern and inquiry. Much of the discussion centers on what Medcalf and Dolbeare (1985) call the "equality–freedom dichotomy." This position has been frequently represented in the work of Kristol. Kristol (1978, 179) contends that the liberal position on equality has the potential of destroying individual liberty—in his view, the highest value in a free society. Consequently, "'social justice' may require a people, whose preferences are corrupt (in that they prefer liberty to equality), to be coerced into equality."

The Reagan administration accepted this logic as an operational assumption. In assessing the current meaning of equality in America, Verba and Orren (1985) summarize the Reagan approach:

> The Reagan presidency, beginning in 1981, ushered the latest spell of anti-egalitarian fervor. Intellectuals—new and old conservatives alike—criticized the egalitarian thrust of previous decades. The Reagan administration tried to turn back the tide, with some success. The administration approached its task, in the tradition of American politics, by seeking to reduce the disparity between ideal and reality. The Reagan ideal, however, was found not in the egalitarian symbols of the Declaration of Independence but in the individualistic symbols of the marketplace (Verba and Orren 1985, 370).

Even more perplexing is the fact that the courts, the guardians of affirmative action in the 1970s, began to challenge many of affirmative action's core assumptions in the late 1980s and 1990s. Beginning with *Richmond v. J. A. Croson*[*] in 1989, the Supreme Court advocated the application of a "strict scrutiny" to all race-based actions by state and local governments. In 1995, the court further restricted such programs in the controversial *Adarand Constructors v. Pena*[†] decision.

---

[*] US 469 (1989).
[†] S.Ct. 2097 (1995).

Concurring in the majority, Justice Scalia summarized the strongest challenge to Title VII in 30 years:

> In my view, government can never have a compelling interest in discriminating on the basis of race in order to make up for past racial discrimination in the opposite direction. Individuals who have been wronged by unlawful racial discrimination should be made whole; but under our Constitution, there can be no such thing as a creditor or debtor race.

More recent decisions, however, indicate that the court remains willing to support limited—narrowly tailored in the legal vernacular—affirmative-action initiatives. In 2003, the court upheld the University of Michigan's Law School admissions policy in *Grutter v. Bollinger.** Writing for the majority, Justice O'Connor explained that race could be used as a plus factor in the context of a balanced, nonmechanical decision making process. Even so, the court's 5–4 split in *Grutter* suggests that affirmative action will remain at the center of judicial controversy for some time to come.

The subject of comparable worth and a concern over gender-based pay inequities continue to generate heated discussion. Of major concern is the attempt to develop equitable compensatory schedules for jobs that require comparable skills and abilities. Opponents challenge the concept's tendency to inflate artificially market values and later wage stability (Livernash 1980). Neuse's (1982) assessment of the controversial topic is comprehensive and provides an understanding of the often acrimonious exchanges among those researching it.

Much of the debate surrounding pay inequities has centered on the use of an absolute or universal standard for evaluating jobs (Remick 1983; Thompkins 1987). Far less abstract in its implication is the realization that women in the public sector frequently face a "glass ceiling" in career advancement opportunities (Naff 1994). The relative dearth of women at the top levels of governmental service remains a recognizable problem (Cornwell and Kellough 1994), and efforts to remedy the problem are too often marked by "three steps forward and two steps backward" (Guy 1993).

The enduring nature of these questions serves as a useful reminder that the effort to promote, create, and sustain a diverse public workforce has taken on a life of its own in public personnel administration. It is also clear that the effort requires a substantial investment of time and energy on the part of agency officials. Lane et al. (2003) emphasize the difficulty of balancing personnel goals with other organizational imperatives:

> A workforce that represents the polity it serves has been a consistent democratic value.... However, this diversity also can create blocks to energy that will have to be addressed as workforce diversity increases. Differences in outlook, approaches to work, and general behavior customs create potential conflicts that easily can divert energy. Energy can get blocked by frustration or be diverted to conflict among groups. At a minimum, differences persist among groups about how they believe they are treated in the system. Perceived inequity clearly undermines motivation to apply energy to agency purposes (Lane et al. 2003, 135).

The quest for representative bureaucracy continues in our society. Yet what seemed an exemplary, even heroic, pursuit three decades ago has now become the focal point for much divisiveness and even derision. One thing appears certain: the future administrators are likely to see even more controversy with this troubled issue.

V. THE GROWTH OF BILATERALISM IN THE PUBLIC SECTOR

The fourth great issue in public personnel administration and labor relations deals with the development of the labor relations process itself and the growth of bilateralism in the public sector.

---

* US 241 (2003).

The right of federal workers to bargain with management, a relatively new occurrence, dates back only to 1962. On January 17, 1962, President John F. Kennedy issued Executive Order 10988 and established the basis for federal employees to organize.

Executive Order 10988 was superseded in 1969 by Nixon's Executive Order 11491, which created the implementation and mediation framework for the federal collective bargaining process, thus "bringing it more into line with practices in the private sector of the economy" (Fox and Shelton 1972, 113). Executive Order 11491 also acknowledged the right of federal employees to join or not join unions, but it prohibited federal strikes.[*]

Lacking explicit federal guidance, state and local governments tended to follow the federal example, despite a climate of greater hostility, fear, and skepticism (Nigro and DeMarco 1980). The single regional exception to this growth trend occurred in the Southeast, where less collective bargaining legislation has been passed and public employees have viewed the prospect of union affiliation with more reluctance (Kearney 1982).

The public personnel system functioned as a crucible for much of this change, with academicians and practitioners alike attempting to appraise the effects. For the first few years, research attempted to identify the differences between public and private sector bargaining (Haber 1968; Immundo 1975; Shaw and Clark 1972), to assess the size of public union membership (Cohany and Dewey 1970; Stieber 1973), and to explore the nature of public unions (Marshall 1974; O'Neill 1970; Stieber 1973).

The effects of public unionization on the personnel system and the public interest were also considered during this early period. Witte (1967) examined the impact of bargaining on the democratic process, while a number of scholars considered the relationships between bargaining and the merit principle (Helburn and Bennett 1972; Lewin and Horton 1975; Stanley 1970), and between bargaining and the civil service system (Feigenbaum 1974).

Throughout the 1970s, the concept of public strikes was a topic of sustained interest. Numerous articles, chapters, and books were published dealing with the topic of strikes, including both pro and con perspectives. An exceptionally negative treatment of strikes was included in Wilson's (1974) *Unions: Who Needs Them?*, while Billings and Greenya's (1974) *Power to the Public Worker* was unabashedly supportive. More moderate and objective views on the topic were provided by Aaron (1972), Barrett and Lobel (1974), and Barton (1970).

Emerging patterns of impasse resolution in the public sector during this period generated interest in the techniques of fact-finding (Doherty 1976), mediation (Ross 1976), and arbitration (Bornstein 1978; Rehmus 1975). Despite the increased sophistication in impasse resolution processes, Wesley's (1976, 3) comprehensive survey of resolution techniques began with the reminder that resolution often requires the "use of human relations skills" along with a determined commitment to "keep trying." Impasse resolution research has recently turned into a consideration of the effectiveness or various styles at different levels of government (Kolb 1983; Rodgers 1986).

Fiscal austerity in governmental budgets in the late 1970s and the late 1980s stimulated inquiry into the economics of public collective bargaining. Efforts have been undertaken to assess the impact of unionization on public wages (Karper and Meckstroth 1976; Mitchell 1978), to determine the effects of taxpayers' revolts on public employment and unions (Kearney 1983), and to explore the implications of the New York City financial crisis on municipal unions in that city (Weitzman 1979). Similarly, substantial attention has been devoted to productivity bargaining in an attempt to ascertain its viability for public employees. The reviews have ranged from the very critical (Horton 1976) to the moderately supportive (Layden 1980).

Despite this research, public bilateralism has traditionally been depicted as an area of relative neglect within personnel administration. This is particularly true in comparison with the other issues presented in this essay. Hays and Reeves (1984, 344–345) attribute the inattention to the

---

[*] C.F.R. 516 (Supp. 1971).

isolation of labor relations staffs and their low status in the organization. They are no doubt correct, but such an assessment warrants qualification. When the collective bargaining process in a jurisdiction breaks down, as it invariably does, the labor relations staff acquires visibility quickly.

Quite possibly the greatest difficulty still thwarting the credibility of public unionization is its basic incompatibility with civil service merit systems (Douglas 1992). Unions, with a strong reliance on the rule of seniority remain incongruous with the merit principle's rule of ability or even affirmative action's rule of accessibility. In the crowded public personnel agenda of the twenty-first century, unions may realize increasing difficulty in cultivating and maintaining a viable audience. This suspicion is supported by survey research. A 1997 study revealed that most personnel directors of federal, state, and local government agencies see union influence waning in the early years of the twenty-first century (Hays and Kearney 2001).

The future of unions in the public sector has become even more uncertain in the wake of the September 2001 terrorist attacks. The centerpiece of the Bush administration's organizational response to the tragedy was the creation of a new cabinet-level Department of Homeland Security (DHS), an entity which absorbed 170,000 federal employees from twenty-two agencies that previously had been dispersed throughout the federal bureaucracy. The new department, third largest in the national structure, was designed to provide better functional integration of government activities designed to protect against terrorist threats.

Significantly, President Bush requested and received congressional authority to impose a distinct set of personnel rules for the DHS. These rules reflect a "decidedly business school approach" (Ryan 2003) and are intended, in the name of national security imperatives, to give the president and his cabinet officer greater managerial latitude over department employees. Leaders of public sector unions are concerned, and with good reason: under the new rules, the Secretary of DHS has substantial authority to alter civil service protections without the consent of bargaining unit representatives (Ryan 2003).

Does the recent example of President Bush and the DHS exaggerate the threat faced by unions? Hardly; indeed, the threat may well be exacerbated. While DHS is an extraordinary agency formed during extraordinary times, public sector collective bargaining is less notable for what it has accomplished over the past thirty-five years than for what it has failed to accomplish. If public unions are to survive, their platforms must be increasingly progressive and their strategies more conciliatory.

VI. THE RECOGNITION OF THE PROFESSIONAL PUBLIC ADMINISTRATOR

The last of the five issues may well be the least concrete, although it is the most decisive in determining the future of public organizations and the public service. The development of professional public administrators and their recognition by society is the desired end of virtually every task that a personnel manager undertakes. Unfortunately, until the past decade, the concept of professionalism has had little more than symbolic meaning. Paradoxically, attacks on the concept have been responsible for much of the attention it has received during this decade.

In Woodrow Wilson's view, the professional character of civil servants depended on their ability to balance a commitment to the principles of the civil service with a commitment to public interest and opinion:

> The ideal for us is a civil service cultured and self-sufficient enough to act with sense and vigor, and yet so intimately connected with the popular thought, by means of elections and constant public counsel, as to find arbitrariness or class spirit quite out of the question (Wilson 1887).

Max Weber's approach to professionalism was considerably more technical, and included such requirements as training, a fixed salary, tenure, career mobility, and a system of certification (Gerth and Mills 1946). Unlike Wilson, however, Weber was skeptical over the lack of educated public opinion, particularly in large cities in the United States where immigrant votes were "corralled."

Over the years, concerns regarding professional status for public administrators have been voiced sporadically, usually coupled with initiatives for reforming the civil service system. Only since the late 1960s and early 1970s has the issue of professionalism focused more definitively on the individual administrator, rather than on the system of administration. Minnowbrook and the new public administration deserve some credit for this by raising concerns about individual bureaucratic responsibility.[*] The Vietnam War and Watergate should not be discounted as influencing factors, either. During the same time period, professional degree programs in public administration were proliferating as student interest in public service careers grew. The National Association of Schools for Public Administration and Affairs (NASPAA) began to develop as a forum for curricular debate, a role that would develop into accreditation review in the subsequent decades.

The passage of the Ethics in Government Act in 1978 raised public consciousness regarding the ethical obligations of the public service. Structurally the legislation created an Office of Government Crimes within the Department of Justice and an Office of Governmental Ethics within OPM. It also required the disclosure of financial information for high-level bureaucrats and placed restrictions on certain post-employment activities.

The Ethics in Government Act also kindled interest in the ethical and moral foundations of professionalism. In the past few years, scholars have examined the prospects and desirability of a code of ethics (Chandler 1983), explored the nature and limitations of moral responsibility for public officials (Thompson 1985), and assessed the ethical dimensions influencing bureaucratic action in a democratic society (Rohr 1978). In 1984, the National Council of the American Society of Public Administration approved a code of ethics for ASPA members. The code, revised once in 1994, remains the subject of considerable discussion, as ASPA members seek to produce a more streamlined document with which professionals can identify (Menzel 2002).

In addition to the interest in ethics, the theme of professionalism has been treated explicitly in professional journals since 1981. In the fall of 1981, Rabin (1981) edited a symposium entitled "Public Administration as a Profession" in the *Southern Review of Public Administration*. The articles focused on a wide range of topics emanating from the broader theme of professionalism, including semantic definitions of profession (Marutello 1981), the characteristics of a profession (Kline 1981), and professional association membership (Yeager 1981). In 1984, *Public Administration Review* devoted an issue to the publication of the Proceedings of the National Conference on Citizenship and Public Service held in April 1983. The section addressing citizenship and the professional public servant included a consideration of the paradox between democratic citizenship and personnel administration (McGregor 1984), a review of the status of bureaucrats as second-class citizens (Rohr 1984), and a discussion of the relationship between citizenship and public administration professionalism (Cooper 1984). Much of this journal's literature has been preoccupied with defining professionalism and rationalizing public administration's claim to professional status.

Much of the recent emphasis on professionalism within public administration has come about as a defensive reaction to the wave of bureaucracy bashing so prevalent in the last decade. It is not surprising, therefore, that public administration has countered such criticisms with contentions underscoring the field's record of administrative excellence, such as those contained in Goodsell (1985) *The Case for Bureaucracy: A Public Administration Polemic*. Goodsell's thesis is unabashedly supportive of the American bureaucracy and the role that bureaucrats have played in the development of American society, but he does caution that:

> [T]he field of public administration must develop the intellectual self-confidence to extend more uninhibitedly its own body of knowledge about public bureaucracy. We need to move beyond forty years of

---

[*] See the essays contained in Marini (1971).

dubious sociology and the antigovernmental biases of market-oriented economists, expose sociologists, and the critical theorists. Bureaucracies should be studied honestly for what they are, rather than for what they are not (Goodsell 1985, 148).

Professionalism differs from the preceding four issues in two aspects. First, the call for professionalism is limitless. Presumably, as practitioners attain a heightened level of professional competency, or as a profession achieves a desired state of development, new standards are prescribed; the paradigm, of necessity, shifts. This is understandable within, but is frequently confusing outside, the profession. Second, professionalism is a terribly amorphous concept. Its meaning has varied with time, circumstance, and opportunity. In sum, the term as applied to the public service has lacked real definition and direction.

This uncertainty and the attendant skepticism have made public administrators easy targets as factional politics become more divisive. Yet, oddly, these are the times during which administrative competence is most sorely needed:

> For politics only gives government its direction in a democratic order. It is commonly left to highly trained officials within the bureaucracy to provide the knowledge and skill that will enable government policy to arrive safely at its destination (Rourke 1992).

A more exacting standard, with barriers to entry, credentialization, and continuing certification is critically needed as this fledgling profession moves tentatively ahead.

VII. CONCLUSION

The enduring public personnel administration concepts presented in this chapter were chosen and argued based on reasonable and logical criteria. Still, the topics, by their very nature, promote controversy and argument. Conceptually, it is essential to understand that many of these concepts are interrelated to some degree, although distinctions, often arbitrary, have been made between each in order to facilitate their presentation.

The field of public administration has progressed substantially over the last one hundred years, driven in large part by the standards and expectations generated through its personnel function. After all, this was the century in which organizations were explored and defined and their personnel analyzed and categorized. While, certainly, the capabilities and limitations of the complex organization in contemporary society are now better understood, there is also enough information to make it clear how very little is known. The twenty-first century will likely see the emergence of new issues and new tensions, and will hopefully bring new wisdom. Still, the admonition of Alexander Hamilton in *Federalist* No. 68 remains timeless:

> Though we cannot acquiesce in the political heresy of the poet who says—'For forms of government let fools contest—That which is best administered is best'—Yet we may safely pronounce, that the true test of a good government is its aptitude and tendency to produce a good administration.

REFERENCES

Aaron, B., Collective bargaining where strikes are not tolerated, In *Collective Bargaining: Survival in the 1970s?*, Rowen, R. L., Ed., University of Pennsylvania Press, Philadelphia, PA, pp. 129–153, 1972.

Argyris, C., *Personality and Organization*, Harper and Row, New York, 1957.

Argyris, C., *Integrating the Individual and the Organization*, Wiley, New York, 1964.

Argyris, C., *Intervention Theory and Method: A Behavioral Science View*, Addison-Wesley, Reading, MA, 1970.

Arnold, P. E., Reform's changing role, *Public Administration Review*, 55, 407–417, 1995

Barnard, C. I., *The Functions of the Executive*, Harvard University Press, Cambridge, MA, 1938.

Barrett, J. T. and Lobel, I. T., Public sector strikes: legislative and court treatment, *Monthly Labor Review*, September, 19–22, 1974.

Barton, J. F. J., Can public employees be given the right to strike?, *Labor Law Journal*, August, 472–478, 1970.

Bennis, W., *Changing Organizations*, McGraw-Hill, New York, 1966.

Bellone, C. J. and Goerl, G. F., Reconciling public entrepreneurship and democracy, *Public Administration Review*, 52, 130–134, 1992.

Billings, R. N. and Greenya, J., *Power to the Public Worker*, Robert B. Luce, Washington, DC, 1974.

Bornstein, T., Interest arbitration in public employment: an arbitrator views the process, *Labor Law Journal*, 29, 77–86, 1978.

Boyne, G., Jenkins, G., and Poole, M., Human resource management in the public and private sectors: an empirical comparison, *Public Administration Review*, 77, 407–421, 1999.

Brayfield, A. H. and Crockett, W. H., Employee attitudes and employee performance, *Psychological Bulletin*, 52, 393–401, 1955.

Campbell, A. K., Civil service reform: a new commitment, *Public Administration Review*, 38, 99–103, 1978.

Cavanagh, M., In search of motivation, *Personnel Journal*, 63(3), 76–82, 1984.

Chandler, R. C., The problem of moral reasoning in American public administration: the case for a code of ethics, *Public Administration Review*, 43, 32–39, 1983.

Cohany, H. P. and Dewey, L. M., Unionism among government employees, *Monthly Labor Review*, July, 15–20, 1970.

Conant, J. K., In the shadow of Wilson and Brownlow: executive branch reorganization in the states, 1965 to 1987, *Public Administration Review*, 48, 892–902, 1988.

Cooper, T., Citizenship and professionalism in public administration, *Public Administration Review*, 44, 143–149, 1984.

Cornwell, C. and Kellough, J. E., Women and minorities in federal government agencies: examining new evidence from panel data, *Public Administration Review*, 54, 265–270, 1994.

Cummings, L., Compensation, culture and motivation: a systems perspective, *Organizational Dynamics*, Winter, 1984.

Davis, P. and Murphy, M. A., *Local Governments and the Fair Labor Standards Act*, Institute for Public Service, University of Tennessee, Knoxville, TN, 1985.

DeMan, H., *Joy in Work*, Trans. E. Paul, Holt, Rinehart and Winston, New York, 1929.

Doherty, R. E., On fact finding: a one-eyed man lost among the eagles, *Public Personnel Management*, 5, 363–367, 1976.

Dometrius, N. C. and Sigelman, L., Assessing progress toward affirmative action goals in state and local government: a new benchmark, *Public Administration Review*, 44, 241–246, 1984.

Douglas, I. M., State civil service and collective bargaining: systems in conflict, *Public Administration Review*, 52, 162–172, 1992.

Elder, P. K. and Miller, H. D., The fair labor standards act: changes of four decades, *Monthly Labor Review*, July, 30–38, 1979.

Elling, R., State bureaucracies, In *Politics in the American States: A Comparative Analysis*, 4th ed., Gray, V., Jacob, H., and Vines, K. N., Eds., Little, Brown, Boston, MA, 1983.

Emery, F. E. and Trist, E. L., The causal texture of organizational environments, *Human Relations*, 18, 21–32, 1965.

Feigenbaum, C., Civil service and collective bargaining: conflict or compatibility?, *Public Personnel Management*, 3, 244–252, 1974.

Follett, M. P., The giving of orders, In *Scientific Foundations of Business Administration*, Metcalf, H. C., Ed., Williams and Wilkins, Baltimore, MD, 1926.

Follett, M. P., *Dynamic administration*, Harper and Brothers, New York, p. 248, 1940.

Fox, M. J. and Shelton, H. E., The impact of executive order 11491 on the federal labor management relations process, *Journal of Collective Negotiations in the Public Sector*, 1, 113–124, 1972.

Frederickson, H. G., Toward a new public administration, In *Toward a New Public Administration: The Minnowbrook Perspective*, Marini, F., Ed., Chandler, Scranton, PA, pp. 309–331, 1971.

Frederickson, H. G., *New Public Administration*, University of Alabama Press, University, Alabama, 1980.

Gerth, H. and Mills, C. W., *From Max Weber: Essays in Sociology*, Oxford University Press, New York, 1946.

Glazer, N., *Affirmative Discrimination: Ethnic Inequality and Public Policy*, Basic Books, New York, 1977.

Goodnow, F. J., *Politics and Administration*, Macmillan, New York, 1900.

Goodsell, C. T., The Grace commission: seeking efficiency for the whole people?, *Public Administration Review*, 44, 196–204, 1984.

Goodsell, C. T., *The case for bureaucracy: A Public Administration Polemic*, Chatham House, Chatham, NJ, 1985.

Guy, M. E., Three steps forward, two steps backward: the status of women's integration into public management, *Public Administration Review*, 53, 285–292, 1993.

Haber, H., The relevance of private sector experience to public sector collective bargaining, *Proceedings of the Conference of the Institute of Management and Labor Relations,* Rutgers Univ., New Brunswick, NJ, 1968.

Harmon, M. M. and Mayer, R. T., *Organization Theory for Public Administration*, Little, Brown, Boston, MA, 1986.

Hays, S. W. and Reeves, T. Z., *Personnel Management in the Public Sector*, Allyn and Bacon, Boston, MA, 1984.

Hays, S. W. and Kearney, R. C., Anticipated changes in human resource management: views from the field, *Public Administration Review*, 61, 585–597, 2001.

Helburn, I. B. and Bennett, N. D., Public employee bargaining and the merit principle, *Labor Law Journal*, 23, 618–629, 1972.

Henry, N. L., *Public Administration and Public Affairs*, 3rd ed., Prentice Hall, Englewood Cliffs, NJ, p. 197, 1986.

Horton, R., Productivity and productivity bargaining in government: a critical analysis, *Public Administration Review*, 36, 407–414, 1976.

Howard, L. C., Civil service reform: a minority and woman's perspective, *Public Administration Review*, 38, 305–309, 1978.

Huddleston, M. W., The Carter civil service reforms, *Political Science Quarterly*, 96, 607–621, 1982.

Immundo, Jr., L. V., Federal government sovereignty and its effect on labor-management relations, *Labor Law Journal*, March, 46–151, 1975.

Ingraham, P. W., *The Foundation of Merit: Public Service in American Democracy*, Johns Hopkins Press, Baltimore, MD, 1995.

Ink, D., What was behind the 1978 civil service reform?, In *The Future of Merit: Twenty Years after the Civil Service Reform Act*, Pfiffner, J. P. and Brook, D. A., Eds., Woodrow Wilson Center Press, Washington, DC, 2000.

Joiner, B., *Fourth Generation Management*, McGraw-Hill, New York, 1994.

Karper, M. D. and Meckstroth, D. J., The impact of unionization on public wage rates, *Public Personnel Management*, 5, 343–346, 1976.

Kearney, R. C., Public employee unionization and collective bargaining in the southeast, *Southern Review of Public Administration*, 5, 477–499, 1982.

Kearney, R. C., Public employment and public employee unions in a time of taxpayer revolt, In *Public Personnel Administration: Problems and Prospects*, Hays, S. W. and Kearney, R. C., Eds., Prentice Hall, Englewood Cliffs, NJ, pp. 189–202, 1983.

Kellough, J. E. and Selden, S. C., The reinvention of public personnel administration: an analysis of the diffusion of personnel management reforms in the states, *Public Administration Review*, 63, 165–177, 2003.

Kettl, D. F., Ingraham, P. W., Sanders, R. P., and Horner, C., *Civil Service Reform: Building a Government That Works*, Brookings Institution Press, Washington, DC, 1996.

Kingsley, J. D., *Representative Bureaucracy*, Antioch Press, Yellow Springs, OH, 1944.

Kline, E. H., To be a professional, *Southern Review of Public Administration*, 5, 58–281, 1981.

Kolb, D. M., *The Mediators*, MIT Press, Cambridge, MA, 1983.

Kranz, H., *The Participatory Bureaucracy: Women and Minorities in a More Representative Public Service*, Lexington Books, Lexington, MA, 1976.

Krislov, S. and Rosenbloom, D. H., *Representative Bureaucracy and the American Political System*, Praeger, New York, pp. 52–57, 1981.

Kristol, I., *Three Cheers for Capitalism*, Basic Books, New York, 1978.

Lane, L. M., Wolf, J. F., and Woodard, C., Reassessing the human resource crisis in the public service, 1987–2002, *American Review of Public Administration*, 33, 123–145, 2003.

Lawler III, E. E. and Porter, L. W., The effect of performance on job satisfaction, *Industrial Relations*, 7, 20–28, 1967.

Layden, D. R., Productivity and productivity bargaining: the environmental context, *Public Personnel Management*, 9, 244–256, 1980.

Levine, C., *The Quiet Crisis of the Civil Service: The Federal Personnel System at the Crossroads*, National Academy of Public Administration, Washington, DC, 1986.

Lewin, D. and Horton, R. D., The impact of collective bargaining on the merit system in government, *Arbitration Journal*, 30, 199–211, 1975.

Lewis, G. B. and Frank, S. A., Who wants to work for government?, *Public Administration Review*, 62, 395–405, 2002.

Light, P.C., To restore and renew. Government Executive, November 1, 2001, http//www.govexec.com/ (accessed February 2, 2004).

Likert, R., *New Patterns of Management*, McGraw-Hill, New York, 1961.

Likert, R., *The Human Organization*, McGraw-Hill, New York, 1967.

Livernash, E. R., Ed., *Comparable Worth: Issues and Alternatives*, Equal Employment Advisory Council, Washington, DC, 1980.

Livingston, J. C., *Fair Game?: Inequality and Affirmative Action*, W.H. Freeman, San Francisco, CA, 1979.

Lynn, N. and Vaden, R. E., Bureaucratic response to civil service reform, *Public Administration Review*, 39, 333–343, 1979.

Marini, F., Ed., *Toward a New Public Administration: The Minnowbrook Perspective*, Chandler, Scranton, PA, 1971.

Marshall, J. F., Public employee associations: roles and programs, *Public Personnel Management*, 3, 415–424, 1974.

Marutello, F., The semantic definitions of profession, *Southern Review of Public Administration*, 5, 246–257, 1981.

Maslow, A., A theory of human motivation, *Psychological Review*, 50, 370–396, 1943.

McGregor, D., *The Human Side of Enterprise*, McGraw-Hill, New York, 1960.

McGregor, Jr., E. B., The great paradox of democratic citizenship and public personnel administration, *Public Administration Review*, 44, 126–131, 1984.

Medcalf, L. J. and Dolbeare, K. M., *Neopolitics: American Political Ideas in the 1980s*, Random House, New York, 1985.

Menzel, D., ASPA's code of ethics: time to change?, *PA Times*, 25, 8, 2002.

Milbourn, G., The relationship of money and motivation, Compensation Review Second Quarter, 1980.

Mitchell, D. J. B., Collective bargaining and wage determination in the public sector: is Armageddon really at hand?, *Public Personnel Management*, 7, 80–95, 1978.

Mosher, F. C., *Democracy and the Public Service*, Oxford University Press, New York, 1968.

Naff, K. C., Through the glass ceiling: prospects for the advancement of women in the federal civil service, *Public Administration Review*, 54, 507–514, 1994.

Nalbandian, J. and Klingner, D., The politics of public personnel administration: towards theoretical understanding, *Public Administration Review*, 45, 541–549, 1981.

Neuse, S. A., A critical perspective on the comparable worth debate, *Review of Public Personnel Administration*, 3, 1–20, 1982.

Nigro, F. A. and Nigro, L., *The New Public Personnel Administration*, 2nd ed., Peacock, Itasca, IL, pp. 11–27, 1981.

Nigro, L. and DeMarco, J. J., Collective bargaining and the attitudes of local government personnel managers, *Public Personnel Management*, 9, 160–168, 1980.

O'Neill, H., The growth of municipal employee unions, In *Unionization of Municipal Employees*, Connery, R. H. and Farr, W., Eds., Academy of Political Science, New York, 1970.

Osborne, D. and Gaebler, T., *Reinventing Government*, Addison-Wesley, Reading, MA, 1992.

Pearce, J. L. and Perry, J. L., Federal merit pay: a longitudinal analysis, *Public Administration Review*, 43, 315–325, 1983.

Perrow, C., *Complex Organizations: A Critical Essay*, 3rd ed., McGraw-Hill, New York, 1986.

Rabin, J., Public administration as a profession: a symposium, *Southern Review of Public Administration*, 5, 237–391, 1981.

Pratchett, L. and Wingfield, M., Petty bureaucracy and woolly-minded liberalism? The changing ethos of local government officers, *Public Administration*, 74, 639–656, 1996.

Rehmus, C. M., Legislated interest arbitration, *Proceedings of the Twenty-Seventh Annual Winter Meeting*, Industrial Relations Research Association, Champaign, IL, pp. 307–314, 1975.

Remick, H., The comparable worth controversy, *Public Personnel Management Journal*, 12, 371–382, 1983.

Rogers, Jr., H.P., Fair employment laws for minorities: an evaluation of federal implementation, In *Implementation of Civil Rights Policy*, Bullock III, C.S. and Lamb, C.M., Eds., Brooks/Cole, Monterey, CA, 1984.

Rodgers, R. C., An interesting, bad theory of mediation, *Public Administration Review*, 46, 67–74, 1986.

Roethlisberger, F. J., *Management and Morale*, chap. 2, Harvard University Press, Cambridge, MA, 1941.

Roethlisberger, F. J. and Dickson, W. J., *Management and the Worker*, Harvard University Press, Cambridge, MA, 1939.

Rohr, J. A., *Ethics for Bureaucrats*, Dekker, New York, 1978.

Rohr, J. A., Civil servants and second class citizens, *Public Administration Review*, 44, 135–139, 1984.

Rose, W. and Chia, T., The impact of the equal employment opportunity act of 1972 on black employment in the federal service: a preliminary analysis, *Public Administration Review*, 38, 245–261, 1978.

Rosen, B., Merit and the president's plan for changing the civil service system, *Public Administration Review*, 38, 301–304, 1978.

Rosenbloom, D. H. and Obuchowski, C. C., Public personnel examinations and the constitution: emerging trends, *Public Administration Review*, 37, 9–18, 1977.

Ross, J. H., Federal mediation in the public sector, *Monthly Labor Review*, 99, 41–45, 1976.

Rourke, F., Responsiveness and neutral competence in american bureaucracy, *Public Administration Review*, 52, 546, 1992.

Ryan, R. W., The department of homeland security challenges the federal civil service system. Public Administration and Management, 8:3 [http://www.pamij.com/], 2003.

Schiesl, M. J., *The Politics of Efficiency: Municipal Administration and Reform in America: 1880–1920*, University of California Press, Berkeley, CA, 1977.

Schriesheim, C. A., Tolliver, J. M., and Behling, O. C., Leadership theory: some implications for managers, *MSU Business Topics*, Summer, 34–40, 1978.

Shaw, L. C. and Clark, Jr., T. R., The practical differences between public and private sector collective bargaining, *UCLA Law Review*, 19, 867–886, 1972.

Siegel, G. B. and Myrtle, R. C., *Public Personnel Administration: Concepts and Practices*, Houghton Mifflin, Boston, MA, p. 23, 1985.

Stahl, O. G., *Public Personnel Administration*, 7th ed., Harper and Row, New York, p.42, 1976.

Stanley, D., What are unions doing to the merit system? *Public Personnel Review*, 31, 141–162, 1970.

Stewart, D. W., Women in top jobs: an opportunity for federal leadership, *Public Administration Review*, 36, 357–364, 1976.

Stieber, J., *Public Employee Unionism: Structure, Growth, Policy*, Brookings Institution, Washington, DC, 1973.

Stogdill, R. M., *Handbook of Leadership: A Survey of Theory and Leadership*, Free Press, New York, 1974.

Swiss, J. E., Adapting total quality management (TQM) to government, *Public Administration Review*, 52, 356–362, 1992.

Taylor, F. W., *The Principles of Scientific Management*, W.W. Norton, New York, 1911.

Thayer, F. C., The president's management "reforms:" Theory X triumphant, *Public Administration Review*, 38, 309–314, 1978.

Thompkins, J., Comparable worth and job evaluation, *Public Administration Review*, 47, 254–258, 1987.

Thompson, D. F., The possibility of administrative ethics, *Public Administration Review*, 45, 555–561, 1985.

US House Committee on Government Reform, *Achieving Diversity in the Senior Executive Service Hearing*, 15 October 2003.

Van Riper, R. P., *History of the United States Civil Service Commission*, Harper and Row, New York, 1958.

Verba, S. and Orren, G. R., The meaning of equality in America, *Political Science Quarterly*, 100, 369–387, 1985.

Vroom, V., *Work and Motivation*, John Wiley & Sons, New York, 1964.

Waldo, D., Development of theory of democratic administration, *American Political Science Review*, 46(1), 81–103, 1952

Waldo, D., *The Enterprise of Public Administration: A Summary View*, Chandler and Sharp, Novato, CA, pp. 81–98, 1980.

Weitzman, J. P., The effect of economic restraints on public sector collective bargaining: the lessons of New York City, In *Government Labor Relations: Trends and Information for the Future*, Jascourt, H. D., Ed., Moore, Oak Park, IL, pp. 334–346, 1979.

Wentworth, K., Development and use of written tests, In *Recruitment and Selection in the Public Service*, Donovan, J. J., Ed., Public Personnel Association, Chicago, IL, pp. 112–122, 1968.

Wesley, R., *Impasse Resolution: An Analysis of Old and New Ways to End Deadlocks*, Labor-Management Relations Service, Washington, DC, 1976.

White, L., *Public Administration*, McMillan, New York, 1926.

Wilson, J., *Unions: Who Needs Them?*, Omni-Print, Sarasota, FL, 1974.

Wilson, W., The study of administration. *Political Science Quarterly*, 2(2), 197–222, 1887.

Wilson, W., President's committee on administrative management, *Report on the Committee on Administrative Management*, Government Printing Office, Washington, DC, 1937.

Witte, E. E., Collective bargaining and the democratic process, In *Unions, Management and the Public*, Bakke, E. W., Kerr, C., and Amos, C., Eds., Harcourt, Brace and World, Chicago, IL, 1967.

Wren, D. A., *The Evolution of Management Thought*, John Wiley & Sons, New York, 1972.

Yeager, S. J., Fostering the development of professionalism: an exchange theory perspective of the decision to join a public organization, *Southern Review of Public Administration*, 5, 314–338, 1981.

Zashin, E. M., Affirmative action, preferential selection, and federal employment, In *Public Personnel Management: Readings in Contexts and Strategies*, Klingner, D. E., Ed., Mayfield, Palo Alto, CA, pp. 366–383, 1981.

Unit 6

Federalism and Intergovernmental Relations

11

Federalism, Intergovernmental Relations, and Intergovernmental Management: The Origins, Emergence, and Maturity of Three Concepts across Two Centuries of Organizing Power by Area and by Function

Deil S. Wright and Carl W. Stenberg

CONTENTS

I. INTRODUCTION

All nations of any size and consequence must confront one of the fundamental problems of governance—how will the competing claims between central and peripheral authority be resolved? Constitutionally the issue is commonly framed in legal terms: Which jurisdiction has power(s) to do what, with what degree of discretion or autonomy? (Bulpitt 1983; Davis 1978; King 1982; Riker 1964; Rose 1982; Wheare 1964). Administratively the "basic theoretical question" was posed by Fesler: "How to relate area and function?" (also Fesler 1949, 1965, 1973; Truman 1940; Ylvisaker 1959). Much like the blending of politics and administration, the two questions overlap, are interrelated, and even merge (Macmahon 1972). The link between constitutional arrangements based on politics and organizational implementation centered on administration is a theme that permeates this chapter. It is hardly new. In fact, the constitutional–administrative theme has a not-so-hallowed tradition that spans the two centuries of American historical experience.

      Our central aim in this essay is to offer a broad historical overview and alternative interpretations of the functioning of the American system of multi-level governance. We pursue this aim guided by a chronological motif that elaborates the three concepts specified in the essay's title: Federalism, Intergovernmental Relations, and Intergovernmental Management. Each concept is traced successively from its origin and development, including its meaning and maturation. Several decades are specified and elaborated during which each concept gained currency, evolved in usage, and attained practical application. The span covered by the three concepts starts with the legal-historical features of the nation's origins and the ambiguous status of administration at the founding of the Republic. It extends to the contemporary scene and includes major policy conflicts and tensions at the opening of the twenty-first century.

Several writers have noted the non-constitutional status of public administration in the mind-sets of the framers at the Philadelphia Convention (Carroll 1982; Heady 1987; Krislov and Rosenbloom 1981; Waldo 1980). Clauses in the Constitution that recognize the administrative function are nearly nonexistent. *The Federalist* does provide a few statements on administration. Despite their brevity and submerged status, the following passages from Hamilton, Madison, and Jay are instructive and pertinent to the purposes of this historical overview.

From Jay (No. 3):

when once an efficient national government is established the best men in the country will not only consent to serve, but also will generally be appointed to manage it; ... Hence it will result that the administration, the political counsels, and the judicial decisions of the national government will be more wise, systematical, and judicious than those of individual states, and consequently more satisfactory with respect to other nations as well as more safe with respect to us.

From Hamilton (No. 27):

Unless we presume at the same time that the powers of the general government will be worse administered than those of the State governments, there seems to be no room for the presumption of ill will, disaffection, or opposition in the people. I believe it may be laid down as a general rule that their confidence in and obedience to a government will commonly be proportioned to the goodness or badness of its administration. It must be admitted that there are exceptions to this rule; but these exceptions depend so entirely on accidental causes that they cannot be considered as having any relation to the intrinsic merits or demerits of a constitution. These can only be judged of by general principles and maxims.

From Madison (No. 46):

If ... the people should in future become more partial to the federal than to the State governments, the change can only result from such manifest and irresistible proofs of a better administration as will overcome all their antecedent propensities.

From Hamilton (No. 68):

... we may safely pronounce that the true test of a good government is its aptitude and tendency to produce a good administration.

From Hamilton (No. 72):

The administration of government, in its largest sense, comprehends all the operations of the body politic, whether legislative, executive, or judiciary; but in its most usual and perhaps most precise signification, it is limited to executive details, and falls peculiarly within the province of the executive department.

While modest in bulk, the ideas are large in importance. Hamilton (in 72) notes both the wide scope and detailed specificity of administration. He links good administration (in 68 and 27) to citizen confidence in and legitimacy according to government. Madison (in 46) also notes the link between good administration *and* citizen respect and loyalty; Jay (in 3) sees the national government attracting the best cadre of persons to manage and administer the new system.

Commentaries and analyses of the framers' views on constitutional federalism are legion (Beer 1993; Diamond 1961; Diamond 1976a, 1976b; Huntington 1959; Jillson 1981; Lienesch 1983a, 1983b; Warren 1968). Less extensive and probing are analyses of the framers' views on administration, although there are a few exceptions (Caldwell 1944; Rohr 1986; White 1948).

One hundred years after *The Federalist*, Woodrow Wilson closely scrutinized both administration and federalism in his well-known (1887) essay "The Study of Administration". Four statements from the essay, two on administration and two on federalism, are noteworthy. Echoing Hamilton's assertions, Wilson (1941, 497) noted that "the study of administration, philosophically viewed, is closely connected to the study of the proper distribution of constitutional authority." Wilson also acknowledged that "it is getting to be harder to *run* a constitution than to frame one." Although Wilson's essay is often noted for creating the politics–administration dichotomy, a full and balanced reading of the essay makes it difficult to support the thesis that Wilson originated and endorsed a neat, simple, and sharp split between the two activities.

The extent to which Wilson discussed federalism in his classic essay is regularly overlooked (Wright 1987). Two passages quoted below are selected from several on the subject in the article. The first indicates Wilson's awareness of the framers' originality and of the constitutional–legal dimensions of federalism. In the second statement he expands on features of national–state–local relationships in language that could be used as a contemporary description of intergovernmental relations without appearing archaic:

> What did we ever originate, except the action of the Federal government upon individuals and some of the functions of the Federal Supreme Court.

> Our duty is, to supply the best possible life to a *federal* organization, to systems within systems: to make town, city, county, state, and federal governments live with a like strength and an equally assured healthfulness, keeping each unquestionably its own master and yet making all interdependent and co-operative, combining independence with mutual helpfulness. The task is great and important enough to attract *the best* minds.

We may debate whether Wilson was a founder or was influential in the development of public administration (Van Riper 1983; Waldo 1948). Regardless of the outcome of that debate, Wilson's reflections and essay were part of the larger social, political, and intellectual ferment near the end of the nineteenth century. His thinking, writing, and action(s) were efforts to address and cope with a rapidly changing economic, social, and political–administrative order (Skowronek 1982).

Wilson's (1887) essay and his statement about federalism 21 years later (Wilson 1908)—that it was the "cardinal question" of our constitutional system—reemphasized the basic issue of center–periphery authority one century after the system had been launched. About a half century after Wilson's essay, Durham (1940, 6) explored the politics–administration link with a specific focus on intergovernmental relations (IGR):

> So what of politics and administration in intergovernmental relations? Their interlocking indicates the unreality of checks, balances, and division into politics and administration. As a guide to a new theory of the division of powers, the idea of *administrative politics*, or the interrelations of public administrators in what appears to be increasingly more permanent offices with tenure, forms a more realistic concept ... Questions of structure and function in the federal system preclude, under present boundaries and constitutional restrictions, the emergence of a more significant factor than the party in clearly defining the policy-phase of a new "administrative politics."

Durham was unquestionably accurate in viewing IGR, conceptually and operationally, as an arena for the permanent blending or merging of politics and administration. His phrase "administrative politics" did not survive and blossom, but it did add impetus to the demise of the dichotomy that Appleby (1949), Long (1949, 1962), Sayre (1951), and others confirmed. Colbert (1983) suggested a politics-in-administration continuum as a reformulation and located more than a half dozen references to such a continuum. Regardless of subsequent developments, the significance of

Durham's critique of the dichotomy as it applied to federalism and IGR should not be underestimated. Waldo, for example, in *The Administrative State* (1948, 128) noted, "There is a close similarity between the rigid politics-administration viewpoint and that philosophy of federalism that pictured state and nation moving noiselessly and without friction each in its separate sphere."

While Durham was moving with the intellectual flow in attacking the politics–administration dichotomy, his analysis was not as prescient or predictive concerning two other variables he identified: political party and professionalism (permanent tenure). Durham (1940, 6) anticipated the "importance of the [political] party" as an instrument in producing "a decentralizing of ... power." In this respect he was a precursor of the more extensive development of the party-as-decentralizer thesis by the Advisory Commission on Intergovernmental Relations (ACIR) (ACIR 1986), Buchanan (1965), Grodzins (1960a), Riker (1964), and Truman (1955). The declines and shifts in party identification, party loyalty, and party efficacy have called into question the broad issue of the relationship, if any, of the party system to centralizing and decentralizing forces.

Durham's oblique reference to professionalism touched on another variable whose effect on federalism and IGR he could, at that juncture (late 1930s), only dimly perceive. The broader and generally centralizing impact of professionalism was not fully appreciated until years later by Beer (1978a), Grodzins (1966), Kaufman (1969), Mosher (1968), Mosher and Stillman (1978), and Wirt (1981).

We conclude this introductory 200-year sketch by drawing on Beer's presidential address to the American Political Science Association (Beer 1978a). His analysis of federalism and IGR was important for several reasons, only two which will be discussed here. The first highlights a political dimension and addresses Beer's idea of "representational federalism." Another element, addressed secondarily by Beer, involved administration and management, a domain from which the concept and practice of intergovernmental management (IGM) emerged.

By focusing on representational federalism, Beer put the final quietus, if one was needed, on the politics–administration dichotomy. He did this by arguing that wholly new forms of influence had evolved in the US political system and that federal arrangements accommodated them in ways consistent with its historic, flexible, and open-ended nature (Leach 1970, 1988).

The two emergent representational interests in Washington were, according to Beer, the "technocrats" and the "topocrats." The former represent the "new professionalism" in government—national, state, and local. They form the "professional bureaucratic complex" of functional program specialists; they are most easily understood as the vertical "pickets" forming the classic graphic of picket fence federalism (Sanford 1967; Wright 1974, 1988).

The topocratic interests revolve around what Beer (1976, 1977, 1978a) called the intergovernmental lobby. This cluster of self-designated public interest groups was composed of the associations of political–administrative generalists at the state and local level. Governors, state and local legislators, mayors, county executives, and city/county managers have mobilized on behalf of varied common concerns to make their presence and influence felt in the halls of Congress, the executive branch, and even the judiciary (Farkas 1971; Haider 1974; *National League of Cities v. Usery* 426 U.S. 833 1976; *Garcia v. San Antonio Metropolitan Transit Authority* 469 U.S. 546 1985; Arnold and Plant 1994).

Tensions and divisiveness between the technocrats and the topocrats were not new in the 1970s. They began to surface even as Durham wrote in the late 1930s (Clark 1938; Hovde 1940; Vieg 1940). Systematic investigation of the cleavages was pursued in the late 1940s by graduate students at the University of Minnesota under the direction of William Anderson (1960). In-depth attention to contrasting attitudes between the two groups was explored by Weidner (1955, 1960), and Ylvisaker (1956).

The normative issue surrounding the conflicts identified by Beer should not be overlooked. What has been the effect of these two new representational forms on other aspects of the democratic process? Have the technocrats and topocrats caused, as Beer (1978a, 20) feared, "dilutions of the popular will?" Have they contributed further to fragmentation of representation and a reinforcement of the image that the nation's capitol is dominated by "special interests?" Despite corporate instead of personal representation, Beer conceded that the two entities "do add real strengths to the modern state." He wondered, however, whether "this may be at some cost to free government."

Beer's acknowledgment of the role(s) of technocrats (program professionals) constituted a secondary set of developments that originated in the 1970s. The operational significance and specialized domain of these administrators (later called policy professionals in the 1980s) were inadequately portrayed even in Beer's perceptive analysis. Not until the 1980s would IGM be elaborated as a concept describing actions that sometimes complemented but often conflicted with federalism and IGR (Agranoff 1986; Peterson et al. 1986; Wright 1983, 1990a; Wright and Krane 1998).

This introductory section has touched lightly on a few critical junctures in the two-century evolution of center–periphery relations in the United States. On a chronological basis we have identified issues, ideas, and concepts surfacing at roughly 200, 100, 50, and 20 years ago. The remainder of this chapter relies on this chronological motif.

Three terms serve as the organizing concepts: federalism (FED), intergovernmental relations (IGR), and intergovernmental management (IGM). Our approach will follow the development sequence mentioned in the essay subtitle—the origins, emergence, and maturity of each concept, beginning with FED and concluding with IGM.

The temporal and developmental strategy adopted for the exposition of these three concepts can be presented in visual form. Figure 11.1 offers a timeline intended to reflect the historical patterns and the respective sub-periods for each concept. Federalism, which began with the founding of the republic, is often characterized as experiencing three broad eras—dual, cooperative, and coercive (Kincaid 1990b, 1993b, 1996). Over the past six decades IGR has been interpreted as passing

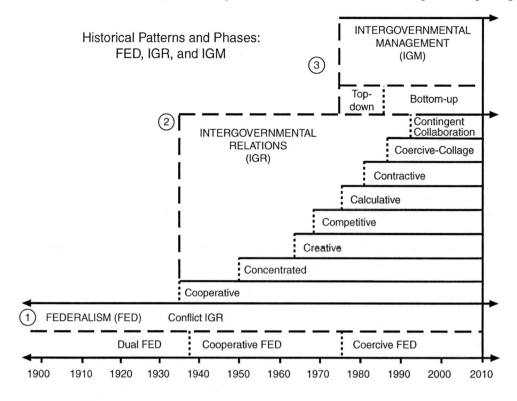

FIGURE 11.1 Historical patterns and phrases: federalism (FED), IGR, and IGM.

through multiple phases. These began with the conflict phase in the pre-1930s and continued to the coercive-collage phase of the 1990s and extended into the twenty-first century with the contingent collaboration phase (Wright 1988, 1997, 2003). Finally, IGM has been subdivided into two distinct periods. They reflect the top-down and bottom-up approaches to intergovernmental problem-solving practices encompassed by the concept (Wright and Krane 1998).

II. ORIGINS OF FEDERALISM

A.   THE PHILADELPHIA CONVENTION

Without a doubt the Philadelphia Convention marks the starting point for an understanding of the origins of federalism and the meaning of the term today. The convention was called to "propose amendments and revisions" to the Articles of Confederation which had governed the former colonies since 1777. To the framers at Philadelphia the articles were "a federal system." In other words, they did not make a distinction between federal and nonfederal arrangements.

Two statements make this clear. Madison writes in *Federalist* No. 39 about ways in which the new constitution incorporated both national and "federal" features. In the latter case he meant features from the Articles of Confederation. He concludes by saying that the new constitution is "neither wholly *national* nor wholly *federal*." Elsewhere, George Mason wrote to his son shortly before the convention convened about the degree of agreement expected to prevail at the sessions (Jillson 1981, 600): "The most prevalent idea in the principal States seems to be a total alteration of the present federal system."

Two points might be noted from these assertions. One is the political and strategic inventiveness of those supporters of the new Constitution. By calling themselves Federalists they laid claim to the least centralized system of links between central and peripheral governing entities. It also put their opponents, the *anti*-Federalists, in the awkward and defensive position of attacking modifications of existing federal arrangements (Storing 1981). The second point, drawn from Mason's letter, is the widely shared set of basic political beliefs that were held in common by those who met in Philadelphia (Bailyn 1967; Benson 1960; Roche 1961; Wood 1969). A majority of the framers were clearly nationalists, although Holcombe (1950) and others have described and probed the various factions among those who agreed on the need for a stronger central government. Most analyses of the Philadelphia Convention dynamics highlight conflicts and crucial compromises. It is important, however, to be clear about two fundamental features that bound the framers together: (1) an underlying nationalism guiding "the first new nation" (Lipset 1963); and (2) a consensus on the need to strengthen the new central/national government (Holcombe 1950; Lienesch 1983b).

In spite of substantial agreement on fundamentals, the dominant mode of analysis of the convention is one that focuses on conflicts and compromises over the content, clauses, and structures of the draft Constitution (Farrand 1911, 1913; Holcombe 1950; Jillson 1981; Smith 1965; Warren 1968). Jillson (1981) applies factor analysis to convention votes at various phases and finds four issues that run through the alignments and realignments. Two of these, state integrity and the power scope of the national government, are federalism related. The broader implication of Jillson's analysis is his effort to link convention constitution-making to theories of conflict and cleavage (Schattschneider 1960) and of critical realignment of the American party system (Burnham 1970; Key 1955; Sundquist 1973).

B.   ADOPTION OF THE CONSTITUTION

The Federalist Papers are the undisputed starting point for understanding (1) the provisions of the Constitution, (2) the rationale of three framers (Hamilton, Madison, and Jay) for those provisions, and (3) the main arguments, pro and con, used during the adoption process. Seven different editions of *The Federalist* offer extended introductory essays that provide helpful orienting discussions

(Ball 2003; Carey and McClellan 2001; Earle 1937; Fairfield 1981; Kesler 1999; Rossiter 1961; Wootton 2003). *The Federalist Papers*, however, do not stand alone as the definitive corpus for constitutional understanding and interpretation, nor are they adequate for a firm grasp of the politics of the adoption process.

The negative side of the debate between the Federalists and the anti-Federalists has long been neglected, and only recently have the anti-Federalists reached a status where they "deserve to be considered founders as well" (Lienesch 1983a). The definitive work in this connection is traceable to the dedicated efforts of Storing (1981). In his exposition of what the anti-Federalists were for, Storing effectively challenged Kenyon's (1955) thesis that the opponents of the Constitution were "men of little faith." Lienesch (1983, 1988) added depth to the thesis with a careful and detailed analysis of the debates in the several state conventions called to consider adoption of the proposed constitution (Elliott 1861–1863). Ball (2003), in his edition of *The Federalist*, provides and cross-references fourteen "Brutus" anti-federalist essays to give readers "the greatest non-violent verbal battle ever waged in America" (xv) Cornell's recent volume provides a full length treatment of the anti-federalist's role "founders" (Cornell 1999).

C. Framers' Intent, Meaning, and Orientation

There has been a revival of interest and debate over the framers' meaning or intent concerning federalism as well as other parts of the Constitution. This can be traced in no small measure to Attorney General Edwin Meese's (1985) stance favoring a "jurisprudence of original intention," in contrast to what he saw as a "jurisprudence of idiosyncrasy." Federalism, and particularly the doctrine of incorporation of the Bill of Rights as limits on the states (through the Fourteenth Amendment), is one of the issues at bar.

What was the framers' original view(s) of federalism? How was federalism linked to the larger philosophical context and framework from which the framers developed their arguments? This chapter cannot answer those questions; it can only identify sources and views from which discussion and debate may proceed (Beer 1993).

The most serious, sustained, and critical appraisal of the framers' views of federalism has been the work of Diamond (1961, 1969, 1971, 1976a, 1976b). His multiple and thorough explorations of the subject are done an injustice by any effort at a condensed summary. One theme, however, that pervaded his incisive analysis was the search for a clear and coherent set of constitutional principles. Diamond was undoubtedly one of the most persistent and rigorous examiners of the *principles* of the framers, confident in the fact that there were such principles and that it was imperative, for our own good, that we comprehend them.

William Anderson, no less of a scholar, was not sanguine about discerning the intention(s) of the framers. He devoted a full chapter to this subject in his thoughtful overview of *The Nation and the States: Rivals or Partners* (1955). Anderson adopted what might be termed an evolutionary view of the origin and meaning of the Constitution, saying that it "simply did not spring forth perfect, complete, and self-explanatory; most likely it never will be complete and perfect" (Anderson 1955). Anderson adds, with regard to the framers' intent, "Indeed, it is merely vain imagining to assume that such a thing as 'the intention' of 'its framers' in the full sense ever existed or ever can be discovered" (Anderson 1955). More recently, Rakove (1990) provided an overview of issues involving original intent.

Beyond the "original intention" debate there is a broad and expanding body of recent critical or rethinking literature on the philosophical foundations of the framers from which federalism, however interpreted, sprang. Three full-length expositions offer formidable challenges: Dahl (1956), Wills (1981), and Elkins and McKitrick (1993). Dahl argues, in part, that Madison (primarily) misread his own time and was not fully consistent in the logic of his arguments, especially in *Federalist* no. 10. Wills, on the other hand, finds a single philosophical base penetrating all of *The Federalist*, even overriding the inconsistencies and differences between Hamilton and

Madison. Recall that when the Virginia Plan was drafted by Madison to take to Philadelphia, Hamilton urged that state governors be appointed and removed by the president; Madison tempered this by including a provision permitting the national Congress to veto any state law. Elkins and McKitrick (1993) probe deeply the entire age (decade) of the "founding generation" with a special emphasis on their "modes of thought and feeling."

Wills argues that what pervaded *The Federalist* and bound it into a single whole was a non-Hobbesian view of human nature, one confident of the presence of public good and virtue among the citizenry. Thus, the fragmented structure of the government, including federalism, was not anti-democratic. Rather it was a way of filtering out through selection processes across large territory those people who would not put the public interest and common good first and foremost (see also Morgan 1981).

The contrast between Dahl and Wills can be usefully mediated by reading the essays of Ostrom (1971, 1987, 1991) and an article by Lienesch (1983b). Ostrom emphasizes the "compound" character of the republic and its consistency as a complex political theory involving federalism.[*] Lienesch contends that the meaning of the Constitution can be constructively interpreted if the framers are seen as relying on a blend of history, philosophy, and science. The science-based character of the framers was further elaborated by Ranney (1976).

One further point requires notation before completing this sketch of the founding of federalism. It can usefully be addressed in terms of the framers' orientation toward change. Were the framers at Philadelphia reactionaries, reformists, or revolutionaries? Cases have been made for all three interpretations.

The classic exposition of the reactionary view was Beard's (1913) *Economic Interpretation of the Constitution*. His view that Madison was the Marx of the ruling class has been broadly challenged (Brown 1956; Warren 1968). The influence of Beard's interpretation persists despite his later recantation (Beard 1945).

A second view of the framers saw them as a reformist group of pragmatic politicians. Perhaps the leading exponent of this view was Roche (1961). There are, however, several others who would share this label and highlight federalism as one of the pragmatic reforms produced by the convention (Elkins and McKitrick 1961, 1993; Holcombe 1950; Jensen 1950; Ranney 1976; Smith 1965). This view of the framers as constructive change agents appears to dominate contemporary thinking.

Perhaps the least attention has been devoted to the framers as radicals or revolutionaries, a group that overthrew the old order. One of the few to address this issue was Earle (1937). Three revolutionary actions were taken by the framers, ones that violated the "rules of the game." First, the convention at Philadelphia had exceeded its authority by writing a whole new constitution, not merely proposing revisions or amendments to the Articles of Confederation. Second, in securing adoption, the framers bypassed the state legislatures and called for the document to be considered by popularly elected special conventions. The third revolutionary element was that the Constitution took effect after adoption by 9 of the 13 state conventions. Earle observes that these unprecedented actions constituted "an act of revolution, a coup d'etat" (1937, ix). Lienesch (1983a, 65) puts the results in appropriate and ironic perspective concerning the anti-Federalists and the Federalists: "Perhaps it is only proper that history is unkind to losers. To the victors go the spoils, including a prominent place in the history books."

While tangential to our central thesis, ratification of the Constitution by the specially-called state conventions merits passing comment. Two points are particularly relevant. One was the

---

[*] Ostrom (1987) later expanded his analysis of the framers' premises concerning choices about the constitutional "rules of the game." The framers' premises, according to Ostrom, included an optimistic view of how constitutional arrangements could constrain selfish interests and encourage or promote actions favoring the common good. This optimism stood in sharp contrast to Hobbesian assumptions. One reviewer of Ostrom's work (Yarbrough 1988, 299) concluded, however, that he (Ostrom) has "a far closer affinity with Hobbes than is in fact the case."

emphasis on state sovereignty as a check on national power(s). A second was the crucial concession made by Constitutional advocates involving the need for a Bill of Rights (Lienesch 1983b, 1988). The first Congress submitted several amendments, ten of which were promptly adopted. Setting the agenda for future controversies that would escalate both sooner and later, the Tenth Amendment provided for "reserved powers" to remain the domain of state governments.

III. EMERGENT FEDERALISM 1790–1890

The phrase *emergent is* used to convey the idea of a period in which a young system grows, evolves, and achieves a well-developed or coherent identity. This stage or phase precedes the *mature* stage in which it reaches its broadest variety, complexity, and sophistication. The somewhat arbitrary time frame established for this emergent phase of federalism is from 1790 to 1890. We look at this span from four standpoints: (1) the nature of the Union and the legal order, (2) politics, (3) administration, and (4) resources.

A. NATURE OF THE UNION

In his 1981 inaugural address, President Ronald Reagan asserted: "The federal government did not create the states; the states created the federal government." His words were quickly challenged by historians and political scientists (Beer 1982, 1993). Their rejoinders were on the grounds of historical inaccuracy and/or interpretation. The point at issue of course was, what was or is the nature of the federal union put in place by the Constitution?

Was the Union a compact among states? Or did the Union rest directly on the consent of the people as the source of legitimate power(s) exercised by both the national and the state governments? The premise behind both these questions derives from the prevailing eighteenth-century social contract theory about the basis for exercising political and governmental authority. The issue was who were parties to the contract—the states or the whole people of the United States? Ardent advocates over two centuries of political and legal constitutional debate have leaned toward one or the other of these state-based compact or people-based nationalist assumptions.[*]

Leaders of the nationalist view ranged from Alexander Hamilton and Daniel Webster to Abraham Lincoln and both Theodore and Franklin Roosevelt. Lincoln, for example, in his first inaugural address (1861) declared that "the Union is older than any of the states, and in fact created them as states.... The Union gave each [state] whatever of independence and liberty it has." Lincoln's choice of words is significant. By Union he is not referring to the national or federal government (in Washington, DC). Rather his reference draws on the abstract idea of the United States of America, a term that transcends (yet includes) all the states as well as the national government.

The compact theorists also featured prominent historical personages—John C. Calhoun, Jefferson Davis, and (earlier) Richard Henry Lee, as well as other anti-Federalists opposing the adoption of the Philadelphia Convention product. The anti-Federalists recognized the major short-comings of the Articles of Confederation but they could not concede the need for such a strong central or national government.

---

[*] There is an alternative to the either/or alternative presented by the nationalist versus compact theories regarding the nature of the union. This might be termed the "mixed" or the "matrix" model of the national-state relations. It has been a focus of attention for Ostrom (1971, 1987), but it has been elaborated most extensively by Elazar (1973, 1981, 1987, 1988). Ostrom and Elazar trace this model directly to Madison's writings, both within and beyond *The Federalist Papers*. They note that, among other things, this matrix model explains why Madison could be both a strong nationalist at the Philadelphia Convention in 1787 and yet 10 years later emerge as a compact advocate in the Kentucky resolutions.

At one time, 1798–1799, the compact advocates even included Thomas Jefferson and James Madison, who, respectively, drafted the Kentucky and Virginia resolutions. These strident state legislative actions were precipitated by the Alien and Sedition Acts passed by Congress in 1798. They used the words *nullification* and *interposition* to identify and justify broad but uncertain powers reserved to the states. The two sets of resolutions claimed that the states could use the powers to oppose (block or nullify) what they (individually or collectively) thought were unconstitutional actions by the national government. The resolutions also laid claim to the right of secession. A nullifying state could leave the union if it disagreed with the will of a majority of states regarding a particular national action.

How has this conflict over the nature of the Union been resolved? It has been settled in practical and probably unalterable terms in favor of the nationalist view, President Reagan to the contrary notwithstanding. The means of settlement have been multiple and varied. The Civil War was one manner of settlement—by violence. Constitutional amendment, especially the Fourteenth Amendment, was a second means. Judicial interpretation has been a particularly prominent third means. Indeed, Chief Justice Chase's view in *Texas v. White 7 Wall* 700 (1869) is perhaps the classic court assertion. The case hinged on the question of whether the State of Texas had actually left the Union when it seceded in 1861:

> When, therefore, Texas became one of the United States, she entered into an indissoluble relation.... The act which consummated her admission into the Union was something more than a compact; it was the incorporation of a new member into the political body. And it was final. The union between Texas and the other States was as complete, as perpetual, and as indissoluble as the union between the original States. The Constitution, in all its provisions, looks to an indestructible Union, composed of indestructible States.

Note that the "Union" here, as in Lincoln's comments, is not the national government. Indeed, the terms used for the governmental entity in Washington, DC, during the first century reflected, for the most part, the multiple descriptors used originally in *The Federalist Papers* written in 1787–1788. These included general government, central government, national government, US government, and federal government. Recall also that during the Civil War the forces of the North were referred to as the Union Army and the soldiers were called Federals.

From a legal, historical, and conceptual standpoint we can treat the nature of the Union as being settled in favor of the nationalist interpretation. To assert, this, however, does not imply that all legal and jurisdictional questions of national–state relations are stable or settled. There is an enormous body of writing and corpus of case law that addresses the past, present, and prospective dimensions of these formal power controversies.

Beyond the abstract question of the nature of the Union, there was a set of economic development forces and efforts that led to an intimate intertwining of federalism, state legal doctrines, economic growth, and federal and state judiciaries. The interplay of these themes is reviewed insightfully and comprehensively by Scheiber (1976, 1978). He refers to the period from 1789 to 1861 as "dual federalism and rivalistic state mercantilism." Scheiber (1976, 71) notes that "precisely because significant policy fields were occupied largely by the states (whether or not all of the policies pursued were consistent with Supreme Court dicta), and because state area jurisdictions were congruent with the functions undertaken, American federalism before 1861 was decentralized."

Scheiber (1978, 636) classifies the period from the Civil War to 1890 as "transitional federalism." Despite three constitutional amendments (Thirteenth, Fourteenth, and Fifteenth), court decisions, economic changes (industrialism), and so forth, there is strong evidence in support of the thesis that "in sum, there was remarkably little shift toward the center in real power" (Scheiber 1978, 637).

B.   Politics

If there was little consequential legal shift in real power toward the center during the nineteenth century, there were some significant political alternatives that added to the stature of emergent federalism. Only one institutional change will be discussed, one that set the stage for subsequent maturation.

The US Senate was originally and generally viewed as a "peripheralizing institution" (Riker 1955, 455). It was expected to be a direct vehicle for the expression and protection of state interests (Riker 1955). Recall, of course, that unless some states chose otherwise, and until the Seventeenth Amendment in 1913 mandated popular election, US senators were selected by votes in each state legislature.

Riker (1955) traces the unsuccessful effort of state legislatures to instruct senators on crucial votes. The "right of instruction" was even proposed for inclusion in the First Amendment but failed to secure House passage. Thus began the demise of the Senate as an instrument of *state* representation. The story is more complex and involved than this brief summary conveys, but the primary point holds. The Senate began as a low-status, "localist" entity. (From 1790 to 1849 a total of 48 US senators actually resigned to accept state offices). It became, during the nineteenth century, a more potent and even powerful body (Wilson 1885). Its power was significantly enhanced when the spoils system became more extensive (and venal) later in the century and when senators, because of patronage, often became informal heads of their state party organizations.

C.   Administration and Resources

In his magnum opus on intergovernmental relations, Graves (1964, 478) notes, "At the risk of over-simplification, one may say that there were four major problems in nineteenth-century America—disposition of the public domain, internal improvements, education, and slavery." The last of these was addressed by the courts and, ultimately, on the battlefield. The other three were addressed first in the Congress by legislation and finally in their implementation by administrative operations.

The definitive history of administration during the emergent phase of federalism is the four-volume work of L. D. White beginning with *The Federalists* and ending with *The Republican Era* (1948, 1951, 1954, 1958). White's focus was not primarily federalism oriented but relevant insights are strewn throughout the books. Elsewhere he developed more fully his thesis about the century-long "administrative settlement" between the national and state governments (White 1953, 6–12). White (1953, 8) described the arrangement as follows: "A dual system of government and administration emerged, each level independent in its own sphere and operating without hindrance from the other, each supported by revenues of which it held full command." He added that "the states and particularly the cities became busy workshops of the administrative world, while the general government performed few functions that had not been commenced in the days of the Federalists" (White 1953, 10).

White's administrative "settlement" or dualism was probably accurate so far as the absence of hindrances was concerned. But the dualism thesis had modest or limited applicability in the realm of advice, technical assistance, and resources. Elazar's (1962) work on nineteenth century cooperative federalism amply documented the support provided to state operations by national officials in such areas as internal improvements, agriculture, banking, elementary education, forestry, higher education, state militia, and social services.

Elazar's thesis was sweeping, namely, "that virtually all the activities of government in the nineteenth century United States were cooperative endeavors, shared by federal and state agencies in much the same manner as government programs are shared in the twentieth century" (1962, 1). Stated this broadly, it invited challenges. Scheiber's (1966, 1980) rejoinders are probably the most significant. The issue(s) centered on the scope and significance of the administrative cooperation in the context of constitutional, legal, political, and battlefield conflict(s). The controversies over states' rights and the compact theory of the union were not moderated or obliterated by the extensive amount of cooperation confirmed by Elazar (1962).[*]

In the resource field, Elazar (1962) and Graves (1964) offer solid and original analyses of the way in which the national government used its major resource—the public domain—to promote its purposes. From 1787 in the Northwest Ordinance, through the Morrill Acts (1862 and 1890) to the 1887 Hatch Act on agricultural research stations, the national government used resources to promote education in particular and internal improvements generally. Graves (1964, 510) lists 18 pieces of legislation that constituted federal aid to education from 1785 to 1890. Public land, of course, was the chief resource of the national government. Over 1 million acres in land grants were made during this period, with about 30% claimed by homesteading, 20% set aside for schools, and around 10% for railroad construction (Graves 1964, 481).

As the end of the nineteenth century approached, federalism in the United States had fully and clearly emerged. It had reached what some theorists of economic development might term a takeoff stage. We choose to call it the beginning of the mature stage.

IV. MATURE FEDERALISM 1890–1940

The half-century period from 1890 to 1940 marked the nation's movement, both domestically and internationally, toward maturity in several domains. The maturation of federalism was an important part of overall domestic development. Changes occurred in the arenas of constitutional law, political realignments, administrative growth, and fiscal innovations. Each of these four arenas will be reviewed briefly.

A. CONSTITUTIONAL LAW

The nature of constitutional interpretation during the five decades prior to 1940 has commonly been referred to as the heyday of "dual federalism" (Corwin 1950). Corwin's thesis was that for much of this period the Supreme Court operated as a super-legislature, sitting in judgment to second-guess the actions of both the national and the various state legislatures. The extremity of judicial activism was so unprecedented, in Corwin's view, that it constituted "Court over Constitution" (Corwin 1938).

The mechanisms of judicial judgment were chiefly twofold: (1) the due process clause of the Fourteenth Amendment and (2) the reserved powers doctrine of the Tenth Amendment. The former provision became a vehicle for Court review of numerous state laws involving economic and social legislation, for example, labor unions, employment, and so forth. In interpreting due process the Court exercised *substantive* judgment about the wisdom and desirability of numerous state actions.

From 1890 to 1940, the Supreme Court considered 2316 cases dealing with federalism that involved the exercise of state authority (Sprague 1968, 62). It is also pertinent to note that during this 50-year period only 21% of the Court opinions on federalism cases were divided. From 1940 to 1960, over 50% of the federalism cases were split decisions (Sprague 1968, 62). The former low percentage suggests a high degree of agreement about the nature of national–state relations characteristic of an advanced stage of development.

The basic posture of the Court was set during the initial part of this half-century under the leadership of Chief Justice Fuller (1888–1910). Of this period Schmidhauser (1958, 139) noted that "two fundamentally important revolutions in federal-state relations can be in large part credited to the Fuller Court. By utilizing doctrines such as reasonableness and liberty of contract, the Fuller Court made the due process clause of the Fourteenth Amendment the lever for a hitherto unprecedented expansion of federal judiciary supervisory power over the legislation and action of the states." Another and somewhat lesser lever for the Court's accomplishing the same end was the use

---

[*] In fairness to Elazar, however, it should be noted that he did not assert that the extensive collaboration he documented either eliminated or reduced to insignificance many aspects of state-national conflict in the nineteenth century.

of the national commerce power as a limit on state action. At the same time the Court beat a hasty and significant retreat on potentially broad interpretations of different Fourteenth Amendment provisions as limitations on the states, for example, the equal protection and privileges and immunities clauses.

It was the expansion of national power through the commerce and taxation powers that marked the "second great revolution" introduced by the Fuller Court. Here, Schmidhauser (1958, 140) concludes, "So far as the federal system is concerned, the Fuller Court wrought a far greater modification of the federal system in the direction of centralization than had any of its predecessors." The Court, it appears, was launched on the way to confirming the maturity of federalism by giving wide latitude for selective national actions and imposing a more limited, restricted role for the states. Viewed from the standpoint of jurisprudence, judicial activism on federalism and other issues was more than merely launched, it was fully commissioned.

There was, however, a diversion or detour on the Court's road to nearly unrestricted approval of national action. This happened when the national government attempted, through the commerce and taxation powers, to regulate such matters as child labor, agriculture, coal mining, and labor–management relations. From 1917 to 1937, in a series of cases, the Supreme Court held unconstitutional *national* legislation on the grounds that it invaded the reserved powers of the states to regulate manufacturing, mining, and so forth. For a brief time, particularly in the 1930s, it appeared that Court doctrines involving the Tenth and Fourteenth Amendments had created a no-man's land where neither the national nor the state governments could effectively regulate some areas of economic and social endeavors. This issue reached its climax in the mid-1930s with the Court's rejection of several major pieces of New Deal legislation.

Starting in 1937, the Court beat a timely retreat, upholding several important statutes involving social security, labor–management relations, and agriculture. The Court's about-face was humorously noted as "the switch in time that saved nine." After this "peaceful revolution" (Schmidhauser 1958, 182) the Tenth Amendment was "but a truism" that no longer operated as a direct restriction on national actions. Schmidhauser concisely summarizes below the legal status of mature federalism at the end of the 1930s:

> After 1937, the doctrine of dual federalism was decisively rejected in the *Darby* case. The formalistic distinction between "direct" and "indirect" effect in commerce clause questions was, in effect, rejected in the *Jones-Laughlin* case. Federal taxing and spending power was construed broadly in the Social Security cases. The net effect of these broad constructionist decisions was a tremendous expansion of federal police power. Many subjects, such as certain aspects of labor relations, which had heretofore been considered well within the reserved powers of the states now fell under the congressional commerce power. The Supreme Court after nearly half a century of "selective" uncertainty viewed the economy of the nation for most purposes as unified one (Schmidhauser 1958, 182).

Corwin reflected on the changes wrought by the court and offered a more sweeping set of judgments:

> ... what was once vaunted as Constitution of Rights, both state and private, has been replaced by a Constitution of Powers. More specifically, the Federal system has shifted based in the direction of a consolidated national power, while within the National government itself an increased flow of power in the direction of the President has ensued (Corwin 1950, 2).

B. POLITICS AND PARTY REALIGNMENT

American politics from 1890 to 1940 were marked by two features that bore a significant relationship to a mature federalism. The first was presidential leadership of the type noted at the end of the preceding quotation from Corwin. The second was the prominence (even dominance) of political party patterns structured by two "critical elections" (Key 1955) occurring in this period.

The "rise of the presidency" is one of the distinctive aspects of institutional change in American politics in the twentieth century (Corwin 1957; Leuchtenburg 1983). The firm foundations of presidential leadership were laid in three presidencies during the first four decades of the century. Theodore Roosevelt, Woodrow Wilson, and Franklin Roosevelt brought energy, vitality, and initiative to a national government that would, in various and subtle ways, confirm the preeminence of national issues over sectional and local ones.

All three offered national programs whose aims and mandates were solidified and sold as new. They were T. Roosevelt's New Nationalism (Leuchtenburg 1961), Wilson's New Freedom (Morison and Commager 1950), and FDR's New Deal (Schlesinger 1959, 1960). The particular content(s) of the three programs varied, of course, in response to the perceived needs of the time. Their common theme, however, was the importance of action by the *national* government on a wide range of domestic problems. In slightly different terms, American politics from 1890 to 1940 had two bookends. At one end was the Progressive movement; at the one and other end was the New Deal. Both represented political surges that coalesced around issues that were perceived as national in scope and required national-level responses. These responses, however, tended to focus on and were filtered through national–state interactions. The state-level base and general structure of the party system ensured a high degree of national-level sensitivity to state-grounded interests and concerns.

Two specific examples will lend concreteness to this otherwise abstract set of assertions. On May 13, 1908, more than 40 governors met in Washington, DC, at the invitation of President T. Roosevelt (Brooks 1961). Although many national officials and public notables were present, "the governors were clearly the center of attention, and the proceedings were designated as a conference of governors without reference to the other participants" (Brooks 1961, 11). After this first conference the governors continued to meet on their own initiative and subsequently became known as the National Governors' Conference (now the National Governors' Association). The impetus for the initial meeting, however, was presidential, and it was convened to build visibility and popular support for TR's *national* conservation policies.

The second illustration is drawn from the New Deal period and was described by Samuel Beer, himself a participant in the process he observed: "Roosevelt's nationalism was a doctrine of federal centralization, and under his administration, in peace as well as in war, the balance of the American federal system swung sharply toward Washington" (Beer 1978b, 7). Beer reflects on his own role in contributing to the maturation of federalism by recounting his experience as a staff assistant to principals in FDR's "Brain Trust": "I vividly recall our preoccupation with persuading people to look to Washington for the solution of problems and our sense of what a great change in public attitude this involved" (Beer 1978b, 8).

Before this section on the politics of a mature federalism is concluded, more than incidental note should be taken of the party and partisan character of this half-century. Its politics were anchored by two critical or realigning elections (Burnham 1970; Key 1955). These anchors, dropped in 1896–1900 and 1928–1932, were ones around which a semblance if not a coherence in "public philosophy" emerged (Beer 1978b). While governed by a dominant Republican party coalition largely from 1896 to 1930, the politics of this era included strong strains of progressivism, reform, and humanitarianism (Morison and Commager 1950). Among the many challenges faced by American democracy in this period, two involved federalism. One was the rise of the city and the attendant demands for new types of political and social (as well as technical) engineering. The second was repairing the breakdowns in honesty and efficiency in the administrative systems of the country—national, state, and local (Morison and Commager 1950). These themes are addressed directly or indirectly in the following sections. They have already been referred to, at least obliquely, in Wilson's (1887) essay where he called for trained and efficient public servants who would help put an end to "the poisonous atmosphere of city government and the crooked secrets of state administration" (Wilson 1941, 485).

C. Administration

L. D. White settled on 1887, the year of Wilson's essay, as the date when the administrative dualism between the national government and the states was breached, claiming that "the original *administrative* settlement existed without substantial alteration until 1887, the date of the passage of the Interstate Commerce Act" (White 1953, 10). This act was neither the singular nor the most significant administrative element in the transition from an emergent to a mature federal arrangement. White later notes, "The breakdown of the original pattern of independent administrative dualism was completed by the growth of the system of conditional grants-in-aid to the states and their subdivisions" (1953, 16).

The year 1887 seemed to be a vintage one for administrative transformation. Besides Wilson's essay and the Interstate Commerce Act, the first annual cash grants to the states were authorized in this year. The Hatch Act of 1887, a prototype for modern grants, created the agricultural experiment stations—entities that quickly became associated with state colleges of agriculture (ACIR 1978a, 15; MacDonald 1928; Walker and Plant 1984).

It would be wrong, however, to think of 1887, or any other single year as the precise date for the transition from an emergent to a mature phase of federalism. This is true whether the shift is administrative, fiscal, political, or constitutional. The movement from one era to another occurred gradually but perceptibly. In few other instances is this progressive transition so well illustrated as in the administrative arena. Documentation on this point comes from a probing review of administrative maturation in the national government by Skowronek (1982).

Skowronek approaches his historical analysis from the theoretical standpoint of state building, where *state* is the generic term for the capacity to govern. His specific time focus is 1877 (the end of Reconstruction) to 1920 (demobilization after World War I). This four-decade period roughly fits the maturation phase of federalism.

The three specific foci of Skowronek's detailed examination are (1) reform of civil administration (civil service reform starting in the 1880s), (2) reorganization of the army (shortly after 1900), and (3) establishment of national railroad regulation (starting in 1887). As he notes, "Taken together, [these three] mark the pivotal turn away from a state organization that presumed the absence of extensive institutional controls at the national level toward a state organized around national administrative capacities" (Skowronek 1982, 4).

The scope and content of Skowronek's analysis are significant at multiple levels, with federalism representing only one element for which his findings have important implications. The general sweep of his approach and a flavor of his findings can be gleaned from two paragraphs:

> Generally speaking, the expansion of national administrative capacities in America around the turn of the century was a response to industrialism. The construction of a central bureaucratic apparatus was championed as the best way to maintain order during this period of upheaval in economic, social, and international affairs. Viewed at this level, the American experience fits a general pattern of institutional development and rationalization in public administration. Indeed, specific and contemporaneous parallels can be found throughout the rapidly industrializing Western states for each of the administrative innovations to be examined here.

> At a deeper level, however, our administrative response to industrialism stands apart and deserves special attention. In America, the modernization of national administrative controls did not entail making the established state more efficient; it entailed building a qualitatively different kind of state. The path that had been traveled in the development of early American government did not anticipate the need for a strong national administrative arm. To embrace the cosmopolitan bureaucratic remedy in meeting new demands on government, America had to alter course and shed already well-articulated

governing arrangements. The expansion of national administrative capacities in the age of industrialism became contingent on undermining the established structure of political and institutional power and on simultaneously forging an entirely new framework for governmental operations. The state that now supports so prominent a central bureaucracy is the product of this precarious politics of negotiating an internal governmental reconstruction (Skowronek 1982, 4).

A thoughtful reading of Skowronek's short introductory chapter and epilogue offers a tour de force for capturing the import of *national* governance capacities. The thesis advanced and confirmed by his study also sets the context for understanding better the nature of fiscal changes that were instrumental in fostering a mature federalism.

D. FINANCIAL RESOURCES

Several fiscal themes were prominent and persistent during the five decades following 1890. Among these were the following: (1) national resources to finance federal aid, (2) authorization and funding levels of grant-in-aid programs, (3) legal status of grants, (4) administration and implementation of grants, and (5) direct aid to cities (bypassing the states). Each theme is described briefly with references indicating opportunities for more detailed description and discussion of major issues.

1. Funds for Financing Federal Aid

During the nineteenth century, the prime resource of the national government was, as indicated earlier, public land. By 1890, a noted historian, Frederick Jackson Turner, and the Superintendent of the Census both announced "that there can hardly be said to be a frontier line" (Morison and Commager 1950, 99). The seemingly inexhaustible revenue resource from land sales was rapidly disappearing. For a variety of revenue reasons, the Congress passed an income tax levy (as part of a tariff measure) in 1894. This tax (of 2% on personal income over $4000) was promptly declared unconstitutional in *Pollock v. Farmers Loan and Trust* 158 US 601 (1895).

It took until 1913 and the approval of the Sixteenth Amendment to overcome this Supreme Court decision. With its adoption the gate was opened for national government access to a major new revenue source. This source was so significant that by 1922 over 60% of all federal receipts came from the income tax (ACIR 1978a, 17). This growing and productive revenue base made it possible for the national government to look for new uses for the revenues. Among the many claimants were interests sponsoring new grant-in-aid programs.

2. Growth in and Funding of Grant Programs

Starting in 1914 and continuing sporadically to 1930 a small number of grant-in-aid programs were created and funded. These few (10–12) programs covered such purposes as agricultural extension (1914), highway construction (1916), vocational education (1917), vocational rehabilitation (1920), maternal and child health (1921), and forestry (1924). Five informative discussions are available on the growing variety and sophistication of grants during this period (ACIR 1978a; Council of State Governments 1949; Key 1937; MacDonald 1928; Report 1928).

Writing shortly before the 1932 presidential election, MacDonald updated his 1928 study of federal aid and reported that the level of funding for the "subsidy system" had remained relatively stable (MacDonald 1931). The figures were (in millions) 1922: $118; 1927: $123; 1930: $135. He anticipated, however, that the aid figure would exceed $200 million in 1932 in response to depression-prompted demands. MacDonald was prescient in other ways:

In various ways, therefore, the grants from the federal treasury to the states are establishing more firmly their claim to a permanent place in the scheme of American administration. Every year they receive the support of additional precedents. They are rapidly becoming a habit. Still more important, they are producing results (MacDonald 1931, 634).

Not only did federal aid surpass $200 million in 1932, it moved on a sharp upward curve before declining during the remainder of the Depression-dominated 1930s. ACIR's (1978a, 19) figures and MacDonald's (1940, 489) review of the 1930s disclose the following pattern of outlays (in millions):

1931:	$180	1936:	$1015
1932:	$214	1937:	$818
1933:	$190	1938:	$790
1934:	$1803	1939:	$583
1935:	$2197		

The number of grant programs precipitated by the domestic economic emergency had risen to 21 in comparison to the few programs authorized and sometimes funded prior to 1930.

3. Legal Status of Grants

Two constitutional issues of major significance involving federal aid were resolved in this maturation period, specifically in 1923 and 1936. Two sources (Council of State Governments 1949; Wright 1968) address the issues raised in Supreme Court decisions rendered in those two years. In 1923, the Court made it difficult, if not impossible, for a taxpayer or a state government to gain legal standing and sustain a suit aimed at blocking the expenditure of funds for a grant program (*Frothingham v. Mellon* 262 US 447; *Massachusetts v. Mellon* 262 US 447).

In 1936, the Supreme Court finally confronted directly a long-standing controversy over the scope of the spending power implied in the "general welfare" clause of the Constitution (*US v. Butler* 297 US 1). Three brief discussions of this case and the spending power can be consulted (*Constitution of the US: Analysis and Interpretation* 1973, 136–140; Council of State Governments 1949, 17–20; Wright 1968, 19–25). There are, of course, extensive analyses of the clause and attendant issues in legal periodicals.

The basic fiscal issue at bar in *US v. Butler* was whether the Hamiltonian or Madisonian view of the spending power would prevail. Hamilton held that the Congress, under the first clause in Article I, Section 8, could spend money for any "general welfare" purpose. Madison took a strict constructionist approach, arguing that the taxing and spending power could be used only to foster the aims of other powers specifically granted to the national government. Following this principle, Madison opposed significant internal-improvements legislation on the grounds that the activities (e.g., roads, canals) were not enumerated as constitutional purposes of the national government. To shorten a long and somewhat complicated story, the Supreme Court in 1936 explicitly endorsed Hamilton's expansive view of the taxing/spending power. Sky (2003) provides a book-length exposition and interpretation of the long and complex history of the "general welfare" clause and spending power.

4. Administration of Grants

Two works offer sustained attention to the administration of grant programs. MacDonald's (1928) work reveals the progressive elaboration of review, approval, auditing, and other administrative components of the few early cash grant programs. He also explored aspects of grant impacts on state officials and intended recipients. MacDonald was active on a Committee on Federal Aid to the States sponsored by the National Municipal League. The committee conducted a questionnaire survey of state grant program administrators (*National Municipal Review* 1928). The survey results indicated that federal grants had "stimulated state activity" in the aided fields, that "federal supervision had improved state standards of administration," and that federal aid had *not* "led to federal interference in state affairs."

The administration of New Deal grant programs came under the probing eye of Key (1937). Key's analysis was extensive, intensive, and magisterial. He found several "mechanisms of federal control" (Key 1937, 369). Among the highlights of his observations were (1) the focus on service rather than regulatory activities, (2) the blending or mixing of federal and state personnel, (3) the autonomy or non-coordinated character of aided activities, (4) the involvement and impact of interest groups on behalf of grants, and (5) the absence of an overall strategy guiding federal grants. Two statements draw these and other administrative themes together:

> The American system of grants has had important effects on the federal-state fiscal system, but incidentally rather than by design.
> The states became in effect, although not in form, agents of the central government in the prosecution of activities deemed by Congress to be clothed with a national interest (Key 1937, 367, 368).

Key's insights are impressive for penetrating and articulating several basic issues surrounding grant programs at a critical juncture. They are also significant because they crystallized issues that have persisted through the several decades following his groundbreaking study.

5.   Federal Aid to Cities

One aspect of the mature stage of federalism did escape Key's attention, undoubtedly because it was defined as external to his state-oriented focus. This was the development of direct links between the national government and localities, specifically with cities. Gelfand (1975, 222) says, "The New Deal marked a new epoch in American urban history; overlooked by the Constitution and ignored in a century-and-a-half on national legislation, the cities finally gained some recognition from Washington." An ACIR (1978a, 17) report notes that during the 1930s, "new links between Washington, DC and city halls were forged; and the legal basis for the expanding intergovernmental partnership [was] clarified." Elsewhere, Martin (1965, 111) called the New Deal a "geologic fault line" in the development of national–local relations. Clark (1938) called the expansion of grants generally and funding directly to cities "the rise of a new federalism."

Our thesis modifies or challenges these assertions—less in terms of the novelty of national–local relations, but more in terms of national–local contacts as a logical extension or enlargement of prior precedents. The urbanizing character of the country presented growing economic, social, and fiscal problems. These problems resulted in demands that some national politicians viewed as an opportunity to build a political coalition. Mollenkopf (1983, 254) devotes a book to support the thesis that "over the five decades since the New Deal, the web of federal urban development programs and the intricate national-local political coalitions woven largely by Democratic political entrepreneurs succeeded in reshaping American cities and in establishing the Democrats as the normal majority party."

Direct national–city contacts, however, antedated the 1930s (Elazar 1967). Here we turn to urban historians for insights on federal–urban partnerships that were well established but long neglected (Mowry and Brownell 1981). This research and writing is variously titled: "the martial metropolis" (Lotchin 1984), "the city and the sword" (Lotchin 1982), and the "municipal-military complex" (Lotchin 1979a, 1979b, 1979c). These terms convey the *alliance* between cities and their associated and/or proximate military installations. A few passages will serve to make the essential points.

> The marriage of a city and the sword in California was a voluntary affair. It was also a very seminal alliance, contributing to the alteration of American governmental structures, encouraging the westward reorientation of American culture, and aiding in the legitimization of the military in American society.

Although the federal urban partnership is usually attributed to the period of the New Deal and to civilian and reform impulses, it goes back at least to the Progressive Era and has military as well as civilian roots (Lotchin 1982, 2).

Lotchin's study of San Diego and its wooing of the Navy reveals the city's success in the 1920s. By the early 1930s, one-third of the area's total employment was Navy dependent.

Perhaps the most significant theoretical point emerging from this literature is the importance of viewing the city as an *independent* variable (Lotchin 1984). This approach argues that cities are more than malleable entities molded like putty by state or national governments. Cities, according to this view, have a measure of influence over their destiny; many municipalities (and urban areas) have exerted significant influence over their future(s), especially during the expansion of peacetime military activities since World War II. Precedents and learning experiences in this skill of urban entrepreneurship, however, were first developed during the period from 1890 to 1940.

Although the states were sometimes bypassed and subordinated during the New Deal, it would be wrong to assume that these capstone years of mature federalism left the states supine and atrophied. One observer (Gulick 1933, 420) thought that the states were moribund: "I do not predict that the states will go, but affirm that they have [already] gone." A more extensive, balanced, and retrospective view was offered by Paterson:

> The New Deal produced neither federal dictation, a completely cooperative federalism, nor a new state progressivism. Instead, it helped create a rather flat mixture of achievement, mediocrity, and confusion. For all the supposed power of the New Deal, it was unable to impose all its guidelines on the autonomous 48 states (Paterson 1969, 202).

All but one of the 15 permanent (continuing) grant programs emerging from the New Deal period were national–state in character (MacDonald 1940). The decentralized character of the party system seemed to assure that state interests would be taken into account even in the severest of economic emergencies. The varied depression-generated emergency actions also produced a significant set of direct national–local relationships that bypassed the states. Just as T.R. Roosevelt had convened state governors (in 1908) that led to the creation of the National Governors Association (NGA), F.D. Roosevelt convened the mayors of large cities (in 1933). That in turn led to the creation of the American Municipal Association–US Conference of Mayors (AMA-USCM).

By the end of the New Deal and the 1930s, the mature phase of federalism was confirmed. By this we mean that the national government had consolidated its constitutional, political, administrative, and fiscal preeminence. The states, while far from vibrant, were at least functional and showed signs of entering the twentieth century, albeit reluctantly in many instances (Goldwin 1961). And cities as well as other localities had exerted a presence and gained national attention on a variety of issues.

Stated differently, this mature stage was more than merely national preeminence. While it held that distinction, the mature stage was also a period and circumstance when most governments—national, state, and local—had become increasingly active politically, fiscally, and administratively. Electoral publics had been galvanized and mobilized to support the promotion and delivery of public services.

This mature stage prompted some commentators to see "the obsolescence of federalism" (Laski 1939). Laski's attack was a pragmatic one: the US federal arrangement did not work; it was obstructionist, negative, ineffective. The states, in particular, were too large to deal with local problems and too small to address regional issues. Various direct and indirect rejoinders to Laski (and other critics) were made in defense of federalism (Benson 1941). In one sense, however, Laski won the conceptual or debating point. As he wrote, a new term, *intergovernmental relations*, had surfaced as an alternate phrase to describe the changing and evolving nature of national–state–local relationships.

Continued use of the term *federalism* was common (Dye 1990; Earle 1968; Elazar 1969, 1987; Friedrich 1968). But more frequently and regularly it appeared in hyphenated form or was preceded by a variety of adjectives. Indeed, by the 1980s one scholar could tally 497 different types of federalism (Stewart 1982, 1984). This progressively varied and even helter-skelter use of the term did two things. First, it diminished the clarity, utility, and precision of the term; like a coin of the realm too long or too much in circulation, it (federalism) lost some of its luster and value (Davis 1978). Second, the conceptual (but not necessarily practical) decline opened the way for the new concept, IGR.

V. INTERGOVERNMENTAL RELATIONS (IGR): ORIGINS AND EMERGENCE 1940–1960

The year 1940 is an arbitrary date for the origin and later emergence of IGR as a term describing the altered character of American federalism. The year's significance attaches to the appearance of *The Annals* (Vol. 207, 1940) titled "Intergovernmental Relations in the United States." The editor (W. Brooke Graves 1940) assembled 26 articles covering not only national–state, interstate, and national–local relations, but also regionalism and inter-local relationships. A nine-page bibliography (Culver 1940) contained over 150 references to books, articles, and reports published almost exclusively in the 1930s.

The multiplicity and concentration of references tend to confirm that IGR, as a concept, originated in the 1930s (Wright 1975). The earliest documented formal use of the phrase was by Snider (1937, 909). The most likely originator and person who popularized the term, however, was William Anderson. Anderson (1970) acknowledged that "there is no one person whose name is more fully associated with the early use of the term (back in the 1930s) than my own." Anderson used the term not only in his American Government and Constitutional Law courses, but in a graduate seminar titled "Federalism and Intergovernmental Relations" (Anderson 1970). From that seminar emerged the extensive research and several monographic studies focusing on IGR in Minnesota (Anderson 1960).

Two passages from Anderson's overview assist in identifying and defining IGR:

> [It] designates an important body of activities or interactions occurring between governmental units of all types and levels within the [US] federal system ...

> It is human beings clothed with office who are the real determiners of what the relations between units of government will be. Consequently, the concept of intergovernmental relations necessarily has to be formulated largely in terms of human relations and human behavior (Anderson 1960, 3).

To this we would only add that, in one sense, there are no intergovernmental relations; there are only relations among officials who govern in different roles in diverse and numerous units of government. The point cannot be pursued here, but it should be noted that this "human" dimension is one important feature that distinguishes IGR from federalism.

It is unnecessary to devote further space to the origin and initial elaboration of IGR as a concept. Sources are readily available (Anderson 1960; Durham 1940; Graves 1964; Wright 1975, 1990b). Indicative of the early self-consciousness about the term was Anderson's (1946) *Federalism and Intergovernmental Relations: A Budget of Suggestions for Research.* Ten years later Graves (1956) prepared an exhaustive (120-page) bibliography (issued as a Committee Print) for the House Subcommittee on Intergovernmental Relations. The classified (but not annotated) set of references to books, reports, articles, pamphlets, and bibliographies contained about 3500 entries. Graves (1958) later completed an annotated chronology of IGR events in US history.

It is also unnecessary to discuss the distinctive features of IGR and the multiple reasons for using IGR instead of federalism for a variety of analytical purposes (Anderson 1960; Wright 1974, 1975, 1982b). Nor is it imperative to offer a detailed disaggregation of the several phases of IGR since the 1930s (Wright 1997). In place of concept clarification and elaboration we focus on how IGR developed in the field during the emergent period of 1940–1960. This focus confirms the strong administrative link emphasized by Durham (1940), a link extensively reflected in articles appearing in the *Public Administration Review (PAR)* during these two decades. (For an assessment of IGR in the 1935–1960 period, see Wright 1985). The 1940s, of course, were dominated by cooperative efforts to prosecute and recover from World War II. The 1950s was a decade of introspection, analysis, and reassessment (Wright and White 1984). During these years, however, the number of new grant program authorizations proceeded at a rapid but relatively little-noted pace. From 1946 to 1960, nearly 100 new grant programs were authorized!

A. WARTIME AND POSTWAR IGR

The epitome of cooperative administration during wartime was captured by Bane (1942) in describing the extensive and impressive national–state–local collaboration in implementing rationing programs. Bane subsequently served as executive director of the Council of State Governments (CSG) and as the first chairman of the ACIR (1959–1969). No one deserves the title of Mr. IGR more than Frank Bane. He noted at this early date that the wartime experience was producing a "new system" that he called "cooperative government" (1942, 95). The blending of national–state–local relations in a smooth and effective mode would later be developed as "marble cake" federalism by McLean (1952, 2) and Grodzins (1960b).

The degree, depth, and dedication of cooperative IGR in wartime was demonstrated by the commodity rationing program put in place following Pearl Harbor on December 7, 1941. White (1942) describes the process and results as follows:

> Legal authority to ration was vested in the War Production Board but delegated by it to the Office of Price Administration (OPA). Four days after Pearl Harbor the former Office of Production Management froze the supplies of rubber; on December 14, 1941, the OPA was given the task of creating a rationing system; and on January 5, 1942, the system was in country-wide operation, an administrative feat due to the genius of Mr. Frank Bane, then director of field operations, OPA.

Another perceptive observer saw the wartime effort as producing a result that was unlike prior patterns or precedents. Bromage (1943, 35) saw IGR as developing an identity or life of its own:

> Like all other aspects of public administration, intergovernmental relations are undergoing constant readjustment to the times and conditions. War so alters conditions in public affairs that federal-state-local realignments are taking place from month to month. Cooperative government by federal-state-local authorities has become a by-word in the prodigious effort to administer civilian defense, rationing, and other wartime programs. Intergovernmental administration, while it is a part of all levels of government, is turning into something quite distinct from them all.

Clearly, IGR and its administrative or operational aspects had emerged in wartime as a distinctive feature of the American system.

Evidence abounds on the growth of the field during the 1940s. Lutz (1949) wrote a review, titled "Intergovernmental Relations at the Grass Roots," of seven reports produced by several councils on intergovernmental relations. These local-level councils were citizen-based groups established in one or more counties within each of four states. A national coordinating committee had illustrious members, for example, William Anderson, Frank Bane, Luther Gulick, Paul McNutt, and Harold D. Smith.

To show where the field stood in the late 1940s it is useful to cite statements underlying the creation of the councils, the problems they considered, and the judgments they made (Lutz 1949, 119–120):

1. The control over local affairs and local government has gradually been more and more centralized into the state and federal governments.
2. That unless checked, this gradual drift will continue.
3. That the rapid expansion of government has confused the minds of people at the "grass roots" and there is no clear-cut understanding as to what phases of government should properly and profitably be federal, state, or local.
4. That unless clarified and the trend reversed it may eventually undermine democratic government.
5. That this gradual centralization of authority and control has been due in part to the feeling by those at the top and in control, that the people at the local level are not capable of handling the problems which arise.
6. That the council does not believe this to be true. It believes that the feeling has arisen, not as a result of the incapacity of the people, but rather is it due to the absence of interagency coordination at the local level and a positive citizen interest and participation in the direction of "our government."
7. That greater responsibility for operating and improving government services should rest in the hands of persons at the local level.

Citizen involvement and inter-level coordination were issues decades ago, as well as later (Browning 1983; Porter 1975). So also was the problem of state budgeting for federal aid. An article by Ader (1950) considered "state budgetary controls of federal grants-in-aid." The author found such controls "woefully lacking" and noted that "perhaps of even greater importance is the fact that requests for grant funds by the state operating departments are not channeled through the state budget offices" (Ader 1950, 92).

A prime example of inter-level exchange was described in an article by Crook (1951), "The Pacific Coast Board of Inter-Governmental Relations." This unique entity was organized on a voluntary, cooperative basis in 1945 under the joint sponsorship of key officials from all levels of government in the West Coast states. It had a membership of 71 officials and held quarterly meetings that rotated among the three regional cities of Seattle, Portland, and San Francisco. Crook, who worked as the administrator of the board, offered the following conclusions about the five-year efforts on the entity:

> In five years of successful operation the Pacific Coast Board of Intergovernmental Relations has demonstrated the feasibility and value of cooperation among all levels of government in the West Coast area. It has fostered a regard for the regional point of view in officials presumed to be confined jurisdictionally to the consideration of problems assumed also to be so confined. In so doing it has been able to bring about a regional point of view concerning basic regional requirements, and thereby to increase the chances for perception of the specialized character of those requirements in Washington, D.C. Finally, it has been successful in promoting good day-to-day working relationships between officials who must consult across government lines on official business. Perhaps the organization and work of the board offers a pattern for intergovernmental cooperation in other regions (Crook 1951, 108).

Despite the apparent success of the board, it was disbanded in 1953 because of national-level domestic budget cuts and officials' declining interest. Its disappearance seems representative of the fragile and fleeting nature of the early IGR administrative efforts.

B.   THE 1950S: THE ACADEMIC DECADE

This period of IGR emergence is called the "academic" decade for a combination of reasons (Wright and White 1984). First, a national commission, launched in 1953, produced extensive studies on IGR. Second, scholars produced a variety of books, monographs, and articles exploring various policy, program, and political dimensions of the topic. Third, the decade was one of relative quiescence from the standpoint of broad national domestic policy initiatives, although numerous new but modest grant programs were put on the statute books.

Two noteworthy IGR national policy actions were dual defense pieces of legislation—the Interstate and Defense Highway Construction Act of 1956 and the National Defense Education Act of 1958. The former established and funded the system of interstate highways, while the latter was a response to Russian space research (the Sputnik launch). In spite of the substantial funding of these two programs, federal aid to the states increased from only $2.4 billion in 1950 to $7.0 billion in 1960. The number of grant authorizations, which had risen from about 30 in 1940 to around 60 by 1950, continued on a constant climb to approximately 130 in 1960.

The midpoint of the decade was punctuated by the appearance of the report of the Eisenhower-sponsored Commission on Intergovernmental Relations (1955) chaired by Chicago business executive Meyer Kestnbaum. The summary report and extensive supporting studies, committee reports, and research documents provided a major impetus to IGR as a concept and a topic worthy of sustained interest. The impetus and interest were expressed in several directions: (1) legislative, (2) institutional, (3) policy/political, and (4) academic.

The report of the Kestnbaum Commission prompted the Intergovernmental Relations Subcommittee of the House Committee on Government Operations to initiate a series of hearings, reports, and staff studies over a four-year period. (See Wright and Peddicord (1973) for a three-decade listing of government documents on IGR, including a full list of House and Senate documents, ACIR publications, and all the reports on the Commission on Intergovernmental Relations.) These legislative-based efforts contributed to a 1959 institutional result—the creation of the ACIR (Wright 1965).

A policy/political product of the presidential commission was an effort to return some functions (and tax sources) to the states. Proposed by President Eisenhower to the Governors' Conference in 1957, the proposal was to revert to the states responsibility for vocational education and waste treatment facility construction programs, together with a tax credit on local telephone service to pay for these programs. This turn-back strategy was aborted by a combination of political, economic, fiscal, and administrative difficulties (Grodzins 1960b; Maxwell 1960, 1962; Shore 1959a, 1959b; Subcommittee on Intergovernmental Relations 1958b). The final report of the joint national–state committee to explore the turn-back proposals acknowledged the obstacles confronting its devolution efforts (Joint Federal-State Action Committee 1960). A general treatment of increasing grant problems appeared as the Joint Committee disbanded and the ACIR came on line. Mushkin (1960) reviewed the experience of the 1950s and the unsuccessful efforts to modify and manage the growing aid programs and the failures to overcome the numerous "barriers to a system of federal grants-in-aid."

After 1959, the ACIR became the official and sometime definitive observer/researcher on IGR. Prior to the ACIR's creation, the presence of organized, focused, and sustained research on IGR was the exception rather than the rule. The main exceptions in the 1950s may be briefly noted and are clearly marked as emerging from the academic arena.

First, 10 volumes appeared from the long-running Minnesota studies of IGR under William Anderson's direction. The various research projects focused on courts (Talbott 1950), highways (Gomez 1950), education (Morlan 1950), public health (Wyatt 1951), social welfare (Raup 1952), employment security (Rourke 1952), local government (Ylvisaker 1956), finances (Anderson 1956), and participants' perspectives (Weidner 1960).

Second, Morton Grodzins initiated the Federalism Workshop at the University of Chicago with support from Meyer Kestnbaum. Grodzins and several associates explored the "new American system" from a variety of approaches and perspectives (Elazar 1962; Elazar et al. 1969; Grodzins 1960a, 1960b, 1966).

A third source of reflections on the system appeared in a Gaus (1956) review essay of four major works on IGR—those by Anderson (1955), the Commission on Intergovernmental Relations (1955), Macmahon (1955), and White (1953). Gaus's evaluations were mature, balanced, and reflective, befitting a person of his academic stature. His concluding comment was "We are an unfinished country, and have yet to know our landscape" (Gaus 1956, 109).

Two aspects of that national landscape were not addressed or sketched by Gaus. One was the future landscape of mature IGR. The other was the urban-metropolitan scene—the focus of considerable attention in the postwar era. This second topic concludes our discussion of the emergent period of IGR.

The topic of metropolitan problems, policies, and reforms was exceptional and distinctive for the amount of sustained attention it received in the postwar period. Significant initial attention to the topic had, however, antedated that war (Jones 1942; Ketcham 1940; Merriam et al. 1933; Reed 1942; Studenski 1930).

In 1953 Jones reviewed several "Metropolitan Studies" (1953) dealing with problems in and reform proposals for Atlanta, Birmingham, Chicago, San Francisco, Toronto, and Washington, DC. Jones, a well-established metropolitan scholar, regretted the fact that there were no more metropolitan governments than in 1942, when his own book on the subject was published. Nor was there progress since 1930 when the first wave of metropolitan interest and reform began. This hard fact remained despite Jones's noting the existence of "many more published and unpublished studies of government in metropolitan areas—official survey reports, doctoral dissertations, prizewinning essays and monographs" (1953, 58). The failure of reform proposals was likely to continue, Jones concluded, until research was done to "supplement the administrative and structural studies of metropolitan communities with studies of the metropolitan organization and relationships of attitude and opinion-forming agencies" (1953, 63).

Jones's synthesis of metropolitan organization and reform issues focused largely on interlocal and indigenous approaches to solving the IGR problems of these burgeoning areas. A broader approach or strategy was emerging, however (Wood 1958, 1959, 1961). This involved national-level actions and policies. It was exemplified by Grant's (1954) article, "Federal-Municipal Relationships and Metropolitan Integration." Grant noted that "virtually all of the metropolitan area studies devote considerable attention to every conceivable alternative solution or device for metropolitan integration, yet omit any consideration of federal intervention in a day when it is customary for frustrated cities to go to the federal government for help in any and all problems" (Grant 1954, 259). Grant's preferences for national involvement to promote metropolitan change emerged near the end of his essay. "The continued failure to evolve even a reasonable facsimile of integrated metropolitan government for any of the 170 standard metropolitan areas in the United States makes it clear that new avenues of integration need to be explored" (Grant 1954, 267).

Grant's call for active and even aggressive national involvement on metropolitan issues landed on productive scholarly turf but on barren political and policy soil in the "academic" 1950s (Proctor 1953). A steady stream of research and recommendations continued for the remainder of the 1950s and into the early 1960s (Bollens 1956, 1957, 1961; Connery and Leach 1960). During the 1950s, no less than 15 *PAR* articles or book review essays treated metropolitan problems directly or indirectly. A major bibliography on metropolitan problems appeared in 1957 (Governmental Affairs Foundation 1957). But deliberate and purposeful national action on urban/metropolitan issues awaited the arrival of the 1960s and a broader base of political support. That support would develop in the mature period of IGR.

VI. IGR: A QUARTER CENTURY OF MATURATION AND METAMORPHOSIS 1960–1985

In 1962, Senator Edmund S. Muskie of Maine described IGR as the "hidden dimension" of government, "performing as almost a fourth branch of government in meeting the needs of our people, it nonetheless has no direct electorate, operates from no set perspective, is under no special control, and moves in no particular direction" (Muskie 1962). Creation of the ACIR in 1959 can be construed as a convenient (albeit arbitrary) transition point marking IGR's passage from a hidden or emergent stage to a mature period. The formal organizational recognition signaled by the ACIR's creation gave IGR a deliberate, continuing, and institutional focus (Wright 1965). The ACIR did not spring suddenly from Zeus's brow, however. Instead, it was the culmination of a decade-long series of events, actions, and recommendations.

The first Hoover Commission (1949a, 1949b) made only incidental mention of IGR, but it did recommend "that a continuing agency on Federal-State relations be created with primary responsibility for study, information, and guidance in the field of Federal-State relations" (Hoover Commission 1949a, 36). This proposal was given added impetus by the temporary Kestnbaum Commission on Intergovernmental Relations, which called for "continuing attention to interlevel relations" (Commission on Intergovernmental Relations 1955, 86).

Attention was devoted to IGR during the late 1950s but it required four years to create a record and build support for establishing a permanent body. Two streams of activity aided the boomlet that resulted in the 1959 passage of Public Law 86-380, which chartered the ACIR. These two sets were mentioned previously: (1) legislative hearings on IGR by the House Subcommittee on Intergovernmental Relations, chaired by Rep. L. H. Fountain, and (2) presidentially inspired turnback efforts channeled through the Joint Federal-State Action Committee (Subcommittee 1956b, 1956c, 1957, 1958a, 1958b).

By 1960, the ACIR was operational and was poised to observe political, policy, administrative, and legal gyrations involving subsequent shifts in IGR. Any effort to chart the changes in IGR since 1960 has faced formidable difficulties. In commenting on IGR developments from the 1960s into the 1980s, Derthick observed that "for a student of federalism to make sense of the events [of this period] is no easy task" (1987, 67).

Any approach to a quarter century of IGR must be selective in two respects. First, it must proceed from some organizing principle. Second, it can sample only a small amount of the activities, actors, events, and research/writing flooding the public agenda under the label of IGR. The organizing principle selected for the following discussion is consistent with this chapter's chronological motif. The sampling criterion is also parsimonious—developments that tend to be national in scope and institutional in focus. The orientation toward national and institutional patterns produces a bias against state–local, interstate, and interlocal relations as elements of IGR. Lack of attention to these IGR patterns is not an oversight; it results from trade-offs made under time and space constraints. An independent and significant chapter could be written (elsewhere) on state-local relations (Zimmerman 1972, 1983, 1995) and on interstate relations (Zimmerman 2002, 2004,; Bowman 2005).

A. MONITORING MATURATION AND METAMORPHOSIS

Prior to a discussion of successive five-year chronological periods, it is useful to reference selective sources that have charted and commented on IGR developments since 1960.

During its first 15 years the ACIR issued yearly reports that not only covered the Commission's activities, research, and recommendations but also commented on annual and longer-term IGR patterns. In 1975, the ACIR initiated a quarterly publication, *Intergovernmental Perspective*. A review of articles and events reported in this periodical offer a continuous education in IGR from the mid-1970s into the 1990s until the demise of the ACIR in 1996 (McDowell 1997).*

The ACIR during its lifetime was the foremost governmental agency whose primary mission involved monitoring of IGR developments. Numerous other agencies of the national government, however, produced research studies, policy analyses, reports, and recommendations affecting IGR (and federalism) matters. An earlier, dated, and provisional list was assembled in a bibliography by Wright and Peddicord (1973). Additionally, over 400 congressional committees and subcommittees were (and are) potential and actual loci for staff studies, hearings, and reports that affect the direction of one or more intergovernmental programs, policies, and politics.

In the 1970s and 1980s, two congressionally based analysis units made their presence known on the intergovernmental scene. The Congressional Budget Office, created in 1974, explores and presents policy options to the Congress on pending legislation, including alternatives on many intergovernmental proposals. Also, from the early 1970s through the 1980s, the General Accounting Office (GAO) became an assertive actor on IGR issues. The GAO at various times organized itself to focus explicitly on intergovernmental questions. In the late 1970s, for example, it developed a "program plan" (GAO 1978) to examine a wide range of intergovernmental policy and fiscal relationships such as grant-in-aid formulas and block grants. During the 1980s, the GAO created an Intergovernmental Relations Group within its Human Resources Division and developed an "intergovernmental research agenda" (GAO 1986). That group has since been disbanded and GAO's focus on IGR was de-emphasized (Kincaid and Stever 1992).

Other sources and publications should be noted as centers for monitoring IGR during recent decades. Prominent are the regular periodicals of the so-called Big Seven public interest groups: National Governors Association (NGA), Council of State Governments (CSG), National Conference of State Legislatures (NCSL), National League of Cities (NLC), U.S. Conference of Mayors (USCM), National Association of Counties (NACO), and International City/County Management Association (ICMA). These include *Public Management* (ICMA, monthly), *Nation's Cities* (NLC, monthly), *Counties* (NACO, monthly), *State Legislatures* (NCSL, monthly), and *State News* (CSG, monthly). The NGA does not publish a separate major periodical but produces a biweekly newsletter called "Governors Bulletin" that was dominated by intergovernmental issues. Accompanying these numerous periodicals, each Big Seven group has a website which provides current, if not extensive, coverage of intergovernmental affairs and their positions on fiscal, regulatory, and program issues.

The activities and periodicals of another relevant association need to be mentioned. The American Society for Public Administration (ASPA) publishes *Public Administration Review (PAR)* bimonthly. From 1940 to 1983, *PAR* published over 350 articles dealing with various aspects of IGR (Wright and White 1984). Since that inventory, the number of IGR-related articles appears to have increased. The ASPA also publishes *PA Times* on a monthly basis, and it consistently reports administrative developments that have IGR ramifications. Another ASPA-based source is the Section on Intergovernmental Administration and Management (SIAM), one of the major sections in the ASPA. It has produced a quarterly newsletter, *SIAM Intergovernmental News* since 1977. Since 1993, it has been a cosponsor, with the Vinson Institute of Government at the University of Georgia, in publishing *State and Local Government Review.*

Three other periodicals deserve mention and emphasis for coverage of IGR matters. First, the *National Civic Review* (formerly *National Municipal Review)* is a monthly (bimonthly since 1987) of long standing, dating back to the municipal reform movement in the early nineteenth century. Its articles tend to be brief and advocacy oriented, befitting its origins. For sheer reportage of events and issues that involve national–state–local interactions, however, it would be difficult to match the *National Civic Review* for long-term scope and illustrative detailed content.

---

*The ACIR was also disbanded (in 1996) because of budget reductions enacted by the 104th Congress.

The second journal is also broad, even catholic, in IGR scope, but is more recent in origin. Appearing first in 1971, *Publius: The Journal of Federalism* is a quarterly publication, originally from Center for the Study of Federalism at Temple University but subsequently shifted to the Meyner State and Local Government Center at Lafayette College. Its substantive strengths, diverse contributors, and innovative contents put it at the center of a scholarly nexus for the critical study of IGR and federalism. Worthy of special note since 1977 is the allocation of one issue of *Publius* to an annual review of the state of federalism.

The third periodical is *Governing: The Magazine of States and Localities*. Published since 1988 by Congressional Quarterly, Inc., this monthly magazine covers current issues of IGR interest, noteworthy work of state and local leaders, program innovations, and assessments of trends and report cards on performance. Regular columns feature developments on the state and local financial, management, technological, and political fronts, among others, as well as a "Potomac Chronicle" and "Urban Notebook." Annually, *Governing* recognizes "Public Officials of the Year" for their contributions.

The prior publications can be regularly monitored or selectively consulted for exposure to a large variety of approaches and analyses of IGR over recent decades. It would be impossible to extract the IGR content of these numerous sources. It is worthwhile, however, to mention two articles that review IGR trends and patterns over a two-decade (1960–1980) span. Stenberg (1980) was an ACIR staff member when he reviewed the impending shift from "the days of wine and roses" to the period of policy redirection and retrenchment called by one wag, "the evening of beer and daisies." Writing in *PAR*, he saw the turn of policy cycle toward what Miller would later refer to as "public sector performance: a conceptual turning point" (Miller 1984). Wright later called this "the contractive phase of IGR" (Wright 1988).

In *Publius*, a trio of authors reflected on the major events and chief trends affecting IGR in the 1960s and 1970s (Cole et al. 1983). Relying on a survey of scores of IGR academic observers, the authors attempted, quite successfully, to chart major events, actions, trends, and impacts prominent during the two-decade span. Table 11.1 and Table 11.2 provide a condensed configuration of their findings.

Both new and experienced/established observers of IGR can benefit from a reflecting reading of articles in *PAR*, *Publius*, and *Governing*. They frame the bulk of the quarter century that we now examine in five-year segments.

B. 1960–1965: POLITICAL PROCESSES, SHARED FUNCTIONS, CHANGING STRUCTURE

The political process and quasi-behavioral approaches of the 1950s had discernible impacts on the research and literature of the early 1960s. Grodzins' focus on the role of the party system as a variable explaining non-centralization in the American system clearly articulated process and behavioral themes (Grodzins 1960a, 1960b). In this respect he developed in greater depth a theme that David Truman had raised a few years earlier (Truman 1955). This theme was explored later in the period from two contrasting perspectives. Riker (1964) essentially subscribed to the party-as-decentralizer thesis in his well-known and highly critical book on federalism, in which he likened states' rights to racism. Buchanan (1965) on the other hand, had doubts about which way the supposed causal relationship ran. In "Politics and Federalism: Party or Anti-Party?" he hypothesized that the structural arrangement of federalism might be the variable that explained why American parties were decentralized. As will be reported later, the role of political parties as decentralizers and the influence of state and local officials in nominating candidates for national office declined steadily from this point onward.

Both the process and behavioral approaches current in this period were represented in articles appearing in the second special issue of *The Annals* (1965) devoted to IGR. In addition to Buchanan's article on parties and federalism, contributions were included on pressure groups (Anderson 1965), public officials' attitudes (McCulloch 1965), and "A Behavioral Approach to the Study of

TABLE 11.1
Major Trends Affecting IGR in the 20 Years 1960–1980

Rank Order	Trend or Development
1	Increased flow of federal dollars to state and local governments
2	Disaffection with government and growing concern for government accountability, manifested in the late 1970s
3	Growing dependence of local governments (particularly cities) on state and federal aid
4	Increased suburbanization and continued loss of population by many inner cities
5	Emergence of Frostbelt–Sunbelt regional competition and growing tensions between haves and have-nots
6	Increasingly significant role of the courts in intergovernmental areas accompanying a concern for equity in the system
7	Increased federal regulation of use of shared revenues
8	Broadening of federal aid, especially general revenue sharing
9	Increase in number and influence of Washington-based public interest groups
10	Blurring of private and public sector
11	Increased use by federal government of formulas to target federal aid dollars
12	Rise and increased influence of regional governing and coordinating bodies (COGs, sub-state national organizations, multi-state regional organizations)
13	Increased state aid to local governments
14	Increased adoption by states of income taxes
15	New or updated state constitutions

Source: From Cole, R.L., Stenberg, C.W., and Weissert, C.S., *Publius*, 13, 113–122, 1983.

Intergovernmental Relations" (Ostrom and Ostrom 1965). The last selection was one of the earliest rational or public choice approaches to IGR.

Grodzins also effectively elaborated the concept of shared functions, beginning with his widely distributed essay for the President's Commission on National Goals (Grodzins 1960b). It was

TABLE 11.2
Ranking of Ten Major Social and Political Events Affecting Intergovernmental Relations: 1960–1980

Rank Order	Event
1	Vietnam War and the resulting inflationary spiral
2	Energy crisis: 1973 and 1979
3	Election of Lyndon Johnson: beginning of the Great Society (1964)
4	Demographic shifts: increasing proportion of young and elderly segments of the population
5	Rise of the Sunbelt states in population and political influence
6	Financial crisis of large cities, including the fiscal default of New York City
7	Urban riots, 1964–1968
8	Environmental movement
9	Election of Richard Nixon: resultant new federalism of the early 1970s
10	Watergate

Source: From Cole, R.L., Stenberg, C.W., and Weissert, C.S., *Publius*, 13, 113–122, 1983.

extended and expanded in his posthumously published book, *The American System* (Grodzins 1966). Others, most notably Daniel Elazar, picked up the theme and applied it to current as well as long-term historical analyses (Elazar 1962, 1965, 1969). Graves, in his magnum opus *American Intergovernmental Relations* (1964), provided further detailed (even exhaustive) descriptive material. In the process Graves produced the first bona fide but ponderous (985 pages) text on IGR.

In other quarters, concerns over structure as well as process were thoughtfully articulated. The urban-metropolitan thrust of the 1950s bore fruit in strong pressures to create a cabinet-level department of urban affairs. Connery and Leach (1960) offered a balanced examination of the controversial issue. It was resolved politically by the creation of the U.S. Department of Housing and Urban Development (HUD) and in the welter of policy actions that were part of the Great Society (Creative Federalism) thrust of the early Johnson presidency (ACIR 1963; Cleaveland 1969).

Structural aspects surfaced in surprising places. The structure of representation in state legislatures had been an intense political issue for years. In *Baker v. Carr* (1962), the Supreme Court produced a landmark decision that extended the court's interpretation and application of the equal-protection clause of the Fourteenth Amendment. The 1962 court decision would eventually result in a significant restructuring and reorientation, from a policy/representational standpoint, of the legislatures of most states. Landau (1965), however, saw the reapportionment case in a different light. In an essay titled, "*Baker v. Carr* and the Ghost of Federalism," he projected the effects of the case as accelerating the decline and atrophy of federalism in the United States (Landau 1965, 1973) largely because it would foster the increased nationalization of many issues.

C.   1965–1970: Finances, the States, and Urban Affairs

The late 1960s recorded numerous and even violent political whirlwinds across the American intergovernmental landscape. The tracking of only three of these storm systems—finances, the states, and urbanization—seems sufficient to give a sense of IGR weather patterns in this volatile period. For some sense of how tense and pressurized this period was, the following offers a flavor of the times:

> The people don't give a damn about "intergovernmental relations." It smacks of the excuse for inaction. The people want bread, not excuses. The people want jobs, not intergovernmental explanations. The people want opportunity for their children, not intergovernmental expiations of guilt (Abrams 1969, 378).

From a fiscal standpoint the shower of federal dollars emerging from the Great Society grant-in-aid programs was sufficient to turn the eyes of many observers and participants, especially state and local officials, into a fixed gaze on Washington. All of the Big Seven Public Interest Groups set up offices in Washington, DC. The ACIR produced a definitive volume of the fiscal balance/imbalance in the IGR system (ACIR 1967). A major argument of the report was the need for a more balanced configuration of federal aid—a shift from categorical/project grants toward block grants and revenue sharing.

This point of view was shared by most, if not all, state and local officials. It was also supported in some academic quarters, although the view was far from unanimous (Anderson 1968; Heller 1966; Perloff and Nathan 1968; Wright 1968). Opinions in the Congress, however, were much more ambivalent, if not adamantly opposed. One senior member of the House of Representatives produced a book that argued that revenue sharing should be conditioned on and require a wholesale reorganization of state and local government (Reuss 1970).

Reuss's views, needless to say, did not carry the day. But his focus on state-level issues was consistent with a significant shift in attention toward state government. The nature of this focus on the states was diverse, disparate, and eclectic. One common theme running through the research and writing by practitioners and academics, however, was the relevance and significance of the states in IGR.

A political and policy focus dominated much of the first wave of state-oriented analyses. Jacob and Vines (1965) put forth "a comparative analysis" in the first edition of their groundbreaking state politics book. Eight editions have subsequently been published (Gray and Hanson 2004). Interstate IGR was a core component of the text, although not explicitly acknowledged. Furthermore, the policy chapters on education, highways, welfare, and so forth, prominently incorporated significant state national and state–local elements.

The policy focus on the states mushroomed as Dye, Sharkansky, and others sought explanations for varying expenditure-based output measures in numerous political and economic variables. Dye's (1966) book seemed to open the floodgates, and in the mainstream was Sharkansky (1968, 1970), looking at inter- as well as intra-governmental factors affecting state expenditures. Sharkansky (1972) followed his heavily statistical analyses with a more interpretive work on state policy accomplishments and opportunities. Lowi's writings (1964, 1972, 1978) accentuated the policy focus, one that would subsequently be explored by many authors, e.g., Anton (1989).

Two interpretive, non-quantitative volumes came on line but were distinctively different from the policy output literature on the states. Both were explicitly and extensively intergovernmental in focus. Elazar (1966) adopted "a view from the states" in looking at IGR in the mid-1960s. Two subsequent revisions (Elazar 1972, 1984) did not falter from this state-based perspective, with a special emphasis on state political cultures (or subcultures).

More activist and advocacy oriented was Governor Terry Sanford's (1967) book *Storm over the States.* This call for state revival originated the famous "picket fence federalism" metaphor to describe the narrow, insular, programmatic/professional loyalties inherent and implicit in federal aid programs. The basic tension between program specialists and policy generalists had, however, been clearly identified somewhat earlier (Advisory Committee on Local Government 1955; Weidner 1955, 1960). Sanford also highlighted the difficult position and stereotypical view of the states in terms of their support for and sensitivity to local governments:

The states are indecisive.
The states are antiquated.
The states are timid and ineffective.
The states are not willing to face their problems.
The states are not responsive.
The states are not interested in cities.
These half-dozen charges are true about all of the states some of the time and some of the states all of the time (Sanford 1967, 1).

The seeds of ideas about the states' strengths strewn through Sanford's book did not land on barren soil. Instead, and in no small part due to Sanford's initiative, two entities were formed to promote a revitalized IGR role for the states. One was the permanent Education Committee of the States promoted jointly by Sanford and Harvard President James B. Conant. The second was the temporary (two-year) Institute for State Programming for the 1970s. A former governor headed the latter group. He discussed both organizations under the rhetorical title "Are the States Here to Stay?" (Campbell 1968).

Few doubted the continued presence of the states. More crucial were questions about the competence and capacity of the states to function as active and effective participants in the expanded partnership. No less a distinguished scholar than Samuel Beer of Harvard was drawn to this subject, and he chose to focus on a policy question that seemed least likely to be a state-level interest—poverty. Beer and his associates found problems but also positive prospects in state actions dealing with poverty, at least in Massachusetts (Beer and Barringer 1970).

An extensive focus on the states did not preclude concern for and attention to urban issues (Mogulof 1971; Long 1972). Indeed, one of the observations that could be made about the late 1960s was that urban problems were uniformly acknowledged to be intergovernmental in character. Roscoe Martin had long recognized this fact but many others had failed to appreciate its significance. Martin's (1965) book *The Cities and the Federal System* both emphasized and crystallized the national–local (urban) nexus while delivering a devastating critique of the "reluctant" states. He called national–local relations "the expanded partnership" (Martin 1965, 109).

The national–urban link was played out more prominently for the public in lengthy, well-orchestrated Senate hearings starting in 1966. A parade of mayors and other local officials testified about urban malaise and sociopolitical conflagrations then called "urban riots" (Subcommittee on Executive Reorganization 1966–1968). The public rebukes, recriminations, and animosity present in national–local exchanges between Senator Robert Kennedy and Los Angeles Mayor Samuel Yorty, for example, are indicative of the tensions surrounding the expanded partnership.

As the decade drew to a close, two volumes seemed to address the mood of the moment and offer some hope for the future. Sundquist assessed the national-level dimension (and much more) in his *Making Federalism Work* (1969). The book's subtitle, "A Study of Program Coordination at the Community Level," accurately conveyed its central focus and content. The title, however, only hints at its more prescriptive dimensions. On this latter point the following is illustrative: "Somewhere in the Executive Office [of the President] must be centered a concern for the structure of federalism—a responsibility for guiding the evolution of the whole system of federal–state–local relations, viewed for the first time as a single system" (Sundquist 1969, 246).

A second volume that in a sense closed the 1960s was Campbell's (1970) book *The States and the Urban Crisis*. The volume emerged from an American Assembly conference on the topic and its state–local focus neatly complemented the primary national–local thrust of Sundquist's analysis. Eight essays appeared in the Campbell volume. Rather than raking the states over the IGR coals, the analyses were more balanced and even positive on the role and prospects for the states. There was, however, an urgency in the message calling for state action:

> Time grows short for America.
> Torn by a divisive war, a generation gap to end all generation gaps, and a polarization of white and black society, America is in the midst of a deepening political, economic, cultural, spiritual and moral crisis perhaps nowhere more strongly felt than in the great urban centers of the country.
> No one individual, institution, system, or level of government can single-handedly solve the urban crisis. The problems that have been allowed to develop unchallenged, and the institutions that have been allowed to disintegrate are too complex to admit of a single simple solution.
> However, the states if they choose can exert strong leverage to break loose vast amounts of available but as yet untrapped resources for community development. By virtue of their position, state governments possess the power, and the obligation, to attack all of those problems which in sum equal the urban crisis (American Assembly 1970, 3).

It is difficult to overemphasize the significance of events for IGR in this period (1965–1970) as well as subsequently. Two volumes written from retrospective stances offer insightful observations on IGR in the later 1960s. Frieden and Kaplan (1975) focus primarily on the urban dimension of the Great Society, especially model cities. Welborn and Burkhead (1989) offer a broad-gauged assessment of the Johnson administration's impact on the American political and administrative systems. They note that, "Perhaps the most important change was the enlarged scope and penetration of national power. A multitude of intergovernmental programs were enacted that thrust the national government [administratively and politically] into much closer and more intimate involvement in the operations of sub-national governments" (Welborn and Burkhead 1989, 1).

D. 1970–1975: Regionalism, Reorientation, and Implementation

If the 1960s were a feisty time for IGR, then the 1970s marked a yeasty period. Important shifts and changes occurred, but they seemed to arise more from the leavened lump of hard work, perseverance, and patience than from dramatic political confrontations and conquests. These shifts in the first part of the decade are classified and linked with three terms—regionalism, reorientation, and implementation.

The regional theme had emerged along two major tracks and a minor one. The minor path involved regional reorganization within national cabinet departments to achieve ten common or standard regional boundaries for the administration of many federal aid programs. From this effort emerged fledgling federal regional councils aimed at coordinating programs and policies between and among national administrative agencies (Derthick 1974). For example, this initiative permitted if not promoted the concept of annual arrangements between national agencies and a single city, under which a lump sum of funds was disbursed pursuant to a contract relating to a citywide development strategy negotiated between the mayor and the US Department of Housing and Urban Development (*National Journal* 1973). From a local or state perspective the standardized federal regions allowed these officials a common one-stop location for dealing with the regional administrative headquarters of major national agencies. This administrative regionalism during the Nixon presidency was, it could be argued, the seed from which the plant, stem, and flower of IGM later grew and blossomed.

On a much broader policy and structural scale were issues associated with statutory multi-state regional bodies such as the Tennessee Valley Authority (TVA), Appalachian Regional Commission, and various river basin and economic development bodies. These agencies, of course, were created during or before the 1960s, but several factors converged to make them a political/policy issue in the 1970s. One precipitating force was President Nixon's aim to reduce or eliminate many of these entities. The most significant works on these agencies were produced near the time of their highest political visibility (ACIR 1972, 1973–1974; Derthick 1974). The ACIR explored several aspects of multi-state regionalism and the federal system (ACIR 1972). The continued relevance of these entities through the 1970s was demonstrated when the ACIR produced a "regionalism revisited" report in 1977 (ACIR 1977d).

The IGR changes percolating in a structural arena via Councils of Governments (COGs) were approaching the boiling point in the federal aid arena (ACIR 1972; Wikstrom 1977).[*] Nathan (1975, 127) referred to these currents as a "new structuralism." Pressures had been building to force some clear, if not sharp, reorientations in the funding and administration of categorical grants-in-aid. Two books by the same author could easily serve as literal book ends for this policy reorientation during the 1970–1975 period.

Derthick (1970) produced a probing analysis of the political dynamics revolving around the categorical public assistance program. In discussing "prospects for the grant systems," she documented with precision and clarity the configurations of influence around grant programs and the tensions associated with proposals for change. She noted:

> If it is easy to exaggerate the defects of the grant system, however, and to attribute to it flaws that are actually general features of contemporary politics, it is also easy to exaggerate its advantages; as a way of dispersing power and safeguarding pluralism—supposedly its chief virtues—it is flawed by a tendency to foster powerful, self-serving intergovernmental alliances between official agencies that share values and interests as well as functions, and that gain autonomy through the system's operation (Derthick 1970, 243).

---

[*] Councils of governments (COGS) have a long (50-year) history as sub-state regional entities for interlocal communication, cooperation, and coordination. By the 1970s there were over 600 COGs in existence across the nation. The number has declined since that date but they remain viable and constructive entities in many states.

To restrict this autonomy the IGR battle cry of the early 1970s was called New Federalism. Ironically, Derthick documented five years later the hazards of rash action in jerking control away from professionals in the social services field. The combination of a loose law, novice political appointees, and other factors in health, education, and welfare produced "uncontrollable spending" for social services grants (Derthick 1975).

The rallying cry among academics for a New Federalism sounded like reveille and it drew many followers. But the bugle notes were also heard by differently tuned ears. For governors, mayors, and other officials engaged in intergovernmental lobbying (Haider 1974), the notes sounded "charge"—especially after general revenue sharing. For at least one skeptical academic the tonal pattern signified a recognition that, "Federalism—old style—is dead. Yet federalism—new style—is alive and well and living in the United States. Its name is *intergovernmental relations*" (Reagan 1972, 3).

General revenue sharing (GRS) passed the Congress and was signed by President Nixon in 1972. Seldom, if ever, has a single national assistance program been subjected to such intensive and extensive analysis. Four substantial works focused on the descriptive, prescriptive, and political aspects of its passage (Beer 1976; Dommel 1974; Stolz 1974; Thompson 1973). Studies of its specific policy impact(s) are legion, as are analyses of its general effects on IGR (*Annals* 1975; Caputo 1975; Caputo and Cole 1974, 1976; Nathan 1975; Nathan et al. 1975; Nathan and Adams 1977; Oates 1975; Wright et al. 1975; Scheffer 1976). The National Science Foundation (NSF) allocated $3 million for research projects to evaluate the formula and process impacts of GRS (Lucas 1976).

Strategies to reorient federal assistance programs spread far beyond GRS, however. Block grants, also called special revenue sharing at this juncture, were part of the New Federalism package, but were destined to lag behind GRS in enactment (Dommel et al. 1978, 1980). But both GRS and block grants, as well as existing categorical grants, raised the issue of state and local policy management capacities. This concern gave rise to a joint NSF/OMB task force that was ultimately called the Study Committee on Policy Management Assistance (SCOPMA) (Executive Office of the President 1975). The most accessible place to review and evaluate the content of SCOPMA is in a special issue of PAR (Clayton et al. 1975; Macaluso 1975).

Reference to policy turns attention to the third and final prominent IGR theme developing in the early 1970s—implementation. The process of getting a program to produce results rarely is far from an intergovernmental administrator's mind. Beginning in the 1970s, however, the concept of implementation commanded the attention of practitioner and scholar alike. (One term that may rival implementation in spanning the often wide gulf between scholar and practitioner is *incrementalism*). The starting point for the burgeoning body of literature on implementation seems clearly identifiable. Pressman and Wildavsky (1973) launched its meteoric rise with their book *Implementation: How Great Expectations in Washington Are Dashed in Oakland*. Pressman (1975) followed with his broad-ranging and insightful analysis of the interaction between federal programs and Oakland's city politics.

One clear consequence of the onset of the implementation literature was to emphasize, even dramatize, the shortfall between performance and promise (expectations). It was almost as if the research literature was saying: "You can't get there from here." The retrospective studies and pessimistic views were not this simplistic, of course (Hanf and Scharpf 1978; Salamon 1976; Warren 1978). There were critical appraisals that probed thoughtfully for lessons for the future. In looking at the model cities program, for example, Frieden and Kaplan (1975, 4) observed, "A careful reading of the federal implementation effort should help to define the future role for the federal government in reducing poverty and inequality, drawing on the experience of the 1960s but without repeating the overly optimistic assumptions and mistakes of that decade."

The federal role issue will be addressed shortly. First, however, acknowledgment should be made of the appearance of a third issue of *The Annals* (1974) devoted to IGR. Edited by

Leach (1974), the volume contained 16 articles organized under the theme "Intergovernmental Relations in America Today." The essays can be read for the purpose of understanding precisely what the title promises, the status of IGR near the midpoint of the 1970s.

E.   1975–1980: EVALUATION AND CODIFICATION

The federal aid policy shifts occurring in the early 1970s and the critical attitudes engendered by the implementation studies combined with other factors to produce new emphases and issues in the late 1970s. Only two themes—evaluation and codification—are discussed here.

Evaluation in the federal aid arena had clear antecedents in the research studies on GRS cited earlier. Indeed, the GRS renewal legislation in 1976 contained a provision requiring the ACIR to pursue broadly based evaluation studies. To say that this mandate was taken seriously is an understatement.

From 1976 through 1978 the ACIR published 14 volumes under its broad project title "The Intergovernmental Grant System: An Assessment and Proposed Policies" (ACIR 1977a,b,c,d, 1978a,b). The major block-grant programs were examined and several specialized studies were conducted, for example, the design and role of categorical grants (ACIR 1978a). The core of the Commission's orientation can be found in a painstakingly thorough analysis on improving the management of federal grants (ACIR 1977b).

A second major ACIR evaluation effort closely followed the first. The Commission's federal role studies were conducted from 1978 to 1980 and produced 11 volumes on the dynamics of national growth and influence in the intergovernmental system (ACIR 1980a,b,c,d,e, 1981, 1982). These exhaustive reports ranged from functional program analyses to ones broadly titled "Confidence and Competence" (ACIR 1980c) and "Collapsing Constraints" (ACIR 1980b). The groundwork laid in these studies led to the oft-quoted assertion that, "American federalism ... is in trouble. The federal government's influence has become more pervasive, more intrusive, more unmanageable, more ineffective, more costly, and, above all, more unaccountable" (ACIR 1980d, 1).

Evaluation of IGR in the late 1970s moved far beyond the confines of the ACIR. The Brookings Institution, the Urban Institute, and the American Enterprise Institute (AEI) were three Washington-based centers of activity from which appraisals emerged. Richard Nathan at Brookings continued and extended his distinctive field research methodology to community development and manpower block grant programs (Nathan et al. 1977). Economic and econometric approaches to federal aid were pursued at the Urban Institute (Mieszkowski and Oakland 1979). More interpretive as well as more critical appraisals came from the AEI (Barfield 1981).

Outside of Washington the examinations of IGR were episodic, eclectic, and numberless. Sources with a strong policy focus may be cited but should not be construed as being fully representative of the mass of materials flowing through the research communities (Anton et al. 1980; Carroll and Campbell 1976; Couturier and Dunn 1977; Gramlich 1977; Jones and Thomas 1976; Larkey 1979; Lyons and Morgan 1977; Muller and Fix 1980; Rosenthal 1979; Stephens 1974; Stephens and Olson 1979; Wright et al. 1975).

The immense corpus of materials on IGR in the 1950s and 1960s had stimulated courses on the subject at some universities. (The authors have, separately and at various institutions, offered graduate and/or undergraduate courses on IGR, begining in 1956 and continuing to the present). The scope and content of the courses were not as extensive as anticipated by a survey of academe (ACIR 1969). The field was ripe, one might say, for codification by a text that would offer the subject some focus, coherence, or synthesis.

Three efforts to fill this need appeared during the approximate period under discussion (Glendening and Reeves 1977; Walker 1981; Wright 1978). The Glendening and Reeves volume adopted a strong institutional interaction approach with chapters on national–state, state–local, national–local, and inter-local relationships. The Walker text gave considerable space to an historical survey of the evolution and adaptation of the IGR system since the eighteenth century. A second priority was on contemporary judicial, fiscal, and political dynamics, with special attention to the problem of system "overload" (Beer 1977; Walker 1979; Wright 1980). Wright's text made a bow in the direction of history, mainly concentrating on "phases" of IGR during the twentieth century. Higher priority was given, however, to matters of finance, policy, and "participants' perspectives." That these texts did not spread eagle the field is evidenced by the appearance later of several text or text-type volumes in the 1980s.

F.   THE 1980S: ELABORATION, REGULATION, RETRENCHMENT/REDIRECTION, AND MANAGEMENT

Efforts to bring cohesion and synthesis to the IGR field through textbooks produced mixed results. On the one hand, the diverse and amorphous character of the field almost guaranteed that no single text would fully and successfully cover the subject. On the other hand, the initial textual efforts prompted other writers to put their hand(s) to the plow handle and till the IGR soil.

In addition to revisions in the Glendening and Reeves (1984) and Wright (1982b, 1988) texts, three edited books of readings on IGR appeared in the 1980s. Furthermore, quasi-texts focusing on federal grants were published (Howitt 1984; Nice 1987; Nice and Frederickson 1995). Of more than passing interest is the fact that the text-type volumes combined federalism and intergovernmental relations in their titles or subtitles.

The three edited volumes attempted to provide both current coverage and broad-ranging exposure to IGR in the 1980s. Leach (1983) enlisted seven specialists to probe the field in the early part of the decade, just after the Reagan policy initiatives took shape. O'Toole in three editions (1985, 1993, 2000) offered a reader consisting of many selections ranging in content from Madison (*Federalist* No. 39) to Reagan's first State of the Union message. A majority of the items came from the 1970s and 1980s. Dilger (1986) assembled fewer (17) but longer selections, all written in the early 1980s.

The persistence of issues associated with federal aid programs remained prominent into the 1980s (Clark 1983; Fossett 1983; Peterson 1981; Williamson 1983, 1990). Two volumes surveyed these issues in text-type fashion. Shapek (1981) offered extensive background material on grants management issues, particularly in the 1970s. Complementing Shapek's managerial focus was a political orientation toward grants by Hale and Palley (1981). They adopted a "regulatory model" of the grants process, a theme addressed in the next few paragraphs.

In one sense the regulatory issues involving IGR are at least as old as the earliest conditional grant programs (circa 1887) and perhaps are as old as the Republic itself (Hanus 1981). Starting in the 1970s, however, and rising to prominence in the 1980s, was an array of issues cataloged under the phrase "regulatory federalism." Perhaps the single most important source on the subject was a volume published by the ACIR (1984b). This thorough study examined the politics, policy issues, process aspects, impacts and reform proposals associated with intergovernmental regulation. A short (50-page) condensation the full report was also published (ACIR 1984a). The continued significance of the topic was confirmed by a reassessment study (ACIR 1993).

A major aim of the Reagan administration was deregulation—a policy thrust that began during the Carter administration. Three essays focused specifically on IGR regulatory reform in the 1980s. Mashaw and Rose-Ackerman (1984) offered an insightful analysis of national deregulation. Fix (1984) examined the conscious transfer of authority from the national government to the states. Elsewhere, Reagan (1987) offered a "marble cake" analysis of IGR regulation within the framework of a volume that attempts a comprehensive view of the politics of regulatory policy. In spite of deregulation rhetoric during the 1980s, the reality was that the greatest growth in federal regulations and preemptions occurred in the 1980s (ACIR 1993; Zimmerman 1991).

The topic of IGR regulation should not be closed without some references to other studies of regulatory issues (Brown 1980, 1981, 1983; Lovell 1981a, 1981b; Lovell and Tobin 1981;

Petkas 1981). Levine and Wexler (1981) provided a focused, readable, advocacy-based study of the enactment and implementation of the Education for All Handicapped Children Act of 1975 (P.L. 94–142). Its value rests mainly in dealing with the politics of lobbying and enacting (rather than implementing) this significant piece of intergovernmental legislation. In contrast to the Levine and Wexler case study, Katzmann (1986) completed a balanced study of implementing Section 504 of the Rehabilitation Act of 1973 as it applied to public transit systems. Katzmann's special concern for IGR emerged not only in his title, "Institutional Disability," but also in the normative question he posed: "Can the structures and incentives of institutions be changed so that policy processes and outcomes are less confused?" (Katzmann 1986a, 14). Another balanced and probing exploration of IGR regulation was Kettl's study of national guidance and direction efforts in the community development block grant program (Kettl 1981a, 1981b, 1983a, 1983b). The difficulties of national oversight and direction are the main messages emerging from much of the research on IGR regulation. A significant counterpoint to the incapacity of national-level direction is Chubb's (1985a,c) longitudinal study of the redistributive implementation of federal aid for elementary and secondary education.

The retrenchment and redirection feature(s) of IGR in the 1980s produced research and writing that nearly overwhelm an observer of recent developments. We refer, of course, to the origins, enactment, and implementation of what has been variously termed "the Reagan revolution" (Nathan 1986) or "the new direction in American politics" (Chubb and Peterson 1985). From an IGR standpoint the case has been made that the Reagan policies have been less than revolutionary and/or reactionary (Glazer 1986; Heclo 1986; Palmer 1986; Wright 1988). A more accurate description of the IGR policy shift might designate it as "redirection" (Wright 1988). A preview of IGR directions appeared in a book edited by Hawkins (1982a), the individual Reagan subsequently selected to chair the ACIR. His term for the direction and content of the administration's IGR proposals was "reform" (Hawkins 1982b).

Regardless of the term employed to describe IGR since 1981, some sense of order and pattern can be imposed on these developments (Conlan 1987, 1988, 1998). One theme that emerged early to describe Reagan's New Federalism ideas was retrenchment, or decrementalism (Wright 1982a). An early, descriptive, and somewhat surface-level review of spending reductions, with specific focus on state–local impacts, was assembled by Ellwood (1982). This was followed by more in-depth analyses of the "consequence of cuts" by Nathan and Doolittle (1983). Continued assessments of "retrenchment and redirection" were contributed by Beam (1984) and Goldenberg (1984).

Time and temporal-oriented analyses gave researchers an opportunity to put the Reagan-induced changes into a longitudinal context. By 1985, Chubb (1985b, 306) could observe that "the centralized system of extensive targeted subsidies [to state and local governments] will not be swept aside by a sea change in national party fortunes; it is institutionalized." At Brookings, Peterson had directed a long-term research project monitoring changes in development, distributive, and redistributive grant programs. More could be said about the originality and significance of the research, but the relevant substantive point stated that "thus far federal policy has changed less than many anticipated" (Peterson et al. 1986, xii).

A major feature of the Reagan administration's policies of retrenchment and redirection was the consolidation of 77 categorical grants into nine block grants through the Omnibus Budget Reconciliation Act of 1981 (Conlan 1988, 172–3). The plethora of research studies and publications cannot be plumbed. Only a single quote is offered from one of several careful studies of block grant implementation: "In a word, the administrative rationale of block grant consolidation, and even the political rationale for returning decision-making authority to the states, has been largely vindicated by the experience since 1981" (Peterson et al. 1986, 29). Separate but complementary research focused on the administrative devolution of the small-cities community development block grant (CDBG) program from the national government to the states (Jennings et al. 1986).

Two other assessments of the Reagan New Federalism adopted an explicit institutional focus. One looked at Reagan and the cities (Peterson and Lewis 1986). The authors noted that "one of the most encouraging developments of the Reagan presidency, yet one that requires a rethinking of city behavior as we understand it, was the favorable economic and fiscal position that cities found themselves in at the beginning of the president's second term" (Peterson and Lewis 1986, 11).

Nathan and Doolittle (1987) centered their attention on Reagan and the states, generally concluding that the states demonstrated significant and constructive resilience and response to Reagan-induced IGR policy changes. These IGR policy changes of whatever shape, substance, and effect, cannot and should not be considered in isolation from the broader economic, social, and political shifts of the 1980s (Yoo and Wright 1993). Fortunately an excellent summary set of perspectives on the Reagan years was produced as part of the Urban Institute's large-scale study on changing domestic priorities (Palmer 1986).

We have pursued a quarter century overview of the maturation of IGR from 1960 to 1985 (Anton 1984). The time period is acknowledged as inexact. Furthermore, closing the discussion at the mid-1980s does not imply that the relevance of the concept and practice(s) of IGR ended or declined. For example, it has been suggested that following the peaking of a "contractive" phase of IGR in the mid-1980s, there was a shift to a "coercive-collage" mode in IGR during the late 1980s and 1990s (Wright 1992, 1997). Additionally, a fourth volume of *The Annals* (1990) devoted to IGR appeared at the end of the decade (Kincaid 1990a).

The continued relevance of national domestic leadership in the 1980s and 1990s must be acknowledged, for example, in the expanded use of national preemption statutes, the rise in unfunded federal mandates, and the greater use of crossover sanctions (conditions) associated with federal aid (Dye 1990; Kenyon and Kincaid 1991; Kincaid 1990a; Walker 2000). Perhaps ironically, at the same time studies called attention to the resurgence of the states (Bowman and Kearney 1986; Stenberg 1985). Nevertheless, the regulatory practices (and others) by the national government enabled critics and commentators to make a strong case that "coercive federalism" replaced cooperative federalism as the prevailing mode of national–state relations (Kincaid 1990b, 1996; Zimmerman 1991, 1992).

The coercive elements of IGR make it more than mere policy and political coincidence that several features of the 1994 Republican Party "Contract with America" attacked the extensive and intrusive use of national power(s) over state and local governments. The significance of the 1994 electoral turnabout for FED and IGR was indicated in a 1995 survey of intergovernmental scholars and practitioners, in which the respondents rated the Republican Party gaining control of both Houses of Congress as well as thirty governorships as the top IGR event since 1980 (Cole et al. 1996, 31). The 1995 survey updated and extended the 1980 study that produced the results reported earlier in Table 11.1 and Table 11.2. Table 11.3 and Table 11.4 list the leading events and trends, respectively, for the 1980 and 1995 period.

A scan of the major IGR events of 1980 to 1995 (Table 11.3) provides the base for three notable observations. First, both political and fiscal events occupy featured roles and prominent status. Second, all of the major events are national in character or content. They involve national institutions, actors, or actions. The reported rankings would need to be extended through the top twenty events before a non-national action was included. Third, the top-ranked events are linked to all three national-level institutions: the Congress, president, and Supreme Court. Each entity attained high rankings for its impact(s) on federalism (FED), IGR, and IGM.

One can imagine the title of a future essay which might address the long-term impact of mid-decade political changes: "From Management to Politics: The Decline of IGM and the Resurgence of FED." The meaning and import of such a prospective essay requires an exposition of the origins, emergence, and maturation of IGM as a concept and of the administrative practices it represents.

TABLE 11.3
Major Intergovernmental Events: 1980–1995

Rank Order	Events
1	Republican party wins control of the US Congress and 30 governorships in 1994
2	The election (1980) and reelection (1984) of Ronald Reagan as president
3	General revenue sharing is not renewed by Congress (1986)
4	Americans with Disabilities Act of 1990 passed, prohibiting discrimination and requiring access in/to all public services and facilities
5	Supreme course decision: *Garcia v. San Antonio Metropolitan Transit Authority* 469 U.S. 546 (1985) overturning *National League of Cities v. Usery* 426 U.S. 833 (1976)
6	Omnibus Budget and Reconciliation Act of 1981 enacted
7	Clean Air Act Amendments of 1990 passed establishing deadlines on state/local governments involving smog, acid rain, and airborne toxins

Source: From Cole R.L., Stenberg, C.W., and Weissert, C.S., *Publius*, 26, 25–40, 1996.

VII. INTERGOVERNMENTAL MANAGEMENT (IGM): 1970s–2000s

Intergovernmental management (IGM) is a term of fairly recent vintage, first employed in the early 1970s. The sections that follow will discuss its meaning, origins, evolution, and comparative maturity. These are followed by concluding comments aimed at highlighting the interconnection(s) among IGM, IGR, and FED.

A. The Meaning of IGM

We acknowledge at the outset that there is no fixed or consensual definition of IGM. Under these conditions there is an advantage to examining the concept from an exclusionary approach (see, however, Wright and Krane 1998).

Some grasp of IGM accrues by clarifying what it is *not*. One notable contributor to the concept's development and clarification identified several features that he placed outside the domain of IGM (Agranoff 1986). The excluded items were cataloged in the context of the delivery of human service programs among multiple local and urban-metropolitan governments.

TABLE 11.4
Major Trends Affecting Intergovernmental Relations: 1980–1995

Rank Order	Trend Development
1	Rising costs of health care and health insurance
2	Federal aid growth rate declines; drops from 1978 peak (26.5%) as a proportion of state–local outlays
3	Shift of US population from greater Northeast to Southeast and West
4	Public disaffection and distrust of government increases
5	Significance of regulatory federalism increases (coercive impacts of court decisions, legislative actions, executive orders)
6	Unfunded and underfunded mandates increasingly incorporated in congressional actions
7	Widening of social and economic disparities continues between central cities and suburbs

Source: From Cole R.L., Stenberg, C.W., and Weissert, C.S., *Publius*, 26, 25–40, 1996.

The elements placed beyond the bounds of IGM were:

Fundamental change in social structure(s), basic power relationships, or fiscal responsibilities;
Realignment(s) in national–state–local relationships;
Major intergovernmental shifts in program or functional activities;
Significant policy revisions or redirection in the scope of service level(s) of existing programs;
Structural change in metropolitan governance (Agranoff 1986, 1–2).

IGM, in other words, takes systems, structures, policies, and programs largely as givens. It concentrates more on incremental and innovative adjustments in managerial activities that enhance service delivery. It focuses less (or not at all) on major changes that alter significant political, economic, and social equilibrium. In place of systemic changes IGM centers attention on networks of effective implementation.

There is an alternate exclusionary approach to clarifying IGM. Simply put, IGM is not FED nor is it IGR. The differences among the three concepts have been discussed elsewhere (Wright 1983, 1987, 1990a). The differences include (1) leading actors/participants, (2) political quotient, (3) value scope, (4) means of conflict resolution, (5) authority relationships, and (6) jurisdictional involvement. The distinguishing features of IGM on each of these characteristics emerge below.

It is possible to highlight historically and compare conceptually the features of IGM in relation to FED and IGR. This task is facilitated by Figure 11.2, using a time line identifying the origin of FED at the founding of the Republic (Circa 1790). The origin of IGR is placed in the 1930s and IGM is identified as originating in the 1970s.

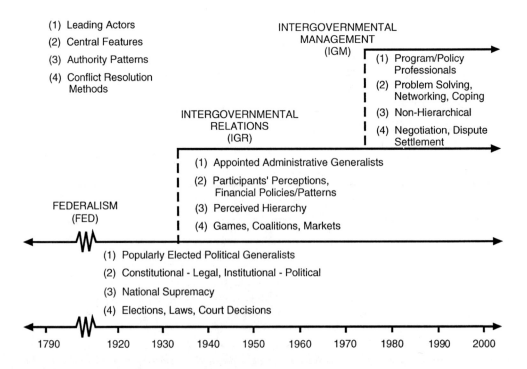

FIGURE 11.2 Historical evolution of interjurisdictional concepts: FED, IGR, and IGM.

Besides historical sequencing, Figure 11.2 provides a summary of four characteristics on which IGM departs from or contrasts with FED and IGR. These comparisons are (1) leading actors, (2) central features, (3) authority patterns, and (4) conflict resolution methods. The following discussion of IGM addresses its distinctive characteristics as well as the origin and emergence of IGM as a significant concept for the practice of public administration in an inter-jurisdictional context.

The most common components initially identified with IGM have been those of problem solving, networks and networking, and coping/managing under uncertainty (Agranoff 1986; 2001; Agranoff and Lindsay 1983; Agranoff and McGuire 2001, 2003; Gage and Mandell 1990; Mandell 1979). Marando and Florestano (1990) subsequently clarified and added noteworthy features in moving "Toward a Theory of IGM." They grounded their assessment within the blending (or continuum) of politics and administration as well as linkages to FED and IGR historically, descriptively, and analytically. They observe, for example, that "neither politics nor management can be minimized by researchers in their effort to understand governmental performance and capacity" (1990, 294). They also note that "the distinguishing feature of IGM is that it emphasizes the management process" (1990, 299).

Marando and Florestano offer a summary judgment: "IGM is a bold step toward recasting the politics/administration issue within the context of contemporary assessments of the American federal system" (1990, 299). This statement frames their substantial (eight-item) comparison of IGM with IGR as well as their questions aimed at clarifying how IGM helps improve the understanding of human and organizational behavior:

> Must all involved parties have visible stake in the outcome for IGM to be successful? How much inequality in the authority, status, and resources among intergovernmental actors can be assumed in the IGM process? To what extent do different problem areas require variations in IGM approaches? (Marando and Florestano 1990, 299).

The central features of IGM can now be summarized through a series of questions and responses:

1. Who are the leading actors or prime participants in IGM? They are the program/policy professionals first, followed closely by administrative generalists, for example, city managers. The central players on the IGM stage are "technocrats" (Beer 1978a) and "policy professionals" (Peterson et al. 1986).
2. What is the level of partisan politics in IGM? The level is modest, if not minimal. Effective program implementation and problem-solving strategies in service delivery are the primary or focal issues.
3. What goals or values tend to dominate IGM? The chief aims involving IGM are achieving positive program results through skillful public management (Wright 1990a).
4. What are the main means of conflict resolution in IGM? In contrast to elections, courts, and legislation for FED, and apart from coalitions, games, and markets for IGR, conflict-sare resolved in the IGM arena through bargaining, negotiation, and dispute settlement methods. When or where conflicts cannot be resolved, the differences are endured, tolerated, accommodated, or "coped with" (Agranoff 1986, 1989; Mandell 1990).
5. What is the distinctive character of authority relationships in IGR? In contrast to national supremacy (contingent hierarchy) for FED and different from the often-perceived hierarchy (asymmetric influence) for IGR, nonhierarchical networks or matrix patterns of influence characterize IGM (Mandell 1990). A level playing field is the most common venue for IGM.
6. What jurisdictional entities are the featured participants in IGM? *All* governmental entities—national, state, and local—are the structures within which IGM functions. In this respect, IGM operates on the same institutional base(s) as FED and IGR. As noted

earlier, however, IGM encompasses more than merely units of government (Agranoff 1986, 1989, 1990). It includes a significant degree of policy making in administration/ management (the policy-in-administration continuum), and the prominent presence of private and/or nonprofit sectors in the service delivery process(es). The latter element has been referred to as the public-private sector mix, or the "array of public and private actors" with "membership in several implementation structures" (Mandell 1990, 35). The mention of non-profit and for-profit entities in connection with IGM incorporates one feature that dramatically contrasts IGM with FED and IGR. The scope, significance, and implications of the participation of these nongovernmental entities in policy/program implementation cannot be explored or developed in this limited space and framework. One brief illustration of its significance comes from a survey of state administrative agency heads in 1998 that included questions about privatization and contracting for service delivery. Of the 800 state agencies that used third parties for service delivery, 60% contracted with other governments, 70% with nonprofits, and over 80% with for-profit organizations (Choi and Wright 2004; Choi et al. 2005).

We have considered what IGM is as well as what it is not. Based on this set of conceptual clarifications and distinctions it is useful to look at IGM across the three decades of its origins and evolution.

B. THE ORIGIN AND EMERGENCE OF IGM: THE 1970s

No single or specific date has been or can be confirmed for the origination of IGM. The approximate time of its gestation and birth, however, can be reasonably fixed as the early 1970s. Two special issues of *PAR* presented substantial manifestations of the problems, issues, and questions connected with a "management" approach to inter-jurisdictional relations (Clayton et al. 1975; Grosenick 1973). Limited space prohibits an attempt to summarize or synthesize the dozen articles in "The Administration of the New Federalism" (Grosenick 1973), or the 21 essays in "Policy Management Assistance" (Clayton et al. 1975).

It is sufficient to note, however, the "top-down" or national-based springboard from which IGM was launched. A joint OMB–NSF management initiative culminated in the 1975 *PAR* issue. The initiative was called SCOPMA (Study Committee on Policy Management Assistance). Its report, *Strengthening Public Management in the Intergovernmental System* (Executive Office of the President 1975), came in several parts in addition to the special issue of *PAR*. These included an OMB document, an NSF volume of 1200 pages containing 40 background papers, and a 40-minute color video cassette. In a curious and ironic twist, the NSF director of this project became persona non grata among national administrative agencies for his role in unleashing (through the various SCOPMA activities) a torrent of state–local criticisms and lobbying for general revenue sharing among other reforms of how "the feds" conducted intergovernmental business.

Apart from personalities, career conflicts, and bureaucratic byplays, a central point remains. The origin of IGM in the 1970s was largely nationally initiated, Washington-based, and hierarchical in tone and temperament. Subsequent activities during the remainder of the 1970s appeared to confirm what Stever (1992, 347) later called "the hierarchical approach to inter-governmental management dominant during the 1970s." A list of reports and activities included the following:

- ACIR, *Improving Federal Grants Management*. (Washington, DC: A-53, February 1977b)

- ASPA, *Strengthening Intergovernmental Management: An Agenda for Reform* (Washington, DC: April 1979)
- Executive Office of the President, Office of Management and Budget, *Managing Federal Assistance in the 1980s*, Report to the Congress pursuant to P.L. 95–224 (Washington, DC: March 1980)
- Creation of the Section on Federalism and Intergovernmental Relations within APSA in 1976
- Creation of SIAM (Section on Intergovernmental Administration and Management) within ASPA in 1978
- Creation of NAMA (National Assistance Management Association) in 1979.

C. IGM Evolution in the 1980s and 1990s: From Top-Down to Bottom-Up

The 1980s reflected a secular if not a sea-change shift in outlook and approach to IGM. The multiple forces at work might be provisionally classified in two categories: practical/political and intellectual/ideological. The first includes the significant intergovernmental policy redirections that accompanied the Reagan administration's New Federalism approach, which featured an ill-fated proposal to federalize Medicaid and Food Stamps in return for the states taking over welfare (Conlan 1987, 1998; Farber 1983; Williamson 1983, 1990; Walker 2000; Yoo and Wright 1993). In the second category are the sharp academic attacks on the concept of IGM. These took to task the hierarchical, technocratic, and non-constitutional dimensions of the term (Elazar 1981; Gordon 1980; Schechter 1981). It is curious but not coincidental that these three referenced critiques of IGM all appeared in *Publius: The Journal of Federalism*.

We take as given (but unproved) that the double-barreled attack of practical politics and academic argument undercut the hierarchical foundations on which IGM was constructed in the 1970s. Two possibilities emerged from those circumstances. One was that the concept might atrophy and disappear as a consequence of having few real-world, empirical referents. The second option was to fill the seemingly vacant conceptual space with new and different real-world operating experience(s). The second option was the path pursued, whether purposely or providentially. Intergovernmental management, in short, lost its national-based, hierarchic connotation. Those elements were replaced by state-local, and especially locally based, bottom-up practice(s), research, and new conceptualization (see Figure 11.1).

The following references reflect the relevance and significance of the bottom-up approach to understanding IGM through the 1980s and the 1990s: Agranoff (1986, 1989, 1990); Agranoff and Lindsay (1983); Gage and Mandell (1990); Jennings and Krane (1994); Jennings and Zank (1993); Johnson and Heilman (1987); Peterson et al. (1986); Rosenthal (1984); and Stoker (1991).

The locally based, community-focused, bottom-up approach to IGM was reflected in the popularization of the term governance to capture the multiple actors involved in pursuing public purposes. Government and IGR actors were involved but were not the exclusive players. According to Dodge governance has evolved into " … a more inclusive term to encompass: (1) all community interests affected by challenges and necessary to their resolution, not just government institutions, and (2) the collaborative problem-solving mechanisms needed to design timely strategies as well as the government institutions and other service-delivery mechanisms needed to implement them" (Dodge 1996, 38).

During the 1990s, the Reinventing Government movement swept the country, and its principles embodied the concept of governance (Brudney et al. 1999; Burke and Wright 2002). Developed by Osborne and Gaebler (1992) and based on their experiences working with local governmental and non-profit organizations, the authors called upon governments at all levels to operate in an entrepreneurial manner and adopt the following 10 principles as features of reinvention (Osborne and

Gaebler 1992; Osborne and Plastrik 1997):

- Government should steer (through policy) rather than row (through implementation) and make greater use of alternatives to in-house service delivery.
- Agencies should be driven by mission rather than rules.
- Agencies and administrators should be outcome and results oriented instead of input and process oriented.
- Citizens should be considered customers, instead of clients.
- Administrators should empower communities to participate in the delivery of services through management councils, teams, and other processes.
- Competition should be encouraged within the public sector (i.e. bidding for tasks) as well as between government and the private sector.
- Agencies should earn money through user fees and profit centers.
- Authority should be decentralized.
- Prevention should be an objective in addition to amelioration or remediation of a problem.
- Governments should leverage the marketplace rather than just create public programs to solve problems.

Although coming from the bottom-up the powerful message conveyed by Osborne and Gaebler was heard at the national level. One consequence was establishment of the National Performance Review (NPR) headed by Vice-President Al Gore to steer the reinvention of federal management practices—from customer service to procurement system reform to work force downsizing—as a means of creating a national government that "works better and costs less" (Gore 1993). By its fifth anniversary, Gore's reinventing government program had attained an overall grade of B by authors of a Brookings Institution study (Carroll 1995; Kamensky 1996; Kettl 1998; Thompson and Ingraham 1996). This emphasis on governmental effectiveness was underscored by Congress' enactment of the Governmental Performance and Results Act of 1993 (P.L. 103-62), which required each federal agency to prepare strategic plans, identify major goals and objectives, establish performance targets and measure progress. An analysis of several IGM strategies that were intimately connected with the "performance movement" of the 1990s was provided by Radin (2000).

The Clinton administration sought to achieve its reinvention goals in a number of interesting inter-jurisdictional ways. One approach, which balanced recipient flexibility with grantor account-ability was the performance partnership. Under this arrangement, states could voluntarily enter agreements with regional offices of the Environmental Protection Agency (EPA) and shift funds across major EPA grant programs. States were held accountable for making progress towards EPA's national environmental goals.

A different example of the bottom-up approach to IGM during the 1990s was the Clinton administration's welfare reform initiative, which included numerous waivers granting states con-siderable discretion in advance of the 1996 legislation. President Clinton had promised "to end welfare as we know it." His signing of the Personal Responsibility Work Opportunity Reconcilia-tion Act of 1996 (P.L. 104-193) signaled bipartisan recognition that the time was opportune to turn over greater responsibility to the states and localities. The cornerstone of welfare reform, the Temporary Assistance to Needy Families (TANF) block grant, replaced the Aid to Families with Dependent Children program, which was established during the New Deal. Significantly, the National Governors Association played an influential role in designing and building political support for the welfare reform legislation, which gave governors considerable discretion in using funds to accomplish the purposes of the legislation.

This new flexibility included setting priorities, determining eligibility, integrating state programs, streamlining and re-engineering delivery systems, creating and experimenting with workfare programs, and engaging private and non-profit organizations in managing cases and delivering services. Although TANF was hailed by some observers as the frontlines of the "devolution revolution" (Nathan 1996) and a return toward a revenue-sharing model, the national government remained a powerful player. It retained a major financial role although contributions were capped at the 1996 level, a cause for great concern on the part of governors when welfare rolls began to grow during the recession starting in 2001. States were required to ensure compliance with minimum national standards and requirements, and to abide by program restrictions such as limiting aid to five years, requiring welfare recipients to find work within two years, curbing benefits for legal and illegal immigrants, and mandates to establish and pursue goals to reduce out-of-wedlock pregnancies and to provide education and training on statutory rape (Walker 2000, 163–164). As a result of this balancing of accountability with discretion, TANF could be viewed at best as a partial and contingent devolution instrument.

The implementation of TANF illustrated in multiple ways the significance of IGM, especially in the several states where second-order (state-to-local) devolution took place (Gainsborough 2003; Kelleher and Yackee 2002; Liebschutz 2000; Weissert 2000). Central to the core component of IGM was the manner in which national objectives incorporated in TANF traversed the multiple intergovernmental boundaries and actors. It gave IGM operational meaning at the local level (Cho et al. 2004). TANF as well as other policy initiatives in the 1990s (and later) prominently illustrated the bottom-up emphasis of IGM.

In Stever's (1992) review of the Gage and Mandell work he captured not only a major theme of that book but also the three-decade reversal thesis in understanding and using IGM. Stever (1992, 347) notes that, "These authors attempt to stimulate the metamorphosis of a new paradigm for intergovernmental management, one that does not depend on central coordination by the federal government." He extracts a further relevant assessment from the volume: "The policy arenas and intergovernmental networks the authors propose are consensually created from the bottom up in incremental fashion by actors in diverse institutional settings" (Stever 1992, 350). If Stever is correct, and we have no basis for doubting him, then IGM represents a further important "hidden dimension" of inter-jurisdictional and inter-organizational activity that is extensive, significant, and largely unrecognized (Muskie 1962). It is a current phenomenon that would fit Woodrow Wilson's (1887) historic phrase, "of systems within systems."

D. IGM: CLOSING OBSERVATIONS

Where does all this leave IGM? Quite simply, it leaves its future uncertain as to direction and significance. It suggests that IGM has yet to mature and that this discussion of IGM, in comparison to FED and IGR, is open ended.

This analysis of IGM has therefore been more exploratory and expository than empirical and explanatory. Few firm conclusions are forthcoming, but a few closing observations may serve as a useful summary. For brevity and focus they are listed below:

1. For three decades IGM has been the subject of controversy and metamorphosis. It has evolved, however, into a useful concept for practical, analytic, and theoretic purposes.
2. It is not surprising that IGM originated and emerged so prominently in the 1970s. The concept of management received endorsement and strong support from the highest office in the land—the presidency. Richard Nixon was one president who took the concept of management most seriously. Witness his initiative (among many) in changing the name of the old Bureau of the Budget to the Office of Management and Budget.
3. Public administration (and public administrators) cannot be separated from politics and policy processes. Neither can public administration be removed or isolated from the multidimensional features of FED, IGR, IGM. Marando and Florestano (1990, 309) "wondered if much of public administration is not now intergovernmental." The gist

of this essay is that nearly all of public administration is inseparable from varying blends and balances of IGM as well as FED and IGR.

4. Good decision making, constructive conflict resolution, and effective policy implementation hinge on a strategic balance between actor roles and institutional responsibilities. One way to understand institutional responsibilities (activities/duties) is through the conceptual framework of IGM. Actor roles can be usefully understood in the three-category scheme of elected generalists, administrative generalists, and program professionals. These three types of officials each occupy significant roles, respectively, in FED, IGR, and IGM (Wright 1990a; Wright and Cho 2000).

5. As IGM evolved it included a wider range of actors, or "rowers," in implementing programs extending beyond IGR to include private firms, non-profit organizations, and individual citizens. This *governance* framework continues to be relevant to the design and delivery of intergovernmental programs, even though the emphasis has shifted from top-down to bottom-up.

In spite of controversy, change, and evolution, IGM has persisted because management has become a pervasive and critical process in our society generally and in the public sector in particular. An expression of management's significance was somewhat surprisingly offered by an historian. Hays (1991) discussed three decades of environmental policy in a section titled, "The Politics of Environmental Management." His language provides an extended exclamation point to this essay's emphasis on the prominence and pervasiveness of management:

> As environmental politics evolved, its context shifted from broader public debate to management. Increasingly one spoke of air quality management, water quality management, forest management, range management, the Bureau of Land Management, Coastal Zone Management, risk management, river management, and wilderness management. Hardly an environmental problem could be dealt with outside the terminology and conceptual focus of management, and, in turn, management played a powerful role in shaping the world of environmental choice. The influence of management grew because of its power and its authority to coordinate discordant elements in the "system" on its own terms, and even more because it constituted the persistent institution of government, with ongoing day-to-day capabilities of communication and action. Institutional power was the stuff of political power; it arose from a continuous presence requiring that others reckon with it day in and day out; it set the bounds of choice if not the actual agenda. While the larger ideological debates in environmental affairs came and went, management shaped the world of day-to-day political affairs (Hays 1991, 49).

The M in IGM gives both symbolic and operational significance to management (and administration) in the larger arenas of politics, policy making, and governance in its broad sense. It expresses in a different manner what one intellectual leader of political science asserted several decades ago. "Bureaucracy," by which Friedrich meant management and administration, "is the core of modern government" (1950, 37). Consistent with the historical context of the above quote and the temporal orientation of this essay, Schechter (1981) posed the issues involving IGM in the following terms:

> The popular acceptance of intergovernmental management is not a historically discrete occurrence. The starting premise of this article is that "intergovernmental management" (as that term has developed since 1974) is best understood not as a president's pipe dream but as the completion of the twentieth century revolution in public administration first enunciated by Woodrow Wilson. For its adherents, "intergovernmental management" is more than merely compatible with federalism; it is both the natural extension and resuscitating element of the twin commitment to federalism and managerialism in a time of scarcity—both of resources and leadership.
> The basic difference between federalism and managerialism, and hence the tension between them, has to do with ends and limits. The end of federalism, in the American system at least, is liberty; the end of

managerialism is efficiency. In this sense, the challenge of public management consists largely in directing the "gospel of efficiency" to the constitutional ends of limited government (Schechter 1981, 127, 136).

We clearly cannot explore, much less revolve, the issues posed above within the context of this chapter. Perhaps a subsequent survey similar to this some years hence will reveal how experience with and analysis of FED, IGR, and IGM have been accommodated.

VIII. THE CONTEMPORARY SCENE: CONFLICTS AND CROSS-CURRENTS

The chronological motif guiding this chapter has produced a leveling or sameness among the numerous issues, events, developments, and shifts covered in this two-century review. It is neither feasible nor useful to recapitulate the temporal patterns woven into FED, IGR, and IGM. It is important, however, to note the undifferentiated status of the topics reviewed by this chronology. If we were to introduce some priority ordering in the maze of issues, problems, and developments sketched above, what underlying elements or dimensions would be among the most important and significant? We mention four dimensions that are explicit or implicit themes within the major sections. Three—constitutional (legal), political (politics), and fiscal (deficits and debt)— are addressed in Sections A and B below. The Fourth, administrative issues targeted towards contingent collaboration across multiple governmental boundaries, is considered in Section C.

A. BASIC DIMENSIONS

One dimension threading its way through the two-century pattern of governance involves *constitutional* questions and judicial interpretations. The constitutional foundations and the legal superstructure of governing constitute a fundamental framework for the functioning of the American political system. Some of the most difficult political questions are recast into legal form and are resolved by the courts in constitutional rulings. Often Supreme Court rulings in federalism cases are close calls. By 5–4 decisions the power balance between the nation and the states has shifted back and forth. Space prohibits an analysis of individual decisions and trends in judicial decision-making. However, scholars as well as state and local leaders generally agree that, with notable exceptions, the Court has usually reaffirmed national power and weakened the Tenth Amendment. According to Walker, the Court has continued to defer to Congress in interpreting the scope of the conditional spending power, the " … most centralizing provision of the United States Constitution" (Walker 2000, 211). State governments individually and collectively, however, have become quite sophisticated, skillful, and successful in pursuing cases in a strategic manner before the Supreme Court when they are parties to various judicial proceedings (Waltenburg and Swinford 1999; Pickering and Clayton 2004).

A second dimension could be labeled *political* in the broad sense of the term, but it takes on a more specific complexion as discussed here. The prime focus of the political dimension in this chapter has been the party system. The relationship between the party system and national–state power distribution remains problematic. Is there a causal link between party structure and decentralization? If there is such a link, in which direction(s) does the causal arrow run? Walker (2000) has provided one penetrating analysis of this issue. In a chapter titled, "A New Political System?," Walker reviews how changed political dynamics in the United States, such as the growing influence of political action committees, escalating costs of campaigns, and other nationalizing forces, have weakened parties and served as conduits for "Slouching Toward Washington."

A third dimension clusters around the dollar sign and is *fiscal* in character. Fiscal questions are clearly and closely related to political ones, but the twentieth century fostered a measure of independent or autonomous significance to intergovernmental financial problems and policies. Indeed, the "fiscalization" of the debate over Ronald Reagan's New Federalism in 1981–1982 could be taken as one indicator of the extent to which FED and IGR issues were drawn in dollar terms. In some quarters this fiscal focus is seen as either undesirable or unproductive, or both. Phraseology attacking this fiscalization tendency includes such terms as "fiscal fixation," "monetary myopia," and "federal aid junkies."

The continued prominence if not centrality of fiscal issues is attested to by several recent developments. One is the culmination during the 1990s of a dramatic shift in federal aid from places (governments) to persons (individual-based entitlements). Articles by Kincaid (1993a, 1993b) placed the shift in both historical and political perspective. The proportion of federal aid going to individual beneficiaries averaged 35% in the 1960s but averaged 61% in the 1990s, with a complimentary decline in aid channeled to places—cities, counties, etc. (Walker 2000, 4–5). Much of this shift was due to the rapid growth of Medicaid, a federal-state open-ended matching program providing health care coverage to low-income beneficiaries.

Another issue crystallized the condition under which finances spill over into the arena of "high politics" (Bulpitt 1983). An example was the proposed constitutional amendment to require a balanced federal budget. In the 1980s nearly two-thirds of the 50 state legislatures petitioned the Congress to call a constitutional convention for the purpose of proposing such an amendment. By the mid-1990s the politics of the issue had changed dramatically. The prospect that the Congress would place the balanced budget amendment before the states gave rise to political second thoughts among governors and state legislators.

The magnitude of federal budget reductions required by adopting the balanced budget amendment caused governors and state legislators to reassess its fiscal consequences for state government(s). Federal aid monies, for example, are among the so-called discretionary funds in the national budget that might experience the largest reductions mandated by a balanced budget requirement. Furthermore, not even the passage of 1995 mandate relief legislation by the Congress could ensure protection of the states (and localities) from a powerful congressional majority bent on imposing unfunded federal mandates in the face of federal budget constraints. In short, the Congress (Fiorina 1977), with the concurrence of the president and the Supreme Court, could pass the fiscal buck to the states with assured legal immunity and perhaps political impunity.

Similarly, state legislatures and governors could decide to "pass the fiscal" buck to localities, by reducing general assistance or school aid, for example, plus impose their own unfunded mandates on municipalities and counties. Local jurisdictions could do little to effectively oppose such actions. These prospective—and sometimes actual—steps by national and state decision-makers have been called "shift and shaft federalism" by local officials. It was explained as follows: "Nobody is innocent here. The feds stiff the states. The states stiff the cities and counties. Whenever one layer of government can push an unpleasant or costly responsibility down to the level below, it nearly always does so. The cities and counties would do it too, except they are on the bottom rung. They can't cut taxes and services and then pin the responsibility on the Salvation Army. Or at least they haven't thought of that yet" (Ehrenhalt 2003, 7). This phenomenon or process has also been identified as the "intergovernmental law of gravity—the buck drops down!" (Wright 1988).

By the late 1990s, pressure for a constitutional amendment was further reduced by the ability of President Clinton and Congress, thanks largely to revenues generated by the booming national economy, to balance the national budget and even generate a surplus. This breakthrough stimulated a different type of debate, one between those who wanted to return the surplus funds to citizens by cutting national (and related state) taxes and those who wanted to invest these monies in public programs.

A second example of the convergence of finance with politics was the Transportation Equity Act for the twenty-first century, TEA-21 (P.L. 105-178), which was passed by Congress in 1997. Building on its predecessor, the Intermodal Surface Transportation Efficiency Act of 1991 ISTEA (P.L. 102-240), the legislation provided substantial federal funds ($218 billion from a trust fund between 1998 and 2003) for a wide range of transportation and related infrastructure needs—from highways to mass transit to bike paths to train stations (Dilger 1992, 1998; Marbach and Lackrone 2002).

Accompanying the inter-modal approach was a strong national policy re-emphasis on regional collaboration through establishment of Metropolitan Planning Organizations to plan for and coordinate TEA-21-funded projects. This strategy had been significantly weakened by the Reagan administration. A large and diverse coalition was responsible for passing TEA-21, including state and local elected and transit officials, the highway lobby, regional planners, environmentalists, and historic site preservationists. The program has been judged a success in establishing a comprehensive approach to planning and funding transportation. Walker, for example, called it a "healthy sign" of balance between units at the center and periphery, emphasizing both IGR and IGM (Walker 2000). Yet when the legislation expired in September 2003, Congress failed to renew it. Special interest pressures, reflecting Sanford's "picket fence federalism" metaphor, sought to remove national funding from non-traditional transportation projects and return to reliance on separate highway, transit, and other wish lists of pork-barrel politics in awarding federal aid. Stopgap funding was provided under a continuing resolution, but in one observer's view advocates will be forced to " … fight the usual rear-guard action and be lucky if they hold their own" (Walters 2003, 14). On August 10, 2005 President Bush signed the new transportation bill P.L. 109-59, the "Safe, Accountable, Flexible, Efficient Transportation Equity Act: A Legacy for Users" (SAFETEA-LU). The $268 billion bill contained a record number of nearly 6,500 individual projects requested by Republican and Democratic members of Congress. These special "earmarks" totaled more than $24 billion.

As indicated above, it is possible to differentiate *fiscal* issues from purely *political* ones. But it is difficult if not impossible to isolate the two. This inseparability is one lesson emerging from the election of the Republican-controlled 104th Congress. The 1995 battle over the balanced budget amendment (which fell short by one vote in the US Senate) was only one of numerous issues in which politics and finances were inextricably intertwined. These linkages are likely to have immense consequences for FED, IGR, and IGM well into the twenty-first century, especially as huge annual deficits and a steadily climbing federal debt are projected for several years ahead.

B.   Toward Contingent Collaboration: Four Examples

Recent election results and presidential initiatives have sent mixed signals about the location and responsibility for actions affecting the US systems of inter-jurisdictional relations. The successes of Republican candidates for national and state executive and legislative offices since the mid-1990s have been noteworthy. Despite the party's philosophy supporting smaller, decentralized government, and the fact that four of the past five presidents have been governors, the current and future configurations of FED, IGR, and IGM are likely to be shaped far more in Washington, DC than in the state capitols, county courthouses, or city and town halls.

Space does not permit elaboration of our broader argument as well as of the politics–finances link. Four examples will suffice as illustrative of both themes, however.

1.   Mandates

The first involves P.L. 104-4, the Unfunded Mandates Reform Act of 1995 (UMRA). This legislation passed in March 1995 by votes of 91–9 in the Senate and 394–28 in the House. It was aimed at reducing the compulsory coercive costs borne by state and local governments as a consequence of national mandates contained in congressional statutes and administrative rules and regulations (Posner 1997, 1998). Prior to 1980 the ACIR had identified a total of 36 federal unfunded mandates; but the 1980s alone added 25 more to the statute books (ACIR 1993). The most galling aspect of these actions for state and local officials was the absence of compensatory money accompanying these mandates. In fact, if federal pass-through aid to individuals is excluded, the real federal value of federal aid (to places) declined by 33% between 1980 and 1990 (Conlan et al. 1995).

This fiscal squeeze made it understandable why state and local officials labeled unfunded mandates as fiscal terrorism, silent subversion, and the undeclared war. A small indication of the fiscal magnitude of unfunded mandates came from a 1990 EPA report. It estimated that federal pollution requirements cost local governments $19 billion from 1970 to 1987 with a projected cost increase to $32 billion in the year 2000 (Conlan et al. 1995). Unfunded mandates, of course, are only one form of coercive IGR. Another coercive mechanism is preemption (Conlan 1991; Zimmerman 1991). The use of these two (and other) coercive instruments reflected, in the 1990s, the "regulatory federalism" shift noted by Elazar in the 1980s (Elazar 1984, 252).

Mandate reform was a key plank in the Republican Party's Contract with America in the 1994 election campaign. A further (but imperfect) indicator of the priority attached to the unfunded mandate issue was the bill numbers of the mandate legislation, S. 1 and H.R. 5, in the 104th Congress. With strong support from the Big Seven Public Interest Groups, the unfunded mandate reform legislation became law and was hailed as a significant victory (Posner 1997, 1998). UMRA has been considered helpful in bringing to the attention of Congress the anticipated compliance costs of proposed legislation, and invoking a point of order procedural threat to halt action on mandates imposing $50 million or more of direct uncompensated annual costs on states and localities. This victory, however, was compromised by significant omissions from coverage under the act, such as exemptions of regulations dealing with Constitutional rights, anti-discrimination, grant conditions, national emergencies, and preemptions, as well as all pre-1995 mandates. Nor does the act deal with the cumulative financial impacts of mandates below the threshold on states and localities. A senior staff member of the General Accounting Office (renamed the Government Accountability Office) described UMRA as a "stop, look, and listen" approach to mandate restraint (Posner 1997, 53). A Congressional Budget Office study found that, over seven years since UMRA's passage, mandates in only 42 out of 4097 bills exceeded the threshold, or 1%, while the remainder was exempt from it (Kettl 2003, 12). According to a close observer, federal agencies are "... just not obeying the law ... so they're not making the estimates of how much it is going to cost states to comply" (Clewett 2003, 7).

2. No Child Left Behind

The second illustration is the No Child Left Behind Act of 2001 (NCLB), signed by President Bush on January 8, 2002 (P.L. 107-110). It greatly expanded the national role in public education, historically a predominantly local and state responsibility, and changed the emphasis toward accountability for results. The NCLB built on the 1994 Goals 2000: Educate America Act, signed by President Clinton, which codified national goals for elementary/secondary education and emphasized standards-based improvement for all children. More than just a reauthorization of the Elementary and Secondary Education Act of 1965 (ESEA), NCLB shifted the national government's role of targeting student groups (or areas of need) to drive general improvement of public education. Strategically, ESEA's distributive, stimulating, and supplementary approach to grants was replaced by a performance-based and penalty-laden system. The bills passed by 81–10 margins in the Senate and 381–41 in the House, with obvious strong bipartisan support.

In exchange for nearly a 25% increase in federal aid (more than $4.3 billion the first year), under NCLB, states must be more accountable for results and develop plans to ensure that no child will be left behind or, as one author put it: "No Child Left Untested," "No Teachers Left Teaching" (Wright 2003, 229). Nearly all children in grades 3 through 8 must be tested and assessed each year in reading and math. Other federal mandates require states to collect and disseminate results of tests, ensure that every classroom has a "highly qualified" teacher (as indicated by having a degree in their field and passing a state test), hold school leadership accountable for performance, establish standards and conduct assessments for science progress, and guarantee that all students achieve a "proficient" education level by the 2014–2015 school year through attaining annual benchmarks. A particularly controversial provision of the law is that schools where only one subgroup of students—such as special education students or students not proficient in English—fail to reach annual improvement targets and are labeled "needs improvement." This stigma is assigned even though all other categories of students attain "adequate yearly progress" (AYP) targets. Where a school's students are failing to make the AYP grade, states may arrange for students to transfer to a higher-achieving school, replace local school personnel, turn operations over to the state education agency, extend the school day or year, make curriculum changes, require tutoring, and reopen the school as a charter school (run by teachers independent from the local school system) or place it under private management.

Testing students has long been a fundamental component of K-12 education, but under NCLB the stakes have been raised enormously. Critics claim that a one-size-fits-all Texas model has been imposed over existing state testing systems. A National Education Association policy analyst (Pons) characterized the AYP: "It's the equivalent of saying every kid should be three feet six when they're in fourth grade" (Andrade 2004, 14).

Other criticisms, concerns, and complications abound. Samples include the following: teachers will be encouraged to teach to the test and emphasize math and science, instead of using a broad well-rounded curriculum; teachers will practice grade inflation and schools will lower standards and "game" AYP targets; schools will treat high- and low-performing students in the same manner; schools that are already performing at high levels will have difficulties showing substantial improvement; and parents will be unable to find suitable alternatives to under-performing schools.

Even with this infusion of new monies, federal funds will still account for only about 10% of total spending on elementary and secondary education. Yet governors and legislators have been reluctant to turn down funds despite the accompanying stringent—and not fully funded—testing and other mandates that generate an estimated additional $35 billion in new costs above the $29 billion annual congressional appropriation. Nevertheless, and somewhat surprisingly, an on-going study by the Education Commission of the States indicated that by March 2003 states were making "significant progress" and were generally "on track" implementing the spirit and requirements of NCLB (Decesare 2003, 14–15). However, in view of the growing national deficit, by 2004, state and local officials were increasingly skeptical of prospects for continued substantial increases in federal education spending under NCLB. A study by the National Conference of State Legislatures found appropriations for NCLB in 2004 to be $9.6 billion below the amounts authorized for mandated state actions (Stauffer and Tubbesing 2004, 22).

3.　Homeland Security

A third example of the contemporary scene is the Department of Homeland Security (DHS) legislation signed by President Bush on November 25, 2002 (P.L. 107-296). The new Cabinet level department represents the most extensive reorganization since creation of the Department of Defense in 1947, involving programs of some 22 federal agencies (Kettl 2004). The mission of DHS is to bolster national capacity in intelligence and warning, border and transportation security, domestic counter-terrorism, critical infrastructure protection, defense against catastrophic terrorism, and emergency preparedness and response. According to the Bush Administration's National Strategy for Homeland Security, state and local governments play primary responsibilities in "funding, preparing, and operating the emergency services that would respond in the event of a terrorist attack" (Krane 2002, 4). An Office of State and Local Coordination was created in the Office of the Secretary to link IGR roles and responsibilities.

In the post-September 11 environment both local and state government spending for security has expanded considerably on their own initiative as well as pursuant to federal mandates and incentives. In addition to making improvements and adding safeguards in transportation, communications, public health, and drinking water infrastructure systems to reduce vulnerabilities, under the USA Patriot Act of 2002 (P.L. 107-56) states and localities are required to collect and disseminate information on the status of immigrants, international students, and driving license applications.

Financial help from Washington, DC has been slow in arriving. Historically, the major sources of assistance to states and localities were the Federal Emergency Management Agency, the Public

Health Service, and the Justice Department's Office of Defense Preparedness (ODP). A new source is the Bush administration's First Responder State/Local Preparedness Grant, totaling about $3.5 billion annually. Funds are available for communications improvements, first response unit support, and training activities and other related purposes. States must prepare a plan, approved by ODP, with strategies for dealing with threats, vulnerabilities, and capabilities. The legislation mandated that states pass-through 75% of their allocation to local governments, with the remainder for use at the states' discretion on such activities as coordinating drivers license standards, terrorism insurance marketing, and money laundering suppression. States also received $1 billion for Public Health Grants for Bioterrorism Preparedness. In the fiscal year 2003–2004 budgets, grants accounted for about 10% of the total homeland security appropriation, far less than state and local leaders claim they need.

Although considerable attention has been given to the advantages of a centralized department, the homeland security system remains fragmented at the national level. For example, 23 federal grants available for first responders, amounting to $20–$22 billion, are administered by three different national agencies (National Academy of Public Administration 2004, 15). Overlap and duplication are apparent, such as in the existence of 16 training grants. Eligible recipients differ, definitions of "first responder" are inconsistent, funds are both targeted and untargeted, some programs are direct national–local and others are channeled through state agencies, and requirements such as matching and maintenance of effort vary from program-to-program (General Accounting Office 2002).

This fragmentation is superimposed over a historically decentralized system. For example, homeland (local) security in the Seattle, Washington area involves coordinating the efforts of 115 signatories to the regional disaster plan, including cities, fire districts, school districts, water and sewer districts, numerous hospitals, and the Port of Seattle (Stenberg 2004, 7). In his analysis of New York's response on September 11, Kettl noted the fundamental coordination challenge raised by Gulick in 1937: "It required the linkage of strong, functionally organized bureaucracies to solve a place-based problem" (Kettl 2004, 69).

At the sub-state regional level, the need for better IGR and IGM communications and coordination has provided a new and potentially valuable role for councils of governments. Yet the "coordination challenge" will severely test their capacity to achieve inter-jurisdictional collaboration. In the aftermath of September 11, there was confusion about who was or should be responsible for functions like airport and port security, protection of possible targets like nuclear power plants and local water systems, routine traffic stops, and bioterrorist attack prevention. There also was little consensus on who should pay for these additional measures. Information sharing about emergency preparedness, suspects, and potential threats was problematic, both among federal agencies and throughout the intergovernmental system. Trust and partnership were often lacking between states and localities, between sub-national and national agencies, and among federal agencies (Wise and Nader 2002). In GAO's judgment, "the federal government will need to effectively respond to significant management and coordination challenges if it is to provide ... leadership and be successful in preventing and responding to any future acts of terrorism" (General Accounting Office 2002, 1). A panel of the National Academy of Public Administration observed: "Fitting this intergovernmental system together coherently will not be easy" (National Academy of Public Administration 2004, 9).

4. Internet Taxation

The fourth example involves the broad domain and overlapping conditions where state taxes impinge on interstate commerce. The Internet Tax Freedom Act, which Congress passed in 1999 (P.L. 105-277), placed a temporary (three-year) moratorium on new state and local telecommunications taxes and prohibition on applying existing utility or gross receipts taxes to access to the Internet, such as franchise and subscription fees for high speed lines or cable-modem service. The ban expired in November 2003. Collection of taxes on mail order sales from remote sellers not having a physical presence in a state was a related aspect of this issue that reached the US Supreme Court in 1967 and 1992 (*National Bellas Hess, Inc. v Department of Revenue* and *Quill v North Dakota*) and had remained a problem since, with taxes rarely being collected. While Congress did not prohibit sales taxes on Internet purchases, collection was impeded by a national requirement that both the buyer and seller must have a physical presence in the state where the buyer resides (Powell 2000).

The Big seven public interest groups, together with organizations representing state and local tax officials, vigorously opposed the 1999 preemption and later legislation. They claimed that not taxing Internet transactions gave an unfair advantage over traditional retail business enterprises operating within a state. The tax avoidance/evasion deprived state and local governments of significant sales tax revenues. One study estimated total state and local government yearly revenue losses from e-commerce on all sales over the Internet to be $15.5 billion in FY 2003, growing to between $21.5 billion and $33.7 billion by 2008 (Bruce and Fox 2004). The losses represent from 2.6 to 9.9% of total state tax collections over this time period.

In April 2003, the temporary moratorium was extended for two years to give state and local leaders an opportunity to address issues associated with telecommunications taxation. One of the key concerns of Congress was the confusing array of 7500 jurisdictions levying state and local sales and use taxes dating from the 1930s. The National Governors Association and others argued that a uniform state sales tax on Internet transactions would be equitable for all parties and eliminate the need for continuation of the moratorium. By the end of 2003, over thirty states had signed the Streamlined Sales and Use Tax Agreement. This provided for model legislation to modernize, simplify, and unify state and local tax code language, administrative systems, and audit processes across the country. The result would be greatly reduced compliance and collection burdens on remote sellers. The collaborative project that gave rise to the agreement was an example of how interstate cooperation, prodded by a looming national prohibition or preemption, can successfully address national issues without the intervention of Congress. Nevertheless, in 2004 Congress passed the Internet Tax Nondiscrimination Act (P.L. 108-435) extending the prohibition on taxing Internet access to November 1, 2007.

In summary, these four programs illustrate the mixed signals being sent from Washington, DC to state and local officials at the turn of the century. On the positive side, President Bush sought to give states more discretion and flexibility by proposing the consolidation of a number of categorical programs into block grants, including Medicaid, low-income housing, Head Start, and child welfare. In 2003, the Bush administration and Congress provided $20 billion in unrestricted federal aid to help compensate states for lost revenues attributed to federal tax cuts. By 2004, total federal aid had reached nearly $400 billion, a record level in terms of overall magnitude, percentage of gross domestic product (3.6%), and percentage of federal spending (18%). In addition, the Supreme Court under Chief Justice William Rehnquist had taken a pro-state persona in decisions in federalism cases (often by a 5–4 majority) that restrained federal authority in prohibiting Indian tribes suing states in federal court to force negotiations over casino gambling on reservations and state personnel suing their employer alleging age discrimination. The Court also took a narrow view of the interstate commerce and the necessary and proper powers. It reasserted Tenth Amendment significance in striking down congressional laws banning sodomy, those requiring local gun-free school zones, state disposal of low-level radioactive waste within their borders, and local law enforcement agencies conducting background checks on handgun purchasers (Kincaid 2001 Pickering and Clayton 2004).

The Supreme Court's decisions reflect the pro-state philosophies of its Republican appointees, as well as the growing proficiency of state attorneys general as litigators before the Court and their increasing willingness to file amicus curiae briefs in behalf of state interests. As one analyst of federalism case litigation concluded: "As a group, the states are more capable Supreme Court litigators, and they win more often." Hence, their participation in cases before the Court "... is a function not only of necessity, but also a strategic calculation that state concerns will receive a positive response within this policy arena combined with an increased ability to take advantage of this arrangement" (Waltenburg and Swinford 1999, 55, 58).

States also acted on their own by confronting or outflanking national authorities where they believed national officials were acting too slowly or contrary to state interests (Provost 2003). Led State attorneys general have been particularly active by forcing major tobacco companies to agree to make $250 billion in compensatory payments for the costs of treating tobacco-related illnesses under state Medicaid programs. They also led opposition to high-cost prescription drugs. States have challenged efforts by the Bush administration to weaken air quality regulations, criticized the Environmental Protection Agency (EPA) for moving slowly in regulating, interstate emissions from coal-fired power plants, and sued EPA for failing to regulate emissions of carbon dioxide. Stung by state retirement system losses in the Enron scandal, the attorneys general led an investigation of fraudulent practices in the securities industry when national officials hesitated to move against dubious and/or illegal Wall Street practices.

Offsetting these positive fiscal, judicial, and legal developments, the widening federal deficit raised fears that grants-in-aid, the most discretionary sector of the federal budget, would be targeted for reduction to help pay defense and homeland security costs and cover entitlement program expenditures. While the block grant proposals would bring welcome discretion, they would be accompanied by caps on or cuts in federal aid. The NGA's executive director (Scheppach) summarized the aid/discretion issue: "Historically, the way they have cut is to offer more flexibility in exchange for less money" (Greenblatt 2004, 86; Posner and Wrightson 1996). Despite UMRA, unfunded and partially funded mandates accompanied each of the Bush block grant programs. Perhaps most disconcerting was the president's proposal in the 2005 budget to eliminate or curtail 128 grant programs. These were identified in an OMB assessment as not demonstrating positive results or being duplicative.

These mixed signals reflect what one of the authors has described as the "coercive-collage" phase of IGR evolution. The coercive features are evident in continued federal preemptions, mandates, grant conditions, and the "consolidate, cap, and cut" strategy of the Bush administration. The collage features are apparent in the complex and confusing dynamics of centralization–decentralization, flexibility–accountability, diversity–uniformity, and vertical–horizontal coordination shown in the above examples.

Reconciling these points of tension could lead to a new phase of IGR, contingent collaboration, emphasizing the need for officials at all levels to be more anticipatory and adaptive in responding to uncertain and unpredictable events. To do so will call for new networks and partnerships spanning across governmental and sectored boundaries and require facilitative rather than command-control leadership styles. The challenges of contingent collaboration place a premium on a willingness to work outside of bureaucratic frameworks and engage citizens, non-governmental organizations, and the private sector in meeting a wide range of governance issues (Wright 2003). In his examination of homeland security, Kettl provides an excellent example of these challenges: " … coordination is a *contingent* problem, and what works best depends on the problem to be solved. What it is, how it works, and how best to create the solution depends on the nature of the issue, the nature of the organization, and the nature of its employees. Structures rarely adapt easily enough and quickly enough to meet the challenges that hard problems present. So the very strategies deployed to improve coordination often become the targets for critics when problems occur—and so the bureaucrats and managers seek to reorganize yet again" (Kettl 2004, 68).

C. The Administrative Dimension

We have devoted considerable space in this concluding section to political and fiscal themes and their interrelationship(s) insofar as they impact on FED, IGR, and IGM. It is not inaccurate or inappropriate to emphasize these foundation factors, together with constitutional–legal features, as central variables in shaping the dynamics of our multi-jurisdictional systems of governance. To these three elements, which have been extensively noted and elaborated in this essay, we add a fourth and final element. This is the *administrative* (managerial and bureaucratic) dimension woven into the fabric of this analysis.

The twentieth century recorded and confirmed in the United States the rise, prominence, and even selective dominance of the "administrative state" (Mosher 1968; Redford 1969; Skowronek 1982; Waldo 1948). There is, of course, no small amount of controversy associated with the constitutional base, legitimacy, and representativeness of that administrative state (Krislov and Rosenbloom 1981; Rohr 1986; Stillman 1991).

The issues associated with the development and status of the administrative state need not and cannot be addressed here. What is noteworthy, however, are the various features of the American administrative state that became more evident as the concepts of IGR and IGM originated, emerged, and matured. Indeed, IGR and IGM have served as concepts that have enabled scholars and practitioners alike to identify and analyze events and actor interactions more systematically. Three distinctive features have emerged from the application of these concepts and analyses.

The first feature associated with American administration is its fragmentation among thousands of governmental jurisdictions. This dispersion and diversity is a given when effective administrative action is expected (Jennings and Krane 1994; Jennings and Zank 1993). This allocation of authority and responsibility among different governmental entities is sometimes called *horizontal fragmentation*.

One label for the second feature of American administration is *functionalism*. This refers to the high degree of specialization and professionalism that has evolved in the course of creating, expanding, and delivering public services in the United States. This functionalism, of course, is a form of fragmentation. But it is programmatic or professionally based in contrast to the jurisdictionally based fragmentation noted above (Choi, Cho, and Wright 2004). This functional fragmentation was noted and challenged in the 1950s and received classic articulation in the 1960s as "picket-fence federalism" (Sanford 1967). This vertical functional focus and the multiple strategies to cope with it that gave rise in the 1970s to the concept of IGM.

The third and final administrative feature to emerge and wend its way through this essay is a reformist one, namely, the need to create a better bridge and balance between jurisdictional (horizontal) fragmentation and functional (vertical) fragmentation. There is a fundamental tension between the two (Fesler 1949, 1973). The former emphasizes separation of responsibilities and accountability by unit, level, or plane of government. The latter tends toward the fusion or condensation of tasks into a singular functional, often hierarchical, framework. The task of the public administrator specifically, and public officials in general, is to resolve these tensions in a responsive and responsible way.

These features are especially significant when considered in the context of *globalization*. This single word stands for a constellation of international and trans-governmental forces that have altered the cultural, demographic, economic, social, and political character of countries and communities (Jun and Wright 1996). The blurring of jurisdictional boundary lines has challenged us to think in terms of global–regional–neighborhood instead of national–state–local relationships (Peirce et al. 1993). Terms such as "intermestic," "perforated sovereignties, "six-pack surprise," and "globalizing the local community" have appeared as ways to express the penetration of international influences at the sub-national and micro-community levels (Brown and Fry 1993; Hobbs 1994). One possible consequence of these developments is that cultural, economic, and other issues will overwhelm management problems and processes as objects worthy of primary attention on the public agenda.

The resolution of such tensions and challenges hinges on the capacity and ability to use power(s) in constructive ways. We have already noted that Friedrich (1950) called bureaucracy "the core of modern government." How constitutional, political, and fiscal powers relate to this "core" is likely to shape the character of American public administration well into the twenty-first century. Only a retrospective view on FED, IGR, and IGM some years hence will provide a clearer picture of how the features of the administrative landscape fit into the hills, valleys, and plateaus of constitutional, political, and fiscal terrains.

REFERENCES

Abrams, A. J., Making public administration relevant, *Public Administration Review*, 29, 378–379, 1969.

Ader, E. B., State budgetary controls of federal grants-in-aid, *Public Administration Review*, 10, 87–92, 1950.

Advisory Commission on Intergovernmental Relations, *Performance of Urban Functions: Local and Area-wide*, US Government Printing Office, Washington, DC, 1963.

Advisory Commission on Intergovernmental Relations, *Metropolitan Councils of Governments*, US Government Printing Office, Washington, DC, 1966.

Advisory Commission on Intergovernmental Relations, *Fiscal Balance in the American Federal System*, US Government Printing Office, Washington, DC, 1967.

Advisory Commission on Intergovernmental Relations, *Federalism and the Academic Community: A Brief Survey*, US Government Printing Office, Washington, DC, 1969.

Advisory Commission on Intergovernmental Relations, *Multistate Regionalism*, US Government Printing Office, Washington, DC, 1972.

Advisory Commission on Intergovernmental Relations, *Substate Regionalism and the Federal System*, Vols. 1–6, US Government Printing Office, Washington, DC, 1973.

Advisory Commission on Intergovernmental Relations, *Federal Grants: Their Effects on State-Local Expenditures, Employment Levels, and Wage Rates*, US Government Printing Office, Washington, DC, 1977a.

Advisory Commission on Intergovernmental Relations, *Improving Federal Grants Management*, US Government Printing Office, Washington, DC, 1977b.

Advisory Commission on Intergovernmental Relations, *The Intergovernmental Grant System as Seen by Local, State, and Federal Officials*, US Government Printing Office, Washington, DC, 1977c.

Advisory Commission on Intergovernmental Relations, *Regionalism Revisited: Recent Areawide and Local Responses*, US Government Printing Office, Washington, DC, 1977d.

Advisory Commission on Intergovernmental Relations, *Categorical Grants: Their Role and Design*, US Government Printing Office, Washington, DC, 1978a.

Advisory Commission on Intergovernmental Relations, *Brief—The Intergovernmental Grant System: An Assessment and Proposed Policies*, US Government Printing Office, Washington, DC, 1978b.

Advisory Commission on Intergovernmental Relations, *Awakening the Slumbering Giant: Intergovernmental Relations and Federal Grant Law*, US Government Printing Office, Washington, DC, 1980a.

Advisory Commission on Intergovernmental Relations, *The Condition of Contemporary Federalism: Conflicting Theories and Collapsing Constraints*, US Government Printing Office, Washington, DC, 1980b.

Advisory Commission on Intergovernmental Relations, *A Crisis of Confidence and Competence*, US Government Printing Office, Washington, DC, 1980c.

Advisory Commission on Intergovernmental Relations, *Brief—The Federal Role in the Federal System: The Dynamics of Growth*, US Government Printing Office, Washington, DC, 1980d.

Advisory Commission on Intergovernmental Relations, *An Agenda for American Federalism: Restoring Confidence and Competence*, US Government Printing Office, Washington, DC, 1980e.

Advisory Commission on Intergovernmental Relations, *Brief—State and Local Roles in the Federal System*, US Government Printing Office, Washington, DC, 1981.

Advisory Commission on Intergovernmental Relations, *State and Local Roles in the Federal System*, US Government Printing Office, Washington, DC, 1982.

Advisory Commission on Intergovernmental Relations, *Brief—Regulatory Federalism: Policy, Process, Impact, and Reform*, US Government Printing Office, Washington, DC, 1984a.

Advisory Commission on Intergovernmental Relations, *Regulatory Federalism: Policy, Process, Impact, and Reform*, US Government Printing Office, Washington, DC, 1984b.

Advisory Commission on Intergovernmental Relations, *The Transformation in American Politics: Implications for Federalism*, US Government Printing Office, Washington, DC, 1986.

Advisory Commission on Intergovernmental Relations, *Federal Regulation of State and Local Governments: The Mixed Record of the 1980s*, US Government Printing Office, Washington, DC, 1993.

Advisory Committee on Local Government, *An Advisory Committee Report on Local Government. Submitted to the Commission on Intergovernmental Relations*, US Government Printing Office, Washington, DC, 1955.

Agranoff, R., *Intergovernmental Management: Human Services Problem Solving in Six Metropolitan Areas*, State University of New York, Albany, NY, 1986.

Agranoff, R., Managing intergovernmental processes, In *Handbook of Public Administration*, Perry, J. L., Ed., Jossey-Bass, San Francisco, CA, pp. 131–147, 1989.

Agranoff, R., Managing federalism through metropolitan human services intergovernmental bodies, *Publius*, 20, 1–22, 1990.

Agranoff, R., Managing within the matrix: do collaborative intergovernmental relations exist?, *Publius*, 31, 31–56, 2001.

Agranoff, R. and Lindsay, V. A., Intergovernmental management: perspectives from human services problem solving at the local level, *Public Administration Review*, 43, 227–237, 1983.

Agranoff, R. and McGuire, M., American federalism and the search for models of management, *Public Administration Review*, 61, 671–681, 2001.

Agranoff, R. and McGuire, M., *Collaborative Public Management*, Georgetown University Press, Washington, DC, 2003.

American Assembly, *Report on the Mid-America Assembly, Time Grows Short for America: The Role of the States in the Urban Crisis*, School of Law. St. Louis University, St. Louis, MO, 1970.

Anderson, T. J., Pressure groups and intergovernmental relations, *Annals*, 359, 116–126, 1965.

Anderson, W., *Federalism and Intergovernmental Relations: A budget of Suggestions for Research*, Public Administration Service, Chicago, IL, 1946.

Anderson, W., *The Nation and the States: Rivals or Partners?*, University of Minnesota Press, Minneapolis, MN, 1955.

Anderson, W., *Intergovernmental Fiscal Relations*, University of Minnesota Press, Minneapolis, MN, 1956.

Anderson, W., *Intergovernmental Relations in Review*, University of Minnesota Press, Minneapolis, MN, 1960.

Anderson, W., The myths of tax sharing, *Public Administration Review*, 28, 10–14, 1968.

Anderson, W. Personal letter to the author, May 20, 1970.

Andrade, J. C., Statewide student tests, *State Legislatures*, 30(February), 32–35, 2004.

Annals, Intergovernmental relations in the United States, 207, 1940.

Annals, Intergovernmental relations in the United States, 359 1996.

Annals, Intergovernmental relations in America today, American Academy of Political and Social Science, Philadelphia, PA, 416, 1974.

Annals, General revenue sharing and federalism, American Academy of Political and Social Science, Philadelphia, PA, 419, 1975.

Annals, American Federalism, The Third Century, 509, 1990.

Anton, T. J., Intergovernmental change in the United States: an assessment of the literature, In *Public Sector Performance: A Conceptual Turning Point*, Miller, T. C., Ed., Johns Hopkins University Press, Baltimore, MD, pp. 15–64, 1984.

Anton, T. J., *American Federalism and Public Policy: How the System Works*, Random House, New York, 1989.

Anton, T. J., Cawley, J., and Kramer, K., *Moving Money: An Empirical Analysis of Federal Expenditure Patterns*, Oelgeschlager, Gunn & Ham, Cambridge, MA, 1980.

Appleby, P. H., *Policy and Administration*, University of Alabama Press, Tuscaloosa, AL, 1949.

Arnold, D. S. and Plant, J. F., *Public Official Associations and State and Local Government: A Bridge Across One Hundred Years*, George Mason University Press, Fairfax, VA, 1994.

Bailyn, B., *The Ideological Origins of the American Revolution*, Harvard University Press, Cambridge, MA, 1967.

Ball, T., Ed., *The Federalist, with Letters of "Brutus,"* Cambridge University Press, New York, 2003.

Bane, F., Cooperative government in wartime, *Public Administration Review*, 2, 95–103, 1942.

Barfield, C. E., *Rethinking Federalism: Block Grants and Federal, State, Local Responsibilities*, American Enterprise Institute, Washington, DC, 1981.

Beam, D. R., New federalism, old realities: the reagan administration and intergovernmental reform, In *The Reagan Presidency and the Governing of America*, Salamon, L. M. and Lund, M. S., Eds., Urban Institute Press, Washington, DC, pp. 415–442, 1984.

Beam, D. R. and Conlan, T., Grants, In *The Tools of Government: A Guide to the New Governance*, Salamon, L. M., Ed., Oxford University Press, New York, 2002.

Beard, C. A., *An Economic Interpretation of the Constitution of the United States*, Macmillan, New York, 1913.

Beard, C. A., *The Economic Basis of Politics*, Knopf, New York, 1945.

Beer, S. H., The adoption of general revenue sharing: a case study in public sector politics, *Public Policy*, 24, 127–195, 1976.

Beer, S. H., Political overload and federalism, *Polity*, 10, 5–17, 1977.

Beer, S. H., Federalism, nationalism, and democracy in America, *American Political Science Review*, 72, 9–21, 1978a.

Beer, S. H., In search of a new public philosophy, In *The New American Political System*, King, A., Ed., American Enterprise Institute, Washington, DC, pp. 5–44, 1978b.

Beer, S. H., The idea of the nation, *New Republic*, 187, 23–29, 1982.

Beer, S. H., *To Make a Nation: The Rediscovery of American Federalism*, Harvard University Press, Cambridge, MA, 1993.

Beer, S. H., Welfare reform: revolution or retrenchment?, *Publius*, 28, 9–16, 1998.

Beer, S. H. and Barringer, R. E., Eds., *The Sate and the Poor*, Winthrop, Cambridge, MA, 1970.

Benson, G. C. S., *The New Centralization: A Study of Intergovernmental Relationships in the United States*, Rinehart, New York, 1941.

Benson, L., *Turner and Beard: American Historical Writing Reconsidered*, Free Press, Glencoe, IL, 1960.

Berman, D. R., *State and Local Politics*, 8th ed., M.E. Sharpe, Armonk, NY, 1997.

Berman, D. R., *Local Government and the States: Autonomy, Politics, and Policy*, M.E. Sharpe, Armonk, NY, 2003.

Bollens, J. C., *The States and the Metropolitan Problem*, Council of State Governments, Lexington, KY, 1956.

Bollens, J. C., *Special District Governments in the United States*, University of California Press, Berkeley, CA, 1957.

Bollens, J. C., *Exploring the Metropolis*, University of California Press, Berkeley, CA, 1961.

Bowman, A., Horizontal federalism: Exploring interstate interactions, *Journal of Public Administration Research and Theory*, 14, 535–546, 2004.

Bowman, A. and Kearney, R. C., *The Resurgence of the States*, Prentice Hall, Englewood Cliffs, NJ, 1986.

Bromage, A. W., Federal-state-local relations, *American Political Science Review*, 37, 35–47, 1943.

Brooks, G., *When Governors Convene: The Governors' Conference in National Politics*, Johns Hopkins University Press, Baltimore, MD, 1961.

Brown, D. M. and Fry, E. H., Eds., *States and Provinces in the International Economy*, Institute of Governmental Studies Press, Berkeley, CA, 1993.

Brown, G. D., The courts and grant reform: a time for action, *Intergovernmental Perspectives*, 7, 6–14, 1981.

Brown, G. D., Federal funds and federal courts—community development litigation as a testing ground for the new law of standing, *Boston College Law Rev*, 21, 525–556, 1980.

Brown, G. D., Federalism from the "Grant Law" perspective, *Urban Lawyer*, 15, ix–xxi, 1983.

Brown, R. E., *Charles Beard and the American Constitution: A Critical Analysis of "An Economic Interpretation of the Constitution"*, Princeton University Press, Princeton, NJ, 1956.

Browning, R., Marshall, D., and Tabb, D., *Protest is Not Enough: The Struggle of Blacks and Hispanics for Equality in Urban Politics*, University of California Press, Berkeley, CA, 1983.

Bruce, D., and Fox, W. F. *State and Local Sales Tax Revenue Losses from E-Commerce: Updated Estimates*, Center for Business and Economic Research, University of Tennessee, Knoxville, TN, 2004.

Brudney, J. L., Hebert, F. T., and Wright, D. S., Reinventing government in the American states: measuring and explaining administrative reform, *Public Administration Review*, 59, 19–30, 1999.

Buchanan, W., Politics and federalism: party or anti-party?, *Annals*, 359, 107–115, 1965.

Bulpitt, J., *Territory and Power in the United Kingdom: An Interpretation*, Manchester University Press, Manchester, UK, 1983.

Burke, B. F. and Wright, D. S., Reassessing and reconciling reinvention in the American states: exploring state administrative performance, *State and Local Government Review*, 34, 7–19, 2002.

Burnham, W. D., *Critical Elections: And the Mainsprings of American Politics*, W.W. Norton, New York, 1970.

Caldwell, L. K., *The Administrative Theories of Hamilton and Jefferson*, University of Chicago Press, Chicago, IL, 1944.

Campbell, A. K., Ed., *The States and the Urban Crisis*, Prentice Hall, Englewood Cliffs, NJ, 1970.

Campbell, J. M., Are the states here to stay?, *Public Administration Review*, 28, 26–29, 1968.

Caputo, D. A., Ed., General revenue sharing and federalism, *Annals*, 419, ix, 1–142.

Caputo, D. A. and Cole, R. L., *Urban Politics and Decentralization: The Case of General Revenue Sharing*, Lexington Books, Lexington, MA, 1974.

Caputo, D. A. and Cole, R. L., Eds., *Revenue Sharing: Methodological Approaches and Problems*, Lexington Books, Lexington, MA, 1976.

Carey, G. W. and McClellan, J., Eds., *The Federalist: The Gideon Edition*, Liberty Fund, Indianapolis, IN, 2001.

Carroll, J. D., The new juridical federalism and alienation of public policy and administration, *American Review Public Administration*, 16, 89–105, 1982.

Carroll, J. D., The rhetoric of reform and political reality in the national performance review, *Public Administration Review*, 55, 302–310, 1995.

Carroll, J. D. and Campbell, R. W., Eds., *Intergovernmental Administration: 1976 Eleven Academic and Practitioner Perspectives*, Syracuse University, Maxwell School of Citizenship and Public Affairs, Syracuse, NY, 1976.

Cho, C. L., Kelleher, C. A., Wright, D. S., and Yackee, S. W., Translating national policy objectives into local achievements across planes of governance and among multiple actors, *Journal of Public Administration Research and Theory*, 15, 31–54, 2005.

Cho, C. L. and Wright, D. S., Managing carrots and sticks: changes in state administrators perceptions of cooperative and coercive federalism during the 1990s, *Publius*, 31, 57–80, 2001.

Choi, Y. S., Cho, C. L., and Wright, D. S., Administrative autonomy among american state agencies: an empirical analysis of fragmentation and functionalism, *International Journal of Public Administration*, 27, 373–398, 2004.

Choi., Y. S. and Wright, D. S., Contracting out as administrative reform; conceptualizing components and measuring dimensions of contracting as a feature in the global transformation of governance, *The Korea Local Administration Review*, 6 (June), 199–232, 2004.

Choi, Y. S. and D. S., Wright, Dimensions of contracting for service delivery by American State Administrative Agencies: Exploring relationships between intergovernmental relations and intersectoral administration, *Public Performance and Management Review*, 29, 46–66, (September), 2005.

Chubb, J. E., Excessive regulation: the case of federal aid to education, *Political Science Quarterly*, 100, 287–311, 1985a.

Chubb, J. E., Federalism and the bias for centralization, In *The New Direction in American Politics*, Chubb, J. E. and Peterson, P. E., Eds., Brookings Institution, Washington, DC, pp. 273–306, 1985b.

Chubb, J. E., The political economy of federalism, *American Political Science Review*, 79, 994–1015, 1985c.

Chubb, J. E. and Peterson, E., Eds., *The New Direction in American Politics*, Brookings Institution, Washington, DC, 1985.

Clark, J. P., *The Rise of a New Federalism: Federal-State Co-operation in the United States*, Columbia University Press, New York, 1938.

Clark, T. and Ferguson, L., *City Money: Political Processes. Fiscal Strain, and Retrenchment*, Columbia University Press, New York, 1983.

Clayton, R., Conklin, P., and Shapek R. Eds., Policy management assistance—a developing dialogue, *Public Administration Review*, 35, 693–818, 1975.

Cleaveland, F., Ed., *Congress and Urban Problems*, Brookings Institution, Washington, DC, 1969.

Clewett, L., Federalism in flux, *State Government News*, 46, 6–8, October, 2003.

Colbert, C. M. An Empirical Analysis of Politics-in-Administration: State Agency and State Agency Head Participation in the Policy Process. PhD dissertation, University of North Carolina, Chapel Hill, NC, 1983.

Cole, R. L., Stenberg, C. W., and Weissert, C. S., Two decades of change: a ranking of key issues affecting intergovernmental relations, *Publius*, 13, 113–122, 1983.

Cole, R. L., Stenberg, C. W., and Weissert, C. S., Reversing directions: a ranking and comparison of key intergovernmental events, 1960–1980 and 1980–1995, *Publius*, 26, 25–40, 1996.

Commission on Intergovernmental Relations, *Report to the President for Transmittal to the Congress*, Government Printing Office, Washington, DC, 1955.

Conlan, T. J., Federalism and competing values in the Reagan administration, *Publius*, 16, 29–48, 1987.

Conlan, T. J., *New Federalism: Intergovernmental Reform from Nixon to Reagan*, Brookings Institution, Washington, DC, 1988.

Conlan, T. J., Intergovernmental mandates and preemption in an era of deregulation, *Publius*, 21, 43–58, 1991.

Conlan, T. J., *From New Federalism to Devolution: Twenty-five Years of Intergovernmental Reform*, Brookings Institution, Washington, DC, 1998.

Conlan, T. J., Riggle, J. D., and Schwartz, D. E., Deregulating federalism? The politics of mandate reform in the 104th Congress, *Publius*, 25, 23–40, 1995.

Connery, R. H. and Leach, L. H., *The Federal Government and Metropolitan Areas*, Harvard University Press, Cambridge, MA, 1960.

Constitution of the United States of America: Analysis and Interpretation. Congressional Research Service, Library of Congress, S. Doc. 92–82. 92nd Cong, 2nd sess, US Government Printing Office, Washington, DC, 1973.

Cornell, S., *The Other Founders*, University of North Carolina Press, Chapel Hill, NC, 1999.

Corwin, E. S., *Court Over Constitution*, Princeton University Press, Princeton, NJ, 1938.

Corwin, E. S., The passing of dual federalism, *Virginia Law Rev*, 36, 1–23, 1950.

Corwin, E. S., *The President — Office and Powers, 1787–1957: History and Analysis of Practice and Opinion*, New York University Press, New York, 1957.

Council of State Governments, *Federal Grants-in-aid: Report of the Committee on Federal-Grants-in-aid*, Council of State Governments, Chicago, IL, 1949.

Couturier, J. J. and Dunn, S. E., Federal colonization of state and local government, *State Government*, 50, 65–71, 1977.

Crook, S. K., The pacific coast board of inter-governmental relations, *Public Administration Review*, 11, 103–108, 1951.

Culver, D. C., A bibliography of intergovernmental relations in the United States, *Annals*, 207, 210–218, 1940.

Dahl, R. A., *A Preface to Democratic Theory*, University of Chicago Press, Chicago, IL, 1956.

Davis, S. R., *The Federal Principle: A Journey Through Time in Quest of Meaning*, University of California Press, Berkeley, CA, 1978.

Decesare, D., NCLB report card, *State Government News*, 46, 14–15, April, 2003.

Derthick, M., *The Influence of Federal Grants: Public Assistance in Massachusetts*, Harvard University Press, Cambridge, MA, 1970.

Derthick, M., *Between State and Nation: Regional Organizations of the United States*, Brookings Institution, Washington, DC, 1974.

Derthick, M., *Uncontrollable Spending for Social Services Grants*, Brookings Institution, Washington, DC, 1975.

Derthick, M., American federalism: Madison's middle ground in the 1980s, *Public Administration Review*, 47, 66–74, 1987.

Diamond, M., What the framers meant by federalism, In *A Nation of States: Essays on the American Federal System*, Goldwin, R. A., Ed., Rand McNally, Chicago, IL, pp. 24–41, 1961.

Diamond, M., The federalist's view of federalism, In *Essays in Federalism*, Benson, G. C. S., Ed., Institute for Studies in Federalism, Claremont College, Claremont, CA, 1961.

Diamond, M., On the relationship of federalism and decentralization, In *Cooperation and Conflict: Readings in American Federalism*, Elazar, D. J., Ed., Peacock, Itasca, IL, pp. 72–81, 1969.

Diamond, M., *Notes on the Political Theory of the Founding Fathers*, Center for the Study of Federalism, Temple University, Philadelphia, PA, 1971.

Diamond, M., The American idea of equality: a view from the founding, *Rev Politics*, 38, 313–331, 1976a.

Diamond, M., The forgotten doctrine of enumerated powers, *Publius*, 6, 187–193, 1976b.

Dilger, R. J., Ed., *American Intergovernmental Relations Today: Perspectives and Controversies*, Prentice Hall, Englewood Cliffs, NJ, 1986.

Dilger, R. J., ISTEA: a new direction for transportation policy, *Publius*, 22, 67–78, 1992.

Dilger, R. J., TEA-21: transportation policy, pork barrel politics, and American federalism, *Publius*, 28, 49–70, 1998.

Dodge, W., *Regional Excellence: Governing Together to Compete Globally and Flourish Locally*, National League of Cities, Washington, DC, 1996.

Dommel, P. R., *The Politics of Revenue Sharing*, Indiana University Press, Bloomington, IN, 1974.

Dommel, P. R., Social targeting in community development, *Political Science Quarterly*, 95, 465–481, 1980.

Dommel, P. R., Nathan, R. P., Liebschutz, S. F., and Wringhtson, M. T., *Decentralizing Community Development*, Department of Housing and Urban Development, Washington, DC, 1978.

Dommel, P. R., *Targeting Community Development*, Department of Housing and Urban Development, Washington, DC, 1980.

Durham, G., Politics and administration in intergovernmental relations, *Annals*, 207, 1–6, 1940.

Dye, T. R., *Politics, Economics, and the Public: Policy Outcomes in the American States*, Rand McNally, Chicago, IL, 1966.

Dye, T. R., *American Federalism: Competition Among Governments*, Lexington Books, Lexington, MA, 1990.

Earle, E. M., Ed., *The Federalist*, Random House Modern Library, New York, 1937.

Earle, V., Ed., *Federalism: Infinite Variety in Theory and Practice*, Peacock, Itasca, IL, 1968.

Ehrenhalt, A., Devolution's double standard, *Governing*, 16, 6–8, April, 2003.

Elazar, D. J., *The American Partnership: Intergovernmental Cooperation in the Nineteenth-Century United States*, University of Chicago Press, Chicago, IL, 1962.

Elazar, D. J., The shaping of intergovernmental relations in the twentieth century, *Annals*, 359, 10–22, 1965.

Elazar, D.J. *American Federalism: A View from the States*. Harper & Row, New York, 1966, 1972, 1984.

Elazar, D. J., Urban problems and the federal government: a historical inquiry, *Political Science Quarterly*, 82, 505–525, 1967.

Elazar, D. J., Ed., *The Politics of American Federalism*, D.C. Heath, Lexington, MA, 1969.

Elazar, D. J., Ed., The federal polity, *Publius*, 3, 1–299, 1973.

Elazar, D. J., Is federalism compatible with prefectoral administration?, *Publius*, 11, 3–22, 1981.

Elazar, D. J., *Exploring Federalism*, University of Alabama Press, Tuscaloosa, AL, 1987.

Elazar, D. J., Cooperative federalism, Paper presented for the Advisory Commission on Intergovernmental Relations—Urban Institute Conference on Interjurisdictional Tax and Policy Competition. Washington, DC, 23–24 March, 1988.

Elazar, D. J., Carroll, R. B., Levine, E. L., and St. Angelo, D., Eds., *Cooperation and Conflict: Readings in American Federalism*, Peacock, Itasca, IL, 1969.

Elkins, S. and McKitrick, E., The founding fathers: young men of the revolution, *Political Science Quarterly*, 66, 181–216, 1961.

Elkins, S. and McKitrick, E., *The Age of Federalism*, Oxford University Press, New York, 1993.

Elliott, J., Ed., *The Debates in the Severalstate Conventions on the Adoption of the Federal Constitution The Debates in the Severalstate Conventions on the Adoption of the Federal Constitution*, Vol. 5, Lippincott, Philadelphia, PA, 1861–1863.

Ellwood, J. W., Ed., *Reductions in US Domestic Spending: How They Affect State and Local Governments*, Transaction Books, New Brunswick, NJ, 1982.

Executive Office of the President, Office of Management and Budget, *Strengthening Public Management in the Intergovernmental System: A Report Prepared for the Office of Management and Budget by the Study Committee on Policy Management Assistance*, US Government Printing Office, Washington, DC, 1975.

Executive Office of the President, Office of Management and Budget, *Managing Federal Assistance in the 1980s*, US Government Printing Office, Washington, DC, 1980.

Fairfield, R. P., Ed., *The Federalist Papers*, Johns Hopkins University Press, Baltimore, MD, 1981.

Farber, S. B., The 1982 new federalism negotiations: a view from the states, *Publius*, 13, 33–38, 1983.

Farkas, S. G., *Urban Lobbying: Mayors in the Federal Arena*, New York University Press, New York, 1971.

Farrand, M., *The Records of the Federal Convention of 1787*, Vol. 3, Yale University Press, New Haven, CT, 1911.

Farrand, M., *The Framing of the Constitution of the United States*, Yale University Press, New Haven, CT, 1913.

Fesler, J. W., *Area and Administration*, University of Alabama Press, Tuscaloosa, AL, 1949.

Fesler, J. W., Approaches to the understanding of decentralization, *J Politics*, 27, 536–566, 1965.

Fesler, J. W., The basic theoretical question: how to relate area and function, In *The Administration of the New Federalism: Objectives and Issues*, Grosenick, L. E., Ed., American Society for Public Administration, Washington, DC, pp. 4–14, 1973.

Fiorina, M., *Congress: Keystone of the Washington Establishment*, Yale University Press, New Haven, CT, 1977.

Fix, M., Transferring regulatory authority to the states, In *The Reagan Regulatory Strategy: An Assessment*, Fix, G. C., Ed., Urban Institute, Washington, DC, pp. 153–179, 1984.

Fossett, J., *Federal Aid to Big Cities: The Politics of Dependence*, Brookings Institution, Washington, DC, 1983.

Frieden, B. J. and Kaplan, M., *The Politics of Neglect: Urban Aid from Model Cities to Revenue Sharing*, MIT Press, Cambridge, MA, 1975.

Friedrich, C. J., *Constitutional Government and Democracy*, Ginn and Company, New York, 1950.

Friedrich, C. J., *Trends of Federalism in Theory and Practice*, Praeger, New York, 1968.

Gage, R. W. and Mandell, M. P., Eds., *Strategies for Managing Intergovernmental Policies and Networks*, Praeger, New York, 1990.

Gainsborough, J., To devolve or not to devolve? Welfare Reform in the States, *Policy Studies Journal*, 31(4), 603–623, 2003.

General Accounting Office, *Management Challenges Facing Federal Leadership*, General Accounting Office, Washington, DC, 2002.

General Accounting Office, *Intergovernmental Policy and Fiscal Relations*, General Government Division, General Accounting Office, Washington, DC, 1978.

General Accounting Office, *Intergovernmental Research Agenda. FY 1987–1988*, Intergovernmental Relations Group, Human Resources Division, General Accounting Office, Washington, DC, 1986.

Gaus, J. M., Federalism and intergovernmental relations, *Public Administration Review*, 16, 102–109, 1956.

Gelfand, M. I., *A Nation of Cities: The Federal Government and Urban America, 1933–1965*, Oxford University Press, New York, 1975.

Glazer, N., The social agenda, In *Perspectives on the Reagan Years*, Palmer, J. L., Ed., Urban Institute Press, Washington, DC, pp. 5–30, 1986.

Glendening, P. N. and Reeves, M. M., *Pragmatic Federalism: An Intergovernmental View of American Government*, Palisades Publishers, Pacific Palisades, CA, 1977.

Goldenberg, E. N., The permanent government in an era of retrenchment and redirection, In *The Reagan Presidency and the Governing of America*, Salamon, L. M. and Lund, M. S., Eds., Urban Institute Press, Washington, DC, pp. 381–404, 1984.

Goldwin, R. A., Ed., *A Nation of States: Essays on the American Federal System*, Rand McNally, Chicago, IL, 1967.

Gomez, R. A., *Intergovernmental Relations in Highways*, University of Minnesota Press, Minneapolis, MN, 1950.

Gordon, G. J., Managing leviathan: the intergovernmental management agenda for 1980, *Publius*, 10, 137–144, 1980.

Gore, A., *Creating a Government that Works Better and Costs Less: Report of the National Performance Review*, US Government Printing Office, Washington, DC, 1993.

Governmental Affairs Foundation, *Metropolitan Communities: A Bibliography with Special Emphasis on Government and Politics*, Public Administration Service, Chicago, IL, 1957.

Gramlich, E. M., Intergovernmental grants: a review of the empirical literature, In *The Political Economy of Fiscal Federalism*, Oates, W. E., Ed., Lexington Books, Lexington, MA, 1977.

Grant, D. R., Federal-municipal relationships and metropolitan integration, *Public Administration Review*, 14, 259–267, 1954.

Graves, W. B., Ed., Intergovernmental relations in the United States. *Annals*, 207, 1–218, 1940.

Graves, W. B., Ed., *Intergovernmental relations in the United States*, Legislative Reference Service, Library of Congress, Intergovernmental Relations Subcommittee (Committee Print). 84th Congr., 2nd sess. US Government Printing Office, Washington, DC, 1956.

Graves, W. B., Ed., *Intergovernmental Relations in the United States: An Annotated Chronology of Significant Events, Developments, and Publications with Particular Reference to the Period of the Last Fifty Years*, Council of State Governments, Chicago, IL, 1958.

Graves, W. B., Ed., *American Intergovernmental Relations: Their Origins, Historical Development, and Current Status*, Scribner's, New York, 1964.

Gray, V. and Hanson, R. L., *Politics in the American States: A Comparative Analysis*, 8th ed., CQ Press, Washington, DC, 2004.

Greenblatt, A., Fallout from the federal deficit, *Governing*, 17, 86, February, 2004.

Grodzins, M., American political parties and the American system, *West Political Q*, 13, 974–998, 1960.

Grodzins, M., The federal system, In *Goals for Americans: The Report of the President's Commission on National Goals*, Prentice Hall, Englewood Cliffs, NJ, pp. 265–282, 1960.

Grodzins, M., In *The American System: A New View of Government in the United States*, Elazar, D. J., Ed., Rand McNally, Chicago, IL, 1966.

Grosenick, L. E., Ed., *The Administration of the New Federalism: Objectives and Issues*, American Society for Public Administration, Washington, DC, 1973.

Gulick, L. H., Reorganization of the states, *Civil Eng*, 16, 420–421, 1933.

Haider, D. H., *When Governments Come to Washington: Governors, Mayors, and Intergovernmental Lobbying*, Free Press, New York, 1974.

Hale, G. E. and Palley, M. L., *The Politics of Federal Grants*, Congressional Quarterly Press, Washington, DC, 1981.

Hamilton, A., Jay, J., and Madison, J., *The Federalist*, Modern Library, New York, 1937. Introduction by Edward M. Earle.

Hanf, K. and Scharpf, F. W., *Intergovernmental Policy Making: Limits to Coordination and Central Control*, Sage, Beverly Hills, CA, 1978.

Hanus, J. J., Ed., *The Nationalization of State Government*, D.C. Heath, Lexington, MA, 1981.

Hawkins, R. B., Ed., *American Federalism: A New Partnership of the Republic*, Institute for Contemporary Studies, San Francisco, 1982a.

Hawkins, R. B., Conclusion: administrative versus political reform, In *American Federalism: A New Partnership of the Republic*, Hawkins, R. B., Ed., Institute for Contemporary Studies, San Francisco, CA, pp. 247–254, 1982b.

Hays, S. P., Three decades of environmental politics: the historical context, In *Government and Environmental Politics: Essays on Historical Developments Since World War Two*, Lacey, M. J., Ed., Johns Hopkins University Press, Baltimore, MD, 1991.

Heady, F., American constitutional and administrative systems in comparative perspective, *Public Administration Review*, 47, 9–16, 1987.

Heclo, H., Reaganism and the search for a public philosophy, In *Perspectives on the Reagan Years*, Palmer, J. L., Ed., Urban Institute Press, Washington, DC, pp. 31–63, 1986.

Heller, W. W., *New Dimensions of Political Economy*, Harvard University Press, Cambridge, MA, 1966.

Hobbs, H. H., *City Hall Goes Abroad: The Foreign Policy of Local Politics*, Sage Publications, Thousands Oaks, CA, 1994.

Holcombe, A. N., *Our More Perfect Union: From Eighteenth-Century Principles to Twentieth-Century Practice*, Harvard University Press, Cambridge, MA, 1950.

Hoover Commission (Commission on Organization of the Executive Branch of Government), *Administration of Overseas Affairs, Federal-State Relations, Rederal Research: A Report to the Congress*, Commission Report 18, US Government Printing Office, Washington, DC, 1949a.

Hoover Commission (Commission on Organization of the Executive Branch of Government). *Federal-sate relations*. S. Doc. 81, 81st Cong., 1st Sess., March 25. US Government Printing Office, Washington, DC, 1949b.

Hovde, B. J., The local housing authority, *Public Administration Review*, 1, 167–175, 1940.

Howitt, A. M., *Managing Federalism: Studies in Intergovernmental Relations*, Congressional Quarterly Press, Washington, DC, 1984.

Huntington, S. P., The founding fathers and the division of powers, In *A Theory of Local Government*, Maass, A., Ed., Free Press, Glencoe, IL, pp. 150–205, 1959.

Jacob, H. and Vines, K. N., Eds., *Politics in the American States: A Comparative Analysis*, Little, Brown, Boston, MA, 1965.

Jennings, E. T. Jr., and Krane, D., Coordination and welfare reform: the quest for the philosopher's stone, *Public Administration Review*, 54, 341–348, 1994.

Jennings, E. T. Jr., and Zank, N. S., Eds., *Welfare System Reform: Coordinating Federal, State, and Local Public Assistance Programs*, Greenwood Press, Westport, CT, 1993.

Jennings, E. T. Jr., Krane, D., Pattakos, A. N., and Reid, B. J., *From Nation to States: The Small Cities Community Development Block Grant Program*, State University of New York Press, Albany, NY, 1986.

Jensen, M., *The New Nation: A History of the United States During the Confederation, 1781–1789*, Knopf, New York, pp. 1781–1789, 1950.

Jillson, C. C., Constitution-making: alignment and realignment in the federal convention of 1787, *American Political Science Review*, 75, 598–612, 1981.

Johnson, G. W. and Heilman, J. G., Metapolicy transition and policy implementation: new federalism and privatization, *Public Administration Review*, 47, 468–478, 1987.

Joint Federal-State Action Committee. *Final report of the Joint Federal-State Action Committee to the President of the United States and to the Chairman of the Governors' Conference*. US Government Printing Office, Washington, DC, 1960.

Jones, C. O. and Thomas, R. D., Eds., *Public Policy Making in a Federal System*, Sage Publications, Beverly Hills, CA, 1976.

Jones, V., *Metropolitan Government*, University of Chicago Press, Chicago, IL, 1942.

Jones, V., Metropolitan studies, *Public Administration Review*, 13, 57–63, 1953.

Jun, J. S. and Wright, D. S., Eds., *Globalization and Decentralization: Institutional Contexts, Policy Issues, and Intergovernmental Relations in Japan and the United States*, Georgetown University Press, Washington, DC, 1996.

Kamensky, J. M., Role of the "Reinventing Government" movement in federal management reform, *Public Administration Review*, 56, 247–255, 1996.

Katzmann, R. A., *Institutional Disability: The Saga of Transportation Policy for the Disabled*, Brookings Institution, Washington, DC, 1986.

Kaufman, H., Administrative decentralization and political power, *Public Administration Review*, 29, 3–15, 1969.

Kelleher, C. and Yackee, S. W., Eds., *Meeting Challenges: North Carolina Responds to Welfare Reform*, The School of Government at the University of North Carolina at Chapel Hill, Chapel Hill, NC, pp. 1996–2001, 2002.

Kenyon, C., Men of little faith: the anti-federalists on the nature of representative government, *William Mary Q*, 12, 1–25, 1955.

Kenyon, D. A. and Kincaid, J., *Competition Among States and Local Governments: Efficiency and Equity in American Federalism*, Urban Institute Press, Washington, DC, 1991.

Kesler, C. R., Ed., *The Federalist Papers*, New American Library, New York, 1999.

Ketcham, R. M., *Intergovernmental Cooperation in the Los Angeles Area*, Bureau of Government Research, University of California, Berkeley, CA, 1940.

Kettl, D. F., The fourth face of federalism, *Public Administration Review*, 41, 366–371, 1981a.

Kettl, D. F., Regulating the cities, *Publius*, 11, 111–125, 1981b.

Kettl, D. F., *The Regulation of Federalism*, Louisiana State University Press, Baton Rouge, CA, 1983a.

Kettl, D. F., The uncertain brides: regulatory reform in Reagan's new federalism, In *Publius: Annual Review of American Federalism, 1981*, Center for the Study of Federalism, Temple University, Philadelphia, PA, 1983b.

Kettl, D. F., *Reinventing Government: A Fifth-Year Report Card*, The Brookings Institution, Washington, DC, 1998.

Kettl, D. F., Mandates forever, *Governing*, 16, 12, August, 2003.

Kettl, D. F., *System Under Stress: Homeland Security and American Politics*, CQ Press, Washington, DC, 2004.

Key, V.O. Jr., *The Administration of Federal Grants to the States*, Public Administration Service, Chicago, IL, 1937.

Key, V. O. Jr., A theory of critical elections, *J Politics*, 17, 3–18, 1955.

Kincaid, J., American federalism: the third century, *Annals*, 509, 9–152, 1990a.

Kincaid, J., From cooperative to coercive federalism, *Annals*, 509, 139–152, 1990b.

Kincaid, J., Constitutional federalism: labor's role in displacing places to benefit persons, *PS: Political Science and Politics*, 26, 172–177, 1993a.

Kincaid, J., From cooperation to coercion in American federalism: housing, fragmentation and preemption 1780–1992, *J Law Politics*, 9, 333–430, 1993b.

Kincaid, J., From dual to coercive federalism in American intergovernmental relations, In *Globalization and Decentralization: Institutional Contexts, Policy Issues, and Intergovernmental Relations in Japan and the United States*, Jun, J. S. and Wright, D. S., Eds., Georgetown University Press, Washington, DC, pp. 21–47, 1996.

Kincaid, J., The state of the US federalism 2000–2001: continuity in crisis, *Publius*, 31, 1–69, 2001.

Kincaid, J., Stever, J.A. *Rise and Decline of the Federal Government's Institutional Capacity for Intergovernmental Analysis: ACIR, OMB, GAO, and the Congress*, Paper presented at the 1992 annual meeting of the American Political Science Association, Chicago, IL, 1992.

King, P., *Federalism and Federation*, Johns Hopkins University Press, Baltimore, MD, 1982.

Krane, D., The state of American federalism 2001–2002: resilience in response to crisis, *Publius*, 32, 1–28, 2002.

Krane, D. and Wright, D. S., Intergovernmental relations, In *International Encyclopedia of Public Policy and Administration*, Shafritz, J., Ed., Vol. 2, Westview Press, Boulder, CO, pp. 1168–1176, 1998.

Krislov, S. and Rosenbloom, D., *Representative Bureaucracy and the American Political System*, Praeger, New York, 1981.

Landau, M., Baker v. Carr and the ghost of federalism, In *Reapportionment*, Schubert, G., Ed., Scribner's, New York, 1965.

Landau, M., Federalism, redundancy, and system reliability, *Publius*, 3, 173–196, 1973.

Larkey, P. D., *Evaluating Public Programs: The Impact of General Revenue Sharing on Municipal Government*, Princeton University Press, Princeton, NJ, 1979.

Laski, H. J., The obsolescence of federalism, *New Republic*, 98, 367–369, 1939.

Leach, R. H., *American Federalism*, W.W. Norton, New York, 1970.

Leach, R. H., Ed., Intergovernmental relations in America today, *Annals*, 416, ix, 1–193, 1974.

Leach, R. H., Ed., *Intergovernmental Relations in the 1980s*, Marcel Dekker, New York, 1983.

Leach, R. H., Federalism and intergovernmental relations: theories, ideas, concepts, In *Handbook of Public Administration*, Rabin, J., Hildreth, W. B., and Miller, G. J., Eds., Marcel Dekker, New York, pp. 387–404, 1988.

Leuchtenburg, W. E., *The New Nationalism: Theodore Roosevelt*, Prentice Hall, Englewood Cliffs, NJ, 1961.

Leuchtenburg, W. E., *In the Shadow of FDR: From Harry Truman to Ronald Reagan*, Cornell University Press, Ithaca, NY, 1983.

Levine, E. L. and Wexler, E. M., *PL 94–142: An Act of Congress*, Macmillan, New York, 1981.

Liebschutz, S. F., Ed., *Managing Welfare Reform in Five States: The Challenges of Devolution*, Rockefeller Institute Press, Albany, NY, 2000.

Lienesch, M., In defense of the anti-federalists, *History of Political Thought*, 4, 65–87, 1983a.

Lienesch, M., Interpreting experience: history, philosophy, and science in the American constitutional debates, *Am Politics Q*, 11, 379–401, 1983b.

Lienesch, M., *New Order of the Ages: Time, the Constitution, and the Making of Modern Political Thought*, Princeton University Press, Princeton, NJ, 1988.

Lipset, S. M., *The First New Nation: The United States in Historical and Comparative Perspective*, Basic Books, New York, NY, 1963.

Long, N. E., Power and administration, *Public Administration Review*, 9, 257–264, 1949.

Long, N. E., *The Polity*, Rand McNally, Chicago, 1962.

Long, N. E., *The Unwalled City: Reconstituting the Urban Community*, Basic Books, New York, 1972.

Lotchin, R. W., The city and the sword: San Francisco and the rise of the metropolitan-military complex 1919–1941, *J Am Hist*, 65, 996–1020, 1979a.

Lotchin, R. W., The Darwinian city: the politics of urbanization in San Francisco between the world wars, *Pacific Hist Rev*, 48, 357–381, 1979b.

Lotchin, R. W., The metropolitan-military complex in comparative perspective: San Francisco Los Angeles, San Diego, 1919–1941, *J West*, 18, 19–30, 1979c.

Lotchin, R. W., The city and the sword in metropolitan California, 1919–1941, *Urban Past Present*, 7, 1–16, 1982a.

Lotchin, R. W., Ed., *The Martial Metropolis: US Cities in War and Peace*, Praeger, New York, 1984.

Lovell, C., Evolving local government dependency, *Public Administration Review*, 41, 189–202, 1981.

Lovell, C., Mandating: operationalizing domination, *Publius*, 11, 59–78, 1981.

Lovell, C. and Tobin, C., The mandating issue, *Public Administration Review*, 41, 318–331, 1981.

Lowi, T., American business, public policy, case-studies, and political theory, *World Politics*, 16, 677–715, 1964.

Lowi, T., Four systems of policy, politics, and choice, *Public Administration Review*, 32, 298–310, 1972.

Lowi, T., The Europeanization of America? From United States to United state, In *Nationalizing Government: Public Policies in America*, Lowi, T. and Stone, A., Eds., Sage Publications, Beverly Hills, CA, 1978.

Lucas, T. M., NSF-sponsored research on general revenue sharing: the formula, In *Revenue Sharing: Methodological Approaches and Problems*, Caputo, D. A. and Cole, R. L., Eds., Lexington Books, Lexington, MA, 1976.

Lutz, E. A., Intergovernmental relations at the grass roots, *Public Administration Review*, 9, 119–125, 1949.

Lyons, W. and Morgan, D., The impact of intergovernmental revenue on city expenditures: analysis over time, *J Politics*, 39, 1088–1097, 1977.

Macaluso, A., Background and history of the study committee on policy management assistance, *Public Administration Review*, 35, 695–700, 1975.

MacDonald, A. F., *Federal Aid: A Study of the American Subsidy System*, Crowell, New York, 1928.

MacDonald, A. F., Recent trends in federal aid to the states, *American Political Science Review*, 25, 628–634, 1931.

MacDonald, A. F., Federal aid to the states: 1940 model, *American Political Science Review*, 34, 489–499, 1940.

Macmahon, A. W., Ed., *Federalism: Mature and Emergent*, Doubleday, Garden City, NY, 1955.

Macmahon, A. W., Ed., *Administering Federalism in a Democracy*, Oxford University Press, New York, 1972.

Mandell, M., Letters to the editor: intergovernmental management, *Public Admin Times*, 2, 2, December 15, 1979.

Mandell, M. P., Network management: strategic behavior in the public sector, In *Strategies for Managing Intergovernmental Policies and Networks*, Gage, R. W. and Mandell, M. P., Eds., Praeger, New York, pp. 29–53, 1990.

Marando, V. L. and Florestano, P. S., Intergovernmental management: the state of the discipline, In *The State of the Discipline*, Lynn, N. B. and Wildavsky, A., Eds., Chatham House, Chatham, NJ, pp. 287–317, 1990.

Marbach, J. R. and Leckrone, J. W., Intergovernmental lobbying for the passage of TEA-21, *Publius*, 32, 45–64, 2002.

Martin, R. C., *The Cities and the Federal System*, Atherton Press, New York, 1965.

Mashaw, J. L. and Rose-Ackerman, S., Federalism and regulations, In *The Reagan Regulatory Strategy: An Assessment*, Eads, G. C. and Fix, M. N., Eds., Urban Institute, Washington, DC, pp. 111–145, 1984.

Maxwell, J. A., Recent developments in federal-state financial relations, *Net Tax J*, 13, 310–319, 1960.

Maxwell, J. A., *Tax Credits and Intergovernmental Fiscal Relations*, Brookings Institution, Washington, DC, 1962.

McCulloch, R. W., Intergovernmental relations as seen by public officials, *Annals*, 359, 127–136, 1965.

McDowell, Bruce D., Advisory commission on intergovernmental relations in 1996: the end of an era, *Publius*, 27, 111–128, 1997.

McLean, J. E., *Politics is What You Make it. Public Affairs Pamphlet*, Public Affairs Committee, New York, 1952.

Meese, E., The attorney general's view of the Supreme Court: toward a jurisprudence of original intention, *Public Administration Review*, 45, 701–704, 1985.

Merriam, C. E. et al., *The Government of the Metropolitan Region of Chicago*, University of Chicago Press, Chicago, IL, 1933.

Mieszkowski, P. and Oakland, W. H., Eds., *Fiscal Federalism and Grants-in-aid*, Urban Institute Press, Washington, DC, 1979.

Miller, T. C., Ed., *Public Sector Performance: A Conceptual Turning Point*, Johns Hopkins University Press, Baltimore, MD, 1984.

Mogulof, M. B., *Governing Metropolitan Areas: A Critical Review of Councils of Governments and the Federal Role*, Urban Institute Press, Washington, DC, 1971.

Mollenkopf, J. H., *The Contested City*, Princeton University Press, Princeton, NJ, 1983.

Morgan, D. R. and Kickham, K., Modernization among the US states: change and continuity from 1960 to 1990, *Publius*, 27, 23–40, 1997.

Morgan, R. J., Madison's analysis of the sources of political authority, *American Political Science Review*, 75, 613–625, 1981.

Morison, S. E. and Commager, H. S., *The Growth of the American Republic*, Vol. 2, Oxford University Press, New York, 1950.

Morlan, R. L., *Intergovernmental Relations in Education*, University of Minnesota Press, Minneapolis, MN, 1950.

Mosher, F., *Democracy and the Public Service*, Oxford University Press, New York, 1968.

Mosher, F. and Stillman, R., Introduction to symposium on the professions in government, *Public Administration Review*, 37, 631–633, 1978.

Mowry, G. E. and Brownell, B. A., *The Urban Nation: 1920–1980*, rev. ed., Hill and Wang, New York, 1981.

Muller, T. and Fix, M., *The Impact of Selected Federal Actions on Municipal Outlays*, Joint Economic Committee of the US Congress, Washington, DC, 1980.

Mushkin, S. J., Barriers to a system of federal grants-in-aids, *Nat Tax Journal*, 13, 193–218, 1960.

Muskie, E. S., The $ and c of federalism, *National Civic Review*, 53, 235–238, 1964.

Muskie, E. S., Problems of Federal-State-Local Relations, *Hearings, 88th Cong., 2nd sess., September 18, 1962, Subcommittee on Intergovernmental Relations of the Senate Committee on Government Operations*, p. 4, 1962.

Nathan, R. P., Federalism and the shifting nature of fiscal relations, *Annals*, 419, 120–129, 1975.

Nathan, R. P., Institutional change under Reagan, In *Perspectives on the Reagan Years*, Palmer, J. L., Ed., Urban Institute Press, Washington, DC, pp. 121–145, 1986.

Nathan, R. P. and Adams, C. F. Jr., *Revenue Sharing: The Second Round*, Brookings Institution, Washington, DC, 1977.

Nathan, R. P. and Doolittle, F. C., *The Consequences of Cuts: The Effects of the Reagan Domestic Program on State and Local Governments*, Princeton Urban and Regional Research Center, Princeton, NJ, 1983.

Nathan, R. P. and Doolittle, F. C., *Reagan and the States*, Princeton University Press, Princeton, NJ, 1987.

Nathan, R. P. et al., *Monitoring Revenue Sharing*, Brookings Institution, Washington, DC, 1975.

Nathan, R. P. et al., *Block Grants for Community Development*, Department of Housing and Urban Development, Washington, DC, 1977.

Nathan, R. P. and Gais, T. L., Early findings about the newest new federalism for welfare, *Publius*, 28, 95–104, 1998.

National Academy of Public Administration, *Advancing the Management of Homeland Security: Managing Intergovernmental Relations for Homeland Security*, The Academy, Washington, DC, 2004.

National Journal, The New Federalism: Theory, Practice, Problems. A Special Report, Government Research Corporation, Washington, DC, 1973.

National Municipal Review, Report of the Committee on Federal Aid to the States, National Municipal League, 619–659, 1928.

Nice, D. C., *Federalism: The Politics of Intergovernmental Relations*, St. Martin's Press, New York, 1987.

Nice, D. C. and Frederickson, P., *The Politics of Intergovernmental Relations*, 2nd ed., Nelson Hall, Chicago, IL, 1995.

Oates, W. E., Ed., *Financing the New Federalism: Revenue Sharing, Conditional Grants, and Taxation*, Johns Hopkins University Press, Baltimore, MD, 1975.

Osborne, D. and Gaebler, T., *Reinventing Government: How the Entrepreneurial Spirit is Transforming the Public Sector*, Addison-Wesley, Reading, MA, 1992.

Osborne, D. and Plastrik, P., *Banishing Bureaucracy: The Five Strategies for Reinventing Government*, Addison-Wesley, Reading, MA, 1997.

Ostrom, V., *The Political Theory of a Compound Republic: A Reconstruction of the Logical Foundations of American Democracy as Presented in "The Federalist,"* Center for Public Choice, Virginia Polytechnic Institute, Blacksburg, VA, 1971.

Ostrom, V., *The Political Theory of the Compound Republic: Designing the American Experiment*, University of Nebraska Press, Lincoln, NE, 1987.

Ostrom, V., *The Meaning of American Federalism: Constituting a Self-governing Society*, Institute for Contemporary Studies, San Francisco, CA, 1991.

Ostrom, V. and Ostrom, E., A behavioral approach to the study of intergovernmental relations, *Annals*, 359, 137–146, 1965.

O'Toole, L. J., Jr., Ed., *American Intergovernmental Relations: Foundations, Perspectives, and Issues*, 1st ed., 1985, 2nd ed., 1993, 3rd ed., Congressional Quarterly Press, Washington, DC, 2000.

Palmer, J. L., Philosophy, policy, politics: integrating themes, In *Perspectives on the Reagan Years*, Palmer, J. L., Ed., Urban Institute Press, Washington, DC, pp. 175–206, 1986.

Paterson, J. T., *The New Deal and the states: Federalism in Transition*, Princeton University Press, Princeton, NJ, 1969.

Peirce, N. R., Johnson, C. W., and Hall, J. S., *Citistates: How Urban America can Prosper in a Competitive World*, Seven Locks Press, Washington, DC, 1993.

Perloff, H. S. and Nathan, R. P., Eds., *Revenue Sharing and the City*, Johns Hopkins University Press, Baltimore, MD, 1968.

Peterson, G. E. and Lewis, C. W., Eds., *Reagan and the Cities*, Urban Institute Press, Washington, DC, 1986.

Peterson, G. E. et al., *The Reagan Block Grants: What have we Learned?*, Urban Institute Press, Washington, DC, 1986.

Peterson, P., *City Limits*, University of Chicago Press, Chicago, IL, 1981.

Peterson, P., Rabe, B. G., and Wong, K. K., *When Federalism Works*, Brookings Institution, Washington, DC, 1986.

Petkas, P. J., The US regulatory system: partnership or maze?, *Nat Civic Rev*, 70, 297–301, 1981.

Pickering, J. M. and Clayton, C. W., The Rehnquist court and the political dynamics of federalism , *Perspectives on Politics*, 2, 233–248, 2004.

Pittenger, J. C., Garcia and the political safeguards of federalism: is there a better solution to the conundrum of the tenth amendment?, *Publius*, 22, 1–20, 1992.

Posner, P. L., Unfunded mandates reform act: 1996 and beyond, *Publius*, 27, 53–71, 1997.

Posner, P. L., *The Politics of Unfunded Mandates: Whither Federalism?*, Georgetown University Press, Washington, DC, 1998.

Posner, P. L., Wrightson, M. T. Block grants: a perennial, but unstable, tool of government, *Publius*, 26, 87–108, 1996.

Porter, D., Responsiveness to citizen-consumers in a federal system, *Publius*, 5, 51–77, 1975.

Powell, D. C., Internet taxation and US intergovernmental relations: from quill to the present, *Publius*, 30, 39–52, 2000.

Pressman, J. L., *Federal Programs and City Politics*, University of California Press, Berkeley, CA, 1975.

Pressman, J. L. and Wildavsky, A. B., *Implementation: How Great Expectations in Washington are Dashed in Oakland*, University of California Press, Berkeley, CA, 1973.

Proctor, D. M., *Federal-City Relations: A Report to the President of the United States*, National Institute of Municipal Law Officers, Washington, DC, 1953.

Provost, C. L., State attorneys general, entrepreneurship, and consumer protection in the new federalism, *Publius*, 33, 37–54, 2003.

Ranney, A., The divine science: political engineering in American culture, *American Political Science Review*, 70, 140–148, 1976.

Radin, B. A., Intergovernmental relationships in the federal performance movement, *Publius*, 30, 143–158, 2000.

Radin, B. A., *The Accountable Juggler: The Art of Leadership in a Federal Agency*, CQ Press, Washington, DC, 2002.

Rakove, J. N., Ed., *Interpreting the Constitution: The Debate Over Original Intent*, Northeastern University Press, Boston, MA, 1990.

Raup, R., *Intergovernmental Relations in Social Welfare*, University of Minnesota Press, Minneapolis, MN, 1952.

Reagan, M. D., *The New Federalism*, Oxford University Press, New York, 1972.

Reagan, M. D., *Regulation: The Politics of Policy*, Little, Brown, Boston, MA, 1987.

Redford, E. S., *Democracy and the Administrative State*, Oxford University Press, New York, 1969.

Reed, T. H., *Federal-State-Local Fiscal Relations*, Municipal Finance Officers Association, Chicago, IL, 1942.

Report of the Committee on Federal Aid to the States, *National Municipal Review* 17(special supplement), 1928.

Reuss, H. S., *Revenue Sharing: Crutch or Catalyst for State and Local Governments?*, Praeger, New York, 1970.

Riker, W. H., The senate in American federalism, *American Political Science Review*, 44, 452–469, 1955.

Riker, W. H., *Federalism: Origin Operation Significance*, Little, Brown, Boston, MA, 1964.

Roche, J. P., The founding fathers: a reform caucus in action, *American Political Science Review*, 55, 799–816, 1961.

Rohr, J. A., *To Run a Constitution: The Legitimacy of the Administrative State*, University of Kansas Press, Lawrence, KS, 1986.

Rose, R., *The Territorial Dimension in Government*, Chatham House, Chatham, NJ, 1982.

Rosenthal, D., *Sticking-Points and Ploys in Federal-State Relations*, Center for the Study of Federalism, Temple University, Philadelphia, PA, 1979.

Rosenthal, S. R., New directions for evaluating intergovernmental programs, *Public Administration Review*, 44, 491–503, 1984.

Rossiter, C., Ed, *The Federalist Papers*, Mentor Books, New York, 1961.

Rourke, F. E., *Intergovernmental Relations in Employment Security*, University of Minnesota Press, Minneapolis, MN, 1952.

Salamon, L., Follow-ups, let downs, and sleepers: the time dimension in policy evaluation, In *Public Policy Making in a Federal System*, Jones, C. and Thomas, R., Eds., Sage Publications, Beverly Hills, CA, 1976.

Salamon, L., Ed, *The Tools of Government: A Guide to the New Governance*, Oxford University Press, New York, 2002.

Sanford, T., *Storm Over the States*, McGraw-Hill, New York, 1967.

Sayre, W. S., Trends in a decade of administrative values, *Public Administration Review*, 11, 1–9, 1951.

Schattschneider, E. E., *The Semi-Sovereign People: A Realist's View of Democracy in America*, Holt, Rinehart, and Winston, New York, 1960.

Schechter, S. L., On the compatibility of federalism and intergovernmental management, *Publius*, 11, 127–141, 1981.

Scheffer, W. F., Ed, *General Revenue Sharing and Decentralization*, University of Oklahoma Press, Norman, OK, 1976.

Scheiber, H. N., *The Condition of American Federalism: An Historian's View*, US Government Printing Office, Washington, DC, 1966, Committee Print. Subcommittee on Intergovernmental Relations, US Senate, 89th Cong., 2nd sess.

Scheiber, H. N., Federalism and the American economic order 1789–1910, *Law Soc Rev*, 10, 57–118, 1976.

Scheiber, H. N., American federalism and the diffusion of power: historical and contemporary perspectives, *Toledo Law Rev*, 9, 619–680, 1978.

Scheiber, H. N., Federalism and legal process: historical and contemporary analysis of the American system, *Law Soc Rev*, 14, 663–722, 1980.

Schlesinger, A. M., *The Age of Roosevelt: The Coming of the New Deal*, Houghton Mifflin, Boston, MA, 1959.

Schlesinger, A. M., *The Age of Roosevelt: The Politics of Upheaval*, Houghton Mifflin, Boston, MA, 1960.

Schmidhauser, J. R., *The Supreme Court as Final Arbiter in Federal-State Relations*, University of North Carolina Press, Chapel Hill, NC, 1958.

Shapek, R. A., *Managing Federalism: Evolution and Development of the Grant-in-aid System*, Community Collaborators, Charlottesville, VA, 1981.

Sharkansky, I., *Spending in the American States*, Rand McNally, Chicago, IL, 1968.

Sharkansky, I., *Regionalism in American Politics*, Bobbs-Merrill, Indianapolis, IN, 1970.

Sharkansky, I., *The Maligned States: Policy Accomplishments, Problems, Opportunities*, McGraw-Hill, New York, 1972.

Shore, W. B., Cooperation grows among government units, *Public Administration Review*, 19, 279–282, 1959a.

Shore, W. B., Intergovernmental relations: satisfactions and problems, *Public Administration Review*, 19, 65–69, 1959b.

Skowronek, S., *Building a New American State: The Expansion of National Administrative Capacities 1877–1920*, Cambridge University Press, Cambridge, UK, 1982.

Sky, T., *To Provide for the General Welfare: A History of the Federal Spending Power*, University of Delaware Press, Newark, DL, 2003.

Smith, D. G., *The Convention and the Constitution: The Political Ideas of the Founding Fathers*, St. Martin's, New York, 1965.

Snider, C. F., County and township government in 1935–1936, *American Political Science Review*, 31, 909–916, 1937.

Sprague, J. D., *Voting Patterns of the United States Supreme Court: Cases in Federalism 1889–1959*, Bobbs-Merrill, New York, 1968.

Stauffer, M. and Tubbesing, C., The mandate monster, *State Legislatures*, 30(May), 22–23, 2004.

Stenberg, C., Beyond the days of wine and roses: intergovernmental management in a cutback environment, *Public Administration Review*, 41, 10–20, 1980.

Stenberg, C., States under the spotlight: an intergovernmental view, *Public Administration Review*, 45, 319–326, 1985.

Stenberg, C., Recent trends in state spending: patterns, problems, prospects, *Publius*, 24, 135–152, 1994.

Stenberg, C., Pulling together, *National Academy of Public Administration Transitioning from Campaigning to Governing*, National Academy of Public Administration, Washington, DC, 2004.

Stephens, G. R., State centralization and the erosion of local autonomy, *J Politics*, 36, 44–75, 1974.

Stephens, G. R. and Olson, G., *Pass-Through Federal Aid and Interlevel Finance in the American Federal System*, University of Missouri at Kansas City, Kansas City, MO, 1979.

Stever, J. A., Intergovernmental management in a revolutionary era, *J Public Admin Res Theory*, 2, 347–350, 1992.

Stewart, W. H., Metaphors and models and the development of federal theory, *Publius*, 12, 5–24, 1982.

Stewart, W. H., *Concepts of Federalism*, University Press of America, Lanham, MD, 1984.

Stillman, R. I. H., *Preface to Public Administration: A Search for Themes and Directions*, St. Martin's, New York, 1991.

Stoker, R. P., *Reluctant Partners: Implementing Public Policy*, University of Pittsburgh Press, Pittsburgh, PA, 1991.

Stolz, O. G., *Revenue Sharing: A Legal and Policy Analysis*, Praeger, New York, 1974.

Storing, H. J., *What the Anti-Federalists were for*, University of Chicago Press, Chicago, IL, 1981.

Studenski, P., *The Government of Metropolitan Areas in the United States*, National Municipal League, New York, 1930.

Subcommittee on Executive Reorganization, Committee on Government Operations, US Senate, *Federal Role in Urban Affairs*, Hearings, 90th Cong. pt. 1–21, US Government Printing Office, Washington, DC, 1966–1968.

Subcommittee on Executive Reorganization, Committee on Government Operations, *Intergovernmental Relations in the United States: A Selected Bibliography*, prepared by W. Brooke Graves, Legislative Reference Service, Library of Congress, at the request of the Subcommittee, Committee Print, 84th Cong., 2nd sess., November 1956, US Government Printing Office, Washington, DC, 1956.

Subcommittee on Executive Reorganization, Committee on Government Operations. Subcommittee on Intergovernmental Relations, Committee on Government Operations, US House of Representatives (Fountain Committee). *Recommendations and Major Statements of the Commission on Intergovernmental Relations, Annotated to Show Method of Implementation and Federal Agency and Program Affected*, prepared by the Bureau of the Budget at the request of the Subcommittee. Committee print, 84th Cong., 2nd sess., August 1956. US Government Printing Office, Washington, DC, 1956.

Subcommittee on Executive Reorganization, Committee on Government Operations, *Staff Report on Replies from Federal Agencies to Questionnaire on Intergovernmental Relations*, US Government Printing Office, Washington, DC, 1956. Committee Print, 84th Cong., 2nd Sess., August, 1956.

Subcommittee on Executive Reorganization, Committee on Government Operations, *Replies from State and Local Governments to Questionnaire on Intergovernmental Relations: Sixth Report*, US Government Printing Office, Washington, DC, 1957. House Report 575, 85th Cong., 1st sess., June 17, 1957.

Subcommittee on Executive Reorganization, Committee on Government Operations, *Federal-State-Local Relations: Federal Grants-in-aid, Thirteenth Report*, US Government Printing Office, Washington, DC, 1958. House Report 2435, 85th Cong. 2nd seas., August 8, 1958.

Subcommittee on Executive Reorganization, Committee on Government Operations, *Federal-State-Local Relations: Joint Federal-State Action Committee, Hearings*, US Government Printing Office, Washington, DC, 1958. 85th Cong., 2nd sess., February 18, 1958.

Sundquist, I. L., *Dynamics of the Party System: Alignment and Realignment of Political Parties in the United States*, Brookings Institution, Washington, DC, 1973.

Sundquist, J. L. and Davis, W., *Making Federalism Work: A Study of Program Coordination at the Community Level*, Brookings Institution, Washington, DC, 1969.

Talbott, F., *Intergovernmental Relations and the Courts*, University of Minnesota Press, Minneapolis, MN, 1950.

Thompson, J. R. and Ingraham, P. W., The reinvention game, *Public Administration Review*, 56, 291–296, 1996.

Thompson, R. E., *Revenue Sharing: A New Era in Federalism?*, Revenue Sharing Advisory Service, Washington, DC, 1973.

Truman, D. B., *Administrative Decentralization*, Public Administration Service, Chicago, IL, 1940.

Truman, D. B., Federalism and the party system, In *Federalism: Mature and Emergent*, Macmahon, A. W., Ed., Doubleday, Garden City, NY, pp. 115–136, 1955.

Van Riper, P., The American administrative state: Wilson and the founder-san unorthodox view, *Public Administration Review*, 43, 477–490, 1983.

Vieg, J. A., Working relationships in governmental agricultural programs, *Public Administration Review*, 1, 141–148, 1940.

Waldo, D., *The Administrative State: A Study of the Political Theory of American Public Administration*, Ronald Press, New York, 1948.

Waldo, D., *The Enterprise of Public Administration: A Summary Wew*, Chandler and Sharp, Novato, CA, 1980.

Walker, D. B., Is there federalism in our future?, *Public Management*, 61, 12, 1979.

Walker, D. B., *Toward a Functioning Federalism*, Winthrop, Cambridge, MA, 1981.

Walker, D. B., *The Rebirth of Federalism: Slouching Toward Washington*, Chatham House, Chatham, NJ, 2000.

Walker, L. and Plant, J. F., Woodrow Wilson and the federal system, In *Politics and Administration: Woodrow Wilson and American Public Administration*, Rabin, J. and Bowman, J. S., Eds., Marcel Dekker, New York, pp. 119–132, 1984.

Walters, J., Road blocks, *Governing*, 16(November), 14, 2003.

Waltenburg, E. N. and Swinford, B., *Litigating Federalism: The States Before the US Supreme Court*, Greenwood Press, Westport, CT, 1999.

Warren, C., *The Making of the Constitution*, Barnes and Noble, New York, 1968.

Warren, R., *The Community in America*, 3rd ed., Rand McNally, New York, 1978.

Weidner, E. E., Decision making in a federal system, In *Federalism: Mature and Emergent*, Macmahon, A. W., Ed., Garden City, NY, pp. 363–383, 1955.

Weidner, E. E., *Intergovernmental Relations as seen by Public Officials*, University of Minnesota Press, Minneapolis, MN, 1960.

Weissert, C. S., Medicaid in the 1990s: trends, innovations, and the future, *Publius*, 22, 93–110, 1992.

Weissert, C. S., Ed., *Learning from Leaders: Welfare Reform Politics and Policy in Five Midwestern States*, Rockefeller Institute Press, Albany, NY, 2000.

Welborn, D. M. and Burkhead, J., *Intergovernmental Relations in the American Administrative State: The Johnson Presidency*, University of Texas Press, Austin, TX, 1989.

Wheare, K. C., *Federal Government*, 4th ed., Oxford University Press, New York, 1964.

White, L. D., *Introduction to the Study of Public Administration*, Macmillan, New York, 1942. Supplement to the 1939 rev. ed., 1–21.

White, L. D., *The Federalists*, Macmillan, New York, 1948.

White, L. D., *The Jeffersonians*, Macmillan, New York, 1951.

White, L. D., *The States and the Nation*, Louisiana State University Press, Baton Rouge, CA, 1953.

White, L. D., *The Jacksonians*, Macmillan, New York, 1954.

White, L. D., *The Republican Era*, Macmillan, New York, 1958.

Wikstrom, N., *Councils of Governments: A Study of Political Incrementalism*, Nelson-Hall, Chicago, IL, 1977.

Williamson, R. S., The 1982 new federalism negotiations, *Publius*, 13, 11–32, 1983.

Williamson, R. S., *Reagan's Federalism: His Efforts to Decentralize Government*, University Press of America, Lanham, MD, 1990.

Wills, G., *Explaining America: The Federalist*, Penguin Books, New York, 1981.

Wilson, W., *Congressional Government: A Study in American Politics*, Johns Hopkins University Press, Baltimore, MD, 1885.

Wilson, W., The study of administration, *Political Science Quarterly*, 2, 197–222, 1887. (Reprinted, *Political Science Quarterly*, 55, 481–506, 1941.)

Wilson, W., *Constitutional Government in the United States*, Columbia University Press, New York, 1908.

Wirt, F., Does control follow the dollar? Value analysis, school policy, and state-local linkages, *Publius*, 10, 69–88, 1980.

Wirt, F., Professionalism and political conflict: a developmental model, *J Public Policy*, 1, 61–93, 1981.

Wise, C. and Nader, R., Organizing the federal system for homeland security: problems, issues, and dilemmas, *Public Administration Review*, 62(September), 44–57, 2002.

Wood, G. W., *The Creation of the American Republic 1776–1787*, W.W. Norton, New York, 1969.

Wood, R. C., *Suburbia: Its People and their Politics*, Houghton Mifflin, Boston, MA, 1958.

Wood, R. C., *Metropolis Against Itself*, Committee for Economic Development, New York, 1959.

Wood, R. C., *1400 Governments*, Harvard University Press, Cambridge, MA, 1961.

Wootton, D., Ed., *The Essential Federalist and Anti-Federalist Papers*, Hackett Publishing, Indianapolis, IN, 2003.

Wright, D. S., The advisory commission on intergovernmental relations: unique features and policy orientation, *Public Administration Review*, 25, 193–202, 1965.

Wright, D. S., *Intergovernmental Action on Environmental Policy: The Role of the States*, Institute of Public Administration, Indiana University, Bloomington, IN, 1967.

Wright, D. S., *Federal Grants-in-aid: Perspectives and Alternatives*, American Enterprise Institute, Washington, DC, 1968.

Wright, D. S., Intergovernmental relations: an analytical overview, *Annals*, 416, 1–16, 1974.

Wright, D. S., Intergovernmental relations and policy choice, *Publius*, 5, 1–24, 1975.

Wright, D. S., *Understanding Intergovernmental Relations*, Duxbury, North Scituate, MA, 1978.

Wright, D. S., Intergovernmental games: an approach to understanding intergovernmental relations, *South Rev Public Admin*, 3, 383–403, 1980.

Wright, D. S., New federalism: recent varieties of an older species, *American Review Public Administration*, 16, 56–73, 1982a.

Wright, D. S., *Understanding Intergovernmental Relations*, 2nd ed., Brooks/Cole, Monterey, CA, 1982b.

Wright, D. S., Managing the intergovernmental scene: the changing dramas of federalism, intergovernmental relations, and intergovernmental management, In *Handbook of Organization Management*, Eddy, W. B., Ed., Marcel Dekker, New York, pp. 417–454, 1983.

Wright, D. S., A quarter-century window on the US federal system: the shift from national-state relations to intergovernmental relations, 1935–1960, In *Patterns in American Federal-State Relations During the 1950s, the 1960s and the 1970s*, Gelfand, L. E. and Neymeyer, R. J., Eds., Center for the Study of the Recent History of the United States University of Iowa, Iowa City, IA, pp. 1–30, 1985.

Wright, D. S., A century of the intergovernmental administrative state: Wilson's federalism, new deal intergovernmental relations, and contemporary intergovernmental management, In *A Centennial History of the American Administrative State*, Chandler, R. C., Ed., Macmillan, New York, pp. 219–260, 1987.

Wright, D. S., *Understanding Intergovernmental Relations*, 3rd ed., Brooks/Cole, Monterey, CA, 1988.

Wright, D. S., Federalism, intergovernmental relations, and intergovernmental management: historical reflections and conceptual comparisons, *Public Administration Review*, 50, 168–178, 1990a.

Wright, D. S., Policy shifts in the politics and administration of intergovernmental relations, 1930s–1990s, *Annals*, 509, 60–72, 1990b.

Wright, D. S., The coercive-collage phase of IGR, *SIAM Intergov News*, 15, 1–3, 1992.

Wright, D. S., Understanding intergovernmental relations, In *Classics of Public Administration*, Shafritz, J. M. and Hyde, A. C., Eds., 4th ed., Harcourt Brace, Fort Worth, TX, pp. 578–594, 1997.

Wright, D. S., Federalism and intergovernmental relations: trauma, tensions, and trends, In *The Book of the States*, The Council of State Governments, Lexington, KY, pp. 227–231, 2003.

Wright, D. S. and Cho, C. L., State administration and intergovernmental interdependency: do national impacts on state agencies contribute to organizational turbulence?, In *Handbook of State Government Administration*, Gargin, J. J., Ed., Marcel Dekker, New York, pp. 33–66, 2000.

Wright, D. S. and Krane, D., Intergovernmental Management, In *International Encyclopedia of Public Policy and Administration*, Shafritz, J., Ed., Vol. 2, Westview Press, Boulder, CO, pp. 1162–1168, 1998.

Wright, D. S. and Peddicord, T. E., *Intergovernmental Relations in the United States: Selected Books and Documents on Federalism and National-State-Local Relations*, Center for the Study of Federalism, Temple University, Philadelphia, PA, 1973.

Wright, D. S. et al., *Assessing the Impacts of General Revenue Sharing in the Fifty States: A Survey of State Administrators*, Institute for Research in Social Science, University of North Carolina, Chapel Hill, NC, 1975.

Wright D. S. and White H. L., Eds., *Federalism and Intergovernmental Relations*, American Society for Public Administration, Washington, DC, 1984.

Wyatt, L. R., *Intergovernmental Relations in Public Health*, University of Minnesota Press, Minneapolis, MN, 1951.

Yarbrough, J., Book review of Vincent Ostrom, the political theory of the compound republic, *American Political Science Review*, 82, 298–300, 1988.

Ylvisaker, P. N., *Intergovernmental Relations at the Grass Roots*, University of Minnesota Press, Minneapolis, MN, 1956.

Ylvisaker, P. N., Some criteria for a "proper" areal division of powers, In *Area and Power: A Theory of Local Government*, Maass, A., Ed., Free Press, Glencoe, IL, pp. 27–49, 1959.

Yoo, J. W. and Wright, D. S., Public policy and intergovernmental relations: measuring perceived change(s) in national influence—the effects of the federalism decade, *Policy Studies J*, 21, 687–699, 1993.

Zimmerman, J. F., *The Federated City*, St. Martin's, New York, 1972.

Zimmerman, J. F., *State-Local Relations: A Partnership Approach*, 2nd ed., Praeger, New York, 1995.

Zimmerman, J. F., *Federal Preemption: The Silent Revolution*, Iowa State University Press, Ames, IA, 1991.

Zimmerman, J. F., Federal preemption under Reagan's new federalism, *Publius*, 21, 7–28, 1991.

Zimmerman, J. F., *The Growth of National Power*, Praeger, New York, 1992.

Zimmerman, J. F., National-state relations: cooperative federalism in the twentieth century, *Publius*, 31, 15–30, 2001.

Zimmerman, J. F., *Evolving State-Local Relations, The Book of the States,* 2002 ed., Council of State Governments, Lexington, KY, pp. 33–39, 2002a.

Zimmerman, J. F., *Trends in Interstate Relations: Political and Administrative Cooperation. The Book of the States,* 2002 ed., Council of State Governments, Lexington, KY, pp. 40–47, 2002b.

Zimmerman, J. F., *Interstate Economic Relations,* State University of New York Press, Albany, NY, 2004.

12 Federalism and Intergovernmental Relations: Theories, Ideas, and Concepts

Dale Krane and Richard H. Leach*

CONTENTS

Any student of or participant in American government quickly understands that it is distinctive in at least three ways: our constitutional system incorporates separation of powers, judicial review, and federalism. All three were manifestations of the founders' concern that power be divided and so limited. Oddly enough, they did not include in the constitution they were drafting any specifics about the three special features they were writing into it. What they intended as far as separation of powers goes can only be gleaned by ex post facto analysis of the multiple relationships implicit in the first three articles of the Constitution. And although judicial review has a taproot in the Supremacy Clause (Article VI, Section 2), its fuller exposition waited for Alexander Hamilton in *Federalist* No. 78 and John Marshall in *Marbury v. Madison* and *McCulloch v. Maryland*.

It is much the same with federalism. The founders came to Philadelphia to deal, in Hamilton's words, with the "risk of our independence" they believed to stem from "the dangers of ... the evils of a precarious Union" (Hamilton 1850). The continuation of that union, which had been formalized in the Articles of Confederation, was taken for granted. What was needed, as they saw it, were alterations in the role and power of the central government—and so inevitably in those of the states which together constituted the union. "It is indispensable to the happiness of the individual States," George Washington wrote to Chancellor Robert Livingstone of New York, "that there should be lodged some where a Supreme Power, to regulate and govern the general Concerns of the

---

* This chapter is a revised version of an essay authored by Richard H. Leach (now deceased) and published in 1998 in the second edition of this Handbook. It is a privilege to have been asked to update Prof. Leach's original contribution. Much of this new version retains his line of reasoning and his language. A long time faculty member in the Dept. of Political Science at Duke University, Richard Leach established a reputation as one of the most insightful students of federalism, and his book *American Federalism* is a classic on the subject.

confederated Republic" (Mason and Leach 1981). It was to that end that the national power-oriented Virginia Plan was put forward, which in turn provoked the New Jersey Plan, which saw as a way of preserving the union a constitution limiting national power in favor of the states. If this suggests that the ensuing debate seeking to reconcile the two plans illuminated the founders' understanding of what the final product would mean in terms of federalism, in fact it did not. Debate focused on the specifics of establishing the various organs of the national government and never touched what they considered to be the nature of the relationship between the strengthened central government and the several states. Thus, as is the case with separation of powers and judicial review, neither the theoretical nor the operational underpinnings of federalism were adumbrated by the founders.

But the lack of a defining conception of federalism at the outset did not mean that no attention was paid to the direction it should take. Debate began immediately, and has continued ever since, on what the Constitution implies as to federalism. The purpose of this writing, indeed, is to attempt to capture the essence of the main directive thrusts in the thinking about federalism that have developed over the more than 200 years of American history since the framing of the Constitution.

The literature on federalism is voluminous and is still growing. If it is agreed that federalism is a way of distributing power among one central or national government (usually called the federal government) and the governments of the smaller jurisdictions into which the country is divided, states or provinces and myriad local government units, all of which levels of government operate directly on the people on the basis of constitutional allocations of authority, agreement on much else remains elusive. That at least five differing conceptions of federalism can be identified is proof of the divergence of opinion that has marked the subject. Those five approaches, briefly, are:

- *Constitutional federalism*: the indeterminate sharing of power among the national government and the states and their local governments.
- *States' rights federalism*: the sharing of power only up to certain barriers protecting the states.
- *Administrative federalism*: the everyday sharing of power on varying partnership bases.
- *Centralized federalism*: the sharing of power with the goals and procedures of the national government dictating implementation.
- *New federalism*: the sharing of power on the basis of defined national and state functions.

Each of these approaches will now be described briefly.

I. CONSTITUTIONAL FEDERALISM

As already noted, our founding fathers did not elaborate on the federal system they put into operation. But if the founders collectively failed to expound on federalism at Philadelphia, two of them tried to remedy the situation almost immediately thereafter. In several of *The Federalist Papers* (Federalist 1981), Alexander Hamilton and James Madison expatiated here and there on federalism in their extensive commentary on the Constitution, which was just then being considered by ratifying conventions in several states.

Thus Hamilton, in *Federalist* No. 15, echoed founder James Wilson's conclusion that the specific declaration in the preamble of the Constitution that it is an emanation of the people rendered state sovereignty, the basis of the Articles of Confederation, no longer possible. It was the people, Hamilton declared in *Federalist* No. 9, who had endowed the national government with vastly increased powers, and it was the people who had ordained "a consolidated system," a "Union under one government" and the "perfect subordination [of the states] to the general authority of the Union."

But as Wills (1982) has pointed out, all three authors of *The Federalist Papers*—Hamilton, Madison, and Jay—had to convince those opposed to ratifying the Constitution—and there were many such anti-Federalists—"that the subordination of the states [to the proposed energized national government] would not lead to their obliteration. So as a kind of sweet talk, Hamilton referred ... to *partial* incorporation or consolidation" of the states into the revised union. In *Federalist* No. 32, Hamilton argued that:

> an intire consolidation of the States into one complete national sovereignty would imply an intire subordination of the parts, and whatever powers might remain in them would be altogether dependent on the general will [of the people]. But ... the plan of the Convention aims only at a partial Union or consolidation ...

As Wills reminds us, however, if Hamilton was for centralization of power, "decentralization existed at the time [and] that was what [he] was fighting." Thus he had to "reassure people that ... 'consolidation' would not mean complete homogenization" (Wills 1982), which Hamilton attempted to do in *Federalist* No. 9, when he posited that those areas of authority not claimed for the new national government in Article I, Section 8, still remained with the states as a kind of residual or concurrent sovereignty, and in *Federalist* No. 34 where he spoke of the states having "co-equal power with the Union" with regard to the power to tax. In *Federalist* No. 23, he denied that the additional powers granted to the national government were "too extensive for the *objects*" confined to it, "or, in other words, for the management of our *national* interests." By implication, there were state interests as well that warranted protection.

Madison, though "his basic argument [was] for more power to the central government" (Wills 1982), in *Federalist* No. 39 asserted that the states would not be "consolidated into one nation" but would retain authority "within their respective spheres"; in *Federalist* No. 43 he spoke of "the residuary sovereignty of the States"; and in *Federalist* No. 45 he worried about danger to "the unsacrificed residue" of sovereignty in the states' possession. The celebrated passage in *Federalist* No. 39 reveals that Madison's ability to "sweet talk" equaled Hamilton's:

> The proposed Constitution ... is, in strictness neither a national or a federal Constitution, but a composition of both. In its foundation it is federal, not national; in the sources from which the ordinary powers of the government are drawn, it is partly federal and partly national; in the operation of these powers, it is national, not federal; in the extent of them, again, it is federal, not national ... in the authoritative mode of introducing amendments, it is neither wholly federal or wholly national; [and] in ratifying the Constitution, [in which case each state] is considered as a sovereign body, independent of all others, and only to be bound by its own voluntary act ... the ... Constitution will, if established, be a *federal* and not a national Constitution.

Nor did Madison let the matter rest there. In *Federalist* No. 51, where he sought to slay the beast of factions, he praised the new constitution for the way it divided power surrendered to government by the people "between two distinct governments." What better way to protect the rights of the people: "The different governments will control each other, at the same time that each will be controlled by itself."

The anti-Federalists were not satisfied with Hamilton's and Madison's "sweet talk." A careful reading of all the substantial anti-Federalist writings at the time of ratification convinced Storing (1981), whose study remains the definitive work on the subject, that while they believed the exigencies of the union in 1787 were not severe enough to justify the extensive changes in the "governmental system suggested by the Constitution," they did agree "that a union was wanted, that it required an efficient government, and that the Articles of Confederation did not provide such a government." It was for them a matter of finding some middle ground between the Articles and the proposed Constitution. The stumbling block for them was their almost unanimous fear that power granted would inevitably become power abused. Thus both the ends of the national government and the powers granted to it to accomplish those ends must somehow be more limited than it appeared to them they were in the draft of the Constitution before them.

Moreover, the anti-Federalists were sure that the Federalists sought to overendow the national government with power so as to make it the instrument of the people for "the pursuit of national riches and glory" (Storing 1981). But the latter were not in their eyes the proper ends of government, especially for America. "You are not to inquire how ... you are to become a great and powerful people," wrote anti-Federalist Patrick Henry. You are to inquire instead "how your liberties may be secured." In that inquiry, the anti-Federalists argued, state governments were of central importance, for it was they that had primary responsibility for the happiness of the citizenry, the national government being properly confined to defense, foreign relations, and general commerce. In short, the federal system ought to be one that contained "parallel governments in a kind of balance or tension with one another." As one anti-Federalist tract (Brutus) put it:

> Neither the general government, nor the state governments, ought to be vested with all the powers proper to be exercised for promoting the ends of government. The powers are divided between them— certain ends to be attained by the one, and other certain ends by the other; and these, taken together, include all the ends of good government. This being the case, the conclusion follows, that each should be furnished with the means, to attain the ends, to which they are designed (Storing 1981).

Or, as Storing concluded from a broader perspective based on the generality of anti-Federalist writings, "the Federalists emphasized the primacy of the national component in the [mixed system], while the Anti-Federalists urged the importance of a strict division of power and even something like a divided sovereignty" (Storing 1981).

In the end, the draft Constitution was accepted as proposed, but shortly thereafter an attempt was made to "ensure the continued independence and vigor of the states, which [was] missing from the Constitution" (Storing 1981). The Tenth Amendment, added as a part of the Bill of Rights in 1791, states that "powers not delegated to the United States by the Constitution, nor prohibited by it to the states, are reserved to the states, respectively, or to the people." In fact, the Tenth Amendment has not offered a satisfactory solution to the problem raised by the anti-Federalists; the inclusion of the last four words have tended to make it an empty statement.

Constitutional federalism, in sum, introduces us to the dancers in the federal reel but does not instruct us or them on the intricacies of their dance.[*] It avoids facing the ultimate theoretical dilemma of definition and so leaves it to the dancers themselves to improvise, and to us to seek understanding of what is happening on the stage. It may be that it did not matter to many of the founders, who may have thought that they had settled on a compromise, "a more or less temporary arrangement in the course of building a genuine national government" (Storing 1981). In any case, constitutional federalism absolutely bars us from arguing for any particular relationship between national and state power.

II. STATES' RIGHTS FEDERALISM

Although a number of threads tie it to anti-Federalist thought at the time of the nation's founding, the roots of *states' rights* federalism really lie in the Kentucky and Virginia Resolutions of 1798 and 1799, authored by Thomas Jefferson and James Madison, respectively. These resolutions were directed at the Alien and Sedition Acts, enacted by the Federalist-dominated Congress in 1798 in response to a perceived possibility of war with France. They would have allowed among other things the president to order out of the country any aliens he judged to be dangerous to the nation's peace and safety, and would have permitted the punishment by fine and imprisonment of any

---

* For a contemporary analysis of the argument over federalism, see Ostrorm (1991).

persons conspiring against any measure of the national government, impeding the operation of any national law, or uttering any malicious statement against an official of the national government. Although their enforcement was lax and they were soon allowed to expire, their execution in some cases and their very presence on the statute books aroused the wrath of many Americans. What is more, they were alleged to be unconstitutional; none of them, however, was ever tested before the Supreme Court. The legislature of Kentucky, predominantly composed of opponents to the Federalist party which controlled the national government, asked Jefferson to draft a series of resolutions for its consideration. Jefferson was happy to comply with the request, and the set of resolutions he wrote moved swiftly to passage and approval by the state's governor before the end of 1798. They were reaffirmed by the legislature in 1799. The resolutions asserted that:

> Whenever the general government assumes undelegated powers, its acts are unauthoritative, void, and of no force; that to this compact [i.e., the Constitution] each State acceded as a State, and is an integral party, its co-States forming, as to itself, the other party; that the government created by this compact was not made the exclusive or final judge of the extent of the powers delegated to itself; … but that, as in all cases of compact among parties, having no common judge, each party has an equal right to judge for itself, as well of infractions as of the mode and measure of redress (Jefferson 1975).

Madison used stronger language in the resolutions he prepared at the request of the Virginia legislature, which were also passed and approved in 1798. In part, Madison's view was that:

> the powers of the Federal Government, as resulting from the compact to which the States [are] parties limited by the plain sense and intention of the instrument constituting that compact, and are no further valid than they are authorized by the grants enumerated in that compact; and … in case of a deliberate, palpable, and dangerous exercise of … powers not granted by the said compact, the States which are parties thereto have the right, and are in duty bound, to interpose, for arresting the progress of the evil, and for maintaining within their respective limits the authorities, rights, and liberties appertaining to them (Madison 1884).

What Jefferson and Madison did in the political heat of the moment, in short, was to introduce a novel notion into the discussion of American federalism: namely, that the Constitution was no more than a compact—an agreement or covenant—entered into by the several states, not an instrument of the people as declared in its own preamble. The word compact was not in general use at the time as far as public law was concerned, except with reference to agreements between two or more states. Both Jefferson and Madison would have been familiar with the Potomac River Compact that was concluded between Virginia and Maryland in 1785 and still in force as they wrote. In that usage, to be sure, the party states, having drawn up and accepted a compact, retained the right to abrogate it. But to carry the idea to the broader context of the Constitution was bizarre, as the lack of support in other states for the resolutions suggests.

More importantly, what Jefferson and especially Madison advocated was state action—interposition and nullification—in protest of alleged violations of the compact by its creation, the national government. Interposition involves the state placing itself "between the citizens and the national government so as to prevent the enforcement of national law upon [them]. According to this doctrine, each state may be the judge of the legality or constitutionality of national action and may 'interpose' its sovereignty to nullify federal action" (Plano and Greenberg 1985). The object of doing so would be to protect states' rights, rights to the unspecified area of authority left to them in the Constitution after the delegation of powers to the national government and the denial of powers to both national and state governments. Perhaps surprisingly, neither Jefferson nor Madison made reference to the Tenth Amendment as the protector of states' rights.

If the Kentucky and Virginia Resolutions were less than important in their own day, the novel ideas in them have been drawn on since, as the concept of states' right they spawned came into maturity. Jefferson and Madison were supplemented later by John C. Calhoun, as he argued his case for the protection of pre-Civil War southern sectionalism; by those a century later who saw in the Supreme Court's rulings on desegregation, the Commerce Clause, and state sedition laws a usurpation of state authority; and by others who saw in federal laws and regulations providing grants-in-aid to the states an element of unauthorized coercion. To many in the states' rights fold, the 10th Amendment had said it all.

States' rights federalism continues to live on. References to "resurgent states" or to the "primary role of the states in domestic policy" often are euphemisms for a state-centered view (Walker 2000, 27). The Republican party, in particular, has actively sought to instill states' rights theory into policy initiatives as exemplified by the 1994 Contract With America. Furthermore, conservative think tanks allied with the Republican party have published philosophical defenses of states' rights and have called for a constitutional convention on federalism with the objective, among others, of reviving the Tenth Amendment (Seay and Smith 1996). More specific attempts to limit federal government preemption of state or local authority include the Tenth Amendment Enforcement Act (S. 1629, 104th Cong. (1996)) and the Federalism Accountability Act (S. 1214, 106th Cong. (1999)). Both bills failed to win passage, but some provisions related to expediting waiver requests by the states were incorporated into Executive Order 13132 (4 August 1999) issued by the Clinton Administration.

The real enemy of the states' righters has been, from the beginning, the doctrine of implied powers; the national government has repeatedly relied on this doctrine to breach the compact between the states by entering willfully into the states' reserved domain. The states' righters believe a halt must be called to that encroachment. As they see it, state powers can be clearly identified as such, and once this has been done, presumably on a case-by-case basis through the threat of interposition and nullification, the state domain should be fenced off from the national Leviathan. If some states' righters see their role as chiefly one of protest, others interpret it as calling for a declaration of war, particularly on the role the Supreme Court has come to play in the federal system, "for the interpositionists hold that the Court is not to be viewed as the final voice in federal problems because this power ultimately rests in the states operating through Congress or by constitutional amendment" (Macdonald et al. 1957). At least the Civil War ruled out the final stratagem, secession.

But the states' righters have not given up. Although they vehemently attacked the US Supreme Court during the 1950s and 1960s because of the Court's rulings on civil and political rights for non-whites, states' righters have been cheerleaders for the so-called Federalism Five consisting of Justices Rehnquist, Kennedy, O'Connor, Scalia, and Thomas. During the past decade, these five justices have handed down a number of rulings that have begun to erect some fences between state and federal governments. Decisions limiting national authority under the Interstate Commerce Clause, Section 5 of the Fourteenth Amendment, the Eleventh Amendment, and the Tenth Amendment all have been based on the argument that "dual federalism was 'embedded in our constitutional structure'... [and] It upholds the 'dignity' of the states as dual sovereigns" (Kettl 2002). Whether these rulings constitute a federalism revolution is a matter of debate, but there is no doubt that this new line of judicial reasoning in support of states' rights has prompted deep disagreements within the Court as well as in the larger political arena over the nature of the US constitutional system (Clayton and Pickerill 2003; Kettl 2002; Peterson 2003). Confirmation hearings for Justice Roberts and Alito gave little indication of their stances on federalism and it remains an open question as to whether the new Roberts court will try to curb congressional power and favor state governments.

III. ADMINISTRATIVE FEDERALISM

Regardless of the impreciseness of constitutional federalism and the longed for, but not achieved, preciseness of states' rights federalism, those at work on the operating side of the federal system have from the beginning been establishing yet another view of federalism. The operators of that system—men and women on local councils and commissions, in state legislatures, and in Congress, governors and state and local executive officers, and bureaucrats at all three levels—have not worried very much about articulating a theory of federalism, leaving that to scholars who have had no trouble describing the administrative federalism they saw developing in practice. One of the first of those scholars was Jane Perry Clark, who in her trailblazing *The Rise of a New Federalism: Federal-State Cooperation in the United States* (1938) described and discussed the panoply of formal and informal cooperative mechanisms which had been developed by the time she wrote, mechanisms which linked the national government and those at the state and local levels in a joint effort to provide for the nation's needs. Among those mechanisms, almost all of them developed pragmatically, were informational exchange, loans of personnel, agreements and contracts, joint regulatory arrangements, and grants-in-aid. A later scholar, Daniel Elazar, related in his monumental *The American Partnership* (1962) how from the very beginning of the Republic all levels of government in the United States had collaborated in performing governmental functions. By 1962 Elazar could point to intergovernmental collaboration as "actually the norm" in American political life and in American federalism.

For as Elazar and others made clear, the facts showed that far from comprising separate and independent spheres of authority—"collateral political spheres" in the words of an early states' righter (Taylor 1820)—federalism necessarily implies cooperation, a blending of governmental efforts in a skein of intergovernmental relations for the furtherance of the public welfare. As Morton Grodzins so eloquently put it, the federal system in the operation of government programs resembles a "rainbow or marble cake, characterized by an inseparable mingling of differently colored ingredients, the colors appearing in vertical and diagonal strands and unexpected swirls. As colors are mixed in the marble cake, so functions are mixed in the American federal system" (Grodzins 1960).

In short, administrative federalism posits a single mechanism of government for the United States, with many centers of action, which between them are to perform all the functions required of government by the American people. Even before the Philadelphia Convention, intergovernmental cooperation was being utilized in a number of functional areas, and the founders were so conscious of "the essential unity of state and federal financial systems" that they provided for the assumption by the national government of the Revolutionary War debts of the states (Grodzins 1960). If they did not say so explicitly, the founders understood that the national government would act in harmony with state and local government programs and policies. During the nineteenth century that understanding was manifest in a steadily increasing intergovernmental cooperation in all the important functional areas of American government that continued through the twentieth century. Thus administrative federalism can be read as cooperative federalism, in that it accepts and operates on the principle that shared programs, without too much regard for neat allocations of responsibility, form the core of American governmental operation, and so of federalism as well.

Intergovernmental relations (IGR)—that is, intergovernmental cooperation—rather than the required priority of one or another level of government, is the working principle of the federal system and is not confined to relations between the national government and the states. IGR also includes relations between (a) the national government and local units of government, (b) two or more states, (c) each state and its own subordinate governments, and (d) two or more governments at the local level. The complex and diverse jurisdictional variation typical of American federalism creates an organizational and functional fragmentation across levels of government which in turn produces equally complex and diverse patterns of administration among and between units of government. The critical challenge, of course, is the production and delivery of public services with reasonable effectiveness and efficiency in a fragmented system that is not hospitable to integration, but is constrained by interjurisdictional dependency. "Consequently, IGR is generally characterized by reciprocal activity and interdependent choices among multiple governmental units and political interests" (Krane and Wright 1998).

The fullest exposition of the concept may be found in the study of Deil S. Wright (1988) in his *Understanding Intergovernmental Relations*. Wright identifies five important dimensions of IGR: (1) the number and types of governmental units, their legal status, and changes over time; (2) the number and types of public officials by jurisdiction and unit, their backgrounds and training, the attitudes and perceptions of their roles and responsibilities, and the actions they normally pursue; (3) the patterns of interaction among and between officials representing various jurisdictions and governmental units; (4) the range of involvement by all public officials—elected and appointed, national and local, executive, legislative, and judicial—especially in the formulation of policies and programs that have impact on more than one unit; and (5) the policies and programs implemented through intergovernmental arrangements with particular concerns about administrative discretion by official and by unit, control over and flow of fiscal resources, and differential effects of policies and programs delivered via different intergovernmental routes. These five dimensions must be understood against the distribution of authority and power which is diffused in the United States. Because "the spheres of autonomous action lack precise definition" (Anton 1989), administrative activity succeeds only if a "working partnership" prevails (Elazar 1972).

Furthermore, these partnerships need not be restricted to relations between governments only. The so-called creative federalism, briefly in vogue in the 1960s and 1970s but now experiencing a revival, was a logical extension of administrative federalism. The phrase was first used and the concept described by Governor Nelson A. Rockefeller of New York in his Godkin Lectures at Harvard University in 1962 (Rockefeller 1962). Later the idea was picked up by President Johnson and made central to his program agenda after his election in 1964. That agenda recognized that private, usually nonprofit, centers of power may appropriately share with governments the job of serving the American people. As extended to creative federalism, administrative federalism incorporates the view that when action is needed in attacking the problems facing the nation, a public–private working team may be among the forces at work in certain problem areas, with the national government not necessarily the senior partner.

The ad hoc proliferation of programs designed and funded by the national program but administered primarily by states and localities brought to the fore the question of program performance. As responsibilities became increasingly shared within a network of government jurisdictions, public agencies, nonprofit organizations, and for-profit enterprises, administrative federalism became intersectoral as well as intergovernmental (Musolf and Seidman 1980; Williams 1980). Concerns about the quality of program administration and the cost of services delivered were expressed by government watchdogs such as the Office of Management and Budget (OMB), the Government Accountability Office (GAO), and the Advisory Commission on Intergovernmental Relations (ACIR), as well as by professional associations such as the National Assistance Management Association and the American Society for Public Administration's Section on Intergovernmental Administration and Management. The need for improved coordination and orchestration of many different organizations (public, nonprofit, for-profit) in the implementation partnerships that became characteristic of public programs ́expanded the work of public managers beyond that of traditional administration—the operation of a bureau—to include the management of an interorganizational network (Gage and Mandell 1990). This shift has been labeled *intergovernmental management* (IGM) to emphasize the management processes inherent in program administration (Marando and Florestano 1990; Wright 1990). But the M in IGM has come to be seen not in terms of top-down hierarchical control, but rather in terms of loosely coupled patterns of interaction and influence that require government officials to rely more on bargaining, negotiation, dispute resolution, informal personal linkages, and trust-building (Agranoff 1986; Agranoff and McGuire 2003; Jennings and Krane 1994).

The concept of administrative federalism, in sum, focuses on those involved in carrying out the service functions required by the American people. For the most part their attention has been devoted from the outset to administering as effectively as possible the functions required of them, not with theoretical niceties.* Thus they see federalism as a process, as a way of doing things, rather than as a set of abstract principles—remembering always the most basic principle of American political thought, limited government. The most frequently occurring words in their vocabulary are function, program, activity, and administration, in all of which collaborative relations are fundamental. If they think about federalism at all, they see it as a method permitting the accomplishment of commonly held objectives, a method whose virtue lies in what it permits to be accomplished rather than in its adherence to a set of binding tenets.

Just as it cannot be shown that theory informs administrative federalism, so it cannot be demonstrated that it demands a certain pattern of intergovernmental relations be followed. Rather, variation and adaptation to different changing needs have been characteristic of American intergovernmental relations. Each particular type of relationship has been determined by the area of activity and the set of actors involved. In some areas, no clear pattern of intergovernmental relations has evolved. In others, programs have tended to follow fairly well-defined sets of relationships. Seldom is the same pattern followed in two action areas; new varieties of relationships are constantly being developed and put into use.

What Luther Gulick had to say about programs in the area of business regulations and control applies with equal pertinence to the development of intergovernmental relations in other areas. The former, Gulick observed:

> did not come about as a matter of social theory. [They] came about because ... problems arose.... The people most affected took what steps they could to establish the controls and the services they found to be needed.... Each move was a pragmatic Yankee solution designed to meet a condition, not a theory (Gulick 1962).

As a result, working federalism—that is, administrative federalism—is marked by diversity, trial and error, and experimentation on the one hand and it is problem-oriented on the other. As new problems are brought under attack by governments, different sets of relationships are established in connection with each. As Walker (1981) put it, what it all amounts to is a "non-system of federal-state-county-city-town-school district-special district-non-profit relationships that comprises the dynamics of ... American federalism."

IV. CENTRALIZED FEDERALISM

Although *centralized* federalism is primarily a product of the 1960s and 1970s, its roots go back to the first years of the Republic. Alexander Hamilton laid the foundation for it in his contributions to *The Federalist Papers* and in his state papers and actions as Secretary of the Treasury under George Washington. Later John Marshall, in his opinions as Chief Justice of the United States, consistently emphasized national power, stressing that the Constitution emanates from the American people as a whole. It followed then that the government created by the whole people is to be the focal point of governmental power in the United States and that it has the primary responsibility for meeting the needs of the American people. Between them, Hamilton and Marshall made the point that, in Marshall's words in *McCulloch v. Maryland* (1819), the national government "is the government of all, its powers are delegated by all; it represents all, and acts for all.... The nation, in those subjects on which it can act, must necessarily bind its component parts." Among those subjects is the responsibility, to paraphrase Chief Justice Salmon P. Chase in *Texas v. White* (1869) of maintaining not only the national government itself but of preserving the states and maintaining the governments thereof.

---

* In an early study of the attitudes of governmental officials concerned with the administration of federal grant programs (Subcommittee on Intergovernmental Relations, 1965) it was found that state and local officials were more apt to take a theoretical stand and to be concerned with balance and parity than were federal officials (pp. 95–97, 99).

Basic to the concept of centralized federalism obviously is reliance on the powers specifically delegated to the national government by the Constitution and perhaps less obviously those powers implied from the former through Article I, Section 8, the "necessary and proper" clause. "Broad construction of this clause by the Supreme Court, defining 'necessary' as meaning appropriate to the end and not explicitly forbidden, so effectively expanded the range of subjects on which the Congress could act that the Court ... came to see the Tenth Amendment as simply stating a truism" (Reagan and Sanzone 1981). The net effect of such judicial interpretation, which has been pretty consistently followed through the years, has been to permit the national government virtually all the latitude it needs to act when and how it sees fit, at least when it feels that the political consensus of the American people is behind it.

If there were few opportunities at first to put centralized federalism into practice, government as a whole not playing much of a part in Americans' lives, the Civil War and the two decades following it, Scheiber (1980) concluded, saw a "vast expansion of the policy responsibilities of the national government and an increase in the jurisdiction of the federal courts [underpinning a] significant centralization of real power," leading him to describe the period as one of "transitional centralization." From 1890 to 1933, Scheiber (1980) saw a period of "accelerating centralization marked by [s]uccessive federal laws advanc[ing] federal regulation" and the "intensive, if temporary, centralization" required by World War I. This period was characterized by a slow but steady growth in federal grants-in-aid from $52 million in 1902 to $596 million in 1927. That new technologies and the emerging national marketplace fueled governmental centralization is exemplified by the rapid rise in federal highway construction aid from none in 1915 to $92 million in 1922 (Walker 2000).

But it was the crisis caused by the Great Depression and the efforts of the New Deal to fight it that provided the opportunity for centralized federalism to become consolidated. Although the New Deal was not consistent in its policies and programs, it tended to view the national government as the engine to drive the country toward economic recovery and reform, and it continued to hold that view during World War II and afterwards. Looking back at the New Deal era, Leuchtenburg (1963) observed that "Roosevelt and the New Dealers almost revolutionized the agenda of American politics" by shifting the balance of federalism from state capitals to Washington and by making the national government, especially the president, "the focus of all government—the fountainhead of ideas, the initiator of action, the representative of the national interest." Such action was possible, in part, because many state governments failed to act or were unable to act effectively in attacking the multiple ills caused by the Depression.

Later the Roosevelt view was even more fully implemented. With the end of World War II the federal government embarked on a major expansion of the nation's physical infrastructure, including an interstate highway system, the Hill-Burton hospital construction program, public housing, and urban development. The recognition of poverty and racial segregation and other dysfunctional social conditions provided the impetus for the creation or enlargement of federal aid programs in economic development, education, environmental protection, law enforcement, medical care, social services, and welfare. Under the rubric of President Johnson's Great Society, centralization blossomed, until by 1969 James Sundquist could declare that "the American federal system [had] entered a new phase," a phase marked by "massive federal intervention in community affairs." Sundquist went on, "Through a series of dramatic enactments the Congress [had] asserted the national interest and authority in a wide range of governmental functions that until then had been the province exclusively or predominantly, of state and local governments" (Sundquist 1969; see also Benson 1941). Again, it is important to note that a wide variety of organized interests demanded national government initiatives because many state governments as late as the mid-1960s were characterized by mismanagement and political corruption (Leach 1970).

The chief tool employed by Congress in doing so was the grant-in-aid, which had begun to be used much earlier. But whereas at the beginning of the 1960s there were only about forty major governmental functions being aided by some billion federal dollars, by the end of the decade there were about 150 such functions to which some $24 billion federal dollars were being directed. And the numbers continued to grow. But it was not merely the proliferation of programs and the remarkable increase in the amount of federal funds to underwrite them that marked the centralization thrust of the Great Society. It was, even more importantly, the taking of the initiative by the national government in identifying what the national objectives were to be and in developing the programs thought necessary to achieve them.

Having identified a broad range of programs as being in the national interest and having provided funds to state and local governments to implement them in whole or in part, the national government, through congressional enactments and administrative rules, placed their administration under close federal control. The 1950s push to build up the country's physical plant included, for the first time, requirements that states and localities submit plans as part of their requests for federal aid dollars. This seemingly modest requirement led to rapid growth in the planning profession; this in turn was followed by growth in the evaluation and policy analysis professions as additional federal regulations demanded accountability for the use of federal funds (Krane 2001). Walker (1981) commented on "the many avenues" through which state and local actions were "circumscribed … by federal statutory and federal court-sanctioned constraints—based on an extraordinarily expansive interpretation of Congress's power to regulate interstate commerce and to spend for the public welfare." It would be a mistake to view the expansion of conditions associated with federal grants-in-aid as solely a bureaucratic product; after all, interest groups pressured Congress and the executive branch to attach rules on federal aid as a means of changing the behavior of state and local officials in areas as diverse as nondiscrimination, environmental and historic protection, access to government information and decision procedures, health, welfare and safety, and general administrative requirements (Walker 2000).

All the foregoing aside, centralized federalism did not crowd the states and their local subdivisions completely off the stage. Certain areas—matters affecting property and business contracts, the law of domestic relations, and the authority of state governments over local governments, for example—were not invaded at all. And despite the ever-widening panoply of nationally conceived and designed programs, the national government, as already suggested, usually worked through state and local governments in the actual administration of those programs. Thus the national bureaucracy remained remarkably stable throughout the period, while those of state and local governments increased enormously. Indeed, it is entirely possible to incorporate cooperative federalism into the concept of centralized federalism, as Vile (1961) concluded when he wrote that "the foremost characteristic of American federalism … is the *inter*dependence of federal and state governments."

Oddly enough, but perhaps not surprisingly, there was little evidence that many, if any, of those most active over time in developing centralized federalism thought in theoretical terms as they proceeded about their business, despite the easy availability of a corpus of theory to turn to. Rather, it appears clear that centralized federalism came about in large part because subnational governments found it easier and more expedient to turn to Uncle Sam for financing: an Uncle Sam who in the 1960s and into the 1970s seemed to be riding the crest of a wave of prosperity and could afford largess to them (and an Uncle Sam who was quickly losing his fear of deficit spending!), instead of meeting program needs out of their own resources. Thus program needs, not theory, propelled the rise of centralized federalism.

National actions from the end of World War II to the late 1970s aimed to overcome differences in life conditions by race, gender, and region as well as to reduce the spillover effects of changes in the economy and living patterns. Federal policies targeted opportunities and resources to populations and places that had not benefited from the explosive economic growth of the period. Similarly, federal actions also sought to establish a national sense of citizenship such that laws and services became more uniform across the fifty states. In this regard, Congressional legislation and US Supreme Court rulings on civil and political rights were crucial.

Political scientist Samuel Beer asserts that centralization was made inevitable by the very nature of the American economy as it came to be after World War II—an economy featuring ever-growing functional differentiation at the hands of professional technocrats, an economy that could only be held together for the overall good by centralized authority. Beer (1983) stressed the centralizing impact of scientific knowledge and of the technology attendant upon it on public policy makers and administrators, all of whom were united across jurisdictional lines in the particular programs or segments thereof in which they could apply their own skills and knowledge. This new professionalism—or "picket fence" federalism to use Wright's term—Beer (1983) contends, accounts for much of the expansionist public sector politics that marked the mid-decades of the twentieth century and contributed to centralization.

V. NEW FEDERALISM

Like states' rights federalism, *new* federalism was informed by a theoretical assumption made by President Nixon, who pledged both in campaigning and from the White House to redirect the actions on the federalism stage. A self-conscious conservative philosophically, Nixon was offended by the rise of centralized federalism and the imbalance he believed it produced in governmental power in the United States. He thought a sorting out of governmental roles and responsibilities and a rearrangement of governmental functions was not only possible but was required to bring about a balanced federal system. He found in a set of published writings just the exposition and synthesis he needed to operate from.* Basically, those writings made a case for a degree of decentralization in domestic policy making and program administration to be accompanied by more selective and refined financial assistance from the national government to the states and local governments. The focus of the latter was to be general revenue sharing (GRS), which once in effect would remove most of the strictures on how monies received from the national government could be spent by the recipient subnational governments. If the decentralization of policy making and administration remained confined mostly to rhetoric, GRS became the law of the land in 1972 and remained so until it was phased out in the middle 1980s.

But if GRS had been conceived as a tool of decentralization, it served as such only in part, for it increased the dependency of state (until 1980, when states were dropped from the list of recipient governments) and local governments on federal funding and, since payments went by right (no applications were necessary) to virtually all subnational jurisdictions in the country, it vastly extended the involvement of the national government in state and local program planning and operation.

Nixon and his successor Gerald Ford did not achieve their stated objective of returning domestic policy responsibility back to the states and localities. Instead, national aid as a percentage of state and local government expenditures increased as the federal government moved into functions traditionally associated with subnational governments. An important new direction in federal aid appeared during this period—newer aid programs targeted national funds toward individuals rather than jurisdictions. The bulk of federal dollars was distributed via entitlements for health care, housing, and income maintenance (Anton 1989). An ironic consequence of the federal shift to finance social services was that under new federalism aid to places peaked in 1978 and has declined since then (Kincaid 1999).

The effort to devolve program responsibility begun by Nixon gained new momentum during the Carter and Reagan administrations. Carter, during his one term, sought to deregulate certain sectors of the economy as well as to reduce the rules attached to federal aid. President Reagan, who

---

*Four papers, written under the pseudonyms of Publius, Cato, Althusius, and Polybius, appeared in *Publius*, 2, 95–146. Another, by Richard P. Nathan, "Federalism and the Shifting Nature of Fiscal Relations," appeared in *The Annals of the American Academy of Political and Social Science*, 419, 120–129.

campaigned on a platform that claimed "government was the problem" holding back the nation's progress, proposed an "even newer" new federalism that explicitly rejected cooperative federalism as well as the Nixon commitment to a national obligation to help states and localities pay for programs transferred from the federal government (Krane 1990). His first budget terminated 60 grant-in-aid programs, reduced funds for several entitlement programs, and consolidated 77 grants into 9 new block grants, and as a result, produced "the first absolute reduction in federal aid outlays recorded in decades" (Beam 1984). Many of the Reagan cuts fell on programs for the working poor and this targeting forced state governments to raise their own revenues to make up for the loss of federal dollars.

As Peirce (1984) observed, "When Reagan came to the presidency, his view of federalism was the strongest of any predecessor in decades." It was his conviction that Washington and the national power it stood for were the enemies both of subnational governments and of the American people and that they must be fought if federalism were to be rebalanced. Reagan (1982) urged a gathering of state legislators, "Together let us restore constitutional government, let us renew and enrich the power and purpose of state and local communities." Reagan carried his dream of reform further by proposing a swap to give the states full responsibility for welfare programs in return for the national government taking over the costs of Medicaid and the food stamp program, the eventual turnback of certain federal programs to the states, and the creation of a trust fund to be funded partially by the assignment of federal excise taxes to it and partially from general federal revenues, its purpose being to finance the transition from federal to state and local funding. Reactions to these proposals both in Congress and by state leaders was so vehemently negative that little was heard of them subsequently.

Undaunted and still in search of action to exemplify theoretical commitment, the Reagan administration came up with four routes to the restoration of the balance in the federal system deemed desirable, two of which were to significantly alter long-time usages in American federalism. Accepting the conclusions of a study by the ACIR (1980) that the federal grant-in-aid program had become overloaded and needed decongestion, Reaganites made the same call for a sorting out of responsibilities among the various levels of government President Nixon had made earlier. As it turned out, however, it was not politically possible to arrive at any generally accepted, precise allocation of level responsibilities. Devolution was also called for—that is, the substitution of state and local decision making for decision making at the national level, largely through the collapse of a number of categorical grants-in-aid into only a few block grants under which the states were to have more discretion in using the funds made available to them. Congress was not willing to go very far along that route, so not much actual devolution took place. Decongestion and devolution were to be joined by decrementalism and deregulation as routes to the new federalism.

Decrementalism was defined as reducing over time the funding levels of many government programs: simply cutting back on the national government's share of financing programs and thus forcing state and local governments to either reduce program services proportionately or fill the gap from their own supposedly ample resources. From fiscal 1982 on, administration budgets, lowering the proportion of the federal contribution to most grant-in-aid programs, and eliminating other programs altogether, were generally accepted by Congress, and the passage in 1985 of the Gramm-Rudman-Hollings bill, which mandated decreasing federal budget deficit levels each year until 1991, when a balanced budget was supposed to have been reached, made adherence to decrementalism the law of the land. The effect on state and local government finances was substantial: in 1980 federal grants-in-aid made up nearly 27% of state and local spending, but by 1987 dropped to 19%—a decline in real terms of 34% (Gleason 1988). The combination of devolution and decrementalism led to a defacto sorting out of functional responsibilities between national and state governments (Stenberg 1988) and produced a condition best labeled by John Shannon (1987) as "fend-for-yourself federalism."

Deregulation was the fourth of the D's proposed by the Reagan administration. It was in response to what were generally seen as overly demanding rules and regulations woven into the specifics of grant programs by Congress and federal administrative departments and agencies which were held to impede state and local governments in the implementation of federal co-funded programs. Executive Order 12291 established a benefit-cost analysis requirement and an OMB review of proposed regulations to slow the growth in federal regulatory burdens. As this increase in presidential oversight was put into place, the Reaganites also terminated the A-95 process of intergovernmental consultation that incorporated states and localities in the notice and review process related to federal grants. However, the Reagan administration abandoned its deregulatory rhetoric and imposed a new round of regulations designed to create uniform national standards on product liability. The intent of these new regulations was to assist corporations who faced compliance with widely varying state government regulations, some of which were more restrictive than national standards. In similar fashion, the Reaganites moved to impose new rules on states and localities in the areas of affirmative action, welfare-to-work programs, and medical care for handicapped infants. Despite its federalism rhetoric, the Reagan administration when "forced to choose between policies supportive of its federalist objectives ... and those supportive of other presidential priorities..., the administration decided to pursue a course that was openly or implicitly contrary to its stated intergovernmental goals" (Conlan 1988).

What is the legacy of Reagan's dream of federalism reform? Alice Rivlin (1992) calls attention to effects beyond the national capital:

> Unexpectedly, the Reagan cuts energized state and local governments. The cuts created what Richard Nathan has called "the paradox of devolution." With less federal help, states, and to some extent localities, were forced to strengthen their own capacities and resources to meet the rising social problems of the 1980s. The federal pullback came at a fortunate moment—after two decades that had greatly enhanced states' ability to move into the breach.

David Walker (2000) argues Reagan's attempts to reverse the centralization in American federalism failed:

> In short, Reagan's and Congress's impacts on intergovernmental relations from 1981 to 1988 were mildly surgical from a conservative perspective, though drastically so from a liberal vantage point. They constituted more a reaction than a revolution because neither the politics undergirding the earlier public expansionism nor most of the major programs that symbolized that activism were eliminated. To achieve a kind of "defacto," "decremental" federalism in some areas by the drastic device of triple-digit (in billions) budget deficits suggests an approach that does not make sense fiscally or, in the long run, for federalism. No return to dual or even simple cooperative federalism of 1960 occurred. When the regulatory, preemptive, political, and judicial developments of the Reagan years are combined, the net result was a greater centralization in the system ...

Perhaps the numbers give the best assessment: the rapidly growing costs of health care and income maintenance programs forced the George H. W. Bush administration to reverse course, and by the end of the first Clinton administration, federal aid as a percentage of state and local expenditures reached near-historic high levels.

VI. EVOLVING FEDERALISM

American federalism in the last years of the twentieth century was significantly more centralized than it was at beginning or the middle of that century and the federal government's impact on the lives of US citizens was more extensive and pervasive (Zimmerman 1992). But states and localities also played a much larger role in people's lives. The relationship between national and state government authority, which is at the heart of any discussion of American federalism, is open-ended and shaped by the larger economic, cultural, and political forces in society. Several influences on how the attributes of US federalism are changing merit comment.

Washington, DC continues to be the principal forum in which important policy directions are established, but the administration of domestic programs has been devolved to the states and localities. Sawicky (1999) points out that "if we exclude Social Security, Medicare, net interest on the federal debt, and defense from the total expenditures of federal, state, and local governments in the United States, 80 percent of what remains is administered by state and local governments." The movement to downsize government at all levels, as exemplified by the Republican party's 1994 Contract with America, is perceived by many as a long overdue readjustment of responsibilities between national and state governments. Critics note that this devolution of program responsibility has not stopped with state governments because states have also devolved programmatic responsibilities to local governments. The result is a second order devolution in which states have transferred federal and state program activities along with federal and state regulations to county and city governments, often without the necessary fiscal support or policy authority (National League of Cities 2003). "Squeeze-down federalism," Jonathan Walters (1996) argues, has relegated to local government "a huge amount of responsibility for some of society's toughest, costliest. and most thankless jobs…, and the results can be overwhelming."

The capacity of state and local governments to fend for themselves has been diminished by two important fiscal trends. Citizen revolts against property taxes beginning in California in the late 1970s led state governments to enact restrictions on local property tax rates or growth. By the late 1990s, 37 states had put in place property tax limits (Mackey 1997), and while the reductions in property tax revenues have been partially offset by other sources of revenues (e.g., sales tax, user fees, state aid), many localities struggle financially. The antigovernment stance espoused by Reagan has also found expression in state-imposed limits on local government expenditures. This combination of tax and expenditure limits (TELs) has reduced local autonomy and increased centralization of state and local finances (Saxton et al. 2002). Some states have increased state aid to localities and/or assumed more responsibility for local services (e.g., K-12 education) to replace lost property tax revenues (Fisher 1996), but the ability of state governments to pay for local services has been seriously undermined by the worst shortfall in state revenues since the Great Depression (Lemov 2002). Faced with huge budget deficits, state governments began in 2001 to slash programs and personnel across the board, exhaust state reserve funds, borrow monies, adopt accounting gimmicks, and even raise taxes. Not even sacred cows such as public education or prisons were exempt. Cities and counties soon found state aid drying up, and they were left with even fewer funds as their local sales tax revenues also declined. But the national government has not stepped in to aid states and localities, reflecting in part the legacy of the Reagan administration's antigovernment policy. Members of the George W. Bush administration, with support from think tanks such as the Heritage Foundation, have argued that "if it is important to shrink the size of the bureaucracy in Washington, it is also important to shrink state government bureaucracy" (Krane 2003). Of course, the lack of federal assistance leaves states and localities with the difficulty of delivering major federal and state programs to citizens, but without sufficient monies to cover the costs. Bruce Katz (2003), an analyst at The Brookings Institution, argues that "it is odd and ahistorical to do nothing for the states and not expect it to hurt the national economy." Nothing could be more indicative of the fend-for-yourself devolutionary legacy of new federalism than the refusal of federal authorities to bail out the states and localities.

An important foundation of Reagan's new federalism was the belief, based in normative economic theory, that public provision of goods and services was inherently more inefficient than private provision because governments did not operate in a competitive market (Schlesinger et al. 1986). Efficiencies could be gained, the remedy prescribed, by privatization of government services, primarily through the use of contracts with private enterprise, but also by the divestiture of services (Savas 1982; Tullock 1965). A long history of government contracting for infrastructure, defense, and administrative supplies has existed, but the more recent movement to downsize the public sector has expanded contracting to areas such as social services where there was little or no previous history. As social service contracting by state and local governments has become more common, the delivery of public programs is characterized increasingly by the use of complex provider networks composed of public agencies (often linked vertically or horizontally), nonprofit organizations, and for-profit enterprises. One important consequence of this shift from a single government agency to a network of diverse organizations is the emergence of *intersectoral administration*. By blurring the boundaries between public, nonprofit, and for-profit sectors in society (Musolf and Seidman 1980), privatization expands administrative federalism by incorporating the intergovernmental management of multi-sectoral networks. Contracted delivery of government services may yield more efficiencies, though the evidence on this claim is still out, but it may also reduce significantly the capacity of public agencies to perform their functions (Milward and Provan 2000), and it definitely poses serious issues of accountability (Romzek and Dubnick 1987).

Not only are the boundaries blurring between public and private sectors, but the boundaries between nations are blurring in regard to the formulation and implementation of public policies. Numerous policy areas are shaped increasingly by decisions made beyond national borders (e.g., international agreements; multinational corporate actions) and these decisions often impose requirements that must be administered locally. Policy issues that result from the interconnections between international and domestic problems have been labeled *intermestic issues* (Manning 1977). Examples encompass the enforcement of international treaties protecting the environment and wildlife, United Nations' agreements on rights for women and for children, the adoption of industrial quality standards, and most recently the imposition of homeland security procedures. Intermestic issues affect federalism because they "constitute a new source of likely IGR tension ... [since] the catalyst causing the conflict can be any one or a combination of different planes of government—international, national, state, local—often located in another country" (Krane and Wright 1998). Whether local industries or local officials wish it, global agreements (e.g., on subsidies or pollutants) can impose unexpected and unwanted mandates that must be enforced.

But intermestic issues are not a one-way street; state and local governments also act internationally. In response to a globalized marketplace, many state and local governments actively promote direct foreign investment, levy taxes on foreign businesses, and even enact regulations requiring ethical and moral actions on the part of other countries or by multinational corporations. The US Constitution's grant of authority in international affairs to the national government has not prevented state and local governments from international involvement (Conlan et al. 2003). What in the past was seen as an inherent power of the federal government is being transformed into a de facto concurrent power.

America's political parties are a product of the nation's federal arrangements and a source of its manner of functioning (Elazar 1972), so how the two parties conceive of federalism and act on their conception critically affects the evolution of federalism. Party positions adopted during the 1950s and 1960s struggle for civil and political rights made federal–state relations an important issue. By 1980 the two parties' perspectives on federalism had diverged to the point that they became a defining aspect of each party's identity. Democrats continued to support a cooperative federalism that relied on a flexible intergovernmental approach to policy problems. Republicans, by contrast, adopted a firm prescription as to how responsibilities between federal and state governments ought to be divided, and they pushed for the creation (or perhaps resurrection) of restraints to insure this division. Stymied by the Democrats' control of Congress, Republican presidents appointed Supreme Court justices who shared the party's federalism vision. The Rehnquist Court's rulings moving away from the New Deal's centralized federalism and giving states some protections from unlimited expansion of federal encroachment, Clayton and Pickerill (2003) argue, are a product of this change in the Republican party's conception of federalism.

In a very real sense, the opposing partisan conceptions of federalism reflect different strategies about how best to maintain federalism within a modern mass democracy. For the Democrats, the Madisonian maneuvering of interests within majority rule institutions offers a set of political safeguards for the position of the states in the federal system. Republicans prefer the judicial safeguard of articulated legal limits which courts would enforce (Kramer 2000; Hamilton 2001).

But whether the two parties will hold fast to their distinct positions on federalism is an open question. Since the Democrats' loss of their congressional majorities, they have increasingly supported giving state governments discretion over important policy decisions such as air pollution, electricity deregulation, health care, financial services, same-sex marriage, and stem cell research. At the same time, Republicans have used their control of Congress to push national standards even in functions traditionally associated with local governments (Krane 2002). The best example of this is President George W. Bush's support for the No Child Left Behind Act of 2001, which has been attacked by critics as "the single largest, and the single most damaging expansion of national power over the nation's school system in history" (Elmore 2003). But how does one account for this seemingly hypocritical stance toward federalism by both parties? It is important to remember "American federalism is a supremely political institution" (Anton 1989) and politicians pursue benefits for themselves and for their supporters by arguing for policy control at one tier of government or another as a means to those benefits. Simply put, federalism principles will be sacrificed for pragmatic policy gains. The ambiguity over assignments of functional responsibility abets battles over which level and institution of government should make a policy decision and which should pay and/or administer a policy. Because "no solution is ever final," "the federal system in the United States ... is always in flux" (Leach 1970). That the political parties will change positions over what some consider to be fundamental principles of American federalism should come as no surprise. After all, changing one's position about federal–state relations began in the early days of the Republic.

VII. CONCLUSION

As the foregoing has demonstrated, the concept of federalism in the American system of government has been undergoing change and adaptation ever since the drafting of the Constitution in 1787. It continues so. For some time now the nation has been in a transitional stage in federalism. The five ideas and concepts that have animated our system of government over the years may well be joined by another set of concepts. None of the original five has disappeared from the stage, however, and may be drawn on as the pendulum continues to swing. As a variation of states' rights federalism, state-oriented federalism, as already suggested, seems likely to be fleshed out, in the course of which process centralized and administrative federalism seem as likely to be significantly altered. And new federalism in the guise of devolution may well become dominant.

Adaptations are already in train, and the plethora of problems which demand government attention in the years just ahead suggest they will continue to be made. Health and welfare reform are perhaps the key areas of action, but curbing environmental abuses, expanding educational quality and opportunities, dealing with hazardous waste, coping with international terrorism, and rising to the challenges of what Drucker (1994) has called "the age of social transformation" will all impact on the federal system.

It is worth remembering that over the years theory has not been a very important element in the actual operation of the American federal system. For the most part, federalism has developed pragmatically rather than in response to a conceptual framework. Two things might be kept in mind: (1) constitutional federalism left it unclear, barring future amendments, as to the precise direction in which the federal ship was to sail, and (2) experience has shown that federalism being in flux is normal, for the founders created an open-ended system. We can only be the losers if we try to close it off by adopting one set of theoretical principles, particular model, or set construct. As in so many areas, in building federalism the founders built better than they knew, and we are the beneficiaries.

REFERENCES

ACIR (Advisory Commission on Intergovernmental Relations), *In Brief—The Federal Role in the Federal System: The Dynamics of Growth*, Vol. 37, Government Printing Office, Washington, DC, 1980.

Agranoff, R. J., *Intergovernmental Management: Human Services Problem Solving in Six Metropolitan Areas*, State University of New York Press, Albany, NY, 1986.

Agranoff, R. J. and McGuire, M., *Collaborative Management: New Strategies for Local Government*, Georgetown University Press, Washington, DC, 2003.

Anton, T. J., *American Federalism & Public Policy: How the System Works*, Random House, New York, 1989.

Beam, D. R., New federalism, old realities: the Reagan administration and intergovernmental reform, In *The Reagan Presidency and the Governing of America*, Salamon, L. M. and Lund, M. S., Eds., Urban Institute Press, Washington, DC, pp. 415–442, 1984.

Beer, S. H., The modernization of American federalism, *Publius*, 3, 53–95, 1983.

Benson, G. C. S., *The New Centralization: A Study of Intergovernmental Relationships in the United States*, Rinehart, New York, 1941.

Clayton, C.W. and Pickerill, J.M., The Supreme Court and federalism: guess what happened on the way to the revolution? Paper presented at the annual meeting of the American Political Science Association, Philadelphia, PA, 2003.

Clark, J. P., *The Rise of a New Federalism: Federal-State Cooperation in the United States*, Columbia University Press, New York, 1938.

Conlan, T., *New Federalism: Intergovernmental Reform from Nixon to Reagan*, The Brookings Institution, Washington, DC, 1988.

Conlan, T., Dudley, R.L., and Clark, J.F., Taking on the world: the international activities of American state legislatures. Paper presented at the annual meeting of the American Political Science Association, Philadelphia, PA, 2003.

Drucker, P. F., The age of social transformation, *Atlantic Monthly*, 53–56, November 1994.

Elazar, D. J., *The American Partnership*, University of Chicago Press, Chicago, IL, p. 336, 1962.

Elazar, D. J., *American Federalism: A View from the States*, Vol. 6, 2nd ed., Crowell, New York, pp. 219–220 1972.

Elmore, R., Quoted in Sam Dillion, States cut test standards to avoid sanctions, *New York Times*, May 22, 2003.

Federalist, *The Federalist Papers*, Bantam Books, New York, 1981.

Fisher, G. W., *The Worst Tax?: A History of the Property Tax in America*, University Press of Kansas, Lawrence, KS, 1996.

Gage, R. W. and Mandell, M. P., Eds., *Strategies for Managing Intergovernmental Policies and Networks*, Praeger, New York, 1990.

Gleason, R., Federalism 1986–1987: Signals of a new era, *Intergovernmental Perspective*, Vol. 14, Advisory Commission on Intergovernmental Relations, Washington, DC, pp. 9–14, 1988.

Grodzins, M., The federal system, In *Goals for Americans, The Report of the President's Commission on National Goals*, Prentice Hall, New York, pp. 265–268, 1960.

Gulick, L. H., *The Metropolitan Problem and American Ideas*, Knopf, New York, pp. 15–16, 1962.

Hamilton, J. C., *The Works of Alexander Hamilton*, Vol. 2, John F. Trow, New York, p. 194, 1850.

Hamilton, M., The elusive safeguards of federalism, *The Annals of the American Academy of Political and Social Science*, 574, 93–103, 2001.

Jefferson, T., The Kentucky resolutions, In *The Portable Thomas Jefferson*, Peterson, M. D., Ed., Penguin Books, New York, pp. 281–289, 1975.

Jennings, E. T., Jr., and Krane, D., Coordination and welfare reform: the quest for the philosopher's stone, *Public Administration Review*, 54, 341–348, 1994.

Katz, B., Quoted in Powell, M., Rescue's just not part of the plan. *Washington Post*, May 4 2003 (Netscape version).

Kettl, D. F., Federalism: dusting off 'dignity,' *Governing*, 15(1), 14, 2002.

Kincaid, J., DeFacto devolution and urban defunding: the priority of persons over places, *Journal of Urban Affairs*, 21, 135–167, 1999.

Kramer, L. D., Putting the politics back into the political safeguards of federalism, *Columbia Law Review*, 100, 215–293, 2000.

Krane, D., Devolution as an intergovernmental reform strategy, In *Strategies for Managing Intergovernmental Policies and Networks*, Gage, R. W. and Mandell, M. P., Eds., Praeger, New York, 1990.

Krane, D., Disorderly progress on the frontiers of policy evaluation, *International Journal of Public Administration*, 24, 95–123, 2001.

Krane, D., The state of American federalism: resilience in response to crisis, *Publius*, 32(4), 1–28, 2002.

Krane, D., The state of American federalism: division replaces unity, *Publius*, 33(3), 1–44, 2003.

Krane, D. and Wright, D. S., Intergovernmental relations, In *International Encyclopedia of Public Policy and Administration*, Shafritz, J., Ed., Vol. 2, Westview Press, Boulder, CO, pp. 1168–1176, 1998.

Leach, R. H., *American Federalism*, W.W. Norton, New York, 1970.

Lemov, P., Deficit deluge, *Governing*, May 22, 2002.

Leuchtenburg, W. E., *Franklin D. Roosevelt and the New Deal*, Harper & Row, New York, p. 326, 1963.

Macdonald, H. M., Webb, M. D., Lewis, E. G., and Strauss, W. L., *Outside Readings in American Government*, 3rd ed., Crowell, New York, pp. 113–116, 1957.

Mackey, S., *Critical Issues in State–Local Fiscal Policy*, National Conference of State Legislatures, Denver, CO, 1997.

Madison, J., The Virginia resolution, In *Letters and Other Writings of James Madison*, Crowell, New York, pp. 113–116, 1884.

Manning, B., The Congress, the executive, and intermestic affairs, *Foreign Affairs*, 55, 306–324, 1977.

Marando, V. L. and Florestano, P. S., Intergovernmental management: the state of the discipline, In *Public Administration: The State of the Discipline*, Lynn, N. B. and Wildavsky, A., Eds., Chatham House, Chatham, NJ, pp. 287–317, 1990.

Mason, A. T. and Leach, R. H., In *Quest of Freedom: American Political Thought and Practice*, Vol. 61, University Press of America, Washington, DC, p. 103, 1981.

Milward, H. B. and Provan, G. K., Governing the hollow state, *Journal of Public Administration Research and Theory*, 10(2), 359–380, 2000.

Musolf, L. D. and Seidman, H., The blurred boundaries of public administration, *Public Administration Review*, 40(2), 124–130, 1980.

National League of Cities, *Cities and the Future of Public Finance: A Framework for Public Discussion*, Washington, DC, 2003.

Ostrorm, V., *The Meaning of Federalism: Constituting a Self-Governing Society*, Institute for Contemporary Studies, San Francisco, CA, 1991.

Peirce, N. R., Ronald Reagan: the states' president?, *Public Administration Times*, 7, 2, 1984.

Peterson, P. E., *The Changing Politics of Federalism Evolving Federalism: The Intergovernmental Balance of Power in America and Europe*, Campbell Public Affairs Institute, The Maxwell School of Syracuse University, Syracuse, NY, pp. 25–41, 2003.

Plano, J. C. and Greenberg, M., *The American Political Dictionary*, 7th ed., Holt, Rinehart and Winston, New York, p. 42, 1985.

Reagan, R., Remarks of President Reagan to the National Conference of State Legislatures, Atlanta, GA, July 30, 1982.

Reagan, M. D. and Sanzone, J. G., *The New Federalism*, 2nd ed., Oxford University Press, New York, p. 10, 1981.

Rivlin, A. M., *Reviving the American Dream: The Economy, the States and the Federal Government*, The Brookings Institution, Washington, DC, 1992.

Rockefeller, N. A., *The Future of Federalism*, Harvard University Press, Cambridge, MA, 1962.

Romzek, B. S. and Dubnick, M. J., Accountability in the public sector: lessons from the challenger tragedy, *Public Administration Review*, 47, 227–238, 1987.

Savas, E. S., *Privatizing the Public Sector: How to Shrink Government*, Chatham House Publishers, Chatham, NJ, 1982.

Saxton, G. D., Hoene, C. W., and Erie, S. P., Fiscal constraints and the loss of home rule: the long-term impacts of California's post-Proposition 13 fiscal regime, *American Review of Public Administration*, 32, 423–454, 2002.

Sawicky, M., The new American devolution: problems and prospects, In *The End of Welfare?: Consequences of Federal Devolution for the Nation*, Sawicky, M., Ed., M.E. Sharpe, Armonk, NY, pp. 3–24, 1999.

Scheiber, R. N., Federalism and legal process: historical and contemporary analysis of the American system, *Law and Society Review*, 14, 679–680, 1980.

Schlesinger, M., Dorwart, R. A., and Pulice, R. T., Competitive bidding and states' purchase of services: the case of mental health care in Massachusetts, *Journal of Policy Analysis and Management*, 5(2), 245–263, 1986.

Seay, D. and Smith, W., *Federalism Issues '96: the Candidate's Briefing Book*, The Heritage Foundation, Washington, DC, 1996.

Shannon, J., The return of fend-for-yourself federalism: the Reagan mark, *Intergovernmental Perspective*, 13, 34–37, 1987.

Stenberg, C. W., *Intergovernmental Ironies. SIAM Intergovernmental News*, Vol. 11, Section on Intergovernmental Administration and Management, American Society for Public Administration, Washington, DC, pp. 4–5, 1988.

Storing, H. J., *What the Anti-Federalists Were For*, Murray Dry, Ed., 28, 30–35, passim, and especially chap. 4: University of Chicago Press, Chicago, IL. See also his (with Murray Dry) *The Complete Anti-Federalist*. 7 Vols. 1982. University of Chicago Press, Chicago, IL, 1981.

Sundquist, J. L. and Davis, D. W., *Making Federalism Work: a Study of Program Coordination at the Community Level*, Vol. 1, Brookings Institution, Washington, DC, 1969.

Taylor, J., *Construction Construed and Constitutions Vindicated*, Shepherd and Pollard, Richmond, VA, 1820.

Tullock, G., *The Politics of Bureaucracy*, Public Affairs Press, Washington, DC, 1965.

Vile, M. J. C., *The Structure of American Federalism*, Oxford University Press, New York, p. 3, 1961.

Walker, D. B., The condition of American federalism. A statement of the Advisory Commission on Intergovernmental Relations before the Subcommittee on Intergovernmental Relations and Human Resources of the Committee on Government Operations, U.S. House of Representatives, 2–4 Xerox, April 7, 1981.

Walker, D. B., *The Rebirth of Federalism*, 2nd ed., Chatham House, New York, 2000.

Walters, J., Cry, the beleaguered county, *Governing*, August, 31–37, 1996.

Williams, W., *The Implementation Perspective: a Guide for Managing Social Service Delivery Programs*, University of California Press, Berkeley, CA, 1980.

Wills, G., *Explaining America: The Federalist*, Penguin Books, New York, 174, pp. 171–172, 1982.

Wright, D. S., *Understanding Intergovernmental Relations*, 3rd ed., Brooks Cole Publications, Pacific Grove, CA, 1988.

Wright, D. S., Federalism, intergovernmental relations, and intergovernmental management: historical reflections and conceptual comparisons, *Public Administration Review*, 50, 168–178, 1990.

Zimmerman, J. F., *Contemporary American Federalism: the Growth of National Power*, Praeger, New York, 1992.

Unit 7

Public Policy

Back to Square One: The History and Promise of the Policy Sciences

Peter deLeon and Danielle M. Vogenbeck[*]

CONTENTS

[*] Prof. E. Samuel Overman, who died in 1986, was a co-author of the first edition of this essay. The current authors gratefully acknowledge their debt to Prof. Overman.

I. INTRODUCTION

The policy sciences are characterized by a long past but a short history. For a discipline whose intellectual seeds were sown in the 1940s, the policy sciences have achieved remarkable success in altering the landscape of academic and government organizations. Clearly, public policies and policy advice can be traced back to the beginnings of history itself, but the contemporary policy sciences have a particularly American and twentieth-century flavor. Pre-World War II aspirations among a small core of American social scientists (such as John Dewey and Charles Merriam) for producing societally relevant knowledge led to the publication of *The Policy Sciences* edited by Lerner and Lasswell (1951). Lasswell's now-famous vision articulated in his contribution, "The Policy Orientation," was of a multidisciplinary, contextual, problem-oriented, and explicitly normative policy science. Achieving these ambitious goals has occupied the policy sciences throughout the remainder of the twentieth century and, indeed, into the twenty-first century.

The articulation and subsequent practice of the policy sciences have depended on the complex interaction of academic and social influences. From within the community of policy science, the struggle has been to expand the scope and uses of the approach. This dynamic, however, has always been tempered by the major social and political events of the day. Thus, the on-going emphasis on policy evaluation must be seen as a direct consequence of the social programs of the 1960s and education controversies, policy termination as a result of resource scarcity in the 1970s, 1980s, and the early 2000s, and the role of ethics and values at least partly attributable to the Watergate affair. As a function of these and other events, the policy sciences grew in both theoretical scope and applicability throughout the 1970s and 1980s. As will be discussed, the 1990s resulted in a partial reformulation, followed by a retrenchment in the early twenty-first century.

Today the policy sciences have moved beyond naive aspirations for societally relevant knowledge. The credibility of policy sciences has justifiably been challenged for failing to produce objective empirical and normative truths. In the 1980s, the emphasis on ethics and values and the inclusion of institutional analysis and public management as central policy concerns improved the scope of the policy sciences but were ultimately injurious to the credibility of their scientific status. Scientific rationality, thought by many to be the cornerstone of policy sciences, is being challenged by a broader concept of reason in society. Thus, the contemporary policy sciences are at a crossroads, wavering between narrow-gauge utility and a more complete understanding, with important amendments still to be made.

II. ASPIRATIONS FOR SOCIETALLY RELEVANT KNOWLEDGE

The policy orientation was not articulated until 1951 by Harold Lasswell, but its origins go back much further. The history of governing has always been marked by the relationships of advisor to ruler on a personalized and circumstantial basis. From Plato's Academy and the courts of the Chinese emperors to the modern policy institutes, people have been trying to bring knowledge to government and the act of governing. Although the American experience still owes much to the history of Western civilization, the conception, birth, and early growth of the policy sciences are in many ways particular to the United States. Early American philosophical orientations (see John Dewey) favored a highly pragmatic and utilitarian concept of knowledge and science. These philosophical positions led both physical and social scientists to search for practical applications of their knowledge and expertise. Applied social science was a pre-World War II vision and, in some cases, a legitimate accomplishment among the nation's social scientists (Lynd 1939; Merton 1936). The policy sciences as described by Lasswell (1951) were the culmination of efforts to define a discipline for producing and applying societally relevant knowledge.

A. POLICY SCIENCES IN WESTERN CIVILIZATION

Policy analysis and its consequent advice have been practiced in one form or another since people have been making political decisions. Dunn (1981) considers the Code of Hammurabi, originating around the eighteenth century BC, to be among the earliest recorded examples of policy analysis. Tuchman (1984) re-creates a debate among the leaders of Troy about whether or not to accept the Greek-proffered Trojan horse as an example of an early episode (and failure) in policy analysis. Policy advice as a political exercise is hardly a new or novel idea. Still, historically, policy analysis and advice were very personalized, idiosyncratic activities, passing from sage to ruler with only scarce and episodic regard for routinizing the activity (Goldhamer 1978).

Systematic policy counsel grew out of the church and state relationship. Like many themes in Western civilization, it was not until the Italian Renaissance that policy advice assumed a more institutionalized basis, the writings of Machiavelli (1515/1959) being the most celebrated illustration. Thomas More's *Utopia* (1516) provided a haven for social contemplation; Bacon's *New Atlantis* (1627) applied scientific knowledge to the circles of government. The worldly philosophers such as Erasmus and the English political philosophers (e.g., Locke and Hobbes) set the intellectual tones for the subsequent study of politics and administration as the partial precursors of the policy sciences. And, of course, Jonathan Swift had the curious Gulliver observe the Academy of Projectors in his voyage to Legado, as its scientists worked to convert cucumbers into solar energy (1726).

Important in this historical progression was the growing political acceptance of knowledge and its substantive application for those with ruling responsibilities, a condition reflected by the influence of the eighteenth-century English political philosophers such as Burke, Locke, and Hume. The increased involvement and interaction of political philosophy with political events was apparent with the French philosophers, e.g., Montesquieu's *The Spirit of Laws* (1748) and Rousseau's *Social Contract* (1762), who preceded the Age of Revolution. The later American *Federalist Papers* (1787/1788) elaborated on the interplay of political doctrine with specific ideas as to how a government should be structured and operate.

However, while there might have been some basic recognition of the need for nominally independent policy advice regularly offered to governing bodies, this counsel was more likely to be tendered on a parochial, personalized basis, largely predicated on political caprice and association. The political philosophers of the day were far from objective, neutral participants. There was scant consideration of intellectual underpinnings, honesty, cumulative knowledge, or independent evaluations as they could be applied to policy issues. In short, there was little reason for these activities to be considered as the intellectual precursors of the policy sciences. There was little conception of a policy process or what composed a good policy; certainly there was no explicit research or literature on these issues. They did, however, provide an intellectual stimulus and some practical precedents to the later development and articulation in the pursuit of societally relevant knowledge.

The growth of applied empirical research in France and England during the nineteenth century coincided with public awareness of acute social problems (Dunn 1981). Descriptive statistics were used to plot the plight of the English urban poor. The English Industrial Revolution and the American Progressive movement both produced widespread demands for improvements in the inchoate social welfare programs. While new policies were initiated to relieve these tensions, they certainly were not brought about by analytic (as opposed to literary) examinations of the conditions and trends. Examples of early research on the documentation and alleviation of social woes were not totally lacking, but were generally isolated and not cumulative (Bulmer 1982). Dickens and Shaw were probably more influential in affecting British social welfare legislation than Booth and the Webbs, just as the Tarbells and Sinclairs were primary movers in the American Progressive movement.

There were some unquestionably important early developments in the academic disciplines, which were later to leave their marks on the policy sciences. Beginning in the mid-eighteenth century, the study of economics began to mature as a set of possible insights into policy issues; Adam Smith's writing in political economy and David Ricardo's influence on English agriculture and free-trade policies are the most prominent examples. Historians were in the vanguard in contextual studies, but their works almost never assumed a prescriptive perspective. The principal intellectual motif of the late nineteenth century was that social laws akin to physical and natural counterparts could be discovered and applied. Social Darwinism—as interpreted by Herbert Spencer and T. H. Huxley—was a cultural phenomenon on both sides of the Atlantic. Finally, the study of politics and public administration was starting to define itself in matters pertaining to governance. In 1887, the academic study of American public administration was established by Woodrow Wilson, who realized that it was "getting to be harder to run a constitution than to frame one" (Wilson 1887). In short, academic disciplines were beginning to apply their skills and insights to social problems, that is, to test cautious notions of societally relevant knowledge.

Thus, even though the systematic and routinized examination of public policy issues and problems was not in existence by the dawn of the twentieth century—certainly not from an organized institutional basis—many disciplinary contributions that would later emerge as central components or stimuli to the policy sciences were starting to fall into place. However, these various approaches were developing their limited policy concerns and insights isolated from one another. They were largely defining themselves as very differentiated disciplines rather than coordinated, integrated approaches addressing social problems. Indeed, as these disciplines struggled for their respective, distinctive identities, they adopted their own intellectual boundaries that jealously precluded other perspectives. This trend affected the policy sciences well into the twentieth century.

B.   AMERICAN PRAGMATISM AND INSTRUMENTALISM

American pragmatic and instrumental philosophies had a profound effect on the development of the social sciences. American philosopher William James, who popularized the term pragmatism, was reacting against an earlier and primarily European rationalist and empirical philosophical insistence on singular and objective truths. He saw the American experience as requiring a philosophy separate from its European antecedents. James (1975) held that truth and, by extension, societally relevant knowledge must conform to much more pluralist notions of reality. To these ends, he developed pragmatism, a philosophy later attacked as reflecting the material, practical, and even commercial values of American society (Ross 1970, xii). Pragmatism allows human perception, multiple interpretation, and debate to become an integral part of theories and meaning of truth and thus the political arena. Knowledge, embedded in a social context and valuable for the type of practical problems, would become a leitmotiv among twentieth century American social scientists. At the turn of the century, pragmatism provided a rationale for extending the application and relevance of the scientific approach to social, political, and economic components of life. As such, it was incorporated in the concept of the policy sciences through the writing of John Dewey.

Dewey extended James' pragmatist notions of truth and meaning to fit his more instrumental orientation. According to Dewey, the goal of scientific inquiry should not be some abstract version of the truth, rather a transformed situation (Dewey 1927). Knowledge and ideas are instruments that lead to action and are to be understood in terms of the consequences of those actions. Science, particularly social science, is to be judged on the basis of its contributions toward improving the human condition. This instrumental view of the role of knowledge in society formed the basic premise of the policy sciences. Lasswell, in his 1951 essay, credited Dewey as an early example of a policy scientist more interested in "evaluating and reconstructing the practices of society than in higher ratiocination about the higher abstractions from which his values are derived" (Lasswell 1951, 12). In his preface to *A Pre-View of Policy Sciences*, Lasswell (1971, xiv) acknowledged, "The policy sciences are a contemporary policy adaptation of the general approach to public policy that was recommended by John Dewey and his colleagues in the development of American pragmatism."

Perhaps even more important, Dewey developed a process of inquiry that still stands at the heart of contemporary policy process. Dewey (1929) outlined an instrumental process of inquiry, in which the investigator begins with a definition of the problem and proceeds through steps analyzing different alternatives ("ordering of suggestions") and evaluating the consequences of each alternative before arriving at the alternative that best solves the problem. In Dewey's words, scientific observation was impelled by active exploration and a sympathetic interest in solving some social and theoretical problem, not an end in itself (Dewey 1933). Finally, Dewey's (1927) unending advocacy for—insistence upon—a democratic order is also reflected in the policy sciences.

Although pragmatism and instrumentalism provide a philosophical underpinning for the goal of producing societally relevant knowledge, they are also the source of the single most perceptive critique of the policy sciences. Specifically, the policy sciences have been attacked for serving as a high-priced apologist to political interests (Horowitz and Katz 1975). Given the open, pluralist ideals that instrumentalism espoused for societally relevant knowledge, it simply was not enough to produce relevant and action-oriented knowledge; one need ask, "Whose interests would knowledge serve?" and "What are the distributive consequences in terms of both power and resources of public policies?" These questions continue to haunt the policy sciences as they reveal the inherently normative nature of an instrumentally driven social inquiry.

As the policy sciences have evolved, so did their uses, intended or not. That good policy analysis can now support political actions as widely divergent as privatization and public ownership is ample evidence that public policy is inevitably also the study of who gets what, when, and how (Fischer 1993). Nevertheless, in the early twentieth century, the study of public policy provided a forum for social scientists to practice their pragmatist ideals of applied social science.

C. Applied Social Science

Most social scientists were initially reluctant to abandon their disciplinary training, but by the late 1930s, the idea that scientific advice and procedures could and should have a direct effect on social problems was no longer an academic fantasy, but was slowly becoming a personal and institutionalized expectation, although not without some friction. It was easier for academic departments to remain isolated from their surrounding communities than to test their knowledge in a social arena. Despite their reluctance, an integrated policy science was foreshadowed by isolated and largely fruitless attempts to foster an applied social science.

Charles Merriam, Lasswell's University of Chicago mentor, was an early proponent of an applied, multidisciplinary social science. His 1925 presidential address before the American Political Science Association is indicative of these leanings:

> Likewise we are likely to see a closer integration of the social sciences themselves, which in the necessary process of differentiation have in many cases become too isolated. In dealing with basic problems such as those of the punishment and prevention of crime, alcoholism, the vexed question of human migration, the relations of the Negro, and a wise variety of industrial and agricultural problems, it becomes evident that neither the facts and the technique of economics alone, nor of politics alone, nor of history alone, are adequate to their analysis and interpretation....

After all, it does not seriously matter what this integration is called, whether sociology or *staatswissenschaft* or anthropology or economics or politics. The essential consideration is that the point of view and the contacts are obtained and sustained in the various fields of social inquiry; that partial treatment does not twist and warp the judgment of social observers and analysts. The problem of social behavior is essentially one problem, and while the angles of the approach may and should be different, the scientific result will be imperfect unless these points of view are at times brought together in some effective way, so that the full benefit of the multiple analysis may be realized (Merriam 1926, 8–9).

However prescient Merriam might have been in his assaults on disciplinary satraps and appeals for applied social science research, his exhortations fell on fallow ground. Few university departments or professional associations followed his lead. They might have been too busy consolidating and protecting their own professional identities and egos, or they might have been too enamored with the hallowed academic tradition of independence from their surrounding communities. Although certainly there were intellectual refinements during the 1930s, most were directed internally toward methodological enhancements rather than externally toward community problems. Political science, for example, became embroiled in the behavioral debate, while economics was thoroughly enmeshed in its own theoretic coils of empiricism, even if this meant distancing itself from Adam Smith's legacy. The emerging field of public administration—one consciously directed toward improving the practice of government—was practically emasculated by its domestic squabbles over the politics versus administration dichotomy and the role of bureaucrats as an instrument of governing (White 1948; Willoughby 1927).

There were, to be sure, individual and institutional exceptions to this disciplinary protectionism: sociologist Robert Merton (1936), economist Wesley Mitchell (1937), the establishment of the Social Science Research Council (incorporated in 1923 under Merriam's tutelage and the sponsorship of the Rockefeller Foundation), and the consolidation of the Brookings Institution (in 1928 with assistance from the Carnegie Foundation) come prominently to mind (see Critchlow 1985; Lyons 1969). However, these exceptions were so striking as to support the observation that multidisciplinary research and its applications to social problems were like foundling children, i.e., largely unappreciated.

Thus it is not surprising that in 1939, Robert Lynd posed the question, *Knowledge for What?* Arguing against what he viewed as excessive empiricism and social detachment, he cautioned, "If the social scientist is too bent upon waiting until all the data are in… the decisions will be made any way without him… by the 'practical' man and by the 'hard-headed' politician chivvied by interest-pressure bloc" (Lynd 1939, 9). What, asked Lynd, in an echo of the pragmatist theme, was the ultimate purpose of knowledge—for its own sake or to better society? The answer was clear in most academic circles: the very idea of societally relevant knowledge was in deliberate neglect. This neglect was profoundly altered by World War II, in which American intellectual resources were mobilized to confront the immediate exigencies at hand.

Immediately after World War II, Congress and the executive branch sought to define the government sponsorship of scientific research as an instrument of public policy. This was a radical concept at the time, one whose discussion grew heated as Congress debated the creation and purview of what was to become the National Science Foundation (NSF) (Lyons 1969; Polsby 1984). The relative disparity between the social and physical sciences was highlighted during the NSF deliberations. The former were excluded from the Foundation's sponsorship when the NSF was mandated in 1950. As Senator William Fulbright commented during the hearings, "People simply don't appreciate the significance of the social sciences, which means your legislators don't either" (Lyons 1969, 33). This attitude hardly boded well for the development of the policy sciences, which might have had a claim on the issue of relevance but had no organized stakeholders to articulate their case.

There were, however, key proponents willing to span academic disciplines and argue forcefully for the necessary application of multidisciplinary research to social problems. Robert Merton, in his landmark 1949 article, called for an "applied social research on applied social research to ferret out the public images of social science, particularly among makers of policy in government, labor and business." Asserting that it was "well-known, a given practical problem requires the collaborative researchers of several social sciences," Merton stated, "[p]ractical problems are many faceted. They can be examined from the perspectives of several different disciplines." Merton challenged social scientists to "sensitize policy-makers to new types of achievable goals... and to more effective means of reaching established goals." He concluded that "a major function of applied research is to provide occasion and pressures for interdisciplinary investigations and for the development of a theoretic system of 'basic social science,' rather than discrete bodies of uncoordinated specialized theory" (Merton 1949, 167 and 171).

III. LASSWELL'S VISION OF THE POLICY SCIENCES: THE EARLY DECADES

Harold Lasswell is considered to be the founder of the policy sciences. His essay on "The Policy Orientation" in *The Policy Sciences*, co-edited with Daniel Lerner (1951), articulated the policy map of social science discipline and practice. The subsequent development of the policy sciences can be traced to three principal defining characteristics, as set forth by Lasswell (1951): *multidisciplinary perspective, contextual and problem-oriented in nature*, and *explicitly normative*. In many ways, these represent different emphases, for they reflect distinct events and conditions. In other ways, they are mutually reinforcing. For purposes of the present exposition and at the risk of some redundancy, they will be discussed individually because each had an identifiable influence on the evolution and acceptance of the policy sciences.

A. MULTIDISCIPLINARY PERSPECTIVE

Lasswell's early admonitions were immediately policy-directed in nature and multidisciplinary in execution:

> A policy orientation has been developing that cuts across the existing specializations. The orientation is twofold. In part it is directed towards the policy process, and in part towards the intelligence needs of policy. The first task, which is the development of a science of policy forming and execution, uses the methods of social and psychological inquiry. The second task, which is the improving of the concrete content of the information and the interpretations available to policy makers, typically goes outside the boundaries of social science and psychology (Lasswell 1951, 3).

Lasswell (1951, 3) stressed that the policy sciences were not to be equated with "applied social science" or "applied social and psychological science." "Nor," he cautioned, "are the 'policy sciences' to be thought of as identical with what is studied by the political scientists" (Lasswell 1951, 4) Dedicated to the "fuller realization of human dignity,... the basic emphasis of the approach...is upon the fundamental problems of man in society" (Lasswell 1951, 8). Finally, after arguing for a closer relationship between the potential adviser and the policy process, Lasswell advised, "in order to bring the academician and the active policy maker into fruitful association, new institutions are needed" (Lasswell 1951, 14).

Like Merriam and Merton before him, the scenarios laid down by Lasswell of the policy sciences approach were seemingly left largely unattended. Except for an occasional review of the Lasswell volume (Kecskemeti 1952), contemporary academicians were just as oblivious to the message as their interbellum counterparts. The obvious audience should have been political scientists, but they were internally focused by their behavioral conflicts and had little inclination to adopt a new disciplinary focus. Many years and reflections later, Lasswell was asked how he might explain this attitude; he responded somewhat ambiguously, "I guess the times just were not right." The policy sciences movement remained basically dormant until the late 1950s and early 1960s.

Operations researchers and economists moved aggressively into the world of application. Lineberry argues that the roots of the policy sciences lay within economics, not political science, and cites Tjalling Koopmans: "efforts during World War II to develop a theory of resource allocation" were he to "locate the origins of policy sciences ... with a person and place" (Lineberry 1982, 7). Operations research and systems analysis applied their methodological tools to a series of discrete problems with some noted successes. Even though the more cognizant systems analysts generally limited the scope of their work, the equating of systems analysis and policy analysis was reflected in much of the literature. Majone and Quade (1980, 5) wrote that "systems analysis and policy analysis are used as essentially synonymous terms for the same activity."

At the same time, system analysis and cost-benefit analysis were enjoying bureaucratic success in certain sectors of government, especially in the Department of Defense (Enthoven and Smith 1971; Hitch and McKean 1960). Although the more perceptive practitioners always warned of their limitations, cost-benefit analysis, systems analysis, program-planning budgeting system (PPBS), and quantitative modeling became prevalent passwords for policy analysis (e.g., Quade and Boucher 1968); the seeming need to reduce all policies to a set of economic or quantitative indicators became pervasive. Analytical techniques and procedures of the defense realm were soon extended to social issues. In 1966, President Lyndon Johnson ordered PPBS as practiced in the Department of Defense to be instituted in the Department of Health, Education, and Welfare. However limited these approaches might have been, it should be admitted that their practitioners were venturing out beyond academe and applying their theories and tools to real world issues.

These approaches were, like their social sciences predecessors, soon seen to have run their bureaucratic course. Systems analysis was seen to be largely insensitive to public policy issues (Hoos 1983). Similarly, economics had its limitations, even in apparently proprietary economic issues (Green 1972; Heller 1975). The inability of PPBS to repeat its Defense Department successes (Wildavsky 1979) were practical evidence that public policy problems often—perhaps typically—refused to be corrected because of their very complex, interactive, and changing natures. The agnostic perspective on policy goals, the stress on optimization, the neglect of process and procedure, and the acceptance of microeconomic assumptions regarding human behavior simply proved to be inadequate bases for treating public policy issues (Mead 1983). As Stone (1997) later emphasized, the general tendency of these theories and programs to exclude normative considerations—to emphasize efficiency to the exclusion of equity—was unacceptable to political policy makers. These growing awareness and sensitivities led policy analysts to propose new conceptual paradigms and methodological approaches to what were coming to be known as "squishy" problems (Strauch 1975, 1976).

At the same time, there was a school of thought that viewed the policy sciences as an opportunity for developing an all-encompassing metatheory of political interactions, whose purpose was to integrate the social and physical sciences, fulfilling Comte's vision of social physics as a means of alleviating society ills. Merton (1949, 171) asserted that "a major function of applied research is to provide occasions and pressure for interdisciplinary investigations and for the development of a theoretic system of 'basic social science'." Dror (1970, 138) was even more emphatic: "Policy sciences must integrate knowledge from a variety of branches of knowledge into a supradiscipline focusing on public policy-making." Although well intended, these efforts were quietly abandoned because they lacked the necessary theoretical foundation and empirical substance to support such an enterprise, as Lasswell (1951) clearly suggested in "The Policy Orientation" and Merton (1949) implied when he formulated his research agenda based on midrange theories. Lasswell and Merton were careful not to force the policy sciences goals and components into premature intellectual and definitional straitjackets that Dror's (1971a, 1971b) approach would have entailed.

Other scholars looked to the nascent policy sciences movement as a means to coordinate several of the social sciences, with each discipline still retaining its individual identity (see Charlesworth 1972; Coleman 1972). An early leading text in the field, written with chapters drawn from the various contributing disciplines and case materials, reflects this orientation (Bauer and Gergen 1968).

Explicit in this theme was the hesitant recognition but still unproven hypothesis that the various disciplines would provide different but complementary perspectives on a given problem. The fact that operations research texts routinely included chapters on policy implementation alongside their technical exegeses (Larson and Odoni 1981) and social psychologists became leaders in policy evaluation (Campbell 1969) reflected the growing acceptance of the limitations of single-discipline policy research and the priority of multidisciplinary policy research.

This is not to suggest that the policy sciences' appeal for multidisciplinary approaches was universally accepted. In place of the unitary disciplinary research approach, these precedents have resulted in a much more thoroughgoing commitment to multidisciplinary research. This commitment appears to be more deep seated than the earlier advocacies for three reasons. First, the initial call for multidisciplinary research was relatively isolated and more threatening to the disciplines' respective identities. Few analysts knew how to engage in multidisciplinary research, for their entire scholastic training was in a single discipline. Lacking the requisite skills, their inclinations and enthusiasms for integrated policy research were understandably reserved. Still, while the contemporary pool may not be particularly well stocked, it is undoubtedly better supplied today than it was 40 years ago. The multidisciplinary training featured in university public policy curricula reinforces research approaches (see Karlqvist 1999). Second, as Heclo (1972) pointed out, policy scholars are "seeking to become more truthful to the complexity of events," a posture that impresses a multidisciplinary set of perspectives on a given social problem for the simple reason that policy issues rarely limit themselves to a single academic discipline. Finally, there is now an increasingly varied number of organizations that specialize in public policy research (Fischer 1993). These can be found within and outside of government circles and services both public and private clients. The relative quality of their product, their distinguishing activities, and the institutional life spans are varied, but these criteria are not at issue here. To the point, multidisciplinary, applied policy research no longer has to rely exclusively on the fractious university setting for its institutional bases. For these reasons, it seems that the multidisciplinary plank of the policy sciences platform is secure.

B. CONTEXTUAL AND PROBLEM-ORIENTED PERSPECTIVE

In Lasswell's initial vision, the policy sciences were explicitly problem oriented and utilized broad contextual approaches. This came in part from his realization that most social problems could not be extracted from their political, economic, social, and cultural environments. A fine example comes from Lasswell's (1951, 3) essay, which begins, "The continuing crisis of national security in which we live..." and uses the Cold War context as a rationale for developing policy orientations. Later, in the same essay, he confirms, "It is against the background of stress," referring to the consequences of depression and war "on improving the sciences of man by sharpening the tools of research that subsequent developments need to be set" Lasswell (1951, 7). (Also, Lasswell (1956) continued to articulate this agenda.)

In regard to the problem-oriented and contextual policy orientation, Lasswell's vision was twofold: "In part it is directed toward the policy process, and in part toward the intelligence needs of policy" (Lasswell 1951, 3). Later he refined his definition of the policy sciences to be "knowledge of and in the policy process" (Lasswell 1971, 1). Although it is safe to assume that Lasswell himself emphasized knowledge of the policy process (after all, he was a political scientist), it is equally clear that he was able to see two separate approaches to the policy sciences: one emphasizing *procedural* knowledge of the policy process and another emphasizing *topical* knowledge for use in the policy process.

This split between knowledge in and knowledge of policy developed during the 1960s and has remained relatively constant to this day. Ranney (1968) built on Easton's (1965) seminal *A Systems Analysis of Political Life* to delineate process and content as foci for political science. The conflicting forces of activism versus scientism had driven political scientists to one of the two approaches. Ranney's preference was to focus on content, as opposed to the post-1945 behavioral emphasis that had stressed process. Garson (1981) traces this dual character of the policy sciences to the joining of scientific analyses (largely behavioralism in Lasswell's case and only later emphasizing systems analysis) to democratic humanism. Lasswell's chosen phrase was "the policy sciences of democracy." The policy sciences, to Garson, were to serve as the synthesis. "These two viewpoints," wrote Garson (1981, 538), "underlie divisions between the empirico-analytic and neo-pluralist orientations toward policy analysis."

The two approaches, although distinctly different in their purpose and method, share the contextual and problem-oriented nature of inquiry, as Dewey's earlier insistence on a formal process of inquiry for his instrumental ideals began to pay dividends. This integrated vision of scientific method and democratic humanism, however, proved operationally and philosophically difficult as the policy sciences moved to achieve status and recognition during the 1960s and 1970s. Instead of integration, these two emphases—one on process and one on content—strengthened their respective identities, each claiming some form of conceptual hegemony.

Pursuing their own separate-but-equal doctrine, each approach staked out its professional territory in universities, institutes, and government offices. Operationally, the two approaches have led to the formulation of two sets of models of public policy: (1) those models emphasizing policy analysis have been dominant among economists and public administrators, relying on Dewey-like procedure of rational inquiry; and (2) those models emphasizing the policy process have been dominant among political scientists and focus on defining stages of the policy process. A brief elaboration follows.

1. Policy Analysis

The operations researchers—fresh from their successes of World War II—and the economists—flush with Keynesian macroeconomic principles and depression-era analyses—were the first disciplines to move into the policy orientation. Their assumptions were that policy problems and their solutions could be defined with comprehensive and rational accuracy and subjected to quantitative and empirical analytical precision. Policy solutions were to be optimal, and consequences of government action could be foreseen with at least probabilistic assurance.

However, their policy approach was largely generic and reductionist, typically applicable regardless of the policy problem. In *A Primer for Policy Analysis*, Stokey and Zeckhauser (1978) provided analysts with models and techniques ranging from differential equations to queuing models to linear programming and cost-benefit analysis. The *modus operandi* of these policy paladins was seemingly "Have technique, will travel." Policy techniques were eventually extended into methodologies and management practice through such innovations as PPBS and management information systems (MIS). But these approaches were characteristically addressed by the intelligence needs and content of specific public policies.

Edward Quade is often recognized as a pioneering proponent of the policy analytical approach. In his *Analysis for Public Decisions*, Quade (1975 and 1982) saw both operations research and systems analysis as synonyms for a policy process framework. The elements of Quade's vision of policy analysis were (1) identification of objectives; (2) specification of alternatives; (3) recommending policy action; (4) monitoring policy outcomes; and (5) evaluating policy performance.

2. Policy Process

At the same time that operations research and economic analysis were gaining influence, a serious criticism of such systems of rational calculation and control was also being voiced. Dahl and Lindblom (1953) attacked the rational-comprehensive approach as both dangerous and unworkable. Democratic and pluralist norms and descriptive reality replaced scientific and rational ideals. Their key assumption was that a pluralist political process, in which a lack of a clear agreement on policy objectives and criteria for choice was far more prevalent than the synoptic approach permitted. In place of comprehensive rationality, Lindblom described the public process as one of disjointed incrementalism and "muddling through." Instead of universal and analytic methods, Lindblom and others (i.e., Simon 1945; Wildavsky 1979) suggested such political strategies as successive limited comparison and partisan mutual adjustment (Lindblom 1959). Jones (1977, 9) echoed Lindblom by outlining the policy process as a "highly relative and pluralistic decision-making system characterized by compromise, incrementalism, and continual adjustment."

The critique of the synoptic approach centered on limited to human and particularly institutional rationality that prevent legitimate claims to knowing all possible alternative solutions or being able to forecast specific policy impacts. In more cases than not, policy analysts forced technical models to fit complex and dynamic policy problems, and therefore ran the risk of yielding solutions that were more often than not wrong. For proponents of the policy process, it was essential to acquire knowledge of the policy process to understand government actions.

Advocates of the policy process had strong descriptive evidence of the superiority of their approach. The assertions of the policy analysts eventually led Wildavsky (1969) to write "Rescuing Policy Analysis from PPBS." In this article, Wildavsky asserted that despite the inevitable problems encountered by rational-analytical techniques like PPBS, this was no reason to assume all policy analysis was bad. Others were not so generous. Hoos (1983, 241) wrote, "We first must recognize systems analysis as more than an assemblage of techniques and methods but rather as a social phenomenon fraught with social significance, perhaps all the more because it is characterized by contradictions, internal and external."

Policy theorists, emanating primarily from political science, developed new models of the policy process. These models have highlighted the contextual and problem-oriented nature of the policy sciences, but their focus is on knowledge of the policy process. In contrast to Quade's or Dunn's models, May and Wildavsky (1978) describe a policy cycle in which they include: (1) agenda setting, (2) issue analysis, (3) implementation, (4) evaluation, and (5) termination. Similarly, Brewer and deLeon (1983) based their understanding of the policy process on a series they define as: (1) initiation, (2) estimation, (3) selection, (4) implementation, (5) evaluation, and (6) termination. Although some have raised validity issues regarding the policy process as a model (Sabatier and Jenkins-Smith 1993), the policy process framework generally stresses the political and operational uses and abuses of policy evaluation.

Despite the actual or perceived entrenchment of the two approaches in their respective locations, neither the models nor their elements are cast in nine yards of typological concrete. In fact, the approaches and stages seep into and inform one another. To isolate them would be unrealistic and harmful. In reality, "public policy is almost never a single, discrete, unitary phenomena. Indeed, the appeal of public policy studies... lies precisely in its richness" (Greenberg et al. 1977, 533; also see Jenkins-Smith 1990). But the approaches and various models of public policy can be used as desiderata, for organizing and illustrating knowledge of and in the policy process.

Finally, numerous efforts have been made to compromise or reach a synthesis of the synoptic and anti-synoptic approaches. Even before the bifurcation of the policy sciences, Simon (1945) had outlined a theory of decision-making bounded by notions of "satisficing" and "bounded rationality," one in which policy-making was constrained by the context and operation in a world of incomplete and imperfect information. Decision makers would nevertheless choose to pursue rational scientific inquiry. Etzioni (1967) claimed the two approaches are both necessary, and he distinguished between types of decision (strategic and operational) and the appropriate approach (see also Beckman 1977). Lately there has been another, more directed effort toward melding the two, one characterized by the phrase "post-positivism" (Ascher 1987; deLeon 1992; Fischer 1998), a topic that will be returned to later.

C. EXPLICITLY NORMATIVE PERSPECTIVE

The policy sciences, almost from their very conception, have been explicitly normative in their content and concern with human value. In Lasswell's (1951, 16) words, "The policy sciences approach... calls forth a very considerable clarification of the value goals involved in policy." Lasswell and Kaplan (1950, xii, xxiv) defined the policy sciences as providing "intelligence pertinent to the integration of values realized by and embodied in interpersonal relations," one which "prizes not the glory of a depersonalized state or the efficiency of a social mechanism, but human dignity and the realization of human capacities."

This emphasis on values has remained a beacon of the policy sciences approach. Equally important is the idea that these values can be recognized and made an explicit part of the analysis of social issues (Kaplan 1963; Lasswell 1971). The normative imperative rings true, even if the means to this end are much in doubt and dispute (Hawkesworth 1988; MacRae 1981; Rein 1983; Stone 1997). Can anybody, the policy scientist would ask, understand civil rights policies, welfare transfer payments, global economics, or comparative-worth legislation without a clear acknowledgment that all persons *ought* to have equal access without regard to race, creed, sex, or religion? The rancorous controversies over the Clinton nominations of Lani Guinier and Zoe Baird were not framed in terms of their professional or legal standings; on these bases, both women were eminently qualified. The virulent debates produced by their nominations and hearings can only be explained by the values these nominations appeared to represent. Similarly no one could fathom the virulence of the Clarence Thomas Supreme Court nomination without an understanding of the underlying values positions.

In spite of these early strictures, the normative aspects of the policy sciences were neglected by virtually all for three reasons. First, some claimed that governments and programs basically muddle through and that an incremental approach to policy would encompass or balance any normative postures that might occur. These might be on a *sub rosa*, unarticulated level, but nevertheless they would be de facto incorporated (Lindblom 1959). Second, others argued that quantitative methodologies, such as practiced in operations research and economics, were essentially value-free and therefore did not have to concern themselves with questions of ethics or values. And third, a sizable number of policy analysts argued that values were the exclusive domain of the policy maker and that for analysts to intrude on that realm, to interject their values, would be unwarranted, beyond their professional competencies, and perhaps even wrong in the sense of the democratic ethic (Amy 1984).

Of course none of these arguments lacks merit, but they clearly deviate from the original enunciation of the policy sciences. Even more cogently, the refusal to consider explicitly the normative and ideological aspects of the policy process has repeatedly resulted in empty analyses that poorly explained what had happened or what might be. A value-free approach might be perhaps sufficient for very limited systems analysis problems such as alternative mass transit systems, but even that assumption is questionable because it does not consider who is served (and why) by the transit system (see Dryzek 1990). What is unquestionable is that the broad, societally relevant contextual issues addressed by the policy sciences simply cannot be understood without the open recognition of pertaining social values. Dror (1964) long ago demonstrated the vulnerability of the incrementalist sleight of hand.

Second, most observers can agree that the strictly quantitative approach to policy problems is insufficient, that matters such as equity must be broached and consciously included. More at dispute are the means to that goal (see Fischer 1980; Rein 1976). Furthermore, it is now widely conceded that even the choice of methodologies implies a powerful set of normative values and analytical assumptions that will shape the analysis. There is no such thing as a value-free study or even methodology, as the postpositivists tell us (Fischer 2003). And third, few analysts would claim that they can resolve normative issues in their analyses, but an increasingly large number will admit that they can at least make such considerations an open element of their work and ultimate advice.

In many ways, this has led analysts to propose a "democratization of the policy sciences" (deLeon 1992, 1997; Dryzek and Torgerson 1993; Fischer 1993).

Examples of normative standards and political ideologies as they apply to and affect policy analysis are readily available. President George W. Bush at least partially defended his invasion of Iraq in 2003 on the precept that it would lead to a democratization of the Middle East. The clamorous transition to the privatization of formerly public services is a certain signal of value judgments that private firms are better suited than public sector organizations for a variety of tasks. Normative overtones and prior persuasions would be hard to overlook in the Reagan adminis-tration's education and energy programs.

The conflict between the public's right to protect its collective self and the sanctity of individual privacy—a dilemma most poignantly revisited by the spreading AIDS epidemic, exacerbated by the post-September 11 fear of terrorism—is constantly being played out. These policies, however objectively presented with quantitative indicators such as weapons of mass destruction, rates of welfare recipients, or infection rates, are directly derived from one's moral and ideological precepts. This is surely the domain of policy sciences, a problem-oriented process of choice among competing alternatives for public action. The normative issue cannot be avoided, and indeed the value question remains at the center of the contemporary policy sciences. The debate over whether or not values are explicitly part of the policy sciences, if ever it were a debate, is over. The field, by the early 1990s, had progressed to the problems of how to include values in policy analysis as a major theoretical and practical analytic issue.

One can thus assume that normative standards are increasingly being made a visible part of political decision-making. If policy analysts wish to continue the quality of their access and advice, then they must be openly and candidly included in their policy analyses. The idea that they could be ignored or subverted to technical sophistications (as is still assumed by many systems analysts) is no longer tenable, if it ever were. More the problem now, of course, is to understand that prior values do not dominate the other elements of the policy sciences. Although the policy scientists may not be able to convince the political policy makers of the rectitude of any given set of norms, analysts can at least explicate the contending values and thereby permit policy makers to make an honest, more transparent judgment. Thus, for a third time, the policy sciences have matured in such a way as to validate the original Lasswellian framework.

IV. GROWTH AND DEVELOPMENT OF POLICY SCIENCES: THROUGH THE 1970s

It is easy to see that the Lasswellian tenets of multidisciplinary, contextual, and problem-oriented normative policy sciences remain in various stages of debate and resolution. But, of course, the historical touchstones and personages changed, and with them, new conditions prevailed. To these new proponents, Lasswell served as the norm; any return to academic irrelevance was to be avoided. The social background of this generation was also different from that of their predecessors. In place of the Great Depression and World War II, the new generation of policy analysts had to contend with their owns wars and crises of a different nature (e.g., Vietnam and the War on Poverty), causing the demand and need for the policy sciences to be greater than ever by the late 1960s and 1970s.

Influence on the pace and direction of the march of the policy sciences took on two forms. One set of influences came from within the community of policy scientists, who struggled to expand the theoretical and political power of their claims and pursuits. A second set of influences came from outside the field, originating in the major social and political events of the period. Both these internal and external influences interacted to contribute to the growth and development of the policy sciences.

A. EXPANDING THE SCOPE OF THE POLICY SCIENCES

A virtual college of policy analysts and scientists had formed by the late 1960s, at least partially as a growth in the area in a number of universities. In reflecting on their own discipline and practice, they recognized both the shortcomings of and the opportunities for their knowledge and skills. Gradually, and with some logic of sequence, if not conclusiveness, the policy sciences expanded in theoretical scope and application. Both the policy analysis and policy process approaches flourished as each rushed to explain some new-found element or stage in the policy process. Through the 1970s, the policy sciences addressed topics of evaluation, utilization, implementation, and termination in a more or less orderly and systematic manner, though never in clear resolve. The development of these stages is reviewed below.

1. Evaluation

The obvious purpose of policy analysis was to learn from public programs so that the social objectives expressed in the early 1960s could be met with new and more effective programs. In many circles (e.g., Nagel 1990), evaluation was considered to be the policy analysis *sine qua non*, where the analytical rubber hit the policy road.

The evaluation community was seemingly well prepared for this opportunity. Rossi and Freeman (1985) comment, "In the modem era, commitment to the systematic evaluation of programs in such fields as education and public health can be traced to efforts at the turn of the century to provide literacy and occupational training by the most effective and economical means, and to reduce mortality and morbidity from infectious diseases." Daniels and Wirth (1983) identify two stages in evaluation research prior to the mid-1960s efforts: "evaluation research as efficiency" (1910 to World War II) and "evaluation as field research" (World War II to 1963). Their third period, "evaluation as social experimentation" (1963–1974) encompasses the present period. Public health scholars such as Suchman (1967) were central in developing systematic program evaluation and evaluation research and, in particular, in urging the application skills to social problems rather than academic exercises.

In the late 1960s and early 1970s, virtually en masse, the policy analysis community focused almost exclusively on policy evaluation, in areas as varied as education, health, crime rates, and public welfare. The evaluation phase of the policy cycle certainly benefited from this concentration of attention. New methodologies, often from social and clinical psychology, were brought to bear while others were adjusted to fit special needs. Federal government and private foundation (especially the Russell Sage Foundation) funding was extensive; much federal legislation was written to provide support for program evaluation. For these reasons, problem-oriented evaluation research stood poised to make substantial contributions to public policy-making. Alice Rivlin's *Systematic Thinking for Social Action* (1971) presents an excellent assessment of the state of the art during this period.

The embarrassment of resource and methodological riches had one serious drawback that was to prove damaging. Most of these evaluators assuming the role of policy researchers had spent their entire professional experience within academic circles. For this reason, they had developed little appreciation for the policy sensitivities of working with public officials or making sure that their findings and recommendations matched the clients' needs. Academic purposes and bureaucratic objectives presented very different agenda. Many evaluators did not recognize these differences, or if they did they were reluctant to assimilate the new protocols. Furthermore, the problems turned out to be much more difficult and significant than originally anticipated, so the results typically fell well short of their promised mark.

As a result, evaluation proved a questionable activity. Not only were the evaluations seldom able to identify with great clarity the sources of programmatic shortcomings, they were rarely able to be responsive to the policy maker's needs for better information. Evaluation *qua* policy analysis received poor ratings from the sponsors who were financially supporting it. Relevance versus rigor controversies undercut numerous evaluations (see the debate between Carol Weiss and Michael Patton in Alkin (1990)). Most critically, they were not able to address the pivotal policy questions: are these programs working and if not, why not and what can be done to improve them? Regardless, for whatever reasons and to whatever outcomes, the policy research community during the later 1960s and early 1970s was fixated on questions of policy evaluation to the deprivation of other aspects of the policy process.

2. Utilization

The perceived shortcomings of law, political science, operations research, sociology, economics, psychology, and the other social sciences as they applied to public policy issues led to a general identity crisis and widespread pessimism. Scott and Shore (1976) raised the specter every discipline was afraid to face. Rein and White (1979) were not alone when they voiced the concern "can policy research help policy?" Weiss (1977) talked in incremental terms about "knowledge creep" and asked whether the social sciences could do little more for public policy makers than fulfill an ambiguous "enlightenment function." Lindblom and Cohen (1979) were even more cynical; they claimed that the likelihood of success for policy analysis (or what they termed "professional social inquiry") alleviating policy problems was little better than random occurrence; subsequent Lindblom (1990) was hardly more sanguine. Caplan et al.'s (1975) study of knowledge use by federal executives gave caution to many and evidence to others as they found users oriented toward "soft knowledge" (non-research-based, qualitative, and couched in lay language), used primarily for the purpose of sensitizing policy makers to social needs. Rivlin (1971) was more balanced, noting how policy research has made great advances in some fields but was still lacking in others.

These sobering assessments surely offered a thoughtful cause to pause; perhaps social complexities were too great to be analytically captured, even by a multidisciplinary approach which, by itself, might be too unwieldy to produce any firm resolutions. However, as the individual disciplinary fountains proved arid, the demand for the integrated policy research only increased with virtually every agency in the federal government establishing its own policy bureau. The policy sciences, without ever reaching closure on the utilization question, would move on to more pressing matters.

3. Implementation

Given the evaluation and utilization concerns, it was not surprising that in the mid-1970s, the focus again switched as policy researchers believed that they had identified the root cause of program failure. In 1973, *A Report on Studies of Implementation in the Public Sector*, published by Harvard's Kennedy School of Government, commented:

> We became increasingly bothered in the late 1960s by those aspects of the exercise of government authority bound up with implementation. Results achieved by the programs of that decade were widely recognized as inadequate. One clear source of failure emerged: political and bureaucratic aspects of the implementation process were, in great measure, left outside both the considerations of participants of government and calculations of formal policy analysts who assisted them (Brewer and deLeon 1983, 249).

In the early 1970s, implementation was a neglected phase—both conceptually and operationally—in the policy process, a commentary on its shortcomings of traditional public administration. Pressman and Wildavsky (1973), in their landmark study, found virtually no antecedent research on implementation. It was professionally reassuring to suspect that the programs themselves, as conceived, were equal to the task and that the real culprit of policy failure was the administrative delivery system. Claiming that the implementation was the missing link separating program formation and program success, the policy research community moved enthusiastically to a wealth of case studies discerning this phase of the policy process (see Hargrove 1975). For instance, Berman and McLaughlin (1974) discussed implementation in the context of federally sponsored education programs, while Derthick (1972) explained the foundering of the new towns-in-town urban renewal programs as multiple failures in implementation politics. The disjuncts between the federal and local governments were seen as especially culpable of implementation crimes. Recognizing the dilemmas presented by policy implementation, Williams (1975) proposed "implementation analysis" that would include implementation strategies in an analysis so that the policy maker could appreciate the problems that faulty or slipshod implementation could engender; armed with such knowledge, the cognizant policy maker would select the most effective policies and programs. Unfortunately, implementation analysis failed to recognize the pervasiveness of Murphy's law, the idea that the unexpected always seems to happen, making implementation prescience often illusionary.

Like the earlier emphases on program evaluation, this focus on implementation was undoubtedly salutary. Great amounts of case study materials were developed and brought to bear, highlighting both the difficulties of policy implementation and how they might be foreseen and reduced. Policy scholars offered implementation typologies (Bardach 1977), while a few proposed tentative first steps toward a general theory of policy implementation (Hargrove 1983; also Mazmanian and Sabatier 1981, 1983). And again, like the earlier problems with utilization and evaluation, this emphasis on implementation produced more confusion than clarification. Implementation turned out to be far more complex and difficult than the implementation analysis proponents had suggested, even to those claiming to represent the third generation (Groggin 1990; Linder and Peters 1987; Wittrock and deLeon 1986). Regardless of the outcome of these efforts, one can safely say that the policy research community during the mid- to late 1970s heavily attended to questions of policy implementation to the relative exclusion of the other phases of the policy process (deLeon and deLeon 2002).

4. Termination

Toward the end of the 1970s, government on all levels was besieged with demands for greater economy, demands reinforced by reduced revenues as taxpayers insisted on reduced government expenditures. California's Proposition 13—which rolled back property taxes and hence local government revenues—was indicative; social welfare programs, suspect during the best of times, came under particular scrutiny (see Bardach 1976). This tendency was further supported by the political inclinations of elected representatives who were ideologically opposed to big government during the Reagan administration. In light of these developments, program termination—under such labels as cutback management, sunset legislation, and fiscal retrenchment—became a prevalent theme in policy research, although not to the extent of the previous emphasis on program implementation and evaluation. Casualties from the war on poverty were rampant. Under the Nixon administration, Howard Phillips fought to eliminate the Office of Economic Opportunity (OEO), even while he was its director. Although the Community Services Act of 1974 officially ended the OEO, many of its programs continued into the 1980s, when they began to succumb to the reductions of the Reagan administration. The financial tribulations of New York City, only one of several financially endangered cities, gave additional credence to and cause for termination studies and proposed tactics (Caralay 1982; Levine et al. 1981), as have the numerous cutbacks in state budgets since 2000. In a limited number of cases, a few authors (e.g., Frantz 1993; Daniels 1997) have tested whether some of the early termination authors (e.g., deLeon 1978a) remain relevant in light of different termination actions.

With bountiful materials and ready clients at their disposal, policy scientists turned their attentions to describing and prescribing termination strategies. But like the other emphases on the different phases of the policy process, termination studies proved similarly unable to provide solid programmatic advice. For a variety of reasons, most of the programs and institutions ticketed for elimination proved remarkably resistant to the policy termination axe, thereby affirming a positive answer to Kaufman's (1976) question, "Are government organizations immortal?" Another policy research trend had come and gone without leaving much in the way of positive, worthwhile recommendations, even as Clinton and Gore's National Performance Review and the Republican Contract with America seemingly present ample evidence.

5. Summary

Certainly none of these concentrations represented wasted effort. Immense literatures have been written, disseminated, and perhaps taken to heart. Much has been learned about each of these areas and their unique characteristics. No doubt the policy communities—both analysts and policy makers—are much wiser than they were in the early 1960s. But what has been largely overlooked from a conceptual vantage point is the need for integration and balance, the initial Lasswellian injunction that these are not discretely separable elements or stages in the policy process. Each of the policy stages is by necessity iteratively tied to the others: initiation is tied to estimation, selection must be advised by implementation, just as evaluation must precede and inform termination (Brewer and deLeon 1983). And initiation and termination—the beginning and the end of the policy cycle—are cut from the very same conceptual and analytical bolts (deLeon 1978a, 1978b). There is a growing acceptance that the policy process is a seamless web rather than a disjointed series of individual stages or phases, and that policy analysis permeates this process at every step. But the downside remains the continual rediscovery of processes seemingly discovered years ago.

Thus, one can see how the evolution of the multidisciplinary nature, problem-oriented elements, contextual nature, and normative emphasis of the policy sciences has come full circle to some of its founding contextual hypotheses. Moreover, it is clear that the policy sciences, perhaps more than any other intellectual pursuit, are intimately affected by exogenous events. They are, by definition, problem oriented, so they cannot absent themselves from the political and social environments without abandoning an integral part of their *raison d'etre*. It is evident that the policy sciences have been profoundly affected by their heritage of problem orientation. There is no ready solution for this situation, for the policy sciences have deliberately set themselves in the midst of the real-world circus and must therefore endure whatever political acts might come down the boardwalk. The discipline's professional challenge, then, is to be able to accommodate in the face of changing conditions.

B. Political Events and the Policy Sciences

The evolution of policy sciences must also be partly attributed to political and social events that surrounded their development. As Lasswell had realized, such political or contextual conditions lay behind the control of the analyst required by the tasks at hand. For instance, the demands for rigorous, or at least systematic, policy and program evaluation were given a tremendous impetus by the need to assay the social welfare programs formulated in the mid-1960s, ultimately leading to the Welfare Reform Act of 1996. Several exogenous phenomena of the post-World War II American experience have had fundamental effects on the policy sciences.

1. The War on Poverty

The belated recognition of systemic, pernicious, racial discrimination and journalistic accounts of pervasive, debilitating poverty in "the other America" (Harrington 1963) led the Kennedy and Johnson administrations to move aggressively and initiate and implement a wide variety of social welfare programs (see Levine 1970). Unquestionably well intended, the panoply of corrective programs ranged from education to housing to nutrition to employment (Kershaw and

Courant 1970). Their common denominator, unfortunately unrecognized at the time, was profound and collective ignorance, both of the cause of the social malaise they were to correct and their possible effects, and, of course, how to alleviate them.

In Moynihan's (1969) telling phrase, the War on Poverty programs were based on "maximum feasible misunderstanding." More telling was the lack of clear or even consensual objectives. Enthusiasm, motivated by political drive, supplanted whatever meager analysis was available, as Williams (1998) has noted. The result, not surprisingly, was a decade of trial, error, and frustration, after which it was arguable if ten years and billions of dollars had produced any discernible, let alone effective, relief (Aaron 1978), or from the vantage point of the mid-1990s, the advent of a Republican Congress largely bent on undoing the War on Poverty.

Whatever the political and socio-economic results of the War on Poverty, its impacts on the policy sciences were notable. The War on Poverty's lessons were applicable to all phases of policy analysis activities. The initiation of many programs was ill informed, estimation was problematic, at best, implementation was ignored as an unimportant afterthought, naively left to supposedly neutral administrators and bureaucrats, and evaluation was neglected until much too late and then discovered to be much more complex than previously realized (Glazer 1983). Comparing the promised with the delivered products, skepticism regarding the ability of the social sciences to alleviate social problems legitimately appeared among both practitioners and sympathetic sponsors (see section 13.IV.A.2 above; also see Rivlin 1971).

The influence of the War on Poverty on the development of the policy sciences can be seen in many reactions and subsequent themes. On the most practical level, it provided social scientists with heretofore unheard of amounts of financial support (from both public and private sources) and ready access to policy makers. On the more conceptual level, partially stimulated and illustrated by the War on Poverty experiences, a major outpouring of policy literature appeared in the late 1960s and early 1970s. Professional journals were started, and several universities (most notably Harvard and the University of California, Berkeley) established professional graduate training programs in policy analysis. In many ways, opportunity seemingly created its own demand, and study and practice of policy analysis rocketed into the policy space, even if its objectives and orbits were unknown.

At the same time, policy researchers had recognized their methodological problems and, most pointedly, the shortcomings of their results. Theoretical assumptions and epistemological sophistication, which had proven so persuasive in the academy, were seen as only first approximations for devising social interventions. Questions regarding the measurement of the quality of education or the application of labor economics to problems of unemployment and poverty were found to be much more complex than previously thought (Aaron 1978; Mead 1992). Empirical research suffered from poor, inadequate data. And, most tellingly, the political parameters that defined the War on Poverty programs were revealed as both an inherent part of the policy problem and therefore an integral part of any problem solution. While this contextual element had been nominally recognized by the policy sciences, the War on Poverty brought this lesson home in unambiguous language. In sum, the War on Poverty simultaneously provided both unprecedented visibility as well as opportunity for the policy sciences and the imperative for considerable intellectual retrenchment.

2. The Vietnam War

The pivotal American political event of the 1960s and 1970s was the Vietnam conflict. Although highly politicized and managed by successive White Houses, the analysis and conduct of the war were the responsibility of the Department of Defense and the military services. Vietnam could have been the foundry and mettle of analysis, for the defense communities had consistently been at the forefront of analytical approaches. Systems analysis and costing techniques had been developed by the RAND Corporation under the sponsorship of the Air Force and the Office of the Secretary of

Defense (see Fisher 1971; Quade and Boucher 1968). The economics of defense were well understood, if not always well practiced (Hitch and McKean 1960). PPBS was first implemented in the Defense Department; yet in retrospect it can be argued that with all its apparent analytical prowess and sophistication, the United States profoundly mismanaged the Vietnam War. Without pausing here to reflect on the controversies and failures of the Vietnam War, one can point to shortcomings in information transmissions, faulty analogies, reluctance to include social and political variables (and a concomitant commitment to quantitative measures), and a myopic adherence to incremental decision-making as contributory factors that undermined the analyses of the conduct of the Vietnam War (FitzGerald 1972; Gelb and Betts 1979; Sheehan 1971; and most important, McNamara 1995).

The policy analysis community could extract at least five critical lessons from the Vietnam engagement. First was the realization that rational decision-making was a necessary but insufficient criterion in this (and maybe most) political arena. The steadfast resolve of the North Vietnamese consistently violated the cost-benefit equations upon which US policy makers justified their decisions. Second, quantitative measures were seen as being crucial for planning purposes; however, later disclosures revealed that the numbers coming out of Vietnam were just as subjective and manipulated (i.e., unreliable) as the more openly interpretative reports. Third, the conservative nature of policy analysis reinforced the commitment to the incremental nature of American decision-making, thus making major departures from existing policy a position advanced only by those out of favor or court. Fourth, Vietnam was a constantly changing arena, a contextual picture that defied static analysis. Yet, most American interpretations of the conflict refused to countenance the changing political landscape until the evidence was inescapable and the only remedies were radical. Finally, the Vietnam War demonstrated just as forcefully as the War on Poverty the normative imperatives, especially in terms of objectives or goals, that must be articulated in any major policy exercise. Whereas some vague political consensus might have supported (or acquiesced to in) US policy during the early days of the war, the steadily eroding political base—fueled by the growing public conviction that the war was morally problematic—was not acknowledged until chasms had appeared in the American social and political strata.

All these conditions forced the more conscientious policy scientists to amend their confidence in systems and quantitative analyses. This is not to suggest that quantitative methodologies were tossed aside like last year's postulates or that situational ethics became the new touchstone, but one can argue that the contextual experiences of the Vietnam War produced a new mix between the quantitative and qualitative aspects of the policy sciences, with a greater emphasis on the latter than might previously have been the case.

3. Watergate

In time, the resignations of President Richard Nixon and Vice President Spiro Agnew in the context of the Watergate scandals may be perceived as little more than an unfortunate warp of the American body politic (Olson 2003). The political system responded as one might hope. The offending parties were effectively removed and, from a functional perspective, quickly replaced, all within the bands of legitimacy and with no lasting traumas to the system. Still, Watergate was a highly visible and public milestone, especially as it raised the unmistakable issue of morality in government. Few will forget President Nixon proclaiming, "I am not a crook," just prior to his resignation, or the Vice President abjectly bargaining before submitting a *nolo contendere* plea of accepting illegal contributions. While the moral courage of Eliot Richardson and Archibald Cox, victims of the Saturday night massacre, suggested that scruples in government were not totally absent, the overall public impression of the Watergate episode was one of immoral behaviors throughout the government, up to and including its highest offices.

Even though the direct effects of Watergate on the American political system may have been brief, its surfacing of the issues of political morality added new evidence to the admonishments of the early policy sciences proponents who had urged the explicit consideration of normative standards as a central criterion. Watergate conferred a new urgency to those concerns, while at the same time enhancing the debate as to how morality and value judgments could, in operational terms, be included in a policy exercise; for instance, Watergate spawned the Office of the Special Prosecutor, which has been (at best) a mixed blessing. Subsequent research revealed that political corruption like Watergate was just as likely to be the result of replacing governmental equity with efficiency (deLeon 1994b). Unlike the previous examples of political conditions that provided substantial reason for the policy sciences to reassess and renew their commitment to norms and values, it would no longer be convenient for the analyst to protect lamely. But equally important, the corruptions of the Reagan administration—up to and including Iran-*contra* with its worrisome implications on presidential integrity—and the tawdry personal indiscretions of President Clinton indicated to all that these lessons were not necessarily lasting (deLeon 1994b).

4. The Energy Crises

The 1973 and 1978 energy crises in the United States and their feared ramifications all but required that energy policy would be a major political issue. To help unravel the complicated relationships, public and private sponsors generated a number of studies that were used as the basis for recommending and formulating energy policy (Greenberger et al. 1983). Many of these studies were based on elaborate computer models in which complex networks of interacting mathematical equations simulated the reaction of the economy given different supply-and-demand levels. Variables included the price of oil and other sources of energy (e.g., nuclear, renewable, and synthetic fuels), demand rates, and allocations of energy among the various end-use sectors (e.g., industry versus residential versus transportation), all of these over time. Mathematical models were a principal tool of investigation, even though an earlier survey of federally funded modeling projects concluded that "perhaps as many as two-thirds of the models failed to achieve their avowed purpose in the form of direct application to policy problems" (Weyant 1980, 212).

The analyses were hardly academic or moot. As gas lines grew, rather technical energy studies could be found in many bookstores; one, *Energy Futures*, by Stobaugh and Yergin (1979) even reached best-seller status. President Nixon mandated Project Independence; President Carter wore sweaters, urged energy conservation, subsidized a solar energy industry, and declared the energy crisis as the "moral equivalency of war" (whose MEOW acronym was priceless). War or not, the energy crises presented the types of political exigencies and debates that had a major influence on the policy sciences.

The energy crises were characterized by at least four features that warrant comment. First, beyond the call for energy independence, there was little agreement on goals, let alone the appropriate means to those objectives. Opposing camps were formed that were in constant opposition because they had so little in common; their basic assumptions, analytical frameworks, methodological approaches, energy supply-and-demand projections, and even data sources were so incompatible that no dialogue or policy convergence should have been expected (Robinson 1982). The controversies between the contending tribes were later described as "examples not of decision making under uncertainty but of decision making under contradictory certainties" (Thompson 1984).

Second, there was an abiding distrust of virtually everything connected with the energy crisis; the public perceived the oil companies as reaping obscene profits, the Arabs as the "bad guys," and the government as meddling middle men. The cynical public saw everybody tainted with energy analysis as either incompetent or fraudulent, if not both.

Third, there were in fact fundamental technical uncertainties, even unknowables, that clouded the analysis and debate. Under the best of analytical circumstances, the problems of accurately estimating supply-and-demand values from energy resources and applications would be monumental; in the politically virulent environment of the energy crises, they were insurmountable (Wildavsky and Tenenbaum 1981). This situation was exacerbated by the government's heavy-handed manipulation of the energy simulation models until they produced results that supported predetermined political positions (Commoner 1979).

Distressingly, these machinations were hidden behind the guise of objective quantitative modeling. Many of these computer models were employed and relied on by policy makers who lacked the technical competence to evaluate them; what reservations they might have had were more intuitive than informed. Yet, there is good reason to believe that the model results, however imperfect or specious, were used to formulate energy policy.

And fourth, the energy crises had tremendous visibility. They left nobody unaffected and were seen to portend dire consequences if left unattended. Energy models were viewed by policy makers as low-cost political actions or easy symbols of government attention to these threats, a quick and costless fix for all that ailed the country (Hammond 1984), up to and including a subsequent war in the Persian Gulf to protect Middle East petroleum. The long-term consequences of this national security rhetoric were later called on by President Bush as a rationale for engaging in the 1990 Persian Gulf War, with distinct echoes to the 2003 Persian Gulf War.

Taken in total, the energy crises presented a symbiotic relationship between policy analysts and policy makers, a condition fraught with significant opportunities and pitfalls for all involved. The energy crises gave policy analysts the opportunity to parade their modeling skills before the highest councils of government; their findings could define and determine policy. Furthermore, they could be assertive in their analyses because the policy makers would not have the technical competence to assess the work. This presented tension within the energy analysis community. There was ample evidence that quantitative models had nowhere near the forecasting precisions ascribed to them by their supporters (Ascher 1978), but to admit to these uncertainties would have severely limited the access to policy-making circles, i.e., the coveted ability to speak truth to power. At the same time, the putatively objective nature of the modeling exercises concealed the reality that their underlying political and social assumptions were what really drove the results. Rather than confess the limitations of their approaches, the energy modelers presented their projections with unwarranted confidences and unconfessed caveats. To be sure, the duplicity was hardly one-sided; policy makers were not hesitant to dictate desired model results or to use their analyses as proof for justification of their policies. The lesson is distinctly negative in tone; the analytical commitment to responsible reporting was sorely strained during the energy crises as was the abuse of their results, derelictions that served nobody's long-range purposes.

As was the case with the previous wars, the energy crisis studies reinforced the need for multidisciplinary approaches, even in the face of massive quantitative computer models. An over-reliance on the technology assessment model led energy analysts to be insensitive to the relationship between technology and social change (Frankel 1981). The political motivations and actions of the OPEC monopoly removed any analysis of energy supplies from the convenient calculus of economic supply and demand. The interaction of the public and private sectors and the dynamics of technology diffusions required still another set of disciplinary perspectives beyond standard marketplace economics. Legal and ecological issues had to be taken into account, as well as philosophical preferences (e.g., as mirrored in the centralized versus decentralized and hard versus soft energy source dichotomies). The multifaceted nature of the energy debate clearly required that the policy sciences retire whatever vestiges of strictly academic research it might still have retained.

A final but increasing central lesson for the policy sciences from the energy crises was the necessity to translate sophisticated, technical analysis into language policy makers could understand and to couch recommendations in the political context in which policy makers must operate (Meltsner 1980). This is surely not an unprecedented observation; analyst–client communications have been a repeated theme in the policy analysis literature, but rarely has the requirement been so badly neglected. This could have been a mixed blessing, for some of the energy studies achieved prominence more as a result of their self-generated publicity than the quality of their research and recommendations. However, that is scant excuse.

5. The End of the Cold War

Perhaps the most epochal political event in the latter half of the twentieth century was the end of the Cold War, and what it portended: the 1989 collapse of the Soviet Union, the loosening of its ties to its Eastern European satellite nations, and the end of the Communist political threat to the nations of the world. While this particular end game has yet to be fully played out (e.g., this hardly represents an "end to history," as Fukuyama (1992) has suggested), the relatively sudden demise of the evil empire does have a number of implications for the policy sciences, the most notable being the reluctance of the American intelligence and policy communities to countenance such a possibility until the evidence was unmistakably in hand. Where this shortfall is particularly apparent was that American advisers and policy makers had little idea as to what the either the domestic or external consequences might be. That is, the fall of the Soviet Union might have been due to its internal dynamics, but the policy advice community in the United States was certainly unprepared.

6. To Review

By the close of the 1970s, Lasswell's original agenda had received much work from within the policy science community and ample testing by the social and political forces of the day. More important, the policy sciences had survived into a second generation and, indeed, have prospered if one notes the growing number of policy shops in the federal government and increasingly in the individual states, to say nothing of the proliferation of policy think tanks. Despite unquestionably mixed results and frequent critical reviews, the policy sciences remained an intellectually viable and popular political strategy. Still, however, greater tests were ahead in the 1980s and 1990s. Conservative political ideologies and a general feeling that government action might not be the preferred way to solve public problems—historically, always an implicit assumption of the policy sciences—forced some policy scientists to envision a less ambitious posture.

V. FROM POLICY SCIENCE TO POLICY INQUIRY: THE 1990s AND BEYOND

When the 1970s came to a close, the policy sciences were in a state of healthy skepticism, one the 1980s did little to relieve. Many were convinced of the benefits of the policy sciences' approach, yet just as many were skeptical of its offerings. Certainly the assessment of the policy sciences was much more complex than the initial enthusiasm for producing societally relevant knowledge that had marked their inception in 1951. That the policy sciences are relevant remains a safe assumption—hardly an office in the federal government exists without an analytic arm—but the nature and the use of the knowledge they produce is today much less certain in either substance or procedure.

When the 1980s began, new concerns were being raised about what some scholars have termed the "credibility" of the policy sciences. The credibility problem is a reaction not just to the internal development of theory and method in the policy sciences, but just as clearly a consequence of a shifting political ideology away from the *hubris* of political reform to the helplessness of government policy to accomplish anything (Downs and Larkey 1986; Stone 1997), a condition exacerbated with increasing calls for the privatization of government services. The credibility of policy sciences has been challenged for failing to produce the objective empirical and normative truth implied by its scientific aspirations. It may be that the policy research still generates the most systematic and critical analyses of complex social problems, but it is also just as evident that policy science represents only one of several rational ideologies competing for social and political advantage (Diesing 1982). And more to the point, other approaches are presenting their cases (see Dryzek 1990; Fischer and Forester 1993).

The development of the policy sciences since the 1980s is one edging, probably incrementally, toward one of comprehensive change based, not surprisingly, on some of its earliest tenets (deLeon 1994a). In the 1980s and 1990s, the policy sciences revisited old themes in an effort to reconcile long-existing conflicts and improve their place among both academic and government audiences. For instance, Brunner (1991) has argued against the idea that they lack a conceptual core. Much within the policy sciences worked very well, but primarily on problems that were well defined and bounded, typically conditions at odds with social reality. The case could be made that what the policy sciences needed was more of the same, only with greater fidelity (see Brewer and Lövgren 1999), but the argument lacked conviction. Yet, in more subtle ways, the policy sciences are expanding their evidentiary bases to include more of a post-positivist orientation (Brunner 1991), as will be proposed below.

A. Old Themes Revisited

Two items of unfinished business have remained on the agenda for the policy sciences since the mid-1980s. First, the policy sciences were to become explicitly (albeit not loudly) normative. The unresolved issue was not whether policy analyses should include values and yield prescriptive advice, but how this was to be accomplished in the face of a tangled web of social, professional, and political ethics and values (Amy 1984). Second, the split between the cognitive and analytical aspects of public policy, on the one hand, and the organizational and procedural aspects, on the other, continued to plague the policy sciences as they searched for some synthesis. To this end, during the 1980s and 1990s, a union of public management to public policy was proposed in an effort to ease these tensions.

1. Ethics and Values in the Policy Sciences

When Lasswell, Kaplan, and others were arguing for an explicitly normative policy analysis, they had in mind a policy sciences inherently based on some theory of choice. That is, the policy sciences, to produce policy prescriptions, would need to make explicit choices among alternatives based on some equally explicit exposition of the criteria for choice, usually defined as part of the policy's objectives. Lasswell's vision has admittedly been difficult from the start for a social science community more accustomed to a detached, nominally objective role, one openly removed from value-based choices. The contemporary normative agenda has moved from a consideration of whether values should be included in the policy sciences—to which the answer was an unequivocal yes—to how to include questions of ethics and values in public policy. As Dunn (1983, 859) asked, "If policy analysts are expected to produce ethical as well as empirico-analytic knowledge, what methods should be employed to assess competing knowledge claims?" This dilemma becomes even more challenging as the American electorate becomes more openly bifurcated along ideological fault lines.

Four general approaches to studying ethics and values in the policy sciences have been forwarded during the 1980s and early 1990s (see Brown 1986; Cahill and Overman 1988). These are: (1) social philosophy and political theory, (2) ethical issues and social morality, (3) professional and administrative ethics, and (4) meta-ethics and ethical analyses. In some ways, they represent an intellectual evolution, yet each is still very much distinguishable as a separate approach to the study of ethics and values in public policy.

Social philosophy and political theory are easily the most entrenched approaches to the study of ethics and values in public policy. A Hastings Center study of public policy curricula around the United States revealed that one-third of the courses surveyed were based on ethical principles of social and political theory. Utilitarianism, communitarianism, and liberalism are most often cited as examples of moral theory; Rawls' (1971) *A Theory of Justice* is the most frequently referenced book. Rawls argued that the dominant system of ethics should be replaced by a system of "distributive justice." Communitarians emphasized doing good in addition to utilitarian norms of doing well, with a definite emphasis on social as opposed to strictly economic welfare. Liberalism framed the debate between liberty and equality in the formation of public policies. It seemed everyone, whether he cites Plato or Rawls, levels his sights on the utilitarian norm as the legitimate basis for social contract. However, Stone (1997) for one has argued that this avails itself of an ambiguous framework, one bound to generate internal confusion and conflict rather than analytic clarity.

The reliance on a social and political order for defining the content of policy values, as well as the process by which ethical and value decisions are made, is characteristic of this approach. The American experience has consistently argued for the democratic/administrative ethos as the source of ethics and values for public policy (cf. Lasswell 1951; Lilla 1981). Separation of politics from administration would theoretically prevent political power from corrupting public services. Similarly, public accountability of top public officials would provide the moral safeguards against ethical transgressions. In public policy-making, the democratic/administrative ethos assumes a pluralistic process in the formulation of public policies and a neutral-competent implementation follow-on, a condition, as Lindblom (1990) has claimed, that heavily biased procedures in favor of incrementalism.

The second approach to develop a *study of ethics and values*, one concentrated on specific issues of ethics and social morality, is a topical approach most suited to the contextually oriented policy sciences. Whereas the broad philosophical approach had neglected specific issues in favor of abstract moral systems, the premise of the topical perspective was that individuals and groups both inside and outside public service are forced to make concrete ethical and value judgments on a regular basis, or what Kaplan (1963) referred to as "situational ethics." Specific ethical issues change to reflect contemporary debate in the political arena, and can easily transform the debate; witness the American phobia toward extreme left-wing groups in the 1960s that transformed into similar fears against extreme right-wing groups in the mid-1990s and later re-aligned itself against any group linked to terrorism. In 1964, Girvetz's *Contemporary Moral Issues* emphasized ethical problems of national security, civil rights, and war. By 1975, Beauchamp's *Ethics and Public Policy* reflected changing public priorities by addressing ethical issues of abortion, capital punishment, and sexual discrimination. In 1984, Gutmann and Thompson examined violence, deception, official disobedience, equal opportunity, liberty, and life as major issues of ethical conflict. And the crux of the debate over American health care or social welfare policies in the 1990s was divided along ethical divides. The focus on the ethical and value content of specific policy issues increases the complexity and accentuates the normative character of the policy sciences, but with little concern paid to the process of problem definition and implementation.

The issue-oriented approach is often criticized for its lack of attention to *administrative implementation and bureaucratic control* in resolution of *ethical conflicts*. A third approach, then, revolves around the administrative ethics orientation, one focused not only on public rights and issues, but on public duties and responsibilities as well (Fleishman et al. 1981). The norms and standards of professional conduct, in particular by public officials and bureaucrats, and the conflict between public duty, personal morality, and private interest developed into "the possibility of an administrative ethics" (Thompson 1985) —historically a central theme in public administration, but less developed in the policy sciences, in part due to the putative neutrality of the policy approach. Public administration scholars, like Appleby (1959), Bailey (1964) and more recently Gawthrop (1984) and Rohr (1978), have labored to develop a perspective by which the ethical behavior and actions of individual public officials could be described and in some cases regulated, but, for the most part, have not found a resonant chord.

A fourth approach to ethics and values in public policy emerged as scholars intensified their efforts to analyze the *ethical content in the study of public policy*. Meta-ethics, or the ethical study of ethics, incorporated in such procedures as MacRae's (1976) "reasoned ethical discourse," and Rein's (1976) "value critical approach" replaced the discredited belief in value-free social science inquiry. Drawing on the work of the Frankfurt School, Fischer and Forester (1993) have argued for an "argumentative turn" to policy analysis, one in which multiple perspectives are argued openly, even if their resolution is not quite as well developed a consensus as one might want.

Much work remains to be done on methods and procedures for ethical analyses, and this will be on top of the policy sciences' agenda as they enter the twenty-first century. New methodological areas focusing on the logic of policy inquiry and the integration of empirical and normative questions of public policy (e.g., deLeon 1997; Dryzek 1990; Fischer 1989) will increasingly replace the assumption that public service is a neutral-competent activity somehow self-regulated by the democratic-administrative ethos. The Republican political *contretemps* of the 1980s and the Democratic fund-raising and personal morals scandals in the 1990s give vivid indication of the weaknesses inherent in that particular component of the policy sciences framework. Issue ethics and administrative ethics will remain strong elements as problems of policy formulation and implementation can only increase the natural conflicts that arise from values and ethics in public affairs. Moreover, a clear value structure pervades the entire "democracy of the policy sciences" movement (deLeon 1997; Dryzek and Torgerson 1993; Fischer 2003), which directly implies that citizen values are central to the policy process, even overriding the traditional beliefs in representative government (Anderson 1993).

2. Public Policy and Public Management

During the 1970s, the policy sciences directed their attention on evaluation, utilization, implementation, and termination. To some degree, each of these topics focused on moving from strategic policy analyses and advice to practical operations and organization. Just because something was defined as policy did not mean that it was automatically accomplished, and almost never, it seemed, was policy accomplished with the intended consequences. Public administration would have been the perfect ally, but in an effort to distinguish themselves from the long history of that field, the policy scientists distanced themselves from the canons of traditional public administration and, not surprisingly, vice versa. Though some (e.g., the editors of this particular volume) would argue that differences between public administration and policy sciences are more a matter of style than substance, it seemed important that the policy scientists develop their own disciplinary rules and safeguards, even if it appears in retrospect that they turned their backs on important bodies of knowledge.

To this end, the field of public management more or less evolved, particularly after the 1978 Civil Service Reform Act (CSRA). Whereas the policy sciences had estranged themselves from traditional public administration, the newer public management approach seemed to provide a convenient transition with public administration to the policy sciences. Public management, like policy, shared a general discomfort for traditional objective, discipline-bound, social science inquiry, and preferred the multidisciplinary, problem-oriented, and explicitly normative nature of its policy-oriented kin. Public management, according to Garson and Overman (1983), adopted the instrumental and pragmatic orientation so successful in the policy sciences, but with a distinct focus on organization, program, and individual performance, rather than entire social and political systems. The public manager is understood to be concerned with the specific functions necessary to the organization and implementation of public policy: planning, organization, directing, and controlling. Policy and management are natural partners, convergent in outcome yet discriminating in focus. They even share the same conceptual divisions. Just as the policy sciences have been divided between process and content, the classic dichotomy in the public management is between the behavioral humanistic orientation and the scientific orientation.

Several contemporary authors have addressed the union of policy and management. Meltsner and Bellavita (1983), in *The Policy Organization*, discuss communication and effective policy management. Their theme is that to improve communication and (implicitly) effective policy, managers need to move beyond a limited conception of policy communication and include an issue-specific view (content), the policy network view (process), and most of all the management view of how an idea can be translated into operational policy. The management view, they claim, "links the world of ideas to the world of feasible actions through the intervention of organizations"

(Meltsner and Bellavita 1983, 46). Lynn (1987), in *Managing Public Policy*, combined theories of managerial and organizational behavior of senior public executives as they pursue their individual contribution to public policy. Managing public policy, according to Lynn (1987, 19), was typically "the result of executive effort directed at affecting governmental outcomes by influencing the processes that design and carry out governmental activity." Lynn (1994) later chronicled a new relationship between public policy scholars and their new-found management colleagues, to the point where policy and management scholars have joined in the New Public Management (NPM) proposals.

From the managerial perspective, Salamon (1981) went as far as "rethinking public management" by requesting a change in the unit of analysis in public management from individual programs and organizations to the generic tools of government. Viewing public management as tools, such as regulation, tax incentives, and government sponsorship or ownership, effectively equated management with policy implementation. As such, implementation served as the featured synergistic union between public policy and public management.

Although this linkage of management and implementation provided many policy scholars with an organizational touchstone, it did not suggest the entire set of management contribution. From a purely business administration perspective, Mintzberg (1977) sees policy strictly as a field of management theory. He argues that policy is really a form of strategic management that focuses on the total organization. The process of strategy (read policy) formulation in the public sector is clearly more diffuse and complex than in the private sector, yet discussions of strategic management and public policy are increasingly found in the public policy literature. Others (e.g., Behn 2001) have focused on issues of leadership and, drawing upon the public administration tradition, accountability.

Perhaps the best evidence of the new marriage between policy and management is institutional. The establishment of the Association for Public Policy Analysis and Management and its *Journal of Policy Analysis and Management* reflects the explicit contributions of policy to management, although the union has been slow to be consummated on an equal basis, judging by the journal's selection of articles. Similarly a number of academic programs across the country either created and added management to their policy curricula or changed their rubric to indicate both. The public policy schools from Harvard to Berkeley and those geographically (and philosophically) in between, have added faculty and classes in public management, or what some preferred to call organizational politics and public policy. Even traditional business schools such as the Wharton School of the University of Pennsylvania created doctoral and master's programs in public policy analysis and management. By the end of the 1990s, the union of policy and management was a foregone conclusion, even as some scholars tacitly (and mistakenly in our opinion) moved away from traditional public administration studies. In the long term, this recognition can only prove rewarding for the policy sciences as they strive to expand their theoretical boundaries to practical applications.

The 1990s brought heightened interest in public management. Perhaps, as never before, the best-selling book on *Reinventing Government* and its subsequent adoption by the Clinton administration pushed an agenda of management reform at all levels of government. One of the themes was deceptively simple: it is not so much that the policies and intentions of government are bad, but it is the way government goes about governing that needs to be more market-like and less command-and-control oriented. It was an old idea of the policy sciences brought home in public management, but it created a new perspective of what some would label the postbureaucratic approach to organizations and government (Barzelay 1992). Moreover, the success of the NPM reforms in nations like New Zealand and Great Britain was evidence that NPM and its intellectual underpinnings (e.g., transaction analysis and decentralization) deserved careful attention by the policy scientists of the 1990s and 2000s; indeed, much of the American Welfare Reform Act was predicated on key parts of the NPM platform. In short, during the 1990s, what were previously policy issues had, in many cases, become management issues; more tellingly, what were the distinctions between the two areas of inquiry became even vaguer and less distinct.

B. New Directions Broached

Predicting the future of an evolving academic activity is akin to nailing Jell-O® to the wall; not only is it difficult to do, but you can look foolish doing it. One safe tactic is to predict the changes and trends in the policy sciences and hope they do not turn out to be passing fancies. The argument can be made that during the 1980s, the attacks on the credibility of the policy sciences resulted in a shift from the policy sciences through policy inquiry to policy design (see Bobrow and Dryzek 1987; Ingram and Schneider 1993; Schneider and Ingram 1997). Policy design, insofar as it is different from the policy sciences, has offered a more synoptic view of what was earlier described as the policy process, with early attention paid to such issues as implementation analysis. Of course, the recognition that implementation is a thorny endeavor does not necessarily mean that it is easily resolved by early attention; would that it were so (see deLeon and deLeon 2002).

At the risk of hurling Jell-O, let us offer a number of emerging issues in the development of the policy science arsenal, specifically exploring the issues of their relevance, the possibility offered by policy inquiry, the emergence of a post-positivist approach, and finally an exploration of (social) network analysis. Special attention is devoted to discussing network analysis because of its relatively limited exposure to date in the policy sciences and its great potential.

1. Increasing Relevance and Application

Although the intellectual and practical shortcomings of the policy sciences are easy to posit, it is much more difficult to debate their successes beyond the analytically ordinary, i.e., first you define the problem, then somebody has to chose a policy option, etc. However, we propose that the policy orientation is relevant for resolving complex social and political issues and doing so in an integrated, policy-relevant manner, if for no other reason than that these are its intellectual benchmarks. Old areas of public concern are continuously subjected to policy analysis—economic development, international trade, health policy, social welfare policies, and defense to name a few. New policy areas also provide ample additional grist for the policy sciences' mills. Genetic engineering and biotechnology, globalization and terrorism, robotics, information policy, and immigration and assimilation policies are only the most recent in a long series of public policy issues that would benefit from the systematic lenses of the policy sciences.

While the policy sciences were providing social and political relevance in varying degrees, some sacrifice in neutrality and objectivity were seemingly necessary. Rising above the earlier partisan claims, the policy sciences were able to accommodate new political ideologies as well. For much of their brief history, the policy sciences appeared to hold an implicit assumption about the benefits of government intervention and public problems. The conservative political movements of the 1980s and 1990s challenged this assumption by querying whether government should even be in the business of social intervention and change. Increasingly, policy analyses could be found to support the wide spectrum of political ideologies. Whether it was Murray (1984) on welfare reform, or Savas (1987) on privatization, it was still the policy sciences. More important, however, has been the recent realization that ideological preferences can pre-empt analytic contributions, as was seemingly the case for the American entry into the second Gulf War (e.g., see Clark 2003), which stood in stark contrast to the depiction of President Clinton and Vice President Gore as "policy wonks" (Woodward 1994).

That the policy sciences are able to address most issues from a number of often competing perspectives lends support to the notion that the policy sciences have become one voice in the chorus of social change. As Paris and Reynolds (1983, 219) note, "The sad truth is that much empirical policy inquiry is actually more like empirical policy warfare," which Jenkins-Smith

(1990) documented in his discussion of US maritime policy. Instead of being the final arbiter of policy issues, the policy sciences have been described as yet another contributor to a polity of competing rational ideologies in which policy makers serve as the ultimate arbiter, using whatever criteria they choose. Whether Lasswell ever intended the policy orientation to be the *sine quo non* of policy sciences is open to debate. His insistence on scientific knowledge, however, as the basis of the policy sciences is more clear; epistemological shifts—such as Dryzek (1990), who argues that the rational foundation of policy analysis finally dooms it to irrelevancy—toward more relativistic forms of inquiry were not within Lasswell's original framework and stand as one of the major changes in the field of the policy sciences since its inception in 1951.

2. From Policy Science to Policy Inquiry

Rationality has always been a central interpretation within the policy sciences, especially among economists. A rational theory of choice assumes both a transitive ordering of preferences and maximization of values. It further assumes that choices are capable of being calculated to an approximation of the scientific method. As such, policy choices based on technical and economic criteria (e.g., cost-benefit analysis) could be counted on for maximizing benefits and minimizing costs. Proponents of the policy process realized that, more often than not, rational expectation failed to meet descriptive realities, but relied almost exclusively on political and organizational imperatives that usually fall beyond the limits of economic rationality to explain the variance (Simon 1985). However, rationality as a theory of choice could not ultimately explain the diversity and richness of the policy phenomena, and whether it is ethics and values or organizational ambiguity and conflict that disturb the rational expectations, some new theory or major amendments need to be developed (cf. Etzioni 1988). Clearly it is not that the rational theory is wrong as much as it has proven to be incomplete.

As a possible amendment, Diesing (1962) developed a theory of reason in society that broadened the traditional conception of rationality from the technical and economic rationality—the easiest to define and apply—to include social, legal, and political rationality. Others who have subsequently taken up his line of reasoning include Fischer (1989), Hawkesworth (1988), and Robinson (1992). Instead of narrowing the focus of application for the policy sciences during the 1970s and 1980s by insisting on economic and technical rationality, Diesing (1962, 247) suggested that "the proper response should have been the opposite one of broadening the conception of rationality to fit the broadened conception of society which was developing. The aim should have been to locate and describe new types of calculation, or quasi-calculation, appropriate to social, political and legal problems." Simon (1983, but as early as Simon 1945) agreed. He proposed a concept of reason in human affairs that includes four visions of rationality: (1) the Olympian model—traditional economic and technical rationality, so named because of the impossibility of achieving its lofty goals, (2) the behavioral model, (3) the intuitive model, and (4) the evolutionary model. Each, according to Simon, contributes to a theory of reason in society and human affairs.

The theoretical broadening of rationality to a theory of reason in society terms remained more an aspiration than an achievement in the policy sciences through into the 1990s. An updated policy analysis orientation, instead of stressing the traditional rational approach, or even a bifurcation of scientific and political rationalities, would rely more on a "polity of rational ideologies" in which reasoned policy inquiry replaces the "objective" model of the policy sciences (Paris and Reynolds 1983). Such an expanded concept of reason has the added advantage of furthering the context-oriented and explicitly normative nature of the policy sciences. Toulmin and his colleagues (1979) unintentionally provided a new definition of the policy sciences: "Reasoning does not create ideas and does not answer once and for all whether those ideas are good or bad, true or false. Rather, the task of reasoning in each situation is to enable the questioner to make the best decision about a particular issue, in particular circumstances, within a particular form or enterprise"

(18). Others have worked to integrate critical theory (Forester 1993), and particularly the idea of an open exchange, into the policy process. These are the proper and prescribed roles of the policy sciences as they possibly move towards a more post-positivist future (deLeon 1994a, 1997), as described below.

An area that warrants special attention deals with what Sabatier and his colleagues (1993, 1999) have termed "policy change and learning" or the conditions and ideas that motivate alterations in policy positions (Baumgartner and Jones 1993; Sabatier 1999; Sabatier and Jenkins-Smith 1993). This emphasis intellectually moves us to yet another emerging frontier in public policy theory, social network analysis (see below).

One such method of reasoning and policy inquiry, known as policy argumentation or forensic policy analysis, has already made substantial inroads into the policy literature. Fischer (1980), drawing on Habermas and others, advocates "a logic of policy questions" that is designed to constitute a complete policy argument. A decade later, Fischer and Forester (1993) have evolved this logic into a local of policy argumentation. As a method this framework of questions does not provide right and wrong answers, but reasons why one policy may be superior compared to another. As a political tool it is intended to stimulate debate and open communication within traditional policy structures. Above all, it is a process of iterative inquiry. Dunn (1981) included a textbook chapter on modes of policy argument in which he illustrates how complex policy arguments can be created and analyzed using a specific argument structure of data, claims, warrants, and backings. Borrowing from the fields of rhetoric (see Brock et al. 1973; Freely 1976; Hambrick 1974) and philosophical reasoning (Toulmin et al. 1979), policy argumentation promises not only to meet the goals set out by a theory of reason in society, but also to integrate the process and content divisions that have arisen within the policy sciences. To be fair, argumentation has been attacked for being relativistic, as Fischer (2003) has acknowledged. In the absence of criteria for judging the validity of policy arguments, policy argumentation could become a forum of debate in which advocacy outweighs analysis (see Majone 1989). Establishment of criteria, such as completeness or cogency, for assessing policy arguments must be a priority if policy inquiry approaches are to advance. Thus argumentation and policy inquiry might represent a new advance, but are neither free of problems nor a dominant solution.

3. Post-Positivism in the Policy Sciences

Another avenue for the contemporary policy sciences concerns the role of post-positivism in general and participatory policy analysis in particular. At first, the post-positivist proponents (e.g., Dryzek 1990) strongly indicated that the analytic heart of the policy sciences (what Dryzek called "instrumental rationality" was not only inaccurate in an analytic sense—i.e., it fundamentally skews the analytic process—but it was also inherently non-democratic (also, see Fischer 2003; deLeon 1997; Durning 1999). While numerous scholars have inveighed against those propositions (see Lynn 1999), a more balanced assessment indicates that a post-positivist orientation holds that both quantitative and qualitative research approaches are legitimate; however, rather than being a particular function of research skills, they need to be determined as a function of the issue being investigated (Bobrow and Dryzek 1987).

The effects of the post-positivist approach have already been seen, for it implies a greater concern for values as they exist—and are influential—outside the rational actor model. A second issues substantiates the post-positivist model in terms of its practical influence, since it argues explicitly that greater public participation in the policy process is necessary for the policy sciences to achieve their Lasswellian goal of the policy sciences of democracy. This realization is critical because the human condition is often temperamentally beyond the ability of the quantitative approaches to capture (deLeon 1992, 1997; Dryzek 1990; Durning 1993). Again, no one should assume that the postpositive approaches answer all questions or resolve all problems. Like the other orientations reviewed above, they too have their shortcomings—for example, how to incorporate public hearings into policy formulation or evaluation exercises or even who should be included—but promise new lines of research in the coming decade.

4.   Social Network Analysis

As mentioned previously, the instrumental notion of the role of knowledge in society has been the basic premise of the policy sciences. The use of alternative methods for policy analysis in the latter part of the century has contributed to the legitimatization and knowledge contributions of the policy sciences. One such notable alternative approach is network analysis, or social network analysis. Many of the discussed approaches to policy analysis are "characterized by political and administrative jurisdictions that are poorly suited for solving many emerging problems" (Schneider et al. 2003, 143). To understand the relevant stakeholders in the policy arena, the most important issues and manners in which these variables are interrelated represented intractable problems using the traditional approaches to policy analysis. Schneider et al. (2003) and Toonen (1998) recognized that the shift from traditional large-scale governmental organizations to new regional governmental institutions and non-profit agencies has created the need to evaluate the formation of public policy in terms of the influence of the network in which it is based.

To Hanf and Scharpf (1978, 12), the policy network approach is a tool to evaluate the "large number of public and private actors from different levels and functional areas of government and society." Other forms of policy analysis have tended to focus on the *hierarchical* process that has characterized the process. The network approach looks at the policy process in terms of the *horizontal* relationships that define the development of public policies (see Hajer and Wagenaar 2003). Carlsson (2000) defines policy networks as "cluster[s] or complexes of organizations connected to each other by resource dependencies and distinguished from other clusters or complexes by breaks in the structure of resource dependencies." Heclo (1978, 187) famously notes that "... it is through networks of people who regard each other as knowledgeable, or at least needing to be answered, that public policy issues tend to be refined, evidence debated, and alternative options worked out—though rarely in any controlled, well-organized way." These horizontal relationships can include individuals, organizations, lobbyists, legislators, or whoever plays a role in policy development.

The structure of the network is the central focus of the approach. To visualize the horizontal connections within a social structure allows one to see the strength of relationships, the availability of resources, the possibility of political influences, and access to otherwise hard to reach populations. Schneider et al. (2003, 143–144) note that network-based structures are characterized by "high levels of interdependence involving multiple organizations, where formal lines of authority are blurred and where diverse policy actors are knitted together to focus on common problems." The network approach has solved the problem of attempting to understand what might otherwise seem to be fragmented networks, can lead to the development of common perspectives on policy issues and norms of cooperation and trust (Lin 2001), and jibes neatly with the prevalent theme of democratic governance (Hajer and Wagenaar 2003). According to Schneider et al. (2003, 144), "the resulting formal and informal interactions have the potential to increase policy effectiveness at less cost than authority-based structural changes arrived at through formal reorganization."

A network approach to policy analysis has been developed in a variety of ways (Carlsson 2000; Heclo 1978; Hjern and Hull 1983; Jordan 1990). For example, in his evaluation of subgovernments, Rhodes (1990, 297) defines them as "small groups of political actors, both governmental and non-governmental that specialize in specific issue areas." He takes a network approach to understanding how these subgovernments, each focused around policy issues, create successful public policy development. In his study of the formation of the new state of Israel, Yishai (1992) found that a policy community was formed around a sequence of concepts, leading to a health policy for the new state.

Policy networks have the ability to increase the likelihood and scope of policy agreements "by increasing available information about potential agreements and enhancing the credibility of commitments to fulfill the agreements" (Schneider et al. 2003, 144). This is done by spanning organizational boundaries, exploring the details of organizational decision-making, and discovering barriers to implementation, thus increasing the likelihood of successful policy-making. Once a policy network is identified, a variety of techniques can be used.

Dowding (1995) argues that the most that can be learned from a policy network comes from a formal approach in which properties of the network can be explained, but nothing more. He states that "while it has proven useful for cataloging policy procedures into different types of networks, it cannot be used to provide a fundamental reassessment of the policy process" (136). However, others state that what is useful for policy-making is the very idea that the structure and how it is designed, can influence the policy process (Carlsson 2000; Provan and Milward 1995). The key to the network approach is understanding how certain relationships are formed and which parts of the network are the strongest and most knowledgeable, i.e., the most connected to others.

Understanding of such characteristics as "structural holes"—that is, a "relationship of nonredundancy between two contacts... a buffer... [that] as a result of the hole between them, the two contacts provide network benefits that are in some degree additive rather than overlapping" (Burt 1992, 18)—are only one of many theoretical developments in the area of network analysis. Numerous researchers (Borgatti et al. 1998; Burt 1979; Granovetter 1982; Prell 2003; Provan and Milward 1995; Scott 1991) have made developments in the theory, going beyond evaluation of the structure of the network alone, and understanding how the placement of actors influences such variables as power, knowledge, brokering of information, and resource sharing.

Carlsson (2000) suggests that a network approach is useful, but claims that, as of now, it is not a viable policy analysis approach because it lacks "a theoretical scaffold" and must find theoretical support from well-defined theories such as collective action theory. Although this is a thoughtful argument, Carlsson has failed to appreciate the explanatory power of network analysis. Not only are the features and structure of networks well explained, but numerous theoretical advancements in terms of social networking have been advanced (Borgatti et al. 1998; Burt 1979; Burt 2000; Carlsson 2000; Cashore and Vertinsky 2000; Granovetter 1982; Milward et al. 1993; Wholey 2002; Wright 1994). Ample empirical research now governs the field in regards to the effects of networks on a variety of social phenomenon including advancements in policy analysis.

VI. SUMMARY: HALF A CENTURY OF POLICY SCIENCES

This chapter has traced the progression of the policy sciences during the last half of the twentieth century. In our review, four central themes mark this progression. First, in the pre-World War II environment, it was the aspirations for societally relevant knowledge among a small group of social scientists that provided greatest impetus to the policy sciences. Second, during the 1950s and 1960s, most efforts were devoted to realizing the vision of the policy sciences as multidisciplinary, contextual, problem-oriented, and explicitly normative. Third, once they achieved initial success in academic and government settings, the objective of the 1970s and 1980s became one of expanding the relevance while clinging to the scientific rigor of the policy sciences. Finally, the future of the policy sciences will depend less on its adherence to the natural science model and ability to produce empirically demonstrable truths and more on its ability to serve the knowledge needs of the administrative and political community in the form of directed policy inquiry (Brunner 1991). This last period thus presents a multitude of either promises or pitfalls (perhaps both) as the policy sciences work toward their goal of providing better information and processes to enlighten and enhance the public good.

REFERENCES

Aaron, H. J., *Politics and the Professors: The Great Society in Perspective*, Brookings Institution, Washington, DC, 1978.

Alkin, M.C, Ed., *Debates on Evaluation*, Sage Publication, Newbury Park, CA, 1990.

Amy, D. J., Why policy analysis and ethics are incompatible, *Journal of Policy Analysis and Management*, 3(4), 573–591, 1984.

Anderson, C. W., Recommending a scheme of reason: political theory, policy science, and democracy, *Policy Sciences*, 26, 215–218, 1993.

Appleby, P. *Administration in Democratic Government*, Louisiana State Univeristy Press, Baton Rouge, LA, 1959.

Ascher, W., Policy sciences and the economic approach in a post-positivist world, *Policy Sciences*, 20, 3–9, 1987.

Bailey, S., Ethics and public service, *Public Administration Review*, 24, 234–243, 1964.

Bardach, E. C., Special issue. *Policy Sciences* 7(2), 1976.

Bardach, E. C., *The Implementation Game*, MIT Press, Cambridge, MA, 1977.

Barzelay, M., *Breaking through Bureaucracy*, University of California Press, Berkeley, CA, 1992.

Bauer, R. A. and Gergen, K. J., Eds., *The Study of Policy Formation*, Free Press, New York, 1968.

Baumgartner, F. R. and Jones, B. D., *Agendas and Instability in American Politics*, University of Chicago Press, Chicago, IL, 1993.

Beauchamp, T., *Ethics and Public Policy*, Prentice Hall, Englewood Cliffs, NJ, 1975.

Beckman, N., ed., (1977). Policy analysis in government: alternatives to " muddling through." *Public Administration Review*. 37(3):221–263.

Behn, R. D., *Rethinking Democratic Accountability*, The Brookings Institution, Washington, DC, 2001.

Berman, P. and McLaughlin, M. W., *Federal Programs Supporting Educational Change: A Model of Educational Change*, Rand Corporation, Santa Monica, CA, 1974.

Bobrow, D. and Dryzek, J. S., *Policy Analysis by Design*, University of Pittsburgh Press, Pittsburgh, PA, 1987.

Borgatti, K. S. *et al.*, *Networks Measures of Social Capital Connections*, 21(2), 27–36, 1998.

Brewer, G. D. and deLeon, P., *The Foundations of Policy Analysis*, Brooks/Cole, Monterey, CA, 1983.

Brewer, G. D. and Lövgren, K., The theory and practice of interdisciplinary research, *Policy Sciences*, 24, 295–331, 1999.

Brock, B., Chesebro, J. W., Cragan, J. F., and Klumpp, J. F., *Public Policy Decision-Making: Systems Analysis and Comparative Advantages Debate*, Harper & Row, New York, 1973.

Brown, P., Ethics and education for public service in a liberal state, *Journal of Policy Analysis and Management*, 6(1), 56–68, 1986.

Brunner, R. D., The policy movement as a policy problem, *Policy Sciences*, 24, 65–98, 1991.

Bulmer, M., *The Uses of Social Research*, George Allen & Unwin, London, 1982.

Burt, R. S., A structural theory of interlocking directorates, *Social Networks*, 1, 415–435, 1979.

Burt, R. S., *Structural Holes*, Cambridge University Press, Cambridge, 1992.

Burt, R. S., *The network structure of social capital In Research in Organizational Behavior*, JAI Press, Greenwich, CT, 2000.

Cahill, A. and Overman, E. S., Contemporary perspectives on ethics and values in public affairs, In *Ethics, Government and Policy: An Anthology of Original Essays*, Bowman, J. and Elliston, F., Eds., Greenwood Press, Westport, CT, 1988.

Campbell, D. T., Reforms as experiments, *American Psychological Review*, 24, 409–429, 1969.

Caplan, N. *et al.*, *The Use of Social Science Knowledge in Policy Decisions at the National Level*, University of Michigan Press, Ann Arbor, MI, 1975.

Caralay, D., *Doing More with Less*, Graduate Program in Public Policy, Columbia University, New York, 1982.

Carlsson, L., Policy networks as collective action. *Policy Studies Journal* 28:502–527, 2000.

Cashore, B. and Vertinsky, I., Policy networks and firm behaviors: governance systems and firm responses to external demands for sustainable forest management, *Policy Sciences*, 33, 1–30, 2000.

Charlesworth, J. C., Ed., *Integration of the Social Sciences through Policy Analysis. Monograph no. 14*, American Academy of Political and Social Sciences, Philadelphia, PA, 1972.

Coleman, J. C., Ed., *Policy Research in the Social Sciences* General Learning Press, Morristown, NJ, 1972.

Commoner, B., *The Politics of Energy*, Knopf, New York, 1979.

Critchlow, D. T., *The Brookings Institution, 1916–1952: Expertise and the Public Interest in a Democratic Society*, Northern Illinois University Press, DeKalb, IL, 1985.

Dahl, R. A. and Lindblom, C. E., *Politics, Economics, and Welfare*, Harper, New York, 1953.

Daniels, M. R., *Terminating Pubic Programs: An American Political Paradox*, M.E. Sharpe, Armonk, NY, 1997.

Daniels, M., and Wirth, C. J., Paradigms of evaluation research: the development of an important policy-making component, *American Review of Public Administration*, 17, 33–45, 1983.

deLeon, P., Public policy termination: an end and a beginning, *Policy Analysis*, 4, 369–392, 1978.

deLeon, P., A theory of policy termination, In *The Policy Cycle*, May, J. and Wildavsky, A., Eds., Sage Publications, Beverly Hills, CA, 1978.

deLeon, P., The democratization of the policy sciences, *Public Administration Review*, 52, 125–129, 1992.

deLeon, P., Reinventing the policy sciences: three steps back towards the future, *Policy Sciences*, 27, 77–95, 1994.

deLeon, P., *Thinking about Political Corruption*, M.E. Sharpe, Armonk, NY, 1994.

deLeon, P., *Democracy and the Policy Sciences*, SUNY Press, Albany, NY, 1997.

deLeon, P. and deLeon, L., Whatever happened to policy implementation: an alternative approach, *Journal of Public Administration Research and Theory*, 12, 467–492, 2002.

Derthick, M., *New Towns-In Town*, Urban Institute, Washington, DC, 1972.

Dewey, J., *The Public and Its Problems*, Alan Swallow, Denver, CO, 1927.

Dewey, J., *The Quest for Certainty*, Putnam, New York, 1929.

Dewey, J., *How We Think*, Henry Regnery, Chicago, IL, 1933.

Diesing, P., *Reason in Society*, University of Illinois Press, Urbana, IL, 1962.

Diesing, P., *Science and Ideology in the Policy Sciences*, Aldine, New York, 1982.

Dowding, K., Model or metaphor? A critical review of the policy network approach, *Political Studies*, 43(1), 136–158, 1995.

Downs, G. W. and Larkey, P. D., *The Search for Government Efficiency: From Hubris to Helplessness*, Random House, New York, 1986.

Dror, Y., Muddling through—"Science" or Inertia?, *Public Administration Review*, 24, 153–157, 1964.

Dror, Y., Prolegomena to policy sciences, *Policy Sciences*, 1, 138, 1970.

Dror, Y., *Design for the Policy Sciences*, American Elsevier, New York, 1971.

Dror, Y., *Ventures in Policy Analysis*, American Elsevier, New York, 1971.

Dryzek, J., *Discursive Democracy*, Cambridge University Press, New York, 1990.

Dryzek, J. and Torgerson, D., Democracy and the policy sciences: a progress report, *Policy Sciences*, 26, 127–137, 1993.

Dunn, W. N., *Public Policy Analysis*, Prentice Hall, Englewood Cliffs, NJ, 1981.

Dunn, W. N., Values, ethics, and standards in policy analysis, In *Encyclopedia of Policy Studies*, Nagel, S., Ed., Marcel Dekker, New York, 1983.

Durning, D., Participatory policy analysis in a social services agency, *Journal of Policy Analysis and Management*, 12, 231–257, 1993.

Durning, D., The transition for traditional to postpositivist policy analysis: a role for Q-methodology, *Journal of Policy Analysis and Management*, 18, 389–410, 1999.

Easton, D., *A Systems Analysis of Political Life*, Wiley, New York, 1965.

Enthoven, A. and Smith, C. W., *How Much is Enough?*, Harper & Row, New York, 1971.

Etzioni, A., Mixed-scanning: a "third" approach to decision making, *Public Administration Review*, 27, 385–392, 1967.

Etzioni, A., *The Moral Dimension*, Free Press, New York, 1988.

Fischer, F., *Politics, Values, and Public Policy: The Problem of Methodology*, Westview Press, Boulder, CO, 1980.

Fischer, F., The rationality project: policy analysis and the postpositivist challenge, *Policy Studies Review*, 17, 941–951, 1989.

Fischer, F., Citizen participation and the democratization of policy expertise: from theoretic inquiry to practical cases, *Policy Sciences Review*, 26, 165–188, 1993.

Fischer, F., Beyond empiricism: policy inquiry in postpositivist perspectives, *Policy Studies Review*, 26, 129–147, 1998.

Fischer, F., *Reframing Policy Analysis*, Oxford University Press, New York, 2003.

Fischer, F. and Forester, J., Eds., *The Argumentative Turn in Policy Analysis and Planning*, Duke University Press, Durham NC, 1993.

Fisher, G. H., *Cost Considerations in Systems Analysis*, American Elsevier, New York, 1971.

FitzGerald, F., *Fire in the Lake*, Little, Brown, Boston, MA, 1972.

Fleishman, J. L., Liebman, L., and Moore, M. H., Eds., *Public Duties: The Moral Obligation of Public Officials*, Harvard University Press, Cambridge, MA, 1981.

Forester, J., *Critical Theory, Public Policy, and Planning Practice*, State University of New York Press, Albany, NY, 1993.

Frankel, E., Energy and social change: an historian's perspective, *Policy Sciences*, 14, 59–73, 1981.

Frantz, J. E., Reviving and revising a termination theory, *Policy Sciences*, 25, 175–190, 1993.

Freely, A. L., *Argumentation and Debate: Rational Decision Making*, 4th ed., Wadsworth, Belmont, CA, 1976.

Fukuyama, F., *End of History and the Last Man*, Free Press, New York, 1992.

Garson, G. D., From policy science to policy analysis: a quarter century of progress? *Policy Studies Journal Special Issue*, 535–545, 1981.

Garson, G. D. and Overman, E. S., *Public Management Research in the United States*, Praeger, New York, 1983.

Gawthrop, L., *Public Sector Management, Systems, and Ethics*, Indiana University Press, Bloomington, 1984.

Gelb, L. H. and Betts, R. K., *The Irony of Vietnam: The System Worked*, Brookings Institution, Washington, DC, 1979.

Glazer, N., *Ethnic Dilemmas: 1964–1982*, Harvard University Press, Cambridge, MA, 1983.

Goldhamer, H., *The Advisor*, Elsevier, New York, 1978.

Granovetter, M. S., *The Strength of Weak Ties in Social Structure and Network Analysis*, Sage, London, 1982.

Green, W., Economists in recession: after an inflation of errors and depletion of theory, *New York Times Magazine*, May 12, 1972.

Greenberg, G., Developing public theory: perspectives from empirical research, *American Political Science Review*, 71, 1532–1543, 1977.

Greenberger, M. *et al.*, *Caught Unawares: The Energy Decade in Retrospect*, Ballinger, Cambridge, MA, 1983.

Groggin, M. L. *et al.*, *Implementation Theory and Practice: Toward a Third Generation*, Scott Foresman, Glenville, IL, 1990.

Gutmann, A. and Thompson, D., Eds., *Ethics and Politics: Cases and Comments*, Nelson Hall, Chicago, IL, 1984.

Hajer, M and Wagenaar, H., *Deliberative Policy Analysis*, Cambridge University Press, Cambridge, UK, 2003.

Hambrick, R. S., A guide for the analysis of policy arguments, *Policy Sciences*, 5, 469–478, 1974.

Hammond, P. B., The energy model muddle, *Policy Sciences*, 16, 227–243, 1984.

Hanf, K. and Scharpf, F., Eds., *Interorganizational Policymaking*, Sage Modern Political Series, London, 1978.

Hargrove, E. C., *The Missing Link: The Study of Implementation*, Urban Institute, Washington, DC, 1975.

Hargrove, E. C., The search for implementation theory, In *What Role for Government?* Zeckhauser, R. J. and Leebaert, D., Eds., Duke University Press, Durham, NC, 1983.

Harrington, M., *The Other America: Poverty in the United States*, Macmillan, New York, 1963.

Hawkesworth, M. E., *Theoretical Issues of Policy Analysis*, State University of New York Press, Albany, NY, 1988.

Heclo, H., Review article: policy analysis, *British Journal of Politics*, 2, 83–108, 1972.

Heclo, H., Issue networks and the executive establishment, In *The New American Political System*, American Enterprise Institute, Washington, DC, 1978.

Heller, W. W., What's right with economics, *American Economic Review*, 65, 1–26, 1975.

Hitch, C. H. and McKean, R. N., *The Economics of Defense in the Nuclear Age*, Harvard University Press, Cambridge, MA, 1960.

Hjern, B. and Hull, C., Implementation structures: a new unit of administrative analysis, In *Realizing Social Science Knowledge*, Holzner, B., Ed., Physica-Verlag, Vienna, pp. 265–277, 1983.

Hoos, I., *Systems Analysis in Public Policy*, Rev. ed., University of California Press, Berkeley, CA, 1972.

Horowitz, I. and Katz, J., *Social Science and Public Policy in the United States*, Praeger, New York, 1975.

Ingram, H. and Schneider, A., Constructing citizenship: the subtle messages of policy design, In *Public Policies for Democracy*, Ingram, H. and Smith, S. R., Eds., Brookings Institution, Washington, DC, 1993.

Jenkins-Smith, H. C., *Democratic Politics and Policy Analysis*, Brooks/Cole, Pacific Grove, CA, 1990.

Jones, C. O., *An Introduction to the Study of Public Policy*, 2nd ed., Duxbury Press, North Scituate, MA, 1977.

Jordan, G., Sub-governments, policy communities, and networks: refilling old bottles?, *Journal of Theoretical Politics*, 2(3), 319–338, 1990.

Kaplan, A., *American Ethics and Public Policy*, Oxford University Press, New York, 1963.

Karlqvist, A., Going beyond disciplines: the meaning of interdisciplinary, *Policy Sciences*, 32, 379–383, 1999.

Kaufman, H., *Are Government Organizations Immortal?* Brookings Institution, Washington, DC, 1976.

Kecskemeti, P., The 'policy sciences': aspiration and outlook, *World Politics*, 5, 520–535, 1952.

Kershaw, J. A. and Courant, P. N., *Government Against Poverty*, Markham, Chicago, IL, 1970.

Larson, R. C. and Odoni, A., *Urban Operations Research*, Prentice Hall, Englewood Cliffs, NJ, 1981.

Lasswell, H. D., The political science of science, *American Political Science Review*, 50, 961–979, 1956.

Lasswell, H. D., The emerging conception of the policy sciences, *Policy Sciences*, 1, 1–15, 1970.

Lasswell, H. D., *A Pre-View of Policy Sciences*, American Elsevier, New York, 1971.

Lasswell, H. D. and Kaplan, A., *Power and Society*, Yale University Press, New Haven, CT, 1950.

Lerner, D. and Lasswell, H. D., Eds., *The Policy Sciences*, Stanford University Press, Stanford, CA, 1951.

Levine, C. H. et al., *The Politics of Retrenchment*, Sage Publications, Beverly Hills, CA, 1981.

Levine, R. A., *The Poor Ye Need not have with You: Lessons from the War on Poverty*, MIT Press, Cambridge, MA, 1970.

Lilla, M., Ethos, ethics, and public service, *Public Interest*, 63, 3–17, 1981.

Lin, N., *Social Capital: A Theory of Social Structure and Action*, Cambridge University Press, London and New York, 2001.

Lindblom, C. E., The handling of norms in policy analysis, In *The Allocation of Economic Resource*, Baran, P. A., Ed., Stanford University Press, Stanford, CA, 1959.

Lindblom, C. E., *Inquiry and Change*, Yale University Press, New Haven, CT, 1990.

Lindblom, C. E. and Cohen, D. K., *Usable Knowledge: Social Sciences and Social Problem Solving*, Yale University Press, New Haven, CT, 1979.

Linder, B. H. and Peters, B. G., A design perspective on policy implementations: the fallacies of misplaced prescription, *Policy Studies Review*, 6, 459–475, 1987.

Lineberry, R.L., Policy analysis, policy sciences, and political science, Paper presented to the American Political Science Association, Chicago, IL, 1982.

Lynd, R. S., *Knowledge for What?*, Princeton University Press, Princeton, NJ, 1939.

Lynn, L. E., *Managing Public Policy*, Little, Brown, Boston, MA, 1987.

Lynn, L. E., Public management: a survey, *Journal of Policy Analysis and Management*, 13, 231–259, 1994.

Lynn, L.E., A place at the table: policy analysis, its postpositivist critics, and the future of practice, *Journal of Policy Analysis and Management*, 18, 411–424, 1999.

Lyons, G. M., *The Uneasy Partnership*, Russell Sage Foundation, New York, 1969.

MacRae, D., *The Social Function of Social Science*, Yale University Press, New Haven, CT, 1976.

MacRae, D., Valuative problems of public policy analysis, In *Research in Public Policy Analysis and Management*, Crecine, J. C., Ed., Vol. 1, JAI Press, Greenwich, CT, 1981.

Majone, G., *Evidence, Argument and Persuasion in the Policy Process*, Yale University Press, New Haven, CT, 1989.

May, J. and Wildavsky, A., Eds., *The Policy Cycle*, Sage Publications, Beverly Hills, CA, 1978.

Mazmanian, D. A. and Sabatier, P. A., Eds., *Effective Implementation Policy*, D.C. Heath, Lexington, MA, 1981.

Mazmanian, D. A. and Sabatier, P. A., Eds., *Implementation and Public Policy*, Scott, Foresman, Glencoe, IL, 1983.

McNamara, R. S. and VanDeMark, B., *In Retrospect*, Times Books/Random House, New York, 1995.

Mead, L. M., The interactive problem in policy analysis, *Policy Sciences*, 16, 45–66, 1983.

Mead, L. M., *The New Politics of Poverty*, Basic Books, New York, 1992.

Meltsner, A., Don't slight communications: some problems to analytic practice, In *Pitfalls of Analysis*, Majone, G. and Quade, E. S., Eds., Wiley, New York, 1980.

Meltsner, A. and Bellavita, C., *The Policy Organization*, Sage Publications, Beverly Hills, CA, 1983.

Merriam, C. E., Progress in political research, *American Political Science Review*, 20, 1–13, 1926.

Merton, R. K., The unanticipated consequences of purposive social action, *American Sociological Review*, 1, 894–904, 1936.

Merton, R. K., The role of applied social science in the formation of policy: a research memorandum, *Philosophy of Science*, 161–181, 1949.

Milward, H. B. and Provan, K. G., What does the "hollow state" look like?, In *Public Management: The State of the Art*, Bozeman, B., Ed., Jossey-Bass, San Francisco, CA, 1993.

Mintzberg, H., Policy as a field of management theory, *Academy of Management Revkiew*, 2, 88–103, 1977.

Mitchell, W. C., *The Backward Art of Spending Money and Other Essays*, McGraw-Hill, New York, 1937.

Polsby, N. W., *Political Innovation in America*, Yale University Press, New Haven, CT, 1984.

Prell, C., Community networking and social capital: early investigations, *JCMC*, 8(3), 1–22, 2003.

Pressman, J. L. and Wildavsky, A., *Appendix A Implementation*, University of California Press, Berkeley, CA, 1973.

Provan, K. G. and Milward, H. B., A preliminary theory of interorganizational network effectiveness: a comparative study of four community mental health systems, *Administrative Science Quarterly*, 40(1), 1–33, 1995.

Olson, K. W., *Watergate: The Presidential Scandal that Shook America*, University of Kansas Press, Lawrence, KS, 32, 2003.

Quade, E. S., *Analysis for Public Decisions*, Elsevier, New York, 1975.

Quade, E. S. and Boucher, W. I., Eds., *Systems Analysis and Policy Planning: Applications in Defense*, Elsevier, New York, 1968.

Ranney, A., Ed., *Political Science and Public Policy*, Markham, Chicago, IL, 1968.

Rawls, J., *A Theory of Justice*, Belknap Press, Cambridge, MA, 1971.

Rein, M., *Social Science and Public Policy*, Penguin Books, Baltimore, MD, 1976.

Rein, M., Value-critical policy analysis, In *Ethics, the Social Sciences, and Policy Analysis*, Callahan, D. and Jennings, B., Eds., Plenum Press, New York, 1983.

Rein, M. and White, S. H., Can policy research help policy?, *Public Interest*, 49, 119–136, 1979.

Rhodes, R. A. W., Policy networks: a British perspective, *Journal of Theoretical Politics*, 2(3), 293–317, 1990.

Rivlin, A., *Systematic Thinking for Social Action*, Brookings Institution, Washington, DC, 1971.

Robinson, J. B., Apples and homed toads: on the framework-determined nature of the energy debate, *Policy Sciences*, 15, 23–45, 1982.

Robinson, J. B., Risks, predictions and other optical illusions: rethinking the use of science in social decision-making, *Policy Sciences*, 25, 237–255, 1992.

Ross, R., Introduction, In *The Meaning of Truth*, James, W., Ed., University of Michigan Press, Ann Arbor, 1970.

Rossi, P. H. and Freeman, H. E., *Evaluation: A Systematic Approach*, Sage Publications, Beverly Hills, CA, 1985.

Sabatier, P. A. and Jenkins-Smith, H. C., Eds., *Policy Change and Learning*, Westview Press, Boulder, CO, 1993.

Sabatier, P. A., Ed., *Theories of the Policy Process*, Westview Press, Boulder, CO, 1999.

Salamon, L., Rethinking public management: third party government and the changing forms of government action, *Public Policy*, 29, 255–275, 1981.

Savas, E. S., *Privatization: The Key to Better Management*, Chatham House, Chatham, NJ, 1987.

Schneider, A. L. and Ingram, H., *Policy Design for Democracy*, University of Kansas Press, Lawrence, KS, 1997.

Schneider, M. et al., Building consensual institutions: networks and the national estuary program, *American Journal of Political Science*, 47, 143–158, 2003.

Scott, J., *Social Network Analysis: A Handbook*, Sage Publications, London, 1991.

Simon, H., *Administrative Behavior*, Free Press, New York, 1945.

Simon, H., *Reason in Human Affairs*, Stanford University Press, Stanford, CA, 1983.

Simon, H., Human nature in politics: the dialogue of psychology with political science, *American Political Science Review*, 79, 293–304, 1985.

Stone, D. A., *Policy Paradox*, HarperCollins, New York, 1997.

Stobaugh, R. and Yergin, D., Eds., *Energy Futures*, Random House, New York, 1979.

Stokey, E. and Zeckhauser, R., *A Primer for Policy Analysis*, Norton, New York, 1978.

Strauch, R. E., "Squishy" problems and quantitative methods, *Policy Sciences*, 6, 175–184, 1975.

Strauch, R. E., A critical look at quantitative methodology, *Policy Analysis*, 2, 121–144, 1976.

Toonen, T. A. J., Networks, management and institutions: public administration as "normal science," *Public Administration Review*, 76(2), 229–253, 1998.

Weiss, C., Ed., *Using Social Science in Public Policy Making* D.C. Health, Lexington, MA, 1977.

White, L., *Introduction of Public Administration*, Macmillian, New York, 1948.

Wholey, D., Managing collaborative networks. Department of health services research and policy, University of Minnesota." Accessed at: http://www.hsr.umn.edu/fac_pages/dwholey/CNET/Net_Text/c1data.html, 2002.

Wildavsky, A., Rescuing policy analysis from PPBS, *Public Administration Review*, 29, 189–202, 1969.

Wildavsky, A., *The Politics of the Budgetary Process*, Little, Brown, Boston, MA, 1979.

Wildavsky, A. and Tenenbaum, E., *The Politics of Mistrust*, Sage Publications, Beverly Hills, CA, 1981.

Williams, W., Implementation analysis of assessment, *Policy Analysis*, 1, 531–566, 1975.

Williams, W., *Dishonest Numbers and Democracy*, Georgetown University Press, Washington, DC, 1998.

Willoughby, F. W., *Principles of Public Administration*, Brookings Institution, Washington, DC, 1927.

Wilson, W., The study of administration, *Political Science Quarterly* 2, 1887.

Wittrock, B. and deLeon, P., Policy as a moving target: a call for conceptual realism, *Policy Studies Review*, 6, 44–60, 1986.

Woodward, B., *The Agenda: Inside the Clinton White House*, Simon & Schuster, New York, 1994.

Wright, R., Policy networks: empirical evidence and theoretical considerations, *West European Journal*, 17(3), 206–208, 1994.

14 The Policy Sciences in Critical Perspective

Matthew R. Auer

CONTENTS

I. INTRODUCTION

Ronald Brunner (1996, 45) declares that the term policy sciences can be traced back to at least 1943 when Harold D. Lasswell crystallized the concept, and Lasswell and his intellectual alter ego, Myres S. McDougal, published the first of many collaborative essays, "Legal Education and Public Policy Professional Training in the Public Interest" (Lasswell and McDougal 1943).

Distinguishing features of the policy sciences, however, are recognizable in even earlier writings of Lasswell. His classic *World Politics and Personal Insecurity* opens with: "Political analysis is the study of changes in the shape and composition of value patterns of society" (Lasswell 1935, 3). From this sentence alone, normative and methodological features of what later became the policy sciences are recognizable. Lasswell makes reference to societal values that are at once instrumental in social and political processes and are ends in themselves. Changing configurations of these values lead to changes in the societal and political order. Lasswell's definition of political analysis also underlies his method. He spent much of his professional life discerning the shapes and composition of societal value patterns. The mapping tools he devised to make sense of values and to relate values to policy decisions are among the most influential parts of his legacy.

That very legacy, however, is the subject of contemporary controversy. More than thirty years after Heinz Eulau remarked on Harold Lasswell's "maddening methods," (Eulau 1969, 119–137) some observers find Lasswell's approach baffling or antiquated, even as it wins new followers, and, ironically, as the critics themselves wonder aloud whether Lasswell's contributions are under-appreciated (Eulau and Zlomke 1999).

Critical reviews of Lasswell's legacy are numerous (Crick 1959, 176–209; Jenkins-Smith and Sabatier 1993; Little 1974; Merelman 1981; Morgenthau 1952; Sabatier 1999).[*] Seldom, however, have these perspectives been carefully examined. Fewer still are explorations of the most recent critiques. This chapter addresses these analyses while enquiring of the practical and intellectual advantages of the policy sciences for policy analysis and public administration generally.

The contributions of Lasswell and his main collaborators are often appraised through derivative work, and critics find fault with the former by way of the latter. In addition, the supposed theoretical and empirical limitations of the policy sciences stem from partial deployment of Lasswell's framework and a misunderstanding of the basic premises of the contextual, problem-oriented, and multi-method approach.

Skeptics have inveighed against Lasswell's decision process schema, in particular, and those criticisms are explored in the next section. Essential, but often underused concepts from Lasswell and his collaborators are considered in part III, with attention to political myths and distinctions between policy outcomes and effects. Part IV documents the convergence of approaches and insights from other fields with those of the policy sciences. That section considers whether convergence on the problem-oriented approach is a welcome or potentially threatening development.

II. DECISION PROCESS AND THE STAGES APPROACH

Lasswell proposed that to improve the development and execution of policy "a crucial step is the formulation of relevant criteria" (Lasswell 1971, 85). Those criteria are found in Lasswell's decision process. Perhaps more so than any other policy sciences schema, the decision process concept is broadly diffused in research on authoritative decision-making. Its categories—*intelligence, promotion, prescription, invocation, application, appraisal,* and *termination*—are the basis for identifying all functional dimensions of the development and enforcement of authoritative norms. As a collection, the categories imply a conceptual wholeness (what with intelligence and termination as seeming book ends) that render any policy context suitable for analysis. Some adherents are persuaded not only by its schematic comprehensiveness, but by an apparent order to the decision process—namely that the functions are actually stages. This re-rendering of the functions as stages is not accepted by mainstream policy scientists. Unfortunately, however, some readers have perceived the decision process and the stages approach as one and the same, casting both into the dustbin of flawed and antiquated policy concepts.

Critics note that real policy-making processes are seldom linear and stage-like and, in that respect, the decision process concept is fallacious. The linearity critique is the first of four common complaints about the decision process proposed by Lasswell and his collaborators. A second charge is that it renders policy-making a uniformly top-down and legalistic process. Third, the decision process is said to be too facile to account for complex webs of ideas, information, and values in the development and implementation of authoritative decisions. Finally, the decision process and the policy sciences, generally, are accused of theoretical emptiness. Each of these charges is considered in sequence, below.

---

[*] Other critical essays include Horowitz (1962); Ross (1991, and especially pp. 455–463); and Falk (1995). I am indebted to Christina Cromley, Rod Muth, Roger Pielke, Jr., and Steven Brown for bringing several of these titles to my attention.

A. THE LINEARITY CRITIQUE

DeLeon writes (1999, 20) that Lasswell's "listing reflects the origins of what has arguably been the most widely accepted concept of the policy sciences, that is the policy process..." Lasswell referred to the seven concepts themselves as "functions and components of the decision process." Re-constituted and modified versions of Lasswell's decision process are many, including Brewer and deLeon's (1983) six-phase approach; Hogwood and Gunn's (1984) nine stages; Stokey and Zeckhauser's (1978) five-part framework; Foyle's (1999) four-stage process; and Anderson's (2000) five-stage process, among others (see also, Jones 1984; Ripley 1984). Objections to these phase- or stage-oriented approaches are that they posit sequential steps when, in fact, real policy processes frequently deviate from a preconceived path (Jenkins-Smith and Sabatier 1993, 3). Uninterrupted, smoothly turning policy cycles are the exception rather than the rule since there are frequent ruptures and rifts between the so-called stages (Colebatch 2002, 52). A second critique is that the stages approach assumes that each stage "develop(s) on its own" and in isolation from the other stages (Sabatier 1999, 7). This second criticism is somewhat puzzling because it verges on contradicting the previous charge, that is, that the stages approach is linear and sequential. If the decision process were truly linear, surely each stage would develop as natural outgrowths of other stages. In any case, Lasswell and his students neither assumed that information flowed uninterruptedly between functions, nor, alternatively, that it was cutoff or quarantined between phases or stages. Nevertheless, policy scientists tend to be alert to disjunctions in information and other resource flows and to recognize these disconnects as symptoms of larger problems, such as undemocratic rule-making processes. Lasswell and McDougal (1992, 1261) contend:

> Unless there are intelligence structures that perform the comprehensive information gathering-planning role, the inclusive frame of reference appropriate to planning is not likely to appear. Unless promotional organs are provided for, the role of outspokenness and controversy may be lost sight of, and at least temporarily forced underground. If the prescribing function is not separated from top organs of invocation and application, the prescriptive codes of the community may be viewed in terms of executive expediency. The appraisal function, unless independently embodied, is lost in a fog of promotional manipulations and applications of circumscribed scope.

Lasswell and his intellectual heirs clearly understood that the decision process could malfunction at any time, particularly from a common-interest standpoint.

Returning to the supposed linearity of the decision process, it is apparent that Lasswell himself did not think of the decision functions as inevitably constituting a sequence nor does he refer to them as stages or steps.[*] In his 1956 monograph *The Decision Process*, he suggests that a cycle is one possible form with "interdependent changes" occurring within and among the functions (Lasswell 1956, 9). Interestingly, his illustration begins with appraisal rather than intelligence. But later in the text, he allows for functions to occur simultaneously or with participants incorporating one function in the act of performing another. With reference to the Supreme Court, he notes, "The appraisal statements made by the Court or made to the Court are typically imbedded with...invocation or final judgment..." (1956, 18) and "The Court performs a positive intelligence function when public attention is focused upon its deliberations and decision" (1956, 17).

More broadly, Lasswell conceptualized all seven decision functions as embedded in the execution of other functions (see also, Brunner 1997a, 202–203; Lasswell and McDougal 1992, 1260). Hence, in performing any given function, For example, the collection and analysis of

---

[*] DeLeon (1999, 20) writes that Lasswell "nominated seven 'stages' of what he was later to call 'the decision process'." However, I have found no reference by Lasswell to "stages" in the decision process. Lasswell's 1956 monograph *The Decision Process*, which Brunner (1997a, 203) identifies as "the original sketch of the conceptual model" describes the parts of the decision process as functional categories.

intelligence, actors might engage in promoting, prescribing, and invoking. Consider a prosecutor's collection of evidence (intelligence): She assembles information pertinent to the case and obtaining that information involves promotional efforts. Specifically, she refers to relevant procedures (prescriptions) to obtain a search warrant. A judge is then summoned to authorize that warrant (invocation). Similarly, Brunner speaks of nested or hierarchical interconnections among decision processes, with single functions in a given decision process encapsulating other, lower level, serial, or parallel decision functions (Ron Brunner, personal communication).

For those who transform functions into stages, the complaint about descriptive inaccuracy may resonate. At least one prominent reinterpreter of the decision process, Peter deLeon, does not accept the charge. He asserts that the phases in his and Garry Brewer's policy process scheme were never intended to be "unidirectional or lack(ing) feedback capabilities…" Feedback and recursive loops, he observes, are quite normal in the policy process such that "estimation can lead back to initiation rather than the next step, selection, and implementation and evaluation insistently feed back and forth on each other…" (1999, 23). Similarly, and with reference to their multi-stage approach, Brian Hogwood and Lewis Gunn warn (1984, 4):

> It should be stressed that this list is not intended as a straightforward description of what actually happens to every issue; rather, it is a framework for organizing our understanding of what happens— and does not happen…The dividing lines between the various activities are artificial and policy-makers are unlikely to perform them consciously or in the implied 'logical' order. To take two examples, it is sometimes only at the implementation stage that questions are raised about the objectives the programme is expected to achieve, and one lesson often learned at the evaluation stage is that the logically prior activity of defining the problem to which the programme is addressed has never been undertaken or perhaps, consensus about the nature of the problem was assumed where none existed.

Hogwood and Gunn's clarification is all the more striking because it appears immediately after they introduce their discursive framework for the policy process. In light of these and other clarifications by reinterpreters of the decision process, we might discount some of the broadsides against the so-called stages heuristic. Those accusing the frameworks of being excessively formulaic and simplistic may have missed the user instructions. Where such instructions are missing (see for example, Bonser et al. 1996, 52–53), the critique may be justified.

B. PUBLIC EXPECTATIONS AND THE POLICY CYCLE

Although the decision process does not assume linearity or circularity as a defining feature of policymaking, there is nevertheless a potentially worthwhile research agenda concerning perceptions of linearity and circularity in the policymaking process. A researchable question is whether and to what extent politicians, experts, and laypeople tend to think of a linear, unidirectional policy process as a preferred way to make and implement policy. Moreover, one might inquire whether and to what extent participants are provoked when that expected pattern is violated. It is plausible that ordinary citizens in a democracy both prefer and expects a logical sequence of steps for policymaking. Conceivably, citizens prefer the expeditious collection and analysis of pertinent intelligence before policy choices are made, particularly when those choices involve significant trade-offs. When police officers use deadly force, the community might expect authorities to justify these actions vis-à-vis relevant prescriptions. When expected protocols are violated, the community may become agitated. The essential point is not whether decision processes follow a sequence of predictable stages. It is that society may *expect* and even demand that a staged approach be employed. Hence, it is worth considering the political consequences of short-circuiting these collective expectations. An apt illustration is the controversial intelligence-gathering activities leading up to the US invasion of Iraq in 2003.

Hersh and Suskind have suggested that senior Pentagon officials were so eager to confront Saddam Hussein that the prescription to prepare for war was developed well before relevant data was assembled (Hersh 2003, 44; Suskind 2004a).[*] The Bush administration truncated the intelligence stage when it refused to wait for United Nations weapons inspectors to complete their work. Moreover, critics contend that when intelligence failed to support the original justification for war—namely that Hussein harbored weapons of mass destruction—a new round of promotion was necessary. The new grounds for war were to eject a brutal tyrant and to transform Iraq into a beachhead for democracy in the Middle East.[†]

By the autumn of 2003, many Americans soured on the war due to setbacks in the reconstruction effort and mounting casualties. But the violation of an idealized policy cycle played a role in the public's disillusionment as well. Reports emerged of an administration distorting intelligence, reinventing the purposes for the invasion (promotion) and deciding on a course of action and moving forward (prescription and invocation) before compelling evidence was available (intelligence) (Hersh 2003).[‡]

A breach in expected policy protocol also partly explains why many Europeans were cool to the war plan. Invocation of the prescription to use force occurred ahead of the Bush administration's coalition-building efforts (promotion). American and British forces assembled in neighboring Kuwait even as the State Department eschewed shuttle diplomacy (promotion). Compared to his American counterparts, UK Prime Minister Tony Blair was more intent on winning over would-be allies in Europe, though Blair had comparatively weaker domestic backing for a war against Iraq. In early March of 2003, President Bush declared the United States to be prepared for war with or without official United Nations support. Two weeks thereafter, the conflict began.

It is apparent that the phases of decisions in this case do not conform to a conventional linear policy process, but this is not surprising in light of our refutation of the stages-heuristic critique. More salient in this case is that the expectations of different actors—including average citizens— were not met for a set of logical, sequential steps in decision-making. Ripe for analysis is whether ordinary citizens, and policy analysts themselves, come to expect a particular order in policymaking and to what extent disturbances of that idealization jeopardize the decision process itself, injure the reputations and undermine the effectiveness of decision-makers, and even harm society. Testing whether citizens have preconceived notions of a step-wise approach to policymaking is more edifying than testing the descriptive accuracy or predictive powers of models of the step-wise approach.

C. Decision Process as Top-Down and Legalistic

Reassuring critics that the decision process is functional and interpretative rather than linear and deterministic will not allay all concerns. With or without assumptions of linearity, some will find the decision process limiting in the types of policy contexts that can be examined. Jenkins-Smith

---

[*] On President George W. Bush's decision to invade Iraq, former Secretary Paul O'Neill remarked, "If you operate in a certain way—by saying this is how I want to justify what I've already decided to do, and I don't care how you pull it off— you guarantee that you'll get faulty, one-sided information" (Suskind 2004b). In other words, the President is being accused of performing a first round of performing after he has already promoted and prescribed a decision.

[†] Friedman (2003, 4:13) quoting Michael Sandel, notes that Bush's midstream change in promotion was not the first by an American president: "It often happens that presidents, under the pressure of events, especially during war, find themselves needing to articulate new and more persuasive rationales for their policies—especially when great sacrifices are involved. This happened to Lincoln during the Civil War. At the outset, the purpose of the Civil War for Lincoln was to oppose secession and preserve the Union. It was really only after the battle at Gettysburg that Lincoln articulated a larger purpose...namely freedom and the elimination of slavery."

[‡] Brunner offers an alternative explanation: the intelligence function was performed early in the decision process. But it was performed poorly, especially with respect to five key criteria that shore up intelligence-gathering and analysis, namely goal clarification, analysis of trends, analysis of conditioning factors that shape trends, projection of possible futures, and exploration of alternatives to prevent undesirable futures (R. D. Brunner, personal communication, 2004).

and Sabatier (1993), for example, contend that the stages approach is undermined by its "legalistic, top-down focus" (Jenkins-Smith and Sabatier 1993, 3). In a similar vein, Mereleman characterizes Lasswell's policy sciences as "'democracy from above,' that is, an effort on the part of the powerful to transfer some power to their subordinates" (1981, 495).

Lasswell and McDougal applied the decision process to myriad legal contexts, in part because scholars and practitioners of law were among the main consumers of their work. However, the decision process has illuminated policymaking contexts that are neither legalistic nor top-down. Garen (2000), for example, explained how two American scientists incorporated local demands into successful programs that at once protected mountain gorillas and fulfilled community expectations in Rwanda. The important prescriptions in this case were not laws *per se* but informed choices made by the project's investigators to invite community participation and to respect community interests. Other, detailed illustrations of unofficial and bottom-up decision processes can be found in Brunner et al.'s (2002) edited volume on governance of natural resources.

Lasswell surely meant for applications of the decision process to include, but not be limited to, formal legal and administrative arenas when he wrote (1971, 1):

> In complex societies the agencies of official decision do not account for many of the most important choices that affect men's lives. In the interest of realism, it is essential to give full deference to the study of semiofficial and nonofficial processes.

Lasswell's scholarship included much work on congressional law-making and American public administration. However, it is clear that Lasswell had something other in mind than articulating and testing a "top-down" decision process. The criteria he offered for the seven decision functions include demands for openness, integrativeness, comprehensiveness, and other requirements for inclusivity (Lasswell 1971, 86–93). Lasswell suggested optimal ways to execute the various decision functions in democratic society. The well-executed promotion function, for example, assures that "all participants in the social and political process are activated with sufficient frequency to permit the formation of programs that reflect the full range of community interests" (Lasswell 1971, 89). Here and elsewhere, Lasswell's concept more nearly resembles a communitarian than a top-down approach.

D. THE INSUFFICIENT COMPREHENSIVENESS OF THE DECISION PROCESS

Theories of the Policy Process is the attempt of editor Paul Sabatier and contributors to offer more descriptively accurate, theoretically grounded, and empirically testable alternatives to the so-called stages model of the policy process. Sabatier's dismissal of the policy sciences is hasty, however, because none of the other main schema from the policy sciences is consulted, and Lasswell and his adherents deemed each part essential to clarifying and redressing policy problems. Lasswell never meant for the decision process to be used in exclusion from other cognitive mapping tools. Hence, when one considers Sabatier's criteria for "better theoretical frameworks" (i.e., better than the stages approach), one must subject all of the main policy sciences schema to scrutiny.

Sabatier (1999, 8) contends that better theoretical frameworks must, among other things:

> ... address the broad sets of factors that political scientists looking at different aspects of public policy-making have traditionally deemed important: conflicting values and interests, information flows, institutional arrangements, and variation in the socioeconomic environment.

We might explore the potential of the policy sciences for clarifying these four aspects of public policymaking, beginning with those aspects that *are* most pertinent to the decision process concept, namely the accounting of information flows and institutional arrangements.

As Lasswell proposed, all of the decision functions are subsumed in the execution of each function of the policy process. Information is integral to the intelligence function, and intelligence is part and parcel of all decision functions. Hence the expert can use the decision process to track "information flows" throughout the life of a policy. More broadly, in any policy context, the decision process can be used to map the development, transformation, manipulation, and instrumental uses and effects of information throughout the life of a policy decision. The decision process does not presuppose, as has been suggested, that streams of information are invented in and confined to the "boundaries" of individualized policy "stages."

"Institutional arrangements," a second aspect of policymaking addressed in "better theoretical frameworks" is clearly the domain of the decision process. Institutions, according to Ostrom in Sabatier's edited volume, refer to rules, norms, and strategies adopted by individuals operating within or across organizations (1999, 37). Central to the decision process is how actors develop and enforce rules that secure organizational or communal interests. Prescription, invocation, and application are the decision process's most obvious descriptive expressions of rule-making, implementation, and enforcement. Other key institutional functions of the decision process are mapping information pertinent to the problem at hand and its potential resolution (intelligence), and how that information is assembled and characterized (promoted) and appraised by various participants.

Accounting for the values of participants in policymaking processes—Sabatier's third dimension for a preferred theoretical framework—is, arguably, the distinguishing feature of cognitive mapping in the policy sciences. Ironically, Sabatier equivocates on the salience of values in policy analysis when he calls for a theoretical framework for policy analysis that "may also contain some explicitly normative elements, but these are not required." The subtitle of the leading academic journal in the field, *Policy Sciences*, is "integrating knowledge and practice to advance human dignity." To my knowledge, every contemporary application of the decision process makes explicit reference to policy participants' values (see, for example, the various contributions to Clark et al. 2000; see also Auer 1998). However, in these cases and others, the policy scientist tends to account for values by complementing the decision process with another mapping tool, namely the *social process*.

In their major expositions on policy constructs, such as *A Pre-View of Policy Sciences*, and *Jurisprudence for a Free Society*,[*] Lasswell and his collaborators focused on the concept of the social process. Lasswell and McDougal (1992, xxi) argued that "making authoritative decisions in the common interest" required:

> …a focus of attention upon both the totality of a community's values and institutional practices and the employment, beyond traditional logical derivation, of a considerable number of distinguishable, though interrelated tasks.

Those tasks are illuminated by deploying the social process, problem orientation, as well as the decision process. Among these schemas, the social process is the most complex, and it is beyond the scope of this chapter to define each of its components and principal functions, though *Jurisprudence* is perhaps the most comprehensive treatment. But conflicting values and interests in policymaking (as per Sabatier) are essential to clarifying policy problems and appraising and selecting potential interventions. Policy scientists use Lasswell's base value/scope value concept to account for the stock of values that participants draw upon (base values) to secure other values (scope values) (Clark 2002, 40–41).

"When we speak of the social process of any community," Lasswell and McDougal declare (1992, 337), "we refer to 'people seeking values through institutions using resources'."

---

[*] *Jurisprudence* was published after Lasswell's death. As explained by McDougal in the book's preface, parts II, III, and IV were written almost entirely by Lasswell (Lasswell and McDougal 1992, xxiii–xxvii).

TABLE 14.1
Values and Outcomes

Value	Example of Outcome
Power	Victory or defeat in fights or elections
Enlightenment	Scientific discovery, news
Wealth	Income, ownership transfer
Well-being	Medical care, protection
Skill	Instruction, demonstration of proficiency
Affection	Expression of intimacy, friendship, loyalty
Respect	Honor, discriminatory exclusion
Rectitude	Acceptance in religious or ethical association

Source: From Lasswell, Harold D., *A Pre-View of Policy Sciences*, American Elsevier, New York, p. 18, 1971.

Lasswell used eight value terms to "classify the nearly infinite number of preferred outcomes" namely, power, enlightenment, wealth, well-being, skill, affection, respect, and rectitude (Lasswell 1971, 18). Distinctive outcomes (Table 14.1) and institutions are associated with each value, though Lasswell and his collaborators assumed that all eight values were, to some degree, shaped and/or shared in every institution.

However, whereas institution is the essence of other theories of collective action and policy decision, such as in the institutional analysis and development framework (Ostrom et al. 1993) and in regime theory (Young 1989a), the many conditioning factors of Lasswell's social process are too varied and functionally diverse to be captured by the term institution alone.

To Lasswell and his students, declaring the primacy of institutions or of authoritative decision processes without reference to social processes would be akin to making rules for society without attention to societal interests and demands. As Lasswell and McDougal (1992, 1137), insisted "...the constitutive process must provide for the performance of all necessary functions of decision (intelligence, recommending, prescribing, invoking...)" such that the decision-maker and policy adviser pose and satisfactorily address all facets of the social process in the context of each function of Lasswell's decision process. Each decision function, then, is affected by answers to constituting questions, namely:

1. Participants: Who shall be authorized to participate in each phase of the decision process? With what skill qualifications? What mode of selection?
2. Perspectives: What policies shall be sought? What expectations, demands, and identifications shall participants have? What mode of selection?
3. Arenas: What organizations shall be authorized to decide? How centralized, concentrated, or pluralized?
4. Base Values: What decision-making power shall be authorized? What authority to obtain what other base values? What control is to be established?
5. Strategies: What authority (including limitations) shall be granted to employ base values as a means of influencing outcomes? By what methods?
6. Outcomes: What mode of deciding shall be authorized? What values may be affected?
7. Effects: For what intended or unintended effects shall there be responsibility (Lasswell and McDougal 1992, 1137–1138)?[*]

---

[*] These categories can be used prescriptively, as in the above illustration, or descriptively. For the latter, the map of participants reveals who is authorized to participate; perspectives indicates whose policies are sought; and so on.

A thorough and integrated map of the social and decision processes should thus provide insights on "contrasting values and interests" of policy-making participants.

Finally, there is Sabatier's fourth criterion for preferred policy frameworks—that they must account for "variation in the socioeconomic environment." The social process model can be construed as an abstract map of any particular socioeconomic environment. Moreover, policy scientists use the intelligence function to account for variation in the socioeconomic environment. Rather than filtering out unmeasurable variables—a step that is required in reductionist approaches like econometrics—the intelligence function demands data on variables that are otherwise difficult to specify, so long as these factors affect actors' behavior and are consequential in shaping social interaction. For policy contexts of almost any degree of complexity, the policy scientist expects variation, and the main empirical demand is to capture that variation, whether in accounting for participants' perspectives, their strategies for achieving value demands, or for changing social or economic conditions bearing on policy processes and outcomes.

But much as accounting for participants' values is the comparative advantage of the social process, mapping variation in policy contexts is a major aim of *problem orientation*. Problem orientation is perhaps the most tractable of the main policy sciences schemas. It posits that in any given problem context, there are particular intellectual tasks to perform. First, the goal or goals of the community must be clarified. Second, interested parties must determine which past and recent events (trends) have led the community to move toward or away from the specified goal or goals. Third, factors that have conditioned (i.e., affected) the direction and magnitude of the trends must be elaborated. Fourth, assuming the *status quo*, parties must consider the likelihood of reaching the goal(s). The fifth task deals with possible strategies for goal attainment. In capsule form, the five intellectual tasks are: goal clarification; trend description; analysis of conditions; projection of developments; and invention, evaluation, and selection of alternatives (Lasswell 1971, 39).

Policy scientists approach problem orientation as an effort to synthesize rather than to sequence. This means relying on knowledge gleaned from one task to inform another task—for example, analysis of trends and conditions affects projections. Not unlike the decision process where all seven functions can be subsumed in any other, all five of the intellectual tasks are used to gather intelligence pertinent to any given task. Hence, for example, goals, trend description, analysis of conditions, and projections are all integral to devising policy alternatives for the community. It is not difficult to imagine how the intellectual tasks can help the analysis uncover variation in the socioeconomic environment, and providing intelligence for each of the decision functions.

Complaints about the supposed inadequacies of the decision process wither on recognizing its *organic* role in policy analysis. By organic, I am referring to the coordinated function performed by this part in the company of the other parts. Together, the schema are designed to clarify for the expert, the decision-maker, and the community alike. They contribute to illuminating the goals of the community including the obstacles and pathways to goal attainment (problem orientation); the social process in which value demands are sought; *and* the relevant decisions leading to preferred policy outcomes. DeLeon (1999, 29) suggests that experts may have "loaded an impossibly heroic stature upon the policy stages framework." In fact, the policy stages in deLeon and Lasswell's decision functions are not identical, but deLeon's observation is nonetheless valid in that some experts have placed undue demands on the decision process, and by extension, on the policy stages heuristic. Recognizing that the decision process serves a complementary function helps resolve a problem for the so-called stages approach. The stages model founders, it is proclaimed, because for any policy, there are multiple goals among multiple interests (Colebatch 2002, 51; Falk 1995, 2000–2001). This condition cries out for weighing not only how decisions are made but how participants identify their interests *vis-à-vis* other policy participants; how they express their demands; and how they go about achieving their goals—all essential elements of the social process. Moreover, the policy scientist will be inclined to search for a common interest amidst the multiple and conflicting demands (Lasswell and McDougal 1992, 23)—an explicitly normative, and hence, quite different approach from the positivist tradition of conventional policy analysis.

E.   DECISION PROCESS AND CAUSAL THEORY

The last of the main charges leveled against the decision process are its supposed theoretical inadequacies. Sabatier (1999, 7) contends that the stages approach (and by extension, the decision process) is not a causal theory:

> ... since it never identifies a set of causal drivers that govern the process within and across stages... In addition, without causal drivers there can be no coherent set of hypotheses within and across stages.

One of the comparative advantages of the policy sciences approach is that, by illuminating the actual practice of policymaking, it clarifies which theories are worth testing in the context of real cases.[*] Brunner observes (1991, 70):

> If taken too seriously, demands for the elaboration of theory could become a diversion from (or even a substitute for) practical policy inquiry. The demands could rationalize the postponement of inquiry into specific practical problems, pending some grand theoretical breakthrough...They could, over a period of time, reduce the policy movement to another ivory tower in the academic landscape, with little relevance to practical problems outside. And even if some latter-day Isaac Newton should achieve a grand theoretical breakthrough, practical relevance would still require the painstaking specification and elaboration of theory through observations on particular, ever-changing contexts.

The implication from Brunner and other policy scientists (see, e.g., Ascher 1987) is that the observation and characterization of policy problems comes first, from which relevant theories are developed and tested—and not vice versa. Hence, in the policy sciences approach, the "causal drivers" emerge from the specification of particular interactions between variables in real cases, and not from universal, first principles or presumptive truths about human behavior.

Confusion about the role of causation in the problem-oriented approach explains only part of the critics' frustration. There are also the supposed shortcomings of the policy sciences framework for the purposes of prediction (DeLeon 1999). Policy scientists counter that their approach allows for better predictions because it maps the trajectories of real problems in context—and not merely those problems that avail themselves to preferred methods of the analyst. In this respect, the policy sciences differ from conventional applied economics. In the policy sciences, the substrate for theory construction and empirical testing is the problem context itself. Brunner argues (1997b, 222) that "From observations on the particular context, one can use the schema to specify testable hypotheses and theories about what is probable and preferable in that context." Among accurate predictions drawn from maps of particular contexts, consider Brunner et al.'s "instability" and "termination" scenarios for the Space Station that were proffered in the early 1990s (Brunner et al. 1992).

Probability theory, the Delphi technique, trend extrapolation, and any number of other technical tools can aid prediction as well. But the policy sciences clarify for the adviser and his/her client the difficult, value-laden questions of what ought to be projected, and why. Conceivably, an organization will make very different decisions about what to forecast if the main decision criteria revolve around costs and efficiency versus Lasswell's demand for "the realization of the human dignity of the many" (1971, 41–42). Lasswell meant the latter to be a goal-clarification task for the policy adviser and his/her client. A policy scientist may concentrate on specifying goals before focusing on predictions, since knowledge and assessment of the community's demands presumably bear on

---

[*] Crick, who is otherwise critical of the policy sciences, insists that Lasswell "did not confuse science with 'fact gathering' or with a purely inductive logic; he grasped both the logical and the practical primacy of theory to observation in natural science" (1959, 177; see also Lasswell and Kaplan 1950, x).

what is worthwhile studying. This has important implications for Colebatch's observation that it can be difficult to ascertain policy goals, and that goals may be vague and ambiguous (2002, 51). Positivist training urges analysts to capitulate on goal clarification (or take goals as given), and instead, focus on problems that are readily clarified by their preferred methods. This approach risks wasting resources by predicting future states that are unimportant to the community, or worse, by presenting policy choices that are inimical to community interests.

Another risk is that prediction and methodological concerns, detached from the details of context, substitute for goals. Lessons from the Vietnam War provide poignant illustrations of this problem. In diagnosing the threat to US national security, policymakers embraced a theory of expansionist Communism bent on world domination. The real problem setting was that of a revolution against French colonialism (Herring 1984, 633). President John F. Kennedy's stark question, "how can we tell if we're winning?" betrayed more than a quandary about how to measure battlefield success. It revealed a fundamental failure to elucidate US (not to mention Vietnamese) goals and objectives and in defining progress toward those ends. As one witness observed (Herring 1984, 633):

> The only answer that could be devised was the notorious body count, as grim and corrupting as it was unreliable as an index of success. In time, the strategy of attrition and the body count came to represent for sensitive G.I.s and for those at home killing for the sake of killing.

It is intriguing to consider, but ultimately unknowable, whether attention to goal clarification and other problem-oriented tasks might have altered the perspectives of Pentagon analysts in the Kennedy and Johnson administrations. Many of these experts were acolytes of the Planning, Programming, and Budgeting System approach to policy analysis. A brief encounter with Lasswell's methods would not supplant this positivist training. But in a late appraisal of the "shortcomings of US decision-making processes," McNamara admits, "...decision-making was not organized to deal effectively with the extraordinarily complex range of political and military issues involved" and that Americans were "ill-equipped" for the combat experience in Vietnam having so little knowledge of the context (McNamara et al. 1999, 388). These and other issues "were not fully explored when the United States initially intervened, and they were not reviewed periodically as conditions changed during ensuing years." This post-mortem certainly resonates with the policy sciences' demands for careful specification of problem contexts and for allowing contextual maps to shape theoretical explanations of what is happening and not vice versa. More-over, McNamara appears to validate an essential facet of the problem-oriented approach, which is to retrace and revise cognitive maps of problems and to treat policy appraisal as a continuous function rather than a one-time exercise.

The call for theory, prediction, and methods of verification to be practice-based and in the service of (and not substituted for) larger community aims seems reasonable—indeed rightful. But without an overarching "theory of human behavior" to guide the analyst's work, some skeptics of the policy sciences will remain unfulfilled. Lasswell's "maximization postulate," which undergirds the various policy sciences components, is unlikely to change opinions either. Lasswell proposed that living forms are predisposed to complete acts in ways that are perceived to leave the actor better off than if he had completed them differently (1971, 16). It has been likened to the utility-maximizing presumptions of rational choice theory (DeLeon 1999, 27), but this is at best an imprecise reading. Indeed, because the maximization postulate is not another evocation of *homo economicus,* it is likely to disappoint many positivists in the academy. What is crucial in Lasswell's postulate is that the actor perceives that his/her act leaves him/her better off—and not that the actor necessarily relies on rational calculus.[*] The actor may behave non-rationally; he nevertheless

---

[*] Lasswell and Kaplan write (1950, 70), "it is entirely possible for a person to be mistaken not only as to means for attaining his values, but even as to what his values are." On this point, see also Clark (2002, 24–25).

deems himself better off than if he/she had completed the act differently. Moreover, perspectives on the same situation may differ; acts that are rational from one actor's perspective are non-rational from another's.

Another key difference between the rationality principle and Lasswell's is that the latter conceived of maximization of value accumulations as a decidedly social undertaking—steeped in particular practices developed by the interaction of people who recognize the institutions themselves as intrinsically valuable. This is quite different from conceiving institutions as epiphenomena or byproducts of individual, selfish acts. Brunner (1997a) argues that there are "normative propositions" and "empirical propositions" of democracy that together form a "central theory" of the policy sciences, and that constitute suitable guides for decision-making practice. Normative propositions "accept the fact that ordinary citizens (like the experts) are boundedly rational, but capable of good judgment when they have direct experience or access to reliable facts and interpretations prepared by experts" (Brunner 1997a, 208; see also DeLeon 1997). Empirical propositions "focus on myth and the dynamics of political and social change associated with them" (Brunner 1997a, 206–207)—a topic addressed in greater depth below. These propositions are universal heuristics: they guide what to look for in any context, but do not predict or prescribe what will be found there.

III. INSIGHTS FROM INSIDE THE SOCIAL PROCESS

The promise of the policy sciences extends beyond merely clarifying the uses of the decision process. The "user instruction" we argue for above is "use all the parts as universal heuristics, in real problem contexts." Elaborating all of the possible uses of the schema is beyond the scope of the present enquiry. Such an undertaking would resemble a course of study. Fortunately, thorough treatments on the pedagogy and practice of the policy sciences are emerging (see for example, Brunner 1997a, 1997b; Clark and Willard 2000a, 2000b). Nevertheless, there remain scores of underappreciated insights from the component parts, and it is perhaps unsurprising that many are aspects of the most complex part, the social process. Here we single out two elements of the social process that could have as much consequence for clarifying the practice of policymaking as do the various functions of the decision process.[*] They are the defining of the political myth and the distinguishing of policy outcomes from effects.

A. POLITICAL MYTH AS POLICY CONSTRUCT

Myth refers to the "basic operating premises, belief systems, frames of reference, outlooks, worldviews, or paradigms" that do nothing less than "hold society together" (Clark 2002, 21) or, indeed, tear them apart. Lasswell and his collaborators conceived of myth as a "stable pattern of personal as well as group perspectives" and that these private or group perspectives are imbued with particular expectations and demands (Lasswell and McDougal 1992, 353). The salience of myth, in this rendering, is not that it is empirically true or false in the conventional sense, but that it is a relatively stable background of perspectives about society and the world at large. The shaping and reinforcing of the myth is a function of "symbol specialists," and in particular, politicians, opinion-makers and other elites. They may also intentionally or inadvertently challenge the myth thereby challenging individuals' or groups' prevailing view of how the world works. The intensity of the backlash may take by surprise those expressing the alternative viewpoint. Not infrequent instances of such surprise suggest that the power of myth is underappreciated.

---

[*] Regarding the influence of the decision process and the stages approach on subsequent scholarship, see DeLeon (1999, 21–22).

Consider, for example, the case of an editorialist who received hateful mail in response to her doubts about President George W. Bush's Moon–Mars space program. She writes, "Although I've grown used to this phenomenon," (i.e., angry mail) "I was nevertheless completely unprepared for the passions sparked by (the previous column)" and which included "insults of the kind that people generally write only to strangers" (Applebaum 2004, A19). She may have underestimated the passion bred by more than four decades of emotive and symbol-laden justifications for the manned space program. The myth, in this case, is imbued with symbols of American heroism, morality, and sacrifice.

Lasswell and Kaplan observed (1950, 104) that political symbols, such as national flags, uniforms, and anthems, are meaningful not merely because they represent objects and ideas but because they arouse feelings and incite actions. Uniformed astronauts are the sacred—and at times, sacrificial—symbols of America's space program, and astronauts' adventures stir a range of intense emotions—from elation to despair, pride to pathos (Auer 2004). The manned space program is not unique in the intensity of its reliance on symbols. What policy scientists can do is make plain— which is to say, make conscious—what are otherwise subconscious appeals to public demands and expectations. Such an endeavor is consistent with the policy sciences' mission to clarify community goals. Here, it is accomplished by illuminating the covert promotion that justifies the use of power and public resources.

B. Distinguishing Outcomes from Effects

Policy scientists recognize that though political myths represent stable perspectives, they are never-theless mutable (Clark 2002, 23). More often, the change occurs gradually and over long periods, as particular policy outcomes cause individuals and groups to revise basic premises about the world around them and their place in it. Even seemingly abrupt shocks to public perspectives do not necessarily lead to permanent changes to the prevailing myth. For example, the ideal of Americans as champions of human rights and democratic pluralism was starkly challenged by the My Lai massacre in Vietnam, and the Vietnam War experience generally. Yet less than a half-century later, politicians justified military intervention and post-conflict reconstruction in Iraq and Afghanistan based on America's unique ability to promote the free will and democratic aspirations of people, everywhere (Bush 2004).

Even as the self-image of America as a beacon of democracy endures, the myth of American innocence has been worn down by inglorious wars in Southeast Asia, military support for anti-Communist autocrats in the developing world, and political scandals and corporate malfeasance at home. In all of these arenas, particular outcomes of policies had long-term effects on institutions, including that of electoral politics (evident in chronic low voter turnout) and participation in multilateral institutions (manifested in isolationist worldviews in Congress), among other effects. This interplay between the short-term consequences of policy outcomes and the long-term impacts on institutions and institutional values is the domain of the outcome and effects categories in the social process. Mastering knowledge of each category requires an accounting of particular policy end-states and these outcomes' reverberations on society. It discourages the albeit easier but ultimately self-defeating alternative of deeming particular policy outcomes as terminal events that are final in their effects.

Per Clark's (2002, 42) interpretation, by outcomes, Lasswell was referring to "short-term, cumulating events that indulge or deprive participants in a given situation." In contrast, effects are long-term impacts that are manifested in changes to institutions and to social practices (Clark 2002, 43). Outcomes in particular contexts may have long-term effects (i.e., cause notable changes) in particular institutional settings or in society at large.

To illustrate how an outcome in a seemingly narrow policy context reverberates noisily in a broader institutional setting, consider the case of Elián González, a young Cuban refugee whose

Florida-bound vessel capsized but who was rescued by American fishermen. Immigration and naturalization regulations provided clear guidance in this case: the boy, whose mother had perished at sea, should have been returned to Cuba to his father's custody. However, US immigration authorities delivered Elián to the custody of relatives in Miami. After months of debate and delay, federal authorities seized Elián in an early morning raid, returning the boy to Cuba. Outcomes in this case, using the metrics of value accumulation and deprivation, were the upholding of the rule of law; indulgence of affection between Elián and his father and a corollary loss for the Miami relatives; and critically, intense feelings of disrespect among the exile community.

Vice-President Al Gore was attuned to the political trade-offs in this case; he broke with the administration to side with Elián's Miami relatives (Falcoff 2003, 267). But this was not enough to assuage Cuban American voters who turned out strongly for Gore's Republican opponent during the 2000 presidential election. In both that test and the 2002 gubernatorial elections, Republican candidates received more than 80 percent of the Cuban American vote (Moreno 2003). Though it was neither the sole nor perhaps the primary reason for Gore's defeat in the general election in Florida, the Democratic Party's reversal of fortunes in Dade County (where large numbers of Cuban exiles reside) certainly made matters worse. In 1996, 40 percent of Cuban Americans—a community that traditionally leans Republican—cast ballots for Bill Clinton after the president pledged early and unambiguously to continue the US embargo of Cuba (Moreno 2003).

In 2002, Janet Reno, Clinton's attorney general and a central figure in the Elián affair, lost in the Democratic gubernatorial primary in Florida. Many expected her to be the party's nominee. No reliable estimate of Cuban American votes is available from that primary race (Dario Moreno, personal communication, November 24, 2003), but there is little doubt about the hangover from the Elián case.

The mutual mistrust that permeated both sides' deliberations in the Elián affair, and the Clinton administration's failure to mend the breach after the boy's return to Cuba suggest that Democrats underestimated the long-term consequences of the custody battle and late-night seizure of the boy. Had party elites thoroughly mapped the social process, they may have better understood the value assets, perspectives (particularly the participants' identifications), and organizational capabilities of a very motivated bloc of voters.

Outcomes and effects do not merely illustrate the law of unintended consequences. When properly mapped, these categories tend to minimize unintended consequences because the analyst anticipates how outcomes in particular contexts affect people, resources, and institutions over the long term. For the affected community, the outcome in the Elián case hardened group identifications, emboldened demands for justice, and galvanized highly disciplined and decisive voting behavior in the years that followed.

IV. CONVERGENCE IN PROBLEM-ORIENTED RESEARCH AND PRACTICE

The ultimate challenge for the policy sciences is to make good on its central aim: to contribute to the realization of human dignity. In the process, it must demonstrate its advantages to analysts, decision-makers, and the communities they serve. Sabatier proclaims that for a policy framework to prove its worth, it "must be the subject of a fair amount of recent conceptual development and/or empirical testing," and that "a number of currently active policy scholars must view it as a viable way of understanding the policy process" (1999, 8). The board of editors of *Policy Sciences* includes numerous adherents to Lasswell's approach. But the policy sciences' mark extends beyond the academy. It is practitioner-friendly, and its users hail from many nations and professions, including many developing nations. For example, among non-US law experts, Falk declares (1995, 1997):

TABLE 14.2
Intellectual Tasks, Foundations, and Approaches

Intellectual Tasks	Intellectual Foundations and Approaches
Goals	Philosophy
Trends	History
Conditions	The scientific approach, e.g., hypothesis testing, modeling
Projections	Forecasting; extrapolation; futures
Alternatives	Optimization; benefit/cost, risk, and feasibility analysis

Source: From Lasswell, Harold D., *A Pre-View of Policy Sciences*, American Elsevier, New York, pp. 40–57; 1971; see also Clark, Tim W., Rutheford, Murray B., Ziegelmayer, Kim, and Stevenson, Michael J., In *Species and Ecosystem Conservation: An Interdisciplinary Approach*, Clark, Tim W., Stevenson, Michael, Ziegelmayer, Kim, and Rutherford, Murray, Eds. *Bulletin Series No. 105*, Yale School of Forestry and Environmental Studies, New Haven, CT, 2001.

...the McDougal and Lasswell framework has had more influence in Third World countries than any other American jurisprudential perspective... This truth illustrates the power of the framework to structure decisions whatever the observational stance of the user.[*]

Somewhat paradoxically, Falk also contends (1995, 2000) that "...the adoption of the jurisprudential orientation as method as well as perspective, has been limited to the scholarly community..." There is considerable evidence to the contrary, including, for example, a World Bank project promoting social capital formation (Brunner 2003); a workshop that explored perspectives of advocates and challengers of wildlife reintroduction policies in the American intermountain west (Brown 2003); an application of problem orientation to promote conservation in the Northern Rocky Mountains (Clark and Gaillard 2001); an effort to share power in a psychiatric hospital (Lasswell and Rubenstein 1966); and a new direction for policy analysis in the arena of nutrition policy (Haddad and Pelletier 2003).

Framing policy problems and possible solutions using the policy sciences, and having that approach deployed by multidisciplinary teams of experts goes back several decades; they include activities involving Lasswell himself, such as a program to diffuse power and enlightenment to campesinos in Vicos, Peru (Dobyns et al. 1964; Holmberg 1958).[†]

Sustained interest in the policy sciences for applied problem-solving results not merely from its explicit problem-orientation, but also its accommodation of multiple methods and bases of knowledge (Ascher 1987). Multidisciplinarity is implicit in the analytic parts themselves, for example, when policy scientists liken intellectual tasks to different intellectual foundations and approaches (Table 14.2).

The value categories—power, wealth, well-being, rectitude, and so on—also have disciplinary analogues: political science (power); economics (wealth); health sciences (well-being); theology (rectitude); etc. One provisional indicator that policy scientists are heeding the call for multidisciplinarity is the diverse membership of the Society for the Policy Sciences. As of 2005, the membership rolls included foreign aid experts, government auditors, international lawyers, wildlife ecologists, foresters, nutritionists, human rights experts, political psychologists, security studies experts, and university administrators to name a few (see member list at www.policysciences. org)—several of whom are professional collaborators. This tendency toward collaboration contrasts

---

[*] On the broad appeal of the policy sciences, Falk adds (1995, 1997): "It is...a tribute to McDougal's extraordinary missionary gift as an engaged teacher."

[†] For a critique of the Vicos project and the Yale Psychiatric Institute experiment, see Merelman (1981, 493–495).

with other fields that pay homage to knowledge integration but are nevertheless deeply balkanized intellectually (Brecher 1999).

Among the latter, consider international relations (IR). Lamenting the "intolerance" and "fratricidal" quality of international relations experts' competing paradigms and approaches, a former president of the International Studies Association beseeched his colleagues to embrace pluralism, synthesis, complementarity, and knowledge cumulation in constructing and using theories and cases (Brecher 1999). Brecher offers his collaborative research on international crisis behavior (i.e., interstate crisis and conflict) as illustrative of the integrative approach he espouses. Notably, part of its success depends on "the values of tolerance, mutual respect and civility" of the participating investigators, themselves.[*]

Scholars and practitioners persuaded by Brecher's philosophy will find company among policy scientists. Knowledge cumulation and integration, pluralism and complementarity in methods, and mutual respect imbue the collaborations between policy scientists and their partners, beginning with Lasswell and McDougal's first interdisciplinary forays to Lasswell, Holmberg et al.'s work in the Peruvian highlands, to the various contemporary, problem-oriented quests mentioned above.

Much as the policy sciences' demands for intellectual tolerance could provide a salve for international relations, Lasswell's demands for problem orientation could increase the practical value of particular analytical tools used by IR experts. Consider, for example, a problem-oriented grounding for game theory. Game theory would appear to promise considerable advantages to international negotiators by helping predict opponents' strategies and by comparing different reward structures. However, the field has been criticized for its tendency toward abstraction, dislocation from problems on the ground, and lack of useful prescriptions (Kadane and Larkey 1983). Habeeb laments (1988, 11): "Clearly game theory has little relevance for the dynamic process of international negotiation, in which power has many sources and dimensions and there are at least as many possible tactics as there are actors." If the different sources and dimensions of power are stripped away from the exercise, then, indeed, what is left is a game, whereas the negotiator demands intelligence that can inform strategies and the selection of choices.

Lasswell and Kaplan's (1950) explication of the sources and functions of power offers a potential antidote to otherwise insufficient or simplistic renderings of power. But there is an equally important reform to consider. To be genuinely useful, games must integrate the negotiators' own perspectives on linkages between issues, stakeholder demands, and notions of mutual respect and fairness (Newsom 1995–1996, 62–66; Young 1989b). More robust—and albeit more complex—simulations of negotiations will locate the negotiator in relevant social contexts, including organizational and inter-organizational settings where the negotiator alternately issues and takes orders. Such an approach would account for the different sources and dimensions of power that are used by or that restrict the negotiator.

The prescription here is neither to co-opt nor conquer game theory with the policy sciences, but rather to reconfigure the approach for problem-oriented research and practice. Were some game theorists to accept the challenge,[†] they would join other experts who do not identify themselves as policy scientists per se, but nevertheless, have converged on the basic formulas of the approach. The origins of the convergence are decades old. To wit, thirty years ago, Lee Cronbach famously

---

[*] On this point, see also Falk (1995, 1997) who mentions professional respect as a basis for shaping and sharing values in policymaking. With reference to Myres McDougal's cultivation of international students, Falk writes (1995, 1997): "Somehow, Mac listened carefully enough to create bonds that endured over great distances and for decades, giving individuals who were then anonymous students that experience of dignity in concrete personal encounter that the jurisprudence promised at the level of social and political intercourse."

[†] Much as game theorists can improve their craft with insights from the policy sciences, convergence can come from the other direction too as the policy sciences draw on the strengths of game theory, such as its insights on zero-sum games, lotteries, and other contexts where rules are well specified and the menu of choices is limited.

questioned the search for and reliance on universal theories of human behavior in psychological research. "Originally," he writes (1975, 124),

> ...the psychologist saw his role as the scientific observation of human behavior. When hypothesis testing became paramount, observation was neglected, and even actively discouraged by editorial policies of journals. Some authors now report nothing save F ratios.

Elsewhere he opines (1975, 123–125),

> The experimenter or the correlational researcher can and should look within his data for local effects arising from uncontrolled conditions and intermediate responses... Instead of making generalization the ruling consideration of our research, I suggest that we reverse our priorities. An observer collecting data in one particular situation is in a position to appraise a practice or proposition in that setting, observing effects in context... As results accumulate, a person who seeks understanding will do his best to trace how the uncontrolled factors could have caused local departures from the modal effect. That is, generalization comes late, and the exception is taken as seriously as the rule.

Like Cronbach, C. S. Holling settles on contextual analysis as an alternative or complement to abstract theorizing. But the reformist agenda of Holling, who is an ecologist, has less drastic consequences for conventional practice than does Cronbach's. Science in the service of managing ecosystems, Holling observed (1995, 13–14) must integrate knowledge derived from reductionist approaches, including hypothesis testing and data collection, with a context-specific "adaptive management" approach that respects complexity, incomplete knowledge of that complexity, and ever-changing conditions. Brunner and Colburn (2002, 242–243) identify other experts who have reached similar conclusions about the need for conceptual and practice-oriented frameworks that are responsive to changes in underlying conditions. Lasswell himself predicted a synthesis of methods and approaches (1971, 58): convergence would be spurred not by the pressures of peer review or flavor-of-the-month intellectual fashions, but due to "the self-correcting impact of experience"—i.e., the requirements of practice, which demand knowledge integration for complex problem-solving.

Craig Nelson, a biologist and recipient of a US Professor of the Year prize from the Carnegie Foundation for the Advancement of Teaching, argues that "contextual decisions" mediated by values are the highest order of cognitive development among undergraduate students (Nelson 1997). At the beginning of their course of study, undergraduates approach learning with a "Sgt. Friday" mentality, inclined to treat knowledge as the exclusive domain of inviolable facts. Sensitivity to scientific uncertainty leads to a new state of cognition, where knowledge is shaped by the learners' perceptions of the opinions of others. Eventually, students learn the importance of probing the intellectual bases of and inherent biases in disparate opinions and viewpoints. The final stage of cognition concerns contextual learning, coping with provisional explanations, and appreciation of the values of affected actors and the students' own (Nelson 1997, 70):

> We come to see knowledge as constructed rather than discovered, as contextual, as based inevitably on approximations, as involving tradeoffs among conflicting values, and as requiring of us that we take stands and actively seek to make the world a better place.

Contextuality, values, and skepticism of the pure rational actor model are prominent in the inner workings of Elinor Ostrom's institutional analysis and development (IAD) framework—a model her students use to clarify complex policy problems, including environmental and natural resource management problems. IAD is often associated with the rational choice school of public policy, but Ostrom cautions readers not to imagine the individual actors at the core of the framework as one-dimensional, utility maximizers. "The most well-established formal model of the individual used in institutional analysis," she observes (1999, 44–45)

> ...is *Homo economicus*. To use *Homo economicus*, one assumes that actors have complete and well-ordered preferences and complete information, and that they maximize the net value of expected returns to themselves... Many institutional analysts tend to use a broader conception of individual actors... one could assume that the individuals who calculate benefits and costs are fallible learners who vary in terms of the number of other persons whose perceived benefits and costs are important to them and in terms of their personal commitment to keeping promises and honoring forms of reciprocity extended to them.

Ostrom contends (1999, 45) that fallibility and the capacity to learn are "assumptions of a more general theory of the individual." The maximization postulate and contextuality, and not rational choice, are closer approximations of how fallible learners behave in the IAD framework. Of fallible learners: "in some settings, the incentives lead them to repeat the mistakes of the past. In others, the rate of effective learning about how to make a resource sustainable over time is rapid" (Ostrom 1999, 45).[*]

V. CONCLUDING REMARKS

There is no singular perspective in the community of policy scientists as to the inherent advantages or risks of other disciplines rediscovering or converging on the central tenets of the policy sciences movement. Rather, there is debate. It concerns the degree of enthusiasm with which policy scientists invite others to join who are already problem-oriented and contextual, or who are predisposed to such approaches, or who are frustrated with the limits of their own approaches to discovery and learning. To clarify, the question is not whether to invite the favorably inclined; new collaborators are always welcome. The sticking point is how to contend with those who are strongly invested in alternative (frequently, positivistic) approaches to policy analysis, but who find advantages in problem-orientation or contextuality or multiple methods, and who partially incorporate the policy sciences into their own approaches.

Many policy scientists will embrace like-minded scholars and practitioners on the basis of shared morality. If counterparts are partially incorporating Lasswell's or other policy scientists' ideas even as they subscribe to other methods and approaches, they nevertheless may be viewed as compatriots in the overarching tasks of clarifying and securing community interests. A second reason that convergence may be welcomed by the many, rather than the minority, is that policy scientists are predisposed to problem-solving using multiple methods. Those experts converging on Lasswell and McDougal's principles from other disciplines are the very allies that policy scientists imagine as partners. Policy scientists already count among their numbers many who came late to the contextual, problem-oriented movement. The price of admissions does not include renunciation of a latecomers' training. Indeed, such a demand would contradict the policy sciences' normative claims to multi-method enquiry.

Some in the policy sciences community may be less accommodating and will contend that Lasswell's constructs are necessarily compromised by half-way or hybrid approaches. Policy scientists' approach to knowledge integration could be threatened if new knowledge exposes the central canons of the policy sciences to the forces of syncretization or even supplantation. However, it is striking that major changes to the policy sciences' cognitive mapping schema have not come to pass which is testament to the comprehensiveness and versatility of Lasswell's, McDougal's, and their collaborators' original formulations. Durability of its working gears aside, the door for new

---

[*] Another core concept in the IAD framework is "levels of analysis and outcomes" in policy processes which track rule making and rule enforcement at different levels of human association. That concept draws explicitly on Lasswell's decision process (see Ostrom 1999, 58–61).

ideas and helpful innovations remains open. This is so because the policy sciences' key testing ground is the world of real problems and not the world of perfect ideas. Freed from having to discover—and then defend—universal laws of human behavior, policy scientists can integrate any idea or tool that advances the movement's central aim: promoting human dignity.

Still, competing claims to superior conceptual rigor and empirical validity are the blood sport of policy analysis. If, indeed, the search for social scientific equivalents of Newton's laws gradually gives way to problem-oriented approaches, then competition among alternative versions of the latter will only stiffen. Admirers of older approaches will borrow liberally even as they declare the unequalled advantages of the new scheme. If the new approach is deemed superior by everyone except the old order, it seems likely that the former will eventually prevail. But unless the main components are at risk of being replaced by something inferior, self-defensive postures and pre-emption by policy scientists are unnecessary.

William Ascher's perspective on the disposition of policy scientists toward like-minded, but nevertheless, divergent approaches is probably the right one. He counsels (1987, 366):

> ... let us not separate ourselves from the other people who agree with us on the fundamentals but use different labels. We need all the true allies we can get, and the work of many others fits these criteria even if it is not called 'policy sciences.'

One of the essential reasons to open the tent flaps wide enough for like-minded approaches is to ward off so-called value-neutral alternative schemes that, for all their normative neutrality, make value-laden decisions about what problems to tackle and in what order (Ascher 1987, 365). This may mean reaching out to positivists who nevertheless express fundamental misgivings about positivism. Consider, for example, microeconomist David W. Bromley's exhortation to his colleagues to rethink the most basic assumptions and intentions of that discipline. He affirms (1990, 99):

> When I say that we must begin to assess policy impacts in terms that are relevant to those affected, I mean only that we must begin to expend more effort to ascertain exactly how individuals regard the benefits and costs of certain policy alternatives. This would stand in contrast to the current approach which regards pertinent benefits and costs to be those that we—as economists—happen to be proficient at measuring.

Bromley's demand for an intellectual orientation that places the affected community's demands and expectations front-and-center is fundamental and obvious to students of Lasswell. But the essential point is not Bromley's rediscovery of Lasswell's participant- and problem-oriented approach. It is that a prominent economist has discovered the normative shortcomings of his own analytical frames of reference and is searching for a new approach. Whether Bromley and other newcomers to post-positivism eventually identify themselves as policy scientists is beside the point. There are multiple pathways to contextual, problem-focused, and multi-method enquiry. What matters is when in one's career such paths are discovered and whether one has the courage to explore them.

REFERENCES

Anderson, James E., *Public Policymaking*, Houghton Mifflin, Boston, MA, 2000.

Applebaum, Anne, Re: 'Mission to nowhere,' *Washington Post*, A19, January 14, 2004.

Ascher, W., The evolution of the policy sciences, *Journal of Policy Analysis and Management*, 5, 365–389, 1987.

Auer, Matthew R., Agency reform as decision process: the reengineering of the agency for international development, *Policy Sciences*, 31, 81–105, 1998.

Auer, Matthew R., The human faces of the space mission, *Indianapolis Star*, A13, January 14, 2004.

Bonser, Charles E., McGregor Eugene B., and Oster, Clinton V., *Policy Choices and Public Action*, Prentice Hall, Upper Saddle River, NJ, 1996.

Brecher, Michael, International studies in the twentieth century and beyond: flawed dichotomies, synthesis, cumulation, *International Studies Quarterly*, 43, 213–264, 1999.

Brewer, Garry D. and deLeon, Peter, *The Foundations of Policy Analysis*, Brooks/Cole, Monterey, CA, 1983.

Bromley, Daniel W., The ideology of efficiency: searching for a theory of policy analysis, *Journal of Environmental Economics and Management*, 19, 86–107, 1990.

Brown, Steven R., Summary of a workshop on clarifying perspectives, paper presented at the Policy Sciences Annual Institute, in New Haven, CT, 16–19, October, 2003.

Brunner, Ronald D., The policy movement as a policy process, *Policy Sciences*, 24, 65–98, 1991.

Brunner, Ronald D., A milestone in the policy sciences, *Policy Sciences*, 29, 45–68, 1996.

Brunner, Robald D., Introduction to the policy sciences, *Policy Sciences*, 30, 191–215, 1997a.

Brunner, Ronald D., Teaching the policy sciences: reflections on a graduate seminar, *Policy Sciences*, 30, 217–231, 1997b.

Brunner Ronald, D., Context-sensitive methods and evaluation for the World Bank, Paper presented at the Policy Sciences Annual Institute, in New Haven, CT, October 16–19, 2003.

Brunner, Ronald D., Colburn, Christine H., Harvesting experience, In *Finding Common Ground: Governance and Natural Resources in the American West*, Brunner, Ronald D., Colburn, Christine H., Cromley, Christina M., Klein, Roberta A., and Olson, Elizabeth A., Eds., Yale University Press, New Haven, CT, 2002.

Brunner, Ronald D., Byerly, Radford, Jr,, and Pielke, Roger A., The future of the space station program, In *Space Policy Alternatives*, Byerly, Radford Jr,, Ed., Westview Press, Boulder, CO, 1992.

Brunner, Ronald D., Colburn, Christine H., Cromley, Christina M., Klein, Roberta A., and Olson, Elizabeth A., Eds., *Finding Common Ground: Governance and Natural Resources in the American West*, Yale University Press, New Haven, CT, 2002.

Bush, George W., "State of the union address." 20, January, 2004. www.whitehouse.gov/news/releases/2004/01/20040120-7.html.

Clark, Tim W, *The Policy Process: A Practical Guide for Natural Resource Professionals*, Yale University Press, New Haven, CT, 2002.

Clark, Tim W. and Willard, Andrew, R., Learning about natural resources policy, In *Foundations of Natural Resources Policy and Management*, Clark, Tim W., Willard, Andrew R., and Cromley, Christina M., Eds., Yale University Press, New Haven, CT, 2000a.

Clark, Tim W. and Willard, Andrew, Analyizing Natural Resources Policy, In *Foundations of Natural Resources Policy and Management*, Clark, Tim W., Willard, Andrew R., and Cromley, Christina M., Eds., Yale University Press, New Haven, CT, pp. 32–44, 2000b.

Clark, Tim W. and Gaillard, David L., Organizing an effective partnership for the Yellowstone to Yukon Conservation Initiative, In *Species and Ecosystem Conservation: An Interdisciplinary Approach*, Clark, Tim W., Stevenson, Michael, Ziegelmayer, Kim, and Rutheford, Murray, Eds., Bulletin Series No. 105, Yale School of Forestry and Environmental Studies, New Haven, CT, 2001.

Clark, Tim W., Willard, Andrew R., and Cromley, Christina M., Eds., *Foundations of Natural Resources Policy and Management*, Yale University Press, New Haven, CT, 2000.

Clark, Tim W., Rutheford, Murray B., Ziegelmayer, Kim, and Stevenson, Michael J., Conclusion: knowledge and skills for professional practice., In *Species and Ecosystem Conservation: An Interdisciplinary Approach*, Clark, Tim W., Stevenson, Michael, Ziegelmayer, Kim, and Rutheford, Murray, Eds. *Bulletin Series No. 105*, Yale School of Forestry and Environmental Studies, New Haven, CT, 2001.

Colebatch, H.K., *Policy*, Open University Press, Buckingham, UK, 2002.

Crick, Bernard., *The American Science of Politics*, University of California Press, Berkeley, CA, 1959.

Cronbach, Lee, Beyond the two disciplines of scientific psychology, *American Psychologist*, 30, 117–127, 1975.

DeLeon, Peter., *Democracy and the Policy Sciences*, State University of New York Press, Albany, NY, 1997.

DeLeon, Peter, In *The Stages Approach to the Policy Process: What Has It Done? Where Is It Going?*, Paul A, Sabatier, Ed., Theories of the Policy Process, Westview, Boulder, CO, 1999.

Dobyns, Henry, Doughty, Paul, and Lasswell, Harold D., Eds., *Peasants, Power and Applied Social Change*, Sage, Beverly Hills, CA, 1964.

Eulau, Heinz, *Micro-Macro Analysis: Accents of Inquiry*, Aldine, Chicago, IL, 1969.

Eulau, Heinz and Zlomke, Susan, Harold D. Lasswell's legacy to mainstream political science: a neglected agenda, *Annual Review of Political Science*, 2, 75–89, 1999.

Falcoff, Mark, *Cuba: The Morning After*, American Enterprise Institute, Washington, DC, 2003.

Falk, Richard A., Casting the spell: the new haven school of international Law, *Yale Law Journal*, 104, 1991–2008, 1995.

Foyle, Douglas C., *Counting the Public In: Presidents, Public Opinion, and Foreign Policy*, Columbia University Press, New York, 1999.

Friedman, Thomas L., Presidents remade by war, *New York Times*, (section 4), 13, December 7, 2003.

Garen, Eva, Appraising ecotourism in conserving biodiversity, In *Foundations of Natural Resources Policy and Management*, Tim W, Clark, Willard R., Andrew, Cromley, Christina M., Yale University Press, New Haven, CT, 2000.

Habeeb, William Mark, *Power and Tactics in International Negotiation: How Weak Nations Bargain with Strong Nations*, The Johns Hopkins University Press, Baltimore, MD, 1988.

Haddad, Lawrence and Pelletier, David, *Nutrition Policy Process: Program Proposal of the Food Consumption and Nutrition Division of the International Food Policy and Research Institute*, IFPRI, Washington, DC, 2003.

Herring, George C., Why the United States failed in Vietnam, In *Major Problems in American Foreign Policy: Documents and Essay, Vol. II: Since 1914*, Thomas C. Patterson, Ed., D.C. Heath, Lexington, MA, 1984.

Hersh, Seymour, Selective intelligence, *New Yorker*, 12, 44, 2003.

Hogwood, Brian W. and Gunn, Lewis A., *Policy Analysis for the Real World*, Oxford University Press, Oxford, 1984.

Holling, C. S., In *What barriers? What bridges?*, Lance, H., Gunderson, Holling, C.S, and Light, Stephen S, Eds., *Barriers and Bridges to the Renewal of Ecosystems and Institutions*, Columbia University Press, New York, 1995.

Holmberg, Allen R, The research and development approach to the study of change, *Human Organization*, 17, 12–16, 1958.

Horowitz, Robert, Scientific propaganda, In *Essays on the Scientific Study of Politics*, Herbert J. Storing, Ed., Holt, Rinehart and Winston, New York, 1962.

Jenkins-Smith, Hank C., and Sabatier, Paul A., The study of public policy process, In *Policy and Change and Learning: An Advocacy Coalition Approach*, Sabatier, Paul A., and Jenkins-Smith, Hank C., Eds., Westview, Boulder, CO, 1993.

Jones, Charles, *An Introduction to the Study of Public Policy*, Wadsworth and Ripley, Belmont, CA, 1984.

Kadane, Jay and Larkey, Patrick, The confusion between is and ought, *Management Science*, 29, 1365–1379, 1983.

Lasswell, Harold D., *World Politics and Personal Insecurity*, McGraw-Hill, New York, 1935.

Lasswell, Harold D., *The Decision Process: Seven Categories of Functional Analysis*, University of Maryland, Bureau of Government Research, College Park, MD, 1956.

Lasswell, Harold D., *A Pre-View of Policy Sciences*, American Elsevier, New York, 1971.

Lasswell, Harold D. and Kaplan, Abraham, *Power and Society*, New Haven Press, New Haven, CT, 1950.

Lasswell, Harold D. and McDougal, Myres S., Legal education and public policy professional training in the public interest, *Yale Law Journal*, 52, 203–295, 1943.

Lasswell, Harold D. and McDougal, Myres S., *Jurisprudence for a Free Society: Science in Law, Science and Policy, Volumes I and II*, New Haven Press and Martinus Nijhoff, New Haven, CT and Dordrecht, The Netherlands, 1992.

Lasswell, Harold D. and Rubenstein, Robert, An application of the policy sciences orientation: the sharing of power in a psychiatric hospital, In *Political Science Annual: An International Review*, Robinson, James A., Ed., Bobbs-Merrill, Indianapolis, IN, vol. 1, 1966.

Little, David, Toward clarifying the grounds of value-clarification: a reaction to the policy-oriented jurisprudence of Lasswell and McDougal, *Virginia Journal of International Law*, 14, 452–461, 1974.

McNamara, Robert S., Blight, James G., and Brigham, Robert K., *Argument without End: In Search of Answers to the Vietnam Tragedy*, Public Affairs, New York, 1999.

Merelman, Richard M., Review article: Harold D. Lasswell's political world: weak tea for hard times, *British Journal of Political Science*, 11(4), 471–497, 1981.

Moreno, Dario. Exit political power: Cubans in the United States political system. Unpublished paper of the Metropolitan Center. Florida International University, Miami, FL, 2003.

Morgenthau, Hans J., Review of power and society, *American Political Science Review*, 46(1), 230–234, 1952.

Nelson, Craig, Tools for Tampering with Teaching Taboos, In *New Paradigms for College Teaching*, Campbell, William E. and Smith, Karl A., Eds., Interaction Book Company, Edina, MN, 1997.

Newsom, David D., Foreign policy and academia, *Foreign Policy*, 101, 52–67, 1995–1996.

Ostrom, Elinor, Institutional rational choice: an assessment of the institutional analysis and development framework, In *Theories of the Policy Process*, Sabatier, Paul A., Ed., Westview, Boulder, CO, 1999.

Ostrom, Elinor, Schroeder, Larry, and Wynne, Susan, *Institutional Incentives and Sustainable Development: Infrastructure Policies in Perspective*, Westview, Boulder, CO, 1993.

Ripley, Randall, *Policy Analysis in Political Science*, Nelson Hall, Chicago, IL, 1984.

Ross, Dorothy, *The Origins of American Social Science*, Cambridge University Press, Cambridge, 1991.

Sabatier, Paul A., The need for better theories, In *Theories of the Policy Process*, Sabatier, Paul A., Ed., Westview, Boulder, CO, 1999.

Stokey, Edith and Zeckhauser, Richard, *A Primer for Policy Analysis*, W.W. Norton, New York, 1978.

Suskind, Ron, *The Price of Loyalty: George W. Bush, the White House and the Education of Paul O'Neill*, Simon and Schuster, New York, 2004a.

Suskind, Ron, Without a doubt, *New York Times Magazine*, 44–51, October 17, 2004b; see also 64, 102, and 106.

Young, Oran, *International Cooperation: Building Regimes for Natural Resources and the Environment*, Cornell University Press, Ithaca, NY, 1989a.

Young, Oran, The politics of international regime formation: managing natural resources and the environment, *International Organization*, 43, 349–375, 1989b.

Unit 8

Comparative and International Relations

15 Comparative and International Administration

George M. Guess and Vache Gabrielyan

CONTENTS

I. INTRODUCTION

The field of comparative public administration (CPA) has bseen redefined by new research demands in response to major global transformations of political and economic systems. From a field drawing largely on academic political science and trends in US foreign aid policies, CPA has been pulled in several directions by new management and policy needs. Comparative public administration is still the study of similarities and differences in organization, management, and policy issues for the purpose of creating an institutionalized knowledge base to aid in making better decisions (Guess 1987a, 477). But with fewer funds available for development assistance in the 1990s, donors have focused attention on obvious administrative inefficiencies that have inhibited implementation of adjustment policies, as well as put greater emphasis on preemption-aimed, systematic surveillance of mostly economic policies of developing countries. As government reform rhetoric became more popular across the globe (Pollitt and Bouckaert 2000; Saint-Martin 2001) and domestic resources dwindled, governments have become increasingly critical of the administration of their own domestic programs. Both donors and host governments have become more open to the possibilities of using comparative administrative lessons to avoid the mistakes of the past.

For governments to improve domestic policy making and implementation, they need to know what systems and skills are needed to make them work. Governments must also display political will. However, in many instances, the will has been weakened by the ready availability of donor funding which buys time to avoid hard choices. In the past, CPA has been able to provide models and frameworks but few empirical conclusions on the appropriateness of systems and skills transfers. In its past role as a field of academic study closely tied to changing foreign assistance programs, CPA was rarely able to provide support for political decisions at the country level. The abstract language of its descriptive models did not provide substantive foundation for reform decisions. This may have contributed to the very lack of administrative reforms recommended in CPA reports and studies.

This chapter argues that world events have forced CPA to provide information for real management and policy problems. As the emphasis has shifted from paradigms and models to rapid-fire testing of hunches, with field confirmation often under makeshift conditions to improve administrative operations, formal deductive theory building has been demoted to second place. Largely inductive work is accumulating from aid missions and academic research which should lead to the development of more realistic descriptions of total systems and explanations through middle-range theories. The inquiry is now geared to problem solving: How can public investment programming be linked to the current budget in Honduras and Nicaragua? What sequence should we use to reform personnel administration in West Africa? The shift has been from systems theory to practice, from cases to field-tested comparative lessons.

Some will say this practical action trend is not new. Riggs (1967, 150) had asked questions about comparative auditing and expenditure controls nearly 40 years ago. But at that time there were no comparative studies for answers. The difference is that applied solutions must now be provided to solve simultaneous country and regional crises of security, democracy, and market in Eastern Europe (Nelson and Bentley 1994, 49). Given the dangers of repeating a totalitarian past (Pomfret 1994) and the long legacy of intractable ethnic and nationalist conflicts in such places as Macedonia and Sudan, leisurely institutional studies and framework building for foreign aid agencies will no longer do. The stakes for making application errors in CPA are much higher today than ever before.

To solve problems for the desperate public practitioners of these new regions requires some combination of local action research and improvisation of reforms carried out elsewhere; this is the kind of work in which most donor missions engage in. While this is unsatisfactory formal scholarship, it usually gets the job done. If the government stays around long enough to implement recommendations, it can even provide a basis for institutionalization of reforms. The dilemma is that early CPA works provided lots of models and few clear, testable propositions of value to decision makers. More recent CPA efforts exude desperate attempts to answer profound questions with small samples and skimpy methods. With the impetus of international organizations actively promoting standards and codes of behavior regarding certain government policies and transparency, there is an overall sense that both longer-term scholarship and quick field studies are revitalizing this field.

The next section briefly reviews the strengths and weaknesses of the period of classical CPA, roughly from the Alliance for Progress program to 1981. The third section, and the bulk of this chapter, will detail the new CPA period that dates from about 1982 to the present.

II. CLASSICIAL COMPARATIVE PUBLIC ADMINISTRATION

A.   FOREIGN AID AND COMPARATIVE PUBLIC ADMINISTRATION

The classical CPA era includes influences from both the *Alliance for Progress* (1961–1972) and *New Directions* (1973–1980) periods of US foreign assistance. These influences to some extent paralleled activities in other bilateral programs by the French and English with former colonies, and of United Nations agencies such as United Nations Development Program (UNDP) and the World Bank. But the driving force of most CPA scholarship during this period was the US foreign aid program. The systemic successes of the postwar Alliance program in Europe, for example, generated optimism and excitement about using administrative means to reform developing societies in the Western image. The emphasis, as indicated by formation of the Comparative Administrative Group in 1962, was on whole systems transformation: exporting political democracy, building legislatures, and designing planning systems.

Academic debates over minutiae arose in the Alliance era and contributed to the slothful evolution of the field. For example, the term development administration largely replaced the term comparative, indicating a bold interest in intervention for societal reform. At the same time, it left wide open the definition of the overall development objective needed for proper program administration. Just like the term development used in development budgets, the term could be used for anything from construction projects to human resource training programs. More importantly, it opened up a debate between those who could easily see what development was (i.e., primary education and rural water supplies) and simply wanted to administer the programs, and those who wanted to develop local capacity to manage their programs and make sound public policies (Riggs 1970, 3, 6–7). The latter view was at odds with the majority during this period because it implied that local traditional qualities would be required to achieve modern Western results. Building management capacity in traditional societies meant that the functional specificity of modern bureaucratic organization would have to be reinforced by informal patterns of association to be effective in practice. In short, CPA in this period stressed transfer of Western technology and systems for modernization and democratic development. Like the Alliance program itself, which applied to advanced industrial nations, the approach to developing countries was top-down and presumptuous.

The *New Directions* emphasis of classical CPA tried to shift gears and move to a less presumptuous approach to development. Under the new perspective, decentralization, deregulation, and democratic decision making would be program targets, using such means as small-scale appropriate technology. Critics of CPA pointed to the superficiality of trying to develop democratic alternatives to Communism via creation of mutual dependencies on Western technology and expertise through foreign aid. More forcefully, it was suggested that an obsession with the transfer of Western functions obscured the real damage done to developing societies by urban sprawl, natural resource depletion, superficial materialist culture, and environmental pollution (as if these were peculiarly Western). The aid relation itself became a cause of administrative incapacity as local program goals were displaced by the need to ask for more foreign assistance (Heady 1979, 104; Morss and Morss 1982, 25). Coming full circle, critics charged New Directions with withholding advanced technology to impede development in favor of small-scale systems.

In principle, New Directions was the polar opposite of the Alliance approach. In practice, programming aid for equity rather than growth or democracy made little difference on the ground. Dependency scholars argued that this was because systems of class privilege maintained the existing inequities and that revolutions were often required to liberate the poor (Chilcote and Edelstein 1974). Others focused on the top-down, inflexible mechanisms of dispensing aid through U.S. Agency for International Development (USAID) and other donors as an obstacle to reform. Because much of CPA research focused on the effects of aid and suggestions for reform, pure country studies of administrative strengths and weaknesses in comparative perspective were not very plentiful. In this sense, following the aid flows contributed to the later irrelevance of the field in providing practical solutions to local problems.

The results of the classical CPA period were useful in stimulating debates that strengthened a broad inquiry into comparative politics and administration. But the utility of lessons and propositions for designing administrative systems, programs, or policies in the field was not very high. The agenda was determined largely by the needs of the major donor (USAID) and particular university research programs, and to a much less extent by those of civil service practitioners, planners, and policy makers in developing societies. As a Honduran intellectual once said to aid in understanding of the new setting: "We are a prismatic society with a highly ascriptive status." This candid (if not canned) comment summed up both the strengths and weaknesses of the two main CPA products in this early period.

As might be expected, the first product of the period was insight into the US foreign aid process itself. Various scholars, either as consultants or researchers, cataloged the constraints impeding development results through transfer of systems and skills abroad. Much of the works focused on the practical realities of USAID in rigid macroplanning, micromanagement, and disinterest in actual results from aid project implementation (Guess 1987b; Montgomery 1986). The aid program moved from the flexible, high-energy operation of the Charles River action intellectuals in the early Alliance period to a rigid, politicized bureaucratic maze by the end of the New Directions period.

This product of early CPA scholarship was extremely valuable. The evolution of this critical literature on foreign aid policy and administration continued into the new CPA period, with studies of how the foreign aid process itself causes local problems in public sector management. For example, Ghai (1991) reviewed the social impact of International Monetary Fund (IMF) adjustment programs in particular African countries. Consistent with the dependency perspective used frequently in the classical CPA period, his major finding was that interference in internal affairs by structural adjustment programs, particularly privatization conditions, have accelerated the capture of national institutions by international capitalism (Ghai 1991, 91). Critical studies of USAID administration have continued. For instance, a recent study focused on the issues of AID personnel incentives, micromanagement, reporting requirements, use of consultants, and the need for mission presence abroad (NPR 1993a).

In the classical CPA period it was unclear whether the research agenda or the aid program itself caused the gap in applied knowledge. But clearly the literature did not appreciate the importance of local bureaucratic incapacity to perform basic government output functions (Packenham 1973, 229). At the same time, the aid program was scored for tinkering at the margins with institution building for budgeting and personnel systems (Packenham 1973, 116–117). In fact, very few positive results in changing systems and skills could be demonstrated here either. There were very few comparative studies of program or policy administration. The field studies that were performed were largely case studies of particular programs, from which comparative lessons were often proffered but rarely followed up on in later studies. The exceptions, such as Danziger's (1978) organizational explanations for British interborough expenditure variations, or the Heidenheimer et al. (1983) study of European and US health, local government, and other policies, only confirmed the rule that most comparative work was still conducted in advanced industrial nations. In developing countries, comparative studies often boiled down to case studies, such as the Braibanti study (1967, 360) of the Pakistani civil service, or formal-legal analyses of particular programs, such as forestry administrations (UNFAO 1975).

B. THE FUNCTIONALIST FRAMEWORK AND OTHER ROADMAPS

The second major product of this period was the academic roadmap or framework that provided broader insights into transitional or mixed societies (first- and third-class roads in one place), structures that performed multiple functions (road agencies that performed social welfare as well as construction and maintenance), and peculiar mixed functions performed by unexpected prismatic structures (local highway rule making by informal group structures or fluctuating networks rather than formal visible organizations like the legislature or national police). The underlying functionalist premise was that to become modern and institutionalized, possibly even democratic, societies would have to pass through and perform a variety of basic functions, such as interest articulation and interest aggregation. Put another way, modernization would produce a "viable civic culture consisting of autonomous and differentiated sectors of society capable of articulating and aggregating interests" (Rahmans 1973, 159).

Similarly, modern bureaucracies would have to include the Weberian attributes of hierarchy, differentiation, discipline, and professionalization (LaPalombara 1967, 10). More usefully, there was debate about the order of developing functional performance (see Hoselitz 1967, 188). It was well recognized that in poor countries, political structures were multifunctional and that bureaucratic functions could be performed elsewhere in the social system. In Nicaragua and Honduras, for example, the auditor-general performs both internal and external expenditure control functions. Clearly, some functions were not even performed at all (Hoselitz 1967, 176–177). Again, in Nicaragua and Honduras, the external control function of economy and efficiency analysis and audit is simply not performed. In Central and Eastern Europe, internal control is still rigid, legalistic, and ignores performance issues (Kirby 1993). The performance or non-performance of basic functions permitted classification of bureaucracies along a scale of traditional to modern.

A modern fiscal analog of the functionalist model in comparative organizational analysis might be the "financial condition" evaluation of US state and local units and public enterprises for issuance of long-term debt. Such units are evaluated on their performance of basic managerial and budgetary functions by bond rating agencies. The performance assessments may indicate underlying debt service and performance problems and provide the basis for assessments of credit risk that are in part subjective. But they serve to increase the level of knowledge about the strengths and weaknesses of each unit for investors and analysts.

Also similar to the fiscal condition framework, not all CPA frameworks concentrated on purely administrative functions. As could be expected, insights into the many cultural, sociological, and institutional variables that affected administrative behavior of transitional societies came from a variety of directions. In addition to anthropology, economics, and sociology, fictional literature was a major source of research hypothesis and cultural insight. In this period, the stories and travels of V. S. Naipaul (Guess 1979; Hamner 1977), as well as Gary (1939) and Forster (1924), provided development researchers valuable roadmaps on the potential clashes of cultures, petty misunderstandings, and complexities lurking beneath the surface of ordinary life.

In probably unmeasurable ways, such books strengthened research and foreign assistance efforts. To continue with the map metaphor for CPA models, a great deal of effort during this period was also spent on developing visionary roadmaps (paradigms, models, middle-range theories, theses, and frameworks) to such destinations as revolution, modernization, and development. Such maps could be followed only if resources were available and the elaborate conditions could be met (Almond 1970; Huntington 1968; Riggs 1964). Prismatic perspectives allowed scholars to see the surface modernization of institutions (rational work rules and organization charts) and the underlying reality of often dysfunctional work practices. The subtlety and sensitivity of these perspectives were useful for more recent appraisals, such as for civil service reform. For instance, the Nepali practice of writing memos on all matters and sending them through the hierarchy for clearance rather than adopting informal face-to-face meetings or using the telephone (World Bank 1993a, 9) is a well-recognized local practice. Proliferation of meaningless memos hampers senior management's ability to plan and budget, as well as mid-level manager's capacity to serve the public effectively. The "multiple-veto system" of files requiring endless clearances operates also in India to inhibit reform from the top (*Economist* 1995d, 7).

Unfortunately, the roadmaps also became confused by the complexity of local meanderings (customs, peculiar institutions, and practices that worked against professionalism and efficient administration). Scholars fascinated by cultural bottlenecks often believed them to be unique and even rational. Images projected by the roadmaps lacked resolution. Structure was not imposed on phenomena, rather the phenomena guided the roadmaps. The result was frequently confused comparative research that offered few empirical insights. Tensions between pro-Western and anti-Western functionalist premises impeded comparative research into how organizations could be adapted to achieve efficiency (which fiscal managers and clients of major services needed) consistent with the relevant features of local culture. For instance, fascination with the intricacies of Nepali cultural constraints to civil service reform seem to have held back reform efforts. While the centralized features of this administrative system are common to many developing countries, particularly Latin America (Harrison 1985), they are hardly unique in how they function to impede efficient and effective service.

To provide evidence of how far CPA studies have come since this period, it may be instructive to illustrate the perils of bottom-up research, or how in one instance political culture got tangled up with performance questions. In a comparative performance evaluation of the *panchayati raj* multi-tiered rural councils in India, for example, Rahman (1973) indicated at the outset that Western theories of administrative and political development would be unsatisfactory. Though evidently local program units of central government ministries, they were also designed to facilitate local democratic participation (Rahman 1973, 158). Despite the absence of linkage with any elected local bodies, Rahman believed that the units were simply too rich and diverse for explanation by the traditional Western politics–administration dichotomy or functionalism. Implicitly, the institutions were beyond Western comprehension.

A common message of much classical CPA work was that outsiders should first spend large portions of their lives studying local institutional complexity before attempting to change organizations that serve complex religious, ethnic, and social functions. The outsider would agree entirely if the shoddy services and arrogantly incompetent officials did not perpetuate so much human misery. The results of the multi-textured cultural complexity of most poor countries often boils down to a simple phenomenon: corruptly inefficient programs and services. The romantic notion of institutional mysticism and complexity was simply an extreme version of the not uncommon premise that institutional performance was impossible to change (Crozier 1964; Nisbet 1970).

The Rahman article provided further insight into classical CPA works on many poor countries from ideological bottom-up perspectives. Here Rahman (1973, 151) applied the Riggsian notion of a "prismatic" institution, where politics and administration are interwoven in an "undifferentiated nonautonomous structure" (Rahman 1973, 163). But few scholars in the West actually buy the old-fashioned politics–administration dichotomy anymore. One often makes the distinction to proceed with governance process, particularly administrative rulemaking. Effective administration requires influencing decisions, which means engaging in politics. Moreover, a theme of this chapter is that functionalism is quite alive and well. Rahman dwelled on the descriptive complexity of local multifunctional systems (which can also be found in regions of advanced societies) and ignores the fact that service improvement requires application of some kinds of normative concepts of efficiency (e.g., cost/unit) and effectiveness (i.e., measurable outcomes).

Along with such criticism, comparative public (and development) administration was critically dissected in two issues of *Public Administration Review* in 1976 and in 1980 (the latter discussing policy and administrative failures in Iran). Challenges were raised both on ethical/political (Loveman 1976), cultural (Siffin 1976), as well as methodological (Jreisat 1976; Jun 1976) grounds. Balanoff, Van Wart, and Pryor (1998, 458) identify five "substantial strains" of this critique:

1. Much like the broader field of public administration, no paradigm or widely accepted model has emerged; research was non-cumulative and lacked focus.
2. The macrolevel studies (especially the most prominent of them—Riggs's (1964) prismatic model) were seen as obscure and linguistically confusing.
3. The subfield was accused of being underdeveloped in terms of theory building and hypothesis testing.
4. Development administration research was seen as detached from useful application.
5. Ethnocentrism has pervaded the literature.

In short, classical CPA studies often denied Western norms and preferred to analyze local complexity. For instance, without making the normative distinction between politics and administration, one had to agree that social security administrators should be allowed to set eligibility requirements. The implication of this value was that either such behavior could not be controlled (via normal internal control systems) or that it should not be because this would be peculiarly Western. By taking the stance that all was politics (Rahman 1973, 163), a self-fulfilling prophecy is put into practice that simply perpetuates administrative chaos. This stance also produces muddled comparative research. Mysticism surrounding the basic unit of evaluation raises the obvious question of whether any systematic pattern of decisions can arise where all variables are caught in the swirl of politics. Was there an administrative system here at all? In fact, these units were mostly power extensions of the central government, set up as in many countries to keep an eye on local activities. Thus weak research design and fascination with mystical organizations obscured the very purposes of this kind of early CPA research.

III. THE NEW COMPARATIVE ADMINISTRATION

The agenda of CPA was profoundly affected by the beginning, in 1981, of a long period of fiscal conservatism and skepticism in the United States, United Kingdom, and elsewhere.[*] The US aid program suffered most from this mood, as typically the most unpopular of annual programs. The period of critical reexamination of foreign aid results began during the Reagan administration and produced a shift in the amount and direction of aid. The critical mood continues to the present day as the Republican leadership enacted the Millennium Challenge Account aiming at rethinking of official development assistance, tying the aid with "economic freedom and just rule" in the country, and using built-in monitoring and greater use of markets in design of the programs (MCC 2004).[†] In the early 1980s CPA was affected by the push of a revamped foreign aid program. In the early 1990s it was also affected by the pull of events in Eastern Europe, the Soviet Union, and Latin America that required new applied knowledge.

The general pattern of reformed foreign aid programs has been to shift funds from direct government assistance to non-governmental organizations (NGOs) and private firms, as well as toward efforts to streamline intrusive state regulatory functions, such as business licensing, and to reduce the state in productive activities through State-owned enterprises (SOEs). Trade and investment were becoming the preferred solutions to nation building. To the extent that government was the focus of aid, it was primarily to downsize the civil service, and to a lesser extent, to revitalize basic government functions of budgeting, personnel, and program management. Under these conditions foreign aid programs became increasingly interested in finding successful applied solutions, if for no other reason than to maintain their own niches and funding sources.

The CPA agenda was affected by the underlying perception that traditional government solutions were not very effective either in the United States and Europe or in developing countries. The focus became models of reform and methods of turning around government agencies. But with popular suspicions of government running high in the United States, many questioned whether the transfer of US and European best practices to fix governments might only make the public bureaucracies more oppressive and ineffective than before. Despite the comparative efficiency of the US model of local government, and many federal programs such as urban mass transit, the mood was that they should be fixed anyway by programs of contracting out and privatization mechanisms, coupled with buyouts and severance programs for personnel in the rest of the bureaucracy. On the bright side, some governments were clearly more effective than others at generating professional incentives and delivering services. They became subjects and models for the new CPA.

---

[*] George Guess would like to note that while he enthusiastically taught the CPA, comparative Latin American political systems, and comparative public budgeting seminars several times, his behavior as a one-time student of CPA was quite inconsistent. He dropped the only CPA course in which he enrolled at USC in 1971. The crusty materials then available could be described as "death warmed over."

[†] Even the choice for the entity administering the account is telling; it is a specially created corporation and not a government agency, supposedly not competing with USAID, but collaborating with it.

Faced with fewer resources and increased skepticism, the new CPA pushed ahead with both theory building and empirical research. This is evident in the major subfields of organization theory, personnel administration, budgetary systems, intergovernmental relations, and public management. In contrast to past bickering over such items as turf or field definition and the quest for middle-range versus systems theory, CPA research began to focus on the application of organization theory to comparative management and policy problems. For the first time, a concerted effort was made on several fronts to examine the determinants of organizational efficiency and effectiveness in comparative perspective. As noted, writers such as Jun (1976) and Tapia-Videla (1976) criticized CPA for failure to do this in the past. In an almost dialectical pattern, CPA theory and research practices have fed on each other to the benefit of the subfield as a whole.

The methodological debate about the maturity of the CPA has not ended. While most academic commentators (Heady 1996; Peters 1988, 1994; Siffin 1991) acknowledge some evident progress, they still do not see a unitary approach to methodology, covered topics and frameworks. On the other hand, there are optimistic assessments as well. Pierre (1995) concurs with Heady (1996), Peters (1994), and Farazmand (1996) about the necessity to concentrate on middle-range theories centered on bureaucracy, but he is also optimistic about the convergence of theory and practice. To him, this is a natural evolution for comparative public administration, much like comparative politics several decades earlier (Neumann 1974), passed through the phases of epic macro-generalizations (nomothetic studies) and micro-behavioral studies (ideographic studies) to the current third phase, when the "theory and empirical studies began to connect more clearly than previously" (Pierre 1995, 6).

In particular, the new CPA was strengthened by (1) more rigorous utilization of older perspectives, such as "functionalism-systems theory," and introduction of new theoretical perspectives, such as "public choice," the "new institutional economics," and "reinvention of government," and (2) focusing research on significant institutional problems of LDCs such as the performance of state enterprises, personnel, and public expenditure management systems. Such theories and research emphases are not new. They have been talked about for 50 years, but for the first time they are being used and performed with the goal of providing information to decision makers who have to deal with these problems on a daily basis. The new CPA is no longer a small pub where public administration and political science academics talk only to each other. There are also development policy experts and pracademics, who have gained extensive experience consulting on behalf of the World Bank, IMF, and USAID, and who often value timeliness of action over methodological perfection The CPA is now an eclectic mix of disciplines contributing diverse hypotheses and findings to a larger body of applied knowledge. Comparative public administration is no longer strictly a subfield of public administration (or public sector management). It is being fed from many sources, and this bodes well for the future.

A. PUBLIC CHOICE AND INSTITUTIONAL ECONOMICS

Public choice was one of the earlier new perspectives that sallowed CPA studies to focus on the decision-making implications of market and non-market incentive structures. It provided a more rigorous, deductive approach to organizing information and policy recommendations. As applied to transitional societies, the choice perspective is still useful in predicting the choice outcomes of particular institutional structures. For example, based on public choice analysis, Maass (1978) argued that local control, a reasonable degree of equity, and the ability to exclude nonmembers were keys to effective irrigation management. While the choice approach has often been condemned for methodological individualism and for its market efficiency premise, here it was demonstrated that although paradoxically a market system of allocation would be more economical for farmers, its cost could be loss of control over resources to outsiders with more power.

Similarly, in Africa, Thomson (1981) explained deterioration of firewood supplies as a product of distorted incentives created by formal and informal land tenure rules. That is, the individual underinvests in tree production because he cannot protect it against encroachment by others. Underinvestment would also be the result of underpricing of the resource. The government attempts to protect the forest resource by regulating access, which cannot protect individual investments (Nicholson 1981, 39). An implication of this choice analysis is that raising the stumpage price of the wood, at the potential short-run costs of higher prices, can preserve the resource and benefit the community. By this perspective, one could view more clearly the determinants of individual and policy failure than perspectives that simply assume the market will work (systems and structural–functional assumptions) or that it will not because of regulatory conflicts of interest (interest group control) or because of permanent flaws in economic incentives (Marxism and dependency).

The new institutional economics challenged public choice theory on its assumptions that acquisition of essential information would produce correct decisions for both individuals and institutions. The problem with the rational choice perspective for CPA is that it linked individual rationality with institutional efficiency. Many noted that information was always more incomplete and the decision environment more complex than neoclassical choice assumptions granted. It was widely suggested that the approach neglected the "heterogeneity of the bureaucracy" (Premchand 1983, 53), and this limited the value of analyses produced by choice theory.

For example, North (1990, 17) suggested that individuals act from widely divergent and subjective decision models which makes the information even more incomplete. Choice theory presumes, like neoclassical economic theory, that institutions are designed to achieve efficient outcomes. In fact, formal institutional rules of the game are created to serve the interests of those with the bargaining power to devise new rules (North 1990, 16). North proposed a "path dependence" model to understand how institutional constraints (e.g., tax structures and regulations) provide incentives for productive or unproductive behavior. He suggested that actors have subjective mental constructs for information processing that overrule the neoclassical assumption that they can correctly identify the reasons for their predicaments, that is, they know the costs and benefits of alternate choices (North 1990, 111).

An important implication of the new institutional critique of choice theory was reinforcement of the classical CPA view that culture and the vagaries of human motivation more profoundly affect institutional arrangements and choice than had been recognized by economists. It was suggested that such informal factors must be recognized and changed for path modification and organizational change. Comparative public administration studies pointed to the informal factors for decades, but had difficulty in finding a rigorous predictive framework (for example, see Israel 1989) or specifying cultural determinants of particular institutional outcomes. The new institutional political economy approach attempted to provide that framework. Its premise is that political economy is not just a question of "getting prices right" but "getting institutions right" (Levi 1994). A great deal of research is already underway that attempts to isolate the institutional effects of informal factors on incentives.

For instance, an emerging CPA question for organizational design in the former Soviet Union and Easter Europe has been: What institutional mechanisms can provide coordination between different organizations without hierarchy and central planning? That is, through what methods and strategies can a culture of authoritarian paternalism and mutual distrust be replaced by professional incentives for service results and accountability? In a study that may provide some insights, Chisholm (1989) isolated formal and informal mechanisms by which coordination can occur through multiple exchanges, in this case interdependence between urban transit agencies. One finding of interest is that formal coordination mechanisms can disrupt existing informalities (between specialized personnel such as operations and maintenance) that make coordination possible (Chisholm 1989, 189).

The Chisholm study was a rich source of hypotheses and suggested that a great deal of CPA research is needed on the effects of management mechanisms within and between organizations. Much work needs to be done on isolating the right bureaucratic structures and institutional mechanisms for administrative reforms. This neoclassical approach is clearly a conceptual advance over the simple interest-group modeling of political science and economics of the past, and can enable more comprehensive explanations of institutional, policy, and management failure. It also provides an innovative framework for comparative research on institutional constraints.

While the advances by CPA scholars have not been very distinct, the effort in this direction has been quite substantive. Mostly using the databases amassed by international organizations, many economists ventured into the territory charted by North. Based on rigorous quantitative analysis of pooled cross country data, the emerging consensus seems to be that for economic growth, institutions matter, albeit with complex causality (Acemoglu 2003; Meier 2000; Rodrik and Subramanian 2003). Such things as market-regulating (e.g., regulatory agencies), market-legitimizing (e.g., pension systems), and market stabilizing (e.g., central banks, fiscal rules) are of particular importance. Although such results are quite important and impressive, they raise the traditional quandary between economics and public administration (Thompson 1997). While everybody would agree that pension systems are important, what does it mean for real-life action? First pillar (pay-as-you-go) reform into a second (mandatory and centralized, but market orientation) or third (voluntary savings), or some combination thereof? Even in cases when there is more guidance on how to measure these institutions, there is a lot left to context and action. For example, the aggregate governance index consists of six dimensions, which, inter alia, include such hard definable and multi-operational concepts as "rule of law" and "freedom from graft" (Edison 2003, 36). Kouzmin, Leivesley, and Korac-Kakabadse (1997, 22) argue that social choice theory is allegedly "strong" on prediction only because of a concentration on behavioral outcomes, at the expense of dismissing issues of how and why. Most public administrators, on the other hand, are primarily interested in how and why questions because they both need prescriptions and to justify their actions in the face of competing value norms.

The problem has been addressed through global standardization of best practices. Drawing from a body of empirical research (neither very systematized nor systematic case studies) and from principal-agent theory on how to resolve possible conflicts of interest, best practices have been codified by several international institutions. There are instances of both hard and soft institutionalization of best practices, depending on prospective impact and available tools of standardization.[*] The IMF and World Bank, together with World Trade Organization (WTO) and Organization For Economic Cooperation and Development (OECD), have been in the forefront of framing institutions as a systematic set of standards and codes.

Initiated in 1998, the Reports on the Observance of Standards and Codes (ROSCs) for individual countries became permanent features of the IMF and World Bank's policy agenda. The codes and standards can be divided into three broad categories relating to: (1) increased transparency of government policymaking and operations and include data dissemination standards and codes of transparency in monetary and financial, and fiscal policies; (2) prevention of crises of financial systems. Standards and codes here relate to banking supervision, securities and insurance regulation, and payments systems. Reports on observance are regularly assessed in the context of a joint IMF–\World Bank program—the Financial Sector Assessment Program (FSAP); (3) enterprise behavior and protection of the integrity of markets, and include principles of corporate governance, accounting and auditing, and insolvency and creditors' rights (IMF 2001).

The list of engaged international organizations is not limited to the World Bank and the IMF. To list a few, the forum for banking supervision and financial stability is Bank for International

---

* Discussing the impact of the West on Eastern European and former Soviet countries, Cooley (2004) finds institutions with higher stakes and higher involvement—NATO and European Union having the most impact, international financial institutions having mixed impact, while multinational corporations and NGOs having low or almost non-existent influence over the processes of the region. Although the requirements of EU were the toughest (a very substantive part of legislation and regulatory practices have gone through a long and detailed twinning process to full correspondence with EU), they have been met with quite enthusiasm, since the prospects of benefits were the most tangible.

Settlements in Basel, while OECD is taking the lead on corporate governance principles, and International Accounting Standards Board in UK on accounting.

Quasi-official research on the status of current public administration practices (though mostly in developing countries) by multilateral institutions fit the pattern of soft standardization. Most active on this front has been the Public Management Service (PUMA) of the OECD (1990, 1995, 1996b). While surveying public management tendencies in the OECD countries for several years, in 1995 PUMA came up with an extensive research report, entitled *Governance in Transition*, where argument is made for reconfiguration of governance structures and public service delivery in a new environment, very much along the lines of the British *new public management* and American *reinventing government* initiatives. Criticizing rigid, excessively regulated and excessively regulating inflexible structures that cannot respond to change and place too much emphasis on process instead of results, the report argues for new public management in an era when "large government debts and fiscal imbalances exacerbated by recession ... place limits on the size of the state," and consumers are demanding "value for money and are increasingly reluctant to pay higher taxes" (OECD 1995, 7).

The 1996 OECD Ministerial Symposium on the Future of Public Services discussed OECD country responses to mounting pressures on the public sector in recent decades. Alice Rivlin, the Chair of the Symposium, identified seven ways OECD countries have responded to pressures for change in the role and structure of the government:

- Decentralization of authority within governmental units and devolution of responsibilities to lower levels of government (i.e., municipalities)
- Re-examination of what government should pay for and do, what it should pay for but not do, and what it should neither pay for nor do
- Downsizing the public service and the privatization or corporatization of activities
- Consideration of more cost-effective ways of delivering services, such as contracting out, market-type mechanisms, and user charges
- Customer orientation, including explicit quality standards for public services
- Benchmarking and measuring performance
- Reforms designed to simplify regulation and reduce its costs (OECD 1996a, 8)

This thinking is synchronous not only with an economics-informed hierarchical conceptualization of governance as a set of principal–agent relationships (largely an Anglo-American phenomenon), but also with conceptualization of the public sector as a web of complex interactions between multiple social and political actors where the state should show guidance (largely a Western European phenomenon). While guidance, control, and evaluation in the public sector have been in the focus of attention for a while in countries with corporatist traditions, and gained wide exposure after the famous Bielfield project (Kaufman 1991), now these issues are being recast in the framework of governance.

The OECD definition of governance is quite interesting in this respect because OECD ministerial symposium report uses the concept of governance to bring clarity into the even fuzzier distinction between public administration and public management. Governance is defined in terms of relationships rather than structures, and "thus includes more than public administration and the institutions, methods and instruments of governing. It also encompasses the set of relationships between governments and citizens, acting as both individuals and as part or through institutions, e.g., political parties, productive enterprises, special interest groups and the media" (OECD 1996a, 11).

According to this definition, *public administration* is the rather mundane task of properly taking care of the organizational side of the government. *Public management*, on the other hand, is concerned with *managing the governance process,* and "encompasses the broad range of techniques and strategies that are used to carry out the responsibilities assigned to governments" (e.g., managing economic development). "It includes, but goes beyond, the structure and administration of the public service. In contrast, the term "public administration" refers to the techniques by which government policies are carried out" (OECD 1996a, 11).

Though many commentators have not been very kind to such assertions (Green and Hubbell 1996; Moe 1994; Newland 1994), such bravura assertions have sparked a host of studies compiling, comparing, and systematizing NPM experiences in OECD countries (Kettl 1997, 1998, 2000; Matheson and Kwon 2003; Pollitt and Bouckaert 2000; Wollman 2001) and their adaptability to developing countries (Schick 1998). While acknowledging the momentum for reform, increased service quality, and greater transparency, most studies concur that (1) management or administrative reform is a process that is here to stay as a permanent feature of government; (2) as such it should be viewed as any other government policy that is subject to changing shifts in value emphasis, stakeholders, and implementation; (3) the rhetoric of reform reaches farther than actual practices; (4) there is not only convergence, but also a significant divergence of reform efforts in various countries; (5) such divergence, as well as failures of reform, often are due to the ignorance of functional and systemic effects of governance structures. Matheson and Kwon, commenting on the shortcomings of "first generation of reforms" (2003, 45) comment:

> ... the third problem was a failure to understand that public management is not only about delivering public services, but it also 'institutionalizes' deeper governance values and is therefore in some respects inseparable from the governance arrangements in which it is embedded.

Such a view brings us back to the systems view and functionalism—another tenet of classic CPA to be revived in the new CPA period.

B. BACK TO FUNCTIONALISM AND SYSTEMS ANALYSIS

In the new CPA period, normative efforts to streamline government had been justified by reference to older functionalist models and newer perspectives that actually boiled down to older paradigms dressed up in new-age management language. While Riggsian terms such as "clects" (Riggs 1964) at least had empirical referents useful for analysis (cliques and sects), modern descriptive terms like virtuality may sell well on the consultant circuit, but they only add to analytic vagueness. It may be recalled that the functionalism and systems analysis of the 1960s and 1970s had been largely discredited as tautological (whatever is is functional) and conservative (systems maintenance, integration, and order as the core functions) (Bill and Hardgrave 1973, 208). The parts of the functionalist framework that have interested CPA studies have been the allocation and implementation systems: interest aggregation, rule making, rule application, and rule adjudication (Almond and Coleman 1960).

By the 1980s, however, it was evident that many political and administrative systems were in fact fragmented and that only integration along several fronts could preserve the value of either individual functions or the operation of the whole system. Questions needed to be asked about which public sector functions were being performed, and how well.

For example, it is clear that the capital maintenance function is critical to the sustainability of rural infrastructure in poor countries (Heggie 1991). One perspective could be that this is a peculiarly Western notion and that local customs are different. But allowing infrastructure to deteriorate and financing current maintenance out of capital budgets are common practices in poor countries that have functional consequences. However, this is usually less an issue of traditional practices than entirely modern local responses to irrational donor incentives. Under conditions of donor financing for new investments, poor countries rationally undermaintain facilities. The question is: what institutional incentives can be designed to encourage local organizations to provide sufficient maintenance for infrastructure in particular areas, such as roads? To answer this question, Schroeder (1993, 11) compared management and financing incentives of a number of Asian and African countries to try and explain agency maintenance performance differences and to design new incentives for improved road maintenance.

Despite such major efforts, the belief continued that CPA studies were still not asking the right questions (Wilson 1994, 667, 671) to explain organizational performance variability. Growing problems of policy design, administration, and impact at all levels of government breathed new life into the works of those who had long argued for partial systems analysis and empirical testing of middle-range propositions before launching into high-flown generalizations about societies (LaPalombara 1979, 137). Most of the typologies and abstractions of the classical CPA period provided little utility to those confronting major problems of policy or operational alternatives.

This was clearly the case with public financial management, for example, which consisted of multiple functions that had to be coordinated to allocate and control resources. Unless the budgeting, accounting, procurement, payroll, treasury management, and auditing/evaluation functions are integrated with information and control mechanisms, proper decisions cannot be made. In fact, debate has erupted between sets of functionalists on whether budgeting is first among equal functions or simply one among many in the financial management system (Miller 1994; Wesberry 1994).

The turf issue is functionally important. In Russia, for instance, nothing less than the battle between the old Russia of collective farms, subsidies, and state firms and the new Russia of stabilization and foreign investment incentives was taking place on the "budget battlefield" (*Economist* 1995c, 45). The arena for translation of politics and policies into financial programs is logically and substantively the budget process, not the accounting department or treasury system. Nevertheless, many argue that budgeting is simply resource allocation and that the rest of the process is the product of accounting and auditing functions (Wesberry 1994). In this sense the functionalist model has been extremely useful in comparing public finance systems cross-culturally. Gray et al. (1993, 3) suggest that the functions of budgeting, accounting, and evaluation, for example, are central to the cohesion of the political system and the sustaining of economic growth. They then compare the operation of all three functions in the United States, United Kingdom, Germany, Canada, Spain, Sweden, and Finland.

Further, the classic comparative budgeting studies by Caiden and Wildavsky (1974) and Wildavsky (1986) represented attempts to use the functionalist and systems approaches for policy and management purposes in both developing and developed countries. These were attempts to both describe functions and to explain their variation due to political structure and cultural patterns. Other studies merely provide comparative descriptions of functions. For example, OECD (1987) compared the budgeting and expenditure control systems of nineteen members. Such works are important for technical design issues, such as whether to install multiyear expenditure planning systems or how to treat reserve funds during the fiscal year.

Over the last two decades, with the advance of computer-aided technology and better standardization, budgeting has made significant advances both in terms of techniques and methodology. Though, as research shows, with every cycle of rationalization drive (Planning, Programming and Budgeting Systems (PPBS), Zero-Based Budgeting (ZBB), target budgeting, etc.), it starts with higher rationality promise, while ends up with not revolutionary, but workable improvements. In their study of introduction of performance-oriented budgeting (POB) in three Latin American countries (Mexico, Colombia, and Venezuela), Arreliano-Gault and Gil-Garcia (2004) come to the conclusion that:

> In practical terms, POB seen as an NPM policy cannot accomplish both its performance and accountability objectives easily. On the side of performance measurements, in many cases those measures are, and have to be, the result of political negotiations between budget control agencies, the rest of the agencies, and in some cases, key legislators. The promise of an objective and technical definition of these performance measurements is almost impossible to achieve, at least in settings like some Latin American countries.

Another issue that has been in the focus of public attention was the impact of globalization. While the popular conception of globalization has been as an inevitable force driving to economic convergence and cultural homogenization across boundaries (e.g., Friedman 1999) through a systematic analysis of organizational change in Argentina, South Korea, and Spain since the 1950s, Guillen (2001) showed how the social, political, and economic conditions preconditioned the role of business groups, small enterprises, and foreign multinationals as the lead actors of development in each country. Thus, together with the global drive for standardization, the new CPA has shifted its attention also to the idiosyncratic responses of countries to limitations and possibilites offered by globalization. As many argue, political and administrative culture is one of the leading determinants of parameters of such a response.

C. BACK TO POLITICAL CULTURE

Earlier fascination with the effects of culture on bureaucratic design and performance did not really move beyond cautionary statements for Westerners and academic typology. The earlier political culture approach offered a method "to look beyond the structures of politics to the beliefs that affect the ways in which people act within these political institutions" (Pye and Verba 1965, 514). But attempts to narrow the concept to "a system of beliefs about patterns of political interaction and political institutions" (Pye and Verba 1965, 516) did not move us very far. The concept of "belief" was almost as vague as "culture." Addition of the word "political" did not add much to its overall tangibility.

More importantly, the political culture approach did not result in studies that linked particular aspects of political culture to specific political outcomes. In particular, culture was not applied to the organizational context to explain administrative or policy-making behavior. Part of the problem is that culture was often treated as a constant. The question then became how to replace culture with attitudes and behavior consistent with what would be needed for local use in modern Western administrative systems. Under these conditions, the gap between expected political cultural practices and resultant democratic administration remained substantial.

For a time the radical presumption that a dominant Western capitalist culture was the real determinant of political behavior injected new life into the concept of political culture. For example, it was held that Latin American culture was not actually composed of isolated and self-sufficient feudal latifundios. Rather, it was the product of capitalist exploitation in service of monopolistic colonialist structures that left the region underdeveloped (Frank 1969, 239). Neo-colonial institutions such as multinational firms (through investments) and multilateral donors like the World Bank (through adjustment programs) continue to dominate the local culture, removing capital and perpetuating backward behavior in the region.

The major insight of this criticism of political culture was that although it presumed an evolution from backward less-developed country (LDC) cultures to Western modernity, in fact stagnation or revolution could occur. But despite such titillating insights, failure to find viable and growing societies under alternative noncapitalist cultures in the 1960s and 1970s, and the fact that radical findings merely confirmed traditional functionalist conclusions (such as Huntington 1968) led to an intellectual dead end for the radical comparative approach to political culture. Internal collapse of the model radical culture (the Soviet Union) and conceptual failure to explain the growth of selected countries (e.g., Chile) despite culture (the authoritarian paternalism of a statist culture) led to its demise in more establishment CPA studies.

Despite these conceptual problems, the rise of viable and growing capitalist economies and societies beyond the West, particularly in Asia, breathed new life into the concept of political culture in the 1980s. Studies began to treat political culture as a variable rather than a constant. The study of political culture became based on the notion that "autonomous and reasonably enduring cross-cultural differences exist and that they have important political consequences." For example, Inglehart (1988, 1205) hypothesized that high levels of political satisfaction, life satisfaction, interpersonal trust, and support for the existing social order would be associated with adoption and maintenance of democratic institutions. In this period, Wildavsky (1986, chap. 11) superimposed political culture as a motivating force for budgetary change. Classification of political cultures into collectivism egalitarian, individualist, and fatalist allowed description of regime types and explanation of budgetary behaviors, for example, proclivities toward balancing budgets varied with culture (Caiden 1994, 53).

But the rise of non-democratic high achievers and the fall of communist political systems forced the cultural question to the fore. How could institutional incentives be designed to maximize particular cultural practices to achieve the universal values of service efficiency and program effectiveness? In East Asia, it may be recalled, Max Weber once held Confucianism to be an obstacle to economic development because of its substitution of tradition (local custom and personal favor of officials) for rational law.

The East Asian region began to grow rapidly, leaving the many cultural obstacles noted by legions of scholars to be explained away. The critical question for CPA was: how did the cultural obstacles suddenly become opportunities? The immediate answer was that culture was an adaptable variable rather than a constant. In contrast with "racist theories that imply culture is inborn and static," according to Harrison (1985, 166), "it is transmitted and received." For instance, the new orthodoxy is that Confucian respect for authority, family loyalty, and commitment to practical education contributes in various ways to the self-confidence and social cohesion that is currently producing the economic miracle (*Economist* 1995a, 39).

The need to define political culture and explain its administrative influence has gained new urgency with the realization that practices in Eastern Europe and the former Soviet Union are ingrained in values and attitudes. Official ways of seeing the world have been driven by the momentum of almost a century. It has been suggested that similar world views described as "antiwork," "antientrepreneurial," and "antidemocratic" impeded the progress of political pluralism and human development in Latin America (Harrison 1985, 165).

Both Latin America and Eastern Europe have been described as "statist cultures" (Veliz 1980; Wynia 1984). In Latin America, elements of this top-down, control-obsessed culture translate into attempted precontrol of public expenditures. But each clearance step creates more opportunities for corruption and the control system delays payments and projects that increase the general level of inefficiency. Based on a small sample and one type of administrative behavior (payments approvals), it was concluded that operational cultures can be changed by paradoxically centralizing certain transactions (payments distribution) in exchange for grants of wider authority to line managers. Ministries gained accountability for program results with funds allocated in broader line items (Guess 1992).

In the former Soviet Union, the cultural legacy was "negative egalitarianism"— disposition to prevent rather than emulate a neighbor's success. "The huge socialist-communist bureaucracy was parasitic, corrupt, and unable to generate any serious institutional innovation after Stalin's death" (Gleason 1992, 32). The same governmental cultures pervades Eastern Europe. Tall organizations controlled sectors of the economy through a rigid command structure. Civil service positions were not well defined and power was derived from personal ties to the party *nomenklatura* and seniority. The rigid rules that inhibited professionalism were subverted by vertical patronage and political pull (World Bank 1993b, 26). Thus the same kinds of cultural forces work against public management and effective expenditure controls in both Eastern Europe and Latin America (Guess 1997). Despite these cultural constraints, it is believed that similar kinds of culturally consistent changes at the margin can change operating behavior and reduce the inhibiting effects of past culture in Eastern Europe as well (Nolan 1997).

The need for an institutional basis for sustainable development had long been recognized. The key is to design local institutions to correspond with likely democratic outcomes rather than around features that will exacerbate conflict. Public sector management and public budgeting assistance programs from the World Bank and IMF are based on this premise. What may not have been recognized is the need for institutional rules of the game that optimize those features of local culture that lead toward stability and democracy. Note that we have come full circle and now recognize some cultural features as constants.

In Uganda, for example, it has been argued that despite cultural consistency, multiparty democracy has had only a superficial relationship to democracy. This is because it was linked to tribe and not class. Multiple parties based on tribe served only ethnic manipulation and led to polarization rather than tolerance and democratic consensus. Conversely, basing multiple parties on class served to cut across ethnic divisions. Berkeley (1994, 24) asked the comparative question of which similarities existed in postcolonial African nations that explain political deterioration into chaos and violence. The major difference for those countries that did not deteriorate was resiliency of administrative and political institutions. An important feature of this strength was political parties that were not aligned with ethnic and sectarian interests and with regimes that represented those interests. That is, the multiple parties were organized horizontally on class and not vertically by tribe (Berkeley 1994, 28).

Similarly, it is well known that African administrative systems were designed functionally to serve the political domination and economic exploitation objectives of colonialists. Newly independent countries inherited these structures and now faced the task of reforming institutions that have been stratified along racial lines and centralized to maintain control from the capital cities. In a comparative study of administrative reform efforts in Tanzania, Kenya, and Zambia, Mutahaba (1989) also assesses the applicability of administrative reform traditions of the United States, Great Britain, France, and Russia to postcolonial Africa. Russia and France are noted for application of scientific management principles. While the British cultural and historical tradition seeks protection of what has already been attained through order and security, the US reform legacy is continuous innovation and managerial invention. The US culture is viewed as the product of exciting adventures based on attempts to survive in the elements. However, such elements do not include the modern government office. Based on his work, it appears that most African countries have followed the US path. But it is clear that the most successful reformers (e.g., Botswana) have followed the British tradition.

The debate about culture was revitalized after the 1998 Asian crisis. As if overnight, Asian values were seen as impediments of innovation and growth, and not the holistic engine of the Asian (mostly Japanese) competitiveness machine. Or, they have been treated as useful in the past, but possibly not as very adequate in the era of globalization (Pye 2000). Research has tackled the links between culture and democracy (Inglehart 2000) and culture and economic development (Porter 2000; Sachs 2000). The leading narrative has been the malleability of culture. In the words of Moynihan, "the central conservative truth is that it is culture, not politics, that determines the success of a society. The central liberal truth is that politics can change a culture and save it from itself" (as quoted in Huntington 2000, xiv).

As opposed to organizational study research that focused how work-related values impact organizations and wealth creation (e.g., Hofstede 1980, 1991; Hampden-Turner and Trompenaars 1994), public administration scholars often focused on malleability of culture. Weiss (1993) has shown how the Japanese corporate employment system, interpreted in the West as the product of centuries-old Japanese culture, has been actively formed by the militarist Japanese state in the first half of the twentieth century, while Li and Karakowski (2002) have argued that government had an indelible impact on business strategy formation and entrepreneurship in Singapore.

D. CIVIL SERVICE REFORM AND PERSONNEL ADMINISTRATION

Nearly all of the major new CPA works represent efforts that build on and actively strengthen the functionalist framework. The World Bank has taken very seriously the comparative study of public sector reforms in basic areas such as public expenditure management and civil service reform. An important finding with intended implications for Russia was that successful reforms in thirteen countries used contractualism (transparent quid pro quos), managed expectations to ensure that traction took place, built on existing institutions, paid attention to the formalistic quality of local political cultures, and took advantage of idiosyncratic developments as they occurred (Manning and Parison 2004). This approach is in contrast to the rigidly scripted and overly ambitious approach that one finds in many reform programs today financed by international donors.

In personnel administration, for instance, a host of comparative studies based on administrative field research have been produced by such international organizations as the World Bank. Caiden (1994, 124) noted critically that though most of the civil service reform ideas—such as downsizing the public sector, privatization, and debureaurcratization—are American in origin, very few of them have been applied in the United States. He suggested that in spite of being tied to outdated theories and antiquated institutions, at least in intent with the Clinton–Gore Commission, the United States has finally joined the global administrative reform movement. But regardless of label, the problems boil down to design and performance of administrative functions. Thus at the core, for good reason, the guiding theory remained functionalist. Most practitioners recognized that for comprehensive public sector reform, analysis should begin with structures of missions, goals, operational methods, and management incentives. Structures are: interlocking sets of systems, roles and responsibilities with authority to perform a function (Shahid and Perry 1998). To reform functions, or the activities which combine to achieve organizational objectives without attention to structural constraints, risks making irrelevant systems efficient. An example would be building e-government portals from existing organizational structures and civil service job descriptions rather than to serve user needs. Reviews of international civil service performance have concentrated on both structures and functions. In Africa, for example, public sector employment has long outstripped revenue growth and productivity (World Bank 1989, 59).

The reaction to this at the World Bank was a logical two-step approach to problem solving. First generation World Bank studies of personnel issues defined problems and offered empirical assessments. Second generation analyses now offer comparative prescriptions and evaluations of many civil service reform programs in the region (Lindauer and Nunberg 1994, 5). For example, deMerode and Thomas (1994, 160) compare the impact of personnel system reforms in Ghana, Gambia, and Guinea on employment reduction, rationalization of compensation, fiscal benefits, and improvements in government performance. Based on experience in Tanzania and other African countries, Stevens (1994, 103) offers a set of instructions on how to conduct pay and employment analyses.[*] Comparative studies of reforms, such as job reviews, are beginning to emerge from private firms which raise major questions about their relationship to public sector job commitment and performance. Some have suggested that occasional conversations unrelated to pay or promotion may be superior to formal performance evaluations (Mathews 1994). Lindauer and Nunberg (1994, 238) review political reactions to civil service reform experiences and conclude that "deeper reforms may be less politically costly than thus far has been assumed."[†]

A similar comparative approach has been taken to civil service reform issues in Latin America (Chaudhry and Reid 1993). For example, in this set of conference papers, Kitchen (1993) reported compensation upgrading practices in the Caribbean civil service. Other papers are based on similar field experiences. Measurement of government functional performance is critical to civil service reform. Based on reviews of agency functional performance and staffing patterns, many studies point to overstaffing, which should be treated with pay decompression and downsizing to bring

---

[*] It should be noted that Stevens and others in the Operations Policy Department of the World Bank have been conducting comparative reviews and analyses of public management and public expenditure systems around the globe since the early 1980s (see World Bank 1994).

[†] Unfortunately, the January 1995 takeover of the El Salvadorian congress and seizure of hostages by soldiers caught in budget cutbacks as *desmovilizados* suggests that such propositions do not extend beyond the civil service into the military (*La Prensa 1995*). This gives support to those who argue that in many ways downsizing programs hit the weakest parts of the government and that most of the secure, high-paid jobs are untouched by reforms.

productivity gains (World Bank 1993a). As enthusiasm for downsizing and governmental reinvention continues, sensible administrative reform decisions will require information on the comparative cost implications of employee buyout and severance packages. Many studies on personnel reduction strategies in multiple jurisdictions with multiple techniques are now being performed (e.g., Congressional Budget Office (CBO) 1993).

Comparative study of civil services across nations also strived for clear methodological principles. In a most systematic effort of comparative study of civil service (though in a limited number of developed countries), Bekke, Perry, and Toonen (1996) identify three levels in their comparative analysis of civil service systems: (1) operational level: civil service as personnel system; (2) collective choice level: civil service as governance institution; and (3) constitutional choice level: civil service as symbol systems. Wise et al. (1996), comparing the capacities of national administrative organizations of the United States and Sweden, identify three analytical dimensions for research: (1) the public interest dimension; (2) the economic dimension; and (3) the management dimension. Such an approach is also being employed by major players in the donor community. A World Bank Discussion paper on civil service reform in Gambia (Pinto 1994, 14) "vertically segments the environment into the following three analytical levels, from the top down: (1) political-structural level (organization of the state); (2) administrative systems level (public bureaucracy); and (3) technical level (service delivery and core economic functions)."

The World Bank has recently started to compile and codify its efforts in the field, and under the title of Administrative and Civil Service Reform (part of broader Governance and Public Sector Reform), covering both country experiences and regional summaries of topics ranging from personnel and budget issues to the design and practice of reform itself (World Bank 2004). Both for the World Bank and OECD PUMA program, electronic publication of best practices and major trends has been an important feature of such efforts. Of the latter, the SIGMA program, aimed at support for governance and institutional reform (with civil service as its core) in Eastern and Central Europe, has been of particular interest in its effort of systematic description of both civil service and central government organization (OECD 2004).

E. Public Budgeting and Financing Management

Building on the earlier comparative frameworks of Caiden and Wildavsky (1975) and Wildavsky (1986) there has been a substantial outpouring of comparative field studies covering all phases of the budget process. Schick (1988), for example, conducted a major comparative study of budgetary behavior under fiscal stress in OECD countries. As indicated above, reformers are still uncertain as to the best methods of cutting back resources. One opinion holds that despite lack of academic respectability, simply delegating across-the-board ceilings to department heads may be the best as well as the most used method (Pearlstein 1995). But Schick's answer explores the use of newer techniques, such as packaging politically sensitive cutbacks (entitlements), as opposed to the old tricks of personnel freezes, delayed filling of vacancies, and lowering adjustments for inflation by removing some prices from the indexation formula. Perhaps the major current problem in most OECD countries is that of fixed expenditures that crowd out new initiatives. Only 36% of fiscal year 1995 US expenditures are actually discretionary. In a common pattern for advanced countries, medicare and social security entitlements are expected to absorb 35% of the budget by 2000 (Classman 1994). Schick (1988, 527) reviews responses to the fixed cost problem, such as Japan's scrap and build rules that allow new programs to be financed out of savings from curtailed programs, and Australia's allocations to broad running cost categories with loosened expenditure controls and devolved authority to line managers. He also explores how budget systems adapt as spending priorities are changed during preparation, analyzed for identification of efficient alternatives, and monitored during the year in comparative perspective. In the new CPA period, field studies have also been conducted on the effects of rigid and flexible financial controls over budget releases in Latin America (Guess 1992).

Perhaps because of the ease of quantification and its role as the central incentive system of government, the varying subtopics of public budgeting have been the subject of most of the new CPA studies. Premchand has been perhaps the most thorough in compiling facts on systems and methods of budgeting in most of the transitional and developed countries of the world. Such major process issues as coverage and classification of expenditures, expenditure planning and forecasting, inflation budgeting, short-term adjustments in public expenditures, and the effects of budget reform have been reviewed in comparative perspective by Premchand and the Fiscal Affairs Department of the IMF for the last 25 years.

A good deal of effort has gone into the subject of budget execution, in particular the release of funds and reporting and accounting systems. For example, Premchand (1983, 358) compared the impacts of fund release systems in Commonwealth, Latin American, and US budget systems on overall expenditure control and agency management incentives. A later work (Premchand 1990) offers ten country studies revealing the major government financial management problems of expenditure planning, budget structures, implementation, and accounting and reporting. Premchand's latest work (1993) is a synthesis of the comparative public expenditure management knowledge needed for reconstruction of systems in the former Soviet Union and Eastern Europe, and reform of existing systems elsewhere.

To a large extent, the World Bank and the IMF have divided their technical assistance work and comparative studies between the budget formulation and execution states, respectively. Thus the IMF has emphasized monitoring and reporting of execution and proper accounting for payments. In a more recent review of the strengths and weaknesses of budgeting and accounting under central planning versus market systems, Premchand and Garamfalvi (1992, 280) found major strengths in the existing system. For example, planners relied more on statistical data (such as budget norms) than accounting data for policy making and monitoring. The payments process was also abridged by assigning banks to each spending agency, which reduced red tape and verification steps required in other systems. They found, however, that budgetary control under central planning was virtually nonexistent: budgets financed plans, but because plans were political, intense bargaining and negotiation was the real process of allocation (confirming Lewis' (1952) assertion that socialist planners had no method to allocate expenditures for program A versus program B either). Central planning also relied heavily on extrabudgetary funds (as in Latin America) which inhibited policy planning and weakened implementation controls even further.

No review of comparative public finances would be complete without noting the work done on fiscal deficits. A large literature comparing the economic effects of fiscal deficits in particular countries began in the early 1980s (Guess and Koford 1984). In the political realm, the belief grew that deficit reduction was no longer a means to the end of policy stability, but an end in itself. Many believe that budgets should be balanced regardless of resultant institutional rigidities that will likely inhibit economic expansion and service delivery (Harris and Chandler 1995). This belief was the basis for the EU Stability Pact that limits EU members to deficits no larger than 3% of GDP. One practical problem with most legal and constitutional proposals for deficit reduction focuses on discretionary expenditures, but it is the mandatory expenditures (mainly social entitlements and debt service costs) and politically uncontrollable defense items that have grown in most countries. As debt service payments eat up substantial amounts of discretionary expenditures in most countries, the question arises of how to force governments to deal with them. Given the political risks of cutting popular programs and raising taxes, how should democracies respond?

The GAO (1994) reviewed the effectiveness of external credit markets and legal and constitutional requirements in reducing deficits in Australia, Germany, Japan, Mexico, and the United Kingdom. The major means of deficit reduction were expenditure control (reducing social benefits, delayed indexing, cost-shifting to lower levels of government, reduction of public sector employment, privatization of functions) and revenue increases (primarily through economic growth and inflation) (GAO 1994, 7). The administrative question is, how can governments manage services and implement policies under the tight legal and constitutional constraints devised to serve the political obsession with balance? What kinds of cutback systems function most effectively where top-down conditions have been imposed by ministries of finance? How do legal and constitutional constraints result in reduced entitlement outlays that are the primary cause of the most fiscal deficits? These are areas of needed future research in comparative fiscal administration.

F.   INTERGOVERNMENTAL RELATIONS AND LOCAL GOVERNMENT

Comparative public administration studies have long focused on intergovernmental relations. Three perennial issues have been (1) the design of intergovernmental administrative systems and allocation of decision-making authority between levels of government, (2) the degree of decentralization of management authority within government levels, and (3) the comparative performance of units at each level of government, such as the propositions explaining local government performance differences. It should be noted first that the (IGR) area is replete with labels that create confusion. There is considerable terminological debate over core terms of decentralization: principal-agent, delegation, devolution, and deconcentration.

For example, in a recent paper, Hofman (1994, 2) uses "delegation" for shifts of functions and accountability from central agencies to subnational units. By contrast, Mutahaba (1989, 70) calls this "deconcentration." Hofman (1994) uses "devolution" to describe the shift of authority beyond central government chain of command to other levels of government subject to national guidelines. This is consistent to other levels of government subject to national guidelines. This is consistent with Mutahaba's use of that term (1989, 70). The problem is that, "The distinction between the types of decentralization is not always clear, and many countries operate with hybrid forms, that may differ from function to function. In the dual leadership of China or the Russian federation, in which subnational functional ministries and bureaus are subordinated to both subnational government and central agencies, there is an amalgam of de-concentration and devolution" (Hofman 1994, 3).

Thus, the terms are often used interchangeably, with hair-splitting, nearly content-free distinctions that add to the confusion. For example, "devolution" is both the means or *process* by which the central government decentralizes authority, and also the most complete degree or *stage* in which autonomous local governments are empowered to raise revenues and operate services under broad national guidelines (World Bank 1994, 42). In Nicaragua, transfer of functions out of ministries by contracting out is considered "delegation" (Coopers 1994, viii). But if localities are empowered to regulate service delivery contracts, how should we distinguish between devolution and delegation? In addition, how can devolution be both a dynamic process and a static stage? One solution is to use delegation for shifts of authority within unitary systems, while reserving devolution for real transfer of functions to other units of government (e.g., creation of a federal system). There seems to be more consensus on devolution than delegation or deconcentration. The brief review of these terms leads back to the obvious question: What empirical value for policy design and implementation is there in the distinction between four types of decentralization? It is evident that here the work of classical CPA was left undone. The new CPA should attempt to forge conceptual consensus on the types of decentralization and the conditions for their success.

Field work in the comparative IGR area is still subject to large doses of democratic ideology and the classical CPA premises of local cultural uniqueness. In Nepal, for instance, good politics is equated with bottom-up, locally initiated projects, separately funded and managed from the traditional line agencies of the central government. A major goal in Nepal is to move away from the Panchayat system of the highly centralized and corrupt Rana feudal order (Nepal National Planning Commission 1992, 2). But few comparative studies have been conducted from which design lessons can be drawn. For example, the process of Brazilian decentralization resulted in massive state and local borrowing and substantial additions to the national fiscal deficit. The resulting inflation has harmed national development efforts. Thus, conditions exist under which decentralization will attain some goals at the expense of others. There may well be a set of stages through which tight fiscal controls at the center can be traded off for expansion of authority by local units to achieve maximum gains for a national decentralization strategy. To provide tested lessons for Nepal and other countries on how to decentralize, further research is needed in this area.

1. Devolution of Functions to Lower Levels of Government and to Private Firms

This first area of comparative IGR studies is of continued and growing importance because political transformations particularly in Latin America and Eastern Europe have forced reappraisals of the governmental balance of power in many countries. Note that the most common IGR questions derive from an implicit functionalist perspective: What administrative functions should be transferred from the central government? Which revenue-raising functions should be devolved to local and regional units? Which functions and state enterprises should be privatized? If there are existing regional units, should their boundaries be changed to be consistent with older units of greater historical and religious significance?

Thus, in a deeper sense, intergovernmental issues reflected underlying tensions between diversity and uniformity, between fragmentation of authority, fiscal imbalances, and overcentralization of authority at the center. In Eastern Europe, previous assignments of fiscal functions and power-sharing arrangements between different levels of government are no longer viable nor desirable (Hewitt 1992, 330). This widespread opinion has forced basic new CPA-type practical questions to the fore, such as, What is the optimal basis for allocating fiscal transfers from the central government to local units? This question has been given comparative treatment in such diverse countries as Poland (Guess et al. 1992) and Nicaragua (Guess and Garzon 1994).

Further, how could local units finance mandates and standards imposed from the center? In this context, Martinez-Vazquez (1993) has examined expenditure and revenue assignment as well as alternative financing options for local governments in Bulgaria. How can the center control excessive debt financing by local units and its accompanying corruption? Wallich (1994) has examined the subnational expenditure control issue in Brazil and Russia. These are all issues of institutional economics and administration. But at the core they are also questions of elite tolerance for redistribution of political power. They are of substantial economic and political importance for impatient populations demanding greater accountability for service delivery and political decisions that affect their lives.

As the economies of the former Soviet Union and Eastern Europe began to collapse in the late 1980s, structural reforms and functional transfers were made under pressure of budgetary scarcity rather than for policy reasons. As noted by Martinez-Vazquez and Wallace (1997, 8), none of the former Soviet and Eastern European countries has taken the time to study which level of government should be responsible for which public goods. Thus major Russian decisions on the vertical structure of government, expenditure and revenue assignment, budgeting systems, and intergovernmental transfers have been made without guidance from comparative studies. Fortunately, recent intergovernmental studies have integrated comparative dimensions. For example, in her discussion of options for fiscal decentralization in Russia, Wallich (1994, 68–69) set off the comparative experiences of Germany, Argentina, Brazil, and China. This revealed the costs in macroeconomic destabilization of intergovernmental arrangements giving subnational governments unfettered borrowing rights, and suggested the need for central government retention of control over major taxes and borrowing instruments.

Other recent studies indicated the growing importance of providing comparative lessons for intergovernmental functional design (Davey 2002). For instance, it was found that expenditure and revenue assignment practices in Brazil have major implications for vertical and horizontal fiscal imbalances. To assess the implications of intergovernmental structures, Shah (1991) compared similar fiscal federalism practices in Australia, Germany, Canada, Mexico, and the United States with Brazil on a range of indicators such as local government responsibilities and local government influence on state policy. Other comparative studies have focused on one level of government. For example, Bahl and Linn (1992) conducted an exhaustive comparative study of urban public finances, including a review of principles and practices of intergovernmental transfers and urban fees/taxes around the world.

As efforts to reduce fiscal deficits by streamlining governments and off-loading functions continued, attention has been focused on privatization of functions and sale of city and state enterprises. Comparative studies in this area are growing. For example, Behr (1995) compared the responses of Washington, DC, and Philadelphia to fiscal crisis. Since 1992, the City of Philadelphia has responded to fiscal crisis by moving twenty-six separate city services to private contractors at an annual savings of $25 million. In contrast, in 1993, Washington adopted one of the most stringent laws on privatization to protect city workers. As will be noted below in the cases of Argentina and Nicaragua, US municipal actions have been no different from contrasting international responses to privatization.

Definitions and classifications of privatization in literature vary based on their rationale or underlying theory. Vickers and Wright (1989), for example, write, "there are many ways of categorizing the various dimensions of privatisation—by intent, by impact, by sector." Jurgen Kuhl (1997) 140) distinguishes three basic forms of privatization according to their "political" logic. The first is *political privatization*, where all citizens are provided with shares or vouchers regardless of their economic viability, capital stock and management. Second, there is *fiscal privatization*, where firms are sold to the highest bidder as a means of increasing public revenues. The last is *economic privatization*, where government restructures the enterprise and negotiates some further agreements. Comparative privatization research thus far has mostly concentrated on different factors that affect privatization decisions in different countries, such as labor market flexibility, accountability, potential windfall profit to the government, or moral and political doctrines (Fuller 1994).

Among the issues examined in privatization research are the political economy of privatization (political and economic causes of privatization), performance issues (public vs. private ownership and performance), problems and prospects of different privatization strategies (e.g., competitive tendering, sale of assets, deregulation) (e.g., Clarke and Pitelis 1993; Clarke 1994; Kwan 1990; Gayle and Goodrich 1990), privatization–nationalization cycles (Hirschman 1982; Siegmund 1997). Zahariadis (1995), in his study of industrial privatization in Britain and France, convincingly shows that most rational choice approaches (public choice, property rights, industry structure) have more a normative appeal rather than an empirical record. Drawing from Cohen et al.'s (1972) garbage can model of decision making and Kingdon's (1984) model of agenda forming, Zahariadis develops a multiple streams model of privatization. In brief, the argument is the following: "privatization is brought about by coupling three factors in critical moments in time: available alternatives generated in policy communities; high government borrowing needs; and the ideology and strategy of governing parties" (Zahariadis 1995, 36). Available alternatives are selected according to two criteria, technical feasibility and value acceptability, while ideology is operationalized as party identification with nationalization. Privatization outcomes depend on coupling these three streams in critical moments called policy windows (Zahariadis 1995, 43). This happens because there is a lack of goal clarity. "The model assumes a situation of problematic preferences where policymakers often do not know what they want" (Zahariadis 1995, 43). What results is a "policy in search of a rationale" (Kay and Thompson 1986).

Employing discursive analysis, Gabrielyan (1998) explores the choice of privatization methods in different countries. The argument is that despite some common objectives (most notably, the desire to increase efficiency), privatization strategies in the UK, United States and Russia take different forms. These strategies are shaped by different factors and reflect the predominant discourse in which the debate on privatization in each country is framed. Particularly, in the United States outsourcing is the most common form of privatization because it is most appropriate for managing the government in an ideologically stable (the debate about the size and functions of the government is mostly stale), politically fragmented, and incremental system. In such a situation, privatization is not a tool for systemic change, but rather a means for optimizing limited government.

Britain under Margaret Thatcher embarked on a large-scale privatization program to reverse "the corrosive and corrupting effects of socialism" (Thatcher 1993, 676). Fixed-price flotation of the shares of public enterprises with provisions for wider share ownership emerged as the main form of privatization because among many goals of privatization, it emphasized wider share ownership as the tool for reshaping the society into popular capitalism. The problem was not confined to dealing with particular inefficient industries and enterprises any more, but had the aim of changing the societal system as a whole.

In Russia, privatization was an essential part of revolutionary transition from socialism, and was heavily influenced by ideological considerations. The revolutionary task of destroying the basis of economic and political power of Communism—an ideology that the reformers blamed for crippling their country—has had a determining influence on the choice of privatization mechanisms. Initially, for various economic reasons, the reformers were opposed to the ideas of both voucher privatization and employee buy-outs as the main form of privatization. But it turned out that exactly this combination emerged as the main form of privatization in Russia. Such a development of events was determined by the fact that, while important, these objections were not central for the overarching political purpose of privatization—deriding the Soviet-type ministries of their power, and as secondary details could be accommodated as a part of political compromise concluded with the parliament.

New CPA studies have focused on three questions vital to public sector cost savings and service efficiency. These provide empirical policy lessons for governments that would take politically risky privatization decisions. First, efforts have been made to narrow the definition of the role and scope of the state-owned sector. Governments must make two sets of initial choices here: (1) classification of firm economic viability and political essentiality, and (2) action to retain or divest the firms (Shirley and Nellis 1991, 19). Are the enterprises strategically essential? If retention is desired, how can we improve performance? Comparative studies of French and Senegalese performance contracts concluded that the quantification of performance targets is actually less important than the process of preparation and negotiation (Shirley and Nellis 1991, 23).

Latin American countries have traditionally held SOEs, such as telecommunications, off limits and deemed them strategically essential for national sovereignty. But a host of successful privatizations have created new precedents for innovative policy decisions. The successful Argentine privatization of ENTel was marred only by the failure to set up a viable regulatory regime before (Hill and Abdala 1993). The recent decision of the Honduran president to propose privatization of HONDUTEL was based largely on comparative economic successes and the absence of major labor responses in the region. The refusal of the Nicaraguan congress to vote for privatization of TELCOR indicates the romantic but costly hold of ancient notions of political sovereignty (La Tribuna 1994).

Second, new CPA studies tackled the question of designing control mechanisms for SOE monopoly power without stifling managerial initiative and accountability. As is well known, poor country and transitional society governments typically intervene in pricing and operational decisions of electricity, water, and transportation SOEs at the expense of efficiency. Central government ministries of finance often resent SOE autonomy (and higher pay scales) and their repeated failure to provide timely, transparent, and accurate fiscal data. Central governments consistently provide subsidies, transfers, and loan guarantees to SOEs, but remain unclear about their use. This pushes central governments to demand a lot of reports and to review the line-item details of SOE budgets. As could be expected, SOE managers resent intrusions from political figures. Some of the debt service costs of loss-making SOEs that must be paid out of future budgets may have been foisted on them by politics at the center. Comparative research indicates that where central governments provide incentives in the form of greater autonomy for greater competitiveness, certain kinds of SOE performance improves. This gets around the common oversight problem that sectoral ministries and SOE ministries usually lack a detailed understanding of their sectors (Shirley and Nellis 1991, 32).

Third, the major practical question is: What sequence should be followed in privatization? As noted, the simplicities of outright sale make good press, but can be the worst of both cost savings and efficiency worlds. New CPA research comparing privatizations in Poland and Hungary with the Czech Republic indicated that a major error was selling intact without breaking state firms up or creating mechanisms to regulate their prices (*Economist* 1995, 61). The successful Poles and Hungarians reorganized SOEs first, then privatized. The Poles also slashed direct state subsidies and forced banks to accept solvency standards. This prevented the kind of hyperinflation that hit Russia during its privatization program. Similarly, the British have learned that an early sale of Railtrack (the operator of British Rail's former tracks and stations) could be a mistake. Comparative public administration privatization research nicely confirmed the effect of governmental structures on the creation of risk aversion by employees (Wilson 1994, 672). It was found that British Rail's top-down, engineering-led management structure was too centralized. The practical lesson was that to empower both employees and customers, Railtrack should first be restructured by devolving authority to move line managers closer to customers. This move brought a better sales price to the treasury (Economist 1995b, 61).

In some cases, after dismal performance of privatized enterprises, some commentators also raised questions of post-privatization policies. Often, to ensure efficiency and better service delivery, a relevant framework for market regulation should be put in place. In the UK, for instance, during the most active phase of Thatcher privatizations, 1983–1987, ten new regulatory agencies were created to monitor and regulate newly privatized companies, or industries (because in many cases these companies lost their monopolistic position in the market).

The same kind of applied comparative analysis is also occurring at the level of municipal enterprises. For example, Aziewicz (1994) interviewed 818 municipal enterprises in the Polish public utility sector. The research was designed to provide basic data on their financial condition to determine their potential for sale. The utility enterprises consisted of public transport, water and sewerage, housing maintenance, road maintenance, parks and garden services, heat, and sanitation refuse. Moving to the explanatory stage, the Gdansk Institute of Market Economics, which performed this study, is readying an impact analysis of successes and failures in Polish municipal privatization.

For privatization, the practical question also arises of how to administer the auction of state shares. Comparative knowledge is also accumulating here. In the command economies of Eastern Europe, for example, the reform of SOEs represents the fundamental transformation of the entire society (Shirley and Nellis 1991, 72). Under these conditions, a poorly designed administrative program could create massive political backlash. In Russia, the problem was that privatization certificates were traded for vodka and other commodities rather than invested. In Russia and Romania, pyramid schemes allowed criminals and bureaucrats to rob investors. Based on these experiences, Poland and Ukraine are tightly regulating their investment fund managers. About 75% of Ukraine's industrial sector (telecommunications and energy not included) is up for auction, and they are attempting to avoid the well-recognized mistakes of other regional privatizers (Rupert 1995).

2. Decentralization of Managerial Authority

The second area of IGR studies focused on comparative practices of decentralizing authority to managers within levels of government. One important issue here has been how to push authority downward within local government units to improve service delivery? This has been a difficult maneuver where management skills are scarce and corruption already exists from weak internal and external expenditure controls. A substantial body of empirical knowledge has been developed on local government management practices in Central and Eastern Europe. Cases and training materials financed by such donors as the Open Society Institute (Local Government and Public Services Reform Initiative), World Bank, and USAID have been developed and tested over the past fifteen years (Wright and Nemc 2002). This has led to the transfer of applied lessons within LGUs and between them on a national and international basis. Thus, the question of how to decentralize management authority also raises larger questions for budgeting and management. As noted, it has long been presumed that decentralization and bottom-up management is good or the correct way to move for the creation of democratic management.

Comparative findings suggested that the means to this end may require differing mixes of authority and control. Australia introduced its "forward estimate" system (Keating and Rosalky 1990) that combines centralized budget formulation, control of expenditures, and payments by the MOF with vastly increased departmental managerial discretion for broad line items necessary to run the ministry. Line managers also receive multiyear budget authority and are evaluated on their ability to combine resources for program results over this period.

The experiences of Australia and Malawi have indicated that simply increasing discretion leads to major control problems. Where internal controls have not been installed and the MOF does not control ministry bids, the result is the usual exaggeration of needs during formulation combined with overexpenditure during execution. The result is poor management and increased national fiscal deficits as the treasury picks up the tab for local overruns. In practice, the issue is often when to decentralize the authority for budget payments as well as the physical issuance of checks. Many Eastern European and former Soviet republics fear the decentralized payments model because it could result in more corruption and fiscal hemorrhaging. Similarly, the top-down financial control perspective of Latin America (Bird 1982; Reid 1994), which stresses centralized payments authority, works against diffusion of increased professional responsibility in the line ministries and local governments. Emphasis is on the rigid legal control of details (control previo), which causes the very control and extrabudgetary problems such systems were designed to prevent.

But the evolutionary experience of the Australian model should be applicable to most transitional and developing countries because it translates into controls first, discretion later. By shifting incentives through mixes of centralized and decentralized obligations and controls, the budget becomes a tool to encourage managing for results. This is the ultimate goal for decentralized management because this leads to greater accountability and the democratic results sought by decentralizers. To date, not many comparative studies of incentive strategies have been conducted. Isolating the most effective incentives to encourage fiscal and program management under varying organizational structures is a critical area for further CPA research.

3. Comparative Performance

The third area of IGR work focused on comparative unit performance. Wilson (1994) is quite correct in his assertion that there have been few explanations of performance differences between public agencies and programs. Despite increasing complaints about performance, scholars have not explained why one agency works better than others (Wilson 1994, 671). Earlier works had in fact focused on comparative urban government performance (Fried 1975). Journalistic accounts have explained the failure of US cities to utilize excellent comparative data for designing personnel redundancy and downsizing programs as a function of institutional price and arrogance. Part of the problem with earlier international studies lay in the tension between ideological presumptions for and against Western culture and notions of modernity. That is, hyper-criticism of Western notions of equity and efficiency and excessive fascination with non-Western, often obscurantist, concepts and theories impeded analysis and development of applied comparative lessons. The same problems impeded US studies, for example, in the debate over the performance of administrative strategies to achieve tribal capitalism in the context of cultural features which encouraged maintenance of the centrally planned poverty found on many Indian reservations (Cohen 1989, 36).

Fortunately, newer CPA studies have defined units and functions designated for comparison and have provided clear empirical lessons for policy and management. In the United States, applied comparative research on performance management at the state and local level has been commonplace for nearly a century. Perry and Babitsky (1986) compared the ownership–management structures of 246 transit agencies in 1980 and 1981 using a series of performance indicators such as labor efficiency, revenue generation, and service consumption. In a study replete with implications for international privatization programs, they compared the performance results of (1) general government ownership, public management; (2) special authority ownership, public management; (3) general government ownership, contract management; (4) special authority ownership, contract management; and (5) private ownership, private management (Perry and Babitsky 1986, 59). They found that privately owned and operated systems were more productive because public systems had to perform a variety of social roles in addition to transit service delivery (Perry and Babitsky 1986, 63). The important point for CPA studies, however, is that methods have become far more sophisticated since the days of phenomenological analysis of prismatic public organizations to determine their existential and cultural properties.

G. NEW CPA PROBLEMS AND OPPORTUNITIES

Two trends in government have been particularly notable over the last fifteen years: (1) efforts to enhance service and program effectiveness in the face of budgetary cutbacks at all levels of government in most countries, and (2) efforts to improve both data quality and transmission efficiency within and between public sector organizations for management and financial information.

H. FROM REORGANIZATION TO GOVERNMENT REINVENTION

Following a decade of criticism of big government in the United States, articles and books on government reinvention began appearing in the early 1990s. Writings of members of the Reinvention Government Network (RON) and Public Strategies Group (PSG) such as Osborne and Gaebler (1992) translated into the what was called the postbureaucratic paradigm. The National Performance Review (NPR) of the Clinton administration seeks to reinvent much of the US government consistent with RON and PSG principles. By the normative postbureaucratic perspective, public organizations should be redesigned to serve customers, empower employees, face competition, produce results, and replace hierarchy with teamwork (Barzelay 1992; Osborne and Gaebler 1992). It should be noted that plans for flattening hierarchies and devolving authority to line managers, opening government to competition via contracting-out services and increasing accountability, and reforming public expenditure management by results measures and program evaluation are all essentially functionalist ideas that have all been around for years. Kaufman (1978), for instance, outlined the differences between administrative systems reform and major reorganization nearly 20 years ago. More usefully, he described the contradictions of reform prescriptions (or proverbs), for example, that delegation of discretion to lower echelons decentralizes authority but risks entrapment of local field offices by private and political interests.

No such empirical division of NPR principles and activities into administrative proverbs has yet taken place. But in contrast with past reforms, this movement has presidential authority in the National Performance Review and has been translated into law in the Government Performance and Results Act of 1993. Many of the Act's provisions were adopted from experiences with corporate restructuring (Drucker 1995). Because the approach focuses on institutional incentives, there is a good common ground between neoinstitutional political economy (described above) and this more atheoretical, hands-on approach. There is also plenty of potential for application of new reform principles abroad and for comparative research on the results of their application.[*]

---

[*] For example, in 1995, Development Alternatives, Inc. (DAI) teamed with RGN on a USAID contract to reinvent government through local public financial management reforms in Estonia.

As could be expected, the entrepreneurial or postbureaucratic paradigm has been roundly criticized for ignoring the existing legal and policy determinants of ineffective administrative processes (Moe 1994, 115) and for being largely untested in the field. Due in part to the recency of events in Eastern Europe and the relative youth of the reinvention movement, few studies to date have asked such questions as, how do we modify statist cultures in Eastern Europe to improve performance? And what sequence of steps would be taken to reinvent their governments? More specifically, the paradigm is charged with being neither an empirical theory nor an action program, and for representing largely a synthesis of older ideas in new language. It is similar, again, to the black box in systems theory. It produces outputs and receives support and demand. But it fails to specify the exact mechanisms by which the inputs (reinvention resources) are converted by the system or process into outputs (improved performance) (Easton 1965).

For example, one of the core reinventing government principles for organizational planning and budgeting has been that resource allocations should link directly with service and performance levels. One recommended output is biennial budgeting. Another is that departments be required to specify outcomes that would be produced for given levels of resources. These and other budget reform principles are drawn directly from ZBB in the 1970s and performance budgeting in the 1950s and 1960s. The only question is, what is the new catalyst that will cause them to work more effectively now?

The black box problem raises the question of how to proceed with actual reinvention of government beyond reintroduction of existing methods and principles in new language. So far, for instance, the NPR methodology begins with critical assumptions about the size of the governmental problem. Under such conditions, downsizing is not the result of careful analysis of functional performance in relation to an assessment of the kind of government that is needed (Barr 1994). The effect of this flawed method is something like streamlining the performance of a tourist ministry which may not be needed in the first place. Moreover, failure to perform staffing analysis could result in cutting the wrong personnel (e.g., contract oversight and internal control people) and weakening program performance further (which will lower effectiveness).

For example, with the highest per pupil but lowest in-class expenditures in the United States, and some of the worst student test performance, any cuts in the Washington, DC, school system should be based on a thorough program review. But common sense would suggest that the focus should be on the bloat at central headquarters rather than on an excessive number of qualified teachers (Horwitz 1995). Determination of where resources should be decreased and increased must be related to program outputs and expected outcomes, not maintenance of existing work flows. Studies suggest that in most poor countries, health ministries are relatively efficient (because they have been targets of various aid programs) and need more rather than fewer workers. Comparative lessons from private firms on how to sequence reforms and to deal with special-interest resistance has started to permeate public sector reorganization efforts with positive results.

Several earlier reinvention lessons should be cited. First, pruning labor, making across-the-board cuts, and outsourcing tasks are traumatic affairs. Companies have often discovered that following massive cuts, the remaining workforce was not consistent with where the firm was headed. Public sector organizations need to redefine missions before, not after, downsizing. Second, downsizing and pruning should occur only after work is reorganized. Failure to do this results in lower productivity, morale, and quality. Managers need to root out causes of inefficiency which may be time wasted in compiling unnecessary reports, generating data not needed for short or medium-term decision making, excessive numbers of meetings, excess layers of management, and even wasting senior-level staff time with excessive information system tasks. Third, survivors from downsizing should see that the organization has been serious about cutting real inefficiency and will reward them for staying with training, equipment, and merit pay (Pearlstein 1995). These lessons have not yet been tested internationally. Needed are comparative studies of the sequences of reform, from which applied reinvention principles and administrative theory can be developed.

Paradoxically, in terms of energizing reforms, combining conceptual popularity with definitional vagueness may be one of the reinvention movement's greatest strengths. Wilson (1994, 668) notes that the NPR could not be more different from the eleven reorganization task forces created since 1904. The NPR ignores theory and takes the normative position that government ought to be more responsive and less bureaucratic. This is far more tangible to the public than the accountability or efficiency that governed previous approaches. Just as most who have applied for a drivers license know about needless queues and red tape, most people in business know the functions and costs of regulatory excess.

The NPR reinvention approach has been extremely valuable in focusing on the machinery (e.g., procurement systems) and results (e.g., overcharging weakening program results) of government operations. It has also given a boost to the new CPA agenda of providing international empirical lessons for management and policy. For instance, the Australian and New Zealand models that have provided incentives for managers to achieve program results, have been repeatedly cited by the NPR as tested examples for the United States (NPR 1993b, 16). In this vein, Mascarenhas (1993) compared the efforts of Australia, New Zealand, and Britain to restructure their public sectors to give managers greater authority and responsibility. With similar hypotheses, Holmes and Shand (1994) have also compared the structural changes in core government functions in Australia, New Zealand, and the United Kingdom. As noted, because the reinvention approach stresses functional revitalization, the approach is clearly also within the functionalist tradition of CPA. Needed are more studies of the results of comparative state reform that follow these ground breaking efforts, as well as those of Schick (1990) and Barzelay and Hassel (1994).

I. COMPARATIVE MANAGEMENT INFORMATION SYSTEMS

A second feature of the late 1990s to 2004 period has been the diffusion of information technology. Public sector organizations have always been hermetic and secretive affairs within levels and between their operations and the public. Clearly, solid leadership and effective management require timely and accurate information to make technical decisions and to anticipate and control their consequences. Thus, better lines of data communication are needed within organizations and the public, as well as incentives for better analysis of raw data, to prevent information overload on decision makers. For management control, information is needed during implementation on budget outlays, for purchase orders and contract commitments, and for payroll activity in relation to public employment. For strategic planning, general managers need non-financial information on employee performance, office operations, and the progress of particular projects. Within the financial management area, functions must be integrated for proper resource allocation, control, and evaluation of results.

To date, there has been little comparative work on many of the core issues in information technology. Based on information theory, it has been presumed that increasing control in organizations is a natural process of information feedback and deviation correction (Overman and Loraine 1984, 194). Recent experience and studies suggest, however, that in the case of public projects there may be less of a connection between control and information than imagined. Managers can be dysfunctionally tied down by their information systems; information itself is governed by managerial behavior and organizational norms (ibid.). Information theory must be deepened to explain the link between information and control more rigorously. For dynamic and unstable systems, such as public organizations, chaos theory is one alternative. In practice, the implication is that given the chaotic relation between information and control, more sophisticated information systems may not be better. In the words of Lao Tsu: "One must know when to stop" (Overman and Loraine 1984, 196).

Such studies raise a number of critical questions on the costs and benefits of information systems and their transfer abroad. For example, should there be separate management and financial management information systems (MIS and FMIS)? Under what conditions should some of the core payroll, personnel, and capital investment programming functions be independent or tightly integrated into one FMIS (Wesberry 1994)? What lessons can be offered for design of information access systems? How can rules avoid policy coordination and internal communication problems, such as the type where nonunion staff will only share certain kinds of financial information with unionized line workers? If management information systems are severed, is there not the danger that softer management systems will take on lives of their own, driving out the productive work of the organization?

The question of how to integrate multiple information systems is related to the issue of how to design systems consistent with the organizational flow of work. Most organizations are faced with goal incongruity problems (contradictory work incentives), meaning that institutional incentives should be examined first. Personnel resources are often wasted performing tasks at the wrong level, for example, managers often waste time on clerical tasks or strategic planning matters instead of maintaining systems of operational control. Organizational division of labor, spans of control, and the implications of behavioral incentives created by defining responsibility centers as profit, revenue, or expense need to be considered before installing systems (Anthony and Young 1988, 8). These are obvious points that are frequently ignored in the rush to sell off-the-shelf information systems.

Throughout Eastern Europe, for example, computerized information systems have been provided by donors and their consultants. Many systems are now incompatible with each other. Consistent with the above discussion, many systems often ignore the flow of organizational authority and power. For example, the respective ministries of finance were mostly irrelevant to planning under socialism, that is, the budget simply executed the plan. Despite the shift in power from macroplanning to microbudgeting, several projects have linked the planning ministry back into budgeting. The need to shift power to line ministries while retaining control of payments (at least initially) has been ignored in many cases by an almost obsessive push toward computerized information systems. Work by Allan and Hashim (1994) suggests that system architecture should link both general public management and financial management functions. But they make it clear that before work begins on the design of computer systems to support fiscal management, the regulatory framework needs to be in place, that is, the accounts classification, reporting requirements, and overall control structure (at both the document and transaction levels) (Allan and Hashim 1994, 3–4).[*]

Second, systems design needs to take into account the question of the role of budgeting in the larger financial management system noted above. Should budgeting simply be one more financial management information function? If so, what financial management function should control the rest of the system?[†] Or should all functions share power? As the link with the political and policy function, as well as the central incentive system for government operations, shouldn't the budget function be considered first among equals? Like the black box of systems theory discussed above in connection with reinvention methods, it is presumed that the system itself is functional. Disequilibrium produced by information defects from any subpart affect financial results in multiple ways. From this perspective, the broad notion of system becomes the unit of analysis. Conversely, inserting budgeting as the lead function, the black box gains meaning as the driving force of public policy and public sector management.

This would be consistent with the widespread view that the role of the budget is central. It "translates political objectives into government programs and constitutes the major part of the incentive system which conditions bureaucratic behavior" (World Bank 1994). The issue might be resolved in part by taking the common-sense view that proper budgeting first requires linkage of

---

*For an excellent discussion of internal and external expenditure control principles applicable for design of systems in Central and Eastern Europe, see Kirby (1993).

†For a recent discussion of conflicting financial management frameworks issues, see Miller (1994).

the budget function to accounting, treasury, procurement, and payroll. Otherwise, functional distortions occur that diminish the role of budgeting. In Honduras, for example, financial management functions such as treasury and accounting are not even linked within the MOF building. In Ghana, the internal control and audit department has taken over budget planning and execution by default. Under these conditions, budgeting is performed in an accounting and policy vacuum, and its credibility as allocator of resources is near zero. In short, the larger budget function should be constructed in an iterative fashion from development of separate financial management components into an integrated system.

Third, is there a management information and data overload point within public sector organizations? Can preoccupation with the acquisition and exchange of management information lead to decay as well as development within organizations? At what point does the existence of equipment and systems, together with the labor required for data entry, become dysfunctional to efficiency? At what stage does accumulation of data for the future distort incentives and jeopardize current staff productivity? Can information technology lead to goal displacement where the data itself becomes more important than its use to solve real problems? More tangibly, how much should be spent on data systems if results cannot be precisely gauged?

More than 30 years ago, Packenham (1973, 258) noted the fascination of CPA with new methods of data handling and esoteric frameworks and concepts. As noted above in the discussion of prismatic approaches, new CPA methods represent major research advances in forging problem-specific solutions. However, the growing technological fascination within organizations may not be leading to better results measured in profitability, service, or real productivity. This is in part because of the large blocks of time required for training and retraining, daily data entry, meetings on system modifications, and systems overload that cause valuable loss of time. Time spent documenting decisions, putting them in proper form, and informing the rest of the organization may be displacing more needed work.

IV. SUMMARY AND CONCLUSION

To summarize, prodded by world events, CPA moved from the theoretical emphasis of the classical era to a new empirical emphasis that tries to solve problems of policy and management. In the classical period, CPA shifted from the top-down emphasis of the Alliance foreign aid period to a bottom-up approach under the New Directions program. The classical era produced mostly rhetorical debate about the true meaning of development and strategies of achieving revolution. Tensions between the Western and purely socialist alternatives were debated, producing an appreciation for the complexities of local cultures and institutions. But lacking the infrastructure and skills of the original Marshall Plan target countries, few Third World countries grew or developed under the influence of either foreign aid or CPA model building.

Skepticism about the size and results of government led to a resurgent interest in performance and structural reform. In principle, spurred by new choice and institutional economic theories, this meant a return to the traditional interest in the creation and revitalization of core government functions, consistent with local values and attitudes (political culture). In practice, the new efforts to apply comparative lessons to energize modern functions within different (but certainly not unique) cultures, were distinguishing features of the classical versus new CPA. The new CPA agenda of the early twenty-first century is less interested in theory building than in application and translation of existing theories into practice. As with past CPA efforts, the new CPA shares only a utilitarian interest in making functions work and stimulating democratic capitalism. With these interests, new CPA studies have poured out in the traditional areas of public budgeting, public personnel management, and intergovernmental relations.

New research areas requiring innovative problem-solving techniques and applied solutions include structural and functional reform of government programs and agencies, and integration of information systems technology with essential work routines and agency missions. As old orders change with the collapse of the former Soviet Union and the rise of religious fundamentalism, new opportunities for research into the political stabilization function of public sector management institutions (building on work performed in Africa) should continue. The CPA agenda is no longer simply determined by the flow of US foreign aid money. Funding for applied public sector administrative studies is now solidly multinational, primarily through such institutions as UNDP, EC-PHARE, the World Bank, and IMF. To conclude, a fortuitous set of circumstances exists for CPA work in the future. While the challenges created by a changing world order have never been greater, the use of applied methods and a growing international interest in the results of public sector reform have created a variety of scholarly resources equal to these new challenges.

REFERENCES

Acemoglu, D., Root Causes: a historical approach to assessing the role of institutions of economic development, *Finance and Development*, 40, 27–30, 2003.

Allan, B. and Hashim, A., Core functional requirements for fiscal management systems, Working paper #JEL 322, International Monetary Fund, Washington, DC, 1994.

Almond, G., *Political Development*, Little, Brown, Boston, MA, 1970.

Almond, G. and Coleman, J. S., *The Politics of Developing Areas*, Princeton University Press, Princeton, NJ, 1960.

Anthony, R. N. and Young, D. W., *Management Control in Nonprofit Organizations*, 4th ed., Irwin, Homewood, IL, 1988.

Arreliano-Gault, D. and Gil-Garcia, J. R., Public management policy and accountability in Latin America: performance oriented budgeting in Colombia, Mexico and Venezuela (1994–2000), *International Public Management Journal*, 7, 49–71, 2004.

Ashford, D. E., Ed., *Comparing Public Policies: New Concepts and Methods*, Sage Publications, Beverly Hills, CA, 1978.

Aucion, P., *The New Public Management: Canada in Comparative Perspective*, IRPP, Montreal, Canada, 1995.

Aziewicz, T., *The Transformation of the Public Utility Sector*, Gdansk Institute of Market Economics, Warsaw, Poland, 1994.

Bahl, R. W. and Linn, J. F., *Urban Public Finance in Developing Countries*, Oxford University Press, New York, 1992.

Balanoff, H., Montgomery, Van Wart, and Kenneth, Pryor, Comparative public administration, In *International Encyclopedia of Public Policy and Administration*, Jay, Shafritz, Ed., Westview Press, Westport, CT, pp. 456–460, 1998.

Barr, S., Midterm exam for 'reinventing', *Washington Post*, A25, August 19, 1994.

Barzelay, M., *Breaking Through Bureaucracy: A New Vision for Managing Government*, University of California Press, Berkeley, CA, 1992.

Barzelay, M. and Hassel, B., Revamping public management: integrating comparative research, Paper presented at International Political Science Association Meeting, Manchester, UK, 1994.

Behr, P., The case for privatization, *Washington Post*, February 13, 1995.

Bekke, H. A. G. M., Perry, J. L., and Toonen, T. A. J., Eds., *Civil Service Systems in Comparative Perspective*, Indiana University Press, Bloomington, IN, 1996.

Berkeley, B., An African success story?, *Atlantic Monthly*, 22–30, September, 1994.

Bill, J. and Hardgrave, R., *Comparative Politics, the Quest for Theory*, Charles Merrill, Columbus, OH, 1973.

Bird, R., Budgeting and expenditure control in Colombia, *Public Budget Finance*, 2, 87–100, 1982.

Braibanti, R., Public bureaucracy and judiciary in Pakistan, In *Bureaucracy and Political Development*, La Palombara, J., Ed., Princeton University Press, Princeton, NJ, 1967.

Caiden, G., Administrative reform: American style, *Public Administration Review*, 54, 123–129, 1994.

Caiden, N., Forward: budgeting in historical and comparative perspective, *Public Budget Finance*, 14, 1, 1994.

Caiden, N. and Wildavsky, A., *Planning and Budgeting in Poor Countries*, Wiley, New York, 1974.

Clarke, T., Ed., *International Privatization: Strategies and Practices*, De Gruyter, New York, 1994.

Clarke, T. and Pitelis, C., Eds., *The Political Economy of Privatization*, Routledge, London, 1993.

Cohen, M. D., March, J. G., and Olsen, J. P., A garbage can model of organizational choice, *Administrative Sciences Quarterly*, 17(1), 1–25, 1972.

Gary, J., Mr. Johnson, *New Directions*, New York, 1939.

Chandler, J. A., Conclusion: globalisation and public administration, In *Comparative Public Administration*, Chandler, J. A., Ed., Routledge, London, pp. 249–265, 2000.

Chaudhry, S. A. and Reid, G. J., *World Bank Conference on Civil Service Reform in Latin America and the Caribbean*, Washington, DC, 1993.

Chilcote, R. H. and Edelstein, J., *Latin America: The Struggle with Dependency and Beyond*, Schenkman, Cambridge, MA, 1974.

Chisholm, D., *Coordination without Hierarchy, Informal Structures in Multiorganizational Systems*, University of California Press, Berkeley, CA, 1989.

Clarke, T., Ed., *International Privatization: Strategies and Practices*, De Gruyter, New York, 1994.

Clarke, T. and Pitelis, C., Eds., *The Political Economy of Privatization*, Routledge, London, 1993.

Cohen, M. D., March, J. G., and Olsen, J. P., A garbage can model of organizational choice, *Administrative Sciences Quarterly*, 17(1), 1–25, 1972.

Cohen, D., Tribal enterprise, *Atlantic Monthly*, 32–43, October, 1989.

Congressional Budget Office (CBO), *Reducing the Size of the Federal Civilian Work Force*, Congressional Budget Office, Washington, DC, 1993.

Considine, M. and Lewis, J. M., Bureaucracy, network, or enterprise? Comparing models of governance in Australia, Britain, the Netherlands, and New Zealand, *Public Administration Review*, 63, 131–141, 2003.

Cooley, A., Western conditions and domestic choices: the influence of external actors on the post-communist transition. In *Freedom House, Nations in Transit 2003*, Freedom House, New York, 25–38. http://www.freedomhouse.org/research/nattransit.htm.

Coopers, L., Institutional Diagnostic and Restructuring Study, Nicaragua, 1994.

Crozier, M., *The Bureaucratic Phenomenon*, University of Chicago Press, Chicago, IL, 1964.

Danziger, J. D., *Making Budgets, Public Resource Allocation*, Sage Publications, Beverly Hills, CA, 1978.

Davey, Kenneth, Ed., *Fiscal Autonomy and Efficiency: Reforms in the Former Soviet Union*, Open Society Institute, Local Government and Public Service Reform Initiative, Budapest, Hungary, 2002.

deMerode, L. and Thomas, C., Experience with civil service pay and employment reform, In *Rehabilitating Government: Pay and Employment Reform in Africa*, Lindauer, D. L. and Nunberg, B., Eds., World Bank, Washington, DC, pp. 119–160, 1994.

Drucker, P., Really reinventing government, *Atlantic Monthly*, 49–62, February, 1995.

Dunleavy, P. and Hood, C., From old public administration to new public management, *Public Money and Management*, 14(3), 9–16, 1994.

Easton, D. A., *Framework for Political Analysis*, Prentice Hall, Englewood Cliffs, NJ, 1965.

The Economist, Confucianism: new fashion for old visdom, *The Economist*, 21, 38–39, January, 1995a.

The Economist, A great train crash, *The Economist*, 21, 20, January, 1995b.

The Economist, Russia, seconds out, round 40, *The Economist*, 28, 45–46, January, 1995c.

The Economist, A survey of India, *The Economist*, 21, 1–30, January, 1995d.

The Economist, tired of capitalism? So soon?, *The Economist*, 21, 61–62, January, 1995e.

Esman, Milton J., *Management Dimensions of Development: Perspectives and Strategies*, Kumarian Press, West Hartford, CT, 1991.

Farazmand, Ali, Development and comparative public administration: past, present, and future, *Public Administration Quarterly*, 20(3), 343–364, 1996.

Farazmand, A., The new world order and global public administration, In *Public Administration in the Global Village*, Jean-Claude, Garcia-Zamor, and Renu, Khator, Eds., Praeger, Westport, CT, pp. 61–82, 1994.

Forster, E. M., *A Passage to India*, Harcourt Brace, New York, 1952 [1954].

Fried, R. C., Comparative urban policy and performance. In *Handbook of Political Science*, Vol. 6, Greenstein, F. I. and Polsby, N. W., Eds., chap. 6., Reading, Addison-Wesley, MA, 1975.

Friedman, T., *The Lexus and the Olive Tree: Understanding Globalization*, Farrar, Straus and Giroux, New York, 1999.

Frank, A. G., *Latin America: Underdevelopment or Revolution?*, Monthly Review Press, New York, 1969.

Fuller, D. E., Privatization: a comparative focus, In *Comparative Public Management: Putting US Public Policy and Implementation in Context*, Baker, R., Ed., Praeger, Westport, CT, pp. 261–270, 1994.

Gabrielyan, V., *Toward a Discursive Comparative Public Management: Study of Privatization in the US, UK and Russia*, Ph.D. thesis, Department of Public Administration, Rutgers University, 1998.

Garcia-Zamor, J.-C. and Renu, K., Eds., *Public Administration in the Global Village*, Praeger, Westport, CT, 1994.

Gayle, D. and Goodrich, J., Eds., *Privatization and Deregulation in Global Perspective*, Quorum Books, New York, 1990.

General Accounting Office (GAO), *Deficit Reduction: Experiences of Other Nations*, U.S. Government Accounting Office, Washington, DC, 1994.

Ghai, D., Ed., *The IMF and the South: The Social Impact of Crisis and Adjustment*, Zed Books, London, 1991.

Classman, J. K., We have the blueprints in hand for a balanced budget, *Washington Post*, 9, November, 1994.

Gleason, A., Russia: the meaning of 1917, *Atlantic Monthly*, 30–34, November, 1992.

Goldsmith, J. and Gunderson, G., *Comparative Local Politics: A Systems-Functional Approach*, Holbrook Press, Boston, MA, 1973.

Gow, J. I. and Dufour, C., Is the new public management a paradigm? Does it matter?, *International Review of Administrative Sciences*, 66, 573–597, 2000.

Gray, A., Jenkins, B., and Segsworth, B., Eds., *Budgeting, Auditing and Evaluation: Functions and Integration in Seven Governments*, Transaction, New Brunswick, NJ, 1993.

Green, R. T. and Hubbell, L., On governance and reinventing government, In *Refounding Democratic Public Administration: Modern Paradoxes, Postmodern Responses*, Wamsley, G. L. and Wolf, J. F., Eds., Sage Publications, Thousand Oaks, CA, pp. 38–69, 1996.

Gregory, P., Dealing with redundancies in government employment in Ghana, In *Rehabilitating Government: Pay and Employment Reform in Africa*, Lindauer, D. L. and Nunberg, B., Eds., World Bank, Washington, DC, pp. 195–211, 1994.

Guess, G. M., V.S. Naipaul and development administration, *Philippine Journal of Public Administration*, 23, 105–117, 1979.

Guess, G. M., Comparative and international administration, In *Handbook on Public Administration*, Rabin, J., Hildreth, W. B., and Miller, G. J., Eds., Marcel Dekker, New York, pp. 477–497, 1987a.

Guess, G. M., *The Politics of United States Foreign Aid*, St. Martin's, New York, 1987b.

Guess, G. M., Centralization of expenditure controls, *Latin America. Public Admin Q.*, 16, 376–394, 1992.

Guess, G. M., Transformation of bureaucratic states in Eastern Europe: public expenditure lessons Latin America, *International Journal of Public Administration*, 1997b.

Guess, G. M. and Garzon, H., *Nicaragua: Financial Management Reform Project, Budget Systems Implementation Plan*, World Bank, Washington, DC, 1994.

Guess, G. M. and Koford, K., Inflation and the federal budget deficit: or blaming economic problems on a statistical mirage, *Policy Sciences*, 17, 385–402, 1984.

Guess, G. M., Frenzen, R., Garzon, H., Serageldin, M., and Winters, J., *Technical Assistance Strategy on Poland in Local Government and Housing Privatization*, International City-County Management Association, Washington, DC, 1992.

Garzon, H., *Nicaragua: Financial Management Reform Project, Budget Systems Implementation Plan*, World Bank, Washington, DC, 1994.

Garzon, H. and Koford, K., Inflation and the federal budget deficit: or blaming economic problems on a statistical mirage, *Policy Sciences*, 17, 385–402, 1984.

Guillen, M. F., *The Limits of Convergence: Globalization and Organizational Change in Argentina, South Korea, and Spain*, Princeton University Press, Oxford, 2001.

Guthrie, James and Olov Olson, Public Sector Management and Financial Management Change in a Group of OECD Countries: Global Warning about Managing Public Services in a Market Environment. Paper delivered at Public Administration in the Transition Economies Conference, St. Petersburg, Russia, 13–16. June, 1996.

Frenzen, R., Garzon, H., Serageldin, M., and Winters, J., *Technical Assistance Strategy on Poland in Local Government and Housing Privatization*, International City–County Management Association, Washington, DC, 1992.

Hali, E., Testing the Links: how strong are the links between institutional quality and economic performance?, *Finance and Development*, 40(2), 35–38, 2003.

Hamner, R. D., Ed., *Critical Perspectives on V.S. Naipaul*, Three Continents Press, Washington, DC, 1977.

Harris, J. F. and Chandler, C., $1.61 trillion budget to hill, *Washington Post*, 7, Al, February, 1995.

Hampden-Turner, C., and Trompenaars, F., *Seven Cultures of Capitalism*, Doubleday, New York, 1994.

Harrison, L. E., *Underdevelopment as a State of Mind, the Latin American Case*, University Press of America, Lanham, MD, 1985.

Heady, Ferrel, *Public Administration: A Comparative Perspective*, 4th ed., Marcel Dekker, New York, 1996.

Heady, F., Comparative and international public administration: building intellectual bridges, *Public Administration Review*, 58, 32–40, 1998.

Heady, F., *Public Administration: A Comparative Perspective*, 2nd ed., Marcel Dekker, New York, 1979.

Heggie, I. G., *Improving Management and Charging Policies for Roads: An Agenda for Reform*, World Bank, Washington, DC, 1991.

Heidenheimer, A. J., Heclo, H., and Adams, C., *Comparative Public Policy, the Politics of Social Choice in Europe and America*, 2nd ed., St. Martin's Press, New York, 1983.

Hewitt, D. and Mihaljek, D., Fiscal federalism, In *Fiscal Policies in Economies in Transition*, Tanzi, V., Ed., International Monetary Fund, Washington, DC, pp. 330–350, 1992.

Hill, A. and Abdala, M. A., *Regulations, Institutions and Commitment: Privatization and Regulation in the Argentine Telecommunications Sector*, World Bank, Washington, DC, 1993.

Hirschman, A., *Shifting Involvements: Private Interest and Public Action*, Basil Blackwell, Oxford, 1982.

Hofman, B., *Decentralization and Financial Management. Background Note for Government Expenditure and Financial Management Course*, World Bank, Washington, DC, 1994.

Hofstede, G., *Culture and Organizations: Software of the Mind*, McGraw-Hill, London, 1991.

Hofstede, G., *Culture's Consequences: International Differences in Work-Related Values*, Sage Publications, Thousand Oaks, CA, 1980.

Holmes, M. and Shand, D., *Management Reform, Some Practitioner Perspectives on the Past Ten Years*, World Bank, Washington, DC, 1994.

Hood, C., Public management for all seasons?, *Public Administration*, 69, 3–19, 1991.

Horwitz, S., D.C. schools may cut 500 teaching positions, *Washington Post*, 19, B4, 1995.

Hoselitz, B. F., Levels of economic performance and bureaucratic structures, In *Bureaucracy and Political Development*, LaPalombara, J., Ed., Princeton University Press, Princeton, NJ, 1967.

Huddleston, M. W., Onto the darkling plain: globalization and the American public service in the twenty-first century, *Journal of Public Administration Research and Theory*, 10, 665–675, 2000.

Huntington, S. P., *Political Order in Changing Societies*, Yale University Press, New Haven, CT, 1968.

International Monetary Fund (IMF), Standards and codes: the IMF's role, An IMF Issues Brief, Also available at URL: http://www.imf.org/external/np/exr/ib/2001/042701.htm, See also related Reports on the Observance of Standards and Codes (ROSCs) http://www.imf.org/external/np/rosc/rosc.asp, April 26, 2001.

Inglehart, R., The renaissance of political culture, *American Political Science Review*, 82, 1203–1231, 1988.

Inglehart, R., Culture and Democracy, In *Culture Matters: How Values Shape Human Progress*, Lawrence, E. H. and Samuel, H., Eds., Basic Books, New York, 2000.

Israel, A., *Institutional Development, Incentives to Performance*, Johns Hopkins University, Baltimore, MD, 1989.

Jreisat, J. E., Comparative public administration and reform, *International Journal of Public Administration*, 855–857, 1999.

Jun, J. S., Renewing the study of comparative administration: some reflections on the current possibilities, *Public Administration Review*, 36, 641–647, 1976.

Kaufman, H., Reflections on administrative reorganization, In *Setting National Priorities: The 1978 budget*, Pechman, J., Ed., Brookings Institution, Washington, DC, 1978.

Kaufman, F. X., Ed., *The Public Sector: Challenge for Coordination and Learning*, Walter de Gruyter, Berlin, 1991.

Kay, J. A. and Thompson, D. J., Privatization: a policy in search of a rational, *Economic Journal*, 96(381), 18–31, 1986.

Keating, M. and Rosalky, D., Rolling expenditure plans: Australian experience and prognosis, In *Government Financial Management: Issues and Country Studies*, Premchand, A., Ed., pp. 72–78, 1990.

Kettl, D. F., *Reinventing Government: A Fifth-Year Report Card. A Report of the Brookings Institution's Center for Public Management*, Brookings Institution, Washington, DC, 1998.

Kettl, D. F., The global revolution in public management: driving themes, missing links, *Journal of Policy Analysis and Management*, 16(3), 446–462, 1997.

Kettl, D. F., Privatization as a tool of reform, *The LaFollette Policy Report*, 7(1), 1–4, 1995.

Kettl, D. F., The myths, realities, and challenges of privatization, In *Revitalizing State and Local Public Service: Strengthening Performance, Accountability and Citizen Confidence*, Thompson, Frank J., Ed. Jossey-Bass, pp. 246–279, 1993.

Kettl, D. F., *The Global Public Management Revolution: A Report on the Transference of Governance*, Brookings Institution Press, Washington, DC, 2000.

Kingdon, J. W., *Agendas, Alternatives, and Public Policies*, Little, Brown, Boston, 1984.

Kirby, G., Overview of governmental financial control systems in OECD Countries, Paris: EC/PHARE, SIGMA-Support for Improvement in Governance and Management in Central and Eastern Europe, 1993.

Kitchen, R., Compensation upgrading in the Caribbean public service: comparative needs and experience. Paper #5, In *Latin America and the Caribbean*, Chaudhry, S. A. and Reid, G. J., Eds., World Bank Conference on Civil Service Reform in 1993, Washington, DC, 1993.

Kouzmin, A., Leivesley, R., and Korac-Kakabadse, N., From managerialism and economic rationalism: toward "re-inventing" economic ideology and administrative diversity, *Administrative Theory & Praxis*, 19, 19–42, 1997.

Kuhl, J., Privatization and its labor market effects in Eastern Germany, In *Lessons from Privatization: Labor Issues in Developing and Transitional Countries*, Rolph, Van der Hoeven and Sziraczki, Gyorgy, Eds., International Labor Office, Geneva, Switzerland, pp. 119–143, 1997.

Kwan, O. Y., Ed., *International Privatization: Global Trends, Policies, Processes, Experiences*, The Institute for Saskatchewan Enterprise, Saskatoon, 1990.

LaPalombara, J., Bureaucracy and political development: notes, queries and dilemmas, In *Bureaucracy and Political Development*, LaPalombara, J., Ed., Princeton University Press, Princeton, NJ, 1967.

LaPalombara, J., Parsimony and empiricism, in comparative politics: an anti-scholastic view, In *The Methodology of Comparative Research*, Holt, R. and Turner, J., Eds., Free Press, New York, 1979.

La Prensa, Problemas con desmovilizados en El Salvador. 25 January, 1995.

La Tribuna, Asamblea Podria Rechazar Privatizacion de TELCOR, 26 January, 1994.

Levi, M., Review of political and economic interactions in policy reform, *American Political Science Review*, 88, 233–234, 1994.

Lewis, V., Toward a theory of budgeting, *Public Administration Review*, Winter, 1952.

Li, J. and Karakowsky, L., Cultural malleability in an east Asian context: an illustration of the relationship between government policy, national culture, and firm behavior, *Administration & Society*, 34(2), 176–201, 2002.

Lindauer, D. L., Introduction: pay and employment reform of the Civil Service, In *Rehabilitating Government: Pay and Employment Reform in Africa*, Lindauer, D. L. and Nunberg, B., Eds., World Bank, Washington, DC, pp. 1–17, 1994.

Lindauer, D. L. and Nunberg, B., Eds., *Rehabilitating Government: Pay and Employment Reform in Africa*, World Bank, Washington, DC, 1994.

Loveman, B., The comparative administration group, development administration, and antidevelopment, *Public Administration Review*, 36(6), 616–621, 1976.

Lynn, L., *Public Management as Art, Science and Profession*, Chatham House Publishers, Chatham, NJ, 1996a.

Lynn, L., The new public management as an international phenomenon: a skeptical view, paper presented at the conference, New Public Management in International Perspective, University of St. Gallen, Switzerland, http://www.willamette.org/ipmn, July, 1996b.

Manning, N. and Parison, N., *International Public Administration Reform: Implications for the Russian Federation*, World Bank, Washington, DC, 2004.

Martinez-Vazquez, J., Intergovernmental fiscal relations in Bulgaria, Research paper #38, Georgia State University Policy Research Center, Atlanta, GA, 1993.

Martinez-Vasquez, J. and Wallace, S., The challenge of design of intergovernmental relations in economies in transition. *International Journal of Public Administration*, 160–184, 1997.

Mascarenhas, R. C., Building an enterprise culture in the public sector: reform of the public sector in Australia, Britain, and New Zealand, *Public Administration Review*, 53, 319–329, 1993.

Maass, A. and Anderson, R., *And the Desert Shall Rejoice*, MIT Press, Cambridge, MA, 1978.

Matheson, A. and Kwon, H. S., Public management in flux: trends and differences across OECD countries, In *Public Management and Governance*, Bovaird, T. and Loffler, E., Eds., Routledge, London, pp. 41–52, 2003.

Mathews, G. J., Do job reviews work?, *Washington Post*, March 20, A16, 1994.

MCC, Millenium Challenge Corporation, Available at www.mcc.gov (Last accessed in 2004).

Meier, G. M., The old generation of development economists and the new, In *Frontiers of Development Economics: The Future in Perspective*, Meier, G. M. and Stiglitz, J. E., Eds., Oxford University Press, pp. 13–51, 2000.

Miller, G. J., What is financial management? Are we inventing a new field here?, *Public Administration Review*, 54, 209–213, 1994.

Moe, R. C., The reinventing government exercise: misinterpreting the problem, misjudging the consequences, *Public Administration Review*, 54, 111–123, 1994.

Montgomery, J. D., *Aftermath: Tarnished Outcomes of American Foreign Policy*, Auburn House, Dover, MA, 1986.

Morss, E. R. and Morss, V. A., *U.S. Foreign Aid: An Assessment of New and Traditional Development Strategies*, Westview Press, Boulder, CO, 1982.

Mutahaba, G., *Reforming Public Administration for Development: Experiences from East Africa*, Kumarian, London, 1989.

National Performance Review (NPR), *Agency for International Development*, NPR, Washington, DC, 1993a.

National Performance Review (NPR), *Mission-Driven, Results-Oriented Budgeting*, NPR, Washington, DC, 1993b.

Nelson, D. N. and Bentley, S., The comparative politics of Eastern Europe, *PS: Political Science & Politics*, 27, 45–53, 1994.

Neumann, S., Comparative politics: a half-century appraisal, In *Comparative Political Systems*, Cantori, L. J., Ed., Holbrook Press, Boston, MA, pp. 8–26, 1974.

Newland, C. A., A field of strangers in search of discipline: separation of public management research from public administration, *Public Administration Review*, 54(5), 486–488, 1994.

Nicholson, N., Applications of public choice theory to rural development—a statement of the problem, In *Public Choice and Rural Development*, Russell, C. and Nicholson, N., Eds., Resources for the Future, Washington, DC, pp. 17–43, 1981.

Nepal National Planning Commission, *The Keys to Democracy, Decentralization and Development in Nepal*, Government of Nepal, Kathmandu, Nepal, 1992.

Nisbet, R. A., *Social Change and History: Aspects of the Western Theory of Development*, Oxford University Press, London, 1970.

Nolan, R. Public sector training in Eastern Europe: problems and opportunitie. *International Journal of Public Administration*, 1997.

North, D. C., *Institutional Change and Economic Performance*, Cambridge University Press, Cambridge, MA, 1990.

North, D. C., *Mission Driven: Results Oriented Budgeting*, NPR, Washington, DC, 1993.

Nunberg, B. and Lindauer, D. L., Conclusion: the political economy of civil service pay and employment reform, In *Rehabilitating Government: Pay and Employment Reform in Africa*, Lindauer, D. L. and Nunberg, B., Eds., World Bank, Washington, DC, 238–244, 1994.

Organization for Economic Cooperation and Development (OECD), *Public Management Developments: Survey*, OECD, Paris, 1990.

Organization for Economic Cooperation and Development (OECD), *Governance in Transition: Public Management Reforms in OECD Countries*, OECD, Paris, 1995.

Organization for Economic Cooperation and Development (OECD), Government of the future, OECD public management policy brief No. 9. June, 2001.

Organization for Economic Cooperation and Development (OECD), *Issues and Developments in Public Management: Survey 1996–1997 on the United Kingdom*, OECD, Paris, http://www.oecd.org/puma/ gvrnance/surveys/pubs/report97/surveyuk.htm 1997.

Organization for Economic Cooperation and Development (OECD), *Ministerial Symposium of the Future of Public Services*, OECD, Paris, 1996a.

Organization for Economic Cooperation and Development (OECD), *Globalization: What Challenges and Opportunities for Governments?*, OECD, Paris, http://www.oecd.org/puma/gvrnance/strat/pubs/ glo96/, 1996b.

Organization for Economic Cooperation and Development (OECD), *Governance in Transition: Public Management Reforms in OECD countries*, OECD, Paris, 1995.

Organization for Economic Cooperation and Development (OECD), *The Control and Management of Government Expenditure*, OECD, Paris, 1987.

Osborne, D. and Gaebler, T., *Reinventing Government*, Addison-Wesley, New York, 1992.

Overman, E. S. and Loraine, D. T., Information for control: another management proverb?, *Public Administration Review*, 54(1), 193–197, 1984.

Packenham, R. A., *Liberal America and the Third World, Political Development Ideas in Foreign Aid and Social Science*, Princeton University Press, Princeton, NJ, 1973.

Pearlstein, S., Eight lessons of downsizing, *Washington Post*, HI, January 1, 1995.

Pechman, J., Ed., *Setting National Priorities, the Budget*, Brookings Institution, Washington, DC, 1978.

Perry, J. L. and Babitsky, T. T., Comparative performance in urban bus transit: assessing privatization strategies, *Public Administration Review*, 46(1), 57–67, 1986.

Peters, B. G., Theory and methodology in the study of comparative public administration, In *Comparative Public Management*, Baker, R., Ed., Praeger, Westport, CT, pp. 67–92, 1994.

Pierre, Jon, Ed., *Bureaucracy in the Modern State: An Introduction to Comparative Public Administration*, Edward Elgar, Aldershot, UK, 1995.

Pinto, R. F., *Projecting the Governance Approach to Civil Service Reform: An Institutional Environment Assessment for Preparing Sectoral Adjustment Loan in the Gambia*, The World Bank, Washington, DC, 1994.

Pollitt, C. and Bouckaert, G., *Public Management Reform: A Comparative Analysis*, Oxford University Press, Oxford, 2000.

Pomfret, J., Reform wins: dissidents lose: Eastern Europe's rebels vanish from post cold-war cabinets, *Washington Post*, Al, October 24, 1994.

Pomfret, J., *Public Expenditure Management*, International Monetary Fund, Washington, DC, 1993.

Pomfret, J., Ed., *Government Financial Management, Issues and Country Studies*, International Monetary Fund, Washington, DC, 1990.

Porter, M. E., Attitudes, values, beliefs, and the microeconomics of prosperity, In *Culture Matters: How Values Shape Human Progress*, Harrison, L. E. and Huntington, S. P., Eds., Basic Books, New York, pp. 14–28, 2000.

Premchand, A., *Government Budgeting and Expenditure Controls, Theory and Practice*, International Monetary Fund, Washington, DC, 1983.

Premchand, A., Ed., *Government Financial Management, Issues and Country Studies*, International Monetary Fund, Washington, DC, 1990.

Premchand, A., *Public Expenditure Management*, International Monetary Fund, Washington, DC, 1993.

Peters, Guy B., *Comparing Public Bureaucratic: Problems of Theory and Method*, University of Alabama Press, Tuscaloosa, 1988.

Premchand, A. and Garamfalvi, L., Government budget and accounting systems, In *Fiscal Policies in Economies in Transition*, Tanzi, V., Ed., International Monetary Fund, Washington, DC, 1992.

Pye, L. W., "Asian Values": from dynamos to dominoes? In *Culture Matters: How Values Shape Human Progress*, Harrison, L. E. and Huntington, S. P. Ed., Basic Books, New York, 2000.

Pye, L. and Verba, S., *Political Culture and Political Development*, Princeton University Press, Princeton, NJ, 1965.

Rahman, A. T. R., Rural institutions in India and Pakistan, In *Comparative Local Politics: A Systems-Functional Approach*, Goldsmith, J. and Gunderson, G., Eds., Holbrook Press, Boston, pp. 150–168, 1973.

Reid, G. J., *Ecuador: Modernization of the State Technical Assistance Project: Public Sector Modernization Component Preappraisal Recommendations*, World Bank, Washington, DC, 1994.

Riggs, F. W., Ed., *Frontiers of Development Administration*, Duke University Press, Durham, NC, 1970.

Riggs, F. W., Bureaucrats and political development: a paradoxical view, In *Bureaucracy and Political Development*, LaPalombara, J., Ed., Princeton University Press, Princeton, NJ, 1967.

Riggs, F. W., *Administration in Developing Countries: The Theory of Prismatic Society*, Houghton Mifflin, Boston, MA, 1964.

Rodrik, D., and Arvind, S., The primacy of institutions (and what this does and does not mean), *Finance and Development*, 40(2), 31–34, 2003.

Rupert, J., Ukraine starts selling state-owned firms, *Washington Post*, January 27.

Russell, C. S., Introduction, In *Public Choice and Rural Development*, Russell, C. S. and Nicholson, N. K., Eds., Resources for the Future, Washington, DC, pp. 1–17, 1981.

Russell, C. S. and Nicholson, N. K., *Public Choice and Rural Development*, Resources for the Future, Washington, DC, 1981.

Saint-Martin, D., How the reinventing government movement in public administration was exported from the U.S. to other countries, *International Journal of Public Administration*, 24(6), 573–605, 2001.

Sachs, J. D., Notes on a new sociology of economic development, In *Culture Matters: How Values Shape Human Progress*, Harrison L. E. and Huntington, S. P., Eds., Basic Books, New York, pp. 29–43, 2000.

Schick, A., Why most developing countries should not try New Zealand reforms, *The World Bank Research Observer*, 13, 123–131, 1998.

Schick, A., Budgeting for results: recent developments in five industrialized countries, *Public Administration Review*, 50, 26–35, 1990.

Schick, A., Micro-budgetary adaptations to fiscal stress in industrialized democracies, *Public Administration Review*, 48, 523–534, 1988.

Shah, A., The New Fiscal Federalism in Brazil, Discussion paper #124, World Bank Washington, DC, 1991.

Shahid, Javed Burki and Guillermo, Perry, *Beyond the Washington Consensus: Institutions Matter*, World Bank, Washington, DC, 1998.

Shirley, M. and Nellis, J., *Public Enterprise Reform, The Lessons of Experience*, World Bank, Washington, DC, 1991.

Schroeder, L., *A Guide to Sustaining Rural Infrastructure Investments*, Associates in Rural Development, Burlington, VT, 1993.

Siegmund, U., *Are there Nationalization-Privatization Cycles? Paper Presented at the Inaugural Conference for the Society for New Institutional Economics, September 19–21*, Washington University-St Louis, MO, 1997.

Siffin, W. J., Two decades of public administration in developing countries, *Public Administration Review*, 36(1), 61–71, 1976.

Siffin, W. J., The problem of development administration, In *Handbook of Comparative and Development Public Administration*, Farazmand, A., Ed., Marcel Dekker, New York, pp. 5–14, 1991.

Stevens, M., Preparing for civil service pay and employment reform, In *Rehabilitating Government: Pay and Employment Reform in Africa*, Lindaur, D. L. and Nunberg, B., Eds., World Bank, Washington, DC, pp. 103–119, 1994.

Stillman, R. J., American vs. European public administration: does public administration make the modern state, or does the state make public administration?, *Public Administration Review*, 57, 332–339, 1997.

Subramaniam, V., Comparative public administration: from failed universal theory to raw empiricism—a frank analysis and guidelines towards a realistic perspective, *International Review of Administrative Sciences*, 66, 557–572, 2000.

Tanzi, V., Ed, *Fiscal Policies in Economies in Transition*, International Monetary Fund, Washington, DC, 1992.

Tapia-Videla, J. L., Understanding organizations and environments: a comparative perspective, *Public Administration Review*, 36, 631–636, 1976.

Thomson, J. T., Public choice analysis of institutional constraints on firewood production strategies in the West African Sahel, In *Public Choice and Rural Development*, Russell, C. S. and Nicholson, N. K., Eds., Resources for the Future, Washington, DC, 1981.

Thompson, F., Public economics and public administration, In *Handbook of Public Administration*, 2nd ed., Rabin, J. et al., Eds., Marcel Dekker, New York, 1997.

United Nations Food and Agricultural Organization (UNFAO), *Estudio Comparativo de las Administraciones Forestales Publicas de America Latina*, UNFAO, Rome, 1975.

Veliz, C., *The Centralist Tradition of Latin America*, Princeton University Press, Princeton, NJ, 1980.

Verheijen, T., Public management in East and Central Europe, In *Innovations in Public Management: Perspectives from East and West Europe*, Verheijen, T. and Coombes, D., Eds., Edward Elgar, Cheltenham, UK, pp. 207–219, 1998.

Vickers, J. and Wright, V., Eds., *The Politics of Privatization in Western Europe*, Frank Cass, London, 1989.

Wallich, C. I., Ed., *Russia and the Challenge of Fiscal Federalism*, World Bank, Washington, DC, 1994.

Weiss, L., War, the state, and the origins of the Japanese employment system, *Politics & Society*, 21(3), 325–354, 1993.

Welch, E. and Wong, W., Public administration in a global context: bridging the gaps of theory and practice between Western and non-Western nations, *Public Administration Review*, 58, 40–50, 1998.

Wesberry, J. P., *Integrated Financial Management in Government*, World Bank, Washington, DC, 1994.

Wildavsky, A., *Budgeting: A Comparative Theory of Budgetary Processes*, Rev. ed., Transaction Books, New Brunswick, NJ, 1986.

Wilson, J. Q., Reinventing public administration, *PS: Political Science and Politics*, 27, 667–673, 1994.

Wollman, H., Public sector reforms and evaluation: trajectories and trends, An international overview, In *Evaluating Public Sector Reforms: An International and Comparative Perspective, Special Issue of Revista International de Estudios Politicos*, Wollman, H., Ed., pp. 11–40, 2000.

World Bank, *Overview of Governance & Public Sector Reform*, Available at URL: http://www1.worldbank.org/publicsector/index.cfm, 2004.

World Bank Governance, *The World Bank's Experience*, World Bank, Washington, DC, 1994.

World Bank Governance, *The Philippines Country Economic Report: Public Sector Resource Mobilization and Expenditure Management*, World Bank, Washington, DC, 1992.

World Bank Governance, *Nepal: Civil Service Reform: An Agenda for Action*, World Bank, Washington, DC, 1993.

World Bank Governance, *Poland: Transforming the State: Issues in Public Administration Reform*, World Bank, Washington, DC, 1993.

World Bank Governance, *Sub-Saharan Africa: From Crisis to Sustainable Growth*, World Bank, Washington, DC, 1989.

Wright, G. and Nemc, J., *Public Management in the Central and Eastern European Transition: Concepts and Cases*, Network of Institutes and Schools of Public Administration in Central and Eastern Europe, Bratislava, 2002.

Wynia, G. W., *The Politics of Latin America Development*, 2nd ed., Cambridge University Press, Cambridge, 1984.

Zahariadis, N., *Markets, States, and Public Policy: Privatization in Britain and France*, University of Michigan Press, Ann Arbor, MI, 1995.

16 Issues in Comparative and International Administration

Ferrel Heady, Bruce Perlman, and Mario Rivera

CONTENTS

I. COMPARATIVE AND INTERNATIONAL PERSPECTIVES

A. HISTORICAL BACKGROUND

The study of public administration has tended historically to concentrate on the administrative systems of individual nation-states. This is particularly characteristic of the discipline as it evolved and gained recognition in the United States. Such parochialism has often been deplored. There have been occasional efforts to broaden the horizon of attention, but only during the last few decades have these efforts produced substantial results.

Two focuses of interest beyond the American system of administration have emerged. The first focus is the set of comparisons among patterns of public administration in different nation-states, often including the United States, while considering a variety of other administrations, both historical and contemporary. Although its origins can be traced to earlier periods, comparative public administration in this sense is mainly the product of a movement that began in the years just after World War II. This movement peaked during the late 1960s and early 1970s, underwent a number of adjustments and reorientations in the 1980s and 1990s, and continues to develop integrally around newly salient concerns in the first decade of the twenty-first century. The second focus is international public administration, historically centered on the administrative operations of agencies created by sovereign nation-states as instrumentalities for international or regional cooperation. First stimulated by the establishment of the League of Nations, international administration has persisted to the present as a distinct field; its driving interests are largely defined by the problems that international organizations, notably the United Nations, have faced.

Comparative public administration did not gain a self-conscious identity until after World War II. Leaders of the comparativist movement were mainly identified with public administration as an academic field of study, and most had gained foreign experience either in military service or in postwar technical assistance programs. They recognized early the need to familiarize themselves with comparative politics as a subfield in political science, and they also found it necessary to draw on sociology, economics, management science, and other disciplines in their effort to make cross-national comparisons among institutions and processes of government.

Interest in international administration emerged between the two world wars as a byproduct of international organization as a field of specialization in political science. The link between students of international administration and political science was primarily through the sub-discipline of international relations. As a consequence, although most students of comparative public administration and international public administration were political scientists, the students tended to be from different subfields in that discipline. This meant that their educational backgrounds were somewhat dissimilar, as were their methodological preferences. Consequently, sizable bodies of literature were generated in both comparative and international administration, but with few close connections between the two fields.

Comparative public administration and international public administration both avoid concentration on the administrative system of a particular nation-state. The fields also share many attributes and confront common issues, which is an indication that treating the two subfields together would be generally advantageous. This assumption links them in this discussion. Even a casual survey of the academic literature on these subjects reveals, however, that whatever the substantive connection between the two, the fields have generally been dealt with separately rather than in tandem.

The explanation seems to be that contributors to comparative public administration, on the one hand, and international public administration, on the other, have drawn on different intellectual sources in their work. The closest association of persons with a primary interest in one or the other of these specializations has been through affiliates of major professional societies, such as the Section on International and Comparative Administration of the American Society for Public Administration and similar groups attached to the American Political Science Association, the National Academy of Public Administration, the National Association of Schools of Public Affairs and Administration, and other umbrella organizations in the United States. The International Political Science Association, the International Institute of Administrative Sciences, and other organizations have provided equivalent support cross-nationally. Despite such support, comparative and international public administration teaching and research have, for the most part, been undertaken along parallel paths rather than collaboratively.

The identification of central common themes is difficult when comparative and international administration are taken together. Much may be gained by the effort, because the two are much more closely linked in substance than they have been in practice. As a prelude to identifying and examining these issues, some attention must be given to variations in perspective between comparative and international public administration due to the differing circumstances affecting the evolutionary development of these areas of specialization. This preliminary overview is followed by further analysis of some of the characteristics of each field.

B. COMPARATIVE ADMINISTRATION

American students and practitioners of public administration have, from the beginning, shown an interest in the administrative experiences of other historical and contemporary political systems (Riggs 1976), but this has never been the dominant focus for a field of study that concentrated for the most part on American problems and American solutions. During the first century after independence, there were sporadic evidences of inquiries into and borrowings from foreign administrative systems by founders such as Madison, Hamilton, and Jefferson. Alexis de Tocqueville, as a foreign commentator on American institutions, constantly made comparisons with European counterparts. The civil service reform movement of the post-Civil War period was guided mainly by British experience in the installation of a merit system. Woodrow Wilson, Frank Goodnow, and others who helped to shape the administrative state and to promote the study of public administration and administrative law, demonstrated their knowledge of European precedents and urged Americans to benefit by adapting these to the needs of the United States. From the turn of the twentieth century to the end of World War II, when American public administration was emerging as a self-conscious and accepted field of academic study and research, the comparative element diminished until it was just a part of the overall effort. Only since World War II has comparative public administration finally become a field within public administration and political science that has demonstrated its own vitality and has gained separate recognition and acceptance. After a remarkable burst of activity during the 1960s and early 1970s, enthusiasm declined and the mood became more introspective and pessimistic, but comparativism has clearly become established over the three intervening decades as an integral disciplinary component of public administration (Heady 1966, 1987).

Characteristics of the post-war comparative administration movement shaped the dimensions of the contemporary comparative perspective. The most important of these characteristics have been an urge to find a framework for analysis that permits comparisons on a global basis among existing nation-states; a special interest in the administrative problems of newly independent and developing countries; confidence in the advantages of transfers of administrative technologies from more advanced to less advanced nations; and a continuing desire to scrutinize and evaluate previous activities to devise more productive methods for comparative studies in the future. In combination, these characteristics explain features of the evolution of comparative administration. An example is the lack of agreement on a disciplinary paradigm, which led to controversy as to how scientific the field could claim to be. The main options for research have been a "general-systems" approach, with Riggs (1964, 1973) as its strongest advocate, and a middle-range approach based on bureaucratic theory, promoted early by Presthus (1959) and Waldo (1964) and later described by Arora (1972) as "the single most dominant conceptual framework in the study of comparative administration." The focus on newly independent countries resulted in a great deal of work on "development administration" (Esman 1991; Gant 1979; Honadle 1982; Huque 1990; Siffin 1991), leading to controversies as to how administrative improvement could be brought about and what the role of technical assistance projects should be in this regard. Both veterans and newcomers to the field have undertaken numerous reassessments, however (Caiden and Caiden 1990; Heady 1996; Peters 1988, 1994; Waldo 1976), indicating that a stage of maturity has arrived.

C. INTERNATIONAL ADMINISTRATION

The international administration perspective must be considered part of the study of international organization, a field of specialization within political science. International public administration never succeeded in establishing a separate identity to the extent that comparative public administration did beginning in the 1950s. As a result, the literature of international administration consists primarily of that part of international organization output that has been produced by what Ruggie (1985) describes as "a steady if low level of interest in the administrative workings of international agencies and programs." Stages in the evolution of international organization as an international relations subfield thus became the focus of interest. Rochester (1986, 779) states that "international organization did not become an identifiable, systematic area of inquiry until the creation of the League of Nations in 1920 ... at a time when the international relations field itself emerged as a distinct academic discipline." During the interwar period and World War II, the literature of international organization was largely descriptive and normative, dealing mostly with the League of Nations and its subsidiary institutions (Yalem 1966). The scholars who took this approach were later characterized as idealists, because their concern was more with potentiality than with actuality in the operations of international institutions.

With the creation of the United Nations in 1945, the idealist school shifted its interest to this new international agency and its subsidiaries, but its concern with institution-building was challenged by the realists who soon became dominant, with Morgenthau (1948) a leading spokesmen. Their focus was on "state sovereignty, the elements of national power, military strategy, diplomacy and other instruments of statecraft, and the nature of national interests" (Rochester 1986, 781). Concern with international organizations was essentially limited to the role of these institutions in the management of balance of power or concert of power politics.

The debate between idealists and realists continued vigorously during the postwar years, tending to exaggerate the disagreements between them and to mask the similarities. As Inis Claude, the author of an influential text (Claude 1956) that attempted to combine the two approaches, observed (Claude 1981, 199), "The major difference between realism and idealism pertains not to what is or what should be but to what is possible." Perhaps more important in the evolution of the field have been the shifts noted by Rochester (1986) and Ruggie (1985) in substantive focus from global to regional issues, nongovernmental organizations (NGOs), and international regimes, and also in methodology from traditionalist to quantitative research techniques, and in modes of research analysis from descriptive and normative toward more theoretical and empirical approaches.

Significantly more than comparative administration, international administration as a field appears to be in a state of chronic disarray, as evaluated by specialist commentators. Rochester (1986) speaks of the "failure" of the international organization field. He found that, by the 1970s, "many observers of international organizations were becoming more interested in studying the politics surrounding international organizations than in studying the organizations themselves." Rochester also found a pattern in the postwar era that led the study of international organization to the brink of collapse in the early 1980s and to a "virtual loss of identity of the field." He recommends as a "first step" that there be a return "to a conception of international organization which distinguishes it clearly from other international relations phenomena."

II. ISSUES IN COMPARATIVE AND INTERNATIONAL ADMINISTRATION

Five issues have been identified, for reasons that will be explained, as the most crucial for the combined field of comparative and international public administration:

1. What is the best framework, or acceptable optional frameworks, for the study, on a comparative basis, of national systems of public administration and the study of administration in public international organizations?
2. What are the current and prospective probabilities for achieving empirical knowledge about improvements in administrative capabilities in these settings?

3. What are the major trends and prospects for development of administrative capabilities in less-developed nations?
4. How can a competent civil service operating in an adequate administrative structure be achieved in international organizations, given the context of a global nation-state system?
5. What are the implications for comparative and international administration of possible future system transformations?

Primary attention will be given to consideration of these major issues as each has appeared in the evolutionary course of comparative international administration. This historical survey will conclude with an assessment of the possibility and desirability of disciplinary convergence, based both on history and on the emergence of certain integrative themes.

A. FRAMEWORKS OF STUDY

A major and continuing concern for both comparative and international public administration has been the search for the most appropriate framework, model, or paradigm for analysis. In no case has this search been successful in the sense of identifying and establishing a single paradigm as standard for the field. Although each field has confronted a common dilemma in seeking consensus, the specifics of the alternatives considered are largely separate, with only minor commonalities.

Most of the options in comparative administration appeared early during the postwar emergence of interest in the field and have remained in contention since, although some of them have seen changes in emphasis over time. By the early 1960s, one of the authors (Heady 1962) identified four categories of cross-national comparative administration studies. The category that differed the least from more parochially based research was labeled modified traditional. It consisted primarily of cases in which studies of such subjects as standard as human resource management or administration, in programmatic areas such as health or agriculture, were extended from particular national administrative systems to comparisons among them; but it also included a number of institutional comparisons of administration in Western developed countries, with emphasis on differences in central government organizational arrangements and civil service systems. Such comparisons continue to be made today, often with useful results, but this is not considered to be a promising pattern for progress in the field.

A more productive and enduring focus has been development administration. The term itself was apparently coined in the 1950s by George Gant, a staff member of the Ford Foundation. It conveniently highlighted a desire to give concentrated attention to improvement in the administrative capabilities of developing countries. This had the advantage of responding to two objectives accepted by most comparative administration pioneers: extending the range of comparison on a global basis beyond advanced Western countries, and assisting newly independent nations in meeting their nation-building needs. The Comparative Administration Group (CAG) was affiliated with the American Society for Public Administration, the organizational base for the movement. For the CAG, this alliance had the additional advantage that it attracted financial support, particularly from the Ford Foundation, which provided grants to the CAG during its most active decade. The outcome was that during the 1960s development administration and comparative administration became almost synonymous terms, and most CAG-sponsored publications included the words development or developmental in their titles.

These considerations masked the built-in problems of development administration as a basic framework for advancement of the field. Ambiguities in the meaning of the term have never been satisfactorily cleared up. The most widely accepted definition is one advocated by Gant (1979), who defined it as "the complex of agencies, management systems, and processes a government establishes to achieve its development goals," centered in "nation-building departments or ministries, in such fields as agriculture, industry, education, and health." This definition had the advantage of focusing on less-developed countries, while recognizing that more developed ones also had developmental problems. It also did not clearly differentiate between development and non-development administration. Commentators found problems of substance and not just semantics in these distinctions. For instance, Esman (1991) conceded that "the concept of development has been and remains imprecise," and "multi-dimensional, with scholars and practitioners disagreeing, however, on relative emphasis, priority, and timing." For Siffin (1991), "development administration" was "the indicative but imprecise label for a set, or at least a potential batch, of problems" and "a subject matter lacking clear boundaries and crisp disciplinary rigor." One difficulty has been that the field, however defined, is rather limited in scope in the context of public administration; and cross-national studies confined to issues of development administration necessarily exclude many legitimate topics from comparison.

Recognition of this shortcoming, along with growing evidence of deficiencies in the performance record of technical assistance programs designed to assist developing countries, has diminished the appeal of the development administration approach as a framework. Interest in development administration endures, but the emphasis has shifted markedly to a reassessment of technical assistance goals and strategies. Interest has moved away from a model that focuses on organizational and procedural reform, and toward one that makes a more direct connection between public policy and administrative capacity, while stressing the importance of decentralization and local participation (Bryant and White 1982; Honadle 1982; Islam and Henault 1979; Korten 1980, 1990).

The leading model builder in comparative public administration has been Fred W. Riggs, whose preference has been for what is usually referred to as general-systems theory. This approach involves as a starting point the comparative analysis of whole societies, which can then be followed by study of societal segments such as the political system and its administrative subsystem. Influenced by structural-functionalism, Riggs (1964, 1973) has formulated and reformulated what he referred to as the "prismatic-sala" set of "ideal-type" models of societies and their component parts, as an analytic lens for contemporary administration, particularly in less-developed states. In his revised presentation, Riggs (1973) offers a framework for characterizing societies in two dimensions: degree of integration and degree of differentiation. Integration means close coordination among constituent social structures, while differentiation refers to the extent of subdivision or segmentation among these structures and the specificity of their functions.

While the "prismatic-sala" framework could be used to rank any society on each of these dimensions, its use by Riggs and others has been mostly limited to societies which he labels "orthoprismatic," and which he posits to correspond closely to those of many developing countries. Riggs has been particularly interested in the sala administrative subsystem of such societies and has speculated in detail as to its characteristics. Riggs has also published a case study (Riggs 1966) of Thailand as a "bureaucratic polity" with typical orthoprismatic features, but he has not attempted to use his model to place a large array of contemporary nations along the two-dimensional typological framework. The only other contemporaneous instance of a general-systems approach was Dorsey's (1962) proposed "information-energy" model, which Dorsey applied in an analysis of political development in Vietnam (Dorsey 1963). Berenson (1977) tested it in a multination study with what he considered disappointing results.

As already mentioned, Presthus (1959) took the lead in suggesting what he referred to as "middle-range" theory as an alternative to the "cosmic dimension" he considered characteristic of general-systems theory. A readily available example of such middle-range theory was the ideal-type model of bureaucracy which had been formulated early in the century by Max Weber, and subsequently revised by other sociologists and political scientists. Berger (1957) pioneered its use in a study of the bureaucracy of contemporary Egypt, and the role of bureaucracy in political development was emphasized in a series of studies published in an influential volume edited by LaPalombara (1963). The public bureaucracies that exist in every contemporary nation-state were chosen as the focus for comparison in the first general text on comparative public administration, which originally appeared in 1966 (Heady 1966). By the early 1970s, bureaucratic middle-range theory had become recognized as the most useful and frequently preferred alternative among the available frameworks of research and study, without establishing itself, however, as the standard analytical framework in a field that continued to value diversity rather than orthodoxy.

The only contemporary innovation that might be considered as an additional alternative is the use of a public policy orientation as the principal basis for comparison. There has been, without question, a marked upsurge since the mid-1970s in comparative public policy studies. This development in many ways replicates the earlier, broader comparative public administration movement (Hancock 1983). Henderson (1981) views this as a significant trend, but public policy is similar to other segmental approaches in its subject-matter limitation to less than the comparison of whole national administrative systems. Hence, comparative public policy does not appear to be a feasible substitute for earlier models that have been competing for recognition, and is unlikely to succeed where these models failed in establishing the basis for a still-elusive disciplinary consensus.

Identification of the competing paradigms in international administration is more difficult and more controversial, with authoritative commentators offering a variety of analyses—including Abi-Saab (1981), Feld et al. (1983), and Rochester (1986). A helpful summary approach, as Rochester suggests, is to review four alternatives that have appeared in successive chronological order during the last half-century as the most popular frameworks for study. These approaches are most commonly referred to as idealism, realism, globalism (or modernism), and neorealism. As already indicated, the long-range competition has been between the idealist and realist schools, while the other two approaches are variations on these two basic options. These labels are shorthand for a cluster of related features having to do with the preferred scope, focus, methodology, and value orientation of each approach. Shifts in the weight of scholarship over time have been due, at least in part, to critical events and contingencies in the international arena.

Idealism has been characterized by the following things: the relatively narrow demarcation of the scope of the field, a focus on the organization and administration of institutions that are clearly international and governmental, a methodology that is traditional and does not stress quantitative techniques, and a value commitment to improvement in the capabilities of these institutions to reduce international tensions and conflicts. Both before and after World War II, the purview of the idealists was limited by the conventional definition of an international organization as "an institutionalized arrangement among members of the international system to solve tasks which have evolved from systemic conditions" (Hanrieder 1971) or as "an association of States, established by agreement among its members and ... whose task it is to pursue objectives of common interest by means of co-operation among its members" (Virally 1981).

The idealist focus was mainly on global organizations—earlier the League of Nations and later the United Nations—or their specialized agencies, such as the International Labor Organization (ILO) and the World Health Organization (WHO). Methods of research were primarily descriptive, resulting in narratives of institutional development or analyses of formal institutional characteristics. Idealists have tended to be highly prescriptive, and aim at the building up of those international organizations that could promote peace and lead to world government. A representative book is Clark and Sohn's (1958) *World Peace Through World Law*.

The realist reaction, initiated by Morgenthau in the 1940s, gained strength in the 1950s and peaked in the 1960s, altering several of these priorities. Although international organizations continued to be the prime subject of study, attention markedly turned to regionalism and regional institutions, particularly related to the European Community, but focused to a lesser extent on Latin America, the Middle East, and other regions. Empiricism in research was emphasized as part of the behavioral movement in the social sciences, and experimentation with quantitative techniques increased. More efforts were made to go beyond descriptive treatments of institutions toward theoretical formulations and empirical testing as a guide to research endeavors. Value neutrality was believed to allow a more realistic perception of the international political domain. Commenting on the general situation in the field of international relations during this period, Holsti (1971) summed it up by saying that "the major preoccupations of theorists... have been to explore specific problems, to form hypotheses or generalizations explaining limited ranges of phenomena, and, particularly, to obtain data to test those hypotheses." Haas (1958) provides a prominent example of such research.

The globalist or modernist reaction, which emerged during the early 1970s variously as a challenge to and refinement of realism, was stimulated by contemporary events such as the 1973 oil embargo and recognition of such worldwide problems as population growth and environmental degradation. The globalist approach had significant impact on international organization studies. The growing complexity of interdependence was believed to necessitate an extension of the scope of attention beyond sovereign nation-states and international organizations to nongovernmental organizations (NGOs), such as international disaster relief agencies and multinational corporations, thus broadening the meaning and reach of international organization as a field beyond formal institutions of international governance like the United Nations.

The importance and effectiveness of regional institutions were questioned by advocates of the new globalist perspective, and interest in regionalism declined. Quantitative research techniques continued to be favored in principle but were not used any more widely in practice than before, and increasing doubt was expressed as to the field's putative quest for the cumulative acquisition of knowledge. Moreover, international organization scholars "were urged to deal more squarely and directly with values, or at the very least make more explicit the normative or prescriptive implications of their research. The post-behavioral call to relate knowledge to action led in the international organization field to an increased policy science perspective" (Rochester 1986).

A more influential disciplinary trend has been neorealism. As the name implies, neorealism is not so much a new model as a reformulation of the realist position, with several significant differences. One has to do with scope. Neorealists have extended the range of international administration by emphasizing the importance of international regimes. This concept has numerous definitions. One is that such regimes are "recognized patterns of practice around which expectations converge" and "may or may not be accompanied by explicit organizational arrangements" (Young 1980). Another is that regimes are "goal-oriented enterprises whose participating members seek benefits through explicit or tacit authoritative allocations of values" (Feld et al. 1983). Rochester (1986) maintains that the amorphous quality of neorealism "has meant almost intellectual chaos" to the international organization field.

Neorealism is more pessimistic and more fatalistic about prospects for the future than are the idealist and globalist strains of international organization studies. Rochester (1986) thinks that the value orientation of neorealism, especially as manifested in some forms of regime analysis, has "an implicit bias against any major changes in the fabric of world politics" and marks "the completion of the postwar odyssey of scholars away from interwar idealism." Whether or not one agrees with Rochester's conclusion, the evidence from the present survey is that there is no consensus in the field as to what its paradigmatic framework should be.

B. THE ACQUISITION OF KNOWLEDGE

In the 1970s and 1980s, comparative and international administration, along with numerous other social and behavioral science specializations, sought to become more scientific in their efforts to acquire knowledge. The often-cited work of Kuhn (1970) was very influential in the interpretation of that shift. Although Kuhn was concerned primarily with hard sciences such as physics and chemistry rather than soft sciences such as political science and sociology, his specifications as to what constitutes a science were widely accepted for a time as criteria for evaluating progress in the social and behavioral sciences. In his formulation, the key requirement for a field to claim to be a normal science is that a standard paradigm or theoretical framework for study emerge and be accepted as appropriate in the given discipline. The urge to conform to Kuhn's criterion of paradigmatic consensus was very strong for those striving to establish scientific credentials for their research activities. An inability to achieve such consensus was often cited as evidence of failure to make satisfactory disciplinary progress.

Another crucial consideration has been the generalizability of professed knowledge resulting from scientific or quasi-scientific research. Dahl (1947, 8) emphasized the importance of comparative aspects of public administration in evaluating claims that there is or can be a "science" of public administration. He pointed out that knowledge applicable only to a particular national system of administration is insufficient, and that the requirement should be "a body of generalized principles independent of their peculiar national setting." Although this admonition has been noted in the literature of comparative public administration, it is equally pertinent to research in international administration. Presumably, scientific knowledge would also have to be applicable not just to one or a cluster of international organizations, but to all of them. Moreover, generalized administrative knowledge should have relevance for both domestic administrative systems and international ones outside the institutional framework of particular nation-states. Finally, comparison is taken to be an inescapable and fundamental trait of all evaluative analysis.

The proposal of paradigmatic options in comparative administration has been an effort to some extent to respond to these calls for acceptance and generality of application. General-systems theorists such as Riggs and Dorsey have stressed the advantages of an ecological approach which places national systems of administration in their respective political and social settings before turning to comparisons among them. In development administration research, Korten (1980), Rondinelli and Ingle (1981), and others have concentrated on formulation of systematic strategies for improving the implementation of development programs and have viewed their effort as the application of principles drawn from a general science of management.

Likewise in international organization/administration, advocates of each proposed model have backed it as the most deserving of general acceptance, and better at promoting the systematic accumulation of knowledge. As previously noted, the behavioral movement to make the study of international organization more scientific peaked in the 1960s, and by the mid-1970s there was a postbehavioral reaction, with the judgment expressed (as quoted by Rochester 1986, 795, 796) that a "science of international organization" had failed to materialize as promised. However, both comparative and international administration have, perhaps inevitably, fallen short of success in settling on an orthodox paradigm and in demonstrating conclusively that they build on Kuhnian scientific principles and protocols—although that does not mean that these fields have failed to make substantial progress or to advance empirical research or cumulative knowledge.

A complaint frequently voiced by critics of comparative administration is that the search for a scientific paradigm enjoying general acceptance has been futile, but those critics differ in their suggestions as to what the defining disciplinary framework should be. Similarly, international organization/administration experts have shifted position from time to time as to what model attracts the most support, without moving to greater consensus. Both fields are apparently floundering in what Kuhn terms a "preparadigmatic" stage.

Again, however, the more important question is how much cumulative buildup of usable knowledge has taken place, whether or not that knowledge qualifies as the product of a science. As Waldo once pointed out (1980, 22), "the root meaning of *science* is *knowledge*." "Scientific" knowledge, he notes, has become "associated with the methods and findings of the natural sciences, more strictly with the physical sciences, and what doesn't fit this pattern is deemed second-rate knowledge or nonknowledge," adding that it is not at all evident that physical science is more advanced than social science in the marriage of its findings with technology to bring about "concrete transformations." A general reaction against the movement toward a hard science benchmark for the social sciences is that it is actually a scientistic and reductionist criterion.

Peter Savage provides a balanced summary of the accomplishments of the comparative administration movement, suggesting that failure to meet earlier expectations had "more to do with the complexities and intractabilities in its chosen domain than with faulty purpose" (1976, 420–422). Even severe critics of the overall results of the movement concede that its vitality and productivity added greatly to available knowledge in a relatively brief span of time. Assessments cited by Rochester (1986, 807–809) of international administration indicate greater variability, leading him to observe that "there is huge discord over even so basic a question as the general degree to which knowledge in the field has been advanced." He concludes that "the cumulative knowledge problem" found across many disciplines seems unusually acute in this field.

C. Administrative Capabilities and Governance in the Less-Developed Countries

In its practical application, knowledge in public administration aims to improve administrative operations and, more generally, the capability of corresponding institutions. In both comparative administration and international administration special attention has been devoted to the enhancement of administrative capabilities in areas selected as having crucial importance to each field. Most observers of the public bureaucratic organizations of nation-states agree that they should meet two basic performance criteria: they should be exhibit efficacy and efficiency, and they should be instrumental. The first criterion requires a public bureaucracy to make effective use of resources to meet public policy objectives. A bureaucracy meets the second criterion if it is instrumental in serving as institutional agent and, not acting as master or principal, responding to political leadership from outside its ranks in the choice of public policy objectives. Countries of the so-called Third World (a term now largely abandoned) were likely to be labeled as developing or modernizing in large part because their bureaucracies were judged neither efficient nor instrumental. A continuing theme in comparative public administration as well as specifically in development administration has been the challenge of improving the capacity of public institutions in less-developed countries as measured by these two standards.

During the 1950s and early 1960s, the rapid buildup of bilateral and multilateral technical assistance programs and the emergence of issues of development administration occurred in response to the perceived necessity for urgent and dramatic social transformation in countries with only rudimentary administrative systems, usually derived from pre-independence antecedents designed by the former colonizing power or powers. Advocates of development administration such as Weidner (1962) stressed the need "to relate different administrative roles, practices, organizational arrangements, and procedures to the maximizing of development objectives." During the same period, general-systems theorists such as Riggs (1964) suggested that there was a direct causal link between the opportunities presented to many of these public bureaucracies to gain political power and their inadequacies in administrative performance.

By the early 1970s, evidence had accumulated that the problem of administrative inefficiency combined with bureaucratic elite political dominance was growing. Administrative reform efforts through technical assistance projects had been disappointing, and often produced unintended, counterproductive outcomes (Siffin 1976). Military regimes became more and more prevalent, with the result that, by the mid-1970s, more than a third of the member states of the United Nations had governments installed by military intervention (Welch 1976). The prevailing pattern was for military and civilian professional bureaucrats to work in concert, with the military having or striving for ultimate control. Such bureaucratic polities or bureaucratic-authoritarian regimes were generally judged by comparativists to fail the aforementioned, twofold capability test.

Significant efforts have been directed at reversing these trends, with mixed results. Special attention has been given to both substance and procedure in technical assistance.

A major controversy has persisted over the issue of whether or not externally generated projects to upgrade administrative performance should be encouraged in countries where the public bureaucracy is already dominant over other political institutions. Supporters of what is labeled the imbalance thesis contend that further strengthening the bureaucratic institutions under such circumstances only aggravates the problems of equilibrium and autonomy, lessening the likelihood of balanced political growth. Its critics argue that, as a rule, requests for technical assistance should be honored by donor countries, even though the polity may appear to be out of balance because of bureaucratic dominance. This essay will return to questions relating to the state of development assistance thinking and practice, in the context of comparative administration, at its conclusion.

Riggs (1963, 1970, 1971) has been a leading spokesman for the first point of view, contending that the objective should be the attainment of a balanced polity with a reasonably stable equilibrium between the bureaucracy and the "constitutive system." The constitutive system is one made up of such elements as an electoral system, an elected legislature and executive, and a party system. External efforts at strengthening a spectrum of social institutions in a bureaucratic polity are opposed for not only contributing to political imbalance but also for impairing administrative performance. Braibanti (1961, 1969) has been a consistent advocate of the contrary view that a competent bureaucracy is a primary requisite for political development, and that strengthening public administration is desirable whatever the overall political balance of power may be. He therefore asserts that the general strategy for external inducement of political development should be to strengthen as many political institutions as possible, including already strong bureaucracies. The hope is for a trickle-down effect, where more mature institutions help to strengthen weaker ones.

The debate about competing strategies for administrative capacity building and balanced political development continues (Heady 1996). Sigelman (1972, 1974) conducted two separate tests of the imbalance thesis, analyzing data on a large group of developing countries, with 57 in one test and 38 in the other, as to the relationship between bureaucratic maturity and political "over-participation." Contrary to the presumption of the imbalance thesis of a positive relationship between bureaucratic development and political dominance, Sigelman found that it was actually the less-developed bureaucracies that tended to seize power. Mabbutt (1979) undertook still another study in which he corrected what he considered to be deficiencies in Sigelman's research, but Mabbutt also concluded that several strains of the imbalance thesis are not supported by empirical research.

In any event, the trend in development administration has been away from administrative reform of central government bureaucracies as such and toward improvement of the decentralized operation of specific, locally targeted development projects. In the Latin American development assistance program, according to authors Perlman and Rivera, the US Agency for International Development has tended to favor aid to municipal governments over central governments on the basis of their relatively greater creativity, innovativeness, and effectiveness, including their propensity to establish often improvised cross-sectoral links and public–private partnerships, thereby doing more with fewer resources than central government institutions.

D. ADMINISTRATIVE CAPABILITIES OF INTERNATIONAL INSTITUTIONS AND AGENCIES

International administration, defined by Weiss (1975) as "the conduct of public affairs through an international body utilizing public resources," can be used, he points out, "to describe collectively the group of officials that administers international organizations." These officials comprise the international civil service, a key concern for students of international administration interested in improving the administrative capabilities of agencies like the United Nations.

International institutions were preceded by national ones, so the natural instinct is to compare the two. Opinions on this issue differ widely. Van Wagenen (1971) expresses the most common view when he states: "The *similarities* overwhelm the differences between national and international administration." At the other extreme is the assertion by McLaren (1980) that "the findings of public administration, concerning the secretariats of national governments, are not applicable to the secretariats of international organizations." Obviously, preexisting national administrative systems have influenced the development of international administration, but the operating environment and the tasks are not the same, so resulting differences should be expected. Claude (1984) argues that there "are no long-established patterns of administrative structure and procedure in the international field, or traditional values of international public service," and that national precedents are "inconsistent with each other and they may be, singly or in combination, inconsistent with the requirements of international administration." Another factor is noted by Jordan (1971), who comments that "whereas domestically there has evolved a variety of means by which bureaucrats carry out their purposes, and [of] national administrative traditions to serve national needs, such has not been the case internationally... The primacy of the state as the major political force in world affairs has been one reason for this situation."

The situation can be described in a phrase as the international secretariat tradition. Its origins are traced to the Congress of Vienna, but the most important precedent was the existence in Great Britain of a secretariat system that originated early in the twentieth century in the Committee of Imperial Defense and extended to the British Cabinet generally by the end of World War I (Jordan 1971). The essence of the secretariat as an institution was that there should be a group of non-political professional civil servants at the service of political, policy-making authorities. This cadre was concerned primarily with the implementation rather than the making of policy.

When the League of Nations was founded, its first secretary general was Sir Eric Drummond, who adapted the British secretariat arrangements with which he was familiar to the needs of the League, by creating an international civil service intended to be loyal to the League as an international organization, rather than to the countries of national origin of the secretariat members. The international secretariat pattern was later copied by the United Nations and the international civil service that ensued was presumed to have four basic characteristics: loyalty to the international organization, impartiality in the execution of policy, independence from allegiances to countries of origin, and personnel recruitment and retention primarily on the basis of merit (Feld et al. 1983). The international organizations in which such a civil service operated were viewed as a hybrid product of nationalism and interdependence as the two main opposing forces in international affairs. Among key differences thought to exist between international and national bureaucratic institutions was the conciliar form of organization of the former, in contrast to the hierarchical form of organization in the latter. Moreover, the international secretariats were further removed from policy-making functions than their national counterparts.

The concept of an international civil service, according to Urquhart (1978), "is at the heart of the possibility, let alone the practicality, of eventually constructing some form of working world order. The international civil service ought to be the point at which expertise, disinterested common sense, far-sightedness, objective judgment, and moderation converge. It should provide the common ground where governments can begin to unify their conflicting viewpoints. It should be the heart of the effort to reach some working balance between national sovereignty and interest, and international responsibility." Reliance on international organizations as a collective means to address global needs has been especially great for developing countries (Feld et al. 1983), but there is also a growing general expectation that these organizations must play an accountable role, and establish a credible performance record in doing so.

Evaluations of the performance record of international organizations have been very mixed. Several assessments appeared in the early 1970s, after the United Nations had completed a quarter century of operations (James 1971; Mailick 1970). Some analysts then expressed optimism.

> Under the United Nations, global international organization has reached an unparalleled comprehensiveness and integration. Its present membership approaches universality, crossing all geographical, political and ideological lines.... Its functions cover virtually every major field of human endeavor.

Separate and isolated agencies of international administration and adjudication have, to a large extent, been brought under one umbrella as part of a single system of international cooperation. Though coordination is far from complete and the authority of the United Nations is limited, it provides the most extensive framework yet achieved for joint action on international problems (Jacob et al. 1972).

A more common pessimistic assessment was tied to what was seen as deterioration of the international civil service, because of a global situation that was becoming ever more nationalistic. A prominent manifestation was what James called the "specter" of the movement for equitable geographical distribution, which he contended had gradually led to establishment of a geographic quota system and appointment of second-rate officials. The conflict-of-loyalty problem was alleged to have been been increasing. The UN Secretariat gradually and painfully made a series of compromises with the original concept of an international career civil service. The question is whether these compromises have not merely undermined the original concept of an international civil service—in any event a very limited one—but also the capability of the Secretariat, to the point that it is incapable of fulfilling its tasks. James (1971) concluded that the demise of the Secretariat was "perilously close." During the intervening years, the problem continued to be whether a competent international civil service could be put in place and maintained in a world dominated by nation-states that put their own interests first and common global interests second.

Commentators during the 1980s generally agreed that the UN agenda had continued to expand, with the emphasis increasingly on management tasks, but were doubtful that its administrative problems were being resolved. Mathiason (1986) stated that "on the whole the United Nations has been asked to deal with an increasing variety of subjects, to perform increasingly complex tasks from an administrative point of view and has been provided with increasing resources for that purpose. The organization has clearly evolved from its initial function of servicing the transactions of nation-states into one of providing and administering global services." Mathiason (1986) nevertheless concluded that the financial and other problems of the United Nations reflected "a general malaise about the organization, its size and its general administration."

Jordan (1981), in a review of personnel policies and practices of the United Nations Secretariat, found evidence of low morale and general discontent in the international civil service, of increasing difficulty for the Secretary General in maintaining a sense of personnel security and commitment to the organization, and of a growing tendency for national governments and members of the international bureaucracy to put their own particular interests ahead of those of the United Nations as an organization. In a survey of the administrative problems of international organizations, Argyriades (1986) asserted that there had been "a great expansion in the scale and complexity of the operations of the United Nations with a less than commensurate increase in its capacity to cope with this situation." He found that nationality factors had become a major impetus in staff career development, along with intensification of "the relative importance of the representational and symbolic over the substantive content of the functions of particular posts, the senior posts especially." The principal casualties were precisely "merit, professionalism, and rationality norms," with the result that the dominant characteristic features of international organizations had become "diffraction, fragmentation, dispersion, [and] diversification."

Reymond and Mailick (1986) agreed with this view, but were somewhat more optimistic. Asserting that the main requirement was "to strengthen the independence and integrity of the international service," they tied the future of the UN service to the future of the organization itself, and urged that the service be adapted to the evolving structure and functions of the United Nations in a continuing process that "will be one of the important tasks of public administration."

As the United Nations neared its 50th anniversary in 1995, new analyses appeared concerning the condition and prospects of international organizations and the international civil service. A few analysts (Barkdull 1995; Krause and Knight 1995; Murphy 1994; Taylor 1993) provided wide-ranging theoretical treatments of the international system and its organizational manifestations. Some concentrated on the UN's operating problems (Eban 1995; Kennedy and Russett 1995; Urquhart and Childers 1990), such as the selection of senior Secretariat officials, and the dilemma posed by sharply increasing demand for services combined with increasingly precarious funding.

The greatest disciplinary interest has been shown in studies concerning bureaucracies in international organizations (Beigbeder 1988; Jordan 1988, 1991; Lengyel 1993; Mouritzen 1990; Pitt and Weiss 1986; Wilson 1994). The most generally accepted conclusion is well expressed by Jordan (1991), who says that "an international UN bureaucracy, composed of politically neutral international civil servants, recruited on the basis of merit, and subject to uniform standards of appointment, promotion, compensation, and retention must be viewed as being more of an ideal than a reflection of reality. The reality more closely approximates the highly politicized civil services of most member states." Lengyel (1993) expresses hope that "political circumstances now at last allow for, if they do not actually impel, moves which would have been unthinkable even five years ago." Even if he is correct, the problem of perfecting a competent international civil service in an increasingly turbulent global system is not likely to be easily solved.

Events implicating senior UN Secretariat levels in the multi-billion-dollar Oil-for-Food Program scandal and other financial crises have been advanced as evidence of an over-politicized and corrupt administration, and have raised questions as to the adequacy and viability of the organization, often in ideologically charged debates. For instance, Helle Dale (2004), who directs Foreign Policy and Defense Studies for the Heritage Foundation, has written in this context "these revelations do not inspire confidence that the United Nations is capable of running anything in Iraq…"

E. PROSPECTS FOR TRANSFORMATION OF A WORLD SYSTEM DOMINATED BY NATION-STATES

A persistent theme in the literature of both comparative and international administration has been speculation on prospective transformations in the existing nation-state world system, which might affect national and international bureaucratic institutions. Few of these conjectures have anticipated, at least in the short run, the disappearance of the nation-state as the dominant form of political order in the world, notwithstanding the global terrorist threat presented by nonstate actors (which rely on the support of national allies), and the apparent inability of international organizations to respond to the challenge. Most analysts have accepted Miller's (1986) view that "for the time being and for as far ahead as we can see," the sovereign state will remain the primary political entity. Attention has turned to significant, anticipated shifts in the characteristics of the nation-state system, including the role of nonstate actors, notably nongovernmental organizations, multilateral lending institutions, foundations, and even terrorist networks.

The common assumptions during the heyday of the founding comparative administration movement of the 1950s and 1960s were that all nations had much the same desire for national development, that less-developed nations would emulate more developed ones by taking the same developmental path, and that they would be assisted in so doing by importing administrative technology to provide crucial leverage in their developmental programs. These assumptions were never fully accepted, and objections to them have persisted for decades, with important challenges being posed by dependency, systems delimitation, and postindustrial theories and visions.

Dependency theorists share the basic views that underdevelopment or lack of development is the consequence of a conditioned state of dependence for some societies on others, and that prospects for improvement are slight without radical alterations in these relationships. The impact of external factors from the metropolitan developed countries on the periphery of developing countries has been judged to be essentially adverse, and these conditioning factors have been usually, though not always, delineated along neo-Marxist, structuralist lines of analysis.

Before the dissolution of the Soviet Union, the cause of dependency was most often said to be capitalist imperialism, at times generally referred to as superpower primacy, the superpowers being the United States and the USSR, depending on the political orientation of the writer. Jaguaribe (1973) offered a comprehensive overview of the dependency literature, including options proposed for escape from or alleviation of the dependency condition. Dependency theorists made a relentlessly negative and pessimistic prognosis, among other things deploring the intent as well as impact of external programs of administrative technical assistance and dismissing the contributions that governmental institutions could make toward national development.

As their influence peaked, dependency writers had to make major adjustments in their arguments to take into account the fall of the Soviet Union, the post-Soviet and East European transitions, the rise of Asian Tiger states such as Hong Kong, Singapore, Taiwan, and South Korea, the relative economic success of neoliberal experiments such as Chile's, and the increasing globalization of political, financial, and cultural institutions. Variants of new dependency theory responding to these events failed to rekindle scholarly or practitioner interest, and they certainly failed to influence public administrationists (dos Santos 1971, 1998; Surin 1998; Tures 1998).

The leading proponent of social systems delimitation has been A. G. Ramos. The message of his "new science of organizations" to developing countries is that the delimitative model would reject the historical experience of developed countries as a guide, and substitute for it what he calls a "paraeconomic paradigm," which would provide a variety of societal enclaves capable of their own development. The role of the state would be to foster a multicentric society with "allocative policies supportive not only of market-oriented pursuits, but of social settings suited for personal actualization, convivial relationships, and community activities of citizens as well" (Ramos 1981, 135). The definition of development would change, and with it the goals of public policy. Forward planning would be emphasized and the role of policy makers and implementers would be expanded. National public bureaucracies would obviously need to be strengthened and reoriented, but Ramos and other delimitation theorists have said little as to how this should be done.

Postindustrialism and similar formulations are social forecasts concerning the present and future of the more developed countries. Bell (1973), Touraine (1971), and other social scientists making these prognostications have been more in agreement that a major transition is in the offing than what the exact characteristics of the new society will be. The thrust is that theoretical knowledge and technology will become increasingly important and that highly educated professional and technical personnel will be dominant. The role of tradition and traditional institutions may also become salient, and the scope of political decision-making and policy implementation might be expanded, but how this might be accomplished has not been a major concern for this literature.

As time passes, the predictive validity of each of these points of view is increasingly in question. The dependency condition now appears to be at best a partial explanation for shortcomings in development. Social systems delimitation proponents have been vague in identifying instances where their views have been adopted. China, Yugoslavia, and Tanzania have been mentioned, but the tendency seems to be away from rather than toward delimitation in these countries. Finally, Etzioni (1980) and others argue that postindustrial society is becoming ever less likely a reality.

Against the background of failed theories, speculation as to what is in the offing for international administration falls into two general categories. One assumes that there will be only minor changes in the existing nation-state system, and the other contemplates a gradual transition toward some kind of world order in which the nation-state will be replaced as the basic political entity. Bennett (1977) representing the first group, argues that the nation-state system "shows no sign of rapid deterioration or transformation into new forms." Bennett's viewpoint leads to emphasis on how an international civil service can be maintained in the face of pressures to subvert it to particularistic national interests. It realistically stresses the distances among groups of nations according to their perceptions of how international organizations should operate.

Among those accepting the continued centrality of the nation-state, while also recognizing the increasing importance of other governmental and nongovernmental actors, there has been a wide difference of opinion. For example, Cleveland (1993) saw an opportunity during the political and economic ferment of the early 1990s to adopt a positive action agenda for shaping the future, while Huntington (1993) expressed pessimism in his now-vindicated warning that cultural and religious—civilizational—conflict would soon dominate global politics, with dire consequences.

Some analysts of international organization still counter with critiques of the nation-state and anticipations of a world system. For example, Alger (1977) asserts that "the nation-state system" is but "*one* historic form of organization for *some* of the activities of humankind," and "existing nation-states are not inevitable territorial components of future global systems." Claude (1984), arguing that "the danger of violent conflict among states possessing vast powers is the overwhelming reality of our time," expresses the hope that "international organization may transform the working of the multi-state system" in "a process of gradual replacement of national governments as the major agencies for the management of human affairs" and that "international organization, considered as an historical process, represents a secular trend toward the systematic development of an enterprising quest for political means of making the world safe."

The specifics of a new world order or system, should one ever emerge, are simply unclear, and its prospects uncertain. The characteristics of an appropriate institutional apparatus for such a system are even more nebulous. Claude (1984) points out that "a kind of institutional loneliness" is one of the burdens of the contemporary international civil service, and that "a civil service is not just a technical achievement but an outgrowth of a political community." Until a global political community other than the nation-state system begins to take shape, critical elements of a corresponding institutional and administrative system can only be dimly outlined.

III. EXPLORING PROSPECTS FOR INTERDISCIPLINARY CONVERGENCE

The historical and disciplinary record shows that comparative administration and international administration, although alike in focusing on a subject other than the administrative system of a single nation-state, nevertheless developed along parallel lines, rather than overlapping ones. For the most part, leading contributors to these subjects have constituted two distinct groups of individuals, drawn from and influenced by different political science specializations. As the preceding survey of the literature of comparative and international administration has shown, however, these two subfields became centrally preoccupied with very similar questions and problems. As a result, primary issues have been identified that are of common concern to students of both comparative and international administration. These include differences of opinion as to the most appropriate paradigm or paradigms for study, debates as to how additions to the store of knowledge can best be attained, differing approaches to the search for strategies to improve administrative capabilities in the public organizations of primary interest, and divergent speculations as to the consequences of fundamental changes in prospect.

What is needed is for the two cognate fields of specialization to combine forces more effectively by greater familiarization on the part of each camp with the work of the other, possibly leading to a gradual convergence that would benefit both the comparative and international components of the study of public administration. The previously explored subspecialty of development administration may serve to indicate ways in which such integration could be sought.

A. DEVELOPMENT ADMINISTRATION OR MANAGEMENT: INTEGRATIVE AND CONVERGENT THEMES

Development administration, or development management, as it is often called today, is proto-typical of the continued unfolding of the subfields of comparative public administration and international administration in ways that promote disciplinary integration or convergence. Development studies are conducive to integration because they are thoroughly interdisciplinary, incorporating a multiplicity of analytical themes.

One of these themes involves appreciation of the role of culture in economic development. This approach, which is consistent with the standpoint of both comparative public administration and comparative economic systems, does not as a rule take a parochial or deterministic view of development, but does examine cultural paths of economic causation in developing countries. It builds on the premise that cultural values, and legal and economic institutions, can either inhibit or promote the transactional trust and entrepreneurial commitment that can spur economic and technological growth, as outlined in the works of Lawrence Harrison (1992, 1998) and Buscaglia and Ratliff (2000). In his Latin American research, Harrison (1998) in particular finds four cultural conditions essential for prosperity: the prevalence of trust 'and sense of community; the quality of the system of public ethics; the incidence of restraint in the exercise of power; and the quality of attitudes about work, innovation, thrift, and commerce.

The themes of trust and community support the concept of social capital, and are thereby linked to both development theory and social network theory—the latter a product of anthropology and sociology. As Sylvia Mitraund (2001) indicates, social capital "is the aggregate of the actual or potential resources which are linked to possession of a durable network of more or less institutionalized relationships of mutual acquaintance and recognition." Mitraund distinguishes between two "strands" or levels of social capital as a "mediational" good built on trust and reciprocity, namely the individual one, as in one's "social capital" in interpersonal networks, and the collective one, of one's social relations. Mitraund places this kind of social capital squarely within the framework of social network theory: "Operationalization of social capital in this strand is centered on the study of social networks and their characteristics." However, both levels of analysis and types of action are of interest to comparative and development research.

Susan Rose-Ackerman (2001) posits a tension between the individual and collective sense of social capital in the instance of post-socialist transitions. Specifically, Rose-Ackerman notes tension "between trust in rules and reciprocal trust," arguing that over-reliance on interpersonal reciprocity rather than institutional arrangements will "undermine reform efforts" aimed at economic and political development. She cites an example: "Russians and Central and East Europeans established dense networks of informal connections to cope with the difficulties of life under socialism and... some of these practices have continued as ways to cope with the present situation." Rose-Ackerman concludes "reliance on interpersonal ties is understandable but may make some types of reform difficult." It is evident that persistence of cultural practice can be at odds with the requirements for institutional reform and development.

Authors Perlman and Rivera (2000) note paradoxes in the way that interpersonal networks both undermine and support institutional reform and development in Cuba. Coping mechanisms found in the underground economy militate against the development of trust in rules and institutions, even if they constitute a kind of market, for example, the black market. Conversely, networked interpersonal and working relationships among managers of multinational enterprises in Cuba foster a culture of pragmatism and professionalism that is conducive to the development of a market-based economic institution. However, these are elite relationships sponsored by a Socialist system that is hostile to the market, as it is hostile to democracy. Social capital, which finds instantiation in the reciprocity and mutuality of social networks, therefore plays an ambiguous role in economic and political development. This is an area that merits further research.

Robert Dahl suggests that two culturally based practices are crucial to democratic transitions: bringing the use of force under the control of elected political leaders, and establishing politico-legal protection and socio-cultural space for dissenting views and beliefs. On the basis of extensive empirical research, Claus Offe argues in the same context (Offe 1999) that trust and trust-generating institutions are critical for the development and consolidation of democracy, particularly in post-authoritarian and post-conflict societies. At another level of analysis, and the other end of the capacity-promotion spectrum, the overwhelming trend has been toward managerial approaches modeled on market mechanisms and performance accountability. This has resulted in the New Public Management, performance management, or government reinvention, and, similarly, the semantic turn from development administration to development management (Hirschmann 1999). However, as suggested in the concluding section that follows, the theoretical and empirical linkages among economic, political, and institutional development and democratization remain to be established.

Certain gaps are evident in the development literature spanning the fields of comparative and international administration. Some propose that the framing of both political transition and of democracy aid has been based largely on Southern European and Latin American cases, and appears less applicable to post-communist transitions (Bunce 2003). Riggs (1998) has argued that scholars and practitioners from the United States would have done better abroad with develop-ment assistance and the promotion of democracy if they had paid closer attention to public administration in the United States in comparative perspective. Had they done so, and also learned a great deal more about the constraints and opportunities of politics and administration in the new successor states, they could have been more successful and developed a fuller under-standing of their own system of government. Riggs was not being ironic when he proposed that a better understanding of the requirements of development assistance be rooted in better national self-understanding, a notion that at other times, or articulated differently, might have been rejected as parochial.

There has been little research to date devoted to comprehensive, comparative studies of reforms aimed at greater, results-based accountability. The study of performance measurement and reporting, prominently the interdisciplinary approach known as comparative performance measurement (CPM), which incorporates performance audit and performance-monitoring prac-tices, has largely taken the form of within-country, cross-agency research, rather than comparison among countries and continents (Jreisat 2002). It is nonetheless an emerging theme and a promising trend. One of the authors, Rivera, has found that in-service or practitioner students in Master of Public Administration and Master of Public Policy programs especially welcome applied approaches like CPM in comparative public administration classes, apparently because these methods help bridge their workaday experience with the broader vistas of comparativism.

B.   The Outlines of an Emerging Research and Practitioner Consensus

Notwithstanding these disciplinary and operational difficulties, the experience of administrative reform and development assistance during the past two and a half decades has resulted in some consensus as to what works. For instance, there is considerable agreement about the need for phased reform that takes into account the endurance of political, cultural, and other constitutive elements of organizational restructuring and institutional reform in ways that are consistent with the idea of *path dependence* in institutional economics. While there is a great deal of situational variation, most successful development initiatives can be plotted along Barzelay's analytic typology of first-, second- and third-generation reforms (Barzelay 2003), a framework that presupposes and accommodates the persistence of institutions, practices, values, and interests.

There is also wide agreement among scholars and practitioners for the need for capacity building in the applied areas of planning and management. Two of the authors (Perlman and Rivera 2003) have questioned the efficacy of formal planning, especially strategic planning, in setting direction for, implementing, and monitoring the effectiveness of governmental action in developing countries. They acknowledged that strategic planning may be valuable in creating and disseminating knowledge among government agencies and in reducing information asymmetry among organizational levels. However, strategic planning, as practiced in both developed and developing countries, seems better suited to large-scale industrial organizations than to the flatter, networked, cross-sectoral operations of contemporary governance. Strategic planning may be prone to formalism in any national or organizational context, but formalism is arguably more damaging to developing countries, where it can only be overcome by the unaccustomed creation of innovative linkages across social sectors and governmental jurisdictions, involving the challenges of what some have called "strategic coalignment" (Venkatraman 1990). Here, the role of nongovernmental organizations and other emerging social actors must be fully acknowledged.

There is, finally, wide agreement that both the perception and the reality of a capable, dedicated, and equitable public sector are key to economic growth and development. Only a professional, competent civil service can provide critical public goods, build up the private sector, and harness private initiative to national development. The model that has emerged as an ideal in much of the developing world, as suggested previously with regard to the international civil service, is that of a professional national civil service recruited and promoted on the basis of openly discussed and agreed-upon criteria of technical competence. Such a service should act in accordance with expectations of administrative rather than political responsibility, pursuant to a rule-based system, in the context of trustworthy institutions and a law-ordered society. In other words, the ideal is a political and economic system that relies on the trust and reciprocity connoted by the concept of social capital, and on well-ordered institutions seen as legitimate because they are worthy of public confidence.

The strongest instrumental reason for good government, however unattainable it may seem in the ideal, is that good government is apt to be the most transforming and enduring form of collective action. Governance programming is essential for all other forms of international cooperation and foreign assistance. Development assistance will not be of benefit if host governments are not capable of ensuring that aid is well absorbed and that development cooperation promotes better governance. In other words, any investment or attempt at active cooperation will fail if it does not contribute significantly to improving the quality of governance. Such an attempt will likewise fail if it does not centrally include an effort to determine that aid is used transparently, effectively, and equitably.

What is required for development administration to succeed is concerted interdisciplinary research, with contributions from both scholars and practitioners, linking comparative and international administration, for instance in exploring ways in which international organizations and multilateral financial institutions may partner with each other and with national governments to improve development assistance programs. As one of the authors (Heady 1998) advocated in an essay in *Public Administration Review*, there should be a redirection of both scholarship and applied research toward the goal of interdisciplinary integration—implicit in the Section on International and Comparative Administration's mission is the task of bringing together the study and practice of comparative public administration and international administration. While a great deal remains to be done in accomplishing closer collaboration among specialists in these two fields, the rationale, need, and opportunity for collaborative work are now compelling.

C. Concluding Considerations on Performance Management Approaches to Development

If the propositions just outlined are justified, comparative administration may be moving toward a reinvigorated functionalism, stimulated by the growth of *public management* as a significant influence in public administration and in development administration in particular (Kettl 1997). Public management—essentially a set of market-modeled approaches to administration that prominently includes performance-based management and institutional reform—is concerned with functional questions about the operational capabilities of institutions and the *what* and *how* of programs, and less so with theoretical propositions about the *why* of institutional systems. Public management has been disparaged as managerialism by some, and as ill-defined economicism by others, who view it as a neoliberal austerity program uncritically oriented toward economic growth at home and abroad, through an array of disparate goals and means that include free trade, privatization, reduction of government spending, and financial liberalization.

The interrelation of such interventions is not fully articulated in the literature, and even less articulated is the relationship between them and democracy. Nonetheless, public management has become a dominant perspective in public and comparative administration. The public management approach is finding acceptance because of its relative clarity and utility, in its operational emphasis, its themes of performance management, improvement, assessment, and accountability, and its concern with programmatic questions that delimit the level and scope of the behavior under study. This approach is consistent with a broader shift away from an emphasis on *administration* and *policy* to a singular stress on *management* as a new mode of governance (Pollitt 1990). This viewpoint, often characterized as the *New Public Management* (NPM), has been particularly influential in English-speaking countries, for example the United Kingdom, Australia, Canada, New Zealand, and the United States, and, with some lag, in European countries such as Belgium, Finland, Germany, and Italy, and in the European Union as such (Pollitt and Bouckaert 2000). As Stubbs (2005, 31) writes, "the emerging [development administration] regime is... a product of the orthodoxy of 'new public management' which applied management concepts originating in the for-profit sector to Western welfare states and, later, to development contexts, as a key element of their 'marketization'." Stubbs adds that the "tenets of the approach have certainly infused development agencies, INGOs and ICCs, [with] the core components of the new public management [being] the de-regulation of line management; the conversion of civil service departments into free-standing agencies and enterprises; performance-based accountability through contracting; and competitive mechanisms including internal markets" (Stubbs 2005, 31).

In the United States, public management has focused on the application of lessons learned from national performance improvement and government reinvention, as previously noted. Therefore, most of contemporary North American thinking in comparative administration has been informed by issues of policy impact and program effectiveness, especially concerning issues of policy implementation and corresponding institutional development. The comparative focus has been on practical issues of policy and administration, ranging from performance-based procurement and contracting to performance budgeting and performance measurement. Theoretical and empirical questions pertaining to large-scale privatization and the divestiture of government functions, institutional restructuring and reform, and democratic accountability, such as in the task of fostering democratic along with economic liberalization, have been largely avoided or forestalled.

These questions are often more insistent in contexts of development assistance and international administration rather than national contexts. One group that has led the way in reinvigorating comparative administration in the direction of a more reflective development administration is the International Public Management Network (IPMN). With its two journals, the print *International Public Management Journal* (IMPJ) and the web-based *International Public Management Review*, and through a yearly conference and workshop so dedicated, IPMN promotes the comparative study of public management as the proper focus for Comparative Administration.

Though this group today is broadly international, it began in the United States, and *IMPJ* is edited at Harvard University. The IPMN's stress is on implementation as that term is used in policy studies in the United States, indicating a driving concern with performance budgeting and performance measurement, but in relation to the management of policy and programmatic complexity. It is the latter theme, that of complexity, that brings IPMN to more probing levels of inquiry. At one IPMN conference in Rio de Janeiro, for instance, the conference program was dominated by practical comparisons among Brazilian programs and by studies of performance measurement, but the research was often framed by issues of policy and program complexity (Perlman, Caperchione, and Virtanen 2005).

Another current in comparative administration that reflects these trends and is worthy of mention is the development of a Chinese public administration literature. It prominently includes publication in the United States of the *Chinese Pubic Administration Review*, sponsored by the Graduate Department of Public Administration at Rutgers University-Newark. A joint ASPA–NASPAA Secretariat for the United States and China sponsors publication of this important journal.

The Europeans have taken a methodologically comparative indicators approach that is driven by the need to do cross-national comparisons in the European Union. Major contributions to this effort have been made at the Public Management Institute at the Catholic University at Leuven, Belgium. By its very nature, the work done at the institute is comparative, looking at the performance of social programs across national institutions. The Public Management Institute has been instrumental in developing a set of performance indicators comparing national-level public sector performance in policy areas such as health and public welfare. What has become an explicit model for judging the policy effectiveness of member governments is particularly useful in evaluating contingencies of institutional development and reform, relying on sources such as cross-national survey research, for example on citizens' attitudes toward national bureaucracy (Bouckaert et al. 2000, 2005).

In addition, the Europeans have taken a broadly comparative approach across organizations by sponsoring the development of the European Common Assessment Framework (CAF). CAF is a computerized data generation and aggregation tool intended to help public-sector organizations across Europe to use performance management techniques, develop common performance indicators, and facilitate benchmarking. The resulting scorecard is being applied throughout Europe to assess program quality and policy performance across public sector organizations. The CAF was developed at the European Institute of Public Administration in Maastricht, Belgium in concert with Public Management Institute researchers (European CAF Resource Centre 2004).

As suggested earlier in this essay, much of the fascination with neoliberalism is due to the success of the Asian Tigers in modernizing their economies. Neoliberal policies of reduced government size and lowered trade barriers are given much credit for these economic miracles, but doubts have been raised about the possibility and desirability of their wide application. On the one hand, the countries undergoing the so-called miracle exhibited particular pre-conditions such as an educated labor force and direct investment, and, on the other, they have seen some undesirable political outcomes. One such outcome has taken the form of repressive governments that systematically violate human and labor rights. Critics point out that, over the long term, the East Asian model is unsustainable in the absence of a balance between economic and social policies. A very similar line of argumentation and critique has been brought to bear on the Chilean miracle.

There are also difficulties with the assumption that the adoption or promotion of neoliberalism as a development assistance philosophy, as in the case of the Bretton Woods institutions such as the World Bank and International Monetary Fund, is apolitical or that the application of any given performance-premised technique is apolitical. In general, these multilateral institutions have particular, refined expectations concerning how reforms will work, and these expectations express both political goals and ideological assumptions. One author argues that the World Bank substitutes rational technical decisions for political vision, although its decisions serve the same purpose in practice. For instance, when analyzed critically, the Bank's perspective is unable to take into account the realities of African development, particularly in comparison with prominent theories of African politics. Accordingly, its governance agenda misses three crucial aspects of African politics: the unity of political and economic power, the extreme openness of African states to external pressures, and the salience of historically embedded cultural and political relations. Others have criticized the Bank's neoliberal institutionalism, in particular for taking management technique to replace what are in fact governance decisions (Kerr 2005).

One might caution, as does Stubbs (2005, 73), that there should not be any "simplistic conflation of new public management with neo-liberal approaches per se," even if "they do have shared origins, shared assumptions, and some shared practices." Nonetheless, it is important to note, with Stubbs, that while "much of the content of neo-liberalism in development has been critiqued and, even, dismantled, practices deriving from its 'little brother' [the NPM] have gone from strength to strength." Managerial approaches to development have grown in influence notwithstanding a "disjunction between processes and effects" in the application of "discourse" originating in the developed world to often very different domains of developing nations (Stubbs 2005, 73).

These various concerns notwithstanding, performance-based managerial approaches to development assistance may well be justified in practice, with the caveat that translation from one national context to another cannot be accomplished uncritically or in a facile manner. Because of its stress on government accountability, performance management can prove to be conducive to institutional responsiveness and responsibility. Significant theoretical and applied consensus in comparative and international administration, and particularly in development administration, may yet be built around this prospect. Normative agreement will depend, however, as Klinger (2003, 23) suggests, on the way that institutional reform efforts, as a kind of technology transfer, "affect democratic values such as decentralization, transparency and citizen participation."

REFERENCES

Abi-Saab, G., Ed., *The Concept of International Organization*, UNESCO, Paris, 1981.

Alger, C. F., Functionalism and integration as approaches to international organization, In *The Concept of International Organization*, Georges, A.-S., Ed., UNESCO, Paris, pp. 122–145, 1977.

Argyriades, D., The Adaptation of Government to Economic Change, *XXth International Congress of Administrative Sciences*, Amman, Jordan, 1986.

Arora, R. K., *Comparative Public Administration*, Associated Publishing House, New Delhi, 1972.

Asmeron, H. K. and Jain, R. E., Politics and administration: some conceptual issues, In *Politics, Administration, and Public Policy in Developing Countries*, Asmeron, H. K. and Jain, R. B., Eds., VU University Press, Amsterdam.

Barkdull, J., Waltz, Durkheim, and international relations: the international system as an abnormal form, *American Politic Science Review*, 89, 669–680, 1995.

Barzelay, M., *Preparing for the Future: Strategic Planning in the US Air Force*, Brookings Institution, Washington, DC, 2003.

Beigbeder, Y., *Threats to the International Civil Service: Past Pressures and New Trends*, Pinter Publishers, London, 1988.

Bell, D., *The Coming of Post-industrial Society: A Venture in Social Forecasting*, Free Press, New York, 1973.

Bennett, A. L., *International Organizations: Principles and Issues*, Prentice Hall, Englewood Cliffs, NJ, 1977.

Berenson, W. M., Testing the information-energy model, *Administration Society*, 9, 139–158, 1977.

Berger, M., *Bureaucracy and Society in Modern Egypt*, Princeton University Press, Princeton, NJ, 1957.

Bouckaert, G., Omond, D., and Peters, G. B., *A Potential Governance Agenda for Finland*, Ministry of Finance Research Report 8, Helsinki, Finland, 2000.

Bouckaert, G., Van de Walle, S., and Kampen, J. K., Potential for comparative public opinion research in public administration, *International Review of Administrative Sciences*, 71, 229–240, 2005.

Braibanti, R., The relevance of political science to the study of underdeveloped areas, In *Tradition, Values, and Socio-economic Development*, Braibanti, R. and Spengler, J. J., Eds., Duke University Press, Durham, NC, 1961.

Braibanti, R., External inducement of political-administrative development: an institutional strategy, In *Political and Administrative Development*, Braibanti, R., Ed., Duke University Press, Durham, NC, pp. 3–106, 1969.

Bryant, C. and White, L. G., *Managing Development in the Third World*, Westview, Boulder, CO, 1982.

Bunce, V., Rethinking recent democratization: lessons from the postcommunist experience, *World Politics*, 55, 167–192, 2003.

Buscaglia, E. and Ratliff, W., *Law and Economics in Developing Countries*, Hoover Institution Press, Washington, DC, 2000.

Caiden, G. E. and Caiden, J. J., Towards the future of comparative public administration, In *Public Administration in World Perspective*, Dwivedi, O. P. and Henderson, K., Eds., Iowa State University Press, Ames, IA, 1990.

Clark, G. and Sohn, L. B., *World Peace Through World Law*, Harvard University Press, Cambridge, MA, 1958.

Claude, I. L., *Swords into Plowshares: The Problems and Progress of International Organization*, Random House, New York, 1956.

Claude, I. L., Comment, *International Studies Q*, 25, 199, 1981.

Claude, I. L., *Swords into Plowshares: The Problems and Progress of International Organization*, 4th ed., Random House, New York, 1984.

Cleveland, H., *Birth of a New World: An Open Moment for International Leadership*, Jossey-Bass, San Francisco, CA, 1993.

Dahl, R. A., The science of public administration: three problems, *Public Administration Review*, 7, I–II, 1947.

Dale, H., *Food for Fraud*, The Heritage Foundation Policy Research and Analysis Webpage, April 21, 2004, available at: http://www.heritage.org/About/Staff/helledalepapers_old.cfm.

Dorsey, I. T., An information-energy model, In *Papers in Comparative Public Administration*, Heady, F. and Stokes, S. L., Eds., Institute of Public Administration, University of Michigan, Ann Arbor, MI, pp. 37–57, 1962.

Dorsey, I. T., The bureaucracy and political development in Viet Nam. In *Bureaucracy and Political Development*, LaPalombara, J., Ed., Princeton University Press, Princeton, NJ, pp. 318–359, 1963.

dos Santos, T., The structure of dependence, In *Readings in US Imperialism*, Dan, K. T. and Hodges, D. C., Eds., Extending Horizons, Boston, MA, 1971.

dos Santos, T., The theoretical foundations of the Cardoso governments: a new stage of the dependency theory debate, *Latin American Perspectives*, 25, 53–70, 1998.

Eban, A., The U.N. idea revisited, *Foreign Affairs*, 74(5), 39–55, 1995.

Esman, M. J., *Management Dimensions of Development: Perspectives and Strategies*, Kumarian Press, Hartford, CT, 1991.

European CAF Resource Centre, *The Common Assessment Framework: Improving and Organisation through Self-assessment*, Institute of Public Administration, Maastricth, Belgium, 2004.

Etzioni, A., Who killed postindustrial society?, *Next*, 1, 20, 1980.

Feld, W. J., Jordan, R. S., and Hurwitz, L., *International Organization: A Comparative Approach*, Praeger, New York, 1983.

Gant, G., *Development Administration: Concepts, Goals, Methods*, University of Wisconsin Press, Madison, WI, 1979.

Graham, H., The World Bank, governance and theories of political action in Africa, *British Journal of Politics and International Religion*, 7, 240–260, 2005.

Haas, E. B., *Uniting of Europe*, Stanford University Press, Stanford, CA, 1958.

Hancock, M. D., Comparative public policy: an assessment, In *Political Science: The State of the Discipline*, Finifter, A., Ed., American Political Science Association, Washington, DC, pp. 283–308, 1983.

Hanrieder, W. F., International organizations and international systems, In *The Process of International Organization*, Wood, R. S., Ed., Random House, New York, pp. 275–295, 1971.

Heady, F., Comparative public administration: concerns and priorities, In *Papers in Comparative Public Administration*, Heady, F. and Stokes, S. L., Eds., Institute of Public Administration, University of Michigan, Ann Arbor, MI, pp. 1–18, 1962.

Heady, F., *Public Administration: A Comparative Perspective*, Prentice Hall, Englewood Cliffs, NJ, 1966.

Heady, F., Comparative public administration in the United States, In *A Centennial History of the American Administrative State*, Chandler, R. C., Ed., Free Press, New York, pp. 477–508, 1987.

Heady, F., *Public Administration: A Comparative Perspective*, 5th ed., Marcel Dekker, New York, 1996.

Heady, F., Comparative public administration: building intellectual bridges, *Public Administrative Review*, 58, 32–49, 1998.

Henderson, K. M., From comparative public administration to comparative public policy, *International Review Administration Science*, 47, 356–364, 1981.

Holsti, K. J., Retreat from utopia: international relations theory, 1945–1970, *Canadian Journal of Politic Science*, 4, 171, 1971.

Honadle, G., Development administration in the eighties: new agendas or old perspectives?, *Public Administrative Review*, 42, 174–179, 1982.

Huque, A. S., *Paradoxes in Public Administration: Dimensions of Development*, University Press, Dhaka, Bangladesh, 1990.

Harrison, L. E., *Who Prospers?*, Basic Books, New York, 1993.

Harrison, L. E., *The Pan-American Dream: Do Latin America's Cultural Values Discourage True Partnership with the United States and Canada?*, Westview Press, Boulder, CO, 1998.

Hirschmann, D., Development management versus Third World bureaucracies: a brief history of conflicting interests, *Development and Change*, 30, 287–305, 1999.

Huntington, S., The clash of civilizations, *Foreign Affairs*, 72(3), 22–49, 1993.

Islam, N. and Henault, G. M., From GNP to basic needs: a critical review of development and development administration, *International Review Administration Science*, 45, 253–267, 1979.

Jacob, P. E., Atherton, A. L., and Wallenstein, A. M., *The Dynamics of International Organization*, Revised ed., Dorsey Press, Homewood, IL, 1972.

Jaguaribe, H., *Political Development: A General Theory and a Latin American Case Study*, Harper & Row, New York, 1973.

James, R. R., The evolving concept of the international civil service, In *International Administration: Its Evolution and Contemporary Applications*, Jordan, R. S., Ed., Oxford University Press, New York, pp. 51–73, 1971.

Jordan, R. S., The influence of the British secretariat tradition on the formation of the League of Nations, In *International Administration: Its Evolution and Contemporary Applications*, Jordan, R. S., Ed., Oxford University Press, New York, pp. 27–50, 1971.

Jordan, R. S., What has happened to our international civil service? The case of the United Nations, *Public Administrative Review*, 41, 236–245, 1981.

Jordan, R. S., 'Truly' international bureaucracies: real or imagined?, In *Politics in the United Nations System*, Finkelstein, L. S., Ed., Duke University Press, Durham, NC, 1988.

Jordan, R. S., The fluctuating fortunes of the United Nations international civil service: hostage to politics or undeservedly criticized?, *Public Administrative Review*, 51, 353–357, 1991.

Jreisat, J., *Comparative Public Administration and Policy*, Westview Press, Boulder, CO, 2002.

Kennedy, P. and Russett, B., Reforming the United Nations, *Foreign Affairs*, 74(5), 56–71, 1995.

Kerr, R., *International Development and the New Public Management: Projects and Logframes as Discursive Technologies of Governance*, Paper presented at the 4th International Critical Management Studies Conference, Cambridge University, UK, July 4–6, 2005.

Kettl, D. F., The global revolution in public management: driving themes, missing links, *Journal of Policy Analysis and Management*, 16, 446–462, 1997.

Klinger, D. E., Technology transfer and the future of public administration: an agenda for study and practice. http://web.uccs.edu/klingner/Articles/2003%20CTTS%20Tech%20Transfer%20&%20PA. doc (accessed September 25, 2005).

Korten, D. C., Community organization and rural development: a learning process approach, *Public Administrative Review*, 40, 480–511, 1980.

Korten, D. C., *Getting to the 21st Century: Voluntary Action and the Global Agenda*, Kumarian Press, West Hartford, CT, 1990.

Krause, K. and Knight, W. A., Eds., *State, Society, and the UN System*, United Nations University Press, Tokyo, 1995.

Kuhn, T., *The Structure of Scientific Revolutions*, 2nd ed., University of Chicago Press, Chicago, IL, 1970.

LaPalombara, J., Ed., *Bureaucracy and Political Development*, Princeton University Press, Princeton, NJ, 1963.

Lengyel, P., Reforming the international civil service in a new world context, *International Social Science of Journal*, 45, 533–547, 1993.

Mabbutt, R., Bureaucratic Development and Political Dominance: An Analysis and Alternative Test of the Imbalance Thesis, Mimeo, 1979.

Mailick, S., Ed., A symposium towards an international civil service. *Public Administrative Review* 30, 206–263, 1970.

Mathiason, J. R., *Evolution of Tasks and Functions in the United Nations and its Implications for Reform*, Paper presented for the National Conference of the American Society for Public Administration, 1986.

McLaren, R. I., *Civil Servants and Public Policy: A Comparative Study of International Secretariats*, Wilfred Laurier University Press, Waterloo, Canada, 1980.

Miller, J. D. B., The sovereign state and its future, *International Journal*, 39, 285–301, 1986.

Mitraund, S., *Promoting conservation and development through social capital: a new name for an old framework*, Paper presented at the Comparative Research Workshop, Yale University, April 9, 2001.

Morgenthau, H. J., *Politics among Nations*, Knopf, New York, 1948.

Mouritzen, H., *The International Civil Service*, Dartmouth Publishing, Aldershot, UK, 1990.

Murphy, C. N., *International Organization and Industrial Change: Global Governance since 1950*, Oxford University Press, New York, 1950.

Offe, C., How can we trust our fellow citizens?, In *Democracy and Trust*, Warren, M., Ed., Cambridge University Press, Cambridge, 1999.

Perlman, B. and Rivera, M., Institutional constraints on market liberalization policies in Cuba, *Policy and Management Review*, 1(1), 2000.

Perlman, B. and Rivera, M., Planeación e integración estratégica: un modelo con estudio de caso del sector judicial, *Estado, Gobierno, Gestión Pública*, 2(4), 2003.

Peters, B. G., *Comparing Public Bureaucracies: Problems of Theory and Method*, University of Alabama Press, Tuscaloosa, AL, 1988.

Peters, B. G., Theory and methodology in the study of comparative public administration, In *Comparative Public Management*, Baker, R., Ed., Praeger, Westport, CT, 1994.

Pitt, D. and Weiss, T. G., Eds., *The Nature of United Nations Bureaucracies*, Westview Press, Boulder, CO, 1986.

Pollitt, C., *Managerialism and the Public Services: The Anglo-American Experience*, Basil Blackwell, Oxford, 1990.

Pollitt, C. and Bouckaert, G., *Public Management Reform: A Comparative Perspective*, Oxford University Press, Oxford, 2000.

Presthus, R. V., Behavior and bureaucracy in many cultures, *Public Administrative Review*, 19, 25–35, 1959.

Ramos, A. G., *The New Science of Organizations: Reconceptualizing the Wealth of Nations*, University of Toronto Press, Toronto, 1981.

Rashoffen-Wertheimer, E. F., *The International Secretariat*, Carnegie Endowment for International Peace, Washington, DC, 1945.

Reymond, H. and Mailick, S., The international civil service revisited, *Public Administrative Review*, 46, 135–143, 1986.

Riggs, F. W., Bureaucrats and political development: a paradoxical view, In *Bureaucracy and Political Development*, LaPalombara, J., Ed., Princeton University Press, Princeton, NJ, pp. 120–167, 1963.

Riggs, F. W., *Administration in Developing Countries—The Theory of Prismatic Society*, Houghton Mifflin, Boston, MA, 1964.

Riggs, F. W., *Thailand: The Modernization of a Bureaucratic Polity*, East–West Center Press, Honolulu, 1966.

Riggs, F. W., Bureaucratic politics in comparative perspective, In *Frontiers of Development Administration*, Riggs, F. W., Ed., Duke University Press, Durham, NC, pp. 375–414, 1970.

Riggs, F. W., *Administrative Reform and Political Responsiveness: A Theory of Dynamic Balancing*, Vol. 1, Sage Publications, Beverly Hills, CA, 1971, Series No. 01–010.

Riggs, F. W., *Prismatic Society Revisited*, General Learning Press, Morristown, NJ, 1973.

Riggs, F. W., *The American Tradition in Comparative Administration*, Paper prepared for the National Conference of the American Society for Public Administration, 1976.

Riggs, F. W., Public administration in America: why our uniqueness is exceptional and important, *Public Administrative Review*, 58, 22–31, 1998.

Rochester, J. M., The rise and fall of international organization as a field of study, *International Organization*, 40, 777–813, 1986.

Rondinelli, D. A. and Ingle, M. D., *Improving the Implementation of Development Programs: Beyond Administrative Reform SICA Occasional Papers Series, no. 10*, American Society for Public Administration, Washington, DC, 1981.

Rose-Ackerman, S., Trust, honesty, and corruption: theories and survey evidence from post-socialist societies—Toward a research agenda for a project of the Collegium Budapest, Presented at the Workshop on Honesty and Trust in Post-Socialist Societies at Collegium Budapest. http://www.colbud.hu/honesty-trust/rose/pub01.doc (accessed November 24, 2004).

Ruggie, J. G., *International Organization: A State of the Art or an Art of the State*, Paper prepared for the American Political Science Association, 1985.

Savage, P., Optimism and pessimism in comparative administration, *Public Administrative Review*, 36, 415–523, 1976.

Siffin, W. J., Two decades of public administration in developing countries, *Public Administrative Review*, 36, 61–71, 1976.

Siffin, W. J., The problem of development administration, In *Handbook of Comparative and Development Public Administration*, Farazmand, A., Ed., Marcel Dekker, New York, 1991.

Sigelman, L., Do modern bureaucracies dominate underdeveloped polities? A test of the imbalance thesis, *American Politics of Scientific Review*, 66, 525–528, 1972.

Sigelman, L., Bureaucratic development and dominance: a new test of the imbalance thesis, *West Politic Q*, 27, 308–313, 1974.

Stubbs, P., International non-state actors and social development policy, http://www.gaspp.org/people/pstubbs/StubbsGSPrevised.doc (accessed September 1, 2005).

Surin, K., Dependency theory's reanimation in the era of financial capital, *Cultural Logic*, 1(2), 1998.

Taylor, P., *International Organization in the Modern World: The Regional and the Global Process*, Pinter, London, 1993.

Touraine, A., In *The Post-industrial Society: Classes, Conflicts and Culture in the Programmed Society*, Trans., Mayhew L.F.W., Random House, New York, 1971.

Tures, J., Development theories in the East European context: the impact of new dependency theory and neo-classical economics, *East European Quarterly*, 32, 281–299, 1998.

Urquhart, B. E., The international civil servant, In *The International Executive*, Gordenker, L., Ed., Princeton University Center of International Studies, Princeton, NJ, pp. 37–48, 1978.

Urquhart, B. and Childers, E., *A World in Need of Leadership: Tomorrow's United Nations*, Dag Hammarskjold and The Ford Foundation, Uppsala, Sweden, 1990.

Van Wagenen, R. W., Observations on the life of an international civil servant, In *International Administration: Its Evolution and Contemporary Applications*, Jordan, R. S., Ed., Oxford University Press, New York, pp. 3–24, 1971.

Venkatraman, N., Performance implications of strategic coalignment: a methodological perspective, *Journal of Management Studies*, 27, 19–41, 1990.

Virally, M., Definition and classification of international organizations: a legal approach, In *The Concept of International Organization*, Abi-Saab, G., Ed., UNESCO, Paris, pp. 50–66, 1981.

Waldo, D., *Comparative Public Administration: Prologue, Problems, and Promise*, American Society for Public Administration, Chicago, IL, 1964.

Waldo, D., Ed. Symposium on comparative and development administration: retrospect and prospect. *Public Administrative Review*, 36, 615–654, 1976.

Waldo, D., *The Enterprise of Public Administration*, Chandler & Sharp, Novato, CA, 1980.

Weidner, E. W., Development administration: a new focus for research, In *Papers in Comparative Public Administration*, Heady, F. and Stokes, S. L., Eds., Institute of Public Administration, University of Michigan, Ann Arbor, MI, pp. 97–115, 1962.

Weiss, T. G., *International Bureaucracy*, D.C. Heath, Lexington, MA, 1975.

Welch, C. E., Ed, *Civilian Control of the Military: Theory and Cases from Developing Countries*, State University of New York Press, Albany, NY, 1976.

Wilson, D. E., Bureaucracy in international organizations: building capacity and credibility in a newly interdependent world, In *Handbook of Bureaucracy*, Farazmand, A., Ed., Marcel Dekker, New York, 1994.

Yalem, R. J., The study of international organization, 1920–1965: a survey of the literature, *Background*, 10, 2–5, 1966.

Young, O. R., International regimes: problems of concept formulation, *World Politics*, 32, 332–333, 1980.

Unit 9

Public Law

17 Administrative Law and Regulation

David H. Rosenbloom

CONTENTS

I. INTRODUCTION

Administrative law generically regulates public administration. It consists of statutes, constitutional law, court decisions, executive orders, and other measures that control administrative processes such as rule making, adjudication, enforcement, public participation, and transparency. Because the law encompasses a great deal, it lacks well-defined boundaries. Much of the literature on administrative law is not well suited to scholars and practitioners of public administration. It is characterized by limited historical analysis, with Stewart (1975) being a leading exception. Law-school textbooks tend to be so disjointed and highly detailed that it is difficult for readers who are interested in public administration to develop a broad understanding of the role of administrative law in administrative practice. These texts and the accompanying law-review literature concentrate very heavily on regulatory commissions, thereby paying little attention to the bulk of contemporary public administrative decision-making and other activity. As Richard Stewart (1975) and Gerald Frug (1984) argue, traditional legal theories of administration are unable to satisfactorily explain the realities of today's complex administrative state. Consequently, public-administration scholars and practitioners are apt to find conventional administrative law texts, articles, and treatises difficult to follow, as well as formalistic and alien to their concerns and experience. Conversely, public-administration texts tend to be of limited help in understanding administrative law, as they typically devote little attention to it and fail to recognize its central role in regulating administrative practice. As Warren (2004, 2) sums up the state of the traditional public administration literature, "social scientists have not given much more than a flirtatious glance at the technical legal aspects associated with public administration. Law schools, in contrast, have been content to produce graduates with a relatively solid understanding of legal doctrines, but only a flimsy grasp of the connection between technical legal doctrines and the normative operational needs of democratic government and society." A few recent texts written specifically for those interested in public administration attempt to overcome these shortcomings (Rosenbloom 2003a; Warren 2004; see also Cann 2002).

This chapter develops a history of US administrative law for public-administration scholars, educators, and practitioners who are broadly concerned with citizenship in the modern American administrative state. It seeks to show how the directions taken by administrative law were influenced by political, economic, social, and technological change, as well as by administrative development and evolving legal theory. In addition, it provides conceptual frameworks for sorting out and analyzing the nation's twentieth-century movement from a liberal to an administrative state.

This chapter views administrative law in the United States as the product of tension between public administrative doctrine and practice and the Constitution's separation of powers and broad guarantees of individual rights. The chapter will consist of six parts: (1) an overview of the central constitutional problem addressed by administrative law; (2) a discussion of the evolving formal definitions of administrative law; (3) an analysis of the relationship between regulatory administration and the development of administrative law; (4) a schema for analyzing administrative penetration of the economy and society; (5) a decade-by-decade historical analysis of the development of contemporary administrative law; and (6) a conclusion that addresses a big question confronting American public administration today: how and when to extend constitutional and administrative law requirements to private individuals and organizations performing functions outsourced to them by government agencies.

II. OVERVIEW: THE ROLE OF ADMINISTRATIVE LAW

The development of administrative law in the United States has been linked to the growing tension between the rising modern administrative state and the framework for constitutional democracy that was established in 1787. Administrative law is critical to both public administration and constitutional democracy, as well as to the relationship between them. It concerns (1) the powers of administrative agencies and the checks against their abuse; (2) the rights and legal immunities of public administrators and their legal obligations and liabilities; (3) the rights of private parties in their encounters with public administration; and (4) the quality of legislative, judicial, executive, and public oversight of agencies' activities. Administrative law also is a tool for defining the public's right to participate in public-administration decision making and for facilitating administrative transparency. As the administrative component of government at all levels has expanded, the importance of administrative law as a means of regulating their authority has increased. Eventually, the development of administrative law also had profound influences on American legal theories.

Public-administration practitioners may find alien the notion that public administration, organized and intended to promote the public interest, may somehow constitute a threat to the constitutional democratic order. Public-administration students seeking to learn and develop better ways of providing public service may also wonder how greater administrative cost-effectiveness can undermine democracy. To appreciate the historical development of administrative law, it is critical that public administrators understand the long-standing perception of many politicians, public officials, jurists, and scholars that the contemporary administrative state poses serious difficulties for the US governmental scheme.

Judicial concern with the tension between public administration and constitutional government has several dimensions. First, it has long been thought that the organization of public administration violates the principles of the separation of powers. As Supreme Court Justice Robert Jackson said in 1952:

> The rise of administrative bodies probably has been the most significant legal trend of the last century and perhaps more values today are affected by their decisions than by those of all the courts, review of administrative decisions apart…. They have become a veritable fourth branch of the Government, which has deranged our three-branch legal theories much as the concept of a fourth dimension unsettles our three dimensional thinking. *Federal Trade Commission v. Ruberoid Co*, 343 US 470, 487 (1952) (dissenting opinion).

In 1976, the Supreme Court reiterated that the development of administrative agencies "has placed severe strain on the separation-of-powers principle in its pristine formulation." *Buckley v. Valeo*, 424 US 1, 280–281 (1976).

Second, jurists contend that public-administration values and actions tend to abridge individuals' constitutional civil liberties and property rights. For instance, in *Spady v. Mount Vernon*, 419 US 983 (1974), Justice William O. Douglas wrote in his dissenting opinion that "today's mounting bureaucracy, both at the state and federal levels, promises to be suffocating and repressive unless it is put into the harness of procedural due process." (419 US 983, 985). Contemporary administrative law addresses such concerns by protecting the constitutional due process and privacy rights of individuals, including public employees, as well as by establishing the liabilities of public administrators for violations of those rights.

Third, the rise of the administrative state places governmental authority in the hands of public officials who are neither elected nor politically appointed. In Justice Lewis Powell's words, "The growth of the civil service system already has limited the ability of elected politicians to effect political change." *Branti v. Finkel*, 445 US 507, 530 (1980) (dissenting opinion).

Finally, governmental reliance on administrative agencies to accomplish its purposes tends to distort constitutional procedures (Fiorina 1977; Arnold, 1979; Nachmias and Rosenbloom 1980). For example, in *Immigration and Naturalization Service v. Chadha*, 462 US 919 (1983), a case dealing with the constitutionality of the US House of Representatives' "legislative veto" of a decision by the attorney general, Chief Justice Warren Burger observed:

The bicameral requirement, the Presentment Clauses, the President's veto, and Congress' power to override a veto were intended to erect enduring checks on each Branch and to protect the people from the improvident exercise of power by mandating certain prescribed steps. To preserve those checks, and maintain the separation of powers, the carefully defined limits on the power of each Branch must not be eroded. To accomplish what has been attempted by one House of Congress in this case requires action in conformity with the express procedures of the Constitution's prescription for legislative action: passage by a majority of both Houses and presentment to the President.

In another case, *Morrison v. Olson*, 478 US 654, 662, 727, 733 (1988), Justice Antonin Scalia complained bitterly that the Court's majority was itself impairing constitutional integrity by allowing Congress to restrict the president's power to dismiss an independent counselor who was appointed by a federal court and who had "full power and independent authority to exercise all investigative and prosecutorial functions and powers of the Department of Justice, the Attorney General, and any other officer or employee of the Department of Justice." Scalia argued that "there are now no lines" regarding "the fragmentation of executive power."

Administrative law developed over the course of several phases during which it was primarily concerned with one or another aspect of the tension between the administrative and constitutional states. In its earliest phase, administrative law concentrated on the rights and obligations of public officers. Bruce Wyman's 1903 administrative law text, which appears to be the first of its kind published in the United States, conceptualized the subject as the law "governing the relations of public officers."

Beginning in the 1910s and continuing through the 1930s, administrative law tended to focus on the proper extent of judicial review of agency decisions, procedures, and powers. In 1914, Roscoe Pound spoke for a large slice of the legal profession when he declared that administrative adjudication was itself improper, calling it "executive justice" and consequently "one of those reversions to justice without law" (Pound 1914, 18). From this perspective, the greater the ability of the courts to substitute their judgment for that of administrators, the better.

The Administrative Procedure Act (APA) of 1946 aimed to set the parameters of judicial review of federal administrative activity and to balance the public's competing concerns. For example, the act precludes judicial review of matters committed by law to agency discretion and sets evidentiary standards for judicial review of administrative rules. Soon after the APA's enactment the judiciary's impact on public administration grew well beyond its statutory framework, however, and the focus turned to fashioning constitutional constraints on administration.

Beginning in the 1950s and continuing to the present, the Supreme Court has articulated many previously undeclared constitutional rights of individuals interacting with administrative agencies. Substantive rights and liberties under the First and Fourteenth Amendments, procedural and substantive due process, individual property rights, and equal protection are now much more extensive than they were when the APA was passed (Rosenbloom and O'Leary 1997; Rosenbloom 1983). Since the mid-1960s, a growing emphasis also has been placed on making public administration more open, more representative of the general public, and participatory (Krislov and Rosenbloom 1981; Rosenbloom 2000, chap. 2; Dolan and Rosenbloom 2003).

As the focus of administrative law shifted, attention was drawn to new questions and diverted from older ones—but few of the earlier concerns disappeared entirely. For instance, fixing the proper scope of judicial review is still of great importance despite previous efforts to reduce judicial oversight by making agencies' adjudicatory procedures more court-like, that is, by the judicialization of public administration. Whether the overall enterprise of administrative law has been successful depends on one's perspective. Is the tension between public administration and democracy a resolvable "problem" or a "fact" that the polity must accept (Waldo 1980, 1984)? Has administrative law tried to solve the "problem" or to make it easier to live with the "fact"? Is the balance between administrative cost-effectiveness and individual liberty appropriate? Is the trade-off between administrative discretion and the rule of law suitable to constitutional government?

III. WHAT IS ADMINISTRATIVE LAW?

Like many aspects of public administration, administrative law lacks a standard definition. It has been many things over the years, and reviewing its evolution can help establish a working definition for this chapter. The obvious place to start is with Wyman's *Principles of the Administrative Law Governing the Relations of Public Officers* (1903). Wyman self-consciously tried to frame, define, conceptualize, and explain the subject matter of administrative law. His definition was far broader than the definition found in more recent texts, and in some respects it presaged the expansion of constitutional rights in administrative law since the 1950s. Wyman wrote that "administrative law... is that body of rules which defines the authority and the responsibility of that department of the government which is charged with the enforcement of the law" (ibid., 1). He later refined this by distinguishing between two aspects of administrative law: external and internal:

> The external administrative law... deals with the relations of the administration, and of officials, with citizens. External administrative law is thus concerned with almost everything, which the government asks of the citizens; and it is concerned with almost everything, which citizens ask of the government....
> [A]ll the law as to the authority of officers is brought into the discussion [a]nd... all the law as to the responsibility of officers is brought in issue (Wyman 1903, 9).

> Internal administrative law as defined deals with the relations of the officers in the administration to each other, and to the administration itself. The position of the officer in its organization and his function in its action is the object of this inquiry (Wyman 1903, 14).

Although different labels have been employed, both the external and internal dimensions are now considered part of administrative law. For example, the external focus encompasses several aspects of agency rule making, among them public notice and opportunity to comment; freedom of information; privacy; and the constitutional rights of individuals as they come into contact with administrative agencies, including matters of entitlement. The internal aspects include such matters as the position of administrative law judges (ALJs) in administrative agencies, doctrines such as *respondeat superior* (i.e., let the hierarchical authority answer), and several aspects of the rights of public employees vis-à-vis their organizations, such as whistle blowing and procedural due process in dismissals and other adverse actions.

Frank Goodnow advanced another early definition of administrative law in *The Principles of the Administrative Law of the United States* (1905). Goodnow's work was informed by his well-known distinction between politics and administration, the former being the expression of the will of the people, and the latter the execution of that will. This dichotomy was ambiguous when applied to a fundamental aspect of administrative law, namely the organization of government agencies. Is the organization, presumably including its establishment and empowerment, an expression of or the execution of the people's will? Goodnow's recognition of the important conceptual problem prompted him to consider the relationship between administrative law and constitutional law. In his words:

> Administrative law not only treats of the function of administration, i.e., the execution of the law, thus determining the competence of the executive or administrative officers of the government, it has also to supplement constitutional law. For while constitutional law in theory should deal with the entire structural organization of the government, as a matter of fact it has to do merely with the general form of the government and the relations of the most important governmental authorities, one with another. Administrative law takes up this work where constitutional law leaves it, and carries out in its minutest details the general plan of governmental organization laid down by constitutional law (Goodnow 1905, 16).

Consequently, administrative law must be informed by constitutional law with regard to the organization, purposes, and powers used in exercising governmental authority. Eventually, cases involving the constitutionality of public-administration operations and actions would become common. Although Goodnow did not stress the point in 1905, if administrative law has such a close relationship to constitutional law, it will inevitably concern the scope of individual rights in administrative encounters. Goodnow's summary definition of administrative law provided for the possibility: "Administrative law is... that part of the law which fixes the organization and determines the competence of the authorities which execute the law, and indicates to the individual remedies for the violation of his rights" (1905, 17).

Wyman and Goodnow were engaged in defining a field, mapping out its boundaries, and demonstrating why it should be considered an important area of legal classification and study. But it was not until the 1930s and 1940s that the term administrative law appeared in various legal digests (Tresolini 1951, 377). The "first general work of an introductory character" on administrative law after Goodnow's was James Hart's *An Introduction to Administrative Law with Selected Cases* (1940, vii). Hart benefited from a vast array of already published works on specific aspects of administrative law as he continued the tradition of devoting considerable space to defining the term. His overall purpose was to educate public-administration students, rather than those in law school, in the substance and significance of administrative law, and his task was informed by a sense of urgency. As he expressed it:

> [D]espite an ever-increasing number of courses on public administration and even of whole curricula for training for the public service, students of public administration have all too often received no sufficient training in the legal matrix of their subject. Administrative law, moreover, is coming to loom so large in the fields of modern government and public law that its implications reach far beyond public administration as a technical subject. The time is at hand when these implications must be brought to the attention of every student of political science and every undergraduate who is preparing for the law (Hart 1940, vii).

With this purpose in mind, Hart was impelled to arrive at a definition of administrative law by synthesizing the works of others. His definition appears in five tightly packed pages, but it can be distilled as follows:

- Broadly conceived, administrative law includes the law that is made by, as well as the law that controls, the administrative authorities of a government. By the term law is here meant all those regulations, orders, and decisions, whether of general or particular applicability, that have consequences in terms of a postulated legal order.
- The administrative law that controls administrative authorities is made by constituent or constitution-making authorities, by legislatures, by the courts, and by administrative superiors in giving directions to their administrative subordinates.... [T]here are all those judicial decisions that construe statutory administrative law and apply to administrative authorities appropriate principles of the common law, of equity, or of a written constitution.
- The law of internal administration, such as the law of public office.
- The law of external administration may conveniently be divided into four parts: first, a survey of those powers and duties of administrative authorities that relate directly to private interests; second, an analysis of the scope and limits of such powers; third, some account of the sanctions attached to, or the means of enforcing, official determinations; and fourth, examination of the remedies against official action.
- [A]dministrative and constitutional law bear the relation of overlapping but nonconcentric circles. On the one hand, administrative law includes judicial decisions that construe statutory administrative law or apply common law principles to administrative

authorities, without involving any constitutional question. On the other hand, constitutional law relates typically to the question whether the national government has the power to regulate a given subject at all, without reference to the administration of congressional statutes.

- [I]n the study of administrative law certain constitutional problems constantly recur. This is especially so with the constitutional problems of due process and the separation of powers.

At least two important points are obvious from this definition. First, that "administrative law is defined in terms of substance rather than form" (Hart 1940). In other words, it consists of a variety of components, such as statutes and court decisions, that affect public administration but are not self-consciously called or thought of primarily as "administrative law." Administrative law is a derivative category into which many legal elements may be placed. Following from this, administrative law "is not one of the traditionally recognized parts of the law, such, for example, as the criminal law, the common law, and equity" (Hart 1940, 3). For Hart, part of the task at hand was to win for administrative law a standard classification in legal thought and education that would make it a central and recognizable field of public law.

The second striking aspect of Hart's definition is the absence of a statement about the coherence of the parts of administrative law. For instance, how are internal and external administrative law related to one another? How is due process or the separation of powers related to internal and external administration? What are the fundamental principles and values that inform administrative law?

The absence of a general theory of administrative law is no small matter. It has been a barrier to the development of an intellectual field of public administrative law that incorporates an adequate and realistic understanding of the field and practice of public administration. The lack of adequate theory also reinforces the tendency of public administrators to treat law as a subfield, such as, but generally of lesser importance than, human-resources management or budgeting. As J. Forrester Davison and Nathan Grundstein noted:

[A]dministrative law has no theory of the proper organization of the whole administrative system: it sees only a congeries of administrative agencies functioning under an umbrella of judicial review. The organization of the administration has been left to public administration, which ignores historical conceptions of law and taught legal traditions, but whose theories of administrative organization are constantly pressing for legal recognition (1968, 10).

Moreover, according to Davison and Grundstein (1968, 9), "In contrast to administrative law, public administration has been impelled towards an administrative system congenial to centralized control in the name of the chief executive." There is perhaps a better working relationship between administrative law and public administration today, and less hostility between specialists in each field. Nevertheless, the view of public administration in American law has serious limitations, and Hart's desire to make administrative law a central aspect of the enterprise of public administration has not been fulfilled (Frug 1984; Stewart 1975; Waldo 1980).

The basic definitions of administrative law as a field of adjudication, practice, and study that evolved from Wyman through Hart were more or less superseded by Kenneth Culp Davis's various works on the subject. Davis's *Administrative Law Treatise* (1958) and the several editions of his *Administrative Law Text* (1951, 1959, 1972) are preeminent sources of authority on administrative law. Davis's definition of administrative law may still be the most commonly accepted one today:

- Administrative law is the law concerning the powers and procedures of administrative agencies, including especially the law governing judicial review of administrative action.

- Administrative law embraces all governmental machinery for carrying out governmental programs.
- American administrative law is limited to the law concerning powers, procedures, and judicial review; it does not include the enormous mass of substantive law produced by the agencies, such as tax law, labor law, antitrust law, public utility law, transportation law, welfare law, zoning law, and the like.
- Administrative law consists of constitutional law, statutory law, common law, and agency-made law. The great bulk of administrative law is judge-made law.
- One uneasy fact about American administrative law in its present stage of development is that for reasons of history and only for such reasons it has excluded criminal administration (1972, 1–2).

At least two additional points should be added to this definition: first, that administrative law does not encompass military law; and second, that it continues to be concerned with the rights, duties, and liabilities of public employees and officials, that is, with the law of public officers.

For the most part, Davis's definition of administrative law exemplifies the contemporary understanding of the field. Most would agree that the substantive law of welfare, taxes, environmental regulation and so forth should not be considered part of administrative law. This understanding was not shared by all members of Congress as they debated the APA in 1946 (Rosenbloom 2000, 31, 33). It is also at odds with Hart's definition and the concept of administrative law in several European countries (Davis 1972, 2). Reluctance to consider substantive regulations as part of administrative law in the United States may be "[d]ue largely to the unfortunate use of the words 'executive' and 'administrative' as almost interchangeable terms" (Willoughby 1934, 115) in a separate-powers system in which the legislative powers are formally granted exclusively to Congress.

Davis (1969) emphasized the extent to which public administrators exercise discretionary authority and dispense "discretionary justice". He noted that a great deal of agency actions rest on informal processes that should be considered within the purview of administrative law. Despite Davis's major contributions to the study of administrative law, his work was unable to bridge the conceptual gap, noted above, between the ways in which scholars in public administration and those in law understand the field.

During the 1970s and 1980s, the traditional model of administrative law that had developed from Wyman through Davis came under increasing attack. In analyzing administrative discretion and informal processes, Davis recognized the weakness of the traditional model of judicial review and judicialization. However, it was Richard B. Stewart who developed the most influential critique of the traditional model of judicial review by recognizing what he called "the reformation of American administrative law." In 1975, Stewart observed that the traditional model of administrative law consisted of the following elements:

1. The imposition of administratively determined sanctions on private individuals must be authorized by the legislature through rules which control agency action (1975, 1672).
2. The decisional procedures followed by the agency must be such as will tend to ensure the agency's compliance with [the above] requirement... (ibid., 1673).
3. The decisional processes of the agency must facilitate judicial review to ensure agency compliance with [both of the above] requirements... (ibid., 1654).
4. Judicial review must be available to ensure compliance with requirements (1) and (2) [above] (ibid., 1674).

The underlying premise of this traditional model was its conception of "the agency as a mere transmission belt for implementing legislative directives in particular cases" (Stewart 1975, 1675). In Stewart's view, the transition belt was a misconception, because Congress broadly delegates its legislative authority to federal agencies: "[F]ederal legislation establishing agency charters has, over the past several decades, often been strikingly broad and nonspecific, and has accordingly generated the very conditions which the traditional model was designed to eliminate" (ibid., 1677). Stewart further stated that "[m]ajor questions of social and economic policy are determined by officials who are not formally accountable to the electorate, and both the checking and validating functions of the traditional model are impaired" (ibid., 1676).

Stewart noted that the federal courts were trying to come to grips with the breadth of delegation: "Faced with the seemingly intractable problem of agency discretion, courts have changed the focus of judicial review... so that its dominant purpose is no longer the prevention of unauthorized intrusions on private autonomy, but the assurance of fair representation for all affected interests in the exercise of the legislative power delegated to agencies" (ibid., 1712). This was accomplished through doctrinal developments creating stronger presumptions in favor of judicial review of agency actions and facilitating the ability of individuals and groups to gain legal standing to obtain such a review. Stewart identified some problems with the representational model, such as its heavy costs in terms of time and case loads and its probable imbalance in favor of organized, entrenched interests. However, he concluded that this might become the basis for the further development of administrative law into a model more in keeping with the realities of the agencies' political power.

In practice, three Supreme Court decisions in the late 1970s and mid-1980s sharply reduced the judicial proclivity to provide a forum for reviewing agency decisions: *Vermont Yankee Nuclear Power Corp. v. Natural Resources Defense Council*, 435 US 519 (1978); *Chevron v. Natural Resources Defense Council*, 467 US 837 (1984); and *Heckler v. Chaney*, 470 US 821 (1985). Together, these decisions weakened judicial review of agency rule making proceedings, statutory interpretation, and decisions not to enforce statutes.

Gerald Frug presented a more fundamental critique of traditional administrative law in "The Ideology of Bureaucracy in American Law," which appeared in the *Harvard Law Review* in 1984. Frug considered several theories or approaches for legitimizing public bureaucratic power and domination of the polity and economy. Using a "critical legal studies" analysis, he concluded that legal doctrines based on concepts of bureaucracy as formal, mechanistic, and essentially Weberian (Weber 1958) organizations are no more than ideologies. The same can be said of other legal models, including those assuming administrative expertise, judicial review, and administrative pluralism as bases for legitimizing administrative authority and autonomous discretion. These ideologies are essentially supportive of bureaucratic organization, but in Frug's view bureaucracy is fundamentally nondemocratic and an inappropriate governmental structure in the United States In his words:

> [W]e can reject the supposedly immutable characteristics of bureaucracy and act instead on the belief that the quest for democracy is possible even within modern structures. Of course, we need energy and courage to overcome the pervasive presence of the status quo in our thoughts, hopes and actions. To gain this determination, it seems helpful to undermine the incessant assurances that there is no need to revise the status quo because the bureaucratic form can protect, even enhance, human freedom. To help us see the possibilities for change, in other words, it seems worthwhile to criticize the ideology of bureaucracy in American law (Frug 1984, 1388).

Stewart's and Frug's positions mark the outer bounds of contemporary mainstream theories of administrative law. Both agree that the traditional model or ideology of administrative law is conceptually and descriptively inadequate. Stewart believes change is possible, and perhaps even inevitable, but that much of the corpus of administrative law can be preserved and incorporated into an approach that better fits the realities of public administration. Frug, by contrast, believes previous theories and approaches must be discarded to bring about a full realization of democracy. If there is consensus on any point, it is perhaps that "[o]ne can... expect almost all critical issues in administrative law to center ultimately on questions of power politics, which are vitally important to the character of any democratic political system" (Warren 2004, 24).

The future is uncertain, of course. But one would assume that experts in public administration can have a significant impact on its directions. Much of the remainder of this chapter is devoted to a discussion of the development of the traditional model of administrative law in the hope that it will provide a useful basis for thinking about future choices.

IV. REGULATORY ADMINISTRATION AND ADMINISTRATIVE LAW

Administrative law in the United States grew out of the strain placed on democratic constitutionalism by the rise of the administrative state. As is evident from the evolving definitions and theories of administrative law, the field has been oriented largely toward the control, review, and judicialization of administrative action. The tension between public administration and democratic constitutionalism is particularly acute in terms of regulatory administration. In the view of many lawyers versed in the common law of the 1880s through the 1930s, governmental intervention in the free-market economy violated the underpinnings of the liberal state upon which US democratic constitutionalism rests (Pound 1914). This perspective is shared by some of the twentieth century's leading political theorists and economists, including Friedman (1962) and Hayek (1944). For the legal community, the emergence of the administrative state presented an especially severe challenge because it threatened the supremacy of the common law. Not only were administrative agencies established and empowered according to statutory law, but their substantive regulations also had the force of law and often superseded the common law. Reliance on the common law was not just a preference among lawyers. It became the fundamental way of thinking about government, society, and legal matters (Johnson 1981; Ackerman 1984).

The legal profession's response to the rise of the administrative state has had a major influence on the development of administrative law. Consequently, it is useful to review those aspects of the emergence of the administrative state and regulatory administration that were seen as particularly problematic from a common-law perspective.

The constitutional regime established in 1789 envisioned and protected what has become known as a "liberal society" (Hartz 1955). Underlying the Constitution is the theory that government is not synonymous with the society, but merely an actor within it. The society predates government and is protected from it by limitations placed on governmental powers. The people forming the society enjoy certain natural rights, which cannot be abridged by government, except under appropriate, and often extraordinary, circumstances. Perhaps the Declaration of Independence (1776) best states the theory behind a liberal society:

> We hold these Truths to be self-evident, that all Men are created equal, that they are endowed by their Creator with certain unalienable Rights, that among these are Life, Liberty and the Pursuit of Happiness.—That to secure these Rights, Governments are instituted among Men, deriving their just Powers from the Consent of the Governed....

The Constitution's Ninth Amendment seeks to protect natural rights from governmental encroachment: "The enumeration in the Constitution, of certain rights, shall not be construed to deny or disparage others retained by the people." For example, natural rights include the right to procreate within the framework of a valid marriage, a right to privacy, and the liberty to engage in homosexual relationships. (*Cleveland Board of Education v. LaFleur*, 414 US 632 [1974]; *Lawrence v. Texas*, 539 US 558 [2003]). The full scope and source of the rights "retained by the people," however, are uncertain.

Clearly the states' constitutions and statutes cannot protect these rights from encroachment by the federal government because the Constitution is the "supreme Law of the Land," with "any thing in the Constitution or Laws of any State to the contrary notwithstanding." In practice, if such unspecified rights were to be enumerated, the most likely place would be in the common law as understood by federal judges. The common law could be seen as providing the legal foundation for a liberal society and a central mechanism for promoting justice by adjusting and defining individuals' rights in relation to one another and to the government. In theory, at least, the common law's broad concepts of individual rights could be protected or made a part of constitutional law through the Ninth Amendment.

Allowing the common law to be supplanted by statutory regulations and administrative rules not only ran the risk of abandoning the wisdom that came through centuries of adjudication, but it also raised the prospect that fundamental rights—especially those relating to private property—would be sacrificed. From a more immediate political perspective, moving away from the common law would change the role of judges in the political system and reduce their ability to make rules for the economy and society. As John Johnson observes, "During the nineteenth century, the American legal system was almost wholly dominated by the judicially administered common law. Appellate judges determined the substance and direction of legal doctrine in grandiloquently written opinions. Although the austere men on the state and federal benches were certainly influenced by everyday events and the currents of opinion, they were loath to admit it" (1981, 10).

The Constitution is an expression of a liberal society in more direct ways as well. In terms of the administrative state, the Fifth and Fourteenth Amendments have been particularly important. Their due-process clauses provide that "nor shall any person... be deprived of life, liberty, or property, without due process of law...." This right was fundamental to an understanding of a liberal society at the end of the nineteenth century. The importance of life requires no elaboration. Liberty was taken to include the right to sell one's labor at whatever rate, in terms of wages and hours, or conditions one saw fit. Of course, such liberty was not absolute—one could be prohibited from engaging in prostitution or murder for hire and much more, but it was pervasive. Each individual was thought to have these liberties and could exercise them rationally in a self-interested fashion, while governmental interference could be considered demeaning to the individual and an abridgment of his or her fundamental rights. Moreover, from a free-market economic perspective, governmental interference could be viewed as inefficient and counterproductive. Social Darwinists considered regulations on the number of hours in the work week as inappropriate, designed to protect weaker workers from competition with stronger ones and thereby interfering with the law of natural selection. These were precisely the theories underlying adjudication in the late nineteenth and early twentieth centuries.

Property rights were an equally central aspect of the economy. The owners of economic enterprises might acquire and use their property more or less as they saw fit. The use of property for industrial production might have harmful effects on the workers and on the society, for example through dangerous conditions or pollution. However, the basic presumption was that the government was restricted by the Constitution with regard to regulation of the use of economically productive property. Additionally, injunctions could be issued to punish striking laborers whose activity threatened an employer's physical property or its economic interests (Leslie 1979; Gregory and Katz 1979). More recently, property rights have gained a boost from Supreme Court decisions regarding the Fifth Amendment's "takings clause" (*Nollan v. California Costal Commission*, 483 US 825 [1987]; *Lucas v. South Carolina Costal Council*, 505 US 1003 [1992]; *Dolan v. City of Tigard*, 512 US 374 [1994], but see *Kelo v. City of New London*, No. 04-108 [2005]).

The Fifth and Fourteenth Amendments allow the abridgment of liberty, property rights, and even life itself with due process of law. Historically, due process has been conceptualized as having two components: (1) procedural due process, and (2) substantive due process. Procedural due process guards against unfair governmental decision making and is perhaps best exemplified by the full-fledged criminal trial. It includes the right to an impartial judge and jury, confrontation and cross-examination, the right to counsel and to present witnesses, and so on. A reduced version might simply be the right to present one's side of the story to a public official whose proposed action would harm one's individual liberty or property interests (*Goss v. Lopez*, 419 US 565 [1975]; *Cleveland Board of Education v. Loudermill*, 470 US 532 [1985]; *Hamdi v. Rumsfeld*, 542 US 507 [2005]).

At present, the minimal extent of procedural due process afforded to an individual generally depends on three factors: (1) the nature of the private interest affected by governmental action, (2) the risk that the governmental action will be erroneous and the expected value of more elaborate procedures that would reduce that risk, and (3) the government's interests, including financial and administrative burdens, that might be affected by additional procedures (*Mathews v. Eldridge*, 424 US 319 [1976]). During the late 1800s and early 1900s, regulation by administrative adjudication ran a substantial risk of being overturned by federal judges who held that administrative procedures violated procedural due process by not sufficiently incorporating procedures used in judicial trials.

Substantive due process has been more controversial and ill defined. It focuses primarily on the meaning of the word "liberty" in the Constitution's due-process clauses. "Liberty" can be defined to include the right to sell one's labor at whatever rate one wants, as well as several rights of greater contemporary interest, such as the freedom to die (*Washington v. Glucksberg*, 521 US 702 [1997]). Under the concept of substantive due process, it is possible to challenge a law that interferes with liberties that are not specifically enumerated or defined in the Constitution. The rights protected by substantive due process must be determined by judges in the context of deciding specific cases. Toward the close of the nineteenth century, substantive due process was defined primarily in terms of economic rights by judges committed to the common law and a free-market economy.

The dominance of the common law, the concepts of a liberal society, procedural due process, and economic substantive due process were all fundamentally challenged by the development of the administrative state during the period from the 1880s to the 1920s. Large-scale public administration can be the result of many factors, including public-works projects, war, or even ideology. Industrialization is most relevant to the discussion here.

Industrialization upsets the notions of a liberal society in which individuals are free to exercise economic liberty and rational economic judgment. In the United States, at least at first, industrialization's scale, competitiveness, and concentration of resources and power led to the following problems and responses:

1. Industrialization made individuals dependent on others whose reliability they were unable to assess independently, as Lawrence Friedman noted:

   The discovery of germs, invisible, insidious, hidden in every spot of filth, had a profound effect on the legal system. To a much greater extent than before [the 1890s], goods—including food—were packaged and sent long distances, to be marketed impersonally, in bulk, rather than to be felt, handled, and squeezed at the point of purchase. This meant that a person was dependent on others, on strangers, on far-off corporations, for necessities of life; that society was more than ever a complex cellular organism; these strangers, these distant others had the capacity to inflict catastrophic, irreparable harm (1973, 458).

   New laws dealing with public health, factory inspections, and pure food and drugs were enacted in response.
2. Industrialization was associated with the failure of markets to coordinate economic activity. For a variety of reasons, markets may not always function to society's satisfaction. In the 1880s and 1890s, the political system became concerned with monopolization, particularly of the railroads. In some areas and towns, their rates were sensitive to competition, but elsewhere they were set at whatever level the traffic would bear, regardless of the actual cost of transporting goods. In one case, the Alabama Midland Railway charged $3.22 per ton of phosphate rock shipped to the town of Troy, but only $3.00 per ton of the same material shipped *through* Troy to Montgomery (*ICC v. Alabama Midland Railway Co.*, 168 US 144 [1897]). Competition in the public-utility field was also viewed as inadequate. The creation of huge trusts was another development not satisfactorily controlled by competitive market forces. Additionally,

competition among doctors, pharmacists, dentists, and members of other professions and sub-professions was thought to provide inadequate protection against malpractice. Labor markets also failed to prevent practices that eventually were viewed as antisocial, such as child labor, long working hours, and dangerous working conditions. Administrative agencies had a variety of regulatory responses to these perceived inadequacies of the market.

3. The scale of industrialism created difficulties with "externalities," that is, aspects of economic activity not a part of market transactions between buyer and seller, such as pollution. Something external to the market cannot be controlled or coordinated by it. During the 1880s through 1919, the regulation of such externalities frequently involved public-health laws and inspections. For instance, although it had limited influence and even less power, the Wisconsin State Board of Health, established in 1876, publicized such externalities as "discolored, odorous, and nauseous-flavored" water pollution (Friedman 1973, 404). If construed broadly enough, externalities also can include social problems, including antisocial behaviors associated with industrialism (Mayo 1933). By the 1960s and 1970s, a variety of externalities prompted the development of more extensive environmental regulation.

These conditions of industrialization were not adequately envisioned in the common law inherited from an earlier age. Some early cases remain instructive. For instance, prior to New York State Judge Benjamin Cardozo's decision in *MacPherson v. Buick Motor Co*, 217 NY 382 (1916), product-liability law was dominated by a concept of privity. In such cases, a direct relationship had to exist between the plaintiff and the defendant, generally the buyer and seller. For a variety of individual and social reasons, however, it might be better to sue the manufacturer of a dangerous product, rather than only its retailer. The threat of such suits ought to create an incentive for the manufacturer, who produces the danger in the first place, to make its products safer. It was precisely such reasoning that led Cardozo to alter the case law and allow MacPherson to sue the Buick Motor Company, which under the concept of privity would be the wrong defendant (the dealer who sold the car being the proper one). Eventually, other state courts followed Cardozo's lead.

The famous fellow servant rule is another example of a common-law approach that was eventually adjudged unsuitable to the industrial era. Dating from the 1840s in the United States, though appearing earlier in English law, the rule held that "an employee has no cause of action against his employer for an injury caused by the negligence of another employee of the same company" (Johnson 1981, 13). By the 1860s, the rule was deeply ingrained in common law, but by the 1880s and 1890s it was increasingly viewed as problematic. After all, in an industrial society, one worker may be harmed by the negligence of another whom he or she has never even seen: the worker down the railroad tracks depends on the proper functioning of the switchman up the tracks, for example, while the operator of a machine, such as a mangle, may be injured because another has failed to keep it in proper operating condition. Imagine applying such a rule in modern plants with mile-long assembly lines. How is the injured worker to assess the behavior of the negligent one? Equally important, in the 1880s and 1890s most workers were poor, and the injured worker could not expect to collect much through a lawsuit against a fellow servant. The employer was in a better position to supervise, train, and compensate workers for their injuries. As Johnson writes, the fellow-servant rule was so out of touch with the real world of industrialism that it was weakened and abandoned for multiple reasons:

> The sheer number and cost of industrial accidents in the late nineteenth century not only alarmed the poor but also troubled a few vocal members of the legal community who agitated for reform. Judges, not comfortable with the arbitrariness of the fellow servant rule, fashioned a myriad of exceptions. The development of the contingent fee system of litigation around 1900 made it worthwhile for

hundreds of attorneys to take the cases of poor workers, thus flooding the courts with employers' liability cases. State legislatures, in response to reform groups such as the Grangers, began to enact laws about 1870 that mitigated and occasionally abrogated the fellow servant rule. Finally, in 1908 the federal government passed the Federal Employers' Liability Act, which had, as one of its provisions, the abolition of the fellow servant rule for railroading (1981, 16).

The common law and the judicial application of substantive due process were not always as readily adjusted to the new economic realities and demands for greater governmental regulation of the changing industrial order. For example, in *Chicago, Milwaukee and St. Paul Railway Co. v. Minnesota*, 134 US 418 (1890), the Supreme Court declared unconstitutional a Minnesota statute creating a public commission to regulate railroad rates. In the process, the Court asserted that such rate regulation, if engaged in at all, ought to be subject to far-reaching judicial review, rather than left to public administrators alone:

> The question of the reasonableness of a rate charge for transportation by a railroad company... is eminently a question for judicial investigations, requiring due process of law for its determination. If the company is deprived of the power of charging reasonable rates for the use of its property, and such deprivation takes place in the absence of an investigation by judicial machinery, it is deprived of the lawful use of its property, and thus, in substance and effect, of the property itself... (*Chicago*, 134 US at 458).

Later, using statutory construction, the Court held that the federal Interstate Commerce Commission (ICC) lacked the authority to establish railroad rates (*ICC v. Cincinnati, New Orleans and Texas Pacific Railroad Co.*, 167 US 479 [1897]).

The famous case *of Lochner v. New York*, 198 US 45 (1905) is probably the leading example of substantive due process informed by common law concepts. New York enacted a law prohibiting the employment of bakery workers for more than ten hours a day or sixty hours a week. The state considered the law to be a public-health measure. Lochner, a Utica baker, was convicted and fined for allowing an employee to work for more than sixty hours a week. The Supreme Court held that the law unconstitutionally interfered with the employee's liberty to contract out his or her labor. In retrospect, its opinion is almost a caricature of judicial reasoning at the time:

> There is no reasonable ground for interfering with the liberty of person or the right of free contract, by determining the hours of labor, in the occupation of a baker. There is no contention that bakers as a class are not equal in intelligence and capacity to men in other trades or manual occupations, or that they are not able to assert their rights and care for themselves without the protecting arm of the State, interfering with their independence of judgment and of action. They are in no sense wards of the State.... The law must be upheld, if at all, as a law pertaining to the health of the individual engaged in the occupation of a baker. It does not affect any other portion of the public than those who are engaged in that occupation. Clean and wholesome bread does not depend upon whether the baker works but ten hours per day or only sixty hours a week.
> We think that there can be no fair doubt that the trade of a baker, in and of itself, is not an unhealthy one to that degree which would authorize the legislature to interfere with the right to labor, and with the right of free contract on the part of the individual, either as employer or employee.... There must be more than the mere fact of the possible existence of some small amount of unhealthiness to warrant legislative interference with liberty....
> Statutes of the nature of that under review, limiting the hours in which grown and intelligent men may labor to earn their living, are mere meddlesome interferences with the rights of the individual.... (198 US 45, 57–61 (1905)).

In dissent, Justice Oliver Wendell Holmes correctly indicated the direction the law would take in the future: "This case is decided upon an economic theory which a large part of the country

does not entertain…. [A] constitution is not intended to embody a particular economic theory…."
(*Id.* at 75).

Judicial decisions embodying a laissez-faire economic theory were not the universal rule, but they were a serious obstacle to administrative regulation of the economy. Approximately two hundred regulations were struck down during what could be called the "Lochner era" (Gunther 1975, 565). Moreover, the application of those statutes that were sustained was restricted by two canons of jurisprudence: first, the "derogation canon" held that statutes running contrary to the common law ought to be interpreted in the fashion so as to least interfere with it (Johnson 1981, 76); and second, the "plain meaning rule" "decreed that the courts should not look past the exact language of a statute unless the words were prima facie confusing or lent themselves to absurd consequences…." (ibid.). In one case, for instance, the Wisconsin Supreme Court declined to apply a statute pertaining to "every railroad company" to an "electric interurban railway," *Jones v. Milwaukee Electric Railway Co*, 147 Wis. 427 (1911).

Apart from these canons, judicial review was itself a barrier to administrative action. As Roscoe Pound, often a severe critic of administrative regulation, admitted, "at the end of the [nineteenth] century administrative agencies had two very real grievances against the common law and judicial review as developed under the common law in the United States" (1942, 28). One was that administrative proceedings were not accepted as producing a reliable record upon which judicial review could be based; rather, "every fact necessary to the administrative determination might have to be shown de novo" in the reviewing court (ibid., 29). The other grievance "was the enforcing upon administrative tribunals of the rules of evidence developed by the common law courts to meet the exigencies of jury trial" (ibid.). Although these grievances were eventually resolved in favor of the administrative agencies, at the time they were indicative of the judiciary's effort to frustrate administrative regulatory authority and activity.

The courts also interpreted the Constitution's commerce clause in ways that limited administrative development at the federal level. By today's standards—even after significant narrowing since 1995 (see Section VI-L)—definitions of interstate commerce were cramped. To be regulated by Congress or federal agencies, economic activity had to cross state lines or enter or significantly affect the stream of interstate commerce. Many aspects of manufacturing, mining, and agriculture were beyond the reach of the commerce clause. Social objectives, such as eliminating child labor, were considered beyond the scope of the federal government's commerce powers (*Hammer v. Dagenhart*, 257 US 251 [1918]). The type of reasoning that dominated interpretation of the commerce clause was well displayed in *Carter v. Carter Coal Co.*:

> The distinction between a direct and an indirect effect turns, not upon the magnitude of either the cause or the effect, but entirely upon the manner in which the effect has been brought about. If the production by one man of a single ton of coal intended for interstate sale and shipment… affects interstate commerce indirectly, the effect does not become direct by multiplying the tonnage, or increasing the number of men employed, or adding to the expense or complexities of the business, or by all combined 289 US 238, 308 (1936).

As C. Herman Pritchett observed, *Carter* "illuminated as by a flash of lightning a judicial dream world of logical abstractions, where there was no difference between one ton of coal and a million tons of coal, where considerations of degree were not cognizable by the law. Production was local. A production crisis in every part of the country simultaneously could never add up to a national problem with which Congress could deal… " (1977, 193).

Judicial opposition to the administrative state as expressed through the common law, substantive due process, and canons such as those mentioned above could not prevent the development of administrative regulation. But opposition did slow things down and present a serious obstacle until matters came to a head in the 1930s. Judicial opposition to the administrative state was transformed then into judicial acquiescence toward public administration through a political contest during the New Deal (which will be discussed later). However, even before the 1930s, it was clear that the judicial perspective on administrative regulation as represented in *Lochner* and other cases could not prevail. The reasons for this were at least threefold.

First, and most directly, as Holmes pointed out, the courts were acting on an economic theory that was increasingly out of vogue among politicians and the politically active public. Holmes correctly stated that "the Fourteenth Amendment does not enact Mr. Herbert Spencer's Social Statics." *Lochner*, 198 US at 75. The Progressive movement (generally dated from 1890 or 1900 to 1924) favored a government whose trained, politically neutral, technically oriented public administrators could intervene in the economy and society to fix problems.

Second, although in the abstract judicial opinions may have been finely reasoned and common-law concepts well honed, they were not necessarily realistic in application. The fellow-servant rule is one example, but the *Lochner* decision was even more striking It is true that in the abstract a person seeking employment as a baker may have the liberty to reach a contract with an employer establishing the hours of work per day or per week; legislative regulation of this liberty can be considered as abridgment of it. However, at a time when modern collective bargaining was in its infancy or nonexistent, the economic reality was often that the worker had no such liberty. He or she either accepted the terms and conditions offered by employers or faced homelessness and star-vation. Industrialism eroded the old safety net—the family farm to which one might return. An employee who chose not to work more than sixty hours a week in Lochner's bakery might soon be unemployed. Moreover, to the extent that industrialization increased the size of firms and the number of jobs calling for unskilled (undifferentiated) labor, the notion of individual workers exercising their liberty of contract with an employer was increasingly unrealistic. Many industrial workers became interchangeable. They had physical strength and stamina, but not scarce skills to sell (Zuboff 1988).

Third, laissez-faire oriented judges chose a path that was politically untenable. In the face of growing economic and social complexity that promoted demands for government regulation, they made it difficult for all levels of government—local, state, and federal—to regulate commercial activity.

The divergence between judicial interpretation and economic reality was challenged by two legal developments that reduced the barriers that judicial review posed to the development of the administrative state. One was the advent of the "Brandeis brief" in *Muller v. Oregon*, 208 US 412 (1908), which argued in favor of an Oregon statute providing that "no female" shall be employed in any factory or laundry for more than 10 hours during any single day. According to Johnson (1981, 29), this marked the beginning of a new era in American law. The Brandeis brief was revolutionary because it drew heavily on sources of information that could not be considered legal authority. As Johnson explains:

> Unlike past appellate arguments that relied upon case precedents, the so-called 'Brandeis brief' in the Muller case alluded strictly to legal authorities on only 3 of its 113 pages. Most of Brandeis's support for his position was drawn from government labor statistics, reports of factory inspectors, and testimony from psychological, economic and medical treatises. Sources such as these had rarely been called to the attention of the appellate courts before 1908, and never had any attorney drawn so heavily upon such extra-legal authorities in a single brief (ibid., 30).

Brandeis presented enough information to convince the Supreme Court that the Oregon legis-lature could reasonably conclude that long hours of work in factories and laundries were harmful to the safety, morals, and health of women. Therefore, even though the regulation interfered with a woman's liberty of contract, it was within the police power of the state to enact it. Today such gender-based protective legislation is viewed as discriminatory (see *J.E.B. v. Alabama ex rel. T.B.*, 511 US 127 [1994]). But the larger point beyond the specifics of *Muller* is that by successfully bringing new sources of information to bear on adjudication, Brandeis opened the door to a jurisprudence that could more readily adjust to a rapidly changing society.

The second development prompting greater judicial acceptance of the administrative state was legal realism, an intellectual approach to analyzing law that emerged in the 1920s and 1930s. Legal realism was not a tightly coherent movement or school of thought. Rather, it was a general outlook that questioned assumptions about the legal system and the empirical premises on which much traditional legal doctrine rested. Realists included judges, lawyers, and scholars (Johnson 1981, 123) who supported legal reforms grounded on social scientific research. Realism can be contrasted with the formalism of *Lochner, Carter*, and similar cases.

Although the influence of legal realism has been hotly contested, in retrospect it appears that the movement facilitated the legal community's acceptance of the administrative state. In a complex argument, Bruce Ackerman maintains that "it was only by assimilating large chunks of Realist wisdom that the profession managed to preserve so much of its traditional common law discourse" (1984, 13). This was in part because "the Realistic lawyers' skepticism about abstraction permitted them to keep invoking particular doctrines inherited from the past without confronting their foundation in laissez-faire legal theory" (ibid., 19).

Realism provided a channel through which administrative law could be discussed and formulated in terms of more traditional American legal concepts. By the late 1930s, the question was no longer whether law would stand as a fundamental obstacle to a full-fledged administrative state. Instead, the issue was how the law could best inform and check administrative rule making, adjudication, and enforcement. The American legal community was ready to bring to fruition the early efforts of Wyman and Goodnow to establish administrative law as a category of law and legal study. Ironically, as Stewart and Frug observe, the model of public administration that was chosen as the basis for administrative law itself became increasingly unrealistic.

V. ADMINISTRATIVE PENETRATION TODAY: A SCHEMA

The relationships between the contemporary administrative state and administrative law can be viewed through many lenses. Some analyses rely on broad categories such as economic regulation, social regulation, and social policy. Others, along with Lowi (1964), categorize administrative behavior according to such policy arenas as distribution, regulation, and redistribution. Yet another approach is to consider administrative processes in terms of representation, participation, transparency, and the protection of individual rights. Each set of lenses yields important insights. In terms of the relationship between administrative law and administrative practice, the following schema offers a broad, yet reasonably detailed, review of how administrative activities are connected to administrative law.

A. ADMINISTRATION TO CREATE SURROGATE MARKETS

Administration of this type is used where it is believed that free markets are an inappropriate means of promoting the public interest. Transportation is the classic case. The Interstate Commerce Commission (ICC) was established in 1887 for the purpose of regulating railroads with a view toward ensuring that "all charges… shall be reasonable and just." Later, in 1938, the Civil Aeronautics Board (CAB) was established to control entry and rates in airline transportation. Public utility commissions and sundry other administrative structures, such as the Federal Communications Commission (FCC), are also commonly used in areas of economic activity affected by a deep public interest and in which it is thought that free markets will be unsatisfactory.

The administration of surrogate markets is typically informed by the economic analysis of rates of return and considerations of the distribution of services. The process frequently requires regulated parties to submit requests for rate increases or changes in the nature of services.

The regulatory agency, generally a commission of some kind, then performs an assessment, usually in the form of an adjudicatory process. The regulated party's request is probed by the legal staff of the commission before a hearing examiner or an ALJ. The latter's decision is submitted to the commissioners, who may accept, modify, or reject it. Typically, the agency's mandate is to balance the public interest with the economic interests of the private concern.

The administrative law pertinent to the administration of surrogate markets will tend to focus on the adjudicatory procedure used by the agency. For example, prominent issues may be the hearing examiner's independence, ex parte (one-sided) communications, and burdens of persuasion. Judicial review of the agency's decision is often more concerned with procedure than substance because the court is deferential to the agency's technical expertise. This is true even though some agencies have a vague statutory mission, such as regulating the use of the airwaves in the public interest, necessity, or convenience. However, the agency's adjudicatory decisions (known as "orders") must be supported by substantial factual evidence. During the late 1970s and 1980s, federal deregulation focused largely on surrogate market administration, most notably in the airline and trucking industries. The CAB was abolished in the mid-1980s, and the ICC was shut down a decade later.

B. ADMINISTRATION TO ENSURE THE PROPER FUNCTIONING OF MARKETS

Antitrust and fair-trade regulations are the preeminent examples of administrative activities aimed at regulating market behavior. The Sherman Anti-Trust Act of 1890 and the Federal Trade Commission Act of 1914 were framed with these purposes in mind. Traditionally, antitrust regulatory activity has been informed by economic analysis of the effect of mergers, acquisitions, and other practices on the competitiveness of markets; contemporary approaches may look to efficiency rather than competition per se. Fair-trade regulation also is informed by economic analysis, but it may be more concerned with the regulation of antisocial economic practices per se, regardless of whether they have a pronounced effect on markets. For instance, the Federal Trade Commission (FTC) has successfully maintained that it can prohibit practices that are unfair even without showing that these practices are harmful to competition (*FTC v. Sperry and Hutchinson*, 405 US 233 [1972]). False or deceptive advertising is a standard concern in fair-trade administration.

The legislative mandate for these regulatory activities is often vague, and the administrative processes employed may vary widely. The Department of Justice's efforts to block mergers or require the breakup of corporations can rely on voluntary settlements or involve full-fledged adjudication in federal court, followed by very probing judicial review on appeal.

The regulation of fair-trade practices by the FTC relies primarily on rule making, adjudication within the agency, and settlements with parties engaged in illegal activity. Its adjudicatory and enforcement procedures are controlled by the APA. Much fair-trade activity is aimed at the resolution of individual complaints, often through the informal processes.

C. ADMINISTRATION TO ENSURE THE SAFETY OF PRODUCTS AND SERVICES

The federal Consumer Product Safety Commission (CPSC), National Highway Traffic Safety Administration (NHTSA), Food and Drug Administration (FDA), and Federal Aviation Agency (FAA) are examples of agencies that regulate safety. Such regulation is informed by the belief that liability law is inadequate to protect consumers against serious harm from the use of unsafe products or services. Agency rule making relies heavily on science and engineering, with economics being a secondary or even lesser concern. Enforcement involves testing and inspection. In some cases, as in new-drug testing and aircraft inspection, regulation is proactive in the sense that the private entity cannot market a product or service until it has been given permission to do so. The agency and the regulated party may work in a cooperative fashion to prevent harm to the public. Although hearings may be held to solicit information and opinion from experts and interested parties, agency procedures tend not to be highly judicialized.

D. REGULATION TO ENSURE THE SAFETY OF NEW TECHNOLOGIES

The Nuclear Regulatory Commission (NRC) is an example. Although related to regulatory activity for consumer safety, the regulation of new and presumptively dangerous technologies is conceptually different. It is aimed at protecting members of the broad public who may not enter into direct economic relationships with the firm that uses the technology. Even people living far away from the site of the technology are potentially at risk, as in the case of radioactive leaks and toxic spills. Genetic engineering and microwave technologies also have been candidates for far-reaching regulation.

The regulation of technologies for safety is largely informed by engineering and science. It relies on inspections, testing, and licensing. Hearings may be held on applications for licenses and renewals, but these may not be highly judicialized in their adjudicatory procedures. The judiciary is likely to be deferential to the technical expertise of the regulatory agency.

E. REGULATION TO PROTECT THE ENVIRONMENT

Federal regulation for the purpose of protecting the environment is a relatively distinct category of administrative law. Much federal substantive environmental law, such as the Clean Air and Clean Water Acts, affect state and local administration (O'Leary 1994). In terms of administrative law, however, the National Environmental Policy Act of 1969 (NEPA) is more important. NEPA has among its purposes "to declare a national policy which will encourage productive and enjoyable harmony between man and his environment; to promote efforts which will prevent or eliminate damage to the environment and biosphere and stimulate the health and welfare of man; to enrich the understanding of the ecological systems and natural resources important to the Nation...." It requires federal agencies to "include in every recommendation or report on proposals for legislation and other major Federal actions significantly affecting the environment, a detailed statement... on... the environmental impact of the proposed action." Such regulation goes beyond what are identified as dangerous technologies to the full panoply of practices that may be damaging to the environment. The sources of harmful pollutants are multifold, and some of the technologies, such as burning coal or even wood for power, are quite old. Taken to its fullest extent, environmental regulation is oriented toward future generations.

Environmental rule making is informed by engineering and a host of sciences. Enforcement relies on testing and inspection. Efforts are made to screen out new threats to the environment through environmental impact statements, the evaluation of which often involves broad public participation or debate. Although internal EPA processes are not judicialized, environmental regulation has been an area of massive litigation (O'Leary 1993).

F. REGULATION OF EMPLOYMENT PROCESSES

Modern wage employment and labor markets are clearly the products of industrialization. Labor relations emerged as a public-policy problem in the 1870s (Rosenbloom and Shafritz 1985). Until the 1930s, regulation of employment, for the most part, was left to the state governments and courts. During the New Deal, however, the National Labor Relations Act of 1935 established a federal administrative agency, the National Labor Relations Board (NLRB), to oversee collective bargaining in private employment generally and to prohibit unfair labor practices. Its mission is to balance the interests of employers and their organized employees. In 1965, the Equal Employment Opportunity Commission (EEOC) began regulating employment to eliminate prohibited discrimination based on race, color, national origin, religion, and sex. In 1967, the category of age was added to this list, and pregnancy followed in 1978. In the early 1970s, the Occupational Safety and Health Administration (OSHA) was created to regulate workplaces in the interest of employees' physical safety and health. In 1993, the Americans with Disabilities Act provided federal protection of the employment interests of handicapped and disabled persons. More specialized regulatory activities exist in the mining industry.

Although regulatory activities for these purposes rely on different procedures and are informed by different specializations, it is useful to combine them under one category because they all deal with one or another facet of employment relationships. Regulation by the NLRB and the EEOC relies heavily on adjudication. Both agencies are judicialized and oriented toward the adjudication of complaints, but the EEOC also has used litigation as a strategy of combating broad patterns and practices of prohibited discrimination by specific employers. OSHA relies more heavily on rule making and inspections. The EEOC and OSHA have jurisdiction in both the public and private sectors. With very few exceptions, the NLRB is concerned only with private employment.

G. THE PROTECTION OF ENTITLEMENTS

The administration of entitlements has become pertinent to contemporary administrative law. Broadly construed, entitlements include a range of programs for income support, nutrition, housing, education, and health. In some contexts, building and zoning permits and occupational and commercial licenses also may be considered entitlements. In terms of administrative law, the withholding of benefits from individuals claiming to be entitled to them is informed largely by the requirements of procedural due process, equal protection, and estoppel. Administrative procedure has been constitutionalized, as entitlements are sometimes treated as property interests. (*Goldberg v. Kelly*, 397 US 254 [1970]; *Cleveland Board of Education v. Loudermill*, 470 US 532 [1985]). Moreover, although public administrators may think of entitlements as providing welfare services to the public, from a legal perspective these benefits may be seen as having a regulatory dimension that interferes with individuals' liberty in some fashion. For instance, as a condition of receiving welfare benefits for their children, parents may have to agree to in-home visits by social workers (*Wyman v. James*, 400 US 309 [1971]), and public-school students engaged in extra-curricular activities may be subject to random drug testing (*Board of Education of Independent School District No. 92 of Pottawatomie County v. Earls*, 536 US 822 [2002]).

It will be useful to keep these categories in mind throughout the remainder of this chapter as the historical development of specific regulatory initiatives is discussed. It is particularly important to note how different regulatory activities raise particular questions about how administrative agencies should be regulated by administrative law.

VI. DECADE-BY-DECADE ANALYSIS 1880s–2000s

A. 1880s

It is customary to date the origins of American administrative law from the 1880s, a decade in which the Civil Service Act (1883; also known as the Pendleton Act) and the Interstate Commerce Act (1887) were enacted. Both acts had important federal or state antecedents. However, together they were a critical part of the broad historical effort, extending from about 1877 to 1920, to develop a greater federal administrative capacity (Skowronek 1982).

The Civil Service Act has had an enduring legacy for the law of public office. It was passed after a protracted struggle by reformers who had multiple goals. Among the most important of these were (1) the elimination of the prevailing practices of patronage hiring and dismissal in the federal service (i.e., the "spoils system"); (2) the development of a system of merit exams as the cornerstone of federal personnel practices; and (3) the removal of considerations of partisanship from the personnel system.

The reformers argued that these changes would bring higher levels of morality and efficiency to the federal service. More generally, they thought that these reforms would lead to fundamental changes in the character of American politics and political leadership (Rosenbloom 1971). Their overall goal was to destroy the power of political machines and bosses by depriving them of patronage appointments in the public service. As one of their leaders, Dorman B. Eaton, asserted, the reformers' most fundamental critique of the spoils system was that under it "we have seen a class of politicians become powerful in high places, who have not taken (and who by nature are not qualified to take) any large part in the social and educational life of the people. Politics have tended more and more to become a trade, or separate occupation. High character and capacity have become disassociated from public life in the popular mind" (Eaton 1880, 392). Ultimately, the reformers hoped "to restore ability, high character, and true public spirit once more to their legitimate spheres in our public life, and to make active politics once more attractive to men of self-respect and high patriotic aspirations," as Carl Schurz, another leading reformer, explained (Schurz 1893, 614). Such men would not be unlike the civil-service reformers themselves.

The fundamental premise of the reform movement and the Civil Service Act was that "the business part of the government shall be carried on in a sound businesslike manner" (Schurz 1894, 3). A distinction between politics and administration (that is, the business part) was drawn. Through the work of Woodrow Wilson (1887), Frank Goodnow (1900), this distinction, now known as the politics–administration dichotomy, eventually became central to American public administrative theory.

The Civil Service Act was passed as a result of several factors. The reformers themselves were undeniably an important force. Eaton actually wrote the act. Public opinion crystallized against patronage when a demented office-seeker assassinated President James Garfield in 1881. Ironically, though, the legislative politics involved in enacting the Civil Service Act were concerned with partisan advantage. The Republican Party, which had fared poorly in the 1882 mid-term congressional elections, supported reform as a means of reducing the amount of patronage that would be available to the Democrats should they win the presidency in 1884 (which they did, when Grover Cleveland triumphed over James Blaine) (Hoogenboom 1961).

The following were the Civil Service Act's most important features:

1. The creation of a three-member, bipartisan Civil Service Commission (CSC) to police personnel practices. Among other responsibilities, the commissioners were charged with aiding the president in preparing rules for the personnel system. They were appointed by the president with the advice and consent of the Senate. Originally, the commissioners held indefinite terms of office and could be dismissed by the president. In 1956, they were given six-year overlapping terms but were still subject to dismissal. The Civil Service Reform Act of 1978 abolished the CSC, effective 1979.
2. The specification that a system of "open, competitive examinations for testing the fitness of applicants for the public service" be developed. The exams were to be practical in nature and job-related.
3. The elimination of partisan politics from personnel actions by providing that "no person in the public service is for that reason under any obligations to contribute to any political fund, or to render any political service, and that he will not be removed or otherwise prejudiced for refusing to do so." The act also outlawed coercion of political action on the part of federal employees and contained a number of other provisions to eliminate partisan intrusion into the federal service.
4. The development or improvement of employee classification systems in the Treasury, Post Office, and other departments.

The act provided a remarkably durable framework for federal personnel in a system that grew from about 100,000 employees in 1880 to approximately 3 million by 1978, when thoroughgoing changes were mandated by the Civil Service Reform Act.

The Interstate Commerce Act has been considered of equal or greater importance in the development of administrative law. It created the ICC, which legal scholars—though not those of public administration—generally consider "the archetype of the modern administrative agency" (Schwartz 1977, 293). The act embodied the federal government's general consensus that private-sector market forces were inadequate to regulate railroad transportation in the public interest.

Specifically, the Interstate Commerce Act established the following:

- A five-member, bipartisan commission. The commissioners, who held six-year overlapping terms, were removable by the president for "inefficiency, neglect of duty, or malfeasance in office";
- A provision that all railroad rates in interstate commerce be "reasonable and just";
- A number of provisions prohibiting "undue preferences to persons, localities, and traffic;" discrimination against connecting lines, and price discrimination for short distances;
- A requirement that common carriers print and post rate schedules for public and ICC inspections;
- A provision for individuals to file complaints with the ICC; and
- A number of penalties for violation, including fines of up to $5,000 and civil liability for damages.

The politics behind the act were perplexing. A movement in favor of regulating the railroads developed in the 1870s as farmers in the Middle West felt victimized by monopolies or quasi-monopolies. Rates were viewed as exorbitant and unrelated to the actual cost of transporting materials. A Granger movement was successful in the 1870s in getting some states, notably Illinois and Wisconsin, to pass laws regulating the railroads. A comprehensive Illinois law for the regulation of railroads, warehouses, and grain elevators by commission was upheld by the Supreme Court in *Munn v. Illinois*, 94 US 113 (1877). The Court accepted the argument that these businesses were "clothed with a public interest" and accordingly could be supervised by the government. The Court's decision seemed to provide impetus for the advocates of railroad regulation elsewhere, and in the late 1870s and early 1880s, South Carolina, Georgia, and New York were among the states adopting such measures.

Despite these victories, the advocates of regulation did not necessarily achieve their overall goal of taming the railroads. Railroad interests were also heard in the state legislatures, and the Grangers' influence began to diminish. For example, Wisconsin's 1874 Potter Law, which authorized a commission to set maximum railroad freight rates within the state, was repealed in 1876 (Friedman 1973, 392; Ranney 2004). More importantly, perhaps, the administration of current laws was sometimes quite weak (Friedman 1973, 392).

Yet the existence of state regulation, and the potential for more such activity, remained a check on the railroads' behavior, until this framework came to an abrupt halt in 1886, with the Supreme Court's decision in *Wabash Railway v. Illinois*, 118 US 557. The Court held that because the Constitution gives the federal government power to regulate interstate commerce, a state was not permitted to regulate commerce coming from or going to another state. This line of reasoning is now called the dormant or negative commerce clause. It prevents states from discriminating against or excessively burdening interstate commerce (*Carbone v. Town of Clarkstown*, 511 US 383 [1994]). *Wabash Railway* made federal regulation virtually inevitable. Even some railroad interests were in favor of balanced federal regulation that would protect them from public hostility. This stance was reflected in the Interstate Commerce Act's vagueness as to whether the ICC could actually set rates. In 1897, the Supreme Court held that it did not have this power

(*ICC v. Cincinnati, New Orleans and Texas Pacific Railroad Co.*, 167 US 479). It was eventually conveyed by the Hepburn Act of 1906.

B.   1890s

Regulation in the 1890s was dominated by another enduring statute, the Sherman Anti-Trust Act of 1890. Unlike the Civil Service Act and the Interstate Commerce Act, the Sherman Act did not establish an administrative agency for its implementation. It relied on the Department of Justice for enforcement through the courts. Moreover, the act was not confined to a specific process, substance, or industry. At least potentially, it cut broadly across interstate commerce throughout the United States.

The breadth of the act notwithstanding, its purpose and language were vague. The CSC and ICC were created to deal with specific problems; the Sherman Act was aimed at a general condition. The act makes illegal "every combination, contract or conspiracy… in restraint of trade" and prohibits monopolization and any efforts to monopolize markets. The term "restraint of trade" had some standing at common law. Such restraints were considered to harm the public interest. Before 1890, several states had adopted antitrust measures. The common thread in the antitrust movement was a pervasive fear or concern with "bigness," that is, the sheer size and concentrated power of large business interests. As Friedman observed, "What the solid middle class wanted, insofar as one can speak of a dominant desire, was not a law to restore pure, unrestricted competition but rather a giant killer, an act to cut down to size the monstrous combinations which had aggregated too much power for the country's good" (1973, 465).

Such a goal is perhaps too general to inform consistent implementation (Weaver 1980). Worse yet, the act's intent seems more mystified than clarified by an analysis of its legislative history. John Sherman, its sponsor, was given to explaining the bill in different ways at different times. At one point, he argued that:

> the popular mind is agitated with problems that may disturb the social order, and among them all none is more threatening than the inequality of condition, of wealth and opportunity that has grown within a single generation out of the concentration of vast combinations of capital to control production and trade and to break down competition (Weaver 1980, 129).

However, he also argued that "if we will not endure a king as a political power we should not endure a king over the production, transportation, and sale of any of the necessaries of life" (ibid.). Whether the primary purpose of the act in his mind was to combat inequality or to constrain power is a moot point, but not an inconsequential one. It is perfectly plausible that, under some conditions, the combinations that he opposed would be powerful but not necessarily detrimental to equality of condition, wealth, and opportunity. Sherman seems to have recognized this to some extent. When challenged as to the vagueness of the bill's language, he responded as follows: "I admit that it is difficult to define in legal language the precise line between lawful and unlawful combinations" (Weaver 1980, 130).

It is debatable whether the Sherman Act and, before it, the Interstate Commerce Act were representative of a general ongoing legislative response to demands for governmental intervention in the economy. Certainly in the case of the Sherman Act it was fully evident, as Friedman notes, that "vague language in a statute is, in effect, a delegation by Congress to lower agencies, or to the executive and the courts; it passes the problem along to these others. Such a law often buys time; it postpones resolution of a problem; it acts as a compromise between those who want sharp, specific action and those who stand on the status quo" (1973, 464–465). Sherman was candid in announcing that "all that we, as lawmakers, can do is to declare general principles, and we can be assured that the courts will apply them so as to carry out the meaning of the law" (Weaver 1980, 130). In other words, it was to "be left for the courts to determine in each particular case" what the law intended (ibid.).

Of course the courts cannot determine anything under such a law unless an appropriate administrative agency or outside party with standing to sue brings a case in the first place. A vague mandate provides administrators with considerable discretion—and discretion to intervene in the marketplace was not something much favored by the courts of the 1890s. Unchecked discretion has been considered abhorrent to the rule of law as well as to the constitutional separation of powers. It has long been a chief concern of US administrative law.

During the decade of the 1890s, both the Department of Justice and the Supreme Court had difficulty dealing effectively and consistently with the Sherman Act. According to Suzanne Weaver (1980, 132), the Department brought an average of fewer than 1.5 cases per year during the period from 1890 through 1904, but an average of 31 per year from 1910 through 1914. In *US v. E. C Knight*, 156 US 1 (1895), the Supreme Court temporarily rendered the act irrelevant to manufacturing. As David Shannon explains:

> In 1895, the Court passed judgment on the law in a way that seriously limited the law's application. [President] Cleveland's Attorney General, Richard Olney, argued a suit against the American Sugar Refining Company, commonly called the Sugar Trust, in a way that showed the Court how to exempt manufacturing from the Act. Although the consolidated Sugar Trust was a 98 per cent perfect monopoly, the Court ruled... that the Trust's acquisition of the stocks of its component corporation did not constitute interstate commerce and was, therefore, not affected by the Sherman Act. The Court made a distinction between manufacturing and commerce and asserted the federal Constitution's interstate commerce clause did not embrace manufacturing. Mergers and consolidations of all kinds came rapidly after the *Knight* case." (1963, 29)

By 1899, however, the Court seemed to have moved away from the view expressed in the *Knight* case (*see US v. Trans-Missouri Freight Assn*, 166 US 290 [1897], and *Addyson Pipe & Steel Co. v. US*, 175 US 211 [1899]). Even so, between 1897 and 1904, trust building was rampant. According to Kenneth Meier, during that period "some 70 major industries merged into monopolies or near monopolies … 4,227 firms merged into 257 combinations that established 'trusts' in over 300 different industries" (1985, 236). In 1914, Congress enacted the Clayton Act as a means of strengthening antitrust policy (discussed in the section on the 1910s below).

C. 1900s

Unlike the 1880s and 1890s, the 1900s were marked less by specific achievements—though there were some—than by the development of a general "administrative culture" that continues to have a strong impact on contemporary public administrative theory, practice, and law. This culture began to develop out of the confluence of the last stages of the nineteenth century civil-service reform movement and the first phases of the Progressive movement. Later, in the 1910s and 1920s, the administrative culture would be crystallized by the influence of the Scientific Management Movement. By the 1930s, the United States had developed a theory and discipline of public administration that considered itself to be grounded in scientific principles and sound business management rather than in law or political science. The chief values were efficiency and economy, which were sought through a scientific approach to managing administrative activities.

Nineteenth century civil service reform, as previously discussed, sought the creation of a merit-oriented, nonpartisan, or even apolitical civil service as a means of achieving not only more effective public administration but also a broad change in the character of the nation's political leadership and electoral politics. The reformers were aware that if government were to be an effective mechanism for promoting the public's economic and social welfare, it would need a much greater administrative capability. For instance, Carl Schurz noted that "as the functions of government grow in extent, importance and complexity, the necessity grows of their being admi-nistered not only with honesty, but also with trained ability and knowledge" (1895, 4). The Progressives shared these concerns, but with a different emphasis.

Between 1900 and 1920, vast social and economic changes occurred in the United States. Perhaps most striking, David Shannon notes, was the extent of immigration:

> [W]ith the twentieth century came the largest immigration wave of all time. Between 1860 and 1900, the total number of immigrants had been slightly less than 14,000,000. Between 1900 and 1915, the total was over 14,500,000, close to one-fifth of what the total population had been in 1900. In 1907 alone, the peak year, immigration amounted to 1,285,000, and in six of the years between 1904 and 1914 the total was over 1,000,000. In 1910, about one-seventh of the total American population had been born abroad and about as many more were offspring of immigrant parents.... In 1910, 78 percent of New York City's population was first- or second-generation immigrant, Chicago's percentage was the same, and in Boston, Philadelphia, Pittsburgh, and St. Louis more than half of the population was no more than one generation away from Europe (1963, 88).

Shannon's data indicate that immigration was an important factor in the growth of the nation's urban population. In 1900, the Bureau of the Census classified 60 percent of the population as rural, that is, living in towns with a population under 2500. In 1910, the figure was 54.2 percent, and in 1920, it was 48.6 percent (Shannon 1963, 73). This was at a time when transportation and com-munication technologies did not have the capacity to promote immediate widespread acculturation and today's no surprises regional and cultural standardization. A wing of the Progressive movement dominated by women sought to help immigrants settle into mainstream American life. These settlement women founded public administration's sibling public-service profession, social work (Stivers 2000).

Business and labor were vastly changing during this period of rapid industrialization and urbanization. The hallmark in business was the Ford Motor Company's development in 1913 and 1914 of mass, assembly-line production. Even earlier, however, in 1911, Frederick Taylor developed what he called "scientific management" as a means of promoting greater industrial efficiency. Taylorism began in the 1890s and emerged as an important aspect of America's indus-trial workplaces by 1920. It gave impetus to industrialization's tendency to simplify jobs and to reduce employees' discretion and control of work processes. It also sought to elevate managerial authority and legitimize it as science. At the same time, perhaps partly as a counterforce, the American labor movement grew and gained greater institutional stability. Unlike earlier large unions, the American Federation of Labor demonstrated staying power. Its membership increased from about 1 million in 1900 to 2 million in 1917 (Shannon 1963, 78).

The Progressive movement sought to control, assimilate, and amalgamate these changes into an America that was politically, economically, morally, and socially wholesome. Progressives saw immigrants as a threat to Anglo-American political, moral, and legal values. Woodrow Wilson worried about "a partial corruption of foreign blood" and the fact that "[w]e are unquestionably facing an ever-increasing difficulty of self-command with ever-deteriorating materials, possibly with degenerating fibre" (Rohr 1986, 72). He also was concerned with preserving "our nationality in its integrity and its old-time originative force in the face of growth and imported change" (ibid., 23n6). The Progressives were relentless in their attacks on political corruption, especially in the urban areas, and they supported pure food and drug legislation and better economic and social conditions for immigrants. They continued the effort to place public administration on a sound, businesslike basis, for example by strongly supporting the concept of city management and the creation of municipal research bureaus. In 1915, New York City's bureau had the following objectives: "to promote efficient and economical municipal government; to promote adoption of scientific methods of accounting and of reporting the details of municipal business...; to collect, to classify, to analyze, to correlate, to interpret and to publish facts as to the administration of municipal government" (Mosher 1976, 45). The concept of a city manager was in itself remarkable in the heyday of political bosses, and even more remarkable was the objective that such a manager should be chosen "solely on the basis of his executive and administrative qualifications" (Mosher 1976, 83; from the second edition of the Model City Charter of 1916).

The mix of nineteenth-century reform and twentieth-century progressivism was clearly the basis of American public administrative theory and preferred practice until the 1940s. Arguably, it still informs a good deal of administrative practice, though it is now considered unenlightened (Gore 1993, 3). As late as the 1990s, advocates of reinventing government identified it as the dominant force in American administrative culture (Gore 1993, 3; Osborne and Gaebler 1992).

The connection between the reformers and Progressives was explained in 1900 by Frank Goodnow in his book *Politics and Administration*. Goodnow was both prescient in his anticipation of the impact that Progressive rumblings would have and reflective of Progressive concerns. He was well versed in the desire of nineteenth-century civil-service reform to separate politics from administration as a means of promoting both good politics and sound administration. He also recognized the Progressive demand for political reforms per se, which would improve politics by weakening or destroying political bosses and machines. These political reforms would create a better environment for efficient and economical administration as well. Eventually, Progressive reforms included primary elections, the short ballot, the referendum, and the recall. For Goodnow, political and administrative reforms were somewhat interdependent. Political reforms would enable the public to express its will; administrative reforms would enable that will to be implemented efficiently. Politics and administration went together in the service of the public—yet they were also separate. If public administrators had virtually no role in expressing the will of the people, then politicians had at best only a very limited role in telling technically competent public administrators how to execute it. Public administration remained a field of business, but it would function in the most businesslike manner only when the political system functioned effectively in expressing the will of the people. This basic framework is still reflected in a great deal of thinking about public administration and administrative law. It is essentially the "transmission belt" theory criticized by Richard Stewart (1975), as discussed earlier.

Goodnow was a leading authority on administrative law, but his framework in *Politics and Administration* was not altogether satisfactory for dealing with the relationship between public administration and law (Goodnow 1893, 1900, 1905). Judicial review of public administration emerged as a key issue in the 1910s and 1920s, and judicialization became central by the 1940s. But where do they stand in terms of expression of the people's will versus its execution? If one assumes that federal judges represent the will of the people, even though they are not elected, then their review of public administration is presumably to be welcomed unless it interferes with the technical execution of the will. By contrast, if one assumes administrative agencies are responsible to the legislature and the chief executive in their interpretation of the expression of the people's will, then judicial review could be highly intrusive in principle.

Judicialization presents a similar problem. If public administrators engage in adjudication, then by any modern conception they must exercise considerable discretion. If this discretion is to be informed by technical considerations of law, then it should be subject to searching judicial review because the courts are presumed to be the repository of legal expertise and binding judgment. If the discretion is to be informed by interpretations of the will of the people, then some political check on its exercise would be highly desirable. Goodnow was aware of some of the difficulties posed by the relationship of public administration to law. However, because his work predated the emergence of a full-fledged administrative state and extensive and judicialization of public administration, he could not have foreseen the limitations of the transmission belt theory or the concepts of bureaucratic expertise and unity of command as bases for administrative law.

Goodnow's work is not only valuable for its ability to bridge the nineteenth-century civil service reform and the twentieth-century Progressive movements. In retrospect, it is equally valuable in pointing to the central problems of modern administrative law. Goodnow, the reformers, and, for the most part, the Progressives were convinced that despite the government's three branches, it really only had two functions: politics and administration. Politics was preeminently the domain of legislatures and elected chief executives. Administration was for apolitical trained managers and specialists in such activities as accounting and personnel. Administration was an executive function, but one that should be insulated from elected executives in important ways, including merit systems and regulations for political neutrality. This scheme fails to deal with two of the most important questions in American administrative law: (1) What is the proper role of the courts with respect to public administrative decisions and other activities? (2) To what extent, and under what conditions, can adjudicatory functions properly be placed in administrative agencies? It was not until the 1940s that the federal government established a unified statutory framework—the APA—for dealing with these issues.

In rounding out the discussion in this section, some specific legal developments should be mentioned. The Pure Food and Drug Act was passed in 1906. It outlawed the use of several specific additives in foods and prohibited false claims about drugs. The act was the culmination of several years of lobbying by Dr. Harvey Wiley, a chemist in the Department of Agriculture. At one point, Harvey created a poison squad of Department employees who were fed food additives under controlled conditions. Wiley's efforts were strongly aided by the publication of Upton Sinclair's *The Jungle* (1905), a novel that brought the disgusting and repulsive conditions in meat-packing plants to the nation's attention. The Pure Food and Drug Act was followed by the Meat Inspection Act of 1907. The latter required the Department of Agriculture to inspect all meat sold in interstate commerce.

Another important development occurred in the law of public officers. In 1907, President Theodore Roosevelt issued an executive order creating a system of restrictions on the political activities of federal employees:

> [P]ersons who by the provisions of these [civil service] rules are in the competitive classified service, while retaining the right to vote as they please and to express privately their opinions on all political subjects, shall take no active part in political management or in political campaigns. (US Civil Service Commission *Annual Report* 1907, 9).

Enforcement was handled by the Civil Service Commission, which interpreted the rule strictly, though in some cases perhaps arbitrarily (Rosenbloom 1971, 108–110). Roosevelt's order was superseded by the Hatch Act of 1939, which extended political neutrality to federal employees outside the competitive service, with limited exceptions. The restrictions were substantially liberalized by the Hatch Act Reform Amendments of 1993, which permitted most federal employees to engage in such partisan campaign activities as stuffing envelopes, giving speeches, making phone calls, and distributing literature. The reform also allowed them to hold offices in political parties. Soliciting funds, however, remains highly regulated.

D. 1910s

The decade from 1910 to 1919 emphasized regulating banking and commerce. Regulatory policy continued to try to reconcile new economic realities with traditional American values. In the case of banking, regulation was seen as a means of protecting stability and independence. The object was to make banks and their clients less vulnerable to failures induced by "panics" or external influences. Although it is inconceivable that the United States would not have adopted banking regulations at some point, regardless of a specific incident, the impetus for this regulation grew out of the Panic of 1907, which occurred when Englishmen began to withdraw their gold from American banks. The banks, in response, began calling loans, which in turn led depositors to withdraw their funds in a panic based on the belief that the banks were failing. The Panic itself caused some banks with insufficient reserves to collapse (Meier 1985, 48–50).

The political response to the Panic was the appointment of a commission to study the banking problem and, eventually, the enactment of the Federal Reserve Act of 1913. The act created a highly independent Federal Reserve Board and twelve regional Federal Reserve Banks. All national banks were required to keep a proportion of their funds in these Federal Reserve Banks and the latter were authorized to help national banks facing liquidity problems. The act also created common accounting procedures and authorized the Comptroller of the Currency to inspect banks (Meier 1985, 49–50). The establishment of the Federal Reserve System predated the use of monetary policy and public budget deficits and surpluses as tools for controlling the booms and busts of the business cycle Eventually, the Federal Reserve Board became a key actor in the economy through its ability to adjust interest rates.

The second major thrust of regulation during the 1910s focused on trust-busting and trade practices. The Clayton Act and the Federal Trade Commission Act were passed in 1914. The former made a number of practices, including price discrimination and exclusionary agreements, illegal in interstate commerce. The Clayton Act also broadly declares a practice to be illegal when its effect may be to substantially lessen competition or to tend to create a monopoly.

The Federal Trade Commission Act created the FTC, with responsibility for enforcing the Clayton Act and preventing unfair methods of competition more generally. The FTC is authorized to combat deceptive practices, including false advertising, and to prevent mergers or acquisitions that tend to create monopoly or substantially reduce competition (Katzmann 1980).

A final noteworthy development of the decade was the enactment of the Lloyd-LaFollette Act of 1912. The act afforded a modicum of statutory protection for federal employees in dismissals. It fit the Progressive interest in establishing an apolitical, technically based, and career-oriented public service. The act established a standard for dismissals that essentially is still in use: "no person in the classified Civil Service of the United States shall be removed there from except for such cause as will promote the efficiency of said service." The act also required agencies to give federal employees in the classified service written notice of the reasons for their dismissals and an opportunity to respond in writing. It specifically provided that no hearing or trial was necessary in such removals. The act further provided that postal workers, and by implication other federal employees, could unionize. However, it contemplated discussions between these unions and members of Congress, rather than modern collective bargaining.

E.   1920s

For the most part, the 1920s were a pause in the development of the contemporary administrative state. They marked the end of the Progressive Era and predated the massive administrative change of the New Deal. The major legal development of the period was an increasing inclination to come to grips with the realities of the emerging administrative state. As noted earlier, the legal community of judges, scholars, and practitioners had shown considerable hostility to administrative intervention in the economy generally, and to administrative adjudication in particular. However, in his presidential address to the American Bar Association in 1916, Senator Elihu Root called attention to the fact that:

> one special field of law development... has manifestly become inevitable.... The Interstate Commerce Commission, the state public service commissions, the Federal Trade Commission, the powers of the Federal Reserve Board, the health departments of the states, and many other supervisory offices and agencies are familiar illustrations. Before these agencies the old doctrine prohibiting the delegation of legislative power has virtually retired from the field and given up the fight. There will be no withdrawal from these experiments. We shall go on; we shall expand them, whether we approve theoretically or not, because such agencies furnish protection to rights and obstacles to wrong-doing, which under our new social and industrial conditions cannot be practically accomplished by the old and simple procedure of legislatures and courts as in the last generation. Yet the powers that are committed to these regulating agencies, and which they must have to do their work, carry with them great and dangerous opportunities

of oppression and wrong. If we are to continue a government of limited powers, these agencies of regulation must themselves be regulated.... A system of administrative law must be developed, and that with us is still in its infancy, crude and imperfect (1916, 368–369).

Root's speech was important because it placed the development of administrative law on the agenda for the community of legal scholars and practitioners. It also added legitimacy to the concept of administrative law and urgency to its development as a legal field. By the latter part of the 1920s, greater support was emerging for the proposition that the rule of law could be preserved even where administrative agencies engaged in adjudication. John Dickinson's book, *Administrative Justice and the Supremacy of Law* (1927, 37), argued that "the question of court review of administrative determinations has come to be of such central importance and has been the focus of so much discussion since the rise of the administrative procedure. For just in so far as administrative determinations are subject to court review, a means exists for maintaining the supremacy of law, though at one remove and as a sort of secondary line of defence." By the 1930s, the issue of judicial review of administrative actions and powers became paramount. In the 1940s, the APA was enacted to regulate federal administrative activity legislatively and to establish standards for judicial review.

In addition to the intellectual developments of the 1920s, at least one important statute was enacted. The Railway Labor Act of 1926 consolidated a few earlier federal regulations for collective bargaining in interstate railroading. It protected the right of railroad employees to unionize and created a positive obligation for employers to engage in collective bargaining with these unions. The act was amended in 1934 to include the airline industry. It served as a model for the National Labor Relations Act of 1935 (Wagner Act), which remains the primary federal labor-relations statute to this day.

Perhaps *J.W. Hampton, Jr., & Co. v. United States* was the most important administrative law case of the 1920s. It involved the constitutionality of a congressional delegation of legislative authority to the president. The Supreme Court formulated the standard that formally remains in effect today: such delegations must contain an "intelligible principle" to which the president or administrative agencies are "directed to conform" 276 US 394, 409 (1928). Since the mid-1930s, "intelligible principle" has been interpreted loosely and has not been a barrier to delegations of legislative authority. In at least one case, *Industrial Union Department, AFL-CIO v. American Petroleum Institute*, 448 US 607 (1980), the Supreme Court upheld a delegation that could rightly be called a "legislative mirage, appearing to some Members [of Congress] but not to others and assuming any form desired by the beholder" *Id.* at 681; see also *Whitman v. American Trucking Ass'ns, Inc.*, 531 US 457 (2001).

F. 1930s

The full-fledged American administrative state emerged during the 1930s. Administrative development was primarily in response to the Great Depression, during which unemployment climbed to about 25 percent of the workforce. The amount of administrative growth was truly phenomenal. During 1933 and 1934, some 60 new agencies were established (Van Riper 1958, 320). The new agencies created by 1936 included the Food and Drug Administration, Federal Home Loan Bank Board, Commodity Credit Corporation, Federal Deposit Insurance Corporation, Federal Communications Commission, Securities and Exchange Commission, and the National Labor Relations Board. By the end of the decade, these were joined by the Agricultural Marketing Service, Civil Aeronautics Board, and others. The Executive Office of the President (EOP), which is vital to the modern presidency, was created in 1939. In addition, the Social Security Act and the Fair Labor Standards Act were enacted, and the Food and Drug Act was strengthened. These developments are obviously too varied and major to be adequately covered here. However, several observations seem appropriate.

First, many of the regulatory activities undertaken during the New Deal were not conceptually different from those developed earlier. However, federal regulation expanded into new fields and became more comprehensive in others. Overall, administrative penetration of the economy and society increased so dramatically that it virtually ushered in a new regime. Post-New Deal politics and administration differed greatly from previous patterns. Although interest groups, legislative committees, and administrative agencies had existed from the earliest days of American constitutional government, a new relationship among them began to develop in the 1930s. As government became more salient to the economy and society, myriad interest groups sought to influence the directions it took. They focused much of their attention on administrative agencies, which were now clearly understood to play important roles in policy-making and implementation.

By the end of the decade, the federal government was considered to have a headless fourth branch of independent regulatory commissions and other administrative units. The task of congressional oversight of federal administration was complicated by the proliferation of agencies. Eventually, during the 1940s, Congress began a pattern of increasing its committee and subcommittee capacity to engage in effective oversight. By the 1960s, harmonious relationships and world views frequently developed among agencies, interest groups, and (sub)committees, creating so-called iron triangles. These triangles became powerful in the development of public-policy agendas and actual policies. They constituted governmental subsystems in agriculture, transportation, and other policy arenas. Broad delegations of legislative authority to administrative agencies fueled the iron triangles' independence from the president and Congress as a whole (see Nachmias and Rosenbloom 1980). Such delegations were a second major change associated with the New Deal.

Delegations of legislative authority to administrative agencies enable public administrators to formulate rules, adjudicatory orders, and policies that effectively have the force of law. These delegations, especially those for rule making, enable agencies to legislate in a generic sense. Delegations are favored for a variety of reasons: they reduce Congress' workload, they take advantage of public administrators' expertise by deferring to their knowledge of specialized policy areas, and they have the advantage of flexibility because agency rule-making processes are generally less cumbersome than Congress's legislative process. However, delegations can threaten the constitutional separation of power by transferring legislative authority to the executive branch.

The Supreme Court's rigorous application of the intelligible principle doctrine in the mid-1930s provoked a confrontation of historic proportions between the Court and the president. The Court struck down three delegations of legislative authority in *Panama Refining Co. v. Ryan*, 293 US 388 (1935), *Schechter Poultry Corp. v. US*, 295 US 495 (1935), and *Carter v. Carter Coal Co.*, mentioned earlier. *Panama* and *Schechter* involved the National Industrial Recovery Act, perhaps *the* key New Deal statute. The act's general purpose was to eliminate destructive economic competition, that is, unfair competition that might result in more business failures and greater unemployment. The *Panama* case involved a delegation allowing the president to prohibit the shipment of "hot oil" (produced in contravention of state laws) into interstate commerce. But the provision did not specify the standards that should guide the president's exercise of the power delegated. For the most part, guidance was limited to the vague objectives of eliminating "unfair competitive practices" and "conserving natural resources." Accordingly, the Court considered the delegation an unconstitutional transfer of legislative power to the president.

Schechter involved an even broader delegation of legislative authority by allowing the president to approve "codes of fair competition" for firms in interstate commerce. These codes could establish binding rules for whole industries, and the rules could be highly detailed, involving selling practices and wages and hours, as in *Schechter*. In the Supreme Court's view, Congress failed utterly to provide an intelligible principle for formulating the codes and therefore unconstitutionally delegated its legislative authority to the executive branch. Even justices who were generally supportive of the New Deal could agree that the delegation was far too broad. Finally, in *Carter*, the Court struck down the Bituminous Coal Conservation Act of 1935. In the Court's view, the Act contained a fatal flaw: "legislative delegation in its most obnoxious form... [t]o private persons whose interests may be and often are adverse to the interests of others in the same business... " *Carter*, 298 US at, 311.

The *Panama, Schechter*, and *Carter* decisions provoked a constitutional crisis. They gave the appearance of unelected Supreme Court justices, holding virtually life-time appointments, steadfastly adhering to hoary constitutional doctrines in a way that frustrated the will of Congress, the president, and a majority of voters. President Franklin Roosevelt countered with a plan to pack the Court by increasing its size by as many as six new seats, but this provoked a storm of political controversy and the plan never reached full fruition. It was obviated when one of the justices, Owen Roberts, switched his voting from essentially anti-New Deal to pro-New Deal, thereby creating a majority on the Court sympathetic to Roosevelt's initiatives. Soon thereafter, vacancies occurred on the Court and Roosevelt was able to appoint several new justices without requiring statutory expansion of the Court's size. Subsequently, as Kenneth Davis explains, "In absence of palpable abuse or true congressional abdication, the nondelegation doctrine to which the Supreme Court has in the past often paid lip service is without practical force" (1975, 39).

It would be difficult to overstate the importance of lax application of the intelligible principle doctrine. It enables the administrative state to flourish. The actual function of legislating has largely shifted to administrative agencies (Kerwin 2003). With it has come the political activities of lobbying and participation by constituencies and stakeholders affected by administrative rules and policies. Public administrators are now clearly engaged in formulating as well as implementing public policies. Congress' role in government has also changed. Rather than the branch that initiates policy, as contemplated in Article I of the Constitution, it now shares that function with the president and administrative agencies. Congressional committees spend much of their time reacting to proposals from the executive branch. Although no longer in good constitutional standing, the legislative veto epitomizes the shifting roles of Congress and the executive (*Immigration & Naturalization Service v. Chadha*, 462 US 919 [1983]).

The expansion of presidential power and responsibility was a related major administrative development of the 1930s. The growth of government and delegation of legislative power to the executive left the president very clearly at the center of American politics. Symbolically, the change is represented by the comparison of the last president before the Depression, Calvin Coolidge, to President Franklin Roosevelt. As the power of the presidency changed, so did the structure. In the late 1930s, the President's Committee on Administrative Management (the Brownlow Committee) was candid in promoting greater presidential power through restructuring the executive branch. It also recommended additional delegations of legislative authority to the president. Aside from the creation of the EOP as an organizational tool for presidential management of the expanded executive branch, the Committee's report was influential in passage of the Reorganization Act of 1939, which allowed the president to reorganize administrative agencies, subject to congressional veto.

G. 1940s

Fundamental and enduring frameworks for US administrative law and congressional involvement in federal administration were developed in the 1940s. The courts and Congress responded to the vast expansion of federal administration created by the New Deal and later World War II. The Supreme Court became acquiescent in the exercise of administrative authority (Pritchett 1948; Shapiro 1968). Most importantly, the Court reformulated the commerce clause to accommodate far greater federal regulatory power. In *United States v. Darby*, 312 US 100 (1941), it upheld the constitutionality of the Fair Labor Standards Act of 1938, which regulated the wages and hours of workers in interstate commerce. The Court went much further in *Wickard v. Filburn*, 317 US 111 (1942), by allowing the federal government to reach almost any activity that, if sufficiently aggregated, could substantially affect interstate commerce. It upheld the federal Agricultural Adjustment Act's imposition of crop quotas on a farmer's wheat grown in one state and "not intended in any part for commerce but wholly for consumption on the farm" (*Id.* at 125). The Court reasoned that "even if [the] activity be local and though it may not be regarded as commerce, it may still, whatever its nature, be reached by Congress if it exerts a substantial economic effect on interstate commerce, and this irrespective of whether such effect is what might at some earlier time have been defined as 'direct' or 'indirect'" (*Id.*).

In 1946, Congress sought to adjust its constitutional role in the post-New Deal administrative state and to develop institutional means for better overseeing, regulating, and controlling administrative activity (Rosenbloom 2000). Institutionally, Congress recognized that in the full-fledged administrative state it would play a less proactive and more reactive role in policy-making and regulatory activity. Of necessity, it would broadly delegate legislative authority to administrative agencies, and, consequently, would also have to strengthen its oversight of agencies and regulate the agencies' use of delegated authority. To serve these ends, Congress enacted four major statutes.

The Legislative Reorganization Act of August 2, 1946, restructured Congress in an effort to promote better oversight. It reorganized the committee system so that jurisdictions were clearer, more distinct, and parallel in each chamber. It also standardized some aspects of committee procedure, provided for more committee staff, and for the first time in Congress' history charged the standing committees to "exercise continuous watchfulness of the execution by the administrative agencies concerned of any laws, the subject matter of which is within the jurisdiction of such committee." Legislative oversight was also enhanced by the creation of the Legislative Reference Service in the Library of Congress and by vesting responsibility in the Comptroller General to conduct expenditure analyses of the agencies. The Act also sought to promote better congressional control of the executive branch by calling on Congress to formulate an annual legislative budget for the federal government. The legislative budget would give Congress a more proactive role in national budgeting and make it less dependent on the president's annual federal budget submission (that is, the executive budget). However, this feature of the Act quickly fell into disuse and was dormant until being revamped by the Congressional Budget and Impoundment Control Act of 1974.

Eventually, the number of committees and subcommittees expanded, Congress became less centralized, and micro-management and subsystem politics became pronounced. Iron or cozy triangles comprised of (sub)committees, administrative bureaus, and interest groups began to dominate substantial policy areas (Lowi 1969; Ripley and Franklin 1976). In the executive branch, agencies have often been largely extensions of legislative committees or responsive and subordinate to them. In time, these structural changes contributed to an "impressive" system of oversight that "...probably improves policy at the margins" (Aberbach 1990, 198).

The Federal Tort Claims Act is Title IV of the Legislative Reorganization Act. Its purpose was consonant with the reorganization's larger objective of making Congress more efficient and focused. As Senator Robert M. La Follette, cosponsor of the Reorganization Act explained, "Congress is overburdened by many... private matters which divert its attention from national policy-making and which it ought not to have to consider.... It serves as a tribunal for the settlement of private claims... " (1946, 46). The Tort Claims Act took some of this pressure off Congress by authorizing the heads of agencies to settle property damage and personal-injury claims not exceeding $1000, "where the United States, if a private person, would be liable to the claimant for such damage, loss, injury, or death...." It also authorized suits by private parties in the federal district courts. The Tort Claims Act waived a considerable amount of the government's sovereign immunity, thereby making the government and its administrative agencies more directly responsible for their injurious actions. Over time, through amendment and judicial interpretation, it has become somewhat easier to sue the federal government and collect money damages for its torts.

The Employment Act of February 20, 1946, ratified the New Deal by making the federal government responsible for promoting "maximum employment, production, and purchasing power" in the nation's economy. The act created the Council of Economic Advisers, which is charged with advising the president on economic policy. In practice, the act formally made the federal budget a fiscal policy tool. Because a major means of pump priming is pork-barrel spending, the act virtually invited Congress to micro-manage some aspects of agencies' spending. Prescient critics charged that implementation would be "honey combed with political expediency" (Donnelly 1945, 665).

The APA (June 11, 1946) is the chief generic statute for the regulation of federal agencies' processes and actions. It was predicated on two concerns of central importance to Congress's effort to establish a clearer role for itself in the post-New Deal administrative state. First, it structures agency rule making pursuant to delegations of legislative authority with a view toward ensuring that rule making is open and somewhat participatory. Second, the APA was aimed at preventing agencies from abusing the powers delegated to them. It places procedural constraints on agencies' dealings with individuals, regulates agency adjudication, and provides for judicial review of much agency activity. The APA has proven quite flexible and able to accommodate new concerns. For instance, it has been augmented by the Freedom of Information Act (1966), the Privacy Act (1974), the Government in the Sunshine Act (1976), the Regulatory Flexibility Act (1980), the Negotiated Rulemaking Act (1990), the Administrative Dispute Resolution Acts (1990, 1996), and the Small Business Regulatory Enforcement Fairness Act (1996).

The APA was a product of the broad effort to subordinate and retrofit the administrative state to the United States constitutional structure. As early as 1933, the Committee on Administrative Law of the American Bar Association (ABA) argued that the judiciary should have a broad scope of review of public administration precisely because "certain fundamental safeguards of notice, opportunity for hearing, and determination or review of issues of fact and of law by an independent tribunal (and eventually, on questions of law at least, by a court) are involved, and, indeed, are necessary if justice is to be done to the individual" (see Woll 1963, 17). By 1934, the ABA became strongly supportive of the establishment of an administrative court system to exercise broad review over federal agencies. According to Peter Woll, "this proposal was destined to be repeated at relatively frequent intervals by various groups, between 1934 and 1960" (1963, 17). For example it was supported by the Brownlow Committee in 1937 and the Hoover Commission in 1955. Understandably, though, the president and the agencies have not been enthusiastic about sharing control of public administration with an independent judiciary. This was especially true during the 1930s. In 1940, President Roosevelt vetoed the Walter-Logan bill, which "provided for judicial review of law and fact with regard to all agency decisions" (Woll 1963, 19). The bill also required public notice and public hearings regarding administrative rule making and provided that a "substantially interested" party could petition for a reconsideration of any rule within a three-year period. Such a party could even demand a hearing on the matter (Brazier 1993, 131–201; Rosenbloom 2000, 30–33; Woll 1963, 18). In his veto message, Roosevelt indicated that the attorney general would soon issue a comprehensive report on the whole matter of federal administrative law.

Although Congress was unable to override Roosevelt's veto, its concern with judicial review of administrative activities remained strong. In 1941, when the attorney general's Committee on Administrative Procedure issued its report, it appeared that a compromise was possible between the extreme judicial review and judicialization sought by Congress and the haphazard patchwork of procedures that had evolved in the agencies during the 1930s. The report noted the need for administrative flexibility and emphasized the extent to which public administration involves informal procedures. The report was instrumental in informing much of the thinking later manifested in the APA (United States Congress 1946).

The APA contains four types of provisions that have been of great importance to federal administrative law since 1946. First, section 3 of the Act (5 U.S.C. 552) requires agencies to make available to the public information about their rules, opinions and orders, and records. Such information must be published in the *Federal Register*, which dates from the mid-1930s and is a daily governmental publication containing executive orders, agency rules and proposed rules, and other executive-branch information. In the latter category are "descriptions of [agencies'] central and field organization and the established places at which... the public may obtain information, make submittals or requests, or obtain decisions" and "statements of the general course and method by which its functions are channeled and determined, including the nature and requirements of all formal and informal procedures available." In 1966, these requirements were amended by the Freedom of Information Act, which gives private individuals a legally enforceable right to access to government records, regardless of any special connection with an agency. The Freedom of Information Act includes nine statutory exemptions, which are discussed below in the section on the 1960s. The Government in the Sunshine Act of 1976 also promotes transparency through open meetings.

Second, the APA establishes procedures for agency rule making (section 3; 5 U.S.C. 553). The act seeks to ensure public notice of agency rule making and rule changing. For the purposes of analyzing the act, it is useful to categorize rules as follows:

1. Legislative or Substantive Rules

Assuming these rules are valid, they have the same legal effect as laws passed by Congress. According to Heffron and McFeeley, a rule can be "substantive" only if it satisfies three criteria: (i) "it must affect individual rights and obligations," (ii) "it must have been properly promulgated through statutorily specified procedures," and (iii) "it must have been made pursuant to a grant of legislative authority by Congress" (1983, 235). The *Federal Register* contains numerous legislative rules, many of which are highly specific and may directly affect only a small number of people, firms, or other entities The APA sets forth three ways of promulgating legislative rules. These are augmented by negotiated rule making, which is discussed in the section on the 1990s (see generally Rosenbloom 2003, chap. 3; Warren 2004, chap. 5). The APA provides for the following.

a.   Formal Rule Making, or Rule Making on the Record

The APA does not require agencies to use formal rule making. Rather, it establishes the procedures agencies must use when voluntarily engaging in formal rule making or when it is required to do so by another statute, unless that statute specifies different procedures. Formal rule making involves a trial-type hearing presided over by one or more members of the agency, such as a hearing examiner of some kind, or an ALJ. An adversary approach is followed, during which time both sides may offer evidence and seek to impugn the information offered by the other. Although courtroom-like rules of evidence may not be followed, there are restrictions on the kind of information that can be received as evidence. The APA requires that "except as otherwise provided by statute, the proponent of a rule or order has the burden of proof. Any oral or documentary evidence may be received, but the agency as a matter of policy shall provide for the exclusion of irrelevant, immaterial, or unduly repetitious evidence." Notice of an agency's intent to engage in formal rule making is published in the Federal Register along with information about the time and place of such hearings.

Ordinarily, ALJs issue one of two types of decisions in formal rule making, neither of which is automatically binding on the agency: (1) "initial" decisions, which become final unless they are appealed, and (2) "recommended" decisions, which are automatically subject to review by the agency head, commission, or governing board. Formal rule-making procedures are obviously time consuming and somewhat inflexible. Consequently, it is unusual for them to be required today. Perhaps their use by the Food and Drug Administration is most familiar (Warren 2004, 219).

b.   Informal Rule-Making Procedures Are More Common

They require the agency to publish information about proposed rules in the *Federal Register*. The issues pertaining to the rule and its general terms or substance are noted. An explanation of the statutory authority for the proposed rule and notice of the time, place, and character of public proceedings, if any, for proposed rule making will also appear. Some opportunity for interested parties to make their views on the proposed rule known is granted. However, because informal rule making does not require adjudicatory proceedings, public participation can be limited to the submission of written or oral comments. The final rule must contain a concise statement of its purpose or basis, and it must be published in the *Federal Register* at least thirty days before taking effect.

c. Rule Making with Limited or No Procedural Requirements

The APA exempts rules concerning military and foreign affairs, agency management and personnel, public property, and loans, benefits, grants, and contracts. It also has a "good cause" exemption for informal rule-making proceedings that would be "impractical, unnecessary, or contrary to the public interest" (section 553[a][3][b]). The "good cause" exemption may be coupled with obtaining public input after the rule is published in the *Federal Register*. "Direct final rules" go into effect at a specified future date unless adverse comments are received. "Interim final rules" are effective immediately but may be withdrawn or revised based on comments received by the agencies.

2. Interpretative Rules

Also called interpretive rules, these are statements of an agency's interpretation of a statute or regulation. They can be used to advise the public and the agency's staff as to what the agency believes the statutes or regulations require. Under the Freedom of Information Act (1966), such rules must be published in the *Federal Register*, but no additional APA procedures are required. Interpretative rules are essentially policy guides for the enforcement of statutes and regulations. It is not always immediately clear how they differ form substantive rules in their impact on regulated parties. However, because they are not promulgated as either formal or informal rules, the courts may interpret them as essentially nonbinding legal opinions of the agencies.

3. Procedural Rules

These regulate the internal organization, operations, and practices of agencies. They must be published in the *Federal Register*, but no other procedural requirements apply. Once they are promulgated, the agencies are bound by them, though they can be changed in a proactive fashion. Procedural rules are useful in informing the public about the workings of agencies.

A third area of administrative practice regulated by the APA is adjudication, or "order making" (sections 5, 7, 11; 5 U.S.C. 554, 556, 557) (see generally Rosenbloom 2003a, chap. 4; Warren 2004, chap. 6). Administrative adjudication covers a range of subjects, including violations of laws and agency rules, the issuance of licenses of various kinds, and the determination of continued eligibility for benefits. In a formal sense, such adjudication ends with an order. Adjudication can be based on statutory requirements, constitutional requirements of due process, or some combination of the two. An elaborate adjudicatory procedure will require a trial-type hearing. Under the APA, adjudicatory procedures require the following: (1) notice of the time, place, and nature of the hearing; (2) the legal authority for the hearing; (3) the matters of fact and law involved; (4) the right to be represented by retained counsel; (5) the conclusion of the hearing within a reasonable amount of time; (6) a decision based on substantial evidence in the record; (7) an impartial decision maker (defined by case law as one whose mind is not "unalterably" or "irrevocably" closed); (8) the right to submit oral or documentary evidence and rebuttal evidence, and to cross-examine as necessary to establish the facts; (9) the maintenance of a complete written record of the proceedings; (10) the right to submit a proposed set of findings, conclusions, and exceptions; and (11) a comprehensive written decision based exclusively on the record. The latter exclusivity requirement prohibits ex parte contacts between the decision maker and only one of the parties to the proceedings. Additional restrictions limit the participation of agency employees and their subordinates who were involved in the investigation, if any, that led to the proceedings. The APA also establishes the right, scope, and standards of judicial review (section 10; 5 U.S.C. chapter 7).

The burden of persuasion generally falls on the agency. Its decision must be supported by "substantial evidence," which in this context refers to the amount or weight of evidence, rather than a standard of proof such as "beyond a reasonable doubt." The APA does not establish a standard of proof for agencies' adjudicatory decisions. However, the Supreme Court has ruled that the minimum standard is a "preponderance of evidence," which means that the decision is more likely correct than not (see *Steadman v. Securities & Exchange Commission*, 450 US 91 [1981]). In misconduct and some other cases, the standard may require "clear and convincing evidence," that is, a roughly 75–80 percent likelihood of being correct. In eligibility cases, the burden of persuasion may fall on private parties. Decisions by ALJs may be appealed to the agency itself. Barring such an appeal or motion to review, the decision becomes the final decision. When the agency itself (e.g., its Commission) presides over the adjudication, its decision is final. In general, the courts will not review an agency action until it is final (see Rosenbloom 2003, 154–155).

Adjudication has been affected by two major developments that occurred after 1946. One is the constitutionalization of administrative law, beginning in the 1950s. The other is the development of position of ALJ. When the APA was enacted, there were 197 incumbent hearing examiners in 18 agencies (Dullea 1973, 43). In 1972, the CSC changed the title of hearing examiner to "administrative law judge." At that time there were about 780 ALJs in 22 agencies (Dullea 1973, 47). By 1980, more than 1,000 ALJs were employed in 29 agencies (Heffron and McFeeley 1983, 273). Most ALJs are in the Social Security Administration and the National Labor Relations Board. ALJs are selected from lists established by the Office of Personnel Management. Discipline is by the Merit Systems Protection Board. By law, ALJs must be independent of the hierarchy of the agency in which the hearing occurs. Consequently, their function is at odds with traditional public administration's concern with unity of command. Because ALJs' decisions concern the rights, status, and property of private parties, they can affect an agencies' resources and budgets. Marshall Dimock (1980, 113) identifies the expanding importance of ALJs as the essence of judicialization of public administration (see also Lubbers 1994).

Judicial review is a fourth area of administrative law deeply affected by the APA (section 10; 5 U.S.C. Chapter 7). However, the act is imprecise. It contains the broad statement that "a person suffering legal wrong because of agency action, or adversely affected or aggrieved by agency action within the meaning of a relevant statute, is entitled to judicial review thereof." It also provides that "agency action made reviewable by statute and final agency action for which there is no other adequate remedy in a court are subject to judicial review." At the same time, though, matters "committed to agency discretion by law" are exempt from judicial review, as are matters that are specifically precluded from judicial review by other statutes. The combined meaning of these clauses has been determined incrementally on a case-by-case basis over the years and remains subject to subtle or substantial change from time to time (see Heffron and McFeeley 1983, 293–317, for a lucid review). This process has yielded some general outlines:

1. Disputes in administrative law are subject to the general justiciability requirements established by the Constitution and case law. Plaintiffs must have standing to sue, and the disputes cannot be political questions, moot, or insufficiently ripe for resolution (see Rosenbloom 2003, 147–153). Under the Declaratory Judgment Act of 1934, however, some matters can be considered ripe for judicial review even though the administrative action has yet to be implemented. For instance, in *Abbott Laboratories v. Gardner*, 387 US 136 (1967), the Supreme Court ruled that certain pharmaceutical companies could gain judicial review of the legality of a Food and Drug Administration labeling requirement before the measure was actually enforced.

2. Generally, an individual must exhaust potential administrative remedies, such as appeals within an agency, and the agency's action must be final before his or her case can be subjected to judicial review.

3. Judicial review will not be immediately available if an administrative agency has primary jurisdiction over the subject matter of adjudication. This is a technical doctrine that requires the courts to look at the specific wording of statutes empowering agencies and to assess the substantive expertise of agencies relative to that of the courts.

Assuming judicial review is available, it may nevertheless vary in scope. Under the APA, the courts are authorized to "compel agency action unlawfully withheld or unreasonably delayed" and "hold unlawful and set aside agency action, findings, and conclusions found to be" in any one of the following categories: arbitrary, capricious, an abuse of discretion, or otherwise unlawful; in violation of the Constitution; in excess of jurisdiction or authority; in violation of procedural requirements; in the cases of adjudication and formal rule making, unsupported by substantial evidence; or so unwarranted by the facts that the matter is subject to a de novo trial in court. Within the framework of these guidelines and requirements, the courts have tended toward more or less rigorous review at various times. In the wake of the court-packing plan of the 1930s, the courts generally avoided probing reviews of administrative action. By the early 1970s, however, a noticeable trend toward deeper and broader review had emerged (Davis 1975, 53–71, 331–346).

As mentioned earlier, a trilogy of Supreme Court decisions subsequently called for more limited judicial review of agency rule-making procedures, statutory interpretation, and decisions not to take enforcement actions (*Vermont Yankee Nuclear Power Corp. v. Natural Resources Defense Council*, 435 US 519 [1978]; *Chevron v. Natural Resources Defense Council*, 467 US 837 [1984]; *Heckler v. Chaney*, 470 US 821 [1985]). Today, the courts apply a hard look (probing review) to: the logic behind and substance of legislative rules, including decisions to rescind rules; denials of Freedom of Information Act requests; and agency discretionary actions. Depending on the circumstances, agency adjudicatory orders may also receive a hard look.

The APA remains the fundamental law of federal administrative procedure generally. Similar laws can be found in the states (Bonfield and Asimow 1989). Appraisals of these acts vary, but overall, it is easy to conclude that the APA has been durable, adaptable, and largely successful in regulating agency procedures in the interests of making federal administration more consonant with the requisites of US constitutional democracy. The APA provides a framework for increasing transparency, fairness, and public participation and representativeness in rule making and agenda setting (see discussion of the Federal Advisory Committee Act in the section on the 1970s).

No discussion of regulation and administrative law in the 1940s would be complete without mention of the Atomic Energy Commission (AEC), established in 1946, and the Loyalty Program, initiated by President Harry Truman's Executive Order 9835 of 1947. The AEC was an example of administration to regulate a new and presumptively dangerous technology. Its mission was to promote the development of atomic energy and to regulate the safety of nuclear power. In the mid-1970s, the AEC was abolished through a reorganization that placed its promotional mission in the Energy Research and Development Agency (now part of the Department of Energy) and its regulatory functions in the Nuclear Regulatory Commission. The Loyalty Program was aimed at preventing subversives from working in the federal government. It was part of the general period now labeled the McCarthy era, after Republican Senator Joseph McCarthy of Wisconsin. The program severely encroached on the ordinary First Amendment rights of federal employees and was procedurally defective in the extreme (Rosenbloom 1971, chap. 6). It was later superseded by a Security Program (Executive Order 10540 [1953]). Together, loyalty–security measures eventually promoted a sweeping change in constitutional doctrine pertaining to public employment, a development that is discussed in the next section.

H.   1950s

Although there were some antecedents, the constitutionalization of American public administration can reasonably be dated back to the 1950s, when, for the first time in American history, constitutional law became broadly salient as a constraint on agency treatment of individuals and private organizations. Constitutionalization grew out of a clash between traditional administrative values, such as efficiency, economy, and organizational effectiveness through hierarchical control, and emerging constitutional values favoring robust substantive rights, procedural due process, and equal protection. The key development in the 1950s was the Supreme Court's embarkation upon a jurisprudence that would eventually broadly attach constitutional rights to the receipt of governmental employment and benefits.

Constitutionalization depended on the Supreme Court's willingness to overturn the historic doctrine of privilege. In essence, this doctrine contained the following premises and conclusion: (1) the government was not constitutionally required to supply public employment or benefits, licenses, and other largess; (2) thus there was no constitutional right to receive largess and it could be dispensed without regard to constitutional requirements for equal protection of the laws; (3) the individual was not required to accept employment and largess, but rather did so voluntarily; (4) therefore, the government could dispense employment and largess as it saw fit and could attach whatever conditions it thought reasonable to an individual's initial and continuing eligibility for such employment and benefits. The best epigram for the doctrine of privilege remains Justice Holmes' famous statement in an 1892 political neutrality case that "the petitioner may have a constitutional right to talk politics, but he has no constitutional right to be a policeman." *McAuliffe v. New Bedford*, 155 Mass. 216, 220.

The doctrine of privilege allowed such decisions as: a person could be dismissed from a public-sector job based on being married or unmarried, of fair complexion or dark, or for being a member of a trade union (*People ex. rel Fursman v. City of Chicago*, 278 Ill. 318 [1917]); high-school students could be barred from certain activities on the basis of being married (*Starkey v. Board of Education*, 381 P.2d 718 [1963]); a person could be faced with the choice of living in conventional housing conditions deemed suitable by a county public-welfare office or losing his old-age-assistance benefits (*Wilkie v. O'Connor*, 25 NYS 2d 617 [1941]), and a Seventh-Day Adventist could be denied unemployment compensation for voluntarily taking herself out of the workforce by adhering to religious principles forbidding work on Saturday (*Sherbert v. Verner*, 374 US 398 [1963], *reversing the holding described*). Such actions could be accomplished without significant procedural safeguards (*Bailey v. Richardson*, 341 US 918 [1951]).

The doctrine of privilege had an appealing simplicity. However, it failed to protect individual rights in the new administrative state (see Reich 1964, for the classic analysis). This was nowhere more evident than in the realm of public employment.

In the early 1950s, the Loyalty Program was broadened into a Loyalty-Security Program under which government employment was denied not only to those who were disloyal, but also to those thought to be security risks for other reasons (Brown 1958; Bontecou 1953; Rosenbloom 1971). The category of security risks included persons who were considered to be particularly vulnerable to blackmail, e.g., homosexuals. One also could be considered a security risk for being careless with classified documents and information. Neither program was particularly clear with regard to the attitudes and behaviors proscribed. In fact, the anti-Communist hysteria of the period had manifest results that would be considered positively bizarre today. For example, formal probes of federal employees included such questions as:

What do you think of female chastity?

Were you a regular reader of *The New York Times?*

Do you and your wife regularly attend any organized church services?

Have you ever had Negroes in your home?

Are your friends and associates intelligent, clever? (Rosenbloom 1971, 163–164).

During the 1950s, the Supreme Court was confronted with a number of cases of individuals who were harmed by such loyalty–security measures at all levels of government and in some fields of private employment requiring governmental security clearances. In *Bailey v. Richardson*, 341 US 918 (1951), the Court faced the case of a woman who was dismissed for disloyalty after several years of adequate federal service. She went through hearings at the Fourth Regional Loyalty Board and subsequently at the national Loyalty Review Board. She was not able to confront or cross-examine the informants against her. The chairman of the Loyalty Review Board indicated that he did not know who these informants were or whether their testimony was sworn. Among other questions, Ms. Bailey was asked, "Did you ever write a letter to the Red Cross about the segregation of blood [by race]?" The court of appeals upheld her dismissal, largely on the logic of the doctrine of privilege: the "plain hard fact is that so far as the Constitution is concerned there is no prohibition against the dismissal of Government employees because of their political beliefs, activities or affiliations…. The First Amendment guarantees free speech and assembly, but it does not guarantee Government employ." *Bailey v. Richardson*, 182 F.2d 46, 59 (1950).

An equally divided Supreme Court affirmed the lower court's holding in *Bailey* without opinion. 341 US 918 (1951). However, two justices, William Douglas and Robert Jackson, expressed views in a related case, *Joint Anti-Fascist Refugee Committee v. McGrath*, 341 US 123 (1951), indicating that they were ready to reject the doctrine of privilege. Justice Black had rejected it earlier in the political neutrality case of *United Public Workers v. Mitchell*, 330 US 75 (1947), and Justice Frankfurter subsequently rejected it in *Garner v. Los Angeles*, 341 US 716 (1951). A year later, in *Weiman v. Updegraff*, a majority of the Court rejected the doctrine of privilege in the following terms: "We need not pause to consider whether an abstract right to public employment exists. It is sufficient to say that constitutional protection does extend to the public servant whose exclusion pursuant to a statute is patently arbitrary or discriminatory." 344 US 183, 192 (1952).

Over the years, the approach begun in *Weiman* grew to encompass the protection of the rights of public employees to due process and equal protection. Eventually, several substantive rights also were afforded greater protection, including freedom of expression (for nonpartisan speech on matters of public concern), freedom of association including the right to join labor unions, protection from unreasonable searches and seizures, protection of the privilege against self-incrimination, and protection of the liberty to marry and procreate (see Rosenbloom 1971, 1983; Rosenbloom and Carroll 1994; Rosenbloom and O'Leary 1997, chap. 6). Moreover, once the doctrine of privilege was rejected with regard to public employment, it did not appear logical to apply it to the receipt of benefits, such as welfare payments, unemployment compensation, or public education (Rosenbloom 1983, chap. 3; Rosenbloom and O'Leary 1997, chap. 4). By the mid-1970s, constitutional requirements of due process, equal protection, and protection of substantive rights greatly affected public personnel management and social administration.

Although usually analyzed from the perspectives of public school desegregation, *Brown v. Board of Education*, 347 US 483 (1954) also weakened the doctrine of privilege by applying equal protection to governmental largess. Subsequently, equal protection was applied by lower courts to public employment (*Brooks v. School District*, 267 F.2d 733 [1959]), prisons (*Holt v. Sarver*, 309 F. Supp. 362 [1970]), infrastructure (*Hawkins v. Town of Shaw*, 437 F.2d 1286 [1971]), and other areas of public administration.

I. 1960s

Unlike the 1940s and 1950s, the 1960s were a decade of intense regulatory activity, a great deal of which carried over into the 1970s. These regulatory developments can be grouped into three broad categories: consumer protection, civil rights, and environmental protection. The 1960s also witnessed the enactment of the Freedom of Information Act.

First and least complex, regulation to protect consumers was strengthened and extended. Among the major enactments were the Drug Amendments of 1962 and the National Traffic and Motor Vehicle Safety Act of 1966. The Drug Amendments required that drugs sold in the United States be efficacious as well as safe. The FDA, which has authority for enforcement, restructured its internal procedures to require more stringent evaluation of drugs. It also undertook a review of the effectiveness of all drugs it had approved since 1938. According to Kenneth Meier, this led to removal from the market of "some 6,000 different brands and products" by the 1970s (1985, 86). The National Traffic and Motor Vehicle Safety Act authorized the establishment of safety standards for automobiles and a system for reporting safety defects. The enactment of both statutes followed mass publicity about the dangers to consumers posed by inadequate regulation. Senator Estes Kefauver publicized the tragic consequence of severe birth defects caused by the use of the drug thalidomide by pregnant women in Europe (Quirk 1980). Ralph Nader's *Unsafe at Any Speed* (1965) helped to raise consciousness and concern about dangerously engineered and designed automobiles. In 1969, the National Traffic and Motor Vehicle Safety Act was amended to cover tires. In 1970, the National Highway Traffic Safety Administration was established within the Department of Transportation as the chief federal regulatory agency for motor vehicle and highway safety.

Second, the Civil Rights Act of 1964 was a landmark in US race relations and gender equality, manifesting a strong governmental commitment to the principle of equal opportunity. The act relied on the federal government's power to regulate interstate commerce to prohibit discrimination based on race, color, creed, national origin, or sex in most private employment (including by unions and employment agencies), in places of public accommodation (such as hotels and restaurants), and by buses and other common carriers. The act also strengthened the government's powers and role concerning school desegregation. Moreover, it included a broad provision outlawing discrimination in any federally assisted program. The act applied to federal personnel management, but not to state and local governmental employment. State and local governments were brought under the federal regulatory regime by the 1972 Equal Employment Opportunity Act, which broadly amended the 1964 act. Other additions to the statutory scheme for protecting civil rights included voting rights (1966) and fair-housing regulations (1968).

Authority to enforce civil rights legislation is dispersed among several federal agencies. The 1964 act established the Equal Employment Opportunity Commission (EEOC), which has enforcement authority for most private employment, and since 1972 for employment in state and local government systems as well. In 1979, the EEOC gained responsibility for equal opportunity in federal employment, which previously had been vested in the CSC. The EEOC has authority to adjudicate complaints of discrimination, to take legal action against employers who engage in broad patterns or practices of illegal discrimination, and to issue guidelines for the interpretation of federal equal employment opportunity law. The agency has been hampered by inadequate resources for its massive mission. Although the Supreme Court has been deferential to the EEOC's guidelines in some key cases, a major ambiguity in the statutes themselves continues to create enforcement problems. While the Civil Rights and Equal Employment Opportunity Acts prohibit discrimination, just how much affirmative action they allow has been the subject of tortuous case-by-case litigation. Additionally, because public employment is regulated by the Constitution's equal-protection clause as well as by civil rights legislation, the federal courts may treat it differently from private employment (Crowley 1985; Rosenbloom 1979; US Commission on Civil Rights 1975). Among the other agencies with authority to implement parts of the

1960s civil-rights legislation are the Departments of Labor, Justice, Housing and Urban Development, Health and Human Services, and Education.

Environmental protection, the third main area of regulatory activity in the 1960s, was promoted through a variety of statutes including the Water Quality Act of 1965 and the Clean Air and Air Quality Acts of 1963 and 1967, respectively (see generally O'Leary 1993, 1994). For the most part, these acts were aimed at establishing standards that would be implemented by the states. The National Environmental Policy Act of 1969 (actually signed on January 1, 1970) is of greater importance to federal administrative law generally.

NEPA created a Council on Environmental Quality, which is housed in the EOP and vested with broad advisory responsibility for evaluating the condition of the environment and any threats to it. The act also placed new procedural requirements on federal agencies. These are consonant with the APA and intended to provide notice of agency activities and an opportunity to comment on them. NEPA's provisions include the following:

1. Agencies are required to develop environmental impact statements. These must address consideration of adverse environmental effects, alternatives to the proposed action, the relationship between short-run uses and long-term productivity, and any irreversible and irretrievable commitments of resources.
2. Agencies are permitted to comment on the environmental impact statements of one another.
3. Citizens are provided with access to the environmental impact statements and an opportunity to comment on them. Comments may be limited to written statements. However, if an agency holds a hearing on its proposed action, it may be required to allow citizen participation. Moreover, NEPA makes it easier for those citizens likely to be injured by agency action to bring suits against the government, either to compel agencies to develop impact statements or to challenge their findings or conclusions.

The Freedom of Information Act of 1966 (FOIA) was also a major addition to administrative law. FOIA provides members of the public with access to all government information that is not excepted under one of the act's nine exemptions. It relies on a requestor model, rather than a dissemination model, for promoting governmental transparency. FOIA requests can be filed with the agencies by individuals, whether citizens or noncitizens (including foreigners), corporations, and associations. Federal agencies cannot "FOIA" one another. Unlike the APA's equivalent provision, requestors are not required to show a particular need for the information sought. The act's coverage is broad, extending to executive departments and agencies (including the Central Intelligence Agency and the Federal Bureau of Investigation), independent regulatory commissions, and government corporations. It also applies to units of the EOP having statutory responsibilities, such as OMB, but not to those with purely advisory functions (e.g., the Council of Economic Advisers). It does not apply to the president, Congress, or the judiciary.

The act covers agency records, not information scattered throughout its files and archives. (Under the Electronic Freedom of Information Act of 1996, agencies are required to maintain certain types of information in electronic form and to make reasonable efforts to produce electronic records on request.) Information is usually disclosed by publication in the *Federal Register*, availability for public inspection and copying in agencies' physical or electronic reading rooms, or by transmission to individuals who describe the records sought and request them in accordance with established agency procedures. Federal district courts have authority to compel agencies to release improperly withheld information. In such cases the burden of persuasion falls on the agency, and reasonable attorney's fees can be awarded to plaintiffs.

Over the years, the main difficulties with the FOIA have been as follows (see generally Vaughn 1994). First, government attitudes have not favored disclosure. Agencies have sometimes obstructed the purpose of the act by refusing to release information unless it is described in highly specific detail by the requestor. Second, agencies do not always have a sufficient budget to deal with the volume of FOIA requests. Third, the nine exemptions are broad and somewhat ambiguous. They include (1) secret defense and foreign-policy information; (2) the "internal personnel rules and practices" of agencies; (3) material prohibited from disclosure by other statutes; (4) privileged or confidential trade secrets, and commercial and financial information; (5) memoranda that would not be available to a party engaged in litigation with the agency; (6) files containing personal information that "would constitute a clearly unwarranted invasion of personal privacy;" (7) some law enforcement records; (8) information on the regulation of financial institutions; and (9) geological and geophysical information. The act itself does not prohibit disclosure of information covered by these exemptions, but rather provides agencies with the discretion to withhold it. However, this discretion is negated when the release of information would violate another statute, such as the Privacy Act of 1974 (discussed under the 1970s).

The diverse developments of the 1960s contain a unifying theme. The regulatory measures and FOIA protect broad and diffuse public interests against established bases of political and economic power. It is unusual for the benefits of regulation to be so widely dispersed while the costs are relatively concentrated (see Wilson 1980, 370). The diffuse interests of minority groups and women in gaining equal opportunity were protected against employers and other entities whose discrimination impeded their interstate economic activity. The broad public interest gained protection against narrower economic interests that might compromise the safety of drugs, vehicles, and environmental quality. FOIA promotes governmental transparency and a form of direct governmental accountability to the public.

J.   1970s

The 1970s were a decade of transition in regulatory policy. The decade began with broad-scale efforts to consolidate and extend federal regulatory activity, but it ended with an emphasis on deregulation. The changing regulatory climate reflected the growing political strength of individuals and political groups who believed the market was more effective and efficient than administrative agencies as a means of organizing and controlling economic activity. The effort to reduce agencies' regulatory role was complemented by measures in administrative law aimed at checking their power.

The early part of the 1970s was remarkable in the extension of traditional forms of regulation. The Occupational Safety and Health Act of 1970 provided the first substantial federal regulatory presence in America's workplaces for the sake of assuring "so far as possible every working man and woman in the Nation safe and healthful work conditions." Previously, such regulation was primarily the domain of the states and collective bargaining agreements. The act created two agencies, the Occupational Safety and Health Administration (OSHA) and the Occupational Safety and Health Review Commission (OSHRC). The latter serves as an independent body to which appeals from OSHA decisions can be made. Perhaps more than any other agency, OSHA has become symbolic of contemporary problems in regulatory administration. In the early 1980s, it was responsible for regulating conditions in some five million workplaces that employed many times more millions of workers (Kagan 1994, 404). Inevitably, its rules are sometimes over-inclusive and its inspections too limited. Moreover, as noted earlier, the key terms of its statutory mission have been called a "legislative mirage." *Industrial Union Department, AFL-CIO v. American Petroleum Institute*, 448 US 607, 681 (1980) (Rehnquist concurring). Within the framework of its broad scope and unclear mission, the OSHA, which is housed in the Department of Labor, has tended to be more favorable to workers than to employers. The OSHA has also favored engineering solutions for eliminating hazardous or toxic substances from workplaces, as opposed to the less costly use of respirators and other protective gear. The OSHA's overall effectiveness has been subject to wide debate (see Kagan 1994, 402; Kelman 1980; Meier 1985, 221–224; Scholz 1994, 455).

The EPA was established in 1970 by means of a reorganization plan consolidating many existing environmental regulatory programs within one organization. At the same time, the scope of environmental regulation was broadened. The Clean Air Act Amendments of 1970 required the EPA to oversee the reduction of harmful automobile emissions by 90 percent by 1975. The Federal Water Pollution Control Act was amended in 1972 in an effort to ensure that the nation's waters would be safe for swimming and fishing by the early 1980s. Like the OSHA, the EPA faces an exceptionally broad mission, sometimes even requiring the use of technologies that have not yet been developed. In 1976, the EPA's problems were complicated by the Resource Conservation and Recovery Act, which gave it responsibility for regulating the disposal of hazardous wastes. Under the direction of Anne Gorsuch Burford, early in President Ronald Reagan's first administration, the EPA was besieged by criticism from environmentalists and fell under scandal for its political favoritism in the use of "Superfund" money and other activities in connection with the elimination of hazardous wastes.

The Consumer Product Safety Commission (CPSC), established by the Consumer Product Safety Act of 1972, was another instance of regulatory continuity. The CPSC was designed to be independent. It is empowered to recall and ban dangerous products from the market and to establish safety standards. According to Meier (1985, 103–104), the CPSC was charged with regulating some 10,000 products—and it failed miserably at this until 1978. A change in leadership and greater support from the Carter administration seems to have saved the agency, which later was the target of an unsuccessful bid for termination early in the first Reagan administration. It fell under attack again in 1995 and 1996 after the Republican party gained control of Congress.

The movement toward deregulation during the 1970s is analyzed by Martha Derthick and Paul Quirk (1985). Perhaps it is best exemplified by the Airline Deregulation Act of 1978. The Civil Aeronautics Board (CAB) had controlled rates, conditions of service, and entry in the interstate air transportation industry since 1938. Safety was placed under the Federal Aviation Administration (FAA) a decade later. Historically, the CAB tended to protect major carriers from competition— both from possible new entrants as well as, to an extent, from each other (Behrman 1980; Gray 1961). Whether this approach was desirable in the early days of the industry is a moot point. By the mid-1970s, the politically predominant view was that air transportation could be organized more efficiently and effectively by market forces. Deregulation was promoted by economists who studied intrastate air transportation in Texas and California. Importantly, the airlines themselves were ambivalent toward the CAB and not uniformly supportive of, or opposed to, deregulation. By 1977, under the leadership of economist Alfred Kahn, the CAB also supported deregulation even though it would eventually lead to the agency's 1985 demise. With the CAB leading the way, trucking, banking, and communications were soon subject to partial deregulation.

Deregulation in the 1970s and 1980s was confined mostly to rates and entry. Its hallmarks were transportation and banking. Efforts to reduce the intrusiveness of agencies such as the FTC, OSHA, and CPSC did not produce wholesale deregulation. Nonetheless, opposition to administrative regulation was successful in promoting a number of regulatory reforms that occurred in the 1980s.

Derthick and Quirk attribute the successes of "pro-competitive" deregulation to a number of factors, including the strength of ideas, the power of microeconomic analysis, and changes in the political system. They believe that national politics became much more fragmented than it had been in the past, and that "pluralism of political leadership and loose definition of administrative and judicial roles are alternative sources of dynamism" (1985, 257). The linking of expert analysis with mass sentiment or the broad public interest enables political leaders in this "new American political system" to "have a good chance of defeating narrow, particularistic interests" that previously may have been served by anticompetitive tendencies in surrogate market regulation (ibid., 257, 258). Even so, pro-competitive regulation is not without substantial costs and strong critics. For instance, Dempsey claims that "under deregulation, the airline industry lost all the money it made since the Wright Brothers' inaugural flight at Kitty Hawk in 1903, plus $2 billion more" (1994, 177)

Dempsey argues that a long-term, public interest perspective should treat airline transportation more like infrastructure than like a consumer good (see also Sternberg 1996).

The major measures in administrative law during the 1970s promoted representativeness, openness, and checks on abuses of authority. The Federal Advisory Committee Act of 1972 improved the use of private advisory committees by federal agencies. The act contains transparency provisions that open committee and agency meetings to public observation. It also seeks to ensure that the membership of committees is representative and reflective of diverse perspectives on the economic or other interest concerned, such as cattle raising, cotton growing, and child nutrition. A number of provisions make the committee system more accountable. (See *Northwest Forest Resource Council v. Espy*, 846 F. Supp. 1009 [1994] for a detailed review of the act's central requirements). The act does not apply to committees composed entirely of federal employees, the CIA, the Federal Reserve System, or local civic groups. In 1998, there were 892 advisory committees associated with 55 agencies, holding 5852 meetings, issuing 973 reports, and totaling 41,259 members (US General Services Administration 1999).

The Privacy Act of 1974 guards against administrative invasions of individuals' personal privacy. It applies to citizens and permanent residents, but not to corporations, associations, or other organizations. The act is intended to prevent the gratuitous collection of personal information by federal agencies, and it provides individuals with a right to review and challenge information in records that agencies may have on them. Law-enforcement records and records kept by the CIA and are excluded. The act establishes procedural and transparency requirements for handling information, including agency notices in the *Federal Register* explaining their policies for access to and storage and disposal of records. The act also limits the release of information about individuals without their prior consent, unless the disclosure falls into one of twelve statutory exemptions. These include disclosure for routine use (defined as the purpose for which the information was collected), to Congress and law enforcement agencies at all levels of government, and for compelling reasons such as someone's health or safety.

The Privacy Act affects FOIA by restricting the release of information that would constitute an unwarranted invasion of personal privacy. In *US Department of Defense v. Federal Labor Relations Authority*, 510 US 487, 495 (1994), the Supreme Court held that the release of information protected by the Privacy Act must be balanced against "the public interest in disclosure," and that "the only relevant public interest to be weighed in this balance is the extent to which disclosure would serve FOIA's core purpose of contributing significantly to public understanding of the Government's operations or activities." Individuals whose rights are violated under the Privacy Act may sue agencies for money damages. Criminal penalties for violation are possible, though very rare.

Transparency was promoted by 1974 amendments to FOIA and by the Government in the Sunshine Act of 1976. The FOIA amendments gave the agencies ten days—later changed to twenty—to tell requesters whether the information they sought would be released. (It did not affect the actual release date.) The amendments also limited to actual costs the fees that agencies can charge for searching and copying, and they strengthened judicial review of requests for information that may be improperly classified.

The Government in the Sunshine Act prohibits multi-headed federal boards and commissions from holding secret meetings and entitles the public to at least one week's notice of all agency meetings, even those that are closed to the public. Such notices must contain the name and phone number of an official who can be contacted for more information about the meeting. Meetings may be closed to the public on a number of grounds, including those paralleling the exemptions in FOIA, but a meeting cannot be closed to protect pre-decisional discussion from public scrutiny. Meetings can be closed when premature disclosure of information would frustrate proposed agency action or create speculation in financial or commodity markets. As with FOIA, these exceptions permit, but do not require, agencies to close meetings. The Advisory Committee and Sunshine Acts are important additions to administrative law that further the trend analyzed by Richard Stewart (1975), and discussed earlier, to promote fair representation in the administrative process.

A major deterrent to abuse of administrative power emerged in the law of public officers. Prior to the 1970s, many public administrators were absolutely immune from civil suits for damages arising from their official actions (Rosenbloom 1983, chap. 6; Rosenbloom and O'Leary 1997, chap. 8). The historic doctrine of official, absolute immunity was based in the common law and drew some support from the US Constitution. It prevented suits against government officials on the rationale that "it would seriously cripple the proper and effective administration of public affairs as entrusted to the executive branch of the government" if public administrators were subjected to "inquiry in a civil suit for damages." *Spalding v. Vilas*, 161 US 483, 498 (1896). Between 1971 and 1975, the doctrine of absolute immunity was largely abandoned in favor of providing qualified immunity only. Under this approach, most public administrators are now liable for compensatory damages if they violate "clearly established [federal] statutory or constitutional rights of which a reasonable person would have known." *Harlow v. Fitzgerald*, 457 US 800, 818 (1982). Punitive damages also may be assessed in some cases (*Smith v. Wade*, 641 US 30 [1983]). Municipalities are liable for actions caused pursuant to their policies that violate federally protected rights (*Owen v. City of Independence*, 445 US 622 [1980]). States and state agencies cannot be sued as persons for money damages, but their employees can be sued in their personal capacities for their constitutional torts committed under color of state authority (*Will v. Michigan Department of State Police*, 491 US 59 [1989]; *Hefer v. Melo*, 502 US 21 [1991]). Although public administrators engaged in legislative and adjudicatory or other judicial functions retain absolute immunity, for the most part the doctrinal change works to compensate victims, deter violations of federally protected rights, and "create an incentive for officials who may harbor doubts about the lawfulness of their intended actions to err on the side of protecting citizens' constitutional rights" *Owen*, 445 US at 651–652. In essence, knowledge of individual constitutional rights has now become an aspect of job competence for public administrators. Those deficient in this respect risk being sued personally for money damages, while local governments can be held liable for failure to train their employees to avoid violating constitutional rights (*City of Canton v. Harris*, 489 US 378 [1989]).

Establishing a connection would be difficult now, but it cannot escape notice that the switch from a general presumption of absolute immunity to one of qualified immunity only occurred at about the same time that several other manifestations of opposition to administrative power were present. Certainly, the Federal Advisory Committee Act, the Privacy Act, the Sunshine Act, FOIA, and NEPA before them, along with the movement toward deregulation, are linked in mood, if not specific substance, to making it easier to hold public administrators liable for their violations of constitutional and other federally protected rights.

The Civil Service Reform Act of 1978 is a development in the law of public officers that should be mentioned. The act abolished the Civil Service Commission and created an Office of Personnel Management and a Merit Systems Protection Board in its stead. Some authority formerly vested in the CSC was transferred to the EEOC, as noted earlier. The Federal Labor Relations Council was replaced by the more independent Federal Labor Relations Authority, which regulates many aspects of federal labor relations and collective bargaining processes. The act also created statutory protections for whistleblowers who make information public about waste, fraud, abuse, misuse of authority, or substantial and specific dangers to the public health or safety in federal administration. The Merit Systems Protection Board is responsible for ensuring that merit-system principles are upheld and that reprisals are not taken against whistleblowers. Another feature of the act was to create a Senior Executive Service (SES) as a means of increasing flexibility at the top of the federal civil service. Of the SES members, 90 percent hold career positions, while 10 percent are political appointees. Because rank is vested in the SES members themselves, rather than in the positions they hold, their responsibilities can be changed without regard to the federal government's cumbersome position-classification requirements. SES members also can be reassigned within agencies more easily than most other federal employees. Finally, the act contributed to the ongoing effort to make the federal bureaucracy representative by declaring that "it is the policy of the United States" to establish a "Federal work force reflective of the Nation's diversity."

K. 1980s

Popular suspicion of public bureaucracies and opposition to their intrusiveness in society and the economy continued throughout the 1980s. Dissatisfaction with public administration was reinforced by a growing concern about the cost of government, the size of budget deficits, and the accumulating national debt. Government regulation increasingly appeared to be clumsy, costly, and un-coordinated. President Reagan was openly and vociferously opposed to the federal bureaucracy, with the exception of national defense. The decade witnessed a number of important reforms in regulatory processes.

In 1980, two statutes of lasting importance to federal regulation were enacted: the Regulatory Flexibility Act and the Paperwork Reduction Act. The Regulatory Flexibility Act provides that "uniform federal regulatory and reporting requirements have in numerous instances imposed unnecessary and disproportionately burdensome demands including legal, accounting and consulting costs upon small businesses...." The act protects small businesses by requiring publication in the *Federal Register* of a "regulatory flexibility agenda." The agenda contains a list of rules that the agency expects to issue that may have a significant economic impact on small businesses. The rules on the agenda must be subject to an "initial regulatory flexibility analysis," consisting of a statement of the rationale for each rule, its objective and legal basis, the anticipated reporting and record-keeping requirements, the identification of any overlapping, duplicative, or contradictory federal rules, and a discussion of possible alternatives. The agency is required to take public comments into account before issuing a final rule. It also must issue a final regulatory flexibility analysis within 180 days of issuing a final rule. This analysis describes the agency's reaction to comments received. In the absence of a final analysis, the rule becomes void after 180 days (Reigel and Owen 1982, 35–37).

The Paperwork Reduction Act of 1980 was enacted in response to the paperwork burden federal programs often thrust on private entities and state and local governments. In 1980, the Office of Management and Budget (OMB) estimated the total paperwork burden at 1.5 billion hours (Skrzycki 1998, G2). Writing in 1977, Herbert Kaufman put a human face on that number:

> A 'Mom and Pop' store with a gross annual income of less than $30,000 had to file tax forms fifty-two times a year. A firm with fewer than fifty employees had to prepare seventy-five or eighty submissions a year for various agencies. A small securities broker-dealer sent thirty-eight submissions a year for various agencies. A plant employing seventy-five people had two of them working half time solely to draw up compulsory plans and reports; a company with a hundred employees made seventy filings or payments each year to the Internal Revenue Service alone; a small radio station assigned two employees full time for four months to supply all the information specified by the Federal Communications Commission for license renewal, and another reported that its application for renewal weighed forty-five pounds. The chairman of the board of a large pharmaceutical firm claimed that his company prepared 27,000 government forms or reports a year at a cost of $5 million. ('We spend,' he added, 'more man-hours filling out government forms or reports than we do on research for cancer and heart disease combined') (1977, 7–8).

The Paperwork Reduction Act's major purposes are to (1) minimize the federal paperwork burden on private parties, states, and local governments; (2) minimize the cost of collecting and using information; (3) maximize the usefulness of information collected by the government; (4) coordinate federal information activities; (5) improve information technology in the federal government; and (6) ensure confidentiality within the framework of the Privacy Act and other federal laws. The act established an Office of Information and Regulatory Affairs (OIRA) within the OMB. OIRA was charged with taking the lead in developing uniform policies for information processing, storage, and transmittal systems; reducing the amount of information collected; and safeguarding privacy. The act prohibits agencies from adopting regulations imposing paperwork requirements on the public when the information is already available within the federal government. Agencies are required to minimize paperwork burdens on the public and to submit "information collection requests" to the OMB for approval.

The act notwithstanding, by 1994 the federal paperwork burden apparently reached 6.5 billion hours and may have cost 9 percent of the nation's gross domestic product (Strauss et al. 1995, 872). Dissatisfaction with OIRA's performance led Congress to allow its authority to lapse in 1983. The Paperwork Reduction Reauthorization Act of 1986 strengthened OIRA's accountability by requiring more transparency in its operations and making its director a presidential appointee subject to Senate confirmation. The ongoing struggle against paperwork was bolstered by the 1995 Paperwork Reduction Act, discussed in the section on the 1990s.

In addition to the Regulatory Flexibility and Paperwork Reduction Acts, there were important regulatory developments in two main areas during the 1980s: (1) agency rule making was put under greater presidential supervision and control; and (2) efforts were undertaken to ensure that regulations met broad generic policy goals such as maintaining US economic competitiveness, strengthening families, and protecting federalism.

Beginning in earnest under President Richard Nixon, presidents have sought to gain greater control over federal regulatory activity. Nixon initiated a regulatory review process under which the OMB conducted quality of life reviews of proposed regulations. These reviews focused on costs, benefits, and alternatives, especially in the area of environmental regulation. President Gerald Ford required agencies to include inflation impact statements in the proposed regulations they sent to the OMB for review. Under both Nixon and Ford, agencies could enact final rules despite the OMB's opposition to them.

President Jimmy Carter went further in reforming regulation. He established a Regulatory Analysis Review Group (RARG), drawn from relevant agencies, to review agency proposals likely to cost at least $100 million per year. Aside from creating RARG, his Executive Order 12044 required (1) proposed regulations to be as simple and clear as possible, (2) agencies to consider and analyze meaningful alternatives before promulgating regulations, (3) public participation in the rule making process, (4) publication of agency regulatory agendas, (5) economic impact analyses for all significant regulations, and (6) periodic review of the efficacy of existing regulations.

President Reagan developed a more complex and comprehensive strategy for controlling agency rule making. Executive Order 12291 (1981) required that, unless otherwise prohibited by law, agencies must subject their regulations to a cost-benefit analysis and achieve their regulatory objectives by the means least costly to society. The OMB received discretion to review any rules that would have a major impact on costs and prices or that adversely affected competition, employment, investment, productivity, or innovation. It could also demand a regulatory impact analysis of both existing and proposed rules. The order required agencies to develop regulatory agendas identifying the rules they were considering proposing. Several independent regulatory commissions were excluded from the order's coverage, though some complied voluntarily (Moreno 1994, 494–499).

The OMB's clearance role under Executive Order 12291 brought greater coordination to federal regulation—but at a price. In 1985, it took the OMB an average of 43 days to review major rules (Havemann 1986, 12). Most proposed rules were approved, but agencies had to draft rules in anticipation of the OMB's reaction, and at times it appeared that the OMB was more responsive to business interests than to other concerns. In 1985, Executive Order 12498 further strengthened the OMB's role by requiring agencies to submit draft regulatory programs before even developing proposed rules. Congress responded to this centralization of rule making under the OMB by threatening to cut off the office's funds if it did not adopt a more open process and balanced perspective in its review of agency actions.

President Reagan also modified the regulatory process in an effort to promote specific policy goals. Executive Order 12606 (1987) required that agencies consider the effect that proposed policies and regulations would have on American families. Executive Order 12612 (1987) required agencies to undertake a "federalism assessment" in actions covered under Executive Order 12291.

President George H. W. Bush (Bush I) promoted deregulation through a Council on Competitiveness, which was chaired by the vice president and comprised of the attorney general, the director of the OMB, the chair of the Council of Economic Advisers, the secretaries of commerce and treasury, and the White House Chief of Staff. Unlike the OMB, the Council could operate outside legislative oversight or influence. However, its effort did not reach independent regulatory commissions.

FOIA was back in the legislative arena in 1986. The act was amended to regulate fees according to how the requested information would be used. Noncommercial information, such as information of value to research, scholarship, media reporting, and the public's understanding of government, receives preferential treatment.

L. 1990s

The 1990s were a decade punctuated by thoroughgoing strategies to reform federal administration. In September 1993, President Bill Clinton and Vice President Al Gore introduced an ambitious agenda for reform with the National Performance Review (NPR). While the NPR's main principles were easily listed, their implementation proved challenging and incomplete. Those principles were: accountability for results rather than processes; cutting unnecessary spending; serving customers; empowering employees; helping communities solve their own problems; fostering excellence by creating a clear sense of mission; steering more and rowing less (that is, providing services indirectly through contracting them out or other means); delegating authority and responsibility within agencies; replacing regulations with incentives; developing budgets based on outcomes; exposing federal operations to competition; searching for market rather than administrative solutions; and using customer satisfaction as a prime measure of success (Gore 1993, 7). The NPR had three broad phases: first, from 1993 into 1995, to change the way the federal government was administered; second, (1995 into 1998), to determine what the federal government should do and what could be done more appropriately by state and local governments and the private sector; third (1998 through January 2001), to diffuse administrative reform throughout the nation's many governments. In 1998, the NPR's name was changed to the National Partnership for Reinventing Government to highlight the shift into the final phase.

The NPR sought to deregulate the government itself, especially in the areas of personnel and procurement. Executive Order 12861 (1993) called for the elimination over a three-year period of at least 50 percent of internal administrative regulations not required by law. The (in)famous 10,000-page *Federal Personnel Manual*—a compendium of detailed personnel regulations—was discarded with great fanfare in 1994. Agencies could still use it for guidance, though, and anecdotal evidence suggests that many field offices did. However, in the new era procurement was simplified. Privatization was emphasized, and agencies were encouraged to act more like corporations competing for customers. Although the extent to which the NPR was successfully implemented is uncertain, its core concepts and language changed the thinking about federal administration and provided a platform similar to the reforms of the administration of President George W. Bush (Bush II), discussed in the section on the 2000s.

The Clinton administration also initiated broad reforms in federal regulatory processes. The administration was not opposed to regulation per se, but rather to "unnecessary" and frivolous regulation. Clinton's Executive Order 12866 (1993) listed twelve principles to guide agency regulatory action: (1) identify the problems addressed; (2) assess the contribution, if any, of existing regulations to those problems; (3) identify alternatives to regulation; (4) consider risks; (5) seek cost-effectiveness; (6) weigh costs and benefits; (7) base decisions on the best information obtainable; (8) assess alternatives among regulatory possibilities; (9) seek the views of state, local, and tribal governments; (10) avoid inconsistency among regulations; (11) impose the least burden on society; and (12) write regulations in simple, understandable language. The order revoked Executive Orders 12291 and 12498. However, it maintained centralized OMB review of much agency rule-making activity. In an important change, the OMB's OIRA was required to operate more openly than in the past. The vice president was charged with settling disputes between agencies and OIRA. Executive Order 12898 (1994) called on agencies to incorporate environmental justice into their policies. Early on, Clinton established a National Economic Council to coordinate and oversee agencies' economic policies (Executive Order 12835 [1993]).

Substantial changes in statutory administrative law also occurred during the 1990s. Legislative initiatives included the Administrative Dispute Resolution Acts of 1990 and 1996 (ADRA), the Negotiated Rulemaking Act of 1990, the Government Performance and Results Act of 1993 (GPRA), the Paperwork Reduction Act of 1995; the Electronic Freedom of Information Act of 1996 (E-FOIA); the Small Business Regulatory Enforcement Fairness Act of 1996 (SBREFA); and the Assessment of Federal Regulations and Policies and Families Act of 1998.

The ADRA authorizes agencies to substitute alternative dispute resolution for adjudication under the APA. Alternative dispute resolution can include the use of ombudsmen and ombudswomen, settlement negotiations, conciliation, facilitation, mediation, fact finding, mini-trials, arbitration, or combinations of these approaches. Arbitration under the ADRA is voluntary: the parties to a dispute cannot be compelled to enter into it. If they choose to do so, however, they may also elect to make the arbitrator's decision binding rather than advisory. The 1996 act requires agencies to set an upper limit on the amount of money that can be awarded through arbitration. The decision to use alternative dispute resolution is not subject to judicial review. Alternative dispute resolution techniques can also be used for rule making and can potentially reduce the litigation that often follows the promulgation of rules. The act requires each agency to appoint a senior official to serve as a Dispute Resolution Specialist.

Like the ADRA, the Negotiated Rulemaking Act of 1990 is aimed at simplifying administrative processes. The act permits agencies to develop rules through negotiation with interested parties. Regulatory negotiation, or reg-neg, is intended to produce better rules, increase rule-making efficiency, and reduce litigation. Broad participation in negotiating rules can better balance competing interests and make rule making less adversarial and more focused on problem solving than the conventional formal or informal rule making. Procedurally, the Negotiated Rulemaking Act calls on agencies to publish in the *Federal Register* notice of their intent to engage in reg-neg and to create rule-making committees of up to twenty-five members based on the comments and expressions of interest they receive from stakeholders and others. The committee should adequately represent the agency, regulated entities, citizen groups, trade associations, unions, and other relevant interests. Committee meetings, which may be managed by a facilitator or mediator, are open to the public. Under the act, successful negotiation requires unanimity on the committee. A committee member who refuses to support a rule being negotiated can block it or withdraw from the committee. After a rule is negotiated, it is published in the *Federal Register* for comment, which may prompt revision by the agency. The act, which originally had a sunset provision, was permanently re-authorized by the ADRA of 1996. Reg-neg offers considerable flexibility and has been used for rules on wood stoves, handicapped parking, direct student loans, and wood furniture coatings (Cognlianese 1997). Evaluations of the reg-neg vary. Critics claim it can obscure the public interest. Proponents believe it can produce better information and promote creative solutions to public-policy problems (see Rosenbloom 2003, 70-71). The impact of reg-neg on timeliness and litigation rates is uncertain (Cognlianese 1997; Kerwin and Furlong 1992).

The GPRA (also known as the Results Act) is more complicated. Its overall purpose is to develop better measures of agency performance and to tie performance to budgeting. The act requires agencies to develop strategic plans in consultation with Congress, the OMB, and interested parties. It instructs agencies to develop quantitative measures of performance wherever possible.

Phase-in occurred over several years, with results-oriented budgeting yet to be established. The GPRA follows the NPR in focusing on results, rather than procedures. At the same time, however, like the APA it views agencies as extensions of Congress. It authorizes deep (sub)committee involvement in agency goal setting and, because what one measures in administration is often what one gets, in the development of performance measures as well (see Rosenbloom 2000, 81–85). To date, though, the act has not achieved its full potential impact on federal administration.

The Paperwork Reduction Act of 1995 recodified the 1980 act discussed earlier. The 1995 act strengthens and clarifies some provisions of the 1980 act while adhering to its overall goals. Most notably, the 1995 act provides greater protection to the public by specifying that no one can be subject to an administrative process or judicial action for failing to respond to a form or other instrument for collecting information that does not have a control number assigned to it by the administrator of OIRA. Failure by the agency to notify the public that such a number must be assigned also negates the legal obligation to submit information. The act enhances the opportunities for public participation in OMB's decision making regarding forms and other information-gathering devices. It also extended OIRA's role to cover agency requirements that private parties, such as businesses, maintain information for the benefit of the public and other third parties.

As mentioned earlier, E-FOIA facilitates the release of electronic information. The act also requires each covered agency to submit an annual FOIA report to the attorney general. These reports, which are available on the Department of Justice's Web site, include the number of: requests for information received by the agency; denials and the reasons for them; days taken to process different types of requests; and full-time staff devoted to FOIA. Agencies also are required to report the total amount of fees collected for processing requests.

The SBREFA strengthens the 1980 Regulatory Flexibility Act by requiring the EPA and OSHA to be proactive in seeking input from small entities on potential rules. It also establishes broader judicial review for aggrieved small entities. A subtitle of Title II of the act is known as the Congressional Review Act. It places rules into two categories: (1) major rules, that is, those expected to have an annual impact of at least $100 million or a substantial effect on costs, prices, employment, and productivity; and (2) ordinary rules, which are not expected to have such effects. With some exceptions, major rules undergo a sixty-day review in Congress, which can seek to nullify them through a joint resolution of disapproval. The joint resolution is subject to presidential veto and potential congressional override. If a joint resolution is successfully passed, the agency cannot issue the same or a similar rule unless specifically afforded statutory authorization to do so. Agencies may publish rules in the *Federal Register* at the same time that they submit them to Congress for review. If a rule is not disapproved, it takes effect as indicated in the *Federal Register.*

Ordinary rules also face congressional disapproval, but they are not submitted to Congress for a sixty day review and take effect as their provisions indicate when they are published in the *Federal Register*. In 2001, OSHA's ergonomics rule, which had been some ten years in the making, became the first rule to be disapproved (Dewar 2001). Congressional review of agency rules was discussed in the 1940s and is in keeping with Congress' 1946 design for treating federal administrative agencies as its extensions for legislative functions and supervising their activities.

The Assessment of Regulations and Policies on Families Act requires federal agencies to consider the impact of their proposed actions on the well-being of families. Specifically, agencies should assess whether the action strengthens or weakens family stability and safety, marital commitments, parental rights, the personal responsibility of youths, independence from government, and economic welfare. The OMB and the Office of Policy Development, another EOP unit, are charged with overseeing implementation.

Two Supreme Court decisions in the 1990s are of particular importance to the national government's power to develop and implement regulations. *United States v. Lopez*, 514 US 549 (1995), fundamentally altered commerce-clause analysis by holding that the act regulated by Congress must be an economic activity. In *Lopez*, the federal Gun-Free School Zones Act of 1990 exceeded Congress' commerce-clause powers because "[t]he possession of a gun in a local school zone is in no sense an economic activity that might, through repetition elsewhere, substantially affect any sort of interstate commerce." *Id.* at 567. *Lopez* was the first Supreme Court decision since the 1930s to limit congressional commerce-clause authority. Any ambiguity in its holding was removed with *United States v. Morrison*, 529 US 598, 617 (2000), in which the Court reiterated that Congress cannot regulate "noneconomic violent criminal conduct based solely on that conduct's aggregate effect on interstate commerce."

Decided under the Tenth Amendment, *Printz v. United States*, 521 US 898 (1997), held that the constitutional system of dual sovereignty prohibits the national government from coercing state officers and employees into implementing federal regulations on gun buyers, sellers, or third parties generally. In other words, the national government may rely on its own employees to implement its regulations or induce the states to implement them voluntarily, but it cannot compel the states to assign its personnel to the enforcement of federal regulations (other than those regulating the states themselves). In what may turn out to be a remarkably prescient dissent, Justice Stevens wrote:

> Indeed, since the ultimate issue is one of power, we must consider its implications in times of national emergency. Matters such as the enlistment of air raid wardens, the administration of a military draft, the mass inoculation of children to forestall an epidemic, or perhaps the threat of an international terrorist, may require a national response before federal personnel can be made available to respond. If the Constitution empowers Congress and the President to make an appropriate response, is there anything in the Tenth Amendment, 'in historical understanding and practice, in the structure of the Constitution, [or] in the jurisprudence of this Court,'... that forbids the enlistment of state officers to make that response effective? More narrowly, what basis is there in any of those sources for concluding that it is the Members of this Court, rather than the elected representatives of the people, who should determine whether the Constitution contains the unwritten rule that the Court announces today? (*Printz*, 521 US at 940).

Lopez, Morrison, and *Printz* were all 5–4 decisions, with Chief Justice William Rehnquist and Justices Anthony Kennedy, Sandra Day O'Connor, Antonin Scalia, and Clarence Thomas in the majority and Justices Richard Breyer, Ruth Bader Ginsburg, David Souter, and John Paul Stevens dissenting. Together, the decisions resurrect dual sovereignty (also called dual federalism) by confining the national government's commerce-clause authority and strengthening the states' autonomy in the federal system. Whether the principles articulated in these cases will prove stable or relatively ephemeral is a matter of conjecture. As Stevens' dissent in *Printz* suggests, however, the requisites of homeland security and the domestic war on terror may prompt a readjustment.

M. INTO THE 2000s

During the presidential election campaign of 2000, Bush II seemed to share the NPR's approach to federal management: "My policies and my vision of government reform are guided by three principles: Government should be citizen-centered, results oriented, and wherever possible, market based" (Bush 2000). However, there is a major difference between his approach and that of the NPR, undoubtedly reinforced by the September 11, 2001, terrorist attacks: Bush II's administration takes a very expansive view of the president's executive power, which inevitably has substantial implications for the separation of powers and administrative law.

The administration's broad assertion of executive power is manifested primarily in three ways: (1) reluctance or refusal to share information with Congress, (2) reliance on "executive privilege" as a basis for opting out of legal requirements, and (3) unilateral action based on executive order and other presidential tools.

Several members of Congress, both Democrats and Republicans, have complained bitterly that obtaining information from the administration—especially from former Attorney General John Ashcroft—is like "pulling teeth" (Victor 2003, 6). In the words of long-time congressional scholar, Thomas Mann, "They [the administration] have cut Congress off" (ibid., 7). Ari Fleischer, then Bush II's press secretary, provided the rationale for the administration's stance. When asked why they refused to release some information to Congress, he replied, "Is it because we have something to hide? No. It's because it's the best way to have a healthy discussion inside an administration and that serves the President" (Simendinger 2002, 7).

Vice President Cheney relied on the constitutional doctrine of executive privilege in refusing to release the names of the members of the National Energy Policy Development Group. The scope of executive privilege is defined by the federal courts and is uncertain. However, it legitimately can shield some presidential documents and his exchanges with his top appointees from disclosure. *Nixon v. Administrator of General Services*, 433 US 425 (1977). Cheney's action faced a variety of legal challenges but the Supreme Court has not ruled on its constitutionality (*Cheney v. US District Court for the District of Columbia*, 542 US 367 [2004].)

Bush II took unilateral action in establishing a White House Office of Homeland Security by Executive Order 13,228 on October 8, 2001. This arrangement gave the president considerable flexibility in appointing and working with the office's director. It also limited congressional oversight because officials in the White House Office do not ordinarily testify before or report to congressional committees. Congress responded by pushing for the statutory creation of a Department of Homeland Security, which would be subject to the same legislative supervision and controls as other executive departments. At first, Bush II resisted, but eventually he supported the Department of Homeland Security Act of 2002 when it became clear that he could obtain a number of personnel-management reforms, both specific to the department and government wide.

Bush II also relied on unilateral action to change implementation of the Presidential Records Act of 1978 in fundamental ways. The act gives the Archivist of the United States custody over presidential materials and an "affirmative duty" to make them public "as rapidly and completely as possible." Former presidents can shield their records for twelve years, and records can be withheld pursuant to the FOIA exemptions. Relying on claims of executive privilege, Bush II issued Executive Order No. 13,233 (2001) to prevent the archivist from granting access to materials that either a former president or the incumbent wants withheld. Additionally, the executive order gives former vice presidents greater control over their papers and in some cases would allow family members of former presidents to block the release of materials. The order shifts the legal burden of persuasion from those who want materials withheld to those seeking their release. The courts have yet to rule on the order's legality.

On its Inaugural Day, January 20, 2001, the Bush II administration took unilateral action to block the implementation of agency rules promulgated late in the Clinton administration. Bush II's White House chief of staff, Andrew Card, issued a memorandum asking the agencies to add sixty days to the date on which final rules that had not yet become effective would go into force. The legality of the Card Memorandum was dubious because the effective date of a rule is part of the rule itself and subject to APA rule-making requirements. However, mounting a successful legal challenge to something like the Card memo would be difficult if not impossible (see Skrzycki 2001).

Two complicated splintered decisions decided on June 28, 2004, the Supreme Court strongly rebuked the Bush II administration's claims of very broad unilateral powers under the Constitution's commander-in-chief clause. (*Rasul v. Bush*, 542 US 466; *Hamdi v. Rumsfeld*, 542 US 507. Overall, the Court held that the president lacks the constitutional authority to hold US citizens and others in indeterminate detention as enemy combatants without affording them an opportunity to seek release in federal court.

The cases mentioned immediately above are emblematic of much of the Supreme Court's decision making in the early 2000s. They produced seven separate opinions; *Hamdi* was decided by a four-justice plurality joined in the judgment by a separate concurring and dissenting opinion to which two justices subscribed, while three other justices rejected the Court's decision in two separate dissents. Trying to find definitive clarity in such splintered decision making is like searching for the philosopher's stone. Administrative law and regulatory cases likewise proved highly divisive. The key cases can be placed in three categories: (1) federalism, (2) judicial review of administrative agencies, and (3) liability for constitutional torts, which is discussed in the conclusion to this chapter.

The Eleventh Amendment figured prominently in the Supreme Court's federalism decisions. Among other features, it limits the opportunity for individuals to sue states for money damages in federal court. The amendment can be overridden by appropriately framed legislation under the Fourteenth Amendment's enforcement clause, but not through Congress' commerce-clause powers. (*Seminole Tribe of Florida v. Florida*, 517 US 44 [1996]).

In the early years of the twenty-first century, the Eleventh Amendment has emerged as a barrier to federal regulatory measures aimed at preventing state governments and agencies from discriminating in employment. In *Kimel v. Florida Board of Regents*, 528 US 62 (2000), the Supreme Court held that the amendment barred a state employee from suing his or her employer in federal court for money damages for violations of the federal Age Discrimination in Employment Act of 1967. Permitting such suits would be an inappropriate use of the Fourteenth Amendment's enforcement clause because the remedy was not congruent and proportional to the injury to equal-protection rights. It is incongruent because preventing age discrimination is only a tertiary interest of the Fourteenth Amendment's equal-protection clause. It is disproportionate because Congress did not show that there was a widespread pattern of irrational age discrimination in state employment.

Kimel was followed by *Board of Trustees of the University of Alabama v. Garrett*, 531 US 356 (2001), in which the Court used the same reasoning to prevent state employees from suing their employers for breaches of the Americans with Disabilities Act of 1990. However, in *Nevada Department of Human Resources v. Hibbs*, 538 US 721 (2003), the Court held that the Family Medical Leave Act of 1993 was a valid exercise of congressional authority under the Fourteenth Amendment's enforcement clause. *Hibbs* differs from the other two cases in that (1) the Family Medical Leave Act is intended to prevent discrimination based on gender, which receives greater protection than age and disability under the equal-protection clause (congruence); and (2) there was widespread evidence of gender-based discrimination in state employment (proportionality). The Court was divided and splintered with concurring and dissenting opinions in *Kimel, Garrett*, and *Hibbs*, but it appears that future decisions will be based on the level of equal protection that the discrimination at issue receives and whether Congress has met its burden of persuasion in basing legislation on empirical findings of widespread patterns of such discrimination. See also *Tennessee v. Lane*, 541 US 509 (2004).

The relief contemplated under the Age Discrimination in Employment Act, the Americans with Disabilities Act, and the Family Medical Leave Act is a private civil suit in federal court against state governmental or other employers. From the standpoint of public administration and administrative law, adjudication by federal agencies is a more important venue for remedying violations of federal regulatory measures. However, in *Federal Maritime Commission v. South Carolina State Ports Authority*, the Supreme Court held that "[s]tate sovereign immunity's preeminent purpose— to accord States the dignity that is consistent with their status as sovereign entities—and the overwhelming similarities between FMC [Federal Maritime Commission] adjudicative proceedings and civil litigation lead to the conclusion that the FMC is barred from adjudicating a private party's complaint against a nonconsenting State" 535 US 743, 744 (2002). The ruling, which is the first of its kind, means that private entities may have no practical recourse for some state governmental violations of their federally protected statutory rights.

Kimel, Garret, South Carolina State Ports, and *United States v. Morrison* (2000), discussed under the 1990s, significantly strengthen dual sovereignty and the states' autonomy in the federal system. *Hibbs* cuts the other way. The Supreme Court was divided 6–3, 5–4, or splintered in each of these decisions. Whether the vision of federalism they embody will endure is an open question. In *Gonzales v. Raich*, 545 U.S. 1 (2005), a majority of the Court seemed to backtrack by accepting Congress' commerce clause power to regulate marijuana that had not entered an economic market and was used exclusively for medical purposes as authorized under California state law.

Judicial review of federal agencies by the federal courts was another area of important Supreme Court decision making in the early years of the twenty-first century. Two cases, *Solid Waste Agency of Northern Cook County (SWANCC)*, 531 US 159 (2001) and *United States v. Mead Corp.*, 533 US 218 (2001), modified the Court's decision in *Chevron v. Natural Resources Defense Council*, 467 US 837 (1984). The *Chevron* rule allows agencies to adopt any permissible interpretation of a statute that fails to speak precisely to an issue under authority Congress has delegated to them. A permissible interpretation is one that is reasonable, not the one a reviewing court might find most reasonable. The rule affords agencies wide latitude in their statutory interpretation and obviates the need to delve deeply into legislative histories and congressional intent. It also calls on the courts to provide only a soft look to the agencies' interpretation of the statutes they implement. *SWANCC* modified *Chevron* by calling on the courts to exercise a more probing review of congressional intent (that is, a "hard look") when an agency's interpretation of a statute raises questions about the law's constitutionality:

> Where an administrative interpretation of a statute invokes the outer limits of Congress' power, we expect a clear indication that Congress intended that result.... This requirement stems from our pruden- tial desire not to needlessly reach constitutional issues and our assumption that Congress does not casually authorize administrative agencies to interpret a statute to push the limit of congressional authority.... This concern is heightened where the administrative interpretation alters the federal- state framework by permitting federal encroachment upon a traditional state power (531 US at 172–173).

Based on these principles, a five-justice majority held that that the Clean Water Act does not give the Army Corps of Engineers jurisdiction over intrastate flooded gravel pits, prairie potholes, ponds, or mudflats, even when these waters are used by migratory birds on interstate journeys. Evoking the commerce-clause interpretations developed in *Lopez* and *Morrison*, the majority hinted that Congress might lack the constitutional authority to regulate noneconomic acts (such as bird migration) associated with such intrastate waters.

Mead limited the *Chevron* rule to instances in which "Congress delegated authority to the agency generally to make rules carrying the force of law, and... the agency interpretation claiming deference was promulgated in the exercise of that authority" 533 US at 218. Neither condition was met by the Customs Service's "ruling letters," such as the one that classified Mead's day planners as dutiable diaries. However, even when the *Chevron* rule does not apply, an agency's statutory interpretation may be entitled to judicial respect and courtesy, something known as "Skidmore deference," after *Skidmore v. Swift & Co.*, 323 US 134 (1944).

In *Norton v. Southern Utah Wilderness Alliance (SUWA)*, 542 US 55 (2004), a unanimous Court provided greater definition to the APA's authorization of suits to "compel agency action unlawfully withheld or unreasonably delayed" 5 U.S.C. 706(1). The Court distinguished between "failure to act" and "denial" in holding that "the only agency action that can be compelled under the APA is action legally required" (Slip opinion:7). Consequently, a claim under this section "can proceed only where a plaintiff asserts that an agency failed to take a discrete agency action that it is required to take" (Slip opinion:8). This interpretation prevents judicial "interference" with agencies' exercise of discretion and "entanglement in abstract policy disagreements which courts lack the expertise and information to resolve" (Slip opinion:2). Taken together, *SWANCC*, *Mead*, and *SUWA* follow a pragmatic approach to judicial review, tailoring "hard," "soft," and "no" looks to the agency action involved. *SWANCC* and *Mead* promote stronger judicial review of agency action whereas *SUWA* does the opposite.

Two Supreme Court decisions in the early years of the twenty-first century clarified important aspects of constitutional tort law. First, in *Correctional Services Corp. v. Malesko*, 534 US 61 (2001), a 5–4 majority held that private contractors performing outsourced functions for federal agencies are not subject to constitutional tort suits. The Court reasoned that if such suits were available, they would undercut the main purpose of constitutional tort law, which is to deter individual public employees from treading on constitutional rights, "[f]or if a corporate defendant is available for suit, claimants will focus their collection efforts on it, and not the individual directly responsible for the alleged injury" *Id.* at 62. This rationale prevents constitutional tort suits against federal agencies themselves (*Federal Deposit Insurance Corp. v. Meyer*, 510 US 471 [1994]). Because Malesko could not sue the federal Bureau of Prisons for violation of his Eighth Amendment rights, by extension he could not sue its contractor, Correctional Services Corporation. The *Malesko* holding applies only to federal contractors, not those performing outsourced functions for state and local agencies. It does not prevent constitutional tort suits against contractors' employees. *(See Richardson v. McKnight*, 521 US 399 [1997]).

In *Hope v. Pelzer*, 536 US 730 (2002), the Court addressed the nagging question of when public employees lose their qualified immunity by violating "clearly established statutory or constitutional rights of which a reasonable person would have known." *Harlow v. Fitzgerald*, 457 US 800, 818 (1982). The Court held that a constitutional right is clearly established when there is "fair warning" that it will be violated by an administrator's action, regardless of whether a case with fundamentally or materially similar facts had already been decided. Fair warning can come from several sources, including legal precedents, agency policies, official legal advice, and the broad values of constitutional law (Rosenbloom 2003b). In effect, *Hope* places a greater burden on individual public administrators to know the constitutional law governing their official functions.

VII. CONCLUSION: THE BIG QUESTION FOR TODAY'S PUBLIC ADMINISTRATION

The development of federal administrative law and regulatory policy since the 1880s is characterized by two broad themes. One is the need to retrofit the administrative state to the nation's constitutional democracy. The other is the need to balance governmental regulation against private-property rights in a market economy. Today, these themes collide as public administrative doctrine favors outsourcing government work to private entities. On the one hand, it is almost axiomatic that the public loses constitutional and administrative-law protections when governmental functions are outsourced. On the other hand, applying constitutional and administrative-law constraints to private contractors encroaches on the independence and autonomy of a growing segment of the private sector. At present, the constitutional state action doctrine is the main vehicle for weighing constitutional protections against private autonomy when government agencies outsource their work. There is not yet an equivalent approach for determining when private contractors should adhere to the requirements of administrative law. The big question for contemporary public administration is how best to protect constitutional and administrative-law norms when outsourcing. A quick look back will indicate what is at stake.

Federal administration is seemingly subject to endless criticism and reform. Yet to a considerable extent the federal government has successfully blended public administration and constitutional democracy. The great fears that administrative adjudication was inherently "justice without law" (Pound 1914, 18), that agency rule making was usurpation of legislative power (Rosenbloom 2003a, 30–35), and that the administrative state was the "road to serfdom" (Hayek 1944) have been allayed. Agencies are regulated by contemporary administrative law in ways that offer considerable opportunities for public representation and participation in administrative rule making and agenda setting. Administrative law provides access to information and the protection of broad constitutional rights and privacy interests. Accountability is maintained in a number of ways, including holding public administrators personally liable for their constitutional torts. Impact statements—whether pertaining to the environment, families, federalism, or environmental justice—force agencies to focus on the potential negative effects of their actions. The tools available for presidential and congressional oversight of administration are increasing in strength.

Judicial review of agency actions remains a powerful tool for continuing constitutionalization of public administration. In short, what were once revolutionary developments, such as the APA, FOIA, congressional standing-committee oversight of federal agencies, judicialization of federal administration, and the massive strengthening of individuals' constitutional rights in the context of public administration, are now routine features of the way the federal government operates. The same cannot be said of the private contractors to which government functions are outsourced.

The state-action doctrine is the major exception to private contractors' freedom from constitutional constraints. It would be better termed the governmental-action doctrine because it pertains to all levels of government in the United States. It is a useful place to ground one's thinking about the big question of how and when to outsource constitutional and administrative-law constraints along with government functions (that is, to apply these constraints to private contractors). Whereas governments at all levels in the United States are regulated by the federal Constitution and constitutional law, only the Thirteen Amendment's prohibition of slavery and involuntary servitude constrains purely private relationships. The state-action doctrine extends constitutional constraints to private entities when their action can be "fairly treated as that of the State [i.e., a US government] itself." *Brentwood Academy v. Tennessee Secondary School Athletic Ass'n*, 531 US 288, 295 (2001). Application of the doctrine requires a balance that protects three major values: individual rights; the autonomy of the private sphere; and assurance that "the most solemn obligations imposed by the Constitution" on government are not circumvented through privatizing, outsourcing, corporatizing, or other means. *Lebron v. National Railroad Passenger Corp.*, 513 US 374, 397 (1995).

In general, a private party will become a state actor if it is: (1) engaged in a public function, such as incarceration, (2) actually controlled by the government; (3) a joint participant with or is otherwise entwined with government in an endeavor; or (4) it is empowered by government *(see Brentwood* and Barron and Dienes 2000, chap. 9). Assessing precisely when state-action doctrine applies is "a matter of normative judgment" and "necessarily fact bound." *Brentwood*, 531 US 288, at 295, 298. However, a private entity will not become a state actor simply because it is paid, subsidized, licensed, regulated, or chartered by government.

Thus far, it has been up to the judiciary to determine when an entity is a state actor. In *Lebron*, the Supreme Court admonished that:

> it is not for Congress to make the final determination of Amtrak's status as a government entity for purposes of determining the constitutional rights of citizens affected by its actions. If Amtrak is, by its very nature, what the Constitution regards as the Government, congressional pronouncement that it is not such can no more relieve it of its First Amendment restrictions than a similar pronouncement could exempt the Federal Bureau of Investigation from the Fourth Amendment (513 US at 392).

The extant case law establishes some parameters. Public functions include incarceration, providing medical care in public or private prisons, administering elections, managing a privately owned town (though not a homeowner association) (*Malesko*; *West v. Atkins*, 487 US 42 [1988] *Terry v. Adams*, 345 US 461 [1953]; *Marsh v. Alabama*, 326 US 501 [1946]). However, it is also evident that "...cases deciding when private action might be deemed that of the state have not been a model of consistency." *Lebron*, 513 US at 378.

Although the courts can also impose administrative-law requirements on government contractors, federal judges have been very reluctant to do so (Guttman 2000). The state courts, however, have been more active in this regard, and some models are emerging with respect to transparency in at least thirty-four states. Overall, the courts are inclined to look at: (1) the nature of the function and records involved; (2) the extent of government funding, regulation, or involvement; and (3) whether the private entity was created by government or is explicitly under freedom of information or related legal requirements (Feiser 2000).

The state-action doctrine and the judicial imposition of administrative-law requirements on private entities provide guidelines from a legalistic perspective. Legislators, executive officials, and public administrators undoubtedly also have views on how and when to impose constitutional constraints and administrative-law norms on government contractors. There is no obvious reason to leave the field to the courts. As early as 1941, President Franklin D. Roosevelt's Executive Order 8802 prohibited federal defense contractors from engaging in employment discrimination based on race, color, creed, or national origin. Contractors can be required to adhere to constitutional and administrative-law norms by executive action, legislation, and agency rules, as well as by court decisions. The rapid growth in outsourcing governmental operations since the reinventing government movement burst on the scene in the early 1990s makes it desirable, if not imperative, for the field of public administration to develop workable theories to guide the inclusion of constitutional and administrative-law norms in contracts (Rosenbloom and Piotrowski 2005).

Books on bureaucracy and democracy are a staple of the literature on public administration (e.g., Hyneman 1950; Gormley and Balla 2004). Administrative law, including its constitutional aspects, has done a great deal to reduce the tensions between the administrative state and America's democratic constitutionalism. Outsourcing without attention to administrative and constitutional-law norms puts this progress at risk. The big question for today's public administration is how to ensure that an outsourced government will also be a democratic-constitutional one.

CASES

Abbott Laboratories v. Gardner, 387 US 136 (1967).

Addyson Pipe and Steel Co. v. United States, 175 US 211 (1899).

Bailey v. Richardson, 182 F.2d 46 (1950).

Bailey v. Richardson, 341 US 918 (1951).

Board of Trustees of the University of Alabama v. Garrett, 531 US 356 (2001).

Bowsher v. Synar, 478 US 714 (1986).

Branti v. Finkel, 445 US 507 (1980).

Brooks v. School District, 267 F.2d 733 (1959).

Brown v. Board of Education of Topeka, 347 US 483 (1954).

Buckley v. Valeo, 424 US 1 (1976).

Carter v. Carter Coal Co., 289 US 238 (1936).

Cheney v. US District Court for the District of Columbia, 542 US 367 (2004).

Chevron v. Natural Resources Defense Council, 467 US 837 (1984).

Chicago, Milwaukee & St. Paul Railway Co. v. Minnesota, 134 US 418 (1890).

City of Canton v. Harris, 489 US 378 (1989).

Cleveland Board of Education v. LaFleur, 414 US 632 (1974).

Cleveland Board of Education v. Loudermill, 470 US 532 (1985).

Correctional Services Corp. v. Malesko, 534 US 61 (2001).

Federal Deposit Insurance Corp. v. Meyer, 510 US 471 (1994).

Federal Maritime Commission v. South Carolina State Ports Authority, 535 US 743 (2002).

Federal Trade Commission v. Ruberoid Co., 343 US 470 (1952).

Federal Trade Commission v. Sperry & Hutchinson, 405 US 233 (1972).

Garner v. Los Angeles, 341 US 716 (1951).

Goldberg v. Kelly, 397 US 254 (1970).

Gonzales v. Raich, 545 US 1 (2005).

Goss v. Lopez, 419 US 565 (1975).

Hafer v. Melo, 502 US 21 (1991).

Hamdi v. Rumsfeld, 542 US 507 (2004).

Hammer v. Dagenhart, 257 US 251 (1918).

Harlow v. Fitzgerald, 457 US 800 (1982).

Hawkins v. Town of Shaw, 437 F.2d 1286 (1971).

Heckler v. Cheney, 470 US 821 (1985).

Holt v. Sarver, 309 F. Supp. 362 (1970).

Hope v. Pelzer, 536 US 730 (2002).

Immigration & Naturalization Service v. Chadha, 462 U.S 919 (1983).

Industrial Union Department, AFL-CIO v. American Petroleum Institute, 448 US 607 (1980).

Interstate Commerce Commission v. Alabama Midland Railway Co., 168 US 144 (1897).

Interstate Commerce Commission v. Cincinnati, New Orleans & Texas Pacific Railroad Co., 167 US 479 (1897).

J. E. B. v. Alabama ex rel. T. B., 511 US 127 (1994).

Joint Anti-Fascist Refugee Committee v. McGrath, 341 US 123 (1951).

Jones v. Milwaukee Electric Railway Co., 147 Wis. 427 (1911).

Kelo v. City of New London, US Supreme Court No. 04-108 (2005).

Kimel v. Florida Board of Regents, 528 US 62 (2000).

Lawrence v. Texa, 539 US 558 (2003).

Lebron v. National Railroad Passenger Corp., 513 US 374 (1995).

Lochner v. New York, 198 US 45 (1905).

Lucas v. South Carolina Coastal Council, 505 US 1003 (1992).

MacPherson v. Buick Motor Co., 217 NY 382 (1916).

Marsh v. Alabama, 326 US 501 (1946).

Mathews v. Eldridge, 424 US 319 (1976).

McAuliffe v. New Bedford, 155 Mass. 216 (1892).

Morrison v. Olson, 478 US 654 (1988).

Muller v. Oregon, 208 US 412 (1908).

Munn v. Illinois, 94 US 113 (1877).

Nevada Department of Human Resources v. Hibbs, 538 US 721 (2003).

Nixon v. Administrator of General Services, 433 US 425 (1977).

Nollan v. California Coastal Commission, 483 U. S. 825 (1987).

Northwest Forest Resource Council v. Espy, 846 F. Supp. 1009 (1994).

Norton v. Southern Utah Wilderness Alliance, 542 US 55 (2004).

Owen v. City of Independence, 445 US 622 (1980).

Panama Refining Co. v. Ryan, 293 US 388 (1935).

People ex rel. Fursman v. City of Chicago, 278 Ill. 318 (1917).

Printz v. United States, 521 US 898 (1997).

Rasul v. Bush, 542 US 466 (2004).

Richardson v. McKnight, 521 US 399 (1997).

Schechter Poultry Corp. v. United States, 295 US 495 (1935).

Seminole Tribe of Florida v. Florida, 517 US 44 (1996).

Sherbert v. Verner, 374 US 398 (1963).

Skidmore v. Swift & Co., 323 US 134 (1944).

Smith v. Wade, 641 US 30 (1983).

Solid Waste Agency of Northern Cook County v. Army Corps of Engineers, 531 US 159 (2001).

Spady v. Mt. Vernon, 419 US 983 (1974).

Spalding v. Vilas, 161 US 483 (1896).

Starkey v. Board of Education, 381 P2d 718 (1963).

Steadman v. Security and Exchange Commission, 450 US 91 (1981).

Tennessee v. Lane, 541 US 508 (2004).

Terry v. Adams, 345 US 461 (1953).

United Public Workers v. Mitchell, 330 US 75 (1947).

United States Department of Defense v. Federal Labor Relations Authority, 510 US 487 (1994).

United States v. Darby, 312 US 100 (1941).

United States v. E. C. Knight, 156 US 1 (1895).

United States. v. Lopez, 514 US 549 (1995).

United States v. Mead Corp., 533 US 218 (2001).

United States v. Morrison, 529 US 598 (2000).

United States v. Trans-Missouri Freight Ass'n., 166 US 290 (1897).

Vermont Yankee Nuclear Power Corp. v. Natural Resources Defense Council, 435 US 519 (1978).

Wabash Railway v. Illinois, 118 US 557 (1886).

Walker v. Cheney, 230 F. Supp. 2d 51 (2002).

Weiman v. Updegraff, 344 US 183 (1952).

West v. Atkins, 487 US 42 (1988).

Whitman v. American Trucking Ass'ns, Inc., 531 US 457 (2001).

Wickard v. Filburn, 317 US 111 (1942).

Wilkie v. O'Connor, 25 NYS 2d 617 (1946).

Will v. Michigan Department of State Police, 491 US 59 (1989).

Wyman v. James, 400 US 309 (1971).

REFERENCES

Aberbach, Joel, *Keeping a Watchful Eye*, Brookings Institution, Washington, DC, 1990.

Ackerman, Bruce, *Reconstructing American Law*, Harvard University Press, Cambridge, MA, 1984.

Arnold, R. Douglas, *Congress and the Bureaucracy*, Yale University Press, New Haven, CT, 1979.

Barron, Jerome and Dienes, C. Thomas, *Constitutional Law in a Nutshell*, West Group, St. Paul, MN, 2000.

Bradley, Behrman, The civil aeronautics board, In *The Politics of Regulation*, Wilson, James Q., Ed., Basic Books, New York, pp. 75–120, 1980.

Bonfield, Arthur and Asimow, Michael, *State and Federal Administrative Law*, West, St. Paul, MN, 1989.

Bontecou, Eleanor, *The Federal Loyalty-Security Program*, Cornell University Press, Ithaca, NY, 1953.

Brazier, James, *Who Controls the Administrative State? Congress and the President Adopt the Administrative Procedure Act of 1946*, UMI, Ann Arbor, MI, 1993.

Brown, Ralph S., *Loyalty and Security*, Yale University Press, New Haven, CT, 1958.

Bryner, Gary, *Bureaucratic Discretion*, Pergammon, New York, 1987.

Bush, George W., Building a responsive, innovative government, *Federal Times*, 15, June 26, 2000.

Cann, Steven, *Administrative Law*, Sage, Thousand Oaks, CA, 2002.

Cognlianese, Cary, Assessing consensus: the promise and performance of negotiated rulemaking, *Duke Law Journal*, 46, 1255–1349, 1997.

Crowley, Donald, Selection tests and equal opportunity: the court and the EEOC, *Administration and Society*, 17, 361–384, 1985.

Davis, Kenneth C., *Administrative Law Treatise*, West, St. Paul, MN, 1958.

Davis, Kenneth C., *Discretionary Justice*, Louisiana State University Press, Baton Rouge, LA, 1969.

Davis, Kenneth C., *Administrative Law Text*, 3rd ed., West, St. Paul, MN, 1972.

Davis, Kenneth C., *Administrative Law and Government*, 2nd ed., West, St. Paul, MN, 1975.

Davison, J. Forrester and Grundstein, Nathan, *Administrative Law and the Regulatory System*, Lerner Law Book Co., Washington, DC, 1968.

Dempsey, Paul, Deregulation and reregulation, In *Handbook of Regulation and Administrative Law*, Rosen-bloom, David and Schwartz, Richard, Eds., Marcel Dekker, New York, pp. 175–206, 1994.

Derthick, Martha and Quirk, Paul, *The Politics of Deregulation*, Brookings Institution, Washington, DC, 1985.

Dewar, Helen, Ergonomics repeal prompts look back, *Washington Post*, A16, March 9, 2001.

Dickinson, John, *Administrative Justice and the Supremacy of Law*, Harvard University Press, Cambridge, MA, 1927.

Dimock, Marshall, *Law and Dynamic Administration*, Praeger, New York, 1980.

Dolan, Julie and Rosenbloom, David H., Eds., *Representative Bureaucracy: Classic Readings and Contemporary Issues*, M.E. Sharpe, Armonk, NY, 2003.

Donnelly, James., US Senate Committee on banking and currency, testimony before the full employment subcommittee, Senate Hearing 763, Aug. 30, Government Printing Office, Washington, DC, pp. 665–668, 1945.

Dullea, Charles, Development of the personnel program for administrative law judges, *Administrative Law Review*, 25, 41–47, 1973.

Eaton, Dorman, *The Civil Service in Great Britain*, Harper & Bros, New York, 1880.

Feiser, Craig, Protecting the public's right to know, *Florida State University Law Review*, 27, 825–864, 2000.

Fiorina, Morris, *Congress: Keystone of the Washington Establishment*, Yale University Press, New Haven, CT, 1977.

Friedman, Lawrence M., *A History of American Law*, Simon & Schuster, New York, 1973.

Friedman, Milton, *Capitalism and Freedom*, University of Chicago Press, Chicago, IL, 1962.

Frug, Gerald, The ideology of bureaucracy in american law, *Harvard Law Review*, 97, 1276–1388, 1984.

Goodnow, Frank, *Comparative Administrative Law*, G.P. Putnam's Sons, New York, 1893.

Goodnow, Frank, *Politics and Administration*, Macmillan, New York, 1900.

Goodnow, Frank, *The Principles of the Administrative Law of the United States*, G.P. Putnam's Sons, New York, 1905.

Gore, Al., *Creating a Government That Works Better and Costs Less*, Government Printing Office, Washington, DC, 1993.

Gormley, William Jr., and Balla, Steven, *Bureaucracy and Democracy*, CQ Press, Washington, DC, 2004.

Gray, Horace M., The airlines industry, In *The Structure of American Industry*, Adams Walter, Ed., Macmillan, New York, pp. 465–508, 1961.

Gregory, Charles O. and Katz, Harold A., *Labor and the Law*, 3rd ed., Norton, New York, 1979.

Gunther, Gerald, *Cases and Materials on Constitutional Law*, 10th ed., Foundation Press, Mineola, NY, 1975.

Guttman, Daniel, Public purpose and private service, *Administrative Law Review*, 52, 859–926, 2000.

Hart, James, *An Introduction to Administrative Law with Selected Cases*, F.S. Crofts, New York, 1940.

Hartz, Louis, *The Liberal Tradition in America*, Harcourt, Brace, New York, 1955.

Havemann, Judith, How do you get OMB's attention?, *Washington Post Weekly Edition*, 12, June 2, 1986.

Hayek, Friedrich, *The Road to Serfdom*, University of Chicago Press, Chicago, IL, 1944.

Heffron, Florence and McFeeley, Neil, *The Administrative Regulatory Process*, Longman, New York, 1983.

Hoogenboom, Ari, *Outlawing the Spoils*, University of Illinois Press, Urbana, IL, 1961.

Johnson, John W., *American Legal Culture 1908–1940*, Greenwood Press, Westport, CT, 1981.

Hyneman, Charles, *Bureaucracy in a Democracy*, Harper & Brothers, New York, 1950.

Kagan, Robert, Regulatory enforcement, In *Handbook of Regulation and Administrative Law*, Rosenbloom, David and Schwartz, Richard, Eds., Marcel Dekker, New York, pp. 383–422, 1994.

Katzmann, Robert, Federal trade commission, In *The Politics of Regulation*, Wilson, James Q., Ed., Basic Books, New York, pp. 152–187, 1980.

Kaufman, Herbert, *Red Tape*, Brookings Institution, Washington, DC, 1977.

Kelman, Steven, Occupational safety and health administration, In *The Politics of Regulation*, Wilson, James Q., Ed., Basic Books, New York, pp. 236–265, 1980.

Kerwin, Cornelius, *Rulemaking: How Government Agencies Write Law and Make Policy*, 3rd ed., CQ Press, Washington, DC, 2003.

Kerwin, Cornelius and Furlong, Scott, Time and rulemaking, *Journal of Public Administration Research and Theory*, 2, 113–138, 1992.

Krislov, Samuel and Rosenbloom, David H., *Representative Bureaucracy and the American Political System*, Praeger, New York, 1981.

La Follette, Robert, Congress wins a victory over Congress, *New York Times Magazine*, 11ff, August 4, 1946.

Leslie, Douglas A., *Labor Law*, West, St. Paul, MN, 1979.

Lowi, Theodore J., Distribution, regulation, redistribution: the functions of government, *World Politics*, 16, 677–715, 1964.

Lowi, Theodore J., *The End of Liberalism*, Norton, New York, 1969.

Lubbers, Jeffrey, Management of federal agency adjudication, In *Handbook of Regulation and Administrative Law*, Rosenbloom, David and Schwartz, Richard, Eds., Marcel Dekker, New York, pp. 287–323, 1994.

Mayo, Elton, *The Human Problems of an Industrial Civilization*, Macmillan, New York, 1933.

Meier, Kenneth J., *Regulation*, St. Martin's Press, New York, 1985.

Moreno, Angel Manuel, Presidential coordination of the independent regulatory process, *Administrative Law Journal of the American University*, 8, 461–516, 1994.

Mosher, Frederick, *Basic Documents of American Public Administration, 1776–1950*, Holmes and Meier, New York, 1976.

Nachmias, David and Rosenbloom, David H., *Bureaucratic Government, USA*, St. Martin's Press, New York, 1980.

Nader, Ralph, *Unsafe at Any Speed*, Grossman, New York, 1965.

O'Leary, Rosemary, *Environmental Change: The Courts and the EPA*, Temple University Press, Philadelphia, PA, 1993.

O'Leary, Rosemary, What every administrator should know about environmental law, In *Handbook of Regulation and Administrative Law*, Rosenbloom, David and Schwartz, Richard, Eds., Marcel Dekker, New York, pp. 139–155, 1994.

Osborne, David and Gaebler, Ted, *Reinventing Government*, Addison-Wesley, Reading, MA, 1992.

Pound, Roscoe, Justice according to law, *Columbia Law Review*, 14, 1–26, 1914.

Pound, Roscoe, *Administrative Law*, University of Pittsburgh Press, Pittsburgh, PA, 1942.

Pritchett, C. Herman, *The Roosevelt Court*, Macmillan, New York, 1948.

Pritchett, C. Herman, *The American Constitution*, McGraw-Hill, New York, 1977.

Quirk, Paul, Food and drug administration, In *The Politics of Regulation*, Wilson, James Q., Ed., Basic Books, New York, pp. 191–235, 1980.

Ranney, Joseph, Imperia in imperiis: law and railroads in Wisconsin, 1847–1910, Wisconsin Lawyer. http://www.wicourts.gov/about/organization/history/article19.html (accessed June 19, 2006), 2004.

Reich, Charles, The new property, *Yale Law Journal*, 73, 733–787, 1964.

Reigel, Stanley and Owen, P. John, *Administrative Law*, Ann Arbor Science, Ann Arbor, MI, 1982.

Ripley, Randall and Franklin, Grace, *Congress, the Bureaucracy, and Public Policy*, Dorsey, Homewood, IL, 1976.

Rohr, John, *To Run a Constitution*, University Press of Kansas, Lawrence, KS, 1986.

Root, Elihu, Presidential address, *American Bar Association Report*, 41, 355–374, 1916.

Rosenbloom, David H., *Federal Service and the Constitution*, Cornell University Press, Ithaca, NY, 1971.

Rosenbloom, David H., Kaiser v. weber: perspectives from the public sector, *Public Personnel Management*, 8, 392–396, 1979.

Rosenbloom, David H., *Public Administration and Law*, Marcel Dekker, New York, 1983.

Rosenbloom, David H., *Building a Legislative-Centered Public Administration: Congress and the Administrative State, 1946–1999*, University of Alabama Press, Tuscaloosa, AL, 2000.

Rosenbloom, David H., *Administrative Law for Public Managers*, Westview, Boulder, CO, 2003.

Rosenbloom, David H., *Hope v. Pelzer*: raising the bar for public administrators' qualified immunity, *Review of Public Personnel Administration*, 23, 255–261, 2003.

Rosenbloom, David H. and Carroll, James, Public personnel administration and law, In *Handbook on Public Personnel Administration and Labor Relations*, Rabin, T.J., Hildredth Vocino, W., Miller, G., Eds., Marcel Dekker, New York, pp. 91–113, 1994.

Rosenbloom, David H. and O'Leary, Rosemary, *Public Administration and Law*, 2nd ed., Marcel Dekker, New York, 1997.

Rosenbloom, David, H. and Piotrowski, Suzanne, J., Reinventing public administration while "deinventing" administrative law: is time for an "APA" for regulating outsourced government work?, *Syracuse Journal of International Law and Commerce*, 33, 175–189, 2005.

Rosenbloom, David H. and Shafritz, Jay, *Essentials of Labor Relations*, Reston, Reston, VA, 1985.

Scholz, John, Managing regulatory enforcement, In *Handbook of Regulation and Administrative Law*, Rosenbloom, David and Schwartz, Richard, Eds., Marcel Dekker, New York, pp. 423–463, 1994.

Schurz, Carl, Editorial, *Harper's Weekly*, 37, 614, 1893.

Schurz, Carl, *The Necessity and Progress of Civil Service Reform*, Good Government, Washington, DC, 1894.

Schurz, Carl, *Congress and the Spoils System*, George G. Peck, New York, 1895.

Schwartz, Bernard, Administrative law: the third century, *Administrative Law Review*, 29, 291–319, 1977.

Shannon, David, *Twentieth Century America*, Rand McNally, Chicago, IL, 1963.

Shapiro, Martin, *The Supreme Court and Administrative Agencies*, Free Press, New York, 1968.

Simendinger, Alexis, Results-oriented president uses levers of power, Government Executive online edition, http://govexec.com (accessed Jan. 25, 2002), 2002.

Sinclair, Upton, *The Jungle*, New American Library, New York, 1905.

Skowronek, Stephen, *Building a New American State: The Expansion of National Administrative Capacities, 1877–1920*, Cambridge University Press, Cambridge, UK, 1982.

Skrzycki, Cindy, Congress: fewer forms or budgets will suffer, *Washington Post*, E1, May 29, 1998.

Skrzycki, Cindy, Critics assail review of 'final' rules, *Washington Post*, E1, April 3, 2001.

Stewart, Richard, The reformation of American administrative law, *Harvard Law Review*, 88, 1609–1813, 1975.

Stivers, Camilla, *Bureau Men, Settlement Women: Constructing Public Administration in the Progressive Era*, University Press of Kansas, Lawrence, KS, 2000.

Strauss, Peter, Rakoff, Todd, Schotland, Roy, and Farina, Cynthia, *Gellhorn and Byse's Administrative Law: Cases and Comments*, 9th ed., Foundation Press, Westbury, NY, 1995.

Taylor, Frederick, *The Principles of Scientific Management*, Norton, New York, 1967/1911.

Tresolini, R. John, The development of administrative law, *University of Pittsburgh Law Review*, 12, 362–380, 1951.

US Civil Service Commission, *Annual Report*, US Government Printing Office, Washington, DC, 1907.

US Commission on Civil Rights, *The Federal Civil Rights Enforcement Effort—1974*, Government Printing Office, Washington, DC, 1975.

US Congress. Senate Committee on the Judiciary, *Administrative Procedure Act: Legislative History*, US Government Printing Office, Washington, DC, 1946.

US General Services Administration, *Twenty-Seventh Annual Report of the President on Federal Advisory Committees, Fiscal Year 1998*, The Administration, Washington, DC, 1999.

Van Riper, Paul, *History of the United States Civil Service*, Row, Peterson, Evanston, IL, 1958.

Vaughn, Robert, Federal information policy and administrative law, In *Handbook of Regulation and Administrative Law*, Rosenbloom, David and Schwartz, Richard, Eds., Marcel Dekker, New York, pp. 467–484, 1994.

Victor, Kirk, Congress in eclipse as power shifts to executive branch, Government Executive online edition, http://govexec.com/ (accessed February 18), 2003.

Waldo, Dwight, *The Enterprise of Public Administration*, Chandler and Sharp, Novoto, CA, 1980.

Waldo, Dwight, *The Administrative State*, 2nd ed., Holmes and Meier, New York, 1984.

Warren, Kenneth, *Administrative Law in the Political System*, 4th ed., Westview, Boulder, CO, 2004.

Weaver, Suzanne, Antitrust division of the Department of Justice, In *The Politics of Regulation*, Wilson, James Q., Ed., Basic Books, New York, pp. 123–151, 1980.

Weber, Max, Bureaucracy, In *Max Weber: Essays in Sociology,* Gerth H. H. and Mills, C. W., Eds., Brookings Institution, Washington, DC, 1958.

Willoughby, W. F., *Principles of Legislative Organization and Administration*, Brookings Institution, Washington, DC, 1934.

Wilson, James Q., The politics of regulation, In *The Politics of Regulation*, Wilson, James Q., Ed., Basic Books, New York, pp. 357–394, 1980.

Wilson, Woodrow, The study of administration, *Political Science Quarterly*, 56, 481–506, 1941/1887.

Woll, Peter, *Administrative Law*, University of California Press, Berkeley, CA, 1963.

Wyman, Bruce, *The Principles of the Administrative Law Governing the Relations of Public Officers*, Keefe-Davidson, St. Paul, MN, 1903.

Zuboff, Shoshana, *In the Age of the Smart Machine*, Basic Books, New York, 1988.

18 Five Great Issues in Public Law and Public Administration

*Julia Beckett**

CONTENTS

There are many important questions concerning law and public administration. Is public adminis-tration legitimate within the constitutional framework? Do courts influence administration? Do lawsuits obstruct efficient administration? What is the scope of administrative law? Is there too

---

* The author would like to thank L. R. Keller, H. O. Koenig, and B. Westbrook for comments and suggestions, and G. J. Miller, D. H. Rosenbloom, and K. B. Gatti for encouragement and support.

much red tape? Are there better ways to regulate? What aspects of law does an administrator need to know?

Public administration and public law have different emphases. Public administration involves the activities of government including implementing policies, overseeing distribution of benefits, collecting taxes, and overseeing programs. In all of these endeavors of governance there are legal components and instruments. Public law includes the Constitution, statutes, regulations and common law decisions that affect government actions. The scope of public law is broad and affects every aspect of governance.

This chapter considers the great issues related to public law and public administration. The great issues are interesting to both theorists and practitioners, have been sources of controversy, and are enduring. The five great issues discussed in this chapter are

1. The legal foundations of administration
2. The role of courts
3. The development of administrative law
4. The extent of regulation
5. Legal influence on administrative practice

I. THE LEGAL FOUNDATIONS OF PUBLIC ADMINISTRATION

The legal foundations of public administration are expressed in the classic definition of public administration as the execution of the law. The legitimacy of public administration is linked to the constitutional foundations. In addition, arguments can be made that the political and legal philosophies in the Constitution, rule of law, and court interpretations must be considered for a balanced approach to the legal foundations of public administration; thus, the issues discussed in this section concern what can be and should be included in the legal foundations of public administration.

A. WHAT ARE THE CONSTITUTIONAL FOUNDATIONS OF GOVERNMENT?

In our democratic republic, public law is necessary for public managers to know because of its constitutive nature. Law relates to the structural and philosophical composition of government. The Constitution is an essential foundation for both public law and public administration. Public law scholars have stressed how law is a philosophical foundation for our society (Moe and Gilmour 1995; Rosenbloom and O'Leary 1997; Rosenbloom 1998); how law pervades and legitimizes administration (Rohr 1986; Wamsley et al. 1990; Wamsley and Wolf 1996); and how positive aspects of law are useful as guidance, as technique, as perspective, and as process (Cooper and Newland 1997; O'Leary and Wise 1991).

Public administrators are to implement policies and be responsive to the public. Administrators should perform these tasks efficiently and equitably. The sources of many administrative obligations and imperatives are found in the Constitution, laws, rules, and executive orders—these sources are called positive law. Trail court decisions interpret and evaluate administrative actions, while appellate court decisions establish binding precedent—these decisions comprise common law. Both types of law are intimately part of public administration. Constitutional and political theory are fundamental parts of public administration. The phrase, "This is a government of laws and not men," stresses the importance of the social context of laws. In other words, this phrase defines government under the rule of law.

The rule of law is a philosophy that includes foundation assumptions for government as well. Within these philosophical discussions are a number of ways for considering and analyzing public administration. The underlying values linked to public law are important for administrative practice. Public law is part of governance.

The Constitution, as a written document and as a founding event, is reflected in the idea of social contract. The social contract contains the powers, duties, rights, and responsibilities of government and the public. Commonly accepted tenets about the structure and powers of American constitutional government are:

- The three branches of government—the legislative, the executive, and the judicial— share power and serve as checks and balances for each other.
- The fragmented government powers of this country are enumerated in the appropriate realms of power to the federal government with the remainder reserved for the states.
- The government must have enumerated powers—that means a government must have power delegated by the Constitution to enact and administer laws, and approved by the executive.
- The federal government has limited and specified powers, and state governments have general powers to protect the health, safety, and welfare of the people.
- The courts were first viewed as the weakest branch, yet they have the power to review the legality and constitutionality of the other branches' actions.
- The Bill of Rights and other constitutional amendments add responsibilities and limits on governmental actions as well as provide rights to individuals.
- The Constitution is a living document that can change and apply to differing situations and eras.

Public administration scholars ground the political and philosophical foundations of governance in the Constitution (Lowi 1993; Moe and Gilmour 1995; Rohr 1993; Rosenbloom and O'Leary 1997; Spicer 1990, 1995; Spicer and Terry 1993; Wise 1993). The Supreme Court's role and decisions affecting policy are also connected to foundation literature (Barclay and Birkland 1998; Rosenbloom and Ross 1998; Wise and O'Leary 1992). Philosophical issues are also the subject of the extremely well-developed legal scholarship and initial attempts have been made to connect these two academic domains of scholarship (Rosenbloom and Schwartz 1994).

B. IS PUBLIC ADMINISTRATION LEGITIMATE WITHIN THE DIRECT CONSTITUTIONAL TEXT?

The legitimacy of government is tied to the founding documents of constitutions and charters. The legislative, executive and judicial branches each have an article defining their powers in the US Constitution. There is the briefest mention of minor offices and appointments, but there is no extensive and focused attention to public administration or public servants in the U.S. Constitution. One approach is to consider that administration is implicit and inferred because government could not exist without people—agents—carrying out its responsibilities.

Since Rohr (1986) drew attention to the lack of explicit constitutional text regarding public administrators, there has been concerted scholarly attention focused on the legitimacy of public administration. This constitutional legitimacy discourse has been particularly focused at the national level. To establish legitimacy, some look to the intent of the founders, and often this only includes the Federalist Papers and omits the Anti-Federalist side of the debate. Others note that the analytical approach of distinct and clear separation of powers as a concept is not analytically consistent with the constitutional scheme and practice (Rohr 1986). Still others argued that public administrators were ultimately responsible to the people and must seek the public good that is consistent with constitutional and democratic values (Spicer and Terry 1993); thus, the question of constitutional legitimacy is an enduring concern.

Scholars have thoroughly considered how constitutional origins affect the legitimacy of public administration, but most of this discussion is focused at the federal level. References to administration differ for governments; state constitutions and local charters define their government powers in greater detail than the federal constitution. State and local founding documents often have specific and detailed references to administrative departments and officers. Yet much of the theoretical and conceptual discussions about constitutional legitimacy apply to every level of government. Constitutions and charters define and enumerate the powers of government; without the direct, express grant of powers, governments have no authority.

These conceptions reflect themes that recur in the definition and role of public administration. The foundational concerns are: sources of power, clear lines of organizational authority, functional results orientation, public representation, and responsiveness. These concerns reflect formal versus functional debates that recur in public administration literature. They often intermingle normative and ideological concerns. These basic conceptualizations are linked most often to modes of legal interpretation, to the delegation doctrine, and to ethics.

C. WHAT ARE THE LEGISLATIVE SOURCES OF AUTHORITY FOR PUBLIC POLICY AND PUBLIC ADMINISTRATION?

The legislative source of authority is an essential part of the legal foundations of government. These grants of statutory powers both enable and limit government actions. The scope of power and authority for administrators occurs through delegation. These delegations are found in statutes called organic or substantive laws. Yet the manner, process, and scope of delegations have been a recurring concern. Policies and programs are decided by the legislature, yet administrators often flesh in the details and carry out the policies. Many statutory schemes are vague to reach general agreement or because of confidence that those administering the law will determine detailed definitions or develop processes to implement the laws. Thus, the second issue becomes, what is the extent of administrative discretion? If administrative powers and responsibilities are both delegated by law and a matter of discretion then there is the concern about how statutes should be interpreted to indicate whether administrators are carrying out the legislative intent.

Within the tradition of express government powers, the legislature passes laws that enable and limit administrative action or that define rights and responsibilities. The delegation doctrine holds that administrative responsibilities and actions are delegated by the legislature. An ongoing debate within academic writings and Supreme Court decisions focuses on how broad administrative delegations should be. Lowi (1979) and others argue delegations should be detailed, specific, and narrow. Other recognize that delegations are broader, general, long lasting and flexible (e.g. Davis 1969). Underlying concerns about delegations focus on representation and democratic accountability because administrators are not directly responsive to the public as are elected legislators or the president.

Legislation that defines roles and responsibilities for agencies and public managers is an aspect of public law. Legislation may be general or vague; it may provide a framework and specifically require agencies to develop modes of administering the law. Thus, there is discretion in how laws are carried out by administrators. The choice to enforce a law can be established in policy directives or, for example, by the individual decision of a street-level bureaucrat who chooses to giving a traffic ticket are types of discretion (Lipsky 1980). The way laws are administered changes with the political focus of a presidential administration, or because of budget, war, or social problems. The scope and extent of discretion are both concerns raised in legal challenges and in administrative practice.

Although legislation defines what government can do, the issue of how legislation is carried out is often the subject of public administration. Organic legislation defines the substantive law of regulated activities such as environmental regulation (O'Leary 1994a; Wise and O'Leary 1997) or entitlements such as social security disability benefits (Kaboolian 1999). Other times statutes define internal operations, such as personnel administration (Crockett and Gilmore 1999; Lee and Greenlaw 1995; Strickland 1995); sometimes the issues raised balance constitutional rights with efficient management (Richman 1997). The enabling and budgetary legislation also provides balance between policy goals and administrative duties. Most often, these analyses are connected to policy rather than law in the literature on governance.

If legislation empowers government to adopt programs and regulations, then the manner in which the statutes are understood is important (Calabresi 1982; Sunstein 1996). Thus, the question of interpretation is a concern, but the approach and manner that laws are interpreted differs between lawyers, ordinary people, and administrators.

The legal doctrine regarding the practice of statutory interpretation is that courts and lawyers should start with the text and apply the plain language of the statute as written. Courts may also use the intent of the framers, or situational interpretation models, when the text is ambiguous or would lead to an absurd result (Llewellyn 1950). It is not clear that this mode of interpretation is used by administrators. An alternative legal view to interpreting statutes using a law-as-purpose approach takes a wider social view into consideration, but again limits authority to the courts to consider and declare which the resources, facts, or scope of review are appropriate (Eskridge 1996). Others contend that courts really take a more pragmatic approach to interpreting authoritative statutes and considering what is appropriate for a given situation (Carter 1994; Frankfurter 1950). The more purposive or pragmatic approach may be closer to what administrators do when they interpret statutes.

The typical academic terminology for the application and interpretation of law in public organizations is to called the legal–rational approach. This is deemed to be a mechanical application of legal rules to given situations which results in lack of flexibility and sophistication. Although the application of clear codes or rules is the dominant approach in Europe, it is not the typical Anglo-American approach to legal decisions. The legal-rational approach does not represent judicial approaches to statutory interpretation. The legal-rational label does not reflect the interpretive, situational, and individual concern of courts evaluating the case before them and how appellate courts evaluate cases within the precedent of the established body of common law (Carter 1994). Whether the legal-rational approach is actually the way American administrators view law and court decisions has drawn some attention (Spicer and Terry 1996; White 1999).

Ordinary people do not have a single view of law and how it should be interpreted. Some people believe laws should be literally enforced; others see laws as situational justice, but most want law used by administrators and government to deal with real problems (Merry 1986). Often ordinary people are confused by the technical language of statutes and regulations, or they may never look to the statutes. The question becomes, how do administrators interpret statutory authority?

In the major public administration textbooks, interpretation of statutes is rarely mentioned. The discussions focus on making policy and implementing policy. However, discussions of policy rarely refer to administrators considering statues to understand what the legislature intended. How administrators interpret statutes is only occasionally evaluated (Spicer and Terry 1996). Other inquiries concern how administrators affect or propose legislation and interact with the legislature (Gill 1995). An administrator's efforts to get legislation enacted are described as clandestine and the actors are organizational deviants; these studies focus on agency hierarchy and politics of the agency setting (O'Leary 1994a).

There is a gap about discussing the techniques of administering legislation in public administration. This gap is sometimes stark when administrative interpretations are successfully challenged in court because what was practiced differed from what was statutorily defined. It seems that public administrators, in the common public administration texts, are closer to the ordinary person's unfocused interpretation than the specific technical interpretation of lawyers. This contrast raises concerns of consistency and accountability.

Issues of legislative foundations are often grouped as issues of delegation, interpretation, and discretion. Often the issues are ideological and normative; they are linked to the power of government, the types of political concerns, and the extent of government. Many of the debates incorporate central constitutional questions of governance. Rather than being resolved or settled by easy answers, the range of discourse and persuasive presentation of ideas and implications makes the delegation question ongoing normative issues about governance.

D. How Do Constitutional Duties Affect Administrative Values?

Another approach to the foundations of public administration is in the connection to ethical obligations for governance. The Constitution is seen as a source of administrative values, as guidance for statesmanship, leadership, and responsibility (Lawler, Shaefer, and Shaefer 1998). The public administration ethics literature often refers to the Constitution as a source of ethical duty but sees this duty as distinct from law (Martinez 1998). There is a narrow and limited view of law when discussing ethics where the legal approach to ethics is represented as rule obeisance or subordination (Van Wart 1998). There is also an underlying ambivalence and antagonism between these representations of ethics and law. These views are more limited than the rigorous and robust presentations in jurisprudence literature and Supreme Court decisions regarding the duties and responsibilities public officials and managers have towards the general public.

Policies, ethics, and democratic obligations of public leaders have public law connections in the specific grants and limitations of power in positive law of the Constitution, statutes, and rules. These public duties are distinct from the source of obligations for businesses (Beckett 2000). The links to the Constitution legitimize administrators and managers (Rohr 1998). The Blacksburg group's contributions to ethics and obligations for public servants explicitly build on the Constitution (Wamsley et al. 1990; Wamsley and Wolf 1996). The debates about delegation and discretion, formal authority, and social norms are seen in the Frederick and Finer debates (Stewart 1985). These norms are repeated elsewhere and they are related to America's two legal traditions of positive law and common law. They are connected to the debates of strict construction versus liberal interpretation of statutes and constitution and to the debates of judicial restraint versus judicial activism.

Governmental duties are particularly located in constitutional amendments. It is not possible to say which Constitutional amendment is the most important; different individual rights affect different types of administrative duties. A brief overview of constitutional rights include: the due process rights in the Fifth and Fourteenth Amendments; the equal protection rights in the Fourteenth Amendment; the right to counsel in the Sixth Amendment; a right to protection against unreasonable search and seizure in the Fourth Amendment; freedom of religion and the press as well as the right to assembly and petition in the First Amendment. These amendments give rights to the people and limit government actions.

Perhaps the constitutional duty that has presented the greatest concern for public managers and administrators is the requirement of due process. Although the general public is familiar with an individual taking the Fifth by refusing to incriminate himself or herself, the Fifth Amendment imposes many requirements on public administrators. It states, "No person... shall be deprived of life, liberty or property without due process of law; nor shall private property be taken for public use without just compensation." Due process also applies to the state and local governments under the Fourteenth Amendment.

Government action taken by administrators must meet tests of substantive and procedural due process. Due process is not narrowly defined; instead, due process has a flexible definition. Due process unlike some legal rules, is not a technical conception with a fixed content unrelated to time, place and circumstance' (*Joint Anti-Fascist Refugee Committee v. McGrath*). The scope of situations that require due process and constitutional competence is broad; it ranges from employment, benefits, criminal process, prisons to taxes, and zoning (Rosenbloom and O'Leary 1997; Rosenbloom, Carroll, and Carroll 1999).

Constitutional values often come in conflict in specific cases and in important social issues. Both administrators and courts are called upon to balance interests. For example, the concern of equal protection versus prohibiting discrimination, both contained in the Fourteenth Amendment, raise conflicting values when considering civil rights laws and implementation of Affirmative Action for past wrongs. Some would consider these intractable issues, others would say they demonstrate the complex range of responsibilities and duties that have to be considered in administration (Frederickson 1990).

Constitutions limit and enable a particular government; thus, most of the federal constitution applies to the federal government. However, parts such as the Fourteenth Amendment place limits and duties on state and local governments. Constitutions and cases brought under constitutional provisions define both ethical and legal relationships. Constitutions impose restraints and restrictions on administrators; in addition, administrators may be personally liable for violating an individual's constitutional rights (Rosenbloom and O'Leary 1997).

II. THE ROLE OF THE COURTS

Law is often synonymous with judges and courts. Courts are seen as independent institutions of government while attorneys are seen as distinct professionals specializing in law. This viewpoint tends to see law as a separate and contentious domain tangential to public administration. Yet both courts and administrators look to the Constitution as source of values and obligations. Often, courts are asked to determine the legality or constitutionality of administrative actions. Two common assertions about lawsuits and government are that there is judicial interference in public administration and that lawsuits raise the cost of government. Related issues consider the role of courts and litigation, the judicial administrative partnership, the cost of litigation, developing public policy through litigation, and the shifting nature of liability. These raise the large and enduring issue of the role of courts and administration. The following sections will consider constitutional cases; appellate courts and administration; the rule of law philosophy; trials, litigation, and costs; and alternatives dispute resolution processes.

A. How Do Courts Interpret the Constitution?

The Supreme Court declared the right to interpret the meaning of laws and the Constitution itself (*Marbury v. Madison*, 5 US 137 [1803]). This gives the courts power to review, approve or reject actions by the other branches. The early administrative decisions by Hamilton in founding the national bank included an expansive view of authority under the Constitution for public administrators. The question of legitimacy of administration and practices was then the subject of a seminal Supreme Court decision. The implied powers of the legislature to undertake "necessary and proper" administration for the nation was decided by Chief Justice John Marshall in *McCulloch v. Maryland* which upheld the formation of the national bank. Marshall's decisions, including *McCulloch* and *Marbury*, established the legal foundations of the administrative state. Hamilton and Marshall both read the Constitution as empowering administration.

The constitutional powers of government are often at issue in cases which challenge specific actions of administrators or statutory schemes. What the Constitution means has been developed in a long line of Supreme Court cases. The extent and scope of constitutional duties developed in constitutional law cases conceptually fit in two categories: the structure and role of government branches and the civil rights litigation. Landmark Supreme Court cases interpreting constitutional duties such as equal protection in public schools may result in radical shifts in legal precedent. The implications of these constitutional decisions can produce a wide range of challenges for administrators.

Conceptually, constitutional cases are often divided between the powers of government and individual rights litigation. Administrators should know aspects of public law such as how to evaluate the way the court decides whether it should narrowly interpret the Constitution or if it can liberally consider the Constitution as a living document. Quite often, the framing of the issue and facts within a particular case affect how a court decides a dispute before them.

The ethical and legal duties under the Constitution are subjects discussed by administrators and judges. The Supreme Court as final arbiter of law determines which duties and rights exist under the law, but administrators must put the laws and decisions into practice. Due process, equal protection, and non-discrimination are three important constitutional concepts relating to justice that permeate government actions and how government treats individuals. These constitutional duties affect public servants because they carry out the law and activities of government. Both courts and administrators flesh out constitutional duties relating to ideals of fairness, justice, rights, and duties.

B. DO COURTS INTERFERE WITH ADMINISTRATION?

There is longstanding debate about the appropriate role of courts in reviewing legislation and actions of the executive branch and administrators. Often courts are portrayed as interfering with administration. These debates are centered on the balance of powers in action rather than in theory. Although the Supreme Court has authority to review the legality and constitutionality of the other branches' actions, the methods, extent of review, and effects have been contentious matters. Part of this debate considers whether judicial policymaking should be narrow or liberal. Others are concerned not just with deference to the other branches, but how courts make policy in their decisions (Barclay and Birkland 1998).

Some public administration scholarship addresses landmark decision of the Supreme Court and analyzes the implications of the cases for public administrators. For example, the 2000 *Bush v. Gore* decision was analyzed in relation to the democratic and practical aspects of election administration (Wise 2001) and the 1995 *Adarand Constructors v. Pena* decision was analyzed in relation to equal opportunity and public contract administration (Rice and Mongkuo 1998). Other scholars may take a line of Supreme Court cases and analyze the cases for the impact on administrative practices (O'Leary and Strausman 1993; O'leary 1989).

Cases where courts have enjoined and supervised administrative practice raise particular concern because these often involve tensions between issues of constitutional rights and acceptable government practices. For example, active judicial supervision of public service provision arose in litigation seeking to remedy discrimination in elementary and secondary schools (Wise and O'Leary 2003). Other examples of cases where there was active judicial supervision of administration include prison conditions or rights of the institutionalized (Rosenbloom and O'Leary 1997). Many of these cases involve important civil rights questions and government approaches to social problems.

Trial and appellate court decisions affect administrative practice. Court decisions may uphold or challenge the legality of existing practices, rights, or relationship. In addition, the results from landmark appellate decisions often affect general administrative processes and procedures beyond those at issue in the case. Administrative practices often shift to address the issue addressed in court decisions, or dominant legal viewpoints. The shift can be radical or incremental. Sometimes major shifts in legal viewpoints have enormous implications on administrators. One shift occurred in the judicial review of legislation and administrative action from a strict interpretation approach before 1930 to a deferential to administrative expertise and delegations approach from the 1930s to 1960s. The shift towards new property has had enormous impact. The shift from viewing jobs as privileges to the legal status of jobs involving property rights held by individuals has come with the attendant requirement on managers to provide due process when disciplining or firing has spawned calls for reform of the procedures. The shift from representing social programs as government largess, or gifts subject to terms and conditions, towards being property also required due process elements of notice, gathering information, and hearings prior to termination found in the cases of *Goldberg* and progeny (Rosenbloom and O'Leary 1997).

Another type of scholarship considers how court decisions affect administration by survey a line of landmark cases by topic area. Some examples of the trends in cases studies are: privacy (Boling 1994); ethics (Roberts 1999); Federalism changes (Wise 2001; Wise and O'Leary 1997);

sex discrimination (Greenlaw, Kohl, and Lee 1998); comparable worth (Moore and Abraham 1994); and the courts' use of the term public service (Richman 1997).

There have been differing ways to categorize how courts approach the review of legislation, regulation, and administrative action. The current approach is to consider this a partnership between administrator and the courts. A historic review and discussion shows this was an uneasy partnership with differing levels of deference by the courts to administrative interpretation of statutes and administrative processes (Cooper 1985). Another view looks at the courts and legislature as partners in establishing values and goals (Rosenbloom 2000b). In subject areas where litigation and legislation affect administrative actions—such as personnel management—the partnership language reflects areas of shared concerns and the ongoing development of legal relationships (O'Leary 1994b).

When discussing courts, scholars often evaluate them as either an institution or individual actor. Each state has its own laws and court system so there may be multiple laws and court decisions affecting administrators. Most of the cases discussed are appellate and federal decisions, with particular emphasis on Supreme Court opinions. Courts make policy in their decisions that interpret, extend or overturn prior court decree, when they uphold or overturn administrative decisions and rulemaking, and when they uphold or strike down legislation.

C. How Does Legal Reasoning of Courts Relate to Administrative Decision-Making?

Common law develops through cases through appellate challenges to the existing doctrine or by distinguishing facts of one case from prior case precedent. As a result, law develops not by looking at the norms, but by reporting the new question or the exception to prior decisions. This attention to established precedent leads to parsing of terms. It focuses on individual or unique circumstances rather than general and stable rules. This approach of legal reasoning is a characteristic of law as a separate profession and discipline. Administrators tend to develop general rules that can be generally applied to a given group which reflects more of a legislative norm towards laws. The mode of analogic reasoning is also distinct from the predominant paradigms of social science research design.

Supreme Court decisions do not follow the empirical or survey-based research approaches so common in social science. Court decisions are decided by using a different type of rationale based on data, facts, context, existing rules, persuasive argument, and deliberation. Both the individual issue and the legal context are evaluated. An appellate case affects the litigants before it; then, as precedent, the decision becomes an authoritative legal rule of general applicability. In public law, a useable and applied history is found in case precedent. In public administration literature, precedent and cases are too often seen as merely anecdotal and not based on empirical or systematic analyses.

Judicial reasoning differs from administrative decision-making. Guiding judicial decisions are these five major principles regarding the conduct of government and society (Altman 1996, 3–7):

1. Law serves to define, enable, constrain, and regulate the power of government and its agents.
2. Government should maintain civil order and peace mainly through a system of general and authoritative rules.
3. Laws should be public and reasonably clear in meaning (with specified sanctions); allow for compliance and prospective (not retroactive), impartial, and consistent application; and be enacted in accordance with preexisting rules.
4. Government must give all persons accused of violating the law and rules a fair chance to defend themselves; fairness includes having an impartial court or arbiter to resolve disputes and add clarity to uncertain areas of law.

5. People must act within the requirements of legality, both as individuals and as government. Government must not act or operate above the law.

These rules of law reflect judicial philosophy (jurisprudence) about government. The elements
of judicial reasoning link decision-making and the rule of law to ideals of fairness, justice, and
integrity. It does not privilege efficiency but it does emphasize a type of accountability. It includes
components about the ethics or expressions of what the institutions of government—legislature,
executive courts, and administrators—should do.

D. Do Lawsuits Interfere with Administration?

Disputes about government actions often result in claims. How to resolve disputes is a longstanding
concern, and litigation is one tactic. Some disputes result in individuals suing government for relief.
The concern of what affect litigation has on government is expressed in both the academic and
practitioner journals. Most of the government litigation writings examine the role of government in
defending lawsuits. There are concerns about litigation regarding budget effects (MacManus 1994;
MacManus and Turner 1993); the time and monetary costs of litigation (Rudman 1999); and how
being sued adds inefficiency or uncertainty to management (Kagan 1991). The shift from sovereign
immunity to official and government liability is a longstanding concern (Lee and Otting 2001).
   Claims and lawsuits may also raise managerial concerns about feedback and managerial
processes. The attention tends to be on the costs rather than the underlying causes of liability.
What administrators do to reduce risks and decrease negligent behavior is worth attention. Lawsuits
have sparked some studies about the long-term effects of litigation on management practices or
policy emphasis (e.g., O'Leary and Strausman 1993). One study examined whether liability limitations affected the level of care in highway maintenance (Clayed 1994). Another view is that tort
litigation caused the move towards formalism and caution—or legalism—that imposed costs on
government and business and lead to rule-bound, cautious behavior (Kagan 1991; Sitkin and Bies
1994). The tort reform movement is very much one of political and special interest arguments.
When some scholars have investigated the assertions of the outrageous costs of tort awards, they
found that empirical data do not support these assertions.
   Lawsuits are brought by aggrieved individuals; it is a constitutional right to bring grievances.
Most grievances, claims, and lawsuits are brought by individuals on claims arising in contract or
torts. As a result of lawsuits, courts declare managers and bureaucrats exceeded authority, wrongly
harmed individuals, failed to follow requirements, and agencies are often liable for monetary
damages awarded in these cases. Courts uphold administrative decisions, approve discretion, and
find government not at fault. In these cases, courts measure accountability, evaluate responsibility,
and decide duties of public managers and their programs. Court challenges by employees, regulated
industries, and private citizens are costs of feedback for democratic accountability (Kelly 1998), but
this role of checks and balances, feedback, and accountability is seldom discussed.
   Many of the social changes and civil rights at the end of the twentieth century were gained
through public interest litigation. Some scholars promote public interest litigation as a mode to
change policy (Schuck 1983). School desegregation, prisoners' rights, entitlements, and new property resulted from court cases that sought to change government practices and public policy. What
is seldom studied is that government, through selective appeals and litigation, establishes policies.
Two examples of government policy making through litigation are the recent public interest
lawsuits against the tobacco and gun industries brought by state Attorneys General (Stone and
Thomas 1999).

E. What Are the Alternatives to Litigation?

Litigation is a common concern. Businesses, individuals, and governments are concerned about
how to avoid it or at least reduce the costs and uncertainty of lawsuits. Lawyers and judges also

have longstanding concerns about litigation. Judges and legal scholars decry crowded dockets and increasing delays in hearing cases. Judges manage the civil cases before them by encouraging settlement before a trial is held.

Government, businesses, and others complain of the high costs of litigation, but disputes continue to occur. Disputes must be resolved in a fair and just manner so administration should be concerned with conflict resolution (Lan 1997). In recent years, the trend has moved toward avoiding lawsuits coupled with the advancement of alternative dispute resolution (ADR) techniques. Some administrative agencies have a depth of experience with ADR (O'Leary and Raines 2001), and many administrative agencies are implementing ADR practices. There is a history of successful use of ADR techniques such as mediation, structured negotiation, and arbitration; recent statutes have encouraged ADR over traditional agency adjudication or litigation (Bingham 1997). Cost is often a justification for ADR. In addition to avoiding the procedures and delay of court trials, ADR is also proposed to be less disputatious and adversarial. ADR is promoted as a way to maintain ongoing relationships and work on common interests through cooperation, rather than encouraging positional attitudes that may damage relationships.

Court cases are expected to be open and notorious; thus, there is more public accountability in them. Court cases allow the underlying laws to be challenged through the appeals process while ADR proceedings do not have an appeals process. Thus, there are strategic and public policy considerations in deciding whether to litigate or to use alternative approaches.

III. THE DEVELOPMENT OF ADMINISTRATIVE LAW

The roots of scholarship on public administration can be traced to Goodnow's 1893 work on administrative law. Goodnow's focus and definition of administrative law is more generous than what lawyers and legal scholars today consider as administrative law. For Goodnow, administrative law included the operations, techniques, and processes that are now seen as public administration. When current public administration scholars discuss law, they often mean the current view of administrative law that is centered on the Administrative Procedure Act (APA).

An early debate about public administration focused on the role and extent of law in the administrative process. It was tied to the expansion and shifting roles of the federal government and is an important part of the history of public administration. It also foreshadows many continuing controversies: the appropriate role of administrative action, the source of authority, the extent of review, and the imposition of rules and procedures. This section will look at two themes in administrative law. The first will be the historic roots of administrative law and debates about the role of law in administration. The second theme addresses the workings and effect of the Administrative Procedure Act (APA) on administrators.

A. How Is Administrative Law Related to the Development of the Field of Public Administration?

Historically, public law was one beginning point for the study and practice of public administration both in Europe and the United States. This was at a time when the division of specialties in the academy was more fluid and law was included in undergraduate curricula. Wilson's famous 1887 essay calling for a science of administration explicitly links law and administration (Wilson 1998). At the close of the nineteenth century, public administration knowledge was extracted by Goodnow in a comparison of US government practices and law to the practices and laws of England, France, and Germany (1893). Yet reading this treatise shows that the operations, not just legal authority, were matters that interested Goodnow. Early classic public administration scholars, particularly Leonard White (1926), advocated moving public administration from law into the area of management study.

Administration is separate and distinct from law became the dominant doctrine of the relationship between public administration and law. Sometimes this doctrine is tacit; law is noticeable by its absence in basic public administration textbooks. At other times scholars argue that law obstructs, interferes, or detracts from administration. Some scholars have raised the issue of whether this doctrine is valid and useful (e.g., Cooper and Newland 1997; Dimock 1936; Rosenbloom 1994); one response to the negative attitude towards law focused on the "neglected foundations of public law" (Moe and Gilmour 1995).

The nineteenth century definition of administrative law, meaning the law and management of government, shifted around 1930 from ordering, structuring, and enabling government action to the current view of administrative regulatory procedure and processes embodied in the APA (Bryner 1998). Legal scholars' and judges' approach to law shifted. The legal realist approach in legal scholarship also led towards considering law—court decisions and legislation—distinct from the operations of government. The development of distinct professions of management, public administration, law, and others also contributed to the separation, specialization, and categorization of responsibilities (Green, Keller and Wamsley 1993). The separation of law and administration is tied to social changes, particularly the professionalization movement.

The APA was proposed to codify administrative procedure that modeled rule making on legislative powers and agency adjudications on judicial practice. The shift away from law was not just to management and social science models; the shift in focus also engendered a hostility to law and legal principles, particularly due process and judicial review. It is ironic that legal concerns were de-emphasized in study just as federal regulatory action was increasing during the New Deal.

There were prominent and important debates early in the twentieth century about the role of administrators and the political and legal context in which they acted (Cooper 2000). These debates considered public interest and the administrative state, and they lead to the development of standardized administrative process. Contemporaries of White, Gulick, and Brownlow considered the role of government and administration in the context of law and the public interest. Dewey's influential *The Public and Its Problems* (1927) considered the role and responsibilities between government and the public. The development of the administrative state was the subject of important debates about the role of government, public problems, administrative process, and the extent of administrative powers (Frank 1942; Frankfurter 1930; Freund 1928; Gaus, White and Dimock 1936; Gellhorn 1941; Landis 1938). Administration, governance, and public service were called "civic art" (White and Smith 1939). These important public interest discussions are seldom reflected in the history of the field, even though law and legal instruments and methods were a central part of the debate. What is best know from this era is the Brownlow Commission report which came in the midst of this 1937 debate and included Gulick's executive duties acronym PODSCORB, which stands for Planning, Organizing, Staffing, Directing, Coordinating, reporting and Budgeting.

Experience with independent regulatory agencies such as the Interstate Commerce Commission (ICC), established in 1887, was well known during these public interest debates. Regulatory agencies could address numerous concerns such as technology and innovation, public problems, inadequate response by states to national problems, the fusion of court and legislative powers, and the use of administrative restraint (Rohr 1986). The need for administrative process and agency flexibility were presented eloquently by Landis (1938). Landis argued that agencies were not just an extension of the executive, but they could cure the flaws of the executive, legislative, and judicial branches. By containing all governmental authority, developing specialized expertise, and establishing long-term employees, agencies could balance the powers of businesses to achieve public goals. Specifically, agency adjudications could cure some of the defects in the legal process. The particular defect of concern was the common law process which relies on individuals' suits to both enforce claims and interests and change the common law through the appeals process. Because the common law was slow, costly and not systematic in addressing problems, the alternative proposed emphasized agencies that could investigate and fashion policies that applied to all. Agencies could propose legislation to advance policies in the public interest. For Landis, the ultimate test of an agency was the policies it developed.

Frank (1942) reached back to Madison's "If men were angels" language to argue that systematic controls and checks were important as well. Frank argued that uniform procedures embodied in an administrative procedures law would provide this structure. The debate about administrative powers reflects concerns of pragmatism and public responsiveness. This debate about forming a framework statute that established regularized administrative process for making rules and adjudicating disputes was included in the early editions of *Public Administration Review* (e.g., Jaffe 1942). Challenges to New Deal programs in pivotal Supreme Court cases such as *Schecter Poultry (1935)* and the Hot Oil case (*Panama Refining 1935*) centered on questions of the extent of administrative power. A central question was how Congress should delegate and define administrative agency powers (Rosenbloom and O'Leary 1997, 38–40). Many scholars refer to the development of these administrative agencies between the 1880s and the 1930s as the development of the administrative state.

Because the breadth of powers and responsibilities granted to agencies, some began to call agencies the fourth branch of government. Many were concerned about whether there was systematic and democratic accountability in these independent boards and agencies. The Attorney General's Committee on Administrative Management, which reported in 1941, considered in-depth concerns about systematic administrative procedures (Rosenbloom 2000a). In part, the form and impetus for the APA can be directly traced to E. Blythe Stason and two other dissenters who included an APA with their dissent to the Attorney General's Report. In large part, this draft became the APA five years later. The development of administrative agencies and administrative powers that were regularized in the APA in 1946 reflected existing innovations and shifts in governmental powers.

The development of the administrative state in the last decades of the nineteenth century and the early decades of the twentieth century also brought a shift in the attention from an age of common law to the age of statutes (Calabresi 1982). When individuals and businesses challenged government regulations, the court's interpretations of government authority to act and the nature of legislation at first was very narrow and limiting. Legislative delegation and language became important, and the court allowed broader power after the *Schecter* and *Panama Refining* cases raised the public debate about the administrative state. Yet the manner and scope of legislative delegation of administrative powers remains a concern in law. However, the focus in public administration writings has been on the executive and agencies carrying out the tasks of government. Often the concerns discussed in the administrative literature about developing programs or agency powers are considered under the auspices of public policy with few references to statues and laws.

The APA regularized the administrative state, yet it also marked the shift towards a legislative-centered public administration (Rosenbloom 2000a). This shift raises the question of whether public administration is accountable both to the legislature and the executive; and an additional question of whether administration is a distinct government institution. An understanding of the history and arguments underlying the development of the administrative state shows the broad intermixture of legal, political, social, and administrative aspects.

B.   What Does Administrative Law Mean Now and How Does It Affect Administrators?

To lawyers and judges, administrative law is a rather narrow classification that now means the APA and cases interpreting it—or the source of administrative procedure. Although there is a great deal of legal scholarship on issues of delegation, interpretation of statues, judicial deference, and legal requirements for due process (see Sargentich 1994), it is rare to take an interdisciplinary approach that includes both legal, political, and administrative concerns (see Shuck 1994). Another common

definition of administrative law is the law created by administrative agencies by way of rules, regulations, or decisions—; or the legal products of agencies. Both the source and product definitions
of administrative law are linked to the APA as a quasi-constitutive statute—; or a statute that
establishes broad guidelines of types of powers and processes. There is public administration
scholarship about the major components of the APA and implications for governance.

Administrative law is now linked to the APA, and the more generous definition that included all
law that affects governance is no longer used. There are numerous textbooks and works about the
APA. Most textbooks are written for law students, so administrative law is often seen from
the "vantage point of a lawyer with a client who faced action by an agency" (Cooper 1990, 258).
The theme of many of these texts is how to successfully challenge administrative process. The
process of adjudication, the minimum standards, the qualification of administrative law judges, the
due process requirements, and standards of court review have often have been the subject of APA
litigation. The informal and discretionary aspects of administrative process that are not subject to
litigation are de-emphasized or nearly ignored in legal texts, and these are the aspects that may be of
most interest to administrators.

The main parts of the APA include: rule making, adjudication, the Freedom of Information Act,
and open government provisions. These have been studied from a public administration viewpoint.
The legal requirements for formal rule making, which include evidentiary hearings, are compared
to informal, notice and comment, rule making. When analyzing rule making there are a number of
factors to discuss: process, substance, management, participation, oversight—by executive, legislative, and judicial branches—and theory. The give-and-take process of informal rule making has
procedures required by law but it also has numerous procedures required by organizational, policy,
and political considerations (Kerwin 2003). What is noteworthy about Kerwin's influential book on
rule making is its subtitle: "How government agencies write law and make policy." This clearly
expresses that agencies are law makers.

Public administration studies regarding APA adjudication or rule making often take the tack of
explaining and interpreting the implications of a lead appellate case. Some take a broader view and
look at administrative and organizational practice. One impressive study across agencies based on
due process standards was by Verkuil in 1976. This study evaluated how forty-two different
agencies used the ten due process factors from *Goldberg v. Kelly (1970)* in hearings and decisions.
Verkuil's four conclusions were: (1) there is a range of administrative adjudication formality even
in a small sample; (2) agencies used their own discretion when adopting procedures, not the
influence of court orders or statutory prescriptions; (3) "determination on the record" and other
Goldberg terms have specific legal meaning, and so an understanding of court decisions on due
process is need by agency personnel; and (4) the determination of which procedures are needed and
the test to decide at any given point is a matter of considering the situation and balancing interests
and needs of the agency and parties.

Administrative law is viewed differently. Legal scholars emphasized how administrative
powers have been defined by the APA and limited through litigation. For the administrator,
often the informal processes that involved developing and enforcing the rules are of greater importance. These informal aspects deal with the governance actions of administration and
implementation of policies.

IV. THE EXTENT OF REGULATION

The common statement of the purpose for governments found in constitutions is: government is to
promote the general health, safety, and welfare of the public. The government accomplishes these
duties through regulation. Defining acceptable and desirable behavior and consequences is one
purpose of rules and regulations; this is external regulation. This regulatory function of government
carried out by agencies and public administrators. There are also regulations addressing the

standard operating procedures and practices that affect the internal operations. The common phrase command and control is used to describe rules and regulations. Yet a persistent issue is the extent of regulations. Quite often this issue considers the negative view of regulation as red tape. To others, there are more theoretical and practical inquiries as to how rules are used and how they might be improved. These aspects of regulation are discussed below.

A.   Is There Too Much Red Tape?

Red tape is a phrase that often means government rules, regulations, and processes. When people rail against red tape they mean they are subjected to too many constraints, that many of the constraints seem pointless, and that agencies seem to take forever to act (Kaufman 1977, 5). Thus, there are many calls to reduce red tape as a way to reform bureaucracy and government. At other times, red tape is a rallying cry for political or strategic purpose. It is next to impossible to answer the beginning question about an appropriate amount of regulation.

The pejorative term red tape is pervasive. Although it once was descriptive and more neutral, red tape, like bureaucracy, is now imbued with negative connotations. Although some critics talk about getting rid of unnecessary or excessive red tape, the term often implies that all government requirements found in statutes, rules, and regulations are red tape and thus unnecessary. The discussion of red tape often begins with why it is wrong. Trying to defend government requirements is met with the single rejoinder: red tape. Then the discussion is over.

There are many attacks on red tape and very few are willing to defend it. Goodsell, in particular, in *The Case for Bureaucracy* (1994) forcefully defends bureaucracy. This defense of bureaucracy explains how the procedures and practices found in established rules and procedures provide accountability, predictability, information, and fairness for both the administrators and the affected public. Thus, bureaucratic practices and regulations are tied to conceptions of public service for citizens. Yet, as Kaufman said, "One person's red tape may be another's treasured safeguard" (1977, 4). For the purposes here, the balance of rules, regulations, and protected rights will be the subject of discussion.

Often when courts review rules and regulations the concerns focus on values of information, accountability, and deliberation. Courts scrutinize notices about proposed action, gather sufficient data to support the decision, present information, deliberate as the decision maker, and then disclose how the decision was reached. These due process expectations comport with public management values of informed decisions. Thus, court cases about regulations may consider the process in which rules were made and whether the regulations are narrowly tailored to meet government purposes, but do not interfere with individuals' rights. Regulation also occurs through adjudication or the case-by-case hearings. The decision process and fairness of adjudication, may also be evaluated in court cases.

Critics suggest that these decision-process requirements embodied in rules interfere with management, impair creativity, and are inefficient. In some public management works, there are calls for deregulating public service and removing legal constraints on management (D'Iulio 1994; Kettl et al. 1996; Barzelay 1992). Although some critics may maintain that external regulation of crime, environment, and public health is legitimate, they want to liberate managers from excessive or unnecessary internal rules. Often these critiques are closely linked to the reinventing government movement and the claim that regulation and red tape interfere with customer orientation.

Some critiques of red tape even suggest that managers should ignore rules and laws because that success requires "circumventing or subverting political and institutional obstacles" (Levin and Sanger 1994, 269). Lawyers are socialized differently about following rules. Lawyers will review existing case law and rules to see if they are still in force and apply to the given situation, and if lawyers are confronted with rules that apply, then they consider it their obligation to either follow or seek to change the rule (Carter 1994). Thus, ignoring a valid and applicable rule would violate professional norms.

The complaints and antagonism towards process and court decisions in some public management literature are often coupled with calls to reduce red tape. Terry (1998) discussed this theme as liberation management, where good managers are impeded by bad rules and bad processes. Others say ambiguous or gray areas of law should not intimidate strategic public management (Landsbergen and Orosz 1996). Although there may be good rules and bad red tape, Kaufman's (1977) analysis of red tape raises three points from a practical viewpoint: (1) society, including public servants and managers, makes red tape; (2) the value of red tape and regulation differs by point of view; and (3) those who make red tape can remove or change it when it is outmoded. The critiques and enumerations of red tape often miss these points.

B. HOW ARE RULES AND REGULATIONS USED AND EVALUATED?

An underlying issue is whether there are more objective ways to discuss rules and regulations. There has been some research and scholarship about how rules and regulation are used and evaluated. In addition to Bozeman's (2000) recent efforts to develop a testable theory of red tape, others have examined how regulation affects administrators. Some have looked at how particular statutes and rules are implemented, for instance, disability law (Koenig 2001). Others may ask if tools, such as cost-benefit analysis, are legal (Zerbe 1998). Still others have focused on areas such as employment law and regulations, and perhaps the most developed area of regulation is in the field of environmental regulations. Others consider whether bureaucratic enforcement of rules and distribution of benefits adequately considers the public, and some ask if there is bureaucratic justice.

There is some research about the effect of red tape. An example: one simulated experiment in assigning benefits by caseworkers defined high red tape as writing explanations for decisions, and low red tape as filling out a checklist (Scott and Pandey 2000). This red tape research lacked considering or connecting the values of accountability and informed clientele that are part of due process. Thus, legal and management rationales for rules and procedures were glossed over. The hopeful sign is the attempt to engage in research on the use of regulations and opinions about red tape, rather than starting from a polemic base.

The need for more objective research on rules and regulations is a concern. There is an increasing scholarship and recognition that rules and regulations are policy instruments. Attention focused on differing tools and techniques in forming, instituting, and accomplishing goals is an approach more common in European studies (see Lane 2000). Stone (1997) discusses inducements, rules, information, rights, and powers. Schneider and Ingram (1997) discuss how policy designs include tools, rules, and rationales. Ostrom and colleagues have looked carefully at rules used to structure patterns of interaction. The focus on rules-in-use rather than rules-in-form is a part of a theory of institutional rational design, where institution is defined as "the shared concepts used by humans in repetitive situations organized by rules, norms, and strategies" (Ostrom 1999, 37).

The shift towards looking at policy instruments and theories of regulation can clearly be linked to both law and administration. This shift also reflects the rise of a more mature public choice body of literature. Public choice scholars now view law as a method of facilitating choices in process as well as goals. The move towards the concern of norms, decision-making, and accomplishing social goals is one approach for public administration discussions to overcome the animosity of the red tape label and look at how administrators, target groups, and the general public are affected by rules and regulations.

V. THE LEGAL INFLUENCE ON ADMINISTRATIVE PRACTICE

Law is very broad and it can be categorized in many ways: public and private law; common and statutory law; procedural and substantive law; and constitutional, administrative, civil, and criminal law. Civil law includes substantive areas of contracts, property, torts, and family law.

A complicating factor is that there may be either federal law or state laws that apply to a given situation. There are two very practical issues to consider. What law does an administrator need to know? How does law contribute to a robust public administration?

A. WHAT LAW DOES AN ADMINISTRATOR NEED TO KNOW?

In law, a fundamental tenet is "Ignorance of the law is no excuse." Yet studies have shown that in general, people do not understand either substantive or procedural law. The public is concerned with fairness, but their preconceptions and understanding about the justice system are in conflict with the technical and legal interpretations (O'Barr and Conle 1988). This raises a similar concern about what administrators understand about the nexus of law and administration. Some would say administrators need to know administrative and constitutional law. Others say that administrators and street-level bureaucrats need to develop expertise in areas of law that affect them.

A general understanding of public law may provide a base, but there are also processes that connect to substantive areas seen as private common law. For example, contract law affects two administrative processes currently being promoted: contracting out and ADR. These contracting and ADR processes are advocated on the grounds of efficiency and cost effectiveness. However, contracting out requires understanding of not just developing agreements but the very real administrative and legal difficulties of contract enforcement. In contracting out services, the long-term relationship between the parties and the ongoing nature of the agreement is important. Thus, when there are problems, they do not fit neatly under contract law which might allow for declaring a breach and suing for damages. ADR may be required but in many instances it is agreed to by the disputants and so trying to obtain court review of ADR problems may be based on contract law principles. Theorists note that ADR processes can intimidate or maintain disparate power relationships, and so they raise questions of the fundamental fairness of ADR.

When it comes to public administrators, knowing the law has been translated into a responsibility: " [A] reasonably competent public official should know the law governing his conduct" (*Harlow v. Fitzgerald*, 487 US 800, 819 (1982)). Reviewing courts expect administrators to develop expertise in interpreting the statutes and laws relating to their programs and duties, and courts give deference to these interpretations. Courts do not yield on administrative interpretations on constitutional questions.

As Rosenbloom has pointed out many times, constitutional competence is a necessary skill for administrators (Rosenbloom, Carroll, and Carroll 1999; Rosenbloom and O'Leary 1997). This leads to another issue: how do administrators gain expertise and maintain an understanding of laws? Although law is a recommended subject for Master of Public Administration degrees, the main texts address administrative law more often from the perspective of legal concerns about due process or judicial restraint. Texts that emphasize constitutional concerns combine both a general understanding of constitutional duties as well as the warning that individual administrators can be individually liable for violating a person's constitutional rights. A corollary to understanding law considers whether there are distinct administrative concerns in evaluating law. "What needs to be examined, the perspective that needs to be remembered is the effect of administrative law practices and procedures on the agency, its people and its operations. We are not surprised when the lawyer ignores this viewpoint" (Dolan 1984, 89).

B. HOW DOES LAW CONTRIBUTE TO A ROBUST PUBLIC ADMINISTRATION?

One common theme is that law is a distinct domain from public administration. Scholarly and practitioner articles quite often begin as arguments or criticisms that emphasize the flaws or limitations that law places on administration. Law is often presented as mechanistic, intrusive, technocratic, inflexible, and expensive. The idea of law as rigid and unchanging is a common conception in public administration scholarship; yet this is not the case. A balanced consideration might address why limits are there and how to best develop administrative processes to be consistent with constitutional, statutory, and policy demands.

When law-related subjects are presented in a more favorable manner in public administration scholarship, the discussion is often regarding democratic or founding values. Decision-making is seen as an administrative skill, but it may not be connected to court decisions. In other areas where there are links, the language often shifts to discuss adopting and implementing policy rather than recognizing law or legal instruments such as statutes or executive orders. Thus, how law in statutes, court decisions, and regulations contributes to the robust practice of democratic administration and governance is seldom addressed in depth.

It is clear that law and administration are linked. "With the revolt against the legal approach to government, the legal aspects of public administration were, as a direct result, given insufficient attention for a considerable time. This was obviously unfortunate because the administration of law necessarily begins with an understanding of law and the policies which are to be enforced" (Dimock 1936, 6). Public law includes statutes, the Constitution, rules, executive orders, and court decisions that affect governance and public administration. A broader conception of the scope of governance puts public law as the foundation for the structure and theory of public administration (Moe and Gilmour 1995). This issue remains unsettled: how to link public law to the mainstream doctrine and practice of public administration.

VI. CONCLUSION

Themes of underlying ambivalence and antagonism towards law occur throughout much of the public administration literature. Law makes administration inefficient is often the subtext. The sheer repetition of these allegations without the balancing concerns of the legal process, fundamental fairness, statutory authority, and constitutional requirements raises concerns about the values in governance. Although the practice of public administration is concerned with efficiency, this is tempered by responsibility to enforce the law in a fair and consistent manner. Unfortunately, law is often presented as distinct from or interfering with public administration. What is needed is integration and balance. Both law and administration are integral parts of government; one does not exist without the other.

The gaps in the critiques and caricatures of law in the administrative scholarship challenge the doctrines of due process and the underlying philosophy of the rule of law. The legal-rational approach to public administration is most often presented as limiting, rule-bound, obstructive, and antagonistic to flexible efficient management. Granted, some of these representations are straw man arguments establishing a need for reform, but too often they do not proposed remedies to the flaws they describe. Some of the critiques seem to be at their core libertarian or anarchistic. In the alternative, when courts consider rational decision-making by administrators, they emphasize the source of the authority, whether actions are consistent, if there are facts that are gathered and disclosed, and if there is deliberation based on the rule and the facts before them. Courts then emphasize that the bases of government decisions are disclosed to the affected parties and to the general public. This deliberative legal rationality takes into consideration both individual facts and the immediate context. This deliberative legal rationality emphasizes process to allow both for flexibility in situations and an expression about what is good management. Deliberative legal rationality requires balancing considerations to serve in the public interest, but court decisions may not consider the long-term social implications and public interest that legislation or administration.

An additional concern in evaluating the great issues in public law and public administration is the concern of understanding the law. The debates about the intent or the pragmatic considerations occur regularly in public law and public administration discourse and scholarship. These text or context positions about interpretation of authoritative documents formed in the democratic process occur in court decisions. Understanding the delegations and established rules are present in the task of administration. But the analysis and colloquy is often within either the legal profession or the administrative realm. There remains a seldom-addressed concern about whether the public understands the technical and formal language of statutes, court decisions, administrative rules, and process. This is not merely a problem of jargon. This problem of complexity and formality affects the accountability and transparency of government. Thus, a question in law and administration is not just how the public understands this written authority, but how to make it more accessible.

Clearly, the connections to constitutional foundations, ethical responsibilities, and legal process can be better integrated into the public administration literature. Statues, rules, and regulations are developed to promote public goals. They can be changed or repealed if they no longer serve the public interest. The critiques often omit these concerns. The critiques of courts and litigation also lack objective balance. They omit the democratic aspects. It is a fundamental right for the public to challenge government actions in courts; it is part of the checks and balances to allow open hearings to provide accountability and public information. Too often the focus is on costs rather than on democratic benefits when law and litigation are discussed.

At their heart the great issues address both the political and philosophical role of government. The issues are enduring and important. Questions of delegation, discretion, and appropriate use of power are not easily resolved. The great issues of justice, fairness, duties, and rights are important in the field of law and administration. Legal disputes are not abstract; litigation involves real individuals with real problems in real situations. Supreme Court cases have profound impacts on administration and governance.

The great issues in public law and public administration address both theory and practice, but it is time to end the longstanding negative undercurrent in public administration literature about law. In the checks and balances of democratic governance, laws do not obstruct, courts do not interfere, and regulations do not impede. Public law and public administration share concerns about practices, actions, procedures, and goals. The important theme in all the great issues is how to balance the shared concerns of law and administration in the serving the public interest.

CASES

Adarand Constructors, Inc. v. Pena., 515 US 200 (1995).
Bush v. Gore, US 98 (2000).
Goldberg v. Kelly, 397 US 254 (1970).
Harlow v. Fitzgerald, 457 US 800 (1982).
Joint Anti-Fascist Refugee Committee v. McGrath, 341 US 123b (1951).
Marbury v. Madison, 5 US 137 (1803).
Mathews v. Eldridge, 424 US 316 (1819).
McCulloch v. Maryland, 17 US 316 (1819).
Panama Refining Co. v. Ryan, 293 US 388 (1935).
Schecter Poultry Co. v. US, 295 US 495 (1935).

REFERENCES

Altman, A., *Arguing about the Law: An Introduction to Legal Philosophy*, Wadsworth, Belmont, CA, 1996.
Barclay, S. and Birkland, T., Law, policy making, and the policy process: closing the gaps, *Policy Studies Journal*, 26, 227–243, 1998.
Barzelay, M., *Breaking through Bureaucracy*, University of California Press, Berkeley, CA, 1992.

Beckett, J., "The government should run like a business" mantra, *The American Review of Public Adminis-trtion*, 30(2), 185–204, 2000.

Bingham, L. B., Alternative dispute resolution in public administration, In *Handbook of Public Law and Administration*, Cooper, P. J. and Newland, C. A., Eds., Jossey-Bass, San Francisco, CA, pp. 546–566, 1997.

Boling, P., Privacy as autonomy versus privacy as familial attachment: a conceptual approach to the right of privacy, *Policy Studies Review*, 13(1–2), 91–110, 1994.

Bozeman, B., *Bureaucracy and Red Tape*, Prentice Hall, Upper Saddle River, NJ, 2000.

Bryner, G. C., Limiting bureaucratic discretion: competing theories of administrative law, In *Active Duty: Public Administration as Democratic Statesmanship*, Schaeffer, R. M. and Schaeffer, D. L., Eds., Rowman and Littlefield, Langham, MD, pp. 237–260, 1998.

Calabresi, G., *A Common Law for the Age of Statutes*, Harvard University Press, Cambridge, MA, 1982.

Carter, L. H., *Reason in Law*, 4th ed., HarperCollins, New York, 1994.

Carter, L. H. and Harrington, C. B., *Administrative Law and Politics: Cases and Comments*, HarperCollins, New York, 1991.

Clayed, S. H., Effect of liability limitations on the level of care in the public sector: the case of highway maintenance, *Public Finance Quarterly*, 22(4), 483–497, 1994.

Cooper, P. J., Conflict or constructive tension: the changing relationship between judges and administrators, *Public Administration Review*, 45(6), 643–652, 1985.

Cooper, P. J., Public law and public administration. In *Public Administration the State of the Discipline*, Lynn, N. B. and Wildavsky, A., Eds., Chatham House, Chatham, NJ, pp. 256–284, 1990.

Cooper, P. J., *Public Law and Public Administration*, 3rd ed., F.E. Peacock Publishers, Itaska, IL, 2000.

Cooper, P. J. and Newland, C. A., *Handbook of Public Law and Administration*, Jossey-Bass, San Francisco, CA, 1997.

Crockett, R. W. and Gilmore, J. A., Retaliation: agency theory and gaps in the law, *Public Personnel Management*, 28, 39–49, 1999.

D'Iulio, J. J. Jr., *Deregulating the Public Service: Can Government be Improved?*, Brookings Institute, Washington, DC, 1994.

Davis, K. C., *Discretionary Justice: A Preliminary Inquiry*, Louisiana State Univ. Press, Baton Rouge, LA, 1969.

Dewey, J., *The Public and Its Problems*, Holt, New York, 1927.

Dimock, M. E., The meaning and scope of public administration, In *The Frontiers of Public Administration*, Gaus, J. M., White, L. D., and Dimock, M. E., Eds., Univ. of Chicago Press, Chicago, IL, pp. 1–12, 1936.

Dolan, M. W., Administrative law and public administration, *Public Administration Review*, 44(1), 86–89, 1984.

Eskridge, W. N., Jr., Interpretation of statutes, In *A Companion to Philosophy of Law and Legal Theory*, Patterson, D., Ed., Blackwell Press, Cambridge, MA, pp. 200–208, 1996.

Frank, J., *If Men Were Angels: Some Aspects of Government in a Democracy*, Harper and Brothers, New York, 1942.

Frankfurter, F., *The Public and Its Government*, Yale University Press, New Haven, CT, 1930.

Frankfurter, F., A symposium on statutory construction: foreword, *Vanderbilt Law Review*, 3, 356–368, 1950.

Frederickson, H. G., Public administration and social equity, *Public Administration Review*, 50(2), 228–237, 1990.

Freund, E., *Administrative Powers over Persons and Property*, University of Chicago Press, Chicago, IL, 1928.

Gaus, J. M., White, L. D., and Dimock, M. E., *The Frontiers of Public Administration*, Univ. of Chicago Press, Chicago, IL, 1936.

Gellhorn, W., *Federal Administrative Proceedings*, Johns Hopkins Press, Baltimore, MD, 1941.

Gill, J., Formal models of legislative/administrative interaction: a survey of the subfield, *Public Administration Review*, 55(1), 99–107, 1995.

Goodsell, C. T., *The Case for Bureaucracy*, 3rd ed., Chatham House, Chatham, NJ, 1994.

Goodnow, F. J., *Comparative Administrative Law: An Analysis of the Administrative Systems National and Local, of the United States, England, France and Germany*, Putnam's Sons, New York, 1893.

Gortner, H. F., Mahler, J., and Nicholson, J. B., The pivotal controversies, In *Introduction to Public Administration: A Book of Readings*, Ott, J. S. and Russell, E. W., Eds., Addison-Wesley Longam, New York, pp. 218–220, 2001.

Green, R. T., Keller, L. R., and Wamsley, G. L., Reconstitution a profession for American public administration, *Public Administration Review*, 53(6), 516–524, 1993.

Greenlaw, P. S., Kohl, J. P., and Lee, R. D. Jr., Title VII sex discrimination in the public sector in the 1990s: the courts' view, *Public Personnel Management*, 27(2), 249–268, 1998.

Gulick, L., Notes on the theory od organization, In *Papers on the Science of Administration*, Gulick, L. and Urwick, L., Eds., Institute of Public Administration, New York, pp. 3–13, 1937.

Jaffe, L. L., The reform of federal administrative procedure, *Public Administration Review*, 2, 41–158, 1942.

Kaboolian, L., Dialogue between advocates and executive agencies: new roles for public management, In *Public Management Reform and Innovation: Research, Theory and Application*, Frederickson, H. G. and Johnston, J. M., Eds., Univ. of Alabama Press, Tuscaloosa, AL, pp. 312–328, 1999.

Kagan, R. A., Adversarial legalism and American government, *Journal of Policy Analysis and Management*, 10(3), 369–406, 1991.

Kaufman, H., *Red Tape: Its Origins, Uses and Abuses*, Brookings Institution, Washington, DC, 1977.

Kelly, R. M., An inclusive democratic polity, representative bureaucracies, and the new public management, *Public Administration Review*, 58(3), 201–208, 1998.

Kerwin, C. M., *Rulemaking: How Government Agencies Write Law and Make Policy*, 3rd ed., CQ Press, Washington, DC, 2003.

Kettl, D. F., Ingraham, P. W., Sanders, R., and Horner, C., *Civil Service Reform: Building a Government that Works*, Brookings Institution, Washington, DC, 1996.

Koenig, H. O., A case study of an exercise in inclusiveness: the americans with disabilities act in local government. *Public Administration & Management: An Interactive Journal* 6(1), http://www.pamij.com/6_1/6_1_s3_koenig.html (accessed August 3, 2004), 2001.

Lan, Z., A conflict resolution approach to public administration, *Public Administration Review*, 57(1), 27–35, 1997.

Landesbergen, D. and Orosz, J. F., Why public managers should not be afraid to enter the "gray zone": strategic management and public law, *Administration & Society*, 28(2), 238–266, 1996.

Landis, J. M., *The Administrative Process*, Yale University Press, New Haven, CT, 1938.

Lane, J., *The Public Sector: Concepts, Models and Approaches*, 3rd ed., Sage, Thoushand Oaks, CA, 2000.

Lawler, P. A., Shaefer, R. M., and Shaefer, D. L., *Active Duty: Public Administration as Democratic Statesmanship*, Rowman and Littlefield, Lanham, MD, 1998.

Lee Y. S., and Otting, G., In defense of the street-level bureaucrats against civil damages liability: twenty years after *Harlow v. Fitzerald*. Paper presented at the 2001 National Conference of the American Society for Public Administrators, 2001.

Lee, R. D. Jr., and Greenlaw, P. S., The legal evolution of sexual harassment, *Public Administration Review*, 55(4), 357–365, 1995.

Levin, M. A. and Sanger, M. B., *Making Government Work: How Entrepreneurial Executives Turn Bright Ideas into Real Results*, Jossey-Bass, San Francisco, CA, 1994.

Lipsky, M., *Street-Level Bureaucracy*, Russell Sage Foundation, New York, 1980.

Llewellyn, Karl N., Remarks on the theory of appellate decision and the rules or cannons about how statutes are to be construed, *Vanderbilt Law Review*, 3, 395–406, 1950.

Lowi, T. J., *The End of Liberalism*, Norton, New York, 1979.

Lowi, T. J., Legitimizing public administration: a disturbed dissent, *Public Administration Review*, 53(3), 261–264, 1993.

MacManus, S. A., Litigation: a real budget buster for many U.S. municipalities, *Government Finance Review*, 10(1), 27–31, 1994.

MacManus, S. A. and Turner, P., Litigation as a budgetary constraint: problem areas and costs, *Public Administration Review*, 53(5), 462–472, 1993.

Martinez, J. M., Law versus ethics: reconciling two concepts of public service ethics, *Administration and Society*, 29(6), 690–722, 1998.

Merry, S. E., Everyday understandings of the law in working-class America, *American Ethnologist*, 13, 253–270, 1986.

Moe, R. C. and Gilmour, R. S., Rediscovering principles of public administration: the neglected foundations of
   public law, *Public Administration Review*, 55(2), 135–146, 1995.
Moore, M. V. and Abraham, Y. T., Comparable worth: is it a moot issue? Part II: the legal and juridical posture,
   Public Personnel Management, 23(2), 263–286, 1994.
O'Barr, W. M. and Conley, J. M., Lay expectations of the civil justice system, *Law and Society Review*, 22(1),
   137–161, 1988.
O'Leary, R., The impact of federal court decisions on the polices and administration of the U.S. Environmental
   Protection Agency, *Public Administration Review*, 49(6), 549–574, 1989.
O'Leary, R., The bureaucratic politics paradox: the case of wetlands legislation in Nevada, *Journal of Public
   Administration Research and Theory*, 4(4), 443–467, 1994a.
O'Leary, R., The expanding partnership between personnel management and the courts, In *New Paradigms for
   Government: Issues for the Changing Public Service*, Ingraham, P. W. and Romzek, B. S., Eds.,
   Jossey-Bass, San Francisco, CA, pp. 168–190, 1994b.
O'Leary, R. and Raines, S. S., Lessons learned from two decades of alternative dispute resolution programs
   and processes at the U.S. Environmental Protection Agency, *Public Administration Review*, 61(6),
   682–692, 2001.
Leary, R. and Strausman, J., The impact of courts on public management, In *Public Management: The State of
   the Art*, Bozeman, B., Ed., Jossey-Bass, San Francisco, CA, pp. 189–205, 1993.
O'Leary, R. and Wise, C. R., Public managers, judges, and legislators: redefining the "new partnership",
   Public Administration Review, 51(4), 316–328, 1991.
Ostrom, E., Institutional rational choice: an assessment of the institutional analysis and development frame-
   work, In *Theories of the Policy Process*, Sabatier, P. S., Ed., Westview Press, Boulder, CO, pp. 35–71,
   1999.
Rice, M. and Mongkuo, M., Did Adarand Kill Minority Set-Asides? *Public Administration Review*, 58(1),
   82–86, 1998.
Richman, R., The Supreme Court and the "integrity of the public service": an interpretation, *American Review
   of Public Administration*, 27(1), 43–60, 1997.
Roberts, R., The supreme court and the law of public service ethics, *Public Integrity*, 1(1), 20–40, 1999.
Rohr, J. A., *To Run a Constitution: The Legitimacy of the Administrative State*, Univ. of Kansas Press,
   Lawrence, KS, 1986.
Rohr, J. A., Toward a more perfect union, *Public Administration Review*, 53(3), 246–249, 1993.
Rohr, J. A., *Public Service, Ethics and Constitutional Practice*, Univ. of Kansas Press, Lawrence, KS, 1998.
Rosenbloom, D. H., Constitutional problems for the new public management in the United States, In *Current
   Public Policy Issues: The 1998 Annals*, Thai, K. and Carter, R. Y., Eds., Academics Press, Boca Raton,
   FL, 1998.
Rosenbloom, D. H., *Building a Legislative-Centered Public Administration: Congress and the Administrative
   State, 1946–1999*, The Univ. of Alabama Press, Tuscaloosa, AL, 2000a.
Rosenbloom, D. H., Retrofitting the administrative state to the constitution: congress and the judiciary's
   twentieth century progress, *Public Administration Review*, 60(1), 39–46, 2000.
Rosenbloom, D. H., *Administrative Law for Public, Managers*, Westview Press, Boulder, CO, 2003.
Rosenbloom, David H., Carroll James D., and Carroll Jonathan D., *Constitutional Competence for Public
   Managers: Cases and Commentary*, Peacock, Itaska, IL, 1999.
Rosenbloom, D. H. and O'Leary, R., *Public Administration and Law*, 2nd ed., Marcel Dekker, New York,
   1997.
Rosenbloom, D. H. and Ross, B. H., Towards a new jurisprudence of constitutional federalism: the Supreme
   Court in the 1990s and public administration, *American Review of Public Administration*, 28(2),
   107–125, 1998.
Rosenbloom, D. H. and Schwartz, R. D., *Handbook of Regulation and Administrative Law*, Marcel Dekker,
   New York, 1994.
Rudman, W., The cost of complaints, *Government Executive*, 52–56, 1999. June
Sargentich, T. O., *Administrative Law Anthology*, Anderson Publishing, Cincinnati, OH, 1994.
Schneider, A. L. and Ingram, H., *Policy Design for Democracy*, Univ. of Kansas Press, Lawrence, KS, 1997.
Schuck, P. H., *Foundations of Administrative Law*, Oxford Univ. Press, New York, 1994.
Schuck, P. H., *Suing Government: Citizen Remedies for Official Wrongs*, Yale Univ. Press, New Haven, CT,
   1983.

Scott, P. G. and Pandey, S. K., The influence of red tape on bureaucratic behavior: an experimental simulation, *Journal of Policy Analysis and Management*, 19(4), 615–633, 2000.

Sitkin, S. B. and Bies, R. J., *The Legalistic Organization*, Sage, Thousand Oaks, CA, 1994.

Spicer, M. W., A contractarian approach to public administration, *Administration & Society*, 22, 303–316, 1990.

Spicer, M. W., *The Founders, the Constitution, and Public Administration: A Conflict in World Views*, Georgetown Univ. Press, Washington, DC, 1995.

Spicer, M. W. and Terry, L. D., Legitimacy, history and logic: public administration and the constitution, *Public Administration Review*, 53(3), 239–245, 1993.

Spicer, M. W. and Terry, L. D., Administrative interpretation of statutes: a constitutional view of the "New World Order" of public administration, *Public Administration Review*, 56(3), 38–47, 1996.

Stewart, D. W., Professionalism vs. democracy: Friedrich vs. Finer revisited, *Public Administration Review*, 45(1), 13–25, 1985.

Stone, A., and Thomas, RD., The new role of state Attorneys General: an assessment of critical costs. Paper presented at the 60th National Conference of the American Society for Public Administration, Orlando, FL, April 10, 1999.

Stone, D., *Policy Paradox: The Art of Political Decision Making*, Norton, New York, 1997.

Strickland, R. A., Sexual harassment: a legal perspective for public administrators, *Public Personnel Management*, 24, 493–513, 1995.

Sunstein, C. R., *Legal Reasoning and Political Conflict*, Oxford University Press, New York, 1996.

Terry, L. D., Administrative leadership, neo-managerialism, and the public management movement, *Public Administration Review*, 58(3), 194–200, 1998.

Van Wart, M., *Change Public Sector Values*, Garland Publishing, New York, 1998.

Verkuil, P., A study of informal adjudication procedures, *University of Chicago Law Review*, 43, 739–771, 1976.

Wamsley, G. L., Bacher, R. N., Kronenberg, P. S., and Rohr, J. A., *Refounding Public Administration*, Sage, Newbury Park, CA, 1990.

Wamsley, G. L. and Wolf, J. F., *Refounding Democratic Public Administration: Modern Paradoxes, Post-modern Challenges*, Sage, Thousand Oaks, CA, 1996.

White, J. D., *Taking Language Seriously: The Narrative Foundations of Public Administration Research*, Georgetown University Press, Washington, DC, 1999.

White, L. D., *Introduction to the Study of Public Administration*, Macmillan, New York, 1926.

White, L. D. and Smith, T. V., *Politics and Public Service: A Discussion of the Civic Art in America*, Harper and Brothers, New York, 1939.

Wilson. W., The study of administration, In *Classics of Public Administration*, 4th ed., Shafritz, J.M. and Hyde, A.C., Eds., The Dorsey Press, Chicago, IL, pp. 10–37, 1997.

Wise, C. R., Public administration is constitutional and legitimate, *Public Administration Review*, 53(3), 257–261, 1993.

Wise, C. R., The future of public law: beyond administrative law and national borders, In *Handbook of Public Law and Administration*, Cooper, P. J. and Newland, C. A., Eds., Jossey-Bass, San Francisco, CA, pp. 569–588, 1997.

Wise, C. R., Election administration in crisis: an early look at lessons from Bush versus Gore, *Public Administration Review*, 61(2), 131–139, 2001.

Wise, C. R. and O'Leary, R., Is federalism dead or alive in the Supreme Court? Implications for public administrators, *Public Administration Review*, 52(6), 559–572, 1992.

Wise, C. R. and O'Leary, R., Intergovernmental relations and federalism in environmental management and policy: the role of the courts, *Public Administration Review*, 57(2), 150–159, 1997.

Wise, C. R. and O'Leary, R., Breaking up is hard to do: the dissolution of judicial supervision of public services, *Public Administration Review*, 63(2), 177–191, 2003.

Zerbe, R. O. Jr., Is cost-benefit analysis legal? Three rules, *Journal of Policy Analysis and Management*, 17(3), 419–456, 1998.

Unit 10

Public Administration Pedagogy

19 A History of Pedagogy in Public Administration

Eleanor V. Laudicina

CONTENTS

I. INTRODUCTION

The history of pedagogy in public administration mirrors the history of public administration itself as both discipline and practice. All the elements of growth, diversification, change, and turbulence characterizing the evolving field of public administration are present in its academic arena. Public service education has been repeatedly shaped and reshaped, responding to the spirit and ethos of the eras through which it has passed. As a consequence, the educational enterprise, as is the case for the field itself, has been built upon a succession of layers, an additive process through which new, competing, contradictory, and often incompatible themes maintain a close but uneasy coexistence. Historical depiction, therefore, takes on something of an archeological quality. Each historical period represents a separate stratum, peripherally related to those above and below but largely independent of them. Each continues, however, to play an important role in defining the character of contemporary education for public service.

The purpose of this chapter is to describe the formation of the multiple, varied, and complex strata providing the foundation for public administration pedagogy today. Within each historical period, political and social currents, economic variables, and other factors external to the educational setting played a critical role in shaping the educational mission. Institutional configurations, curricular development, and pedagogical approaches emerged in response to these forces. As the environment changed, new educational approaches emerged but rarely supplanted older models. Over time, therefore, the educational landscape took on the same character as many of the older university campuses within which public administration programs are found: a polyglot assortment of architectural styles, each clearly characteristic of the particular era in which it was built. Nevertheless, each structure remains serviceable in its own way, and the particular combination lends a certain unique dimension, creating a whole more complete than any of the parts.

II. THE FORMATIVE YEARS: 1880–1920

The emergence of public administration education as a self-conscious enterprise is irrevocably linked to the Progressive Era (Mosher 1975; Waldo 1955). The underlying spirit of the time was one of profound optimism, an unshakable faith in progress and in the capacity of mankind to direct and control its environment and destiny for the better (Mosher 1975). Despite differences in approach and emphasis, the early reformers, those who shaped our modern-day administrative state, shared a common moral vision founded in a Calvinistic sense of individual and civic responsibility. Public Administration scholars have paid little attention to this period, although during this time the intellectual core of the field emerged (Stivers 2000). Of even greater import for the educational enterprise, the basic curricular structures and emphases that would dominate the field to the present day had their origins in these early years.

The reform movement introduced the "essential preconditions" for the systematic study and teaching of administration: awareness of administrative management as an essential function of government (Stone and Stone 1975). For reform to succeed, the tasks of government had to be carried out by a new public servant who was not only honest, but also knowledgeable in the operation of administrative functions, systems, policies, and processes. The origins of public administration education emerged as an inevitable consequence of the campaign for administrative reform (Stone and Stone 1975).

Publication of Woodrow Wilson's (1880) "The Study of Administration" provides an identifiable starting point for the systematic inquiry into the operative principles of governmental organization. Wilson's essay resonates with the Progressive themes prevalent at the time. The essay also, and for the first time, expressed the need for a "scientific" and systematic study of administration (Wilson 1880). In addition, Wilson established the terms on which public service education would be based for decades to come, namely the notion that the science to which Wilson referred was an intrinsic part of the orderly, organized, and efficient world of business, far from the "hurry and strife of politics."

Wilson's essay gave impetus to the systematic study and teaching of administration. The first curriculum devoted specifically to educating American public servants took shape at Johns Hopkins University between 1884 and 1896. Wilson himself joined Herbert Baxter Adams, James Bryce, Richard Ely, and Albert Shaw in offering a broad foundation of courses in politics, economics, history, and law. Based loosely on the European model, the program emphasized local government and aimed at building a justification for a distinctly American form of public administration. Despite the prominence of its founders, the program failed to become a model for other institutions. Its broad, normative framework was soon eclipsed by the practical, applied, and efficiency-minded framework of administrative management (Hoffman 2002).

Critical to this approach was the emergence of the concept of professional education as an important task of higher education. The first third of the century was a period in which the professions and professional education were born (Mosher 1975). Accounting, business administration, city planning, engineering, nursing, journalism, social work, teaching, and many other fields emerged as legitimate objects of academic attention. Establishment of the American Academy of Political and Social Science in 1889 and the American Political Science Association in 1903 provided the disciplinary identity, conceptual foundations, and financial base upon which the new science of administration would emerge.

Within several years professional associations began to form: the International City Management Association in 1913, followed a year later by the Society for the Promotion of Training for Public Service, forerunner of the American Society for Public Administration (ASPA). In time these associations demanded higher standards of professionalism and an enhanced knowledge base, fueling curricular and programmatic growth in universities now ready to welcome those demands.

Courses preceded programs as the new model of public service education emerged. The Wharton School of the University of Pennsylvania first offered courses specifically focused on public management topics. Reflecting the school's mission, these courses emphasized finance. This emphasis also reflected the contemporary preoccupation with corruption and with imposing honest, "businesslike" practice in municipal affairs (Blunt 1989, 612). Before long, public administration courses appeared elsewhere. In 1892, the University of California began a series of offerings, mostly in local government and finance. Other courses followed. Within the decade courses in comparative administration, city government, administrative law, and state and federal administration appeared in college catalogs. In 1900, another milestone for the newly emerging field appeared: the publication of Frank Goodnow's *Politics and Administration*, generally regarded as the first true textbook in public administration. Beyond offering new courses, some universities in the early years of the century assumed another role: establishing research bureaus to support the work of urban reform movements. In 1909, the Wisconsin and Kansas Municipal Information Bureaus were established, administered by university extension services. In 1911, the New York Bureau of Municipal Research began operation. By 1913, research bureaus had been set up in eight states. In keeping with the spirit of Progressive reform, their emphasis was practical and pragmatic: the provision of direct, useful assistance to support efficient operation in the day-to-day affairs of government. Some of these bureaus soon would become the springboard for complete degree programs.

Universities, however, were slow to respond to the emerging need for professional training. In fact, the "first genuine professional school of public administration" (Stone and Stone 1975, 28) began outside of academia. Mary Averill Harriman in her travels abroad had been impressed by the English civil service model. Upon returning home, she sought unsuccessfully to interest the presidents of Harvard, Yale, and Columbia in developing an American counterpart for training able and ambitious young men for public service. Ultimately, she turned her beneficence to the New York Bureau of Municipal Research, founded in 1906 as part of the reform movement in that city. In 1911, the Bureau established the Training School for Public Service, buoyed by a quarter of a million dollars from Mrs. Harriman and subsequent financial support from other equally wealthy and generous benefactors, including Andrew Carnegie and John D. Rockefeller (Roberts 1994).

The early curriculum of the Training School for Public Service embodied the predominant themes of the era. The approach was pragmatic, interdisciplinary, and problem-oriented, sustained by a faith in progress, efficiency, and meritocracy. The concept of learning by doing played a central role in the curriculum. Students were set to work immediately on current projects. Research, public service, and pedagogy were tightly entwined. In 1915, the curriculum became more formalized with the introduction of regularly scheduled lectures and seminars as core features of a two-year program, although the practical, applied element remained. Courses covered such topics as law and municipal government, legislative drafting and administration, municipal highway engineering, municipal accounting, police and fire administration, and principles of management. Between 1911 and 1930, almost 1600 men and a few women had passed through the program, with 80% of the graduates entering government or some other form of public service (Stone and Stone 1975, 269–271).

Camilla Stivers, in her landmark study of the Progressive era, argues that the curricular emphasis on "scientific method," neutral competence, and techniques of management drew selectively from the multiple intellectual and political currents of the time. In their quest for legitimacy and credibility and to counter attacks on their masculinity by machine politicians, the reformers sought metaphors in the accepted male arenas of science and business. As the bureaus became increasingly dependent on private philanthropy, the need to avoid controversial policy issues further strengthened the emphasis on presumably neutral and objective principles of management. As a result the men of the municipal research bureaus became increasingly estranged from the concerns of the women who labored on behalf of the in the poor in the settlement houses. Emphasis on meaningful outcomes gave way to the ideology of scientific method and objective efficiency, an intellectual framework persisting to this day. The curriculum of the period focused largely on scientific and businesslike administrative procedures. Broader questions of public purpose were largely ignored (Stivers 2000).

By 1920, the foundation had been laid for the direction that public service education sub-sequently followed for more thsan thirty years. The energy, optimism, and faith in progress that infused the Progressive era would continue to inspire an educational enterprise dedicated to trans-forming society through enlightened professionalism. The underlying themes of technocratic reformism, heavily aligned with the twin values of efficiency and economy, focused primarily on education for local-government management through much of this period. Later, the same themes would characterize academic programs focused on the national level.

Most fundamental to the definition of curriculum for decades to come was the basic planning, organizing, directing, staffing, co-ordinating, reporting, and budgeting (PODSCORB) formula, an emphasis on teaching management as a series of skills (Ellwood 1985, 6). Management throughout this period was perceived as "a single process wherever found," the teaching of which, much like the practice, could eventually be conducted in a scientific manner. The essential "principles of management" emerging in the literature of the period became a guiding beacon for the emerging educational enterprise (Waldo 1955, 39).

Education for management increasingly coalesced within the disciplinary bounds of political science. The reason for this development lies in the emphasis at the time on "locus" rather than "focus," as Nicholas Henry has suggested. Early writing, research, and teaching emphasized "locus," the governmental setting. Focus, the essential functions of management, although still integral to the curriculum, became less central as guiding elements in defining the discipline (Henry 1998). The result was a growing isolation of public administration from related and emerging fields such as business administration and social work, which at the time were beginning their own fruitful explorations into the nature of organizations. At the same time, however, the seeds of what would become a growing schism within political science were planted. The politics/administration dichotomy provided the rationale for an analytic carving up of the territory between public admin-istration and political science, fostering curricular disputes and internecine battles evident to the present day.

III. THE 1920s: EMERGENCE OF PUBLIC ADMINISTRATION AS A SEPARATE FIELD OF STUDY

In the decade between 1920 and 1930, solid institutional housings and accepted curricular models for public administration education emerged. Institutional growth, beginning slowly but proceeding at an ever-accelerating pace, characterized the period, with private philanthropy the engine propel-ling much of the growth.

Throughout the 1920s training programs, research bureaus, and university-based courses in public administration expanded. Relatively few, however, developed into formal degree programs. In addition to programs initiated at the University of California at Berkeley (1920) and at Stanford University (1921), the decade saw the emergence of two programs whose formative influences epitomized the major themes of the decade, the Maxwell School of Citizenship and Public Affairs at Syracuse University and the School of Citizenship and Public Administration at the University of Southern California (USC). Both were pioneering efforts in the establishment of public adminis-tration as a separate and distinct field of study.

In the early years of the decade, George A. Maxwell, a wealthy entrepreneur and alumnus of Syracuse University, expressed interest in establishing a new school dedicated to the dual purposes of educating better citizens and combining education and research in the social sciences with professional education for public service. George Davenport, appointed first dean of the Maxwell School, turned for advice on the training of experts for public service to Luther Gulick, who headed the National Institute for Public Administration, formerly the New York Bureau of Municipal Research. At the time, the Institute was in the throes of serious financial difficulties. Recognizing the opportunity, Gulick suggested that instead of starting from scratch, Syracuse should absorb the activities of the Training School. In 1924, the Maxwell School opened its doors to its initial class of six students, all supported by fellowships.

Establishment of the Maxwell School exemplifies the close ties between the emergence of public administration education and the Progressive era. The founders of the school, George Maxwell, Frederick Davenport, Luther Gulick and William Mosher (Davenport's successor as dean) were linked individually to several different strands of the Progressive era, but all shared the belief that the major enemies of the common good were political corruption and administrative inefficiency. Their common goal was the creation, through appropriate graduate education, of a corps of professional public administrators. Their educational philosophy was pragmatic, instrumentalist, and experimentalist. All shared a profound belief in the need for a vast expansion of governmental power to regulate the economy and police political and social abuses (Johnson no date).

Transfer of the Training School to Syracuse brought to a university setting the ethos of practical application as the bedrock of pedagogy for public administration. The curriculum emphasized visits to water works, sewage treatment plants, police headquarters, and a host of other municipal agencies. Internships were essential to those without managerial experience. The focus of the school was on city management, but with a distinct emphasis on substantive policies and operations. The absence of textbooks, especially during the early years, encouraged an inductive approach to coursework, a focus on problem solving, and the development of pragmatic skills (Stone and Stone 1975, 45–46).

Several years after the founding of the Maxwell School, the USC established its own professional school in public administration. The school had its beginnings in 1928 with a series short courses for practitioners. The offerings soon expanded into a full curriculum. On February 28, 1929, the School of Citizenship and Public Administration opened its doors. In common with most emerging educational enterprises of the day, the curriculum focused on local government, stressed the prevailing norms of efficiency and economy, and relied on the importation of successful techniques from the business world (Olson 1955, 10).

Unlike the Maxwell School, the School of Citizenship and Public Administration offered both bachelor's and master's degrees. Courses were offered in the day and the evening, with no difference in the content of courses given in the regular and extension divisions. The curriculum was broadly multidisciplinary, including courses in politics, economics, sociology, psychology, anthropology, history, and science. Unlike the Maxwell School, the USC program was deeply rooted in its local community. The business sector in particular actively participated in the definition of curriculum, policies, and procedures.

In the similarities and differences of the Maxwell and USC experiences, it is possible to identify the early outlines of two very different approaches to education for public service. The Maxwell School provided an early model for the education and training of a relatively small and elite cadre of full-time graduate students. The USC program was the forerunner of the many diverse, multi-purpose programs serving state and local governments today. Dedicated to the education of both full- and part-time students, preservice and in-service, graduate and undergraduate, these programs are deeply rooted in the local community and region.

The emergence of an educational infrastructure to support the new profession of public administration was strengthened by the simultaneous establishment of complementary professional associations and research institutes. Among the most important was the Public Administration

Clearing House. Initially located on the campus of the University of Chicago, the Clearing House brought together at one location a total of fifteen public service organizations, including the International City Management Association, the Municipal Finance Officers' Association, the Civil Service Assembly, the American Municipal Association, and the American Public Works Association. Under the leadership of Louis Brownlow for much of its formative period, the Clearing House repeatedly stressed the need for in-service training and preservice education by universities and developed many of its own training materials.

In an era of parsimonious governmental support for all but the most basic services, financial support for education, training, and research had to come from private sources. A variety of philanthropies supported education, training, and research in public administration. By far the most influential was the Rockefeller Foundation. Rockefeller support directly fueled the expansion of many teaching programs. From 1927 to 1930, the Foundation contributed more than a million dollars to support new academic programs in public administration, including those at Syracuse, Harvard, the University of Chicago, and the University of California at Berkeley (Roberts 1994).

The size and scope of Rockefeller funding and the conditions under which it was granted had a significant influence over the course of both research and education during this period. Rockefeller Foundation funding for the infant enterprise of public service education reinforced the conceptual separation of politics and administration and the search for an objective science of administration. In its concern to avoid scandal and any taint of controversy, the foundation adamantly refused to support projects involving policy questions or the merest hint of partisanship (Roberts 1994, 224).

The detachment of administration from politics, the use of science metaphors, and the search for objective principles of administration also characterized early textbooks. These themes suffuse the first textbook entirely devoted to public administration, Leonard D. White's *Introduction to the Study of Administration*. Published in 1926, it is considered by some to have "spawned public administration as a separate field of study" (Chandler and Plano 1982). The book was the first to systematically organize the study of administration. It developed concepts and approaches defining the field well into the 1940s. In 1927, W. F. Willoughby's *Principles of Public Administration* came out. Willoughby adopted many of the same Progressive themes as White but more strongly emphasized the development and application of scientific principles.

By the conclusion of the decade, commonly accepted definitions of curriculum, course content, and disciplinary direction had begun to emerge. Four central doctrines were by now deeply inscribed in the literature and in the curriculum: (1) the process of government consists of only two parts, decision and execution; (2) administration can be made into a science; (3) scientific study leads to the discovery of principles of administration; and (4) economy and efficiency are the central, if not sole, goals of administrative study (Waldo 1955). By this time it was also clear that the emerging educational model would have a decidedly managerial emphasis (Ellwood 1985). The American approach to education for public service would, therefore, differ from the law-dominated European model and the general-education emphasis of the British model. The authorship of early texts and writings also confirmed the tendency, evident almost from the start, for the field to be dominated by political scientists and their disciplinary perspectives.

IV. THE 1930s AND 1940s: EDUCATION FOR THE ADMINISTRATIVE STATE

The two decades between the late 1920s and late 1940s were a golden age for academic public administration. The combined impact of the New Deal and World War II created a massive expansion of governmental power at the national level. Much of this expansion was supported, justified, engineered, and rationalized by academicians within the public administration community. Never before or since has academic public administration been so closely tied to seats of power (Egger, in Mosher 1975).

These also were the decades within which public administration, as academic enterprise and professional practice, finally achieved external recognition: "A person could not have spoken about the field of public administration in 1925 and had confidence that the audience knew what was meant. In 1937, the situation was quite different" (Roberts 1994, 222). Much of the institutional foundation for research and practice in the field was laid during these decades. Moreover, the degree of unanimity on the fundamental values, premises, content, and purpose of education for public service would not be seen again.

Academic programs grew at a slow but regular pace throughout the period. By 1933, some twenty-five new programs in public administration emerged. In addition, thirty-nine training schools and twelve or more university research bureaus had started up (Stone and Stone 1975). Employment opportunities expanded, commensurate with the expansion of governmental activities. The University of Minnesota reported that fully one-third of all graduates went into public service between 1928 and 1936 (Graham 1941).

Despite expanding credibility of public administration as an academic field, doubts remained about the efficacy or wisdom of training specifically for public service. The very first issue of the *Public Administration Review* featured a dialogue between Robert M. Hutchins, then president of the University of Chicago, and Dean William E. Mosher of the Maxwell School. Hutchins, adhering to the British model, argued that a broad foundation in the liberal arts provided the only necessary base for administrative work. Fortunately for the future of public administration education, Mosher's view prevailed, and academic programs continued their slow but steady growth.

Throughout the twenty-year period, the academic curriculum adjusted to changing circumstances, but always within the framework of its Progressive era foundations. Among the most significant curricular shifts was a move away from the earlier local/municipal focus and toward a greater concern with administration at the federal level. Similarly, the very pragmatic, practical, and largely hands-on skill-building emphasis of the early years declined in favor of more classroom instruction, with a thrust toward development of broad managerial and administrative competencies (Egger 1975). Following the work of Elton Mayo and associates, and supported by Chester Barnard's earlier writings, human relations now became a common curricular element, although hardly supplanting PODSCORB or the ubiquitous efficiency norms.

In 1935 the first review and evaluation of public administration education took place. The Public Administration Clearing House sponsored a conference to consider appropriate models for education and training. The report of conference proceedings describes the several forms of preparation for public service then emerging: preliminary education, internships or apprenticeships, and in-service or post-entry training (Lambie 1935, 11). The report articulated for the first time the notion that specific preparation for managerial roles in the public sector should be limited to the post-baccalaureate experience. That view would largely characterize perceptions of the under-graduate/graduate distinction for many decades to come. For in-service training, the report identified no fewer than eleven types of training, ranging from conferences and short courses to "organized curricula." One theme common to all types, however, was the need for close interaction of academics and practitioners (Lambie 1935).

Clearly the conferees were far less concerned with the distinction between degree and nondegree programs than they were with the need to assure close, continuous working relationships between the university and the practitioner communities. The report clearly expresses the sense of an emerging career service for which students might be educated at many levels. Beyond its significance as the first of a genre, the report also has some continuing resonance as the first to sharply delineate the types of education appropriate for prebaccalaureate preparation and those specific to post-baccalaureate training.

Throughout the 1930s support for professional training grew (White 1933). At the local level leagues of municipalities often assumed responsibility for training, frequently with the aid of local philanthropies. At the national level the 1937 report of the President's Committee on Administrative Management, the Brownlow Committee, argued for a professionally trained cadre of administrators in whose hands many of the procedural reforms recommended in the report could be accomplished.

Establishment of ASPA provided yet another indication of an emergent professional identity. The Society was to serve as a focal point around which the newly formulated art and science of administration would be nurtured. Formation of ASPA helped to legitimize the developing academic discipline (Blunt 1989). As Dwight Waldo noted, "The sense that political science as an academic discipline did not adequately represent and nurture the needs of those interested in improving performance in public administration was a strong motivating force in creating the new organization. In retrospect, it is clear that ASPA represented above all an attempt to loosen public administration from the restraints of political science" (Waldo in Mosher 1975, 13–14).

As the 1930s ended and the 1940s began, concern for educational capacity to serve the rapidly growing ranks of government officials increased. In 1941, the Committee on Public Administration of the Social Science Research Council published the first comprehensive study of educational preparation: *Education for Public Administration.* The report identified five distinct activities for universities: professional preparation, promoting research and the natural sciences, promoting research and social sciences, strengthening auxiliary staff agencies, and developing managerial functions (Graham 1941). This report, like the earlier conference report, clearly differentiated undergraduate and graduate preparation, advocating liberal education exclusively at the undergraduate level. For the graduate level, the report recommended comprehensive offerings including personnel and fiscal management, organizations, and courses in related disciplines such as economics, political science, and statistics. English, psychology, history, and public speaking also were considered appropriate topics, consistent with a strongly interdisciplinary thrust.

A comparison of this study with the earlier conference report shows a definite alteration in emphasis. Unlike the 1930s conferees, Graham saw public administration education as firmly lodged within a university setting and closely tied to conventional degree programs. The 1935 report described, in essence, a partnership between universities and practitioners. If either were to be seen as the junior partner in this model, it would be the university, which was viewed as little more than an instrument through which the pragmatic, practical needs of the public service could be met. By the 1940s, however, a sea change had occurred. Now the university became the senior partner, with the practitioner community as adjunct and in support. A major conceptual split between degree-based education and nondegree "practical" training for public service had begun.

By 1940, more than seventy academic programs of various types had been established. Some were mere collections of courses; some were undergraduate majors. Syracuse University and the University of Cincinnati offered well defined degree programs with a tightly structured curriculum. Others, like the University of Michigan and Harvard, allowed students considerable latitude in course selection. All programs of the period were designed to prepare administrative generalists, and all adhered to the intellectual core of "administrative science" (Whitaker 1998).

The war years had a major impact on public administration programs, setting the stage for the cataclysmic changes that the postwar years would bring. The most immediate and obvious impact of the war was a visible alteration in the characteristics of the student body (Egger 1975, 86). As in many other fields, the war years opened access and new opportunities to women. An influx of foreign students also occurred in some programs, especially at Syracuse, adding a level of demographic diversity that would not be evident again for many years to come. These changes were largely temporary, however, and would disappear once the war ended and seats once again could be filled with men.

Of greater significance for the future of public administration as discipline and academic enterprise was the exodus of university faculties from the campus and into line and policymaking functions. Experience in the federal bureaucracy introduced a far more sophisticated understanding of policy processes. The association of policy development with partisan controversy, the legacy of the field's early dependence on Rockefeller funds, gave way to a new sense of policy as a response to overriding national interests. Returning to the campus, academics now sought to portray an accurate and optimistic picture of the possibilities for achieving "good" results through administration (Ellwood 1985). Many of these faculty-turned-administrators were political scientists. Their newfound energy and voice, combined with the collapse of the conceptual foundation that had maintained the separation of public administration from political science, strengthened the influence of political science on the development of the discipline.

The war years and immediate postwar era also were a time in which the educational seeds of the past decade began to bear fruit at the national level. Many graduates of the infant programs of the 1920s and 1930s remained in Washington after the war. A significant number achieved positions of power (Ellwood 1985, 9). As a result the academic community experienced an unprecedented sense of importance. At the same time, however, the unity of perspective that had fueled earlier progress was about to dissolve. Toward the end of the decade a series of challenges to prevailing views of public administration emerged. Publication in 1946 of Fritz Morstein Marx's book of readings initiated the challenge to prevailing views. It was followed by Dahl's 1947 article, "The Science of Administration: Three Problems," and capped that same year by the appearance of Simon's *Administrative Behavior*.

In 1948, Dwight Waldo's seminal study, *The Administrative State*, was published (Waldo 1948). Waldo's work explored the intellectual premises of the administrative science movement and revealed its theoretical and normative presumptions. Waldo did not reject these ideas but challenged them and set out their limitations. "With publication of *The Administrative State* the prewar POSDCORB world of public administration would never be the same" (Carroll and Fredrickson 2001).

These were but opening volleys in an attack that would alter forever the teaching of public administration and open the way for the dominance of political science throughout the 1950s and into the 1960s. The academic study of public administration no longer would feature learning by and through practice. It would become an abstract science whose objectivity depended on remoteness from practice.

V. THE 1950s: DECLINE AND FRAGMENTATION

Academic public administration was not well equipped to deal with the mounting number of challenges with which it was confronted as the 1950s began. Left in intellectual disarray by the fatal assault against its most sacred precepts, the field now grappled with new forces sweeping through academia, forces that would further erode whatever tenuous sense of identity remained. The result, by the conclusion of the decade, was an academic field with minimal sense of purpose, disparaged by colleagues in related disciplines, and departmentally isolated from alternative models and methodologies that might have promoted revitalization. Public administration had begun a long downhill spiral (Henry 1987).

The signs of decline were not apparent at first. Indeed, the experience of the preceding decades initially appeared to have had a very positive impact on the curriculum. The combined effect of the New Deal and World War II experiences produced four major shifts in curricular emphasis (Fesler 1975). The first was a move away from administrative staff specialties, such as personnel and purchasing, in favor of line operations concerned with achieving public purposes. The second was a change of emphasis from the chief executive and major auxiliary and control agencies to administrative problems at the department and bureau levels. The third entailed a turning away from general, abstract principles to an appreciation of the varying contexts of individual departments and programs. Finally, the field shifted from a concern with economy and efficiency as guiding norms to a broader sense of how public administration is or should be affected by the political values and processes of its democratic setting. Even as the field was losing its major conceptual underpinnings, a richer and more variegated view of the administrative arena emerged.

Several new texts conveyed the impact of the Depression and war years. These included *The Elements of Public Administration*, edited by Fritz Morstein Marx, and *Big Democracy, Policy and Administration*, and *Morality and Administration in Democratic Government*, by Paul Appleby. These new texts, perhaps the last in the tradition of the academic/practitioner, attempted to convey the rich reality of administrative life. The underlying theme was the concept that government is intrinsically different from all other forms of administrative organization. Methodologically, these works departed radically from the earlier aim of developing universal or scientific principles of administration. In 1953, publication of two new texts, by Pfiffner and Presthus and by Dimock and Dimock, confirmed the major shift taking place. Both placed less emphasis on staff or housekeeping functions than on political context. To an even greater extent than evident just a few years earlier, these texts focus less on the structural aspects of administration than on processes, particularly within the interplay of political dynamics (Waldo 1955).

But just as public administration began to encompass a broader, more sophisticated view of administrative complexity, attacks on its methods, credibility, mission, and very raison d'etre (Henry 1995). A major blow came with the emergence of the behavioral movement. Behavioralism scorned the study of governmental and political institutions, the very essence of academic public administration at that time. Rooted in logical positivism with its rigid fact/value distinction, behavioralism challenged normative prescriptions in teaching and learning. Behavioralism called for severe standards of scientific research; it demanded rigor in the design of theories and models, explicitness in definitions and assumptions, operationalism in and empirical testing of hypotheses, and the primacy of quantitative methods. As Fesler later lamented, "Government seemed to have become only a dependent variable and administration an irrelevancy" (Fesler 1975, 115).

Some adaptation to the new academic mood did occur within the ranks of known public administration scholars. A 1950 text, *Public Administration*, by Herbert Simon, Donald Smithburg, and Victor Thompson demonstrated a rigorous commitment to logical positivism. Efforts to adapt to behavioral imperatives were evident in other textbooks as well (Waldo 1955, 31). A 1958 symposium on public service education emphasized the importance of studying the psychological and social aspects of organization and the roles of public agencies in the policy-making process (Sweeney 1958).

These adaptations were, however, exceptions. In general, courses and curricula continued to reflect the traditional emphasis on organization and management, administrative technique, public personnel, budgeting, and finance. Only a few programs required a course in statistics; only half required an internship (Whitaker 214). Public administration faculty housed within political science departments increasingly lost stature and students to presumably more exciting, state-of-the-art appeals of mainstream political science.

In the face of rapidly diminishing status, public administration scholars struggled to find new teaching approaches. The case study method soon became a popular and, in many ways, distinct innovation in public administration pedagogy. The growing attractiveness of case studies reflected general dissatisfaction with the textbook approach to teaching and training. For the time, they were the closest articulation of the connection between public administration and public policy (Waldo 1955). The principles approach, still evident in many texts, overstated the firmness of supposedly scientific generalizations about administration. Procedurally, texts conveyed little sense of the realities of administrative life. Cases, by contrast, were an effort to reconstruct real administrative events, made significant because of the problems and activities exhibited. Case examination also provided an opportunity to reintroduce values into the curriculum despite their proscription in the ranks of behaviorally oriented texts.

The case method received a major boost in 1948 with the inauguration of the Interuniversity Case Program (ICP). Begun under the sponsorship of Cornell, Harvard, Princeton, and Syracuse Universities, the ICP benefited in its early years from generous assistance by the Carnegie Corporation of New York. The ICP cases were distinctive in their focus on important decisions with substantial economic and social dimensions.

Despite its value and popularity as a pedagogical tool, the case method aroused some ambivalence among public administration scholars. Reliance on case research and writing emphasized the growing gulf between political science and public administration. While their colleagues in political science diligently attempted to move toward scientific generalization and theory building, public administration faculties, aligned in precisely the opposite direction, focused on individual phenomena and diversity of administrative experience (Henry 1987, 52).

Just as academic public administration had become isolated within the boundaries of political science, its location within those boundaries provided further isolation from potentially valuable influences in disciplines such as economics, sociology, and psychology. In later decades the value of research beyond the bounds of political science would be recognized by the public administration community and result in a range of interdisciplinary curricular approaches. The seeds for many of the programmatic and curricular changes that would occur in the future were planted during the 1950s. The perspectives of Simon and others would spawn the policy movement of the 1970s and 1980s. Occurring even sooner, the human relations movement would create such evocative concepts as participatory democracy, higher needs actualization, and authenticity in interpersonal relations. These concepts set the stage for the arrival of a new public administration in the late 1960s.

Even during the 1950s there were clear indications of dissatisfaction with the political science model of public administration education. At midpoint in the decade Cornell University founded the School of Business and Public Administration, the first example at a major institution of a new generic approach to the study of management. This approach emphasized the techniques of management, with the presumption that technical skill, not contextual awareness, was the most critical ingredient for managerial success in the public and private sectors. In 1954, a new textbook, John D. Millett's *Management in the Public Sector: The Quest for Effective Performance*, adopted the generic approach, emphasizing the common denominators of management problems across agencies and using a multidisciplinary focus. The generic management trend, once begun, would assume substantial momentum in the coming decade.

Another important exception to the prevailing political science model of public administration education thrived in the large, separate schools of public administration founded in the 1930s. These included the public administration schools at Syracuse University and USC as well as the Woodrow Wilson School at Princeton University. In the mid-1950s the deans of these and other large schools established the Committee on Graduate Education for Public Administration (CGEPE) as a subgroup within ASPA. For much of its early history, CGEPA was little more than an informal get-together of senior university leaders, often deemed a dean's club by outsiders (Henry 1995). Meeting for a few days before or after the annual ASPA conference, CGEPA initially served only as a forum for systematic attention to issues relevant to these schools and as an organized voice for them within ASPA. In years to come, however, it would assume far greater significance.

By the end of the decade, centrifugal forces set in motion with the demise of public administration's guiding principles and by its disciplinary fragmentation were taking their toll. A 1961 survey of graduate education in public administration found a great variety of forms and emphases, but no comprehensive intellectual framework (Stewart 1961). Clearly, the conceptual unity binding the field together prior to World War II was lost, and public administration became, as John Ellwood has suggested, an "umbrella term," covering a heterogeneous mix of programs (Ellwood 1985, 11).

VI. THE 1960s: OLD PROBLEMS AND NEW DIRECTIONS

The decade of the 1960s has been characterized as period of enormous expansion of the periphery, but without retention or creation of a unifying center (Waldo 1975, 185). As Alan Schick put it,

"Matters that were unsettled a generation earlier remained unsettled. Public administration had come apart and could not be put together again" (Shick 1975, 157). None of the strains characterizing this period first appeared in the 1960s, but none was healed during the decade, either. Nonetheless, this period spawned important new additions to the curriculum, new program models, and fledgling initiatives that later would have a significant impact. By the end of the decade, there was some indication of a resurgence of identity and focus (Henry 1987).

One indicator of continuing entropic tendencies was the fact that no new textbooks were published during this period, marking a nadir in creative energy. A report prepared for ASPA in the mid-1960s noted the widespread lack of status and resources characterizing much of academic public administration, confusion about intellectual direction, and concerns about the professional competence of graduates (Honey 1966). Although there were now more than seventy graduate programs, many were quite small, and the total number of degrees awarded annually numbered only about 400 (Whitaker 214).

Nevertheless, important developments occurred during the decade, sometimes through importation of work initiated in other disciplines, sometimes as a consequence of innovations in administrative practice. A good example of the former was the incorporation of organization theory and organization development as topics in the curriculum. Renewal of interest in organization studies in some ways harkened back to earlier concerns with structure and control, although the context and approach were quite different in the 1960s. This interest also was part of a more generalized outreach to other social sciences and a growing commonalty of interest with sociology, psychology, economics, and business management.

Another new curricular emphasis during this period was comparative administration, denoting an international perspective and movement away from the parochialism characterizing the field since its founding. In 1960 the Comparative Administration Group was founded. Two years later it received major philanthropic support from the Ford Foundation. The primary interest of the group was the use of comparative studies to strengthen theory in public administration, not to conduct area studies or to improve practice (Henry 1987, 54). The comparative administration initiative attracted considerable attention in its first years, and membership increased to about 500 by 1968. Within another decade, however, interest declined precipitously.

As public administration began to reach out to other disciplines in an effort to find new theoretical and conceptual grounding, its standing within the ranks of political science continued to erode. Meanwhile, the generic-management model flourished. Clearly, the standard public administration courses found in political science-based curricula did not appear adequate to equip students with the competencies necessary for the management of large organizations, particularly in its inattention to modern analytic and informational technologies.

In the mid-1960s, the Graduate School of Management at the University of California at Irvine proclaimed itself the first consciously created school of administrative science. The School offered master's degrees only in "administration" and "management" (Henry 1987). New programs at the University of California at Riverside, Willamette University, and Yale University soon followed. Other institutions began to offer public administration as an area of specialization within the business program. The philosophical premise for all of these programs was that phenomena common to all fields of management are more important than those that characterize specific venues, public or private. Often these programs demonstrated a strong inclination toward quantitative and financial analysis, rather than the softer social science disciplines.

Despite its initial attraction, administrative housing within a generic program or in one heavily slanted toward business soon appeared as problematic in its own way as housing within political science. Few courses turned out to be truly generic. This approach clearly reinforced the early normative emphasis on economy and efficiency (albeit in new garb), but it gave short shrift to new normative concerns. The promise of higher salaries and higher status in the business sector lured students away from public service. Public administration faculties often found that business-sector colleagues took little interest in governmental issues. As a consequence, and with a few notable exceptions, the momentum of the generic-school movement soon began to slow.

Although the generic movement failed to achieve broad support, it left a lasting legacy for the future of academic public administration. The serious challenge presented by the generic schools underscored the limitations intrinsic in the teaching of public administration at the time. The management emphasis also forced a renewed consideration of the meaning of public in public administration, particularly from the perspective of its unique moral and ethical concerns (Henry 1987). Alterations in the curriculum inevitably resulted. Courses in evaluation research and program evaluation, greater emphasis on statistics and quantitative analysis, and integration of management control techniques in budgeting courses became relatively commonplace.

The generic management challenge also supported the emergence of one of the few truly innovative developments of the era: policy studies. In some ways the policy movement was a natural synthesis: a resolution of the competing claims for greater attention to the uniqueness of the public context in business-focused curricula, and the need for greater attention to the techniques and methodologies of management in government-focused curricula. Emerging from the clash was a new hybrid, bearing the stamp of many disciplines but unique in its own right.

For the public administration community, the concept of public policy presented a new and unprecedented opportunity to apply rigorous analytical techniques to significant public issues. With the growing popularity of sophisticated analysis in Washington, the demand for graduates with new skills and capabilities also increased. Few traditional programs had the proper mix of expertise and skills within their faculties to meet the demand. The policy focus appeared to offer everything: an opportunity for public administration once again to achieve importance and status within political science, a vehicle both for integrating a broad multidisciplinary emphasis in the curriculum and to match the quantitative rigor of the business schools, a way, once more, to play an integral role in governmental decision making, and, as well, a chance to deal with the significant social issues of the time. The promise of the latter provided the motivation for the Ford Foundation to support the development of courses, curriculum, and institutional underpinnings for the new movement. By the end of the 1960s eight new schools of public policy had been established.

The later years of the decade also witnessed the beginnings of a wholly new view of public administration, one that would have a considerable impact on courses and curricula for several decades to come. In 1968, Dwight Waldo convened a conference of promising young scholars to consider the state of public administration as it was then taught and practiced. The result of that meeting, the "Minnowbrook Perspective," presented an entirely new challenge to education for public service. The true impact of this meeting would not be felt for several more years.

By the end of the 1960s the dissolution of the traditional foundations for the study and practice of public administration was complete. Significant fragments remained in the curriculum, but the unanimity of purpose characterizing earlier eras was gone. In its place, a variety of new perspectives appeared, but none could be considered a unifying model. Instead, the process of layering-on that would characterize the field for the remainder of the century was well underway. Within and among public administration programs, new perspectives competed with earlier ones. Elements of the policy and generic models competed with political science-based approaches and even earlier PODSCORB elements. Some vitality clearly had returned, but the currents were running in multiple, diffuse, and contradictory directions. At the same time the practitioner community and civic and business groups expressed growing alarm with the inability of academic public administration to respond effectively to the needs of a burgeoning public service (CED 1964).

VII. THE 1970s: RENEWAL AND GROWTH

The 1970s were characterized by vast growth in student populations and academic programs, curricular and pedagogical innovation, and increasing differentiation and diversity in programmatic options. Public administration assumed greater popularity as a course of study at both the graduate and undergraduate levels. Two contradictory movements, however, dominated the decade. The first was a continued enlargement in the number and scope of academic programs, albeit with no commonly accepted intellectual paradigm or public philosophy. The second was an acceleration in efforts to introduce some degree of uniformity and standardization into the curriculum. Paradoxically, the success of this latter effort helped to legitimize rather than erase the multiplicity of approaches.

The decade witnessed an unprecedented growth in the number of degree programs in public administration. From 1970 to 1978 the number of master's degrees awarded grew by 153%, mostly because of the establishment of new programs and an increase in the number of part-time enrollees (Ellwood 1985, 27–28; Zumeta and Solomon 1982). The number of bachelor's degrees increased at an astonishing rate, from 425 in 1970 to 2034 in 1978. The number of doctoral degrees awarded during the same period grew from 36 to 153. The number of separate professional schools increased 21%, while separate departments of public administration or public affairs grew by 53%.

Programs, new and old, exhibited a remarkable diversity in administrative housing. There were schools, institutes, divisions, departments, programs, and centers (Waldo 1972). Program titles also displayed great variety, including such terms as policy, management, administration, public service, government, and public affairs (Conant 1992). A marked tendency toward increased curricular specialization also became apparent during this period. Social service administration, judicial administration, health administration, recreation administration, and other variants appeared (Waldo 1975, 202).

In the absence of an agreed-on framework to guide programmatic or curricular development, the proliferation of new programs not only led to great diversity in mission and approach, but also to wide variation in the quality of offerings and capabilities of graduates. Concerned with the future of the field and its capacity to respond effectively to the growing need for professionalism, the deans and directors of large and established programs saw the need for a new organizational framework to guide the future direction of public service education. The Committee for Education in Public Administration (CGEPA), a largely informal gathering of academic public administrators, had been formed during the 1960s as a vehicle within ASPA for discussing the mutual concerns of those with responsibility for academic program leadership. Leadership within CGEPA gravitated toward the larger programs, some of which began referring to themselves as "comprehensive professional schools." The rank-and-file membership tended to be from smaller programs, many within political science departments and having minimal organizational foundation (Henry 1995).

By the late 1960s the movers and shakers in CGEPA, alarmed in equal measure about the proliferation of small programs of questionable quality and the emergence of large and powerful generic schools, came together in April of 1970 to create a new organization, the National Association of Schools of Public Affairs and Administration (NASPAA). Like its predecessor, NASPAA was an association of institutions with programs of varying size and emphasis.

During its formative discussions, the NASPAA faced critical decisions on issues of inclusiveness and equality versus exclusiveness and differentiation. Despite the efforts of some of the larger programs to impose membership criteria and bylaws that would insure the dominance of the established elite institutions, the organization ultimately opted for an inclusive approach, with membership open to all programs whose purpose was in the largest and most general sense professional education for public service. That decision would have major implications for the future of the discipline. By 1973, NASPAA encompassed 101 member schools. Together they awarded 2403 master's degrees, up from about 400 less than ten years earlier.

Establishment of NASPAA signaled a new determination among public administration educators, particularly those within large, established schools, to take responsibility for upgrading the educational background and technical competence of public managers. Supporters of the concept of public administration as a profession recognized that enhanced professionalism in the practice of public administration was inextricably linked to enhancement of the rigor and credibility of graduate education (Schott 1976). This was the challenge to NASPAA.

Few of NASPAA's founders envisioned accreditation as the core function of the Association. The principal goal of the founders was to ensure that NASPAA would encourage growth and that it would somehow influence universities to offer larger and better programs (Henry 1995). A number of the founders also saw NASPAA as the vehicle for securing foundation and governmental support for university programs. NASPAA's leadership worked diligently to secure funding of federal grants to public affairs schools under Title IX of the Higher Education Act passed in 1968. The Ford Foundation in 1970 awarded $1 million for a three-year program to provide graduate fellowships to minority students in urban administration. Despite the hopes of its founders, however, NASPAA never became a wellspring of institutional or fellowship support. Even the modest programs initiated in the 1970s would largely dissipate by the early 1980s.

In the aftermath of the contentious struggles over membership criteria that had occurred in Princeton, NASPAA moved slowly in the development of curricular standards. The opening salvo in the struggle for credibility in graduate public administration education was fired in 1974 when the membership of NASPAA formally adopted curricular standards for master's degree programs in public administration and public affairs. For the first time a commonly accepted, if broadly defined, framework existed to guide curricular and programmatic development. Despite the concerns of some of the smaller programs about standards related to faculty size and institutional housing, the membership accepted the new guidelines without a dissenting vote (Henry 1995, 28).

One reason for widespread acceptance of the new "Standards and Guidelines" was the assurance of the leadership that implementation would rest solely on voluntary self-evaluation studies. The emphasis on voluntarism was persuasive. It was also clear, however, that few in NASPAA, even those who feared the encroachment of AACSB into public affairs programs, envisioned accreditation as the next step. Accreditation was rejected as a move toward standardization and conformity at a time when the nascent field needed to encourage flexibility and diversity in academic programming.

The new guidelines emphasized the need for a professional focus in contrast to one on liberal arts, included a matrix of professional competencies to be developed within the curriculum, and identified the distinctive attributes of public service management. The emphasis was on the content of learning rather than institutional characteristics. The new standards encouraged programs to model their curricula around five major knowledge and skill areas: (1) the political, social and economic context of public administration; (2) analytic tools, both quantitative and nonquantitative; (3) individual, group, and organizational dynamics; (4) policy analysis; and (5) administrative/management processes (NASPAA 1974).

Three years later, despite earlier disclaimers, NASPAA took the next step. At its annual meeting in Colorado Springs, the membership voted to undertake a process of peer review followed by publication of a roster of programs judged to be in substantial conformity with the standards. The vote capped several days of intense debate, with agreement coming only after assurances that multiple approaches to public service education could be encompassed within the broad framework of the standards. The Broadmoor Pledge assured that diverse approaches established an organizational commitment to avoid stifling creativity and innovation in pursuit of uniformity and coherence. By July of 1979, sixty-seven programs had submitted self-study reports. Forty-five appeared on the first roster of approved programs (Poore 1982, 92).

The argument in favor of standards and peer review centered around the need to more clearly define the parameters of public service education, strengthening its credibility and legitimacy as professional preparation. In making the decision to adopt standards, the leadership of NASPAA faced a dilemma. The very existence of standards logically implies some degree of uniformity. Given the wide array of programs within NASPAA, however, agreement could be reached only by defining the standards at a level of generality sufficiently broad to alleviate the genuine fear of some programs that one or another approach would be ruled unacceptable. The standards, therefore, became a broad umbrella accommodating a wide and disparate array of approaches, functions, specialties and educational philosophies. The need to achieve agreement precluded argument on underlying principles or philosophical foundations. Quite the contrary, acceptance of diversity in programmatic emphases came to be seen as a positive attribute of NASPAA's accreditation philosophy, a source of vitality and creativity in a youthful, energetic new field.

Soon, however, there was evidence of a growing uniformity among programs, particularly in required foundation-course offerings. These included advanced quantitative methods and financial management. Public administration curricula more heavily emphasized statistical analysis, especially as applications in courses such as program evaluation and policy analysis (Meier and Brudney 1981). The number of credits in required courses increased from fewer than thirty-nine in 1974 and 1975 to more than forty-one in 1980.

The 1970s also saw the ascendancy of public policy programs. Policy studies became a new center for teaching, research, and practice. The *Policy Studies Journal* and *Policy Studies Review* appeared. In 1972, the Policy Studies Organization was formed. For the first time in several decades, policy studies united political scientists and public administrators within a single intellectual frame of reference (Henry 1987, 65). Public policy programs, frequently offering a Master's of Public Policy (MPP) degree, emphasized microeconomics, benefit/cost analysis, statistics, and systems analysis. The Association for Policy Analysis and Management (APPAM) was organized to provide a forum for developing and disseminating the new approach (Whitaker 1998, 215). While policy studies entered an era of growth, comparative administration experienced a precipitous demise. Comparative administration courses either disappeared from the curriculum entirely or were relegated to the status of seldom-offered electives.

The popularity of the case method also began to falter in the 1970s despite valiant efforts to keep it alive. This decline might have been linked to the decline in popularity of the generic management approach or to increasing numbers of in-service students whose personal work experience served as the foil against which theory and concepts could be tested. The case method also may have fallen victim to a plethora of new learning techniques beginning to invade academia. These included universities without walls, use of work experience as a substitute for classroom instruction, off-site locations to meet the needs of working students, and experimentation with new, hands-on classroom techniques. Internships, long a staple of the curriculum, received new attention as the demand for relevance became an engine driving curricular change. States and municipalities established formal programs, many in urban settings. In 1977, the Presidential Management Internship Program began, presaging what many hoped would be a new era of cooperation between the academic community and federal agencies.

Emergence of the New Public Administration accelerated the trend away from traditional teaching techniques and normative assumptions. The full impact of the Minnowbrook movement on program emphases, courses, or overall curriculum during the decade is difficult to assess. Unquestionably, advocates raised issues and concerns that dominated much of the scholarly dialogue of the era and challenged conventional beliefs in multiple ways. Younger faculty surely brought the new perspective into the classroom, and many later texts reflected the influence of the young Turks of the time. Arguably, later changes in curricular emphasis, particularly a renewed focus on ethics, on the moral purposes of public service, on equity and responsiveness as core values can be traced directly to this period. Certainly the movement encouraged a greater openness in the curriculum, a willingness to experiment with new pedagogical forms and techniques. Use of fiction, imagination, subjective interpretation, and Jungian psychology injected a new vitality and energy into the classroom.

The fact that the New Public Administration failed to develop a coherent intellectual or curricular framework should not detract from an assessment of its importance to public service education. The Minnowbrook influence runs like a thread through the fabric of academic public administration as it evolved from the 1970s into the 1980s. Rather than adding a layer or strata to those introduced earlier by the political science, policy, or generic approaches, the New Public Administration influenced them all.

VIII. THE 1980s: CONSOLIDATION AND CHANGE

During the 1980s earlier initiatives began to have a major impact; at the same time, new concerns emerged. While education at the master's level continued to dominate pedagogical concerns, new issues relating to doctoral level and, to a lesser extent, undergraduate education surfaced. Rampant expansion in the number and size of academic programs slowed, but questions about demographic diversity among faculties and student bodies assumed new prominence. As the decade drew to a close, a disturbing new paradox appeared. Just as it seemed that a minimal level of curricular consensus had emerged for the first time in decades, the very foundations of public administration, as both discipline and practice, came into question.

By 1983, NASPAA had 186 member programs awarding 6209 master's degrees (Whitaker 1998). Curricular diversity continued, however, to characterize education at the master's level. A 1984 NASPAA-sponsored study identified no fewer than five distinct models of graduate education for public service (Ellwood 1985). Each of the five models defined a separate stratum in the historical evolution of the educational enterprise, the end result of distinctive forces impacting the field at specific points in time. The existence of five very different approaches also demonstrated the absence of a single coherent disciplinary focus within the field. Each of the five models displayed not only a different curricular framework, but differences in content and emphases within courses, even those bearing identical or similar titles. Moreover, within each model were obvious differences in the level, scope, and application of quantitative tools; in the disciplinary backgrounds of faculty; and in the nature of the student body. The five models encompassed: (1) political science-based programs; (2) separate units or departments of public administration; (3) comprehensive schools or programs; (4) public policy programs; and (5) generic management programs.

The Ellwood study was a snapshot in time, capturing the state of public administration education when its basic outlines were relatively clear. Over the course of the next two decades elements in that configuration would change under the impact of NASPAA review processes and the inevitable tendency of programs to borrow from one another. The popularity of some would wane, especially those based on the generic model. Many political science-based programs would separate into independent organizational units. Nevertheless, the essential configuration identified in the early 1980s would remain remarkably constant through the decade and well into the 1990s.

Some new curricular trends influenced virtually all programs during the 1980s. Interest in program evaluation and policy analysis exploded. Perhaps in response to the imperatives of NASPAA accreditation standards, perhaps as an attribute of growing interest in policy analysis and program evaluation, public administration curricula, particularly at the master's level, devoted increasing attention to research methods. In the early 1980s, the first research-methods texts with a public sector focus appeared (Gohagan 1980; Meier and Brudney 1981; Welsh and Comer 1983).

Concern with the pace of progress in teaching computer applications for public administration followed close on the heels of increased interest in research methods. Despite the growing importance of computers in the practice of public administration, the academic field throughout the 1980s generally didn't prepare students well for the information age. A 1983 study found that microcomputing was rarely taught within academic programs (Garson 1983). Three years later, NASPAA's Ad Hoc Committee on Computers in Public Management Education found public administration programs well behind other disciplines in bringing computer skills into the curriculum.

While program faculty struggled to adapt the curriculum to rapid changes in the technological underpinnings of public policy and public administration, enrollments suddenly assumed a new and unexpected volatility. Between 1978 and 1983, the number of graduates of Master of Public Administration (MPA) programs declined by about 25%, from 28,191 to 21,138. The one exception was in public policy programs, where the number of graduates actually increased by 15.4% (Conant 1992, 228). Between 1981 and 1983, the number of graduate programs within NASPAA decreased for the first time from 192 to 186, but by the end of the decade a selective recovery had occurred. Throughout the decade, public policy programs displayed the greatest vitality, increasing enrollments by 78% from 1982 to 1989. During the same period comprehensive school enrollments declined 18%. The most dramatic reversal came, however, in the generic management programs, where total enrollments declined by over 73%. Four of the five major generic schools decided to eliminate their public sector focus altogether. Clearly, with the exception of the policy programs, the period of rapid growth and expansion characterizing the 1970s was over.

One outgrowth of declining enrollment was the development of new and innovative approaches to curriculum delivery. Needs unique to the growing number of part-time adult students altered the manner in which courses were taught. A 1982 study found that three-quarters of the programs surveyed offered courses in the evening. Many also used late-afternoon periods and lunchtimes. Weekend-intensive programs and Executive MPA programs and off-campus courses also became commonplace in the search for new and more attractive scheduling alternatives (Daniels, Darch, and Swain 1982).

In a climate of intense competition for students, recognition as a program in substantial conformity with NASPAA's master's degree standards assumed ever greater importance. As NASPAA's peer review process acquired wider acceptance, the membership agreed that the time had come to move away from the somewhat ambiguous process of rostering approved programs and toward full-fledged accreditation. By this time approximately seventy programs had been rostered, that is, given the functional equivalent of accreditation. In 1983, therefore, NASPAA successfully petitioned the Council on Postsecondary Accreditation for recognition as an authorized accrediting agency.

Concern with enrollments had the additional effect of focusing attention on the demographics of the student body. Nationwide, pressures for increased access and opportunity for women and minorities in all academic fields compelled programs to examine student recruitment and faculty representation. In 1984, a report of the NASPAA Diversity Committee pointed out that representation of women students in MPA programs increased from 20% in 1976 to 43% in 1984; African American student representation increased from 9% to 11% in that same period. Nevertheless, female faculty members constituted only 14.4% of faculty in NASPAA-member schools, and African Americans only 5%. Both remained largely concentrated at instructor and assistant professor levels, and at lower average salaries. Almost half of NASPAA-member programs had no minority faculty, 22% had no women, and 13.4% had neither women nor minority faculty (NASPAA, Interim Report of the Diversity Committee 1984). A later study found that women and minority faculty encountered substantial institutional obstacles constraining their careers. Isolation, the absence of mentors, and a lack of informal support from colleagues limited career mobility (Cicin-Sain et al. 1988).

NASPAA responded in several ways to the concerns raised by the Diversity Committee. At one level, NASPAA attempted to strengthen the accreditation standard requiring programs to demonstrate that they had plans to increase the racial and gender diversity of full-time faculty. In 1988 NASPAA, in cooperation with thirty-two participating doctoral-granting institutions, inaugurated a fellowship program to increase the number of minority doctoral candidates. A 1990 survey found, however, continuing under-representation of women and, especially, minorities in doctoral programs (Overman 1990).

Doctoral education itself had become the focus of increasing attention and a source of some alarm in the 1980s, although such qualitative concerns were not new. The first NASPAA policy statement on doctoral education was issued in 1975. The original statement was amended in 1983 and again in 1987 (Overman 1990; NASPAA 1987). The central issue concerned the quality of doctoral-level preparation in public administration as compared to that in related disciplines. Major problems included the overall quality of dissertation research, the level of rigor in instructional content of doctoral-level courses, and the quality of interaction with and supervision by faculty.

Concern for the quality of doctoral programs was part of a coming-of-age process for public administration as a separate discipline. For public administration to assume its place on an equal footing with established social science disciplines the quality and rigor of doctoral education would have to be strengthened. One critical first step was to establish the doctorate as a research degree and not an advanced credential for professional practice. This principle was affirmed in the first NASPAA policy statement and reiterated in subsequent versions.

Inextricably tied to the issue of doctoral education was an equally pressing concern with the overall quality of research. Critics regularly cited the low quality of research as evidence of the failure of doctoral programs to prepare students adequately (Stallings 1986; White 1986;). Throughout the 1980s a regular succession of studies criticized the quality and sophistication of public administration research. (Cleary and McCurdy 1984; Garson and Overman 1983; Perry and Kraemer 1986, 1989). A 1990 study, for example, found research in public administration largely underfunded in relation to other disciplines, nonempirical, and with little theory testing. It ended with the dispirited conclusion that a cumulative knowledge base was not being developed (Houston and Delavan 1990).

The debate on doctoral education and research set in motion during the 1980s would last well into the 1990s and beyond. Meanwhile, at the other end of the spectrum, new concerns with undergraduate education emerged. In 1976, NASPAA approved guidelines for baccalaureate-level programs in public administration. Several decades of profound neglect followed as the Association's attention fixed on accreditation for master's level programs. A study undertaken by the Undergraduate Section of NASPAA in the early 1980s found approximately 225 under-graduate programs at universities across the country. Only sixty-seven, however, were located in NASPAA-affiliated institutions, with most of those connected to graduate-level programs in some way. By the mid-1980s virtually all of the institutions having solely undergraduate programs had withdrawn from NASPAA. The Undergraduate Section itself slowly withered and finally was disbanded.

Publication of the Volcker Commission report provided some impetus for a reexamination of undergraduate preparation for public service. Among other findings, the report noted serious difficulty in recruiting the best and brightest college students into public service. The portrayal of government and public service in the classroom, the report suggested, leads to a highly critical and negative view of government service, discouraging career interest. A study of the treatment of bureaucracy in introductory American government textbooks, for example, found a clearly negative and derogatory slant (Cigler 1991).

Resurgence of interest in doctoral and undergraduate education indicated a growing sense that main task of NASPAA in its early years, to strengthen the master's degree in public affairs and public administration, had been successfully completed. Initial confirmation emerged from the results of a 1989 survey of 215 NASPAA-affiliated institutions. The results demonstrated a growing commonalty in the required core course component in the curriculum among both accre-dited and nonaccredited programs. Specific course titles differed, but an inner core of six areas characterized many of the programs surveyed. These six areas included: (1) a general overview or introduction to public administration, (2) research methods, (3) public finance, (4) policy analysis, (5) personnel, and (6) political institutions and processes. These areas appeared in required course offerings in over half of the programs, although not necessarily in the same courses. For the first time since the end of the 1940s, there appeared to be fairly widespread agreement on a general body of knowledge central to the field (Cleary 1990).

Despite clear evidence of commonalties in core curricula, there was no evidence that accred-itation was leading to a uniform or standardized pattern. Considerable variation among programs continued to be the norm. Credit-hour requirements, for example, varied greatly, from a low of twenty-four to a high of sixty-four. Programs in political science departments not only were smaller than the norm, but they were less likely to be accredited. Public policy programs, with their emphasis on economic models and analytic techniques, were very different from the others.

Ironically, just as academic public administration, at least at the master's level, seemed to have achieved a modicum of curricular consensus, new waves of criticism from within and outside academia were about to break. Ultimately these would challenge not only the complacency of the academic community, but also the very foundations of the enterprise upon which education for public service was built.

The NASPAA Committee on Careers and Marketing issued a report in 1989, which, although not widely noted at the time, contained startling and in many ways disheartening news for graduate programs. The fundamental conclusion can be summarized in one statement: "Even in government, employers are shockingly ignorant of the MPA curriculum and education." After close to a century of growth, ferment and debate, the fundamental academic credential for public sector management still lacked recognition. The report expressed concern for the identity and value of the MPA degree, noting that the degree was neither well known nor clearly understood by prospective employers within or outside of government. Most significant for the decade to come was the apparent lack of congruence between NASPAA accreditation standards and the diverse roles graduates would play in the changing world of the future.

The report of the Committee on Careers and Marketing is important in that it was one of the earliest notes in what would become a growing chorus of concern about the capacity of education in public administration to meet the changing needs of the public service. At about the same time, and with far greater public fanfare, the National Commission on the Public Service, commonly known as the Volcker Commission, released its unsettling two-volume report. The main conclusion was that the federal government was in the throes of a "quiet crisis," a persistent erosion in the quality of the public service, particularly at the senior administrative and professional levels. The Commission called upon educational institutions and agencies of government to work together cooperatively to enlarge the pool of young talent with a commitment to public service.

Implicit in the Commission report was a devastating commentary on education for public administration, specifically on the failure of the academic community in its most critical responsibility; i.e., to assure a steady and reliable stream of well-trained, capable recruits for government service. The report challenged the academic community to do better. Considerable discussion and debate followed, punctuated by a series of reports within NASPAA urging reconsideration of undergraduate and secondary school teaching about government and public service; suggesting methods to enhance recruitment of students for public service; and examining the adequacy of midcareer education (NASPAA 1991). Following publication of the Winter Commission Report on the state and local public service, a similar set of recommendations ensued, albeit with a greater focus on the need to strengthen in-service education and training (NASPAA 1992; Dunn 1994).

Running through all of the responses to the Winter and Volcker Commission reports was the sense of a genuine public crisis of confidence in American governmental institutions. In vivid contrast to the 1930s, public opinion at the end of the 1980s viewed government as an adversary, a morass of costly, redundant, and ineffective institutions administered by remote, unresponsive, and inefficient bureaucrats. Discussions having to do with strengthening government service had, therefore, a faintly anachronistic quality. Despite the interest, even zeal within the academic community to improve the quality of government management, the national tide clearly was running in a different direction.

As the 1980s drew to a close, people recognized that the nature of public service was changing dramatically and that those changes would have profound implications for both teaching and practice in public administration. Activities and operations previously confined to government now fell within the province of other sectors (NASPAA 1989, 9). By the end of the decade, a combination of widespread moves to privatize government services, demands to downsize government, reinventing and reengineering initiatives, rising concerns with budgetary deficits at the federal level and rising taxes pointed to a radically changed environment for public service.

These changes, part of a rising tide of distrust and disbelief in the efficacy of government at all levels, would continue well into the next decade and would provide the backdrop against which education for public administration would confront fundamental challenges to its very purpose. Just when some consensus on curriculum finally emerged, the capacity of that curriculum and of public service education in general to meet the needs of the future was seriously in doubt.

IX. THE DECADE OF THE 1990s: INTO A STRANGE NEW WORLD

For public service education, the final decade of the twentieth century represented both the best and the worst of times. Curricular consensus on a common core of knowledge and a rich diversity of approaches and concentrations characterized education at the master's level. Enrollments were on the rise, and unprecedented levels of external recognition and respect had been achieved. Advancing technologies gave rise to new pedagogical tools both within and beyond the bounds of the traditional classroom. Beneath the surface, however, changes were occurring that would threaten the very foundations of the discipline upon which the educational enterprise was based. By the conclusion of the decade every aspect of education, from the nature and goals of the students to the basic definitions of public in public administration, would have changed. As both academic discipline and operational enterprise, public administration was about to confront a major identity crisis, the ramifications of which would be felt well into the next millennium.

By the early 1990s, public administration had come into its own as a separate, identifiable field of study. Organizational and institutional separation from political science and from management was well underway. In 1991, for the first time, separate public administration departments were a plurality of NASPAA-member programs (Henry 1995, 45). Organizational separation of public administration programs indicated an increase in perceived effectiveness, a quality long attributed to MPA programs within independent schools or departments (Baldwin 1989). Also notable, however, was the decline in the percentage of separate professional schools within NASPAA. To some extent this decline may reflect the demise of the generic school concept and subsequent withdrawal of several generic schools from NASPAA membership. It also reflects the growing diversity of programmatic emphases within the association, the growth of newer, smaller programs through the 1980s, and NASPAA's shift from its origins as a Dean's Club to an organization serving a broad spectrum of program types. Between 1983 and 1993 the number of NASPAA-member programs had grown from 186 to 218.

In 1995 the first journal devoted solely and specifically to public service education appeared. The *Journal of Public Administration Education* initially was sponsored jointly by ASPA's section on Public Administration Education, the University of Kansas, and the University of Akron. Several years later, NASPAA assumed responsibility for it, and the renamed *Journal of Public Affairs Education* (JPAE) became the central forum for the discussion of a wide range of educational issues: from pedagogical approaches and new instructional technologies to the educational impact of the larger trends and forces on the profession. Publication of *JPAE* was yet another indication of the growing independent identity of public administration as a separate and distinct field of study. It also reflected continued dissatisfaction with the capacity of ASPA and the *Public Administration Review* to effectively serve the needs of the academic community.

Evidence continued to accumulate on the impact of accreditation. The trend toward broader curriculum coverage in topics and skills not previously included in the core continued. The traditional distinction between the policy analysis and institutional management approaches became increasingly blurred as a broadly similar common core of required courses came to characterize all NASPAA-accredited programs (Roeder and Whitaker 1993). Attitudinal surveys of MPA students and graduates found few notable distinctions between those in public policy or those in public administration programs (DeSoto, Opheim, and Tajalli 1999). Although not always with great success, many programs intensified efforts to increase the numbers of members of previously unrepresented groups, both as faculty members and students. At an institutional level, clearer arrangements for program governance were evident at many institutions. Accreditation processes also seemed to generate more resources for program use, more accurate admissions decisions, and greater "truth in advertising" (NASPAA 1992; COPRA 1992).

By the early 1990s it was also clear that MPA enrollments were on the rise. The number of master's degrees awarded had increased from 6209 in 1983 to 7867 in 1993 and by 1997 had surged to over ten thousand. That number would remain relatively stable through the remainder of the decade. Undergraduate enrollments, however, declined precipitously, from a high of 11,518 in 1995 to 8355 in 1999.

Increasing gender diversity characterized MPA enrollments. In 1993, for the first time, slightly over half of the master's level students were female, although that number had declined slightly by the end of the decade. The number of African-American students, however, remained level, and the number of Hispanic students increased only slightly (NASPAA 2000). Despite accreditation mandates and aggressive outreach and recruitment efforts by some programs, progress toward increasing the representation of minority students was slow.

New constituencies for programs in public affairs and public administration also emerged in the early 1990s. The changing international environment increased demand for education in public administration from foreign students and foreign countries. The need was especially great in the newly emerging democracies of Eastern Europe and among nations attempting to move toward free market economies. Requests for technical assistance provided exciting new opportunities for American faculty to work with their counterparts in Eastern Europe, China, and other parts of the world. Rising expectations, however, also presented a challenge to individual programs and to the academic community in general. The fragmented nature of requests for assistance created a call for a more coordinated and strategic response (NASPAA, February, 1994). The need to develop curricula for administration in governments and cultures unlike those in the United States also highlighted a creative tension between the particularistic and universalistic content of traditional MPA degree programs, raising again a long-standing concern with the fundamentally parochial nature of American public administration (Maggiotto 1997).

Bringing public management teaching cases to newly democratizing and developing nations emphasized the importance of the democratic context so often taken for granted in American institutions (Husock 1995). In the absence of such crucial instruments as contract law, the concept of property rights and civil liberties, instruction in the fundamentals of western public administration proved particularly problematic (Eliason 1995). Faculty teaching in newly emerging or newly democratizing nations confronted the difficulty of establishing the fundamental constructs of critical thinking and free exchange of ideas in students subject to decades, even centuries of cultural and political repression (Boyd 1997).

By midpoint in the decade new technologies were beginning to have a major impact on public service education. First, these technologies opened up vast new opportunities for distance education. Second, they expanded the range of classroom pedagogy through various forms of online and internet-mediated instruction. The widespread availability of distance learning technologies promised access to new student populations as well as expanding enrollments. This availability also raised concerns about instructional quality, learning outcomes, and accreditation (Banas 1998; Brower and Klay 2000; Rahm and Reed 1997, 1999). The results of two surveys undertaken in the middle of the decade indicated growing interest in the use of distance technologies, although at that point only 10% to 12% of institutions contacted actually offered distance learning courses (NASPAA 1995; Leavitt and Richman 1997). Despite predictions early in the decade that the growth of distance education might spell the demise of many traditional programs, by the end of the 1990s it seemed clear that for most programs distance and online instruction would serve as a useful tool and adjunct rather than a replacement for conventional forms of instruction. Use of distance technologies continued to be limited by equipment and training costs and by the quality of interaction between students and faculty.

While widespread use of distance learning may have been limited to a relatively small numbers of programs, other technologies were influencing virtually all institutions. Tools such as email, listservs, the Internet, teleconferencing, electronic bulletin boards, home pages, which were almost unknown in 1990 were transforming teaching and research by 1995. The vision of "cyberschools" of public administration, i.e., electronically linked learning communities characterized by a seamless web of communication and information access, seemed a realistic possibility by midpoint in the decade (Cahill and Overman 1996). During the 1990s, with astonishing rapidity, electronic media literally transformed the way in which students learned and changed the way that information was gathered, organized, and presented (Labaree 1996).

The case method, often maligned but still a staple instructional medium in many MPA programs, received renewed attention in the 1990s, often in conjunction with efforts to improve the scope and impact of ethics education (Winston 2000), as a tool for aggregating and generalizing organizational experiences, e.g., "best practices" (Hannah 1995), or as a means of introducing preservice students to the realities and dilemmas of administrative life (Massic 1994). Electronic access to case materials and new forms of instructional software almost certainly facilitated the renewal of interest (Brock 1994; Saint-Germain 1998).

Of all curricular topics, concern with the teaching of ethics seemed to dominate thought and discussion throughout the decade. Some of this discussion focused on pedagogical approaches to teaching ethics in the classroom, such as through cases, literature (Marini 1992), or historical reference (Edmondson 1995). Much more of the discussion, however, examined the underlying purpose of ethics education and the extent to which ethics instruction can change underlying values, attitudes, and behaviors (Bowman and Menzel 1998; Garofalo 1994; Lee and Paddock 1992;). In an effort to answer the latter question, a study of MPA graduates was undertaken in 1996. The findings were ambiguous. Course assessments were generally favorable, with most students noting that the course had made them more ethically sensitive. One in three respondents, however, reported that the course had made no difference in their ethical outlook or behavior. Less than half (43%) of those who reported facing an ethical dilemma found that their educational experience had been helpful (Menzel 1997).

A wide and growing range of elective concentrations characterized the MPA curriculum in the 1990s. These ranged from such traditional areas as human resources and finance to newly emerging fields such as information technology or even such specialized fields such as defense procurement. Particularly notable during this period was the proliferation of programs devoted to the management of nonprofit organizations. Beginning with fewer than a dozen such offerings in the early 1990s, the number had grown to over eighty by the end of the decade. Programs of this type were found not only within MPA programs, but also in within MSW and even MBA curricula. Considerable debate focused on the appropriate housing for such programs (Mirabella and Wish 2000) and on appropriate curricular design (Young 1999), discussion that undoubtedly continued well into the next decade. The most telling aspect of these new programs, however, rested with their growth and rapid expansion. Clearly, several decades of privatization, cutbacks, and devolution of governmental services had led inexorably to new venues for the provision of public services and new constituencies for graduate degree programs devoted to the management of such services.

The early 1990s also witnessed the beginnings of several significant alterations in accreditation processes and procedures. The first occurred following a new mandate issued by the Council on Postsecondary Accreditation (COPA). The mandate required all accrediting associations to demonstrate a relationship between the standards applied to programs and the outcomes produced. As a result, NASPAA now expected all programs applying for accreditation to develop some means for determining the effectiveness of their educational efforts. The COPA mandate shifted the emphasis of accreditation from traditional input measures such as number of credit hours required, number of full-time faculty, and core course components, to an examination of results: the actual capacity of graduates to assume the responsibilities for which their education supposedly prepares them (Poister 1991). Emphasis on outcomes redirected attention toward ways to measure the skills and competencies of graduates and prompted renewed attention to experiential or skill-building aspects of the curriculum as well as to development of specific, course-related skills such as those in quantitative methods. Studies of the latter, long an object of concern, indicated that, while the teaching of quantitative methods by the early 1990s had become almost universal in MPA programs, the level of sophistication in such courses remained low (Waugh and Hy 1994).

Discussion of outcome measures also became part of a larger dialogue within NASPAA centered around the question of whether accreditation processes had lost the flexibility and respon- siveness to programmatic diversity that had been a hallmark of their creation. To some, accreditation had become fixated on narrow, quantitative measures of conformity, losing sight of broader measures of quality and success. (COPA Report October 23, 1992). Expressing a collective belief that creative pluralism should be a prime characteristic of education for public adminis- tration, the NASPAA membership voted in 1992 to accept proposed changes in the standards and peer review process to move toward a mission-directed accreditation process. The change to program mission as the central focus of accreditation was the first major change in accreditation procedures in twenty years, but one that was welcomed by the vast majority of NASPAA members.

The shift in accreditation emphasis demonstrated the growing influence of organizations and agencies outside the traditional sphere of public administration education. A further indicator, one appearing less benign to many, appeared when MPA programs for the first time were included in *U.S. News and World Report*'s annual examination of "America's Best Graduate Schools." The published rankings produced glee among in some programs and consternation in others. While the results occasioned angry denunciations of the study's approach and methodology (Teasley 1995), they also were seen by some as indicative of a growing legitimacy and professionalism in the field (Perry 1995) and by others as a vehicle for reconsidering qualitative indicators for MPA programs (Ventriss 1995).

One topic of perennial concern, the quality of dissertation research, continued to bedevil the academic community throughout the 1990s. The number of universities granting the doctorate in public administration had increased from fifty-seven in 1981 to seventy-three in 1998. Neverthe- less, the number of dissertations listed by Dissertation Abstracts had increased only slightly, from 142 in 1981 to 168 in 1998. The number of dissertations written by women, however, more than doubled during the same period, from twenty to fifty-six (Cleary 1998).

There was some cause for optimism. Follow-up studies undertaken by Robert Cleary in1992 and in 1998 found considerable improvement in the quality of doctoral dissertations (Cleary 1992, 1998). Attaching the same criteria used in 1981, both studies found that later dissertations in general demonstrated a better defined research purpose, stronger methodology, and greater attention to causality. Both studies also noted a decline in the number of purely descriptive and single case study dissertations as well as "practitioner projects." Even this more optimistic assessment, noted, however, with some concern that many of the topics were of peripheral interest to the field.

During the same period, Adams and White compared dissertation research in public adminis- tration with five other fields and concluded that public administration research was not inferior to that undertaken in the other disciplines (Adams and White 1994). The authors did note the preva- lence of "practice research," studies of organizational change or policy implementation confined to the author's own agency. This type of study appeared to be almost nonexistent in other fields, but comprised almost a quarter of all dissertations in public administration. Descriptive and nontheore- tical, these dissertations ranked among the lowest in quality.

The issue of dissertation quality inevitably led to broader discussions of research quality within the discipline as a whole (White and Adams 1994). The use of the case study in dissertation research revived perennial debates as to the worth of this kind of research in general (Jensen and Rodgers 2001). Several studies led inescapably to the conclusion that both dissertation quality and sub- sequent research productivity were closely linked to faculty research productivity and exposure to research opportunities (Brewer et al. 1999; Douglas 1996).

By the conclusion of the decade, there appeared to be little agreement even on such fundamental questions as whether or not there exists a coherent intellectual body of knowledge for doctoral students to master or the appropriate definition of the doctorate within the field of public administration (Felbinger et al. 1999). The distinction between the Ph.D. and D.P.A. degrees remained murky at best, and the debate continued as to whether a distinction should be made between doctoral programs oriented toward the needs of practitioners and those designed to prepare future academicians (Sherwood 1996; Clayton 1995). Prospects for NASPAA accreditation of doctoral programs, an issue under discussion for several decades, remained uncertain. The only certainty was that a multiplicity of approaches and methodologies would continue to characterize dissertation research well into the foreseeable future.

The early 1990s would provide evidence at many levels of a growing distance between the concerns of academics and practitioners. Indeed, the Golden Age of the 1930s and 1940s may have been the only time in which the academic study and professional practice of public administration were fully aligned. By the end of the 1980s, however, the historical tension between the two had reached a new level. For academics, the field of public administration needed to move toward a new level of theory building and theory development if ever it could assume the status of a credible academic discipline. Academics within ASPA increasingly demanded a room of their own. In 1990 a new journal appeared, the *Journal of Public Administration Research and Theory*, with an "avowedly scholarly" editorial objective. *J-PART*, as it became known, set as its task the promotion of research and theory building in public administration (*Journal of Public Administration Research and Theory* 1993). The growing disenchantment of academics with the traditional professional associations in public administration was demonstrated also by the number of public administration faculty turning back to political science as a forum for publication and discussion.

Even as longstanding battles between academic and practitioner and theory and practice continued to characterize the internecine landscape, far more ominous storm clouds gathered on the outside. Relentless attacks on government at all levels accelerated and intensified throughout the decade as both Republican and Democratic administrations sought ways to downsize, privatize, outsource, and otherwise reduce the size, scope, and cost of government. Compounding the environmental challenges was an unprecedented crisis of identity within the discipline itself. Nowhere was that point more starkly and dramatically evident than in the fact that the two most influential movements shaping the behavior of governmental organizations throughout the decade, Total Quality Management and the Reinventing Government movement, had their origins far from what could be considered mainstream public administration (Osborne and Gaebler 1993). Further underscoring the growing isolation of academic public administration from the world of practice, the Clinton administration undertook the most ambitious managerial reform in decades with virtually no involvement or participation from the professional or academic communities (Gore 1993).

Meanwhile, the nature of the public service, even the nature of public itself was experiencing radical transformation. The trend toward contraction of middle management was evident throughout the decade as public sector resources continued to shrink. Not only did this contraction threaten the traditional pool from which prospective MPA students had been recruited, it imposed new demands and pressures on those middle managers remaining in government. Management in the newly emerging hollow state demanded skills and competencies not traditionally considered part of the MPA curriculum. As the report of the Winter Commission noted, future managers would be called upon far less to manage bureaucracies in the traditional sense, and far more to arrange networks. Traditional emphases on matters such as supervision, discipline, and oversight. were giving way to the need for skills in coaching, benchmarking, mentoring, and championing (National Commission on the State and Local Public Service 1993). Despite indisputable evidence that government and the public service in the twenty-first century would be very different from those in earlier times, there was little indication in the final years of the 1990s that educational organizations or institutions were prepared to respond in any systematic or concerted fashion. Clearly, there was evidence of greater openness and flexibility in accreditation processes and of a conceptual broadening of the field. Emphasis in general was shifting away from education exclusively for career government service and toward education for diverse and mobile careers across sectors (NASPAA 1994). Nevertheless, as the decade drew to a close academic public administration confronted a future clouded with uncertainty.

X. EDUCATION AND THE CHALLENGES OF A NEW MILENNIUM

As the United States entered a new millennium, critics in government, the media, and even the discipline itself questioned the efficacy, values, and philosophical foundations upon which the enterprise of public administration had rested for the past century. An unprecedented crisis of legitimacy and loss of confidence, which were the cumulative result of reinvention, the primacy of market models, and multiple assaults on government, confronted the discipline (Denhardt and Denhardt 2000). The catastrophic events early in the new decade would pose still greater challenges to a profession and discipline struggling to define itself in a dramatically changed environment.

Some responsibility for the crisis was laid to rest directly on the doorstep of academia. Critics argued that educators themselves had played an important contributory role in the crisis through their failure to make the moral case for government or to give adequate consideration to the ethical duties of public servants (Brown 1998). Moreover, they argued, the willingness on the part of at least some in the educational community to adopt the language of the marketplace and to accept the premises of reinvention undermines the fundamental constructs of democratic citizenship.

Whatever the source of the problem, however responsibility might be established, the nature of the public service clearly was changing. Fewer and fewer graduates of the country's most prestigious MPA programs entered the public sector. More and more found more exciting or more lucrative opportunities with nonprofit organizations or with private sector contracting and consulting firms (Swope 2001). Of serious import for the future of the federal government were the results of one study of first-year graduate students that found federal jobs to be a priority for only about one-fourth of the respondents, while more than half looked to the nonprofit and private sectors for future employment (Adams et al. 1999).

Paul Light, in the most comprehensive study to date on the public service at the turn of the new millennium found, "… government is becoming the employer of last resort, one that caters more to the security-craver than the risk-taker" (Light 1999). Concluding that a government-centered public service is a thing of the past, Light defined four characteristics of the new public service: (1) greater diversity in age, race, and gender among students; (2) a rising interest in nongovernmental career options, especially in the nonprofit sector; (3) higher levels of job mobility within and among sectors; and (4) a deep commitment to making a difference in the world. While the commitment to making the world a better place remained, government no longer appeared the most likely tool for doing so. In both recruitment and retention of graduates, government lagged farther and farther behind.

Light's study posed important new questions for public service education. While most students noted general satisfaction with the quality of their education, they also noted gaps in the curriculum. These included areas such as conflict and change management, information and communication technology as well as leadership and ethics. The study underscored the absence of attention within the curriculum to the different organizational settings making up the new public service and challenged the individual institutions as well as NASPAA and APPAM to address the need for curricular change and to become more actively involved in addressing the needs of the new public service.

Even as it struggled to cope with the changing nature of the public service, NASPAA itself faced new demands for openness and accountability. Under new mandates from the Council on Higher Education Accreditation, the work of NASPAA's Commission on Peer Review and

Accreditation operated increasingly as an autonomous and independent body. Only accredited institutions, not the full membership, as in the past, were permitted to vote on changes in the MPA Standards. Council for Higher Education Accreditation (CHEA) began to require COPRA to provide more information on interpreting the Standards to institutions pursuing accreditation and, in turn, to require the institutions themselves to provide more public disclosure on important outcome measures such as placement and success rates of graduates. In direct contravention of prior practice, COPRA faced pressures for full disclosure of its actions, an accounting both of accredited programs as well as those not successful in satisfying accreditation requirements. A longstanding tradition of collegiality wrestled with new pressures for accountability and public disclosure.

As public administration struggled with its crisis of confidence, some scholars began to rethink the lessons of the past. In doing so they found new insights into the past and new visions for the future of public service education. Camilla Stivers (2000) in her groundbreaking study of the urban reform movement, suggested that the efficiency norms and managerial focus that dominated both the reform movement and professional education in public administration reflected the values of an essentially masculine view of public improvement. An alternative view, one emphasizing norms of responsiveness and compassion, was embodied in the settlement work of women, but this work was largely ignored by history and in the evolution of academic training for the profession. Richard Stillman (1998) taking a different approach, explored the religious and moral convictions of the early reformers and stressed the need to reestablish a new value-based foundation in order for the discipline to thrive. Hindy Schachter (1997) retrieved the notion of active citizenship embodied in the early reform movements to counter the ethos of reinvention and customer-driven public administration.

In the early years of the decade, however, there were few indications that the field had found new groundings or that public service education had discovered a new center. Enrollments in master's and doctoral programs continued to rise but, paradoxically, students and graduates sought the satisfactions of public service outside of and sometimes far from the realm of government. Most notably, almost a century after the first formal instruction in public administration began, academicians still found it necessary to try to define the "big questions" of public administration education (Denhardt 2001). Clearly, big answers were not readily apparent.

XI. THE FUTURE OF EDUCATION AND PUBLIC SERVICE IN THE NEW MILLENNIUM

From its beginnings the character of the educational enterprise has been shaped by events in the surrounding environment. Curricular and programmatic growth blossomed under the benign influence of Progressivism and the urban reform movement, followed quickly by expansion of the administrative state in the 1930s and 1940s. As the range and scope of governmental activism diminished in the 1950s and early 1960s, academic public administration waned as well. The societal turbulence and change characterizing the period from the late 1960s to the 1980s boosted the fortunes of academic programs and led to curricular and pedagogical transformation. By the end of the 1980s to the present time, however, as the scope of governmental activity diminished and the very purpose of government faced growing scrutiny, both the academy and public administration faced perhaps their greatest challenge.

Responding to the changing character of the public sector will demand considerable curricular transformation. New competencies in team building, communication, employee involvement, cultural awareness and labor relations, to name a few, will be needed by managers in the future. Meeting these challenges may well require faculty to radically reconsider the core curriculum and the range of skills it imparts to graduates (Dunn 1994). New teaching methods also may be needed, with a greater focus on experiential opportunities to assist students in mastering interpersonal and managerial skills. The interdisciplinary quality that always has characterized public service education will need to be expanded still further as graduates increasingly move across sectors in the course of their careers.

Throughout its history, the strength and vitality of education for public service derived from its capacity to respond to changing times, needs, and values. While the nature of that response has led less to consistency than to multiplicity, it has enabled the field to respond effectively to changing and ever more complex demands. By all indications, the response to the foreseeable and unforeseeable demands of the future will follow the same pattern, continuing the process of layering-on that has characterized the past. Those who seek a neat synthesis or a universal paradigm probably are doomed to disappointment. In all likelihood an even greater multiplication of educational approaches will occur as academic public administration becomes still more multidisciplinary and as new educational experiments respond to the changing nature of public service, to emerging pedagogical technologies, and to new expectations.

REFERENCES

Adams, G. B. and White, J. D., Dissertation research in public administration and cognate fields: an assessment of methods and quality, *Public Administration Review*, 54(6), 565–575, 1994.

Adams, W. C. et al., *Attitudes Toward Public Service Careers: NASPAA/GWU Survey Results*, National Association of Schools of Public Affairs and Administration, Washington, DC, 1999.

Ad Hoc Committee on Computers in Public Management Education, Curriculum recommendations for public management education in computing, *Public Administration Review*, 46(6), 595–602, 1986.

Baldwin, J. N., Comparison of perceived effectiveness of MPA programs administered under different institutional arrangements, *Public Administration Review*, 48, 876–884, 1989.

Banas, E. J., History and issues of distance learning, *Public Administration Quarterly*, 22(3), 365–383, 1998.

Blunt, B. E., Developments in public administration pedagogy: 1880 to the present, In *Handbook of Public Administration*, Rabin, J., Hildreth, W. B., and Miller, G. I., Eds., Marcel Dekker, New York, 1989.

Bowman, J. and Menzel, D., Eds., *Teaching Ethics and Values in Public Administration Programs: Innovations, Strategies, and Issues*, State University of New York Press, Albany, NY, 1998.

Boyd, K. J., Practice makes perfect: the art of American public management, *Journal of Public Administration Education*, 3(1), 93–96, 1997.

Brewer, G. A., Douglas, J. W. and Fazer, R. L., Determinants of graduate research productivity in doctoral programs of public administration, *Public Administration Review*, 59(5), 373–382, 1999.

Brock, J., An electronic hallway: desktop case access becomes available, *Journal of Political Analysis and Management*, 13, 778–784, 1994.

Brower, R. and Klay, W. E., Distance learning: some functional questions for public affairs education, *Journal of Public Affairs Education*, 6(4), 215–231, 2000.

Brown, P. G., The legitimacy crisis and the new progressivism, *Public Administration Review*, 58(4), 1998.

Cahill, A. G. and Overman, E. S., The cyberschool vision: living on planet PA, *Journal of Public Administration Education*, 2(1), 67–75, 1996.

Carroll, J. D. and Fredrickson, H. G., Dwight Waldo 1913–2000, *Public Administration Review*, 61(1), 2–8, 2001.

Chandler, R. C. and Plano, I. C., *The Public Administration Dictionary*, Wiley, New York, 1982.

Chapman, R. L. and Cleaveland, F. N., *Meeting the Needs of Tomorrow's Public Service: Guidelines for Professional Education in Public Administration*, The National Academy of Public Administration, Washington, DC, 1973.

Church, R. L., History of universities in the united states, In *The Encyclopedia of Education*, Deighton, L., Ed., Macmillan, New York, pp. 341–354, 1971.

Cicin-Sain, B., Newcomer, K. E. and Sampson, C., *The Status and Concerns of Women and Minority Faculty in Public Administration: Results from a National Survey*, National Association of Schools of Public Affairs and Administration, Washington, DC, 1988.

Cigler, B. A. and Neiswender, H. L., 'Bureaucracy' in the introductory American government textbook, *Public Administration Review*, 51, 442–450, 1991.

Clayton, R., The DPA: contributing to society's need for scholarship and leadership, *Journal of Public Administration Education*, 1(1), 61–65, 1995.

Cleary, R., What do public administration master's programs look like? do they do what is needed?, *Public Administration Review*, 50(6), 663–673, 1990.

Cleary, R., Revisiting the doctoral dissertation in public administration: an examination of the dissertations of 1990, *Public Administration Review*, 55(6), 55–61, 1992.

Cleary, R., The public administration doctoral dissertation reexamined: an evaluation of the dissertations of 1998, *Public Administration Review*, 60(5), 446–455, 1998.

Committee for Economic Development, *Improving Executive Management in The Federal Government*, Committee for Economic Development, Washington, DC, 1964.

Conant, I. K., Enrollment trends in schools of public affairs and administration: a search for winners and losers, *Public Administration Review*, 52(3), 288–297, 1992.

Daniels, M. R., Darch, R. E., and Swain, J., Public administration extension activities by American colleges and universities, *Public Administration Review*, 422, 56–65, 1982.

Denhardt, R. B., The big questions of public administration education, *Public Administration Review*, 61(5), 526–534, 2001.

Denhardt, R. B. and Denhardt, J. V., The new public service: serving rather than steering, *Public Administration Review*, 60(5), 549–559, 2000.

DeSoto, W., Opheim, C., and Tajalli, H., Apples and oranges? comparing the attitudes of public policy versus public administration students, *American Review of Public Administration*, 29(1), 77–91, 1999.

Douglas, J. W., Faculty, graduate student, and graduate productivity in public administration and public affairs programs, 1986–1993, *Public Administration Review*, 56(5), 433–440, 1996.

Dunn, D. D., Public affairs, administrative faculty and the winter commission report, *Public Administration Review*, 54(2), 109–110, 1994.

Edmondson, H. T., Teaching administrative ethics with help from Jefferson, *Political Science Policy*, 28, 226–229, 1995.

Egger, R., The period of crisis: 1933–1945, In *American Public Administration: Past, Present and Future*, Moscher F. C., Ed., University of Alabama Press, Tuscaloosa, AL, pp. 49–96, 1975.

Eliason, L., Public administration education in democratizing societies, *Journal of Policy Analysis and Management*, 14(4), 149–155, 1995.

Ellwood, J. W., *A Morphology of Graduate Education for Public Service in the United States*, National Association of Schools of Public Affairs and Administration, Washington, DC, 1984.

Felbinger, C., Holzer, M. and White, J. D., The doctorate in public administration: some unresolved questions and recommendations, *Public Administration Review*, 59(5), 459–464, 1999.

Fesler, J. W., Public administration and the social sciences: 1946–1960, In *American Public Administration: Past, Present and Future*, Mosher, F. C., Ed., University of Alabama Press, Tuscaloosa, AL, pp. 97–141, 1975.

Garofalo, C., Ethics education and training in the public service, *American Review of Public Administration*, 24(3), 283–292, 1994.

Garson, G. D., Microcomputer applications in public administration, *Public Administration Review*, 43, 453–458, 1983.

Garson, G. D. and Overman, S., *Public Management Research in the United States*, Praeger, New York, 1983.

Gohagan, J. K., *Quantitative Analysis for Public Policy*, McGraw-Hill, New York, 1980.

Gordon, R. A. and Howell, J. E., *Higher Education for Business*, Columbia University Press, New York, 1959.

Gore, A., *Creating a Government That Works Better and Costs Less*, US Government Printing Office, Washington, DC, 1993.

Graham, G. A., *Education for Public Administration*, Committee on Public Administration of the Social Science Research, Public Administration Service, Chicago, IL, 1941.

Gulick, L. and Urwick, L., *Papers on the Science of Administration*, Institute of Public Administration, New York, 1937.

Hannah, S. B., The correlates of innovation: lessons from best practice, *Public Productivity and Management Review*, 19, 216–228, 1995.

Henry, L. L. Early NASPAA history, Summary report from NASPAA historical project, prepared for NASPAA's, 25th anniversary conference, Austin, TX, October, 18–21, 1995.

Henry N., The emergence of public administration as a field of study, In *A Centennial History of the American Administrative State*, Chandler R., Ed., Free Press, New York, pp. 37–78, 1987.

Henry, N., *Public Administration and Public Affairs*, 6th ed., Simon and Schuster, Englewood Cliffs, NJ, 1998.

Hoffman, C. M., Paradigm lost: public administration at Johns Hopkins University, 1884–1896, *Public Administration Review*, 62, 12–23, 2002.

Honey, J. C., *Higher Education for Public Service*, American Society for Public Administration, Washington, DC, 1966.

Houston, D. J. and Delevan, S. M., Public administration research: an assessment of journal publications, *Public Administration Review*, 50(6), 674–681, 1990.

Husock, H. Democracy and public management cases, *Journal of Policy Analysis and Management*, 14(4), 145–148, 1995.

Hutchins, R. M., Shall we train for public administration? 'Impossible', In *Ideas and Issues in Public Administration*, Waldo, D., Ed., McGraw-Hill, New York, pp. 225–227, 1953.

Jensen, J. L. and Rodgers, R., Cumulating the intellectual gold of case study research, *Public Administration Review*, 61(2), 235–246, 2001.

Johnson, P. I., *The Progressive Movement, Municipal Reform, and the Founding of the Maxwell School Review*, The Maxwell School of Citizenship and Public Affairs, New York.

Kraemer, K. and Perry, J., Institutional requirements for academic research in Public Administration, *Public Administration Review*, 49(1), 9–16, 1989.

Kraemer, K. and Perry, J., Editorial comment, *Journal of Public Administration Research and Theory*, 3(1), 1–3, 1993.

Labaree, R. V., Teaching public administration in the information age, *Journal of Public Administration Education*, 2(1), 76–85, 1996.

Lambie, M., *Training for the Public Service*, Public Administration Clearing House, Chicago, IL, 1935.

Leavitt, W. M. and Richman, R. S., The high tech MPA: distance learning technology and graduate public administration education, *Journal of Public Administration Education*, 3(1), 13–27, 1997.

Lee, D. and Paddock, S. C., Improving the effectiveness of teaching public administration ethics, *Public Productivity Management Review*, 15(4), 487–495, 1992.

Light, P., *The New Public Service*, Brookings Institution, Washington, DC, 1999.

Maggiotto, M. A., Transferring the american experience: rethinking an old question, *Journal of Public Administration Education*, 3(1), 65–68, 1997.

Marini, F., Literature and public administration ethics, *American Review of Public Administration*, 22(2), 111–120, 1992.

Martin, R., Political science and public administration: a note on the state of the union, *American Political Science Review*, 46, 665, 1952.

Massie, C. F., Teaching introduction to public administration via the case method, *Journal of Public Administration Education*, 1, 102–115, 1995.

McCurdy, H. and Cleary, R., Why can't we resolve the research issue in public administration?, *Public Administration Review*, 44(1), 49–55, 1984.

McKenna, C. K., *Quantitative Methods for Public Decision Making*, McGraw-Hill, New York, 1981.

Meier, K. and Brudney, J. L., *Applied Statistics for Public Administration*, Duxbury Press, Boston, MA, 1981.

Menzel, D. C., Teaching ethics and values in public administration: are we making a difference?, *Public Administration Review*, 57(3), 224–230, 1981.

Miller, I. P., Graduate education, In *The Encyclopedia of Education*, Deighton, L. D., Ed., Macmillan, New York, pp. 185–190, 1971.

Mirabella, R. M. and Wish, N. B., The 'best place' debate: a comparison of graduate education programs for nonprofit managers, *Public Administration Review*, 60(3), 219–229, 2000.

Morstern-Marx, F., Ed., *Elements of Public Administration*, Prentice Hall, Englewood Cliffs, NJ, 1946.

Mosher, F. C., *Democracy and the Public Service*, Oxford University Press, New York, 1968.

Mosher, F. C., Ed., *American Public Administration: Past, Present and Future*, University of Alabama Press, Tuscaloosa, AL, 1975.

Murphy, T., *Government Management Internships and Executive Development*, Lexington Books, Lexington, MA, 1973.

Murphy, T., *Democracy and the Public Service*, Oxford University Press, New York, 1982.

National Association of Schools of Public Affairs and Administration, *Standards for Masters Degree Programs in Public Affairs and Administration*, NASPAA, Washington, DC, 1974.

National Association of Schools of Public Affairs and Administration, *NASPAA Policy on Doctoral Education in Public Affairs/Public Administration*, NASPAA, Washington, DC, October 16, 1983.

National Association of Schools of Public Affairs and Administration, *Interim Report on Diversity Committee*, NASPAA, Washington, DC, September 26, 1984.

National Association of Schools of Public Affairs and Administration, *Task Force Report on the future of NASPAA*, NASPAA, Washington, DC, February 10, 1984.

National Association of Schools of Public Affairs and Administration, *NASPAA Policy on Doctoral Education in Public Affairs/Public Administration*, NASPAA, Washington, DC, October 24, 1987.

National Association of Schools of Public Affairs and Administration, *Final Report of the NASPAA Committee on Careers and Marketing*, NASPAA, Washington, DC, October 28, 1989.

National Association of Schools of Public Affairs and Administration, *Report of the NASPAA Task Force on Revitalizing the Public Service*, NASPAA, Washington, DC, December, 1991.

National Association of Schools of Public Affairs and Administration, *Improving Public Service in State and Local Governments*, NASPAA, Washington, DC, August, 1992.

National Association of Schools of Public Affairs and Administration, *Report of the Ad Hoc Commitee on the Future of Public Service Education and Accreditation*, NASPAA, Washington, DC, April, 1992.

National Association of Schools of Public Affairs and Administration, *Commission on Peer Review and Accreditaiton, Annual Report to NASPA Members*, NASPAA, Washington, DC, 1992.

National Association of Schools of Public Affairs and Administration, *Report on the Meeting of NASPAA Deans and Directors on International Public Administration, Education, Training and Research*, NASPAA, Washington, DC, 1994.

National Association of Schools of Public Affairs and Administration, *Report of the First Meeting of the Task `Force on the Future of NASPA*, NASPAA, Washington, DC, 1994.

National Association of Schools of Public Affairs and Administration, *Report of the Standards Committee: survey Results on Distance Learning Technologies*, NASPAA, Washington, DC, 1995.

National Association of Schools of Public Affairs and Administration, *Attitudes toward Public Service Carreers: NASPAA/GWV Survey Resuits*, NASPAA, Washington, DC, 1999.

National Commission on the State and Local Public Service, *Hard Truths/Tough Choices: An Agenda for State and Local Reform*, Nelson A. Rockefeller Institute of Government, Albany, NY, 1993.

National Commission on the Public Service, *Leadership for America: Rebuilding the Public Service*, US Government Printing Office, Washington, DC, 1989.

Nelson, L., Public administration and training in the former Soviet and communist countries, *Journal of Public Administration Education*, 3(1), 61–64, 1997.

Olson B. E., Challenge and response: the history of the school of public administration, In *Twenty-Five Years of Building Better Government: A Report of the Proceedings, Twenty-Fifth Anniversary Celebration, School of Public Administration*, Olson F. P., Ed., XX. University of Southern California Press, Los Angeles, CA, 1955.

Osborne, D. and Gaebler, T., *Reinventing Government*, Addison-Wesley, Reading, MA, 1993.

Overman, B. S., Perry, J., and Radin, B. A. *Doctoral Education in Public Affairs and Administration: Issues for the 1990s*, Paper prepared for NASPAA annual conference, October 27, 1990.

Perry, J., Ranking public administration programs, *Journal of Public Administration Education*, 1, 132–135, 1995.

Perry, J. and Kraemer, K., Research methodology in the public administration review, 1975–1984, *Public Administration Review*, 46(3), 215–226, 1986.

Pierson, F., *The Education of American Businessmen*, Carnegie Corporation, New York, 1959.

Poister, T. R., *Public Program Analysis: Applied Research Methods*, University Park Press, Baltimore, MD, 1978.

Poister, T. R, Ed., Symposium on outcomes assessment, *American Review of Public Administration*, 21(3), 1991.

Poore, D. M., The impact of NASPAA's standards on defining the field of public administration, In *Public Administration: History and Theory in Contemporary Perspective*, Uveges, J. A., Ed., Dekker, New York, pp. 85–104, 1982.

Rahm, D. and Reed, B. J., Going remote: the use of distance learning, the world wide web and the internet in graduate programs in public affairs and administration, *Public Productivity Management Review*, 20(4), 459–474, 1997.

Rahm, D. and Rydl, T., Internet-mediated learning in public affairs programs: issues and implications, *Journal of Public Affairs Education*, 5(3), 213–223, 1999.

Roberts, A., Demonstrating neutrality: the Rockefeller philanthropies and the evolution of public administration, 1927–1936, *Public Administration Review*, 54, 3, 1994.

Roeder, P. W. and Whitaker, G., Education for the public service: policy analysis and administration in the MPA core curriculum, *Public Productivity and Management Review*, 24(4), 512–529, 1993.

Saint-Germain, M. A., Does new media software improve MPA student performance?, *Public Productivity Management Review*, 21(3), 309–323, 1998.

Sass, S. A., *The Pragmatic Imagination: A History of the Wharton School*, University of Pennsylvania, Philadelphia, PA, 1983.

Schachter, H. L., *Reinventing Government or Reinventing Ourselves*, State University of New York Press, New York, 1997.

Schott, R. L., Public administration as a profession: problems and prospects, *Public Administration Review*, 36, 253–259, 1976.

Schick, A., The trauma of politics: public administration in the 1960s, In *American Public Administration: Past, Present and Future*, Mosher, F. C., Ed., University of Alabama Press, Tuscaloosa, AL, pp. 142–180, 1975.

Sherwood, F., Revisiting the premises of the DPA after 25 years, *Journal of Public Administration Education*, 2, 107–115, 1996.

Siffin, W. L., The new public administration: its study in the United States, *Public Administration*, 34, 357, 1956.

Simon, H. A., *Administrative Behavior: A Study of Decision-Making Processes in Administrative Organizations*, Free Press, New York, 1947.

Stallings, R., Doctoral programs in public administration, *Public Administration Review*, 46(3), 235–240, 1986.

Stewart, W., *Graduate Study in Public Administration*, US Office of Education, Washington, DC, 1961.

Stillman, R., *Creating the American State: The Moral Reformers and the Modern Administrative World they Made*, University of Alabama Press, Tuscaloosa, AL, 1998.

Stivers, C., *Bureau Men, Settlement Women: Constructing Public Administration in the Progressive Era*, University Press of Kansas, Lawrence, KS, 2000.

Stone, A. B. and Stone, D. C., Early development of education in public administration and appendix: case histories of early professional education programs, In *American Public Administration: Past, Present, and Future*, Mosher, F. C., Ed., University of Alabama Press, Tuscaloosa, AL, pp. 11–48, 1975.

Sweeney, S. B., Ed., *Education for Administrative Careers in Government Service*, University of Pennsylvania Press, Philadelphia, PA, 1958.

Swope, C., Ways to sway an MPA, *Governing*, 14(9), 30–31, 2001.

Teasley, C. E., The bad (U.S.) news ranking of MPA programs, *Journal of Public Administration Education*, 1, 136–141, 1995.

Ventriss, C., The rating system: determining what constitutes a quality public administration program, *Journal of Public Administration Education*, 1, 142–153, 1995.

Waldo, D., *The Administrative State*, The Ronald Press, New York, 1948.

Waldo, D., Ed., *Ideas and Issues in Public Administration*. McGraw-Hill, New York, 225–254, 1953.

Waldo, D., *The Sudy of Public Administration*, Random House, New York, 1955.

Waldo, D., Public administration, In *Political Science: Advance of the Discipline*, Trish, M. D., Ed., Prentice Hall, Englewood Cliffs, NJ, pp. 153–189, 1968.

Waldo, D., Developments in public administration, *Annals of the American Academy of Political and Social Science*, 404, 217–245, 1972.

Waldo, D., Education for public administration in the seventies, In *Public Administration: Past, Present and Future*, Mosher, F. C., Ed., University of Alabama Press, Tuscaloosa, AL, pp. 181–232, 1975.

Waldo, D., *The Enterprise of Public Administration: A Summary View*, Chandler and Sharp, Novato, CA, 1980.

Waugh, W. L. and Hy, R. J., Quantitative analysis and skill building in public administration graduate education, *Public Administration Quarterly*, 18(2), 204–210, 1994.

Welsh, S. and Comer, I. C., *Quantitative Methods for Public Administration*, Dorsey Press, Homewood, IL, 1983.

Whitaker, G., Segmentation, decentralization and diversity: public administration education in the United States, In *Serving the State: Global Public Administration and Training*, Davies, M., Ed., Ashgate Press, Brookfield, VT, pp. 211–223, 1998.

White, J. D., Dissertations and publications in public administration, *Public Administration Review*, 46(3), 227–234, 1986.

White, J. D. and Adams, G. B., Eds., *Research in Public Administration: Reflections on Theory and Practice*, American Society for Public Administration/Sage Publications, Thousand Oaks, CA, 1994.

White, L. D., *Introduction to the Study of Public Administration*, Macmillan, New York, 1926.

Wildavsky, A., *The Politics of the Budgetary Process*, Little Brown, Boston, MA, 1964.

Wilson, W., The study of administration, *Political Science Quarterly*, 2, 197–222, 1887.

Winston, K., Teaching ethics by the case method, *Journal of Political Analysis and Management*, 19, 153–160, 2000.

Young, D., Nonprofit management Studies in the United States: current developments and future prospects, *Journal of Public Affairs Education*, 5, 13–24, 1999.

Zumeta, W. and Solmon, L. C., Professions education, In *Encyclopedia of Educational Research*, Mitzel, H. E., Ed., Free Press, New York, pp. 1458–1466, 1982.

20 Public Administration Pedagogy: What Is It?

Norma M. Riccucci

CONTENTS

I. INTRODUCTION

Public administration education in the United States began in large part as a reaction to corruption, fraud, and moral perversions in government service. As tensions grew around the perceived incompetence and inefficiency of this service, government reformers sought to make government run more like a business; to make it function, in the words of Wilson (1887, 197) "with the utmost possible efficiency and at the least possible cost either of money or of energy." Indeed, the first piece of civil service legislation, the Pendleton Act, passed in 1883, sought to create an administrative service that was competent and devoid of politics. It was from these reform initiatives that educational programs in public administration began to emerge in this country.

It is virtually impossible to separate public administration pedagogy and andragogy from the history of public administration as a field of study. While early educational programs in public administration may not have reflected a self-conscious or self-aware concern for the field (see Waldo 1980, 10–12), contemporary education in public administration reflects the field's or, more appropriately, subsets of the field's definition of what public administration is.

This chapter begins with a brief overview of the evolution of the first public administration educational programs in the United States. It then looks at how various areas of study or of academic inquiry have sought to stake a claim in public administration, and as a corollary, its pedagogical orientation. The eclectic nature of the field of public administration illustrates that there is no single, cookie-cutter approach to teaching public administration. The focus of the chapter is on public administration education at the master's, as opposed to doctoral, level. While the master's degree (e.g., MPA) is geared toward practice, the doctoral degree is geared toward study and research, and hence has an entirely different pedagogical approach.

A. The Genesis of Public Administration Education

Scholarly attention to the administrative apparatus in government in the United States is generally attributed to Woodrow Wilson's seminal 1887 piece, "The Study of Administration." This was an intellectualized response to a slow train wreck produced by patronage and spoils in the federal government. The now well-cataloged (or well-maligned) politics–administration dichotomy was a theoretic call to purge politics and its ensuing corruptions from the practice of public administration. But the popularity of Wilson's treatise to the field of public administration was perhaps not extant when educational programs emerged in this country. That is to say, educational programs were more a practical response to the corruption in government; the focus was thus on the preparation of professionals in public service or administration. The intent was to train practitioners to be effective and efficient public administrators, much like the aim of the curricula of the eighteenth-century Cameralists[*] and later the nineteenth-century Prussians (Waldo 1980). Education for public service, then, was not encumbered by the various expositions of "what is public administration?" Even though national and state developments signaled the need to create a trained cadre of public administrators, it was at the municipal level that the first training ground for public servants emerged. As Stone and Stone (1975, 19) observed:

> Greater access to information and use of communications made it easier for citizen groups to ferret out local scandals and to press for reform than to affect the national government.

Corruption in New York City, they go on, was particularly formidable, thus providing a fertile setting for change that ultimately brought into flower the profession of public administration and the creation of variously titled educational programs in public affairs and administration (Stone and Stone 1975, 19–20).

In 1906, the New York Bureau of Municipal Research was established in response to the abuses and corruption plaguing New York City government. Initially founded to study and expose the political excesses of New York City government, the Bureau also established the first professional school of public administration: The Training School for Public Service, founded outside of academe in 1911. Although formally separate, the Training School functioned as a part of the New York Bureau of Municipal Research (Stivers 2002). The applied-focused curricula were intended to provide those already trained in a particular profession (e.g., social work or civil engineering) with education in the processes, functions, and management of government, as well as in research techniques. Examples (Stone and Stone 1975) of the courses offered include:

- Law and Municipal Government
- Legislative Drafting and Administration
- Elements of Municipal Accounting
- Municipal Highway Engineering
- Politics and Administration
- Principles of Management
- Police and Fire Administration
- Budget-Making, Accounting, and Reporting

The first distinctly professional graduate program in public administration[†] was not offered until 1914. It began when the University of Michigan's political science department launched

---

[*] See Wagner 2005, who explores the relevance of a Cameralist orientation for contemporary scholarship in public finance.
[†] Certainly, however, universities had been offering programs in civil engineering that were among the first of public service education.

a one-year master's program in municipal administration that, in addition to course work, required three months of field work.[*] After that, the department of political science at the University of California, Berkeley began offering seminars and courses in public administration in 1920. Then, in 1921, Stanford University began a three-year program in public administration within its political science department (Stone and Stone 1975).

But America's oldest separate school of public affairs and administration is the Maxwell School of Citizenship and Public Affairs, established at Syracuse University in 1924, with William E. Mosher as its first dean (Lane, undated manuscript). A large part of the Training School for Public Service was transferred to the Maxwell School, and graduate work required courses not only in public administration, but in all the social sciences (Stone and Stone 1975). The University of Southern California, like Syracuse, established a separate professional school between 1928 and 1929: the School of Public Administration. These are important developments because these schools positioned public administration as a field separate and distinct from political science. Additionally, the actual location of a public administration program or department may be indicative of its approach to pedagogy, as will be discussed later.

In the 1930s, a number of other universities began to offer course work in public administration, many within political science departments, and from all of these early efforts, a basis for public administration education emerged.

B. Public Administration: Its Scope and Its Place

Waldo states that:

> By accident or necessity—who can way which?—Public Administration became identified with the new academic discipline of Political Science (1980, 12).

As a field of study, this seems clear. Although, as noted above, educational programs in public administration first emerged within political science departments,[†] early writings linked to public administration suggest with certainty that public administration was seen as more than a political science endeavor. Frank Goodnow's (1893) *Comparative Administrative Law*, his *The Principles of the Administrative Law of the United States* (1905), and Frederick Taylor's *Principles of Scientific Management* (1911), to name but a few, would place public administration squarely in the fields of law or industrial engineering. These influential discourses and the history of the field hint lack of consensus and, indeed, outright disagreement over the scope of public administration. Again, all these factors have implications for public administration educational programs.

C. The Organizational Chart

The physical location of public administration programs within university settings tells us something about pedagogical approach. Programs housed in political science departments, for example, might emphasize course work in intergovernmental relations; urban politics; bureaucracy and society; public policy; and state and local government. Those teaching in these programs will likely have a philosophical bent, twisting as far as an academic degree, toward political science as opposed to something like organizational behavior.

---

[*] The program later evolved into the Institute of Public Administration, and then the Institute of Public Policy Analysis.

[†] See, however, the second note on the previous page.

Public administration programs, in particular those accredited by the field's accreditation body, the National Association of Schools of Public Affairs and Administration (NASPAA),[*] are organized into universities in a variety of manners. For example, there are free-standing schools of public administration or affairs that house, as one department, public administration. Syracuse University's Maxwell School of Public Affairs and Citizenship has under its wings about a half a dozen departments and programs, one of which is the Department of Public Administration. The University of Georgia's School of Public and International Affairs has three departments, one of which is the Department of Public Administration and Policy.

Some public administration programs or departments are located within business schools. For example, the MPA program[†] at Golden Gate University in California is housed in the Ageno School of Business; it offers such courses as Public Enterprise Management E. Public Sector Business Relations, and Public Service Law. Other institutional arrangements for public administration programs can be seen as follows:

- Social Science Departments or Schools (e.g., the University at Texas at Dallas)
- Public Management Departments or Schools (e.g., Suffolk University, Boston)
- Urban Affairs Schools or Colleges (e.g., Cleveland State University)
- Management & Urban Policy Departments or Schools (e.g., The New School in New York)
- Public Policy & Management Schools or Departments (e.g., Carnegie Mellon University in Pennsylvania)
- Public Service Schools (e.g., New York University)

The point here is that the way in which public administration programs or departments are organized into the university setting will reflect the unique pedagogical approaches to public administration. The orientation may be geared toward business administration, generic management, urban affairs, political science, government, or public administration, and, so forth. In this sense, there is no uniformity in master's degrees in public administration. Because NASPAA's accreditation process is mission-based,[‡] a master's degree in public administration, affairs, or policy from Carnegie Mellon will look very different from that from Syracuse University.

D. DEFINING THE FIELD

Chapter 1 in this book addresses more fully the history of the field of public administration and what this signifies for efforts to clearly define the field. Suffice it to say here that there is no consensus in the field as to what the academic enterprise of public administration comprises (see Frederickson 1991; Frederickson and Smith 2003; Rosenbloom 1983; Rosenbloom and Kravchuck 2004; Riccucci 2001, 2005). Public administration has historically been pulled towards different disciplinary areas or fields of inquiry, each seeking to stake a claim in the field. This is one explanation for the varied physical locations of public administration programs. The different orientations have led to a patchwork of educational programs in public administration. Is the heart of public administration political science? Is it organizational behavior? Perhaps it could be management of the

---

[*] NASPAA, formerly known as the Council on Graduate Education for Public Administration (CGEPA), first began as a satellite of the American Society for Public Administration (ASPA), the professional association of public administration. By 1975, it had become independent of ASPA (see, for example, Frederickson 2004).

[†] The degree is called EMPA, or executive master of public administration.

[‡] Mission-based accreditation requires departments or programs of public administration to tie their curricula directly to their specified mission. NASPAA also recommends that public administration degree programs cover such topics as budgeting, human resources, ethics and so forth.

public and generic type? Could it even be economics (policy analysis)[*] or decision-making? Is public administration the creation of public policy, or is it policy implementation?

In one sense, public administration is all of the above, and then some. By its very nature, public administration is a multidisciplinary endeavor. As Waldo (1980, 58) observes, because public administration is multidisciplinary, "no single, agreed, and authoritative definition" of public administrative pedagogy is possible. "Nor," he adds, "would it be desirable" (Waldo 1980, 58). He goes on to say that:

> Among those engaged in education for the M.P.A. there would be almost no dissent from the proposition that any *one* academic discipline is inadequate to the task of supplying the needed knowledge and skills (Waldo 1980, 59, emphasis in original).

In this sense, professional training in public administration is strengthened by the variegated nature of the field and its related pedagogical approaches.

In addition to the multidisciplinary nature of public administration and its implications for pedagogy, the question has often been asked, "Is public administration an art or a science?" The answer to this question begets another question: Are administrators born or are they trained? The answer here is that public administration is both art and, taken loosely, science. It is an art because persons who become leaders or exemplary managers are understood to possess innate talent. That is, there is a belief that some people may be naturally predisposed or inclined to leadership roles as compared with others; although disputable, they are referred to as natural born leaders.

The practice of public administration, despite the teachings of Taylor (1911) and Gulick and Urwick (1937), can never be a science, where principles formulating one best way can be methodically reproduced and adhered to. Yet, on the other hand, the practice of public administration can be thought of as requiring some scientific training insofar as persons need some technical preparation to become public administrators. Indeed, by virtue of the very existence of the MPA degree, public administration from the standpoint of practice represents, in part, a scientific or policy analytic endeavor, although never, of course, entirely sans politics. As Leonard White (1955) predicted, our society has become so complex and mutable that it must continually rely on technical and scientific training of government administrators.

Lynn (1996) seeks to make some sense out of the different labels that have been ascribed to public administration and public administrative education. Specifically, he provides some definitions for the domain of public management as a field and as a practice, urging universities to provide educational training to foster public management as both study and practice. He points out that public management did not originate as a term of scholarship, a way to define or clarify. Instead, it began as a term of art expressing a jurisdictional claim by new graduate programs in public policy to a domain owned until the 1970s, when public policy programs began to proliferate, by another field, so-called traditional public administration (Lynn 1996, 1–2).

Lynn goes on to say that issues of jurisdiction inform the teaching and research enterprise of public management. The term public management "has been appropriated by teachers and scholars in the academic community to provide a theme for their work" (Lynn 1996, 2). Ultimately, as Lynn (1996, 86) admits, when members of the public administration community and the public policy community refer to public management, they are not speaking the same language, nor are they pursuing the same intellectual agenda. The leaders of the effort to create a new field of public policy analysis proclaimed a decisive break with traditional public administration. Public policy's public management community has shown little subsequent inclination toward comity with its sister province in public administration.

---

[*] See Weiner (1980) and Behn (1980) for discussions of the rise of policy analysis programs and their relationship to public administration and public management.

Again, all of these ruminations, proclamations, and imperialist proclivities, in effect have implications for how public administration—or public management or public policy, or public policy analysis—is taught. One approach is not better than the others; it is merely a reflection of the orientation of those studying and teaching public administration, and laying claim to it from their personal intellectual, philosophical, or ideological frames of reference.

It is also worth noting, *vis-à-vis* labels, that the appellation of the degree program itself reflects the lack of agreement in the field over what public administration is. Again, the upshot here is that there is no uniform, one best pedagogical approach to public administration. The array of different degree programs, from MPA to MSPPM (see below), further reflects the biases in public administrative educational programs. Some examples will be examined here (the degree titles and acronyms come directly from each institution's website):

1. The Heinz School of Public Policy and Management at Carnegie Mellon University
   - Master of Science in Public Policy and Management (MSPPM)
   - Master of Science in Information Security Policy and Management (MSISPM)
   - Master of Public Management (MPM)
   - Master of Science in Information Technology (MSIT)
2. The University of Massachusetts at Amherst's Center for Public Policy and Administration
   - Master's Degree in Public Policy and Administration (MPPA)
3. The University of California in Los Angeles (UCLA) School of Public Affairs
   - Master of Public Policy (MPP)
4. The University of Southern California's School of Policy, Planning and Development
   - Master of Planning (MPL)
   - Master of Public Administration (MPA)
   - Master of Public Policy (MPP)
   - Master of Health Administration (MHA)
   - Master of Real Estate Development (MRED)
   - Master of International Public Policy and Management (IPPAM)
   - Executive Master of Health Administration (Executive MHA)
5. The Bush School of Government and Public Service at Texas A&M
   - Master of Public Service and Administration (MPSA)
   - Master's Program in International Affairs (MPIA)
6. New York University's Wagner Graduate School of Public Service
   - Master of Science in Management (MS in Management)
   - Master of Urban Planning (MUP)
   - MPA in Public and Nonprofit Management and Policy (PNP)
   - MPA Health Policy and Management (HPAM)

These are but a sampling of the various master's degree programs in public administration, illustrating the various ways in which the programs are conceptualized, articulated, and packaged, from A to Z. In some cases, the course work between an MPA and MPP may be very similar. In other cases, it may be completely different. In addition, the MPA or the MPP may look very different from one institution to the next. For example, one program's MPP may be geared more toward political science, whereas another's may be geared more toward economics.[*] Again, the locations of the department, program, or school within the university, as well as the orientation of the teaching faculty, are factors that may influence the substantive content of each degree program.

---

[*] Future studies might examine the courses offered in each degree program.

E. TEACHING PUBLIC ADMINISTRATION

The way in which one defines the field, and hence teaches public administration, is also a function of one's academic training in a doctoral program. The varied master's degree programs, and the departments or schools that house them, were discussed previously. A brief examination will be made of who teaches in public administration programs or departments accredited by NASPAA. The following is meant to be illustrative, based on a nonprobability, purposive sample. Although somewhat crude, it provides some information on who teaches public administration.

In general, faculty who teach in public administration,[*] affairs, or policy departments have doctoral training in a host of disciplines, from management science to nuclear engineering. Looking at the faculty members teaching in the institutions discussed earlier indicates the following:

1. The Heinz School of Public Policy and Management at Carnegie Mellon University
   A relatively high proportion of the faculty hold PhDs in Economics (roughly 30%), followed by around 20% holding PhDs in management science/information technology/operations research. Others hold degrees in applied physics, biotechnology, business administration or management, social psychology, urban planning, and theater.
2. The University of Massachusetts at Amherst's Center for Public Policy and Administration
   The highest concentration of doctorates held by faculty is in political science (about 37%), followed by economics (22%) and sociology (11%). Others (one or two) hold doctorates in law, anthropology, geography, communication and public policy, and education and public policy.
3. The School of Public Affairs at the University of California in Los Angeles (UCLA)
   Faculty members in the Department of Public Policy hold doctorates in economics (about 25%) and political science (about 21.4%), in addition to at least one or two faculty members holding degrees in nuclear engineering, medicine, law, geography, public policy, and urban planning.
4. The University of Southern California's School of Policy, Planning and Development
   Two of the 34 or so faculty[†] have doctorates in public administration (DPAs), two in public policy, and one in government. In addition, about 26.5% hold PhDs in economics, 11.6% in political science, and 8.8% in sociology. Other degrees held by one or two faculty members include civil engineering, physics, mathematical psychology, urban planning, and history.
5. The Bush School of Government and Public Service at Texas A&M
   Out of over 30 faculty members, two hold PhDs in public administration. About 30% hold degrees in political science, 16.7% in economics, and the remainder of faculty have degrees in such fields as law, educational administration, and history.
6. New York University's Wagner Graduate School of Public Service
   Faculty at the Wagner School hold degrees in economics (about 20%), political science (12.5%), business administration or management (about 10%), and public administration (about 10%). Others have degrees in medicine, law, clinical psychology, urban studies, sociology, and public policy.

In short, faculty members teaching in departments of public administration, policy, or affairs hold a host of different degrees. In the schools and departments profiled in this chapter, there is

---

[*] NASPAA does collect profile data on faculty members teaching at accredited institutions, but the data do not include field of study in doctoral programs (e.g., PhD in economics, political science and so forth).

[†] In some cases, the field of study was not listed for faculty, and, hence, they were excluded from the total count. In addition, here as elsewhere, only full-time faculty members are included.

generally a relatively high percentage of faculty holding PhDs in economics, followed next by political science. Interestingly, in this rudimentary, to be sure nonrandom review, extraordinarily few faculty members hold degrees in public administration. There were a total of two DPAs, and five PhDs in public administration out of more than 200 faculty members represented at these six institutions. Again, the training and background of those teaching public administration will certainly influence the approach to pedagogy.

F. SPAE AND *JPAE*

In 1979, the primary professional association of public administration, the American Society for Public Administration (ASPA), established the Section on Public Administration Education (SPAE), aimed at promoting excellence in the teaching of public administration. Over the years, efforts were made to encourage SPAE to launch a journal in public administration education, but the section never moved forward with the initiative (Frederickson 2004, 84).

The push to create to such a journal, however, did not diminish. One scholar in particular invested an enormous amount of time to establish a journal devoted to public administration education: H. George Frederickson. In the early 1990s, Frederickson devised a strategy to house and financially support a journal of public administration education within the academy, specifically in a school or department of public administration. Two universities, Akron and Kansas, supported such an idea, and together they launched the *Journal of Public Administration Education*. The first issue of *JPAE* appeared in May of 1995.

In 1997, facing problems in attracting subscriptions, *JPAE* was acquired by NASPAA, and the first issue of the journal, renamed *Journal of Public Affairs Education,* appeared in January of 1998 (Frederickson 2004). Today, *JPAE* fills an important gap in the field of public administration by providing a scholarly outlet for those who study public administrative education. Published quarterly, *JPAE* includes articles on curriculum content, pedagogy, and educational philosophy.

II. CONCLUSIONS

Public administration is a dynamic field that continues to draw students from all disciplinary backgrounds. The master's degrees offered are wide and varied, as reflected in the names of the degree programs and the fields of training of those who teach the courses. As noted throughout this chapter, public administration pedagogy cannot be separated from the history of public administration as a field of study, and more specifically, the manner in which public administration is conceptualized. In this sense, there is no single way to develop and teach the courses that comprise master's degrees in public administration, affairs, management, policy, and so forth. In the end, this adds strength to a field that is multidisciplinary in nature, encompassing aspects of both art and science; an area of study that means different things to different people.

REFERENCES

Behn, R. D., Policy analysis and public management: what should Jones do?, In *Education for Public Service*, Birkhead, G. S. and Carroll, J. D., Eds., Maxwell School of Citizenship and Public Affairs, Syracuse University, Syracuse, NY, 1980.

Frederickson, H. G., Toward a theory of the public of public administration, *Admin. Soc.*, 22(4), 395–417, 1991.

Frederickson, H. G., The journal of public affairs education at age ten: history, content and prospects, *J. Public Aff. Educ.*, 10(2), 83–89, 2004.

Frederickson, H. G. and Smith, K. B., *The Public Administration Theory Primer*, Westview Press, Boulder, CO, 2003.

Goodnow, F. J., *Comparative Administrative Law: An Analysis of the Administrative Systems National and Local, of the United States, England, France and Germany*, G.P. Putnam's Sons, New York, 1893, 1902.

Goodnow, F. J., *The Principles of the Administrative Law of the United States*, G.P. Putnam's Sons, New York, 1905.

Gulick, L. and Urwick, L., Eds., *Papers on the Science of Administration*, Institute of Public Administration, New York, 1937.

Lane, F. S., *The Baruch MPA and Public Affairs Education in the United States: A Short History*, School of Public Affairs, Baruch College, City University of New York, New York, Undated, unpublished manuscript.

Lynn, L. E., Jr., *Public Management as Art, Science, and Profession*, Chatham House, Chatham, NJ, 1996.

Riccucci, N. M., The 'old' public management v. the 'new' public management: where does public administration fit in?, *Public Admin. Rev.*, 61(2), 172–175, 2001.

Riccucci, N. M., The criteria of action in reforming and advancing the administrative state: how do we determine or "know" effectiveness? In *Revisiting Dwight Waldo's Administrative State*, McCurdy, H. and Rosenbloom, D. H. Eds., Georgetown University Press, Washington, DC, pp. 55–70, 2005.

Rosenbloom, D. H., Public administrative theory and the separation of powers, *Public Admin. Rev.*, 43, 219–227, 1983.

Rosenbloom, D. H. and Kravchuck, R. S., *Public Administration: Understanding Management, Politics and the Law in the Public Sector*, 6th ed., McGraw-Hill, New York, 2004.

Stivers, C., *Bureau Men, Settlement Women Constructing Public Administration*, University Press of Kansas, Lawrence, KS, 2002.

Taylor, F., *The Principles of Scientific Management in the Progressive Era*, W.W. Norton & Company, New York, 1911.

Stone, A. B. and Stone, D. C., Early development of education in public administration, In *American Public Administration: Past Present, Future*, Mosher, F. C., Ed., University of Alabama Press, Tuscaloosa, AL, pp. 11–48, 1975.

Wagner, R. E., *The Cameralists: Fertile Sources for a New Science of Public Finance*, Department of Economics, George Mason University, Fairfax, VA, 2005, http://mason.gmu.edu/-rwagner/cameralist.pdf (accessed, February 7, 2005).

Waldo, D., *The Enterprise of Public Administration*, Chandler & Sharp, Novato, CA, 1980.

Weiner, H., Policy analysis and public administration: convergent courses?, In *Education for Public Service*, Birkhead, G. S. and Carroll, J. D., Eds., Maxwell School of Citizenship and Public Affairs, Syracuse University, Syracuse, NY, pp. 13–16, 1980.

White, L. D., *Introduction to the Study of Public Administration*, 4th ed., Macmillan, New York, 1955.

Wilson, W., The study of administration, *Polit. Sci. Q.*, 2, 197–222, 1887.

Unit 11

Information Technology

21 The Evolution of Information Technology in the Public Sector

James Melitski

CONTENTS

I. INTRODUCTION: DATA, INFORMATION, AND KNOWLEDGE

Before discussing the history of information technology (IT) and how it has been applied in the public sector, it is necessary to discuss how we collect, organize, and retain data, information, and, ultimately, knowledge. In his text, *Managing the Public Sector*, Grover Starling (2002) offers the following definitions:

- *Data* are raw, unannotated and unanalyzed facts.
- *Information* is data that are meaningful and that alter the receiver's understanding; it is the data that managers actually use to interpret and understand events in the organization and the environment.
- *Knowledge* is the body of information or the comprehension and understanding that comes from having acquired and organized a great deal of information, e.g., knowledge of medicine.

In other words, data represent descriptive facts and figures. Transforming data into information requires placing it into a broader context so that it can be interpreted and used for making decisions. Knowledge represents framed experiences, values, contextual information, and expert insight that provide a framework for information (Davenport and Prusak 2000).

Having defined information, one can examine information technology that broadly is concerned with "technologies related to a restricted view of information: the generation, processing, and distribution of representations of information" (Zorkoczy 1982). Other experts add that IT "consists of more than just computers; managers must conceive of it broadly to encompass a wide spectrum of linked technologies" (Starling 2002). It is important to note that IT is associated with the technical devices that allow information to be generated analyzed and distributed. Information systems include information technologies but are broader and represent "the people, procedures, inputs, outputs, and processing all working together to produce accurate and timely information" (O'Leary and Williams 1989).

This chapter discusses how data information and knowledge are related from three related perspectives: hardware development, application development, and network development. Since the end of World War II, each of these three perspectives has become mutually dependent while competing for dominance as trends in IT in the public sector have shifted. In recent years, these perspectives have become even more integrated, profoundly affecting the way public organizations plan, implement, evaluate, and generally administer public programs. This discussion will begin by examining the three frameworks. How the perspectives have shaped managerial changes in the field of public administration will be discussed, as will current public sector trends in the application of IT.

II. HARDWARE DEVELOPMENT

A discussion of the history of those technologies designed to count things and create data is typically traced back to the abacus in Babylonia in the fourth century BC (Cringley 1996). In the United States, the public sector made use of technology to generate data as early as 1890, when the US Census Bureau adapted Charles Babbage's punchcard-based computing machine for mass data processing (Davis, Alderman, and Robinson 1990). However, the history of IT and computing in the United States begins in 1942 with the Atanasoff-Berry Computer (ABC), the world's first electronic digital computer (Burks and Burks 1988). A few years later, the ABC was refined and the Electronic Numerical Integrator Analyzer and Computer (ENIAC) was deployed to assist in the preparation of firing tables for artillery (Cringley 1996; Mollenhoff 1988).

However, it was not until after World War II that computers began to replace traditional methods of accounting and record keeping. During the 1950s, as transistors replaced vacuum tubes, the reliability of computers increased (Kroenke 1992). This was an important step that led electrical engineers to create the first Universal Automatic Computer (UNIVAC) that stored 12,000 digits in random access mercury tubes (Mahoney 1988). Again, the government was one of the first organizations to employ the new technology, and, in 1951, the UNIVAC system was used by the US Census Bureau for data storage, retrieval, and counting (Shelley and Cashman 1984). According to Swain and White (1992), using the UNIVAC greatly decreased reporting time, reported accurate data, reduced the Bureau's reliance on staff, and represented the first non-scientific, non-military, and non-engineering use of the computer. The Bureau's use of the UNIVAC system for electronic data processing (EDP) signified the beginning of a public organization's use of IT.

EDP remained the primary focus of public sector computing and spread from the federal to state and local levels by the 1960s. From a managerial perspective, EDP placed emphasis on using hardware to automate and economize traditional methods of processing data. Price and Mulvihill (1965) report that in the fifteen years following the US Census Bureau's use of the UNIVAC, EDP became a mainstay at the federal, state, and local levels in government. Their survey of forty-three states found that agencies at the state level were becoming increasingly dependent on EDP in areas such as law enforcement, employment security, and motor vehicle services. Furthermore, they noted that while computers were used primarily for clerical activities, they were increasingly used in managerial realms. During the hardware development stage, engineering and the electrical engineers that developed the hardware devices heavily influenced the dominant mindset for IT, both in the public and private sectors.

III. APPLICATION DEVELOPMENT

Even though it is now common to think of hardware and software together, historically they evolved a bit differently. Electrical engineers developed the hardware, but there was not a need for new software or application development until organizations required that each new generation of computing technology be adapted and applied in business and government. Once computers left the labs, they needed to be adapted for each specific application, and computer programmers filled this need. Unlike the development of computer hardware, the field of computer programming is not derived from engineering but rather from logical mathematics, mathematical linguistics, and George Boole's algebra of thought (Mahoney 1988). The historical evolution of software application development coincides with several interesting management reforms in the public sector and begins the evolution of management reporting. Starting in the 1960s, individuals applying technology in organizations sought to move the public sector beyond data processing by engaging managers (Holden 2003).

This shift away from strictly data processing toward creating information relevant to managers marks the beginning of the management information systems (MIS) movement (O'Brien 1993). Simply put, an MIS puts data in a context that is applicable to managers. Dock and Wetherbe (1988) note that "a management information system uses computers to provide management information for decision-making. The goal of MIS is to get correct information to the appropriate manager at the right time, in a useful form." However, in a practical sense, the MIS movement fell short in the public sector because it failed to recognize the need to integrate systems. This was due, in large part, to the MIS tendency to view IT developments one application at a time (Holden 2003).

IV. NETWORK DEVELOPMENT

In 1957, the Union of Soviet Socialist Republics (USSR) launched Sputnik, the first space satellite, and the ensuing science gap propelled the United States to investment in science and technology. Following Sputnik and in the midst of the Cold War, the United States saw space exploration and the development of defense-related science and technology as critical to national interests (Hafner and Lyon 1996). In addition to the Cold War rivalry referred to above, Janet Abbate (2000) credits the film *Dr. Strangelove* as another possible catalyst for the development of network technologies that would eventually become the Internet. Abbate argues that the film exposed the vulnerability of the United States' communication networks due to their reliance on centralized telephone systems.

In 1962, the Air Force contracted with the nonprofit Rand Corporation to develop a distributed communication system that employed a technique for transmitting data across telephone lines using a technology that became known as packet switching. The development of packet switching is a useful anecdote for two reasons: first, packet switching technology was adapted in 1969 by the US Department of Defense's Advanced Research Projects Agency in the development of ARPANET—the first computer network and precursor to the Internet; second, and perhaps more importantly, packet switching moved IT beyond processing power and demonstrated its potential for communication (Hafner and Lyon 1996). No longer were information technology specialists concerned solely with technology's ability to process data or calculate pi to thousands of decimal places. Now, IT specialists also needed to be concerned with how computers (and eventually people) exchange data and information.

Ultimately, the technological capabilities of computers and new software applications grew, and the need arose to connect them together. Methods for networking computers became more prevalent. Networking technology facilitated increased processing capabilities and also the sharing of information and communication. In addition, the convergence of hardware, software, and networking along with decreasing costs and the increasing processing capabilities made technology more accessible to managers, not just computer technicians and engineers. Today, managing information across networks of computers has become an integral component of managing in the public sector. Practitioners and public administration researchers alike now recognize that managing information is as vital to the success of their organization as managing a budget or people. The day has passed when public managers could rely on their organizations' technology staffs to manage vital program information (Starling 2002).

Advances in hardware, software, and networking increased the need for organization, transmission, and storage of data. The result was the field of computer science that sought to study the system. While computer scientists were designing new and efficient ways to create networks of computer information systems, managers were applying the systems in organizations. In the 1970s and 1980s, a renewed emphasis was placed on providing managers with information relevant for making decisions and decision support systems (DSS) were developed.

The use of networks in organizations also served as a catalyst for several management reforms. For example, systems analysis was once perceived as a rational decision-making model, coupled with the parallel network technologies, resulting in rapid growth of Tayloresque operations research (Mahoney 1988). In recent years, the confluence of technology, software applications, and networks also catalyzed management reforms such as business process reengineering (BPR), aim to innovate organizational processes and have clear roots in system analysis (Handy 1978). In an interesting juxtaposition, some managers now view organizations as networks, giving rise to the popularity of social network theory (O'Toole 1997; O'Toole and Meirer 2004).

As DSS gained popularity in the private sector between the 1970s and 1980s, managers in the public sector began to recognize that while traditional MISs reinforced organizational silos, the new model, information resource management (IRM), emerged to make use of networking technologies. IRM advocated a holistic approach to the entire organization and emphasized planning as a means for integrating and managing (Caudle 1987).

We are currently managing IT in an information age where public information systems have become integrated and accessible to multiple stakeholders (Holden 2003). Public organizations need to recognize that IT can make the internal processing of data more efficient, but it can also provide timelier and higher quality services by reaching out to stakeholders and using the technology for deliberation and communication.

Table 21.1 represents a comparison of different accounts of the development of computing technologies. Column A represents a history of the evolution of information systems. Column B represents the tripartite nature of computing and examines the historical origins of computing technologies that came together in the 1960s to form a basis, eventually becoming the modern IT movement. Column C gives a timeline of key events in electrical engineering, computer, and network histories leading to the development of the Internet. Combined, these frameworks provide the theoretical foundation for the three paradigms: technology development, application development, and network development.

Table 21.2 examines how public organizations have implemented new information technologies.

A comparison of Table 21.1 and Table 21.2 yields several similarities. As one would expect, parallels exist in the history of IT and computing and the application of those technologies in public organizations. Grounded in the epistemologies of electrical engineering and mathematics, most early information technology initiatives (in both Table 21.1 and Table 21.2) are rational attempts to increase efficiency, automation, and centralization, and decrease costs. In other words, the comprehensive rational techniques derived from mathematics and engineering seek to discover the one best way to accomplish a particular task. Equaliy striking is that as the epistemologies of math and engineering converge with networking, the information processing paradigm is augmented by one of communication and information sharing. The history of networking demonstrates that communication and decentralization were essential to the development of networking technologies and reinforces the significance of networking technologies in public organizations.

The history of e-mail on ARPANET provides an example of how networking facilitated communication in a system that was designed for its processing capabilities rather than its

TABLE 21.1
Frameworks for Examining the History of Computing Technologies

A. Evolution of Information Systems (O'Brien 1993)	B. Tripartite Framework for Computing (Mahoney 1988)	C. History of the Computer Timeline (Cringley 1996)
1950–1960s Data processing Transaction processing, record keeping traditional accounting applications **1960–1970s Management reporting** Besides data processing in the 1960s there is a trend to engage managers and provide them with data for making decisions. This marks the beginning of the MIS movement **1970–1980s Decision support** More emphasis is placed on providing managers with relevant information for making decisions. The renewed emphasis on decisions leads to the development of DSS **1980–1990s Strategic and end-user support** The development of microcomputer software engineering, and computer science breathes new life into applied management techniques like operations research that provides a platform for applying Tayloresque mathematical models for rational decision-making The development of microcomputer enables widespread use of desktop computing, and organizations begin managing their own networks. Widespread use of technology throughout organizations leads to increased need for supporting end users and planning	**Electrical engineering** Hardware development begins as machines designed for high-speed automatic calculation capable of significant reasoning are developed **Software engineering** Mathematical logic like Booles' algebra of thought is applied to technical advances in hardware and the field of software development begins **Computer science** As advances in hardware technology and software are applied the increased need for organization, transmission, and storage of data gives birth to computer science The convergence of electrical engineering,	**Electronics** 1951: UNIVAC is developed and can store 12,000 digits in random access mercury-delay tubes 1959: The integrated circuit is developed by Texas Instruments and Fairchild **Mini computers** 1965: An integrated circuit costing $1000 in 1959 costs $10 in 1965, prompting Gordon Moore to predict exponential growth in processing capabilities combined with equally decreasing costs (Moore's law) 1968: The first word processor, an early version of hypertext, and a collaboration application are developed by Doug Englebart 1969: Xerox creates a research center to explore the architecture of information 1970 and 1972: Intel introduces the first four- and eight-bit microprocessors **Micro computers** 1975: The MITS Altair 8800 is hailed as the first "personal computer" 1975: Paul Allen and Bill Gates develop BASIC for the Altair 8800 and Microsoft is born 1980: Microsoft is approached by IBM to develop BASIC for its IBM PC 1981: The first IBM PC is released	**Networks** 1962: The backbone of networking and eventually the Internet, packet switching, is developed by Paul Baran of the Rand Corporation 1969: The US Department of Defense's Advanced Research Projects Agency goes online with ARPANET 1974: The acoustics consulting firm Bolt, Beranek and Newman opens Telnet, the first public network 1982: Transmission control protocol and Internet protocol (TCP/IP) are established for ARPANET 1991: The first Internet server is developed by Tim Berners-Lee and the world wide web is born 1994: The National Science Foundation's NSFNET reverts back to a research network, and U.S. Internet traffic is routed through commercial providers

TABLE 21.2
Frameworks for Implementing Information Technology (IT) in the Public Sector

A. Evolution of Federal Information Technology Management (Holden 2003)	B. Approaches to Computer Management (Northrop 1982)	C. Stages of E-Government (Moon 2002)	D. Strategic Uses of IT in the Public Sector (Yang 2004)
Stage one: Management information systems (1960–1970s). In conjunction with the private sector, public organizations begin using IT to automate aspects of their back offices to make the organization more efficient. As applied in the public sector, this stage looked at IT development one application (or related applications) at a time	**Technological development** Advanced technology versus appropriate technology	1. Information dissemination/ catalogue	I. Service and financial transactions
	Structural arrangements Classic hierarchal structures or decentralized participatory structures	2. Two-way communication	II. Vertical integration
		3. Service and financial transactions	III. Horizontal Integration
Stage two: Information resources management (1970–1980s). As individual applications developed, the need arose to connect the various systems and manage them as a strategic resource. This stage also allowed managers to realize that they could use IT for more than simply automation and increasing efficiency. Where stage one reinforced organizational silos, IRM forced agencies to look at the entire organization. Stage two also saw growth in planning information systems, a rational process that was generally not part of previous efforts	**Socio-technical design** Task efficiency versus human relations design that has a positive impact on work environment and morale	4. Vertical and horizontal Integration	IV. Public participation
	Organizational context Impartial professional administration versus administration that is sensitive to employee, citizen, and political concerns	5. Political participation	
Stage three: Managing IT in an information age (1980s–Present). As public information systems became more integrated and accessible to multiple stakeholders, stage three emerged. This stage also applies strategic management concepts in the form of business process reengineering and other rational approaches to performance improvement. Stage three builds on IRM and recognizes that IT can be used to make government operations more efficient for internal processing and provide more timely and higher quality services by reaching out to stakeholders			

interactivity. According to Spinello (2002), the primary goal of ARPANET was to connect geographically disbursed sites to share processing power; however, researchers working on the project soon began using the network for another purpose—communicating via e-mail. From their inception, networks were significant, not only because they allowed researchers to access nodes in a different geographical location, but also because they allowed early users of ARPANET to engage other researchers and develop a new medium of communication—e-mail. This example illustrates the convergence of hardware and software applications on a network, resulting in a greater processing power and increased human interaction.

As the frameworks in each table progress, the multiple technologies converge and are applied throughout organizations. The framework for implementing technology in the public sector illustrates that as technology was applied in an organizational context, managers saw its potential for implementing management reforms that emphasize increased planning, integration, decentralization, communication, and participatory management.

This convergence of technology and management predates the later response to the application of the electronic dimension to citizen empowerment. Appearing around the turn of the last century, early observers of its development and usefulness formulated a series of stages to show the evolution of various electronic capabilities. This linear progression led to employing the concepts of e-government and e-governance interchangeably. Both relatively routine and highly complex activities were plotted as moving in tandem. Thus, at the first stage, simple cataloging of agency services on a Web site and use of an Intranet for off-site communications was pooled. At a later stage, citizen participation and vertical integration of agency services online were folded together. The underlying argument of this chapter is that use of the electronic dimension in the public sector embodies two distinct components—namely, e-government and e-governance—that can be displayed as curvilinear trajectories characterized by different features over time.

V. IMPLEMENTING APPROPRIATE TECHNOLOGY EFFICIENTLY AND ENSURING QUALITY

From a managerial perspective, the tug-of-war between bureaucratic tendencies to maximize efficiency through centralization and reform efforts to decentralize authority and engage in participatory management are always in a state of tension. Max Weber (1946) first described centralized decision-making in hierarchical organizations where information flows upward to facilitate executive decision-making. Early management theorists feared that the increased use of computers and emphasis on EDP would have a centralizing effect on organizations.

They feared that employees at lower levels of organizations would become dissatisfied by menial tasks like data entry, and these early prognosticators felt that computerization would funnel decision-making to the top of organizational hierarchies. In such situations, "managers struggle to retain their traditional sources of authority that have depended in an important way on their exclusive control of the organization's knowledge base. They use the new technology to structure organization experience in ways that help reproduce the legitimacy of [its] traditional role" (Zuboff 1988).

Alternatively, reform efforts calling for decentralized, participatory management can be seen throughout the history of public administration. Osborne and Gaebler (1993) propose decentralized decision-making as a way for public institutions to become more flexible, effective, innovative, and productive and to encourage higher morale. Reform advocates that favor participatory management often view technology as a facilitator of decentralized decision-making (Heeks 2001).

Zuboff (1988) cautions that decentralized, participatory management can be achieved through increased implementation of management technology, but it also requires a conscious choice by managers. In other words, managers must consciously choose whether to use technology for the purposes of increasing centralized control or decentralizing and empowering employees. In a similar vein, some argue that the use of computers and IT in the workplace merely enforces the status quo or reinforces existing management practices and decision-making structures within the organization (Peled 2001).

Still others like Peters and Waterman (1982) endorse a loose-tight management theory that echoes a perspective similar to that of Dwight Waldo who, in 1948, addressed the issue of centralization by concluding that managers could not rely exclusively on centralized or decentralized decision-making but rather some combination of the two. Table 21.1 and Table 21.2 illustrate an incremental evolution of management and technology grounded in engineering and mathematics that start with centralization and move toward decentralized and applied network applications.

There have also been public sector approaches to computer management that examine the impact of centralized and decentralized reforms. Northrop, Dutton and Kraemer (1982) identify four perspectives (technological development, structural arrangements, socio-technical design, and organization context) that can be examined through centralized (reform) and decentralized (post-reform) lenses. Technological development in centralized organizations typically involves the automation of applications, whereas decentralized organizations are often concerned with the appropriateness of technology.

Structurally, centralized organizations are more hierarchical when compared with decentralized ones that adopt more humanistic participatory management that engages the end-users of technology. From a socio-technical design perspective, centralized organizations often focus on task efficiency, whereas decentralized ones highlight human relations and design data tasks so that they have a positive impact on the work environment and morale. Centralized organizations are characterized by professional administration contexts that attempt to make impartial decisions, while political administration that is sensitive to stakeholder demands when making decisions typifies decentralized organizations. In the end, Northrop, Dutton and Kraemer (1982) conclude, similar to Waldo, that the most successful organizations mix combinations of centralized and decentralized approaches to implementing technology. It appears that the implementation of new IT initiatives in the public sector needs to be developed by those most familiar with its business practices, while taking advantage of rational mechanisms like strategic planning, centralized architectures, increased efficiency, and reduced costs while increasing effectiveness and the quality of services provided.

In looking to the future, we need to consider whether the combined descriptive histories of technology and their applications in organizations that evolved from centralize to decentralized are normative. That is, as we look to implement new technologies, should organizations first seek to centralize authority through their use of technology and then use it to decentralize, or is some other approach more advisable?

VI. APPLIED INFORMATION TECHNOLOGY IN THE PUBLIC SECTOR: e-GOVERNMENT

In the late 1990s, public expenditures for IT ballooned as public organizations prepared for what was called the Y2K threat. In essence, the Y2K threat arose because the internal calendars and clocks developed by programmers underlying most applications in the public and private sector used only two digits to represent the year. So, the year 1984 was represented by two digits—eight and four. In the late 1990s, there was a need to reconfigure the internal clocks and calendars so that they used all four digits to represent the date before December 31, 1999. In preparation for Y2K, IT managers in the public sector had risen to prominence in their organizations. Where computers and the public employees responsible for them once resided in the basement of many government offices, Y2K demonstrated just how dependent public organizations had become on technology for their everyday operations. To properly upgrade all of the necessary systems, IT managers became well versed in strategic information system planning, and technology managers rose to positions of prominence in public organizations.

Sometime before the turn of the millennium, public managers of IT realized that they would meet their goal, and they did not want to become relegated back to the bowels of their respective organizations. At the time, the tech bubble was booming, the Internet was blossoming as a ubiquitous source of information that could be accessed twenty-four hours a day, seven days a week, and the private sector was raving about e-commerce. Enter e-government (Melitski 2003).

An early e-government survey conducted by the United Nations and the American Society for Public Administration (2001) in conjunction with the e-Governance Institute at Rutgers University defines e-government as: "A permanent commitment by government to improve the relationship between the private citizen and the public sector through enhanced, cost-effective and efficient delivery of services, information, and knowledge. It is the practical realization of the best that government has to offer."

Descriptive research examining government use of Web sites revealed that public Web sites followed a predictable evolution along a continuum. The process typically begins as agencies place descriptive information on official government Web pages. Early champions of e-government were typically technology-savvy managers or management-savvy technologists, and initial Web sites of public organizations most often reflected an agency's organizational chart as it was perceived by the Web site's developers. E-Government's clients became all the more important as the World Wide Web became more mature, and the use of portals or customizable access points to Web sites became prevalent in the private sector. The result for e-government was a renewed emphasis on the need to design their Web sites for the users and not the developers.

As agencies became proficient at providing up-to-date content in a usable format on their Web sites, they began developing mechanisms for interacting with other government agencies, businesses, and individual citizens using the Internet. Initially, public organizations made telephone and e-mail directories available in internal Intranets and sometimes on the Internet to encourage the public to use e-mail to interact with public managers. Public organizations continued to develop a more interactive and dynamic Internet presence often moved on to automate some of their transactions and provide government services over the Internet.

The automation of transactional services was first accomplished by placing government forms online that could be accessed, printed, completed, and returned by fax or mail. Placing forms online decreased printing costs and increased business and citizen satisfaction with public agencies because they could be accessed twenty-four hours per day, seven days a week without making a trip to a government office and often standing in line. Soon, public organizations began allowing their clients to complete and submit online forms that were stored in online databases while the form was processed. Data entry errors reduced because users (i.e., citizens) enter the data directly into the form themselves, and the applications are sent electronically wherever needed for processing. Examples of transactional services that became the first online services are: dog license applications, environmental permits, driver's license renewals, zoning permits, the payment of parking tickets, and even picnic site reservations.

The process of automating transactional public services also encouraged agencies to re-examine and streamline their business processes. As Web sites for public organizations have become more sophisticated the term e-government has sometimes become synonymous with online transactional services. In fact, many local government Web sites have an e-government link on their home pages that direct individuals to a list of online transactional services offered.

A. LINEAR E-GOVERNMENT MODELS

Up to this point, the development of e-government has followed a trajectory similar to the development of technology and its applications that is similar to the hardware/software phases of technology development dependent on the engineering and mathematical worldview. Similarly, e-government has focused rational initiatives to automate, centralize authority, decrease costs, and increase efficiency. However, much like the evolution of IT development, the application of such technologies by managers has refocused new efforts on the use of technology for communication. Consistent with this evolution, many e-government researchers have developed a continuum of e-government stages. Column C in Table 21.2 lists Moon's (2002) e-government stages, and they have been echoed by other researchers (Layne and Lee 2001; UN/ASPA 2001). Each of these linear-type models typically emphasizes the organizational efficiencies that can be gained by placing material online and automating services. These are consistent with the early history of technology development and the dominant engineering and mathematics paradigm.

Similar to the early history of networking, the use of e-mail, or rather the listing of e-mail addresses online, is typically one of the first e-government initiatives that involves communication. Over and above e-mail communication, e-government advocates also call for organizational transformation that involves both horizontal and vertical integration. Beyond integration, many researchers have hypothesized that Internet technologies can be used to encourage political participation and facilitate a dialogue between citizens and government. Indeed, many view e-government as a mechanism for encouraging democratic processes by empowering and engaging citizens at the grassroots level. This process is clearly aligned with decentralizing management reforms and the networking paradigm of applying technology in organizations. Unfortunately, much of the promise of the network paradigm in e-government has yet to be realized. With a few notable exceptions, such as regulations.gov, EPA's national dialogue of public involvement, and CitizenSpace in the United Kingdom (Holzer et al. 2004), the theory of digital democracy seems more promising than its practice.

B.   E-GOVERNMENT AND E-GOVERNANCE AS DISTINCT DIMENSIONS

Other experts have viewed e-government not as a series of stages but rather as a set of competing value preferences (Yang and Melitski 2004). In other words, it is not a necessary precursor for agencies to automate and integrate their administrative systems before engaging citizens online. Some suggest that the term e-government has perhaps been used too broadly to define initiatives and programs that should rightly be deemed e-governance. Such criticisms demonstrate that the term e-governance should distinguish itself by describing the networking paradigm and its decentralizing and communicatory implications. Alternatively, e-government should be used when discussing the efforts to centralize authority, reduce costs, and increase efficiency and other initiatives that fall under the technology and application development paradigms.

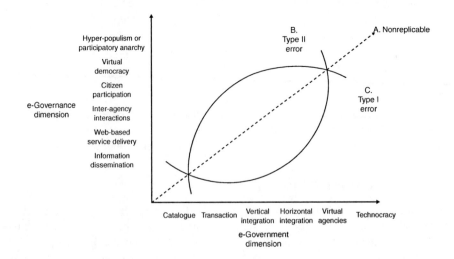

FIGURE 21.1 The e-gov dichotomy.

Melitski and Calista (2005) view e-government and e-governance as competing paradigms that intersect at times during their development. As illustrated in Figure 21.1, they conclude that the overlap between e-government and e-governance allows for mutually inclusive goals, but they warn of unintended consequences. Carried to extremes, e-government's propensity to emphasize administrative efficiency can lead toward technocratic organizations manipulated by elites and disenfranchising lower organizational levels. Conversely, e-governance taken to its extreme has the potential to lead to what Kettl (2002) refers to as hyperpluralism whereby decision makers in public organizations become overwhelmed by their information, thereby inhibiting their abilities to make effective decisions.

VII. CONCLUSION

The history of IT demonstrates that the generation of information and knowledge through digital means facilitates communication and can lead to increases in organization performance. As hardware, software, and network technologies have become increasingly integrated, they have also been applied in organizational settings as managers adapted the technologies in ways to support their agencies' vision. Managers interested in controlling the flow of information in their organizations and increasing efficiency found IT just as useful as collaborative managers who were interested in sharing ideas, empowering employees, and reaching out to citizens.

Despite competing managerial and technical perspectives, organizations have adapted information technology to serve a mutually inclusive goal whose lineage begins with the Cold War following World War II and runs through recent calls for e-government and e-governance. The application of IT in the public sector serves to illustrate the influence of IT over management reforms in the public sector. Further, managers must view IT as a strategic organizational asset. Only after managers recognize that IT is a strategic asset that greatly influences how they manage their organizations can they leverage it across their organizations. In this way IT can serve as both a change agent and asset for achieving the complex and competing mission of public organizations.

REFERENCES

Abbate, J., *Inventing the Internet,* MIT Press, Cambridge, MA, 2000.

Burks, A. R. and Burks, A. W., *The First Electronic Computer: The Atanasoff Story,* University of Michigan Press, Ann Arbor, MI, 1988.

Calista, D. and Melitski, J., *E-Gov Reform: Negative Consequences of Revisiting the Politics-Administration Dichotomy Paper Presented at the International Association of Schools and Institutes of Administration Conference,* Working Group III—Public Sector Reform, Lake Como, Italy, 2005.

Caudle, S. L., *Federal Information Resources Management: Bridging Vision and Action,* National Academy of Public Administration, Washington, DC, 1987.

Cringley, R., *Accidental Empires: How the Boys of Silicon Valley Make their Millions, Battle Foreign Competition, and Still Can't Get a Date,* Harper Business, New York, 1996.

Davenport, T. H. and Prusak, L., *Working Knowledge,* Harvard Business School Press, Cambridge, MA, 2000.

Davis, J., Alderman, C. W., and Robinson, L., *Accounting Information Systems,* Wiley, New York, 1990.

Dock, T. V. and Wetherbe, J. C., *Computer Information Systems for Business,* West Publishing, St. Paul, MN, 1988.

Hafner, K., *Where Wizards Stay up Late: The Origins of the Internet,* Simon and Schuster, New York, 1996.

Handy, C., *Gods of Management,* Oxford University Press, New York, 1978.

Heeks, R., *Reinventing Government in the Information Age,* Routledge, New York, 2001.

Holden, S. H. The evolution of information technology management at the federal level: implications for public administration, *Public Information Technology: Policy and Management Issue,* Garson, G. D., Ed., Idea Group Publishing, Hershey, PA, pp. 53–73, 2003.

Holzer, M., Melitski, J., Rho, S.-Y., and Schwester, R., *Restoring Trust in Government: The Potential of Digital Citizen Participation,* IBM Center for Business of Government, Washington, DC, 2004.

Kettl, D. F., *The Transformation of Governance: Public Administration in the Twenty-First Century,* The Johns Hopkins Press, Baltimore, MD, 2002.

Kroenke, D., *Management Information Systems,* McGraw-Hill, New York, 1992.

Layne, K. and Lee, J., Developing fully functional e-government: a four stage model, *Government Information Quarterly,* 18(2), 122–136, 2001.

Mahoney, M., The history of computing in the history of technology, *Annals of the History of Computing,* 10(2), 113–123, 1988.

Melitski, J., Capacity and e-government performance: an analysis based on early adopters of internet technologies, *New Jersey Public Performance and Management Review,* 26(4), 376–390, 2003.

Mollenhoff, C., *Atanasoff, Forgotten Father of the Computer,* Iowa State University Press, Ames, IA, 1988.

Moon, M. J., The evolution of e-government among municipalities: rhetoric or reality?, *Public Administration Review,* 62(4), 424–433, 2002.

Northrop, A. et al., The management of computer applications in local government, *Public Administration Review,* 42(3), 234–244, 1982.

O'Brien, J., *Management Information Systems: A Managerial and End Perspective,* Irwin, Boston, MA, 1993.

O'Leary, T. J. and Williams, B., *Computers and Information Systems,* Benjamin/Cummings, New York, 1989.

Osborne, D. and Gaebler, T., *Reinventing Government,* Penguin Group, New York, 1993.

O'Toole, L., Treating networks seriously: practical and research based agendas in public administration, *Public Administration Review,* 57(1), 45–53, 1997.

O'Toole, L. and Meirer, K., Desperately seeking selznick: cooptation and the dark side of public management in networks, *Public Administration Review,* 54(6), 681–694, 2004.

Peled, A., Do computers cut red tape?, *American Review of Public Administration,* 31(4), 2001.

Peters, T. and Waterman, R., *In Search of Excellence,* Warner Books, New York, 1982.

Price, D. G. and Mulvihill, D. E., The present and future use of computers in state governments, *Public Administration Review,* 25(2), 142–151, 1965.

Shelley, G. B. and Cashman, T. J., *Computer Fundamentals for an Information Age,* Anaheim Publishing, Brea, CA, 1984.

Spinello, R., *Regulating Cyberspace,* Quorum Books, Westport, CT, 2002.

Starling, G., *Managing the Public Sector,* Thomson Wadsworth, Belmont, CA, 2002.

Swain, J. W. and White, J. D., Information technology for productivity: maybe, maybe not: an assessment, In *The Public Productivity Handbook,* Holzer, M., Ed., Marcel Dekker, New York, pp. 643–663, 1992.

United Nations and the American Society for Public Administration, *Benchmarking E-government: A Global Perspective,* New York, 2001.

Waldo, D., *The Administrative State: A Study of the Political Theory of American Public Administration,* Holmes and Meier, New York, 1948.

Weber, M., Bureaucracy, In *Classics of Public Administration,* Shafritz, J. and Hyde, A., Eds., Wadsworth, Belmont, CA, 1946.

Yang, K. and Melitski, J., *A Comparative Analysis of State Strategic Plans for Information Technology,* American Society for Public Administration Annual Conference, Milwaukee, WI, 2004.

Zorkoczy, P., *Information Technology: An Introduction,* Knowledge Industry Publications, White Plains, NY, 1982.

Zuboff, S., *In the Age of the Smart Machine,* Basic Books, New York, 1988.

22 Strategically Managing Information Technology: Challenges in the e-Gov Era

David Coursey

CONTENTS

I. INTRODUCTION

Even after many decades of experience with information technology (IT), public management researchers and administrators find it challenging to obtain the many promised benefits. Various technologies and management schemes have waxed and waned over the decades with attached promises of cost savings, improved efficiency, better and more representative decision-making, streamlined organizational structures, and many others. Yet, research evidence of these benefits is surprisingly lacking, or at best mixed (cf., Danziger 1977; Heintze and Bretschneider 2000; Northrup et al. 1990); for an alternative view, see Lee and Perry (2002). The literature is dominated by questionably representative best practices or exemplars, and is noticeably sparse with instructive failures (Bozeman 2002; Coursey and Killingsworth 2000).

Electronic-government (e-gov) is the latest IT associated with productivity promises. Over the last few years, governments have hurriedly adopted e-gov technologies and ideas from simple, online communication of government information to real-time, secure transactions for various processes and payments. Demands generated from political leadership, other associated governments, capacity building needs, and perceived citizen expectations all contribute. Certainly, there are numerous reported success stories.

Yet, the existing evidence is that e-gov, at least for now, is arguably over-promised like so many earlier ITs. Experience is that many e-gov projects become unwieldy (Holden and Fletcher 2001; Kaylor et al. 2001; Vriens and Achterbergh 2004), especially as they seek to restructure how work is done across agencies (business re-engineering). For example, survey results of American e-government efforts at the local level by the International City/County Management Association (ICMA) indicate far less advanced application development than might be expected from best practice studies. Few local governments actually have online transactional processes noting demonstrable, hard benefits like cost savings (Coursey 2005; Moon 2002), although more intangible ones such as improved customer service are claimed by government representatives. Not only are expected benefits often intractable, but unexpected negative implications and costs are possible. For example, in the 2004 ICMA survey, chief administrators were more likely to indicate that their e-gov efforts increase, not decrease, staff demands (Moon 2002).

With all the attention, money, and time devoted to e-gov, it is fair to surmise that more should be expected. The lack of notable and widespread hard benefits, such as cost savings, can be associated with the growing pains of any new technology. New ideas must diffuse for experiences, good and bad, to better instruct implementation and governance. At the local level, larger jurisdictions with greater technical staff and financial resources report more success (Moon 2002), but, the IT innovation history of alleging that e-gov experiences are due simply to diffusion patterns and associated resources is, at best, questionable. Another common claim, especially in the popular press, is that government employees are technophobes and resist new technology. However, research findings question this assumption, and even suggest that public officials are more open to IT innovations than their private counterparts (Bretschneider and Wittmer 1993; Moon and Bretschneider 2002).

II. e-GOV IN CONTEXT: THE EVOLUTION OF IT IN GOVERNMENT

e-Gov should not be considered something brand new. Like other new IT technologies before it, e-gov must be managed in the government context, with its assorted political, financial, personnel, and organizational challenges (Stevens and McGowan 1985). Unfortunately, this lesson is commonly missed in the government IT literature with almost every new, major technological change. Classic government IT research, such as the URBIS studies (Danziger 1982; Kraemer et al. 1981) demonstrates that technology does not change the organization as much as the organization and those with political power shape it. This may at first depress those who believe that new technologies can change the world, but in reality, technology should be the organization's servant.

It is important to understand e-gov in the historical context of government IT.[*] Andersen et al. (1994) define three eras of public computing. The first, which includes the late 1950s and early 1960s, was mostly experimental. Few government agencies had major computing operations. What did exist mainly involved large, repetitive batch processing. Applications such as tax processing, accounts payable/receivable, and census taking dominated.

Success lead to the second era, the mid-1960s through most of the 1970s, which featured mainframe operations and greater diffusion among and within governments. Typically, government units purchased services from a central computing facility and any direct access given to agencies was limited to dummy terminals without independent storage or processing capabilities. Federal government programs, particularly in law enforcement, incited a dramatic increase in computing use among local governments. Most IT management was central, usually within budgeting units,

---

[*] For additional reviews of the history of government IT, see Holden (2003) and Garson (2005).

given that most government IT operations began there and financial transactions were the dominant demand.

The third era came with microcomputers in the early 1980s. Computing prices plummeted and there was a rapid decentralization of processing and management within governments, often with very incompatible hardware and software. Standardization at the microcomputer level around IBM and Microsoft Windows helped, but agencies were still left with often inconsistent data storage applications (e.g., different database software, different naming conventions for data such as names and addresses) that defied data sharing. Dissatisfaction with the costs, especially as the promised benefits became difficult to document, led to movements back to more centralized control and purchasing as well as IT perspectives, such as information resource management (IRM), in an attempt to collectively manage all IT resources—personnel and technical—toward public problems.

The arrival of e-gov in the early 1990s is often viewed as a new era challenged by the legacy of problems from microcomputing. This perspective confuses the technology's diffusion and technical side with its actual application. There is a major difference between a city using e-gov just to post some official phone numbers, business hours, and park locations versus one taking building permits, job applications, and fine payments online. Most e-gov literature argues that the best benefits derive from using the technology to re-engineer—rethink and reorganize—the way an existing process is conducted. This usually means spanning existing organizational missions and structures. Applications such as geographic information systems (GIS) also represent this perspective of interoperability and networking.

Such perspectives represent the fourth generation of IT in government where interoperability and networking of data systems are key to generating information applicable to public problems (Landsbergen and Wolken 2001). For example, what if a community wished to determine if a perceived high rate of infant cancer is related to cancer-causing facilities such as leaky industrial plants? Such data would need to be merged from several sources, such as census, business location, and public health records. Each source would, almost assuredly, be stored by a different agency (example adapted from Landsbergen and Wolken 2001).

Consider a state-level example. Many states require licensed drivers to carry automobile insurance. Yet, driver license data are usually handled by a highway safety or motor vehicles department. Insurance is often confirmed at vehicle purchase, but afterwards drivers often simply cancel their coverage. Actually tracking and enforcing such policies is notoriously difficult. One possibility would be for insurance carriers to directly note dropped coverage into the state licensing databases via an e-gov application (viz., Extranet), but again, that requires networking and very complex legal and political issues given a private/public sector sharing.

Such fourth generation thinking and technologies present special challenges to organizations. Over the first three generations of government IT, the presumption has been based on research such as URBIS (Danziger 1982)—that technology has far less influence on organizational structures and political power than often presumed. The fourth generation, however, is more about an idea, a philosophy, than a technical component such as a microcomputer. The very goal is to reshape how work is done, despite historical organizational divisions. There is a notable shift from a technical component to a process perspective. Hence, maybe e-gov will be different?

III. THE LITANY OF STRATEGIC MANAGEMENT PERSPECTIVES IN PUBLIC IT

Like in previous eras, e-gov as part of the fourth generation faces special challenges. Perhaps the most important of these is strategic management, given the value placed on networking across agencies towards finding novel ways to address public problems. Getting organizations to share information requires mutual trust (Dawes 1996), technical compatibility, some centralized purchasing or approval of projects across organizations, bid processes that stress more long-term goals than low bid orientations, resolving public data privacy issues, and others (cf., Landsbergen and Wolken 2001). These problems require significantly improved strategic coordination and planning.

Over the eras of government IT, a classically claimed reason for the perceived limited effect of IT is lack of solid planning, or more specifically, strategic management. Strategic management, though viewed in many divergent ways (Bryson and Roering 1996; Nutt and Backoff 1992), can be roughly defined as the review of goals and objectives along with planning based on related strengths, weaknesses, and externalities such as stakeholders and general societal conditions (Rainey 2003). General strategic management and planning, at least in some form, is common (Berry and Wechesler 1995). Public agencies, however, are challenged by a greater diversity of interests and stakeholders, unstable political leadership due to election cycles, and arguably broader impact of programs (Nutt and Backoff 1995). Studies of government administrators generally support such differences in strategic management within the public sector (Coursey and Bozeman 1990; Hickson et al. 1986). Still, the perception is that despite these issues, strategic management and planning in some form is a useful process (Berry and Wechesler 1995).

Strategic IT management is also hardly novel, with its own set of approaches (Andersen et al. 1994; Caudle et al. 1991; Holley et al. 2002). Over the years, many governments have implemented various reforms seeking a more rational, comprehensive approach to IT planning. Previous IT experience, such as with the information resource management (IRM) planning movement in the 1980s (Caudle 1990), is, at best, mixed in terms of clear, demonstrable results (cf., Pollitt and Bouckaert 2000). While many governments cite strategic IT plans, too often they are simply burdensome reports with little clear indication of actual decision-making use.

Within e-gov, calls for more unified, centralized evaluation and management of resources are commonplace. This is partly due to the expectation that many e-gov applications require spanning existing organizational structures and modifying processes (re-engineering) where a higher level view and coordination are deemed necessary. For example, applications such as procurement systems, benefit payments, and various environmental permit filings all potentially involve multiple agencies and jurisdictions. The perceived need for a more comprehensive planning process for such challenging work induces more strategic planning efforts and reforms. At the federal level, reforms such as the Information Technology Management Reform Act (ITMRA) of 1996 (P.L. 104-106) and the Government Performance and Results Act (GRPA) of 1993 (P.L. 103-62) stress more strategic, centralized decision-making and performance measurement. These initiatives, among others (Beachboard 1997), are met skeptically and success is questionable (Breul 2003). Beachboard (1997) found that bureau-level IT managers do not believe such reforms are very different from past, failed efforts and that many of the requirements will usher in another era of burdensome reporting, oversight, and overly restrictive centralized policies. Efforts to develop highly centralized procurement coordination and strategic planning in state governments are often viewed and assessed as political power grabbing by governors, more so than real meaningful reform (Coursey and Killingsworth 2005). The Government Accountability Office (GAO) also reports significant problems with the federal government's large e-gov initiatives in human resource management, pursuant to the E-Government Act of 2002 (Barr 2003).

Such strategic efforts presume that much of the problem is lack of coordination and systematic planning. Balutis (2001, 43) typifies the strategic reformers' view, suggesting that "government must have a single voice that provides a clear strategy and image to the entire e-gov movement." However, much of the public management IT literature suggests that the variety, power, and number of influences, internal and external, on projects are primary predictors of success. Fountain (2001) argues that the mix of cultural, mission, stakeholder, technical, structural, and legal differences plagues implementation. Holley and colleagues (2004) report in a study of the forty largest US counties that various structural features, including the common dispersion of county functions across elected officials such as sheriffs, clerks, property appraisers, and commissioners, inhibit strategic efforts.

Most strategic planning efforts note these concerns, as they are partly why such reforms are deemed necessary, but the difficulty is whether the typical, top-down IT models are realistic for public sector work with arguably greater complexity and instability. Moreover, while reforms such as ITMRA stress more control (Pollitt and Bouckaert 2000), notable project problems of delay and cost overruns at the Internal Revenue Service (IRS) and Federal Aviation Administration (FAA) were not for a lack of strong oversight mechanisms. The initial leading success of Florida in e-gov compared to most states is also contradictory. Florida's pioneering efforts were aided by political competition between two agencies reporting to differing elected officials of varying parties—hardly the coordinated effort deemed necessary by many reformers (Coursey and Killingsworth 2000).

With all this criticism of strategic IT planning, it is important to note that government implementation of such reforms rarely coincides well with much of the prescriptive literature in general public management. Many implemented reforms are very top-down, centralized systems that are heavy on reporting and paperwork. How to tailor strategic planning reform is a complex issue. Few scholars deny that a more comprehensive, rational process for IT decision-making can yield benefits. The problem is, in what form can such a process be meaningful given the realities of public sector work? There are two important questions for the e-gov era for such reforms:

1. How does e-gov differ from traditional IT in terms of difficulties in strategic planning?
2. Given these differences, in what form can strategic planning and management benefit e-gov efforts?

This chapter addresses the first question. Beyond the usual issues such as mission fragmentation, diverse interests and stakeholders, and control-orientated management associated with traditional IT public management, what limits e-gov efforts?

In explaining these issues, I rely heavily on personal participant observation. Since, 1993—the real beginning of the modern Web with the release of the first graphical browser (NCSA Mosaic)—I have developed and supervised about sixty e-gov applications at all levels of complexity for a variety of governments by heading an e-gov development unit within our school and through my own private company. These projects cut across agencies and governments, reorganized work, and while most were quite successful, there were a few failures as well. Many were leading (some would say bleeding) edge applications in online transactions, elections, permitting, and other areas. I have seen the pains of transition from traditional, paper-based or IT processes to online ones and witnessed the complexity of organizational and political factors influencing, for good or bad, the benefits of technological change. I was trained in public IT, both as a scholar and a practitioner, with the knowledge to expect such difficulties and how to handle them, but my opinion is that e-gov presents some special challenges in strategic planning. It is these experiences that are stressed in the following sections. While such personal experience has obvious epistemological concerns, this approach complements a literature heavy on single, exemplary cases and survey data often dependent on singular agency representatives to describe practices.

Most of these experiences are with local and state agencies in Florida. Florida governments were the leading early e-gov innovators, winners of Best of Web for state governments in *Government Technology* magazine so often in the early years of e-gov that they were eliminated from the competition for a brief period. The state simply has more history with e-gov applications than most others, across missions and levels of government. Since then, the state has continued to be highly regarded in various comparative evaluations (e.g., West 2003). Hence, if the focus is on one state, Florida is a prime choice. The state government also has a noted history for its work in pioneering information resource management practices in the 1980s and entered e-gov after much dissatisfaction with those IT management efforts and processes, primarily as individual agencies rebelled against centralized reporting and control procedures.

IV. CHALLENGES TO E-GOV STRATEGIC MANAGEMENT AND PLANNING

There are two primary differences between traditional IT and e-gov with respect to strategic planning: increased attention of political officials and a changing, more directive vendor role. Both of these significantly reduce the level of control necessary to set a reasonably stable planning horizon. Obviously, political officials and vendors have always been involved in IT. Even in traditional IT, it is argued that more than a 2–3 year planning horizon can be difficult to obtain due to public exposure (Bozeman and Bretschneider 1986). However, for reasons explained in each of the following sections, the fundamental relationships are significantly more challenging than historically presumed in public IT management.

A. INCREASED ATTENTION OF POLITICAL OFFICIALS

Historically, politically elected leadership has had limited interest in IT. Seen as more of a cost-center than a resource, and mostly limited to internal processing, IT had little public exposure or direct ties to service delivery. Hence, unless there was a colossal project failure, most public officials left IT issues well enough alone to the hired civil servants. For example, the recent influx of political interest money and requirements for new voting systems came only after the serious problems with antiquated voting technology, such as punch card balloting, garnered huge public outcry after the 2000 presidential election. Otherwise, interests typically focus on controlling costs and accountability. Moreover, the volatile nature of political appointments and elections, coupled with the perceived need for technical and organizational experiences and skills, encourages researchers to suggest that leading IT decision-making roles should not be at the top of the organizational hierarchy, but preferably headed by a career civil servant (Bozeman and Bretschneider 1986). Ideally, to many, elected officials should support IT efforts with resources—political and financial—but abstain from key technical decisions.

For example, in evaluating the reasons for the rather massive failure of the IRS's technology modernization efforts in the late 1980s and early 1990s, Bozeman (2002) recommended, in part, a reduction in the agency's political exposure (*TechTopics* 1997). Suggestions included getting Congress and the president to take the IRS out of political wars over tax policy and the creation of an external commission to guide technology by objectives.

The e-gov era has seen a dramatic increase in IT interest among elected officials. This partly comes from a receptive political climate frustrated with notable, large-scale project failures in the 1980s such as the IRS Tax System Modernization program (Bozeman 2002), but the dominant likely reason is that e-gov directly delivers services and exposes government processes to the public. This is a major change. IT is no longer just a supporting, internal service—it becomes the service. How well IT does what it chooses to do becomes a major source of perceived political gain. In some ways, this is not too surprising. The classic URBIS studies from the 1970s and 1980s found that political leadership tends to understand the power implications of technologies and supports personally favorable arrangements (Danziger 1982; Kraemer et al. 1981).

Publicity and visibility are additional factors. e-Gov has been closely associated with prominent, politically popular, government reform literature such as Osborne and Gaebler's *Reinventing Government*. The mass exposure of the Web itself draws political attention. Political leaders value association with such new, innovative technology and fear any perception that they are behind the times (cf., Northrup and Kraemer 2000). Florida's e-gov beginnings can be traced to Governor Lawton Chiles' concern over an influential state business magazine criticism of the state's e-gov progress during a close 1994 gubernatorial re-election campaign against Jeb Bush (which Chiles won). Jeb Bush, the next Florida chief executive (1998–present), wanted to be known as the e-governor and promoted e-gov efforts on his government reform résumé.

As the Web becomes less novel, political attention may wane. However, the role e-gov will play in directly delivering many services suggests that public IT management will be subject more to the interest and involvement of elected officials. This foretells potentially greater problems with producing a meaningful, followed strategic plan of action for any reasonable period with increased exposure to the political environment.

Within e-gov, there are three primary implications for strategic management and planning attributable to increased political interest:

- Publicity and propaganda desire distort project goals and selection
- Rushed innovations and projects
- The chief information officer (CIO) and political leadership models of centralized IT control and planning

1. Publicity and Propaganda

Political officials understand that Web services offer significant, potentially positive publicity. Much has been made of Howard Dean's success in raising money via the Web for his unsuccessful campaign to secure the Democratic nomination for president in 2004. There are numerous studies detailing the use of the Web to promote political mobilization (Bimber 1998; Bonchek 1995). However, the issue here is when such political uses conflict with the presumably neutral administration of information services by elected representatives as office holders bound by public duty. The temptation to use e-gov for publicity and confuse public information with political spin is almost irrepressible.

Especially in the early years of the graphical Web, even the most basic Web page launch or application would yield significant press coverage. Competition, within limits, between political leaders to trump each other can be healthy, as it was in Florida's early efforts, but the long term favors applications more on technical merit than real usefulness. Many political leaders also view, often incorrectly, a strong demand by citizens for government services online, such as payments for various permits and fees.

Adoption of new ideas is also more likely if they have positive publicity implications. Development of Web portals—centralized interfaces across agencies for e-gov operations borrowed from private sector models—serves the useful purposes of creating a one-stop government and facilitating access outside the formal organizational structure. But do not underestimate the role portals play in providing significant public exposure for the chief executive usually controlling such sites. In the case of state governments, such portals are commonly under the control of governors and are often used, to varying degrees, to promote the governor's policy objectives. Alternatively, many citizens reasonably expect portals to represent the entire government, not just one of the three branches and its political head. They also expect portals to be somewhat politically neutral.

The desire to obtain positive publicity from e-gov exposure can yield bad investment and management decisions. For example, one of Florida Governor Jeb Bush's early directives was to make all state agencies under his control place a link to e-mail him at the top of every Web page. This took hundreds of hours to process (at the time few agencies had automated content management systems). Clearly, Bush valued creating the perception of citizen responsiveness. Various IT professionals with the state government warned him that the policy would yield thousands of e-mails to process. A few months later, agencies received a new directive to remove the governor's e-mail address along with several hundred, in some cases thousands, of e-mails specific to agency business that had been directed to the governor and languished in his mailbox.

Web-based broadcasts of government sessions, such as state legislative and city council meetings, are another example. Such applications are technically challenging and expensive, but there is little evidence of significant public use to justify the costs. Video, in most cases, is not that necessary (and significantly raises costs and complexity unless fed from an existing cable television broadcast), but political representatives almost always insist on including video for obvious publicity purposes. However, public exposure from such services is, at best, questionable. In Florida, the first state to provide Web-based streaming media of legislative sessions in the mid-1990s, the general experience has been that the service is used more by legislative staff, lobbyists, and government officials than the public at large.

Political officials also carefully consider the negative implications of services, and not always in the public interest. For example, the Florida Correctional Medical Authority (FCMA) developed a Web site to provide downloadable reports on the quality of medical services at state prisons. Several politically appointed board members objected to the online provision, saying that the already public reports were too controversial—code for really being politically damaging to a conservative political résumé. The FCMA was ordered to only provide a reference to its reports and provide public records requests by mail only. In developing the Florida's legislative website, many legislators objected to listing their e-mail addresses, and in some cases even their basic information from fear of being swamped with citizen queries.

Even something as simple as e-mailed newsletters and stored addresses can be tempting targets for political use. In Florida, Speaker of the House Johnnie Byrd (R) used a list of Choose Life auto license tag owners to send a mailing that advocated a parental-notice abortion law just a few days after announcing his US Senate campaign. A Byrd spokesperson defended the expense and use of such public addresses: "The speaker is the speaker for the entire state of Florida. State government has a responsibility to inform Floridians about things that affect their daily lives" (Bousquet 2003).

2. Rushed Innovations and Projects—The Cult of Innovation Renewed

Despite the typical public perception to the contrary, research suggests that public employees value IT innovation at least as much as their private counterparts (e.g., Bretschneider and Wittmer 1993; Moon and Bretschneider 2002). Among government employees, the lack of resources for implementation and support is often perceived as more of a barrier than technophobia or bureaucratic limitations (Coursey 2005). Few citizens remember that governments were far more likely to go online than businesses in the early years of graphical Web applications and that the very Web itself is derived from government activity, not business.

If anything, there may be too much emphasis on innovation, rushing into technologies before they are stable. One commonly cited prescription for public IT is for governments to avoid first-to-market strategies due to public exposure (West 2003). Even worse, agencies rush into massive innovation projects without the necessary technical expertise, goal setting, and project management skills—some of the major reasons for the IRS modernization difficulties (Bozeman 2002). Much of public IT's commonly optimistic view of new technological benefits follows what Garson (2000) dubs "decentralization/democratization" theory. Advocates of e-democracy, a term used to denote use of the Web to foster increased participation in government decision-making by the public in a variety of forms, follow this optimistic picture.

e-Gov is no exception from traditional IT in terms of having many government officials stress innovation. But given the newness of the technology and challenging re-engineering and organizational issues, it is perhaps more concerning. In many cases, projects are simply presumed to have positive payoffs and few, if any, performance measures are articulated. Political leadership, like with traditional IT, often demands unrealistic e-gov project timelines to fit election cycles. This is especially taxing to e-gov efforts where the common assertion is that the greatest benefits derive from potentially massive re-engineering efforts, cutting across inter-organizational and inter-governmental processes and structures with all the technical, political, and organizational issues that must be settled. Political officials expect results triumphed from best practices and glowing testimonials, especially cost savings. To date, e-gov has received a bit of a free ride in justifying its financial success. However, as many such efforts are funded from general revenues at the presumed expense of other government interests and supportive groups, the reality is that cost savings assertions will need some reasonable justification.

Florida's first major attempt at online permitting is instructive. One of the first e-gov proposals of Governor Bush's administration was one-stop permitting, a project which aimed to place virtually all state permit processes online. Agencies were given no additional resources to convert to online applications (as Bush and the Legislature expected cost savings to pay for the development). If that was not enough, the entire project was expected to take approximately six months and agencies were even prohibited from charging their normal application and permit fees (presumably to encourage citizens to convert to the cost saving Web application).

Though Florida, as of 2005, now has a handful of permit processes online, the project in its time was almost a complete failure. The Bush administration failed to recognize the enormous difficulty in simply identifying permit processes (most agencies could not even provide a list of their permit processes to even begin the project) and the wide variation in their length and complexity (viz., there is a big difference between requesting a hunting license and filing an environmental permit, both in terms of information volume and involved agencies and governments). The decision to remove charges effectively froze many agencies' e-gov efforts as well. Privately, IT managers stonewalled the project as they feared the online form would dramatically reduce operating revenues derived from the existing, paper-based processes. Moreover, for those permits that did go online, Florida has found, like many governments, that Web-based submissions rarely replace traditional services, either out of public choice or necessity, because of legal and access-equity reasons. Hence, costs savings largely presumed from retiring legacy, paper-based services are far more difficult to obtain than expected.

The lesson from Florida's massive online permitting attempt is that IT innovation is difficult. That knowledge has long been available in the public IT literature. However, the Florida case exemplifies how the e-gov rush towards faster innovation and ever more complex applications, coupled with all-too-often scant project evaluation and thought about the realities of public operations, seriously hinders e-gov efforts. Such cases are far from strategically planned or managed, by almost any definition of the concept, and the tendency for such projects to come from rather unpredictable political mandates makes e-gov planning quite taxing.

3. The CIO and Political Leadership Models of IT Centralized Control

Direct political appointee management of IT operations is traditionally viewed as undesirable among public administration scholars (West 2003). Among the primary reasons are concerns about the qualifications of such appointees and political turnover endangering professional management of a complex area. e-Gov, however, has been closely associated with the popularity of the CIO—often a political appointee charged with supervision and responsibility for government-wide IT projects and operations. The CIO concept, like many management reforms, is derived from business models and presumes that a central, politically connected position is necessary to effectively cross the various organizational units to re-engineer various processes and discover potentially shared applications. But there is considerable question as to whether the CIO role is really effective. Do CIOs really improve IT planning and management, or does their political exposure, as often feared in the past, seriously limit their effectiveness?

There is a noted paucity of research on the background and effectiveness of CIOs but existing literature presents cause for skepticism. At the federal level, McClure and Bertot (2000) question the management effectiveness of agency CIOs established under ITMRA after reviewing the experiences with the office after three years of implementation. At the state level, in contrast to the federal level where a government-wide post is the norm, CIOs have significant turnover, even more than a normal political cycle would predict. Between August 2003 and February 2004, five state CIOs resigned, one after being blamed for not delivering on expected cost savings from e-gov, one due to a change in governor, and three to pursue private sector jobs. A study by the National Association of State Chief Information Officers (NASCIO) in 2001 found 16 of the 48 reporting CIOs were new that year (NASCIO 2002). CIO tenures less than a couple of years are too common.

It is rather difficult to expect any realistic strategic planning under such short tenures. Additionally, the political power, even with the backing of a chief executive, to instill coordination across agencies is highly limited when agency IT and program staff expect short CIO tenures.

There is also a growing concerning with a revolving door between high-level government CIOs and private companies, especially CIOs taking jobs at companies to whom they previously awarded contracts. To many companies, hiring such people is a logical move to improve corporate marketability to government. Yet, even if there are no shady employment offers for contracts being arranged, the practice seriously undermines public confidence in the objective professionalism of the CIO role.

For example, Florida CIO Kim Bahrami awarded BearingPoint a $126 million contract to overhaul and manage the state's primary computer operations. After resigning in February 2004 following a scathing audit on the vagueness and financial risk associated with the project, Bahrami was hired by BearingPoint in July. Under state ethics laws, Bahrami would have been prohibited from employment for two years with vendors who had contracts she oversaw as a government employee. However, BearningPoint claimed that her work in their corporate office in Virginia did not include the Florida agreements. Meanwhile, the state's primary law enforcement agency is investigating, and the contracts were terminated in October 2004 (James 2004).

The potential political power and resource control may be useful to comprehensive and more strategically orientated planning, but Bahrami's case is a stern warning about the potential dangers. Coupled with short tenures due to political cycles and being politically susceptible to blame for e-gov perceived failures, or unrealized benefits, claims of CIO productivity should meet healthy skepticism.

Besides tenure and vendor connections, CIOs may also suffer from their backgrounds. Many CIOs, whose appointments are high level and political, have questionably qualified professional backgrounds (e.g., Breul 2003). Often they come from private sector work and are simply not prepared for the complexity and differences in government operations, often exacerbated by traditional business IT instruction where management approaches are presumed generic and sector makes little, if any, difference (Campbell 2003). CIO roles are also changing. As more services are contracted out and governments face questions about their vendor relations, there is a greater need for legal expertise. In 2004, Florida appointed a new CIO, Simone Marstiller, a lawyer by trade who served as a general counsel for various agencies under the Bush administration and has, even by the governor's own admission, little IT background.

B. CHANGING VENDOR ROLES AND INCREASED POWER

Public agencies have long relied on outside contractors to assist in IT operations and development, but such consultants traditionally worked mostly through the IT staff rather than political officials. For example, an internal database development or imaging system might be deemed necessary to support an agency task. The IT staff would develop the request for proposals and technical deliverables and handle most of the contract negotiations and management. Of course, there is significant variation in how vendors work with public agencies, but the point is that in traditional IT, this operational perspective is commonly assumed.

One of the most notable changes in IT management under e-gov is the increasingly powerful role of vendors in decision-making. This is partly attributable to privatization or outsourcing efforts among many governments and the huge, sudden influx of money for e-gov development, but many governments have arguably become far more reliant on outside consultants under e-gov than traditional IT. A recent national survey reports that US local governments are more likely to rely on vendors for estimating potential project costs than their own estimates or the work of other local governments (Coursey 2005), though larger jurisdictions are notably less reliant on vendors.

The reason is so many governments were faced with a sudden, strong political demand to develop e-gov services but they lacked crucial staff expertise and resources for internal development. Hence, the choice was to outsource such work, often with little realization that such development was not just a database or an imaging system, but a completely different, defining architecture to managing work. Such massive vendor dependence is dangerous. Bozeman (2002) argues that the lack of internal management of outsourcing activity was a significant problem in the grandiose IRS modernization efforts. Under e-gov, vendors have also been far more aggressive in seeking government work, partly as a business strategy to expand their client base given an economic downturn, and also due to the perception of significant profits from large-scale e-gov development.

In the e-gov era, the role of vendors has changed significantly for many governments. Outsourcing various operations, and not building internal capacity, weakens the ability of governments to strategically control IT resources. This is a historical concern, but with e-gov, vendors appear far more powerful in the decision-making process, not just in operations. The control many vendors can exert over how potential systems are assessed, chosen, planned, developed, and maintained seriously jeopardizes any realistic strategic planning. Specifically, there are three major concerns with vendors under e-gov:

- Preference for political leadership over career officials
- Determining IT direction
- Support for centralization

1. Preference for Political Leadership over Career Officials

While cozy relationships between vendors and political officials certainly existed in traditional IT, the e-gov era may find them more commonplace. The occasional contract for campaign donations is still often alleged. However, it is too simple to label vendors as somewhat sleazy for going directly to elected officials to pitch their products and services. There are just too many incentives to do so. First, vendors know elected officials control the money for the large-scale e-gov projects far more than career IT officials. Few major projects come from existing IT budgets. Second, given politicians' attention to e-gov, vendors find access to elected officials far easier than has normally been the case with government IT. Third, vendors know claims such as cost savings and other tangible benefits are far more readily accepted by politicians compared to career IT staff, who have learned to be a bit more skeptical of project promises. Fourth, the movement towards sole source and no-bid contracts, presumably to reduce contractual red tape and costs and speed project development, encourages vendors to work more directly with political leadership to obtain contracts. The famed political scandal over a $95 million no-bid contract with Oracle for unneeded software under California Governor Gray Davis (Patton 2004) is an often-cited example of the inherit dangers of politically connected vendors. Fifth, vendors favor elected officials for e-gov projects who cut across agency lines because they can help ensure agreement and compliance on system design and management.

As vendors work more with political leadership than career IT staff, governments potentially face serious, negative implications for IT planning and management. Vendors can, and do, use their political connections to intimidate career staff and reduce their ability to supervise projects. Even under a traditional bid system for reviewing contracts, IT staffs respond to the powerful political connections of the various competing vendors.

In Florida, where much of civil service protection was eliminated under Governor Jeb Bush's administration, this is especially troubling. Privately, many career IT staffers have expressed grave concerns that their technical objectivity in reviewing bids is mitigated by fear, justifiably or not, of punishment for not selecting a politically favored vendor. Employees have also noted concerns about their jobs being outsourced to such companies and, if they are seen as antagonistic, that the company may not retain them for the converted, private sector operation.

The more powerful relationship of vendors with elected officials has potentially enormous consequences for strategic planning and management. Vendors have arguably more control over key decisions regarding project selection, development, and assessment than before. In Florida, the power of vendors to shape IT decision-making has even been noted by a House Appropriations Committee head, Republican Representative Carols Lacasa, who stated: "If you try to fire [them], they will come in with an army of lobbyists and try to extend the deadlines and change the law. It's a nightmare" (quoted in Patton 2004). Additionally, the role of career IT staff and their expertise is significantly reduced. Privatization and outsourcing compounds the problem as government has less direct control over their critical IT resources.

2. Determining IT Directions

The greater access of vendors to elected officials suggests a greater role in determining the directions of IT operations and management. Too often under e-gov, project ideas come not from anything close to a systematic evaluation of government needs, but from a vendor proposal to an elected official who suddenly announces a new, major initiative much to the surprise of career IT staff. Such problems are not new to IT. The very lack of setting goals and objectives in relation to technology decisions was a major cause of the problems in IRS modernization during the late 1980s and early 1990s (Bozeman 2002).

In many cases, e-gov projects are from previously implemented private sector applications with the questionable presumption that they can be readily converted to government tasks. Such is the case with Florida's seven-year, $280 million People First project which outsourced much of the state's personnel administration and replaced an antiquated twenty-year-old state application. The project met considerable delays and problems, despite Convergys Corporation's previous experience with such systems in private management (Coursey and McCreary 2004).

Touch screen voting systems, while not e-gov per se, are another good example of where vendors have effectively made major government IT investment decisions. After the 2000 presidential election, such vendor proposals are almost always pitched directly to political leadership and many local governments adopted them, despite the reality that such systems had never been used in a significantly sized election and other existing technologies are cheaper (like optical scan forms) and known to be quite successful. Under a traditional IT evaluation considering costs, technological maturity, and risk, it is very doubtful many of these systems would have been implemented. Touch screens have faced a mixed reception, with reports of significant implementation and security problems, as well as concerns over auditing capabilities, especially in Ohio and Florida. The combination of political leadership involvement (and the usual bias towards new technology) yields a questionable investment decision.

3. Favoring Centralization

For years, government IT scholars and officials have debated the relative merits of centralized IT procurement. Favoring centralization are possible economies of scale and standardization of systems. Decentralization advocates note the importance of agencies developing rather personal, long-term working relationships with vendors who understand their unique needs. Plus, in the case where projects are smaller at the agency level, and where smaller companies can handle the work, agencies may find vendors more responsive as they may be more dependent on the agency for work than a large private firm.

e-Gov, with the often proposed large-scale projects, tends to benefit larger companies over smaller ones. Moreover, the very idea that e-gov benefits best accrue from cross-organizational projects suggest agency-level contracts are less germane. Even so, there is an inherent incentive for large companies to favor centralized decision-making. It is far easier and cheaper for vendors to propose, obtain, and manage a project with one client as opposed to several.

This tendency is exemplified in the battle over federal money for election technology allocated to states under the Help America Vote Act of 2002 (P.L. 107-252). Control over investment decisions varies across states, some use county governments and their supervisors of elections, others utilize the state agency charged with overseeing election systems, and in others there is a mix of responsibility. It is hardly surprising that voting technology companies like Diebold prefer and lobby for more centralized decision-making, at least in terms of setting standards for voting machines that limit the choices available to county governments.

Additionally, large-scale companies use their political clout via centralized decision-making to force smaller companies, especially local IT firms, out of the market. A growing dependence on single, large-scale vendors suggests government agencies may have far less control over assuring vendor contract performance.

e-Gov is big business and other major recent investments in more traditional IT, like voting systems, attract and favor large firms. Larger firms have major advantages in fights over bidding rules and outcomes, which is evident in the continuing battles across states purchasing new voting technology. It is clearly advantageous to such firms to centralize procurement decisions, especially when under the control of politically influenced elected officials. Competition becomes more of a political market than one based on technical and managerial capabilities. Consider this telling paradox: centralized IT planning models are supposed to provide governments more control over resources to produce better strategic plans. But the very nature of a centralized process encourages dependence on a few, powerful vendors limiting the ability of government IT professionals to perform strategic planning.

V. CONCLUSION AND SUMMARY

IT, like many areas of public service, is historically faced with significant problems in applying strategic perspectives. This essay argues that e-gov presents some additional challenges. Specifically, e-gov encourages more political official and vendor intervention—challenging the ability to realistically assess medium to long-term needs, set goals and objectives, and evaluate the necessary resources, stakeholders, and environmental factors involved. Many of the ideas presented here defy the common e-gov mantra, especially the rather pessimistic view of the CIO role, but their bases are on experiences with dozens of real e-gov projects across several governments.

Readers should not presume the intent is to claim any of these assertions as gospel. To some extent, this review plays devil's advocate or anti-polemic. For researchers, the claims concerning political leadership and vendors present fodder for future study. Is e-gov really that different and if so, to what extent are the alleged problems applicable to other projects and efforts? The relative power of vendors to set the IT agenda, the effects of the CIO model, and the influence of political officials on the quality of IT work are all significant concerns warranting study. What are the implications? Are the increased involvement of vendors and political officials simply temporary, given the level of funding and newness of the technology?

For example, how will government respond to e-gov failures and associated contract problems? Commonly, evaluations of major IT failures and successes have stressed some removal of political controls. Yet it will be very tempting for elected officials to presume that contracting failures are from a lack of political oversight, not too much public exposure as commonly presumed in the literature. For example, the 2005 Florida Legislature responded to the perceived contractual problems under Governor Jeb Bush by passing a bill to abolish the core IT management unit behind previous centralized efforts, the State Technology Office (STO). The bill was vetoed by Governor Bush, justified on the basis that the proposed changes encroached on executive authority. If the bill had become law, the STO would have been replaced by a new council, with members appointed by the governor. The council, however, would have been required to confer with CIOs of various agencies as well as pass the existing review requirements with a legislative workgroup.

Such proposed changes are likely in the future, and not only in Florida, but council is unlikely to fix the political problems, given the gubernatorial appointments that provide even greater opportunities for golden parachute jobs with contracted vendors for the politically connected appointees. The CIO requirements may offer some increased administrative control, yet CIOs are increasingly less technical and rather political themselves (as noted earlier). The legislative workgroup arguably becomes more important and it would not be surprising to see even more vendor lobbyists, this time targeting the Legislature, not just the executive agencies. Such reforms may, in the end, do more harm than good.

The lessons from Florida and other governments both challenge and complement much of our traditional conceptions of public sector IT administration. The examples here illustrate where political officials and vendors may be more influential than traditionally assumed. However, these are vital research questions not solely related to whether these findings hold for varying levels of government and are more generalizable, but also to what possible mediating variables may alter these changes. For example, it may be the case that as e-gov becomes more commonplace, political interest will dissipate. Also, concerns over insuring contractual accountability may encourage varying and new administrative structures. The role and effectiveness of the CIO model is in serious question given its typically close ties to political-over-professional responsibility and turnover rates.

Vendor relations are also important for future research. Models predicting the level of vendor influence are as equally essential as more practical, grounded, experienced-based suggestions for proper control of vendor contracts. The revolving door problem—high-ranking IT officials leaving for government vendors—is also a major administrative and ethical question needing serious examination. One possibility is that vendors will be more influential for large projects where there are less professional IT capacity and staff, more pro-business and powerful executive branches, and few legal restrictions on vendor contracting. This not only concerns ethical behavior, but bidding rules such as no-bid contracts which might streamline bidding, but unfortunately encourage improper contractual arrangements based on political connections.

Where e-gov will be most successful, perhaps, is where the focus is not on e-gov itself. e-Gov is a technology to help solve problems. Where agencies stress the development of coherent organizational missions and strategies and link e-gov to those concepts by finding, educating, and encouraging supportive political leadership dedicated to public service and not their own career advancement, more success should be evident. This is a daunting assignment, yet success is possible. Thompson and Rainey (2003), in reviewing the modernization of the IRS human resource management system after passage of the IRS Restructuring and Reform Act of 1998, found solid evidence of success linked to these very ideas. Of course, being able to achieve organizational and political agreement and support for missions and goals is always challenging within the public sector.

These ideas, closely linked with strategic planning in its various forms, are hardly new to government IT. Over the years, the management answers have been there, but actually implementing them has usually proven extremely challenging. Political leadership becomes critical in re-engineering efforts under fourth-generation technologies such as e-gov, and often requires changed organizational responsibilities, shared roles, and interagency cooperation. Until such research, or history, provides more definitive answers, let the warning be heeded by those in practice. The optimistic view of the great, brave new world of e-gov solutions, as part of the fourth generation of IT, is questionable at best.

ACKNOWLEDGMENTS

This article originated as a series of invited university lectures in the People's Republic of China during 2004. The author gratefully acknowledges the comments of faculty and students at Huazhong, Renmin, and Zhejiang.

REFERENCES

Andersen, D., Belardo, S., and Dawes, S., Strategic information management: conceptual frameworks for the public sector, *Public Productivity and Management Review*, 17, 335, 1994.

Balutis, A., E-government 2001, Part II: evolving strategies for action, *The Public Manager*, 41, 2001.

Barr, S., Savings uncertain from electronic tracking of employees, *Washington Post*, 24, B2, September, 2003.

Beachboard, J., Assessing the information technology management reform act from a bureau's perspective, *Government Information Quarterly*, 14, 291, 1997.

Berry, F. and Wechesler, B., State agencies' experience with strategic planning: findings from a national survey, *Public Administration Review*, 55, 159, 1995.

Bimber, B., The internet and political mobilization: research note on the 1996 election season, *Social Science Computer Review*, 16, 391, 1998.

Bonchek, M., A grassroots in cyberspace: using computer networks to facilitate political participation, Paper presented at the Midwest Political Science Association, Annual Meeting, Chicago, IL, 1995.

Bousquet, S., Speaker used license tag list, *Saint Petersburg Times*, 21, 1B, August, 2003.

Bozeman, B., *Government Management of Information Mega-technology: Lessons from the Internal Revenue Service's Tax Systems Modernization*, IBM Endowment for the Business of Government, Arlington, VA, 2002.

Bozeman, B. and Bretschneider, S., Public management information systems: theory and prescriptions, *Public Administration Review*, 46, 475, 1986.

Bretschneider, S. and Wittmer, D., Organizational adoption of microcomputer technology: the role of sector, *Information Systems Research*, 4, 88, 1993.

Breul, J., The government performance and results act—10 years later, *Journal of Government Financial Management*, 52, 58, 2003.

Bryson, J. and Roering, W., Strategic planning options for the public sector, In *Handbook of Public Administration*, 2nd ed., Perry, J., Ed., Jossey-Bass, San Francisco, CA, 1996.

Campbell, W., How to survive in the public sector, *CIO*, 16, 1, 2003.

Caudle, S., Managing information resources in state government, *Public Administration Review*, 50, 515, 1990.

Caudle, S., Gorr, W., and Newcomer, K., Key information systems management issues for the public sector, *MIS Quarterly*, 15, 171, 1991.

Coursey, D., E-government: trends, benefits, and challenges, In *The Municipal Yearbook*, Vol. 14, ICMA, Washington, DC, 2005.

Coursey, D. and Bozeman, B., Decision making in public and private organizations: a test of alternative concepts of "publicness," *Public Administration Review*, 50, 525, 1990.

Coursey, D. and Killingsworth, J., Managing government web services in florida: issues and lessons, In *Handbook of Public Information Systems*, Garson, D., Ed., Marcel Dekker, New York, p. 331, 2000.

Coursey, D. and Killingsworth, J., Managing e-gov in florida: further lessons from transition and maturity, In *Handbook of Public Information Systems*, Garson, D., Ed., Taylor & Francis, Boca Raton, FL, p. 335, 2005.

Coursey, D. and McCreary, S., Using technology in the workplace, In *Handbook of Human Resource Management in Government*, Condrey, S., Ed., Jossey-Bass, San Francisco, CA, 189, 2004.

Danziger, J., Computers and local governments and the litany of EDP, *Public Administration Review*, 36, 28, 1977.

Danziger, J., *Computers and Politics: High Technology in American Local Government*, Columbia University Press, New York, 1982.

Dawes, S., Interagency information sharing: expected benefits, manageable risks, *Journal of Policy Analysis and Management*, 15, 377, 1996.

Fountain, J., *Building the Virtual State: Information Technology and Institutional Change*, Brookings Institution, Washington, DC, 2001.

Garson, D., Information systems, politics, and government: leading theoretical perspectives, In *Handbook of Public Information Systems*, Garson, D., Ed., Marcel Dekker, New York, p. 591, 2000.

Garson, D., Public information technology and e-government: a historical timeline, In *Handbook of Public Information Systems*, Garson, D., Ed., Taylor and Francis, Boca Raton, FL, 27, 2005.

Hauserman, J., Bush may privatize personnel operation, *Saint Petersburg Times*, 7, 1B, September, 2001.

Heintze, T. and Bretschneider, S., Information technology and restructuring in public organizations does adoption of information technology affect organizational structures, communications, and decision-making?, *Journal of Public Administration Research and Theory*, 10, 801, 2000.

Hickson, D., et al., *Top Decisions: Strategic Decision-making in Organizations*, Jossey-Bass, San Francisco, CA, 1986.

Holden, S., The evolution of information technology management at the federal level: implications for public administration, In *Public Information Technology: Policy and Management Issues*, Garson, D., Ed., Idea Group Publishing, Hershey, PA, pp. 479–498, 2003.

Holden, S. and Fletcher, P., Introduction, *Government Information Quarterly*, 18, 75, 2001.

Holley, L., Dufner, D., Reed, B., and Got, SISP?, Strategic information systems planning in U.S. state governments, *Public Performance and Management Review*, 25, 398, 2002.

Holley, L., Dufner, D., and Reed, B., Strategic information systems planning in US. county governments: will the real SISP model please stand up?, *Public Performance and Management Review*, 27, 102, 2004.

James, J., State kills disputed contracts, *Saint Petersburg Times*, 1, 1A, October, 2004.

Kaylor, C., Deshazo, R., and Van Eck, D., Gauging e-government: a report on implementing services among American cities, *Government Information Quarterly*, 18, 293, 2001.

Kraemer, K., Dutton, D., and Northrop, A., *The Management of Information Systems*, Columbia University Press, New York, 1981.

Landsbergen, D. and Wolken, G., Realizing the promise: government information systems and the fourth generation of information technology, *Public Administration Review*, 61, 206, 2001.

Lee, G. and Perry, J., Are computers boosting productivity? A test of the paradox in state governments, *Journal of Public Administration Research and Theory*, 12, 77, 2002.

McClure, C. and Bertot, J., The chief information officer (CIO): assessing its impact, *Government Information Quarterly*, 17, 7, 2000.

Moon, M., The evolution of e-government among municipalities: rhetoric or reality?, *Public Administration Review*, 62, 424, 2002.

Moon, M. and Bretschneider, S., Does the perception of red tape constrain IT innovativeness in organizations? Unexpected results from a simultaneous equation model and implications, *Journal of Public Administration Research and Theory*, 12, 273, 2002.

NASCIO, NASCIO releases 2002 compendium of digital government in the states, *Journal of Government Financial Management*, 51, 64, 2002.

Northrup, A., Kraemer, K., Dunkle, D., and King, J., Payoffs from computerization: lessons over time, *Public Administration Review*, 50, 505, 1990.

Northrup, A. and Kraemer, K., The information age: which countries will benefit?, In *Handbook of Public Information Systems*, Garson, D., Ed., Marcel Dekker, New York, Vol. 265, 2000.

Nutt, P. and Backoff, P., *Strategic Management of Public and Third-sector Organizations: A Handbook for Leaders*, Jossey-Bass, San Francisco, CA, 1992.

Nutt, P. and Backoff, P., Strategy for public and third-sector organizations, *Journal of Public Administration Research and Theory*, 5, 189, 1995.

Osborne, D. and Gaebler, T., *Reinventing Government*, Addison-Wesley, MA, 1992.

Patton, S., *Reforming California IT*, CIO Magazine, December 1, 2004, http://www.cio.com/archive/120104/reform.html (accessed April 3, 2005).

Pollitt, C. and Bouckaert, G., *Public Management Reform: A Comparative Analysis*, Oxford University Press, New York, 2000.

Rainey, H., *Understanding and Managing Public Organizations*, Jossey-Bass, San Francisco, 2003.

Stevens, J. and McGowan, R., *Information Systems in Public Management*, Praeger, New York, 1985.

TechTopics (a Georgia Tech alumni magazine), http://gtalumni.org/Publications/techtopics/fall97/taxing.html, 1997.

Thompson, J. and Rainey, H., *Modernizing Human Resource Management in the Federal Government: The IRS Model*, IBM Endowment for the Business of Government, Arlington, VA, 2003.

Vriens, D. and Achterbergh, J., Planning local e-government, *Information Systems Management*, 21, 45, 2004.

West, J., State and federal e-government in the United States, 2003, Policy report, http://www.insidepolitics.org/egovt03us.pdf (accessed April 3, 2004), 2003.

23 Five Great Ideas in Public Information Technology Literature

Alexei Pavlichev and G. David Garson

CONTENTS

I. INTRODUCTION

Information and communication technology (ICT) has been a major research focus in public administration for over two decades. ICT has come to be seen as central to the improvement of productivity and better delivery of services in the public sector. A milestone was reached when, in 1986, an entire issue of the leading journal in the discipline, *Public Administration Review*, was devoted to the discussion of information technology. Since then, significant research progress has been made during a period in which there was a transition from cumbersome and expensive mainframe computers with attached monochrome monitors to elegant, affordable, and often more powerful PCs and laptops with broadband and even wireless connection to organizational networks and the World Wide Web.

When used effectively, many ICTs, such as the Internet, have been proven to improve government performance in many areas. They also allow for a more customer-centric approach to service provision. By transferring the provision of information (such as forms and brochures) as well as many services (driver's license renewal and permit applications) online, the government provides its customers with opportunity to use these services any time of the day from any location that is equipped with Internet access. One can renew one's driver's license while on a business trip in a different state or even a different country. ICT enables government agencies to create one-stop integrated portals that make it possible for citizens to access government services online in "no more than three clicks" (OMB 2003b). ICT has the potential to make public services accessible to remote rural areas where they were previously unavailable (Edmiston 2003). Migrating online not only allows government to make its services more customer-centric and convenient for citizens, but also more beneficial for government agencies themselves, sometimes reducing costs by 70% compared to providing the same services over the counter (NECCC 2000).

On all levels, government agencies are recognizing the potential of ICT and rushing to implement these technologies. e-Government is one of the key elements in the five-part President's Management Agenda for improving performance of the federal government. An e-government survey conducted by the International City/County Management Association and Public Technology Inc. shows that 85.3% of municipal governments have their own web sites, and 57.4% have an Intranet (Moon 2002). The best indicator of this is the amount of spending on ICT. By 2004, ICT investments are expected to account for 40% of all capital investment in the United States (GAO 2000). According to the Office of Management and Budget, considering only the federal government, investment in information technology is estimated to be $59 billion for 2040, which is up from the budget request of $53 billion in 2003 (OMB 2003a).

For the purpose of improving government services by moving them online, government initiatives are well justified. The use of ICT, such as the Internet, is becoming increasingly widespread among businesses and the general public. According to a comScore Media Metrix Press Release (2003), in September 2003 the number of Internet users in the US passed the 150 million mark. Results of a survey conducted recently by Hart-Teeter on behalf of the Council for Excellence in Government and Accenture indicate that nearly seven in ten respondents use the Internet every day for information searches and e-mail, and 66% also use it for online transactions (Hart-Teeter 2003). According to the research conducted by the Pew Foundation, 71 million Americans have used government websites (OMB 2003b).

ICT undoubtedly holds great potential for increasing the efficiency and quality of government services and for broadening public access at the same time. Moreover, ICT can change the entire mechanism of interaction between citizens and government. It is argued that ICT can have a significant potential for democratization of governance, because citizens, including those who had difficulties of doing so before, are provided with opportunities to interact with government instantaneously at any time through one-stop electronic portals. However, in popular debate and academic literature, these optimistic, even utopian, prognoses regarding the role of technology in society have always been paralleled by more cautious, even dystopian, visions with respect to the consequences of ICT implementation. Dystopians argue that ICT implementation will exacerbate the stratification of society by increasing the digital divide, infringe upon personal privacy, lead to individual isolation, and make it easier for those in power to exercise political manipulation of socially isolated groups (Fountain 2001a; Frissen 1998; Garson 2003; Kamarck 2002; Kling 1996; Margetts 1999; Norris 2001). The reality probably lies somewhere in between, gravitating toward each extreme under different circumstances.

To better understand the impact of ICT on the field of public administration, it is useful to examine five of the major ideas that have played a prominent role in research on ICT in the public sector:

1. *ICT is political.* A continuing theme in public sector research on information technology has been the finding that what appears to the public to be a technical matter, is at its core a fundamentally political process in which human factors are paramount.
2. *ICT is an engine of organizational change in public agencies.* Research in the 1980s on public productivity and in the early 1990s on reinvention of government came to focus increasingly in the late 1990s on ICT as the critical element in transforming governance.

3. *ICT has the potential to lead to de-territorialization.* The rise of ICT commoditizes information and in the information marketplace, information flow does not follow the old geopolitics of hierarchical agencies on up to nation states. Instead, research suggests a blurring of jurisdictional lines at agency, regional, and even global levels.
4. *ICT creates digital divide.* If information is power, then it matters who the haves and have-nots are in the information society. Although universal service equalizes the playing field in terms of computer hardware and Internet access in advanced countries, the global digital divide looms as a major policy issue, as do differentials in the quality of access even within industrially advanced nations.
5. *Public ICT management is different from private sector ICT management.* The fifth major idea guiding ICT research in the public sector arises from a seminal article by Bozeman and Bretschneider (1986) appearing in the aforementioned 1986 special issue of the *Public Administration Review,* in which it was argued that sectoral differences in the management of information technology required two different lines of research.

These five ideas, taken together, form the mainstream of public administration research on ICT: that information technology is a fundamentally political phenomenon that holds the potential to transform governmental processes for the better, but in the process raises issues of structural evolution of organizational forms as well as differential comparative advantage from the individual level to the level of nation-states—and that the IT cannot be well understood simply by assuming that lessons of the private sector apply to the public. Each of these five ideas is now examined in turn.

II. ICT IS POLITICAL

Redistricting illustrates how political considerations are embedded in technical systems. For the 1990 census, the Census Bureau used a database called Topologically Integrated Geographic Encoding and Referencing (TIGER). The database was developed to automate production of Census cartographic products and to perform geographic analyses of Census data. Soon after TIGER was developed, political geographers and redistricting experts started using the database in combination with Geographic Information Systems (GIS) to redefine voting districts. According to the Constitution, congressional and legislative districts have to be reconfigured every ten years. In the 1960s the Supreme Court ruled that in the process of districts reconfiguring, variation among districts in population size should be kept to a minimum (Monmonier 2001). The process of districts' reconfiguration is also regulated by the Voting Rights Act of 1965, which prohibits redistricting from splitting a district in which representatives of a minority group constitute a majority. GIS software algorithms and decision trees that use the TIGER data to redefine voting districts have to be designed in such a way that they take into account the decisions of the Supreme Court and the provisions of Voting Rights Act. According to Monmonier, there is more than one way to transfer these provisions into algorithms executable by GIS. The new voting districts produced as the result of executing these algorithms would depend, among other things, on how the algorithms measure population density and whether or in what way they define minority groups. Monmonier concluded, "This variation affords a diverse suite of solutions, undermining claims that automated, algorithmic redistricting is neutral, nonpartisan, and inherently objective. Because party leaders, judges, or Justice Department officials can choose the solutions they like, manipulation is inevitable..."

In other words, using technology for redistricting makes the process more efficient but in no way more objective or neutral. The results continue to reflect the values and attitudes of people who control the technology. At the same time, using technology to execute political decisions makes it more difficult to hold responsible parties accountable for outcomes. This is because the application of technology creates an illusion of objectivity and because verifying the results produced by ICT would require a certain degree of technological expertise. That is, technology provides a mystification factor which is useful in the exercise of political discretion.

Very few, if any, would disagree with the notion that political factors underlie the use of seemingly technical redistricting software. However, much social science research on ICT implementation has demonstrated that political factors (defined as normative choice not technologically determined, whether at organizational or governmental levels) characterize a broad range of ICT arenas and the redistricting example is the rule, not the exception. In this way the body of social science research stands rather in contrast to the mainstream official position maintained by formal government entities, such as the General Accounting Office (GAO) and the Office of Management and Budget (OMB), whose policy guidance and directives generally hold an optimistic, technocratic perspective on the way ICT increases efficiency of government operations. This optimism is shared by some academics, while others exercise a more cautious approach.

The many social scientists who have pointed to the importance of political factors in technological undertakings generally fall into two schools. The minority position is held by those who believe that not only is ICT political, but that technocratic power is increasingly important in the policy-making process. The majority position is associated with enhancement theory—that ICT reinforces the policies of the prevailing power structure of the organization and, correspondingly, the technocrats themselves do not represent a new, independent class of power.

Questions of information technology and power have been a major concern for over three decades (Mowshowitz 1976; Weizenbaum 1976). As early as 1967 Downs raised the issue of technical experts gaining power at the expense of elected officials or corporate CEOs simply because such experts had control over the means of information (Downs, 1967). Writers such as Field (1970) predicted that computerization might eventually mean that top management would become "programmed" by technocrats at lower levels, "stripping the power of the mighty." David Burnham (1983) painted a picture of a high-tech city of the future in which a privileged class ruled through computerized business, education, entertainment, and security.

Frank Fischer in his book *Technocracy and the Politics of Expertise* (1990) staked out the position that ICT expands the political role of technocracy in the policy-making process. Fischer defines technocracy as "a system of governance in which technically trained experts rule by virtue of their specialized knowledge and position in dominant political and economic institutions." According to Fischer, ICT affects policy making by contradicting the democratic nature of the process and narrowing policy options and choices. Despite the fact that ICT has the potential to improve government efficiency, in many instances technocrats constrain the direction and the scope of democratic discourse by shaping feasible and appropriate courses of action, where the constraints are given by the nature of information systems. As a result, policy making adjusts current institutions and practices to the nature and capabilities of available technology. Under these circumstances, the expertise of technical experts—or technocrats—becomes increasingly important. Technocrats come to be able to influence the direction and development of the policy-making process, all of which leads to creation of technocratic politics. Although technocrats remain formally subordinate to politicians and administrators, they are able to exercise influence over the definitions of specific issues and feasibility of solutions. The ultimate choice of policy is still made by policy makers, but it is increasingly the technocrats who determine the limit of available choices from which policy makers choose.

The context for concern over technocratic power in America is not so much about technocrats as a social class but about their role in organizations. The concern is that database management is part of a larger process of collecting, processing, manipulating, exchanging, and using information within and among commercial and governmental units (King and Kraemer 1984). By performing these functions, information workers define the categories by which the organization perceives everything from the behavior of its staff to its external environment. Like the historians of Orwell's *1984*, there is the potential for recreating the history and memory of an organization or even society along lines that conform to guidelines set by information technocrats (Weizenbaum 1976, 238). Even more important, information system design may institutionalize certain evaluative standards and long-term organizational goals.

Some early empirical studies did indeed show that computing can produce what some might call an information elite who benefit from increased power as a result of their position in information systems (IS) (see Kraemer and Danziger 1984; Danziger and Kraemer 1987). However, others saw that the more technologically advanced the society, the more power is dispersed among functional organizations and specialized interest groups rather than being concentrated in a single social class—technocratic, military, bureaucratic, or otherwise (Ferkiss 1970).

An important potential of ICT mentioned by Fischer (1990) is that technology can be antagonistic to democratic politics. ICT involves the application of rational analytical methodologies to problem solving. From this perspective, democratic politics is too contradictory and irrational, which leads to complications in finding solutions. Fischer further argues that ICT leads to political transformations that result in creation of competing political and economic elites, technocratic strata of experts, and a depoliticized mass public. He argues that political agendas are shaped by elites who have access to technical experts who in turn, to a certain degree, determine policy direction. The public, it is argued, has very little influence because it does not have the necessary skills to understand technocratic components of political decisions.

While it is true that ICT and the Internet provide the public with opportunities to exercise political activity on a scale never seen before (obtaining information from FirstGov.gov, online lobbying by MoveOn.org, and interest group organization by SierraClub.org, to name a few examples), Fisher is concerned less with the political *uses* of the Internet than with the political *nature* of ICT. That nature, Fischer argues, is to allow the framing of alternatives to be shaped by those who control information in the organization—the technocrats.

Even in terms of political uses of the Internet, those who see a new American revolution wrought by e-democracy in its many forms exaggerate the power of the public. Empowered by ICT, citizens can increase their political activity, make more informed decisions, and directly impact democratic processes. "But would they want to?" asks Yuval Levin (2002). His answer is: not necessarily. Low levels of political activity occur not because the information is hard to find, but because most citizens are not interested in finding it. The Internet makes it easier for people to access political information, but it does not increase people's interest in politics (Levin, 2002; Norris 2002). Moreover, according to Levin, the Internet can actually narrow a person's political awareness by shielding him or her from information on alternative solutions about the issue that interests the person. That is, unlike traditional broad-spectrum media, the Internet promotes narrow-spectrum partitioning of the information marketplace, allowing (some would say encouraging) individuals to use only specialized channels. This isolating tendency of the Internet may lead to fragmentation of a political community into many isolated communities that have narrow perspectives on policy issues. Such techniques as narrowcasting (Nye 2002) that allow political actors to deliver specific messages to each particular segment of their audience they target may exacerbate fragmentation even further.

The majority view of social scientists on the political nature of ICT is not the earlier-cited view based on arguments about technocratic power and public disengagement. For the majority, the effect of ICT is contingent upon the social setting in which implementation takes place. Thus ICT may facilitate centralization and even totalitarian elements as well as act to empower and liberate democratic forces, depending on the setting in which it is used. That is, the majority view has been that ICT implementation is a political process in which the net contribution of technocrats and their information systems reinforces the powers-that-be within the organization or governmental jurisdiction.

As Danziger (1986) noted, by the 1980s a survey of research on ICT showed little evidence of significant impact on political power within organizations. Although computerization often increases managerial control (e.g., Rule and Attewell 1989, 237–239) and affects the control structure of organizations in complex ways, studies of computer programmers and their managers revealed little interest in unionization or other forms of organization to assert interests as a class (Fidel and Garner 1987). There appeared to be little evidence of technocrats acting like a class, much less an elite.

Scholars found more evidence lying on the side of viewing IT primarily as a tool like other tools, conferring power on the wielder of the tool—namely, the powers that be within any organization. At the societal level, Gattiker (2001) found that the Internet does offer additional avenues for political participation but mostly functions simply as one more communications medium, in addition to print, radio, and television, equally prone to manipulation by lobbyists and well-funded interests with the resources and motives to invest in the medium. At the organizational level, other researchers found that IT implementation does not disrupt the persistence of existing political structures within organizations, including Danziger et al. (1982); Kraemer (1991); Kolleck (1993); Pinsonneault and Kraemer (1993); Robertson and Seneviratne (1995); Riedel et al. (2000). For instance, Davis (1999), Margolis and Resnick (2000), Agre (2002) all uphold the amplification model (an institution's participants' appropriate technology to enhance preexisting organizational goals and relationships) in their research, finding that the Internet is rapidly amplifying existing political relationships, not overthrowing them. Moreover, it should be noted that studies of other technologies, such as the telephone, have likewise found a lack of substantial impact of these other technologies on the distribution of power, organizationally or societally (Fischer 1992).

III. ICT IS AN ENGINE OF ORGANIZATION CHANGE

In what Warshofsky (1989) called the "battle for the world of tomorrow," national governments must position themselves in the new information economy. In the context of the 1980s, much attention was given to the Japanese-subsidized Fifth Generation artificial intelligence project and other ICT initiatives of the Ministry of International Trade and Industry (MITI), as well as to similar efforts in Taiwan and Korea. In Europe, the Council of European Communities established a plan for constructing a common information services market and the Commission of the European Communities funded the European Strategic Programme of Research and Development in Information Technology.

In the United States, Edward Feigenbaum and Pamela Corduck's *The Fifth Generation: Artificial Intelligence and Japan's Computer Challenge to the World* (1985) reacted to such developments with alarm: "We are writing this book because we are worried…. America needs a national plan of action, a kind of space shuttle program for the knowledge systems of the future" (xvii). A Brookings Institution study likewise called for sharp cuts in military research and development funding in favor of financing cutting-edge information technology geared to global competitiveness (Flamm 1987). Congressional task forces on science policy in the 1980s and 1990s placed increasing emphasis on computing as a tool of global competition. Efforts, for example, took the form of supercomputer centers connected by networks such as NREN and the creation of a new technology development center under the National Institute of Standards and Technology.

In early 1993, the incoming Clinton administration was dismayed by IBM cutbacks in research and development at a time of global challenge in ICT industries. Most commentators expected new initiatives toward establishment of a national information technology policy to be forthcoming in the 1990s. While this was mitigated somewhat by the relative failure of the Japanese Fifth Generation project, which ended in 1992, and by the continued decline of the European semiconductor industry, the fact that Clinton had chosen Al Gore as his running mate was critical. In the words of then Senator Al Gore, NREN and the High Performance Computer Act were seen explicitly as a way to "allow us to leapfrog the Germans and the Japanese" (Schwartz 1992, 56).

Gore was placed in charge of President Clinton's primary management initiative, the National Performance Review (NPR), created in 1993. The NPR represented the Clinton administration's emphasis on information technology as a tool to reform government. In its report, "Creating a Government that Works Better and Costs Less: Reengineering Through Information Technology," the NPR report illustrated that the reinventing government movement, originated with a focus on decentralization/devolution, came to see e-government as a major reform thrust. NPR was later renamed the National Partnership for Reinventing Government (NPRG). The focus on reinvention was partly a proclamation that ICT was officially seen as an agent of governmental transformation and partly reflected the thinking of managerial scholars at this time.

Michael Porter, in an influential 1985 essay titled "How Information Gives You Competitive Advantage," was one of many scholars of the period arguing that ICT was an engine of organizational and even societal transformation. Peter Drucker predicted in 1988 that within twenty years information technology would lead to more efficient organizations with half the levels of management compared to the present. A special issue of the *Harvard Business Review* in 1990 was devoted to authors articulating the excitement over the potential transformative effects of ICT. Likewise, in the public sector, Northrop et al. (1990) documented the productivity payoff of ICT to American city governments. Norris's study of 65 local government units found time savings of 25% to 300% on computerized tasks as well as ability to do work that had not been feasible before (Norris 1989, 143). Early research led scholars in public administration to share the excitement of their private sector counterparts in the transformative potential of ICT.

However, the optimistic view of ICT as the agent of transformation is not without its cautionary detractors. The functioning of bureaucratic agencies often involves multiple stakeholders who bring to the table numerous constraints. Under these circumstances, any change, including the change triggered by information technology, is possible only when there is agreement. This in turn means that the propensity of most agencies faced with change, including change triggered by ICT implementation, is to maintain the status quo and preserve existing organizational processes in place (Fountain 2001b; Fountain 2002; Garson 2003; Margetts 1999; O'Looney 2002; Seneviratne 1999; Wilson 1989).

Although ICT holds a great potential for improving government services, various authors have pointed out the problematic nature of ICT investment. The OMB itself has noted that out of the $59 billion in the 2004 Budget for ICT, 35.4% of projects are in the at-risk category, meaning they do not demonstrate sufficient potential for success (OMB 2003a). Other research indicates that more than 80% of ICT initiatives fail to achieve their objectives or to be implemented at all (Center for Technology in Government 1999). Public employees and managers resist implementation of the ICT, side-stepping, undermining, or ignoring technological initiatives (Heeks 1999; Heeks and Davies 1999; Loader 1998; O'Looney 2002). Poor pay in comparison with the private sector companies is another important factor in government's inability to attract and retain sufficient and capable staff.

A consensus has developed in the evaluation literature on ICT that the productivity potential of ICT initiatives will not be achieved as long as government agencies merely automate existing processes. The OMB refers to this as "paving a cowpath" (OMB 2003a). Most scholarly writers now agree that to develop ICT potential, agencies may have to reevaluate their mission, management practices, and the way their existing tasks are carried out (Allen 1996; Atkinson and Ulevich 2000; Fountain 2001b; Kling and Margetts 1999; OMB, 2002a, 2002b, 2003a; Seneviratne 1999).

The importance of integrating ICT with management practices and organizational processes has been consistently brought up in the President's Management Agenda and in OMB reports. Even more significantly, it has been embedded in executive and legislative documents. OMB Circular A-11, the Clinger-Cohen Act, and the Government Performance and Results Act require federal agencies to establish performance goals for ICT and to link these goals to their strategic plans. The E-Government Act of 2002 expands these requirements and mandates agencies to develop performance measures for e-government and ICT that focus on improving productivity and quality of services provided to citizens. Following OMB policy guidance, implementing these provisions requires public agencies to address organizational restructuring issues. Some believe that the restructuring will lead to new forms of bureaucratic organization.

In 1994 Dutch academic Arre Zuurmond defended a dissertation thesis in which he argued that there is a possibility that bureaucracy will in fact be replaced—at least partially—with a new organizational structure which he called *inforcratie*, or infocracy. Zuurmond followed his dissertation with several articles, some of which were published in the US, where he further developed the idea of infocracy. He argued that, like Weberian bureaucracy, infocracy is an ideal-type theoretical construct, which may never materialize in its pure, absolute form. Zuurmond does not argue that infocracy will necessarily become the new form of organization that will completely replace bureaucracy, but that infocracy and bureaucracy differ in ways that illustrate the transformative effect of ICT.

In 2002, two other Dutch academics, Mark Bovens and Stavros Zouridis, published an article in *Public Administration Review*, where they argued that under the influence of ICT, traditional bureaucracy will be transformed into a "system-level" bureaucracy, which will preserve most of the characteristics of the traditional Weberian bureaucracy, but will also bring changes illustrating organizational transformation.

In the US, one of the most comprehensive discussions of the influence of ICT on bureaucracy was Jane E. Fountain's book *Building the Virtual State: Information Technology and Institutional Change*. In her book and subsequent works (Fountain 2001b, 2002), Fountain focused on many of the same issues as previous scholars. She argued that ICT implementation will not lead to the demise of bureaucracy but instead will create a modified bureaucratic structure, which she referred to as "virtual bureaucracy." Some of the prominent characteristics of the traditional bureaucratic structure will vanish, she asserted, while others will be reinforced.

Whether described as infocracy, system bureaucracy, or virtual bureaucracy, major emphasis is given to three types of organizational change: flattening organizational structures, development of interorganizational networks, and change in the degree of public employee discretion. Table 23.1 outlines the major differences between traditional and virtual/system bureaucracy, or infocracy.

A. FLATTENING ORGANIZATIONAL STRUCTURES

When James Q. Wilson (1989) described the structure of bureaucratic hierarchy, he classified public employees into three major categories: operators, managers, and executives. Operators are front-line employees, or "street-level bureaucrats" who interact with customers of the public agencies on a regular basis and policies that govern functioning of the government agencies. Responsibilities of managers usually involve preliminary data analysis and producing reports for executives. Finally, career executives are involved in making major organizational decisions, creating organizational policies, and standard operating procedures, and representing organizations externally.

According to the literature, ICT most seriously affects operators and middle managers. As more government services become available online, the functions previously performed by front-line employees are automated. Providing citizens with an opportunity to renew car registration online, at any convenient time, means that the Department of Motor Vehicles office does not need as many window clerks to perform the duties associated with the registration renewal. The same is true of the functions of middle managers. Expert systems and decision trees embedded in modern ICT have powerful capabilities of data analysis and reporting. In addition, ICT systems are able to perform analyses in a real time and make the results immediately available to decision makers in a required format through the networks. ICT is also significantly more error-proof than human data analysis. The time and resources that traditional managers have to spend on coordinating acquisition from various departments the data necessary for their analyses are no longer necessary after processes

TABLE 23.1
Traditional Bureaucracy versus Infocracy

Weberian (Traditional) Bureaucracy	Infocracy
Fixed and official jurisdictional areas, which define areas and scope of organizational activities, resources (budget), and overall legitimacy and responsibility	Jurisdictional areas may extend beyond single organization
Monocratically organized hierarchy of offices and personnel, which define organizational responsibilities and accountabilities of organizational members, as well as the channels through which information travels into, from, and within the organization	Information and data may travel upward and downward in an organization regardless of hierarchical layers. In a networking organization, when databases are updated, the data become available for all levels at the same time. Organizations become flatter. Middle management disappears, but overall hierarchical structure does not completely vanish. Bosses will remain, though fewer
	In networked organizations, information may become available simultaneously to the members of the organization where it was generated and to the organizations that are part of the network. This may cause a certain degree of conflict because in traditional bureaucracy organizations may lose monopoly on information
Office management is based on written documents (files). Document originals are archived. The files determine rules of professional behavior. Some of the rules are followed; however, sometimes, when reality is more complex than it is defined by the rules, bureaucrats may exercise discretion and step outside the boundaries of the rules	Rules and standard operating procedures may not be written, but instead are programmed into the databases and software. Though employees may be more empowered, it is much harder to exercise discretion outside of what is allowed by the programmed SOPs. Even in cases where it may be possible, any smallest violation would be noticed, and therefore infocrats are less likely to exercise discretion
Employees are neutral and impersonal because they are required to be; however, there are exceptions, such as with street-level bureaucrats, who bend the rules to exercise discretion	Employees are neutral and impersonal because there are fewer possibilities or no possibility for discretion. Even if they decide to bend the rules, the systems may not allow them to do so
Information is processed slowly due to the inefficiency of channels, and it takes a long time to provide the feedback to the clients/customers	Information is provided quickly, in most cases instantly. Oftentimes, no human processing of information is required. The feedback to customers may be instant

become automated. The result is elimination of middle management positions and, in general, cost savings through flattening of organizations. Empirical evidence since the 1990s upholds this theory of ICT effects in both the public and private sectors.

B. INTERORGANIZATIONAL NETWORKS

The emergence of interorganizational networks stimulated by ICT represents the most significant difference between traditional and virtual bureaucracy. In government, interorganizational networks carry the potential for dramatically increasing efficiency of operation for all agencies within the network. They are also much more customer-centric than the traditional way of providing services over the counter. Network efficiency results from sharing organizational databases. Many public organizations have to collect the same or very similar data about their customers. The process of data collection is generally very expensive and takes a long time. In characterizing interorganizational networks, Fountain (2001a) mentions that enabling organizations that are part of the same network to access each other's databases eliminates the necessity to spend resources on collecting redundant data.

Another important benefit of increasingly integrated networking is that all organizational levels—from headquarters to field offices and within and across the agencies—members of the network have instant access to the most current information. A networked environment also prevents information losses that normally occur as information gets filtered when passed in physical form through traditional hierarchical structures. Customers also potentially benefit from networks as they receive opportunities to access government services online through a single web portal, without being concerned about organizational boundaries or limited jurisdiction of different agencies. A formal OMB (2003b) goal is for citizens and businesses to be able to access online government services and information "within three clicks." Full-scale government portals are supposed to be set up in such a way that government customers do not have to input required information more then once, after which the information is automatically entered or updated in all databases that use it.

Government networks present two major challenges, however. The first is technical in nature and is related to the issue of data standardization. Initially, databases of most public agencies were created without the goal of being shared with outside organizations. Therefore, they were designed in various formats and for different computer platforms. For agencies to be able to seamlessly share data, their databases have to be converted into a standard format (Fountain 2001a). The second challenge goes back to the bureaucratic structure of public agencies. Networks may challenge such fundamental concepts of traditional government as jurisdiction, accountability, and command-and-control hierarchy, as well as undercut monopoly of bureaucratic organizations on information they collect (Bekkers 1998; Fountain 2001a, 2001b; Nye 2002).

According to Bekkers and Fountain, an agency's jurisdiction is a central concept of the modern Weberian bureaucracy that defines organizational structure of the agency, its legal and political authority and accountability, as well as the budget process. This bureaucratic emphasis on agency jurisdiction promotes institutional autonomy and discourages cross-agency interactions. Traditional bureaucracies adopt vertical, stove-pipe approaches toward information flow that include information traveling through each layer of organizational hierarchy on its way upward or downward in the organization. In the process of competing with others for limited resources, agencies consider information they collect to be a valuable commodity that can be used as leverage during budget requests or to gain political power. For this reason many agencies are very reluctant to lose their information monopoly by sharing data with others.

C. CHANGE IN THE DEGREE OF PUBLIC EMPLOYEE DISCRETION

It has been long recognized that no matter how sophisticated a public policy is, it cannot account for all the complexities and intricacies of the real world. Therefore, front-line employees of public agencies, who are the main agents of policy implementation, exercise a substantial degree of discretion. By doing so, these employees, who Michael Lipsky once called "street-level bureaucrats," become policy makers themselves. Whether street-level bureaucracy as a phenomenon results in positive or negative impact on policy implementation is a matter of opinion. Some believe that interference of street-level bureaucrats with implementing of public policies creates idiosyncrasies in government operations and promotes unequal treatment of clients, while such factors as personal prejudices and biases affect the decisions of street-level bureaucrats. On the other hand, others believe that, because street-level bureaucrats interact with the agency customers on a regular basis, they have the most comprehensive knowledge about these customers and their issues. Besides, no two clients are the same, so an individualized approach may be justified under certain circumstances. Moreover, some policies are unclear to begin with, contradictory, or even in conflict with yet other policies. In these cases, whoever executes policies inevitably has to face making choices and the exercise of discretion. Street-level bureaucrats may be the most equipped for making these choices because of their unique knowledge and experience.

The vast majority of literature recognizes that ICT will affect street-level bureaucracy. However, authors are divided with regard to what exactly this effect will be. Three possible scenarios have been offered (Bovens and Zouridis 2002; Fountain 2001a, 2002; Frissen 1998; Taylor 1998; Van de Donk 1998; Zuurmond 1998). First, there is a belief that ICT leads to empowerment of employees and increases their discretion in handling clients. According to a second scenario, ICT leads to increased rationalization of organization processes, which makes public agencies more resemble classic bureaucracy. Employees' discretion decreases not because they decide to remain neutral, but because, after many of the organizational rules and decision processes are programmed into computer systems, employees are given fewer or no opportunities for discretion. Finally, a third possibility discussed by the literature is that discretion in implementing policies will remain but be shifted from street-level bureaucrats to systems designers and programmers who encode operating rules into management systems governing what agencies do.

Those who represent the point of view that ICT will lead to an increase of public employees' discretion argue that such components of ICT as e-mail, the Internet, agency Intranets, and web portals enhance the abilities and skills of employees to provide high-quality services to agencies' customers. Thus, for example, some argue that e-mail promotes direct, more informal communication and can even encourage employees to come forward with and express their opinion in situations when they would not do so in a face-to-face context or even when using other media, such as telephones or faxes. ICT-based organizational networks encourage employees to communicate across internal and external organization boundaries and hierarchical layers (O'Looney 2002). ICT enables employees to access in real time data and information generated not only by their agencies but also by other agencies linked in interorganizational networks. Thus, employees feel more informed, in control of the problems they are trying to solve, and are therefore able to make better judgments. Employees can address the issues they are dealing with by performing data mining, or if necessary, can consult with colleagues inside and outside their agencies using such media as e-mail, listservs, chat rooms, and web portals. In making decisions, information-rich public employees will need to check with supervisors less frequently and will be less subject to overt command-and-control practices.

On the opposite end of the continuum are those who believe that in the process of ICT implementation employees are losing a significant portion of their traditional discretion. As the result of ICT, as public agencies become increasingly information-based, street-level bureaucracy is being transformed into something that Bovens and Zouridis are calling system-level bureaucracy. Algorithms and decision trees that are used to automate organizational processes create infrastructures and digital architectures that make system bureaucracy invisible. Rationalization and standardization of decision-making processes seem to vanish from information-based agencies, but in reality they are embedded into information systems of agencies. Contrary to the arguments presented in the previous scenario, theorists in this scenario believe that ICT causes agencies to become not less, but more rule-based and rationalized than was previously possible.

In this second view, the invisible bureaucracy embedded in ICT determines and constrains behavior of public employees, especially those who are considered operators or street-level bureaucrats. The personal experience, judgments, and idiosyncrasies of the street-level bureaucrats that previously affected their discretion are no longer relevant. Decision trees and algorithms would allow employees to choose a solution only within pre-programmed options. Policy execution no longer constitutes the application of rules to *individual* cases (Bovens and Zouridis 2002). Instead, individual cases are collapsed into the several most common categories, and, after information about a case is entered into the systems, algorithms and decision trees assign this case to the category it fits the best. In the process, some of the individual peculiarities of each case will inevitably be ignored either by algorithms not processing the data or, most likely, not allowing the customer to enter the information the system is not prepared to handle. Qualitative considerations in particular may well be suppressed. Decision-making under infocracy may come to rely on information missing important facts pertaining to any given individual case.

Some literature suggests that as front-line or street-level employees lose their discretion in favor of ICT systems, power shifts to systems designers and analysts. Bovens and Zouridis argue that just as Lipsky's street-level bureaucrats participate in the policy-making by exercising discretion during interaction with agency customers, systems analysts do so by making choices about the way ICT should affect practical implementation of policies through algorithms they design to execute it. The example of using GIS for political redistricting provided at the beginning is an illustration.

The rules embedded into algorithms replace overt supervisory controls (Fountain 2001a, 2002). It is likely that public employees will continue to be given a certain degree of marginal discretion. However, it is increasingly likely that this discretion will be strictly within boundaries allowed by ICT systems. ICT systems make the behavior of employees very transparent, which diminishes the necessity for their overt physical supervision. As long as the cases employees are dealing with are standard, they might feel more empowered, or at least less weighed down by redundant paperwork. However, when employees encounter non-standard cases, ICT systems will impose constraints which will make employees feel powerless.

In some cases ICT-based rationalization of work processes may even lead to professional deskilling of public employees (Fountain 2002; Zuurmond 1998). It is possible that fewer employees will receive the same level of professional training as they did before the ICT were introduced. Reliance on ICT systems and transfer of policy decision making to technocrats encoding oversight systems, creates for many organizations vague, conflicting, and possibly shifting goals and missions that result from compromise between multiple stakeholders. It is very difficult, if possible at all, for rationally designed ICT systems to be able to take into consideration all conflicting intricacies of agencies' missions (Fountain 2002; Kling and Allen 1996). Whole-hearted embrace of infocracy, without organizational provision for a more holistic approach, ironically could mean that the quality of decision making in full-blown infocracies is diminished, contrary to the intentions of its advocates.

IV. DETERRITORIALIZATION

ICT adoption by public agencies redefines fundamental bureaucratic principles such as accountability, hierarchical structure, and geographical jurisdiction. Donk and Snellen (1998), for example, are among those who have argued that because of ICT, the state is losing its territorial basis. They refer to this phenomenon as "deterritorialization," characterized by the erosion of jurisdictional boundaries among government agencies. Above, it was noted that Fountain (2001a) argued that since Weber, the concept of jurisdiction has served as a normative and theoretical basis of government operations. Jurisdictional boundaries guide the structure of public agencies, their executive and legal authority, as well as organization of budget process and congressional committees. Likewise, the free cross-border flow of data in the age of the information economy means that not only knowledge, but also work and even assets may be transferred in ways which are difficult for the traditional nation-state to regulate.

Government initiatives with regard to ICT may be classified (and are commonly abbreviated as) government-to-government (G2G), government-to-business (G2B), and government-to-citizens (G2C) (OMB, 2003c). Deterritorialization affects all three types of these initiatives.

Creation of interorganizational networks linking public agencies, discussed above, is the primary effect of deterritorialization on G2G relationships. The ability to share electronic databases in real time diminishes geographical and temporal constraints. With electronic networks, cost and speed of transmitting information among agencies over the Internet is independent of their physical locations or proximity to each other. This allows creating geographically distributed partnerships and performing collaborative problem solving (Fountain 2001a). Though these possibilities improve speed, accuracy, and efficiency of government transactions, they also create a number of problems. Agencies may have to reconsider their proprietary attitude toward information under their control. They may have to overcome their competitive attitude towards other agencies; and even give up some of their budgetary autonomy. The gains agencies receive from networked collaboration may not seem obvious, creating problems in securing full cooperation. Organizational culture must change. Instead of the comforting clarity of traditional hierarchical structures, inter-organizational partnerships across jurisdictional boundaries would require agencies to develop cooperative behavior and the ability to coordinate their activities without a clear governance structure (Fountain 2001b).

Transactions and communications that are performed through the Internet often cut across local and national geographical borders, making it difficult, if not impossible, to make them subject to laws based on geographic boundaries (Biegel 2001; Goldsmith 1998; Johnson and Post 1996; Swartz 2003). Some authors argue that the application of a geographically based approach to legal regulation of the a-geographical nature of the Internet makes no sense and may lead to confusion. Johnson and Post (1996) argue that the Internet "is destroying the link between geographical location and: (1) the power of local governments to assert control over online behavior; (2) the effects of online behavior on individuals or things; (3) the legitimacy of a local sovereign's efforts to regulate global phenomena; and (4) the ability of physical location to give notice of which sets of rules apply." Many forms of online activity are outside the scope of the traditional territorially based legal systems.

e-Commerce is the most discussed setting for problems associated with deterritorialization. In particular, state and local government face severe issues in connection to levying sales and use taxes on Internet purchases made by their residents from online vendors. The Internet Tax Freedom Act (ITFA) of 1998 and the Supreme Court case, *Quill Corporation v. North Dakota* (1992), prohibit state and political subdivisions from imposing use tax collection and remittance obligations on remote sellers lacking a substantial nexus with the taxing state. As of November, 2003, legislation to make the tax moratorium permanent was pending and thought likely to pass. State and local governments may still require remote sellers to collect and remit use taxes in cases when there is a substantial nexus between the remote seller and the state where the purchase was made. Buyers may also be required to pay use taxes according to the tax code of the particular jurisdiction when the online remote seller lacks physical presence (Swartz 2003). However, government has no mechanism of enforcing these tax collections on Internet purchases. As a result, government loses significant revenue. This e-tax situation exacerbates the digital divide because consumers who do not have access to the Internet must purchase the same products from a traditional bricks-and-mortar retailer, in which case they would pay a sales tax (Swartz 2003).

Just as state regulation of industry has been undermined by intra-state competition as fleeing bricks-and-mortar companies fled first to the non-unionized South and then offshore altogether, so the ease of movement of e-business has meant an erosion of state power and acquiescence to deterritorialization of the economy. Proponents of taxes on online purchases argue that exempting online retailers from the duty to collect use tax would give them an unfair advantage in comparison with Main Street retailers and would attract consumers to making purchases online. Alternatively, opponents argue that imposing tax collection obligations on retail sellers would create an unbearable administrative and financial burden. Currently, about 7600 taxing jurisdictions exist in the US, which means that if Internet sellers are required to collect use taxes they would have to comply with thousands of tax codes, which would put them at a disadvantage in comparison with Main Street retailers who need to comply only with the tax code of the jurisdiction where they are physically present (Swartz 2003). Requiring consumers to pay the use tax on the Internet purchases is ineffective because there are no enforcement mechanisms in place and because consumers are often unaware of their obligations with regard to such taxes.

What works for e-commerce works for e-crime. Both exhibit tendencies toward deterritorialization and erosion of state power. There are many examples of unlawful conduct that can be conducted through the Internet. For example, one can post materials, such as photos, pictures, or text that may be regarded as obscene in certain jurisdictions. Where once many communities asserted control to be relatively pornography free, now access to pornography is nearly universal. The ability to dispense pornography from offshore makes even national regulation difficult at best, even should lawmakers be willing to cede tax revenue to foreign countries. Biegel (2001), Johnson and Post (1996) as well as others argue that it might not make any sense to base jurisdiction on the physical location of the Internet server that hosts the website with questionable materials, because "a website physically located in Brazil has no more an effect on individuals in Brazil than does a website physically located in Belgium" (Johnson and Post, 1996).

This controversy has generated a series of legal disputes, the main question of which is: If certain online materials are accessible in a jurisdiction where they are considered obscene, or inappropriate in other way, does this jurisdiction have the right to prosecute the person who put them on the Internet even if the server that hosts the website is located in another jurisdiction where materials in questions are not considered inappropriate? In the US, one of the most well known cases in which this problem was addressed is the *U.S. v. Thomas (1996)* case. In this federal court (not Supreme Court) case, the Thomases, who ran an adult content bulletin board service (BBS) from Northern California, were indicted by the US District Court for the Western District of Tennessee in response to a complaint of a person from this state about sexually explicit images on the service (Biegel 2001). The Thomases were convicted, but their conviction raised many issues.

In the Thomas case, the argument is made that if the 1973 Supreme Court community standards rule is applied to the Internet, then juries in the most conservative areas of the country could determine Internet content. The appeals court ruled against the Thomases, on the dubious argument that they should have been able to determine which jurisdictions were more conservative than theirs in California, and then to deny access to subscribers from those jurisdictions. However, people who post information online often do not know who will access this information. It is impossible to tell whether given information produces effects in a particular jurisdiction, and those who post information online are unfamiliar with the laws of each jurisdiction and hence cannot conform their behavior to these laws (Goldsmith 1998).

Even a simple email message sent to a neighbor across the street may travel outside the border of the state or even the country before it gets to its final destination. If the content of the message is found offensive or inappropriate, the person who sent it may be prosecuted under the federal statute with more stringent penalties because it crossed the borders of two or more states. There is no simple solution to this problem because it is often impossible to predict, much less control, from which jurisdiction can access a website or what path an electronic message will travel before it reaches its final destination (Biegel 2001).

Jurisdictional issues become even more complicated in the international arena. In 1995, the Justice Ministry of Bavaria, Germany, threatened to prosecute CompuServe for allowing circulation of information that contained neo-Nazi propaganda and violated German anti-pornography laws. CompuServe ended up blocking access to this information. Because it was unable to block the access only to German users, it blocked it for all of CompuServe users worldwide. In this spillover effect, it is possible for one jurisdiction to regulate extraterritorial conduct in such a way that it affects behaviors and regulations in other jurisdictions.

Similar jurisdictional problems are related to defamatory messages and copyright violations. To quote Johnson and Post: "Whose substantive legal rules apply to a defamatory message that is written by someone in Mexico, read by someone in Israel by means of an Internet server located in the United States, injuring the reputation of a Norwegian?" Goldsmith similarly quotes Perritt with regard to online copyright law violation:

> Which of the many plausibly applicable bodies of copyright law do we consult to determine whether a hyperlink on a World Wide Web page located on a server in France and constructed by a Filipino citizen, which points to a server in Brazil that contains materials protected by German (but not Brazilian) copyright law, which is downloaded to a server in the United States and reposted to a newsgroup, constitutes a remediable infringement of copyright?

Opinions vary with regard to what should be done to address the jurisdictional effects of deterritorialization. One of the proposed solutions is to leave cyberspace to self-regulation (Black 1998; Weber 1997). Johnson and Post (1996) argue that because the Internet has no territorially based boundaries, it requires designing laws different from those that regulate geographically defined territories of physical world. For legal purposes, they propose to conceive of cyberspace as a distinct place, similar to the concept of virtual community where people engage in various activities that can be regulated by specifically designed rules. Goldsmith, on the other hand, argues that differences between cyberspace transactions and transactions of the physical world are overstated, and the solution may be in amending current laws to include cyberspace activities.

While writers vary in their policies toward the Internet, the common thread is the rising threat of deterritorialization in an information economy. The problem is most visible for those dimensions of the economy one might most like to regulate: Internet pornography, piracy, gambling, consumer fraud, and other e-vices. However, the more significant element is e-commerce, not c-vice. Instantaneous international electronic funds transfer (EFT), for example, can have profound effects on the global economy and on individual nation states, as the destabilizing effects of EFT on the Asian economy in 1997 bore witness. The issue of deterritorialization is put forcefully in the Cato Institute report, "The Future of Money in the Information Age" (Cato 1996):

> [A]ny authority that asserts sovereignty over actions that take place entirely within cyberspace must resort to acts of physical coercion or threats thereof. That, however, requires that the target be identified and located. It will always be possible to identify and locate Fortune 500 companies, whose vast visible assets make them conspicuously vulnerable. But it is going to get very difficult to keep track of the growing number of individuals who are rapidly learning to ply their trades on the Internet. In practice, that means that ordinary people will be able to create and exchange wealth away from the prying eyes and grasping hands of sovereign powers. That possibility is going to be treated as a grave threat by most national governments.

However, the new freedom of deterritorialization does not accrue just to individuals but also to corporations with global reach. These new ITC-based economic entities come to be able to compromise local and even national regulation and to assume some of the characteristics of private government.

V. THE DIGITAL DIVIDE

Many have argued that the revolution in ICT is democratizing in nature. GIS technology provides one example. Applying GIS to address planning needs of local communities has proven to be an effective practice. Since relatively recently, the use of GIS on local level has been used to solicit opinions from the general public about planning projects that are affecting their communities. This practice, known as public participation GIS (PPGIS), it is argued, has a democratizing effect on local communities by broadening public participation in planning projects. With PPGIS, digital maps that display planning projects and the results of spatial analysis that demonstrate effects of these projects on communities are made available online so that citizens can access them at any convenient time and express their opinion with regard to desirability of a particular project in their communities.

Supporters of using web-based PPGIS for the planning purposes identify several advantages of the practice. According to Kingston et al. (2000), PPGIS may be superior to traditional planning meetings that often take place in an atmosphere of conflict, and which may discourage participation by the less outspoken. The restricted time and the actual location of public meetings can further restrict the possibility of widespread attendance. PPGIS eliminates these restrictions. Access to information on planning projects is available at any time from any location that has Internet access. Citizens can post their comments online without feeling intimidated or criticized, and everyone's opinion will be considered.

On the other hand, it has been argued that PPGIS would create a division between computer literate and illiterate (Al-Kodamny 2000). People who do not have Internet access, have slow Internet connections, or simply are less familiar with computers would be excluded or may feel intimidated by the technology and may withdraw from participation. The pros and cons of ICT-facilitated democratic participation in the case of PPGIS is repeated in dozens of other ICT arenas. The digital divide issue goes beyond hardware ownership differentials or differences in Internet connections. It extends to questions of citizen computer literacy or, indeed, literacy itself insofar as the average reading level of American adults is 8th grade. West (2003) has found that governmental websites average about 11th grade in readability; two-thirds were at 12th grade level. Then there is the issue of bilingual availability, especially for the growing Spanish population, and the lack of access for the millions who are incarcerated (the US is by far the highest proportionally in the world) or institutionalized. Beyond this, the digital divide raises issues of differential perceptions of efficacy and empowerment among different subpopulations, and issues of differential feedback and reinforcement of effects of ICT-facilitated democratic participation.

The gap in opportunities to benefit from ICT between the information-rich and information-poor is at the center of the digital divide. There is even a potential for ICT to diminish services to the disadvantaged. As public administration authors such as Fountain (2001a) acknowledge, once an agency has established an active Internet presence, it may be more difficult for it to justify providing in-person services, even though many citizens still lack Internet access. Rocheleau (2003) points out that employees of public agencies that provide online services may face conflict when allocating their workload when they have to face the decision whether they should give priority to in-person or phone requests or to lower transaction cost electronic requests.

The National Telecommunications & Information Administration (NTIA) and Economics and Statistics Administration have conducted extensive research on the digital divide and have published four comprehensive reports on the issue (NTIA 1995, 1998, 1999, 2000). The digital divide was also a focus of the Hart-Teeter (2003) report on e-government, which summarizes the findings of the study Hart-Teeter conducted on behalf of Council of Excellence in Government. Reports from both organizations consider digital divide to be a serious problem. The statistics show an improvement of access by all groups in society, but with the width of the gap between information-rich and information-poor diminishing only for some categories (such as gender) while widening for others (racial divide for some ethnic categories). In spite of higher levels of connectivity, the problem of digital divide persists. Thus, according to NTIA (2000), urban high-income households ($75,000 and higher) are more than twenty times more likely to have access to the Internet than low-income rural households, and more than nine times as likely to have a computer at home. Table 23.2 summarizes more recent data by Hart-Teeter (2003) comparing percentages of access to the Internet between some of the major categories of ICT haves and have nots.

The information in Table 23.2 shows the disparity among various socioeconomic groups with respect to Internet access within the US. Virtually all countries, even where a sizeable population has Internet access, are facing the problem of digital divide. Though not always clearly distinguished in the literature, digital divide takes two forms. The first one, discussed above, may be defined as the domestic digital divide and relates to the gap between information-rich and information-poor population groups within one country. However, there is also an international version

---

TABLE 23.2
Internet Access for Different Categories

Categories	Percentage with Access to the Internet
Education	
College graduate	87
High school graduate	48
Employment	
Professional	86
Blue-collar	58
Age	
18–34 years old	78
≥ 65 years old	43
Ethnicity	
Caucasian	70
Black	59
Sex	
Male	68
Female	69

Source: From Hart-Teeter, *The New e-Government Equation: Ease, Engagement, Privacy and Protection*, Report prepared for the Council for Excellence in Government, http://www.excelgov.org, 2003.

---

of the digital divide, which relates to inequalities between various countries with regard to the number of people with Internet access (Drori and Jang 2003). Thus, in 2001 in the US and Canada, on average 57.2% of the population had Internet access, while in African countries the number was only 0.5% (Warschauer 2003). In this section, the domestic digital divide will be referred to as digital divide 1 (DD1), and the international divide will be referred to as digital divide 2 (DD2). Though many of the mechanisms that cause DD1 and DD2 are the same, as well as potential solutions, there are some additional considerations with regard to DD2.

Despite the fact that the costs have considerably decreased, for many people hardware, software, and fees associated with maintaining Internet access are still prohibitively expensive even in the US and especially worldwide. Therefore, the most obvious approach to close the digital divide that has been widely discussed among academics and practitioners is to provide people who cannot afford private Internet access with the opportunity to get online at no or minimal cost via community access centers (CAC) or Internet kiosks that can be installed in public places, such as libraries, shopping malls, transportation terminals, employment centers, etc. (Edmiston 2003; NTIA 2000). However, a CAC approach can only provide fragmented and temporary solution. Thomas and Wyatt (2000) point out that after a person has started taking advantage of online government services by accessing the Internet through a CAC, this practice may stop when the CAC ceases to function or the person moves to a new place with no CAC in proximity. But a more important reason why the CAC approach alone will likely be ineffective is because the digital divide has much deeper roots than simple lack of online access—roots that extend to computer literacy, information competency, and political efficacy.

Education and literacy are factors that affect the digital divide in a way equally important to technical access (Norris 2001; Warschauer 2003). Advanced reading, writing, and analytical skills are important for being able to use the Internet effectively (Warschauer 2003). Besides, the complexity and volume of online government information require people who access this information to be able to search for the information or services they need as well as to evaluate the results of their search (Fountain 2001a). The data from research demonstrate that education, socio-economic status, and the use of the Internet are positively correlated with each other. People of lower socioeconomic status who cannot afford Internet access tend also to be less literate. Merely providing them with access would get them online but would not guarantee they would reap all the benefits of e-government. Thus, the digital divide provides an additional reason in favor of access of socially (i.e., digitally) disadvantaged groups to education (Warschauer 2003), including lifelong education.

English monolingualism on the web is another common digital divide issue raised in the literature (Norris 2001; Warschauer 2003). Warschauer notes that while only 6% of the world's population speak English a native language, 81% of international websites are in English. In case of the US, at first glance, this may seem more as a DD2 problem. However, more and more state and local government jurisdictions have a significant number of residents who do not speak English as the first language. In such cases, having a Spanish-language (for some communities, other languages too) version of government websites would be a big step towards eliminating this form of digital divide. West (2003), however, found only 13% of governmental websites offered any form of foreign language access, and often this was partial and minimal.

Many authors who mention dominance of the English language on the Internet internationally often do so with a negative connotation, because it might exclude non-English speakers or at the least be a form of cultural imperialism. The counter-argument is that the information society we live in is becoming increasingly global, and English assumes the role of the unifying global language of ICT-facilitated communication. Maintaining websites in English promotes more interaction and communication among citizens and governments of different countries, much more so than exclusive reliance by each citizen and government on their own native language alone. For example, in Eastern Europe, the Estonian government has made tremendous progress towards establishing an online presence, and providing services and information online. It might be much easier for other countries in the region to benefit from learning about Estonian success if at least part of the information were in English. Of course, it might not always make sense for local government websites to have an English version, but it would be beneficial to do so for national governments and many do.

VI. PUBLIC INFORMATION TECHNOLOGY MANAGEMENT IS DIFFERENT FROM PRIVATE SECTOR IT MANAGEMENT

In 1986, a special issue of *Public Administration Review* published an article by Barry Bozeman and Stuart Bretschneider, in which the authors argued that because government agencies operate in an environment "that is much different from that faced by public business organizations," they have to be very cautious in trying directly to apply business ICT models. Instead, they argued, public agencies have to develop different, unique approaches to managing ICT, which they labeled "public management information systems" (PMIS). Today, after almost two decades, many ICT government initiatives are still focused on improving government performance by adopting explicitly business models. Has theory changed since the Bozeman and Bretschneider article? Not according to academic literature (Fountain 2001a; Garson 2003; Heeks and Bhatnagar 1999; O'Looney 2002). However, OMB officials and others who have led ICT initiatives in government continue to be trained in business schools or come from corporate backgrounds or simply recognize the legitimating power of labeling what one does as a business case even when what is actually done differs from most private sector models.

There is nothing wrong with emulating the best practices in the private sector per se. Bozeman and Bretsneider warned in 1986 that "[p]rescriptions developed for the private-sector or for 'generic' management may be valid for the public sector context. The problem is in determining which findings and prescriptions are applicable to public management and which are not."

TABLE 23.3
Difference between Public and Private Sector Organizations

Private	Public
Property may be shared and transferred between individuals	Property may not be shared and transferred
Clear link between performance and rewards, such as pay and promotion	No clear link between performance and rewards, which may lead to lower productivity
Authority rests on economic incentives. Market is viewed as the most efficient device for allocation of goods and services	Authority is political; it is reflected in fundamental values and the psychological commitments of individuals to the government; legitimacy of political authority is embodied in legal and constitutional structure
Private firm is driven by internal goals related to profit	Goals of public organizations are, at least to some extent, set externally
Business managers work fast with less accountability to external actors	Public managers are subjects to scrutiny by the mass media, interest groups, and general public
Working environment is not affected by periodic changes	Work is affected by political cycles (annual appropriations, two-year Congress, four-year presidency)

Source: From Bozeman, B. and Bretschneider, S., *Public Administration Review*, 46, 475–487, 1986.

They outlined several major areas where public and private agencies are different (Table 23.3). Subsequent research by Bretschneider (1990) also found that IT directors are lower in the organizational hierarchy in the public sector and experience more delays in getting purchasing approval, among other differences. These differences remain true today.

The most important current US initiatives in ICT arose from the National Performance Review (NPR) under the Clinton administration, later renamed the National Partnership for Reinventing Government (Fountain 2001a; Garson 2003). NPR and the ensuing Bush administration Presidential Management Agenda have been criticized by some academic writers for lacking a theoretical basis, violating the principles of public administration, and even contradicting constitutional values. In particular, the NPR has been portrayed with displaying an overwhelming emphasis on increasing the efficiency of agency operations and making the delivery of public services as fast and convenient for public customers as possible—objectives very similar to that of a private company. While such objectives seem laudable, the charge was raised that in practice ICT was used as a legitimating cloak for massive, largely traditional meat-ax downsizing of agency staff and for outsourcing for ideological reasons having little to do with efficiency. That is, critics have argued that business efficiency and business models of ICT have overlooked the differences between the environment in which public and private agencies operate. Critics have contended that it might not be possible or even desirable to reach the levels of efficiency many business-oriented practitioners aim for. Democratic values and constitutional principles—rather than efficiency—should be the primary concern for public agencies in this view.

In public agencies, property may not be shared and transferred between employees. This means that there is little incentive to be efficient if an agency has to return all surplus revenues for the fiscal year. If an agency runs a surplus, its budget for the next year may be reduced, punishing the agency for being efficient. In the light of this dynamic, Osborne and Plastrik (2000) proposed a model which would allow the agency to keep its entire surplus or a part of it arising from efficiencies, which are often ICT-based. However, this practice makes sense only for a short-term period. An agency may save some money and may be allowed to keep it as a reward for being efficient in a given year. The agency may still be given the same amount for additional efficiencies the next year. However, if this agency keeps underspending several years in a row, no logic would justify a legislative body keeping the budget of this agency at the same level. Because public resources are always limited, it would be considered inefficient to provide an agency with a budget that exceeds its spending. The money would rather be appropriated to departments that run deficits, even if these deficits are caused by their not being efficient. The result of increased efficiency due to the ICT implementation would follow the same logic in the public sector, whereas in the private sector a division which increased efficiency year after year would be rewarded indefinitely through promotions, profit sharing, bonuses, and other flexible forms of remuneration not available in the public sector. Public employees are often promoted based on seniority rather than performance and it is more difficult to fire or demote employees who lag behind with regard to new ICT skills, just as it is more difficult to reward technological innovators. In fact, for the technologically savvy, the public sector is commonly used as a training springboard to more lucrative positions in the private sector.

The writers who compare public and private agencies often mention that activities of private companies are driven by the bottom line, which is profit, while government agencies, to use the expression of James Q. Wilson, are driven by constraints. These constraints dictate that public administration, unlike business, requires more than efficient use of economic, material, and human resources. In fact, efficiency should not necessarily be the goal of public administration if it conflicts with founding democratic values (Rohr 1986; Rosenbloom and O'Leary 1997; Waldo 1948). Democratic values reflected in such documents as the Bill of Rights, the Due Process Clause, and the principles of separation of powers, to name a few, should be the primary guidance for public administrators' actions and should not be sacrificed for the sake of a merely efficient approach. To illustrate this point, Rosenbloom and O'Leary (1997) provide quotes from the two Supreme Court cases. The first one, from *Stanley v. Illinois*, states:

> [T]he Constitution recognizes higher values than speed and efficiency. Indeed, one might fairly say of the Bill of Rights in general, and the Due Process Clause in particular, that they were designed to protect the fragile values of a vulnerable citizenry form the overbearing concern for efficiency and efficacy that may characterize praiseworthy government officials no less, and perhaps more, than mediocre ones.

Similarly, *Immigration and Naturalization Service v. Chadha* states:

> The choices we discern as having been made in the Constitutional Convention impose burdens on governmental process that often seem clumsy, inefficient, even unworkable, but those hard choices were consciously made by men who had lived under a form of government that permitted arbitrary governmental acts to go unchecked. There is no support in the Constitution or decisions of this Court for the proposition that cumbersomeness and delays often encountered in complying with explicit constitutional standards may be avoided.... With all the obvious flaws of delay, untidiness, and potential for abuse, we have not yet found a better way to preserve freedom than by making the exercise of power subject to the carefully crafted restraints spelled out in the Constitution.

Transferring government services online without creating corresponding opportunities for those without effective Internet access with a mechanism to conveniently take advantage of these same services provides a perfect illustration of how "the overbearing concern for efficiency" could interfere with democratic values by depriving information have-nots with equal opportunities to benefit from government services.

Private companies are free to set up and modify their goals, which are usually relatively narrow financial focus. In contrast, the mission and goals of public agencies are typically broader and encompass political, social, and economic factors (Heeks and Bhatnagar 1999). These goals are often the result of a compromise among various stakeholders of public agencies, many of which have different, often conflicting, views of how the mission of the agency should be achieved. As the result, often the mission and goals of public agencies are vague and inconsistent. There may be more than one strategy to achieve these goals, and later it is hard to measure whether the goals have actually been achieved (Fountain 2001a; Wilson 1989). Under these circumstances it may be difficult to agree on what an efficient approach is, much less design a system that would improve efficiency. ICT literature stresses the importance of linking ICT to the mission and goals of public agencies, but a rational business systems approach applied to the ICT design assumes that organizational goals and processes are clear, resources are ample and steady, and members and stakeholders are cooperative.

Private sector organizations are, of course, accountable to their shareholders, customers, and employees. However, their organizational processes are not usually subject to close scrutiny unless private companies are involved in some unethical or controversial activity. For the most part, accountability of private companies is limited to results: profit to their shareholders, satisfactory product or service for customers, and adequate compensation for employees. By comparison, public agencies have to consider a broader spectrum of political and legal accountability. Organizational processes of public agencies are under close examination and criticism by diverse political constituencies, the media, interest groups, and the public at large.

Public organizations operate in different time frames from their private sector counterparts and have to deal with political cycles that are related to changes in appropriation processes and to congressional and presidential changes (Bozeman and Bretschneider 1986). With respect to the ICT initiatives, this unstable environment marked by changes in legislation, policy, political parties, and so on, can create contradictory or short-term information needs to which considerable resources have to be devoted (Heeks and Bhatnagar 1999). ICT personnel from web designers to systems managers frequently face political and non-technical demands which alter what they would have done in a business environment.

How much difference do sectoral differences make? A lot. The mantra of the business model for large-scale ICT initiatives, first under Clinton–Gore's NPR and now under the Bush–OMB President's Management Agenda, is that ICT can be used to leverage organizational changes, restructuring and reengineering government processes. Heintz and Bretschneider (2000) studied the use of information technology in relation to restructuring in public organizations, asking whether adoption of information technology affected organizational structures, communications, and decision making? They found that there is little empirical relationship between ICT adoption and subsequent agency restructuring in the public sector. In the cases where restructuring occurs, managers reported only minimal effects on performance. While ICT may improve performance directly it did not appear that ICT changes public organizational structure. There seems to be more evidence for ICT as a control strategy in public organizations than as a restructuring strategy as, for example, in research by Henman and Adler (2003), who found that in the case of the Social Security Administration, computerization has generally increased management control over both staff and claimants, contrary to ICT empowerment theory.

VII. SUMMARY

In this short essay, we have outlined five of the great ideas which are found in the literature of public sector ICT. It is the purpose of such ideas to generate discussion, controversy, and insight into policy direction. What emerges from this constellation of ideas, as seen in public administration literature, is a view of information technology implementation as a fundamentally political process which has the potential to transform governance and to erode traditional jurisdictional territories. It is also a process which raises domestic and global issues of equity. And because implementation in the public sector is fundamentally different from that in the private sector, structural inertia is great and issues of control paramount.

If these conclusions seem reasonable, one should not that this view is strongly at variance with the perspective of the OMB and others inured in the ideology of the business model of ICT. This counter-perspective holds that information technology implementation can be treated as a primarily technical process that strengthens agencies, whose heads need be little concerned with issues of control, deterritorialization, inequitable empowerment, and similar matters raised in the scholarly literature of public administration. For the counter-perspective, there is no dark side, no politics, no conflict, and no struggle. There are only enlightened managers who embrace the business model of ICT and bureaucratic dead wood who resist change and need to be bypassed by the forces of progress along the one correct path of ICT development.

It has been the contribution of political science to management to teach that conflict is not a bad thing, that progress is less linear than an unfolding of force, counterforce, and synthesis, and that in any policy arena, on must ask, as Harold Lasswell (1958) did long ago, "Who gets what, when, and how?" Issues such as organizational transformation, the digital divide, deterritorialization, and the political forces that govern the public sector are the most interesting ones in the study of ICT. While the perspective research these issues encompasses is not always ascendant over the uncritical salesmanship of the counter-perspective, in the long run administrators who attend to the true issues of ICT will be those who most fulfill the aspirations of those who wish ICT to be an engine for the improvement of governance in this country and around the world.

REFERENCES

Agre Philip, E., Realtime politics: the internet and the political process, *The Information Society*, 18(5), 311–331, 2002.

Al-Kodamny, K., Extending geographic information systems to meet neighborhood planning needs, *URISA Journal*, 12(3), 19–37, 2000.

Atkinson, R. D. and Ulevich, J., *Digital Government: The Next Step to Reengineering the Federal Government*, Progressive Policy Institute, Washington, DC, 2002, http://www.dlcppi.org (accessed August 15, 2002).

Bekkers, V. J. J. M., Wiring public organizations and changing organizational jurisdictions, In *Public Administration in an Information Age*, Snellen, I. T and van de Donk, W. B. H. J., Eds., IOS Press, Amsterdam, The Netherlands, pp. 57–77, 1998.

Biegel, S., *Beyond Our Control? Confronting the Limits of Our Legal System in the Age of Cyberspace*, MIT Press, Cambridge, MA, 2001.

Black, G. Call for controls: the Internet must regulate itself, *Financial Times*, April 1, p. 12, 1998.

Bovens, M. and Zouridis, S., From street-level to system-level bureaucracies: how information and communication technology is transforming administrative discretion and constitutional control, *Public Administration Review*, 62(2), 174–184, 2002.

Bozeman, B. and Bretschneider, S., Public management information systems: theory and prescription, *Public Administration Review*, 46, 475–487, 1986.

Bretschneider, S., Management information systems in public and private organizations: an empirical test, *Public Administrative Review*, 50(5), 536–545, 1990.

Burnham, D., *The Rise of the Computer State*, Pantheon Books, NY, 1983.

Cato Policy Institute, The future of money in the information age, *Cato Policy Report*, 18(4), http://www.cato.org/pubs/policy_report/v18n46.html (accessed November 15, 2003, 1990).

Center for Technology in Government, Some assembly required: building a digital government for the 21st century, http://www.ctg.albany.edu/resources/abstract/abdgfinalreport.html (accessed August 14, 2002), 1999.

comScore Media Metrix, Press release: comScore media metrix announces top 50 U.S. internet property rankings for September 2003, http://www.comscore.com/press/release.asp?id = 360 (accessed October 26, 2003).

Danziger, J. N., Computing and the political world, *Computers and the Social Sciences*, 2(4), 183–200, 1986.

Danziger, J. N., Dutton, W. H., Kling, R., and Kraemer, K. L., *Computers and Politics*, Columbia University Press, New York, 1982.

Danziger, J. N. and Kraemer, K. L., *People and Computers: The Impact of Computing on End Users in Organizations*, Columbia University Press, New York, 1987.

Davis, R., *The Web of Politics: The Internet's Impact on the American Political System*, Oxford University Press, Oxford, UK, 1999.

Downs, A., A realistic look at the final payoffs from urban data systems, *Public Administration Review*, 77(3), 204–210, 1967.

Drori, G. S. and Jang, Y.S, The global digital divide: a sociological assessment of trends and causes, *Social Science Computer Review*, 21(2), 144–161, 2003.

Drucker, P., The coming of the new organization, *Harvard Business Review*, 66(1), 45–53, 1988.

Edmiston, K. D., State and local e-government: prospects and challenges, *American Review of Public Administration*, 33(1), 20–45, 2003.

Feigenbaum, E. and McCorduck, P., *The Fifth Generation: Artificial Intelligence and Japan's Computer Challenge to the World*, New American Library, New York, 1985.

Ferkiss, V., *Technological Man: The Myth and the Reality*, New American Library, New York, 1970.

Fidel, K. and Garner, R., *Computer Professionals: Career Lines and Occupational Identity*, Society for the Study of Social Problems, Annual Meeting, Chicago, IL, 1987.

Field, G. A., Behavioral aspects of the computer, *MSU Business Topics*, 18(3), 27–33, 1970.

Fischer, C. S., *America Calling: A Social History of the Telephone to 1940*, University of California Press, Berkeley, CA, 1992.

Fischer, F., *Technocracy and the Politics of Expertise*, Sage Publications, Inc., Newbury Park, CA, 1990.

Flamm, K., *Targeting the Computer: Government Support and International Competition*, Brookings Institution Press, Washington, DC, 1987.

Fountain, J. E., *Building the Virtual State: Information Technology and Institutional Change*, Brookings Institution Press, Washington, DC, 2001a.

Fountain, J. E., The virtual state: transforming American government?, *National Civic Review*, 90(3), 241–251, 2001b.

Fountain, J. E., Toward a theory of federal bureaucracy for the twenty-first century, In *Governance.com: Democracy in the Information Age*, Kamarck, E. C. and Nye, J. S. Jr., Eds., Brookings Institution Press, Washington, DC, pp. 117–140, 2002.

Frissen, P. H. A., Public administration in cyberspace, In *Public Administration in an Information Age*, Snellen, I. Th. and van de Donk, W. B. H. J., Eds., IOS Press, Amsterdam, The Netherlands, pp. 33–46, 1998.

Garson, G. D., Toward and information technology research agenda for public administration, In *Public Information Technology: Policy and Management Issues*, Garson, G. D., Ed., Idea Group Publishing, Hershey, PA, pp. 331–357, 2003.

Gattiker, Urs. E., *The Internet as a Diverse Community: Cultural, Organizational, and Political Issues*, Lawrence Erlbaum, Mahwah, NJ, 2001.

General Accounting Office, *Electronic Government. Federal Initiatives are Evolving Rapidly but they Face Significant Challenges*, U.S. Government Printing Office, Washington, DC, 2000. (GAO/T-AIMD/GGD-00-179, May 2000)

Goldsmith, J. L., Against cyberanarchy, *The University of Chicago Law Review*, 65(4), 1199–1250, 1998.

Hart-Teeter. The new e-government equation: ease, engagement, privacy and protection, Report prepared for the Council for Excellence in Government, http://www.excelgov.org (accessed August 25, 2003).

Heeks, R. and Bhatnagar, S., Understanding success and failure in information age reform, In *Reinventing Government in the Information Age: International Practice in Public Sector Reform*, Heeks, R., Ed., Routledge, London, 1999.

Heeks, R. and Davies, A., Different approaches to information age reform, In *Reinventing Government in the Information Age: International Practice in Public Sector Reform*, Heeks, R., Ed., Routledge, London, 1999.

Heintz, T. and Bretschneider, S., *Journal of Public Administration Research and Theory*, 10(4), 801–830, 2000.

Henman, P. and Adler, M., Information technology and the governance of social security, *Critical Social Policy*, 23(2), 139–164, 2003.

Johnson, D. R. and Post, D., The rise of law in cyberspace, *Stanford Law Review*, 48, 1367, 1996.

Johnson, D. R. and Post, D., The new 'Civic Virtue' of the internet, In *The Emerging Internet*, The Aspen Institue, Institute for Information Studies, Washington, DC, 1998.

Kamarck, E. C., Political campaigning on the internet: business as usual?, In *Governance.com: Democracy in the Information Age*, Kamarck, E. C. and Nye, J. S. Jr., Eds., Brookings Institution Press, Washington, DC, pp. 81–103, 2002.

Kingston, R., Carver, S., Evans, A., and Turton, I., Web-based participation geographical information systems: an aid to local environmental decision-making, *Computer, Environment and Urban Systems*, 24, 109–125, 2000.

King, J. L. and Kraemer, K. L., Information systems and intergovernmental relations, In *Public Sector Performance: A Conceptual Turning Point*, Miller, T. C., Ed., Johns Hopkins University Press, Baltimore, MD, pp. 102–130, 1984.

King, John Leslie and Kraemer, Kenneth L., Evolution and organizational information systems: an assessment of Nolan's stage model, *Communications of the ACM*, 27(5), 466–475, 1984.

Kling, R., A reader's guide to computerization and controversy, In *Computerization and Controversy: Value Conflicts and Social Choices*, Kling, R., Ed., Academic Press, San Diego, CA, pp. 108–132, 1996.

Kling, R. and Allen, J. P., Can computer science solve organizational problems? The case for organizational informatics, In *Computerization and Controversy: Value Conflicts and Social Choices*, Kling, R., Ed., Academic Press, San Diego, CA, pp. 261–276, 1996.

Kolleck, B., Computer information and human knowledge: new thinking and old critique, In *Technology in People Services: Research, Theory, and Applications*, Leiderman, M., Guzetta, C., Struminger, L., and Monnickendam, M., Eds., Haworth Press, New York, pp. 455–464, 1993.

Kraemer, K. L., Strategic computing and administrative reform, In *Computerization and Controversy*, Dunlop, C. and King, R., Eds., Academic Press, New York, pp. 167–180, 1991.

Kraemer, K. L. and Danziger, J. N., Computers and control in the work environment, *Public Administration Review*, 44, 32–42, 1984.

Lasswell, H., *Politics: Who Gets What, When, and How*, Meridian Books, Cleveland, OH, 1958.

Levin, Y., Politics after the internet, *Public Interest*, 149, 80–94, 2002.

Loader, B. D., Cyberspace divide: equality, agency and policy in the information society, In *Cyberspace divide: Equality, Agency and Policy in the Information Society*, Loader, B. D., Ed., Routledge, London, pp. 3–16, 1998.

Margetts, H., *Information Technology in Government: Britain and America*, Routledge, New York, 1999.

Margolis, M. and Resnick, D., *Politics as Usual: The Cyberspace "Revolution,"* Sage Publications, Thousand Oaks, CA, 2000.

Monmonier, M., *Bushmanders and Bullwinkles: How Politicians Manipulate Electronic Maps and Census Data to Win Elections*, University of Chicago Press, Chicago, IL, 2001.

Moon, M. J., The evolution of e-government among municipalities: rhetoric or reality?, *Public Administration Review*, 62(4), 424–433, 2002.

Mowshowitz, A., *Conquest of the Will: Information Processing in Human Affairs*, Addison-Wesley, Reading, MA, 1976.

National Electronic Commerce Coordinating Council, Critical business issues in the transformation to electronic government. NECCC Annual Conference, Las Vegas, NV, December 13–15, 2000, http://www.ec3.org/InfoCenter/02_WorkGroups/2001_Workgroups/2001_White_Papers_&_EDs.htm (accessed August 16, 2002).

National Telecommunications and Information Administration and Economics and Statistics Administration, US Department of Commerce, *Falling Through the Net: A Survey of the "have nots" in Rural and Urban America*, http://www.ntia.doc.gov/ (accessed October 14, 2003), July 1995.

National Telecommunications and Information Administration and Economics and Statistics Administration, US Department of Commerce, *Falling Through the Net II: New Data on the Digital Divide*, http://www.ntia.doc.gov/ (accessed October 14, 2003), July 1998.

National Telecommunications and Information Administration and Economics and Statistics Administration, US Department of Commerce, *Falling Through the Net: Defining the Digital Divide*, http://www.ntia.doc.gov/ (accessed October 14, 2003), November 1999.

National Telecommunications and Information Administration and Economics and Statistics Administration, US Department of Commerce, *Falling Through the Net: Toward Digital Inclusion*, http://www.ntia.doc.gov/ (accessed October 14, 2003), October 2000.

Norris, Donald F., High tech in city hall: uses and effects of microcomputers in United States local governments, *Social Science Computer Review*, 7(2), 137–146, 1989.

Norris, P., *Digital Divide: Civic Engagement, Information Poverty, and the Internet Worldwide*, Cambridge University Press, Cambridge, MA, 2001.

Norris, P., Revolution, what revolution? The internet and U.S. elections, 1992–2000, In *Governance.com: Democracy in the Information Age*, Kamarck, E. C. and Nye, J. S., Eds., Brookings Institution Press, Washington, DC, 2002.

Northrop, A., Kraemer, K. L., Dunkle, D., and King, J. L., Payoffs from computerization: lessons over time, *Public Administration Review*, 50(5), 505–514, 1990.

Nye, J. S. Jr., Information technology and democratic governance, In *Governance.com: Democracy in the Information Age*, Kamarck, E. C. and Nye, J. S., Eds., Brookings Institution Press, Washington, D.C, pp. 1–16, 2002.

O'Looney, J. A., *Wiring Governments: Challenges and Possibilities for Public Managers*, Quorum Books, Westport, CT, 2002.

Office of Management and Budget, E-government strategy: simplified delivery of services to citizens, http://www.whitehouse.gov/omb/inforeg/egovstrategy.pdf (accessed August 14, 2002), 2002a.

Office of Management and Budget, The President's management agenda, http://www.whitehouse.gov/omb/budintegration/pma_index.html (accessed August 17, 2002), 2002b.

Office of Management and Budget, Analytical perspectives: budget of the United States Government, Fiscal Year 2004, 2003a. http://www.whitehouse.gov/omb/budget/fy2004/pdf/spec.pdf

Office of Management and Budget. E-government strategy: implementing the president's management agenda for e-government, http://www.whitehouse.gov/omb/egov/downloads/2003egov_strat.pdf (accessed October 17, 2003), 2003b.

Office of Management and Budget, The official web site of the president's e-government initiatives, http://www.whitehouse.gov/omb/egov/index.html (accessed November 3, 2003), 2003c.

Orwell, G., *1984*, Signet Classic, New York, 1950.

Osborne, D. and Plastrik, P., *The Reinventor's Fieldbook: Tools for Transferring Your Government*, Jossey-Bass, San Francisco, CA, 2000.

Pinsonneault, A. and Kraemer, K. L., The impact of information technology on middle managers, *MIS Quarterly*, 17, 271–292, 1993.

Porter, Michael E., *Competitive Advantage: Creating and Sustaining Critical Performance*, Free Press, New York, 1985.

Quill Corp. V. North Dakota (91-0194), 504 US 298, 1992.

Riedel, E., Wagoner, M. J., Dresel, L., Sullivan, J. L., and Borgida, E., Electronic communities: assessing equality of access in a rural Minnesota community, In *Social Dimensions of Information Technology: Issues for the New Millennium*, David Garson, G., Ed., Idea Group Press, Hershey, PA, pp. 86–108, 2000.

Rocheleau, B., Politics, accountability, and governmental information systems, In *Public Information Technology: Policy and Management Issues*, Garson, G. D., Ed., Idea Group Publishing, Hershey, PA, pp. 20–52, 2003.

Robertson, P. J. and Seneviratne, S. J., Outcomes of planned organizational change in the public sector: a meta analytic comparison to the public sector, *Public Administration Review*, 55(6), 547–558, 1995.

Rohr, J. A., *To Run a Constitution*, University Press of Kansas, Lawrence, KS, 1986.

Rosenbloom, D. H. and O'Leary, R., *Public Administration and Law*, 2nd ed., Marcel Dekker, New York, 1997.

Rule, J. D. and Attewell, P., What do computers do?, *Social Problems*, 36(3), 225–241, 1989.

Schwartz, J., The highway to the future, *Newsweek*, 56–57, January 13, 1992.

Seneviratne, S. J., Information technology and organizational change in the pubic sector, In *Information Technology and Computer Applications in Public Administration*, Garson, D. G., Ed., Idea Group Publishing, Hershey, PA, pp. 41–61, 1999.

Snellen, I. Th. M. and van de Donk, W. B. H. J., *Public Administration in an Information Age: A Handbook*, IOS Press, Amsterdam, The Netherlands, 1998.

Swartz, R. J., The imposition of sales and use taxes on e-commerce: a taxing dilemma for states and remote sellers, *Journal of High Technology Law*, 2, 143, 2003.

Taylor, J., Informatization as x-ray: what is public administration for the information age?, In *Public Administration in an Information Age*, Snellen, I. T. and van de Donk, W. B. H. J., Eds., IOS Press, Amsterdam, The Netherlands, pp. 21–32, 1998.

Thomas, G. and Wyatt, S., Access is not the only problem: using and controlling the internet, In *Technology and In/Equality: Questioning the Information Society*, Wyatt, S., Henwood, F., Miller, N., and Senker, P., Eds., Routledge, London, 2000.

United States vs. Thomas, 74 F.3d 701 (6th Cir.), 1996.

Waldo, D., *The Administrative State*, The Ronald Press, New York, 1948.

Warschauer, M., *Technology and Social Inclusion: Rethinking the Digital Divide*, MIT Press, Cambridge, MA, 2003.

Warshofsky, F., *The Chip War: The Battle for the World of Tomorrow*, Scribner, New York, 1989.

Weber, T. E., The internet (a special report): debate: does anything go? Limiting free speech on the net, *Wall Street Journal*, December 8, R29, 1997.

Weizenbaum, J., *Computer Power and Human Reason: From Judgment to Calculation*, W.H. Freeman, San Francisco, CA, 1976.

West, Darrell, *State and Federal E-Government E-Government in the United States, 2003*, http://www.insidepolitics.org/egovt03us.pdf (accessed November 25, 2003), 2003.

Wilson, J. Q., *Bureaucracy: What Government Agencies Do and Why They Do It*, Basic Books, Inc., New York, 1989.

Zuurmond, A., From bureaucracy to infocracy: are democratic institutions lagging behind?, In *Public Administration in an Information Age*, Snellen, I. T. and van de Donk, W. B. H. J., Eds., IOS Press, Amsterdam, The Netherlands, pp. 259–271, 1998.

Unit 12

The Conduct of Inquiry

24 A History of the Conduct of Inquiry in Public Administration

Robert K. Whelan

CONTENTS

I. THE ERA UP TO 1945

Many scholars date the modern study of public administration from the publication of Woodrow Wilson's famous essay in the first volume of *Political Science Quarterly* (Wilson 1887). It is more difficult to set a precise date for modern efforts in data administration and research methods.

Some might choose the establishment of a permanent Bureau of Census in 1902 as a key date. For more than one hundred years, the census had been conducted by staffs that were responsible for major innovations in this area in the nineteenth century. In 1879, the census introduced the use of tallying machines in compiling systems, allowing large groups of figures to be handled efficiently (Lyons 1969, 23–24).

Others might vote for several efforts associated with the excellent work of the turn-of-the-century reformers. As in so many areas of public administration, the efforts of the American reformers of the early twentieth century were vital in the fields of data administration and research methods. As early as 1894, Richmond Mayo-Smith established a statistical laboratory at Columbia University for the "accumulation and analysis of data concerning social conditions in the city" (Karl 1974, 31). Columbia students of that era were also involved in field projects with many of New York City's charitable organizations. In the classroom, Thorstein Veblen taught a course called "Scope and Methods of Political Economy" at the University of Chicago in the early years of the century (Karl 1974, 45).

A. The Efforts of Municipal Research Bureaus and Rural Reformers

There are many who might date modern public administration efforts in this era from the establishment of the New York Bureau of Municipal Research. The bureau was founded in 1907 by William H. Allen, Henry Bruere, and Frederick Cleveland. Funding for the Bureau's work came from wealthy businessmen, especially Andrew Carnegie, R. Fulton Cutting (an investment banker), and John D. Rockefeller. The founders of the Bureau were "confident that if the citizenry only knew the facts about government it would take the right steps." Thus, they decided to "determine and disseminate such facts" (Caro 1974, 61). The employees of the Bureau had backgrounds in engineering, accounting, statistics, and administration. They used statistical methods to compare and classify the activities of municipal agencies and departments. Bureau staff would survey an agency, and, after collecting data on an agency, they would examine it and make recommendations for change. The Bureau published bulletins describing economic and social conditions in New York City (Schiesl 1977). To cite an example, one Bureau study was a detailed report on the rating of the efficiency of civil service employees. Bureau staffers spent days watching people at their jobs, breaking their jobs down into quantifiable components.

Recent research indicates that the Bureau was utilizing reasonably sophisticated tools of performance measurement in the early decades of the twentieth century. These tools came from such diverse fields as accounting, social surveys, work records, and municipal statistics. In an excellent and thorough article, Daniel Williams (2003) concludes that performance measurement exhibited many of the features associated with modern practice, including the measurement of input, output, and results. The early performance measurement was part of a shift of power from legislative to executive branches of government in that era.

In 1913, the Bureau organized the Training School for Public Service, a forerunner of today's MPA programs. Mrs. E. H. Harriman provided the initial funds, and Charles Beard was the first director of the Training School. Robert Moses was the most notable employee of the Bureau and the Training School in its early years. The Bureau's reports didn't gather dust on shelves; they were used as the basis for major governmental reforms. The Bureau's 1915 report, *Government of the State of New York*, served as the basis for a major reorganization of the state government undertaken by Moses on behalf of Governor Alfred E. Smith after Smith's election in 1918. In addition, the Bureau worked in other cities around the country, including Philadelphia and Cincinnati. The Bureau's work in other cities was a major source of income.

In many respects the Bureau's work represented the application of Frederick W. Taylor's philosophy of scientific management to municipal administration. As set out by Taylor (1911) and his followers, scientific management included specialization, planning, quantitative measurement, and standardization. These concepts added up to efficiency, which basically meant the maximization of output for a given input. As Schiesl (1977) points out, the Bureau reorganized government offices based on accurate data and rationalization of operations in the Taylor manner. In particular, Bureau personnel employed statistical methods as they compared and classified municipal activities. Not all Bureau staffers were enamored with the efficiency emphasis. Robert Moses, probably the Bureau's most famous alumnus, was responsible for building much of the New York City and State infrastructure from the 1920s to the 1960s. Moses was known for his effectiveness rather than his efficiency in a lengthy, successful, and controversial public sector career.

Charles Merriam's work in Chicago in the early part of the century is also illustrative. The City Club of Chicago received money from a philanthropist, Miss Helen Culver, to aid in the "investigation and improvement of municipal conditions in the city of Chicago." Merriam skillfully used his academic interests and community connections to undertake a study of Chicago's municipal revenue system using City Club monies. Merriam's thorough comparative study, done in 1906, was well received by urban reformers in Chicago and nationally. In the final analysis the activities of municipal research bureaus consistently encouraged better accounting and budgeting systems, more systematic record keeping, and standardized data collection by cities. The municipal research bureaus formed part of a network of urban reform that also included the developing professional organizations of that era.

Along with Merriam, the name of Charles Beard should be mentioned as a founder of public administration research. Beard was a professor at Columbia and served as the director of training for the New York Bureau of Municipal Research. Like Charles Merriam, Beard was a graduate student of Frank Goodnow's at Columbia. Beard left academics in a dispute over academic freedom during the World War I era, and became the director of the New York Bureau of Municipal Research. Beard believed in an empirical and activist approach. His most significant work in public administration is considered to be his study of the administration and politics of Tokyo, published in 1923 (Smith 1994).

Recent scholarship has illuminated some neglected aspects of the reform effort. Stivers (1995) points out that scholars have emphasized the "efficiency" approach of the "bureau men," who wanted improvement in governmental procedures. The reform movement also included "settlement house women" who sought substantive progress in solving social problems. Schachter (1995) notes the utility of the citizen owner model that stemmed from the work of the Bureau of Municipal Research. The Bureau brought information to citizens in a readily usable form. Moreover, the Bureau's efforts encouraged widespread citizen involvement in the local budgetary process in the early decades of the twentieth century.

Federal government efforts in this regard should also be mentioned. US Census Bureau reports at the turn of the century provided all cities with populations of 30,000 or more with detailed analyses of their annual expenditures for several essential government functions. Thus, cities had information on variations in per capita expenditures and information on whether cities were responsible for essential services (as opposed to other units of government).

Paralleling the urban reform effort was similar work in cooperative extension in rural areas. The US Department of Agriculture and the Morrill Act that set up land-grant colleges, were established in 1862. In 1914, Congress passed the Smith-Lever Act that created Cooperative Extension as a partnership of the US Department of Agriculture and the land-grant educational institutions. The purpose of this partnership was to facilitate the "diffusion among the people of the United States useful and practical information on agriculture and home economics." This information was brought to farmers through the county agent system.

B. DEVELOPMENT OF PROFESSIONAL ORGANIZATIONS

Even before the turn of the century, public administrators were organized for the exchange of experience and information. Organizations such as the American Public Health Association and the

International Association of Chiefs of Police existed before 1900. Many state leagues of municipalities formed in the early years of the twentieth century. The International City Managers Association (ICMA) was founded in 1913. On the academic side, the American Political Science Association (APSA) began in 1903.

Central to this effort was the concentration of public interest organizations in 1313 East Sixtieth Street in Chicago. This grouping occurred in the late 1920s and early 1930s and was facilitated by the efforts of Charles Merriam, then chairman of political science at the University of Chicago. Merriam brought Louis Brownlow to Chicago and aided him in creating the Public Administration Clearing House. Joint appointments and joint research projects were examples of cross-fertilization between the university and 1313 organizations. These organizations included such groups as the International City Managers Association, the Council of State Governments, the American Public Works Association, and the Municipal Finance Officers Association. In 1933, these groups established the Public Administration Service (PAS), a joint effort that provided consulting, research, and publications to communities. Some of these organizations offered training programs.

Any discussion of professional organizations should also include the American Society for Public Administration (ASPA) that was founded in 1939. ASPA was founded to promote better management in the public sector and to provide a place for academic–practitioner interaction.

C.   THE INFLUENCE OF WORLD WAR I

Although US involvement in World War I was brief, it was clearly important to the history of data administration. The mobilization and conduct of the war effort demanded more and manageable statistics. Later, there would be pressures for better government statistics during the Depression and World War II.

From our perspective in public administration, World War I was important because psychologists came into government for the first time. Psychology had been around for some thirty or forty years, but World War I saw the initiation of psychologists into government, where they worked on military testing and personnel problems. Later, some of the psychologists who worked with the Army established the Research Division of the US Civil Service Commission in 1922. These psychologists devised methods of personnel testing and selection for the old Civil Service Commission (Lyons 1969).

In addition to psychology, statistics were introduced in a more rigorous fashion as part of the World War I mobilization effort. Edwin Gay, dean of the Harvard Business School, headed a division of statistics for the Army. Gay collected information on the Army's requirements and the nature of shipping and tonnage. In 1918, Gay became head of planning and statistics for the war industries and head of Central Planning and Statistics (an independent war-time agency reporting to the president). This bureau set up a clearinghouse of statistical work, coordinated statistical efforts for war bonds, and centralized the data production process for the war bureaucracy. For the first time, there was movement toward systematic organization of federal statistics. These efforts could have provided the basis for peacetime economic planning. After the war, Wesley Mitchell (who worked with Gay) headed the National Bureau of Economic Research that became the center for theoretical work in the field (Alchon 1985).

D.   SOCIAL SCIENCE RESEARCH COUNCIL

Charles Merriam was instrumental in the founding of the Social Science Research Council (SSRC) in 1923. The SSRC provided badly needed funds for academic research and served as a coordinating body for much of the major foundations' funding of social science research. In one of its earliest efforts, the Committee on Human Migration of the SSRC voted to seek relationships with workers in the development of a "correlation computing mechanism" for dealing with new statistical data (Karl 1974, 130). The SSRC formed a Committee on Public Administration.

In the 1930s, the Committee aimed at upgrading academic research and bringing it into closer contact with the latest administrative methods. Before World War II the Committee funded numerous studies of newly developing administrative subjects. In addition, the Committee's publications greatly influenced research subjects and methods (Egger 1975, 66–67). The first volume in the SSRC series on "Studies in Administration" was Key's *The Administration of Federal Grants to States* (1937). Key gathered detailed information on administrative practices from federal agencies in Washington and state administrators. His interviews produced a mass of data on the administration of federal aid. Some of the information in Key's tables can be obtained easily from federal agencies today. In 1937, however, Key was breaking new ground. There were no sophisticated statistical analyses in the study.

In the development of the SSRC, some more recent debates were foreshadowed. In particular, Robert Crane (later the director of the SSRC) joined Charles Merriam in a debate that would today be recognized as pure versus applied research. In a 1924 report in *American Political Science Review*, Crane was extremely critical of the research bureau method of research. Crane believed that the scientific nature of the work was undermined by the bureau's dependence on the production of results, the emphasis on economy and efficiency, and the need to produce propaganda (Karl 1974). This debate haunts us to the present day at many universities.

E. Institute of Government Research and Brookings Institution

The Institute of Government Research was founded in 1910 in the aftermath of the Taft Commission on Economy and Efficiency in Government. Frederick Cleveland, from the New York Bureau of Municipal Research, directed the Taft Commission. In brief, the participants believed there was a need for municipal research bureau-type operation at the national level. With support from the Rockefeller Foundation, the first staff director of the institute was William F. Willoughby. The national budget and budgetary reform was the major interest of the institute in its early years.

The institute staff worked with government agencies on improving administrative procedures. These included the drafting of personnel manuals, the establishment of modern accounting systems, and the creation of office files. The thrust of the institute's work was to bring government agencies in line with modern business practices. As Smith (1991) points out, the institute's scholars were collecting facts and data for the foundation of a science of public administration as well as improving civil service practices.

In 1928, the Institute of Government Research was combined with the Institute of Economics and the Graduate School of Economics and Government into the Brookings Institution. Brookings was a St. Louis financier who had helped to fund many of these efforts. Typical of the work of the Institute of Government Research was a survey of the organization and administration of Mississippi's state and county governments under W.F. Willoughby's direction. The study has four major components: studies of the revenue system, the state's financial administration, state government, and county government.

The study is extremely rich as a data source. There are tables and charts detailing the sources of state revenue and expenditure and explaining such state governmental functions as education and public health. Data are also presented on administrative and governmental costs at the county level. These studies paved the way for today's routine publication of this same sort of information. Such studies were a significant and innovative achievement more than seventy years ago. It must be remembered that while massive amounts of data were collected and presented, this was largely descriptive material. There is little that would be recognized as contemporary statistical analysis (Institute of Government Research 1930).

In a similar fashion, the New York Bureau of Municipal Research conducted management studies in states and localities. O'Toole (1986) analyzes one of their efforts in an outstanding article on the role of the bureau in the reorganization of Virginia government during Harry Byrd's administration in the 1920s. The Bureau (which later changed its name to today's Institute of Public Administration) was directed by Luther Gulick. The research studies conducted were very similar to the Brookings studies mentioned above. The interesting conclusion is that the reformers (Gulick and his staff) acted with a great deal of political skill and that the machine politicians (Byrd and his associates) were strongly interested in reform. This provides a different view of the politics–administration dichotomy in this era than the usual historical view.

F. THE NEW DEAL

The New Deal was important in this field for many reasons. Large numbers of social scientists entered government for the first time. During the New Deal era, statistical agencies grew and were systematically coordinated through a Central Statistical Board that was established in 1933. The Board tried to develop effective methods for collecting information through sampling techniques and to improve machine tabulation (Lyons 1969). The research units in such agencies as the Bureau of Indian Affairs and the Department of Agriculture played an important role in the policy-making process. The President's Committee of Administrative Management, with Charles Merriam, Louis Brownlow, and Luther Gulick as members, was another example of social science expertise in the New Deal era. The Committee's recommendation created the Executive Office of the President, and the modern Presidency.

A recent recollection by James W. Fesler, then a young staff member for the Brownlow Committee, observes that the Committee's most significant accomplishments were the creation of the Executive Office of the President and the provision of six administrative assistants to the president. Fesler notes the Committee's concern with administrative management. The executive office would have "central agencies for the great managerial functions of the government that affect all the administrative departments" (Fesler 1987). These functions were personnel management, fiscal and organizational management, and planning management.

Another milestone in the 1930s was the publication of *Papers on the Science of Administration* (Gulick and Urwick 1937). Most students of public administration are very familiar with such concepts as span of control and the POSDCORB description of the work of a chief executive that were discussed in *Papers*. There are three points in *Papers* that concern us here. One is Gulick's optimistic mention of the effort by Buck, Ridley, Simon, and others to find "measurements of administration." If students of public administration could make accurate measurements of government results, executives with modern technologies would have greater opportunities for effective control, with new possibilities for the organization (Gill and Kenneth 2000, 32–33). The second point is made by Henry Dennison in one of the lesser-known papers in the volume. Dennison calls for "beginnings to be made in the application of scientific knowledge and method to the art of governing in the development of an objective and realistic Political Science Engineering" (Gulick and Urwick 1937, 142). Gulick's concluding paper on "Science, Values, and Public Administration" raises the third point of interest. Gulick was extremely interested in measurement and was involved in the invention and development of calculators, voting machines, and other statistical machinery. Gulick concludes that what is needed in social sciences is "analysis of phenomena, development of extensive scientific documentation based upon these angles, and the encouragement of imaginative approaches," combined with the testing of hypotheses (Gulick 1937, 194). Looking to the future, with his usual prescient perceptions, Gulick notes that "surely we have in the punch card, the instantaneous electrical transmission of information, automatic accounting, the electrical scoring of examination and schedules...and similar well-known devices, the basic instrumental equipment which in necessary for the advance of the social sciences (Gulick 1937, 195)."

The National Resources Planning Board, with Charles Merriam as a member, collected much useful data on natural resources, industrial locations, and transportation systems and produced significant reports on these issues. Congress refused funds for the Board's continued existence in 1943.

There were many social research projects conducted by New Deal agencies, especially under the auspices of the Federal Emergency Relief Agency and the Works Progress Administration. In 1935, a small interviewing division was established in the Department of Agriculture to ascertain farmers' opinions. In 1939, Rensis Likert became director of this unit. This Division of Program Surveys examined farmers' views on USDA programs such as domestic allotments and soil conservation. Likert emphasized standardization and quantification. In a short time he was conducting surveys throughout the Agriculture Department and for other government agencies (Converse 1987).

G. WORLD WAR II

World War II provided important breakthroughs in the area of data administration, as it did in other areas of the social sciences. Economists became increasingly important in government, as they staffed such agencies as the Office of Price Administration (OPA) and the Office of War Mobilization (OWM). The collection, sorting, analysis, and projection of economic infor- mation were central to wartime economic efforts such as price control and rationing. Despite the improvement in government statistical services during the New Deal, economic adminis- trators needed better data. Economic agencies such as the Bureau of Labor Statistics refined their data-collection techniques. The Census Bureau, under wartime pressure, employed more and better statistics and developed new systems of sampling, questionnaire design, and machine tabulation. As Lyons (1969, 88) concludes, the war "forced the government to develop a complex set of economic and social statistics and new methods of economic and social analysis that took into account the whole of the economy, not only as an integrated system but also in detailed terms of its parts."

In 1938, Ridley and Simon published *Measuring Municipal Activities: Survey of Suggested Criteria for Appraising Administration*. They identified five types of necessary measurement: needs, results, costs, effort, and performance. They examined obstacles to measuring needs and results and combined costs, efforts, and performance into a measure of administrative efficiency. It was probably the most advanced expression of methods in this area before cost-benefit analysis and systems analysis became widely used.

In his work with Ridley, Simon had an early encounter with computers. Simon mechanized the statistical work of the *Municipal Year Book*. This activity was important not only for its practical implications but because Simon developed a fascination with computers that stimulated his later work on artificial intelligence. The practical work of the ICMA also stimulated Simon's (1991) inquiries into administrative behavior.

Although perhaps more appropriately discussed in the next section because of its 1947 publication date, it is useful to discuss Simon's *Administrative Behavior* at this juncture. Simon himself notes that the bulk of the work was written in 1942. This landmark work literally stood the study of public administration on its head because traditional concepts and approaches were challenged throughout. In overhauling the "proverbs of administration," Simon called for "empirical research and experimentation to determine the relative desirability of alternative administrative arrangements" (Simon 1997, 42). The methodological framework was already there in the principle of efficiency, as outlined earlier by Ridley and Simon. Simon noted two conditions for successful research in this vein: "the objectives of the organization under study must be defined in terms so that results, expressed in terms of these objectives may be accurately measured, and that sufficient experimental control be exercised to make possible the isolation of the particular effect under study from other disturbing factors that might be operating on the organization at the same time" (Simon 1997, 42).

The use of survey research, a newly developing field before World War II, became more widespread during the war. Pioneers such as Paul Lazarsfeld, Hadley Cantril, and Rensis Likert employed survey research in projects during the 1930s. During the war, public opinion and attitude surveys were used in price control and rationing and with war bond drives. The war also provided the impetus for the development of social psychology, a development that had tremendous significance for public administration.

In a similar vein, psychological research techniques developed during the war. While there were numerous efforts, the most important was the work of the Army's Research Branch of the Information and Education Division, under the direction of Samuel Stouffer. Stouffer's unit employed surveys and experiments to study such topics as the adjustment of Americans to Army life, the effectiveness of troops in combat, and servicemen's expectations of society after the war. In 1949, Stouffer and his associates published their research in the classic study *The American Soldier* (Stouffer et al. 1949). The study was important not only for its survey research techniques but also for its insights into human behavior in organizations.

Any discussion of World War II and research methods should include content analysis. Using the methods of content analysis, scholars working in defense and intelligence agencies studied press reports, radio broadcasts, and propaganda materials to examine foreign political systems and to predict the behavior of foreign governments. Harold Lasswell's work pioneered in this field.

Problems of data administration were discussed in *Public Administration Review* as early as the summer 1944 issue. Joel Gordon, the director of statistics for the Federal Public Housing Authority, wrote on the growth of statistical units in government and the need for coordination with executive management (Gordon 1944). Gordon noted some of the problems in the collection of data, such as the need to synthesize administrative and statistical reports, and problems in compiling, analyzing, and presenting data. Gordon saw a need for operating research to encompass progress reporting and progress analysis, statistical measurement and analysis of administrative performance (including analyses of workload, comparative unit costs, and time requirements of administrative operations), and statistical measurement and analysis of program results.

This was followed in the next issue by an article on the use of statistics in the Army during World War II. Colonel John Witten, the chief of the statistics aid progress branch of the Army Service Forces, discussed the use of statistics as a management tool (Witten 1944). Witten described the preparation of the Army's monthly progress report that included statistics on procurement, contract price changes, storage and issue, ammunition supply, storage operations, transportation, construction terminations, and property disposition. Witten spoke favorably of the decentralization of the preparation of the progress report to lower echelons. He concluded that, for a reporting system to function effectively, the activities of the agency had to be susceptible to statistical measurement and that the statistics developed had to be used in the direction of activities.

One final development that should be mentioned in regard to World War II is the development of operations research. In brief, large-scale data analysis and data collection were used to project the uses of new military technologies. British efforts were notable in such areas as anti-aircraft studies. American success stories in operations research included new patterns of search patrols for detection of ships by planes, alternative ways of sighting for range in bomber formations, and mine-laying tactics. What was most significant was that the wartime experiences established the basis for efforts in operations research and management science that occurred in the years after World War II (White 1983).

II. THE POSTWAR PERIOD, 1946–1960

A. The Case Study Method

One of the notable intellectual developments of the postwar period in public administration is the abandonment of the politics–administration dichotomy. Closely associated with this development is the beginning of the case method of teaching and study.

The case method has been associated with Harvard University in several academic fields. In public administration, Harvard experimented with public administration cases at the end of World War II. Along with Cornell, Princeton, and Syracuse Universities, and with financial aid from the Carnegie Corporation, Harvard began the Committee on Public Administration Cases in 1948. The staff director of the program was Harold Stein. This became the Interuniversity Case Program (IUCP) in 1951. The IUCP produced public administration cases for many years.

Twenty-six of these cases, many of them written by leading scholars in the field, were compiled and published by Stein in *Public Administration and Policy Development: A Case Book* (1952). Stein's introduction serves as one of the best overviews of the case method in public administration. In Stein's view, a public administration case is "a narrative of the events that constitute or lead to a decision or group of related decisions by a public administrator or group of public administrators" (Stein 1952, xxvii). Most of the cases in the collection are written from the "perspective of the detached observer" (Stein 1952, xxvii).

In addition to the Stein case book, several classic individual case studies were published in this era. One such study was Kaufman's *The Forest Ranger* (1960). Stimulated by Herbert Simon, Kaufman chose five forest ranger districts for intensive study. In addition to detailed background research, Kaufman conducted lengthy interviews in each district. Perhaps the most significant contribution of Kaufman's work is his examination of the organization from the bottom upward. His pioneering work paved the way for later students such as Michael Lipsky, who studied city bureaucracies from the "street level" (Lipsky 1980).

Another classic case is Selznick's *TVA and the Grass Roots* (1949). Like Kaufman, Selznick had access to TVA personnel and files while conducting the study. The significance of Selznick's empirical analysis is that it transcends the mere case, as it illuminates general concepts of organizational behavior. The importance of leadership, in this instance H.A. Morgan's development of TVA's grassroots program, is demonstrated by Selznick. Moreover, Selznick shows how the organization made itself more stable and gained support by absorbing various constituencies into the policy-making structure of the TVA. This process, known as co-optation, is a familiar concept today but was introduced by Selznick in his TVA study (Selznick 1949).

The IUCP cases and other public administration cases published in this era provided a source of data of diverse types about public administration decisions. Nonetheless, the case method was widely criticized in the discipline for many years. Davis and Weinbaum (1969, 84) have observed that "most of these criticisms focus upon either dramatic tome, research procedures, or social-scientific relevance." Other critics have also faulted case study methods in public administration. Fesler (1962, 75) noted that cases have the "tendency to stress the pathological situation, for the drama of conflict and its resolution via decision is naturally more lively than the common-place adjustments of administrative life."

The research methods of case study writers have often been condemned. Davis and Weinbaum (1969, 4) cite several deficiencies in research methods that frequently occur in case studies: data resources are superficial or misleading; the selection of information is haphazard; and impressionistic and "inside dopester" evidence may be employed.

Perhaps the most widespread and most serious criticism of case studies is their alleged failure to make a theoretical contribution to public administration. In particular, cases are faulted for failing to provide us with comparative materials for analysis of administrative behavior. A comment by Fesler, in his history of the era, is typical:

> Each case focused on a single decision (or set of interconnected decisions) and the emphasis was on the behavior of particular organizations, groups, and individuals. Neither individually nor in the aggregate did the case provide the empirical foundation for scientific generalizations. They were probing but not probative. We had not yet learned to use the scientifically respectably word "heuristic," and so few but the already converted acknowledged that the abundance of hypotheses derivable from the cases helped advance toward a "science" of public administration (Fesler 1975, 107–108).

Below, some later efforts by case study writers will be examined to answer these criticisms.

B. THE INTRODUCTION OF OPERATIONS RESEARCH AND SYSTEMS ANALYSIS

After World War II, the military services continued many of their research efforts. In 1948, the Army established an Operations Research Office (ORO), with Johns Hopkins University as the contractor. Later, the Army supported the Human Resources Research Office at George Washington University. These two offices engaged in operational studies of logistics, troop movements, and combat behavior during the Korean War (Lyons 1969, 141–142).

After World War II the Air Force established Project RAND to conduct operations research. RAND became a separate nonprofit corporation in 1948. Although the RAND staff was comprised mainly of mathematicians, scientists, and engineers, the Air Force was impressed enough by wartime social science research to establish a Social Science and Economics Division at RAND. It was the work of the economics division that led to the widespread use of systems analysis in the management of the Defense Department. In the 1960s, this in turn led to the employment of systems analysis and the planning–programming–budgeting system (PPBS) approach in all agencies of the federal government.

RAND staff members were allowed to undertake research on their own initiative and to expand research inquiries. Perhaps the most famous instance of this is a study of overseas air bases. Congress authorized $1.5 billion for overseas air base construction in fiscal 1952. RAND was asked for help in determining how to spend the money. The study ultimately examined the vulnerability of aircraft on the ground to surprise atomic attack and demonstrated that preserving a second strike capability was essential to a policy of deterrence. The final result was a change in our policy on nuclear deterrence.

In the postwar years, the reports of the first Hoover Commission were a highly significant public administration milestone. Recognizing our diverse governmental statistical system, the Hoover Commission recommended that "greater use should be made of the Census Bureau for the repetitive, large-scale tasks of primary collection and tabulation of statistical data." The Commission also recommended that the Division of Statistical Standards of the Office of the Budget should make an effort to simplify forms and questionnaires sent to the public.

C. TEXTBOOKS IN THE FIELD

Certainly the state of public administration in any era can be assessed by an examination of the textbooks that are published. The postwar era is no exception. *Public Administration* (Simon et al. 1950) is the preeminent example. The authors realized that they faced two major instructional problems: "to make sure that what we teach about public administration accurately reflects what goes on in the real world—that it makes sense when applied to the actual experiences of administrators" and "to convey these experiences to the student in such a way as to give him concrete pictures of how people behave in governmental organizations" (Simon et al. 1950, v). The authors observed three major areas of interest in public administration: the organization and reorganization of government at all three levels, a growing concern with human behavior, and a reexamination of the politics–administration relationship. Simon et al. realized that public administration was emerging as a scientific field and that research methods left much to be desired. The authors noted that "in starting generalizations about administration, we have tried to present the evidence on which these generalizations are based, where such evidence exists. Where evidence is adequate, we have sometimes tried to indicate what empirical studies are needed to test out propositions.... We have tried to illuminate, wherever possible, the generalizations that we make" (Simon et al. 1950, vi). The chapter headings indicate the new behavioral and empirical work in the field. The authors discuss such subjects as the building blocks of organization, dividing the work, securing teamwork, large-scale organizations, selection of the team, the struggle for existence, and the tactics of execution.

The other landmark text of this era was *Elements of Public Administraiton* (Morstein-Marx 1959). Fourteen scholars with World War II government experiences jointly authored the book. The contributors read like a who's who of public administration: James Fesler, George Graham, V.O. Key, Avery Leiserson, Milton Mandell, Harvey Mansfield, John Millett, Fritz Morstein-Marx, Don Price, Henry Reining, Wallace Sayre, Donald Stone, John Vieg, and Dwight Waldo. Perhaps most significant for our purposes here is the chapter on "Applying Management Knowledge" by Donald C. Stone. Stone begins with a history of public administration efforts in this area, and analyzes the government response in such efforts as the Brownlow Committee and the Hoover Commissions. After a section on how to organize for administrative improvement, Stone discusses survey and analysis techniques in the administrative agency. He concludes with a discussion of other tools for administrative improvement, including operations research and automatic data processing systems (Morstein-Marx 1959, 406–434).

D. THE STATE OF PUBLIC ADMINISTRATION RESEARCH

Certainly there was much vigor in public administration research in the decade following World War II. It is easy to think of numerous classic studies that appeared in that decade. Research proceeded in two broad directions: research concerned with immediate problem solving, and research concerned with gaining basic understanding. Nonetheless, as early as 1956, Mosher sounded a warning in *Public Administration Review*—a warning that echoes today. Mosher suggested that public administration was in danger of "senescence." First, Mosher noted that there was little systematic articulation of the scattered research in the field. Second, Mosher observed that "a more significant deficiency is the relative absence of correlations, syntheses, or summaries of the findings of research of the past and present" (Mosher 1956, 171). Mosher felt that public administration research fell short of its potential effectiveness because there was not enough research performed; areas of crucial concern were neglected; there was insufficient communication within the field; and there was inadequate communication with related fields.

Mosher's concerns were taken up by John C. Honey of the Carnegie Corporation in a follow-up article (Honey 1957). Honey asked, "How can theoretical and practical problems be identified, hypotheses formulated, and research techniques applied, if we have been unable to demarcate our area of interest?" Honey viewed public administration as a practical art rather than as a scientific field or discipline. Honey saw a substantial demand for research of a utilitarian bent, for research that revealed the complexity of government processes, for research that dealt with problems of concern to government in their functional context, and for research of truly fundamental character.

In discussing the environment of big social science in this postwar period, Jean Converse (1987) notes three major developments. First, there were the new capacities of computer technology. New kinds of analyses could be performed at much greater speed. Second, new data archives were available. Machine-readable data became readily available to academicians and practitioners. Finally, there was the development of research organizations. A complex politics of research administration emerged in the development and sustenance of these organizations (Converse 1987).

III. THE 1960s

In an article published in conjunction with the celebration of ASPA's twenty-fifth anniversary in 1964, Simon reviewed developments in administrative decision making. Simon noted the development of many quantitative decision-making tools during World War II. For example, Simon cited the inventors of linear programming, including Koopman, who worked on the efficient scheduling of tanker operations, and Dantzig and Wood, who scheduled a then-hypothetical Berlin airlift. Charles Hitch brought many of the operations research tools to the Defense Department when he served with Robert McNamara in the 1960s. PERT (or critical path scheduling) was another technique developed in the early 1960s that has widespread government usage. In an experimental vein, the System's Research Laboratory of the RAND Corporation studied decision making by simulating an entire air defense control center with associated early warning stations and was staffed by thirty people over a time span of several months (Simon 1965).

A. THE RISE OF PPBS

In the mid-1960s, the Bureau of the Budget announced the introduction of the comprehensive PPBS and ordered its installation in every federal agency. This approach grew out of systems analysis. In brief, this approach is based on the idea that an organization's activity can be viewed as the production of defined products or objectives. Costs and benefits can be determined. In bringing these concepts to federal agencies, students and practitioners were aware that program objectives had to be clearly defined and then related to a quantifiable result. Again, practitioners were aware that valid and reliable program statistics are often hard to find in government agencies. Similar efforts were made in the states and localities, with New York State as one of the leaders.

The growing concern with PPBS led to the publication of a *Public Administration Review* symposium in December 1966. Two of the articles have attained the status of classics. Schick's (1966) "The Road to PPB: The Stages of Budget Reform" traces the evolution of budgetary reform through a control-oriented era, a management-oriented stage, and finally, a planning orientation in PPB. From our perspective, Schick notes the importance of the development of new decisional and informational technologies, such as operations research, cost-benefit analysis, and systems analysis. These techniques provided a methodology for the analysis of alternatives and made it possible to deal with the informational and analytic burdens imposed by PPBS (Schick 1966).

The second article is Wildavsky's (1966) "The Political Economy of Efficiency: Cost-Benefit Analysis, Systems Analysis, and Program Budgeting." It is difficult to do justice to Wildavsky's rich paper in a short space, but Wildavsky showed that much more than economics was involved in these approaches. Wildavsky demonstrated that there was a political theory underlying these techniques, and he also pointed out some of the limitations involved in their use. In noting the difficulties in making calculations in systems analysis, Wildavsky noted the merger of quantitative techniques with "rules of thumb." Wildavsky set out some of the difficulties with the concept of program budgeting. In conclusion, Wildavsky suggested that not only the economic "but the *political* costs and benefits turn out to be crucial" (Wildavsky 1966, 308).

Incredibly, the same issue included findings from Ida Hoos' research on the state of California's experience in applying systems analysis in five policy areas: crime, transportation, waste management, information handling, and welfare. In brief, Hoos noted new patterns of intergovernmental relationships and the need for new kinds of staff capability and called for the guarding of human values by public administrators (Hoos 1966).

Many in that era were highly skeptical of such techniques and methods of PPBS and systems analysis. Yehezel Dror, for example, noted some of the weaknesses of systems analysis: dependence upon quantification, an incapacity to deal with conflicting noncommensurate values, the requirement of clear-cut criteria for decisions, neglect of the problems of political feasibility, lack of treatment of extranational decision elements (such as judgment), inability to deal with large and complex systems, and a lack of instruments for taking human behavior into account. Dror feared "boomerang effects" (a revolt against all rational-type techniques) and suggested that we move into policy analysis. In Dror's usage, policy analysis included attention to the political aspects of public decision making, a broad conception of decision making and policy making, an emphasis on the encouragement of creative and innovative thinking, a reliance on tact and understanding, an emphasis on futuristic thinking, and, overall, a looser and less rigid but still systematic approach (Dror 1967).

B. URBAN AND REGIONAL GOVERNMENT EFFORTS

Efforts to professionalize and systematize the work of local governments in the 1960s should also be mentioned. Stimulated by the efforts of the federal government, local governments were able to conduct basic research studies, to develop comprehensive plans, and to acquire computer capability.

One of the best-known federal efforts was the urban planning assistance program, known as the 701 program because it was established by section 701 of the Housing Act of 1954. The special importance of the act was its effort to encourage state and local governments to establish and improve planning staffs. With the national government paying two-thirds of the costs, smaller local governments (especially suburban municipalities) were able to hire trained professional planners who could develop comprehensive plans in such areas as transportation. Later, in the Housing Act of 1965, the federal government provided grants to regional organizations composed of public officials representing the governments within a metropolitan area or region. Federal money was a great inducement for councils of governments (COGS) to form. HUD 701 money promoted technical assistance and the diffusion of management improvements.

Later, Great Society legislation such as the Model Cities Act of 1966 and the Intergovernmental Cooperation Act of 1968 added to this regional stimulus. The Office of Management and Budget, in its Circular A-95 review process set up a network of clearinghouses that would receive and distribute information about proposed projects in the area and assess their regional value (Goodall and Sprengel 1975). Again, the key is that professional planners were hired. In every major metropolitan area, planners conducted all sorts of research studies and brought urban governments into the computer age. Although the Reagan administration abolished the A-95 review process, most metropolitan areas still have a council of governments and/or a regional planning commission with a professional staff.

A parallel effort occurred in the health care field. In 1964, amendments to the Hill-Burton Act established local health facilities and planning councils. These agencies were replaced by comprehensive health planning agencies in 1966. There were over 200 area-wide health planning agencies by 1974, but they were perceived as ineffective as Medicare and Medicaid expenses rose. Health Systems Agencies were created by the Health Planning and Resources Development Act of 1974. These units were to be primarily private, nonprofit organizations funded by the federal government. In an attempt to foster economy and efficiency, the US Department of Health, Education, and Welfare attempted to set quantitative health standards in basic areas of health care. Like regional planning commissions, HSAs were doomed to failure because they lacked the resources necessary to affect supply and distribution of medical services (Thompson 1981, 45–64).

IV. THE 1970s

A. The Study of Urban Service Delivery

Like the literature on the growth of computer usage, the literature on urban service delivery expanded greatly in the 1970s. This expansion reflected increased federal dollars for urban programs and research in the late 1960s and much of the 1970s, attempts to decentralize federal programs, and a concomitant concern by students of urban politics and public administration.

What is most important from our perspective is that scholars collected data that attempted to measure the outputs and outcomes of urban governmental performance. Then they analyzed these findings with reference to classic public administration concerns (such as efficiency) and to the concerns of the "new public administration" of the 1970s (such as equality and discrimination).

To summarize this diverse literature in a short space is a challenging task. In brief, public agencies have limited resources in money and personnel. Agencies have neither the time nor the money to treat every situation as a unique case. Instead, agencies develop routines and devise rules for the allocation of their resources and the determination of their service priorities. These decision rules largely determine which individual or area receives what kind of service benefits (see, in particular, Jones et al. 1980; Lineberry 1977). In many respects these decision rules are based on technical considerations—how to perform a task efficiently. Some are based on criteria derived from professional associations; some are simply guidelines for coping with the pressures of a heavy workload—emergency rooms, for example, take life-threatening cases first (see Prottas 1979).

A brief review of the complicated findings of the urban service delivery literature follows. Researchers found some class inequalities in facilities, but this was usually not the case. Even with equal facilities, there may be inequality in maintenance and in the quality of services provided. While most decision rules are based on technical or professional criteria, there are cases of political intervention by organized and influential groups. Some decisions reflect conscious efforts to promote urban economic development and to retain affluent taxpayers (see Levy et al. 1974). Some decision rules reflect preferences for avoiding work with lower-class clientele (see Levy et al. 1974; Prottas 1979). Some decision rules based ostensibly on professional and technical criteria reinforce inequalities in distribution, resulting in a pattern of "the more, the more." However, some programs are deliberately compensatory, especially in the area of education. These are often based on state and federal directives, and sometimes they are resisted by local communities. Some decision rules ration scarce resources by concentrating on those with the greatest need. Occasionally, decision rules based on racial prejudice (such as property tax assessment in San Antonio; see Lineberry 1977) or employee-negotiated benefits (such as teacher-union contracts in New York City that reduce student load in compensatory education classes) work to the distribution advantage of the lower strata. (This section is based on Stone et al. 1986, 335–363.)

B. The More Systematic Use of Case Studies

Scholars in the late 1960s and 1970s developed a more rigorous approach to the case study method. Robert Yin, perhaps the leader in the effort, claims that there is no reason to be defensive about the use of the case method. Some of the classics of social science were mere case studies. For example, Whyte's *Street Corner Society* (1943) is a descriptive case study that has been cited widely by students of urban neighborhoods and political machines.

One such rigorous effort was the series of cases on government reorganization edited by Mosher (1967). These cases were undertaken "primarily for scientific research purposes" and for the purpose of systematically exploring or validating hypotheses about administrative behavior (Mosher 1967, iii). Mosher's introduction provides an excellent discussion of the case method, and generates hypotheses on reorganization. The case studies themselves are divided into three parts: agencies engaged in public services and regulation procedures (e.g., the Public Health Service), agencies engaged in research, development, or education (e.g., the Ballistics Division of the Department of Defense), and agencies engaged in management and services within the government (e.g., the California State Personnel Board). Cases from federal, state, and local levels are included. Mosher concludes with an extensive analytical commentary on public organizations, organization changes, and participation and reorganization.

Allison's *Essence of Decisions: Explaining the Cuban Missile Crisis* (1971) is an example of a case study that pursues explanatory purposes. Allison posits three competing organizational theories to explain the events of the 1962 Cuban missile crisis: the rational actor model, the organizational process model, and the governmental politics model. Allison suggests that the governmental politics model provided the best explanation for this sort of crisis. Allison further suggests that this explanation can be applied to other foreign policy situations, such as United States involvement in Vietnam.

In a most rigorous and thorough discussion of case study methodology, Yin (1984) observes that case studies must be able to meet the same tests as other social science research. Case studies must have construct validity—the concepts studied should have correct operational measures; internal validity—explanatory and causal studies must have an established causal relationship; external validity—the extent to which a study's findings can be generalized must be established; and reliability—the operations of the study can be repeated with the same results (Yin 1984, 36).

Yin suggests three tactics for researchers who want to increase construct validity: the use of multiple sources of evidence, the establishment of a chain of evidence, and the review of the case study report by key informants. Specific techniques for achieving internal validity are hard to identify, but Yin believes that pattern matching, explanation building, and time-series analysis can be useful. In discussing external validity, Yin notes that the often-cited analogy to survey research is inappropriate. Yin employs the example of Jacobs' *The Death and Life of Great American Cities* (1961). Jacobs drew primarily on New York City, especially Greenwich Village, in writing her book. Yet the book stimulated widespread debate in urban planning theory. To achieve reliability, Yin suggests the documentation of procedures, the use of a case study protocol to deal with the documentation of procedures, the use of a case study protocol to deal with the documentation problem, and the development of a case study database.

Yin employs this approach in his own research. In *Tinkering With the System* (Yin et al. 1977), Yin and his research team reviewed case studies of technological innovations in state and local services. Yin reviewed 140 case studies undertaken by other scholars and subjected them to quantitative analysis. After the analysis, Yin offered conclusions about the process of innovation in local government. In a later work, *Changing Urban Bureaucracies* (Yin 1979), Yin analyzed the life history of innovations in urban bureaucracies. In this instance, the study of six types of innovations was based on nineteen on-site case studies, supplemented by telephone interviews in ninety more cities. The six innovations studied were computer-assisted instruction, police computer systems, mobile intensive care units, closed-circuit television systems, breath-testing for driver safety, and Jet-Axc (an explosive device used by fire departments). Yin's conclusions discuss how new service practices become routinized.

V. INQUIRY IN PUBLIC ADMINISTRATION, 1980–2005

A. CRITIQUE OF RESEARCH METHODS IN THE FIELD

Despite the numerous advances mentioned above, many scholars are unhappy with the state of research methodology in public administration. The volume *Research in Public Administration* (White and Adams 1994) conveniently brings together many of these critiques. The chapters in the book appeared in *Public Administration Review* between 1986 and 1993, save for the foreword and introduction.

A first set of criticisms center around the nature and scope of research in the field. Scholars urge the exploration of different frameworks and approaches. Adams calls for greater attention to public administration history, a criticism that has been addressed by the scholars in this volume. White calls for interpretive and critical research as complements to explanatory research. Daneke proposes an advanced systems theory paradigm. Box asks if the ideal scientific method is appropriate for a practice-oriented discipline (all in White and Adams 1994).

A second set of criticisms derives from the actual published work in the field, as evidenced by doctoral dissertations and articles in reference journals. McCurdy and Cleary (1984) analyzed abstracts from public administration doctoral dissertations and found that most dissertations did not deal with significant issues. Moreover, one could not be confident in the findings because of the lack of rigorous methodology. The lack of progress, in their view, could be attributed to inadequate standards in doctoral programs, as well as to the often muddled state of the field. White's (1986) update of the McCurdy and Cleary (1984) study found that dissertation research is not a major source of knowledge for the field. Very little dissertation research is later published. The knowledge does not get past the committee, whatever the possible reasons (such as poor quality or lack of interest in publishing the dissertation). In a later study Adams and White (1994) compare public administration doctoral dissertations to those in similar fields. The public administration dissertations are characterized by the abundance of "practice research" (research that asks "how?" but not "why?"), a foreign focus (i.e., studies of single countries outside the United States), and a case study approach. The authors criticize dissertation research for "mindless empiricism," for being a "theoretical wasteland," and for parochialism.

Perry and Kraemer (1986) studied articles published in *Public Administration Review* from 1975 to 1984. Over half of the articles (52%) were empirical research. Most of this was at a fairly low level. Of this 52%, 37% were of the case study variety and 52% were cross-sectional and correctional analysis. Very little of the empirical research involved field experiments, structural equations, or longitudinal studies. In addition to increased support, Perry and Kraemer call for more extensive use of meta-analysis, further refinements in case study methods, greater proficiencies in qualitative methodologies, and use of more advanced quantitative methodologies, such as causal analysis, structural equation models, and longitudinal statistical methods. Stallings and Ferris (1988) extended this work by analyzing research published in *Public Administration Review* from 1940 to 1984. Much of the research was at the early stage of conceptualizing problems. Little of the research involved an analysis of causal relationships or of theory testing. Even in the 1980s, conceptualizations provided the main form of research (70%) in *Public Administration Review* articles.

A final set of concerns focus on the extent to which knowledge and theory development are different in an applied, professional field. Bailey argues on behalf of the properly structured case study, in the vein of authors mentioned in the case study section above. Kelly and Maynard-Moody call for understanding agency operations from insiders' or shareholders' perspectives, in their study of the nationwide Economic Development Districts program. Hummel contends that the "stories managers tell" (i.e., the way they interpret their world) is a valid means of producing and accumulating knowledge (all in White and Adams 1994).

B. CONCERN WITH GOVERNMENTAL PERFORMANCE

Throughout the 1980s and 1990s, scholars and practitioners have been very concerned with governmental performance. This is to be expected in an era characterized by fiscal scarcity, governmental retrenchment, and efforts to balance governmental budgets and limit governmental growth. As the title of her book suggests, Miller (1984) believes that our understanding of public sector performance has reached a conceptual turning point.

An attempt to measure governmental performance that bridges the theory–practice gap, can be found in the work of the Urban Institute. The Institute has developed several types of performance measures: effectiveness/quality measures, efficiency measures, and productivity indices. The Institute employs three types of data collection procedures: use of governmental records, trained observer ratings, and citizen/client surveys (Hatry 1985). If there is progress in performance measurement, it is slow. One wonders how the work of today's Urban Institute investigators compares with the work of the Bureau of Municipal Research staffers 75 years ago.

On a practical level, criticism of public sector inefficiency reached a high point with the publication of the report of the President's Private Sector Survey (PPSS) on Cost Control in 1984. The PPSS, popularly called the Grace Commission (after its chairman, shipping executive J. Peter Grace), offered recommendations that would save $424 billion in three years, and $1.9 trillion per year by the year 2000. The Commission concluded that "one-third of all our taxes is consumed by waste and inefficiency in the Federal Government" (Grace Commission 1984, vii). The Commission suggested many cost-saving measures, including the adjustment of federal pension plans and the closing of many military bases.

The Commission worked in line with classic public administration tradition, although it was largely staffed by private sector executive volunteers. In a thoughtful critique of the Commission's work, Goodsell (1984) notes that the inquiry was unprecedented in size, scope, and method. Thousands of interviews were conducted. The reports themselves, including sections on methodology, are so extensive as to be almost impenetrable. Goodsell finds the reports of mixed quality. He also believes that the reports include a certain amount of misrepresentation. Goodsell (1984, 200) detects a "distinctly business-oriented bias that should be recognized for what it is." Goodsell is ultimately concerned with erosion of federal civil service morale and the Commission's secretive methods. However, the Commission's methods of operation and concerns can be traced to such earlier scholars and practitioners as Taylor, Gulick, the Brownlow Commission, and the Hoover Commission.

One of the most controversial areas of the Grace Commission report was the section on automatic data processing and office automation. The Commission "found Federal automated data processing activities to be disorganized and inefficient, falling far short of the potential for productivity improvements and consequent savings that exist in state-of-the-art computer systems. More than half of all Federal ADP systems are obsolete, with an average age about twice that in the public sector" (Grace Commission 1984, 81). Echoing a criticism that was noted at the beginning of the computer era, the Grace Commission noted that "ADP systems are not acquired with coordinated planning and the Government's computer systems are, therefore, generally incompatible. In addition, the Government's ADP performance has been impaired by the inability to attract and retain qualified personnel" (Grace Commission 1984, 81). The Commission recommended the establishment of a Federal Information Resources Manager who would direct a coordinated government-wide effort to upgrade existing systems and personnel.

Downs and Larkey, two academic experts on governmental efficiency, note some of the difficulties with the Commission's proposals. Although the Commission's overall recommendations aimed at lowering government expenditures, the costs of reducing the age of the government's computers could be astronomical. Downs and Larkey (1986, 231) observe that "simply because a computer is old does not mean it is inefficient, wasteful, or inappropriate for the task to which it is being applied." Downs and Larkey argue that coordination of the government effort would be difficult to achieve. Technical problems are difficult because of the differences among computer manufacturers. Organizational problems are also difficult. Data-processing operations are traditionally centralized in governmental organizations. The microcomputer revolution made it possible for the computing function to be distributed throughout organizations.

The concern with government performance has continued through the recent Republican administrations to the Democratic presidency of Bill Clinton. The National Performance Review began in March 1993, when President Clinton announced a six-month review, headed by Vice President Al Gore. Discussion of this report and its implementation has been widespread. The focus here is the recommendations related to this chapter.

One recommendation is that "all agencies will begin developing and using measurable objectives and reporting results" (Gore 1993a). A related recommendation is for upgraded federal training for information technology for all employees. Other pertinent recommendations include the creation of a coherent financial management system, development of a set of accounting standards for the federal government, the issuing of an annual accountability report to citizens, and the development of a strategic plan for using information technology in the federal government.

One of the review's accompanying reports focused on the federal government's efforts in information technology. The federal government lags behind the private sector, as it "lacks appropriate access to the most efficient, cost-effective information technology products and services" Gore (1993b) looks to the implementation of electronic government, including integrated electronic benefit transfer, the creation of a national law enforcement/public safety network, the development of a national environmental data index, and government-wide electronic mail. An interagency customer service improvement team was appointed to oversee implementation of these recommendations.

The scholarly community continues to recognize problems in performance measurement and assessment. Williams et al. (1994) notes that today's public managers are consumers of many different kinds of research. They are optimistic that management information systems will be applied in evaluation of government performance. VanWart (1995) suggests that serious assessment is necessary before government performance can be improved. He discusses seven different types of assessment strategies: mission; values, planning, and vision statement assessments; ethics assessments; customer and citizen assessments; employee assessments; benchmarking; and quality assessments. Schachter (1995) contrasts the citizen-as-consumer model with the citizen-owner model posited by the Bureau of Municipal Research. Schachter believes that there is merit in the creation of a more active citizenry through education and information exchange. This could lead to improved government performance. In a related vein, Ammons (1995) argues that increased emphasis on relevant performance comparisons could capture media and citizen attention and thereby bring greater accountability. Ammons divides performance measures into four broad categories: workload, efficiency, effectiveness, and productivity measures. He employs these in an examination of library and leisure services that leads to the encouraging conclusion cited above. Behn (1995) observes that measurement is one of the big questions facing public administration as we look to the next century: How can public managers measure the achievements of their agencies in ways that help to increase those achievements?

C.   Recent Research Trends

The case study method is a hardy perennial of public administration research and teaching. In the last decade, through increased computer use, case materials for classes are more readily available. The excellent cases of the John F. Kennedy School of Government at Harvard University are accessed easily. The creation of the Electronic Hallway Network at the University of Washington is noteworthy. The Electronic Hallway offers classes for academics in the teaching and writing of case studies. Its cases, chosen from all levels of government and non-profit agencies, are used by network numbers on an ongoing basis.

As noted above, case study research is a dominant mode in public administration doctoral dissertations. Many articles, monographs, and books in the field are case studies. Some of the critics of contemporary public administration research have been very hard on the case method. One example is Jameson Doig's magnificent study of the Port of New York Authority (2001). Four major themes in public administration are illuminated by Doig's study: the search in efficiency, the need for vigorous executive action to overcome the fragmentation of the American political system government program, as handmaidens for private economic development, and the problem-solving ability of the US system. Case studies are often criticized for being ahistorical. Doig's study emphasizes the development of the Port Authority from its inception in 1921 until the 1950s.

The work has a particular timeliness and poignancy because of the destruction of the Port Authority offices in its World Trade Center building on September 11, 2001.

Case study research has been criticized because knowledge in the field is not being cumulated and because the research is of low quality. In a provocative and suggestive article, Jensen and Rodgers (2001) suggest that meta-analysis can be used to cumulate case study knowledge. By analyzing many case studies, meta-analysis can "examine the same phenomena in different settings, at different times, and utilizing different methodologies." Jensen and Rodgers also note that the criteria used by the critics of case study research may be overly stringent. They note that two classics of public administration based on doctoral dissertations, Herbert Simon's *Administrative Behavior* (1945) and Dwight Waldo's *The Administrative State* (1948), would not score on the criteria used by the methodologists.

Another recent effort to provide better understanding of the case study is focused on the work of John Gerring (2004). He defines a case study as "an intensive study of a single unit for the purpose of understanding a larger class of units" (342). Gerring discusses a number of ambiguities in case study research design. He sees case studies as being particularly useful in forming descriptive inference and notes that many social science classics are primarily descriptive in nature.

Another project with widespread implications for public administration research is the Policy Agendas Project of political scientists Frank Baumgartner and Bryan Jones. With support from the National Science Foundation, these researchers have assembled five data sets tracing public attention to issues in the post World War II era. The data sets are a congressional hearings record, a *Congressional Quarterly Almanac* record, a Public Laws data set, a *New York Times Index* data set, and a federal budget data set. All provide relevant research avenues for public administration scholars, as an extensive set of topics involving federal agencies and policies are coded. Perhaps the most useful from a public administration perspective are the budgetary studies, in which the authors have coded sixty-six detailed topical categories of spending in seventeen major areas of government activity (Baumgartner and Jones 2002).

Baumgartner and Jones note three major problems in research studies using data bases of this type. Most information systems are based on retrieval rather than trend recognition. The first problem is backward compatibility; most data bases add and subtract categories and do not maintain consistency over time. A second problem is over-categorization. A single legislative proposal, for example, may be included in many different categories. The researcher must be able to distinguish between when the keyword is a main topic and when it is one of a long list of possible topics with limited relevance. A third problem is uniqueness. How do you compare among data sets? The Baumgartner and Jones data sets aim at pattern recognition instead of information retrieval. The data sets allow for systematic comparison, and the case studies in their volume, *Policy Dynamics*, provide concrete examples of their utility (Baumgartner and Jones 2002).

Perhaps some of the criticisms of past research in public administration are being addressed. Many recent research efforts aim at systematization and rigor. One recent issue of the *Public Administration Review*, chosen randomly from a pile of materials being used in the compilation of this chapter, contained *five* articles that utilized regression analyses. These articles examined such topics as: assessing the effects of public participation (Halvorsen 2003); public policy and contribution to public radio (Brooks 2003); presidential preferences in the distribution of empowerment zones and enterprise communities (Wallace 2003); the measurement of organizational performance (Rubenstein et al. 2003), and economic development policies in council-manager cities (Feiock et al. 2003).

While the research may be of better quality, there has been increased concern about the disconnect between theory and practice. Among others, Donald Kettl (2002) has illuminated this problem. Kettl notes that, historically, the public administration research community was involved in government reorganization efforts such as the Brownlow Commission and the various Hoover Commissions in the 1950s. By the 1990s, the prestige of the academic public administration community had slipped. In discussing the reinvention movement, Kettl observes that academics had little to do with Osborne and Gaebler's book, *Reinventing Government* (1992), or its implementation in the federal government through the work of the Gore Commission. In an interview with Kettl, Vice President Gore's chief policy adviser said she couldn't think of any academic contribution that was used in the reinvention project.

The disconnect between theory and practice has been noted from the practitioner side also. Two authors with many years of state and local government experience discuss the "specious relevance of academic research" (Bolton and Stoleis 2003). They note that the theory–practice disconnect is a recent one, and they offer constructive suggestions for bridging the perceived gap. The director of a local government social service agency notes that theory and practice are two halves of a whole. Each needs the other. From her perspective (Englehart 2001), the scientific model of theory often puts off practitioners. Two public administration academics suggest that the theory–practice dichotomy is in some senses a false one. They believe that some of the difference might be resolved through the application of the ideas of the British social theorist, Anthony Giddens. Giddens' structuration theory aims at understanding the patterns and norms of everyday practice. In applying these ideas, practical theory results (Miller and King 1998).

One of the most critical pieces on research methods is the attack by Gill and Meier (2000) that appeared in the tenth anniversary issue of the *Journal of Public Administration Research and Theory*. In brief, Gill and Meier (2001) argue that "public administration has ignored its technical side" and that "a serious upgrading of methodological skills is needed" (157). The authors believe that public administration scholars need to invest heavily in developing their own research methods. The six methodological developments they think essential to public administration are independent data archives, avoidance of the null hypothesis significance test, increased use of time-series analysis, adoption of Bayesian methods, use of substantive weighted analytical techniques (SWAT), and use of the general linear model (GLM). In conclusion, the authors offer a strong assessment: "The current mean methodological level of journals in the field is significantly lower than in every other social science... the core issue is that many journals pander to the lower levels of research sophistication held by public administration practitioners. The so-called flagship journal of the field is the most flagrant offender in this regard" (2000, 194).

D. GOVERNANCE AND NETWORK RESEARCH

Another research trend in the last decade is the emphasis on governance. Indeed, at times, the term governance seems to have replaced public administration or public management in the literature. This same trend is also evident in the urban literature in the study of regimes and metropolitan governance. It is evident in titles such as Kettl's *The Transformation of Governance* (2002), Box's *Public Administration and Society: A Critical Issue in American Governance* (2004), and Lynn et al.'s *Improving Governance* (2001).

It is difficult to find a commonly agreed upon definition of the term governance. Rhodes (2000) lists seven different definitions of governance. Most definitions, however, center on the idea that in today's interdependent world, public agencies must create networks for coordination to deliver services and to solve policy problems. Public agencies cannot simply command and control within their own agencies. In the twenty-first century they must reach out to nonprofit agencies and to the private sector in delivering services. This seems to be a common phenomenon in Western industrial democracies.

Peters' observations are typical: "Contemporary public organizations also must negotiate societal compliance with their decisions and negotiate compliance with contracts for service delivery, instead of implementing public programs directly through law and other authoritative means... Governing in most industrialized democracies has become a process of bargaining and mediating rather than of applying roles" (2001, 8). The dominant feature of the governance model is said to be that networks dominate public policy (Peters and Pierre 1998).

In studying governance, public administration scholars utilize network research and analysis. Frances Berry and her colleagues (2004) note that there have been three major strains in network research: social network analysis, used in sociology since the 1930s; policy change and the impact of networks on policy outcomes, used in political science since the 1970s; and the study of public management networks, used in public administration since the mid-1990s. They compare these three strains along three dimensions: their assumptions about human motivation, the research methods used, and the principal research questions. The authors believe that the social network analysis tradition can be used to provide research insights for scholars who focus on public management networks.

Blair (2002) notes a fundamental difficulty in carrying out research related to governance and/ or networks. Public service delivery is no longer an exclusive and direct responsibility of people on the government payroll. Implementation is now indirect, as complex organization network of public, nonprofit, and private providers deliver services. These program delivery networks have arguably become the dominant feature of the new policy implementation model" (2002, 162).

E. Research Paths/Scholarly Success

Some interesting research sheds light on the process of inquiry in public administration research. Rodgers and Rodgers (1999) evaluated seven years of publication activity for a panel of eighty assistant professors accepting appointments in public administration programs beginning in 1990. A best-fit causal model was developed, taking into account the faculty member's ability, the prestige of the graduate program, research support, publications, and citations. The model also recognizes the influence of graduate school publications and six of the researchers. They use the term "sacred spark," which means that some faculty members have an intrinsic joy in doing their research. Rodgers and Rodgers conclude that "a key path to publishing success is motivated by a sacred spark (1999, 490)."

A really thoughtful piece of research comes from the Successful Scholars Project (SSP) at Syracuse University. Larry Schroeder and his coauthors (2004) first compiled a list of the top public administration scholars alive today. These scholars were surveyed and were asked to rank a set of characteristics and behaviors that might have contributed to their success. Good methodological training and quality mentoring were found to be significant. Successful scholars stressed choosing important subjects and publishing quality works. Presenting research at national conferences was highly recommended, while administrative positions should be avoided. Advice to young scholars included the following: "Be yourself... Research what you like... You must publish... but aim for quality, quality, quality" (2004, 1–3).

From our perspective here, the importance of good methodological training was frequently mentioned in open-ended responses. Nearly 90% of the scholars surveyed stated that their success was attributable to hard work. Another strong conclusion was that students should be exposed to the research process thoroughly while in graduate school. This includes broad exposure to research topics, methods and journals, as well as journal-article critiquing science. In addition, students should be encouraged in terms of feedback from research memoirs and in attending conferences.

F. Qualitative Methods: Memoirs, Stories and Cases

Above, there was a brief mention of a trend in the 1980s and early 1990s to use managers' stories and bureaucrats' interpretations of their own world as the basis for research studies. This research has emerged from in-depth qualitative interviews and/or detailed analysis of textual materials.

For example, Dobel (2003) demonstrate that the memoirs of public officials are a very rich source for understanding the ethical and political challenges faced by senior governmental officials. He examined ten memoirs by former officials of the Clinton administration. The memoirs illustrate the conflict between officials' ideals and daily political realities: Dobel draws a picture of the world of senior public service that includes the chief executive, the influence of elections, court politics, the feeling that your agency is peripheral, and the influence of the media. Dobel analyzes the ethical dilemmas resulting from the view of politics held by the officials. The costs of services and how to survive are also part of the discussion. Clearly, memoirs provide another means of enriching or understanding of public administration.

Feldman and her colleagues (2004) use an interpretative methodology of narrative analysis to examine data about change in city administration. Data came from fifteen extensive interviews of mid-level and high-level local government administrators in Charlotte, North Carolina, and Grand Rapids, Michigan. The interviews yielded 154 stories. These data were then coded thematically. These data are being used to generate a theory of organizational change in local government. The authors think that they have been able to gain a deeper understanding of the process of change through this approach.

An excellent example of the use of qualitative case techniques is provided by Romzek and Johnson's (2002) research on state contracting for social services for the elderly. The authors identified and analyzed key variables associated with social service contract implementation. They chose five program areas and interviewed state officials, legislators, federal officials, and contractors. In the interviews, officials responded to a list of questions hoping to identify key issues. The authors conclude that successful contracting "requires an extraordinary amount of advance planning, negotiation and on-going collaboration among contracting partners" (2002, 448).

VI. CONCLUSION

It is clear from even this cursory examination that decision makers today have access to vast amounts of data that their predecessors did not have. At all levels of government, computers produce data of all sorts. Decision makers, elected and appointed, are literally inundated with information. The problem is, of course, how to use this information effectively. Even with today's capabilities, decision makers satisfice. Still, it seems that decisions that are better informed with data should be superior to those that are made simply on the basis of biases. Of course, the rationalist approach can go too far; one recalls Jimmy Carter sitting in the White House totaling points for and against a missile system. Today's decision makers have greater access to information and analytical capability. Sometimes this leads to confusion and complexity, but certainly it can also lead to more intelligent and informed decisions.

On the academic side, it is clear that today's students and scholars can be much more sophisticated than their predecessors. In some respects, the field has progressed immensely. Still, there are occasions when it seems as if we have not gone far beyond the methods of the turn-of-the-century researchers at the Bureau of Governmental Research. Today's researchers learn sophisticated techniques, but they do not always bring them into their research. Again, there has been a great deal of progress, but the research path has been an uneven one, particularly in a field that is still undergoing a process of definition. At present, there seems to be a great deal of questioning of the traditional, rationalist approaches, both in practice and in theory, under the guise of postmodernism and postpositivism.

REFERENCES

Adams, G. B. and White, J. D., Dissertation research in public administration and cognate fields: an assessment of methods and quality, *Public Administration Review*, 54, 565–576, 1994.

Alchon, G., *The Invisible Hand of Planning: Capitalism Social Science, and the State in the 1920s.*, Princeton University Press, Princeton, NJ, 1985.

Allison, G. T., *Essence of Decision: Explaining the Cuban Missile Crisis*, Little, Brown, Boston, MA, 1971.

Ammons, D. N., Overcoming the inadequacies of performance measurement in local government: the case of libraries and leisure services, *Public Administration Review*, 55, 37–47, 1995.

Baumgartner, F. R. and Jones, B. D., Eds., *Policy Dynamics*, University of Chicago Press, Chicago, IL, 2002.

Behn, R. D., The big questions of public management, *Public Administration Review*, 55, 313–324, 1995.

Berry, R. D., Brower, R. S., Choi, S. O., Goa, W. X., Juna, H. S., Kwan, M., and Wood, J., Three tradition of network research: what the public management research agenda can learn from other research communities, *Public Administration Review*, 64, 539–552, 2004.

Blair, R., Policy tools theory and implementation networks: understanding state enterprise zone partnerships, *Journal of Public Administration Research Theory*, 12, 161–190, 2002.

Bolton, M. J. and Stoleis, G. B., Ties that do not bind: musings on the specious relevance of academic research, *Public Administration Review*, 63, 626–630, 2003.

Box, R. C., *Public Administration and Society: Critical Issues in American Governance*, M.E. Sharpe, Armonk, NY, 2004.

Brooks, A. C., Taxes, subsidies, and listeners like you: public policy and contributions to public radio, *Public Administration Review*, 63, 554–561, 2003.

Caro, R., *The Power Broker: Robert Moses and the Fall of New York*, Knopf, New York, 1974.

Converse, J. M., *Survey Research in the United States: Roots and Emergence, 1890–1960*, University of California Press, Berkeley, CA, 1987.

Davis, M. and Weinbaum, M., *Metropolitan Decision Processes*, Rand McNally, Chicago, IL, 1969.

Dobel, J. P., The odyssey of senior public service: what memoirs can teach us, *Public Administration Review*, 63, 16–29, 2003.

Doig, J. W., *Empire on the Hudson: Entrepreneurial Vision and Political Power at the Port of New York Authority*, Columbia University Press, New York, 2001.

Downs, G. W. and Larkey, P. D., *The Search for Governmental Efficiency: From Hubris to Helplessness*, Random House, New York, 1986.

Dror, Y., Policy analysis: a new professional role in government services, *Public Administration Review*, 27, 187–203, 1967.

Egger, R., The period of crisis: 1933–1945, In *American Public Administration: Past, Present, Future*, Mosher, F. C., Ed., University of Alabama Press, Tuscaloosa, AL, 1975.

Englehart, J. K., The marriage between theory and practice, *Public Administration Review*, 61, 371–374, 2001.

Feiock, R. C., Jeong, H. G., and Kim, J., Credible commitment and council-manager government: implications for policy instrument choices, *Public Administration Review*, 63, 616–623, 2003.

Feldman, M. S., Making sense of stories: a rhetorical approach to narrative analysis, *Journal of Public Administration Research Theory*, 14, 147–170, 2004.

Fesler, J. W., The Brownlow Committee: fifty years later, *Public Administration Review*, 47, 217–296, 1987.

Fesler, J. W., The case method in political science, In *Essays in the Case Method in Public Administration*, Bock, E. A., Ed., International Institute of Administrative Sciences, Brussels, Belgium, pp. 64–88, 1962.

Fesler, J. W., Public administration and the social sciences, 1946 to 1960, In *American Public Administration: Past, Present, Future*, Mosher, F. C., Ed., University of Alabama Press, Tuscaloosa, AL, pp. 97–141, 1975.

Gerring, J., What is a case study and what is it good for?, *American Political Science Review*, 98, 341–354, 2004.

Gill, J. and Meier, K. J., Public administration research and practice: a methodological manifests, *Journal of Public Administration Research and Theory*, 10, 157–199, 2000.

Goodall, L. E. and Sprengel, D., *The American Metropolis*, 2nd ed., Charles E. Merrill, Columbus, OH, 1975.

Goodsell, C. T., The Grace Commission: seeking efficiency for the whole people?, *Public Administration Review*, 44, 196–204, 1984.

Gordon, J., Operating statistics as a tool of management, *Public Administration Review*, 4, 189–196, 1944.

Gore, A., *From Red Tape to Results: Creating a Government that Works Better and Costs Less. Report of the National Performance Review*, Government Printing Office, Washington, DC, 1993a.

Gore, A., *From Red Tape to Results: Creating a Government that Works Better and Costs Less-Reengineering Through Information Technology. Accompanying Report of the National Performance Review*, US Government Printing Office, Washington, DC, 1993b.

Grace Commission (President's Private Sector Survey on Cost Control), *War on Waste*, Macmillan, New York, 1984.

Gulick, L. L. and Urwick, L., *Papers on the Science of Administration*, Institute of Public Administration, New York, 1937.

Halvorsen, K. E., Assessing the effects of public participation, *PAR*, 63, 535–543, 2003.

Hatry, H., State and local government productivity and performance measurement, In *State and Local Government Administration*, Rabin, J. and Dodd, D., Eds., Marcell Dekker, New York, pp. 121–142, 1985.

Honey, J. C., Research in public administration: a further note, *Public Administration Review*, 17, 238–243, 1957.

Hoos, I. R., Automation, systems, engineering, and public administration: observations and reflections on the California experience, *Public Administration Review*, 26, 31–319, 1966.

Institute of Government Research, *Report on a Survey of the Organization and Administration of State and County Government in Mississippi*, Research Commission on the State of Mississippi, Jackson, MS, 1930.

Jacobs, J., *The Death and Life of Great American Cities*, Vintage Books, New York, 1961.

Jensen, J. L. and Rodgers, R., Cumulating the intellectual gold of case study research, *Public Administration Review*, 61, 235–246, 2001.

Jones, B., Greenberg, S., and Drew, J., *Service Delivery in the City*, Longman, New York, 1980.

Karl, B. D., *Charles E. Merriam and the Study of Politics*, University of Chicago Press, Chicago, IL, 1974.

Kaufman, H., *The Forest Ranger: A Study in Administrative Behavior*, Johns Hopkins University Press, Baltimore, MD, 1960.

Kettl, D. F., *The Transformation of Governance: Public Administration for Twenty-First Century America*, The Johns Hopkins University Press, Baltimore, MD, 2002.

Key, V. O. Jr., *The Administration of Federal Grants to States*, Public Administration Service, Chicago, 1937.

Levy, F. S., Meltsner, A. S., and Wildavsky, A., *Urban Outcomes: Schools, Streets, and Libraries*, University of California Press, Berkeley, CA, 1974.

Lineberry, R. L., *Equality and Urban Policy*, Sage, Beverly Hills, CA, 1977.

Lipsky, M., *Street-Level Bureaucracy*, Russell Sage, New York, 1980.

Lynn, L. E. Jr., Heinrich, C. J., and Hill, C. J., *Improving Governance: A New Logic for Empirical Research*, Georgetown University Press, Washington, DC, 2001.

Lyons, G. M., *The Uneasy Partnership: Social Science and the Federal Government in the Twentieth Century*, Russell Sage, New York, 1969.

McCurdy, H. E. and Cleary, R., Why can't we resolve the research issue in public administration?, *Public Administration Review*, 44, 49–55, 1984.

Miller, H. T. and King, C. S., Practical theory, *American Review of Public Administration*, 28, 42–60, 1998.

Miller, T. C., Ed., *Public Sector Performance: A Conceptual Turning Point*, Johns Hopkins University Press, Baltimore, MD, 1984.

Morstein-Marx, F., Ed., *Elements of Public Administration* 2nd ed., Prentice Hall, Englewood Cliffs, NJ, 1959.

Mosher, F. C., Ed., *Governmental Reorganization: Cases and Commentary*, Bobbs-Merrill, Indianapolis, IN, 1967.

Mosher, F. C., Research, in public administration: some notes and suggestions, *Public Administration Review*, 16, 169–178, 1956.

Osborne, D. and Gaebler, T., *Reinventing Government*, Addison-Wesley, Reading, MA, 1992.

O'Toole, L. J. Jr. and Harry, F. B. Sr., The New York bureau of municipal research: lessons from an ironic alliance, *Public Administration Review*, 46, 113–123, 1986.

Perry, J. L. and Kraemer, K. L., Research methodology in the public administration review 1975–1984., *Public Administration Review*, 46, 215–226, 1986.

Peters, B. G., *The Future of Governing*, 2nd ed., University Press of Kansas, Lawrence, KS, 2001.

Peters, B. G. and Pierre, J., Governance without government: rethinking public administration?, *Journal of Public Administration Research and Theory*, 8, 223–243, 1998.

Prottas, J. M., *People-Processing*, Lexington, Lexington, MA, 1979.

Rhodes, R. A. W., Governance and public administration, In *Debating Governance: Authority Steering and Democracy*, Pierre, J., Ed., Oxford University Press, Oxford, pp. 54–90, 2000.

Rodgers, Robert and Rodgers, Nanette, The sacred spark of academic research, *Journal of Public Administration Research and Theory*, 9, 473–492, 1999.

Romzek, B. S. and Johnston, J. M., Effective contract implementation and management: a preliminary model, *Journal of Public Administration Research and Theory*, 12, 423–453, 2002.

Rubenstein, R., Schwartz, A. E., and Stiefel, L., Better than raw: a guide to measuring organizational performance with adjusted performance measures, *Public Administration Review*, 63, 607–615, 2003.

Schachter, H. L., Reinventing government or reinventing ourselves: two models for improving government performance, *Public Administration Review*, 55, 530–537, 1995.

Schick, A., The road to PPB: the stages of budget reform, *Public Administration Review*, 26, 243–258, 1966.

Schiesl, M. J., *The Politics of Efficiency: Municipal Administration and Reform in America, 1890–1920*, University of California Press, Berkeley, CA, 1977.

Schroeder, L., Routes to scholarly success in public administration: is there a right path?, *Public Administration Review*, 64, 92–105, 2004.

Selznick, P., *TVA and the Grass Roots: A Study in the Sociology of Formal Organization*, University of California Press, Berkeley, CA, 1949.

Simon, H. A., *Administrative Behavior: A Study of Decision-Making Processes in Administration Organization*, 4th ed., Free Press, New York, 1997. Originally published 1947.

Simon, H. A., Administrative decision making, *Public Administration Review*, 25, 31–47, 1965.

Simon, H. A., *Models of My Life*, Basic Books, New York, 1991.

Simon, H. A., Smithburg, D., and Thompson, V., *Public Administration*, Knopf, New York, 1950.

Smith, J. A., *Brookings at Seventy-Five*, Brookings Institution, Washington, DC, 1991.

Smith, M. C., *Social Science in the Crucible: The American Debate Over Objectivity and Purpose, 1918–1941*, Duke University Press, Durham, 1994.

Stallings, R. A. and Ferris, J. M., Public administration research: work in PAR 1940–1984, *Public Administration Review*, 48, 580–587, 1988.

Stein, H., Ed., *Public Administration and Policy Development: A Case Book*, Harcourt, Brace and World, New York, 1952.

Stivers, C., Settlement women and bureau men: constructing a usable past for public administration, *Public Administration Review*, 55, 522–529, 1995.

Stone, C. N., Whelan, R. K., and Murin, W. J., *Urban Policy and Politics in a Bureaucratic Age*, 2nd ed., Prentice Hall, Englewood Cliffs, NJ, 1986.

Stouffer, S., Suchman, E. A., De Vinney, L. C., Star, S. A., and Williams, R. M. Jr., *The American soldier*, Princeton University Press, Princeton, NJ, 1949.

Taylor, F. W., *The Principles of Scientific Management*, W.W. Norton, New York, 1911.

Thompson, F. J., *Health Policy and the Bureaucracy: Politics and Implementation*, MIT Press, Cambridge, MA, 1981.

VanWort, M., The first step in the reinvention process: assessment, *Public Administration Review*, 55, 429–438, 1995.

Wallace, More A., An analysis of presidential preferences in the distribution of empowerment zones and enterprise communities, *Public Administration Review*, 63, 562–572, 2003.

White, J., Dissertations and publications in public administration, *Public Administration Review*, 46, 227–234, 1986.

White, J. and Adams, G. B., Eds., *Research in Public Administration: Reflections on Theory and Practice*, Sage, Thousand Oaks, CA, 1994.

White, M. J., Policy analysis and management science, In *Encyclopedia of Policy Sciences*, Nagal, S. W., Ed., Marcel Dekker, New York, 1983.

Whyte, W. F., *Street Corner Society: The Social Structure of an Italian Slum*, University of Chicago Press, Chicago, IL, 1943.

Wildavsky, A., The political economy of efficiency: cost-benefit analysis, systems analysis, and program budgeting, *Public Administration Review*, 26, 292–310, 1966.

Williams, D. W., Measuring government in the early twentieth century, *Public Administration Review*, 63, 643–649, 2003.

Williams, F. P., McShane, M. D., and Sechrest, D., Barriers to effective performance review: the seduction of new data, *Public Administration Review*, 54, 537–542, 1994.

Wilson, W., The study of administration, In *Classics of Public Administration*, Shafritz, J. M. and Hyde, A. C., Eds., Moore, Oak Park, IL, 1887.

Witten, J. D., Statistics as a tool of measurement, *Public Administration Review*, 4, 279–286, 1944.

Yin, R. K., *Case Study Research: Design and Methods*, Sage, Beverly Hills, CA, 1984.

Yin, R.K, *Changing Urban Bureaucracies: How New Practices Become Routinized*, Lexington, Lexington, MA, 1979.

Yin, R. K., Healt, K. A., and Vogel, M. E., *Tinkering With the System: Technological Innovations in State and Local Services*, Lexington, Lexington, MA, 1977.

FURTHER READING

Agranoff, R. and McGuire, M., *Collaborative Public Management: New Strategies for Local Governments*, Georgetown University Press, Washington, DC, 2003.

Arnold, Douglas R., Overtilled and undertilled fields in American politics, *Political Science Quarterly*, 97, 91–103, 1982–1983.

Barzelay, M., *The New Public Management: Improving Research and Policy Dialogue*, University of California Press and Russell Sage, Berkeley, CA and New York, 2001.

Behn, R. D., Why measure performance? different purposes require different measures, *Public Administration Review*, 63, 586–606, 2003.

Bendor, Jonathan, The fields of bureaucracy and public administration: basis and applied research, *J-PART*, 4, 27–39, 1994.

Bayne, G. A., Sources of public service improvement: a critical review and research agenda, *Journal of Public Administration Research and Theory*, 13, 367–394, 2003.

Brudney, J. L., O'Toole, L. J. Jr., and Rainey, H. G., Eds., *Advancing Public Management: New Developments in Theory Methods and Practice*, Georgetown University Press, Washington, DC, 2001.

Charlesworth, J. C., Ed., *Theory and Practice of Public Administration: Scope, Objectives and Methods*, American Academy of Political and Social Science, Philadelphia, PA, 1968.

Fesler, J. W., The higher public service in Western Europe, In *A Centennial History of the American Administrative State*, Chandler, R. C., Ed., Free Press, New York, pp. 509–539, 1987.

Kettl, D. F., Public administration at the millennium: the state of the field, *J-PART*, 10(1), 7–34, 2000.

McGregor, E. B. Jr., Primed for public administration theory, *J-PART*, 14(2), 253–257, 2004.

Meier, K. J. and Bohtu, J., Span of control and public organization: implementing Luther Gulick's research design, *Public Administration Review*, 63, 61–70, 2003.

Moe, T. M., Integrating politics and organization: positive theory and public administration, *J-PART*, 4(1), 17–25, 1994.

Perry, J. L. and Kraemer, K. L., Research methodology in public administration: issues and patterns, In *Public Administration: The State of the Discipline*, Lynn, N. and Wildavsky, A., Eds., Chatham House, Chatham, NJ, pp. 347–372, 1990.

Peters, B.G., *Institutional Theory in Political Science: The 'New Institutionalism.'* Pinter, London, 1999.

Raab, J. and Milward, H. B., Dark networks as problems, *Journal of Public Administration Research and Theory*, 13, 413–429, 2003.

Raadschelders, J. C. N., A coherent framework for the study of public administration, *J-PART*, 9, 281–303, 1999.

Raadschelders, J. C. N., *Government: A Public Administration Perspective*, M.E. Sharpe, Armonk, NY, 2003.

Scott, J. C., *Seeing Like a State: How Certain Schemes to Improve the Human Condition Have Failed*, Yale University Press, New Haven, CT, 1998.

Waldo, Dwight, Public administration, In *International Encyclopedia of the Social Sciences*, Sills, D., Ed., Macmillan, New York, pp. 145–156, 1968.

West, William E., Formal procedures, informal processes, accountability, and responsiveness in bureaucratic policy making: an institutional policy analysis, *PAX*, 64(1), 66–80, 2004.

Wise, L. R., Bureaucratic posture: on the need for a composite theory of bureaucratic behavior, *Public Administration Review*, 64, 669–680, 2004.

25 Classic Methods in Public Administration Research

Samuel J. Yeager

CONTENTS

I. INTRODUCTION

This chapter on methods used in public administration research contains five sections focusing on case studies, interviews, unobtrusive methods and records, participant observation, and surveys. These methods were selected because they are widely used in the study of public administration. For example, in 2004, the *Public Administration Review (PAR)* published fifty-nine articles, whose authors utilized eighty-two research methods. One researcher used four methods in a single article, although most authors used just one method. The most frequent approaches, in descending order, were archival materials/organizational decisions and documents/literature-based (17), survey(s) including primary and secondary analyses (17), agency data (15), interviews (14), and case studies (11). Two studies used focus groups or group interviews. In addition, there were three participant observation studies/fieldwork, a single content analysis, one Delphi exercise, and a simulation.

Two of the surveys were conducted by phone, three surveys were secondary analyses of data originally collected by someone else, four of the survey-based studies used more than one survey, and ten were mail-back surveys. It appears that none of the surveys were conducted by e-mail/ Internet, although it is not clear how all of the surveys used in secondary analysis were conducted.

Certain explanations and caveats apply to this analysis of research methods used in the most recent full year of *PAR*. Every article contained a literature review. Those listed as literature-based used no other research methods besides drawing on a literature review to support their argument. Although only three authors identify their research as a participant observation/fieldwork study, several articles were prepared by individuals working in the field they studied. Obviously, each of them owes something to participant observation/fieldwork, even if they chose not to acknowledge it.

Discussion of these topics is limited to a few carefully selected aspects of the larger topics they represent, and these sections differ considerably in substance and format. This is necessary so that this chapter could be finished in a reasonable amount of time and in an acceptable number of pages. For example, the section on unobtrusive methods focuses on the use of documents and secondary sources, rather than on a cursory examination of a more comprehensive list of different facets of these research methods. Early efforts to write this section focused more comprehensively, and became bogged down in the morass of techniques. The seemingly endless list of unobtrusive measures ranges in nature from assessment of the relative popularity of museum displays based on examination of floor tile wear and the number of nose prints found on glass display cases, to estimating the number of alcoholics in a small community by examining the contents of garbage cans on Sunday mornings while residents were in church. Limiting discussion of unobtrusive measures to documents and archival sources reflects the methodology and content of a large percentage of published studies containing public administration research.

Similarly, the section on survey research focuses on the problem of increasing response to mail-back surveys. Certainly, use of mail-back surveys in public administration research has increased during the last 50 years. Increasing response to mail-back surveys is examined here because this is a difficult and important part of survey research. Many surveys have poor response rates, and, consequently, their results are of limited validity. Sophisticated quantitative analyses cannot make up for incomplete and inaccurate data. This aspect of survey research is too often completely ignored in public administration and in published research in general.

These topics overlap in some ways and they represent different levels of analysis. For instance, case studies can potentially employ any of the other methods discussed here, and participant observation can include results from interviews as well as other sources. Surveys are often based on initial background work consisting of examinations of records, observation in the field, and interviews. However, the reverse is not necessarily true. Interviews and field observations may be used in but are not necessarily part of case studies. Issues of concern in more than one of these methods are not discussed in each section of this chapter, since this would cause too much overlap. These issues are acknowledged at appropriate points in the chapter.

This chapter is not like an introductory methods textbook that very briefly summarizes and evaluates many methods of potential use. By the same token, this chapter is not an all-encompassing summary of methods used in public administration. This chapter does not suggest that any method is better than another, although it very clearly describes and illustrates the uses of each method, and also examines their strengths and weaknesses.

Each section of this chapter examines a specific methodology utilized in public administration research. However, since the focus of this chapter is methodology, a comprehensive review of the various methods used in the public administration literature is not presented. Instead, the task undertaken is only to demonstrate that the technique in question has been used by a substantial number of those doing research in public administration and other related fields. Consequently, most of the content of each section is an examination of the methods themselves rather than their use.

Readers interested in a broader and more general summary of methods used in public administration research can consult a series of articles published in the *PAR* that attempt this prodigious feat. These articles include Perry and Kraemer's "Research Methodology in the *Public Administration Review* 1975–1984" (1986) and the more comprehensive work by Stallings and Ferris, "Public Administration Research Work in *PAR*, 1940–1984" (1988). Other reviews of methods used have examined published abstracts of dissertations in public administration. This is a quite different database than the articles published in *PAR*. These articles include McCurdy and Cleary's article, "Why Can't We Resolve the Research Issue in Public Administration?" (1984), White's "Dissertations and Publications in Public Administration" (1986), Cleary's "Revisiting the Doctoral Dissertation in Public Administration: An Examination of the Dissertations of 1990," (1992) and Adams and White's "Dissertation Research in Public Administration and Cognate Field: An Assessment of Methods and Quality" (1994). These articles identify patterns within public administration research. Criticisms such as "methodological problems," "qualitative rather than quantitative," "invalid," "mindless empiricism," "practice research," "atheoretical," and "fail to test theory" are disturbing.

The reader might well ask why this chapter on research methods in public administration includes case studies, interviews, unobtrusive methods and records, participant observation, and surveys rather than other methods. Simply put, it is the author's belief that these methods have been used in public administration research more than any others. This belief is based on the fact that the literature of public administration contains thousands of case studies, and also on the author's examination of books, dissertations, and journal articles on public administration published in the last 125 years. Reference is made within each section to the types of methods used in the in the *PAR* since its initial publication in 1940. The rationale for using this journal as a referent is explained in the section on case analyses, and a more complete discussion is found in recent surveys of methods usage in *PAR* (Perry and Kraemer 1986; Stallings and Ferris 1988).

Additionally, the reader might wonder why sections of this chapter do not focus on statistics, which are widely used methodological tools, and on evaluation, which an earlier study of methods in public administration indicates is widely used (Perry and Kraemer 1986). They are not examined here because these topics are too general and all-encompassing. Each of these topics is worthy of a chapter or, more appropriately, a handbook of its own. Some may suggest that a different set of methods might be more appropriate: so be it. Alternative lists are inevitable, because everyone involved in public administration research has a favorite method or set of methods. No doubt some of these methods have been overlooked. The author offers his apologies for this oversight and neither asserts nor implies that the methods examined here are better than any others for public administration research. Others, cited above, have been quite willing to undertake that task. The fact remains that five topics will not stretch to become ten despite the author's efforts to include related issues with each topic. For that matter, even if this chapter examined ten methods instead of five, that number would not be enough. The author knows this problem firsthand, since most of the methods he has recently used and the statistics used throughout his career are not included here.

II. CASE STUDIES

Single and multiple case studies are among the most widely-used methodological techniques in public administration research (Brower et al. 2000; Jensen and Rodgers 2001; Perry and Kraemer 1986). The case study method was popularized and legitimized for students and practitioners of public administration by Harold Stein, whose classic essay "On Public Administration and Public Administration Cases" was published in 1952. Since Stein's early work, three trends have occurred. First, the case study approach has been widely used. For example, in its 66-year history, every issue of the *Public Administration Review* has included one or more articles that use the case study method either wholly or in part. Second, the case study has been harshly critiqued for its inherent limitations. Third, this method has been staunchly defended and extended. Given the methodo-logical focus of this chapter, this section examines the second and third of these trends. Stein's essay was the initial chapter in his case book, entitled *Public Administration and Policy Develop-ment*, and was reprinted along with other original essays on the case method in Bock et al. (1962). Stein (1952) defines the case method as follows:

> A public administration case may be defined as a narrative of the events that lead to a decision or group of related decisions by a public administrator or group of public administrators. Some account is given of the numerous personal, legal, institutional, political, economic, and other factors that surrounded the process of decision but there is no attempt to assert absolute causal relationships.

Two more recent definitions differ only slightly from Stein's. A case is a description of a management situation based on interview, archival, naturalistic observation, and other data, constructed to be sensitive to the context in which management behavior takes place and to its temporal restraints. These are characteristics shared by all cases (Bonoma 1985). As a research strategy, the distinguishing characteristic of the case study is that it attempts to examine: (a) a contemporary phenomenon in its real-life context, especially when (b) the boundaries between phenomenon and context are not clearly evident (Yin 1981a).

A case is analogous to the physician's clinical examination and relies on a similar appeal to multiple data sources for reliable diagnosis (Leenders and Erskine 1978; MacLeod 1979; Stein 1952). Case studies used in classrooms usually focus on some problem of interest to organizational management and have strong pedagogical appeal (see, for example, Briscoe and Leonardson 1980; Golembiewski 1976; Golembiewski and Stevenson 1998; Golembiewski et al. 1997; Golembiewski and Varney 1999; Golembiewski and White 1976, 1980, 1983, 1987; Henry 1978, 1982, 1991; Holzer and Roser 1981; Meyer et al. 1983; Meyer and Brown 1988; Stillman 1976, 1984, 1992, 2004; Uveges 1978; Watson 2001). Cases can be constructed without a problem focus to learn about the management of a healthy organization (Waldo 1962).

Following in Stein's footsteps, Laurence Lynn (1999) identifies use of teaching cases in helping students acquire the following skills:

- To help students acquire the habit of being analytical in areas of political and bureaucratic life where analysis is thought to be of questionable value
- To increase students' facility in using specific analytic concepts and techniques that have been helpful in analyzing policy problems
- To familiarize students with the intellectual and political context of public policy formulation, that is, with the experiential basis of policy-making and implementation

Lynn's book contains detailed advice on how to integrate cases into the classroom. The sections on case discussion and on closure (making the point of the lesson) are particularly useful guides. In addition, there is a section on researching and writing a case.

Cases are available in a wide variety of convenient places. For instance, The *Journal of Policy Analysis and Management* publishes a multi-page teaching case, and has done so since spring 1983. These cases focus on current issues in public administration. Readers are invited to submit comments on the cases, and some of these comments are published in later issues. Similarly, the International City/County Management Association (ICMA)'s journal *Public Management* began including a one-page ethics scenario/case in nearly every issue in 1994, and sometimes publishes commentary on these cases. This journal began publishing question-and-answer discussions of ethics issues in 1987, some of which make excellent mini-cases for teaching purposes. Similarly, the *PA Times* publishes an "Ethics Minute" in each issue. Some of these notes are cases suitable for teaching cases. The *Public Productivity and Management Review* publishes a case with comments in each issue. The author hopes that the *Journal of Public Administration Education* (*JPAE*) and *Public Integrity* will begin publishing teaching cases in each issue.

Cases for teaching are available online through The Electronic Hallway and Harvard University's Case Program. The Case Teaching Resources section of The Electronic Hallway (URL: https://hallway.org/) is located at the Evans School of Public Affairs. Many Hallway cases include teaching notes that help instructors determine how to use them. Videos are available for some cases that show the case being taught by an experienced teacher. The Hallway also provides excellent annual Case Teaching and Writing Workshops. A recent Hallway case study is entitled "Donald Rumsfeld and Prisoner Abuse at Abu Ghraib" and can be located at The Kennedy School of Government's Case Program (URL: http://www.ksgcase.harvard.edu/). There are nearly 2000 cases available from the public and private sectors. The case catalog is searchable, and teaching notes are available for many cases. A recent Harvard case is entitled "Rudy Guiliani: The Man and His Moment." In addition, there are multiple publications on using cases in teaching.

Cases are a ubiquitous phenomenon in public administration. For instance, there are now several hundred cases prepared under the guidance of the Inter-University Case Program. Many of the best-known works in public administration or in the study of administration in general are case studies. For example, Kaufman's book *The Forest Ranger: A Study in Administrative Behavior* (1960) is a classic case study in the field of public administration. This case was revisited and updated in a *PAR* article (Tipple and Wellman 1991). Other examples abound, including Derthick's (1972) study of federal funding of programs at the state level, Redman's (1973) case study of the Congressional origins of the National Health Service Corps, Neustadt and Fineberg's study of the swine flue national immunization program (1983), Baumgartner and Jones' (1993) assessment of policy-agenda setting and policy change in government agencies and their follow-up work (Baumgartner and Jones 2002; Jones 1994; Jones et al. 1998; Jones and Baumgartner 1993, 2005). The Policy Agendas Project continues to follow-up on this work (URL: http://www.policyagendas. org/). Other examples include McCurdy's (1991) appraisal of National Aeronautics and Space Administration bureaus; Moe's (1985) study of the National Labor Relations Board, Romzek and Ingraham's (2000) and Romzek and Dubnick's (1987) excellent studies of accountability in the Challenger and Ron Brown plane crash disasters; Scholz and Wei's (1986) examination of the Occupational Safety and Health Administration; Rodgers and Hunter's (1991, 1992); studies of leaders in government organizations Ban (1995), Moore (1995) and Riccucci (1995) studies of management by objectives' impact on organizational productivity; Rodgers et al.'s (1993) examination of the effects of top management commitment on organizational success; Warwick's (1975) study of an effort to de-bureaucratize the State Department; Wood's (1988) treatise on the Environmental Protection Agency; and Pressman and Wildavsky's (1973) study of economic development efforts. Nonacademic books also document cases (Lovell and Kluger 1995; Vaughn 1996). Case material has often been used to provide evidence in other classic works, such as Wildavsky's (1984) classic *The Politics of the Budgetary Process*. Thus, although a management problem often is the stimulus for case construction, a problem focus is not required.

Second, unlike some other qualitative methods, case methodology draws on numerous other data sources to triangulate these findings within a broader context. This requirement is not new. Waldo (1962) identified the need for cross and multiple checking and review to reduce the likelihood of "special pleading and idiosyncratic perspective." Case construction usually requires use of multiple data sources, such as personal interviews and unobtrusive observation. For example, two welfare reform case studies in Kansas are based on an extensive set of interviews (Snyder 1992, 1995). Usually other data sources, including quantitative data, serve as a means of "perceptual triangulation" and provide a fuller picture of the organization under study. These sources include financial data (budgets, operating statements, auditors' reports), performance data (annual reports on work accomplished and workloads), and planning documents and data (plans, special studies, and census data). Additional data sources consulted include written archives (records, memoranda, judicial decisions) and direct observations of management activities.

Third, cases should reflect and be sensitive to the context within which management activities occur and to the temporal dimension through which events unfold. They go beyond providing a static snapshot of events and cut across the temporal and contextual dimensions of situations (Bonoma 1985; Stein 1952; Waldo 1962).

Finally, cases involve direct observation of management behavior by a trained observer who applies his or her own understanding of events while also trying to understand the perceptions of the actors. This method is often called ethnography. The case method requires skilled judgment about what to watch and what these observations mean. Thus, like other qualitative methods, the case method is concerned with the researcher's interpretation of management's and other appropriate persons' perceptions of events, information, and reality, not some "objective reality" (Bonoma 1985; Stein 1952; Waldo 1962).

A. CRITIQUE

Criticism of the case study method has taken many forms. One of the most thorough and most frequently-cited of these critiques is that of Matthew Miles (1979), who identified the following limitations: (1) analysis is "essentially intuitive, primitive, and unmanageable" within cases, (2) "even less well formulated" across cases, and (3) interviewees object to the results of case analyses more strenuously than to results based on survey research.

A fourth problem is that case studies usually rely heavily on qualitative data. This fact is "often regarded as prima facie evidence that [their] validity is questionable. The burden is on the case study researcher to prove otherwise" (Lee 1985), and the results of case studies are then summarily dismissed as unscientific (Lee 1985; Morgan and Smircich 1980; Perry and Kraemer 1986). Without doubt, reliance on qualitative data limits ability to generalize (Louis 1982; Patton 1980; Sampson 1972). Consequently, the labels qualitative and case have become pejorative terms.

Unfortunately, the basis for these observations is too often left unexplained. Quantitatively based methodologies are preferred by many researchers because generalization to a population is desirable, and because statistical techniques permit the researcher to estimate the ability to generalize their findings. With proper sampling techniques, the variance of the sample can be used to estimate the variance of the population. A single case study cannot meet this criterion. And without an estimate of population variability, no basis exists for statistical inference about the population (Edgington 1967; McNemar 1940).

Fifth, case studies involve unique and nonrecurring phenomena. Hence, case studies are not replicable and not subject to verification through replication (Datta 1982; Louis 1982; Miles 1979, 1982; Yin 1981a, 1981b, 1981c, 1982b). Separate case studies are difficult to aggregate meaningfully because they differ in many ways, including focus, methods, settings, and timeframe; all of which limit meaningful comparison of their findings (Kennedy 1979).

Sixth, case studies have been critiqued as a theoretical and unable to support hypothesis testing or theory disconfirmation (Dunn 1984; Waldo 1962). An important part of this problem is the fact that few researchers using the case method formulate appropriate hypotheses, much less attempt to test them, as part of their research (Lee 1985; Yin 1981a).

Seventh, case studies suffer from the risk of measurement bias and error due to researcher subjectivity (Datta 1982; Gordon 1976; London 1964; Susman and Evered 1978; Waldo 1962). Concerns about data integrity or error and bias in research results raise issues affecting internal validity (Campbell and Stanley 1963), "statistical conclusion validity" (Cook and Campbell 1979), and reliability (Guilford 1954; Sellitz et al. 1959) and force researchers to choose methods based on the inductive statistical mode of explanation (Susman and Evered 1978).

These difficulties have negative consequences for academics who find that publication of case study results may be comparatively more difficult than publication of research results based on other methodologies. This may discourage use of this method (Bonoma 1985; Das 1983).

Given these problems, it is not surprising that case study results are considered suspect and even "unscientific" when researchers are concerned about causality, quantification, statistically-measurable internal and external validity, and hypothesis falsification (Van Maanen 1979a).

Even as these problems were identified and defined, the case study approach fell into decline with the rise of the positivist approach to science (Lee 1985). Within public administration, this decline has been attributed to the bias against case studies in political science, one of the parent disciplines of public administration. Like their peers within the parent discipline, public administration scholars sought more-sophisticated methodologies that would support development and testing of theory. Consequently, the case approach, which was critiqued as "descriptive and virtually atheoretical," became less widely-used and no longer was a method of choice (Dunn 1984). It has been devalued by scholars within the field of public administration (Bailey 1992).

This trend was not wholly due to changes within political science alone. Driven by positivism, social science as a whole evolved in this manner, and change within political science was just part of this evolution. Positivism, with its emphasis on empirical analysis of concrete relationships in an external social world, encouraged concern for an "objective" form of knowledge that specified the precise nature of laws, regularities, and relationships among phenomena measured in terms of social "facts" (Pugh and Hickson 1976; Skinner 1953, 1957). Consequently, case studies were replaced by a strong preference for quantitative research methods (Bailey 1992; Mitroff 1974; Van Maanen 1979b).

Given these and other problems, Miles (1979) concluded that without methodological improvements in case analysis, "qualitative research on organizations cannot be expected to transcend storytelling." Despite this grim conclusion, reasons exist for using case studies, and techniques exist that make them a more tenable approach to certain types of research problems.

B. Defense and Extension

This defense of the case method is multifaceted. First, quantitative methods as an alternative suffer from inherent flaws and limitations of their own. Second, the case method and quantitative methods have different objectives, strengths, and weaknesses, and hence can be used to supplement one another. Third, a specific series of steps exist which provide a general design for case research. Fourth, specific technical practices also exist, which the researcher can build into the case analysis process in order to overcome some of the pitfalls identified in the preceding section.

1. Quantitative Warts

First, all methods—including surveys and quantitative analysis techniques—have strengths and weaknesses. None of them can meet all research needs equally well. Strength in one respect may be a weakness in other ways because of multiple threats to validity and differing research purposes (Campbell and Stanley 1963; Jensen and Rodgers 2001; McGrath 1982). For example, the study that seeks a high degree of data integrity requires a precise operationalization of the research variables, a relatively large sample size and quantitative data for statistical power, and the ability to exercise control over persons, settings, and other factors to prevent causal contamination. Quantitative methods used in the social sciences, such as survey research and multivariate statistical analyses, draw on the natural sciences and assume that a lawful structure exists between elements (such as persons, groups, organizations, things, behaviors) which can be discovered. Those using these methods also assume that the world lends itself to an objective form of measurement, and that accurate definition and measurement require that these elements can be abstracted from their context (Morgan and Smircich 1980). Consequently, these quantitative measurements are merely snapshots of reality taken at one point in time in a limited setting and therefore have limited external validity.

Quantitative research has been criticized for analyzing a few isolated variables apart from the real world, since situations cannot be meaningfully segmented in this way (Rist 1977). Hence, the paradigm underlying quantitative social science, which assumes a static model of causality, rather than the possibility of a dynamic world full of complex causal connections between actors, organizations, clients, politicians, and programs, is inadequate (Bryck and Weisberg 1978; Glaser 1978; Glaser and Backer 1972). An alternative view assumes that the world is in some form of open-ended process, or, to use Argyris's term, in a state of becoming, and that a priori elimination of some methodological alternatives in favor of approaches that focus narrowly on limited points in time and limited settings cannot do justice to most research topics (Morgan and Smircich 1980; O'Dempsey 1976).

Dissatisfaction with quantitative research methods and strategies has emerged, particularly as they are applied to phenomena not easily operationalized or easily observable outside their natural settings (see, for instance, the special issue of the *Administrative Science Quarterly* (1979), or the Sage Series in Qualitative Research (Van Maanen et al. 1982, or Yin 1984, 1994, 2003)). Van Maanen (1982a) summarizes reasons for the reemergence of qualitative research in the social science disciplines and disenchantment with quantitative research tools as follows: "the relatively trivial amount of explained variance, the abstract and remote character of key variables, the lack of comparability across studies, the failure to achieve much predictive validity... and the causal complexity of multivariate analysis, which, even when understood, makes change oriented actions difficult to contemplate."

Questions have been raised about the assumptions underlying popular social science research methods, such as survey research, and, in turn, about the nature and adequacy of the knowledge resulting from research based on these methods. Traditional quantitative methods have been challenged as inadequate and inappropriate (Burrell and Morgan 1979; McGuire 1986; Mitroff and Kilmann 1978; Morgan and Smircich 1980). Management research has been criticized because of its limited utility for management practice (Hakel et al. 1982; Lawler et al. 1985; Shrivasta and Mitroff 1984) and because of its focus on fads and "quick fixes" (Byrne 1986; Kilmann 1984). Treatments are hard to define or manipulate. Confounding influences include Hawthorne effects and extenuating circumstances which can interfere with the researcher's ability to draw valid conclusions. These influences are difficult to identify, and naturally, even more difficult to avoid (Anderson 1976; Gold 1997; Kennedy 1978).

Other problems with traditional quantitative methods also limit their usefulness. In particular, the frequent use of and, in some cases, over-reliance on survey research has led several persons to question the nature and quality of the variables used in organizational research. For example, it has been pointed out that even minor variations in survey design can affect response rates (Houston and Nevin 1977; Wiseman 1973) and response patterns (Blair et al. 1977). Similarly, others have found that even in a well-planned interview, interviewer effects sometimes account for a significant proportion of the variance of the dependent variables (McKenzie 1977). Case studies conducted longitudinally enable a researcher to examine changes that occur and factors influencing those changes (DiIulio 1994; Ross and Staw 1986; Wood 1988).

Validity issues also result from semantic problems, problems of unwilling interviewees, interviewer effects, and other challenges commonly faced during interviewing (Becker and Greer 1957; Burstein et al. 1985; DeMaio 1980; O'Neil 1979; Steeh 1981; Wiener et al. 1972).

Consequently, a growing number of researchers in economics (Piore 1979), medicine (Feinstein 1977), management (Mintzberg 1978), organizational behavior (Fombrun 1982; Van Maanen 1979b), public administration (Bailey 1992; Jensen and Rodgers 2001), sociology (McGrath et al. 1982; Mitroff 1974), and psychiatry have advocated and helped foster rebirth of qualitative research in the social sciences.

This increasing interest in qualitative research techniques began in the mid 1970s and includes participant observation, ethnography, case analysis and the cluster method, and other qualitative approaches (see, for example, Bogdon and Taylor 1975; Downey and Ireland 1979; Greenhalgh and Jick 1979; Manning 1977; McClintock 1978; Millman 1977; Mintzberg 1978, 1979; Pettigrew and Bumstead 1980; Turner 1974). Qualitative research is becoming respectable.

2. An Impossible Burden

The eleven criteria of research quality developed by McCurdy and Cleary (1984) and White (1986) impose a heavy judgmental burden on public administration research. All of the criteria are not equally important, and no study can meet all the criteria. Classics such as Simon's *Administrative Behavior* (1945) and Waldo's *The Administrative State* (1948), and all fifty-one of the studies contained in Shafritz and Hyde's *Classics of Public Administration* (1992), would fail on almost all of these criteria. Hence, none would be judged to be "high-quality" research (Bailey 1992; Jensen and Rodgers 2001).

3. Objectives, Strengths, and Choice of Method

The case method supports different research objectives and has different strengths than those already identified for survey-based quantitative research. Substantial differences exist between case research and methods, which emphasize higher data integrity. First, the goal of data collection in case research is not quantification or even enumeration, but (1) description, (2) classification (typology development), (3) theory development, and (4) limited theory testing. In short, as in all social science, the goal is understanding.

Second, most enumeration is of little value in case research. The goal is not breadth or representativeness of research, but depth of understanding. The risks of relatively lower data integrity are traded for currency and contextual richness of what is learned. Once researchers are confident of their understanding of a phenomenon explored with case research, other, more traditional. deductive approaches may be applied to the problem.

Third, using the case study method does not require the use of ethnography, participant observation, or any other particular type of methodology. Case study evidence may come from fieldwork, archival records, verbal reports, observations, and quantitative sources, or any combination of these sources. For example, Allison's (1971) study of the Cuban missile crisis does not rely on either ethnography or observational techniques. Gross et al.'s (1971) organizational case study and Vietorisz and Harrison's (1970) study of economic development in urban areas combine qualitative with quantitative evidence. For that matter, ethnography and participant observation methods have been the basis for research on the organizational behavior of police and other individuals, which has not resulted in published case studies (see, for example, studies by Jacobs 1970; Reiss 1971; Rubenstein 1973; Van Maanen 1979b).

Moreover, even by itself, a purely qualitative case research project can be the basis for a valuable and valid scientific attack on certain classes of important problems. When researchers are interested in theory-building rather than verification or extension, use of case studies involving description, classification, and comparison is an appropriate research technique. Research using the case method can provide a "deep understanding" (Geertz 1973), a fuller contextual sense of the phenomena under study (Miles 1979), and detailed descriptions of events, situations, and interactions between people and things providing depth and detail (Patton 1980). In the words of Jensen and Rodgers (2001), case studies contain "intellectual gold that is absent from a large-sample study of many agencies, because detailed information is reported about specific conditions that are present and critical events that occur... and the processes of a single entity" (237). This information enables researchers to take an explicit step toward theory-building as opposed to theory testing, which often is missing from both simple descriptive work and most cause and effect research (Bailey 1992; Mchuire 1969; Van Maanen 1982a).

Fourth, case studies may not provide findings that are universally generalizable, but they do provide insightful and significant knowledge that may be useful for building substantive theory (Glaser and Strauss 1967). Qualitative observations from case studies have and will continue to generate unexpected findings, which form the basis of new hypotheses and grounded theories (Glaser and Strauss 1967; Lundberg 1976). For example, quantitative results of the well-known bank wiring room experiment in the Hawthorne study (Roethlisberger and Dickson 1939) could not be explained without using qualitative data—the observed informal group norms. Similarly, case studies that span a lengthy period of time can reveal developmental information that other methods, such as one-shot surveys, are unable to reveal (Agranoff and Radin 1991). Since the researcher using qualitative methods is more likely to be aware of various aspects of the subject matter under investigation at the practitioner's or field level, it may be easier for that person to suggest alternative explanations for conflicting evidence that can form the basis of further inquiry.

The decision to use the case method as a research strategy should be influenced by the research objectives and by the nature of the data needed during the research project. The investigator should specify research objectives before case development and before the case method is chosen as the research strategy (Bonoma 1985; Waldo 1962). Interest in theory development, the complex nature of the problem or situation, and the need to study phenomena in their natural context should determine the applicability of the case method (Feagin et al. 1991). Since research objectives may change during a research project, the case method may be appropriate for one but not another stage of the research (Van Maanen et al. 1982, 1984).

Certain organizational phenomena cannot be validly measured without using qualitative techniques. Case study research can provide depth of understanding of phenomena and their contexts, which quantitative analysis may lack (Agranoff and Radin 1991; Bailey 1992; Geertz 1973; Miles 1979; Sjoberg et al. 1991; Van Maanen 1982a). Another aspect of this problem is that "blind research for quantifiable regularities... can lead to ignorance of those aspects of man—the most important ones—that are intrinsically nonquantitative" (Nicosia and Rosenberg 1972). The "objective" researcher is likely to "fill in the process of interpretation with his own surmises in place of catching the process as it occurs in the experience of the acting unit which uses it" (Blumer 1962), and, in that process, may risk being highly subjective. Case studies may facilitate the understanding of complex social interactions typical of all organizations, since they provide a means of synthesizing knowledge emerging from different disciplines.

C. A PROCESS FOR CASE RESEARCH

A four-stage process labeled drift, design, prediction, and disconfirmation can be used to guide and explain applications of the case method in research. During the initial, or drift, stage of a research project, the investigator attempts to learn the concepts, locale, and jargon of phenomena and begin integration from literature, a priori notions about the phenomenon's operation, and critical components of observed practices. Most research methods involve this sort of situation analysis, or drift stage. During this stage, contexts are observed to develop as accurate a perspective as possible (Sjoberg et al. 1991; Van Maanen et al. 1982, 1988).

One of the critical and difficult tasks of the researcher in the drift stage is to suspend judgment and ignore preconceived biases to be able to learn from the phenomena encountered. For example, Piore (1979) illustrated what occurs during the drift stage in describing his first attempt to do case research in economics. Much of his early research was not data collection, but focused on learning to cope with the discrepancies between his prior beliefs of manning levels in plants and the way the issue was thought about in the field. It took time to overcome his reluctance to listen to managers' stories about manning levels as anything other than useless mythology, and to consider such accounts as perhaps a more-useful approach to his research interest than his original, theoretically legitimate view. Without these stories, he probably would have treated management behavior as model deviations that required a correction factor instead of as the stimulus for building a more correct understanding.

The design stage begins with the development of tentative explanations of the observations collected up to this point. These tentative explanations lead to the development of theory. In the design stage, the object of data collection is to assess and define major areas of inquiry suggested by the preliminary model. Information is gathered to flesh out the model and permit the development of some generalizations to account for divergences in observations. The critical skill for the qualitative researcher at this point is to be willing to let further data recycle his or her thinking back to the drift stage if initial conceptualizations do not hold up against new situations, or as better conceptualizations suggest themselves or are developed.

The third stage of case research, prediction, or generalization formation, occurs in the middle of a case research project. By this point, the researcher has a model suggesting generalizations to test, a good understanding of the characteristics that make separation of field data into relatively well-defined separate categories, and is trying to evaluate initial predictions (Sjoberg et al. 1991; Van Maanen 1988).

The researcher might compile more cases from sites that are different from but conceptually similar to those sites used to arrive at the generalizations. This step usually requires evaluating the generalization in organizations or settings not yet explored. Thus, a large number of cases can be collected to test the predictive power of a generalization and to learn about its parameters. This stage requires that the researcher (1) take into account the fact that many generalizations are not widely applicable, since they are based on and only accurately describe or fit particular situations, settings, or activities, and (2) be willing to use new disconfirming evidence as a basis for development of new generalizations and modifying earlier ones (Agranoff and Radin 1991; Bailey 1992; Lofland 1971; Van Maanen 1988; Yin 1994, 2003).

The fourth stage, disconfirmation, consists of further testing the limits of generalizations not rejected in the prediction stage. An attempt is made to disconfirm tentative generalizations by applying them to a broader set of cases than in the prediction stage. This stage in case research is a surrogate for the falsification procedures used in deductive analysis. The blending of initial discomfirming efforts in the prediction stage and the more complete falsification attempts in the disconfirmation stage illustrates an important point: these four stages do not form a rigid sequential hierarchy, but an iterative series of steps designed to lead to understanding of the phenomena examined (Yin 1994, 2003).

D. APPROACHES TO CASE ANALYSIS

According to Miles (1979), the analyst faced with qualitative data has "few guidelines for protection from selfdelusion." In contrast, clear guidelines exist for the researcher working with quantitative data regarding data characteristics, choice of statistics, and their interpretation. Reviewing the literature on the case method identified five ways in which evidence from a single case or within case evidence can be analyzed. These are narrative, question and answer, explanatory, case cluster, and quantitative formats.

1. Narrative

Narrative preparation is a longstanding and traditional method of imposing order on a case analysis. Construction of a narrative may be helpful when theoretical propositions do not exist. For example, Pressman and Wildavsky (1973) used this technique to describe possible causal links between events.

A variety of specific techniques exist which can be used to assist with case narrative construction and in other case-preparation approaches. Miles and Huberman (1984) suggest using the following methods to impose order on case materials: putting information in chronological order; putting information into different arrays or groups; creating a matrix of categories and placing the evidence within these categories; creating data displays such as flow charts, which make step-by-step processes clearer and which may also help organize other information; tabulating the frequency of different events; and using appropriate statistics, such as means, variances, cross-tabulations, and measures of interrelationships between variables, to examine the complex interrelationships within these data.

Miles (1979) found that narrative preparation was not useful because of the complexity of the task. Case study narratives are often lengthy and follow no predictable structure (Yin 1981a, 1984, 1994, 2003). Consequently, case analyses are difficult to write and hard to understand. This problem can be avoided if a case study is built around a clear conceptual framework in which special characteristics and intervening circumstances are identified (Bailey 1992).

A case study analysis in narrative and other forms can be organized around the specific substantive propositions, questions, and activities of the case. As pointed out in the discussion of a research design for the case method, the central questions of the case need to be identified early in the study (Agranoff and Radin 1991; Bailey 1992; Bonoma 1985; Stein 1952; Yin 1981a, 1984, 1994, 2003). Theory helps impose order on a case study by suggesting the how and why questions that guide the analysis. This does not mean that a rigid conceptual framework must be used. Since case studies often begin with little conceptual framework, modifications to these conceptualizations usually must be made as the analysis progresses.

Development of a conceptual framework may limit the all-too-common tendency of those preparing case studies to assume that anything might be relevant, so one ought to observe and code everything. During initial phases of the research such openness is warranted, but as conceptualizations develop, notes should reflect meaningful events rather than all events in a case study. These generalizations apply equally well to both qualitative and quantitative data.

A conceptual framework may also limit the tendency for analysts to spend an inordinate amount of time and effort constructing readable narratives for separate data sources such as individual interviews, meetings or other major events, logs of daily or weekly activities, and individual documents or reports. Each narrative portion should integrate evidence from different data elements, which must be recorded accurately, though in the form of notes rather than narratives. Data that address the same topic should be assembled together; for instance, interview segments from different respondents on the same topic should be integrated (Jick 1979; Yin 1980). In preparing a narrative and in every other technique used in case research, the researcher must build and present a chain of evidence consisting of the citation of particular pieces of evidence. Most case study research has failed to establish any explicit chain, and consequently critics question how specific conclusions were reached (Yin 1979, 1981a).

Two techniques may help formulate the central questions of a case. One requires narrowing the case focus and the other broadening it. First, the case study's focus can be limited to a restricted time period and only briefly summarize background and aftermath. Emphasis should be on the focal decision, either as an act or as a process, and extraneous matters should be ignored (Stein 1952). Second, the degrees of freedom of the typical case study can, in fact, be increased. Campbell (1975) discusses how the richness of case analysis can be significantly improved by looking for multiple implications of the theoretical ideas under investigation. Given these different purposes, they can perhaps both be used sequentially or on different parts of a single case study where appropriate. Certainly there is room for both these procedures in the four-part cycle for case research previously described.

2. Questions and Answers

A series of open-ended questions and accompanying answers can replace a case study narrative. It is simpler to collect and integrate information in this format than in relatively less-structured formats. Consequently, cases based on this format are simpler to produce than a narrative, and the reader can usually find desired information easily.

Two excellent case studies illustrate the question-and-answer approach. The US National Commission on Neighborhoods (1979) case studies of forty community organizations provides an example of the question-and-answer approach. Nearly sixty open-ended questions were developed early in the project; these questions were used to guide collection of the data. Fieldworkers prepared two or three paragraphs in response to each question. These questions and answers were used as the basis for preparing the final report entitled "People, Building Neighborhoods" (US National Commission on Neighborhoods, 1979). Similarly, Yin and White (1984) used 50 open-ended questions to gather data about computer utilization in twelve different schools. Interviewers sought information from subjects that would answer these questions as completely as possible. The interviewers' notes were the basis for individual case reports and the cross-case analysis. Numerous other public administration case studies using multiple cases exist (Agranoff and Radin 1991; Korosec and Mead 1996; *Public Citizen* 2001; Yin, 1981c).

3. Explanatory

A third technique is to use a case study to explain a phenomenon. An explanatory case study consists of (1) an accurate rendition of the facts, (2) consideration of alternative explanations of these facts, (3) an evaluation of these alternatives, and (4) a conclusion based on the single explanation that appears most congruent with the facts. This approach lends itself to exploring both rejected and accepted hypothetical alternatives, which Stein (1952) recommended.

Some of the best-known case studies in public administration, including works by Allison (1971), Derthick (1972), Gross et al. (1971), and Pressman and Wildavsky (1973) used this explanatory technique. For example, Allison's (1971) study examined three alternative explanations of the Cuban missile crisis and found that one explanation was more satisfactory than the others. Similarly, a case study of the usefulness of research compared the facts of a case against several competing models of the research utilization process (Yin and Heinsohn 1980).

4. Case Cluster

McClintock et al. (1979) describe a technique for the analysis of a single case called the case cluster method. This technique relies on data that are usually collected from a variety of sources on the same event or "activity, process, feature, or dimension of organizational behavior." These data come from stratified samples drawn from appropriate sources, although informants are often used as data sources. For example, data are gathered on one topic from a variety of different individuals using responses to an identical set of questions. Several studies have used this technique. One of the earliest studies to use this approach was McClintock's (1978) examination of planning processes in state agencies. Brannon's (1979) study of decision-making in a public welfare agency also used the case cluster method. McClintock et al.'s (1979) study of task predictability within a university also used this approach. All three of these studies used informants.

The case cluster technique differs from the case survey method of Yin (1979) or Yin and Heald (1975), described below, in focus. The case survey method relies on different case studies focusing on the same topic. In contrast, the case cluster method of McClintock et al. (1979) used data from a variety of sources focusing on a single case or incident.

5. Quantitative

Another traditional technique designed to impose order on case analysis is analysis of quantitative data. Once events are coded into numerical form (Hodson 1999), standard statistical techniques can be used in the analysis (Pelz 1981). Well-known case studies have made significant use of quantitative data. For example, Pressman and Wildavsky's (1973) study of policy implementation contains quantitative data—a count of the number of decisions that had to be made in order for a policy to be implemented. Similarly, Yin (1981a) used quantitative data in his study of the life histories of innovations.The quantitative data were based on tabulations of different organizational events, which were coded for each case study.

Not all efforts to include quantitative data in case analyses have been successful. Miles found that this technique was not useful: "We developed an elaborate coding scheme. Fieldworkers, including the coding specialist, hated the job." As a result, "the coding stopped," and the coded data were not used in subsequent analyses (Miles 1979). Despite Miles' experience, coding is a useful method in which the information can be analyzed using meta-analysis (Hodson, 1999).

Possible causes of these problems include use of coding categories that are too narrow and too numerous. This problem is exacerbated by the fact that it is difficult to define categories accurately in advance. This situation creates difficulties for the case study analyst, who has neither the training nor the inclination to serve as a mechanical recording device (Yin 1981a). One solution to this problem is to combine initial response categories as experience develops during the coding process. For instance, different events or actions that are essentially synonymous but were initially identified with unique terms can be combined.

E. METHODOLOGICAL ISSUES—VALIDITY

Much of the subjectivity in case analysis can be eliminated by using one or more (without a doubt, using more than one of these techniques usually is better than using just one) of the following methods:

1. Validation of the data by comparing it with outside sources and known facts (Foreman 1948; Sjoberg et al. 1991; Van Maanen 1988; Yin 1994, 2003). This approach can help clear up the problem of conflicting evidence from multiple sources of information, especially individuals, who were involved in the case.

2. Validation by self-confrontation and checking the internal consistency of the data (Agranoff and Radin 1991; Bailey 1992; Foreman 1948; Sjoberg et al. 1991; Yin 1994, 2003). This can be accomplished by comparing different segments of the information collected. Cross-checking may also be accomplished by coding it and using meta-analysis to identify patterns (Hodson 1999).

Using either or both of these different (1) external and (2) internal sources of data and using data from different methods in this way is called *triangulation*. This process is also called the multitrait multimethod approach, and it is often used to corroborate findings within case studies (Campbell and Fiske 1959). Unfortunately, time constraints, technological problems, and the cost of gathering and analyzing data often limit or preclude the use of multiple methods or triangulation efforts (Martin 1982).

3. Validation by review of the researcher's interpretations by the subjects involved in the study (Foreman 1948; Sjoberg et al. 1991). For example, Alkin et al. (1979), in preparing their study of school districts, had the individuals whom they interviewed in each school district review a draft of their case. A set of open-ended questions was used to facilitate their reviews. Comments and suggestions from participants were used in modifying the drafts, and content from the open-ended questionnaires was used in the final study.

Miles (1979) pointed out the problem of informants reacting more negatively to the results of case studies than to survey results. This problem is not due to the use of case methodology. Negative reactions are caused by participants reacting to evidence about themselves. Similar hostile reactions occur when survey respondents are asked to review their results. Regardless of the research methodology employed, negative reactions are less likely when informants are asked to review results in aggregate or summary form (Yin 1981a). An approach that often leads to reinterpretation and correction is treat ones subjects as collaborators (Whyte 1973).

When confronted with individual data, respondents complain about not having enough time to explain their actions and statements, being misunderstood, and being misinterpreted (Yin 1981a). Stein (1952) suggested the following strategies to prevent these problems: avoid psychological speculation, focus on repetitive patterns of behavior, and quote or summarize interpretations by participants of their actions.

An alternative and less-reactive review procedure is to use a panel of experts. Between 1980 and 1981, the US Office of Technology Assessment used twenty or more reviewers to examine each of seventeen different case studies of medical technologies. The wide variety of backgrounds of the reviewers provided a variety of different insights about the cases.

4. Validation by predictive discrimination or hypothesis formulation and testing (Foreman 1948).

5. Validation of the data by allowing several investigations to come independently to their conclusions, thus increasing the number of observations of the same event (Foreman 1948; Van Maanen 1988; Yin 1994, 2003). Patton (1990) suggests examining rival explanations thoroughly by carefully collecting as extensive data as possible. In this manner, another form of triangulation occurs across projects. "Interproject triangulation," as Bonoma (1985) calls it, or separate studies of the same phenomena in different contexts by researchers using different methods, can produce confirmatory results. This technique is limited by comparability problems between studies.

F. ANALYSIS OF EVIDENCE FROM MULTIPLE CASES

The case survey technique is one of the best-defined and most-utilized approaches to between case analysis and multicase studies, which are frequently used in public administration research

(Brower et al. 2000), even though the case survey method is not so well-defined as to serve as the formal, fully developed set of rules for multicase analysis that Kennedy (1979) called for ago.

The case survey approach requires identification of similar behaviors and events in different cases. This process starts with the selection of behaviors and events that are central to the research topic. This is followed by identification of a number of case studies dealing with this common topic. The number of cases must be large enough to support cross-case tabulations.

How many cases are enough? There is no definite answer to this question, but this requirement cannot always be satisfied. Large numbers of cases have been available for some studies where the case survey technique has been used. For example, Yin and Heald (1975) studied 269 case studies in their examination of urban decentralization, and Yin et al. (1976) used data from 140 cases in their study of urban innovations. Some successful studies have used far fewer cases. For example, Bigelow and Stone (1995) used four cases in their study of pressures on community health care centers. Derthick (1972) used seven cases in her study of new towns. DiMaggio and Useem (1979) examined twenty-five cases in their study of research utilization, and Yin and White's (1984) study of computer utilization in schools is based on only twelve cases. Other case surveys either have used too few cases or have suffered from the fact that too few cases with relevant content existed. For instance, Miles' (1979) project attempted to follow the case survey approach, but the results were difficult to interpret because there were too few cases to do this successfully.

Once a number of cases have been identified, common behaviors and events are tabulated. This facilitates comparison of results and the search for common patterns of behavior. A multicase study may synthesize material from each of the cases into a more meaningful whole rather than present material from each of the cases separately.

Numerous examples of multicase-based research exist both in the public administration literature and in studies having a more general management focus than just the public sector. For instance, Kaufman's (1981) study of six federal bureau chiefs contains a synthesis of materials from each of the individuals studied. The focus is on important topics, such as how they review information, make decisions, and interact with and motivate staff. In dealing with these topics, examples are drawn from the behaviors of the individual administrators, but these specific cases are not the major focus. Synthesis and material unique to separate cases may be used in the same study (Agranoff and Radin 1991; Bailey 1992; Coggin 1986; Patton 1990; Sjoberg et al. 1991; Yin 1994, 2003). Herriott and Gross' (1979) book *The Dynamics of Planned Educational Change* contains ten chapters, five describing change in five different school systems and the other five chapters describing cross-case issues. Similarly, Peters and Waterman's (1982) now-famous book, entitled *In Search of Excellence*, contains materials drawn from case studies of sixty successful, large corporations. Each substantive chapter is a cross-case analysis.

The case survey approach has not been perfected yet. First, the number of factors worth examining is usually large relative to the number of relevant case studies available. This results in a shortage of sampling points, which makes problematic if not impossible the identification of statistical interaction effects that might confound analytical results. Second, focusing on single factors in isolation from their case study context may oversimplify the phenomenon being studied. Third, the case survey method treats case studies as individual data points or observations to be tabulated.

G. META-ANALYSIS OF CASES

In 1975 Yin and Yates employed meta-analysis of 48 case studies as a basis for their study of urban services and citizen participation. More recently, Jensen and Rodgers (2001) proposed using meta-analysis as a means of cumulating the findings of case studies. Since Glass (1976) introduced meta-analysis, this methodology has become a widely used method for summarizing research. Meta-analysis emphasizes objective observation and critical evaluation. It has been adopted in a wide variety of fields, ranging from social science to medicine

(Cooper 1998; Davey Smith 2001; Eden 2002; Egger et al. 2001; Glass 1983; Hunt 1997; Hunter and Schmidt 1990, 1996, 2004; Hunter et al. 1982; Lipsey and Wilson 2001; Mulrow and Cook 1998; Petitti 2000; Rosenthal 1991; Schulze 2004; Schulze et al. 2003; Stangl and Berry 2000; Stanley and Jarrell 1989; Sutton et al. 2000; Van der Bergh et al. 1997; Whitehead 2002; Wolf 1986). This method is widely used in the social sciences (Bausell et al. 1995).

Meta-analysis enables a researcher to analyze findings from multiple studies in an effort to assess their generalizability. It also enables the researcher to make a more objective appraisal of the evidence, which can resolve uncertainty and disagreement about the meaning of cases not possible with single case analyses. Heterogeneity between study results may be explored and sometimes explained. Meta-analysis can reduce the probability of false negative results. Use of a large number of individual studies in meta-analysis makes it possible to test a priori hypotheses. Promising research questions to be addressed in future studies may be generated, and the sample size needed in future studies may be calculated accurately (Hedges and Olkin 1985; Hunter et al. 1982; Jensen and Rodgers 2001; Lipsey and Wilson 2001; Miller et al. 1991).

There are a few examples of meta-analysis in the *PAR*. For example, Wolf (1993) used meta-analysis to examine forty-four case studies (85 observations) of bureaucratic effectiveness. Wolf (1997) examined entrepreneurial reforms in 170 case studies conducted in federal agencies. Studies appearing in other venues also give some idea of the number of studies analyzed. Pinello (1999) analyzed eighty-four studies that examined the link between judges' political party affiliation and the judicial ideology. Wise (2001) analyzed 109 studies of effects of diversity in the workplace.

Meta-analyses exist in the public administration and related literatures, but comparatively speaking, there are not large numbers of them. They include the cost-effectiveness of public and private prisons (Pratt and Maahs 1999); leadership effectiveness and gender (Eagly et al. 1995); the spiral of silence (Glynn et al. 1997); motor vehicle safety inspection effectiveness (Thompson et al. 1991); effectiveness of workplace heterogeneity programs (Wise, 2001); the impact of funding on public school student achievement (Greenwald et al. 1996); modeling public sector performance (Moynihan and Pandey 2003); impacts of charismatic leaders on organizations (DeGroot et al. 2000); team effectiveness (Gully et al. 2002); work team homogeneity needs (Bowers 2000); ethics education (Haws 2001); the impact of job satisfaction and individual job performance (Petty et al. 1984); incentive effects on survey response (Church 1993); effectiveness of pregnancy prevention programs for teens (Franklin et al. 1997); the effectiveness of HIV interventions (Logan et al. 2002); how the presence or absence of fathers affects children (Amato and Gilbreth 1999); and the impact of ideology on judicial decisions (Pinello 1999). Of interest to MPA programs is Kuncel et al. (2001) examination of GRE prediction of graduate student performance. Googling meta-analysis on June 4, 2005 produced 1,600,000 hits; meta-analysis AND public administration produced 8,930 hits on June 3, 2005.

To use meta-analysis, a researcher starts by defining a research question whose nature defines applicable cases (Wyatt and Guly 2002). For example, we might want to determine the effectiveness of public sector organizational development procedures. Next, case studies, which fit the research question would be identified. Each case is a data point for the meta-analysis. Then, the information in each case would be content-analyzed so that it could be coded. Imprecise reporting of results could make this process difficult. In organization development, whether in the public or private sector, many studies do not report outcome measures consisting of hard data. Standardization requirements might remedy some of these problems (Brower et al. 2000; Denzin and Lincoln 1994, 2000; Jensen and Rodgers 2001; Hodson 1999).

Statistical findings, such as the relationship between two variables, can be convertible into a common measure of effect size—the Pearson product–moment correlation (Cohen 1988; Cooper 1998; Rosenthal et al. 2000; Wolf 1986). Usually, relationships between two variables based on percentages or proportions, cross-tabulations, correlation coefficients, partial-correlation coefficients, regression coefficients, and probit analysis can be converted into effect sizes. However, failure to report data necessary to make these calculations means that a study or case must be excluded from the meta-analysis. For example, if standard errors, t statistics, or degrees of freedom are not reported for regression coefficients, then conversion is not possible. Similarly, if statistics are used that cannot be converted, such as discriminate function analysis, path analysis, or difference of medians, then these cases cannot be included in a meta-analysis.

Adjustments are made for sample size and sampling error (Hunter and Schmidt 1990, 2004). Common analyses include the analysis of exact probabilities (p values) (Rosenthal 1991), analysis of effect sizes d (Glass 1976; Hedges and Olkin 1985), and analysis of effect sizes r (Hunter and Schmidt 1990, 2004; Rosenthal et al. 2000, 2000; Schulze 2004, Schulze et al. 2003). Confidence intervals are calculated for the population effect size (Shadish and Haddock 1994). Results are reported with blobbograms and odds ratios, or 95% credibility and confidence intervals (Whitener 1990). Heterogeneity statistics indicate if the effect sizes all come from one distribution. If there is a significant amount of heterogeneity, then moderator analyses can be done to explain the variance (Hedges 1994). Two different kinds of statistical analyses are used to confirm moderator variables. One method disaggregates studies into subpopulations suggested by the prospective moderators and then examines the credibility intervals of the subgroups (Whitener 1990). Fixed-effect models are used more than random-effect models (Hedges 1994; Hedges and Vevea 1998; Overton 1998). Another method is meta-regression analysis (Steel and Ovalle 1984; Stanley and Jarrell 1989; Phillips and Goss 1995). Other sources discussing statistics used in meta-analysis include Lipsey and Wilson (2001) and Wang and Bushman (1999).

Meta-analysis is not a simple, easy answer or a panacea. There are instances in which meta-analyses have produced wrong answers and have resulted in some combination of the following issues. Problems existing with meta-analysis include having an adequate number of cases, positive bias in publication (Rosenthal 1979), availability of unpublished studies, quality of cases selected, heterogeneity of cases, and bias in case selection. The rationale involved in making decisions about the inclusion and exclusion of cases should be included with the analysis. Funnel analysis can be used to determine if bias exists in case selection. Issues such as the number of cases or their size, size of subgroups, and effect sizes are concerns. Sensitivity analyses can be done to assess the adequacy of subgroup analyses, and validity concerns must be addressed in multiple ways (Davey Smith and Egger 1999; Davey Smith et al. 1997a, 1997b; Egger and Davey Smith 1995, 1997, 1998; Egger et al. 1996, 1998, 2002, 2003; Greenhalgh 1997; Hunter and Schmidt 1990; Le Lorier et al. 1997; Murphy 2003; Naylor 1997; Naylor and Smith 1998; Rosenthal and DiMatteo 2001; Weed 2001; Wyatt and Guly 2002).

H. Conclusion

Case research offers significant opportunities to the public administration researcher. First, it allows investigation of a number of important public administration problems that are not amenable to investigation with other techniques because of their complexity.

Second, such indepth analyses promote understanding of details and theory-building. Third, the depth of knowledge gained from case research feeds back into other activities, such as teaching and consulting, and also to theory development and testing efforts beyond the initial research project itself. Fourth, case research can bring public administration scholars into closer contact with public administration practitioners. In addition, case-cluster, multi-case, and meta-analysis can add methodological support to the use of case analyses.

Significant problems remain for researchers using case research methods to study public administration phenomena. These difficulties include conceptual, executional, and political problems. Conceptually, it is easy to advocate a high-quality research judgment, but difficult to cultivate or improve judgment except by doing research projects. Moreover, each data point in case research (a case study) can be an extensive and expensive venture, making the acquisition of expertise arduous and time-consuming. Access to organizations appropriate for the research objectives may not be as easy as obtaining a mailing list or the resources necessary to send out a mail-back survey. Individual case studies are not necessarily as expensive as a major survey project, but the necessity for repeated case development in the theory–data–theory validation cycle often requires a more substantial investment of time and funds than other methods. Politically, because the major thrust of much recent public administration research is toward deductive, quantitative, and causally directed research, the researcher may have a greater challenge in demonstrating the benefits and necessity of qualitative methods for the problem studied.

In sum, there is a need for more use of the case method in public administration research. This is particularly appropriate when complex observational tasks exist and where little theoretical material exists to use as a starting point.

III. INTERVIEWS

Interviews are frequently used to collect data in public administration research. This method of gathering data has been used throughout the history of public administration research. For example, references to interviews began to appear in the *Public Administration Review* from its beginning and are still used as a reference tool today, albeit usually along with other research methods. One reason for the popularity of interviewing is that this technique can be used within other methodological approaches such as case analysis, participant observation, and survey research.

The term interview is commonly used in two different ways. Often interview refers to a face-to-face or telephone interview used to collect survey data. This is a widely-used technique. In survey interviews, each subject or individual interviewed is asked an identical set of questions, which are presented in the same order. Usually, probes or follow-up questions are limited in number, if they are used at all. In addition, probes are usually predefined, which may limit their appropriateness and usefulness. Major differences between a survey interview and a mail-back survey are that the interviewer can make sure that the right person participates in the survey, and that the questions are answered completely and in the proper order. The interviewer can also present questions to individuals that are difficult to present in written form.

The second type of interview is sometimes called elite or specialized interviewing (Burgess 1988; Dexter 1970). This type of interview is used to collect data from a more-limited group of individuals called key informants. Key informants are individuals who, because of their position, are likely to have been involved either in making a decision of interest or in carrying it out. The special knowledge and unique experience they are likely to have distinguishes key informants from other organizational members and the public in general. This special knowledge may enable them to comment on or verify the accuracy of a researcher's initial interpretations of information gathered during the course of a research project (Dexter 1970; Fetterman 1989, 1998; Heard 1950; Lofland and Lofland 1995; McCracken 1988; Seldon and Pappworth 1983; Spector 1980).

The specialized interview differs from the survey interview in at least four ways. First, the number of subjects is usually limited. Rather than interview many subjects selected in a sample designed to guarantee a statistically acceptable level of accuracy in describing a population of some kind, subjects are selected because of the position they have held or because of their experiences. Second, the questions asked in each interview are not necessarily the same, and are in fact likely to differ in significant ways, depending on the different positions and experiences of each subject. For instance, questions are often open-ended and designed to get the subject to talk in his or her own terms about a topic. Topics and details are likely to focus on what the subject believes is significant. Third, probes are not predefined, and probes differ in number and content from subject to subject. Fourth, the interviewer can adjust the interview in a variety of ways and can help the respondent by answering his or her questions as well (Burgess 1988; Cassell 1988; Dexter 1970; Downs et al. 1980; Fetterman 1989, 1998; Heard 1950; Lofland and Lofland 1995; McCracken 1988; Moyser 1988; Spector 1980; Thomas 1995).

The type of interview of interest here is the elite or specialized interview, since it has been widely used in public administration research. This section examines the following aspects of interviewing: advantages of face-to-face interviewing, disadvantages of interviewing, training interviewers, background work, who should conduct an interview, interview settings, gaining access, the interview process, establishing rapport, neutrality and rapport, interview formats, types of questions, the need for probes, types of probes, sources of error, multiple sessions, sensitive questions, confrontation, and recording and note taking.

A. ADVANTAGES OF INTERVIEWING

Face-to-face interviews offer the following significant advantages: first, rapport with the respondent may be easier to establish than through other research techniques, and hence respondent co-operation may be relatively high. Second, it is more difficult for a respondent to terminate a face-to-face interview than to end some other kind of data-gathering effort. For this reason, personal interviews usually last much longer than telephone interviews. Third, visual aids can be used. This means that complex questions can be asked which either cannot be asked or are awkward to ask in mail-back or telephone interviews. Face-to-face interviews are usually more accurate than other data-collection methods.

Face-to-face interviews are more effective than telephone interviews. Significant differences include higher response rates, longer interviews, fewer unanswered questions, and more detailed responses to open-ended questions (Groves and Kahn 1979; Jordan et al. 1980; Lofland and Lofland 1995; McCracken 1988; Quinn et al. 1980). Personal interviews may result in interviewees giving more complete answers than telephone interviews, especially for sensitive or controversial topics such as alcohol and drug use (Aquilino and LoSciuto 1990; Johntson et al. 1989; Mensch and Kandel 1988).

These differences may occur because face-to-face interviews proceed at a slower pace, allow more personal interaction between interviewer and interviewee, and give the interviewer the opportunity to provide more feedback to the subject than any other research media (Groves 1978; Groves and Kahn 1979; Singer 1981; Thomas 1995). This is an opportunity for the interviewer to encourage reflection and to draw them out. These differences occur for all subjects, but are even more pronounced for older subjects than younger ones (Herzog et al. 1983).

Personal interviews are more enjoyable for the interviewee and produce more complete data than mail or telephone surveys. However, personal interviews are much more expensive than mail or telephone surveys (Dillman 1978). Interviewees often find the experience satisfying (Coleman 1996; Oakley 1981, 2000). These differences of enjoyment and completeness are both larger and even more important when collecting sensitive data (Lee 1993; Mangione et al. 1982). These facts may justify the additional cost of face-to-face interviews.

Interviews can be used to connect with hard-to-reach populations. For example, members of violent youth gangs were interviewed to determine where they hang out as a basis for mapping gang locations (Tita et al. 2005). Similarly, homeless persons lack a permanent address and phone number. Contacting them may require face-to-face interviews because other methods are impractical (Calsyn et al. 1993; Mensch and Kandel 1988; Rosenheck et al. 2001; Roll et al. 1999; Zlotnick et al. 1999).

Most important, perhaps, is the wealth of information interviews produce. Results from interviews and oral histories include personal narratives and stories, in addition to straightforward question–answer materials. Personal narratives and stories may be more detailed than information gleaned in question–answer sessions. Often, they place content in a unique personal context and include a wealth of detail and priceless examples. It seems to the author that everyone has a story to tell. Whether they are willing to tell it or not is another matter.

Personal narratives and stories are of increasing value and frequency in public administration research and have value in connecting research with practice (Brower et al. 2000; Dobel 2003;

Dodge Ospina and Foldy 2005; Hummel 1991; Kelly 1994; Kelly and Maynard-Moody 1993; Lin 1998; Maynard-Moody and Musheno 2003; Newland 2000; Rubin and Rubin 1995; Schmidt 1994; White 1999). Examples of the use of narratives abound in public administration and organizational behavior (Allen 1990; Ban 1995; Bryson and Crosby 1992; Burns 1978; Chrislip and Larson 1994; Coble-Vinzant and Crothers 1998; Cohen et al. 1997; Crosby 1999; Cunningham et al. 2005; Czarniawska 1997; Drath and Palus 1994; Ewick and Silbey 1995; Fiske 1993; Gaskell and Bauer 2000; Heifetz 1994; Herzon and Claunch 1997; Hummel 1991; Hunt 1984; Huxham and Vangen 2000; Jennings 1987; Kellerman 1999; Kelly 1994; Kelly and Maynard-Moody 1993; Lipsky 1980; Luke 1998; Lynn and Heinrich 2000; Maynard-Moody and Musheno 2003; Meindl 1995; Pfeffer 1997; Prottas 1979; Roe 1994; Rubin 1992; Rubin and Rubin 1995; Schall 1997; Schram and Neisser 1997; Stafford 1996; Terry 2003; Tetreault 2000; Tierney 1987; Yanow 1996; Yeager 2005).

B.   DISADVANTAGES OF INTERVIEWING

Problems also exist in interviewing. Interviewers need to be aware of several potential problems, including the possibility of leading the subject and communicating their own attitudes and biases to the subject. For instance, something as simple as a frown or a raised eyebrow can convey a sense of disagreement or skepticism. Tone of voice and statements which are neutral to the interviewer may appear to the interviewee to be judgmental, biased, offensive, and that roused suspicion can negatively affect an interview or precipitously end it (Heard 1950; Spencer 1982).

Social desirability explains the tendency of interview and survey respondents to shape their answers to please or satisfy the interviewer. Social desirability is exacerbated by the stereotyping threat can occur when an individual is interviewed by a person of a different race, which generates pressure to disconfirm and to avoid being judged by negative and potentially degrading stereotypes. Stereotype threat interferes with the processing of information (Davis and Silver 2003). Davis and Silver believe that social desirability adequately explains attitudinal and opinion questions, but not factual issues.

Sensitive questions may affect an interviewee's willingness to answer, as well as the extent and accuracy of the answers. Subjects may withhold negative information from an interviewer based on perceived sensitivity of the topic and social desirability of their answers (Krysan et al. 1994; Sudman and Bradburn 1974). One solution to this problem is use of a self-administered questionnaire (SAQ) during the interview. Research shows that during interviews, subjects may give more complete answers to SAQs about sensitive topics than direct questioning (Tourangeau and Smith 1996).

When sensitive topics are involved, results are affected by the data-collection method used. For example, reported drug use of interviewees was highest when obtained through a SAQ included in a personal interview, next-highest when obtained through questions asked in a personal interview, and lowest when data were collected through telephone interviews (Aquilino 1994; Fendrich and Vaughn 1994; Gfroerer and Hughes 1991; Turner, Lessler, and Devore 1992; Turner, Lessler, and Gfroerer 1992).

Face-to-face interviewing is time-consuming and expensive. This is especially true when subjects are geographically dispersed and when multiple visits with subjects are required to complete each interview (Rainey, Pandey, and Bozeman 1995). For these reasons, face-to-face interviewing is more expensive than most other research techniques.

C.   TRAINING INTERVIEWERS

Interviewers should be trained by using role-play or simulated interviews, video-recording their performances, and then critiquing their performances (Jones 1959). Several practice sessions work better than just one session. Training sessions in which neophyte interviewers get to see an experienced interviewer at work (either live or on videotape), followed by a critique or review session, are extremely effective preparation for would be interviewers.

Training for interviewers needs to include information about the speed and ease with which subjects make judgments about interviewers. The basis for these judgments need be no more than the tone of voice or pitch; amount of variation in pitch; rate of speech, volume, or degree of loudness; and the number and duration of the pauses the interviewer makes (Sharf and Lehman 1984). The interviewer's speech patterns affect the subject's reactions to him or her, and, in turn, the interviewer's ability to successfully conduct interviews (Dillman et al. 1976; O'Neil et al. 1979). Speech patterns also affect other forms of human behavior, such as patient referrals (Milmoe et al. 1967) and patient–psychiatrist interaction (Goldman-Eisler 1952). Nonverbal behavior and idiosyncrasies can also affect the effectiveness of any communicator, including interviewers (Mehrabian and Williams 1969; Wiener et al. 1972). Interviewer training might include feedback and corrective training based on an analysis of the interviewer trainee's speech patterns.

Training will raise the capabilities of interviewers and their expectations of success. These expectations are important because they affect an interviewer's success rate. Positive expectations about the ease of getting individuals to participate results in both a higher level of participation and more complete interviews. Positive expectations increase with the amount of experience of the interviewer (Singer et al. 1983).

A variety of techniques can be used in training interviewers. Some of these training techniques include individual study in which trainees administer the interview to themselves, written exercises, demonstration interviews, roundrobin interviewing, trial interviews for pairs and trios of trainees, interviews with uninformed respondents, and interviews with prearranged respondents (Parten 1966; Weinberg 1983).

Individual study involves the interviewer reviewing the interview guide and any other material by him- or herself. If an interviewee needs specialized substantive knowledge in order to be able to intelligently discuss the study topic with an interviewee, this is an effective way to acquire that knowledge. Weinberg (1983) provides the example of the interviewer of drug-users having to learn about drug paraphernalia, dosages, and supply sources in order to be able to interview addicts. One way of learning the questions is for the trainees to administer the questionnaire to themselves. This results in familiarity with and understanding of these materials (Weinberg 1983). Ideally, each interviewer will have these materials virtually memorized before they conduct their first interview. Knowing relevant background impresses the subject, since the interviewer knows what he or she wants, speaks knowledgeably of the subject, and understands what the subject is saying. In addition, this knowledge eliminates the task of having to keep up with an interview guide while taking notes, and it eliminates loss of eye contact and distraction while trying to converse or listen and simultaneously read the next question (Heard 1950). This is especially important, because listening carefully and giving the interviewee one's undivided attention are noticed by the interviewee, leading to more willing participation and detailed answers (Anderson and Jack 1991; Hess 2001; Undheim 2003).

Written and oral exercises can be used to determine what the interviewer has learned from individual study. These exercises also serve as a review and give the interviewer a chance to apply what they have learned in answering questions about hypothetical situations. The trainer should be able to tell from an exercise if the would-be interviewer has read the material and remembers it, and if desired skills have been mastered (Weinberg 1983).

In a demonstration interview, a role-player takes the part of the subject and an instructor conducts the interview while students watch. This is followed by a critique and discussion, in which positive and negative aspects of the interview are pointed out and student questions are answered. The critique session is valuable, because trainees are more adept at picking up the obvious positive and negative aspects of the interview process, but lack the experience to notice the more subtle events. These include facial expressions and other forms of body language, voice tone, and the phraseology used by the interviewer and subject. Every new interviewer should have the opportunity to conduct trial interviews before conducting real interviews in the field (Parten 1966).

The critique process and amount of trainee learning will be enhanced if the trial interviews are audio- or videotaped and the trainees can either hear or see and hear what they did during each session. Weinberg (1983) suggests using tape recorders so that interviewers will become more conscious of and improve the pace at which they present interview questions and the rate at which they move through the interview. In addition, use of audio- and videotapes is an effective means of training interviewers how to recognize when probes or follow-up questions are needed and how to effectively phrase follow-up questions.

Roundrobin interviewing involves the trainer or a role-player acting as the subject, with each interviewer trainee asking some of the questions in turn. The whole group of trainees listens to the interview. This is followed by a critique and a feedback session (Weinberg 1983).

One way to conduct trial interviews is to have students work in pairs, with one trainee taking the role of the subject while the other works as the interviewer. Interviewing in trios involves a third trainee acting as an observer and providing feedback after each session. Trainees switch roles in these designs until each trainee has played each role at least once (Weinberg 1983). These techniques can be used to review sections of the interview guide or individual questions that a trainee had problems with or wants to practice again.

Practice interviews with uninformed respondents, with prearranged, recruited, and paid subjects, and with paid role-players are real interviews except that the subject is not one of those who would be included in the actual study (Weinberg 1983). The interviewee must be someone whom the trainee does not know. Subjects usually are friends of the trainer or of other trainees and paid role-players.

D. BACKGROUND WORK

Those who have conducted some interviews suggest using other sources rather than interviews to gain factual information that the subject will expect the interviewer to know. Often, background information can be gained from published sources, such as newspaper accounts and official records. For example, much can be learned about prominent subjects and their activities from public records (Heard 1950; Van Schendelen 1984). The major weakness of these sources is that they do not cover everything, all topics are not covered equally well, and they are usually not indexed. If background information is not available from newspaper reports and other published reports, then interviews can be used to gather this information. However, these interviews should be with persons other than the key or most important interview subjects. Key subjects should be saved for questions that no one else can answer (Dexter 1970; Fetterman 1989, 1998; Heard 1950). For example, rather than conduct initial interviews with key decision-makers, it would be more effective to start with members of their staff.

Background information can be just as important as information gained from an interview. The interviewer needs this information to convey to the subject that he or she is prepared and seriously interested in the topic. In addition, having background information in hand before an interview means that the time of the interviewer and of the subject will not be wasted on background questions. This information is needed in order to ask intelligent questions of the subject and to understand the subject's statements. Background information makes it possible to maintain the flow of the interview without having to interrupt by asking background questions, and to concentrate on meaningful follow-up questions (Ball 1967; Cassell 1988; Dexter 1970; Fetterman 1989, 1998; Heard 1950; Lee 1993; McCracken 1988). Background information should make it easier to identify additional information and details needed, such as the explanations of how and why decisions were made. Moreover, background information may contain details that the subject skips or cannot remember. This is especially likely when the topic is a technical matter, such as a budget or a schedule.

E. Who Should Conduct an Interview?

Substantial evidence suggests that the quality of an interview's content is affected by the interviewer. Prior experience affects the interviewer's ability to get individuals to participate in an interview and the completeness of the interview. Interviewers with more experience do better (Burstein et al. 1985; Groves et al. 1992), but there appears to be a threshold effect beyond which large amounts of improvement do not occur. Improvement in interview performance occurs across the first year of experience. More than one year of experience does not add a significant amount of additional improvement to the interviewer's performance (Singer et al. 1983).

Interviews conducted by an individual of the same gender, race, and social status as the interviewee are more accurate than those conducted by others. This is especially the case when questions of a sensitive nature are asked. Some studies report that matching interviewer–interviewee race and gender results in higher response rates or cooperation (Brunswick 1984, 1991). Gender of interviewer has shown significant effects on reported sexual behavior reports (Catania et al. 1996). Similarly, some studies have repeatedly shown that white interviewers cannot get accurate interviews from blacks when sensitive questions are asked (Grimshaw 1969, 1970; Schaffer 1980; Williams 1964, 1968).

Interviewer characteristics make a difference in interview results, and these effects may be quite large. Some researchers report that men and women answer questions differently depending on the gender of the interviewer (Groves and Fultz 1985; Johnson and DeLamater 1976; Kane and Maculay 1993; Morin 1990). Men and women were more likely to state more egalitarian, gender-related attitudes and more criticism of gender-related inequalities to female interviewers than to male interviewers (Huddy and Bracciodieta 1992; Kane and Maculay 1993). In addition, Kane and Maculay (1993) found that men and women gave more feminist, Democratic, liberal, and anti-authoritarian responses to women than to male interviewers. Similarly, Huddy et al. (1997) found that respondents were more likely to provide pro-feminist answers to female interviewers, and this effect was stronger for controversial issues. When interviewed by women, both male and female respondents report more symptoms of depression, substance abuse, and conduct disorders than respondents interviewed by men (Pollner 1998). Pollner believes that these differences in interview results occur because "female interviewers may create conditions more conducive to disclosure and be perceived as more sympathetic than male interviewers" (1998). Other researchers found no difference in answers to questions based on gender of the interviewer. However, they also reported differences in the amount and nature of information volunteered by interviewees, with women volunteering much more information to female interviewers than to their male counterparts (Padfield and Procter 1996).

Race of interviewer can strongly affect interview results (Anderson et al. 1988a, 1988b; Campbell 1981; Cotter et al. 1982; Davis 1997a, 1997b; Finkel, Guterbock, and Borg 1991; Hatchett and Schuman 1975–1976; Hyman et al. 1954; Schaffer 1980; Schuman and Converse 1971). Some researchers report that blacks respond differently to white than to black interviewers, and that whites respond differently to white interviewers than to black ones. For example, Anderson et al. (1988b) found that when blacks were interviewed by whites, they were much more likely to express warmth and closeness toward whites than when blacks were interviewed by blacks. Similarly, black respondents were more accommodating and deferential to white interviewers, even to the point of taking contradictory stances in evaluations of political figures and political parties. In same-race interviews, their responses were reversed (Davis 1997a; Meislin 1987). Likewise, race-of-interviewer effects occurred in an election poll during the 1989 Virginia gubernatorial election between a black Democrat and a white Republican. White respondents interviewed by black interviewers were significantly more likely to state a preference for Wilder than their peers who were questioned by white interviewers (Finkel, Guterbock, and Borg 1991). Campbell (1981) found that race affected interview responses only on race-related issues. Black interviewees give responses that are more pro-white with white interviewers than with black interviewers, and the opposite is true for the white interviewees. Similar effects occur when whites are interviewed by blacks (Hurtado 1994; Reese et al. 1986; Weeks and Moore 1981).

Similarly, black and white subjects tend to avoid responses that will offend an interviewer of the other race, and they tend to be franker with an interviewer of their own race. However, these differences are likely to occur only when questions are asked that deal with race or race relations (Athey et al. 1960; Bailey et al. 1978; Campbell 1981; Chandler 1990; Cotter et al. 1982; Dohrenwend et al. 1968; Fetterman 1989, 1998; Groves and Kahn 1979; Groves and Magilavy 1980; Hanson and Marks 1958; Hatchett and Schuman 1975; Hyman et al. 1954; Kish 1962; Lee 1993; Schuman and Converse 1971; Singer and Kohnke-Aguirre 1979; Stock and Hochstim 1951; Sudman and Bradburn 1974; Sudman et al. 1974; Tucker 1983; Weiss 1975).

One explanation for race affecting interview results is social desirability. This occurs when an interviewee tailors their responses to please or satisfy the interviewer. Davis and Silver (2003) provide an alternative explanation called "stereotype threat." Stereotype threat consists of pressure to disconfirm and avoid being judged by negative and degrading stereotypes. They found that black respondents gave fewer correct answers to questions about politics when interviewed by a white interviewer than when questioned by someone of the same race. They believe that "stereotype threat" caused this by interfering with the interviewee's ability to process information or think clearly.

Race-of-interviewer effects also occur for other racial combinations of interviewee and interviewer, including Asians, Cubans, Hispanics, and Native Americans, when racially-sensitive questions are asked. For example, Reese et al. (1986) reported that interviewer ethnicity (white versus Hispanic) affected responses to questions relating to the culture of the interviewer. When Anglos were asked questions by Hispanics about aspects of Mexican-American life, they responded more sympathetically than when they were asked the same questions by fellow Anglos. In addition, the language used by the interviewer can affect interview results. Lee (2001) found that respondents' answers differed depending on whether the interview was conducted in Spanish or English. Race-of-interviewer effects usually do not occur when less-sensitive questions are involved (Weeks and Moore 1981).

The issue of race of interviewer and interviewee affected the Works Project Administration (WPA) collection of slave narratives in 1936–1938 and slave narratives collected under other auspices. This collection is housed at the Library of Congress and is available online (2001). When race of interviewer and interviewee differ, interview responses may be more positive or acceptable than when race of the interviewer and subject race are the same. This bias does not always occur, but depends on the subject and how questions are asked. Multiple scholars using the WPA interviews point out that the interviewer may be a source of bias when race of interviewer and subject differ if the interviewer interprets, edits, and censors responses so that they will be more positive and acceptable to society at large (Blassingame 1972, 1975, 1977; Rawick 1977, 1979; Yetman 2001).

An interviewer's clothing and personal grooming can have important impacts on the interview process and affect interview content. Long hair and sideburns, a beard and moustache may serve as a basis for the subject drawing conclusions about the interviewer's political preferences and personal habits (Babbie 1983). Whether these conclusions are correct or not is beside the point. These characteristics are enough to support a set of stereotypic conclusions which cause changes in the subject's responses to the interviewer that otherwise would not occur. This may occur because the subject's conclusions about the interviewer affect the amount of trust that the subject has in the interviewer (Fetterman 1989, 1998; Johnson 1975; Lee 1993; Van Schendelen 1984; Williams 1964). To avoid or minimize this potential problem, the dress and grooming of the interviewer should be congruent with those of the subject (Groves et al. 1992; Van Schendelen 1984; Williams 1964).

Interviewer appearance is important because it can affect the interviewee reactions and interview results. For example, Bateman and Mawby (2004) found that altering the appearance of an interviewer (wearing either formal or casual clothing) and changing the amount of information provided can have significant impacts on interview responses.

F. Interview Settings

Both Dexter (1970) and Douglas (1976) emphasize the importance of the interview setting in establishing and maintaining rapport. Interviews should be conducted one-on-one in private. A comfortable setting, free from interruptions, works best. Subjects are not as candid as they otherwise would be when there is someone else present or when other persons can wander into the room (Downs et al. 1980; Parten 1966). A person's office or home may be suitable if potential interruptions can be controlled. This is difficult, because there are some persons whom the subject cannot or will not refuse to see or accept a phone call from (Dexter 1970; Van Schendelen 1984). Some individuals have work commitments, which preclude their ignoring interruptions. This conclusion is based on the author's experience interviewing fire and police chiefs, and high-ranking military officers with command responsibility that had to repeatedly stop and re-start interviews as they handled work responsibilities. For these reasons, an interviewee's office or a conference room will usually work better than a private home. An even better alternative may be quiet surroundings away from the respondent's place of work, which will put the subject at ease and avoid interruptions (Van Schendelen 1984). A quiet setting is essential for a successful interview. A telephone ringing in the background will destroy both the subject's and the interviewer's concentration (Parten 1966). Restaurants are too noisy, and it is impossible to control interruptions (Dexter 1970).

G. Gaining Access

Access can sometimes be a problem. Important persons may have little free time and may have already been interviewed by one or more other researchers. Those currently serving in office often will not grant interviews, especially on topics that could harm their careers. Occasionally, an individual will not grant interviews because of his or her own plans for the lecture circuit or a book.

The literature indicates that gaining access or 'entering the field' can be a difficult, time-consuming process (Chandler 1990; Fox and Lundman 1974; Johnson 1975; Lofland and Lofland 1995; Rossman and Rallis 1998). Establishing rapport with the subject may help (Clifford and Marcus 1986; Garfinkel 1967; Hammersley and Atkinson 1983; Hannerz 1969; Jorgensen 1989; Lee 1993; Marshall and Rossman 1995; Nader 1972; Seldon and Pappworth 1983; Van Maanen 1988). Background research may make this process easier (Coleman 1996; Hertz and Imber 1995; Lofland and Lofland 1995; Nader 1972; Ostrander 1993). Threatening information and questions that are likely to embarrass the interviewee should be avoided (Moyser 1988).

In addition, the interviewing literature suggests using professional and social contacts, social skills, inside connections, your status as a researcher and your employer's or sponsor's prestige to help gain access (Brannen 1987; Fox and Lundman 1974; Galaskiewicz, 1987; Hoffmann 1980; Thomas 1995; Winkler 1987). An influential person's introduction or request for cooperation to the subject may be effective (Spencer 1982). Friends and acquaintances or "allies," especially if powerful themselves, may provide introductions (Latour 1987; Lofland and Lofland 1995). Identity and trust play a key role in getting access (Johnson 1975; Lee 1993). Knowing someone, such as a common friend, or having common background or a common experience can establish a connection (Bernard 1994; Hoffmann 1980).

Sometimes name-dropping can be helpful. This might involve the name of a sponsor or the names of other elite subjects participating in the study. For example, Undheim (2003) suggests that "You need to praise, explain, impress, and respect all parties involved. Tell the secretary that you are currently talking to a lot of important people, and that you thought it would be fair to give your boss a chance to voice his opinion on this, as well."

Arranging to meet people in order to ask them for an interview face-to-face is effective (Winkler 1987). Meeting at the end of business hours for a drink may be effective with some individuals, but can be expensive (Winkler 1987).

If you have a person's name and contact information, then you can get in touch with them directly. Use multiple communications tools to contact elites, including the Internet, e-mail, cell phone, and other media (Castells 1996; Taylor 2000; Undheim 2003).

Public and private organizations use gatekeepers, such as secretaries, to protect the time of powerful persons. Gaining access requires overcoming their skepticism (Bernard 1994; Broadhead and Rist 1976; Castells 1996; Hammersley and Atkinson 1983; Jackall 1988; Smith 2001; Thomas 1995). Gatekeepers try to keep you out because they do not know who you are or what you want. Your task is to make your case and gain access. This can be accomplished by sending an interview proposal, consisting of a brief description of the project and of the researchers and a brief explanation of why it is important that a particular person talk with the interviewer (Undheim 2003). Gatekeeper effects are a source of bias (Groger Mayberry and Straker 1999). Gatekeepers are important decision-makers controlling access to people, information, and facilities and other resources (Mechanic 1962). The rule of thumb is always be friendly and polite to secretaries.

Persistence is important. "They will give in if you take the time. This happened several times with me. Once, after fifteen phone calls, three faxes, and three emails by two team-members, we finally got through. The secretary admitted she got 'tired' of us, and had to ask her boss at last" (Undheim 2003).

Subjects are not all equally important. They may differ in rank, responsibility, and involvement in the activities of interest. Obviously, one wants to interview the major participants or persons involved in the focal issues. Who these persons are is not always clear. For example, in doing research on the IranContra affair, interviews with the major participants would be crucial. Who are the major participants? (They are not listed in order to get to the point). There has been much debate about the importance of then-Vice President George H.W. Bush's role in the IranContra affair. Was he an important or influential participant or not? Would he be willing to be interviewed or not? If not, would it matter? Whether an interview with a former vice president is as important as an interview with other subjects is unclear. See the discussion of elite interviews and key informants in this chapter for more detail.

All subjects do not have the same knowledge of events. Some potential subjects are reflective and have excellent memories. They learn from their experiences and from what they observe around them. Others have either poor or selective memories. Some subjects may dissemble for one reason or another, refusing to share information or trying to spin the information they share. Regardless of the subjects' cooperation and apparent knowledge or lack of it, everything they share needs to be verified through other sources (Dexter 1970; Douglas 1976; Fetterman 1989, 1998; Heard 1950; McCracken 1988; Seidler 1974).

H. The Interview Process

The interview process consists of the following steps: sell the interview while introducing yourself and the project, establish rapport, follow the interview outline or questionnaire, make the interview process a pleasant experience for the subject, probe answers to minimize your own input, and thank the interviewee for his or her time and cooperation. This list is an outline which can be embellished in a variety of ways. For instance, follow-up visits can be used to check points that are unclear, to ask additional probes or additional questions that have occurred to you since the initial interview, to ask items that were missed, and to seek information about new questions (Dexter 1970; Downs et al. 1980; Fetterman 1989, 1998; Heard 1950; McCracken 1988).

Introducing yourself and the project and selling the potential interviewee or convincing him or her to participate are essential if an interview is going to occur. Each of the following items and combinations of items have been found useful in setting up an interview and convincing a potential interviewee to participate: sending a letter of introduction describing the project and introducing yourself, calling ahead to introduce yourself and the project and set up an appointment, using a letter of introduction from a friend or colleague of the subject or a reference to him in a letter or call of your own, and using a letter of introduction from an appropriate sponsor (Brannen 1987; Dexter 1970; Downs et al. 1980; Fetterman 1989, 1998; Hoffmann 1980; Holstein and Gubrium 1995; Lofland and Lofland 1995; Spencer 1982; Thomas 1995; Winkler 1987).

Specific appeals that can be used effectively in convincing a potential interviewee to participate include telling the individual that you need his or her help; telling him or her that their opinion is important and that is why it is sought; telling an individual that a friend, neighbor, or colleague has participated or suggested his or her name; telling the interviewee that the results will be published; telling him or her that the results will be used in making important decisions; and promising to share a copy of the results with them (Dexter 1970; Downs et al. 1980; Heard 1950; McCracken 1988; Undheim 2003).

Some subjects will agree to be interviewed only if the interviewer promises that nothing they say will be attributed to them. If a respondent wishes that they and their responses should remain anonymous, then the interviewer must be prepared to make such guarantees or forego the interview (Dexter 1970; Finch 1984; Heard 1950; Van Schendelen 1984; Spector 1980; Taylor and Bogdon 1984). Attribution and anonymity should always be discussed explicitly, and a specific agreement should be reached on these matters early in the interview process. It is helpful to send the interviewee a letter stating this understanding after the interview process has been completed (Dexter 1970).

1. Establishing Rapport

The reason for establishing rapport with the subject is so that the subject will feel comfortable enough that he or she will tell the interviewer information that is needed. Hopefully this information is more accurate, candid, and complete than what might otherwise be shared (Dexter 1956). Writing and calling the subject in advance to set up the interview can help establish rapport (Bergsten et al. 1984; Brunner and Carroll 1969; Dexter 1970; Sudman 1966; McCracken 1988). Tone and manner, or how one speaks and acts, can affect rapport. Explaining what the research project is about and why it is being done may ease a subject's anxiety about participating. Assuring the subject that his or her responses will be kept confidential and not used in a manner that will identify him or her also can help put him or her at ease. Asking subjects to talk about themselves and what they do usually relaxes them and causes them to open up. The subject matter is familiar to them, and they are comfortable with it and with the idea that the researcher is interested in them. An easy transition like this from familiar matters to the topics of the interview is far more effective than a barrage of questions from a total stranger (Dexter 1970; Fetterman 1989, 1998; Heard 1950; Kahn and Cannell 1963; McCracken 1988).

Another technique that may foster candor on the part of the respondent is for the interviewer to treat the subject as an equal or as a co-researcher (Dexter 1970; Heard 1950; London 1975; London and London 1966; Weiss 1994). An inappropriate superior attitude will destroy rapport between the interviewer and the subject (Dexter 1970).

2. Neutrality and Rapport

It is easier to say, "Start by establishing rapport with the subject," than it is to do it. For example, when she starts talking with a subject, an interviewer usually tries to establish that she holds a neutral view on the topic or that she has an open mind. This may be a good social science research practice, as making one's own position known will bias interview results (Heard 1950; Lenski and Leggett 1960; McCracken 1988; Smith and Hyman 1950; Wyatt and Campbell 1950), but it can create difficulty in establishing rapport. The reason for this is that subjects who are deeply and emotionally committed to their position on an issue may view any other position as being against them. This conclusion will bias their answers accordingly.

Another technique for establishing neutrality is to not tell, hint, say, or do anything that might inform the subject about how one feels or what one's position is on an issue (Dexter 1970; Fetterman 1989, 1998; Heard 1950; McCracken 1988; Williams 1968). Unfortunately, overcoming the difficulty of establishing that one is neutral on an issue is difficult, because subjects often make judgments about the interviewer's position on an issue before the interviewer says anything. These judgments may be based on how the interviewer is dressed and on his institutional affiliation. For example, a college professor may be viewed by some as a liberal simply because of his or her job, and the subject's answers to interview questions may reflect what he believes this liberal college professor wants to hear. The opposite can occur as well. A subject may see the college professor as part of the establishment and therefore as a conservative and give answers that reflect this bias. A hairstyle considerably longer than the subject's and wearing blue jeans on the job, or use of a job title and wearing a suit and tie, may be enough to create either of these impressions in the subject's mind and cause him or her to say what he thinks the interviewer wants to hear (Dexter 1956; Fetterman 1989, 1998; Thibaut and Kelley 1959).

Establishing rapport is more than putting someone at ease. It is a matter of getting them to share information with you. It is answering the question "Why should I talk with you?" Perhaps, it is getting them to tell their unique story for the first time, or to tell it again for the "umpteenth" time. Dexter (1956), Dollard (1937), Douglas (1976), and Kinsey (1948) suggest listening to the subject's speech and carefully choosing and using the terminology that the subject uses. Use of these key words tells the subject that the interviewer shares her perspective. The rationale underlying this approach is the fact that the interviewer can be neutral for most subjects only within the subject's frame of reference (Dexter 1956). Unfortunately, this approach is not without risk, since it involves loss of neutrality and deception of the subject. The more the subject's words and phrases are used, the more this may bias interview results. It may be true that a neutral position is viewed as a hostile one, and that the subject may not share as much information and that the content of information shared will differ, but suppose the subject changes their responses in order to agree with the interviewer in these circumstances and takes an even more extreme position than they normally would. How can the researcher tell whether this has happened? The simple fact is that he or she cannot tell. As harmless as using a few words may seem, there is no guarantee that this will not bias the interview results too.

Neutrality is necessary in asking questions to avoid biasing interview results (Brenner et al. 1985; McCracken 1988; Mishler 1986). For instance, leading questions usually give predictable results. An inappropriate leading question may offend the subject and damage rapport.

Another means of establishing rapport is by using a sponsor, an acquaintance, or a colleague of the subject to provide an introduction. This can involve a letter of introduction, a phone call, an e-mail, or a personal introduction. Introductions have worked in a variety of disparate settings with all kinds of subjects (Dexter 1970; Douglas 1976; Fetterman 1989, 1998; Heard 1950; Lofland and Lofland 1995; Spencer 1982). However, use of personal introductions can be overdone. Care must be taken to avoid creating the perception that you work for someone you do not, or that a letter of introduction implies a depth of friendship that does not exist, or that the interviewer shares the beliefs of the person providing the introduction. Any of these misinterpretations could lead subjects to change their answers in some way. Typically, subjects would be more prone to tell the researcher what they thought he or she wanted to hear (Dexter 1970; Fetterman 1989, 1998; Heard 1950).

Other techniques for establishing rapport with a subject include being open with the subject and sharing information with him. This may include information indicating that the interviewer is sympathetic with the subject (Douglas 1976; Fetterman 1989, 1998; Goffman 1973; Heard 1950). Statements of sympathy raise the issue of neutrality already discussed. It is possible to establish rapport with a subject to such an extent that it interferes with the interview and research process. Rapport can be developed to such an extent that the subject thinks of the interviewer as a close friend and confidant. This relationship becomes an impediment in several senses. First, the interviewee may share information with the interviewer that would be harmful to the subject if it were revealed. Second, sensitive negative topics cannot comfortably be explored. Third, it is difficult, if not impossible, to back off to a lower level of rapport. Fourth, a high level of rapport with some subjects may make it difficult, if not impossible, to establish rapport with or interview other subjects who hold different positions or attitudes. The interviewer may be identified with a particular group. Continuous interaction and the continued development of rapport can mean that the interviewer takes on the attitudes, values, and perspectives of the subject or of a group of subjects. Objectivity and impartiality may be difficult to establish and to maintain (McCracken 1988; Miller 1952; Mishler 1986).

The notion of over doing rapport and its consequences raises many ethical questions. For instance, revealing information gained because of friendship with a subject, if public knowledge of that information would harm the subject, is unethical. This would be even more the case if rapport were established with the intent of manipulating the victim. Heard (1950) discusses protecting interviewees by limiting access to transcripts and using pseudonyms for individual subjects and organizations. Deception in the interview process has ethical implications (Dexter 1970; Fetterman 1989, 1998; Lofland and Lofland 1995; Spector 1980).

3. Interview Formats

Three different formats can be used in elite or specialized interviews. A structured interview uses an interview schedule or set of questions that are asked of each subject. Each individual is asked the same set of questions. The wording of the questions, the order of the questions, and any follow-up questions are identical in each case. The intent of this format is to make sure that differences between respondents are the result of actual differences rather than variations in the way the interviews are conducted. Use of an interview schedule assumes that subjects have a common vocabulary so that it is possible to phrase questions that will mean the same thing to each of them, and that the interview context, including prior questions, must be identical for each respondent (Richardson et al. 1965).

A second type of interview format is called a focused or nonscheduled structured interview. Typically, this type of interview involves collecting information from individuals who participated in the making of a decision or in its implementation. The decision or situation is known and has been analyzed prior to the interview, resulting in formulation of a set of research questions and tentative hypotheses. The researcher uses these questions and tentative hypotheses as a guide, or source of structure, in questioning subjects. The form and order of questions is the same for each subject, but the specific content of follow-up questions varies with the nature of the responses received from the subjects. Subjects are encouraged to answer expansively. Personal reactions, perceptions, beliefs, and interpretations of events are sought. Revelation of new materials, perspectives, and interpretations may result in the researcher returning to partially reinterview a previous subject (Fetterman 1989, 1998; Heard 1950; Merton and Kendal 1946).

A third type of interview is the nonscheduled or nondirective interview. No preconceived set of questions is developed in advance. The form and order of questions vary from subject to subject. Respondents are encouraged to describe their experiences and their interpretations of events. Research questions, tentative hypotheses, generalizations, or observed patterns, such as similarities and differences, are used in subsequent interviews of other subjects to verify or test them. Research done in this manner takes shape or develops as it progresses (Fetterman 1989, 1998; Lofland and Lofland 1995; McCracken 1988; Van Maanen 1988).

I. Types of Questions

Regardless of the type of interview conducted, questions used in the interview process may be of the same type. Both closed questions, requiring choice of a specific alternative answer and open-ended questions, in which the respondent answers in her own words, are used in interviews.

One of the best techniques is to ask open-ended questions that prompt long, detailed answers from the participant. McCracken (1988) calls questions that lead the interviewee to tell their story in an expansive, detailed manner "grand tour questions." A series of open-ended questions or series of topic statements to use in the interview can be prepared based on background information. The most effective questions are clear in meaning and short in length (Van Schendelen 1984). Additional questions of an open-ended nature can be developed from and during each interview. These can be used to provide a starting place in the interview, to provide some sense of order to the interview, and to make sure that no important matter is overlooked. Probes or more specific follow-up questions can be used when needed after any open-ended question.

1.   The Need for Probes and Follow-Ups

Probes or follow-up questions must be used when answers to questions are inadequate. Inadequate answers occur in a variety of ways, including nonresponse; an incomplete answer; an irrelevant answer; an inaccurate answer; a poorly organized answer; jargon or words that the interviewer does not understand; references to people, places, and events that are unknown to the interviewer; and when the interviewer simply does not understand what is said or is confused (Downs et al. 1980; Fetterman 1989, 1998; Kahn and Cannell 1963). Background research might enable the interviewer to understand more of the subject's conversation (Coleman 1996; Hertz and Imber 1995; Lofland and Lofland 1995; Nader 1972).

These problems occur for as many different specific reasons as there are individuals interviewed. In general, these reasons boil down to the following three problems: the interviewee may not know what you want, may neither remember nor know the answer to the question, or may be unwilling to answer a question. First, an interviewee may misunderstand a question or what kind of answer the interviewer wants. The interviewer needs to repeatedly provide information to his subject about how much detail is needed in the answer. For example, rephrasing a question sometimes helps the interviewee remember. Asking for more detail or asking another question about part of a previous answer is an effective way to do this.

Second, an interviewee may be unable to answer a question because he does not know or does not remember the answer. The subject may have no information about a particular question because he was not present when an event took place, did not read the record if one existed, and heard nothing about it. An accurate and satisfactory answer is that he does not know. Nothing can be done about this except to ask the subject who else might know the answer or where an answer might be found. Many people do not remember details, even shortly after an event occurs, and this problem increases with the amount of time since an event happened. This is a common problem. Even researchers who conduct interviews are told that they should tape record each session in order to get the most accurate record possible. One sometimes-successful solution to this problem occurs naturally. Given some time to think about a question, an interviewee may remember an answer. Sometimes an interviewee may interrupt themselves later in the interview process to provide an answer to an earlier question. If follow-up sessions are used, an interviewee may remember an answer between sessions. Sometimes rephrasing a question helps someone remember.

Third, a subject may not want to answer a particular question. An interviewee may be unwilling to share information about confidential matters, personnel matters, personal matters, anything potentially embarrassing, politically sensitive events, and matters under dispute, or events that reflect negatively on an agency, program, others, and especially on themselves (Anderson and Jack 1991; Spencer 1982). When information on such topics is shared, dissembling may occur. Inaccurate and incomplete information may be shared. Individuals with something at risk, something to gain or lose, and something to hide often emphasize the positive and filter out negative information. This type of behavior is intensified when the information might be used against an individual or when someone might get even (Brannen 1987; Fetterman 1989, 1998; Heard 1950; Jablin 1979; Lee 1993; Muchinsky 1977; O'Reilly and Roberts 1974; Penley and Hawkins 1985;

Read 1962; Roberts and O'Reilly 1974; Roberts et al. 1974; Spencer 1982; Zand 1972). It may be legally and ethically out-of-bounds to share information on some topics. Examples of these items include personnel matters, ongoing investigations, and legal cases. Human subject guidelines may suggest limits as well.

2. Types of Probes or Follow-Up Questions

Several different kinds of questions or probes can be asked when following up an answer to an earlier question. These include silence, neutral statements, repetition, clarification, elaboration, internal summaries, and confrontation (Downs et al. 1980; Fetterman 1989, 1998; Heard 1950).

Silence during short pauses or waiting for the interviewee to begin talking again allows the subject to reflect on questions and prepare answers and to set the pace of the interview at a comfortable level. Moreover, it allows the interviewer to evaluate the answers received and to think of additional questions and probes that may be needed. Silence accompanied by eye contact, an expression of interest, and appropriate body language, such as a nod, indicates a willingness to listen and that more information is sought (Anderson and Jack 1991; Downs et al. 1980).

Neutral statements such as "Uh-huh," "Yes," "Okay," and "I see" tend to encourage a subject to continue to talk. Statements of this kind occur in all conversation and convey a sense of interest and attention.

Repeating a question that was not answered or was not answered correctly or completely is one way to elicit an answer to it. Many techniques are used to do this, including rephrasing a question, making it more specific, including an example, and breaking a difficult question down into simpler component parts.

Clarification involves asking for further explanation because something is unclear or incomplete. If the interviewer does not understand what a subject says, then requests for clarification are appropriate. Vague statements, generalizations, using people's first names, special terminology, and technical explanations often lead to lack of understanding and misunderstandings. Interviewees often assume that the interviewer has more knowledge than they do. Personnel textbooks mention an explanation for this in the context of performance evaluation known as the "like me" error. This amounts to assuming that "since I know it everyone else knows it too" (Decotiis and Petit 1978; Tyer 1983). Statements such as "Do you mean this or that?" or "I don't understand" and simply asking an interviewee to repeat something are appropriate examples of this type of probe. Another technique is to repeat a statement made by the subject and ask them to explain it. Care must taken in doing this, since an interviewee could be put on the defensive (Jorgensen 1989).

Elaboration is simply asking for more information. Questions such as "What else happened?," "Do you know anything else about it?," "How did you feel about that?" and "Tell me more about it" are examples of an interviewer asking for elaboration of an earlier answer. A statement made by the subject may be repeated and she may be asked to add to it. Requests for elaboration on earlier answers are a natural part of follow-up sessions. The interviewer may ask the subject for an example to illustrate a point. Obviously, elaboration may result in clarification, too (McCracken 1988).

Occasionally, pausing to review what has been said or to check your interpretation of what has been said can improve the quality of interview responses. One way to do this is to stop and summarize what you have heard and ask if your understanding is correct. Internal reviews allow the interviewee the chance to verify that the interviewer's perceptions are correct, lead to clarification of earlier answers and other types of probes, demonstrate that the interviewer has been listening and thus build rapport between the researcher and subject, and serve as transitions to new topics (Fetterman 1989, 1998). If the interviewer is not taping the session and is taking notes, this technique provides a few minutes in which to catch up. If he is neither taping nor taking notes, then this technique will fix the main points of the interview more firmly in his mind until notes can be prepared. It is an effective interview technique to end discussion of each different topic with a brief review or summary session.

J. Sources of Error

Sources of error include distortion and overstatement, omission and underreporting, telescoping and overreporting, lack of communications skills, lack of language skills, and failure to determine if a subject understood a question and if the interviewer's understanding of the subject's answers is correct. Subjects are more likely to distort or overstate their answers to questions with answers that are socially desirable or have prestige value (Hyman 1944). Verification through other sources and by double-checking with the subject may provide answers to these problems.

Some common errors affect interview and survey results. Subjects forget events, persons, and details as time passes. The longer the time since an event occurred, the more subjects will forget (Sudman and Bradburn 1973). Forgetting an event, person, or detail results in omission and underreporting. Another type of error is telescoping. This problem is caused by forgetting when events occurred, how much time elapsed between events, and the order of events. Telescoping usually results in overreporting because the respondent honestly believes that events occurred closer together or more frequently than they actually did (Bradburn 1983). One solution to the problem of telescoping is use of a procedure called bounded recall (Neter and Waksberg 1964; Sudman et al. 1984). Unfortunately, this procedure works only when there are repeated interviews, as in a panel of subjects that is repeatedly interviewed across time. During a second or later interview, the subject is reminded of her previous answers during questioning. It is not surprising that use of bounded recall markedly increases the accuracy of subject responses.

Lack of awareness of metacommunications can make an interviewer ineffective. Lack of knowledge about acceptable forms of comportment and acceptable ways of asking questions can cause problems. Inappropriate questions, errors in phraseology, asking questions of the wrong person, socially-unacceptable questions, offensive statements, and improper forms of address can lead to errors in communication, offend the subject and their associates, and bring an interview to an abrupt end (Briggs 1984; Grimshaw 1969; Heard 1950). Interviewer training should contain material on metacommunications, including unique language usages and the social norms of the group that will be interviewed. This is especially important when ethnic minorities and those who do not speak fluent English are going to be interview subjects (Briggs 1983, 1984; Grimshaw 1970; Strauss and Schatzman 1955). Every interviewer needs to undergo orientation in the terminology and cultural background of the subjects so that they will understand the referents of the subject (London 1975).

Lack of language facility may create problems for the interviewer, who then has to rely on an interpreter. Something may be lost in translation as the translator imposes his own words, interpretations, and values on both the interviewer's questions and the subject's answers. Even if carefully trained, the interviewer may filter, transform, distort, and create material (London 1975; Sudman and Bradburn 1983). Lack of language facility increases the possibility of this problem occurring, eliminates spontaneity, and limits the use of follow-up questions.

The interviewer needs some sense of whether or not and how the subject understood each question. Reasonable answers do not always mean that the respondent understood the question. Unfortunately, interviewers rarely attempt to find out how a subject interprets any given question (London 1975).

When an interviewer fails to verify his understanding of what the subject has said by checking it with the subject, communications between them can deteriorate rapidly. A subject may realize that the interviewer does not understand and thereafter try to simplify answers or give answers that will be understood (London 1975). This problem means loss of detail and accuracy. Moreover, the most interesting, useful, and new materials are the most likely to be lost. This problem is somewhat similar to the ubiquitous problem of subjects telling the interviewer what they think he or she would like to hear.

K. MULTIPLE SESSIONS

Multiple sessions may be necessary to obtain a great deal of detailed information from a subject. This is especially likely when fatigue is a factor and when long interview sessions are difficult to arrange (Dexter 1970; Heard 1950; London and London 1966; Sudman and Bradburn, 1983). Multiple sessions give the interviewer a chance to develop more questions and to follow-up or seek clarification of answers that were unclear in earlier sessions. The interviewer can summarize or present an interpretation and get feedback from the subject (Dexter 1970).

Multiple interviews can be used to verify the accuracy of material from earlier sessions. Apparent contradictions can be cleared up by tactfully asking the subject about them (Agar 1980; Bernard 1994; Dexter 1970; Heard 1950; Kingdon 1984; London 1974; Mead 1953; Paul 1953; Van Schendelen 1984). Another technique to verify the accuracy of interview content is to interview multiple subjects on the same topics (Fetterman 1989, 1998; London 1974; McCracken 1988; Merton 1947; Seidler 1974; Williams 1968). These can be done individually or in focus groups (Krueger 1998a, 1998b; Stewart and Shamdasani 1990).

L. SENSITIVE QUESTIONS

Difficult, sensitive, potentially threatening questions should be left until later in an interview. Rapport should be established first and the subject should be comfortable interacting with the interviewer. Rapport and trust are established over time through interaction, and there is no shortcut method to create these characteristics (Bernard 1994; Coleman 1996; DeMunk and Sobo 1998; DeWalt and DeWalt 2002; Dexter 1970; Hertz and Imber 1995; Lincoln and Guba 1985; Lofland and Lofland 1995; Van Maanen 1988). Some individuals are more open and trusting than others and it is easier to get them to talk. Others will never be completely candid (Dexter 1970; Douglas 1976; Fetterman 1989, 1998).

Questions with threatening content cause responses to be distorted (Sudman and Bradburn 1974). No method of correcting for this, including the randomized response model, eliminates the errors in answers caused by threatening questions. Randomized response is a technique developed by Warner (1965) in which the respondent is given a nickel to flip to determine whether he will answer a threatening question or a nonthreatening question that is paired with it. The interviewer does not know which of the two questions the subject answers, but by knowing the total number of yes and no responses, the sample size, and the probability of subjects answering each question, the proportion of the population giving a given answer can be calculated. Variations of the randomized response technique have been developed in order to improve respondent co-operation and honesty (Horvitz et al. 1967). The randomized response technique fails because it is applicable only in situations where large samples of subjects can be interviewed, as in sample surveys, and because it does not eliminate the large errors that result from threatening questions (Locander et al. 1976). There are some topics about which any particular interviewee simply will not disclose information (Anderson and Jack 1991; Fetterman 1989, 1998; Heard 1950; Lee 1993; London 1974).

M. CONFRONTATION

Dexter suggests that confrontation is the only way it is possible to get some subjects to "open up" and "level" with the interviewer. They appreciate candor and a chance to have their say or to try to convince the interviewer that they are right (Dexter 1956, 1970). Negative questions are sometimes used to catch a subject off-guard and get them to talk about things he usually would not discuss (Minor 1970). This technique may work, but it is not recommended because it is likely to end an interview and destroy the trust that exists between the interviewee and the subject. The subject will always be on guard and candor will be limited. Also, there is no guarantee that information revealed under stressful circumstances is accurate (Douglas 1976).

Confrontation or asking questions about apparent contradictions or questions that may embarrass the interviewee or make them uncomfortable are often left out of interviews. Interviewers may not ask these questions because they are afraid they will result in the interview being cut short. Asking questions about apparent inconsistencies is important, because they often can be cleared up. An incomplete answer or lapse of memory may clarify the apparent inconsistency. Failure to resolve inconsistencies can cast a shadow of doubt over a whole interview. Some facts can be checked elsewhere. Potentially confrontational questions must be tactfully phrased. "You said this about X. It obviously isn't true." This blunt judgmental approach is likely to be offensive and to destroy rapport. Seeking elaboration or clarification on that item is less likely to offend anyone. Thus, "Can you tell me more about X?" is likely to be a far-more-effective and -less-risky technique.

Aggressive confrontational behavior is sometimes used in a deliberate and calculated manner to get information from a subject who otherwise would be uncommunicative (Bernstein and Woodward 1974). This technique may be especially effective if the subject is emotionally burdened by other problems (Levine 1980).

N. RECORDING AND NOTE-TAKING

Interviews should be taped in order to gather the greatest amount of accurate and detailed information possible. If the interviewer cannot record an interview, then he or she must settle for second-best, taking notes during each interview. Note-taking often distracts both the interviewer and the subject, but notes provide a record of major points. Exact quotes are often lost this way, since the interviewer cannot write as fast as the subject speaks. Note-taking makes it harder to maintain eye contact, formulate the next question, and make judgments about when probes are needed. On the other hand, some subjects are uncomfortable being taped and readily accept note-taking (Dexter 1970; Fetterman 1989, 1998; Lofland and Lofland 1995; McCracken 1988; McMahan and Rogers 1994; Morton-Williams 1993). In fact, the interviewer's note-taking helps some subjects to accept the interview process (Bernstein and Woodward 1974). Taking notes after the interview is a distant third choice since the interviewer will forget some things and miss details. For instance, exact wordings or expressions and almost all quotes are lost. However, each of these alternatives is better than not recording or taking any notes at all and relying only on memory.

Recording the respondent's exact words is important so that the researcher knows exactly what was said and how it was said. Exact quotations contain this information, and there is no substitute for them. This is important in trying to determine exact meanings. Quotations or recordings are a safeguard against forgetting, misquoting, and taking material out of context. Quotations serve as evidence to support the interviewer's or researcher's conclusions. Quotations can be used to provide examples that give a sense of depth (Dexter 1970; Douglas 1976; Fetterman 1989, 1998; Heard 1950; London 1961, 1974; London and London 1966; McCracken 1988).

An effective alternative is to interview a subject while a third person takes notes. The note-taker can ask questions in order to make sure that the record being assembled is complete and clear. Both the interviewer and the note-taker can later participate in interpreting the notes (London 1974).

IV. UNOBTRUSIVE MEASURES—USE OF ARCHIVAL DATA

After 40 years, the bestknown work on unobtrusive measures is Webb et al.'s (1966, 1972, 1976) classic work, *Unobtrusive Measures: Nonreactive Research in the Social Sciences*. They point out that the most commonly used means of gathering social science data are surveys and interviews. The validity of data gathered solely by these methods is threatened by the limitations inherent in survey and interview methods. Using these threats as a springboard, they then survey alternative methods of collecting data.

These threats include the following problems: interviews and surveys "create as well as measure attitudes, they elicit atypical roles and responses, they are limited to those who are accessible and will cooperate, and the responses obtained are produced in part by dimensions of individual differences irrelevant to the topic at hand" (Webb et al. 1966, 1972). These threats lead to questions about the internal and external validity of research results.

The question of internal validity usually focuses on whether a difference exists in any given comparison. The issue of external validity focuses on the problem of interpreting observed differences, of generalizing or explaining the results so that they can be applied more broadly. Distinctions between internal and external validity are vague, because factors that threaten internal validity often threaten external validity, too. The potential sources of invalidity that Webb et al. (1966, 1972) identify are numerous, and include reactive measurement effects or the error produced by the respondent. This is a pervasive problem, since even a well-intentioned, cooperative research subject knows that he is participating in a research project. This knowledge may cause the subject to behave in such a way that inaccuracies occur in the data. These errors take four different forms: awareness of being tested, or the guinea pig effect; role selection; measurement as a change agent; and response sets. Further, heavy reliance on self-report-based methods excludes crucial populations from examination (Daft and Widgington 1979; Webb and Weick 1979).

Webb et al.'s major complaint, however, is the fact that interviews and surveys are too often used alone. Other methods are ignored and, consequently, corroborating evidence is not gathered. As they point out, "No research method is without bias. Interviews and questionnaires must be supplemented by methods testing the same... variables but having different methodological weaknesses" (Webb et al. 1966, 1972). They do not advocate elimination of surveys and interviews. Instead, they advocate use of multile different methods, so that triangulation in the measurement process can occur. Findings from studies using identical methods raise the possibility that research findings are method specific. Achieving similar results from different methods makes it possible to rule out the plausible rival hypothesis of research results being due to methodology. Development and application of unobtrusive measures should offset the tendency to satisfice in data collection or to delay cross-checking of findings and should produce a wider variety of observations that reflect more accurately what actually happens in organizations (Daft and Widgington 1979; Webb et al. 1966, 1972; Webb and Weick 1979).

Every would-be researcher should read the methodological discussion in Webb et al. (1966) Similar methodological discussions of traditional mainstream data collection techniques and use of unobtrusive measures as alternatives are found in Brandt (1972) and Denzin (1970).

Webb et al. (1966) developed four large classes of unobtrusive measures: physical traces, archives, simple observations, and measures gathered with hardware. One of these classes— archival sources of information—has been widely used in public administration, and is described in the next section.

A. ARCHIVES

Archival sources of data include materials that are available from public and private records.

1. Public Records

Archives include the ongoing records of society, such as actuarial records, voting records, government budgets, and communications media, which are produced and paid for by someone other than the researcher. Data from these sources are relatively nonreactive, readily available, and inexpensive to collect. For example, a study of the construction and impacts of the Erie Canal (Sheriff 1966), a detailed examination of the public sector activities of the Rockefeller Foundations (Roberts 1994), and an assessment of the roles of men and women in early municipal research bureaus and settlement houses, respectively (Stivers 1995) rely heavily on archival data.

Actuarial records take many forms, including birth, marriage, and death certificates, census reports, and organizational membership lists. These records can provide data on age, gender, life expectancy, occupation, religion, marriage, and other topics. These records can be used creatively. For example, by examining marriage records at various points in history, it is possible to determine the extent of literacy by noting the proportion of people signing their name as X (Webb et al. 1966, 1972).

Political records, such as election records and legislative rollcall votes, are examples of political archives. Federal and state laws mandate that those running for certain offices keep records of donations and expenditures and file these documents with the appropriate election commission. Some of these materials are published in newspapers. Legislative rollcall votes are often used by political scientists for their studies. Unfortunately, it is impossible to tell how individuals voted on voice votes, and voice votes are often intentionally used to avoid recording how individuals voted on controversial measures. Other sources for studying politicians are the content of their speeches and letters. Presidential speeches are published in collected volumes. Newspapers regularly print presidential and gubernatorial speeches. Media coverage of a lesser political figure's public utterances is much more likely to be a hit-and-miss proposition.

Court records and published decisions provide information for the study of courts. For example, these sources have been used in studying factors that affect sentencing. Court records have been used to study racial differences (Blacks vs. Whites, and Hispanics vs. Whites) in criminal sentencing (Bridges and Crutchfield 1988; Bridges et al. 1987; Georges-Abeyie 1992; Hagan 1974; Mumola 1999; Muñoz 1999; Tonry 1995; Zatz 1987), gender and sentencing (Daly 1994; Snell 1991, 1994), sentencing in family violence cases (Daly, 1989; Gannon and Brzozowski, 2004; Ursel, 2003), gender differences in sentencing of minors (Johnson and Scheuble 1991; Zingraff and Thomson 1984; Steffensmeier Kramer and Streifel 1993), trends in drug sentences (Bowman and Heise 2001, 2002; Kuklinski and Stanga 1979), and use of alternatives to prison in sentencing juveniles (Gottfredson and Barton 1993; Macallair 1994). Data for prison populations has been used for similar studies (Beck and Harrison 2004; Greenfield and Snell 1999; Harrison and Karberg 2004; Snell and Maruschak 2002).

Government records can be used to study the operations and impacts of federal, state, and local programs. For example, government data are the basis for studies of commuting (Aronsson and Brännäs 1996; Cropper and Gordon 1991; Fuguitt 1991; Hamilton 1989; Hamilton and Roell 1982; Krout 1983; Small and Song 1992; Srinivasan 2002; White 1988), and transportation and land use (O'Sullivan 1990; Pickrell 1999; Renkow 2003; Singletary et al. 1995).

Public reactions to politicians and government activities can be assessed using letters to the editor, a popular and widely used form of self-expression and public debate (Hill 1981; Renfro 1979). Those who use letters to editor for research purposes need to ask the question, "How representative is this letter?" Historically, most cities had multiple competing newspapers that printed letters agreeing with their editorial and political stance. In any case, letters to the editor go through an editorial staff member's winnowing process. Most are not printed, and usually only selected parts appear in print (Hill 1981; Renfro 1979). Some research indicates that letters to the editor reflect the range of public opinion and that this is especially likely when people are divided about an issue and feel strongly about it (Buell 1975; Hill 1981; Sigelman and Walkosz 1992). Other studies conclude that those who write letters to the editor are better educated, older, more conservative, more likely to be Republican, and more pessimistic than the general public (Buell 1975; Forsythe 1950; Foster and Friedrich 1937; Grey and Brown 1970; Rosenau, 1974; Tarrant 1957; Vacin 1965; Volgy et al. 1977).

Other government records include data on weather patterns, the time of year, phases of the moon, patents, economic trends, manufacturing trends, labor force data and trends, census of population records and projections, tax data, power failures, patents, municipal water pressure, parkingmeter collections, welfare payments, crimes committed and crime rates, and traffic fatalities. Use of these data is most often quite straightforward. Almost every issue of *PAR* in recent years has either contained tables of data from a government data collection program, or reported the results of analyses based on such data. If an original analysis has not been performed, then the work of another scholar or government agency has been cited.

In some instances, government data do not directly measure what an investigator is interested in, so data from different sources may be compiled to support the analysis of interest. For instance, Berry et al. (1976) compiled data from different sources in analyzing urbanization in the Chicago area.

Published records have been used as a source of data in community power studies (Aiken 1970; Alford 1973; Clark 1968; Hawley 1963; Smith 1976; Summers and Bloomquist 1982; Walton 1976; Warren 1983). Data has also been gathered from official documents for studies of economic development (Fuguitt and Deeley 1966; Richardson and Larson 1976; Summers et al. 1976), program implementation (Kovner 1996; Luloff and Wilkinson, 1979; Moore and Cantrell, 1976; Pressman and Wildavsky 1973), personnel matters (Cornwell and Kellough 1994; Kim 1996; Kim and Lewis 1994; Mesch and Shamayeva 1996; Newman 1994; Tang and McCollum 1996; Thompson 1975), population changes (Fuguitt and Beale 1978; Hassinger 1957; Humphrey et al. 1977; Humphrey and Sell 1975), the relative status of different places (Logan 1976; Logan and Schneider 1981; Logan and Semyonov 1980), and tax trends (Fisher 1996).

In other research projects, government data do not exist that directly measure variables of research interest. In these cases, use of government data can be quite innovative. Policy studies have often used one variable as a pseudomeasure of a variable of interest. For example, parking-meter collections were used to determine the impact of a newspaper strike in one city. In another study, traffic fatalities were used to determine the impact of changes in speed limits. Variance in water pressure was used to determine when people retired for the night (Webb et al. 1966, 1972). The weight of portable television sets has even been used as a predictor of burglary trends (Felson and Cohen 1980), and data from the Internal Revenue Service has been used to measure marijuana consumption (Felson 1983).

The mass media also provide a continuous and easily available record of current and historical events. Use of their records is limited primarily by availability and imagination. Media content has been used to determine politicians' policy positions by studying content of press conferences and press releases. Media content has also been used to assess societal values at different points in time.

2. Private Records

Archival materials also include episodic and private records. These sources of archival data are more discontinuous, and often are not part of the public record. For example, data on private corporations are selectively reported to the public, and some kinds of corporate data (personnel records, for instance) are not reported at all. With the exception of private data collected by government agencies, these sources are difficult to access. They are more difficult to identify and gain access to, unless the researcher is a member of the organization producing these records. These records are usually more difficult and expensive to acquire than public records, and the data is often not available for reasons such as security and the fact that data is stored for short periods and then destroyed because of the expense involved in keeping it. In some instances private archival materials or even whole archives are donated to public repositories such as the Smithsonian Institution which results in easier accessibility (Yeager and Blyth 2004, 2005).

Although difficult to acquire, private archival data often provides specificity of content and less dross than public data. Any study of the past that includes assessment of the perspectives, attitudes, motives, and experiences of a population requires examination of historical records. Personal documents may be the only extant sources of data regarding organizations and movements no longer in existence (Mariampolski and Hughes 1978). Three types of private data have been used regularly—financial and sales records, institutional records, and personal documents. Financial and sales records are a common form of data that has been used in a wide variety of ways.

For example, data on sales of alcoholic beverages has been used as a measure of stress. Commemorative stamp sales data has been used to measure the popularity of events and individuals, and the sales value of an individual's autograph has been used as a measure of his or her popularity.

Industrial and institutional records include data on such things as the amount and quality of output, grievances, and use of sick leave. These data have been used to cross-check supervisory ratings, to develop work standards, to predict job turnover and absenteeism, and to create a wide variety of proficiency measures for different types of jobs, work conditions, and work groups. For example, rating data has been used to measure the validity of assessment centers (Neidig and Neidig 1984; Sackett and Dreher 1982, 1984).

The usefulness of private and institutional records is illustrated by Bernstein and Woodward (1974), who made imaginative use of a wide variety of public and private documents in doing the research for their book *All the President's Men*. Their materials included address books, library slips, bills, long-distance phone records, bank records, canceled checks, credit card records, and telephone lists. Use of all of these materials would raise interesting ethical and legal issues for a social scientist, since some of these materials were obtained surreptitiously from sources. Today, obtaining records from a credit bureau without proper clearance could result in serious legal problems.

Personal documents are widely used sources. A personal document is any item that reveals the participant's view of experiences in which he or she has been involved (Angell 1947). These documents include diaries and personal letters, stenographic records, business papers, memoranda, newspaper reports, autobiographies, certain kinds of government documents, works of fiction, films, handbills, flyers, manifestos, family Bibles, artwork, and photographs (Bouchard 1976a, 1976b; Gottschalk et al. 1947; Sechrest 1976; Webb et al. 1966). Use of letters, diaries, and other sources is limited primarily by availability. Most of these materials are thrown out on a regular basis. For example, letters to political figures are often studied. This mail can give misleading impressions of public opinion, because it includes letters from persons who are not constituents, and simulated mail. Simulated mail occurs when some organization encourages its members or the public to write spontaneous letters. Simulated mail can be detected by the use of form letters on which individuals have only filled in their name and address or signed their name, or when many letters contain identical phrases and arguments or use identical sentence structure, and when multiple letters on the same topic come from a small number of individuals. Similarly, innovative use was made of the letters and diaries of German troops to captured during World War II. These personal documents were analyzed to determine the impact of propaganda and to assess troop morale (Webb et al. 1966, 1972). Diaries have also been used to study communications behavior in organizations (Higgins et al. 1985; Irving and Elton 1986).

Brandt (1972) and Bouchard (1976a, 1976b) have identified a variety of different kinds of routine records and documents and suggest a number of uses for them. Their list, which draws heavily from Webb et al. (1966, 1972), and more recent materials from a variety of different sources identified by other individuals, are described in Table 25.1.

A variety of other specific studies illustrate the breadth of use of unobtrusive measures. For instance, Weiner (1973) studied the effects of an imposed deadline on organizational decision-making. Weiner used Cohen et al.'s (1972) garbage can model to trace the appearance of the desegregation issue, the lack of decisive action, and the final organizational decision triggered by a federal court judge's imposing a 50-day deadline for submitting a desegregation plan (Weiner 1973).

Organizational charts define formal organizational structure, power, and communications relationships. Organizational charts are efforts to control expectations, requests, and accountability. These have been used to identify those who had been bypassed in informal networking (Webb and Weick 1979).

A unique source of archival data in the communications industry consists of out-takes, field interviews and other material gathered by television and radio networks, but never broadcast or

TABLE 25.1
Public Records

Kind of Record	Variable(s) Being Measured
Federal, state, and local laws	Official societal restrictions
Legislative and committee reports	Organizational status, activities, institutional modification attempts
Board minutes	Official institutional policies and decisions
Published speeches	Political, social, and economic attitudes
Content analysis of speeches	NAchievement and Npower (Donley and Winter 1970)
Letters exchanged between nations	Friendship–hostility dimension between nations (Inoguchi 1972)
Legislative roll calls	Actions taken by individual legislators, measures of liberalism/conservativism (Sechrest 1969)
Congressional record and similar records for state and local bodies	Statements of position on particular issues
Judicial records	Patterns in sentencing, antisocial behavior, impacts of judicial decisions
Tax records	Regional differences in patterns of living
Federal, state, and local government budgets	Perceived value and extent of support for various activities
Government agency records	Government activities and their impacts
	Living and commercial trends
Organizational charts	Formal organizational structure, power, control, and communication arrangements
Employee handbooks	Formal rules, emphasis on control
Work flowcharts	Formal work procedures
Production and output figures	Performance of individuals and departments
Number of program clients, consumption levels of goods and services	Public demand for support for program, effectiveness of publicity campaign
Seating at meetings	Informal power
Arrival and departure times	Control emphasis in an organization (Webb and Weick 1979)
List of unsolicited complaints or of commendations about employees	Client perceptions and reactions
Absentee and tardiness records	Work habits or motivation
Sick call rates	Morale
Military reenlistment and longevity figures	Morale
Salaries of teachers or government employees	Community support
Pay increase and promotion lists	Perceived value of individuals to an organization
Want ads	Employer inducements
Grievance board records	Index conflict among minorities (Stuart 1963)
Number of people one supervises	Measure of responsibility
Desk calendars	Establish time frames and sequences of events
Officials' notebooks	Often contain useful observation relevant to matters other than what the notebook was primarily used for
Diaries	Establish sequence of events, such as first contact
Organizational membership and clientele lists	Indicator of segment of society involved/served
Sales slips at Delegations' Lounge bar in United Nations	Tensions indicator
Air trip insurance figures	Public concern before and after air crashes

(continued)

Table 25.1 *(Continued)*

Kind of Record	Variable(s) Being Measured
Actuarial records, birth, baptismal, time data records, marriage licenses	Comparative demographic data (occupation, religion, cause of death, and other variables)
Cemetery documents, burial lot records	Family membership
Admission rate in psychiatric hospitals	General overall anxiety in society
Reader's Digest	Mathematics vocabulary in common usage
Associated Press releases	Details of news events of various sorts
Newspaper headlines	Press coverage and biases
Obituary columns	Charity preferences
Society section of metropolitan newspaper	Upper-, middle-, and lower-class activities
Telephone directories	Community ethnic group membership
Moody's Handbook	Corporate financial structure, well-being of a state or local government
Who's Who in America	Nature of accomplishments of successful persons
Children's books	Qualities of role models (heroes and heroines)
Property transfer listings	Commercial activity of individuals
Change-of-address forms in post office	Mobility data
Library files and circulation records	Used to check on who read assignments, motivation, level of interest, impact of teaching methods (Robinson et al. 1966)
	Used in organizational contexts—Who is interested in what?
Literacy analysis of letters	Level of literacy of senders (Plog 1966; Routh and Rettig 1969)
Sale price of autographs	Popularity indicator
Number of patents	Industrial creativity (Taylor et al. 1963)
Out-takes (unused film held by TV stations)	May be used for documentary construction, testing for media bias, establishing base rates for certain behaviors of groups or individuals in the past (Matarazzo et al. 1964; Westerbeck 1970)
Personal documents and letters	Observations and reflections on events; attitudes of people away from home, e.g., immigrants (Thomas and Znaniecki 1918)
Phone bills	Contact networks: who was contacted and when, how long they talked
Promptness and frequency of use of new drugs and new procedures by hospitals	Innovativeness of hospitals (Rosner 1968)
Peanut sales at ballgames	Excitement indicator (greater after than before seventh inning)
Mail-order catalogs	Apparel trends, merchandise as reflections of living patterns

published. The fact that there are attempts to subpoena this material indicates its potential import-ance (Westerbeck 1970). Film material gathered for one specific purpose, such as the evening news, may be useful to a researcher for many other purposes. For those hardy souls bent on making their own films or videotapes, Cary (1982) offers sound technical advice.

Udy (1964) made use of the Human Relations Area Files for cross-cultural comparative studies of organizations. A list of the institutions at which these files are located is given in Whiting (1968). Schoenfeldt (1970) gives a list of the major data archives in the Western world available to researchers. Trochim (1981) identifies a variety of government archives, which contain vast amounts of data. Hamer (1961) identifies archives and their contents in the United States. Publications of the National Archives and Records Administration (1987) and the National Historical Publications and Records Commission (1988) provide access to vast amounts of information either produced by or in the keeping of the federal government. Andriot (1990) indexes U.S. government publications and reports. Access to federal government statistics is facilitated by several other publications (Andriot et al. 1995; Evinger 1988). Some of the large reference works, such as the County and City Data Book (US Department of Commerce 1994) and most Department of the Census data are available on CD-ROM.

Virtually every federal and state government agency has a website that makes vast amounts of material available either directly on-line or facilitates access through other means. Many of these sites include tables of contents with links to subsections, indexes, search engines, help, and frequently asked questions (FAQs) support. The amount of material directly available through and the ease of use in locating appropriate material and a copy of it is particularly impressive at the National Archives and Records Administration, the Library of Congress, the Government Accountability Office, the Smithsonian Institution, and the Department of Justice. States vary widely in what they provide online, both in terms of ability to identify and obtain copies of materials. Cities and counties, especially those in large urban areas, have emulated federal and state governments to some extent, but there is tremendous variation.

Access to the Library of Congress catalog and the catalogs of most large university and public libraries is available on the Internet. Materials designed to teach customers how to search and access the collection is usually available. Indices, such as those produced by the W. W. Wilson Company with both general and narrower more specific foci, are available through libraries. In some cases, indices are linked to library holdings. In a few short minutes, a journal article might be found in an index and a copy in Portable Document Format (PDF) or other format can be obtained from an electronic subscription held by the library or from the indexing or information service without leaving your desk. For that matter, many publishers, such as SAGE and Blackwells, make issues of many journals available in on-line in searchable databases. Copies of the most recent articles usually require a subscription to gain access, or articles are available for a fee. Materials in older issues of some journals are free. References from 2004 and more recent journal articles are downloadable to reference management software. Some journals make their content available on the Internet, and authors often make copies of either their manuscripts or the published versions of them available on the Internet. As a result, the problem with an Internet search often is not that there are too few hits, but too many.

Unlike many of the on-line databases and indexes, which focus on only a limited time period for the journals they cover, indices exist that provide access to information in every year of some of the public administration journals. These include the Index of the Public Administration Review 1940–1994 (Yeager 1995), "Index of the International Journal of Public Administration: Volumes 1 (1979) through 13 (1990)" (Yeager 1991), "Index of the Public Administration Quarterly: Volumes 1 (June, 1977) through 14 (Winter, 1991)" (Yeager 1992), "Index of the Journal of Health and Human Resources Administration: Volumes 1/1 (August, 1978) through 15/1 (Summer, 1992; Yeager 1993), and the "Index of the Proceedings of the National Conferences on Teaching Public Administration: 1978–1989" (Yeager and Manns 1990). Similar indexes are being completed for other public administration and political science journals.

Secondary sources, as historians call them, include the published books, articles, studies, papers, and lectures of academics and other writers. Use of secondary sources is widespread. A cursory examination of forty issues of the *PAR*, the oldest, most widely read, and most-cited public administration journal (Colson 1990), indicates that secondary sources of these kinds are cited far more often than primary or original sources. In fact, it is not uncommon for an author who uses a large number of primary sources to use an equal or greater number of secondary materials.

The content of these secondary documents may sometimes be reactive and interpretive, despite social science prescriptions of neutrality and accuracy. However, once published, these sources are fixed in time. These secondary sources become part of the historic record and part of the history of ideas examined by subsequent scholars. Wholly accurate or not, these documents represent the latest thinking at one point in time—roughly when they are published. There are immense advantages to standing on the shoulders of Galileo and DaVinci or Weber and Wilson in terms of the development of scientific methods or public administration theory, respectively. Secondary documents, such as the contributions to the *Handbook of Public Administration*, are useful because they identify primary source materials, synthesize those materials, and reflect and build on them. This makes the tasks of learning, education, and administrative practice faced by the student, faculty member, and practitioner easier and contributes to better outputs and outcomes from these individuals.

As a routine first step in any project, a researcher should become familiar with the literature in their field of interest. Reasons for doing this include the fact that secondary sources identify many, if not all, of the primary information sources, identify critical issues related to the research topic, and identify questions about and problems with the research materials. Also, they serve as a baseline for evaluating primary materials by helping identify materials and data that were overlooked or were either under or overemphasized, and serve as a source of theoretical hunches that can be used as guidelines during initial stages of research (Stanfield 1987).

B. PROBLEMS WITH ARCHIVAL DATA

Those who use archival materials need to be aware of and guard against several potential problems with these data sources. First, archives may contain errors and may be incomplete. These errors can be guarded against by checking for internal consistency and by use of multiple sources. Second, some archival materials suffer from selective deposit. For example, study of the longevity of Romans based on birth and death dates taken from tombstones is confounded by gender and social class differences in likelihood of having a tombstone. Wives who died after their husbands, and the poor, were not very likely to have tombstones.

Third, errors in interpretation of data can occur because of changes in bookkeeping practices of which the researcher is not aware. Bias may exist within archival data because of editing. For instance, the *Congressional Record* contains the edited text of speeches and is not a verbatim record (Bouchard 1976a; Webb et al. 1966, 1972).

Fourth, even if the records are accurate, errors can occur because of selective survivability. Materials may be missing and some kinds of materials are systematically more likely to survive than others. For example, as Webb et al. (1966) point out, "it is no accident that archeologists are pottery experts." Several factors affect what gets saved. Rock (1976) notes that there are broad areas of experience that inevitably escape documentation. For example, because they do not necessarily parallel verbal expression, emotions exemplify experiences that may not become accurately recorded. Experience is rarely put in writing immediately. Almost always, writing about an event or experience occurs retrospectively, and consequently, important details may be forgotten. This delay may partially explain why experience is very selectively recorded. Another reason that historical materials are selective is because education was not widespread until the twentieth century (Mariampolski and Hughes 1978).

Records may be systematically destroyed. Survival may be affected by occasional systematic purges of materials from the record. For example, a political administration may remove records that reflect negatively on individuals and events they wish to conceal. A wide variety of shameful or intimate experiences escape documentation for no other reason than to guard the respectability of the author, some other person, or an organization (Rock 1976).

A more common, and hence, more likely event is that records are casually discarded. This problem, casually discarding materials, is becoming more pervasive with the advent of electronic communications, especially cell phones and e-mail. Hard copies of memoranda almost always survive better than their electronic counterparts. Many individuals use a private phone or private e-mail account in order to bypass their official communications devices. Others have replaced hard drives when they changed offices and destroyed backup records. Unfortunately storage devices of all kinds have legitimately failed too.

Great care must be taken in the choice of data sources when the intent is to exclude reactive measurement effects. There is a tendency to think that reactivity is restricted to verbal (interview) and test (questionnaire) behavior. This is short-sighted. People can and do dissemble. Furthermore, reactivity is not always a response to the researcher. Routine records and documents which, on their face, might appear to be unbiased are often reactive to political considerations (Dalton 1959). Materials may disappear and then be changed to either improve or eliminate the record. For example, activities of this kind occurred on a grand scale during the Iran-Contra affair of 1986–1987. Similar actions have occurred at high levels since then. In fact, destruction of relevant documents continued during initial stages of Justice Department investigations of these events. When this occurs, much of the data that one would normally consider to be nonreactive is contaminated prior to the investigator's examination of the materials.

Data from archival records are affected by a variety of factors that the researcher needs to keep in mind in order to avoid potential problems. First, extraneous events of history affect these records. For example, this country's population is continually growing and changing its characteristics. These trends affect historical events and interpretation of them. Thus, as Webb et al. (1966, 1972) state, "It gives Mr. Nixon little comfort, we are sure, to know that he garnered more votes in 1960, as a loser, than did any preceding winning candidate except Eisenhower." Similarly, the number of members in the U.S. House of Representatives and in the U.S. Senate is stable over time, but the characteristics of these bodies change. For instance, reapportionment has had a dramatic effect on the background and interests of House members. These differences are nowhere more apparent than in studies using voting indices.

Other problems with archival records include selective survival, changes in record-keeping methods, and the sheer mass of archival material. Selective survival is a threat to the validity of these records. Some may be casually discarded; others may be deliberately destroyed. Changes in record-keeping criteria can also be a problem. For example, "suicides in Prussia jumped 20% between 1882 and 1883" was the result of a change in record-keeping criteria (Webb et al. 1966, 1972). Another problem with archives is that their records may be so numerous that they overwhelm the researcher. One answer to this problem is random sampling. Glassner and Corzine (1982) suggest strategies for sampling within and across archives, which may help solve this difficulty. As a data source, personal documents have many potential limitations, of which the researcher needs to be aware. First, these resources are, for the most part, privately owned, and it is difficult to locate them and then gain access to them. Second, letters may not exist on a particular topic or there may be very few of them. One reason for this is the fact that letters are usually not written unless individuals are separated from one another. Third, letters typically show only one side of an issue. Fourth, personal materials are subject to the problem of selective survival. Personal letters are especially likely to be casually discarded. Materials that reflect negatively on the recipient and those with extremely personal content, such as love letters, are, on the one hand, unlikely to survive, and on the other, if they do survive, unlikely to be released for public examination. Finally, both the producer and the repository may contaminate these materials. A person's awareness of present or future image can generate validity problems as they manipulate and manage record keeping to ensure that they have a positive image. According to Stanfield (1987), "Such manipulation and management of record keeping includes writing and responding to letters as if responding to a future audience, destroying records revealing negative personal qualities, doctoring up records, and placing records in the hands of a devoted heir." Even if a subject does not do these things, surviving family members may manipulate private records to protect and improve the image of their deceased relative. Since the descendants of historical personages are usually concerned about propriety and respectability, they must be treated as potential sources of distortion. Changing codes of morality and/or the upward mobility achieved by the heirs may lead them to either hide and destroy or edit and distort records. The respectability of subsequent generations can be influenced by the reputation of an ancestor. Custodians of public and private records need not distort these records. Nevertheless, custodians affect the records they hold in many ways. For example, as Erikson (1970, 1971) points out:

> [T]he one quality all these documents have in common is their survival; and even though a researcher has complete faith in the authenticity and reliability of the documents, he must wonder by what law or accident they came to be preserved. They are not the random remains of a dead age, like the debris found at an archaeological site. Every generation of men that has lived meantime has served for a period as custodian of those records, and thus the surviving library of materials is in many ways a record of all the intervening years as well.

Documents and records can be very useful to a field researcher, but their use has been very circumspect because they can never be taken at face value. Even elementary statistics, such as operating costs, are juggled for political reasons (Dalton 1959). Angell and Fredman (1953), Madge (1965), Mann (1968), and Webb et al. (1966, 1972) all have excellent discussions of the serious limitations of various kinds of documents. Studies of government databanks have found that they usually contain a significant amount of erroneous information (Kruskal 1977; Roos et al. 1979). Roos et al. (1979) suggest using a series of internal cross-checks and audits to reduce the error rate within government archives.

Researchers sometimes gain access to confidential and personal records. The researcher who uses personal materials should have a clear agreement in writing about what will or will not be published (Selznick 1949; Whyte 1959).

C. Remedies

Given these problems with archival materials, personal records, and other sources, practical guidelines for working with these materials are of value to public administration scholars. Blumer (1939) identifies four criteria for evaluating data source: representativeness of data, adequacy of data, reliability of the data, and validity of data interpretation.

1. Representativeness of Data

It is difficult in public administration research to evaluate how adequately-available materials represent the universe of activities, behaviors, and attitudes that characterized a particular event. Although difficult, the identification and location of public and personal documents is a process similar to historical bibliographical research. Excellent guides to historical research by Barzun and Graff (1977), Shafer (1974), Gottschalk et al. (1947), Trochim (1981), and Winks (1968) provide a starting point.

Unfortunately, there is no reliable test that indicates whether or not the surviving data are a representative sample of experiences. Consequently, the researcher should remain skeptical and assume that enormous biases pervade the historical remnants (Barzun and Graff 1977).

2. Adequacy of Data

There is no way to evaluate the comprehensiveness of the materials that have been identified. However, there are several means by which the public administration researcher can make educated guesses about their adequacy. First, the researcher should critically examine the scope of material available to determine whether it reflects the full range of perspectives. In short, the researcher must always and repeatedly ask the question "Is the coverage of events balanced?" Since a completely adequate sample of materials is rarely available, the researcher should identify and evaluate the gaps in coverage and suggest areas that need further examination in future studies or when additional sources of data are found (Cahnman and Boskoff 1964; Mariampolski and Hughes 1978).

3. Reliability of Data

Examination of both public and private documents and archival materials for authenticity, either in whole or in part, is a necessary and constant task (Barzun and Graff, 1977). Some would argue that social scientists do not scrutinize their source materials enough. For example, historians sometimes criticize other social scientists for being insufficiently critical and skeptical about materials that they put through analysis (Erikson 1970, 1971).

The reliability of data involves (1) the credibility of the data source and (2) the accuracy of the data recorder. It is impossible to eliminate distortions in historical records and difficult to assess the extent and consequences of distortion. However, guidelines may be established for evaluating the degree of distortion and estimating the reliability of the historical record (Mariampolski and Hughes 1978).

Several factors can result in distortions of the data. The political or ideological orientations of the data source or recorder may bias his or her perspective and thus leave open the possibility of mistaken inferences. Distortion may also follow from the perspective generated by the particular organizational role, personal involvement, and personality of the data source or record keeper whether that person is a civil servant, political appointee, or some other type of government employee, or not (Mariampolski and Hughes 1978).

Although the issue of reliability may never be completely laid to rest, there are guidelines to help the researcher detect the presence of distortion, estimate the amount of distortion, and avoid this pitfall (Erikson 1970, 1971). One of the most useful statements on the evaluation of evidence for reliability was made by Gottschalk et al. (1947). They identified four tests to use in determining how dependable any body of personal documents may be:

1. Was the ultimate source of the detail (the primary witness) able to tell the truth?
2. Was the primary witness willing to tell the truth?
3. Is the primary witness accurately reported with regard to the detail under examination?
4. Is there any external corroboration of the detail under examination?

While information or evidence extracted from a document by the process described so far is presumably trustworthy, Gottschalk et al. (1947) do not regard it as reliable or accurate until it has been confirmed by two or more independent sources. When it is impossible to locate two independent documents reporting the same facts, the investigator must look for other kinds of corroboration, such as the absence of contradictions in other contemporary sources, the general reliability of the document, the reputation of the author for veracity and completeness, a lack of self-contradiction within the document, and the way the document conforms to, coincides with, or fits into the otherwise-known facts. Contradictory statements may have equal reliability if the researcher understands the basis or evidence underlying the differing statements (Mariampolski and Hughes 1978).

4. Validity of Interpretation

Unfortunately, social scientists frequently base elaborate arguments on sketchy and fragmentary data or on only secondary data sources. Every social scientist should develop a healthy skepticism about archival materials (Erikson 1970, 1971; Mariampolski and Hughes 1978).

It is usually impossible to apply statistical methods that permit interpretive judgments based on the logic of probability to documents because of data sampling problems, including adequacy and reliability, and their qualitative nature. Consequently, social scientists are forced to use other means to explain their findings.

A careful argument, supported by the cautious use of evidence that has gone through a skeptical analysis, is an acceptable means of analyzing these materials. This approach is no substitute for an analysis based on statistical inference. However, given the nature of the materials being examined, it is the only viable approach. Three processes are critical in the development of a sound argument: (1) a sensitive commitment to a theoretical perspective; (2) thorough familiarity with the documentary material; and (3) the ability to imaginatively interrelate evidence and theory. The researcher must ultimately develop a sense of balance and proportion concerning the data and capacity for judgment when synthesizing these materials. The procedures suggested in the validity section above are useful in this regard—especially the need to have multiple independent sources confirming findings.

The researcher may use an existing model or theory and evaluate the "fit" between archival evidence and the expectations generated by the theory (Smelser 1967). Theory can be a useful guide in determining the relevance of materials for use in a project, or the researcher may develop an explanation or theory from information found in the archival materials being examined (Cahnman and Boskoff 1964). In either case, the theoretical principles being used or developed should be flexible. Theory should be "a guide, not a master" (Cahnman 1976).

Many documents can be subjected to content analysis, a technique that has undergone extensive growth and sophistication since the development of computers. If a document is relatively free of reactive measurement effects, use of content analysis will produce results that are to some degree unobtrusive. Two of the early discussions of this technique are by Holsti (1968) and Gerbner et al. (1969). An early computer content analysis program was the General Inquirer, which is a set of computer programs designed to "(a) identify systematically, within text, instances of words and phrases that belong to categories specified by the investigator; (b) count occurrences and specified cooccurrences of these categories; (c) print and graph tabulations; (d) perform statistical tests; and (e) sort and regroup sentences according to whether they contain instances of a particular category or combination of categories" (Stone et al. 1966). Text must be coded before it can be analyzed, and to some extent this process can be automated (Hodson 1999). Some computer programs available for content analysis include Atlas/ti (Scolari Software), Intext and TextQuest, QSR NUD*IST (Scolari Software), QUALRUS (Idea Works), TextSmart (SPSS, Inc.). These and other programs and their capabilities are described in detail in Weitzman and Miles' (1998) publication. Stone et al. (1966) describe the General Inquirer. Klein (1999) describes INTEXT/PC (1991). NUD*IST is described by Richards and Richards (1991).

Computer analyses produce concordances (alphabetical lists of words occurring in a text), word organizing information through data reduction into lists, indexes, and cognitive maps Brent and Slusarz 2003; Hockey 1980; Mangabeira et al. 2004; Neuman 1994; Oakman 1980; Weber 1990; Wood 1984). The frequency of word or phrase usage and patterns of usage can reveal trends or tendencies and policy concerns. Content analysis can be used to check for internal consistency and to identify changes within documents or sets of documents across time (Weber 1990; Woodrum 1984). Several recent books provide more-detailed information about different aspects of content analysis (Neuendorf 2002; Popping 1999; Roberts 1997; Weber 1990).

Although use of content analysis programs is not widespread in public administration research, some examples in which it has been used do exist. For example, Brunner and Livornese (1982) have encoded and analyzed the State of the Union addresses of the U.S. presidents since 1945. Nazi propaganda (George 1959) and the content of soldiers' letters and diaries have also been subject to content analysis (Webb et al. 1966, 1972). Without a doubt, this analytical approach may be useful to others.

D. Summary

In summary, those doing research on public administration make frequent use of archival materials. These materials are used by themselves when other data collection procedures are inappropriate and when there is need to substantiate findings from other methodologies through triangulation.

Archival materials offer many advantages, such as allowing the researcher to use one source to cross-check another and to see how things change over time, suggesting explanations about why these changes occurred. In addition, the stability of archival materials makes it possible to test a hypothesis, modify the hypothesis, and test it again across time and in different situations.

No source of data or measure is perfect. Hence, all measures can and should be supplemented with information from other sources. Unobtrusive measures, especially archival materials in public administration research, are often used as supplemental measures in triangulation (using data gathered through multiple techniques) efforts to exclude plausible rival hypotheses. Unobtrusive measures are neither a panacea for measurement problems in public administration, nor are they the measure of choice in many research contexts. Nevertheless, their judicious and flexible use can result in improvement of the overall quality of public administration research.

V. PARTICIPANT OBSERVATION

Participant observation is an old and widely-used research method, both in public administration and in other fields of study. Today, the term participant observation subsumes a variety of techniques, including observation in one form or another, use of key informants, ethnography, and controlled observation techniques. Participant observation includes material that the observer gains directly from personally seeing or hearing an event occur. Often, the participant observer establishes personal relationships with subjects and maintains those relationships over a period of time. The duration of these relationships is longer than in other research techniques, such as surveys and interviews. Rapport and trust are established with subjects to a far greater extent than in other methods. Typically, more exhaustive data are gathered from fewer subjects using participant observation than with other methods. Data may be available through participant observation that are not available through other methods (Sjoberg et al. 1991).

In addition to information they gather themselves, participant observers often make use of information obtained from key informants. Material from key informants is necessary because an observer cannot be everywhere to cover simultaneous events, or may not have access to certain individuals or events and may need information about events that occurred before he or she began gathering information.

Historically, ethnography was the realm of the anthropologist, who used participant observation as just one of several data collection techniques in fieldwork. Today, the term ethnography is used both as a synonym for participant observation and in a broader sense to include participant observation together with any other methods the researcher uses to study a society, organization, group, or individual. These methods include use of informants, interviews and surveys (Denzin and Lincoln 1994, 2000; Fetterman 1989, 1998; Gold 1997; Rist 1980; Stocking 1983).

More recently, Controlled observation techniques have been developed to impose order on the observational process. For instance, observers in many studies of leadership have used these techniques (Busson et al. 1981; Feilders 1979; Fieldler 1967; Guest 1956; Jasinski 1956; Kaplan 1979; Kelley 1964; Kmetz and Willower 1982; Kurke and Aldrich 1979; Landsberger 1961; Larson et al. 1981; Lau et al. 1980; Martin and Willower 1981; Martinko and Gardner 1984a, b; Mintzberg 1968, 1970, 1971, 1973, 1975, 1979; Morris et al. 1981; O'Neil and Kubany 1959; Peterson 1977; Pitner 1978; Ponder 1957, 1959; Snyder and Glueck 1980; Sproul 1981).

A.   CHARACTERISTICS OF PARTICIPANT OBSERVATION

Participant observation has the following characteristics: first, observation takes place in a natural setting. The only difference is the presence of the observer. Second, observation over an extended period produces a large volume of information. Third, the observer is able to include their own and the subjects' reactions. Introspection or reflection on their experience is a legitimate source of data from participant observers (Balaban 1973). For example, a participant observer can report on his experience when calling a social service agency for information or their feelings while waiting in line for a case worker to conduct an unemployment compensation eligibility interview (Balaban 1978). Fourth, the observer can record the context in which the subject's statements and other behaviors occurred, thus making them more meaningful. Fifth, if the observer can establish rapport and trust with the subject(s), then she may be able to obtain information that the subject(s) normally would not share with a researcher conducting an interview or survey whose contact with them is comparatively fleeting, shallow, and impersonal (Jorgensen 1989).

Sometimes, it is assumed that participant observers passively watch what goes on around them. This is a mistaken impression. Certainly, participant observers see and hear much of what occurs in a research setting; however, the participant observer must ask questions too. What the observer does in the field is primarily based on talking with those around him, since the observer can personally see and hear only a small part of what occurs and is unlikely to understand significant parts of this material. Understanding events that are observed in the field depends to a large extent on finding out what these events mean to participants and informants (Becker 1958; Bittner 1973; Clough 1998; Coffey 1999; Gertz 1973; Goodenough 1971; Malinowski 1935; Pelto, 1970; Tremblay 1957; Van Maanen 1979b, 1988). These exchanges can result in the observer discovering things—meanings and patterns, for instance—of which the subject or informer normally is not aware or does not consciously think about (Malinowski 1922). Unless subjects and informants volunteer an explanation, there is no other way for a participant observer to learn why someone did something, why a particular event occurred, or what the events mean to them. The need to ask questions is great, because subjects usually do not volunteer explanations without being asked. This happens because subjects often assume that the researcher either knows why an event occurred, understands it just as they do, or that the researcher is not interested in it. Additionally, subjects expect the observer to ask questions and tend to wait for this to happen. The major disadvantage of the participant observation process is that too much is assumed or taken for granted on both sides. As a result, subjects volunteer too few explanations and observers ask too few questions (Kvale 1996; Lofland and Lofland 1984, 1995; Patton 1980).

Participant observation is a useful alternative to methods that rely almost entirely on self-report measures, such as interviews and surveys. These measures have dominated social science research for several decades despite their shortcomings (Selltiz et al. 1976; Webb et al. 1966, 1972). Recent studies indicate that the accuracy of selfreport measures in group and organizational settings is affected by a variety of factors such as the subject's knowledge of performance and perceptions of the environment (Binning and Lord 1980; DeNisi and Pritchard 1978; Downey et al. 1979; McElroy and Downey 1982; Staw 1975). McElroy and Downey (1982) report that both group-related and task-related factors affect observer results in controlled experiments. Observers are less influenced by outside factors than by the persons, groups, and organizations they study (Jones and Nisbett 1972). McElroy and Downey (1982) report similar results for both group and task-related information and for individuals fitting each of the four varieties of participant observer roles identified by Gold (1958), Junker (1960), and Bouchard (1976b).

B.   HISTORY AND USAGE

Participant observation has been used to gather data for more than 150 years. For example, Lewis Cass and Henry Rowe Schoolcraft used this method to study American Indians living on the

Michigan Upper Peninsula (Hinsley 1981; Schoolcraft 1846; Stocking 1983). Participant observation was used by Schoolcraft in 1846 in his study of the Iroquois. Frank Hamilton Cushing used this technique between 1879 and 1884 in studying the Zuni Indians (Brandes 1965; Green and Mitchell 1979; Hinsley 1981, 1983; Mark 1976; Stocking 1983). Boas used this technique on Baffin Island in 1883–1884 (Cole 1983) and in other studies during the 1890s (Boas 1897). Two early studies of child laborers and their working conditions, Hunter's (1904) publication and Spargo's in 1906, used participant observation. Early reports of committees of visitation to poorhouses, orphanages, asylums, and prisons were based on participant observation techniques too, and these have a long history in this and other countries (Bremner 1970–1971; Rist 1981).

Although not known as a proponent of participant observation, Jesse Walter Fewkes developed a useful tool for those who collect field data. His work between 1890 and 1894 included gramophone recordings of Zuni Indian behavior (Hinsley 1981, 1983). This is the earliest use of a sound recording device to supplement field observations and notes that the author has found.

Participant observation has been used throughout the history of public administration research. For example, early issues of the *PAR* contained large numbers of articles that are essentially case studies based primarily either on an observer's experiences as an employee or on his or her work as an externally-based researcher examining a particular agency or program. Articles of this kind can be found in every issue of *PAR* throughout its history. Similarly, many of the cases published by the Inter-University Case Program during the past 50 years are based either completely or in part on the work of participant observers. The trend across time in the research published in both these sources has been to use other methods too in a single study rather than to rely on just participant observation.

Recent studies have used participant observers to gather data along with other methods on a wide variety of research topics. For example, these topics include hospital information usage and patient care (Georgopoulos and Mann 1962); managerial communications patterns (Lawler et al. 1968); decision-making styles in welfare agencies (Aiken and Hage 1968); decisionmaking and authority patterns (Inkson et al. 1970); interaction patterns within a government agency (Blau 1954); managerial behavior (Hodgson et al. 1965; Sayles 1964); police recruit socialization (Van Maanen 1973, 1975); decision-making within the policy implementation process (Pressman and Wildavsky 1973); personnel processes (Thompson 1975); sources of information used in decision-making (Blau 1968); evaluation of a family planning clinic (Glaser and Humphries 1985); state capacity building programs (Madley 1981); federal dissemination of materials and school activities (Huberman and Crandall 1982); parental involvement in schools (Smith and Robbins 1982); police behavior on the street (Banton 1964; Buckner 1967; Cain 1973; Fox and Lundman 1974; Harris 1973; Lundman and Fox 1974; Manning 1972, 1976a, 1976b, 1977; McCall 1975; Reiss 1968, 1971; Rubenstein 1973; Skolnick 1966; Van Maanen 1974, 1978b, 1988; Westley 1970); police careers (Van Maanen 1978a; Van Maanen and Schein 1977); rural experimental schools (Herriott 1982); social movements (Gusfield 1955); the treatment of women in corporations (Kanter 1977); urban subcultures (Polsky 1967; Whyte 1955b); and the use of research in schools (Louis 1982).

Participant observation studies have evolved from single case studies (Blau 1960) to studies of multiple organizations (Blau and Schoenherr 1971; Huberman and Crandall 1982; Dalton 1950; Simpson and Gulley 1962) and from studies relying primarily on either a single or a small number of observers and informants into studies utilizing large numbers of them (Boas 1897; Datta 1982; Malinowski 1922; Mead 1953; Opler and Singh 1948; Osgood 1940; Paul 1953; Rist 1980; Yang 1945). These trends have occurred as participant observation evolved from being part of ethnography used primarily by anthropologists to a widely used technique employed by a variety of different kinds of social scientists (Lofland and Lofland 1995; Rist 1980; Van Maanen 1983).

C. KEY INFORMANTS

Key informants have been widely used in participant observation studies and their use has been increasing for some time (Inkson et al., 1970). Use of key informants has advantages, including control of costs and maintaining the focus of a study (Seidler 1974). One of the easiest ways to learn anything is to ask someone whom you believe knows something about it.

Key informants have been used to gather information about a wide variety of different topics. For instance, key informants have been used in traditional ethnographic studies of whole societies (Mead 1953). In addition, key informants have been used along with documentary sources of data in studies comparing different communities (Burt, 1981; Summers and Bloomquist 1982) and in research on related topics such as community power and decision-making (Aiken 1970; Clark 1968; Crain et al. 1969; Hawley 1963; Hunter 1953; Smith 1976); relative community status (Logan 1976; Logan and Schneider 1981; Logan and Semyonov 1980); economic and industrial development (Fuguitt and Deeley 1966; Krannich 1981; Richardson and Larson 1976; Summers et al. 1976); community involvement in environmental protection (Bridgeland and Sofranko 1975); community growth and population trends (Fuguitt and Beale 1978; Hassinger 1957; Humphrey and Krannich 1980; Humphrey et al. 1977; Humphrey and Sell 1975; Johansen and Fuguitt 1984; Krannich and Humphrey 1983; Maurer and Christensen 1982); community growth control (Baldassare 1981; Baldassare and Protash 1982); and program implementation (Luloff and Wilkinson 1979; Moore and Cantrell 1976). One explanation of the increasing use of key informants in studies comparing communities is the fact that available data often does not measure the variables that researchers need to examine in their studies. The adequacy of surrogate measures, such as available census data, as substitutes for actual variables of interest has been seriously questioned (Alford 1973, 1975; Summers and Bloomquist 1982; Walton 1976; Warren 1983).

Key informants are selected in a different manner than survey subjects. Subjects are selected for surveys as part of a probability sample designed to accurately represent a particular population. Key informants in participant observation studies are selected because of the work they do or the positions they hold and the experiences they are likely to have had. The experience, knowledge, and expertise of the informant are the basis for selecting them, rather than their being selected at random (Seidler 1974; Tremblay 1957). If informants are keen observers with good memories and are articulate, so much the better, since this makes the data more easily available than the researcher otherwise would be unlikely to find (Boas 1897; Paul 1953). Unfortunately, there is no guarantee that an able informant can be found. Individuals who would make appropriate informants may refuse to talk. All informants are not equal, since they do not have the same quantity or quality of information (Lofland and Lofland 1984, 1995; Van Maanen 1979b). Consequently, finding informants with knowledge and appropriate skills and gaining access to them have been major difficulties and limitations (Krannich and Humphrey 1986; Osgood 1940; Parrish and Whyte 1978; Tremblay 1957; Van Maanen 1979b, 1983, 1988; Whyte 1984). Gaining access is discussed at length in the interviewing section of this chapter.

Informants and subjects can function either as respondents or as informants. Respondents are asked to describe their own behavior, attitudes, and feelings. Often, informants report information about other persons and events, not themselves, and about events that occurred when the researcher was not present (Zelditch 1962). Informants are used to gather data that otherwise would be inaccessible. In addition, researchers sometimes ask the same subjects to function as respondents at one point in time and as observers at another point in a research project (Aiken and Hage, 1968).

Gathering data from informants has been accomplished by talking informally with them, by interviewing them, and by use of surveys. These techniques are not identical. A fixed question-and-answer format is not as effective as an informal discussion with one or two other persons (Malinowski 1935). This point is also made in Section III on the use of interviews. In some instances, all three techniques have been used in the same study. There are numerous examples of studies in which surveys were used to gather data from individuals who earlier had served as informants, or in which surveys were used after initial exploratory work was done by personally interviewing informants (Simpson and Gulley 1962; Smith et al. 1969; Tremblay 1957; Williams et al., 1959).

D. Types of Data in Participant Observation

Participant observation research can focus on a variety of kinds of information. One typology of participant observation data includes meanings, practices, episodes, encounters, roles, relationships, groups, organizations, and settlements (Lofland and Lofland 1984, 1995). Meanings include language, idiom, oral and written statements, cultural norms, and formal rules. Practices and behaviors of one kind or another are observed and reported. Episodes are specific, identifiable, discrete events with beginning and ending points that are usually well defined. Examples include an illness, divorce, crime, and the visit of a client to an office. Encounters differ from episodes in that they involve two or more people meeting and interacting face-to-face. Roles are the positions individuals occupy and the behaviors of individuals in those positions. Relationships are pairs or sets of roles such as teacher–pupil, superior–subordinate, committee members, coworkers, and caseworker–client. Groups, especially small groups, include work groups. Small-group behavior including subsets of this type of research, such as group decision-making (Allison 1971; DeWalt and DeWalt 2002; Janis 1983), is one of the most prolific areas of social science research. Groups as a focus of participant observation research include study of informal organizations. In contrast, the study of organizations usually means study of formal organizations: units within larger organizations, such as departments and programs, their structure and operations. Settlements include studies of towns, cities, and segments of them, such as neighborhoods.

E. Ethnography

Historically, ethnography and participant observation required long-term commitment of a researcher to a setting where he or she would literally live as he worked. Early work of this kind is associated with the Chicago School (Agar 1980, 1996; Becker 1966; Lee, 1993; Lindner 1996; Smith 1988; Whyte 1943). Today, even the Government Accountability Office uses ethnographic research in its assessments of federal programs (GAO, 2003).

In performing ethnographic research, the investigator typically immersed himself in the activities around him while maintaining enough distance from the setting and those around him to be able to make impartial judgments about the events and activities observed (Agar 1980; Asad 1973; Bernard 1994; Cesara 1982; Clifford 1983; Datta, 1982; Denzin and Lincoln 1994, 2000; Epstein 1967; Fetterman 1989, 1998; Foster et al. 1979; Gaunt 1982; Hinsley 1983; Kaberry 1957; Leach 1965; Lincoln and Guba 1985; Lofland and Lofland 1994, 1995; Malinowski 1954, 1967; Mandelbaum 1980; Powdermaker 1970; Rist 1980, 1981; Sanday 1979; Sontag 1970; Stocking 1968, 1982, 1983; Tremblay 1957; Whyte 1960). This time requirement has changed drastically, despite the admonitions and advice of experts. One expert recommends that at least a year be spent in observation for the study of a school system or program (Wolcott 1975). Multiple other researchers suggest spending a significant amount of time nearly a year or more (Bernard 1994; DeWalt and DeWalt 2002; Doheny-Farina 1985; Fetterman 1989; Lauer and Asher 1988; Wolcott 2001). Others point out that research is done more quickly in most observational studies today, such as Bowker's investigation of online communities (2001). This happens despite practical difficulties, such as the fact that establishing rapport and trust requires a substantial amount of interaction across time (Lofland and Lofland 1984, 1995; Rist 1980; Van Maanen 1979a, 1983, 1988; Wolcott 1975).

The rapid increase in the use of ethnography and associated techniques, such as participant observation, has been caused in part by demands of federal grant agencies requiring this type of research and by tortuous, multistage research proposal review and approval processes developed under regulations restricting and guiding access to human subjects (Boruch and Cordray 1980; Rist 1980; Raizen and Rossi 1981). Given a research history that includes abuse of human subjects and other problems, reviews and prior approval of research proposals by human subjects review bodies are used to prevent research that might be embarrassing or have potential legal ramifications (Datta 1982; Rist 1980; Van Maanen 1983). These requirements and difficulties have resulted in the relative decline of survey and experimental research as evaluation tools, which almost always require human subjects review of the entire study. This difficulty is more likely to occur and to be more extensive for experiments and surveys. These trends and difficulties have resulted in the ascendancy of methods, such as participant observation and ethnography, which are somewhat less likely to cause problems. One basis for this difference is that observation requires fewer subjects (Datta 1982; Rist 1980). Ethical behavior of researchers and appropriate treatment of subjects are ethical issues deserving careful attention (Fetterman 1989, 1998).

F. Roles of the Observer

Participant observation requires that the researcher fill numerous research and evaluation roles and use a wide variety of data sources (McCall and Simmons 1969). Junker (1960) and Bouchard (1976a) identified four sources of data from observers, including the complete participant, the participant as observer, the observer as participant, and the complete observer. McElroy and Downey (1982) linked Junker's (1960) typology to the amount of involvement that an observer has with the group being observed and to the amount of involvement that the observer has with the group's task. Thus, a complete participant is highly involved with the group and with their tasks. The participant-as-observer is highly involved with the group but less involved with their tasks. The observer-as-participant is highly involved with the group's tasks, but less involved with the group or its members. Finally, the complete observer is less involved with both the group and the group's tasks and focuses almost entirely on observation (Schwartz and Schwartz 1955).

One of the most common research roles for the participant observer is that of the participant-asobserver who informs subjects of his or her research aims (Gold, 1958; Junker 1960). Studies using this approach include the work of Becker et al. (1961) and Merton et al.'s (1957) studies of the socialization of medical students. Skolnick (1966) and Van Maanen's (1978a, 1988) studies of police behavior are examples of research based on the participant-as-observer model.

Another widely used research role in participant observation is that of the complete participant, who acts like an actual member of the group or organization under study and does not reveal either that a research study is in process or the purposes of the research to his or her subjects (Gold 1958; Junker 1960). An unusual and widely known example of this form of participant observation is found in Rosenhan's (1973) study of a state hospital, "On Being Sane in Insane Places." This approach results in the researcher having data that include both his own experiences in the research setting, as well as observations of the actions of those around him. In addition, this method provides access to settings and persons that otherwise would not be available (Riecken 1956; Riesman and Watson 1964).

G. Common Problems

Researchers using participant observation techniques to gather data encounter some common problems. These include difficulties with entry into the research setting; pressures on subjects; involvement in the research setting, rapport and language; over-involvement/over-rapport, methods of recording data; potential limitations of the participant observation methodology; and causes of inaccuracy.

1. Entry into the Research Setting

Potential problems encountered by participant observers when entering a research setting include obtaining permission to conduct research, suspicions of the subjects, and gaining acceptance by the subjects. In order to do research in most organizations, permission must be obtained from those in leadership positions. Official permission only gives the researcher legitimate access; it does not guarantee success. Even with permission from those in leadership positions and an introduction from them, the appearance of a stranger in the organization may arouse suspicion and anxiety among those whom the researcher wants to observe. Potential subjects may fear that the research will result in negative repercussions for them (Dollard 1937; Heffernon 1972; Van Maanen 1979b, 1983, 1988; Wax 1960). Similarly, employees might suspect that the researcher was hired by management to spy on them (Blau 1964). The problem of gaining access is discussed at length in the interviewing section of this chapter.

A participant observer often has some feelings of anxiety when first entering a new research setting (Powdermaker 1967). These feelings may be intensified if individuals around the participant observer indicate that they are suspicious and anxious about the researcher's purpose and if they act in a hostile manner. For instance, those in the work setting may avoid the researcher or not talk with him or her. Wilson (1956) provides an extreme example of subjects behaving in a hostile manner when he describes a stranger who concluded that he had been accepted because, after many years, the subjects had stopped spitting when they encountered him in public. It may take a good deal of time to gain acceptance from those being observed and during this time the researcher may become frustrated about the small amount of useful information initially gathered. Also, the participant observer may suffer some anxiety about the success or failure of the research project (Blau 1964; Coffey 1999; DeWalt and DeWalt 2002; Leach 1965; Powdermaker 1967, 1970; Van Maanen 1979b, 1983; Wax 1960; Wolcott 2001). Lack of initial success may cause anxiety about organizational leaders canceling the project (Balaban 1978).

Entering a new organization or research setting for the first time is a stressful experience for the observer. Suelzle and Borzak (1981) describe the researcher as a stranger unknown to those in the organization, with the process of entering the organization ultimately resulting in the observer being accepted in the role of guest. A guest or neophyte is expected to not know much, to ask many questions, to need help, and to make mistakes (Suelzle and Borzak 1981; Van Maanen 1979b). This strategy may offend elite or key informants and cause them to treat the interview as unimportant. In the words of Undheim (2003), "You risk losing respect, getting little or no time to talk, and you might be unable to steer the interview in the direction you want."

2. Pressures on Subjects

Subjects in participant observation studies are pressured to talk with strangers and to answer questions that make them feel uncomfortable. Normally, most people share little information about their lives and innermost feelings with other persons, especially strangers. Regardless of reassurances from a researcher, they will not believe what a stranger says, especially when either real or imagined personal risks are involved (Wax 1971).

Some questions may cause anxiety among most people. For example, questions about income, sexual behavior, and work performance are threatening to most people. Questions about personal matters and questions about topics that the subject knows little or nothing about can cause anxiety. A subject who cannot answer a question or answer a question well may be bothered by this fact. Few people want to appear ignorant. Even the fact that someone is asking questions can be bothersome. Subjects may experience pressure to answer questions. The fact that they are being asked by a researcher from the government or a university or the fact that other persons whom they know have participated or nominated them for participation may result in their feeling pressure to participate when they normally would not (Useem and Marx 1983). Feelings of pressure to participate and to answer questions may be so strong that individuals make up answers and even answer questions about nonexistent matters (Bishop et al. 1980, 1986; Collette and O'Shay 1976; Kolson and Green 1970; Orne 1962; Schuman and Kalton 1985; Schuman and Presser 1981).

As a result of these pressures, the following sequence of events often occurs during participant observation studies: first, the observer becomes increasingly better informed and more adept during the research project. Second, in many studies, the researcher is increasingly more accepted by research subjects from the beginning to a point well into the project. This depends on the subjects and the observer getting to know, respect, and trust one another, and sustaining these feelings over a substantial amount of time. Neither of these developments always or automatically happens. Consequently, what often happens is that subjects begin to routinely discuss with the participant observer things that they would either not talk about or would not be candid about earlier. These patterns result in differences in the quality of the data across time, which raises questions about the validity of earlier observations (Balaban 1978; Levine 1974; Patton 1980; Rist 1980; Van Maanen 1979b, 1983, 1988; Webb et al. 1966, 1972; Wolcott 2001). One answer to this problem is to examine general issues first and sensitive issues later in the research project. Another solution is to make note of issues that subjects are hesitant to discuss and raise these topics later.

3. Involvement in the Research Setting

Active involvement in the research setting is an excellent way to gather data without disturbing individuals or events. Contact between the researcher and subject is natural and unguarded (Bryun 1966; Dollard 1937; Liebow 1967; Wax 1960). Usually, initial data-collection efforts are devoted to gaining background information; getting to know the people, the processes, and the setting; and identifying and defining likely research topics. The researcher's own experience as a participant is one of the best sources of this information. Spending time with subjects helps the participant observer build an understanding of them, their feelings, and their perceptions (Coffey 1999; Dollard 1937; Fetterman 1989, 1998; Liebow 1971; Polsky 1962; Van Maanen 1988).

The participant observer may have to ask questions because he or she has no other alternatives. Asking questions may heighten subjects' fears, especially if a great many questions are asked and if any of the questions are about sensitive and threatening matters (Richardson 1960). Some subjects simply do not like to be asked questions, especially by people they do not know very well, and they usually like answering questions even less (Bain 1960). The best strategy during the early portion of a research project is to try to establish rapport, to rely on one's own observations, and to ask few questions of others. By asking questions before he or she has an understanding of the people and their situation in an organization, the researcher risks inadvertently asking embarrassing and threatening questions (Bogdon and Taylor 1975; Dalton 1964; Lofland and Lofland 1984, 1995; Van Maanen 1983, 1988). More questions can be asked when the participant observer and subjects get to know each other, assuming that the subjects like and respect the observer. Many researchers indicate that rapport with subjects is so important it can literally make or break a research project (Douglas 1976; Lofland and Lofland 1984, 1995; Van Maanen 1983; Whyte 1955a). Even after rapport is established, when a subject resists questioning, it is best to drop this approach and collect data by other means, including asking the same questions of other persons.

4. Establishing Rapport

A variety of techniques can be used to overcome subjects' anxiety about the participant observer and the research project. Answering questions may be a better initial strategy than asking questions, since questions may exacerbate subjects' fears (Richardson 1960). This is especially likely early in the research project. Asking subjects to explain what you have observed is a useful way to build rapport, since this shows interest in the subjects and their activities, ensures greater accuracy, and involves subjects in the project. Some of these techniques include explaining the purpose of the project to each subject, answering their questions about the project, and assuring each individual that what is observed and heard will not be attributed to them or any other individual and that anything they share in confidence will not be disclosed (Balaban 1978; Bogdon and Taylor 1975; Douglas 1976; Fetterman 1989, 1998; Patton 1980). Developing interpersonal relationships with subjects, especially with informal leaders, is another way to gain their confidence. Some of the things that observers have done to develop these relationships include not acting in an officious manner, talking with individuals and acting in a friendly manner toward them, spending time during breaks together, discussing nonbusiness and personal matters, and socializing after work (Fox and Lundman 1974; Lofland and Lofland 1984, 1995; Van Maanen 1983, 1988; Whyte 1943, 1955).

Developing trust may be the most important part of these interpersonal relationships (Zand 1972). Promising subjects and informants that what they say will be kept confidential may help (Bain 1960; Becker 1967; Gullahorn and Strauss 1960). The researcher may tell subjects that confidentiality can be maintained by disguising persons, places, and events in research reports (Geer 1964; Lynd and Lynd 1937; Van Maanen 1979a, 1983) and by not using information that could only have come from just one person (Berreman 1962; Dexter 1970; Whyte 1983). Using specific examples from the observer's experience with the subject in these discussions is effective, because the subject understands the content of the example.

The researcher needs to pay careful attention to protecting subjects from embarrassment and from more serious harm (Salancik 1979). Disguising names of persons, organizations, and places, and changing dates and times are useful and effective ways to protect sources from the general public. However, informed readers, such as other members of the organization the subject works for and other persons who may have been involved in an event, can see through these facile efforts to disguise and protect informants (Becker 1964; Lofland and Lofland 1984, 1995; McCall and Simmons 1969; Ruebenhausen and Brim 1965; Van Maanen 1983, 1988).

5. Involvement, Rapport, and Language

The observer's ability to understand his or her subjects and to be understood by subjects depends on their speaking a common language. This may be a matter of learning the jargon and usages of a profession or cultural group (Jorgensen 1989; Van Maanen 1979b, 1983, 1988), or it may be a matter of learning a new foreign language (Cole 1983; Hinsley 1983; Lowie 1940). Either limitation prevents the researcher from fully understanding and being understood, with obvious implications for research results. Without language facility, the researcher is dependent on an interpreter and the willingness of the subjects to learn and speak his or her language. Ability to speak the language is a necessity for rapport to develop. Without language facility, the observer is viewed as an outsider, and remains so because he or she can take few of the actions already described for building rapport and trust. Forcing others to communicate through an interpreter or to speak the observer's language communicates a negative message to the subjects about the observer's view of them, their language, and the research topic. These practices place the observer in a superior and the subjects in an inferior position relative to one another. With rapport and accuracy at risk, the observer must develop language facility.

6. Over-Involvement/Over-Rapport

Over-involvement and over-rapport negatively affect participant observation in two different ways. First, the observer may be unable to do his or her job. The participant observer needs to understand how the people observed think, feel, and behave, while remaining neutral and emotionally detached so that he can accurately record his observations. The observer can allow himself to become so deeply involved with the subjects and events that he is unable to accurately observe what is happening (Coffey 1999; Fetterman 1989, 1998; Gullahorn and Stauss 1960; Miller 1952; Powdermaker 1967; Tosenthal 1976; Vidich 1955). Forms of over-involvement include succumbing to a desire to help people in need, involvement in competition for status, taking sides in internal conflicts, and participation in ethically unacceptable activities (Bogdon and Taylor 1975; Bouchard 1976b; Patton 1980; Van Maanen 1983, 1988). Moreover, the observer may feel that he cannot ask sensitive questions because this would damage his personal relationship with the subject(s) (Argyris 1952; Douglas 1976; Lofland and Lofland 1984, 1995; Miller 1952; Schwartz-baum and Gruenfeld 1969; Van Maanen 1983, 1988; Whyte 1983). Second, subjects may literally "put on a show" for the observer by doing things that they normally would not do and by concentrating on activities they think the observer would like to see in the time the observer is present (Van Maanen 1983, 1988). Possible reasons for "putting on a show" include the subjects' desire to demonstrate their competence, knowledge, special skills; pride in their work; and their desire to either educate an ignorant observer, or make their case. All of these actions are examples of observer effects. They result from the observer's presence affecting the people they are observing and interacting with (Spano, 2006).

7. Note-Taking and Recording Data

The major purpose of observation is to gather information, and note-taking and taping are tools for making a permanent record of these observations. Some experts believe that the observer who fails to do this might as well quit trying to do research (Lofland 1971).

What the observer sees and hears should be recorded as soon as possible so that details will not be forgotten (Bogdon and Taylor 1975; Lofland 1971; Van Maanen 1983, 1988; Whyte 1983). Notes can be recorded during the day or after work. Notes taken during the day are usually in an abbreviated form, since there generally is no time for anything more detailed. These brief notes need to be expanded as soon as possible to minimize what is forgotten or confused (Dollard 1937). Notes should include descriptions of persons and events, quotations, the observer's own feelings, and the researcher's thoughts about what various observations mean and how they should be interpreted. The researcher's thoughts can be added to the notes at any time (Balaban 1978; Dalton 1964; Patton 1980). If the researcher expects certain things to happen because of past experiences and they do not occur, then this fact should be included in the record (Patton 1980).

Subjects usually accept note-taking and tape-recording because they expect the observer to do these things (Lofland and Lofland 1984, 1995). If the researcher wants to tape record informal discussions or formal interviews, it is a good idea to ask the subject for permission to make a recording. This may make the subject more comfortable (Davis 1961; Lofland and Lofland 1984, 1995). In addition, a discussion of taping provides an opportunity for the researcher to reassure the subject by explaining why she wants to make a tape or what the tape will be used for, and to provide a guarantee of anonymity.

Observers need to review their notes while the research project is in progress to identify unanswered questions, new questions, and patterns in and potential explanations of what they are observing. Any material of this kind must be added to the written record so that it will not be forgotten. This information can be used as a guide in subsequent observation sessions, and may be useful in report preparation. One authority suggests that as much time should be spent in these review sessions as is spent collecting data in the field (Lofland and Lofland 1984, 1995).

8. Potential Limitations of the Participant Observation Method

Limitations of this method include validity and reliability problems caused by (1) the random observations by fieldworkers or observers; (2) the generally passive nature of the participant observation process; (3) the observer's biases and selectivity; (4) over-involvement in the research site or with the subjects; (5) the observer's taking things for granted; (6) limitations inherent in the research/observer's role, including the form of observation, the observer's impact on the situation caused by others reacting to his or her presence, and conflict between the participant and observer roles; and (7) the amount of time and energy the participant observer devotes to ensuring that the information collected is accurate.

First, participant observation is beset by the lack of reliability resulting from random observations by the researcher. It is unlikely that two separate observers will see, hear, and record the same events in the same way. Moreover, there is no guarantee that two researchers will interpret a set of observations gathered by a fieldworker in the same way. Possible solutions for most of these problems are discussed in Section H, "Remedies."

Second, observers usually wait passively for desired events or behaviors to occur. There is no guarantee that the events of interest will occur when the observer is present. Two observers' experiences may be totally different. This can be limited by spending more time observing, by using multiple observers, by taking actions designed to stimulate behavior and reactions from subjects (Salancik 1979), and by using some form of structural observation (Martinko and Gardner 1985).

Third, biases and selective perception of observers cause unreliability and threaten validity. This problem can be exacerbated by an observer's having prior knowledge of and commitment to a theory and set of topics of interest. This problem is even worse when the research topic and significant questions are completely defined in advance before any fieldwork is done (Rist 1980; Van Maanen 1983, 1988). This knowledge can cause observers to concentrate on behaviors or events that relate to these questions or are consistent with them and to pay less attention to other events. Biases and preconceptions can affect the researcher's interpretation of the observations. When only one observer is used, this source of potential bias is more likely to occur and more likely to go undetected.

The biases of an observer and of his or her subjects are especially likely to affect reporting of negative information. Participant observers are likely to underreport or not record negative events, especially events that reflect badly on themselves (Balaban 1978) and their subjects (Van Maanen 1983, 1988). This will also occur because subjects are unwilling and unlikely to share this kind of information with them. Development of rapport and trust may reduce this problem over time.

Fourth, the observer may become so involved in the group that he or she identifies or sympathizes with them and loses objectivity—a process called "going native." As already indicated, over-involvement and over-rapport can be severe problems. This is a special form of bias. Complete or partial withdrawal from the research setting is the solution to this problem.

Fifth, observers often fail to record information because they take it for granted. One reason this occurs is that observers take routine events which they have heard and seen many times in the past for granted. They build up expectations over time about sequences of events and are not prepared for deviations from these long-established and expected patterns. Another way in which observers take things for granted is by ignoring the physical setting in which events occur (Bogdon and Taylor 1975; Friedman 1990; Patton 1980; Whyte 1984).

Sixth, limitations inherent in the researcher's role and gender can create problems. The form of observation or role taken by the observer defines the potential range of his or her experiences. For example, a covert observer serving as an office clerk usually cannot ask the agency head for personal information, and an employee-as-observer cannot disappear anytime he wants to take notes, much less take them openly. For others, a strong sense of frustration results from the fact that covert observation interferes with their ability to take notes (Dalton 1959). Freedom of movement throughout the organization is restricted by their role and gender, as is the range of topics the covert observer can ask about (Bernard 1994; Connelly and Clandinin 1990; DeWalt and DeWalt 2002; Schensul, Schensul, and LeCompte 1999).

Another problem inherent in the observer's role is that the presence of a known participant observer may sensitize subjects so that they change their behavior. Some researchers see this as less of a problem than others, because they see no reason for subjects to change their behaviors when an observer is present (Skolnick 1966). Nevertheless, it is widely believed that the presence of an observer can cause subjects to change their behavior in some way. Others see this as a difficult problem to prevent, detect, and correct (Van Maanen 1979b, 1983, 1988). Solutions to this problem include the observer's being present for a significant amount of time and the building of rapport and trust between subjects and the observer(s). Avoiding persons who exhibit changed or intensified behaviors is another way to deal with this problem, even though it depends on other persons being available (Agar 1980; Bernard 1994; DeWalt and DeWalt 2002; Van Maanen 1983, 1988).

Conflict between the participant and observer roles results in significant stress for observers. Some stress on observers may result from ethical difficulties. These feelings may be so strong that they affect the observers' work. Observers may see subjects participate in illegal acts. They may be pressured to engage in these acts themselves, and they may actually commit illegal acts. For example, some researchers report observing police officers beat a suspect and other persons engage in a variety of other illegal acts (Becker 1970; Chevigny 1968, 1972; Irwin 1972; Kitsuse 1962; Polsky 1967; Skolnick 1966). Illegal and ethically questionable events many be observed (heard or seen) by the observer. In addition, the observer often hears from subjects about the illegal activities of others. Other observers have been pressured to participate in the subject's activities. For example, an observer was pressured to help verbally and physically abuse patients (Bogdon and Taylor 1975). Some have even engaged in illegal acts such as voting fraud (Whyte 1960) and the keeping and hiding of weapons used to commit crimes (Polsky 1967), in order to maintain their relationship with a group. Subjects have also been put in positions where they are expected to choose sides in internal organizational conflicts and office politics (Bogdon and Taylor 1975; Bouchard 1976b; Douglas 1976; Patton 1980; Van Maanen 1983, 1988).

Being an accessory, complicitly concealing information, guilty knowledge, and moral conflicts are heavy and difficult burdens for the observer to bear (Becker 1964, 1967). Observation can lead to legal problems, because an observer and his or her sources are not protected by law in the same way that attorneys and their clients and physicians and their patients are privileged (Becker and Friedson 1964; Carroll 1973; Klockers, 1974; Lewis 1994; Nejelski and Lerman 1971; Rainwater and Pittman 1967; Ruebenhausen and Brim 1965; *Social Problems* 1967; Vidich et al. 1964; Yablonsky 1968a, 1968b). In fact, at least one social scientist served a short jail term for failure to answer court directed questions (Carroll 1973), and charges were filed and later dropped against another social scientist for refusing to answer questions and turn over research records (Van Maanen 1983).

The rationale for using a covert rather than an overt approach during participant observation is that some information could not be collected at all or less accurate information would be collected. Some observers are disturbed by their covert observation activities. Deception bothers some observers so much that they report feelings of frustration, anger, resentment, and disgust with the research process (Hsu 1979; Schwartz and Schwartz 1955; Van Maanen 1983, 1988). These feelings may even cause some observers to quit the researcher project (Bogdon and Taylor 1975; Lofland and Lofland 1984, 1995; Patton 1980; Van Maanen 1983).

9. Causes of Inaccuracy

The researcher bears the burden of evaluating the informant's information. It is both important and difficult to detect lies and other kinds of inaccuracies. Obviously, detection of falsehoods is important in order to have accurate information on which to base one's findings. In addition, detection is useful in order to know what subjects are so concerned about that they will lie or try to cover it up, and it is useful for filtering purposes to know who is likely to lie to you and who is not.

Detection of inaccuracies is a difficult task, because the observer can be misled in many ways. First, the subject or informant may deliberately mislead the observer. Subjects may not want to share certain information, or they may want to create a particular impression so they lie, partially answer a question, or evade answering a question. Subjects make selfserving errors because they, like most other individuals, naturally want to present themselves in as favorable a way as possible (Goffman 1973). Emphasis is placed on the positive and negative content is either eliminated or minimized. Social desirability, competition, desire to avoid blame, and bias are some of the explanations for this behavior (Sudman and Bradburn 1974).

Bias and prejudice exist because people have different values and needs, and because of inaccurate perceptions of the other persons and situations. Often, biases are assumptions based on ignorance rather than facts. Stereotypes, racism, sexism, ageism, and religious prejudice are examples of common biases. Sometimes these biases are obvious and easily detected by the observer, who can then take them into account in subsequent analyses. For example, a subject who makes racist and sexist remarks reveals their feelings. However, subjects sometimes are biased and are careful not to reveal these things. The observer may hear statements and observe behaviors that could be attributed to bias or prejudice, but are attributed by the subject or by an informant to other acceptable or legitimate beliefs and values. The observer has no means of determining their accuracy or motivation. Continued observation over a long period of time and analysis of patterns of behavior may shed some light on this type of problem. For instance, an observer might draw the conclusion that the individual in each of the following examples is biased in a particular way. A subject says that he is an independent, but he has never failed to vote a straight party ticket for the same party year after year. A personnel officer who hires large numbers of persons for management positions says that they are not biased, but they have never hired a woman or a black or a member of a religious minority for one of these positions.

Second, lying is sometimes done for humorous reasons. A subject may want to have some fun or see how much misinformation an observer will accept before realizing that someone is pulling-their leg. This may be a form of hazing that all new group members endure.

Third, the informant may tell the truth as they know it but has been misled themselves, or have inaccurate and incomplete information. For example, in recent years, presidential press secretaries and other official spokesmen have occasionally made statements that they believed were true, but which later proved inaccurate. On occasion, others have deliberately manipulated these spokesmen by not telling them the truth so that they would lie convincingly.

Plain and simple errors of fact often are accepted without question, rather than being tested for accuracy. This problem exists in many settings. For example, current research often accepts prior research findings without question. Reanalysis of existing data is rare, although noteworthy examples exist, such as reanalysis of the famed Hawthorne experiments (Franke and Kaul 1978). These reanalyses are statistical in nature and the participant observation portion of the studies has not been completely reanalyzed; critiques, yes, but not completely reanalyzed. Similarly, but in a different context, budget decisions usually perpetuate the priorities and agreements of the past (Barber 1966; Wildavsky 1984). The source may have his or her facts wrong. Even sources with a record of being honest and reliable inadvertently forget and confuse facts sometimes. Participant observers can contribute to this error by not listening attentively, by misinterpreting what they hear and see, by not noticing the events occurring around them, and by making errors in recording their observations.

Fourth, informants are sometimes unaware of the facts. They answer because they want to please the observer and do not want to appear ignorant.

Fifth, fear of reprisals also results in subjects providing inaccurate information. Often they will leave things out, deal with non-threatening questions and information, and present only positive information (Griaule 1957; Van Maanen 1979b, 1988). Internal organizational evaluations and exit interviews, whether based on interviews or surveys, are subject to this problem, and positively biased as a result. Both these problems were discussed in detail earlier.

Other sources of error include the directness of the material, the spatial location of the observer, and social-locational skewing of opinion. Directness refers to the source of the information. Did the participant observer see or hear an event themselves? Did a source personally hear or see it? Or, is the information second or third hand? The more persons the information passes through, the more likely it is that material has been added or deleted. A good story often becomes better as it is passed along. Rumors and subsequent riots have started this way. The observer must be concerned with the reliability of each source and, on occasion, must even verify his or her own observations.

The spatial location of the observer determines what he or she will see and hear. Location can account for the perspective of an observer. If the observer was not present, then the material he or she has must have come from a secondary source of some kind (Malinowski 1926). Additionally, this error can occur because an observer might forget when and where an event occurred or, worse yet, remember it incorrectly. Unfortunately, other possibilities exist too, such as the observer either assuming things or making them up.

Social-locational skewing of opinion occurs in every group of people, whether that group is formal or informal in nature. The observer may go completely native and accept, without question, the opinions, attitudes, and perspectives of their subjects. Differences in subjects' attitudes and behaviors and conflict between subjects may limit the possibility of an observer going native. For example, an observer working with two department heads in a city found that they had totally different perspectives on and attitudes toward productivity assessment and improvement projects (Yeager 1983). Awareness of the danger of going native and use of multiple perspectives are means of countering this problem.

H.   Remedies

A variety of techniques are used to assure that the quality of information from participant observation or to overcome these difficulties. Answers to these problems include training of observers, use of protocols and field guides, remaining open-minded, use of a field coordinator, use of multiple observers and comparing their results, triangulation or comparison of the observer's information with data from other sources, and secondary analysis by other researchers (DeWalt and DeWalt 2002). The final segment of this section (I) assesses the accuracy of participant observation when compared to other data collection methods.

1.   Training

It is often difficult to find persons with the background and skills to function as observers (Smith and Robbins 1982). Experienced observers are even more difficult to find. Hence, training of observers is usually necessary.

Training of inexperienced observers is essential if their data are going to be accurate, complete, and useful (Pelto 1970; Sanday 1979; Wolcott 1975). Useful training techniques include classroom, field, and post-observation feedback sessions. In the classroom, the trainee can be given background about the project, the field setting, and the subjects. The trainee can be exposed to examples of subject matter and examples of appropriate and inappropriate statements to record and things to ignore. They can practice observation, interviewing, and notetaking techniques. Video is useful in these sessions, both to demonstrate methods and provide feedback on trainee practice. The trainee can accompany an experienced observer and have that person explain what and why he or she is collecting certain information. The experienced observer can coach the neophyte during his or her first few field sessions. Feedback sessions following practice or training observations can be used to review the individual observer's notes. Sessions like this can also include comparisons of one person's observations with those of other trainees and of experienced observers. Since participant observers often ask questions of the people around them and may even interview key informants, training in open-ended interviewing techniques and in using follow-up questions or probes is appropriate. Training of interviewers is discussed in the section on interviewing.

2. Balanced Subjects

A second method of preventing problems with observational data is to ensure that the subjects represent a cross-section of those who could be appropriate subjects. The question "How representative are the informants?" should always be asked. Balance among subjects is important, since several authors report that initial contacts are likely to be with marginal group members and those who are disgruntled (Douglas 1976; Glaser and Strauss 1967; Kluckholn 1940; Lofland 1976; Merton 1947; Patton 1980; Van Maanen 1979a, 1983, 1988).

Individuals vary considerably in their willingness to serve as informants. For instance, Seidler (1974) points out that marginal members of an organization or group and those who are dissatisfied will often be the first to make contact with a researcher. Several studies indicate that public officials are more willing to serve as key informants than officials in private-sector companies (Burt 1981; Johansen and Fuguitt 1984; Krannich and Humphrey 1986; Maurer and Christenson 1982). These sources of potential bias—first contacts and marginal and disgruntled informants—need to be guarded against. Awareness is a first step. More specific remedial actions include interacting with multiple subjects, those in formal and informal power positions as well as other individuals, making an effort to interact with persons in all segments of the research setting, and trying to interact with a balanced and representative group of subjects.

In order to assess balance among subjects, the researcher can gather background information from the informants and other sources (Seidler 1974). The researcher can select informants who hold particular formal titles and positions, since they may have desired experiences and access to information (Campbell 1955; Cartwright and Schwartz 1973; Clark 1968; Krannich and Humphrey 1986; Sjoberg et al. 1991; Tremblay 1957; Williams 1973). However, just because individuals hold similar positions is not a sufficient reason to assume they will be equally willing and capable informants (Krannich and Humphrey 1986; Yeager 1983).

The observer should not settle just for the first few subjects with whom they have contact, volunteers and those who are cooperative and with whom it is relatively easy to converse. Multiple work or community groups and multiple individuals should be contacted, not just one group or one person as a representative of that group. Similarly, if initial subjects present mostly cynical and negative information, the observer needs to make multiple other contacts to see if subsequent sources present similar or different perspectives. Working with a balanced group of subjects is especially important, but is sometimes difficult to do when some subjects refuse to interact with the observer (Festinger et al. 1956). Informants can be asked to nominate other knowledgeable persons who, in turn, may be used as informants (Seidler 1974; Tremblay 1957). This is snowball sampling (Berg 1988; Hendricks et al. 1992; Griffiths et al. 1993; Thompson 1997; Van Meter 1990; Vogt 1999). Overlap in these lists is an indicator of the relative involvement and visibility of each individual in the research setting. Multiple interactions or visits and contact over a substantial length of time with the subjects may help too (Griaule 1957; Rist 1980; Van Maanen 1983, 1988).

3. Field Guides

Using written protocols and field guides that tell the observer what to look for, questions to ask and answer, guidance about what to record, and general rules covering a variety of different contingencies may be helpful. Examples provided in these guides can be especially useful to an inexperienced observer (Datta 1982; Louis 1982; Smith and Robbins 1982). It is inappropriate to develop these guides too early in a research project. Rist (1980) reports that some researchers develop these guides before making their first visit to the field. This a priori approach seems bound to impose inappropriate biases on observers. In fact, one of the purposes of initial field visits usually is to develop an initial sense of the existing situation, definitions, boundaries, and potential problems (Tremblay 1957). Ongoing revision of field guides seems appropriate for most studies.

4. Remaining Open-Minded

The observer needs to be both open-minded and non-judgmental. To do so, the observer needs to guard against being unduly influenced by first impressions, whether good or bad. Making up one's mind too quickly and being too certain about things result in failure to ask questions and to seek advice and help. As a result, important events and behaviors might be overlooked or taken for granted, and the meaning of these events and behaviors to subjects misunderstood (Suelzle and Borzak 1981; Van Maanen 1979b, 1988).

5. Field Coordinators

A field coordinator can answer questions that observers have, on site and in a timely manner. Information gained from one observer, such as an explanation or a question, can be shared with other observers. The field coordinator helps lessen the impact of unforeseen contingencies, such as the effects of the participant observation process on the observer. A field coordinator can also help ensure consistency within and between observers by reviewing their notes. A field coordinator can use feedback and encouragement to improve observer performance (Tremblay 1957). Further evidence about the efficacy of feedback and advice is given in Yeager et al. (1985).

6. Pairs of Observers

Another researcher who does not act as an observer sometimes works with a participant observer to help maintain his or her sense of purpose, objectivity, and reality (Levine 1974). The term a "knowledgeable other" is sometimes used to describe this person (Balaban 1978). Whyte (1951) points out that all researchers have "blind spots" and that a knowledgeable other may make the participant observer aware of these blind spots. Obviously, it is far better if this awareness occurs early in a research project, when appropriate adjustments can be made, rather than after most of the data have been collected. Yin (1994) recommends ongoing discussion of preliminary findings with knowledgeable colleagues as a means of discovering meaning and maintaining perspective.

A knowledgeable other can help the researcher deal with conflicts between the roles of participant and observer. For example, researchers sometimes feel that they are exploiting the people around them from whom they are gathering data. Feelings of guilt about this can make it difficult to continue with a research project. The knowledgeable other can help them maintain a sense of purpose (Jorgensen 1989; Powdermaker 1967; Riesman and Watson 1964). Additionally, over-involvement in the research setting can distract the observer; a knowledgeable other can help overcome this problem (Balaban 1978; Sullivan et al. 1958). Another researcher can serve as an "adversary," "gadfly," or reviewer to question observations and interpretations of the participant observer (Levine 1974; Yin 1994). The other researcher's detachment can balance the observer's participation in the research setting. Both this individual and the participant observer can independently interpret all notes from the research project and then compare their interpretations. This technique will help prevent the participant observer from overlooking possible multiple alternative, and equally plausible, interpretations.

7. How Does the Informant Know?

It is helpful for the researcher to gather information from the informant about how he knows a particular fact or piece of information. For instance, did he see or hear it himself? Or did he hear about it from someone else? Accuracy may decrease as information passes from one person to another. For example, stories and rumors get better as they move from one person to another. Similarly, the researcher should determine how long ago the informant saw or heard an event. As the amount of time since an event occurred lengthens, memory usually becomes increasingly more fallible. With the passage of time, loss of detail and the likelihood of confusion increase, unless the informant has done something to refresh his or her memory, such as mentally reviewing the details and sequences of the event, keeping a diary, recounting the event to others, and discussing it with others who may or may not have been present.

The researcher should always ask, "How accurate is the information the informant supplied?" The researcher can judge the accuracy of his or her informant's information (Vidich and Bensman 1954; Vidich and Shapiro 1955). An informant who is ignorant of events of interest should be avoided. Similarly, Seidler (1974) suggests not using individuals who take extreme and obviously biased positions. If this is impossible, then select a set of informants whose biases balance one another. The researcher can use multiple informants in one setting and ask them identical questions, emulating an interview to some extent (Bridgeland and Sofranko 1975; Clark 1968; Humphrey and Krannich 1980; Krannich and Humphrey 1983, 1986; Merton 1947; Williams 1973). Single informants can be used and their responses checked against those of similarly placed individuals in the same and other organizations (Baldassare 1981; Baldassare and Protash 1982; Caputo and Cole 1977; Cartwright and Schwartz 1973; Johansen and Fuguitt 1984; Maurer and Christiansen 1982). Multiple informant information can be checked by outside experts, by comparing their statements for consistency, and by cross-checking their information with written records and other sources (Kendall and Lazarsfeld 1950; Pennings 1973; Seidler 1974). Also, the researcher can judge their statements against the amount of time required for an event to occur, a sequence or timeline of events, and the likelihood that a particular action or event occurred in a particular way (Mead 1953). Examples of questions the researcher could ask herself about an informant's testimony include, "Could the informant have been present? Could the individual have participated in the event? Could he or she have said and done or observed what is claimed?"

8. Agreement among Observers

Multiple observers can cross-check one another's observations (Griaule 1957; Levine 1974; Poggie 1972; Riesman and Watson 1964; Whyte 1951; Young and Young 1962). This is an effective means of establishing the consistency of results. Comparison of different observer's notes may reveal dissimilar perspectives, biases, oversights, and alternative interpretations. Hopefully, comparisons will reveal more similarities than differences. Once researchers are aware of differences, especially patterns in their differences, they can take them into account in interpreting their data and in planning further research. Multiple observers can watch each other in the field and note how subjects and the other observer interact (Whyte 1951).

Agreement between informants can be measured and assessed statistically. A useful statistic for this type of analysis, measuring agreement across observers and informants, is Cohen's (1960) kappa. Use and interpretation of this measure are explained by several authors (Cohen 1968; Fleiss 1981; Krannich and Humphrey 1986; Landis and Koch 1977; Maclure and Willett 1987; McBride 2005; Posner et al. 1990; Spitzer and Fleiss 1974; Spitzer et al. 1967; Whyte and Finlay 1995). Inter-rater agreement on interval-level ratings can be examined using higher order statistics. Rater agreement or association can be determined using factor analysis; rater bias using one-way analysis of variance, and rating distributions can be compared by plotting them (Uebersax 1988, 1992).

Participant observers differ in what they notice and record. These differences occur because of each individual's values, biases, and interests; differences in location and time; and differences in whether one is lucky enough to be present when major events occur. Multiple events occur simultaneously, and the observer cannot be everywhere at the same time. In addition, sometimes events occur so rapidly that a single observer simply cannot see and hear, much less record everything that happens. Use of multiple observers will give greater coverage because they will be able to see, hear, and record more than a single observer (Balaban 1978; Blau 1964; Dalton 1964; Epstein 1967; Griaule 1957; Malinowski 1926).

Discarding observations that cannot be substantiated by some other means is one way of avoiding problems of reliability (Louis 1982; Tremblay 1957). A variant of this technique is to use teams of observers and require them to discuss their findings and reach consensus before data are accepted. Involving the observers directly in the cross-checking and interpretation processes can be a powerful learning and motivational experience (Louis 1982).

9. Reflection

Researcher can spend time reflecting on their experiences and notes trying to identify real and potential biases prior to, during, and after a research project. This effort may include reflection on the research topics, the human subjects, and the research setting. Reflection can identify existing and potential problems, and the researcher can attempt to develop solutions to these problems. Awareness and compensation are potential solutions. In addition, this reflective process should follow each portion of the research process. For example, following a day spent observing the activities of a group of subjects, the researcher should review each interaction with or between subjects to identify biases and other problems, issues, or questions to follow-up, and ways to improve the research process or avoid mistakes, as well as examine successes (Dexter 1970; Krieger 1985).

The observer can look for implausible material and contradictions and check new information for accuracy against prior observations and established facts. Apparent inconsistencies and other problems can be checked with the subject in subsequent contacts (Griaule 1957). Once questions about the credibility of a subject exist, then more careful attention and cross-checking should be given to information from this source. The researcher might decide not to use any information that cannot be verified by more than one source. These techniques can be used with other methods such as interviewing.

10. Commitment to Quality

The researcher can commit him or herself to not using the shortcut methods known as blitzkrieg ethnography. Participant observation compressed into a very short period of time, such as a week or two, and involving a limited number of site visits (as few as one or two) is unlikely to produce accurate and meaningful results. Time constraints limit the quantity and quality of data that can be gathered. Rapport and trust are difficult, if not totally impossible, to establish in a day or two of fieldwork. The terminology of ethnography is sometimes used as a defense of such shoddy methodological work: for example, a research report's contents that were "real to the subjects," "phenomenological in nature," "unique personal experiences," and "the beginnings of grounded theories." Such explanations are an ineffective defense, since they fail to make the unknown comprehensible (Rist 1980). Discussions of the requirements of meaningful efforts to conduct participant observation or ethnography are found in many sources (Adams and Priess 1960; Bernard 1994; Bogdon and Taylor 1975; Bryun 1966; Clifford 1983; DeWalt and Dewalt 2002; DeMunck and Sobo 1992; Filstead 1970; Freilich 1970; Glazer 1972; Gusfield 1955; Johnson 1975; Kaberry 1957; Leach 1965; Lincoln and Guba 1985; Lofland and Lofland 1984, 1995; Marshall and Rossman 1995; Merriam 1988; Patton 1980; Powdermaker 1970; Riess 1968; Rist 1980; Ward 1964; Wolcott 2001).

11. Triangulation

Another means of verifying data from participant observations is to use multiple kinds of data gathered in a variety of ways from different kinds of sources, including interviews, published records, surveys, earlier secondary studies, and any other sources available. For example, information can be used from other sources, such as newspapers and the writings of other individuals who are not trained researchers, ethnographers, or participant observers (Sanday 1979). Using multiple data sources in this way is called triangulation (Denzin 1978; Janesick 1994; Jick 1978, 1979; Louis 1982; Patton 1987; Sypher et al. 1985; Vidich and Lyman 1994; Yin 1994, 2003). Smith points out multiple ways in which triangulation could help resolve disputed research findings (1997).

Another helpful source may be biographies, autobiographies, and diaries. Autobiographies and diaries may contain information available nowhere else (Sjober and Kuhn 1989; Sjoberg et al. 1991). In a somewhat similar but more systematic fashion, several participant observation studies have used prior studies as a starting point and source of comparative data (Summers et al. 1976; Summers and Bloomquist 1982). Some of these data may be collected by participant observers if they are able to use recording devices, cameras, and video cameras, and by researchers using other methods such as surveys and formal interviews. For example, observations, surveys, and interviews were used to collect data in an evaluation of Salvation Army programs (Glaser et al. 1987). Triangulation is discussed at greater length in the section on the case study method.

12. Structured Observation

Observation can be made at least somewhat systematic by using structured observation techniques in the field. For instance, it is sometimes helpful for the observer to have a set of categories or classification system to help them impose order on what is observed and to guide the recording of data. This is especially true when there is a large amount of information and it comes about in a short period of time. For example, Robert Bales (1950) developed a set of twelve well-defined categories for use in classifying the behaviors of group members. These categories are as follows: shows solidarity, shows tension release, agrees, gives suggestion, gives opinion, gives orientation, asks for orientation, asks for opinion, asks for suggestion, disagrees, shows tension, and shows antagonism. Another example is provided by Mintzberg (1973), who developed an observational scheme for the study of chief executive officers which included the location, the number and kind of participants (e.g., client, subordinate, director), the type of activity (e.g., desk work, scheduled meeting, tour), the communications media used (e.g., verbal face-to-face, telephone, written), who initiated the contact with the chief executive officer, and the purpose of each event (e.g., giving information, scheduling, action request).

The advantages and disadvantages of structured observation have been examined in a number of places (Busson et al. 1981; DeWalt annd DeWalt 2002; Miles 1979; Penfield 1974; Stewart 1976; Weick 1968; Wilpert 1982; Wolcott 2001). These limitations include small sample sizes, which exacerbate the impact of unusual cases (outliers) and nonparticipants, and limit the use of inferential statistics and reliability checks. Lack of inferential statistics and reliability checks is also a major criticism of studies using structured observation methods. Another criticism is that studies using structured observation methods are not conceptually well developed. For instance, Mintzberg's work on managerial roles (1973) has been criticized for being simplistic, mechanistic (failing to take environmental effects and individual differences into account), focused on minute details rather than the meanings of these details, for not being theoretically based, for failing to adequately code data, and for failing to differentiate effective and ineffective managerial behaviors (Gronn 1982; Pitner 1982). These difficulties have been surmounted, at least in part, in more recent studies of management (Burgoyne and Hodgson 1984; Gronn 1982; Huff et al. 1982; Martinko and Gardner 1984a, b; Snyder and Glueck 1980).

Unfortunately, as Mintzberg's (1973) work illustrates, a complete, carefully developed, theoretically based, pre-tested instrument like Bales' is not available in advance for most participant observation studies. Nevertheless, given the difficulties of observing and recording complex behaviors which may occur rapidly, and the desirability of a uniform method of recording data, it may well be worth the effort to develop a guide of some kind to help observers. A guide can be revised and improved as the project progresses, and a guide, once developed, can be modified for future work. Even the lack of an adequate guide, as in Mintzberg's work (1973), may stimulate subsequent researchers, such as Martinko and Gardner (1984a), to develop a guide based on the findings of their immediate predecessors.

13. Secondary Analysis

In addition to these techniques, researchers can perform secondary analyses on the original data from participant observation studies and thus attempt to verify the original results. Several obstacles limit the applicability of secondary analysis to participant observation studies. First, it is unethical to turn raw data containing the names and confidences of subjects over to others (Datta 1982). If guarantees of confidentiality are made, the researcher has a moral obligation to meet these guarantees. Researchers also have obligations to not harm their subjects and to prevent others from using their research data to harm them.

To abide by these obligations, the researcher would have to heavily edit the written record. All names of persons and places would have to be disguised. This might not be enough. Future users will know who did the research, where, and when it was done. They will have copies of reports and publications based on the research and they will have other relevant public records as well. Information from these and other sources may make it easy for someone else to determine who the subjects were, who and what they talked about, and where and when the events described in the record occurred. Consequently, information that was potentially harmful and sensitive in nature, either to the subjects who supplied it or to other persons whom the subjects talked about, might have to be removed from the record. For example, if a subject's statement is libelous and it is left in the record, many kinds of problems can result for the researcher, the subject, and the person the subject talked about. These editing tasks are monumental. How many active researchers have the time to prepare their records in this way for public access? Help with this task would be difficult to obtain for who else has the knowledge necessary to make the judgments needed to identify critical contents that need to be deleted. This problem is compounded by the fact that once the research records are no longer under the researcher's control and are part of the public record, they can then be examined by anyone and used for any purpose.

Second, secondary analysis of participant observation studies has not been performed in many instances because archives containing raw data from this type of study virtually do not exist (Datta 1982). The data from the Western Electric Hawthorne studies are in exception to this generalization. Some authors jealously guard their data and will not share it with others. Some scholars view research as a competitive business. For instance, the author has observed at least a dozen instances of scholars who, when nearing the end of a research project, found a newly published article by someone else who was working on a similar project. When these data exist, they are not readily available. To have access, the researcher must travel to the facility housing these materials. In contrast, several archives exist containing survey and other forms of quantitative data. One of these is the Survey Research Center at the University of Michigan.

Third, analysis of masses of qualitative data is prohibitively expensive in terms of both time and money (Datta 1982). The need to go to the facility housing the research records and stay there for a long period of time magnifies the expense of a project like this. Typically, a project like this takes years. A one- or two-semester sabbatical is not long enough. Faculty who would do this research are often under pressure to either publish or perish. Institutional rewards and professional recognition for secondary analyses are not as great as for primary or original research. The odds of developing major new findings or a significant reinterpretation of earlier data are slim, unless major errors or unused materials are found. Imagine the difficulties confronting the scholar and would be author who has spent five years on a research project that confirms the findings of a study done 20 years earlier.

A final reason for the paucity of secondary analyses of participant observation studies is the limited number of persons who have the skills and resources necessary to perform these analyses

(Datta 1982). The impact of this limitation is exacerbated by the fact that the concept of opportunity costs applies here. Simply put, many of those who have the necessary skills are working on other, perhaps easier, and perhaps more timely, and even more interesting projects.

I. ACCURACY OF PARTICIPANT OBSERVATION

A variety of empirical studies have been done assessing the accuracy of data gathered by the participant observation/key informant method. Often, these studies have compared data from key informants with data gathered by other means, such as surveys and documents (Honigmann and Carrera 1957; Honigmann and Honigmann 1955; Johansen and Fuguit, 1984; Pennings 1973; Poggie 1972; Tremblay 1957; Young and Young 1962). The results indicate that key informants were more likely to be reliable when what they were reporting on was directly observable by them, was noncontroversial, and was public knowledge. Informants were not as accurate when what they were reporting on was not directly observable, was controversial, might make them or someone they know and like or their organization look bad, and required more than a little inference, evaluation, or judgment. Events occurring within a building or within a person's head cannot be observed (Poggie 1972; Young and Young 1962). Moreover, participant observers or key informants were reliable sources of information on matters which were relatively stable or which changed very slowly.

VI. SURVEY RESEARCH

Survey data is collected using structured face-to-face interviews, structured telephone interviews, by having subjects fill out surveys in controlled situations, and by sending surveys to subjects by e-mail/Internet and by mail, who then fill out the survey. Examples of each of these respective methods include the face-to-face General Social Surveys conducted by the National Opinion Research Center (Steinhaus and Perry, 1996), the numerous telephone surveys conducted during primaries and election, and the evaluations of Drug Resistance Education (DARE) programs that are given to students in classroom settings (Dukes et al., 1996, 1997). Internet and e-mail surveys are discussed later in this section. This section focuses primarily on mail-back surveys.

The mail-back survey is an increasingly popular method used in public administration research. Evidence of this increasing popularity is found in *PAR*. The annual volume for 1971 contains three articles based on survey methodology, or 5.9% of the articles published in that volume. The 1976 volume contains four articles that use survey research methods, or 6% of the articles in that volume. The 1986 volume contains ten articles whose authors used a mail survey to gather their data, or 18% of the articles published that year. In 1995, six articles, or 11.8% of the fifty-one articles were based on surveys. In 2004, surveys were more widely used than in the past. Authors of seventeen of the fifty-nine articles, or 28.8% of them, relied either completely or in part on surveys as a source of data. This evidence indicates that surveys are being increasingly used for public administration research. No doubt this pattern reflects the heavy emphasis given to surveys in public administration and political science research methods courses (Schwartz-Shea 2001).

Mail-back surveys have also been used to study a vast range of public administration topics, including managerial attitudes about business–government relations (Stevens et al. 1991), information flows from staff to state legislative committees (Lewis and Ellefson 1996), the experiences of political appointees (Michaels 1995), community power (Clark 1968; Crain et al. 1969), local government decision-making (Caputo and Cole 1977); local government compliance with state mandates (May and Burby 1996), local government ethics practices (West et al. 1993), how local government officials cope with ethics stress (Miller et al. 2005), implementation of environmental policies (Bridgeland and Sofranko 1975), industrial development (Krannich 1981), economic development (Glaser et al. 1997; Humphrey and Krannich 1980; Johansen and Fuguitt 1984; Maurer and Christensen 1982; Krannich and Humphrey 1983), assessment of the impacts of set-aside programs (May and Burby 1996; Myers and chan 1996), employee attitudes towards pay (Scott et al. 1996), why senior executives leave the federal service (Wilson 1994), organizational commitment (Balfour and Wechsler 1996), training needs of state employees (Guthrie and Schwoerer 1996), community growth control policies (Baldassare 1981; Baldassare and Protash 1982), and assessment of professional journals (Forrester and Watson 1994; Vocino and Elliott 1982 1984). Surveys are used by state and local governments to increase citizen participation and assess the quality of government programs (Brown and Fish 1973; Daneke and Kobus-Edwards 1979; Ferris 1982; Glaser and Hildreth 1996; Poister and Henry 1994; Watson et al. 1991). Even the ranking of public administration and cognate programs is accomplished by use of mail-back surveys.

The most popular form of survey technique used in this public administration research is a mail-back survey, rather than either a face-to-face, telephone interview or an e-mail/Internet based survey to gather data. In the 1971, 1976, and 1986 annual volumes of the *PAR*, only one telephone survey-based article appears, and that was published in the 1986 volume. In 2004, two of 17 surveys were conducted by phone and none were conducted by e-mail/Internet.

Users of mail surveys are beset with the ubiquitous disadvantage of nonresponse and the problems it can cause. This section examines nonresponse, the problems it causes, and solutions to these difficulties. Important as this topic is for survey validity, it is virtually ignored in the public administration literature.

A. NONRESPONSE

Since the 1950s, response rates to all kinds of surveys have declined, because it is more difficult to contact people and because people are more likely to refuse to participate. This has occurred despite the development and use of more elaborate and extensive survey procedures (Atrostic et al. 2001; Biemer and Lyberg 2003; Groves and Couper 1998; Groves et al. 2002; Goyder 1982b; Keeter et al. 2000; Pearl and Fairley 1985; Spaeth 1992; Steeh 1981).

Need for a high response rate is considered a decisive argument in favor of face-to-face interviews over mailed questionnaires, since it is common knowledge that response rates to mailed questionnaires usually are much lower than those to personal interview questionnaires. One argument for this generalization is that it is far more difficult for a potential respondent to refuse a caller at the door than a letter in the mail (Babbie 1973; Sanders and Pinhey 1983; True 1983). To refuse an interview is to incur the psychic cost arising from the fieldworker's disapproval. Noncompliance costs less when contact is by mail and a questionnaire can easily be lost or forgotten. This view of nonresponse is consistent with the exchange theory espoused in Gallegos (1974) and Dillman (1978, 2000).

Despite these advantages, during the past thirty-five years, the percentage of interviewer contacts resulting in refusals has been increasing. This has eroded response rates in interview surveys and enhanced the competitive position of questionnaires (Koenig et al. 1977; Steeh 1981). For some topics, a mailed questionnaire may produce a higher response rate than a personal interview (Dillman 1978, 2000; Nachmias and Nachmias 1976).

Similarly, although response rates to telephone surveys are generally higher than to mail-back surveys, telephone survey response rates have become more problematic and have declined in recent years also. More elaborate sampling, callback, and case replacement methods have been required to produce acceptable levels of response, much less levels of response that used to be taken for granted (Cummings 1979; Dillman 1978, 2000; Dillman et al. 1976; Groves and Kahn 1979).

The number of prior surveys that an individual has been exposed to in the recent past affects their willingness to participate in a survey. A significant number of people are over-surveyed (Goyder 1987; Schleifer 1986). The author believes that this over-surveyed effect is exacerbated by unscrupulous mass marketing/fund raising organizations disguising their mailings and phone contacts as surveys. These manipulations may reduce public trust of surveys and those who do surveys, reducing responses to surveys (Butz 1985).

Although the problem of declining response rates is common to all survey methods, common knowledge has it that mail-back surveys produce lower response rates than either face-to-face or telephone interviews. Few studies have directly compared response rates in face-to-face surveys with those obtained by mail and telephone. Substantial evidence indicates that it is possible to produce similar response rates using each of these methods (Dillman et al. 1974; Dillman 1978, 2000). At least one researcher found higher response rates for telephone and mail surveys and concluded that potential respondents prefer the anonymity and impersonality of these methods (Steeh 1981). Also, some evidence exists that FAX-based surveys are cheaper to administer and provide response rates similar to those of mail-back surveys (Schreckhise 2006).

Methodology textbooks indicate a wide variety of typical response rates that can be expected from mail-back surveys. Several texts indicate that mail surveys of members of the general population will not exceed about 30% (Black and Champion 1976; Labovitz and Hagedorn 1971; Meyers and Grosson 1974). Williamson et al. (1982) point out that "return rates of 10% or less are common." Babbie (1986) and Bailey (1978, 1982) call a 50% response rate adequate. Other authors indicate that this is perhaps the upper limit to be expected from mail surveys of the general population (Guy et al. 1987; Kidder 1981; Nachmias and Nachmias 1987; Orenstein and Phillips 1978). Others indicate that higher upper limits are possible. These estimates include 60% (Fitzgerald and Cox 1975) and 70% (Cole 1980; Goode and Hatt 1952; True 1983). Others indicate that even higher response rates are possible (70–80%), especially if multiple follow-up contacts are used (Bailey 1978, 1982; Dillman et al. 1974; Dillman 1978, 2000; Miller 1977; Sanders and Pinhey 1983; Weisberg and Bowen 1977).

In addition, no single method of conducting a survey (mail, face-to-face interview, telephone interview, e-mail/Internet and FAX-based) is the single best technique for gathering all forms of survey data. A variety of studies show tremendous variation in the direction of differences between these methods and in the direction and amount of variance in data gathered on the same topics using these different techniques (Bradburn 1983; Dillman 1978, 2000; Jonsson 1957; Cannel and Kahn 1979; Freeman and Butler 1976; Marks and Maudlin 1950; Sudman and Bradburn 1974; Yammarino et al. 1991).

Sources of error in survey research include sampling error, coverage error, measurement error, and nonresponse error. Sampling error occurs when a sample is not large enough. Coverage error results from all persons in the population not having an equal chance of being selected for the survey. Measurement error results from inappropriately constructed questions and question-order effects. Finally, nonresponse error occurs when individuals in a sample fail to participate or return surveys (Biemer and Lyberg 2003; Dillman 2000; Groves 1989; Salant and Dillman 1994).

B. NONRESPONSE BIAS

Given that nonresponse occurs in all surveys regardless of the method used, what is known about it? The problem of nonresponse biasing mail surveys was noted as early as 1838 (Porter 1838). Nonresponse is a major source of survey error. The problem of nonresponse is important because the unknown opinions of those who do not respond cannot be used to estimate a population's perceptions, preferences, or attitudes. Unless there is a 100% response rate, we can never be 100% certain that distortion does not occur (Erdos 1983).

Nonresponse bias occurs when there is a difference between the attitudes, opinions, or preferences of those who responded and those who did not respond. The size of this difference multiplied by the proportion of nonrespondents indicates the expected amount of nonresponse bias. Thus, a low response rate in mail polls amplifies any nonresponse bias that exists (Eisinger et al. 1974; Pearl and Fairley 1985). The problem is particularly acute for mail surveys, which, though popular because they are inexpensive, sometimes have response rates well below 50% (Bradburn 1983; Dillman 1978, 2000; Pearl and Fairley 1985).

Results from any survey with a response rate of less than 50% can never be considered reliable unless it is demonstrated that nonrespondents do not differ statistically from respondents. This does not mean that a response rate greater than 50% is necessarily adequate, for this depends on the nature of each individual study. Nor does this mean that nonrespondents and respondents who do not differ on demographic items are sufficiently alike, since they may differ only on substantive questions (Erdos 1983).

Nonresponse bias is less likely to occur when nonrespondents are similar to respondents. Unfortunately, most current evidence indicates that respondents and those who refuse differ in significant ways. This increases the likelihood of response bias occurring (Dillman 1978, 2000).

Bias in mail surveys is often due to the fact that people who have a particular interest in the subject of the survey are more likely to return a mail questionnaire than those who are less interested. This means that the results of mail surveys with low response rates will usually be biased in ways that are directly related to the survey's topic (Bradburn 1983; Donald 1960). The most famous example of nonrespondents affecting the accuracy of a mail survey in this way is the frequently cited *Literary Digest* presidential election poll of 1936, which predicted a victory for Alf Landon. Franklin Roosevelt won that election by a landslide. Over time, the story has developed that the failure of this survey was caused by drawing a sample from telephone books and calling those in the sample on the phone. Republicans, members of Landon's party, the comparatively economically well-off, were more likely to have a telephone than Democrats in 1936. This story is incorrect, since that survey was conducted by mail and it failed because of nonresponse. Most of those who received a questionnaire did not return it. Those who wanted the underdog to win were more likely to want to express their views (Bryson 1976; Squire 1988).

Many studies have found that those who do not respond are significantly different from those who respond to a survey. For instance, those who refuse are far more likely to live in central cities rather than inner suburbs or outer suburbs of central cities, small cities, or small towns (Dillman, 1978, 2000; Goyder 1985; Riche 1987). Similar nonresponse patterns for urban residents were found in earlier studies by Hawkins (1977), Kish (1965), and Mayer (1964). Other studies indicate that response rates are inversely related to size of place. In addition, they indicate that response rates have been dropping for all types of respondents since the 1950s because of increasing refusals, and that differences in response rates between larger and smaller areas have been widening (DeMaio 1980; Goyder 1985; Hirst and Goeltz 1984; House and Wolf 1978; Steeh 1981).

People who are 50 years of age or older are more likely to refuse than younger persons (DeMaio 1980; Goyder 1985; Groves 1977, 1989; Herzog and Rodgers 1988; Kish 1965; Palmer 1968). This relationship is stronger in large cities than in smaller locations. A greater proportion of those who fail to return surveys are people with lower levels of education (Goudy 1976). Married and separated individuals are more likely to refuse than people who are widowed, divorced, or never married (Goyder 1985; Hawkins 1977). People living in highrise apartments, duplexes, and town or row houses are more likely to refuse than those living in either single-family houses or low-rise apartments (Goyder 1985). Other studies report different relationships between housing and refusal tendencies. These differences may be due to the fact that dwelling types have been classified in many different ways in these studies (Lagay 1969). For example, Hawkins (1975, 1977) found that residents of single-family dwellings were more likely to refuse than those living in any other type of dwelling.

Males, non-whites, less-educated, and wealthier persons are less likely to respond to surveys (Groves 1989). This pattern of response is likely to result in errors in survey results. However, other studies report inconsistent relationships between age, income, race and gender and willingness to respond to a survey (Brehm 1990; Brown and Bish 1982; DeMaio 1980, 1977; Goyder 1985, 1987; Groves 1977, 1989; Herzog and Rogers 1988; Lagay 1969; Schuman and Gruenberg 1970;

Schuman and Kalton 1985; Smith 1979, 1983). One explanation for blacks being less likely to respond is that they are over-surveyed.

Several reasons for declining response rates, especially in cities, have been suggested. These include suspicion of strangers, fear of crime, lifestyle changes, and the desire to avoid involvement in anything unusual. Fear of crime is a major reason for the elderly not participating in surveys, especially in urban areas (Clemente and Kleiman 1976). There seems to be an increasing desire for privacy and unwillingness to reveal personal information, which respondents feel they do not have to share since they have a right to privacy (DeMaio 1980). A common reason for not filling out surveys is a desire to keep personal information confidential (Tomaskovic-Devey et al. 1994).

Nonrespondents commonly give a variety of different reasons for not returning a mail survey. These include the fact that they mislaid it, overlooked it, believe that they have already filled out or returned a questionnaire, were too busy at the time, were away from home, never received it, were not interested in the topic, never answer questionnaires, were ill when it arrived, and enjoyed the questionnaire so much that they kept it (Robinson and Agisim 1951). In addition to these reasons for not returning a survey, nonrespondents sometimes are individuals who cannot be located. If those who cannot be located are the most mobile individuals in a sample, this fact may bias survey results (Mayer and Pratt 1966).

Mail surveys have the problem of subjects moving and mail not being forwarded successfully to them. Some people either do not file change-of-address cards or do not fill these cards out correctly. The U.S. Postal Service keeps change-of-address cards active for only six months and does not forward mail once that time elapses. Mailing lists whether purchased from professional organizations or the services which handle these lists may not be completely up-to-date or accurate. In the author's experience working with mailing lists provided by professional associations and state agencies that license members of professional associations, these lists contained 8–10% errors. These are organizations that annually update their mailing lists and have multiple contacts per year with their members. Other sources may contain even more out-of-date addresses. Some studies exist that indicate that it is not unusual to find that 10% of surveys mailed cannot be delivered (Brennan and Hoek 1992; Sosidian and Sharp 1980).

Those conducting mail surveys may have some idea about the accuracy of their mailing list based on the number of returns that they receive. However, returns are made only for first-class mail. If surveys are sent bulk-rate, then mail that cannot be delivered will not be returned. Even when first-class postage is used, undeliverable mail may not be returned. For instance, a letter delivered to a last known address may be thrown away by the current resident rather than marked "Moved," "Addressee Unknown," "Not this address," or "Return to sender" and put in a mail box so that it can be returned.

C. RESEARCH ON IMPROVING RESPONSE TO MAIL SURVEYS

Because nonresponse is a fact of life for those conducting surveys, the problem involves finding ways to increase response to surveys. In the last forty-five years, there have been several comprehensive reviews of factors affecting response to mail surveys. The earlier review articles summarized empirical studies of response rate including Scott's (1961) review of nearly 100 empirical studies, Kanuk and Berenson's (1975) review of over eighty empirical studies, Linsky's (1975) examination of approximately 58 studies, Duncan's (1979) review, and Edwards et al.'s (2002) review of 292 studies.

Some recent review articles have limited their analyses to studies reporting the results of experiments designed to determine, in a controlled and meaningful way, the effects of different practices on survey returns. These authors have also performed quantitative analyses on data from the studies of surveys they examined. In their review of ninety-eight separate experiments on factors affecting mail surveys, Heberlein and Baumgartner (1978) identified ten variables that affect response to mail surveys. These ten factors predicted 66% of the variability in response rate in the studies they reviewed. Since then, Goyder (1982a) replicated their study with a sample of 330 surveys, and Eichner and Habermehl (1981) used a sample of 152 surveys conducted in Austria and West Germany to replicate their work. Baumgartner and Heberlein (1984), Yammarino et al. (1991), and Edwards et al. (2002) report results based on data from subsequent studies of survey practices. The effects of the following eleven factors on mail survey return rates are examined here: the number of contacts including follow-up contacts, sponsorship, the nature of the respondent population, salience, incentives, length, anonymity, personalization, types of appeals, postage, and deadlines.

1. The Number of Contacts Including Follow-Up Contacts

The number of contacts consistently results in improved response rates. Use of extensive follow-ups is not a new technique. Rigorous follow-ups have been a standard procedure for interview surveys for more than forty years (Gaudet and Wilson 1940). Follow-ups can range from a reminder postcard to Dillman's (1978) total design method (TDM), which utilizes an elaborate follow-up scheme that takes into account careful timing of no less than four follow-ups, increasingly stronger letters of appeal, a second, third, and, if need be, fourth copy of the questionnaire, and the use of registered mail. Dillman (1978) reports that returns for surveys using the total design method varied between 58 and 94%. The TDM is based on paying careful attention to detail in all parts of the survey process from beginning to end. The TDM results in both a higher response rate than would otherwise be achieved and a higher rate of completion of items in the survey. Other authors espouse close attention to detail, too, even though they do not adhere to the TDM format. For instance, Altschuld and Lower (1984) indicate that they paid careful attention to detail as Dillman suggests. Their survey was revised five times before it was sent out, and multiple contacts were used to stimulate returns.

Dillman (2000) revised his prescribed method for maximizing survey response, replacing the TDM with a tailored design method (TD). The tailored design consists of four contacts. These are a pre-notice; an initial mailing containing a cover letter, incentive, and a copy of the survey; a reminder postcard; and a follow-up contact, containing a different cover letter and a copy of the survey, which are sent by registered mail.

Multiple contacts are essential to obtain a high response rate (Scott 1961; Heberlein and Baumgartner 1978; Dillman 1991, 2000). Heberlein and Baumgartner (1978) found that number of contacts was the single best predictor of a survey's response rate, accounting for 42% of the variance in response rates in the surveys they examined. Multiple contacts, including prenotification, multiple cover letters and surveys, and reminder postcards, will enhance response rate. Prenotification is an effective means of increasing the response rate (Brehm 1994; Dillman et al. 1995; Dillman 2000; Dillman and Bowker 2001; Fox et al. 1988, Goldstein and Jennings 2002; Yammarino et al. 1991; Yu and Cooper 1983). In addition, multiple contacts comprise repeated mailings that include cover letters and a copy of the survey (Goyder 1982; Heberlein and Baumgartner 1978; James and Bolstein 1990; Smith and Bers 1987). Sending a second copy of the survey to nonrespondents increased the likelihood of their responding significantly (Edwards et al. 2002).

Many studies have reported that follow-up contacts are an effective way to increase response rates. Edwards et al. (2002), Eichner and Habermehl (1981), Goyder (1982b 1985), Kasprzyk et al. (2001); Yammarino et al. (1991), Yu and Cooper (1983), and Ziegler (2006) report similar strong relationships between follow-up contacts and response rates, and that the effect of follow-up contacts on response rate is even greater for institutional than for individual respondents.

Securing survey response is largely a matter of overcoming resistance or even educating those contacted (Cannell and Kahn 1968; Young 1949). These techniques vary widely along the following dimensions: type, frequency, and timing. Regardless of format, most studies using one or more follow-up techniques resulted in higher response rates than singleshot surveys produced

(Dillman et al. 1974; Dillman 1978, 1991, 2000; Duncan 1979; Edwards et al. 2002; Fox et al. 1988; Goyder 1982a; Groves et al. 2000; Heberlein and Baumgartner 1978; James and Bolstein 1990, 1992; Kanuk and Berenson 1975; Kish 1965; Levine and Gordon 1958; Lindsey 1921; Linsky 1975; Scott 1961; Survey Research Center 1976; Trussell and Lavrakas 2004; Willimack et al. 1995; Yammarino et al. 1991; Yu and Cooper 1983).

A method of following up that has produced high response rates is use of multiple phone calls soliciting participation in addition to multiple follow-up mailings (Altschuld and Lower 1984; McClosky 1983). Comer and Kelly (1980) found that telephone follow-ups produced higher response rates (46%) than mail follow-ups (33%). Similarly, Brennan and Hoek (1992) and Yammarino et al. (1991) report significant effects for telephone follow-ups.

Those conducting surveys by phone have indicated repeatedly that personification either by mail or by phone helps increase response rate (Bergsten et al. 1984; Dillman et al. 1996; Groves 1989; Pol 1992; Traugott et al. 1987). Use of either media to prenotify mail survey recipients increases response rate too (Fox et al. 1988; Goyder 1982a; Heberlein and Baumgartner 1978; Yammarino et al. 1991; Yu and Cooper 1983).

Repeating the message in the first cover letter is not effective with a second mailing of the survey because it did not work the first time with these nonrespondents. The second letter may be more effective if it contains a different message. It could emphasize the importance of the research, the fact that many other individuals have already participated, and the fact that their opportunity to participate will soon vanish may increase the likelihood of their responding (Cialdini 1984; Dillman 2000).

Several researchers report that including a copy of the questionnaire with the follow-up request will increase response rates. This seems to be more effective when the questionnaire is included with a second or later follow-up rather than an initial one (Dillman et al. 1974; Dillman 1978, 2000; Swan et al. 1980; Heberlein and Baumgartner 1981a, 1981b). Special classes of postage (first-class and registered mail) have also been found to influence response rates to follow-up appeals (Dillman 1978; Goyder 1982a; Heberlein and Baumgartner 1978), but more recent research indicates that postage makes no difference except on the return envelope, and then only if stamps are used (Dillman 2000).

Assertive methods designed to get the attention of the subject are sometimes used such as stamping "second notice" on the envelope or cover letter. These practices are not recommended. A negative message, like "second notice," may backfire by angering potential respondents and result in a lower response rate (Dillman 2000).

Prenotification is one way of doing this. Prenotification can occur through a postcard in the mail telling the potential respondent that a survey will soon follow, or through a phone call soliciting participation (Armstrong and Lusk 1987; Church 1993; Dillman 1978 2000; Fox et al. 1988; James and Bolstein 1990; Willimack et al. 1995; Yammarino et al. 1991; Yu and Cooper 1983), or a FAX (Schreckhise 2006). A wide variety of studies summarized in Duncan (1979), Edwards et al. (2002), Goyder (1982a, 1985), Kanuk and Berenson (1975), Linsky (1975), and Scott (1961) report that prenotification increases response to most surveys.

2. Sponsorship

Heberlein and Baumgartner (1978) report that sponsorship or the nature of the organization conducting the survey has a substantial impact on mail survey response rates. For instance, university and government organization sponsorship had a positive impact (about a 10% increase) on response, while market research organization sponsorship had a negative impact (about a 10% decline). One meta-analysis reports that surveys from universities were more likely to be returned than when sent by other sponsors such as businesses (Edwards et al. 2002). Similar results have been reported on government and university sponsored surveys in a variety of other studies (Armstrong and Lusk 1987; Brunner and Carroll 1969; Dillman 2000; Fox et al. 1988;

Goyder 1982b; Houston and Nevin 1977; Jones 1979; Jones and Lang 1980, 1982; Jones and Linda 1978; Peterson 1975; Scott 1961; Willimack et al. 1995; Yu and Cooper 1983). Finally, some studies contain results showing no difference in response rates of surveys sponsored by government or universities and marketing firms (Hawkins 1979). Jones (1979) indicates that sponsorship decisions should be based on using a sponsor that has the highest possible status with the population to be surveyed. In their meta-analysis, Yammarino et al. (1991) report mixed results for sponsorship. This may reflect differing interactions of sponsors and samples.

In their study of schoolteachers and administrators, Lower and Altschuld (1982) indicate that sponsorship may not be as effective when anonymity of respondents and confidentiality of responses are guaranteed as they might be when such guarantees do not exist and a coercion factor can take effect. Both Dillman (1978, 2000) and Heberlein and Baumgartner (1978) believe that sponsorship works at least in part because individuals are concerned about potential negative consequences of failure to comply by filling out and returning a survey. This threat seems more realistic for employees of the sponsoring organization than for others.

3. Nature of the Respondent Population

Return rates are affected by the nature of the population surveyed. Surveys are better suited for use with some populations than others. Heberlein and Baumgartner (1978) report that lower returns were achieved when surveys tapped the general population than when school, government, military, and employee populations were surveyed. Other researchers report similar results for general population surveys (Eichner and Habermehl 1981; O'Neil 1979). Goyder (1982b) reported a similar positive result for populations of government employees, and Altschuld and Lower (1984) report very high returns for schoolteachers and principals.

There are vast differences in the level of difficulty that exists in obtaining responses from specialized or homogeneous populations and from general population samples. The wide variety of individuals found in a general population sample will differ in almost every possible combination of characteristics. Hence, they are much more difficult than a homogeneous sample to identify, contact, and persuade to participate (O'Neil 1979).

Some organizations, both public and private, forbid employees participating in surveys or research projects without permission and even identify this behavior as potential grounds for dismissal. Participating without permission in some cases is an offense meriting termination. Others allow participation, but only after the project or survey instrument has been approved. A survey would have to be accompanied by a copy of the permission letter. Access in these cases is limited.

4. Salience

Salience, or the perceived importance of the survey topic to the potential respondent, is an extremely important factor affecting response rate. The importance of this factor is argued in other review articles on questionnaire response (Dillman 2000; Edwards et al. 2002; Goyder 1982a; Heberlein and Baumgartner 1978; Kish 1965; Levine and Gordon 1958; Linsky 1975; Survey Research Center 1976; Yu and Cooper 1983). People who feel strongly about the issues examined in a survey are more likely to respond. Special purpose surveys that are highly salient to a specific target population or sampling frame can produce response rates over 90% (deVaus 1986). Salience can also produce nonresponse bias when the strength of opinion is related to the reply on issue preference a survey topic or question is of low salience, vague or sensitive in nature (Armstrong and Overton 1977; Baur 1947; Benson 1946; Burt 1981; Couper 1997; Dillman 1978, 2000; Donald 1960; Erdos 1983; Groves 2004; LaHaut et al. 2002; Pfeffer and Salancik 1978; Scott 1961).

Heberlein and Baumgartner (1978) found that response rate was significantly linked to perceived salience of the questionnaire's topic. They reported that surveys judged not salient or of low salience obtained only a 42% average response rate, surveys deemed to be possibly or moderately salient obtained a 66% response rate, and surveys judged to be highly salient resulted in a 77% response rate. These are large and statistically-significant differences. Results of their multivariate analysis indicated that each one-point increase in the salience scale resulted in a 7.3% increase in response. Both Eichner and Habermehl (1981) and Goyder (1982b) report that response rates are affected in substantial ways by the perceived salience of the questionnaire.

Designing the survey so that it is more interesting to respondents will increase response rate. In contrast, including questions of a sensitive nature will decrease response rate (Dillman 2000; Edwards et al. 2002). The researcher can use other aspects of survey design and administration to overcome low salience. For example, the length of the survey can be reduced and the number of contacts can be increased (Edwards et al. 2002).

It is up to the researcher to convince the subject that the research topic is important and that the questionnaire is worth completing and returning. An advance letter describing the research project's purposes and soliciting the subject's help, a carefully prepared cover letter with an endorsement from an appropriate sponsor, multiple mailings at appropriate points in time, and multiple personal contacts via the telephone are effective ways to enhance the subject's perceptions of the salience of a particular survey (Altschuld and Lower 1984; Dillman 1978 2000; Edwards et al. 2002).

5. Incentives

Incentives can be provided, either as prepayments included with the survey or as contingent payments made after the survey is returned. Which of these techniques, prepayment or the promise of future payment, is most effective? Some early research on incentives reported that a promised monetary incentive contingent on completion of a survey was just as effective as prepayment for improving survey response rates in general populations (Armstrong 1975; Bevi's 1948; Baumgartner and Heberlein 1984; Dohrenwend 1970; King 1979; Sudman and Ferber 1974).

Today most studies report that a prepaid cash incentive, one that is delivered with the survey and not conditional upon completing the survey, has a substantial positive effect on response rate. In fact, this effect is great than that of a conditional payment, even if the conditional payment is somewhat larger than the prepaid or unconditional one (Armstrong and Lusk 1987; Baumgartner and Heberlein 1984; Dillman 1978, 2000; Duncan 1979; Fox et al. 1988; Goodstadt et al. 1977; Goyder 1982a, 1985; Hansen 1980; Heberlein and Baumgartner 1978; Houston and Ford 1976; Jobber and Saunders 1988; Kanuk and Berenson 1975; Kulka 1994; Linsky 1975; McDaniel and Rao 1980; Mizes et al. 1984; Scott 1961; Sudman and Ferber 1974; Warriner et al. 1996; Willimack et al. 1995; Yammarino et al. 1991; Yu and Cooper 1983). A recent meta-analysis found that the odds of response almost doubled when incentives were immediate rather than conditional on response (Edwards et al. 2002).

In addition, prepaying individuals who are members of populations whose members often refuse to participate in mail surveys and who are difficult to contact, executives, physicians, and lawyers in large public and private organizations, where traditional follow-up may be expensive, can be very effective in increasing response rates and lowering total survey costs because fewer follow-up contacts are needed (Berk et al. 1987; Berry and Kanouse 1987; Dillman 2000; Edwards et al. 2002; Ferber and Sudman 1974; Gunn and Rhodes 1981; James and Bolstein 1992; Tedin and Hofstetter 1982; Walsh 1977; Weber et al. 1982).

Most studies indicate that monetary incentives are more effective than other types of incentives, such as a gift (Edwards et al. 2002; Goodstadt et al. 1977; Hansen 1980; Willimack et al. 1995). A recent meta-analysis reported that the odds of response more than doubled when a monetary incentive was used instead of some other form of incentive (Edwards et al. 2002). A few exceptions to this generalization exist, including one study which reported that whether the incentive was cash or a gift made no difference in response rate (Church 1993). A promised contribution to a charity produced a higher response rate than a cash incentive in one study (Robertson and Bellenger 1978), but a replication effort did not support the earlier findings (Furse and Stewart 1982).

A monetary incentive could be in the form of either cash or a check. Whether the payment is in cash or a check makes no difference in generating response (Berry and Kanouse 1987; Dillman 2000; Furse et al. 1977; James and Bolstein 1992). However, cash is more cost-effective than a check. Use of a check is not recommended because of the costs of issuing and handling the checks (Dillman 2000). As for cashing the check or keeping cash without filling out the questionnaire, norms of equity in social exchange may make the respondent feel uncomfortable with the idea of getting something for nothing (Adams 1956; Homans 1961). Very few subjects cash a check without returning a survey and the opposite contingency occurs as well—a significant number of survey respondents fail to cash their check (Dillman 2000).

Early studies examining the question of whether it is more effective to include an incentive in the first or a subsequent mailing found that it makes no difference (Furse et al. 1977). Most researchers report that including the incentive in the first mailing is far more effective than placing it in subsequent ones (Armstrong 1975; Baumgartner and Heberlein 1984; Berk et al. 1987; Church 1993; Dillman 1978, 2000; Edwards et al. 2002; Gelb 1975; Goodstadt et al. 1977; Gunn and Rhodes 1981; Isen 1987; James and Bolstein 1992; King 1979; Linsky 1975; Weber et al. 1982; Willimack et al. 1995; Wotruba 1966; Yammarino et al. 1991; Yu and Cooper 1983).

Why is prepayment so much more effective than the promise of a future payment? Two theoretical explanations exist for a prepaid or unconditional monetary incentive increasing response rate. Dillman (1991, 2000) believes that it is a matter explained by exchange theory (Blau 1964; Cialdini 1988; Homans 1961; Thibaut and Kelley 1959), and a norm of reciprocity (Gouldner 1960; Groves 1989). According to exchange theory, a monetary gift creates a sense of social obligation that increases the likelihood of the subject completing and returning the survey. In contrast, when a respondent is asked to fill out a questionnaire with a promise of subsequent payment, control over the initiation of an exchange is left to that individual. Until the questionnaire has been filled out, no obligation exists on either side. Research by Dillman (1978, 2000) supports this rationale.

Dillman (2000) also believes that this sense of obligation can be diminished by an imbalance between the size of the incentive (small reward) and of the task (long and difficult survey to complete). Response will increase when rewards or what one hopes to gain exceeds the cost of participating and when the potential subject trusts the surveyor to deliver the rewards (Dillman 1978; Gallegos, 1974; Goyder 1987). Social exchange is not an economic exchange. Payment that is contingent on completing the survey before the payment is sent is equivalent to paying someone for their time, which is an economic exchange. Social exchange is less precise, but a more effective means of generating survey responses (Dillman 1978, 2000).

Another explanation called leverage-salience theory is offered by Groves et al. (2000). They suggest that the size of the incentive accompanying the survey must match the demands of completing the survey. A longer and more difficult-to-complete survey must be accompanied by a larger monetary incentive than a shorter and more easily completed survey.

These theoretical considerations raise the question of "how large a cash incentive would be to be most effective?" On the one hand, today, a dollar incentive is the minimum amount (Dillman 2000), but how much more could effectively be given? Answering this question might enable researchers to achieve some form of efficiency, such as generating the maximum number of surveys returned for the fewest possible number of dollars. They would give each subject an incentive large enough to prompt their responding, but not waste money by giving anyone more than necessary. This is a difficult question to answer, given the interaction of survey and respondent characteristics. How much is enough?

Armstrong (1979) called for research on this topic, and Godwin (1979) performed such research with mixed results. Many early studies used a prepaid incentive of 25 cents, and some of them told the subject that this was a token of appreciation (Baumgartner and Heberlein 1984). Today, the minimum practical size of an incentive is one dollar. Smaller amounts are not as effective, because they increase the cost of the survey by adding significantly to the cost of postage (Dillman 2000). Some early research on the impact of different size incentives on response rates produced mixed results (Godwin 1979). One study found that there was no difference in response rates of those receiving $1.00 and $5.00 incentives (Mizes et al. 1984).

Research indicates that a sum of $1.00 is very effective (Dillman 1978, 2000; James and Bolstein 1990, 1992; Kephart and Bressler 1958; Mizes et al. 1984; Schewe and Cournoyer 1976; Willimack et al. 1995; Yammarino et al. 1991). A recent meta-analysis found that including a $1 incentive more than doubled the response obtained with no incentive (Edwards et al. 2002).

Larger amounts produce rapidly diminishing returns or "bang for the buck." Dillman (2000) found that $1 produced the largest increment in survey response. Additional dollars increased response further, but at a declining rate. Armstrong (1975), Fox et al. (1988), James and Bolstein (1990, 1992), and Willimack et al. (1995) report similar results. Roberts et al. (2000) report that an incentive of five English pounds increased the response rate by only 12% over that obtained with one pound. In their meta-analysis, Edwards et al. (2002) report that increasing the incentive resulted in a diminishing return for each additional $1 increase. Their regression model predicts that a $15 incentive will be only 2.5 times as effective as no incentive.

Recent research by Trussell and Lavrakas (2004) addresses the question of "how much is enough?" They studied incentives ranging in size from $1 though $8, and $10. No $9 incentive was used. They found that the largest impact on response rate occurred with the first dollar, and that the effectiveness of additional dollars declined progressively.

This experiment also examined the simultaneous impact of prior contact determining agreement to participate in the study or not, and no prior contact. Groves et al. (2000) indicated that the impact of a monetary incentive is affected by prior contact (contacted or not) and the results of the contact (willingness or unwillingness to participate in a survey). Trussell and Lavrakas (2004) report that those who previously agreed to participate did so at higher levels than those who refused or who had not previously been contacted, regardless of the size of monetary incentive. For those who had agreed to participate, a dollar or more incentive significantly increased the likelihood of response (from 42.7 to 56.9%). Larger amounts did not increase response significantly.

Many of those who previously said they would not participate changed their minds when offered a monetary incentive. Two dollars produced a significant increase in response and this effect increased until four dollars produced maximum response. Larger amounts did not make a significant difference.

Incentives were less effective for those who were not contacted in advance. In addition, it took a larger incentive ($5 or more) to produce a significant increase in participation. The response rate was 20.3% for $5 and 30.6% for $10.

Simply put, larger incentives can produce greater response. However, there is a diminishing return and a cap beyond which additional dollars make no difference (Trussell and Lavrakas 2004). These findings also tell us that prior contact is a useful filter when conducting survey research. If a person says they will not participate, it will take substantially more money to obtain cooperation of fewer of them than for their more-agreeable peers. These findings suggest that a substantial incentive may be useful in improving response from hard-to-reach populations and that sample weighting may be needed to insure that an adequate number of respondents is obtained.

One study indicates that large incentives ($25.00) result in a very high response rate (98%) (Carter et al. 1983). In contrast to the idea of large incentives generating an automatic increase in response, some studies indicate that heavy-handed blatant manipulation can generate a negative backlash (Berry and Kanouse 1987; Brehm 1966; Brehm and Brehm 1981; Weiner and Brehm 1966;

Wicklund 1974; Willimack et al. 1995). For example, Church (1993) found that 10% of the studies he examined reported lower response rates with an incentive than without.

Finally, use of incentives can have negative effects. For instance, using an incentive of equal size for all subjects who differ widely in terms of their relative income might increase response disproportionately from lower income respondents, since the incentive, typically a dollar, means more to them than to wealthier potential respondents. This could result in a less representative sample (Schweitzer and Asch 1995).

6. Length

The length of a survey has a negative impact on its response rate. Long surveys result in lower response rates than shorter surveys. A recent meta-analysis found that predicted response to a one-page survey will be twice that obtained with a three-page questionnaire (Edwards et al. 2002). A decade earlier, another meta-analysis found that a length of four pages was a meaningful upper bound affecting response rates (Yammarino et al. 1991).

Earlier research on length's impact on survey response rates produced mixed results. Some report that length had a weak negative effect on response rate and that the number of questions was a significant but minor factor affecting response to mailed questionnaires (Goyder 1982b; Heberlein and Baumgartner 1978; Yu and Cooper 1983). Others report that length had no impact (Childers and Ferrell 1979; Lockhart and Russo 1981). One study found a positive association between length and response rate (Hornik 1981). Heberlein and Baumgartner (1978) offer the following explanation for these mixed results: although a longer questionnaire costs a respondent more time and effort to complete and may cause a lower response rate, length may also indicate to potential respondents that the study is important.

Length can be measured in a variety of ways, including the number of pages, the number of questions, how difficult it is to answer questions, and the estimated time of completion. Length is also a matter of perception. Length, or the appearance of length, can result from bulk and formatting that create the impression that a questionnaire is lengthy and will take a significant amount of time and effort to complete. These problems of length will lower the response rate (Asch et al. 1998; Bogen 1996; Dillman 1978, 2000; Dillman et al. 1993; Heberlein and Baumgartner 1978; Thran and Hixson 2000; Yammarino et al. 1991; Yu and Cooper 1983).

It seems that length, real or imagined, creates an impression in the mind of the subject that this survey will take a significant amount of time and effort to complete. On the list of things the subject has to do on a particular day, time-consuming and difficult activities, such as that long survey, lose out to "must do" activities and to more appealing, perhaps shorter, less demanding, more interesting and pleasurable, activities.

Given the negative impact of length on survey response rates, what is to be done about it? The first and most important means of reducing the cost to the subject of completing a survey is to keep the survey short. This can be accomplished by asking oneself what you want to know from the respondents, and asking only the questions necessary to obtain this information. A second alternative is to avoid long, complex questions that are difficult and tiring to answer. Multipart tabular questions and open-ended questions take time to complete and can tire the respondent (Dillman 2000).

A third alternative is to change the questionnaire's format in appropriate ways. Typesetting it in booklet format using ten-point type, thin paper, and other appropriate design elements may completely alter the impression a questionnaire makes and result in a higher response rate (Dillman 1978, 2000; Dillman et al. 1993; Heberlein and Baumgartner 1978; Leslie 1997). In sum, a survey that is shorter or that looks and feels shorter will have a higher response rate.

Another alternative is to compensate for length by using the TD (Dillman 2000) or the TDM (Dillman 1978), or other methods designed to maximize survey response, such as including a comparatively large incentive. For example, Dillman (1978) reports achieving relatively high response rates (around 70%) with surveys of ten and eleven pages. There is no doubt that successful administration of long surveys will cost more to conduct than short ones.

7. Anonymity/Confidentiality

Anonymity and confidentiality are important aspects of survey research. Anonymity means not being able to identify the subjects. Confidentiality means not revealing what an individual said. Both anonymity and confidentiality are usually guaranteed in the cover letter with the intention of reassuring respondents about how information they provide, including their name, will be used. The widely shared rationale for doing this is that respondents will provide more detailed and accurate responses. In addition, a researcher has an ethical obligation to protect a subject from harm, and providing anonymity and confidentiality in handling information is one way to do this. Institutional review bodies help researchers enact this obligation.

Assurance of anonymity and confidentiality are commonly described as having a beneficial effect on response rate and on other response characteristics, including item omission, response bias, and quality of item responses. However, significant evidence indicates that anonymity and confidentiality make only a small difference in response rates (Singer et al. 1995).

Most studies have found that anonymity is not necessary for a high response rate, and that it increases response rate only slightly (Frey 1986; Heberlein and Baumgartner 1978; Singer 1978; Singer et al. 1995; Skinner and Childers 1980; Yammarino et al. 1991; Yu and Cooper 1983). In a recent meta-analysis, neither anonymity nor confidentiality was among the practices found to consistently enhance response rate to mail surveys (Edwards et al. 2002).

In fact, some studies indicate that over-emphasis on anonymity in the cover letter seems to sensitize subjects and negatively affect response rates (Berman et al. 1977; Reamer 1979; Singer et al. 1995).

How should anonymity and confidentiality be handled? These issues should be addressed in the cover letter. Simple straightforward statements suffice, such as "Anonymity and confidentiality are guaranteed," and "Results will only be reported in summary form."

The presence of an identification number on the survey so that follow-up mailings will not be sent to those who have already returned a survey does not significantly affect response rate (Dillman 1978, 2000; Futrell and Swan 1977). If identification numbers are used, they can be explained in the cover letter. The author has placed identification numbers in the upper-right-hand corner of many surveys conducted over the past thirty years. In very rare instances, a subject has marked it out or clipped it off. One effective alternative practice is to enclose a self-addressed post card with an identification number on it with the survey, which the respondent can mail back separately. Another effective alternative is to ask the subject to enclose a business card if they would like a summary of the results mailed to them. Business cards are separated from the surveys when they are opened to preserve anonymity. With public and private professionals, this practice has resulted in more than 90% of the subjects returning a business card. Use of a hidden or disguised identification number on the survey is discouraged, because it is unethical to do this when the cover letter contains assurance of anonymity and confidentiality.

Other factors may mask or make it difficult to determine the effects of anonymity and confidentiality upon survey response, since they directly affect response themselves. For example, some studies indicate that use of prepaid monetary incentive may result in completion of more questions and giving more complete individual answers (Willimack et al. 1995). Similarly, certain demographic variables may affect the relationship between anonymity and item completion rate. For instance, Ferber (1966) found that females, older individuals, and lower-educated respondents had significantly lower item completion rates than other respondents. Moreover, Downs and Kerr (1986) report that item completion rates were affected by lack of anonymity. Self-identified respondents who were older, had low incomes, owned their own homes, or were minority group members had lower item completion rates than anonymous respondents.

8. Personalization

Personalization takes many forms and involves attention to small details. For example, Dillman (1978, 2000) reports addressing envelopes to individuals by name on an outgoing envelope, rather than using mailing labels. Today, personally addressed mail is easily achieved, given mailing lists and computer programs. Another way to achieve personalization is using first-class mail on outgoing and return envelopes instead of bulk-rate postage; this makes a substantial difference in how a potential respondent initially reacts to a mail survey. A survey that is sent bulk-rate may be treated like an unsolicited advertisement and be discarded unopened. Use of postage to increase survey response is discussed in detail in the Section VI.C.9. A third method involves formatting the survey in an appealing, easy-to-use manner. Another commonly-used method of enhancing personalization is to increase the number of contacts with potential respondents. This topic is discussed in detail earlier in this chapter, in Section VI.C.1.

The TDM and its successor, the TD, of Dillman both rely heavily on a high degree of personalization in every aspect of survey construction and administration and produce relatively high response rates (Dillman 1978 2000). One issue addressed in the TD is the cost of personalization. Personally signing each survey by hand can be foregone in favor of saving time and money.

Results of studies of the effects of personalization on response rates are mixed. Reviews of empirical studies by Duncan (1979) and Scott (1961) and meta-analyses by Worthen and Valcarce (1985) and Yammarino et al. (1991) conclude that personalization enhances response rate.

In contrast, a recent meta-analysis did not list personalization as a factor that consistently and significantly increased response rate to mail surveys (Edwards et al. 2002), and several other studies have found no relationship between personalization and response rate (Heberlein and Baumgartner 1978; Kanuk and Berenson 1975; LaBreque 1978; Roberts et al. 1978). One explanation of difference in personalization results is the fact that vast differences exist in how this methodology is defined. For example, Dillman defines personalization strategies more broadly and inclusively than many other researchers, who may limit their definition to addressing survey mailings to a specific person.

9. Postage

First-class postage increases the return rate of mail surveys, but how this effect occurs is unclear. On the one hand, recent meta-analyses indicate that use of first-class postage has a positive effect on survey response (Edwards et al. 2002; Willimack et al. 1995). On the other hand, some studies indicate that the effect depends upon use of stamps on the return envelope, increasing the response rate, while use of stamps on the outgoing survey mailing makes no difference (Armstrong and Luske 1987; Dillman 1991, 2000).

It is especially important to include a stamped, self-addressed return envelope with the survey. Dillman (1978, 2000) points out that return postage on a self-addressed return envelope is a necessity. Likewise, Ferriss (1951) indicates that a self-addressed return envelope must be included with the survey, because lack of a return envelope with sufficient postage will have a disastrous impact on response rate. Respondents cannot reasonably be expected to bear either the additional burden of paying postage or the cost of supplying a return envelope. In addition, including first-class postage is an act of trust on the part of the surveyor that helps establish the exchange relationship discussed under incentives above. The potential respondent could use the stamps on the envelope for other purposes of their own rather using them to return the survey (Dillman 2000).

Earlier studies focusing on the effects of postage examined different forms of postage on the envelope used to mail a survey to the respondent and different forms of postage used on the return envelope. The type of postage used on the envelope for mailing a survey to respondents is important; surveys should always use first-class postage (Dillman 1978, 2000). Use of either first-class or airmail postage increases response rates in most cases (Armstrong and Lusk 1987; Church 1993; Duncan 1979; Finn 1983; Fox et al. 1988; Kanuk and Berenson 1975; Linsky 1975; Scott 1961; Willimack et al. 1995; Yammarino et al. 1991; Yu and Cooper 1983). Armstrong and Lusk (1987) report that first-class postage yielded an average of 9% more responses than business reply postage, stamps averaged 3.4% more returns than metered postage, and commemorative stamps averaged 1.6% more responses than surveys using regular stamps on their return envelopes. Armstrong and Lusk (1987) recommend "use of either commemorative or a set of small denomination stamps on the return envelope."

Dillman (1978, 2000) justified the higher expense of first-class postage by pointing out that first-class mail is forwarded when possible and returned when it cannot be delivered, and any survey mailed third class may be mistaken for junk mail and discarded unopened. Use of more expensive forms of postage, such as certified mail, has resulted in higher response rates than use of regular first-class postage (Tedin and Hofstetter 1982; Willimack et al. 1995) and may double the response rate (Edwards et al. 2002). Similarly, a final mailing might be sent by registered mail to ensure that it reaches the subject and gets attention (Dillman 1978). However, other studies are less sanguine about the effectiveness of first-class and other special mailing rates. Tests of different kinds of postage (regular first-class stamps and commemoratives, third-class, metered first-class, metered third-class) produced no differences in response rates (McCrohan and Lowe 1981).

Other factors may confound these philatelic arguments. Baumgartner and Heberlein (1984) indicate that use of third-class postage will have a negative impact on response rates unless the mailing list is up to date. Dillman (1978, 2000) extends this qualifier to all survey mailings, regardless of the type of postage used. Mailing lists go out-of-date quickly. The older a mailing list, the higher the number of nonresponses.

10. Deadlines

Studies of the influence of deadlines by which a survey needs to be completed on response rates are mixed. Vocino (1975) reported that a two-week deadline had no effect on response rate. Another study found that use of a three-week deadline had a substantial impact on response rate to first mailing and first and second follow-ups (Roberts et al. 1978). A recent meta-analysis did not identify use of deadlines in the cover letter as an effective means of increasing survey response (Edwards et al. 2002).

11. Types of Appeals

Appeals that will benefit respondents have a more positive impact on response rates than appeals to help a researcher (Armstrong and Lusk 1987; Childers et al. 1980; Church 1993; Fox et al. 1988; Jones and Linda 1978; Yammarino et al. 1991; Yu and Cooper 1983). Personalized appeals are more effective than impersonal ones. For instance, the studies just cited report mixed results for appeals to help the researcher or research sponsor. These researchers also indicate that asking for help is effective. An appeal from a university is more effective than one from a business or market research firm. Abstract appeals such as for the benefit of humanity are ineffective.

Appeals from high-profile individuals, such as a mayor or president of a professional organization—especially if that individual is quite visible and highly regarded—may increase response. Whether it is because the appeal comes from the high-profile individual or because that person's name increases perceptions of the importance of the survey is unclear.

12. Reflections on Increasing Response Rates

Using this assortment of techniques to increase response rate is not a simple matter. Given the variety of techniques, it might seem that you could increase response to 50% by using multiple contacts and then increase it to 75% by using an incentive, and then make the survey short and interesting to achieve a total response of 90%. Unfortunately, a survey researcher's life is not so easy. Even those who follow Dillman's TDM usually do not reach 80%. Unfortunately, using multiple strategies together does not have an additive effect, because they overlap and interact in a variety of ways. Which strategies will work best together to gather data about a given topic from a specific population has to be determined on a case-by-case basis.

D. WEIGHTING

Alternative approaches exist which can be used instead of making an effort to increase response rates. One of these methods attempts to reduce response bias by using sample weights to adjust survey results (sample estimates of population parameters).

The most common method of weighting uses data on other variables in the survey for which the population distribution is nearly known, such as sex, race, age, and income. Often, this knowledge comes from census data. A variety of weighting schemes have been used to implement this strategy. For instance, survey results are adjusted based on such known data through ratio estimation (Bailar et al. 1978; Bourque and Clark 1992). Others have simply extrapolated from the responses of respondents who have the same or similar demographic characteristics as nonrespondents (Fuller 1974; O'Neil 1979; Taylor 2000). For example, in a sample that under represents older persons, responses of older respondents might be weighted to approximate their known distribution in the population or sampling frame.

Another method gives greater weight to responses from participants who were more difficult to bring into the sample or took longer to decide to participate on the assumption that they more closely resemble the nonrespondents (Goudy 1976; O'Neil 1979; Pace 1939; Platek et al. 1978; Politz and Simmons 1949). A fourth technique bases weighting calculations on the strength and direction of respondent opinions on an issue (Pearl and Fairley 1985). Issues affecting weighting decisions are discussed briefly in Erdos (1983) and in Goyder (1985).

All of these methods are based on the assumption that the relationship among the variables that are weighted and dependent variables of interest is the same for those who refuse to participate as it is for respondents. Whether this assumption is appropriate or not has rarely been tested. This assumption is often inappropriate for two reasons. First, the estimates will correctly approximate the true population parameter only when the dependent variable is strongly correlated with the demographic variables about which the researcher has information. Second, this assumption does not correct for any biasing effects of refusals on the relationship between variables—a factor that is both likely to occur and is unknown. Third, weighting works best when the proportion of non-respondents is small. Bourque and Clark (1992) report that "the use of weights does not substantially change estimates of the sample mean unless nonrespondents are appreciably different from respondents and there is a substantial proportion of nonrespondents."

Since studies examining how nonrespondents differ from respondents have considered non-response only in relation to a particular sample drawn at a given time in one place to investigate a given problem, some authors conclude that it is futile to try to identify typical nonrespondents or those likely to not respond (Cannell 1964; Hawkins 1977; Palmer 1968). Others disagree. For instance, Goyder (1985) and Pearl and Fairley (1985) point out that commonality exists despite these different survey characteristics.

Weighting differs from other efforts to increase response rates significantly, in that it occurs after data have been collected. As indicated in the preceding paragraphs, weighting suffers from methodological difficulties which cannot be overcome. In contrast, stimulating response rates can increase the likelihood that survey response more closely resembles the sampling frame or population surveyed.

E. INTERNET AND E-MAIL SURVEYS

Experts believe that Internet surveys will be the method of choice in the future (Couper 2000; Couper et al. 2001; Dillman 2000; Illeva, Baron, and Healey 2002; Sills and Song 2002). This conclusion rests on an assessment of relative convenience, speed, lower costs, and effectiveness. Up-to-date, accurate contact information may be easier and less expensive to obtain. The cost of delivering the survey and other contacts may be easier, more reliable, and cheaper. Ability to create a dataset for analysis may be more accurate and easier, as well (Taylor 2000).

Increased use of the Internet and e-mail for survey research will also result from difficulty in conducting telephone surveys. Large numbers of sales and fund-raising campaigns, salespersons masquerading as surveyors, unlisted numbers, and use of screening and blocking technology have made it increasingly difficult to conduct telephone surveys. To reach an individual may require a large numbers of contact attempts (Hox and de Leeuw 1994). The writer's experience indicates that reaching a sample of a desired size may require over-sampling by a factor of 6–10 times the number of desired cases and that this problem has been getting worse during the last 20 years.

E-mail and Internet surveys are developing and their use is becoming widespread. However, they have not surpassed mail-back surveys as the most popular form of survey. Reasons for this include response rates, limitations on the ability to use some effective methods that foster survey response, lower response rates than mail-back surveys, and limitations tied to length and the time it takes to complete a survey. Contact problems exist for e-mail and Internet surveyors created by spammers (Mehta and Sivadas 1995; Sheehan and Hoy 1999), just as mass marketers and fund-raisers create problems for telephone and mail surveyors. These problems make achieving contact with subjects and obtaining a response more difficult. Nevertheless the use of e-mail/Internet surveys has increased dramatically. Whether they supplant mail-back surveys as the survey method of choice depends on overcoming the following research problems and others yet to be discovered.

Questions have to be resolved about delivery of a token payment with a survey. Loss of this key element of the social exchange mechanism could impact survey response negatively. Similarly, it appears that use of e-mail addresses and ability to track or identify persons who visit websites make it more difficult to provide an absolute guarantee of anonymity (Couper et al. 2001; Dillman 2000; Dommeyer and Moriarty 2000; Illeva, Baron, and Healey 2002; Sills and Song 2002). These anonymity or privacy issues can result in lower e-mail/Internet survey response (Bradley 1999; Couper et al. 1997; Illeva, Baron, and Healey 2002; Mehta and Sivadas 1998; Schaefer and Dillman 1998; Sheehan and Hoy 1999; Sheehan and McMillan 1999).

In addition, Internet surveys have some response problems. First, Internet surveys may produce more positive responses than mail surveys for certain types of questions (Carini et al. 2003). Since e-mail/Internet surveys are richer media than paper and pencil (Coyle and Thorson 2001; Dillman 2000) they may elicit more detailed and comprehensive responses especially to open-ended questions (Bachman et al. 1996; Mehta and Sivadas 1995; Schaefer and Dillman 1998; Stanton 1998). Second, Internet surveys may have lower response rates than mail surveys (Roscoe et al. 2002). This may reflect design issues. For instance, how can a token cash incentive that is not contingent on making a response of some kind be included with an Internet survey? The frequent practice of using a lottery is not as effective as cash, especially if entry in the lottery is contingent on completing the survey (Mehta and Sivadas 1995). To date, results of studies comparing results of paper and Internet surveys are mixed, with some showing mail surveys producing better response rates (Shannon and Bradshaw 2002), others producing more positive results for Internet surveys (Cobanoglu et al. 2001), and still others not differing significantly (Schaffer and Dillman 1998; Weible and Wallace 1998). Also, some studies report that results from mail-back and web-based surveys are not significantly different either in completion rates or response content (Denscombe 2006; Kaplowitz et al. 2004).

Internet access is also an issue. Not everyone has Internet access or high-speed access. Internet surveys requiring complex access procedures have lower response rates than surveys that are easy to access (Crawford et al. 2001; Schaefer and Dillman 1985). Likewise, Internet surveys having a colorful, fancy, or complex design have lower response rates than plainer ones (Dillman et al. 1998). A wide variety of method exist for conducting surveys such as within the body of an email, as an attachment to an email, including a link to a website, and using mail, phone and FAX methods to convey information about the survey and how to access it (Dommeyer and Moriarty 2000; Illeva, Baron, and Healey 2002; Roos 2002; Swartz and Hancock 2002; Taylor 2000). Using mixed or multimode strategy can increase response to e-mail/Internet surveys (Dillman 2000; Illeva, Baron, and Healey 2002; Roos 2002; Schaefer and Dillman 1998).

As with mail surveys, use of multiple contacts including both an invitation and reminders increase email/Internet survey response (Cook et al. 2000; Mehta and Sivadas 1995; Schaefer and Dillman 1998; Smith 1997; Trouteaud 2004). Sending of pre- and post-survey postcards can significantly enhance response to Internet-based surveys (Kaplowitz et al. 2004).

The author agrees with Dillman and others who believe that Internet and e-mail surveys are here to stay, and their use will continue to expand. Like mail and telephone surveys that have long developmental histories, Internet and e-mail survey researchers will continue to identify and resolve problems. The *PAR* content analysis indicates that Internet and e-mail surveys are not widely used in public administration research. Without doubt, the next edition of the *Handbook of Public Administration* will address this topic in detail.

F. SUMMARY

Mail-back surveys are widely used in public administration research to gather data, and their use is increasing. Evidence examined from *PAR* for 1971, 1976, 1986, 1995, and 2004 shows this pattern.

It is difficult to generalize about nonresponse, because there is a tremendous amount of variability in survey response caused by differences in factors, such as level of salience of the survey's topic, the survey's sponsor, and the nature of the target population, among other factors (Heberlein and Baumgartner 1978; Yammarino et al. 1991). There is evidence that nonresponse has increased for all types of surveys during the last 40 years. This problem has become more difficult to overcome.

Since survey research methods are increasingly being used, this section has reviewed a series of factors that affect survey response rates. These factors are follow-up contacts, sponsorship, the nature of the respondent population, salience, incentives, length, anonymity, personalization, types of appeals, postage, and deadlines. Knowledge of these methodological options is crucial if this widely used method of collecting data in public administration research is to produce valid and reliable results.

Like many of those who have examined the factors affecting mail survey response rates (Dillman et al. 1974; Dillman 1978, 2000; Edwards et al. 2002; Willimack et al. 1995; Yammarino et al. 1991; Yu and Cooper 1983), this review reaches the conclusion that no aspect of survey preparation or administration can be safely ignored. A single ill-considered decision, such as failing to enclose a pre-addressed return envelope bearing sufficient first-class postage, or failure to use multiple contacts and follow-ups, can have disastrous consequences for the response rate for a survey.

VII. CONCLUSION

In conclusion, the author offers few generalizations about research methods. The choice of a method or methods must be determined by the research questions and setting. No method fits every question and setting. The possibility of method specific results is a threat to validity and reliability. Hence, use of multiple methods is suggested. Replication is necessary in a variety of settings and with a variety of methods to establish the validity and reliability of findings. When they are appropriate, new methods should be used to reexamine questions already studied by other means.

The author believes that the debate over whether quantitative or qualitative methods are superior has consumed too much time and energy. It is more worthwhile to use both kinds of methods where and when they are appropriate. Methods that are usually associated with quantitative and qualitative analyses are not mutually exclusive, as they are sometimes portrayed. For instance, many have called for triangulation or using one method to corroborate and supplement another (Denzin 1978, Janesick 1994, Jick 1978, Patton 1987, Sypher et al. 1985 and Vidich and Lyman 1994, Yin 1994, 2003), and many examples of triangulation exist. Triangulation is examined in more detail in the section on case studies, and to a lesser extent in the section on participant observation. Despite the criticisms in the literature, it is a good sign that a number of recent public administration studies cited in this chapter make use of multiple methods.

REFERENCES

Adams, G. B. and White, J. D., Dissertation research in public administration and cognate fields: an assessment of methods and quality, *Public Administration Review*, 54, 565–576, 1994.

Adams, J. S., An experiment on question and response bias, *Public Opinion Quarterly*, 20, 593–598, 1956.

Adams, R. N. and Priess, J. J., *Human Organizational Research*, Dorsey, Homewood, IL, 1960.

Agar, M., *The Professional Stranger: An Informal Introduction to Ethnography*, Academic Press, New York, 1980.

Agar, M., *The Professional Stranger: An Informal Introduction to Ethnography*, 2nd ed., Academic Press, New York, 1996.

Agar, M. H., *The Professional Stranger: An Informal Introduction to Ethnography*, Academic Press, San Diego, 1980.

Agranoff, R. and Radin, B. A., The comparative case study approach in public administration, In *Research in Public Administration*, Perry, J. L., Ed., JAI Press, Greenwich, CT, pp. 203–231, 1991.

Aiken, M., The distribution of community power: structural bases and social consequences, In *The Structure of Community Power*, Aiken, M. and Mott, P., Eds., Random House, New York, pp. 487–525, 1970.

Aiken, M. and Hage, J., Organizational interdependence and intra-organizational structure, *American Sociological Review*, 33, 912–930, 1968.

Alford, R. R., Quantitative indicators of the quality of life: a critique, *Comparative Urban Research*, 3, 5–8, 1973.

Alford, R. R., Ideological filters and bureaucratic responses in interpreting research: community planning and poverty, In *Social Policy and Sociology*, Demerath, N. J. et al., Eds., Academic Press, New York, pp. 25–36, 1975.

Alkin, M., Dillak, R., and White, P., *Using Evaluation: Does Evaluation Make a Difference?*, Sage Publications, Beverly Hills, CA, 1979.

Allen, K. E., *Diverse Voices of Leadership: Different Rhythms and Emerging Harmonies*, UMI, Ann Arbor, MI, 1990.

Allison, G. T., *Essence of Decision: Explaining the Cuban Missile Crisis*, Little, Brown, Boston, MA, 1971.

Altschuld, J. W. and Lower, M. A., Improving mailed questionnaires: analysis of a 96 percent return rate, In *Making Effective Use of Mailed Questionnaires*, Lockhart, D. C., Ed., Jossey-Bass, San Francisco, CA, pp. 5–18, 1984.

Amato, P. R. and Gilbreth, J. G., Nonresident fathers and children's well-being: a meta-analysis, *Journal of Marriage and the Family*, 61, 557–573, 1999.

Anderson, A. B., Policy experiments: selected analytic issues, In *Validity Issues in Evaluative Research*, Bernstein, I. N., Ed., Sage, Beverly Hills, CA, pp. 17–34, 1976.

Anderson, B. A., Silver, B. D., and Abramson, P. R., The effects of race of the interviewer on measures of electoral participation by blacks in SRC national election studies, *Public Opinion Quarterly*, 52(1), 53–83, 1988a.

Anderson, B. A., Silver, B. D., and Abramson, P. R., The effects of the race of the interviewer on race-related attitudes of black respondents in SRC/CPS national election studies, *Public Opinion Quarterly*, 52(3), 289–324, 1988b.

Anderson, K. and Jack, D. C., Learning to listen, In *Women's Words: The Feminist Practice of Oral History*, Gluck, S. B. and Patai, D., Eds., Routledge, New York, pp. 11–26, 1991.

Andriot, D., *Guide to United States Government Publications*, Documents Index, McLean, VA, 1990.

Andriot, D., Andriot, J., Andriot, J., and Andriot, L., *Guide to United States Government Statistics*, Documents Index, Manassas, VA, 1995.

Angell, R., A critical review of the development of the personal document method in sociology, 1920–1940, In *The Use of Personal Documents in History, Anthropology, and Sociology*, Gottschalk, L., Kluckhohn, C., and Angell, R., Eds., Social Science Research Council, New York, pp. 177–232, 1947.

Angell, R. C. and Fredman, R., The use of documents, records, census materials, and indices, In *Research Methods in the Behavioral Sciences*, Festinger, L. and Katz, D. D., Eds., Holt, Rinehart, and Winston, New York, pp. 300–326, 1953.

Aquilino, W. S., Interview mode effects in surveys of drug and alcohol use: a field experiment, *Public Opinion Quarterly*, 58, 210–240, 1994.

Aquilino, W. S. and LoSciuto, L. A., Effects of interview mode on self-reported drug use, *Public Opinion Quarterly*, 54, 362–395, 1990.

Argyris, C., Diagnosing defenses against the outsider, *Journal of Social Issues*, 8, 24–34, 1952.

Armstrong, J. S., Monetary incentives in mail surveys, *Public Opinion Quarterly*, 39, 111–116, 1975.

Armstrong, J. S., Advocacy and objectivity in science, *Management Science*, 25, 423–428, 1979.

Armstrong, J. S. and Lusk, E. J., Return postage in mail surveys: a meta-analysis, *Public Opinion Quarterly*, 51, 231–248, 1987.

Armstrong, J. S. and Overton, T. S., Estimating nonresponse bias in mail surveys, *Journal of Marketing Research*, 14, 397–402, 1977.

Aronsson, T. and Brännäs, K., Household work travel time, *Regional Studies*, 30(6), 541–548, 1996.

Asad, T., Ed., *Anthropology and the Colonial Encounter*, Humanities, London, 1973.

Asch, D. A., Christakis, N. A., and Ubel, P. A., Conducting physician mail surveys on a limited budget: a randomized trial comparing $2 bill versus $5 bill incentives, *Medical Care*, 36, 95–99, 1998.

Athey, K. R., Coleman, J. E., Reitman, A. P., and Tang, J., Two experiments showing the effect of the interviewer's racial background on responses to questionnaires concerning racial issues, *Journal of Applied Psychology*, 44, 244–246, 1960.

Atrostic, B. K., Bates, N., Burt, G., and Silberstein, A., Nonresponse in U.S, *Journal of Official Statistics*, 17(2), 209–226, 2001.

Babbie, E., *Survey Research Methods*, Wadsworth, Belmont, CA, 1973.

Babbie, E., *The Practice of Social Research*, 3rd ed., Wadsworth, Belmont, CA, 1983.

Babbie, E., *Practicing Social Research*, 4th ed., Wadsworth, Belmont, CA, 1986.

Bachman, D., Elfrink, J., and Vazzana, G., Tracking the progress of email versus snail-mail, *Marketing Research*, 8, 31–35, 1996.

Bailar, B., Bailey, L., and Colby, C., A comparison of some adjustment and weighting procedures for survey data, In *Survey Sampling and Measurement*, Namboodiri, N. K., Ed., Academic Press, New York, pp. 175–198, 1978.

Bailey, K. D., *Methods for Social Research*, Free Press, New York, 1978.

Bailey, K. D., *Methods for Social Research*, 2nd ed., Free Press, New York, 1982.

Bailey, L., Moore, T. F., and Bailar, B., An interview variance study for the eight impact cities of the national crime survey's cities sample, *Journal of the American Statistical Association*, 73, 16–23, 1978.

Bailey, M. T., Do physicists use case studies? Thoughts on public administration research, *Public Administration Review*, 52, 47–54, 1992.

Bain, R. K., The researcher's role: a case study, In *Human Organization Research*, Adams, R. N. and Preiss, J. J., Eds., Dorsey Press, Homewood, IL, pp. 140–152, 1960.

Balaban, R. M., The contribution of participant observation to the study of process in program evaluation, *The International Journal of Mental Health*, 2, 59–70, 1973.

Balaban, R. M., Participant observation—rediscovering a research method, In *Research Methods for Counselors*, Goldman, L., Ed., Wiley, New York, pp. 155–175, 1978.

Baldassare, M., *The Growth Dilemma*, University of California Press, Berkeley, CA, 1981.

Baldassare, M. and Protash, W., Growth controls, population growth, and community satisfaction, *American Sociological Review*, 47, 339–346, 1982.

Bales, R. F., *Interaction Process Analysis*, Addison-Wesley, Cambridge, MA, 1950.

Balfour, D. L. and Wechsler, B., Organizational commitment: antecedents and outcomes in public organizations, *Public Productivity and Management Review*, 19, 256–277, 1996.

Ball, J. C., The reliability and validity of interview data obtained from 59 narcotic drug addicts, *American Journal of Sociology*, 72, 650–654, 1967.

Ban, C., *How do Public Managers Manage? Bureaucratic Constraints, Organizational Culture, and the Potential for Reform*, Jossey-Bass, San Francisco, CA, 1995.

Banton, M., *The Policeman in the Community*, Anchor, Garden City, NJ, 1964.

Barber, J. D., *Power in Committees: An Experiment in the Governmental Process*, Rand-McNally, Chicago, IL, 1966.

Barzun, J. and Graff, H., *The Modern Researcher*, 3rd ed., Harcourt Brace Jovanovich, New York, 1977.

Bateman, I. J. and Mawby, J., First impressions count: interviewer appearance and information effects in stated preference studies, *Ecological Economics*, 49, 47–55, 2004.

Baumgartner, F. and Jones, B., Eds., *Policy Dynamics*, University of Chicago Press, Chicago, IL, 2002.

Baumgartner, F. R. and Jones, B. D., *Agendas and Instability in American Politics*, University of Chicago Press, Chicago, IL, 1993.

Baumgartner, R. M. and Heberlein, T. A., Recent research on mailed questionnaire response rates, In *Making Effective Use of Mailed Questionnaires*, Lockhart, Daniel C., Ed., Jossey-Bass, San Francisco, CA, pp. 65–76, 1984.

Baur, E. J., Response bias in a mail survey, *Public Opinion Quarterly*, 11, 594–600, 1947.

Bausell, R. B., Li, Y., Gau, M., and Soeken, K. L., The growth of meta-analytic literature from 1980 to 1993, *Evaluation and the Health Professions*, 18, 238–251, 1995.

Beck, Allen J. and Harrison, Paige M., *Prisoners in 2003*, Bureau of Justice Statistics, US Department of Justice, Washington, DC, 2004.

Becker, H. S., Problems of inference and proof in participant observation, *American Sociological Review*, 23, 652–660, 1958.

Becker, H. S., Problems in the publication of field studies, In *Reflections on Community Studies*, Vidich, A., Bensman, J., and Stein, M., Eds., John Wiley, New York, pp. 267–284, 1964.

Becker, H. S., *Outsiders: Studies in the Sociology of Deviance*, Free Press, New York, 1966.

Becker, H. S., Whose side are we on?, *Social Problems*, 14, 239–247, 1967.

Becker, H. S., Practitioners of vice and crime, In *Pathways to Data*, Habenstein, R. W., Ed., Aldine, Chicago, IL, pp. 30–49, 1970.

Becker, H. S. and Friedson, E., Against the code of ethics, *American Sociological Review*, 29, 409–410, 1964.

Becker, H. S. and Greer, B., Participant observation and interviewing: a comparison, *Human Organization*, 16, 28–32, 1957.

Becker, H. S., Greer, B., Hughes, E. C., and Strauss, A., *Boys in White: Student Culture in Medical School*, University of Chicago Press, Chicago, IL, 1961.

Benson, L. E., Mail surveys can be valuable, *Public Opinion Quarterly*, 10, 234–241, 1946.

Berg, S., In *Snowball Sampling*, Kotz, S. and Johnson, N. L., Eds., *Encyclopaedia of Statistical Sciences*, Vol. 8, Wiley & Son, New York, 1988.

Bergsten, J. W., Weeks, M. F., and Bryan, F. A., Effects of an advance telephone call in a personal interview survey, *Public Opinion Quarterly*, 48, 650–657, 1984.

Berk, M. L., Mathiowetz, N. J., Ward, E. P., and White, A. A., The effect of prepaid and promised incentives: results of a controlled experiment, *Journal of Official Statistics*, 3, 449–457, 1987.

Berman, J., McCombs, H., and Boruch, R. F., Notes on the contamination method, *Sociological Methods and Research*, 6, 45–62, 1977.

Bernard, H. R., *Research Methods in Anthropology: Qualitative and Quantitative Approaches*, 2nd ed., AltaMira Press, Walnut Creek, CA, 1994.

Bernstein, C. and Woodward, B., *All the President's Men*, Warner Books, New York, 1974.

Berreman, G., *Behind Many Masks: Impression Management in a Himalayan Village Hindus of the Himalayas,* xvii-lvii, University of California Press, Berkeley CA, 1962.

Berry, B. J. L., Cutler, I., Draine, E. H., Kians, Y. C., Tocalis, T. R., and deVise, P., *Chicago: Transformation of an Urban System*, Ballinger, Cambridge, MA, 1976.

Berry, S. H. and Kanouse, D. E., Physician response to a mailed survey: an experiment in timing of payment, *Public Opinion Quarterly*, 51, 102–114, 1987.

Bevis, J. C., Economical incentive used for mail questionnaire, *Public Opinion Quarterly*, 12, 492–493, 1948.

Biemer, P. P. and Lyberg, L. E., *Introduction to Survey Quality*, Wiley, New York, 2003.

Bigelow, B. and Stone, M. M., Why don't they do what we want? An exploration of organizational responses to institutional pressures in community health centers, *Public Administration Review*, 55, 183–192, 1995.

Binning, J. F. and Lord, R. G., Boundary conditions for performance cue effects on group process rating: familiarity versus type of feedback, *Organizational Behavior and Human Performance*, 26, 115–130, 1980.

Bishop, G. F., Oldendick, R. W., Tuchfarber, A. J., and Bennett, S. E., Pseudo-opinions on public affairs, *Public Opinion Quarterly*, 44, 198–209, 1980.

Bishop, G. F., Tuchfarber, A. J., and Oldendick, R. W., Opinions on fictitious issues: the pressure to answer survey questions, *Public Opinion Quarterly*, 50, 240–250, 1986.

Bittner, E., Objectivity and realism in sociology, In *Phenomenological Sociology*, Psathas, G., Ed., Wiley, New York, pp. 108–125, 1973.

Black, J. A. and Champion, D. J., *Methods and Issues in Social Research*, Wiley, New York, 1976.

Blair, E., Sudman, S., Bradburn, N. M., and Stocking, C., How to ask questions about drinking and sex: response effects in measuring consumer behavior, *Journal of Marketing Research*, 14, 316–321, 1977.

Blassingame, J. W., *The Slave Community: Plantation Life in the Ante-Bellum South*, Oxford University Press, New York, 1972.

Blassingame, J. W., Using the testimony of ex-slaves: approaches and problems, *Journal of Southern History*, 41, 490, 1975.

Blassingame, J. W., *Slave Testimony*, Louisiana State University Press, Baton Rouge, 1977.

Blau, P. M., Patterns of interaction among a group of officials in a government agency, *Human Relations*, 7, 337–338, 1954.

Blau, P. M., Orientation toward clients in a public welfare agency, *Administration Science Quarterly*, 5, 341–361, 1960.

Blau, P. M., The research process in the study of "The dynamics of bureaucracy," In *Sociologists at Work*, Hammond, P. E., Ed., Basic Books, New York, pp. 16–49, 1964.

Blau, P. M., The hierarchy of authority in organizations, *American Journal of Sociology*, 73, 453–467, 1968.

Blau, P. M. and Schoenherr, R. A., *The Structure of Organizations*, Basic Books, New York, 1971.

Blumer, H., *Critiques of Research in the Social Sciences: 1: An Appraisal of Thomas and Znaniecki's The Polish Peasant in Europe and America*, Social Science Research Council, New York, 1939.

Blumer, H., Society as symbolic interactionism, In *Human Behavior and Social Processes*, Rose, A., Ed., Houghton-Mifflin, Boston, pp. 179–192, 1962.

Boas, F., The social organization and the secret societies of the Kwakiutl Indians, In *Report of the US National Museum for 1895*, Washington, DC, pp. 311–337, 1897.

Bock, E. A., Fessler, J. W., Stein, H., and Waldo, D., Eds., *Essays on the Case Method*, International Institute of Administrative Science and the Inter-University Case Program, Paris, 1962.

Bogdon, R. and Taylor, S. J., *Introduction to Qualitative Research Methods: A Phenomenological Approach to the Social Sciences*, Wiley, New York, 1975.

Bogen, K., The effect of questionnaire length on response rates—a review of the literature, *Proceedings of the Section on Survey Research Methods*, American Statistical Association, pp.1020–1025, 1996.

Bonoma, T. V., Case research in marketing: opportunities, problems, and a process, *Journal of Marketing Research*, 22, 199–208, 1985.

Bouchard, T. J., Unobtrusive measures: an inventory of uses, *Sociological Methods and Research*, 4, 267–300, 1976.

Bouchard, T. J., Field research methods: interviewing, questionnaires, participant observation, systematic observation, unobtrusive measures, In *Handbook of Industrial and Organizational Psychology*, Dunnette, M. D., Ed., Rand-McNally, Chicago, pp. 289–328, 1976.

Bourque, L. B. and Clark, V. A., *Processing Data: The Survey Example*, Sage, Thousand Oaks, CA, 1992.

Bowers, C., When member homogeneity is needed in work teams: a meta-analysis, *Small Group Research*, 31, 305–327, 2000.

Bowker, I. R., Understanding online communities through multiple methodologies combined under a postmodern research endeavour, *Qualitative Social Research*, 2, 1, 2001. http://www.qualitative-research.net/fqs-texte/1-01/1-01bowker-e.htm

Bowman, F. O. and Heise, M., Quiet rebellion? Explaining nearly a decade of declining federal drug sentences, *Iowa Law Review* 88, No. 4, http://papers.ssrn.com/sol3/papers.cfm?abstract_id = 281798 (accessed), 2001.

Bowman, F. O. and Heise, M., Quiet rebellion II: an empirical analysis of declining federal drug sentences including data from the district level, *Iowa Law Review* 87(2), http://ssrn.com/abstract = 301649, 2002.

Bradburn, N.M, Response effects, In *Handbook of Survey Research*, Rheas, P. H., Wright, J. D., and Anderson, A. B., Eds., Academic Press, New York, pp. 289–328, 1983.

Bradley, N., Sampling for internet surveys. An examination of respondent selection for internet research, *Journal of the Market Research Society*, 41(4), 387–395, 1999.

Brandes, R. S., *Frank Hamilton Cushing: Pioneer Americanist*, Unpublished doctoral dissertation, University of Arizona, Tucson, AZ, 1965.

Brandt, R. M., *Studying Behavior in Natural Settings*, Holt, Rinehart and Winston, New York, 1972.

Brannon, D., *Choice Behavior in a Public Welfare Agency*. Unpublished manuscript, Department of Human Service Studies, Cornell University, Ithaca, NY, 1979.

Brannen, P., Working on directors: some methodological issues, In *Research Methods for Elite Studies*, Moyser, G. and Wagstaffe, M., Eds., Allen and Unwin, London, pp. 166–180, 1987.

Brehm, J. W., *A Theory of Psychological Reactance*, Academic Press, New York, 1966.

Brehm J. W., *Opinion Surveys and Political Representation*, Unpublished doctoral dissertation, University of Michigan, MI, 1990.

Brehm, J., Stubbing our toes for a foot in the door? Prior contact, incentives and survey response improving response to surveys, *International Public Opinion Research*, 6, 45–64, 1994.

Brehm, S. S. and Brehm, J. W., *Psychological Reactance: A Theory of Freedom and Control*, Academic Press, New York, 1981.

Bremner, R., Ed., *Children and Youth in America*, Harvard University Press, Cambridge, MA, Vol. 1, 1600–1865, Vol. 2, 1866–1932, Vol. 3, 1933–1973, 1970–1971.

Brennan, M. and Hoek, J., The behavior of respondents, nonrespondents, and refusers across mail surveys, *Public Opinion Quarterly*, 56, 530–535, 1992.

Brenner, M. C., Brown, J., and Canter, D., *The Research Interview: Uses and Approaches*, Academic Press, London, 1985.

Brent, E. and Slusarz, P., "Feeling the Beat": intelligent coding advice from metaknowledge in qualitative research, *Social Science Computer Review*, 21, 281–303, 2003.

Bridgeland, W. M. and Sofranko, A., Community structure and issue-specific influences: community mobilization over environmental quality, *Urban Affairs Quarterly*, 11, 186–214, 1975.

Bridges, G. S. and Crutchfield, R. S., Law, social standing, and racial disparities in imprisonment, *Social Forces*, 66, 699–724, 1988.

Bridges, G. S., Crutchfield, R. D., and Simpson, E. E., Crime, social structure and criminal punishment: white and nonwhite rates of imprisonment, *Social Problems*, 34, 345–361, 1987.

Briggs, C. L., Questions for the ethnographer: a critical examination of the role of the interview in fieldwork, *Semiotica*, 46, 233–261, 1983.

Briggs, C. L., Learning how to ask: native metacommunicative competence and the incompetence of field-workers, *Language in Society*, 13, 1–28, 1984.

Briscoe, D. R. and Leonardson, G. S., *Experiences in Public Administration*, Duxbury Press, North Scituate, MA, 1980.

Broadhead, R. and Rist, R., Gatekeepers and the social control of social research, *Social Problems*, 21, 52–64, 1976.

Brower, R. S., Abolafia, Mitchel Y., and Carr, J. B., On improving qualitative methods in public administration research, *Administration and Society*, 32, 363–397, 2000.

Brown, P. R. and Bishop, G. F., Who refuses and resists in telephone surveys? Some new evidence, Paper presented at the Annual Conference of the Midwest Association for Public Opinion Research, 1982.

Brown, R. and Fish, D., *Recreation Planning and Analysis in Local Government 1973 Municipal Year Book*, International City Management Association, Washington, DC, pp. 54–60, 1973.

Brunner, A. and Carroll, S. J., The effect of prior telephone notification on the refusal in fixed address surveys, *Journal of Advertising Research*, 9, 42–44, 1969.

Brunner, R. D. and Livornese, K. M., *Subjective Political Change: A Prospectus*, Center for Public Policy Research, University of Colorado, Boulder, CO, 1982.

Brunswick, A. F., Health consequences of drug use: a longitudinal study of urban Black youth, In *Handbook of Longitudinal Research in the US*, Mednick, S. A., Harway, M., and Finello, K. M., Eds., Praeger Press, New York, pp. 290–314, 1984.

Brunswick, A. F., Health and substance use behavior, *Journal of Addictive Diseases*, 11, 119–137, 1991.

Bryck, A. and Weisberg, H., An alternative paradigm for evaluation individualized demonstration programs, Presented at the Annual Meeting of the American Educational Research Association, Toronto, ON, Canada, April, 1978.

Bryson, J. and Crosby, B., *Leadership for the Common Good: Tackling Public Problems in a Shared-Power World*, Jossey-Bass, San Francisco, 1992.

Bryson, M. C., The literary digest poll: making of a statistical myth, *American Statistician*, 30(4), 184–185, 1976.

Bryun, S., *The Human Perspective in Sociology*, Prentice Hall, Englewood Cliffs, NJ, 1966.

Buckner, H. T., The police: the culture of a social control agency, Unpublished Ph.D., dissertation, University of California, Berkeley, CA, 1967.

Buell, E. H., Eccentrics or gladiators? People who write about politics in letters to the editors, *Social Science Quarterly*, 56, 440–449, 1975.

Burgess, R. G., Ed., *Studies in Qualitative Methodology*, JAI Press, Greenwich, CT, 1988.

Burgoyne, J. G. and Hodgson, V. E., An experimental approach to understanding managerial action, In *Leaders and Managers: International Perspective on Managerial Behavior and Leadership*, Hunt, H. G., Hosking, D. M., Schriesheim, C., and Stewart, R., Eds., Pergamon, Elmsford, NY, pp. 163–178, 1984.

Burns, J., *Leadership*, Harper and Row, New York, 1978.

Burrell, G. and Morgan, G., *Sociological Paradigms and Organizational Analysis*, Heinemann, London, 1979.

Burstein, L., Freeman, H. E., Sirotnik, K. A., Delandshere, G., and Hollis, M., Data collection: the Achilles heel of evaluation research, *Sociological Methods and Research*, 14, 65–80, 1985.

Burt, R. S., Comparative power structures in American communities, *Social Science Research*, 10, 115–176, 1981.

Busson, R. S., Larson, L. L., Vicars, W. M., and Ness, J. J., *The Nature of Police Executive's Work: Final Report*, Southern Illinois University, Carbondale, IL, 1981.

Butz, W. P., *Data Confidentiality and Public Perceptions: The Case of the European Censuses Proceedings of the Section on Survey Research Methods*, American Statistical Association, Washington, DC, pp. 90–97, 1985.

Byrne, J., Business fads: what's in-and out, Executives latch onto any management idea that looks like a quick fix, *Business Week*, Jan 20, 52–55, 58, 60–61, 1986.

Cahnman, W. J., Historical sociology: what it is and what it is not, In *The New Social Sciences*, Varma, B. N., Ed., Greenwood Press, Westport, CT, pp. 107–122, 1976.

Cahnman, W. J. and Boskoff, A., *Sociology and History: Theory and Research*, Free Press, New York, 1964.

Cain, M., *Society and the Policeman's Role*, Routledge and Kegan Paul, London, 1973.

Calsyn, R. J., Kohfeld, C. W., and Roades, L. A., Urban homeless people and welfare: who receives benefits?, *American Journal of Community Psychology*, 21, 95–112, 1993.

Campbell, B., Race-interviewer effects among Southern adolescents, *Public Opinion Quarterly*, 45, 231–244, 1981.

Campbell, D. T., The informant in quantitative research, *American Journal of Sociology*, 60, 339–342, 1955.

Campbell, D. T., Degrees of freedom and the case study, *Comparative Political Studies*, 8, 178–193, 1975.

Campbell, D. T. and Fiske, D. W., Convergent and discriminant validation by the multitrait-multimethod matrix, *Psychological Bulletin*, 56, 81–105, 1959.

Campbell, D. T. and Stanley, J. C., *Experimental and Quasi-Experimental Designs for Research*, Rand-McNally, Chicago, IL, 1963.

Cannell, C. F., Factors affecting the refusal rate in interviewing, Working paper, Survey Research Center, University of Michigan, Ann Arbor, MI, 1964.

Cannell, C. F. and Kahn, R. L., In *Interviewing*, Lindzey, G. and Aronson, E., Eds., 2nd ed., *Handbook of Social Psychology*, Vol. 2, Addison-Wesley, Reading, MA, pp. 526–595, 1968.

Cannell, C. F., Miller, P. V., and Oksenberg, L., Research on interviewing techniques, *Sociological Methodology*, 12, 389–437, 1981.

Caputo, D. A. and Cole, R. L., City officials and mailed questionnaires: an investigation of the response bias assumption, *Political Methodology*, 4, 271–287, 1977.

Carini, R. M., Hayek, J. C., Kuh, G. D., Kennedy, J. M., and Ouimet, J. A., College student responses to web and paper surveys: does mode matter?, *Research in Higher Education*, 44, 1–19, 2003.

Carroll, J. D., Confidentiality of social science research sources and data: the Popkin case, *Political Science*, 6, 11–24, 1973.

Carter, G. M., Robyn, A., and Singer, A. M., *The Supply of Physician Researchers and Support for Research Training, Part I of an Evaluation of the Hartford Foundation Fellowship Program N2003-HF*, Rand Corporation, Santa Monica, CA, 1983.

Cartwright, B. C. and Schwartz, R. D., The invocation of legal norms: an empirical investigation of Durkheim and Weber, *American Sociological Review*, 38, 340–354, 1973.

Cary, M. S., Data collection: film and videotape, *Sociological Methods and Research*, 11, 167–174, 1982.

Cassell, J., The relationship of observer to observed when studying up, In *Studies in Qualitative Methodology*, Burgess, R. G., Ed., JAI Press, Greenwich, CT, pp. 89–108, 1988.

Castells, M., *The Rise of the Network Society*, Blackwell, London, 1996.

Catania, J. A., Binson, D., Canchola, J., Pollack, L. M., Hauck, W., and Coates, T. J., Effects of interviewer gender, interviewer choice, and item wording on responses to questions concerning sexual behavior, *Public Opinion Quarterly*, 60, 345–375, 1996.

Cesara, M., *Reflections of a Woman Anthropologist*, Academic Press, New York, 1982.

Chandler, J., Researching and the relevance of gender, In *Studies in Qualitative Methodology*, Burgess, R. G., Ed., Vol. 2, JAI Press, Greenwich, CT, pp. 119–140, 1990.

Chevigny, P., *Police Power: Police Abuses in New York City*, Pantheon, New York, 1968.

Chevigny, P., *Cops and Rebels*, Pantheon, New York, 1972.

Childers, T. L. and Ferrell, O. C., Response rates and perceived questionnaire length in mail surveys, *Journal of Marketing Research*, 16, 429–431, 1979.

Childers, T. L., Pride, W. M., and Ferrell, O. C., A reassessment of the effects of appeals on response to mail surveys, *Journal of Marketing Research*, 17, 365–370, 1980.

Chrislip, D. D. and Larson, C. F., *Collaborative Leadership: How Citizens and Civic Leaders Can Make a Difference*, Jossey-Bass, San Francisco, CA, 1994.

Church, A. H., Estimating the effect of incentives on mail survey response rates: a meta-analysis, *Public Opinion Quarterly*, 57, 62–79, 1993.

Cialdini, R. B., *Influence: Science and Practice*, Scott, Foresman, Glenview, IL, 1988.

Clark, T. N., Community structure, decision-making and urban renewal in 51 American communities, *American Sociological Review*, 33, 576–593, 1968.

Cleary, R. E., Revisiting the doctoral dissertation in public administration: an examination of the dissertations of 1990, *Public Administration Review*, 52, 55–61, 1992.

Clemente, F. and Kleiman, M. B., Fear of crime among the aged, *Gerontologist*, 16, 207–210, 1976.

Clifford, J., Power and dialogue in ethnography: Marcel Griaule's initiation, In *Observers Observed: Essays on Ethnographic Fieldwork*, Stocking, G. W. Jr., Ed., University of Wisconsin Press, Madison, WI, pp. 121–156, 1983.

Clifford, J. and Marcus, G. E., Eds., *Writing Culture: The Poetics and Politics of Ethnography*, University of California Press, Berkeley, CA, 1986.

Clough, Patricia Ticineto, *The End(s) of Ethnography: From Realism to Social Criticism*, 2nd ed., Sage, Thousand Oaks, CA, 1998.

Cobanoglu, C., Warde, B., and Moreo, P., A comparison of mail, fax and web-based survey methods, *International Journal of Market Research*, 43(4), 441–452, 2001.

Coble-Vinzant, J. and Crothers, L., *Street-Level Leadership: Discretion and Legitimacy in Front-Line Public Service*, Georgetown University Press, Washington, DC, 1998.

Coffey, Amanda, *The Ethnographic Self: Fieldwork and the Representation of Identity*, Sage Publications, Thousand Oaks, CA, 1999.

Coggin, M., The 'too few cases/too many variables' problem in implementation research, *Western Political Quarterly*, 39, 328–347, 1986.

Cohen, C., Jones, K., and Tronto, J., *Women Transforming Politics: An Alternative Reader*, New York University Press, New York, 1997.

Cohen, J., A coefficient of agreement for nominal scales, *Educational Psychology Measurement*, 20, 37–46, 1960.

Cohen, J., Weighted kappa: nominal scale agreement with provision for scaled disagreement or partial credit, *Psychological Bulletin*, 70, 213–220, 1968.

Cohen, M. D., March, J. G., and Olsen, J. P., A garbage can model of organizational choice, *Administrative Science Quarterly*, 17, 1–25, 1972.

Cohen, J., *Statical Power Analysis for the Behavioral Sciences*, 2nd ed., Lawrence Eribaum, New Jersey, 1988.

Cole, D., The value of a person lies in his herzensbildung: Franz Boas' Baffin Island letter-diary, 1883–1884, In *Observers Observed: Essays on Ethnographic Fieldwork*, Stocking, G. W. Jr., Ed., University of Wisconsin Press, Madison, WI, pp. 13–52, 1884.

Cole, S., *The Sociological Method: An Introduction to the Science of Sociology*, 3rd ed., Rand-McNally, Chicago, IL, 1980.

Coleman, S., Obstacles and opportunities in access to professional work organizations for long-term fieldwork: the case of Japanese laboratories, *Human Organization*, 55(3), 334–343, 1996.

Collette, P. and O'Shea, G., Pointing the way to a fictional place: a study of direction giving in Iran and England, *European Journal of Social Psychology*, 6, 447–458, 1976.

Colson, H., Citation ranking of public administration journals, *Administration and Society*, 21, 452–471, 1990.

Comer, J. M. and Kelly, J. S., Follow-up techniques: the effect of methods and source appeal, Working paper, University of Cincinnati, Cincinnati, OH, 1980.

Connelly, F. M. and Clandinin, D. J., Stories of experience and narrative inquiry, *Educational Researcher*, 19, 2–14, 1990.

Cook, T. D. and Campbell, D. T., *Quasi-Experimentation: Design and Analysis for Field Settings*, Houghton-Mifflin, Boston, MA, 1979.

Cook, C., Health, F., and Thompson, R. L., A meta-analysis of response rates in web or Internet-based surveys, *Educational and Psychological Measurement*, 60, 821–826, 2000.

Cooper, H., *Integrating Research: A Guide for Literature Reviews*, Sage, Thousand Oaks, CA, 1998.

Cornwell, C. and Kellough, J. E., Women and minorities in federal government agencies: examining new evidence from panel data, *Public Administration Review*, 54, 265–270, 1994.

Cotter, P. R., Cohen, J., and Coulter, P. B., Race-of-interviewer effects in telephone interviews, *Public Opinion Quarterly*, 46, 278–284, 1982.

Couper, M. P., Survey introductions and data quality, *Public Opinion Quarterly*, 61(2), 317–338, 1997.

Couper, M. P., Web surveys: a review of issues and approaches, *Public Opinion Quarterly*, 64, 464–494, 2000.

Couper, M. P., Traugott, M. W., and Lamias, M. J., Web survey design and administration, *Public Opinion Quarterly*, 65, 230–253, 2001.

Crain, R. L., Katz, E., and Rosenthal, D., *The Politics of Community Conflict: The Fluoridation Issue*, Bobbs-Merrill, Indianapolis, IN, 1969.

Crawford, S. D., Couper, M. P., and Lamias, M. J., Web surveys: perception of burden, *Social Science Computer Review*, 19, 146–162, 2001.

Cropper, M. and Gordon, P., Wasteful commuting: a re-examination, *Journal of Urban Economics*, 29, 2–13, 1991.

Crosby, B., *Leadership for Global Citizenship: Building Transnational Community*, Sage, Thousand Oaks, CA, 1999.

Cummings, K., Random digit dialing: a sampling technique for telephone surveys, *Public Opinion Quarterly*, 43, 233–244, 1979.

Cunningham, B., Riverstone, L., and Roberts, S., Scholars, teachers, practitioners, and students: learning by fishing, storytelling, and appreciative inquiry, *Journal of Public Affairs Education*, 11, 45–52, 2005.

Czarniawska, B., *Narrating the Organization: Dramas of Institutional Identity*, University of Chicago Publishing, Chicago, IL, 1997.

Daft, R. L. and Widgington, J. C., Language and organizations, *Academy of Management Review*, 4(2), 179–191, 1979.

Daly, K., Neither conflict nor labeling nor paternalism will suffice: intersections of race, ethnicity, gender, and family in criminal court decisions, *Crime and Delinquency*, 35, 136–168, 1989.

Dalton, M., Conflict between staff and line managerial officers, *American Sociological Review*, 15, 342–351, 1950.

Dalton, M., *Men Who Manage: Fusions of Feelings and Theory in Administration*, Wiley, New York, 1959.

Dalton, M., Preconceptions and method in "Men Who Manage", In *Sociologists at Work*, Hammond, P. E., Ed., Basic Books, New York, pp. 50–95, 1964.

Daly, Kathleen, *Gender, Crime, and Punishment*, Yale University Press, New Haven, CT, 1994.

Daneke, G. A. and Kobus-Edwards, P., Survey research for public administrators, *Public Administration Review*, 39, 421–426, 1979.

Das, T. H., Qualitative research in organizational behavior, *Journal of Management Studies*, 20, 301–314, 1983.

Datta, L., Strange bedfellows: the politics of qualitative methods, *American Behavioral Scientist*, 26, 133–144, 1982.

Davey Smith, G., Ed., *Clinical Meta-Analysis*, Wiley, New York, 2001.

Davey, Smith G. and Egger, M., Meta-analyses of observational data should be done with due care, *British Medical Journal*, 318, 56, 1999.

Davey, Smith G., Egger, M., and Phillips, A. N., Meta-analysis: principles and procedures, *British Medical Journal*, 315, 1533–1537, 1997a.

Davey, Smith G., Egger, M., and Phillips, A. N., Meta-analysis: beyond the grand mean?, *British Medical Journal*, 315, 1610–1614, 1997b.

Davis, F., Deviance disavowal: the management of strained interaction by the visibly handicapped, *Social Problems*, 9, 120–132, 1961.

Davis, D. W., Nonrandom measurement error and race of interviewer effects among African Americans, *Public Opinion Quarterly*, 61, 183–207, 1997a.

Davis, W., The direction of race of interviewer effects among African-Americans: donning the black mask, *American Journal of Political Science*, 41(1), 309–322, 1997b.

Davis, D. W. and Silver, B. D., Stereotype threat and race of interviewer effects in a survey on political knowledge, *American Journal of Political Science*, 47, 33–45, 2003.

Decotiis, T. and Petit, A., The performance appraisal process: a model and some testable propositions, *Academy of Management Review*, 3, 635–646, 1978.

DeGroot, T., Kiker, D. S., and Cross, T. C., A meta-analysis to review organizational outcomes related to charismatic leadership, *Canadian Journal of Administrative Sciences*, 17, 356–371, 2000.

DeMaio, T. J., Refusals: who, where and why, *Public Opinion Quarterly*, 39, 223–233, 1980.

DeMunck, V. C. and Sobo, E. J., Eds., *Using Methods in the Field: A Practical Introduction and Casebook*, AltaMira Press, Walnut Creek, CA, 1998.

DeNisi, A. S. and Pritchard, R. D., Implicit theories of performance as artifacts in survey research: a replication and extension, *Organizational Behavior and Human Performance*, 21, 358–366, 1978.

Denscombe, M., Web-based questionnaires and the mode effect, *Social Science Computer Review*, 24, 246–254, 2005.

Denzin, N., *The Research Act*, Aldine, Chicago, IL, 1970.

Denzin, N. K., *The Research Act: A Theoretical Introduction to Sociological Methods*, 2nd ed., McGraw-Hill, New York, 1978.

Denzin, N. K. and Lincoln, Y. S., *Handbook of Qualitative Research*, Sage Publications, Thousand Oaks, CA, 1994.

Denzin, N. K. and Lincoln, Y. S., *Handbook of Qualitative Research*, 2nd ed., Sage Publications, Thousand Oaks, CA, 2000.

Derthick, M., *New Towns in-Town: Why a Federal Program Failed*, Urban Institute, Washington, DC, 1972.

DeVaus, D. A., *Surveys in Social Research*, George Allen and Unwin, London, 1986.

DeWalt, K. M. and DeWalt, B. R., *Participant Observation: A Guide for Fieldworkers*, AltaMira Press, Walnut Creek, CA, 2002.

Dexter, L. A., Role relationships and conceptions of neutrality in interviewing, *American Journal of Sociology*, 62, 153–157, 1956.

Dexter, A., *Elite and Specialized Interviewing*, Northwestern University Press, Evanston, IL, 1970.

DiIulio, J. D., Principled agents: the cultural basis of behavior in a federal government bureaucracy, *Journal of Public Administration Research and Theory*, 4, 277–318, 1994.

Dillman, D. A., *Mail and Telephone Surveys: The Total Design Method*, Wiley, New York, 1978.

Dillman, D. A., *Mail and Internet Surveys: The Tailored Design Method*, 2nd ed., Wiley, New York, 2000.

Dillman, D. A., Christenson, J. A., Carpenter, E. H., and Brooks, R. M., Increasing mail questionnaire response: a four-state comparison, *American Sociological Review*, 39, 744–756, 1974.

Dillman, D. A., Gallegos, J. G., and Frey, J. H., Reducing refusal rates from telephone interviews, *Public Opinion Quarterly*, 40, 66–78, 1976.

Dillman, D. A., The design and administration of mail surveys, *Annual Review of Sociology*, 17, 225–249, 1991.

Dillman, D. A., Clark, J. R., and Sinclair, M. A., How prenotice letters, stamped return envelopes, and reminder postcards affect mailback response rates for census questionnaires, *Survey Methodology*, 31, 1–7, 1995.

Dillman, D. A., Sangster, R. L., Tarnai, J., and Rockwood, T., Understanding differences in people's answers to telephone and mail surveys. In *Current Issues in Survey Research, New Directions for Program Evaluation Series*, Braverman, M. T. and Slater, J. K., Eds., chap. 4, Jossey-Bass, San Francisco, pp. 45–62, 1996.

Dillman, D. A., Totora, R. D., Conradt, J., and Bowker, D., Influence of plain versus fancy design on response rates for web surveys, Paper presented at the Annual Meeting of the American Statistical Association, Dallas, TX, 1998.

DiMaggio, P. and Useem, M., Decentralized applied research: factors affecting the use of audience research byart organizations, *Journal of Applied Behavioral Science*, 15, 79–93, 1979.

Dobel, J. P., The odyssey of senior public service: what memoirs can teach us, *Public Administration Review*, 63, 16–20, 2003.

Dodge, J. S. M., Ospina, and Foldy, E. G., Integrating rigor and relevance in public administration scholarship: the contribution of narrative inquiry, *Public Administration Review*, 65, 286–300, 2005.

Doheny-Farina, S., Writing in an emerging organization: an ethnographic study, *Written Communication*, 3, 158–185, 1986.

Dohrenwend, B. S., An experimental study of payments to respondents, *Public Opinion Quarterly*, 34, 620–624, 1970.

Dohrenwend, B. S., Colombotos, J., and Dohrenwend, J., Social distance and interviewer effects, *Public Opinion Quarterly*, 32, 410–422, 1968–1969.

Dollard, J., *Caste and Class in a Southern Town*, Yale University Press, New Haven, CT, 1937.

Dommeyer, C. J. and Moriarty, E., Comparing two forms of an e-mail survey: embedded vs. attached, *International Journal of Market Research*, 42, 39–50, 2000.

Donald, M. N., Implications of nonresponse for the interpretation of mail questionnaire data, *Public Opinion Quarterly*, 24, 99–114, 1960.

Donley, E. and Winter, G., Measuring the motives of public officials at a distance: an exploratory study of American Presidents, *Behavioral Science*, 15, 222–236, 1970.

l-Douglas, J. D., *Investigative Social Research: Individual and Team Field Research*, Sage, Beverly Hills, CA, 1976.

Downey, H. K., Chacko, T., and McElroy, J. C., Attribution of the "causes" of performance: a constructive, quasi-longitudinal replication of the Staw study (1975), *Organizational Behavior and Human Performance*, 24, 287–299, 1979.

Downey, H. K. and Ireland, R. D., Quantitative versus qualitative: environmental assessment in organizational studies, *Administrative Science Quarterly*, 24, 630–637, 1979.

Downs, C. W., Smeyak, G. P., and Martin, E., *Professional Interviewing*, Harper and Row, New York, 1980.

Downs, P. E. and Kerr, J. R., Recent evidence on the relationship between anonymity and response variables for mail surveys, *Journal of the Academy of Marketing Science*, 14, 72–82, 1986.

Drath, W. H. and Palus, C. J., *Making Common Sense: Leadership as Meaning-Making in a Community of Practice*, Center for Creative Leadership, Greensboro, NC, 1994.

Dukes, R. L., Ullman, J. B., and Stein, I. A., A three-year follow-up of Drug Abuse Resistance Education (DARE), *Evaluation Review*, 20, 49–66, 1996.

Dukes, R. L., Stein, J. A., and Ullman, J. B., Long-term impact of Drug Abuse Resistance Education (DARE), *Evaluation Review*, 21, 483–500, 1997.

Duncan, W. J., Mail questionnaires in survey research: a review of response inducement techniques, *Journal of Management*, 5, 39–55, 1979.

Dunn, D. D., Blinders on research in public sector performance, *Public Administration Quarterly*, 8, 313–324, 1984.

Eagly, A. H., Karau, S. J., and Makhijani, M. G., Gender and the effectiveness of leaders: a meta-analysis, *Psychological Bulletin*, 117, 125–145, 1995.

Edgington, E. S., Statistical inference from $N = 1$ experiments, *Journal of Psychology*, 65, 195–199, 1967.

Eden, D., Replication, meta-analysis, scientific progress, and AMJ's publication policy, *Academy of Management Journal*, 45(5), 841–846, 2002.

Edwards, P., Roberts, L., Clarke, M., DiGuiseppi, C., Pratap, S., Wentz, R., and Kwan, I., Increasing response rates to postal questionnaires: systematic review, *British Medical Journal*, 324, 1183–1185, 2002.

Egger, M. and Davey Smith, G., Misleading meta-analysis: lessons from "an effective, safe, simple" intervention that wasn't, *British Medical Journal*, 310, 752–754, 1995.

Egger, M and Davey Smith, G., Meta-analysis: potentials and promise, *British Medical Journal*, 315, 1371–1374, 1997.

Egger, M and Davey Smith, G., Misleading meta-analysis: bias in location and selection of studies, *British Medical Journal*, 316, 61–68, 1998.

Egger, M., Davey Smith G., and Altman, D. G., Eds., *Systematic Reviews in Health Care: Meta-Analysis in Context,* 2nd ed., BMJ Publications, London, 2001.

Egger, M., Davey Smith G., Schneider, M., and Minder, C., Bias in meta-analysis detected by a simple, graphical test, *British Medical Journal*, 315, 629–634, 1996.

Egger, M., Ebrahim, S., and Smith, G. D., Where now for meta-analysis?, *International Journal of Epidemiology*, 31(1), 1–5, 2002.

Egger, M., Juni, P., Bartlett, C., Holenstein, C., and Sterne, J., How important are comprehensive literature searches and the assessment of trial quality in systematic reviews, *Health Technology Assessment*, 7(1), 2003.

Egger, M., Schneider, M., and Davey, Smith G., Meta-analysis spurious precision? Meta-analysis of observational studies, *British Medical Journal*, 316, 140–144, 1998.

Eichner, K. and Habermehl, W., Predicting response rates to mailed questionnaires (comment on Heberlein and Baumgartner, ASR, August 1978), *American Sociological Review*, 46, 361–363, 1981.

Eisinger, R., Janicki, W., Stevenson, R., and Thompson, W., Increasing returns in international mail surveys, *Public Opinion Quarterly*, 38, 124–130, 1974.

Epstein, A., Ed., *The Craft of Social Anthropology*, Tavistock, London, 1967.

Erdos, P., *Professional Mail Surveys*, Kreiger, Malabar, FL, 1983.

Erikson, K. T., Sociology and the historical perspective, *The American Sociologist*, 5, 331–338, 1970.

Erikson, K. T., Sociology and the historical perspective, In *The Sociology of the Future*, Bell, W. and Mau, J. J., Eds., Russell Sage, New York, pp. 61–67, 1971.

Evinger, W. R., *Federal Statistical Data Bases: A Comprehensive Catalog of Current Machine-Readable and Online Files*, Oryx Press, Phoenix, AZ, 1988.

Ewick, P. and Silbey, S. S., Subversive stories and hegemonic tales: toward a sociology of narrative, *Law and Society Review*, 29, 197–226, 1995.

Feagin, J. R., Orum, A. M., and Sjoberg, G., Eds., *A Case for the Case Study*, University of North Carolina Press, Chapel Hill, NC, 1991.

Feilders J. F., *Action and Reaction: The Job of an Urban School Superintendent*, Unpublished doctoral dissertation, Stanford University, Stanford, CA, 1979.

Feinstein, A. R., The haze of Bayes, the aerial palaces of decision analysis, and the computerized Ouija board, *Clinical Pharmacology and Therapeutics*, 21, 482–496, 1977.

Felson, M., Unobtrusive indicators of cultural change, *American Behavioral Scientist*, 26, 534–542, 1983.

Felson, M. and Cohen, L. E., Human ecology and crime: a routine activity approach, *Human Ecology*, 8, 397–406, 1980.

Fendrich, M. and Vaughn, C. M., Diminished lifetime substance use over time, *Public Opinion Quarterly*, 58, 96–123, 1994.

Ferber, R., Item nonresponse in a consumer survey, *Public Opinion Quarterly*, 30, 399–415, 1966.

Ferber, R. and Sudman, S., Effects of compensation in consumer expenditure studies, *Annals of Economic and Social Measurement*, 3, 319–331, 1974.

Ferriss, A. L., A note on stimulating response to questionnaires, *American Sociological Review*, 16, 247–249, 1951.

Ferris, J. A., A theoretical framework for surveying citizens' fiscal preferences, *Public Administration Review*, 42(3), 213–219, 1982.

Festinger, L., Reicken, H. W., and Schacter, S., *When Prophecy Fails*, University of Minnesota Press, Minneapolis, MN, 1956.

Fetterman, D. M., *Ethnography: Step-by-Step*, Sage Publications, Newbury Park, CA, 1989.

Fetterman, D. M., *Ethnography Step-by-Step*, 2nd ed., Sage Publications, Thousand Oaks, CA, 1998.

Fieldler, F. E., *A Theory of Leader Effectiveness*, McGraw-Hill, New York, 1967.

Filstead, W. J., *Qualitative Methodology: First Hand Involvement in the Social World*, Markham, Chicago, IL, 1970.

Finch, J., "It's great to have someone to talk to": the ethics and politics of interviewing women, In *Social Researching: Politics, Problems, Practice*, Bell, C. and Roberts, H., Eds., Routledge & Kegan Paul, London, pp. 70–87, 1984.

Finkel, S. E., Guterbock, T. M., and Borg, M. J., Race-of-interviewer effects in a preelection poll, *Public Opinion Quarterly*, 55, 313–330, 1991.

Finn, D. W., Response speeds, functions, and predictability in mail surveys, *Journal of the Academy of Marketing Science*, 11, 61–70, 1983.

Fisher, G. W., *The Worst Tax? A History of the Property Tax in America*, University Press of Kansas, Lawrence, KS, 1996.

Fiske, J., *Power Play, Power Works*, Verso, London, 1993.

Fitzgerald, J. D. and Cox, S. M., *Unravelling Social Science: A Primer on Perspectives, Methods, and Statistics*, Rand-McNally, Chicago, IL, 1975.

Fleiss, J. L., *Statistical Methods for Rates and Proportions*, 2nd ed., Wiley, New York, 1981.

Fombrun, C. J., Strategies for network research in organizations, *Academy of Management Review*, 7, 280–291, 1982.

Foreman, P. B., The theory of case studies, *Social Forces*, 26, 408–419, 1948.

Forrester, J. P. and Watson, S. S., An assessment of public administration journals: the perspective of editors and editorial board members, *Public Administration Review*, 54, 474–482, 1994.

Forsythe, S. A., An exploratory study of letters to the editor and their contributors, *Public Opinion Quarterly*, 14, 143–144, 1950.

Foster, G. M., Scudder, T., Colson, E., and Kemper, R. V., Eds., *Long Term Research in Social Anthropology*, Academic Press, New York, 1979.

Foster, H. S. Jr., and Friedrich, C. J., Letters to the editor as a means of measuring the effectiveness of propaganda, *American Political Science Review*, 31, 71–79, 1937.

Fox, J. C. and Lundman, R. J., Problems and strategies in gaining access in police organizations, *Criminology*, 12, 52–69, 1974.

Fox, R. J., Crask, M. R., and Kim, J., Mail survey response rate: a meta-analysis of selected techniques for inducing response, *Public Opinion Quarterly*, 52, 467–491, 1988.

Franke, R. H. and Kaul, J. D., *American Sociological Review*, 43, 623–639, 1978.

Franklin, C., Grant, D., Corcoran, J., Miller, P. O., and Bultman, L., Effectiveness of prevention programs for adolescent pregnancy: a meta-analysis, *Journal of Marriage and the Family*, 59, 551–567, 1997.

Freeman, J. and Butler, E. W., Some sources of interviewer variance in surveys, *Public Opinion Quarterly*, 40, 79–91, 1976.

Freilich, M., *Marginal Natives: Anthropologists at Work*, Harper and Row, New York, 1970.

Frey, J. H., An experiment with a confidentiality reminder in a telephone survey, *Public Opinion Quarterly*, 50, 267–269, 1986.

Friedman, N. L., Conventional covert ethnographic research by a worker, In *Studies in Qualitative Methodology*, Burgess, R., Ed., Vol. 2, JAI Press, Greenwich, CT, pp. 189–204, 1990.

Fuguitt, G., Commuting and the rural-urban hierarchy, *Journal of Rural Studies*, 7(4), 459–466, 1991.

Fuguitt, G. V. and Beale, C. L., Population trends of nonmetropolitan cities and villages in subregions of the United States, *Demography*, 15, 605–620, 1978.

Fuguitt, G. V. and Deeley, N. A., Retail service patterns and small town population change: a replication of Hassinger's study, *Rural Sociology*, 31, 53–63, 1966.

Fuller, C. H., Weighting to adjust for survey nonresponse, *Public Opinion Quarterly*, 38, 239–246, 1974.

Furse, D. H. and Stewart, D. W., Monetary incentives versus promised contributions to charity: new evidence on mailed survey response, *Journal of Marketing Research*, 19, 375–380, 1982.

Furse, D. H., Stewart, D. W., and Rados, D. L., Effects of foot in the door, cash incentives, and follow-ups on survey response, *Journal of Marketing Research*, 14, 611–616, 1977.

Futrell, C. M. and Swan, J. E., Anonymity and response by salespeople to a mailed questionnaire, *Journal of Marketing Research*, 14, 611–616, 1977.

Galaskiewicz, J., The study of a business elite and corporate philanthrophy in a United States metropolitan area, In *Research Methods for Elite Studies*, Moyser, G. and Wagstaffe, M., Eds., Allen and Unwin, London, pp. 147–165, 1987.

Gallegos, J. C., An experiment in maximizing response to telephone interviews through the use of a preliminary letter, based on the principles of exchange theory, M.A. Thesis, Washington State University, 1974.

Gannon, M. and Brzozowski, J., Sentencing in cases of family violence, In *Family Violence in Canada: A Statistical Profile*, Brzozowski, J., Ed., Statistics Canada, Ottawa, Canada, 2004.

GAO, *Federal Programs: Ethnographic Studies Can Inform Agencies' Actions*. GAO-03-455, Available at http://www.gao.gov/cgi-bin/getrpt?GAO-03-455, March 2003.

Garfinkel, H., *Studies in Ethnomethodology*, Prentice Hall, Englewood Cliffs, NJ, 1967.

Gaskell, G. and Bauer, M. W., Towards public accountability: beyond sampling, reliability and validity, In *Qualitative Researching with Text, Image and Sound*, Bauer, M. W. and Gaskell, G., Eds., Sage, Thousand Oaks, CA, pp. 336–350, 2000.

Gaudet, H. and Wilson, E. C., Who escapes the personal investigator?, *Journal of Applied Psychology*, 24, 773–777, 1940.

Gaunt, D., *Memoir on History and Anthropology*, Swedish Council for Research in the Humanities and Social Sciences, Stockholm, Sweden, 1982.

Geer, B., First days in the field, In *Sociologists at Work*, Hammond, P. E., Ed., Basic Books, New York, pp. 322–344, 1964.

Geertz, C. A., *The Interpretation of Cultures*, Basic Books, New York, 1973.

Gelb, B. D., Incentives to increase survey returns: social class considerations, *Journal of Marketing Research*, 12, 107–109, 1975.

George, A. L., *Propaganda Analysis: A Study of Inferences Made from Nazi Propaganda in World War II*, Greenwood Press, Westport, CT, 1959.

Georges-Abeyie, D. E., Defining race, ethnicity, and social distance: their impact on crime, criminal victimization, and the criminal justice processing of minorities, *Journal of Contemporary Criminal Justice*, 8, 100–113, 1992.

Georgopoulos, B. S. and Mann, F. C., *The Community General Hospital*, Macmillan, New York, 1962.

Gerbner, G. O., Holsti, O. R., Krippendorff, K., Paisley, W. J., and Stone, P. J., Eds., *The Analysis of Communication Content: Development in Scientific Theories and Computer Techniques*, Wiley, New York, 1969.

Gfroerer, J. C. and Hughes, A. L., The feasibility of collecting drug abuse data by telephone, *Public Health Reoorts*, 106, 384–393, 1991.

Glaser, B., *Theoretical Sensitivity*, Sociology Press, Mill Valley, CA, 1978.

Glaser, B. G. and Strauss, A. L., *The Discovery of Grounded Theory: Strategies for Qualitative Research*, Aldine, Chicago, IL, 1967.

Glaser, E. and Backer, T., A clinical approach to program evaluation, *Evaluation*, 1(1), 541–549, 1972.

Glaser, M. and Humphries, K., Eds., In *An Evaluation of the Wichita-Sedgwick County Department of Community Health Family Planning Clinic*, Hugo Wall Center for Urban Studies, Wichita State University, Wichita, KS, 1985.

Glaser, M., McKinney, J., and Urbom, D., Eds., In *An Evaluation and Needs Assessment of the Wichita-Sedgwick County Salvation Army*, Hugo Wall Center for Urban Studies, Wichita State University, Wichita, KS, 1987.

Glaser, M. and Hildreth, W. B., A profile of discontinuity between citizen demand and willingness to pay taxes: comprehensive planning for park and recreation investment, *Public Budgeting and Finance*, 16, 96–113, 1996.

Glass, Gene V., Primary, secondary, and meta-analysis of research, *Educational Researcher*, 5, 3–8, 1976.

Glass, Gene V., Synthesizing empirical research: meta-analysis, In *Knowledge Structure and Use*, Ward, S. A. and Reed, L. J., Eds., Temple University Press, Philadelphia, PA, 1983.

Glassner, B. and Corzine, J., Library research as fieldwork: a strategy for qualitative content analysis, *Sociology and Social Research*, 66, 305–319, 1982.

Glazer, M., *The Research Adventure: Promise and Problems of Fieldwork*, Random House, New York, 1972.

Glynn, C. J., Hayes, A. F., and Shanahan, J., Perceived support for one's opinions and willingness to speak out: a meta-analysis of survey studies on the "spiral of silence," *Public Opinion Quarterly*, 61, 452–463, 1997.

Godwin, R. K., The consequences of large monetary incentives in mail surveys of elites, *Public Opinion Quarterly*, 43, 378–387, 1979.

Goffman, E., *The Presentation of Self in Everyday Life*, Overlook Press, Woodstock, NY, 1973.

Gold, R. L., Roles in sociological field observations, *Social Forces*, 36, 217–223, 1958.

Gold, R. L., The ethnographic method in sociology, *Qualitative Inquiry*, 3(4), 388–402, 1997.

Goldman-Eisler, F., Individual differences between interviewers and their effect on interviewees' conversational behavior, *Journal of Mental Science*, 98, 660–671, 1952.

Golembiewski, R. T., Ed., *Perspectives on Public Management: Cases and Learning Designs*, Peacock, Itasca, IL, 1976.

Golembiewski, R. T. and Stevenson, J. G., Eds., *Cases and Applications in Nonprofit Management*, Wadsworth, Belmont, CA, 1998.

Golembiewski, R. T. and Varney, G. H., Eds., *Cases in Organization Development*, Wadsworth, Belmont, CA, 1999.

Golembiewski, R. T. and White, M., Eds., *Cases in Public Management* 2nd ed., Rand-McNally, Chicago, IL, 1976.

Golembiewski, R. T. and White, M., *Cases in Public Management*, 3rd ed., Rand-McNally, Chicago, IL, 1980.

Golembiewski, R. T. and White, M., *Cases in Public Management*, 4th ed., Houghton-Mifflin, Boston, MA, 1983.

Golembiewski, Robert T., Stevenson, J., and White, M., Eds., *Cases in Public Management*, 5th ed., Wadsworth, Belmont, CA, 1997.

Goode, W. J. and Hatt, P. K., *Methods in Social Research*, McGraw-Hill, New York, 1952.

Goodenough, W., *Culture, Language, and Society*, Addison-Wesley, Reading, MA, 1971.

Goodstadt, M. S., Chung, L., Kronitz, R., and Cook, G., Mail survey response rates: their manipulation and impact, *Journal of Marketing Research*, 14, 391–395, 1977.

Gordon, R., Ethnomethodology—radical critique, *Human Relations*, 29, 193–202, 1976.

Gottfredson, D. C. and Barton, W., Deinstitutionalization of juvenile offenders, *Criminology*, 31, 591–608, 1993.

Gottschalk, L., Kluckhohn, C., and Angell, R., *The Use of Personal Documents in History, Anthropology, and Sociology*, Social Science Research Council, New York, 1947.

Goudy, W. J., Nonresponse effects on relationships between variables, *Public Opinion Quarterly*, 40, 360–369, 1976.

Gouldner, A. W., The norm of reciprocity: a preliminary statement, *American Sociological Review*, 25, 161–178, 1960.

Goyder, J., Nonresponse: the opinion surveyor's dilemma, *Queen's Quarterly*, 89, 569–582, 1982a.

Goyder, J., Further evidence on factors affecting response rates to mailed questionnaires, *American Sociological Review*, 47, 550–553, 1982b.

Goyder, J., Face-to-face interviews and mailed questionnaires: the net difference in response rate, *Public Opinion Quarterly*, 49, 234–252, 1985.

Goyder, J., *The Silent Minority: Nonrespondents on Sample Surveys*, Westview Press, Boulder, CO, 1987.

Green, S. G. and Mitchell, T. R., Attributional processes of leaders in leader-member interactions, *Organizational Behavior and Human Performance*, 23, 429–458, 1979.

Greenfield, L. A. and Snell, T. L., *Women Offenders. Bureau of Justice Statistics*, US Department of Justice, 1999.

Greenhalgh, L. and Jick, T. D., The relationship between job security and turnover and its differential effects on employee quality level. Paper presented in the Academy of Management Conference, Atlanta, GA, 1979.

Greenhalgh, T., How to read a paper: papers that summarise other papers systematic reviews and meta-analyses, *British Medical Journal*, 13 September, 1992.

Greenwald, R., Hedges, L., and Laine, R., The effect of school expenditures on school achievement, *Review of Educational Research*, 66, 361–396, 1996.

Grey, D. L. and Brown, T., Letters to the editor: Hazy reflections of public opinion, *Journalism Quarterly*, 47, 450–471, 1970.

Griaule, M., *Methode de l'ethnographie*, Paris, 1957.

Griffiths, P., Gossop, M., Powis, B., and Strang, J., Reaching hidden populations of drug users by privileged access interviewers: methodological and practical issues, *Addiction*, 88, 1617–1626, 1993.

Grimshaw, A. D., Language as data and as obstacle in sociological research, *Items*, 23, 17–21, 1969.

Grimshaw, A. D., Some problematic aspects of communication in crossracial research in the United States, *Sociological Focus*, 3, 67–85, 1970.

Groger, L., Mayberry, P., and Straker, J., What we didn't learn because of who would not talk to us, *Qualitative Health Research*, 9, 829–835, 1999.

Gronn, P. C., Methodological perspective: Neo-Taylorism in educational administration?, *Educational Administration Quarterly*, 18, 17–35, 1982.

Gross, N., Giacquinta, J. B., and Bernstein, M., *Implementing Organizational Innovations*, Basic Books, New York, 1971.

Groves, R. M., An experimental comparison of national and personal telephone surveys, *Social Statistics Section Proceedings of the American Statistical Association*, pp. 232–241, 1977.

Groves, R. M., On the mode of administering a questionnaire and responses to open-ended items, *Social Science Research*, 7, 257–271, 1978.

Groves, R. M., *Survey Errors and Survey Costs*, Wiley, New York, 1989.

Groves, R. M., Cialdini, R. B., and Couper, M. B., Understanding the decision to participate in a survey, *Public Opinion Quarterly*, 56, 475–495, 1992.

Groves, R. M. and Couper, M. P., *Nonresponse in Household Interview Surveys*, Wiley, New York, 1998.

Groves, R. M., Dillman, D. A., Eltinge, J. L., and Little, R. J. A., Eds., *Survey Nonresponse*, Wiley, New York, 2002.

Groves, R. M. and Fultz, N. H., Gender effects among telephone interviewers in a survey of economic attitudes, *Sociological Methods and Research*, 14, 31–52, 1985.

Groves, R. M. and Kahn, R. L., *Surveys by Telephone: A National Comparison with Personal Interviews*, Academic Press, New York, 1979.

Groves, R. M. and Magilavy, L. J., Estimates of interviewer variance in telephone surveys, *Proceedings of Survey Research Methods Section*, American Statistical Association, 622–627, 1980.

Groves, R. M., *Survey Errors and Survey Costs*, Wiley, New York, 1989.

Groves, R. M., Singer, E., and Corning, A. C., Leverage-salience theory of survey participation: description and an illustration, *Public Opinion Quarterly*, 2000.

Groves, R. M., Presser, S., and Dipko, S., The role of topic interest in survey participation decisions, *Public Opinion Quarterly*, 68, 2–31, 2004.

Guest, R. H., Of time and the foremen, *Personnel*, 32, 478–486, 1956.

Guilford, J. P., *Psychometric Methods*, 2nd ed., McGraw-Hill, New York, 1954.

Gullahorn, J. and Strauss, G., The field worker in union research, In *Human Organization Research*, Adams, R. N. and Preiss, J. J., Eds., Dorsey Press, Homewood, IL, pp. 153–165, 1960.

Gully, S. M., Incalcaterra, K. A., Joshi, A., and Beaubin, J. M., A meta-analysis of team-efficacy, potency, and performance: interdependence and level of analysis as moderators of observed relationships, *Journal of Applied Psychology*, 87, 819–832, 2002.

Gunn, W. J. and Rhodes, I. N., Physician response rates to a telephone survey: effects of monetary incentive on response level, *Public Opinion Quarterly*, 45, 109–115, 1981.

Gusfield, J. R., Field work reciprocities in studying a social movement, *Human Organization*, 14, 29–33, 1955.

Guthrie, J. P. and Schwoerer, C. E., Older dogs and new tricks: career stage and self-assessed need for training, *Public Personnel Management*, 25, 59–72, 1996.

Guy, R. F., Edgley, C. E., Arafat, I., and Allen, D. E., *Social Research Methods: Puzzles and Solutions*, Allyn and Bacon, Inc., Boston, 1987.

Hagan, J., Extra-legal attributes and criminal sentencing: an assessment of a sociological viewpoint, *Law and Society*, 8, 357–383, 1974.

Hakel, M., Sorcher, M., Beer, M., and Moses, J., *Making it Happen: Designing Research with Implementation in Mind*, Sage Publications, Beverly Hills, CA, 1982.

Hamer, P. M., *A Guide to Archives and Manuscripts in the United States*, Yale University Press, New Haven, CT, 1961.

Hamilton, B., Wasteful commuting again, *The Journal of Political Economy*, 97(6), 1497–1504, 1989.

Hamilton, B. and Roell, A., Wasteful Commuting, *The Journal of Political Economy*, 90(5), 1035–1053, October 1982.

Hammersley, M. and Atkinson, P., *Ethnography*, Routledge, London, 1983.

Hannerz, U., *Soulside: Inquiries into Ghetto Culture and Community*, Columbia University Press, New York, 1969.

Hansen, R. A., A self-perception interpretation of the effect of monetary and non-monetary incentives on mail survey respondent behavior, *Journal of Marketing Research*, 17, 77–83, 1980.

Hanson, R. H. and Marks, E. S., Influence of the interviewer on the accuracy of survey results, *Journal of the American Statistical Association*, 53, 635–655, 1958.

Harris, R. N., *The Police Academy: An Inside View*, Wiley, New York, 1973.

Harrison, Paige, M., Jennifer, C., and Karberg, *Prison and Jail Inmates at Midyear 2003*, Bureau of Justice Statistics, US Department of Justice, 2004.

Hassinger, E., The relationship of trade-center population change to distance from larger centers in an agricultural area, *Rural Sociology*, 22, 131–136, 1957.

Hatchett, S. and Schuman, H., White respondents and race of interview effects. *Public Opinion Quarterly*, 39, 523–528, 1975–1976.

Hawkins, D. I., *Nonresponse in Detroit Area Study Surveys: A Ten Year Analysis. Working Papers in Methodology*, Institute for Research in Social Science, University of North Carolina, Chapel Hill, NC, 1977.

Hawkins, D. I., The impact of sponsor identification and direct disclosure of respondent rights on the quantity and quality of mail survey data, *Journal of Business*, 52, 577–590, 1979.

Hawley, A. H., Community power and urban renewal success, *American Journal of Sociology*, 68, 422–431, 1963.

Haws, David R., Ethics instruction in engineering education: a (mini) meta-analysis, *Journal of Engineering Education*, 223–229, 2001.

Heard, A., Interviewing southern politicians, *American Political Science Review*, 44, 886–896, 1950.

Heberlein, T. A. and Baumgartner, R. M., Factors affecting response rates to mailed questionnaires: a quantitative analysis of the published literature, *American Sociological Review*, 43, 447–462, 1978.

Heberlein, T. A. and Baumgartner, R. M., Is a questionnaire necessary in a second mailing?, *Public Opinion Quarterly*, 45, 102–108, 1981a.

Heberlein, T. A. and Baumgartner, R. M., The effectiveness of the Heberlein-Baumgartner models for predicting response rates to mailed questionnaires: European and U.S. examples, *American Sociological Review*, 46, 361–363, 1981b.

Hedges, L. V., Fixed effects models, In *The Handbook of Research Synthesis*, Cooper, H. and Hedges, L. V., Eds., Sage, New York, pp. 285–300, 1994.

Hedges, L. V. and Olkin, I., *Statistical Methods for Meta-Analysis*, Academic Press, San Diego, CA, 1985.

Hedges, L. V. and Vevea, J. L., Fixed- and random-effects models in meta-analysis, *Psychological Methods*, 3, 486–504, 1998.

Heffernon, E., *Making It in Prison*, Wiley-Interscience, New York, 1972.

Heifetz, R., *Leadership without Easy Answers*, Harvard University Press, Cambridge, MA, 1994.

Hendricks, V. M., Blanken, P., and Adriaans, N., *Snowball Sampling: A Pilot Study on Cocaine Use*, IVO, Rotterdam, The Netherlands, 1992.

Henry, N., Ed., *Doing Public Administration: Exercises, Essays, and Cases*, Allyn and Bacon, Boston, MA, 1978.

Henry, N., *Doing Public Administration: Exercises, Essays, and Cases*, 2nd ed., Allyn and Bacon, Boston, MA, 1982.

Henry, N. L. Ed., *Doing Public Administration: Exercises in Public Management*, 3rd ed., Brown and Benchmark, Madison, WI, 1991.

Herriott, R. E., Tensions in research design implementation: the rural experimental schools study, *American Behavioral Scientist*, 26, 23–44, 1982.

Herriott, R. E. and Gross, N., Eds., *The Dynamics of Planned Educational Change*, McCutchan, Berkeley, CA, 1979.

Hertz, R. and Imber, J. B., *Studying Elites Using Qualitative Methods*, Sage, London, 1995.

Herzog, A. R. and Rodgers, W. L., Age and response rates to interview sample surveys, *Journal of Gerontology*, 43, 200–205, 1988.

Herzog, A. R. and Rodgers, W. L., Age and response rates to interview sample surveys, *Journals of Geronotology*, 43, S200–S205, 1988.

Herzog, A. R., Rodgers, W. L., and Kulka, R. A., Interviewing older adults: a comparison of telephone and face-to-face modalities, *Public Opinion Quarterly*, 47, 405–418, 1983.

Herzon, R. J. and Claunch, R. G., Stories citizens tell and how administrators use types of knowledge, *Public Administration Review*, 57, 374–379, 1997.

Hess, D., Ethnography and the development of science and technology studies, In *Handbook of Ethnography*, Atkinson, P., Coffey, A., Delamont, S., Lofland, J., and Lofland, L., Eds., Sage, London, pp. 220–233, 2001.

Higgins, C. A., McClean, R. J., and Conrath, D. W., The accuracy and biases of diary communication data, *Journal of Social Networks*, 7, 173–187, 1985.

Hill D. B., Letter opinion on ERA: a test of the newspaper bias hypothesis, *Public Opinion Quarterly*, 45, 384–392, 1981.

Hinsley, C., *Savages and Scientists: The Smithsonian Institution and the Development of American Anthropology*, Smithsonian Institute Press, Washington, DC, 1846–1910, 1981.

Hinsley, C., Ethnographic charisma and scientific routine: Cushing and Fewkes in the American Southwest, In *Observers Observed: Essays on Ethnographic Fieldwork*, Stocking, G. W., Ed., University of Wisconsin Press, Madison, WI, pp. 53–69, 1879–1893, 1983.

Hirst, E. and Goeltz, R., Testing for nonresponse bias: evaluation of utility energy conservation programs, *Evaluation Review*, 8, 269–278, 1984.

Hockey, S. A., *A Guide to Computer Applications in the Humanities*, Johns Hopkins University Press, Baltimore, MD, 1980.

Hodson, R., *Analyzing Documentary Accounts*, Sage, Thousand Oaks, CA, 1999.

Hodgson, R. C., Levinson, D. J., and Zaleznik, A., *The Executive Role Constellation: An Analysis of Personality and Role Relations in Management*, Harvard Business School, Boston, MA, 1965.

Hoffmann, J. E., Problems of access in the study of social elites and boards of directors, In *Fieldwork Experience: Qualitiative Approaches to Social Research*, Shaffir, W. B., Stebbins, R. A., and Turowetz, A., Eds., St. Martin's Press, New York, pp. 45–56, 1980.

Holstein, J. A. and Gubrium, J. F., *The Active Interview*, Sage, Thousand Oaks, CA, 1995.

Holsti, O. R., Content analysis, In *The Handbook of Social Psychology*, Lindzey, G. and Aronson, E., Eds., Addison-Wesley, Reading, MA, Vol. 2, 596–693, 1968.

Holzer, M. and Rosen, E. D., *Current Cases in Public Administration*, Harper and Row, New York, 1981.

Homans, G. C., *Social Behavior: Its Elementary Forms*, Harcourt Brace, New York, 1961.

Honigmann, J. and Carrera, R., Another experiment in sample reliability, *Southwestern Journal of Anthropology*, 13, 99–102, 1957.

Honigmann, J. and Honigmann, I., Sampling reliability in ethnological field work, *Southwestern Journal of Anthropology*, 11, 282–287, 1955.

Hornik, J., Time cue and time perception effect on response to mail surveys, *Journal of Marketing Research*, 18, 243–248, 1981.

Horvitz, D. G., Shah, B. V., and Simmons, W. R., The unrelated question randomized response model, *Proceedings of the American Statistical Association Social Statistics Section*, 67–72, 1967.

House, J. S. and Wolf, S., Effects of urban residence on interpersonal trust and helping behavior, *Journal of Personality and Social Psychology*, 36, 1029–1043, 1978.

Houston, M. J. and Ford, N. M., Broadening the scope of methodological research on mail surveys, *Journal of Marketing Research*, 13, 397–403, 1976.

Houston, M. J. and Nevin, J. R., The effects of source and appeal on mail survey response patterns, *Journal of Marketing Research*, 14, 374–378, 1977.

Hox, J. J. and de Leeuw, E. D., A comparison of nonresponse in mail, telephone, and face-to-face surveys, *Quality and Quantity*, 28, 329–344, 1994.

Hsu, F. L. K., The cultural problem of the cultural anthropologist, *American Anthropologist*, 81, 517–532, 1979.

Huddy, L., Billig, J., Bracciodieta, J., Hoeffler, L., Moynihan, P. J., and Pugliani, P., The effect of interviewer gender on the survey response, *Political Behavior*, 19, 197–220, 1997.

Huff, S. M., Lake, D., and Schaalman, M. L., *Principal Differences: Excellence in School Leadership and Management*, McBer, Boston, MA, 1982.

Huberman, A. M. and Crandall, D. P., Fitting words to numbers: multisite/multimethod research in educational dissemination, *American Behavioral Scientist*, 26, 62–83, 1982.

Hummel, R., Stories managers tell: why they are as valid as science, *Public Administration Review*, 51, 31–34, 1991.

Humphrey, C. R. and Krannich, R. S., The promotion of growth in small urban places and its impact on population change, *1975–1978 Social Science Quarterly*, 61, 581–594, 1980.

Humphrey, C. R., Krout, J., and Gillaspy, R. T., Net migration turnaround in Pennsylvania nonmetropolitan minor civil divisions, *1960–1970 Rural Sociology*, 42, 332–351, 1977.

Humphrey, C. R. and Sell, R. R., The impact of controlled-access highways on population growth in nonmetropolitan communities, *1940–1970 Rural Sociology*, 40, 323–343, 1975.

Hunt, S., The role of leadership in the construction of reality, In *Leadership: Multidisciplinary Perspectives*, Kellerman, B., Ed., Prentice-Hall, Englewood Cliffs, NJ, 1984.

Hunt, M., *How Science takes Stock: The Story of Meta-Analysis*, Russell Sage Foundation, New York, 1997.

Hunter, F., *Community Power Structure: A Study of Decision Makers*, University of North Carolina Press, Chapel Hill, NC, 1953.

Hunter, J. E. and Schmidt, F. L., *Methods of Meta-Analysis: Correcting Error and Bias in Research Findings*, Sage, Beverly Hills, CA, 1990.

Hunter, J. E. and Schmidt, F. L., Cumulative research knowledge and social policy formulation: the critical role of meta-analysis, *Psychology, Public Policy and Law*, 2, 324, 1996.

Hunter, J. E. and Schmidt, F. L., *Methods of Meta-Analysis: Correcting Error and Bias in Research Synthesis*, 2nd ed., Sage, New York, 2004.

Hunter, J. E., Schmidt, F. L., and Jackson, G. B., *Meta-Analysis: Cumulating Research Findings across Studies*, Sage, Beverly Hills, CA, 1982.

Hunter, R., In *The Child in Poverty: Social Conscience of the Progressive Era*, Hunter, R. and Jones, P., Eds., Harper and Row, New York, 1904.

Hurtado, A., Does similarity breed respect? Interviewer evaluations of Mexican-descent respondents in a bilingual survey, *Public Opinion Quarterly*, 58, 77–95, 1994.

Huxham, C. and Vangen, S., Leadership in the shaping and implementation of collaboration agendas: how things happen in a not quite joined-up world, *Academy of Management Journal*, 43, 1159–1175, 2000.

Hyman, H., Do they tell the truth?, *Public Opinion Quarterly*, 8, 557–559, 1944.

Hyman, H. H., Cobb, W. J., Feldman, J. J., Hart, C. W., and Spencer, C. H., *Interviewing in Social Research*, Aldine, Chicago, IL, 1954.

Ilieva, J., Baron, S., and Healey, N. M., Online surveys in marketing research: pros and cons, *International Journal of Market Research*, 44, 361–376, 2002.

Ingraham, P. W., Thompson, J. R., and Eisenberg, E. F., Political management strategies and political/career relationships: where are we now in the federal government?, *Public Administration Review*, 55, 263–272, 1995.

Inkson, J. H. K., Pugh, D. S., and Hickson, D. J., Organizational context and structure: an abbreviated replication, *Administrative Science Quarterly*, 15, 318–329, 1970.

Inoguchi, T., Measuring friendship and hostility among communist powers: some unobtrusive measures of esoteric communication, *Social Science Research*, 1, 79–105, 1972.

Irving, R. and Elton, M. C. J., The use of diaries to measure discretionary behavior: hypothesis and results, *Evaluation Review*, 10, 95–113, 1986.

Irwin, J., Participant-observation of criminals, In *Research on Deviance*, Douglas, J. D., Ed., Random House, New York, pp. 117–138, 1972.

Isen, A. M., Positive affect, cognitive processes, and social behavior, In *Advances in Experimental Social Psychology*, Berkowitz, L., Ed., Academic Press, New York, Vol. 20, pp. 203–253, 1987.

Jablin, F. M., Superiorsubordinate communication: the state of the art, *Psychological Bulletin*, 86, 1201–1222, 1979.

Jackall, R., *Moral Mazes: The World of Corporate Managers*, Oxford University Press, New York, 1988.

Jacobs, G., Ed., *The Participant Observer: Encounters with Social Reality*, Braziller, New York, 1970.

James, J. M. and Bolstein, R., The effect of monetary incentives and follow-up mailings on response rate and response quality in mail surveys, *Public Opinion Quarterly*, 54, 346–361, 1990.

James, J. M. and Bolstein, R., Large monetary incentives and their effect on mail survey response rates, *Public Opinion Quarterly*, 56, 442–453, 1992.

Janesick, V. J., The dance of qualitative research design: metaphor, metadolatry, and meaning, In *Handbook of Qualitative Research*, Denizen, N. K. and Lincoln, Y. S., Eds., Sage, Thousand Oaks, CA, 1994.

Janis, I. L., *Groupthink: Psychological Studies of Policy Decisions and Fiascoes*, 2nd ed., Houghton-Mifflin, Boston, MA, 1983.

Jasinski, F. J., Foremen relationships outside the work group, *Personnel*, 33, 130–136, 1956.

Jennings, B., Interpretive social science and policy analysis, In *Ethics, the Social Sciences and Policy Analysis*, Callahan, D. and Jennings, B., Eds., Sage, Newburg Park, CA, pp. 3–36, 1987.

Jensen, J. L. and Rodgers, R., Cumulating the intellectual gold of case study research, *Public Administration Review*, 61, 235–246, 2001.

Jick, T. D., Mixing qualitative and quantitative methods: triangulation in action, *Administrative Science Quarterly*, 24, 602–611, 1979.

Jobber, D. and Saunders, J., Modeling the effects of prepaid monetary incentives on mail-survey, *The Journal of Operational Research Society*, 39, 365–372, 1988.

Johansen, H. E. and Fuguitt, G. V., *The Changing Rural Village in America*, Ballinger, Cambridge, MA, 1984.

Johnson, D. R. and Scheuble, L. K., Gender bias in the disposition of juvenile court referrals: the effects of time and location, *Criminology*, 29, 677–699, 1991.

Johnson, J., *Doing Field Research*, Free Press, New York, 1975.

Johnson, W. T. and DeLamater, J. D., Response effects in sex surveys, *Public Opinion Quarterly*, 40, 165–181, 1976.

Johnston, L. D., O'Malley, P. M., and Bachman, J. G., *Drug Use Drinking, and Smoking: National Survey Results from High School, College, and Young Adult Population, 1975–1988*, (DHHNS Publication No.[ADM] 89–1638), National Institute on Drug Abuse, Rockvile, MD, 1989.

Jones, B., *Reconceiving Decision-Making in Democratic Politics: Attention, Choice, and Public Policy*, University of Chicago Press, Chicago, IL, 1994.

Jones, B. D. and Baumgartner, F. R., *The Politics of Attention: How Government Prioritizes Problems*, University of Chicago Press, Chicago, 2005.

Jones, B. D., Baumgartner, F., and Talbert, J., The destruction of issue monopolies in Congress, *American Political Science Review*, 87, 657–671, 1993.

Jones, B. D., Baumgartner, F. R., and True, J. L., Policy punctuations: US budget authority, *1947–95 Journal of Politics*, 60, 1–30, 1998.

Jones, C., Notes on interviewing members of the House of Representatives, *Public Opinion Quarterly*, 23, 404–406, 1959.

Jones, E. E. and Nisbett, R. E., The actor and the observer: divergent perceptions of the causes of behavior, In *Attribution: Perceiving the Causes of Behavior*, Jones, E. E., Kanouse, D. E., Kelly, H. H., Nisbett, R. E., Valins, S., and Weiner, B., Eds., General Learning Press, Morristoen, NJ, 1972.

Jones, W. H., Generalizing mail survey inducement methods: population interactions with anonymity and sponsorship, *Public Opinion Quarterly*, 43, 102–111, 1979.

Jones, W. H. and Lang, J. R., Sample composition bias and response bias in a mail survey: a comparison of inducement methods, *Journal of Marketing Research*, 17, 69–76, 1980.

Jones, W. H. and Lang, J. R., Reliability and validity effects under mail survey conditions, *Journal of Business Research*, 10, 339–353, 1982.

Jones, W. H. and Linda, G., Multiple criteria effects in a mail survey experiment, *Journal of Marketing Research*, 15, 280–284, 1978.

Jonsson, C. O., *Questionnaires and Interviews: Experimental Studies Concerning Concurrent Validity on Well-Motivated Subjects*, The Swedish Council for Personnel Administration, Stockholm, Sweden, 1957.

Jordan, L. A., Marcus, A. C., and Reeder, L. G., Response styles in telephone and household interviewing: a field experiment, *Public Opinion Quarterly*, 44, 210–222, 1980.

Jorgensen, D. L., *Participant Observation: A Methodology for Human Studies*, Sage Publications, Newbury Park, CA, 1989.

Junker, B. H., *Field Work: An Introduction to the Social Sciences*, University of Chicago Press, Chicago, IL, 1960.

Kaberry, P., Malinowski's contribution to field-work methods and the writing of ethnography, In *Man and Culture: An Evaluation of the Work of Bronislaw Malinowski*, Firth, R., Ed., Routledge and Kegan Paul, London, pp. 71–92, 1957.

Kahn, R. and Cannell, C., *Dynamics of Interviewing*, Wiley, New York, 1963.

Kane, E. W. and Maculay, L. J., Interviewer gender and gender attitudes, *Public Opinion Quarterly*, 57, 1–28, 1993.

Kanter, R. M., *Men and Women of the Corporation*, Basic Books, New York, 1977.

Kanuk, L. and Berenson, C., Mail surveys and research rates: a literature review, *Journal of Marketing Research*, 12, 440–453, 1975.

Kaplan, A.L., *Management Activities in an Organized Anarchy and a Rational Organization: Community Mental Health Centers Contrasted to Branch Banks*, Unpublished doctoral dissertation. Stanford University, Stanford, CA, 1979.

Kaplowitz, M. D., Hadlock, T. D., and Levine, R., A comparison of web and mail survey response rates, *Public Opinion Quarterly*, 68, 94–110, 2004.

Kaufman, H., *The Forest Ranger: A Study in Administrative Behavior*, Johns Hopkins University Press, Baltimore, MD, 1960.

Kaufman, H., *The Administrative Behavior of Federal Bureau Chiefs*, Brookings Institution, Washington, DC, 1981.

Keeter, S., Miller, C., Kohut, A., Groves, R. M., and Presser, S., Consequences of reducing non-response in a national telephone survey, *Public Opinion Quarterly*, 64, 125–148, 2000.

Kellerman, B., *Reinventing Leadership: Making the Connection between Politics and Business*, State University of New York Press, New York, 1999.

Kelley, J., The study of executive behavior by activity sampling, *Human Relations*, 17, 277–287, 1964.

Kelly, M., Theories of justice and street-level discretion, *Journal of Public Administration Research and Theory*, 4, 119–140, 1994.

Kelly, M. and Maynard-Moody, S., Policy analysis in the post-positivist era: engaging stakeholders in evaluating the Economic Development Districts Program, *Public Administration Review*, 53, 135–142, 1993.

Kendall, P. L. and Lazarsfeld, P. F., Problems of survey analysis, In *Continuities in Social Research*, Merton, R. K. and Lazarsfeld, P. F., Eds., Free Press, Glencoe, IL, pp. 133–196, 1950.

Kennedy, M. M., Findings from the follow through planned variation study, *Educational Researcher*, 7(6), 3–11, 1978.

Kennedy, M. M., Generalizing from single case studies, *Evaluation Quarterly*, 3, 661–678, 1979.

Kennedy School of Government's Case Program, http://www.ksgcase.harvard.edu/.

Kephart, W. M. and Bressler, M., Increasing the responses to mail questionnaires: a research study, *Public Opinion Quarterly*, 22, 123–132, 1958.

Kidder, L. H., Qualitative research and quasi experimental frameworks, In *Knowing and Validating: A Tribute to Donald T. Campbell*, Brewer, M. B. and Collins, B. E., Eds., Jossey-Bass, San Francisco, CA, 1981.

Kilmann, R., *Beyond the Quick Fix*, Jossey-Bass, San Francisco, 1984.

Kim, P. S., Disability policy: an analysis of the employment of people disabilities in the American federal government, *Public Personnel Management*, 25, 73–88, 1996.

Kim, P. S. and Lewis, G. B., Asian Americans in the public service: success, diversity, and discrimination, *Public Administration Review*, 54, 285–290, 1994.

King, D. N., The effects of incentives on response rates on the national longitudinal survey of education effects, Paper presented at the 34th Annual Conference for Public Opinion Research, Buck Hill Falls, PA, 1979.

Kingdon, J., *Agendas, Alternatives, and Public Policies*, Little, Brown, Boston, MA, 1984.

Kinsey, A., *Sexual Behavior in the Human Male*, W.B. Saunders Company, Philadelphia, PA, 1948.

Kish, L., Studies of interviewer variance for attitudinal variables, *Journal of the American Statistical Association*, 57, 92–115, 1962.

Kish, L., *Survey Sampling*, Wiley, New York, 1965.

Kitsuse, J. I., Societal reaction to deviant behavior: problems of theory and method, *Social Problems*, 9, 247–256, 1962.

Klein, Harald, INTEXT/PC—A program package for the analysis of texts in the humanities and social sciences, *Literary and Linguistic Computing*, 6, 108–111, 1991.

Klockers, C. B., *The Professional Fence*, Free Press, New York, 1974.

Kluckholn, F. R., The participant observer technique in small communities, *American Journal of Sociology*, 46, 331–343, 1940.

Kmetz, J. T. and Willower, D. J., Elementary school principals' work behavior, *Educational Administrative Quarterly*, 18, 62–78, 1982.

Koenig, D. J., Martin, G. R., and Seiler, L. H., Response rates and quality of data: a re-examination of the mail questionnaire, *Canadian Review of Sociology and Anthropology*, 14, 432–438, 1977.

Kolson, K. L. and Green, J. J., Response set bias and political socialization research, *Social Science Quarterly*, 51, 527–538, 1970.

Korosec, R. L. and Mead, T. D., Lessons from privatization task forces: comparative case studies, *Policy Studies Journal*, 24, 641–648, 1996.

Kovner, A. R., Assessing medicaid managed care in eastern state, *Journal of Policy Analysis and Management*, 15, 276–284, 1996.

Krannich, R. S., Socioeconomic impacts of power plant developments on nonmetropolitan communities: an analysis of perceptions and hypothesized impact determinants, *Rural Sociology*, 46, 128–142, 1981.

Krannich, R. S. and Humphrey, C. R., Local mobilization and community growth: toward an assessment of the 'growth machine' hypothesis, *Rural Sociology*, 48, 60–81, 1983.

Krannich, R. S. and Humphrey, C. R., Using key informant data in comparative community research, *Sociological Methods and Research*, 14, 473–493, 1986.

Krieger, S., Beyond 'subjectivity': the use of the self in social science, *Qualitative Sociology*, 8, 309–324, 1985.

Krout, J., Intercounty commuting in nonmetropolitan America in 1960 and 1970, growth and change, *Canadian Journal of Administrative Sciences*, 14(1), 9–19, 1983.

Krueger, R. A., *Developing Questions for Focus Groups*, Sage, Thousand Oaks, CA, 1998a.

Krueger, R. A., *Moderating Focus Groups*, Sage, Thousand Oaks, CA, 1998b.

Kruskal, W. H., Issues and opportunities, In *Statistics and Public Policy*, Fairley, W. B. and Moesteller, F., Eds., Addison-Wesley, Reading, MA, pp. 3–20, 1977.

Krysan, M., Schuman, H., Scott, L. J., and Beatty, P., Response rates and response content in mail versus face-to-face surveys, *Public Opinion Quarterly*, 58, 381–399, 1994.

Kuklinski, J. H. and Stanga, J., Political participation and government responsiveness: the behavior of California superior courts, *American Political Science Review*, 73, 1090–1099, 1979.

Kuncel, N. R., Hezlett, S. A., and Ones, D. S., A comprehensive meta-analysis of the predictive validity of the graduate record examinations: implications for graduate student selection and performance, *Psychological Bulletin*, Sage, Thousand Oaks, CA, 127, pp. 162–181, 2001.

Kurke, L. B. and Aldrich, H. E., Mintzberg was right! A replication and extension of "The Nature of Managerial Work," *Academy of Management Proceedings*, Atlanta, GA, August, 1979

Kvale, Steinar, *Interviews: An Introduction to Qualitative Research Interviewing*, Sage Publications, Thousand Oaks, CA, 1996.

Labovitz, S. and Hagedorn, R., *Introduction to Social Research*, McGraw-Hill, New York, 1971.

LaBreque, D. P., A response rate experiment using mail questionnaires, *Journal of Marketing*, 42, 82–83, 1978.

Lagay, B. W., Assessing bias: a comparison of two methods, *Public Opinion Quarterly*, 33, 615–618, 1969.

LaHaut, V. M., Jansen, H., van de Mheen, D., and Garretsen, F. L., Non-response bias in a sample survey on alcohol consumption, *Alcohol and Alcoholism*, 37, 256–260, 2002.

Landis, J. R. and Koch, G. G., The measurement of observer agreement for categorical data, *Biometrics*, 45, 255–268, 1977.

Landsberger, H. A., The horizontal dimension in bureaucracy, *Administrative Science Quarterly*, 6, 299–332, 1961.

Larson, L. L., Busson, R. S., and Vicars, W. M., *The Nature of a School Superintendent's Work: Final Technical Report*, Southern Illinois University, Carbondale, IL, 1981.

Latour, B., *Science in Action*, Open University Press, Milton Keynes, UK, 1987.

Lau, A. W., Newman, A. R., and Broedling, L. A., The nature of managerial work in the public sector, *Public Administration Review*, 40, 513–520, 1980.

Lauer, J. M. and Asher, J. W., Ethnographies, In *Composition Research: Empirical Designs*, Lauer, J. M. and Asher, J. W., Eds., Oxford University Press, New York, pp. 39–53, 1988.

Lawler, E. E., Mohrman, A., Mohrman, S., Ledford, G., Cummings, T., and Associates, Eds., *Doing Research That Is Useful for Theory and Practice*, Jossey-Bass, San Francisco, CA, 1985.

Lawler, E. E., Porter, L. W., and Tannenbaum, A., Managers' attitudes toward interaction episodes, *Journal of Applied Psychology*, 52, 432–439, 1968.

Le Lorier, J., Gregoire, G., Benhaddad, A., Lapierre, J., and Derderian, F., Discrepancies between meta-analyses and subsequent large randomized controlled trials, *New England Journal of Medicine*, 337, 537–542, 1997.

Leach, E., Introduction, In *Coral Gardens and their Magic*, Malinowski, B., Ed., Bloomington University Press, Bloomington, IN, Vol. I, vii–xvii, 1965.

Lee, A., The scientific basis for conducting case studies of organizations, *Academy of Management Proceedings, 45th Annual Meeting of the Academy of Management*, San Diego, CA, 320–324, August 1985.

Lee, R. M., *Doing Research on Sensitive Topics*, Sage, London, 1993.

Lee, T., Language-of-interview effects and Latino mass opinion, Paper presented at the Annual Meeting of the Midwest Political Science Association, Chicago, IL, 19–22, April, 2001.

Leenders, M. R. and Erskine, J. A., *Case Research: The Case Writing Process Research and Publications Division, School of Business Administration*, 2nd ed., The University of Western Ontario, London, ON, Canada, 1978.

Lenski, G. E. and Leggett, J. C., Caste, class, and deference in the research interview, *American Journal of Sociology*, 65, 463–467, 1960.

Leslie, T. F., Comparing two approaches to questionnaire design: official government versus public information design, *Proceedings of the Section on Survey Research Methods, American Association of Political Opinion Research*, American Statistical Association, Alexandria, VA, pp. 336–341, 1997.

Levine, M., Scientific method and the adversary model: some preliminary thoughts, *American Psychologist*, 29, 661–677, 1974.

Levine, M., Investigate reporting as a research method: an analysis of Bernstein and Woodward's *All the President's Men*, *American Psychologist*, 35, 626–638, 1980.

Levine, S. and Gordon, G., Maximizing returns on mail questionnaires, *Public Opinion Quarterly*, 22, 568–575, 1958.

Lewis, B. J. and Ellefson, P. V., Evaluating information flows to policy committees in state legislatures: forest and natural resources as a case, *Evaluation Review*, 20, 29–48, 1996.

Lewis, G. B., Women, occupations, and federal agencies: occupational mix and interagency differences in sexual equality in federal white-collar employment, *Public Administration Review*, 54, 271–276, 1994.

Library of Congress, Born in slavery: slave narratives from the Federal Writers' Project, http://memory.loc.gov/ammem/snhtml/snhome.ht, 1936–1938, 2001.

Liebow, A. A., *Encounter with Disaster: A Medical Diary of Hiroshima 1945*, Norton, New York, 1971.

Liebow, E., *Talley's Corner: A Study of Negro Streetcorner Men*, Little, Brown, Boston, MA, 1967.

Lin, A. C., Bridging positivist and interpretivist approaches to qualitative methods, *Policy Studies Journal*, 26, 162–180, 1998.

Lincoln, Y. S. and Guba, E. G., *Naturalistic Inquiry*, Sage, Beverly Hills, CA, 1985.

Lindsey, E. E., Questionnaires and follow-up letters, *Pedagogical Seminary Journal*, 28, 303–307, 1921.

Linsky, A. S., Stimulatory responses to mailed questionnaires, *Public Opinion Quarterly*, 39, 82–101, 1975.

Lindner, R., *The Reportage of Urban Culture: Robert Park and the Chicago School*, Cambridge University Press, Cambridge, 1996.

Lipsey, M. W. and Wilson, D. B., *Practical Meta-Analysis*, Sage Publications, Thousand Oaks, CA, 2001.

Lipsky, M., *Street Level Bureaucrats: Dilemmas of the Individual in Public Services*, Russell Sage, New York, 1980.

Locander, W., Sudman, S., and Bradburn, N., An investigation of interview method, threat and response distortion, *Journal of the American Statistical Association*, 71, 269–275, 1976.

Lockhart, D. C., *Making Effective Use of Mailed Questionnaires*, Jossey-Bass, San Francisco, CA, 1984.

Lockhart, D. C. and Russo, J. R., The effect of length of questionnaire and type of follow-up on the return rate of a mailed questionnaire, Paper Presented at the Annual Conference of the Evaluation Network and the Evaluation Research Society, Austin, TX. October, 1981.

Lofland, J., *Analyzing Social Settings: A Guide to Qualitative Observation and Analysis*, Wadsworth, Belmont, CA, 1971.

Lofland, J., *Doing Social Life*, Wiley, New York, 1976.

Lofland, J. and Lofland, L. H., *Analyzing Social Settings*, Wadsworth, Belmont, CA, 1984.

Lofland, J. and Lofland, L. H., *Analyzing Social Settings*, 3rd ed., Wadsworth, Belmont, CA, 1995.

Logan, J. R., Industrialization and the stratification of cities in suburban regions, *American Journal of Sociology*, 82, 333–348, 1976.

Logan, J. R. and Schneider, M., The stratification of metropolitan suburbs: 1960–1970, *American Sociological Review*, 46, 175–186, 1981.

Logan, J. R. and Semyonov, M., Growth and succession in suburban communities, *Sociological Quarterly*, 21, 93–105, 1980.

Logan, T. K., Cole, J., and Leukefeld, C., Women, sex, and HIV: social and contextual factors, meta-analysis of published interventions, and implications for practice and research, *Psychological Bulletin*, 128, 851–885, 2002.

London, I. D., Respondent evaluation applied to quotational analysis: a case study, *Psychological Reports*, 9, 615–621, 1961.

London, I. D., The revenge of heaven: a brief methodological account, *Psychological Reports*, 34, 1023–1030, 1974.

London, I. D., Interviewing in sinology: observations on methods and fundamental concepts, *Psychological Reports*, 36, 683–691, 1975.

London, I. D. and London, M. B., A research-examination of the harvard project on the soviet social system. Part 1: The basic written questionnaire, *Psychological Reports*, 19, 1011–1109, 1966.

London, P., *The Modes and Morals of Psychotherapy*, Holt, Rinehart and Winston, New York, 1964.

Louis, K. S., Sociologist as sleuth: integrating methods in the RDU study, *American Behavioral Scientist*, 26, 101–120, 1982.

Lovell, J. and Kluger, J., *Apollo 13*, Simon and Schuster, New York, 1995.

Lower, M. A. and Altschuld, J. W., *A Study of Attitudes and Perceptions of the Evaluation of Teaching*, Ohio State University, Columbus, OH, 1982.

Lowie, R. H., Native languages as ethnographic tools, *American Anthropologist*, 42, 81–89, 1940.

Luke, J. S., *Catalytic Leadership: Strategies for an Interconnected World*, Jossey-Bass, San Francisco, CA, 1998.

Luloff, A. E. and Wilkinson, K. P., Participation in the national flood insurance program: a study of community activeness, *Rural Sociology*, 44, 137–152, 1979.

Lundberg, C. C., Hypothesis creation in organizational behavior research, *Academy of Management Review*, 1, 5–12, 1976.

Lundman, R. J. and Fox, J. C., Maintaining research access in a commonwealth bureaucracy, Unpublished paper presented to the American Society of Criminology, 1974.

Lynd, R. S. and Lynd, H. M., *Middletown in Transition*, Harcourt Brace Jovanovich, New York, 1937.

Lynn, L. E. and Heinrich, C. J., *Governance and Performance: New Perspectives*, Georgetown University Press, Washington, DC, 2000.

Lynn, L. E. Jr., *Teaching and Learning with Cases: A Guidebook*, Chatham House, Seven Bridges Press, LLC, New York, 1999.

Macallair, D., Disposition case advocacy in San Francisco's juvenile justice system: a new approach to deinstitutionalization, *Crime and Delinquency*, 40, 84–95, 1994.

Maclure, M. and Willett, W. C., Misinterpretation and misuse of the kappa statistic, *American Journal of Epidemiology*, 126, 161–169, 1987.

Michaels, J. E., A view from the top: reflections of the bush administration presidential appointees, *Public Administration Review*, 55, 273–283, 1995.

MacLeod, J., *Clinical Examination*, Churchill Livingstone, Edinburgh, UK, 1979.

Madge, J., *The Tools of Social Science*, Anchor, New York, 1965.

Madley, D.L., Some benefits of integrating qualitative and quantitative methods in program evaluation. *Education Evaluation and Policy Analysis*, 1981.

Malinowski, B., *Argonauts of the Western Pacific*, Duton, New York, 1922.

Malinowski, B., Myth in Primitive Psychology, In *Magic, Science and Religion*, Malinowski, B., Ed., Beacon, Boston, MA, 1926.

Malinowski, B., *Coral Gardens and their Magic*, Bloomington University Press, Bloomington, IN, Vol. 2, 1935.

Malinowski, B., *A Diary in the Strict Sense of the Term*, Harcourt, Brace and World, New York, 1967.

Mandelbaum, D., Some shared ideas, In *Crisis in Anthropology: View from Spring Hill*, Hoebel, E. A., Currier, R. L., and Kaiser, S., Eds., Garland Publishing, New York, pp. 35–50, 1980.

Mangabeira, W. C., Lee, R. M., and Fielding, N. G., Computers and qualitative research: adoption, use and representation, *Social Science Computer Review*, 22, 167–178, 2004.

Mangione, T. W., Hingson, R., and Barrett, J., Collecting sensitive data: a comparison of three survey strategies, *Sociological Methods and Research*, 10, 337–346, 1982.

Mann, P. H., *Methods of Sociological Enquiry*, Basil Blackwell, Oxford, UK, 1968.

Manning, P. K., Observing the police: deviants, respectables and the law, In *Research on Deviance*, Douglas, J. D., Ed., Random House, New York, pp. 213–268, 1972.

Manning, P. K., Rules, colleagues and situationally justified actions, In *Colleagues in Organization*, Blankenship, R. A., Ed., John Wiley, New York, pp. 263–289, 1976a.

Manning, P. K., The researcher: an alien in the police world, In *The Ambivalent Force*, Neiderhoffer, A. and Blumberg, A., Eds., 2nd ed., Dryden Press, Chicago, IL, 1976b.

Manning, P. K., *Police Work: The Social Organization of Policing*, MIT Press, Cambridge, MA, 1977.

Mariampolski, H. and Hughes, D. C., The use of personal documents in historical sociology, *The American Sociologist*, 13, 104–113, 1978.

Mark, J., Frank Hamilton Cushing and an American science of anthropology, *Perspectives on American History*, 10, 449–486, 1976.

Marks, E. S. and Maudlin, W. P., Response errors in census research, *Journal of American Statistical Association*, 45, 424–438, 1950.

Marshall, C. and Rossman, G. B., *Designing Qualitative Research*, 2nd ed., Sage, London, 1995.

Martin, J., A garbage can model of the research process, In *Judgement Calls in Research*, McGrath, J. E., Martin, J., and Kulka, R. A., Eds., Sage, Beverly Hills, CA, pp. 17–40, 1982.

Martin, W. J. and Willower, D. J., The managerial behavior of high school principals, *Educational Administration Quarterly*, 17, 69–90, 1981.

Martinko M. J. and Gardner W. L., The observation of high performing educational managers: an observational study, Department of Management, Florida State University, Unpublished papaer, 1984a.

Martinko, M. J. and Gardner, W. L., The observation of high performing educational managers: methodological issues and managerial implications, In *Leadership and Managers: International Perspective on Managerial Behavior and Leadership*, Hunt, J. G., Hosking, D. M., Schriesheim, C., and Stewart, R., Eds., Pergamon, Elmsford, NY, pp. 142–162, 1984b.

Martinko, M. J. and Gardner, W. L., Beyond structured observation: methodological issues and new directions, *Academy of Management Review*, 10, 676–695, 1985.

Matarazzo, J. D., Wiens, A. N., Saslow, G., Dunham, R. M., and Voas, R. B., Speech duration of astronaut and ground communicator, *Science*, 143, 148–150, 1964.

Maurer, R. C. and Christensen, J. A., Growth and nongrowth orientations of urban, suburban and rural mayors: reflections on the city as a growth machine, *Social Science Quarterly*, 63, 350–358, 1982.

May, P. J. and Burby, R. J., Coercive versus cooperative policies: comparing intergovernmental mandate performance, *Journal of Policy Analysis and Management*, 15, 171–201, 1996.

Mayer, C. A., The interviewer and his environment, *Journal of Marketing Research*, 1, 24–31, 1964.

Mayer, C. S. and Pratt, R. W. Jr., A note on nonresponse in a mail survey, *Public Opinion Quarterly*, 30, 639–646, 1966.

Maynard-Moody, S. and Musheno, M., *Cops, Teachers, Counselors: Stories from the Front Lines of Public Service*, University of Michigan Press, Ann Arbor, MI, 2003.

McBride, G. B., *Using Statistical Methods for Water Quality Management: Issues, Problems and Solutions*, Wiley, New York, 2005.

McCall, G. J., *Observing the Law*, US Government Printing Office, Washington, DC, 1975.

McCall, G. J. and Simmons, J. L., *Issues in Participant Observation: A Text and Reader*, Addison-Wesley, Reading, MA, 1969.

McClintock, C. C., Evaluation of human services planning at state and local levels, *Journal of Human Service Abstracts*, 3, 26, 1978.

McClintock, C. C., Barnard, D., and Maynard-Moody, S., Applying the logic of sample surveys to qualitative case studies: the case cluster method, *Administrative Science Quarterly*, 24, 612–629, 1979.

McColsky, W. H., Identifying predictors of information utilization by secondary school principals, Ohio State University, Unpublished Dissertation, 1983.

McCrohan, K. F. and Lowe, L. S., A cost benefit approach to postage used in mail questionnaires, *Journal of Marketing*, 45, 130–133, 1981.

McMahan, E. M. and Rogers, K. L., *Interactive Oral History Interviewing*, Lawrence Erlbaum, Hillsdale, NJ, 1994.

McCracken, G., *The Long Interview*, Sage, London, 1988.

McCurdy, H. E., Organization decline: NASA and the life-cycle of bureaus, *Public Administration Review*, 51, 308–315, 1991.

McCurdy, H. E. and Cleary, R. E., Why can't we resolve the research issue in public administration?, *Public Administration Review*, 44, 49–55, 1984.

McDaniel, S. W. and Rao, C. P., The effect of monetary inducement on mailed questionnaire response quality, *Journal of Marketing Research*, 17, 265–268, 1980.

McElroy, J. C. and Downey, H. K., Observation in organizational research: panacea to the performance-attribution effect?, *Academy of Management Journal*, 25, 822–835, 1982.

McGrath, J. E., Dilemmatics: the study of choice and dilemmas, In *Judgement Calls in Research*, McGrath, J. E., Martin, J. J., and Kulka, R. A., Eds., Sage Publications, Beverly Hills, CA, pp. 69–102, 1982.

McGrath, J. E., Martin, J., and Kulka, R. A., Some quasi-rules for making judgement calls in research, In *Judgement Calls in Research*, McGrath, J. E., Martin, J., and Kulka, R. A., Eds., Sage Publication, Beverly Hills, CA, pp. 103–118, 1982.

McGuire, J., Management and research methodology, *Journal of Management*, 12(1), 5–17, 1986.

McGuire, W. J., Theory oriented research in natural settings: the best of both worlds for social psychology, In *Interdisciplinary Relationships in the Social Sciences*, Sherif, M. and Sherif, C. S., Eds., Aldine, Chicago, IL, pp. 21–51, 1969.

McKenzie, J. F., An investigation into interviewer effects in market research, *Journal of Marketing Research*, 14, 330–363, 1977.

McNemar, Q., Sampling in psychological research, *Psychology Bulletin*, 37, 331–365, 1940.

Mead, M., The study of culture at a distance, In *The Study of Culture at a Distance*, Mead, M. and Metraux, R., Eds., University of Chicago Press, Chicago, IL, pp. 3–53, 1953.

Mechanic, D., Sources of power of lower participants in complex organizations, *Administrative Science Quarterly*, 7, 349–364, 1962.

Mehrabian, A. and Williams, M., Nonverbal concomitants of perceived and intended persuasiveness, *Journal of Personality and Social Psychology*, 13, 37–58, 1969.

Mehta, R. and Sivadas, E., Comparing response rates and response content in mail versus electronic mail surveys, *Journal of the Market Research Society*, 37(4), 429–439, 1995.

Meindl, J., The romance of leadership as a follower-centric theory: a social constructionist approach, *Leadership Quarterly*, 6, 329–341, 1995.

Meislin, R. J., January Racial divisions seen in poll on Howard Beach attack, *New York Times*, B2, January, 1987.

Mensch, B. S. and Kandel, D. B., Under-reporting of substance use in a national longitudinal youth cohort: individual and interviewer effects, *Public Opinion Quarterly*, 52, 100–124, 1988.

Merriam, S. B., *Qualitative Research and Case Study Applications in Education*, Jossey Bass, San Francisco, 1988.

Merton, R. K., Selected properties of field work in the planned community, *American Sociological Review*, 12, 304–312, 1947.

Merton, R. K. and Kendal, P. L., The focused interview, *American Journal of Sociology*, 51, 541–557, 1946.

Merton, R. K., Reader, G. G., and Kendall, P. L., Eds., *The Student-Physician: Introductory Studies in the Sociology of Medical Education*, Harvard University Press, Cambridge, MA, 1957.

Mesch, D. J. and Shamayeva, O., Arbitration in practice: a profile of public sector arbitration cases, *Public Personnel Management*, 25, 119–132, 1996.

Meyer, C. K. and Brown, C. H., Eds., *Practicing Public Management: A Casebook,* 2nd ed., St. Martin's Press, New York, 1988.

Meyer, C. K., Brown, C. H., Beville, M. J., Scheffer, W. F., and Preheim, R. L., *Practicing Public Management: A Casebook*, St. Martin's Press, New York, 1983.

Meyers, L. S. and Grosson, N. E., *Behavioral Research: Theory, Procedure, and Design*, W.H. Freeman, San Francisco, CA, 1974.

Miles, M. B., Qualitative data as an attractive nuisance, *Administrative Science Quarterly*, 24, 590–601, 1979.

Miles, M. B., A mini-cross-site analysis: commentary on these studies, *American Behavioral Scientist*, 26, 121–132, 1982.

Miles, M. B. and Huberman, A. M., *Analyzing Qualitative Data: A Source Book for New Methods*, Sage Publications, Beverly Hills, CA, 1984.

Miller, C. C., Glick, W. H., Wang, Y. D., and Huber, G. P., Understanding technology-structure relationships: theory development and meta-analytic theory testing, *Academy of Management Journal*, 34, 370–399, 1991.

Miller, D. C., *Handbook of Research Design and Social Measurement*, David McKay, New York, 1977.

Miller, G., Yeager, S. J., Hildreth, W. B., and Rabin, J., *Public Administration Review*, 65, 301–312, 2005.

Miller, S. M., The participant observer and 'over-rapport', *American Sociological Review*, 17, 97–99, 1952.

Millman, M., *The Unkindest Cut: Life in the Backrooms of Medicine*, William Morrow, New York, 1977.

Milmoe, S., Rosenthal, R., Blane, H. T., Chavetz, M. E., and Wolf, I., The doctor's voice: postdictor of successful referral of alcoholic patients, *Journal of Abnormal Psychology*, 72, 78–84, 1967.

Minor, D., *The Information War*, Hawthorne Books, New York, 1970.

Mintzberg, H., The manager at work—determining his activities, and programs by structured observation, Unpublished doctoral dissertation, M.I.T. Sloan School of Management, Cambridge, MA, 1968.

Mintzberg, H., Structured observation as a method to study managerial work, *Journal of Management Studies*, 7, 87–104, 1970.

Mintzberg, H., Managerial work: analysis from observation, *Management Science*, 97–110, 18B, 1971.

Mintzberg, H., *The Nature of Managerial Work*, Harper and Row, New York, 1973.

Mintzberg, H., The manager's job: folklore and fact, *Harvard Business Review*, 5, 49–61, 1975.

Mintzberg, H., Patterns in strategy formulation, *Management Science*, 24, 934–948, 1978.

Mintzberg, H., An emerging strategy of 'direct' research, *Administrative Science Quarterly*, 24, 582–589, 1979.

Mishler, E. G., *Research Interviewing: Context and Narrative*, Harvard University Press, Cambridge, MA, 1986.

Mitroff, I. M., *The Subjective Side of Science*, Elsevier, New York, 1974.

Mitroff, I. M. and Kilmann, R., *Methodological Approaches to Social Science*, Jossey-Bass, San Francisco, CA, 1978.

Mizes, J. S., Fleece, E. L., and Roos, C., Incentives for increasing return rates: magnitude levels, response bias, and format, *Public Opinion Quarterly*, 48, 794–800, 1984.

Moe, T. M., Control and feedback in economic regulation: the case of the NLRB, *American Political Science Review*, 79, 1094–1116, 1985.

Moore, D. E. and Cantrell, R., Community response to external demands: an analysis of participation in the federal flood insurance program, *Rural Sociology*, 41, 484–508, 1976.

Moore, M., *Creating Public Values: Strategic Management in Government*, Harvard University Press, Cambridge, MA, 1995.

Morgan, G. and Smirich, L., The case of qualitative research, *Academy of Management Review*, 5, 491–500, 1980.

Morris, V. C., Crowson, R. L., Hurwitz, E., and Porter-Gehnie, C., The urban principal: discretionary decision-making in a large educational organization, University of Illinois, Unpublished Manuscript, Chicago, IL, 1981.

Morton-Williams, J., *Interviewer Approaches*, Dartmouth Publishing Company, Brookfield, VT, 1993.

Moynihan, D. and Pandey, S. K., Testing a model of public sector performance: how does management matter?, Paper prepared for the National Public Management Research Conference, Georgetown University, October 9–11, 2003.

Moyser, G., Non-standardized interviewing in elite research, In *Studies in Qualitative Methodology*, Burgess, R., Ed., Vol. 1, JAI Press, Greenwich, CT, pp. 109–136, 1988.

Muchinsky, P. M., Organizational communication: relationships to organizational climate and job satisfaction, *Academy of Management Journal*, 20, 592–607, 1977.

Mulrow, C. D. and Cook, D., Eds., *Systematic Reviews: Synthesis of Best Evidence for Health Care Decisions*, American College of Physicians, Philadelphia, PA, 1998.

Mumola, Christopher, *Substance Abuse and Treatment, State and Federal Prisoners 1997*, Bureau of Justice Statistics, U.S. Department of Justice, Washington, DC, 1999.

Muñoz, E. A., Racial disparities in imprisonment rates in nebraska: a case study of panhandle county, JSRI Research Report #22, The Julian Samora Research Institute, Michigan State University, East Lansing, MI, 1999.

Murphy, K. R. Ed., *Validity Generalization: A Critical Review*, Erlbaum, Mahwah, NJ, 2003.

Myers, S. and Chan, T., Who benefits from minority business set-asides? The case of New Jersey, *Journal of Policy Analysis and Management*, 15, 202–226, 1996.

Nachmias, D. and Nachmias, C., *Research Methods in the Social Sciences*, St. Martin's Press, New York, 1976.

Nachmias, D. and Nachmias, C., *Research Methods in the Social Sciences*, 3rd ed., St. Martin's Press, New York, 1987.

Nader, L., Up the anthropologist: perspectives gained from studying up, In *Reinventing Anthropology*, Hymes, D., Ed., Pantheon, New York, 1972.

National Archives and Records Administration, *Guide to the National Archives of the United States*, National Archives and Records Administration, Washington, DC, 1987.

National Historical Publications and Records Commission, *Directory of Archives and Manuscript Repositories in the United States*, Oryx Press, Phoenix, AZ, 1988.

Naylor, C. D., Meta-analysis and the meta-epidemiology of clinical research, *British Medical Journal*, 315, 617–619, 1997.

Naylor, C. D. and Smith, G. D., Test meta-analyses for stability, *British Medical Journal*, 317, 206, 1998.

Neidig, R. D. and Neidig, P. J., Multiple assessment center exercises and job relatedness, *Journal of Applied Psychology*, 69, 182–186, 1984.

Nejelski, P. and Lerman, L. M., A researcher-subject testimonial privilege: what to do before the subpoena arrives, *Wisconsin Law Review*, 1086–1103, 1971.

Neter, J. and Waksberg, J., A study of response error in expenditures data from household interviews, *Journal of the American Statistical Association*, 59, 18–55, 1964.

Neuendorf, K. A., *The Content Analysis Handbook*, Sage Publications, Thousand Oaks, CA, 2002.

Neuman, W. L., *Social Research Methods: Qualitative and Quantitative Approaches*, Allyn and Bacon, Boston, 1994.

Neustadt, R. E. and Fineberg, H., *The Epidemic That Never Was: Policy-Making and the Swine Flu Affair*, Vintage Books, New York, 1983.

Newland, C. A., The public administration review and ongoing struggles for connectedness, *Public Administration Review*, 60, 20–38, 2000.

Newman, M. A., Gender and Lowi's thesis: implications for career advancement, *Public Administration Review*, 54, 277–284, 1994.

Nicosia, F. H. and Rosenberg, B., Substantive modeling in consumer attitude research, In *Attitude Research in Transition*, Haley, R. I., Ed., American Marketing Association, Chicago, Chicago, IL, pp. 213–247, 1972.

Oakley, A., Interviewing women: a contradiction in terms, In *Doing Feminist Research*, Roberts, H., Ed., Routledge, London, pp. 30–61, 1981.

Oakley, A., *Experiments in Knowing: Gender and Method in the Social Sciences*, The New Press, New York, 2000.

Oakman, R. L., *Computer Methods for Literature Research*, University of South Carolina Press, Columbia, SC, 1980.

O'Dempsey, K., Time analysis of activities, work patterns and roles of high school principals, *Administrator's Bulletin*, 7, 1976.

O'Neil, M. J., Estimating the nonresponse bias due to refusals in telephone surveys, *Public Opinion Quarterly*, 43, 218–232, 1979.

O'Neil, M. J., Groves, R. M., and Cannell, C. F., Telephone interview introductions and refusal rates: experiments in increasing respondent cooperation, Presented at the American Statistical Association Meeting, 1979.

O'Neil, H. E. and Kubany, A. J., Observation methodology and supervisory behavior, *Personnel Psychology*, 12, 85–95, 1959.

Opler, M. and Singh, R. D., The division of labor in an Indian village, In *A Reader in General Anthropology*, Coon, C. S., Ed., Holt and Co., New York, pp. 464–496, 1948.

O'Reilly, C. A. and Roberts, K. H., Information filtration in organizations: three experiments, *Organizational Behavior and Human Performance*, 11, 253–265, 1974.

Orenstein, A. and Phillips, W. R. F., *Understanding Social Research: An Introduction*, Allyn and Bacon, Boston, MA, 1978.

Orne, M. J., On the social psychology of the psychology experiment: with particular reference to demand characteristics and their implications, *American Psychologist*, 17, 776–783, 1962.

Osgood, C., Informants, In *Ingalik Material Culture*, Osgood, C., Ed., Yale University Publications in Anthropology, New Haven, CT, pp. 50–55, 1940.

Ostrander, S. A., Surely you're not in this just to be helpful: access, rapport, and interviews in three studies of elites, *Journal of Contemporary Ethnography*, 22, 1–27, 1993.

O'Sullivan, A., *Urban Economics*, Richard D. Irwin, Inc., Homewood, IL, 1990.

Overton, R. C., A comparison of fixed-effects and mixed (random-effects) models for meta-analysis tests of moderator variable effects, *Psychological Methods*, 3, 354–379, 1998.

Parrish, W. L. and Whyte, M. K., *Village and Family in Contemporary China*, University of Chicago Press, Chicago, IL, 1978.

Pace, R. C., Factors influencing questionnaire returns from former university students, *Journal of Applied Psychology*, 23, 388–397, 1939.

Padfield, M. and Procter, I., The effect of interviewer's gender on the interviewing process: a comparative enquiry, *Sociology*, 30, 355–366, 1996.

Palmer, S., On the character and influence of nonresponse in the current population survey, *Proceedings of the Social Science Statistics Section, American Statistical Association*, 10, 73–80, 1968.

Parten, M., *Surveys, Polls, and Samples: Practical Procedures*, Cooper Square, New York, 1966.

Patton, M. Q., *Qualitative Evaluation Methods*, Sage Publications, Beverly Hills, CA, 1980.

Patton, M. Q., *How to Use Qualitative Methods in Evaluation*, Sage, Newbury Park, CA, 1987.

Patton, M. Q., *Qualitative Evaluation and Research Methods*, 2nd ed., Sage, Thousand Oaks, CA, 1990.

Paul, B. D., Interview techniques and field relationships, In *Anthropology Today*, Kroeber, A. L., Ed., University of Chicago Press, Chicago, IL, pp. 430–451, 1953.

Pearl, D. K. and Fairley, D., Testing for the potential for nonresponse bias in sample surveys, *Public Opinion Quarterly*, 49, 553–560, 1985.

Pelto, P. J., *Anthropological Research: The Structure of Inquiry*, Harper and Row, New York, 1970.

Pelz, D. C., *Use of Innovation in Innovating Processes by Local Governments*, CRUSK, Institute for Social Research, University of Michigan, Ann Arbor, MI, 1981.

Penfield, R. V., Time allocation patterns and effectiveness of managers, *Personnel Psychology*, 27, 245–255, 1974.

Penley, L. E. and Hawkins, B., Studying interpersonal communication in organizations: a leadership application, *Academy of Management Journal*, 28, 309–326, 1985.

Pennings, J., Measures of organizational structure: a methodological note, *American Journal of Sociology*, 79, 686–704, 1973.

Perry, J. L. and Kraemer, K. L., Research methodology in the public administration review, 1975–1984, *Public Administration Review*, 46, 215–226, 1986.

Peters, R. J. and Waterman, R. H., *In Search of Excellence*, Harper and Row, New York, 1982.

Peterson, K. D., The principal's tasks, *Administrator's Notebook*, 26, 1–4, 1977.

Peterson, R. A., An experimental investigation of mail survey response, *Journal of Business Research*, 3, 199–210, 1975.

Petitti, D. B., *Meta-Analysis, Decisions Analysis, and Cost-Effectiveness Analysis: Methods for Quantitative Synthesis in Medicine*, 2nd ed., Oxford University Press, New York, 2000.

Pettigrew, A. M. and Bumstead, D. C., Strategies of organization development in differing contexts, In *Organizational Change and Development in Europe*, Clark, P. A., Guiot, J., and Thirry, H., Eds., Wiley, London, 1980.

Petty, M. M., McGee, G. W., and Cavendar, G. W., A meta-analysis of the relationship between individual job satisfaction and individual performance, *Academy of Management Review*, 9, 712–721, 1984.

Pfeffer, J., The ambiguity of leadership, *Academy of Management Review*, 2, 104–112, 1997.

Pfeffer, J. and Salancik, G. R., *The External Control of Organizations: A Resource Dependence Perspective*, Harper and Rowe, New York, 1978.

Phillips, J. M. and Goss, E. P., The effect of State and local taxes on economic development: a meta-analysis, *Southern Economic Journal*, 62, 320, 1995.

Pickrell, D., Transportation and land use, In *Essays in Transportation Economics and Policy*, Gomez-Ibanez, J., Tye, W. B., and Winston, C., Eds., Brookings Institution, Washington, DC, 1999.

Pinello, Daniel R., Linking party to judicial ideology in American courts: a meta-analysis, *The Justice System Journal*, 20, 219–254, 1999.

Piore, M. J., Qualitative research techniques in economics, *Administrative Science Quarterly*, 24, 560–569, 1979.

Pitner, N. J., Descriptive study of the everyday activities of suburban school superintendents: the management of information. Unpublished doctoral dissertation, Ohio State University, Columbus, OH, 1978.

Pitner, N. J., *Training of the School Administrator: State of the Art*, College of Education, Center for Educational Policy and Management, University of Oregon, Eugene, OR, 1982.

Platek, R., Singh, M. P., and Tremblay, V., Adjustment for nonresponse in surveys, In *Survey Sampling and Measurement*, Namboodiri, N. K., Ed., Academic, New York, pp. 157–174, 1978.

Plog, S. C., Literary index for the mailbag, *Journal of Applied Psychology, PM Public Management*, 50, 86–91, 1966.

Poggie, J. J., Toward quality control in key informant data, *Human Organization*, 31, 23–30, 1972.

Poister, T. H. and Henry, G. T., Citizen ratings of public and private service quality: a comparative perspective, *Public Administration Review*, 54(2), 155–160, 1994.

Pol, L. G., A method to increase response when external interference and time constraints reduce interview quality, *Public Opinion Quarterly*, 56, 356–359, 1992.

Politz, A. and Simmons, W., An attempt to get not-at-homes into the sample without callbacks, *Journal of the American Statistical Association*, 44, 9–31, 1949.

Pollner, M., The effects of interviewer gender in mental health interviews, *Journal of Nervous and Mental Disease*, 186, 369–373, 1998.

Polsky, H. W., *Cottage Six*, Russell Sage Foundation, New York, 1962.

Polsky, N., *Hustlers, Beats, and Others*, Aldine, Chicago, IL, 1967.

Ponder, Q. D., *The Effective Manufacturing Foremen*, Proceedings of the Tenth Annual Meeting, Industrial Relations, Research Association, Madison, WI, pp. 41–54, 1957.

Ponder, Q. D., *Supervisory Practices of Effective and Ineffective Foremen*, Doctoral Dissertation, Columbia University, New York, Dissertation Abstracts, 20, 3983, 1959.

Popping, Roel, *Computer-Assisted Text Analysis*, Sage, Thousand Oaks, CA, 1999.

Porter, G. R., Agricultural queries, with returns from the County of Bedford, *Journal of the Statistical Society of London*, 1, 89–96, 1838.

Posner, K. L., Sampson, P. D., Caplan, R. A., Ward, R. J., and Cheney, F. W., Measuring inter-rater reliability among multiple raters: an example of methods for nominal data, *Statistics in Medicine*, 9, 1103–1115, 1990.

Powdermaker, H., *Stranger and Friend: The Way of an Anthropologist*, Norton, New York, 1967.

Powdermaker, H., Further reflections on Lesu and Malinowski's diary, *Oceania*, 40, 344–347, 1970.

Pratt, T. C. and Maahs, J., Are private prisons more cost effective than public prisons? A meta-analysis of evaluation research studies, *Crime and Delinquency*, 45, 3, 1999.

Pressman, J. L. and Wildavsky, A., *Implementation: How Great Expectations in Washington Are Dashed in Oakland; Or, Why It's Amazing That Federal Programs Work at All This Being a Saga of the Economic Development Administration*, University of California Press, Berkeley, CA, 1973.

Prottas, J. M., *People-Processing: The Street-Level Bureaucrat in Public Service Bureaucracies*, Lexington Books, Lexington, MA, 1979.

Public Citizen, Water privatization: a broken promise, Case histories from throughout the United States, Public Citizen's Critical Mass Energy and Environment Program, Washington, DC, October, 2001.

Pugh, D. S. and Hickson, D. J., *Organizational Structure in Its Context*, Saxon House, Farnborough, Hants, UK, Vol. 1, 1976.

Quinn, R. P., Gutek, B. A., and Walsh, T., Telephone interviewing: a reappraisal and a field experiment, *Basic and Applied Social Psychology*, 1, 127–153, 1980.

Rainey, H. G., Pandey, S., and Bozeman, B., Research note: public and private managers' perceptions of red tape, *Public Administration Review*, 55, 567–574, 1995.

Rainwater, L. and Pittman, D. J., Ethical problems in studying a politically sensitive and deviant community, *Social Problems*, 14, 357–366, 1967.

Raizen, S. and Rossi, R., Eds., *Program Evaluation in Education: When? How? To What Ends?*, National Academy Press, Washington, DC, 1981.

Rawick, G. P., *The American Slave, Supplement Series 2*. Westport, CT, 1979.

Rawick G. P., *The American Slave, Supplement Series 1*. Westport, CT, 1977.

Read, W. H., Upward communication in industrial hierarchies, *Human Relations*, 15, 3–15, 1962.

Reamer, F. G., Protecting research subjects and unintended consequences: the effect of guarantees of confidentiality, *Public Opinion Quarterly*, 43, 497–506, 1979.

Redman, E., *The Dance of Legislation*, Simon and Schuster, New York, 1973.

Reese, S. D., Danielson, W. A., Shoemaker, P. J., Chang, T.-K., and Hsu, H.-L., Ethnicity-of-interviewer effects among Mexican-Americans and Anglos, *Public Opinion Quarterly*, 50, 563–572, 1986.

Reiss, A. J., Stuff and nonsense about social surveys and observation, In *Institutions and the Person*, Becker, H. S., Greer, B., Riesman, D., and Weiss, R. S., Eds., Aldine, Chicago, pp. 351–367, 1968.

Reiss, A. J., *The Police and the Public*, New Haven, Yale University Press, 1971.

Renfro, P. C., Bias in selection in letters to the editor, *Journalism Quarterly*, 56, 822–826, 1979.

Renkow, M., Employment growth, worker mobility, and rural economic development, *American Journal of Agricultural Economics May*, 85(2), 503–513, 2003.

Riccucci, N. M., *Unsung Heroes: Federal Execucrats Making a Difference*, Georgetown University Press, Washington, DC, 1995.

Richards, T. J. and Richards, L., The NUD.IST qualitative data analysis system, *Qualitative Sociology*, 14, 307–324, 1991.

Richardson, J. L. and Larson, O. F., Small community trends: a 50-year perspective on social-economic change in 13 New York communities, *Rural Sociology*, 41, 45–59, 1976.

Richardson, S. A., A framework for reporting field-relations experiences, In *Human Organization Research*, Adams, R. N. and Preiss, J. J., Eds., Dorsey Press, Homewood, IL, pp. 124–139, 1960.

Richardson, S., Dohrenwend, B. S., and Klein, D., *Interviewing: Its Forms and Functions*, Basic Books, New York, 1965.

Riche, M. F., Who says yes, *American Demographics*, 9(2), 8, 1987.

Riecken, H. W., The unidentified interviewer, *American Journal of Sociology*, 62, 210–212, 1956.

Riesman, D. and Watson, J., The sociability project: a chronicle of frustration and achievement, In *Sociologists at Work*, Hammond, P. E., Ed., Basic Books, New York, pp. 235–321, 1964.

Rist, R. C., On the relations among educational research paradigms: from disdain to detente, *Anthropology and Education*, 8, 42–49, 1977.

Rist, R. C., Blitzkrieg ethnography: on the transformation of a method into a movement, *Educational Researcher*, 9, 8–10, 1980.

Rist, R. C., *Earning and Learning: Youth Employment Policies and Programs*, Sage Publications, Beverly Hills, CA, 1981.

Roberts, A., Demonstrating neutrality: the Rockefeller philanthropies and the evolution of public administration, *1927–1936, Public Administration Review*, 54, 221–228, 1994.

Roberts, C. W. Ed., *Text Analysis for the Social Sciences: Methods for Drawing Inferences from Texts and Transcripts*, Lawrence Erlbaum, Mahwah, NJ, 1997.

Roberts, K. and O'Reilly, C., Failures in upward communication: three possible culprits, *Academy of Management Journal*, 17, 205–215, 1974.

Roberts, K., O'Reilly, C. A., Bretton, G. A., and Porter, L. W., Organizational theory and organizational communication: a communication failure?, *Human Relations*, 27, 501–524, 1974.

Roberts, P. J., Roberts, C., Sibbald, B., and Torgerson, D. J., The effect of a direct payment or a lottery on questionnaire response rates: a randomised controlled trial, *Journal of Epidemiology and Community Health*, 54, 71–72, 2000.

Roberts, R. E., McCrory, O. F., and Forthofer, R. N., Further evidence on using a deadline to stimulate responses to a mail survey, *Public Opinion Quarterly*, 42, 407–410, 1978.

Robertson, D. H. and Bellenger, D. N., A new method of increasing mail survey responses: contributions to charity, *Journal of Marketing Research*, 15, 632–633, 1978.

Robinson, R. A. and Agisim, P., Making mail surveys more reliable, *Journal of Marketing*, 15, 415–424, 1951.

Robinson, J. A., Anderson, L. F., Hermann, M. G., and Snyder, R. C., Teaching with inter-nation simulation and case studies, *American Political Science Review*, 60, 53–65, 1966.

Rock, P., Some problems of interpretive historiography, *British Journal of Sociology*, 27, 353–369, September, 1976.

Rodgers, R. and Hunter, J. E., Impact of management by objectives on organizational productivity, *Journal of Applied Psychology*, 76, 322–336, 1991.

Rodgers, R. and Hunter, J. E., A foundation of good management practice in government: management by objectives, *Public Administration Review*, 52, 27–39, 1992.

Rodgers, R., Hunter, J. F., and Rogers, D., Influence of top management commitment on management program success, *Journal of Applied Psychology*, 78, 151–155, 1993.

Roe, E., *Narrative Policy Analysis: Theory and Practice*, Duke University Press, Durham, NC, 1994.

Roethlisberger, F. J. and Dickson, W. J., *Management and the Worker*, Harvard University Press, Cambridge, MA, 1939.

Roll, C. N., Toro, P. A., and Ortola, G. L., Characteristics and experiences of homeless adults: a comparison of single men, single women, and women with children, *Journal of Community Psychology*, 27, 189–198, 1999.

Romzek, B. and Ingraham, P. W., Cross pressures of accountability: initiative, command, and failure in the Ron Brown plane crash, *Public Administration Review*, 60, 240–253, 2000.

Romzek, B. S. and Dubnick, M. J., Accountability in the public sector: lessons from the Challenger tragedy, *Public Administration Review*, 47, 227–238, 1987.

Roos, M., Methods of Internet data collection and implications for recruiting respondents, *Statistical Journal of the United Nations Economic Commission for Europe*, 19, 175–186, 2002.

Roos, L. L., Nichol, J. P., Johnson, C. F., and Roos, N. P., Using administrative data banks for research and evaluation: a case study, *Evaluation Quarterly*, 3, 236–255, 1979.

Roscoe, H. S., Terkla, D. G., and Dyer, J. A., Administering Surveys on the web: methodological issues, Paper presented at the Annual Conference of the Association of Institutional Research, Toronto, Canada, June 2002.

Rosenau, J., *Citizenship between Elections*, Free Press, New York, 1974.

Rosenheck, R., Morrissey, J., Lam, J., Calloway, M., Stolar, M., Johnsen, M., Randolph, F., Blasinsky, M., and Goldman, H., Service delivery and community: social capital, service systems integration, and outcomes among homeless persons with severe mental illness, *Health Services Research*, 36, 691–710, 2001.

Rosenhan, D. L., On being sane in insane places, *Science*, 179, 250–258, 1973.

Rosenthal, R., The "file drawer problem" and tolerance for null results, *Psychological Bulletin*, 86, 438–461, 1979.

Rosenthal, R., *Meta-Analytic Procedures for Social Research*, Revised ed., Sage, Newbury Park, CA, 1991.

Rosenthal, R., Rosnow, R. L., and Rubin, D. B., *Contrasts and Effect Sizes in Behavioral Research: A Correlational Approach*, Cambridge University Press, Cambridge, UK, 2000.

Rosenthal, R. and DiMatteo, M. R., Meta analysis: recent developments in quantitative methods for literature reviews, *Annual Review of Psychology*, 52, 59–82, 2001.

Rosner, M. M., Administrative controls and innovation, *Behavior Science*, 13, 36–43, 1968.

Ross, J. and Staw, B. M., Expo 86: an escalation prototype, *Administrative Science Quarterly*, 31, 274–297, 1986.

Rossman, G. B. and Rallis, S. F., *Learning in the Field*, Sage, Thousand Oaks, CA, 1998.

Routh, D. K. and Rettig, K., The mailbag literacy index in a clinical population: relation to education, income, occupation, and social class, *Education and Psychological Measurement*, 29, 485–488, 1969.

Rubenstein, J., *City Police*, Farrar, Strauss and Giroux, New York, 1973.

Rubin, H. J. and Rubin, I. S., *Qualitative Interviewing: The Art of Hearing Data*, Sage, Thousand Oaks, CA, 1995.

Rubin, I. S., Budget reform and political reform: conclusions from six cities, *Public Administration Review*, 52, 454–466, 1992.

Ruebenhausen, G. and Brim, O. G., Privacy and behavioral research, *Columbia Law Review*, 65, 1184–1908, 1965.

Sackett, P. and Dreher, G. F., Constructs and assessment center dimensions: some troubling empirical findings, *Journal of Applied Psychology*, 67, 401–410, 1982.

Sackett, P. and Dreher, G. F., Situation specificity of behavior and assessment center validation strategies: a rejoinder to Neidig and Neidig, *Journal of Applied Psychology*, 69, 182–190, 1984.

Salancik, G. R., Field simulations for organizational behavior research, *Administrative Science Quarterly*, 24, 638–649, 1979.

Salant, P. and Dillman, D. A., *How to Conduct Your Own Survey*, Wiley, New York, 1994.

Sampson, P., Qualitative research and motivational research, In *Consumer Market Research Handbook*, Worcester, R. M. and Downham, J., Eds., McGraw-Hill, London, pp. 25–48, 1972.

Sanday, P. R., The ethnographic paradigms, *Administrative Science Quarterly*, 24, 527–538, 1979.

Sanders, W. B. and Pinhey, T. K., *The Conduct of Social Research*, Holt, Rinehart and Winston, New York, 1983.

Sayles, L. R., *Managerial Behavior: Administration in Complex Organizations*, McGraw-Hill, New York, 1964.

Schaefer, D. and Dillman, D. A., Development of a standard e-mail methodology: results of an experiment, *Public Opinion Quarterly*, 62, 378–397, 1985.

Schaffer, N. C., Evaluating race-of-interviewer effects in a national survey, *Sociological Methods and Research*, 8, 400–419, 1980.

Schall, E., Notes from a reflective practitioner of innovation, In *Innovation in American Government: Challenges, Opportunities and Dilemmas*, Altshculer, A. A. and Behn, R. D., Eds., Brookings Institution, Washington, DC, pp. 360–377, 1997.

Schaeffer, D. R. and Dillman, D. A., Development of standard e-mail methodology: results of an experiment, *Public Opinion Quarterly*, 62, 378–397, 1998.

Schaefer, D. R., Don, A., and Dillman, D. A., Development of a standard e-mail methodology: results of an experiment, *Public Opinion Quarterly*, 62(3), 378–397, 1998.

Schensul, S. L., Schensul, J. J., and LeCompte, M. D., *Essential Ethnographic Methods: Observations, Interviews, and Questionnaires*, AltaMira Press, Walnut Creek, CA, 1999.

Schewe, C. D. and Cournoyer, N. G., Prepaid versus promised monetary incentives to questionnaire response: further evidence, *Public Opinion Quarterly*, 40, 105–107, 1976.

Schleifer, S., Trends in attitudes toward and participation in survey research, *Public Opinion Quarterly*, 50, 17–26, 1986.

Schmidt, M. R., Grout: alternative kinds of knowledge and why they are ignored, In *Research in Public Administration: Reflections on Theory and Practice*, White, J. D. and Adams, G. B., Eds., Sage, Thousand Oaks, CA, pp. 213–224, 1994.

Schoolcraft, H. R., An address delivered before the Was-Ah-Ho-De-No-Son-Ne, or new confederacy of the Iroquois, at its third annual council, Rochester, NY, August 14, 1846. Cited by Hinsley (1983).

Schoenfeldt, L. F., Data archives as resources for research instruction, and policy planning, *American Psychologist*, 25, 609–616, 1970.

Scholz, J. and Wei, F. H., Regulatory enforcement in a federal system, *American Political Science Review*, 80, 1249–1270, 1986.

Schram, S. F. and Neisser, P. T., *Tales of the State: Narrative in Contemporary U.S. Politics and Public Policy*, Rowman and Littlefield, Lanham, MD, 1997.

Schreckhise, W. D., The costs and benefits of mail, fax, and mixed-mode surveys in organizational research, *Public Administration Quarterly*, 29, 492–510, 2006.

Schulze, R., *Meta-Analysis: A Comparison of Approaches*, Hogrefe and Huber, Göttingen, 2004.

Schulze, R., Holling, H., and Bohning, D., *Meta-Analysis: New Developments and Applications in Medical and Social Sciences*, Hogrefe and Huber, Göttingen, 2003.

Schuman, H. and Converse, J., The effects of black and white interviewers on black respondents in 1968, *Public Opinion Quarterly*, 35, 44–68, 1971.

Schuman, H. and Gruenberg, B., *The Impact of City on Racial Attitudes*, Institute for Social Research, University of Michigan, Ann Arbor, MI, 1970.

Schuman, H. and Kalton, G., Survey methods, In *Handbook of Social Psychology*, Aronson, G. L. A. E., Ed., Random House, New York, 1985.

Schuman, H. and Presser, S., *Questions and Answers in Attitude Surveys*, Academic Press, New York, 1981.

Schwartz, M. S. and Schwartz, C. G., Problems in participant observation, *American Journal of Sociology*, 60, 343–354, 1955.

Schwartz-Shea, P., Curricular visions: doctoral program requirements, offerings, and the meanings of political science, Presented at the Annual Meeting of the American Political Science Association, San Francisco, CA, 2001.

Schwartzbaum, A. and Greunfeld, L., Factors influencing subject observer interaction in an organization study, *Administrative Science Quarterly*, 14, 443–449, 1969.

Schweitzer, M. and Asch, D. A., Timing payments to subjects of mail surveys: cost-effectiveness and bias, *Journal of Clinical Epidemiology*, 48, 1325–1329, 1995.

Scott, C., Research on mail surveys, *Journal of the Royal Statistical Society (part 2)*, 124, 143–195, 1961.

Scott, K. D., Markham, S. E., and Vest, M. J., The influence of a merit pay guide chart on employee attitudes toward pay at a transit authority, *Public Personnel Management*, 25, 103–117, 1996.

Sechrest, L., Nonreactive assessment of attitudes, In *Naturalistic Viewpoints in Psychological Research*, Willems, E. P. and Raush, H. L., Eds., Holt, Rinehart and Winston, New York, 1969.

Sechrest, L., Another look at unobtrusive measures, In *Perspectives on Attitude Assessment: Surveys and their Alternatives*, Sinaiko, H. W. and Broeding, L. A., Eds., Pendleton, Champaign, IL, pp. 97–107, 1976.

Seidler, J., On using informants: a technique for collecting quantitative data and controlling measurement error in organization analysis, *American Sociological Review*, 39, 816–831, 1974.

Seldon, A. and Pappworth, J., *By Word of Mouth: Elite Oral History*, Methuen, New York, 1983.

Sellitz, C., Jahoda, M., Deutsch, M., and Cook, S. W., *Research Methods in Social Relations*, Holt, Rinehart and Winston, New York, 1959.

Selltiz, C., Wrightsman, L. S., and Cook, S. W., *Research Methods in Social Relations*, 3rd ed., Holt, Rinehart, and Winston, New York, 1976.

Selznick, P., *TVA and the Grass Roots: A Study of Politics and Organization*, University of California Press, Berkeley, CA, 1949.

Shadish, W. R. and Haddock, C. K., Combining estimates of effect size, In *The Handbook of Research Synthesis*, Cooper, H. and Hedges, L. V., Eds., Sage, New York, 1994.

Shafritz, J. M. and Hyde, A. C., Eds., *Classics of Public Administration*, Brooks/Cole, Pacific Grove, CA, 1992.

Shannon, D. M. and Bradshaw, C. C., A comparison of response rate, speed and costs of mail and electronic surveys, *Journal of Experimental Education*, 70, 179–192, 2002.

Sharf, D. J. and Lehman, M. E., Relationship between the speech characteristics and effectiveness of telephone interviewers, *Journal of Phonetics*, 12, 219–228, 1984.

Sheehan, K. B. and Hoy, M. G., Using e-mail to survey internet users in the United States: methodology and assessment, *Journal of Computer Mediated Communication*, 4(3), 1999 http://wwwascuscorg/jcmc/vol4/issue3/sheehan.html

Sheehan, K. B. and McMillan, S. J., Response variation in email surveys: an exploration, *Journal of Advertising Research*, 39, 45–54, 1999.

Sheriff, C., *The Artificial River: The Erie Canal and the Paradox of Progress, 1817–1862*, Hill and Wang, New York, 1996.

Shrivasta, P. and Mitroff, I., Enhancing organizational research utilization, *Academy of Management Review*, 9, 18–26, 1984.

Sigelman, L. and Walkosz, B., Letters to the editor as a public opinion thermometer, *Social Science Quarterly*, 73, 938–946, 1992.

Sills, S. J. and Song, C., Innovations in survey research: an application of web surveys, *Social Science Computer Review*, 20, 22–30, 2002.

Simon, H. A., *Administrative Behavior*, The Free Press, New York, 1945.

Simpson, R. L. and Gulley, W. H., Goals, environmental pressures, and organizational characteristics, *American Sociological Review*, 27, 344–351, 1962.

Singer, E., Informed consent: consequences for response rate and response quality in social surveys, *American Sociological Review*, 43, 144–162, 1978.

Singer E., Telephone interviewing as a black box, In *Health Survey Research Methods, Research Proceedings from the Third Biennial Conference*, U.S. Department of Health and Human Services, National Center for Health Services Research, Reston, VA, 1981.

Singer, E. and Kohnke-Aguirre, L., Interviewer expectation effects: a replication and extension, *Public Opinion Quarterly*, 43, 245–260, 1979.

Singer, E., Frankel, M. R., and Glassman, M. B., The effect of interviewer characteristics and expectations on response. response, *Public Opinion Quarterly*, 47, 68–83, 1983.

Singer, E., Von Thurn, D. R., and Miller, E. R., Confidentiality assurances and response, *Public Opinion Quarterly*, 59, 66–77, 1995.

Singletary, L., Henry, M., Brooks, K., and London, J., The impact of highway investment on new manufacturing employment in South Carolina: a small region spatial analysis, *Review of Regional Studies*, 25(1), 37–55, 1995.

Sjoberg, G. and Kuhn, K., Autobiography and organizations: theoretical and methodological issues, *Journal of Applied Behavioral Science*, 25, 309–326, 1989.

Sjoberg, G., Williams, N., Vaughan, T. R., and Sjoberg, A. F., The case study approach in social research: basic methodological issues, In *A Case for the Case Study*, Feagin, J. R., Orum, A. M., and Sjoberg, G., Eds., University of North Carolina Press, Chapel Hill, NC, pp. 27–79, 1991.

Skinner, B. F., *Science and Human Behavior*, Macmillan, New York, 1953.

Skinner, B. F., *Verbal Behavior*, Macmillan, New York, 1957.

Skinner, S. J. and Childers, T. L., Respondent identification in mail surveys, *Journal of Advertising Research*, 20(6), 57–61, 1980.

Skolnick, J., *Justice without Trial*, Wiley, New York, 1966.

Small, K. and Song, S., Wasteful commuting: a resolution, *The Journal of Political Economy*, 100(4), 888–898, 1992.

Smelser, N. J., Sociological history: the industrial revolution and the British working class family, *Journal of Social History*, 1, 17–35, 1967.

Smith, A. G. and Robbins, A. E., Structured ethnography: the study of parental involvement, *American Behavioral Scientist*, 26, 45–61, 1982.

Smith, D., *The Chicago School: A Liberal Critique of Capitalism*, Macmillan, London, 1988.

Smith, H. L. and Hyman, H., The biasing effect of interviewer expectations on survey results, *Public Opinion Quarterly*, 14, 491–506, 1950.

Smith, P. C., Kendall, L. M., and Hulin, C. L., *The Measurement of Satisfaction in Work and Retirement*, Rand-McNally, Chicago, IL, 1969.

Smith, R. A., Community power and decision-making: a replication and extension of hawley, *American Sociological Review*, 41, 691–705, 1976.

Smith, T. W., *Sex and the GSS. General Social Survey Technical Report Number 17*, National Opinion Research Center, Chicago, IL, 1979.

Smith, T. W., The hidden 25 percent: an analysis of nonresponse on the 1980 general social survey, *Public Opinion Quarterly*, 47, 386–404, 1983.

Smith, C. B., Casting the net: surveying an Internet population, *Journal of Communication Mediated by Computers*, 3(1), 1997. http://www.ascuse.org/jcmc/vol3/issue1/

Smith, T. W., A call for truce in the DGU war, *Journal of Criminal Law and Criminology*, 87(4), 1462–1469, 1997.

Smith, V., Ethnographies of work, work of ethnographers, In *Handbook of Ethnography*, Atkinson, P., Coffey, A., Delamont, S., Lofland, J., and Lofland, L., Eds., Sage, London, pp. 220–233, 2001.

Snell, T. L. and Morton, D. C., *Women in Prison, Survey of State Inmates, 1991*, Bureau of Justice Statistics, US Department of Justice, 1991.

Snell, T. L. and Morton, D. C., *Women in Prison: Survey of State Prison Inmates* (NCJ 145321), U.S. Department of Justice, Washington, DC, 1994.

Snell, T. L. and Maruschak, L. M., Capital punishment 2001, *Bulletin*. NCJ 197020, United States Department of Justice, Bureau of Justice Statistics, Washington, DC, 2002.

Snyder, N. and Glueck, W. F., How managers plan—the analysis of managers' activities, *Long Range Planning*, 13, 70–76, 1980.

Snyder, N. M., Managerial and organizational impediments to effective welfare reform, *Journal of Health and Human Resources Administration*, 14, 445–464, 1992.

Snyder, N. M., Organizational culture and management capacity in a social welfare organization: a case study of Kansas, *Public Administration Quarterly*, 19, 243–265, 1995.

Social Problems, 14(2), 1967, Entire Issue.

Sontag, S., The anthropologist as hero, In *Claude Levi Strauss: The Anthropologist as Hero*, Hayes, E. N. and Hayes, T., Eds., MIT Press, Cambridge, MA, pp. 184–197, 1970.

Sosidian, C. P. and Sharp, L. M., Nonresponse in mail surveys: access failure or respondent resistance?, *Sociology and Social Research*, 66, 348–361, 1980.

Spaeth, M. A., Response rates at academic survey research organizations, *Survey Research*, 23, 18–20, 1992.

Spano, R., Observer behavior as a potential source of reactivity: describing and quantifying observer effects in a large-scale observational study of police, *Sociological Methods and Research*, 34, 521–553, 2006.

Spargo, J., *The Bitter Cry of Children*, Macmillan, New York, 1906.

Spector, M., Learning to study public figures, In *Fieldwork Experience: Qualitiative Approaches to Social Research*, Shaffir, W. B., Stebbins, R. A., and Turowetz, A., Eds., St. Martin's Press, New York, pp. 45–56, 1980.

Spencer, G., Methodological issues in the study of bureaucratic elites: a case study of West Point, In *Field Research: a Sourcebook and Field Manual*, Burgess, R. G., Ed., George Allen and Unwin, London, pp. 23–30, 1982.

Spitzer, R. L. and Fleiss, J. L., A reanalysis of the reliability of psychiatric diagnosis, *British Journal of Psychiatry*, 125, 341–347, 1974.

Spitzer, R., Cohen, J., Fleiss, J., and Endicott, J., Quantification of agreement in psychiatry diagnosis: a new approach, *Archives of General Psychiatry*, 17, 83–87, 1967.

Sproul, L. S., Managing education programs: a microbehavioral analysis, *Human Organization*, 40, 113–122, 1981.

Squire, P., Why the 1936 literary digest poll failed, *Public Opinion Quarterly*, 52, 125–133, 1988.

Srinivasan, S., Quantifying spatial characteristics of cities, *Urban Studies*, 39(11), 2005–2028, 2002.

Stafford, W., Black civil society: fighting for a seat at the table, *Social Policy*, 27, 11–16, 1996.

Stallings, R. A. and Ferris, J. M., Public administration research: work in *PAR*, 1940–1984, *Public Administration Review*, 48, 580–587, 1988.

Stanfield, J. H., Archival methods and race relations research, *American Behavioral Scientist*, 30, 366–380, 1987.

Stangl, D. K. and Berry, D. A., Eds., *Meta-Analysis in Medicine and Health Policy*, Marcel Dekker, New York, 2000.

Stanley, T. D. and Jarrell, S. B., Meta-regression analysis: a quantitative method of literature surveys, *Journal of Economic Surveys*, 3, 161, 1989.

Stanton, J. M., An empirical assessment of data collection using the Internet, *Personnel Psychology*, 51, 709–726, 1998.

Staw, B. M., Attributions of the 'causes' of performance: a general alternative interpretation of cross-sectional research on organizations, *Organizational Behavior and Human Performance*, 13, 414–432, 1975.

Steeh, C., Trends in nonresponse rates, *1952–1979 Public Opinion Quarterly*, 40, 40–57, 1981.

Steel, R. P. and Ovalle, N. K., A review and meta-analysis of research on the relationship between behavioral intentions and employee turnover, *Journal of Applied Psychology*, 69(4), 673, 1984.

Steffensmeier, D., Kramer, J., and Streifel, C., Gender and imprisonment decisions, *Criminology*, 31, 411–438, 1993.

Stein, H., Case method and the analysis of public administration, In *Public Administration and Policy Development*, Stein, H., Ed., Harcourt Brace Jovanovich, New York, xx–xxvi, 1952.

Steinhaus, C. S. and Perry, J. L., Organizational commitment: does sector matter?, *Public Productivity & Management Review*, 19, 278–288, 1996.

Stevens, J. M., Wartick, S. L., and Bagby, J. W., Managerial attitudes on business-government relations, In *Research in Public Administration*, James L. P., Ed., JAI Press, Greenwich, CT, 1991.

Stewart, D. W. and Shamdasani, P. N., *Focus Groups: Theory and Practice*, Sage, Newbury Park, CA, 1990.

Stewart, R., *Contrasts in Management: A Study of the Different Types of Managers Jobs: Their Demands and Choices*, McGraw-Hill, London, 1976.

Stillman, R. J., Ed., *Public Administration: Concepts and Cases*, Houghton-Mifflin, Boston, MA, 1976.

Stillman, R. J., *Public Administration: Concepts and Cases*, Houghton-Mifflin, Boston, MA, 1984.

Stillman, R. J., *Public Administration: Concepts and Cases*, 5th ed., Houghton-Mifflin, Boston, MA, 1992.

Stillman, R. J., *Public Administration: Concepts and Cases*, 8th ed., Houghton-Mifflin, Boston, MA, 2004.

Stivers, C., Settlement women and bureau men: constructing a usable past for public administration, *Public Administration Review*, 55, 522–529, 1995.

Stock, J. S. and Hochstim, J. R., A method of measuring interviewer variability, *Public Opinion Quarterly*, 15, 322–334, 1951.

Stocking, G. W., From physics to ethnology, In *Race, Culture and Evolution: Essays in the History of Anthropology*, Free Press, New York, 1968.

Stocking, G. W., Anthropology in crisis? A view from between the generations, In *Crisis in Anthropology: View from Spring Hill, 1980*, Hoebel, E. A., Currier, R. L., and Kaiser, S., Eds., Garland Publishing, New York, pp. 407–419, 1982.

Stocking, G. W., History of anthropology: whence/whither, In *Observers Observed: Essays on Ethnographic Fieldwork*, Stocking, G. W., Ed., University of Wisconsin Press, Madison, WI, pp. 3–12, 1983.

Stone, P. J., Dunphy, D. C., Smith, M. S., Ogilvie, D. M., and with associates, *The General Inquirer: A Computer Approach to Content Analysis*, MIT Press, Cambridge, MA, 1966.

Strauss, A. and Schatzman, L., Cross class interviewing: an analysis of interaction and communication styles, *Human Organization*, 14, 28–31, 1955.

Stuart, I. R., Minorities vs. minorities: cognitive, affective, and conative components of Puerto Rican and Negro acceptance and rejection, *Journal of Social Psychology*, 59, 93–99, 1963.

Sudman, S., New uses of telephone methods in survey research, *Journal of Marketing Research*, 3, 163–166, 1966.

Sudman, S. and Bradburn, N. M., Effects of time and memory factors on response in surveys, *Journal of the American Statistical Association*, 69, 805–815, 1973.

Sudman, S. and Bradburn, N. M., *Response Effects in Surveys: A Review and Synthesis*, Aldine, Chicago, 1974.

Sudman, S. and Bradburn, N. M., *Asking Questions. A Practical Guide to Questionnaire Design*, Jossey-Bass Publishers, London, 1983.

Sudman, S., Bradburn, N. M., Blair, E., and Stocking, C., Modest expectations: the effects of interviewers' prior expectations on response, *Sociological Methods and Research*, 6, 177–182, 1974.

Sudman, S. and Ferber, R., A comparison of alternative procedures for collecting consumer expenditure data for frequently purchased products, *Journal of Marketing Research*, 11, 128–136, 1974.

Sudman, S., Finn, A., and Lannom, L., The use of bounded recall procedures in single interviews, *Public Opinion Quarterly*, 48, 520–524, 1984.

Suelzle, M. and Borzak, L., Stages of Field Work, In *Field Study: A Sourcebook for Experiential Learning*, Borzak, L., Ed., Sage, Beverly Hills, CA, pp. 136–154, 1981.

Sullivan, M. A., Queen, S. A., and Patrick, R. C., Participant observation as employed in the study of a military training program, *American Sociological Review*, 23, 660–667, 1958.

Summers, G. F., Evans, S. D., Clemente, F., Beck, E. M., and Minkoff, J., *Industrial Invasion of Nonmetropolitan America: A Quarter Century of Experience*, Praeger, New York, 1976.

Summers, G. F. and Bloomquist, L. E., Votes count, but resources decide, *Presented at the International Conference on Energy Resource Communities*, Calgary and Edmonton, Canada, 22–30, June, 1982.

Survey Research Center, *Interviewer's Manual*, revised ed., The University of Michigan, Ann Arbor, MI, 1976.

Susman, G. I. and Evered, R. D., An assessment of the scientific merits of action research, *Administrative Science Quarterly*, 23, 582–603, 1978.

Sutton, A. J., Abrams, K. R., Jones, D. R., Sheldon, T. A., and Song, F., *Methods for Meta-Analysis in Medical Research*, Wiley, Chichester, UK, 2000.

Swan, J. E., Epley, D. E., and Burns, W. L., Can follow-up response rates to a mail survey be increased by including another copy of the questionnaire?, *Psychological Reports*, 47, 103–106, 1980.

Swartz, R. W. and Hancock, C., Data collection through web-based technology, *Statistical Journal of the United Nations Economic Commission for Europe*, 19, 153–159, 2002.

Sypher, B. D., Applegate, J., and Sypher, H., Culture and communication in organizational contexts, In *Communication, Culture, and Organization Processes*, Gudykunst, W., Stewart, L., and Ting-Toomey, S., Eds., Sage, Beverly hills, CA, p. 1329, 1985.

Tang, T. L. and McCollum, S. L., Sexual harassment in the workplace, *Public Personnel Management*, 25, 53–58, 1996.

Tarrant, W. D., Who writes letters to the editor?, *Journalism Quarterly*, 34, 501–502, 1957.

Taylor, C. W., Smith, W. R., and Ghiselin, B., The creative and other contributions of one sample of research scientists, In *Scientific Creativity: Its Recognition and Development*, Taylor, C. W. and Barron, F., Eds., Wiley, New York, pp. 53–76, 1963.

Taylor, S. J. and Bogdan, R., *Introduction to Qualitative Research*, Wiley, New York, 1984.

Taylor, H., Does internet research work?, *International Journal of Market Research*, 42, 51–63, 2000.

Tedin, K. L. and Hofstetter, C. R., The effect of cost and importance factors on the return rate for single and multiple mailings, *Public Opinion Quarterly*, 46, 122–128, 1982.

Terry, L. D., *Leadership in Public Bureaucracies: The Administrator as Conservator*, 2nd ed., M.E. Sharpe, Armonk, NY, 2003.

Tetreault, M. A., *Stories of Democracy: Politics and Society in Contemporary Kuwait*, Columbia University Press, New York, 2000.

The Electronic Hallway. https://hallway.org/.

Thibaut, J. W. and Kelley, H. H., *The Social Psychology of Groups*, Wiley, New York, 1959.

Thomas, R. J., Interviewing important people in big companies, In *Studying Elites Using Qualitative Methods*, Hertz, R. and Imber, J. B., Eds., Sage, London, pp. 3–17, 1995.

Thomas, W. I. and Znaniecki, F., *The Polish Peasant in Europe and America*, University of Chicago Press, Chicago, IL, 1918.

Thompson, F., *Personnel Policy in the City*, University of California Press, Berkeley, CA, 1975.

Thompson, S. K., Adaptive sampling in behavioral surveys, In *The Validity of Self-Reported Drug Use: Improving the Accuracy of Survey Estimates*, Harrison, L. and Hughes, A., Eds., NIDA Research Monograph 167, National Institute of Drug Abuse, Rockville, MD, pp. 296–319, 1997.

Thompson, F., Wolfe, A., Jones, L.R., The Effectiveness of Motor Vehicle Safety Inspection: A Meta-Analysis. *Research in Public Administration: A JAI Annual*. ed., J. Perry, Vol. 1, 175–202, 1991.

Thran, S. L. and Hixson, J. S., Physician surveys: recent difficulties and proposed solutions, *American Statistical Association 2000 Proceedings*, pp. 233–237, 2000, http://www.amstat.org/sections/srms/Proceedings/papers/2000_035.pdf.

Tierney, W., The semiotic aspects of leadership: an ethnographic perspective, *American Journal of Semiotics*, 5, 223–250, 1987.

Tipple, T. J. and Wellman, J. D., Herbert Kaufman's forest ranger thirty years later: from simplicity and homogeneity to complexity and diversity, *Public Administration Review*, 51, 421–428, 1991.

Tita, G. E., Cohen, J., and Engberg, J., An ecological study of the location of gang 'set space,' *Social Problems*, 52, 272–298, 2005.

Tomaskovic-Devey, D., Leiter, J., and Thompson, S., Organizational survey nonresponse, *Administrative Science Quarterly*, 39, 439–457, 1994.

Tonry, M., *Malign Neglect—Race, Crime, and Punishment in America*, Oxford University Press, New York, 1995.

Tourangeau, R. and Smith, T. W., Asking sensitive questions, *Public Opinion Quarterly*, 60, 275–304, 1996.

Traugott, M. W., Govers, R. M., and Lepkowski, J. M., Using dual frame designs to reduce nonresponse in telephone surveys, *Public Opinion Quarterly*, 51, 523–539, 1987.

Tremblay, M. A., The keyinformant technique: a nonethnographic application, *American Anthropologist*, 59, 688–701, 1957.

Trochim, W. M. K., Resources for locating public and private data, In *Reanalyzing Program Evaluations*, Boruch, R. F., Wortman, P. J., Cordray, D. S., and Associates, Eds., Jossey-Bass, San Francisco, CA, pp. 57–67, 1981.

Trouteaud, A. R., How you ask counts: a test of Internet-related components of response rates to a web-based survey, *Social Science Computer Review*, 22, 385–392, 2004.

True, J. A., *Finding Out: Conducting and Evaluating Social Science Research*, Wadsworth, Belmont, CA, 1983.

Trussell, N. and Lavrakas, P. J., The influence of incremental increases in token cash incentives on mail survey response: is there an optimal amount?, *Public Opinion Quarterly*, 68, 349–367, 2004.

Tucker, C., Interviewer effects in telephone surveys, *Public Opinion Quarterly*, 47, 84–95, 1983.

Turner, C. F., Lessler, J. T., and Devore, J., Effects of mode of administration and wording on reporting of drug use, In *Survey Measurement of Drug Use*, Turner, C., Lessler, J. T., and Gfroerer, J. C., Eds., National Institute on Drug Abuse, Rockville, MD, 1992.

Turner, C. F., Lessler, J. T., and Gfroerer, J. C., Future directions for research and practice, In *Survey Measurement of Drug Use*, Turner, C. F., Lessler, J. T., and Gfroerer, J. C., Eds., National Institute on Drug Abuse, Rockville, MD, 1992.

Turner, R., Ed., In *Ethnomethodology*, Penguin, Markham, ON, Canada, 1974.

Tyer, C. B., Employee performance appraisal: process in search of a technique, In *Public Personnel Administration: Problems and Prospects*, Hays, S. W. and Kearney, R. C., Eds., Prentice Hall, Englewood Cliffs, NJ, pp. 118–136, 1983.

Udy, S. H., Cross-cultural analysis: a case study, In *Sociologists at Work*, Hammond, P. E., Ed., Basic Books, New York, pp. 161–183, 1964.

Uebersax, J. S., Validity inferences from interobserver agreement, *Psychological Bulletin*, 104, 405–416, 1988.

Uebersax, J. S., A review of modeling approaches for the analysis of observer agreement, *Investigative Radiology*, 27, 738–743, 1992.

Undheim, T. A., Getting connected: how sociologists can access the high tech elite, *The Qualitative Report*, 8, 104–128, 2003.

Ursel, J., Using the justice system in Winnipeg, In *Family Violence in Canada: A Statistical Profile 2003*, Johnson, H. and AuCoin, K., Eds., Ottawa, Statistics Canada, 2003.

US Department of Commerce, *County and City Data Book, CD-ROM*, US Bureau of the Census, Washington, DC, 1994.

US National Commission on Neighborhoods, *People, Building Neighborhoods*, US Government Printing Office, Washington, DC, 1979.

Useem, M. and Marx, G. T., Ethical dilemmas and political considerations, In *An Introduction to Social Research: Volume I of Handbook of Social Science Methods*, Smith, R. B., Ed., Ballinger, Cambridge, MA, pp. 169–200, 1983.

Uveges, J. A., *Cases in Public Administration: Narratives in Administrative Problems*, Holbrook Press, Boston, MA, 1978.

Vacin, G. L., A study of letter-writers, *Journalism Quarterly*, 42(464–465), 510, 1965.

Van der Bergh, J. C. J. M., Button, K. J., Nijkamp, P., and Pepping, G. C., *Meta-Analysis in Environmental Economics*, Kluwer, Dordrecht, the Netherlands, 1997.

Van Maanen, J., Observations on the making of police, *Human Organization*, 32, 407–418, 1973.

Van Maanen, J., Working in the street, In *The Potential for the Reform of Criminal Justice*, Jacob, J., Ed., Sage Criminal Justice System Annuals, Beverly Hills, CA, pp. 83–130, 1974.

Van Maanen, J., Police socialization, *Administrative Science Quarterly*, 32, 207–228, 1975.

Van Maanen, J., *Organizational Careers: Some New Perspectives*, Wiley, New York, 1977.

Van Maanen, J., The asshole, In *Policing*, Manning, P. K. and Van Maanen, J., Eds., Goodyear, Pacific Palisades, CA, pp. 221–238, 1978a.

Van Maanen, J., Policing, In *On Watching the Watchers*, Manning, P. K. and Van Maanen, J., Eds., Goodyear, Pacific Palisades, CA, pp. 309–349, 1978b.

Van Maanen, J., Reclaiming qualitative methods for organizational research: a preface, *Administrative Science Quarterly*, 24, 520, 1979a.

Van Maanen, J., The fact or fiction in organizational ethnography, *Administrative Science Quarterly*, 24, 539–550, 1979b.

Van Maanen, J., Fieldwork on the beat, In *Varieties of Qualitative Research*, Van Maanen, J., Dabbs, J. M., and Faulkner, R. R., Eds., Sage, Beverly Hills, CA, pp. 103–151, 1982a.

Van Maanen, J., On the Ethics of Fieldwork, In *An Introduction to Social Research, Volume I of Handbook of Social Science Methods*, Smith, R. B., Ed., Ballinger, Cambridge, MA, pp. 227–251, 1983.

Van Maanen, J., *Qualitive Methodology*, Sage Publications, Beveriy Hills, CA, 1984.

Van Maanen, J., *Tales of the Field: On Writing Ethnography*, The University of Chicago Press, Chicago, IL, 1988.

Van Maanen, J., Dabbs, J. M., and Faulkner, R. R., Eds., *Van Maanen Varieties of Qualitative Research*, Sage Publications, Beverly Hills, CA, 1982.

Van Maanen, J. and Schein, E. H., Improving life at work, In *Career Development*, Hackman, J. R. and Suttle, J. L., Eds., Goodyear, Pacific Palisades, CA, pp. 30–95, 1977.

Van Meter, K., Methodological and design issues: techniques for assessing the representatives of snowball samples, *NIDA Research Monograph*, 31–43, 1990.

Van Schendelen, M., Interviewing members of parliament, *Political Methodology*, 10, 301–321, 1984.

Vaughn, Diane, *Challenger Launch Decision: Risky Technology, Culture, and Deviance at NASA*, University of Chicago Press, Chicago, IL, 1996.

Vidich, A. J., Participant observation and the collection and interpretation of data, *American Journal of Sociology*, 60, 354–360, 1955.

Vidich, A. J. and Bensman, J., The validity of field data, *Human Organization*, 13, 20–27, 1954.

Vidich, A. J., Bensman, J., and Stein, M. A., *Reflections on Community Studies*, Wiley, New York, 1964.

Vidich, A. J. and Shapiro, G., A comparison of participant observation and survey data, *American Sociological Review*, 20, 28–33, 1955.

Vidich, A. J. and Lyman, S. M., Qualitative methods: their history in sociology and anthropology, In *The Landscape of Qualitative Research*, Denzin, N. K. and Lincoln Y. S., Eds., 2nd ed., chap. 2, Sage, Thousand Oaks, CA, 2000.

Vietorisz, T. and Harrison, B., *The Economic Development of Harlem*, Praeger, New York, 1970.

Vocino, T., Three variables in stimulating response to mailed questionnaires, *Journal of Marketing*, 41, 76–77, 1975.

Vocino, T. and Elliott, R. H., Journal prestige in public administration: a research note, *Administration and Society*, 14, 5–14, 1982.

Vocino, T. and Elliott, R. H., Public administration journal prestige: a time series analysis, *Administrative Science Quarterly*, 29, 43–51, 1984.

Vogt, W. P., *Dictionary of Statistics and Methodology: A Nontechnical Guide for the Social Sciences*, Sage, London, 1999.

Volgy, T. J., Krigbaum, M., Langan, M. K., and Moshier, V., Some of my best friends are letter writers: eccentrics and gladiators revisited, *Social Science Quarterly*, 58, 321–327, 1977.

Waldo, D., *The Administrative State*, Ronald Press, New York, 1948.

Waldo, D., Five perspectives on the cases of the inter-university case program, In *Essays on the Case Method*, Bock, E. A., Fessler, J. W., Stein, H., and Waldo, D., Eds., The Inter-University Case Program, New York, pp. 39–63, 1962.

Walsh, T. C., Selected results from the 1972–73 diary surveys, *Journal of Marketing Research*, 14, 344–352, 1977.

Walton, J., Community power and the retreat from politics, *Social Problems*, 23, 292–303, 1976.

Wang, M. C. and Bushman, B. J., *Integrating Results through Meta-Analytic Review Using SAS Software*, SAS Institute, Cary, NC, 1999.

Ward, R. E., *Studying Politics Abroad: Field Research in the Developing Areas*, Little, Brown, Boston, MA, 1964.

Warner, S. L., Randomized response: a survey technique for eliminating error answer bias, *Journal of the American Statistical Association*, 60, 63–69, 1965.

Warren, R. L., Observations on the state of community theory, In *New Perspectives on the American Community*, Warren, R. and Lyon, L., Eds., Dorsey, Homewood, IL, pp. 76–79, 1983.

Warwick, D. P., *A Theory of Public Bureaucracy: Politics, Personality, and Organization in the State Department*, Harvard Press, Cambridge, MA, 1975.

Watson, D. J., Juster, R. J., and Johnson, G. W., Institutionalized use of citizen surveys in the budgetary and policy-making processes: a small city study, *Public Administration Review*, 51(3), 232–239, 1991.

Watson, R. P., *Public Administration: Cases in Managerial Role-Playing*, Longman, New York, 2001.

Wax, R. H., Twelve years later: an analysis of field experience, In *Human Organization Research*, Adams, R. N. and Preiss, J. J., Eds., Dorsey Press, Homewood, IL, pp. 166–178, 1960.

Wax, R. H., *Doing Fieldwork: Warnings and Advice*, University of Chicago Press, Chicago, IL, 1971.

Webb, E. J., Campbell, D. T., Schwartz, R. D., and Sechrest, L. L., *Unobtrusive Measures: Nonreactive Research in the Social Sciences*, Rand-McNally, Chicago, IL, 1966.

Webb, E. J., Campbell, D. T., Schwartz, R. D., and Sechrest, L. L., *Unobtrusive Measures: Nonreactive Research in the Social Sciences*, Rand-McNally, Chicago, IL, 1972.

Webb, E. J. and Ellsworth, P. C., On nature and knowing, In *Perspectives on Attitude Assessment: Surveys and their Alternatives*, Sinaiko, H. W. and Broedling, L. A., Eds., Pendleton, Champaign, IL, pp. 223–238, 1976.

Webb, E. J. and Weick, K. E., Unobtrusive measures in organizational theory: a reminder, *Administrative Science Quarterly*, 24, 650–659, 1979.

Weber, R. P., *Basic Content Analysis*, 2nd ed., Sage, Newbury Park, CA, 1990.

Weber, S. J., Wycoff, M. L., and Adamson, D. R., *The Impact of Two Clinical Trials on Physician Knowledge and Practice*, Market Facts, Arlington, VA, 1982.

Weed, D. L., Methods in epidemiology and public health: does practice match theory?, *Journal of Epidemiology and Community Health*, 55, 104–110, 2001.

Weeks, M. F. and Moore, R. P., Ethnicity-of-interviewer effects on ethnic respondents, *Public Opinion Quarterly*, 45, 245–249, 1981.

Weible, R. and Wallace, J., Cyber research: the impact of the Internet on data collection, *Marketing Research*, 10, 19–23, 1998.

Weick, K. E., Systematic observational methods, In *Handbook of Social Psychology*, Lindzey, G. and Aronson, E., Eds., Addison-Wesley, Reading, MA, Vol. 4, pp. 357–451, 1968.

Weinberg, E., Data collection: planning and management, In *Handbook of Survey Research*, Rossi, P. H., Wright, J. D., and Anderson, A. B., Eds., Academic Press, New York, pp. 329–358, 1983.

Weiner S. S., Deadlines and school desegregation in San Francisco, In *Papers for the March 1973 Deadline Conference:* Unpublished Manuscript, E. J. Webb., Ed., Graduate School of Business, Stanford University, 1973.

Weiner, S. S. and Brehm, J. W., Buying behavior as a function of verbal and monetary inducements, In *A Theory of Psychological Reactance*, Brehm, J. W., Ed., Academic Press, New York, 1966.

Weisberg, H. F. and Bowen, B. D., *An Introduction to Survey Research and Data Analysis*, W.H. Freeman, San Francisco, CA, 1977.

Weiss, C. H., Interviewing in evaluation research, In *Handbook of Evaluation Research*, Streuning, E. L. and Guttentag, M., Eds., Vol. 1, Sage, Beverly Hills, CA, 1975.

Weiss, R. S., *Learning from Strangers*, The Free Press, New York, 1994.

Weitzman, E. A. and Miles, M. B., *Computer Programs for Qualitative Data Analysis. A Software Sourcebook*, 2nd ed., Sage, Thousand Oaks, CA, 1998.

West, J. P., Berman, E., and Cava, A., *Ethics in the Municipal Workplace the Municipal Yearbook*, ICMA, Washington, DC, 1993.

Westerbeck, C.J., Some outakes from radical filmmaking: Emile de Antonio, *Sight and Sound*, Summer, 1970.

Westley, W. A., *Violence and the Police: A Sociological Study of Law, Custom and Morality*, MIT Press, Cambridge, MA, 1970.

White, J. D., Dissertations and publications in public administration, *Public Administration Review*, 46, 227–234, 1986.

White, J. D., *Taking Language Seriously: The Narrative Foundations of Public Administration Research*, Georgetown University Press, Washington, DC, 1999.

White, M., Urban commuting journeys are not "wasteful," *The Journal of Political Economy*, 96(5), 1097–1110, 1988.

Whitehead, A., *Meta-Analysis of Controlled Clinical Trials*, Wiley, Chichester, UK, 2002.

Whitener, E. M., Confusion of confidence intervals and credibility intervals in meta-analysis, *Journal of Applied Psychology*, 75, 315, 1990.

Whiting, J. W. M., Methods and problems in cross-cultural research, In *Handbook of Social Psychology*, Lindzey, G. and Aronson, E., Eds., Addison-Wesley, Reading, MA, Vol. 2, pp. 693–728, 1968.

Whyte, W. F., *Street Corner Society*, The University of Chicago Press, Chicago, IL, 1943.

Whyte, W. F., Observational field-work methods, In *Research Methods in Social Relations*, Jahoda, M., Deutsch, M., and Cook, S. W., Eds., Dryden Press, New York, Vol. 2, pp. 493–513, 1951.

Whyte, W. F., *Street Corner Society*, revised ed., University of Chicago Press, Chicago, IL, 1955.

Whyte, W. F., *Learning from the Field: A Guide from Experience*, Sage Publications, Beverly Hills, CA, 1955.

Whyte, W. F., *Man and Organization*, Irwin, Homewood, IL, 1959.

Whyte, W. F., Interviewing in field research, In *Human Organization Research*, Adams, R. N. and Preiss, J. J., Eds., Dorsey Press, Homewood, IL, pp. 352–374, 1960.

Whyte, W. F., On making the most of participant observation, *The American Sociologist*, 14, 56–66, 1979.

Whyte, W. F., On studying China at a distance, In *The Social Sciences and Field Work in China*, Thurston, A. F. and Pasternack, B., Eds., Westview Press, Boulder, CO, pp. 63–80, 1983.

Whyte, W. F., *Learning from the Field: A Guide from Experience*, Sage, Beverly Hills, CA, 1984.

Whyte, R. and Finlay, R., Monitoring the microbiological quality of drinking-waters, *Water and Wastes in New Zealand*, 60, 43–45, 1995.

Wicklund, R. A., *Freedom and Reactance*, Erlbaum, Hillsdale, NJ, 1974.

Wildavsky, A. B., *The Politics of the Budgetary Process*, Little, Brown, Boston, MA, 1984.

Wiener, M., Devoe, S., Rubinow, S., and Geller, J., Nonverbal behavior and nonverbal communication, *Psychology Review*, 79, 185–214, 1972.

Williams, J. A., Interviewer-respondent interaction: a study of bias in the information interview, *Sociometry*, 27, 338–352, 1964.

Williams, J. A., Interviewer role performance: a further note on bias in the information interview, *Public Opinion Quarterly*, 32, 287–294, 1968.

Williams, J. A., The ecological approach in measuring community power concentration: an analysis of Hawley's MPO ratio, *American Sociological Review*, 38, 230–242, 1973.

Williamson, J. B., Karp, D. A., and Dalphin, J. R., *The Research Craft*, Little, Brown, Boston, MA, 1982.

Willimack, D. K., Schuman, H., Pennell, B., and Lepkowski, J. M., Effects of a prepaid nonmonetary incentive on response rates and response quality in a face-to-face survey, *Public Opinion Quarterly*, 59, 78–92, 1995.

Wilpert, B., Various paths beyond establishment views, In *Leadership beyond Establishment Views*, Hunt, J. G., Sekaran, U., and Schriesheim, C. A., Eds., University of Illinois Press, Carbondale, IL, pp. 68–74, 1982.

Wilson, P. A., Power, politics, and other reasons why senior executives leave the federal government, *Public Administration Review*, 54, 12–19, 1994.

Winkler, J., The fly on the wall of the inner sanctum: observing company directors at work, In *Research Methods for Elite Studies*, Moyser, G. and Wagstaffe, M., Eds., Allen and Unwin, London, pp. 129–146, 1987.

Winks, R. W., *The Historian as Detective: Essays on Evidence*, Harper and Row, New York, 1968.

Wise, L. R., Managing for diversity research: what we know from empirical research about the consequences of heterogeneity in the workplace, Paper presented at the Metropolis Conference, November 27-30, Rotterdam, 2001.

Wiseman, F., Factor interaction effects in mail survey response rates, *Journal of Marketing Research*, 41, 74–79, 1973.

Wolcott, H., Criteria for an ethnographic approach to research in schools, *Human Organization*, 34, 111–128, 1975.

Wolcott, H. F., *The Art of Fieldwork*, AltaMira Press, Walnut Creek, CA, 2001.

Wolf, F. M., *Meta-Analysis: Quantitative Methods for Research Synthesis*, Sage, Beverly Hills, CA, 1986.

Wolf, P. J., A case survey of bureaucratic effectiveness in U.S. cabinet agencies: preliminary results, *Journal of Public Administration Research and Theory*, 3, 161–181, 1993.

Wolf, P. J., Why must we reinvent the federal government? Putting historical development claims to the test, *Journal of Public Administration Research and Theory*, 7, 353–388, 1997.

Wood, B. D., Principals, bureaucrats, and responsiveness in clean air enforcement, *American Political Science Review*, 82, 214–234, 1988.

Wood, M., Methodological observations on applied behavioral science, *Journal of Applied Behavioral Science*, 20, 289–297, 1984.

Woodrum, E., 'Mainstreaming' content analysis in social sciences: methodological advantages, obstacles, and solutions, *Social Science Research*, 13, 1–19, 1984.

Worthen, B. R. and Valcarce, R. W., Relative effectiveness of personalized and form covering letters in initial and follow-up mail surveys, *Psychological Reports*, 57, 735–744, 1985.

Wotruba, T. R., Monetary inducements and mail questionnaire response, *Journal of Marketing Research*, 3, 398–400, 1966.

Wyatt, D. F. and Campbell, D. T., A study of interviewer bias as related to interviewer's expectations and own opinions, *International Journal of Opinion and Attitude Research*, 4, 77–83, 1950.

Wyatt, J. and Guly, H., Identifying the research question and planning the project, *Emergency Medicine Journal*, 19, 318–321, 2002.

Yablonsky, L., Experiences with the criminal community, In *Applied Sociology*, Gouldner, A. W. and Miller, S. M., Eds., Free Press, New York, pp. 55–73, 1968a.

Yablonsky, L., On crime, violence, LSD, and legal immunity for social scientists, *American Sociologist*, 3, 148–149, 1968b.

Yammarino, F. J., Skinner, S. J., and Childers, T. L., Understanding mail survey response behavior, *Public Opinion Quarterly*, 55, 613–639, 1991.

Yang, M., *Taitou: A Chinese Village*, John Day, New York, 1945.

Yanow, D., *How Does a Policy Mean? Interpreting Policy and Organizational Actions*, Georgetown University Press, Washington, DC, 1996.

Yeager, S. J., Applying research on productivity improvement in local government, Paper presented at the Annual Conference, National Association of Schools of Public Affairs and Administration, Minneapolis, MN, 1983.

Yeager, S. J., Index of the international journal of public administration: volumes 1 (1979) through 13 (1990), *International Journal of Public Administration*, 14, 439–498, 1991.

Yeager, S. J., Index of the public administration quarterly: volumes 1 (June, 1977) through 14 (winter, 1991), *Public Administration Quarterly*, 18(1), 1–156, 1992.

Yeager, S. J., Index of the journal of health and human resources administration: volumes 1/1 (august, 1978) through 15/1 (summer, 1992), *Journal of Health and Human Resources Administration*, 15(4), 379–610, 1993.

Yeager, S. J., *Index of the Public Administration Review 1940-1994*, Bratton-Yeager Publishing, Inc., Wichita, KS, 1995.

Yeager, M. E. B., *The Story Behind Rosie the Riveter: A Study of Life Magazine Advertisements and Oral Histories from 1939 and 1947*, A thesis submitted in partial fulfillment of the requirements for the Master of Arts in Communication, Wichita State University, Wichita, KS, 2005.

Yeager, S. J. and Manns, E. K., *Index of the Proceedings of the National Conferences on Teaching Public Administration: 1978–1989*, Section on Public Administration Education, American Society for Public Administration, Washington, DC, 1990.

Yeager, M. E. and Blythe, L., Hot doughnuts! Krispy Kreme's rise to the top, 2004 Popular Culture Association Conference, San Antonio TX, 2004.

Yeager, M. E. and Blythe, L., Online archives of the Smithsonian, *American Journalism Historians Association Conference*, San Antonio, TX, 2005.

Yeager, S. J., Rabin, J., and Vocino, T., Feedback and administrative behavior in the public sector, *Public Administration Review*, 45, 570–575, 1985.

Yetman, N.R., An introduction to the WPA slave narratives, A special presentation essay accompanying library of congress, Born in slavery: slave narratives from the federal writers' project, 1936–1938. http://memory.loc.gov/ammem/snhtml/snintro00.html and the collection of narratives, http://memory.loc.gov/ammem/snhtml/snhome.html, 2001

Yin, R. K., *Changing Urban Bureaucracies: How New Practices Become Routinized*, Lexington Books, Lexington, MA, 1979.

Yin, R. K., The federal impact on the structure and function of local government, In *The Urban Impact of Federal Policies*, Glickman, N. J., Ed., Johns Hopkins University Press, Baltimore, MD, pp. 595–618, 1980.

Yin, R. K., The case study as a serious research strategy, *Knowledge: Creation, Diffusion, Utilization*, 3, 97–114, 1981a.

Yin, R. K., The case study crisis: some answers, *Administrative Science Quarterly*, 26, 58–65, 1981b.

Yin, R. K., Life histories of innovations: how new practices become routinized, *Public Administration Review*, 41, 21–28, 1981c.

Yin, R. K., *Conserving America's Neighborhoods*, Plenum, New York, 1982a.

Yin, R.K, Studying the implementation of public programs, In *Studying Implementation: Methodological and Administrative Issues*, Williams, W. et al., Eds., Chatham House, Chatham, NJ, pp. 36–72, 1982b.

Yin, R. K., *Case Study Research: Design and Methods*, Sage, Beverly Hills, CA, 1984.

Yin, R. K., *Case Study Research: Design and Methods*, 2nd ed., Sage, Beverly Hills, CA, 1994.

Yin, R. K., *Case Study Research: Design and Methods*, 3rd ed., Sage, Thousand Oaks, CA, 2003.

Yin, R. K., Bingham, E., and Heald, K. A., The difference that quality makes, *Sociological Methods and Research*, 5, 139–156, 1976.

Yin, R. K. and Heald, K. A., Using the case survey method to analyze policy studies, *Administrative Science Quarterly*, 20, 371–381, 1975.

Yin, R. K. and Heinsohn, I., *Case Studies in Research Utilization*, American Institutes for Research, Washington, DC, 1980.

Yin, R. K. and White, J. L., *Micro Computer Implementation in Schools*, COSMOS Corporation, Washington, DC, 1984.

Yin, R. K. and Yates, D., *Street Level Governments: Assessing Decentralization and Urban Services*, Lexington Books, Lexington, MA, 1975.

Young, P. V., *Scientific Social Surveys and Research: An Introduction to the Background, Content, Methods, and Analysis of Social Studies*, Prentice Hall, New York, 1949.

Young, F. W. and Young, R. C., Key informant reliability in rural Mexican villages, *Human Organization*, 20, 141–148, 1962.

Yu, J. and Cooper, H., A quantitative review of research design effects on response rates to questionnaires, *Journal of Marketing Research*, 20, 36–44, 1983.

Zand, D., Trust and managerial problem solving, *Administrative Science Quarterly*, 17, 229–240, 1972.

Zatz, M. S., The changing forms of racial/ethnic biases in sentencing, *Journal of Research in Crime and Delinquency*, 24(1), 69–92, 1987.

Zelditch, M., Some methodological problems of field studies, *American Journal of Sociology*, 67, 566–576, 1962.

Ziegler, S. J., Increasing response rates in mail surveys without increasing error, *Criminal Justice Policy Review*, 17, 22–31, 2006.

Zingraff, M. and Thomson, R., Differential sentencing of women and men in the USA, *International Journal of the Sociology of Law*, 12, 401–413, 1984.

Zlotnick, C., Robertson, M. J., and Lahiff, M., Getting off the streets: economic resources and residential exits from homelessness, *Journal of Community Psychology*, 27, 209–224, 1999.

Unit 13

Judicial Administration

26 Judicial Administration: Modernizing the Third Branch

Steven W. Hays and James W. Douglas

CONTENTS

I. INTRODUCTION: THE REFORM OF TRADITION

Since it first emerged as an identifiable specialization within the management field, judicial administration has been preoccupied with a clear goal: modernization of court organization and practice. While this objective might seem relatively simple, given the small size of most court organizations, it has proven to be a laborious task. As one of the most famous proponents of judicial administration noted in 1949, modernization of the courts "is no sport for the short winded" (Vanderbilt 1949, 54). Later events have repeatedly emphasized the veracity of this observation. Court management as both an academic and practical exercise has gone through many peaks and valleys. Although the *practice* of court administration has progressed in a relatively steady manner in contemporary times, the academic component of the equation has not always kept pace.

In a very real sense, the history of judicial administration has revolved around the issue of *court reform*. Instead of merely tinkering with the minutiae of court administrative routines, practitioners and theorists within the field have often recommended ambitious structural and procedural reforms that, if adopted, would radically transform most judicial organizations. The reform fervor has ebbed and flowed, often in response to high-profile litigation—such as the Rodney King, O.J. Simpson, and Michael Jackson trials—that either shake the public's faith in the justice system or point to imperfections that beg for attention. High levels of public dissatisfaction with both the process and outcomes of the courts occasionally lead to calls for massive changes in the structure and procedures of courts at all levels of government. Yet, in recent years, the volume of the "reform clarion" has actually declined, even while an undercurrent of steady change has improved judicial practices throughout most of the United States.

Although all institutions of government have undergone dramatic changes over the past century, few (if any) public organizations have been asked to implement the types of sweeping changes that are routinely suggested for our nation's courts. Herein lies a supreme irony: the judicial system is targeted for a plethora of fundamental changes in its operation and structure, yet it is easily the stodgiest and most tradition-bound branch of government. The clash between these conflicting forces has resulted in a reform process that, at best, has been slow and irregular.

To appreciate the inherent difficulties in modernizing the courts, it is helpful to travel the well-worn path of reviewing the specific reasons *why* the judicial system is so attached to tradition (see, e.g., Fish 1973; Frank 1949), and why it has proven to be so reluctant to welcome administrative reform (Dubois 1982; Friesen 1971; Stupak 1991). Foremost among these reasons is the simple fact that courts are, and will continue to be, the special province of attorneys. No other public organization is so dominated by a single profession. As a consequence, court reform is typically controlled by members of the legal community. Although lawyers are by no means a homogeneous or cohesive group (a topic that will be addressed more thoroughly below), their domination over the judiciary produces a number of intended and unintended effects.

Several of the behavioral and professional characteristics that typify judges and attorneys exert a direct impact upon efforts to modernize the courts. As a byproduct of their legal training and professional experiences, judges and attorneys ordinarily value their independence highly, and thus are repelled by bureaucratic tendencies (Wheeler and Whitcomb 1977, 17–19). They jealously guard against any external threats to their autonomy, as they greatly value the freedom to decide the law relatively "unrestricted by external pressures or dictates" (Cannon 1982, 670). Similarly, they tend to resolve problems in a collegial fashion, and they "prize the tradition of civility and camaraderie associated with their profession" (Cannon 1982, 670). In summary, judges and attorneys are not accustomed to such bureaucratic trappings as hierarchical chains of command and norms of impersonality. Like most members of high-status professional groups, they have a strong predilection to be left alone to do their jobs as they were taught, without meddlesome interference from "the outside" (see Wice 1995).

Another set of impediments to court modernization springs from the adversarial process that predominates in American jurisprudence. Having borrowed much of the English common law tradition, our legal system places a great deal of emphasis upon precedent (*stare decisis*). This orientation leads lawyers and judges to look to the past for guidance in dealing with contemporary problems. Moreover, it has imbued the legal profession with a strong attachment to the *process* by which justice is dispensed.

Originating from ancient customs involving trial by battle and/or confrontation, adversary proceedings are characterized by "verbal jousting" before an impartial decider (the judge). It is believed that, through an impressive array of procedural protections and guarantees, justice and fairness (or the proper interpretation of the law) will result from the proceedings. The judicial process has thus evolved into "an elaborate ritual" (Friesen 1971, 122) that requires the careful orchestration of dozens of individuals, including attorneys, judges, witnesses, jurors, court clerks, bailiffs, and the like. The obvious difficulties encountered in staging this judicial drama are exacerbated by the fact that most of the actors are not employees of the court and thus are not subject to the direct control of judges. In addition to creating a serious administrative dilemma, the adversarial process fosters an additional professional predilection among attorneys and judges. Specifically, practitioners of the legal art are not generally concerned about time, efficiency, or other values that are near and dear to the hearts of administrators. To many judges and attorneys, it would be unthinkable to rush justice, to surrender to administrative expediency, when the rights of litigants are at risk. Even when the length and cost of a trial swells to ludicrous proportions, as was clearly evident in the O.J. Simpson fiasco, very few members of the legal profession call for expedited procedures. They perceive a fundamental conflict between justice and efficiency. As one jurist expressed it, "Due process is inefficient, deliberately so!" (Greene 1972, 250).

It can thus be seen that court modernization was never simply a matter of teaching eager judicial actors how to do their jobs more effectively and efficiently. Before substantial changes could be made in the court system, a long and concerted educational process had to be accomplished. Judges and attorneys needed to be convinced that there was a better way of doing things, and that administrative reforms would lead to an improved quality of justice for America's litigants. Not surprisingly, the job of carrying this message to legal practitioners fell almost solely on the shoulders of law professors, eminent jurists, and other enlightened members of the legal community. This fact is reflected in James A. Gazell's summary of the judicial management literature up to the 1970s (Gazell 1975). After discovering that legal periodicals contained 98% of all the journal articles published in the field between 1910 and 1969, he concluded that judicial management "has been an almost exclusive preoccupation of the legal profession" (Gazell 1975, 12). Of the 1400 articles dealing with judicial administration topics published during those six decades, only 28 appeared in political science, public administration, or other types of journals. Not surprisingly, this trend continued into the 1990s, and even worsened (as will be discussed in later sections). A huge majority of the research conducted in the field of court management is published in law reviews and specialized journals targeted at the legal community. The only major exceptions to this phenomenon are *Judicature* and *Justice System Journal*, two journals that count numerous social scientists among their audiences. The generic public management literature, however, rarely mentions the third branch of government.

As a consequence of this unique situation, the history of judicial management does not always parallel that of the broader discipline of public administration. Due to the inertia of tradition, administrative change did not come quickly to the courts. And, just as reform was slow in coming, so too did the theory of judicial management lag behind the intellectual ferment in other subdisciplines of the field. Whereas the intellectual tides within public administration ebbed and flowed over the past century, the theory of judicial administration remained relatively unchanged for nearly 100 years. Although new topics were occasionally added to the reform agenda, the central core of judicial management thought was not seriously influenced or altered by the changes that were occurring elsewhere. In effect, judicial reformers locked onto an idealized model of judicial management early in the field's development; with only minor changes, that original vision persists even today. The essential institutions of justice remain in place, and modernization often appears to be a process of tinkering around the margins.

II. THE EARLY HISTORY: PRECURSORS TO POUND

A. THE REVOLUTIONARY PERIOD TO 1900

A cursory reading of the judicial administration literature will almost certainly leave one with the impression that this subdiscipline of public administration began in 1906 with Roscoe Pound's controversial and iconoclastic speech to the American Bar Association. Breaking a long tradition of comity and gentility, Pound used his keynote address before the ABA convention to lambaste the courts (and, by association, his legal colleagues) for outmoded and inefficient administrative practices. In so doing, he established the reform agenda for decades to come.

Although it is certainly true that Pound's comments immediately shocked at least a few members of the legal community out of their complacency, the concerns that he articulated were not entirely new. In fact, debates relating to the operation and staffing of the court system had long been "a fairly consistent element of American history" (Wheeler and Whitcomb 1977, 26).

For much of the nineteenth century, three issues tended to dominate political discussions concerning the courts: methods of selection of the judiciary; the level of judicial access that was available to everyday citizens; and judicial structure, including the number and jurisdictions of lower courts. Although all of these issues resurfaced continually throughout the 1800s, the most enduring was (and, according to some reformers, still is) judicial selection. The controversy surrounding the best way to staff the courts dates back to the Revolutionary War period. One of the colonists' original complaints about the rule of King George III was that judges of that era served at the pleasure of the colonial governors. As was specifically noted in the Declaration of Independence, this practice threatened the judges' decision-making objectivity by making them dependent upon the executive branch of government for their livelihoods. The colonists' solution to the problem of judicial neutrality appeared in the "tenure during good behavior" provision of the US Constitution.

While the means of selecting federal judges was resolved very early in the nation's history, the controversy over the staffing of *state* courts has never subsided. Major quantities of fuel were added to this fire during the 1830s and 1840s, when Jacksonian democracy was in full bloom. The most immediate effect of this grassroots political movement was to open government up to the "common man" (see Crenson 1975; Kaufman 1965), a phenomenon that ushered in the long ballot. Once it was decided that the voters ought to elect just about every public official imaginable, popular election of judges became the norm in state government. Relatedly, state legislatures began to take a much more active role in monitoring and controlling the judicial machinery. The tenure of judges was severely restricted (many being elected to four-year terms to make them coincide with their state's gubernatorial elections), and judicial organization and procedures came under increased scrutiny.

Consistent with the ambitions of Jackson's populist ideals, an important goal of many state legislatures during much of the mid-to-late 1800s was to increase the common man's access to courts. Legislatures therefore often took the lead in engineering structural reforms of their states' court systems, as well as in prescribing judicial procedures. According to one analysis, "radicals... wanted... a cheap, simple, easily available and speedy system of administering justice, one that would ensure equality and provide security with only a minimum of contact with the legal profession" (Ellis 1971, 121). Where Jacksonians (who were given the non-pejorative title of radicals) were in charge, new courts were often created to provide greater public access. Additionally, the radicals' goals were pursued through the appointments of justices of the peace and the expansion of their jurisdictions.

The general trend toward the proliferation of courts and judicial officers picked up momentum during the late 1800s and early 1900s. As the population grew, and as society became more complex, the number of cases presented to judges for resolution swelled dramatically. This required an expansion in the size of judicial bureaucracies at all levels of government. At the federal level, the judicial structure was permanently fixed in 1891 with the adoption of the Court of Appeals Act (see Richardson and Vines 1970, 16–35). After decades of feuding over the proper number and distribution of federal courts, the act established the three-tiered judicial system: Supreme Court, Circuit Courts of Appeal, and District Courts (see Wasby 1993).

The situation at the state level was never as neat and clean. In response to the social demands occasioned by urbanization, the decline of the agrarian economy, the advent of the automobile and related trends, state legislatures engaged in an orgy of court creation. Specialized judicial bodies were established to contend with ever-increasing numbers of divorces, landlord–tenant disputes, traffic violations, municipal code infractions, and a plethora of other types of litigation that had previously been handled informally. And, because these courts were created sporadically to meet critical needs, the judicial system grew in an uncontrolled and essentially undisciplined fashion. By the dawn of the twentieth century, "state courts were complex but disorganized... Overlapping jurisdictional boundaries were common, and no two state-court systems had identical structures" (Wheeler and Whitcomb 1977, 28).

Another consequence of this judicial history was the legislative domination of judicial procedures and resources. In contrast to the other branches of government, the judiciary did not function autonomously within the governmental system. In addition to being dependent upon the executive and legislative branches for its resources (including its buildings, operating revenues, and personnel), the judicial system's very mode of operation was governed by procedures that were dictated by legislative bodies (see Barr 1975; Biden 1994; Friesen 1971; Tobin 1999). Instead of being the masters of their own administrative and procedural domains, judges were compelled to participate in the political process to win appropriations and to manage the judicial household. This situation was complicated by the fact that, in creating new courts, legislatures generally would either prescribe new sets of civil and criminal procedure, or permit the affected judges to manufacture their own procedures as needed (thereby leading to confusing diversities in court practices and legal requirements within and between jurisdictions). Moreover, they would usually give cities and counties the responsibility for funding and staffing the courts located within their jurisdictions. One obvious byproduct of this situation was that wide variations existed in the procedures, operating practices, jurisdictions, and funding levels of courts in different locations. The court system was truly evolving into a non-system of disjointed parts.

Despite the apparent chaos of the pre-1900 period, early court reformers provided their successors with an occasional object lesson and/or victory during their struggles to rationalize the judicial process. One of the most influential reformers of the day was the jurist David Dudley Field (1805–1895), who agitated endlessly for the codification of state laws relating to judicial procedures. His goal was to establish a simple, expeditious, and inexpensive system of litigation so that citizens would be encouraged (rather than *dis*couraged) to turn to the courts to resolve private disputes (Aumann 1969, 208). Field's efforts were ultimately rewarded with the passage of New York's Field Code of Civil Procedure. Adopted in 1848, this code represented a huge improvement over the procedural anarchy of the day. It was so effective at standardizing and regularizing civil procedure that it became a model that continues to be used in almost all of the states today (Aumann 1969; Mayers 1964, 227). Although Field lost several later battles that were intended to regularize criminal and administrative laws and procedures, his pioneering efforts proved that the forces of tradition could be overcome with perseverance.

Two decades after Field's codification efforts bore fruit, elite members of the legal profession joined together to improve the public image of attorneys and to "promote widespread public acceptance of law practice" (Glick 1982, 20). The first city bar associations were formed in New York City and Chicago in the early 1870s, and the ABA was created shortly thereafter (1878).

One of the chief concerns of these professional associations was to improve the image of justice that was prevalent during the last half of the nineteenth century. Through long involvement in partisan politics—during a period in which such politics were notoriously corrupt—the reputations of both judges and attorneys had been badly tarnished. Thus, one of the earliest goals of the ABA was to improve public respect for the courts by "getting judges out of politics" (Glick 1982, 20). This goal was ultimately translated into a number of specific reform proposals, including *nonpartisan* election of judges (an objective that was later amended to promote the neutral *appointment* of judges), standardization of judicial procedures (to reduce favoritism and corruption), and increased judicial system autonomy from legislative influence. As any student of public administration will readily note, this movement in judicial administration dovetailed almost completely with the concurrent efforts that were occurring in the 1870s and 1880s to de-politicize (neutralize) the civil service.

At the same time that American attorneys were organizing in an effort to promote needed judicial reforms, a major restructuring of the English judicial system was taking place. The Judicature Act of 1873 represented a British attempt to systematize their judicial system by standardizing court jurisdictions, regularizing appellate procedures, and minimizing the amount of wasted judicial time by providing for the transfer of judges to different venues, depending upon case loads. The centerpiece of this reform was the concept of *court unification* that established the highest tribunal in the land as the bureaucratic, as well as the legal, authority for the entire judicial system. By vesting administrative authority and responsibility at the pinnacle of the judicial hierarchy, it was assumed that the courts could be made to function more like formal organizations than had been the case previously. This concept ultimately became a central component of the theory and practice of American judicial administration.

Thus, events that occurred long before the birth of modern judicial administration provided many cues to the reformers of the twentieth century. The courts labored under a heavy burden of historical baggage, including chaotic structures, excessive involvement in politics, procedural confusion, and near-total resource dependency. Moreover, they were further constrained by the absence of an administrative tradition. Whereas management considerations had been at least marginally relevant within the other branches, and were taking on increased importance during the latter part of the nineteenth century, the words "court" and "management" were rarely mentioned in the same breath until 1906. Instead, decisions concerning the structure, composition, and procedures of the nation's courts were all viewed as political concerns that were the province of legislatures, not judges or administrators.

Yet, despite a weighty list of problems, the nineteenth century had provided the judicial system with a small (and largely ignored) reform agenda. Movements were afoot to reduce political influences in the courts, and the benefits of procedural standardization were recognized by progressive elements of the legal profession. Finally, a vaguely defined concept of court unification had been introduced to America, although its potential significance had not yet been formally acknowledged by anyone within the legal community.

III. JUDICIAL ADMINISTRATION GETS ITS START: 1900–1909

By the turn of the century, governmental reform was taking place on a broad front under the banner of the Progressive Movement. This consisted of a variety of "good government" campaigns that were intended to help America "come to terms with the vast transformations produced by the preceding century's Industrial Revolution" (Wheeler and Whitcomb 1977, 47). The Progressive dogma held that government needed to be purged of special interests, that citizen access to public institutions should be greatly broadened, and that public resources ought to be mobilized to relieve the social and economic difficulties of the masses (Wheeler and Whitcomb 1977, 28–29).

The Progressive movement's direct impact upon court operations was, for the most part, nominal. One of its chief goals *vis-à-vis* the judicial system was, at least initially, to broaden access to the courts by creating small claims courts in which minor disputes could be resolved quickly and cheaply. Although the Progressives were very effective at getting state legislatures to create these courts, they did not represent a major advance in court management practice. Another goal of the Progressives was to give the voting public the ability to recall errant judges, as well as to negate unpopular judicial decisions through the ballot box. Neither of these reforms was enthusiastically received by state legislatures.

A. POUND'S ABA ADDRESS: JUDICIAL ADMINISTRATION IS BORN

Despite its marginal influence on the specifics of judicial administration, the Progressive Movement deserves much of the credit for providing the intellectual environment that produced the field's seminal theorist. The cross-fertilization between classical management theory and the ideals of Progressivism provided the catalyst that motivated Roscoe Pound to deliver his famous plea to the 1906 annual convention of the ABA. Pound, who later became Dean of the Harvard Law School, detailed "the major causes of popular dissatisfaction" with American courts (Pound 1937). Daily experiences with injustice, delay, and excessive expense had created "a deep-seated desire to keep out of court, right or wrong, on the part of every sensible businessman in the community" (Pound 1937, 179; see also Downie 1972, 205). Having noted this gloomy reality, he listed the shortcomings of the American courts and provided a framework for systemic reform.

The bulk of Pound's remarks were focused on the "archaic" nature of American judicial organization and procedure (Pound 1937, 1962, 62). Three specific shortcomings of the judicial system were then singled out. First, he argued that there were simply *too many courts*; their very existence was seen as proof that the judicial system contained excessive amounts of duplication, waste, and inefficiency (Berkson 1977, 7). Second, he maintained that, by preserving *concurrent jurisdictions* (which means that more than one court has the authority to hear a case), American courts were squandering judicial resources and confusing litigants. Finally, Pound complained of the *"inherent waste of judicial manpower"* that was occasioned by the other two traits, as well as by rigid jurisdictional boundaries that prohibited the transfer of judges between and among courts. He observed that some judges were idle much of the time, yet they were precluded from lending aid to other judges whose dockets were overly congested (Berkson 1977, 7). "The judicial organizations of the several states exhibit many differences in detail," he noted, "but they agree in these three respects" (Pound 1962, 62).

The evils that Pound attacked are best understood in the context of local justice during the early part of this century. When his speech was delivered, most large cities contained a bewildering variety of courts, including orphans' courts, courts of oyer and terminer (higher criminal courts), general sessions courts, mayors' courts, hustings courts (that were comparable to today's municipal courts), land courts, police courts, recorders' courts (that are also termed justice of the peace courts), alderman's courts, small claims courts, probate courts, tax courts, family courts, and juvenile courts (Berkson 1980, 18; Tobin 1999). Some of these judicial bodies would ordinarily be badly backlogged with cases, while others seldom heard disputes. Moreover, the tangle of overlapping jurisdictions served to confuse litigants, and permitted attorneys to judge shop (i.e., take their cases from court to court until they found an appropriately sympathetic and/or friendly judge). The only control over the quality of justice was that litigants who were displeased with the outcome of their cases often had a right to a trial *de novo* (a completely new trial on the merits) in a higher court. Thus, the same case might occasionally be heard anew in several courts before it was finally resolved. Lawrence Friedman summarized the situation as follows: "No administrator ran, controlled, or coordinated the judicial system. No one could shift judges about as needed from a crowded to an empty docket; or monitor the flow of litigation; or set up rules to tell the courts how to behave. Higher courts controlled lower courts weakly and partially through the power to reverse decisions—but only in the event of an appeal" (Friedman 1973, 336).

In articulating his reform proposals, Pound relied heavily upon the English Judicature Act of 1873. One reason why he was attracted to the British method of judicial administration was that it was widely known to process cases more expeditiously than its American counterpart. The characteristic of the English court system that he found most appealing was its hierarchical, unified structure.

Pound suggested that all states consolidate their trial and appellate courts into a two-tier system consisting of a court of first instance and a court of appeals. This structural configuration would, according to Pound, provide the following benefits: (1) it would "focus the judiciary's attention on litigants' causes of action rather than on techniques of appellate procedure" (Ashman and Parness 1974, 3); (2) it would reduce the number of errors in the choice of forums, thereby minimizing case dismissals; and (3) the amount of wasted judicial manpower would be reduced through the elimination of idleness and unnecessary retrials (Ashman and Parness 1974, 3).

The underlying premise of Pound's comments was that the courts needed to be *managed*. That is, they needed to adopt an administrative style that was patterned after other public organizations. The proposed reforms implicitly contained two broad components. First, Pound believed that each state judicial system ought to be *consolidated* structurally. All lower specialized courts should be abolished, with their jurisdictional responsibilities being assigned to the new unified court. All cases would be heard originally in the trial branch of the unified system, and any subsequent appeals would go to the appellate branch (thereby foreclosing the possibility of trials *de novo*). Second, the unified court structure would be under the administrative supervision of a single entity. *Administrative centralization* was perceived as a path out of the wilderness of conflicting procedures, wasted judicial manpower, and inconsistent standards of justice. Stated more simply, Pound merely wanted to impose a classical bureaucratic structure on the courts, complete with fixed responsibility, unity of command, a chain of authority, and the other fixtures that were believed to be responsible for the efficiency of bureaucracy.

Although Pound's ideas were iconoclastic, to say the least, they were not as foreign to the American judicial scene as one might imagine. Several months prior to the 1906 ABA convention, the Illinois legislature had consolidated Chicago's municipal court in a manner that was remarkably similar to Pound's pronouncements. The court had "an administrative head with power to control its administrative agencies [bailiffs, clerks, etc.], utilize its personnel for the speedy disposition of business, and adjust its organization periodically to meet existing workloads" (Ashman and Parness 1974, 4). In a journal article that appeared a few years after his speech, Pound was very complimentary of this array of administrative powers, and was especially struck by the Chicago court's unbridled power to make rules of procedure without interference from any legislative body (Pound 1913). Thus, freedom from legislative involvement in judicial administration quickly became an additional component of Pound's reform program.

B. THE LEGAL PROFESSION'S ROLE IN REFORM

As he probably expected, Pound's comments were initially received unenthusiastically by most of the legal community. In fact, the reaction of some of the ABA audience can almost be termed hostile. Immediately after his speech was concluded, a series of speakers took the podium to rebut Pound's indictment of the courts. One elder statesman from the audience accused Pound of "attempting to destroy that which the wisdom of the centuries had built up" (as quoted in Vanderbilt 1938, 5–6). James Andrews, a respected New York attorney, proclaimed that "a more drastic attack upon the system of procedure employed by the courts in the United States could scarcely be devised". Others later characterized their reactions as "astonished" and "resentful" (Wigmore 1962, 52–53).

Despite this inauspicious start, the judicial reform movement began in earnest soon after Pound's angry colleagues had left the assembly hall. For, despite the opposition of the bar's rank and file members, powerful forces within the legal community were silently nodding in agreement as Pound spoke. Indeed, Pound's speech articulated a point of view that had long been germinating within the ABA's upper crust. From the very beginning, the major proponents of judicial administration came from the very summit of the law profession. Pound had not been speaking for the vast majority of attorneys who practiced in the legal trenches. Instead, he represented a small group of legal elites that feared serious repercussions if attorneys and courts did not become more responsive to the needs of litigants. Over time, these influential elements of the legal community were able to win converts among the rank and file. Before the reform agenda became a mass movement, however, the elite bar forged a path that was not widely embraced by the ABA's broader membership.

According to one insightful analysis, their motives were not always selfless. Lawrence Friedman has argued that the elite bar's support of court management was (and is) intended to help the legal profession justify its own market monopoly by minimizing public antipathy for the judicial process and "institutionalizing mechanisms that create a favorable public image" (1969, 358). Court reform was seen as a means of strengthening the legal community's hold on its market, as well as a convenient method of gaining even greater autonomy by reducing the politicians' influence over court procedures and the practice of law. Thus, bar leaders, prominent law professors, and "organizations created specifically by leading members of the bar" assumed a virtual stranglehold over the business of court reform (Munger 1982, 53). As will be discussed, external groups did not become significantly involved in the court modernization movement until much later.

For obvious reasons, it is not meaningful or appropriate to apply a normative yardstick to the elite bar's early control of judicial administration. Whatever their motivations, the goals they set for court reform were a huge improvement over the structural and procedural confusion of the day. The legal establishment's role did, however, exert a critical influence upon the way that the reform program was defined and pursued. Almost without exception, the specifics of the reform agenda were hammered out in various committees of the ABA and/or by special organizations that were controlled by legal elites. Thus, judicial administration during the first sixty or seventy years of the past century came to be defined in terms of the formal pronouncements and reform proposals of the legal establishment. Moreover, the reform goals that were established came to be viewed by the elite legal community as components of a holy grail of judicial administration (Gazell 1978, 5). Reform became something of a crusade (albeit a slow and irregular one), and the movement's principles were transformed into articles of faith that were seldom questioned by individuals of any intellectual or professional persuasion.

C. The Reform Agenda Takes Shape

The first official response of the legal community to Pound's call for a unified court system came in 1909. In that year, an ABA study committee (Special Committee to Suggest Remedies and Formulate Proposed Laws to Prevent Delay and Unnecessary Cost in Litigation) that had been appointed to analyze Pound's complaints issued its report. After examining the problems of court delay and excessive expense in litigation, the Committee identified four primary factors in the subject of judicial administration: judicial organization; the law of procedure; the means of selecting and tenuring judges; and the "organization, training and tradition of the Bar" (Special Committee to Suggest Remedies and Formulate Proposed Laws to Prevent Delay and Unnecessary Cost in Litigation 1909, 588). To resolve problems in judicial organization, the Committee stated: "The whole judicial power of each state... should be vested in one great court, of which all tribunals should be branches, departments or divisions. The business, as well as the judicial administration of the court, should be thoroughly organized, so as to prevent not merely waste of judicial power, but all needless clerical work, duplication of papers and records, and the like, thus obviating expense to litigants and cost to the public" (Special Committee to Suggest Remedies and Formulate Proposed Laws to Prevent Delay and Unnecessary Cost in Litigation 1909, 589).

In slight contrast to Pound's original view of a two-tier court, the Committee suggested that state legislatures create *three* branches within their "great court": county courts (to include municipal courts, as well), with exclusive jurisdiction over all petty matters; a superior court of first instance (a trial court of general jurisdiction); and a single court of appeals. The Committee had added a county court, a change that Pound quickly embraced. Management of the great court would be the responsibility of a single "high official" who would assign cases and otherwise handle the administrative supervision of the system.

Other recommendations of the Committee focused on extending the tenure of judges, making their selection as neutral and nonpartisan as possible, and improving the management awareness of judges and attorneys. Also, the Committee held that "procedural details should be left to rules of court instead of being prescribed by legislative action" (Ashman and Parness 1974, 11). Statutes, it said, should only establish a general outline, leaving the details of procedures to be fixed by rules of court. This would enable the court to tailor procedures to meet unanticipated developments, and to alter court practices as experience dictated.

Although some of the most important components of the Committee report were never submitted to the ABA membership for a formal vote (partly out of fear that they would be rejected by the rank and file), a concise and reasonable reform agenda had been articulated and publicized. After having nearly been driven from the podium in 1906, Pound's ideas became the centerpiece of an ABA Committee report in 1909. In addition to borrowing many of his recommendations, the committee came forth with a broader reform agenda than Pound had originally proposed. Thanks to the sponsorship of the elite bar, court reform had been successfully launched.

IV. ALLIES ARE ENLISTED: 1910–1919

The ABA Committee's report played a dual role in the early development of judicial administration. In addition to enhancing the legitimacy of some of the goals of judicial reformers, it heightened the visibility of court management issues among "good government" and other public interest groups. Although few skeptics were converted to the doctrines of court reform (law journals of the day regularly carried as many articles that were critical of the reform efforts as they did supportive ones), the publicity did raise the level of public consciousness and attract broadened support for the cause. The job of educating the public was further aided in 1912, when Roscoe Pound was appointed Dean of the Harvard Law School. From that "position of national prominence," he fine-tuned his thesis of court reform and attracted many notable allies (Lowe 1973, 317).

Perhaps Pound's most influential ally of the decade was former President Taft. As president of the ABA, he lobbied extensively for structural and procedural changes that would contribute to "the dispatch of judicial business" (as quoted in Wiebe 1967, 167). At a 1914 commencement address before the University of Cincinnati Law School, he admonished the American courts to learn from the English experience. He criticized Congress for "being derelict in its duty" to remedy the system's shortcomings (Berkson 1977, 8). Taft then tendered five recommendations for the improvement of the federal system of justice (Berkson 1977, 8–9): (1) Abolish the system that separates law and equity, thereby creating unnecessary litigation and confusion; (2) Give either the Supreme Court or a council of judges complete control over the rules of procedure; (3) Minimize the costs of litigation, even if it involves making the government (rather than litigants) responsible for the expense; (4) Confer upon the head of the federal judicial system (presumably, the Chief Justice of the US Supreme Court) the authority to redistribute judges to reduce case backlogs; and

(5) Enact a federal workmen's compensation law (the presence of which would reduce the amount of worker–employer litigation).

Interestingly, Taft's proposals combine procedural, administrative, and *caseload* solutions to the courts' problems. His suggestions concerning the merging of law and equity had been around for nearly a century, and most of the administrative reforms that he identified can be traced to Pound. By calling for reductions in the number and types of cases that must be judicially decided, however, Taft broke ground that had only been slightly cultivated in the immediate past (although Pound, too, had made this an agenda item). In so doing, he initiated a long-term discussion of the relative merits of delegating disputes to quasi-judicial and/or administrative bodies for resolution (i.e., the concept of *alternative dispute resolution* (ADR) was on the reform table at an early date). In essence, his sixth recommendation was for the creation of an administrative, rather than judicial, response to the thousands of cases arising from work-related injuries. This focus on *input* solutions—i.e., reducing the input of cases into the judicial system by diverting them to quasi-judicial bodies—would later assume increased importance.

According to Peter Fish, Taft's efforts were clearly an attempt to blunt the thrust of the Progressives, who at the time were agitating for the total democratization of the courts. They wanted a version of pure democracy that would have allowed the people to be the ultimate deciders of statutory meaning and constitutional intent. Taft saw this as one path to socialism; he complained that, under such a system, law would become dependent upon "the momentary passions of a people" expressed via initiatives, referenda, and recalls of judicial officials and decisions (Fish 1973; Pringle 1939). By making the courts work more efficiently, Taft apparently believed that he could deflect some of the Progressives' criticisms of the judicial process. As such, Taft was very much a "classic conservative reformer" (Fish 1975, 4), striving to channel change onto a reasonable (i.e., not too disruptive) path.

The fact that Pound was able to successfully attract other important allies is reflected in a court reform document that he coauthored in 1914. Among his collaborators were Louis D. Brandeis (later appointed to the Supreme Court), Charles Eliot (who had recently retired from the presidency of Harvard University), and Moorfield Storey (past president of the ABA and founder of the National Association for the Advancement of Colored People). Their *Preliminary Report on Efficiency in the Administration of Justice* (1914) was prepared for the National Economic League that had been one of the first good government groups to jump on the court reform wagon (Wheeler and Whitcomb 1977, 47–48). In addition to calling for the usual reform platform (unified courts, extended judicial tenure, procedural autonomy), the *Report* emphasized the need for *professional court managers* and a system of *merit selection of judges*. Another segment of the report discussed the difficulties that ensue from allowing elected court clerks and other independent officers to exercise authority over many facets of court operations. Although these ideas and concerns were not well defined at this stage of the reform process, they were precursors of important later movements in judicial administration. As will be discussed below, calls for the employment of trained court managers, as well as for the merit selection of all judicial personnel, eventually became important components of ABA reform proposals (see American Bar Association 1962, 1971, 1974, 1990).

A related development in 1914 soon gave greater texture to the concept of merit selection. Albert M. Kales, an avid opponent of the Progressives' recall plan, proposed an alternative means of selecting judges that combined both election and appointment. He proposed that the public elect the head of the unified court to a short term, during which that person would be authorized to fill judicial vacancies by appointment. Then, the judges who were appointed through this procedure would run unopposed "on their records" in a "retention election" (Kales 1914). Elements of this judicial selection strategy ultimately became part of the "Kales plan," the most famous merit selection technique currently used (see Harley 1936).

The judicial administration movement received perhaps its biggest boost of the decade (and perhaps of its history, next to Pound's speech) with the formation of the American Judicature

Society (AJS) in 1913. Richard S. Chiles, founder of the short-ballot movement and intellectual leader of the related city management movement, provided the funding that allowed a small but "cohesive group of people" to initiate the activities of this most influential court reform organization (Wheeler and Whitcomb 1977, 47). The AJS started out as a tiny interest group that was founded "To Promote the Efficient Administration of Justice," the logo that appears on its publications.

Initially, its only activities consisted of the publication of several bulletins that described court reform issues. *Bulletin I*, for example, outlined a set of proposals that was intended to serve "as a basis of discussion." Albert Kales, the *Bulletin's* author, listed such topics as jury selection, rules of practice, the selection and disciplining of judges, and the selection of non-judicial court personnel. One of AJS's most ambitious early publications was *Bulletin IV* (1914) that contained a model Metropolitan Court Act. This, in turn, was followed by a model State-Wide Judicature Act. These documents faithfully clung to the reform agenda that Pound had identified, although more and more meat had begun to add form to the skeleton. Kale's merit selection plan, for instance, was originally contained as part of the Metropolitan Court Act (*Bulletin IV*). The body of court reform literature then began in earnest in 1917, when the *Journal of the American Judicature Society* began publication. That journal, now called simply *Judicature*, is by far the most authoritative chronicle of judicial administration in American. Its pages contain discussions of every debate and issue that has ever surfaced in the contemporary history of the field. As such, its influence on the subdiscipline has been extraordinary. During the first several years of its existence, the journal was distributed free of charge to libraries, members of the bar, and academics throughout the nation. No other publication approaches the journal's significance in educating the public to the need for modern judicial administration (see Harley 1936), although the *Justice System Journal* has more recently emerged as a predominantly academic outlet for relevant research.

V. JUDICIAL ADMINISTRATION TAKES HOLD: 1920–1929

In its first issue, the AJS journal noted that "there can be no patented scheme for judicial salvation" (Harley 1917, 4). The prescience of this observation was demonstrated in 1920, when the second major model of judicial administration was developed. The National Municipal League, another group of good government activists, joined forces with the AJS in promoting the Model Judiciary Article.

A. THE MODEL JUDICIARY ARTICLE OF 1920

This model's primary contribution to reform thought was to recommend a *method* by which a unified court system should be instituted in the various state governments. Characterizing state judicial systems as "extensive institutions without brains" (*Journal of the American Judicature Society* 1920, 132), it maintained that court unification ought to be accomplished by way of *constitutional revisions* rather than through statutory means. The model asserted that state legislatures had been doing a poor job of directing their court systems, and that further legislative intervention through statutes would merely worsen the situation. Moreover, statutory control over the judicial system was viewed as a violation of the separation of powers doctrine; it placed the courts in an inferior position relative to the legislature, and severely restricted judges' administrative flexibility (Ashman and Parness 1974, 6).

In offering a proposed remedy to legislative involvement in court practice, the model embellished an earlier concept of the judicial council. All rules of practice and procedure would be the exclusive responsibility of the court system, and these powers would be exercised through the rule-making authority of a judicial council. This body would be composed of representative judges from the three courts (following the 1909 model of judicial structure). The council's management responsibilities would be extensive, including powers to regulate all non-judicial personnel in the courthouse, to reduce the numbers of justice of the peace, to control the assignment of judges, and to manage the court calendar. The system's chief justice would be the chief administrative officer of the system. Among his other duties as presiding officer of the judicial council, this "Chief Judicial Superintendent" (Wigmore 1917) would be responsible for compiling judicial statistics and for publishing an annual report of the courts' activities. These efforts would be essential in providing the judicial system with a *planning* capability through which future staffing and case assignment decisions could be made.

Another noteworthy proposal arising from the 1920 Model Judiciary Article was that all court officers be paid by the state, with all fines and fees collected by the courts being returned to the state treasury. This would ensure a measure of uniformity within the system, in contrast to the diversity that prevailed when each local jurisdiction was responsible for the financial upkeep of the courts within its boundaries.

B.   THE FEDERAL AND STATE RESPONSES

Although no state embraced the entire range of reforms contained in the model article, several states adopted some of its more important components during the 1920s and 1930s. The article "was instrumental in the creation of several state judicial councils, the return of much of the rule-making power to the state courts, and in several other areas of judicial administration" (Ashman and Parness 1974, 7). However, as the AJS opined in 1937, the National Municipal League's preoccupation with city and county governmental reform meant that the Model Judiciary Article did not receive the publicity that it deserved (*Journal of the American Judicature Society* 1937, 189).

While the League's model was serving as a guide for state court reform, Taft's 1914 reform agenda was receiving a positive welcome in the United States Congress. In 1922, for example, Congress established the Conference of Senior Circuit Judges that was intended to comply with Taft's suggestion that a council of judges be given authority over the court system's procedures. Later renamed the Judicial Conference of the United States, this body was given authority to assign judges, monitor the operation and effect of rules and procedures, and to plan for future contingencies in judicial workload. Moreover, it was (and is) empowered to "promulgate rules of procedure for the federal courts which take effect upon adoption by the Supreme Court unless rejected by Congress within 90 days" (Berkson 1977, 9).

A related move occurred in 1925, when Congress enacted the Judiciary Act. Usually called the Judge's Bill, this act was a response to Taft's request for a reduction in the appellate jurisdiction of the Supreme Court. The act eliminated all but a small amount of obligatory appellate jurisdiction (making *writs of certiorari* the primary avenue of appeal), thereby reducing the Court's caseload and backlog (Berkson 1977, 9). Additionally, it resulted in "a complete codification of federal appellate jurisdiction...and set up the basic scheme of organization under which the federal courts now operate" (Wheeler and Whitcomb 1977, 42).

C.   RESEARCH ACTIVITIES

In addition to major legislative initiatives, the 1920s witnessed the first significant research efforts to assess the actual condition of the nation's courts. Until the AJS began its *Bulletin* series, there had been no systematic effort to examine courts from anything but an anecdotal or exposé perspective. While almost everyone acknowledged that Pound's description of the courts was generally accurate, there had not been many attempts to evaluate the impact or consequences of the existing administrative practices. This began to change, albeit slowly, during the 1920s.

One of the first empirical studies in what was to become a long tradition of judicial management research focused on the Cleveland criminal courts. Completed in 1921, the findings of that study led Roscoe Pound to comment that "the professional criminal and his advisers have learned rapidly to use this machinery and make devices intended to temper the application of criminal law to the occasional offender a means of escape for the habitual offender" (Pound 1921, 45). Pound attributed this problem to chaotic organization, inept judges, and "haggling lawyers" (Downie 1972, 205). The ability to link poor court management practices to serious social problems (i.e., the freeing of dangerous criminals), boosted the cause of court reform considerably (see Pound 1913).

Pound and other court reformers managed to exploit such themes fairly effectively. In 1927, for example, Pound wrote an article that traced the historical background of state judicial systems with an eye toward convincing the reader that the United States had borrowed most of the bad points, and few of the good, from the English and French judicial systems. Making liberal references to certain horror stories about urban and state courts, he noted: "the model was English judicial organization at its worst, and the circumstances of time in which our judicial system was wrought did not make against the primitive policy of multiplying courts. Hence, in a time when unification is sorely needed, we go on making new courts" (Pound 1927, 75).

A similar type of literature also began to appear in the social science community during the 1920s, although it was rare indeed. Some social scientists teamed up to conduct interdisciplinary studies of urban trial courts. Many of these studies were very descriptive, almost journalistic, in content. They regaled the reader with details concerning the foibles of judicial actors, and pointed out obvious flaws in the process of justice. Almost inevitably, the court systems that were analyzed were compared unfavorably with the ideals of court consolidation and unification. Two examples are Albert Lepawsky's *The Judicial System of Metropolitan Chicago* (1932) and Raymond Moley's *Our Criminal Courts* (1930). This vein in the literature of political science (narrow though it may be) is referenced in such dated bibliographies as Kuhlman's *A Guide to Material on Crime and Criminal Justice* (1939).

VI. FURTHER REFINEMENTS, FEWER ACTIONS: 1930–1939

Despite the impressive progress that was made in reforming the state and federal court systems in the 1920s, interest in judicial administration had begun to peak by 1930. As the Progressive Movement's popularity waned, the court reform agenda lost much of its mass appeal. Similarly, the Great Depression was a serious distraction that bled the enthusiasm of the members of many reform movements (yet which, parenthetically, launched *other* types of reform initiatives). Although the tight-knit group of judicial reformers continued its unrelenting reform campaign, the victories became fewer and fewer as the decade of the 1930s progressed. One dramatic reflection of this fact can be found in the experience of the Chicago Municipal Court that Pound had referred to fondly in 1906. By the early 1930s, "new judicial layers had been added, and the Chicago area found itself with more than two and one-half times as many courts as it had had before the 'reform'" (Wheeler and Whitcomb 1977, 29). Along with the progress up the slippery slope of court reform, a good bit of backsliding had occurred.

A. JUDICIAL ADMINISTRATION LITERATURE AS BOOSTERISM

Much of the judicial administration literature of the early 1930s consisted of descriptions of the reforms that had been implemented up to that point. Given the fact that judicial councils were the most popular component of most state reform efforts (by 1949, 37 states had created such bodies; however, by 1995 only six states continued to use them), many researchers focused on their activities and modes of operation. This was especially true in the social science literature, where most of the very few articles that were written dealt with judicial councils (Aumann 1930; Grant 1928; Sikes 1935). Other researchers recounted the experiences surrounding the rare examples of unified (loosely speaking) state court systems, such as the one that had been implemented in Missouri, and the ones that were being discussed in the states of Kansas, Georgia, Idaho, New Jersey, and Wisconsin (Harley 1932). Another favorite topic of journal articles was the how-to piece that usually concentrated on an after-the-fact look at how reform was achieved in a specific location (and which almost inevitably concluded with the observation that the case study findings were readily applicable elsewhere).

Perhaps the best way to encapsulate the content of judicial administration literature of this (and later) periods is to refer to it as cheerleading for the unified court concept. According to Henry Glick, "most writing about court reform is more like a sales pitch or boosterism than a cool evaluation of the impact of change on court operations" (1982, 28). This phenomenon is largely attributable to the fact that the individuals who were writing about judicial administration were almost always the same ones who were integrally involved in the reform movement itself (except, of course, for the opponents of court reform, whose arguments were often equally non-analytical).

B. Arthur T. Vanderbilt Boosts the Boosters

The court reform movement received a much-needed shot in the arm during the latter part of the 1930s when Arthur T. Vanderbilt emerged as an articulate champion of judicial administration. As president of the ABA, he created a Section on Judicial Administration to study seven distinct topics: the improvement of pre-trial procedures; jury selection; trial practice; the law of evidence; appellate procedure; the control of state administrative agencies; and court organization and procedure. In an article titled "Section of Judicial Administration Launches Program on Wide Front," he argued "the courts exist not for the benefit of either judges or lawyers, but for the sake of citizens who are obliged to litigate their interests" (Vanderbilt 1938, 6). He went on to specify the litigants' "fundamental rights," including (1) a prompt and efficient trial, (2) at a reasonable cost, (3) representation by a competent attorney, (4) before an impartial and competent judge, and (5) with the privilege of review by an appellate tribunal that will render a decision within four months after the appeal is initiated (Vanderbilt 1938, 6).

These rights were used as guiding principles in the Section's assigned task of promulgating standards that were to be adopted by state and local bar associations. Ultimately, the ABA House of Delegates approved 66 resolutions that were presented by the Section, prompting the AJS to call this development "the most important thing that has occurred in respect to civil procedure in our generation" (*Journal of the American Judicature Society* 1938, 66). Reflecting Roscoe Pound's legacy, as well as Vanderbilt's imprint, the resolutions covered such elements as court unification, the need for quarterly judicial statistics, full rule-making power for the courts, and the provision of adequate administrative assistance to the judiciary.

This latter point was soon formalized into one of Vanderbilt's chief reform goals, the establishment of an administrative arm for the courts. Later, as Chief Justice of the New Jersey Supreme Court, Vanderbilt would see this ideal realized with the creation of the Administrative Director of the Courts in 1947.

Vanderbilt was not the first, however, to enjoy the services of a professional administrative arm for the judicial system. Over the grudging acquiescence of Chief Justice Charles Evan Hughes, Congress created the Administrative Office of the United States in 1939. This entity was partly the consequence of the diminished prestige that the federal courts experienced during the Great Depression. The Supreme Court's perceived role in hastening the depression through economically conservative rulings, aggravated by its attempt to kill the New Deal, had created much bad press for the courts and led directly to Franklin D. Roosevelt's famous court packing scheme. Roosevelt's claim that the federal courts were inefficient naturally resulted in his proposal for the creation of a national court administrator, a proposal that Vanderbilt and other court reformers generally supported.

Ultimately, the compromise that was struck resulted in the creation of the Administrative Office that became an agency of the Judicial Conference. While Roosevelt had initially envisioned a powerful court administrator, the Office was not provided with real policy-making authority. Rather, it is termed "the judiciary's housekeeping agency" (Fish 1973, 124). Its director serves at the pleasure of the Supreme Court, and its responsibilities are limited to budget preparation, financial auditing, personnel management (excluding the management of judges), statistical compilation and analysis, space utilization and allocation, and planning (Carp and Stidham 1985, 66–68).

Thus, on the eve of World War II, judicial administration was gradually adding formal organizations, although actual reform progress had slowed considerably since the preceding decades. The reform agenda, however, continued to flourish. Despite a relatively weak and non-empirical body of literature, the quality of thought within the field of judicial administration progressed steadily. Thanks to the intellectual involvement of Vanderbilt, coupled with the ABA's enthusiastic support, court reform stood on the threshold of becoming a much more broad-based movement than had been the case previously.

VII. THE DISTRACTED DECADE: 1940–1949

As was the case with so many intellectual and governmental endeavors in the 1940s, most judicial administration activities were put on hold during the United States' involvement in World War II. For nearly a six-year period, there was a virtual absence of concrete reform attempts, and journal article output lagged behind even the anemic pace that prevailed prior to the war. This fact is aptly illustrated by Gazell's finding that only 139 articles were published during the entire decade, compared to the 224 that appeared during the 1930s. Of the 139, all but three were contained in legal journals (Gazell 1975, 13).

Had the hostilities not interrupted the reform movement, the 1940s may well have been a banner decade for judicial administration. The publication of the ABA's standards of judicial administration in 1938 had reignited interest in the court reform movement within the legal community. With the encouragement of Vanderbilt, the Junior Bar Conference of the ABA initiated a nationwide survey of the administration of justice in 1940. In particular, the survey was intended to assess the judicial administration practices of the 48 states in terms of the ABA's 1938 proposals. The survey examined the status of state judicial systems in all of the seven areas specified by the Section, and added questions probing such topics as judicial selection and tenure and traffic courts.

Near the end of the decade, the findings of this survey were incorporated into an enormous document authored by Vanderbilt. Published in 1949, *Minimum Standards of Judicial Administration* is credited with "breathing life into the ABA standards" and "paving the way toward the actual meaning of the unified court concept" (Ashman and Parness 1974, 18–19). In addition to providing a compendium of information concerning state judicial practices, the document provides an immensely detailed explication of the various components of judicial administration. As such, it is probably the best statement of the conventional wisdom of court management that has ever surfaced.

Another clarification of the unified court concept also appeared during the decade. In a 1940 article titled "Principles and Outline of a Modern Unified Court Organization," the ubiquitous Roscoe Pound articulated his "controlling ideas" of unification. These included unification, conservation of judicial manpower, flexibility, and responsibility. To promote these goals, he recommended a single structured court system divided into "two or three levels or branches," an administrative chief judge assisted by an executive manager and a professional staff (the "court manager"), centralized procedural and rule-making authority (to be vested in the Supreme Court, *not* a judicial council), and the *specialization of judges*, rather than the creation of specialized courts to resolve varying types of disputes (Pound 1940). By this time, Pound had relegated judicial councils to essentially an oversight role involving the monitoring of the chief judge's administrative performance.

For the most part, the remaining judicial administration literature of the decade consisted of numerous court studies in which researchers took close looks at the operation and management of various state and local judicial bodies. Typical of this genre were studies that examined the entire range of court problems (including interagency coordination problems, congestion, inadequately trained support personnel) and which proposed various solutions, most of which sprung from the ABA standards and/or other accepted principles of court unification (see, e.g., Citizens Reform Committee 1948; Lawson 1974, 18; Virtue 1950).

Although social scientists were only peripheral actors in most of this type of research, judicial administration panels first began to appear on the agenda of American Political Science Association meetings during the 1940s. As Russell Wheeler noted in 1975, a "Judicial Administration Round-table" was held at the 1940 APSA convention, and the participants discussed the general topic of "Current Administrative Problems of Federal and State Courts" (Colgrove 1941). Then, in 1946, Arthur Vanderbilt chaired an APSA panel on "The Manpower of the Courts," "with papers by a court administrator, a 'judicial administration consultant,' a state and federal judge, and discussion by Glenn Winters of the American Judicature Society" (Griffith 1950; Wheeler 1975, 1). Thus, at least a few social (and management) scientists were interested in judicial administration by the latter half of the 1940s. Their numbers would later swell, thanks partly to the publication of a "popular press" book that appeared in 1949. Jerome Frank's *Courts on Trial: Myth and Reality in American Justice* attracted an unusual degree of scholarly and popular attention because it described many of the most egregious shortcomings of the judicial system in a stirring commentary. By popularizing the notion that inefficient courts affect almost all of us, Frank's work established an important precedent that was later emulated by many others.

One last event of the 1940s deserves at least a passing mention. After years of activism, punctuated by effective legislative lobbying, Arthur Vanderbilt was finally successful in 1947 at getting his home state of New Jersey to accept a new judicial article. Although this reform did not create a truly unified judicial system, it did engineer a greatly improved structure with centralized management responsibility. Additionally, it created the position of Administrative Director of the Courts, a concept that Vanderbilt had long supported. As Chief Justice of this reformed judicial system, Vanderbilt's hand was strengthened in his relentless attempt to unify the nation's courts. By the end of the decade, the New Jersey example was already making its mark. When the Conference of Commissioners of Uniform State Laws met in 1948, it included provisions for a state court administrator in its model statute. By 1956, sixteen states had created such offices, although their duties varied significantly from state to state (Lawson 1974).

VIII. THE MODERN ERA BEGINS: 1950–1959

The 1950s mark the beginning of what has been called the modern era of judicial administration (Saari 1980). Although the court reform agenda did not change discernibly during the decade, the number and types of individuals who were involved in the field began a slow yet significant expansion. As this more broad-based movement spread, judicial administration ultimately began to spill over its traditionally narrow borders.

A. THE LEGAL GRIP LOOSENS

One of the most important modernizing influences on the field was the creation of the Institute of Judicial Administration in 1952. Founded under the leadership of Arthur Vanderbilt, and affiliated with the New York University School of Law, the Institute immediately began an ambitious research and publications series. Aided by a large research staff, the Institute published reports on an impressive array of issues, including "Checklist Summary of Developments in Judicial Administration" (1954–1958), "A Guide to State Court Systems" (1959), "Judicial Articles— Selected Recent Proposals with Explanatory Comment" (1958), and numerous specialized reports that focused on individual state court systems (see Klein 1963). In addition to spreading the word concerning court reform to a wider academic and professional audience than had previously received the message, the Institute occasionally utilized the services of social scientists and management specialists.

The involvement of increasing numbers of non-legal specialists in judicial administration research had a number of important effects on the subdiscipline. Over time, court reform topics, along with the precepts of unification and consolidation, began to appear in textbooks that were intended for public administration and political science students. W. B. Graves' (1953) text in American state government, for example, included almost 180 pages (out of approximately 950) on such topics as the jury system, judicial organization, administrative dilemmas, and judicial selection and tenure. Similarly, books written for judicial process and constitutional law students in the social sciences began to discuss court structure, state constitutional articles, and the progress of reform (see Berman 1958; Blume and Joiner 1952). In a very real sense, these textbook references to judicial administration reflected the fact that the subject matter was finally becoming a legitimate concern for non-attorneys.

Another important sign of the de-legalization of judicial administration was the renewed interest shown by the American Academy of Political and Social Sciences. After a twenty-year hiatus (see American Academy 1933) in examining judicial administration, the Academy's *Annals* series published a lengthy tome entitled *Judicial Administration and the Common Man* (1953). Individual articles within the volume addressed family court problems, workers' compensation concerns, traffic court operations, probate, accident litigation, jury management, and a variety of administrative and structural concerns.

The chief significance of this work, and others like it (Crane and Elliot 1953), is that it exemplifies a new wave of "legal realism" in academic circles (for a discussion of legal realism, see Frank 1930; Llewellyn 1930). Professors and students came to realize that the *lower courts* have a far greater impact upon the lives of American citizens than do appellate courts. But, due to a phenomenon termed the "upper court myth" (Frank 1949, 222–224), the attention of most scholars had long been fixed on the appellate courts in the belief that the rest of the judicial system was trivial and inconsequential. Thus, most social science research of the period focused on judicial decision making, abstract rules and propositions of law, and attempts to discern the true meaning of appellate decisions (see Munger 1982). By attempting to dismantle this philosophical bias, the legal realists of the 1950s began to shift the attention of researchers away from appellate tribunals and toward trial courts, where the need for administrative improvements happened to be more acute.

Once the attention of non-attorneys was focused on the conditions of lower courts, a number of startling realities surfaced. Urban trial courts were found to have civil jury case delays of up to *five years* (Institute of Judicial Administration 1956), owing in large part to the high rate of automobile-related litigation. The *quality* of local justice also became a major concern, especially as it related to the performance of justices of the peace, mayors' courts, and other judicial officers who generally lacked law degrees. Horror stories concerning the antics of these layperson judges abounded; accounts of judges who could not read and write were common, as were reports that not guilty verdicts were almost unheard of in some judges' chambers because of the fee system—only litigants who were found guilty were required to pay fines and fees, from which the judges often derived their only income (see Sunderland 1945; Tobin 1999; Weygandt 1956). Moreover, inept managerial practices received increased attention in the popular and scholarly presses. In an exposé titled *Courts of Injustice*, Callison (1956) found the administration of justice in America to be a "tragic failure" due to the negative influences of its inadequate administrative infrastructure, poorly qualified judges, and mercenary attorneys. After nearly fifty years of court reform, in 1950 "most state courts had about the same structure and powers that they had one hundred years before" (Hurst 1950, 85).

B. PROFESSIONALIZATION BEGINS

The second major move toward the modernization of judicial administration came with the advent of *professional* court managers during the 1950s. Prior to that time, the legal community's stranglehold on the courts was so complete that even the few court managers who were employed had law backgrounds and biases. As stated by David J. Saari (1980, 6–7): "Within the courts up to approximately 1950, there was little or no room for contemporary management thinking about management problems. The courts used lawyer-like thinking about management problems ... Management was thought to involve primarily 'getting papers filed' and 'sharpening pencils' for the use of the judges on the bench."

Saari attributes a major change in this attitude to the first two truly professional court managers in the country, Edward B. McConnell and Edward C. Gallas. McConnell was appointed Director of the Courts of the State of New Jersey by Arthur Vanderbilt in 1953. A few years later, Gallas assumed the post of Executive Officer of the Los Angeles Superior Court, a position that had been created following a recommendation by Chief Justice Earl Warren. Unlike previous court managers, these two individuals possessed professional management skills: McConnell had degrees in both law and management, while Gallas was a public administrator with no legal background.

The pioneering mark that these two individuals made on the field of judicial administration can scarcely be overstated. Their presence as successful court managers demonstrated to the legal community that "administrative knowledge, in addition to law, was relevant to administering a court system" (Saari 1980, 7). By assuming responsibility over calendaring, public relations, jury management, and a legion of related activities, they freed the judges from time-consuming and distracting tasks. Moreover, they were able to introduce a "management perspective" into their court systems, thereby upgrading the budgeting, staffing, planning, and control functions that typify all complex organizations. Their impact on the discipline was enhanced by the fact that they practiced in two of the largest urban areas in the country, highly visible locations that contributed to the rapid spread of the lessons they learned.

Thus, one of the major new directions in the study of judicial administration had begun. As Gazell mentions in the next chapter in this volume, discussions concerning the proper role, training, education, and duties of professional court managers now occupy center stage in the literature of judicial administration.

IX. THE TURBULENT DECADE: 1960–1969

If the 1950s initiated a de-legalization trend in judicial administration, then the 1960s can be credited with *popularizing* court reform goals. Without question, public awareness and concern about judicial administration was at its zenith during that period. The high level of popular interest was directly attributable to the social turmoil that characterized this cathartic stage in our nation's history. Among the many crises that the nation faced during these years were an unprecedented crime wave, huge increases in divorce rates and juvenile delinquency, President Kennedy's assassination, and widespread social strife brought on by the Civil Rights Movement and opposition to the Vietnam War. Each of these forces and events exerted pressure on the criminal justice system that was terribly overloaded and proved to be inadequate to meet the challenge (Downs 1972; Seymore 1973). As Lawrence Friedman later concluded, "the system of justice was rotten. The left considered it oppressive and unjust; the right complained that it did not work" (1973, 595).

The consequences of this so-called crisis in the courts were predictable. In addition to spawning dozens of study commissions and conferences (Brownell 1970), government began to devote increasing amounts of financial resources to the operation and improvement of the criminal justice system. Throughout it all, however, the theoretical underpinnings of judicial administration changed little.

A. DEVELOPMENTS IN THE PRINCIPLES OF JUDICIAL ADMINISTRATION

For the most part, the judicial administration literature of the 1960s emphasized (1) analyses of court maladies, (2) enthusiastic justifications for court reform, and/or (3) summaries of the changes that were planned, or already implemented, in various locales (see Klein 1976). Court delay was a favored topic (see American Academy of Political and Social Sciences 1960), along with automation and information management applications (Adams 1972; Popp and Kuyendall 1977), jury management (Klein 1976, 476–508), and alternatives to court adjudication (see Pearson 1982). Almost without exception, the authors relied heavily upon either the 1938 ABA standards, *or* a 1962 version of the standards that departed from the earlier draft in a few important respects.

The 1962 model state judicial article included strong language concerning the need for an administrator of the unified court system. It even went so far as to propose that the court administrator be given *constitutional* responsibility for the judicial system's budget, statistics, and related functions. Judicial councils were notably de-emphasized in the standards (they were mentioned only as one less-than-optimal alternative), as were other types of judicial policy-making bodies. Instead, the Supreme Court was vested with rule-making authority over all procedures, jurisdictional issues, rules of evidence, and rules governing bar admissions and conduct (Ashman and Parness 1974, 13–14; ABA 1962). In effect, then, the state Supreme Court was now supreme in every sense of the word. This was a controversial suggestion, especially as it concerned the Supreme Court's control over rules of evidence. Finally, in contrast to earlier two- and three-tier models, the 1962 standards called for a four-tier court system consisting of a supreme court, an intermediate court of appeals, a trial court of general jurisdiction, and a trial court of limited jurisdiction (the magistrate's court).

Another important guide to reformers appeared a few years after the ABA issued its new standards. The President's Commission on Law Enforcement and the Administration of Justice compiled a compendium of court reform suggestions called *Task Force Report: The Courts* (1967). This document relied extensively on the conventional wisdom of court unification, following the lead of the ABA, the AJS, and the National Municipal League. Additionally, professional (expert) court managers were prominently mentioned, as were the needs for "business management practices," modern technology, improved jury management techniques, centralized budgetary control, and more efficient clerical practices (President's Commission on Law Enforcement and the Administration of Justice 1967). As is clearly reflected in this *Report*, improving the management capability of judicial systems, regardless of their overall structures, had become almost as important a goal as systemic reform (although the commission certainly hoped that states would adopt the unified and centralized model that was viewed as the most expeditious route to administrative nirvana). This report, it was later claimed, "served as the impetus for states to revise and reform what can only be termed as extremely outdated and archaic judicial systems" (Berkson 1977a, 12).

B. INSTITUTION BUILDING

Perhaps the most important judicial administration trend that occurred during the 1960s was the *institution building* that took place. In a 1970 summary of the past decade's events, Justice Tom Clark called the 1960s "A Historic Decade in Judicial Improvement" (Clark 1970). Much of the credit is given to the numerous organizations that were created during the 1960s to further the theory and practice of judicial administration. For example, in 1963 the National College of the State Judiciary was established for the purpose of providing continuing education programs to state and local jurists. Through an extensive network of regional and state programs, it now provides educational services to tens of thousands of judges annually. Another important move toward the professionalization of legal services came in the mid-1960s, when the National Association of Trial

Court Administrators and the National Association for Court Administration were founded (the two organizations ultimately merged in 1985).

In 1967, the federal government also added an immensely important organization to its judicial bureaucracy. Under the supervision of Chief Justice Earl Warren, the Judicial Conference sponsored the creation of a research arm for the federal judiciary. Upon its founding, the Federal Judicial Center was given four functions: conducting research and studying the operation of US courts; developing and presenting recommendations to the Judicial Conference; creating, developing, and conducting programs of continuing education for all judicial and quasi-judicial (clerks, etc.) personnel; and providing staff, research, and planning assistance to the Judicial Conference (Berkson 1977, 12). Among its many programs and activities, the Center sponsors New Judges Seminars for newly appointed jurists, it publishes handbooks for judges and ancillary personnel (most notably *The Judge's Bench Book*, that first appeared in 1969), and it routinely summarizes new legal developments and disseminates the information to judicial personnel (see Carp and Stidham 1985, 68–72). Its research staff is multidisciplinary, and issues reports on topics ranging from the impact of management innovations to "reviews of the psychology literature dealing with a jury's competency to evaluate complex fact situations" (Carp and Stidham 1985, 70).

One final event of the 1960s deserves special note. At the conclusion of the decade, newly appointed Chief Justice Warren Burger announced his personal support for a diverse program of court reform and judicial administration initiatives. In speech after speech, he reiterated Roscoe Pound's criticisms of the judicial system and called for both old and new solutions. Among other things, his reform agenda included: procedural standardization and clarification; elimination of diversity jurisdiction; reexamination of the twelve-person jury (with an eye toward reducing its number and/or eliminating the need for unanimity in criminal verdicts); cost reductions in probate proceedings; speedy trial rules (i.e., requiring jurisdictions to bring defendants to trial within a certain period of time); and the increased utilization of technology to expedite the process of justice (see Tamm and Reardon 1981). To these mainly management solutions, he added calls for the expanded use of arbitration, coupled with reductions in the number of malpractice, tort, marriage, custody, and adoption proceedings that end up in court. Thus, he returned to a theme that Chief Justice Taft had sounded in 1914—reducing the courts' burden by minimizing their *inputs* as well as through improving their management capability.

In summary, by the end of the 1960s, the judicial administration pot was boiling wildly. The public was convinced that the courts were poorly managed, and political pressure was being exerted at all levels for systemic reform. Numerous organizations existed to promote judicial administration objectives, and more were on the way. Moreover, an energetic new champion of judicial administration had emerged. Court reform had finally arrived.

X. THE REFORM ONSLAUGHT: 1970–1979

Early in his term as chief justice, Warren Burger added his support to a piece of pending legislation that would create court administrator positions in each of the circuit courts of appeal (that, at the time, numbered eleven; a twelfth and thirteenth were added in 1981 and 1982, respectively). Regarding his congressional testimony on the topic, Burger noted:

> The United States currently has 38 trained astronauts … [but] if this legislation were passed at once we would not begin to fill the positions. We should indeed pass the legislation but we must also take immediate steps to ensure a supply of administrators. We cannot legislate court administrators any more than we can legislate astronauts; they must be trained (Burger 1971a, 4).

The year was 1971. This observation, more than any other single quote, demonstrates just how quickly the field of judicial administration progressed. In 1971, astronauts outnumbered court managers by a ratio of three or four to one. By the end of the decade, professionally trained court managers numbered in the thousands (Saari et al. 1993).

As was noted above, this extraordinary change in the status of judicial administration was signaled repeatedly during the preceding decades. After fifty years of plodding growth, events of the 1960s provided the catalyst that generated an explosion of activity during the 1970s. In addition to creating a completely new profession almost from scratch, theorists and practitioners of judicial administration transformed numerous state court systems, and in the process generated a rich and varied literature.

A. COURT UNIFICATION SPREADS

By far the most visible trend in court reform during the aggressive 1970s was a fairly single-minded pursuit of court unification and consolidation (see Berkson and Carbon 1978; Gazell 1978). Although few states wholeheartedly embraced the components of court unification, most initiated moves in that direction. For the most part, these efforts included consolidation of trial courts, centralization of rule-making and procedural authority with the judicial system, and state assumption of responsibility for the courts' financial and personnel systems. In so doing, the states made major strides toward reducing the number of specialized courts, eliminating overlapping jurisdictions, and standardizing judicial procedures.

When evaluated according to the orthodox yardsticks of judicial performance—i.e., rates of court delay and case backlog, procedural consistency, ease of citizen access to the courts, and efficient use of judges' time—the unification movement seemed to have a highly salutary effect on court management (see, for example, Baar 1980; Cannon 1982). Plotting the path of this progress became a major preoccupation of the field's literature.

The evaluation benchmark for all court reforms during the latter decades of the twentieth century was the ABA's *Standards Relating to Court Organization* (1974; revised again in 1990). The 1974 version of this reform bible was patterned after the 1978 Parker-Vanderbilt Standards, yet it was far more comprehensive. Using the unified court concept as "the axis on which the other recommendations revolve" (Volcansek 1977, 23), the *Standards* departed from previous pronouncements by recommending a three-tier court system consisting of a supreme court, intermediate appellate court, and trial courts of general jurisdiction. Earlier models had generally provided for two tiers, to which the *Standards* added the intermediate appellate tribunal. The Supreme Court was given total control over its input of cases through the elimination of any rights of appeal; all cases come to the court through discretionary avenues (*certiorari*).

The remaining provisions of the *Standards* elaborated on earlier themes of the reform movement. Merit selection of judges was a primary goal, as was the relatively new concept of using a board of judicial inquiry to recommend removal of disabled and/or corrupt judges (Braithwaite 1971; Frankel 1970; Swain 1976). This contrasts with the traditional methods of judicial discipline and removal—impeachment, address, and resolution. According to virtually all commentators, such legislatively based techniques are unduly cumbersome, politically motivated, and infrequently invoked (Abraham 1986, 40–50). By empowering the judicial system to punish its own members through an internal investigation process, it was hoped that the judiciary will be more effectively (and neutrally) policed.

Another major refinement contained in the 1974 ABA *Standards* was the attention paid to the need for the judiciary to determine its own rules of procedure; this power was vested entirely in the state's Supreme Court. Relatedly, the system's chief justice was designated as the chief administrative officer of the court. His powers were to extend to such areas as the assignment of judicial and non-judicial personnel, supervision of planning and financial matters, and defining the policy agenda.

Grounded on the classical principle of unity of command, the chief administrative officer concept quickly displaced all alternative managerial configurations that have intermittently been advanced. It was perceived as being a logical outgrowth of the Supreme Court's pre-eminent role in the administrative structure; as the first among equals within the Supreme Court, the chief justice occupies the ideal vantage point from which to coordinate the system's activities. While some thought was devoted to having the Supreme Court make administrative decisions *en banc*, or to assign oversight functions to a judicial council composed of judges drawn from throughout the court system (a format employed in only a few states and the federal government), arguments against this rule-by-committee format were usually persuasive. Ease and simplicity of action, as well as uniformity in result, are the anticipated advantages. Moreover, centralization of authority is made more palatable by the fact that the chief justice is not intended to be a boss in the classical bureaucratic sense. Instead, the role is meant to be that of a facilitator and coordinator. Implicit in the arrangement is the expectation that the chief justice will devote a great deal of energy to consensus building and consultation prior to action. To do otherwise in a professional organization, especially one with highly pronounced norms of independence and autonomy, would invite disaster.

The role of the professional staff was also much more succinctly defined in the 1974 *Standards*. Specified duties of the court administrator were to include calendar management, supervision of non-judicial personnel, budgeting, administration of auxiliary services, monitoring of court operations, planning, statistics gathering, and operation of the management information system (ABA 1974; Volcansek 1977, 23). In effect, the administrative office of the court came to be viewed almost as an administrative assistant to the chief justice and Supreme Court. The office was expected to handle housekeeping functions and to provide whatever support services are necessary; it was not intended to play any substantive role in the purely judicial or policy-making functions of the Supreme Court.

Within this exciting reform milieu, it is not surprising that most of the court management literature consisted of panoramic national surveys (Berkson and Carbon 1978; Gazell 1978) or state-based case studies (Hays 1977; Powell 1980) of court reform. Another large body of literature consisted of the hundreds of case studies that dealt with minor structural revisions of individual courts and/or court systems. This type of study most often appeared in law journals and bar association publications. Its focus was usually "to describe the legal, organizational and political contexts in which campaigns to unify courts occur and to describe the structural and procedural changes that have occurred as a result" (Henderson and Kerwin 1982, 452).

Late in the decade, some attention turned to what might be called the discovery of non-judicial personnel in the courthouse. The fact that the courts have not traditionally controlled the clerks, bailiffs, and recorders on whom they depend for critical services became more troublesome as judicial systems attempted to come to grips with their administrative problems. Due to the absence of a direct line of administrative authority between the chief judge and all employees in the courthouse, coordination and cooperation often suffer. This issue is especially acute in locations where court clerks, sheriffs, and other officials who provide essential administrative support to the courts are popularly elected. Thus, giving judges control over all of their support staffs became an additional component of the reform agenda, as did the suggestion that state governments eliminate the antiquated practice of electing court clerks (Berkson and Hays 1976; ABA *Standards* 1974; Fetter and Scott 1980). And, as court administrators began to challenge the managerial influence of court clerks and other non-judicial personnel, many researchers took a look at the resulting conflicts (Berkson and Hays 1976b; Mort and Hall 1980).

A representative example of the research that was conducted in this area is that of (Berkson and Hays 1976; see also Hays 1978). Their study focused on the political and administrative warfare that broke out between elected court clerks and appointed court administrators in the Florida judicial system. The conflict initially arose when Law Enforcement Assistance Administration (LEAA) funds made it possible for the chief judges in the newly unified court system to appoint professional court managers as their administrative assistants. Because their functions and duties significantly overlapped the traditional responsibilities of court clerks (e.g., courthouse management, record keeping, jury management), many clerks felt that their turf was being invaded. And, due to the clerks' more established political base, and their traditional stranglehold on the county judicial machinery, most clerks were able (at least temporarily) to ward off the challenge that the court administrators represented. Thus, the administrators were not immediately able to assume the expansive managerial role that was envisioned for them in the ABA *Standards*. Instead, many performed only tangential functions (data gathering and analysis, for example) that did not truly involve them in the administrative life of the court system. Studies of this type represented the initial efforts to *evaluate* the impacts of specific reform measures, a trend that accelerated in later years.

B. MANAGEMENT REFORMS

While structural changes were certainly the most visible outgrowth of the reform movement, the field's most pervasive impact probably came in the area of improved management practices. Judicial administration's focus on upgrading the internal management capability of individual court systems led David Saari to term the 1970s the "infrastructure decade" (Saari 1980, 27). In essence, it was judicial administration's task to assist court systems in catching up with the managerial and technical accomplishments of other public bureaucracies. To accomplish this feat, judicial administration was compelled to create "an infrastructure of organizations, a research base, and a method of publishing and disseminating new knowledge" and of educating practitioners (Saari 1980, 7). One indication of the seriousness of this struggle is found in Downie's comment that, as late as 1965, "it took Chief Justice (Earl) Warren three years to get a typewriter in the clerk's office of the U.S. Supreme Court and to stop the making of docket entries in longhand there" (Downie 1972, 140).

Given their slow start on the road toward administrative modernism, the courts' accomplishments during the decade were remarkable. Many court systems concentrated on computer and technological applications, paper flow improvements, and enhanced space and architectural design, including ergonomics. These types of reforms, in turn, prompted a flood of explanatory and promotional literature detailing the dimensions and methods of records management (Carbon 1977; Soloman and Doan 1981), the design and maintenance of courthouse space (Sobel 1972; Wong 1973), and management information system (MIS) applications (Freed 1972; Gazell 1977).

More important, the core management functions were significantly improved. In contrast to past practices, most courts started to utilize modern planning (State Court Project 1977; Wheeler 1977a, 1977b, 1979), staffing (Gazell 1974; Lawson, Ackerman, and Fuller 1979), budgeting (Baar 1975; Lawson, Ackerman, and Fuller 1979) and control (Anderson 1977) techniques. And, remarkably, a number even made use of relatively sophisticated strategies, such as the application of queuing theory to jury management problems (Winters 1971) and the use of management science techniques to solve space allocation, resource distribution, and an array of other dilemmas that confront the courts (Flanders 1978; Nagel, Neef, and Munshaw 1978).

A related trend in the literature dealt with management solutions to court delay. Numerous authors discussed various "jury management" strategies (AJS 1971; Church 1982; Zeisel 1973), while others focused on "the courtroom workgroup" as "the starting point for improvements in the efficiency of court proceedings" (Henderson and Kerwin 1982, 454). Integration and coordination of the tasks performed by the participants in the courtroom came to be seen as relevant to judicial performance, as did the informal associations and customs that largely dictate their behavior (Eisenstein and Jacob 1977; Nardulli 1978).

For obvious reasons, these efforts to enhance the administrative capability of the judicial system were largely bottom-up in nature. Instead of imposing change from the outside, the field's focus was (and continues to be) to *train and educate* a cadre of professional managers to upgrade administrative practices in the courts. Similarly, continuing education has been a chief concern, as has the provision of technical assistance through publication and consultant services. During the

1970s, funds provided by the LEAA were instrumental in furthering these pursuits, as well as providing many court systems with the money to hire their first professional managers (Fisher 1981). These efforts received a major boost in 1970, when the Institute for Court Management formally began its intensive educational program for court executives. The following year, the National Center for State Courts was established to provide policy guidance, as well as to engage in research, publication, and technical assistance activities. Both entities soon began to publish their own journals—ICM's *Justice System Journal* and the National Center's *State Court Journal*—as a means of disseminating the message to a wider audience.

Although specialized institutes continued to train the bulk of our professional court managers, a few formal Masters of Judicial Administration (MJA) programs were thriving by the 1980s. The MJA programs at American University and the University of Southern California were best known, but nearly forty other schools offered coursework in the field by the end of the decade.

The development of these programs was an important (if fleeting) step in the progress of the discipline, for they provided a *core faculty* of court management scholars, as well as a readily identifiable market for further publications in the field. Since the appearance of the first text in judicial administration—Friesen, Gallas, and Gallas' groundbreaking *Managing the Courts* that came out in 1971—several other texts and readers surfaced. These books made an important contribution to the field by organizing the discipline and by defining its basic components. Among the most noteworthy were: Nelson's huge casebook, *Judicial Administration and the Administration of Justice* (1974); Gazell's *State Trial Courts as Bureaucracies* (1975); Berkson, Hays and Carbon's text (with readings) *Managing the State Courts* (1977); Wheeler and Whitcomb's text (with readings) *Judicial Administration* (1977); and Saari's *American Court Management: Theory and Practice* (1982).

Once significant numbers of court managers had been trained and placed in judicial organizations, a natural trend in the literature was to describe their activities and assess their progress. Commencing with Saari's *Modern Court Management: Trends in the Role of the Court Executive* (1970), numerous studies and analyses appeared. Most resembled show and tell exercises, in which court managers from various locations would relate war stories about life in the courthouse (Hays and Berkson 1977; Malech 1973). Much more thought-provoking writings also became common, however. Discussions of role conflicts (e.g., the Hays and Berkson study discussed earlier), change strategies, and the pitfalls that one encounters in attempting to reform a traditional bureaucracy appeared frequently (Butler 1977; Corso 1980; Dubois 1982c; Martineau 1974). These were precursors to the critical assessments that blossomed during more contemporary times.

XI. MATURATION AND FINE TUNING: THE LATE TWENTIETH AND EARLY TWENTY-FIRST CENTURIES

After the halcyon days of the 1970s, the court reform field entered a relatively turbulent phase in its continuing (and uncertain) development. The sources of this turbulence are varied and complex, but most can be traced to the economic and political forces that still shape the broader field of public administration. Terms such as reinvention, retrenchment, downsizing, TELS (tax and expenditure limitations), and the conservative revolution had as much relevance to court administrators as they did (and do) to city managers and state agency directors. All of these groups faced unrelenting pressures to achieve greater efficiency, to do more with less, and to devise imaginative new ways to accomplish old tasks.

Although the era of fiscal stress certainly complicated the professional lives of court managers, in many cases depriving judicial systems of all but the barest necessities for continued operation (DeBenedictis 1994; Orrick 1990), it may be only indirectly to blame for a discernable slackening of progress toward court unification and consolidation. By the beginning of the 1980s, every state court system had already adopted many of the recommendations of the ABA. The relatively easy reforms had largely been accomplished, leaving in most cases the much more difficult (and politically charged) structural and procedural changes that are the prerequisites to true unification. Hundreds of specialized courts had been eliminated, thousands of court managers had been hired, tens of thousands of computers had been bought, and hundreds of thousands of management practices had been upgraded. A notable gap in the reform agenda, however, was the complete centralization of judicial bureaucracies that was emphasized in the ABA *Standards.*

Part of the reluctance to centralize judicial bureaucracies was attributable to the fact that decentralization—making government more responsive to the people by addressing problems closer to home—became the rage in the late twentieth century. Allowing bureaucrats (even if they happen to be chief justices) in distant state capitals to make decisions for local judges was not as politically acceptable as it may once have been. Devolution of authority to lower and lower levels of government became a reality, even in many court systems. And because the structural and procedural reforms that had already been implemented did not appear to be the panaceas that were once hoped, politicians began to look for quicker fixes to the problems of the justice system. Under extreme pressure to make the courts more efficient, the legal community found itself contending with an ever-expanding array of reform proposals emanating from politicians and the public. As will be seen, this increasingly led to externally imposed reforms that, in most cases, reduced the caseloads that courts must process. A final detour on the way to court centralization was provided by the academic community. For those who were already somewhat skeptical about the unification agenda, theoretical and empirical support could be found in the evaluative literature that had begun to emerge during the 1970s and which subsequently blossomed.

A. THE EVALUATIVE LITERATURE: QUESTIONING THE CONVENTIONAL WISDOM

As has been repeatedly noted, the court management literature's close ties to the reform movement resulted in a corpus of work that was largely descriptive and promotional. Reform was (and is), by its basic nature, "more advocacy than evaluation" (Wheeler 1979, 135). Thus, until the 1980s, the central core of the field—the unified court concept and its various good government components— was treated as if it had been handed down on one of Moses' tablets. Commentators inside and outside of the legal community came to accept the conventional wisdom of court reform with barely a whisper of opposition or true inquiry. The advantages of centralization, consolidation, merit selection of judges, and the like were automatically *assumed*, even though almost no empirical studies had been conducted to determine whether these reforms actually exert beneficial effects on court operations or the quality of justice.

One of the first individuals to question the conventional wisdom was (Gallas 1976, 1979; Gallas and Rausch 1982). He used concepts from *contingency theory* to question whether or not centralization is the appropriate organizational arrangement for courts. Contingency theory's major focus is to explain the impact that numerous variables have on the structures, processes, and behaviors of complex organizations. In so doing, theorists have successfully identified a number of organizational relationships that seem to hold together after repeated empirical tests. For example, hierarchical (centralized) organizations tend to perform best in stable environments, while flat (decentralized) structures are most appropriate in rapidly changing environments. Using contingency theory's claim that there is *no* "one best way" to organize a bureaucracy, Gallas analyzed the environmental and structural components of courts and concluded that a *decentralized* format may well be more consistent with contemporary organizational theory. This conclusion was predicated on the judicial system's professional nature, coupled with its heterogeneous environment and complex internal composition. According to Mintzberg (1979), Galbraith (1973) and other contingency theorists, these conditions would ordinarily call for a *flexible* organizational structure and a decentralized decision-making apparatus.

Once Gallas first emerged as a voice in the wilderness, an expanding group of social scientists joined the chorus. Carl Baar (1982), for example, maintained that the conventional wisdom has caused reformers to commit a grave error: "… creative solutions devised to deal with distinctive managerial and political problems are discouraged in favor of adopting uniform models propounded by national bodies" (1982, 284). Baar cited several examples in which "cookbook" solutions have proven to be terribly naive, as when one reform group recommended the "complete state takeover of court financing, in spite of a highly charged political environment and the absence of adequate evidence that funding was either a problem or a means to improving court operations". Other researchers concluded that effective court reform requires aggressive planning *which involves the people who are most directly affected* (see, e.g., Holmes 1994). Implicit in this conclusion is the realization that courts are largely *local* institutions, and their reform needs to be tailored accordingly.

Dahlin (1986), meanwhile, provided a broad review of the research that both supported and refuted court unification. Borrowing from Gallas' contingency discussion, he concluded that *both* centralization and decentralization "can be taken too far" (Dahlin 1986, viii). In effect, he called for a more cautious approach to court reform in which each judicial system's unique character is taken into account before any quick-fix solutions are prescribed. At a minimum, reformers needed to recognize that a variety of useful court structures can exist within environments characterized by high decentralization. "Unavoidably, courts have to accommodate local peculiarities, problems, and circumstances" (Graham 1993, 117).

In essence, then, critics in recent decades have argued that the criminal justice system should design *local* responses to idiosyncratic local problems, thereby necessitating a flexible organizational arrangement (Broder, Porter, and Smathers 1981). Still other researchers wondered aloud why court reformers had not been more attentive to the political and social implications of court reform (Good 1980; Sarat 1981). In the process of centralizing and unifying judicial systems, aren't some groups losing while others gain? As Broder, Porter, and Smathers (1981) concluded in their study of a city–county court merger in Athens, Georgia, the consolidation had several "hidden consequences" for different groups of citizens. Specifically, the rural (county) residents were advantaged by the reorganization, while the city residents suffered a relative disadvantage. This resulted from the fact that the average cost per case increased for city residents and decreased for county residents; moreover, the rural citizens were found to have much higher levels of policy compatibility (i.e., higher levels of satisfaction with the court's policies) than their urban counterparts.

In a similar examination of trial court practices in several states, Carl Baar (1993) concluded that the blind adherence to ABA *Standards* on trial court consolidation generates unwanted and unanticipated consequences. By upsetting delicate political accommodations, collapsing a two- or three-tier court system into one all-purpose court (which is what the ABA proposes) might "undermine the rule of law by subjecting the trial courts to even more partisan pressures than currently exist" (Baar 1993, 184). Baar concluded that the ABA's prescribed model is "unnecessary and insufficient… the ABA standards are more likely to curb creative efforts to improve the courts than to spur implementation of needed reforms" (Baar 1993, 184). Barr's irritation seems to be especially inflamed because the ABA revised its *Standards* in 1990. Despite widespread questioning of the unification model, the basic thrust of the ABA's 1974 recommendations was not altered. Other than several relatively insignificant revisions concerning such topics as alternative dispute resolution (ADR), the expanded use of technology, and the imposition of judicial performance evaluation programs (ABA 1990), the ABA's love affair with the centralized model of court management remained intact.

Thanks partly to these many expressions of concern, evaluation, and assessment of specific court reforms spiked for a short while in the 1980s and 1990s. Expansion in this type of scholarly attention led to a 1989 Conference on Empirical Research in Judicial Administration (Nelson 1989), and to various Roundtables focusing on the remaining gaps in the research record

(Boyum 1992). Case studies of unified court systems appeared (Baar 1993; Tarr 1981), as did empirical analyses of specific structural and procedural reforms (Flango 1981; Hudzik 1985).

Although much of this literature was highly critical of dogmatic reform prescriptions, some of the research supported the proposition that unification has positive effects on the quality of court services and community attitudes concerning judicial practices (Winberry 1980). Where highly fragmented courts are extant, or where overlapping jurisdictions prevail, some level of consolidation is usually an essential prerequisite before other reforms can make much headway. In these situations, almost all analyses concluded that consolidation and unification have reduced overlapping jurisdictions, minimized the waste of judicial manpower, and simplified the process of justice in state and local government (Lawson and Howard 1991).

Despite the existence of some support for the unified model, there was no real consensus among court reformers about the proper way to proceed. Many academics and practitioners argued that all court systems should feel free to experiment with alternative structural and procedural configurations if their local environments warrant. Others continued to embrace the conventional wisdom of unification. To this point in time, neither side has emerged victorious. A major contribution of the research was, notably, that the literature began to recognize the existence of a "post-unification approach to organizational design" (Lipscher and Conti 1991). Eschewing simplistic prescriptions, this post-unification model "seeks statewide cohesiveness and coordination without heavy reliance on command and control mechanisms" (Lipscher and Conti 1991, 668). Through the use of broad performance standards that are complemented with decentralized decision networks, the new model promotes a bottom-up approach to court reform. Flexibility and responsiveness to local needs are valued (by some, anyway) more than conformity to an externally imposed ideal.

Interestingly enough, this new vision is far more than just a theoretical construct. It found legislative expression in the Civil Justice Reform Act of 1990, the most significant piece of federal law concerning the court system in at least a decade (the nearest competitor was the 1983 change in the Federal Rules of Civil Procedure that greatly increased district court judges' control over scheduling and case management). Intended as a partial solution to the problems of high costs and excessive delay in the federal courts, the act implemented reform "from the bottom up" (Plotnikoff 1991, 232). In effect, each court was empowered to design and implement civil justice expense and delay reduction plans, and to introduce case-tracking systems. The act emphasized the value of decentralized decision making and the benefits of local solutions targeted at local problems. The systematic use of judicial councils and combined meetings of court administrators and chief judges are implied as a means to promote coordination. This approach to "coordinated decentralization" (Lipscher and Conti 1991, 668) was also employed in the US Circuit Courts of Appeal and in several state court systems (Cavanagh 1993; Lamber and Luskin 1992).

Another vein in the empirical literature that seems to refute facets of the conventional wisdom also appeared in the 1990s. Merit selection of judges had attracted a considerable amount of attention because it was so widely accepted as a cornerstone of court reform. Although merit selection has a great deal of intuitive and visceral appeal, no one has demonstrated that judges selected through a merit procedure are somehow better than those who reach the bench by other means (Hays 1993). Invariably, politics surrounds even merit appointment processes, causing most merit selections to be gamed by the participants. As a result, critics often complain that merit plans favor "politically and professionally connected attorneys" (Knutson 2002, 206). Unfortunately for proponents, there is precious little evidence supporting the ABA's adamant position that merit selection improves the quality of justice and lessens political influence on state courts. Indeed, recent research by Hanssen (2002) suggests a more selfish explanation for lawyers' support for the merit plan. Hanssen reports that merit procedures increase the political influence of attorneys by placing them in prominent positions on selection committees. Furthermore, merit selection helps fill the coffers of law firms by increasing the amount of litigation in state courts. Lawyers, therefore, have self-interested reasons to promote merit plans, making their altruistic arguments for such plans less credible.

Levin's (1977) comparison of judges in Pittsburgh and Minneapolis produced more surprising results regarding merit selection. It was observed that those selected through a merit procedure (the Minneapolis judges) were far harsher on defendants than were judges who made their way to the bench through political channels (the Pittsburgh judges). A major portion of the variance was attributed to the fact that almost all of the judges in Minneapolis had been in private practice before being elevated to the bench, while most of the Pittsburgh judges had been employed in low-level political offices. Levin concluded that this aspect of their backgrounds caused the Minneapolis judges to apply universalistic criteria ("to protect society") to their sentencing decisions, while the Pittsburgh judges were prompted to apply particularistic criteria ("concern for the defendant as an individual"). As a consequence of these findings, enthusiasm for merit selection procedures has tapered off significantly since 1980 (Knutson 2002).

B. DEFINING LEADERSHIP ROLES: 1980–1994

Perhaps the only group of ABA recommendations that received broad support from the empirical record is the use of professional court administrators. Although there was plenty of evidence that court managers were not living up to the exalted image that is presented in the reform literature (Gallas and Gallas 1991; Tobin 1999), most commentators began to realize that the earlier model was unrealistic. Those who earnestly believed that court managers could ultimately function as the key decision makers in judicial organizations—such as is sometimes the case with, for example, hospital administrators—did not fully understand the nature of courthouse operations. Judges are extremely reluctant to relinquish their hold on the internal life of the courthouse, and almost always insist that their court administrators play a relatively restricted (if not passive) role of assistant to the chief judge.

Once this less ambitious view of the court administrator achieved wide currency, the profession was in a better position to talk realistically about the contributions that court managers *could* make to the judicial bureaucracy. Within this context, the record improved. Court management established itself (more or less) as an accepted professional category, and its practitioners could be found in almost every court system of reasonable size in the United States by the 1990s (Saari et al. 1993). Many were making significant strides in legitimizing and enriching their positions within the traditionalistic court setting (Dahlin 1986; Saari 1982; Stott 1982). Much of the progress came on the heels of the technological revolution that placed a premium on up-to-date management expertise. And where the offices of (elected) court clerks had not been abolished, court managers and clerks often worked out compromises concerning their relative areas of responsibility. Clerks, for the most part, retained authority over courthouse space, county records, and the quasi-judicial staff (deputy clerks, primarily), while court executives increasingly were entrusted with jury functions, data management, budgeting, and other support activities that directly related to court (not county) business. In effect, a truce was called in many judicial circuits. Just as other new and emerging professions once went through painful and turbulent births, court management's passage through its embryonic stage was stressful for the people who were directly affected. Given the court system's firm grip on tradition, it was quite predictable that change would come only grudgingly.

Not all theorists, however, were comfortable with the minimalist vision of the court administrator's role that emerged in both theory and practice. Stott (1982) for instance, argued that the literature advocates an excessively narrow and constrained role for court managers. To remedy the dilemma, he recommended that judges and administrators form a management team in which responsibility is shared. Notably, Stott was one of the first researchers to suggest that court managers need to assume increased responsibility over some functions that are essentially "judicial" in nature, including "distribution of jurisdiction," judicial performance, and "the quality and quantity of litigation" (Stott 1982, 171). Drawing on the proposition that the legal profession does not have a monopoly on wisdom concerning the court system, he believes that court managers can enter into a *partnership* with judges. This view of an expanded role for the court manager became a frequent discussion topic within the professional literature (Zaffarano 1985, 1988), yet the number of success stories is not very high. Many judicial officials argue that court managers need significant amounts of independence to be effective courthouse performers, but only the truly fortunate (and/or extraordinarily competent) court executives seemed to achieve this ideal (Orrick 1990).

Once the reformers began to lower their sights in regard to the intended role of professional court managers, the issue of *judicial leadership* assumed critical importance. If judges are going to be the *de facto* conductors of the court reform orchestra, then the legal profession needs to recognize that fact and deal with it accordingly. Stated bluntly, court modernization is unlikely to occur in the absence of effective leadership by chief judges and their associates (Faerman, DiPadova, and Quinn 1993).

For this reason, more and more attention began to be paid to the attitudes, capabilities, and output of the judiciary. In addition to providing greatly expanded training opportunities (Gallas 1987), court systems routinely began to provide judges and court administrators with consultative assistance concerning their administrative styles and/or "best practices" (Hendrickson 1996; McConnell 1991; Stupak 1991). Moreover, to stimulate improved performance, formal output measures and performance evaluation instruments surfaced (Graham 1993). These trends are all evident in the 1990 version of the ABA *Standards* that advocate greatly upgraded judicial education programs and sophisticated systems of judicial performance measurement. Related developments included a growing propensity among legislators and state supreme courts to rely more heavily on the contributions of lower court judges. Also, many states began to tighten their requirements for such posts as magistrate and justice of the peace. Recognizing the risks associated with incompetent judicial officials, the states began to require higher educational credentials for appointment. Likewise, standardized training programs and the dissemination of procedural manuals (Bench Books) became common. As was noted above, decentralization of some judicial activities has thrust a spotlight into the offices of trial court judges. By enlisting the lower court judiciary in efforts to enhance judicial performance, reformers hope to add variety and creativity to the court modernization movement.

C. TINKERING AT THE MARGINS: 1995–2005

The development and maturation of functional administrative structures and professional norms throughout the state and federal judiciaries prompted scholars interested in court administration to shift their attention away from large-scale, comprehensive reforms such as unification in favor of more narrowly focused research on topics important to court administrators such as case management, jury systems, high-tech innovations, and therapeutic justice. This scholarship produces information that allows judicial officers to fine tune their existing operational structures and procedures to improve the administration of justice. As a result, such scholarly works are well received by the court community. The research conducted over the past decade can be divided into two broad categories: (1) evaluating traditional structures and practices, and (2) analyzing innovations and reform efforts. Each will be discussed in more detail later in this section.

1. The Academic Component: Where Have All the Scholars Gone?

Despite the need to address a myriad of important questions, academic interest in judicial administration diminished significantly in the late twentieth century. This phenomenon is evident in the small number of journal articles devoted to the topic since the early 1980s, the majority of which have been single-case studies of particular courts or state judicial systems. Furthermore, a large percentage of this published work was not authored by academics interested in studying questions in a systematic manner, but by practitioners writing about the experiences of their local jurisdictions. One reason for the paucity of research produced by academics is the attrition of old guard university faculty who exhibited an interest in court administration. Since the 1970s, there has been a notable lack of new blood coming into the discipline. And, as faculty retired or otherwise became inactive, no group of disciples had been trained to take their place.

The causes of this striking trend are murky (to say the least), but are probably related to the status of academic programs devoted to training the next generation of court managers. Stated simply, these too have undergone an extreme case of atrophy. The premier programs of old—such as those at the University of Southern California and American University—had essentially disappeared by the year 2000 (Hartley and Bates 2005). For the most part, judicial administration is merely taught as a single course, or as part of a more generic program that is not expressly designed to train court managers. Predictably, the result has become a self-fulfilling prophecy. With few academic programs focusing on the preparation and placement of court managers, there is not much of a demand for faculty in the field. Moreover, the few students who elect to specialize in court administration exit their programs with only ill-defined career opportunities. There are still a large number of court administrators in practice, but very few academic programs that cater to their needs. Instead, the demand appears to be filled through more traditional avenues. Most court managers are attorneys who have been hired by chief judges. They refine their skills, to the extent possible, by attending certificate programs such as those offered by the Institute of Court Management ((ICM), which now focuses on helping practitioners upgrade their skills through workshops and short seminars). Except for a very small number of degree opportunities, the Master of Judicial Administration (MJA) degree is nearly defunct.

Another cause for the decline in academic interest is likely the partial split between political science and public administration. Since the 1970s, most public administration programs separated from their parent political science departments and established themselves as stand-alone units. Public administration scholars saw themselves as working in a new discipline outside of political science and devoted themselves to studying the operations of executive branch agencies. To these scholars, the judiciary was viewed as an external principle (somewhat like the legislature) that influenced executive agency decision making and operations, but seldom warranted study as a unique public institution. This is not surprising given the newness and small size of judicial administration compared to the executive branch bureaucracy. For political science scholars, the split with public administration relegated scholarship on administrative issues within their discipline as largely tertiary. Successful careers in political science were difficult to build on the study of bureaucracy and public administration. As a result, public law scholars within the discipline focused their energies elsewhere. The split most probably also contributed to a lack of interaction between public law and public administration faculty, making knowledge of each others' subfields and collaborative projects less likely.

The lack of academic interest does not mean that scholarship on court administration has fallen off the map. In fact, the last 10 years have yielded some encouraging signs. Several younger scholars have rediscovered judicial administration and begun to publish articles on the topic in major public administration, public law, and multidisciplinary journals such as *Public Administration Review, Law and Society Review,* and *Public Choice.* While the numbers of articles are small, their appearance in prestigious academic outlets is recognition by university scholars that studying the administration of justice is important within their disciplines. Regardless of this newfound interest by some academics, the scholarly contributions made by practitioners should not be overlooked. The fact that court administrators and judges are imparting their insights and experiences in scholarly journals such as *Judicature* and *Justice System Journal* (both of which are more likely than the more prestigious academic journals to be read by other practitioners) can only help to improve the practice of administering justice as well as offer starting points for larger-scale academic studies. Should academics' interest continue to grow in coming years, a relationship between practitioner and academic scholars such as is found in the larger field of public administration may develop that can work to improve both theory and practice. A discussion of the research conducted over the last decade follows.

2.   Evaluating Traditional Structures and Practices

As mentioned earlier, a significant portion of the scholarship published over the past 10 years evaluates traditional administrative structures and practices in the judiciary. With this research, scholars attempt to find out what works, where problems exist, and what solutions might be effective at eliminating or reducing any shortcomings that are identified. For the most part, this research is devoid of theory, concentrating instead on substantive issues and the practical relevance of the findings produced.

One vein of this research examines judicial leadership. This is a natural progression given the focus during the previous 15 years on leadership roles and boundaries in the judiciary. The most recent research has centered on the managerial dilemmas faced by judges in leadership positions as well as the activities of individual judges carrying out their management functions.

In regards to managerial difficulties facing judges, it is well documented that the decentralized nature of the judiciary, where no one actor sits at the top of a hierarchy with direct control over all aspects of the institution, makes it difficult for judges in leadership positions to gain compliance from and cooperation with important actors working within their jurisdictions (see Tobin 1999). Herbert Jacob (1997) adds that the leadership role of judges is complicated even further by the *loosely coupled* nature of many of the tasks they perform. Loose coupling in this context refers to the inability of leaders to produce predictable responses when they take action. For example, judges are fairly insulated from each other on a day-to-day basis. When one judge takes an action intended to change the way others behave, many judges will never become aware of it. Others, because they know the leader is unlikely to observe whether they change their behavior, will simply ignore the action. As a result, it is difficult for judicial leaders to know how and to what extent they are having an impact on court operations. Jacob argues that loose coupling makes broad changes nearly impossible, forcing judicial leaders to settle for incremental change; and causes local courts to be more responsive to powerful local clients than to their judicial supervisors.

Despite the difficulties judge supervisors have in controlling many of their subordinates, judges can be effective managers. Paul Wice's account of the innovative leadership provided by Judge George Nicola, a state court judge in New Jersey (Wice 1995a), provides one example. Wice shows that through aggressive and creative leadership, one judge can make profound improvements in the system of justice. During his twenty-year career in the New Jersey courts, Nicola designed and introduced a rich array of innovative programs, not the least of which were: the "Scared Straight" program that discourages juvenile delinquency by exposing young offenders to hardened felons and the rigors of prison life; and "vertical case management," by which cases are expedited through the court system through the assignment of "case supervisors." Judge Nicola's extraordinary legacy of administrative innovations offers eloquent testimony to the centrality of judicial leadership to the court reform enterprise (Wice 1995b). Wice's work is complemented by Stephen L. Wasby's examination of the leadership of Judge Alfred T. Goodwin, Chief Judge of the Ninth US Circuit (2002). Wasby takes a detailed look at the multitude of tasks chief judges must perform, revealing that judicial leaders cannot command but must persuade to achieve their goals because their positions do not provide them with the authority to force compliance. This reality suggests that judicial leaders would be wise to adopt more bottom-up leadership tools such as self-directed work teams (see Zaffarano 1995) and total quality management (see Hendrickson 1996).

Another avenue of research in recent years has focused on measuring judicial performance, with particularly emphasis on the performance of judges. Judicial supervisors, attorneys, and citizens all have an interest in ensuring that judges are competent to hold office and free from bias. Because it is impossible to come up with objective measures of performance along these dimensions, the primary mechanism for evaluating judges has been surveys administered to lawyers, litigants, citizens, and/or other court participants (such as jurors or witnesses). Surveys are by no means perfect—the wording of questions and the rating scales employed can bias results

(Bernick and Pratto 1995); bias can also occur if response rates are low or if surveys are sent to a single group, such as lawyers (Esterling 1999). Biased measures are a real concern because research shows that citizens use survey results to help them decide how to vote during judicial elections (Esterling 1999; Greenstein et al. 2002). Additionally, surveys generally provide judges with their only feedback concerning their performance. Thus, judges interested in improving their performance often change their behaviors in ways suggested by the survey data (Brody 2004; Esterling 1999). Erroneous results, obviously, have the potential to cause citizens and judges to make bad choices that could damage the effectiveness of the courts. Court administrators, therefore, must be careful in how they construct their measures and implement their survey programs.

Surveys are not the only way to evaluate judicial performance. A particularly effective method involves asking volunteers from outside of the court system to sit in on court proceedings and provide feedback. Gary S. Brown's (1997) study of volunteers in New York's court system reveals that volunteers have had a tremendous impact on the administration of justice. Just a few of the changes implemented due to the volunteers' suggestions included creating child care facilities for litigants, staggering daily calendars to reduce wait times, civility training for court personnel, providing judges with microphones, improving security, and encouraging judges to start on time. Brown shows that without the volunteers' efforts, the court likely would not have become aware of many of its shortcomings or how to correct them.

Aside from judges, scholars have also been interested in the performance of public defenders. Their interest, however, has not so much been on how to measure this performance, but on factors that affect performance. David R. Lynch (2004), for example, concludes that undue stress on public defenders damages their performance. He cites several sources of stress that judicial officers have some control over, and recommends that efforts be made to reduce these stressors. They include large caseloads, uncertainty about when cases will be brought to trial, judges showing favoritism, and judges handing out large sentences to punish defendants who exercise their right to a trial when they have no chance of winning. Other scholars have examined the extent to which structural elements of indigent defense affects defense attorney's performance. Surprisingly, and pleasantly so, the amount of compensation provided to court-appointed counsel was found to have no impact on lawyers' efforts on behalf of their clients (Priehs 1999). Another counter-intuitive finding revealed that indigent defendants received the most pre-sentencing jail time when represented by public defenders and the least under assigned counsel (Fender and Brookings 2005). These latter findings show once again that conventional wisdom is not always accurate, and research is essential to decipher which administrative mechanisms are most likely to produce desired results.

The effectiveness of individual actors is not the only type of performance that scholars have focused on. A considerable amount of research has been spent analyzing the performance of the jury system as well, a topic that has occupied scholars for many years (for example, see Feeley 1983). Contemporary studies have analyzed several aspects of the jury system. Jury pools have traditionally been drawn from voter registration roles. Critics of this system complain that it produces juries that are not representative, being more white and wealthier than the population at large. In response, several jurisdictions have begun to supplement or replace their voter registration lists with drivers' license records. William D. Schreckhise and Charles H. Sheldon (1998) found that Washington state's transition produced jury pools that were more representative of the general population, although this translated into juries that were less educated and younger. In contrast, Ted C. Newman's (1996) study of an experiment using drivers' license records in Illinois found that the racial diversity of jury pools improved for Hispanics but not for African Americans (whose representation actually declined). So, it appears that the jury is still out concerning the effectiveness of using drivers' license records.

Other scholars have sought to uncover how effective jury systems are at getting potential jurors to actually show up to serve. The concern here is that if jurors are not appearing on the dates they are called, then some citizens are avoiding their duty to serve, placing the burden on others. Additionally, failing to appear can cause the pool of potential jurors to become unrepresentative of the population. Research shows that jurors confronted with child care issues, uncooperative employers who will not compensate them for the time lost while on duty, uncomfortable surroundings at the court house, or previous commitments on the call-up dates have low appearance rates (Boatright 1999; Seltzer 1999). Other individuals do not report for jury duty simply because a summons never reached them. Richard Seltzer (1999) discovered that 35% of the addresses on file in the Washington, DC court system were incorrect. Courts interested in reducing the non-compliance rates in their jury pools are well advised to use these findings to develop appropriate solutions.

Critics of the jury system have also complained that the rules dictating jury proceedings are too archaic, forbidding jurors from asking questions during the trial, taking notes, or receiving better instructions on their responsibilities. They argue that a fair search for the truth would permit jurors to use these tools. Several studies have analyzed these devices, finding that when they are used they tend to have at least some positive benefits. Note taking improves memory recall in some, but not all, cases (Heuer and Penrod 1996; ForsterLee and Horowitz 2003). Providing better pre-instructions or employing a jury facilitator to explain the proceedings and answer questions produces better informed jurors who know what is required of them and deliberate cases more effectively (Field et al. 1996; ForsterLee and Horowitz 2003). Finally, permitting jurors to ask questions during the trial clarifies issues and better informs jurors about the facts of the case (Heuer and Penrod 1996). Interestingly, none of the studies found evidence that these tools change the outcomes of cases in terms of which party prevails.

Another issue of recent interest to scholars is the extent to which certain aspects of court administration are subject to or involve inter-branch politics. The judiciary is traditionally seen as the non-political branch of government, designed by the founding fathers to uphold the rule of law and protect individual and minority rights against the whims of the majority. Scholars have found, however, that some elements of court administration can expose the judicial branch to political influence, while other aspects allow it to enter the political arena to protect its prerogatives and independence. In a fascinating study on rule making within the federal judiciary, Lori Johnson (2003) shows how, since the 1970s, Congress has moved away from its hands-off policy of permitting the judicial branch to establish and amend the rules of procedure for the federal courts without interference. Instead, Congress has become increasingly involved in developing and approving rules that are more to its liking. Critics complain that such activities threaten judicial independence by taking judicial rule making out of the hands of the experts and subjecting them to political manipulation. Proponents, however, argue that Congress plays an important role in overseeing the courts, and involving itself in rule making ensures that the courts do not stray too far from the values of the people (Johnson 2003).

James W. Douglas and Roger E. Hartley (2003) reveal that legislatures can threaten judicial independence in other ways as well. In their survey of court and budgeting personnel in the states, they find that state judiciaries are often pressured by elected officials to raise more revenue through fee and fine collections. While failing to properly monitor outstanding collections increases non-compliance rates which allows offenders to go unpunished (see Burrell 1997), Douglas and Hartley (2003) argue that pressuring the courts to raise money can result in biased judgments (i.e., handing out the maximum fine for offenses or giving fines in lieu of jail time) and court systems that are inaccessible to the poor. Doing so may serve the political interests of legislators by raising revenue without increasing taxes, but its consequences are to limit court discretion and effectiveness.

Perhaps the most ominous political threat to judicial independence comes via the legislature's control over court budgets. The courts must receive adequate appropriations to carry out their constitutions functions. Donald W. Jackson (1999) explains that receiving sufficient resources is a necessary condition for judicial independence. Unfortunately for the courts, the judicial branch has little budgetary authority of its own. It must rely largely upon legislative appropriations. Because court rulings can have a major impact upon government policy, and because legislators have a vested interest in policy outcomes, an incentive exists for legislatures to use their budgetary powers to influence court rulings. Should judges allow budgetary concerns to affect their decisions, then legislative prerogatives rather than the rule of law would be determining outcomes—a serious threat to judicial independence. The research in this regard is not encouraging. Scholars have found that budgetary powers have been used at both the federal (Toma 1991, 1996) and state (Douglas and Hartley 2003) levels to influence judicial outcomes.

How does the non-political branch respond to political encroachments upon its independence? The answer is by entering the political arena. The administrative capacity of courts enables the judicial branch to lobby elected officials to protect its prerogatives. Administrative offices play an important lobbying role for the judiciary (Douglas 2002; Douglas and Hartley 2001a, 2001b; Winkle 2003). Judges, particularly chief justices, can also be effective lobbyists for the courts (Douglas 2002; Douglas and Hartley 2001a, 2001b). Mobilizing political allies such as judge and lawyer associations to put pressure on elected officials is another option (Barnes 1997; Douglas and Hartley 2001a). Lobbying can be an effective strategy for the courts. However, judges are sometimes reluctant to lobby or pursue other political strategies too aggressively, fearing that doing so will lose them credibility as neutral interpreters of the law. Indeed, Douglas and Hartley (2001a) found that during the budgetary process the courts tend to emphasize much more passive strategies, such as submitting conservative requests. They argue that the courts may be doing themselves a disservice by failing to asserting themselves more during the budgetary process (Douglas and Hartley 2004a). The support of legislators and chief executives is of major importance in determining court success in the budget process (Hartley and Douglas 2003). If the courts do not aggressively attempt to persuade these elected officials of the necessity of respecting judicial independence, then who will?

Several other scholars have studied a diverse range of issues regarding traditional administrative structures in the judiciary. Richard C. Kearney and Holly Taylor Sellers (1997) found gender bias to be a real problem in the judiciary. Women working for the courts tend to be in low-level jobs and receive little support in the form of family-friendly benefits, such as child care. Furthermore, court systems tend to have poorly developed sexual harassment policies. Thomas E. Willging and colleagues (2000) examined judges' use of special masters (also known as court-appointed experts) in the federal courts. They revealed that special masters tend to be appointed to handle complex matters in high-stakes cases, and are effective in performing their duties. By and large, judges and attorneys are satisfied with the work of special masters. However, special masters are rarely used (appointed to work on less than 0.2% of cases), and can be very expensive to both the plaintiffs and defendants, who typically pay their fees (Willging et al. 2000). Neal R. Vance and Ronald J. Stupak (1997) compared the organizational cultures of courts and jails. They concluded that the culture of the courts make them a more appropriate location for pre-trial agencies. Finally, Paul Brace and Melinda Gann Hall (2001) examined state Supreme Courts, finding that courts that were more professionalized better protected the rights of less powerful parties in private civil disputes by giving them a better chance to get their cases on the docket and win once their cases went to trial. While a significant body of research has yet to develop for each of these topics, these studies, like the others in this section, offer practitioners useful information about important administrative issues.

3. Analyzing Innovations and Reform Efforts

As discussed earlier, scholars have shifted their attention away from broad, comprehensive reforms in the past decade. This does not mean that the study of court reforms has been abandoned. To the contrary, roughly half of the published research over the last 10 years has focused on various reform efforts. The innovations examined by scholars, however, have been narrower in scope than the reforms of earlier decades that dealt with the creation of administrative structures in the judiciary as well as the unification of judicial institutions. Instead, research has been centered on innovations that can improve and complement the efficiency and effectiveness of the existing administrative apparatus. Before continuing to discuss the literature, it should be noted that adopting and implementing reforms successfully in the courts is a difficult task. Wice (1995b) lists several characteristics of the judiciary that make this so. First, the courts as conservative institutions give great importance to precedent and, therefore, are leery of and resistant to change. Second, little pressure is placed upon the courts to reform because they are largely isolated from public scrutiny (although this appears to be changing as elected official draw more attention to what they perceive to be shortcoming in the judicial branch). Third, the fragmented structure of the judicial system leads to large disagreements over objectives and goals. And, finally, the idiosyncratic nature of local courts means that few reforms are well suited for all jurisdictions. Current reform efforts must contend with these obstacles if they are to gain acceptance in the larger court community. As with the literature presented in the previous section, most of the work cited below focuses on substantive rather than theoretical issues.

Much of the judicial reform literature has centered on approaches designed to make the courts more efficient or accessible. By and large, such innovations have dealt with improving case management and introducing technology into the judiciary. Not surprisingly, research on the latter has generally shown technology to be beneficial to court operations. The presence of television cameras in the courtroom was found to increase juror attentiveness and encourage attorneys to be better prepared (Kirtley 1995). Court web sites have proven to provide citizens and court officials with improved access to information and court documents (Martin and Schmidt 2003). Computer technology in the form of jury management software, electronic storage, and connections to state and national information networks has also helped court administrators handle their increasing caseloads (Domino 1997; Dahlin 1996). However, judicial officials are warned in the literature that they must be careful when adopting new technology because computer security problems can threaten the privacy rights of litigants (Dahlin 1996; West 2002).

In regard to case management, David C. Steelman (1997) argues that case backlogs are inevitable in many courts simply because they lack resources. If a state refuses to add a sufficient number of judges to a particular court, there is little the court can do to eliminate or reduce delay. In jurisdictions where resources are available, Steelman maintains that the success of case management reforms depends upon the commitment of judges and staff to reducing delay, coordination with the local bar association as well as other relevant actors, proper training, and the use of case flow management improvement plans. According to Steelman, the extent to which these conditions exist in local court systems will determine the success or failure of case flow management reforms.

Should the proper circumstances be present in a local court, scholars have shown a variety of case-management techniques to be useful. These include case-scheduling techniques (Michels 1995), civil mediation (Clarke and Gordon 1997; but see Hartley 2002), arbitration (Gatowski et al. 1996), computerized management systems (Domino 1997), and judicial continuity, which is the keeping of a case in the same court with the same judge from the moment it enters the system to the time it is closed (Festinger and Pratt 2002). Interestingly, in their study of New York City's housing court, Seron et al. (2001) found that cases where poor tenants were provided with legal representation tended to get processed faster than those where no representation existed. This goes against conventional wisdom because it shows that lawyers actually speed up the process rather than slow it down with multiple motions, appeals, and requests for extensions. Given the increasing backlogs in many courts, scholars are likely to remain heavily involved in the study of case management techniques for some time to come.

By far, the reforms receiving the most attention in the literature in recent years are ADR that consists mostly of mediation and arbitration techniques, and therapeutic justice (also known as problem-solving courts). These reform efforts can lead to efficiency gains, but they also are designed to improve judicial effectiveness by providing alternative, and perhaps more appropriate, options to adjudication. Mediation and arbitration are reforms that have gained widespread acceptance in the court community over the past 25 years. Both techniques are designed to improve litigant satisfaction in resolving their disputes by reducing the cost of litigation, increasing the speed of the process, and tailoring solutions to meet the needs of both parties (Meyerson 2002, 328).

The research on ADR is mixed. Some studies have found that ADR is ineffective at achieving its goals. Steven H. Clarke and Elizabeth Ellen Gordon (1997) examined civil mediation in North Carolina and found that it did not improve levels of satisfaction, reduce the trial rate, nor reduce litigation costs. On the bright side, they did find that mediation reduced processing times. Roger E. Hartley (2002) studied ADR in civil cases in Mountain County, Georgia. He found that few cases were ever referred to mediation, cost savings did not materialize, and ADR cases tended to take more time than regular civil cases. Hartley did note that ADR removed especially complex cases from the general docket, possibly reducing delay for cases on that docket. Finally, Jona Gold-schmidt and Michael Hallett (1997) revealed from their study of Arizona's ADR program that many lawyers and judges are reluctant to use the program, often perceiving it to be a "waste of time" (225).

In contrast to these studies, Roselle L. Wissler (1995) found mediation in small claims civil cases to be superior to adjudication along several dimensions. Wissler discovered that litigants perceived mediation to provide them with more control over the process, to be less hurried, to be more fair, and to lead to a better understanding of the other party's point of view. Litigants also viewed mediators to be less biased than judges and "more interested in understanding the dispute" (351). Sophia I. Gatowski et al. (1996) added that court annexed arbitration in Clark County, Arizona, was faster and less expensive than general procedures for civil cases. The debate over the usefulness of ADR will go on until more definitive results are produced.

Therapeutic justice is a more recent development for the courts. Frustrated by offenders continually cycling through the system, court officers began to search for ways to end the revolving door of justice. The result was the establishment of problem-solving courts. These courts represent a dramatic change in court operations because they are not adversarial in nature, but therapeutic. They do not seek to punish or sentence offenders, but rehabilitate them. The first problem-solving courts focused on drug abuse cases (see Nolan 2001). Drug courts, as they became known, allow non-violent drug-addicted offenders to plead guilty in exchange for admittance into the drug court program. Under the supervision of a judge, participants receive drug treatment and are monitored by the court. They have a strong incentive to adhere to the treatment program because any violation of the drug court's rules can result in their dismissal from the program, landing them a jail sentence for the crime they pled guilty to. The implementation of drug courts requires a great deal of cooperation between the prosecutor, defense counsel, police, treatment providers, and the court. Spurred on by Department of Justice start-up grants, drug courts began to spread across the country after the inception of the first court in Dade County, Florida, in 1989. The drug court movement has also encouraged the establishment of other types of problem-solving courts, including domestic violence courts, community courts, and mental health courts (Lurigio et al. 2001; Casey and Rottman 2005).

Most of the evidence to date shows problem-solving courts to be effective at both graduating participants from their treatment programs and reducing recidivism rates (Deschenes et al. 1995; Applegate and Santana 2000; Casey and Rottman 2005). However, most of these courts were established only recently, so it is too early to label them a smashing success (Casey and Rottman 2005). Therapeutic justice is also not without its problems. Certain groups of participants have high failure rates (Torres and Deschenes 1997). In particular, lower-income individuals, non-whites, and crack users tend to have more difficulty graduating from drug court programs (Schiff and Terry 1997). Laura D'Angelo and Robert Victor Wolf (2002) have also discovered that women benefit less from drug court programs than men. This is due to the fact that most programs, quite unintentionally, were set up to deal with men's treatment needs. Unfortunately, early drug court administrators did not recognize that women tend to be different in terms of the addictions they have, the reasons for those addictions, and their treatment needs. D'Angelo and Wolf acknowledge that court officials are now beginning to realize this oversight, and are taking steps to correct it.

Another problem facing therapeutic justice programs is lack of resources. These programs often get started with federal grant money, but once the grants run out, many have a difficult time finding sufficient resources to maintain their service levels. Indeed, the problem of finding stable funding over the long term sometimes forces courts to shut down or prevents them from taking on effective caseloads (see Douglas and Hartley 2004b). Funding problems in conjunction with low success rates for certain groups means that problem-solving courts need to identify which groups are most likely to succeed in their programs, and target those groups for services (Torres and Deschenes 1997). Doing so should maximize the use of scarce resources.

The study of judicial administration began with the evaluation of court reforms. As this section shows, scholars continue to analyze reforms today. The fact that many of the research findings are contradictory or inconclusive indicates that much work needs to be done on this topic in the future. Without the contributions of scholars, both from within the judicial profession and academia, the courts will find it difficult to assess the utility of their reform efforts.

XII. CONCLUSION

Much of the court reform movement appears to be moving along a different path than the one marked by Roscoe Pound in 1906. Whereas Dean Pound blazed a trail—one followed for nearly a century without many detours—toward structural consolidation and centralization of judicial authority, the modern reform dialogue focuses increasingly on alterations in the *process* of justice. Today's reformers are more concerned with improving the efficiency and effectiveness of the judicial branch than with organizational niceties. Reducing the courts' workload, providing judges with the powers and tools to expedite justice, and devising new ways to solve disputes occupy the lion's share of the reform agenda.

If one were to compare the reality of court management today to that which existed only a few decades ago, the conclusion would be inescapable—the field of judicial administration continues to exert a profound impact on court systems throughout the country. It is probably safe to suggest that every single court in the United States has been influenced by innovations springing out of the judicial administration movement. And, notably, efforts to consolidate courts, to install merit selection of judges, to eliminate duplication, and to establish consistency in judicial procedure continue unabated in many areas.

Insofar as court administrators are concerned, there is no question that they will be active participants irrespective of the direction that the reform movement takes. In court systems that continue along the traditional path of centralization and consolidation, professional court executives are routine fixtures who have achieved a high level of legitimacy. In court systems that focus more on the process issues that have just been discussed, court administrators will likely (and somewhat ironically) be even busier than before. As ADR techniques, problem-solving courts, case tracking, differentiated case management, and related reforms spread, courts will require talented managers to oversee and coordinate these new activities. Trained court managers are the logical recipients of these new responsibilities.

Finally, the involvement of social scientists and other researchers in the description and evaluation of the court reform movement can only expand. The emergence of empirical research within the field of judicial administration has already produced some interesting results, many of which are counter-intuitive or otherwise surprising. Although most findings are not yet conclusive, they indicate that the full array of court reforms—structural, procedural, and process— require careful analysis. Attempting to ascertain the consequences and implications of structural and procedural alterations in the court system is clearly an important enterprise. This significance is compounded by the public's apparent willingness to alter long-standing means of dispute resolution. To the extent that new means are employed to limit the courts' caseload, and to the extent that internal judicial procedures are manipulated to accelerate the wheels of justice, then the researchers' role becomes all the more important. These types of changes obviously influence the most basic question in politics, Who gets what? Determining how various court structures, procedures, and reforms affect the answer to that question will no doubt occupy the careers of many social scientists for decades to come. The recent burst of scholarly activity on issues important to the administration of justice is encouraging. Should it continue, the judiciary can only benefit.

REFERENCES

Abraham, H., *Judicial Process*, Allyn and Bacon, Chicago, IL, 1986.

Adams, E., *Courts and Computers*, American Judicature Society, Chicago, IL, 1972.

American Academy of Political and Social Sciences, Administration of judicial administration, *The Annals*, 167, 1–256, 1933.

American Academy of Political and Social Sciences, Judicial administration and the common man, *The Annals*, 287, 1–243, 1953.

American Academy of Political and Social Sciences, Lagging justice, *The Annals*, 328, 1–227, 1960.

American Bar Association, Model state judicial article, *ABA Report*, 87, 392–399, 1962.

American Bar Association, *The Improvement of the Administration of Justice*, ABA, Chicago, IL, 1971.

American Bar Association, *Standards Relating to Court Organization*, ABA, Chicago, IL, 1974.

American Bar Association, *Standards Relating to Court Organization*, ABA, Chicago, IL, 1990.

American Judicature Society, Introduction, *Judicature*, 1, 3–4, 1917a.

American Judicature Society, The unified state court, *Judicature*, 1, 5–7, 1917.

American Judicature Society, Draft judiciary article, *Judicature*, 3, 132–149, 1920.

American Judicature Society, Judicature article in model state constitution, *Judicature*, 20, 189, 1937.

American Judicature Society, Standards of judicial administration adopted, *Judicature*, 22, 66, 1938.

American Judicature Society, The professionalization of court administration, *Judicature*, 50, 256–259, 1967.

American Judicature Society, *The Jury: Selected Readings*, AJS, Chicago, IL, 1971.

Anderson, E. S., Management control in the courts, *State Court Journal*, 1, 12–14, 1977.

Applegate, B. K. and Santana, S., Interviewing with youthful substance abusers: a preliminary analysis of a juvenile drug court, *Justice System Journal*, 21, 281–300, 2000.

Ashman, A. and Parness, J. A., The concept of a unified court system, *DePaul Law Review*, 24, 1–41, 1974.

Aumann, F. R., The Ohio Judicial Council embarks on a survey of justice, *American Political Science Review*, 24, 416–425, 1930.

Aumann, F. R., *The Changing American Legal System: Some Selected Phases*, Da Capo Press, New York, 1969.

Baar, C., *Separate but Subservient: Court Budgeting in the American States*, D.C. Heath, Lexington, MA, 1975.

Baar, C., The scope and limits of court reform, *Justice System Journal*, 5, 274–290, 1980.

Baar, C., Trial court unification in practice, *Judicature*, 76, 179–184, 1993.

Barnes, J. E., Bankrupt bargain? Bankruptcy reform and the politics of adversarial legalism, *Journal of Law and Politics*, 13, 893–935, 1997.

Berkson, L., A brief history of court reform, In *Managing the State Courts*, Berkson, L., Hays, S., and Carbon, S., Eds., West Publishing, St. Paul, MN, 1977a.

Berkson, L., Emerging ideal of court unification, *Judicature*, 60, 327–339, 1977b.

Berkson, L. and Carbon, S., *Court Unification: History, Politics, and Implementation*, National Institute of Law Enforcement and Criminal Justice, Washington, DC, 1978.

Berkson, L. and Hays, S. W., Court clerks: the forgotten politicians, *University of Miami Law Review*, 30, 499–516, 1976.

Berkson, L., Hays, S. W., and Carbon, S., *Managing the State Courts: Texts and Readings*, West Publishing, St. Paul, MN, 1977.

Berman, H. J., *Nature and Functions of Law*, Foundation Press, Brooklyn, NY, 1958.

Bernick, E. L. and Pratto, D. J., A behavior-based evaluation instrument for judges, *Justice System Journal*, 18, 173–184, 1995.

Biden, J., Congress and the courts: our mutual obligation, *Stanford Law Review*, 46, 1285–1302, 1994.

Blume, W. W. and Joiner, C. W., *Jurisdiction and Judgments*, Prentice Hall, New York, 1952.

Boatright, R. G., Why citizens don't respond to jury summonses, *Judicature*, 82, 156–164, 1999.

Boyum, K., Roundtable: an agenda for judicial administration research, *Justice System Journal*, 16, 1–18, 1992.

Braithwaite, W. T., *Who Judges the Judges?*, American Bar Association Foundation, Chicago, IL, 1971.

Brace, P. and Hall, M. G., "Haves" versus "have nots" in state supreme courts: allocating docket space and wins in power asymmetric cases, *Law and Society*, 35, 393–418, 2001.

Broder, J. M., Porter, J. F., and Smather, W. M., The hidden consequences of court unification, *Judicature*, 65, 11–17, 1981.

Brody, D. C., The relationship between judicial evaluations and judicial elections, *Judicature*, 87, 168–177, 2004.

Brown, G. S., Court monitoring: a say for citizens in their justice system, *Judicature*, 80, 219–221, 1997.

Brownell, H., A developmental program for court administration, *Judicature*, 54, 99–103, 1970.

Burrell, D., Financial analysis of traffic court collections in Ada County, Idaho, *Justice System Journal*, 19, 101–116, 1997.

Butler, B. W., Presiding judges' role in perceptions of trial court administrators, *Justice System Journal*, 3, 181–197, 1977.

Burger, W., Address to the American bar association: state of the federal judiciary, *American Bar Association Journal*, 57, 855–865, 1971a.

Burger, W., Bringing the judicial machinery up to the demands made on it, *Pennsylvania Bar Association Quarterly*, 42, 262–267, 1971b.

Callison, I. P., *Courts of Injustice*, Twayne, New York, 1956.

Cannon, M. W., Judicial administration: why should we care?, *Arizona State Law Journal*, 521–535, 1974.

Cannon, M. W., Innovation in the administration of justice, 1961–1981: an overview, *Policy Studies Journal*, 10, 668–679, 1982.

Carbon, S., Records management: obscure components requisite to efficient court administration, In *Managing the Sate Courts*, Berkson, L., Hays, S., and Carbon, S., Eds., West Publishing, St. Paul, MN, 1977.

Carp, R. A. and Stidham, R., *The Federal Courts*, Congressional Quarterly Press, Washington, DC, 1985.

Casey, P. M. and Rottman, D. B., Problem-solving courts: models and trends, *Justice System Journal*, 26, 35–56, 2005.

Cavanagh, E., The Civil Justice Reform Act of 1990 and the 1993 amendments to the Federal Civil Rules of Civil Procedure, *St. Johns Law Review*, 67, 721–763, 1993.

Church, T. W., The 'old and new' conventional wisdom of court delay, *Justice System Journal*, 7, 395–412, 1982.

Citizens Reform Committee, *Analysis of Court Structure in South Carolina*, University of South Carolina Law School, Columbia, SC, 1948.

Clark, T. C., The sixties: a historic decade in judicial improvement, *Brooklyn Law Review*, 36, 331–338, 1970.

Clarke, S. H. and Gordon, E. E., Public sponsorship of private settling: court ordered civil case mediation, *Justice System Journal*, 19, 311–339, 1997.

Colgrove, K., Thirty-sixth annual meeting of the APSA: Program, *American Political Science Review*, 45, 132, 1941.

Corso, J. W., Three political theories for court administrators, *Judicature*, 63, 427–435, 1980.

Crane, B. F. and Elliot, S. D., Progress in judicial administration, *State Government*, 26, 261–262, 1953, see also 271–272.

Crenson, M. A., *The Federal Machine*, Johns Hopkins Press, Baltimore, MD, 1975.

Dahlin, D. C., *Models of Court Management*, Associated Faculty Press, Millwood, NY, 1986.

Dahlin, D. C., Technology court administration in the twenty-first century: hurtling toward?, *Technological Forecasting and Social Change*, 52, 227–239, 1996.

D'Angelo, L. and Wolf, R. V., Women and addiction: challenges for drug court practitioners, *Justice System Journal*, 23, 385–400, 2002.

DeBenedictis, D., Struggling toward recovery, *American Bar Association Journal*, 50–55, August, 1994.

Descjenes, E. P., Turner, S., and Greenwood, P. W., Drug court or probation? An experimental evaluation of maricopa county's drug court, *Justice System Journal*, 18, 55–74, 1995.

Domino, J. C., The adoption of court technology in the Texas trial courts, *Justice System Journal*, 19, 245–266, 1997.

Douglas, J. W., Court strategies in the appropriations process: the Oklahoma case, *Public Budgeting, Accounting, and Financial Management*, 14, 117–136, 2002.

Douglas, J. W. and Hartley, R. E., State court strategies and politics during the appropriations process, *Public Budgeting and Finance*, 21, 35–57, 2001a.

Douglas, J. W. and Hartley, R. E., State court budgeting judicial independence: clues from Oklahoma and Virginia, *Administration and Society*, 33, 54–78, 2001b.

Douglas, J. W. and Hartley, R. E., The politics of court budgeting in the states: is judicial independence threatened by the budgetary process?, *Public Administration Review*, 63, 441–454, 2003.

Douglas, J. W. and Hartley, R. E., Making the case for court funding: the important role of lobbying, *The Judges' Journal*, 43, 35–37, 2004a.

Douglas, J. W. and Hartley, R. E., Sustaining drug courts in Arizona and South Carolina: an experience in hodgepodge budgeting, *Justice System Journal*, 25, 75–88, 2004b.

Downie, L., *Justice Denied*, Penguin, Baltimore, MD, 1972.

Dubois, P. L., *The Politics of Judicial Reform*, D.C. Heath, Lexington, MA, 1982.

Eisenstein, J. and Jacob, H., *Felony Justice: An Organizational Analysis of Criminal Courts*, Little, Brown, Boston, MA, 1977.

Eliot, C. W., Brandeis, L. D., Storey, M., Rodenbeck, A. J., and Pound, R., *Preliminary Report on Efficiency in the Administration of Justice*, National Economic League, Boston, MA, 1914.

Ellis, R. E., *The Jeffersonian Crisis: Courts and Politics in the Young Republic*, Oxford University Press, New York, 1971.

Esterling, K. M., Judicial accountability the right way, *Judicature*, 82, 206–215, 1999.

Faerman, S., DiPadova, L., and Quinn, R., Judicial leadership in court management, In *Handbook of Court Administration and Management*, Hays, S. and Graham, C., Eds., Marcel Dekker, New York, 1993.

Feeley, M. M., *Court Reform on Trial: Why Simple Solutions Fail*, The Twentieth Century Fund, New York, 1983.

Fender, B. F. and Brookings, S., A profile of indigent defense and pre-sentencing jail time in Mississippi, *Justice System Journal*, 25, 209–225, 2005.

Festinger, T. and Pratt, R., Speeding adoptions: an evaluation of the effects of judicial continuity, *Social Work Research*, 26, 217–224, 2002.

Fetter, T. and Scott, E. K., Court administration in rural areas, *Public Administration Review*, 40, 34–40, 1980.

Field, K. H., Zaffrano, M. A., and Liou, Y. I., Bringing technology to the jury deliberation table, *Justice System Journal*, 18, 317–331, 1996.

Fish, P., *The Politics of Federal Judicial Administration*, Princeton University Press, Princeton, NJ, 1973.

Fish P., William Howard Taft and Charles Evan Hughes: politicians as Chief Judicial Reformers, Paper presented to the annual meeting of the Southern Political Science Association, New Orleans, LA, 1975.

Fisher, J. R., Prospects of court reform after LEAA, *Court Management Journal*, 3, 13–15, 1981.

Flanders, S., Case management in federal courts: some controversies and some results, *Justice System Journal*, 4, 147–164, 1978.

Flango, V., Is court unification a uni-dimensional construct?, *Justice System Journal*, 6, 254–261, 1981.

ForsterLee, L. and Horowitz, I. A., The effects of jury-aid innovations on juror performance in complex civil trials, *Judicature*, 86, 184–190, 2003.

Frank, J., *Law and the Modern Mind*, Anchor, New York, 1930.

Frank, J., *Courts on Trial: Myth and Reality in American Justice*, Princeton University Press, Princeton, NJ, 1949.

Frankel, J. E., Judicial discipline and retirement—the California Plan, *Illinois Bar Journal*, 58, 510–520, 1970.

Freed, A. N., Computers in judicial administration, *Judicature*, 52, 419–421, 1972.

Friedman, L., Law reform in historical perspective, *St. Louis Law Journal*, 13, 351–389, 1969.

Friedman, L., *A History of American Law*, Simon and Schuster, New York, 1973.

Friesen, E., Constraints and conflicts in court administration, *Public Administration Review*, 31, 121–124, 1971.

Friesen, E., Gallas, E., and Gallas, N., *Managing the Courts*, Bobbs-Merrill, New York, 1971.

Galbraith, J., *Designing Complex Organizations*, Addison-Wesley, Reading, MA, 1973.

Gallas, G., The conventional wisdom of court administration: a critical assessment and alternative approach, *Justice System Journal*, 2, 35–55, 1976.

Gallas, G., Court reform: has it been built on an adequate foundation?, *Judicature*, 63, 28–38, 1979.

Gallas, G., Judicial leadership excellence: a research prospectus, *Justice System Journal*, 12, 39–60, 1987.

Gallas, G. and Gallas, E., Court management past, present, and future: a comment on Lawson and Howard, *Justice System Journal*, 15, 605–616, 1991.

Gallas, G. and Rausch, A., *Proceedings of the First National Symposium on Court Management*, National Center for State Courts, Williamsburg, VA, 1982.

Gatowski, S. I., Dobbin, S. A., DeWitt, J. S., Capenter, J. F., Dillehoy, R. C., Richardson, J. T., and Carns, D., Court-annexed arbitration in Clark county, Nevada: an evaluation of its impact on the pace, cost, and quality of civil justice, *Justice System Journal*, 18, 288–304, 1996.

Gazell, J. A., *State Trial Courts as Bureaucracies*, Dunellen, New York, 1975.

Gazell, J. A., *The Future of State Court Management*, Kennikat, Port Washington, New York, 1978.

Gazell, J. A., A taxonomy of state court personnel managers, *St. Johns Law Review*, 46, 74–96, 1974.

Glick, H. R., The politics of state court reform, In *The Politics of Judicial Reform*, Dubois, P., Ed., D.C. Heath, Lexington, MA, 1982.

Goldschmidt, J. and Hallett, M., Implementing a statewide ADR program, *Judicature*, 80, 222–229, 1997.

Good, D. W., Court reform: do critics understand the issues?, *Judicature*, 63, 365–375, 1980.

Graham, C., Reshaping the courts: traditions, management theories, and political realities, In *Handbook of Court Administration and Management*, Hays, S. and Graham, C., Eds., Marcel Dekker, New York, pp. 3–25, 1993.

Grant, J. A., The judicial council movement, *American Political Science Review*, 22, 922–941, 1928.

Graves, W. B., *American State Government*, D.C. Heath, Boston, 1953.

Greene, H. H., Court reform: what purpose?, *American Bar Association Journal*, 58, 245–252, 1972.

Greenstein, M. N., Hall, D., and Howell, J., Improving the judiciary through performance evaluations, In *The Improvement of the Administration of Justice*, Griller, G. M. and Stott, E. K., Eds., American Bar Association, Chicago, IL, 2002.

Griffith, E. S., Forty-fifth annual meeting of the APSA: program, *American Political Science Review*, 44, 152, 1950.

Hanssen, F. A., On the politics of judicial selection: lawyers and state campaigns for the merit plan, *Public Choice*, 110, 79–97, 2002.

Harley, H., Introduction, *Judicature*, 1, 3–4, 1917.

Harley, H., Progress in unifying state courts, *Judicature*, 16, 79–85, 1932.

Harley, H., Concerning the AJS: an attempt to give a brief history of a unique organization and to explain its objectives, *Judicature*, 20, 9–12, 1936.

Hartley, R. E., *Alternative Dispute Resolution in Civil Justice Systems*, LFB Scholarly Publishing, New York, 2002.

Hartley, R. E. and Douglas, J. W., Budgeting for state courts: the perceptions of key officials regarding the determinants of budget success, *Justice System Journal*, 24, 251–264, 2003.

Hartley, R.E. and Bates, K., The place of judicial administration in higher education: what court managers can do to (re)establish an academic center for the profession. Presented at the National Association for Court Management annual meeting, San Francisco, CA, 10–14, July, 2005.

Hays, S., *Court Reform: Ideal or Illusion?*, D.C. Heath, Lexington, MA, 1978.

Hays, S., Staffing the bench: personnel managment and the judiciary, In *Handbook of Court Administration and Management*, Hays, S. and Graham, C., Eds., Marcel Dekker, New York, 1993.

Hays, S. and Berkson, L., The new managers: court administrators, In *Managing the State Courts*, Berkson, L., Hays, S., and Carbon, S., Eds., West Publishing, St. Paul, MN, pp. 188–198, 1977.

Hays, S. and Graham, C., The principal facets and goals of court management: a sketch, In *Managing the State Courts*, Berkson, L., Hays, S., and Carbon, S., Eds., West Publishing, St. Paul, MN, 1977.

Hays, S. and Graham, C., Eds., *Handbook of Court Administration and Management*, Marcel Dekker, New York, 1993.

Henderson, T. A. and Kerwin, C. N., The changing character of court organization, *Justice System Journal*, 7, 449–469, 1982.

Hendrickson, D. K., Maximizing productivity: improving service in the federal courts, *Federal Probation*, 60, 11–20, 1996.

Heuer, L. and Penrod, S., Increasing juror participation in trials through note taking and question asking, *Judicature*, 79, 256–262, 1996.

Holmes, F. O., Courts and futures planning: justice 2020, *Justice System Journal*, 16, 101–112, 1994.

Hudzik, J., Rethinking the consequences of state financing, *Justice System Journal*, 10, 135–153, 1985.

Hurst, J. W., *The Growth of American Law*, Little, Brown, Boston, MA, 1950.

Institute for Judicial Administration, *Checklist Summary of Developments in Judicial Administration*, New York University Law School, New York, 1954–1958.

Institute for Judicial Administration, *Assignment Status in Civil Cases, Continuances, and Judicial Vacations*, New York University Law School, New York, 1956a.

Institute for Judicial Administration, *Assignment Status in Civil Cases, Continuances, and Judicial Vacations*, New York University Law School, New York, 1956b.

Institute for Judicial Administration, *Judicial Articles—Selected Recent Proposals with Explanatory Comments*, New York University Law School, New York, 1958.

Institute for Judicial Administration, *A Guide to State Court Systems*, New York University Law School, New York, 1959.

Jackson, D. W., Judicial independence in cross-national perspective, In *Judicial Independence: Essays, Bibliography, and Discussion Guide*, American Bar Association, Division for Public Education, Ed., American Bar Association, Chicago, IL, 1999.

Jacob, H., The governance of trial judges, *Law and Society Review*, 31, 3–30, 1997.

Johnson, L. A., Creating rules of procedure for federal courts: administrative prerogative or legislative policy-making?, *Justice System Journal*, 24, 23–42, 2003.

Journal of the American Judicature Society, Draft judiciary article, *Judicature*, 3, 132–135, 1920.

Journal of the American Judicature Society, Judiciary article in model state constitution, *Judicature*, 20, 189–193, 1937.

Journal of the American Judicature Society, Standards of judicial administration adopted, *Judicature*, 22, 66, 1938.

Kales, A. M., *Bulletin I*, American Judicature Society, Chicago, IL, 1914.

Kuhlman, A. F., *A Guide to Material on Crime and Criminal Justice*, H.W. Wilson, New York, 1939.

Kaufman, H., The growth of the federal personnel system, In *The Federal Government Service*, American Assembly, Ed., Prentice Hall, Englewood Cliffs, NJ, 1965.

Kearney, R. C. and Sellers, H. T., Gender bias in court personnel administration, *Judicature*, 81, 8–14, 1997.

Kirtley, J. E., "A leap not supported by history": the continuing story of cameras in the federal courts, *Government Information Quarterly*, 12, 367–389, 1995.

Klein, F. J., *Judicial Administration and the Legal Profession: A Bibliography*, Oceana Publications, Brooklyn, NY, 1963.

Klein, F. J., *The Administration of Justice in the Courts: Book One*, Oceana Publications, Dobbs Ferry, NY, 1976.

Knutson, J. F., Judicial selection in the states: historical context and ongoing debates, In *The Improvement of the Administration of Justice*, Griller, F. M. and Stott, E. K. Jr., Eds., American Bar Association, Chicago, 2002.

Lamber, J. and Luskin, M., Court reform: a view from the bottom, *Judicature*, 75, 295–299, 1992.

Lawson, H. O., *Overview of Court Administration: A Commentary*, American University, Washington, DC, 1974.

Lawson, H. O., Ackerman, H. R., and Fuller, D. F., *Personnel Administration in the Courts*, Westview Press, Boulder, CO, 1979.

Lawson, H. O. and Howard, D., Development of the profession of court management: a history with commentary, *Justice System Journal*, 15, 580–604, 1991.

Lepawsky, A., *The Judicial System of Metropolitan Chicago*, University of Chicago Press, Chicago, IL, 1932.

Levin, M. A., Urban politics and the criminal courts, *Judges' Journal*, 16, 16–21, 1977, see also 56.

Lipscher, R. and Conti, S., A post-unification approach to court organization design and leadership, *Justice System Journal*, 15, 667–676, 1991.

Llewellyn, K., A realistic jurisprudence—the next step, *Columbia Law Review*, 30, 431, 1930.

Lowe, R. S., Unified courts in America: the legacy of Roscoe Pound, *Judicature*, 56, 316–323, 1973.

Lurigio, A. J., Watwon, A., and Luchins, D. J., Therapeutic jurisprudence in action: specialized courts for the mentally ill, *Judicature*, 84, 184–189, 2001.

Lynch, D. R., The nature of stress among public defenders, *Justice System Journal*, 19, 17–36, 2004.

McConnell, E., What does the future hold for judges?, *Judges' Journal*, 30, 8–14, 1991.

Malech, A. M., A glass house: court administration from the inside, *Judicature*, 56, 249–254, 1973.

Martin, P. and Schmidt, P., The new public face of courts: state judicial systems and the internet as political resource, *Justice System Journal*, 24, 118–136, 2003.

Martineau, J., The federal court executives: an initial report, *Judicature*, 57, 438–445, 1974.

Mayers, L., *The American Legal System*, Harper & Row, New York, 1964.

Meyerson, B. E., Alternative dispute resolution: two decades of movement toward the mainstream, In *The Improvement of the Administration of Justice*, Griller, G. M. and Stott, E. K., Eds., American Bar Association, Chicago, IL, 2002.

Michels, M. J., Case management techniques that work, *Justice System Journal*, 18, 75–88, 1995.

Mintzberg, H., *The Structuring of Organizations*, Prentice Hall, Englewood Cliffs, NJ, 1979.

Moley, R., *Our Criminal Courts*, Milton Balch, New York, 1930.

Mort, G. and Hall, M. D., Trial court administrators: court executive of administrative aide, *Court Management Journal*, 4, 9, 1980.

Munger, F., Movements for court reform: a preliminary interpretation, In *Politics of Judicial Reform*, Dubois, P., Ed., D.C. Heath, Lexington, MA, 1982.

Nagle, S., Neef, P., and Munshaw, R., Bringing management science to the courts to reduce delay, *Judicature*, 62, 128–137, 1978.

Nardulli, P. F., *The Courtroom Elite: An Organizational Perspective on Criminal Justice*, Ballinger, Cambridge, MA, 1978.

Nelson, D., Commentary on the conference on empirical research in judicial administration, *Arizona State Law Journal*, 21, 161–171, 1989.

Nelson, D., *Judicial Administration and the Administration of Justice*, West Publishing, St. Paul, MN, 1974.

Newman, T. C., Fair cross-selections and good intentions: representation in federal juries, *Justice System Journal*, 18, 173–184, 1996.

Nolan, J. L., *Reinventing Justice: The American Drug Court Movement*, Princeton University Press, Princeton, NJ, 2001.

Orrick, D., Court administration in the United States: the on-going problems, *Anglo-American Law Review*, 19, 36–54, 1990.

Pearson, J., An evaluation of alternative to court adjudication, *Justice System Journal*, 7, 420–444, 1982.

Plotnikoff, J., Case control as social policy: civil case management legislation in the United States, *Civil Justice Quarterly*, 10, 230–245, 1991.

Popp, W. H. and Kuykendall, C. M., Computers in the courts, *State Court Journal*, 1, 6–11, 1977.

Pound, R., Justice according to the law, *Columbia Law Review*, 14, 696–713, 1913a.

Pound, R., The administration of justice in the modern city, *Harvard Law Review*, 26, 302–318, 1913b.

Pound, R., Generation of improvements in the administration of justice, *New York University Law Quarterly*, 22, 369–388, 1921.

Pound, R., Organization of courts, *Judicature*, 11, 69, 1927.

Pound, R., The causes of popular dissatisfaction with the administration of justice, *Judicature*, 20, 178–189, 1937, Reprinted in Pound, R, *Judicature*, 46, 55, 1962.

Pound, R., Principles, and outline of a modern unified court organization, *Judicature*, 23, 225–233, 1940.

Powell, L., *Court Reform in Seven States*, American Bar Association Press, Chicago, IL, 1980.

President's Commission on Law Enforcement and the Administration of Justice, *Task Force Report: The Courts*, US Government Printing Office, Washington, DC, 1967.

Priehs, R. E., Appointed counsel for indigent criminal appellants: does compensation influence effort?, *Justice System Journal*, 21, 57–79, 1999.

Pringle, H. F., *The Life and Times of William H. Taft: A Biography*, Farrar and Rinehart, New York, 1939.

Richardson, R. J. and Vines, K. N., *The Politics of the Federal Courts*, Little, Brown, Boston, MA, 1970.

Saari, D. J., *Modern Court Management: Trends in the Role of the Court Executive*, Law Enforcement Assistance Administration, Washington, DC, 1970.

Saari, D. J., Historical perspectives of modern court management, *Court Management Journal*, 2, 6–8, 1980, see also 27–28.

Saari, D. J., *American Court Management: Theories and Practices*, Quorum Books, Westport, CT, 1982.

Saari, D. J., Planet, M., and Reinkensmeyer, M., The modern court managers: who they are and what they do, In *Handbook of Court Administration and Management*, Hays, S. and Graham, C., Eds., Marcel Dekker, New York, 1993.

Sarat, A., The role of courts and the logic of court reform: notes on the justice department's approach to improving justice, *Judicature*, 64, 300–311, 1981.

Schiff, M. and Terry, W. C., Predicting graduation from broward county dedicated drug treatment court, *Justice System Journal*, 19, 291–310, 1997.

Schreckhise, W. D. and Sheldon, C. H., The search for greater juror diversity: the case of the US district court for the eastern district of Washington, *Justice System Journal*, 20, 95–112, 1998.

Seltzer, R., The vanishing juror: why are there not enough available jurors?, *Justice System Journal*, 20, 203–218, 1999.

Seron, C., Van Ryzin, G., and Frankel, M., The impact of legal counsel on outcomes for poor tenants in New York city's housing court: results of a randomized experiment, *Law and Society Review*, 35, 419–434, 2001.

Seymore, W. N., *Why Justice Fails*, Morrow, New York, 1973.

Sikes, P. S., The work of judicial councils, *American Political Science Review*, 29, 456–464, 1935.

Sobel, W. H., The American courthouse: planning and design for judicial process, *Judicature*, 56, 115–123, 1972.

Solomon, M. and Doan, R., Design and implementation of manual case management systems for misdemeanor courts, *Justice System Journal*, 6, 117–134, 1981.

Special Committee to Suggest Remedies and Formulate Proposed Laws to Prevent Delay and Unnecessary Cost in Litigation, *Report*, American Bar Association, Chicago, IL, 1909.

State Court Planning Capabilities Project, Planning in the state courts, *State Court Journal*, 1, 17–21, 1977.

Steelman, D. C., What have we learned about court delay, "local legal culture," and caseflow management since the late 1970s?, *Justice System Journal*, 19, 145–166, 1997.

Stott, E. K., The judicial executive: toward greater congruence in an emerging profession, *Justice System Journal*, 7, 152–179, 1982.

Stupak, R., Court leadership in transition: fast forward toward the year 2000, *Justice System Journal*, 15, 617–627, 1991.

Sunderland, E. R., Qualifications and compensation for minor court judges, *Judicature*, 29, 111–116, 1945.

Swain, J. T., The procedures of judicial discipline, *Marquette Law Review*, 59, 196–224, 1976.

Tamm, E. A. and Reardon, P. C., Warren E. Burger and the administration of justice, *Brigham Young University Law Review*, 447–552, 1981.

Tarr, G. A., Court unification and court performance: a preliminary assessment, *Judicature*, 64, 356–368, 1981.

Tob, R. W., *Creating the Judicial Branch: The Unfinished Reform*, National Center for State Courts, Williamsburg, VA, 1999.

Toma, E. F., Congressional influence and the supreme court: the budget as a signaling device, *Journal of Legal Studies*, 20, 131–146, 1991.

Toma, F., A contractual model of the voting behavior of the supreme court: the role of the chief justice, *International Review of Law and Economics*, 16, 433–447, 1996.

Torres, S. and Deschenes, E. P., Changing the system and making it work: the process of implementing drug courts in Los Angeles county, *Justice System Journal*, 19, 267–290, 1997.

Vance, N. R. and Stupak., R. J., Organization culture and the placement of pre-trial agencies in the criminal justice system, *Justice System Journal*, 19, 51–76, 1997.

Vanderbilt, A. T., Section on judicial administration launches program on wide front, *American Bar Association Journal*, 24, 5–6, 1938, see also 78.

Vanderbilt, A. T., *Minimum Standards of Judicial Administration*, New York University Law Center, New York, 1949.

Virtue, M. B., *Survey of Metropolitan Courts in the Detroit Area*, University of Michigan Law School, Ann Arbor, MI, 1950.

Volcansek, M. L., Conventional wisdom of court reform, In *Managing the State Courts*, Berkson, L., Hays, S., and Carbon, S., Eds., West Publishing, St. Paul, MN, 1977.

Wasby, S., Judicial administration in the federal courts, In *Handbook of Court Administration and Management*, Hays, S. and Graham, C., Eds., Marcel Dekker, New York, pp. 121–138, 1993.

Wasby, S., The work of a circuit's chief judge, *Justice System Journal*, 24, 63–90, 2002.

West, R., Tradition, security stall court technology, *American City and County*, 117, 7–13, 2002.

Weygandt, C. V., Our challenged bench and bar, *Louisiana Bar Journal*, 3, 221–232, 1956.

Wheeler, R. R, What is judicial administration? Paper presented at annual meeting of the American Political Science Association, San Francisco, 1975.

Wheeler, R. R., Broadening participation in the courts through rulemaking and adjudication, *Judicature*, 62, 280, 1977a.

Wheeler, R. R., Planning in the state courts, In *Managing the State Courts*, Berkson, L., Hays, S., and Carbon, S., Eds., West Publishing, St. Paul, MN, 1977b.

Wheeler, R. R., Judicial reform: basic issues and references, *Policy Studies Journal*, 8, 134–153, 1979.

Wheeler, R. R. and Whitcomb, H. R., *Judicial Administration: Text and Readings*, Prentice Hall, Englewood Cliffs, NJ, 1977b.

Wice, P., *Court Reform and Judicial Leadership*, Praeger, Westport, CT, 1995a.

Wice, P., Court reform and judicial leadership: a theoretical discussion, *Justice System Journal*, 17, 309–321, 1995b.

Winkle, J., Interbranch politics: the administrative office of the U.S. courts as liaison, *Justice System Journal*, 24, 43–62, 2003.

Wiebe, R. H., *The Search for Order: 1877–1920*, Hill and Wang, New York, 1967.

Wigmore, J. H., The spark that kindled the white flame of progress—Pound's St. Paul address of 1960, *Judicature*, 46, 50–58, 1962.

Wigmore, J. H., Wanted—a chief judicial superintendent, *Judicature*, 1, 7–9, 1917.

Willging, T. E., Hooper, L. L., Leary, M., Miletich, D., Reagan, R. T., and Shapard, J., *Special Masters' Incidence and Activity. Report to the Judicial Conference's Advisory Committee on Civil Rules and its Subcommittee on Special Masters*, Federal Judicial Center, Washington, DC, 2000.

Winberry, P. B., Washington state court reform, *State Court Journal*, 4, 3–5, 1980.

Winters, G., *The Jury: Selected Readings*, American Judicature Society, Chicago, IL, 1971.

Wissler, R. L., Mediation and adjudication in small claims court: the effects of process and case characteristics, *Law and Society Review*, 29, 323–358, 1995.

Wong, M., Space management: building new life into old courthouses, *Judicature*, 57, 154–158, 1973.

Zaffarano, M., Understanding leadership in state trial courts: a review essay, *Justice System Journal*, 10, 229–242, 1985.

Zaffarano, M., The professional court manager—have the traditional roles changed?, *The Court Manager*, 5, 6–9, 1988.

Zaffarano, M., Team leadership: using self-directed work teams, *Justice System Journal*, 17, 339–355, 1995.

Zeisel, H., Reflections on experimental techniques in the law, *Journal of Legal Studies*, 2, 107–124, 1973.

27 Five Great Issues in Judicial Administration

James A. Gazell

CONTENTS

I. INTRODUCTION

The practice of public administration long preceded this study. The enterprise of this field dates from antiquity, centuries before scholars and practitioners recorded, examined, and codified its basic concepts and facets and traced its evolution (Waldo 1980). In fact, the rise of self-awareness in public administration is little more than a century old, marked from the time of Wilson's (1887) celebrated essay "The Study of Public Administration," which charted its history, defined its essence, and illuminated its comparative side. This effort was paradigmatic in weaving a heuristic mosaic, but inevitably leaving numerous gaps to be filled by generations of future academics and practitioners who expanded, adapted, and reinterpreted this embryonic field.

Public administration steadily developed through the twentieth century, until by the 1970s its reach had encompassed the area of judicial administration among others (Friesen et al. 1971). Until that decade, this absorbed facet of public administration had been ensconced in overlapping fields of law and criminal justice administration, its twin home since the early 1900s (Willoughby 1929). Before this century, the practice of judicial administration had flourished for several thousand years. For example, the Bible (Exodus 18:13–18:27) reports Jethro's instructions to his son-in-law, Moses, on the subject of establishing and running a judicial system. However, one finds only scattered recorded hints about the efficacy of court administration, most of which are critical of it. For instance, Scripture (Luke 11:45–11:46) threatens lawyers. At roughly the same time, two Roman emperors, Augustus Caesar and Vesperian, viewed judicial delay as a problem (Goerdt 1997). Shakespeare's *Hamlet* (3.1.64) also bewails such delay, and Dickens (1853) chronicled the human misery spawned by such inaction in Victorian England, engendering a massive reorganization of the British court system two decades later. Goethe and Voltaire, too, suggested the need for a more efficient judicial system (Cannon 1974; Pound 1906).

Conscious judicial administration arrived when famed legal scholar Roscoe Pound did for it what Wilson had done for public administration (Steelman et al. 2004). Influenced by United Kingdom's judicial reform and by his service as a member of the Nebraska Law Revision Commission, Pound turned his attention increasingly to this subject (Clark 1964). His most celebrated contribution came in 1906 when he spoke to the American Bar Association (ABA) and enumerated his complaints about the management of America's state and federal courts. "Our system of courts," he charged, "is archaic in three respects: (1) In its multiplicity of courts; (2) in preserving concurrent jurisdiction, [and] (3) in the waste of judicial power which it involves." His first allegation centered on the proliferation of state trial courts, which impaired judicial efficiency for a spate of reasons, including redundant adjudication, needless costs, onerous record keeping, and substantive injustice wrought by the procedural error of filing cases in what on appeal turned out to have been the wrong trial court. His second protest focused on the overlapping jurisdiction exercised by the mélange of trial courts and such resulting concomitants as multiple filings of the same case, duplication of judicial decision making, congestion, and delay in resolving legal disputes. His third concern was the maintenance of judicial institutions through greater efficiency, which to him was being dissipated in three respects: (1) by the lack of legal authority for judges in lightly congested courts to assist their colleagues in heavily burdened jurisdictions; (2) by the spending of what he regarded as excessive time on procedural matters, diverting attention from the substance of cases; and (3) by a proliferation of what he considered to be superfluous retrials—those stemming from reversal of judicial decisions as a result of minor procedural errors.

Although Pound continued to excoriate the condition of the nation's courts during his long legal career, he also rendered another notable service, a delineation of a new specialty: judicial administration (Pound 1906, 1927, 1940, 1958; Wheeler and Pound 1909). His work in this area requires at least passing attention because it clearly foreshadowed what became the five great issues in this field: (1) congestion and delay, (2) unification (or centralization), (3) professionalization, (4) education and training, and (5) technology.

Consider briefly his published thoughts about each of these subjects:

1. Pound's condemnation of congestion and delay reflected the ethos of the Progressive era (1890–1920) in American history, one aspect of which stressed honest, efficient government in the executive branches at all levels—federal, state, and local—by separating it as much as possible from politics (Goldman 1955; Hofstadter 1955). Pound applied this outlook to another branch of government: the judiciary. To him court congestion and ensuing delay in the settlement of legal matters were inefficient. Justice was a byproduct of efficiency which would be maximized if courts were run in a businesslike fashion. Consequently, he emphasized the faster termination of cases—cases were to be disposed of, not merely decided, as if accelerated results were patently just. So evident was this connection that it was unnecessary for him to explore its validity. In his view, judicial inefficiencies derived from several sources: superfluous retrials, cumbersome procedures, and misallocations of judicial personnel (the inability to assign underworked judges in various districts to overworked courts in other jurisdictions). Furthermore, he saw much incompetence flowing from the choice of judges on the basis of politics (elections) rather than merit (appointment).

2. Most importantly, Pound attributed judicial inefficiencies, such as delay and congestion, to organizational fragmentation, once appropriate for a lightly populated rural society but not for an urbanized industrial nation. Trial courts typically had operated as islands, independent not only of other courts on this level but also of appellate courts (Friedman 1985). His proposed remedy was structural (or organizational) and administrative unification (or centralization), which encompassed at least two noteworthy aspects. First was the establishment of a single set of trial courts in each state—one per district—with exclusive comprehensive original jurisdiction and with divisions to handle various types of litigation, such as bankruptcies, divorces, probate matters, and intermediate appeals. Second was bureaucratization, for Pound implicitly believed that judicial systems should be organized like pyramids with the following characteristics: (1) a hierarchy running from the state court of the last resort, which would exercise strong supervisory powers and promote uniform procedures for the equitable administration of justice; (2) specialization based on the performance of all judicial functions within each geographical unit and judges concentrating on particular areas of the law but available for other work; and (3) uniform, comprehensive rules promulgated by the highest state court and applicable to all lower courts except for a degree of necessary local discretion. The chief justice (or judge) would supervise the operations of such a bureaucracy with the aid of court administrators and presiding judges for each of the trial courts. To Pound, structural and administrative unification complemented each other. Efficiency, he believed, would redound from a pyramidal organization design (Ostrom 1974), a belief that made him a kindred spirit of such classical administrative theorists as Wilson, Taylor, Weber, and Gulick.

3. Pound was a harbinger of the eventual professionalization of judicial administration. He helped to imbue it with the characteristics of a profession: a body of knowledge, a pantheon of luminaries, organizations for scholars and practitioners, and autonomy (Somit and Tanenhaus 1964). He applied bureaucratic analyses to the courts. He was the first in a long parade of notables that included Herbert Harley, Arthur T. Vanderbilt, William Howard Taft, Charles Evans Hughes, Tom Clark, and Warren Burger. His writings on proper court structure and administration undoubtedly inspired his votaries to establish such organizations as the American Judicature Society, the Institute of Judicial Administration, the National College of the State Judiciary (now the National Judicial College), the Federal Judicial Center, the Institute for Court Management, and the National Center for State Courts. Such knowledge, seminal work, and occupational societies enabled the nation's courts to develop the capacity to take care of their own business, to become far less dependent on other horizontal divisions of government or other levels of government, to move closer toward becoming a genuinely coordinate branch in a system of separation of powers, and thus to help turn constitutional theory into an operational reality.

4. Pound saw education and training as a concomitant of professionalization. Both would result mainly from on-the-job experience and would embrace judges and their staffs. To help develop maximum judicial competence, he favored task specialization rather than assignment rotation. He criticized the latter practice as a waste of court power. Specifically, he saw it as a detrimental judicial acquisition of substantial knowledge and experience in particular areas of the law, a deficiency that tended to make judges uncertain, tentative, and slow in the handling of litigation.

Pound (1940) called for the strict supervision of court staffs (in particular, the historically elected and autonomous clerks) by chief (or presiding) judges as a prerequisite to their education and training. He commented that "scientific management is needed in a modern court no less than in a modern factory." This managerial philosophy, devised by Taylor (1911), advocated the use of what he termed "functional foreman" to teach employees the one best way of doing their jobs. Applying this approach to court systems would cast chief judges at the state and local levels in the role of "functional foremen" with clerks and stenographers (the only staff categories mentioned in his earlier writings) in the role of students. Bureaucratically, the result would be a top-down transfer of the chief judge's on-the-job experience to staff members.

5. Finally, Pound hinted at a need for technology and behavioral research, which in a judicial context suggested the use of computers, management information systems, intra- and inter-court information networks, and eventually an informationally integrated justice system for court security, efficient caseflow management, optimal assignment of human resources (or personnel) and space, achievement of cost effectiveness in handling finances, and ultimately more just dispute resolutions. Two possible applications engendered his interest (Pound 1940). First, he inveighed against "much unnecessary duplication, copying and recopying and general prolixity of records in the great majority of our courts." These problems had resulted from what he called "archaic business methods." Because he wanted courts to be managed like corporations, he envisioned no insurmountable obstacles in adapting the latter's techniques to the former. Second, he advocated the gathering of "reliable and intelligently organized" judicial statistics to promote the formulation of efficient court administration policies, a task whose fulfillment increasingly depended on technology, especially in its state-of-the-art form. Management of this category, like education, was to be a responsibility of state and local chief judges.

This introduction to five greatly important issues in judicial administration supplies us with the background for more adequately reviewing the parallel evolution of each of them since the time of Roscoe Pound. Although these rubrics overlap considerably in theory and practice and, in effect, form a rich mosaic, a seamless web of tasks, let us separate them solely for the purpose of orderly analysis.

II. CONGESTION AND DELAY

The revulsion of Pound and later judicial reformers to congestion and delay has been epitomized in an oft-repeated slogan: "Justice delayed is justice denied." A dim view of these related concepts—congestion and delay—dominated the embryonic field of judicial administration and was repeatedly cited by numerous national commissions and by many reformers as a patent justification for far-reaching structural and administrative changes. However, by the 1950s the conventional wisdom usually applied to these subjects began to undergo reexamination, a process that still continues.

The initial reconsideration did not center on the subject of congestion that was generally equated with a court's backlog or inventory and which was created and aggravated by delay (Trotter and Cooper 1982). Instead, the reappraisal focused on court delay, which was generally equated with unnecessary delay. For instance, researchers from the National Center for State Courts (NCSC), defined "'court delay' as case-processing time beyond that which is necessary for a fair resolution of a case" (Ostrom and Kauder 1999, 106). But they and notable professional organizations (such as the ABA, the Conference of Chief Justices, and the Conference of State Court Administrators) recognized that what constituted unnecessary delay depended on the particular circumstances of a case and that no one time-disposition standard could validly be applied to all cases.

Before 1977, there had been little serious discussion in the legal profession as to exactly what delay or unnecessary delay denoted operationally. Almost invariably, the terms were used without accompanying definitions, as if judicially knowledgeable persons understood the concepts and thought about them in about the same way (Steelman et al. 2004). Zeisel et al. (1959) illuminated ambiguities in the concept of delay by noting that it might refer to several periods in the processing of cases. It might signify (1) the time from case filing to trial date, (2) the time from the filing of an answer to a complaint to the commencement of a trial, (3) the period from case filing to the time when a judge deemed a suit to be at issue (that is, ready for trial), (4) the span from the at-issue stage to trial, (5) the time from answer to trial, or (6) the duration from filing to a final resolution on appeal. These time periods were the most common ones to bring a case to a delay.

Between 1964 and 1974, the Institute of Judicial Administration published annual calendar status reports, compilations of the delays experienced by litigants in state trial courts across the country, especially in metropolitan areas. This New York-based organization relied on two criteria to measure the concept of delay: the median time from the filing of an answer to the start of a trial and the median period from the at-issue stage in a case to the beginning of a trial. However, these efforts suffered from a tendency among some jurisdictions to operationize the concept of delay differently and thus to supply the Institute with what proved to be less than fully comparable statistics. Moreover, other states failed to measure delay at all. They simply tabulated congestion, or backlog, the number of cases in various civil and criminal categories pending over specified periods—for instance, three months, six months, two years, or five years.

Although insufficient funds compelled this privately funded agency to discontinue this project in 1974, its work served as a precedent for the efforts of NCSC in 1975 to achieve uniformity among the states in their compilations of judicial statistics. The goal entailed close cooperation between NCSC officials and state court administrators and yielded a periodic flow of information, thus allowing valid nationwide comparisons. Since 1975, the gathering of court data has become a joint project involving not only the NCSC, but also the Conference of State Court Administrators (COSCA) and the State Justice Institute (SJI). The annual reports provide an overview of the nation's judicial systems, especially the growing volume of litigation handled at the trial levels. By 2003, the size of the state court caseload had risen to a record of 96.2 million. To handle this volume were 29,428 judges in 15,588 courts. The increase in the filing of criminal, civil, domestic, juvenile, and traffic cases appears to be inexorable (National Center for State Courts 2005).

This undertaking parallels the work of the Administrative Office of the United States Courts (AOUSC), which has been garnering data on all federal courts since 1939 when it assumed this duty from the Department of Justice (Fish 1973). Moreover, since 1946, this office has been intermittently measuring delay in the federal courts of appeal and district courts. The Supreme Court has been exempt from analysis because of its unique power since 1925 to control its own docket and thus to avert congestion and delay. The AOUSC conducted its analysis of the problem by asking judges to record the time spent over several months on various types of cases. By 1980, such research enabled the AOUSC to discover the median time spent on handling numerous kinds of litigation, to weigh the caseloads of the judges as a method of deriving their workloads, and to determine whether or not their workloads necessitated additional judgeships (AOUSC 1980). Furthermore, the AOUSC extended its research to encompass federal court-support offices, such as those for district-court clerks, bankruptcy-court clerks, probation, and pretrial services to devise sound staffing formulas and intermittently revise them (AOUSC 2001).

Even without such analyses, however, a common view was that virtually all cases could, and should, be tried within six months of the filing date. When Earl Warren was Chief Justice of the United States, he espoused this view as a line of demarcation between acceptable and intolerable delay in the termination of federal judicial litigation (Warren 1958). In 1972, the Supreme Court approved a change in the Rules of Criminal Procedure (Rule 50b), ordering federal district courts to promulgate plans for trying criminal cases within six months after indictment

(92 S.Ct. 2912–2913). However, in 1974, Congress compressed this time span much further by passing the Speedy Trial Act, which superseded this rule and required, with some exceptions, the adjudication of such business by federal benches within one-hundred days from arrest and sixty from indictment (18 U.S.C. secs. 3161–3174). The exceptions centered on justifiable delays, which might accompany complex cases, time-consuming discovery proceedings, and difficulties in retaining adequate counsel. Because of a five-year transition to full implementation turned out to be unrealistic, Congress relented by amending the statute to allow federal district court judges to suspend the timetable in the interests of justice and, in effect, proceed as they had done under Rule 50b. The less stringent law still virtually forced the national trial courts to give precedence to criminal matters rather than civil suits. Most states have codified this priority, which typically reduces delay in criminal cases while aggravating it in civil litigation and which looms more significantly in urban areas than in rural localities, where judges are sometimes underworked (Gazell 1971, 1972).

Efforts to measure and reduce judicial delay have presupposed a direct, linear relationship between delay and injustice and have assumed that the former is detrimental to justice. Some analysts have questioned the validity of this nexus in civil and criminal cases. Instead, they have posited a curvilinear (or parabolic) relationship whereby some delays may further the interests of justice to a point beyond which further dilatoriness gradually undermines the pursuit (Frank 1964). For instance, in sensational murder or sex crimes, delay often functions to cool popular feelings and to increase the prospects of a fair trial and a just verdict. However, to most of the public, repeated judicially ordered postponements in the carrying out of the death penalty wreak injustice (Jacob 1984).

In civil cases, whether or not long delays yield injustices frequently depends on whether or not one is a plaintiff or a defendant. Illustrative of this divergence in perspective is the most common type of civil business: automobile accident compensation cases. As defendants, insurance companies typically favor repeated delays in resolving such suits as a method of pressuring litigants into accepting settlements at a fraction of the filed claim. By contrast, plaintiffs usually need large sums of money quickly to compensate for their injuries and property damage and thus cannot afford to wait several years for their suits to come to trial. A notable exception centers on insurance companies and other corporations suing for damages (Frank 1964; Jacob 1984; Walter E. Meyer Research Institute of Law 1968; Winters 1960). Similarly, such corporate giants as Microsoft have viewed protracted court delay as an ally in fighting antitrust actions, for they employ teams of lawyers on retainer, who hold advantages in motivation, knowledge, and experience over teams of Department of Justice attorneys who change with successive administrations and need time to master the intricacies of complex litigation even if they want to pursue it. In addition, judicial delays in probate matters often enable attorneys to receive exorbitant fees.

However, in the early 1980s, some analysts began to see judicial delay not as a bane to many litigants, but as a latent public benefit. The most notable exponent of this outlook was jurist Richard Neely (1981, 983), who contended that the persistence of delay in the nation's metropolitan trial courts is partly a result of deliberate but tacit local government policy. Such courts have the technology necessary to eliminate congestion and delay through computerized caseflow management, as exemplified by differential case management (DCM), which involves the classification of incoming cases according to their nature (criminal and civil) and degree of complexity, as well as their placement into a fast, normal, complex, or special tracks with their own set of deadlines for the expeditious movement of a case through a court. DCM often utilizes a judicial automated calendaring system (JACS). Despite such innovations, suits against local government agencies often drag on for years because, if such cases were to reach trial quickly, municipalities and counties would often be found liable, and the monetary judgments against them would accumulate into a severe financial drain, entailing reductions in some local services, higher taxes, or possibly both. Consequently, for local governments, the protracted handling of these cases yielded at least one important benefit: lower financial liability because many plaintiffs suing local government units, like their counterparts in automobile accident litigation, needed some money quickly and thus accepted settlements for a portion of the claimed amount. Remaining cases went to trial but were fewer and dispersed over time. As a result, government setbacks in court and the fiscal impacts (damages and legal fees) declined and thus became less burdensome. New York City was a prime example of a metropolis allegedly benefiting from this practice.

Finally, studies of delay yielded at least four important conclusions for those courts genuinely seeking to combat delay. One was that a detailed mapping of a court's case-processing system was a prerequisite for identifying the events likely to slow or stop the flow of business. The installation of a judicial management information system facilitates this process and makes possible management control. An increasingly common illustration is the adoption of a DCM system, as mentioned above. A second conclusion was that there was a need for augmenting management control when judges abandon their traditional reactive position—that is, having cases proceed at a pace favored by opposing counsel—and for adopting a proactive stance whereby the judges enforce the various deadlines at a minimum or, better yet, take the lead in consistently pushing for a fair and expeditious resolution of cases. Over time such proactive style of management fosters an attitude among courtroom workgroup members (such as judges, attorneys, and court staffers who regularly work together), thus favoring accelerated case handling. It usually takes about six months for such members to adapt to such deadlines. A third conclusion was that more than 200 anti-delay programs, all of which stressed proactive case management, had succeeded in reducing case-processing time and backlogs in twenty-five states and the District of Columbia. However, there is also a concomitant price: litigation costs have risen because attorneys, required to meet deadlines, have had to spend more time on cases and thus charge higher fees (Goerdt 1997; Trotter and Cooper 1982).

A fourth conclusion was the emergence of a consensus, no doubt aided by much empirical research into judicial workloads and the performance of effective courts, about a time frame that should generally guide courts in deciding their volume of business. For example, COSCA, the Conference of Chief Justices (CCJ), and the American Bar Association (ABA) publicly recommended criminal and civil disposition standards as possible models against which trial courts can measure and thereby compare their performance. Because criminal cases (alleged offenses against society) are viewed more seriously than civil cases (mostly private disputes) and thus have priority over them, their recommended standards for criminal-case disposition were listed first. Their standards overlapped but were still distinctive. For the COSCA and the CCJ, all felony cases should be decided within six months of arrest, and all misdemeanors within three months. For the ABA, 90% of the felony cases should be decided within four months of arrest, 98% within six months, and 100% within a year; differently, 90% of the misdemeanors should be decided within thirty days, and all of them within ninety days. For the COSCA and the CCJ, trial courts should adjudicate all civil jury trials within a year and a half, all civil non-jury trials within a year. For the ABA, 90% of civil cases should be decided within one year of their filing, 98%, within a year and a half, and 100% within two years. In addition, for the ABA, trial courts should handle all summary proceedings, small claims, and landlord–tenant cases within thirty days of filing. Overall, for the ABA, 90% of all cases, criminal and civil, should be decided within three months, 98%, within six months, and all within a year. For the COSCA and the CCJ, there was no overall set of standards (National Center for State Courts 2003b).

The most populous state to adopt these standards was California, which has reported substantial compliance with them. Ninety-five percent of the criminal cases in its five largest counties were decided within a year of arrest. Ninety-three percent of civil cases in these counties were processed within two years from the filing date (JCC 2001). By contrast, the national picture of compliance with these standards has not been so positive, although still favorable. In a 1995 study of seventeen large, urban trial courts, the National Center for State Courts found that none of them had measured up to these standards, although they were fairly close. Sixty-six percent of cases were resolved within six months, and 88% within a year. The median criminal case-processing time was slightly more than four months (126 days) from arrest to resolution (Ostrom and Kauder 1999). However, not all jurisdictions have adopted these standards. Many simply rely on their clearance rate: the total number of cases filed divided by the total number of cases decided. Thus, a clearance of one means that a court is keeping up with its caseflow. Under this criterion, most states reported clearing over 90% of their cases (Ostrom et al. 2001, 21, 2nd citation).

III. UNIFICATION (OR CENTRALIZATION)

Pound (1906, 1927, 1940) favored a quasi-Weberian bureaucratization of state and federal court systems. To describe this type of bureaucracy, he used the concept of *unification*, which denoted structural (or organizational) and administrative centralization to achieve a higher level of effectiveness. For him this concept was easy to comprehend, involving only several dimensions: a single set of trial courts with full original jurisdiction within their geographical domains, judicial councils as statewide rulemaking bodies, and chief justices and presiding judges as supervisors with the authority to assign other judges to other branches or courts on the basis of need. Today, however, most analysts divide this concept into structural and administrative aspects. The structural aspect involves mainly trial-court consolidation to eliminate overlapping jurisdiction, to provide oversight, and to promote efficiency. Lawson (1982) pointed out that it was important to distinguish between the structural and administrative aspects because of a tendency of the states to improve their judicial systems relative to one facet but not the other or to proceed serially from one aspect to the other. Differently, judicial reformers advocate simultaneous progress along both aspects, or, failing that prospect, the achievement of structural consolidation before administrative centralization.

Since Pound's time, the idea of court unification has undergone substantial changes. Its meaning has broadened considerably, incorporating additional facets. It has become sensitive to degrees of consolidation. It has gained sophistication, discarding a posited direct relationship with court performance and recognizing the probability that centralization beyond a particular point will turn out to be dysfunctional (Flaherty 1983; Gallas 1976). In addition, consolidation at the final or intermediate appellate levels because only two states have a biramous court of last resort and only three states are bifurcated at the intermediate appellate level (Court Statistics Project 2001).

Having considered the subject of unification generally, let us briefly consider six of its important aspects of unification, beginning with the structural side (one level of trial courts, judicial councils or conferences, and court administrator's offices) and then proceeding with the administrative facets (judicial assignment authority, judicial fiscal consolidation, and judicial human resources).

A. SINGLE-TIER TRIAL COURT

Six states have consolidated their trial courts into a single tier with exclusive original jurisdiction: California, Illinois, Iowa, Minnesota, Rhode Island, and South Dakota. These states have no limited-jurisdiction courts. California is the latest state to complete this step, which proceeded gradually over a half century. In 1950 it compressed the types of trial courts from eight to three: superior, municipal, and justice. Their domains of authority were exclusive. The superior courts were countywide units deciding felonies and civil cases with claims exceeding $25,000. The municipal and justice courts handled preliminary felony hearings, misdemeanors, and infractions as well as civil suits under $25,000. The municipal courts functioned in urban areas, and the justice courts, in the rural areas of the state. In 1995 the justice courts were absorbed into the municipal courts. In 1998, a statewide initiative passed, allowing municipal and superior courts in each of the fifty-eight counties to merge if a majority of judges in both courts voted in favor of such a change. By 2001, all counties had opted for this change, which led to the establishment of a single set of trial courts: superior courts (JCC 2001).

However, other states have opted for a system of two trial-court levels: one with a single general trial court to handle major criminal and civil cases and the other with a range of two-to-eight types of limited-jurisdiction courts to process both kinds of minor cases. The prototype is one general trial court and one limited-jurisdiction court. In 2000, Arkansas became the latest state to adopt such a court system (Steelman 2002). Nevertheless, while thirty-eight states follow this model by featuring one general trial court, only thirteen observe this prototype by authorizing only one limited-jurisdiction court. A mélange prevails in other states. Nine states have two such courts; eleven states, three; six states, four; one state, five; two states, six; and another two states had eight (Court Statistics Project 2001). Such states used criteria such as geography, dollar limits, and type of case to eliminate overlapping jurisdiction. It is noteworthy that except for a few specialized (that is, limited-jurisdiction) courts, the federal judiciary has operated with one level of trial courts: the district courts, of which there are ninety four, with at least one in each state, the District of Columbia, and Puerto Rico (US Courts 2003).

Moreover, within unified court systems, there has been the establishment of divisions, often called problem-solving (or collaborative justice) courts, seeking to focus official attention (typically, a single judge) on causal inveterate behaviors of defendants in criminal cases and creating a new infrastructure to administer what is frequently called therapeutic (or restorative) justice. Examples include courts for domestic violence, driving under the influence of alcohol (DUI), drugs (adults, juveniles, and re-entry), family treatment, guns, homeless, mental health (adult and juvenile), neighborhoods (or communities or folks), reentry, tobacco, and youth (also called peer or teen courts) (National Center for State Courts 2003e, 30; Martin and Wagenknecht-Ivey 2003, 1). In recent years such divisional courts have proliferated across the country. California alone has 248 in operation (JCC 2003). It is noteworthy that drug and youth courts have spread across the nation. The National Center for State Courts reports that there are more than 1200 drug courts in the country (National Center for State Courts 2003e, 30, 83, 93, 99); the National Youth Court Center, about 900 youth courts (Woodson 2003; National Center for State Courts 2003e, 37–38).

B. JUDICIAL COUNCILS (OR CONFERENCES)

The second facet of unification, the establishment of judicial councils (or conferences), deserves considerable attention. Among the earliest states to set up such organizations were California, Kansas, Massachusetts, Michigan, New Jersey, and New York (Pound 1940). The judicial councils, typically consisted of a wide-ranging membership: judges from all levels of the state court system, legislators, bar association representatives, and lay persons. The members met regularly, gathered judicial statistics, and issued reports. Most important, they sought to further the degree of court unification in their states by recommending uniform rules of procedure (for instance, criminal, civil, evidentiary, and appellate among others) to legislatures, which retained such authority as a check on judicial power and which, for the most part, hesitated to relinquish this role until the 1970s (Berkson and Carbon 1980a, b; Glick and Vines 1973). The expansion of work facing state legislatures and their lack of sufficient time spurred them to transfer such authority to the highest state courts, which promulgated judicial standards that took effect until reversed by statutes with a fixed time period, usually 60–90 days (Gazell 1974). Such reversals have been rare, however.

The original federal counterpart to the state judicial councils was the Conference of Senior Circuit Judges, established in 1922 to serve as the policymaking organ of the federal courts. Chaired by the Chief Justice of the United States and composed of the chief judge of the court of appeal in each federal circuit, this organization sought to promote a higher degree of unification in the national judiciary by monitoring the activities of federal appellate and trial court judges, by proposing rules to Congress and lobbying for them, by urging underworked judges to volunteer for assignments in congested districts or circuits, and by encouraging courts to gather relevant statistics. In 1948, this organization became the Judicial Conference of the United States with the extension of its membership to include all courts of appeal and, eight years later, all district and special court judges (Fish 1973). Contemporaneously, Congress further empowered the federal judiciary by gradually ceding its judicial rulemaking authority to the Supreme Court. It did so for civil rules in 1938, criminal procedure in 1946, appellate procedure in 1968, and evidentiary rules in 1975. However, in 1984, Congress sought to reclaim some of its rulemaking influence by establishing a federal commission and requiring it to set guidelines to restrict judicial discretion in sentencing.

C. Court Administrator's Offices

The third aspect of unification involved the creation of court administrator's offices at the federal and state levels. This structural innovation began at the federal level in 1939 when the AOUSC was established. Its director was an appointee of the Supreme Court, acting on the recommendation of the Chief Justice but serving at the former's pleasure. The head of this office performed a myriad of national judicial housekeeping duties, including the collection of pertinent statistics; recommendations for the appointment of federal judicial staff members (such as clerks, librarians, probation officers, secretaries, and stenographers); the handling of judicial assignments to jurisdictions; and the annual preparation of a single federal judicial budges for submission to Congress. The establishment of this office was a move toward federal judicial unification not only because it provided a degree of oversight but also because other functions (especially fiscal and personnel) were removed from the executive branch, which, through its Department of Justice, had traditionally performed them. Furthermore, the creation of the AOUSC ended the conflict of interest experienced by the Department of Justice as the chief litigant in the federal courts, and ultimately accelerated the progress of the national judiciary toward becoming a bona fide coordinate branch of the federal government and helping to turn the constitutional theory of separation of powers (or checks and balances) into an operational reality (Fish 1973). Moreover, state court administrator's offices serve as the operational arm of the highest court, helping it to supervise the rest of the judicial hierarchy by carrying out and monitoring its policies. The directors of such offices typically work closely with the chief justice, who communicates the policies formulated by the court of last resort. Between 1948, when New Jersey became the first state to establish this position, and 1980, when New Hampshire became the last state to create such an office, all the states set up this kind of organization (Farthing-Capowich 1984).

D. Judicial Assignment Authority

The fourth characteristic of unification focused originally on the authority of presiding (or chief) judges in the local trial courts of a state court system to assign other judges from one of their branches to another on the basis of need. Later, at the state level, judicial assignment authority was established to provide the chief justice, operating through the court administrator, with the power to shift trial judges temporarily from uncongested rural courts to overburdened metropolitan benches. Such transfers frequently take place in summer to offset shortages caused by vacationing urban judges. The assigned judges make their greatest contribution by reducing the backlog of trials (Hays and Graham 1993).

The judicial assignment power is far stronger at the state level than in the federal judiciary. Some state chief justices may order judicial reassignments under legally specified circumstances, whereas federal judges, with their de facto lifetime appointments, may be shifted only with their consent. The latter do not face the prospect of disciplinary proceedings as state judges do if they refuse without legally approved reasons.

E. JUDICIAL FISCAL CONSOLIDATION

The fifth component of unification involved judicial fiscal consolidation, which consisted of two aspects: state court financing and a single statewide judicial budget. (The federal court system has the equivalent of both.) Under the first aspect, the legislature became the sole source of funds for state judicial operations as it assumed a responsibility once dispersed among several government units: cities, counties, and local courts, which also raised funds through fines, fees, and forfeitures. State judicial financing embraced numerous costs, including those of the final and intermediate courts, trial courts, judicial and administrative salaries, retirements, and construction and maintenance of court buildings, equipment, travel, judicial councils and conferences, as well as attorney fees for indigent claimants and defendants. The extent of state judicial funding may be viewed in two ways: (1) by activity whose cost may be defrayed by the state, localities, or shared payment; or (2) by percentage of overall court expenses paid for by the state.

Various overlapping justifications have been advanced for state court financing. First, it represented an effort to promote equal justice throughout a state rather than to allow the quality of justice to fluctuate according to local affluence (Baar 1975). Second, it sought to discourage the practice by local trial courts of varying the assessment of traffic and parking fines as their fiscal needs change. Third, because local government resources were greatly reduced in the late 1970s and 1980s due to a widespread tax revolt, state assumption of trial court costs helped to take up the slack. Fourth, such financing promoted the independence of local trial courts from city and county legislative bodies, before which they have had to present and justify budgetary requests. However, one may point out that statewide judicial financing simply shifts their dependency from one level to another, since proposed judicial budgets also had to be presented and supported before state legislatures (Tobin 1999). Fifth, such funding, if combined with a single statewide judicial budget (unitary budgeting), enhanced court management and planning. Sixth, state court financing promotes greater citizen access to local courts where filing fees (in California, for instance) have been mushrooming. Seventh, state judicial fiscal responsibility enhanced the ability of localities to divert more of their revenues toward other matters of public importance, such as property tax relief, police and fire protection, roads, and schools.

Moreover, state court financing was a blow to the remnants of the notorious fee-office system, whereby the income of some judges in minor trial courts (justices of the peace, police magistrates, and constables) depended not on governmentally paid salaries, but on money collected from defendants. Such judges had a vested financial interest in finding defendants guilty. It was not surprising that the abbreviation J.P. stood not only for justice of the peace but also for judgment for plaintiff. It is noteworthy that Pound's advocacy for a single set of trial courts with exclusive, comprehensive original jurisdiction presumed the abolition of fee offices. However, twelve states (Arizona, Delaware, Louisiana, Mississippi, Montana, Nevada, New York, Oregon, Pennsylvania Texas, Utah, and Wyoming) still retain such judicial positions, although sometimes under the name *justice court* (Ostrom, Kauder and La Fountain 2001, 3rd citation). Common victims of fee officers have been automobile drivers with out-of-state license plates caught in speed traps. However, most states have eliminated this kind of judgeship or put its compensation on a salaried basis. Such changes have been difficult to implement because of the political power of some judges. But states have been slowly emulating what Congress did in 1944 when, in one stroke, it transformed its own judicial fee officers (United States Commissioners) into salaried personnel (Fish 1973; Gazell 1975).

Although state court financing may facilitate the preparation of a single judicial budget, the two concepts are not necessarily concomitants of one another. It is possible for a state to defray all judicial expenses while still allowing individual courts to prepare their own budgets for legislative consideration. By 2005, thirty states had assumed substantial financial control of their courts. Florida became the latest in 2000, which involved a gradual shift to full state funding by 2004 (Dew 2000). Arkansas has also begun to move in this direction (Steelman 2002). State court financing need not result in excessive judicial unification if local courts are allowed the option of remaining on a shared funding basis with the state or turning over their filing fees, fines, forfeitures, and penalty assessments to the state in exchange for a state assumption of full monetary responsibility. Finally, during recessions, strong pressure on states to supply monetary relief for counties provides or renews momentum for state judicial financing (Hays and Graham 1993).

F. JUDICIAL HUMAN RESOURCES

The sixth and final aspect of unification pertains to the establishment of a state judicial human resources (or personnel) system, one incorporating judges and other court officials and separate from state and local civil service systems. Such a human resource system (like the federal one directed by the AOUSC) would operate under the direction of the highest state court or judicial council and have the authority within constitutional limits to set its own standards for the recruitment, compensation, promotion, disciplining, removal, and retirement of judicial support personnel (or staff members), such as court security officers, court executives, clerks, secretaries, stenographers, librarians, bailiffs, psychiatrists, probation officers, and public defenders. The trend has been toward discrete civil (or public) service systems, which New Jersey, Colorado, and Iowa have adopted and which have been proposed in numerous other states. In 2001, California became the most recent state to adopt such a system. It covered the issues typical of judicial civil service systems: employee classification, salaries, benefits, retirement, a meet-and-confer process (collective bargaining), access of employees to personnel files, and employee protection (due process) (Judicial Council of California 2002, 2003). Detracting from the ability of states to enact such a system as the status of some local courts' clerks, which perform some important tasks of judicial administration (such as record keeping and the gathering of statistics), but which are elective rather than appointive and thus outside of judicial control. Furthermore, other states, such as Maryland, have chosen to incorporate their judges and staff members into an overall state personnel system, a task that becomes complicated with the advent of state court financing and the need to integrate local judicial personnel into one system (Fish 1973; Gazell 1974a, 1974b).

IV. PROFESSIONALIZATION

Since the time of Roscoe Pound the field of judicial administration has undergone massive professionalization at the state and federal levels. As mentioned in Section III, every state features a court administrator's office, although the job title varies considerably among the jurisdictions. For example, Colorado uses the title State Court Administrator; Arkansas, Executive Secretary, Judicial Department; California, Hawaii, Idaho, Illinois, New Jersey, Ohio, and Oklahoma, Administrative Director for the Courts; Wisconsin, Director of State Courts; and Wyoming uses Court Coordinator. What is more, most metropolitan areas have local versions of these offices.

Despite variations in title, these officers perform similar functions. Basically, these executives seek to bring to their state court systems the greatest degree of uniformity in procedures that is feasible within the law and is managerially efficient. In general, these staff agencies of the highest state court or judicial council help formulate rules and other policies to promote equal justice throughout the state. They monitor the assignment of judges from one place to another within their states. They supervise the garnering and maintenance of numerous statistics relevant to the courts. They oversee the preparation of their state judicial budgets, as well as court personnel practices. In addition, they perform numerous ad hoc tasks at the behest of the chief justice (or judge). Overall, most observers accept Saare's (1970) typology describing eight overlapping kinds of management performed by these offices: (1) "Calendar" (now, caseflow); (2) "Data Processing" (now, management information systems); (3) "Financial"; (4) "Personnel" (now, human resources); (5) "Jury and Witness"; (6) "Space and Equipment"; (7) "Public Information and Report[s]"; and (8) "General" (or miscellaneous). However, these staff agencies lack the daily involvement in calendar and jury and witness management that trial court administrators experience.

Of these deeply entwined functions, perhaps the most significant one at the trial court level is caseflow management, which seeks to move litigation steadily toward a form of resolution (pretrial conferences, plea bargains, out-of-court settlements, case withdrawals, and trials). Trial court administrators tend to be proactive in this regard—that is, to exercise docket control rather than permit the contending attorneys to govern the pace of litigation. One method of exercising such control consists of employing more stringent policies on the granting of continuances. Some law firms accept far more cases than they can handle, which results in conflicting court-room engagements, inevitable requests for delays, and congested dockets. Another method is the establishment of a case assignment system whereby the court administrators or other judicial support officials disperse cases to judges chronologically immediately after their availability to hear them. This practice fosters speedier resolutions as well as a higher degree of equity in the distribution of legal business among the judges. However, it also increases uncertainty among lawyers that their cases will be heard by judges favorable to them. Yet a third method involves the monitoring of assigned cases to ascertain their proximity to resolution, or a periodical checking of individual judicial calendars in system to avoid operating on an assignment basis. The latest technique for increasing docket control and reducing delays in adjudication is, as mentioned in Section II, DCM, which entails the sorting of judicial filings and their placement in various tracks with separate procedures and time frames for their disposition. Civil and criminal cases are classified on the basis of their complexity, which depends on at least four factors: the type of suit or charge, the number of parties, the amount in controversy, and the lawyers' evaluation of the time required to handle the litigation. Beginning with New Jersey in 1986, ten states and the District of Columbia have used DCM in their trial courts (Alliegro et al. 1993; Goerdt 1997; Hays and Graham 1993; Pankey 1992).

Trial court administrators cannot fulfill their caseflow management function without also spending their time on other responsibilities that have become part of their professional role. Coping with a rising stream of judicial business requires, at least in metropolitan trial courts, the establishment of a management information system (computerization), as discussed in Section VI of this chapter. Such a system enables court executives not only to monitor civil and criminal cases to detect incipient backlogs and apportion cases more evenly among the judges, but also to improve fiscal and personnel management. Thus court administrators may better oversee the flow of their expenditures, stay within budgetary constraints, and analyze their priorities, spending patterns, and relationships between fiscal requests and appropriations. In addition, judicial organizations may more efficiently process salary checks and keep records of vacations, disabilities, seniority, pay increases, retirements, and vacancies among other matters.

Computerization greatly influences the remaining forms of management, listed by Saare (1970) that constitute a court administrator's role: "Jury and Witness Management," "Space and Equipment Management," "Public Information and Report Management," and "General Management." Court administrators can more readily maintain up-to-date lists of eligible jury members so that, if litigants are ready for trial, impanelment becomes easier. Such lists enable judges holding pretrial conferences to settle cases and to confront opposing attorneys with the prospect of an immediate trial if they fail to reach an agreement in the judges' chambers. If a trial ensues, court administrators may better monitor the whereabouts of witnesses. These officials know more about rooms available for trial and their efficient use, as well as the location of tape recorders, film projectors, and videotaping machines. They may also improve their ability to maintain the records needed by the state judicial administrator's office to keep itself informed about local operations, to prepare annual reports and timely press releases, and to fulfill requests for data from legislators and other interested groups. General management is a catchall rubric for miscellaneous problems, often unforeseen, that may arise in the course of a work day: for instance, a judge comes in drunk; the courthouse restrooms have to be closed; or an employee alleges sexual harassment. The most significant part of these problems lies, as Saare (1970) contends, in "coordinating the parts of the [judicial] organization."

The number of state trial court administrators grew nationally from a mere six at the end of the 1950s to forty-six by the close of the next decade. By 1977, the figure had reached 420. At the federal level all thirteen circuits have hired court executives since 1971; numerous metropolitan district courts have recruited such managers since 1982. The AOUSC, founded in 1939, has served as a prototype for state and local judicial managers' offices, beginning with New Jersey in 1948 and the Superior Court of the County of Los Angeles exactly one decade later.

The role of the court administrators at the state and federal levels has recently become more complex, not only because of their numerous interlocking functions, but also because of their work environment, which resembles that of other executives in the public, nonprofit, and business sectors. Most analysts agree with Saare (1982) who argues that Mintzberg's (1973) framework for understanding the essence of managerial work in corporations is also apropos for illuminating the work of public executives, including judicial administrators. In general, the activities of these managers exhibit at least a half-dozen characteristics: (1) a variety of duties, (2) little time for any specific work, (3) frequent interruptions, (4) tendency to perform many tasks superficially, (5) strong reliance on verbal communications (such as informal meetings and telephone calls), and (6) proclivity toward overwork. Table 27.1 summarizes the activities of court administrators within broad categories.

Among all the activities performed by court executives, the tasks of helping to represent their organizations and negotiating judicial budgets may be the most significant, because these branches of government have increasingly had to function in open systems, sensitive to frequently hostile public and political milieus, rather than in their traditional manner—that is, as closed Weberian bureaucracies. Furthermore, such responsibilities have become increasingly valuable as courts have faced intense competition for scarce resources in the wake of drastic anti-tax measures (for instance, Proposition 13 in California and Proposition 2 1/2 in Massachusetts) and a reduction in the size of the public sector. This trend has even seeped into state court systems, as exemplified by California's rent-a-judge practice, which enable litigants under some circumstances to hire retired judges to hear their cases.

Moreover, the professionalization of court administrators has influenced them in other respects as well. First, it has increased their sensitivity to various types of bias, those based on race, ethnicity, gender, sexual orientation, disabilities, and language (Low 1994; New Jersey Committee on Women in the Courts 1993). Second, it has made them more receptive to modern management practices, such as total quality management (TQM) to improve court performance and user satisfaction through greater employee participation in setting operational policies (Aikman 1993; Fleischman and Aikman 1993). Third, it has often advanced the educational levels of court administrators, who now frequently hold master's degrees in business administration as well as have law credentials. Their managerial and legal expertise helps them to internalize their duties, thus obviating the formulating of their responsibilities as organizational requirements. Their education and training have also fostered their ability to operate in a collegial work environment (Sargent and Stupak 1993). Fourth, the salary level for court administrators has risen to the point where it approximates that of many judges. By 2004, for example, a judicial salary survey conducted by the National Center for State Courts reported that state court administrators made almost as much in salary as general trial court judges. The respective mean salaries were $113,139 and $113,504; median salaries, $108,288

TABLE 27.1
Categorization of Court Administrator's Activities

Interpersonal	Informational	Decisional
a. Serving as figureheads on ceremonial occasions	a. Monitoring information flowing into courts	a. Propose court policies
b. Guiding and collaborating	b. Observing work environments	b. Assisting chief judges 1. To formulate organizational strategies and tactics, especially for budget battles 2. To design and initiate projects to improve court efficiency
c. Performing liaison role between courts and external world	c. Disseminating knowledge through impromptu and formal meetings	c. Handling daily crises
	d. Helping to represent their courts before governmental, legal, civic, and professional bodies	d. Assigning organizational resources (e.g., funds, space, cases, personnel) e. Negotiating for the court f. Operating as a technical expert in directing projects and facilitating the solution of any concomitant problems

and $110,330; and ranges, $85,000–$175,728 and $88,164–$158,100 (National Center for State Courts 2004a).

In addition, these officials have formed organizations to reinforce their growing professionalization. Among the most prominent have been the National Association of Trial Court Administrators (NATCA) and the National Association for Court Administrators (NACA), which merged in 1984 into the National Association of Court Management (NACM) and now operate under the aegis of the National Center for State Courts. The NACM has approximately three-thousand members. Other notable professional societies include COSCA, and the National Association of Appellate Court Clerks (NAACC). Furthermore, these groups regularly publish newsletters, journals, or both to promote a greater exchange of effective management ideas and practices and to assist their members in keeping abreast of the latest developments in their field (especially technological innovations in management information systems) through seminars and workshops. The best known professional outlets are *The Court Manager*, a quarterly publication of the NACM, and *Court Technology Bulletin*, a bimonthly publication of the NCSC. Sometimes court administration articles even appear in *Judicature*, the monthly publication of the American Judicature Society (AJS) and *RAND Review*, a publication of the Rand (Research and Development) Corporation. All these outlets appear in print and online.

Court administrators at the state and federal levels disseminate and exchange information mostly by newsletters in published and website versions. At the former level, examples include California's *Court News*, a bimonthly publication; Florida's *Full Court Press*, another bimonthly publication; *Justice Matters*, a quarterly publication; and Texas' *Benchmarks*, another quarterly publication. They all announce, among other matters, seminars and workshops as well as judicial rule changes. At the federal level, the preeminent outlet is *The Third Branch*, a printed and online monthly newsletter published by the AOUSC (the staff arm of the federal judiciary). However, unlike its state counterparts, it is more thorough in its coverage. For instance, it includes excerpts from speeches by the Chief Justice of the United States; lengthy interviews with judges, members of Congress, officials in the executive branch, and legal scholars (in short, anyone with a strong interest and expertise in the substantive or administrative facets of the judicial process; news of research developments (particularly in the areas of caseload management and computerization); and human resource (or personnel) changes (nominations, confirmations, applications among federal judges for senior or semi-retired status, resignations, and deaths).

V. EDUCATION AND TRAINING

Another important issue in judicial administration is education and training. The first concept is theoretical, the second, practical. However, because they differ more in degree than in kind, they deserve joint treatment. Both apply to court support personnel and judges. Both are aspects of professionalization, a means to this end, which includes modes of transmitting knowledge systematically to prospective and current judicial managers. Furthermore, both contain informal and formal aspects. The latter involves on-the-job learning and sharing of occupational experiences; the former involves instructional programs offered by law schools, universities, the private sector, and the court systems themselves. Both types of instruction have become increasingly important to meet the performance needs of future court managers in at least nine areas: (1) budgets, (2) community and customer service, (3) ethics, (4) facilities and security, (5) information management, (6) juries, (7) personnel (human resources) and workforce, (8) organization vision and values, and (9) technology (National Center for State Courts 2003e, 86–98).

Numerous law schools have incorporated judicial administration courses into their curricula. Among the notable examples are the legal programs at New York University, the University of Denver, Yale University, the University of Arkansas, and the University of Houston. In fact, law schools offered the first known classes in this field. As early as 1929, Matthew G. Hale conducted such a course at the Oregon College of Law. Five years later, Maynard E. Pirsig headed a similar class at the University of Minnesota law School. Both may have been influenced by the publication of the first textbook in the field of judicial administration, Willoughby's (1929) *Principles of Judicial Administra*tion that affirmed Pound's views toward the subject, but related them to the rest of the criminal justice system. *The Journal of the American Judicature Society* (now *Judicature*) was available as an updating supplement.

Today, more than fifty universities offer courses in judicial management, albeit in different departments. Such classes are segments of programs in public administration, criminal justice, political science, and business administration. Students can receive certificates in this field at such institutions as the University of Southern California, the University of Denver, Central Missouri State University, Indiana University, American University, and Adelphi University. These courses typically cover most subjects of interest to federal, state, and local judicial administrators.

However, educational opportunities in judicial administration lie as much in the private sector as in the state and federal court systems themselves. The Institute for Court Management (ICM), originally located in Denver, Colorado (now in Williamsburg, Virginia) is the chief nongovernmental organization for education in this field. Between 1970, the year of its founding, and 2005, 1020 persons from forty-eight states and twelve foreign countries have received certificates for completing the ICM's Court Executive Development Program (CEDP), which includes both classroom education through a variety of seminars (the most important of which involves caseflow management and delay management) and intensive examination of (and report on) a significant managerial problem facing a court close to the respective candidate's home. Enrollment in this program has attracted those seeking, from the start, a career in court management and persons interested in a career change, veterans of other professions who have novel experiences and insights to bring to the field of judicial administration.

At least five trends in the orientation of ICM have become pronounced since 1980. One is the added instructional attention to the external world of the courts—the public and the other organizations in the civil and criminal justice system—to complement the traditional concern with the internal world. The future of courts is thought to rest on the development of public trust as well as the achievement of intra-court efficiencies. A second trend has been to put a stronger effort in workshops to relate the issues facing local courts to national judicial issues and to place them in that context. A third development has been to globalize the American court administration by comparing it with such administration abroad and through international court official exchange programs. A fourth trend centers on the expanding role of judges in workshops from their initial role as students to that of instructors so that both are now in evidence. A fifth trend has been the shift of orientation from an elitist to an egalitarian one. During the 1970s, those seeking education in court administration had to go to the ICM headquarters for the workshops and for the certificate programs. However, in the 1980s, the ICM began to come to those who were interested by scheduling numerous workshops around the country and steadily expanding the number and kind of workshops, thus making it easier for people to attend them, by distance learning, video-conferencing, and interactive online computer programs, and by setting up certificate programs based on how deeply the participants want to go into the subject.

Therefore, it became possible for people to involve themselves with the ICM to a considerable extent on their terms, not the ICM's. For instance, in 2002 the ICM offered twenty-six courses in sixteen cities, suburbs, or towns within thirteen states or the District of Columbia. It offered courses on managing court finances and human resources, electronic (or e-)filing, imaging documents, court innovation, reengineering, strategic planning and management, and technology. By 2003, the ICM offered twenty-four selections in ten cities, suburbs, or towns within nine states and the DC and added courses on court security, emergency management, and customer service.

Prospective court employees may simply want to complete a course or two to improve their marketability; current court staffers may do the same thing to increase their chances for lateral movement or advancement within their organization or for being hired by another court. Again, those who begin this program are not obligated to complete it, and may improve their marketability even if they move only a part of the way through it. In fact, persons may elect to take one workshop or two related to their current or prospective court employment. For example, they could take a beginning course in court performance standards, caseflow management, or research methods and follow it with an advanced course in these respective topics. Individual choices are on the rise because of the growing availability of workshops and alternate modes of instruction (Institute for Court Management 2002–2005).

However, persons interested in proceeding all the way through the ICM pursue its extensive, four-phase Court Executive Development Program (CEDP) and complete it within five years. In Phase I, participants develop their knowledge and talents in six key areas within court administration by completing courses, that is, workshops, usually lasting three days and conducted over weekends to avoid conflicts with the work schedules of the enrollees. These courses involve understanding court performance standards and research methods as well as managing caseflows, finances, personnel, and information. Each workshop varies in cost, but by 2005 approached $800, making the overall expenditure for Phase I close to $5000.

In Phase II, those certified as having successfully finished the first phase take a three-week course in Williamsburg, Virginia, the headquarters of the ICM. This phase is offered every June for the convenience of participants, many of whom who may schedule it concurrently with their vacations. In this phase they seek to enhance their skills in five areas: (1) the purposes and roles of courts, (2) conceptual and interpersonal skills, (3) internal and external environments, (4) modern leadership and management theory, and (5) appraisal of court operations and programs. The cost of this phase has held steady at $3000.

If this phase is successfully completed, participants may continue to Phase III, during which the enrollees conduct a thorough research project in a court near their home. The project has to be approved by the Director of the CEDP and must involve at least fifty hours of work over a nine-month period and a quality of research and writing equivalent to what is required for master's degree theses. If the Director approves the Phase III paper, the participants enter Phase IV, which entails their coming to Washington, DC for several days to present their reports to the other participants who have also reached this stage, to exchange knowledge with their peers' reports, to discuss leadership questions and future trends in the field of court management, and to attend a graduation ceremony at the Supreme Court of the United States.

At that gathering, the Chief Justice of the United States presents the participants with their certificate of completion for the CEDP. The cost of each of the last two phases has remained unchanged at $1000. By 2005, the tuition for the entire program, due to rising Phase I course costs, had risen to approximately $10,000 spread over five or fewer years. It is possible that courts, as employers, may defray some or all of the expenses in return for an employee's or prospective employee's commitment to serve the court for a specified time period. It is no exaggeration to state that the achievement of such a certificate—an average of only thirty-two are awarded per year—enhances the marketability of the recipients immeasurably over the short term and long run. Nor is it an overstatement to say that those starting the CEDP program but not finishing it still enhance their professional value. This benefit accrues even if they have merely completed one course or two in Phase I.

An alternative to the CEDP is the Court Management Program (CPM), which consists of two phases instead of four. The first phase is identical in course content and cost with that for the CEDP. The second phase, which in 2005 cost $1200, involves a one-week course in lieu of the three-week CEDP second phase. The CPM second phase enables participants to learn in six overlapping areas: (1) conceptual and interpersonal skills, (2) judicial independence and inter-dependence, (3) leadership and management approaches, (4) team-building and communication, (5) efficacious methods of handling specific court issues, and (6) National Association of Court Managers' (NACM) ten core competencies. These interrelated competencies encompass the following: (1) understanding the purposes of courts and court systems; (2) leadership; (3) resource allocation, acquisition, budget, and finance; (4) vision and strategic planning; (5) case-flow management; (6) information technology management; (7) public information and media relations; (8) employee training and development; (9) ancillary services and programs (super-seded by essential components, such as adjudication, alternatives to it, the enforcement of judicial orders, and court facilities); and (10) human resources management (National Associ-ation of Court Managers 1998, 2003). After the two phases are completed, there is a formal graduation ceremony where CMP diplomas are awarded. In 2005, the cost of the CMP was about 60% of that of the CEDP, making the CMP diploma more affordable but less valuable in the job market.

Warren Burger, Chief Justice of the United States, was the catalyst behind the ICM's establish-ment, having introduced the topic in an address to the ABA in 1969. He had been influenced by an analogy between hospitals and courts. By the start of World War II, the effective management of modern hospitals had become so complex that doctors and nurses (whose profession was medicine, not management) could no longer handle administrative responsibilities nearly as well as they once had. As programs in hospital administration burgeoned, those with training in this area were hired to run such institutions, allowing physicians and nurses to concentrate on medicine.

Similarly, those who ran the nation's courts (usually chief justices and presiding judges) faced growing difficulties in coping with their steadily increasing caseloads, personnel, and budgets. Such judges were almost invariably lawyers, not executives, whose training lacked management coursework. In their curricula, law schools presupposed that most of their graduates would be solo practitioners or partners in law firms, neither of which entailed substantial administrative responsibilities. Consequently Burger envisioned the development of court administrators as a *sina qua non* for improving court efficiency. Within a few months after his public call for such education, the ABA, the American Judicature Society, and the Institute of Judicial Administration pooled their resources to help bring the ICM into existence. In 1984 the ICM became part of the NCSC.

At the federal level, education and training in judicial management has extended far beyond court administrators to other court staff members, especially librarians, stenographers, probation officers, bailiffs, secretaries, and psychiatrists. Such instruction was one of the salient functions performed by the Federal Judicial Center, established in 1967 at the behest of Chief Justice Earl Warren and initially headed by another proponent of its creation, retired Associate Justice Tom C. Clark. Since its inception, the Center has regularly offered pre-service and in-service programs, usually several times a year. These courses have enabled judicial support officials to remain conversant with the latest developments in their specialties.

No one seriously disputes the proposition that judges, along with their staff, ought to receive periodic instruction in the managerial and substantive aspects of their roles to enhance their performance and to operate more efficiently and justly. Several institutions have been formed to this widely desired goal. For instance, since its establishment in 1970, the American Academy of Judicial Education (AAJE)—a part of the Judicial Division of the American Bar Association, headquartered in University, Mississippi—has offered extensive instruction across the country mainly to new judges in the form of courses lasting six or seven days. The courses embrace numerous subjects, including some relevant to judicial administration: case flow, and trial management, delay, filing motions, setting trial dates, pretrial conferences, continuances, discovery, judicial independence and the separation of powers, and judicial accountability. If judges complete specified sets of courses, they receive a diploma in humanities and judging or in judicial skills (American Academy of Judicial Education 2005). If judges do not attend the AAJE, they will still probably have to complete pre-service and in-service courses because most states have set up their own agencies and requirements for both kinds of judicial instruction (Rottman et al. 2000).

Despite the eminence of the AAJE, the chief organization for judicial instruction at the state level is the National Judicial College (NJC). Founded in 1963 and located at the University of Nevada, Reno, it had provided, by 2005, education and training for over seventy-thousand judges from all fifty states, the District of Columbia, the territories of the United States, and from over 150 nations. The NJC annually offers an average of ninety courses attended by more than 2700 judges. The enrolled judges run the gamut from those in limited-jurisdiction courts to those in courts of last resort. In fact, over 2000 judges from 150 countries have attended the College. Such instruction typically culminates in the awarding of certifications of completion in one or more of the following five skill areas: (1) administrative law adjudication, (2) court management, (3) disputes resolution, (4) general jurisdiction trials, and (5) special court trials. More than fifty programs are offered each year, and enrollment exceeds three thousand annually. In 2005, forty-five courses were offered, some of which pertained to judicial administration: civil mediation, computer use, decision-making, dispute resolution, presiding-judge management skills, problem-solving, small claims, settlements, and traffic cases. By 2005, tuition for most courses had risen to nearly a $1000. The courses varied in length from two days to twelve and were conducted in state-of-the-art courtrooms, which allowed the video and audio taping of the entire class sessions. Currently, the NJC also offers master's and doctoral programs in judicial studies (National Judicial College 2005).

Each year its faculty (generally in the 250–300 range) provides courses lasting between two-and-one-half days and three weeks for new and experienced judges (National Judicial College 1999 4; 2005). The courses offered include such topics as non-judicial alternatives to dispute resolution (ADR), evidence, great questions in American law, the roles of medicine and science in law, technology (computers), and victim's rights. Well-known attorneys, law professors, and jurists have volunteered to lead classes at the College. Similarly, communications experts, medical doctors, psychologists, and sociologists have contributed their aid without charge. In 1986, the

NJC established a Master of Judicial Studies program, the country's only advanced degree program for trial judges, in cooperation with the University of Nevada, Reno. In 1995, there were more than ninety judges seeking this degree. (The current figure is not available.) A variety of corporations and foundations (most notably the Max C. Fleischmann Foundation) have financially underwritten the operations of this organization. Supplementary assistance has come from federal and state grants, as well as association and individual contributions.

At the federal level, the instructional offerings of the Federal Judicial Center (FJC)—the research, development, education, and training arm of the nation's courts—merit attention. Established in 1967, as mentioned earlier, it has been providing entry-level and in-service instruction not only to a potpourri of court staffers at the appellate and trial levels but also to new and veteran federal judges at both levels. Courses delving into the numerous facets of court management are offered throughout the year, as the annual reports of the Center make evident. In 2004 the FJC offered 410 educational programs (including those telecast on the Federal Judicial Television Network (JNET)), for more than 12,400 federal court staff members and judges, and held seminars or briefings for 290 foreign judges and officials representing sixty-six countries.

The FJC's educational efforts fall into four categories: (1) seminars (for orientation of newly confirmed federal judges and executive management seminars for chief district court judges), (2) workshops (for continuing education of veteran judges), (3) conferences (for chief district court judges), and (4) four kinds of distance learning: computer-based instruction using CD-ROMs, Web-based training conducted over computer networks, satellite broadcasting, and video conferencing (Federal Judicial Center 2001). Foreign judges and offices are included because in 1999 the FJC's mandate was enlarged to provide information to improve the administration of justice in other countries and thus to promote international security and that of Americans traveling abroad for governmental, business, or personal reasons (Federal Judicial Center 1999).

Newly confirmed district judges usually assemble for one week in Washington, DC, to attend a once-a-year seminar and to explore such topics as antitrust cases, calendar management, class actions, employment discrimination suits, evidentiary problems, fraud, judicial ethics, jury administration, search and seizure issues, securities cases, the sentencing process, and stress management. Through regional workshops the FJC also offers continuing education to these judges. In addition, it offers special sessions each summer for appellate as well as trial judges, one-week seminars seeking to update their knowledge of litigations involving economic matters and the increasingly salient matter of statistical proof in such litigation.

Besides the ICM, the NJC, and the FJC, there are other noteworthy institutional programs—for instance, the Institute of Judicial Administration and the University of Virginia School of Law Graduate Program for Judges. Such programs do not warrant much attention because they are largely for appellate judges, not trial judges and court administrators. The Institute of Judicial Administration (IJA), which is a branch of the New York University School of Law, was founded in 1952 and is the oldest such program (Institute of Judicial Administration (US) 2003). The IJA should not be confused with the eponymous Birmingham (UK) organization, which was founded in 1986 and devoted primarily to research in court management (Institute of Judicial Administration (UK) 2003). The University of Virginia program merits some comments since it is similar to the judicial studies programs of the NJC (Judicial Education 2003). Established in 1980, with the aid of the Appellate Judges Conference of the American Bar Association, the Virginia program features seminars attended by thirty federal and state appellate judges for twelve weeks over two consecutive summers (six weeks per summer). During the first year, the judges examine the following subjects: the development of Anglo-American jurisprudence, the links between law and economics, and one or two salient constitutional law questions. During the second year, the judges explore three additional issues that overlap the first three topics: (1) the applicability of social science research to law, (2) the role of medicine (particularly, psychiatry) in criminal cases, and (3) comparative legal systems. By 1992, six groups of judges had passed through the program—a total of 178 participants from forty-five jurisdictions. (The current comparable figures are not available.) They received their degrees after writing an acceptable thesis and passing a three-hour examination devised by the law school faculty. The successful completion of the program culminated in the awarding of a Master of Laws (L.L.M) in the Judicial Process. As of 2003, this program remained the same in content and is still the only one of its kind in the nation (Master of Laws 2003).

VI. TECHNOLOGY

The final important issue confronting the field of judicial administration has been the role of technology (notably, but not exclusively, automation or the use of computers), especially at the trial court level. Court officials find a steady stream of information in this area by reading the National Center for State Court's bimonthly publication, *Court Technology Bulletin*, in print or by accessing it online through the Center's homepage. Also available is its annual compilation, *Court Technology Report*. It is common knowledge that the nation's courts, regardless of level, have lagged behind the federal and state executive and legislative branches as well as the private sector in technological developments. For instance, in 1970, Chief Justice Burger publicized the magnitude of this gap by stressing that most of the country's judicial systems were administratively antiquated, using methods for keeping records, managing litigation, and planning that had not changed since the late nineteenth century and that were inadequate then, as Pound had contended. In effect, Burger was calling for the application of modern business methods, especially management information systems, to the nation's judiciaries rather than simply the traditional remedies of additional judges and higher budgets, although he undoubtedly knew that such technological change required a massive infusion of money, at least at the start. A year later, he reinforced his critique by declaring: "In terms of methods, machinery and equipment, the flow of paper—and we know [that] the business of courts depends on the flow of papers—most courts have changed very little fundamentally in a hundred years or more" (Burger 1970).

This lag stemmed from several causes. One was that many judges viewed the spirit of technology as a threat to their tradition of autonomy. A second was that, until the last three decades, few judges had seen the problem of court congestion and delay as serious enough to seek the aid of computers. A third consideration was that numerous judges feared a substantial loss of power to members of their staff (especially, court administrators), who alone possessed the expertise to run computers successfully. A fourth reason was that most judges knew little about the potentiality of technology, because their frequently heavy workloads had kept them from learning much about it. A fifth cause was that judicial computerization was usually expensive, particularly at the outset (Gazell 1970, 1972).

Nevertheless, state and federal courts have been gradually closing the technology gap. At the state level, such modernization is believed to have started in 1960 when the St. Louis County Probate Court used pre-punched cards to record the possible contingencies influencing its caseflow and to print fee statements. In 1961, the Court of Common Pleas of Allegheny County, Pennsylvania (Pittsburgh), installed computers to determine and monitor the status of all its litigation, to inform attorneys about its oversight, and to urge them into settling at least some of their cases expeditiously. In 1965, analysts devised simulations of the criminal litigation flow through the Court of General Sessions in Washington, DC, and demonstrated the reductions in delay that would probably follow if particular legal matters, such as preliminary hearings in federal felony cases, were removed from this judicial body. Between 1967 and 1969, the Rand Institute of New York City performed similar work in the criminal trial courts of Manhattan and simulated the effects of specific proposals (such as the addition of judges and the elimination of grand jury indictments) on the stream of judicial business.

Moreover, technology embraces much more than computers. It also includes behavioral research, which is done through the use of computers that simulate the conduct of those who use the courts. Such research may facilitate the settlement of cases and lead to an expedited case flow. For instance, since 1979 the Institute for Civil Justice (ICJ) (a division of the Rand Corporation of Santa Monica, California) has fostered such research. In its first five-year report, the ICJ summarized the findings of its work in five broad rubrics: (1) delay, (2) costs, (3) outcomes, (4) strategies and tactics, and (5) alternative modes for settling cases. Although the conclusions under each category are far too numerous to encapsulate within the space allotted for this chapter, one may still cite several of them, albeit in general terms. Here are some of the major findings of ICJ's research (Institute for Civil Justice 1985, 14–15):

1. It learned that delay in the handling of litigation depended more on the local legal culture or on what are often called courtroom workgroups, especially the efforts of judges and attorneys and the political skills of the former and their staffs, than on specific remedies, such as alterations in the court calendar or case assignment system, increases in the number of judges, reductions in continuances, and restrictions on discovery proceedings. These particular steps benefited courts only in the short run.
2. It found that court costs depended most heavily on the percentage of litigants taking advantage of jury trials, the length of those proceedings, the percentage of pretrial settlements, judicial salary levels, the size of court staffs, and the caseloads of individual judges.
3. It reported numerous outcomes, including an increase in the chances of plaintiffs for success with the passage of time in business tort, malpractice, and product liability cases, although in the latter two kinds of suits their prospects were still only 40%. In addition, during the 1970s, the average awards for plaintiffs doubled, with product liability cases producing the largest verdicts.
4. It probed into numerous strategies and tactics, including a federal judicial policy (Rule 68 of the Federal Code of Civil Procedure), which sought to discourage plaintiffs from rejecting defendants' formal settlement offers by requiring the former to pay the latter's legal costs incurred after submission of the offer if the plaintiff went ahead with a trial and then received an award less than the offer. However, the researchers found that the policy actually engendered the opposite result, spawning additional litigation for a variety of reasons, including a tendency of the defendants to make nominal settlement offers in the hope that plaintiffs would mistakenly assess their chances for receiving a higher award from going to trial. Institute researchers, in examining alternate modes for settling disputes, learned that voluntary arbitration inside and outside courts proved efficient in reducing congestion because this procedure was widely seen as fair. They found that such arbitration had been underutilized.

However, in 1993, the ICJ reported that arbitration seldom brought about important reductions in judicial costs and average case-disposition time because it diverted few suits from trial. Nor did arbitration significantly lower costs for litigants, who nonetheless were satisfied with this method of increasing access to adjudication; it gave them an opportunity to present their claims and receive a judgment instead of submitting to a settlement (Institute for Civil Justice 1993, 27–28). The ICJ has an extensive research agenda, which includes a continuing interest in the administration of justice—particularly how well the nation's courts resolve cases in a just, speedy, and inexpensive manner—and in the utility of growing court reliance to ADR to decide minor cases (Institute for Civil Justice 2003).

Today court technology extends far beyond case management and behavioral research. Statewide judicial information systems have come into vogue. Judicial technology is a part of a far larger phenomenon: the international public management movement, which has been spreading globally since the 1970s. This movement has involved governments throughout much of the world, which try to do more with less—greater accomplishments with lower revenues. It came about as a result of people's complaints in many countries. Those people had come to believe that they were paying more and more in taxes while receiving less and less in public services. In the United States, for instance, tax revolts swept through the country in the late 1970s and during the 1980s, which also led to the election of conservative governments in much of the world. The people demanded more effective and less costly government. Some responses to these demands involved various forms of government decentralization, such as privatization, devolution, and deregulation. A concomitant response involved electronic (or, more commonly, e-)government, which sought to automate as many government functions as possible to improve performance and reduce costs. Along with the executive and legislative branches, judiciaries have also felt pressure for e-government, to make themselves more cost effective in dispensing justice. They have done so by seeking to become part of what one may call an electronic (or e-)justice system.

The formation of such a system includes the establishment of an electronic (or e-)court system, which embraces informational integration within state and federal court systems at the trial and appellate levels as well as between court systems. It also includes a comparable integration between all courts and all other components of the nation's justice system: police, prosecutors, probation offices, prisons, jails, parole boards, and juvenile justice agencies. The integration is vertical, horizontal, and diagonal within and between these organizations. Because information from any one component of the system is readily available to all other components, it is increasingly difficult for persons in criminal and civil cases to fall through the interstices within the system. For instance, it is less probable for a defendant to be in court on one charge without that court knowing that there is a warrant for the arrest of that person on another charge in a different jurisdiction. In 1998, Pennsylvania and Colorado became the first state to establish such a system. In the former, the system was called JNET, the acronym for Justice NETwork (Wells 2002). In the latter, it was labeled CICJIS (Colorado Integrated Criminal Justice Information System) (Poulos 1998). The acronym *JNET* also applies to the federal court system's judicial network, an intranet established in 1999 and used largely to provide thousands of judicial employees with ready access to training. Since its inception, the federal JNET has broadcast more than 110 different courses (Administrative Office of the United States Courts 2000).

Within the e-court systems are electronic (or e-)courts, often called cybercourts (alternatively, paperless or virtual courts). They are computerized to manage numerous vital functions more effectively. These include caseflows (dominated by Judicial Automated Calendaring Systems (JACS)), finances, security, human resources, facilities, juries, research, document storage (imaging), electronic (or e-)filings (including small claims cases) and responses, the payment of traffic fines and signups for traffic schools, legal assistance for pro se (self-represented) litigants, online postings of cases and court opinions, and general public access. e-Filings represent one of the earliest forms of computerization. Colorado became the first jurisdiction to set up a statewide system. County-wide systems came originally to Fulton County, Georgia (the Atlanta area) and King County, Washington (the Seattle area). Citywide systems came to San Diego first. Such filings were popular with attorneys because they could be used around the clock to pay the required fees electronically. Court clerks liked e-filings because they typically eliminated a half-dozen steps in the paper-handling process (Kenworthy 2000; Winters 2002). By 2004, most federal courts had implemented e-filing through the CM/ECF (Case Management/Electronic Case Files) system (Administrative Office of the United States Courts 2004). This filing mode has also spread abroad—for instance, to the Supreme Court of Canada (Beaulieu 2002). The advent of the system generated pressure for uniform e-filing standards in all jurisdictions. Furthermore, by 2004, Public Access to Court Electronic Records (PACER) had become the principal means for the federal court system to enable people to gain judicial data. This access permitted users to find case and docket information from federal district, bankruptcy, and appellate courts and from the US Party/Case Index (Administrative Office of the United States Courts 2004).

Within the e-courts are electronic (or e-)courtrooms, modeled after the famous Courtroom 21, a mock state-of-the-art high-technology courtroom set up in 1993 at the Marshall-Wythe School of Law of the College of William and Mary, in Williamsburg, Virginia (Lederer 1994). In the e-courtrooms, all proceedings are video and audio taped from a half-dozen overhead cameras. The cameras are voice activated, and the microphones are self-adjusting. The proceedings are captured on Digital Video (or Versatile) Disks (DVD) to an increasing extent or on Video Cassette Recorder (VCR) tapes. The latter is fast becoming obsolescent. There are computers on the bench of the presiding judge, the tables of the opposing counsel and jury, and the table of the jury deliberation annex. These computers provide the participants with instant transcripts and permit them to take notes on their monitors, to move back for reviewing testimony and forward to catch up with the proceedings, and to do research if necessary. The disks become the court records for each case. On appeals, the disks are simply played, making them superior in accuracy to written documents, which cannot convey, for instance, the demeanor and appearance of the participants.

In 2002, Courtroom 21 became the site of a real court proceeding: a jury trial in a federal manslaughter case. In that case several frontiers in legal technology were crossed: a key witness testified from the United Kingdom; holographic medical evidence and medical animation were presented; the jury viewed evidence electronically while also using computers in their deliberations; and a counsel used instant wireless messaging to communicate with assistants outside the courtroom and, when outside, with court official inside (Gaudreaux 2002). In 2003, this courtroom also served as the site for the trial of a United States citizen accused of trying to provide funds for a terrorist strike against a city in Virginia. The trial involved the same technology as the federal manslaughter case but extended legal technology further through videoconferencing, which included participants from three continents (Flythe 2003). Courtroom 21 has attracted visitors from many nations. There are approximately 500 such courtrooms worldwide (McKay 2002). Nevertheless, not much is known about global e-courts or e-justice systems outside the United States, Australia, and Canada, even in Europe (Fabri 2003).

As mentioned in Section V, the National Judicial College (NJC) established such courtrooms as model forums for conducting its classes. Florida adopted this model in 1998 on a limited basis when it established Courtroom 23, named after the twenty-third floor of the Orange County Courthouse for its ninth judicial circuit (Dussault 1999). Michigan took Florida's prototype further by applying it statewide in 2001 through the establishment of cybercourts that were used to settle real disputes in cyberspace (that is, judicial proceedings and evidence were shared over computers, over the Internet, and through videoconferencing). Cybercourts in this state have jurisdiction over business disputes in excess of $25,000, but only if all parties consent to its application in lieu of the usual jury or bench trials (Douglas 2001).

The emergence of cybercourts (or e-courts), e-court systems, and e-justice systems represented the culminations of developments that, on other than isolated and sporadic scale, stem from the 1970s. For instance, Delaware and New Jersey are notable early examples of states that implemented judicial technological development. The former ran a computerized network encompassing in its trial courts, public defenders offices, and the state department of justice. The system generated court calendars, controled the issuance of subpoenas, and transferred cases from one judicial body to another pursuant to law. The latter featured a system designed not only to improve the management of litigation but also to store case files and to improve the collection of fees and fines. In addition, three states (California, Ohio, and Wisconsin) experimented with the videotaping of trials or portions of such proceedings. Four other states (Alaska, Idaho, Nevada, and Pennsylvania) used this technology in preliminary hearing and arraignments. Among the reported benefits of such taping were time savings, reduced security risks, access to unavailable witnesses, more efficient jury utilization, and improved quality of appellate review, which relied heavily on the written records of trial court proceedings. Because the preparation of such documents was time consuming, and thus a principal source of appellate delay, another state (Texas) sought to expedite appeals by experimenting with computer-assisted transcript and videotaping.

However, the most pervasive technological change was television. The use of video court reporting (operatorless recording equipment for making trial records) and closed-circuit television (CCTV) (a split-screen device to enable all case participants to view and talk with one another) spread across the country. CCTV was used to provide a two-way audio–video link between courts and detention centers (Low 1994). In addition, at least forty-seven states authorized, on an experimental or permanent basis, such coverage of courtroom proceedings (Farthing-Capowich 1984; Hays and Graham 1993), although the federal courts now bar such reporting. Moreover, in 1995 a turning point was reached. The nationally televised O.J. Simpson double-murder case was widely seen as sensationalist and as more entertaining than just. Consequently, although state judges were still allowed to authorize television coverage of trials, they feared that such proceedings would turn into another media circus or soap opera instead of a forum for doing justice. Not surprisingly, most state trial judges have remained unwilling to open their courts to television. The same reluctance is observed at the federal level. For instance, in the trials of Timothy McVeigh and Terry Nichols for the Oklahoma City bombing, which took place in 1995 and killed 169 persons (the worst carnage until 9/11), the United States District Court Judge, Richard Matsch refused to permit cameras inside the courtroom.

Undoubtedly, the increasing efforts to apply technology to state courts in the1990s and the early years of the twenty-first century have derived not only from the pressures of increasing caseloads and limited resources, but also from its seminal and successful applications at the federal judicial level in the 1970s and 1980s. AOUSC took advantage of computers to facilitate district court workload studies by researching the time spent by the judges of these benches on the numerous types of criminal and civil cases. Such analyses served as a means for predicting judicial personnel needs. Another force behind the recent technological change in the federal courts has been the Federal Judicial Center (FJC), which encouraged such development in three areas. One was the continuation of the time studies—in 1969 and 1979—with methodological refinements to enhance the value of their results to the Judicial Conference of the United States, which relied on such analyses as the basis for its judgeship recommendations to Congress. A second facet involved the further pursuit of valid civil and criminal caseload forecasting. Researchers sought to anticipate overall levels of judicial business and in each category of litigation over periods of five, ten, and twenty years. They built caseload models as a result of their search for demographic, economic, and social variables that explained the volume and kinds of legal matters that had entered the federal trial courts during the period between 1950 and 1970.

Such models enabled researchers to test proposed changes in a simulated judicial environment before deciding whether or not to apply them in federal courts. For instance, in 1975 analysts used 158 variables from the above-mentioned general categories to construct models that accounted for the incidence of forty-two modes of litigation in the federal circuit and district courts. They tried to predict caseload impacts under several contingencies—for instance, the establishment of a national no-fault automobile insurance law, the growth of prepaid legal insurance, and restrictions on diversity-of-citizenship jurisdiction permitting residents of one state to sue those of another state in federal court.

However, one year later, FJC researchers came to doubt whether the discerned patterns of litigation entering the national judiciary would continue and whether they could foresee changes in conditions outside this system, such as alteration in the country's economy. By 1981, the Center admitted that research in federal judicial forecasting had not advanced to the stage of permitting valid projections in specific categories of litigation within the district courts under study. Instead, Center analysts restricted their efforts by concentrating on making valid forecasts of caseload trends for the national court system as a whole.

The third and most important area of technology development pertained to the spread of computers throughout the federal judiciary, especially at the trial level where workloads were heaviest. This trend started in 1971 with the computerization of federal trial courts in the District of Columbia and in northern Illinois. These jurisdictions utilized a particular mode of technology: Courtran (superseded by Courtran II) and its applications. Both generations of computerization helped the federal courts cope better with their mounting caseloads as all ninety-four district courts gained either computer terminals of their own or access to them (Federal Judicial Center 1971).

The FJC developed seven applications and transfered them, along with Courtran, to the AOUSC, which assumed operational responsibility for them and thus freed the Center to pursue additional development efforts. The most critical application was the Speedy Trial Act Accounting and Reporting System (STARS), which allowed the district courts to meet all the time requirements of this legislation. Another was the District Court Index System (INDEX), which retrieved such basic data as the filing dates, the names of the litigants, the number of defendants per case, and the judge handling the legal action. A third was the Central Violations Bureau System (CVB), which processed thousands of minor offenses, such as traffic fines on federal properties. Others included the Criminal Caseflow Management System, the Word Processing and Electronic Mail application, and the Appellate Information Management System (AIMS).

After 1983, the rising costs of maintaining a centralized hardware and software system, such as Courtran II, and the development of autonomous microcomputers (such as notebooks, laptops, and hand computers) prompted the FJC and the AOUSC to collaborate on decentralizing their hardware while keeping standardized software. Their plan achieved this computerization goal in five years. The initial effort in that direction was the Small and Medium Court Automation Project (SAMCAP), which provided valuable information for improved case management, jury administration, finance, lawyer admissions, personnel, property inventory, and word processing systems. Shortly following this step was the Large Metropolitan Court Automation Project (LAMCAP), which provided the same breadth of utility (Federal Judicial Center 1983, 1994).

VII. CONCLUSION

The field of judicial administration, which owes much of its development to the landmark efforts of Roscoe Pound, has been dominated by five great, interlocking issues: (1) delay and congestion, (2) unification (or centralization), (3) professionalization, (4) education, and (5) technology. Together, they form a single body of knowledge and practice, although their discrete treatment facilitates clear analysis. Furthermore, a particular behavior or set of behaviors of judges, court executives, and other court staff members may fall under more than one category.

Moreover, although Pound's typology is far reaching, it does not encompass all the important issues facing judicial administration. Six others are certainly important as well. One is a widely perceived need to improve public access to the courts, particularly at the trial level. Response to this alleged need takes the form of what are often called open courts (or multi-door courthouses), which focus increasingly on the pursuit of therapeutic (or collaborative) justice (National Center for State Courts 2003e, 30, 37–38, 40, 93; Martin and Wagenknecht-Ivey 2003, 6). Consequently, a spate of specialized courts, such as those described in Section IIIA, has come into existence. Much of the public has become disenchanted with courts because of access difficulty, their treatment of minority-group members, and their independence and responsiveness, although still viewing them positively with regard to their honesty and fairness in their decisions and their willingness to meet their constitutional obligations. Moreover, there is still a traditional but important issue concerning the cost of filing claims and slowness of courts in deciding them. The net effect to give them only an average grade (National Center for State Courts 2003d, 7, 22).

A second issue is comparative court management, which focuses on the operations of court systems in other nations and on what American and foreign judiciaries can learn from one another's management practices. As suggested in Section V, foreign students have become an important part of the ICM's Court Executive Development Program. The need for more effective judicial administration at home and abroad is becoming increasingly salient in the wake of the terrorist attacks on September 11, 2001.

A third issue, not surprisingly, is courthouse security, which, although now imperative, was a continuing problem before the 9/11 catastrophe (NCSC, annual trend reports under various titles, 2001–2005). For instance, most security incidents take place in state criminal and domestic relations courts. More than half of such experiences involve person-to-person assaults (National Center for State Courts 2002, 2). State courts have been seriously addressing the matter of security in virtually all its dimensions (Bouch 2005; Steadman 2005). Moreover, federal courts face a growing security problem, especially with inflammatory political and public threats from judicial decisions engendering widespread disagreement (Rehnquist 2005). By 2005, this matter had become so serious that virtually every issue of the federal court system's monthly newsletter, *The Third Branch*, contained articles on the subject. However, the need for increased court security conflicts with the need for increased access. A critical challenge facing judges and court administrators is to find a fair and practical balance between these needs.

A fourth issue is judicial accountability—in particular, with the use of suitable methods for disciplining judges, short of removal from office or facilitating their removal. The issue also encompasses rising public pressure for improved judicial performance on an individual and systems basis (Martin and Wagenknecht-Ivey 2003, 7).

A fifth issue is strategic planning at several levels—individual courts, judicial systems, and justice systems—in the short and long term to make optimal use of their human, financial, educational, and technological resources and to provide a higher quality of justice consistent with heightened security needs. Such planning is ubiquitous throughout the federal court system and widespread in state judiciaries.

A sixth issue centers on the ethics of judges who attend judicial education seminars with all expenses paid. These seminars are often held at high-priced resorts and paid for by those with current or likely future business before their courts. Such practices raise problems of conflict of interest in substance and appearance, as well as in judicial economic dependence, which may impair judicial independence (American Judicature Society 2002).

What follows are extensive references, which, because of the inclusion of website addresses (or uniform resource locators (URLs)), may also be partly viewed as a cyberography (or webliography). The references served as the foundation for this chapter, but one should note that many references in the text were omitted because much of the information presented here may be found in several sources and is thus close to becoming common knowledge. Moreover, cluttering the text with citations to all relevant sources detracts from its readability. Finally, although spatial limitations and increasingly voluminous writings in print and online preclude comprehensiveness, the enumerations are patently wide enough to represent a cross-section of the important work that has taken place in the field of judicial administration.

REFERENCES

Administrative Office of the United States Courts, *Report of the Director 1980*, United States Government Printing Office, Washington, DC, 1980.

Administrative Office of the United States Courts, *Report of the Director 2000*, http://www.uscourts.gov/library/dirrpt00/indix.html, 2000.

Administrative Office of the United States Courts, *Report of the Director 2001*, http://www.uscourts.gov/
      library/dirrpt01/index.html, 2001.
Administrative Office of the United States Courts, *Annual Report of the Director 2004*, http://www.uscourts.
      gov/library/dirrpt04/index.html, 2004.
Aikman, A. B., Total quality management in the courts: the time is now, *State Court Journal*, 17(2), 3–7, 1993,
      see also 55.
Alliegro, S., Bright, B., Chacko, J., Cooper, C., Gish, G., Laurence, D., Rutigliano, J., and Torkelson, L.,
      Beyond delay reduction: using diffentiated case management, *Court Manager*, 8(2), 12–18,
      1993a.
Alliegro, S., Bright, B., Chacko, J., Cooper, C., Gish, G., Laurence, D., Rutigliano, J., and Torkelson, L.,
      Beyond delay reduction: using diffentiated case management, *Court Manager*, 8(3), 23–30,
      1993b.
American Academy of Judicial Education (AAJE), http://www.aaje.org/, 2005.
American Judicature Society, Economic independence for judges, http://www.ajs.org/ajs/ajs_editorial-
      template.asp?content_id = 20, 2002.
Baar, C., *Separate But Subservient*, D.C. Heath, Lexington, MA, 1975.
Beaulieu, D., E-filing in the Supreme Court of Canada 2002, *Court Technology Bulletin*, 14(4), 6, 2002.
Berkson, L. C. and Carbon, S. J., *Court Unification: History, Politics and Implementation*, American Judi-
      cature Society, Chicago, 1980a.
Berkson, L. C. and Carbon, S. J., *Literature on Court Unification: An Annotated Bibliography*, American
      Judicature Society, Chicago, IL, 1980b.
Bouch, J., Leadership in uneasy times, *Court Manager*, 20(1), 24–25, 2005.
Burger, W. E., Court administrators: where would we find them?, *Lincoln Law Review*, 5, 1–4, 1969.
Burger, W. E., The state of the judiciary—1970, *American Bar Association Journal*, 56, 929–934, 1970.
Cannon, M., Judicial administration: why should we care?, *Arizona State Law Journal*, 1974(4), 525–553,
      1974.
Clark, T. A., Tribute to Roscoe Pound, *Harvard Law Review*, 78, 1–3, 1964a.
Clark, T. A., Roscoe pound: the man who struck the spark, *Journal of the American Judicature Society*, 48,
      45–49, 1964b.
Court Statistics Project, State Court caseload Statistics, National Center for State Courts, Williamsburg, VA,
      http://www.ncsconline.org/D_Research/csp/2001_Files/2001_sccs.html, 2001.
Dew, J. D., Revision 7 transition: judicial branch moving forward, *Full Court Press* 7(5), 1, http://www.
      flcourts.org, 2000.
Dickens, C., *Bleak House*, Signet, New York, 1853/1964.
Douglas, M., Order in the cyber court, *Government Technology*, http://wwwgovtech.net/magazine/story.
      phtml?id = 3030000000003173.0, 2001.
Dussault, R., Exit robocop, enter cyberjudge, *Government Technology*, 12, 34, 1999, see also 36.
Fabri, M., Judicial electronic data interchange [JEDI] in europe: applications, policies, and trends, *Court
      Technology*, 15(1), 2, 2003, see also 8–9.
Farthing-Capowich, D., In *State of the Judiciary the Book of the States 1984–1985*, Purcell, L., Morrisette, S.,
      and Murray, B., Eds., Council of State Governments, Lexington, KY, pp. 142–163, 1984.
Federal Judicial Center, *The 1969–1970 Federal District Court Time Study*, Federal Judicial Center,
      Washington, DC, 1970.
Federal Judicial Center (FJC), *Annual Report 1982*, Federal Judicial Center, Washington, DC, 1983.
Federal Judicial Center (FJC), *Annual Report 1993*, Federal Judicial Center, Washington, DC, 1994.
Federal Judicial Center (FJC), *2004 Annual Report of the Federal Judicial Center*, http://www.fjc.gov/, 2005.
Fish, P. G., *The Politics of Federal Judicial Administration*, Princeton University Press, Princeton, NJ,
      1973.
Flaherty, F. S., Move to court reform just keeps rolling along, *National Law Journal*, 6(1), 26–28, 1983.
Fleishman, A. L. and Aikman, A. B., Total quality management: where the courts are now, *State Court
      Journal*, 17(3), 17–22, 1993.
Flythe, T., Courtroom 21 lab trial centers on terrorism funding, *Court Technology*, 15(3), 7, 2003, see also 9.
Frank, J. P., *American Law: The Case for Radical Reform*, MacMillan, New York, 1964.
Friedman, L. M., *A History of American Law*, 2nd ed., Simon and Schuster/Touchstone Books, New York,
      1985.

Friesen, E. C. Jr., Gallas, E. C., and Gallas, N. M., *Managing the Courts*, Bobbs-Merrill, Indianapolis, IN, 1971.

Gallas, G. E.,, The conventional wisdom of state court administration: a critical assessment and alternative approach, *Justice System Journal*, 2(1), 35–51, 1976.

Gaudreaux, A., Courtroom trial lab uses ground breaking UR technology, *Court Technology Bulletin*, 14(4), 11, 2002.

Gazell, J. A., Leadership competition in judicial management at the state level, *DePaul Law Review*, 19, 737–750, 1970.

Gazell, J. A., State trial courts: an odyssey into faltering bureaucracies, *San Diego Law Review*, 8, 275–332, 1971.

Gazell, J. A., Developmental syndromes in judicial management, *Brooklyn Law Review*, 38, 587–627, 1972.

Gazell, J. A., Lower-court unification in the american states: is the capture of the holy grail imminent?, *Arizona State Law Journal*, 1974a(4), 653–687, 1974a.

Gazell, J. A., A taxonomy of state court personnel management: problems, prototypes, and prophecies, *St. John's Law Review*, 49, 74–96, 1974b.

Gazell, J. A., A national perspective on justices of the peace: time for an epitaph?, *Mississippi Law Journal*, 46(4), 795–816, 1975.

Glick, H. R. and Vines, K. N., *State Court Systems*, Prentice Hall, Englewood Cliffs, NJ, 1973.

Goerdt, J., Slaying the dragon of delay: findings from a national survey of recent court programs, *Court Manager*, 12(3), 30–38, 1997.

Goldman, E. A., *Rendezvous with Destiny*, Vintage, New York, 1955.

Hays, S. W. and Graham, C. B. Jr., Eds., *Handbook of Court Administration and Management*, Marcel Dekker, New York, 1993.

Hofstadter, R., *The Age of Reform*, Vintage, New York, 1955.

Institute for Civil Justice, *Overview of the First Five Program Years*, Rand, Santa Monica, CA, April 1980–March 1985, 1985.

Institute for Civil Justice, *Annual Report*, Rand, Santa Monica, CA, 1993.

Institute for Civil Justice, *Research Agenda*, http://wwwrand.org/icj/research/, 2003.

Institute for Court Management (ICM), *CEDP Program Description*, http://www.ncsconline.org/D_Icm/icmcedp_program#2003.html, 2003.

Institute for Court Management (ICM), *2002 Catalog*, National Center for State Courts, Williamsburg, VA, http://wwwncsd.dni.us/icm, 2002.

Institute for Court Management (ICM), *2003 Catalog*, http://www.ncsconline.org/D_ICM/icmcourses_catalog.html), Exclusively online from 2003.

Institute for Court Management (ICM), *2004 ICM Catalog*, http://www.ncsconline.org/D_ICM/icmcourses/icmcourses_catalog.2004.html, 2004.

Institute for Court Management (ICM), *2005 ICM Catalog*, http://www.ncsconline.org/D_ICM/icmcourses/icmcourses_catalog 2005.html, 2005.

Institute of Judicial Administration (UK), http://www.law.bham.ac.uk/ija.htm, 2003.

Institute of Judicial Administration (US), http://www.law.nyu.edu/institutes/judicial/, 2003.

Jacob, H., *Justice in America*, Little, Brown, Boston, MA, 1984.

Judicial Council of California (JCC), *Annual Report*, http://www.courtinfo.ca.gov/reference/1_annual reports.htm#2001, 2001.

Judicial Council of California (JCC), *Annual Report*, Improving Justice: the Business of the Courts, http://www.courtinfo.ca.gov/rules/2002/title/1500-end-195.htm, 2002.

Judicial Council of California (JCC), *Annual Report*, Creating the infrastructure for the New California Court System. http://www.courtinfo.ca.gov/reference/2_annual.htm, 2003.

Kenworthy, T., Colo[rado] courts cut work with a click, *USA Today*, 3A, October 9, 2000.

Lawson, H., State court system unification, *American University Law Review*, 31, 273–289, 1982.

Lederer, F. I., Courtroom 21: a model courtroom of the 21st century, *Court Technology Bulletin*, 6(1), 1, 1994, see also pages 5 and 7.

Lederer, F. I., Courtroom 21: the legal and practical implications, *Court Technology Bulletin*, 6(2), 1, 1994, see also pages 5 and 7.

Low, E. B., *Accessing the Judicial System: The States' Response The Book of the States 1994–1995*, Council of State Governments, Lexington, KY, 1994.

Martin, J. A., and Wagenknecht-Ivey, B. J., *Courts 2010: Critical trends shaping the courts in the next decade*, http://www.ncsconline.org/WCDS/index.htm, 2003.

Master of Laws in the Judicial Process, University of Virginia School of Law, http://www.law.virginia.edu/home 2002html/prospectives/judges/judges.htm, 2003.

McKay, J., Technology on trial: the influence of courtroom 21 is felt in real-life courtrooms around the world, *Government Technology*, 15, 82–83, 2002.

Mintzberg, H., *The Nature of Managerial Work*, Harper & Row, New York, 1973.

National Association for Court Management, Core competency curriculum guidelines: what court leaders need to know and be able to do, *Court Manager*, 18(2), 1–66, 2003.

National Association for Court Management, Professional development advisory committee, core competency curriculum guidelines: history, overview, and future uses, *Court Manager*, 13(1), 6–19, 1998.

National Center for State Courts (NCSC), *Annual Report on the Trends in the State Courts, 2001 Edition*, http://www.ncsconline.org/WC/Publications/KIS_CtFutu_Trends01_Pub.pdf, 2002.

National Center for State Courts (NCSC), *Trial Court Performance Standards & Measurement System (Measure 2.1.1: Time to Disposition at fig. 1)*, http://www.ncsconline.org/D_Research/TCPS/Measures/me_2.1.1.htm, 2003b.

National Center for State Courts (NCSC), *How the Public Views the State Courts: A 1999 National Survey*, http://www.ncsconline.org/WC/Publications/Res_AmtPTC_Public ViewCrtsPub.pdf, 2003d.

National Center for State Courts (NCSC), *2002 Report on Trends in The State Courts*, http://www.ncsconline.org/D_KIS/Trends/Trends02MainPage.html, 2003e.

National Center for State Courts (NCSC), *Survey of Judicial Salaries*, http://www.ncsconline.org/D_KIS/Salary_Survey/, 2004a.

National Judicial College (NJC), http://www.judges.org/, 2003/2005.

National Judicial College (NJC), *2000–2001 Course Catalog*, The National Judicial College, Reno, NV, 1999.

Neely, R., *How Courts Govern America*, Yale University Press, New Haven, CT, 1981.

Neely, R., The politics of crime, *Atlantic Monthly*, 250, 27–31, 1982.

Neely, R., *Why Courts Don't Work*, McGraw-Hill, New York, 1983.

New Jersey Committee on Women in the Courts, A guide to using gender-neutral Language, *Court Manager*, 8(3), 31–32, 1993.

Ostrom, B. J. and Kauder, N. B., *Examining the Work of State Courts*, NCSC, Williamsburg, VA, 1999.

Ostrom, B. J., Kauder, N. B. and La Fountain, R. C., *Examining the Work of State Courts, 2001*, http://www.ncsconline.org/D_Research/csp/2001_Main_Page.html, 2001.

Ostrom, V., *The Intellectual Crisis in American Public Administration*, University of Alabama Press, Tuscaloosa, AL, 1974.

Pankey, K. G. Jr., *State of the Judiciary the Book of the States 1992–1993*, Council of State Governments, Lexington, KY, 1992.

Pound, R., The causes of popular dissatisfaction with the administration of justice, *Reports of the American Bar Association*, 29(1), 395–417, 1906.

Pound, R., Organization of courts, *Journal of the American Judicature Society*, 69–83, October, 11, 1927.

Pound, R., Principles and outline of a modern unified court organization, *Journal of the American Judicature Society*, 23, 225–233, 1940.

Pound, R., Toward an adequate administration of justice, *Chicago Bar Record* 247–257, March, 39, 1958.

Poulos, C., Colorado pulls off criminal justice integration, *Government Technology*, 11(7), 39, 1998.

Reardon, R. C., Introduction to state court reform, *American University Law Review*, 31, 207–212, 1982.

Rehnquist, W., 2004 year-end report on the federal judiciary, *The Third Branch*, 37(1), 1–7, 2004.

Rottman, D. B., Flango, C. R., Cantrell, M. T., Hansen, R., and La Fountain, N., *State Court Organization 1998*. Office of Justice Programs, Bureau of Justice Statistics, United States Department of Justice, Washington, DC, http://www.ojp.usdoj.gov/bjs/, 2002.

Saare, D. J., *American Court Management*, Quorum, Westport, CT, 1982.

Saare, D. J., *Modern Court Management: Trends in the Role of the Court Executive*, National Institute of Law Enforcement and Criminal Justice, Washington, DC, 1970.

Sargent, A. G. and Stupak, R. J., Managing in the 90's: the androgynous manager, *Court Manager*, 8(3), 13–18, 1993.

Shakespeare, W., In *Hamlet*, Wright, L. B. and LaMar, V. A., Eds., Washington Square Press (Pocket Books), New York, 1958.

Somit, A. and Tanenhaus, J., *American Political Science: Profile of a Discipline*, Atherton, New York, 1964.

Steadman, S., Weller, S., Pierce, R., and Hamel, C., Improving courthouse safety in Pennsylvania, *Court Manager*, 20(1), 26–30, 2005.

Steelman, D. C., *Post-Amendment 80 Case Management Seminar: Trial Court Administration and Management in State Courts: Viewing Arkansas in a National Context*, http://www.ncsconline.org/WCDS/ Index.htm, 2002.

Steelman, D. C., Goerdt, J., and McMillan, J., *Caseflow Management*, NCSC, Williamsburg, VA, 2004.

Taylor, F.W., *The Principles of Scientific Management*, Norton, New York, 1967, Orginally published in 1911.

Tobin, R. W., *Creating the Judicial Branch: The Unfinished Reform*, National Center for State Courts, Williamsburg, VA, 1999.

Trotter, J. A. and Cooper, C. S., State trial court delay: efforts at reform, *American University Law Review*, 31, 213–236, 1982.

University of Virginia, Graduate program for judges http://www.law.Virginia.edu/home2002/html/prospective/ judges.htm.

United States District Courts, http://www.uscourts.gov/district courts.html, 2003.

Waldo, D., *The Enterprise of Public Administration: A Summary View*, Chandler and Sharp, Novato, CA, 1980.

Walter, E., *Meyer Research Institute of Law Dollars, Delay and the Automobile Victim*, Bobbs-Merrill, Indianapolis, IN, 1968.

Warren, E.A., The problem of delay: a task for bench and bar alike. *American Bar Association Journal*, 44, 1043–1048, 1958.

Wells, M., A model system, *Government Technology* May 1, http://www.govtech.net/magazine/story. phtml?id = 10427#top, 2002.

Wheeler, E. P. and Pound, R., Report of the special committee to suggest remedies and formulate proposed laws to prevent delay and unnecessary cost in litigation, *Reports of the American Bar Association*, 34, 578–602, 1909.

Willoughby, W. F., *Principles of Judicial Administration*, Brookings Institution, Washington, DC, 1929.

Wilson, W., The study of administration, *Political Science Quarterly*, 2, 199–222, 1887.

Winters, G., Ed., Lagging justice, *The Annals*, 328, 1–163, 1960.

Winters, R., Electronic court records in king county, WA, *Court Technology Bulletin*, 14(2), 1, 2002, see also page 4.

Woodson, J., Teen courts give youths lesson in law, *Los Angeles Times*, B2, May 23, 2003.

Zeisel, H., Kalven, H., and Buchholz, B., *Delay in the Court*, Little, Brown, Boston, MA, 1959.

Unit 14

Political Economy

28 The Political Economy of Public Administration

Fred Thompson

CONTENTS

I. INTRODUCTION

Public administration and economics have always overlapped. Efficiency was the Holy Grail of the progressive officials and academics who created the modern discipline of public administration in America. They sought to place public affairs "on a strict business basis," directed "not by partisans, either Republican or Democrat, but by men... skilled in business management and economics." Consequently, they created a professional bureaucracy to manage "the increased importance of the public functions of the twentieth century city. Streets had to be paved for newly developed motor vehicles; harbors had to be deepened for big, new freighters. In addition, electric lighting systems, street railways, sewage disposal plants, water supplies, and fire departments had to be installed or drastically improved to meet the needs of inhabitants, human and commercial, of hundreds of rapidly growing industrial centers" (Weinstein 1968, 93–95). Moreover, establishing a professional bureaucracy at the municipal level led to higher levels of investment in infrastructure and, thereby, to significant increases in economic growth (Rauch 1995).[*]

Organizational efficiency once meant the Weberian bureaucratic paradigm, codified for the public sector in the Taft, Brownlow, and Hoover Commission reports (Barzelay and Armajani 1992; Blau and Meyer 1971). In the years following publication of the first Hoover Commission report, public administration specialists did not abandon the bureaucratic paradigm, yet they drifted away from economics. Some public administration experts discovered organizational psychology and behavior; many rejected the rhetorical differentiation of administration from politics, together with its stress on neutral competence; a few rejected the traditional goals of economy and efficiency on ideological grounds or were intimidated by the mathematics used increasingly by economists.

The drift away from economics was not entirely one-sided. At mid-century, most English-speaking economists accepted Pigouvian welfare economics and Keynesian macroeconomics. They generally believed that government should set goals and objectives for the economy as a whole. Many admired the system of detailed centralized planning and control used by Gosplan in the Soviet Union to implement its long-term policies and strategic plans—Weberian bureaucracy carried to its ultimate conclusion. Indeed, Gosplan's approach was not unlike the planning and control mechanisms used in the United States and the United Kingdom to fight World War II.

Gradually, however, most economists came to appreciate the dysfunctions produced by state allocation of productive assets and central planning and control, and to recognize the impossibility of a Pigouvian social welfare function. For many, this appreciation was reflected in a commitment to markets over almost any system of hierarchy or command. It is hardly surprising that this commitment was inimical to the idea and practice of bureaucracy—or any other kind of organization or regulation, for that matter.

Public administration's distancing from economics was interrupted temporarily by the flurry of excitement generated during the 1960s and early 1970s by program-budgeting and systems analysis, the former grounded primarily in applied economics and the latter in operations research and management science, both rational-choice disciplines. This period witnessed the publication of the work of Charles Hitch and Roland McKean (1960) as well as Jesse Burkhead and Jerry Miner's (1971) landmark text, *Public Expenditure*, both of which focused on the supply and demand for governmentally provided goods and services.[†] These texts and others were concerned primarily with questions of resource allocation in the public sector and focused on defense. This body of literature represents a vein of scholarship that still has not been adequately incorporated into public administration. At the same time, the topics raised by Hitch and McKean and their contemporaries have since been largely abandoned by economists and now find only occasional mention in standard textbooks of public finance and economics.[‡]

In the meantime, two distinct intellectual factions proposed to replace public administration with economics. The first of these factions emerged in 1965 with the creation of what has since come to be known as the Public Choice Society. In its first two meetings, the participants of the Public Choice Society included James Buchanan, Gordon Tullock, John Rawls, William Riker, Vincent Ostrom, Toby Davis, James Coleman, and Charles Plott. Public choice, one of the great success stories of modern social and economic science, stands for the application of economic logic—methodological individualism and rational, self-interested decision-making—to questions

---

[*] See also Rubin (1993) and Mauro (1995).

[†] For other works by these same authors, see also Hitch (1965) and McKean (1968).

[‡] For a few examples of defense-related works in the same vein as Hitch and McKean, see Novick (1954, 1956), Niskanen (1967), Enke (1967), Quade and Boucher (1968), and Fisher (1970). For discussions of resource-allocation in non-defense sectors see, for example, Schultze (1968), Haveman and Margolis (1970), Hirsch (1970), Margolis (1970), Williamson (1970), Merewitz and Sosnick (1971), Rivlin (1971, 1972), and Quade (1975).

and issues that have traditionally been the concern of political scientists and public administration experts.

The second of these factions followed the establishment of schools of public policy at some of America's most prestigious universities: Harvard, Chicago, UC Berkeley, Duke, Carnegie-Mellon. These schools placed the rational-choice disciplines of economics and operations research and management science at the center of their curricula.

Given the intellectual success of public choice and the prestige of the rational-choice disciplines in schools of public policy, it was once possible to imagine—or fear—that the discipline of public administration was undergoing a paradigm shift, and that a rational-choice, economics-based paradigm might emerge preeminent (Moe 1997). Ten years ago, economic imperialism (of the academic variety) was marching from triumph to triumph and to many it seemed that nothing stood in the way of its complete hegemony.

The conviction of the rational choice theorists that they had all the answers to questions of collective choice, assignment of institutional responsibility, design of programmatic organizations, organizational leadership, direction and control, and the like turned out to be somewhat presumptuous. In addition to making us think seriously about incentives and opportunity costs, their main contribution has been a set of theorems proving the impossibility of rational, self-interested cooperative action. In other words, rational-choice theorists have thoroughly demonstrated the theoretical impossibility of all sorts of things that can be observed in practice every day (Miller 1992).This fact has tended to chasten even the most ardent rational-choice theorist and has led many of them to reconsider the insights offered by other social science disciplines having to do with behavior, process, mechanism, and institutional learning (Gibbons 2003).

Consequently, at the beginning of the twenty-first century, we have come almost full circle to where we were at the start of the twentieth century. Both economists and public administration specialists understand that there is a lot that is not known, and, to the extent that they share a common interest in efficiency and economy, both groups recognize that much can be learned from each other by pursuing convergence and interplay between economic models and long-standing insights from public administration.

II. PUBLIC ADMINISTRATION IS NOT ECONOMICS

In retrospect, that a rational-choice, economics-based paradigm did not emerge preeminent in the study of public management and administration is not at all surprising. There are at least three reasons why public administration cannot be economics (Zorn 1989).

A.   PUBLIC ADMINISTRATION IS PRESCRIPTIVE

First, there is the basic distinction between engineering and science (Behn 1996). Public administration is concerned with prescription—the identification of normative rules for decision-makers that would lead them to make optimal decisions from the standpoint of the citizenry as a whole. Economics is concerned with prediction—the identification of rules decision-makers are likely to follow, given their incentives. Bluntly put, public administrators solve problems while economists explain choices.

Economic theory is useful to public administrators when it provides them with concepts they can use to diagnose problems accurately and to prescribe effective solutions. Examples of these are concepts like opportunity costs, incentives, or capitalization, which can be profitably applied to an array of problems frequently encountered by public administrators. However, real-world problem solving also frequently raises questions of right and wrong. Economic logic, on the other hand, recognizes no good but efficiency, no evil aside from inefficiency (Box 1992; see also Hood 1995). Fitness or fairness, what James March (1996) calls the logic of appropriateness, ought to play an important role in the conduct of the public's business; economists often have trouble accepting this simple fact.

B.   Public Administration Is Realistic, Empirically Grounded, and Practical

Secondly, economics is a theoretical discipline, while public administration is concerned with pragmatic reform. Economists build elegant, logically consistent deductive models, while public administrators deal with messy, real-world problems. Indeed, it can be argued that economists prefer rational choice theories to models that incorporate bounded rationality primarily because they are conclusive, rather than because they are right. Decision-makers can be approximately rational in a nearly infinite number of ways, they can be rational in only one.

This difference between economists and public administrators is illustrated by the way they deal with the problem of voluntary provision of collective goods. Economists define a collective (or public) good in terms of two properties: jointness of supply and impossibility of exclusion. This means that once a collective good is supplied by some of the members of a group, it may be enjoyed by all. From this premise they deduce that the decision of some of the members of a group to provide the good or some quantity of it for themselves presents each of the other members with an opportunity for strategic behavior. Because the other members of the group can profitably engage in strategic behavior, economists conclude that they will. If members of the group can share in the good regardless of their contributions, economists predict that the members will withhold or reduce their own contributions to its provision. Hence, the decision by some of the members of a group to supply a quantity of a collective good leads other members to free-ride on their contributions. In other words, economists argue that if contributions are voluntary, collective goods will be under-provided or, in the extreme, not provided at all. Moreover, this problem does not go away simply because the problem is internalized within an organization or publicly provided (Breton 1989; Gittons 2003).

Crime control aptly illustrates this situation. Citizens can affect the level of crime in their community in two ways: by limiting their exposure to risk and protecting their property, and by helping the police fight crime. If their possessions or personal security matter enough to them, individuals may see a direct material benefit from investing in locks, guns, guard dogs, or security systems. They may even see the benefit from participating in volunteer citizen block watches, banding together to patrol their own streets or financing a private security force to do so. The authorities can encourage these kinds of activities by providing guidance and technical assistance, by passing out police whistles, by urging people to mark their property so that it can be more easily identified when stolen, by helping to organize block watches, by setting up emergency call systems tied to rapid response, and by positioning themselves to provide back-up to private efforts.

However, self-defense alone will not control crime. Criminals must be identified, apprehended, and convicted. The police necessarily depend upon the citizenry to alert them to crime and to aid them in the conviction of criminals. Unfortunately, only where their safety or that of their loved ones is at risk, or where their property is threatened, will private citizens realize a direct benefit from intervening to stop crimes in progress. Even when they have been personally victimized, citizens rarely individually benefit from helping the police identify, apprehend, and convict their assailants because the harm has already been done and the criminal justice system seldom provides restitution. In these instances, the behavior expected of citizens, though of great value to their community, is not personally rewarding in any obvious way. Hence, individuals often shirk these onerous civic responsibilities, trying to free-ride on the efforts of their neighbors.

Many economists insist that, in the presence of collective goods, citizens must be coerced to perform their civic responsibilities; otherwise, jointly provided services will necessarily be under-supplied (Breton 1989). This mindset reflects in part the propensity of rational choice theorists to confuse a perfectly useful analytic construct—economic man—with living, breathing humans. Economic man is a rational fool. Given the opportunity to ride free, he will. Because economic man will not voluntarily cooperate with his neighbors to provide public or collective goods, he must be forced to do so. This mindset also reflects a propensity to overlook the vitality of human ingenuity in designing social arrangements, and to ignore the availability of motivational alternatives to coercion or rewards.

In contrast, public administrators recognize that citizens often free-ride on the efforts of their neighbors, but they interpret this as a problem to be solved rather than a necessary fact of life. Beekeeping provides the classic example of the failure to distinguish between economic theory and reality. Once upon a time, economists taught that beekeeping is a collective good and that, because fruit growers can rely on their neighbors' bees to pollinate their blossoms, most growers will. Hence, beekeeping must be under-supplied.

S.N.S. Cheung, then an assistant professor of economics at the University of Washington, did something rather extraordinary: he left his armchair to find out whether beekeeping is actually under-supplied. After a careful study of beekeeping and apple-growing practices in Washington State, Cheung found a long history of contractual relationships between apple growers and beekeepers. These contracts provided for beekeepers to be compensated for their contribution to the growers' apple crops. He also found that apple growers implicitly covenanted with their neighbors to keep the same ratio of bees to trees. Apple growers who did not abide by the covenant were ostracized and treated to inconveniences by those who did. Consequently, Cheung concluded that free riding may not be a serious problem among real apple growers and beekeepers (Cheung 1973; Ostrom 1990; see also Ostrom et al. 1994; Breton 1989).

The primary point that Cheung was trying to make is that real people are not rational fools. They often do contribute voluntarily to the provision of collective goods (Ostrom 1990). Furthermore, social conventions or group norms can discourage free-riding and reduce shirking. These conventions can take the form of ethical precepts, regularities imposed by institutions, or simply fixed rules of thumb for individual behavior. Group norms can be collectively enforced through the ostracism of those who fail to contribute, and praise of those who do.

A second lesson to be drawn from the fable of the bees is that neither community norms, nor the collective enforcement of those norms just happens. Knowledge of what to do and how to do it was provided by field agents of the United States Department of Agriculture's (USDA's) Extension Service. This information gave apple growers a solid technical basis for group norms governing the behavior of individual growers. The field agents determined how many hives were needed and fairly apportioned responsibility for their provision. They also played a role in monitoring compliance with group norms and in passing that information along to growers. In doing so, the field agents could identify shirkers and the subsequent shortfall in the provision of bees that had to be made good by the rest of the community. Moreover, USDA provided growers with a powerful collective sanction against free-riders in the form of marketing orders and quota. Free-riders were not merely subject to social ostracism; the other growers could have actually denied them access to the most lucrative markets.

The point is not that voluntary contributions to the provision of public goods occur spontaneously; opportunities for collectively beneficial action must be identified, individual contributions established, performance monitored, and defectors sanctioned (Heckathorn and Maser 1990; Maser 1986). This is, of course, the last and most important lesson of the fable of the bees: voluntary provision can be organized and must be managed. Because management implies a manager, it follows that someone, usually a public official, must be charged with mobilizing the community on behalf of the public good, organizing provision of the good, creating incentives, and supervising enforcement of community norms (Powers and Thompson 1994).

C. Public Administrators Are Preoccupied with Technical Efficiency

There is a third reason why public administration is not economics. As a normative discipline, public administration is preoccupied with identifying decision-making rules that citizens would unanimously support. In practice this means that, just as economists do not like to make value judgments, public administrators are usually more comfortable condemning technical rather than allocative efficiency. Technical inefficiency is the failure to minimize cost or maximize output because managers are not using the best available technology. Technology here refers not only to plant and equipment, but also to the methods used to coordinate activities and to motivate performance; it has to be the best available technology in practice, not merely in theory.

A comparison of how Ford Motors Company accounts for its purchases with how the Navy handles accounts payable illustrates technical inefficiency. Not so long ago, Ford cut the required number of manual accounting transactions to pay for goods from nine to three, permitting a 75% staff reduction in its accounts payable department (Hammer 1990). In contrast, it takes the Navy twenty-six manual accounting transactions and nine reconciliations—thirty-five steps in all—to process and pay for things (Hemingway 1993). This system is not only time consuming, it often leads to bad service and excessive investment in inventories. According to the National Performance Review, it causes delays in obtaining repair parts that keep a high proportion of the Navy's cars and trucks out of commission, and forces taxpayers to fund 10% more vehicles than the Navy really needs (Gore, 1993).

Computerization could eliminate more than half of the steps in the Navy's accounts payable process (Hemingway 1993). But why are fourteen, let alone thirty-five, accounting records needed where Ford gets by with three? One answer is that Navy fails to capture information once and at the source. Instead, each step in the supply process—requisition, receipt, certification of invoice, reconciliation, and revision—is repeated at every level of the organization. Moreover, the people who produce information do not process it. Processing is handled by financial management specialists from the bottom of the organization to the top. Finally, the Navy does not build financial control into its job designs. Naval officers have little discretion as to the mix or quantity of resources used by their commands. Even in peace time their effectiveness in managing resources often has little or no bearing on the evaluation of their performance.

Until recently, most economists assumed that technical efficiency was someone else's concern: engineers, maybe accountants, organization theorists, or even public administrators. Nowadays, they understand that technical inefficiency is often far more important than allocative inefficiency, but they tend to explain it in terms of structural or other factors (e.g., lack of competitive pressure) that are beyond the control of managers. While the efforts of economists to understand managerial failure have in recent years produced some powerful new theories and concepts that can help public administrators deal with a variety of problems, economists still tend to overlook the most common cause of technical inefficiency: ignorance. Ignorance is Protean. As they say in the Navy, there are only a few ways to do right, there are an infinite number of ways to screw up. For example, the Navy's system of accounting is arguably an unintended consequence of the Anti-Deficiency Act (1905). The system was designed to insure that neither local commanders, nor higher level authorities exceeded the obligational authority granted them by Congress. That authority is now divided into scores of separate accounts, hundreds of management codes, and thousands of accounting lines.

At the same time it should, perhaps, be acknowledged that a preoccupation with technical efficiency leads public administration to slight allocative efficiency. Allocative efficiency has to do with matching supply to demand. It is of special concern to economists, who object to private monopolies, for example, not because their prices are too high, but because they produce less than they would under competition. Why is this bad? It is bad, even where production is technically efficient, because consumers would willingly pay more for the things that are not being produced than it would cost to make them. Hence, net benefits are forfeited (where net benefits = willingness and ability to pay-cost > 0). Economists refer to foregone net benefits as "deadweight loss."

It is not hard to find instances of allocative inefficiency in government, or to identify some fairly common pathologies that induce it. Economics teaches, for example, that in the presence of a capital market where funds can be obtained at a price, the welfare of the citizenry will be maximized by the implementation of all projects offering positive net present values. This means that the timing of benefit/cost flows usually does not matter, so long as future benefits and costs are properly discounted. But governments often appear to be obsessed with the timing of outlays. They give too much weight to current costs and benefits and too little to future ones. Consequently, they often put off investment programs that would produce net benefits or they stretch out programs, thereby increasing their costs, to comply with arbitrary spending constraints.

For example, the Department of Defense has often reduced production rates for a variety of weapons systems below minimum optimal scale. In several instances this has had the result of increasing the present value costs of the total production run by more than 100%. The reason for this action? To reduce the annual deficit. In which case, the federal government was willing to trade large future liabilities for small current reductions in the growth of the national debt, the interest upon which is now less than 5% per year.

Government's propensity to disregard questions of feasibility, especially administrative and economic feasibility, also often results in allocative inefficiency. For example, John Mendeloff (1988) has shown how this propensity leads the Occupational Safty and Health Administration (OSHA) to over-regulate, and how over-regulation leads to under-regulation. Both over- and under-regulation are examples of allocative inefficiency. According to Mendeloff, OSHA over-regulates exposures to harmful chemicals in the workplace because it often sets standards without regard to the benefits and costs of reducing hazards to those levels. John F. Morrall III (1986) estimates that, as a consequence, OSHA's proposed standards impose costs on industry that typically exceed benefits by a factor of ten. In the case of its proposed formaldehyde standard, costs were 25,000 times greater than benefits. Not surprisingly, these costs have inspired industry to embrace every legal, administrative, or political measure that might conceivably prevent, delay, or overturn promulgation of new standards. Consequently, nearly all of OSHA's discretionary resources have been dedicated to defending standards that govern a mere handful of hazardous substances. The opportunity cost of over-regulation is passed on to workers who are exposed to hundreds of under-regulated substances because the resources needed to revise standards are simply not available.

Government also has a propensity to disregard the incentive effects of the prices it sets, which necessarily results in allocative inefficiency. Fortunately, this propensity seems to be waning. Nevertheless, some people still have trouble seeing a relationship between low grazing fees on public land and overgrazing, between low prices for agricultural water and wasteful farm irrigation practices or urban water scarcity, between low timber harvest fees and over-logging, between the low landing fees charged private planes and airport overcrowding, or between agricultural price supports and food surpluses.

Public administrators ignore allocative efficiency at their peril. A preoccupation with technical efficiency, like Tevye said of poverty, is "no sin, but it is no great honor either."

III. THE RENEWAL OF INTEREST IN ECONOMICS

Perceptive observers would not have imagined that public administration was in danger of being taken over by economics, unless the perception reflected a kernel of truth. A paradigm shift seems to be in the works; at the very least, many practitioners now reject the traditional bureaucratic paradigm. Moreover, economics seems much more directly relevant to the concerns of public administration than in the recent past. There are three not entirely unrelated reasons for these changes: changing theories in political science, changes in the environment of public adminis-tration, and advances in economic science. I will deal with the first of these two issues briefly. The remainder of this essay will focus on the last.

A. POLITICAL SCIENCE

It is perhaps not too strong a statement to say that a rational-choice, economics-based paradigm has gained considerable influence in American political science, including bureaucracy and public policy, subfields that are closely related to public administration. In my opinion this is a healthy turn of events. An unbiased observer would have to acknowledge, however, that political science, like most of the humanities and social sciences, is prone to academic fads. They come and go, often leaving little or nothing behind in the way of accumulated knowledge. It is natural that academics think of themselves as the tip of the arrow of progress, yet intellectual history demands a more humble interpretation. Just as academics of past generations usually seem wrong-headed by today's standards, so too are today's academics likely to appear to the next. Nevertheless, for good or ill, when political science sneezes, public administration more often than not catches a cold. Political science sneezed.

B.   CHANGES IN THE ENVIRONMENT OF PUBLIC ADMINISTRATION

The new public management has also influenced public administration in the United States (Gore 1993). The new public management emphasizes "performance appraisal and efficiency; the disaggregation of public bureaucracies into agencies which deal with each other on a user-pay basis; the use of quasi-markets and contracting out to foster competition; cost-cutting; and a style of management which emphasizes amongst other things, output targets, limited term contracts, monetary targets and incentives, and freedom to manage" (Rhodes 1991; see also Dunleavy and Hood 1994).

The new public management is a worldwide movement (Rhodes 1991).[*] Arguably, it represents one aspect of a post-Weberian paradigm transformation in public administration. Herman Schwartz (1994), for example, claims that government is undergoing "a profound shift toward a new kind of regime... not simply a shift towards less state, but also a shift to a different kind of state." Schwartz attributes this shift to international market pressures and stresses that many of the governments that embraced the new public management are or were dominated by social democrats. New Zealand, which under Labour governments went further than any other country in embracing the new public management, is a prominent example (Boston et al. 1996; Quiggin 1998).

The driving force behind the new public management is technological change. Reductions in information costs brought about by computers and computer networks, and our increased capacity to use them have caused four major shifts in the comparative advantage of governance mechanisms and institutional arrangements (Reschenthaler and Thompson 1996). These are:

1. The efficacy of the market has increased relative to government provision and control.
2. The efficacy of the market and other self-organizing systems has increased relative to hierarchically coordinated systems.
3. The efficacy of decentralized allocation of resources and after-the-fact control has increased relative to centralized allocation and before-the-fact control.
4. The efficacy of process-oriented structures has increased relative to functional structures.

These changes are hardly surprising. As will be explained below, the comparative advantage of any institutional arrangement boils down to a question of information or transaction costs. Changes in information costs should, and have dramatically altered the relative advantage of governance mechanisms and institutional arrangements.

Thus, large organizations were once justified by economies of scale and scope. Economies of scale are produced by spreading fixed expenses, especially investments in plant and equipment and the organization of production lines, over larger volumes of output, thereby reducing unit costs. Economies of scope are produced by exploiting the division of labor—sequentially combining highly specialized functional units in multifarious ways to produce a variety of products.

---

[*] For further discussion of the global scope of the new public management, see also Hood (1991), Schedler (1995), Osborne and Gaebler (1992), Barzelay (2001), and Hood and Peters (2004).

Economies of scale and scope were made possible by hierarchy and bureaucracy that broke tasks down into their simplest component parts and recombined them to produce complex goods and services, allocated scarce resources to administrative units, and established product–market strategies.

In turn, hierarchy and bureaucracy were made possible by innovations in organizational design, administrative controls, and operational engineering (Chandler 1962). As Rosenberg and Birdsall (1986) explain, most of the entrepreneurs of the Industrial Revolution were merchants and financiers—they knew little or nothing about production. Business did not learn how to organize and supervise large numbers of workers until the mid-nineteenth century. As late as 1892, for example, Carnegie Steel avoided the problem of organizing and managing the work of its production employees. "The organization of the work of large numbers of employees was a new management function, and direct employment could not have become a general practice until recruiting, organizing, and supervising factory workers been sorted out and fitted into a hierarchical scheme" (Rosenberg and Birdsall 1986, 235–237). Of course, only very large organizations could take full advantage of the bureaucratic revolution. Only they could be completely vertically integrated or afford to devote substantial amounts of resources to gathering and processing quantities of data necessary for top management to coordinate activities, allocate resources, and set strategy—these are, after all, fixed costs, they contribute nothing directly to output.

The computer is rapidly eroding economies of scale in administration, production, and marketing and, thereby, the comparative advantage of hierarchy and bureaucracy. Today, any organization that can afford a computer workstation and software can have first-class administrative systems, ranging from purchasing and inventory control to human resources management, financial planning and capital budgeting, marketing and logistics. Thirty years ago these systems were available only to giant organizations. Moreover, computerized production (which consists of machine tools or other equipment for fabrication, assembly or treatment, linked by a materials-handling system to move parts from one work station to another, and operating as an integrated system under full programmable control) now permits organizations to produce customized services at mass-production prices.

In computerized production facilities, overheads are more important than production volume. In these facilities, direct manufacturing labor often accounts for less than 5% of costs; materials and purchased components typically account for 30–40% more. This leaves at least 35% for overhead costs, most of which are transaction or information costs. Overheads involve activities such as product development and design, purchasing, materials handling, marketing, accounting, and asset utilization. Overhead costs are driven by an organization's policies, its operating and administrative procedures, and its customer relationships—not output volume, rate, or even mix.

To control overheads, including the costs of holding inventories of materials, parts, and finished goods, many organizations have adopted techniques like lean manufacturing and just-in-time delivery of parts and materials. They have also modified their managerial cost accounting systems to focus the attention of responsibility center managers, marketing and manufacturing teams, and especially product designers and engineers on controlling overheads. Two tools have been critical to this effort: cycle-time burdening and transaction cost accounting (activity-based costing). Again, not surprisingly, this is feasible because technology generates information about underlying productive processes. Computer-assisted-design programs also produce cycle-time and transactions cost estimates. Universal product codes and optical scanning devices permit continuous monitoring and, therefore, real-time reprogramming of the production process.

As a result of the declining importance of economies of scale in production, the average size of the workplace has been falling throughout the industrialized world for the last thirty years. Large companies are "mimicking their smaller competitors by shrinking their head offices, removing layers of bureaucracy and breaking themselves up into constellations of profit centers... [t]hey are 'sticking to their knitting'—concentrating on their core businesses and contracting everything else out... [and] they are putting a computer on every desk and giving power to front-line workers."

Economist, June 24, 1995: 4–6 Survey. As Shoshana Zuboft (1988: 204) explains, efficient operations in the modern workplace call for a more equal distribution of knowledge, authority, and responsibility. To create value from information, members of the organization must be given the opportunity to know more and do more. This means "dismantling the very same managerial hierarchy that once brought greatness" (Zuboff 1988, 204).

All of this looks like economics to many non-economists, but it is not. The intellectual justification for these changes comes primarily from management thinkers such as Peter Drucker (1973), Theodore Levitt, and Thomas Peters (1982), Joseph Bower (1970), and Robert Anthony (1965) (see also Anthony and Govindarajan 1995), Robert Kaplan and Robin Cooper, Henry Mintzberg, Alfred Chandler, Kenichi Ohmae, Gary Hamel, and Prahaladad (1994), and Peter M. Senge. The informational and organizational tools used in making these changes are described in the *Harvard Business Review*, *Sloan Management Review*, and *Strategic Finance*, not the *American Economic Review* or even the *Journal of Economic Behavior and Organization*. Many public administrators now read these journals and have tried to use the new tools in their organizations, hence the new public management.

Borrowing from the business management literature is an old custom, as well as a recent phenomenon, for the discipline of public administration. Business administration and public administration are both prescriptive, pragmatic disciplines (Hammond 1990; Fitch 1990). Moreover, business schools and schools of public administration once shared the same proverbs of administration, just as the Weberian bureaucratic paradigm and a common intellectual foundation in the works of Chester Barnard, Henri Fayol, Mary Parker Follett, Luther Gulick, Phillip Selznick, Frederick Taylor, and others were shared. Both disciplines taught that bureaucracy is the solution to the problem of maximizing organizational efficiency, that bigger is better, that organizations should be functionally differentiated and vertically integrated, and that top management always knows best. Besides, large organizations in both the public and the private sectors were fundamentally alike. Most were hierarchies that distinguished between high-level management tasks (planning, organizing, staffing, and developing) and low-level management tasks (controlling, operating, reporting, and budgeting), and centralized resource allocation and staff services.

Now changes are taking place in what managers do and how organizations are put together—even in what they are. The new public managers are interested in the way businesses do things not because they are better than government, but because they face similar problems and because the business management literature is full of ideas that seem relevant to meeting these new challenges.

C. Advances in Economics

While the business management literature is central to the new public management, three bodies of economic literature have also profoundly influenced its reception and its implementation: public choice theory, modern corporate finance and the contemporary macroeconomics it has inspired, and the new economics of organization.

Public choice theory has changed the way people think about government and how it works. Moreover, in explaining the rules that voters, elected officials, and bureaucrats are likely to follow given their incentives, public choice theory has given public administrators some useful new normative information. The same is true, although to less of an extent, of the new corporate finance. Nevertheless, when public administrators look to advances in economic science for help, it is not primarily to the public choice literature or to the new macroeconomics that they turn, but to the new economics of organization.

The new economics of organization focuses on incentive and control structures and on the allocation of property rights and ownership so as to minimize intraorganizational externalities or spillovers. It includes concepts like the Coase Theorem, transaction costs, externality, asymmetric information, agency theory, contract theory, search and signaling theory, team theory, and incentive compatibility, that are directly relevant to managerial problems. It is the legacy of economists like

Kenneth Arrow, Armen Alchian, William Baumol, Harold Demsetz, and Victor Goldberg (1976), Paul Milgrom and John Roberts, William Niskanen, and Gordon Tullock (1971), and especially Ronald Coase (1974) and Oliver Williamson. It provides the new public management with the beginnings of the analytical foundation needed to understand how, when, and where to delegate authority, replace rules and regulations with incentives, develop budgets based upon results, expose operations to competition, search for market rather than administrative solutions, or use quasi-markets and contracting out to foster competition.

The economics of organization has already influenced the design of a variety of institutional arrangements (ranging from emissions trading and bubbles to outright deregulation of the airlines and interstate trucking) in the United States and the privatization and securitization of an astonishing array of government-owned assets (and some liabilities) in the rest of the world. Moreover, the evidence is accumulating that some of these arrangements work. It is partly because of this evidence that the ideas of the new public managers command the attention they do.

IV. PUBLIC CHOICE THEORY

Public choice theory, like the older normative theory of public finance from which it evolved, starts with the demand for, and the supply of collectively provided goods and services. With two exceptions, the theory of demand for a collectively provided good is identical to the theory of consumer demand for a private good. In both instances, demand reflects individual willingness and ability to pay to consume a good or service. Total demand for the service is, therefore, assumed to be a decreasing function of the price of the good, an increasing function of consumer income, and the size of the market for the good. The two differences between the theory of demand for a collectively provided good and the theory of consumer demand for a private good are that the quantity of service provided within a jurisdiction is determined by a political process, usually assumed to be some form of majority rule, and is necessarily uniform throughout the jurisdiction.

Hence, the quantity demanded of a collectively provided service will depend upon its price (P), the permanent income of the citizenry (Y), and population size (C):

$$D_i = f(P^e, Y^a, C^b) \tag{28.1}$$

where e is the price elasticity of demand for good i, a is the income elasticity of demand for good i, and b is a value from 0 to 1, representing the degree of publicness of good i (Borcherding 1977).[*]

The functional relationship that would obtain in any particular case would, of course, reflect existing political institutions as well as culturally mediated tastes and preferences (Breton and Wintrobe 1982). There is a fair amount of evidence that this model of voter demand for collectively provided goods works reasonably well in practice. Literally hundreds of studies have demonstrated that family/per capita income, tax price, community size, and population served explain cross-sectional variations in collectively supplied service levels better than any other set of determinants (Oates 1994; Duncombe 1991; Romer and Rosenthal 1992). These variables work best where service levels are determined by direct referenda (Holcombe 1977; Romer and Rosenthal 1992). The one bug in the ointment is the "flypaper effect," so called because intergovernmental transfers tend to stick where they land (Oates 1994; Ladd 1994). That is, intergovernmental grants appear to produce far larger increases in the output of government services than predicted by the income and price elasticities of the basic demand model.

---

[*] See also Bergstrom and Goodman (1972).

A. THE MEDIAN VOTER AND BOWEN EQUILIBRIUM

In democracy, D_i should reflect the tastes and elasticities of the median voter (Bowen 1943) and would be in equilibrium, where

$$V_m = T_m, \tag{28.2}$$

where V_m is the marginal benefit of good or service i to the median voter m, T_m is the marginal cost of good or service i to the median voter m.

Then, where the cost of the good is equally shared by all voters (n), it follows that the marginal cost of the good to all voters is

$$MC = \sum_{j=1}^{n} T_j. \tag{28.3}$$

Because the Samuelsonian (1954, 1955) efficiency condition, where the sum of the marginal costs of providing the collective good equals the sum of marginal benefits to all contributors, is

$$\sum_{j=1}^{n} V_j = \sum_{j=1}^{n} T_j, \tag{28.4}$$

it follows that, for Bowen equilibrium to be efficient, the marginal cost/benefit to the average voter would have to be equal to the marginal benefit/cost to the median voter, i.e., the following condition would have to be satisfied:

$$\frac{V_m}{\sum_{j=1}^{n} V_j} = \frac{T_m}{\sum_{j=1}^{n} T_j}. \tag{28.5}$$

Consequently, Bowen equilibrium will be efficient if and only if marginal net benefits sum to zero at the output or supply level preferred by the median voter. This is something of a knife-edged condition, except where the tastes, willingness, and ability to pay of all the voters in a jurisdiction are practically identical. One mechanism that might lead to the satisfaction of this condition is Tiebout sorting (Tiebout 1956) in which voters move to the communities whose governments best satisfy their preferences for collectively provided goods and services (Zax 1989; Deller 1990a, 1990b; Taylor 1991; Hoyt 1990). While most economists grant that Tiebout sorting takes place, there is little consensus as to its significance. William Fischel (1992) for example, claims that the evidence from zoning and voting demonstrates that it is fairly complete; John Yinger et al. (1988), however, claim that the evidence from tax-capitalization is equivocal.

This is a significant claim, because, at the local level, to the extent that service and tax levels are capitalized in real property values, reliance on the property tax reduces differences between the mean and the median voter even in the absence of Tiebout sorting. Reliance on proportional or progressive income taxes probably has a similar effect at state and, perhaps, federal levels of government. The key point to be stressed here is, as Bowen explained, the average voter's demand for collectively provided goods will normally exceed the preferred consumption level of the median voter (Downs 1960). This means that in a democracy, where costs are equally shared or, where taxes are proportional to income, collectively provided goods will tend to be under-supplied.

There is evidence that Bowen/Downs undersupply does occur. For example, Fabio Silva and Jon Sonstelie (1995) recently tested William Fischel's (1989, see also 1995) hypothesis that, by requiring equal spending per pupil across all school districts in the state, and thereby reducing Tiebout sorting and widening the gap between the preferences of the average and the median voter, the California Supreme Court in *Serrano v. Priest* caused a reduction in public spending to support elementary and secondary education. Before Serrano, California ranked eleventh among states in public school spending per pupil, 13% above the average of all other states. By 1990, California had fallen to thirtieth, 10% below the average. Silva and Sonstelie found that one-half of this spending decline could be attributed to Serrano. They attributed the remainder to rapid enrollment growth during the 1980s.

B. LINDAHL EQUILIBRIUM

There is a second condition whereby the knife-edged condition described earlier might obtain, at least in theory: where decisions about collective provision are made unanimously. Unanimity can be satisfied under Lindahl equilibrium, a special case of the Samuelsonian efficiency condition (Feldman 1980). Formally, Lindahl equilibrium is defined as a vector of expenditure shares $(S_1, S_2,..., S_n)$ and a level of provision (D^*) such that for all i, where i's expenditure share is S_i, the quantity of the good desired is D^* (because i's expenditure, or T_i, is S_iD^*, $\Sigma S_i = 1$). Furthermore:

$$V_i'(D) = S_i, \tag{28.6}$$

$$V_i''(D^*) = S_i, \quad \text{for all } i, \tag{28.7}$$

$$\sum V_i'(D^*) = \sum S_i = 1. \tag{28.8}$$

Under this formulation, demand for all i is presumed to be normal, i.e., the higher i's share S_i, the less D_i that i will want. Hence, if the Lindahl equilibrium were D_1 and one i reduced their contribution to the provision of the good, the share of all other i would increase and $D_1 > D_2$.

This voting rule is seldom used, however, because of the transactions costs associated with fining Lindahl equilibrium—search, bargaining, and monitoring costs (Heckathorn and Maser 1990; Maser 1986). Because of this fact, James Buchanan and Gordon Tullock (1962) suggest that an optimal constitution would minimize the sum of the costs imposed upon dissatisfied minorities, a decreasing function of the size of required majorities, and transactions costs, an increasing function. Indeed, Americans have tried to design a constitutional order with this goal, albeit not this formulation, in mind. The founding fathers designed the federal Constitution to protect lives, liberties, and property from the overweening ambitions of a reckless and extravagant executive, the passions of minorities, and the interests of narrow or temporary majorities. This structure was intended to insure that the United States would have a government of law and that the law would change slowly and incrementally, and only when the direction of change was endorsed by a large majority of the citizenry. The founding fathers relied upon partisanship, jealousy between the two chambers of Congress, and the particularities of committee interests to make the federal government an agent of negotiation and compromise that would reach its decisions through the discovery of a lowest common denominator (Thompson 1979).

C.   LEGISLATIVE DECISION-MAKING

Representation promotes efficiency in two other ways. First, it minimizes the transactions costs of political participation (economists see participation as a cost, not a benefit). Second, it transforms some public goods, where each individual voter's preferences are known only to himself or herself and costs are shared into private goods, where benefits and costs are denominated in dollars and knowledge of the net-benefit schedule of each voter/legislator is equally available to all (Shepsle and Weingast 1984). Once the public goods problem is laid to rest, efficiency should be easy to achieve. According to the Coase Theorem (Coase 1960), where private goods are dealt with and decisions are made one good at a time, any decision rule will produce an efficient outcome, except where prevented by restrictions on side payments, transactions costs, or just plain ignorance (Dahlman 1979).

Consider, for example, the following problem: there are three legislators: X, M, and N. Each represents a smog producing district; however, X's constituents export all their smog to M's; M's export all theirs to N's; and N's keep all the smog they produce, plus that which they import from M's constituents. The problem that X, M, and N must deal with is underinvestment in maintenance of automotive smog control devices. This is a real market failure: smog control devices work properly only when they are properly maintained; the cost of maintaining this equipment is very low, at least compared to other equally effective means of abating pollution. Unfortunately, because individuals bear the cost of maintenance, but the benefit accrues primarily to others, they have no incentive to do so. The result is underinvestment.

Compulsory inspection and maintenance (I&M) is one way to deal with this market failure. It is an attractive example for our purposes for a number of reasons, one of which is that it can be assumed to impose roughly equal costs on voters in each constituency. Figure 28.1 illustrates the political calculus associated with a typical compulsory I&M option. In this example, the efficient solution is at x_{opt}, where the vertical sum of V_x, V_m and V_n equals MC. But because each legislator prefers the I&M option that equates T and V for the median voter in their constituencies, the efficient solutions are: zero for X, x_{med} for M, and x_{hi} for N. This example also clearly illustrates the typical gap between x_{med} and x_{opt} (Nelson 1990; Bell 1989).

What happens when this problem is approached in a Coasian manner, searching at the margin for Pareto superior moves? For example, I&M does not have to be compulsory to be effective. Automobile operators could be bribed to have their vehicles inspected and to achieve high maintenance scores at inspection. These bribes could be financed by a property tax levied on N's district. Under these circumstances, the situation outlined in Figure 28.2 would be obtained. (Figure 28.3 shows the same circumstances in preference space and demonstrates that the efficient solution obtained in Figure 28.2 is also the Bowen equilibrium.)

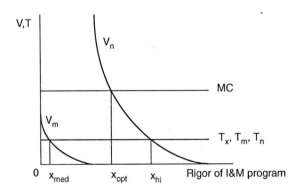

FIGURE 28.1 Bowen equilibrium for I&M policy, constrained case.

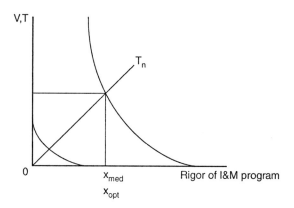

FIGURE 28.2 Bowen equilibrium for I&M policy, unconstrained case.

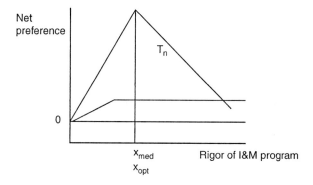

FIGURE 28.3 Unconstrained I&M policy equilibrium in preference space.

Note that this solution has the attractive quality of making all three legislators better off than they would have been under the solutions shown in Figure 28.1, but it is only one of possibly many Coasian solutions to the problem of underinvestment in the maintenance of smog control equipment. The Coase theorem merely states that when decision-makers are not constrained in their search for a solution the solution they choose will be efficient.

Of course, real legislators do not always behave like Coasian paragons. Simple human fallibility goes a long way toward explaining this fact. Information on the incidence of benefits and costs of a proposal may be equally available to all, but it may also be available to none. It is easy to conceptualize a Coasian solution to a problem of market failure; it is frequently far harder to design a practical program than to implement one (Hahn and Noll 1982). Hence, it is not surprising that legislators fail to behave like Coasian paragons. Like the rest of us, individually, and consequently collectively, they make mistakes.

D. EXPLAINING OVERSUPPLY

The basic model for a collectively provided good implies the likelihood of undersupply. To many public choice theorists this likelihood appears to fly in the face of reality. What they want to do is explain what they observe: an excess of government (Coughlin 1990). Two serious attempts to explain government excess have been mounted and, while neither entirely succeeds, both have taught us something about government. These are the interest-group theory of politics and William

Niskanen's theory of spending coalitions, which introduced the notions of structurally induced equilibrium and agency theory to the study of politics and bureaucracy.

The economic theory of interest-group politics is largely the creation of the Chicago school of regulatory theorists: George Stigler (1971, 1981), Richard Posner (1971, 1974), and Sam Peltzman (1976). They argued that a variety of government programs (agricultural subsidies, military procurement, tariffs and import quotas, most regulation of business, and the structure of the tax system) are the product of an exchange between elected officials, who receive votes and campaign contributions, and members of groups, who reap higher incomes from their political investment. The theory predicts that politicians will use their power to transfer income from those with less political power to those with more: from the rich and the poor to the middle class, and from disorganized, diffuse interests to well-organized, concentrated interests, e.g., geographically targeted benefits and predominantly federally financed costs (Ferejohn 1974; Shepsle and Weingast 1981; Hird 1991). Who gets what depends both upon the costs from participating in the political process as a member of a group and the ability of groups to influence policy makers.

Political scientists have known about interest groups for generations. What did the Chicago school of regulatory theorists have to say about interest-group politics that was new or original? First, as economists they better understood the costs and benefits of government actions and their distributional consequences, which focused attention on the size of individual payoffs rather than the wealth of the player. Second, they brought Mancur Olson's (1965) theory of collective action to bear upon the question of interest group influence on the public policy process. Olson demonstrated that political participation (interest-group activity, voting, etc.) imposes private costs upon participants but tends to create benefits that are non-exclusive (i.e., group members benefit whether they bear the costs of participation or not), which in turn leads to free-riding and the "exploitation of the great by the small" (see also Olson and Zeckhauser 1966). Olson's theory of collective action focused attention on the design of public policies that could deny benefits to non-participants, the concentration of benefits produced by those policies, and the support thresholds required to claim those benefits. Third, Chicago school economists based their theory on an assumption that is often wrong, but still might be of considerable utility in partial equilibrium analysis, that elected officials are exclusively concerned with maximizing the probability of their reelection. The probability of reelection is an increasing function of interest group support because citizens won't even vote unless they are persuaded to do so by campaign advertising and workers.

The biggest problem with the economic theory of interest-group politics is that, while it often tells a plausible story about existing public policies, empirical tests of its basic assumptions and predictions seldom work very well compared, say, to the presumption that legislators pursue their own notions of the common good (Coates and Munger 1995; Graddy 1991a, 1991b; Kalt and Zupan 1990; Mayer 1991; Peltzman 1984, 1990). In addition, one should be mindful that the economic theory of interest-group politics was created primarily to explain government regulation of prices and entry in industries like trucking and airlines, both of which have been subsequently deregulated.

The one central claim of the economic theory of interest-group politics that has gone unchallenged is that many of the benefits of government action, such as tariffs, agricultural marketing orders, import quota, various types of price and entry control regulation, tariffs, pork barrel spending, and the like, do not accrue to their nominal recipients (Buchanan and Tullock 1962). Instead, the rents created by government action are capitalized in asset prices, especially real property values, or competed away. Government-created rents are often competed away because their existence leads to rent-seeking behavior aimed at getting or keeping rents. Most of these activities are directly unproductive and are, beyond some point, entirely wasteful.

Gordon Tullock (1967) was probably the first scholar to think systematically about the consequences of rent-seeking. He argued that, if everyone could freely participate in the rush for the spoils, each rent-seeker would expend the full amount of the potential transfer in its pursuit. In such case, the rents created by government would be dissipated by the directly unproductive activities incurred to capture them. In an implicit analogy to the effect of product differentiation in the economics of imperfect competition, Tullock hypothesized that the waste involved in capturing rents could actually exceed the rent to be captured. In a related vein, Mancur Olson (1982) argued that, if rents are extensive and efforts to retain them pervasive, the inevitable result is a kind of policy gridlock, which devours ever more resources in defense of the economic status quo, stultifies change, and, by diverting investment away from productive activities and inhibiting the process of creative destruction, reduces the rate of economic growth.

An outsider cannot help but notice the amounts of money spent on campaigns for public office in this country or the resources employed to influence the legislative, administrative, and judicial processes. What seems remarkable about the American political system is not that it produces more rents than in other countries because that does not seem to be the case (Krueger, 1974), but that the creation, maintenance, and distribution of rents attract so much more effort here than elsewhere.

E. WILLIAM NISKANEN AND THE BUDGET MAXIMIZING BUREAUCRAT

In a second attempt to explain government excess, William Niskanen (1971), chairman of the Cato Institute and former head of the President's Council of Economic Advisors, showed that a revenue-maximizing, single-product bureau with absolute monopoly and agenda-setting powers would be technically efficient but produce up to two times the optimal quantity of output. While there are perhaps too many monopoly bureaus (Carroll 1989, 1990), their agenda-setting powers are often limited; most use a variety of technologies to provide an array of services, and technical inefficiency is widespread. Hence, anyone who leaps from the presumed monopoly power of bureaus to the allocative efficiency of government is undoubtedly over-reaching.

Having said that, one must still recognize the remarkable scientific contribution made by Niskanen. First of all, he more than anyone else demonstrated that the behavior of government officials, like corporate bureaucrats, could be deduced from their tastes and opportunities, and that this approach is more effective than assuming that they are merely well-trained robots. Second, Niskanen showed how the ability to control agendas presented to median voters could shift outcomes from their preferred positions. For example, confronted with a choice between nothing and a higher than preferred spending level (i.e., $V_m < T_m$), the median voter should prefer the higher spending level, as long as total benefits exceeded total costs ($\int V_m > \int T_m$). This same mechanism in the hands of a different agenda setter could lead to undersupply, but Niskanen argued that in the American congressional system, committees and subcommittees, the effective legislative and budget agenda setters, are likely to be dominated by program advocates (Shepsle 1979, 1978; Munger 1984). Finally, Niskanen adapted the structure-conduct-performance paradigm from industrial organization theory to the behavior of government bureaus, demonstrating, among other things, that monopoly supply is a necessary but insufficient condition for allocative inefficiency. Niskanen's strictures against bureaucratic agents have probably had more influence on the theory and practice of public administration than any other idea drawn from the public choice literature (Ezzamel 1993; Ferris and Graddy 1991; Mayston 1993; Miranda 1994, 1995; Rogerson 1990).

Political scientists have embraced Niskanen's notions of structurally induced equilibrium, primarily because those notions resonate with their interest in political institutions and their fascination with games of strategy. There is now an extensive literature on structurally induced equilibrium (Bendor 1990; McKelvey 1976; Shepsle 1979).[*] One conclusion that can be drawn from this literature is that, if referenda are not carefully restricted to a single issue dimension, initiative writers or drafters can manipulate them to produce almost any outcome desired. Another widely accepted conclusion is that an inability on the part of the legislature to achieve a stable collective choice could be a source of considerable bureaucratic discretion, even were there no

---

[*] For a less scholarly discussion, see Thompson and Green (2004).

problems measuring bureaucratic performance or designing incentive mechanisms (Hill 1985; Knott and Miller 1987; Miller 1981).[*]

Both economists and political scientists have also recognized the decisive role played by individually motivated agents in the determination of bureaucratic outcomes. Most, however, question Niskanen's assumption that bureaucrats are revenue maximizers (Blais and Dion 1991). In the meantime, new theories have been developed that rely on a more careful, or perhaps more imaginative description of bureaucratic tastes and opportunities. Contemporary models of bureaucracy stress the informational endowments of bureaucrats, the implicit and explicit contracts that link their actions to rewards, and their discretionary powers. The presumption that individuals within the State's administrative apparatus are single-mindedly driven to expand and protect existing programs and develop new programs of intervention has given way to the presumption that their utility functions might include some or more of the following arguments: effort and risk aversion, perquisite consumption, control and other non-pecuniary benefits, and reputation (Laffont and Tirole 1993; Gonzalez and Mehay 1984; Mehay 1986; Migue and Belanger 1974; Antoci 1995; De Fraja 1993; Gemmell 1990; Santerre 1990; Whynes 1993; McFadden 1976, 1977). Moreover, the dichotomy between competitors and monopolists proposed by the structure–conduct–performance paradigm—price takers versus price setters—has been largely superseded in the industrial organization literature by a new technology of games under incomplete information (Tirole 1988).

The newer models of bureaucratic behavior often seem inherently plausible. However, like the economic theory of interest-group politics, they generally fail to yield successful empirical predictions beyond the ones for which they were custom tailored (Conybeare 1984). For example, Thompson and Jones (1986) proposed a bilateral monopoly model of the budget process, with the central control office on one side and agencies on the other. It was assumed that budgeters were primarily interested in cutting budgets (that is after all what they are paid to do) and that agency officials were motivated by a variety of considerations (task accomplishment, perquisite consumption, control benefits and other non-pecuniary benefits, and reputation) (Thompson and Williams 1979). The typical outcomes of this model were less than optimal budgets and outputs, and higher than minimum unit costs. If this model were generally valid, however, both budgeters and agency heads would consistently oppose competition whenever it raised its head. That does not always seem to be the case, however. In both New Zealand and Australia, for examples, officials in central control agencies have taken the lead in promoting competition within government.

Another example is due to Terry M. Moe (1990), who argues that political authorities, especially legislators, favor administrative controls that are ineffective by design. He claims that legislators shun serious policy control, and instead seek particularized control because they "want to be able to intervene quickly, inexpensively, and in ad hoc ways to protect or advance the interests of particular clients in particular matters" (140). Detailed rules that impose rigid limits on an agency's discretion and its procedures help to satisfy this appetite. Consequently, detailed object-of-expenditure budgets are the norm, for example, not for historical reasons, but because they are suited to the needs of temporary governing coalitions, which are likely to be far more concerned with who gets public monies and where it goes, than with what it buys for the public at large. Furthermore, Moe argues that the rigidity characteristic of the American administrative process is largely the product of the efforts of temporary ruling coalitions to prevent future majorities from interfering with their handiwork.[†]

---

[*] See also Langbein (2000), McCubbins and Schwartz (1984), and McFadden (1976, 1977).

[†] Also see Moe (1989), Tabellini and Alesina (1990), Cooley and Smith (1989), and McCubbins et al. (1989), and Krause and Meier (2003), especially the articles by Daniel P. Carpenter and John Brehm, Scott Gates, and Brad Gomez.

F. Summing Up

Public choice theorists are often cynical about politics and pessimistic about the workings of government. They disallow any role for what Steve Kelman (1987) calls public, or civic, spirit, except to the extent that self-interest is defined to include an interest in the welfare of others (a tactic which has the effect of denying to public choice any Popperian bite whatsoever). Moreover, as Michael Trebilcock (1994) explains, public choice theorists implicitly reject the notion that ideas have power, although the recent trend of privatization, deregulation, and tax reform can hardly be explained any other way. As Trebilcock puts it, these policies show that ideas have force and that "politics, to an important extent, is partly about what are thought to be good ideas as well as what are thought to be politically salient interests."

These problems aside, and they are not small problems, what public choice theorists say about coalition formation, free riding, agenda setting, and bureaucracy is important, if for no other reason than because it has been useful in promoting a healthy skepticism (not cynicism) about government and interest group demands. It is not a bad thing to look beneath the packaging (Stanbury 1993). Individuals and groups do often turn to government to obtain or preserve economic rents that would otherwise be unavailable to them. Government activities often are designed to interfere with efficient market solutions to resource allocation problems. Society has several common pools of wealth: (1) personal and business net assets; (2) government's net real and financial assets, not including natural resources; (3) publicly owned natural resources; (4) the stock human capital; (5) an environment pool that reflects the overall quality of the environment; and (6) the wealth of the future generations. The wealth of future generations is largely dependent upon the expansion of the first five pools.

Politics, at its worst, is merely a means by which stakeholder groups use the collective, coercive power of government to tilt these pools in their direction. This produces a lot of sloshing about and considerable leakage. Moreover, some groups are especially vulnerable to losses—the young and the unborn, for instance, must bear the consequences of the failure of current generations to expand resource pools, but are excluded from political processes. Consumers and taxpayers, individually and collectively, are similarly, although not so completely disadvantaged, in political arenas. It seems likely that increased skepticism about existing institutional arrangements and governance mechanisms has encouraged experimentation with alternatives and increased receptivity to the lessons of the new macroeconomics, as well as the new economics of organizations and institutions.

V. THE NEW MACROECONOMICS

Arguably, the most dramatic advances in economic understanding of the past forty years have taken place in financial economics. There are two reasons for this success: first, modern financial markets have characteristics that make them particularly amenable to understanding via the economists' beloved mathematical tools of partial equilibrium analysis (i.e., many buyers and sellers and standardized products). Second, financial economics is a highly practical discipline. There is a direct and immediate pecuniary payoff to a better understanding of financial markets.

Much of this new understanding has taken the form of appreciation of the consequences of decisions that have future effects, in terms of their present values. Because the future is necessarily uncertain, much of this new learning is concerned with modeling risk and uncertainty, and with the design of institutional arrangements that allow risks to be precisely formulated and priced. Among the most influential of the new financial theories are the capital asset pricing model, portfolio theory, derivatives pricing models and financial engineering, and the theory of real options.

Eventually these theories will probably come to play a dominant role in public financial management. These topics are increasingly evident in periodicals such as *Public Budgeting and Finance* and the *Municipal Finance Journal*. However, their main influence on the field of public finance has come through macroeconomics, especially monetary economics, where they directly bear upon the formulation of interest rates, both real and nominal, and their meaning. More recently these theories have also influenced the way fiscal policy is thought about, as well as the understanding of the nature of fiscal stimulus and drag. In turn, those ideas have materially influenced our understanding of how government spending, taxing, and borrowing ought to be measured.

Most macroeconomists would now agree that the best way to think about spending and taxing decisions that have long-term consequences for the American people is in net present value (NPV) terms. Many budget pundits have forgotten that the executive branch of the US government adopted a consolidated cash budget in the 1960s primarily for macroeconomic reasons: Keynesians held that the public sector borrowing requirement, or annual cash deficit, was the key to sound fiscal management (Meyers 2004). These days, few if any macroeconomists any longer believe that the annual cash deficit is the key to sound fiscal management.

It is now well known that there is little if any correlation between the cash deficit and interest rates, savings and investment, or productivity growth. This is not because, as Robert Barro of Harvard once claimed, fiscal policy does not matter (the basis for that claim, Ricardian equivalence, has been decisively rejected on empirical grounds), but because the deficit has been incorrectly defined. Three of the most influential of the economists taking this position are the late Robert Eisner of Northwestern University, Stanford's Michael Boskin, chairman of the President's Council of Economic Advisers under George H.W. Bush, and Boston University's Laurence Kotlikoff (Trebilcock 1994). They make several important points:

1. The government's official debt measures only the government's liabilities. It completely ignores the government's assets. Using the government's debt figures to assess its financial position is, in their view, akin to calling the owner of a $1 million property a debtor because he has a large mortgage on the property.
2. The conventional deficit measure fails to correct for inflation.
3. The government's official debt ignores government liabilities from transfer programs, such as Social Security, and its implicit commitments to other federal expenditures. The conventional deficit omits changes in the government's liabilities and assets as a result of spending and taxing decisions.

In other words, the current measure of the deficit is based on arbitrary choices of how to label government receipts and payments. If the government labels receipts as taxes and payments as expenditures, it will report one number for the deficit. If it labels receipts as loans and payments as return of principal and interest, it will report a very different number. As Kotlikoff (1986) explains, social security is a good example of this phenomenon. Social Security "contributions" are called taxes, and Social Security benefits are called expenditures. If the government taxes Mr. X by $1000 this year, and pays him $1500 in benefits ten years from now, this year's deficit falls by $1000 and the deficit ten years hence will be $1500 higher. But the taxes could just as plausibly be labeled as a forced loan to the government, and the benefits could be labeled as repayment of principal plus interest. In that case there would be no consequences for the deficit as it is currently measured.

Most contemporary macroeconomists would argue that to measure fiscal stimulus or drag properly, the change in government's net worth must be measured. That means measuring the value of all current and projected payments and receipts in inflation-adjusted (constant) dollars, which is to say government's liabilities and assets should be measured in terms of the discounted present value of the current commitments to individuals to make future payments to, and take receipts from.

Focusing fiscal stimulus and drag in terms of the change in net worth from year to year—what might be called the real deficit—leads to a radically different interpretation of postwar economic policy than does reliance on the cash deficit. From this perspective, the fifties, sixties, and seventies were periods of quite loose fiscal policy. The reason was the build-up of our unfunded, pay-as-you-go Social Security, civil service, and military retirement programs. The eighties and nineties, in contrast, were marked by rather tight fiscal policy. The Reagan tax cuts and military build-up provided considerable fiscal stimulus, but other policies, particularly the 1983 Social Security reform, largely offset them. By raising the retirement age in stages to sixty-seven from sixty-five, and by gradually subjecting retirees' Social Security benefits to income taxation, the 1983 reforms reduced the present value of Social Security benefits to be paid by about $1.1 trillion at that time and nearly $4 trillion now. This perspective, combined with a better understanding of monetary policy and the role of endogenous technological change, allows us to explain most of the variation in economic performance observed over the past 100 years.

Over and above concerns about fiscal stimulus or drag, one theoretical reason contemporary macroeconomists are concerned about the present value of the government's spending and receipts is that policies which reduce the government's net worth can increase national consumption, lower savings, lower investment, raise interest rates, and exacerbate trade deficits—in short, do many of the bad things that have been ascribed to cash deficits. For example, redistribution from younger to older generations will reduce savings and increase consumption because older people have a greater propensity to consume than do young ones.

The present value of the gap between America's long-term entitlement promises and its expected tax revenues looks to be more than $70 trillion. President Bush's tax cuts have made the problem worse. The real deficit shows that controlling entitlement spending is the real challenge; by contrast, tax cuts add only about $3–$5 trillion to the fiscal gap. But, when it comes to the entitlements issue, the president has been largely silent. Though he has talked about diverting payroll taxes to individual accounts, he has said nothing about reducing Social Security benefits. Far from controlling entitlement spending, Bush has expanded it, notably by increasing federal spending on prescription drugs for social security recipients, a measure which, alone, has increased America's long-term fiscal gap by $17 trillion. Bush's recent opponent, John Kerry, was no better. He was silent on Social Security reform and proposed to spend more than Bush on health care.

In the end, these concerns must lead to substantial changes in national income and product accounts, and in how government spending, taxing, and borrowing are measured. At a minimum, it should lead to substantial changes in government budgeting and accounting, issues that are at the heart of traditional public administration (Boskin 2000; Eisner 1986; Kotlikoff 1986; Kotlikoff and Burns 2004).

VI. THE NEW ECONOMICS OF ORGANIZATION

The basic idea of the new economics of organization is that the comparative advantage of governance mechanisms boils down to a question of information or transaction costs "and to the ability and willingness of those affected by information costs to recognize and bear them" (Arrow 1969, 48).[*] Hence, the circumstances that create market failures and justify government action in a capitalist economy: public goods, natural monopolies, externalities, moral hazard and adverse selection, etc., are all fundamentally information failures. Markets could deliver public goods, for example, if information technology existed that would permit free-riders to be profitably excluded from enjoying them. Monopolies could be compensated to behave like competitors, if information costs were lower. And, bargaining between self-interested individuals could eliminate externalities, without the intervention of government, if transaction costs were zero. Much the same logic applies to the choice between organizations and markets and the kinds of governance mechanisms used within organizations.

A corollary to this basic Coasian insight is that information costs—typically search, bargaining, logistics, or enforcement costs—can be reduced by carrying them out through organizations rather

---

[*] Ultimately these ideas derive directly from Coase (1937). See also Alchian and Demsetz (1972) and Barzel (1982).

than markets, or through government rather than private organizations. Reduction does not imply elimination, however. This fact implies a second, perhaps less obvious, corollary to the basic Coasian insight: the conditions that wreck markets will also impair organizations and governments. Consequently, as Robert Gibbons (2003) explains, the organizations that are observed will be tend to be less efficient than observed markets, even though they are more efficient than the markets they replace; observed government agencies will tend to be less efficient than the observed private organizations, even though they are more efficient than the private organizations they replace.

Gibbons' corollary to the basic Coasian insight is illustrated in Figure 28.4, which plots the declining efficacy of markets, organizations, and government as transactions difficulty increases. At the critical values of transaction difficulty shown by the intersection of the lines, markets and organizations and organizations and governments are both equally efficacious; to the right of the first intersection, organizations are more efficient than markets; to the right of the second, government is more efficient than private organizations.

The evidence seems to support Gibbons' corollary. Where the production of privately consumed goods and services—steel, banking, even telecommunications—is concerned, private organizations are usually observed to be more efficient than state-owned enterprises (Mueller, 2003). Dennis Mueller comprehensively surveyed the literature comparing the performance of state-owned enterprises to private organizations, and found that fifty-six reported that private companies were more efficient, ten reported equivalent performance, and only five reported that state-owned enterprises outperformed private companies. Sumit Majumdar's study of Indian industrial companies is illustrative of the findings reported by Mueller. Majumdar (1998) ranked every large-scale industrial enterprise in the country on an efficiency scale of zero to one, with one indicating a perfectly efficient company. He found that state-owned companies averaged about 0.65, mixed ownership companies 0.91, and privately owned companies 0.975. There is a large body of literature which shows that privatization of state-owned enterprises typically produces substantial productivity gains (de Fraja, 1993; Vining and Boardman 1992; Megginson and Netter 2001). Many of these studies conclude that the productivity gain is associated with replacing government-appointed bureaucrats with a new, profit-oriented management team.

On the other hand, it does not seem that private provision of social services, such as health insurance, benefit payments, or public safety is more efficient than public provision (Blank 2000;

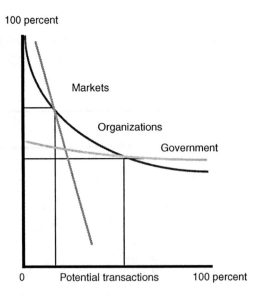

FIGURE 28.4 The relative efficacy of alternative governance mechanisms.

Tirole 1994). One well known example of the problem of private provision of social services is provided by Oliver Hart, Andrei Shleifer, and Robert Vishny (1997), who compared private to public prisons. They found that private prisons are roughly 10% cheaper per prisoner, but that those savings are achieved by paying lower wages to prison guards. The low pay leads to staffing with lower quality guards, resulting in higher instances of violence and in one case a major riot. Thus, lower costs come at the expense of quality.

Finally, it might be noted that Gibbons' corollary is consistent with the notion presented earlier that reducing the cost of information would increase the efficacy of markets relative to organizations, and of non-governmental organizations relative to government. Because improved communications technology, logistics, and information technology (IT) have all reduced the cost of information, it is reasonable to propose that both of the vertical lines shown in Figure 28.4 have also shifted to the right in recent decades.

It is hard to argue with the new economics of organization at this level. The Coasian insight and its corollaries are little more than literary conceits, although profound ones. Problems arise only when these insights are converted into formal models. No argument is made here against formal, mathematical models which can contribute to clear thinking in a variety of ways (by keeping one's logic straight, simplifying relationships, and sorting things out so they can be tested). Moreover, formal models also contribute to our ability to talk to each other. Scholars from different disciplines or traditions within disciplines find it difficult to make sense of each other's verbal models. The terms, constructs, and means of expressing relationships all differ, while models provide the translatability of the mathematical structure. Hence, formalization makes it easier for members of various disciplines to communicate with each other. Recognition that all of the dilemmas underlying the choice of governance mechanisms or the design of programmatic organizations are fundamentally divisible prisoner's dilemma types of games, for example, must surely increase the ability of economists, political scientists, management theorists, students of budgeting and administrative controls, as well as public administrators to talk to one another.

However, while the practitioners of the new economics of organization have provided several elegant, logically consistent deductive models, these models are, for the most part, not very practical or useful. The main contribution rational choice theorists have made to the understanding of organizations and the behavior that takes place within them has been a set of theorems demonstrating the impossibility of various events, many of which are seen in everyday life. Indeed, rational choice theorists often seem more interested in saying what cannot be, rather than what should be done, and in demonstrating that circumstances give rise to inefficiencies, rather than in how one might go about minimizing them.

Consider their approach to market failures resulting from asymmetric information: agency, moral hazard, and adverse selection problems. Economists fixate on problems with a high degree of conflict between principal and agent, which usually leads to a substantial gap between what principals get and what they could get if they were better informed. However, intellectual interest should not obscure reality and many, perhaps most, asymmetric information problems seem to have reasonably satisfactory solutions (Baker 1992; Baker et al. 1994; Bates 1993; Campbell, Chan, and Marino 1989; De Groot 1988; Hemmer 1993; Itoh 1993; Mayston 1993; Wallis 1991; Williamson 1985). Evidence that a potential problem is a real one requires information about magnitudes, rather than just proof of existence. Agency, moral hazard, and adverse selection problems are common in corporate governance because the interests of corporate managers are also not necessarily identical to those of the stockholders, yet many businesses survive and prosper nonetheless. Furthermore, these conflicts do not completely undermine the value of the theories that ignore them.

The difference between potential and real agency problems is demonstrated by James Buchanan's (1969) conjecture that risk-averse public officials will exploit their superior understanding of the production of government services to extract higher budgets from the public. Buchanan argues that from the public official's standpoint it may be more costly to finance public spending with taxes than with debt, in which case borrowing would lead to higher than optimal levels of government spending and services. Consequently, Buchanan concludes that pay-as-you go financing serves as a check on public officials, bringing their actions into line with the tastes of the citizenry. Pay-as-you go financing has much to recommend it but, as it turns out, the risk-aversion problem that is at the heart of Buchanan's conjecture is strictly incentive-compatible—either it is not a problem, or it is easily solved (Breton and Wintrobe 1975; Choate and Thompson 1988, 1990; Wittman 1989).

A preoccupation with problems in which there is a high degree of conflict is not merely a matter of taste. This interest also derives from the kinds of models that are available to the practitioners of the new economics of organization. Traditional structure–conduct–performance formulations will not suffice; they are no more satisfying in economics than they are in sociology or political science. Moreover, existing formal economic models of behavior within organizations perform poorly with regard to the passage of time, path dependence, and irreversibility. They perform equally poorly with certain endogenous mechanisms and processes (such as learning, especially social learning and discovery). Yet, presumably, these mechanisms are fundamental to achieving cooperative collective action. Gibbons (2003) argues that what is needed are game-theoretic formulations of the behavior of individuals in organizations, but acknowledges that the game-theoretic models now available will not suffice. Unfortunately, there is no assurance that the game-theoretic models we need will ever be developed.

Another problem with the models created by the practitioners of the economics of organization is that they are seldom empirically grounded. Until very recently, the economics of organization was a classic example of theory without data. This situation is changing (Frant 1993, 1997), but not very rapidly. One reason for this state of affairs is that tinkering is required to make a satisfactory positive theory of public sector supply arrangements. One cannot, for example, simply presume that governance arrangements have been selected because they minimize the sum of operating and transaction costs, or that the arrangements one observes are optimal (De Groot 1988; Ferris 1984; Ferris and Graddy 1991; Moe 1984). So far, very little careful, comparative research of best practices has been done.

A. FROM THE NEW ECONOMICS OF ORGANIZATION TO NETWORKS

How would one go about empirically grounding these models? To provide context and meaning to this discussion, the idea of a value chain, one of the central organizing concepts in the contemporary management literature, is useful. A value chain is simply an arrangement of activities or tasks undertaken to add or create value, where individual willingness and ability to pay for the services rendered through the chain measures its final value. Some value chains are simple, others complex. Economists presume that governance arrangements make value chains more efficient. That is, that value chains are a means of managing the sum of transaction—search, bargaining, negotiation, and enforcement—and holding costs. Though an oversimplification, this is often a useful starting place in the analysis of institutional arrangements.

As discussed, the traditional transaction cost framework posits two polar types of institutional arrangements:

- The market, which at the limit is a completely deconstructed value chain
- The hierarchical, vertically integrated organization, which at the limit is a completely self-contained value chain

Most real value chains are composed of both markets and organizations.

There is often a tacit assumption in this sort of analysis that the mass production of manufactured goods is the normal mechanism through which organizations create value. Under this mechanism, the lion's share of the value created derives from the production or fabrication process, a repetitive or cyclical process. Consequently, most of the costs incurred in creating value vary directly with the rate and/or volume of output. These assumptions imply a particular division of labor, one in which like activities or tasks are grouped together and performed sequentially, and where each node in the value chain or network is an event signifying completion of a discrete task. Hence, value chains are typically portrayed as linear networks of activities in which events follow sequentially from one to the next until the process culminates in the enjoyment of the good or service in question. A complex value chain might have many tributaries, but its flow is unidirectional. Except where so-called overhead services contribute to the value chain, its activities can be coordinated via simple push–pull mechanisms, with communication concentrated at the links in the process. The other important tacit assumption is that information is very costly and must be carefully husbanded. Consequently, this assumption further implies that the main issue confronted in the governance of value chains is vertical integration, not only to maximize economies of scale, but also to minimize overheads through economies of scope.

In one of the most widely accepted formulations incorporating this perspective, two attributes of primary and intermediate products or services suffice to answer the question of how their place in the value chain should be governed: excludability and exhaustibility. Both non-excludability and non-exhaustibility give rise to divisible prisoner's dilemma games, which often preempt efficient voluntary governance arrangements and, where that is the case, call for coordination by fiat or hierarchy.

The main normative prescription that flows from this perspective is that goods or services that are characterized by excludability and exhaustibility, so-called pure private goods, ought to be supplied via voluntary exchange, i.e., markets. Goods or services that are both non-excludable and non-exhaustible, so-called pure public goods, ought to be subject to hierarchical control. It is usually further presumed that a public-goods value chain involving final goods and services that benefit a large share of the citizenry should be managed by the state or one of its subsidiaries. This formulation logically suggests two additional patterns: excludable, non-exhaustible goods and services, so-called toll goods, and non-excludable, exhaustible goods and services, so-called commons goods, externalities, or spillovers. Under the old structure–conduct–performance paradigm the former called for some form of administered contract (at the limit, government regulation of price and entry) and the latter an M-form organizational design* or, at the limit, government process controls to increase the spillover when a good, or decrease it when a bad (Goldberg 1976; Goldin 1977; Milgrom and Roberts 1992; Vining and Weimer 1998; Williamson 1985). Table 28.1 depicts the traditional normative logic of vertical integration.

The final assumption of the structure–conduct–performance approach to transaction-cost-oriented value-chain analysis is that the coordination of interdependent cooperative activities is easier under an organizational hierarchy than in markets. In turn, the coordination advantages of organizations supposedly derive from the internal homogeneity of their systems of internal contracts: communication systems, including budgets, incentive regimes and authority structures. A corollary of this assumption is that organizations that rely on a small number of suppliers or distributors can write contracts that will, at some cost, constrain the opportunistic behavior of those with whom they deal (Besselman, Arora, and Larkey 2000; Che and Gale 2003; Kovacic 1998).

---

* Because value-creation strategies are usually conceived along product-market lines (single product, differentiated products, multiple products), and because the M-form structures provide a general manager for each product line (rather than for regions or functions), the M-form is broadly endorsed as the mode of organizing and managing large, multiproduct organizations whose products are by definition heterogeneous. The broad outline of the M-form structure is one where substantial decisional authority is decentralized to agents, within the context of well-specified rules determining how agents will be rewarded for their efforts. According to this perspective, the management process mainly involves acquiring and deploying assets and, to influence this process, principals must establish a consistent set of delegated decisions, performance measures, and rewards. Organizational units in such a setup participate in quasi-voluntary value chains linked by transfer prices. Managerial rewards are based on economic quantities of interest to principals, such as returns on capital employed (holding plus embedded transaction costs).

TABLE 28.1
The Traditional Logic of Vertical Integration

Service Characteristics	Excludable	Non-Excludable (Economies of Scope)
Exhaustible (constant or increasing costs)	Market	M-form organization
Non-exhaustible (economies of scale)	Administered contract	Hierarchy

There is a fair amount of evidence supporting the logic of this formulation. Arguably, for example, the main thrust of the regulatory reform movement of the 1970s and 1980s in the United States and the privatization of state-owned enterprises elsewhere was to align governance mechanisms with characteristics of the goods and services produced. In the private sector, mergers and acquisitions that conform to the dictates of this formulation are usually successful. Those that do not, almost inevitably destroy stockholder value. Finally, in a study of defense businesses, Scott Masten (1984) showed that non-exhaustibility (economies of scale) and non-excludability (economies of scope) directly influenced vertical integration. Where intermediate products were both complex and highly specialized (used only by the buyer), there was a 92% probability that they would be produced internally; even 31% of all simple, specialized components were produced internally. The probability dropped to less than 2% if the component was unspecialized, regardless of its complexity.

Nowadays, however, it is increasingly apparent that the principles of hierarchy, levels of graded authority, and a firmly ordered system of super- and subordination and formal contractual mechanisms are at best imperfect solutions to the problems caused by divisible prisoner's dilemma types of games. One of the best ways to conserve on transaction costs is through the elaboration of trust-based relationships of mutual dependency. These can be reflected in intra-organizational cooperation or take the form of inter-organizational alliances. For example, Toyota's legendary just-in-time manufacturing process, which produces dramatic reductions in components, work-in-progress, and finished goods inventories and thereby holding costs, does not depend on vertical integration. Instead, Toyota relies on a few suppliers that it nurtures and supports (Womack, Jones, and Roos 1990). The members of the Toyota alliance have substantial cross-holdings in each other and Toyota often acts as its suppliers' banker. Toyota maintains tight working links between its manufacturing and engineering departments and its suppliers, intimately

TABLE 28.2
The Logic of Horizontal Integration

Project Characteristics	Developmental Process	Known Process
Multiple core competencies required	Alliances (voluntary collaborations involving multiple organizations)	Systems management (hierarchical coordination involving multiple organizations)
Multiple personal competencies required	Teams (voluntary collaborations within a single organization)	Project management (hierarchical coordination within a single organization)

involving them in all aspects of product design and manufacture. It often lends them personnel to deal with production surges, and in return its suppliers accept Toyota people into their personnel systems.

Toyota's alliance members share much more than a marketplace relationship with each other. In a very real sense, Toyota and its suppliers share a common purpose and destiny. Yet, Toyota has not integrated its suppliers into a single, large bureaucracy. It wants its suppliers to remain independent companies with completely separate books—real profit/investment centers, rather than merely notional ones—selling to others whenever possible. Toyota's solution to the cooperative games created by spillovers and toll goods appears to work just fine. Note that the means of reinforcing trust-based alliances often includes the exchange of hostages—surety bonds, the exchange of debt or equity positions, or quasi-vertical integration. Quasi-vertical integration is common in both the automobile and the aerospace industries, and it is standard procedure for the Department of Defense to provide and own the equipment, dies, and designs that defense firms use to supply it with weapons systems and the like (Monteverde and Teece 1982).

Modern information technology has made it economically feasible in a number of cases to exclude users and to design and apply demand-based multi-part tariffs to deal effectively with problems of non-exhaustibility, thereby deconstructing vertically integrated value chains. Under multi-part transfer prices, the service delivered is decomposed to reflect underlying cost drivers and priced accordingly (your home phone bill is an excellent example of a multi-part tariff). Even where sequential value chains remain bounded by a single organization, these innovations often allow intra-organizational exchanges of services, tangible assets, knowledge, and skills to be governed by *laissez faire* transfer prices, in which the buying and selling units are completely free to negotiate prices and to deal or not to deal.[*] The point is that there is more than one way to skin a cat, to cite a familiar value-chain problem.

More significant, given my purpose, is the fact that technology, primarily information technology, but also the technology of social cooperation (mechanisms, processes, doctrines), has rendered traditional mass production methods obsolete by removing value added from the fabrication stage of many value chains. For many final goods and services, direct labor costs at the fabrication stage are now trivial and raw materials and components do not add value at that stage of the process. This means that most of the costs incurred in creating value do not vary directly with the rate or volume of output, but have other drivers. Moreover, modern fabrication technologies are largely available to any producer willing to make the necessary investment.

In a typical modern hi-tech value chain, most of the value is added in product development and design, logistics, materials handling, delivery, post-delivery servicing and maintenance, and in customer relations. In other words, overheads and purchased services and components account for 90% of costs. Consequently, value is now defined more in terms of the quality and heterogeneity of goods and services, their availability and convenience of use, and consumer awareness and knowledge of product or service attributes, rather than in terms of cost or price.

This transformation reflects the fact that mass production entailed costs, in addition to benefits. Costs took the form of mismatches between individual tastes and preferences and product

---

[*] Formerly, in most large complex organizations in the private sector, value chains were typically governed by centralized resource-requirements planning systems. Even where transfer prices were used, the financial performance of a processing unit that contributed directly to a value chain was typically measured against a standard unit-cost target; staff units were not a direct component of the value chain and were typically treated as discretionary expense centers. Only final product-market lines were evaluated in terms of return on investment or economic value added. The reasons for this are complex, but they go to difficulties associated with expensing intermediate and joint products. Consequently, attempts to find the costs of intermediate and joint products or to price them were often either excessively arbitrary or prohibitively costly. In contrast, final products have always been relatively easy to price and expense following generally accepted accounting practice. Recent advances in information technology, managerial accounting, and organizational design have made it possible and, in some cases, beneficial to treat every responsibility center in an organization as an investment center, including those providing overhead services.

characteristics. The classic illustration of this phenomenon is Henry Ford's dictum that customers could have any color Model T they wanted, as long as it was black. This potential misallocation of resources arising from the mismatch between tastes and the product homogeneity induced by mass production is directly comparable to the problem of providing public goods in a jurisdiction where people have different preferences for the good (i.e., where people cannot vote with their feet and zoning doesn't achieve efficient sorting), but face an identical tax price. In that case, where the quantity of the good provided is democratically determined, reflecting the preferences of the median voter, half of the citizens get more of the good than they want (they would rather not buy as much of the public good as they are made to) and half less (they would be willing and able to buy more). Technological changes mean that in many cases it is no longer necessary to bear these costs to obtain the benefits of productive efficiency, even where value chains are concerned with manufactured goods.

Elsewhere, the standard model of the value chain, based as it was upon the technical and social imperatives of the mass-production of manufactured goods, was probably never the best way to think about value creation. The delivery of services, for example, has generally involved at least some accommodation to the needs of the individual recipient. Treating service delivery, especially government service delivery, like manufacturing almost necessarily meant trying to fit it into a Procrustean bed. Much the same could be said about the building and construction trades. Consequently, it may be argued that what has changed in recent years is that manufacturing has simply become more like other value-creating activities.

If true, these facts ought to change how value chains are thought about in some fundamental ways. Instead of linear networks of sequentially dependent activities, it now often makes more sense to think of value chains as parallel networks involving reciprocally interdependent relationships through which activities are simultaneously carried out. Consequently, critical paths, or PERT, networks are better metaphors for these value chains than are directed or linear graphs. This is the case because holding costs can often be minimized by parallel processing where all the participants in the value chain have full access to information about every aspect of the process. The activities and tasks that comprise a value chain, and the technologies used to perform them still determine its optimal arrangement and its governance structure, but the main coordination problems to be solved nowadays typically involve horizontal, rather than vertical integration (Considine and Lewis 1999; O'Toole 1997).

Unfortunately, the logic of horizontal integration is not very well developed or understood, in part because students of management haven't fully appreciated the need to rethink the problem of coordinating activities when information costs are low, or of organizing to create value via parallel processes. Organizational economists have been especially resistant to rethinking received doctrine. Fortunately, however, there exists a lot of empirical knowledge about managing projects, which is the closest analogue to the more general problem of horizontal integration.

The logic of transactions or information cost implies that networks are neither a distinct kind of relationship, nor necessarily superior in performance to other kinds of value chains, nor even uniquely more difficult to sustain than value chains comprehended by single organizations. Nevertheless, work is central to our lives, which implies an important relational difference. At work, people are often silenced: the principles of hierarchy, levels of graded authority, and a firmly ordered system of super-and subordination are inimical to democracy. They are also increasingly inimical to high performance. Nowadays, high performing entities are more likely to be designed around team-based collaborations that successfully spread authority and responsibility throughout the organization, and thereby mobilize the collective intelligences of their members.

Decompartmentalization has led to smaller, flatter organizations, organized around a set of generic value-creating processes and specific competencies. Some single-mission organizations are now organized as virtual networks, some multi-mission organizations as alliances of networks. Philip Evans and Thomas Wurster (1997) refer to both of these kinds of organizational arrangements as hyperarchies, after the hyperlinks of the World Wide Web. Evans and Wurster assert that these kinds of organizations, like the Internet itself, the architectures of object-oriented software programming, and packet switching in telecommunications, have eliminated the need to channel information, thereby eliminating the tradeoff between information bandwidth (richness) and connectivity (reach). Evans and Wurster describe virtual networks (structures designed around fluid, team-based collaboration within the organization) as deconstructed value chains, and alliances of networks (the pattern of "amorphous and permeable corporate boundaries characteristic of companies in the Silicon Valley") as deconstructed supply chains, in which "everyone communicates richly with everyone else on the basis of shared standards" (Table 28.2).

IBM's Dallas, Texas facility is an example of such a network. It mimics a market. Everyone is either a customer or a provider, depending on the transaction, thereby transforming the facility into a network of exchanges. Each exchange is a closed loop involving four steps: request from a customer and offer from a provider, negotiation of the task to be performed, and definition of success, performance, and customer acceptance. Until the last step is completed, the task is unfinished. IBM uses powerful computers to track these loops and monitor the progress of each transaction. The result has been to empower workers, eliminate boundaries and bottlenecks, and boost productivity through the ceiling (Hammer 1990).

Some government organizations have copied well-managed businesses by organizing themselves into similar alliances of networks, sharing their top management, core competencies, and a common culture, and using computers to chart activities and operational flows. Their control systems are like those of centralized bureaucracies in that they collect a lot of real-time information on operations. Unlike the control systems of stove-piped centralized bureaucracies, however, which passed the exercise of judgment up the managerial ranks, this information is used to push it down into the organization, to wherever it is most needed—at delivery, in production, or to the client.

How far hyperarchy will go is an open question. Evans and Wuster (1997) claim that it will dstroy all hierarchies, whether of logic or of power, "with the possibility (or the threat) of random access and information symmetry." If hyperarchy is where we are all heading, M-form structures are at best an intermediate stage to a fundamentally different kind of deceontralization. It is now apparent, as it really was not before, that M-form structures tend to restrict the upward flow of operating information within organizations, thus making decentralization a necessity as well as an ideal (Otley, Broadbent, and Berry 1995).[*] In contrast, networks and alliances are information-rich environments. For the most part, access to information is symmetrical in fully networked organizations, equally available to all the people in the organization.

VII. FINAL THOUGHTS

Economic modeling usually makes two assumptions: methodological individualism, and rational choice. Economists can do without with the latter, but not without the former. Lacking the kinds of game-theoretic models needed to fully pursue the rational-choice agenda with respect to organizational design, perhaps the time has come to reconsider alternatives. Among the most attractive of these are the organizational-process models elaborated by scholars in the 1960s and 1970s: Herbert Simon, John Patrick Crecine, John Padgett, and others (Bendor 2003; Green and Thompson 2001; Jones 2002, 2003). They deserve a second look.

It is also possible that formal modeling of organizational processes and mechanisms is premature, at least insofar as our ends are fundamentally managerialist in nature. I once believed that a good normative model was merely a good empirical model run backwards. I also tended to believe that we could rely on linear models in which $y = f(x)$. That is, given condition set x, outcome y will occur, all other things equal; absent set x, y will not occur; hence, if you want y, do set x.

---

[*] See also Simons (1995), Bruggeman (1995), Otley (1994), and Bunce et al. (1995).

One of the more insightful discussions of this perspective is Larry Lynn's (1996) reworking of Simon's "Proverbs of Administration," which distinguishes between proverbs, or principles, and rules (see also Simon 1946). Principles are universal truths—they always apply, but are largely devoid of specific content. Thus, pay attention to people; do first things first; do what has to be done. In contrast, rules are contingent propositions: if you encounter a problem of the form A, do A' (but don't do A' if the problem is B, because it won't work). In other words, rules are based on robust distinctions. Lynn further argues that formal models help us to deduce distinctions; we do empirical work is to test their validity with real data; and then we teach the resulting rules to our students, making certain that, if they are curious, they can find out how the rules were produced. His conclusion is that what is needed are diagnostic and prescriptive tools, enabling students to tell A from B, and to know what to do, A' or B', or what questions to ask in each situation (presuming that one can first sort out the rules).

I am now inclined to question the praticality or feasibility of Lynn's agenda. Perhaps proverbs of administration should be sought, rather than attempt to deduce rules from first principles. Good clinical analysis may be a better way to find principles—once one has good principles to work with, good theorizing can (and probably will) follow.

The fundamental conceit of clinical research is that the important concepts of management cannot be grasped if treated in merely formal relationship to one another. As Karl Weick explains in *Making Sense of the Organization* (2001:80):

> Typically, environmental change is viewed as something largely outside the influence of organizations. The position being developed suggests a different conclusion. Justifications, assembled into paradigms, can be enacted into a changing environment, thereby imposing some stability on it. Perception guided by a coherent paradigm can prefigure an environment. And confident action based on that prefiguring can actually move the environment in the direction of those paradigmatic preconceptions. That possibility is the important design point that is implicit in serial self-fulfilling prophesies.

My experience suggests that there is a fundamental truth embedded in this conceit. When management principles become the objects of commitment and action, consequential relationships—responsibility and authority, knowledge and organization, incentives and cooperation—look different from the way they do in the doctoral seminar room. To understand relationships of this kind one must perhaps experience them, either directly or indirectly through a narrator's ability to make sense of a particular time and context and convey that understanding to the reader (Barzelay and Campbell 2003).

Consequently, I accept the core of Lynn's argument that any serious attempt to move from principles to practical reasoning requires a conceptual frame. Clinical research is especially in need of sound conceptual frames. However, the developmental arc of my thinking about public management research goes in precisely the opposite direction of most public administration experts. I was trained in positive science and methodological individualism, empirical testing of carefully specified models derived from first principles; that is the kind of research I used to do and occasionally still do. My experience leads me to conclude that, at this time, it is not a practical way to go about answering the kind of questions about public management that should be answered.

Perhaps my newfound appreciation of narrative methods is ingenuous, reflecting my inexperience with them. There is a big difference between reading about, or even teaching, something and doing it. I confess my concluding methodological inferences here are largely conjectural. Ultimately, the proof of the pudding is in the eating, and the only unqualified advice I would presume to offer the prospective public management scholar is: Do good work! Interest, delight, persuade, and amaze us. Remember that every kind of discourse has its rules. Abide by them. Cultivate a richer appreciation for alternative discourses and a shared sense of our subject matter, whose boundaries are probably a greater source of conflict within the field than the rules of discourse.

REFERENCES

Alchian, A. and Demsetz, H., Production, information costs, and economic organization, *American Economic Review*, 62, 777–795, 1972.

Anthony, R. N., *Planning and Control Systems: A Framework for Analysis*, Harvard Business School Press, Boston, MA, 1965.

Anthony, R. N. and Govindarajan, V., *Management Control Systems*, 8th ed., Irwin, Chicago, IL, 1995.

Anti-Deficiency Act. 1905. 1257. 33rd Cong.

Antoci, A., A public contracting evolutionary game with corruption, *Zeitschrift Fuer Nationaloekonomie*, 61, 89–122, 1995.

Arrow, K. The organization of economic activity, In *The Analysis and Evaluation of Public Expenditure: The PPB System*. U.S. Congress. Joint Economic Committee, US GPO, Washington, DC, 1969.

Baker, G. P., Incentive contracts and performance measurement, *Journal of Political Economy*, 100, 598–614, 1992.

Baker, G. P., Gibbons, R., and Murphy, K. J., Subjective performance measures in optimal incentive contracts, *Quarterly Journal of Economics*, 109, 1125–1156, 1994.

Barzel, Y., Measurement costs and the organization of markets, *Journal of Law and Economics*, 25, 27–48, 1982.

Barzelay, M., *The New Public Management*, University of California Press, Berkeley, CA, 2001.

Barzelay, M. and Armajani, B. J., *Breaking through Bureaucracy: A New Vision for Managing in Government*, University of California Press, Berkeley, CA, 1992.

Barzelay, M. and Campbell, C., *Preparing for the Future: Strategic Planning in the U.S. Air Force*, Brookings Institution, Washington, DC, 2003.

Bates, L. J., Property tax collector performance and pay, *National Tax Journal*, 46, 23–31, 1993.

Behn, R., Public management: should it strive to be art, science, or engineering, *Journal of Public Administration Research and Theory*, 6, 91–193, 1996.

Bell, C. R., Between anarchy and leviathan, *Journal of Public Economics*, 39, 207–221, 1989.

Bendor, J., Formal models of bureaucracy, In *Public Administration: The State of the Discipline*, Lynn, N. B. and Wildavsky, A., Eds., Chatham, Chatham, NJ, 1990: 373–441.

Bendor, J., Herbert, A., and Simon, *Annual Review of Political Science*, 6, 433–471, 2003.

Bergstrom, T. and Goodman, R., Private demands for public goods, *American Economic Review*, 63, 280–296, 1972.

Besselman, J., Arora, A., and Larkey, P., Buying in a businesslike fashion, *Public Administration Review*, 60, 421–434, 2000.

Blais, A. and Dion, S., Eds., *The Budget-Maximizing Bureaucrat*, University of Pittsburgh Press, Pittsburgh, PA, 1991.

Blank, R., When can public policy makers rely on private markets?, *Economic Journal*, 110, C34–C39, 2000.

Blau, P. M. and Meyer, M. W., *Bureaucracy in Modern Society*, 2nd ed., Random House, New York, 1971.

Borcherding, T. E., *Budgets and Bureaucrats: The Sources of Government Growth*, Duke University Press, Durham, NC, 1977.

Boskin, M. J., Economic measurement, *American Economic Review*, 90, 247–252, 2000.

Boston, J., Martin, J., Pallot, J., and Walsh, P., *Public Management: The New Zealand Model*, Oxford University Press, London, 1996.

Bowen, H. R., The interpretation of voting in the allocation of resources, *Quarterly Journal of Economics*, 58, 27–48, 1943.

Bower, J., *The Resource Allocation Process*, Harvard Business School Press, Boston, MA, 1970.

Box, R., Public choice and public administration, *Public Administration Review*, 52, 303–304, 1992.

Breton, A., The growth of competitive governments, *Canadian Journal of Economics*, 22, 717–750, 1989.

Breton, A. and Wintrobe, R., The equilibrium size of a budget-maximizing bureau, *Journal of Political Economy*, 83, 195–207, 1975.

Breton, A. and Wintrobe, R., *The Logic of Bureaucratic Conduct*, Cambridge University Press, New York, 1982.

Bruggeman, W., The impact of technological change on management accounting, *Management Accounting Research*, 6, 241–252, 1995.

Bunce, P., Fraser, R., and Woodcock, L., Advanced budgeting, *Management Accounting Research*, 6, 253–265, 1995.

Buchanan, J. M., *Cost and Choice: An Inquiry into Economic Theory*, University of Chicago Press, Chicago, IL, 1969.

Buchanan, J. M. and Tullock, G., *The Calculus of Consent: Logical Foundations of Constitutional Democracy*, University of Michigan Press, Ann Arbor, MI, 1962.

Burkhead, J. and Miner, J., *Public Expenditure*, Aldine-Atherton, Chicago, IL, 1971.

Campbell, T. S., Chan, Y., and Marino, A. M., Incentive contracts for managers who discover and manage investment projects, *Journal of Economic Behavior & Organization*, 12, 353–364, 1989.

Carroll, K. A., Industrial structure and monopoly power in the federal bureaucracy, *Economic Inquiry*, 27, 683–703, 1989.

Carroll, K. A., Bureau competition and inefficiency, *Journal of Economic Behavior & Organization*, 13, 21–40, 1990.

Chandler, A., *Strategy and Structure: Chapters in the History of Industrial Enterprise*, MIT Press, Cambridge, MA, 1962.

Che, Y. K. and Gale, I., Optimal design of research contests, *American Economic Review*, 93, 646–671, 2003.

Cheung, S. N. S., The fable of the bees, *Journal of Law & Economics*, 16, 11–33, 1973.

Choate, G. M. and Thompson, F., Budget makers as agents: an investigation of discretionary behavior under state-contingent rewards, *Public Choice*, 58, 13–20, 1988.

Choate, G. M. and Thompson, F., Biased budgets, *Journal of Economic Behavior & Organization*, 14, 425–434, 1990.

Coase, R., The nature of the firm, *Economica*, 4, 386–405, 1937.

Coase, R., The problem of social cost, *Journal of Law and Economics*, 3, 1–44, 1960.

Coase, R., The lighthouse in economics, *Journal of Law and Economics*, 17, 357–376, 1974.

Coates, D. and Munger, M., Legislative voting and the economic theory of politics, *Southern Economics Journal*, 61, 861–872, 1995.

Conybeare, J. A. C., Bureaucracy, monopoly and competition: a critical analysis of the budget-maximizing model of bureaucracy, *American Journal of Political Science*, 28, 479–502, 1984.

Cooley, T. F. and Smith, B. D., Dynamic coalition formation and equilibrium policy selection, *Journal of Monetary Economics*, 24, 211–233, 1989.

Considine, M. and Lewis, J. M., Governance at ground level, *Public Administration Review*, 59, 467–480, 1999.

Coughlin, P. J., Electoral politics, interest groups, and the size of government, *Economic Inquiry*, 28, 682–705, 1990.

Dalhman, C., The problem of externality, *Journal of Law and Economics*, 23, 140–162, 1979.

De Fraja, G., Productive efficiency in public and private firms, *Journal of Public Economics*, 50, 15–30, 1993.

De Groot, H., Decentralization decisions in bureaucracies as a principal-agent problem, *Journal of Public Economics*, 36, 323–337, 1988.

Deller, S. C., An application of a test for allocative efficiency in the local public sector, *Regional Science & Urban Economics*, 20, 395–406, 1990a.

Deller, S. C., Pareto-efficiency and the provision of public goods within a rural setting, *Growth & Change*, 21, 30–39, 1990b.

Downs, A., Why the government budget is too small in a democracy, *World Politics*, 12, 541–563, 1960.

Drucker, P., *Management: Tasks, Responsibilities, Practices*, Harper & Row, New York, 1973.

Duncombe, W. D., Demand for local public services revisited: the case of fire protection, *Public Finance Quarterly*, 19, 412–436, 1991.

Dunleavy, P. and Hood, C., From old public administration to new public management, *Public Money & Management*, 1, 9–16, 1994.

Eisner, R. *How Real Is the Federal Deficit?*, Springer, New York, 1986.

Enke, S., Ed, *Defense Management*, Prentice Hall, Englewood Cliffs, NJ, 1967.

Evans, P. B. and Wurster, T. S., Strategy and the new economics of information, *Harvard Business Review*, September-October-1997, 71–82, 1997.

Ezzamel, M., Corporate governance and financial accountability, *Accounting Auditing & Accountability Journal*, 6, 109–132, 1993.

Feldman, A. M., *Welfare Economics and Social Choice Theory*, Martinus Nijhoff, Boston, MA, 1980.

Ferejohn, J. A., *Pork Barrel Politics: Rivers and Harbors Legislation, 1947–1968*, Stanford University Press, Stanford, CA, 1974.

Ferris, J. M., Coprovision: citizen time and money donations in public service provision, *Public Administration Review*, 44, 324–333, 1984.

Ferris, J. M. and Graddy, E., Production costs, transaction costs, and local government contractor choice, *Economic Inquiry*, 19, 541–554, 1991.

Fischel, W. A., Did Serrano cause proposition 13?, *National Tax Journal*, 42, 465–473, 1989.

Fischel, W. A., Property taxation and the tiebout model, *Journal of Economic Literature*, 30, 171–177, 1992.

Fischel, W. A., Property taxes and tax revolts, *Journal of Economic Literature*, 33, 239–240, 1995.

Fisher, G. H., *Cost Considerations in Systems Analysis*, Rand, Santa Monica, CA, 1970.

Fitch, L. C., Luther gulick, *Public Administration Review*, 50, 604–608, 1990.

Frant, Howard, Rules and governance in the public sector, *American Journal of Political Science*, 37, 990–1007, 1993.

Frant, Howard, Reconsidering the determinants of public authority use, *Journal of Public Administration Research and Theory*, 7, 57–590, 1997.

Gemmell, N., Public employees' preferences and the size of the public sector, *Journal of Economic Behavior and Organization*, 14, 393–402, 1990.

Gibbons, R., Team theory, garbage cans and real organizations, *Industrial and Corporate Change*, 12, 753–787, 2003.

Goldberg, V., Regulation and administered contracts, *Bell Journal of Economics*, 7, 425–448, 1976.

Goldin, K. D., Equal access vs. selective access, *Public Choice*, 29, 53–71, 1977.

Gonzalez, R. A. and Mehay, S. L., Bureaucracy and the divisibility of local public output, *Public Choice*, 45, 89–102, 1984.

Gore, A. *The Gore Report on Reinventing Government*, Times Books, New York, 1993.

Graddy, E., Toward a general theory of occupational regulation, *Social Science Quarterly*, 72, 676–695, 1991a.

Graddy, E., Interest groups or the public interest, *Journal of Health Politics, Policy, and Law*, 16, 25–49, 1991b.

Green, M. and Thompson, F., Organizational process models of budgeting, *Research in Public Administration*, 7, 55–81, 2001.

Hahn, R. W. and Noll, R. G., Implementing tradable emissions permits, In *Reforming Social Regulation*, Graymer, L. and Thompson, F., Eds., Sage, Beverly Hills, CA, 1982.

Hamel, G. and Prahalad, C. K., *Competing for the Future*, Harvard Business School Press, Boston, MA, 1994.

Hammer, M., Reengineering work, *Harvard Business Review*, 68, 104–112, 1990.

Hammond, T. H., In defense of Luther Gulick's 'Notes on the Theory of Organization,' *Public Administration*, 68, 143–173, 1990.

Hart, O., Shleifer, A., and Vishny, R. W., The proper scope of government: theory and applications to prisons, *Quarterly Journal of Economics*, 112, 1127–1161, 1997.

Haveman, R. H. and Margolis, J., Eds., *Public Expenditures and Policy Analysis*, Rand McNally, Chicago, IL, 1970.

Heckathorn, D. and Maser, S. M., The contractual architecture of public policy: a critical reconstruction of lowi's typology, *Journal of Politics*, 52, 1101–1123, 1990.

Hemingway, A. W., Cost center financial management, *Navy Comptroller*, 3, 2–26, 1993.

Hemmer, T., Risk-free incentive contracts, *Journal of Accounting and Economics*, 16, 447–473, 1993.

Hill, J., Why so much stability?, *Public Choice*, 46, 275–287, 1985.

Hird, J. A., The political economy of pork, *American Political Science Review*, 85, 429–456, 1991.

Hirsch, W. Z., *The Economics of State and Local Government*, McGraw-Hill, New York, 1970.

Hitch, C. J., *Decision Making for Defense*, University of California Press, Berkeley, CA, 1965.

Hitch, C. J. and McKean, R., *The Economics of Defense in the Nuclear Age*, Harvard University Press, Cambridge, MA, 1960.

Holcombe, R. G., The Florida system: a Bowen equilibrium referendum process, *National Tax Journal*, 30, 77–84, 1977.

Hood, C., A public management for all seasons, *Public Administration*, 69, 3–20, 1991.

Hood, C., Emerging issues in public administration, *Public Administration*, 73, 165–183, 1995.

Hood, C. and Peters, G., The middle aging of new public management, *Journal of Public Administration Research and Theory*, 14, 267–282, 2004.

Hoyt, W. H., Local government inefficiency and the tiebout hypothesis, *Southern Economic Journal*, 57, 481–496, 1990.

Itoh, H., Coalitions, incentives, and risk sharing, *Journal of Economic Theory*, 60, 410–427, 1993.

Jones, B. D., Bounded rationality and public policy, *Policy Sciences*, 35, 269–284, 2002.

Jones, B. D., Bounded rationality and political science, *Journal of Public Administration Research and Theory*, 13, 395–412, 2003.

Kalt, J. and Zupan, M., The apparent ideological behavior of legislators, *Journal of Law and Economics*, 33, 103–132, 1990.

Kelman, S., *Making Public Policy: A Hopeful View of American Government*, Basic Books, New York, 1987.

Knott, J. H. and Miller, G., *Reforming Bureaucracy: The Politics of Institutional Choice*, Prentice Hall, Englewood Cliffs, NJ, 1987.

Kotlikoff, L. J., Deficit delusion, *Public Interest*, Summer, 53–65, 1986.

Kotlikoff, L.J. and Burns, S., *The Coming Generational Storm: What You Need to Know about America's Economic Future*, MIT Press, Boston, 2004.

Kovacic, W. E., Law, economics, and the reinvention of public administration, *Administrative Law Review*, 50, 141–156, 1998.

Krause, G. A. and Meier, K. J., Eds., *Politics, Policy, and Organizations: Frontiers in the Study of Bureaucracy*, University of Michigan Press, Ann Arbor, MI, 2003.

Krueger, A. O., The political economy of the rent-seeking society, In *Toward a Theory of the Rent-Seeking Society*, Buchanan, Tollison, and Tullock, Eds., University of Michigan Press, Ann Arbor, MI, First published in American Economic Review, 64, pp. 291-303, June, 1974.

Ladd, H. F., Comments on chapter 5, In *Modern Public Finance*, Quigley, J. and Smolensky, E., Eds., Harvard University Press, Cambridge, MA, 1994.

Laffont, J. and Tirole, J., *A Theory of Incentives in Procurement and Regulation*, MIT Press, Cambridge, MA, 1993.

Langbein, L., Ownership, empowerment, and productivity: some empirical evidence on the causes and consequences of employee discretion, *Journal of Policy Analysis and Management*, 19, 427–449, 2000.

Lynn, L. E., *Public Management as Art, Science, and Profession*, Chatham House, Chatham, NJ, 1996.

Majumdar, S. K., Assessing comparative efficiency of the state-owned mixed and private sectors in Indian industry, *Public Choice*, 96, 1–24, 1998.

March, J. G., Continuity and changes in theories of organizational action, *Administrative Science Quarterly*, 41, 278–287, 1996.

Margolis, J., Ed., *The Analysis of Public Output*, Columbia University Press, New York, 1970.

Maser, S. M., Transaction costs in public administration, In *Bureaucratic and Governmental Reform*, Calista, D., Ed., JAI Press, Greenwich, CT, 1986.

Masten, S. E., The organization of production, *The Journal of Law and Economics*, 27, 403–417, 1984.

Mauro, P., Corruption and growth, *Quarterly Journal of Economics*, 110, 681–712, 1995.

Mayer, Kenneth R., *The Political Economy of Defense Contracting*, Yale University Press, New Haven, CT, 1991.

Mayston, D., Principals, agents and the economics of accountability in the new public sector, *Accounting Auditing & Accountability Journal*, 6, 68–96, 1993.

McCubbins, M. D. and Schwartz, T., Congressional oversight overlooked, *American Journal of Political Science*, 28, 165–179, 1984.

McCubbins, M. D., Noll, R. G., and Weingast, B. R., Structure and process, politics and policy, *Virginia Law Review*, 75, 431–508, 1989.

McFadden, D., Revealed preferences of a government bureaucracy. Parts 1 and 2, *Bell Journal of Economics*, 6, 401–416, 7,52-72, 1976 & 1977.

McKean, R. N., *Public Spending*, McGraw-Hill, New York, 1968.

McKelvey, R., Intransitivities in multidimensional voting models and some implications for agenda control, *Journal of Economic Theory*, 12, 427–482, 1976.

Megginson, W. L. and Netter, J. M., From state to market, *Journal of Economic Literature*, 39, 321–389, 2001.

Mehay, S. L., Economic incentives under contract supply of local government services, *Public Choice*, 46, 79–86, 1986.

Mendeloff, J. M., *The Dilemma of Toxic Substance Regulation: How Overregulation Causes Under-regulation*, MIT Press, Cambridge, MA, 1988.

Merewitz, L. and Sosnick, S. H., *The Budget's New Clothes: A Critique of Planning-Programming-Budgeting and Benefit-Cost Analysis*, Markham, Chicago, IL, 1971.

Meyers, R.T., It's time for a second commission on budget concepts. Paper presented at the third annual Congressional Budget Office Director's conference, US Senate, 14, September, 2004.

Migue, J. L. and Belanger, G., Toward a general theory of managerial discretion, *Public Choice*, 17, 27–42, 1974.

Milgrom, P. and Roberts, J., *Economics, Organization and Management*, Prentice Hall, Englewood Cliffs, NJ, 1992.

Miller, G. J., *Cities by Contract*, MIT Press, Cambridge, MA, 1981.

Miller, G. J., *Manageria Dilemmas: The Political Economy of Hierarchy*, Cambridge University Press, Cambridge, MA, 1992.

Miranda, R., Privatization and the budget-maximizing bureaucrat, *Public Productivity & Management Review*, 17, 17–34, 1994.

Miranda, R., Bureaucracy, organizational redundancy, and the privatization of public services, *Public Administration Review*, 55, 193–200, 1995.

Moe, T. M., The new economics of organization, *American Journal of Political Science*, 28, 739–777, 1984.

Moe, T. M., The politics of bureaucratic structure, In *Can the Government Govern?*, Chubb, J. E. and Peterson, P. E., Eds., Brookings Institution, Washington, DC, 1989.

Moe, T. M., The politics of structural choice, In *Organization Theory*, Williamson, O. E., Ed., Oxford University Press, New York, 1990.

Moe, T. M., The positive theory of public bureaucracy, In *Perspectives on Public Choice*, Mueller, D., Ed., Cambridge University Press, New York, 1997.

Monteverde, K. and Teece, D. J., Appropriable rents and quasi-vertical integration, *The Journal of Law and Economics*, 25, 403–418, 1982.

Morra, J. F., A review of the record, *Regulation*, 10, 25–43, 1986.

Mueller, D. C., *Public Choice III*, Cambridge University Press, New York, 2003.

Munger, M., On the mutuality of interests between bureaus and high demand review committees, *Public Choice*, 43, 211–215, 1984.

Nelson, M. A., Decentralization of the subnational public sector, *Southern Economic Journal*, 57, 443–457, 1990.

Niskanen, W. A., The defense resource allocation process, In *Defense Management*, Enke, S., Ed., Prentice Hall, Englewood Cliffs, NJ, 1967.

Niskanen, W. A., *Bureaucracy and Representative Government*, Aldine-Atherton, Chicago, IL, 1971.

Novick, D., *Efficiency and Economy in Government through New Budgeting and Accounting Procedures*, Rand, Santa Monica, CA, 1954.

Novick, D., *A New Approach to the Military Budget*, Rand, Santa Monica, CA, 1956.

O'Toole, L. J., Treating networks seriously, *Public Administration Review*, 57, 45–52, 1997.

Oates, W. E., Federalism and government finance, In *Modern Public Finance*, Quigley, J. and Smolensky, E., Eds., Harvard University Press, Cambridge, MA, 1994.

Olson, M., *The Logic of Collective Action*, Harvard University Press, Cambridge, MA, 1965.

Olson, M., *The Rise and Decline of Nations*, Yale University Press, New Haven, CT, 1982.

Olson, M. and Zeckhauser, R., An economic theory of alliances, *Review of Economics & Statistics*, 48, 266–279, 1966.

Osborne, D. and Gaebler, T., *Reinventing Government*, Addison-Wesley, Reading, MA, 1992.

Ostrom, E., *Governing the Commons: The Evolution of Institutions for Collective Action*, Cambridge University Press, New York, 1990.

Ostrom, E., Gardner, R., Walker, J., and Agarwal, A., *Rules, Games, and Common-Pool Resources*, University of Michigan Press, Ann Arbor, MI, 1994.

Otley, D. J., Management control in contemporary organizations, *Management Accounting Research*, 53, 289–299, 1994.

Otley, D. J., Broadbent, J., and Berry, A., Research in management control, *British Journal of Management*, 6, 31–44, 1995.

Peltzman, S., Toward a more general theory of regulation, *Journal of Law and Economics*, 14, 109–148, 1976.

Peltzman, S., Constituent interest and congressional voting, *Journal of Law and Economics*, 27, 181–210, 1984.

Peltzman, S., How efficient is the voting market?, *Journal of Law and Economics*, 33, 27–63, 1990.

Peters, T. J. and Waterman, R. H., *In Search of Excellence: Lessons Form America's Best-run Companies*, Harper & Row, New York, 1982.

Posner, R. A., Taxation by regulation, *Bell Journal of Economics and Management Science*, 2, 22–50, 1971.

Posner, R. A., Theories of economic regulation, *Bell Journal of Economics and Management Science*, 5, 335–358, 1974.

Powers, K. A. and Thompson, F., Managing coprovision: using expectancy theory to overcome the free-rider problem, *Journal of Public Administration Research and Theory*, 4, 179–196, 1994.

Quade, E. S., *Analysis for Public Decisions*, American Elsevier, New York, 1975.

Quade, E. S. and Boucher, W. I., *Systems Analysis and Policy Planning*, American Elsevier, New York, 1968.

Quiggin, J., Social democracy and market reform in Australia and New Zealand, *Oxford Review of Economic Policy*, 14, 76–95, 1998.

Rauch, J. E., Bureaucracy, infrastructure, and economic growth, *American Economic Review*, 85, 968–979, 1995.

Reschenthaler, G. B. and Thompson, F., The information revolution and the new public management, *Journal of Public Administration Research and Theory*, 6, 124–143, 1996.

Rhodes, R. A. W., The new public management, *Public Administration*, 69, 1991.

Rivlin, A. M., *Systematic Thinking for Social Action*, Brookings Institution, Washington, DC, 1971.

Rivlin, A. M., *New Approaches to Public Decision-Making*, Information Canada, Ottawa, ON, Canada, 1972.

Rogerson, W. P., Quality vs. quantity in military procurement, *American Economic Review*, 80, 83–92, 1990.

Romer, T. and Rosenthal, H., Economic incentives and political institutions, *Journal of Public Economics*, 49, 1–33, 1992.

Rosenberg, N. and Birdsall, L. E., *How the West Grew Rich: The Economic Transformation of the Industrial World*, Basic Books, New York, 1986.

Rubin, I. S., Who invented budgeting in the United States?, *Public Administration Review*, 53, 438–444, 1993.

Samuelson, P. A., The pure theory of public expenditure, *Review of Economics and Statistics*, 36, 387–389, 1954.

Samuelson, P. A., A diagrammatic exposition of a theory of public expenditure, *Review of Economics and Statistics*, 37, 350–356, 1955.

Santerre, R. E., A test of executive behavior in the local public sector, *Review of Economics & Statistics*, 72, 546–550, 1990.

Schedler, K., *Ansatze Einer Wirkungsorientierten Verwaltungsfuhrung: Von Der Idee Des New Public Managements (Npm) Zum Konkreten Gestaltungsmodell*, Paul Haupt, Bern, Germany, 1995.

Schultze, C. L., *The Politics and Economics of Public Spending*, Brookings Institution, Washington, DC, 1968.

Schwartz, H., Small states in big trouble, *World Politics*, 46, 527–555, 1994.

Shepsle, K. A., *The Giant Jigsaw Puzzle: Democratic Committee Assignments in the Modern House*, University of Chicago Press, Chicago, IL, 1978.

Shepsle, K. A., Institutional arrangements and equilibrium in multidimensional voting models, *American Journal of Political Science*, 23, 27–43, 1979.

Shepsle, K. A. and Weingast, B. R., Political preferences for the pork barrel, *American Journal of Political Science*, 25, 96–111, 1981.

Shepsle, K. A. and Weingast, B. R., Political solutions to market problems, *American Political Science Review*, 78, 417–434, 1984.

Silva, F. and Sonstelie, J., Did Serrano cause a decline in school spending?, *National Tax Journal*, 48, 199–215, 1995.

Simon, H. A., The proverbs of administration, *Public Administration Review*, 6, 53–67, 1946.

Simons, R., *Levels of Control: How Managers Use Innovative Control Systems to Drive Strategic Renewal*, Harvard Business School Press, Boston, MA, 1995.

Stanbury, W. T., A skeptic's guide to the claims of so-called public interest groups, *Canadian Public Administration*, 36, 580–605, 1993.

Stigler, G. J., Comment on Joskow and Noll, In *Studies in Public Regulation*, Froman, G., Ed., MIT Press, Cambridge, MA, 1981.

Survey, *Economist*, 4–6, June, 1995.

Tabellini, G. and Alesina, A., Voting on the budget deficit, *American Economic Review*, 80, 37–49, 1990.

Taylor, L. L., Government budgets and property value, *Economic Review*, 27, 1–7, 1991.

Thompson, F., American legislative decision making and the size principle, *American Political Science Review*, 73, 1100–1108, 1979.

Thompson, F. and Williams, R., A horse race around a Mobius strip, *Policy Sciences*, 11, 119–142, 1979.

Thompson, F. and Jones, L. R., Controllership in the public sector, *Journal of Policy Analysis and Management*, 5, 547–571, 1986.

Thompson, F. and Green, M., Vox populi: tax and expenditure limitation initiatives in oregon, *Public Budgeting & Finance*, 24, 73–88, 2004.

Tiebout, C. M., A pure theory of local expenditures, *Journal of Political Economy*, 64, 416–424, 1956.

Tirole, J., *The Theory of Industrial Organization*, MIT Press, Cambridge, MA, 1988.

Tirole, J., The internal organization of government, *Oxford Economic Papers*, 46, 1–29, 1994.

Trebilcock, M. J., *The Prospects for Reinventing Government?*, C.D. Howe Institute, Toronto, ON, Canada, 1994.

Tullock, G., The welfare costs of tariffs, monopolies and theft, *Western Economic Journal*, 5, (June 1967), pp. 224–232, 1980b.

Vining, A. R. and Boardman, A. E., Ownership versus competition, *Public Choice*, 73, 205–239, 1992.

Vining, A. and Weimer, D. L., Passive use benefits: existence, option, and quasi-option value, In *Handbook of Public Finance*, Thompson, F. and Green, M., Eds., Dekker, New York, 1998.

Wallis, J. J., The political economy of new deal fiscal federalism, *Economic Inquiry*, 29, 1991.

Weick, K., *Making Sense of the Organization*, Blackwell, Oxford, 2001.

Weinstein, J., *The Corporate Ideal in the Liberal State: 1900–1918*, Beacon, Boston, MA, 1968.

Whynes, D. K., Can performance monitoring solve the public services' principal-agent problem?, *Scottish Journal of Political Economy*, 40, 434–446, 1993.

Williamson, O. E., Administrative decision making and pricing, In *The Analysis of Public Output*, Margolis, J., Ed., National Bureau of Research, distributed by Columbia University Press, New York, pp. 115–135, 1970.

Williamson, O. E., *The Economic Institutions of Capitalism*, Free Press, New York, 1985.

Wittman, D., Why democracies produce efficient results, *Journal of Political Economy*, 9, 1395–1424, 1989.

Womack, J. P., Jones, D. T., and Roos, D., *The Machine That Changed the World*, Rawson, New York, 1990.

Yinger, J., Bloom, H. S., Borsch-Supan, A., and Ladd, H. F., *Property Taxes and House Values: The Theory and Estimation of Intrajurisdictional Property Tax Capitalization*, Academic Press, Boston, MA, 1988.

Zax, J. S., Is there a leviathan in your neighborhood?, *American Economic Review*, 79, 560–583, 1989.

Zorn, C. K., The economic perspective on public administration, *Public Administration Review*, 49, 213–214, 1989.

Zuboff, S., *In the Age of the Smart Machine: The Future of Work and Power*, Basic Books, New York, 1988.

29 Some Developments in the Study of Market Choice, Public Choice, and Institutional Choice

Vincent Ostrom

CONTENTS

I. INTRODUCTION

In the 1950s and early 1960s, several publications appeared that used the rudiments of economic reasoning to address basic aspects of governmental, or public sector, organization. Among these were Arrow's (1951) *Social Choice and Individual Values*, Buchanan and Tullock's (1962) *The Calculus of Consent*, Downs' (1957) *An Economic Theory of Democracy*, Olson's (1965) *The Logic of Collective Action*, Riker's (1962) *The Theory of Political Coalitions*, and Tullock's (1965) *The Politics of Bureaucracy*. Two journal articles might be added to this list: Ostrom et al.'s (1999) "The Organization of Government in Metropolitan Areas: A Theoretical Inquiry" and Tiebout's (1956) "A Pure Theory of Local Expenditures."

These works constituted the core of what has preoccupied the community of scholars associated with the public choice tradition. Work growing out of the Arrow and Riker traditions has become the dominant preoccupation of a subset of scholars in this tradition who tend to identify themselves with social choice as a variant of public choice. Thus, some ambiguity exists in identifying scholars with public choice as distinguished from social choice.

Early work in these traditions tended to identify human choice as operating in the context of particular types of choice mechanisms as reflected in the institutions of voting, exchange arrangements, and hierarchies. Alternative institutional arrangements, that is, arrangements for making choices, were assumed to be available in human societies, and the availability of alternatives presumed some potential for choice among institutional arrangements in contrast to choices among goods and services. When arrangements for making choices are themselves conceived as being the subject of choice, we recognize a realm of choice that might be called institutional choice.

The identifying characteristic of the public choice approach has been the application of economic reasoning to nonmarket decision making. The approach has provoked considerable controversy in the social sciences, especially among students of public administration (e.g., Golembiewski 1977). The most extensive critique is made in Green and Shapiro (1994). My own critique is offered in an essay entitled "Epistemic Choice and Public Choice," published in the twenty-fifth anniversary edition of the journal *Public Choice* (V. Ostrom 1993).

Much of the criticism within public administration has been directed at a particular model of man used in various forms of economic reasoning. Some public choice theorists posit an extreme rational-choice model of the individual in their work. But as this essay shall discuss later, that particular model is not the only model of rational behavior used in economic reasoning. The extreme rational-choice model has been useful for some types of inquiry, but much of the inquiry in contemporary economics has treated the basic elements entering into a rational-choice model of man as based on variable, rather than fixed, assumptions. This is especially true of some work in the public choice tradition, where the focus shifts to nonmarket decision structures. Although less attention has been given to similar assumptions in public policy analysis, the same problems exist there (Majone 1986).[*] When we reflect on which assumptions to use, we need to recognize that scholarship in the social sciences and related professional fields of study requires the use of multiple levels and foci of analysis to cope with the problems of complexity that exist in modern societies; choices occur in different contexts and at different levels.

In what follows, this discussion shall turn first to the extreme rational-choice model and some of its contributions. This discourse will then proceed to variable assumptions in the study of market arrangements and similar assumptions in the study of nonmarket institutions. An attempt to clarify the relationship of frameworks to theories and to models will be made. Finally, this essay will draw some concluding observations about the use of basic elements that serve as a foundation for inquiries that move to multiple levels and foci of analysis in complex configurations of relationships.

II. THE EXTREME RATIONAL-CHOICE MODEL AND ITS CONTRIBUTIONS

Most of the work in public choice can be viewed as using one form or another of rational-choice models. All choice models examine individuals in the context of specific situations (Popper 1964, 147–159; 1967). Rational-choice approaches presume varying degrees of (1) concern for others (as the foundation for norms distinguishing "goods" from "bads" (Buchanan 1970; V. Ostrom 1986); (2) knowledge about the world; (3) consistency in valuation; and (4) internal mechanisms for making choices (see Kekes (1976) for a general discussion of rationality). The rational-choice model that has been subjected to the most criticism is one that presumes (1) extreme selfishness, (2) complete information, (3) an unambiguous capacity to attach utility to all outcomes and actions

---

[*] Giandomenico Majone (1986, 61–70) offers a critique of what he calls the "received view" of policy analysis. His criticisms of "decisionism," "unitarianism," and "intellectualism" focus on extreme rationality assumptions that pervade much policy analysis. I shall not pursue those issues here, but refer the reader to Majone's essay. Majone's concluding paragraph, with which I concur, advances the following contention:

> Thus, policy scientists must learn to base their analyses on institutionally rich models of the policy process, just as students of political processes and institutions have learned to use several formal techniques developed by decision and policy analysis. To paraphrase Kant, policy analysis without institutional analysis is empty; institutional analysis without policy analysis is blind (70).

and to rank all alternatives in a consistent manner, and (4) maximization of expected utility (see Riker and Ordeshook (1973) for a clear exposition of this model).

In evaluating rational-choice models, it is important first to consider them in the context for which they were originally developed—situations involving considerable information and high levels of certainty relative to the choices that individuals were making. In this context, the use of an extreme rational-choice model has led to counterintuitive results about counterintentional outcomes. These results are extremely important foundations for the study of all social institutions. Second, it is important to recognize that many variants of rational-choice theories and models have been developed. The extreme rational-choice model is used in public choice, but it is not the only version of rationality adopted in that tradition of work. Less stringent assumptions about individual choice behavior are frequently used. A closer examination is merited by the first issue—the contribution of an extreme rational-choice approach in its original context.

As Sen (1977) has pointed out, this initial model was worked out to address a theoretical puzzle that arose in the early history of modern economic thought. The puzzle was posed in Mandeville's (1962) *The Fable of the Bees* and is concerned with whether it is possible for individuals strongly motivated by egoistic self-interest ("private vices") to serve the public good, or common welfare ("publick benefits"), or a larger community. For some scholars, the self-serving pursuit of individual self-interest would be conceived as creating pure chaos. Instead, this course of inquiry led to a clarification of the emergent properties of competitive market economies to indicate how orderly and predictable relationships would occur.

Given the assumptions of a perfectly competitive market, a stable price indicates an equilibrium between supply and demand. If these balancing tendencies are allowed to work themselves out in a perfectly competitive market situation, there will be a general equilibrium established in relation to all goods where price is equal to marginal cost at any given level of demand and income distribution.

These implications are counterintuitive and counterintentional. The results are counterintuitive in that orderly and predictable relationships emerge rather than the expected chaos. The results are counterintentional in that individuals who are strongly motivated to maximize profits are led—by the force of market competition—to reduce potential profit and to allow economic advantage to accrue to others as consumer surplus. In a competitive market, the relative advantage shifts from egoistic profit maximizers to consumers seeking least-cost opportunities.

The extreme assumptions associated with neoclassical economic theory have yielded important intellectual contributions in understanding competitive market arrangements. Prices generated in competitive markets evoke levels of information that enhance rational calculations in economic relationships. The extreme assumptions made in the neoclassical approach to economic reasoning have proved productive in understanding an emergent order that is characteristic of competitive markets.

The application of extreme rational-choice models to the problem of collective choice has been productive in quite a different way. In collective choice, individuals face the circumstance where each member of a collectivity participates in making choices that become binding on all members of that collectivity. Arrow (1951) shows that when individual preference orderings are highly divergent, there is no feasible decision rule for arriving at a collective outcome with all the advantageous properties of a market equilibrium that enhance social welfare. Majority vote, or other voting arrangements, does not produce the optimal outcomes in collective-choice situations that market arrangements produce in exchange situations. Furthermore, majorities will cycle depending on the order in which voting occurs. Equilibria cannot be expected; minimum-winning coalitions will be unstable (Riker 1962, 1982).

As Shubik (1982, 122–124; 1984) has pointed out, the Arrow problem would not exist as a theoretical problem if Arrow had assumed cardinal utility instead of ordinal utility. The problem then would have been resolved by summing utilities and opting for the "greatest happiness," as Jeremy Bentham would have articulated that standard. Not all values or all goods are amenable to measures that can be manipulated like numbers in arithmetic. Problems of dealing with incommensurables among collective goods are probably better represented by Arrow's formulation, and Arrow's impossibility theorem reflects basic tensions that exist in collective-choice situations. An immense literature has been stimulated, and we have increasingly come to recognize that individual rationality can yield perverse patterns of social relationships that might be characterized as social irrationalities. Barry and Hardin's (1982) *Rational Man and Irrational Society?* and Schelling's (1978) *Micromotives and Macrobehavior,* as the titles of these books indicate, are concerned with disparities between individual motives or intentions and social outcomes (see also Elster 1977).

These results have been productive in indicating the fundamental dilemmas we face in formulating traditions of inquiry in the social sciences. The emergent patterns of relationships in human societies are likely to be counterintuitive or counterintentional. If such problems did not exist, common sense would suffice in addressing problems of social relationships, and there would be no inherent difficulties requiring recourse to critical methods of scientific inquiry.

III. VARYING ASSUMPTIONS IN THE STUDY OF MARKET RELATIONS

Before turning to nonmarket situations, it would be useful to review some developments in the study of markets that are particularly relevant for the study of nonmarket situations. The strong assumptions made about economic man and the emphasis on equilibrium analysis, characteristic of the Anglo-American, neoclassical tradition of inquiry, have not been universally adhered to by all economists. The Austrian school shares common ties with the Scottish school of moral philosophy, but has preferred to work with assumptions of limited information and focus on equilibrating mechanisms rather than equilibrium states (Kirzner 1973, 1979). Some American scholars, in turn, have emphasized transaction cost calculations to explain the rise of firms in markets. The rise of firms is accompanied by asymmetries in information and in authority relationships. When these elements assume variable proportions, economic relationships are subject to variable institutional structures.

The emphasis in Austrian economics is on market structures as providing incentives for innovation and generating information that is relevant to dynamically changing circumstances. F. A. von Hayek is the best-known contemporary representative of this tradition. Von Hayek (1973, chap. 1) assumes that information is necessarily incomplete because the generation of new knowledge contributes to the development of new technologies and to new economic opportunities. He further assumes that distinctions need to be made between knowledge that applies to generalized relationships—as articulated in scientific knowledge—and time and place information, which takes on variably specific values in particular situations (von Hayek 1945).

Much of the focus in Austrian economics then, is on entrepreneurship, as Kirzner emphasizes. Entrepreneurs have an incentive to search out new possibilities. Such activities disturb any presumed equilibrium, placing burdens on others to acquire similar capabilities in a market economy. Entrepreneurship and innovation create a competitive dynamic that has to do with advances in knowledge, the extension of technological capabilities, and an opening of new economic opportunities. This is a form of competition that can only occur in a world of incomplete information rather than in a world of complete information. The competitive dynamics associated with the Austrian school are quite different than, but not contradictory to, the traditional equilibrium analyses of Anglo-American economists.

Work in the Austrian school is also consistent with Simon's (1972, 1978, 1981) work on "bounded rationality." Nelson and Winter's (1982) *An Evolutionary Theory of Economic Change* is built on assumptions that have to do with limited information and potentials for learning (see also Nelson 1977). Dosi (1984), in a study of *Technical Change and Industrial Transformation,* is critically concerned with the place of advancing knowledge and technological innovation as a competitive process that affects market structures in different ways than would be expected to occur in competitive markets with complete information. Russell and Thaler (1985), in an article on "The Relevance of Quasi-Rationality in Competitive Markets," demonstrate how varying the rationality assumption yields a different equilibrium solution with different market characteristics than would be expected from complete information and perfect competition.

Other related analyses, which treat information asymmetry as being characteristic of some markets, indicate how such characteristics can be expected to affect market structures. Akerlof (1970) shows how information asymmetries in used-car markets create problems when buyers find it difficult to distinguish between peaches and lemons. These information asymmetries create incentives for some to differentiate themselves as vendors of peaches from vendors of lemons. Factors of reputation and trust enter into such markets in place of the impersonality, or nontuism, assumed to be characteristic of perfectly competitive markets. Popkin (1981), whose work on *The Rational Peasant* (1979) is well known, examines problems of information asymmetry that are characteristic of agricultural productivity and how information asymmetries yield different institutional arrangements, such as those involved in sharecropping, piecework, fixed-fee wages, or fixed-fee rental arrangements.

These traditions of analysis that rely on assumptions of incomplete information of one type or another have a close parallel to a somewhat different tradition of analysis that has grown out of a problem posed by Coase (1937) in an essay on "The Nature of the Firm." Coase was concerned with why firms, organized more on hierarchical principles, occur in market economies that rely on buying and selling among individuals having equal standing in relation to one another. Why do individuals move to nonmarket patterns of organization within markets?

To account for this apparent anomaly, Coase conjectured that organizing transactions across markets entails costs. These costs might reflect the costs of getting information about going prices, costs of negotiation, and so forth. There might then be costs to transactions across markets that could yield savings by having recourse to other patterns of organization. The basic structure of transactions within a firm would be altered to include reference to a long-term employment contract where an employer in the new relationship could assign and reassign employees to a variety of different tasks. A superior–subordinate relationship was established within the operation of a firm subject to the longer-term employment contract.

Coase conjectures that savings in transaction costs across markets would reach some point of equilibrium in relation to increases in management costs. The net advantage of moving to a firm would be reached where the increase in management costs equals the savings in transaction costs. We have an explanation, then, for why hierarchies would arise within firms that operate in market structures. Williamson (1975) has built, in part, on the Coase analysis to indicate how differential reliance on either quasi-market or shadow-market structures can be built into the management of subdivisions within a firm. Components in a larger production process can be organized in relation to subdivisions that function as profit centers as though they were firms in markets. Management can then rely on the competitive dynamics of market arrangements to enhance efficiency among subdivisions in a larger organization.

Alchian and Demsetz (1972) address the problem that Coase raised in the context of limited information and the way that limits on information relate to organizational structures. Alchian and Demsetz offer teamwork as an explanation for the development of firms in a market. Individuals working together as teams can accomplish tasks that cannot be accomplished by acting alone. Teamwork implies, then, that joint effort has potentials for yielding increased productivity. In these circumstances, a puzzle arises. When each worker receives a fixed share of the joint effort as wages, a temptation arises for each worker to enjoy more leisure on the job, and the yield from teamwork declines.

This circumstance suggests that limits on information exist even in regard to the contribution of each participant to the joint product. It then becomes necessary to make provisions for someone to monitor performance and reduce shirking in order to maintain the productive potential derived from teamwork. This can be done by having recourse to a single contracting party that assumes proprietary responsibility for organizing the enterprise, monitoring performance, and receiving the residual earnings that derive from joint productivity. The margin of residual earnings will be constrained because competitive dynamics in a product market will drive down profits and yield increased consumer surplus.

The form of enterprise that Alchian and Demsetz characterize with reference to a single contracting party is a sole proprietorship. They demonstrate, however, that the structure of incentives in different forms of organization will be affected by the way that the residual earnings derived from increased productivity are distributed, and responsibility is allocated for monitoring performance in order to reduce shirking and enhance productivity.

The analysis of shirking in Alchian and Demsetz points to temptations that arise for some to exploit others. Williamson (1975) characterizes such temptations as opportunism and as hazards. This is analogous to the temptations to pursue noncooperative, rather than cooperative, strategies in the so-called prisoner's dilemma, and in the commons dilemma problem that yields the tragedy of the commons (E. Ostrom 1990). The Alchian and Demsetz solution for relying on a single contracting party is only one way to address this type of problem. These problems occur in many aspects of human relationships, and they are not likely to yield to simple solutions. Successful resolutions of shirking problems may yield other temptations and hazards that have perverse implications. The single contracting party that resolves Alchian and Demsetz's shirking problem may now pursue temptations to exploit others.

At this point it is important to point out that this tradition of inquiry, which is usually characterized as transaction cost economics (Williamson 1979), takes elements that would have been subsumed under fixed assumption in the neoclassical Anglo-American approach to economic analysis and treats those elements as variables. Coase assumes that there are costs to organizing transactions across markets. Among those costs are information costs. Alchian and Demsetz assume limits on information that now require an investment of time and effort in monitoring performance. These problems are subject to potential resolution by moving toward different patterns of organization. This implies differential assignments of authority. A differential assignment of authority in turn implies distinctions among positions that involve management and monitoring responsibilities with differential compensation.

Also implicit in these analyses is a multiple-level problem. A long-term labor contract that is constitutive of the firm lays the basis for differential assignments of authority that pertain to the exercise of shorter-term managerial, monitoring, and entrepreneurial functions. Competitive dynamics can be reintroduced among units within a firm, as Williamson (1975) suggests, to yield more complex structures that simplify management tasks and monitoring problems. The structures of contractual arrangements in economic relationships become much more complex than the quid pro quo arrangements assumed in the neoclassical model of perfect competition (Cheung 1969; De Alessi 1980).

Krüsselberg (1986), in an essay on "Markets and Hierarchies," raises questions about the twofold distinction of markets and hierarchies as affording an appropriate characterization of the organizing principles that differentiate firms from transactions across markets. There is a strong tendency to move from associations between markets and hierarchies to associations between markets and states. These dichotomies introduce simplifications that are likely to obfuscate the analysis of market and nonmarket decision-making arrangements in societies.

Krüsselberg argues that making employment contracts in a factor market pertaining to labor services is quite different from dealing in product markets with standardized and substitutable commodities. Labor markets involve quite different economic relationships than product markets. The organization of firms, then, becomes a part of the organizational technologies appropriate to the proportioning of labor as a factor entering into production processes.

Krüsselberg's analysis provides us with another critique of the neoclassical model of perfect competition. The dynamics of the market are assumed to have a general equilibrating tendency with regard to everything that is subject to exchange in a market economy. But human labor is not simply another commodity in a market. Contracting for labor services will occur under different conditions than those that apply to standardized commodities in product markets (cf., Taylor 1966). Krüsselberg cites Cheung (1983) approvingly when Cheung indicates that the employment contract may be as simple as a piece-rate contract or as complex as the establishment of a Communist regime as a dictatorship of the proletariat.

Entrepreneurs who want to make effective use of their human capital are confronted with all of the puzzles that are inherent in dealing with human relationships. This turns critically on the potential for each person to enter into voluntary exchange relationships that leave each party better off for having entered into employment relationships as a mutually productive endeavor. Standards of productivity, fairness, and liberty cannot be ignored. Employers and employees have rights and duties in relation to one another, and their productive potential depends on shared understanding and volition. The self-serving entrepreneur is required to take account of the interests of others in light of a larger range of opportunities that are available when each is free to pursue alternative employment opportunities.

The thrust of Krüsselberg's analysis is to indicate that employment markets have quite different characteristics than standardized product markets. Contingencies affecting entrepreneurship are required to take account of the variable factor markets and product markets. Differential conditions applicable to factor and product markets imply that highly differential structures will occur. These principles are dramatically illustrated by Picht (1985) with reference to the relationship of monetary institutions to market economies. Money as media for exchange has at least two distinguishable characteristics. One is to offer a unit of account that is standardized for all transactions in a given monetary arrangement. This attribute has the characteristic of a purely public good. Money as a medium of exchange also performs a liquidity function, where given units of money can be exchanged for particular goods. This aspect of money meets the criterion of being a purely private good. Monetary institutions in a society are required to take account of both the unit-of-account and liquidity services afforded by a medium of exchange. The two aspects of monetary systems have different institutional implications that are closely linked to one another and cut across private and public sectors. When monetary policies yield unstable unit-of-account services, market arrangements become highly unstable.

Krüsselberg is associated with the German school of economists who identify themselves with *Ordnungstheorie* (theory of order). Their focus is on the comparative study of economic systems that takes account of different structural arrangements within any given economy and extends its analyses to economies with different ordering principles, such as the Soviet type of centrally planned and directed economy, as contrasted with other economies that rely predominantly on market organization (see Montias (1976) and Pryor (1973) for close English-language approximations). Anglo-American parallels occur in studies of industrial organization where there is a strong effort to use theory in the context of empirical inquiries where variations in institutional structures become independent variables in studies that emphasize structure, conduct, and performance (Bain 1959; Bain et al., 1966; Caves 1980). Theoretical conjectures growing out of the industrial organization tradition have addressed problems of market organization where perfect competition does not exist. The work of Baumol et al. (1982) on contestable markets indicates how competitive pressures can be affected by the way that economic relations are structured in industries that tend toward natural monopolies. This work has been used in policy initiatives, for example, to deregulate the airline industry.

When different traditions in economic inquiry are viewed as complementary to one another, much of the rigidity and apparent arbitrariness of the basic assumptions in the microeconomic theory of perfect competition with complete information begins to take on the characteristics of analytical elements that can be specified to operate as variables. When limited information is treated as a variable rather than being assumed away under conditions of complete information, a variety of problems come to the foreground that require variable attention to authority structures and to the nature of both factors and products that enter into economic relationships.

Limited information may take on highly variable characteristics that become the object of attention in entrepreneurship to yield innovation and a competitive dynamic that focuses on innovation. Differential access to knowledge may yield characteristic asymmetries like those in the used-car market; in health, educational, and professional services; or in employment relationships. Market structures can occur in different patterns of organization and equilibria when the condition of information is treated as a variable. Information can also be viewed as a product of differently structured institutional arrangements. Market prices generate information, and the meaning of that information depends on its use in a computational logic derived from economic theory.

Extreme assumptions such as those of complete information, although useful in giving us a basic understanding of the nature of order when great multitudes of actors independently pursue economic opportunities, have tended to cut economists off from productive collaboration with other scholars who have been concerned with other attributes of order in human societies. The shift away from extreme assumptions to analytical elements that can be treated as variables opens more extended opportunities for collaboration across the different social sciences and professional fields of study.

IV. VARYING ASSUMPTIONS IN THE STUDY OF NONMARKET ARRANGEMENTS

When the public choice tradition is characterized as the application of economic reasoning to nonmarket decision making, as it was earlier conceived, the key to specifying a referent turns on what is meant by economic reasoning and how market arrangements might be distinguished from nonmarket arrangements. If by economic reasoning we mean the use of the intellectual apparatus associated with perfect competition, there would not be much relevance for applying that mode of reasoning to nonmarket decision making. The dominance of that mode of analysis in Anglo-American microeconomic theory has not exhausted the possibilities for economic analysis in the rest of the world or for important strands of economic analysis in the Anglo-American tradition.

As we come to appreciate Krüsselberg's observations about the human factor that enters into employment relationships, we begin to understand that the nexus of economic relationships is one where market and nonmarket arrangements converge. Dichotomies between private and public, markets and hierarchies, or market and nonmarket institutional arrangements become conceptual distinctions that may be useful for limited analytical purposes in distinguishing some attributes of social reality. Any presumption that social reality exists in two separable domains isolated from one another would be an obvious conceptual error. Living in this world entails choices about how to relate to others in situations that are complexly nested in social space and time continuities, as one variably deals with others where conceptual distinctions such as private–public, markets–hierarchies, and market–nonmarket arrangements have only limited usefulness (Shubik 1986).

The next section shall indicate how public choice studies of bureaucracy have been built on assumptions that diverge from the assumptions used in the microeconomic theory of perfect competition in much the same way that has occurred in the work associated with Austrian economics, the transaction cost approach, and the German approach to the comparative study of economic systems. The exposition shall then turn to the place of constitutional choice in an analytical tradition that permits one to anticipate how Arrow's paradox may be potentially addressed in multiple levels of analysis where it is recognized that choices exist about institutional arrangements apart from choices about goods and services.[*]

A. BUREAUCRACIES

What has been called the span-of-control principle in the public administration literature reflects an important consideration in bureaucratic patterns of organization. If we were to postulate populations with complete information but limited capabilities, we might formulate bureaucracy as an ideal-type organization where it would be possible for obedient and knowing individuals with complete information to maintain a uniform rule of law across some domain that was subject to a bureaucratically ordered system of rulership. Such an act of the imagination would enable us to account for Max Weber's characterization of bureaucracy as being an ideal form of organization capable of maintaining a rational legal order in a society.

The span-of-control problem suggests limited information as well as limited capabilities. In the traditional theory of public administration, it was assumed that the span-of-control problem could be resolved if the number of subordinates was confined to a small number at each level of organization. Simon (1946, [1947] 1957, 1959), however, offered a critique that indicated that the loss of information and control is a function of the number of levels in a hierarchy of organization as well as the superior–subordinate ratio at any one level of organization.

Tullock (1965) shifts the focus to a positive theoretical analysis where each individual is assumed to be motivated by aspirations for career advancement. Tullock posits limited information and capabilities on the part of each individual functioning in a hierarchically ordered structure of superior–subordinate relationships where promotions are predominantly influenced by the recommendation and decision of superiors. Tullock anticipates that movement of information up a hierarchy will be systematically biased to repress adverse information and facilitate the movement of favorable information. Analogous processes can be expected in carrying out commands that either indulge or deprive others. Systematic distortions occur in flows of information and commands such that promise and performance are subject to increasing divergence as bureaucracies become larger and organizational links more extended (see also Williamson 1967). Tullock's theory of bureaucracy turns critically on limited information and what can be expected to happen to information flows within a hierarchically structured organization. The structure performs a transformational function that is likely to bias and distort information. In this case, organization yields a perverse transformation that is counterintuitive and counterintentional to those who may have assumed that bureaucracies were an ideal-type organization capable of maintaining a rational legal order in society. Peachy assumptions can yield bitter fruit, and we face the task of fashioning alternative methods of organization that are more trustworthy. The implications of a Williamson-type approach to the generation, transmission, and use of information as an organizational function have been rudimentarily pursued in works like Nelson and Winter's (1982) *An Evolutionary Theory of Economic Change*, but many frontiers remain to be explored. Tullock's work is not the last word, but merely a beginning.

In a review essay on "Multiorganizational Arrangements and Coordination: An Application of Institutional Analysis," Elinor Ostrom (1986) shows how different models of representative government, bureaucratic organization, and the budget bargain yield different logical implications when analytical elements are specified as assumptions that take on variable values in different modeling efforts. The Downs (1957) model of representative government is contrasted to the Niskanen (1971, 1975) model of representative government. These are juxtaposed in relation to a budget bargain (see also Borcherding 1977) where the outcome of that bargain varies in relation to assumptions

---

[*] I shall not attempt to examine in this chapter the vast literature on voting and representative institutions by public choice theorists. Several major reviews are available in the literature (Mueller 1979). For public administration scholars, the theory of bureaucracy and the theory of constitutional choice are most relevant.

made about information asymmetries, reversion rules that apply in the absence of agreement, and degrees of competitive exposure. Issues that are sometimes addressed as indicating deficiencies in an effort to model institutional arrangements associated with representative government, bureaucracies, and budget bargains can be treated as elements in an analysis that are allowed to take on variable values in different models. Niskanen's (1971) effort can then be juxtaposed with Downs' (1957) analyses and the critiques of Romer and Rosenthal (1978) to yield models of multiorganizational arrangements that offer alternative implications (see also Orzechowski 1977). The different theoretical arguments and their divergent implications can then be treated as hypothetical conjectures that are subject to empirical inquiry in the large number of natural experiments that exist in the diversely organized world that has been constructed in human societies (E. Ostrom 1999; Parks and Ostrom 1999; Pommerehne and Frey 1977; Savas 1974, 1977, 1979, 1982). The work of Tullock, Downs, Niskanen, and others can be built on by treating basic elements in their analysis as variables rather than assuming that initial models are to be treated with fixed assumptions, having some ultimate truth value.

Similarly, Olson's (1965) *The Logic of Collective Action* can be built on by conceptualizing alternatives to an exclusive reliance on hierarchical principles of bureaucratic organization in the public sector, when the provision of collective goods and services is the focus of inquiry. Olson explicitly ties the problem of collective organization to a theory of public or collective goods as distinguished from private goods. He recognizes the failure of exclusion as occurring in the collective good situation. He also recognizes, as a result of Head's (1962) work, that jointness of use or consumption is an attribute of public goods. Size becomes an important variable, but the problem of limited information associated with noticeability is not given strong enough emphasis in Olson's analysis. The basic thesis is that efforts to supply collective goods will fail unless accompanied by selective incentives to enforce compliance, either through coercion or through some associated benefit that is subject to exclusion and to which a price can be attached.

The same problem that gave rise to shirking in the organization of productivity gains from teamwork in the Alchian and Demsetz (1972) analysis gives rise to the holdout or free-rider problem in the case of collective goods. The basic difference is that the jointness problem occurs on the consumption side of economic relationships rather than on the production side. Just as there are various ways of organizing the monitoring function to reduce shirking in teamwork, there are various ways of organizing collectively to avoid the holdout or free-rider problem in the provision of public goods and services. The essential problem is one of collective organization of consumption functions rather than production functions (Ostrom and Ostrom 1999).

If it is assumed that the material conditions of the world that are relevant to human welfare refer to many different goods and services that are subject to joint use or consumption and that the jointness of use or consumption impinges on many different domains, we have problems that arise in organizing collective consumption for many diversely sized communities of people (Bish 1971; V. Ostrom 1973, 1983). These might be resolved by the organization of diverse collectivities of varying jurisdictions that are capable of internalizing the domain that is subject to joint use or consumption by different communities of people. Such patterns of organization would be consonant with a highly federalized political system that has reference to a multitude of different units of government of varying domains (Gregg 1974; V. Ostrom 1973, 1983; Tullock 1969).

Because problems associated with the failure of exclusion and jointness of use apply to consumption functions, these can be resolved by organizing a unit of government capable of levying taxes and taking collective decisions through devices such as public discussion, voting, representation, the taking of collective decisions by plurality vote, and regulation of patterns of use. Once the collective-consumption functions are organized through structures capable of taking binding collective decisions to avoid the holdout or free-rider problem, diverse options are available for organizing production functions. Apart from relying on its own bureau, a unit of government organized as a collective-consumption unit might contract either with private vendors or with other public vendors to supply a public good or service. So long as the collectivity can monitor the performance of the supplier, there is no reason to rely on an exclusive bureau to supply a collective good or service (E. Ostrom 1986; Ostrom and Ostrom 1999).

This possibility permits contracting for services and the development of quasi-market conditions in the public sector (V. Ostrom et al., 1999; Warren 1964). Quasi-markets are distinguishable from private markets because collectivities are the purchasing units, not individuals. Privatization is an inappropriate term to apply to public economies relying on contractual relationships between collective-consumption units and production units. Privatization may occur on the production side of economic relationships, but collective organizations capable of taxing and regulating patterns of use are also necessary for collective-consumption goods. So long as multiple vendors are available, competitive options provide alternatives to an exclusive reliance on bureaucratic principles of organization in the public sector. Contestable quasi-market arrangements are feasible in the public sector.

To understand how such mixed structures work in public economies requires a shift of attention away from the internal structure of units of government to patterns of relationships across quasi-markets. This is the reverse of the Coase problem of explaining why firms rise in markets. The problem instead is determining why quasi-markets and other patterns of interorganizational and intergovernmental arrangements arise in the public sector. The explanation turns on collective organizations being largely concerned with problems of organizing consumption functions in a public economy. Modern public sectors can be characterized, as Kaufmann (1986b, 211) did, as one of "multi-bureaucracies" rather than "megabureaucracies," where the larger order of complexity is organized by reference to networks of interorganizational arrangements.

The neoclassical model of perfectly competitive markets does not provide appropriate assumptions for reasoning about public economies that have reference to types of goods and services that are subject to jointness of use or consumption, failure of exclusion, and other attributes of goods that contribute to market weaknesses and market failures. Elements such as information, preference ordering and aggregation, authority relationships, and distinguishable attributes of goods and services can accommodate varying assumptions that can be used to derive inferences that serve as theoretical conjectures about alternatively conceptualized possibilities. Even though the conclusions indicate no more than equilibrating tendencies, such conjectures can be used as the source of competing hypotheses for empirical inquiries in relation to quasi-experimental and experimental research designs occurring in the variable exigencies of human experience (E. Ostrom et al., 1994).

We can now take the Krüsselberg (1986) critique of the transaction-cost approach and recognize that collective-consumption facilities, such as public streets and highways, supply infrastructures or factors essential to entrepreneurship in market economies. Any entrepreneur is required to take these factors into account in the organization of an enterprise. The tasks that private entrepreneurs face may require them to engage in public entrepreneurship wherever some factor or infrastructure necessary to the viability of an enterprise is subject to joint use by some larger community of people. There is a sense in which all economies become mixed economies involving diverse forms of private and public institutional arrangements (V. Ostrom et al., [1988] 1993).

The close tie between private and public is indicated by the circumstance that markets as institutions permit multitudes of buyers and sellers to engage in transactions with one another. Exclusion applies to these potential linkages. For transactions to occur, agreement must exist and an exchange must take place. If one shifts attention away from the buying and selling among participants in the market to the milieu in which this buying and selling occurs, one would then find that markets are themselves subject to joint use by buyers and sellers. Exclusion from the market itself does not prevail in free markets. The conditions of market organization have the characteristics of collective goods, in contrast to the buying and selling that occur within markets (V. Ostrom 1983). Berman (1983, 557), in the concluding chapter of *Law and Revolution*, makes the following observation that suggests that law is itself an essential factor for any entrepreneur or economic agent:

> Law is as much a part of the mode of production of a society as farmland or machinery; the farmland or machinery is nothing unless it operates, and law is an integral part of its operation. Crops are not sown and harvested without duties and rights of work and of exchange. Machinery is not produced, moved from the producer to the user, and used, and the costs and benefits of its use are not valued, without some kind of legal ordering of these activities. Such legal ordering is itself a form of capital.

Models of competitive market economies are clearly unsatisfactory for addressing problems of economic development anywhere in the world. In the same way, the concept of the state and hierarchical principles of organization are clearly unsatisfactory for addressing problems of collective organization in human societies. Patterns of diversity and interdependence are such that models grounded in presuppositions applicable to pure competition or pure hierarchies are of limited utility.

B.   Constitutional Choice

Among the early contributions to the public choice tradition is Buchanan and Tullock's (1962) *The Calculus of Consent*. As the subtitle "Logical Foundations of Constitutional Democracy" indicates, the concern is with constitutional choice. Arrow's (1951) work on social choice was the occasion for deriving an impossibility theorem. Given assumptions in the extreme rational-choice tradition, it is *impossible* to derive a collective choice that is consistent with the diverse preferences of individuals comprising a collectivity. The Buchanan and Tullock approach recognizes that the radical asymmetries in the structure of rule–ruler–ruled relationships can be subject to constraint. Who are to invent, design, reform, or reinvent government (Osborne [1992] 1993): people in a democracy or the government? Who are principals and who are agents? Arrow's impossibility theorem might be used to suggest that dictatorship is one way to achieve stability. When dictatorship is conceived as an option, human beings might still explore other possibilities for reducing the costs of that form of rulership.

By shifting the level of analysis, Buchanan and Tullock suggest the possibility that individuals participating in the structure of choice situations where winning and losing will occur, may constitute such situations by reference to rules that meet conditions of fairness that are agreeable to all players. This is the basis for constituting a fair game, as Hobbes ([1651] 1960, 227) recognized when he observed: "It is in the laws of a commonwealth, as in the laws of gaming: whatsoever the gamesters all agree on, is injustice to none of them."

Buchanan and Tullock's shift in the analytical context is not a solution to the Arrow paradox, but a way of reducing the costs that are entailed when collective decisions cannot meet the condition of conforming to the diverse preferences of individuals comprising collectivities. Buchanan and Tullock make important contributions in advancing a cost calculus that is applicable to the choice of aggregation rules that apply to the taking of collective decisions. They assume that collective organization depends on an implicit agreement about the benefits or values to be derived from taking collective action. Without this condition, which diverges from Arrow's assumptions, there is no ground for collective organization. When joint benefits are recognized, there is a logic that can be used to contemplate the choice of a least-cost aggregation rule (an aggregation rule indicates the agreement or concurrence necessary to take collective decisions) given potential decision costs (expenditures on time and effort) and potential external costs (deprivations suffered from adverse decisions).

The constitutional level of choice is analogous to the long-term contracts that are constitutive of the internal arrangement within Coase's firm for assigning differential authority to managers and workers (V. Ostrom 1999b). However, the Buchanan and Tullock effort is explicitly related to the more general problem of governance in human societies. Analogous problems of governance arise in all human efforts at teamwork. Oliver Williamson (pers. comm.) has conceptualized the task of working out contractual arrangements that specify institutional arrangements as economizing on bounded rationality while simultaneously safeguarding transactions from hazards and opportunism.

An explicit recognition that a logic of constitutional choice applies to different levels of analysis in the governance of human societies is one of the important implications of the Buchanan and Tullock formulation. A constitution can be viewed as setting the terms and conditions of government: making, monitoring, and carrying out collective decisions. Issues about what those terms and conditions should be are different from issues about what governments should do at the collective-choice level of analysis. In turn, what a government should do is a different question than what occurs at an operational level of analysis as a consequence of collective decisions having been made. Problems of institutional analysis reflected in constitutional choice are then linked to problems of policy analysis, which in turn are linked to an operational level of analysis. Studies of implementation and service delivery need to be viewed in the context of both institutional analysis and policy analysis. Exploring questions about the nature and constitution of order in human societies that would be relevant to a political science and the practice of public administration would require reference to multiple levels and foci of analysis (V. Ostrom [1971] 1987, especially chaps. 1 and 9). Human beings face many different levels of choice—not just choices from among some array of goods and services.

The problems of governance in human societies can be conceptualized in different ways. However, concepts are never enough to suffice in the governance of human relationships. Instead, differential assignment of authority needs to be made in ways that are appropriate to different conceptions that apply to the design of systems of governance. Much of the speculation in political theory from the seventeenth century onward and in the design of systems of governance in the contexts of the British, American, French, and Russian revolutions has been critically concerned with problems of constitutional choice. The Buchanan and Tullock efforts to clarify the problem of constitutional choice open us to a much longer tradition of political inquiry.

Theories of sovereignty relying on some single center of ultimate authority yield structures of governance where a sovereign is the source of law, above the law, and not accountable to the law. A federal system of governance where constitutions specify the terms and conditions of government and where constitutions serve as enforceable rules of law can yield a system of authority relationships where all authority is subject to limits and no one exercises unlimited authority. The one gives rise to circumstances where a sovereign rules over society; the other to circumstances where all citizens participate in processes of constitutional decision making in creating, maintaining, and monitoring diverse instrumentalities of governance. Under these circumstances, societies have the potential for becoming self-governing rather than relying on states to rule over societies.

At this point we need to recognize that the theories of sovereignty formulated in the Hobbes tradition, where sovereign authority is conceived as *unlimited, inalienable, absolute,* and *indivisible,* imply a *unity of power*—a monopoly of the prerogatives of government. Other theoretical traditions exist where the term *sovereignty* is either given a different meaning or where the prerogatives of sovereigns are conceived as being limited by the organic nature of society. Alexis de Tocqueville ([1835] 1945, 1:123) defines sovereignty as the right to make laws. This leads to a conceptualization in which a much wider range of structural characteristics applies to systems of government than in Hobbes' formulation.

Many European writers also argue that different patterns of organization are indigenous to society and function autonomously from the state. State interference with these relationships can be disruptive of fundamental socialization and acculturation processes, and destructive of society. Hegel advances such an argument for the family. Similar arguments have been advanced relative to religious and educational institutions, economic institutions, including guilds and economic associations and relationships of different types, and to institutions of local government.

Herre (1982, 171–181) indicates how Constantin Frantz fashioned a theory of federalism from a theory of a state that views various forms of organization as *Urzelle* (indigenous) to society.

Hobbes' concept of a unity of power is unambiguous; it is a monopoly of power. European traditions that recognize an institutional specialization associated with a differentiation of legislative, executive, and judicial instrumentalities of government, while proclaiming a unitary system of government, are subject to greater ambiguities (V. Ostrom 1985). These ambiguities can be resolved in part by conceptualizing societies as organic systems where aspects of those societies are viewed as indigenous to the society and autonomous from the state.

Although aggregation rules (rules for aggregating votes into decisions) are important in the governance of democratic societies, they are only one of several essential types of rules. Elinor Ostrom (2000), in drawing on game-theoretical traditions, has specified the minimal set of rules as referring to boundary rules, scope rules, position rules, authority rules, information rules, and payoff rules, in addition to aggregation rules. If aggregation rules are placed within the constraints afforded by authority rules, one can begin to appreciate how voting rules pertain to veto rules in creating equilibrating tendencies among decision processes in systems of governance (Herzberg and Ostrom 2000; see also Shepsle 1979). Voting rules, veto rules, equal-protection-of-the-law rules, and due-process rules work together in configurations of rules that are constitutive of diverse communities of relationships in democratic societies.

Rules, then, need to be viewed as being interrelated in configurations of relationships where any change in a given rule will affect opportunities for strategic choices within the larger configuration of rules. Though rules themselves are configurational in nature, we must also recognize that rules, as such, are no more than words articulated in human language (V. Ostrom 1997). For such words to have meaning, human beings require access to methods of normative inquiry that enable them to make interpersonal comparisons in establishing norms and criteria of choice (Harsanyi 1977; V. Ostrom 1986) and to contingency calculations that involve institutional arrangements of diverse sorts in relation to the material conditions of the world (V. Ostrom 1976, 1999a). If human beings are to have a critical awareness of the world in which they live and of the opportunities for choices that are available, we are required to address multiple levels, facets, and foci of analysis that relate to (1) human valuation, (2) production possibilities, (3) arrays of goods and services, (4) rule-ordered relationships, and (5) shared levels of common understanding that enable people to communicate and act meaningfully with one another.

V. THE PEOPLE PROBLEM

If one looks back on the recent history of the twentieth century, epic events such as the Russian Revolution, Marxist struggles, and the emergence of new states with the end of European colonialism in Africa have been marked by failures of overwhelming proportions. Marxist and Leninist prophets anticipated the liberation of mankind. Collectivization of agriculture in the Union of Soviet Socialist Republics and the Great Leap Forward in the People's Republic of China came at the cost of tens of millions of lives amid famines induced by public policies. In Africa, nation-states dominated by military forces engaged in forms of pillage and plunder of tragic importance amid substantial destruction of human capital by arming children with weapons of warfare. The use of slogans to shape thinking and the formulation of what passes for public policy without the openness of the *res publica* (open society) condition have heaped tragedies upon tragedies despite the promise of the United Nations.

In the late eighteenth century, Alexander Hamilton (Hamilton et al., [1788] n.d., 3), in addressing the People of the State of New York, raised the question—which could only be decided by the people—of "whether societies of men are really capable or not of establishing good government from reflection and choice, or whether they are forever destined to depend for their political constitutions on accident and force." Promises of the liberation of mankind, struggles for socialism and the destruction of capitalism, and the achievement of liberty, equality, and fraternity by armed struggle were destined to fail, as were independent nation-states exercising the prerogatives of sovereignty. If people are to become self-governing, it is they who are required to become knowledgeable about the science and art of association, including market choice, public choice, and institutional choice.

The science and art of association need to be grounded in knowledge and shared communities of understanding among peoples existing in human communities wherever we find them. It is they who face the challenge of creating good government by reflection and choice. The meaning of value terms such as liberty, fraternity, and justice are artifices that people can establish as a result of their joint effort grounded in the practice of normative inquiry taught by Moses in his formulation of God's law. The constitution of order in Africa must begin with an understanding of the indigenous institutions of the African peoples (Shivakumar 2003). *Democracy in America* ([1835, 1840] 1990), according to Tocqueville, was about a self-governing society, not a state-governed society. The free cities of Europe were self-governing communities and the passage to modernity in Europe was grounded in the exercise of such self-governing capabilities (Sabetti 2003). The exercise of self-governing capabilities among diverse units of government requires recourse to public entrepreneurship (Kuhnert 2001). Public enterprises in public economies are necessary complements to private enterprises in market economies. The liberation of mankind in socialist societies is the tragic illusion of intellectuals and aspiring revolutionaries. Only people grounded in a warrantable art and science of association can create good government from reflection and choice.

VI. FRAMEWORKS, THEORIES, AND MODELS

When the diverse elements that are included in a model are treated as factors that are themselves treated as variables, we no longer have a model. The usual pattern in economic reasoning was to specify certain assumptions and then deal with assumptions as exogenous variables. These were set by stipulation. The activating factor was located in a somewhat similar way, but since it was the active factor, its governing principle was formulated as a postulate implying a principle of selection. By varying some endogenous variable, there were grounds for anticipating how reliance on an activating principle would yield hypothetical consequences. Such an approach is vulnerable to error when the reference is to some ambiguous set identified as nonmarket decision making. These problems are especially serious when efforts are made to engage in forms of analysis applicable to practical exigencies arising in human societies.

A primary task in resolving a puzzle is to attempt to identify the source of some problematic in an existing state of affairs that has yielded perverse effects—engendering conflicts or other manifestations of what is considered to be pathological. When a problematic can be identified, the relevant field of effects needs to be indicated as implicating those who are affected, revealing a hypothetical action arena. Affecting the domain of that action arena are three broad types of factors that need consideration. The first is the physical environing conditions, as these pertain to the relevant technologies and types of resources and goods that are implicated. The second factor is the people who are affected and the shared community or communities of understanding—or their absence thereof—that exist among the people involved. A third general factor is to identify the existing structure of institutional arrangements as rule-ordered relationships that are the basis for structuring the choices people make (e.g., Crawford and Ostrom 2005; E. Ostrom et al., 1994, chap. 2). A clarification of these features and how they interact with one another is an effort to clarify the structure of the action situation. If actors whose actions contribute to the problematics of that characteristic situation can be identified in light of the structure of incentives that are at work, a basis exists for postulating an action tendency. These are the grounds for making a diagnostic assessment. Remedial actions might then be explored. From the perspective of institutional analysis, possible modifications in patterns of rule-ordered relationships would need to be considered. Technological features may also bear on potentials for development. If those technologies will have an effect on the larger community of relationships, then modifications in the system of rule-ordered relationships would also be involved.

Wherever potential for change exists, attention needs to be given to the way that all of those hypothetically involved may function as participants in how the processing of an inquiry affects potential for achieving conflict resolution. Essential features in such a process involve the elucidation of information, the clarification of anticipated consequences, and the essential logics that are applicable to the type of situation in which people find themselves in light of the environing conditions. An incidental feature of such processes, in addition to working out a particular resolution, is the generation of a level of common knowledge, a shared community of understanding, including reference to patterns of accountability, and levels of confidence and trustworthiness that may accrue from the process of inquiry and the promise afforded by the resolutions achieved. Transformations are occurring that may have technological, institutional, and cultural significance, which all reach well beyond purely economic or narrowly construed political calculations.

Eucken ([1940] 1951) engaged in a fundamental critique of neoclassical economic theory when he argued that efforts to formulate a universal model of competitive market economy had the effect of increasingly distancing economic theorists from what might be called economic "reality". His critique of the empirical inquiries undertaken by economic historians was that in the absence of theory, their work involved heaping facts on facts. These dual tendencies created a great antinomy. Empirical inquiry was not being informed by theory, and theoretical formulations were not being informed by empirical applications. This is an affliction that has been characteristic of public administration: an unbridged gap between theory and practice.

A way of bridging this gap between theory and practice is to shift attention away from model thinking and to recognize that beginning with basic elements of a framework—material conditions, technologies, goods; rules and rule-ordered relationships; shared communities of understanding—in which hypothetical actors are acting in action situations, is a way to *frame* an inquiry. As soon as a scholar relates an understanding of the structure of an action situation and postulates applicable to human agency, we have the rudiments necessary for deriving theoretical inferences. This requires learning how to do theory rather than just *talking about* theory as a purely abstract enterprise. We can address the *logic* of actions in situations. The more carefully the logic of an action situation can be specified, the more closely one can approach a fully specified model capable of yielding a determinate outcome.

The framework–theory–model way of thinking is opening new vistas for empirical inquiry. Game theory in the extensive form becomes a complement to the various models for applying economic reasoning to the choices that human beings make. Public choice theory, the new institutional economics, and institutional analysis and development are now being complemented by empirical inquiries conducted in field settings and laboratories. By using a common approach to address different contexts, levels, and foci of analysis, a greater degree of complementarity can be achieved among all of the sciences that impinges on policies and their implementation as working rules of going concerns.

VII. SUMMARY AND CONCLUSIONS

This chapter has constituted an attempt to show how different methods that are broadly viewed as economic reasoning can be used in the analysis of diverse institutional arrangements. If one takes the extreme model used in the neoclassical approach to perfectly competitive markets, the result is an explanation for how egoistic individuals seeking their own good are led by competitive dynamics to a general equilibrium where supply equals demand at prices that cover marginal costs. This outcome is counterintuitive or counterintentional in at least two ways. First, individual self-serving activities in a market yield orderly patterns of relationships. Second, the pressure of competitive dynamics reduces the gain to be realized by producers with a commensurate increase in consumer surplus. The presumptions of complete information, though glaringly false, are most closely approximated in competitive markets where people habitually engage in repetitive transactions on a continuing basis.

Perfect competition can, however, become a "nirvana" model (Demsetz 1969) that cuts economists off from problems that many in the field find to be of interest. Many economists now substitute an assumption of limited information to replace that of complete information. As varying degrees of ignorance are postulated in economic analysis, we see how consideration being given to institutional variables fits in the context of contracting about patterns of human relationships. Complete information drives out most problems of institutional analysis. It is uncertainties about how others can be expected to act and about what the future holds that require human beings to place reliance on rules in ordering their relationships with one another (Heiner 1983). Reliance on varying assumptions about the basic elements in economic relationships yields capabilities for addressing analogous types of problems in both market and nonmarket decision-making arrangements. Problems of exchange relationships and jointness in production and consumption have their analogs in both the private and public sectors. These interdependencies become such that the conceptual distinctions between the private and public sectors need to be viewed with caution (Kaufmann 1986a, especially 131–134).

Thus, one must face the problem of exploring what it is that is common to all human societies so that variable features in different societies can be better understood. The field has barely begun to explore which elements are constitutive of organization in human societies and how discrete patterns of organization could be characterized as meta-types that function at different levels of analysis in relation to other meta-structures that include reference to societies, to civilizations, and to processes of acculturation that enable human beings to develop a critical self-consciousness of what it means to live in self-governing societies and contribute to the unfolding of human civilizations (V. Ostrom 1997; Taylor 1966; Teilhard de Chardin 1961; Tocqueville [1835 and 1840] 1945; Turchin 1977; von Hayek 1960). These efforts require us to move to meta-theoretical syntheses of different approaches to institutional analysis where we attempt to understand the terms on which alternatives become available for different levels of choice in human societies (Kiser and Ostrom 2000), including the levels of choice applicable to the analytical tools used in the study of public administration.

ACKNOWLEDGMENTS

Peter Bogason, Roberta Herzberg, Gayle Higgins, Elinor Ostrom, Hartmut Picht, and Jeanne Schaaf have been most helpful in eliminating some of the ambiguities in my use of language. Key distinctions are important to what I have to say. Whatever ambiguities remain result from my own failure to make appropriate distinctions.

REFERENCES

Akerlof, G., The market for 'lemons': quality, uncertainty and the market mechanism, *Quarterly Journal of Economics*, 84, 488–500, 1970.

Alchian, A. and Demsetz, H., Production, information costs, and economic organization, *American Economic Review*, 62, 777–795, 1972.

Arrow, K. J., *Social Choice and Individual Values*, Wiley, New York, 1951.

Bain, J. S., *Industrial Organization*, University of California Press, Berkeley, CA, 1959.

Bain, J. S., Caves, R. E., and Margolis, J., *Northern California's Water Industry: The Comparative Efficiency of Public Enterprise in Developing a Scarce Natural Resource*, Johns Hopkins University Press, Baltimore, MD, 1966.

Barry, B. and Hardin, R., Eds., *Rational Man and Irrational Society?: An Introduction and Sourcebook*, Sage, Beverly Hills, CA, 1982.

Baumol, W. J., Panzar, J. C., and Willig, R. D., *Contestable Markets and the Theory of Industry Structure*, Harcourt Brace Jovanovich, New York, 1982.

Berman, H., *Law and Revolution: The Formation of the Western Legal Tradition*, Harvard University Press, Cambridge, MA, 1983.

Bish, R. L., *The Public Economy of Metropolitan Areas*, Markham, Chicago, IL, 1971.

Borcherding, T. E., Ed., *Budgets and Bureaucrats*, Duke University Press, Durham, NC, 1977.

Buchanan, J. M., Public goods and public bads, In *Financing the Metropolis*, Crecine, J. P., Ed., Sage, Beverly Hills, CA, pp. 51–71, 1970.

Buchanan, J. M. and Tullock, G., *The Calculus of Consent: Logical Foundations of Constitutional Democracy*, University of Michigan Press, Ann Arbor, MI, 1962.

Caves, R. E., Industrial organization, corporate strategy and structure, *Journal of Economic Literature*, 18, 64–92, 1980.

Cheung, S. N. S., Transaction costs, risk aversion, and the choice of contractual arrangements, *Journal of Law and Economics*, 12, 23–42, 1969.

Cheung, S. N. S., The contractual nature of the firm, *Journal of Law and Economics*, 26, 1–21, 1983.

Coase, R. H., The nature of the firm, *Economica*, 4, 386–405, 1937.

Crawford, S. and Ostrom, E., A grammar of institutions, In *Understanding Institutional Diversity*, Ostrom, E., Ed., Princeton University, Princeton, NJ, pp. 137–174, 2005.

De Alessi, L., The economics of property rights: a review of the evidence, *Research in Law and Economics*, 2, 1–47, 1980.

Demsetz, H., Information and efficiency: another viewpoint, *Journal of Law and Economics*, 12, 1–22, 1969.

Dosi, G., *Technical Change and Industrial Transformation*, St. Martin's, New York, 1984.

Downs, A., *An Economic Theory of Democracy*, Harper & Row, New York, 1957.

Elster, J., *Ulysses and the Sirens*, Cambridge University Press, New York, 1977.

Eucken, W., *The Foundations of Economics*, University of Chicago Press, Chicago, IL, Reprinted, [1940] 1951.

Golembiewski, R. T., A critique of "democratic administration" and its supporting ideation: observations on "doing political theory": a rejoinder, *American Political Science Review*, 71, 1526–1531, 1977.

Green, D. P. and Shapiro, I., *Pathologies of Rational Choice Theory: A Critique of Applications in Political Science*, Yale University Press, New Haven, CT, 1994.

Gregg, M., Units and levels of analysis: a problem of policy analysis in federal systems, *Publius*, 4, 59–86, 1974.

Hamilton, A., Jay, J., and Madison, J., In *The Federalist*, Earle, E., Ed., Modern Library, New York, [1788] n.d.

Harsanyi, J. C., Rule utilitarianism and decision theory, *Erkenntnis*, 11, 25–53, 1977.

Head, J. G., Public goods and public policy, *Public Finance*, 17, 197–219, 1962.

Heiner, R. A., The origin of predictable behavior, *American Economic Review*, 73, 560–595, 1983.

Herre, F., *Nation Ohne Staat: Die Entstehung Der Deutschen Frage*, Bastei-Lubbe-Taschenbuch, Gladbach, Germany, 1982.

Herzberg, R. and Ostrom, V., Votes and vetoes, In *Polycentric Games and Institutions: Readings from the Workshop in Political Theory and Policy Analysis*, McGinnis, M., Ed., University of Michigan Press, Ann Arbor, MI, pp. 168–183, 2000.

Hobbes, T., *Leviathan or the Matter, Forme and Power of a Commonwealth Ecclesiasticall and Civil*, Oakeshott, M., Ed., Basil Blackwell, Oxford, Reprinted, [1651] 1960.

Kaufmann, F. X., The blurring of the distinction "state versus society" in the idea and practice of the welfare state, In *Guidance, Control, and Evaluation in the Public Sector*, Kaufmann, F.X., Majone, G., and Ostrom V. Eds., Walter de Gruyter, Berlin and New York, pp. 127–138, 1986a.

Kaufmann, F. X., The relationship between guidance, control, and evaluation, In *Guidance, Control, and Evaluation in the Public Sector*, Kaufmann, F. X., Majone, G., and Ostrom, V., Eds., Walter de Gruyter, Berlin and New York, pp. 211–228, 1986b.

Kekes, J., *A Justification of Rationality*, State University of New York Press, Albany, NY, 1976.

Kirzner, I. M., *Competition and Entrepreneurship*, University of Chicago Press, Chicago, IL, 1973.

Kirzner, I. M., *Perception, Opportunity, and Profit: Studies in the Theory of Entrepreneurship*, University of Chicago Press, Chicago, IL, 1979.

Kiser, L. L. and Ostrom, E., The three worlds of action: a metatheoretical synthesis of institutional approaches, In *Polycentric Games and Institutions: Readings from the Workshop in Political Theory and Policy Analysis*, McGinnis, M., Ed., University of Michigan Press, Ann Arbor, MI, pp. 56–88, 2000.

Krüsselberg, H. G., Markets and hierarchies, In *Guidance, Control, and Evaluation in the Public Sector*, Kaufmann, F. X., Majone, G., and Ostrom, V., Eds., Walter de Gruyter, Berlin and New York, pp. 349–386, 1986.

Kuhnert, S., An evolutionary theory of collective action: schumpeterian entrepreneurship for the common good, *Constitutional Political Economy*, 12, 13–29, 2001.

Majone, G., Policy science, In *Guidance, Control, and Evaluation in the Public Sector*, Kaufmann, F. X., Majone, G., and Ostrom, V., Eds., Walter de Gruyter, Berlin and New York, pp. 61–70, 1986.

Mandeville, B., In *The Fable of the Bees, or Private Vices, Publick Benefits*, Primer, I., Ed., Capricorn Books, New York, 1962.

Montias, J. M., *The Structure of Economic Systems*, Yale University Press, New Haven, CT, 1976.

Mueller, D., *Public Choice*, Cambridge University Press, Cambridge, 1979.

Nelson, R. R., *The Moon and the Ghetto: An Essay on Public Policy Analysis*, Norton, New York, 1977.

Nelson, R. R. and Winter, S. G., *An Evolutionary Theory of Economic Change*, Harvard University Press, Cambridge, MA, 1982.

Niskanen, W., *Bureaucracy and Representative Government*, Aldine-Atherton, Chicago, IL, 1971.

Niskanen, W., Bureaucrats and politicians, *Journal of Law and Economics*, 18, 617–643, 1975.

Olson, M., *The Logic of Collective Action: Public Goods and the Theory of Groups*, Harvard University Press, Cambridge, MA, 1965.

Orzechowski, W., Economic models of bureaucracy: survey, extensions and evidence, In *Budgets and Bureaucrats: The Sources of Government Growth*, Borcherding, T. E., Ed., Duke University Press, Durham, NC, pp. 229–259, 1977.

Osborne, D., *Reinventing Government: How the Entrepreneurial Spirit is Transforming the Public Sector*, Plume, New York, Reprinted, [1992] 1993.

Ostrom, E., Multiorganizational arrangements and coordination: an application of institutional analysis, In *Guidance, Control, and Evaluation in the Public Sector*, Kaufmann, F. X., Majone, G., and Ostrom, V., Eds., Walter de Gruyter, Berlin and New York, pp. 495–510, 1986.

Ostrom, E., *Governing the Commons: The Evolution of Institutions for Collective Action*, Cambridge University Press, New York, 1990.

Ostrom, E., Metropolitan reform: propositions derived from two traditions, In *Polycentricity and Local Public Economies: Readings from the Workshop in Political Theory and Policy Analysis*, McGinnis, M., Ed., University of Michigan Press, Ann Arbor, MI, pp. 139–160, 1999.

Ostrom, E., An agenda for the study of institutions, In *Polycentric Games and Institutions: Readings from the Workshop in Political Theory and Policy Analysis*, McGinnis, M., Ed., University of Michigan Press, Ann Arbor, MI, pp. 89–113, 2000.

Ostrom, E., Gardner, R., and Walker, J., *Rules, Games, and Common-Pool Resources*, University of Michigan Press, Ann Arbor, MI, 1994.

Ostrom, V., Can federalism make a difference?, *Publius*, 3, 197–238, 1973.

Ostrom, V., Some paradoxes for planners: human knowledge and its limitations, In *The Politics of Planning: A Review and Critique of Centralized Economic Planning*, Chickering, L., Ed., Institute for Contemporary Studies Press, San Francisco, CA, pp. 243–254, 1976.

Ostrom, V., Reflexions on public administration in Europe, In *The Development of Research and Training in European Policy-Making*, Papers presented at the Inaugural Colloquium of the European Institute of Public Administration, Maastricht, The Netherlands, 122–169, 1983.

Ostrom, V., Multiorganizational arrangements in the governance of unitary and federal systems of governance, In *Policy Implementation in Federal and Unitary Systems*, Hanf, K. and Toonen, T., Eds., Martinus Nijhoff, Dordrecht, The Netherlands, pp. 1–16, 1985.

Ostrom, V., A fallabilist's approach to norms and criteria of choice, In *Guidance, Control, and Evaluation in the Public Sector*, Kaufmann, F. X., Majone, G., and Ostrom, V., Eds., Walter de Gruyter, Berlin and New York, pp. 229–249, 1986.

Ostrom, V., *The Political Theory of a Compound Republic: Designing the American Experiment*, 2nd ed., Institute for Contemporary Studies Press, San Francisco, CA, [1971] 1987.

Ostrom, V., Epistemic choice and public choice, *Public Choice*, 77, 163–176, 1993.

Ostrom, V., *The Meaning of Democracy and the Vulnerability of Democracies: A Response to Tocqueville's Challenge*, The University of Michigan Press, Ann Arbor, MI, 1997.

Ostrom, V., Artisanship and artifact, In *Polycentric Governance and Development: Readings from the Workshop in Political Theory and Policy Analysis*, McGinnis, M., Ed., University of Michigan Press, Ann Arbor, MI, pp. 377–393, 1999a.

Ostrom, V., A forgotten tradition: the constitutional level of analysis, In *Polycentric Governance and Development: Readings from the Workshop in Political Theory and Policy Analysis*, McGinnis, M., Ed., University of Michigan Press, Ann Arbor, MI, pp. 151–165, 1999b.

Ostrom, V., Feeny, D., and Picht, H., Eds., *Rethinking Institutional Analysis and Development: Issues, Alternatives, and Choices,* 2nd ed., Institute for Contemporary Studies Press, San Francisco, CA, [1988] 1993.

Ostrom, V. and Ostrom, E., Public goods and public choices, In *Polycentricity and Local Public Economies: Readings from the Workshop in Political Theory and Policy Analysis*, McGinnis, M., Ed., University of Michigan Press, Ann Arbor, MI, pp. 75–103, 1999.

Ostrom, V., Tiebout, C. M., and Warren, R., The organization of government in metropolitan areas: a theoretical inquiry, In *Polycentricity and Local Public Economies: Readings from the Workshop in Political Theory and Policy Analysis*, McGinnis, M., Ed., University of Michigan Press, Ann Arbor, MI, pp. 31–51, 1999.

Parks, R. B. and Ostrom, E., Complex models of urban service systems, In *Polycentricity and Local Public Economies: Readings from the Workshop in Political Theory and Policy Analysis*, McGinnis, M., Ed., University of Michigan Press, Ann Arbor, MI, pp. 355–380, 1999.

Picht, H., Monetary arrangements for economic development, *Working Paper* Workshop in Political Theory and Policy Analysis, Indiana University, Bloomington, IN, 1985.

Pommerehne, W. and Frey, B. S., Public versus private production efficiency in Switzerland: a theoretical and empirical comparison, In *Urban Affairs Annual Reviews*, Ostrom, V. and Bish, F. P., Eds., Vol. 12, Sage, Beverly Hills, CA, pp. 221–242, 1977.

Popkin, S., *The Rational Peasant*, University of California Press, Berkeley, CA, 1979.

Popkin, S., Public choice and rural development—free riders, lemons, and institutional design, In *Public Choice and Rural Development*, Russell, C. S. and Nicholson, N. K., Eds., Johns Hopkins University Press, Baltimore, MD, pp. 43–80, 1981.

Popper, K. R., In *The Poverty of Historicism*, Harper & Row, New York, 1964.

Popper, K. R., La rationalite et le statut due principe de rationalite [Rationality and the status of the rationality principle], In *Le Fondements Philosophiques Des Systems Economiques: Textes De Jacques Rueff Et Essays Rediges En Son Honneur*, Classen, E. M., Ed., Payot, Paris, pp. 145–150, 1967.

Pryor, F. L., *Property and Industrial Organization in Communist and Capitalist Nations*, Indiana University Press, Bloomington, IN, 1973.

Riker, W., *The Theory of Political Coalitions*, Yale University Press, New Haven, CT, 1962.

Riker, W., *Liberalism against Populism*, W.H. Freeman, San Francisco, CA, 1982.

Riker, W. H. and Ordeshook, P., *An Introduction to Positive Political Theory*, Prentice Hall, Englewood Cliffs, NJ, 1973.

Romer, T. and Rosenthal, H., Political resource allocation, controlled agendas, and the status quo, *Public Choice*, 33, 27–43, 1978.

Russell, T. and Thaler, R., The relevance of quasi-rationality in competitive markets, *American Economic Review*, 75, 1071–1082, 1985.

Sabetti, F., Achieving self-governing capabilities in societies with federal potentials, Paper presented at international conference on "Which Federalism?" at Savelletri, Brindisi, 2003.

Savas, E. S., Municipal monopolies versus competition in delivering urban services, In *Urban Affairs Annual Reviews*, Hawley, W. D. and Rogers, D., Eds., Vol. 5, Sage, Beverly Hills, CA, pp. 473–500, 1974.

Savas, E. S., An empirical study of competition in municipal service delivery, *Public Administration Review*, 37, 717–724, 1977.

Savas, E. S., Public vs. private refuse collection: a critical review of the evidence, *Urban Analysis*, 7, 1–12, 1979.

Savas, E. S., *Privatizing the Public Sector*, Chatham House, Chatham, NJ, 1982.

Schelling, T. C., *Micromotives and Macrobehavior*, Norton, New York, 1978.

Sen, A. K., Rational fools: a critique of the behavioral foundations of economic theory, *Philosophy and Public Affairs*, 6, 317–344, 1977.

Shepsle, K., Institutional arrangements and equilibrium in multidimensional voting models, *American Journal of Political Science*, 23, 27–59, 1979.

Shivakumar, S., The place of indigenous institutions in constitutional order, *Constitutional Political Economy*, 14, 3–21, 2003.

Shubik, M., *Game Theory in the Social Sciences: Concepts and Solutions*, MIT Press, Cambridge, MA, 1982.

Shubik, M., *Game Theory in the Social Sciences*, Vol. 2, *A Game-Theoretic Approach to Political Economy*, MIT Press, Cambridge, MA, 1984.

Shubik, M., The games within the game: modeling politico-economic structures, In *Guidance, Control, and Evaluation in the Public Sector*, Kaufmann, F. X., Majone, G., and Ostrom, V., Eds., Walter de Gruyter, Berlin and New York, pp. 571–591, 1986.

Simon, H. A., The proverbs of administration, *Public Administration Review*, 6, 53–67, 1946.

Simon, H. A., *Administrative Behavior: A Study of Decision-Making Processes in Administrative Organization*, 2nd ed., Free Press, New York, [1947] 1957.

Simon, H. A., Theories of decision making in economics and behavioral science, *American Economic Review*, 49, 253–283, 1959.

Simon, H. A., Theories of bounded rationality, In *Decision and Organization: A Volume in Honor of Jacob Marschak*, McGuire, C. B. and Radner, R., Eds., North Holland, Amsterdam, 1972.

Simon, H. A., Rationality as process and as product of thought, *American Economic Review*, 68, 1–16, 1978.

Simon, H. A., *The sciences of the artificial*, 2nd ed., MIT Press, Cambridge, MA, 1981.

Taylor, J. F. A., *The Masks of Society—An Inquiry into the Covenants of Civilization*, Appleton-Century Crofts, New York, 1966.

Teilhard de Chardin, P., *The Phenomenon of Man*, Harper & Row, New York, 1961.

Tiebout, C., A pure theory of local expenditures, *Journal of Political Economy*, 64, 416–424, 1956.

Tocqueville, A., In *Democracy in America*, Vol.2, Bradley, P., Ed., Vintage Books, New York, [1835, 1840] 1945.

Tullock, G., *The Politics of Bureaucracy*, Public Affairs Press, Washington, DC, 1965.

Tullock, G., Federalism: the problem of scale, *Public Choice*, 6, 19–29, 1969.

Turchin, V. F., *The Phenomenon of Science*, Columbia University Press, New York, 1977.

von Hayek, F. A., The use of knowledge in society, *American Economic Review*, 35, 519–530, 1945.

von Hayek, F. A., *The Constitution of Liberty*, University of Chicago Press, Chicago, IL, 1960.

von Hayek, F. A., *Law, Legislation and Liberty*,Vol.3, University of Chicago Press, Chicago, IL, 1973, 1976, 1979.

Warren, R. O., A municipal services market model of metropolitan organization, *Journal of the American Institute of Planners*, 30, 193–204, 1964.

Williamson, O., Hierarchical control and optimal firm size, *Journal of Political Economy*, 75, 123–138, 1967.

Williamson, O., *Markets and Hierarchies: Analysis and Antitrust Implications*, Free Press, New York and London, 1975.

Williamson, O., Transaction-cost economics: the governance of contractual relations, *Journal of Law and Economics*, 22, 233–261, 1979.

Unit 15

Public Administration as a Profession

30 The Public Administration Community and the Search for Professionalism

John J. Gargan

CONTENTS

I. INTRODUCTION: ON THE CONCEPT OF PROFESSION

Societal capacity is a function of the ability to marshal and organize knowledge and skill. In contemporary developed societies, knowledge in many domains and technology-related skills are requisites of influence and bases of power. This chapter is concerned with one dimension of societal capacity, that of public administration professionalism.

Over the past century and a quarter there have been changes in the structure of occupations, mobility of white-collar workers into professions, and dramatic growth in professional elites (Brint 1994, 5). Given its significance for contemporary life, professionalism has been a topic of concern in a variety of fields, including public administration.

A conventional notion of profession is that of an occupational classification involving relatively abstract or esoteric knowledge and related skills. Presumably professional status is based on competency, achieved not ascribed. At minimum, professionals translate "knowledge into action" and "use their knowledge or experience in helping people meet problems which they cannot handle themselves" (Eulau 1973, 172–173). Representative of scholarly definitions of profession would be:

> *A profession is a relatively 'high status' occupation whose members apply abstract knowledge to solve problems in a particular field of endeavor.* The definition identifies three elements as critical to the idea of a profession: highstatus, ...; applied abstract knowledge, the source of expertise; and a field of endeavor or jurisdiction for problem-solving (Burk 2002, 21).

Or:

> professions are somewhat exclusive groups of people applying somewhat abstract knowledge to particular cases (Abbott 1988, 318).

Despite the relative clarity of these definitions, interpretations of the meaning of profession and related terms have varied. Professions are socially constructed in that societal values at a given time and in a given context will determine which problems are deemed sufficiently serious to be included in the jurisdiction of a particular profession and, by that inclusion, which kinds of professional knowledge and skills are relevant to problem solutions.

Literature reviews of research on professions, professionalism, and professionalization summarize efforts to develop typologies and shifts in conceptual focus. Initial studies in the post World War II years involved historical analyses and case studies of individual professions; subsequent work focused on such topics as specific criteria of professionalism (Kline 1981, 260–276); stages of the process of professionalism, and critical events in the push toward professionalization (Wilensky 1964, 142).

The conceptual focus and the substantive views of professionalization in these studies changed through time. Andrew Abbott has classified the substantive views in four basic categories: functional, structural, monopolist, and cultural. Several scholars analyzed professions in functional terms, the ways professionals used knowledge and skill to assist clients with problems; "[p]rofession was ... a means to control the asymmetric expert-client relation." A structuralist school paid less attention to work and expert–client interactions but focused on forces shaping structure and models of the professionalization process; [p]rofession was merely a form of occupational control. A monopoly approach to the professions argued that the emergence of professional structures such as associations and schools and functions performed (credentialing, licensing, regulation, expulsion) could be attributed not to a natural process but to a desire for dominance or authority; [p]rofessions were corporate groups with 'mobility projects' aimed at control of work. Researchers in the cultural category assessed the "cultural authority of professions" and the central process by which cultural legitimacy designates certain occupations as professions (Abbott 1988, 14–15).

Some shifts in conceptual focus had potential implications for core values of the public administration community.* Early works on the professions, including those produced in the initial post-World War II years, emphasized a public service ideal where the professional's technical solutions would be related to a clientele's needs (Goode 1969); professional obligation to the client "overrode the dictates of the marketplace and self-interest" and was to be met "even if that required an element of self-sacrifice" (Burk 2002, 23–24).

This public service ideal began to be downplayed, according to some authors, during the 1960s. Commenting on the writing on professions during the period, Freidson (1986, 28) noted:

> a shift in both the emphasis and interest developed both in the United States and in the United Kingdom. The mood shifted from one of approval to one of disapproval, from one that emphasized virtue over failing to one that emphasized failings over virtues. The very idea of profession was attacked, implying, if not often stating, that the world would be better off without professions.

A new body of work reflected scholarly attention to political, cultural, and power influences on professional behavior and the relation of professions to the state, the market and the class system (Freidson 1986, 29). In a similar vein Brint has argued that in recent decades the professions have been more disconnected from functions perceived to be central to the public welfare and more exclusively connected to the idea of 'expert knowledge' with the rise of an "ideal of expert professionalism [which] emphasized the instrumental effectiveness of specialized, theoretically grounded knowledge, but included comparatively little concern with collegial organization, ethical standards, or [excepting the public and nonprofit sectors] service in the public interest" (Brint 1994, 8, 37).

A theory of professions developed by sociologist Andrew Abbott focuses on professional work dealing with human problems amenable to expert service (Abbott 1988, 35). Professionals claim

---

* The choice of terminology for any study of public administration is difficult. Throughout this chapter, reference is made to a public administration community. As used, the term community includes academics and scholars whose primary teaching and research interests are the operations and practice of government. Also included are those in government whose primary responsibilities are administration and management and those in staff positions that support administration and management.

expertise in three aspects of practice: diagnosis, to classify a problem; inference, to reason about it; and treatment, to take action on it. The three tasks are obviously related; "diagnosis takes information into the professional knowledge system and treatment brings instructions back from it" (Abbott 1988, 40) and "[i]nference is undertaken when the connection between diagnosis and treatment is obscure" (49).

By Abbott's theory, professions perform their work within a jurisdiction "defined by the boundaries of the domain within which expert knowledge is applied. It is sometimes an actual place, like a hospital, court room or battlefield, and sometimes a slice or aspect of life" (Burk 2002, 29). An individual profession engages in those activities that link it to its jurisdiction but, given that the links are neither absolute nor permanent, at any given time individual professions are elements in a system of professions.

Professions and alternative approaches within a profession compete for absolute control of a jurisdiction or for superior or subordinate positions within the jurisdiction. Examples of this competition would be that among religious, medical, and law enforcement professionals seeking dominance in the treatment of alcoholism; that of the military services (Army, Navy, Air Force) when each sought control of an aspect of the new nuclear weaponry during the 1950s; that between doctors and nurse practitioners over which professionals would have responsibility for what medical procedures. Through time, the general history of the professions is determined by the success or failure of particular professions in the jurisdiction competition.

Jurisdiction is a feature of the context of professional practice. Another distinguishing characteristic of the context, cited by essentially all observers, is autonomy. The premise is that, if professionals are to be held accountable for their decisions, they must be allowed discretion and discretion presupposes freedom from meticulous supervision and direction by others (Freidson 1986, 147). Autonomy is crucial if professionals are to apply judgment and skill to inference making when faced with unfamiliar problems.

Individual professionals, however, are never completely autonomous in that some oversight of professional behavior is necessary. The question is more one of who is to oversee than whether to oversee. Professional practitioners favor maximum autonomy with any regulation and control handled by peers. Standards for credentials and entry into a profession, accreditation of academic programs, conditions of employment, codes of ethical behavior, and policing of untoward practices can all be handled by a professional association through its standing committees, boards, or conventions. The profession at-large also has real economic and power interests in controlling the quality and number of entrants to the profession.

Others outside the profession also have an interest in regulating professional behavior. To protect citizens from charlatans and to promote a public interest, government, including American state government, claims some responsibility to license occupations, including professions. Public officials must also be concerned with significant policy issues: matching the production of professionals with societal needs, assuring clientele access to services by market or non-market mechanisms, and ensuring the enforcement of suitable regulations (Trebilcock 1978, 7).

II. PROFESSIONS, PROFESSIONALISM, AND THE PUBLIC SECTOR

Like professional communities generally, the public administration community has been aware of the importance of professional recognition and has sought the status, prestige, and autonomy accorded other fields. Over time, public administrators periodically have indicated concerns about their core knowledge and skills, unique competencies, ethical obligations, and the legitimacy of their autonomy in a democratic political system. Throughout the political system governments are major employers of professionals of all stripes and public officials seek out professionals for advice when confronted with unfamiliar problems. As Brint (1994, 129) points out:

> Certainly, no government in the developed world finds itself able to do without the armies of experts who conduct research on matters of consequence to public policy, consult and advise decision makers, and develop policy options for the future.

The effectiveness of professionals in public and quasi-public bureaucracies has been of interest to academics in their studies of state capacity to carry through interventionist policies (Skocpol and Finegold 1982, 260–261) and of "the processes by which [the public administration community] ... participates in creating and interpreting law with how such creating and interpreting can be done 'correctly,' 'wisely,' or in the 'public interest'" (Waldo 1968a, 145). Determining the efficacy of these bureaucracies at the several levels of government and as elements in networks of public, private, and nonprofit organizations has been a primary challenge to those seeking to understand the behavior of public administration professionals (Buchanan 1985; Ostrom 1974; O'Toole 2003; Wilson 1989).

A. PROFESSIONALS IN AND OF GOVERNMENT

In discussing the professions and government some clarification is required as to terminology. References to professionals, as used here, are to two generic categories. One category involves professionals in government, those who have the required "knowledge in a field of science or learning characteristically acquired through education or training equivalent to a bachelor's or higher degree with major study in or pertinent to the specialized field, as distinguished from general education" (US Equal Employment Opportunity Commission 2002, Appendix I).

Frederick Mosher (1982, 116) has labeled two classes of professionals in government. The first is a class of general professionals, those who are employable in both the public and private sectors (lawyers, doctors, engineers, accountants). The second class is one of public service professionals, (military officers, foresters, meteorologists, diplomats, intelligence agents) who are concentrated in government positions. Traditionally, career opportunities for public service professionals have been primarily, if not exclusively, in government (Levine 1986, 202). However, recent emphasis on privatization of aspects of public functions has resulted in a transfer of previously governmental activities, including even the organizing and training of military professionals, to private sector firms (Singer 2003).

The second generic category involves professionals of government, those engaged in the supervision, management, and administration of public business. The equal Opportunity Commission makes use of the Office of Personnel Management definition of Administrative Occupational Category occupations "involving the exercise of analytical ability, judgment, discretion, and personal responsibility, and application of a substantial body of knowledge of principles, concepts, and practices applicable to one or more fields of administration or management. These positions do not require specialized educational majors..." (US Equal Employment Opportunity Commission 2002, Appendix I).

Students and practitioners need to be attentive to both generic categories of professionals. Elected officials rely on professionals for recommendations for treatment of issues and, equally or more important, for effective implementation of policies adopted to deal with those issues. The conduct of government and the public's judgments of its adequacy are molded by the performance of professionals of government in policy implementation.

While the boundaries of categories of public sector professionals are clear, the categories are dynamic and the qualities of professionalism within each category change. The press of external events alters the critical tasks of bureaucracies and their professional cadres. Creation of the federal Department of Homeland Security in 2002 called for a major reorganization within the executive branch, resulting in the movement to the department of personnel and programs from Departments of Justice, Transportation, and Treasury and the Federal Emergency Management Agency. The new mix of programs and personnel is not simply the sum of their earlier forms. Rather, in light of the unprecedented war on terrorism, the professionals brought to the new department have had to deal with a new set of missions requiring unique skills—prevent terrorist attacks within the United States, reduce America's vulnerability to terrorism, and minimize the damage from potential attacks and natural disasters (Department of Homeland Security 2004).

Political and organizational dynamics also redefine the professionalism qualities and critical tasks of professionals *of* government. So, for example, in the not too distant past those professionals responsible for personnel matters utilized a traditional civil service model concerned with testing, promotion on merit, neutral competence, and political independence. Currently, those professionals are urged to adopt a human capital model which places human resource management at the very center of agency strategic direction and management, not as a technical activity removed from daily management, as does the traditional civil service model (Ingraham 2003, 50).

Because of the level of knowledge and skill needed to satisfy statutory obligations and political expectations, individual agencies may employ several types of professionals—both types of professionals *in* government (general professionals and public service professionals) as well as professionals *of* government. The professional culture of an agency will be defined by a professional elite who has won jurisdictional competition for dominance (lawyers in the state attorney general's offices, public health doctors in health offices, engineers in highway departments, etc.). The work of the elite professionals is usually supported by subordinate line professionals, staff and administrative professionals (Abbott 1988, chaps 5 and 6).

B. Federal Employment (Including Professionals in Government)

While the public sector professional workforce is diverse, the greater part of public employment is concentrated in a limited number of functions at each level of government. Conforming to the rationales of public goods and functional assignment in a federal system, national defense and delivery of the mail continue to be primary purposes of employment in the federal government, just as in the nineteenth century. Active duty military personnel and Postal Service employees were 53% of total federal employment in FY 2000. Through the 1960s, active duty military personnel, among the most highly professionalized of professionals *in* and *of* government, comprised just over half of total federal employment; by 2000 the share had declined to just under one-third.

Another perspective on professionalism in the national government can be gained from Table 30.1 that reports, by executive department for 2003, the number of civilian employees,

TABLE 30.1
Executive Branch Civilian Employment by Department, 2003

Department	Total number (000)	Total (%)	Cumulative
Defense	636	34.0	34.0
Veterans Affairs	226	12.0	46.0
Homeland Security	153	8.1	54.1
Treasury	132	7.0	61.1
Health and Human Services	131	6.9	68.0
Justice	102	5.4	73.4

Source: *Budget of the United States*, 2005, Historical Tables, Tables 17.1 and 17.2.

departmental employment as a percentage of total executive branch employment, and a cumulative percentage for 2003 (U.S. Office of Management and Budget 2004).

Although the six departments listed in Table 30.1 deal with only selected national functions, they employ nearly three-quarters of executive branch civilian workers. Over half of executive branch civilian employment is related to preparing for future wars (Department of Defense), preventing attacks on the homeland (Department of Homeland Security), or coping with the human costs of past wars (Department of Veterans Affairs). Lesser numbers of professionals and support employees are involved in the three other departments which collect taxes, direct social welfare programs, and oversee the administration of justice.

Involved in the work of the departments listed in Table 30.1 is the full range of Mosher's general and public service professionals, from security strategists, to attorneys, to accountants, to contract negotiators, to medical doctors. The civilian employees of the federal government, like their military counterparts, represent well the concept of professionals *in* and of government. And the levels of professionalism are increasing. The Congressional Budget Office reported in 2001 that the federal workforce had become better educated and more professional than in 1985. The upper echelon white collar component of that workforce had grown to 24% professional, 32% administrative, and 19% technical (Congressional Budget Office 2001).

C. State–Local Employment (Including Professionals in Government)

Despite scholarly attention to professionals in the national government, any reference to professionalism in the civilian public sector is, in the main, a reference to the state–local sector. This is because state–local employment surpasses federal employment by multiples of four to five to one. Within the state–local sector the local sector is two to three times greater than that of the state. Because of the significant interstate variation in the functional assignment of responsibility,[*] combined state and local government employment in the major functions are rank ordered in Table 30.2 by full-time employment per 10,000 population, percent of total state–local employment, and cumulative percent of total state-local employment.

Most state–local public employment is concentrated in few functions, as at the national level. Over half the total is in education—elementary, secondary, and higher. By training, experience, traditions, and codes of ethics, those employed in education represent a major segment of the professionals in government. Aside from those in education, professionals in considerable numbers are engaged in other state–local functions. Many of these professionals, along with technical and semi-skilled workers, are involved in custodial work—caring for those who are ill or need help in coping in contemporary society (hospitals) or controlling people who have broken the law (corrections). Police protection accounts for nearly 6% of state–local employment. Maintaining basic transportation systems (streets and highways) accounts for another major group of workers. The six functions listed in Table 30.2 account for 72.2% of state–local public employment.

Another perspective on the penetration of state–local employment by the professions can also be seen in earlier data (Table 30.3) gathered by the Equal Employment Opportunities Commission (US Equal Employment Opportunity Commission 1992). For each state, EEOC reported employment in several occupation categories, *exclusive of education*, by the state and its local governments.

The EEOC category labels are descriptive. Criteria used to designate jobs holders as professionals are familiar to those who have worked with the scholarly literature. Professionals possess "specialized and theoretical knowledge which is usually acquired through college training or through work experience and other training which provides comparable knowledge"

---

[*] Because of differences among the states as to the assignment of functional responsibilities to state and/or local governments, it is necessary to combine state and local employment for comparative purposes. Table 30.2 lists the major, but not all, state–local functions.

TABLE 30.2
State and Local Public Employment by Major Function, 2002

Function	Full-time Employment Per 10,000 Population 2002	Percent Total State–Local Employment	Cumulative Percent
Elementary/secondary education	223.44	40.3	40.3
Higher education	68.32	12.3	52.6
Hospitals	32.58	5.9	58.5
Police	31.52	5.7	64.2
Corrections	24.96	4.5	68.7
Streets and highways	19.37	3.5	72.2

Source: U.S. Bureau of the Census, 2002.

(US Equal Employment Opportunity Commission 1992, xxxv). The occupations included in the category cover the gamut of professionalism. Among them are social workers, doctors, registered nurses, economists, dieticians, lawyers, system analysts, engineers, vocational rehabilitation counselors, librarians, management analysts, airplane pilots, and navigators.

Even with education excluded, professionals *in* government dominate state–local employment. The Professional category is the largest in Table 30.3 and accounts, on average, for 23.2% of the state–local total. There is interstate variation in the employment of professionals but the variation is generally less than in the other categories as the coefficient of variation for professionals is the next to smallest in the table.

D. ASSESSING PROFESSIONALS OF GOVERNMENT

In their appraisal of federal personnel, Lane and Wolf (1990, 63) cited three types of competencies which were relevant to discussions of public sector professionalism:

> First, there are the technical competencies—the basic occupational skills necessary to execute the varied tasks of governance. Next are the program and agency competencies—those capabilities required to activate administrative processes which create and deliver programs and execute public policies. Third, there is governance competency—that composite of special abilities which federal workers must possess in order to work effectively in and among political institutions at all levels of governmental activity.

TABLE 30.3
State and Local Non-Education Public Employment by Major Job Category, 1991

Job Category	State Mean (N = 49)	Coefficient of Variation
Officials and administrators	6.2	21.9
Professionals	23.2	14.2
Technicians	9.2	22.7
Protective service workers	15.5	18.1
Paraprofessionals	7.7	30.6
Administrative support	17.6	12.7
Skilled craft workers	8.6	22.2
Service–maintenance	12.0	22.0

Source: U.S. Equal Opportunity Commission, 1992.

The first competencies, involving technical skills, are the domain of professionals in government. The second and third competencies, involving agency administration, policy implementation, and interorganizational communication and negotiation, have been perennial concerns of professionals of government.

Professionals of government have come to occupy pivotal decision and action posts in American government and politics. The quality of the decisions and actions is shaped by the talents of those in managerial and administrative leadership positions. Understanding the behavior of these leaders has been a central interest of public administration scholars, including those interested in public sector professionalism.

Professionals of government are the supervisors, managers, and executives from the career service who play a central role in determining the success or failure of government policies. The long-term performance of the modern administrative state is fundamentally determined by their talents. Responsibilities of professionals of government include, but are not limited to, components of program management (effective coordination of the implementation of public programs and the networks of program stakeholders involved), resource management (oversight of well-developed budgeting, accounting, information, and personnel systems), and policy management (guidance of strategic planning, priority setting, and system design and transformation).[*] Each of the management components includes technical and political elements, though in differing combinations. Over the course of a career the individual professional of government typically moves through a series of positions in which the skill and knowledge requirements shift from the more specialized and technical to the more conceptual and political.

Professionals of government are important because of their positions in governmental organizations rather than their numbers. As a proportion of the public sector workforce, the professionals of government component is limited. The Office of Personnel Management reports that in 1999 11.9% of the federal government's white-collar employees were managers and mainly supervisors and 10.0% of blue-collar employees were in supervisory jobs (Office of Personnel Management 1999).

Despite their limited numbers, professionals *of* government have received sustained attention at the senior levels and particularly in the Senior Executive Service. The attention is warranted. Those who achieve the upper grades of the civil service accept major responsibilities for policy management. Often they are expected to carry institutional memory, to be able to invoke intricate bureaucratic expertise, and to exhibit well-honed political dexterity. To be successful these higher civil servants need to become specialists in generalization (Smith 1984, 16).

This is easier said than done. Constitutional provisions for the separation and sharing of powers among the branches of government blur lines of authority and responsibility for civil servants. Though personnel systems have generally been designed to favor specialists over generalists, changes in the properties of generalization complicate matters. As federal policy has devolved delivery of services responsibility to state and local governments, promoted privatization of public functions, and supported contracts with third-party providers, senior managers have had to alter their approaches to government (Kettl 2002; Lane and Wolf 1990).

III. THE EVOLUTION OF PUBLIC ADMINISTRATION PROFESSIONALISM

Professionalism in the public sector has matured when it has been viewed as meeting particular needs. The view and the definition of needs have been determined by the political mood of the times, the content of issues dominating the public agenda, and the capabilities of professionals in

---

[*] The primary management categories—program management, resource management, and policy management—are drawn from Burgess (1975). Though Burgess was concerned primarily with management in local governments, his categories are obviously applicable to other levels.

and *of* government. Political mood, issue substance, and professional capability have not remained constant. Understanding public administration professionalism in the twenty-first century is facilitated by consideration of the domains of activity which determine professional capabilities and specific historic developments which have affected the emergence of the abstract knowledge and exemplary practices of professions.

A. DOMAINS OF PROFESSIONAL ACTIVITY

The structure of professions is supported by abstract knowledge. Utilization of abstract knowledge to define problems and to develop practical skills distinguishes professional occupations from craft occupations (Abbott 1988, 8). For any problem, the quality of the three modes of professional practice—diagnosis, inference, treatment—will be related to the professional's mastery of the extant body of abstract knowledge.

Abstract knowledge is developed and is sustained within the parameters of the theory based dominant paradigm guiding a profession or its subfields. Paradigms offer an overview of an area of inquiry. They provide a set of assumptions and givens that facilitate understanding the area of inquiry and instruct a professional how to deal with problems. Paradigms involve beliefs and forms of "disciplined inquiry, concerned with how we explore the world, how it is we come to systematize or order knowledge about the world, and what methods might be most appropriate for accomplishing that end" (Lincoln 1985, 31).

In a significant work, *The Structure of Scientific Revolutions*, Thomas Kuhn (1962) developed the thesis that, despite conventional thought, the history of the natural sciences was not one of linear, incremental additions to the accumulated knowledge in particular fields. Instead, a scientific field was dominated by a paradigm which tells the scientist about the entities that nature does and does not contain and about the way in which those entities behave (Kuhn 1962, 109). Episodic crises occur in the scientific field with the accumulation of disconfirming evidence in the conduct of normal science within the prevailing dominant paradigm. Such crises may lead to periods during which new paradigms emerge and compete to replace the prevailing dominant paradigm. The pattern is an ongoing one of dominant paradigm to normal science to expanded abstract knowledge to disconfirming evidence to paradigm crisis to competition for a new dominant paradigm.

The pattern has serious implications for a science or, by extension, a profession. Acceptance of a new dominant paradigm will initiate fresh questions deemed topics of relevant research, new methodologies, and new standards of proof. In time, academic programs, professional journals, and exemplary or best practices will adjust to conform to the logic of the new dominant paradigm. Those adhering to the displaced dominant paradigm will, in time, be viewed as obsolete and irrelevant to the science or profession.

For professions, the pattern of evolving paradigm to dominant pattern status to paradigm obsolescence is the product of developments within three domains of activity: paradigm generation, paradigm translation and advocacy, and paradigm implementation.

1. Paradigm Generation

Paradigm generation consists of intellectual activities leading to knowledge systems of a profession which describe phenomena, explain causal relationships, and lead to useable exemplary practices better than the knowledge systems of competing professions. Early in its development, a profession's abstract knowledge system may be rough and incomplete. New paradigms may be based upon insights gained from disconfirming evidence in normal science research related to the prevailing dominant paradigm. Or the new paradigms may result from a borrowing of concepts and approaches from other fields, as public administration theorists have borrowed from business administration, economics, psychology, and organizational theory. Regardless of source, the resulting paradigms are whole or partial and involve explicit or implicit statements of how professionals should relate to the context of practice.

Paradigm shifts often lead to periods of competition and even conflict within professions, as in medicine and law in the past (Freidson 1970; Larson 1977). The recent history of public administration has been marked by competition between such alternative approaches to governing as market government, participative government, flexible government, and deregulated government (Peters 1996). The competition and conflict may be beneficial to a profession's future performance but disruptive in the short term. Ostrom (1974, 11–12) notes:

> If the methods of studying, teaching and practicing the subject matter… have become problematical, then the profession can*not* have much confidence in what it professes. The practice of a profession rests upon the validity of the knowledge which it professes. When the confidence of a profession in the essential validity of its knowledge has been shattered, that profession should be extraordinarily modest about the professional advice it renders while keeping up its appearance.

For some professionals in government new paradigms have emerged from the confluence of certain critical factors. Thus, for example, the character of military professionalism in the United States and other nations has been shaped by revolutions in military affairs (RMA). Such revolutions involve a paradigm shift in the nature and conduct of military operations. An RMA typically comes about from the proper combination of technology, organization, and doctrine, resulting in a transformation of warfare and the core competencies of warfare (Hundley 1999, chap. 2). So with the combination of airplane and aircraft carrier technologies, carrier fleet organization, and new doctrine, sea warfare was transformed. Similarly, the evolution of nuclear weapons, long range delivery systems, and mutual assured destruction doctrine, the nature and character of post-World War II warfare was fundamentally and qualitatively different from pre-World War II warfare.

2.   Paradigm Translation and Advocacy

The generation of new paradigms and abstract knowledge frequently has been done in very select research universities and independent research institutions which have primary responsibility for a profession's academic knowledge system. The system "excels at invention precisely because it is organized along abstract lines, rather than syndromic ones. It can make connections that seem nonsensical within practical professional knowledge, but that may reveal underlying regularities that can ultimately reshape practical knowledge altogether" (Abbott 1988, 54).

Practicing professionals in their day to day work rely less on abstract knowledge than on concrete recipes for concrete cases (Goode 1969, 282). If the academic knowledge system, based on the Paradigm Generation domain, is to be of relevance to practitioners it must be translated into a useable form, that of doctrine. Professional doctrine provides principles of action and "teaches what to think and what to do, rather than how to think and how to be prepared to do it." Academic scholars are apt to forget about the vital intermediary function that doctrine plays between ideas and behaviour. Scholars write theory, they do not write doctrine (Gray 1999, 36).

In the Paradigm Translation and Advocacy domain abstract knowledge is translated into professional doctrine through academic curricula, professional associations, textbooks, and in-service training programs. In the domain, representatives of key institutions become intellectual bridges between paradigm generators and paradigm implementers. The bridging function becomes ever more salient as information and knowledge increasingly become power resources and relevant to client issues.

Cases of expanded translation-advocacy activity in professions illustrate the domain. In the post-Civil War years internal pressures for more mature professionalism led the military services to form branch schools for in-service officers, and the Naval War College (1884) and Army War College (1901) for advanced training for senior officers. Early in the twentieth century a number of universities established public administration programs to train individuals for work in municipal administration (1914–1930) and national administration (1933–1941) (Keyssar and May 2003). More recently (1960s to the present), many such programs shifted focus from more traditional public administration to public management and public policy analysis (Stokes 1996).

The most significant institutions in this domain have been universities and their professional schools. Within universities, neophyte professionals receive the accumulated abstract knowledge and the state of the art of the profession, are socialized to professional norms, and develop some sense of professional identity. Training and experience inculcate an orientation to the world, a vocabulary, and common ways of perceiving and structuring problems and of attacking and of solving them (Mosher 1978, 147).

The university and its faculty serve a number of additional profession-related functions. In evaluating the student's presentation of self and intellectual ability, the university performs an initial screening operation, weeding out individuals who do not fit prevailing professional norms or criteria. Faculty members in professional schools, free of the constraints of real world practice, are able to articulate normative visions of how the profession might serve the world. As centers of basic research, major universities have expanded professions' core knowledge systems and innovative practices. The new core knowledge is translated and transmitted to new students in the regular curriculum and to professionals in the field through mid-career training programs.

3. Paradigm Implementation

If the outcomes of the first and second domains prove appropriate, the success or failure of a particular paradigm will be determined by the quality of the implementation of derived doctrine and practices by a profession's practitioners. The derived doctrine and practices must work, must be as useful, or more useful, than those in effect. Acceptance of the new doctrine and practices in a variety of field settings are prerequisites of paradigm implementation.

As in the public and private policy realms, implementation success for professional practice is contingent on a number of factors. Most fundamental is the validity of the theory and related assumptions of the paradigm. The absence of disconfirming evidence during the implementation of the paradigm's doctrine and practices strengthens the claims of its supporters; the more disconfirming the evidence, the weaker their claims.

Also important for implementation success is the delivery performance of implementers (Winter 2003, 206) shaped by the training, experience, and skill level of practitioners. Exemplary practices based on a valid paradigm doctrine but carried out by less competent practitioners may lead to unsatisfactory results. Alternatively, unsatisfactory results may result when competent practitioners working in networks of professions or organizations find successful implementation of exemplary practices thwarted by insufficient resources, varying levels of organizational commitment, or coordination complexity (O'Toole 2003). Where unsatisfactory results are too frequent, a profession may reject the paradigm and derived practices or a clientele may question the competence of the practitioners and look to other professions for help.

To a significant degree, the progress of a profession seeking or maintaining jurisdictional dominance will be determined by clients' perceptions and judgments as to which of available professions is most qualified to deal with their problems. Again, professions compete for control or a share of control of problem jurisdiction. Inter- and intra-profession competition continues for jurisdiction control even when a problem remains essentially the same. Clients, and their society's culture, can transfer their allegiance from one profession's (or faction within a profession) modes of diagnosis, treatment, and inference to another's. This has been the case, on occasion, for public administration professionalism as for medicine, law, and religion.

The three domains of professional activities, as presented, are rarely precise steps in an exercise beginning with the formulation of a paradigm and concluding with practitioners using translated abstract knowledge and derived skills. In professional work the sources of new knowledge and skills are many. New approaches to problems may bypass the first two domains and come out as policies are implemented; "... practitioners are continually designing and taking action, as is increasingly being realized, on the basis of 'theories-in-use' that are often tacit and taken for granted" (Argyris 1991, 338).

B. Public Administration as Paradigms in Effect

Advancing cooperation in a complex and globally interdependent society is a primary task before public administration professionals. The state of public administration professionalism confronting the task in the early years of the twenty-first century is the end product of fits and starts over the past century and a quarter in the three domains outlined. Understanding of the contemporary field will be heightened by consideration of the major fits and starts.

Limiting the assessment to a century and a quarter is to some extent artificial. The study and practice of public administration did not begin in the nineteenth century. Some form of administration has been present in all societies. As James Fesler (1982) has reminded, financial administration, development of a career service, and field office oversight had roots in twelfth-century England and thirteenth-century France. Early in the history of the United States, issues of proper administrative arrangements were studied and debated (Rohr 1986), an administrative structure was established by Federalists and Jeffersonians (Van Riper 1958), and administrative practices were implemented (Crenson 1975; White 1951, 1954).

In the following sections, reference is made to dominant paradigm, public administration, and management practices. The references to a dominant paradigm indicate that, for purposes of the analysis, a paradigm was in place which, with modifications, underpinned the professional public administration community until the latter decades of the last century. On this, Frederickson and Smith (2003, 207) point out that "[f]or virtually all the twentieth century, public administration was synonymous with bureaucracy, hierarchy, and accountability."

The paradigm and the public administration orthodoxy that it generated viewed government as the primary and logical instrument for solutions to social, economic, and foreign problems. These problems were to be solved or ameliorated by way of public law, regulations, and financing. Public administration professionals—professionals in government and professionals of government—served as agents of the paradigm and were accountable for administration of the public sector. The legitimacy of the dominant paradigm was supported by the politics–administration dichotomy, a separation of the formulation of policy, the responsibility of the elected office holder, and the implementation of policy as efficiently as possible under the law, the responsibility of the professional public administrator.

The resulting bureaucratic structure presumed the importance of a single center of public power and authority. From that came precepts for guiding public administration professionals. The precepts were espoused by such figures as Wilson, Goodnow, Taylor, White, Willoughby, Gulick, and Urwick, and were evident in the 1937 report of the President's Committee on Administrative Management. The precepts emphasized hierarchical arrangements, clear lines of authority, technical proficiency, and political neutrality of career administrators.

Advanced by the paradigm was the importance of developing administrative capacity and promoting democratic control as well as "recognition of the policy-making roles of civil servants, the inevitability of administrative discretion, the importance of persuading the courts to formally recognize the necessity for administrative discretion [and] the concomitant requirement for responsible conduct by managers and civil servants ..." (Lynn 2001, 151). Attention was also directed to what modern scholars refer to as public management structures and processes of executive government (Pollitt and Bouckaert 2004, 13). This included basic management skills in such areas as planning, staffing, coordinating, and budgeting.

Through the century there were numerous modifications in the dominant paradigm. Some related to basic assumptions, others to management practices. Following World War II was an assault on traditional thinking (Lynn 2001, 145), initially by Herbert Simon and Robert Dahl and subsequently by Dwight Waldo. These scholars and others offered criticisms and new perspectives on public administration and the expansive administrative state. They rejected as simplistic the pre-war guiding principles and found the politics–administration dichotomy contrary to empirical evidence, "in practice, administration [was] not a technical and value-neutral activity separable form politics. Administration is politics" (Frederickson and Smith 2003, 41).

The criticisms and new perspectives were important and stimulated contributions to theory building. Nonetheless, they were more in the form of disconfirming evidence about the dominant paradigm than to articulation of a new paradigm. Arguments were to the validity of the precepts of the existing paradigm and the need for new analytical approaches for understanding behavior within it. Both in theory and practice the hierarchical bureaucratic state was accepted as still the primary and logical instrument for solutions to societal problems. For Frederickson and Smith (2003, 207–208): "The theoretical landscape of public administration changed, but its professional and empirical reality remained stable."

In the following analysis developments are discussed relative to the prevailing dominant paradigm as portrayed above. For competing paradigms discussion centers on three—new public administration, public choice, and new public management. Also assessed are two major management innovations—the Planning, Programming, Budgeting System (PPBS) and Network Management in intergovernmental relations. If fully adopted and implemented either would be, or would have been, a major change in approaches to administration, possibly constituting a new dominant governing paradigm.

C.   DELINEATING THE BOUNDARIES OF THE FIELD: 1880–1910

The 1880s is a timely starting point for any assessment of public administration professionalism. Events of that decade led to theoretical thinking on professionals of government and fundamental alterations in the conditions of government employment. Though the theory guiding the alternations was partial and underdeveloped, action on applied problems was taken.

The Pendleton Act of 1883 was one such action, significant for creating a legal arrangement for professionalism to develop in the public sector. Providing for competitive examinations, tenure, and political neutrality, the act set into place the minimal requisites for a career service (Van Riper 1958, chap. 5). From the outset, the service was to be one in which individuals were recruited and tested for abilities instead of political patron support.

Adoption of the Pendleton Act marked the merger of paradigm assumptions and political forces supportive of reform for disparate reasons. The nineteenth-century regime of political parties and courts as the principal institutions of governing was overtaken by the Progressive Movement. Agitation for a career civil service, in the European model or some American variant, was of long standing. Emerging business and professional classes recognized the need for state building and a national administration more competent than that of political parties and courts to cope with the interdependencies of an urbanizing and industrializing society (Skowronek 1982; Wiebe 1967). Those opposing city political leaders and party organizations supported civil service reform more as a means of eliminating patronage than of increasing administrative competence or management professionalism.

Because professionalism requires a structure of merit, tenure, rules, and career paths, the Pendleton Act was of fundamental importance to the public administration field. Its importance was as much symbolic as real. Protection of employees was limited, involving clerks and technicians but only 11% of federal personnel. The Act affected federal government employees in an era when most governing was at the state and local levels. When the act passed, many reformers, who would later play major political roles and define the field of public administration, were outside the governmental apparatus. Dominant factions of the major political parties were not committed to neutral competence and merit in all governmental positions. According to Skowronek (1982): "The merit system was born a bastard in the party state. The support it had gained among the party professionals was that of another weapon in the contest for party power. The status of a merit civil service in the heyday of American party government remained uncertain at best."

If the 1883 Pendleton Act stands as a major case of policy action affecting public administration professionalism, Woodrow Wilson's (1887) essay The Study of Administration stands as a major early effort at articulating the essential ideation and dominant paradigm for the profession. Though the essay "wasn't widely read or cited until it was reprinted in 1941" (Lynn 2001), it serves as a benchmark in the development of the field's discrete body of abstract knowledge. For Wilson, a paradigm of administration had been developed in France and Germany which could be transferred to the United States.

Such a paradigm of administration was essential for government in action, for the executive branch of government to run a constitution. The paradigm was concerned with government as a field of business (Wilson 1887, 209) and the effective and efficient performance of the machinery of government. Attention was to be directed to important matters apart from the "hurry and strife of politics" or the debatable ground of constitutional study (Wilson 1887, 209–210). Essential for the improvement of governmental performance and the utilization of good business practices was a cadre of professionals in administration. To Wilson (1887, 216), "[a] body of thoroughly trained officials serving during good behavior we must have in any case; that is a plain business necessity."

Design of a field and science of administration presented major intellectual dilemmas for the emerging paradigm. Viewing administration as the province of executive bureaucracies required Wilson and others to deal with fundamental constitutional issues of the separation of conflicting values of democracy and efficiency. If thoroughly trained officials and public administration professionals were to practice the science of administration, it was necessary to distinguish the boundaries between their activities and those of elected and appointed political leaders.

Effective administration was important to Wilson. The mode of operations of existing governments was not geared for an interdependent industrial society (Skowronek 1982, 35). A public sector confronting the emerging social and economic changes of the United States in the late nineteenth century needed to support the development of practitioners of administration and to permit them to apply scientific techniques to public problems. Along with his fellow reformers, Wilson "was caught up in the pressing issues of the day, namely, how to make politics less open to the influence of the spoilsmen, less prone to political abuse, and more representative of the general public interest rather than of special interests" (Stillman 1973, 585). While practitioners had to recognize that public opinion guided their actions, they were to be protected from the excesses of democracy and from meddling by politicians. Undue public involvement in administration would be a clumsy nuisance and akin to a rustic handling delicate machinery (Wilson 1887, 215).

A more fully developed theoretical statement on the place of administration in government was Frank J. Goodnow's *Politics and Administration*. Goodnow (1900, 22) delineated the principal functions of government:

> There are… in all governmental systems two primary or ultimate functions of government, viz. the expression of the will of the state and the execution of that will. There are also in all states separate organs, each of which is mainly busied with the discharge of one of these functions. These functions are, respectively, Politics and Administration.

Activities are to one or the other of these ultimate functions. Legislatures busy themselves with politics and the expression of the state's will. Administration as execution of the state's will is carried out by the judicial and executive branches. Within the executive branch, a distinction is to be made between executive authorities engaged in executive functions and certain administration authorities engaged in distinctly administrative functions. Among the distinctly administrative functions are, for example, the "semi-scientific, *quasi*-judicial and *quasi*-business or commercial activity—work which has little if any influence on the expression of the true state will" (Goodnow 1900, 85).

Because executive authorities are responsible for carrying out the will of the state, they must be subject to the political control of the legislature. Those in the higher divisions of the administrative system who have a determining influence on questions of policy (Goodnow 1900, 91) should also be subject to political control and not have tenure. However, the work of lesser administrative authorities and clerical and ministerial employees is such that political influence over their conduct must be avoided.

Goodnow proposed that distinctly administrative activities be carried out by a force of governmental agents absolutely free from the influence of politics. The administrative agents would enjoy tenure because expertise and excellent work could result only from long experience on the job. They would thus be able to carry out their mission: "the exercise of foresight and discretion, the pursuit of truth, the gathering of information, the maintenance of a strictly impartial attitude toward the individuals with whom they have dealings, and the provision of the most efficient possible administrative organization" (Goodnow 1900, 85).

That turn-of-the-century government was in need of improvement is hardly debatable; Wilson (1887, 201) referred to the poisonous atmosphere of city government as well as to "the crooked secrets of state administration, the confusion, sinecurism, and corruption ever and again discovered in the bureaux at Washington." Wilson and Goodnow articulated a logic for the emergence of professionals *in* government and professionals *of* government. If there was to be a public administration professionalism, there first had to be some notion of the content of that professionalism. Drawing upon democratic and non-democratic European systems for illustrations of the successful use of administrative practices, Wilson and Goodnow gave an argument for a United States based public administration.

The Wilson–Goodnow argument was important. Significant administrative capacity building called for a governing paradigm which supported a jurisdiction, in Abbott's terms, wherein the separation of politics and administration was viewed as legitimate. With the separation, an emphasis could be placed on a politically neutral professionalism, science, and rationality in problem diagnosis, inference, and treatment. The paradigm and jurisdiction would be essential for an expanded national government during the New Deal, later in the twentieth century.

The locus of concern, however, from the late nineteenth century until well into the twentieth century, was not national but local government. Academics, journalists, and reformers, aligned in the Progressive Movement and interested in public issues, focused much of their attention on city governments.[*] There were episodic and dramatic strains on the national and state governments— wars, depressions, and scandals. And there were responsibilities of the national and state governments that significantly affected the pace of social and economic development—foreign affairs, fiscal policy, postal service, regulatory activities, and judicial decisions. But in the aggregate— personnel, expenditures, programs—to refer to governing and governmental capacity prior to 1930 was to refer to local governments.

The attention paid by reformers to the governing of larger cities was justified. At the time, the distribution of patronage was a major dynamic of national politics which led to the assassination of a president. The dispersion of executive authority impeded business-like administration at the national and state levels, but the absence of rational, efficient, and effective government was most apparent in growing cities. The big-city political boss, controlling jobs, contracts, and party organization, was able to provide a structure for overcoming administrative fragmentation and get things done. When reformers attempted to remove the boss, they proved to be mornin' glories

---

[*] At the time of major publications by Wilson and Goodnow, the governments receiving the most attention and viewed as most in need of administrative expertise were at the local level. Before and after *Politics and Administration*, Goodnow wrote extensively on city government and politics (Goodnow 1897, 1904)

(Riordon 1963, 17); they came to office but did not remain. Even when good men were elected, their best intentions were subverted by autonomous city agencies, personnel loyal to the political party organizations, and the lack of a usable science of administration.

The contributions of urban America to public administration were substantial. Ideas applied initially to concrete issues in local governments influenced subsequent developments in the entire field. Advances in budgeting and financial management, for example, would be tested at the local level before they were adopted at other levels. Mosher (1975, 8) notes, "Public administration as practice, as field of study and as self-conscious profession, began in the cities." Activists in the Progressive and municipal reform movements heightened civic awareness of the administration, management, and policies of larger cities.

It was recognition of the need for a source of accurate data and innovative solutions to city problems that led to the establishment of the New York Bureau of Municipal Research. Training at the Bureau and at university-based public administration programs (Syracuse, Michigan, Columbia, Stanford, and others) was directed to the preparation of experts qualified to deal with urban management issues (Stone and Stone 1975). The intellectual and experiential bases brought by Charles Merriam, Louis Brownlow, and Luther Gulick to the reorganization of the presidency in the 1930s were the result of professional careers spent on theoretical and applied issues of municipal government and administration (Karl 1963).

Adaptations from the Progressive Movement through the New Deal contributed to the coming of age the modern administrative state (Luton 2003, 172). A belief in the curative potency of empirical knowledge and scientific methods emerged in the public and private sectors of the late 1800s and early 1900s. On the period, Karl (1963, XI) states:

> The more 'scientific' the study of society became, both in method and in principle, the less 'political' it could be, the less subject to compromise and the tradition of the 'deal.' Scientific truth, if it were indeed scientific, could not be made more or less true by agreement, or by majority decision, or, above all, by personal preference.

The belief, coupled with heightened middle-class aspirations and improvements in technologies, was supportive of professionalism in many local government fields. Education, public health, law enforcement, and engineering were increasingly staffed by functional professionals who, in turn, were controlled by professional norms and professional organizations. Thus began the growth in the number of professionals in government.

A major advance for professionals of government was the formulation and promotion of the city manager plan in the first two decades of the century. The city manager was not and never has been either an ideal type or the typical case of public administration professionalism. The city manager plan did, though, incorporate the concepts of those concerned with a science of administration and public administration professionalism. Separation-of-powers issues, so bothersome to students of national government, were dealt with by allocating political and policy powers to a non-partisan city council, a single elective board of directors; responsibility for administration was vested in a professional manager. The advantages of such an arrangement were assumed to be clear to any businessman. "For counsel, many minds are needed; for execution, a single head is required" (Childs 1914, 96).

The city manager plan, as it evolved, structured boundaries of sorts between politics and administration as called for by major scholars of public administration (Stillman 1974, 11). Sophisticated theorists, James Svara (1985, 1990) in particular, have pointed out that the distinction was never a simple politics–administration dichotomy but a continuum—mission, policy, administration, and management. City council was to dominate the mission/policy end of the continuum and the manager the administration, management end. Like their counterparts in the corporate world, city managers were to bring to issues their training in and knowledge of the principles of effective management. They were to recognize the relationship between good government and planning, organization, and detailed issue research. In government, the policy process understandably involved conflict but the neutrally competent manager was charged with implementing policies as effectively, efficiently, and economically as possible. Though the manager's term was controlled by city council, tenure in office was contingent on meritorious performance.

The nature and severity of problems determined the level of expertise a manager brought to a city. Government in smaller communities was primarily about physical development and utility matters; therefore, the city manager should be a practical city engineer. For larger communities, "broad executive experience would of course be a major requirement. Regardless of community size, skill in municipal administration was to be the primary criterion for employment (Childs 1914, 96).

The city manager plan was a major development in the evolution of public administration professionalism (Nalbandian 1991). Embodied in the plan was a faith that, independent of political factors, effective management could enhance the administrative capacity of communities. This faith remained intact long after many in the public administration field had changed perspectives on the separation of politics and administration. Attesting to the continuing strength of the faith has been the production of a voluminous literature on urban administration by scholars and the managers' professional association and establishment of academic and in-service training programs for city managers.*

D. The Transformation of Public Administration: From Reform to Professionalism: 1910–1930

Highlighting the city-manager plan oversimplifies a complex reality. Even in the mature years of the plan, from the end of World War II to the 1980s, city managers constituted a minority of public administration professionals. Yet the highlighting is useful. In its formative years, the plan embraced early tenets of a public administration paradigm. The manager's primary responsibility was to execute policy decided by members of city council as elected representatives of the community. Possessing the necessary knowledge, skills, and talents, and operating in a centralized and hierarchical organization, the city manager could assure the council and the community effective and efficient policy execution. The importance of the emerging paradigm and the city manager plan should be emphasized. During the presidency of Franklin Roosevelt, Dimock (1937, 261) wrote:

> The city-manager form of government provides a model for state and federal administrations. They need the dual executive, the figurehead elective official and the efficient appointive manager, much more than does the municipality. After all, what city-manager cities have done is what almost every country outside the United States has found necessary and desirable. The elective head is a symbol of popular rule, of national unity; he relieves the efficient executive of most of the ceremonial obligations attached to political life, while the executive really gets the work done.

Emphasis on better city management was indicative of the pace of societal change. A robust, expansive capitalist economy made the businessman a folk hero and the private corporation a model of effective organization. Relevant or not, the standard for comparison of government's accomplishments would become, and into the future continue to be, the private corporation (Allison 1980; Downs and Larkey 1986). The period from 1910 to 1930 marked a transition in the extant body of abstract knowledge for a paradigm shift from one supportive of parties and courts and a local focus to one supportive of professional administration and, in time, a more national focus. By the mid-1920s, a field of public administration was identifiable. According to

---

* Good practices in general and functionally specific management are covered in the green book and other series of the International City Management Association.

Waldo (1968a, 146–147) this involved the confluence and mixture of three main currents—governmental reform, scientific management, and empirical political science.

The contributions of the scientific management current were especially great. Scientific management, as an ideology and an approach, grew out of the seminal work by Frederick W. Taylor on industrial production technology. During his career as a mechanical engineer, Taylor experimented with methods of identifying basic work elements so as to raise efficiency and productivity in manufacturing plants and ordinance arsenals. Eventually, Taylor's principles of scientific management and his belief in the efficacy of expert judgment were disseminated, in simplified form, to a larger audience through lectures and publications (Taylor 1911).

Whether or not Taylor's principles were valid to the world outside manufacturing plants, they were enthusiastically received. Expressly to those working for governmental reform (Nelson 1980, 173):

> His call for 'science' administered by experts was an appeal for the 'mechanism' of scientific management and the services of the expert, but it was also a formula for achieving the progressives' goal of eliminating the evils of American society without fundamentally altering institutions and values. Scientific knowledge, administered by objective, political neutral experts, would eliminate the waste associated with the factory, the corporation, the government bureau, and the school.

That efficiency goals could be achieved by scientific means justified the professionalization of management. During the inter-war period, progress was made in the institutionalization of expertise and the reduction of amateur and political control of such public functions as education, social work, law enforcement, and the military (Knott and Miller 1987, chap. 4). Scientific management altered general approaches to the structure and organization of government and specific approaches to more limited, though key, activities within government. The focus of personnel administration shifted from eliminating political machinations to testing for classified positions and identifying the most qualified, most expert candidates for those positions. Increasingly, the public service of professionals *in* government "began to revolve around positions rather than people, and the rank was securely vested in the former rather than in the latter" (Shafritz et al. 1986, 36). Status was to be a function of job characteristics rather than of individual characteristics; an individual would be a professional if a professional job was held.

Introduction of scientific management to the public sector would have long-term consequences for public administration professionalism. Functionally specific management training, as for school superintendents and police chiefs, complicated definitions of a generic field of public administration for education and training purposes. Emphasis by civil service agencies on position classification and searches for the one best individual for a given job would impede a career system for mobile general managers.

There were also positive effects. If the distinction between politics and administration drawn by Wilson and Goodnow was primarily a normative or analytical distinction, scientific management provided a basis for making the distinction operational. Politics and administration were separable in that they involved different criteria and goals. For professionals in public administration, as in scientific management generally, there was a primary focus and it centered on the "acceptance of 'efficiency' as both criterion and goal" (Waldo 1948, 60). That the focus and its implications were significant is suggested by Roscoe Martin (1952, 667):

> As applied to public administration, the credo of scientific management came in time to be characterized by attention to administration as administration without much stress on the *public* part of the term, by faith in 'principles,' by emphasis on science in administration, and by divorce of administration and values.

The focus on goals and criteria indicates that by the 1920s there was in the United States substance to a paradigm of public administration, another prerequisite to any public administration professionalism. A second indicator was the publication of introductory public administration textbooks by Leonard D. White (1926) and W. F. Willoughby (1927). Publication of the texts was a benchmark. In any professional field, textbooks perform the critically important function of paradigm translation and advocacy by transmitting basic information, interpreting specialized literature, and describing professional experiences. Textbooks also facilitate the socialization process by exposing students to the profession's jurisdiction and core analytic knowledge and techniques expected of those who would be professionals.

Although the White and Willoughby texts differed in fundamental respects, there were general similarities. Summarized in each was the substantial body of literature that had been produced on the business side of government (White 1926, 9) and on the actual conduct of governmental affairs (Willoughby 1927, 1). Though legal and political factors were recognized as important in determining policy (the legislature was, for Willoughby, a board of directors which dominated administrators), they were less significant than management in executing policy. In both texts, management was central to the objectives of public administration, the most efficient utilization of the resources at the disposal of officials and employees (White 1926, 2) and securing economy and efficiency in the actual administration of governmental affairs (Willoughby 1927, viii).

White and Willoughby pointed out to their colleagues and students that, while public and private organizations differed, within the public sector it was meaningful to speak of a public administration. To White (1926, 2), distinctions for levels of government were unnecessary because "the administrative process is a unit, … a process common to all levels of government." For Willoughby (1927, 1), administration "denotes the work involved in the actual conduct of governmental affairs, regardless of the particular branch of government concerned."

Conveyed to students by White and Willoughby were the dominant paradigm and jurisdiction of public administration in the 1920s. Problems before the public and legislative bodies could be resolved only through the efforts of the technically competent because the problems "are often entangled with, or become exclusively technical questions which the layman can handle only by utilizing the services of the expert" (White 1926, 6). To these technical questions would be brought the expert and a science of administration since (Willoughby 1927, ix):

> in administration, there are certain fundamental principles of general application analogous to those characterizing any science which must be observed if the end of administration, efficiency in operation, is to be secured, and… these principles are to be determined and their significance made known only by the rigid application of the scientific method to their investigation.

The 1910s and 1920s marked a transition from political reform supported by amateur civic activists to efforts on behalf of rationality and expertise in government. Public sector expertise became structured in university training programs and in organizations such as the City Managers' Association. The analytical and knowledge bases of public administration were expanded by municipal and state research bureaus, the Brookings Institution, the Social Science Research Council, and, by the early 1930s, the Public Administration Clearing House. Evidence of the practical effects of the period could be seen in the reorganization of state and local governments, centralization of executive authority, and sustained attention to budgeting and financial management, future major subfields of public administration professionals.

The most important outcome of the period was a perspective on the role of management expertise in government. This perspective drew from scientific management, related to the model of the private corporation, and sought empirically based principles. Research and publication were underway—including that of Mary Parker Follett, Elton Mayo, and Fritz Roethlisberger (Gross 1964, chap. 7)—which, along with later work by Chester Barnard (1938) and others, would significantly modify the perspective. For a time there was a paradigm and an orthodoxy that shaped theory and action. Caiden (1984, 62) notes, "…it appeared on the eve of the Great

Depression that the American study of public administration was firmly committed to the search for an apolitical science based on nomothetic management principles."

E. Public Administration Professionalism and the Interaction of Orthodoxy and Political Reality: The 1930s

In the development of public administration professionalism, the 1930s and 1940s were years of profound change. The press of events during the Depression and World War II led to a major growth of government and forced attention of scholars and practitioners to broad questions of constitutional law and to practical matters of structure, organization, and staffing. Experience with the broad questions and practical matters produced, in time, significant debates over the abstract knowledge and dominant paradigm guiding the field. The period began with general acceptance of theories of public administration; the period ended with disagreements over the prevailing orthodoxy and fundamental principles.

In response to the depression, the Roosevelt administration sponsored a number of innovative and experimental programs and agencies. Much was done outside of normal channels. Nearly 60 new agencies and 100,000 persons were exempted from the merit system by Congress in the first two years of the New Deal (Van Riper 1958, 32); during Roosevelt's first term, 80% of 250,000 new workers were exempted from civil service (Polenberg 1966, 22). The innovation and experimentation required creative use of the commerce, general welfare, and necessary and proper clauses of the US Constitution to legitimate supremacy of the national government in the federal system and of the presidency within the national government (Rohr 1986, chap. 8). Constitutional matters were one aspect of the overall challenge of the 1930s to the continued emergence of a fully developed administrative state. The challenge also brought forth efforts to modernize the nation's civil service, to strengthen the president's management powers, and to provide federal aid in support of services administered by state and local governments. Substantial theoretical and applied research during the 1930s centered on these efforts.

The meaning of professionalism in public administration, as in all fields, is determined by the interaction of professional practices and jurisdictions in which the practices are employed. In light of the magnitude of demands and the resulting need for competent personnel, proposals were put forth to overhaul public personnel systems. To observers, existing civil service structures were antiquated, designed to eliminate patronage abuses rather than to promote excellence. Testing procedures pigeonholed ambitious individuals and tenure provisions prevented the removal of deadwood. After extensive research and surveys, the Commission of Inquiry of Public Service Personnel (1935, 16) observed: "It is apparent that the weakest link in American democracy, the point at which we fall most conspicuously behind the other self-governing peoples, is in the appointive services where the great bulk of the work of modern government is carried on."

According to the Commission and scholars (White 1935, 18), weaknesses in the civil service could be overcome by developing a career service like those of Great Britain, Germany, and France. Career ladders would allow the ambitious to demonstrate their abilities. The special character of the career ladders is seen in the Commission's (Commission of Inquiry of Public Service Personnel 1935) differentiation of government work into five categories: unskilled, skilled and trades, clerical, professional, and administrative.

While the principle of equal opportunity prescribes that individuals be allowed to transfer between categories and even between levels of government, the Commission assumed that most would pursue careers in a single category. Careers would be defined by the knowledge and skill brought to a position. Those in the professional category—doctors, engineers, lawyers, chemists, teachers—make use of "special scientific knowledge and techniques" (Commission of Inquiry of Public Service Personnel 1935, 26) which are important but not particularly relevant to administrative positions.

Career administrators would carry institutional memories and control facts and technical information, making them indispensable to elected and appointed officials engaged in policy formulation. The primary contributions of administrators to governing were in policy execution; for once a new policy is adopted:

> it is the administrator who translates the decision into reality through planning, organizing, and delegating, staffing, directing, coordinating, and budgeting for the execution of the program within the limits assigned. In this process there are many important decisions of administrative policy to be made. ... Under a career administrative service, the administrator becomes extremely skillful in making the nice distinctions between political questions of policy and administrative questions of policy, because he rises in a service devoted to these matters (Commission of Inquiry of Public Service Personnel 1935, 34–35).

Familiarity with management practices, administrative experience, and sensitivity to the subtlety of the lines separating political and administrative matters were to set apart the administrative career service or corps recommended by the Commission and Leonard White from other professionals in government.

That devising entry-level tests for career administrators would be difficult was recognized. Emphasis was to be placed on general knowledge and training in such fields as economics, statistics, public administration, and political science (White 1935, 42). Higher education would prepare future administrators in a general way; mastery of the art of administration would come with training and experience (Friedrich 1935). Precedent for the combination of general education, training, and experience for such an elite group could be found in the Foreign Service of the State Department. And there were other precedents for the initial in-service training of young career administrators. Suggested White (1935, 60): "The discipline of the training period should be strict and exacting, comparable to that found at West Point or Annapolis, but without the regimentation characteristic of a military academy."

The Great Depression and New Deal policies raised issues beyond personnel. The public administration community also gave considerable thought to the problems of administrative management in the executive branch. An exposition of that thought was presented in a set of papers (Gulick and Urwick 1937) used in preparation of the report of the President's Committee on Administrative Management (1937). As viewed in the papers, public administration is a part of the more encompassing science of administration. That science, fundamentally, has to do with getting things done; with the accomplishment of defined objectives. Effectively practiced, administration increases efficiency, axiom number one in the value scale of administration. Achievement of efficiency depends on the division and organization of work so that group tasks are done "with the least expenditure of man-power and materials" (Gulick 1937b, 191–192).

The division and organization of governmental work is to be guided by principles that can be "arrived at inductively from the study of human experience of organization, which should govern arrangements for human association of any kind" (Urwick 1937a, 50). Of these principles the most central is the coordination of functions and activities, vertically and horizontally (Mooney 1937). The central principle dictates the overall pattern of authority and control. From it are derived other main principles—span of control, functional specialization, and division of activities into line and staff components. These principles provided frameworks and guidance for structuring the "major duties of the chief executive": planning, organizing, staffing, directing, coordinating, reporting, and budgeting or POSDCORB (Gulick 1937a, 13; Urwick 1937b).

The principles were applied by Brownlow, Merriam, and Gulick in the 1937 report of the President's Committee on Administrative Management. If the president was to be "the Chief Executive and administrator within the Federal system and service" (President's Committee on Administrative Management 1937, 2), it was necessary to enlarge his management capabilities and to restructure the executive branch as his domain. The president needed a small number of assistants as "arms of the Chief Executive" for budgeting, efficiency research, personnel management, and planning. So that the president would be the Executive as opposed to only one of many executives, treading his way around obstacles which he has no power to overcome, he would be authorized to continually reorganize the division of work among departments; and all governmental functions, including the activities of independent regulatory commissions, would be concentrated in twelve major departments.

Although the Committee's recommendations were not all accepted by Congress, the Report of the President's Committee on Administrative Management (the Brownlow Report) stands as a major policy statement. Mosher (1984, 66) states: "The tenets of the Brownlow report would soon become basic doctrine for students and practitioners of public administration and would so remain for decades to come." According to the report, public administration related to the executive branch of government. Organization of the branch was to be hierarchical, with clear lines of authority and responsibility to keep the executive's span of control limited. To assure efficient operations, the president could draw on career civil service employees for key line and staff positions for the White House staff, Bureau of the Budget, National Resources Board, or other jobs. The dynamic center of public administration professionalism was the executive branch, with the chief executive as the main actor at the center.

The language of the Brownlow report was that of the science of administration, emphasizing efficiency, expertise, and effective management. Staff assistance to the president was to be nonpolitical and provided by neutrally competent administrative experts (Hart 1987, 186). The language of the report was also nonpartisan. Nonpartisanship was not the equivalent of political neutrality and nonpartisanship proposals would not always lead to nonpartisan effects. There were immense political implications in the reasoning of the Brownlow Report and, to a lesser degree, in the earlier report of the Commission of Inquiry on Public Service Personnel. Extension of civil service coverage throughout the government, called for in both reports, meant New Deal appointees would become career government employees predisposed to New Deal social programs after Roosevelt left office. If chief executives and administrative structures were to control public policy in formulation and execution, given the concentration of substantive knowledge, technical expertise, and policy clientele in executive departments, linkages of the executives and structures to the citizenry would become more direct and primary in the political system. Other political institutions, such as legislatures and political parties, would decline in importance (Milkis 1987).

The relationship between changes in administrative form and changes in politics was complex. The relationship was recognized throughout the Brownlow Report in references to democratic values: "The forward march of American democracy at this point of our history depends more upon effective management than upon any other single factor" (President's Committee on Administrative Management 1937, 47).

Despite such statements, for some 1930s proponents of effective public administration a distinction had to be made between political and administrative concerns. Students of administration were to recognize and take into account the ways in which political conditions and frameworks impinge on and affect the practice of administration. But for a science of administration to be fully developed, such conditions and frameworks had to be viewed as a part of the environment of activities and practices related to the achievement of efficiency, the single ultimate test of value in administration. Only by concentrating on efficiency, and treating political and other factors as environmental, would it be possible to approximate more nearly the impersonal valueless world in which exact science has advanced with such success (Gulick 1937b, 193).

Evidenced in the academic writings and studies of applied governmental problems of the 1930s was a paradigm of administration most salient for public administration professionalism. The paradigm allowed for the delimitation of professional jurisdiction and professional concern and responsibility. Once these primary concerns and responsibilities were made explicit, subsidiary matters could be addressed. The acronym POSDCORB, describing the functional elements (planning, organizing, staffing, directing, coordinating, reporting, and budgeting) of executive work, could be the curriculum basis for educational programs to train individuals for the profession. Indeed, Stillman (1999, 52) notes:

> The field would no longer be simply scattered techniques of 'economy' and 'efficiency' *a la* Taylorism. Rather, POSDCORB laid a respectable intellectual basis for a far-broader, more unified American Administrative Sciences to grapple with the crises of the 1930s and 1940s.

A heightened sense of public administration professionalism was evidenced in other ways during the 1930s. The Public Administration Clearing House, incorporated in 1930, became an important source of information on advances in administrative subfields (Karl 1963, 118). Major research projects were undertaken by the Committee on Public Administration of the Social Science Research Council (Anderson and Gaus 1945; Clapp 1946). The expansion of the national government and the arrival of a fully developed administrative state gave to professors and their students' new short- and long-term career opportunities. A number of colleges and universities offered course work in public administration, training programs, and technical assistance to local officials by way of university-based research bureaus (Egger 1975, 56–57). A measure of the developing shared sense of professionalism and a united community of interests within a diverse public administration community was the founding of the American Society for Public Administration in 1939 (Pugh 1985, 476; Stone 1975). Commencing in 1940, the *Public Administration Review* became a major publication for theoretical and applied research.

F.   From Orthodoxy to Heterodoxy in Public Administration: 1940–1960

As field and profession in the late 1930s, public administration was characterized by clarity of purpose and focus. Field and profession were dedicated to efficiency in the conduct of government by trained professionals. Responsible to a chief executive who managed a holding company kind of operation, professionals performed best in a rationally designed organization. Their work was directly administrative or, in offices such as the Division of Administrative Management in the Bureau of the Budget, supportive of administrators. Those involved in administration were guided by a set of principles related to a theory and science of administration. Considerable effort was devoted to the formulation of definitions, propositions, and axioms supportive of the theory and the science (Gulick and Urwick 1937; Stene 1940).

Cautions were raised as to the legitimacy and feasibility of the paradigm of administration championed in the writings of Gulick, Urwick, Mooney, and others (Gaus et al. 1940). At the theoretical level, Dwight Waldo (1948) in *The Administrative State* claimed that little had been contributed, classical theory was crude, presumptuous, incomplete—wrong in some of its conclusions, naïve in its scientific methodology, parochial in its outlook. As to pedagogy and paradigm translation derived from the orthodoxy, Wallace Sayre stated that the White (1926) and Willoughby (1927) texts advocated "a closely knit set of values, confidently and incisively presented"; along with Waldo, Sayre "declared these values obsolete and applauded the field's movement toward heterodoxy" (quoted in Lynn 2001, 146). Broader critiques were made in literature on the actual operations of governmental agencies and the experiences of academics in administration; for the academics "the view from the inside looked dramatically different from the classical theories of Goodnow's, White's and Gulick's 'principles'" (Stillman 1982, 25).

The challenges and critiques resulted from a questioning of the influences of values, politics, and political power on, and in, administration. Close observation revealed, in Kuhnian terms, disconfirming evidence in the slippage between paradigm assumptions and the actual conduct of government. Professionals were not simply experts in techniques and substance; they were also participants in the policy process and, as officials in individual agencies, sought to augment their specific interests.

In a rapidly expanding public sector, particularistic strategies by professionals to protect their own specialties complicated central policy coordination. Direct involvement by administrative agencies in the policy process raised fundamental questions of professional accountability and the separability of policy development and implementation. Any empirically valid theory of public administration had to account for the effects of the triad described by Key (1942, 152): "The close communion of pressure group, congressional bloc, and subordinate elements of the administrative hierarchy obstructs central direction in the general interest."

Another body of thought, of long standing and related to the basics of public administration professionalism, concerns the exercise of discretion by public sector administrators. A common organizational arrangement, extending mainly from the 1930s on, is the administrative agency wherein career professionals are given considerable discretionary power to deal with very specialized areas such as communications and pharmaceutical drugs. In many instances, the discretionary powers combined investigative, prosecutorial, and adjudicative functions (Freedman 1978, 139) so as to assemble technical expertise and experience in dealing with very intricate problems. The career professional was thus able to serve the public interest by overriding the intrinsic limitations of the separation of powers doctrine.

As noted earlier, autonomy and independence are assumed to be crucial to all professionals by the very nature of their work—the application of special technical knowledge, judgment, and skill to problems. In the public sector this can create difficulties. Because legislative bodies cannot foresee all possible contingencies, the conduct of government requires that some power over decisions be delegated from legislators, as principals, to technical professionals of the career service, as their agents. Exercising independent judgment as to what should be done under particular circumstances in the implementation of policies, these professionals effectively make policy. A quandary of the public administration community has been the legitimacy of the discretionary authority delegated by elected officials to unelected professionals in and of government.

A general outline of positions on the quandary was drawn in the early 1940s in an exchange between Carl Friedrich (1940) and Herman Finer (1941). Both maintained that "responsible government required that public administrators be held accountable for serving the public interest" (Harmon 1995, 48). The essential issue was *how* to hold administrators accountable. Friedrich favored forms of self-control, Finer political controls. To assure responsible behavior by administrators exercising discretion, Friedrich looked to two factors: "… the responsible administrator is one who is responsive to…: technical knowledge and popular sentiment." For their use of technical knowledge, administrators are held to an objective or technical responsibility in that they must answer to professional colleagues in the fellowship of science, those fellows who are capable of judging his policy in terms of the scientific knowledge bearing upon it (Friedrich 1940, 13).

The second of Friedrich's factors, popular sentiment, relates to responsibility. The administrator exercising discretion in the policy process needs to be responsive to political forces as well as the technical. Responsible administrators are also responsive to subjective forces by anticipating reactions to their proposals from the media, public, and legislators.

For Finer, control of the career service and its exercise of discretion was essential to the survival of democratic government. The power of the state had so expanded that the weight and immensity of this behemoth, for our good as well as for our control, are well known to all of us. In democratic regimes, public officials are held responsible on the basis of three doctrines (Finer 1941, 336–337):

mastership of the public, in the sense that politicians and employees are working… [to meet]… the *wants* of the public as expressed by the public.

recognition that this mastership needs institutions, and… the centrality of an elected organ for its expression and the exertion of its authority.

the function of the public and of its elected institutions is not merely the exhibition of its mastership by informing governments and officials of what it wants, but the authority and power to exercise an effect upon the course which the latter are to pursue, the power to exact obedience to orders.

Following from these three doctrines, administrators are to be held responsible to the hierarchy of their agencies, the courts, and the authority of their superiors based on sanctions exercised by the representative assembly.

Answers to the quandary were reasonably clear to observers in the 1940s. The special nature of public administration made the linkages of administration and politics direct. Precisely because it deals with *public* concerns, public administration is called on to accomplish simultaneously multiple and sometimes conflicting goals. In a democratic government, values such as equity and citizen participation compete with efficiency (Appleby 1945, 1949; Dahl 1947; Waldo 1948). Diversity of goals and visibility separate public and private administration (Appleby 1945, 7):

> Government administration differs from all other administrative work to a degree not even faintly realized outside, by virtue of its public nature, the way in which it is subject to public scrutiny and public outcry. An administrator coming into government is struck at once, and continually thereafter, by the press and public interest in every detail of his life, personality, and conduct. This interest often runs to details of administrative action that in private business would never be of concern other than inside the organization.

To succeed in such an environment, the administrator coming into government and the career professional should have special qualities—"the ability to handle relationships in their larger and broader terms—the quality of philosophy"; 'governmental sense,' the ingrained disposition to put the public interest first; and the quality of public-relations or political sense (Appleby 1945, 43).

The qualities suggested by Appleby for top-level administrators indicated the centrality of political factors. A science of public administration had to account for political influence as an endogenous, rather than as an exogenous, variable. It is this influence that potentially reduces the applicability of a general science of administration to government. If administration is about efficient movement toward given ends, "in most societies, and particularly in democratic ones, ends are often in dispute; rarely are they clearly and unequivocally determined" (Dahl 1947, 3).

The fundamental issue is broader than ends and values. Bureaucratic resistance to central control and coordination, agency promotion of policy interests of clientele groups, and departmental pursuit of conflicting objectives reflected the dispersion of power in American society and the absence of a disciplined political party system. Determinants of effective public administration were based less in abstract principles than in power. In fact, "[t]he lifeblood of administration is power. Its attainment, maintenance, increase, dissipation, and loss are subjects the practitioner and student can ill afford to neglect. Loss of realism and failure are almost certain consequences" (Long 1949, 257).

During the 1940s, issues of politics, political power, and governmental performance were addressed in the research of V.O. Key (1949) on the southern states. Key's methods were adopted by scholars analyzing state politics in other regions (Fenton 1957; Lockard 1959; Munger 1966). Though tangential to theories to public administration and public administration professionalism, the findings of the state-based studies were, or should have been, troublesome. Cleavage bases in state politics were rooted in historic patterns of race relations, political party factionalism, and the timing of ethnic settlement. In such a setting, state politics were often little related to issues of the general public interest and effective administrative procedures. Judgments of public administration professionals were often not simply constrained, but were irrelevant to government practices.

G. Herbert Simon and New Concepts of Administration

Thinking on public administration professionalism during and after World War II was reshaped in basic ways by consideration of the place of values, politics, and political power in a science of administration. The reshaped thinking was, in turn, fundamentally challenged by the work of Herbert Simon. For purposes of this analysis of paradigm development and change, two aspects of Simon's manifold contributions are significant. The first is his reaction to the science of administration critiques related to values, politics, and power. The second is his specification of decision making as the critical unit of analysis for a true administrative science.

In his 1947 essay, Robert Dahl raised objections to the field's orthodoxy relating public administration to a set of principles of presumed universal validity; "basic problems of *public* administration as a discipline and as a potential science are much wider than the problem of mere *administration*" (Dahl 1947, 2). Definitions of universal principles of administration were handicapped by the importance of normative values in public administration, the complexity of human behavior, and the lack of knowledge regarding social and cultural influences on administration in different national settings.

Responding to Dahl, Simon (1947) argued the importance of distinguishing science from its applications. Theorists and students should focus on public administration as science and the creation of "a pure science of human behavior in organizations—and, in particular, governmental organizations, … and … raise a more solid theory on the foundations of social psychology." The alternative, for those concerned with applied problem solving and consideration of all relevant values, is to become public policy experts. The implications of the alternative for public administration professionalism are great, however. Noted Simon (1947, 202):

> For him who proposes to do work in the applied area, it will condemn a narrow specialization in any one area of political science, or even in the whole of it, in favor of both a broad and a deep training in political science, economics, and sociology—a return to the original meaning of political economy.

The emphasis by Simon on the relationship of public administration to an encompassing science of administration, as opposed to public administration as applied public policy or as political process, involved a shift within the dominant paradigm and an altered professional jurisdiction. Principles of administration from the 1930s were attacked for being like proverbs, internally inconsistent and contradictory (Simon 1946). For Simon, value and fact decision premises were the basic unit of analysis because "decision-making is the heart of administration, and… the vocabulary of administrative theory must be derived from the logic and psychology of human choice" (Simon 1957, xlvi).

It is through organizations, private and public, and administrative processes that individuals and groups cooperate to accomplish common goals (Simon et al. 1950). To describe and understand administration in terms of tested if–then relationships, it is necessary to study individuals in organizational settings. Organizational efficiency is ultimately determined by decisions and the factual premises of the decisions. The decisions are shaped by the qualities individuals bring to the organization and the incentives they gain relative to contributions made. Decisions are also affected by the formal and informal structures—the psychological bases of cohesion (Simon 1952, 1133)—of the organization; and the "environment of 'givens'—premises that are accepted …as bases for… choice" (Simon 1957, 79; Gore 1981).

Presented with problem stimuli, an organization's response is determined by its problem-solving capacity relative to the details of the stimuli. A familiar problem will elicit a performance program, a response—sometimes very elaborate—that has been developed and learned at some previous time as an appropriate response for a stimuli of this class (March and Simon 1958, 139). Unfamiliar problem stimuli call forth greater efforts and more extensive solution searches. These searches are bounded by human intellective capacities (March and Simon 1958, 169) and the realities of organizational behavior. Bounded rationality constrains the discovery of optimal solutions to problems. Limits on attention span, knowledge, time, and processes prevent consideration of all possible alternatives and result in a satisficing strategy, use of "a set of criteria that describes minimally satisfactory alternatives ..." (March and Simon 1958, 140).

Simon's work has had major implications for the study of public administration and the practice of public administration professionalism. His publications in the late 1940s and through the 1950s called for a change in research focus. Anyone seriously interested in the field was to use a scientific approach and the tools of science to describe and to evaluate, rather than to prescribe and to recommend, decision-making and organizational behavior. Participation in such research required immersion in psychology, sociology, and social psychology as well as sophisticated methodologies and techniques of data analysis.

These points of knowledge, methodologies, and techniques encompassed more than the work of Herbert Simon or of political science and public administration. The points reflect epistemological issues of the behavioral movement throughout the social sciences of the 1950s. Emphasis was on the unity of the social sciences and the need to cross disciplinary lines for conceptual frameworks, analytical approaches, and laws of behavior (Waldo 1954, 1956a). Professionals of public administration had to see the relationships between their goals and the frameworks of Weber and Barnard, findings of the Hawthorne experiments, Keynesian economics, Likert's use of survey research, and mathematical modeling. Such substantive knowledge was beyond the traditional areas of political science and the prevailing public administration paradigm.

Calls for a more scientific approach to public administration were not universally accepted. For some, the new approaches were unrealistic or basically flawed (Banfield 1957; Storing 1962). Others were more interested in the ethics of democratic administration and representative bureaucracy than in statistical validity. While the benefits of a fully developed causal model of public administration were recognized, so too were the difficulties of its attainment. If government was different from other enterprises, better descriptions and greater understanding of the differences might come from the insights of governmental experience than from controlled experiments. Post-World War II writings which furnished insightful speculation about the world of administrative reality were, in many instances, by political scientists who had served; they were "not closet philosophers, but men with experience as public administrators or consultants and with a background of direct observation of the phenomena which they seek to order for purposes of analysis" (Fesler 1957, 143).

Developments of the 1940s and 1950s were disconcerting to members of the profession. Those interested in a professional career faced difficult choices in their academic training. They were to become familiar with subjects ranging from political science and the other social sciences to mathematics, history, biology, literature, economics, and systems theory. The familiarity was necessary because administration is so large a subject, and still in many ways so dark, we should open upon it all the windows we can find (Waldo 1956b, 49). The breadth of knowledge relevant to public administration raised difficult pedagogical questions about any new paradigm translation Case studies, though of limited use for providing overarching frameworks, did give students a sense of the rich and variegated context of policy and decision making, as in business administration (Kaufman 1958). The teaching of mathematical modeling and operations research gave students the tools necessary for improving decisions and expanding the boundaries of bounded rationality (Simon 1960).

A diversity of knowledge, methodologies, and teaching methods was reflected in debates carried on in the field. To the extent any profession rests on a core body of analytic knowledge and a special technology, the debates suggested the absence of an accepted core for public administration professionals. Mosher (1956, 177) wrote of public administration in the mid-1950s:

> Perhaps it is best that it not be defined. It is more an area of interest than a discipline, more a focus than a separate science. Like administration itself, the study of administration must employ a variety of methods and approaches. It is necessarily cross-disciplinary.

Intense disciplinary debate may appear to outsiders as little more than esoteric arguments among academics. This is sometimes the case. However, over the long term, as the debates generate new paradigms and theories which are translated into journal articles and textbooks, the education and training of young professionals are reshaped. Perspectives from the education and training are carried into professional roles. Reality testing or senior colleague resistance may force the young professional to drop the perspective. Alternatively, if accepted, the new paradigm will redefine professional norms and eventually be incorporated into advice from consultants and staff to clients and superiors. The specialization of knowledge that characterizes professions is such that seemingly esoteric debates are of fundamental relevance as the stages of paradigm generation, translation and advocacy, and implementation are completed.

Proponents' claims on behalf of one or another approach did not halt the practice of public administration in the 1950s as policies were adopted, decisions made, and governing structures reorganized. The connection of public administration paradigms to practice in these matters is not easily stated because lags between paradigms and practice were in both directions. Some activities in the public sector were based on premises considered outmoded by particular academics. Other activities were ahead of dominant academic thinking. As in the past, the content of public administration professionalism was the product of the interplay of theorizing and real world activities.

Following World War II and into the 1950s there was much governmental reorganization and restructuring in response to a changing environment and conscious designs to improve governmental performance. Two commissions chaired by former President Herbert Hoover from 1947 to 1949 and from 1953 to 1955 characterized attempts to improve the capacity of government by conscious application of paradigms and principles of good administration. The bipartisan commissions studied, analyzed, and recommended changes in federal governmental structure and practices. Among the many contributions of the Hoover commissions to an understanding of public administration professionalism, two were especially important: the demonstrable use of theoretical frameworks in applied problem solving and consideration of a career civil service system with an elite corps of administrators.

Members of the commissions brought to their tasks great experience and a general perspective on government.[*] The commissions' reports reflected a belief in the close relationship between the structure of government and what government does. To improve what was being done, it was first necessary to develop an administrative system that gave the president appropriate organizational power and control. There was a best way to organize the executive branch and economy and efficiency would be brought about only by strict adherence to sound principles of executive branch organization (Seidman and Gilmour 1986, 4). The Hoover Commission Report of 1949 enunciated a philosophy of government and management, similar to that of the Brownlow Report of 1937: "As a statement of administrative philosophy, the goals of the first Hoover Commission were definitely in the tradition of the Scientific Management movement and of earlier reform efforts" (Moe 1982, 34). The focus on hierarchical structure, grouping of functions, avoidance of duplication and overlap, and the applicability of business practices in government were repeated in the work of the second Hoover Commission and in much of the work of little Hoover commissions at the state and local levels from the 1950s to the 1980s.

From the Hoover commissions also came analyses and recommendations regarding governmental employment, a career service, and senior administrators. The analyses and recommendations were to very practical matters in the management of large-scale government.

---

[*] In making a general point, this section may appear simplistic. There were important differences between the two commissions. The first was formed during a Democratic administration, the second during a Republican administration. In addition to the altered political milieu, there were changes in membership, staffs, mandates, and emphases of the commissions (Moe 1982).

At the national level alone, civilian employment increased from 580,000 in 1930, to 1,000,000 in 1940, over 3,700,000 in 1945, and 2,600,000 in 1952. The increases made for serious issues of management and control of more specialized technical employees. The issues were sufficiently serious that "during the decade from 1946 through 1956, there were more studies and analyses of various aspects of the federal service, both civil and military, than in the previous century" (Van Riper 1958, 516).

The changing size and scope of government through the New Deal and World War II heightened awareness of program interdependencies, interagency communications, and vertical and horizontal coordination, the stuff of management. At the city government level, such management was performed by the professional city manager. However, the federal service was based on fitting the technically proficient to specific jobs. Promotion to administrative positions often went to technicians with competence in fields far removed from administration, thus raising definitional questions about public administration as a true profession.

The technically proficient who were promoted faced difficulties; "educated as a specialist, recruited as a specialist, and honored as a specialist by his professional colleagues, he becomes uncomfortable with executive responsibilities for which he has had little preparation" (Randall 1956, 28). Typically proposed to reduce the discomfort were educational opportunities and programs to assist the specialist in gaining the knowledge and skills of the generalist administrator (Dimock 1958; Harder and Stephens 1956).

To deal with the inherent limitations of a position-based civil service the second Hoover Commission pressed for a senior civil service of 1500 to 3000 careerists, nominated by agency heads and appointed to the service by a special board (Macneil and Metz 1956, 36). As envisioned, the service would resemble the American military and the British administrative class. The imagery of military was drawn on in support:

> A general is a general, in full possession of rank, emoluments, and status whether he is in command of a division or army in the field, stationed at a garrison at home or on occupation duty, sitting behind a desk in Washington with duties large or small, or awaiting orders. He may be assigned to various types of mission, to varying responsibilities, at any place. ... Applying these standards to high-ranking civil officers, it would follow that an incoming administration would have available a corps of highly qualified civilian executives with protected status, ready for assignment wherever the political command thought advisable (White 1955, 330).

Despite discussions and steps initiated by executive orders during the 1950s, establishment of a senior service would be delayed until 1978. Adjustments were made to improve the existing system. The pool of recruits into the federal service, including entry-level management positions, was expanded and made potentially more diverse by the adoption in 1955 of the Federal Service Entrance Examination. Enactment of the Government Employees Training Act of 1958 legitimated and strengthened "the forms and varieties of in-service and out-training for staff improvement" (Stahl 1963, 31).

The second Hoover Commission's recommendation for a senior service raised issues pertaining to the essence of public administration professionalism. Among the most critical of the issues was (and is) the political constraint on strengthening the leadership group of the executive branch: "political executives, who would represent ... policy positions; senior civil servants, who would provide expertise and continuity in administration; program executives, who would contribute expertise and energy to new programs" (Sayre 1960, 294). While most discussion of improving the leadership group related to demands on the presidency, the fundamental issues related to executives throughout the federal system. At all levels of government, structuring the leadership core would prove more difficult than pointing up its need.

H. Even Greater Paradigm Diversity, Continued Public Sector Expansion, and Public Administration Professionalism in the 1960s

The heterodoxy facing professional students and practitioners of public administration during the 1950s increased even more dramatically in the 1960s. The pace and, on occasion, turbulent nature of demographic, social, economic, and political changes in domestic affairs and heightened Cold War tensions in foreign policy led to a challenging of basic assumptions of the prevailing dominant paradigms. Innovative management practices such as the PPBS and dramatic expansion of the federal government's involvement, by way of intergovernmental grants, in policy areas traditionally the province of state and local governments raised concerns about the adequacy of practitioner core knowledge and training.

Reflecting the field's diversity was a continuation of the debate on the nature of public administration. In a presentation late in the decade, Waldo (1968b, 10) urged his colleagues to consider a professional perspective as a way of countering a crisis of identity:

What I propose is that we try to act as a profession without actually being one, and perhaps even without the hope or intention of becoming one in any strict sense. ...

My favorite analogy is to medicine. By common consent, this is a profession; but it is also a congeries of professions, subprofessions, and occupational specializations, ramifying in fantastic complexity. It is science and art, theory and practice, study and application. It is not based on a single discipline, but utilizes many. It is not united by a single theory, but is justified and given direction by a broad social purpose.

The call to act as a profession without actually being one was to a distinguished group convened in 1967 to assess the scope, objectives, and methods of public administration. All did not concur with Waldo's crisis of identity. It was pointed out that the literature of public administration demonstrated progress in the building of partial theories (Sayre 1968). Others urged more theoretical, scientific, and comparative work on the administrative function in government and basic thinking on government as a total system (Riggs 1968).

Disagreements on the particulars of scope and objectives aside, conference participants recognized the enduring stresses in public administration. Theoretical and methodological emphases on behavioralism in political science made an applied public administration less welcome as a subfield of the parent discipline (Altshuler 1968). Even in a political science framework, the interdisciplinary concerns of public administration scholars raised questions as to how well their interests were served in that framework.

Tensions at play within the public administration community of the 1960s and beyond were most fundamental. A significant development of the period was the increased separation of the domains of paradigm generation and paradigm implementation. Stillman (1999, 69) notes that while in the pre- and post-World War II years there was "generally a close collaboration between practitioners and academics, during the 1966–1986 period, by comparison, a much sharper differentiation between theory and practice became evident throughout the field. ...[E]ntire academic careers developed within Public Administration [theoreticians] with little or no exposure to public administration [practitioners]." Further, within the community itself there were pockets of opposition to government and administration as practiced; "no recent era in US Administration Sciences witnessed a more intense outpouring of antistatist literature than from the late 1960s to the mid-1980s" (Stillman 1999, 60).

Competing paradigms evolved which, if not in direct conflict, were not complementary. In the academy, many faculty and students articulated a new public administration and redirected their attention from a fairly narrow definition of management and a primarily social–psychological focus on public organizations to a broader concern for system performance and humanistic concerns

(Golembiewski 1977a, chap. 2). Other faculty and students looked to economics and public choice for a theoretical basis for government action and a rationale for public policy.

I. THE NEW PUBLIC ADMINISTRATION

Humanistic concerns were related to the full gamut of issues that crowded public sector agendas and competed vigorously, and on occasion violently, for the attention of elected officials and the career bureaucracy. Governmental responses to the issues and the capacity of government to respond were questioned, particularly by younger university based members of the public administration community. To the academics, inadequacy of public responses to problems of poverty in the United States and to the morality of a system analysis based war in Vietnam reflected, in part, the inadequacy of the current dominant public administration paradigm. Needed were new paradigms, assumptions, and exemplary practices—a new public administration.

A seminal event in the formation of the new public administration was a 1968 conference at Minnowbrook, a conference center of Syracuse University. Brought together at Minnowbrook were scholars concerned with the theoretical foundations, research foci, and methodological sophistication of public administration as an academic field and those who were more action directed, more concerned with the impacts or failures of public policies. Presentations from Minnowbrook yielded the texts and intellectual bases for a period of spirited debate.

Briefly summarizing the texts and bases of Minnowbrook and beyond is difficult; the views and positions of the new public administration were diverse and to several ends. However, they did reflect pessimism about the state of public administration and its organizing values, conceptual frameworks, and definitions of good practices inherited from the 1940s and 1950s. The inherited field, it was claimed, adhered to a positivistic approach to phenomena and a limited view of rationality, emphasized efficiency and economy to the exclusion of other values, and promoted centralized and hierarchical forms of organization. The old public administration was unable, according to its new critics, to deal with rapidly changing social, economic, and political orders.

The prevailing public administration was not only limited in its responses, it was itself a source of problems: "There is growing evidence that the institutions of public administration have failed to finish what they set out to do and, worse, are now suspected of aggravating or intensifying the very problems they were designed to solve" (Savage 1971, 46). The academic pessimism was not immutable. A regenerated public administration could become relevant to an agitated society and serve as the instrument for guiding social change (White 1971). By a new public administration those in public organizations could be liberated from organizational constraints, be self-actualized, and become champions of the politically powerless.

Regeneration meant comprehensive change, including change in epistemologies and philosophies (Guerreiro-Ramos 1980). Movement toward intersubjective and away from positivistic learning and knowing implied a new paradigm and jurisdiction oriented to policy and action based on knowledge gained from an interchange of views of administrators and clients. The interchange required new institutions of structured nonhierarchy (Thayer 1980) and consociated organizations which lacked permanent hierarchy, recognized leadership as situational, and relied on project teams to meet objectives (Kirkhart 1971, 160). Public administration was to be less insular with more consideration given to the external relationships of public organizations and to the effects of the organizations' actions.

Proponents of the new public administration made much of value emphases and normative foundations. The orthodox values of the field—"economy, efficiency, effectiveness, responsiveness to elected officials, responsibility"—were not wrong (Frederickson 1980a, 49; cf., Frederickson 1980b); they were necessary but not sufficient. Other deserving values were "citizen responsiveness, worker and citizen participation in decision making, the equitable distribution of public services, the provision of a range of citizen choices, and administrative responsibility for program effectiveness" (Frederickson 1980a, 49). With greater sensitivity to these values public administration would become truly relevant and satisfy its primary normative premise: "*the purpose of public organization is the reduction of economic, social, and psychic suffering and the enhancement of life opportunities for those inside and outside the organization*" (LaPorte 1971, 32).

In a regenerated discipline, academic public administration programs would enlist and train 'short-haired' radicals as change agents (Frederickson 1971, 331). A new breed of administrator would finally lay to rest the politically useful myth of a separation of politics and administration. By dint of heightened sensitivity in administrators, continued organizational development, and a desire for change, new Public Administration might well foster a political system in which elected officials speak basically for the majority and for the privileged minorities while courts and the administrators are spokesmen for disadvantaged minorities (Frederickson 1971, 329).

The new public administration stimulated paradigm competition among academics of the 1960s and 1970s and generated yet another intrafield debate as to the newness, feasibility, and purpose of the contemplated changes (Campbell 1972; Meade 1971; Mosher 1971; Wilbern 1973). Scholars such as Victor Thompson (1975) argued vigorously that the new paradigm betrayed the public interest by subverting the authority of legitimately elected officials. For the professional practitioner, the new value emphases and liberation from then field's orthodoxies carried costs, especially legitimacy costs:

> Liberation, ..., poses a serious problem for the way in which the orthodoxy deals with administrative legitimacy. Liberation makes it impossible to insist that civil servants are politically neutral in a policy sense. They may be blatant and open advocates of policy positions, ... Moreover, when they disagree with one another, it is clear that their technical expertise cannot be the basis for their exercise of public authority. Where then, will the liberated public service find its legitimacy? The New Public Administration explicitly argued that legitimacy would flow from advancing social equity. (Ingraham and Rosenbloom 1989, 118)

Effects of the new public administration are difficult to decipher. Minnowbrook ideas that inspired young academics in 1968 did not always help the line administrator. On the policy and administrative turbulence of the late 1960s and early 1970s, Campbell (1972, 344) reflected:

> As the students of administration are questioning the very foundations of their discipline, the practitioners of the art are being confronted by those affected by their actions. Unable to hide behind claims of professionalism, expertise, and political neutrality, the administrator ... found himself daily challenged by those whom he supposedly served.

At its base the New Public Administration proposed a new dominant paradigm which mandated the reordering of political power and political roles. In the existing order, administrators were aware that they influenced policy and political processes, their influence was contextually determined, and their interests and the interests of the political system were served by the rhetoric and symbolism of a separation of politics and administration. Administrators' power was derived from extant praxis. "Like the Federalists, the Jacksonians, and the civil service reformers and progressives before them, then, the New Public Administration, focused upon administrative reform as a means of redistributing political power" (Ingraham and Rosenbloom 1989, 118).

Longer term effects of new public administration thinking on public administration professionalism can be speculated upon, if not proven to be causal. Through the 1960s, 1970s, and 1980s elements of the paradigm were incorporated in administrative practice. Policy makers experimented with initiatives that were drawn from, or ideologically related to, the new public administration essays—citizen participation requirements, decentralized service delivery arrangements, and expansive interpretations of rights and entitlements.

In an introduction to a symposium on a second conference (Minnowbrook II) Frederickson (1989, 97) summarized nine major themes developed at the first Minnowbrook Conference that had became important aspects of public administration…:

1. The field has shifted focus in significant measure from the management of agencies to policy issues.
2. Social equity has been added to efficiency and economy as the rationale or justification for policy positions.
3. Ethics, honesty, and responsibility in government have returned again to the lexicon of public administration.
4. The Minnowbrook perspective argued that, as public needs change, government agencies often outlive their purposes.
5. Change, not growth, has come to be understood as the more critical theoretical issue.
6. Effective public administration has come to be defined in the context of an active and participative citizenry.
7. Implementation moved center stage in studies of decision making in the 1950s and 1960s, but in the 1970s it came to be better understood that the more difficult challenge is to carry out decisions.
8. Correctness of the rational model and the usefulness of the strict concept of hierarchy has been severely challenged.
9. While pluralism continues to be widely accepted as a useful device for explaining the exercise of public power, it has ceased to be the standard for the practice of public administration.

The themes implied that disconfirming evidence had weakened the legitimacy of existing approaches. They also suggested changing foci of public administration professionalism, new core knowledge, and expanded jurisdiction of professional practice. Moving beyond the management of public agencies, decision-making models, and the use of updated POSDCORB techniques, professionals of the new public administration school were to be more attuned to public policy issues, their implementation, and their social equity consequences. Professionals were to be managers of change, both growth and decline. In meeting their responsibilities, professionals would support open organizations, citizen participation in the policy and administrative processes, and political representation of the politically weak and unrepresented.

As at Minnowbrook I, assorted views were offered at Minnowbrook II on the state of public administration as academic and professional fields. Some participants, such as Brown (1989, 215) asserted that twenty years of developments had not eliminated primary problems and that germane materials continued to be left out of the field's prevailing paradigm:

> As a result, the core of the field is not adequately nourished or integrated so that it can provide anchoring for the many diverse strands of interest that public administration now has or that might become a responsibility in the future.

The views of other participants echoed the social equity-human development points of Minnowbrook I. Suggestive of these views were the following.

> The problem for public servants is [that] … most of their attention must be given to the practical, day-to-day operations of government. But included in their responsibilities should be concern for enhancing the civic character of all involved (Hart 1989, 103).

> Designing more responsible organizations is an especially difficult task given that the aims of bureaucratic organization are often biased in favor of efficiency and effectiveness rather than responsible action (Burke 1989, 184).

An inner life is essential so that meanings generated there can provide conscious guidance to the affairs of the outer world.

Implicit in this is the axiom that the purpose of human life is development, not simply survival and continued procreation of the species.... What is primarily entailed in the life project is the resolution of self alienation at the level of the individual but through social relations (McSwain and White 1989, 198).

Although emphasized in these remarks, social equity and human development concerns did not dominate Minnowbrook II. Other participants addressed topics related to more traditional concerns of public administration professionals. The continued centrality of public management as a determinant of effective institutional performance was considered (DiIulio 1989). Also considered was the possibility of structuring public administration as a design science as suggested years earlier by Herbert Simon (Shangraw and Crow 1989). New topics were suggested for professional work, such as the administration of the relations between government and universities in science and technology projects.

In an assessment of particular relevance to students of public administration professionalism, Ingraham and Rosenbloom (1989, 117) reviewed developments in public personnel policy very much in keeping with the central concerns, if not the specific techniques of the new public administration. By their judgment, three developments deserving of attention involved liberation of employees, increased representation of social groupings in the public workforce, and greater participation by public employees in administrative decisions.

The causes of the developments relevant to professionalism were manifold. Liberation of public employees from hierarchical authority structures was a result of extensive unionization of public employees and legal decisions favoring employee constitutional rights during the 1960s and 1970s. Increased representation of disadvantaged groups, and therefore, presumably, increased representation of diverse values and interests, was made possible by changes in federal law, court decisions, and societal attitudes. Greater participation by employees in decision making was facilitated by union contract provisions but also by changes in the culture of administration which made managers more receptive to employee views (Ingraham and Rosenbloom 1989, 117–119).

Some of the goals sought by advocates of a new public administration in 1968 had been achieved by the 1980s, at least a partial victory for elements of their paradigm. However, from the 1960s to the 1980s the political context had also changed from one generally supportive of, or not actively resistant to, activism and policy experimentation on behalf of social equity, to one skeptical of the capacity of government to solve social problems.

J.   ANOTHER ALTERNATIVE PARADIGM: PUBLIC CHOICE AND PUBLIC ADMINISTRATION PROFESSIONALISM

One more challenge to the intellectual foundations of public administration professionalism came from the public choice school. Though from a grandly different perspective, public choice, like new public administration, questioned the basic assumptions of the profession's dominant paradigm and its accepted jurisdiction. The school has been described as being made up of, during the 1960s and 1970s, "a rather loose community of economists and political scientists who, increasingly, have adopted theoretical variants of classical political economy as a means of studying how scarce public goods and services might best be allocated in society" (Baker 1976, 42). Since then, the school has had considerable impact on academic-based paradigm generators; public policy formulation, adoption, and implementation (including new public management discussed later), and citizen-voters.

Separating public choice from the main body of public administration thought are judgments on the motivations and behaviors of individuals, the nature of public sector responsibilities, and the efficiency and efficacy of structural arrangements. Public choice theory is primarily deductive, "draws its analytical tools from formal logic and probability theory, as well as economics" (Abrams 1980, 1). A starting premise of public choice "is that politics is inextricably involved with the act of choosing. ...[A]ctors (individuals, states, organizations, etc.) make purposive, goal-seeking choices based on their own preferences—they are rational. It is assumed that an individual is able to rank alternatives from best to worst. ...Actors are thought to choose according to what is best for them given their *own* preferences or tastes" (Lalman et al. 1993, 79).

For public choice theorists the public good or public interest has no meaning apart from choices by individuals; "any methodology that seeks to explain and predict political action must be premised on the assumption of rational individuals pursuing their own interests" (Harmon and Mayer 1986, 244). These theorists hypothesize that individuals operating in public economies behave rationally, as do individuals in market economies. Voters choose parties and candidates whose position on the issues are closest to their own; public employees adopt strategies that facilitate promotion to higher rank within an organization and that increase the organization's size and budget (Borcherding 1977; Niskanen 1971; Tullock 1965); and the elected official engages in activities, such as dealing with constituency requests, which enhance the probability of reelection (Fiorina 1977). These behaviors complicate the use of governmental policies to solve problems. When government intervenes there is a very real probability of government failures. The failures are due to problems inherent in direct democracy, representative government, bureaucratic supply, and decentralization (Weimer and Vining 1999, chap. 8).

Individuals satisfy most of their preferences in the private market because society's social surplus, the net benefits consumers and producers receive from participation in markets, is maximized in an ideally competitive economy (Weimer and Vining 1999, 61). It is in this economy that a Pareto efficient distribution of goods and prices is generated such that "no one could be better-off without making anyone else worse-off" (Weimer and Vining 1999, 59–60).

Because actual market operations do not always meet the criteria of the ideally competitive economy, market failure, a situation where an unregulated market fails to reach a Pareto optimum (McLean 1987, 196) may develop and collective public action is required. Generally, four generic market failures are recognized (Weimer and Vining 1999, 74–115; Mitchell and Simmons 1994, chap. 1).

1. Public Goods

Goods and services can be located in a matrix defined by two dimensions, one of the extent of joint consumption and the other of the feasibility of exclusion from the good or service. At the point where joint consumption is possible and exclusion is not feasible the good or service must be treated as a public or common good and provided by government or some governmental arrangement.

2. Externalities

Condition holds when the effects, positive or negative, of an action—water and air pollution, second hand smoke, poorly educated students—are felt beyond the jurisdiction in which the action was produced. The spillover costs of an action are those that are passed on to others (Mitchell and Simmons 1994, 7). To deal with externalities government can persuade producers to reduce externalities, regulate through market incentives or through direct controls, use government expenditures to reduce effects.

3. Natural Monopolies

Develop when conditions are such that "a single firm can produce the output at a lower cost than any other market arrangement, including competition" (Weimer and Vining 1999, 100). Examples of natural monopoles include utilities, pipe lines between cities and cable television. Because natural monopolies are unconstrained by competition, they may attempt to underproduce so as to maximize profits thus requiring governmental regulation or some form of subsidy to increase production.

4. Information Asymmetry

Results when one party in a transaction such as the seller in a buyer–seller situation or the producer of an externality—has monopoly or near monopoly control of information regarding the issue at hand. Information asymmetry can result in cases involving, for example, pharmaceuticals, medical advice, or environmental pollution (Weimer and Vining 1999, 107–115). If the information asymmetry is sufficiently serious, government may provide information to parties in need or support non-governmental efforts to reduce the asymmetry.

Once the decision is made for collective action to deal with market failure, there are social and political consequences. The coercive powers of government will be used to punish any "free riders," those enjoying the benefits of the action without bearing fair shares of the costs. As the size of the collectivity increases, there is an increased probability that some individual preference orderings will be violated. Both of these negatives of collective action, coercion and preference thwarting, are mitigated by opportunities for the expression of views—voting, interest groups, voluntary associations, independently elected officials, autonomous units of government. Where public choice prevails, politics (decisions about which policies are to be adopted) and administration (decisions about what organizational arrangements are to be used for their implementation) are not separate but intimately related because "the structure of public administration cannot be organized apart from processes of political choice…" (Ostrom 1974, 66).

Public choice and traditional public administration have a common interest in governmental performance measured by efficiency, though not invariably by the same measurement tests. According to Ostrom (1974, 48), public administration has tended to judge efficiency indirectly by an administrative structure criterion which presumes "the greater the degree of specialization, professionalization, and linear organization in a unitary chain of command, the greater the efficiency."

To the public choice school, efficiency is most appropriately measured by a cost calculus, "accomplishment of a specifiable objective at least cost; or, a higher level of performance at a given cost." (Ostrom 1974, 48). If efficiency so defined is to be raised and citizen preferences respected, alternative arrangements for the production and provision of public goods and services must be considered. The form and scale of the arrangements are dictated by the nature of a good or service. By separating production and provision decisions (Ostrom et al. 1961), political decision makers have numerous options in responding to constituency demands. Among the options are arrangements—public, private, and public/private combinations—which encourage competition among service providers and assure greater choice for service consumers (Savas 1987). A potential consequence of the options is a diverse, fragmented, and overlapping delivery system.

A public sector depicted by diversity, fragmentation, and overlap can be quite efficient (Ostrom et al. 1973) and capable of optimizing citizen preferences. Moreover, diversity, fragmentation, and overlap provide the additional benefit of inhibiting public organization growth. Certain inefficiencies are associated with organizational size. In large centralized bureaucracies, subordinates seeking to please their superiors may transmit inaccurate information, thereby making decisions and policies more error prone. Other things being equal, as size increases fewer organizational resources are allocated to the primary mission of service delivery and more resources are devoted to management and control activities (Ostrom 1977, 30).

The joining of extensive functional professionalism, professionals in government, and large-scale organization administered by professionals *of* government often produces negative results. This is especially the case in those functions where policy effectiveness success is dependent on coproduction, cooperative exchanges between service providers and service consumers—teachers, students, and families; public health workers and smokers; etc. The difficulties are indicated by Ostrom (1977, 35–36):

> Professionalization of public services can be accompanied by a serious erosion in the quality of those services. This is especially true when professionals presume to know what is good for people rather than provide people with opportunities to express their own preferences, and when they fail to regard citizens as essential coproducers of many public goods and services. Higher expenditures for public services supplied exclusively by highly trained cadres of professional personnel may contribute to a 'service paradox,' where the better that services are, as defined by professional criteria, the less satisfied that citizens are with those services. An efficient system of public administration will depend upon professionals working under conditions where they have incentives to assist citizens as essential coproducers rather than assume that citizens are incompetent to realize their own interests.

Vincent Ostrom and his colleagues have attacked the hegemony of bureaucratic administration of the past fifty years and have presented the thesis of bureaucratic administration as a source of crisis in democratic society. As a result, the study and practice of public administration have been influenced by public choice theory virtually on a global basis. Derived from the theory have been prescriptions that constitute major, and in some instances radical, departures from conventional thinking on public administration professionalism. Though the theory's logic has been criticized for supporting vested interests and for underestimating the implications for the rights of minorities (Baker 1976; Golembiewski 1977b), an extensive body of normative and empirical literature was produced (King 1987).

Movement from traditional bureaucratic administration and toward public choice's democratic administration constitutes a major paradigm shift and modifications of the criteria of exemplary performance and the direction of public administration research and training. Most fundamentally, with the satisfaction of citizen preferences as a predominant concern, professionals of government study alternative means of service production and delivery and examine anew how the constitutional order and federal arrangements contribute to citizen satisfaction. The professional's reputation would be judged more by citizen consumers than by the standards of professional organizations. Those who best satisfy the demands of citizen as customers will be accordingly rewarded.

K.   INNOVATIVE MANAGEMENT PRACTICE AND PARADIGM IMPLICATIONS

On occasion during the 1960s practical policy problems gave rise to adaptations in administrative practices, adaptations which fundamentally altered approaches to governing and therefore had implications for public administration professionalism. One such adaptation was the PPBS, an innovative approach to budgeting adopted early in the Kennedy Administration. Adoption of PPBS involved academic and practitioner members of the public administration community and a convergence of factors—transition in national security policy; need for more sophisticated approaches to analysis of organizational capacity; ascension to Secretary of Defense of an activist administrator committed to empirical data based decision making.

National security policy during the 1950s was based primarily upon a strategy of massive retaliation through nuclear weapons. A New Look strategy took advantage of the United State's initial monopoly of nuclear technology. Reliance upon that technology allowed for reductions in spending for service personnel and related weapons systems. It also ameliorated a major concern of President Eisenhower, that national defense not negatively affect economic growth. By all accounts, defense spending was capped. The permissible level of spending during the Eisenhower years was the residual of estimated revenues minus the sum of mandated expenditures, domestic spending, and foreign aid (Boll 1988, 121).

This approach to strategy and budgeting had policy and administrative consequences. Among other things, given the emphasis on massive retaliation and fiscal ceilings, the military services competed to develop independent plans for nuclear related weapons and a greater share of defense spending. President Eisenhower's secretaries of defense generally operated as mediators among the services, worked to assure service adherence to budget ceilings, and tended to defer to the experience and wisdom of the professional military on matters of military policy and strategy (Boll 1988, 121).

By the time the Kennedy administration took office in 1961 the policy context had changed fundamentally. Constraints on defense financing were loosened; quoting President-elect Kennedy's comments to his Secretary of Defense nominee Robert McNamara, Theodore Sorensen has written (1965, 603): "Under no circumstances should we allow a predetermined arbitrary financial limit to establish either strategy or force levels." With successful nuclear tests by the Soviet Union, the United States lost its technology monopoly. Moreover, United States commitments to post-World War II allies required strategies to carry out missions in many regions.

Replacing the Eisenhower New Look strategy was a Kennedy Flexible Response strategy. Advocated during the late 1950s by then Army Chief of Staff General Maxwell Taylor (Chairman of the Joint Chiefs of Staff 1962–1964 and ambassador to South Vietnam, 1964–1965), Flexible Response held that there was a "need for a capability to react across the entire spectrum of possible challenge, for coping with anything from general atomic war to infiltrations and aggressions" (Taylor 1960, 6–7).

Developing this capability mandated an optimal mix of forces and weapons that would best achieve military objectives. Because the mix of elements would vary from mission to mission, developing capability necessitated close cooperation and coordination of the individual service strategies. Close cooperation and coordination were not readily assured. Under procedures in effect 1947-1960 the individual services developed their own strategic plans (Jordan et al. 1999, 199) and budgets were formulated without participation by the Joint Chiefs of Staff. The two functions were carried out by different people, planning by the military planners and the budgeting by the civilian Secretaries and the comptroller organizations (Hitch 1966, 67). Taylor (1960, 70) noted on budget formulation:

> With the Chiefs out of the picture, the budget was put together in the usual way, each service producing its budget in isolation from the others. ... [A]t no time to my knowledge were the three service budgets put side by side and an appraisal made of the fighting capabilities of the aggregate military forces supported by the budget. This so-called 'vertical' (rather than 'horizontal') approach to building the budget has many defects and accounts in a large measure for the inability thus far to develop a budget which keeps fiscal emphasis in phase with military priorities. It is not an exaggeration to say that nobody knows what we are actually buying with any specific budget.

Changing these procedures and installing a new approach was one major task facing Secretary of Defense McNamara in 1961. The secretary was able to draw upon experienced analysts, several of whom had worked on operation research and systems analysis type security problems during World War II and at the RAND Corporation in the postwar years (Kaplan 1983, 252–257). Notable among there were two economists—Charles Hitch who became the department's Comptroller and was instrumental in transferring PPBS concepts from RAND to the Department of Defense (DOD) (Quade 1968, 6) and Alain Enthoven, a young scholar who had achieved a reputation for his analytical work and was made head of a systems analysis office in the department.

Common to both Secretary McNamara and those who joined him were an intellectual orientation to problem solving and a faith in the power of quantitative analysis over history and career experiences. Writing of the Secretary's reaction to reading *The Economics of Defense in the Nuclear Age*, coauthored by Hitch and McKean (1960), Fred Kaplan (1983, 252) points out:

> Here was someone who was doing the same sort of thing that McNamara had done during the war—applying the principles of microeconomics, operations research and statistical analysis to defense issues—but doing it on a much broader scale, covering the whole gamut of national security, including comparing and choosing weapons systems, restructuring the defense budget, formulating military strategy.

Between 1961 when he came to office and 1968 when he left, McNamara significantly altered the administration of the DOD. The locus of critical decision making shifted from the service departments and the career officer corps toward the Office of the Secretary of Defense. Among the implications of the shift was that greater attention would be given to total military capability rather than specific service capability. The need to measure total capability emphasized the importance of the Hitch–McKean recommendation for "the reorganization of planning and budgeting into suitable categories or programs and the continuous operation of a forward plan for a long period so that, as far as possible, systems could be compared over their whole life cycle" (Palmer 1978, 59).

The PPBS was an instrument used by Robert McNamara to expand the role of the secretary and his office in defining national security policy. Implementation of PPBS drew upon new management tools to emphasize system outputs, determine total costs of forces participating in major missions, and assess and compare options for achieving objectives (Hitch 1966, 70–71). Engaging PPBS was to consider military problems from a perspective involving particular elements (Hitch and McKean 1960, 118–120):

1. An objective or objectives. What military ... aim are we trying to accomplish with the forces, equipments, projects, or tactics that the analysis is designed to compare?
2. Alternatives. By what alternative forces, equipments, projects, tactics, and so on may the objective be accomplished?
3. Costs or resources used. Each alternative method of accomplishing the objective, ... involves the incurring of certain resources.
4. A model or models. ... In systems analyses models of one type or another are required to trace the relations between inputs and outputs, resources and objectives, for each of the systems to be compared, so that we can predict the relevant consequences of choosing any system.
5. A criterion. ... In principle, the criterion we want is clear enough: the optimal system is the one which yields the greatest excess of positive values (objectives) over negative values (resources used up, or costs).

1. Planning

Some of these perspective elements were familiar, in general form, to the military establishment. Planning, the first stage of PPBS, had been conducted by the staff arms of the service departments and the Joint Chiefs of Staff. The work did identify objectives to be achieved and potential individual service strategies to achieve their specific objectives. Nonetheless, as envisioned by PPBS advocates planning was to be more comprehensive, ongoing, and open to all relevant departmental stakeholders. Planning results were to be more than individual service requirement studies. Systems analysis was to be engaged to compare options for achieving objectives and "to determine the one that contribute[d] the most for a given cost or achieve[d] a given objective at the least cost" (Hitch 1966, 73–74).

2. Programming

The second stage of PPBS, programming, was somewhat more problematic in that, while planning and budgeting were established functions, programming was less familiar though it was to provide a bridge between the two (Hitch 1966, 72). The intent was to enable decision makers to comprehensively appraise the multi-year fiscal and capability implications of decisions.

Initial programming efforts were to formulating means of updating data and grouping all existing (pre-PPBS) defense activities into programs—combinations of forces, weapons systems, and support elements related to strategic objectives (Hitch 1966, 75). This required some means of grouping DOD activities across the military services into a workable set of categories. The means developed was the Five Year Defense Plan (FYDP). In format, the FYDP gave a number of force tables providing an eight-year projection of forces and a five-year projection of costs and manpower, displayed in mission-oriented programs (Enthoven and Smith 1971, 48).

Military forces were clearly related in the plan to their multi-year total costs and to budget implications thus giving financial planning the same output orientation as force planning. With the FYDP the implications of decisions were more discernable than earlier because the Secretary of Defense had "a record of current cost and manpower but also projections of this information far enough ahead to enable him to estimate the main consequences of today's decisions" (Enthoven and Smith 1971, 48–50).

The FYDP grouping categories covered ten primary military programs. Illustrative of these programs were strategic forces, general-purpose forces, intelligence and communications, airlift and sealift, guard and reserve forces, research and development, central supply and maintenance, training and medical services. Each program consisted of all related program elements comprising a military capability (carriers, divisions, air wings) directed to a common mission (Enthoven and Smith 1971, 48–49).

3. Budgeting

Secretary McNamara's administrative world was multifaceted and required creative coordination. His PPBS innovations in planning and programming had to be synchronized with the Defense Department's budget which, in turn, was to be a device for integrating military strategy, military forces, and defense costs (Grant 1994, 1969). With assistance from Charles Hitch, Secretary McNamara was able to submit to Congress in January 1962 a reoriented budget which divided weapons systems and forces into mission-related programs, incorporated the "cost and force projections for each program in a" Five Year Defense Program, and created a programming process linking the planning and budgeting processes (Jordan et al. 1999, 204).

Individual members of Congress were impressed with the McNamara innovations (Enthoven and Smith 1971, 41–42). Nonetheless, modifications were necessitated by congressional practices. The planning and programming phases of PPBS were dominated by political officials, civil servants, and career military officers in the executive branch, primarily in the DOD. For the budgeting phase key participants were in the legislative branch, most especially in the financial authorization and appropriations committees of the House and Senate.

Given the locus of budgetary decision making in congressional committees it was necessary for executive branch PPBS supporters to modify their approach to conform to congressional preferences. The Defense Department's planning and programming were to system outputs—missions and strategies. The House Appropriation Committee concentrated on inputs and structured its budget decisions in terms of resource categories: (1) military personnel; (2) operations and maintenance; (3) procurement; (4) research, development, test, and evaluation; and (5) military construction. This required a major effort to convert the approximately 1000 program elements into the relevant appropriation accounts (Hitch 1965, 29–34).

4. Summary

The PPBS brought new methodologies and technologies to decision making. The system, as initially structured, was to make greater use of empirical data and modes of analysis to reduce the risk and uncertainty of the decision context. A distinction was made (in theory if not in practice) between the sequencing and content of the planning and programming phases:

> In PPBS, it can be argued that the proper product of the planning phase is not plans, but the decisions as to what ought to be programmed and then budgeted. The product of the programming phase is plans— program plans.... Planning is mostly about ends; programming is mostly about means to those ends. One side deals with decision uncertainties, the other with design uncertainties (Builder and Dewar 1994, 6–7).

The originators of PPBS were based in economics, operations research, and systems analysis rather than in traditional public administration. Origins aside, PPBS received considerable attention from the public administration community. Scholarly articles and symposia were devoted to the system's comprehensiveness and fundamental logic. For a while, PPBS was promoted as a means for improving decision making and performance throughout the national government and, by extension, to other levels of government (Mushkin et al. 1969; Schick 1971).

President Lyndon Johnson was sufficiently impressed with PPBS that in 1965 he directed its adoption by all domestic agencies. The president's confidence in the relation between budgeting and quality of life not withstanding, the role of PPBS in national government proved to be limited. Adoption of the system by all federal agencies was mandated in 1965; by 1971 the mandate was lifted. Experience demonstrated several practical limitations in the use of PPBS in applied decision settings (Schick 1973; Wildavsky 1969). These limitations included the complexity of measuring and evaluating programs to assess costs and benefits, the size of staffs needed to prepare documentation, and training necessary to develop basic skills.

The record of PPBS as an innovative management practice or as a potential public administration paradigm has been mixed. It entered the profession's discourse with great promise. PPBS was designed to redirect budgeting and policy making. Budgets were to be mechanisms for public sector investment and used primarily for planning rather than management purposes. Whatever its promise, PPBS was relatively short lived. After much initial activity, interest waned. By the Carter administration in the 1970s professional interest had refocused on Zero Base Budgeting as a management reform.

Reasons for declining interest in PPBS are many, including the complexity and resource demands cited. Also, it was a major change affecting public administrators but a reform, as on other occasions, which was externally imposed rather than internally generated. None of the developments cited by Schick (1966, 253) as contributing to changes in budgeting—economic analysis, information and decision technologies, convergence of planning and budgetary processes—was due exclusively or even primarily to contributions of members of the public administration community.

The PPBS record does include many positive contributions. Approaches to problem solving— cost-benefit analysis, multi-year forecasting, priority setting, horizontal rather than vertical treatment of organizational mission contributions—were tested and refined in the PPBS experience. These and related approaches continue to be taught to and applied by public administration researchers and practitioners.

Perhaps most significant is that the PPBS continues to be used by the DOD four decades after it was introduced. Comments by Chu and Berstein (2003, 20) on the relevance of the system echo those of McNamara and Hitch in the 1960s:

> PPBS gives the secretary of defense the essential tool to control the department's key decisions, each of which requires resources to implement: the structure of forces, their training and readiness, the

equipment with which they are armed, and the provisions set aside to sustain them in operations....
... The fact that the secretary of defense can begin the process with a reasonably clean sheet of paper gives him wide latitude to reshape the department as circumstances dictate, albeit at the expense of established programs and priorities. And because the service secretaries run a similar process within their areas of responsibility ... they, too, enjoy considerable latitude.

In the twenty-first century, the fundamental purpose of planning, programming, and budgeting continues to be the rational allocation scarce resources for security operations, including investments in future weapons systems. While modifications in the system have been made over time, the general approach, vocabulary, and process stages are essentially the same as in the 1960s. The function of paradigm translation and advocacy is maintained by sophisticated descriptions of the PPBS approach on the website of the Comptroller of the DOD and in on-line tutorials for officers moving into budgeting and policy analysis positions (paradigm implementation) furnished by the military services. Symposia on the process continue to be sponsored by RAND and other organizations. Proposals for reform of the process or its phasing are regularly put forth by professional groups and non governmental organizations.

L. INTERGOVERNMENTAL PUBLIC POLICY AND ALTERED MANAGEMENT PARADIGMS

Attention to PPBS was a manifestation of a broader movement shaping the public administration community in the 1960s and 1970s. Difficulties encountered in coping with national security and domestic situations forced new searches for optimizing strategies and optional approaches to policy choice. Search responses included sophisticated quantitative and economic techniques as well as extensive research on the policy process (Brewer and deLeon 1983; Wildavsky 1979). Major universities transformed established or proposed public administration and public affairs schools into public policy programs (Stokes 1996, 160).

Giving rise to a need for better analysis techniques and a clearer understanding of the policy process was the spectrum of issues facing post-World War II public administration academics and practitioners. Demographic and economic changes across American society prompted the issues and increased calls for action at all levels of government.

The more salient of the demographic and economic changes are readily identifiable in retrospect. Births rates of the 1950s, 1960s, and 1970s were much higher than those of earlier decades and produced a large population cohort which would affect all aspects of life as it moved through the life cycle. The availability of rural undeveloped land for housing tracts made possible a migration of primarily white, middle-class families, and subsequently retail and wholesale firms to serve them, from central cities to new, relatively homogenous, suburbs. The need for horizontal space for the technology of assembly line production and proper climate for certain industries created a similar migration of manufacturing plants from central cities to outside central city areas and from north eastern and north-central regions to southern and western regions.

The demographic and economic changes had differential impacts on metropolitan areas and regions. Most generally, and allowing for considerable internal variation, an expanding population and economic base heightened political and administrative issues associated with growth; conversely, a declining population and economic base heightened political and administrative issues associated with decline.

So during the 1950s, 1960s, and 1970s, again allowing for considerable internal variation, political leaders, professionals *in* government, and professionals *of* government in suburban jurisdictions and growing regions faced more local revenue sources and needs for, among others, new infrastructure of all types, regulations on land use, hiring and training of employees, measures for dealing with congestion, pollution, and other externalities, and opportunities for a participatory civic culture.

Their counterparts, political leaders, professionals *in* government and professionals of government in older central cities and declining regions faced fewer local revenue sources and the realities of, among others, decaying infrastructure of all types, vacant land, displacement of the most recently hired employees, worsening congestion, pollution, and other externalities, and the emergence of radical political movements or a politically isolated and alienated minority population.

Proposals to cope with conditions in both growing and declining communities were developed at the local, state, and federal levels of government. Especially important were the federal proposals. Enacted during the 1960s were programs financing infrastructure construction projects in newer and older communities, employment training, income security and medical care.

Greater federal penetration of the state–local sector resulted from several factors, three of which were paramount:

> The elasticity of the income tax (dominated by the national government) exceeded those of sales and property taxes (dominated by state and local governments). During periods of economic growth national, but not state and local, revenues grew at a faster rate than the economy.

> Of the three levels of government, the national government, the national government is generally best able to incur a deficit in its operating budget.

> The 1960s have been characterized as a period of heightened expectations as to entitlements, that individuals of all stripes were entitled to sets of legal, social, and political rights financed by the public sector.

Federal aid grew in importance and played an increasingly significant part in American politics as well as state–local finance and administration. From the 1960s onward, federal grants were an increasingly important element of state and local government finances. Grants were 19% of total state–local expenditures in 1960, 30% in 1980, and 25% in 1999.

The aggregate percentages do not indicate the policy priorities supported by the grants. Four policy areas—income security; transportation; education, training, employment, and social services; and health—account for between 75% and 91% of total grants between 1960 and 2000. Some changes have occurred in the relative ranking of the four policy areas. In 1960, transportation ranked first and accounted for 43% of total grants, reflecting the national commitment to construction of the interstate highway system. By 2000, transportation ranked fourth and payments for individuals, most importantly health care, ranked first and accounted for 62% of the total.

The level and purpose of federal grants is a product of political forces at play during a given period. Writing in the late 1970s, Samuel Beer made the case that the growth of federal grants was due, in part, to the influence and promoting efforts of two grouping in the modern state (Beer 1978, 17):

> One results from functional specialization ... I call it the professional bureaucratic complex ... The other results from territorial specialization and I call it the intergovernmental lobby ...

The professional bureaucratic complex, technocrats, was made up of technical functional professionals, equivalent to professionals in government, who by education, training, and experience have expertise in such specific functional areas as health, transportation, poverty, and energy. Technocrats in a particular function at the federal, state, and local governmental levels share a common world view regarding their policy concerns, current issues, and exemplary professional practices. Their shared professional views facilitates cooperation in program administration, reduces inter-governmental level conflict, and promotes a unified stand in resistance to jurisdictional intrusions from technocrats from other functions and professionals *of* government.

The intergovernmental lobby, topocrats, are more political generalists: "governors, mayors, county supervisors, and other officeholders usually elective, who exercise general responsibilities in state and local governments" (Beer 1978, 18). The world view and representation concerns of the topocrats, like the professionals of government, are to their area defined jurisdictions and the interests of constituents within their jurisdictions, rather than specific functions. Tensions between federal, state, and local level official are not inevitable but may result when federal program requirements and regulation interfere with the policy and political preferences of diverse state and local constituencies.

Differences in the world views and functional and policy orientations of Beer's technocrats and topocrats and between professional in government and professionals of government have been reflected in decisions over the forms legislated for federal grants.

Much of the political controversy that has centered on federal aid to state and local governments has involved, not surprisingly, the amounts of money to be allocated but also the form in which the aid was to be distributed (Conlan 1998, chaps 7 and 8). For the public administration community, academic and practitioner, debates over aid form were debates over aid substance as well as the relative influence of professionals in government and professionals of government in the use of the funds.

Federal grants vary in form from specific purpose grants, to formula based categorical grants, to functional block grants, to general purpose finance grants. The grant forms vary in the amount of decision discretion available to the grant maker and the grant recipient. Federal authorities have greatest control over the specific purpose grants, medium control over the block grants, and minimal control over the general purpose finance grants. Control exercised by grant recipients at the state and local levels increases in reverse order (Wright 1988, chap. 6),

For the public administration community federal grant form has been significant for reasons more complex that the degree of general control at the granting and receiving levels. Specific purpose and narrowly focused categorical grants are generally more favorable to the functionally specific interests of professionals in government (health specialties, social service programs for targeted populations, rehabilitation of housing for mentally retarded adults, etc.). Congressional committee and subcommittee chairs with jurisdiction over legislation to the specific substance of the categorical grants were resistant to changes in grants. Block grants and general purpose finance grants, best exemplified by the former General Revenue Sharing, were more favorable to the broader responsibilities and interests of professionals of government and the intergovernmental lobby.

With some regularity, efforts have been made by political coalitions to increase the flexibility or discretion available to state and local officials by greater devolution of program responsibility, frequently by integrating several categorical grants into individual block grants. Among many examples, President Nixon supported a New Federalism of block grants and revenue sharing; President Reagan worked to reduce federal program involvement in the state-local system by advocating federal assumption of Medicaid in return for state government assumption of federal welfare programs (Conlan 1998, chap. 8); the Report of the National Performance Review included recommendations, among others, to Consolidate 55 categorical grants into broader 'flexible grants' and Increase state and local flexibility in using the remaining categorical grants in order to Empower State and Local Governments (National Performance Review 1993, 38–39); and President Bush's proposed 2005 budget recommended converting a number of social welfare, transportation, and housing programs to block grants (Finegold et al. 2004).

Practical experience with intergovernmental programs and process brought new insights to public administration academics and practitioners and bases for consideration of paradigm modifications. Particularly important were insights on policy implementation. Implementation requires institutions to carry the burden of transforming general policy intent into an array of rules, routines and social processes that can convert policy intention into action. This process is the core of what is meant by implementation (O'Toole 2003, 234).

At play in policy implementation were new levels of complexity in objectives, value priorities, and organizational structures. Programs designed to achieve the objectives increasingly involved combinations of federal, state, and local governmental agencies, private for profit firms, nonprofit organizations, and representatives of program clientele. Increasingly, these multiple units involved in program implementation constituted networks, structures of interdependence involving multiple organizations or parts thereof, were one unit is not merely the formal subordinate of the others in some larger hierarchical arrangement (O'Toole 1997, 45).

The reality of networks complicates administrative–management arrangements for program implementation. The traditional paradigms of administration—where managers in hierarchical structures held higher organizational rank than those whom they supervised and utilized instruments of command and control, leadership, accountability, and strategic planning—proved inadequate. National officials, and by extension their administrative counterparts at the other levels, responsible for achieving policy objectives had to deal with conditions of indirect management including—partial accountability, mixed objectives, and inter-organizational activity (Rosenthal 1984, 470).

Such conditions, and the interconnectedness they reflected, necessitate a new approach which supports new collaborative mechanisms and collective strategies (Luke 1992, 19) for [p]rogram management in a networked world (O'Toole 1996, 256). For the contemporary policy world, implementation success depends on the actions of networks and requires the use of inducements of authority (such as exists), common interest, and exchange. These serve to influence interdependencies across the network or among clusters of participants within the network in support of essential cooperative efforts (O'Toole 2003, 237–239).

Paradigm generation efforts have been forthcoming from academics and research organizations in the professional community to improve policy implementation, formulate an Intergovernmental Management approach, and cope with the proliferation of interorganizational connections (O'Toole 2003, 235). Emphasized has been a problem-solving focus, a means of understanding and coping with systems as they are, and an emphasis on contacts and the development of communication networks (Agranoff 1996, 211).

These emphases require new approaches to governing by professional administrators and managers and are made real through skillful use of formal and less formal resources. Basic to the formal is legislation structuring policies and programs, the better their design the greater the probability of implementation success. Programs provided by the legislation must have valid theoretical bases and be technically, fiscally, and politically feasible. At the operational level, another formal resource is the fiscal, the amount of money allocated to a program, the form of program financing, and reporting and accounting requirements shape participant behavior. For administrators and network managers Agranoff (1996, 214) observes that "[u]nderstanding financing patterns is key to understand the system because intergovernmental transfers and tax policies are important orchestrators of intergovernmental connections."

Regulations constitute another formal resource of intergovernmental management available to national or state officials to achieve necessary cooperation or coordination among governments, organizations, and policy and program participants. Regulations may prohibit some activities or require others as conditions for funding; they may override existing state regulations or provide waivers or exemptions to federal regulations when equivalent state or local initiatives achieve national policy objectives.

Federal regulations take several forms. They can be specific to a given program. Or they can apply across a number of state and local activities, receipt of funds for federal program A requires adherence to federal regulations in state–local programs B, C, and D. A variant of familiar

regulations is the unfunded mandate where the national government requires
governments and state governments require (mandate) local governments to car
programs without financial assistance. The burden of mandates, such as those as
Clean Air Act and the Americans with Disabilities Act, came to be resisted b
officials. Conlan (1998, 261) indicates that by the 1990s "For the first time federal *regulations*
rather than federal *spending* became the preeminent intergovernmental issue for many state and
local officials and their national associations."

Less formal resources which contribute to successful intergovernmental administration and
network management are political skills and administrative capacity. Basic decisions as to the
purpose and form of intergovernmental programs are made by political officials at the national
level (including presidents, members of Congress, and department secretaries) and implemented
under the direction of a political officials at the state and local levels (including governors, mayors,
state legislators, and members of city councils). Among these, collaboration of short and longer-
term political interests can be a resource in promoting cooperation and coordination of key program
participants (Agranoff 1996, 216). Political party leaders, fixers who arrange deals to facilitate
implementation, associations of elected officials, and public interest groups assist in the political
aspects of intergovernmental management.

With the national government as the main source of funding and state and local governments as
service providers, federal program success has depended on the abilities of professionals of government and administrators outside the immediate control of federal officials. Timothy Mead's
assessment of factors defining high capacity cites included the administrative sophistication and
skill of elected officials and important administrators (Mead 1981, 8). Such administrators further
network learning by widespread sharing of program information on incentives and coordination.

Recognition of the significance of professional state and local administrators and management
skill to program success, was evident in a number of federally sponsored capacity building initiatives by way of technical assistance, technology transfers, and reports on state of the art
management practices. In general, the initiatives focused on area wide jurisdictions and the
management capabilities of topocrats and professionals of government. Included were initiatives
related to policy management (to *Strategic* functions of providing *guidance* and *leadership*),
resource management (*Routine* support functions to ensure *organizational maintenance*, …), and
program management (*Technical* functions of *executing* administrative directives and policy
guidance …) (Burgess 1975, 709). From the initiatives applied and theoretical research projects
and publications were generated in the public administration community (Gargan 1981; Honadle
1981; Mead 1981). And work on the topic of governing capacity in state and local governments has
continued (Campbell Public Affairs Institute 2002).

M. Paradigms, Reform, and the New Public Management

The decade of the 1980s marked the coming of age of a new paradigm of administration that, if fully
adopted, would transform public administration professionalism with regard to missions, strategies,
and management skills. Labeled New Public Management (NPM), the approach rapidly diffused as
a global public management reform movement (Frederickson and Smith 2003, 214) and has been a
major topic of interest to public administration practitioners and researchers.

Management reforms have varied from case to case but generally have followed either of two
models. The Westminster model, covering most cases (Great Britain, Australia, Canada, etc.), in
broad outline is reflected in the experience of New Zealand from the mid-1980s to the present.
The Reinvention model, which covers the single case of the United States, was an initiative of
the Clinton–Gore administration during the 1990s (Kettl 2000, 7). Overall, management reforms
in the NPM mold have been instigated by governments large and small, headed
by liberal and conservative regimes, and located in a variety of geographic regions.

Owen Hughes (1998, 59), these reforms represent a *transformation* of the public sector and its relationship with government and society.

Summarizing the canons of the Westminster–Reinvention reform approach, Theo A.J. Toonen (2001, 185) lists six:

- "[A] business-oriented approach to government
- [A] quality and performance oriented approach to public management;
- [A]n emphasis on improved service delivery and functional responsiveness;
- [A]n institutional separation of public demand functions ..., public provision ... and public service productions functions ...;
- [A] linkage of public demand, provision and supply units by transactional devices ... and quality management; and
- [W]herever possible, the retreat of (bureaucratic) government institutions in favour of an intelligent use of markets and commercial market enterprises .... or virtual markets ..."

Sharing the canons, the two primary models differ in particular ways. The Westminster model, which has made basic and major changes in the New Zealand political system, is more a top-down approach and is more deductive theory based.

The Reinvention model, drawing concepts from Osborne and Gaebler's *Reinventing Government* (1992) and explicated in National Performance Review (NPR) reports, was more bottom-up, more experientially based, and generated reforms addressing specific issues "rather than transforming the fundamental fiber of government's structure and processes" (Kettl 2000, 15).

The models do, however, share foci and concerns. Both relate to elements of public choice theory, discussed above, which emphasize containment and reduction of the public sector by way of deregulation and privatization and the use of market, or market like, competition among service providers to boost program efficiency and effectiveness. Recognized too are the implications of steering rather than rowing, where steering means setting broad policy objectives and rowing means actually taking the actions that fulfill those objectives (Frederickson and Smith 2003, 218). The models support the transferability from the private to the public sector of proven management practices and an emphasis on accountability to customers.

Developments in the United States and New Zealand are discussed in the following section. Treatment of the United States experience relates almost exclusively to the Clinton–Gore years though the management reform motivation has continued into the administration of George W. Bush. The purpose of the discussion is to highlight the nature of reform generated by the Reinvention and Westminster models, recognizing that the discussion is limited in coverage and the fact that the New Zealand case is but one of several of the Westminster type.

1. Reinventing in the United States

At the most general level, the government to be reinvented during the Clinton–Gore administration was much in line with the prevailing public administration paradigm and was described as one dominated by arrangements of hierarchical, centralized, and permanent organizations. Managed by a cadre of career administrators and political appointees, the organizations have been the basis for the conduct of programs by functional professionals and technical specialists (Peters 1994, 316).

Evolving from the arrangements was a national government which did not perform adequately and, by its performance, reinforced public distrust. Recognized early in the NPR assessment was a performance deficit:

The federal government is filled with good people trapped in bad systems: budget systems, personnel systems, procurement systems, financial management systems, information systems (National Performance Review 1993, 2).

Elimination of the performance deficit was to come from NPR recommendations based on four principles. First was Cutting Red Tape by using incentives rather than regulations to achieve objectives and by reducing federal regulations and mandates on operations of federal agencies, and state and local governments. Second was Putting Customers First by collecting data on customer-citizen attitudes on services, by competing with each other and the private sector for customers, and, where feasible, transferring government functions to private firms. Third was Empowering Employees to Get Results by giving employees at lower levels in agencies an expanded role in decision making, by holding them accountable for decisions, and by using performance agreements for department executives. Fourth was Cutting Back to Basics which called for elimination of unneeded federal activities, reengineering programs to greater productivity, and elimination of fraud (National Performance Review 1993, 12).

By enacting the recommendations, outmoded bureaucracies were to be transformed into innovative organizations that measure performance success by customer satisfaction. Substantial savings were projected ($108 billion over five years) along with a federal civilian workforce that was to be reduced by 12% (252,000 positions). Fundamental to the transformation and the savings was a new perspective, an altered mind set supportive of a culture capable of sustaining fundamental change (National Performance Review 1993, 12).

Donald Kettl (2000, 16–19) views the Reinvention process as taking place in three phases over six years. Phase I was a period of data gathering during which teams of government employees surveyed the bureaucracy to identify opportunities for decreasing waste and improving management, the basis for specific reform proposals. Phase I also produced legislation to improve procurement procedures.

In Phase II the pace of reform was slowed when Republicans gained control of Congress in the 1994 elections. Faced with political constraints, Vice President Gore refocused NPR from attending to how government could better perform what it was doing to rethinking what government was doing. Managers were instructed to assess what they were managing, to decide if they should continue doing it, and to consider the implications of eliminating what they were managing. Recommendations regarding the assignment of functional responsibilities were blocked by congressional Republicans and the battle ended in a draw with little sorting out of government's functions, reorganizing of its operations, or minimizing of its role (Kettl 2000, 17–18).

Phase III, with a new name (National Partnership for Reinventing Government), marked continuation of earlier themes of effective administration, quality of life improvements, customer services, as well as themes of linking information technology and capacity building so that the federal government is managed as well as America's best companies. Better customer-citizen service was to result from changes in the organizational culture of high-impact agencies like Internal Revenue Service, Food and Drug Administration, and the Postal Service. Performance goals were assigned to agencies; for example, the Federal Drug Administration was to complete the new drug approval process within a year and the Postal Service was to deliver 90% of local first class mail overnight (Kettl 2000, 18–19).

Through the 1990s proposals were developed to guide the reinvention of government and the reengineering of agencies. Market-like competition among providers was to be increased by separating provision of services decisions from production and delivery, a concept advocated by public choice supporters for some time (Savas 1987). More than 300 reinvention laboratories worked on innovative approaches to public service delivery (Kettl 2000, 20). Action recommendations were also taken from reviews of earlier studies, suggestions of federal employees, focus groups, and reinventing government meetings.

Action proposals ranged from significant policy changes (institute biennial budgets and appropriations and Congress should allow states and localities to consolidate separate grant programs from the bottom up) to the very specific (eliminate federal price supports for honey and consolidate a single civilian polar satellite system). The recommendations dealt with problems and issues in specific agencies (the Department of the Interior, National Aeronautic and Space Administration,

Office of Personnel Management) and addressed ideas applicable across agencies (streamlining management control, improving customer service, rethinking program design).

The Clinton–Gore reform efforts resulted in additional successes. In 1993, the administration supported Republican sponsored Government Performance and Results Act which required federal departments and agencies to develop strategic plans directed to performance goals and priorities, to prepare annual performance plans, and to initiate capacity building in performance management, including performance based budgeting.

Reinventing government legislation was enacted in 1994 to simplify federal purchasing, to revise federal administrative procedures, to reorganize the Department of Agriculture and to reform Federal Crop Insurance (Light 1997, 252).

Several of the reform themes of the Clinton–Gore administration were continued by President George W. Bush. The Bush administration's efforts, as announced in The President's Management Agenda, 2001, are based on three principles, not significantly different from those of the Clinton–Gore years. The principles hold that government should be: "Citizen-centered, not bureaucracy centered; Results-oriented; Market-based, actively promoting rather than stifling innovation through competition" (U.S. Office of Management and Budget 2001, 4).

Guided by the principles are five government-wide goals [that] are mutually reinforcing: strategic management of human capital, competitive sourcing, improved financial performance, expanded electronic government, and budget and performance integration. Additionally, the management agenda includes nine agency-specific reforms targeted to serious problems. Examples are Faith-Based and Community Initiative, Housing and Urban Development Management and Performance, Broadened Health Insurance Coverage through State Initiative, A "Right-Sized" Overseas Presence. These are described as test case reforms. With experience, additional agency problems would be addressed.

Implementation of the reforms has emphasized management practices that link resources to specific outputs and results. In 2001, the Office of Management and Budget announced that diffusion of performance based budgeting throughout the federal government was the administration's highest management priority (Kamensky 2003; Lunney 2001). To oversee reform, chief operating officers were appointed in each department and agency to have responsibility for day-to-day operations and the President's Management Council was reestablished to provide an integrating mechanism for policy implementation within agencies and across government. Agenda progress is tracked by way of an Executive Branch Management Scorecard. Quarterly, the Office of Management and Budget assigns to each department and agency a score of success, mixed results, or unsatisfactory as to its current status and progress on implementation of the five government wide goals.

Because the Bush administration's management agenda is a work in progress at this writing, its overall success is not known. The complexity of some issues, such as performance based budgeting generally and the measurement of outputs and results specifically, constrains implementation. Nonetheless, available evidence suggests that departments and agencies have made efforts to meet the president's reform charges.

Examples of the efforts made can be seen in a DOD memorandum from Under Secretary David S. Chu to his administrative colleagues. In the memorandum he relates DOD involvement with the president's program. Covered are arrangements for program implementation (established a Senior Steering Group ... to coordinate action among the principals and ensure compliance to the PMA and integrating the Scorecard requirements with the Department's Balanced Scorecard for risk management).

More directly to the Management Agenda, for each of the five government-wide goals the under secretary provided a synopsis of the department's past involvement with the goal's issues and current measures to reach the goal. For example, to the goal of Strategic Management of Human Capital the department's general personnel philosophy and operations as the Nation's largest employer are described. Actions taken to align department strategy with agenda goal are presented along with probable consequences. These included:

> In 2002, the Department deployed an enterprise HR transaction and information system supporting over 800,000 Defense employee records ... Within one year, this system was updated to an internet platform This has allowed the Department to decrease HR processing requirements and provide strategic information for workforce planning.

As a result, the DOD is better positioned to respond and attend to the personnel needs and expectations of job applicants; attract and appoint high quality, diverse candidates using shortened and streamlined processes; and retain a strong workforce using competitive compensation strategies.

The DOD memorandum by Under Secretary Chu is representative of reports by other departments and agencies outlining what has been done in strategic policy and management tactical terms to support the administration's vision on performance management. With national security matters competing for attention and priority status, maintaining a performance management vision and strategic and tactical support will be difficult, albeit critically important.

The Reinvention model of management reform, begun in the Clinton administration and continued by a different name in the Bush administration, fits into one of Light's (1997, 1) tides or philosophies of governmental reform—that of liberation management, with its cry of let the managers manage, albeit with a bit of market pressure. In the Clinton and Bush versions prominence has been given to increasing performance based management practices (especially budgetary), program outputs that relate to strategic goals, customer-citizen satisfaction, policy decision devolution, and decreasing levels of bureaucratic structure, federal regulations and mandates, federal personnel, and unneeded programs. In both administrations successes have been achieved. Market concepts are an ongoing dimension of governing discourse and mandate some fundamental changes in the management skills required of public administration professionals. But success has also been limited. A useful assessment of the wins and losses of the reinvention experience, at least for the Clinton–Gore era, was provided by Donald Kettl (2000, 28–29):

> it showed genuine accomplishment ... It saved a significant amount of money, brought substantial managerial reforms (especially in customer service and procurement processes), and promoted a more performance—based discussion about the functions of government.

> However, the shortcomings of the NPR are as instructive as its early successes. ... The NPR demonstrated, in its achievements and its failures, that the federal government is no longer organized for the job that law and the Constitution charge it to do. ... Both Democrats and Republicans have been politically burned on megapolicy initiatives, and neither side has shown much stomach for further adventures.

2. Transforming

As the Kettl quote indicates, in the United States there has been bipartisan reluctance to take on megapolicy initiatives. To gain a fuller appreciation of the implications of the new public management for the public administration community it is necessary to consider developments outside the United States.

The most striking megapolicy initiatives and far reaching changes in governmental arrangements have been those adopted in New Zealand since the mid-1980s. Upon winning control of government in 1984 the Labour Party faced an economy in decline and lacked sufficient resources to fund public programs at their current levels. An expansive welfare state had developed since World War II which placed growing demands on a constrained budget. For New Zealand, as for other welfare states, Lane (1997, 13–14) notes, "There [was] increasingly a realization that a big public sector not only offers a set of tools for solving social problems but has efficiency problems of its own."

Complicating the New Zealand political, governmental, and economic situations was the central government's control of major segments of the national economy. Over time, an interventionist government had taken control of enterprises and services including telecommunications, transportation, oil, insurance, and airlines. In the judgment of some analysts, many of these businesses were in general poorly managed, used to expand public employment, and largely captured by provider interests, which substantially controlled advice about funding and service configurations (Scott et al. 1997, 358).

The need for changes in economic policy and the effects of low capacity public management on economic conditions were widely recognized. By 1984, there was growing support inside the bureaucracy for change (Scott 1996, 11). Leadership of reform efforts came from within the Labour Party and with intellectual guidance from Minister of Finance Roger Douglas and senior professional staff in the Treasury. A 1987 Treasury brief, *Government Management* included comprehensive criticism of the management systems for central government administration... This was followed by detailed proposals from that department and the State Services Commission over the coming years (Scott 1996, 11). Basic principles that the brief (The Treasury 1987) counseled the Government to follow in organizing were seven: (i) *Clarify objectives*; (ii) *Transparency*; (iii) *Avoidance of capture*; (iv) *Incentives*; (v) *Informatio*; (vi) *Accountability*; (vii) *Contestability*.

The major reforms New Zealand adopted had a theoretical base in institutional economics. There was a special focus on transaction costs, the costs incurred in formulating and maintaining arrangements necessary to conducting business, such as information gathering, developing and negotiating contracts, and monitoring activities. The special concern for the Treasury's seven organizing principles and the focus on transaction costs in formulating management reforms indicated a true paradigm shift from traditional ideas of administration that advocated orderly hierarchies and elimination of duplication or overlap (Hood 1991, 5).

The economic theory guiding reform holds that the design of public sector arrangements is a function of the transaction costs involved: "The transactions approach suggests that legislators choose those administrative arrangements that best address the transaction problems they encounter. More precisely, they choose from among the available intuitional arrangements to minimize the sum of the transaction costs they face in any given situation" (Horn 1995, 24). Depending upon the level of costs, arrangements can rely on private firms and market like conditions or take the form of governmental hierarchical bureaucracies. When transaction costs in a case are relatively low, public authorities can enter into short term contracts with private firms or organizations for production and/or delivery of a good or service. Short-term contracts specify exactly what is to be provided and the payments to be made (Weimer and Vining 1999, 183).

Alternatively, as transaction costs reach a level of complexity and volume that lowers efficiency, it leads to the rational creation of hierarchical organizations (and incomplete contracts) in lieu of markets (and complete contracts) (Lynn et al. 2001, 64). In these situations the hierarchical organizations internalize a range of activities so as to reduce all the uncertainties and difficulties of doing business (Parsons 1995, 329). Reliance on the long term contract helps achieve stability and facilitates the exercise of command and control. According to Lane (2000, 133–134):

> The long-term relational contact has been typical of public organisations, especially the bureaux but also of the traditional public enterprises. Employment was basically lifetime, and the employees were instructed what to do by means of administrative law. The Weberian ideal type of a rational bureaucracy emphasises the positive consequences of long-term contracting for the evolution of expertise, agency independence and the Rule of Law.

In the traditional large-scale bureaucracy, internal control was exercised by way of networks of contracts (Kettl 2002, 86). Public employees were protected directly by long-term contracts of civil service laws and regulations. Typically, employees could also enjoy some flexibility in their on the job behavior and the more involved the tasks of the job the greater the flexibility.

The flexibility in actual job behavior was a manifestation of another matter of theoretical interest and practical concern to the new public management reformers, the principal-agent problem drawn from public choice theory. Most basically, authorities empowered to adopt policies and programs (principals) must rely on holders of specialized knowledge and technical expertise (agents) to implement the projects. This results in a knowledge–information asymmetry between the principal and the agent. In light of the asymmetry, the government needs to avoid being captured by external lobbying groups and its internal bureaucracy. Because of their detailed familiarity with issues, their interest, and organization, lobbying groups enjoy a strategic advantage over the general public and will attempt to manipulate public policies in their favor at the expense of the wider public interest (Scott et al. 1997, 359).

Bureaucrats in public agencies not only have a knowledge–information advantage over their principals, they also are motivated by self-interest such as larger budgets and staff or particular policies. This means that they will seek to optimize their positions, but within a framework of imperfect information and may thwart their agencies' missions and the public will. The problem facing a government then is one of contracting efficiently between principals and agents in a way that minimizes the so-called 'agency costs' of setting up and monitoring that contractual relationship (Scott 1996, 12). This is often difficult because neither short nor long-term contracts can feasibly cover all contingences. Nonetheless, efforts should be made through the contracts for "making managers manage" by contracting in as specific terms as possible.

The paradigm adopted by the New Zealand reformers mirrored the principles in the 1987 Treasury brief and the theoretical groundings outlined. Overall, the thrust of the reforms was to a transformation of institutional arrangements for political–economic matters from a highly centralized hierarchical structure with transaction costs internalized to a significantly deregulated, market oriented arrangement with transaction costs externalized and managed by way of short term contracts.

Supporting the reforms were several acts adopted by the Parliament from the mid-1980s into the early 2000s. Among the most important were as follows.

a. State Owned Enterprises Act 1986

This act made fundamental changes in the legal basis and principles for conducting commercial type programs housed in government departments. By the Act, "the principal objective of every State enterprise [was]…to operate as a successful business." State enterprises were expected to be "as profitable and efficient as comparable businesses that are not owned by the Crown; a good employer; an organization that exhibits a sense or social responsibility by having regard to the interests of the community in which it operates…" (State Services Commission 1998).

b. State Sector Act 1988

This act restructured the basics of departmental and public service administration. Emphasis was placed on bringing business management practices to the public sector. Heads of departments were designated chief executives and the relationship between the chief executives, Ministers, and the State Services Commissioner was delineated. Chief executives were given significantly greater authority over departmental operations and were to be responsible by contract for specific outputs. Functions of the Human Services Commissioner and aspects of human resource management were covered (State Services Commission 1998; Scott 1996, section VII).

c. Public Finance Act 1989

This act complemented reforms initiated by the State Sector Act by fundamentally restructuring the New Zealand financial management system. Fiscal responsibilities of ministers and chief executives were clarified by separating the purchase of services (responsibility of ministers) from the provision of services (responsibility of chief executives and their departments). The method of contracting between purchasers and providers was structured. And the character of information and the type of accounting to be used in reporting on departmental operations was outlined (State Services Commission 1998; Schick 2001, 8–9).

The three acts constitute a substantial portion of the legal basis of New Zealand's new public management reforms. Other measures contribute to that legal basis. For example, adding to the provisions of the Public Finance Act was the 1994 Fiscal Responsibilities Act. The 1994 Act extends reporting on public finances by setting legal standards for transparency of fiscal policy and reporting, and [holding] the government formally responsible to the public for its fiscal performance. In meeting its responsibilities the Government is to publish a Budget Policy Statement specifying short-term fiscal intentions, and long-term fiscal objectives. Periodic reports on economic and fiscal conditions are to include estimates of fiscal decision impacts (International Monetary Fund 2001, 1–2; Schick 2001, 6–7).

Also mandated by the Act was the charge to the Government to present long term (up to twenty years) budget estimates and forecasts. The combined information and data contained in the annual budget and long term forecasts are assumed to enhance the quality and accuracy of public finance decision making.

Brief summaries of, and references to, important legislation, as above and in subsequent sections, mask the dynamics of the interplay of determinants. All reform acts that have been adopted by New Zealand's Parliament reflect, in varying degrees, the combined effects of paradigm assumptions, ideology, and political party interests. This can be seen in recent legislative approaches to labor relations.

After gaining control of the Government in1990, the National Party passed the Employment Contracts Act of 1991. The Act marked a major departure from the historic pattern of labor relations in New Zealand and, according to one assessment, took economic reform of the market place to a new level (Auckland District Law Society 2002, 1–3). Nonetheless, the Act did relate generally to the contractual emphasis of reform initiatives and the National Government's attention to deregulation in the economy.

The Act aimed to promote an efficient labor market by recognizing a right of employees and employers to choose the type of employment relationship they would engage. More specifically, under the law, employees would be free to negotiate a contract individually with an employer or to accept terms of a collective contract the employer had entered. Similarly, employers, who were not obligated to recognize trade unions or to accept collective bargaining, could agree to specific contracts with individual employees or accept a collective contract for employees. Whether individual or collective contracts, or a combination, would be used was to be decided by negotiations between the parties (Auckland District Law Society 2002, 1–3).

The Employment Contracts Act was short lived. In 2000, the Coalition Government, an alliance of Labour and Alliance Parties, enacted the Employment Relations Act of 2000 with the objective of building productive employment relationships through the promotion of mutual trust and confidence in all aspects of the employment environment and of the employment relationship (Auckland District Law Society 2002, 3). In effect, this act mandated the status quo ante and a step back from heavy reliance on contracts in most employer-employee relations. A summary noted, "The Employment Relations Act 2000 is seen in many ways as a return to the principles of employment law developed prior to the 1991 Act" (Auckland District Law Society 2002, 4). Under the law unions were recognized as legitimate organizations to promote employees interests, employees are given the right to strike, and unions and employers are the only parties recognized for collective bargaining (The Treasury 2004).

3. New Zealand NPM Implementation

Articulation of theoretical frameworks (Paradigm Generation) and adoption of laws based on the frameworks (Paradigm Translation) are crucially important. But it is in real operations (Paradigm Implementation) that the public administration community, and especially its practitioner wing, comes to judgment on the validity and utility of competing paradigms of administration and management. Though a comprehensive discussion of reforms is not feasible, consideration of aspects of selected reform effects indicates how the new public management has developed in New Zealand.

Organizational arrangements of the New Zealand public sector are of three generic forms. The core public sector consists of departments and ministries responsible for more basic and traditional services; examples of such units include the Department of Conservation, Department of Labour, Ministry of Health, Ministry of Defence. A second form is the Crown entity, organizations performing specialized tasks under particular governing legislation; some crown entities are Crown research institutes, School boards of trustees, New Zealand Lotteries Commission, New Zealand Fire Service Commission. The third form is the State Owned Enterprise, commercial businesses owned and controlled by the Government; among State Owned Enterprises are Airways Corporation of New Zealand Limited, New Zealand Railways Corporation, Mighty River Power Limited, and New Zealand Post Limited. The following discussion concentrates on the core public sector and State Owned Enterprises.

Core public sector management reforms have been, by and large, of two types relating to administration-management professionalism, those that seek to introduce managerial discretion and accountability, and those that seek to introduce contract-like arrangements in government (Schick 1996, 19). Drawn from different theoretical perspectives, these two types of reform involve different assumptions about how and why managers behave and how their administrative and political superiors view them. From the discretionary perspective, the manager is assumed to be committed and motivated to achieve organizational goals and the reform intent is *freeing* managers to manage; the manager's superiors are expected to shape a context that encourages activism and reasonable risk taking. From the contractual perspective, the manager is assumed to be motivated to seek individual goals and to behave opportunistically, hence the reform intent is "*making* managers manage"; here the managers' superiors are expected to closely observe and control developments (emphasis added, Schick 1996, 23).

Regardless of whether New Zealand managers were to be freed or made to manage, reforms were necessary to enable them. If they were to be innovative and responsible for carrying out strategies for departmental goals, it was essential that they had the authority and power to manage. Managerial power and authority and flexibility over budget, personnel, organizational, and policy implementation decisions had been lacking in the traditionally highly centralized bureaucratic system.

With the 1988 State Sector Act and the 1989 Public Finance Act, managerial power, authority, and flexibility were increased and long standing aspects of public administration professionalism were modified. In place of permanent tenure, departmental chief executives were to be appointed for five year terms subject to renewal. They were given greater direct control over personnel (hiring, firing, promoting), budgeting (how and where resources were to be allocated), and departmental organization and operations. By the 1989 Public Finance Act, chief executives were made responsible for departmental financial management, including accrual based accounting and budgeting (Scott 1996, section VII; Kettl 2000; Halligan 1997).

Also rearranged and formalized, in line with the new guiding paradigm, were relations between political authorities (government ministers) and managerial authorities (departmental chief executives). To avoid the capture problem inherent in the principal-agent relationship the department chief executive was to be held responsible and accountable for service and output delivery, any policy advising function was to be assigned to experts outside the department. Annual performance agreements between ministers and departmental chief executives present departmental objectives and clear ex ante agreements, about performance expectations (Scott 1996, 32).

Ministers, as political authorities, are responsible for outcomes, the societal, economic, and political effects or consequences of policies and governmental initiatives. Department chief executives are responsible for outputs, units of goods or services to be produced by the department that contribute to the achievement of outcomes. Purchase agreements between the two stipulate the quantity of outputs to be produced and their price, quality, and timing. Executives are both held accountable and evaluated on the basis of their success in meeting performance and purchase agreement rather than more traditional adherence to process requirements and control of the use of inputs (Kettl 2000).

4. State Owned Enterprises

As noted, a primary inducement for reform in New Zealand was the condition of the nation's economy. Inhibiting economic development was government participation in virtually all sectors from manufacturing to extraction to transportation. Institutional arrangements for the conduct of business took several forms including government departments, public corporations, and limited liability corporations with shares held by government ministers (Scott 1996, section VI).

In dealing with economic questions New Zealand decision makers confronted elemental questions of governing in the late twentieth century. How much of the extensive economic regulation could be reduced? Which economic activities under governmental control should be retained but conducted under a different arrangement? Alternatively, which economic activities under governmental control would be more efficiently and effectively conducted in the private sector? What constituted a core public sector?

The strategy for economic reform included deregulation, corporatization, and privatization. Early on, efforts centered on deregulation, modification of the tax structure, and the lowering of subsidies to industry to improve the competitive advantage of firms in several sectors. Those initially affected by moves towards a free market context were in transportation and banking and finance; further deregulation affected those in utilities, postal services, and telecommunications (Scott and Gorringe 1989; State Services Commission 1998).

Corporatization put into effect provisions of the 1986 State Owned Enterprises Act. Commercial activities of government department were separated out and restructured as State Owned Enterprises (SOE). Examples of the SOEs are Airways Corporation of New Zealand Limited, Electricity Corporation of New Zealand Limited, and Timberlands West Coast Limited. The enterprises operate as if they were private firms and are evaluated in terms of their efficiency and profitability. Loans made by an enterprise are its responsibility without government guarantees. Like firms in the private sector, SOEs are required to pay taxes and are expected to pay dividends to Ministers holding shares in the enterprise.

Policy for SOEs is made by boards of directors comprised of individuals with pertinent private sector commercial experience. Boards report corporate intent, business objectives, and performance goals to relevant ministers. For operations, managers are given control over resource inputs while decisions on pricing and marketing are made by enterprise board members.

From the mid-1980s onward, the New Zealand government has reduced its participation in the economy by selling assets to private investors. In a number of cases, SOE status has been an intermediate step from commercial type activity in a department towards sale by the government to buyers in the private sector. William Eggers (1997) describes one such case:

> With more than 12,000 employees, New Zealand's Ministry of Public Works used to be one of the country's largest departments.... In 1990, the ministry was split up. All policy advice functions were

transferred to other departments Commercial oriented agencies—property services, computer services, architectural and engineering consulting, construction and maintenance and road sign production—were converted into state-owned enterprises (SOEs) and reorganized along business lines. Each was required to pay taxes, raise capital on the market (with no government backing-explicit or implicit) and operate according to commercial principles. At the same time, the SOEs were freed from civil service, procurement, and financial management regulations.

Over time, each of the new SOEs was sold to the private sector. New Zealand no longer has any government in-house capability to design, build or repair infrastructure. When these services are needed, they are purchased on the open market.

5. Some Consequences of New Public Management for New Zealand

The transformation of the New Zealand political system has been central to the strategy of economic adjustment (Scott 1996, section XI). Clearly the governmental regime of the early twenty-first century is fundamentally different from that of the late twentieth century. The effects of such regime change are of interest firstly to New Zealanders and elites in other societies considering governmental reform and secondly to the more specialized audience of the academic and practitioner member of the public administration community.

Demonstrating the effects of governmental and economic reforms is difficult. Implying a causal relationship between a reform and a positive or negative outcome may be tempting but dangerous when the effect is due to a third factor or interactions among factors. Nonetheless, some summary statements can be made about the results of reform. Not surprisingly, the reform results are mixed—significant improvements in several areas, inadequate or incomplete changes in some areas, and unanticipated or paradoxical results in still others.

In general, by the judgment of expert observers, reforms have significantly affected performance in fiscal policy and administration broadly considered. Improvements have been made in budget processes and financial management and reporting, with the adoption of accrual accounting, as one example of the comprehensiveness and quality of information reported available to parliament. More fiscal transparency and quality data mean that parliament is better positioned to understand the longer term impacts of public policy. The same developments have improved the ability of the cabinet to exercise fiscal control in macromanagement of the economy (Scott 1996, 2001).

Other reforms have similarly had positive results. Privatization of assets had two fold consequences—it took the government out of activities where it no longer belonged and, given the returns from sale of the assets, furthered the government's financial condition. Through the policy on state owned enterprises the government took resource-hungry, government-owned businesses out of the budget sector and forced them to raise their efficiency, in part by competing for finance in the private sector (Scott 1996, 78).

New Zealand has probably been more creative and innovative than other countries in constructing a management context which drew upon private sector experiences and which allowed managers to manage. In that context managers have enjoyed authority and flexibility in personnel and budgetary matters, free from undue central office control. The use of performance contracts and purchase agreements make explicit the criteria that are to be used for managerial assessment (Schick 2001, 4). Advancement and professional growth in such a context rewards the committed, competitive, and ambitious. The successes of the New Zealand experiment are real and looked to by other nations for guidance.

Along with the experiment's successes have been inadequate and unanticipated results. The negative results have been due in part to the arrangements resulting from new public management doctrine. The separation of policy advice from service delivery to avoid agency capture of principal and assignment of outcomes to ministers and outputs, enforced by performance contracts and purchase agreements to chief executives, have consequences. The short-term focus of department chief executives necessitated by the reality of performance contracts distracts attention from longer range strategic planning. Even more fundamentally, contractual arrangements may impose limits on policy discussion between those most knowledgeable. Schick (2001, 5) illustrates:

> While mangers focus on the minutiae of internal operations, ministers are interested in how to use their authority and resources to shape New Zealand's future. The connection between the political and managerial world is impaired if each side remains absorbed in it own narrow concerns and the two do not share enough in common to make for a satisfying relationship.

Unanticipated negative results can follow from initiatives like those designed to enhance the management performance of chief executives and others. The devolution of personnel decision making from a central office to the department level and the use of employment contracts, thereby allowing managers to manage, may well have reduced the government-wide unity and public regarding ethos of public employees and the authority of the State Service Commission the government's central civil service agency. With passage of the 1988 State Sector Act, note Ingraham, Peters, and Moynihan (2000, 392) the State Service Commission was reconfigured from a strongly standardized central personnel agency to a much more modest consultant and adviser.

6. Some Consequences of New Public Management for the Public Administration Community

As a significant intellectual development, new public management takes its place among many other developments even since World War II as Toonen (2001, 184) points out:

> NPM has been to the public sector reform movement of the late twentieth century, what PPBS and 'Policy Analysis' were to the administrative reform movement in the late 1960s, and 1970s, 'rationalisation and democratisation' in the 1960s, and 'Scientific management' in some countries briefly before and just after the Second World War.

The new public management consists of a combination of the theoretical and technical familiar and new. For example, elements of the traditional meaning of public administration professionalism continue in NPM. Andrew Stark (2002, 141–145) cites four pillars or principles of Westminster-style public service—anonymity, merit, permanence, and neutrality. The ideal professional public servant reflects all four principles but other participants in the governing process (protégés, mandarins, consultants, aide-bureaucrats) reflect only two of the principles, From Stark's perspective, the career professional in the NPM system, consider the chief executive in a the New Zealand core public sector, does not hold to the principles of anonymity (by contract the executive is held personally accountable for his performance) or on permanence (the executive is appointed for a five year term). The career professional in the NPM system does, however, adhere to the principles of merit and neutrality. By Stark's (2002, 144–145) terms, "There is nothing about NPM that requires or even allows public servants, …, to be hired on any principle other than merit." And "[n]or is there anything about NPM that requires new public managers to be anything other than neutral implementers …"

Also familiar to the public administration community would be the continued significance of management as process and technology in the implementation of public problems. However obvious, it is worth reminding the community that it has long given attention to such management topics as strategic planning, personnel development, financial management, organizational structure, and information systems. These functions are basic to the conduct and maintenance of public, private, and nonprofit organizations. They also continue to be core subject matters in most public administration graduate programs preparing new public administration professionals.

Many of the core public sector management functions, processes and technologies resemble those in the private sector. Since the early twentieth century in the Progressive Movement and the city manager plan the public administration community has periodically looked to private sector management for models and advice on organizational arrangements and technical issues. And Peters and Pierre (2003, 7) indicate: "Administrative reforms of the past several decades have placed a substantial emphasis on the similarities of public and private management and there has been a good deal of borrowing from business management to transform government." With new public management, adherence to both private sector theories and values, in addition to the processes and technologies, the long-standing public–private relationship has continued.

Noting elements common to traditional public administration and new public management is interesting but should not be overdone. As the abbreviated discussion of New Zealand indicates, with changes in the law formal relations between political authorities and management executives were defined by contractual provisions rather than more traditional common understandings of objectives, informal agreements, or consensual adjustments in past practices. The contracts, enforceable in the courts, entail formal statement of executive responsibilities and consequences of executive performance with regard to departmental objectives, and output production. Involved is establishment of a new public order where NPM puts in place a contracting state [in which] ... contracting would replace public law or public administration as the coordination mechanism in the public sector. The reason that this is done is the basic belief that contracting enhances efficiency (Lane 2000, 147).

To maximize efficiency the public administrator as professional must be taught and socialized to think and operate as a manager. For Larry Terry (1998), this has profound implications for the professional public administration community. According to Terry, contemporary approaches to management, especially liberation and market-driven versions with their emphasis on the values of competition, private sector management practices, and the need to free managers from red tape and bad systems, have a theoretical basis in neo-managerialism which draws upon updated interpretations of Frederick Wilson Taylor as well as a complex mixture of public choice theory, agency theory, and transaction-cost economics (Terry 1998, 194).

The basic assumptions of public choice and organizational economics about human motivations and behavior structure neo-managerialism such that it (Terry 1998, 197) "fosters the idea that public managers are (and should be) self-interested, opportunistic, innovators and risk-takers who exploit information and situations to produce radical change." By the underlying theory public managers must assume the role of entrepreneur in policy and governance. For public administration professionals considering the new public management, the mind sets and motivations of such managers raise doubts regarding democratic accountability of managers and make it unlikely that they would support the notions of the public interest and the public good (Terry 1998, 197–198). Notions of the public interest and public good have been basic elements of the ethics and guiding principles of the modern public administration community.

V. LEGAL, ETHICAL, AND MORAL CONCERNS OF THE PUBLIC ADMINISTRATION COMMUNITY

All professional communities must be concerned with three types of membership behavior. The first is the legal behavior—professionals should conform to the civil and criminal codes generally and to laws relating to the professions specifically. Second is the professional behavior—professionals should follow standards of good professional practices and those profession specific criteria depicted in codes of ethics. The third is moral behavior—professionals should be guided by principles derived from a moral structure. Demonstrating acceptable behavior of all three types is integral to a profession's long-term interests and the well being of the society beyond the profession's membership.

The legitimacy and stability of a political system is likely enhanced when appointed administrators and career civil servants obey the law and adhere to high professional standards and moral precepts. Adherence to the rules elevates the work of the individual public administrator and supports the American public administration community's historical commitment to the goals of building institutional capacity and supporting citizen control (Lynn 2001). Adherence to the rules also helps to prevent charges of misfeasance, embarrassing media exposure, or actual indictments, court cases, and prison sentences, thereby diminishing political and legal embarrassments to those in power and public cynicism.

Professionals in and of government operate in a variety of settings where they are subject to controls on their behavior. DeLeon (2003, 572) identifies four generic types of organizational settings—hierarchies, competitive pluralism, community and anarchy. While the combination of controls varies from setting to setting, each uses external controls to constrain behavior within acceptable limits, but each also relies on internalized controls, the sense of individual responsibility.

So long as behavior is within acceptable limits and social and political support is sustained, professionals function relatively unfettered. Deviations from the external controls may trigger calls for further constraints on professional autonomy. A growing distrust of professions generally, specific professions, or individual professionals also precipitate demands for more stringent controls. Illustratively, a Hastings Center Report pointed out in the 1980s that "...the tenor of discourse on professional ethics changed drastically, amid a growing concern with the rights of clients and a backlash against professional paternalism" (Jennings et al. 1987, 1). Under such circumstances, increased external oversight will often be imposed through new laws, regulations, and court decisions.

Professions contribute to the development of internal controls on the conduct and behavior of their members. Among the mechanisms used is the code of ethics (Griener 1993; Jennings et al. 1987; Sanders 1993). Codes typically spell out ideals of professional performance, principles guiding such performance, ethical obligations and responsibilities to clients, profession, institutions, and the broader public.

Additionally, codes bond and inspire professionals by striving to capture the essence of the character and style that animates the self-image common among practitioners. Professions, and their codes, mean something to practitioners that is not shared with outsiders (Sanders 1993, 93). This is evident in the experience of professional army officers. As a part of their pre-professional training, cadets at the United States Military Academy are exposed to material on army values and the Cadet Honor Code produced by the Academy's Center for the Professional Military Ethic. Throughout their careers Army officers will find articles on values and ethics in professional journals (Brinsfield 1998; Peters 1996). Advanced military education programs, such as those at the US Army War College, periodically publish monographs and extensive bibliographies on professional ethics and values (Shope 2003).

Despite attention to both external and internal controls in organizational settings, for the past few decades the public administration community and the general public has attended to accounts of untoward actions by elected, appointed, and career service officials. Many of the high visibility cases have entangled national figures—members of Congress, armed services officers, high-ranking career employees of defense and intelligence agencies. The unacceptable behavior has not been limited to Washington, DC and has included all levels, branches, and functions of government. In recent years governors have been forced to resign from office for the awarding of contracts to political supporters and for unethical personal behavior. Local newspapers periodically carry stories dealing with venal bribe taking by city inspectors or unprofessional conduct by law enforcement professionals.

Although the incidence in recent years of corrupt and unprofessional behavior has not necessarily been higher than in the past, key conditions have changed. A more intrusive media reports on incidents that, by gentlemen's agreements, may have gone unreported. Middle class expectations have been heightened as to how professionals, including those in government, should perform. With internet access non-professionals can obtain information on medical, legal, and educational issues that traditionally were considered the esoteric domain of professionals.

There are practical consequences of the interplay of changed conditions and unethical behavior. New laws have been adopted to promote ethical behavior generally. Ethics commissions have been established in state governments. Magazine articles, scholarly publications, and handbooks address such topics as "citizenship and democratic theory, virtue, ..., the organizational context, ethics education, and philosophical theory and perspectives" (Cooper 1994, 17). A significant literature continues to advocate ethical and value positions for public administration professionals that are well beyond conflict of interest or corruption matters (Menzel 1999; Rohr 1998). The American Society for Public Administration Section on Ethics publishes a quarterly newsletter, *Ethics Today*, dealing with current issues. Ethics topics have been included in the curriculum of public administration programs and workshops for in-service public employees are regularly conducted. Such audiences are regularly reminded that "[a]dministrative ethics involves the application of moral principles to the conduct of officials in organizations" (Thompson 1985, 555).

A noteworthy development in the recent history of public administration was adoption of a code of ethics by the American Society for Public Administration in 1984. This was an event of particular importance for the community's progress toward professional status and followed years of study, discussion, and debate. Articulated in the code are commitments to the public interest, political regime, practitioner integrity, organizational ethics, and professional excellence. Five principles (and illustrative goals) set forth are:

- Serve the Public Interest
  - Exercise discretionary authority to promote the public interest.
  - Involve citizens in policy decision making.
  - Be prepared to make decisions that may not be popular.
- Respect the Constitution and the Law
  - Understand and apply legislation and regulations relevant to their professional role. Respect and protect privileged information.
  - Promote constitutional principles of equality, fairness, representativeness, responsiveness and due process in protecting citizens' rights.
- Demonstrate Personal Integrity
  - Maintain truthfulness and honesty and to not compromise them for advancement, honor, or personal gain.
  - Zealously guard against conflict of interest or its appearance: e.g., nepotism, improper outside employment, misuse of pubic resources, or the acceptance of gifts.
  - Conduct official acts without partisanship.
- Promote Ethical Organizations
  - Enhance organizational capacity for open communication, creativity, and dedication.
  - Subordinate institutional loyalties to the public good.
  - Promote merit principles that protect against arbitrary capricious actions.
- Strive for Professional Excellence
  - Provide support and encouragement to upgrade competence.
  - Accept as a personal duty the responsibility to keep up to date on emerging issues and potential problems.
  - Encourage others, throughout their careers, to participate in professional activities and associations.

Adoption of the code reflected some sensitivity to the short term factors of public discontent and a desire for the status of professionalism implied by a code of ethics. However, the effects of the short term factors are limited. The legal, professional, and ethical behaviors dealt with in the code had long been concerns of the professional public administration community.

A. DISCRETION AND ITS IMPLICATIONS

As discretion is central to the issue of bureaucratic accountability in democratic societies, the issue debated by Friedrich and Finer and their successors, discretion is also one underlying cause of ethical problems in government. The exercise of discretion is conspicuous at elite levels of the career service where boundaries between politics and administration are virtually non-existent. It is also evident in the work of the street level bureaucrat who determines the quality of public service received by most citizens. Dealing with the consequences of discretion in practice is especially burdensome in the United States where power is structurally separated and dispersed. Goodsell (1989, 575) explains that:

> In some countries, a system of administrative law or even administrative corruption is sufficiently rigid that the discretion of the administrator is minimal. In others, external political control is so strong that the administrator is given ample guidance. In contrast to these situations, the American public admin-istrator operates with wide discretion, within the constitutional context of separation of powers.

Probably a significant percentage of professional practice quandaries or ethical predicaments that arise for the elites and the street level bureaucrats are over discretion situations. Choices are rarely between absolute good and absolute evil. Instead, the choices are about matters where the ethical manager or service provider can decide, one way or another, with equal validity—to approve or disapprove the request for a waiver, to pursue to prosecution or to overlook an incident, to award the contract to firm A instead of firm B. In such practical situations, administrators "often face the dilemma of honoring one legitimate value orientation over another" (Goodsell 1989, 576) and the dilemma can be compounded by such subtle influences as racial–ethnic–religious attitudes or political ideologies. Such is the stuff of discretion, ethical quandaries, and decision making in the modern administrative state.

How the public administration community deals with discretion has consequences for the study of ethics and morality as they pertain to its members. On the point, Rohr (1990, 119) contends that discretion is the central ethical problem of the career civil service. Controlling discretion raises fundamental considerations of democratic theory and political power. Put starkly, who shall govern under what circumstances? Rosenbloom (1989, 464) raises the most basic questions of responsive-ness, accountability, power, and control in asking:

> If public administrators are in fact the 'permanent branch' of government, the guardians of the long-term public interest, and the keepers of the public trust, then who guards the guardians?

B. ETHICS AND MORALITY OF ADMINISTRATION AND THE POLITICAL CONTEXT

The debate over administrative discretion and its ethical implications is likely to continue given long standing opposing positions such as Herman Finer's external (or objective and political) controls versus Carl Friedrich's internal (or subjective and personal), or some combination of external and internal. Alternatively, several public administration theorists (Cooper 1987, 1990; Denhardt 1991; Harmon 1995) have made use of Alasdair MacIntyre's concept of practice as an explanation of what should constitute public administration and thereby public administration professionalism. According to MacIntyre (1984, 187), a practice is

> any coherent and complex form of socially established cooperative human activity thorough which goods internal to that form of activity are realized in the course of trying to achieve those standards of excellence which are appropriate to, and partially definitive of, that form of activity, with the result that human powers to achieve excellence, and human conceptions of the ends and goods involved, are systematically extended.

Two kinds of goods may be obtained from a practice—external (those gained from the practice but obtainable elsewhere—wealth, prestige, station) and internal (those gained from the practice and not obtainable elsewhere—excellence of performance in the specific practice, commitment and obedience to rules associated with the practice) (MacIntyre 1984, 188–190). Practice carries moral content in that it provides "the arena in which the virtues are exhibited." Virtues are inclinations that predispose individuals to act morally and on principles. The internal goods of a practice "can only be achieved by subordinating ourselves within the practice in our relationship to other practitioners" (MacIntyre 1984, 191).

Appraising public administration as a practice, rather than as a profession, requires alterations in customary thinking about balancing internal and external controls of administrative discretion as well the field's core knowledge and skills. To date, public administration has been viewed essentially as a technical field emphasizing instrumental rationality. Any consideration and adoption of a practice perspective of necessity will be preceded by sustained thought on the internal goods and the virtues that constitute the practice. Most basically, a life spent in public administration practice would probably be viewed as a vocation, reflecting a calling more than a job or career (Wolf and Bacher 1989). The responsible administrator would draw upon the traditions of performance in public administration and follow its rules and norms. The traditions, rules, and norms are subject to change because, in public administration as in all fields:

> No one can really predict the progress and outcome [of a practice]. Over time accepted standards of excellence... alter, and the rules... change. These indeterminacies and changes occur through participants' conscious efforts and arguments about what the practice, and the tradition, is—that is, by what we might call a process of interpretive criticism or critique. Our social identities are structured by the prior existence of practices and the practices are constituted by social actors (Frazer and Lacey 1994, 271).

In the public administration practice, emphasis would be placed on achievement of internal goods and virtues rather than such external goods as organizational size, personal income, or professional status. In seeking the public interest (an obligation of the practice) the practitioner would realize the internal goods of justice (a primary virtue), charity, and kindness to citizens and exhibit the virtues of courage, prudence, rationality and fair-mindedness, among others (Cooper 1987, 324).

Disagreements on matters as basic as constitutional interpretation and virtues to be sought, as well as differences in emphases, should not overshadow common concerns of some modern-day theorists. They have directed attention from internal versus external control over the discretion exercised by unelected bureaucrats. Articulated instead are arguments for the autonomy of public administration as an institution separate from legislative, executive, and judicial offices. The importance of this institution to the long-term well being of the political order, in the opinion of some, is considerable: "We see no way of arresting the pathologies of our political system and coming to grips with the sizeable problems of our nation's political economy without a new way of thinking about, speaking of, and acting toward The Public Administration"

(Wamsley et al. 1990, 34). As an institution, the Public Administration smoothes rough edges of the political order when it links the three branches:

> When it does this, the Public Administration plays a crucial role in softening the harsh logic of separation of powers and proves itself a worthy successor to the courts and political parties that provided the same service in the nineteenth century. Parties, courts, and agencies have emerged as the institutional expression of Publius's caution against a doctrinaire interpretation of the principle of separation of powers (Rohr 1986, 184).

Despite the very creative thinking underway, there is no clear agreement on a philosophical position for political administrators and professionals of and in government. Disagreements between contending positions play out in very specific ways.

So the Senior Executive Service, as envisioned, was to include career administrators who had regularly exercised discretion and who were to bring their experience and technical skills to the highest levels of government. A goal of the service, according to Alan K. Campbell (1972), was "appropriate responsiveness to the government's political leadership, while resisting improper political influence." To aid those in the service faced with potential ethical dilemmas, such as "improper political influence," John Rohr recommended an ethical training program which would emphasize: recognition of the ethical implications of the oath of office to support the constitution, knowledge of agency program and institutional history, and awareness of the political vision and political goals of the president they were serving (Rohr 1980, 1998).

The ethics–morality–public administration professionalism linkage is of long standing. Widespread evidence of illegal, unprofessional, and immoral practices in government contributed to the rise of public administration as a field of academic study and as an applied practice (Pugh 1991). Episodic reform movements have served as vehicles of protest against corrupt political practices and in support of innovations that would make government more efficient by way of better management and more moral by way of bringing a better class of people to office and to power. Late nineteenth century reforms of city government and amelioration of urban poverty were guided by principles of social Christianity and concern for personal salvation. According to Pugh (1991, 11):

> Imbued with a 'social gospel' that offered reform of social institutions as the key to personal salvation, this movement endorsed instrumental rationality and bureaucratic means as the key to personal moral salvation, this movement endorsed instrumental rationality and bureaucratic means in pursuit of the 'heavenly city' on earth.

Alternative ethical frameworks have been proposed to steer the profession (or practice). On occasion, scholars have been explicit about the normative basis of public administration. For much of the twentieth century, neutral competence and efficiency, as values to be maximized, were the lodestone of the profession. The New Public Administration, drawing upon the philosophical work of John Rawls, argued that the achievement of social equity should be a mission. Juxtaposed have been the Public Choice school and the more recent New Public Management whose members, drawing from economic theory, have sought to optimize efficiency and to satisfy citizen preference orderings. Denhardt (1991, 92) has held that the discipline of public administration is built on a coherent set of moral principles and virtues of which honor, benevolence, and justice should serve as "moral guideposts." And Terry Cooper (1987, 325) has claimed that:

> The practice of public administration involves more than the simple subordination of the administrative role to that of the politician and the dominance of functional rationality as the only legitimate style of

thought for the administrator. Rather, the role of the public administrator as a fiduciary for the citizenry gives rise to certain internal goods and virtues associated with carrying out the trust inherent in that role.

In a similar vein, Stephen K. Bailey, complementing Paul Appleby's insights on the ethics enhancing potential of system level processes and structural arrangements, stressed the importance of individual characteristics. Bailey asserted that public sector ethics are a composite of mental attitudes and moral qualities. The most essential of the moral qualities are ... optimism,...courage, and... fairness tempered by charity" (Bailey 1965, 285–286).

The values and moral qualities advocated by the new public administrationists, public choicers, new public managers, Denhardt, Bailey, Cooper, and others, are well within the mainstream of American and Western political thought. Nonetheless, the values and qualities do not inherently link to the work of public administration practitioners. A critical question is the extent to which the points covered by the scholarly discussions are derived from observations of *values applied in concrete situations* or expressions of individual visions of how government *ought to operate* and which normative values should be sought.

If the points covered are derived from observations of values applied in concrete situations, the scholarly discussions constitute an impressive foundation for guidance to newcomers to administrative positions. Given the technical specialist bias in recruitment and promotion in the US career service, individuals coming to such positions, though technically competent, may lack experience in dealing with competing ethical claims or ethically ambiguous problems. Attention in training programs to legal conformance and awareness of the ethical problems of ambiguity is important and fundamental to the effective performance of public agencies.

Points covered by scholarly discussions, however, may not be grounded in descriptions of ethical and moral principles observed in practice but instead consist of normative goals sought by scholars. Then the scene becomes more convoluted as alternative definitions of the good compete for dominance. Under these circumstances the difficulty of making visions real and the possibility of value paradoxes should not be underestimated.

Proponents of "Public Administration [playing] a crucial role in softening the harsh logic of separation of powers" or serving as the "fiduciary for the citizenry" need first address a fundamental political question. That is the one which faced reformers a century ago and has become even more pressing as discretionary authority expands. The question is wisely identified by Rohr (1998, 6): "how can a democratic regime justify substantial political power in the hands of people who are exempt by law from the discipline of the ballot box?" Though conditions may change, at this point in America's development, the political regime, subject to discipline of the ballot box, and the administrative regime, subject to legislative and fiscal controls, are not equals. The latter and its ethical and moral preferences are subordinate to the former. To alter this structure to make them equal would require a further transformation of constitutional interpretation, political culture, and power distribution.

C.   THE PHILOSOPHICAL–POLITICS INTERFACE

The challenge to public administration professionalism is the daunting one of specifying a class of ethical and moral principles to guide professionals and about which there is general consensus in the community. If taken seriously, the challenge would force attention to topics that are significant points of controversy among professional philosophers. As one illustration, the community would need to decide which of two tracks to follow—foundationalist (which holds that there are fundamental objective rules that can be discovered, including those for ethical behavior and moral obligation) or postmodernist (which holds to a conventionalistic view of normative principles, that ethical behavior and moral obligation are not rooted in social convention or cultural practice but are products of individual choice).

Foundationalists are, in turn, subdivided into teleological and deontological orders on the derivation of rules for ethical behavior and moral obligation (Chandler 1994). The teleological position holds that an act is judged for its actual or expected consequences (Pops 1994, 157). For utilitarianism, the most familiar example of a teleological position, an act is morally obligatory if the rule under which it is subsumed leads to the greatest overall balance of good over evil (Fox 1994, 86). The deontological position relates to explicitly linking a value with some general procedure or practice (Chandler 1994, 149) and holds that acts are based on duties or principles that are either right or wrong in themselves, the results being irrelevant to moral judgment (Frederickson 1993, 248).

Evidence of the impact of both positions—teleological and deontological—on the workings of the public administration community has been pointed out by a number of scholars. The bureaucratic ethos, which supports the community's dominant and traditional framework, is teleological, emphasizing instrumental rationality, efficiency, and expertise (Pugh 1991). Alternatively, many of the codes of ethics adopted by public administration groups "are primarily deontological—... [based upon]... assumptions... that there are absolute principles of right and wrong, independent of results or consequences, and that public administrators will adhere to these values" (Frederickson 1993, 249).

Obviously, disagreements among professional philosophers on fundamentals impede selection of a single class of ethical and moral principles to guide public administration. There are other, compounding factors. The conduct of public policy sometimes dictates actions which create ethical quandaries and make ethical codes problematic. Michael Walzer (1973) and Dennis Thompson (1987) have gone to the teachings of Machiavelli to remind students of politics and morality of the paradox of dirty hands. This paradox concerns the political leader who for the sake of public purposes violates moral principles (Thompson 1987, 11). Professionals in and of government (elected, appointed, career) can ignore conventional morality and gain dirty hands for the noblest of reasons—lying to preserve national security, torture to gain information to save a population, assassination of despots. When the weight of harmful consequences to many others is sufficiently great, unwillingness to take the necessary (albeit unethical) action may be "moral self-indulgence" (Thompson 1987, 52).

Dirty hands are also acquired for ignoble reasons. Professionals in and of government on occasion might approve actions involving substantial risk where the risk is for neither the public good nor individual goodness "but power and glory. If the politician succeeds, he is a hero; eternal praise is the supreme reward for not being good" (Walzer 1973, 176). The breaking of the law which frequently accompanies dirty hands action is not to be confused with the breaking of the law which accompanies civil disobedience:

> In most cases of civil disobedience the laws of the state are broken for moral reasons, and the state provides the punishment. In most cases of dirty hands moral rules are broken for reasons of state, and no one provides the punishment. There is rarely a Czarist executioner waiting in the wings for politicians with dirty hands, even the most deserving among them (Walzer 1973, 179).

Scholarly attention to philosophical controversies is meaningful and, over the long haul, regulates the terms of political debate. In the interim, professionals in and of government need practical guidance. For public administration professionals, difficult ethical situations are rarely ones in which the moral or ethical issues are sharply drawn and the public interest explicit. Most ethical situations with which administrators and career professionals must deal are morally ambiguous. In these cases the professional challenge is one of courage and a sense of duty.

Coping with ambiguous and complex problems requires ethical flexibility and avoidance of moral rigidity. Ethical flexibility is not a lack of principle or chameleon like morals, it denotes sensitivity to the reality that the relative importance of principles varies from situation to situation.

Morgan and Kass found in focus groups with practicing administrators that three languages were used to explain administrative actions: a language of neutral competence which emphasizes efficiency and technical skill; a language of pluralist politics which appreciates the importance and legitimacy of balancing competing interests; and a language of public interest which emphasizes the administrator's responsibility to protect the public interest, primary community values, even in the face of majority opposition. No one of the languages was preferred to the exclusion of others. A language prevailed when it fit a decision making context "filled with complexity;... uncertainty; [and]... considerable potential for *conflict*, which, if not kept in manageable bounds, will prevent managers from getting their jobs done" (Morgan and Kass 1991, 288). The Morgan–Kass findings may connote, to some purists, moral relativity and situation ethics (and therefore be troubling) or, to more experienced practitioners, the flexibility and adaptability of true professionals (and therefore be laudable).

Absent agreement on specific values to be binding on government or criteria for selecting the values (MacIntyre 1984, chap. 2), some mechanism must be adopted for choosing priority values. This is not easily done. Values take many forms. Laswell (1971, 42–43) borrows from the Universal Declaration of Human Rights and lists values related to human dignity—power, enlightenment, wealth, well-being, skill, affection, respect, rectitude. Gormley (1989, 42) enumerates more explicitly political values of reformers, among them responsiveness, efficiency, consistency, rationality, accountability.

The values offered by Laswell and Gormley may be mutually reinforcing, maximizing one maximizes others. Frequently, the reverse is true. Values are mutually exclusive, maximizing one precludes maximizing others. Thus, the consequences of a decision by the public administration community to be guided by John Rawls and a principle of equality with respect to needs are likely very different from those of a decision to be guided by Robert Nozick and a principle of equality with respect to entitlement (MacIntyre 1984, 248). Though the positions of both Rawls and Nozick are rationally derived, they are, in MacIntyre's judgment, incompatible and incommensurable. Nonetheless, in a political system tolerant of diversity, public administrators presumably could be allowed to choose to be guided in their professional work by the value position most ethical to them personally. The different choices might result in administrative chaos, dramatic service disparities from one jurisdiction to another, and different decisions in like circumstances from one professional administrator to another.

However intellectually appealing, proposals to permit such free choice in moral positions are not likely to succeed. Political cultures which define bureaucrats not as independent agents but as servants are likely to resist free choices and the substantive outcomes they produce (Elazar 1984). A political order wherein power accrues from electoral success and control of strategic decision points may not tolerate administrative chaos nor permit free wheeling decisions about morals and ethics which threaten the well being of the dominant governing coalition.

Claims of a lack of criteria for ranking values by their virtuousness are in many ways irrelevant. Politics in its most raw or noble senses is ultimately concerned with the authoritative allocation of values for a society (Easton 1965), producing decisions regarding which individuals and interests will gain materially from policy decisions, and whose values are to prevail and be legally binding on society members, whatever their individual moral preferences. Administrative capacity, and therefore the quality of public administration professional's performance, is tested in the implementation of policies incorporating the authoritative allocation of values. Confronting issues of ethics, values, and morals in administration and management compels the public administration community to deal with questions of normative political theory and political philosophy. As generations long gone would remind us, the questions have confounded the community from its earliest days and have complicated development of a profession of public administration.

VI. CONCLUDING OBSERVATIONS

Students of the professions frequently list benchmark criteria of growth and development. Among the more basic are organization, education criteria, knowledge base, code of ethics, and service orientation. At least on these criteria, public administration has achieved professional status.

Since 1939, the American Society for Public Administration (ASPA) has functioned as a national professional organization and has represented the movements, circumstances, personalities, and pressures that have sculpted American public administration (Pugh 1985, 475). ASPA provides members with a variety of professionally related services, conferences, websites, and publications. Through organizational activities in regional chapters and substantive sections ASPA members are regularly able to update interests and skills and interact with professional colleagues.

The public administration community has also had a long established relationship with professional training and educational programs. From the early decades of the last century institutes and universities have been preparing men and women for careers as professionals in and of government. For generations, the Masters of Public Administration (MPA) has served as the terminal professional degree.

Like other professions, public administration has worked to assure and maintain the quality of professional training. Since the 1970s the National Association of Schools of Public Affairs and Administration (NASPAA) has supported a program of peer review and, since the 1980s, the accreditation of "Professional Master's Degree Programs in Public Affairs, Policy and Administration." Currently, the accreditation process involves submission of a self-study report by the program seeking accreditation; technical review of the report by staff of NASPAA's Commission on Peer Review and Accreditation; review of the self-study study report and recommendation by the Commission on the conduct of a site visit; appointment of a Site Visit Team; a site visit and submission of a report to the Commission; a Commission decision on accreditation. (National Association of Schools of Public Affairs and Administration 2003, 1–3).

During the accreditation process, a program's Common Curriculum Components are assessed. Of concern is whether the components are designed to produce professionals capable of intelligent, creative analysis and communication, and action in public service. The three common components and related substantive course topics are: Management of Public Service Organizations (human resources, budgeting and financial processes, information management); Application of Quantitative and Qualitative Techniques of Analysis (policy and program formulation, implementation and evaluation, decision-making and problem-solving); Understanding of Public Policy and Organizational Environment (political and legal institutions and processes, economic and social institutions and processes, organization and management concepts and behavior) (National Association of Schools of Public Affairs and Administration 2003, 8–9).

A case might be made that these Common Curriculum Components constitute a core knowledge system for the public administration profession. The first component covers key management topics—personnel, financial management, and information technology—required for the maintenance of any public organization. The second component provides the requisite analytical skills needed for the three aspects of professional practice—diagnosis, inference, and treatment. The third component addresses factors—political, legal, social, economic, institutional—that form the context of professional practice.

In combination, the components are basic to analyzing, understanding, and dealing with complexity. That professionals of government must be proficient in these matters for major undertakings and routine services, regardless of competing paradigms, structural forms, or definitions of purpose, is obvious. Mastery of these basics is, and will continue to be, a necessary but not sufficient condition of professionalism.

But the major issues yet to be adequately addressed are not related to basic management skills. Instead, they are to the generation and acceptance of a new dominant paradigm to guide professional practice. The grounds for the paradigm search derive from perceptions of a decline in the historic authority of the state. More directly, the perceptions hold that "the idea that national governments are the major actors in public policy and that they are able to influence the economy and society thorough their actions now appears to be in doubt" (Peters and Pierre 1998, 223).

Arguments made to explain these fundamental changes are several. Peters and Pierre (1998, 225–227) cite four:

- "[N]etworks have come to dominate public policy. The assertion is that these amorphous collections of actors—not formal policy-making institutions in government—control policy. ...[T]he real action occurs within the private sector."
- The state has lost "the capacity for direct control ...Government actors are conceptualized as in a continuous process of bargaining with the members of their relevant networks."
- The use of networks ...leads to a blending of public-sector and private-sector resources. ...[by] "the creation of more or less formal partnerships between actors in government and actors in the private sector."
- "The utilization of public–private partnerships for policy indicates the willingness of a government operating within the governance framework to develop alternative means of making and implementing policy."

As a result of the decline in traditional state authority, greater attention has been directed to new modes of governance and related matters of accountability, public–private sector relations, inter- and intra-sector competition, emphasis on outputs, and techniques of societal steering (Peters and Pierre 1998, 227–228). These constitute issues before the public administration community.

Among the scholars working on the contemporary issues are Laurence Lynn, Carolyn Heinrich, and Carolyn Hill. They define governance (2001, 7) as regimes of laws, rules, judicial decisions, and administrative practices that constrain, prescribe, and enable the provision of publicly supported goods and services. To expand the knowledge base on governance and public management under new conditions they outline a comprehensive research agenda.

Recognized, however, is the complexity of the topics and the difficulty of carrying out the required body of work. Proposed to deal with the complexity is a "schematic or heuristic framework that suggests how the elements of governance—...—might be linked through a dynamic and interactive process." The proposed framework from a "political economy" base and is expected to utilize developed theory, quantitative and qualitative research methodologies, and empirical data (Lynn et al. 2001, 30, 36).

Studying and understanding governance in all its dimensions is a complex project involving several levels of analysis. A formula which provides a framing device for this complexity particularly in the management of human services is presented (Lynn et al. 2001, 81):

$$O = f\,(E, C, T, S, M)$$

where O is outputs/outcomes, E is environmental factors, C is client characteristics, T is treatments, S is structures, and M is managerial roles and actions.

The levels of governance included by Lynn, Heinrich, and Hill (2001, 37) for analysis are:

Global/National/Cultural Environment → Institutional (Public Choice) Level → Managerial Level

→ Technical (Primary Work) Level → Political Assessment

Research at and between these levels is conducted because behaviors or activities at various levels might be linked through a dynamic and interactive process That is, conditions at any given level may be affected by developments (culture, mandates, fiscal resources, etc.) at other levels and failure to take these developments into account can lead to incorrect or incomplete analysis. By recognizing these levels, governance research is more likely to produce usable knowledge about governing instead of ignoring contexts and processes that are fundamental elements of governance in practice (Lynn et al. 2001, 36).

Discussions of contemporary public organizational change or institutional restructuring typically include references to governance and new public management. This is understandable because there are many similarities between the mainstream debate on the emerging forms of governance and the overarching philosophy behind the NPM (Peters and Pierre 1998, 227).

Primary similarities between the two can be cited. Significantly, governance and NPM hold that current public administration and the state are increasingly separated from and out of touch with the rest of society. The two approaches see a diminished role for elected officials and the replacement of political power derived from legal mandates or elected office with an entrepreneurial style of leadership ...." For both, this leadership is to advocate greater emphasis on new techniques of steering. Concerned primarily with results, both favor a shift in control emphasis from inputs to outputs. And to increase sensitivity to customer preferences and efficiency governance and NPM look to competition within the public sector and between potential public and private service providers (Peters and Pierre 1998, 227–231).

Governance and new public management overlap but are not congruent. Despite the similarities at the operational level, the two approaches do differ in underlying philosophy (Peters and Pierre 1998, 231). Peters and Pierre identify five differences between them. First, governance is a long-standing concept related to the functions of democratic systems and the importance of public interest; NPM seeks mainly the transfer of corporate practices to better produce and deliver a public product.

A second difference is principal focus. As exemplified by Lynn, Heinrich, and Hill, governance is concerned with analyzing process, interactions, and policy actor influence; NPM focuses on outcomes and management practices that improve efficiency and better meet customer preferences. Third, governance may be viewed as political theory; NPM stands as a theory of organizations. Fourth, governance seeks strategies for retaining political control of public resources, building state capacity, and coordinating public–private initiatives; NPM favors strategies which emphasize transference of private sector techniques to public agencies and enhance provider–customer exchanges. Fifth, because governance is less ideological in orientation and continues many traditional administrative practices, its reforms can adapt to most jurisdictions without significant cultural change; NPM, on the other hand, is highly ideological advocating "a unilateral infusion of corporate-sector values and objectives into the public sector and public-service production and delivery" (Peters and Pierre 1998, 231–233; Frederickson and Smith 2003, chap. 9).

Governance and new public management are competing for acceptance as the dominant public administration paradigm. Either would provide a core body of professional knowledge, analytical skills, and exemplary practices for professionals in and of government. This competition is in the tradition of paradigm competition of the past.

Vitality in the generation of new paradigms may be evidence of a profession's commitment to growth, innovation, and intellectual renewal. Alternatively, the ongoing debates for one paradigm over another may suggest that the profession has not yet decided what constitutes its core knowledge, its essential technical skills, or its ethical standards. It makes a good deal of difference to the training of neophyte public administrators, the actual practice of governance, and the professional ethical standards whether the dominant paradigm of professional education and practice is new public administration, public choice, or new public management. Or, as the PPBS and intergovernmental policy experiences demonstrated, for successful government-wide paradigm implementation, even when paradigm generation and translation have been carried out, it is necessary to have enough trained professionals in place with requisite skills and organizational objectives and critical tasks that are amenable to the paradigms.

Continued debate over paradigm qualities is essential to the strength of the public administration profession and the well-being of the democratic polity.

REFERENCES

Abbott, A., *The System of Professions*, The University of Chicago Press, Chicago, IL, 1988.

Abrams, R., *Foundations of Political Analyses: An Introduction to the Theory of Collective Choice*, Columbia University Press, New York, 1980.

Agranoff, R., Managing Intergovernmental Processes, In *Handbook of Public Administration*, Perry, J. L., Ed., 2nd ed., Jossey-Bass, San Francisco, CA, pp. 210–231, 1996.

Allison, G. T., Public and private management: are they alike in all unimportant respects?, In *Proceedings for the Public Management Research Conference: OPM Document 127-53-1*, Office of Personnel Management, Washington, DC, 1980.

Altshuler, A. A., The study of American public administration, In *The Politics of the Federal Bureaucracy*, Altshuler, A. A., Ed., Dodd, Mead, New York, 1968.

Anderson, W. and Gaus, J. M., *Research in Public Administration*, Social Science Research Council, Public Administration Service, Chicago, IL, 1945.

Appleby, P. H., *Big Democracy*, Knopf, New York, 1945.

Appleby, P. H., *Policy and Administration*, University of Alabama Press, Tuscaloosa, AL, 1949.

Argyris, C., The use of knowledge as a test for theory: the case of public administration, *Journal Public Administration Research Theory*, 1, 337–345, 1991.

Auckland District Law Society Making a Change, 2002, Auckland, NZ, http://www.adls.org.nz/publilc/public50/nzls03/nzls31.asp (accessed March 9, 2004).

Bailey, S. K., Ethics and the public service, In *Public Administration and Democracy*, Martin, R. C., Ed., Syracuse University Press, Syracuse, NY, pp. 283–298, 1965.

Baker, K. G., Public choice theory: some important assumptions and public-policy implications, In *Public Administration: Readings in Institutions, Processes, Behavior, Policy*, Golembiewski, R. T., Gibson, F. G. Y., and Cornog, G. Y., Eds., Rand McNally, New York, pp. 41–60, 1976.

Banfield, E. C., The decision-making schema, *Public Administration Review*, 17, 278–285, 1957.

Barnard, C. I., *The Functions of the Executive*, Harvard University Press, Cambridge, MA, 1938.

Beer, S. H., Federalism, nationalism, and democracy in America, *American Political Science Review*, 72, 9–21, 1978.

Boll, M. M., *National Security Planning*, The University Press of Kentucky, Lexington, KY, 1988.

Borcherding, T. E., Ed., *Budgets and Bureaucrats: The Sources of Government Growth*, Duke University Press, Durham, NC, 1977.

Brewer, G. D. and deLeon, P., *The Foundations of Policy Analysis*, Dorsey, Homewood, IL, 1983.

Brinsfield, J. W., Army values and ethics: a search for consistency and relevance, *Parameters*, 28, 69–82, 1998.

Brint, S., *In an Age of Experts*, Princeton University Press, Princeton, NJ, 1994.

Brown, B., The search for public administration: roads not followed, *Public Administration Review*, 49, 215–216, 1989.

Buchanan, J. M., *Liberty, Market, and State*, New York University Press, New York, 1985.

Budget of the United States Fiscal Year 2005, US Government Printing Office, Washington, DC, 2004.

Builder, C. H. and Dewar, J. A., A time for planning? if not now, when?, *Parameters*, 24, 4–15, 1994.

Burgess, P. M., Capacity building and the elements of public management, *Public Administration Review*, 35, 705–716, 1975.

Burk, J., Expertise, jurisdiction, and legitimacy of the military profession, In *The Future of the Army Profession*, Matthews, L. J., Ed., McGraw-Hill, Boston, MA, pp. 19–38, 2002.

Burke, J. P., Reconciling public administration and democracy: the role of the responsible administrator, *Public Administration Review*, 49, 180–185, 1989.

Caiden, G. E., In search of an apolitical science of American public administration, In *Politics and Administration: Woodrow Wilson and American Public Administration*, Rabin, J. and Bowman, J. S., Eds., Marcel Dekker, New York, pp. 51–76, 1984.

Campbell, A. K., Old and new public administration in the 1970s, *Public Administration Review*, 32, 343–347, 1972.

Campbell Public Affairs Institute, *Paths to Performance in State and Local Government*, Government Performance Project, Syracuse, NY, 2002.

Chandler, R. C., Deontological dimensions of administrative ethics, In *Handbook of Administrative Ethics*, Cooper, T. L., Ed., Marcel Dekker, New York, pp. 147–156, 1994.

Childs, R. S., Commission government and the city-manager plan, *Annals American Politic Social Science* 841–849; Mosher, F. C., Ed., *Basic Literature of American Public Administration* 1787–1950, Holmes & Meier, New York, 1914.

Chu, D.S., Memorandum for Secretaries of the Military Departments, Department of Defense, Washington, DC. http//:www.dod.mil/prhome/docs/Results_Final.pdf (accessed December 16, 2004).

Chu, D. S. C. and Berstein, N., Decisionmaking for defense, In *New Challenges New Tools for Defense Decisionmaking*, Johnson, S. E., Libicki, M. C., and Treverton, G. F., Eds., RAND, Santa Monica, CA, pp. 13–32, 2003.

Clapp, G. R., The long road to profession, *Public Administration Review*, 6, 171–174, 1946.

Commission of Inquiry of Public Service Personnel, *Better Government Personnel*, McGraw-Hill, New York, 1935.

Congressional Budget Office, *Changes in Federal Civilian Employment: An Update*, US Government Printing Office, Washington, DC, 2001.

Conlan, T. J., *From New Federalism to Devolution: Twenty-Five Years of Intergovernmental Reform*, Brookings Institution, Washington, DC, 1998.

Cooper, T. L., Hierarchy, virtue, and the practice of public administration: a perspective for normative ethics, *Public Administration Review*, 47, 320–328, 1987.

Cooper, T. L., *The Responsible Administrator*, Jossey-Bass, San Francisco, CA, 1990.

Cooper, T. L., The emergence of administrative ethics as a field of study in the United States, In *Handbook of Administrative Ethics*, Cooper, T. L., Ed., Marcel Dekker, New York, pp. 3–30, 1994.

Crenson, M. A., *The Federal Machine: Beginnings of Bureaucracy in Jacksonian America*, Johns Hopkins University Press, Baltimore, MD, 1975.

Dahl, R. A., The science of public administration: three problems, *Public Administration Review*, 7, 1–11, 1947.

deLeon, L., On acting responsibly in a disorderly world: individual ethics and administrative responsibility, In *Handbook of Public Administration*, Peters, B. G. and Pierre, J., Eds., Sage Publications, London, pp. 569–580, 2003.

Denhardt, K. G., Unearthing the moral foundations of public administration: honor, benevolence, and justice, In *Ethical Frontiers in Public Management*, Bowman, J. S., Ed., Jossey-Bass, San Francisco, CA, pp. 91–113, 1991.

Department of Homeland Security, Washington, DC, http://www.dhs.gov (accessed November 23, 2004).

DiIulio, J. J., Recovering the public management variable: lessons from schools, prisons, and armies, *Public Administration Review*, 49, 127–133, 1989.

Dimock, M. E., *Modern Politics and Administration: A Study of the Creative State*, American Book Co, New York, 1937.

Dimock, M. E., Executive development after ten years, *Public Administration Review*, 18, 91–97, 1958.

Downs, G. W. and Larkey, P. D., *The Search for Government Efficiency: From Hubris to Helplessness*, Temple University Press, Philadelphia, PA, 1986.

Easton, D., *A Framework for Political Analysis*, Prentice Hall, Englewood Cliffs, NJ, 1965.

Egger, R., The period of crisis: 1933 to 1945, In *American Public Administration: Past, Present, Future*, Mosher, F. C., Ed., University of Alabama Press, Tuscaloosa, AL, pp. 49–96, 1975.

Eggers, W.D., The wonder down under, GovExec.com, March 1, 1997.

Elazar, D. J., *American Federalism: A View from the States*, 3rd ed., Harper & Row, New York, 1984.

Enthoven, A. C. and Smith, K. W., *How Much Is Enough?*, Harper & Row, New York, 1971.

Eulau, H., Skill revolution and the consultative commonwealth, *American Political Science Review*, 67, 169–191, 1973.

Fenton, J. H., *Politics in the Border States*, Hauser Press, New Orleans, LA, 1957.

Fesler, J. W., Administrative literature and the second Hoover Commission reports, *American Political Science Review*, 51, 135–157, 1957.

Fesler, J. W., The presence of the administrative past, In *American Public Administration: Patterns of the Past*, Fesler, J. W., Ed., American Society for Public Administration, Washington, DC, pp. 1–27, 1982.

Finer, H., Administrative responsibility in democratic government, *Public Administration Review*, 1, 335–350, 1941.

Finegold, K., Wherry, L., and Schardin, S., *Block Grants: Details of the Bush Proposals*, The Urban Institute, Washington, DC, 2004.

Fiorina, M. P., *Congress: Keystone of the Washington Establishment*, Yale University Press, New Haven, CT, 1977.

Fox, C. J., The use of philosophy in administrative ethics, In *Handbook of Administrative Ethics*, Cooper, T. L., Ed., Marcel Dekker, New York, pp. 83–105, 1994.

Frazer, E. and Lacey, N., MacIntyre, feminism and the concept of practice, In *After MacIntyre*, Horton, J. and Mendus, S., Eds., University of Notre Dame Press, Notre Dame, IN, pp. 265–282, 1994.

Frederickson, H. G., Toward a new public administration, In *Toward a New Public Administration*, Marini, F., Ed., Chandler, Scranton, PA, 1971.

Frederickson, H. G., The lineage of new public administration, In *Organization Theory and the New Public Administration*, Bellone, C. J., Ed., Allyn and Bacon, Boston, MA, pp. 33–51, 1980a.

Frederickson, H. G., *New Public Administration*, University of Alabama Press, Tuscaloosa, AL, 1980b.

Frederickson, H. G., Minnowbrook II: changing epochs of public administration, *Public Administration Review*, 49, 95–100, 1989.

Frederickson, H. G., Ethics and public administration: some assertions, In *Ethics and Public Administration*, Frederickson, H. G., Ed., E Sharp, Armonk, NY, pp. 243–261, 1993.

Frederickson, H. G. and Smith, K. B., *Public Administration Theory Primer*, Westview Press, Boulder, CO, 2003.

Freedman, J. O., *Crisis and Legitimacy: The Administrative Process and American Government*, Cambridge University Press, Cambridge, IC, 1978.

Freidson, E., *Profession of Medicine: A Study of the Sociology of Applied Knowledge*, Dodd, Mead, New York, 1970.

Freidson, E., *Professional Powers: A Study of the Institutionalization of Formal Knowledge*, University of Chicago Press, Chicago, IL, 1986.

Friedrich, C. J., Responsible government service under the American constitution, In *Problems of the American Public Service: Five Monographs on Specific Aspects of Personnel Administration*, Friedrich, C. J., Beyer, W. C., Spero, S. D., Miller, J. F., and Graham, G. A., Eds., McGraw-Hill, New York, 1935.

Friedrich, C. J., Public policy and the nature of administrative responsibility, In *Public Policy 1940*, Friedrich, C. J. and Mason, E., Eds., Harvard University Press, Cambridge, MA, pp. 3–24, 1940.

Gargan, J. J., Consideration of local government capacity, *Public Administration Review*, 41, 649–658, 1981.

Gaus, J. M., White, L. D., and Dimock, M. E., *The Frontiers of Public Administration*, Russell and Russell, New York, 1940.

Golembiewski, R. T., A critique of 'democratic administration' and its supporting ideation, *American Political Science Review*, 71, 1488–1507, 1977a.

Golembiewski, R. T., *Public Administration as a Developing Discipline. Part 1, Perspectives on Past and Present*, Marcel Dekker, New York, 1977b.

Goode, W. J., The theoretical limits of professionalization, In *The Semi-Professions and Their Organization: Teachers, Nurses, Social Workers*, Etzioni, A. l., Ed., Free Press, New York, pp. 266–313, 1969.

Goodnow, F. J., *Municipal Problems*, Macmillan, New York, 1897.

Goodnow, F. J., *Politics and Administration: A Study in Government*, Macmillan, New York, 1900.

Goodnow, F. J., *City Government in the United States*, Century, New York, 1904.

Goodsell, C. T., Balancing competing values, In *Handbook of Public Administration*, Perry, J. L., Ed., Jossey-Bass, San Francisco, CA, pp. 575–584, 1989.

Gore, W. J., Administrative behavior, In *The Handbook of Political Behavior*, Long, S. L., Ed., Plenum, New York, pp. 113–194, 1981.

Gormley, W. T., *Taming the Bureaucracy: Muscles, Prayers, and Other Strategies*, Princeton University Press, Princeton, NJ, 1989.

Grant, A. V., Operations research and systems analysis, In *Encyclopedia of the American Military*, Jessup, J. E., Ed., Vol. 3, Scribner's, New York, 1957–1985, 1994.

Gray, C. S., *Modern Strategy*, Oxford University Press, Oxford, UK, 1999.

Griener, G. G., Moral integrity of professions, *Profession Ethics*, 2, 15–37, 1993.

Gross, B. M., *The Managing of Organizations: The Administrative Struggle*, Free Press, New York, 1964.

Guerreiro–Ramos, A., A substantive approach to organizations: epistemological grounds, In *Organization Theory and the New Public Administration*, Bellone, C. J., Ed., Allyn and Bacon, Boston, MA, pp. 140–168, 1980.

Gulick, L., Notes on the theory of organization, In *Papers on the Science of Administration*, Gulick, L. and Urwick, L., Eds., Institute of Public Administration, New York, pp. 1–45, 1937a.

Gulick, L., Science, values, and public administration, In *Papers on the Science of Administration*, Gulick, L. and Urwick, L., Eds., Institute of Public Administration, New York, pp. 189–195, 1937.

Gulick, L. and Urwick, L., *Papers on the Science of Administration*, Institute of Public Administration, New York, 1937.

Halligan, J., New public sector models: reform in Australia and New Zealand, In *Public Sector Reform: Rationale, Trends and Problems*, Lane, J. E., Ed., Sage, London, pp. 17–46, 1997.

Harder, K. C. and Stephens, J. C., Management education for professional personnel, *Personnel Administrative*, 19, 37–43, 1956.

Harmon, M. M., *Responsibility as Paradox*, Sage, Thousand Oaks, CA, 1995.

Harmon, M. M. and Mayer, R. T., *Organization Theory for Public Administration*, Little, Brown, Boston, MA, 1986.

Hart, J., *The Presidential Branch*, Pergamon Press, New York, 1987.

Hart, D. K., A partnership in virtue among all citizens: the public service and civic humanism, *Public Administrative Review*, 49, 101–105, 1989.

Hitch, C. J. and McKean, R. N., *The Economics of Defense in the Nuclear Age*, Harvard University Press, Cambridge, MA, 1960.

Hitch, C. J., *Decision-Making for Defense*, University of California Press, Berkeley, CA, 1965.

Hitch, C. J., Development and salient features of the programming system, In *A Modern Design for Defense Decision: A McNamara-Hitch-Enthoven anthology*, Tucker, S. A., Ed., Industrial College of the Armed Forces, Washington, DC, pp. 64–85, 1966.

Honadle, B. W., A capacity-building framework: a search for concept and purpose, *Public Administrative Review*, 41, 574–580, 1981.

Hood, C., A public management for all seasons?, *Public Administrative*, 69, 3–19, 1991.

Horn, M. J., *The Political Economy of Public Administration*, Cambridge University Press, Cambridge, 1995.

Hughes, O. E., *Public Management and Administration*, 2nd ed., St. Martin's Press, New York, 1998.

Hundley, R. O., *Past Revolutions Future Transformations*, Rand, Santa Monica, CA, 1999.

Ingraham, P. W., Human resources management: introduction, In *Handbook of Public Administration*, Peters, B. G., Ed., Sage, London, pp. 49–52, 2003.

Ingraham, P. W. and Rosenbloom, D. H., The new public personnel and the new public service, *Public Administrative Review*, 49, 116–125, 1989.

Ingraham, P. W., Peters, B. G., and Moyniham, D. P., In *Governance in the Twenty-First Century: Revitalizing the Public Service*, Peters, B. G. and Savoie, D. J., Eds., McGuill-Queen's University Press, Montreal, Canada, pp. 385–422, 2000.

International Monetary Fund, IMF manual on fiscal transparency II, Public Availability of Information, 2001.

Jennings, B., Callahan, D., and Wolf, S. M., The professions: public interest and common good, *A Hastings Center Report Special Supplement*, 3–10, 1987.

Jordan, A. A., Taylor, W. J., and Mazarr, M. J., *American National Security*, The Johns Hopkins Press, Baltimore, MD, 1999.

Kamensky, J., OMB must focus performance-based budget effort. Federaltimes.com, February 17, 2003.

Kaplan, F., *The Wizards of Armageddon*, Simon and Schuster, New York, 1983.

Karl, B. D., *Executive Reorganization and Reform in the New Deal*, Harvard University Press, Cambridge, MA, 1963.

Kaufman, H., The next step in case studies, *Public Administration Review*, 18, 52–59, 1958.

Kettl, D. F., *The Global Public Management Revolution*, Brookings Institution, Washington, DC, 2000.

Kettl, D. F., *The Transformation of Governance*, Johns Hopkins Press, Baltimore, MD, 2002.

Key, V. O., Politics and administration, In *The Future of Government in the United States*, White, L. D., Ed., University of Chicago Press, Chicago, IL, pp. 145–163, 1942.

Key, V. O., *Southern Politics in State and Nation*, Knopf, New York, 1949.

Keyssar, A. and May, E. R., Education for public service in the history of the United States, In *For the People: Can We Fix Public Service?*, Donahue, J. D. and Nye, J. S., Eds., Brookings Institution, Washington, DC, pp. 225–237, 2003.

King, D. S., *The New Right*, Dorsey, Chicago, IL, 1987.

Kirkhart, L., Toward a Theory of Public Administration, In *Toward a New Public Administration*, Marini, F., Ed., Chandler, Scranton, PA, pp. 127–164, 1971.

Kline, E. H., To be a professional, *South Review Public Administrative*, 5, 258–281, 1981.

Knott, J. H. and Miller, G. H., *Reforming Bureaucracy: The Politics of Institutional Choice*, Prentice Hall, Englewood Cliffs, NJ, 1987.

Kuhn, T. S., *The Structure of Scientific Revolutions*, University of Chicago Press, Chicago, IL, 1962.

Lalman, D., Oppenheimer, J., and Swistak, P., Formal rational choice theory: a cumulative science of politics, In *The State of the Discipline II*, Finifter, A. W., Ed., American Political Science Association, Washington, DC, pp. 77–104, 1993.

Lane, J. E., Introduction: only deregulation, privatization and marketization, In *Public Sector Reform: Rationale, Trends and Problems*, Lane, J. E., Ed., Sage, London, pp. 1–16, 1997.

Lane, J. E., *New Public Management*, Routledge, London, 2000.

Lane, L. M. and Wolf, J. F., *The Human Resource Crisis in the Public Sector*, Quorum Books, New York, 1990.

LaPorte, T. R., The recovery of relevance in the study of public organizations, In *Toward a New Public Administration*, Marini, F., Ed., Chandler, Scranton, PA, pp. 17–48, 1971.

Larson, M. S., *The Rise of Professionalism: A Sociological Analysis*, University of California Press, Berkeley, CA, 1977.

Laswell, H. D., *A Pre-View of Policy Sciences*, American Elsevier, New York, 1971.

Levine, C. H., The federal government in the year 2000: administrative legacies of the Reagan years, *Public Administrative Review*, 46, 195–206, 1986.

Light, P. C., *The Tides of Reform: Making Government Work, 1945–1995*, Yale University Press, New Haven, CT, 1997.

Lincoln, Y. S., Introduction, In *Organizational Theory and Inquiry: The Paradigm Revolution*, Lincoln, Y. S., Ed., Sage, Beverly Hills, CA, pp. 29–40, 1985.

Lockard, D., *New England State Politics*, Princeton University Press, Princeton, NJ, 1959.

Long, N. E., Power and administration, *Public Administration Review*, 9, 257–264, 1949.

Luke, J. S., Managing interconnections: the new challenge for public administration, In *Public Management in an Interconnected World*, Bailey, M. T. and Mayer, R. T., Eds., Greenwood, New York, pp. 13–32, 1992.

Lunney, K., OMB deputy says performance-based budgeting is top priority, GovExec.com, June 20, 2001.

Luton, L. S., Administrative state and society: a case study of the United States of America, In *Handbook of Public Administration*, Peters, B. G. and Pierre, J., Eds., Sage GE Publications, London, pp. 169–176, 2003.

Lynn, Jr., L. E., The myth of the bureaucratic paradigm: what traditional public administration really stood for, *Public Administration Review*, 61, 144–160, 2001.

Lynn, L. E., Heinrich, C. J., and Hill, C. J., *Improving Governance*, Georgetown University Press, Washington, DC, 2001.

MacIntyre, A., *After Virtue*, 2nd ed., University of Notre Dame Press, Notre Dame, IN, 1984.

McLean, I., *Public Choice: An Introduction*, B. Blackwell, Oxford, 1987.

Macneil, N. and Metz, H., *The Hoover Report 1953–1955*, Wiley, New York, 1956.

March, J. G. and Simon, H. A. *Organizations*, Wiley, New York, 1958.

Martin, R. C., Political science and public administration: a note on the state of the union, *American Political Science Review*, 46, 669–676, 1952.

McSwain, C. J. and White, O., Transforming the golem: technicism, human-relations technology, and the human project, *Public Administration Review*, 49, 197–199, 1989.

Mead, T. D., Identifying management capacity among local governments, *Urban Affairs Papers*, 3, 1–12, 1981.

Meade, M., 'Participative' administration-emerging reality or wishful thinking?, In *Public Administration in a Time of Turbulence*, Waldo, D., Ed., Chandler, Scranton, PA, pp. 169–187, 1971.

Menzel, D. C., Rediscovering the lost world of public service ethics: do we need new ethics for public administration?, *Public Administration Review*, 59, 443–447, 1999.

Milkis, S. M., The New deal, administrative reform, and the transcendence of partisan politics, *Administrative Society*, 18, 433–472, 1987.

Mitchell, W. C. and Simmons, R. T., *Beyond Politics*, Westview, Boulder, CO, 1994.

Moe, R. C., *The Hoover Commissions Revisited*, Westview, Boulder, CO, 1982.

Mooney, J. D., The principles of organization, In *Papers on the Science of Administration*, Gulick, L. and Urwick, L., Eds., Institute of Public Administration, New York, pp. 88–98, 1937.

Morgan, D. F. and Kass, H. D., Legitimizing administrative discretion through constitutional stewardship, In *Ethical Frontiers in Public Management*, Bowman, J. S., Ed., Jossey-Bass, San Francisco, CA, pp. 286–307, 1991.

Mosher, F. C., Research in public administration: some notes and suggestions, *Public Administration Review*, 16, 169–178, 1956.

Mosher, F. C., The public service in the temporary society, In *Public Administration in a Time of Turbulence*, Waldo, D., Ed., Chandler, Scranton, PA, pp. 234–256, 1971.

Mosher, F. C., Introduction: the American setting, In *American Public Administration: Past, Present, Future*, Mosher, F. C., Ed., University of Alabama Press, Tuscaloosa, AL, pp. 1–10, 1975.

Mosher, F. C., Professions in public service, *Public Administration Review*, 38, 144–150, 1978.

Mosher, F. C., *Democracy and the Public Service*, 2nd ed., Oxford University Press, New York, 1982.

Mosher, F. C., *A Tale of Two Agencies: A Comparative Analysis of the General Accounting Office and the Office of Management and Budget*, Louisiana State University Press, Baton Rouge, LA, 1984.

Munger, F., Ed., *American State Politics: Readings for Comparative Analysis*, Crowell, New York, 1966.

Mushkin, S. J. et al., *Implementing PPB in State, City, and County: A Report on the 5-5-5 Project*, State-Local Finance Project, George Washington University, Washington, DC, 1969.

Nalbandian, J., *Professionalism in Local Government*, Jossey-Bass, San Francisco, CA, 1991.

National Association of Schools of Public Affairs and Administration. Standards—General Information and Standards For Professional Masters Degree Programs, National Association of Schools of Public Affairs and Administration, January, 2003, Washington, DC, http://www.naspaa.org/accreditation/seeking/reference/standards.asp (accessed November 16, 2004).

National Performance Review, *From Red Tape to Results: Creating a Government that Works Better and Costs Less*, US Government Printing Office, Washington, DC, 1993.

Nelson, D. and Frederick, W., *Taylor and the Rise of Scientific Management*, University of Wisconsin Press, Madison, WI, 1980.

Niskanen, W. A, Jr., *Bureaucracy and Representative Government*, Aldine-Atherton, Chicago, IL, 1971.

Osborne, D. and Gaebler, T., *Reinventing Government*, Addison-Wesley, Reading, MA, 1992.

Ostrom, E., Baugh, W. H., and Guarasci, R., *Community Organization and the Provision of Police Services*, Sage, Beverly Hills, CA, 1973.

Ostrom, V., *The Intellectual Crisis in American Public Administration*, University of Alabama Press, Tuscaloosa, AL, 1974.

Ostrom, V., Structure and performance, In *Comparing Urban Service Delivery Systems: Structure and Performance*, Ostrom, V. and Bish, F. P., Eds., Sage, Beverly Hills, CA, pp. 19–44, 1977.

Ostrom, V., Tiebout, C., and Warren, R., The organization of government in metropolitan areas, *American Politic Science Review*, 55, 831–842, 1961.

O'Toole, L. J., Jr., Implementing public programs. In *Handbook of Public Administration*, 2nd ed., Perry, J.L., Ed., Jossey-Bass, San Francisco, CA, 250–262, 1996.

O'Toole, L. J. Jr., Treating networks seriously: practical and research-based agendas in public administration, *Public Administration Review*, 57, 45–52, 1997.

O'Toole, L. J. Jr., Interorganizational relations in implementation, In *Handbook of Public Administration*, Peters, B. G. and Pierre, J., Eds., Sage, London, pp. 234–244, 2003.

Palmer, G., *The McNamara Strategy and the Vietnam War*, Greenwood Press, Westport, CT, 1978.

Parsons, W., *Public Policy*, Edward Elgar, Cheltenham, UK, 1995.

Peters, B. G., New visions of government and the public service, In *New Paradigms for Government*, Ingraham, P. W. and Romzek, B. S., Eds., Jossey-Bass, San Francisco, CA, pp. 295–334, 1994.

Peters, B. G. and Pierre, J., Governance without government? Rethinking public administration, *J-PART*, 2, 223–242, 1998.

Peters, B. G. and Pierre, J., Introduction: the role of public administration in governing, In *Handbook of Public Administration*, Peters, B. G. and Pierre, J., Eds., Sage Publications, London, pp. 1–9, 2003.

Peters, R., Revolution in military ethics?, *Parameters*, 26, 102–108, 1996.

Polenberg, R., *Reorganizing Roosevelt's Government: The Controversy over Executive Reorganization*, Harvard University Press, Cambridge, MA, 1966.

Pollitt, C. and Bouckaert, G., *Public Management Reform: A Comparative Analysis*, 2nd ed., Oxford, New York, 2004.

Pops, G. M. A teleological approach to administrative ethics, In *Handbook of Administrative Ethics*, Cooper, T. L., Ed., Marcel Dekker, New York, pp. 157–166, 1994.

President's Committee on Administrative Management, *Administrative Management in the Government of the United States*, US Government Printing Office, Washington, DC, 1937.

Pugh, D., ASPA's history: prologue!, *Public Administration Review*, 45, 475–484, 1985.

Pugh, D. L., The origins of ethical frameworks in public administration, In *Ethical Frontiers in Public Management*, Bowman, J. S., Ed., Jossey-Bass, San Francisco, CA, pp. 9–33, 1991.

Quade, E. S., Introduction, In *Systems Analysis and Policy Planning: Applications in Defense*, Quade, E. S. and Boucher, W. I., Eds., American Elsevier, New York, pp. 1–19, 1968.

Randall, R. L., The federal career executive in transition, *Personnel Administrative*, 19, 23–28, 1956.

Riggs, F. W., Professionalism, political science, and the scope of public administration, In *Theory and Practice of Public Administration: Scope, Objectives, and Methods*, Charlesworth, J. C., Ed., American Academy of Political and Social Science, Philadelphia, PA, pp. 32–62, 1968.

Riordon, W. L., *Plunkitt of Tammany Hall*, Dutton, New York, 1963.

Rohr, J. A., Ethics for the senior executive service, *Administrative Society*, 12, 203–216, 1980.

Rohr, J. A., *To Run a Constitution: The Legitimacy of the Administrative State*, University Press of Kansas, Lawrence, KS, 1986.

Rohr, J. A., Ethics in public administration: a state-of-the-discipline report, In *Public Administration: The State of the Discipline*, Lynn, N. B. and Wildavsky, A., Eds., Chatham House, Chatham, NJ, pp. 97–123, 1990.

Rohr, J. A., *Public Service, Ethics and Constitutional Practice*, University Press of Kansas Press, Lawrence, KS, 1998.

Rosenbloom, D. H., *Public Administration*, 2nd ed., Random House, New York, 1989.

Rosenthal, S. R., New directions for evaluating intergovernmental programs, *Public Administrative Review*, 44, 469–476, 1984.

Sanders, J. T., Honor among thieves: some reflections on professional codes of ethics. *Professional Ethics*, 2, 83–103, 1993.

Savage, P., Contemporary public administration: the changing environment and agenda, In *Public Administration in a Time of Turbulence*, Waldo, D., Ed., Chandler, Scranton, PA, pp. 43–58, 1971.

Savas, E. S., *Privatization: The Key to Better Government*, Chatham House, Chatham, NJ, 1987.

Sayre, W. S., The public service, In *Goals for Americans: The Report of the President's Commission on National Goals and Chapters Submitted for the Consideration of the Commission*, Prentice Hall, New York, pp. 285–296, 1960.

Sayre, W. S., Comment on Waldo's paper, *Theory and Practice of Public Administration: Scope, Objectives, and Methods*, Charlesworth, J. C., Ed., American Academy of Political and Social Science, Philadelphia, pp. 27–31, 1968.

Schick, A., The road to PPB: the stages of budget reform, *Public Administration Review*, 26, 243–258, 1966.

Schick, A., *Budget Innovation in the States*, Brookings Institution, Washington, DC, 1971.

Schick, A., A death in the bureaucracy: the demise of federal PPB, *Public Administration Review*, 33, 146–156, 1973.

Schick, A., *The Spirit of Reform: Managing the New Zealand State Sector in a Time of Change*, A Report Prepared for the State Services Commission and The Treasury, New Zealand, August, 1996.

Schick, A., Reflections on the New Zealand model, Based on a lecture at the New Zealand Treasury, August, 2001.

Scott, G. C., *Government Reform in New Zealand*, International Monetary Fund, Washington, DC, 1996.

Scott, G.C., *Managing Governments for Better Performance and Results: Some Lessons of Experience Rome*, Workshop on Financial Management and Accountability, 28–20, November, 2001.

Scott, G., Ball, I., and Dale, T., New Zealand's public sector management reform: implications for the United States, *Journal Policy Analysis Management*, 16, 357–381, 1997.

Scott, G. and Gorringe, P., Reform of the core public sector: the New Zealand experience, *Australian Journal Public Administration*, 48, 81–92, 1989.

Seidman, H. and Gilmour, R., *Politics, Position, and Power*, Oxford University Press, New York, 1986.

Shafritz, J. M., Hyde, A. C., and Rosenbloom, D. H., *Personnel Management in Government: Politics and Process*, Marcel Dekker, New York, 1986.

Shangraw, R. F., Jr., and Crow, M. M., Public administration as a design science, *Public Administration Review*, 49, 153–158, 1989.

Shope, V. C., *Ethics: A Selected Bibliography*, US Army War College Library, Carlisle, PA, 2003.

Simon, H. A., The proverbs of administration, *Public Administration Review*, 6, 53–67, 1946.

Simon, H. A., A comment on "the science of public administration," *Public Administration Review*, 7, 200–203, 1947.

Simon, H. A., Comments on the theory of organizations, *American Political Science Review*, 46, 1130–1139, 1952.

Simon, H. A., *Administrative Behavior: A Study of Decision-Making in Administrative Organizations*, Free Press, New York, 1957.

Simon, H. A., *The New Science of Management Decision*, Harper & Row, New York, 1960.

Simon, H. A., Smithburg, D. W., and Thompson, V. A., *Public Administration*, Knopf, New York, 1950.

Singer, P. W., *Corporate Warriors*, Cornell University Press, Ithaca, NY, 2003.

Skocpol, T. and Finegold, K., State capacity and economic intervention in the early New Deal, *Political Science Quarterly*, 97, 255–278, 1982.

Skowronek, S., *Building a New American State: The Expansion of National Administrative Capacities*, Cambridge University Press, Cambridge, pp. 1877–1920, 1982.

Smith, B. L. R., The US higher civil service in comparative perspective, In *The Higher Civil Service in Europe and Canada*, Smith, B. L. R., Ed., The Brookings Institution, Washington, DC, pp. 1–19, 1984.

Sorensen, T. C., *Kennedy*, Harper & Row, New York, 1965.

Stahl, O. G., Do present public servants approach the ideal?, In *Achieving Excellence in Public Service*, Sweeney, S. B. and Charlesworth, J. C., Eds., American Academy of Political and Social Science, Philadelphia, PA, pp. 25–40, 1963.

Stark, A., What is the new public management?, *J-PART*, 1, 137–151, 2002.

State Services Commission, *New Zealand's State Sector Reform: A Decade of Change*, 1998.

Stene, E. O., An approach to a science of administration, *American Politic Science Review*, 34, 1124–1137, 1940.

Stillman, R. J., Woodrow Wilson and the study of administration: a new look at an old essay, *American Politic Science Review*, 67, 582–588, 1973.

Stillman, R. J., *The Rise of the City Manager: A Public Professional Local Government*, University of New Mexico Press, Albuquerque, NM, 1974.

Stillman, R. J., The changing patterns of public administration theory in America, In *Public Administration: History and Theory in Contemporary Perspective*, Uveges, J. A., Ed., Marcel Dekker, New York, pp. 1–37, 1982.

Stillman, R. J., Public administration in the United States, In *The Modern State and Its Study*, Kickert, W. J. M. and Stillamn, R. J., Eds., Edward Elgar, Cheltenham, UK, pp. 39–79, 1999.

Stokes, D. E., Presidential' address: the changing environment of education for public service, *Journal Policy Analysis Management*, 15, 158–170, 1996.

Stone, D. C., Birth of ASPA-A collective effort in institution building, *Public Administration Review*, 35, 83–93, 1975.

Stone, A. B. and Stone, D. C., Early development of education in public administration, In *American Public Administration: Past, Present, Future*, Mosher, F. C., Ed., University of Alabama Press, Tuscaloosa, AL, 11–48, 1975.

Storing, H. J., The science of administration: Herbert A. Simon, In *Essays on the Scientific Study of Politics*, Storing, H. J., Ed., Holt, Rinehart, & Winston, New York, pp. 63–150, 1962.

Svara, J. H., Dichotomy and duality: reconceptualizing the relationship between policy and administration in council-manager cities, *Public Administration Review*, 45, 221–232, 1985.

Svara, J. H., *Official Leadership in the City: Patterns of Conflict and Cooperation*, Oxford University Press, New York, 1990.

Taylor, F. W., *The Principles of Scientific Management*, Norton, New York, 1911.

Taylor, M. D., *The Uncertain Trumpet*, Harper & Brothers, New York, 1960.

Terry, L. D., Administrative leadership, neo-managerialism, and the public management movement, *Public Administration Review*, 38, 194–200, 1998.

Thayer, F. C., Organization theory as epistemology: transcending hierarchy and objectivity, In *Organization Theory and the New Public Administration*, Bellone, C. J., Ed., Allyn and Bacon, Boston, MA, pp. 113–139, 1980.

The Treasury, *Government Management: Brief to the Incoming Government*, Vol. 1, 1987.

The Treasury, *The Economy of New Zealand*, 2004.

Thompson, D. F., The possibility of administrative ethics, *Public Administration Review*, 45, 555–561, 1985.

Thompson, D. F., *Political Ethics and Public Office*, Harvard University Press, Cambridge, MA, 1987.

Thompson, V. A., *Without Sympathy or Enthusiasm: The Problem of Administrative Compassion*, University of Alabama Press, Tuscaloosa, AL, 1975.

Toonen, T. A. J., The comparative dimension of administrative reform, In *Politicians, Bureaucrats and Administrative Reform*, Peters, B. G. and Pierre, J., Eds., Routledge, London, pp. 183–201, 2001.

Trebilcock, M. J., The professions and public policy: the nature of the agenda, In *The Professions and Public Policy*, Slayton, P. and Trebilcock, M. J., Eds., University of Toronto Press, Toronto, Canada, pp. 1–12, 1978.

Tullock, G., *The Politics of Bureaucracy*, Public Affairs Press, Washington, DC, 1965.

Urwick L., Organization as a technical problem, In *Papers on the Science of Administration*, Gulick, L. and Urwick, L., Eds., Institute of Public Administration, New York, 47–88, 1937a.

Urwick L., The function of administration with special reference to the work of Henri Fayol, In *Papers on the Science of Administration*, Gulick, L. and Urwick, L., Eds., Institute of Public Administration, New York, 115–130, 1937b.

US Census Bureau, *Census of Governments*, 2002.

US Equal Employment Opportunity Commission, *Job Patterns for Minorities and Women in State and Local Government 1991*, Equal Employment Opportunity Commission, Washington, DC, 1992.

US Equal Employment Opportunity Commission, *Annual Report on the Federal Work Force, Fiscal Year 2002*, Equal Employment Opportunity Commission, Washington, DC, 2002.

US Office of Management and Budget, *President's Management Agenda Fiscal Year 2002*, Governments Printing Office, Washington, DC, 2001.

US Office of Management and Budget, *Budget of the United States Government, Fiscal Year 2005*, Governments Printing Office, Washington, DC, 2004.

US Office of Personnel Management, *Civilian Workforce Statistics*, Office of Personnel Management, Washington, DC, 1999.

Van Riper, P. P., *History of the United States Civil Service*, Greenwood Press, Westport, CT, 1958.

Waldo, D., *The Administrative State: A Study of the Political Theory of American Public Administration*, Roland Press, New York, 1948.

Waldo, D., Administrative theory in the United States: a survey and prospect, *Politic Study*, 2, 70–86, 1954.

Waldo, D., *Perspectives on Administration*, University of Alabama Press, Tuscaloosa, AL, 1956a.

Waldo, D., *Political Science in the United States of America: A Trend Report*, UNESCO, Paris, France, 1956b.

Waldo, D., Public administration, In *International Encyclopedia of the Social Sciences*, Sills, D. L., Ed., Macmillan and Free Press, New York, Vol. 13, pp. 145–156, 1968a.

Waldo, D., Scope of the theory of public administration, In *Theory and Practice of Public Administration: Scope, Objectives, and Methods*, Charlesworth, J. C., Ed., American Academy of Political and Social Science, Philadelphia, PA, pp. 1–26, 1968b.

Walzer, M., Political action: the problem of dirty hands, *Philosophy and Public Affairs*, 2, 160–180, 1973.

Wamsley, G. L. et al., *Refounding Public Administration*, Sage, Newbury Park, CA, 1990.

Weimer, D. L. and Vining, A. R., *Policy Analysis*, 3rd ed., Prentice Hall, Upper Saddle River, NJ, 1999.

White, L. D., *Introduction to the Study of Public Administration*, Macmillan, New York, 1926.

White, L. D., *Government Career Service*, University of Chicago Press, Chicago, IL, 1935.

White, L. D., *The Jeffersonians: A Study in Administrative History, 1801–1829*, Macmillan, New York.

White, L. D., *The Jacksonians: A Study in Administrative History, 1829–1861*, Macmillan, New York.

White, L. D., *Introduction to the Study of Public Administration*, 4th ed., Macmillan, New York, 1955.

White, O. F., Social change and administrative adaptation, In *Toward a New Public Administration*, Marini, F., Ed., Chandler, Scranton, PA, pp. 59–83, 1971.

Wiebe, R. H., *The Search for Order: 1877–1920*, Hill and Wang, New York, 1967.

Wilbern, Y., Is the new public administration still with us?, *Public Administration Review*, 33, 373–378, 1973.

Wildavsky, A., Rescuing policy analysis from PPBS, *Public Administration Review*, 29, 189–202, 1969.

Wildavsky, A., *Speaking Truth to Power*, Little, Brown, Boston, MA, 1979.

Wilensky, H., The professionalization of everyone?, *American Journal Sociology*, 70, 142–146, 1964.

Willoughby, W. F., *Principles of Public Administration*, Brookings Institution, Washington, DC, 1927.

Wilson, J. Q., *Bureaucracy*, Basic Books, New York, 1989.

Wilson, W., The study of administration, *Politic Science Quarterly*, 2, 197–222, 1887.

Winter, S. C., Implementation: introduction, In *Handbook of Public Administration*, Peters, B. G. and Pierre, J., Eds., Sage Publications, London, pp. 205–211, 2003.

Wolf, J. F. and Bacher, R., The public administrator: the worlds of public service occupations, In *Refounding Public Administration*, Wamsley, G. L., et al., Ed., Sage, Newbury Park, CA, pp. 163–181, 1989.

Wright, D. S., *Understanding Intergovernmental Relations*, 3rd ed., Brooks/Cole, Monterey, CA, 1988.

31 Five Great Issues in the Profession of Public Administration

David John Farmer

CONTENTS

I. INTRODUCTION

Traditional concerns about the field of public administration (PA) are now encountering post-traditional frameworks. The five great issues must nowadays be discussed in this fresh context. The PA field has been obsessed throughout its history, more than most fields, by questioning about its identity, for example. In the past, it has seemed enough to discuss such questions of identity in a repetitive and same old, same old way. A main motivation has been the matter of academic turf, escaping the grip of being a subfield of political science and—a self-serving aim—maintaining independence from other avaricious fields. Now this is inadequate. Such great issues must be discussed in the context of the relationship between the traditional and the post-traditional frameworks.

Post-traditional PA seeks to emphasize radically imaginative thinking and action in government. This is reminiscent of an important element in the report of the 9/11 *National Commission Report on Terrorist Attacks Upon the United States* (2004). The Commission wrote about the role of imagination in government. Yet traditional bureaucracy is frequently accused of being unimaginative.

The post-traditional framework, like the traditional, takes a multiplicity of forms (for simplicity's sake, the singular form will be used in the rest of this chapter). The varieties include post-structuralism, postmodernism, feminism, queer theory, post-colonialism, ecologism and other isms. There are significant differences between varieties and sub-varieties. Some varieties run contrary to parts or all of others. For instance, critical theory is post-traditional, although it is modernist in character. These perspectives originated outside of PA and independently of PA.

With post-traditional aiming for a quantum leap toward the radically imaginative, post-traditional and traditional PA differ on at least five opposing polar features. Within the variety and sub-varieties of perspectives, these selected five alternative features are alternative visions (A) of knowing, (B) of the human, (C) of understandings versus explanations, (D) of attitudes toward including marginalized and excluded phenomena, and (E) of norms. These are sketched as part of the discussion of the great issues. Feature A is treated within the first issue, feature B within the second issue, and so on. The post-traditional framework challenges traditional public administration in at least two respects. As explained later, it challenges the traditional consciousness's responsiveness to intellectual perspectives, and it claims that the traditional framework is poor in terms of practical relevance. The relevance of the post-traditional is itself now a great issue for the profession of public administration. In addition, the post-traditional contributes significantly to shaping the other great issues.

This chapter presents an exploration of five great issues, each of which reflects this contestation between the traditional and the non-traditional. In the second edition of this *Handbook*, these issues were listed as the politics–administration dichotomy, the public–private dichotomy the quest for a science of administration, professionalization, and ethics (Fry and Nigro 1998). In the first edition, four of these categories were the same, but ethics was excluded and education was included (Fry 1989). Much in this essay relies on those excellent summaries of traditional concerns, and original quotes appearing in them have been used. The older terms are such well-trodden topics that the contemporary naming will seem odd to those well entrenched in the traditional framework. In the current interaction of frameworks, the parallel issues are identity, radical imagination, quest for hermeneutics, anti-administration, and justice turn.

II. IDENTITY

Traditional PA expresses the issue of identity in such terms as the politics–administration dichotomy. This dichotomy has been one of the signature issues of traditional PA. The post-traditional consciousness transforms this traditional conversation about the dichotomy, shifting the shape of the problem and the available opportunities for coping.

A. SIGNATURE DICHOTOMY

It is traditional to open a discussion of the politics–administration dichotomy by invoking Woodrow Wilson (1887) and his *The Study of Administration*. Within the traditional framework, there are at least two reasons why this significant move can be questioned.

Waldo (1984) explains that Wilson proposes a separation of politics and administration, suggesting the development of a generic science that will make PA more efficient. On the separation, Wilson (1887, 210–211) claims that "administration lies outside the proper sphere of politics... The discrimination between administration and politics is now, happily, too obvious to need further discussion." He has previously said that, the "field of administration is the field of business" (Wilson 1887, 209). On the generic science, Wilson wants to establish a science of PA "upon foundations laid deep in stable principle" (Wilson 1887, 210).

It has been pointed out that Wilson is ambiguous on this dichotomy because he describes how the politician and the administrator each become involved in the work of the other. Also it is said that the dichotomy does not reflect the realities of political–administrative life (Riggs 1991). These are not serious objections, however, because such a dichotomy can be recognized for theoretical or thinking purposes, even if such a dichotomy does not occur in reality. To provide an illustration, it is reasonable to discuss phenomena solely in (say) economic terms, even if it is the case that in reality economics and (say) politics cannot be separated. The same is true for administration, even if administration on the ground is inseparable from politics. It has been often claimed, for instance by Thomas Aquinas, that knowledge inevitably "abstracts" from phenomena.

One reason why starting with Wilson and his dichotomy is questionable is that administrative thinking long precedes Wilson. It goes back to ancient times (e.g., Gladden 1972). Martin (1987) has shown that "virtually every significant concept that existed in American public administration literature by 1937 (half the history of the field since Wilson's essay) had already been published in France by 1852. Most had been published by 1812" (Martin 1987, 297). As Waldo writes, "American self-aware Public Administration needs to be viewed as part of the very long history that has been sketched. So viewed, it is not something altogether new and different, but another chapter in a millennia-length story" (Waldo 1980, 10). On starting with the dichotomy, it is as if there were an attempt to establish the PA discipline as a peculiarly American phenomenon. Such parochialism is not necessary; for example, it is not found in some other fields like economics.

Another reason for questioning is that speaking about this dichotomy glides over the nature of PA's foundation, obscuring the way that American PA was founded. The issue of refounding, as it was termed, was raised in Wamsley et al. (1987, 1990) and later. It has been noted that the form of PA that was founded was essentially ideological. For instance, O. C. McSwite claims that, "although the positive side of Anti-Federalism did indeed provide the inspiration for the founding of public administration, this founding was soon aborted, in something like the way that Federalism overwhelmed Anti-Federalism during the writing of the official Constitution" (McSwite 1997a, 1997b, 118).

However, it is a mistake to dismiss the dichotomy. It is true that it can be doubted whether the politics–administration dichotomy was ever as important as later conversations said that it was (see Fry and Nigro 1998). At the same time, PA as a discipline has been conducted without playing a significant role in the sociopolitical environment, and possibly this has been encouraged in a field that limits itself to the merely administrative. The silence of traditional PA on thorny major sociopolitical issues of the day is deafening.

It is in this sense that the legacy of Wilson and his dichotomy has been important. Yet Fry and Nigro (1998) are right in characterizing the legacy as uncertain, and they list three paradigms that were influential in the field of PA in subsequent years—Wilson's, management, and policy making. Goodnow (1900) is reported as having a view similar to Wilson's. "Politics has to do with policies or expression of state will. Administration has to do with the execution of these policies (Goodnow 1900, 18). Then there was a management orientation by the 1920s. Dimock (1933, 261) describes PA as "a study of the powers and problems, the organization and personnel, and the methods of management involved in carrying out the laws and policies of government authorities." In the 1940s Wilson's position was denied. Claimed Appleby (1949, 29), "Public administration is policy-making." The number of paradigms that dominate PA has since grown, and Fry and Nigro (1998) go on to list others. To these, the listing of types of PA theory specified in Harmon and Mayer (1986) are added. The latter distinguish between neo-classical theory, systems theory, later human relations theory, market theories, interpretive and critical theories, and theories of emergence.

B. DIFFERING CONTEXTS

The situation shifts when insights are applied from post-traditional perspectives like postmodernism, post-structuralism, feminism, ecologism, queer theory, post-colonialism, and critical theory. A postmodern view of knowing embraces philosophical skepticism about expecting certain knowledge of the absolute and complete truth about some or all things. One example from within the postmodern discourse will now be considered: Deleuze and Guattari (1987) on the nature of knowing.

The traditional politics–administration dichotomy has been discussed in the intellectual perspective of what Deleuze and Guattari (1987) call the arborescent view of knowledge. Without this perspective, the dichotomy has different implications for PA. On the arborescent model, knowledge is described as having the characteristics of a tree. It is understood as hierarchical, divided into branches and sub-branches. As explained in the PA context (Farmer 1995, 220), the arborescent model assumes that there "is an essential rootedness of knowledge, and there is a unity of knowledge." Deleuze and Guattari (1987) contrast this model with the rhizomatic. A rhizome is a root-like and typically horizontal stem that grows along or underneath the ground, sending out a confusion and profusion of roots and other stems. The rhizomatic model decenters knowledge into divergent discourses. It destroys roots and binaries, producing multiplicities of differences. Yes, it dates uni-perspectival discussion of the politics–administration dichotomy.

III. RADICAL IMAGINATION

Recall the discussion of imagination in the report of the 9/11 Commission (2004), noted in the Introduction. Radical imagination is intended here in a fuller sense as post-traditional consciousness. It is also understood to apply not just to anti-terrorism but also to all governance functions.

Recall differences between the post-traditional and traditional frameworks as including at least five contrasting or polar features. These features are alternative visions of knowing (noted as part of Section II), of the nature of the human (discussed in this section), of understandings and explanations, of attitudes toward including marginalized or excluded phenomena, and of norms. Such alternative polar visions can be related to a variety of intellectual perspectives. These are perspectives like the contest of the culture wars or the debate between modernism and postmodernism. Deriving the polar visions from the culture wars has the advantage of locating the differences in an ongoing struggle that is live for most of the readers. Deriving them from a contrast between modernism and postmodernism carries baggage, e.g., the terms are often seen in PA as foreign. But the traditional and the post-traditional views of the five polar features (e.g., what it is to be human) are not grounded in the culture wars either. The descriptions of the culture wars are often ideological and narrow-minded, carrying baggage hardly less misleading. It is clearer, it is suggested, if these differences are linked to the radically imaginative.

The emergent post-traditional consciousness is reflected organizationally within the PA field by the growth and activity of the Public Administration Theory Network (PATNet). The history of this association has been described by Harmon (2003). Established in 1978, this is an association of PA theorists with a large variety of views, but membership is motivated by a wish for something more intellectual and more practical beyond the limits of traditional PA. Although many participate in the activities of the American Society for Public Administration (ASPA), most PATNet members see ASPA as traditional and moribund.

Post-traditional perspectives each have powerfully positive visions of society, and they are able to offer positive—albeit distinctive—understandings of PA phenomena. The vision in postmodernism, at its political core, is concerned with radical liberation; at the philosophical core, it is skeptical. Feminism is concerned with the oppression of women and with improving the lot of women. And so on. These varieties share a common negative characteristic, and that is dissatisfaction with the inadequacies of the traditional framework.

In this negative tone, this section notes the slowness of traditional PA to grasp external intellectual ideas. It then discusses a prime motivation of the post-traditional, and this is the belief that traditional PA exhibits a lack of practicality. Then it sketches contrasting views of the human, indicating the post-traditional view that radical imagination is required in government to provide for the individual-in-herself in-her-differences.

A. IMAGINATION AND LATENESS

Failure of imagination may well be reflected in the slowness with which post-traditional perspectives have made their ways to public administration.

Consider deconstruction as an example. Deconstruction has been widely influential in the United States and elsewhere, especially since Jacques Derrida's participation in the seminal 1966 seminar at The Johns Hopkins University. It had significant impact, in the 1980s and 1990s, on a number of social sciences like political science. It found its way into PA only in 1995 (Farmer 1995). Therefore, the complication arises that some post-traditional frameworks probably will have, but have not yet had, substantial impact on traditional PA. These are post-traditional frameworks that are well established in other disciplines but not yet in PA. For example, queer theory finds itself treated with respect and understanding in, say, Lacanian psychoanalysis, but it is foreign to PA. Similar claims can be made for other post-traditional perspectives, like post-colonialism (Thadhani 2005).

This slowness conflicts with a traditional PA self-perception that PA has been porous in admitting ideas from other disciplines, e.g., ideas from psychology and economics. It is true that PA has been more open to, say, parts of psychology, than have other disciplines like economics. One reason for being porous is that PA, unlike economics, lacks a strong central theoretical core. Further, it is questionable whether all the perspectives that have been ingested have been thoroughly digested. For instance, postmodernism has certainly been given short shrift within traditional PA. The situation is further complicated by the fact that parts of post-traditional perspectives are found within PA, but others are not. For example, McGinn and Patterson (2005) question how far PA has come in analyzing and understanding gender and feminism in PA.

B. PRACTICALITY

Post-traditional PA is motivated in part by what it suggests is traditional PA's impotence and lack of practical relevance in a world that increasingly needs help in addressing large scale issues of bureaucracy. There has been in traditional PA a privileging of thinking that is of immediate and short-run practical benefit, especially to middle-level practitioners.

The post-traditional supports the claim that there has been a fundamental misconception of the nature of practicality in traditional PA. It indicates that the notion of macro-PA is virtually neglected in the traditional PA framework. In this respect, PA stands in contrast with disciplines like economics and social work. Macroeconomics and microeconomics are well-recognized sub-fields in economics, and macro and micro social work are well-established categories. Economics and social work literatures and education have long recognized the importance of both macro and micro. Not so in PA, and the results strengthen the post-traditional challenge to traditional PA on the thorny topic of practicality. The solutions in each case have been diametrically opposed. Post-traditional PA distrusts what is described as a theory-scarce and theory-poor traditional PA. Traditional PA harbors a distrust of mere theory as impractical, and it tends to scoff at theory that does not immediately demonstrate short-term micro practicality.

C. ALTERNATIVE VISIONS OF THE HUMAN

What is the nature of the human as human? What is the human who governs or who is governed? What is the human bureaucrat or client? Two alternative characterizations can be briefly identified. Again, it is best to conceptualize the alternatives as at the extreme of what it is to be fully human, with the intermediate positions on the range populated by types that share in varying degrees characteristics from both of the extremes. At one pole is the traditional; at the other is the post-traditional.

The traditional extreme could be described in terms of a person's sense of identity and the relationship of that identity to the person's group. One icon for this understanding of what it is to be human is economic man and his derivative, administrative man—and other derivatives like welfare man or woman. Such men have unchanging identities; for example, economic man relentlessly trucks, barters, and exchanges. They are defined in relation to the group function, receiving their identities respectively from the administrative and economic mechanisms. Neither economic man nor administrative man (nor welfare man, and so on) has any life apart from his mechanisms. These stick figures are constantly what they are. There is another icon where the human is subject to innate or fixed propensities, e.g., biologically derived or divinely dispensed inclinations like hetero-sexuality or sticking to her man and nurturing. Those on the conservative side of the culture wars tend to hold such views.

The post-traditional extreme understands a human as a person-in-herself in-her-differences. Some would use another disquieting term, the postmodern person—where the person recognizes her life as fragmented, as disjointed, as failing to form the kind of unity that looks coherent in an obituary. This conceptualization does not center governing on systems but on the libidinal and life-affirming force of the individual human. The centering is, in Max Weber's (1958, 182) famous phrase on the individual, "in her full and beautiful humanity."

IV. QUEST FOR HERMENEUTICS

Developing a science of administration has long been an aspiration. The aim has been elusive. The aspiration has also been counterproductive to the extent that it has impeded the quest for herme-neutic understanding. It is in the area of hermeneutics where PA has made its greatest achievements and where there is the greatest potential.

The post-traditional framework emphasizes quests for hermeneutics. Through hermeneutics, it seeks the radically imaginative.

A. A SCIENCE OF ADMINISTRATION

The aspiration for a science of administration is described by Fry and Nigro (1998) in terms of two often-mentioned developments. One is the classical science of administration, and the subsequent is the behavioral science of administration. Whether much hangs on such a distinction is a different matter, however.

About the classical science, Luther Gulick asks, "Must we not discover the principles and laws which govern men through the same techniques that we have used to discover the laws which govern atoms?" (Gulick 1928, 102). This attempt to reduce all of PA to the natural science model encounters the problem that values cannot be treated *scientifically*, and writers like Dwight Waldo and Robert Dahl are right in holding that PA thinking and practice should be replete with value considerations.

The behavioral science of administration is described as seeking a scientific theory of organiz-ations. With roots in disciplines like psychology and sociology, the objective is reported to focus on developing a scientific *theory of organizations* that focuses on the individual in organizations. Herbert Simon's influential book (1944, 1976) on *Administrative Behavior: A Study of*

Decision-Making Processes in Administrative Organization articulates his fact–value distinction. For him, administrative decisions have a value and a factual component, and his view is that a *science* of administration should focus on the factual component. As Simon writes, "... every decision involves elements of two kinds, which are called 'factual' and 'value' elements respectively ... The distinction proves to be a very fundamental one for administration" (Simon 1976, 45).

Simon's fact–value distinction is based on an uncritical acceptance of the logical positivist view. As Simon explains, "the conclusions reached by a particular school of modern philosophy—logical positivism—will be accepted as the starting point, and their implications for the theory of decisions examined" (1976, 45). Simon directs his readers to a footnote that lists publications by various logical positivists. Bad luck for Simon's view! The views of the logical positivists are no longer prominent in philosophy of science. Dwight Waldo was again a primary critic of Simon's view. He criticizes Simon's selection of one view of the conception of science as not itself scientific, and—again—there is the problem of values.

Simon underlines his argument for a science of administration with a later pungent comment on the quality of PA. Simon writes that his "academic career started in an academic backwater: public administration. However important that field was and is to public affairs, it attracted few scholars with real understanding of what research was about, or how to construct the theoretical foundations for an applied field. Viewed by the norms of science, many of the books published in public administration (and management generally) are positively embarrassing ..." (Simon 1991, 114).

Unfortunately, philosophy of science is not a routine body of knowledge required in PA curricula. This tends to reduce the quality of discussions of the character of PA. The complexity of the status of scientific propositions is reflected in Boyd et al. (1993, xiii), where the editors report that "it will be apparent that the new consensus (in *Philosophy of Science*) is much more complex than that achieved in late positivism. In part this is simply a reflection of the fact that there is no doctrinal consensus but rather a consensus that identifies three distinct alternative general approaches—scientific realism, neo-Kantian constructivism, and post-positivist empiricism—as the major competitors."

B. A HERMENEUTICS OF ADMINISTRATION

In both quality and quantity, the best work in PA—including Wilson's essay—has been hermeneutic. Providing what he considered to be a satisfactory basis for a science of administration, even Simon's book is hermeneutic. Hermeneutics, it will be recalled, refers to work that is concerned with developing understandings, rather than explanations. It aims to give reasons, rather than to explicate causes (see Diesing 1991).

Hermeneutics does provide for a wide diversity in methods and interests. It has existed, as indicated, in American PA since the foundation. Within the past half-century, hermeneutics was emphasized in the New Public Administration (NPA) that followed the 1968 Minnowbrook Conference, and it was dominated by what McSwite calls questions of epistemology and ontology. "Any new public administration, if it were to live up to its name, has to transcend the idea that the bureaucrat was an expert whose only involvement beyond technique was to resolve analytically the ambiguities of policy issues" (McSwite 1997a, 1997b, 206). The idea of a positive fact was challenged (see McSwite 1998, 17–36). The NPA ended about 1980. Before that date in 1978, the PATNet was established by thinkers like Guy Adams and others. Much of the work of the members associated within the PATNet has been in the hermeneutic tradition, and *Administrative Theory and Praxis* contains significant hermeneutic studies.

A variety of important hermeneutic books were produced. They included Harmon's *Action Theory for Public Administration* (1981) and Hummel's *Bureaucratic Experience* (1977). Later books would certainly include Wamsley (1990). In the 1990s came other books; for instance, some wrote about PA theory in terms of modernity and postmodernity. Speaking of this entire period,

McSwite (1997a, 1997b, 153–237) describes the field of organization as shifting away from the idea that the rational model is the best approach.

Such hermeneutic works ran (and continue to run) against the mainstream PA trend which remains in the grip of the traditional; for instance, the effects of the Wilsonian dichotomy still live (and live). It was also against one important intellectual development. For example, there was Vincent Ostrom's *The Intellectual Crisis in Public Administration* (1973), a hermeneutic book if ever there was.

The post-traditional perspective now favors a shift toward hermeneutic play, emphasizing poetic imagination (e.g., Farmer 1998). This view holds that the play of poetry and the discipline of scholarship are not mutually exclusive categories. An example of such play is the interest in PA in the later 1990s and early 2000s in the relevance of Lacanian psychoanalysis in understanding PA phenomena (e.g., McSwite 1997a, 1997b). Play is often trivialized in a false dichotomy between work and play in our work-oriented culture. On the contrary, it has been argued that a problem in the work of governing is a failure to play. A failure in the work of running a democracy is a failure to imagine. Play is not intended as in *playing around* or in *playing the fool*. It means play in the sense of unleashing the poetic imagination, the artistry of wonder, through openness to the play of events. It was in this sense that there is value in the talk about bureaucratic *failure of imagination*.

V. ANTI-ADMINISTRATION

Post-traditional frameworks emphasize radical imagination that is nourished by a critically open attitude toward wisdom from a wide variety of extra-PA sources. Part of this is openness to anti-administration. Traditional PA has maintained an ambivalent attitude toward openness, as reflected in the public–private and other dichotomies. Yet it has been susceptible to economic and political panaceas like New Public Management.

Consider three examples, discussed below, of a post-traditional perspective that seeks to include neglected approaches and phenomena. The first is rhetoric and the symbolic. A second is governance. A third is the societal production of organizations and (mis)organizations.

A. TRADITIONAL PA: TOWARD NEW PUBLIC MANAGEMENT

A great issue in traditional PA is said to have been whether PA is really different from private administration. When this was discussed in the second edition of this Handbook, Fry and Nigro (1998, 1178–1186) spoke of dissimilarities and similarities. Differences highlighted for the public sector were relative ambiguity of goals (including worker motivation and efficiency), discretion, and flexibility. On the other side, the similarities section included Lorch's claim that "in a sense all large scale organizations today are public, are compelled to address public goals and use methods prescribed by laws and rules" (Lorch 1978). Principal motivations behind the pro-difference lobby include principle and turf.

The principle is the inadequacy of efficiency as the prime governmental value. It is false that a PA free of politics is value-free; instead, it is a PA that maintains a business value of efficiency. As Baechler (1975, 113) has commented, "the specific feature that belongs only to the capitalist system is the privileged position accorded to the search for economic efficiency." Privileging efficiency is, as is well established, a business or commercial value.

Since the 1980s, traditional PA practice has become even more dominated by the business model. Since the Reagan revolution, the emphasis on business values has accelerated. In the United States and in countries influenced by the ideas and practices of America, arguably the dominant mindset is neo-liberal economics or economic fundamentalism. The values of business and of the free market tend to be glorified, reflected in the everyday adage that making money is the American way. This tendency was encouraged by the prominence—reflected in Ostrom (1973) mentioned earlier—of the rational choice or economics paradigm within political science. *Public Choice*

Economics (Mueller 2003) exhibited appeal and benefits in terms of understanding political and bureaucratic phenomena.

PA practice has been impacted significantly by New Public Management, driven by belief in the beneficence of the free market, by what are seen as the imperatives of international economic changes, and by what are judged to be the benefits of computer technology. Symbolic of this impact was the prominence of the 1993–2000 National Partnership for Reinventing Government, directed by Vice President Albert Gore. The major text for this national agency was Osborne and Gaebler (1992). The New Public Management was described as a world wide movement. For instance, the New Zealand government was the poster child for New Public Management. New Public Management has been described as a paradigm shift in PA— "a profound shift toward a new kind of regime... not simply a shift toward less state, and also a shift to a different kind of state" (Schwartz 1994, 527). New Public Management is described as emphasizing "performance appraisal and efficiency; the disaggregation of public bureaucracies into agencies which deal with each other on a user-pay basis; the use of quasi-markets and contracting out to foster competition; cost cutting" and so on (Dunleavy and Hood 1991, 9). Within its narrow fragment of turf, traditional PA soldiers on—armed now with the mixed benefits of New Public Management.

B. POST-TRADITIONAL PA: TOWARD ANTI-ADMINISTRATION

A post-traditional framework can intensify focus on the imagination through anti-administration (Farmer 2002). Anti-administration is a theory about admitting, into administrative thinking and practice, perspectives now either marginalized or excluded. It is a theory about PA theorizing and thinking. It aims to achieve a change in PA consciousness. It also aims for such a change in other social science and action subjects, like economics.

The anti-administrative consciousness has been described (Farmer 2001) as consisting of an anti-impulse and a pro-impulse. The anti-impulse is against limitations that discourage openness in ways of thinking and doing PA. It is against unduly limiting assumptions embedded in PA concepts. Prominently, the anti-impulse is against the assumption that PA truth claims (including this claim) can be made with complete assurance. For example, it favors authentic hesitation—not to be confused with passing the buck or not being serious—in maintaining our own (or our group's) opinions about the right thing to be done.

The pro impulse is for concepts that open up ways of thinking and doing PA. These are the concepts of *imaginization, deconstruction, deterittorialization, alterity,* and *reflexive language. Imaginization* has been described as thinking as playing. The appeal here is to a large literature that includes thinkers like John Huizinga and Hans Gadamer (1975, 96). *Deconstruction* seeks the insights that come from loosening the limitations of metaphors and binary opposites embedded in PA concepts and related language (Farmer 1997, 12–27). *Deterritorialization* wants to loosen the coding or grid that a discipline imposes. Jacobs (2001) illustrates this by claiming that the language of traditional PA marginalizes ecology. *Alterity* is described in terms of the authentic hesitation (again) in the moral relationship with the other (see Farmer 1995, 227–245). *Reflexive language* refers to the large literature that includes Neitzsche, Heidegger, Wittgenstein, and Derrida. It embraces the idea that propositions cannot be made except from a particular perspective. There is no Archimedean point independent of the proposition maker.

The ideas of anti-administration have been explicated and developed by a variety of writers. Box (2001) draws the connection between anti-administration and private lives. Cunningham and Schneider (2001) discuss witnessing and gifting as anti-administrative strategies. Hutchinson (2001) discusses anti-administration and anti-melancholy, suggesting multi-gendering as a possible remedy. McSwite (2001) discussed the nature of anti-administration in terms of Lacanian psychoanalysis. Patterson (2001) speaks of play in terms of the Trickster, who challenges the traditional culture. Spicer (2001) discusses the advantages of moral pluralism.

C. EXAMPLES OF THE MARGINALIZED

Rhetoric, governmentality, and the societal constitute examples of realities that are marginalized or excluded in traditional PA. Anti-administration seeks their inclusion, and yes, other examples could be added, like insights from literature and philosophies from other cultures (see Fitzpatrick 2005).

1. Rhetoric and Symbols

We live in a world of symbols. Yet that symbolizes little for traditional PA thinking. The phenomena of rhetoric and symbolism have been excluded from traditional discourse.

In contrast, the post-traditional framework embraces the New Rhetoric and the linguistic turn, the latter a hot topic in analytical and Continental philosophy over the past century. The New Rhetoric of the twentieth and twenty-first centuries is more like sociology, exploring how a society gives rise to what is written-and-said and how what is written-and-said helps shape a society. This New Rhetoric, as David Fogarty (1959) summarizes it, is the study of what he calls symbolic ways of reaching mutual understanding among individuals aiming towards patterns of cooperative action. This is a long way from empty rhetoric. At the margins of fields related to PA, there has been a long-standing interest in rhetoric and symbols (e.g., Deidre McClosky (1998) on the rhetoric of economics; Murray Edelman (1971) on the rhetoric of politics; Deborah Stone (1998) on the rhetoric of policy analysis). Recently, there have been PA articles in American Public Administration on the rhetoric of PA (e.g. Farmer 2003a, 2003b; Farmer and Patterson 2003). No less than in the political and economic worlds, the PA sphere abounds in the symbolic; rhetoric is the stock in trade of PA practice.

2. Governance

Including a long-tem consideration for the problems of total governance (public, private, not-for-profit; all that gave a governance relationship to the individual) as part of thinking about the narrowly framed topic of bureaucracy would admit a new category of phenomena in PA. There is a move toward what Michel Foucault discussed under the heading of *governmentality*.

A tailored or ad hoc way of transcending traditional social science disciplines, embracing all that impacts on the governance of the individual-in-herself in-her-differences, has been discussed (e.g., Farmer 2005). This is in the tradition of a long-standing discourse and urge to reestablish a unity of knowledge—exemplified in Kant, Comte, Hegel, and others. Huge sums and energies have been expended during the past century on unifying disciplines. Disappointingly for some, the proliferation has only intensified, as new archipelagos have been created. The ad hoc way is in the discourse, not extensive within PA itself, to address the balkanization that has given us a hodgepodge of social sciences (like economics) and action subjects (like American PA) that are relevant to the human condition. Unfortunately, those in the best position to make an informed judgment about the success of their own narrow disciplines and fields are themselves trapped within those subject areas, economically and psychologically.

3. Relevance

It is becoming increasingly recognized that traditional PA fails to recognize the practical relevance of conscious and unconscious societal urges in producing administrative (mal)formations. This links with the claim made in Section III (on radical imagination) about the new understanding of practicality as requiring macro-PA. It is becoming noted that it is counterproductive to claim that major administrative problems can be resolved by no more than mere administrative tinkering, mere technicism. Part of the functioning of bureaucracy—an unconscious functioning, typically—is to execute some conscious and unconscious societal wishes, without necessarily requiring society in the latter case to admit that it has such wishes. As Gibson Burrell (1997, 250) points out, the focus of organization theory has been on the organization of production. He holds that organization theory should give more attention to the production of organizations.

VI. JUSTICE TURN

The traditional PA framework continues to emphasize administrative ethics largely in the tradition of analytical philosophy. In these terms, it has a long history of considering, say, codes of conduct and other items. Unfortunately, these considerations have added less than one might wish toward an understanding of the human condition in bureaucracy. The post-traditional framework *turns* PA more emphatically from a concern with administrative ethics toward justice concerns. It is troubled by the impression that administrative ethics gives the false impression that there is a coherent and operationally meaningful body of ethical knowledge about bureaucracy and bureaucratic functioning. It seeks greater openness to the self in relation to the other.

A. ADMINISTRATIVE ETHICS

Administrative ethics is situated in a context that is paradoxical in at least two respects. First, it is paradoxical in wanting to deal in core values that reconcile democratic ideals with what have been described as bureaucratic ideals. Second, being an applied subject in an action area, it wants to arrive at definite and sure prescriptions. But the difficulty is that it cannot do that to the extent that it is philosophical, because moral and other philosophy do not reach moral conclusions that are beyond questioning. Being such an applied subject, administrative ethics wants solid grounding for its positions; that too is widely recognized as unavailable.

First, the opposing tugs between some democratic ideals and the traditional bureaucratic ideal of hierarchy have been recognized since the beginning of American PA as a subject. Wilson is quoted as asking about our "series of governments within governments" and how they should be administered so "that it shall always be to the interest of the public officer to serve, not only his superior alone but the community also" (Wilson 1887, 16). How this can be resolved is not at all clear, and no one has proposed a viable and complete solution. Part of the problem is the assumption that hierarchy is essential to bureaucracy. This has been questioned (e.g., in Box 2003; Farmer 2003a; Howe 2005; McSwite 2003, 2003b; Patterson 2003; Zanetti 2003). It has been suggested that traditional PA theory is both a celebration and an apology for speaking from power.

Core values have been at the core of administrative ethics, but their problematic character has been noted. K. Denhardt (1991, 8, 23, 26) provides six or seven models. Her model for the 1950s provided that an administrator should ensure that the standards involved in administrative decisions should "reflect to some degree the core values of our society though not relying exclusively on custom or tradition." Her model for "After Rohr" provides in part that "the contents of the new standards may change over time as social values are better understood, or new social concerns are expressed. An administrator should be ready to adapt decisions standards to these changes, always reflecting a commitment to the core values of our society." All these PA models, as described by Denhardt, stress core values.

Where it is recognized that a multicultural society contains multiple differences between humans and where it is intended that governance should respect each person-in-herself in-her-differences, the notion of "core values" appears problematic. It rests on several fictions. One is that society basically—stress basically—has a set of core values that continues throughout history. At one point in history, slavery was a core value of the United States; now it is not. Another fiction is that society is a unitary entity, where people think alike on critical issues. Critical theorists might object that values often represent the ideas or interests of the dominant group in society, for instance. Another fiction is that it is straight forward to pick out core values. Some may look at a nation's history and identify caring-for-others as a core value, for instance, while others might note militarism as a core value in the same society. These arguments are, in my view, compelling. Yet there is support for core values in the shift that Warnke, noted below, describes.

The appeal to universal grounding for moral claims has been abandoned by many significant thinkers in the tradition of analytical philosophy. Warnke (1993) describes a shift in moral philosophy. She explains that many political theorists no longer justify norms of action on Kantian or universalistic grounds such as formal reason, character of human action, or the neutral procedures of human choice. She discusses philosophers making the hermeneutic turn, and they include John Rawls, Michael Walzer, and Charles Taylor. This shift represents an abandonment by those thinkers of any universal grip or grounding for moral behavior.

Second, administrative ethics wants to arrive at definite and sure prescriptions. But the difficulty is that it cannot do this to the extent that it is philosophical. Moral philosophy and philosophy in general cannot reach conclusions that are beyond questioning, because philosophy is a kind of unconstrained science where all foundations are open to questioning. It is also a kind of scholarship where there is a debate over whether there has been any progress over the past millennia, and thinkers like Bertrand Russell can take the position that there has been no progressivity.

On moral philosophy, there are competing ethical systems or ethical grounds. They include the deontological, the consequentialist, the intuitionist, the divine, the cultural, the subjectivist, the cultural relativist, and other positions, and each of these positions have sub-varieties. There are excellent arguments for each of these positions. There are also excellent arguments against each of these positions. There is no decisive winner. How much more obvious is the absence of a winner in the case encountered by those making the shift that Warnke describes.

B.   Beyond Administrative Ethics

Limiting ethical discussion to administrative ethics avoids larger and more important issues like justice considerations, such as those about the role of government in creating norms and ethics, for citizens and for itself, in a free choice or pluralistic situation. It also make it easier for an official following orders (or doing what she was trained to do) to avoid accepting responsibility for any harm her organization may be perpetrating.

In the post-traditional framework, a more emphatic normative *turn* is suggested from administrative ethics to justice concerns. There is also a shift in normative thinking and ethical substance, with the aim of greater openness to the self and to the other. Authentic hesitation, reticence to accept the judgments of one's own group and even one's own, was discussed earlier. At the traditional extreme, the ethic established is typically non-hesitant or assertive (e.g., "life in prison without the possibility of parole" for X, "don't ask, don't tell" for Y). At the post-traditional extreme, a major value is to encourage authentic hesitation in judging. The post-traditional alternative can be realized only when, in governance and in society, the very activity of norming itself is re-normed.

Then there is the additional problem of expanding the range of PA's ethical thinking beyond the analytical tradition in philosophy. For one thing, there is the vast literature of Continental philosophy. Popular in the fringes of PA (e.g., Howe 2003) and now in many philosophy departments, the latter may soon come to mainstream PA.

VII. CONCLUSION

"It is therefore crucial to find a way of routinizing, even bureaucratizing, the exercise of imagination" (9/11 Report 2004, 344). The final report of the *9/11 National Commission on Terrorist*

Attacks upon the United States (2004, 339) spoke of four kinds of failures in government: "in imagination, policy, capabilities, and management." Featured first was lack of imagination in government. The commission, as noted earlier, spoke of a failure of imagination, of the desirability of imagination.

PA is at a crossroads on this issue of radical imagination. Traditional PA is not imagination-friendly. Post-traditional PA is largely about the imagination. In saying this, it is repeated that the 9/11 Commission has a narrow view of the nature of imagination. Imagination at its fullest is not about mere technical capabilities like doing a better job of connecting the dots. It is about infusing government with the poetry of thinking as playing, justice and seeking and action as art (Farmer 2005). It is described as developing a post-traditional consciousness.

Two reasons are imperative for this shift, and they have been described in this chapter. The first is that PA is slow in its receptivity to fresh and challenging intellectual perspectives. It was mentioned earlier that postmodernism came late to PA, for example; it was badly understood; and the mainstream was happy to try to show it the door, even though it offers some very commonsensical ideas of great practical relevance. The basis for this *anti-intellectualism* requires critical self-analysis within PA. This self-analysis should also be conducted in university PA departments.

The second reason is the relative lack of enduring practical relevance in traditional PA thinking. As explained, part of the problem is the absence of a suitable macro-PA. It was noted that traditional PA aims primarily at the short run and particular needs of the middle-level practitioner. In this circumstance, it is not possible to consider larger questions like, for instance, the relationship of intelligence and law enforcement functions throughout the nation. The additional problem is that micro problems cannot be properly addressed to the extent that they are manifestations of the macro situation. The basis for this *anti-relevance* in traditional PA also requires critical self-examination. This also should be done in university PA departments.

The problem of the deadening hand of bureaucracy is very important in society, especially in one where bureaucracy is growing. PA has been the victim of fads like New Public Management. But PA has also victimized reforming politicians, e.g., by being unable to present the ideas of a radically imaginative macro-PA. The national administration is being shortchanged in this way. The long-term future viability of PA, it is suggested, depends on a shift toward post-traditional consciousness.

REFERENCES

Appleby, P., *Policy and Administration*, University of Alabama Press, Tuscaloosa, AL, 1949.

Baechler, J., *The Origins of Capitalism*, Blackwell, Oxford, 1975.

Boyd, R., Gasper, P., and Trout, J. D., *The Philosophy of Science*, MIT Press, Cambridge, 1993.

Box, R. C., Private lives and anti-administration, *Administrative Theory and Praxis*, 23(4), 541–558, 2001.

Box, R. C., Contradiction, utopia, and public administration, *Administrative Theory and Praxis*, 25(2), 243–260, 2003.

Burrell, G., *Pandemonium: Toward a Retro-Organization Theory*, Sage, Thousand Oaks, CA, 1997.

Cunningham, R. and Schneider, R. A., Anti-administration: redeeming bureaucracy by witnessing and gifting, *Administrative Theory and Praxis*, 23(4), 573–588, 2001.

Deleuze, G. and Guattari, F., *A Thousand Plateaus*, University of Minnesota Press, Minneapolis, MN, 1987.

Denhardt, K. G., *The Ethics of Public Service: Resolving Moral Dilemmas in Public Organizations*, Greenwood Press, New York, 1991.

Diesing, P., *How Does Social Science Work? Reflections on Practice*, University of Pittsburgh Press, Pittsburgh, PA, 1991.

Dimock, M. E., What is public administration?, *Public Management*, 15, 259–262, 1933.

Dunleavy, P. and Hood, C., From old public administration to new public management, *Public Money Management*, 1(3), 9–16, 1991.

Edelman, M., *Politics as Symbolic Action*, Academic Press, New York, 1971.

Farmer, D. J., *The Language of Public Administration: Bureaucracy, Modernity, and Postmodernity*, University of Alabama Press, Tuscaloosa, AL, 1995.

Farmer, D. J., Derrida, deconstruction and public administration, *American Behavioral Scientist*, 41(1), 12–27, 1997.

Farmer, D. J., Public administration discourse as play with a purpose, In *Papers on the Art of Anti-Administration*, Farmer, D. J., Ed., Chatelaine Press, Burke, VA, 1998.

Farmer, D. J., Mapping anti-administration: introduction to the symposium, *Administrative Theory and Praxis*, 23(4), 475–492, 2001.

Farmer, D.J., Medusa: Helene Cixous and the writing of laughter." *Administrative Theory and Praxis* 23(4), 559–572.

Farmer, D. J., The discourses of anti-administration, In *Rethinking Administrative Theory: The Challenge of the New Century*, Jun, J. S., Ed., Praeger, Westport, CT, pp. 271–287, 2002.

Farmer, D. J., The allure of rhetoric and the truancy of poetry, *Administrative Theory and Praxis*, 25(1), 9–36, 2003a.

Farmer, D. J., Because my father bathes me, *Administrative Theory and Praxis*, 25(2), 205–232, 2003b.

Farmer, D. J., *To Kill the King: Post-Traditional Governance and Bureaucracy*, M.E. Sharpe, Armonk, NY, 2005.

Farmer, D. J. and Patterson, P. M., The reflective practitioner and the uses of rhetoric, *Public Administration Review*, 63(1), 105–111, 2003.

Fitzpatrick, S. Open-ended tangled hierarchies: zen koans and paradox in public administration, *International Journal of Public Administration*, 28(7), 2000.

Fogarty, D., *Roots for a New Rhetoric*, Teachers College of Columbia University, New York, 1959.

Fry, B., Five great issues in the profession of public administration, In *Handbook of Public Administration*, 1st ed., Rabin, J., Hildreth, W., and Miller, G. J., Eds., Marcel Dekker, New York, pp. 1027–1075, 1989.

Fry, B. and Nigro, L. G., Five great issues in the profession of public administration, In *Handbook of Public Administration*, 2nd ed., Marcel Dekker, New York, pp. 1163–1221, 1998.

Gadamer, H. G., *Truth and Method*, Seabury, New York, 1975.

Gladden, E. N., *A History of Public Administration*, Frank Cass and Co., London, 1972.

Goodnow, F., *Politics and Administration*, Macmillan, New York, 1900.

Gulick, L., *National Institute of Public Administration*, National Institute of Public Administration, New York, 1928.

Harmon, M., *Action Theory for Public Administration*, Longman, New York, 1981.

Harmon, M., PAT-Net turns twenty-five: a short history of the public administration theory network, *Administrative Theory and Praxis*, 25(2), 157–172, 2003.

Harmon, M. and Mayer, R. T., *Organization Theory for Public Administration*, Chatelaine Press, Burke, VA, 1986.

Howe, L. E., Ontology and refusal in subaltern ethics, *Administrative Theory and Praxis*, 25(2), 277–298, 2003.

Howe, L.E. Power, knowledge and virtuous organizations: virtuous college and virtuous war. *International Journal of Public Administration* 29(7), 2005.

Hummel, R., *The Bureaucratic Experience*, St. Martin's Press, New York, 1977.

Hutchinson, J. R., Multigendering PA: anti-administration, anti-blues, *Administrative Theory and Praxis*, 23(4), 589–604, 2001.

Jacobs, D., Alterity and the environment: making the case for anti-administration, *Administrative Theory and Praxis*, 23(4), 605–620, 2001.

Lorch, R. S., *Public Administration*, West Publishing, St. Paul, MN, 1978.

Martin, D. W., Déjà vu: French antecedents of American public administration, *Public Administration Review*, 47(4), 298–301, 1987.

McClosky, D., *The Rhetoric of Economics*, 2nd ed., University of Wisconsin Press, Madison, WI, 1998.

McGinn, C., Patterson P., A long way toward what? Sex, gender, feminism and the study of public administration, *International Journal of Public Administration*, 28(7), 2005.

McSwite, O. C., *Legitimacy in Public Administration: A Discourse Analysis*, Sage, Thousand Oaks, CA, 1997a.

McSwite, O. C., Jacques Lacan and the theory of the human subject: how psychoanalysis can help public administration, *American Behavioral Scientist*, 41(1), 43–63, 1997b.

McSwite, O. C., Stories from the 'real' world: administering anti-administratively, In *Papers on the Art of Anti-Administration*, Farmer, D. J., Ed., Chatelaine Press, Burke, VA, 1998.

McSwite, O. C., The psychoanalytic rationale for anti-administration, *Administrative Theory and Praxis*, 23(4), 493–506, 2001.

McSwite, O. C., Now more than ever—refusal as redemption, *Administrative Theory and Praxis*, 25(2), 183–204, 2003.

Mueller, D., *Public Choice III*, Cambridge University Press, New York, 2003.

National Commission, The 9/11 Commission report: final report of the National Commission report on terrorist attacks upon the United States, W.W. Norton, New York.

Osborne, D. and Gaebler, T., *Reinventing Government: How the Entrepreneurial Spirit is Transforming the Public Sector from Schoolhouse to Statehouse, City Hall to the Pentagon*, Addison-Wesley, Reading, MA, 1992.

Ostrom, V., *Intellectual Crisis in American Public Administration*, University of Alabama Press, Tuscaloosa, AL, 1973.

Patterson, P. M., Imagining anti-administration's anti-hero (antagonist? protagonist? agonist?), *Administrative Theory and Praxis*, 23(4), 529–540, 2001.

Patterson, P. M., "Interpretation, contradiction and refusal: the best lack all conviction?", *Administrative Theory and Praxis*, 25(2), 233–242, 2003.

Riggs, F., Public administration: a comparativist framework, *Public Administration Review*, 51, 473–477, 1991.

Schwartz, H., Small states in big trouble, *World Politics*, 46, 527–555, 1994.

Simon, H. A., *Administrative Behavior: A Study of Decision-Making Processes in Administrative Organization*, Free Press, New York, 1944.

Simon, H. A., *Models of My Life*, Basic Books, New York, 1991.

Spicer, M., Value pluralism and its implications for American public administration, *Administrative Theory and Praxis*, 23(4), 507–528, 2001.

Stone, D., *Policy Paradox and Political Reason*, HarperCollins, New York, 1988.

Thadhani, R., Between monocles and veils: thinking postcolonial public administration, *International Journal of Public Administration*, 28(7), 2005.

Waldo, D., *The Enterprise of Public Administration*, Chandler and Sharp, Novato, CA, 1980.

Waldo, D., *The Administrative State*, 2nd ed., Holmes and Meier, New York, 1984.

Wamsley, G. L., Goodsell, C. T., Rohr, J., White, O. F., and Wolf, J. F., The public administration and the governance process: refounding the American dialogue, In *A Centennial History of the American Administrative State*, Chandler, R. C., Ed., Free Press, New York, pp. 291–317, 1987.

Wamsley, G. L., Goodsell, C. T., Rohr, J. A., White, O. F., Wolf, J. F., and Stivers, C., *Refounding Public Administration*, Sage, Newbury Park, CA, 1990.

Warnke, G., *Justice and Interpretation*, MIT Press, Cambridge, MA, 1993.

Weber, M., *The Protestant Ethic and the Spirit of Capitalism*, Trans. Talcott Parsons, Scribner, New York, 1958.

Wilson, W., The study of administration, *Political Science Quarterly*, 2, 197–222, 1887.

Zanetti, L. A., Holding contradictions: Marcuse and the idea of refusal, *Administrative Theory and Praxis*, 25(2), 261–276, 2003.

Index